Annotated Sample Student Papers

Annotated Student Research Papers

Appendix: Sample Student Paper

Making Literature Matter

AN ANTHOLOGY
FOR READERS AND WRITERS

Making Literature Matter

AN ANTHOLOGY
FOR READERS AND WRITERS

SIXTH EDITION

John Schilb
Indiana University

John Clifford
University of North Carolina at Wilmington

BEDFORD / ST. MARTIN'S   Boston   ▪   New York

For Bedford/St. Martin's

Vice President, Editorial, Macmillan Higher Education Humanities: Edwin Hill
Editorial Director for English and Music: Karen S. Henry
Publisher for Composition and Business and Technical Writing: Leasa Burton
Senior Executive Editor: Stephen A. Scipione
Publishing Services Manager: Andrea Cava
Senior Production Supervisor: Lisa McDowell
Marketing Manager: Jane Helms
Project Management: Jouve
Director of Rights and Permissions: Hilary Newman
Senior Art Director: Anna Palchik
Text Design: Jean Hammond
Cover Design: William Boardman
Cover Photo: Underneath the Cherry Tree, NYC, 1999 (oil on canvas), Bill Jacklin / Private
  Collection / The Bridgeman Art Library
Composition: Jouve
Printing and Binding: Quad/Graphics

Manufactured in the United States of America.

9   8   7   6   5   4

f   e   d   c   b   a

For information, write: Bedford/St. Martin's, 75 Arlington Street, Boston, MA 02116
  (617-399-4000)

ISBN 978-1-4576-7415-0

Acknowledgments

Preface for Instructors

Preparing the sixth edition of *Making Literature Matter* reminds us that we began work on the first edition more than two decades ago. We designed our book for college courses needing a text that could play dual roles: as a literature anthology and as a writing guide. Given the book's many adoptions, instructors appear to find that it achieves both purposes. Yet with each new edition, we aim to do more than maintenance. We re-tailor the book to address emerging trends. One of the trends we have grappled with in recent years is how to capture the sustained attention of students who are incessantly beguiled by their smartphones and the abundant distractions of the Internet. What can a book or teacher do to make literature matter for a digital generation—students who move fast and revel in various media? In choosing literature for our book, we hunt for works that will engage them. We strive to provoke their thoughts, stir their imaginations. Similarly, we aim to ensure that our advice about writing helps students articulate their ideas, even if they do this through a mélange of postmodern devices. We survey teachers who have actually used our text, asking them how it can better serve their classes. At the same time, we track new movements in literature and in literary criticism. We note changes in composition studies, including innovative technologies in the field. We observe what's now occurring in introductory college courses. Above all, we study how they teach writing, reading, and research. In short, we conduct research of our own.

This edition does retain key elements of its predecessors. Basically, Part One performs the functions it has fulfilled before. The opening chapters define *literature* and identify strategies for reading it closely. The rest of the section chiefly presents ways to *write* about literature. Throughout, Part One offers guidance in this art, drawing on numerous student essays for examples. We focus especially on composing *arguments*. As in previous editions, we point out that arguments needn't be mere rants. We note that when college courses ask students to write arguments, usually they want more than screeds. Rather, they seek essays that are civil, thoughtful, and well supported, so that readers can see how the writer's main claim makes sense. We describe how, in their encounters with literature, students can move from their initial responses into this process of persuasion. We identify for them specific steps that arguing about literature involves. We teach them how to pinpoint an issue, take a position, tap evidence, and spell out their logic, so that other people will respect their view. As in previous editions, Part One then turns to the main kinds of literature featured in Part Two: poetry, short stories, plays, and essays. We identify each genre's typical elements, stressing the major role these can play in literary interpretation. Once again, Part One concludes by providing detailed assistance with research-based papers, which courses in literature and composition often require. We discuss various sorts of investigative projects, explaining how to find, deploy, and cite sources.

Part Two of the book remains essentially a collection of literature. Again, the selections appear in chapters focused on thematic topics: families; love; freedom and confinement; crime and justice; and journeys. These subjects quickly interest students due to their obvious relevance. As before, we organize each chapter into small clusters of works. This arrangement encourages comparison and contrast: students grow more aware of similarities *and* more conscious of a text's distinct traits. Every cluster in Part Two remains packed with questions and writing assignments, offering students numerous issues to pursue. Each chapter retains four types of clusters that promote special kinds of inquiry. One type gathers works by the same author, such as Kate Chopin and Langston Hughes. In a second group, a single work, such as Sylvia Plath's "Daddy," is followed by professional critics' comments on it. A third cluster puts a work in cultural context by juxtaposing it with other documents; a favorite example is Ralph Ellison's story "Battle Royal" with accompanying texts by Booker T. Washington, W. E. B. Du Bois, and Gunnar Myrdal. The fourth type presents a work along with "re-visions" of it—texts that transform or translate it in striking ways, as Charles Perrault, the Brothers Grimm, and Angela Carter reinterpret the story of Little Red Riding Hood.

This sixth edition, however, mixes continuity with change. In other words, we have engaged in re-vision ourselves. The book includes several new features, which reflect our attention to developments in literature, curricula, technology, and the larger world.

New to the Sixth Edition

Expanded advice about the process of argument.   At the first-year and sophomore levels, many college programs in composition now emphasize argument. In part, their aim is to help students become better public advocates. Given this trend, we have significantly expanded our advice on writing arguments about literature. We say more about how making a case involves explaining assumptions and showing careful reasoning, not just pointing to bits of evidence. We define more extensively the concept of a rhetorical situation. We enlarge our treatment of the classic rhetorical appeals: logos, ethos, and pathos. We provide an additional example of an argument paper, a student's essay on Jamaica Kincaid's story "Girl."

Updated help with the research process.   We have revised our chapter on the research process in recognition of three emerging facts: (1) students now rely on the Internet when they have to do research; (2) their courses often entail study of visual images; and (3) many courses require research-based class presentations, which may employ various media and involve collaboration with other students. Although we still point out the benefits of turning to physical libraries and their staffs, we provide new guidance in making Internet searches productive. Also, we have added a visual analysis essay to our set of sample student papers on Charlotte Perkins Gilman's "The Yellow Wallpaper." This new paper examines illustrations that originally accompanied Gilman's story. The chapter now concludes with advice for preparing multimedia class presentations that demonstrate research, incorporate images, and depend on group work.

A more streamlined discussion of literary genres in Part One.   Previous versions of Part One devoted a separate chapter to each of the book's four main literary genres. We have concluded, however, that teachers and students will find it easier to consult a single chapter about them. The chapter still presents detailed information about each genre's typical elements so that students grow more able to spot these and write about them.

Much literature that is new to the book.   Bearing in mind the world's ever-increasing diversity, we have added stirring contemporary selections by writers such as Lynn Nottage, Richard Blanco, Victoria Chang, Dagoberto Gilb, Nathan Englander, Robin Becker, Jose Antonio Vargas, Lydia Davis, and Neil Gaiman. We also revive older texts that merit renewed notice — classic works by the likes of Jonathan Swift, Willa Cather, August Strindberg, Elizabeth Barrett Browning, and Pablo Neruda. An entire cluster pivots around Oscar Wilde's comic masterpiece *The Importance of Being Earnest*, presenting the play along with published interpretations of it.

Several new topics for clusters.   Each chapter in our literature anthology has at least one cluster focused on a topic new to the book. With some of these subjects, we emphasize current world issues. For example, we group essays that contemplate governmental surveillance. Other new clusters touch on perpetual human concerns. For example, a pair of stories, one by Ernest Hemingway and one by Louise Erdrich, depict the blend of anguish and freedom that returning war veterans have often experienced. Essays by Ruth Reichl, David Sedaris, and Chang-Rae Lee reflect on the role that food plays in family life. Poems by Alfred Lord Tennyson and Adrienne Rich describe mythic journeys.

An additional kind of special cluster, "Across Genres."   Instructors report to us that, at least occasionally, they want their students to compare works in different genres. To each chapter in Part Two, therefore, we have added a new special cluster that invites such analysis. For example, a poem about immigrant brides by Chitra Banerjee Divakaruni appears with a story on the same subject by Julie Otsuka. Similarly, we pair Sophocles' tragic drama *Antigone* with Martin Luther King Jr.'s essay "Letter from Birmingham Jail," both of them classic works on civil disobedience.

An expanded appendix on critical approaches to literature.   Many instructors tell us that they appreciate how the appendix efficiently explains major schools of literary criticism, from new critical formalism to new historical and postcolonial approaches. Given the increasing popularity of the critical movement known as queer theory, we have added a discussion of it.

An Instructor's Manual Is Available for Download

You may want to access the instructor's manual, *Resources for Teaching Making Literature Matter: An Anthology for Readers and Writers*, Sixth Edition, through the online catalog page; visit **macmillanhighered.com/makinglitmatter /catalog**. Prepared by John Schilb, John Clifford, Joyce Hollingsworth, and Laura Sparks, these instructor resources include sample syllabi; advice (including an annotated bibliography for further research) on teaching literature, composition, and argumentation; and, especially, substantial commentaries on the individual literary works throughout the book to aid class preparation and discussion.

Acknowledgments

As always, the staff at Bedford/St. Martin's has coached us with a rare blend of insight, vision, practicality, wit, and warmth. The utter epitome of these virtues is Senior Executive Editor Steve Scipione, who remains our invaluable mentor and friend. Editorial Director, English, Karen Henry is also a stalwart and perceptive guide, and we are grateful as well to two hardworking editorial assistants, Rachel Greenhaus and Arrin Kaplan. For their editorial vision in earlier editions of *Making Literature Matter*, we thank Charles Christensen, Joan Feinberg, and Denise Wydra. In production, we are grateful to Susan Brown, Andrea Cava, Elise Kaiser, and Sam Spofford. In the permissions department, text permissions manager Kalina Ingham, permissions editor Arthur Johnson, photo researcher Rona Tuccillo, and photo research manager Martha Friedman expertly and efficiently negotiated and obtained reprint rights.

Once more, we thank Janet E. Gardner, formerly of the University of Massachusetts at Dartmouth, for her contributions to the chapter on research; Joyce Hollingsworth of the University of North Carolina at Wilmington for her previous work on the instructor's manual; and Laura Sparks for the work on the instructor's manual for this edition.

As always, John Schilb is indebted to his former University of Maryland colleague Jeanne Fahnestock and his current colleagues at Indiana University, especially Christine Farris, Kathy Smith, and Lisa Ottum. He also thanks Gary Weissman from the University of Cincinnati for calling his attention to Ira Sher's story "The Man in the Well." John Clifford would like to thank Sheri Malman for her invaluable assistance with this project, especially her professional editing.

Of course, we remain grateful as well to the instructors who have commented on various editions over the years — especially to those who have adopted the book, some for many editions. For their extremely helpful responses, we thank Liz Ann Aguilar, San Antonio College; Jonathan Alexander, University of Southern Colorado; Donna Allen, Erie Community College; Julie Aipperspach Anderson, Texas A&M University; Virginia Anderson, University of Texas at Austin; Liana Andreasen, South Texas College; Sonja L. Andrus, Collin County Community College; Joe Argent, Gaston College; Andrew Armond,

Belmont Abbey College; Carolyn Baker, San Antonio College; Rance G. Baker, San Antonio College; Barbara Barnard, Hunter College; Charles Bateman, Essex County College; Linda Bensel-Meyers, University of Tennessee, Knoxville; Elaine Boothby, South River High School; Colleen Brooks-Edgar, South Texas College; Christy Brown, Mission College; Susan Buchler, Montgomery County Community College; Elizabeth L. Cobb, Chapman University; Robin Coffelt, University of North Texas; Chauna Craig, Indiana University of Pennsylvania; Timothy R. Cramer, Santa Monica College; Jacob Crane, Bentley University; Michael A. Cronin, Northern Oklahoma College; Janet Dale, Georgia College; Rosemary B. Day, Central New Mexico Community College–Montoya Campus; Thomas Deans, Kansas State University; Kevin J. H. Dettmar, Pomona College; Jennifer Diffley, Orange Coast College; Jennifer Dorfield, Westfield State College; Michael Doyle, Blue Ridge Community College; Penelope Dugan, Richard Stockton College of New Jersey; Thomas Dukes, University of Akron; Mary Dutterer, Howard Community College; Kelly Edmisten, University of North Carolina at Wilmington; Leigh Edwards, Florida State University; Monika Elbert, Montclair State University; Irene R. Fairley, Northeastern University; John Funk, Bishop Chatard High School; Joli Furnari, Montclair State University; Selma Goldstein, Rider University; Martha K. Goodman, Central Virginia Community College; Christopher Gould, University of North Carolina at Wilmington; Maureen Groome, Brevard Community College; Chad Hammett, Texas State University; Martin Harris, Belmont Abbey College; William Harrison, Northern Virginia Community College; Iris Rose Hart, Santa Fe Community College; Glenn Hatcher, Gaston College; Denise Haughian, University of Wisconsin-Stout; Carol Peterson Haviland, California State University, San Bernardino; H. Suzanne Heagy, Fairmont State University; Ana Hernandez, Miami-Dade College–Wolfson; John Heyda, Miami University–Middletown; Jeff Hoogeveen, Lincoln University; Richard Dean Hovey, Pima Community College; Karen Howard, Volunteer State Community College; Clark Hutton, Volunteer State Community College; Joan Kellerman, University of Massachusetts–Dartmouth; Sabine A. Klein, Purdue University; Sonya Lancaster, University of Kansas; Kasee Clifton Laster, Ashland University; Marianne Layer, Armstrong Atlantic State University; Margaret Lindgren, University of Cincinnati; Donna Long, Fairmont State University; Linda Lovell, Northwest Arkansas Community College; Irma Luna, San Antonio College; Betty Mandeville, Volunteer State Community College; Kelly Martin, Collin County Community College; Phillip Mayfield, Fullerton College; Miles S. McCrimmon, J. Sargeant Reynolds Community College; Christopher McDermott, University of Georgia; Mandy McDougal, Volunteer State Community College; Rebecca Millan, South Texas College; Sharmila Nambiar, South Texas College; Steven Newman, University of Nebraska–Omaha; Dana Nichols, Gainesville State College; Jim O'Loughlin, University of Northern Iowa; Gordon O'Neal, Collin County Community College; Christine Peter, University of Massachusetts–Dartmouth; Brenton Phillips, Cloud County Community College; Nancy Lawson Remler, Armstrong Atlantic State University; David Rollison, College of Marin; Jane Rosecrans, J. Sargeant Reynolds Community College; Teri Rosen,

Hunter College; Lisa Roy-Davis, Collin County Community College; Donna Samet, Broward Community College; Jamie Sanchez, Volunteer State Community College; Daniel Schierenbeck, University of Central Missouri; Meryl F. Schwartz, Lakeland Community College; Pauline Scott, Alabama State University; Julie Segedy, Chabot College; Lucia Seranyan, Northern Virginia Community College, Woodbridge Campus; Kimberly Alford Singh, Northern Virginia Community College; Jason Skipper, Miami University at Oxford; Jennifer Smith, Miami University at Oxford; Debra L. Snyder, Livingstone College; Jamieson Spencer, St. Louis Community College; Pam Stinson, Northern Oklahoma College; Douglas Strayer, Henry Ford Community College; Sarah Syrjanen, Florida State University; Jonathan Taylor, Ferris State University; Julie Tilton, San Bernardino Valley College; Larry A. Van Meter, Texas A&M University; William Verrone, University of North Carolina at Wilmington; Phillippe (Phil) West, Concordia University; Sharon Winn, Northeastern State University; Bertha Wise, Oklahoma City Community College; Pauline G. Woodward, Endicott College; Gulnar Zaman, Northern Virginia Community College.

   Through all editions of *Making Literature Matter*, three things have stayed the same: what matters most to John Schilb is Wendy Elliot; what matters most to John Clifford is Janet Ellerby; and we dedicate this book to them.

John Schilb, Indiana University
John Clifford, University of North Carolina at Wilmington

You Get More Resources for *Making Literature Matter*

Making Literature Matter doesn't stop with a book. Online, you'll find resources to help students get even more out of the book and your course. You'll also find convenient instructor resources, and even a nationwide community of teachers. To learn more about or order any of the products below, contact your Bedford/St. Martin's sales representative, e-mail sales support (macmillanhighered.com/getsupport), or visit the online catalog at **macmillanhighered.com/makinglitmatter/catalog**.

Visit *Re:Writing for Literature* at bedfordstmartins.com/rewritinglit

Get online help for your students in composition and literature:

- Videos of real writers
- Sample documents in design
- Help on building a bibliography
- Checklists for better writing
- Exercises for grammar and writing
- Tutorial on visual analysis
- Glossary of literary terms
- MLA-style student papers
- A sampler of author videos and additional literature
- Help for finding and citing sources

Access video interviews with today's writers. *VideoCentral: Literature*, our growing library of more than 50 video interviews with today's writers, includes Ha Jin on how he uses humor, Chitra Banerjee Divakaruni on how she writes from experience, and T. C. Boyle on how he works with language and style. Biographical notes and questions make each video an assignable module. See **bedfordstmartins.com/videolit/catalog**.

This resource can be packaged for free with new student editions of this book. An activation code is required and must be purchased. To order *VideoCentral: Literature* with this print text, use ISBN 978-1-319-01084-3.

Access Your Instructor Resources at macmillanhighered.com/makinglitmatter/catalog

You have a lot to do in your course. Bedford/St. Martin's wants to make it easy for you to find the support you need—and to get it quickly.

Download your instructor's manual. *Resources for Teaching Making Literature Matter: An Anthology for Readers and Writers*, Sixth Edition, includes sample syllabi; advice (including an annotated bibliography for further research) on teaching literature, composition, and argumentation; and substantial commentaries on the literary works throughout the book to aid class preparation and discussion. For the PDF, go to **macmillanhighered.com/catalog/makinglitmatter**.

Get teaching ideas you can use today. Are you looking for professional resources for teaching literature and writing? How about some help with planning classroom activities?

- **Teaching Central.** We've gathered all of our print and online professional resources in one place. You'll find landmark reference works, sourcebooks on pedagogical issues, award-winning collections, and practical advice for the classroom — all free for instructors and available at **bedfordstmartins.com/teachingcentral**.

- **LitBits Blog: Ideas for Teaching Literature and Creative Writing.** *LitBits* — hosted by a growing team of instructors, poets, novelists, and scholars — offers a fresh, regularly updated collection of ideas and assignments. You'll find simple ways to teach with new media, excite your students with activities, and join an ongoing conversation about teaching. Go to **bedfordstmartins.com/litbits /catalog** and **bedfordstmartins.com/litbits**.

Package one of our best-selling brief handbooks at a discount. Do your students need a pocket-sized handbook for your course? Package *Easy Writer* by Andrea Lunsford or *A Pocket Style Manual* by Diana Hacker and Nancy Sommers with this text at a 20% discount. For more information, go to **bedfordstmartins.com/easywriter/catalog** or **bedfordstmartins.com /pocket/catalog**.

Package multimodal tutorials that bring argument to life. There are things you can't do in a book. You can't analyze a video, listen to a speech, or scroll through a photo essay. Through six multimodal tutorials and an illustrated glossary, *i-claim: visualizing argument* brings argument to life for students by showing them how to analyze and compose arguments in words, images, and sound. Visit **bedfordstmartins.com/catalog/product/i•claim20 -secondedition-clauss:** To package *Making Literature Matter* with *i•claim 2.0*, use package ISBN 978-1-319-01083-6.

Teach longer works at a nice price. Our literary reprints series — the Case Studies in Contemporary Criticism series, Bedford Cultural Edition series, and the Bedford Shakespeare series — can be shrink-wrapped with *Making Literature Matter*. For a complete list of available titles, visit **bedfordstmartins .com/literaryreprints/catalog**.

Package works from our video and DVD library. Qualified adopters can choose from selected videos and DVDs of plays and stories included in *Making Literature Matter*. To learn more, contact your Bedford/St. Martin's sales representative or e-mail sales support **macmillanhighered.com/getsupport**.

Trade up and save 50%. Add more value and choice to your students' learning experiences by packaging their Bedford/St. Martin's textbook with one of a thousand titles from our sister publishers, such as Farrar, Straus and Giroux and St. Martin's Press — at a discount of 50% off the regular price.

Brief Contents

Contents

5. Writing about Literary Genres   115

Portfolio: Comparing Poems and Pictures [between pages 184 and 185]

6. Writing Researched Arguments   187

■ PART TWO   Literature and Its Issues

9. Freedom and Confinement

Contents by Genre

Stories

Poems

Plays

Essays

Critical Commentaries

Cultural Contexts

Full-Color Images

Making Literature Matter

AN ANTHOLOGY
FOR READERS AND WRITERS

Working with Literature

CHAPTER 1

What Is Literature? How and Why Does It Matter?

The title of this book, *Making Literature Matter*, may seem curious to you. Presumably your school assumes that literature already matters, for otherwise it would hardly offer courses in the subject. Quite possibly you are taking this course because you think literature is important or hope it will become so for you. But with our title, we want to emphasize that literature does not exist in a social vacuum. Rather, literature is part of human relationships; people *make* literature matter to other people. We are especially concerned with how you can make literature matter to others as well as to yourself. Above all, we point out ways you can argue about literature, both in class discussions and in your own writing.

Here is a poem that has engaged many readers, judging by how often it has appeared in literature anthologies since its first publication in 1963. The author is James Wright (1927–1980), who was born and raised in the industrial town of Martin's Ferry, Ohio, and won the Pulitzer Prize for poetry in 1972. Many of Wright's poems deal with the working-class life he experienced. Early in his career as a poet, he wrote in conventional forms, but later he became much more experimental. The following poem, perhaps Wright's most famous, is a case in point. The poem's speaker, you will see, comes to a judgment about whether he's managed to make his very existence matter.

JAMES WRIGHT

Lying in a Hammock at William Duffy's Farm in Pine Island, Minnesota

Over my head, I see the bronze butterfly,
Asleep on the black trunk,
Blowing like a leaf in green shadow.
Down the ravine behind the empty house,
The cowbells follow one another
Into the distances of the afternoon.
To my right,

5

In a field of sunlight between two pines,
The droppings of last year's horses
Blaze up into golden stones.
I lean back, as the evening darkens and comes on.
A chicken hawk floats over, looking for home.
I have wasted my life.   *[1963]*

Did the last line startle you? For many readers, Wright's poem is memorable because its conclusion is unexpected, even jarring. At first glance, nothing in the speaker's description of his surroundings justifies his blunt self-condemnation at the end. If anything, the previous lines evoke rural tranquility, so that a more predictable finish would be "I am now at peace." Instead, the speaker suddenly criticizes himself. Intrigued by this mysterious move, readers usually look at the whole poem again, studying it for signs of growing despair. Often they debate with one another how the ending does relate to preceding lines. Thus, although the poem's speaker implies his life hasn't mattered, the poem itself has mattered to readers, plunging them into lively exchanges over how to interpret Wright's text.

We present Wright's poem to begin pointing out how literature can matter to people. We will keep referring to the poem in this introduction. But now we turn to three big questions:

- How have people defined *literature*?
- Why study literature in a college writing course?
- What can *you* do to make literature matter to others?

How Have People Defined *Literature*?

Asked to define *literature*, most people would include Wright's text, along with other poems. In addition to poetry, they would say *literature* encompasses fiction (novels as well as short stories) and drama. But limiting the term's scope to these genres can be misleading, for they are rooted in everyday life. Often they employ ordinary forms of talk, although they may play with such expressions and blend them with less common ones. Someone lying in a hammock may, in fact, recite details of the landscape — especially if he or she is talking to someone else on a cell phone, as is common nowadays. And quite possibly you have heard someone proclaim "I have wasted my life" or m.ake a similar declaration. In any case, surely much of Wright's language is familiar to you, even if you haven't seen it arranged into these particular phrases and lines.

The genres regarded as literary are tied in other ways to everyday behavior. For instance, things function as symbols not only in poems but also in daily conversation. Even people who aren't poets have little trouble associating shadows, evening, darkness, and hawks with death. (In the case of Wright's poem, the issue then becomes whether the text supports or complicates this association.) Hammocks, too, are often treated as meaningful images. They are familiar symbols of "taking it easy." (With Wright's poem, the issue again becomes whether the speaker's hammock signifies *more* than just leisure.)

Throughout the day, then, it can be said that people put literary genres into practice. Perhaps you have commented on certain situations by quoting a song lyric or citing words from a poem, story, or play. Surely you are poetic in the sense that you use metaphors in your everyday conversations. After all, most of us are capable, as Wright's speaker is, of comparing a butterfly to a leaf (even if we aren't apt to compare horse droppings to "golden stones"). Probably you are often theatrical as well, carrying out various kinds of scripts and performing any number of roles. Furthermore, probably you are engaged in storytelling no matter how little fiction you actually write. Imagine this familiar situation: you are late for a meeting with friends because you got stuck in traffic, and now you must explain to them your delay. Your explanation may well become a tale of suspense, with you the hero racing against time to escape the bumper-to-bumper horde. As writer Joan Didion has observed, "We tell ourselves stories in order to live." Almost all of us spin narratives day after day because doing so helps us meaningfully frame our lives. (Unfortunately, the story that Wright's speaker tells is "I have wasted my life." Nevertheless, it's a means for interpreting his existence, and maybe somehow it helps him keep on living.)

You may admit that literature is grounded in real life and yet still tend to apply the term only to written texts of fiction, poetry, and drama. But this tendency is distinctly modern, for the term *literature* has not always been applied so restrictively. *Literature* was at first a characteristic of *readers*. From the term's emergence in the fourteenth century to the middle of the eighteenth, *literature* was more or less a synonym for *literacy*. People of literature were assumed to be well read.

In the late eighteenth century, however, the term's meaning changed. Increasingly it referred to books and other printed texts rather than to people who read them. At the beginning of this shift, the scope of literature was broad, encompassing nearly all public writing. But as the nineteenth century proceeded, the term's range shrank. More and more people considered literature to be imaginative or creative writing, which they distinguished from nonfiction. This trend did take years to build; in the early 1900s, literature anthologies still featured essays as well as excerpts from histories and biographies. By the mid-1900s, though, the narrower definition of literature prevailed.

This limited definition has become vulnerable. From the early 1970s, a number of literature faculty have called for widening it. In 1979, for instance, a National Endowment for the Humanities–Modern Language Association institute entitled "Women's Nontraditional Literature" applied the term *literature* to genres that had not been thought of as such. Participants studied essays, letters, diaries, autobiographies, and oral testimonies. To each of these genres, women have contributed much; in fact, the institute's participants concluded that a literature curriculum slights many works by women if it focuses on fiction, poetry, and drama alone.

Of course, even within these three categories, the term *literature* has been selectively applied. Take the case of novelist and short-story writer Stephen King, whose books have sold millions of copies. Despite his commercial success, a lot of readers — including some of his fans — refuse to call King's writing literature. They assume that to call something literature is to say that it has artistic merit, and for them King's tales of horror fall short.

Yet people who use the term *literature* as a compliment may still disagree about whether a certain text deserves it. Plenty of readers do praise King's writing as literature, even as others deem it simply entertainment. In short, artistic standards differ. To be sure, some works have been constantly admired through the years; regarded as classics, they are frequently taught in literature classes. *Hamlet* and other plays by William Shakespeare are obvious examples. But in the last twenty years, much controversy has arisen over the *literary canon*, those works taught again and again. Are there good reasons why the canon has consisted mostly of works by white men? Or have the principles of selection been skewed by sexism and racism? Should the canon be changed to accommodate a greater range of authors? Or should literary studies resist having any canon at all? These questions have provoked various answers and continued debate.

Also in question are attempts to separate literature from *nonfiction*. Much nonfiction shows imagination and relies on devices found in novels, short stories, poems, and plays. The last few years have seen the emergence of the term *creative nonfiction* as a synonym for essays, autobiographies, histories, and journalistic accounts that use evocative language and strong narratives. Conversely, works of fiction, poetry, and drama may center on real-life events. For example, beginning with James Wright's "Lying in a Hammock," several of the poems in our book can easily be seen as autobiographical. Perhaps you have suspected already that the speaker in Wright's poem is Wright himself. In numerous interviews, Wright admitted as much. He acknowledged that he based the poem on his own experience of lying in a hammock, which really did lead him to think "I have wasted my life."

A note of caution is in order. While testimony such as Wright's can be illuminating, it should be used prudently. In crucial respects, Wright's poem still differs from Wright's life. The text is a representation of his experience, not the experience itself. His particular choice and arrangement of words continue to merit study, especially because he could have depicted his experience in plenty of other ways. As critic Charles Altieri notes, important to specify are the ways in which a poem is "binding the forms of syntax to the possibilities of feeling." Keep in mind, too, that the author of a work is not always the ideal guide to it. After all, the work may matter to its readers by raising for them issues and ideas that the author did not foresee. Besides, often the author's comments about the text leave certain aspects of it unexplained. Though Wright disclosed his poem's origins, readers must still decide how to connect its various images to its final line. Even so, "Lying in a Hammock" confirms that a literary work can stem from actual circumstances, whatever use the reader makes of facts about them.

Some people argue, however, that literature about real events is still "literary" because it inspires contemplation rather than action. This view of literature has traditionally been summed up as "art for art's sake." This notion brushes aside, however, all the poems, novels, short stories, and plays that encourage audiences to undertake certain acts. Included in our book, for example, is Sherman Alexie's "Capital Punishment," a poem designed to spark resistance to the death penalty. True, not every poem is so conspicuously action-oriented. Wright's "Lying in a Hammock" seems more geared toward reflection, especially because the speaker is physically reclining while he observes nature and ponders his life. But readers may take even this poem as an incitement to change their behavior, so that they can feel they have not wasted their own lives.

In our book, we resist endorsing a single definition of *literature*. Rather, we encourage you to review and perhaps rethink what the term means to you. At the same time, to expand the realm of literature, we include several essays in addition to short stories, poems, and plays. We also present numerous critical commentaries as well as various historical documents. Throughout the book, we invite you to make connections among these different kinds of texts. You need not treat them as altogether separate species.

What Makes Literature "Literature"?

We have suggested that, in some respects, literature can resemble other writing. So, too, can it resemble ordinary speech. Still, literature can be viewed as a distinct category, even if controversies arise over what specific texts belong to it. Usually, works classified as literature permit the reader to treat their characters as imaginary. Just as often, these works' use of language is especially skillful and challenging. Through their style, they dramatically depict people, situations, and settings, emotionally drawing their readers in. At the same time, many of the words in such texts can have more than one meaning. They might be ambiguous, symbolic, or metaphorical. Furthermore, the main characters are often complicated, even mysterious. Their acts, relationships, and motives defy simple diagnosis. Typically, just as complex is any "lesson" these works teach. They illuminate life, but they do so by showing how it resists reduction to clichés or other slogans. Furthermore, the basic design of these works may not be immediately clear. Their patterns may be detectable only after repeated reading. Overall, a literary work tends to make its readers *analyze* it, *interpret* it. They may then disagree about its meaning and impact. Indeed, we hope that our own literary selections will spark debates in your class.

To point out a literary work's special features, we turn to a poem that dramatizes the exasperation many people feel when wildlife destroys their farms, gardens, or yards. Entitled "Woodchucks," the poem is by Maxine Kumin (1925–2014) and appears in her 1992 collection *Our Ground Time Here Will Be Brief.*

MAXINE KUMIN

Woodchucks

Gassing the woodchucks didn't turn out right.
The knockout bomb from the Feed and Grain Exchange
was featured as merciful, quick at the bone
and the case we had against them was airtight,
both exits shoehorned shut with puddingstone,°   5
but they had a sub-sub-basement out of range.

Next morning they turned up again, no worse
for the cyanide than we for our cigarettes
and state-store Scotch, all of us up to scratch.
They brought down the marigolds as a matter of course   10
and then took over the vegetable patch
nipping the broccoli shoots, beheading the carrots.

The food from our mouths, I said, righteously thrilling
to the feel of the .22, the bullets' neat noses.
I, a lapsed pacifist fallen from grace   15
puffed with Darwinian° pieties for killing,
now drew a bead on the littlest woodchuck's face.
He died down in the everbearing roses.

Ten minutes later I dropped the mother. She
flipflopped in the air and fell, her needle teeth   20
still hooked in a leaf of early Swiss chard.
Another baby next. O one-two-three
the murderer inside me rose up hard,
the hawkeye killer came on stage forthwith.

There's one chuck left. Old wily fellow, he keeps   25
me cocked and ready day after day after day.
All night I hunt his humped-up form. I dream
I sight along the barrel in my sleep.
If only they'd all consented to die unseen
gassed underground the quiet Nazi way.   *[1972]*   30

5 puddingstone: Cement mixed with pebbles.   **16 Darwinian:** Charles Darwin (1809–1882), an English naturalist who first theorized about evolution and natural selection.

≡ THINKING ABOUT THE TEXT

Here are just a few of the questions that "Woodchucks" provokes. Choose one of them. Then, take ten minutes or so and freewrite an answer to it, supporting your statements with specific words from the poem.

1. In line 4, the word *case* evidently refers to a method of entrapping the woodchucks, but probably it also refers to the speaker's reasons for hunting them. How good are her reasons? What might be the "case" for *not* killing these animals?

2. What key changes — psychological as well as physical — does the speaker go through in her campaign to get rid of the woodchucks?

3. To what extent does the speaker suggest that her feelings are mixed and even in conflict?

4. Presumably the last line alludes to the mass exterminations of the Holocaust. What would you say to someone who argues that this is an inappropriate, even tasteless, way to end a poem about woodchucks?

Of course, Kumin is by no means the only person who has ever written about the ethical and practical issues involved in killing woodchucks. For example, in a lengthy June 5, 2008, *New York Times* article entitled "Peter Rabbit Must Die," reporter Joyce Wadler tells stories about various people she interviewed who had to decide whether and how to exterminate woodchucks or other invaders of their turf. In 2013, a Wisconsin legislator drafted legislation that would remove woodchucks from the state's protected species list and permit hunting or trapping of them ten months out of the year. As you might expect, his proposed bill proved controversial; numerous bloggers argued for and against his proposed bill, the fate of which remains hanging at the moment we write. But Kumin's poem differs from a news report, a statute, or an opinion piece about woodchucks in ways that for many readers would establish it as more literary:

- While news articles such as Wadler's are arranged in paragraphs, "Woodchucks" proceeds through stanzas. This kind of structure, common in poetry, draws attention to words that begin and end lines.

- Like many poems, Kumin's also includes words that stand out because they rhyme (e.g., "scratch" and "patch," "grace" and "face"), virtually echo (e.g., "Gassing" and "gassed"), or begin with the same sound, a pattern known as alliteration (e.g., "bomb" and "bone," "food" and "feel," "neat" and "noses").

- In addition, some words in this poem seem to have multiple meanings. For example, "right" in the first line can mean not only "efficient" but also "ethical," just as "airtight" can mean "perfect" in a *practical* sense as well as "indisputable" in a *philosophical* sense.

- In reading Wadler's article or the legislator's bill or the blogs debating it, you are apt to be chiefly aware of these texts' *content*. Most readers of Kumin's poem are at least as concerned with its *form*. Most of them would linger over the language of "Woodchucks" more than they would over the news report's style. Noteworthy, for instance, is how the speaker looks back ironically on her own language ("The food from our mouths, I said, righteously thrilling"), thereby casting doubt on its logic. And of course, her concluding analogy to the Nazis jolts;

it pushes readers to wonder how much the entire poem has been about Hitler's genocidal regime.

- Many news articles describe their subjects' thoughts rather broadly. For instance, the typical person in Wadler's piece is someone who wants to get rid of intrusive woodchucks but looks for humane ways of doing the deed. Kumin's speaker, on the other hand, seems to go through a complex series of psychological stages; her thoughts seem more intricate than those of Wadler's interviewees.

- Kumin's speaker, like many characters in literature, is hard to pigeon-hole. Wadler identifies her interview subjects as particular individuals, but like many reporters she ultimately seems more interested in them as examples of basic human types. Describing an artist who actually spoke to the woodchucks on his property — warning them to flee before he shot them — she says that this man's tale "is not as unusual as some would like to believe." She thereby suggests that he is a common sort of person afflicted by pests: the sensitive soul driven to fight back. Similarly, in describing some opponents of the proposed Wisconsin bill who attended a hearing about it, Associated Press reporter Todd Richmond labeled them as merely "a handful of animal lovers" who were "blasting the measure." Hardly a profile of psychological depth! Given the words that Kumin's speaker uses and the various patterns they take, her speaker requires more figuring out.

- Whereas news writers surely expect you to assume that their interviewees are real, you don't have to take Kumin's speaker as such. This figure may reflect the poet's own experience to some extent, for Kumin operated a farm in New Hampshire and so perhaps hunted pests herself. Still, you are free to see her central character as fictive. This possibility enables you to speculate long and broadly about the speaker's psyche — including ideas and feelings of hers that she may not be quite aware of. Notice that after referring to "we," she eventually shifts to "I," a change that may be unconscious but that nonetheless implies she has become personally obsessed. Because you can see the poem's speaker as imaginary, you are also free to entertain various responses to her. If she were an actual person — someone you knew or might someday meet — you might feel compelled to make a single, fast judgment about her. The poem, however, lets you access her thinking while not pressuring you to decide quickly how ethical she is. Your attitudes toward her can shift, clash, and blend more than if her acts had real-life effects. In this respect, "Woodchucks" is a thought experiment, as are most literary works. Still, in exercising your interpretive powers, such texts help you cope with the world. They heighten your awareness of the ways in which it, too, demands careful study.

We are *not* saying that poems are always superior to news reports and other true-life texts. That would be an excessive claim. But, as "Woodchucks" demonstrates, literary works often lead you to grapple with more extensive and trickier questions—thereby offering you much to address in your own writing.

To help you think further about what may distinguish a work of literature from other kinds of writing, let's turn to a very short story. Its author, Lydia Davis (b. 1947), has translated a number of French masterpieces, including the novels *Madame Bovary* and *Swann's Way*. But she herself is a writer of fiction. Above all, she has produced many brief stories, all of them examples of what several literary critics today call "microfiction," "sudden fiction," "short shorts," or "flash fiction." "The Outing" appeared in her 1997 collection *Almost No Memory*, and subsequently she included it in her retrospective volume *The Collected Stories of Lydia Davis* (2009). As you read, consider these questions: Do you consider Davis's text to be *literature?* Why, or why not? You might bear in mind a comment that Davis made in a 2008 interview with *The Believer* magazine. "It's a hard thing to define," she remarked, "but to be simple about it, I would say a story has to have a bit of narrative, if only 'she says,' and then enough of a creation of a different time and place to transport the reader." By your own standards, is "The Outing" indeed a *story?* Why, or why not?

LYDIA DAVIS
The Outing

An outburst of anger near the road, a refusal to speak on the path, a silence in the pine woods, a silence across the old railroad bridge, an attempt to be friendly in the water, a refusal to end the argument on the flat stones, a cry of anger on the steep bank of dirt, a weeping among the bushes.   *[1997]*

Why Study Literature in a College Writing Course?

We assume you are reading this book in a course aimed at helping you write. Quite likely the course is meant to prepare you for writing assignments throughout college, including papers in fields beyond English. It's natural to wonder how reading literature serves this purpose.

Much academic writing is, in fact, based on reading. You'll find the two interconnected in course after course. Many classes will ask you to produce essays that analyze published texts. To *analyze* means going beyond your first impressions, carefully noting a text's ideas, techniques, and effects. You'll also find yourself needing to *synthesize*: that is, to trace how the text is patterned, as well as how it relates to other works. Together, these acts of analysis and synthesis have been called reading *closely*, a process we explain and model in Chapter 2. We encourage you to practice this method with the selections in our book.

Often, college courses will ask you to write about some text that isn't easily understood. The purpose of your paper will be to help other readers of the text grasp its meanings and, perhaps, judge its worth. Literature is a good training ground for these skills of interpretation and evaluation. The poems, stories, plays, and essays in this book repeatedly invite inquiry. They don't settle for delivering simple straightforward messages. Rather, they offer puzzles, complications, metaphors, symbols, and mysteries, thereby recognizing that life is complex. In particular, literary works encourage you to ponder the multiple dimensions of language: how, for example, a word's meaning can vary depending on context. Furthermore, much literature can help you understand your own life and conduct it better. In this capacity, literature serves as "equipment for living," scholar-critic Kenneth Burke's description of its function.

Some people *dislike* literature because they find it too vague and indirect. They resent that it often forces them to figure out symbols and implications when they would rather have ideas presented outright. Perhaps you wish the speaker in Wright's poem had made clear why his observations prompted him to criticize himself. But in life, truth can be complicated and elusive. In many ways, literature is most realistic when it suggests the same. Besides, many readers — perhaps including you — appreciate literature most when it resists simple decoding, forcing them to adopt new assumptions and learn new methods of analysis. Indeed, throughout this book we suggest that the most interesting and profitable conversations about literature are those in which the issues are not easily resolved. One of the best things your course can provide you and your classmates is the chance to exchange insights about texts such as Wright's.

We have been suggesting that one value of studying literature in a writing class is that it often engages not just thought but feeling. The two interweave so that readers find themselves engaging in interpretation and evaluation because they *care* about lives depicted in the text. Most of the works in this book appeal to your emotions, encouraging you to identify with certain characters, to be disturbed by others, and to wonder what happens next in the plot. Indeed, many readers of literature prize the moments that make them them laugh or cry or gasp as well as think. To be sure, it can be argued that the most worthwhile literature gets us to comprehend, and perhaps even appreciate, certain kinds of people who would normally confuse or disturb us. Perhaps you would never say to yourself, "I have wasted my life"; all the same, you may find it valuable to analyze how Wright's speaker reaches this conclusion. "When it's the real thing," critic Frank Lentricchia suggests, "literature enlarges us, strips the film of familiarity from the world; creates bonds of sympathy with all kinds, even with evil characters, who we learn are all in the family." This "enlargement" is both intellectual *and* emotional.

Finally, writing about literature is good training for other fields because literary analysis often involves taking an interdisciplinary perspective. A typical interpretation of James Wright's poem, for example, will bring in principles of psychology to explain the speaker's frame of mind. Similarly, to evaluate his statement "I have wasted my life," readers find themselves grappling with the philosophical question of what constitutes a "productive" or "good" life. Moreover, the poem's farm setting has economic, political, historical, and sociological significance, for much less of the world's population performs agricultural labor than was the case a century ago. Wright's brief text can even play a role in studies of cross-cultural relationships, for as Sven Birkerts has pointed out, the poem is one of several experiments the poet tried with Chinese literary forms.

What Can *You* Do to Make Literature Matter to Others?

In an 1895 essay called "The Art of Fiction," the American novelist, short-story writer, and critic Henry James wrote, "Art lives upon discussion, upon experiment, upon curiosity, upon variety of attempt, upon the exchange of views and the comparison of standpoints." Certainly James was suggesting that the creators of literature play a big role in making it matter. But he was suggesting, too, that plenty of other people contribute to literature's impact. Today, these people include publishers, printers, agents, advertisers, librarians, professional reviewers, bookstore staff, Internet chat groups, and even show-business figures such as Oprah Winfrey, who has interested millions of viewers in participating in her "book club." Teachers of literature also make it mat-ter — or at least they try to. Perhaps your parents or other family members have contributed to your appreciation of certain literary texts; many adults introduce their children and grandchildren to books they loved when young. Moreover, friends often recommend works of literature to one another.

Again, we concede that some people think of literature negatively, believ-ing that it matters in a way they don't like. The ancient Greek philosopher Plato wanted to ban poets from his ideal republic because he thought they merely imitated truth. Throughout subsequent history, various groups have tried to abolish or censor much literature. In communities across the contemporary United States, pressure groups have succeeded in removing particular novels from library shelves, including classics such as Mark Twain's *Adventures of Huckleberry Finn* and J. D. Salinger's *The Catcher in the Rye*. History has also seen many writers killed, jailed, or harassed for their work. In recent years, the most conspicuous example of such persecution has been the Ayatollah Khomeini's indictment of author Salman Rushdie. In 1989, the ayatollah was so enraged by the portrayal of Islam in Rushdie's novel *The Satanic Verses* that he com-manded his followers to hunt Rushdie down and slay him. Even after the ayatollah died, Rushdie was in danger, for the *fatwa* against him remained in effect. Not until eight years after the original edict did the Iranian government back away from it. At present, Rushdie still enjoys only a limited measure of safety, and the affair stands as a reminder that some writers risk their lives. Ironically, the ayatollah's execution order was a sort of homage to literature, a fearsome way of crediting it with the power to shape thinking.

Our book aims to help you join the conversations that Henry James saw as nourishing literature. More specifically, our book focuses on helping you argue about literature, whether your audience is your classmates, your teacher, or other people. While arguments involve real or potential disagreement, they need not be waged like wars. When we use the term *argument* in this book, we have in mind civilized efforts through which people try to make their views persuasive. When you argue about literature, you are carefully reasoning with others, helping them see how a certain text should matter to them.

In particular, we have much to say about you as a writer. A key goal of your course, we assume, is to help you compose more effective texts of your own. By writing arguments about literature, you make it matter to others. Moreover, you learn about yourself as you analyze a literary text and negotiate other readers' views of it. We emphasize that, at its best, arguing is a process of inquiry for everyone involved. Both you and your audience may wind up changing your minds.

≡ WRITING ASSIGNMENTS

1. Write a brief essay in which you explain what you value in literature by focusing on why you like a particular literary work. Don't worry about whether you are defining *literature* correctly. This exercise will help you begin to review the values you hold as you read a work that you regard as literary.

2. Sometimes a literary work matters to you in one way when you first read it and in another way when you read it again. Write a brief essay in which you discuss a work that you interpreted differently when you re-read it. What significance did it have for you the first time? What was its significance later? What about your life changed between the two readings? If you cannot think of a literary work, choose a film you have seen.

3. Write a brief essay in which you identify the values that a previous literature teacher of yours seemed to hold. Be sure to identify, too, ways in which the teacher expressed these values. You may want to bring up one or more specific events that took place in the teacher's classroom.

4. Many bookstores sell computer-instruction manuals. Examine one of these. Do you consider it literature? Write a brief essay answering this question. Be sure to explain how you are defining *literature* and to refer to the manual's specific features.

5. Visit a bookstore at your school or in your town. Spend at least half an hour looking at books in various sections of the store, noting how the publishers of these works try to make them matter. Look at such things as the books' physical formats, the language on their covers, and any introductory material they include. Write a brief essay in which you identify and evaluate the strategies for "mattering" used by at least three of these books.

6. Visit a Web site that includes readers' comments about particular works of fiction. A good example is www.amazon.com, a commercial online "bookstore." Another good site is Oprah Winfrey's, www.oprah.com, which features extensive exchanges about novels she has chosen for her "book club." At whatever site you visit, choose a novel or short-story collection that has attracted many reader comments. Write a brief essay in which you identify the values that seem reflected in the comments. In

what respects does literature seem to matter to these readers? What do they evidently hope to find in it?

≡ SUMMING UP: WHAT IS LITERATURE?

- **Literature encompasses poetry, fiction, and plays — but may also encompass other genres, such as nonfiction essays.** This book does not endorse a single definition of *literature* but encourages you to review and perhaps rethink what the term means to you. (pp. 4–7)

- **Literary texts tend to show certain characteristics more than other texts, such as news articles, do.** For example, they call attention to their form; they explore the multiple meanings of words; they present psychological complexity; and they require interpretation. (pp. 7–11)

- **Studying literature in a college writing course makes sense for several reasons.** Many other courses require you to write about reading; literature offers you ground for developing skills of interpretation and evaluation that many college writing assignments demand; literature serves as "equipment for living"; reading it engages both thought and feeling; and literary analysis is often interdisciplinary. (pp. 11–13)

- **The *literary canon* — works taught again and again as great art — is nowadays being reevaluated**. (p. 6)

- **Understanding literature involves collaboration with other readers and comparison with other texts.** (pp. 12–14)

- **Thinking about literature is enhanced and clarified by writing about it.** (p. 12)

- **The most effective arguments about literature involve inquiry, not rancor and battle.** (p. 13)

CHAPTER 2

How to Read Closely

Courses in many disciplines ask for *close reading*. But literature classes strongly emphasize it — one reason they are good preparation for other fields. Nevertheless, the steps involved in close reading are not always clear to students. Perhaps you have been told to engage in this process without knowing what it entails. Because close reading is central to literary studies, plays a big role in other courses, and yet remains murky for many students, this chapter both explains it and models it.

If you are taking a course that asks you to *write* about the literary works you study, close reading of them will help you form ideas about them worth spreading to *your* audiences. Such reading will also help you decide what details of these texts will best support your points about them. So, as we proceed to explain close reading, we treat it mainly as what some would call a method of invention. It's a way for you, as a *writer*, to discover things to say about literature.

Basic Strategies for Close Reading

Actually, close reading consists of not one strategy but several. All of them can help you gain insights into a literary work, which you might then convey through your writing. You need not follow these strategies in the order we list them here, but try each of them.

1. Make predictions as you read. That is, guess what will happen and how the text will turn out. If you wind up being surprised, fine. You may get a richer understanding of the text as you reflect on how it *defies* your expectations.

2. Reread the text. Reread the text several times, focusing each time on a different element of the text and using at least one of these occasions to read aloud. Few readers of a literary work can immediately see everything important and interesting in it. You greatly increase your chances of getting ideas about a text if you read it again and again. At first, you may be preoccupied with following the plot or with figuring out the text's main theme. Only by examining the text repeatedly may you notice several of its other aspects, including features that really stir your thoughts. But don't try to study everything in the text each time you look at it. Use each reading of it to study just one characteristic. In an early stage, for example, you might trace the text's repetitions, and then you might use a later reading to pinpoint its ambiguous words. This division of labor can, in the end, generate many insights that a less focused approach would not.

Reading all of the text or portions of it out loud gives you a better sense of how the text is manipulating language. Reading aloud is especially useful in the case of poems, for you may detect rhymes or soundalike words that you would not notice when reading silently.

3. Test the text against your own experiences.   Keep in mind your experiences, beliefs, assumptions, and values as you read the text, but note ways that it challenges or complicates these things. When you first read a particular literary work, your interpretations and judgments are bound to be influenced by your personal background. This includes your beliefs, assumptions, and values, as well as things that have happened to you. Indeed, many people read a literary work hoping they can personally identify with the characters, situations, and views it presents. This is an understandable goal. Pay attention, though, to details of the text that do *not* match your life and current thinking. After all, the author may be deliberately challenging or complicating readers' habitual attitudes. In any case, parts of the text that are hard to identify with will often provide you with great subjects when you write about the work. Bear in mind, though, that you will not interest your readers if you simply criticize characters in the work or sneer at other elements of it. In particular, try not to sum up characters with negative labels such as *immoral*, *weird*, or *sick*. These terms often strike readers as reflecting mere prejudice — a poor substitute for careful analysis of human complexity.

4. Look for patterns in the text and disruptions of them.   Many a literary work is organized by various patterns, which may not be evident on first reading. In fact, you might not detect a number of these patterns until you read the text several times. You may even see these better if you move back and forth in the text instead of just reading it straight through. Typically, a literary work's patterns include repetitions of words and of actions; oppositions; words similar or related in meaning; and technical methods of organization (such as rhyme schemes or frequent use of flashbacks). Just as important to note are moments in the text that are inconsistent with one or more of its patterns. Locate and think about places where the work makes a significant shift in meaning, imagery, tone, plot, a character's behavior, narrative point of view, or even physical format (for example, a change in rhyme scheme).

5. Note ambiguities.   These are places where the text's meaning is not crystal clear and therefore calls for interpretation: for example, words that can have more than one definition; symbols that have multiple implications; and actions that suggest various things about a character.

6. Consider the author's alternatives.   That is, think about what the author *could* have done and yet did not do. The author of a literary work faces all sorts of decisions in composing it. And as you study the work, you will have more to say about it if you think about those choices. Try, then, to compare the author's handling of particular passages to other possible treatments of them. By considering, for example, why the author chose a certain word over others, you may better detect implications and effects of the author's actual language. Similarly, by reflecting on how the author *might* have portrayed a certain character more simplistically, you strengthen your ability to analyze the character's variety of traits.

7. Ask questions.   As you read, generate questions that have more than one possible answer. When we first read a literary work, most of us try to get comfortable with it. We search for passages that are clear; we groan when we encounter ones that are mysterious or confusing. Sooner or later, though, we must confront puzzles in the text if we are to analyze it in depth. Furthermore, if we plan to *write* about the text, we are more likely to come up with ideas worth communicating to our readers if we present ourselves as helping them deal with matters *not* immediately clear. After all, our audience will not need our analysis if it centers on what's obvious. Therefore, list multiple questions that the work raises for you, especially ones that have various possible answers. Then, if you focus on addressing one of these questions in your writing—providing and supporting your own particular answer to it—your readers will find value in turning to *your* text. Furthermore, when you come across literary passages that seem easy to understand, consider how they might actually involve more than one possible meaning. Even little words may prove ambiguous and, therefore, worth analyzing in your writing. Of course, you may have to consult a dictionary in order to see the different meanings that a word can have.

The questions you come up with need hardly be restricted to matters of the work's "theme." After all, most any literary text worth studying can't be reduced to a single message. Often, such texts play with multiple ideas, perhaps emphasizing tensions among them. Therefore, it may make more sense for you to refer to a work's *themes*. Actually, as we have been suggesting throughout our catalog of reading strategies, any literary text has several other features. As a writer, you may wind up with much more to say about a literary work if you consider one or more of these other elements: for example, facts obscured or absent in the text; possible definitions of key words; symbols; patterns; evaluations to be made of the characters or the overall work; the text's historical and cultural context; the text's genre; its relevance to current political debates; and cause-effect relationships. In the next chapter, we explain these elements at greater length, identifying them as *issues* you might write about.

8. Jot down possible answers.   Even while reading the text, begin developing and pulling together your thoughts by informally writing about it. See if you can generate not only good questions but also tentative answers to them. Writing need not be the final outcome of your reflections on a literary work. You can jot down ideas about the text even as you first encounter it. Such informal, preliminary writing can actually help you generate insights into the text that you would not have achieved simply by scanning it. The following are some of the specific things you might do:

- *Make notes in the text itself.*   A common method is to mark key passages, either by underlining these passages or by running a highlighter over them. Both ways of marking are popular because they help readers recall main features of the text. But use these techniques moderately if you use them at all, for marking lots of passages will leave you unable to distinguish the really important parts of the text. Also, try "talking back" to the text in its margins. Next to particular passages, you might jot down words of your own, indicating any feelings and questions you have about those parts. On any page of the text, you might circle related words and then draw lines between these words to emphasize their connection. If a word or an idea shows up on numerous pages, you might circle it each time. Furthermore, try cross-referencing by listing on at least one page the numbers of all those pages where the word or idea appears.
- *As you read the text, occasionally look away from it and jot down anything in it you recall.*   This memory exercise lets you review your developing impressions of the text. When you turn back to its actual words, you may find that you have distorted or overlooked aspects of it that you should take into account.
- *At various moments in your reading, freewrite about the text for ten minutes or so.*   Spontaneously explore your preliminary thoughts and feelings about it, as well as any personal experiences the text leads you to recall. One logical moment to do freewriting is when you have finished reading the text. But you do not have to wait until then; as you read, you might pause occasionally to freewrite. This way, you give yourself an opportunity to develop and review your thoughts about the text early on.
- *Create a "dialectical notebook."*   So named by composition theorist Ann Berthoff, it involves using pages of your regular notebook in a particular way. On each page, draw a line down the middle to create two columns. In the left column, list various details of the text: specifically, words, images, characters, and events that strike you. In the right column, jot down for each detail one or more sentences indicating *why* you were drawn to it. Take as many pages as you need to record and reflect on your observations. You can also use the two-column format to carry out a dialogue with yourself about the text. This is an especially good way to ponder aspects of the text that you find confusing, mysterious, or complex.
- *Play with the text by revising it.*   Doing so will make you more aware of options that the author rejected and will give you a better sense of the moves that the author chose to make. Specifically, you might rearrange parts of the text, add to it, change some of its words, or shift its narrative point of view. After you revise the text, compare your alternative version with the original, considering especially differences in their effects.

Close Readings of a Poem

To demonstrate what it means to read closely, we present observations that various students made about a poem. Even before you look at the students' comments, try doing what they did. We asked each of them to read the poem several times (step 2, pp. 16–17). More specifically, they devoted each of their readings to a particular element of the poem:

- First, they focused on how it fulfilled or defied their predictions.
- Then, they considered how the poem matched and diverged from their personal backgrounds.
- They then traced the poem's patterns, as well as breaks from these.
- They noted places where the poem is puzzling, ambiguous, or unclear.
- Next, they identified at least one choice that the poem's author faced.
- They then settled on questions that have more than one possible answer and that therefore might be worth addressing in a formal essay about the poem.
- Finally, pulling their thoughts together, they came up with tentative answers to these questions, which they might then have developed in a formal essay.

Again, the order of these stages is not the only one possible; the important thing is to go through them all. At each stage of their reading, the students also did a few minutes of freewriting, using this strategy to develop thoughts about whatever element was their focus. Following the poem are excerpts from these informal reflections.

The poem is by Sharon Olds (b. 1942), who teaches at New York University and has produced many volumes of verse. "Summer Solstice, New York City" appears in her 1987 book, *The Gold Cell*. Again, like most of the other literature we include in Part One, the poem deals with work — in this case, efforts by New York City police to prevent a suicide.

SHARON OLDS

Summer Solstice, New York City

By the end of the longest day of the year he could not stand it,
he went up the iron stairs through the roof of the building
and over the soft, tarry surface
to the edge, put one leg over the complex green tin cornice
and said if they came a step closer that was it.   5
Then the huge machinery of the earth began to work for his life,
the cops came in their suits blue-gray as the sky on a cloudy evening,
and one put on a bullet-proof vest, a
black shell around his own life,
life of his children's father, in case   10

the man was armed, and one, slung with a
rope like the sign of his bounden duty,
came up out of a hole in the top of the neighboring building
like the gold hole they say is in the top of the head,
and began to lurk toward the man who wanted to die.   15
The tallest cop approached him directly,
softly, slowly, talking to him, talking, talking,
while the man's leg hung over the lip of the next world
and the crowd gathered in the street, silent, and the
hairy net with its implacable grid was   20
unfolded near the curb and spread out and
stretched as the sheet is prepared to receive at birth.
Then they all came a little closer
where he squatted next to his death, his shirt
glowing its milky glow like something   25
growing in a dish at night in the dark in a lab and then
everything stopped
as his body jerked and he
stepped down from the parapet and went toward them
and they closed on him, I thought they were going to   30
beat him up, as a mother whose child has been
lost will scream at the child when it's found, they
took him by the arms and held him up and
leaned him against the wall of the chimney and the
tall cop lit a cigarette   35
in his own mouth, and gave it to him, and
then they all lit cigarettes, and the
red, glowing ends burned like the
tiny campfires we lit at night
back at the beginning of the world.   *[1987]*   40

Applying the Strategies

MAKE PREDICTIONS

KATHERINE: I was really tense as I read this poem because I thought the
man would jump at the end and then we would get a horrible description
of him splattering on the sidewalk. I didn't predict the cops would
succeed in talking him out of it. When the poet says he "jerked," that
could easily have been the start of his jumping, but thank God he is
instead stepping back. I'm glad that they persuaded him to remain alive.

MARIA: I was like the poem's speaker expecting that they would physically
grab him and treat him roughly, and so I was surprised when they were
nice to him and even offered him a cigarette.

TREVOR: I predicted that the poem would end with the man still on the edge
of the building deciding whether or not to jump off, because I think that

in a way it would be neat to leave us guessing whether he's really going to do it. I wasn't all that surprised when he pulled back and joined the cops, because that was certainly one possible outcome. However, I was surprised when the author had them smoking cigarettes at the end like "at the beginning of the world." I didn't expect that image of prehistoric people to show up here at the end.

REFLECT ON ONE'S PERSONAL BACKGROUND

JAMES: It's hard for me to sympathize with someone who commits suicide, especially because someone at my high school killed himself and all of his friends and family were terribly saddened by what he did. I think that no matter how bad things get for you, there's a way out if only you look for it. Suicide is no answer, and it hurts the people you leave behind. So I'm glad that the man in this poem winds up not committing suicide. If he had, I would have thought less of him.

CARLA: I vaguely remember seeing some movies in which a character stands on a ledge and thinks about jumping off it. In real life, I've never seen something like that. What this poem most brings to my mind are reports I heard about people jumping off the World Trade Towers to escape being killed by fire. Of course, they died anyway. As I recall, TV didn't show these people jumping, out of respect for them I guess, and I'm glad that I didn't have to see this happen. Still, I'm aware that it did. Anyway, the man thinking about suicide in this poem isn't facing the same situation. He can easily live if he wants to.

BOB: I guess the police are obligated to try rescuing the man even if they have to risk their own lives. I've never been in this position, so I'm not sure how I'd feel if I'd been assigned to save the man in this poem. Though I disapprove of suicide, maybe I wouldn't have the guts to try confronting him on the edge of the building, and I'm not sure I could talk to him calmly, because if he did jump he might take me down with him. I admire the ability of these cops to stay cool and talk him into joining them. I'm also impressed that they then treat him like a friend instead of like a potentially violent nutcase that they have to get under control through force. If it were me, I think I might want to throw him to the ground and pin his arms so that he wouldn't try something like that again.

READ FOR PATTERNS AND FOR BREAKS IN PATTERNS

DOMINICK: This may be too little a thing to think about, but I notice that the word "it" is repeated in the beginning section of the poem. The first line ends with "it," and line 5 does also. I'm not sure what is meant by "it" in "he could not stand it." Obviously on one level "it" here means his life, but he seems to have something specific about his life in mind when he says this, but we don't learn what he's specifically thinking of. The second "it" seems to refer to the fact that he will kill himself if they come closer. But that reference too isn't as clear as it might be. I see that later on "it" comes up again as a word for the cigarette that the cop gives to the man (after lighting it in his own mouth, yuck!). Maybe we're supposed to connect this "it" to the "its" at the start.

BOB: After the middle of the poem we start to get a lot of birth imagery. The word "birth" is even stated, and a little later there's the image of something "growing" in a lab dish.

JARED: "World" is repeated. In the middle of the poem, there's a reference to "the next world," and the very last word of the poem is "world," meaning the world where we currently live.

COURTNEY: I found a number of references to children. There are the words "his children's father," and then toward the end the word "child" is repeated, though this time it's a mother's child. And then the last line refers to "the beginning of the world," as if the world is a child that has just been born.

FRANK: It's funny that the word "end" is one of the first words of the poem, and then the word "beginning" is one of its last words. I can more easily imagine the reverse. Anyway, "end" and "beginning" are opposites that the poet seems to want us to think about. Come to think of it, there is mention of "ends" near the conclusion, but these are the "ends" of the men's cigarettes and not the end of the world.

ALEX: The word "day" appears in the first line (it's "the longest day of the year"), but later there is the word "night" ("growing in a dish at night"), and then "night" is in the next-to-last line. Ironically, things get brighter (the man decides to live) as the poem moves from "day" to "night."

PAUL: As the poem moves along, there's a shift in pronouns. In the first half or so, we get forms of "he" and "they." Then the word "I" suddenly appears, and then the next-to-last line has the word "we."

READ FOR PUZZLES, AMBIGUITIES, AND UNCLEAR MOMENTS

KATHERINE: I just don't learn enough about this man's thinking to know why he's even planning to kill himself. This is something the poem doesn't make clear. But I guess the "I" of the poem doesn't know the man's thinking either, and meanwhile she's in the position of possibly witnessing the man falling to the pavement! Maybe the author doesn't tell us exactly why the man wants to commit suicide because we can then identify more easily with him. We can think about moments when we were incredibly unhappy, whether or not we were depressed by the same things he is.

TIM: We're told that the cop approaching the man is doing a lot of talking, but we don't find out what he specifically says, even though this may have played a big role in getting the man to step back and live.

HILLARY: The gold hole sounds like something from folklore, but I don't know the background.

RACHEL: I'm wondering how much we're supposed to focus on the speaker's reactions to what's going on, or whether we should think more about the man and the policemen.

READ FOR THE AUTHOR'S CHOICES

KATHERINE: Olds could have had the man jump and die. Even if this poem is based on a real incident where the man decided to live, she could have changed what happened. Also, if she still went with the rescue version, she could have had the policemen treat the man roughly after they rescued him.

PAUL: The word "I" could have appeared more often throughout the poem, especially because the poem is written from the point of view of someone observing this suicide attempt.

TIM: We might have been told why the man was thinking of killing himself and what the cops said to him. I realize this information would be hard for the speaker of the poem to give us, since she's just observing the whole business from the street below. Still, maybe Olds could have found a way of telling us at least a little more about what the men on the roof were saying and thinking.

BOB: The author didn't have to use birth images. She could have described this event without them. In fact, death imagery seems more appropriate when a poem is about a possible suicide.

GENERATE QUESTIONS THAT HAVE MORE THAN ONE POSSIBLE ANSWER

JENNIFER: What might the poet be trying to convey when she ends the poem with the image of "the beginning of the world"? The last line really captures my attention.

PAUL: What should we conclude when the pronouns shift from "he" and "they" to "I" and finally "we"?

VICTORIA: How should we interpret the poem's repeated references to children and to parents (both father and mother)?

BOB: How important are the cops as characters in this poem?

STATE TENTATIVE ANSWERS

JENNIFER: Maybe the poet is telling us that each time you overcome depression and decide to go on living, it's like the rebirth of the world, and you're rejoining a "we" in the sense of rejoining the rest of humanity.

PAUL: I believe that the speaker comes to identify with the man and his rescuers and then sees herself and them as all part of a common humanity, as if we all have to decide when to risk our lives and when to preserve them.

VICTORIA: In a paper, I could argue that these child and parent references are used by Olds to suggest that even as adults, we sometimes act like children and sometimes have to act like a parent, but Olds evidently prefers that we not act like a very stern parent.

BOB: The cops are very important in this poem. So much of it is about what they do and how they maybe feel. They're required to save the guy, they're part of "huge machinery," and one of them might end up sacrificing the "life of his children's father" just in order to rescue someone who wants to kill himself anyway, but then the cops turn out to be quite sympathetic toward the guy. There's even this odd religious-type moment with the sharing of a cigarette and then all the men lighting up. I think I would focus my paper on how the cops do their duty to preserve life even when they probably didn't want to, and then something spiritual happens because they didn't give up on the job they were assigned.

DAN: If I'm remembering correctly, the summer solstice is a turning point in the year, and you could say that there's a turning point in this poem when the man steps down from the ledge and chooses not to die. After the summer solstice we're heading toward winter, which is associated with death, but psychologically the poem goes in the opposite direction.

Think about your own developing understanding of Olds's poem. What aspect of it might you focus on in a formal essay? What's a claim that you might make? To us, the students' claims we have quoted seem promising topics for papers. Nevertheless, they could probably stand some polishing and further reflection. After all, they are the outcome of freewriting—an exploratory phase. In any case, what we want to stress is that you are more likely to get ideas about a literary work if you use the reading strategies that this group of students applied.

Reading Closely by Annotating

When you use such strategies, you may come up with several observations about the literary work you are reading. You may even find it helpful to record them directly on the text. Then, by reviewing the points you have annotated and connecting them to one another, you will provide yourself with a solid foundation for a paper. Here we demonstrate this process by showing how student Kara Lundquist annotated a poem by the noted writer and editor X. J. Kennedy (b. 1929) and then composed a possible opening paragraph for an essay about it.

X. J. KENNEDY
Death of a Window Washer

He dropped the way you'd slam an obstinate sash,
— Window washer is given no name.

His split belt like a shade unrolling, flapping.
— Did his body "split" when he hit the ground? Poem avoids gruesome details to focus mostly on bystanders.

Forgotten on his account, the mindless copying

Machine ran scores of memos no one wanted.

Heads stared from every floor, noon traffic halted   5

As though transformed to stone. Cops sealed the block
— Alliteration: What do "c" words suggest?

With sawhorse barricades, laid canvas cover.
— Nuns' reaction different from insects'. But are the humans here much more sensitive?

Nuns crossed themselves, flies went on being alive,

A broker counted ten shares sold as five,
— Echoes "account" in line 3. Did the dead man count (matter)?

And by coincidence a digital clock   10

Stopped in front of a second it couldn't leap over.
— Do people prefer to "leap over" deaths like this?

Struck wordless by his tumble from the sky

To their feet, two lovers held fast to each other

Uttering cries. But he had made no cry.
— At first seems to mean "experience pain," then seems to mean "put up with."

He'd made the city pause briefly to suffer   15

His taking ample room for once. In rather
— "Tedious" to whom? People soon get impatient for the body to go.

A tedious while the rinsed street, left to dry,

Unlatched its gates that passersby might pass.
— Unusual to ask why he lived in the first place.

Why did he live and die? His legacy
— Relates to "wordless" in line 12 and "no cry" in line 14.

Is mute: one final gleaming pane of glass.   20
— "Pane of glass" (clear vision) seems opposite of "mute." Connect "pane" to "pain"?

[2007]

Here is the paragraph that Kara composed, based on her annotations.

X. J. Kennedy's poem "Death of a Window Washer" emphasizes
not the title character's horrible accident, but rather how bystanders
react to it. The poem suggests that although people may be *momentarily* affected by the death of an ordinary person whom they do not
know, eventually they want to resume their own lives and pay him
little attention. The specific situation that the poem dramatizes
is the accidental plunge of a window washer from a city building.
Certainly this incident shocks, at first, the passersby who witness
it. Even though "flies went on being alive," various human beings
are disturbed by the man's sudden death. But as the poem proceeds,
the city's inhabitants want to go back to their personal pursuits. A
turning point in the poem is the word "suffer," which the speaker
uses to describe the city dwellers at the end of line 15. This word
might, at first, lead the reader to believe that they are tormented by
the window washer's accident. But in the next line, it becomes clear
that they are "suffering" in the sense that they are impatiently waiting for his corpse to be removed. Rather than permanently grieve
over his having "passed" (i.e., died), they want to "pass" his body
(line 18) and take up their daily existence once again. Therefore,
although his death has been highly visible to them, they don't really
bother to learn anything about him. His life is *not* revealed to them
like the reality behind a "gleaming pane of glass." The speaker's
concluding use of this image is, in fact, ironic.

Further Strategies for Close Reading
IDENTIFY CHARACTERS' EMOTIONS

Your feelings about the characters in a literary work can help you write a paper
about it. Especially useful to consider is *why* you view these people as you do.
What specific aspects of their thinking and conduct affect your attitudes toward them? You will have more material for the paper, though, if you also examine how the characters feel. With this strategy of close reading, you patiently
and carefully identify *their* emotions, not simply your own. This analysis can
even wind up giving you your paper's key idea — what, in our next chapter, we
will call its *main claim*.

As you pinpoint the characters' passions and moods, try not to judge these
right away. Emotions that may at first seem obnoxious or odd can have interesting roots. Also, they may be stages in complex mental journeys. A character
may display numerous feelings, including ones that conflict, and undergo major changes of heart. Bear in mind, too, that many people in literature repress
or mask their real desires, so the reader must infer their true inner states. Identify as well any emotions that characters significantly *lack*. Noting what feelings they *might* have had helps you pinpoint those they express.

We invite you to practice this method of analysis with the following poem. "Execution" is by the veteran poet Edward Hirsch (b. 1950) and appeared in his 1989 book *The Night Parade* as well as in a 2010 retrospective on his career, *The Living Fire: New and Selected Poems*. As you read the text, try to specify the emotions of the speaker and his main subject, his former coach. We follow up the poem with specific questions about their feelings. Then, to demonstrate the potential benefit of this approach to literature, we present a few ideas that student Courtney Reeves came up with when she applied it to "Execution." The insights she gained helped her eventually construct the introduction to an essay she wrote on the poem.

EDWARD HIRSCH

Execution

The last time I saw my high school football coach
He had cancer stenciled into his face
Like pencil marks from the sun, like intricate
Drawings on the chalkboard, small *x*'s and *o*'s
That he copied down in a neat numerical hand   5
Before practice in the morning. By day's end
The board was a spiderweb of options and counters,
Blasts and sweeps, a constellation of players
Shining under his favorite word, *Execution*,
Underlined in the upper right-hand corner of things.   10
He believed in football like a new religion
And had perfect unquestioning faith in the fundamentals
Of blocking and tackling, the idea of warfare
Without suffering or death, the concept of teammates
Moving in harmony like the planets — and yet   15
Our awkward adolescent bodies were always canceling
The flawless beauty of Saturday afternoons in September,
Falling away from the particular grace of autumn,
The clear weather, the ideal game he imagined.
And so he drove us through punishing drills   20
On weekday afternoons, and doubled our practice time,
And challenged us to hammer him with forearms,
And devised elaborate, last-second plays — a flea-
Flicker, a triple reverse — to save us from defeat.
Almost always they worked. He despised losing   25
And loved winning more than his own body, maybe even
More than himself. But the last time I saw him
He looked wobbly and stunned by illness,
And I remembered the game in my senior year
When we met a downstate team who loved hitting   30
More than we did, who battered us all afternoon

With a vengeance, who destroyed us with timing
And power, with deadly, impersonal authority,
Machine-like fury, perfect execution.   *[1989]*

≡ THINKING ABOUT THE TEXT

1. To what extent does the speaker seem grief-stricken about his coach's mortal illness? Point to specific words in the text that influence your answer.

2. In line 11, the speaker says of the coach, "He believed in football like a new religion." What values would someone like the coach need to have in order to feel so passionately about this sport? Why might someone who regards "football like a new religion" not necessarily feel the same way about baseball or basketball?

3. In line 25, the speaker says that the coach "despised losing." How, if at all, did he reveal this attitude to his players? Identify specific words that help you address this question.

4. What other words in the poem indicate to you how the coach, during the speaker's youth, felt about high school football?

5. Where, if anywhere, does the speaker indicate how the players felt about the coach back then? Where, if anywhere, is the speaker evasive about what the players' attitudes toward the coach were?

6. In line 28, the speaker says that the coach now "looked wobbly and stunned by illness." What, evidently, was the coach feeling about his misfortune?

7. How does the speaker seem to feel about the football game he recalls at the end of the poem?

8. The title word, "execution," appears twice in the poem. Do these two appearances reflect the same emotion, or different ones? Explain.

9. If the title of this poem were the name of an emotion, what emotion would you think appropriate?

After examining the characters' emotions, Courtney Reeves formed these ideas for her paper on the poem. We italicize her references to emotions.

> The speaker does not openly express *sorrow* for his former coach when he finds him both *physically and mentally suffering* from cancer. Nor is it clear that the speaker was ever extremely *fond* of the coach, although probably he *respected* him when he played for him. In general, the poem is not a blatant *sympathy* card for the coach. Instead, it seems chiefly a philosophical reflection, carried out with some *sadness*. The speaker seems mostly to *brood* about the ironies of the coach's present situation, including how these ironies apply to the speaker himself. Noticing that the coach now looks "*wobbly and*

stunned," the speaker obviously thinks that a big reason he appears this way is that cancer has physically attacked him. The speaker also seems to believe that the disease has *psychologically thrown the coach off balance*, in at least two respects. First, although the coach is surely aware that his cancer may kill him, he cannot know for certain how long he actually has to live. The title of the poem, "Execution," refers in one sense to killing that is swift and scheduled, but the coach has now entered a period of *scary* unpredictability about his fate. Second, the coach's look of *unsteadiness and confusion* results from his lifelong belief that people can overcome their limits through skillful physical performances, another sense of the word "execution." This was a goal that the coach *strived for* when he pushed the speaker and his fellow players to achieve a perfect "execution" of plays that would enable them to defeat all opposing teams. Having cancer *shocks* the coach by showing him that he was naive in making football "a new religion" in which proper training of the body would mean success not only on the field but throughout life. He discovers that even though the game of football usually lacks real "suffering and death," these things strike all of us eventually, and that even though he "loved winning more than his own body," he depended on his body's health. The speaker, on the other hand, does not seem "wobbly and stunned" by what has happened to the coach. He suggests that during his boyhood he himself saw the reality of human limits with greater clarity and *detachment* than the coach did. Perhaps, though, the speaker is with *at least a bit of desperation* trying to ward off death by writing this well-"executed" poem about it, just as the coach *frenziedly* wrote marks on the blackboard to help the team "execute" plays.

IDENTIFY SPEECH ACTS

Another way to read a literary text closely and get ideas about it is to identify the **speech acts** in it. Speech acts are things that the characters *do* with words. Try to specify what types of behavior characters engage in as they talk, as well as the effects they aim to have on their listeners. These performances often reveal key aspects of their personalities, features you might overlook if you focus just on their physical acts. When you study their verbal expressions as dramatic gestures, you also provide yourself with more material for a paper — including, perhaps, for its main claim.

Of course, for many speech acts in literature — and for many in real life — there is no single, clearly correct label. How best to describe them is a matter of interpretation. When you read about one of these acts, several terms for it may occur to you, leaving you to decide which fits best.

For examples of speech acts, let's return briefly to Sharon Olds's poem "Summer Solstice, New York City." In line 5, the man on the roof who contemplates suicide tells the people attempting to stop him that "if they came a step closer that was it." You can easily call his words a *warning.* Later, the poem's speaker admits that she wondered whether the police officers would react angrily to the man,

> . . . as a mother whose child has been
> lost will scream at the child when it's found . . . (lines 31–32)

You might say that she envisions their strongly *scolding* him. Actually, though, their behavior toward him is gentler from the start. Early on, the poem's speaker observes that

> The tallest cop approached him directly,
> softly, slowly, talking to him, talking, talking (lines 16–17)

Although neither you nor the poem's speaker knows what exactly the officer is saying, you can guess what he is *doing* as he talks to the man. What label would you apply to this speech act? What does he evidently hope to achieve through it?

Theorists of speech acts have compiled long lists of them, and probably you can think of plenty on your own. Below, we list just a few kinds. For clarity's sake, all of our sample sentences begin with "I," but each of these acts can take other forms.

- The speaker maintains that something is in fact the case.

  Claiming: I *claim* that Brad and Angelina are on the brink of splitting up.

  Concluding: I *conclude* from the data that gender differences are trivial.

  Arguing: I *argue* that victim impact statements deserve more attention in trials.

- The speaker tries to make the hearer carry out the speaker's wish.

  Requesting: I *request* that you turn off your cell phones.

  Demanding: I *demand* that you stop seeing him.

  Recommending: I *recommend* that you drive us home by taking the shortcut.

- The speaker states an intention to do something.

  Promising: I *promise* to get home by 5:00 p.m.

  Guaranteeing: I *guarantee* that I will fix your car by tomorrow.

  Warning: I *warn* you I will call the police if you do not leave right now.

- The speaker establishes a new state of affairs.

  Declaring: I *declare* you the winner of the race.

  Firing: I hereby *fire* you from this company.

  Approving: I hereby *approve* your application for a driver's license.

- The speaker acknowledges that he or she holds a particular attitude toward something.

  Apologizing: I *apologize* to you for my behavior last night.

Congratulating: I *congratulate* you on your promotion.

Protesting: I *protest* your decision to extend the school year.

In addition, many speech acts are best identified by their actual effect on the listener, whether or not it is the impact that the speaker was striving for. Here are some examples: *humiliation, intimidation, scaring, harassment, persuading,* and *misleading.*

A few other things are important to bear in mind:

- Someone may pretend to engage in a particular kind of speech act and yet not fulfill one of its normal conditions: for example, an *apology* may not be sincere; the speaker may not really have the authority to *fire* workers.

- A speech act may not be the kind that it first appears to be: for example, when the head of a corporation seems to make a *suggestion,* the staff might take it as an *order.*

- Often you can better grasp the nature of a particular speech act if you identify options that the speaker rejected — things that the speaker *might* have done but decided not to. For instance, the police officers in Olds's poem *might* have scolded the man on the roof; instead, they chose to talk with him in a friendlier way.

- Most scholars who study "speech acts" extend this term to cover *various* media (not just speech) and *various* communicative signs (not just words). For examples of how broadly the term can be applied, look at photographs that you and other people have posted on Facebook or similar sites. Which of these images strike you as performing the following acts? (Note that an image can have more than one function.)

commemorating	advertising
mourning	denying
announcing	protesting
arguing	bragging
joking	warning

To practice analyzing speech acts in literature, read the following story, "Orientation." As you read, try to come up with names for the speech acts you find in it. Afterward, we will pose some questions that help you do this. Then, to demonstrate the potential benefit of this approach, we present a few ideas that student Eva Berlin came up with when she applied it to "Orientation." The insights she gained helped her eventually construct the introduction to an essay she wrote on the story.

DANIEL OROZCO
Orientation

The son of Nicaraguan immigrants, California-born Daniel Orozco (b. 1957) currently teaches at the University of Idaho. His award-winning short fiction has appeared in a variety of magazines, including Harper's *and* Zoetrope, *and has been collected in* Orientation and Other Stories *(2011). He received a B.A. from Stanford University, an M.A. from San Francisco State University, and an M.F.A. from the University of Washington. He has also held a writing fellowship at Stanford. "Orientation" was originally published in a 1994 issue of* Seattle Review *and was subsequently selected for* The Best American Short Stories 1995.

Those are the offices and these are the cubicles. That's my cubicle there, and this is your cubicle. This is your phone. Never answer your phone. Let the Voicemail System answer it. This is your Voicemail System Manual. There are no personal phone calls allowed. We do, however, allow for emergencies. If you must make an emergency phone call, ask your supervisor first. If you can't find your supervisor, ask Phillip Spiers, who sits over there. He'll check with Clarissa Nicks, who sits over there. If you make an emergency phone call without asking, you may be let go.

These are your IN and OUT boxes. All the forms in your IN box must be logged in by the date shown in the upper left-hand corner, initialed by you in the upper right-hand corner, and distributed to the Processing Analyst whose name is numerically coded in the lower left-hand corner. The lower right-hand corner is left blank. Here's your Processing Analyst Numerical Code Index. And here's your Forms Processing Procedures Manual.

You must pace your work. What do I mean? I'm glad you asked that. We pace our work according to the eight-hour workday. If you have twelve hours of work in your IN box, for example, you must compress that work into the eight-hour day. If you have one hour of work in your IN box, you must expand that work to fill the eight-hour day. That was a good question. Feel free to ask questions. Ask too many questions, however, and you may be let go.

That is our receptionist. She is a temp. We go through receptionists here. They quit with alarming frequency. Be polite and civil to the temps. Learn their names, and invite them to lunch occasionally. But don't get close to them, as it only makes it more difficult when they leave. And they always leave. You can be sure of that.

The men's room is over there. The women's room is over there. John LaFountaine, who sits over there, uses the women's room occasionally. He says it is accidental. We know better, but we let it pass. John LaFountaine is harmless, his forays into the forbidden territory of the women's room simply a benign thrill, a faint blip on the dull flat line of his life.

Russell Nash, who sits in the cubicle to your left, is in love with Amanda Pierce, who sits in the cubicle to your right. They ride the same bus together after work. For Amanda Pierce, it is just a tedious bus ride made less tedious by

5

the idle nattering of Russell Nash. But for Russell Nash, it is the highlight of his day. It is the highlight of his life. Russell Nash has put on forty pounds, and grows fatter with each passing month, nibbling on chips and cookies while peeking glumly over the partitions at Amanda Pierce, and gorging himself at home on cold pizza and ice cream while watching adult videos on TV.

Amanda Pierce, in the cubicle to your right, has a six-year-old son named Jamie, who is autistic. Her cubicle is plastered from top to bottom with the boy's crayon artwork—sheet after sheet of precisely drawn concentric circles and ellipses, in black and yellow. She rotates them every other Friday. Be sure to comment on them. Amanda Pierce also has a husband, who is a lawyer. He subjects her to an escalating array of painful and humiliating sex games, to which Amanda Pierce reluctantly submits. She comes to work exhausted and freshly wounded each morning, wincing from the abrasions on her breasts, or the bruises on her abdomen, or the second-degree burns on the backs of her thighs.

But we're not supposed to know any of this. Do not let on. If you let on, you may be let go.

Amanda Pierce, who tolerates Russell Nash, is in love with Albert Bosch, whose office is over there. Albert Bosch, who only dimly registers Amanda Pierce's existence, has eyes only for Ellie Tapper, who sits over there. Ellie Tapper, who hates Albert Bosch, would walk through fire for Curtis Lance. But Curtis Lance hates Ellie Tapper. Isn't the world a funny place? Not in the ha-ha sense, of course.

Anika Bloom sits in that cubicle. Last year, while reviewing quarterly reports in a meeting with Barry Hacker, Anika Bloom's left palm began to bleed. She fell into a trance, stared into her hand, and told Barry Hacker when and how his wife would die. We laughed it off. She was, after all, a new employee. But Barry Hacker's wife is dead. So unless you want to know exactly when and how you'll die, never talk to Anika Bloom.   10

Colin Heavey sits in that cubicle over there. He was new once, just like you. We warned him about Anika Bloom. But at last year's Christmas Potluck, he felt sorry for her when he saw that no one was talking to her. Colin Heavey brought her a drink. He hasn't been himself since. Colin Heavey is doomed. There's nothing he can do about it, and we are powerless to help him. Stay away from Colin Heavey. Never give any of your work to him. If he asks to do something, tell him you have to check with me. If he asks again, tell him I haven't gotten back to you.

This is the Fire Exit. There are several on this floor, and they are marked accordingly. We have a Floor Evacuation Review every three months, and an Escape Route Quiz once a month. We have our Biannual Fire Drill twice a year, and our Annual Earthquake Drill once a year. These are precautions only. These things never happen.

For your information, we have a comprehensive health plan. Any catastrophic illness, any unforeseen tragedy is completely covered. All dependents are completely covered. Larry Bagdikian, who sits over there, has six daughters. If anything were to happen to any of his girls, or to all of them, if all six were to simultaneously fall victim to illness or injury—stricken with a hideous degenerative muscle disease or some rare toxic blood disorder, sprayed with semiautomatic gunfire while on a class field trip, or attacked in their bunk beds by some prowling nocturnal lunatic—if any of this were to pass, Larry's girls would all be taken care of. Larry Bagdikian would not have to pay one dime. He would have nothing to worry about.

We also have a generous vacation and sick leave policy. We have an excellent disability insurance plan. We have a stable and profitable pension fund. We get group discounts for the symphony, and block seating at the ballpark. We get commuter ticket books for the bridge. We have Direct Deposit. We are all members of Costco.

This is our kitchenette. And this, this is our Mr. Coffee. We have a coffee pool, into which we each pay two dollars a week for coffee, filters, sugar, and CoffeeMate. If you prefer Cremora or half-and-half to CoffeeMate, there is a special pool for three dollars a week. If you prefer Sweet 'n Low to sugar, there is a special pool for two-fifty a week. We do not do decaf. You are allowed to join the coffee pool of your choice, but you are not allowed to touch the Mr. Coffee.

This is the microwave oven. You are allowed to *heat* food in the microwave oven. You are not, however, allowed to *cook* food in the microwave oven.

We get one hour for lunch. We also get one fifteen-minute break in the morning, and one fifteen-minute break in the afternoon. Always take your breaks. If you skip a break, it is gone forever. For your information, your break is a privilege, not a right. If you abuse the break policy, we are authorized to rescind your breaks. Lunch, however, is a right, not a privilege. If you abuse the lunch policy, our hands will be tied, and we will be forced to look the other way. We will not enjoy that.

This is the refrigerator. You may put your lunch in it. Barry Hacker, who sits over there, steals food from this refrigerator. His petty theft is an outlet for his grief. Last New Year's Eve, while kissing his wife, a blood vessel burst in her brain. Barry Hacker's wife was two months pregnant at the time, and lingered in a coma for half a year before dying. It was a tragic loss for Barry Hacker. He hasn't been himself since. Barry Hacker's wife was a beautiful woman. She was also completely covered. Barry Hacker did not have to pay one dime. But his dead wife haunts him. She haunts all of us. We have seen her, reflected in the monitors of our computers, moving past our cubicles. We have seen the dim shadow of her face in our photocopies. She pencils herself in in the receptionist's appointment book, with the notation: To see Barry Hacker. She has left messages in the receptionist's Voicemail box, messages garbled by the electronic chirrups and buzzes in the phone line, her voice echoing from an immense distance within the ambient hum. But the voice is hers. And beneath her voice, beneath the tidal *whoosh* of static and hiss, the gurgling and crying of a baby can be heard.

In any case, if you bring a lunch, put a little something extra in the bag for Barry Hacker. We have four Barrys in this office. Isn't that a coincidence?

This is Matthew Payne's office. He is our Unit Manager, and his door is always closed. We have never seen him, and you will never see him. But he is here. You can be sure of that. He is all around us.

This is the Custodian's Closet. You have no business in the Custodian's Closet.

And this, this is our Supplies Cabinet. If you need supplies, see Curtis Lance. He will log you in on the Supplies Cabinet Authorization Log, then give you a Supplies Authorization Slip. Present your pink copy of the Supplies Authorization Slip to Ellie Tapper. She will log you in on the Supplies Cabinet Key Log, then give you the key. Because the Supplies Cabinet is located outside the Unit Manager's office, you must be very quiet. Gather your supplies quietly. The Supplies Cabinet is divided into four sections. Section One contains letterhead stationery, blank paper and envelopes, memo and note pads, and so on. Section Two contains pens and pencils and typewriter and printer ribbons, and the like. In Section Three we have erasers, correction fluids, transparent tapes, glue sticks, et cetera. And in Section Four we have paper clips and push pins and scissors and razor blades. And here are the spare blades for the shredder. Do not touch the shredder, which is located over there. The shredder is of no concern to you.

Gwendolyn Stich sits in that office there. She is crazy about penguins, and collects penguin knickknacks: penguin posters and coffee mugs and stationery, penguin stuffed animals, penguin jewelry, penguin sweaters and T-shirts and socks. She has a pair of penguin fuzzy slippers she wears when working late at the office. She has a tape cassette of penguin sounds which she listens to for relaxation. Her favorite colors are black and white. She has personalized license plates that read PEN GWEN. Every morning, she passes through all the cubicles to wish each of us a *good* morning. She brings Danish on Wednesdays for Hump Day morning break, and doughnuts on Fridays for TGIF afternoon break. She organizes the Annual Christmas Potluck, and is in charge of the Birthday List. Gwendolyn Stich's door is always open to all of us. She will always lend an ear, and put in a good word for you; she will always give you a hand, or the shirt off her back, or a shoulder to cry on. Because her door is always open, she hides and cries in a stall in the women's room. And John LaFountaine—who, enthralled when a woman enters, sits quietly in his stall with his knees to his chest—John LaFountaine has heard her vomiting in there. We have come upon Gwendolyn Stich huddled in the stairwell, shivering in the updraft, sipping a Diet Mr. Pibb and hugging her knees. She does not let any of this interfere with her work. If it interfered with her work, she might have to be let go.

Kevin Howard sits in that cubicle over there. He is a serial killer, the one they call the Carpet Cutter, responsible for the mutilations across town. We're not supposed to know that, so do not let on. Don't worry. His compulsion inflicts itself on strangers only, and the routine established is elaborate and unwavering. The victim must be a white male, a young adult no older than thirty, heavyset, with dark hair and eyes, and the like. The victim must be chosen at random, before sunset, from a public place; the victim is followed home, and must put up a struggle; et cetera. The carnage inflicted is precise: the angle and direction of the incisions; the layering of skin and muscle tissue; the rearrangement of the visceral organs; and so on. Kevin Howard does not let any of this interfere with his work. He is, in fact, our fastest typist. He types as if he were on fire. He has a secret crush on Gwendolyn Stich, and leaves a red-foil-wrapped Hershey's Kiss on her desk every afternoon. But he hates Anika Bloom, and keeps well away from her. In his presence, she has uncontrollable fits of shaking and trembling. Her left palm does not stop bleeding.

In any case, when Kevin Howard gets caught, act surprised. Say that he seemed like a nice person, a bit of a loner, perhaps, but always quiet and polite.   25

This is the photocopier room. And this, this is our view. It faces southwest. West is down there, toward the water. North is back there. Because we are on the seventeenth floor, we are afforded a magnificent view. Isn't it beautiful? It overlooks the park, where the tops of those trees are. You can see a segment of the bay between those two buildings there. You can see the sun set in the gap between those two buildings over there. You can see this building reflected in the glass panels of that building across the way. There. See? That's you, waving. And look there. There's Anika Bloom in the kitchenette, waving back.

Enjoy this view while photocopying. If you have problems with the photocopier, see Russell Nash. If you have any questions, ask your supervisor. If you can't find your supervisor, ask Phillip Spiers. He sits over there. He'll check with Clarissa Nicks. She sits over there. If you can't find them, feel free to ask me. That's my cubicle. I sit in there.   *[1994]*

≡ THINKING ABOUT THE TEXT

1. Let's return to the story's first paragraph. It seems to feature a variety of speech acts. How would you describe what the speaker is doing in each sentence?

2. What are the various speech acts that the speaker performs in paragraph 3?

3. Discussing Colin Heavey, the speaker says, "We warned him about Anika Bloom" (para. 11). Where in this orientation does the speaker seem to be *warning* the listener? List some specific examples of this speech act.

4. Where, if anywhere, in the story does the speaker seem to engage in the speech act of *gossiping*? Define what this term means to you. How would you distinguish *gossiping* from mere reporting of information?

5. In paragraph 7, the speaker recommends that the listener "comment on" the artwork of Amanda Pierce's son. Presumably it would be impolite to *criticize* these drawings. What other speech acts might the new employee perform when observing them? The speaker also orders the listener to "not let on" that Amanda suffers from spousal abuse. What speech acts could occur if "letting on" were allowed? To whom might they be addressed?

6. In paragraph 13, the speaker praises the firm's "comprehensive health plan." In explaining how it might apply to Larry Bagdikian, however, what else is he doing besides *praising*?

7. In paragraph 18, what might the speaker be doing when he tells the listener that Barry Hacker's deceased wife "haunts all of us"? He claims that "She pencils herself in in the receptionist's appointment book, with the notation: To see Barry Hacker." What speech act might this notation be?

8. What kind of speech act is the statement at the end of paragraph 22, "The shredder is of no concern to you"?

9. In paragraph 23, the speaker says of Gwendolyn Stich that "every morning, she passes through all the cubicles to wish each of us a *good* morning." What kind of speech act is she performing when she does this? In the same paragraph, the speaker reports that Gwendolyn has moments of great emotional distress. What, if anything, does his account of her suffering make you think about the wish she expresses to everyone each day?

10. Why, in paragraph 24, might the speaker tell the listener not to "let on" that Kevin Howard is a serial killer? When the speaker then says "Don't worry," why might he want to reassure the listener that Kevin poses no threat to the office staff?

11. The last sentence in the story is "I sit in there." What would you say to someone who argues that Orozco should have ended not with a simple declaration of fact but with a more dramatic speech act?

12. Orozco reports that since his story was published, "it has even been included in an employee orientation manual, which is either very funny or very disturbing." Why might a company use the story this way? How might it expect new employees to react? Does the orientation in this story resemble other orientations with which you are familiar? In what ways? Consider the kinds of advice given and language used.

13. What assumptions do you make about the speaker's audience, that is, the listener being oriented? Imagine this person's reaction at a few particular moments of the story.

After considering the speech acts that occur in the story, Eva Berlin formed these ideas for her paper on it. We italicize her references to verbal behavior.

> An orientation is something like a course syllabus. Usually, someone who *orients* a company's new employees *explains* to them the firm's policies; *points out* various areas and facilities of the office; *introduces* them to other members of the staff; and in general *welcomes* them to their new workplace while *teaching* them about it. The speaker in Orozco's story does these things, but he performs

more specific speech acts that together might disturb his listener and a lot of the story's readers. Although he *praises* the listener for *asking* "a good question" and *encourages* this person to *raise* even more, he immediately *warns* the listener not to go overboard with inquisitiveness: "*Ask* too many questions, however, and you may be let go" (para. 3). The last four words even become a refrain in the story as it proceeds. At other times, his warnings come across as *threats* that are especially sinister in their vagueness: "If you abuse the lunch policy, our hands will be tied, and we will be forced to look the other way. We will not enjoy that" (para. 17). At other times, he *commands* the listener to perform, or avoid performing, certain acts: for example, "You must pace your work" (para. 3); "Be sure to *comment* on" Jamie's artwork (para. 7); "Stay away from Colin Heavey" (para. 11); "You have no business in the Custodian's Closet" (para. 21); "Gather your supplies quietly" (para. 22); "Do not touch the shredder" (para. 22); "act surprised" (para. 25). Perhaps some readers will regard him as *giving advice*, but he makes these statements so crisply and authoritatively that they seem more like *orders*. Curiously, he doesn't always follow these *orders* himself. Right after *disclosing* to the listener awful details of how Amanda Pierce's husband abuses her, he *commands* the listener to "not *let on*" about these details, even though he himself has just "*let on*" about them (para. 8). Overall, he seems to enjoy *gossiping* about the mostly horrible lives of his co-workers, as if he relishes their misery. Even as he *praises* the company's health plan, *citing* as an example the good coverage that Larry Bagdikian receives, he energetically *elaborates* gruesome details of the calamities that may strike Larry and his family. Interestingly, he *calmly reports* Kevin Howard's murders without *expressing alarm* about them, as if the crimes entertain him rather than scare him. The same goes for his *account* of how Barry Hacker's wife haunts the office. Besides *sketching* eerie biographies of his colleagues, the speaker proves capable of *criticizing* them; he seems to *express outright contempt* when he *labels* John LaFountaine's visits to the women's room as "a faint blip on the dull flat line of his life" (para. 5).

It seems significant that although the speaker *describes* the office as if he is in charge of it, he works in a cubicle, just as his listener will. He does not occupy the suite that a top executive would. In fact, there is no solid indication that the speaker has much power in the company. His rank is certainly lower than that of his Unit Manager, Matthew Payne, whom he has never even had the privilege of seeing. Through his *warnings*, *commands*, *gossiping*, and *criticizing*, he may be trying to *assert through words* a power that he does not really hold within the company's hierarchy. In a sense, his verbal behavior may be a series of *attempts to console himself* for his actual lack of power.

Using Topics of Literary Studies to Get Ideas

You can also get ideas about the text if, as you read it, you consider how it deals with **topics** that have preoccupied literary studies as a profession. Some of these topics have interested the discipline for many years. One example is work, a common subject of the literature in Part One. Traditionally, literary studies has also been concerned with the chapter topics in Part Two: family relations, love, freedom and confinement, justice, and journeys. Moreover, the discipline has long called attention to topics that are essentially classic conflicts: for example, innocence versus experience, free will versus fate or determinism, the individual versus society, nature versus culture, and eternity versus the passing time.

Over the last few years, however, literary studies has turned to several new concerns. For instance, quite a few literary critics now consider the ways in which literary texts are often *about* reading, writing, interpretation, and evaluation. Critics increasingly refer to some of the following subjects in their analysis of literature:

- Traits that significantly shape human identity, including gender, race, ethnic background, social class, sexual orientation, cultural background, nationality, and historical context
- Representations of groups, including stereotypes held by others
- Acknowledgments — or denials — of differences among human beings
- Divisions, conflicts, and multiple forces *within* the self
- Boundaries, including the processes through which these are created, preserved, and challenged
- Politics and ideology, including the various forms that power and authority can take; acts of domination, oppression, exclusion, and appropriation; and acts of subversion, resistance, and parody
- Ways that carnivals and other festivities challenge or preserve social order
- Distinctions between what's universal and what's historically or culturally specific
- Relations between the public and the private, the social and the personal
- Relations between the apparently central and the apparently marginal
- Relations between what's supposedly normal and what's supposedly abnormal
- Relations between "high" culture and "low" (that is, mass or popular) culture
- Economic and technological developments, as well as their effects
- The role of performance in everyday life
- Values — ethical, aesthetic, religious, professional, and institutional
- Desire and pleasure
- The body
- The unconscious
- Memory, including public commemorations as well as personal memory

If you find that a literary text touches on one of these topics, try next to determine how the work specifically addresses that topic. Perhaps you will consider the topic an element of the text's themes. In any case, remember that, by itself, a topic is not the same as a theme. While a topic can usually be expressed in a word or a short phrase, a theme is a whole claim or assertion that you believe the text makes.

Actually, the topics we have identified may be most worth consulting when you have just begun analyzing a literary text and are far from establishing a theme. By using these topics, you can generate preliminary questions about the text, various issues you can then explore.

To demonstrate how these topics can stimulate inquiry, we apply some of them to the following poem, "Night Waitress." It is from the 1986 book *Ghost Memory*, by the late American poet Lynda Hull (1954–1994). Hull had been developing an impressive career in literature when she died in a car accident. This poem is also about work, the speaker being the night waitress of the title.

LYNDA HULL

Night Waitress

Reflected in the plate glass, the pies
look like clouds drifting off my shoulder.
I'm telling myself my face has character,
not beauty. It's my mother's Slavic face.
She washed the floor on hands and knees   5
below the Black Madonna, praying
to her god of sorrows and visions
who's not here tonight when I lay out the plates,
small planets, the cups and moons of saucers.
At this hour the men all look   10
as if they'd never had mothers.
They do not see me. I bring the cups.
I bring the silver. There's the man
who leans over the jukebox nightly
pressing the combinations   15
of numbers. I would not stop him
if he touched me, but it's only songs
of risky love he leans into. The cook sings
with the jukebox, a moan and sizzle
into the grill. On his forehead   20
a tattooed cross furrows,
diminished when he frowns. He sings words
dragged up from the bottom of his lungs.
I want a song that rolls
through the night like a big Cadillac   25
past factories to the refineries

squatting on the bay, round and shiny
as the coffee urn warming my palm.
Sometimes when coffee cruises my mind
visiting the most remote way stations,   30
I think of my room as a calm arrival
each book and lamp in its place. The calendar
on my wall predicts no disaster
only another white square waiting
to be filled like the desire that fills   35
jail cells, the old arrest
that makes me stare out the window or want
to try every bar down the street.
When I walk out of here in the morning
my mouth is bitter with sleeplessness.   40
Men surge to the factories and I'm too tired
to look. Fingers grip lunch box handles,
belt buckles gleam, wind riffles my uniform
and it's not romantic when the sun unlids
the end of the avenue. I'm fading   45
in the morning's insinuations
collecting in the crevices of buildings,
in wrinkles, in every fault
of this frail machinery.   *[1986]*

≡ A WRITING EXERCISE

After you read "Night Waitress," do a ten-minute freewrite in which you try
to identify how the poem relates to one or more of the topics mentioned
on page 40.

We think that several of the topics now popular in literary studies are relevant to Hull's poem. Here are a few possibilities, along with questions that
these topics can generate.

Gender.   The speaker alludes to conventional roles through which men and
women relate to each other. When the speaker declares that "at this hour the
men all look / as if they'd never had mothers," she indicates that women have
often played a maternal role for men. Furthermore, she implies that often
women have been the primary caretaker of their sons. (Notice that she makes
no reference to fathers.) What is the effect of this attention to women as mothers of men? In most of the poem, the speaker refers to men as potential lovers.
Yet even as she suggests she would like a sexual relationship with a man, she
suggests as well that she has had trouble establishing worthwhile attachments.
Why has she had such difficulty, do you think? Does the problem seem due to
her personality alone, or do you sense larger forces shaping her situation? Notice, too, that the poem refers to the factory workers as male, while the woman

who speaks is a waitress. To what extent does American society perpetuate a gendered division of labor?

Ethnic background.   Near the start of the poem, the speaker refers to her "mother's Slavic face" and points out that her mother served "the Black Madonna," a religious icon popular in Central European countries such as the Czech Republic and Poland. What is the effect of these particular ethnic references? To pursue this line of inquiry, probably you will need to do research into the Black Madonna, whether in a library or on the Internet.

Social class.   In part, considering social class means thinking about people's ability to obtain material goods. When the speaker compares her ideal song to "a big Cadillac," she implies that she doesn't currently possess such a luxurious car. At the same time, she is expressing her desire for the song, not the car. Why might the song be more important to her right now? Social class is also a matter of how various workplaces are related to one another. This poem evokes a restaurant, factories, refineries, and bars. How are these settings connected as parts of American society? Think, too, about how you would label the social class of the various occupations the poem mentions. What would you say is the social class of a waitress? To what classes would you assign people who work in factories and refineries? Who, for the most part, are the social classes that have to work at night?

Sexual orientation.   The speaker of "Night Waitress" seems heterosexual, an orientation often regarded as the only legitimate one. Because almost all societies have made heterosexuality the norm, a lot of people forget that it is a particular orientation and that not everyone identifies with it. Within literary studies, gay and lesbian critics have pointed out that a literary work may seem to deal with sexuality in general but may actually refer just to heterosexuality. Perhaps "Night Waitress" is examining heterosexuality as a specific social force. If so, how might the speaker's discontent be related to heterosexuality's influence as a particular institution? Keep in mind that you don't have to assume anything about the author's sexuality as you pursue such a question. In fact, heterosexuality may be a more important topic in Hull's poem than she intended.

Divisions, conflicts, and multiple forces within the self.   The poem's beginning indicates that the speaker experiences herself as divided. The first four lines reveal that she feels pride and disappointment in her mirror image: "I'm telling myself my face has character, / not beauty." Later she indicates that within her mind are "remote way stations" that she visits only on occasion. Furthermore, she seems to contradict herself. Although she initially refers to her room as "a calm arrival," she goes on to describe that place negatively, as empty and confined. Early in the evening, she seems sexually attracted to the man playing the jukebox ("I would not stop him / if he touched me"), but by morning her mood is "not romantic" and she is "too tired / to look" at the male factory workers. What may be the significance of these paradoxes?

Boundaries.   In the first line, the speaker is apparently looking at a window, and later she reveals that at times she feels driven to "stare out the window" of her room. What should a reader make of these two references to such a common boundary? When the speaker observes that the men in the restaurant "do not see me," she indicates that a boundary exists between them and her. Do you think she is merely being paranoid, or do you suspect that the men are indeed ignoring her? If they *are* oblivious to her, how do you explain their behavior? Still another boundary explored in the poem is the line between night and day. What happens when the speaker crosses this line? What can night, day, and the boundary between them signify? You might also consider what the author of a literary work does with its technical boundaries. Often a poem creates boundaries in its breaks between stanzas. Yet "Night Waitress" is a continuous, unbroken text; what is the effect of Hull's making it so? At the same time, Hull doesn't always respect sentence boundaries in her lines. At several points in the poem, sentences spill over from one line to another. This poetic technique is called **enjambment**; what is its effect here?

Politics and ideology.   When, in referring to the jukebox man, the speaker declares that "I would not stop him / if he touched me," she can be taken to imply that male customers often flirt with waitresses. How might flirtation be seen as involving power, authority, and even outright domination? Do you see the poem as commenting on such things? Earlier we raised issues of social class; these can be seen as political issues, too. How would you describe a society in which some people have "a big Cadillac" and others do not?

Carnivals and other festivities.   Although the poem does not refer to a "carnival" in any sense of that word, it does mention bars, which today are regarded by many people as places of festive retreat from work. What adjectives would you use to describe the speaker when she says that sometimes she wants "to try every bar down the street"?

Distinctions between what is universal and what is historically or culturally specific.   Try to identify anything that is historically or culturally specific about this poem's setting. Certainly the word *Slavic* and the reference to the Black Madonna indicate that the speaker has a particular background. You might also note her description of the restaurant, her use of the Cadillac as a metaphor, and her mention of the "factories" and the "refineries" that are "squatting on the bay." Although a wide range of places might fit these details, the poem's setting does not seem universal. Indeed, many readers are attracted to literature *because* it deals with specific landscapes, people, and plots. Nevertheless, these same readers usually expect to get some larger, more widely applicable meanings out of literature even as they are engaged by its specific details. Are you inclined to draw general conclusions from "Night Waitress"? If so, what general meanings do you find in it? What sorts of people do you think might learn something about themselves from reading this poem?

Relations between the public and the private, the social and the personal.   The speaker of "Night Waitress" works in a very public place, a restaurant. Yet she seems to feel isolated there, trapped in her own private world. How did she come to experience public life this way, do you think? Later, she initially seems to value her room as a private retreat, calling it "a calm arrival," but then she describes it as a place so lonely that it leads her to "stare out the window or want / to try every bar down the street." How, then, would you ultimately describe the relations between the speaker's public life and her private one? In addressing this issue, probably you need to consider whether the speaker's difficulties are merely personal or reflect a larger social disorder. When, at the end of the poem, she refers to "this frail machinery," is she referring just to herself, or is she suggesting that this phrase applies to her society in general? If she is indeed making a social observation, what do you sense are the "faults" in her society? Who else might be "fading"?

Relations between "high" culture and "low" culture.   Although the speaker does not identify the "songs / of risky love" playing on the jukebox, surely they are examples of what is called low, mass, or popular culture. Just as a lot of us are moved by such music when we hear it, so the jukebox player and the cook are engaged by it. In contrast, the poem itself can be considered an example of high culture. Often poetry is regarded as a serious art even by people who don't read it. In what ways, if any, does this poem conceivably resemble the songs it mentions? Given that author Lynda Hull is in essence playing with combinations of words, can we compare her with "the man / who leans over the jukebox nightly / pressing the combinations / of numbers"? (Actually, *numbers* has been a poetic term; centuries ago, it was commonly used as a synonym for the rhythms of poems.)

The role of performance in everyday life.   The most conspicuous performer in this poem is the cook, who "sings words / dragged up from the bottom of his lungs." But in everyday life, people often perform in the sense of taking on certain roles, even disguising their real personalities. Do you see such instances of performing in this poem? If so, where? Notice that the speaker wears a uniform; can that be considered a costume she wears while performing as a waitress?

Religious values.   The speaker clearly refers to religion when she recalls her mother's devotion to the Black Madonna, behavior that involved "praying / to her god of sorrows and visions." And although that god is "not here tonight," the speaker's description of waitressing has ritualistic overtones reminiscent of religious ceremonies. When she says, "I bring the cups. / I bring the silver," she could almost be describing preparations for Communion. In fact, she depicts the cook as wearing a religious emblem: "On his forehead / a tattooed cross furrows, / diminished when he frowns." What do you make of all this religious imagery? Might the speaker be trying to pursue certain religious values? Can she be reasonably described as looking for salvation?

Desire and pleasure.   The speaker explicitly mentions the word *desire* when she describes the emptiness she feels in her room, a feeling of desolation "that makes me stare out the window or want / to try every bar down the street." These lines may lead you to believe that her desire is basically sexual. Yet when the speaker uses the words *I want* earlier in the poem, she expresses her wish for "a song that rolls / through the night like a big Cadillac." Here, her longing does not appear sexual in nature. Is the speaker referring to at least two kinds of desire, then? Or do you see her as afflicted with basically one kind?

The body.   A notable feature of this poem is its attention to body parts. The speaker mentions her "shoulder," her "face," her mother's "face," her mother's "hands and knees," the cook's "forehead," his "lungs," her "palm," the "way stations" of her "mind," her "mouth," the factory workers' "fingers," and their "belt buckles." At the same time, the speaker never describes any particular body as a whole. What is the effect of this emphasis on mere parts? Does it connect in any way to the speaker's ultimate "fading"?

Memory.   Already we have noted the speaker's reference to her mother at the start of the poem. In what way, if any, is it significant that she engages in recollection? What circumstances in her life might have prompted the speaker to look back at the past?

≣ A WRITING EXERCISE

We have applied several topics from our list to Lynda Hull's poem "Night Waitress." Now see how you can apply topics from the list to another poem about work in Part One. Try to come up with several questions about the poem you choose, referring to topics on our list. Then select one of the questions you have formulated, and freewrite for ten minutes in response to it.

≣ SUMMING UP: READING CLOSELY

- *Close reading* **is a process that consists of several strategies, all of which can help you get ideas about a literary work for an essay you will write.** These strategies include making predictions as you read; rereading the text with a different focus each time; reading aloud; comparing the text with your personal experience; tracing patterns and breaks from them; noting ambiguities; considering the author's alternatives; generating questions; and formulating a tentative claim. (pp. 16–17)

- **Close reading is aided by several *writing* strategies.** These include commenting in the text's margins; note-taking; freewriting; creating a "dialectical notebook"; and playfully revising the text. (pp. 20–25)

- **To generate ideas about a literary text, consider its characters' emotions and speech acts, as well as how the text deals with topics that have preoccupied literary studies.** (pp. 27–46)

CHAPTER 3

How to Make Arguments about Literature

The fourth word in this chapter's title may puzzle you. Why would we want you to *argue*? Are we really inviting you to yell or sneer? The word *arguing* may remind you of spats you regret. Most everyone has suffered arguments like these. They arise in the media all the time. Talk-radio hosts and their callers mix strong opinion with insult. Television's political panels routinely lapse into squabbles; guests feel required to clash. Quarrels explode on daytime talkfests; couples fight over who's cheated on whom. Online forums are plagued by "trolls," writers who crudely mock others' posts. No wonder many people define *arguing* as combat. It often seems like war.

What Is Argument?

In this book, we define *arguing* in a positive sense. We ask you to think of it as a calm, courteous process in which you

identify a subject of current or possible debate;

analyze why you view the subject the way you do;

address others who may not share your view;

and try to persuade them that your view is worth accepting or at
least makes sense.

This better kind of arguing occurs at various times and places. You may try to coax friends who dread horror films into joining you at *Saw 12*. In class, you may need to explain the logic of your stand on climate change. Beyond campus, you may advocate for social causes. For instance, you might petition your city to launch recycling sites.

Let's face it: to argue *is* to disagree, or to air views not all may hold. Still, at its best, arguing is an *alternative* to war. It's *not* a contest you try to "win" by insisting you're right. To argue well is to state your ideas, support them, and negotiate objections to them, all the while maintaining a civil tone. In an ideal argument, you note principles you share with your critics. You treat fairly ideas different from yours. When these seem wise, you adjust your thinking. The whole process leads you to test your beliefs. "The real argument," Phillip Lopate observes, "should be with yourself." Columnist David Brooks goes even further: "If you write in a way that suggests combative certitude," he warns, "you may gradually smother the inner chaos that will be the source of lifelong freshness and creativity." In their own fashion, these writers point to something important about argument: at its best, it teaches you about yourself and your world, while alerting you to what you still must learn.

Students regularly encounter this kind of arguing in college. Academic subjects aren't just pools of information. They go beyond proven facts. Disciplines grapple with uncertainties: problems, questions, and conflicts they haven't yet solved. Physicists disagree about the origins of the universe. Historians write conflicting accounts of Hitler's Germany; they debate how much his extreme anti-Semitism was traditional there. Two sociologists may scan the same figures on poverty and make different inferences from them. Typically, scholars draw conclusions that are open to challenge. They must explain why their judgments are sound. They expect to engage in reasoned debate with their colleagues. They see this as their field's best chance for truth.

In your classes, expect disagreements. They're crucial to learning in college. Often, classmates will voice ideas you don't immediately accept. Just as often, they'll hesitate to adopt some opinion of yours. Authors you read will deal with controversies, from their own points of view. As a writer yourself, you will enter debates and have to defend your stands.

No one naturally excels at this type of arguing. It takes practice. Our book is a series of opportunities to become skilled in this art. In Part Two, each chapter ends with arguments about a single subject. We then invite you to add your slant. Our book's chief springboard for argument, though, is works of literature. Those we include don't deliver simple, straightforward messages. They offer puzzles, complications, metaphors, symbols, and mysteries. In short, they stress life's complexity. They especially encourage you to ponder multiple dimensions of language: how, for example, shifts of context can change a word's meaning. Each of our literary works calls for you to interpret. As you read the text, you must figure out various features of it. Then, other readers may not see the text as you see it. So next, you'll *argue* for your view. Often you'll do so by composing essays and perhaps online posts. In the rest of this chapter, we offer strategies you can employ to argue about literature as a writer.

As we discuss this process, we refer to arguments that might be made about the following story, Jamaica Kincaid's "Girl." It first appeared in *The New Yorker* in 1978 and was later reprinted in her first book, a 1984 collection of short stories entitled *At the Bottom of the River*.

JAMAICA KINCAID
Girl

Originally named Elaine Potter Richardson, Jamaica Kincaid (b. 1949) was born on the island of Antigua in the West Indies. At the time, Antigua was a British colony. Kincaid lived there until she was seventeen, when she emigrated to the United States. Soon she became a nanny for the family of Michael Arlen, television critic for The

New Yorker. *Eventually, the magazine published her own short stories and, during the early 1990s, her gardening columns. Although she continues to live in the United States, almost all of her writing deals with her native land. In particular, she has written about Antiguan women growing up under British domination. She has published the novels* Annie John *(1985),* Lucy *(1990),* Autobiography of My Mother *(1996), and* Mr. Potter *(2002). Her books of nonfiction include* A Small Place, *an analysis of Antigua (1988); a memoir,* My Brother *(1997);* My Garden (Book) *(1999); and* Talk Stories *(2001), a collection of brief observations that she originally wrote for* The New Yorker. *In 2009, she was inducted into the American Academy of Arts and Sciences and is currently a professor of literature at Claremont McKenna College in California. Her latest book is a novel,* See Now Then *(2013).*

Wash the white clothes on Monday and put them on the stone heap; wash the color clothes on Tuesday and put them on the clothesline to dry; don't walk barehead in the hot sun; cook pumpkin fritters in very hot sweet oil; soak your little cloths right after you take them off; when buying cotton to make yourself a nice blouse, be sure that it doesn't have gum on it, because that way it won't   5
hold up well after a wash; soak salt fish overnight before you cook it; is it true that you sing benna° in Sunday school?; always eat your food in such a way that it won't turn someone else's stomach; on Sundays try to walk like a lady and not like the slut you are so bent on becoming; don't sing benna in Sunday school; you mustn't speak to wharf-rat boys, not even to give directions; don't   10
eat fruits on the street — flies will follow you; *but I don't sing benna on Sundays at all and never in Sunday school*; this is how to sew on a button; this is how to make a button-hole for the button you have just sewed on; this is how to hem a dress when you see the hem coming down and so to prevent yourself from looking like the slut I know you are so bent on becoming; this is how you iron your fa-   15
ther's khaki shirt so that it doesn't have a crease; this is how you iron your father's khaki pants so that they don't have a crease; this is how you grow okra — far from the house, because okra tree harbors red ants; when you are growing dasheen,° make sure it gets plenty of water or else it makes your throat itch when you are eating it; this is how you sweep a corner; this is how you   20
sweep a whole house; this is how you sweep a yard; this is how you smile to someone you don't like too much; this is how you smile to someone you don't like at all; this is how you smile to someone you like completely; this is how you set a table for tea; this is how you set a table for dinner; this is how you set a table for dinner with an important guest; this is how you set a table for lunch;   25
this is how you set a table for breakfast; this is how to behave in the presence of men who don't know you very well, and this way they won't recognize immediately the slut I have warned you against becoming; be sure to wash every day, even if it is with your own spit; don't squat down to play marbles — you are not a boy, you know; don't pick people's flowers — you might catch something;   30
don't throw stones at blackbirds, because it might not be a blackbird at all; this

benna: Calypso music.   **dasheen:** A kind of tarot plant.

is how to make a bread pudding; this is how to make doukona;° this is how to make pepper pot; this is how to make a good medicine for a cold; this is how to make a good medicine to throw away a child before it even becomes a child; this is how to catch a fish; this is how to throw back a fish you don't like, and that   35
way something bad won't fall on you; this is how to bully a man; this is how a man bullies you; this is how to love a man, and if this doesn't work there are other ways, and if they don't work don't feel too bad about giving up; this is how to spit up in the air if you feel like it, and this is how to move quick so that it doesn't fall on you; this is how to make ends meet; always squeeze bread to   40
make sure it's fresh; *but what if the baker won't let me feel the bread?*; you mean to say that after all you are really going to be the kind of woman who the baker won't let near the bread?   [1978]

doukona: A spicy plantain pudding.

≡ THINKING ABOUT THE TEXT

1. Is "Girl" really a story? What characteristics of a story come to mind as you consider this issue?

2. Describe the culture depicted in "Girl" as well as the role of females in that culture. Is either the culture or the role of females in it different from what you are familiar with? Explain.

3. Do you think that the instructions to this girl are all given on the same occasion? Why, or why not? Who do you suppose is giving the instructions? Would you say that the instructor is oppressive or domineering? Identify some of the assumptions behind your position.

4. What effect does Kincaid achieve by making this text a single long sentence? By having the girl speak at only two brief moments?

5. At one point, the girl is shown "how to make a good medicine to throw away a child before it even becomes a child" (lines 33–34). What do you think of the instructor's willingness to give such advice? What do you conclude from its position in the text between "how to make a good medicine for a cold" (line 33) and "how to catch a fish" (line 35)? Does the order of the various pieces of advice matter? Could Kincaid have presented them in a different order without changing their effects?

Strategies for Making Arguments about Literature

Arguing is a form of **rhetoric**. This is a term from ancient Greek. It means writing, speech, and visual images used for a certain purpose: to affect how people think and act. Rhetorical texts don't just convey a message. They aim to *shape* beliefs and conduct. Often they're efforts to *alter* these things. Say you write an essay interpreting Jamaica Kincaid's "Girl"; you will be engaging in rhetoric if you try to change the minds of people who currently hold views of the story other than yours.

A related term is **the rhetorical situation**. It's the specific context you have in mind when you engage in rhetoric. Major circumstances include the following:

- **The particular topic you choose.** If you are writing about "Girl" for your teacher and classmates, have they previously discussed the story? If they have, you won't be introducing a new subject to them. If they haven't, you may have to explain why you are bringing up the story now.

  Of course, the topic of an argument may already interest the public at large. The December 2012 massacre of children in Newtown, Connecticut, immediately provoked disputes over gun control, school safety, mental illness, and screen violence. Other writers must alert their readers to their subject or remind them of it. This was the situation for legal scholars Woodrow Hartzog and Evan Selinger in 2013, when they posted an online argument about Facebook. At the time, people worried about Facebook's dangers to privacy. They felt the site wouldn't securely protect users' personal data. In their argument, Hartzog and Selinger deliberately shift to another subject. They recommend thinking less about *privacy* and more about *obscurity*, which they note is a word "rarely used" in debates about Facebook's risks. To them, *privacy* is so vague a concept that brooding about how the site guards it is futile. They call for pushing Facebook to keep personal facts *obscure*: "hard to obtain or understand" when cyberstalkers hunt for them.

- **The main readers, listeners, or viewers you decide to address.** As we have suggested, these people may be other members of the class you're currently in. In the wider world, writers often have to decide to what specific groups they are directing their arguments. In 2003, for example, architecture critic Paul Goldberger wrote an article complaining that cell phones made their users less sensitive to the physical realities of urban settings. Goldberger chose to publish his argument in *Metropolis*, a city-oriented magazine. Its mission statement declares that it "examines contemporary life through design," featuring articles that "range from the sprawling urban environment to intimate living spaces to small objects of everyday lives." This magazine also seeks to put design in "economic, environmental, social, cultural, political, and technological contexts." Readers of *Metropolis* would not be surprised, therefore, for the magazine to include an opinion piece about cell phones' impact on cities. Perhaps Goldberger hoped his piece would someday circulate more widely, as it now does on the Web. But surely his target group loomed in his mind as he decided on content, form, and words.

- **Possible "channels" for the text.** These include available institutions, media, and genres. To spark a crusade against guerilla leader Joseph Kony—who has kidnapped children and made them serve in his army—Jason Russell chose to make a video documentary exposing his atrocities. (As you may know, the film went viral when Russell posted it online.) Even if you write an interpretive essay about "Girl" for a college class, you might do more than submit it in print to your teacher. Other possibilities include submitting it electronically; posting it online in a class forum; using it as the basis for a YouTube video; or incorporating parts of it into a multimedia class presentation (an activity we discuss at the end of Chapter 6).

Current politicians fling the word "rhetoric" as an insult. They accuse their rivals of indulging in it. They treat the word with contempt because they think it means windy exaggeration. But before the modern age, it meant something nobler. Rhetoric was the valuable attempt to *influence* readers, listeners, or viewers. In this sense, almost all of us resort to rhetoric daily. We need to learn rhetorical strategies if we're to have impact on others. For centuries, then, schools have seen rhetoric as a vital art. They've deemed it important to study, practice, and teach. In ancient Greece and Rome as well as Renaissance Europe, it was a core academic subject. American colleges of the nineteenth century also made it central. This focus survives in many courses today, especially ones about writing or speech. Our book reflects this commitment to rhetoric, especially through our advice about writing.

Within the field of rhetoric, arguments are a more specific category. Those you make about literature involve eight basic elements. You attempt to **persuade** an **audience** to accept your **claims** regarding an **issue**. To achieve this aim, you present **evidence**, explain your **reasoning**, rely on **assumptions**, and make other kinds of **appeals**. The boldfaced words play key roles in this book; we mention them often. Here we explain what we mean by each, beginning with *issue* and then moving to *claims, persuasion, audience, evidence, reasoning, assumptions,* and *appeals.* Throughout our discussion, we refer to Kincaid's story "Girl."

IDENTIFY AN ISSUE

An **issue** is something about which people have disagreed or might disagree. Even as you read a text, you can try to guess what features of it will lead to disagreements in class. You may sense that your own reaction to certain aspects of the text is heavily influenced by your background and values, which other students may not share. Some parts of the text may leave you with conflicting ideas or mixed feelings, as if half of you disagrees with the other half. At moments like these, you come to realize what topics are issues for you, and next you can urge the rest of your class to see these topics as issues, too.

An issue is best defined as a question with no obvious, immediate answer. Thus, you can start identifying issues by noting questions that occur to you as you read. Perhaps this question-posing approach to texts is new for you. Often readers demand that a text be clear, and they get annoyed if it leaves them puzzled. Certain writing ought to be immediately clear in meaning; think of operating instructions on a plane's emergency doors. But the value of a literary work often lies in the work's complexities, which can lead readers to reexamine their own ways of perceiving the world. Also, your discussions and papers about literature are likely to be most useful when they go beyond the obvious to deal with more challenging matters. When your class begins talking about a work, you may feel obliged to stay quiet if you have no firm statements to make. But you can contribute a lot by bringing up questions that occurred to you as you read. Especially worth raising are questions that continue to haunt you.

In any case, when you write an argument about a literary text, readers should find your main issue *significant*. It must be a question they believe is worth caring about. Sometimes they'll immediately see its value. But often you'll need to explain what's *at stake*—how the answer to this question can significantly affect one's understanding of the text. Scholars of rhetoric describe this task as establishing the issue's *exigence*.

A possible issue with Jamaica Kincaid's "Girl" concerns how much affection the main speaker has for the girl she addresses. A logical hypothesis is that these two are mother and daughter, but to what degree is the speaker showing motherly love? In fact, people may disagree over how to define this term. What does it mean to *you*?

You may feel unable to answer questions like these. But again, you achieve much when you simply formulate questions and bring them up in class. As other students help you ponder them, you will grow better able to explore issues through writing as well as through conversation.

You are more likely to come up with questions about a text if you assume that for every decision the writer made, alternatives existed. In "Girl," Kincaid might have given her title character more of a speaking voice. She might have divided the story into multiple sections rather than present it in one long paragraph. When you begin to explore why authors made the choices they did, you also begin to examine the effects of those choices.

Next we identify ten kinds of issues that arise in literature courses. Our list will help you detect the issues that come up in your class and discover others to bring up in discussions or in your writing. The list does not include every kind of issue; you may think of others. Moreover, you may find that an issue can fit into more than one of the categories we name. But when you do have an issue that seems hard to classify, try to assign it to a single category, if only for the time being. You will then have some initial guidance for your reading, class discussions, and writing. If you later feel that the issue belongs to another category, you can shift your focus.

1. Issues of fact.   Rarely does a work of literature provide complete information about its characters and events. Rather, literature is usually marked by what literary theorist Wolfgang Iser calls "gaps," moments when certain facts are omitted or obscured. At such times, readers may give various answers to the question, What is happening in this text? Readers tackle questions of fact only if they suspect that their answers will affect their overall view of a text. It may not matter, for example, that we fail to learn the exact age of Kincaid's title character. More consequential seems the question of whether the story's main speaker actually presented all her lessons at the same time. Imagine a reader who believes this is indeed the case. Imagine a second reader who believes that the speaker delivered these lessons at various times but that the girl is remembering them as one continuous monologue. How might these two readers see the whole story differently because of their different assumptions?

2. Issues of theme.   You may be familiar with the term **theme** from other literature courses. By *theme* critics usually mean the main claim that an author seems to be making with his or her text. Sometimes a theme is defined in terms of a single word — for example, *work* or *love*. But such words are really mere topics. Identifying the topics addressed by a text can be a useful way of starting to analyze that text, and earlier in Part One we list several topics that currently preoccupy literary studies. A text's theme, however, is best seen as an assertion that you need at least one whole sentence to express.

With many texts, an issue of theme arises because readers can easily disagree about the text's main idea. In literature classes, such disagreements often occur, in part because literary works tend to express their themes indirectly. This is especially the case with a story like "Girl," in which the main speaker's views are not necessarily the same as the author's. Readers of the story may give various answers to the question, What is the author ultimately saying? Perhaps some readers will take Kincaid to imply that mothers always know best. Other readers may conclude that Kincaid thinks that excessively controlling mothers are damaging to children.

If you try to express a text's theme, avoid making a statement that is so general that it could apply to many other works. Arguing that Kincaid's theme is "Girls are pressured to fit stereotyped roles" does not get at her story's details. On the other hand, do not let a text's details restrict you so much that you make the theme seem relevant only to a small group. If you argue that Kincaid's theme is "Antiguan women are domineering," then the many readers who are *not* from Antigua will wonder why they should care. In short, try to express themes as *midlevel generalizations.* With Kincaid's story, one possible theme is "In some cultures, women prepare girls for adulthood by teaching them to follow conventions *and* to assert themselves." A statement like this seems both attentive to Kincaid's specific text and applicable to a large portion of humanity. You are free to challenge this version of Kincaid's theme by proposing an alternative. Moreover, even if you do accept this statement as her theme, you are then free to decide whether it is a sound observation. Identifying a theme is one thing; evaluating it is another.

Keep in mind that a theme ties together various parts of a text. Focusing on a single passage, even if it seems thematic, may lead you to ignore other passages that a statement of theme should encompass. For instance, the last words of "Girl" may tempt you to believe that its theme is "Be the kind of woman who feels the bread." Yet in other parts of the story, the main speaker seems to be calling for a compliant attitude. You need to take these moments into account as well.

Often you will sense a work's theme but still have to decide whether to state it as an **observation** or as a **recommendation**. You would be doing the first, for example, if you expressed Kincaid's theme as we did above: "In some cultures, women prepare girls for adulthood by teaching them to follow conventions *and* to assert themselves." You would be doing the second if you said Kincaid's theme is "Women should teach girls to follow conventions *and* to assert themselves." Indeed, people who depict a theme as a recommendation often use a word like *should.* Neither way of expressing a theme is necessarily better than the other. But notice that each way conjures up a particular image of the author. Reporting Kincaid's theme as an observation suggests that she is writing as a psychologist, a philosopher, or some other analyst of human nature. Reporting her theme as a recommendation suggests that she is writing as a teacher, preacher, manager, or coach: someone who is telling her readers what to do. Your decision about how to phrase a theme will depend in part on which image of the author you think is appropriate.

You risk obscuring the intellectual, emotional, and stylistic richness of a text if you insist on reducing it to a single message. Try stating the text's theme as a problem for which there is no easy solution, which suggests that the text is complex. For instance, if you say that Kincaid's theme is "In some cultures, women who prepare girls for adulthood are caught in a contradiction between wanting to empower them and wanting to keep them safe," you position yourself to address various elements of the story.

Also weigh the possibility that a text is conveying more than one theme. If you plan to associate the text with any theme at all, you might refer to *a* theme of the text rather than *the* theme of the text. Your use of the term *theme* would still have implications. Above all, you would still be suggesting that you have identified one of the text's major points. Subsequently, you might have to defend this claim, showing how the point you have identified is indeed central to the text.

Issues of theme have loomed large in literary studies. We hope that you will find them useful to pursue. But because references to theme are so common in literary studies, students sometimes forget that there are other kinds of issues. As you move through this list, you may find some that interest you more.

3. Issues of definition.   In arguments about literature, issues of **definition** arise most often when readers try to decide what an author means by a particular word. Consider the title of Kincaid's story; what does it mean to be a "girl" in this particular culture? Notice that an issue of definition can arise even with ordinary language.

4. Issues of symbolism.   In literary studies, an issue of **symbolism** usually centers on a particular image. In question are the image's meaning and purpose, including whether the image is more than just a detail. Notice that "Girl" concludes with the image of bread; indeed, "bread" is the story's very last word.

You can take this reference literally, thinking just about the physical product that bread is, but you might want to argue that Kincaid is prodding her readers to consider symbolic associations often made with this food. For example, bread has traditionally been taken to represent the very spirit of life itself.

5. Issues of pattern.   With issues of **pattern**, you observe how a text is organized and try to determine how certain parts of the text relate to other parts. But think, too, about the meaning and purpose of any pattern you find, especially since readers may disagree about the pattern's significance. Also ponder the implications of any moment when a text *breaks* with a pattern it has been following. Disruptions of a pattern may be as important as the pattern itself.

A conspicuous pattern in "Girl" is the main speaker's series of commands, which includes repeated use of the words *this is how*. Indeed, **repetition** is a common pattern in literature. Yet at two points in Kincaid's story, the speaker is interrupted by italicized protests from the girl: "*but I don't sing benna on Sundays at all and never in Sunday school*" (lines 11–12) and "*but what if the baker won't let me feel the bread?*" (line 41). What should we conclude about the main speaker from her string of orders? What should we conclude about the girl from her two disruptions? Readers may have various answers to these questions.

A text's apparent oppositions are also patterns that may be debated. An example in "Girl" is the distinction that the main speaker makes in lines 8–9 between being "a lady" and being a "slut." What contrasting values and behavior does she seem to associate with these terms? What sorts of young woman might these two categories leave out? Again, different answers to such questions are possible.

6. Issues of evaluation.   Consciously or unconsciously, **evaluation** always plays a central role in reading. When you read a work of literature, you evaluate its ideas and the actions of its characters. You judge, too, the views you assume the author is promoting. Moreover, you gauge the artistic quality of the text.

Specifically, you engage in three kinds of evaluation as you read. One kind is *philosophical*: you decide whether a particular idea or action is wise. Another kind is *ethical*: you decide whether an idea or action is morally good. The third kind is *aesthetic*: you decide whether the work as a whole or parts of the text succeed as art. Another reader may disagree with your criteria for wisdom, morality, and art; people's standards often differ. It is not surprising, then, that in the study of literature issues of evaluation come up frequently.

Sometimes you may have trouble distinguishing the three types of judgment from each other. Philosophical evaluation, ethical evaluation, and aesthetic evaluation can overlap. Probably the first two operate in the mind of a reader who is judging the advice given by the main speaker in "Girl." This reader may, for instance, find the speaker insensitive: that is, neither smart nor humane. Moreover, if this reader thinks Kincaid sympathizes with the speaker, then he or she may consider "Girl" flawed as a work of art. Keep in mind, however, that you can admire many aspects of a literary work even if you disagree with the ideas you see the author promoting. Someone may relish Kincaid's colorful language regardless of the views presented in the story.

But whose works should be taught? Many scholars argue that literary studies have focused too much on white male authors, and some refuse to assume that the works of these authors are great and universally relevant. They criticize the long neglect of female and minority writers like Kincaid, a black woman born and raised in the West Indies. In part because of these scholars' arguments, "Girl" now appears in many literature anthologies. Yet other people continue to prize "classics" by William Shakespeare, John Milton, and William Blake. This ongoing debate about the literature curriculum includes disagreements about the worth of recent texts. After all, contemporary literature has yet to pass a "test of time." Does Kincaid's 1978 story deserve to be anthologized and taught? We think so and have included "Girl" in our own book. What, though, is *your* evaluation of it? Also, what particular standards have you used to judge it?

7. Issues of historical and cultural context. Plenty of literary works have engaged readers who are quite unlike their authors. These readers may include much-later generations and inhabitants of distant lands. Nevertheless, an author's own **historical and cultural context** may significantly shape his or her text. Consider Jamaica Kincaid's use of her past in "Girl." Though she has lived in the United States since she was seventeen, she evidently tapped memories of her childhood on Antigua to write this story and to represent the island's culture. Since many of the story's readers would be unfamiliar with Antigua, she had to decide what aspects of it to acquaint them with. What features of it does she emphasize, and what features does she downplay or omit? When Kincaid was born, Antiguans were under British control, and many labored hard for little money. Do these historical facts matter in "Girl"? If so, in what conceivable ways? Notice that answering such political and economic questions usually requires research. Even then, answers may be complicated. Indeed, rarely does a literary text straightforwardly reflect its author's background. Debate arises over how text and context relate.

We provide some background for each literary work we present to help you begin to situate it historically and culturally. In Chapter 6, we explain how to put literature in context, especially by doing research in the library and on the Internet. For now, we want to emphasize that contextualizing a work involves more than just piling up facts about its origin. In the study of literature, issues of historical and cultural context are often issues of *relevance*: *which* facts about a work's creation are important for readers to know, and *how* would awareness of these facts help readers better understand the work? Readers can inform themselves about a particular author's life, for instance, but they may disagree about the extent to which a given text is autobiographical.

Perhaps you like to connect a literary work with its author's own life. The author of the story we have been discussing apparently drew to some extent on her personal experiences. You may be tempted, therefore, to think that "Girl" consists of advice Kincaid herself received. Yet when you assert that a work is thoroughly autobiographical, you risk overlooking aspects of the text that depart from the author's own experiences, impressions, and beliefs. We are not urging you to refrain from ever connecting the author's text to the author's life. Rather, we are pointing out that whatever links you forge may be the subject of debate.

Even the term *history* can be defined in various ways. When you refer to a work's historical context, you need to clarify whether you are examining (1) the life of the work's author; (2) the time period in which it was written; (3) any time period mentioned within the text; (4) its subsequent reception, including responses to it by later generations; or (5) the forms in which the work has been published, which may involve changes in its spelling, punctuation, wording, and overall appearance.

8. Issues of genre.   So far, we have been identifying categories of issues. Issues of **genre** are *about* categorization, for they involve determining what *kind* of text a particular work is. You might categorize "Girl" as belonging to the short-story genre, but someone might disagree because it seems to lack a conventional plot. This debate would involve deciding what the essential characteristics of a "short story" are. Even if you argue that Kincaid's text belongs to this genre, you can attempt to classify it more precisely by aiming for a term that better sums up its content and form. Issues of genre often arise with such further classification.

A literary text may relate in some way to a characteristic of ordinary, real-life interactions. In key respects, "Girl" belongs to the parental-advice genre. Try, though, to distinguish between text genre and real-life genre. Kincaid's story can be categorized as *an exploration of how gender roles are reinforced.* In any case, you may find that two or more labels are appropriate for a particular text. For instance, besides the category we've just mentioned, you might label "Girl" as *assembled memories* — if, that is, you believe the title character is *recollecting* bits of advice she received on various occasions. You would then have to decide whether these two labels are equally helpful. Much of the time, issues of genre are issues of priority. Readers debate not whether a certain label for a work is appropriate but whether that label is the best.

9. Issues of social policy.   In many works of literature, writers have attempted to instigate social reform by exposing defects in their cultures and encouraging specific cures. A famous example is Upton Sinclair's 1906 novel, *The Jungle*, which vividly depicts horrible conditions in Chicago's stockyards and thereby led the meat-processing plant owners to adopt more humane and hygienic practices. Even a work of literature that is not blatantly political or that seems rooted in the distant past may make you conscious of your own society's problems and possible solutions to them. Yet you and your classmates may propose different definitions of and solutions for cultural problems. The result is what we call issues of **social policy**.

Sometimes your position on an issue of social policy will affect how you read a certain literary work. For example, your view on how girls and boys should be educated may affect your response to Kincaid's story. Even if current issues of social policy do not influence your original reading of a work, you can still use the work to raise such issues in your writing or in class discussion. Imagine discussing Kincaid's story at a meeting of junior high school teachers. What policies might the story be used to promote there?

10. Issues of cause and effect.   Issues of **causality** are common in literary studies. Often they arise as readers present different explanations for a character's behavior. Why does the girl in Kincaid's story protest at two particular moments? Remember that even a work's narrator or main speaker is a character with motives worth analyzing.

Such questions can be rephrased to center on the author. For instance, you can ask why Kincaid ends her story by having the characters speak about feeling the bread. If you look back at our discussion of these ten types of issues, you may see that most issues can be phrased as questions about the author's purposes. But remember your options. Focusing on authorial intent in a given case may not be as useful as sticking with another type of issue. Or you may turn a question about authorial intent into a question about authorial **effect**. How should readers react when Kincaid ends her story the way she does? You can address questions like this without sounding as if you know exactly what the author intended.

MAKE A CLAIM

You may not be used to calling things you say or write *claims*. But even when you utter a simple observation about the weather — for instance, "It's beginning to rain" — you are making a claim. Basically, a **claim** is a statement that is spoken or written so that others will consider it to be true. With this definition in mind, you may start noticing claims everywhere. Most of us make lots of them every day. Furthermore, most of our claims are accepted as true by the people to whom we make them. Imagine how difficult life would be if the opposite were the case; human beings would be perpetually anxious if they distrusted almost everything they were told.

At times, though, claims do conflict with other claims. In a literature course, disagreements inevitably arise. Again, try not to let disagreements scare you. You can learn a lot from encountering views other than yours and from having to support your own. Moreover, exciting talk can occur as your class negotiates differences of opinion.

Recall that we defined an *issue* as a question with various debatable answers. *Claims*, as we use the term, are the debatable answers. For examples of claims in literary studies, look back at our explanations of ten kinds of issues. In that discussion, we mentioned possible claims about "Girl": e.g., that Kincaid's theme is "Women should teach girls to follow conventions *and* to assert themselves," that the final image of bread is symbolic, and that the story's genre is assembled memories. These claims are debatable because in each case at least one other position is possible.

In literature classes, two types of claims are especially common. To criticize Kincaid's main speaker is to engage in **evaluation**. To identify themes of "Girl" is to engage in **interpretation**. Conventionally, interpretation is the kind of analysis that depends on hypotheses rather than simple observation of plain fact. Throughout this book, we refer to the practice of interpreting a work or certain aspects of it. Admittedly, sometimes you may have trouble distinguishing interpretation from evaluation. When you evaluate some feature of a work or make an overall judgment of that work, probably you are operating with a certain interpretation as well, even if you do not make that interpretation explicit. Similarly, when you interpret part of a work or the text as a whole, probably you have already decided whether the text is worth figuring out. Nevertheless, the two types of claims differ in their emphases. When you attempt to interpret a work, you are mostly analyzing it; when you attempt to evaluate the work, you are mostly judging it.

In class discussions, other students may resist a claim you make about a literary work. Naturally, you may choose to defend your view at length. But remain open to the possibility of changing your mind, either by modifying your claim somehow or by shifting completely to another one. Also, entertain the possibility that a view different from yours is just as reasonable, even if you do not share it.

In much of your writing for your course, you will be identifying an issue and making one main claim about it, which can be called your **thesis**. As you attempt to support your main claim, you will make a number of smaller claims. In drafts of your paper, welcome opportunities to test the claims you make in it. Review your claims with classmates to help you determine how persuasive your thinking is. You will be left with a stronger sense of what you must do to make your paper credible.

AIM TO PERSUADE

As we have noted, argument is often associated with arrogant insistence. Many assume that if two people are arguing, they are each demanding to be seen as correct. At its best, however, argument involves careful efforts to persuade. When you make such an effort, you indicate that you believe your claims, even if you remain open to revising them. You indicate as well that you would like others to agree with you. Yet to attempt **persuasion** is to concede that you must support your claims if others are to value them.

As you have probably discovered on many occasions, swaying people who hold views different from yours can be difficult. You will not always be able to change their minds, yet you may still convince them that your claims are at least reasonable. Moreover, the process of trying to persuade others will compel you to clarify your ideas, to review why you hold them, and to analyze the people you aim to affect.

CONSIDER YOUR AUDIENCE

When you hear the word **audience**, perhaps you think first of people attending plays, concerts, movies, or lectures. Yet *audience* also describes readers, including the people who read your writing. Not everything you write is for other people's eyes; in this course, you may produce notes, journal entries, and even full-length drafts that only you will see. From time to time in the course, however, you will do public writing. On these occasions, you will be trying to persuade your audience to accept whatever claims you make.

These occasions will require you to consider more than just your subject matter. If you are truly to persuade your readers, you must take them into account. Unfortunately, you will not be able to find out everything about your audience beforehand. Moreover, you will have to study the ways in which your readers differ from one another. Usually, though, you will be able to identify some of their common values, experiences, and assumptions. Having this knowledge will strengthen your ability to make a case they appreciate.

In analyzing a work of literature, you may try to identify its *implied reader*: that is, the type of person that the work seems to address. Remember, too, that people may have read the work in manuscript or when it was first published. Finally, the work may have had innumerable readers since. Often we ask you to write about a text's effect on you and to compare your reaction with your classmates'.

You can introduce your essay's main claim by referring to the audience you're focusing on:

- Readers you disagree with

  While some readers may feel that the main speaker in "Girl" loves the title character, the tone of this adult woman suggests that she does not care much for the girl at all.

- Hasty, superficial readers

  Because the main speaker in "Girl" gives many instructions that suggest she is very much in control of her life, readers may overlook signs that she *hasn't* entirely mastered her existence but instead is trying to cope as best she can.

- Puzzled readers

  Many readers may wonder why the girl's father is barely mentioned in Kincaid's story. Kincaid evidently wants us to think more about how mother-daughter relationships treat men, including fathers, as outsiders.

- Your own divided self

  While at first I thought that the main speaker is a cold and perhaps even bitter "teacher," I have concluded that she does feel warm toward the title character and genuinely cares about the girl's welfare.

Above all, you may wonder how familiar your readers already are with the text you are analyzing. Perhaps your teacher will resolve your uncertainty, telling you exactly how much your audience knows about the text. Then again, you may be left to guess. Should you presume that your audience is totally unfamiliar with the text? This approach is risky, for it may lead you to spend a lot of your paper merely summarizing the text rather than analyzing it. A better move is to write as if your audience is at least a bit more knowledgeable. Here is a good rule of thumb: *assume that your audience has, in fact, read the text but that you need to recall for this group any features of the text that are crucial to your argument.* Although probably your paper will still include summary, the amount you provide will be limited, and your own ideas will be more prominent.

GATHER AND PRESENT EVIDENCE

Evidence is the support that you give your claims so that others will accept them. What sort of evidence you must provide depends on what your audience requires to be persuaded. When you make claims during class discussions, your classmates and instructor might ask you follow-up questions, thereby suggesting what you must do to convince them. As a writer, you might often find yourself having to guess your readers' standards of evidence. Naturally, your guesses will be influenced by any prior experiences you have had with your audience. Moreover, you may have opportunities to review drafts with some of its members.

When you make an argument about literature, the evidence most valued by your audience is likely to be details from the work itself. Direct quotations from the text are powerful indications that your claims are well grounded. But when you quote, you need to avoid willful selectivity. If, when writing about Kincaid's story, you quote the girl's question *"but what if the baker won't let me feel the bread?"* without acknowledging the main speaker's response, you may come across as misrepresenting the text. In general, quoting from various parts of a text will help you give your readers the impression that you are being accurate.

If you make claims about the historical or cultural context of a work, your evidence may include facts about its original circumstances. You may be drawn to the author's own experiences and statements, believing these shed light on the text. But again, use such materials cautiously, for they are not always strong evidence for your claims. People are not obliged to accept the author's declaration of his or her intent as a guide to the finished work. Some people may feel that the author's statement of intention was deliberately misleading, while others may claim that the author failed to understand his or her own achievement.

EXPLAIN YOUR REASONING

Philosopher Gary Gutting observes that "facts alone are necessary but not sufficient for a good argument. As important as getting the facts right is putting the facts into a comprehensible logical structure that supports your conclusion." This advice can help you as you strive to persuade others through writing. Besides evidence, your readers will expect you to show careful **reasoning**. Ideally, they'll come away feeling that your ideas truly connect. They should sense that your main claim derives from your other ones. The steps in your logic should be clear in your essay's organization. Otherwise, you may confuse your audience — especially if you crawl through the literary work chronologically, commenting on each of its lines. Perhaps your main claim is that although "Girl" is a collection of the title character's assorted memories — bits of advice that the main speaker gave her on multiple occasions — these bits resemble one another so much that they have come to haunt her as a single monologue. An essay that simply plods through the story won't help you develop this idea. Probably you should first identify for your audience some ways in which the speaker's instructions do seem to have been uttered at various times rather than at a single moment. You should then explain the psychological nature of the girl's memory — her recalling these directions as a single speech. In general, alert your audience to your stages of thought.

IDENTIFY YOUR ASSUMPTIONS

Assumptions behind an argument may be numerous and debatable. That's why we single them out as an element here. One category is beliefs about the audience's experiences. If you suspect that your readers are quite unfamiliar with cultures like Antigua's, then your essay will have to spell out explicitly at least some of its distinctive features.

Another potentially significant set of assumptions has to do with your values, which often reflect your own particular life. For instance, you may want to condemn the speaker in "Girl" as a "bad" mother because your own is nicer. But this criticism would require more support than just your personal experience. You'd need to explain why *various* people should apply it to the speaker — whatever their particular mothers are like. In general, be cautious with the labels you give literary figures. If you describe characters with strongly judgmental words like *bad*, *crazy*, *normal*, or *good*, your readers may think you are showing your own prejudices and upbringing. Often they'll seek more precise and moderate language, believing it is more faithful to the actual text.

A third type of assumption is what rhetorical theory calls *warrants*. This term refers to the writer's beliefs about what can serve as evidence. Imagine, for example, that a paper of yours on Kincaid's story cites the main speaker's final phrase ("the kind of woman who the baker won't let near the bread") as evidence that she basically desires the girl to become an assertive adult. You would be relying on at least two warrants: (1) the assumption that, in a short story, a speaker's concluding words probably convey her central goal; and (2) the assumption that demanding to feel a merchant's wares is a show of strength. Of course, your readers might question these premises; you need to anticipate whether you'll have to state and defend them.

Once you state your warrants for a claim you are making, your audience may go further, asking you to identify assumptions supporting the warrants themselves. But more frequently you will have to decide how much you should mention your warrants in the first place. In class discussion, usually your classmates' and instructor's responses to your claims will indicate how much you have to spell out your assumptions. When you write, you have to rely more on your own judgment of what your audience requires. If you suspect that your readers will find your evidence unusual, you should identify your warrants at length. If, however, your readers are bound to accept your evidence, then a presentation of warrants may simply distract them. Again, reviewing drafts of your paper with potential readers will help you determine what to do.

MAKE USE OF APPEALS

To make their arguments persuasive, writers employ three basic kinds of appeals. Rhetorical theory calls them **logos**, **ethos**, and **pathos**, terms drawn from ancient Greek. In practice, they don't always play equal roles. An argument may depend on one or two of these strategies, not the entire trio. But all three are potential resources.

In a way, we've already introduced **logos**. The term refers to the logical substance of an arguer's case. When you rely on logos, you focus on showing that your claims are sound. You do this by emphasizing your evidence and your reasons. Most audiences will demand anyway that these features be strong. No surprise, then, that logos is the most common type of appeal.

Ethos often operates, too. When applied to writing, this term refers to the image you project as an author. Actually, there are two types of ethos. One is your audience's image of you before you present your analysis. It's your prior reputation. When Paul Goldberger published his article in *Metropolis*, many of its readers already knew that he is a leading, Pulitzer Prize–winning critic of architecture. Their awareness would incline them to respect his argument against cell phones, whether or not they agreed with him. Advertisers have reputational ethos in mind when they hire celebrities for endorsements. The hope is that you'll join Weight Watchers because Jennifer Hudson did. This ethos also comes into play with self-help manuals. Often their covers boast that the writer is an academic. You're supposed to buy *How to Find Lovers by Loving Yourself* because its author has a Ph.D.

Sadly, most of us aren't famous or highly credentialed. Yet there's a second kind of ethos. It's the picture of you that people form as they read your text. To gain their trust, you should patiently lay out your claims, reasons, and evidence. When arguers are scornful, some of their audience may object. John Burt points out a problem that Stephen Douglas's ethos created in his famous debates with Abraham Lincoln. When the two men competed for a U.S. Senate seat in 1858, the main issue was slavery. On this topic, Douglas planned to come across as a seeker of compromise. But on stage, he fiercely insulted Lincoln, showing nastiness and no tact. As Burt observes, "Douglas's own management of his case was so intemperate, so inflammatory, and so personal that whatever case one could make for his position, he himself was the last person who could plausibly carry the day for that case." Sometimes anger *is* right, especially when injustice must be noticed and stopped. But for much of your writing, especially in college, a less combative tone will serve better.

Writers enhance their ethos through **concessions** and **qualifications**. Concessions are kind acknowledgments of interpretations other than yours. Your readers will appreciate your noting in the first place that these views can exist. You will look even better if you treat such alternatives with respect. Try to admit that they're not entirely wrong. For instance, you may want to argue that Kincaid's main speaker holds men in contempt. Even so, consider granting that other readers of the story may see the character differently. You might admit that at moments she suggests her listener should accept male power. Of course, you would still proceed to argue your own claim about her. But you'll have dealt admirably with a rival idea.

In the same spirit, you might *qualify* your generalizations so that you don't come across as proclaiming them to be absolute facts. In rhetorical theory, qualifications aren't credentials for a job. They are two kinds of words. One kind helps writers strengthen their claims. A common example is the word *very*, as in a sentence like "Cell phones are very bad for cities' sense of community." The second kind of qualification has the opposite effect. Words in this category weaken a claim. They help writers sound cautious, often an attractive trait. Rather than declare that "the speaker is scornful toward men," you might say that this is *probably* her attitude or that it *seems* to be her stance. Similar terms that have the nice effect of making you sound careful include *maybe*, *perhaps*, and *possibly*. These words suggest that the writer isn't self-righteously certain; with them, you project restraint.

Pathos is an appeal to the heart. You find it in charities' ads. Many show photos of suffering children — kids who are hungry, injured, or poor. These pictures are meant to rouse pity. If they succeed, viewers sob and donate. At other times, pathos stirs fear. Activists warn that if society ignores them, apocalypse will come. Pathos-filled arguments aren't dry in tone. Their language expresses *moods*. It targets its audience's *emotions*. When you write such arguments, you push readers to *feel* the stakes of your issue. You hope they'll *passionately* favor your claims. Sure, you risk sounding excessive: too sad, too mad, too scared, or too hurt. But pathos can be a respectable tool, as well as a powerful one. Plenty of subjects even demand an emotional tone. Readers expect essays on genocide to anguish over the victims. Further, pathos can join logos and ethos. Arguments that move readers may also awe them with logic; the author's image may impress them, too.

So, in writing an essay about Kincaid's story, you might refer to the "intimidating" voice of the main speaker. But keep such language limited. If you constantly vent your own passions, you may weaken your argument about the story. If you say that you find the speaker "creepy" and "monstrous" and "inhuman" and "despicable" and "loathsome" and "absolutely un-motherly," you may bother your readers. They might think that language like this conveys far more about *you*. Probably they'd want more details of the story and fewer bursts of your feelings. Again, emotional words *can* play a role in your argument. They may well add to its force. But they're effective only when you supply them in small doses.

A Sample Student Argument about Literature

The following essay demonstrates several of the strategies we have discussed. Its student author had read Kincaid's "Girl" in a course on composition and literature. Her assignment was to write an argument paper about a specific element of the story. She chose to raise an issue and develop a claim about its ending.

Ann Schumwalt
English 102
Professor Peretti
3 February ----

The Mother's Mixed Messages in "Girl"

In Jamaica Kincaid's story "Girl," the speaker is evidently a mother trying to teach her daughter how to behave. The story is basically a single-paragraph speech in which the mother gives various commands, instructions, and lessons, apparently in an effort at training her child to become what their culture considers a proper young woman. Only twice does the daughter herself interrupt the mother's monologue. It's interesting that the second break occurs near the end of the story. Right after the mother orders her to "always squeeze bread to make sure it's fresh," the daughter asks, *"but what if the baker won't let me feel the bread?"* (lines 40–41). There is only one more sentence before the story concludes: the mother responds by asking, "you mean to say that after all you are really going to be the kind of woman who the baker won't let near the bread?" (41–42). Faced with this final exchange, many readers may wonder why author Kincaid chooses to make it the story's conclusion. It could have appeared earlier in the text, and Kincaid might have ended with any of the mother's statements that now come before it. This ending also feels *in*conclusive, for the very last words are a question that does not receive an answer. What, therefore, is Kincaid trying to emphasize with this puzzling finish? A closer look at its language, as well as at other words of the text, suggests that Kincaid is deliberately making us uncertain about whether the mother's stern training will indeed help her daughter become strong enough to survive in their society. The mother may *believe* that she is providing sufficient survival skills, but Kincaid encourages readers to suspect that she is actually *dis*empowering her daughter, not letting her develop the willpower she needs to endure.

Refers to puzzled readers, as a way of bringing up the main issue. The essay will help these readers with the "closer look" it proceeds to offer.

Introduces the essay's main issue (a cause and effect one) as a question.

The essay's main claim.

When the mother commands her daughter to squeeze the bread, probably she sees herself as pushing her to take charge of her life rather than meekly accept other people's treatment of her. To squeeze something is to perform a vigorous, self-assertive action, and in this case it would involve testing the baker's product instead of just accepting it. Earlier in the text, the mother offers a few other hints that she wishes the daughter to be aggressive, not passive. For example, she advises her on "how to make a good medicine to throw away a child before it even becomes a child" (33–34); on "how to bully a man" (36); and on "how to spit up in the air if you feel like it" (39). A number of readers may infer, too, that even when she is telling the daughter how to perform house-hold chores like washing, ironing, setting meals, and sweeping, she is fostering her independence by enabling her to handle basic demands of daily existence.

But in crucial ways, the mother presses her daughter to play a subservient role in society. More specifically, she attempts to imprison her in a model of femininity that allows for men to dominate. Emphasizing that "you are not a boy, you know" (29–30), she demands that she "try to walk like a lady" (8) and take care of her father's clothes. The various chores that she expects her daughter to perform would make life easier for the male head of the household. Moreover, they seem duties that a boy would not be required to fulfill. Similarly, the mother hopes to restrict the daughter's sexual behavior. Repeatedly she warns her "to prevent yourself from looking like the slut I know you are so bent on becoming" (14–15). Again, it is doubtful that a boy would receive warnings like this. Like the United States, perhaps the culture reflected in this story even lacks a masculine equivalent of the derogatory term "slut."

At the end, I admit, the mother seems to associate her daughter with an image of power. She implies that the girl should become "the kind of woman" whom the baker *does* "let near the bread" so that she can test it by squeezing it (41–42). But even here, actually, the mother does not envision her daughter as actively taking charge. In the scenario she sketches, the baker *allows* the girl to feel the bread. In order to touch it, she must get his permission, rather than straightforwardly exert her own authority. Moreover, she first has to be a certain sort of woman; otherwise, she has not earned the right to examine his product. What type of woman is this? While some readers may argue that the mother wants her daughter to be an *assertive* female, many of the directions she has already given her would greatly limit her sphere of

Because Ann is mainly concerned with the story's ending, she starts her paper with it, rather than moving chronologically through Kincaid's text.

Qualifies this statement rather than expressing it as an absolute fact.

Draws evidence from the text's actual words.

Acknowledges existence of another possible interpretation.

Pathos used with the negatively emotional words presses, subservient, imprison, and dominate. Evidence then offered to support such language.

A reasonable assumption.

An assumption, though qualified with the word perhaps.

Concession.

action, leaving her to be a relatively unadventurous house-keeping "lady." Evidently the mother feels that the baker will give her daughter access to the bread only if she is a basically tame and polite version of womanhood.

The mother may not realize that she is conveying mixed messages to her child. If we, as readers, take her to be hoping that her daughter becomes empowered *and* subservient, we may be spotting a contradiction that the mother herself is not conscious of. But the daughter may be aware of it. Perhaps the daughter is, in fact, now a grown-up woman who is trying to make sense of the paradoxical pieces of advice her mother gave her during her adolescence. The mother may have offered these supposed bits of wisdom at various different times, but the daughter is now remembering them all as one speech and struggling to figure out their implications. Kincaid's decision to conclude the story with a question mark may be her way of indicating that even in adulthood, the daughter still has not determined whether her mother wanted to *liberate* her or *confine* her. We can regard the daughter as someone who is still attempting to "read" her mother's intentions. As actual readers of this story, we would then be in the same position as she is, having to come up with our own interpretation of what her mother wanted her to do and be.

"May not" is a qualification, indicating that Ann is less than sure what the mother thinks.

Even the text's punctuation may be significant.

Works Cited

Kincaid, Jamaica. "Girl." *Making Literature Matter: An Anthology for Readers and Writers*. Ed. John Schilb and John Clifford. 6th ed. Boston: Bedford, 2015. 48–50. Print.

Looking at Literature as Argument

Much of this book concerns arguing *about* literature. But many works of literature can be said to present arguments themselves. Admittedly, not all of literature can be seen as containing or making arguments, but occasionally you will find that associating a literary text with argument opens up productive lines of inquiry. Moreover, as you argue about literature, arguments *within* literature can help you see how you might persuade others.

Some works lay out an argument that the author obviously approves of. For an example, let us turn to the following poem. It was written around 1652 by John Milton (1608–1674), a poet who played a leading role in England's Puritan revolution. Seeking to make dominant their own version of Christianity, the Puritans executed King Charles I and installed their leader, Oliver Cromwell, as head of state. Milton wrote "When I consider how my light is spent" while working as an official in Cromwell's government. This is an autobiographical poem and refers to Milton's growing blindness, which threatened to prevent him from serving both his political leader and his religious one, God.

JOHN MILTON

When I consider how my light is spent

When I consider how my light is spent,
   Ere half my days in this dark world and wide,
   And that one talent which is death to hide
Lodged with me useless, though my soul more bent
To serve therewith my Maker, and present   5
   My true account, lest He returning chide;
   "Doth God exact day-labor, light denied?"
I fondly ask. But Patience, to prevent
That murmur, soon replies, "God doth not need
   Either man's work or His own gifts. Who best   10
   Bear His mild yoke, they serve Him best. His state
Is kingly: thousands at His bidding speed,
   And post o'er land and ocean without rest;
   They also serve who only stand and wait."   *[c. 1652]*

The speaker does not actually spell out his warrants. Consider, however, his reference to Christ's parable of the talents (Luke 19:12–27). In the ancient Middle East, a *talent* was a unit of money. In the parable, a servant is scolded by his master for hoarding the one talent that his master had given him. By telling this story, Christ implies that people should make use of the gifts afforded them by God. For the speaker in Milton's poem, the parable has a lot of authority. Evidently he feels that he should carry out its lesson. In effect, then, the parable has indeed become a warrant for him: that is, a basis for finding his blindness cause for lament.

Who, exactly, is the speaker's audience? Perhaps he is not addressing anyone in particular. Or perhaps the speaker's mind is divided and one side of it is addressing the other. Or perhaps the speaker is addressing God, even though he refers to God in the third person. Given that the speaker is answered by Patience, perhaps he means to address *that* figure, although Patience may actually be just a part of him rather than an altogether separate being.

At any rate, Patience takes the speaker for an audience in responding. And while Patience does not provide evidence, let alone warrants, Patience does make claims about God and his followers. Furthermore, Milton as author seems to endorse Patience's claims; apparently he is using the poem to advance them. Besides pointing out *how* God is served, Milton suggests that God *ought* to be served, even if God lets bad things happen to good people like Milton.

Every author can be considered an audience for his or her own writing, but some authors write expressly to engage in a dialogue with themselves. Perhaps Milton wrote his poem partly to convince himself that his religion was still valid and his life still worth living. Significantly, he did not publish the poem until about twenty years later. Yet because he did publish it eventually, at some point he must have contemplated a larger audience for it. The first readers of the poem would have been a relatively small segment of the English population: those literate and prosperous enough to have access to books of poetry. In addition, a number of the poem's first readers would have shared Milton's religious beliefs. Perhaps, however, Milton felt that even the faith of this band had to be bolstered. For one thing, not every Protestant of the time would have shared Milton's enthusiasm for the Puritan government. Recall that this regime executed the king, supposedly replacing him with the rule of God. Milton's words "His state / Is kingly" can be seen as an effort to persuade readers that the Puritans did put God on England's throne.

Certain arguments made in literary texts may or may not have the author's endorsement. Faced with a conflict of ideas, readers must engage in interpretation, forced to decide which position is apt to be the author's own view. A classic example is "Mending Wall," a famous poem by Robert Frost (1874–1963), from his 1914 book, *North of Boston*. Troubled by his neighbor's desire to repair the wall between their farms, the poem's speaker argues against its necessity, but literary critics have long debated whether Frost agrees with the speaker's claims and reasons. How persuasive do you find them?

ROBERT FROST

Mending Wall

Something there is that doesn't love a wall,
That sends the frozen-ground-swell under it,
And spills the upper boulders in the sun;
And makes gaps even two can pass abreast.
The work of hunters is another thing: 5
I have come after them and made repair
Where they have left not one stone on a stone,
But they would have the rabbit out of hiding,
To please the yelping dogs. The gaps I mean,
No one has seen them made or heard them made,   10
But at spring mending-time we find them there.
I let my neighbor know beyond the hill;
And on a day we meet to walk the line
And set the wall between us once again.
We keep the wall between us as we go.   15
To each the boulders that have fallen to each.
And some are loaves and some so nearly balls
We have to use a spell to make them balance:
"Stay where you are until our backs are turned!"
We wear our fingers rough with handling them.   20
Oh, just another kind of outdoor game,
One on a side. It comes to little more:
There where it is we do not need the wall:
He is all pine and I am apple orchard.
My apple trees will never get across   25
And eat the cones under his pines, I tell him.
He only says, "Good fences make good neighbors."
Spring is the mischief in me, and I wonder
If I could put a notion in his head:
"Why do they make good neighbors? Isn't it   30
Where there are cows? But here there are no cows.
Before I built a wall I'd ask to know
What I was walling in or walling out,
And to whom I was like to give offense.
Something there is that doesn't love a wall,   35
That wants it down." I could say "Elves" to him,
But it's not elves exactly, and I'd rather
He said it for himself. I see him there
Bringing a stone grasped firmly by the top
In each hand, like an old-stone savage armed.   40
He moves in darkness as it seems to me,
Not of woods only and the shade of trees.
He will not go behind his father's saying,

And he likes having thought of it so well
He says again, "Good fences make good neighbors."   *[1914]*   45

Other literary works, though, present an argument that the author is unlikely to endorse. In such cases, we might describe the work as *ironic* because we sense a distance between the position being expressed and the author's own view. Probably one of the most famous examples in literature of an ironic argument is the 1729 essay "A Modest Proposal." Its author, Jonathan Swift (1667–1745), is today chiefly known for his satirical fantasy *Gulliver's Travels* (1726). He also wrote political journalism and served as dean of St. Patrick's Cathedral in Dublin. Swift was moved to write his "Proposal" by the widespread poverty and hunger in his native Ireland, which was then completely under English control. To him, this suffering had human causes, including neglect by the country's absent English landlords, indifference from its government officials, and economic restrictions established in its laws. The solution that Swift puts forth in his essay is not one he actually favored. Indeed, he thought it would shock most people. By making such an outlandish argument, he aimed to disturb his readers so that they would work to solve Ireland's crisis in more realistic and humane ways.

JONATHAN SWIFT
A Modest Proposal

For preventing the children of poor people in Ireland,
from being a burden on their parents or country,
and for making them beneficial to the public.

It is a melancholy object to those, who walk through this great town, or travel in the country, when they see the streets, the roads, and cabin-doors crowded with beggars of the female sex, followed by three, four, or six children, all in rags, and importuning every passenger for an alms. These mothers, instead of being able to work for their honest livelihood, are forced to employ all their time in strolling to beg sustenance for their helpless infants who, as they grow up, either turn thieves for want of work, or leave their dear native country, to fight for the Pretender° in Spain, or sell themselves to the Barbadoes.

I think it is agreed by all parties that this prodigious number of children in the arms, or on the backs, or at the heels of their mothers, and frequently of their fathers, is in the present deplorable state of the kingdom, a very great additional grievance; and therefore whoever could find out a fair, cheap, and easy method of making these children sound and useful members of the commonwealth, would deserve so well of the public, as to have his statue set up for a preserver of the nation.

Pretender: Son of England's King James II; exiled in Spain but sought his country's throne.

But my intention is very far from being confined to provide only for the children of professed beggars: it is of a much greater extent, and shall take in the whole number of infants at a certain age, who are born of parents in effect as little able to support them, as those who demand our charity in the streets.

As to my own part, having turned my thoughts for many years, upon this important subject, and maturely weighed the several schemes of our projectors, I have always found them grossly mistaken in their computation. It is true, a child just dropped from its dam, may be supported by her milk, for a solar year, with little other nourishment: at most not above the value of two shillings, which the mother may certainly get, or the value in scraps, by her lawful occupation of begging; and it is exactly at one year old that I propose to provide for them in such a manner, as, instead of being a charge upon their parents, or the parish, or wanting food and raiment for the rest of their lives, they shall, on the contrary, contribute to the feeding, and partly to the clothing of many thousands.

There is likewise another great advantage in my scheme, that it will prevent those voluntary abortions, and that horrid practice of women murdering their bastard children, alas! too frequent among us, sacrificing the poor innocent babes, I doubt, more to avoid the expense than the shame, which would move tears and pity in the most savage and inhuman breast.

The number of souls in this kingdom being usually reckoned one million and a half, of these I calculate there may be about two hundred thousand couple whose wives are breeders; from which number I subtract thirty thousand couple, who are able to maintain their own children, (although I apprehend there cannot be so many, under the present distresses of the kingdom) but this being granted, there will remain a hundred and seventy thousand breeders. I again subtract fifty thousand, for those women who miscarry, or whose children die by accident or disease within the year. There only remain a hundred and twenty thousand children of poor parents annually born. The question therefore is, How this number shall be reared, and provided for? which, as I have already said, under the present situation of affairs, is utterly impossible by all the methods hitherto proposed. For we can neither employ them in handicraft or agriculture; we neither build houses (I mean in the country), nor cultivate land: they can very seldom pick up a livelihood by stealing till they arrive at six years old; except where they are of towardly parts, although I confess they learn the rudiments much earlier; during which time they can however be properly looked upon only as probationers: As I have been informed by a principal gentleman in the county of Cavan, who protested to me, that he never knew above one or two instances under the age of six, even in a part of the kingdom so renowned for the quickest proficiency in that art.

I am assured by our merchants, that a boy or a girl before twelve years old, is no saleable commodity, and even when they come to this age, they will not yield above three pounds, or three pounds and half a crown at most, on the exchange; which cannot turn to account either to the parents or kingdom, the charge of nutriments and rags having been at least four times that value.

I shall now therefore humbly propose my own thoughts, which I hope will not be liable to the least objection.

I have been assured by a very knowing American of my acquaintance in London, that a young healthy child well nursed, is, at a year old, a most delicious nourishing and wholesome food, whether stewed, roasted, baked, or boiled; and I make no doubt that it will equally serve in a fricassee or a ragout.

I do therefore humbly offer it to public consideration, that of the hundred   10
and twenty thousand children, already computed, twenty thousand may be reserved for breed, whereof only one-fourth part to be males; which is more than we allow to sheep, black cattle, or swine, and my reason is, that these children are seldom the fruits of marriage, a circumstance not much regarded by our savages, therefore, one male will be sufficient to serve four females. That the remaining hundred thousand may, at a year old, be offered in sale to the persons of quality and fortune, through the kingdom, always advising the mother to let them suck plentifully in the last month, so as to render them plump, and fat for a good table. A child will make two dishes at an entertainment for friends, and when the family dines alone, the fore or hind quarter will make a reasonable dish, and seasoned with a little pepper or salt, will be very good boiled on the fourth day, especially in winter.

I have reckoned upon a medium, that a child just born will weigh 12 pounds, and in a solar year, if tolerably nursed, increase to 28 pounds.

I grant this food will be somewhat dear, and therefore very proper for landlords, who, as they have already devoured most of the parents, seem to have the best title to the children.

Infant's flesh will be in season throughout the year, but more plentiful in March, and a little before and after; for we are told by a grave author, an eminent French physician, that fish being a prolific diet, there are more children born in Roman Catholic countries about nine months after Lent, the markets will be more glutted than usual, because the number of Popish infants, is at least three to one in this kingdom, and therefore it will have one other collateral advantage, by lessening the number of Papists among us.

I have already computed the charge of nursing a beggar's child (in which list I reckon all cottagers, laborers, and four-fifths of the farmers) to be about two shillings per annum, rags included; and I believe no gentleman would repine to give ten shillings for the carcass of a good fat child, which, as I have said, will make four dishes of excellent nutritive meat, when he has only some particular friend, or his own family to dine with him. Thus the squire will learn to be a good landlord, and grow popular among his tenants, the mother will have eight shillings neat profit, and be fit for work till she produces another child.

Those who are more thrifty (as I must confess the times require) may flay   15
the carcass; the skin of which, artificially dressed, will make admirable gloves for ladies, and summer boots for fine gentlemen.

As to our City of Dublin, shambles may be appointed for this purpose, in the most convenient parts of it, and butchers we may be assured will not be wanting; although I rather recommend buying the children alive, and dressing them hot from the knife, as we do roasting pigs.

A very worthy person, a true lover of his country, and whose virtues I highly esteem, was lately pleased, in discoursing on this matter, to offer a refinement upon my scheme. He said, that many gentlemen of this kingdom, having of late destroyed their deer, he conceived that the want of venison might be well supplied by the bodies of young lads and maidens, not exceeding fourteen years of age, nor under twelve; so great a number of both sexes in every country being now ready to starve for want of work and service: And these to be disposed of by their parents if alive, or otherwise by their nearest relations. But with due deference to so excellent a friend, and so deserving a patriot, I cannot be altogether in his sentiments; for as to the males, my American acquaintance assured me from frequent experience, that their flesh was generally tough and lean, like that of our schoolboys, by continual exercise, and their taste disagreeable, and to fatten them would not answer the charge. Then as to the females, it would, I think, with humble submission, be a loss to the public, because they soon would become breeders themselves: And besides, it is not improbable that some scrupulous people might be apt to censure such a practice (although indeed very unjustly), as a little bordering upon cruelty, which, I confess, hath always been with me the strongest objection against any project, how well soever intended.

But in order to justify my friend, he confessed, that this expedient was put into his head by the famous Salmanaazor, a native of the island Formosa, who came from thence to London, above twenty years ago, and in conversation told my friend, that in his country, when any young person happened to be put to death, the executioner sold the carcass to persons of quality, as a prime dainty; and that, in his time, the body of a plump girl of fifteen, who was crucified for an attempt to poison the Emperor, was sold to his imperial majesty's prime minister of state, and other great mandarins of the court, in joints from the gibbet, at four hundred crowns. Neither indeed can I deny, that if the same use were made of several plump young girls in this town, who without one single groat to their fortunes, cannot stir abroad without a chair, and appear at a playhouse and assemblies in foreign fineries which they never will pay for; the kingdom would not be the worse.

Some persons of a desponding spirit are in great concern about that vast number of poor people, who are aged, diseased, or maimed; and I have been desired to employ my thoughts what course may be taken, to ease the nation of so grievous an encumbrance. But I am not in the least pain upon that matter, because it is very well known, that they are every day dying, and rotting, by cold and famine, and filth, and vermin, as fast as can be reasonably expected. And as to the young laborers, they are now in almost as hopeful a condition. They cannot get work, and consequently pine away from want of nourishment, to a degree, that if at any time they are accidentally hired to common labor, they have not strength to perform it, and thus the country and themselves are happily delivered from the evils to come.

I have too long digressed, and therefore shall return to my subject. I think the advantages by the proposal which I have made are obvious and many, as well as of the highest importance.

20

For first, as I have already observed, it would greatly lessen the number of Papists, with whom we are yearly overrun, being the principal breeders of the nation, as well as our most dangerous enemies, and who stay at home on purpose with a design to deliver the kingdom to the Pretender, hoping to take their advantage by the absence of so many good Protestants, who have chosen rather to leave their country, than stay at home and pay tithes against their conscience to an episcopal curate.

Secondly, The poorer tenants will have something valuable of their own, which by law may be made liable to a distress, and help to pay their landlord's rent, their corn and cattle being already seized, and money a thing unknown.

Thirdly, Whereas the maintainance of a hundred thousand children, from two years old, and upward, cannot be computed at less than ten shillings a piece per annum, the nation's stock will be thereby increased fifty thousand pounds per annum, besides the profit of a new dish, introduced to the tables of all gentlemen of fortune in the kingdom, who have any refinement in taste. And the money will circulate among ourselves, the goods being entirely of our own growth and manufacture.

Fourthly, The constant breeders, besides the gain of eight shillings sterling per annum by the sale of their children, will be rid of the charge of maintaining them after the first year.

Fifthly, This food would likewise bring great custom to taverns, where the vintners will certainly be so prudent as to procure the best receipts for dressing it to perfection; and consequently have their houses frequented by all the fine gentlemen, who justly value themselves upon their knowledge in good eating; and a skillful cook, who understands how to oblige his guests, will contrive to make it as expensive as they please.

Sixthly, This would be a great inducement to marriage, which all wise nations have either encouraged by rewards, or enforced by laws and penalties. It would increase the care and tenderness of mothers toward their children, when they were sure of a settlement for life to the poor babes, provided in some sort by the public, to their annual profit instead of expense. We should soon see an honest emulation among the married women, which of them could bring the fattest child to the market. Men would become as fond of their wives, during the time of their pregnancy, as they are now of their mares in foal, their cows in calf, or sow when they are ready to farrow; nor offer to beat or kick them (as is too frequent a practice) for fear of a miscarriage.

Many other advantages might be enumerated. For instance, the addition of some thousand carcasses in our exportation of barreled beef: the propagation of swine's flesh, and improvement in the art of making good bacon, so much wanted among us by the great destruction of pigs, too frequent at our tables; which are no way comparable in taste or magnificence to a well grown, fat yearly child, which roasted whole will make a considerable figure at a Lord Mayor's feast, or any other public entertainment. But this, and many others, I omit, being studious of brevity.

Supposing that one thousand families in this city would be constant customers for infants' flesh, besides others who might have it at merry meetings, particularly at weddings and christenings, I compute that Dublin would take off annually about twenty thousand carcasses; and the rest of the kingdom (where probably they will be sold somewhat cheaper) the remaining eighty thousand.

I can think of no one objection that will possibly be raised against this proposal, unless it should be urged that the number of people will be thereby much lessened in the kingdom. This I freely own, and 'twas indeed one principal design in offering it to the world. I desire the reader will observe that I calculate my remedy for this one individual Kingdom of Ireland, and for no other that ever was, is, or, I think, ever can be upon Earth. Therefore let no man talk to me of other expedients: Of taxing our absentees at five shillings a pound: Of using neither clothes, nor household furniture, except what is of our own growth and manufacture: Of utterly rejecting the materials and instruments that promote foreign luxury: Of curing the expensiveness of pride, vanity, idleness, and gaming in our women: Of introducing a vein of parsimony, prudence, and temperance: Of learning to love our country, wherein we differ even from Laplanders, and the inhabitants of Topinamboo: Of quitting our animosities and factions, nor acting any longer like the Jews, who were murdering one another at the very moment their city was taken: Of being a little cautious not to sell our country and consciences for nothing: Of teaching landlords to have at least one degree of mercy toward their tenants. Lastly, of putting a spirit of honesty, industry, and skill into our shopkeepers, who, if a resolution could now be taken to buy only our native goods, would immediately unite to cheat and exact upon us in the price, the measure, and the goodness, nor could ever yet be brought to make one fair proposal of just dealing, though often and earnestly invited to it.

Therefore I repeat, let no man talk to me of these and the like expedients, till he hath at least some glimpse of hope, that there will ever be some hearty and sincere attempt to put them into practice.

But, as to myself, having been wearied out for many years with offering vain, idle, visionary thoughts, and at length utterly despairing of success, I fortunately fell upon this proposal, which, as it is wholly new, so it hath something solid and real, of no expense and little trouble, full in our own power, and whereby we can incur no danger in disobliging England. For this kind of commodity will not bear exportation, and flesh being of too tender a consistence, to admit a long continuance in salt, although perhaps I could name a country which would be glad to eat up our whole nation without it.

After all, I am not so violently bent upon my own opinion as to reject any offer, proposed by wise men, which shall be found equally innocent, cheap, easy, and effectual. But before something of that kind shall be advanced in contradiction to my scheme, and offering a better, I desire the author or authors will be pleased maturely to consider two points. First, As things now stand, how they will be able to find food and raiment for a hundred thousand useless mouths and backs. And secondly, There being a round million of creatures in human figure throughout this kingdom, whose whole subsistence put into a common stock, would leave them in debt two million of pounds sterling,

30

adding those who are beggars by profession, to the bulk of farmers, cottagers and laborers, with their wives and children, who are beggars in effect; I desire those politicians who dislike my overture, and may perhaps be so bold to attempt an answer, that they will first ask the parents of these mortals, whether they would not at this day think it a great happiness to have been sold for food at a year old, in the manner I prescribe, and thereby have avoided such a perpetual scene of misfortunes, as they have since gone through, by the oppression of landlords, the impossibility of paying rent without money or trade, the want of common sustenance, with neither house nor clothes to cover them from the inclemencies of the weather, and the most inevitable prospect of entailing the like, or greater miseries, upon their breed forever.

I profess, in the sincerity of my heart, that I have not the least personal interest in endeavoring to promote this necessary work, having no other motive than the public good of my country, by advancing our trade, providing for infants, relieving the poor, and giving some pleasure to the rich. I have no children, by which I can propose to get a single penny; the youngest being nine years old, and my wife past child-bearing.   *[1729]*

A contemporary version of an ironic literary argument is the following brief story by British author Neil Gaiman (b. 1960), who first published it in a 1994 edition of the graphic art magazine *Taboo*. Compare this story to Swift's essay. Do you see Gaiman as being "Swiftian"? What, by writing this piece, is Gaiman apparently trying to achieve? What do you suspect he wants his readers to think or do?

NEIL GAIMAN
Babycakes

A few years back all of the animals went away.

We woke up one morning, and they just weren't there anymore. They
    didn't even leave us a note, or say goodbye.

We never quite figured out where they'd gone.

We missed them.

Some of us thought that the world had ended, but it hadn't. There just   5
    weren't any more animals. No cats or rabbits, no dogs or whales, no
    fish in the seas, no birds in the skies.

We were all alone.

We didn't know what to do.

We wandered around lost, for a time, and then someone pointed out that
    just because we didn't have animals anymore, that was no reason to
    change our lives. No reason to change our diets or to cease testing
    products that might cause us harm.

After all, there were still babies.

Babies can't talk. They can hardly move. A baby is not a rational,   10
    thinking creature.

And we used them.

Some of them we ate. Baby flesh is tender and succulent.

We flayed their skin and decorated ourselves in it. Baby leather is soft and comfortable.

Some of them we tested.

We taped open their eyes, dripped detergents and shampoos in, a drop at a time.   15

We scarred them and scalded them. We burned them. We clamped them and planted electrodes into their brains. We grafted, and we froze and we irradiated.

The babies breathed our smoke, and the babies' veins flowed with our medicines and drugs, until they stopped breathing or their blood ceased to flow.

It was hard, of course, but necessary.

No one could deny that.

With the animals gone, what else could we do?   20

Some people complained, of course. But then, they always do.

And everything went back to normal.

Only . . .

Yesterday, all the babies were gone.

We don't know where they went. We didn't even see them go.   25

We don't know what we're going to do without them.

But we'll think of something. Humans are smart. It's what makes us superior to the animals and the babies.

We'll figure something out.   [1994]

≡ SUMMING UP: MAKING ARGUMENTS ABOUT LITERATURE

- The art of arguing is part of the tradition known as *rhetoric*. The *rhetorical situation* includes your particular topic, your audience, and the "channels" you employ. (pp. 51–52).

- When you argue, you attempt to *persuade* an *audience* to accept your *claims* regarding an *issue* by presenting *evidence*, explaining your *reasoning*, relying on *assumptions*, and making other kinds of *appeals*. (p. 52)

- An *issue* is something about which people have disagreed or might disagree. Defined as questions with no obvious, immediate answers, ten kinds of issues that arise in literature courses are those of (1) fact, (2) theme, (3) definition, (4) symbolism, (5) pattern, (6) evaluation, (7) historical and cultural context, (8) genre, (9) social policy, and (10) cause and effect. (pp. 53–59)

(continued on next page)

- *Claims* **are the debatable answers to an issue.** In literature classes, two common types of claims are those of interpretation and those of evaluation. (pp. 47–70)

- **The art of persuasion involves trying to change people's minds.** You should convince them that your claims are at least reasonable. (p. 60).

- **The term** *audience* **applies to the people who read your writing.** If you are to persuade them, you must take into account their common values, experiences, and assumptions, not just focus on your subject matter. To introduce your main claim about a literary work, you might refer to readers of it who disagree with you; hasty, superficial readers; puzzled readers; or your own divided self. (pp. 60–61)

- *Evidence* **is the support that you give your claims so that others will accept them.** When you make an argument about a literary work, your readers expect you to support your case with details in the text. (p. 62)

- **To persuade your audience, you need to show clearly your process of reasoning.** Methodically lay out your claims as well as the logic that connects them. (p. 60)

- *Assumptions* **are beliefs of yours that support your argument and that you may have to acknowledge as well as defend.** They include (1) beliefs about your audience's experiences; (2) values you hold; and (3) warrants, which are reasons you have for considering certain things evidence. (pp. 63–64)

- *Appeals* **in arguments fall into three main categories.** These are *logos*, the logical substance of the case; *ethos*, the image of the arguer that the audience gets; and *pathos*, the stirring of emotion. To create a positive ethos, you might make several concessions and qualifications. (pp. 64–66)

- **Some literary works can be said to present arguments themselves.** Certain characters make claims, often in debate with one another, through characterization, plot, and image, and other works indicate that the author is arguing for a certain position. (pp. 69–78)

CHAPTER 4

The Writing Process

In Chapter 5, we discuss how to write about each of the four literary genres featured in this book. Here, however, we suggest how to write about a literary work of any genre. To make our advice concrete, we mostly trace what one student did as she worked on a writing assignment for a course much like yours. Each student chose a single poem from the syllabus and wrote a 600-word argument paper on it for a general audience. We focus on the writing process of a student named Abby Hazelton.

Ultimately, Abby chose to write about William Wordsworth's "The Solitary Reaper." In his own day, Wordsworth (1770–1850) was poet laureate of England, and he continues to be regarded as a major British Romantic poet. He and fellow poet Samuel Taylor Coleridge collaborated on *Lyrical Ballads* (1798), a collection of verse that became a landmark of Romantic poetry. In his preface to the second edition two years later, Wordsworth famously defined *poetry* as "emotion recollected in tranquillity," contended that it should draw on "common life," and called for it to incorporate "language really used by men." Like many other Romantics, Wordsworth celebrated scenes of nature and country life, while deploring the increasing spread of cities. "The Solitary Reaper" appeared in his 1807 *Poems in Two Volumes*.

Before examining Abby's writing process, read Wordsworth's poem.

WILLIAM WORDSWORTH

The Solitary Reaper

Behold her, single in the field,
    Yon solitary Highland Lass!
Reaping and singing by herself;
    Stop here, or gently pass!
Alone she cuts and binds the grain,   5
And sings a melancholy strain;
O listen! for the Vale profound
Is overflowing with the sound.

No Nightingale did ever chaunt
    More welcome notes to weary bands   10
Of travellers in some shady haunt,
    Among Arabian sands:

A voice so thrilling ne'er was heard
In spring-time from the Cuckoo-bird,
Breaking the silence of the seas   15
Among the farthest Hebrides.

Will no one tell me what she sings? —
    Perhaps the plaintive numbers flow
For old, unhappy, far-off things,
    And battles long ago: 20
Or is it some more humble lay,
Familiar matter of to-day?
Some natural sorrow, loss, or pain,
That has been, and may be again?

Whate'er the theme, the Maiden sang   25
    As if her song could have no ending;
I saw her singing at her work,
    And o'er the sickle bending; —
I listen'd, motionless and still;
And, as I mounted up the hill,   30
The music in my heart I bore,
Long after it was heard no more.   *[1807]*

Once she chose to write about Wordsworth's poem for her paper, Abby engaged in four sorts of activities: (1) exploring, (2) planning, (3) composing, and (4) revising. As we describe each, keep in mind that these activities need not be consecutive. Abby moved back and forth among them as she worked on her assignment.

Strategies for Exploring

As you read a literary work, you are bound to interpret and judge it. Yet not all reading is close reading, which can also be called **critical reading**. This process involves carefully and self-consciously analyzing various aspects of a text, including its meanings, its effects, and its treatment of typical elements of its genre. When you read a work closely and critically, you also note questions it raises for you — issues you might explore further in class discussion and writing. Indeed, close reading is a process of self-reflection. During this process, you monitor your own response to the text and try to identify why you see the text the way you do.

Exploring, the first stage of writing an essay about literature, is this particular process of reading. As we explain in Chapter 2, it specifically involves the following:

- Making predictions as you read
- Rereading the text with a different focus each time, including at least one stage in which you read aloud
- Comparing the text with your personal experience
- Tracing patterns and breaks from these patterns

- Noting ambiguities
- Considering the author's alternatives
- Generating questions
- Considering how the text deals with topics that have preoccupied literary studies
- Formulating a tentative claim
- Using informal writing to move through all these steps, including commenting in the text's margins; note-taking; freewriting; creating a "dialectical notebook"; and playfully revising the text

≡ A WRITING EXERCISE

Do at least ten minutes of freewriting about Wordsworth's poem, keeping it nearby so that you can consult it if you need to. In particular, try to raise questions about the poem, and consider which of these may be worth addressing in a more formal paper.

Here is an excerpt from Abby's freewriting.

I see that this poem consists of four stanzas, each of which is eight lines long. But these stanzas have different emphases. The first stanza is a series of commands. The speaker tells people to "Behold," "Stop here, or gently pass," and "listen." The second stanza mainly describes the reaper. The third stanza is basically a bunch of questions. The fourth is the speaker's recollection of his experience in general. So I could write a paper about how this poem changes as it moves along and why the stanzas shift in emphasis. But one problem with a paper like that is that it might get me bogged down in mechanically moving from stanza to stanza. I don't want that to happen. Another thing I could do is answer one of the speaker's own questions, which are about what kind of song the reaper is singing. Evidently this "Highland Lass" is using a Scottish dialect that he doesn't understand. But I'm just as ignorant as he is about the song. I guess I'm more likely to contribute some analysis of my own if I come up with a question myself. I'm struck by the fact that he doesn't give us much sense of the reaper's song. There's no way that a printed poem could convey the reaper's tune, but still. And the words are foreign to the speaker. But I'm surprised that he doesn't make a little effort to convey at least some of the song's lyrics even if they're foreign words that he might hear wrong or misspell. How can I as a reader join him in experiencing the beauty of her song if I don't learn any of its words? I wonder if we're supposed to see the poem as being more about the speaker than about the reaper. More specifically, maybe we're supposed to be a little disturbed that he's a British intellectual who is making a spectacle out of a foreign woman from the working class. At any rate, he seems bent on controlling this experience even as he invites us to share it. Another question for me is, Why does he shift from present tense to past tense in the last stanza? This change is really curious to me. I don't see anything earlier on that prepares me for it. First, we're led to believe that the speaker is observing the reaper right then and there, but at the end he speaks as if this occurred in the past, though maybe the recent past. This inconsistency in the time frame makes me think that in some important way the overall poem is about time. At any rate, I'm drawn to the inconsistency because it's so blatant. If I wrote about it, I might still devote a paragraph to each stanza, but I'd be starting with the last one and referring back to the others in order to explain that stanza. What I still have to figure out, though, is what exactly the poem is saying about time when it makes the shift of tense.

Freewriting enabled Abby to raise several questions. At the same time, she realized that her paper could not deal with everything that puzzled her. When you first get an assignment like hers, you may fear that you will have nothing to say. But you will come up with a lot of material if, like Abby, you take time for exploration. As we have suggested, it's a process of examining potential subjects through writing, discussion, and just plain thinking. One of your challenges will be to choose among the various issues you have formulated. At the end of this excerpt from her freewriting, Abby is on the verge of choosing to analyze the poem's shift of tense in its final stanza. For her, this shift is an interesting change from a pattern, the poem's previous uses of present tense. Abby has not yet decided how to explain this shift; at the moment, it remains for her a mystery. But her paper would achieve little if it focused just on aspects of the poem that are easy to interpret. Though Abby has more thinking to do about the poem's shift of tense, it seems a promising subject for her precisely because it puzzles her.

Strategies for Planning

Planning for an assignment like Abby's involves five main activities:

1. Choosing the text you will analyze
2. Identifying your audience
3. Identifying the main issue, claim, and evidence you will present
4. Identifying your assumptions
5. Determining how you will organize your argument, including how you will demonstrate your process of reasoning

CHOOSE A TEXT

Abby considered several poems before choosing one for her paper. She settled on Wordsworth's for five reasons. First, it was a text that left her with plenty of questions. Second, she believed that these questions could be issues for other readers. Third, she felt increasingly able to *argue* about the poem — that is, to make and support claims about it. Fourth, she believed that she could adequately analyze the poem within the assignment's word limit. Finally, Wordsworth's poem drew her because she had heard about the Romantic movement in English literature and was curious to study an example of it.

Faced with the same assignment, you might choose a different poem than Abby did. Still, the principles that she followed are useful. Think about them whenever you are free to decide which texts you will write about. With some assignments, of course, you may need a while to decide which text is best for you. And later, after you have made your decision, you may want to make a switch. For example, you may find yourself changing your mind once you have done a complete draft. Frustrated by the text you have chosen, you may realize that another inspires you more. If so, consider making a substitution. Naturally, you will feel more able to switch if you have ample time left to write the paper, so avoid waiting to start your paper just before it is due.

IDENTIFY YOUR AUDIENCE

To determine what your readers will see as an issue and to make your claims about it persuasive to them, you need to develop an audience profile. Perhaps your instructor will specify your audience. You may be asked, for example, to imagine yourself writing for a particular group in a particular situation. If you were Abby, how would you analyze "The Solitary Reaper" for an orchestra wanting to know what this poem implies about music? Even when not required of you, such an exercise can be fun and thought-provoking for you as you plan a paper.

Most often, though, instructors ask students to write for a "general" audience, the readership that Abby was asked to address. Assume that a general audience is one that will want evidence for your claims. While this audience will include your instructor, let it also include your classmates, since in class discussions they will be an audience for you whenever you speak. Besides, your class may engage in peer review, with students giving one another feedback on their drafts.

IDENTIFY YOUR ISSUE, CLAIM, AND EVIDENCE

When you have written papers for previous classes, you may have been most concerned with coming up with a thesis. Maybe you did not encounter the term *issue* at all. But good planning for a paper does entail identifying the main issue you will address. Once you have sensed what that issue is, try phrasing it as a question. If the answer would be obvious to your readers, be cautious, for you really do not have an issue if the problem you are raising can be easily resolved.

Also, try to identify what *kind* of issue you will focus on. For help, look at our list of various types (pp. 42–46). Within "The Solitary Reaper," the speaker raises an issue of fact: he wants to know what sort of song the reaper is singing. But as someone writing about Wordsworth's poem, Abby wanted to focus on another kind of issue, which she decided is best regarded as an issue of pattern. More precisely, she thought her main question might be, What should we conclude from the inconsistency in pattern that occurs when the final stanza shifts to past tense? To be sure, Abby recognized that addressing this issue would lead to issues of theme and of cause and effect, for she would have to consider why Wordsworth shifts tenses and how the shift relates to his overall subject.

Now that she had identified her main issue, Abby had to determine her main claim. Perhaps you have grown comfortable with the term *thesis* and want to keep using it. Fine. Bear in mind, though, that your thesis is the main *claim* you will make and proceed to support. And when, as Abby did, you put your main issue as a question, then your main claim is your answer to that question. Sometimes you will come up with question and answer simultaneously. Once in a while, you may even settle on your answer first, not being certain yet how to word the question. Whatever the case, planning for your paper involves articulating both the question (the issue) and the answer (your main claim). Try actually writing both down, making sure to phrase your main issue as a question and your main claim as the answer. Again, Abby's main issue was, What should we conclude from the inconsistency in pattern that occurs when the final stanza shifts to past tense? After much thought, she expressed her main claim this way:

> One possible justification for the shift to past tense is that it reminds us of the speaker's inability to halt the passage of time. He would like to freeze his encounter with the reaper, keeping it always in the present. But as the shift in tense indicates, time goes on, making the encounter part of the speaker's past. Perhaps, therefore, the poem's real subject is the idea that time is always in flux.

Audiences usually want evidence, and as we noted earlier, most arguments you write about literature will need to cite details of the work itself. Because direct quotation is usually an effective move, Abby planned to elaborate her claim by citing several of Wordsworth's references to time. Remember, though, that you need to avoid seeming willfully selective when you quote. While Abby expected to quote from Wordsworth's last stanza, she also knew she had to relate it to earlier lines so that her readers would see her as illuminating the basic subject of the whole poem. In particular, she looked for language in the first three stanzas that might hint at the speaker's lack of control over time, thereby previewing the last stanza's emphasis.

IDENTIFY YOUR ASSUMPTIONS

Often, to think about particular challenges of your paper is to think about your assumptions. Remember that a big category of assumptions is warrants; these are what lead you to call certain things evidence for your claims. Abby knew that one of her warrants was an assumption about Wordsworth himself — that he was not being sloppy when he shifted tenses in his last stanza. Rarely will your paper need to admit all the warrants on which it relies. Most of the time, your task will be to guess which warrants your readers do want stated. Abby felt there was at least one warrant she would have to spell out — her belief that the poem's verb tenses reveal something about the speaker's state of mind.

DETERMINE YOUR ORGANIZATION

To make sure their texts seem organized and demonstrate the process of reasoning, most writers first do an **outline**, a list of their key points in the order they will appear. Outlines are indeed a good idea, but bear in mind that there are various kinds. One popular type, which you may already know, is the **sentence outline**. As the name implies, it lists the writer's key points in sentence form. Its advantages are obvious: this kind of outline forces you to develop a detailed picture of your argument's major steps, and it leaves you with sentences you can then incorporate into your paper. Unfortunately, sentence outlines tend to discourage flexibility. Because they demand much thought and energy, you may hesitate to revise them, even if you come to feel your paper would work better with a new structure.

A second, equally familiar outline is the **topic outline**, a list in which the writer uses a few words to signify the main subjects that he or she will discuss. Because it is sketchy, this kind of outline allows writers to go back and change plans if necessary. Nevertheless, a topic outline may fail to provide all the guidance a writer needs.

We find a third type useful: a **rhetorical purpose outline**. As with the first two, you list the major sections of your paper. Next, you briefly indicate two things for each section: the effect you want it to have on your audience, and how you will achieve that effect. Here is the rhetorical purpose outline that Abby devised for her paper.

INTRODUCTION

The audience needs to know the text I'll discuss.	I'll identify Wordsworth's poem.
The audience must know my main issue.	I'll point out that the poem is puzzling in its shift of tenses at the end.
The audience must know my main claim.	I'll argue that the shift to past tense suggests that the poem's real subject is the inability of human beings to halt the passage of time.

ANALYSIS OF THE POEM'S FINAL STANZA

The audience needs to see in detail how the final stanza's shift to past tense signals the speaker's inability to control the passage of time.	I will point out not only the shift of tense but also other words in the last stanza that imply time moves on. I will note as well that music is an especially fleeting medium, so the reaper's song was bound to fade.

ANALYSIS OF THE PRECEDING STANZAS

To accept that the passage of time is the poem's real concern, the audience must see that the preceding stanzas hint at this subject.	I will analyze the first three stanzas in turn, showing how each implies the speaker is frustrated over his inability to control time.

CONCLUSION

The audience may need to be clearer about what I consider the ultimate *tone* of the poem.	I will say that although the poem can be thought of as a warm tribute to the singing reaper, the final emphasis on the passage of time is pessimistic in tone, and the speaker winds up as "solitary" as the reaper.

For your own rhetorical purpose outlines, you may want to use phrases rather than sentences. If you do use sentences, as Abby did, you do not have to write all that many. Note that Abby wrote relatively few as she stated the effects she would aim for and her strategies for achieving those effects. Thus, she was not tremendously invested in preserving her original outline. She felt free to change it if it failed to prove helpful.

Strategies for Composing

Composing is not always distinguishable from exploring, planning, and revising. As you prepare for your paper, you may jot down words or whole sentences. Once you begin a draft, you may alter that draft in several ways before you complete it. You may be especially prone to making changes in drafts if you use a computer, for word processing enables you to jump around in your text, revisiting and revising what you have written.

Still, most writers feel that doing a draft is an activity in its own right, and a major one at that. The next chapter presents various tips for writing about specific genres, and Chapter 6 discusses writing research-based papers. Meanwhile, here are some tips to help you with composing in general.

DECIDE ON A TITLE

You may be inclined to let your **title** be the same as that of the text you discuss. Were you to write about Wordsworth's poem, then, you would be calling your own paper "The Solitary Reaper." But often such mimicry backfires. For one thing, it may lead your readers to think that you are unoriginal and perhaps even lazy. Also, you risk confusing your audience, since your paper would actually be *about* Wordsworth's poem rather than being the poem itself. So take the time to come up with a title of your own. Certainly it may announce the text you will focus on, but let it do more. In particular, use your title to indicate the main claim you will be making. With just a few words, you can preview the argument to come.

MAKE CHOICES ABOUT YOUR STYLE

Perhaps you have been told to "sound like yourself" when you write. Yet that can be a difficult demand (especially if you are not sure what your "self" is really like). Above all, the **style** you choose depends on your audience and purpose. In writing an argument for a general audience, probably you would do best to avoid the extremes of pomposity and breezy informality. Try to stick with words you know well, and if you do want to use some that are only hazily familiar to you, check their dictionary definitions first.

At some point in our lives, probably all of us have been warned not to use *I* in our writing. In the course you are taking, however, you may be asked to write about your experiences. If so, you will find *I* hard to avoid. Whether to use it does become a real question when you get assignments like Abby's, which require you chiefly to make an argument about a text. Since you are supposed to focus on that text, your readers may be disconcerted if you keep referring to yourself. Even so, you need not assume that your personal life is irrelevant to the task. Your opening paragraph might refer to your personal encounters with the text, as a way of establishing the issue you will discuss. A personal anecdote might serve as a forceful conclusion to your paper. Moreover, before you reach the conclusion, you might orient your readers to the structure of your paper by using certain expressions that feature the word *I*: for example, *As I suggested earlier, As I have noted, As I argue later.* In general, you may be justified in saying *I* at certain moments. When tempted to use this pronoun, though, consider whether it really is your best move.

Arguments about literature are most compelling when supported by quotations, but be careful not to quote excessively. If you constantly repeat other people's words, providing few of your own, your readers will hardly get a sense of you as an author. Moreover, a paper full of quotation marks is hard to read. Make sure to quote selectively, remembering that sometimes you can simply paraphrase. When you do quote, try to cite only the words you need. You do not have to reproduce a whole line or sentence if one word is enough to support your point.

When summarizing what happens in a literary work, be careful not to shift tenses as you go along. Your reader may be confused if you shift back and forth between past and present. We suggest that you stick primarily to the present tense, which is the tense that literary critics customarily employ. For example, instead of saying that the speaker *praised* the lass, say that he *praises* her.

DRAFT AN INTRODUCTION

As a general principle, use your introduction to identify as quickly and efficiently as possible

- the main text that you will analyze;
- the main issue about it that you will address; and
- the main claim that you will develop in response to that issue.

Don't waste time with grand philosophical statements such as "Society doesn't always appreciate the work that everyone does," or "Over the centuries, much literature has been about work," or "William Wordsworth was a great British Romantic poet."

Remember that your main issue should be a significant question with no obvious answer. Try using one or more of the following strategies to establish that issue at the start of your essay:

- **State the issue as, indeed, a question.** For example: "Why, conceivably, does Wordsworth shift to the past tense in his poem's final stanza?"
- **Apply a word like** *puzzling, confusing, mysterious,* **or** *curious* **to whatever feature your issue will be about.** For example: "Because Wordsworth uses present tense for much of the poem, it is puzzling that he turns to past tense at the very end."
- **Through personal reference, state that you were first puzzled by a particular feature of the work but are now able to interpret it.** For example: "At first, I was confused when Wordsworth shifted to the past tense, but now I have arrived at a possible explanation for this move."
- **Indicate that you aim to help other readers of the work, who may have trouble understanding the feature of it you will focus on.** For example: "Quite a few readers of Wordsworth's poem may have difficulty seeing why he shifts to the past tense at the end. There is, however, a possible explanation for this move."
- **Indicate that you will express disagreement with existing or possible interpretations.** For example: "While some readers of Wordsworth's poem may feel that his shift to the past tense shows a wonderful ability to preserve his experience with the reaper, a more plausible interpretation is that it shows his isolation after meeting her."

LIMIT PLOT SUMMARY

Short stories and plays spin tales. So do many poems and essays. But if you are writing about a literary text that is narrative in form, don't spend much of your paper just summarizing the narrative. Developing a genuine argument about the work involves more than recounting its plot. Here are strategies you can use to limit this:

- Assume that your reader knows the basic plot and needs only a few brief reminders of its key elements.
- Keep in mind that your main purpose is to put forth, explain, and support a *claim* about the text — your answer to some question you raise about it.
- After your introduction, try to begin each new paragraph with a subclaim that helps you develop your main claim. Use the rest of the paragraph to elaborate and provide evidence for this subclaim. *Don't* begin a paragraph simply by recording a plot incident, for doing so is liable to bog you down in sheer summary.
- Instead of reciting plot details, write about how the work you are analyzing is *constructed*. Make observations about specific methods that the author uses to present the story, including techniques of organization and characterization. For example, rather than say "The speaker in Wordsworth's poem wonders what the woman is singing," state and develop a point like "Wordsworth chooses not to translate the woman's song for us; instead, he depicts the speaker as not knowing her words, so that the poem becomes mostly about the effect of her song as sheer musical notes."
- Instead of turning frequently to plot details, try to linger on some of the author's specific language, exploring possible definitions of particular words. For example, rather than say "The speaker in Wordsworth's poem remembers the woman's music," examine possible meanings of the word *bore* in the poem's next-to-last line, "The music in my heart I bore." *Bore* can simply mean "carried," and probably that is one meaning that Wordsworth has in mind here. But it can also mean "engraved, deeply inscribed," and perhaps Wordsworth wants us to think of this definition, too.

DECIDE HOW TO REFER TO THE AUTHOR'S LIFE AND INTENTIONS

Be cautious about relating the work to the author's life. Sometimes a certain character within the work may indeed express the author's own views, but don't simply assume that a character speaks for the author. Even the *I* of a first-person poem may differ significantly from its creator. True, many literary works are at least somewhat autobiographical, based on one or more aspects of the author's life. Nevertheless, even works that are largely autobiographical may not be entirely so. Besides, knowledge of the author's life won't always help you figure out his or her text. Wordsworth may have derived "The Solitary Reaper" from a personal encounter, but we must still interpret the particular poem he proceeded to write. So,

- Be careful in linking a work to the author's own circumstances. Such connections can be legitimate, but the more you push them, the more you may risk distorting the work's exact design. You also risk neglecting the author's artistic achievement. Not everyone who hears a reaper sing could turn this event into a poem!

Much of what you write about a literary work will reflect your understanding of its author's intentions. Needless to say, you can't peer into the author's mind. Rather, you'll make hypotheses about the author's aims. So,

- **Sometimes, at least, admit that you are guessing at what the author thought.** Often, your reader will assume that you are speculating about the author's aims, but your argument about them can be more persuasive if, at times, you acknowledge that you're trying to come up with the best hypothesis rather than stating an absolute fact. Take care, however, to explain why your guesses are logical.
- **If you suspect that the author might object to your view of the text, feel free to acknowledge such possible disagreements.** In fact, many theorists argue that a literary work may differ from how its author sees it. They refuse, therefore, to treat the author as an absolute authority on the work. D. H. Lawrence's advice was "Trust the tale, not the teller." Even if Lawrence is right, of course, you must show how *your* interpretation of a text manages to make sense of it.
- **Feel free to concede that your analysis of the work isn't the only reasonable one.** You can develop your main claim about a literary work partly by noting and addressing ways in which other readers may disagree with you about it. Bear in mind, though, that you will annoy your own audience if you come across as dogmatic. Be as fair as you can to views different from yours. Actually, your readers will appreciate it if at times you concede that yours is not the only reasonable interpretation. You can even specify one or more alternatives. Of course, you would still try to make a case for *your* explanation, perhaps by saying why it is *more plausible* or *more helpful* than its rivals. But speak of these competitors with respect, instead of just dismissing them with scorn.

RECOGNIZE AND AVOID LOGICAL FALLACIES

Although arguments presented in literary texts are often not logical, your arguments about these texts should be. Readers do not expect a poem's speaker, for example, to present cogently reasoned arguments to her lover, nor do they expect a lament for the lost passions of youth to be anything but subjective. But different kinds of writing have different conventions. What works in poetry may not be appropriate in an argument. The kinds of serious arguments you are expected to create cannot be successful using heartfelt emotion alone. When you write about literature, shaky thinking might cause your audience to dismiss your ideas. Your claims and the assumptions behind them should be clear and reasoned. If they are not, you might be committing a **fallacy**, a common term for unsound reasoning.

In the next several paragraphs, we discuss typical logical fallacies. Some of them are especially relevant to literary studies, and for all of them we provide examples related to "The Solitary Reaper." We do not want you to brood over this list, seeing it as a catalog of sins to which you might fall prey. If you constantly fear being accused of fallacies, you might be too paralyzed to make claims at all! In our discussion of fallacies, we also identify circumstances in which your audience might *not* object to a particular fallacy. In addition, we suggest how a writer might revise such claims to be more persuasive. Indeed, the main value in studying fallacies is to identify ways you might develop arguments more effectively.

One of the most common fallacies, ***ad hominem*** (Latin: "toward the man"), is probably the easiest to commit because it is the hardest to resist. Instead of doing the hard work of analyzing the claim and the evidence, we simply ignore them and attack the character of the person making the argument. Instead of trying to figure out what is going on in a complex work of literature, we say, "How can you take seriously a poem about love written by a manic depressive who commits suicide?" It is best to focus on the message, not the messenger.

A related fallacy, **begging the question** (a kind of circular reasoning in which the statement being argued is already assumed to have been decided) is also involved in this example since it is assumed (not proved) that unstable poets cannot have cogent insights about love.

In writing about "The Solitary Reaper," a classmate of Abby's ignored whatever argument the poem is making and focused on Wordsworth's credibility as an observer: "British intellectuals have been either romanticizing or degrading country people for centuries. Whatever Wordsworth thinks about the 'Highland Lass' is almost certainly wrong." First of all, the speaker of the poem should not be automatically equated with the poet. When they write, poets and fictional writers construct personae that may or may not reflect their own views. Second, attacking Wordsworth is a fallacy for several reasons. It first has to be demonstrated that the poet is a British intellectual, that intellectuals have consistently misrepresented rural people, and that the speaker has done so in this particular case. The classmate should revise her claim so that it deals with the words in the text, not her view of the poet's credibility.

Professional historians, mathematicians, and philosophers usually cite other professionals working in their field; that is, they **appeal to authority** to bolster their credibility. Disciplinary knowledge is created by a community of scholars who cite the ideas of its members as evidence for their claims. The warrant is that recognized authorities know what they are talking about. Quoting them is persuasive. But not completely: appeals to authority can also be fallacious. Literary critics, like other thinkers, often disagree. Just citing an expert does not conclusively prove your claim. A classmate of Abby's, for example, quoted a critic, Ian Lancashire, who says that the narrator "transcends the limitations of mortality," but the student did not give his own reasons or his own evidence for thinking this way. This appeal to critical authority without giving reasons or evidence is a fallacy because a sound argument would at least have to consider other critics. An argument is a reasoning process in which claims are supported, not simply asserted, even if they come from an expert.

A related fallacy involves using quotations from unreliable sources. Although the Internet is often a valuable tool, students sometimes use it uncritically. If you went to the search engine Google and entered Wordsworth's "The Solitary Reaper," you would quickly find Ian Lancashire's essay; and since he is a professor at the University of Toronto with many publications on this and other Romantic topics, citing him is appropriate. But some of the commentators noted by the Google search are students, perhaps English majors who have written a paper for a course on the Romantic poets. Using them as authorities would damage your judgment and credibility.

Equally harmful to the soundness of your argument is to rely too heavily on personal experience as evidence for your claim. Personal experience can sometimes be compelling and authoritative. Indeed, many critics have successfully used their own experiences with discrimination to create cogent arguments. But they rarely rely exclusively on personal experience. Instead they blend relevant experience with textual and critical specifics. Telling your readers that "The Solitary Reaper" is factually flawed because you never saw harvesters work alone when you worked on your uncle's farm would be a fallacy.

Actually, the previous example of using personal experience as authority is also unsound because the personal sample is too small to warrant a reasonable conclusion. It is hard to convince your audience if you claim too much based on limited experience. A student arguing that "The Solitary Reaper" demonstrates that field workers are melancholy would be committing a **hasty generalization** fallacy. Simply claiming less would improve the argument. In fact, this student might change the focus of her argument by doing research on other poems by Wordsworth, finding several that deal with young women in nature. Using "She Dwelt among Untrodden Ways" and "She Was a Phantom of Delight," the student might argue that Wordsworth is so enraptured by the natural world that he often blurs the boundaries between people and nature.

Another common fallacy is *post hoc, ergo propter hoc* (Latin: "because of this, then that"). Few of us escape this error in cause and effect. Many superstitions probably began because of this fallacy. A man breaks a mirror and bad luck follows. Did the mirror cause the bad luck? Logic says no, but the next day he breaks a leg, and a week later his car is stolen. The coincidence is often too tempting to resist. Does smoking marijuana lead to hard drugs? Logic says no, since you could argue just as plausibly that almost anything (carrots, beer, coffee) that comes before could be said to cause what comes after. Unless a clear, logical link between the two events is demonstrated, you might be accused of the *post hoc* fallacy.

In writing about "The Solitary Reaper," you might want to argue that the "melancholy strain" the traveler heard caused him to have a deeper appreciation for the beauty and mystery of rural people. But perhaps the narrator held such an opinion for a long time, or perhaps this is just one of dozens of such encounters that the poet remembers fondly. A sounder argument would focus on the cause and effect that do seem to be in the text: the mystery of the song's content adds to the emotional response the poet has.

Most of us commit a version of the **intentional fallacy** when we defend ourselves against someone we offended by saying, "That's not what I meant. It was just a joke." The problem arises because we are not always able to carry out our intentions. Perhaps our language is not precise enough, or perhaps our intention to be sincere or honest or witty gets mixed up with other intentions we have to sound intelligent, confident, or impressive. Students are often surprised when teachers tell them that a writer's stated intentions cannot be taken as the final word on a poem's meaning. "Wordsworth knows the poem better than anyone else" is an understandable retort. But that might not be the case. Wordsworth might not be the most astute reader of his own work. And he may not be fully aware of all that he intended. A student would be committing an intentional fallacy by arguing that "The Solitary Reaper" is written in the language used by the common man because Wordsworth says so in his preface to *Lyrical Ballads.* While this student should be commended for doing extra research, another student might point out that "Vale profound," "plaintive numbers," and "humble lay" seem conventionally poetic. Like others, this fallacy is easily revised by claiming less: "Most of 'The Solitary Reaper' is written in simple diction to approximate the language used by ordinary people."

When you try to destroy someone's argument by ignoring their main point and focusing on something marginal, you are attacking a **straw man**. The student who argues that we should dismiss Wordsworth's credibility as an observer because of "his absurd declaration that 'a voice so thrilling ne'er was heard'" is committing the straw man fallacy. While it is probably true that the song he hears is not the most thrilling in the history of the world, this is hardly Wordsworth's main point. Writers gain more credibility if they deal with a writer's strongest or main claim.

A favorite tactic of traditionalists trying to hold the line against change, the **slippery slope** fallacy is used to claim that if we allow one thing to happen, then slipping into catastrophe is just around the corner. If we do not prevent students from wearing gangsta rap fashions, gangs will eventually roam the hallways; if we allow the morning-after pill, sexual anarchy will follow. A small step is seen as precipitating an avalanche.

The following claim by a student anticipates something that simply is not logically called for: "Although Wordsworth probably means well, his praise for the 'Highland Lass' is a dangerous move since she is probably illiterate and full of rural biases and superstitions. His failure to discriminate will lead to loss of judgment and standards." Again, claiming less improves the argument: Wordsworth is less interested in the content ("Whate'er the theme") than in the "music in my heart," an emotional response that we hope does not carry over into his views on medicine, engineering, and economics.

We are all guilty at times of the fallacy of **oversimplification** — of not seeing the inevitable complexity of things. At the risk of committing a hasty generalization ourselves, it is probably the case that your instructor will be impressed if you look for complexity in literary texts and in your arguments. Seeing complexity is a consequence of hard thinking. There are rarely two sides to a question. More likely, there are a dozen plausible and reasonable perspectives. The cliché that the truth often appears in shades of gray rather than in black and white gets at the idea that simple solutions are often the result of shallow thinking.

Complexity is not what the following claim reveals: "'The Solitary Reaper' is a poem about a traveler who hears a young girl 'singing by herself,' and like a catchy ad, the tune stays with him." Being exposed to other viewpoints in class discussions and in peer-group revision can help this student avoid oversimplifying the experience Wordsworth has, one that touches on issues of mortality, the mysteries of emotional response, the purpose of poetry, and the power of the natural world. When Henry David Thoreau, the author of *Walden* (1854), urged his contemporaries to live simply, he was talking about their lifestyles, not their thinking.

Non sequitur is a general catchall fallacy that means "it does not follow." Some principle of logic has been violated when we make a claim that the evidence cannot support. In "The Solitary Reaper," it does not follow that because the Highland Lass "sings a melancholy strain," she herself is sad. She could be happy, absentminded, or simply bored. Perhaps the song is a conventional ballad typically sung by workers to pass the time. Revising this fallacy, like many of the others, involves setting aside time in the revision process to look again at your claims and the assumptions behind them, carefully and objectively making a clear connection between your claim and the evidence you say supports it.

First Draft of a Student Paper

The following is Abby's first complete draft of her paper. Eventually, she revised this draft after a group of her classmates reviewed it and after she reflected further on it herself. For the moment, though, read this first version, and decide what you would have said to her about it.

Abby Hazelton
Professor Ramsey
English 102
4 March - - - -

The Passage of Time in
"The Solitary Reaper"

William Wordsworth, one of the most famous writers in the movement known as British Romanticism, liked to write about beautiful features of the countryside. In his poem "The Solitary Reaper," the speaker enthuses over a girl who sings as she works in the fields. Yet although he is enraptured by her "melancholy strain," (line 6), he is unsure what it is *about* because she is using a Scottish dialect that he cannot understand. By contrast, the subject of the poem seems much clearer. The very title of the poem refers to the singing girl, and the subsequent lines repeatedly praise her song as wonderfully haunting. Nevertheless, the poem has puzzling aspects. Many readers are likely to wonder if they are supposed to find the speaker guilty of cultural and class superiority when he, as a British intellectual, treats a Scottish peasant girl as a spectacle. Another issue, the one I focus on in my paper, arises when the final stanza shifts to past tense. In the first three stanzas, the speaker uses present tense, as if he is currently observing the singer whom he describes. In the concluding stanza, however, the speaker uses verbs such as "sang" (25), "saw" (27), and "listen'd" (29), as if he is *recalling* his encounter with her. How can we explain this inconsistency? One possible justification for the final shift to past tense is that it reminds us of the speaker's inability to halt the passage of time. Even though he would like to freeze the encounter, time goes on. Perhaps, therefore, the poem's real subject is the idea that time is always in flux. Indeed, even before the final stanza, the speaker betrays an awareness that he can't bend time to his will.

Simply by virtue of the shift to past tense, the last stanza indicates that time goes on despite the speaker's wishes. But other elements of this stanza convey the same notion. Recalling his experience of the girl's singing, the speaker reports that he was "motionless and still" (29), yet in the very next line he admits that he eventually moved: "I mounted up the hill" (30). When the speaker says that "the Maiden sang / As if her song could have no ending" (25–26), the words "As if" are significant, implying that the song did end for him in reality. Similarly, the poem itself has to end at some point. In fact, it concludes with the words "no more," which stress that the singer and her song now belong to the speaker's past (32). Only in his "heart" (31), apparently, can he retain them. Furthermore, the medium of print can never convey the sound of music. In fact, prior to recording technology, music was the most fleeting of media, its notes fading with each new moment. By seeking to transmit music, the speaker ensures that he will wind up being frustrated by time.

Even if the final stanza's shift of tense is jarring, the first three stanzas give hints that the speaker will end up defeated by time. Significantly, the poem's very first word is "Behold" (1). In issuing this command, the speaker evidently hopes that other people will abandon all motion and gaze at the singer, basking in her song. The speaker reinforces this call for paralysis with the command that begins line 4: "Stop here." Yet, as if acknowledging limits to his control, he adds "or gently pass!" (4). Besides referring to other human beings, these commands seem directed at time itself. The speaker hopes that time, too, will "Stop" and "Behold." Even at this point in the poem, however, he realizes that time is inclined to "pass," in which case he hopes that it will at least move on "gently" (4).

The second stanza is chiefly concerned with space. Comparing the girl's song to other sounds, the speaker ranges from "Arabian sands" (12) to "the seas / Among the farthest Hebrides" (15–16). In the third stanza, however, he focuses again on time. Trying to determine the subject of the song, he expresses uncertainty about its time frame. He wonders whether the song concerns "old, unhappy, far-off things / And battles long ago" (19–20) or instead deals with "Familiar matter of to-day" (22). Moreover, even if he suspects the song's subject is "Some natural sorrow, loss, or pain" (23), he is unsure whether this experience of despair is confined to the past ("has been") or will reoccur ("may be again") (24). Whichever of the possibilities he raises is true, the speaker is clearly limited in his ability to figure out the song's relation to time. In other words, he cannot force time into a meaningful pattern, let alone prevent its passing.

By the end of the poem, the speaker seems as "solitary" as the reaper. In addition to losing his experience with her as time moves on, he is isolated in other ways.

This situation seems to leave the speaker as "solitary" as the reaper. Throughout the poem, actually, we don't see him in the company of others. His opening "Behold" is directed at no one in particular. Furthermore, we can't be sure he is speaking to actual passersby or, rather, to the poem's hypothetical future readers. Nor, for all his praise of the singer, does he apparently talk to her. Rather, he gives the impression that he keeps at a distance. Even if he did try to converse with the reaper, he himself would still be "solitary" in the sense of failing to understand her language and failing to communicate her song to his readers. He does not even bother trying to reproduce some of the song's words. Therefore, despite the speaker's enchantment over the reaper, this poem is ultimately pessimistic. The speaker is left only with his memories of a wonderful experience. He has lost the experience itself.

Works Cited

Wordsworth, William. "The Solitary Reaper." *Making Literature Matter: An Anthology for Readers and Writers*. Ed. John Schilb and John Clifford. 6th ed. Boston: Bedford, 2015. 81–82. Print.

Strategies for Revising

Most first drafts are far from perfect. Even experienced professional writers often have to revise their work. Besides making changes on their own, many of them solicit feedback from others. In various workplaces, writing is collaborative, with coauthors exchanging ideas as they try to improve a piece. Remain open to the possibility that your draft needs changes, perhaps several. Of course, you are more apt to revise extensively if you have given yourself enough time. Conversely, you will not feel able to change much of your paper if it is due the next day. You will also limit your ability to revise if you work only with your original manuscript, scribbling possible changes between the lines. This practice amounts to conservatism, for it encourages you to keep passages that really ought to be overhauled.

You may have trouble, however, improving a draft if you are checking many things in it at once. Therefore, read the draft repeatedly, looking at a different aspect of it each time. A good way to begin is to outline the paper you have written and then compare that outline with your original one. If the two outlines differ, your draft may or may not need adjusting; perhaps you were wise to swerve from your original plan. In any case, you should ponder your departures from that plan, considering whether they were for the best.

If, like Abby, you are writing an argument paper, our Checklist for Revising box has some topics and questions you might apply as you review your first draft. Some of these considerations overlap. Nevertheless, take them in turn rather than all at once.

▤ A CHECKLIST FOR REVISING

Logic

- Will my audience see that the issue I am focusing on is indeed an issue?

- Will the audience be able to follow the logic of my argument?

- Is the logic as persuasive as it might be? Is there more evidence I can provide? Do I need to identify more of my assumptions?

- Have I addressed all of my audience's potential concerns?

(continued on next page)

≣ A CHECKLIST FOR REVISING *(continued)*

Organization

- Does my introduction identify the issue that I will focus on? Does it state my main claim?

- Will my audience be able to detect and follow the stages of my argument?

- Does the order of my paragraphs seem purposeful rather than arbitrary?

- Have I done all I can to signal connections within and between sentences? Within and between paragraphs?

- Have I avoided getting bogged down in mere summary?

- Will my conclusion satisfy readers? Does it leave any key questions dangling?

Clarity

- Does my title offer a good preview of my argument?

- Will each of my sentences be immediately clear?

- Am I sure how to define each word that I have used?

Emphasis

- Have I put key points in prominent places?

- Have I worded each sentence for maximum impact? In particular, is each sentence as concise as possible? Do I use active verbs whenever I can?

Style

- Are my tone and level of vocabulary appropriate?

- Will my audience think me fair-minded? Should I make any more concessions?

- Do I use any mannerisms that may distract my readers?

- Have I used any expressions that may annoy or offend?

- Is there anything else I can do to make my paper readable and interesting?

≡ A CHECKLIST FOR REVISING

Grammar

- Is each of my sentences grammatically correct?

- Have I punctuated properly?

Physical Appearance

- Have I followed the proper format for quotations, notes, and bibliography?

- Are there any typographical errors?

We list these considerations from most to least important. When revising a draft, think first about matters of logic, organization, and clarity. There is little point in fixing the grammar of particular sentences if you are going to drop them later because they fail to advance your argument.

As we noted, a group of Abby's classmates discussed her draft. Most of these students seemed to like her overall argument, including her main issue and claim. Having been similarly confused by the poem's shift of tense, they appreciated the light that Abby shed on it. They were impressed by her willingness to examine the poem's specific words. They especially liked her closing analogy between the reaper and the speaker himself. Nevertheless, the group made several comments about Abby's paper that she took as suggestions for improvement. Ultimately, she decided that the following changes were in order.

1. She should make her introduction more concise. The first draft is so long and dense that it may confuse readers instead of helping them sense the paper's main concerns. This problem is common to first drafts. In this preliminary phase, many writers worry that they will fail to generate *enough* words; they are hardly thinking about how to restrain themselves. Moreover, the writer of a first draft may still be unsure about the paper's whole argument, so the introduction often lacks a sharp focus. After Abby finished and reviewed her first draft, she saw ways of making her introduction tighter.

2. She should rearrange paragraphs. After her introduction, Abby discussed the poem's last stanza in more detail. Then she moved back to stanza 1. Next, just before her paper's conclusion, she analyzed stanzas 2 and 3. Abby thought that the structure of her paper moved logically from the obvious to the hidden: the poem's last stanza emphasized the passage of time, and the earlier stanzas touched on this subject more subtly. Yet Abby's method of organization frustrated her classmates. They thought her paper would be easier to follow if, after the introduction, it moved chronologically through the poem. For them, her discussion of stanzas 2 and 3 seemed especially mislocated. Though she had positioned this discussion as her paper's climax, her classmates did not sense it to be her most significant and compelling moment of insight. Most important, they believed, were her comments on the *final* stanza, for that seemed to them the most important part of Wordsworth's poem. In other words, they thought the climax of the paper would be stronger if it focused on the climax of the poem. Abby hesitated to adopt her classmates' recommendation, but eventually she did so. When you read her final version, see if you like her rearrangement of paragraphs. Sometimes, though not always, a paper about a literary work seems more coherent if it does follow the work's chronological structure. And papers should indeed build to a climax, even if readers disagree about what its content should be.

3. She should reconsider her claim that "this poem is ultimately pessimistic."   Abby's classmates thought this claim did not fully account for the poem's last two lines: "The music in my heart I bore, / Long after it was heard no more" (31–32). While they agreed with her that the words "no more" emphasize that the singer has faded into the past, they disagreed that her song is lost as well, for it remains in the speaker's "heart." They noted that Abby had acknowledged this fact, but they felt she had done so too briefly and dismissively. In addition, one student encouraged her to think about poetry and music as ways of keeping memories alive. More specifically, he suggested that the speaker of "The Solitary Reaper" is Wordsworth himself, who is using this poem to preserve his memory of an actual encounter. After studying the poem again, Abby decided that her classmates' ideas had merit, and she incorporated them into her revision. Of course, such advice is not always worth heeding. Still, writers should accept the invitation to look more closely at whatever text they are analyzing.

Revised Draft of a Student Paper

Here is the new version of the paper that Abby wrote. Attached to it are marginal comments by us that call your attention to her strategies.

Abby Hazelton
Professor Ramsey
English 102
11 March ----

The Passage of Time in
"The Solitary Reaper"

In William Wordsworth's poem "The Solitary Reaper," the speaker enthuses over a girl who sings as she works in the fields. Throughout the poem, his rapture is evident. Yet in the last stanza, he makes a puzzling move, shifting to past tense after using present tense in the previous three stanzas. No

Title clearly indicates the particular work being analyzed and the aspect to be focused on.

Immediately refers to specific detail of text.

With "puzzling," signals issue to be addressed.

longer does he seem to be currently observing the singer he describes; rather, now he seems to be *recalling* his encounter with her. One possible justification for this shift in tense is that it reminds us of the speaker's inability to halt the passage of time. Even though he would like to freeze the encounter, time goes on. Perhaps, therefore, the poem's real theme is that time is always in flux. Indeed, even before the final stanza, the speaker betrays an awareness that he can't bend time to his will.

Identifies the main claim.

Connects feature of the poem to be focused on to other parts of it.

Significantly, the poem's very first word is "Behold" (line 1). In issuing this command, the speaker evidently hopes that other people will abandon all motion and gaze at the singer. The speaker reinforces this call for paralysis with the command that begins line 4: "Stop here." Yet, as if acknowledging limits to his control, he adds "or gently pass!" (4). Besides referring to other human beings, these commands seem directed at time itself. The speaker hopes that time, too, will "Stop" and "Behold." Even at this point in the poem, however, he realizes that time is inclined to "pass," in which case he hopes that it will at least move on "gently."

Analyzes an implication of the poem's particular language rather than just beginning with a plot detail.

Develops point that even the poem's early stanzas show concern about the passage of time that final stanza emphasizes.

The second stanza is chiefly concerned with space. Comparing the girl's song to other sounds, the speaker ranges from "Arabian sands" (12) to "the seas / Among the farthest Hebrides" (15–16). In the third stanza, however, he focuses again on time. Trying to determine the subject of her song, he expresses uncertainty about its time frame. He wonders whether the song concerns "old, unhappy, far-off things / And battles long ago" (19–20) or instead deals with "Familiar matter of to-day" (22). Moreover, even if he suspects the song's subject is "Some natural sorrow, loss, or pain" (23), he is unsure whether this experience of despair is confined to the past ("has been") or will reoccur ("may be again") (24). Whichever of the possibilities he raises is true, the speaker is clearly limited in his ability to figure out the song's relation to time. In other words, he cannot force time into a meaningful pattern, let alone prevent its passing.

Moves chronologically through the poem, carefully pointing out how second stanza differs from the first.

Makes distinctions among stanzas' topics. Returns to main claim of the essay.

Refers to actual words of poem to support points.

Ends paragraph by reminding us what main claim is.

Simply by virtue of the shift to past tense, the last stanza indicates that time goes on despite the speaker's wishes. But other elements of the stanza convey this same notion. Recalling his experience of the girl's singing, the speaker reports that he was "motionless and still" (29), yet in the very next line he admits that he eventually moved: "I mounted up the hill" (30). When the speaker says that "the Maiden sang / As if her song could have no ending" (25–26), the words "As if" are significant, implying that the song did end for him in reality. Similarly, the poem itself has to end at some point. In

Directs attention to part of poem with which she is most concerned.

Traces implications of poem's words, especially as these are related to main issue and claim.

fact, it concludes with the words "no more" (32), which stress that the singer and her song now belong to the speaker's past. Only in his "heart" (31), apparently, can he retain them.

This situation seems to leave the speaker as "solitary" as the reaper. Throughout the poem, actually, we don't see him in the company of others. His opening "Behold" is directed at no one in particular. Furthermore, we can't be sure he is speaking to actual passersby or, rather, to the poem's hypothetical future readers. Nor, for all his praise of the singer, does he apparently talk to her. Rather, he gives the impression that he keeps at a distance. Even if he did converse with the reaper, he himself would still be "solitary" in the sense of failing to understand her dialect and failing to communicate her words to his readers. As things stand, he is apparently unable or unwilling to reproduce any of the song's lyrics. Just as important, the medium of print can never convey the sounds of music. In fact, prior to recording technology, music was the most fleeting of media, its notes fading with each new moment. By seeking to transmit music, the speaker ensures that he will wind up being frustrated by time.

Connects last stanza to other parts of poem.

Several observations support idea that the speaker is isolated.

Concludes climactic paragraph with substantial analysis.

Yet perhaps the singer and her song are preserved in more than just the speaker's "heart." It can be argued that they are also preserved by the poem, if only to a limited extent. More generally, we can say that literature is a means by which human beings partially succeed in perpetuating things. This idea seems quite relevant to "The Solitary Reaper" if we suppose that the speaker is the poet himself and that he actually witnessed the scene he describes. If we make such assumptions, we can see Wordsworth as analogous to the speaker. After all, both engage in commemorative verbal art. Because time passes, the "strain[s]" that Wordsworth and the singer produce in their efforts to preserve time are bound to be "melancholy" (6). Still, their art matters, for through it they are imaginatively "[r]eaping" (3) experiences that would otherwise fade.

Signals that she is simply making a suggestion here, rather than asserting a definite new point.

Concluding paragraph reminds us of main issue and claim, but goes beyond mere repetition to bring up some new suggestions.

Works Cited

Wordsworth, William. "The Solitary Reaper." *Making Literature*
    Matter: An Anthology for Readers and Writers. Ed. John
    Schilb and John Clifford. 6th ed. Boston: Bedford, 2015.
    81–82. Print.

To us, Abby's revision is more persuasive and compelling than her first draft. In particular, she has nicely complicated her claim about the poem's "pessimism." Nevertheless, we would hesitate to call this revision the definitive version of her paper. Maybe you have thought of things Abby could do to make it even more effective. In presenting her two drafts, we mainly want to emphasize the importance of revision. We hope, too, that you will remember our specific tips as you work on your own writing.

Strategies for Writing a Comparative Paper

Much writing about literature *compares* two or more texts. After all, you can gain many insights into a text by noting how it resembles and differs from others. In this section we offer specific advice for writing a comparative paper, a task you may be assigned in your course. We also present a sample paper that models strategies of comparative writing.

To aid our discussion, we ask that you read the following two poems. The first, "Two Trees," appears in the 2009 verse collection *Rain* by Don Paterson (b. 1963), a Scottish writer who is also a jazz musician, a professor at the University of St. Andrews, and the poetry editor for the publisher Picador Macmillan. Next comes "Regarding History," a poem from the 2005 book *Trill & Mordent* by Luisa A. Igloria (b. 1961), a Filipina American writer who is a professor of English and creative writing at Old Dominion University in Norfolk, Virginia.

DON PATERSON

Two Trees

One morning, Don Miguel got out of bed
with one idea rooted in his head:
to graft his orange to his lemon tree.
It took him the whole day to work them free,
lay open their sides, and lash them tight.   5
For twelve months, from the shame or from the fright
they put forth nothing; but one day there appeared
two lights in the dark leaves. Over the years
the limbs would get themselves so tangled up
each bough looked like it gave a double crop,   10
and not one kid in the village didn't know
the magic tree in Miguel's patio.

The man who bought the house had had no dream
so who can say what dark malicious whim
led him to take his axe and split the bole   15
along its fused seam, and then dig two holes.
And no, they did not die from solitude;
nor did their branches bear a sterile fruit;
nor did their unhealed flanks weep every spring
for those four yards that lost them everything   20
as each strained on its shackled root to face
the other's empty, intricate embrace.
They were trees, and trees don't weep or ache or shout.
And trees are all this poem is about.   *[2009]*

LUISA A. IGLORIA
Regarding History

A pair of trees on one side of the walk, leaning
now into the wind in a stance we'd call involuntary —
I can see them from the kitchen window, as I take meat
out of the oven and hold my palms above the crust, darkened
with burnt sugar. Nailed with cloves, small earth of flesh   5
still smoldering from its furnace. In truth I want to take it
into the garden and bury it in soil. There are times
I grow weary of coaxing music from silence, silence
from the circularity of logic, logic from the artifact.
Then, the possibilities of sunlight are less attractive   10
than baying at the moon. I want to take your face
in my hands, grow sweet from what it tells, tend
how it leans and turns, trellis or vine of morning-glory.
I wish for limbs pared to muscle, to climb away from
chance and all its missed appointments, its half-drunk   15
cups of coffee. Tell me what I'll find, in this
early period at the beginning of a century.
Tell me what I'll find, stumbling into a boat
and pushing off into the year's last dark hours.   *[2005]*

LIST SIMILARITIES AND DIFFERENCES

A class like yours sensed value in comparing Paterson's poem with Igloria's. So the students proceeded to brainstorm lists of specific similarities and differences — something you might do to start analyzing texts you bring together. For these two poems, the class came up with the following comparisons:

SIMILARITIES

In both poems, a prominent role is played by a real pair of trees, and their relation to each other seems important.

Both poems describe labor. In Paterson's, it's the labor of joining and then separating the trees; in Igloria's, it's the labor of cooking, burying, coaxing, climbing, and "pushing off."

The word *limbs* appears in both poems.

Both poems contain many words that have negative connotations. Paterson's poem includes such words as *shame, fright, dark malicious whim, die, sterile, unhealed, weep, strained, shackled, empty,* and *ache,* while Igloria's poem includes such words as *darkened, burnt, Nailed, bury, weary, missed,* and *dark.*

More specifically, both poems contain words associated with death.

Both poems refer to the time frame of a year, with Paterson's mentioning "twelve months" and Igloria's concluding with "the year's last dark hours."

DIFFERENCES

The speaker in Igloria's poem uses first person, indicated by the pronoun *I,* while the speaker in Paterson's poem is no specific, identifiable person.

Paterson's poem does, however, name a particular character (Don Miguel) and refers to several other people (kids in the village, the man who chopped apart the trees), while the only people in Igloria's poem seem to be "I" and "you."

Paterson's poem centers on a particular image, the two trees, whereas Igloria's poem has other images besides the pair of trees.

Paterson's poem seems more like a narrative; it tells a story. Igloria's poem seems to be more the expression of the speaker's mood.

While Igloria's speaker is clearly interested in the pair of trees as metaphors for her relationship with "you," Paterson's poem leaves readers to interpret whether and how the two trees have metaphorical implications.

"Two Trees" rhymes, but "Regarding History" does not.

"Regarding History" seems in many respects a love poem, but "Two Trees" is hard to see in that way.

"Two Trees" comments on the fact that it is a poem, but "Regarding History" does not.

"Regarding History" ends with its speaker wanting to know something ("Tell me what I'll find"), but "Two Trees" may leave its readers wanting to know something: whether we're supposed to accept its speaker's claim that "trees are all this poem is about."

As you plan your own comparative paper, lists such as these can help you organize your thoughts. To be sure, this class did not immediately think of all the similarities and differences it ended up noting. Usually, going beyond obvious points of comparison is a gradual process, for which you should give yourself plenty of time. Similarly, once you have made lists such as the one above, take time to decide which similarities and differences truly merit your attention. At most, only a few can be part of your paper's main issue and claim.

CONSIDER "WEIGHTING" YOUR COMPARISON

Unfortunately, many students writing a comparative analysis are content to put forth main claims such as these:

> There are many similarities and differences between "Two Trees" and "Regarding History."
>
> While "Two Trees" and "Regarding History" have many similarities, in many ways they are also different.
>
> While "Two Trees" and "Regarding History" are different in many ways, they are similar in others.

Several problems arise with these common methods of introducing a comparative paper. For one thing, they give the reader no preview of the specific ideas to come. Indeed, they could have been written by someone who never bothered to read the two poems, for any two texts are similar in certain ways and different in others. Furthermore, these sorts of claims leave no meaningful and compelling way of organizing the paper. Rather, they encourage the writer to proceed arbitrarily, noting miscellaneous similarities and differences on impulse. More precisely, claims such as these fail to identify the *issue* driving the paper. Why compare Paterson's and Igloria's poems in the first place? Comparison is a means to an end, not an end in itself. What important question is the writer using these two texts to answer? In short, what's at stake?

A more fruitful approach, we think, is to write a *weighted* comparative analysis — that is, an argument chiefly concerned with *one* text more than others. When professional literary critics compare two texts, often they mainly want to answer a question about just one of them. They bring in the second text because they believe that doing so helps them address the issue they are raising about their key text. True, a good paper can result even when you treat equally all texts you discuss. But you might write a paper that seems more purposeful and coherent if you focus basically on one work, using comparisons to resolve some issue concerning it.

A Student Comparative Paper

The following paper by student Jeremy Cooper demonstrates weighted comparative analysis. The author refers to Igloria's "Regarding History" along with

Paterson's "Two Trees," but he is mostly concerned with Paterson's poem. He brings up Igloria's poem not to do comparison for its own sake but to address a question he has about Paterson's text.

Jeremy Cooper
Professor Budnoy
English 102
15 October - - - -

Title does not merely repeat title of the poem to be analyzed. Moreover, title specifies what aspect of that poem he will examine.

Don Paterson's Criticism of Nature's Owners

Until its last two lines, Don Paterson's poem "Two Trees" tells a fairly straightforward story. The title refers to an orange tree and a lemon tree that stood next to each other on an estate. The speaker in the poem recalls how these trees were treated by two different owners of the property. The first owner, Don Miguel, successfully grafted the trees together. The next owner, a man unnamed by the speaker, separated them with an axe. Given the speaker's clear description of these events, most readers would probably have no trouble understanding what happened to the trees. But the poem's concluding pair of lines is puzzling:

First sentence refers to poem he will focus on, his primary text.

> They were trees, and trees don't weep or ache or shout.
> And trees are all this poem is about. (23–24)

On the surface, the word "all" seems equivalent to "merely." If this is the case, readers might feel that Paterson is encouraging them to take a limited view of his poem, seeing it as concerned with nothing more than trees. They would then feel *dis*couraged from looking for additional significance or meaning in his text. But this interpretation of Paterson's focus risks making his poem appear relatively trivial, an impression that he surely does not want to create. A likelier possibility is that the speaker is being ironic in his final declaration, stating the word "all" sarcastically. Such a tone might then move readers to question whether the poem is simply about trees. They might feel compelled to consider how its real subject is something else. Indeed, the poem's actual main topic seems to be the regrettable attitudes that human beings take toward nature when they are able to own it.

Signals issue that the paper will address.

Trees play a major role in Paterson's poem, as their presence in the title suggests. In the first of the poem's two stanzas, the speaker describes Don Miguel's effort to fuse the orange tree and the lemon tree together, something that he evidently managed to accomplish so well that the trees became hard to distinguish from each other: "the limbs would get themselves so tangled up / each bough looked like it gave

Introductory paragraph ends by stating the claim about the primary text that the paper will support and develop.

a double crop" (9–10). In the second stanza, the speaker turns to describing how the next owner of the trees did the opposite thing to them, splitting them apart (15–16). The poem presents no other scenic feature to compete with the two trees for the reader's attention. The speaker just briefly mentions a bed (1), a patio (12), a house (13), and an axe (15).

That the focus is very much on the trees becomes even more apparent if we compare this poem with another in which two trees figure, Luisa A. Igloria's "Regarding History." Igloria's poem begins with "A pair of trees on one side of the walk, leaning / now into the wind in a stance we'd call involuntary" (1–2). Later, the speaker seems to have these two trees still in mind when she says that she wants to hold her lover's face and feel "how it leans and turns, trellis or vine of morning-glory" (13). The close relation of the word "leans" in this line to "leaning" (1) in the earlier one implies that the trees remain a meaningful symbol for her throughout the poem. But, unlike Paterson's speaker, Igloria's turns her thoughts to a number of images other than trees. For example, besides her beloved's face, she thinks of food she has just prepared ("meat / out of the oven" [3–4], which she has evidently "Nailed with cloves" [5]), her garden (7), sunlight (10), the moon (11), muscle (14), coffee (16), and a boat (18). Basically, the two trees in this poem are just part of its many elements. By contrast, the pair of trees in Paterson's poem is much more prominent.

This is a secondary text, which he uses to reinforce the point he has just made about his primary text.

The question then becomes what we as readers should make of their central role in that poem. Some of us may be inclined to see Paterson's trees as a metaphor, their physical existence being less significant than something else they represent. The pair of trees in "Regarding History" do seem metaphorical, functioning in the speaker's mind as stand-ins for a human relationship. When she observes that the trees are "leaning / now into the wind in a stance we'd call involuntary" (1–2), she appears to be actually thinking of her relationship with her beloved. Specifically, she seems worried about pressures on their relationship that threaten their ability to keep it steady. This concern of hers comes up again later, when she expresses a desire "to take your face" (11) and "tend / how it leans and turns" (12–13). Here, too, she evidently feels that her connection to her loved one is challenged by outside forces. As in her earlier remark about the trees, she fears that she will not be able to protect her relationship from influences that will make her and her lover do "involuntary" (2) things. In comparison, though, the two

He has identified a possible interpretation but now offers a different one, which he proceeds to argue for.

trees in Paterson's poem do not appear to have a metaphorical function. In the first place, the speaker of "Two Trees" lacks a distinct personality, so that the poem does not encourage readers to interpret the trees he mentions as representing thoughts or feelings of his. Whereas Igloria's speaker dominates "Regarding History" with her clearly marked hopes and concerns, Paterson's speaker writes largely like a reporter narrating news events. Moreover, when he tells what the two property owners did to the trees, he describes these actions so precisely and concretely that he makes it hard for readers to consider the trees as symbolic rather than physical. Also, in such lines as "they did not die from solitude" (17) and "nor did their unhealed flanks weep every spring" (19) the speaker seems to be reminding the reader that they are, in fact, basically vegetation rather than images of something in the human mind. If anything, these lines discourage the reader from interpreting the trees as metaphors.

He uses comparison with his secondary text to support his argument about his primary text.

But if the two trees in Paterson's poem come across mainly as real elements of nature, the attitudes that their owners show toward them are nevertheless significant. Actually, the poem's main subject is not the trees of the title, but the intense and disturbing emotions that drove Don Miguel and the later owner to handle them roughly. The feelings that led the second owner to separate the trees seem villainous. The speaker suggests that this man "had had no dream" (13) but instead acted on some mysterious "dark malicious whim" that compelled him to "split" them apart (14–15), leaving their flanks "unhealed" (19) and their roots "shackled" (21). This language gives the impression of a plantation owner in the pre–Civil War American South, the type of person who cruelly divided slave families and kept their members separated in bondage. Because the poem ends with the physical stress inflicted upon the trees by their second owner, some readers may be more bothered by this man's behavior than they are by Don Miguel's. They might even appreciate Don Miguel's interest in uniting the trees, especially because his labor resulted in the heartening picture of "two lights in the dark leaves" (8). But the language used to describe his actions, too, is mostly negative. The words "lay open" (5), "lash them tight" (5), "shame" (6), "fright" (6), and "tangled up" (9) imply traumatic destruction, even rape, rather than blissful harmony. In his willingness to manipulate the trees, Don Miguel therefore seems no better than the man who replaced him. Furthermore, Don Miguel's behavior toward the trees did not have the excuse of being carefully thought-out and planned. He simply awoke "with one idea rooted in his head:

He is working with the claim he put forth in his introduction.

Again, he acknowledges the possibility of an interpretation different from his, before advancing his view.

/ to graft his orange to his lemon tree" (2–3). Just as the word "Don" in the first line is an indication that he is a man of power in his community, so the repetition of the word "his" in this line suggests that he felt able to perform surgery on the trees merely because he owned them. Both of the men in the poem avoided thinking of what was best for the trees. Instead, both preferred to exercise the authority they had as possessors of the trees, no matter how abusive their handling of the trees might be. The speaker in Igloria's poem calls attention to what she currently *lacks* or is *unable* to do, through statements like "I want to take your face" (11), "I wish for limbs pared to muscle" (14), and "Tell me what I'll find" (18). Furthermore, she does not possess the two trees that figure in "Regarding History." Rather, she is a mere observer of them: "I can see them from the kitchen window" (3). In Paterson's poem, on the other hand, Don Miguel and the second man treat their trees violently and are able to do so because the trees are legally theirs.

Once more, he uses comparison with his secondary text to reinforce his argument about his primary text.

Paterson does not end his poem by directly indicating what he thinks is the proper way of treating trees like those of his title. He does not clearly offer some sort of prescription for their care. Many readers may, nevertheless, come away from the poem concluding that human beings should avoid tampering with trees and, more generally, should leave nature alone as often as possible. In any case, Paterson's central purpose seems to be to make us more aware that when humans own some of nature, they may treat it arrogantly, whether in the pursuit of unity (Don Miguel's aim when he fuses the trees) or separation (the second man's goal when he breaks them apart).

He suggests that this interpretation is possible but that he is more interested in getting his readers to accept his main claim about the poem: the idea he returns to in his final sentence.

Works Cited

Igloria, Luisa A. "Regarding History." Schilb and Clifford 106.

Paterson, Don. "Two Trees." Schilb and Clifford 105–106.

Schilb, John and John Clifford, eds. *Making Literature Matter:*
   An Anthology for Readers and Writers. 6th ed. Boston:
   Bedford, 2015. Print.

Jeremy gains much from comparing "Two Trees" with "Regarding History." In paragraph 3, the analysis of the modest role that trees play in Igloria's poem bolsters Jeremy's claim that they are the core of Paterson's poem. In paragraph 4, the discussion of how Igloria uses trees as metaphors strengthens Jeremy's point that Paterson's trees are literal. In paragraph 5, the observation that Igloria's speaker is *not* an owner of trees helps Jeremy stress that Paterson's men possess them. Obviously, though, Jeremy focuses his paper on Paterson's poem, not on both. By concentrating chiefly on "Two Trees," he enables himself to develop a tight and logical argument, whereas focusing on both poems would encourage him to roam through similarities and differences at random.

Perhaps you know the advice usually given about how to organize a comparative paper. Traditionally, writers aiming to compare two texts learn of two options: (1) discuss one text and then move to the other, comparing it with the first; (2) discuss the texts together, noting each of their similarities and differences in turn. Both of these alternatives make sense and provide a ready-made structure for your paper; either can result in a coherent essay. Still, a weighted analysis such as Jeremy's — an analysis that focuses on one text more than another — is more likely than either of the alternatives to seem the logical evolution of a pointed claim.

☰ SUMMING UP: THE WRITING PROCESS

- **Writing an argument about a literary work involves *exploring, planning, composing,* and *revising.*** (pp. 99–101)

- ***Exploring* requires you to read the work closely, noting questions it raises for you.** Does the text confirm your predictions about it? Does rereading it change your mind? How does it compare with your personal experience? What patterns, and breaks from these patterns, do you find? What ambiguities? What were the author's alternatives? How does the text deal with common topics in literary studies? What is a tentative claim you can make about it? (pp. 82–83)

(continued on next page)

≡ **SUMMING UP: THE WRITING PROCESS** *(continued)*

- *Planning* **combines several activities.** These include selecting a text to write about; envisioning your audience; identifying your main issue, claim, and evidence as you anticipate challenges to them; deciding what warrants to use; and determining how you will organize your argument. (pp. 84–87)

- **Keep in mind the following tips when you are** *composing* **a draft.**

  Decide on a title that previews your main claim. (pp. 88–89)

  Choose a style that fits your audience and purpose. (p. 89)

  Draft an introduction that identifies as quickly and efficiently as possible the main text you will analyze, your main issue, and your main claim. (p. 90)

  Limit plot summary. (pp. 90–91)

  Decide how you will refer to the author's life and intentions. (pp. 91–92)

  Recognize and avoid logical fallacies. (pp. 92–96)

- *Revising* **is a process.** Read your draft repeatedly, looking at a different aspect of it each time, in particular its logic, organization, clarity, emphases, style, grammar, and physical appearance. (pp. 99–105)

- **Be cautious about relating the work to its author's life, and be alert to fallacious reasoning in your arguments and those of others.** (pp. 91–92)

- **Feel free to concede that your analysis of a literary work is not the only reasonable interpretation of it.** (p. 92)

- **Favor** *weighted* **comparison if you are writing a paper that compares two or more literary works.** (pp. 108–113)

CHAPTER 5

Writing about Literary Genres

At the beginning of Chapter 1, we discussed how literary works are often understood as examples of particular **genres** (kinds or types of writing). While acknowledging that most readers think of literature as comprising the genres of fiction, poetry, and drama, we invited you to think of nonfiction (such as historical writing), creative nonfiction (such as autobiography and memoir), and essays (sometimes including argumentative prose) as literature, too. In this chapter, we present elements of literary analysis for the genres of fiction, poetry, drama, and the essay, and show how various students have used those elements to generate writing about literary works. You will notice that many of these elements are useful in thinking about most genres, but different genres make different use of elements, emphasizing some more than others. We also devote a section to writing about poems and pictures; over the centuries, many poets have been prompted to create their art in response to visual images created by other kinds of artists.

Writing about Stories

Short stories can be said to resemble novels. Above all, both are works of fiction. Yet the difference in length matters. As William Trevor, a veteran writer of short stories, has observed, short fiction is "the art of the glimpse; it deals in echoes and reverberations; craftily it withholds information. Novels tell all. Short stories tell as little as they dare." Maybe Trevor overstates the situation when he claims that novels reveal everything. All sorts of texts feature what literary theorist Wolfgang Iser calls "gaps." Still, Trevor is right to emphasize that short stories usually tell much less than novels do. They demand that you understand and evaluate characters on the basis of just a few details and events. In this respect, short stories resemble poems. Both tend to rely on compression rather than expansion, seeking to affect their audience with a sharply limited number of words.

Short stories' focused use of language can make the experience of reading them wonderfully intense. Furthermore, you may end up considering important human issues as you try to interpret the "glimpses" they provide. Precisely because short stories "tell as little as they dare," they offer you much to ponder as you proceed to write about them.

In discussing the writing process, we refer often to the story that follows.

Published in 1941, "A Visit of Charity" is by a pioneer of American short fiction, Eudora Welty (1909–2001). She spent her life chiefly in her hometown of Jackson, Mississippi, and most of her writing is set in the American South.

EUDORA WELTY
A Visit of Charity

It was mid-morning—a very cold, bright day. Holding a potted plant before her, a girl of fourteen jumped off the bus in front of the Old Ladies' Home, on the outskirts of town. She wore a red coat, and her straight yellow hair was hanging down loose from the pointed white cap all the little girls were wearing that year. She stopped for a moment beside one of the prickly dark shrubs with which the city had beautified the Home, and then proceeded slowly toward the building, which was of whitewashed brick and reflected the winter sunlight like a block of ice. As she walked vaguely up the steps she shifted the small pot from hand to hand; then she had to set it down and remove her mittens before she could open the heavy door.

"I'm a Campfire Girl. . . . I have to pay a visit to some old lady," she told the nurse at the desk. This was a woman in a white uniform who looked as if she were cold; she had close-cut hair which stood up on the very top of her head exactly like a sea wave. Marian, the little girl, did not tell her that this visit would give her a minimum of only three points in her score.

"Acquainted with any of our residents?" asked the nurse. She lifted one eyebrow and spoke like a man.

"With any old ladies? No—but—that is, any of them will do," Marian stammered. With her free hand she pushed her hair behind her ears, as she did when it was time to study Science.

The nurse shrugged and rose. "You have a nice *multiflora cineraria°* there," she remarked as she walked ahead down the hall of closed doors to pick out an old lady.   5

There was loose, bulging linoleum on the floor. Marian felt as if she were walking on the waves, but the nurse paid no attention to it. There was a smell in the hall like the interior of a clock. Everything was silent until, behind one of the doors, an old lady of some kind cleared her throat like a sheep bleating. This decided the nurse. Stopping in her tracks, she first extended her arm, bent her elbow, and leaned forward from the hips—all to examine the watch strapped to her wrist; then she gave a loud double-rap on the door.

"There are two in each room," the nurse remarked over her shoulder.

"Two what?" asked Marian without thinking. The sound like a sheep's bleating almost made her turn around and run back.

One old woman was pulling the door open in short, gradual jerks, and when she saw the nurse a strange smile forced her old face dangerously awry.

multiflora cineraria: A houseplant with brightly colored flowers and heart-shaped leaves.

Marian, suddenly propelled by the strong, impatient arm of the nurse, saw next the side-face of another old woman, even older, who was lying flat in bed with a cap on and a counterpane° drawn up to her chin.

"Visitor," said the nurse, and after one more shove she was off up the hall.   10

Marian stood tongue-tied; both hands held the potted plant. The old woman, still with that terrible, square smile (which was a smile of welcome) stamped on her bony face, was waiting. . . . Perhaps she said something. The old woman in bed said nothing at all, and she did not look around.

Suddenly Marian saw a hand, quick as a bird claw, reach up in the air and pluck the white cap off her head. At the same time, another claw to match drew her all the way into the room, and the next moment the door closed behind her.

"My, my, my," said the old lady at her side.

Marian stood enclosed by a bed, a washstand, and a chair; the tiny room had altogether too much furniture. Everything smelled wet—even the bare floor. She held on to the back of the chair, which was wicker and felt soft and damp. Her heart beat more and more slowly, her hands got colder and colder, and she could not hear whether the old women were saying anything or not. She could not see them very clearly. How dark it was! The window shade was down, and the only door was shut. Marian looked at the ceiling. . . . It was like being caught in a robbers' cave, just before one was murdered.

"Did you come to be our little girl for a while?" the first robber asked.   15

Then something was snatched from Marian's hand—the little potted plant.

"Flowers!" screamed the old woman. She stood holding the pot in an undecided way. "Pretty flowers," she added.

Then the old woman in bed cleared her throat and spoke. "They are not pretty," she said, still without looking around, but very distinctly.

Marian suddenly pitched against the chair and sat down in it.

"Pretty flowers," the first old woman insisted. "Pretty—pretty . . ."   20

Marian wished she had the little pot back for just a moment—she had forgotten to look at the plant herself before giving it away. What did it look like?

"Stinkweeds," said the other old woman sharply. She had a bunchy white forehead and red eyes like a sheep. Now she turned them toward Marian. The fogginess seemed to rise in her throat again, and she bleated, "Who—are—you?"

To her surprise, Marian could not remember her name. "I'm a Campfire Girl," she said finally.

"Watch out for the germs," said the old woman like a sheep, not addressing anyone.

"One came out last month to see us," said the first old woman.   25

A sheep or a germ? wondered Marian dreamily, holding on to the chair.

"Did not!" cried the other old woman.

"Did so! Read to us out of the Bible, and we enjoyed it!" screamed the first.

counterpane: Bedspread.

"Who enjoyed it!" said the woman in bed. Her mouth was unexpectedly small and sorrowful, like a pet's.

"We enjoyed it," insisted the other. "You enjoyed it—I enjoyed it."   30

"We all enjoyed it," said Marian, without realizing that she had said a word.

The first old woman had just finished putting the potted plant high, high on the top of the wardrobe, where it could hardly be seen from below. Marian wondered how she had ever succeeded in placing it there, how she could ever have reached so high.

"You mustn't pay any attention to old Addie," she now said to the little girl. "She's ailing today."

"Will you shut your mouth?" said the woman in bed. "I am not."

"You're a story."   35

"I can't stay but a minute—really, I can't," said Marian suddenly. She looked down at the wet floor and thought that if she were sick in here they would have to let her go.

With much to-do the first old woman sat down in a rocking chair—still another piece of furniture!—and began to rock. With the fingers of one hand she touched a very dirty cameo pin on her chest. "What do you do at school?" she asked.

"I don't know . . ." said Marian. She tried to think but she could not.

"Oh, but the flowers are beautiful," the old woman whispered. She seemed to rock faster and faster; Marian did not see how anyone could rock so fast.

"Ugly," said the woman in bed.   40

"If we bring flowers—" Marian began, and then fell silent. She had almost said that if Campfire Girls brought flowers to the Old Ladies' Home, the visit would count one extra point, and if they took a Bible with them on the bus and read it to the old ladies, it counted double. But the old woman had not listened, anyway; she was rocking and watching the other one, who watched back from the bed.

"Poor Addie is ailing. She has to take medicine—see?" she said, pointing a horny finger at a row of bottles on the table, and rocking so high that her black comfort shoes lifted off the floor like a little child's.

"I am no more sick than you are," said the woman in bed.

"Oh, yes you are!"

"I just got more sense than you have, that's all," said the other old woman,   45
nodding her head.

"That's only the contrary way she talks when *you all* come," said the first old lady with sudden intimacy. She stopped the rocker with a neat pat of her feet and leaned toward Marian. Her hand reached over—it felt like a petunia leaf, clinging and just a little sticky.

"Will you hush! Will you hush!" cried the other one.

Marian leaned back rigidly in her chair.

"When I was a little girl like you, I went to school and all," said the old woman in the same intimate, menacing voice. "Not here—another town . . ."

"Hush!" said the sick woman. "You never went to school. You never   50 came and you never went. You never were anything—only here. You never were born! You don't know anything. Your head is empty, your heart and hands and your old black purse are all empty, even that little old box that you brought with you you brought empty—you showed it to me. And yet you talk, talk, talk, talk, talk all the time until I think I'm losing my mind! Who are you? You're a stranger—a perfect stranger! Don't you know you're a stranger? Is it possible that they have actually done a thing like this to anyone—sent them in a stranger to talk, and rock, and tell away her whole long rigmarole? Do they seriously suppose that I'll be able to keep it up, day in, day out, night in, night out, living in the same room with a terrible old woman—forever?"

Marian saw the old woman's eyes grow bright and turn toward her. This old woman was looking at her with despair and calculation in her face. Her small lips suddenly dropped apart, and exposed a half circle of false teeth with tan gums.

"Come here, I want to tell you something," she whispered. "Come here!"

Marian was trembling, and her heart nearly stopped beating altogether for a moment.

"Now, now, Addie," said the first old woman. "That's not polite. Do you know what's really the matter with old Addie today?" She, too, looked at Marian; one of her eyelids dropped low.

"The matter?" the child repeated stupidly. "What's the matter with her?"   55

"Why, she's mad because it's her birthday!" said the first old woman, beginning to rock again and giving a little crow as though she had answered her own riddle.

"It is not, it is not!" screamed the old woman in bed. "It is not my birthday, no one knows when that is but myself, and will you please be quiet and say nothing more, or I'll go straight out of my mind!" She turned her eyes toward Marian again, and presently she said in the soft, foggy voice, "When the worst comes to the worst, I ring this bell, and the nurse comes." One of her hands was drawn out from under the patched counterpane—a thin little hand with enormous black freckles. With a finger which would not hold still she pointed to a little bell on the table among the bottles.

"How old are you?" Marian breathed. Now she could see the old woman in bed very closely and plainly, and very abruptly, from all sides, as in dreams. She wondered about her—she wondered for a moment as though there was nothing else in the world to wonder about. It was the first time such a thing had happened to Marian.

"I won't tell!"

The old face on the pillow, where Marian was bending over it, slowly gathered   60
and collapsed. Soft whimpers came out of the small open mouth. It was a sheep that she sounded like—a little lamb. Marian's face drew very close, the yellow hair hung forward.

"She's crying!" She turned a bright, burning face up to the first old woman.

"That's Addie for you," the old woman said spitefully.

Marian jumped up and moved toward the door. For the second time, the claw almost touched her hair, but it was not quick enough. The little girl put her cap on.

"Well, it was a real visit," said the old woman, following Marian through the doorway and all the way out into the hall. Then from behind she suddenly clutched the child with her sharp little fingers. In an affected, high-pitched whine she cried, "Oh, little girl, have you a penny to spare for a poor old woman that's not got anything of her own? We don't have a thing in the world—not a penny for candy—not a thing! Little girl, just a nickel—a penny—"

Marian pulled violently against the old hands for a moment before she was   65 free. Then she ran down the hall, without looking behind her and without looking at the nurse, who was reading *Field & Stream* at her desk. The nurse, after another triple motion to consult her wrist watch, asked automatically the question put to visitors in all institutions: "Won't you stay and have dinner with *us*?"

Marian never replied. She pushed the heavy door open into the cold air and ran down the steps.

Under the prickly shrub she stooped and quickly, without being seen, re-trieved a red apple she had hidden there.

Her yellow hair under the white cap, her scarlet coat, her bare knees all flashed in the sunlight as she ran to meet the big bus rocketing through the street.

"Wait for me!" she shouted. As though at an imperial command, the bus ground to a stop.

She jumped on and took a big bite out of the apple.   *[1941]*   70

A Student's Personal Response to the Story

Here is some freewriting a student did about the story you just read. By simply jotting down some observations and questions, she provided herself with the seeds of a paper.

I'm not sure which character I should be sympathizing with in Wel-ty's story. Right away I disliked the girl because she wasn't really in-terested in seeing the old women. I don't know why the story is called "A Visit of Charity," since she just wanted to get more points. And yet I have to admit that when I was younger I was sort of like her. I remember one time when my church youth group had to sing Christmas carols at an old folks' home, and I was uneasy about hav-ing to meet all these ancient men and women I didn't know, some of whom could barely walk or talk. It's funny, because I was always comfortable around my grandparents, but I have to confess that be-ing around all those old people at once spooked me a little. I smiled a lot at them and joined in the singing and helped hand out candy canes afterward. But I couldn't wait to leave. Once I did, I felt proud of myself for going there, but I guess I also felt a little guilty be-cause I didn't really want to be there at all. So, maybe I'm being hypocritical when I criticize the girl in Welty's story for insensitivity. Anyway, I expected that Welty would present in a good light any old women that Marian encountered, just to emphasize that Marian was being unkind and that it's really sad for people to have to live in a retirement home (or senior citizens' center or whatever they're calling such places nowadays). And yet the two old women she meets are cranky and unpleasant. Even the receptionist doesn't come off all that good. If I were Marian, I probably would have left even sooner than she did! Maybe Welty didn't want us to sympathize with anyone in the story, and maybe that's OK. I tend to want a story to make at least some of the characters sympathetic, but maybe it's unfair of me to demand that. Still, I'm wondering if I'm not appreciating Welty's characters enough. When the two old women argue, should we side with one of them, or are we supposed to be bothered by them both? Are we supposed to think any better of the girl by the time she leaves? The apple she eats immediately made me think of the Adam and Eve story, but I don't know what I'm supposed to do with that parallel.

The Elements of Short Fiction

Whether discussing them in class or writing about them, you will improve your ability to analyze stories like Welty's if you grow familiar with typical elements of short fiction. These elements include plot and structure, point of view, characters, setting, imagery, language, and theme.

PLOT AND STRUCTURE

For many readers, the most important element in any work of fiction is **plot**. As they turn the pages of a story, their main question is, What will happen next? In reading Welty's story, quite possibly you wanted to know how Marian's visit to the rest home would turn out. Indeed, plots usually center on human beings, who can be seen as engaging in actions, as being acted upon, or both. You might describe Marian as acting, noting among other things that she "jumped off the bus" (para. 1); that "she shifted the small pot from hand to hand" (para. 1); that "she pushed her hair behind her ears" (para. 4); that her "face drew very close" to Addie's (para. 60); that she "jumped up and moved toward the door" (para. 63); that she "pulled violently against the old hands" of the other elderly woman (para. 65); that "she ran to meet the big bus" (para. 68); and that she "jumped on and took a big bite out of the apple" (para. 70). But you might also describe her as being affected by other forces. For example, she is "suddenly propelled by the strong, impatient arm of the nurse" (para. 9); the "claw" of the first old woman "drew her all the way into the room" (para. 11); and she repeats the two women's language "without realizing that she had said a word" (para. 31). In any case, most short stories put characters into high-pressure situations, whether for dark or comic effect. To earn the merit points she desires, Marian has to contend with the feuding roommates.

Besides physical events, a short story may involve psychological developments. Welty's heroine goes through mental changes during her visit. One is that her interest in the two women grows; they are no longer just a dutiful task to her. This change is indicated best by a particular word: "wondered." When the women discuss a previous visitor, Marian "wondered" about the animal imagery suddenly filling her mind (para. 26). When the first old woman perches the plant "high on the top of the wardrobe," the girl "wondered how she had ever succeeded in placing it there" (para. 32). Then, as Marian gazes upon the bedridden Addie, "She wondered about her—she wondered for a moment as though there was nothing else in the world to wonder about" (para. 58). As if to emphasize that the girl is experiencing a psychological transition, the narrator reports: "It was the first time such a thing had happened to Marian" (para. 58). Many stories do show characters undergoing complete or partial conversions. Meanwhile, a number of stories include characters who stick to their beliefs but gain a new perspective on them.

Does Marian's encounter with the two women have something to do with her ultimately biting the apple and leaping onto the bus? If so, what's the specific connection? Questions like these bring up relations of cause and effect, terms that often figure in discussions of plot. The novelist and short-story writer E. M. Forster refers to them in defining the term *plot* itself. To Forster, a plot is not simply one incident after another, such as "the king died and then the queen died." Rather, it is a situation or a whole chain of events in which there are reasons *why* characters behave as they do. Forster's example: "The king died, and then the queen died of grief."

Writers of short stories do not always make cause and effect immediately clear. Another possible plot, Forster suggests, is "The queen died, no one knew why, until it was discovered that it was through grief at the death of the king." In this scenario, all of the characters lack information about the queen's true psychology for a while, and perhaps the reader is in the dark as well. Indeed, many short stories leave the reader ignorant for a spell. For instance, only near the conclusion of her story does Welty reveal that before entering the rest home, Marian had put an apple under the shrub. Why does the author withhold this key fact from you? Perhaps Welty was silent about the apple because, had she reported it right away, its echoes of Eve might have overshadowed your interpretation of the story as you read. Worth considering are issues of effect: what the characters' behavior makes you think of them and what impact the author's strategies have on you.

When you summarize a story's plot, you may be inclined to put events in chronological order. But remember that short stories are not always linear. Alice Adams, author of many short stories, offered a more detailed outline of their typical **structure**. She proposed the formula ABDCE: these letters stand for **action, background, development, climax,** and **ending**. More precisely, Adams's formula begins a story with an action, follows that action with some background information, and then moves the plot forward in time through a major turning point and toward some sort of resolution. Not all writers of short stories follow this scheme. In fact, Adams did not always stick to it. Certainly a lot of short stories combine her background and development stages, moving the plot along while offering details of their characters' pasts. And sometimes a story will have several turning points rather than a single distinct climax. But by keeping Adams's formula in mind, if only as a common way to construct short stories, you will be better prepared to recognize how a story departs from chronological order.

The first paragraph of Welty's story seems to be centered on *action*. Marian arrives at the Old Ladies' Home and prepares to enter it. Even so, Welty provides some basic information in this paragraph, describing Marian and the rest home as if the reader is unfamiliar with both. Yet only in the second paragraph do you learn Marian's name and the purpose of her visit. Therefore, Welty can be said to obey Adams's formula, beginning with *action* and then moving to *background*. Note, however, that the second paragraph features *development* as well. By explaining to the receptionist who she is and why she is there, Marian takes a step closer to the central event, her meeting with the two roommates. The remainder of the story keeps moving forward in time.

What about *climax*, Adams's fourth term? Traditionally, the climax of a story has been defined as a peak moment of drama appearing near the end. Also, it is usually thought of as a point when at least one character commits a significant act, experiences a significant change, makes a significant discovery, learns a significant lesson, or perhaps does all these things. With Welty's story, you could argue that the climax is when Marian asks Addie her age, meets with refusal, sees Addie crying, and tries to bolt. Certainly this is a dramatic moment, involving intense display of emotion resulting in Marian's departure. But, as we noted, Marian also experiences inner change. When she looks on Addie "as though there was nothing else in the world to wonder about," this is "the first time such a thing had happened to Marian."

Adams's term *ending* may seem unnecessary. Why would anyone have to be reminded that stories end? Yet a story's climax may engage readers so much that they overlook whatever follows. If the climax of Welty's story is Marian's conversation with the tearful Addie, then the ending is basically in four parts: the plea that Addie's roommate makes to Marian as she is leaving; Marian's final encounter with the receptionist; Marian's retrieval of the apple; and her escape on the bus, where she bites into the apple. Keep in mind that the ending of a story may relate somehow to its beginning. The ending of Welty's "A Visit of Charity," for instance, brings the story full circle. Whereas at the start Marian gets off a bus, hides the apple, and meets the receptionist, at the conclusion she rushes by the receptionist, recovers the apple, and boards another bus. However a story ends, ask yourself if any of the characters have changed at some point between start and finish. Does the conclusion of the story indicate that at least one person has developed in some way, or does it leave you with the feeling of lives frozen since the start? As Welty's story ends, readers may have various opinions about Marian. Some may find that she has not been changed all that much by her visit to the home, while others may feel that it has helped her mature.

A common organizational device in short stories is **repetition**. It takes various forms. First, a story may repeat words, as Welty's story does with its multiple uses of the word "wondered." Second, a story may repeatedly refer to a certain image, as you see with Welty's images of the plant and the apple. Third, a story may involve repeated actions. In "A Visit of Charity," the two roommates repeatedly argue; Marian travels by bus at the beginning and at the end; and the nurse consults her wristwatch both when Marian arrives and when she leaves.

POINT OF VIEW

A short story may be told from a particular character's perspective or **point of view**. When it is written in the **first person**—narrated by someone using the pronoun *I* or, more rarely, *we*—you have to decide how much to accept the narrator's point of view, keeping in mind that the narrator may be psychologically complex. How objective does the narrator seem in depicting other people and events? In what ways, if any, do the narrator's perceptions seem influenced by his or her personal experiences, circumstances, feelings, values, and beliefs? Does the narrator seem to have changed in any way since the events recalled? How reasonable do the narrator's judgments seem? At what moments, if any, do you find yourself disagreeing with the narrator's view of things?

Not every short story is narrated by an identifiable person. Many of them are told by what has been traditionally called an **omniscient narrator**. The word *omniscient* means "all-knowing" and is often used as an adjective for God. An omniscient narrator is usually a seemingly all-knowing, objective voice. This is the kind of voice at work in Welty's story, right from the first paragraph. There, Marian is described in an authoritatively matter-of-fact tone that appears detached from her: "Holding a potted plant before her, a girl of fourteen jumped off the bus in front of the Old Ladies' Home." Keep in mind, though, that a story may rely primarily on an omniscient narrator and yet at some points seem immersed in a character's perspective. This, too, is the case with Welty's story. Consider the following passage about Marian:

> Everything smelled wet—even the bare floor. She held on to the back of the chair, which was wicker and felt soft and damp. Her heart beat more and more slowly, her hands got colder and colder, and she could not hear whether the old women were saying anything or not. She could not see them very clearly. How dark it was! The window shade was down, and the only door was shut. Marian looked at the ceiling. . . . It was like being caught in a robbers' cave, just before one was murdered.

The passage remains in the third person, referring to "she" rather than to "I." Nevertheless, the passage seems intimately in touch with Marian's physical sensations. Indeed, the sentence "How dark it was!" seems something that Marian would say to herself. Similarly, the analogy to the robbers' cave may be Marian's own personal perception, and as such, the analogy may reveal more about her own state of mind than about the room. Many literary critics use the term **free indirect style** for moments like this, when a narrator otherwise omniscient conveys a particular character's viewpoint by resorting to the character's own language.

Throughout this book, we encourage you to analyze an author's strategies by considering the options that he or she faced. You may better understand a short story's point of view if you think about the available alternatives. For example, how would you have reacted to Welty's story if it had focused on Addie's perceptions more than on Marian's?

CHARACTERS

Although we have been discussing plots, we have also referred to the people caught up in them. Any analysis you do of a short story will reflect your understanding and evaluation of its **characters**. Rarely does the author of a story provide you with extended, enormously detailed biographies. Rather, you see the story's characters at select moments of their lives. To quote William Trevor again, the short story is "the art of the glimpse."

You may want to judge characters according to how easily you can identify with them. Yet there is little reason for you to read works that merely reinforce your prejudices. Furthermore, you may overlook the potential richness of a story if you insist that its characters fit your usual standards of behavior. An author can teach you much by introducing you to the complexity of people you might automatically praise or condemn in real life. Many of us would immediately condemn someone reluctant to help old women, but Welty encourages us to analyze carefully the girl in her story rather than just denounce her. You may be tempted to dismiss the roommates in Welty's story as unpleasant, even "sick"; in any case, take the story as an opportunity to explore *why* women in a rest home may express discontent.

One thing to consider about the characters in a story is what each basically desires. At the beginning of Welty's story, for example, Marian is hardly visiting the Old Ladies' Home out of "charity," despite that word's presence in the story's title. Rather, Marian hopes to earn points as a Campfire Girl. Again, characters in a story may change, so consider whether the particular characters you are examining alter their thinking. Perhaps you feel that Marian's visit broadens her vision of life; then again, perhaps you conclude that she remains much the same.

Reading a short story involves relating its characters to one another. In part, you'll need to determine their relative importance. Even a seemingly minor character can perform some noteworthy function; the nurse in "A Visit of Charity" not only ushers Marian in and out but also marks time. Nevertheless, any reader will try to identify a story's *main* figures. When a particular character seems the focus, he or she is referred to as the story's **protagonist**. Many readers would say that Marian is the protagonist of "A Visit of Charity." When the protagonist is in notable conflict with another character, this foe is referred to as the **antagonist**. Because Marian initially finds both roommates unpleasant, you may want to call them her antagonists. But it's not a word that you *must* apply to some character in a story; the work can have a protagonist and yet *not* include an opponent. Moreover, as a story proceeds, characters may alter their relationships with one another. Marian grows more conscious of the tensions *between* the roommates, and then for a moment she sympathizes with Addie. It is possible, too, for one character to be ambivalent toward another, feeling both drawn *and* opposed to that person. Perhaps the roommates have a love-hate relationship, needing each other's company even as they bicker. As perhaps you have found in your own experience, human relationships are often far from simple. Works of literature can prove especially interesting when they suggest as much.

What power and influence people achieve may depend on particular traits of theirs. These include their gender, social class, race, ethnic background, nationality, sexual orientation, age, and the kind of work they do. Because these attributes may greatly affect a person's life, pay attention to them as you analyze characters. For instance, in Welty's story, all the characters are female. How might their gender matter? How might the story's dynamics have differed if it had featured at least one man? Another element of the story is its gap in ages: while the roommates are old, Marian is barely a teenager. What, over their years of living, might the two women have learned that the girl doesn't know yet?

Typically, characters express views of one another, and you have to decide how accurate these are. Some characters will seem wise observers of humanity. Others will strike you as making distorted statements about the world, revealing little more than their own biases and quirks. And some characters will seem to fall in the middle, coming across as partly objective and partly subjective. On occasion, you and your classmates may find yourselves debating which category a particular character fits. One interesting case is Welty's character Addie. Look again at the speech in which she berates her roommate:

> "Hush!" said the sick woman. "You never went to school. You never came and you never went. You never were anything—only here. You never were born! You don't know anything. Your head is empty, your heart and hands and your old black purse are all empty, even that little old box that you brought with you you brought empty—you showed it to me. And yet you talk, talk, talk, talk, talk all the time until I think I'm losing my mind! Who are you? You're a stranger—a perfect stranger! Don't you know you're a stranger? Is it possible that they have actually done a thing like this to anyone—sent them in a stranger to talk, and rock, and tell away her whole long rigmarole? Do they seriously suppose that I'll be able to keep it up, day in, day out, night in, night out, living in the same room with a terrible old woman—forever?"

Some may argue that this speech is merely an unreasonable rant, indicating Addie's dour mood rather than her roommate's true nature. (For one thing, contrary to Addie's declaration, the roommate must have been born!) Yet it can also be argued that Addie shrewdly diagnoses her situation. Perhaps statements like "you never were born," "your head is empty," and "you're a stranger" are true in a metaphorical sense.

SETTING

Usually a short story enables readers to examine how people behave in concrete circumstances. The characters are located in a particular place or **setting**. Moreover, they are shown at particular moments in their personal histories.

Sometimes the story goes further, referring to them as living at a certain point in world history.

As the word *sometimes* implies, short stories vary in the precision with which they identify their settings. They differ as well in the importance of their setting. Sometimes location serves as a mere backdrop for the plot. At other times, the setting can be a looming presence. When Welty's character Marian visits the Old Ladies' Home, we get her vivid impressions of it. Even when a story's setting seems ordinary, it may become filled with drama and meaning as the plot develops. One way of analyzing characters is to consider how they accommodate themselves—or fail to accommodate themselves—to their surroundings. The two roommates in Welty's story are evidently frustrated with living in the Old Ladies' Home, and they take out their frustration on each other.

IMAGERY

Just like poems, short stories often use **imagery** to convey meaning. Sometimes a character in the story may interpret a particular image just the way you do. Some stories, though, include images that you and the characters may analyze quite differently. One example is the apple in Welty's story. Whereas Marian probably views the apple as just something to eat, many readers would make other associations with it, thinking in particular of the apple that Adam and Eve ate from the tree of knowledge in the Garden of Eden. By the end of Welty's story, perhaps Marian has indeed become like Adam and Eve, in that she has lost her innocence and grown more aware that human beings age. At any rate, many readers would call Marian's apple a **symbol**. Traditionally, that is the term for an image seen as representing some concept or concepts. Again, Marian herself probably does not view her apple as symbolic; indeed, characters within stories rarely use the word *symbol* at all.

Images may appear in the form of metaphors or other figures of speech. For example, when Marian enters the Old Ladies' Home, she experiences "a smell in the hall like the interior of a clock." Welty soon builds on the clock image as she describes the receptionist checking her wristwatch, an action that this character repeats near the end. Welty's whole story can be said to deal with time and its effects, both on the old and on the young.

Images in short stories usually appeal to the reader's visual sense. Most often, they are things you can picture in your mind. Yet stories are not limited to rendering visual impressions. They may refer to other senses, too, as when Welty's young heroine notices the odor in the hall.

LANGUAGE

Everything about short stories we have discussed so far concerns **language**. After all, works of literature are constructed entirely out of words. Here, however, we call your attention to three specific uses of language in stories: title, predominant style, and dialogue.

A story's **title** may be just as important as any words in the text. Not always will the relevance of the title be immediately clear to you. Usually you have to read a story all the way through before you can sense fully how its title applies. In any case, play with the title in your mind, considering its various possible meanings and implications. In analyzing the title of Welty's "A Visit of Charity," you may find it helpful to think about this famous passage from the King James translation of the New Testament: "And now abideth faith, hope, charity, these three; but the greatest of these is charity" (1 Corinthians 13:13). You may also want to look up the word *charity* in a dictionary.

Not all short stories have a uniform **style**. Some feature various tones, dialects, vocabularies, and levels of formality. Welty's story incorporates different types of speech almost from its start. When, using rather formal language, the nurse asks Marian, "Acquainted with any of our residents?" (para. 3), the girl puts this question more plainly: "With any old ladies?" (para. 4). Stories that do have a predominant style are often told in the first person, thus giving the impression of a presiding "voice." Charlotte Perkins Gilman's "The Yellow Wallpaper (pp. 231–244) teems with the anguished expressions of its beleaguered narrator.

Dialogue may serve more than one purpose in a short story. By reporting various things, characters may provide you with necessary background for the plot. In Welty's story, it's only from the roommates' fragmentary remarks that Marian — and the reader — can learn anything about their lives up until now. Actually, dialogue can also be thought of as an action in itself, moving the plot along. Try to identify the particular kinds of acts that characters perform when they speak. When the first roommate asks the departing Marian for a coin, she seems to be begging, but perhaps she is also doing whatever she can to hold the girl there; her having "clutched the child" (para. 64) suggests as much. Indeed, dialogue may function to reveal shifts in characters' relations with one another.

THEME

We have already discussed the term **theme** on pages 42–46. There, we identified issues of theme as one kind of issue that comes up in literary studies. At the same time, we suggested that the term *theme* applies to various literary genres, not just short stories. Later in this chapter, we examine theme in connection with poems, plays, and essays. Here, though, we consider theme as an element of short fiction. In doing so, we review some points from our earlier discussion, applying them now to Welty's story.

Recall that we defined the theme of a work as the main claim it seems to make. Furthermore, we identified it as an assertion, a proposition, or a statement rather than as a single word. "Charity" is obviously a *topic* of Welty's story, but because it is just one word, it is not an adequate expression of the story's *theme*. The following exercise invites you to consider just what that theme may be.

1. Try to state a text's theme as a midlevel generalization.   If you were to put it in very broad terms, your audience would see it as fitting a great many works besides the one you have read. If you went to the opposite extreme, tying the theme completely to specific details of the text, your audience might think the theme irrelevant to their own lives.

The phrase "the moral of the story" suggests that a story can usually be reduced to a single message, often a principle of ethics or religion. Plenty of examples can be cited to support this suggestion. In the New Testament, for instance, Jesus tells stories—they are called *parables*—to convey some of his key ideas. In any number of cultures today, stories are used to teach children elements of good conduct. Moreover, people often determine the significance of a real-life event by building a story from it and by drawing a moral from it at the same time. These two processes conspicuously dovetailed when England's Princess Diana was killed in a car crash. Given that she died fleeing photographers, many people saw her entire life story as that of a woman hounded by the media. The moral was simultaneous and clear: thou shalt honor the right to privacy.

It is possible to lose sight of a story's theme by placing too much emphasis on minor details of the text. The more common temptation, however, is to turn a story's theme into an all-too-general cliché. Actually, a story is often most interesting when it *complicates* some widely held idea that it seemed ready to endorse. Therefore, a useful exercise is to start with a general thematic statement about the story and then make it increasingly specific. With "A Visit of Charity," for example, you might begin by supposing that a theme is "Everyone must give up their dreams of innocence and paradise, just as Adam and Eve did." Your next step would be to identify the specific spin that Welty's story gives this idea. How does her story differ from others on this theme? Note, for instance, that Marian comes literally face to face with the mortality of women much older than she is, and that the experience fills her momentarily with "wonder." Try to rephrase our version of Welty's theme so that it seems more in touch with these specific details of the text.

2. A theme of a text may be related to its title.   It may also be expressed by some statement made within the text. But often various parts of the text merit consideration as you try to determine its theme.

In our discussion of a short story's language, we called attention to the potential significance of its title. The title may serve as a guide to the story's theme. What clues, if any, do you find in the title "A Visit of Charity"? Of course, determining a story's theme entails going beyond the title. You have to read, and usually reread, the entire text. In doing so, you may come across a statement that seems a candidate for the theme because it is a philosophical generalization. Nevertheless, take the time to consider whether the story's essence is indeed captured by this statement alone.

3. You can state a text's theme either as an observation or as a recommendation.   Each way of putting it evokes a certain image of the text's author. When you state the theme as an **observation**, you depict the author as a psychologist, a philosopher, or some other kind of analyst. When you state the theme as a **recommendation**—which often involves your using the word *should*—you depict the author as a teacher, preacher, manager, or coach. That is, the author comes across as telling readers what to do.

As we have noted, stories are often used to teach lessons. Moreover, often the lessons are recommendations for action, capable of being phrased as "Do X" or "Do not do X." The alternative is to make a generalization about some state of affairs. When you try to express a particular story's theme, which of these two options should you follow? There are several things to consider in making your decision. First is your personal comfort: do you feel at ease with both ways of stating the theme, or is one of these ways more to your taste? Also worth pondering is the impression you want to give of the author: do you want to portray this person as a maker of recommendations, or do you want to assign the author a more modest role? Which of these two identities do you prefer for Welty?

4. Consider stating a text's theme as a problem.   That way, you are more apt to convey the complexity and drama of the text.

We have suggested that short stories often pivot around conflicts between people and conflicts within people. Perhaps the most interesting stories are ones that pose conflicts not easily resolved. Probably you will be more faithful to such a text if you phrase its theme as a problem. In the case of Welty's story, for example, you might state the theme as follows: "Young people may sense an older person's infirmity, but, especially if that person is a stranger, they may as yet lack sufficient maturity and confidence to stay and help."

5. Rather than refer to *the* theme of a text, you might refer to *a* theme of the text, implying that the text has more than one.   You would still be suggesting that you have identified a central idea of the text. Subsequently, you might have to defend your claim.

Unlike the average novel, the typical short story pivots around only a few ideas. Yet you need not insist that the story you are analyzing has a single theme. The shortest piece of short fiction may have more than one, and your audience may well appreciate your admitting this. One theme of Welty's story may be that none of us can escape the passage of time. The old roommates aside, teenaged Marian seems on the brink of adulthood, and her concluding bus ride suggests that she is moving further into it. But additional themes are possible. A second idea, dramatized by the roommates' feud, may be that old age can test a person's spirit even as it hurts the person's body. Of course, to call either of these ideas a theme of the story is still to make a claim that requires support.

Perhaps the biggest challenge you will face in writing about short stories is to avoid long stretches of plot summary. Selected details of the plot will often serve as key evidence for you. You will need to describe such moments from the story you are discussing, even if your audience has already read it. But your readers are apt to be frustrated if you just repeat plot at length. They will feel that they may as well turn back to the story itself rather than linger with your rehash. Your paper is worth your readers' time only if you provide insights of your own, *analyzing* the story rather than just *summarizing* it.

To understand what analysis of a short story involves, let's turn to student Tanya Vincent. Assigned to write an argument paper about a short story, Tanya decided to focus on Welty's. She realized that for her paper to be effective, she had to come up with an issue worth addressing, a claim about that issue, and evidence for that claim. Moreover, she had to be prepared to identify her process of reasoning and her assumptions.

For most writing assignments, settling on an issue will be your most important preliminary step. Without a driving question, you will have difficulty producing fresh, organized, and sustained analysis. For her paper on "A Visit of Charity," Tanya chose to address this issue: What does the story suggest *charity* can mean? In part, she was drawn to this question because the word *charity* appears in the story's title and because it comes up in the famous passage from 1 Corinthians 13 that we quoted earlier. But the question also enticed her because Welty's protagonist doesn't appear truly compassionate. A conventional definition of *charity* is that it is an expression of a sincere desire to help people. Given that Marian appears to lack this desire, is Welty's title ironic? Or does charity in some *other* sense of the word operate in the story? Tanya realized that she would be tackling an issue of definition. She would need to examine various possible meanings of "charity" and determine which are relevant to specific details of Welty's text.

A paper about a short story doesn't have to mention explicitly all the elements of short fiction we've identified. Nevertheless, thinking of these elements can help you plan such a paper, providing you with some preliminary terms for your analysis. Tanya perceived that her paper would be very much about characters and plot; it might also dwell upon imagery and language. She knew, too, that she would be more apt to persuade her readers if she included quotations from the story. Yet, as with plot summary, quoting should be limited, so that the paper seems an original argument—not a recycling of the literary work's own words. Tanya sensed that practically every sentence of Welty's story could be quoted and then interpreted. At the same time, she realized that she should quote only *some* words, not all.

Final Draft of a Student Paper

Here is Tanya's final draft of her paper about "A Visit of Charity." As you read it, keep in mind that it emerged only after she had done several preliminary drafts, in consultation with some of her classmates as well as her instructor. Although Tanya's paper is a good example of how to write about a short story, most drafts can stand to be revised further. What do you think Tanya has done well in her paper? If she planned to do yet another revision, what suggestions would you make?

Tanya Vincent
Professor Stein
English 1A
3 November - - - -

The Real Meaning of "Charity"
in "A Visit of Charity"

Many people would define the word "charity" as an act in which an individual or institution sincerely offers material or

An assumption, but seems a reasonable one.

spiritual comfort to someone less fortunate. In this respect, charity is a form of love. Such is the meaning implied in the King James translation of the most famous statement about charity, 1 Corinthians 13:13: "And now abideth faith, hope, charity, these three; but the greatest of these is charity." In fact, some other translations of this biblical passage use "love" instead of "charity," thereby suggesting that the two terms are more or less equivalent. But Marian, the protagonist of Eudora Welty's short story "A Visit of Charity," does not appear to demonstrate this concept of charity when she visits the Old Ladies' Home. She gives no indication that she sincerely cares about any of its residents. Rather, she approaches the visit as a mechanical task that she must perform to raise her standing as a Campfire Girl. Nor does she seem to become much more empathetic after spending time at the Home. Several readers of the story, therefore, might think its title ironic.

Starts to introduce her issue and claim by referring to readers who are possibly superficial.

This view may, however, be too limited. Welty may be encouraging us to move past our familiar concept of "charity" and give the word a meaning that *can* apply to her text in a nonironic way. It is true that Marian does not act lovingly or even compassionately on her trip to the Home. Yet maybe her brief moments with the two elderly roommates provide charity to Marian herself, making her a beneficiary of it rather than a donor of it. After all, her encounter with the two women helps to make her at least a bit more aware of the stresses that old age can bring. Charity in *this* sense would mean the providing of a necessary lesson about what life can be like as an adult. Even though the two roommates do not intend to be benevolent teachers of the girl, her meeting with them has some value, for it gives her a preview of realities she will have to deal with more extensively as she grows up.

A qualification. Tanya holds back from claiming certainty about Welty's intentions.

Introduction ends with main issue (a definitional kind) and main claim.

When we first meet her in the story, Marian seems anything but passionately devoted to improving life for the Home's inhabitants. Probably "Old Ladies' Home" is not the building's real name to begin with, but instead Marian's own insensitive designation. Clearly she looks upon her visit as a chore. To her, it is just something she must do to earn points. Later, we readers learn that she has even computed the specific amounts available to her: "She had almost said that if Campfire Girls brought flowers to the Old Ladies' Home, the visit would count one extra point, and if they took a Bible with them on the bus and read it to the old ladies, it counted double" (118). When, back at the story's start, she introduces herself to the nurse, she does not even pretend to be a true Angel of Mercy pursuing a higher spiritual purpose: "I'm a

Concession to readers who have trouble finding "charity" in the story.

Campfire Girl. . . . I have to pay a visit to some old lady" (116). So indifferent is she to the Home's aged occupants that she candidly announces "any of them will do" (116). When she does meet with the two roommates, she chooses not to stay long with them. Nor does she offer charity in a traditional sense when one of the roommates begs. While the woman asks, "have you a penny to spare for a poor old woman that's not got anything of her own?" (120), Marian is anxious to flee. Nor, when she does leave the pair, is her exit gradual, patient, and kind: she "jumped up and moved toward the door"; "pulled violently against the old hands"; "ran down the hall, without looking behind her and without looking at the nurse"; "quickly . . . retrieved a red apple"; "ran to meet the big bus"; "shouted" at the bus; and "jumped on" (120). These frenzied motions indicate that Marian is ultimately *repelled* by the two women, not drawn to them as clients for her kindness.

Here and elsewhere in the paper, Tanya quotes from Welty's text.

Nevertheless, perhaps Marian's experience with them confers a sort of charity upon *her* by alerting her to facts she will eventually have to face. When she first meets the roommate who is supposedly healthier, she is struck by the "terrible, square smile (which was a smile of welcome) stamped on her bony face" (117). This seems more an image of death than of life, suggesting that Marian is beginning to grow conscious of mortality. This implication gets even stronger when Marian comes to the bed of the sicker woman, Addie: "She wondered about her — she wondered for a moment as though there was nothing else in the world to wonder about. It was the first time such a thing had happened to Marian" (119). More precisely, Marian seems to discover that people soon to die may become a mixture of helplessness and fierce self-assertion. To the girl, Addie repeatedly comes across as a sheep or lamb, a species of animal traditionally associated with innocence. Even before she enters the room, Marian twice experiences Addie's voice as that of a sheep "bleating" (116), and at Addie's bedside she mentally compares the tearful, suffering woman to "a little lamb" (119). Yet Addie is also someone capable not only of refusing to tell her age, but also of berating her roommate: "And yet you talk, talk, talk, talk, talk all the time until I think I'm losing my mind!" (119). In turn, the object of this scorn displays to Marian a similar blend of powerlessness and ferocity. "In an affected, high-pitched whine," this roommate refers to herself as "a poor old woman," but at the same time "she suddenly clutched the child with her sharp little fingers" (120). Indeed, if Addie comes across to Marian as a sheep or lamb, the girl senses right from the start of the meeting that the other woman is an aggressive

Transition to development of main claim.

As earlier, with "wondered," Tanya shows attention to repetition.

bird: "Suddenly Marian saw a hand, quick as a bird claw, reach up in the air and pluck the white cap off her head" (117). In general, neither of the roommates fits the sentimental stereotype of the sweet old lady. But their difference from this image is precisely what can be educational for Marian. Their nearness to death, and the complex behavior they show in response to their fate, are matters that the girl will have to contend with a lot once she herself becomes a full-fledged adult.

While admitting that the sentence about "the first time" appears significant, some readers may doubt that Marian learns anything from this experience. Their skepticism would be understandable, given that she does not philosophize at length about the visit and ends it rather speedily. Welty does, however, suggest the stirrings of mental change in Marian by drawing our attention to the bodily disorientation she goes through in the old women's room. Immediately upon meeting them, she "stood tongue-tied" (117). Soon, "her heart beat more and more slowly, her hands got colder and colder, and she could not hear whether the old women were saying any-thing or not" (117). Moreover, "she could not see them very clearly" (117). A moment later, she winds up "pitched against the chair" (117) and forgets her own name. Eventually "her heart nearly stopped beating altogether" (119). These disabil-ities, though temporary, indicate that at *some* level of con-sciousness, Marian is having perceptions that she did not have before. Specifically, she seems to have glimmers of how death increasingly enters people's lives as they age.

Concession to readers with a different view.

The story's very last sentence further suggests that Marian either learns this lesson or vaguely intuits it. By tak-ing "a big bite out of the apple" (120), she resembles Adam and Eve, whose own eating of an apple resulted in their be-coming mortal. But in writing her story, Welty may also have had in mind a second biblical passage. Occurring just two lines before the famous statement about charity I have quoted, it is a well-known review of life's journey: "When I was a child, I spake as a child, I understood as a child, I thought as a child: but when I became a man, I put away childish things" (1 Corinthians 13:11). Although Marian is female, the line can still apply to her. Before her visit to the Home, she has been "a child," and she acts that way for much of her time there. But the visit may make her more inclined to "put away childish things," in which case she herself would receive a form of charity from it.

Again, acknowledges that she can't be certain about Welty's thinking.

Works Cited

Welty, Eudora. "A Visit of Charity." *Making Literature Matter: An Anthology for Readers and Writers.* Ed. John Schilb and John Clifford. 6th ed. Boston: Bedford, 2015. 116–120. Print.

≡ SUMMING UP: WRITING ABOUT SHORT STORIES

- **Short stories require you to understand and evaluate them on the basis of just a few details and events.**

- **Think carefully about the title and its possible meanings and implications.**

- **The elements of short fiction include *plot* and *structure*, *point of view*, *characters*, *setting*, *imagery*, *language*, and *theme*.**

- ***Plot* and *structure* are related, but plots usually center on human beings and their actions, and structure often follows the ABDCE formula (action, background, development, climax, ending).** (pp. 121–124)

- ***Points of view* vary and include first person and omniscient.** (pp. 124–125)

- **As you analyze and evaluate the *characters* in a short story** (pp. 125–126), **consider these questions:**

  What does each character desire?

  How do the characters, even minor characters, relate to one another?

  Can you identify a protagonist and an antagonist?

  How are the characters' lives affected by traits such as gender, class, race, ethnicity, nationality, sexual orientation, and occupation?

  Can you trust the accuracy of the views the characters have of one another?

  How does the characters' dialogue function — does it provide background, advance the plot, reveal shifts in characters' relations, or what?

- ***Setting* provides a context for actions.** One way of analyzing characters is to consider how they do or do not accommodate themselves to their surroundings. (pp. 126–127)

(*continued on next page*)

≡ **SUMMING UP: WRITING ABOUT SHORT STORIES**
(continued)

- *Images* appeal to the reader's senses — usually the visual sense — and may appear in the form of metaphors and other figures of speech. (p. 127)

- The language of a short story may have various meanings and implications. Think about the potential significance not only of its title, but also of its style and dialogue. (pp. 127–128)

- A *theme* of a short story is a claim it seems to make, best identified as an assertion, a proposition, or a statement. In your writing, try to state the theme as a midlevel generalization, either as an observation, as a recommendation, or as a problem. (pp. 128–131)

- In writing an argument about a short story, remember to formulate an issue worth addressing. (p. 130)

Writing about Poems

Some students are put off by poetry, perhaps because their early experiences with it were discouraging. They imagine that poems have deep hidden meanings they can't uncover. Maybe their high-school English teacher always had the right interpretation, and they rarely did. This need not be the case. Poetry can be accessible to all readers.

The problem is often a confusion about the nature of poetry, since poetry is more compressed than prose. Poetry focuses more on connotative, emotional, or associative meanings and conveys meaning more through suggestion, indirection, and the use of metaphor, symbol, and imagery than prose does. It seldom hands us a specific meaning. Poetic texts suggest certain possibilities, but the reader completes the transaction. Part of the meaning comes from the writer, part from the text itself, and part from the reader. Even students who are the same age, race, religion, and ethnicity are not duplicates of one another. Each has unique experiences, family histories, and emotional lives. If thirty people read a poem about conformity or responsibility, all thirty will have varying views about these concepts, even though they will probably have some commonalities. (Most societies are so saturated with shared cultural experiences that it is nearly impossible to avoid some overlap in responses.)

In a good class discussion, then, we should be aware that even though we might be members of the same culture, each of us reads from a unique perspective, a perspective that might also shift from time to time. If a woman reads a poem about childbirth, her identity as a female will seem more relevant than if she were reading a poem about death, a more universal experience. In other words, how we read a poem and how significant and meaningful the poem is for us depends both on the content of the poem and on our specific circumstances. Suppose you are fourteen when you first read a poem about dating; you would likely have very different responses rereading it at nineteen, twenty-five, and fifty. We read poems through our experiences. As we gain new experiences, our readings change.

One reason to respond in writing to your first reading is to be able to separate your first thoughts from those of your classmates. They too will bring their own experiences, values, and ideas to the discussion. In the give-and-take of open discussion, it may be difficult to remember what you first said. Of course, the point of a classroom discussion is not simply to defend your initial response, for then you would be denying yourself the benefit of other people's ideas. A good discussion should open up the poem, allow you to see it from multiple viewpoints, and enable you to expand your perspective, to see how others make sense of the world.

This rich mixture of the poet's text, the reader's response, and discussion among several readers can create new possibilities of meaning. Even more than fiction or drama, poetry encourages creative readings that can be simultaneously true to the text and to the reader. A lively class discussion can uncover a dozen or more plausible interpretations of a poem, each backed up with valid evidence both from the poem and the reader's experience. You may try to persuade others that your views about the poem are correct; others may do the same to you. This negotiation is at the heart of a liberal, democratic education. In fact, maybe the most respected and repeated notion about being well-educated is the ability to empathize with another's point of view, to see as another sees. Reading, discussing, and writing about poetry can help you become a person who can both create meaning and understand and appreciate how others do. This is one important way literature matters.

The following three poems are about work — about the joys and sorrows, the satisfactions and frustrations of physical labor. Some people might think of poets as intellectuals who are far removed from the experiences of the working class, but this is not the case. Indeed, many poets were themselves brought up in working-class homes and know firsthand the dignity and value of such work. Even among poets who do not toil with their hands, few lack the imaginative empathy that would allow them to write perceptively about firefighters and factory workers, cleaning women and mill workers. These three poems are especially relevant today when physical work is becoming less and less a reality among middle-class Americans. Poems that matter are poems about real life — about love and death, about pain and loss, about beauty and hope. These three poems about work are about all of these and more.

The first poem, Mary Oliver's (b. 1935) "Singapore," appeared in *House of Light* (1992). She has won a Pulitzer Prize for her poetry. "Blackberries" is by Yusef Komunyakaa (b. 1947), who has become known for exploring various aspects of African American experience; the poem is from *Magic City* (1992). Edwin Arlington Robinson's "The Mill" is the oldest poem in the cluster. Robinson (1869–1935) is considered the first major poet of twentieth-century America.

MARY OLIVER

Singapore

In Singapore, in the airport,
a darkness was ripped from my eyes.
In the women's restroom, one compartment stood open.
A woman knelt there, washing something
    in the white bowl.   5

Disgust argued in my stomach
and I felt, in my pocket, for my ticket.

A poem should always have birds in it.
Kingfishers, say, with their bold eyes and gaudy wings.
Rivers are pleasant, and of course trees.   10
A waterfall, or if that's not possible, a fountain
    rising and falling.
A person wants to stand in a happy place, in a poem.

When the woman turned I could not answer her face.
Her beauty and her embarrassment struggled together, and   15
    neither could win.
She smiled and I smiled. What kind of nonsense is this?
Everybody needs a job.
Yes, a person wants to stand in a happy place, in a poem.
But first we must watch her as she stares down at her labor,   20
    which is dull enough.
She is washing the tops of the airport ashtrays, as big as
    hubcaps, with a blue rag.
Her small hands turn the metal, scrubbing and rinsing.
She does not work slowly, nor quickly, but like a river.   25
Her dark hair is like the wing of a bird.

I don't doubt for a moment that she loves her life.
And I want her to rise up from the crust and the slop
    and fly down to the river.
This probably won't happen.   30
But maybe it will.
If the world were only pain and logic, who would want it?

Of course, it isn't.
Neither do I mean anything miraculous, but only
the light that can shine out of a life. I mean   35
the way she unfolded and refolded the blue cloth,
the way her smile was only for my sake; I mean
the way this poem is filled with trees, and birds.   *[1992]*

YUSEF KOMUNYAKAA

Blackberries

They left my hands like a printer's
Or thief's before a police blotter
& pulled me into early morning's
Terrestrial sweetness, so thick
The damp ground was consecrated   5
Where they fell among a garland of thorns.

Although I could smell old lime-covered
History, at ten I'd still hold out my hands
& berries fell into them. Eating from one
& filling a half gallon with the other,   10
I ate the mythology & dreamt
Of pies & cobbler, almost

Needful as forgiveness. My bird dog Spot
Eyed blue jays & thrashers. The mud frogs
In rich blackness, hid from daylight.   15
An hour later, beside City Limits Road
I balanced a gleaming can in each hand,
Limboed between worlds, repeating *one dollar.*
The big blue car made me sweat.
Wintertime crawled out of the windows.   20
When I leaned closer I saw the boy
& girl my age, in the wide back seat
Smirking, & it was then I remembered my fingers
Burning with thorns among berries too ripe to touch.   *[1992]*

EDWIN ARLINGTON ROBINSON

The Mill

The miller's wife had waited long,
    The tea was cold, the fire was dead;
And there might yet be nothing wrong
    In how he went and what he said:
"There are no millers any more,"   5
    Was all that she had heard him say;
And he had lingered at the door
    So long that it seemed yesterday.

Sick with fear that had no form
    She knew that she was there at last;   10
And in the mill there was a warm
    And mealy fragrance of the past.

What else there was would only seem
        To say again what he had meant;
And what was hanging from a beam   15
        Would not have heeded where she went.

And if she thought it followed her,
        She may have reasoned in the dark
That one way of the few there were
        Would hide her and would leave no mark: 20
Black water, smooth above the weir
        Like starry velvet in the night,
Though ruffled once, would soon appear
        The same as ever to the sight.   [1920]

A Student's Personal Responses to the Poems

The following are selections from the response journal of student Michaela
Fiorucci, who chose to focus on boundaries—on the various divisions we set
up between ourselves and other people, such as income, race, gender, sexual
preference, and religion. It seemed to her an interesting way to talk about work
since Michaela had observed barriers of all kinds between workers at her job at
the university.

Using an explorative strategy, Michaela did some freewriting on the three
poems, hoping to discover an argument about boundaries that might fit. The
following are selections from her response journal.

> In "Singapore," there is a clear boundary between the middle-
> class American tourist and the cleaning lady, so much so that at first
> the narrator says, "Disgust argued in my stomach." The cleaning
> woman also seems to believe in a barrier and continues to work in
> a steady way. The narrator finally sees beauty in her dedication to
> her work. When the narrator does see beauty in her work habits, it
> helps close the barrier between them. There are also the issues of
> boundaries between fantasy and reality and between a world of
> pain and logic and one with birds and rivers. But at the end these
> boundaries also seem to be closing.
>
> In "Blackberries," the young boy seems to be living in a rural
> paradise, beyond the city boundaries, outside the usual urban and
> suburban environment. He lives in a land of bird dogs, jays, thrash-
> ers, and mud frogs. He makes comparisons between blackness and
> light that seem to anticipate the economic boundary that appears in
> the last stanza, the one between the poor boy and the rich kids in
> the car. It is this division between the children in air-conditioned
> comfort and the narrator on the outside looking in that seems to be
> the main point of this poem. Some boundaries cause us pain.
>
> "The Mill" tells the sad story of a miller who could not see a

boundary between himself and his job. When he tells his wife "there are no millers any more," he is really saying that his life is over; he has no reason to live. And so he crosses the boundary between life and death. Tragically, his wife also has difficulty seeing herself outside her role as wife and housekeeper, and so she also crosses that ultimate boundary. She does so, however, in a completely different way: she drowns herself, so no one will know. She passes through life's boundary without leaving a trace.

After reading these brief freewrites to her response group, Michaela still didn't have a focus, but she liked the idea that boundaries, like walls, sometimes serve a purpose and sometimes they don't. She remembered a discussion of Robert Frost's "Mending Wall" from another course that focused on negotiating the walls we build between us. Her professor liked this idea since it helped her considerably narrow the concept of boundaries.

After reviewing her freewriting, Michaela wrote the following first draft and read it to her response group. She then discussed with her instructor her plans for a revision. Her instructor made a number of specific and general comments. After reading her first draft, what feedback would you give Michaela? Her revision appears later in this chapter on pp. 000–00.

First Draft of a Student Paper

Michaela Fiorucci
Mr. Hardy
English 102
15 April - - - -

Boundaries in Robinson, Komunyakaa, and Oliver

Although most sophomores I know at school value their privacy, they also want to create intimate relationships. It is often hard to reconcile these two impulses. Most middle-class students are lucky enough to have their own rooms, private enclaves against annoying sisters and brothers, intrusive mothers and fathers. But a room is also more than a physical boundary; it is also a symbolic assertion of identity. It says, "I'm separate from others, even within the closeness of the family." Such a commitment to physical privacy might be innocent enough, but it does contain dangerous seeds, especially when extended beyond the home to neighborhoods. When different ethnic groups want boundaries between them, it is no longer innocent. When the upper classes need to be separated from workers because they see each other as radically different, a dangerous boundary has been erected.

It would be reductive, however, to say all boundaries need to be erased. Edwin Arlington Robinson's "The Mill" is a good example of the dangerous consequences of a missing boundary. The poem narrates the sad story of a farm couple who commit suicide — the husband because he feels useless, the wife because she can't imagine life without her husband. During my first few readings, I was struck by the lack of communication between the couple. He must have been depressed for a long time, but it seems they never discussed his feelings. Keeping an emotional distance from others was probably a typical part of the way men and women dealt with each other a hundred years ago. It was a boundary not to be crossed. Apparently he could not say, "I feel terrible that I am going to lose my job." And his wife accepts his reticence, even though he might have been having second thoughts as he "lingered at the door" (line 7). Clearly this is a boundary that should have been breached. But after several readings I began to realize that the boundary that should have been established wasn't — the idea that a person's value or worth is synonymous with his or her identity is dehumanizing. And it probably isn't something that just happened in the past. Nor is the equally dehumanizing idea that a wife is nothing without her husband. When the miller's wife decides to "leave no mark" (20) by jumping into the pond, she is admitting she is not a worthwhile person by herself. Both identify totally with a role that in my view should be only one aspect of a complex human life. The final barrier she crosses, from life to death, is symbolically represented in the poem as a feminine domestic gesture: she doesn't want to leave a mess. The boundaries of person and occupation should be made clear; the arbitrary boundaries between genders should not.

When the narrator in Yusef Komunyakaa's "Blackberries" claims that he is "Limboed between worlds" (18), he means the rural paradise of "Terrestrial sweetness" (4) and "rich blackness" (15) he temporarily lives in versus the commercial, urban work that "made me sweat" (19). He has constructed a boundary between the ancient picking of berries and the technology of automobiles, between a natural closeness with nature and the artificial "Wintertime crawled out of the windows" (20). Even though the narrator is only ten, he senses the sensual joys of being one with nature. He seems to reject "old lime-covered / History" (7–8) in favor of "mythology" (11), which seems to suggest a conscious rejection or maybe repression of the contemporary world. But this boundary cannot stand. He needs the outside world to survive, and when the car approaches, it is the modern world and all its pluses and minuses that draw near. When he looks in, he sees "Smirking" (23) children; he sees class prejudice, hierarchy, and economic reality. The smirkers of the world are in charge. This realization dissolves the protective boundary around his Garden of Eden, and he feels physical pain. But really he feels the pain of initiation, the pain of having to cross a boundary he wanted to delay as long as possible. Although we can sympathize with the young narrator, he would probably have fared better by not making his boundary so extreme.

The narrator in Mary Oliver's "Singapore" at first sees a significant boundary between herself as a middle-class traveler and a cleaning woman washing a toilet. It is a separation we might all make, given our socialization to see this kind of physical labor as degrading. College-educated people in America have a tendency to see themselves as distinct from workers. For most, a woman washing something in a compartment is beyond the pale, a clear indication that the woman is other. But Oliver does have some conflicting ideas since she says a "Disgust argued in my stomach" (6). Since we are also socialized to be tolerant and open-minded, she knows she shouldn't think this way. And since she is also a writer with ideas about how a poem should "always have birds in it" (8), she looks harder at the cleaning woman, finally seeing in her face, in her hair, and in the way she works slowly, "like a river" (25), the positive aspects she probably wants to find. Oliver does not simply accept the boundaries that her culture constructs but negotiates with herself, eventually seeing that "light . . . can shine out of a life" (35) even where we do not expect it. In the woman's careful folding and unfolding of her blue work cloth and in her smile, Oliver eclipses the social boundary and ends up with a life-affirming vision "filled with trees, and birds" (38).

Works Cited

Komunyakaa, Yusef. "Blackberries." Schilb and Clifford 139.

Oliver, Mary. "Singapore." Schilb and Clifford 138.

Robinson, Edwin Arlington. "The Mill." Schilb and Clifford
139–140.

Schilb, John, and John Clifford, eds. *Making Literature Matter:
An Anthology for Readers and Writers,* 6th ed. Boston:
Bedford, 2015. Print.

The Elements of Poetry

SPEAKER AND TONE

The voice we hear in a poem could be the poet's, but it is better to think of the speaker as an artistic construction—perhaps a **persona** (mask) for the poet or perhaps a character who does not resemble the poet at all. For example, the speaker in Lynda Hull's "Night Waitress" (p. 41) is not the poet herself but a struggling worker. In large part, to describe any poem's speaker is to pinpoint the person's tone or attitude. Sometimes this is hard to discern. The tone could be ironic or sentimental, joyful or morose, or a combination of emotions. To get a precise sense of it, read the poem aloud, actually performing the speaker's role. Bear in mind that his or her tone may change over the course of the poem. For instance, as the speaker in Yusef Komunyakaa's "Blackberries" recalls a day in his childhood when he picked fruit and then tried to sell it on a highway, he shifts from nostalgia (remembering "Terrestrial sweetness") to bitter recognition of class bias (the "Smirking" of the children who passed him in their car).

The narrator of "The Mill" immediately creates a somber, foreboding tone of anxiety and dread with the tea is "cold" and the fire is "dead," which also foreshadows the death of the miller. Likewise, his brief statement that "there are no millers any more" reinforces and intensifies the sense of impending doom that permeates the plot and theme of the poem. And, of course, such a grim tone is warranted by the dual suicides. Interestingly, the ominous tone of the poem noticeably shifts in the last four lines to one of quiet smooth repose as the once ruffled pond appears "like starry velvet in the night." Perhaps the miller and his wife are finally at peace.

DICTION AND SYNTAX

Although we would all agree that poets rely on the meaning of words to express their feelings and their ideas, what words mean is no simple matter. Perplexed over what a poet might have intended, we often consult a dictionary. And that certainly might help demystify a puzzling passage. But poetry is often more about complicating than clarifying. Most poets are more interested in opening up words than pinning them down. Unlike journalists or science writers, poets often intend to be ambiguous. They like a word's possibilities, its rich emotional overtones. That's one reason readers see in poems different things; one reader may think of the line "Wintertime crawled out of the window" as meaning air conditioning and another as meaning the chilly arrogance and distaste of the privileged for laborers. Komunyakaa knows exactly what he meant by "wintertime."

Looking up "wintertime" in the dictionary would give us the denotative meaning, which wouldn't be much help here. But the emotional overtones or associations for individual readers give us the complex multiplicity that poets hope will enrich the poem's meaning. When in "Singapore," for example, the narrator says "a darkness was ripped from my eyes," the objective denotative meaning is probably not what she is after. More likely Oliver is counting on the more subjective, emotional associations of "darkness." Perhaps lack of understanding or ignorance is suggested. Perhaps intolerance or fear of otherness comes to mind. And in the background lie all the negative associations of the unknown, the uncertainty and the danger of things unseen. These are the word's connotations, and they are crucial to the evocative suggestiveness of poems. Oliver wants readers to allow connotation to do its work in expanding and personalizing the meaning of words. In this sense, the word *darkness* contains within it infinite subjective and cultural possibilities.

The same is true for "light" in line 38 of the last stanza. It is the connotative possibilities that infuse "light" with significance, especially when contrasted with the darkness of the first stanza. Seen in the context of the poem, "light" might suggest beauty or integrity or perhaps dedication, commitment, or the ability to find in work something valuable and beautiful. For religious readers, "light" might suggest the beauty and worthiness of each human soul, while for the political thinkers, the dedication and skill of laborers might come to mind. What other connotations can you suggest for these two words?

The last line of the poem offers a clear distinction between denotation and connotation when Oliver says, "this poem is filled with trees, and birds." Literally, of course, trees and birds do not fill the page (except for the actual words), but if we think of trees and birds connoting or suggesting delicate beauty or the majesty of nature or perhaps simply positive and pleasant thoughts, then through her diction, Oliver's meaning is both clarified and expanded.

FIGURES OF SPEECH

When we use figures of speech, we mean something other than the words' literal meaning. In the first sentence of "Singapore," Mary Oliver writes that "a darkness was ripped from my eyes." This direct comparison is a **metaphor**. Had she been more indirect, she might have written "it was like a darkness . . . ," a common literary device called a **simile**. Poets use metaphors and similes to help us see in a fresh perspective. Comparing love to a rose encourages us to think differently about love, helping us see its delicate beauty. Of course, today that comparison is no longer novel and can even be a cliché, suggesting that a writer is not trying to be original and is settling instead for an easy comparison. When Robert Burns wrote "my love is like a red, red rose" more than two hundred years ago, it was a fresh comparison that excited new ways of looking at love. Indeed, some theorists, like the contemporary American philosopher Richard Rorty, think that metaphors can change our ways of looking at the world. Our thinking about time, for example, might be different if we didn't think with linear metaphors about the past being behind us and the future up ahead. What if, as some American Indian languages do, ours used a circular metaphor, having just one day that constantly repeated itself? Would our perceptions of time change?

What if Mary Oliver had begun her poem by saying that "a misunderstanding was corrected," instead of "a darkness was ripped from my eyes"? Her metaphor is not only more dramatic and memorable but also more suggestive. Darkness deepens the idea of lack of knowledge, suggesting not only intellectual blindness but also a host of negative connotations that readers might associate with the dark. Fresh metaphors can be expansive and illuminating. They help us understand the world differently.

Oliver creatively uses metaphors and similes throughout "Singapore." "Disgust argued" is an interesting metaphor or perhaps a **personification**, in which the speaker's stomach is given the ability to argue. She interrupts her observation of the cleaning woman in the third stanza to make a comment on the function of poetry itself, claiming that poems should have birds, rivers, and trees in them. Is she suggesting metaphorically that poems should be pleasant? Is that the only thing birds, rivers, and trees suggest to you?

She returns to the woman, and they exchange glances. Apparently the speaker is struggling with her own socialization that sees this kind of physical labor as demeaning. She directly describes the woman's "scrubbing and rinsing" but then returns to similes, describing her work as being "like a river" and her hair "like the wing of a bird." These comparisons seem for a moment to clarify the event for the speaker, helping her see this seemingly oppressive job positively. Amazingly, she wants the woman actually to become a bird and "rise up from the crust and the slop and fly."

But in the final stanza, she reminds us that she isn't really expecting that kind of physical miracle; instead, she wants to remind us that how we describe the woman working controls how we feel about her. If we see the folding and unfolding of her washcloth metaphorically, then we might see her differently; we might see her natural dignity, her beauty, and how her "light" was able to illuminate the speaker's "darkness."

Sometimes the poet chooses words like *darkness* and *light* that are so rich in texture that they can be examined as both metaphor and connotation. Such words might also be thought of as examples of synecdoche or metonymy. **Synecdoche** substitutes part of something for the whole, as in "I love my new wheels" referring to a car. **Metonymy** substitutes something associated with a thing, as in "Hollywood is resisting censorship" for the entire film industry. Oliver's "eyes" might be a synecdoche for her mind, and "darkness" and "light" can be metonymies for ignorance and beauty. Locate examples in our three poems of metaphor, connotation, synecdoche, and metonymy, if you can.

Although students often seem perplexed when professors find hidden **symbols** in poems, writers rarely plant such puzzling images deep in the recesses of their texts. The best symbols grow naturally out of the meaning-making process that readers go through. In the context of a particular poem, symbols are usually objects that can stand for general ideas. And like metaphors and similes, they suggest different things to different readers. The whale in *Moby-Dick*, for example, can be read as a symbol for implacable evil or perhaps the mysteries of the universe. In "Singapore," the specific event of the speaker watching a woman washing ashtrays in a toilet could be symbolic of anything we find unpleasant or strange or alien. And the whole event, including her eventual understanding, could easily be an **allegory** or extended symbol for the necessity for all of us to transcend our cultural socialization to understand other cultures and other attitudes toward working.

SOUND

The English poet Alexander Pope hoped that poetry's **sound** could become "an echo to [its] sense," that what the ear hears would reinforce what the mind understands. To many people, **rhyme** is the most recognizable aspect of poetry. The matching of final vowel and consonant sounds can make a poem trite or interesting. The now-familiar rhyming of "moon" and "June" with "swoon" suggests a poet who will settle for a cliché rather than do the hard work of being fresh. Rhyme, of course, is pleasing to the ear and makes the poem easier to remember, but it also gives the poem psychological force. Most contemporary poets choose not to rhyme, preferring the flexibility and freedom of free verse. But sound is still a high priority.

One of the most famous and effective examples of how sound can "echo" its sense is found in Robert Frost's "Stopping by Woods on a Snowy Evening," especially in the last two stanzas:

He gives his harness bells a shake

To ask if there is some mistake.

The only other sound's the sweep

Of easy wind and downy flake.

The woods are lovely, dark and deep,

But I have promises to keep,

And miles to go before I sleep,

And miles to go before I sleep.

Skilled poets like Frost use **alliteration** to connect words near each other by repeating the consonant sound. A variation, **assonance**, repeats vowel sounds. Frost obviously and subtly employs these sound techniques to echo both theme and mood. The alliterative -*s*'s in "shake," "some," "sound's," and "sweep" also connect the meaning of these words, which are also reinforced by the -*s*'s in "gives," "his," "harness," "bells," "asks," "is," "mistake," "sound's," and "easy." And when alliteration is combined with the assonance of "sweep" and "easy," as well as "downy" and "sound's," visual, tactile, and aural images are joined to create a soothing, restful, and idyllic scene of beauty and peace. All of these choices prepare the reader for the -*e*'s of "keep" and "deep" and the -*s*'s of the repeated "woods," "promises," "miles," and "sleep." In this way, the serenity and retreat of the woods are verbally and thematically contrasted with the demands of life's duties, culminating in the deadly temptation to escape responsibility by entering the winter woods.

Notice how Mary Oliver uses alliteration in her first stanza to link "women's," "woman," "washing," and "white." Komunyakaa's first stanza, too, links "printers," "police," and "pulled" as well as "they," "thief's," "Terrestrial," "thick," and "thorns." What effect do these and other elements of sound have on the impact and meaning of the poems?

RHYTHM AND METER

Many poets in the early twentieth century chose to have their poems rhyme. Edwin Arlington Robinson's "The Mill" employs a typical **rhyme scheme** in which in each stanza the last words in lines 1 and 3 sound the same and the last words in lines 2 and 4 sound the same. We indicate such a pattern with letters—*abab*. The second half of the first stanza would then be *cdcd* and so forth.

Rhythm in poetry refers to the beat, a series of stresses, pauses, and accents. We are powerfully attuned to rhythm, whether it is our own heartbeat or the throb of the bass guitar in a rock band. When we pronounce a word, we give more **stress** (breath, emphasis) to some syllables than to others. When these stresses occur at a regular interval over, say, a line of poetry, we refer to it as **meter**. When we scan a line of poetry, we try to mark its stresses and pauses. We use ´ to indicate a stressed syllable and ˘ for an unstressed one. The basic measuring unit for these stressed and unstressed syllables in English is the **foot**. There are four usual feet: *iambic, trochaic, anapestic,* and *dactylic.* An **iamb** is an unstressed syllable followed by a stressed one, as in "thĕ woóds." Reversed we have a **trochee**, as in "tígĕr." An **anapest** contains three syllables that are unstressed, then unstressed, then stressed, as in "Whĕn thĕ blúe / wăve rŏlls níghtlў / ŏn deép Gălĭlee." The reverse, the **dactyl**, can be heard in the Mother Goose rhyme, "Pússў cát, / pússў cát / whére hăve yŏu / beén?" If you look at the first four lines of "The Mill" again, you can hear a regular beat of iambs:

> Thĕ míll / er's wífe / hăd waít / ĕd lóng,
>
> Thĕ téa / wăs cóld, / thĕ fíre / wăs deád;
>
> Ănd thére / mĭght yét / bĕ nóth / ĭng wróng
>
> Ĭn hów / hĕ wént / ănd whăt / hĕ saíd:

Depending on the number of feet, we give lines various names. If a line contains one foot, it is a **monometer**; two, a **dimeter**; three, a **trimeter**; four, a **tetrameter**; five, a **pentameter**; six, a **hexameter**; seven, a **heptameter**; and eight, an **octometer**. So Robinson's lines are iambic tetrameter. Most lines in Shakespeare's sonnets are iambic pentameter, or five iambs.

Note the punctuation in Robinson's poem. When a line ends with a comma, we are meant to pause very briefly; when a line ends with a period (end stop), we pause a bit longer. But when there is no punctuation (line 7), we are meant to continue on until the end of the next line. This is known as **enjambment**. These poetic techniques improve the sound and flow of the poem and enhance the thoughts and feelings that give poetry its memorable depth and meaningfulness.

THEME

Some readers are fond of extracting ideas from poems, claiming, for example, that the theme of "Blackberries" is the loss of innocence or that the theme of "The Mill" is the loss of identity. In a sense, these thematic observations are plausible enough, but they are limiting and misleading. "Blackberries" certainly seems to have something to do with the interruption of a certain view about physical labor, but the significance for each reader might be much more specific, having to do with the Garden of Eden; hierarchy in society; the arrogance of the rich; or sensitivity, cruelty, and dignity. "The Mill" could also be about gender relations, economic cruelty, or the responsibility of communities. Reducing a complex, ambiguous poem to a bald statement robs the poem of its evocative power, its mystery, and its art.

Some critics stress the response of readers; others care only for what the text itself says; still others are concerned with the social and cultural implications of the poem's meaning. Psychoanalytic readers may see poems as reflections of the psychological health or illness of the poet; source-hunting or intertextual readers want to find references and hints of other literary works hidden deep within the poem. Feminist readers may find sexism, Marxists may find economic injustice, and gay and lesbian readers may find heterosexual bias. Readers can and will find in texts a whole range of issues. Perhaps we find what we are looking for, or we find what matters most to us.

This does not mean that we should think of committed readers as biased or as distorting the text to fulfill their own agenda, although biased or distorted readings are not rare. In a literature course, readers are entitled to read poems according to their own interpretations as long as they follow the general convention of academic discourse. That is, it is possible to make a reasonable case that "Blackberries" is really about rejecting contemporary technology in favor of rural life. The reason that some themes sound more plausible than others is that these critics marshal their evidence from the text and their own experience. Usually the evidence that fits best wins: if you can persuade others that you have significant textual support for your theme and if you present a balanced and judicious persona, you can usually carry the day. Poems almost always have several reasonable themes. The critic's job is to argue for a theme that seems to make the most sense in relation to the support. Often the same evidence can be used to bolster different themes because themes are really just higher-level generalizations than the particulars found in the text. Critics use the concrete elements of a poem to make more general abstract statements. In "Blackberries," for example, the same textual support could be used to uphold a theme about the cruelty of children or the more general notion of an initiation in a class-conscious culture or the even more general idea of the inevitable loss of innocence.

Revised Draft of a Student Paper

Michaela Fiorucci
Mr. Hardy
English 102
25 April - - - -

Negotiating Boundaries

Although most college students value their privacy, they also want to create intimate relationships; it is often hard to reconcile these two impulses. Most middle-class students are lucky enough to have their own bedrooms, private enclaves against annoying sisters and brothers, intrusive mothers and fathers. But such boundaries are more than physical barriers; they are also a symbolic assertion of identity. They say, "I'm separate from you even within the closeness of our family." Such a commitment to physical privacy might be innocent enough, but it does contain dangerous seeds, especially when extended beyond the home to neighborhoods. When different ethnic groups want boundaries between them, it is no longer innocent. When the upper classes want to be separated from workers because they see each other as radically different, a dangerously undemocratic boundary has been erected. Boundaries clearly serve a protective function, but unneeded ones can also prevent us from helping and understanding each other. Writers like Edwin Arlington Robinson, Yusef Komunyakaa, and Mary Oliver understand that we must negotiate boundaries, building them when they increase privacy and self-worth and bridging them when human solidarity can be enhanced.

Creates context about boundaries, moving from the personal to neighborhoods and beyond.

Announces her focus on need to negotiate.

It would be reductive to say that boundaries are either good or bad, since their value depends so much on context. Robinson's "The Mill" is a good example of the dangerous consequences of a failure to cross a boundary that should not exist and then a failure to establish a boundary where one should exist. The poem narrates the sad story of a farm couple who commit suicide — the husband because he feels useless, the wife because she can't imagine life without her husband. A contemporary reader is struck by the lack of communication between the couple. He must have been depressed for a long time, but it seems they never discussed his feelings. Keeping such an emotional boundary between husband and wife was probably typical of the way men and women dealt with each

Begins first concrete supporting example.

other one hundred years ago. Apparently it was a constructed barrier that few could cross. He simply could not bare his heart by saying, "I feel terrible that I am going to lose my job." And his wife accepts his reticence, even though he might have been having second thoughts as he "lingered at the door" (line 7). Clearly this is a boundary that should have been breached. The time for their solidarity was before he kills himself, not after.

Example of harmful tradition boundary.

After several readings it is clear that the boundary that should have been established wasn't. The miller is the victim of the demeaning idea that a person's worth is synonymous with his or her occupation. When his job disappears, so must he. Although Robinson's tone is flat, we sense his frustration with the inevitability of this grim tragedy, one that is compounded by the equally dehumanizing idea that a wife cannot exist without her husband. When the miller's wife decides to "leave no mark" (20) by jumping into the pond, she is admitting that she is useless outside her matrimonial role. Both identify with a role that should be only one aspect of a complex human life. The final barrier she crosses, from life to death, is symbolically represented in the poem as a feminine domestic gesture: she doesn't want to leave a mess. She continues as a housewife even in death. The boundaries between a person and occupation should be clear, but the arbitrary boundaries between husbands and wives should continue to be eradicated.

Concrete reference to poems strengthens argument.

Concludes paragraph with example of a boundary needing negotiating.

When the ten-year-old narrator in "Blackberries" claims that he is "Limboed between worlds" (18), he means the rural paradise of "Terrestrial sweetness" (4) and "rich blackness" (15) he temporarily lives in versus the commercial urban world that seems to make him anxious. He has constructed a boundary between the ancient task of picking berries and the modern technology of automobiles, between a closeness with nature and the artificial air-conditioning of the car. Although the narrator enjoys being one with nature, he seems to be cutting himself off from the realities of the world. He seems to reject "old lime-covered / History" (7–8) in favor of "mythology" (11), which seems to suggest a conscious rejection of the present. But this is a boundary that cannot stand. He needs the outside world to survive financially, and so when the car approaches, it is the modern world and all its complexity that draws near. When he looks into the car, he sees "Smirking" (23) children; he sees class prejudice, hierarchy, and economic reality. The smirkers of the world are in charge. It is this realization that dissolves the protective boundary around his Garden of Eden; consequently, he feels physical pain, but it is really the pain of initiation into reality that

Second concrete example of problematic boundary.

Notes consequences of not negotiating.

he feels. He must now cross a boundary he tried to delay. Although we can sympathize with the young narrator, like the couple in "The Mill," he would have been better off not making his boundary so extreme.

Connection to previous poem increases essay's unity.

The narrator in Mary Oliver's "Singapore" also imagines that she sees a significant boundary, here between herself as a middle-class traveler and a cleaning woman laboring over a toilet. It is a separation we might all make, given our socialization in America to consider this kind of physical labor as degrading. College-educated people have a tendency to see themselves as distinct from the working class. For many, a woman washing an ashtray in a toilet bowl is beyond the pale, a clear indication that the woman is Other. But Oliver does not simply give into her cultural conditioning; she contests the boundary, asserting that a "Disgust argued in my stomach"(6). Since part of our democratic socialization is also to be tolerant and open-minded, Oliver knows that she shouldn't stereotype workers. And since she is also a writer with ideas about how a poem should "always have birds in it" (8), she looks hard at the cleaning woman, finally seeing in her face, in her hair, and in the way she works, slowly "like a river" (25), the positive aspects of the woman that most of us would probably miss.

Third concrete example of boundaries.

Explicit example of negotiating a boundary.

Oliver does not simply accept the boundaries that her culture constructs. Instead, she negotiates internally, eventually seeing that a "light . . . can shine out of a life" (35) even where we would not expect it. In the woman's careful folding and unfolding of her blue work cloth and in her smile, Oliver sees a beauty that helps her eclipse a social boundary, ending with a life-affirming vision "filled with trees, and birds" (38). Such an insight does not come easily to us because we usually accept our given cultural boundaries. The miller and his wife are tragically unequipped to bridge the divide between them. Likewise, the boy in "Blackberries" is unable to sustain his fantasy boundaries. Oliver's traveler, however, struggles to negotiate boundaries and is thereby able to increase human solidarity even across class structures and cultures.

Notes benefits of breaching a boundary.

Concludes by uniting all 3 poems in support of claim.

Works Cited

Komunyakaa, Yusef. "Blackberries." Schilb and Clifford 139.

Oliver, Mary. "Singapore." Schilb and Clifford 138.

Robinson, Edwin Arlington. "The Mill." Schilb and Clifford 139–140.

Schilb, John, and John Clifford, eds. *Making Literature Matter:*
An Anthology for Readers and Writers. 6th ed. Boston:
Bedford, 2015. Print.

≡ SUMMING UP: WRITING ABOUT POEMS

- **The elements of poetry include *speaker* and *tone*, *diction* and *syntax*, *figures of speech*, *sound*, *rhythm* and *meter*, and *theme*.**

- **Identify the speaker and tone.** The voice we hear in a poem is often a *persona* — a "mask" that could be the poet's real voice or a complete fiction. Paying attention to the speaker's tone — his or her attitude — illuminates a poem's meaning. (p. 140)

- **Be aware of the complexities of *diction* and *syntax*.** In poetry, the connotations or emotional and personal associations of the diction — word choice — often suggest more than the literal meaning of the words. Poetry is more compressed and indirect than prose, so meaning is often suggested through connotation, metaphor, and imagery and is seldom finite. The order of the words — syntax — can be varied and experimented with to amplify and complicate meaning. (pp. 144–145)

- **Major figures of speech include *metaphor* and *symbols*.** A metaphor is a dramatic direct comparison — "Love is a rose," "Faith is a sea" — that poets use to help readers see and think differently and creatively. Similes ("My love is like a red, red rose") are more indirect, but no less suggestive. Symbols suggest general ideas. They reinforce or extend the poem's possible meanings and rarely point in one direction. (pp. 145–147)

- ***Sound*, *rhythm*, and *meter* work together to give a poem psychological force.** How a poem sounds is often overlooked, perhaps because modern poems often do not rhyme. *Alliteration*, for example, connects words and enhances meaning. As in music, rhythm adds to the meaning of poetry, encircling the thoughts and feeling that give poetry depth and meaning. (pp. 147–149)

- **Don't expect a poem's theme to be straightforward or clear-cut.** Strong poems are rich, complex, and often ambiguous. Narrow theme statements such as " 'Blackberries' is about the loss of innocence" are often misleading and limiting. Although this statement

(continued on next page)

≡ **SUMMING UP: WRITING ABOUT POEMS** *(continued)*

> is plausible enough, a number of other ideas are certainly possible. Be wary of reducing a poem's theme to a bold statement that robs the poem of its subtlety and evocative power. (pp. 149–150)
>
> - **Arguing successfully that your interpretation is worth considering depends largely on the validity of your evidence.** Poems almost always have several reasonable themes. We can argue strongly for a theme, however, if we can support our claim. The critic who presents the best evidence for a particular theme in a balanced and judicious way is often the most persuasive. (pp. 148–149)

Writing about Plays

Most plays incorporate elements also found in short fiction, such as plot, characterization, dialogue, setting, and theme. But, in contrast to short fiction and other literary genres, plays are typically enacted live, in front of an audience. Theater professionals distinguish between the written *script* of a play and its actual *performances*. When you write about a play, you may wind up saying little or nothing about performances of it. When you first read and analyze a play, however, try to imagine ways of staging it. You might even research past productions of the play, noting how scenery, costumes, and lighting—as well as particular actors—were used.

Because a play is usually meant to be staged, its readers are rarely its only interpreters. Audiences at productions of the play also ponder its meanings. So, too, do members of the casts; no doubt you have heard of actors "interpreting" their parts. When a play is put on, even members of the backstage team are involved in interpreting it. The technical designers' choices of sets, costumes, and lighting reflect their ideas about the play, while the director works with cast and crew to implement a particular vision of it. No matter what the author of the script intended, theater is a collaborative art: all of the key figures involved in a play's production are *active* interpreters of the play, in that they influence the audience's understanding and experience of it. Therefore, you can develop good ideas when you read a play if you imagine yourself directing a production of it. More specifically, think what you would say to the actors as you guide them through their parts. As you engage in this thought experiment, you will see that you have options, for even directors keen on staying faithful to the script know it can be staged in any number of ways. Perhaps your course will give you and other students the chance to perform a scene together; if so, you will be deciding what interpretation of the scene to set forth.

To help you understand how to write about plays, we will refer often to the one-act play that follows. *The Stronger* was first performed in 1889. Its Swedish author, August Strindberg (1849–1912), is widely acknowledged as a founder of modern drama. Throughout his career, Strindberg experimented with a variety of theatrical styles. With this particular play, an encounter between two actresses, he dared to have one of the women speak and the other remain silent.

AUGUST STRINDBERG

The Stronger

Translated by Edith and Warner Oland

CHARACTERS

MRS. X, *an actress, married*
MISS Y, *an actress, unmarried*
A WAITRESS

SCENE: *The corner of a ladies' café. Two little iron tables, a red velvet sofa, several chairs. Enter Mrs. X, dressed in winter clothes, carrying a Japanese basket on her arm.*

Miss Y sits with a half-empty beer bottle before her, reading an illustrated paper, which she changes later for another.

MRS. X: Good afternoon, Amelie. You're sitting here alone on Christmas eve like a poor bachelor!

Miss Y looks up, nods, and resumes her reading.

MRS. X: Do you know it really hurts me to see you like this, alone, in a café, and on Christmas eve, too. It makes me feel as I did one time when I saw a bridal party in a Paris restaurant, and the bride sat reading a comic paper, while the groom played billiards with the witnesses. Huh, thought I, with such a beginning, what will follow, and what will be the end? He played billiards on his wedding eve! *(Miss Y starts to speak.)* And she read a comic paper, you mean? Well, they are not altogether the same thing.

A waitress enters, places a cup of chocolate before Mrs. X, and goes out.

MRS. X: You know what, Amelie! I believe you would have done better to have kept him! Do you remember, I was the first to say "Forgive him"? Do you remember that? You would be married now and have a home. Remember that Christmas when you went out to visit your fiancé's parents in the country? How you gloried in the happiness of home life and really longed to quit the theater forever? Yes, Amelie dear, home is the best of all, the theater next and children — well, you don't understand that.

Miss Y looks up scornfully.

   Mrs. X sips a few spoonfuls out of the cup, then opens her basket and shows Christmas presents.

MRS. X: Now you shall see what I bought for my piggywigs. *(Takes up a doll.)* Look at this! This is for Lisa, ha! Do you see how she can roll her eyes and turn her head, eh? And here is Maja's popgun. *(Loads it and shoots at Miss Y.)*

Miss Y makes a startled gesture.

MRS. X: Did I frighten you? Do you think I would like to shoot you, eh? On my soul, if I don't think you did! If you wanted to shoot *me* it wouldn't be so surprising, because I stood in your way—and I know you can never forget that—although I was absolutely innocent. You still believe I intrigued and got you out of the Stora theater, but I didn't. I didn't do that, although you think so. Well, it doesn't make any difference what I say to you. You still believe I did it. *(Takes up a pair of embroidered slippers.)* And these are for my better half. I embroidered them myself—I can't bear tulips, but he wants tulips on everything.

Miss Y looks up ironically and curiously.

MRS. X *(putting a hand in each slipper)*:   What little feet Bob has! What? And you should see what a splendid stride he has! You've never seen him in slippers! *(Miss Y laughs aloud.)* Look! *(She makes the slippers walk on the table. Miss Y laughs loudly.)* And when he is grumpy he stamps like this with his foot. "What! damn those servants who can never learn to make coffee. Oh, now those creatures haven't trimmed the lamp wick properly!" And then there are draughts on the floor and his feet are cold. "Ugh, how cold it is; the stupid idiots can never keep the fire going." *(She rubs the slippers together, one sole over the other.)*

Miss Y shrieks with laughter.

MRS. X: And then he comes home and has to hunt for his slippers which Marie has stuck under the chiffonier—oh, but it's sinful to sit here and make fun of one's husband this way when he is kind and a good little man. You ought to have had such a husband, Amelie. What are you laughing at? What? What? And you see he's true to me. Yes, I'm sure of that, because he told me himself—what are you laughing at?—that when I was touring in Norway that that brazen Frédérique came and wanted to seduce him! Can you fancy anything so infamous? *(Pause.)* I'd have torn her eyes out if she had come to see him when I was at home. *(Pause.)* It was lucky that Bob told me about it himself and that it didn't reach me through gossip. *(Pause.)* But would you believe it, Frédérique wasn't the only one! I don't know why, but the women are crazy about my husband. They must think he has influence about getting them theatrical engagements, because he is connected with the government. Perhaps you were after him yourself. I didn't use to trust you any too much. But now I know he never bothered his head about you, and you always seemed to have a grudge against him someway.

Pause. They look at each other in a puzzled way.

Come and see us this evening, Amelie, and show us that you're not put out with us,—not put out with me at any rate. I don't know, but I think it would be uncomfortable to have you for an enemy. Perhaps it's because I stood in your way or—I really—don't know why—in particular.

Pause. Miss Y stares at Mrs. X curiously.

MRS. X *(thoughtfully)*:   Our acquaintance has been so queer. When I saw you for the first time I was afraid of you, so afraid that I didn't dare let you out of my sight; no matter when or where, I always found myself near you—I didn't dare have you for an enemy, so I became your friend. But there was always discord when you came to our house, because I saw that my husband couldn't endure you, and the whole thing seemed as awry to me as an ill-fitting gown—and I did all I could to make him friendly toward you, but with no success until you became engaged. Then came a violent friendship between you, so that it looked all at once as though you both dared show your real feelings only when you were secure—and then—how was it later? I didn't get jealous—strange to say! And I remember at the christening, when you acted as godmother, I made him kiss you—he did so, and you became so confused—as it were; I didn't notice it then—didn't think about it later, either—have never thought about it until—now! *(Rises suddenly.)* Why are you silent? You haven't said a word this whole time, but you have let me go on talking! You have sat there, and your eyes have reeled out of me all these thoughts which lay like raw silk in its cocoon—thoughts—suspicious thoughts, perhaps. Let me see—why did you break your engagement? Why do you never come to our house any more? Why won't you come to see us tonight?

Miss Y appears as if about to speak.

MRS. X: Hush, you needn't speak—I understand it all! It was because—and because—and because! Yes, yes! Now all the accounts balance. That's it. Fie, I won't sit at the same table with you. *(Moves her things to another table.)* That's the reason I had to embroider tulips—which I hate—on his slippers, because you are fond of tulips; that's why *(Throws slippers on the floor.)* we go to Lake Mälarn in the summer, because you don't like salt water; that's why my boy is named Eskil—because it's your father's name; that's why I wear your colors, read your authors, eat your favorite dishes, drink your drinks—chocolate, for instance; that's why—oh—my God—it's terrible, when I think about it; it's terrible. Everything, everything came from you to me, even your passions. Your soul crept into mine, like a worm into an apple, ate and ate, bored and bored, until nothing was left but the rind and a little black dust within. I wanted to get away from you, but I couldn't; you lay like a snake and charmed me with your black eyes; I felt that when I lifted my wings they only dragged me down; I lay in the water with bound feet, and the stronger I strove to keep up the deeper I worked myself down, down, until I sank to the bottom, where you lay like a giant crab to clutch me in your claws—and there I am lying now.

I hate you, hate you, hate you! And you only sit there silent—silent and indifferent; indifferent whether it's new moon or waning moon, Christmas or New Year's, whether others are happy or unhappy; without power to hate or to love; as quiet as a stork by a rat hole—you couldn't scent your prey and capture it, but you could lie in wait for it! You sit here in your corner of the café—did you know it's called "The Rat Trap" for you?— and read the papers to see if misfortune hasn't befallen someone, to see if someone hasn't been given notice at the theater, perhaps; you sit here and calculate about your next victim and reckon on your chances of recompense like a pilot in a shipwreck. Poor Amelie, I pity you, nevertheless, because I know you are unhappy, unhappy like one who has been wounded, and angry because you are wounded. I can't be angry with you, no matter how much I want to be—because you come out the weaker one. Yes, all that with Bob doesn't trouble me. What is that to me, after all? And what difference does it make whether I learned to drink chocolate from you or someone else. *(Sips a spoonful from her cup.)*

Besides, chocolate is very healthful. And if you taught me how to dress— *tant mieux!*° —that has only made me more attractive to my husband; so you lost and I won there. Well, judging by certain signs, I believe you have already lost him; and you certainly intended that I should leave him—do as you did with your fiancé and regret as you now regret; but, you see, I don't do that—we mustn't be too exacting. And why should I take only what no one else wants?

Perhaps, take it all in all, I am at this moment the stronger one. You received nothing from me, but you gave me much. And now I seem like a thief since you have awakened and find I possess what is your loss. How could it be otherwise when everything is worthless and sterile in your hands? You can never keep a man's love with your tulips and your passions—but I can keep it. You can't learn how to live from your authors, as I have learned. You have no little Eskil to cherish, even if your father's name was Eskil. And why are you always silent, silent, silent? I thought that was strength, but perhaps it is because you have nothing to say! Because you never think about anything! *(Rises and picks up slippers.)*

Now I'm going home—and take the tulips with me—*your* tulips! You are unable to learn from another; you can't bend—therefore, you broke like a dry stalk. But I won't break! Thank you, Amelie, for all your good lessons. Thanks for teaching my husband how to love. Now I'm going home to love him. *(Goes.)*   *[1889]*

---

tant mieux: So much the better (French).

A Student's Personal Response to the Play

Trish Carlisle was enrolled in a class that read and discussed Strindberg's *The Stronger*. Below is some freewriting that Trish did about the play.

> Near the end of Strindberg's play, Mrs. X says that "I am at this moment the stronger one." But is she? I guess that depends on what Strindberg meant by "the stronger" when he gave his play that title. As I was reading, I started to think that the stronger woman is actually the silent one, Miss Y, because she seems to have more self-control than Mrs. X does. I mean, Miss Y doesn't apparently feel that she has to make long, loud speeches in defense of her way of life. I can even believe that with her silence she is manipulating Mrs. X into getting fairly hysterical. Also, I guess we're to think that Amelie has managed to lure away Mrs. X's husband, at least for a while. Furthermore, we don't have to believe Mrs. X when at the end she claims that she has triumphed over Miss Y. Maybe people who have really succeeded in life don't need to proclaim that they have, as Mrs. X does.
>
> Nevertheless, I can see why some students in this class feel that Mrs. X is in fact the stronger. If she has her husband back and wants her husband back, and if Miss Y is really without companionship at the end and has even lost her job at the theater, then probably Mrs. X is entitled to crow. Was Strindberg being deliberately unclear? Did he want his audience to make up their own minds about who is stronger? Maybe neither of these women is strong, because each of them seems dependent on a man, and Mrs. X's husband may not even be such a great person in the first place. If I were Mrs. X, maybe I wouldn't even take him back. I guess someone could say that it's Mrs. X's husband who is the stronger, since he has managed to make the two women fight over him while he enjoys his creature comforts. Anyway, Strindberg makes us guess what he is really like. Because he's offstage, he's just as silent as Miss Y is, although his wife imitates his voice at one point.
>
> In a way, I feel that this play is too short. I want it to go on longer so that I can be sure how to analyze the two women and the man. But I realize that one of the reasons the play is dramatic is that it's brief. I might not be interested in it if it didn't leave me hang-ing. And it's also theatrical because Miss Y is silent even as Mrs. X lashes out at her. I wonder what the play would be like if we could hear Miss Y's thoughts in a sort of voice-over, like we find in some movies. It's interesting to me that the play is *about* actresses. I wonder if these characters are still "performing" with each other even if they're not acting in a theater at the moment.

Trish's freewriting would eventually help her develop ideas for a paper in which she had to analyze Strindberg's play. Compare your responses to the play with hers. Did the same issues come up for you? How do you feel about the women characters? What, if anything, do you wish the playwright had made clearer? What would you advise Trish to think about as she moved from freewriting to drafting a paper?

The Elements of Drama

You strengthen your ability to write about plays if you grow familiar with typical elements of drama. These elements include plot and structure, characterization, stage directions and setting, imagery, language, and theme.

PLOT AND STRUCTURE

Most plays, like most short stories, have a **plot**. When you read them, you find yourself following a narrative, a sequence of interrelated events. Even plays as short as *The Stronger* feature a plot, though the onstage action occurs in just one place and takes just a little while. As with short fiction, the reader of a play is often anxious to know how the events will turn out. The reader may especially feel this way when the play contains a mystery that characters are trying to solve. In Strindberg's play, for example, Mrs. X is apparently bent on discovering what relation her husband has had with her friend.

In summarizing the play, you might choose to depict the plot as a detective story. Then again, you might prefer to emphasize the characters' emotional conflicts as you describe how the play proceeds. In fact, there are various ways you can describe Strindberg's plot; just bear in mind that your account should be grounded in actual details of the text. However you summarize a play will reflect your sense of which characters are central to it. Is the offstage husband Bob in *The Stronger* as important as the two women onstage? More important than they are? Less important? Your summary will also reflect your sense of which characters have power. Do you think the two women in Strindberg's drama equally influence that play's events? In addition, your summary ought to acknowledge the human motives that drive the play's action. Why do you think Mrs. X feels compelled to confront Miss Y?

Summarizing the plot of a play can mean arranging its events chronologically. Yet bear in mind that some of the play's important events may have occurred in the characters' pasts. In many plays, actually, characters learn things about the past that they did not know and must now try to accept. For example, important events mentioned in *The Stronger* take place before the play begins. By the time the curtain rises, Miss Y's close relationship with Bob is well in the past. A typical summary would begin with the events on stage, but you could also summarize Strindberg's play as a chronicle of the relationship that precedes the scene in the café.

In discussing the structure of short stories, we noted that many of them follow Alice Adams's formula *ABDCE* (Action, Background, Development, Climax, and Ending). This scheme, however, does not fit many plays. In a sense, the average play is entirely Action, for its performers are constantly engaged in physical movement of various sorts. Furthermore, as we have been suggesting, information about Background can surface quite often as the play's characters talk. Yet the terms Development, Climax, and Ending do seem appropriate for many plays. Certainly the plot of *The Stronger* develops, as Mrs. X becomes increasingly hostile to Miss Y. Certainly the play can be said to reach a Climax, a moment of great significance and intensity, when Mrs. X moves to another table and declares her hatred for Miss Y. The term *Ending* can also apply to this play, although readers may disagree about exactly when its Climax turns into its Ending. Certainly Mrs. X is in a different state of mind at the play's last moment; at that point, she stops haranguing Miss Y and leaves, declaring that she will save her own marriage.

Like short stories, plays often use repetition as an organizational device. The characters in a play may repeat certain words; Mrs. X's variations on "silence" multiply as Miss Y retreats from interacting with her. Also, a play may show repeated actions, such as Mrs. X's interruptions of Miss Y. In addition, a play may suggest that the onstage situation echoes previous events, as when Mrs. X alludes to confrontations between her husband and Miss Y in the past.

The Stronger is a short, one-act play. But many other plays are longer and divided conspicuously into subsections. The ancient Greek drama *Antigone* alternates choral sections with scenes involving only the title character and her uncle Creon. All of Shakespeare's plays, and most modern ones, are divided into acts, which are often further divided into scenes. Even within a one-act play, however, you can detect various stages in the action. This task is easier when the one-act play is fairly lengthy, but even a very short play like *The Stronger* can be broken down into stages, although you will have to decide exactly what those stages are.

CHARACTERS

Many short stories have a narrator who reveals the characters' inner thoughts. Most plays, however, have no narrator at all. To figure out what the characters think, you must study what they *say* and how they *move*, if the author has indeed provided stage directions. To be sure, some characters say a great deal, leaving you with several clues to their psyche. If you are familiar with Shakespeare's lengthy play *Hamlet*, you may recall that it contains thousands of lines. Moreover, when the title character is alone on stage making long speeches to the audience, he seems to be baring his very soul. Yet despite such moments, Hamlet's mental state remains far from clear; scholars continue to debate his sanity. Thus, as a reader of *Hamlet* and other plays, you have much room for interpretation. Often you will have to decide whether to accept the judgments that characters express about one another. For example, how fair and accurate does Strindberg's Mrs. X seem to you as she berates Miss Y?

As with short stories, a good step toward analyzing a play's characters is to consider what each desires. The drama or comedy of many plays arises when the desires of one character conflict with those of another. Strindberg's Mrs. X feels that Miss Y has been a threat to her marriage, and while we cannot be sure of Miss Y's thoughts, evidently she is determined not to answer Mrs. X's charges. At the end of the play, the women's conflict seems to endure, even though Mrs. X proclaims victory. Many other plays end with characters managing to resolve conflict because one or more of them experiences a change of heart. Whatever the play you are studying, consider whether any of its characters change. Is any character's thinking transformed? If so, whose?

The main character of a play is often referred to as its **protagonist**, and a character who notably opposes this person is often referred to as the **antagonist**. As you might guess without even reading Shakespeare's play, Prince Hamlet is the protagonist of *Hamlet*; his uncle Claudius, who succeeded Hamlet's father to the throne of Denmark, serves as his antagonist. To be sure, applying these terms may be tricky or impossible in some instances. The two women in *The Stronger* oppose each other, but each can be called the protagonist and each can be called the antagonist. Can you think of other plays you have read in which the protagonist and antagonist are not readily identifiable?

In discussing the elements of short fiction, we referred to point of view, the perspective from which a story is told. Since very few plays are narrated, the term *point of view* fits this genre less well. While it is possible to claim that much of Shakespeare's *Hamlet* reflects the title character's point of view, he is offstage for stretches, and the audience may focus on other characters even when he appears. Also, do not overlook the possible significance of characters who are not physically present. A character may be important even when he or she never appears onstage. In *The Stronger*, the two women's conflict is partly about Mrs. X's unseen husband.

In most plays, characters' lives are influenced by their social standing, which in turn is influenced by particular traits of theirs. These may include their gender, their social class, their race, their ethnic background, their nationality, their sexual orientation, and the kind of work they do. Obviously *The Stronger* deals with gender relationships. Mrs. X defines herself in gendered terms: wife, mother, and insecure lover in competition with a rival for her husband's affections. But there are elements of social class too—of the circumstances of upper-middle-class Swedish women in Stockholm in the late nineteenth century—that may require research.

STAGE DIRECTIONS AND SETTING

When analyzing a script, pay attention to the staging directions it gives, and try to imagine additional ways that the actors might move around. Through a slight physical movement, performers can indicate important developments in their characters' thoughts. When Mrs. X fires a popgun at Miss Y, audience members may flinch in surprised sympathy with Miss Y's "startled gesture." But they may be just as startled by Miss Y's mirthful response, culminating in a "shriek of laughter," when Mrs. X uses her husband's slippers to mime and mock him. Is Miss Y's laughter hysterical, or knowing, or something else? How does it set up the "puzzled," curious looks Mrs. X and Miss Y exchange moments later?

You can get a better sense of how a play might be staged if you research its actual production history. Granted, finding out about its previous stagings may be difficult. But at the very least, you can discover some of the theatrical conventions that must have shaped presentations of the play, even one that is centuries old. Consider Sophocles' classical tragedy *Antigone* and Shakespeare's *Hamlet*, canonical plays that you may have read or seen performed in films or theater. While classical scholars would like to learn more about early performances of *Antigone*, they already know that it and other ancient Greek plays were staged in open-air arenas. They know, too, that *Antigone*'s Chorus turned in unison at particular moments, and that the whole cast wore large masks. Although the premiere of *Hamlet* was not videotaped, Shakespeare scholars are sure that, like other productions in Renaissance England, it made spare use of scenery and featured an all-male cast. By contrast, *The Stronger* is anchored in the nineteenth-century realist tradition that values in literary works an accurate and plausible presentation of everyday life and events.

Some plays can be staged in any number of styles and still work well. Shakespeare wrote *Hamlet* back in Renaissance England, but quite a few successful productions of it have been set in later times, such as late-nineteenth-century England. Even modern plays that seem to call for realist productions can be staged in a variety of ways. Note Strindberg's description of the setting for *The Stronger*: "The corner of a ladies' café. Two little iron tables, a red velvet sofa, several chairs." Many productions of this play have remained within the conventions of realism, striving to make the audience believe that it is seeing a late-nineteenth-century Stockholm café. But a production of *The Stronger* may present the audience with only a few pieces of furniture that barely evoke the café. Furthermore, the production might have Mrs. X's husband physically hover in the background, as if he were a ghost haunting both women's minds. You may feel that such a production would horribly distort Strindberg's drama; a boldly experimental staging of a play can indeed become a virtual rewriting of it. Nevertheless, remember that productions of a play may be more diverse in style than the script would indicate.

Remember, too, that a particular theater's architecture may affect a production team's decisions. Realism's illusion of the "fourth wall" works best on a proscenium stage, which is the kind probably most familiar to you. In brief, a proscenium is a boxlike space where the actors perform in front of the entire audience. In a proscenium production of *The Stronger*, the ladies' café can be depicted in great detail. The performing spaces at some theaters, however, are "in the round": that is, the audience completely encircles the stage. What would have to be done with the café then? List some items in the café that an "in the round" staging could accommodate.

In referring to possible ways of staging a play, we have inevitably been referring as well to its setting. A play may not be all that precise in describing its setting; Strindberg provides set designers with few guidelines for creating his Stockholm café. More significant, perhaps, than the place of the action is its *timing*: Mrs. X finds Miss Y sitting alone on Christmas eve. Yet a play may stress to its audience that its characters are located in particular places, at particular moments in their personal histories, and/or at a particular moment in *world* history. For example, *The Stronger* calls attention to the fact that it is set in a ladies' café, a female space. Are there gendered public arenas today where Mrs. X might play out her conflict with Miss Y? Could the play be set in a women's locker room? What would happen if the setting were not for women only?

You can learn much about a play's characters by studying how they accommodate themselves—or fail to accommodate themselves—to their settings. When Strindberg's Mrs. X can no longer bear sitting next to Miss Y, her shift to another table dramatically signifies her feelings. Of course, much of the drama in Strindberg's play occurs because there is a *single* setting, in which at least one character feels confined. Other plays employ a wider variety of settings to dramatize their characters' lives.

IMAGERY

When plays use images to convey meaning, sometimes they do so through dialogue. At the beginning of *The Stronger*, for instance, Mrs. X recalls "a bridal party in a Paris restaurant," where "the bride sat reading a comic paper, while the groom played billiards with the witnesses." The play proceeds to become very much about divisions between husband and wife; moreover, the two women engage in a tense "game" that seems analogous to billiards. But just as often, a play's meaningful images are physically presented in the staging: through gestures, costumes, lighting, and props. For instance, consider the slippers embroidered with tulips that Mrs. X flourishes early in the play. The slippers and the tulips gain meaning as the play progresses. The audience may be ever more inclined to see them as *symbolic*. *Symbol* is the term traditionally used for an image that represents some concept or concepts.

Keep in mind that *you* may interpret an image differently than the characters within the play do. When Strindberg's Mrs. X refers to billiards, she may not think at all that she will be playing an analogous game with Miss Y. You, however, may make this connection, especially as the play proceeds.

LANGUAGE

As we have been suggesting, a play's meaning and impact may be apparent only when the play is physically staged. Nevertheless, you can learn much from studying the language in its script. For example, the play's very title may be important. At the climax of Strindberg's play, Mrs. X even refers to herself as "the stronger." Obviously the playwright is encouraging audiences to think about the title's implications. Yet not always will the meaning of a play's title be immediately clear. In her freewriting, Trish wonders how to define "stronger" and which of Strindberg's characters fit the term. Even if you think the title of a play is easily explainable, pause to see whether that title can actually lead to an issue of definition. In other words, don't take the title for granted.

In most plays, language is a matter of dialogue. The audience tries to figure out the play by focusing on how the characters address one another. But remember that the pauses or silences within a play may be just as important as its dialogue. In fact, a director may *add* moments of silence that the script does not explicitly demand. In many plays, however, the author does specify moments when one or more characters significantly fail to speak. *The Stronger* is a prominent example: Miss Y is notably silent throughout the play, and as a reader you probably find yourself wondering why she is. Ironically, the play's *absence* of true dialogue serves to remind us that plays usually *depend* on dialogue.

Consider this moment in *The Stronger* when Miss Y fails to speak:

> MRS. X: . . . Why are you silent? You haven't said a word this whole time, but you have let me go on talking! You have sat there, and your eyes have reeled out of me all these thoughts which lay like raw silk in its cocoon—thoughts—suspicious thoughts, perhaps. Let me see—why did you break your engagement? Why do you never come to our house any more? Why won't you come to see us tonight?

> *Miss Y appears as if about to speak.*

> MRS. X: Hush, you needn't speak—I understand it all! . . .

An interesting discussion might result from imagining what Miss Y might have said had she not been cut off. It's also worth reflecting on what Strindberg conceivably gains by *not* having Miss Y speak at that moment.

THEME

We have already discussed *theme* in short fiction (pp. 54–55), and here we will build on some points from our earlier discussion. Again, a *theme* is the main claim—an assertion, a proposition, or a statement—that a work seems to make. As with other literary genres, try to state a play's theme as a midlevel generalization. If expressed in very broad terms, it will seem to fit many other works besides the one you have read; if narrowly tied to the play's characters and their particular situation, it will seem irrelevant to most other people's lives. With *The Stronger*, an example of a very broad theme would be "Women should not fight over a man." At the opposite extreme, a too-narrow theme would be "Women should behave well toward each other on Christmas eve, even if one of them has slept with the other's husband." If you are formulating Strindberg's theme, you might *start* with the broad generalization we have cited and then try to narrow it to a midlevel one. You might even think of ways that Strindberg's play *complicates* that broad generalization. What might, in fact, be a good midlevel generalization in Strindberg's case?

As we have noted, the very title of *The Stronger* seems significant. Indeed, a play's theme may be related to its title or to some other parts of the text. Nevertheless, be wary of couching the theme in terms drawn solely from the title or from some passage within the text. The play's theme may not be reducible to these words alone. Remember that the title of Strindberg's play can give rise to issues of definition in the first place.

You can state a play's theme as an observation or as a recommendation. With Strindberg's play, an observation-type theme would be "Marriage and career may disrupt relations between women." A recommendation-type theme would be either the broad or narrow generalization that we cited above. Neither way of stating the theme is automatically preferable, but remain aware of the different tones and effects they may carry. Consider, too, the possibility of stating the theme as a problem, as in this example: "We may be inclined to defend our marriages when they seem threatened, but in our defense we may cling to illusions that can easily shatter." Furthermore, consider the possibility of referring to *a* theme of the play rather than *the* theme, thereby acknowledging the possibility that the play is making several important claims.

When you write about a play, certainly you will refer to the text of it, its **script**. But probably the play was meant to be staged, and most likely it has been. Thus, you might refer to actual productions of it and to ways it can be performed. Remember, though, that different productions of the play may stress different meanings and create different effects. In your paper, you might discuss how much room for interpretation the script allows those who would stage it. For any paper you write about the play, look beyond the characters' dialogue and study whatever stage directions the script gives.

Undoubtedly your paper will have to offer some plot summary, even if your audience has already read the play. After all, certain details of the plot will be important support for your points. But, as with papers about short fiction, keep the amount of plot summary small, mentioning only events in the play that are crucial to your overall argument. Your reader should feel that you are analyzing the play rather than just recounting it.

To understand more what analysis of a play involves, let's return to Trish Carlisle, the student whose freewriting you read earlier. Trish was assigned to write a 600-word paper about Strindberg's *The Stronger*. She was asked to imagine herself writing to a particular audience: performers rehearsing a production of the play she chose. More specifically, she was to identify and address some question that these performers might have, an issue that might be bothering them as they prepared to put on the play. Trish knew that, besides presenting an issue, her paper would have to make a main claim and support it with evidence. Moreover, the paper might have to spell out some of the warrants or assumptions behind her evidence.

Because finding an issue was such an important part of the assignment, Trish decided to review her freewriting about Strindberg's play, noting questions she had raised there about it. Trish saw that the chief issue posed for her by *The Stronger* was "Which character is the stronger?" Nevertheless, Trish recognized that the issue "Which character is the stronger?" still left her with various decisions to make. For one thing, she had to decide what kind of an issue she would call it. Trish saw that it could be considered an issue of fact, an issue of evaluation, or an issue of definition. Although it could fit into all of these categories, Trish knew that the category she chose would influence the direction of her paper. Eventually she decided to treat "Which character is the stronger?" as primarily an issue of definition, because she figured that, no matter what, she would be devoting much of her paper to defining *stronger* as a term.

Of course, there are many different senses in which someone may be "stronger" than someone else. Your best friend may be a stronger tennis player than you, in the sense that he or she always beats you at that game. But you may be a stronger student than your friend, in the sense that you get better grades in school. In the case of Strindberg's play, Trish came to see that a paper focused on which character is *morally* stronger would differ from one focused on who is *emotionally* stronger, and these papers would differ in turn from one focused on which character is *politically* stronger, more able to impose his or her will. These reflections led Trish to revise her issue somewhat. She decided to address the question "Which particular sense of the word 'stronger' is most relevant to Strindberg's play?" In part, Trish came up with this reformulation of her issue because she realized that the two women feuding in the play are actresses, and that they behave as actresses even when they are not professionally performing. Trish's answer to her revised question was that the play encourages the audience to consider which woman is the stronger *actress*—which woman is more able, that is, to convey her preferred version of reality.

When you write about a play, you may have to be selective, for your paper may not be able to accommodate all the ideas and issues that occur to you. Trish was not sure which woman in Strindberg's play is the stronger actress. She felt that a case can be made for Mrs. X or Miss Y; indeed, she suspected that Strindberg was letting his audience decide. But she decided that her paper was not obligated to resolve this matter; she could simply mention the various possible positions in her final paragraph. In the body of her paper, Trish felt she would contribute much if she focused on addressing her main issue with her main claim. Again, her main issue was "Which particular sense of the word 'stronger' is most relevant to Strindberg's play?" Her main claim was that "The play is chiefly concerned with which woman is the stronger actress, 'stronger' here meaning 'more able to convey one's version of reality.'"

Although a paper about a play need not explicitly mention the elements of plays we have identified, thinking about these elements can provide you with a good springboard for analysis. Trish saw that her paper would be very much concerned with the title of Strindberg's play, especially as that title applied to the characters. Also, she would have to refer to stage directions and imagery, because Miss Y's silence leaves the reader having to look at her physical movements and the play's props for clues to her thinking. The play does not really include dialogue, a term that implies people talking with each other. Nevertheless, Trish saw that there are utterances in the script that she could refer to, especially as she made points about the play's lone speaker, Mrs. X. Indeed, a persuasive paper about a play is one that quotes from characters' lines and perhaps from the stage directions, too. Yet the paper needs to quote selectively, for a paper chock full of quotations may obscure instead of enhance the writer's argument.

Final Draft of a Student Paper

Here is Trish's final draft of her paper about *The Stronger*. It emerged out of several drafts, and after Trish had consulted classmates and her instructor. As you read this version of her paper, note its strengths, but also think of any suggestions that might help Trish make the paper even better.

Trish Carlisle
Professor Zelinsky
English 102
28 April - - - -

Which Is the Stronger Actress
in August Strindberg's Play?

You have asked me to help you solve difficulties you may be experiencing with August Strindberg's script for *The Stronger* as you prepare to play the roles of Mrs. X and Miss Y. These female characters seem harder to judge than the three women who are the focus of Susan Glaspell's play *Trifles*, the play you are performing next month. Obviously, Glaspell is pushing us to think well of Mrs. Hale, Mrs. Peters, and Minnie Wright. The two women in Strindberg's play are another matter; in particular, you have probably been wondering which of these two women Strindberg thinks of as "the stronger." If you knew which character he had in mind with that term, you might play the roles accordingly. As things stand, however, Strindberg's use of the term in his title is pretty ambiguous. It is not even clear, at least not immediately, which particular sense of the word *stronger* is most relevant to the play. I suggest that the play is chiefly concerned with which character is the stronger actress. In making this claim, I am defining *stronger* as "more able to convey one's version of reality."

You may feel that Strindberg is clarifying his use of the word *stronger* when he has Mrs. X bring up the word in the long speech that ends the play. In that final speech, she declares to Miss Y that "I am . . . the stronger one" (158) and that Miss Y's silence is not the "strength" that Mrs. X previously thought it was. At this point in the play, Mrs. X is evidently defining *stronger* as "more able to keep things, especially a man." She feels that she is the stronger because she is going home to her husband, while Miss Y is forced to be alone on Christmas Eve. Yet there is little reason to believe that Mrs. X is using the word *stronger* in the sense that the playwright has chiefly in mind. Furthermore, there is little reason to believe that Mrs. X is an accurate judge of the two women's situations. Perhaps she is telling herself that she is stronger because she simply needs to believe that she is. Similarly, perhaps she is telling herself that she now has control over her husband when in actuality he may still be emotionally attached to Miss Y. In addition, because Miss Y does not speak and because Mrs. X sweeps out without giving her any further opportunity to do so, we don't know if Miss Y agrees with Mrs. X's last speech.

Since Mrs. X's final use of the word *stronger* is so questionable, we are justified in thinking of other ways that the term might be applied. In thinking about this play, I have entertained the idea that the stronger character is actually Mrs. X's husband Bob, for he has two women fighting over him and also apparently has the creature comforts that servants provide. But now I tend to think that the term applies to one or both of the two women. Unfortunately, we are not given many facts about them, for it is a brief one-act play and one of the major characters does not even speak. But as we try to figure out how Strindberg is defining the term *stronger*, we should notice one fact that we are indeed given: each of these women is an actress. Both of them have worked at Stockholm's Grand Theater, although apparently Mrs. X got Miss Y fired from the company. Furthermore, Mrs. X engages in a bit of theatrical illusion when she scares Miss Y by firing the toy pistol at her. Soon after, Mrs. X plays the role of her own husband when she puts her hands in the slippers she has bought for him and imitates not only his walk but also the way he scolds his servants. Miss Y even laughs at this "performance," as if she is being an appreciative audience for it. In addition, if Mrs. X is right about there being an adulterous affair between her husband and Miss Y, then those two people have basically been performing an act for Mrs. X. It is possible, too, that Mrs. X has not been quite so naïve; perhaps she has deliberately come to the café in order to confront Miss Y about the affair and to proclaim ultimate victory over her. In that case, Mrs. X is performing as someone more innocent than she really is. On the other hand, Miss Y might be using her silence as an actress would, manipulating her audience's feelings by behaving in a theatrical way.

Because we do know that these women are professional actresses, and because Strindberg gives us several hints that they are performing right there in the café, we should feel encouraged to think that he is raising the question of which is the stronger *actress*. Of course, we would still have to decide how he is defining the term *stronger*. But if he does have in mind the women's careers and behavior as actresses, then he seems to be defining *stronger* as "more able to convey one's version of reality." Obviously Mrs. X is putting forth her own version of reality in her final speech, although we do not know how close her version comes to the actual truth. Again, we cannot be sure of Miss Y's thoughts because she does not express them in words; nevertheless, she can be said to work at influencing Mrs. X's version of reality by making strategic use of silence.

I realize that the claim I am making does not solve every problem you might have with the play as you prepare to perform it. Frankly, I am not sure who *is* the stronger actress. I suspect that Strindberg is being deliberately ambiguous; he wants the performers to act in a way that will let each member of the audience arrive at his or her own opinion. Still, if you accept my claim, each of you will think of yourself as playing the part of an actress who is trying to shape the other woman's sense of reality.

Works Cited

Strindberg, August. "The Stronger." Trans. Edith and Warner Oland. *Making Literature Matter: An Anthology for Readers and Writers*. Ed. John Schilb and John Clifford. 6th ed. Boston: Bedford, 2015. 155–158. Print.

≡ SUMMING UP: WRITING ABOUT PLAYS

- **Consider the differences between page and stage.** Theater professionals distinguish between a play's written script and its actual performances, so consider how any play you are analyzing has been or might be staged. Try to imagine yourself as its director, thinking about how you would guide the actors through their parts. (pp. 154–155)

- **The elements of drama include** *plot* **and** *structure, characters, stage directions* **and** *setting, imagery, language,* **and** *theme.*

- **The** *plot* **and** *structure* **of plays often resemble those of stories.** Like short stories, plays often feature plot development, a climax, a significant ending, and repetitions of words and situations. (pp. 160–161)

- *Characters* **in plays function like characters in stories.** As such, they can often be analyzed by asking the same questions (see Summing Up on pp. 161–162). A difference is that most plays lack a narrator and even a central point of view; you have to figure out the characters' thoughts from dialogue and movement.

- **When analyzing a script, pay attention to its** *stage directions,* **and imagine other ways that the actors might move around.** (pp. 162–164)

- **While some plays do not describe their** *setting* **precisely, others stress that they are occurring in particular places or moments.** As with short stories, you can learn much about a play's characters by examining how they accommodate themselves — or fail to accommodate themselves — to their settings. (pp. 163–164)

- *Images* **are often conveyed through words and stagecraft** — through dialogue, gestures, costumes, lighting, and props. (p. 164)

- **Most plays rely on dialogue as their most important** *language,* making their audience figure things out from how the characters address one another. Pauses or silences may be important as well. (pp. 164–165)

- **The** *theme* **of a play is the main claim — an assertion, a proposition, or a statement — that it seems to make.** As when writing

≡ SUMMING UP: WRITING ABOUT PLAYS

about short stories, try to state the theme as a midlevel generalization, either as an observation or as a recommendation. By specifically wording the theme as a problem, you may better convey the
complexity and drama of the play. (pp. 165–167)

- **When you write about a play, remember to formulate an issue
  worth addressing, a claim about that issue, and evidence for that
  claim, besides preparing to identify your warrants.** Keep in mind
  that you will refer to its script, but you might also discuss how much
  room for interpretation the script allows those who would stage it.

Writing about Essays

Many readers do not realize that nonfiction is a literary genre. They believe that
writing about information and facts, science and technology, history and biography, memories and arguments is far different from writing traditional literary works such as sonnets, short stories, and plays. But what counts as
literature is often more a matter of tradition and perspective than a matter of
content, language, or merit. Many contemporary critics have noticed that definitions of literature are quite subjective, even arbitrary. We are told that literature must move us emotionally; it must contain imaginative, extraordinary
language; it must deal with profound, timeless, and universal themes. If these
claims are true of poems, stories, and plays, they might also be true of essays,
autobiographies, memoirs, speeches, and historical writing.

Essays demand as much of a reader's attention as fiction, drama, and poetry do. They also demand a reader's active participation. And as with more
conventional literature, the intellectual, emotional, and aesthetic rewards of
attentively reading essays are significant.

Writing about essays in college is best done as a process that begins with
careful reading and a first response and ends with editing and proofreading.
Author Henry David Thoreau once noted that books should be read with the
same care and deliberation with which they were written. This is as true for
essays as it is for complex modern poetry. Few people, even professionals, can
read a text and write cogently about it the first time. Writing well about essays—actively participating in a cycle of reading, reflecting, and writing—
takes as much energy and discipline as writing about other genres. And the
results are always worth it.

The essay presented here deals with women and work—more specifically,
with the struggles of gifted African American women in a context of poverty
and oppression. "Many Rivers to Cross" by June Jordan (1936–2002) was the
keynote address at a 1981 conference on "Women and Work" held at Barnard
College in New York City. In the speech, Jordan recalls the suicide of her mother
fifteen years earlier. Her essay uses an autobiographical narrative as evidence

for her argument about the necessity for women to be strong. In this sense, the essay is inductive as it moves from specifics to a generalization rather than the more typical deductive approach, which begins with a claim that is then supported. What are the advantages and disadvantages of Jordan's structure?

JUNE JORDAN
Many Rivers to Cross

When my mother killed herself I was looking for a job. That was fifteen years ago. I had no money and no food. On the pleasure side I was down to my last pack of Pall Malls plus half a bottle of J and B. I needed to find work because I needed to be able fully to support myself and my eight-year-old son, very fast. My plan was to raise enough big bucks so that I could take an okay apartment inside an acceptable public school district, by September. That deadline left me less than three months to turn my fortunes right side up.

It seemed that I had everything to do at once. Somehow, I must move all of our things, mostly books and toys, out of the housing project before the rent fell due, again. I must do this without letting my neighbors know because destitution and divorce added up to personal shame, and failure. Those same neighbors had looked upon my husband and me as an ideal young couple, in many ways: inseparable, doting, ambitious. They had kept me busy and laughing in the hard weeks following my husband's departure for graduate school in Chicago; they had been the ones to remember him warmly through teasing remarks and questions all that long year that I remained alone, waiting for his return while I became the "temporary," sole breadwinner of our peculiar long-distance family by telephone. They had been the ones who kindly stopped the teasing and the queries when the year ended and my husband, the father of my child, did not come back. They never asked me and I never told them what that meant, altogether. I don't think I really knew.

I could see how my husband would proceed more or less naturally from graduate school to a professional occupation of his choice, just as he had shifted rather easily from me, his wife, to another man's wife—another woman. What I could not see was how I should go forward, now, in any natural, coherent way. As a mother without a husband, as a poet without a publisher, a freelance journalist without assignment, a city planner without a contract, it seemed to me that several incontestable and conflicting necessities had suddenly eliminated the whole realm of choice from my life.

My husband and I agreed that he would have the divorce that he wanted, and I would have the child. This ordinary settlement is, as millions of women will testify, as absurd as saying, "I'll give you a call, you handle everything else." At any rate, as my lawyer explained, the law then was the same as the law today; the courts would surely award me a reasonable amount of the father's income as child support, but the courts would also insist that they could not enforce their own decree. In other words, according to the law, what a father owes to his child is not serious compared to what a man owes to the bank for a car, or a vacation. Hence, as they say, it is extremely regrettable but nonetheless true that the courts cannot garnish a father's salary, nor freeze his account, nor seize his property on behalf of his children, in our society. Apparently this is because a child is not a car or a couch or a boat. (I would suppose this is the very best available definition of the difference between an American child and a car.)

Anyway, I wanted to get out of the projects as quickly as possible. But I was going to need help because I couldn't bend down and I couldn't carry anything heavy and I couldn't let my parents know about these problems because I didn't want to fight with them about the reasons behind the problems—which was the same reason I couldn't walk around or sit up straight to read or write without vomiting and acute abdominal pain. My parents would have evaluated that reason as a terrible secret compounded by a terrible crime; once again an unmarried woman, I had, nevertheless, become pregnant. What's more I had tried to interrupt this pregnancy even though this particular effort required not only one but a total of three abortions—each of them illegal and amazingly expensive, as well as, evidently, somewhat poorly executed.

My mother, against my father's furious rejections of me and what he viewed as my failure, offered what she could; she had no money herself but there was space in the old brownstone of my childhood. I would live with them during the summer while I pursued my crash schedule for cash, and she would spend as much time with Christopher, her only and beloved grandchild, as her worsening but partially undiagnosed illness allowed.

After she suffered a stroke, her serenely imposing figure had shrunk into an unevenly balanced, starved shell of chronic disorder. In the last two years, her physical condition had forced her retirement from nursing, and she spent most of her days on a makeshift cot pushed against the wall of the dining room next to the kitchen. She could do very few things for herself, besides snack on crackers, or pour ready-made juice into a cup and then drink it.

In June, 1966, I moved from the projects into my parents' house with the help of a woman named Mrs. Hazel Griffin. Since my teens, she had been my hairdresser. Every day, all day, she stood on her feet, washing and straightening hair in her crowded shop, the Arch of Beauty. Mrs. Griffin had never been married, had never finished high school, and she ran the Arch of Beauty with an imperturbable and contagious sense of success. She had a daughter as old as I who worked alongside her mother, coddling customer fantasy into confidence. Gradually, Mrs. Griffin and I became close; as my own mother became more and more bedridden and demoralized, Mrs. Griffin extended herself—dropping by my parents' house to make dinner for them, or calling me to wish me good luck on a special freelance venture, and so forth. It was Mrs. Griffin who closed her shop for a whole day and drove all the way from Brooklyn to my housing project apartment in Queens. It was Mrs. Griffin who packed me up, so to speak, and carried me and the boxes back to Brooklyn, back to the house of my parents. It was Mrs. Griffin who ignored my father standing hateful at the top of the stone steps of the house and not saying a word of thanks and not once relieving her of a single load she wrestled up the stairs and past him. My father hated

Mrs. Griffin because he was proud and because she was a stranger of mercy. My father hated Mrs. Griffin because he was like that sometimes: hateful and crazy.

My father alternated between weeping bouts of self-pity and storm explosions of wrath against the gods apparently determined to ruin him. These were his alternating reactions to my mother's increasing enfeeblement, her stoic depression. I think he was scared; who would take care of him? Would she get well again and make everything all right again?

This is how we organized the brownstone; I fixed a room for my son on the   10
top floor of the house. I slept on the parlor floor in the front room. My father slept on the same floor, in the back. My mother stayed downstairs.

About a week after moving in, my mother asked me about the progress of my plans. I told her things were not terrific but that there were two different planning jobs I hoped to secure within a few days. One of them involved a study of new towns in Sweden and the other one involved an analysis of the social consequences of a huge hydro-electric dam under construction in Ghana. My mother stared at me uncomprehendingly and then urged me to look for work in the local post office. We bitterly argued about what she dismissed as my "high-falutin" ideas and, I believe, that was the last substantial conversation between us.

From my first memory of him, my father had always worked at the post office. His favorite was the night shift, which brought him home usually between three and four o'clock in the morning.

It was hot. I finally fell asleep that night, a few nights after the argument between my mother and myself. She seemed to be rallying; that afternoon, she and my son had spent a long time in the backyard, oblivious to the heat and the mosquitoes. They were both tired but peaceful when they noisily re-entered the house, holding hands awkwardly.

But someone was knocking at the door to my room. Why should I wake up? It would be impossible to fall asleep again. It was so hot. The knocking continued. I switched on the light by the bed: 3:30 A.M. It must be my father. Furious, I pulled on a pair of shorts and a t-shirt. "What do you want? What's the matter?" I asked him, through the door. Had he gone berserk? What could he have to talk about at that ridiculous hour?

"OK, all right," I said, rubbing my eyes awake as I stepped to the door and   15
opened it. "What?"

To my surprise, my father stood there looking very uncertain.

"It's your mother," he told me, in a burly, formal voice. "I think she's dead, but I'm not sure." He was avoiding my eyes.

"What do you mean," I answered.

"I want you to go downstairs and figure it out."

I could not believe what he was saying to me. "You want me to figure out if   20
my mother is dead or alive?"

"I can't tell! I don't know!!" he shouted angrily.

"Jesus Christ," I muttered, angry and beside myself.

I turned and glanced about my room, wondering if I could find anything to carry with me on this mission; what do you use to determine a life or a death? I couldn't see anything obvious that might be useful.

"I'll wait up here," my father said. "You call up and let me know."

I could not believe it; a man married to a woman more than forty years and   25
he can't tell if she's alive or dead and he wakes up his kid and tells her, "You
figure it out."

I was at the bottom of the stairs. I halted just outside the dining room
where my mother slept. Suppose she really was dead? Suppose my father was
not just being crazy and hateful? "Naw," I shook my head and confidently entered the room.

"Momma?!" I called, aloud. At the edge of the cot, my mother was leaning
forward, one arm braced to hoist her body up. She was trying to stand up! I
rushed over. "Wait. Here, I'll help you!" I said.

And I reached out my hands to give her a lift. The body of my mother was
stiff. She was not yet cold, but she was stiff. Maybe I had come downstairs just
in time! I tried to loosen her arms, to change her position, to ease her into lying
down.

"Momma!" I kept saying. "Momma, listen to me! It's OK! I'm here and everything. Just relax. Relax! Give me a hand, now. I'm trying to help you lie
down!"

Her body did not relax. She did not answer me. But she was not cold. Her   30
eyes were not shut.

From upstairs my father was yelling, "Is she dead? Is she dead?"

"No!" I screamed at him. "No! She's not dead!"

At this, my father tore down the stairs and into the room. Then he braked.

"Milly?" he called out, tentative. Then he shouted at me and banged
around the walls. "You damn fool. Don't you see now she's gone. Now she's
gone!" We began to argue.

"She's alive! Call the doctor!"   35

"No!"

"Yes!"

At last my father left the room to call the doctor.

I straightened up. I felt completely exhausted from trying to gain a response from my mother. There she was, stiff on the edge of her bed, just about
to stand up. Her lips were set, determined. She would manage it, but by herself.
I could not help. Her eyes fixed on some point below the floor.

"Momma!" I shook her hard as I could to rouse her into focus. Now she fell   40
back on the cot, but frozen and in the wrong position. It hit me that she might
be dead. She might be dead.

My father reappeared at the door. He would not come any closer. "Dr. Davis
says he will come. And he call the police."

The police? Would they know if my mother was dead or alive? Who would
know?

I went to the phone and called my aunt. "Come quick," I said. "My father
thinks Momma has died but she's here but she's stiff."

Soon the house was weird and ugly and crowded and I thought I was losing
my mind.

Three white policemen stood around telling me my mother was dead.   45
"How do you know?" I asked, and they shrugged and then they repeated

themselves. And the doctor never came. But my aunt came and my uncle and they said she was dead.

After a conference with the cops, my aunt disappeared and when she came back she held a bottle in one of her hands. She and the police whispered together some more. Then one of the cops said, "Don't worry about it. We won't say anything." My aunt signalled me to follow her into the hallway where she let me understand that, in fact, my mother had committed suicide.

I could not assimilate this information: suicide.

I broke away from my aunt and ran to the telephone. I called a friend of mine, a woman who talked back loud to me so that I could realize my growing hysteria, and check it. Then I called my cousin Valerie who lived in Harlem; she woke up instantly and urged me to come right away.

I hurried to the top floor and stood my sleeping son on his feet. I wanted to get him out of this house of death more than I ever wanted anything. He could not stand by himself so I carried him down the two flights to the street and laid him on the backseat and then took off.

At Valerie's, my son continued to sleep, so we put him to bed, closed the   50
door, and talked. My cousin made me eat eggs, drink whiskey, and shower. She would take care of Christopher, she said. I should go back and deal with the situation in Brooklyn.

When I arrived, the house was absolutely full of women from the church dressed as though they were going to Sunday communion. It seemed to me they were, every one of them, wearing hats and gloves and drinking coffee and solemnly addressing invitations to a funeral and I could not find my mother anywhere and I could not find an empty spot in the house where I could sit down and smoke a cigarette.

My mother was dead.

Feeling completely out of place, I headed for the front door, ready to leave. My father grabbed my shoulder from behind and forcibly spun me around.

"You see this?" he smiled, waving a large document in the air. "This am insurance paper for you!" He waved it into my face. "Your mother, she left you insurance, see?"

I watched him.   55

"But I gwine burn it in the furnace before I give it you to t'row away on trash!"

"Is that money?" I demanded. "Did my mother leave me money?"

"Eh-heh!" he laughed. "And you don't get it from me. Not today, not tomorrow. Not until I dead and buried!"

My father grabbed for my arm and I swung away from him. He hit me on my head and I hit back. We were fighting.

Suddenly, the ladies from the church bustled about and pushed, horrified,   60
between us. This was a sin, they said, for a father and a child to fight in the house of the dead and the mother not yet in the ground! Such a good woman she was, they said. She was a good woman, a good woman, they all agreed. Out of respect for the memory of this good woman, in deference to my mother who had committed suicide, the ladies shook their hats and insisted we should not fight; I should not fight with my father.

Utterly disgusted and disoriented, I went back to Harlem. By the time I reached my cousin's place I had begun to bleed, heavily. Valerie said I was hemorrhaging so she called up her boyfriend and the two of them hobbled me into Harlem Hospital.

I don't know how long I remained unconscious, but when I opened my eyes I found myself on the women's ward, with an intravenous setup feeding into my arm. After a while, Valerie showed up. Christopher was fine, she told me; my friends were taking turns with him. Whatever I did, I should not admit I'd had an abortion or I'd get her into trouble, and myself in trouble. Just play dumb and rest. I'd have to stay on the ward for several days. My mother's funeral was tomorrow afternoon. What did I want her to tell people to explain why I wouldn't be there? She meant, what lie?

I thought about it and I decided I had nothing to say; if I couldn't tell the truth then the hell with it.

I lay in that bed at Harlem Hospital, thinking and sleeping. I wanted to get well.

I wanted to be strong. I never wanted to be weak again as long as I lived. I thought about my mother and her suicide and I thought about how my father could not tell whether she was dead or alive.   65

I wanted to get well and what I wanted to do as soon as I was strong again, actually, what I wanted to do was I wanted to live my life so that people would know unmistakably that I am alive, so that when I finally die people will know the difference for sure between my living and my death.

And I thought about the idea of my mother as a good woman and I rejected that, because I don't see why it's a good thing when you give up, or when you cooperate with those who hate you or when you polish and iron and mend and endlessly mollify for the sake of the people who love the way that you kill yourself day by day silently.

And I think all of this is really about women and work. Certainly this is all about me as a woman and my life work. I mean I am not sure my mother's suicide was something extraordinary. Perhaps most women must deal with a similar inheritance, the legacy of a woman whose death you cannot possibly pinpoint because she died so many, many times and because, even before she became your mother, the life of that woman was taken; I say it was taken away.

And really it was to honor my mother that I did fight with my father, that man who could not tell the living from the dead.

And really it is to honor Mrs. Hazel Griffin and my cousin Valerie and   70
all the women I love, including myself, that I am working for the courage to admit the truth that Bertolt Brecht has written; he says, "It takes courage to say that the good were defeated not because they were good, but because they were weak."

I cherish the mercy and the grace of women's work. But I know there is new work that we must undertake as well: that new work will make defeat detestable to us. That new women's work will mean we will not die trying to stand up: we will live that way: standing up.

I came too late to help my mother to her feet.

By way of everlasting thanks to all of the women who have helped me to stay alive I am working never to be late again.   [1985]

A Student's Personal Response to the Essay

Isla Bravo wrote in her journal:

> It was shocking to read about Jordan's mother's suicide in the first sentence of "Many Rivers to Cross." I expected the rest of the essay to be about only that one event, but she went on to talk about everything else that was going on in her life around that time first. It is hard to understand how she managed everything in her life. She is out of money and needs to find a way to improve her financial status in just three months. My family may not have everything we've ever wanted, but we've always done pretty well, and I never worried about where we lived.
>
> Even though I have never had to struggle the way Jordan did, I can relate to her descriptions of her friends and neighbors. They all help her out the best they can when her husband leaves her and then when her mother dies. These are the people that she really appreciates in her life. They are the same kind of people that brought food to my parents when my grandmother died. These are the people that she loves, and she creates her own sort of family despite the fact that her father is so mean to her. These are people with whom she creates relationships that aren't defined by specific standards created by society.
>
> When Jordan says that her mother's death may not be extraordinary, that maybe every woman watches someone die over and over, she is really talking about all the little things that can wear a lot of women down and cause their deaths a long time before they actually die. She can't even tell that her mother is dead because she's been wearing down for so long. The image of her mother looking as if she was "just about to stand up" made me think of my grandmother's funeral and how she looked like she was sleeping rather than dead. For Jordan the image of her mother in that sort of paralysis is also an image of her possible future. It is strange to think of someone whose life has been so hard on them that their death doesn't create a jarring difference.
>
> Jordan seems to be trying to keep herself from wearing down just like her mother at the end. Women are given roles by society that prevent them from being able to really enjoy their lives. She uses her other friends and family as models for how to survive. She has a friend who calms her down on the phone, a cousin that gives her advice in the hospital, and more that take care of her son when

she can't. Mrs. Griffin is a good example of the type of person she wants to be. She has to work hard to avoid becoming her mother. It seems as if she is motivated by guilt because she wasn't able to help her mother when she says, "I came too late to help my mother to her feet." Even though it wasn't her fault that her mother put up with so much, it certainly makes her determined to prevent her life from ending up the same way her mother's did.

The Elements of Essays

First impressions are valuable, but writing intelligently about essays should not be completely spontaneous. We can be personal and insightful, but persuading others about the validity of our reading takes a more focused and textually informed presentation. The following discussion of the basic elements of the essay is meant to increase your ability to analyze and write about essays. The elements include voice, style, structure, and ideas.

VOICE

When we read the first few sentences of an essay, we usually hear the narrator's **voice**: we hear a person speaking to us, and we begin to notice if he or she sounds friendly or hostile, stuffy or casual, self-assured or tentative. The voice might be austere and technical or personal and flamboyant. The voice may be intimate or remote. It may be sincere, hectoring, hysterical, meditative, or ironic. The possibilities are endless.

We usually get a sense of the writer's voice from the **tone** the writer projects. In the first paragraph of Jordan's essay, we get a sense of the speaker's voice through the direct and forthright tone that she takes, beginning with the disturbing assertion that her mother killed herself and that she herself was destitute. She is also not afraid to admit that her cigarettes and scotch were running low and informal enough to use "big bucks" and "okay" (para. 1). This is not someone who will be putting on airs or who will skirt the bare-bones truth of her situation, however unflattering or unpleasant.

Given the situation she describes, it is not surprising that Jordan's tone would occasionally be sarcastic and ironic, as when she describes the "difference between an American child and a car" (para. 4) and her abortions as "somewhat poorly executed" (para. 5).

Jordan's concerned and bewildered voice over the death of her mother and the revelation of her suicide turns to anger and outrage over the insensitive and selfish response of her father. And then while recovering in the hospital, Jordan's voice and tone shift drastically with "I wanted to be strong" (para. 65). She is now assertive, confident, and committed. Rejecting any sentimental thoughts of her deceased mother, she is determined not to be as weak as her mother. And so she boldly promises that she is now committed to the "new work that we must undertake" (para. 71). This new work, she asserts in a voice brimming with hope and determination, means that she will live "standing up" (para. 71).

When we speak of a writer's persona, we mean a kind of performance mask or stance the writer assumes. Writers are trying to construct a persona that will serve their purposes. Voice and tone are techniques that help writers create an appropriate persona.

STYLE

We all have stylish friends. They look good. Their shoes and pants and shirts seem to complement each other perfectly. It's not that they are color-coordinated — that would be too obvious for them — it's something more subtle. They seem to make just the right choices. When they go to a party, to the movies, or to school, they have a personal style that is their own.

Writers also have **style**. They make specific choices in words, in syntax and sentence length, in diction, in metaphors, even in sentence beginnings and endings. Writers use parallelism, balance, formal diction, poetic language, even sentence fragments to create their own styles.

Jordan's first three dramatic sentences are a good example of how she adapts her style to the content. Here she uses short, direct sentences to announce her predicament, but then her sentences get longer and more complex. Notice in the second paragraph her cumulative sentence ("Those same neighbors . . ."). In this pattern, writers make a statement and then add modifiers after a colon or a comma that can be words (as in this case) or long phrases. Notice the next long, compound sentence. She then ends the paragraph with a short simple assertion. Skilled writers like Jordan vary their sentence length and type as well as the imaginative ways they begin their sentences. Notice, for example, the different ways Jordan begins her paragraphs. Also notice the way Jordan crafts transitions between paragraphs, sometimes with a simple word ("Anyway" in para. 5), or a pronoun ("This" in para. 10), or a conjunction ("And" in paras. 67–70), or a phrase ("About . . ." in para. 11).

STRUCTURE

The way essayists put their work together is not mysterious. The best writers create a **structure** to fit their needs. Most do not have a prearranged structure in mind or feel the need to obey the composition rules many students think they have to follow: topic sentence first and three examples following. Writers of essays aren't inclined to follow formulas. Essayists begin and end as they see fit; they give explicit topic sentences or create narratives that imply themes; they begin with an assertion and support it, or vice versa. Essayists are inventors of structures that fit the occasion and their own way of seeing the world. The thought of the essay significantly influences its structure. Like the relationship between mind and body, form and thought are inseparable.

Jordan's plan, of course, is to begin her argument with a detailed autobiographical narrative focused on her mother's suicide. After setting the scene with her husband abandoning her and the necessity to move into her childhood home, Jordan focuses on the relationship between her egregious bullying father and her weak mother. And then, after detailing in excruciating detail the night of her mother's death, Jordan begins the generalizations that are at the heart of her argument, which is, essentially: my mother was weak and that cost her her life, and I'm not going to let that happen to me.

IDEAS

All writers have something on their minds when they write. That seems especially true when writers decide to put their **ideas** into a nonfictional form such as the essay. Of course, lots of ideas fill poems and short stories too, but they are usually expressed more indirectly. Although essays seem more idea-driven, this does not mean that as readers we have a responsibility to extract the precise idea or argument the writer had in mind. That may not even be possible since in the creative process of all writing, ideas get modified or changed. Sometimes a writer's original intention is significantly transformed; sometimes writers are not fully conscious of all their hidden intentions. Regardless, readers of essays are not simply miners unearthing hidden meanings; they are more like coproducers. And in creating that meaning, ideas are central.

Of course, Jordan has been developing ideas from the very beginning of her essay. It seems as if she becomes more focused on ideas per se when her narrative concludes at the hospital, but her comments about her husband starting in paragraph 2 clearly develop the idea that choice has been systematically eliminated from her life, and by implication the lives of all working-class women. Paragraph 4 also focuses on the unfairness of the courts and their favorable bias toward men. But the primary emphasis on ideas happens with "I wanted to be strong" in paragraph 65, with Jordan's manifesto-like assertion in the same paragraph that she was never going to "be weak again as long as I lived." Interestingly, she cites the fight with her father, who could not tell the difference between the living and the dead, as a metaphor for the larger fight of all women to assert that a change is coming in the lives of women, that new women will live "standing up" (para. 71). And Jordan's concluding idea in the last sentence announces a new solidarity, a new community of women who will help each other be independent. And now, some thirty years later, Jordan's ideas have proven to be prescient.

Final Draft of a Student Paper

After writing journal entries and a freewrite, Isla planned her essay and then wrote a draft. She used responses from several students in a small-group workshop and from her instructor to help her revise her essay, sharpening her focus and supporting her claims more explicitly. Here is Isla's final version.

Isla Bravo
Ms. Hollingsworth
English 201
21 April - - - -

Resisting Women's Roles

June Jordan takes a strongly feminist stance against the
roles women are forced to contend with in her essay "Many
Rivers to Cross." She begins the essay from her experience as
a woman who has conformed to the social expectations of a
wife, daughter, and mother. Her commitment to these roles
has left her as a single mother who is contending with an unwanted pregnancy, forced to care for a dying mother and a
belligerent father, and without a place of her own to live or
work. This essay supports my argument that women need to *Clear, explicit claim with her*
establish their independence and not allow society to control *plan to support.*
their lives. This argument is substantiated by Jordan's exploration of her own defiance of society's conventions regarding
the roles for women as wife, daughter, and mother in an attempt to preserve herself from the restrictions that destroyed
her mother.

Women are expected by society to place their families *Gives concrete examples of*
before their careers, and part of this sacrifice includes aiding *negative consequences of*
their husband's careers in lieu of their own. Jordan portrays *following convention.*
herself as an example of how this convention is detrimental
to a woman's ability to survive on her own. Jordan sacrifices
her own professional ambition to her husband's pursuit of his
career. The ensuing complications depict the limitations and
perils of the idea that women must always place their own careers behind their husbands'. Rather than specifically condemning this social expectation, she provides an illustration
of the destruction it can cause. Her own career is a secondary
priority, subjugated to her roles as a supportive wife and
mother, while her husband pursues graduate school in another
city and has an affair with another man's wife. Jordan squan-
ders a year of her life waiting for her husband's return and becomes "a mother without a husband, . . . a poet without a
publisher, a freelance journalist without assignment, a city
planner without a contract" (172). She abides by the social *Qualifies her objections.*
conventions that insist she support her husband, and her life
remains in stasis until he steps out of his own commitments.
By living her life under the social guidelines for a wife, she
allows herself to be exploited for her husband's convenience.
Her needs are supplanted by her husband's, and his abandon- *Another concrete example*
ment leaves her embarrassed and destitute. *supporting need for*
independence.

Jordan's depiction of her parents' relationship illustrates

the generational quality of these social conventions. Her parents' relationship foreshadows the potential outcome of her marriage if it continues. Her parents' relationship is wholly restricted to the typical gender roles they both inherit from society. Her mother subjugates her own life only to the needs of her husband, a sacrifice he expects from her. This historical relationship becomes clear when Jordan describes her father's response to her mother's fatal illness when she says, "I think he was scared; who would take care of him? Would she get well again and make everything all right again?" (174). The fact that his concern was about his own life — "who would take care of him?" — makes it clear that their relationship revolved around only his own comfort. Jordan is desperate to prevent her own life from following this path.

Concludes paragraph with reference to claim.

Jordan's relationship with her father explores another aspect of the expectations placed on women by society, that of a daughter. Jordan's father's reliance on her mother for all of his comfort turns onto Jordan when her mother is no longer able to fulfill these duties. Jordan's role as his daughter, her most important function, is dynamically portrayed when her father forces her to check her mother's body to see if she is alive because he is incapable or unwilling to do it himself. He says to her, "I'll wait up here. . . . You call up and let me know" (175), only to yell at her inaccurate determination. His anger appears to stem more from the disruption to his own life rather than from the loss of his wife; he is angry rather than sad. He appears almost offended by her death and his daughter's failure to provide him with the level of comfort he craves for his life. His own expectations for the superior role in the household have been created by a male-dominated society and have been enforced by the manner in which his wife seems to have fulfilled those expectations as well. The role of a dutiful child is not by itself destructive until it begins to take precedence in this destructive manner. His expectation is that Jordan should take on the role of caregiver, waiting on him despite any reluctance on her part and regardless of the animosity that exists between them.

Another concrete example of societal expectations.

Qualifies her objections before reinforcing objections to harmful social convention.

Jordan also defies social conventions by her unwillingness to become a mother again to the new baby she's carrying. She attempts to abort the child several times until she finally does lose the baby. Jordan describes the advice she receives from a friend in the hospital: "Whatever I did, I should not admit I'd had an abortion or I'd get her into trouble, and myself in trouble" (177). The possibility that Jordan does not want to be a mother to another child is abhorrent to the social standards that have formed her life and surroundings.

Another concrete example supporting her claim.

Motherhood is the expected career for a woman, and her choice to not have another baby is a direct rejection of those standards.

As a woman in this particular culture, she has certain designated assignments of work that include being a daughter, wife, and mother. She rejects a caretaker role for her father, her marriage has dissolved, and she has an abortion. These portrayals do not suggest a rejection of these roles in their entirety; rather, they explicitly show how they can become harmful if they force women into situations they might have avoided if not for these societal pressures. From this point, she is able to look toward her own career and her own needs. The role society imposes on her as a woman puts her in a position that deemphasizes her own ambitions and preferences. The end of her mother's life is the catalyst that forces her to fully recognize the restrictions that she has been living with and that her mother succumbed to until her death. Jordan says, "I came too late to help my mother to her feet. . . . I am working never to be late again" (178). She wants to free herself from the limiting standards for women in society and hopefully free other women to be independent and assertive.

Reviews her assigned roles and her objections.

Gives context for her defiance of social expectations.

Concludes by reinforcing and extending her claim to all women.

(continued on page 185, after the insert)

≡   ≡

Comparing Poems and Pictures

Although literature and visual art may seem quite different media, they have often been closely connected. For one thing, any page of literature is a visual image, whether or not readers are always conscious of this fact. Also, most publishers of literature carefully design the covers of their books, aiming to lure readers in. Specific genres and authors, however, have forged even stronger relations between literature and art. Beginning in classical times and continuing today, many poems have precisely described existing paintings and sculptures; this tradition of verse is called **ekphrasis**. In the late eighteenth century, William Blake made highly ornamental engravings of his poems, so that they were striking works of art and not just written texts. In the nineteenth century, many novels included illustrations, a tradition evident today in children's picture books. At present, perhaps you are a fan of **graphic novels**: comic books that combine words and images to tell stories aimed at adults.

Aside from this history of connections, comparing a literary text with an image is a good mental exercise. The process can help you acquire more insights into each work. Given this possibility, we present several pairings of poems and works of art. Every pairing deals with one of the topics addressed in Parts One and Two of this book: work, family, love, freedom and confinement, crime an justice, and journeys. In some cases, the literary text was written in response to its accompanying image. In other cases, we connect a poem and an image for the first time, inviting you to trace their similarities and differences. With any of these pairings, comparison can help you generate ideas for writing, a principle we stress throughout this book.

Analyzing Visual Art

You can better understand a work of visual art — and develop ideas for an essay about it — if you raise certain questions about it and try to answer them. These questions apply to various types of pictures. Bear in mind that even photographs are not mere reproductions of reality. People who create them are, consciously or not, choosing their subject and figuring out how best to represent it. Especially in the age of digital technologies such as Photoshop, images caught by the camera can be tweaked in all sorts of ways. Moreover, the scene depicted might be a staged fantasy in the first place.

A

Here are questions to ask yourself as you examine a picture with an eye to analyzing it:

1. **What details do you see in the picture?** Besides recognizable objects and figures (human beings or animals), consider shapes, colors, lighting, and shading. Do not list just the picture's most prominent elements, for those that at first seem trivial may turn out to be important for you.

2. **What are aspects of the picture's *style* — the artist's particular way of handling the subject?** Among other things, consider what the artist does and does not allow the viewer to see; how realistic or abstract the work seems; and whether anyone in the picture looks directly at the viewer.

3. **How has the artist organized the picture?** Note especially patterns of resemblance and contrast. Think, too, about whether the picture's design directs the viewer's attention to a particular part of it.

4. **What mood does the picture evoke?** Consider emotions that you experience as a viewer, as well as those that seem to be felt by any living figures in the scene.

5. **What is at least one detail of the picture that strikes you as puzzling (and therefore especially in need of interpretation)?**

6. **Does the picture seem to tell a story or appear to be part of a story that has already begun and will continue?**

7. **How does the picture relate to its title and (where applicable) to its caption?**

8. **What are some options that the artist could have explored but did not pursue?**

Writing an Essay That Compares Literature and Art

Before you write an essay comparing a work of literature with a work of art, collect as many details as you can about each. The questions above can help you do this with the artwork. For aid in gathering observations about the literary text, see Chapter 2, How to Read Closely, especially the section on Basic Strategies for Close Reading. Then, as you proceed to write, keep the following principles especially in mind:

- **You do not have to give equal space to each work.** Rather, you may prefer to come up with an issue and a main claim by focusing on interpreting *one* of the works: either the literary text *or* the visual image. Your secondary work will still play some role in the essay, but your primary one will receive greater attention. The result will be what in Chapter 4 we call a *weighted* comparison. (See that chapter for more tips.)

- **Assume that your reader is at least somewhat familiar with both the literary work and the image but needs to be reminded of their basic details.** In particular, help your audience *visualize* the art you discuss.

■ **Refer at least sometimes to the author of the literary work and to the artist who created the image.** Doing so will help you analyze how their productions involve particular strategies of representation — attempts to affect audiences in particular ways.

A Sample Paper Comparing a Poem and a Picture

To give you a better idea of what an essay comparing literature and art looks like, we present a paper by student Karl Magnusson. He connects Edward Hopper's painting *Office at Night* to a prose poem of the same title by Rolando Perez. This pairing is the first in our color plates section. As you will see, Karl's essay is a weighted comparison; it focuses mostly on Perez's poem.

Karl Magnusson
Professor Kemper
English W350
May 16, ----

Lack of Motion and Speech in
Rolando Perez's "Office at Night"

Edward Hopper's painting *Office at Night* depicts a man and a woman working in the kind of setting indicated by the title. The man is apparently the boss of the woman, who seems to be his secretary. He sits at a desk by an open window, studying a document that he holds in front of him. She is positioned to the left and slightly to the rear of him. More precisely, she stands at a filing cabinet with her right hand resting on an open drawer. Their respective postures suggest that she is waiting to hear what he will say next. Perhaps she has just asked him a question and he is thinking about how to answer, or perhaps she is simply expecting him, as her superior, to issue her a new order. In any case, viewers of the painting are free to interpret their interaction, and different spectators might come up with different ideas about what these people really mean to each other. Indeed, not everyone would conceive their relationship to be what Rolando Perez imagines it as being in his poem about Hopper's artwork. Also entitled "Office at Night," Perez's poem speculates that the man and woman have a romantic interest in each other that neither he nor she can express. Furthermore, the poem conveys their reticence in terms that have often been used to describe the medium of painting in general.

Immediately refers to the painting and then proceeds to summarize its key details.

Now turns to the poem, which will be the primary work in this weighted comparison.

This is the essay's main claim, which is about the poem.

The poem draws attention more to the self-repression of the boss. The secretary, too, evidently does not feel able to speak frankly about their emotions, perhaps because she is after all his employee. But the text tends to focus on *his* reluctance to reveal that he is enamored of her. This mixture of lust and hesitation is evident right near the start of the poem. There, just before describing the secretary's alluring clothes, the poem's speaker wonders, "How many times did he [the boss] dream of this very same scenario" (lines 1–2). The implication is that the boss has entertained sensual visions of his employee in his mind while doing nothing to bring them about. He merely fantasizes a romance with her, not actually helping it come to life. Soon after, the reader learns that *she* had to prompt *him* to "open the window" (line 5) and let fresh air in. Evidently she wishes to stimulate their senses and admit their real feelings, but this is behavior that he apparently would never "have dared" (line 4) to engage in on his own. Later, he resists actually inviting her to take their office working relationship in a romantic direction. Although he apparently considers the possibility that "he would do something, he would act, produce the right combination of words" (lines 14–15) to initiate a courtship, he remains silent and still. The implication is that he is restrained by the memory of his previous disappointments in love — "too many truths in the past" (line 17). Whatever specific episodes in his past he is thinking of, the result is that "now history holds him back" (line 17). Rather than "suggest[ing] that they lock up and go for a drink somewhere" (line 16), he stays emotionally locked up, not letting his true attachment to her emerge.

> *Proceeds to support the main argument with specific lines from the poem.*

In describing physical details of the office, the poem's speaker sums up the couple's inability to be emotionally open with each other. In part, the speaker does this by sometimes using images of motion that underscore by contrast how the man and woman fail to act on their feelings. The "patch of light" that "touches them both . . . lightly, very lightly . . . as with fingertips" (lines 10–12) is a reminder that these two people do not physically touch each other at all. The phrase "gently carried there by the wind" (line 8) — used in reference to a piece of paper on the floor — indirectly emphasizes that the couple will not let themselves be carried away by passion. When, however, near the end of the poem, the speaker describes the paper as "timidly undisturbed" (line 20), the symbolism is more direct: the word "timidly" seems to fit the couple as well, for they have been too scared to confess their emotional bond. Moreover, the speaker's observation that "he hasn't moved, and she hasn't moved" (lines 18–19) directly reinforces their *psychological* paralysis. The poem's final phrase, "wounded and frozen infinity" (line 20), is not just an overview of this late-night office environment. The speaker is also indicating the basic state of the couple's relationship. They are "wounded" in the sense that they suffer unfulfilled desires for each other. They are "frozen" in the sense that they cannot reveal these desires. The word "infinity" implies that, given their inertia, their situation is unlikely to change.

Not every poem about Hopper's *Office at Night* painting would necessarily focus on its two human figures. Nor would every poem about the painting necessarily depict their relationship in the way that Perez's does. Indeed, a distinctive feature of his poem is that his portrait of the couple attributes to them characteristics often associated with the medium of painting itself. Aware, like most people, that figures in a painting do not move, Perez takes this fact and makes it an element of the couple's behavior. The static nature of painting in general is echoed in their paralytic inhibition. Furthermore, just as people in paintings do not speak aloud, so the couple in Perez's poem resist articulating what they really feel. Also, just as viewers of a painting have to guess the thoughts of anyone shown in it, so Perez's man and woman force themselves to guess what is on each other's mind.

Perez could be seen as tolerating and even encouraging affairs between bosses and their secretaries. In this respect, his text seems more in keeping with the world of 1940, the year Hopper painted *Office at Night*. Back then, expressions of love between a manager and a subordinate might have been smiled upon, perceived as what the poem's speaker calls "the correct combination of words" and "the correct series of reactions" (lines 15–16). The same expressions now, however, might be condemned as politically and even legally *in*correct. Certainly government and company policies on sexual harassment warn executives not to seduce the employees who serve them. Nevertheless, it would be unfair simply to dismiss Perez's poem or Hopper's painting as outdated, especially because the audiences for these works do not have to take them as being just about romance in the office. Both the poem and the painting allow for interpretations that see the couple as universal — as people who might exist anywhere. In this case, their reticence toward each other would be a widespread human problem: the difficulty of communicating the stirrings of one's heart.

The concluding paragraph does not simply repeat what has already been said. It touches on a new subject: changes in policies on office affairs.

Works Cited

Hopper, Edward. *Office at Night*. 1940. Oil on canvas. Walker Art Center, Minneapolis. Schilb and Clifford *Portfolio A*.

Perez, Rolando. "Office at Night." Schilb and Clifford G *Portfolio G*.

Schilb, John, and John Clifford, eds. *Making Literature Matter: An Anthology for Readers and Writers*. 6th ed. Boston: Bedford, 2015. Print.

Edward Hopper, *Office at Night*. 1940. Oil on canvas. 30-5/16 × 33-15/16 × 2-3/4″ framed. Collection Walker Art Center, Minneapolis. Gift of the T. B. Walker Foundation, Gilbert M. Walker Fund, 1948.

ROLANDO PEREZ
Office at Night

It is past nine o'clock, and she has stayed late to help him. How many times did he dream of this very same scenario: her standing there in her tight blue dress, with her black pumps and flesh-colored stockings. And now it has finally happened. Without him having to ask — not that he would have dared — she volunteered all on her own.

He had to "open the window."   5
"This office at night is a bit stuffy."

A sheet of paper that once lay on top of other papers on his desk, now lies on the green carpet — to his right — gently carried there by the wind. Standing at a black filing cabinet, searching for some old bills, she has noticed the paper lying on the floor. The desk lamp throws a shadow on the desk, and illuminates his hands. And a patch   10
of light, reflected on the wall, touches them both . . . lightly, very lightly . . . as with finger tips.

Will she bend over to pick it up?

If only the phone beside him would ring, then he would do something, he would act, produce the correct combination of words that would elicit the correct series of re-   15
actions from her. He might even suggest that they lock up and go for a drink somewhere. But having heard too many truths in the past, now history holds him back. In his suit, with his shirt buttoned to the top, and his tie still on, he hasn't moved, and she hasn't moved; and the wind-swept paper will stay on the floor, halfway between his desk and her cabinet, timidly undisturbed, in this wounded and frozen infinity.   *[2002]*   20

Edward Hopper, *Conference at Night*. The Roland P. Murdock Collection, Wichita Art Museum, Wichita, Kansas.

VICTORIA CHANG
Edward Hopper's *Conference at Night*

The man sitting on the desk seems to have no eyes or they are closed or they have
been dug out the man sitting on the table sits in a way of a boss or perhaps he wants

to be the boss and the woman and man can help him the desks have nothing on
them but two wooden boards they hold shadows and the man no papers no tacks

the man has no stacks of anything the room can't be his office it is a morgue for   5
desks people that have left laid off fired sacked axed let go why let go of the past

why must the past too be given a notice why can't we live in the past in our best
dresses the woman looks like a man maybe she will be a boss or maybe

it's better to look like a woman but act like a man a boss once told me never to
act like a woman the woman stares beyond the man the man on the desk looks   10

between the man and woman whatever they are conferencing about has passed is
the past the pair helped the man become the boss he lost touch with the pair who

lost touch with each other who were both laid off   *[2011]*

Gustav Klimt, *The Kiss*.
1907–1908. Oester-
reichische Galerie im
Belvedere, Vienna,
Austria. Photo Credit:
Erich Lessing/Art
Resource, NY.

LAWRENCE FERLINGHETTI

Short Story on a Painting of Gustav Klimt

They are kneeling upright on a flowered bed
  He
    has just caught her there
          and holds her still
  Her gown   5
     has slipped down
         off her shoulder
He has an urgent hunger
    His dark head
      bends to hers   10
       hungrily
And the woman the woman
  turns her tangerine lips from his
    one hand like the head of a dead swan
      draped down over   15
        his heavy neck
    the fingers
     strangely crimped
      tightly together
   her other arm doubled up   20
    against her tight breast

her hand a languid claw
   clutching his hand
 which would turn her mouth
     to his   25
her long dress made
  of multicolored blossoms
   quilted on gold
her Titian hair
  with blue stars in it   30
And his gold
  harlequin robe
    checkered with
     dark squares
Gold garlands   35
  stream down over
    her bare calves &
    tensed feet
Nearby there must be
  a jeweled tree   40
   with glass leaves aglitter
   in the gold air
It must be
  morning
   in a faraway place somewhere   45
They
 are silent together
    as in a flowered field
 upon the summer couch
   which must be hers   50
And he holds her still
   so passionately
 holds her head to his
   so gently so insistently
 to make her turn   55
   her lips to his
Her eyes are closed
  like folded petals
She
 will not open   60
  He
   is not the One   *[1976]*

Edvard Munch, *The Scream*. © 2014 The Munch Museum/The Munch-Ellingsen Group/Artists Rights Society(ARS), NY. Photo credit: The Art Archive at Art Resource, NY.

MAY MILLER
The Scream

I am a woman controlled,
Remember this; I never scream,
Yet I stood a form apart
Watching my other frenzied self
Beaten by words and wounds   5
Make in silence a mighty scream—
A scream that the wind took up
And thrust through the bars of night
Beyond all reason's final rim.
Out where the sea's last murmur dies   10
And the gull's cry has no sound,
Out where city voices fade,
Stilled in a lyric sleep
Where silence is its own design,
My scream hovered a ghost denied   15
Wanting the shape of lips.   *[1975]*

Larry Rivers,
*Washington Crossing
the Delaware.* 1953.
Art © Estate of Larry
Rivers/Licensed by
Vaga, New York, NY.
Photo credit: Digital
Image © The Museum
of Modern Art/
Licensed by Scala/Art
Resource, NY.

FRANK O'HARA

On Seeing Larry Rivers' "Washington Crossing the Delaware" at the Museum of Modern Art

Now that our hero has come back to us
in his white pants and we know his nose
trembling like a flag under fire,
we see the calm cold river is supporting
our forces, the beautiful history.   5

To be more revolutionary than a nun
is our desire, to be secular and intimate
as, when sighting a redcoat, you smile
and pull the trigger. Anxieties
and animosities, flaming and feeding   10

on theoretical considerations and
the jealous spiritualities of the abstract
the robot? they're smoke, billows above
the physical event. They have burned up.
See how free we are! as a nation of persons.   15

Dear father of our country, so alive
you must have lied incessantly to be
immediate, here are your bones crossed
on my breast like a rusty flintlock,
a pirate's flag, bravely specific   20

and ever so light in the misty glare
of a crossing by water in winter to a shore
other than that the bridge reaches for.
Don't shoot until, the white of freedom glinting
on your gun barrel, you see the general fear.   *[1955]*   25

Frida Kahlo, *Frida and Diego Rivera*. 1931. Oil on canvas. 99 × 78.7 cm. San Francisco Museum of Modern Art, Albert M. Bender Collection, gift of Albert M. Bender; © Banco de Mexico Diego Rivera & Frida Kahlo Museums Trust, Mexico, D.F./Artists Rights Society (ARS), New York.

DAVID DOMINGUEZ
Wedding Portrait

Yesterday afternoon, I hung a framed print in the living room—
a task that took two head-throbbing hours.
It's a wedding portrait that we love: *Frida and Diego Rivera*.
I wonder how two people could consistently hurt each other,
but still feel love so deeply as their bones turned into dust?   5
Before Frida died, she painted a watermelon still life;
before his death, Diego did too.
I want to believe that those paintings were composed
during parallel moments because of their undying devotion.
If I close my eyes, I can see melon wedges left like   10
centerpieces except for the slice
Diego put on the table's corner—
one piece of fruit pecked at by a dove
that passed through a window.
I know that I won't be building a bookshelf anytime soon   15
and that the chances of me constructing a roll-top desk
are as slim as me building an Adirondack chair that sits plumb,

but I'm good with the spackle and putty knives in my tool belt.
The knots in my back might not be there
if I had listened to her suggestions,   20
and I could well have done without two hours of silence
over a few holes in the wall.
But somehow, life has its ways of working things out.
This afternoon, I shut the blinds,
turned off the TV, lights, and phone,   25
and massaged my wife's feet to fight off a migraine—
her second one this week despite
the prophylactics and pain killers that we store in the breadbox.
For once, I'd like to experience what she feels:
nausea, blindness, and pain that strike   30
when the cranial vessels dilate,
fill with blood, leak, and make the brain swell.
Earlier, an MRI triggered the reaction as it mapped her head
with electrical current, gradient magnets, and radio waves
hammering her floundering eyes.   35
For now, we have our room, the bed frame, and the mattress
where she lies as I knead her toes.
Come nightfall, I hope that we'll sit in the patio and watch
the breeze stirring the lemon, lime, and orange trees
that I planted along the back fence.   40
On certain nights, the moon turns our lawn
into green acrylic where we sip Syrah and mint tea
until all we know is the sound
of our breathing among the whispering leaves.   *[2010]*

Rembrandt van Rijn, *Self Portrait at the Age of 63.* 1669. Oil on canvas, 86 × 70.5 cm. National Gallery, London. Photo Credit: © National Gallery, London/Art Resource, NY.

LINDA PASTAN

Ethics

In ethics class so many years ago
our teacher asked this question every fall:
if there were a fire in a museum
which would you save, a Rembrandt painting
or an old woman who hadn't many   5
years left anyhow? Restless on hard chairs
caring little for pictures or old age
we'd opt one year for life, the next for art
and always half-heartedly. Sometimes
the woman borrowed my grandmother's face   10
leaving her usual kitchen to wander
some drafty, half-imagined museum.
One year, feeling clever, I replied
why not let the woman decide herself?
Linda, the teacher would report, eschews   15
the burdens of responsibility.
This fall in a real museum I stand
before a real Rembrandt, old woman,
or nearly so, myself. The colors
within this frame are darker than autumn,   20
darker even than winter — the browns of earth,
though earth's most radiant elements burn
through the canvas. I know now that woman
and painting and season are almost one
and all beyond saving by children.   *[1980]*   25

Pieter Brueghel the Elder, *Landscape with the Fall of Icarus*. Musee d'Art Ancien, Musees Royaux des Beaux-Arts, Brussels, Belgium. Photo Credit: Scala/Art Resource, NY.

W. H. AUDEN
Musée des Beaux Arts

About suffering they were never wrong,
The old Masters: how well they understood
Its human position: how it takes place
While someone else is eating or opening a window or just walking dully along;
How, when the aged are reverently, passionately waiting   5
For the miraculous birth, there always must be
Children who did not specially want it to happen, skating
On a pond at the edge of the wood:
They never forgot
That even the dreadful martyrdom must run its course   10
Anyhow in a corner, some untidy spot
Where the dogs go on with their doggy life and the torturer's horse
Scratches its innocent behind on a tree.

In Brueghel's *Icarus*, for instance: how everything turns away
Quite leisurely from the disaster; the ploughman may   15
Have heard the splash, the forsaken cry,
But for him it was not an important failure; the sun shone
As it had to on the white legs disappearing into the green
Water, and the expensive delicate ship that must have seen
Something amazing, a boy falling out of the sky,   20
Had somewhere to get to and sailed calmly on.   *[1940]*

Works Cited

Jordan, June. "Many Rivers to Cross." *Making Literature Matter: An Anthology for Readers and Writers*. Ed. John Schilb and John Clifford. 6th ed. Boston: Bedford, 2015. 172–178. Print.

☰ SUMMING UP: WRITING ABOUT ESSAYS

- **Essays (and nonfiction) use language as imaginatively and effectively as other genres of literature.** Essays should — like stories, poems, and plays — be read with care and deliberation and written about with energy and discipline. (p. 171)

- **The elements of essays include *voice, style, structure,* and *ideas*.**

- **In essays, *voice* is important.** The writer's voice (which might be sincere, ironic, or meditative) can convey the tone a writer projects. But even in essays, writers might assume a persona that serves their purposes. (pp. 179–181)

- **The *style* and *structure* of essays often provide useful models for writers.** Noticing how essays are put together, how sentences and paragraphs follow one another logically, can lead to the writing of well-organized and stylish essays. (pp. 180–181)

- **As in all genres, *ideas* are crucial, but they seem especially prominent in essays.** (p. 181)

- **Argumentative essays model effective ways to make arguments.** It is often valuable to analyze argumentative essays for the ways that writers make claims about issues, support their claims with evidence, and project a good image of themselves. (pp. 179–181)

CHAPTER 6

Writing Researched Arguments

At the conclusion of this chapter, we discuss five specific kinds of research papers, in each case providing a sample student essay on Charlotte Perkins Gilman's short story "The Yellow Wallpaper." (See pp. 231–234.) We also offer advice for making a multimedia presentation on a literary work. But first we explain in general the research process and how it can lead to successful writing. You may imagine that writing a research paper for your literature class is a significantly different, and perhaps more difficult, assignment than others you have faced. Because more steps are involved in their writing (for example, additional reading and analysis of sources), research papers tend to be long-range projects. They also tend to be more formal than other kinds of papers because they involve integrating and documenting source material.

These differences, however, are essentially of magnitude and appearance, not of substance. Despite the common misconception (cause of much unnecessary anxiety) that writing a research paper requires a special set of knowledge and skills, it draws principally on the same kind of knowledge and skills needed to write other types of papers. You will still need to begin with an arguable **issue** and a **claim**, still need to marshal **evidence** to defend that claim, and still need to display a sound process of **reasoning**, so that your audience will think your claim has merit. The main difference between a researched argument and other types is that the evidence for it comes from a wider variety of sources.

The literary text you focus on is your **primary source**. The other materials you consult for your essay are your **secondary sources**. They may include historical documents along with present-day scholarship. These materials may consist as well of visual artifacts, such as photographs, films, and maps. You may even investigate music recordings or other types of sound. Whatever your sources, your essay will need to **synthesize** them. This means drawing connections between them, explaining how they harmonize or clash. It also means relating your secondary materials clearly to the literature you're analyzing. In a sense, synthesis involves putting the literature and these sources in "conversation" with one another, so your reader can tell how they all bear on your essay's main argument.

Identify an Issue and a Tentative Claim

Your first task in writing most researched arguments is to identify an issue that you genuinely want to think and learn more about. The more interested you are in your issue, the better your essay will be. But here, too, the word *conversation* may apply, for your issue may be a controversy that's come up in class discussions—some topic that you and other students don't agree on. If your essay will focus on literature, any of the types of issues described on pages 53–59 will suit. In any case, read carefully the literary work you choose as your springboard. If it's in this book, review the information we provide about its author; take a look at the questions or commentaries we include along with it. Then, ask questions of your own about it, trying to figure out what really interests you about the text. Don't settle for an issue or a question that you can easily answer with a few factual statements. Strive to come up with a subject that requires serious research.

Before you begin searching for sources, formulate a tentative claim. Consider it a hypothesis to test. Don't worry if it seems a little vague or obvious; you'll have many opportunities to refine it as your research proceeds. Even if you end up changing the claim, having one in mind at the start will help you manage your investigation. It will keep you from feeling overwhelmed by the multitude of sources available.

Search for Sources in the Library and Online

Once you have your topic in mind and have sketched a tentative claim, begin looking for research sources. Many different types of sources for literary research are available, and the types you will need will depend largely on the type of claim you choose to defend. If your issue is primarily one of interpretation—about the theme, patterns, or symbolism of the text, for instance—you will most likely need to consult literary criticism to see what has been said in the past about the literature you are discussing. If your issue concerns historical or cultural context, including issues of social policy, you may need to consult newspapers, magazines, and similar sorts of cultural documents. Some topics might require several different types of sources.

Not many years ago, for most people the word *research* was synonymous with hours spent in the library hunting for books and articles. For many students today, *research* has become synonymous with the Internet, which they turn to in the belief that everything is available online. But this is simply not true. Many of the best and most reliable sources are still available just in print. In particular, lots of potentially useful books haven't been digitized yet. They remain in your school library, so you'll have to go there if you hope to read them. The library may also house relevant documents and scholarly journals that aren't online. The library's computerized **catalog** will alert you to its holdings, helping you locate useful texts. Typically, the catalog entry for a book lists various subject headings for it. By clicking on a heading, you'll find other books on that topic. When you go to the library's shelves for a book, browse through neighboring volumes, for perhaps they also address your subject of study.

Of course, a wealth of information is available on the Internet. As with the library, your goal is to find useful information efficiently, evaluate it carefully, and employ it effectively in your paper. Unfortunately, and unlike a library's sources, information on the Internet is not indexed and organized to make it easily accessible to researchers. Many students go right away to Wikipedia, hoping to find most of their needed data there. Indeed, a Wikipedia entry may contain some useful facts. Nevertheless, you shouldn't accept on faith everything that the entry says. It's the product of anonymous people, many of whom may not really be experts on the subject they claim to know. Wikipedia can be a decent *starting* point for online searches, especially because it provides links to Web sites that may be more authoritative. But many teachers will object if you depend on Wikipedia itself as a source. Consider it a launch pad, not a destination.

You will need to do a certain amount of "surfing" if you are to find appropriate online materials for your project. A number of **search engines** (programs for finding information) are designed to help you track down materials on the Web. If you are an old hand on the Internet, probably you can depend on search engines that have served you well in the past. Bear in mind, however, that relying on just one search engine may not lead you to all the sources that would benefit you. Many students pursuing a research topic go immediately to Google. They type their subject into the box, click a mouse, and expect to see terrific sources pop right up on-screen. Yet often this search method proves exasperating. For one thing, it may suceed all *too* well in generating items. Our five sample researched arguments discuss "The Yellow Wallpaper"; a Google search using this title elicits around 628,000 results. The first paper also deals with postpartum depression; if you Google this term, you'll come up with roughly 3,820,000 results. Even if you combine "The Yellow Wallpaper" with "postpartum depression," you'll get roughly 6,110 results. It can take forever to sift through these avalanches for whatever gems they contain. Faced with such landslides, some writers just pounce on the first few results they obtain. But "first" doesn't necessarily mean "best." An ideal article may surface late in a Google list.

You can narrow your results by adding words to your search, making it more exact. Or, you might turn to Google Scholar, which sticks with academic texts. There, combining "The Yellow Wallpaper" with "postpartum depression" produces about 125 results. This is certainly a more manageable number. Still, Google addiction will limit you as a researcher. See what other Web sites can do for you. If your college or university makes available to you sites such as *JSTOR*, *Academic Search Premier*, and *Project Muse*, these will give you access to hundreds of scholarly journals and books. The Internet service *LexisNexis* offers current articles from newspapers and magazines, as well as transcripts of radio and TV broadcasts. For literary research, a great service is the *MLA International Bibliography*. Sponsored by the Modern Language Association and carried by many schools, it lists books and articles on a wide range of topics in literary criticism, history, and theory.

When you discover a book or article that fits with your research agenda, examine its bibliography. There, perhaps you'll find listed other texts useful to you. In general, scholars refer to previous works on their subject. They extend, challenge, or refine their predecessors' claims. Notice how they treat these prior views. You'll thereby get a sense of the "conversation" your topic has already stirred. You may also see how to join this "dialogue" with ideas of your own.

Evaluate the Sources

Whatever method you use to locate your research materials, remember that not all sources are created equal. Take care to **evaluate** those you come across. When tempted to use a writer's work, ask yourself the following: What do I want my audience to think about this person? Often, you'll hope your readers will accept him or her as some sort of authority. In a way, you have to think about **ethos**, a term we discussed in Chapter 3. There, you may recall, we defined *ethos* as the image that an author projects. Many writers try to be persuasive by constructing an admirable ethos — a version of themselves that will impress their readers. Similarly, when you incorporate sources into a researched argument, you will often want your audience to respect them. These sources may not agree with one another — heck, *you* may not agree with them all — but they'll need to reflect recognizable expertise. Otherwise, why should your readers pay attention to them?

Suppose you plan to write a research paper on "The Yellow Wallpaper." An online search leads you to an analysis of the story. You might refer to this study in your essay. But you need to determine whether the author is someone your readers would take seriously. You have to look for credentials. Perhaps the writer is a professor publishing in a scholarly journal. Maybe, like Paul Goldberger in Chapter 3, this person is an award-winning authority in a certain field (in this case, architecture). Sometimes you can learn writers' professional status by visiting the Web sites of institutions they work for. At any rate, be skeptical when a Web post's author is shrouded in mystery. The views expressed may be interesting, but if their advocate is a phantom, you can't expect your readers to care about them. Useful to bear in mind is the famous *New Yorker* magazine cartoon about the digital age. One canine, perched at a computer, tells another that "on the Internet, nobody knows you're a dog." In short, the Web can fool you. Although someone posting on it is probably human, hunt for details of the person's background. Your audience will expect you to have this information about a source, even if you don't include every bit of it in your paper.

A teacher may require a number of your sources to be articles from "peer-reviewed" academic journals. Such journals publish a manuscript only after it has been evaluated by experts in its subject. Usually, a journal's Web site will indicate whether it falls into this category. Some search engines have a feature that, when you activate it, confines your results to peer-reviewed works. For example, both *Academic Search Premier* and the *MLA International Bibliography* enable you to restrict your search this way. Most books published by academic and unversity presses have also been peer reviewed. Of course, even when it doesn't come with this label, a book or an article may still be worth consulting. In many popular newspapers (such as the *New York Times* and the *Washington Post*) and magazines (such as *The New Yorker* and the *Atlantic*), you'll find thoughtful, well-grounded reports and opinion pieces.

In general, you should ask the following basic questions of your sources: (1) Is the information recent, and if not, is the validity of the information likely to have changed significantly over time? (2) How credible is the author? Is he or she a recognized expert on the subject? (3) Is the source published by an established, respectable press, or does it appear in a well-respected journal or periodical (the *Los Angeles Times* has more credibility than the *National Enquirer*, for example) or Web site (one supported by a university or library, for instance)? (4) Based on what you've learned about responsible argument, do the arguments in your source seem sound, fair, and thoughtful? Is the evidence convincing? Is the development of the argument logical?

You increase your own credibility with your audience by using the most reliable research materials available to you, so do not just stick with whatever comes to hand if you have the opportunity to find a stronger source.

Strategies for Working with Sources

Once you have identified a number of sources for your paper and tracked down the books, periodicals, or other materials, it is time to begin reading, analyzing, and taking notes. At this point, it is especially important to keep yourself well organized and to write down *everything* that may be of use to you later. No matter how good your memory, do not count on remembering a few days (or even hours) later which notes or quotations come from which sources. Scrupulously write down page numbers and Web addresses, and double-check facts and spellings. Some researchers find it useful to record this information on a stack of note cards, with one entry per card. Many others prefer to do their recording on a computer file. Whatever your method, you will need this information for your paper's bibliography, called **Works Cited**.

Many researchers find it easier to stay organized if they divide the notes they take into three basic categories: summaries, paraphrases, and quotations. (A fourth category is notes of your own ideas, prompted by your research. Write these down as well, keeping them separate and clearly labeled, as you would any other notes.)

Student researchers often rely too heavily on **quotations**, copying verbatim large sections from their research sources. Do not make this mistake. Instead, start your note-taking with a **summary** of the source in question — just one or two sentences indicating in your own words the author's main point. Such summaries guarantee that you understand the gist of an author's argument and (since they are your own words) can readily be incorporated in your paper. You might think of a summary as a restatement of the author's principal claim, perhaps with a brief indication of the types of supporting evidence he or she marshals. You can also write summaries of supporting points — subsections of an author's argument—if they seem applicable to your paper. A summary should not, however, include quotations, exhaustive detail about subpoints, or a list of all the evidence in a given source. A summary is meant to provide a succinct overview—to demonstrate that you have grasped a point and can convey it to your readers.

Chances are you will want to take more specific notes as well, ones that **paraphrase** the most germane passages in a particular source. Unlike a summary, a paraphrase does not condense an argument or leave out supporting evidence; instead it puts the information into new words. A paraphrase is generally no shorter than the material being paraphrased, but it still has two advantages over a quotation. First, as with a summary, an accurate paraphrase proves that you understand the material you've read. Second, again as with a summary, a paraphrase is easier to integrate into your paper than a quotation, since it is already written in your own words and style. When you include a paraphrase in your notes, indicate on the note the page numbers in the original source.

The rule of thumb about summarizing or paraphrasing is that you must always clearly indicate which ideas are yours and which are those of others. It is **plagiarism**—a serious violation of academic standards—to accept credit for another's ideas, even if you put them in your own words. Ideas in your paper that are not attributed to a source will be assumed to be your own, so to avoid plagiarism, it is important to leave no doubt in your reader's mind about when you are summarizing or paraphrasing. Always cite the source.

To see better what we mean, look first at the following sentence, which is about the heroine of Charlotte Perkins Gilman's short story "The Yellow Wallpaper." The sentence comes from page 523 of Greg Johnson's article "Gilman's Gothic Allegory: Rage and Redemption in 'The Yellow Wallpaper,'" published in a 1989 issue of the Journal *Studies in Short Fiction*. Many readers of Gilman's story believe that its ending is negative. They think the protagonist goes completely mad, to her terrible misfortune. Johnson, however, disagrees:

> Her experience should finally be viewed not as a final catastrophe but as a terrifying, necessary stage in her progress toward self-identity and personal achievement.

Imagine that you are writing a paper on Gilman's story and that you want to express your approval of Johnson's view. You might quote at least part of his statement and give him credit for it:

> A more useful way to interpret the ending is to regard it optimistically, as Greg Johnson does when he says that although the heroine's behavior is "terrifying," it is also a "necessary stage in her progress toward self-identity and personal achievement" (523).

Alternatively, you can paraphrase Johnson's claim, acknowledging that he is the source of it and noting the page where it appears:

> Greg Johnson points out helpfully that at the end of the story, the
> heroine may seem doomed but actually is not, for she has to engage
> in such frightening behavior if she is eventually to become a ful-
> filled, accomplished individual (523).

You would be committing plagiarism, however, if you presented Johnson's claim as your own. This would be the case if you reproduced his exact statement without admitting that it's his. But you would also be plagiarizing if you paraphrased his idea without noting it's his:

> At the end of the story, the heroine may seem doomed but actually is
> not, for she has to engage in such frightening behavior if she is
> eventually to become a fulfilled, accomplished individual.

What *does not* need to be referenced is **common knowledge**: factual information that the average reader can be expected to know or that is readily available in many easily accessible sources. For example, it is common knowledge that Charlotte Perkins Gilman was an American writer. It is also common knowledge that she was born in 1860 and died in 1935, even though most people would have to look that information up in an encyclopedia or a biographical dictionary to verify it.

Of course, during your process of research, you will sometimes want to copy quotations directly from a source. Do so sparingly, copying quotations only when the author's own words are especially succinct and pertinent. When you write down a quotation, enclose it in quotation marks, and record the *exact* wording, right down to the punctuation. As with a paraphrase, make note of the original page numbers for the quotation, as you will need to indicate this in your final paper.

Each time you take a note, be it summary, paraphrase, or quotation, take a moment to think about why you wrote it down. Why is this particular note from this source important? Write a brief commentary about the note's importance, maybe just a sentence or a few words, perhaps on the back of a note card (if you are using note cards). When the time comes to draft your paper, such commentaries will help you remember why you bothered to take the note and may restart your train of thought if it gets stuck.

And do not forget: if something you read in a source sparks an original idea, write it down and label it clearly as your own. Keep these notes with your notes from the primary and secondary sources. Without your own ideas, your paper will be little more than a report, a record of what others have said. Your ideas will provide the framework for an argument that is your own.

Strategies for Integrating Sources

With your research completed (at least for the moment), it is time to get down to drafting the paper. At this point, many students find themselves overwhelmed with information and wonder if they are really in any better shape to begin writing than they were before starting their research. But having read and thought about a number of authors' ideas and arguments, you are almost certainly more prepared to construct an argument of your own. You can, of course, use any method that has worked for you in the past to devise a first draft of your paper. If you are having trouble getting started, though, you might look to Chapters 4 and 5 of this book, which discuss general strategies for exploring, planning, and drafting papers as well as more specific ideas for working with individual literary genres.

Start by revisiting your tentative claim. Refine it to take into account what you have learned during your research. With your revised and refined claim at hand, examine your assembled notes, and try to subdivide them into groups of related ideas, each of which can form a single section of your paper or even a single piece of supporting evidence for your claim. You can then arrange the groups of notes according to a logical developmental pattern — for example, from cause to effect or from weakest to strongest evidence — which may provide a structure for the body of your essay. As you write, avoid using your own comments as a kind of glue to hold together other people's ideas. Instead, you are constructing an argument of your own, using secondary sources to support your own structure of claims and evidence.

Anytime you summarize, paraphrase, or quote another author, it should be clear how this author's ideas or words relate to your own argument. Keep in mind that, in your final paper, it is quite unlikely that every note you took deserves a place. Be prepared to discard any notes that do not, in some fashion, support your claim and strengthen your argument. Remember also that direct quotations should be used sparingly for greatest effect; papers that rely too heavily on them make for choppy reading. By contrast, summaries and paraphrases are in your own words and should be a clean and easy fit with your prose style.

When you quote directly from either primary or secondary sources, you will need to follow special conventions of format and style. When quoting up to four lines of prose or three lines of poetry, integrate the quotation directly into your paragraph, enclosing the quoted material in double quotation marks and checking to make sure that the quotation accurately reflects the original. Longer quotations are set off from the text by starting a new line and indenting one inch on the left margin only; these are called **block quotations**. For these, quotation marks are omitted since the indention is enough to indicate that the material is a quotation. Examples of the correct format for both long and short quotations appear in Katie Johnson's paper (pp. 213–216).

When a short quotation is from a poem, line breaks in the poem are indicated by slash marks, with single spaces on either side. The following example demonstrates the format for a short quotation, in this case from Yusef Komunyakaa's poem "Blackberries" (featured in Chapter 5). The numbers in parentheses specify which lines in the poem are being quoted:

> The poem's speaker recalls the scene as sinister, noting: "The big blue car made me sweat. / Wintertime crawled out of the windows" (19–20).

While it is essential to quote accurately, sometimes you may need to alter a quotation slightly, either by deleting text for brevity or by adding or changing text to incorporate it grammatically. If you delete words from a quotation, indicate the deletion by inserting an ellipsis (three periods with spaces between them), as demonstrated by the following quotation from Robert Frost's poem "Mending Wall" (Chapter 3):

> The speaker makes his neighbor sound warlike, describing him as "Bringing a stone . . . / In each hand, like an old-stone savage armed" (39–40).

If you need to change or add words for clarity or grammatical correctness, indicate the changes with square brackets. If, for instance, you wanted to clarify the meaning of "They" in Komunyakaa's opening line "They left my hands like a printer's," you could do so like this:

> The speaker recalls that "[the blackberries] left my hands like a printer's" (1).

In addition to these format considerations, remember a few general rules of thumb as you deploy primary and secondary sources in your paper. First, without stinting on necessary information, keep quotations as short as possible—your argument will flow more smoothly if you do. Quotations long enough to be blocked should be relatively rare. Second, never assume that a quotation is self-sufficient or its meaning self-evident. Every time you put a quotation in your paper, take the time to introduce it clearly and comment on it to demonstrate why you chose to include it in the first place. Finally, quote fairly and accurately, and stick to a consistent format (such as the MLA style explained in the next section) when giving credit to your sources.

Strategies for Documenting Sources (MLA Format)

Documentation is the means by which you give credit to the authors of all primary and secondary sources cited within a research paper. It serves two principal purposes: (1) it allows your readers to find out more about the origin of the ideas you present, and (2) it protects you from charges of plagiarism. Every academic discipline follows slightly different conventions for documentation, but the method most commonly used for writing about literature is the format devised by the Modern Language Association (MLA). This documentation method encompasses **in-text citations**, which briefly identify within the body of your paper the source of a particular quotation, summary, or paraphrase, and a bibliography, called **Works Cited**, which gives more complete publication information.

While mastering the precise requirements of MLA punctuation and format can be time-consuming and even frustrating, getting them right adds immeasurably to the professionalism of a finished paper. More detailed information, including special circumstances and documentation styles for types of sources not covered here, will be found in the *MLA Handbook for Writers of Research Papers*, Seventh Edition (New York: Modern Language Association, 2009). Of course, if your instructor requests that you follow a different documentation method, you should follow his or her instructions instead.

MLA IN-TEXT CITATION

Each time you include information from any outside source—whether in the form of a summary, a paraphrase, or a quotation—you must provide your reader with a brief reference indicating the author and page number of the original. This reference directs the reader to the Works Cited list, where more complete information is available.

There are two basic methods for in-text citation. The first, and usually preferable, method is to include the author's name in the text of your essay and note the page number in parentheses at the end of the citation. The following paraphrase and quotation from "The Yellow Wallpaper" show the format to be followed for this method. Note that the page number (without the abbreviation "pg." or additional punctuation) is enclosed within parentheses and that the final punctuation for the sentence occurs after the parenthetical reference, effectively making the reference part of the preceding sentence. For a direct quotation, the closing quotation marks come before the page reference, but the final period is still saved until after the reference.

> Gilman's narrator believes her husband trivializes her disorder (230).

> Gilman's narrator sadly reports that her husband considers her disorder to be just "a slight hysterical tendency" (230).

The method is similar for long quotations (those set off from the main text of your essay). The only differences are that the final punctuation mark comes before the parenthetical page reference, and that the quotation is not enclosed within quotation marks.

In those cases where citing the author's name in your text would be awkward or difficult, you may include both the author's last name and the page reference in the parenthetical citation. The following example draws a quotation from Greg Johnson's article about Gilman's story.

> According to one interpreter of the story, the heroine's final behavior is a "necessary stage in her progress toward self-identity and personal achievement" (Johnson 523).

Knowing the last name of the author is enough to allow your reader to find out more about the reference in the Works Cited, and having the page number makes it easy to find the original of the quotation, summary, or paraphrase should your reader choose to. The only time more information is needed is if you cite more than one work by the same author. In this case, you will need to specify from which of the author's works a particular citation comes. Electronic sources, such as CD-ROMs and Internet sources, are generally not divided into numbered pages. If you cite from such a source, the parenthetical reference need include only the author's last name (or, if the work is anonymous, an identifying title).

MLA WORKS CITED

The second feature of the MLA format is the Works Cited list, or bibliography. This list should begin on a new page of your paper and should be double-spaced throughout and use hanging indention, which means that all lines except the first are indented one-half inch. The list is alphabetized by author's last name (or by the title in the case of anonymous works) and includes every primary and secondary source referred to in your paper. The format for the most common types of entries is given below. If any of the information called for is unavailable for a particular source, simply skip that element and keep the rest of the entry as close as possible to the given format. An anonymous work, for instance, skips the author's name and is alphabetized under the title.

Books

Entries in your Works Cited for books should contain as much of the following information as is available to you. Follow the order and format exactly as given, with a period after each numbered element below (between author and title, and so on). Not all of these elements will be needed for most books. Copy the information directly from the title and publication pages of the book, not from a library catalog or other reference, because these sources often leave out some information.

1. The name of the author (or editor, if no author is listed, or organization in the case of a corporate author), last name first.
2. The full title, in italics. If the book has a subtitle, put a colon between title and subtitle.
3. The name(s) of the editor(s), if the book has both an author and an editor, following the abbreviation "Ed."
4. The name(s) of the translator or compiler, following the abbreviation "Trans." or "Comp.," as appropriate.
5. The edition, if other than the first.
6. The volume(s) used, if the book is part of a multivolume set.
7. The city of publication (followed by a colon), name of the publisher (comma), and year.
8. The medium of publication (Print, Web, etc.), followed by a period.
9. The name of any series to which the book belongs.

The examples below cover the most common types of books you will encounter.

A book by a single author or editor.   Simply follow the elements and format as listed above. The first example below is for a book by a single author; note also the abbreviation "UP," for "University Press." The second example is a book by a single editor. The third is for a book with both an author (Conrad) and an editor (Murfin); note also that it is a third edition and a book in a series, so these facts are listed as well.

> Cima, Gay Gibson. *Performing Women: Female Characters, Male Playwrights, and the Modern Stage*. Ithaca: Cornell UP, 1993. Print.
>
> Tucker, Robert C., ed. *The Marx-Engels Reader*. New York: Norton, 1972. Print.
>
> Conrad, Joseph. *Heart of Darkness*. Ed. Ross C. Murfin. 3rd ed. Boston: Bedford, 2011. Print. Case Studies in Contemporary Criticism.

A book with multiple authors or editors.   If a book has two or three authors or editors, list all names, but note that only the first name is given last name first and the rest are in normal order. In cases where a book has four or more authors or editors, give only the first name listed on the title page, followed by a comma and the phrase "et al." (Latin for "and others").

> Leeming, David, and Jake Page. *God: Myths of the Male Divine*. New York: Oxford UP, 1996. Print.
>
> Arrow, Kenneth Joseph, et al., eds. *Education in a Research University*. Stanford: Stanford UP, 1996. Print.

A book with a corporate author.   When a book has a group, government agency, or other organization listed as its author, treat that organization in your Works Cited just as you would a single author.

> National Conference on Undergraduate Research. *Proceedings of the National Conference on Undergraduate Research*. Asheville: U of North Carolina P, 1995. Print.

Short Works from Collections and Anthologies

Many scholarly books are collections of articles on a single topic by several different authors. When you cite an article from such a collection, include the information given below. The format is the same for works of literature that appear in an anthology, such as this one.

1. The name of the author(s) of the article or literary work.
2. The title of the short work, enclosed in quotation marks.
3. The title of the anthology, italicized.
4. The name(s) of the editor(s) of the collection or anthology.
5. All relevant publication information, in the same order and format as it would appear in a book citation. Include edition number if not the first.
6. The inclusive page numbers for the shorter work.
7. The medium of publication.

A single work from a collection or an anthology.   If you are citing only one article or literary work from any given collection or anthology, simply follow the format outlined above and demonstrated in the following examples.

Kirk, Russell. "Eliot's Christian Imagination." *The Placing of T. S. Eliot*. Ed. Jewel Spears Brooker. Columbia: U of Missouri P, 1991. 136–44. Print.

Silko, Leslie Marmon. "Yellow Woman." *Making Literature Matter: An Anthology for Readers and Writers*. Ed. John Schilb and John Clifford. 6th ed. Boston: Bedford, 2015. 632–639. Print.

Multiple works from the same collection or anthology.   If you are citing more than one short work from a single collection or anthology, it is often more efficient to set up a **cross-reference**. This means first writing a single general entry that provides full publication information for the collection or anthology as a whole. The entries for the shorter works then contain only the author and title of the shorter work, the names of the editors of the book, and the page numbers of the shorter work. The example below shows an entry for a short story cross-referenced with a general entry for this book; note that the entries remain in alphabetical order in your Works Cited, regardless of whether the general or specialized entry comes first.

Faulkner, William. "A Rose for Emily." Schilb and Clifford 000–00.

Schilb, John, and John Clifford, eds. *Making Literature Matter: An Anthology for Readers and Writers*. 6th ed. Boston: Bedford, 2015. Print.

Works in Periodicals

The following information should be included, in the given order and format, when you cite articles and other short works from journals, magazines, or newspapers.

1. The name(s) of the author(s) of the short work.
2. The title of the short work, in quotation marks.
3. The title of the periodical, italicized.
4. All relevant publication information as explained in the examples below.
5. The inclusive page numbers for the shorter work.
6. The medium of publication.

A work in a scholarly journal.   Publication information for works from scholarly and professional journals should include the volume number and the issue number, separated by a period; the year of publication in parentheses, followed by a colon; the page numbers of the shorter work; and the medium of publication.

Charles, Casey. "Gender Trouble in *Twelfth Night*." *Theatre Journal* 49.2 (1997): 121–41. Print.

An article in a magazine.   Publication information for articles in general-circulation magazines includes the month(s) of publication for a monthly (or bimonthly), or the date (day, abbreviated month, then year) for a weekly or bi-weekly, followed by a colon, the page numbers of the article, and the medium of publication.

> Cowley, Malcolm. "It Took a Village." *Utne Reader* Nov.–Dec. 1997:
> 48–49. Print.
> Levy, Steven. "On the Net, Anything Goes." *Newsweek* 7 July 1997:
> 28–30. Print.

An article in a newspaper.   When citing an article from a newspaper, include the date (day, abbreviated month, year) and the edition if one is listed on the masthead, followed by a colon, the page numbers (including the section number or letter, if applicable), and the medium of publication.

> Cobb, Nathan. "How to Dig Up a Family Tree." *Boston Globe* 9 Mar.
> 1998: C7. Print.

CD-ROMs

CD-ROMs come in two basic types: those published in a single edition—including major reference works like dictionaries and encyclopedias—and those published serially on a regular basis. In a Works Cited list, the first type is treated like a book and the second like a periodical. Details of citation appear in the following examples.

Single-edition CD-ROMs.   An entry for a single-edition CD-ROM is formatted like one for a book, but with "CD-ROM" as the medium of publication. Most CD-ROMs are divided into smaller subsections, and these should be treated like short works from anthologies.

> "Realism." *The Oxford English Dictionary*. 2nd ed. Oxford: Oxford UP,
> 1992. CD-ROM.

Serial CD-ROMs.   Treat information published on periodically released CD-ROMs just as you would articles in print periodicals, but also include the title of the CD-ROM, italicized; the word *CD-ROM*; the name of the vendor distributing the CD-ROM; and the date of electronic publication. Many such CD-ROMs contain reprints and abstracts of print works, and in these cases, the publisher and date for the print version should be listed as well, preceding the information for the electronic version.

> Brodie, James Michael, and Barbara K. Curry. *Sweet Words So Brave:*
> *The Story of African American Literature*. Madison: Knowledge Un-
> limited, 1996. CD-ROM. *ERIC*. SilverPlatter. 1997.

The Internet

Internet sources fall into several categories—World Wide Web documents and postings to newsgroups, listservs, and so on. Documentation for these sources should include as much of the following information as is available, in the order and format specified.

1. The name of the author(s), last name first (as for a print publication).
2. The title of the section of the work accessed (the subject line for e-mails and postings) in quotation marks.
3. The title of the Web site in italics.
4. The name of the sponsor or publisher of the Web site.
5. The date the material was published or updated.
6. The medium of publication.
7. The date you access a site.

The examples below show entries for a Web site and a newsgroup citation, two of the most common sorts of Internet sources.

> Brandes, Jay. "Maya Angelou: A Bibliography of Literary Criticism."
>   Troy University, 20 Aug. 1997. Web. 10 June 2009.
> Broun, Mike. "Jane Austen Video Package Launched." *Google groups*.
>   Google, 1 Mar. 1998. Web. 10 June 2009.

Personal Communication

In some cases you may get information directly from another person, either by conducting an interview or by receiving correspondence. In this case, include in your Works Cited the name of the person who gave you the information, the type of communication you had with that person, the date of the communication, and the medium if other than a personal interview.

> Aburrow, Clare. Message to the author. 15 Apr. 2004. E-mail.
> McCorkle, Patrick. Personal interview. 12 Mar. 2004.

Multiple Works by the Same Author

If you cite more than one work (in any medium) by a single author, the individual works are alphabetized by title. The author's full name is given only for the first citation in the Works Cited, after which it is replaced by three hyphens. The rest of the citation follows whatever format is appropriate for the medium of the source. The following two entries are for a work in an anthology and a book, both by the same author.

> Faulkner, William. "A Rose for Emily." *Making Literature Matter: An An-*
>   *thology for Readers and Writers*. 6th ed. Ed. John Schilb and John
>   Clifford. Boston: Bedford, 2015. 000–00. Print.
> - - - . *The Sound and the Fury*. New York: Modern Library, 1956. Print.

Occasionally, you may have an idea or find a piece of information that seems important to your paper but that you just cannot work in smoothly without interrupting the flow of ideas. Such information can be included in the form of **endnotes**. A small superscript number in your text signals a note, and the notes themselves appear on a separate page at the end of your paper, before the Works Cited.

Five Annotated Student Researched Arguments

A PAPER THAT USES A LITERARY WORK TO EXAMINE SOCIAL ISSUES

Some research papers mention a literary work but then focus on examining a social issue related to that work. An example of such a paper is the following essay by student Sarah Michaels. To prepare for writing her paper, Sarah consulted numerous sources, and she turns to them during the course of her essay. The chief danger in a project like this is that it will become a mere "data dump" — that is, a paper in which the writer uncritically cites one source after another without really making an original argument. In writing an essay like Sarah's, be sure to identify your main issue and claim clearly. Present yourself as someone who is genuinely *testing* your sources, determining the specific ways in which they are relevant to your argument. Keep in mind that even if you are representing a source as useful, you can indicate how its ideas need to be further complicated. With at least some of your sources, analyze specific terms they employ, lingering over their language. Moreover, try to relate your sources to one another, orchestrating them into a well-organized conversation. We think Sarah accomplishes all these objectives. Even if you disagree, aim to practice them yourself.

Sarah Michaels
Professor Swain
English L202
21 May - - - -

"The Yellow Wallpaper" as a Guide
to Social Factors in Postpartum Depression
    In 2005, actor Brooke Shields's memoir *Down Came the Rain: My Journey through Postpartum Depression* drew much public attention to the psychological problem mentioned in its subtitle.[1] But during the last couple of decades, postpartum depression has been the subject of reports by many medical institutions and media outlets. By now, lots of people other than health professionals are aware of this problem and can at least roughly define it. If asked, most of them would probably say that although it can exhibit varying degrees of severity, postpartum depression is basically a state of despair suffered by a significant number of women who have just given birth. This is, in fact, the main image of it presented in a recent document about it, an October 2010 report by Marian Earls and a committee of the American Academy of Pediatrics.

Calls attention to an endnote.

Quickly identifies social issue that the paper will focus on.

Besides explaining what postpartum depression is, the report urges pediatricians and other primary care providers to screen new mothers for it. Given that many members of the public already know that the problem is widespread, the report has not sparked much disagreement. Responding to it in the on-line magazine *Slate*, however, Emily Anthes does challenge its almost total emphasis on mothers. She argues that the Academy's committee makes a questionable assumption in writing as if only females are traumatized by birth. In her article entitled "Dads Get Blue, Too," she criticizes the report's authors for not acknowledging at greater length that new fathers can experience postpartum depression as well.[2] More generally, her article suggests that discussions of this disorder can be skewed by ideological views that need to be recognized. But, more than a century ago, Charlotte Perkins Gilman's story "The Yellow Wallpaper" made pretty much the same point, by showing how a woman diagnosed with a label like postpartum depression is a victim of her domestic circumstances and her society's ideas about gender, not just a person who has become ill on her own. When juxtaposed with the Academy's report, Gilman's 1892 tale is a reminder that today's doctors should look beyond an individual woman's symptoms of post-birth distress, because the social arrangements in which she lives may significantly affect her health.

Introduces the literary work that the paper will relate to the social issue.

The term *postpartum depression* has for a long time appeared in analyses of "The Yellow Wallpaper" and of the personal experience that Gilman based the story on. Veronica Makowsky points out that this clinical phrase has even "become a critical commonplace" (329) in studies of the relationship between the story and Gilman's life. Gilman does not, however, actually use the term *postpartum depression* in the tale. Instead, the heroine's husband, John, declares that she suffers from "temporary nervous depression — a slight hysterical tendency" (233), and the character herself refers to her "nervous troubles" (235). Nor does Gilman bring up the term in her accounts of the real-life despair she went through when she gave birth to her daughter. In her essay "Why I Wrote 'The Yellow Wallpaper,'" she recalls being tormented much of her life by "a severe and continuous nervous breakdown tending to melancholia" (245). In her book-length autobiography *The Living of Charlotte Perkins Gilman*, she describes herself as suffering from "nervous prostration" (90). Indeed, the *Oxford English Dictionary*'s entry for *postpartum depression* indicates that the term was not recorded until 1929, when it showed up in an issue of the *American Journal of Psychiatry*.

Concedes that the term is used by scholars rather than by the author herself.

Nevertheless, the phrase does seem to fit the condition of Gilman's narrator. According to the American Academy of Pediatrics report, the symptoms of postpartum depression can range from "crying, worrying, sadness, anxiety, and mood swings" to more disturbing signs like "paranoia, mood shifts, hallucinations, [and] delusions" (1033). Gilman's character can be said to display most of these things once her child is born. At the estate that is the story's setting, she has trouble sleeping, she comes to doubt her husband's love, and, most dramatically, she rips off the wallpaper in her bedroom to free a woman whom she imagines wanting to creep away.

Directly connects language of the report to the story.

But simply labeling the heroine's distress as postpartum depression risks ignoring the conditions surrounding her that contribute to her suffering. Commenting on "The Yellow Wallpaper," literary critic Paula A. Treichler points out that a medical diagnosis can block understanding of "social, cultural, and economic practices" (69), even though these may support the doctor's claim to expertise, play a role in the patient's anguish, and become more important to confront than the patient's individual pain. In Gilman's story, John uses his social authority as physician and husband to control his wife. Specifically, he isolates her on the estate and makes her give up real activity, just as Gilman's real-life doctor, S. Weir Mitchell, demanded that she rest. As a result, the heroine feels obligated to surrender to the stereotypical passive female role, even though she would welcome more interaction with others and suspects that "congenial work, with excitement and change, would do me good" (233). When she proceeds to hallucinate the woman in the wallpaper, this is something that she is *driven* to do by John's assertion of masculine power, just as Weir Mitchell's prescription for inertia drove Gilman "near the border line of utter mental ruin" ("Why" 245).

Uses another interpreter of the story to advance this paper's argument.

Key quote from the story.

With "The Yellow Wallpaper" in mind, readers of the American Academy of Pediatrics report might examine how it downplays what Treichler calls "social, cultural, and economic practices" in its focus on diagnosing postpartum depression in women. Although the report does note that "Paternal depression is estimated at 6%" (1032), it does not linger on this fairly significant figure. In addition, the committee mentions only in passing that while "as many as 12% of all pregnant or postpartum women experience depression in a given year," the percentage is twice as much "for low-income women" (1032). Similarly brief is the recognition that "Eighteen percent of fathers of children in Early Head Start had symptoms of depression" (1033), a distinctly high figure that again suggests one's social class can affect one's health. Nor

Uses the story to examine the issue raised by the report.

Paper works with specific examples and language from the report.

does the report develop its brief notice that possible causes
of postpartum depression include "domestic violence" (1034),
which would be a serious problem in the patient's environment rather than a malfunction within the patient herself.
Instead of insisting that "Treatment must address the mother-
child dyad relationship" (1036), the committee might also
have called for addressing the chance that the mother suffers
from a lack of money or the presence of an abusive partner.

Juxtaposing Gilman's story with the Academy's report
does not mean that readers of this recent document about
postpartum depression have to declare its authors evil. The
attitudes and recommendations of the committee are not as
morally disturbing as those of Gilman's character John. But
her story should encourage the report's readers to notice
where, in its call for screening women for postpartum depression, it risks screening *out* social influences on people diagnosed with this clinical problem.

*Heads off possible
misunderstanding.*

Endnotes

[1] Shields also discussed her postpartum depression in a *New
York Times* op-ed column, in which she defended herself
against actor Tom Cruise's charge that she should have relied
on vitamins and exercise rather than on the prescription drug
Paxil.

[2] For an article that supports Anthes's attention to fathers
even though she does not mention it, see Kim and Swain.

*The endnotes provide
additional information not
easily incorporated into the
paper's main text.*

Works Cited

Anthes, Emily. "Dads Get Blue, Too." *Slate.com*. Slate, 4 Nov. 2010. Web. 9 Nov. 2010.   *Citation for an online article.*

Earls, Marian F., and the Committee on Psychosocial Aspects of Child and Family Health. "Clinical Report: Incorporating Recognition and Management of Perinatal and Postpartum Depression into Pediatric Practice." *Pediatrics. org*. Pediatrics, 25 Oct. 2010. Web. 9 Nov. 2010.

Gilman, Charlotte Perkins. *The Living of Charlotte Perkins Gilman: An Autobiography*. New York: Arno Press, 1972. Print.   *Citation for a book.*

---. "Why I Wrote 'The Yellow Wallpaper.'" Schilb and Clifford 245–246.   *Note style for multiple works by same author. Note, too, that when you cite more than one work from the same book, you give each book its own entry and cite each work from it in the shorthand form you see here.*

---. "The Yellow Wallpaper." Schilb and Clifford 231–244.

Kim, Pilyoung, and James E. Swain. "Sad Dads: Paternal Postpartum Depression." *Psychiatry* Feb. 2007: 36–47. Print.

Makowsky, Veronica. "Fear of Feeling and the Turn-of-the-Century Woman of Letters." *American Literary History* 5.2 (1993): 326–34. Print.

Schilb, John, and John Clifford, eds. *Making Literature Matter: An Anthology for Readers and Writers*. 6th ed. Boston: Bedford, 2015. Print.

Shields, Brooke. *Down Came the Rain: My Journey through Postpartum Depression*. New York: Hyperion, 2005. Print.

---. "War of Words." *New York Times* 1 July 2005, late ed.: A17. Print.

Treichler, Paula A. "Escaping the Sentence: Diagnosis and Discourse in 'The Yellow Wallpaper.'" *Tulsa Studies in Women's Literature* 3.1/2 (1984): 61–77. Print.   *Citation for a print article.*

A PAPER THAT DEALS WITH EXISTING INTERPRETATIONS OF A LITERARY WORK

A research paper assignment may require you to develop a claim about a literary work by relating your analysis to previous interpretations of the text. An example of a paper like this is the following essay, in which student Katie Johnson makes an argument about Charlotte Perkins Gilman's story "The Yellow Wallpaper" by incorporating statements made by people who have already written about it. To prepare for writing her paper, she especially consulted the *MLA International Bibliography*, through which she located several published articles about Gilman's tale. The bibliographies of these articles led her to still more interpretations of the story. The biggest challenge in writing a paper like this is to stay focused on developing an idea of your own, rather than just inserting and echoing opinions held by others. Katie ended up examining an element of Gilman's story that she felt had not been adequately noted, let alone properly interpreted, by literary critics. As her essay proceeds, therefore, she does not simply agree with all the interpreters she cites. She treats with respect, however, those she finds fault with, civilly pointing out how her own thoughts differ. In addition, she clearly takes seriously the specific language of the critics she mentions, pondering their actual words rather than superficially summarizing their views.

Katie Johnson
Professor Van Wyck
English L141
5 May - - - -

The Meaning of the Husband's Fainting
in "The Yellow Wallpaper"

At the end of Charlotte Perkins Gilman's short story "The Yellow Wallpaper," the narrator is in a state that many people observing her would consider madness. She has torn off the wallpaper in her room and now seems proud of being able to "creep smoothly on the floor" (000). Her outwardly bizarre behavior at this point, along with her telling of the whole story beforehand, has led most literary critics to focus on analyzing her final conduct, as if it was the only really noteworthy feature of this concluding scene. Just as striking, however, is the final behavior of the narrator's husband, John. Up until the ending, he has acted as an authority on his wife's medical condition, and he has tried to assert power by always telling her what to do. At the conclusion, though, his mastery plainly vanishes. After finding the key to his wife's room, letting himself in, and beholding her crawling, he faints. Both the narrator and her husband end up on the floor. The narrator herself is highly aware of John's collapse, as she shows when she complains that "I had to creep over him every time!" (244). Because John's fainting is a dramatic reversal of his previous behavior and resembles the narrator's final physical position, it is surprising that only some literary critics have bothered to comment on John's breakdown, and even then the comments are relatively few. This neglect is a shame because, through John's fainting, Gilman seems to imply that he is left without any clear gender role to support him when his wife defies his manly effort to keep her what his society would consider sane.

Concisely summarizes the story's conclusion in first paragraph, which ends by stating main claim the essay will develop.

Until the last scene, John has repeatedly attempted to control his wife in the way that his society would expect of a man. This effort of his is reinforced by the professional standing he has achieved as a doctor. His masculine authority is interconnected with his medical authority. As we readers are made aware, he does not succeed in thoroughly bending his wife's will to his. Much of her narration is about her secret rebellion against him, which takes the form of imagining women trapped in the wallpaper of her room. Despite her hidden thoughts, however, he is often issuing commands to her, and she finds it hard to resist his domination. She admits to us that "I take pains to control myself — before him, at least, and that makes me very tired" (234). His attempts at enforcing his power over her include shutting her up in an odd country house in the first place. When she expresses suspicion of the estate, he simply "laughs" and "scoffs" (233), as he seems to do whenever she reveals independent thinking. She also says that he "hardly lets me stir without special direction" and gives her "a schedule prescription for each hour in the day" (234). Furthermore, he discourages her from writing, does not want to let her have visitors, and refuses to leave the estate when she informs him that she is not getting any better. Actually, he treats her more like his child than his wife, which is revealed when he asks "What is it, little girl?" (239) one night when she wakes up bothered by the wallpaper. All in all, he fits the nineteenth-century image of the ideal man as someone who gives his wife orders and expects her to follow them, though John tries to disguise his bossiness by declaring that he loves her and is looking out for her best interests.

The literary critics who do write about John's fainting at the end of the story tend to see it as a moment of irony, because in their view this masculine authority figure winds up physically collapsing in a way that is stereotypically associated with women. For example, Carol Margaret Davison states that when John faints, he is "assuming the traditional role of frail female" (66). Greg Johnson describes John's fall as "Gilman's witty inversion of a conventional heroine's confrontation with Gothic terror" (529), and similarly, Beverly A. Hume says that what happens is that John is "altering his conventional role as a soothing, masculine figure to that of a stereotypically weak nineteenth-century female" (478). These comments are not unreasonable, because during the nineteenth century, fainting was indeed something that women were believed to do more often than men. But a pair of literary critics has made another observation that, even though it sounds like the ones I have just quoted, points in a different direction that seems worth pursuing. Sandra M. Gilbert and Susan Gubar refer to John's fainting as an "unmasculine swoon of surprise" (91). They sound as if they are saying that he now seems feminine, but actually the word "unmasculine"

Synthesizes comments from critics, combining them to indicate the pattern she finds in interpretations of the story.

Does not flatly declare critics "wrong" but will develop an idea they have not mentioned.

simply indicates that he is no longer acting like a stereotypical male, so that readers of the story have to wonder whether he has any kind of identity left to him now. In fact, John's fainting seems like a total falling apart, as if he has become incapable of performing any further role at all, whether it is stereotypically feminine or masculine. Though his wife is creeping, at least she is still able to move, whereas he lies paralyzed. Overall, he appears to suffer a complete loss of identity rather than take on a female identity. Because his wife has fallen into what he sees as madness despite his efforts to control her, he experiences a shattering of his male ego, the result being not that he is left with a "womanly" self but that he now lacks any sense of self at all. Just as he has only leased the estate instead of owning it, so too has his personhood proven impermanent because his ability to treat his wife as his property has apparently gone. At the very end of the story, the narrator even refers to her husband merely as "that man" (244), suggesting that he is no longer recognizable as an individual human being.

Carefully analyzes a particular word that this pair of critics uses. Rest of paragraph develops main claim.

More than one literary critic has argued that John has suffered a loss of power only momentarily and that he will soon dominate his wife just as much as he did before. Judith Fetterley contends that "when John recovers from his faint, he will put her in a prison from which there will be no escape" (164), and Paula Treichler claims that

> As the ending of her narrative, her madness will no doubt commit her to more intense medical treatment, perhaps to the dreaded Weir Mitchell of whom her husband has spoken. The surrender of patriarchy is only temporary; her husband has merely fainted, after all, not died, and will no doubt move swiftly and severely to deal with her. Her individual escape is temporary and compromised. (67)

Because quotation from Treichler is somewhat lengthy, Katie puts it in block form.

Unfortunately, Gilman did not write a sequel called "The Yellow Wallpaper: The Next Day" to let us know exactly what happens to the couple after the husband wakes up. Fetterley and Treichler might have been right if the events of this story had taken place in real life and involved a real married couple. Though it was based on Gilman's actual situation,[1] the story should be treated as a work of fiction, and Gilman has chosen to conclude it by showing John as physically overcome. If she had wanted to suggest that he will quickly regain power, presumably she would have done so. As the text stands, the final scene emphasizes his new weakness, not signs of a strength that will soon be restored to him.

Synthesizes two critics' observations, putting them together as examples of a view that she questions.

Directs readers to endnote.

Disagrees with two critics but carefully explains why and avoids using hostile tone.

Although both the husband and the wife are in a bad physical state at the end, we as readers do not have to sympathize with them equally. Especially by having the wife narrate the story, Gilman has designed it so that we are encouraged to care far more about her than about John. A lot of readers might even feel joy at his collapse, regarding it as the bringing down of a tyrant. In any case, his fainting is worth paying attention to as a sign that he has experienced a loss of masculine power that leaves him unable to function as any kind of self.

Uses final paragraph not only to restate main claim but also to add the point that readers of story do not have to feel as sorry for John as they do for his wife.

Endnote

[1] Gilman recalls the personal experience that motivated her to write her story in her essay "Why I Wrote 'The Yellow Wallpaper.'"

Endnote provides information that could not be easily integrated into main text of essay.

Works Cited

Davison, Carol Margaret. "Haunted House / Haunted Heroine: Female Gothic Closets in 'The Yellow Wallpaper.'" *Women's Studies* 33.1 (2004): 47–75. Print.   *Citation for article in scholarly journal.*

Fetterley, Judith. "Reading about Reading: 'A Jury of Her Peers,' 'The Murders in the Rue Morgue,' and 'The Yellow Wallpaper.'" *Gender and Reading: Essays on Readers, Texts, and Contexts*. Ed. Elizabeth A. Flynn and Patrocinio P. Schweickart. Baltimore: Johns Hopkins UP, 1986. 147–64. Print.   *Citation for work in anthology.*

Gilbert, Sandra M., and Susan Gubar. *The Madwoman in the Attic: The Woman Writer and the Nineteenth-Century Literary Imagination*. New Haven: Yale UP, 1979. Print.   *Citation for book.*

Gilman, Charlotte Perkins. "Why I Wrote 'The Yellow Wallpaper.'" Schilb and Clifford 245–246.   *Note style for multiple works by the same author. Note, too, that when you cite more than one work from the same book, you give the book its own entry and then cite each work from it in the shorthand form you see here.*

- - - . "The Yellow Wallpaper." Schilb and Clifford 231–244.

Hume, Beverly A. "Gilman's 'Interminable Grotesque': The Narrator of 'The Yellow Wallpaper.'" *Studies in Short Fiction* 28.4 (1991): 477–84. Print.

Johnson, Greg. "Gilman's Gothic Allegory: Rage and Redemption in 'The Yellow Wallpaper.'" *Studies in Short Fiction* 26.4 (1989): 521–30. Print.

Schilb, John, and John Clifford, eds. *Making Literature Matter: An Anthology for Readers and Writers*. 6th ed. Boston: Bedford, 2015. Print.   *Citation for anthology.*

Treichler, Paula A. "Escaping the Sentence: Diagnosis and Discourse in 'The Yellow Wallpaper.'" *Tulsa Studies in Women's Literature* 3.1/2 (1984): 61–77. Print.

A PAPER THAT ANALYZES A LITERARY WORK THROUGH THE FRAMEWORK OF A PARTICULAR THEORIST

In the appendix, we explain how to write a research paper that takes one of the critical approaches now popular in literary theory. Some research papers, however, make an argument about a literary work by applying to it the ideas of a single theorist. Often, this is someone whose concepts have already influenced many scholars. Perhaps this person has even pioneered an entire field of thought. Examples include the father of psychoanalysis, Sigmund Freud; the founder of Marxist theory, Karl Marx; leading voices of existentialism such as Friedrich Nietzsche and Martin Heidegger; and the modern feminist writer Virginia Woolf.

If you attempt a paper like this, the theorist you choose might not have read the literary work you discuss. Even so, his or her ideas can illuminate it. Of course, you need to summarize the theorist's thinking in a manner that is both helpful and concise. Instead of just offering scattered, random passages from this person's writing, try to provide an efficient overview of the theorist's basic *framework*: that is, the main ideas that this figure contributes. You will especially want to specify the ideas that are most helpful for interpreting your chosen literary text. In essence, you will be using these concepts as a *lens*. Your paper can, however, admit that the theorist's principles do not cover *everything* important in the text. Probably you will be more credible to your reader if you concede that while the theorist's framework is useful, it provides a less-than-exact explanation. In fact, you will be seen more as developing a claim of your own if you point out the *limits* of the theorist's ideas along with their strengths. This is what student Jacob Grobowicz does in the following paper. His essay applies to "The Yellow Wallpaper" the ideas of the late Michel Foucault, a French theorist whose writings about modern power relations have inspired scholars in the social sciences and humanities. But Jacob does not simply quote from Foucault's writings. Instead, he critically examines the lens he provides, arguing that it clarifies major parts of the story but does not account for them all.

Jacob Grobowicz
Professor Burke
English L202
10 May - - - -

Using Foucault to Understand Disciplinary Power
in Gilman's "The Yellow Wallpaper"

Michel Foucault provides a useful framework for understanding the narrator's experiences in Charlotte Perkins Gilman's 1892 short story "The Yellow Wallpaper." More specifically, the theory of power that Foucault puts forth in his book *Discipline and Punish*[1] sheds light on the narrator's frustration with the "rest cure" that her husband makes her undergo. Of course, any perspective on a literary work may neglect some aspects of it. As a slant on Gilman's story, Foucault's book does have limits. In particular, *Discipline and Punish* does not pay much attention to gender, a significant element of the narrator's life. Still, quite relevant to her situation is Foucault's central argument in the book, which is that "discipline" is the main form of power in the modern age.

When Foucault refers to "discipline" in his book, he has two meanings of the term in mind, though he sees them as closely related to each other. First, human beings have become "disciplined" in the sense that they feel pressured to follow the standards held by all sorts of authorities. According to his historical account, power was previously associated with the figure of the king. Judges were a narrow group of

Directs reader to an endnote.

Immediately establishes what literary work the paper will focus on, as well as what theorist and what specific text by that theorist.

The paper's main claim, which identifies which of the theorist's concepts the paper will apply to the story.

Begins a two-paragraph section that summarizes relevant details of theorist's framework and defines a key term of his.

officials who carried out the will of the monarch by punishing
blatant violators of the law. Foucault also points out that the
punishment usually took the form of physical imprisonment.
The emphasis was on confinement of the criminal's body, not
on reform of the criminal's soul. Foucault views the modern
era, however, as a major shift from this state of affairs. He
declares that nowadays, the administrators of power are more
widespread: "The judges of normality are everywhere. We are
in the society of the teacher-judge, the doctor-judge, the
educator-judge, the 'social-worker' judge" (304). Furthermore,
these figures look beyond sheer criminals and try to control
all humanity. In fact, they aim to mold human beings' basic
thinking, a goal they pursue by getting people to adopt
conformist ideas and values promoted by various fields of
expertise. Increasingly, Foucault claims, human beings are
kept in place through forms of training, knowledge, and
examination that are developed and advanced by academic
and professional specialties — "disciplines" in the second
sense of the word. Foucault argues that although these fields
pose as benevolent "sciences of man," they actually participate in "the modern play of coercion over bodies, gestures
and behavior" (191).

   Discipline and Power stresses this idea by spending many
pages on the image of the Panopticon. This is a model for a
prison, proposed in the nineteenth century by British philosopher Jeremy Bentham. He envisioned a penitentiary with a
central tower whose guards could observe all of the surrounding cells. The prisoners would feel constantly threatened by
the tower's gaze, even though they could not be sure when
the building was actually occupied. Eventually, their insecurity would drive them to monitor and restrict their conduct on
their own, thereby doing the guards' work. Foucault brings up
the Panopticon to argue that while institutions still engage in
external surveillance — watching people in various ways —
fields of expertise now serve dominant forces by leading
people to engage in *self*-surveillance. In this respect, power
can be said to *produce* the self rather than simply repress it.

   Of all the experts that Foucault mentions in *Discipline and
Power*, the one most significant to the narrator of "The Yellow
Wallpaper" is "the doctor-judge." Suffering from a depression
that seems related to her having recently given birth, she is
in the hands of a physician named John who is also her
husband. His diagnosis of her is reinforced by her brother,
who is a doctor as well. Moreover, when the narrator fails to
get physically better as fast as John would like, he threatens
to deliver her over to S. Weir Mitchell, the real-life medical

*Paper now begins directly
connecting theorist's ideas
to specific details of the
story.*

expert whose rest cure proved unendurable to Gilman herself.
By linking three physicians to each other — John, the brother,
and Weir Mitchell — Gilman suggests that her heroine must
cope with principles and values imposed on her by the field
of medicine in general, which Foucault calls attention to as a
discipline that manipulates people's identities in the name of
health. In John's view, his spouse is not experiencing any
serious discontentment with her life, even though the reader
senses that she is, in fact, distressed at having to accommodate herself to the roles of wife and mother as defined by the
field of medicine specifically and by society overall. Proclaiming that she is afflicted by simply "a slight hysterical tendency" (233), John prevents himself from learning "how much
I really suffer" (235). Relying on his alleged expertise as a
representative of his profession, he values his own clinical
precision over her vague reports of unease: "He has no
patience with faith, an intense horror of superstition, and he
scoffs openly at any talk of things not to be felt and seen and
put down in figures" (233). Foucault might say that John
wishes for his wife to discipline herself, which involves her
obeying the policies that John derives from his scientific
background. Indeed, at two different points in the story,
she comments that he is basically focused on her achieving
"self-control" (234).

It is important for the reader to note that John is not an
outright monster in his treatment of the narrator. He does not
physically abuse her, at least not in any dramatic way. In fact,
even when he is condescending toward her, he seems to believe sincerely that he has her best interests at heart. In an
article that interprets the story with Foucault's ideas in mind,
John S. Bak overstates the case when he argues that the
narrator's husband subjects her to "a dehumanizing imprisonment" (40) and "resembles the penal officers of the
eighteenth-century psychiatric wards or penitentiaries"
(42). Although he isolates her on a country estate, he does
not virtually lock her up and physically torment her, as Bak
implies. While much of the plot takes place in a single room,
she is free to roam the estate, and it is *she* who denies *him*
access to the room for a brief spell at the end. Explaining in
his book how power now operates, Foucault points out that it
tends to present itself not as a crude, blatant instrument of
punishment but as a means of enlightened reform.

Foucault does believe, however, that agents of power like
John are presumptuous in assuming that they can produce
better human beings through their guidance. So, too, Gilman's
narrator does not find that her husband's professional advice

Heads off possible misunderstanding.

Takes a position on an article that has already applied the theorist's ideas to the story.

Resumes connecting the theorist's ideas directly to the story.

is helping her to grow healthier. Inwardly, she disagrees with him when he commands her to avoid physical activity, for she supposes that "congenial work, with excitement and change, would do me good" (233). Though "he hates to have me write a word" (234), she defies him by secretly writing down the story of her lingering unhappiness and tension. Similarly, she tries to conceal from him her inability to comply with his demand that she get plenty of sleep. Eventually, rather than automatically following his prescriptions, she finds herself "getting a little afraid of John" (240). She moves from believing that "he loves me so" (238) to suspecting that in his interrogations of her, he has merely "pretended to be very loving and kind" (242). Of course, the most dramatic form that her alienation from him takes is her preoccupation with the woman she sees lurking behind her room's wallpaper. The narrator's effort to free the woman — including her violent tearing of the paper — vividly demonstrates that Gilman's heroine hopes to escape the forces of domination that her husband symbolizes. She is not as capable as Foucault is of coming up with a full-fledged theory of the modern disciplinary society that her husband represents, but intuitively she associates him with this kind of world, and in essence she protests against it as she strips the paper off.

While Foucault's *Discipline and Punish* provides much context for Gilman's story, it does not offer an adequate account of how lives like the narrator's are affected by their gender. In order to be complete, an analysis of "The Yellow Wallpaper" would have to acknowledge that the narrator's womanhood does matter to the plot. When she originally comes to the estate, clearly she is distressed by her society's expectation that as a mother she will be the prime nurturer of her newborn child. Then, the patriarchal authority that John enjoys in that society as her husband encourages him to tell her what is good for her. His demand that she rest instead of work is no doubt supported by their culture's belief that women of her upper-middle-class standing are not supposed to perform much physical labor in the first place. Most likely Foucault was aware that gender has usually been a key variable in modern society's power structures, and there is no reason to think he would simply ignore how it bears on Gilman's story. But because *Discipline and Punish* does not give gender much attention, its significance for Gilman's narrator is a topic that Foucault leaves other, more explicitly feminist perspectives to discover.

Points out limits of this framework, rather than simply matching it to the story.

Some feminist theorists have criticized Foucault not only for neglecting gender but also for failing to develop any

Concluding paragraph connects the theorist to the story by briefly bringing up new topic, resistance.

model of resistance to domination. For example, Nancy C. M. Hartsock faults him for leaving people with no method of escaping "passivity and immobility," no "hope of transcendence" over "the ways humans have been subjugated" (45). Nor does Gilman offer in her story a clear notion of what resistance to unjust power would look like. One feature of "The Yellow Wallpaper" that has much been debated is whether the narrator's destruction of the wallpaper and her crawling on the floor are a truly effective challenge to disciplinary society. Readers who might otherwise agree on many elements of the story have disagreed on this issue. While Bak, for example, claims that ultimately the narrator "is successful at freeing herself from her male-imposed shackles" (40), Paula A. Treichler argues that "the surrender of patriarchy is only temporary" and that "her madness will no doubt commit her to more intense medical treatment, perhaps to the dreaded Weir Mitchell of whom her husband has spoken" (67). It is possible that Gilman was being deliberately ambiguous with her ending, wishing to provoke discussion about how to define worthwhile resistance instead of attempting to settle the question herself. In any case, Foucault's *Discipline and Punish* sheds light on a lot of her story even if it keeps Gilman's readers wondering exactly what her narrator should have done.

Endnote

[1] *Discipline and Punish* is not the only text by Foucault that can help in analyzing Gilman's story. Another possible work is his book *Madness and Civilization: A History of Insanity in the Age of Reason*, which can be useful for understanding the psychological problems of Gilman's narrator. *Discipline and Punish* is especially good, however, at explaining how power relationships throughout modern societies like the narrator's involve academic and professional disciplines of various sorts.

Endnote provides additional information that is not easily incorporated into main body of the paper.

Works Cited

Bak, John S. "Escaping the Jaundiced Eye: Foucauldian Panopticism in Charlotte Perkins Gilman's 'The Yellow Wallpaper.'" *Studies in Short Fiction* 31.1 (1994): 39–46. Print.   *Citation for scholarly article.*

Foucault, Michel. *Discipline and Punish: The Birth of the Prison.* Trans. Alan Sheridan. New York: Vintage, 1979. Print.   *Citation for book. Note style for multiple works by same author.*

– – – . *Madness and Civilization: A History of Insanity in the Age of Reason.* Trans. Richard Howard. New York: Vintage, 1988. Print.

Gilman, Charlotte Perkins. "The Yellow Wallpaper." *Making Literature Matter: An Anthology for Readers and Writers.* Ed. John Schilb and John Clifford. 6th ed. Boston: Bedford, 2015. 231–244. Print.   *Citation for work in an anthology.*

Hartsock, Nancy C. M. "Postmodernism and Political Change: Issues for Feminist Theory." *Feminist Interpretations of Michel Foucault.* Ed. Susan J. Hekman. University Park: Pennsylvania State UP, 1996. 39–55. Print.

Treichler, Paula A. "Escaping the Sentence: Diagnosis and Discourse in 'The Yellow Wallpaper.'" *Tulsa Studies in Women's Literature* 3.1/2 (1984): 61–77. Print.

A PAPER THAT PLACES A LITERARY WORK IN HISTORICAL AND CULTURAL CONTEXT

When scholars do research on a literary work, often they are trying to place it in its original situation. They wish to identify how it relates to the historical and cultural context in which it emerged. If you write a research paper aiming to provide such background for a literary text, you will probably incorporate various sources. But your essay needs to focus on developing a claim of your own about the text. This is what the following paper by student Brittany Thomas does. Her essay connects Gilman's "The Yellow Wallpaper" to its original time. To prepare for the paper, Brittany examined autobiographical writings by Gilman as well as a lecture by S. Weir Mitchell, Gilman's own real-life doctor. She also investigated scholarship on nineteenth-century medical treatments of women. Becoming interested in the "rest cure" on which Gilman's story was based, Brittany realized that Gilman's plot leaves out the massages that were normally part of this therapy. In her paper, Brittany states and elaborates the claim that this omission was probably intentional—an effort by Gilman to emphasize the narrator's isolation from human touch.

Brittany Thomas
Professor Schneebaum
English L202
25 April - - - -

The Relative Absence of the Human Touch
in "The Yellow Wallpaper"

In her essay "Why I Wrote 'The Yellow Wallpaper,'"
Charlotte Perkins Gilman reveals that her famous story was inspired by a personal depression that got worse when she underwent a "rest cure" prescribed to her by "a noted specialist
in nervous diseases, the best known in the country" (245).
Though she does not name this doctor in the essay, we are
aware today that he was S. Weir Mitchell, a name that she actually brings up briefly in "The Yellow Wallpaper." The rest
cure that the story's narrator goes through, however, does not
seem to have all the features that Weir Mitchell's did. Interestingly, neither by reading the essay nor by reading Gilman's
story would you realize that Weir Mitchell's treatment involved massage. The question for an interpreter of the story
thus becomes, Why did Gilman leave massage out of "The Yellow Wallpaper"? Because we can only guess at her intentions,
perhaps a better way of putting the question is this: What is
the effect of omitting massage from the story? One important
consequence is that there is less of a literal human touch in
the story than there might have been, and so the heroine's
alienation from others and her withdrawal into fantasy seem
stronger than they might have been.

Weir Mitchell himself seems to have regarded massage as
a very big component of his rest cure. He gives it a lot of attention in his 1904 lecture "The Evolution of the Rest Treatment." There he describes at length two cases, one of a man
and one of a woman, where he found out that rubbing the
body helped the person overcome depression. He recalls arriving at the conclusion "that massage was a tonic of extraordinary value" (249), and he continues his lecture by giving a
brief account of the larger world history of what he terms
"this invaluable therapeutic measure" (250). Evidently Weir
Mitchell did not perform massage himself; in his lecture, he
describes having others do it for him. Perhaps he thought
that if he personally rubbed a patient's body, he would run
the risk of being accused of a sexual advance. Despite his use
of stand-ins for him, he clearly considered massage a necessary feature of his rest cure. One reason was that he thought
the depressed person's body needed some form of physical
stimulation, which the person would not otherwise be getting

*Immediately mentions one of
her sources, but only to set
up main claim about Gilman's
story, which she states at
end of paragraph.*

*Using question form helps
signal cause/effect issue
that the essay will address.*

This is the essay's main claim.

*Briefly summarizes Weir
Mitchell's lecture, focusing on
his remarks about massage
rather than spending
additional time on other
topics of his speech.*

by lying around so much of the time. He states in his lecture that massage was something that "enabled me to use rest in bed without causing the injurious effects of unassisted rest" (249). Probably this method also reflected a more general belief of his, which Jane F. Thrailkill describes as the assumption "that the efficacy of his cure lay in its treatment of a patient's material body, not in what we might now term the psychological effects of isolation or of his own charismatic presence" (532). Thrailkill goes on to point out that Weir Mitchell was not alone in this belief: "[T]he medical wisdom of the day . . . conceived of a patient as a conceptually inert bundle of physiological processes" (552).[1] Massage was a means of helpfully manipulating the physique, which for Weir Mitchell and other doctors of his era was the main source of difficulties that today might be seen as chiefly mental.

Analyzes at length one particular source, Weir Mitchell's lecture.

Square brackets indicate alteration of text being quoted. Ellipses indicate words deleted from original text.

Given that massage was so important to Weir Mitchell, it is significant that Gilman's references to it are not consistent. She does recall being massaged when she discusses how Weir Mitchell treated her medically in her autobiography *The Living of Charlotte Perkins Gilman*. In that book, she says that besides being "put to bed and kept there," she was "fed, bathed, [and] rubbed" (96). She does not refer to massage, however, in "Why I Wrote 'The Yellow Wallpaper.'" More important for interpretations of the story, she does not make massage part of "The Yellow Wallpaper" itself. It plays no role at all in the plot. The elements of the rest cure that come up in the story are, instead, physical seclusion and forced abandonment of work.

Synthesis of three texts, comparing what they do with the topic of massage. More specifically, compares Gilman's autobiography, Gilman's essay on writing the story, and the story itself.

If massage were a major element of the rest cure that the narrator goes through in "The Yellow Wallpaper," the story would probably feature a lot more human touching than it presently does. The way the story is written, the heroine experiences relatively little physical contact with other people, or at least she does not tell us that she is having much of this. What is especially interesting is that we do not find many instances of her being physically touched by her husband, John. There are, in fact, a few places in the text where he does touch her. She says that when she informs him that she is disturbed by the wallpaper, "he took me in his arms and called me a blessed little goose" (235). When she weeps because he will not leave the house to visit relatives, "dear John gathered me up in his arms, and just carried me upstairs and laid me on the bed, and sat by me and read to me till it tired my head" (238). When she complains that he is wrong to think she is getting better, he gives her "a big hug" and says "'Bless her little heart! . . . she shall be as sick as she

In effect, admits it would be misleading to claim there are no instances of touching in the story. Proceeds to bring together (to synthesize) various examples of such contact.

pleases!'" (239). Yet his moments of touching her not only are very few but also reflect his insensitivity toward her. His folding her in his arms seems an effort to control her and trivialize her protests, not an expression of genuine love. Moreover, she takes no real comfort from his touch. If this amounts to rubbing her, then from her point of view, he is rubbing her the wrong way. Again, however, massage is significantly absent from this story, and because what touches there are seem so few and inhumane, readers are led to feel that the narrator is pretty much alone in her concerns. She has only the imaginary woman in the wallpaper to bond with, and she seems drawn to that woman in large part because her human companions have no true understanding of the distress that caused her to need some sort of cure in the first place.

Accounts for details of story that might seem to conflict with main claim.

In calling attention to the role of massage in S. Weir Mitchell's rest cure, I do not mean to minimize the importance of his treatment's other components. The physical rest he demanded of his patients was certainly a big element of the cure, so that we can easily see why Gilman made it central to her story. In his lecture, Weir Mitchell also points out that he applied electrical charges to the patient's body. Historians of women's health Barbara Ehrenreich and Deirdre English argue that Weir Mitchell relied heavily as well on "the technique of healing by *command*" (119, emphasis in original), constantly and firmly giving orders to his patients so that they felt obligated to obey his wishes and to get better on the precise schedule he had in mind. Massage certainly figured, however, in Weir Mitchell's mode of treatment, including his handling of Gilman's own case, so that her omission of it from "The Yellow Wallpaper" seems a deliberate strategy for giving other things emphasis. Above all, the quite limited role of human touching in the story serves to make readers highly aware that the narrator is without the loving, intimate company she really needs to recover from her depression.

Heads off possible misunderstanding of argument; dealing with it enables her to write a concluding paragraph that does more than just repeat main claim.

Endnote

[1] Thrailkill spends much of her article tracing how an emphasis on treating depression through physical means (the approach taken by Weir Mitchell) gave way late in the nineteenth century to a more psychological and verbal form of therapy (such as Sigmund Freud practiced).

Endnote provides information that could not be easily integrated into main text of the essay.

Works Cited

Ehrenreich, Barbara, and Deirdre English. *For Her Own Good: 150 Years of the Experts' Advice to Women*. Garden City: Doubleday-Anchor, 1978. Print.

Gilman, Charlotte Perkins. *The Living of Charlotte Perkins Gilman*. New York: Arno Press, 1972. Print.

- - - . "Why I Wrote 'The Yellow Wallpaper.'" Schilb and Clifford 245–246.

- - - . "The Yellow Wallpaper." Schilb and Clifford 231–244.

Schilb, John, and John Clifford, eds. *Making Literature Matter: An Anthology for Readers and Writers*. 6th ed. Boston: Bedford, 2015. Print.

Thrailkill, Jane F. "Doctoring 'The Yellow Wallpaper.'" *ELH* 69.2 (2005): 525–66. Print.

Weir Mitchell, S. Excerpt from "The Evolution of the Rest Treatment." 1904. Schilb and Clifford 246–250.

Citation for book.

Note style for multiple works by same author.

When you cite more than one work from the same book, you give the book its own entry and cite each work from it in the shorthand form you see here.

Citation for anthology.

Citation for scholarly article.

A PAPER THAT PLACES A LITERARY WORK IN A MULTIMEDIA CONTEXT

Increasingly, scholars do research on a literary work by tracing its appearances in, or connections to, various media. These modes can include visual forms such as photographs, films, electronic screens, and print advertisements or illustrations. Music and other kinds of sounds may prove relevant as well. At the start of this book's color portfolio, we present a sample paper that analyzes a poem based on a specific painting. Here, though, is a student essay that develops a claim about "The Yellow Wallpaper." It does so by referring to illustrations that appeared in the January 1892 issue of *The New England Magazine*, where Gilman's story was first published. The paper's author, Kyra Blaylock, was able to access this long-ago issue on the Web. She then examined all of the pictures in it. Of course, she was especially interested in the illustrations that accompanied Gilman's work. But she realized that she could usefully compare one of the Gilman images with another picture: an illustration for the story that preceded Gilman's in the magazine. Kyra reproduces both images at the end of her paper. Alternatively, she might have included them *within* her text, perhaps by reducing their size. Important to notice, in any case, is that she does not simply lay out these pictures for her reader to study. Her essay carefully describes them and probes implications of their details.

Kyra Blaylock
Professor Michaels
English L202
16 May - - - -

Different Kinds of Horrifying Images in
"The Yellow Wallpaper" and "A Salem Witch"

Charlotte Perkins Gilman's short story "The Yellow Wallpaper" was originally published in the January 1892 issue of the
New England Magazine. At the time, many people saw it as a
tale of horror. In a 1996 article that traces the history of the
story's reception, Julie Bates Dock and her coauthors report
that several of its initial readers were scared by Gilman's text.
For example, reviewer Anne Montgomerie found the story "a
perfect crescendo of horror," and famous literary critic William
Dean Howells observed that Gilman manages to "freeze our
young blood" (qtd. in Dock et al. 59).[1] But not all horror stories are alike. They may differ in their means of making their
audiences shudder. This possibility becomes evident if we
compare Gilman's story to the one immediately preceding it
in the same issue of the *New England Magazine*, Edith Mary
Norris's "A Salem Witch."

Uses a source to document first reactions; directs this paper's reader to an endnote.

Like Gilman, Norris centers her story on an oppressed
woman. She sets her tale in late-seventeenth-century Salem,
during that city's notorious witch trials. The heroine,
Margaret, is unjustly charged with witchcraft, after being
accused of it by a rival for her fiancé's affections. Although
the fiancé, Rafe, cannot prevent Margaret from dying of despair, he is an attractive figure who genuinely cares for her.
By contrast, Gilman sets her tale in what is for her the present age, the late nineteenth century. Furthermore, her narrator is persecuted by her husband, a doctor who forbids her to
do meaningful work and who consequently helps drive her
mad. Unlike Rafe, he proves insensitive to the heroine, and in
the end, he collapses in fright when she asserts female power.
In general, "A Salem Witch" situates horror in the nation's
distant past, and it disturbs its audience by depicting a
woman who unfairly and fatally suffers despite a good man's
love. "The Yellow Wallpaper," on the other hand, locates horror in contemporary times and disturbs its audience by presenting a woman who subdues an obnoxious husband. In
other words, the horror evoked by Gilman's story had *feminist*
implications for her era, whereas other examples of the horror
genre — including one in the very same magazine issue —
were not as politically daring. This difference shows up in the

Briefly summarizes Gilman's story and the other that the paper will focus on.

This is the paper's main claim, which involves comparing two particular visual images.

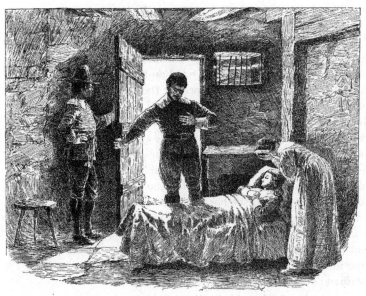

" His strong frame shook with an agony too deep for words."

Figure 1

Courtesy of Cornell University Library, Making of America Digital Collection.

illustrations that accompanied Norris's and Gilman's stories
when they appeared together. The contrast emerges especially
in the pictures depicting the stories' climaxes.

The *New England Magazine*'s illustration for the climax
of "A Salem Witch" (645, fig. 1)[2] juxtaposes male dominance
with female passivity. Rafe stands imposingly inside Margaret's
prison door as she lies dead in bed. Having been declared
guilty of witchcraft, she was scheduled to be executed; no
matter what, she was doomed. But Rafe finds her already destroyed by psychological pain. The tableau seems to bear out
Edgar Allan Poe's famous remark that "the death . . . of a
beautiful woman is unquestionably the most poetical topic in
the world." Of course, Poe's comment would trouble many
people today, for it suggests that good literature depends
upon female characters playing the victim role. In the picture
for Norris's story, Rafe is certainly a victim as well, for he has
lost his beloved. Nevertheless, he remains vividly alive, as is
noted by the picture's caption: "His strong frame shook with
an agony too deep for words." Physically, he remains erect
and mighty, looming at the picture's center, while Margaret is
stretched out lifeless below him. Even her sister, Dorcas, who
has been nursing Margaret and now leans over her body, bows
beneath Rafe rather than standing at his level. To be sure,

*Directs the reader to an
endnote, and the paragraph
proceeds not only to describe
one of the images but also to
analyze its details.*

*Ellipses indicate words
deleted from original text.*

Margaret seems bathed in light, as if she is bound for heaven, while Rafe is consumed by a darkness that signifies abiding sorrow. But Rafe still seems more powerful than Margaret in this continuing capacity to *feel*. Indeed, he dramatically expresses his mental "agony" by placing his hand on his heart and gazing with grief at his beloved's corpse. At the same time, his inability to verbalize his emotions — their being "too deep for words" — fits another masculine stereotype: the stoic, reserved John Wayne figure that many of us know from Western films. Rafe and Margaret do appear similarly pious: Rafe's hand-on-heart gesture seems religiously inspired, and Margaret's dead hands are folded in a prayerful way. But if she is headed toward divine reward, she has nonetheless been mortally punished on earth, while Rafe can still protest against the society that condemned her. By the end of the story, his protest takes the form of abandoning Salem for Europe. In the illustration, however, he serves as a living witness of Margaret's tragedy. As we look at him in the picture, we also see the horror of her death through his eyes.

The illustration for the climax of "The Yellow Wallpaper" (656; fig. 2) reverses this gender dynamic. It shows the female narrator leaning over, and gazing down at, her husband John's sprawled body. Frustrated by her supposedly "therapeutic" confinement, she has been tearing down her room's wallpaper to free the woman she detects in it. Distressed by her action, John has fainted, no longer capable of coolly playing the self-confident medical expert. He hardly displays Rafe's "strong frame"; rather, he seems as stricken as Margaret. His outstretched hands seem to grasp for help. As the narrator bends over him, placing her hands on his ribcage and head, she may even be viewed as a champion wrestler determined to keep him pinned down. Long strands of her hair dangle across his torso, as if to confirm that *she* is in control. Only *her* face is fully visible, while his is partly squashed on the floor. Moreover, we cannot tell from her face whether she even recognizes him. Indeed, within the text itself, she seems to regard him as a bothersome stranger: "Now why should that man have fainted? But he did, and right across my path by the wall, so that I had to creep over him every time!" (244). Because the illustration is a static image, it is unable to depict the narrator's "creeping"; inevitably it must show her as frozen rather than as striving to move past John. In this respect, the picture does not quite convey her sense that he is now just a barrier to her progress. Nevertheless, the drawing implies that she is subverting the social order, for at least temporarily, this woman is exerting power over a man.

Transition to description and analysis of the second image.

Figure 2
Courtesy of Cornell University Library, Making of America Digital Collection.

She enacts a fantasy of woman's liberation that many readers of the magazine would surely find shockingly new.

In their horror at the heroine's revolt, some of these readers may have wished that patriarchy be restored. That is, they may have viewed the illustration as a warning that bizarre and awful consequences will occur if men fail to keep women in their "proper" place. This response would turn "The Yellow Wallpaper" into a cautionary *anti*-feminist tract. But such a reaction would ignore much of Gilman's written text: in particular, her clear effort to show John as oblivious to the emotional needs of the heroine. John not only "laughs at" his wife, but also tells her that "the very worst thing [she] can do is to think about [her] condition" (233) and that her restless discontent "is a false and foolish fancy" (239). In Norris's story, by contrast, Margaret is chiefly betrayed by another *woman*, who calls her a witch in an attempt to steal Rafe away from her. Although the husband in Gilman's story is not an outright, moustache-twirling villain, he is a major source of her distress. When Gilman has him faint at the end of the story, his collapse seems the comeuppance of a husband who has been arrogant, not kind, toward his spouse. He has failed to demonstrate the love that Rafe shows Margaret in "A Salem Witch." With "The Yellow Wallpaper," therefore, Gilman seems chiefly out to horrify her readers by dramatizing how masculine authority thwarts women's freedom to the point where they must gain power in whatever way they can, even if their self-assertion comes at men's expense. By placing "A Salem Witch" in the distant past, by killing Margaret off, and by leaving Rafe alive with his "strong frame," Norris does not challenge her present society nearly as much as Gilman does.

Acknowledges an interpretation different from the paper's own.

Concludes by explaining how the paper's interpretation accounts for more of the story's written text.

Comparing the two climactic illustrations makes the difference in their political stances apparent.

Endnotes

[1]Dock and her coauthors add that at least some early readers of "The Yellow Wallpaper" did not see it *only* as a horror story. Indeed, these scholars argue that a number of readers found feminist messages in Gilman's tale well before the present women's movement did.

[2]The deathbed scene is not the *final* illustration for Norris's story in the magazine. At the conclusion of the story, there appears a picture of the coastal cottage in England where Rafe and Dorcas eventually go to live.

Endnotes provide information that could not be easily integrated into main text of the essay.

Works Cited

Dock, Julie Bates, et al. "'But One Expects That': Charlotte Perkins Gilman's 'The Yellow Wallpaper' and the Shifting Light of Scholarship." *PMLA* 111.1 (1996): 52–65. Print.

Gilman, Charlotte Perkins. "The Yellow Wallpaper." *New England Magazine* Jan. 1892: 647–56. *Making of America.* Cornell University Library. Web. 27 Nov. 2013. Also in Schilb and Clifford, eds. *Making Literature Matter: An Anthology for Readers and Writers.* 6th ed. Boston: Bedford, 2015. 231–244. Print.

Norris, Edith Mary. "A Salem Witch." *New England Magazine* Jan. 1892: 638–46. *Making of America.* Cornell University Library. Web. 27 Nov. 2013.

Poe, Edgar Allan. "The Philosophy of Composition." 1846. *Project Gutenberg Ebook of Edgar Allan Poe's Complete Poetical Works.* Project Gutenberg, 10 Nov. 2003. Web. 27 Nov. 2013.

Citation for article in scholarly journal.

Two citations of the work needed here: (1) Its location in this print anthology; (2) the work's original publication, now available on the Web, which features an illustration that the paper refers to.

Citation for work available on the Web.

MAKING A MULTIMEDIA PRESENTATION ABOUT A LITERARY WORK

College courses often require class presentations. Besides writing about a work of literature, you may have to make a speech about it. Moreover, your talk might employ media other than your spoken words. Kyra Blaylock's paper on "The Yellow Wallpaper" examines drawings that accompanied Gilman's story when it debuted. If Kyra gave a speech based on her essay, she could display these sketches during it. Similarly, a speech by you can use visual images to illustrate, support, or connect your ideas. These images might include photographs, paintings, film clips, YouTube videos, advertisements, diagrams, or screen captures from Web sites. They might include, too, bits of text you want your audience to notice, such as literary quotations, dictionary entries, timelines, headlines, captions, and tweets. An additional medium you can turn to is sound, including music recordings and historic news broadcasts. Don't forget, either, the possibility of using props. American Girl dolls can vividly demonstrate how nineteenth-century women like Gilman's narrator were expected to look.

Whatever media you enlist, a speech about a literary work demands careful planning. Here are some specific tips:

- You may annoy your audience if you just loosely string together assorted facts, images, and details. You need to decide on a structure for your talk — a way to make it seem organized and compelling. One good plan is to frame your speech as an *argument*. This would involve stating an issue and main claim at the outset. Then you would develop and support the claim, pointing out your evidence and reasons. You may also need to admit and defend certain assumptions you hold. Alternatively, you might frame your talk as a *mystery*. You might begin by identifying a difficult question or problem, and then lead your listeners to a solution.

- Visual technology, such as PowerPoint or Prezi, can prove valuable. But make sure that all of your slides play meaningful roles in your presentation. Don't waste time on displays that just amuse or dazzle; each image needs to serve a clear and genuine purpose. Keep in mind that the slides in your talk may not merit equal attention. Some you might show quickly; others you might linger on. In general, planning your speech entails deciding how you will *pace* it. Which parts of it can you race through? Which require longer discussion?

- Limit the number of words you put on a slide, for otherwise your audience may need to spend much time and effort to read them. Make the words large enough to be visible in the first place; don't make people squint. If you do have to show lengthy passages, you might distribute them on handouts.

- Determine how to maintain eye contact with your audience. You may lose their interest if you constantly look at a script or just repeat words already up on screen. You might speak instead from notes written on cards.

- Your presentation will engage people more if you involve them in an activity. It can be one that also helps you understand your audience better. For example, they might briefly freewrite on your topic, jotting down things they currently know or assume about it. You might then have volunteers read a few of their sentences aloud.

- You may want to have a bottle of water at hand, in case your mouth gets dry. Your audience is unlikely to be bothered by an occasional sip. But don't indulge in prolonged, dramatic swigs, as if giving a speech is the same as running a marathon.

- Rehearse your speech several times. This practice will enable you to gauge how long your presentation will take—an important matter if you must stick to a certain time limit. If you plan to use technology, test it beforehand, making sure that it will actually function.

Perhaps your presentation will be a *group* effort rather than a speech you make on your own. Here are some suggestions to help you and your partners collaborate:

- When you first meet as a group, be sure to exchange contact information (e.g., e-mail addresses and phone numbers). Also, try to set up at least a tentative schedule: dates and times when you will meet in person or share work-in-progress through e-mails.

- As early as possible, the group should decide what each member's tasks will be, both in preparing the speech and in actually making it. The goal should be a roughly equal division of labor, based on what each member specifically wants to research and speak about. The group may find value in appointing a "team manager": someone who will monitor the planning and keep everyone informed about how this process is going.

- Rehearsal is always important, but especially for a group. If each member of your team prepares part of the presentation, everyone should then gather for several run-throughs of it, to make sure that its various elements mesh.

- Ideally, each member will come to the group's meetings, take on tasks, and perform them well. But this doesn't always happen. Someone may wind up missing in action. If a member skips meetings or assigned duties, the rest of the group can do more than simply wring their hands. They can adjust their plans, proceed without the person, and tell their instructor what's happened.

≡ SUMMING UP: WRITING RESEARCHED ARGUMENTS

- *Plan* **your research.** (pp. 187–202)

  Identify an issue to pursue.

  Investigate electronic sources such as Internet Web sites, using more than one search engine; investigate print sources as well.

  Take time to evaluate the materials you discover.

  Keep yourself well organized.

  Record everything that may prove useful later — do not risk plagiarism by failing to distinguish between your own ideas and those of others.

- **Start composing by revisiting your tentative main claim, taking into account what you have learned through research.** (p. 202)

  Keep organized, and subdivide and arrange your notes in logical order.

  Focus on constructing an argument of your own, using secondary sources to support your claims and evidence.

  Follow MLA conventions for format and style.

- **Document your sources by following MLA guidelines.** (pp. 195–202)

- **For a research paper that uses a literary work to examine social issues, deals with existing interpretations of it, interprets it through the framework of a particular theorist, places it in a historical or cultural context, or relates it to visual images, be sure to make an argument of your own. This entails raising an issue and making a claim about the work.** (p. 202)

(continued on next page)

≡ **SUMMING UP: WRITING RESEARCHED ARGUMENTS**
(continued)

- For a multimedia presentation on a literary work, aim to engage your audience by clearly organizing your remarks; using technology in helpful and meaningful ways; maintaining eye contact; and perhaps incorporating an activity. For a group presentation, establish a planning schedule and try to divide labor fairly. For any presentation you give, rehearse. (pp. 227–229)

≡ Contexts for Research: Charlotte Perkins Gilman's "The Yellow Wallpaper" and Mental Illness

CHARLOTTE PERKINS GILMAN, "The Yellow Wallpaper"

CULTURAL CONTEXTS:
CHARLOTTE PERKINS GILMAN, "Why I Wrote 'The Yellow Wallpaper' "

S. WEIR MITCHELL, From *"The Evolution of the Rest Treatment"*

JOHN HARVEY KELLOGG, From *The Ladies' Guide in Health and Disease*

When doctors make a medical or psychiatric diagnosis, they pinpoint their pa-tient's condition but also often accept or reject their society's definition of *health.* The social context of diagnoses seems especially worth considering when a particular condition afflicts one gender much more than the other. To-day, many more women than men appear to suffer from depression, anorexia, bulimia, and dissociative identity disorder. Why? Perhaps traditional female roles encourage these illnesses; perhaps gender bias affects how doctors label and treat them. Charlotte Perkins Gilman raised both these possibilities in her 1892 short story "The Yellow Wallpaper." In her own life, the consequences from her egregious treatment were serious if not as horrible as she depicts in her story. But Gilman was the exception. Many women of her time suffered ter-ribly at the hands of doctors who ignored the cultural causes of depression. Besides Gilman's story, we include her account of why she wrote it, an excerpt from a lecture by S. Weir Mitchell about his "cure," and some advice about motherhood from John Kellogg, another influential doctor of the time.

≡ BEFORE YOU READ

How is mental illness depicted in movies and television shows you have seen? Which representations of mental illness have you appreciated the most? Which have you especially disliked? State your criteria for these judg-ments.

CHARLOTTE PERKINS GILMAN
The Yellow Wallpaper

Charlotte Perkins Gilman (1860–1935) was a major activist and theorist in Amer-ica's first wave of feminism. During her lifetime, she was chiefly known for her 1898 book Women and Economics. *In it she argued that women should not be confined to the household and made economically dependent on men. Gilman also advanced such ideas through her many public-speaking appearances and her magazine* The Fore-runner, *which she edited from 1909 to 1916. Gilman wrote many articles and works of fiction for* The Forerunner, *including a tale called* Herland *(1915) in*

Charlotte Perkins
Gilman. Getty Images.

which she envisioned an all-female utopia. Today, however, Gilman is best known for her short story "The Yellow Wallpaper," which she published first in an 1892 issue of the New England Magazine. The story is based on Gilman's struggle with depression after the birth of her daughter Katharine in 1885. Seeking help for emotional turmoil, Gilman consulted the eminent neurologist Silas Weir Mitchell, who prescribed his famous "rest cure." This treatment, which forbade Gilman to work, actually worsened her distress. She improved only after she moved to California, divorced her husband, let him raise Katharine with his new wife, married someone else, and plunged fully into a literary and political career. As Gilman noted in her posthumously published autobiography, The Living of Charlotte Perkins Gilman (1935), she never fully recovered from the debilitation that had led her to Dr. Mitchell, but she ultimately managed to be enormously productive. Although "The Yellow Wallpaper" is a work of fiction rather than a factual account of her experience with Mitchell, Gilman used the story to criticize the doctor's patriarchal approach as well as society's efforts to keep women passive.

It is very seldom that mere ordinary people like John and myself secure ancestral halls for the summer.

A colonial mansion, a hereditary estate, I would say a haunted house and reach the height of romantic felicity—but that would be asking too much of fate!

Still I will proudly declare that there is something queer about it.

Else, why should it be let so cheaply? And why have stood so long untenanted?

John laughs at me, of course, but one expects that in marriage.   5

John is practical in the extreme. He has no patience with faith, an intense horror of superstition, and he scoffs openly at any talk of things not to be felt and seen and put down in figures.

John is a physician, and *perhaps*—(I would not say it to a living soul, of course, but this is dead paper and a great relief to my mind)—*perhaps* that is one reason I do not get well faster.

You see, he does not believe I am sick!

And what can one do?

If a physician of high standing, and one's own husband, assures friends   10
and relatives that there is really nothing the matter with one but temporary nervous depression—a slight hysterical tendency°—what is one to do?

My brother is also a physician, and also of high standing, and he says the same thing.

So I take phosphates or phosphites—whichever it is, and tonics, and journeys, and air, and exercise, and am absolutely forbidden to "work" until I am well again.

Personally, I disagree with their ideas.

Personally, I believe that congenial work, with excitement and change, would do me good.

But what is one to do?   15

I did write for a while in spite of them; but it *does* exhaust me a good deal—having to be so sly about it, or else meet with heavy opposition.

I sometimes fancy that in my condition if I had less opposition and more society and stimulus—but John says the very worst thing I can do is to think about my condition, and I confess it always makes me feel bad.

So I will let it alone and talk about the house.

The most beautiful place! It is quite alone, standing well back from the road, quite three miles from the village. It makes me think of English places that you read about, for there are hedges and walls and gates that lock, and lots of separate little houses for the gardeners and people.

There is a *delicious* garden! I never saw such a garden—large and shady,   20
full of box-bordered paths, and lined with long grape-covered arbors with seats under them.

There were greenhouses, too, but they are all broken now.

There was some legal trouble, I believe, something about the heirs and co-heirs; anyhow, the place has been empty for years.

---

hysterical tendency: It was common among Victorian doctors to believe women had an innate tendency to be overly emotional; now a discredited assumption.

That spoils my ghostliness, I am afraid, but I don't care—there is something strange about the house—I can feel it.

I even said so to John one moonlight evening, but he said what I felt was a *draught*, and shut the window.

I get unreasonably angry with John sometimes. I'm sure I never used to be   25
so sensitive. I think it is due to this nervous condition.

But John says if I feel so, I shall neglect proper self-control; so I take pains to control myself — before him, at least, and that makes me very tired.

I don't like our room a bit. I wanted one downstairs that opened on the piazza and had roses all over the window, and such pretty old-fashioned chintz hangings! but John would not hear of it.

He said there was only one window and not room for two beds, and no near room for him if he took another.

He is very careful and loving, and hardly lets me stir without special direction.

I have a schedule prescription for each hour in the day; he takes all care   30
from me, and so I feel basely ungrateful not to value it more.

He said we came here solely on my account, that I was to have perfect rest and all the air I could get. "Your exercise depends on your strength, my dear," said he, "and your food somewhat on your appetite; but air you can absorb all the time." So we took the nursery at the top of the house.

It is a big, airy room, the whole floor nearly, with windows that look all ways, and air and sunshine galore. It was nursery first and then playroom and gymnasium, I should judge; for the windows are barred for little children, and there are rings and things in the walls.

The paint and paper look as if a boys' school had used it. It is stripped off — the paper—in great patches all around the head of my bed, about as far as I can reach, and in a great place on the other side of the room low down. I never saw a worse paper in my life.

One of those sprawling flamboyant patterns committing every artistic sin.

It is dull enough to confuse the eye in following, pronounced enough to   35
constantly irritate and provoke study, and when you follow the lame uncertain curves for a little distance they suddenly commit suicide—plunge off at outrageous angles, destroy themselves in unheard of contradictions.

The color is repellant, almost revolting; a smouldering unclean yellow, strangely faded by the slow-turning sunlight.

It is a dull yet lurid orange in some places, a sickly sulphur tint in others.

No wonder the children hated it! I should hate it myself if I had to live in this room long.

There comes John, and I must put this away, — he hates to have me write a word.

We have been here two weeks, and I haven't felt like writing before, since that   40
first day.

I am sitting by the window now, up in this atrocious nursery, and there is nothing to hinder my writing as much as I please, save lack of strength.

John is away all day, and even some nights when his cases are serious.

I am glad my case is not serious!

But these nervous troubles are dreadfully depressing.

John does not know how much I really suffer. He knows there is no *reason*   45
to suffer, and that satisfies him.

Of course it is only nervousness. It does weigh on me so not to do my duty
in any way!

I meant to be such a help to John, such a real rest and comfort, and here I
am a comparative burden already!

Nobody would believe what an effort it is to do what little I am able, — to
dress and entertain, and order things.

It is fortunate Mary is so good with the baby. Such a dear baby!

And yet I *cannot* be with him, it makes me so nervous.   50

I suppose John never was nervous in his life. He laughs at me so about this
wallpaper!

At first he meant to repaper the room, but afterward he said that I was letting it get the better of me, and that nothing was worse for a nervous patient
than to give way to such fancies.

He said that after the wallpaper was changed it would be the heavy bedstead, and then the barred windows, and then that gate at the head of the
stairs, and so on.

"You know the place is doing you good," he said, "and really, dear, I don't
care to renovate the house just for a three months' rental."

"Then do let us go downstairs," I said, "there are such pretty rooms there."   55

Then he took me in his arms and called me a blessed little goose, and said
he would go down cellar, if I wished, and have it whitewashed into the bargain.

But he is right enough about the beds and windows and things.

It is an airy and comfortable room as anyone need wish, and, of course, I
would not be so silly as to make him uncomfortable just for a whim.

I'm really getting quite fond of the big room, all but that horrid paper.

Out of one window I can see the garden, those mysterious deep-shaded   60
arbors, the riotous old-fashioned flowers, and bushes and gnarly trees.

Out of another I get a lovely view of the bay and a little private wharf belonging to the estate. There is a beautiful shaded lane that runs down there
from the house. I always fancy I see people walking in these numerous paths
and arbors, but John has cautioned me not to give way to fancy in the least. He
says that with my imaginative power and habit of story-making, a nervous
weakness like mine is sure to lead to all manner of excited fancies, and that I
ought to use my will and good sense to check the tendency. So I try.

I think sometimes that if I were only well enough to write a little it would
relieve the press of ideas and rest me.

But I find I get pretty tired when I try.

It is so discouraging not to have any advice and companionship about my
work. When I get really well, John says we will ask Cousin Henry and Julia
down for a long visit; but he says he would as soon put fireworks in my pillow-
case as to let me have those stimulating people about now.

I wish I could get well faster. 65

But I must not think about that. This paper looks to me as if it *knew* what a vicious influence it had!

There is a recurrent spot where the pattern lolls like a broken neck and two bulbous eyes stare at you upside down.

I get positively angry with the impertinence of it and the everlastingness. Up and down and sideways they crawl, and those absurd, unblinking eyes are everywhere. There is one place where two breadths didn't match, and the eyes go all up and down the line, one a little higher than the other.

I never saw so much expression in an inanimate thing before, and we all know how much expression they have! I used to lie awake as a child and get more entertainment and terror out of blank walls and plain furniture than most children could find in a toy-store.

I remember what a kindly wink the knobs of our big, old bureau used to 70 have, and there was one chair that always seemed like a strong friend.

I used to feel that if any of the other things looked too fierce I could always hop into that chair and be safe.

The furniture in this room is no worse than inharmonious, however, for we had to bring it all from downstairs. I suppose when this was used as a play-room they had to take the nursery things out, and no wonder! I never saw such ravages as the children have made here.

The wallpaper, as I said before, is torn off in spots, and it sticketh closer than a brother—they must have had perseverance as well as hatred.

Then the floor is scratched and gouged and splintered, the plaster itself is dug out here and there, and this great heavy bed, which is all we found in the room, looks as if it had been through the wars.

But I don't mind it a bit—only the paper. 75

There comes John's sister. Such a dear girl as she is, and so careful of me! I must not let her find me writing.

She is a perfect and enthusiastic housekeeper, and hopes for no better profession. I verily believe she thinks it is the writing which made me sick!

But I can write when she is out, and see her a long way off from these windows.

There is one that commands the road, a lovely shaded winding road, and one that just looks off over the country. A lovely country, too, full of great elms and velvet meadows.

This wallpaper has a kind of sub-pattern in a different shade, a particularly 80 irritating one, for you can only see it in certain lights, and not clearly then.

But in the places where it isn't faded and where the sun is just so—I can see a strange, provoking, formless sort of figure, that seems to skulk about behind that silly and conspicuous front design.

There's sister on the stairs!

Well, the Fourth of July is over! The people are all gone and I am tired out. John thought it might do me good to see a little company, so we just had mother and Nellie and the children down for a week.

Of course I didn't do a thing. Jennie sees to everything now.

But it tired me all the same.

John says if I don't pick up faster he shall send me to Weir Mitchell° in the fall.

But I don't want to go there at all. I had a friend who was in his hands once, and she says he is just like John and my brother, only more so!

Besides, it is such an undertaking to go so far.

I don't feel as if it was worthwhile to turn my hand over for anything, and I'm getting dreadfully fretful and querulous.

I cry at nothing, and cry most of the time.

Of course I don't when John is here, or anybody else, but when I am alone.

And I am alone a good deal just now. John is kept in town very often by serious cases, and Jennie is good and lets me alone when I want her to.

So I walk a little in the garden or down that lovely lane, sit on the porch under the roses, and lie down up here a good deal.

I'm getting really fond of the room in spite of the wallpaper. Perhaps *because* of the wallpaper.

It dwells in my mind so!

I lie here on this great immovable bed — it is nailed down, I believe — and follow that pattern about by the hour. It is as good as gymnastics, I assure you. I start, we'll say, at the bottom, down in the corner over there where it has not been touched, and I determine for the thousandth time that I *will* follow that pointless pattern to some sort of a conclusion.

I know a little of the principle of design, and I know this thing was not arranged on any laws of radiation, or alternation, or repetition, or symmetry, or anything else that I ever heard of.

It is repeated, of course, by the breadths, but not otherwise.

Looked at in one way each breadth stands alone, the bloated curves and flourishes — a kind of "debased Romanesque" with *delirium tremens* — go waddling up and down in isolated columns of fatuity.

But, on the other hand, they connect diagonally, and the sprawling outlines run off in great slanting waves of optic horror, like a lot of wallowing seaweeds in full chase.

The whole thing goes horizontally, too, at least it seems so, and I exhaust myself in trying to distinguish the order of its going in that direction.

They have used a horizontal breadth for a frieze, and that adds wonderfully to the confusion.

There is one end of the room where it is almost intact, and there, when the crosslights fade and the low sun shines directly upon it, I can almost fancy radiation after all, — the interminable grotesques seem to form around a common center and rush off in headlong plunges of equal distraction.

It makes me tired to follow it. I will take a nap I guess.

Weir Mitchell: Dr. S. Weir Mitchell (1829–1914) was an eminent Philadelphia neurologist who advocated "rest cures" for nervous disorders. He was the author of *Diseases of the Nervous System, Especially of Women* (1881).

*   *   *

I don't know why I should write this.   105

    I don't want to.

    I don't feel able.

    And I know John would think it absurd. But I *must* say what I feel and think in some way—it is such a relief!

    But the effort is getting to be greater than the relief.

    Half the time now I am awfully lazy, and lie down ever so much.   110

    John says I mustn't lose my strength, and has me take cod liver oil and lots of tonics and things, to say nothing of ale and wine and rare meat.

    Dear John! He loves me very dearly, and hates to have me sick. I tried to have a real earnest reasonable talk with him the other day, and tell him how I wish he would let me go and make a visit to Cousin Henry and Julia.

    But he said I wasn't able to go, nor able to stand it after I got there; and I did not make out a very good case for myself, for I was crying before I had finished.

    It is getting to be a great effort for me to think straight. Just this nervous weakness I suppose.

    And dear John gathered me up in his arms, and just carried me upstairs   115 and laid me on the bed, and sat by me and read to me till it tired my head.

    He said I was his darling and his comfort and all he had, and that I must take care of myself for his sake, and keep well.

    He says no one but myself can help me out of it, that I must use my will and self-control and not let any silly fancies run away with me.

    There's one comfort, the baby is well and happy, and does not have to occupy this nursery with the horrid wallpaper.

    If we had not used it, that blessed child would have! What a fortunate escape! Why, I wouldn't have a child of mine, an impressionable little thing, live in such a room for worlds.

    I never thought of it before, but it is lucky that John kept me here after all,   120 I can stand it so much easier than a baby, you see.

    Of course I never mention it to them any more—I am too wise, but I keep watch of it all the same.

    There are things in the wallpaper that nobody knows but me, or ever will.

    Behind that outside pattern the dim shapes get clearer every day.

    It is always the same shape, only very numerous.

    And it is like a woman stooping down and creeping about behind that pat-   125 tern. I don't like it a bit. I wonder—I begin to think—I wish John would take me away from here!

It is so hard to talk with John about my case, because he is so wise, and because he loves me so.

    But I tried it last night.

    It was moonlight. The moon shines in all around just as the sun does.

    I hate to see it sometimes, it creeps so slowly, and always comes in by one window or another.

John was asleep and I hated to waken him, so I kept still and watched the 130
moonlight on that undulating wallpaper till I felt creepy.

The faint figure behind seemed to shake the pattern, just as if she wanted
to get out.

I got up softly and went to feel and see if the paper *did* move, and when I
came back John was awake.

"What is it, little girl?" he said. "Don't go walking about like that — you'll
get cold."

I thought it was a good time to talk, so I told him that I really was not gaining here, and that I wished he would take me away.

"Why, darling!" said he, "our lease will be up in three weeks, and I can't see 135
how to leave before.

"The repairs are not done at home, and I cannot possibly leave town just
now. Of course if you were in any danger, I could and would, but you really are
better, dear, whether you can see it or not. I am a doctor, dear, and I know. You
are gaining flesh and color, your appetite is better, I feel really much easier
about you."

"I don't weigh a bit more," said I, "nor as much; and my appetite may be
better in the evening when you are here but it is worse in the morning when
you are away!"

"Bless her little heart!" said he with a big hug, "she shall be as sick as she
pleases! But now let's improve the shining hours by going to sleep, and talk
about it in the morning!"

"And you won't go away?" I asked gloomily.

"Why, how can I, dear? It is only three weeks more and then we will take a 140
nice little trip of a few days while Jennie is getting the house ready. Really dear
you are better!"

"Better in body perhaps —" I began, and stopped short, for he sat up
straight and looked at me with such a stern, reproachful look that I could not
say another word.

"My darling," said he, "I beg you, for my sake and for our child's sake, as well
as for your own, that you will never for one instant let that idea enter your mind!
There is nothing so dangerous, so fascinating, to a temperament like yours. It is
a false and foolish fancy. Can you trust me as a physician when I tell you so?"

So of course I said no more on that score, and we went to sleep before long.
He thought I was asleep first, but I wasn't, and lay there for hours trying to
decide whether that front pattern and the back pattern really did move together
or separately.

On a pattern like this, by daylight, there is a lack of sequence, a defiance of law,
that is a constant irritant to a normal mind.

The color is hideous enough, and unreliable enough, and infuriating 145
enough, but the pattern is torturing.

You think you have mastered it, but just as you get well underway in following, it turns a back-somersault and there you are. It slaps you in the face,
knocks you down, and tramples upon you. It is like a bad dream.

The outside pattern is a florid arabesque, reminding one of a fungus. If you can imagine a toadstool in joints, an interminable string of toadstools, budding and sprouting in endless convolutions—why, that is something like it.

That is, sometimes!

There is one marked peculiarity about this paper, a thing nobody seems to notice but myself, and that is that it changes as the light changes.

When the sun shoots in through the east window—I always watch for   150
that first long, straight ray—it changes so quickly that I never can quite believe it.

That is why I watch it always.

By moonlight—the moon shines in all night when there is a moon—I wouldn't know it was the same paper.

At night in any kind of light, in twilight, candlelight, lamplight, and worst of all by moonlight, it becomes bars! The outside pattern I mean, and the woman behind it is as plain as can be.

I didn't realize for a long time what the thing was that showed behind, that dim sub-pattern, but now I am quite sure it is a woman.

By daylight she is subdued, quiet. I fancy it is the pattern that keeps her so   155
still. It is so puzzling. It keeps me quiet by the hour.

I lie down ever so much now. John says it is good for me, and to sleep all I can.

Indeed he started the habit by making me lie down for an hour after each meal.

It is a very bad habit I am convinced, for you see I don't sleep.

And that cultivates deceit, for I don't tell them I'm awake—O, no!

The fact is I am getting a little afraid of John.   160

He seems very queer sometimes, and even Jennie has an inexplicable look.

It strikes me occasionally, just as a scientific hypothesis,—that perhaps it is the paper!

I have watched John when he did not know I was looking, and come into the room suddenly on the most innocent excuses, and I've caught him several times *looking at the paper*! And Jennie too. I caught Jennie with her hand on it once.

She didn't know I was in the room, and when I asked her in a quiet, a very quiet voice, with the most restrained manner possible, what she was doing with the paper—she turned around as if she had been caught stealing, and looked quite angry—asked me why I should frighten her so!

Then she said that the paper stained everything it touched, that she had   165
found yellow smooches on all my clothes and John's, and she wished we would be more careful!

Did not that sound innocent? But I know she was studying that pattern, and I am determined that nobody shall find it out but myself!

Life is very much more exciting now than it used to be. You see I have something more to expect, to look forward to, to watch. I really do eat better, and am more quiet than I was.

John is so pleased to see me improve! He laughed a little the other day, and said I seemed to be flourishing in spite of my wallpaper.

I turned it off with a laugh. I had no intention of telling him it was *because* of the wallpaper—he would make fun of me. He might even want to take me away.

I don't want to leave now until I have found it out. There is a week more, and I think that will be enough. 170

I'm feeling ever so much better! I don't sleep much at night, for it is so interesting to watch developments; but I sleep a good deal in the daytime.

In the daytime it is tiresome and perplexing.

There are always new shoots on the fungus, and new shades of yellow all over it. I cannot keep count of them, though I have tried conscientiously.

It is the strangest yellow, that wallpaper! It makes me think of all the yellow things I ever saw—not beautiful ones like buttercups, but old foul, bad yellow things.

But there is something else about that paper—the smell! I noticed it the moment we came into the room, but with so much air and sun it was not bad. Now we have had a week of fog and rain, and whether the windows are open or not, the smell is here. 175

It creeps all over the house.

I find it hovering in the dining-room, skulking in the parlor, hiding in the hall, lying in wait for me on the stairs.

It gets into my hair.

Even when I go to ride, if I turn my head suddenly and surprise it—there is that smell!

Such a peculiar odor, too! I have spent hours in trying to analyze it, to find what it smelled like. 180

It is not bad—at first, and very gentle, but quite the subtlest, most enduring odor I ever met.

In this damp weather it is awful, I wake up in the night and find it hanging over me.

It used to disturb me at first. I thought seriously of burning the house—to reach the smell.

But now I am used to it. The only thing I can think of that it is like is the *color* of the paper! A yellow smell.

There is a very funny mark on this wall, low down, near the mopboard. A streak that runs round the room. It goes behind every piece of furniture, except the bed, a long, straight, even *smooch*, as if it had been rubbed over and over. 185

I wonder how it was done and who did it, and what they did it for. Round and round and round—round and round and round—it makes me dizzy!

I really have discovered something at last.

Through watching so much at night, when it changes so, I have finally found out.

The front pattern *does* move—and no wonder! The woman behind shakes it!

Sometimes I think there are a great many women behind, and sometimes   190
only one, and she crawls around fast, and her crawling shakes it all over.

Then in the very bright spots she keeps still, and in the very shady spots she
just takes hold of the bars and shakes them hard.

And she is all the time trying to climb through. But nobody could climb
through that pattern—it strangles so; I think that is why it has so many heads.

They get through, and then the pattern strangles them off and turns them
upside down, and makes their eyes white!

If those heads were covered or taken off it would not be half so bad.

I think that woman gets out in the daytime!   195

And I'll tell you why—privately—I've seen her!

I can see her out of every one of my windows!

It is the same woman, I know, for she is always creeping, and most women
do not creep by daylight.

I see her in that long shaded lane, creeping up and down. I see her in those
dark grape arbors, creeping all around the garden.

I see her on that long road under the trees, creeping along, and when a   200
carriage comes she hides under the blackberry vines.

I don't blame her a bit. It must be very humiliating to be caught creeping
by daylight!

I always lock the door when I creep by daylight. I can't do it at night, for I
know John would suspect something at once.

And John is so queer now, that I don't want to irritate him. I wish he would
take another room! Besides, I don't want anybody to get that woman out at
night but myself.

I often wonder if I could see her out of all the windows at once.

But, turn as fast as I can, I can only see out of one at one time.   205

And though I always see her, she *may* be able to creep faster than I can turn!

I have watched her sometimes away off in the open country, creeping as
fast as a cloud shadow in a high wind.

If only that top pattern could be gotten off from the under one! I mean to try it,
little by little.

I have found out another funny thing, but I shan't tell it this time! It does
not do to trust people too much.

There are only two more days to get this paper off, and I believe John is be-   210
ginning to notice. I don't like the look in his eyes.

And I heard him ask Jennie a lot of professional questions, about me. She
had a very good report to give.

She said I slept a good deal in the daytime.

John knows I don't sleep very well at night, for all I'm so quiet!

He asked me all sorts of questions too, and pretended to be very loving
and kind.

As if I couldn't see through him!   215

Still, I don't wonder he acts so, sleeping under this paper for three months.

It only interests me, but I feel sure John and Jennie are secretly affected by it.

*   *   *

Hurrah! This is the last day, but it is enough. John is to stay in town over night, and won't be out until this evening.

Jennie wanted to sleep with me—the sly thing! But I told her I should undoubtedly rest better for a night all alone.

That was clever, for really I wasn't alone a bit! As soon as it was moonlight and   220
that poor thing began to crawl and shake the pattern, I got up and ran to help her.

I pulled and she shook, I shook and she pulled, and before morning we had peeled off yards of that paper.

A strip about as high as my head and half around the room.

And then when the sun came and that awful pattern began to laugh at me, I declared I would finish it to-day!

We go away to-morrow, and they are moving all my furniture down again to leave things as they were before.

Jennie looked at the wall in amazement, but I told her merrily that I did it   225
out of pure spite at the vicious thing.

She laughed and said she wouldn't mind doing it herself, but I must not get tired.

How she betrayed herself that time!

But I am here, and no person touches this paper but me,—not *alive*!

She tried to get me out of the room—it was too patent! But I said it was so quiet and empty and clean now that I believed I would lie down again and sleep all I could, and not to wake me even for dinner—I would call when I woke.

So now she is gone, and the servants are gone, and the things are gone,   230
and there is nothing left but that great bedstead nailed down, with the canvas mattress we found on it.

We shall sleep downstairs to-night, and take the boat home to-morrow.

I quite enjoy the room, now it is bare again.

How those children did tear about here!

This bedstead is fairly gnawed!

But I must get to work.   235

I have locked the door and thrown the key down into the front path.

I don't want to go out, and I don't want to have anybody come in, till John comes.

I want to astonish him.

I've got a rope up here that even Jennie did not find. If that woman does get out, and tries to get away, I can tie her!

But I forgot I could not reach far without anything to stand on!   240

This bed will *not* move!

I tried to lift and push it until I was lame, and then I got so angry I bit off a little piece at one corner—but it hurt my teeth.

Then I peeled off all the paper I could reach standing on the floor. It sticks horribly and the pattern just enjoys it! All those strangled heads and bulbous eyes and waddling fungus growths just shriek with derision!

I am getting angry enough to do something desperate. To jump out of the window would be admirable exercise, but the bars are too strong even to try.

Besides I wouldn't do it. Of course not. I know well enough that a step like   245
that is improper and might be misconstrued.

I don't like to *look* out of the windows even—there are so many of those
creeping women, and they creep so fast.

I wonder if they all come out of that wallpaper as I did?

But I am securely fastened now by my well-hidden rope—you don't get *me*
out in the road there!

I suppose I shall have to get back behind the pattern when it comes night,
and that is hard!

It is so pleasant to be out in this great room and creep around as I please!   250

I don't want to go outside. I won't, even if Jennie asks me to.

For outside you have to creep on the ground, and everything is green instead of yellow.

But here I can creep smoothly on the floor, and my shoulder just fits in that
long smooch around the wall, so I cannot lose my way.

Why, there's John at the door!

It is no use, young man, you can't open it!   255

How he does call and pound!

Now he's crying for an axe.

It would be a shame to break down that beautiful door!

"John dear!" said I in the gentlest voice, "the key is down by the front steps,
under a plantain leaf!"

That silenced him for a few moments.   260

Then he said—very quietly indeed, "Open the door, my darling!"

"I can't," said I. "The key is down by the front door under a plantain
leaf!"

And then I said it again, several times, very gently and slowly, and said it so
often that he had to go and see, and he got it of course, and came in. He stopped
short by the door.

"What is the matter?" he cried. "For God's sake, what are you doing!"

I kept on creeping just the same, but I looked at him over my shoulder.   265

"I've got out at last," said I, "in spite of you and Jane. And I've pulled off
most of the paper, so you can't put me back!"

Now why should that man have fainted? But he did, and right across my
path by the wall, so that I had to creep over him every time!   *[1892]*

≣ THINKING ABOUT THE TEXT

1. What psychological stages does the narrator go through as the story
   progresses?

2. How does the wallpaper function as a symbol in this story? What do
   you conclude about the narrator when she becomes increasingly interested in the woman she finds there?

3. Explain your ultimate view of the narrator, by using specific details of the
   story and by identifying some of the warrants or assumptions behind

your opinion. Do you admire her? Sympathize with her? Recoil from her? What would you say to someone who simply dismisses her as crazy?

4. The story is narrated in the present tense. Would its effect be different if it were narrated in the past tense? Why, or why not?

5. In real life, Gilman's husband and her doctor were two separate people. In the story, the narrator's husband is her doctor as well. Why do you think Gilman made this change? What is the effect of her combining husband and doctor?

CHARLOTTE PERKINS GILMAN
Why I Wrote "The Yellow Wallpaper"

Gilman published the following piece in the October 1913 issue of her magazine, The Forerunner.

Many and many a reader has asked that. When the story first came out, in the *New England Magazine* about 1891, a Boston physician made protest in *The Transcript*. Such a story ought not to be written, he said; it was enough to drive anyone mad to read it.

Another physician, in Kansas I think, wrote to say that it was the best description of incipient insanity he had ever seen, and—begging my pardon—had I been there?

Now the story of the story is this:

For many years I suffered from a severe and continuous nervous breakdown tending to melancholia—and beyond. During about the third year of this trouble I went, in devout faith and some faint stir of hope, to a noted specialist in nervous diseases, the best known in the country. This wise man put me to bed and applied the rest cure, to which a still good physique responded so promptly that, he concluded there was nothing much the matter with me, and sent me home with solemn advice to "live as domestic a life as far as possible," to "have but two hours' intellectual life a day," and "never to touch pen, brush, or pencil again as long as I lived." This was in 1887.

I went home and obeyed those directions for some three months, and came   5
so near the border line of utter mental ruin that I could see over.

Then, using the remnants of intelligence that remained, and helped by a wise friend, I cast the noted specialist's advice to the winds and went to work again—work, the normal life of every human being; work, in which is joy and growth and service, without which one is a pauper and a parasite; ultimately recovering some measure of power.

Being naturally moved to rejoicing by this narrow escape, I wrote *The Yellow Wallpaper*, with its embellishments and additions to carry out the ideal (I never had hallucinations or objections to my mural decorations) and sent a copy to the physician who so nearly drove me mad. He never acknowledged it.

The little book is valued by alienists° and as a good specimen of one kind of literature. It has to my knowledge saved one woman from a similar fate — so terrifying her family that they let her out into normal activity and she recovered.

But the best result is this. Many years later I was told that the great specialist had admitted to friends of his that he had altered his treatment of neurasthenia since reading *The Yellow Wallpaper.*

It was not intended to drive people crazy, but to save people from being   10 driven crazy, and it worked.   *[1913]*

alienists: Nineteenth-century term for psychiatrists.

☰ THINKING ABOUT THE TEXT

1. S. Weir Mitchell was the "noted specialist in nervous diseases" (para. 4) whom Gilman mentions. Yet she does not identify him by name. Why not, do you think? Some historians argue that, contrary to Gilman's claim here, Mitchell continued to believe his "rest cure" valid. Does this issue of fact matter to your judgment of her piece? Why, or why not?

2. Look again at Gilman's last sentence. Do you believe that her story could indeed "save people from being driven crazy"? Why, or why not?

3. Does this piece as a whole affect your interpretation and opinion of Gilman's story? Why, or why not? In general, how much do you think readers of a story should know about its author's life?

S. WEIR MITCHELL
From *The Evolution of the Rest Treatment*

Charlotte Perkins Gilman sought help from Silas Weir Mitchell (1829–1914) because he was a well-known and highly respected physician who had treated many women's mental problems. Weir Mitchell developed his "rest cure" while serving as an army surgeon during the Civil War. Ironically, like Gilman he was also a writer. Besides producing numerous monographs on medical subjects, he published many short stories and novels. The following is an excerpt from a lecture that Weir Mitchell gave to the Philadelphia Neurological Society in 1904, twelve years after "The Yellow Wallpaper" appeared. As you will see, Weir Mitchell was still enthusiastic about his "rest cure," although he had changed it in certain respects since devising it.

I have been asked to come here to-night to speak to you on some subject connected with nervous disease. I had hoped to have had ready a fitting paper for so notable an occasion, but have been prevented by public engagements and private business so as to make it quite impossible. I have, therefore, been driven to ask whether it would be agreeable if I should speak in regard to the mode in which the treatment of disease by rest was evolved. This being favorably received, I am here this evening to say a few words on that subject.

You all know full well that the art of cure rests upon a number of sciences, and that what we do in medicine, we cannot always explain, and that our methods are far from having the accuracy involved in the term scientific. Very often, however, it is found that what comes to us through some accident or popular use and proves of value, is defensible in the end by scientific explanatory research. This was the case as regards the treatment I shall briefly consider for you to-night.

The first indication I ever had of the great value of mere rest in disease, was during the Civil War, when there fell into the hands of Doctors Morehouse, Keen, and myself, a great many cases of what we called acute exhaustion. These were men, who, being tired by much marching, gave out suddenly at the end of some unusual exertion, and remained for weeks, perhaps months, in a pitiable state of what we should call today, Neurasthenia. In these war cases, it came on with strange abruptness. It was more extreme and also more certainly curable than are most of the graver male cases which now we are called on to treat.

I have seen nothing exactly like it in civil experience, but the combination of malaria, excessive exertion, and exposure provided cases such as no one sees today. Complete rest and plentiful diet usually brought these men up again and in many instances enabled them to return to the front.

In 1872 I had charge of a man who had locomotor ataxia° with extreme pain in the extremities, and while making some unusual exertion, he broke his right thigh. This confined him to his bed for three months, and the day he got up, he broke his left thigh. This involved another three months of rest. At the end of that time he confessed with satisfaction that his ataxia was better, and that he was, as he remained thereafter, free from pain. I learned from this, and two other cases, that in ataxia the bones are brittle, and I learned also that rest in bed is valuable in a proportion of such cases. You may perceive that my attention was thus twice drawn towards the fact that mere rest had certain therapeutic values.

In 1874 Mrs. G., of B——, Maine, came to see me in the month of January. I have described her case elsewhere, so that it is needless to go into detail here, except to say that she was a lady of ample means, with no special troubles or annoyances, but completely exhausted by having had children in rapid succession and from having undertaken to do charitable and other work to an extent far beyond her strength. When first I saw this tall woman, large, gaunt, weighing under a hundred pounds, her complexion pale and acneous, and heard her story, I was for a time in a state of such therapeutic despair as usually fell upon physicians of that day when called upon to treat such cases. She had been to Spas, to physicians of the utmost eminence, passed through the hands

5

---

ataxia: An inability to control muscular movements that is symptomatic of some nervous diseases.

of gynecologists, worn spinal supporters, and taken every tonic known to the books. When I saw her she was unable to walk up stairs. Her exercise was limited to moving feebly up and down her room, a dozen times a day. She slept little and, being very intelligent, felt deeply her inability to read or write. Any such use of the eyes caused headache and nausea. Conversation tired her, and she had by degrees accepted a life of isolation. She was able partially to digest and retain her meals if she lay down in a noiseless and darkened room. Any disturbance or the least excitement, in short, any effort, caused nausea and immediate rejection of her meal. With care she could retain enough food to preserve her life and hardly to do more. Anemia, which we had then no accurate means of measuring, had been met by half a dozen forms of iron, all of which were said to produce headache, and generally to disagree with her. Naturally enough, her case had been pronounced to be hysteria, but calling names may relieve a doctor and comfort him in failure, but does not always assist the patient, and to my mind there was more of a general condition of nervous excitability due to the extreme of weakness than I should have been satisfied to label with the apologetic label hysteria.

I sat beside this woman day after day, hearing her pitiful story, and distressed that a woman, young, once handsome, and with every means of enjoyment in life should be condemned to what she had been told was a state of hopeless invalidism. After my third or fourth visit, with a deep sense that everything had been done for her that able men could with reason suggest, and many things which reason never could have suggested, she said to me that I appeared to have nothing to offer which had not been tried over and over again. I asked her for another day before she gave up the hope which had brought her to me. The night brought counsel. The following morning I said to her, if you are at rest you appear to digest your meals better. "Yes," she said. "I have been told that on that account I ought to lie in bed. It has been tried, but when I remain in bed for a few days, I lose all appetite, have intense constipation, and get up feeling weaker than when I went to bed. Please do not ask me to go to bed." Nevertheless, I did, and a week in bed justified her statements. She threw up her meals undigested, and was manifestly worse for my experiment. Sometimes the emesis° was mere regurgitation, sometimes there was nausea and violent straining, with consequent extreme exhaustion. She declared that unless she had the small exercise of walking up and down her room, she was infallibly worse. I was here between two difficulties. That she needed rest I saw, that she required some form of exercise I also saw. How could I unite the two?

As I sat beside her, with a keen sense of defeat, it suddenly occurred to me that some time before, I had seen a man, known as a layer on of hands, use very rough rubbing for a gentleman who was in a state of general paresis.° Mr. S. had asked me if I objected to this man rubbing him. I said no, and that I should like to see him do so, as he had relieved, to my knowledge, cases of rheumatic stiffness. I was present at two sittings and saw this man rub my patient. He kept him sitting in a chair at the time and was very rough and violent like

---

emesis: Vomiting.   **paresis:** Brain syphilis.

the quacks now known as osteopaths. I told him he had injured my patient by his extreme roughness, and that if he rubbed him at all he must be more gentle. He took the hint and as a result there was every time a notable but temporary gain. Struck with this, I tried to have rubbing used on spinal cases, but those who tried to do the work were inefficient, and I made no constant use of it. It remained, however, on my mind, and recurred to me as I sat beside this wreck of a useful and once vigorous woman. The thought was fertile. I asked myself why rubbing might not prove competent to do for the muscles and tardy circulation what voluntary exercise does. I said to myself, this may be exercise without exertion, and wondered why I had not long before had this pregnant view of the matter.

Suffice it to say that I brought a young woman to Mrs. G.'s bedside and told her how I thought she ought to be rubbed. The girl was clever, and developed talent in that direction, and afterwards became the first of that great number of people who have since made a livelihood by massage. I watched the rubbing two or three times, giving instructions, in fact developing out of the clumsy massage I had seen, the manual of a therapeutic means, at that time entirely new to me. A few days later I fell upon the idea of giving electric passive exercise and cautiously added this second agency. Meanwhile, as she had always done best when secluded, I insisted on entire rest and shut out friends, relatives, books, and letters. I had some faith that I should succeed. In ten days I was sure the woman had found a new tonic, hope, and blossomed like a rose. Her symptoms passed away one by one. I was soon able to add to her diet, to feed her between meals, to give her malt daily, and, after a time, to conceal in it full doses of pyro-phosphates of iron. First, then, I had found two means which enabled me to use rest in bed without causing the injurious effects of unassisted rest; secondly, I had discovered that massage was a tonic of extraordinary value; thirdly, I had learned that with this combination of seclusion, massage, and electricity, I could overfeed the patient until I had brought her into a state of entire health. I learned later the care which had to be exercised in getting these patients out of bed. But this does not concern us now. In two months she gained forty pounds and was a cheerful, blooming woman, fit to do as she pleased. She has remained, save for time's ravage, what I made her.

It may strike you as interesting that for a while I was not fully aware of the enormous value of a therapeutic discovery which employed no new agents, but owed its usefulness to a combination of means more or less well known. 10

Simple rest as a treatment had been suggested, but not in this class of cases. Massage has a long history. Used, I think, as a luxury by the Orientals for ages, it was employed by Ling in 1813. It never attained perfection in the hands of the Swedes, nor do they to-day understand the proper use of this agent. It was over and over recognized in Germany, but never generally accepted. In France, at a later period, Dreyfus, in 1841, wrote upon it and advised its use, as did Recamier and Lainé in 1868. Two at least of these authors thought it useful as a general agent, but no one seems to have accepted their views, nor was its value as a tonic spoken of in the books on therapeutics or recommended on any text-book as a powerful toning agent. It was used here in the Rest

Treatment, and this, I think, gave it vogue and caused the familiar use of this invaluable therapeutic measure.

A word before I close. My first case left me in May, 1874, and shortly afterwards I began to employ the same method in other cases, being careful to choose only those which seemed best suited to it. My first mention in print of the treatment was in 1875, in the Sequin Lectures, Vol. 1, No. 4, "Rest in the Treatment of Disease." In that paper I first described Mrs. G.'s case. My second paper was in 1877, an address before the Medico-Chirurgical faculty of Maryland, and the same year I printed my book on "Rest Treatment." The one mistake in the book was the title. I was, however, so impressed at the time by the extraordinary gain in flesh and blood under this treatment that I made it too prominent in the title of the book. Let me say that for a long time the new treatment was received with the utmost incredulity. When I spoke in my papers of the people who had gained half a pound a day or more, my results were questioned and ridiculed in this city as approaching charlatanism. At a later date in England some physicians were equally wanting in foresight and courtesy. It seems incredible that any man who was a member of the British Medical Association could have said that he would rather see his patients not get well than have them cured by such a method as that. It was several years before it was taken up by Professor Goodell, and it was a longer time in making its way in Europe when by mere accident it came to be first used by Professor William Playfair.

I suffered keenly at that time from this unfair criticism, as any sensitive man must have done, for some who were eminent in the profession said of it and of me things which were most inconsiderate. Over and over in consultation I was rejected with ill-concealed scorn. I made no reply to my critics. I knew that time would justify me: I have added a long since accepted means of helping those whom before my day few helped. This is a sufficient reward for silence, patience, and self-faith. I fancy that there are in this room many who have profited for themselves and their patients by the thought which evolved the Rest Treatment as I sat by the bedside of my first rest case in 1874. Playfair said of it at the British Association that he had nothing to add to it and nothing to omit, and to this day no one has differed as to his verdict.

How fully the use of massage has been justified by the later scientific studies of Lauder Brunton, myself, and others you all know. It is one of the most scientific of remedial methods.   *[1904]*

≣ THINKING ABOUT THE TEXT

1. How would you describe Weir Mitchell's tone in this lecture? What self-image does he seem to cultivate? Support your answers by referring to specific words in the text.

2. Why does Weir Mitchell consider Mrs. G.'s case significant? In what ways does she resemble Gilman and the narrator of Gilman's story?

3. Weir Mitchell indicates that his patients have included male as well as female hysterics. Are we therefore justified in concluding that gender did not matter much in his application of the "rest cure"? Why, or why not?

JOHN HARVEY KELLOGG
From *The Ladies' Guide in Health and Disease*

John Harvey Kellogg (1852–1943) was an American physician who wrote much advice about how to discipline one's sexual desires and, in the case of women, how to be a good mother. As founder and superintendent of the Battle Creek Sanitarium in Michigan, Dr. Kellogg urged that his patients eat cereals as part of their treatment, and eventually his brother established the cereal company that bears their family name. Dr. Kellogg's keen interest in cereals and health foods is satirized in T. Coraghessan Boyle's 1993 novel, The Road to Wellville, *and the film based on that book. The following piece is an excerpt from Kellogg's 1882* Ladies' Guide in Health and Disease: Girlhood, Maidenhood, Wifehood, Motherhood. *In this selection, he virtually equates womanhood with motherhood and discusses what a woman must do to produce outstanding children. Kellogg's advice reflects the view that much of his society held about women — or at least about middle- and upper-class white women. His discussion of "puerperal mania" is especially relevant to Gilman's story.*

The special influence of the mother begins with the moment of conception. In fact it is possible that the mental condition at the time of the generative act has much to do with determining the character of the child, though it is generally conceded that at this time the influence of the father is greater than that of the mother. Any number of instances have occurred in which a drunken father has impressed upon his child the condition of his nervous system to such a degree as to render permanent in the child the staggering gait and maudlin manner which in his own case was a transient condition induced by the poisonous influence of alcohol. A child born as the result of a union in which both parents were in a state of beastly intoxication was idiotic.

Another fact might be added to impress the importance that the new being should be supplied from the very beginning of its existence with the very best conditions possible. Indeed, it is desirable to go back still further, and secure a proper preparation for the important function of maternity. The qualities which go to make up individuality of character are the result of the summing up of a long line of influences, too subtle and too varied to admit of full control, but still, to some degree at least, subject to management. The dominance of law is nowhere more evident than in the relation of ante-natal influences to character.

The hap-hazard way in which human beings are generated leaves no room for surprise that the race should deteriorate. No stock-breeder would expect anything but ruin should he allow his animals to propagate with no attention to their physical conditions or previous preparation.

Finding herself in a pregnant condition, the mother should not yield to the depressing influences which often crowd upon her. The anxieties and fears which women sometimes yield themselves to, grow with encouragement, until they become so absorbed as to be capable of producing a profoundly evil impression on the child. The true mother who is prepared for the functions of maternity, will welcome the evidence of pregnancy, and joyfully enter upon the Heaven-given task of molding a human character, of bringing into the world a new being whose life-history may involve the destinies of nations, or change the current of human thought for generations to come.

The pregnant mother should cultivate cheerfulness of mind and calmness   5
of temper, but should avoid excitements of all kinds, such as theatrical performances, public contests of various descriptions, etc. Anger, envy, irritability of temper, and, in fact, all the passions and propensities should be held in check. The fickleness of desire and the constantly varying whims which characterize the pregnant state in some women should not be regarded as uncontrollable, and to be yielded to as the only means of appeasing them. The mother should be gently encouraged to resist such tendencies when they become at all marked, and to assist her in the effort, her husband should endeavor to engage her mind by interesting conversation, reading, and various harmless and pleasant diversions.

If it is desired that the child should possess a special aptitude for any particular art or pursuit, during the period of pregnancy the mother's mind should be constantly directed in this channel. If artistic taste or skill is the trait desired, the mother should be surrounded by works of art of a high order of merit. She should read art, think art, talk, and write about art, and if possible, herself engage in the close practical study of some one or more branches of art, as painting, drawing, etching, or modeling. If ability for authorship is desired, then the mother should devote herself assiduously to literature. It is not claimed that by following these suggestions any mother can make of her children great artists or authors at will; but it is certain that by this means the greatest possibilities in individual cases can be attained; and it is certain that decided results have been secured by close attention to the principles laid down. It should be understood, however, that not merely a formal and desultory effort on the part of the mother is what is required. The theme selected must completely absorb her mind. It must be the one idea of her waking thoughts and the model on which is formed the dreams of her sleeping hours.

The question of diet during pregnancy as before stated is a vitally important one as regards the interests of the child. A diet into which enters largely such unwholesome articles as mustard, pepper, hot sauces, spices, and other stimulating condiments, engenders a love for stimulants in the disposition of the infant. Tea and coffee, especially if used to excess, undoubtedly tend in the same direction. We firmly believe that we have, in the facts first stated, the key to the constant increase in the consumption of ardent spirits. The children of the present generation inherit from their condiment-consuming, tea-, coffee-, and liquor-drinking, and tobacco-using parents, not simply a readiness for the acquirement of the habits mentioned, but a propensity for the use of stimulants which in persons of weak will-power and those whose circumstances are not the most favorable, becomes irresistible.

The present generation is also suffering in consequence of the impoverished diet of its parents. The modern custom of bolting the flour from the different grains has deprived millions of infants and children of the necessary supply of bone-making material, thus giving rise to a greatly increased frequency of the various diseases which arise from imperfect bony structure, as rickets, caries, premature decay of the teeth, etc. The proper remedy is the disuse of fine-flour bread and all other bolted grain preparations. Graham-flour bread, oatmeal, cracked wheat, and similar preparations, should be relied upon as the leading articles of diet. Supplemented by milk, the whole-grain preparations constitute a complete form of nourishment, and render a large amount of animal food not only unnecessary but really harmful on account of its stimulating character. It is by no means so necessary as is generally supposed that meat, fish, fowl, and flesh in various forms should constitute a large element of the dietary of the pregnant or nursing mother in order to furnish adequate nourishment for the developing child. We have seen the happiest results follow the employment of a strictly vegetarian dietary, and do not hesitate to advise moderation in the use of flesh food, though we do not recommend the entire discontinuance of its use by the pregnant mother who has been accustomed to use it freely.

A nursing mother should at once suspend nursing if she discovers that pregnancy has again occurred. The continuance of nursing under such circumstances is to the disadvantage of three individuals, the mother, the infant at the breast, and the developing child.

Sexual indulgence during pregnancy may be suspended with decided benefit to both mother and child. The most ancient medical writers call attention to the fact that by the practice of continence° during gestation, the pains of childbirth are greatly mitigated. The injurious influences upon the child of the gratification of the passions during the period when its character is being formed, is undoubtedly much greater than is usually supposed. We have no doubt that this is a common cause of the transmission of libidinous tendencies to the child; and that the tendency to abortion is induced by sexual indulgence has long been a well-established fact. The females of most animals resolutely resist the advances of the males during this period, being guided in harmony with natural law by their natural instincts which have been less perverted in them than in human beings. The practice of continence during pregnancy is also enforced in the harems of the East, which fact leads to the practice of abortion among women of this class who are desirous of remaining the special favorites of the common husband.

The general health of the mother must be kept up in every way. It is especially important that the regularity of the bowels should be maintained. Proper diet and as much physical exercise as can be taken are the best means for accomplishing this. When constipation is allowed to exist, the infant as well as

10

continence: Chastity, abstinence, or restraint.

the mother suffers. The effete products which should be promptly removed from the body, being long retained, are certain to find their way back into the system again, poisoning not only the blood of the mother but that of the developing fetus. . . .

Puerperal Mania. —This form of mental disease is most apt to show itself about two weeks after delivery. Although, fortunately, of not very frequent occurrence, it is a most serious disorder when it does occur, and hence we may with propriety introduce the following somewhat lengthy, but most graphic description of the disease from the pen of Dr. Ramsbotham, an eminent English physician: —

"In mania there is almost always, at the very commencement, a troubled, agitated, and hurried manner, a restless eye, an unnaturally anxious, suspicious, and unpleasing expression of face; —sometimes it is pallid, at others more flushed than usual; —an unaccustomed irritability of temper, and impatience of control or contradiction; a vacillation of purpose, or loss of memory; sometimes a rapid succession of contradictory orders are issued, or a paroxysm of excessive anger is excited about the merest trifle. Occasionally, one of the first indications will be a sullen obstinacy, or listlessness and stubborn silence. The patient lies on her back, and can by no means be persuaded to reply to the questions of her attendants, or she will repeat them, as an echo, until, all at once, without any apparent cause, she will break out into a torrent of language more or less incoherent, and her words will follow each other with surprising rapidity. These symptoms will sometimes show themselves rather suddenly, on the patient's awakening from a disturbed and unrefreshing sleep, or they may supervene more slowly when she has been harassed with wakefulness for three or four previous nights in succession, or perhaps ever since her delivery. She will very likely then become impressed with the idea that some evil has befallen her husband, or, what is still more usual, her child; that it is dead or stolen; and if it be brought to her, nothing can persuade her it is her own; she supposes it to belong to somebody else; or she will fancy that her husband is unfaithful to her, or that he and those about her have conspired to poison her. Those persons who are naturally the objects of her deepest and most devout affection, are regarded by her with jealousy, suspicion, and hatred. This is particularly remarkable with regard to her newly born infant; and I have known many instances where attempts have been made to destroy it when it has been incautiously left within her power. Sometimes, though rarely, may be observed a great anxiety regarding the termination of her own case, or a firm conviction that she is speedily about to die. I have observed upon occasions a constant movement of the lips, while the mouth was shut; or the patient is incessantly rubbing the inside of her lips with her fingers, or thrusting them far back into her mouth; and if questions are asked, particularly if she be desired to put out her tongue, she will often compress the lips forcibly together, as if with an obstinate determination of resistance. One peculiarity attending some cases of puerperal mania is the immorality and obscenity of the expressions uttered; they are often such, indeed, as to excite our astonishment that women in a respectable station of society could ever have become acquainted with such language."

The insanity of childbirth differs from that of pregnancy in that in the latter cases the patient is almost always melancholy,° while in the former there is active mania. Derangement of the digestive organs is a constant accompaniment of the disease.

If the patient has no previous or hereditary tendency to insanity, the prospect of a quite speedy recovery is good. The result is seldom immediately fatal, but the patient not infrequently remains in a condition of mental unsoundness for months or even years, and sometimes permanently.

Treatment: When there is reason to suspect a liability to puerperal mania from previous mental disease or from hereditary influence, much can be done to ward off an attack. Special attention must be paid to the digestive organs, which should be regulated by proper food and simple means to aid digestion. The tendency to sleeplessness must be combatted by careful nursing, light massage at night, rubbing of the spine, alternate hot and cold applications to the spine, cooling the head by cloths wrung out of cold water, and the use of the warm bath at bed time. These measures are often successful in securing sleep when all other measures fail.

The patient must be kept very quiet. Visitors, even if near relatives, must not be allowed when the patient is at all nervous or disturbed, and it is best to exclude nearly every one from the sick-room with the exception of the nurse, who should be a competent and experienced person.

When the attack has really begun, the patient must have the most vigilant watchcare, not being left alone for a moment. It is much better to care for the patient at home, when possible to do so efficiently, than to take her to an asylum.

When evidences of returning rationality appear, the greatest care must be exercised to prevent too great excitement. Sometimes a change of air, if the patient is sufficiently strong, physically, will at this period prove eminently beneficial. A visit from a dear friend will sometimes afford a needed stimulus to the dormant faculties. Such cases as these of course require intelligent medical supervision.

[1882]

melancholy: Mental state characterized by severe depression, somatic problems, and hallucinations or delusions.

≡ THINKING ABOUT THE TEXT

1. What specific responsibilities does Kellogg assign to women? What are some key assumptions he makes about them?

2. Quite possibly Kellogg would have said that the narrator of Gilman's story suffers from puerperal mania. What details of the story would support this diagnosis? What significant details of the narrator's life, if

any, would Kellogg be ignoring if he saw her as *merely* a case of puerperal mania?

3. If Kellogg's advice were published today, what parts of it do you think readers would accept? What parts do you think many readers would reject?

≡ WRITING ABOUT ISSUES

1. After reading the three essays given here, research women's psychological disorders of the nineteenth century and write an essay that argues that those "disorders" were the result of male attitudes toward women.

2. Research the term "female hysteria" and write a report that includes the ideas of S. Weir Mitchell and other prominent nineteenth-century doctors. Include in your report your evaluation of their credibility.

3. Research mental illness in America from the Puritans to the present. Write an essay that argues that mental illness is connected to the culture it occurs in.

4. Research such contemporary psychological problems as depression, bulimia, anorexia, and dissociative identity disorders. Write an essay that tries to explain why these diseases seem to affect mostly women.

Literature and Its Issues

CHAPTER 7

Families

In the not-too-distant past, family life was the focal point of our emotional existence, the center of all our important psychological successes and failures. It was common for several generations to live together in the same town and even the same home. Grandparents, aunts, and uncles were an intimate part of daily life, not just relatives one saw during the holidays. Besides the usual emotional drama that always takes place between parents and children, there were the additional tensions that inevitably arise when the values of the old clash with those of the young. Of course, there was also the comforting emotional support available from more than just a mother and father as well as the sense of belonging and bonding with the many aunts, uncles, and cousins that usually lived nearby.

As extended families become less common, the emotional stakes of home life seem higher than ever. Since we rely on one another more in today's nuclear family, our sense of disappointment, our sense of rejection, and our sense of unworthiness can be more acute. During childhood, the drama of family life can stamp an indelible mark on our psyches, leaving psychological scars that make safe passage into adulthood difficult. Our status within the family can also offer us a sense of worth and confidence that leads to contentment and success later on. For all of us, however, family life is composed not of psychological and sociological generalities but, rather, of our one-to-one relationships with fathers, sisters, grandmothers. Writers often give us imaginative, honest, and illuminating charts of their successes and failures in negotiating both the calm and the choppy waters of our family journeys. The following clusters do not hope to be complete or representative of your experiences. We do hope, however, that in reading and discussing these poems and stories, you will find them an interesting and provocative catalyst for you to delve into the joys and sorrows of your own life in a family.

The chapter opens with four poems about reconnecting with fathers, followed by four critical commentaries on Sylvia Plath's brilliant classic, "Daddy." The third cluster gives us loving, honest, and humorous snapshots of grandparents. Next is a collection of poems by Sharon Olds as she meditates on her family. The fourth cluster contains four poems that record difficulties of gays and lesbians in families. The sixth group examines stories that reveal the tensions that often arise between mothers and daughters. Next, two stories deal with two boys' searches for a responsible father. Brothers in conflict is the focus of two stories by Tobias Wolff and James Baldwin in the eighth cluster, followed by Tennessee Williams' classic play, *The Glass Menagerie*, along with a humorous revision by Christopher Durang. Lorraine Hansberry's memorable *A Raisin in the Sun* is seen in its cultural context in the tenth cluster. Three memoirs about food and families comprise the penultimate grouping, which is followed by a fictional and nonfictional narrative about fateful decisions concerning parenthood.

≡ Reconciling with Fathers: Poems

LUCILLE CLIFTON, "forgiving my father"

ROBERT HAYDEN, "Those Winter Sundays"

THEODORE ROETHKE, "My Papa's Waltz"

LI-YOUNG LEE, "My Father, in Heaven, Is Reading Out Loud"

In childhood, our emotions are often intense. Fears about life arise because we feel so powerless. For some of us, our fathers held all the power. Fathers may use their power in various ways — some to control or abuse, others to comfort and protect. We form perceptions about our fathers from these early memories. Often we become judgmental about their failures in the world or their failures as parents. As we grow older, we sometimes come to terms with our fathers and see them simply as human beings with strengths and weaknesses. But it is not always simple; some wounds may be too deep for us to reconcile. The five poets in this cluster approach memories of their fathers with different perspectives and purposes: to forgive their fathers and perhaps themselves, to remember fondly, to come to a closure, to relive a past that still haunts them, to come to terms with loss.

≡ BEFORE YOU READ

Make a list of four strong memories about your father from your childhood. Are the memories positive or not? Can you remember how you felt then? Is it different from how you feel now? How can you explain the difference?

LUCILLE CLIFTON
forgiving my father

Lucille Clifton (1936–2010) was born in a small town near Buffalo, New York. She attended Howard University and Fredonia State Teacher's College and taught poetry at a number of universities. Her numerous awards for writing include two creative writing fellowships from the National Endowment for the Arts (1970 and 1973), two Pulitzer Prize nominations (for Good Woman: Poems and a Memoir *and for* Next, *both in 1988), several major poetry awards, and an Emmy. The mother of six, Clifton has written fifteen children's books. She was a former poet laureate of Maryland and the Distinguished Professor of Humanities at St. Mary's College. "Forgiving my father" is from her 1980 book,* Two-Headed Woman. Voices, *her most recent book, was published in 2008.*

it is friday. we have come
to the paying of the bills.
all week you have stood in my dreams
like a ghost, asking for more time
but today is payday, payday old man,   5
my mother's hand opens in her early grave
and i hold it out like a good daughter.

there is no more time for you. there will
never be time enough daddy daddy old lecher
old liar. i wish you were rich so i could take it all   10
and give the lady what she was due
but you were the son of a needy father,
the father of a needy son,
you gave her all you had
which was nothing. you have already given her   15
all you had.

you are the pocket that was going to open
and come up empty any friday.
you were each other's bad bargain, not mine.
daddy old pauper old prisoner, old dead man   20
what am i doing here collecting?
you lie side by side in debtor's boxes
and no accounting will open them up.   *[1980]*

≣ THINKING ABOUT THE TEXT

1. How might you answer the question in line 21? Are the last two lines of
   the poem a kind of answer? Is there some way we can "collect" from the
   dead?

2. Should we bury the dead — that is, should we let the past go and let
   bygones be bygones? Or is it necessary to settle old scores? What do you
   think Clifton's answer would be?

3. How consistently does Clifton use the payday analogy? Make a list of
   words that reinforce her overall scheme.

4. Would you think differently about the speaker's father if Clifton had
   written "elderly one" instead of "old man" (line 5) or "old playboy / old
   fibber" instead of "old lecher / old liar" (lines 9–10)?

5. Some readers look for tensions or contradictions early in a poem, hoping they will be resolved at the end. Does this poem end in a resolution
   of paying up and forgiving?

ROBERT HAYDEN
Those Winter Sundays

Born in Detroit, Michigan, African American poet Robert Hayden (1913–1980) grew up in a poor neighborhood where his natural parents left him with family friends. He grew up with the Hayden name, not discovering his original name until he was forty. Hayden attended Detroit City College (now Wayne State University) from 1932 to 1936, worked in the Federal Writer's Project, and later earned his M.A. at the University of Michigan in 1944. He taught at Fisk University from 1946 to 1968 and at the University of Michigan from 1968 to 1980 and published several collections of poetry. Although his poems sometimes contain autobiographical elements, Hayden is primarily a formalist poet who preferred that his poems not be limited to personal or ethnic interpretations. "Those Winter Sundays" is from Angle of Ascent (1966).

Sundays too my father got up early
and put his clothes on in the blueblack cold,
then with cracked hands that ached
from labor in the weekday weather made
banked fires blaze. No one ever thanked him.   5

I'd wake and hear the cold splintering, breaking.
When the rooms were warm, he'd call,
and slowly I would rise and dress,
fearing the chronic angers of that house,

Speaking indifferently to him,   10
who had driven out the cold
and polished my good shoes as well.
What did I know, what did I know
of love's austere and lonely offices?   [1962]

≡ THINKING ABOUT THE TEXT

1. Is the concluding question meant rhetorically — that is, is the answer so obvious that no real reply is expected? Write a response that you think the son might give now.

2. Why did the children never thank their father? Is this common? What specific things might you thank your father (or mother) for? Do parents have basic responsibilities to their children that do not warrant thanks?

3. Is there evidence that the son loves his father now? Did he then? Why did he speak "indifferently" (line 10) to his father? Is it clear what the "chronic angers" (line 9) are? Should it be?

4. How might you fill in the gaps here? For example, how old do you think the boy is? How old is the father? What kind of a job might he have? What else can you infer?

5. What is the speaker's tone? Is he hoping for your understanding? Your sympathy? Are we responsible for the things we do in childhood? Is this speaker repentant or simply explaining?

≡ MAKING COMPARISONS

1. What degrees of forgiveness do you see in Clifton's and Hayden's poems?
2. Writing a poem for one's father seems different from writing a poem about him. Explain this statement in reference to these poems.
3. Compare the purpose of the questions in each poem. How might each poet answer the other poet's questions?

THEODORE ROETHKE
My Papa's Waltz

Born in Saginaw, Michigan, Theodore Roethke (1908–1963) was strongly influenced by childhood experiences with his father, a usually stern man who sold plants and flowers and who kept a large greenhouse, the setting for many of Roethke's poems. Roethke was educated at the University of Michigan, took courses at Harvard, and taught at several universities before becoming poet-in-residence at the University of Washington in 1948. Roethke's books include The Lost Son and Other Poems *(1949), the source for "My Papa's Waltz";* The Waking *(1953), which won a Pulitzer Prize; and* Words for the Wind *(1958), which won the National Book Award. Roethke's intensely personal style ensures his place among the most influential postmodern American poets.*

The whiskey on your breath
Could make a small boy dizzy;
But I hung on like death:
Such waltzing was not easy.

We romped until the pans   5
Slid from the kitchen shelf;
My mother's countenance
Could not unfrown itself.

The hand that held my wrist
Was battered on one knuckle;   10
At every step you missed
My right ear scraped a buckle.

You beat time on my head
With a palm caked hard by dirt,
Then waltzed me off to bed   15
Still clinging to your shirt.
                                                                [1948]

☰ THINKING ABOUT THE TEXT

1. Is the narrator looking back at his father with fondness? Bitterness?

2. Would the poem make a different impression if we changed "romped" (line 5) to "fought" and "waltzing" (line 4) to "dancing"?

3. Why did the boy hang on and cling to his father? From fear? From affection?

4. What is the mother's role here? How would you characterize her frown?

5. Readers often have a negative view of the relationship represented here, but many change their minds, seeing some positive aspects to the father and son's waltz. How might you account for this revision?

☰ MAKING COMPARISONS

1. Would you have read this poem differently if the poet had used Clifton's title "forgiving my father"?

2. How would you compare the tone of Roethke's poem with that of Hayden's? Do they miss their fathers?

3. Would you say that Roethke has more complex feelings about his father, whereas Clifton and Hayden seem clearer?

LI-YOUNG LEE

My Father, in Heaven, Is Reading Out Loud

Li-Young Lee (b. 1959) was born in Indonesia to Chinese parents. His father taught medicine and philosophy in Jakarta. During a purge of ethnic Chinese, Lee's father was imprisoned because of his Western interests. He eventually escaped, and the family finally settled in Pittsburgh, where his father became a Presbyterian minister. Lee graduated from the University of Pittsburgh in 1979. He has won many prizes for his poetry, from Rose *(1986) to* Book of My Nights *(2001). He lives in Chicago with his wife and two sons.*

> My father, in heaven, is reading out loud
> to himself Psalms or news. Now he ponders what
> he's read. No. He is listening for the sound
> of children in the yard. Was that laughing
> or crying? So much depends upon the   5
> answer, for either he will go on reading,
> or he'll run to save a child's day from grief.
> As it is in heaven, so it was on earth.
>
> Because my father walked the earth with a grave,
> determined rhythm, my shoulders ached   10

from his gaze. Because my father's shoulders
ached from the pulling of oars, my life now moves
with a powerful back-and-forth rhythm:
nostalgia, speculation. Because he
made me recite a book a month, I forget   15
everything as soon as I read it. And knowledge
never comes but while I'm mid-stride a flight
of stairs, or lost a moment on some avenue.

A remarkable disappointment to him,
I am like anyone who arrives late   20
in the millennium and is unable
to stay to the end of days. The world's
beginnings are obscure to me, its outcomes
inaccessible. I don't understand
the source of starlight, or starlight's destinations.   25
And already another year slides out
of balance. But I don't disparage scholars;
my father was one and I loved him,
who packed his books once, and all of our belongings,
then sat down to await instruction   30
from his god, yes, but also from a radio.
At the doorway, I watched, and I suddenly
knew he was one like me, who got my learning
under a lintel; he was one of the powerless,
to whom knowledge came while he sat among   35
suitcases, boxes, old newspapers, string.

He did not decide peace or war, home or exile,
escape by land or escape by sea.
He waited merely, as always someone
waits, far, near, here, hereafter, to find out: 40
is it praise or lament hidden in the next moment?   *[1990]*

≡ **THINKING ABOUT THE TEXT**

1. Lee begins his poem by speculating that his father is either reading
   or listening. What does this suggest about the narrator's view of his
   father?

2. What influence does Lee suggest his father had on him in stanza 2? Is it
   positive or negative or both?

3. When Lee says that his father awaited "instruction / from his god, yes,
   but also from a radio" (lines 30–31), what is he suggesting?

4. Does Lee finally identify with his father? In what way?

5. Would you interpret the last stanza as reconciliation? Be specific about
   the resolution that Lee comes to.

≣ MAKING COMPARISONS

1. Unlike Hayden and Roethke, Lee explicitly says he loved his father. What other differences do you note?

2. Is this view of his father more or less balanced than the other three poets?

3. Which of the previous three fathers does Lee's seem most like?

≣ WRITING ABOUT ISSUES

1. Choose one of the four preceding poems to argue that our feelings for our fathers are complex, not simple.

2. In *Words* (1964), Jean-Paul Sartre writes that "there is no good father, that is the rule." Use examples from the five poems to argue that this is, or is not, the case.

3. Do you think all children leave childhood or adolescence with unresolved tensions in their relationships with their fathers? Write a personal narrative that confronts this idea.

4. Locate at least three more poems that deal with memories of fathers. Write a brief report, noting the similarities to the four poems presented here.

◼ Exorcising the Dead: Critical Commentaries on a Poem

SYLVIA PLATH, "Daddy"

CRITICAL COMMENTARIES:
MARY LYNN BROE, From *Protean Poetic: The Poetry of Sylvia Plath*

LYNDA K. BUNDTZEN, From *Plath's Incarnations*

STEVEN GOULD AXELROD, From *Sylvia Plath: The Wound and the Cure of Words*

TIM KENDALL, From *Sylvia Plath: A Critical Study*

As contradictory as it might seem, we sometimes get angry when someone close to us dies. Psychologists tell us that anger is a healthy emotion in the mourning process, following sorrow and preceding acceptance: it is painful to miss loved ones, and we resent it. We might even direct the anger at them, feeling as if they are responsible for depriving us of their love. Sometimes, however, this anger lingers on long after the normal grieving process is over. Perhaps the attachment was abnormally strong, or perhaps the survivor's own life is too unstable to allow him or her to reach the final acceptance stage.

In the following poem, Sylvia Plath writes about her dead father as if he were a terrible person, even though as a young girl she seems to have adored him. Perhaps she is trying to expel his memory so she can find peace; perhaps she is using the poem as an occasion to express a deeper meaning about authority or influence from the past. Regardless, the poem is a powerful, strange, and passionate work of art. Following the poem, we include four critical essays that focus on autobiographial questions while also extending the critical discussion to include feminist issues, symbolic exorcism, and Freudian therapy.

◼ BEFORE YOU READ

Does it make sense to you that we might get angry at those who die because they have somehow deserted us? Do you think we have to "work out" the tensions between us and our parents before we can move into adulthood? Might it be healthy to exaggerate the difficulties of our childhood in poems and stories?

SYLVIA PLATH

Daddy

Born to middle-class parents in suburban New York, Sylvia Plath (1932–1963) became known as an intensely emotional "confessional" poet whose work is primarily autobiographical. Her father, a professor of biology and German, died when she was

© Bettmann/Corbis

*eight, the year her first poem was published. She graduated with honors from Smith
College in 1950, after an internship at* Mademoiselle *and a suicide attempt in her
junior year, experiences described in her novel* The Bell Jar *(1963). She won a Fulbright Scholarship to study at Cambridge University, in England, where she met and
married poet Ted Hughes. The couple had two children; the marriage ended the year
before her suicide in 1963. "Daddy" is from* Ariel, *published posthumously in 1965.*

You do not do, you do not do
Any more, black shoe
In which I have lived like a foot
For thirty years, poor and white,
Barely daring to breathe or Achoo.   5

Daddy, I have had to kill you.
You died before I had time —
Marble-heavy, a bag full of God,
Ghastly statue with one gray toe
Big as a Frisco seal   10

And a head in the freakish Atlantic
Where it pours bean green over blue
In the waters off beautiful Nauset.°   *Cape Cod inlet*
I used to pray to recover you.
Ach, du.°   *Oh, you*   15

In the German tongue, in the Polish Town°
Scraped flat by the roller
Of wars, wars, wars.
But the name of the town is common.
My Polack friend   20

Says there are a dozen or two.
So I never could tell where you
Put your foot, your root,
I never could talk to you.
The tongue stuck in my jaw.   25

It stuck in a barb wire snare.
Ich, ich, ich, ich,°   *I, I, I, I*
I could hardly speak.
I thought every German was you.
And the language obscene   30

An engine, an engine
Chuffing me off like a Jew.
A Jew to Dachau, Auschwitz, Belsen.°
I began to talk like a Jew.
I think I may well be a Jew.   35

The snows of the Tyrol, the clear beer of Vienna
Are not very pure or true.
With my gypsy-ancestress and my weird luck
And my Taroc° pack and my Taroc pack
I may be a bit of a Jew.   40

I have always been scared of *you,*
With your Luftwaffe,° your gobbledygoo.
And your neat mustache
And your Aryan eye, bright blue.
Panzer-man, panzer-man,° O You —   45

Not God but a swastika
So black no sky could squeak through.

16 Polish Town: Plath's father was born in Granbow, Poland.   **33 Dachau . . . Belsen:**
Nazi death camps in World War II.   **39 Taroc:** Tarot cards used to tell fortunes. The practice may have originated among the early Jewish Cabalists and was then widely adopted by
European Gypsies during the Middle Ages.   **42 Luftwaffe:** World War II German air
force. **45 panzer-man:** A member of the German armored vehicle division.

Every woman adores a Fascist,
The boot in the face, the brute
Brute heart of a brute like you.   50

You stand at the blackboard, daddy,
In the picture I have of you,
A cleft in your chin instead of your foot
But no less a devil for that, no not
Any less the black man who   55

Bit my pretty red heart in two.
I was ten when they buried you.
At twenty I tried to die
And get back, back, back to you.
I thought even the bones would do   60

But they pulled me out of the sack,
And they stuck me together with glue.
And then I knew what to do.
I made a model of you,
A man in black with a Meinkampf° look   65

And a love of the rack and the screw.
And I said I do, I do.
So daddy, I'm finally through.
The black telephone's off at the root,
The voices just can't worm through.   70

If I've killed one man, I've killed two —
The vampire who said he was you
And drank my blood for a year,
Seven years, if you want to know.
Daddy, you can lie back now.   75

There's a stake in your fat black heart
And the villagers never liked you.
They are dancing and stamping on you.
They always *knew* it was you.
Daddy, daddy, you bastard, I'm through.   [1962]   80

65 Meinkampf: Hitler's autobiography (*My Struggle*).

≡ THINKING ABOUT THE TEXT

1. Can this poem be seen as a series of arguments for why Plath has to forget her father? What complaints does the speaker seem to have against her father?

2. Some psychologists claim that we all have a love-hate relationship with our parents. Do you agree? Would Plath's speaker agree?

3. How effective is it for the speaker to compare herself to a Jew in Hitler's Germany? What other similes and metaphors are used to refer to her father? Do they work, or are they too extreme? Perhaps Plath wants them to be outrageous. Why might she?

4. Plath combines childhood rhymes and words with brutal images. What effect does this have on you? Why do you think Plath does this? What odd stylistic features can you point to here?

5. Why do you think it is necessary for the speaker to be finally "through" with her father? Is it normal young adult rebelliousness? What else might it be?

MARY LYNN BROE

From *Protean Poetic: The Poetry of Sylvia Plath*

Mary Lynn Broe (b. 1946) is Caroline Werner Gannett Professor of Humanities emerita at the Rochester Institute of Humanities in New York. She received her B.A. from St. Louis University and her M.A. and Ph.D. from the University of Connecticut. She publishes and travels extensively and is an international voice in the fields of women's studies and modern literature. Her books include Women's Writing in Exile *(1989);* Silence and Power: A Reevaluation of Djuna Barnes *(1991); and* Black Walking: Selected Letters of Djuna Barnes to Emily Holmes Coleman, 1934–1938 *(Wagenbach, 2002; Archinto, 2004). She is currently at work on a book of poetry,* With Edges Slightly Foxed, *and a creative nonfiction memoir.*

Among the other poems that display the performing self, "Daddy" and "Lady Lazarus" are two of the most often quoted, but most frequently misunderstood, poems in the Plath canon. The speaker in "Daddy" performs a mock poetic exorcism of an event that has already happened — the death of her father who she feels withdrew his love from her by dying prematurely: "Daddy, I have had to kill you. / You died before I had time — ."

The speaker attempts to exorcise not just the memory of her father but her own *Mein Kampf* model of him as well as her inherited behavioral traits that lead her graveward under the Freudian banner of death instinct or Thanatos's libido. But her ritual reenactment simply does not take. The event comically backfires as pure self-parody: the metaphorical murder of the father dwindles into Hollywood spectacle, while the poet is lost in the clutter of the collective unconscious.

Early in the poem, the ritual gets off on the wrong foot both literally and figuratively. A sudden rhythmic break midway through the first stanza interrupts the insistent and mesmeric chant of the poet's own freedom:

> You do not do, you do not do
> Any more, black shoe
> In which I have lived like a foot

> For thirty years, poor and white,
> Barely daring to breathe or Achoo.

The break suggests, on the one hand, that the nursery-rhyme world of contained terror is here abandoned; on the other, that the poet-exorcist's mesmeric control is superficial, founded in a shaky faith and an unsure heart—the worst possible state for the strong, disciplined exorcist.

At first, she kills her father succinctly with her own words, demythologizing him to a ludicrous piece of statuary that is hardly a Poseidon or the Colossus of Rhodes:

> Marble-heavy, a bag full of God,
> Ghastly statue with one grey toe
> Big as a Frisco seal
>
> And a head in the freakish Atlantic
> Where it pours bean green over blue
> In the waters off beautiful Nauset.
> I used to pray to recover you.
> Ach, du.

Then as she tries to patch together the narrative of him, his tribal myth (the "common" town, the "German tongue," the war-scraped culture), she begins to lose her own powers of description to a senseless Germanic prattle ("The tongue stuck in my jaw. / It stuck in a barb wire snare. / Ich, ich, ich, ich"). The individual man is absorbed by his inhuman archetype, the "panzer-man," "an engine / Chuffing me off like a Jew." Losing the exorcist's power that binds the spirit and then casts out the demon, she is the classic helpless victim of the swastika man. As she culls up her own picture of him as a devil, he refuses to adopt this stereotype. Instead he jumbles his trademark:

> A cleft in your chin instead of your foot
> But no less a devil for that, no not
> Any less the black man who
>
> Bit my pretty red heart in two.

The overt Nazi-Jew allegory throughout the poem suggests that, by a simple inversion of power, father and daughter grow more alike. But when she tries to imitate his action of dying, making all the appropriate grand gestures, she once again fails: "But they pulled me out of the sack, / And they stuck me together with glue." She retreats to a safe world of icons and replicas, but even the doll image she constructs turns out to be "the vampire who said he was you." At last, she abandons her father to the collective unconscious where it is *he* who is finally recognized ("They always *knew* it was you"). *She* is lost, impersonally absorbed by his irate persecutors, bereft of both her power and her conjurer's discipline, and possessed by the incensed villagers. The exorcist's ritual, one of purifying, cleansing, commanding silence, and then ordering the evil spirit's departure, has dwindled to a comic picture from the heart of darkness. Mad villagers stamp on the devil-vampire creation.

In the course of performing the imaginative "killing," the speaker moves through a variety of emotions, from viciousness ("a stake in your fat black heart"), to vengefulness ("you bastard, I'm through"), finally to silence ("The black telephone's off at the root"). It would seem that the real victim is the poet-performer who, despite her straining toward identification with the public events of holocaust and destruction of World War II, becomes more murderously persecuting than the "panzer-man" who smothered her, and who abandoned her with a paradoxical love, guilt, and fear. Unlike him, she kills three times: the original subject, the model to whom she said "I do, I do," and herself, the imitating victim. But each of these killings is comically inverted. Each backfires. Instead of successfully binding the spirits, commanding them to remain silent and cease doing harm, and then ordering them to an appointed place, the speaker herself is stricken dumb.

The failure of the exorcism and the emotional ambivalence are echoed in the curious rhythm. The incantatory safety of the nursery-rhyme thump (seemingly one of controlled, familiar terrors) also suggests some sinister brooding by its repetition. The poem opens with a suspiciously emphatic protest, a kind of psychological whistling-in-the-dark. As it proceeds, "Daddy"'s continuous life-rhythms — the assonance, consonance, and especially the sustained *oo* sounds — triumph over either the personal or the cultural-historical imagery. The sheer sense of organic life in the interwoven sounds carries the verse forward in boisterous spirit and communicates an underlying feeling of comedy that is also echoed in the repeated failure of the speaker to perform her exorcism.

Ultimately, "Daddy" is like an emotional, psychological, and historical autopsy, a final report. There is no real progress. The poet is in the same place in the beginning as in the end. She begins the poem as a hesitant but familiar fairy-tale daughter who parodies her attempt to reconstruct the myth of her father. Suffocating in her shoe house, she is unable to do much with that "bag full of God." She ends as a murderous member of a mythical community enacting the ritual or vampire killing, but only for a surrogate vampire, not the real thing ("The vampire who said he was you"). Although it seems that the speaker has moved from identification with the persecuted to identify as persecutor, Jew to vampire-killer, powerless to powerful, she has simply enacted a performance that allows her to live with what is unchangeable. She has used her art to stave off suffocation and performs her self-contempt with a degree of bravado.   *[1980]*

LYNDA K. BUNDTZEN

From *Plath's Incarnations*

Educated at the University of Minnesota, where she earned a B.A. in 1968, and the University of Chicago, where she earned a Ph.D. in 1972, Lynda Bundtzen (b. 1947) teaches at Williams College. A Renaissance scholar with a strong interest in women's issues, she teaches and writes on subjects that range from Shakespeare to

Thelma and Louise. Plath's Incarnations *was published in 1983. Her latest book is* The Other Ariel *(2001).*

In "Daddy," Plath is conscious of her complicity in creating and worshiping a father-colossus.

> You stand at the blackboard, daddy,
> In the picture I have of you,
> A cleft in your chin instead of your foot
> But no less a devil for that, no not
> Any less the black man who
>
> Bit my pretty red heart in two.
> I was ten when they buried you.
> At twenty I tried to die
> And get back, back, back to you.
> I thought even the bones would do.

The photograph is of an ordinary man, a teacher, with a cleft chin. She imaginatively transforms him into a devil who broke her heart, and she tells her audience precisely what she is doing. As Plath describes "Daddy," it is "spoken by a girl with an Electra complex. Her father died while she thought he was God. Her case is complicated by the fact that her father was also a Nazi and her mother very possibly part Jewish. In the daughter the two strains marry and paralyze each other — she has to act out the awful little allegory once over before she is free of it." The poem is a figurative drama about mourning — about the human impulse to keep a dead loved one alive emotionally. And it is about mourning gone haywire — a morbid inability to let go of the dead. The child was unready for her father's death, which is why, she says, she must kill him a second time. She resurrected Daddy and sustained his unnatural existence in her psyche as a vampire, sacrificing her own life's blood, her vitality, to a dead man. The worship of this father-god, she now realizes, is self-destructive.

There is nothing unconscious about the poem; instead it seems to force into consciousness the child's dread and love for the father, so that these feelings may be resolved. Plath skillfully evokes the child's world with her own versions of Mother Goose rhymes. Like the "old woman who lived in a shoe and had so many children she didn't know what to do," she has tried to live in the confines of the black shoe that is Daddy. Like Chicken Little, waiting for the sky to fall in, she lives under an omnipresent swastika "So black no sky could squeak through." And Daddy is a fallen giant toppled over and smothering, it seems, the entire United States. He has one grey toe (recalling Otto Plath's gangrened appendage) dangling like a Frisco seal in the Pacific and his head lies in the Atlantic.

The Mother Goose rhythms gradually build to a goose step march as the mourning process turns inward. She feels more than sorrow, now guilt, for Daddy's death and this guilt leads to feelings of inadequacy, acts of self-abasement, and finally self-murder. Nothing she can do will appease the guilt: she tries to learn his language; she tries to kill herself; she marries a man in his image. It will not do.

The self-hatred must be turned outward again into "*You* do not do" by a very self-conscious transformation of a mild-mannered professor into an active oppressor. Her emotional paralysis is acted out as a struggle between Nazi man and Jewess, and, I would argue, the Jewess wins. The poem builds toward the imaginary stake driving, the dancing and stamping and "Daddy, daddy, you bastard, I'm through." Not necessarily through with life, as many critics have read this line, but through with the paralysis, powerlessness, guilt. At last Daddy — the Nazi Daddy she frightened herself with, and not the real one, the professor — is at rest.

Plath's control over ambivalent feelings toward her father is probably the   5
result of their availability for conscious artistic manipulation. She had already written several poems about her dead father when she composed "Daddy," and we also know from a conversation recorded by Steiner that she had "worked through" her emotions in therapy. "She talked freely about her father's death when she was nine and her reactions to it. 'He was an autocrat,' she recalled. 'I adored and despised him, and I probably wished many times that he were dead. When he obliged me and died, I imagined that I had killed him.'" The result in "Daddy" is a powerful and remarkably accessible allegory about her adoration and dread, which ends in emotional catharsis.   *[1983]*

STEVEN GOULD AXELROD
From *Sylvia Plath: The Wound and the Cure of Words*

An expert in nineteenth- and twentieth-century American poetry, Steven Gould Axelrod (b. 1944) was educated at the University of California at Los Angeles and served as chair of the English Department at the University of California at Riverside, where he received a Distinguished Teaching Award in 1989. His publications include book-length works on modern and contemporary poets. Sylvia Plath: The Wound and the Cure of Words *was published in 1990.*

The covert protest of "The Colossus" eventually transformed itself into the overt rebellion of "Daddy." Although this poem too has traditionally been read as "personal" or "confessional," Margaret Homans has more recently suggested that it concerns a woman's dislocated relations to speech. Plath herself introduced it on the BBC as the opposite of confession, as a constructed fiction: "Here is a poem spoken by a girl with an Electra complex. Her father died while she thought he was God. Her case is complicated by the fact that her father was also a Nazi and her mother very possibly part Jewish. In the daughter the two strains marry and paralyze each other — she has to act out the awful little allegory once over before she is free of it." We might interpret this preface as an accurate retelling of the poem; or we might regard it as a case of an author's estrangement from her text, on the order of Coleridge's preface to "Kubla Khan" in which he claims to be unable to finish the poem, having forgotten what it was about. However we interpret Plath's preface, we must agree that "Daddy" is dramatic and allegorical, since its details depart freely from the facts of her biography. In this poem she again figures her unresolved conflicts with paternal authority as a textual issue. Significantly, her father was a published writer, and his successor, her husband, was also a writer. Her preface asserts that the poem concerns a young woman's paralyzing self-division, which she can defeat only through allegorical representation. Recalling that paralysis was one of Plath's main tropes for literary incapacity, we begin to see that the poem evokes the female poet's anxiety of authorship and specifically Plath's strategy of delivering herself from that anxiety by making it the topic of her discourse. Viewed from this perspective, "Daddy" enacts the woman poet's struggle with "daddy-poetry." It represents her effort to eject the "buried male muse" from her invention process and the "jealous gods" from her audience.

Plath wrote "Daddy" several months after Hughes left her, on the day she learned that he had agreed to a divorce. George Brown and Tirril Harris have shown that early loss makes one especially vulnerable to subsequent loss, and Plath seems to have defended against depression by almost literally throwing herself into her poetry. She followed "Daddy" with a host of poems that she considered her greatest achievement to date: "Medusa," "The Jailer," "Lady Lazarus," "Ariel," the bee sequence, and others. The letters she wrote to her mother and brother on the day of "Daddy," and then again four days later, brim with a sense of artistic self-discovery: "Writing like mad. . . . Terrific stuff, as if domesticity had choked me." Composing at the "still blue, almost eternal hour before the baby's cry, before the glassy music of the milkman, settling his bottles," she experienced an enormous surge in creative energy. Yet she also expressed feelings of misery: "The half year ahead seems like a lifetime, and the half behind an endless hell." She was again contemplating things German: a trip to the Austrian Alps, a renewed effort to learn the language. If "German" was Randall Jarrell's "favorite country," it was not hers, yet it returned to her discourse like clockwork at times of psychic distress. Clearly Plath was attempting to find and to evoke in her art what she could not find or communicate in her life. She wished to compensate for her fragmenting social existence by investing herself in her texts: "Hope, when free, to write myself out of this hole." Desperately eager to sacrifice her "flesh," which was "wasted," to her "mind and spirit," which were "fine," she wrote "Daddy" to demonstrate the existence of her voice, which had been silent or subservient for so long. She wrote it to prove her "genius."

Plath projected her struggle for textual identity onto the figure of a partly Jewish young woman who learns to express her anger at the patriarch and at his language of male mastery, which is as foreign to her as German, as "obscene" as murder, and as meaningless as "gobbledygoo." The patriarch's death "off beautiful Nauset" recalls Plath's journal entry in which she associated the "green seaweeded water" at "Nauset Light" with "the deadness of a being . . . who no longer creates." Daddy's deadness — suggesting Plath's un-willingness to let her father, her education, her library, or her husband inhibit her any longer — inspires the poem's speaker to her moment of illumination. At a basic level, "Daddy" concerns its own violent, transgressive birth as a text, its origin in a culture that regards it as illegitimate — a judgment the speaker hurls back on the patriarch himself when she labels *him* a bastard. Plath's un-accommodating worldview, which was validated by much in her childhood and adult experience, led her to understand literary tradition not as an expand-ing universe of beneficial influence . . . but as a closed universe in which every addition required a corresponding subtraction — a Spencerian agon in which only the fittest survived. If Plath's speaker was to be born as a poet, a patriarch must die.

As in "The Colossus," the father here appears as a force or an object rather than as a person. Initially he takes the form of an immense "black shoe," ca-pable of stamping on his victim. Immediately thereafter he becomes a marble "statue," cousin to the monolith of the earlier poem. He then transforms into Nazi Germany, the archetypal totalitarian state. When the protagonist men-tions Daddy's "boot in the face," she may be alluding to Orwell's comment in *1984*, "If you want a picture of the future, imagine a boot stomping on a hu-man face — forever." Eventually the father declines in stature from God to a devil to a dying vampire. Perhaps he shrinks under the force of his victim's de-nunciation, which de-creates him as a power as it creates him as figure. But whatever his size, he never assumes human dimensions, aspirations, and rela-tions — except when posing as a teacher in a photograph. Like the colossus, he remains figurative and symbolic, not individual.

Nevertheless, the male figure of "Daddy" does differ significantly from that of "The Colossus." In the earlier poem, which emphasizes his lips, mouth, throat, tongue, and voice, the colossus allegorically represents the power of speech, however fragmented and resistant to the protagonist's ministrations. In the later poem Daddy remains silent, apart from the gobbledygoo attributed to him once. He uses his mouth primarily for biting and for drinking blood. The poem emphasizes his feet and, implicitly, his phallus. He is a "black shoe," a statue with "one gray toe," a "boot." The speaker, estranged from him by fear, could never tell where he put his "foot," his "root." Furthermore, she is herself silenced by his shoe: "I never could talk to you." Daddy is no "male muse," not even one in ruins, but frankly a male censor. His boot in the face of "every woman" is presumably lodged in her mouth. He stands for all the elements in the literary situation and in the female ephebe's internalization of it, that pre-vent her from producing any words at all, even copied or subservient ones. Ap-propriately, Daddy can be killed only by being stamped on: he lives and dies by force, not language. If "The Colossus" tells a tale of the patriarch's speech, his grunts and brays, "Daddy" tells a tale of the daughter's effort to speak.

Thus we are led to another important difference between the two poems. The "I" of "The Colossus" acquires her identity only through serving her "fa-ther," whereas the "I" of "Daddy" actuates her gift only through opposition to

5

him. The latter poem precisely inscribes the plot of Plath's dream novel of 1958: "a girl's search for her dead father — for an outside authority which must be developed, instead, from the inside." As the child of a Nazi, the girl could "hardly speak," but as a Jew she begins "to talk" and to acquire an identity. In Plath's allegory, the outsider Jew corresponds to "the rebel, the artist, the odd," and particularly to the woman artist. Otto Rank's *Beyond Psychology*, which had a lasting influence on her, explicitly compares women to Jews, since "woman . . . has suffered from the very beginning a fate similar to that of the Jew, namely, suppression, slavery, confinement, and subsequent persecution." Rank, whose discourse I would consider tainted by anti-Semitism, argues that Jews speak a language of pessimistic "self-hatred" that differs essentially from the language of the majority cultures in which they find themselves. He analogously, though more sympathetically, argues that woman speaks in a language different from man's, and that as a result of man's denial of woman's world, "woman's 'native tongue' has hitherto been unknown or at least unheard." Although Rank's essentializing of woman's "nature" lapses into the sexist clichés of his time ("intuitive," "irrational"), his idea of linguistic difference based on gender and his analogy between Jewish and female speech seem to have embedded themselves in the substructure of "Daddy" (and in many of Plath's other texts as well). For Plath, as later for Adrienne Rich, the Holocaust and the patriarchy's silencing of women were linked outcomes of the masculinist interpretation of the world. Political insurrection and female self-assertion also interlaced symbolically. In "Daddy," Plath's speaker finds her voice and motive by identifying herself as antithetical to her Fascist father. Rather than getting the colossus "glued" and properly jointed, she wishes to stick herself "together with glue," an act that seems to require her father's dismemberment. Previously devoted to the patriarch — both in "The Colossus" and in memories evoked in "Daddy" of trying to "get back" to him — she now seeks only to escape from him and to see him destroyed.

Plath has unleashed the anger, normal in mourning as well as in revolt, that she suppressed in the earlier poem. But she has done so at a cost. Let us consider her childlike speaking voice. The language of "Daddy," beginning with its title, is often regressive. The "I" articulates herself by moving backward in time, using the language of nursery rhymes and fairy tales (the little old woman who lived in a shoe, the black man of the forest). Such language accords with a child's conception of the world, not an adult's. Plath's assault on the language of "daddy-poetry" has turned inward, on the language of her own poem, which teeters precariously on the edge of a preverbal abyss — represented by the eerie, keening "oo" sound with which a majority of the verses end. And then let us consider the play on "through" at the poem's conclusion. Although that last line allows for multiple readings, one interpretation is that the "I" has unconsciously carried out her father's wish: her discourse, by transforming itself into cathartic oversimplifications, has undone itself.

Yet the poem does contain its verbal violence by means more productive than silence. In a letter to her brother, Plath referred to "Daddy" as "gruesome," while on almost the same day she described it to A. Alvarez as a piece of "light verse." She later read it on the BBC in a highly ironic tone of voice. The poem's unique spell derives from its rhetorical complexity: its variegated and perhaps bizarre fusion of the horrendous and the comic. . . . [I]t both shares and remains detached from the fixation of its protagonist. The protagonist herself seems detached from her own fixation. She is "split in the most complex fashion," as Plath wrote of Ivan Karamazov in her Smith College honors thesis. Plath's speaker uses potentially self-mocking melodramatic terms to describe both her opponent ("so black no sky could squeak through") and herself ("poor and white"). While this aboriginal speaker quite literally expresses black-and-white thinking, her civilized double possesses a sensibility sophisticated enough to subject such thinking to irony. Thus the poem expresses feelings that it simultaneously parodies — it may be parodying the very idea of feeling. The tension between erudition and simplicity in the speaker's voice appears in her pairings that juxtapose adult with childlike diction: "breathe or Achoo," "your Luftwaffe, your gobbledygoo." She can expound such adult topics as Taroc packs, Viennese beer, and Tyrolean snowfall; can specify death camps by name; and can employ an adult vocabulary of "recover," "ancestress," "Aryan," "*Meinkampf*," "obscene," and "bastard." Yet she also has recourse to a more primitive lexicon that includes "chuffing," "your fat black heart," and "my pretty red heart." She proves herself capable of careful intellectual discriminations ("so I never could tell"), conventionalized description ("beautiful Nauset"), and moral analogy ("if I've killed one man, I've killed two"), while also exhibiting regressive fantasies (vampires), repetitions ("wars, wars, wars"), and inarticulateness ("panzer-man, panzer-man, O You — "). She oscillates between calm reflection ("You stand at the blackboard, daddy, / In the picture I have of you") and mad incoherence ("Ich, ich, ich, ich"). Her sophisticated language puts her wild language in an ironic perspective, removing the discourse from the control of the archaic self who understands experience only in extreme terms.

The ironies in "Daddy" proliferate in unexpected ways, however. When the speaker proclaims categorically that "every woman adores a Fascist," she is subjecting her victimization to irony by suggesting that sufferers choose, or at least accommodate themselves to, their suffering. But she is also subjecting her authority to irony, since her claim about "every woman" is transparently false. It simply parodies patriarchal commonplaces, such as those advanced . . . concerning "feminine masochism." The adult, sophisticated self seems to be speaking here: Who else would have the confidence to make a sociological generalization? Yet the content of the assertion, if taken straightforwardly, returns us to the regressive self who is dominated by extravagant emotions she cannot begin to understand. Plath's mother wished that Plath would write about "decent, courageous people," and she herself heard an inner voice demanding that she be a perfect "paragon" in her language and feeling. But in the speaker of "Daddy," she inscribed the opposite of such a paragon: a divided self whose veneer of civilization is breached and infected by unhealthy instincts.

Plath's irony cuts both ways. At the same time that the speaker's sophisti-   10
cated voice undercuts her childish voice, reducing its melodrama to comedy,
the childish or maddened voice undercuts the pretensions of the sophisticated
voice, revealing the extremity of suffering masked by its ironies. While demonstrating the inadequacy of thinking and feeling in opposites, the poem implies
that such a mode can locate truths denied more complex cognitive and affective systems. The very moderation of the normal adult intelligence, its tolerance of ambiguity, its defenses against the primal energies of the id, results in
falsification. Reflecting Schiller's idea that the creative artist experiences a
"momentary and passing madness" (quoted by Freud in a passage of *The Interpretation of Dreams* that Plath underscored), "Daddy" gives voice to that madness. Yet the poem's sophisticated awareness, its comic vision, probably wins
out in the end, since the poem concludes by curtailing the power of its extreme
discourse. . . . Furthermore, Plath distanced herself from the poem's aboriginal
voice by introducing her text as "a poem spoken by a girl with an Electra complex" — that is, as a study of the *girl's* pathology rather than her father's — and
as an allegory that will "free" her from that pathology. She also distanced herself by reading the poem in a tone that emphasized its irony. And finally, she
distanced herself by laying the poem's wild voice permanently to rest after
October. The aboriginal vision was indeed purged. "Daddy" represents not
Dickinson's madness that is divinest sense, but rather an entry into a style of
discourse and a mastery of it. The poem realizes the trope of suffering by means
of an inherent irony that both questions and validates the trope in the same
gestures, and that finally allows the speaker to conclude the discourse and to
remove herself from the trope with a sense of completion rather than wrench-
ing, since the irony was present from the very beginning.

Plath's poetic revolt in "Daddy" liberated her pent-up creativity, but the
momentary success sustained her little more than self-sacrifice had done.
"Daddy" became another stage in her development, an unrepeatable experiment, a vocal opening that closed itself at once. The poem is not only an elegy
for the power of "daddy-poetry" but for the powers of speech Plath discovered
in composing it.

When we consider "Daddy" generically, a further range of implications
presents itself. Although we could profitably consider the poem as the dramatic
monologue Plath called it in her BBC broadcast, let us regard it instead as the
kind of poem most readers have taken it to be: a domestic poem. I have chosen
this term, rather than M. L. Rosenthal's better-known "confessional poem" or
the more neutral "autobiographical poem," because "confessional poem" implies a confession rather than a making (though Steven Hoffman and Lawrence
Kramer have recently indicated the mode's conventions) and because "autobiographical poem" is too general for our purpose. I shall define the domestic
poem as one that represents and comments on a protagonist's relationship to
one or more family members, usually a parent, child, or spouse. To focus our
discussion even further, I shall emphasize poetry that specifically concerns a
father.   *[1990]*

TIM KENDALL

From *Sylvia Plath: A Critical Study*

Tim Kendall edits Thumbscrew *and is the author of* Paul Muldoon *(2004). He received an Eric Gregory Award for his poetry in 1997 and appears in the* Oxford Poets 2000 *anthology. He was the Thomas Chatterton British Academy Lecturer for 2001 at the University of Bristol and is currently a professor of English literature at the University of Exeter. In 2005, Kendall was awarded the lucrative Philip Leverhulme Prize. This selection is from a book he published in 2001.*

Plath's journals . . . indicate that as late as December 1958, the poet was seriously considering a Ph.D. in psychology: "Awesome to confront a program of study which is so monumental: all human experience."[1] The previous day Plath had discovered in Freud's *Mourning and Melancholia* "an almost exact description of my feelings and reasons for suicide."[2] She felt creatively vindicated when she found parallels between her own life and writings and those of Freud and Jung: "All this relates in a most meaningful way my instinctive images with perfectly valid psychological analysis. However, I am the victim, rather than the analyst."[3] In these examples, experience precedes the psychoanalytical explanation; Freud and Jung confirm what Plath already knows. Despite her emphasis on victimhood, such passages show how she transforms herself into her own case history, becoming simultaneously victim and analyst. The same dual role is apparent in "Daddy," which Plath introduces for BBC radio in terms of Freudian allegory:

> Here is a poem spoken by a girl with an Electra complex. Her father died while she thought he was God. Her case is complicated by the fact that her father was also a Nazi and her mother very possibly part Jewish. In the daughter the two strains marry and paralyze each other — she has to act out the awful little allegory once over before she is free of it.

"Daddy," built on poetic repetition, is therefore a poem about a compulsion to repeat, and its psychology is characterized according to Freudian principles. Repetition necessitates performance — the speaker must "*act out* the awful little allegory once over" in order to escape it. Whether she does succeed in escaping depends on the poem's ambivalent last line: "Daddy, daddy, you bastard, I'm through." "I'm through" can mean (especially to an American ear) "I've had enough of you," but it also means "I've got away from you, I'm free of you," or "I'm done for, I'm beaten," or even "I've finished what I have to say." The speaker's ability to free herself from the urge to repeat remains in the balance.

These dilemmas and uncertainties can be traced back, as Plath suggests, to Freud's accounts of compulsive behavior. "Daddy" adopts a Freudian understanding of infantile sexuality (the Electra complex), a Freudian belief in transference (the vampire-husband "said he was you," and the father also shifts identities), and a Freudian attitude towards repetitive behavior. In a passage from *Beyond the Pleasure Principle* which might conveniently serve to diagnose the speaker of "Daddy," Freud argues that,

> The patient cannot remember the whole of what is repressed in him, and what he cannot remember may be precisely the essential part of it. Thus he acquires no sense of the conviction of the correctness of the construction that has been communicated to him. He is obliged to *repeat* the repressed material as a contemporary experience instead of, as the physician would prefer to see, *remembering* it as something belonging to the past. These reproductions, which emerge with such unwished-for exactitude, always have as their subject some portion of infantile sexual life — of the Oedipus complex, that is, and its derivatives; and they are invariably acted out in the sphere of the transference, of the patient's relation to the physician.[4]

This illuminates Plath's attempts to persuade the dead father to communicate. The refusal of the father-figure, in his various transferred roles of colossus, Nazi, teacher, and vampire, to become "something belonging to the past" is evident in the speaker's need to kill him repeatedly. He must be imaginatively disinterred in order to be killed again, and even as one of the undead, he must be destroyed with a stake in his heart. This repetitive pattern of disappearance and return represents Plath's version of the *fort-da* game as famously described in *Beyond the Pleasure Principle*, where the child's repeated and "long-drawn-out 'o-o-o-o' " is only a slight vowel modulation away from the "oo" repetitions of "Daddy." The father-figure is a "contemporary experience," not a memory; and, as Freud explains, the reason for his continuing presence lies in the speaker's "infantile sexual life." The father's early death ensures that she cannot progress, and her sense of selfhood is stutteringly confined within a compulsion to repeat:

> I never could talk to you.
> The tongue stuck in my jaw.
>
> It stuck in a barb wire snare.
> Ich, ich, ich, ich,
> I could hardly speak.

Repetition occurs when Plath's speaker gets stuck in the barb wire snare of communication with her father. She is unable to move beyond the self. This proposes a more fundamental understanding of repetitive words and phrases than those suggested by Blessing or Shapiro. "Daddy" implies that each local repetition, whatever its microcosmic effects, symptomizes a larger behavioral pattern of repetition compulsion. The poem's title, the "oo" rhymes, and the nursery-rhyme rhythms all reinforce this suggestion of a mind struggling to free itself from the need to repeat infantile trauma. Such infantilism, exhibited by an adult persona, contributes to the poem's transgressive humor: Plath read "Daddy" aloud to a friend, reports Anne Stevenson, "in a mocking, comical voice that made both women fall about with laughter."[5]

Psychoanalyzing the speaker of "Daddy" in the Freudian terms proposed by Plath herself is a valuable exercise which carries important implications for

Ariel's use of repetition, but it still does not settle the nature of the poet's complex relationship to the "girl with an Electra complex." Plath's introduction for radio seems to reverse the pattern in her journals: now Freud becomes a source as much as an explanation. Her introduction also reverses the reader's experience of the poem. "Daddy" conveys a power and an intimacy which challenge any hygienic separation of poet and poetic voice. With such contradictory evidence, the gulf between poet and persona, cold-blooded technique and blood-hot emotion, analyst and victim, seems unbridgeable. If these divisions can be successfully reconciled, it is through Plath's emphasis on performance and repetition. Freud's account of repetition compulsion shares with Plath's description of "Daddy" a crucial verb: just as Plath's persona must "act out the awful little allegory," so Freud notes that the Oedipus complex and its derivatives are "invariably acted out in the sphere of the transference." Repetition guarantees performance, and performance requires an audience. Freud notes, as if glossing "Daddy," that "the artistic play and artistic imitation carried out by adults, which, unlike children's, are aimed at an audience, do not spare the spectators (for instance, in tragedy) the most painful experiences and can yet be felt by them as highly enjoyable." Plath categorized "Daddy" as "light verse,"[6] a genre which W. H. Auden considered to be "written for performance."[7] "Daddy" may be written for performance, but it pushes the "painful experiences" and the entertainment value to extremes which many readers find intolerable. Freud's Aristotelian concern — why is tragedy pleasurable? — also seems a valid question to ask of Plath's poem: "Daddy" derives its aesthetic pleasures from incest, patricide, suicide, and the Nazi extermination camps.

These taboo-breaking juxtapositions of personal and private realms help explain the poem's notoriety. However, controversy over "Daddy" always returns eventually to Plath's relationship with her persona. Seamus Heaney's principled objection, for example, discerns no difference at all:

> A poem like "Daddy," however brilliant a *tour de force* it can be acknowledged to be, and however its violence and vindictiveness can be understood or excused in light of the poet's parental and marital relations, remains, nevertheless, so entangled in biographical circumstances and rampages so permissively in the history of other people's sorrows that it simply withdraws its rights to our sympathy.[8]

Heaney's pointed phrase "rampages so permissively" might be disputed as an unfair rhetorical flourish, especially in the context of Plath's hard-earned Emersonian desire to assimilate and her wider theological explorations. But Heaney's most revealing word is his last: "sympathy." Heaney refers to one aspect of Aristotelian catharsis — pity for the suffering of others — which he claims that "Daddy" fails to earn. It is not surprising that his critical decorum should come into conflict with a poem which is so consciously and manifestly indecorous. Heaney reads "Daddy" purely as the protest of the poet-victim, who behaves vindictively because of her difficult parental and marital relations. This fails to credit Plath with the self-awareness to be acting deliberately — to be performing. In "Daddy" Plath seeks no one's "sympathy"; she has once more become victim and analyst, the girl with the Electra complex and the physician who diagnoses her condition. Plath wonders in her journal whether "our desire to investigate psychology [is] a desire to get Beuscher's [her psychiatrist's] power and handle it ourselves."[9] "Daddy," as her introduction makes clear, represents a poetic handling of that power. Freud states that the patient must acquire "some degree of aloofness."[10] "Daddy" is the work of a poet so aloof as to render allegorical, act out, and psychoanalyze, her own mental history.   *[2001]*

Notes

1. Sylvia Plath, *The Journals of Sylvia Plath, 1950–1962*, ed. Karen V. Kukil (London: Faber & Faber, 2000), p. 452.
2. Ibid., p. 447.
3. Ibid., p. 514.
4. S. Freud, *Beyond the Pleasure Principle*, tr. and ed. J. Strachey (Hogarth, 1961), p. 12.
5. A. Stevenson, *Bitter Fame: A Life of Sylvia Plath* (Viking, 1989), p. 277.
6. A. Alvarez, "Sylvia Plath," in C. Newman (ed.), *The Art of Sylvia Plath* (Indiana UP, 1970), p. 66.
7. W. H. Auden (ed.), *The Oxford Book of Light Verse* (OUP, 1938), p. ix.
8. S. Heaney, "The Indefatigable Hoof-taps: Sylvia Plath," *The Government of the Tongue* (Faber, 1988), p. 165.
9. *Journals*, p. 449.
10. *Beyond the Pleasure Principle*, p. 13.

≡ MAKING COMPARISONS

1. "Daddy" seems to be a protest, but some critics see it as more than that. Which of the four commentaries makes the best case that it is more than a revolt against the speaker's father?

2. Which critic seems to answer most of the perplexing questions of this poem — for example, the father as Nazi, the father as vampire, the child-like rhythms, the speaker's vengefulness, her viciousness?

3. Do these critics make any similar points? How might you describe them? What is their most striking difference?

≡ WRITING ABOUT ISSUES

1. Choose one of the critical commentaries in this cluster and argue that the textual evidence supporting its assertions is, or is not, adequate.

2. Imagine you are Sylvia Plath. After reading these four essays, write a letter to a literary journal either attacking or praising these critics.

3. Write an essay arguing that your own reading of "Daddy" makes more sense than those of Broe, Bundtzen, Axelrod, or Kendall. Assume that the audience for the criticism is your class.

4. There are dozens of critical commentaries on Plath's "Daddy." Some were written soon after the poem's publication; others are quite recent.

Locate an early piece of criticism, and compare it to one published in the past two years. Do these critics make similar or different points? Is one more concerned with the text, with gender issues, with cultural concerns, or with what other critics say? Write a brief comparison of the two, explaining your evidence.

☰ Grandparents and Legacies: Poems

NIKKI GIOVANNI, "Legacies"

LINDA HOGAN, "Heritage"

GARY SOTO, "Behind Grandma's House"

ALBERTO RÍOS, "Mi Abuelo"

JUDITH ORTIZ COFER, "Claims"

In contemporary middle-class America, the influence, even the presence, of our grandparents has waned. They often live elsewhere, perhaps in retirement communities or nursing homes. But this was not always the case. Grandparents in the past, and in traditional households even today, were active members of the family, exerting influence on the daily decisions of everyday life, from diet to child-rearing. Some of this was beneficial: grandparents gave children a personal understanding of their cultural traditions as well as the benefit of their accumulated wisdom. But they could also create tension in families where change and progress conflicted with the habits and attitudes of the past. The following five poets present us with different perspectives on their grandparents, some loving and proud, others less positive, and one quite funny.

☰ BEFORE YOU READ

What specific memories do you have of your grandparents? What role do you think they should play in a family's life? What effects might the segregation of the elderly have on a society?

NIKKI GIOVANNI
Legacies

Raised near Cincinnati, Ohio, Nikki Giovanni (b. 1943) returned as a teenager to her birthplace and spiritual home in Knoxville, Tennessee, where she experienced the strong influence of her grandmother, Louvenia Watson. She studied at the University of Cincinnati from 1961 to 1963 and earned a B.A. at Fisk University in 1967. She also attended the University of Pennsylvania School of Social Work (1967) and Columbia University School of the Arts (1968). She has taught at a number of universities, since 1987 at Virginia Polytechnic Institute, where she is a professor of English. Her poetry, essays, and works for children reflect her commitment to African American community, family, and womanhood. Her books include Quilting the Black-Eyed Pea: Poems and Not Quite Poems *(2002). Her most recent books are* On My Journey Now: Looking at African American History through the Spirituals *(2006) and* Acolytes *(2007). "Legacies" is from Giovanni's 1972 book,* My House.

her grandmother called her from the playground
   "yes, ma'am"
   "i want chu to learn how to make rolls," said the old
woman proudly
but the little girl didn't want   5
to learn how because she knew
even if she couldn't say it that
that would mean when the old one died she would be less
dependent on her spirit so
she said   10
   "i don't want to know how to make no rolls"
with her lips poked out
and the old woman wiped her hands on
her apron saying "lord
   these children"   15
and neither of them ever
said what they meant
and i guess nobody ever does   *[1972]*

≡ THINKING ABOUT THE TEXT

1. Does the dialogue in Giovanni's poem reveal the true feelings of the grandmother and the girl? Be explicit about what is really going on in their minds. Is the girl superstitious?

2. Is it true that "nobody" (line 18) says what she really means? Do you? Is this an indication of honesty or something else — say, tact or convention? Are poets more likely to tell the truth?

3. What makes this piece a poem? Would you prefer more metaphors or similes, allusions, or flowery language? Is *proudly* (line 4) an important word here?

4. Change the grandmother's words to those that reflect more of what is in her heart. Might the girl respond differently if the grandmother were more forthright?

5. The title is only referred to obliquely. Why? What does it refer to? Is contemporary society concerned with legacies? Are you? Are they important or irrelevant?

LINDA HOGAN

Heritage

Born in 1947 in Denver, Colorado, Linda Hogan calls on her Chickasaw heritage to interpret environmental, antinuclear, and other spiritual and societal issues. Her published works include poems, stories, screenplays, essays, and novels. Her novel Power

*(1998) has been praised for its beauty of language, mythical structure, and allegori-
cal power. Her works include* The Woman Who Watches Over the World: A
Native Memoir *(2001) and* Sightings: The Gray Whales' Mysterious Journey
(2002). Her many honors include an American Book Award for Seeing through
the Sun *(1985), a Colorado Book Award and a Pulitzer nomination for* The Book of
Medicines *(1993), fellowships from the Guggenheim Foundation and the National
Endowment for the Arts, and a Lannan Award. Hogan received her M.A. from the
University of Colorado at Boulder, where she currently teaches creative writing.
"Heritage" is from her 1978 book titled* Calling Myself Home.

From my mother, the antique mirror
where I watch my face take on her lines.
She left me the smell of baking bread
to warm fine hairs in my nostrils,
she left the large white breasts that weigh down   5
my body.

From my father I take his brown eyes,
the plague of locusts that leveled our crops,
they flew in formation like buzzards.

From my uncle the whittled wood   10
that rattles like bones
and is white
and smells like all our old houses
that are no longer there. He was the man
who sang old chants to me, the words   15
my father was told not to remember.

From my grandfather who never spoke
I learned to fear silence.
I learned to kill a snake
when you're begging for rain.   20

And Grandmother, blue-eyed woman
whose skin was brown,
she used snuff.
When her coffee can full of black saliva
spilled on me   25
it was like the brown cloud of grasshoppers
that leveled her fields.
It was the brown stain
that covered my white shirt,
my whiteness a shame.   30
That sweet black liquid like the food
she chewed up and spit into my father's mouth
when he was an infant.

It was the brown earth of Oklahoma
stained with oil.   35
She said tobacco would purge your body of poisons.
It has more medicine than stones and knives
against your enemies.
That tobacco is the dark night that covers me.

She said it is wise to eat the flesh of deer   40
so you will be swift and travel over many miles.
She told me how our tribe has always followed a stick
that pointed west
that pointed east.
From my family I have learned the secrets   45
of never having a home.   *[1978]*

≡ THINKING ABOUT THE TEXT

1. The last sentence seems to contain a contradiction. "From my family I
   have learned the secrets" might lead you to expect something positive.
   But maybe the last phrase is not meant to be positive. What is your
   reading of Hogan's conclusion?

2. What does the narrator learn from her mother? Her father? Her uncle?
   Her grandfather? Her grandmother? What kinds of things did you learn
   from your family members? Use concrete images.

3. Why does she say "my whiteness a shame" (line 30)? Is this a racial
   comment?

4. Examine the "black saliva" section in lines 21 to 39. Does it start off
   negatively? Does it change? Explain.

5. We all learn things from our families, both positive and negative. Is
   Hogan giving a balanced account? Should she? Would you? Do poets
   have any responsibility to the larger culture? Or should they just follow
   their own inner vision?

≡ MAKING COMPARISONS

1. Compare Hogan's grandfather to Giovanni's grandmother.

2. Describe the ways the tone of "Heritage" differs from Giovanni's poem.

3. What indications of cultural differences do you find in these two poems?

GARY SOTO
Behind Grandma's House

Born in 1952 in Fresno, California, Gary Soto gives voice to San Joaquin Valley agricultural workers whose deprivations have been part of his experience and social awareness from an early age. After graduating with honors from California State University in 1974, Soto went on to earn an M.F.A. in creative writing from the University of California at Irvine in 1976 and to teach in the university system. He has received numerous writing awards, including the distinction of being the first writer identifying himself as Chicano to be nominated for a Pulitzer Prize. A young adult novel, The Afterlife, *was published in 2003. A book of poems,* One Kind of Faith *(2003), was cited as confirming Soto's "immense talent." His Mexican American heritage continues to be central to his work. The poem reprinted here is from Soto's 1985 book,* Black Hair.

At ten I wanted fame. I had a comb
And two Coke bottles, a tube of Bryl-creem.
I borrowed a dog, one with
Mismatched eyes and a happy tongue,
And wanted to prove I was tough   5
In the alley, kicking over trash cans,
A dull chime of tuna cans falling.
I hurled light bulbs like grenades
And men teachers held their heads,
Fingers of blood lengthening   10
On the ground. I flicked rocks at cats,
Their goofy faces spurred with foxtails.
I kicked fences. I shooed pigeons.
I broke a branch from a flowering peach
And frightened ants with a stream of piss.   15
I said "Shit," "Fuck you," and "No way
Daddy-O" to an imaginary priest
Until grandma came into the alley,
Her apron flapping in a breeze,
Her hair mussed, and said, "Let me help you,"   20
And punched me between the eyes.   *[1985]*

≡ THINKING ABOUT THE TEXT

1. Were you glad or disturbed when the narrator's grandmother hit him? Does he deserve it? Are you angry or sympathetic to his attempts to be tough? Do you understand why he wants to appear older? Is this normal?

2. What did you want at age ten? Did your grandparents know your desires? Did they support you? Did they ever set you straight? Are our grandparents' values too dated to matter?

3. Are the concrete details meaningful to you? Does the profanity help Soto achieve authenticity, or is it unnecessary?

4. Does the speaker learn something here, or is this just a snapshot of an event?

5. How would you describe our culture's ideas of the different roles of parents and grandparents? Do grandparents in today's culture have less influence than in the past? Is this a good thing or not?

≡ MAKING COMPARISONS

1. Is Soto more or less respectful of his grandparent than the writers of the previous two poems?

2. Is this a gendered poem? That is, could a female see herself in a comparable situation? Are the Giovanni and Hogan poems gendered?

3. How might the portraits of grandmothers given here be stereotypical or not?

ALBERTO RÍOS
Mi Abuelo°

Alberto Ríos (b. 1952) has said that being bilingual is like going through life with a pair of binoculars; having at least two words for everything opens one's eyes to the world. Ríos is a person of the border in several ways: his father was from Chiapas, Mexico, and his mother from Lancashire, England. He grew up in the city of Nogales, Arizona, where he could stand with one foot in the United States and the other in Mexico; as a writer, he crosses the line between poetry and prose, having written seven books of poetry, three collections of short stories, and a memoir. He is an instructor of creative writing and since 1994 the Regents Professor of English at Arizona State University, where he has taught since 1982. He received his B.A. (1974) and his M.F.A. in creative writing (1979) from the University of Arizona. His work appears in 175 anthologies, including the Norton Anthology of Modern Poetry, *and his awards include fellowships from the Guggenheim Foundation and the National Endowment for the Arts and the 1982 Walt Whitman Award for* Whispering to Fool the Wind. *A recent book of poems,* The Smallest Muscle in the Human Body *(2002), was a finalist for the National Book Award. His latest work,* The Theatre of Night *(2006), was reviewed as "rhapsodic."*

Where my grandfather is is in the ground
where you can hear the future
like an Indian with his ear at the tracks.
A pipe leads down to him so that sometimes
he whispers what will happen to a man   5

Mi Abuelo: My grandfather (Spanish).

in town or how he will meet the best
dressed woman tomorrow and how the best
man at her wedding will chew the ground
next to her. Mi abuelo is the man
who speaks through all the mouths in my house.   10
An echo of me hitting the pipe sometimes
to stop him from saying *my hair is a*
sieve is the only other sound. It is a phrase
that among all others is the best,
he says, and *my hair is a sieve* is sometimes   15
repeated for hours out of the ground
when I let him, which is not often.
An abuelo should be much more than a man
like you! He stops then, and speaks: *I am a man*
who has served ants with the attitude   20
of a waiter, who has made each smile as only
an ant who is fat can, and they liked me best,
but there is nothing left. Yet I know he ground
green coffee beans as a child, and sometimes
he will talk about his wife, and sometimes   25
about when he was deaf and a man
cured him by mail and he heard groundhogs
talking, or about how he walked with a cane
he chewed on when he got hungry.
At best, mi abuelo is a liar.   30
I see an old picture of him at nani's with an
off-white yellow center mustache and sometimes
that's all I know for sure. He talks best
about these hills, *slowest waves*, and where this man
is going, and I'm convinced his hair is a sieve,   35
that his fever is cooled now underground.
Mi abuelo is an ordinary man.
I look down the pipe, sometimes, and see a
ripple-topped stream in its best suit, in the ground.   *[1990]*

≣ THINKING ABOUT THE TEXT

1. The narrator seems ambivalent about his abuelo. What specific things does he know about him? Can you tell his attitude toward him? How do you read the line "At best, mi abuelo is a liar" (line 30)? What might the worst be?

2. When the grandfather speaks from the grave ("*I am a man . . .*") (lines 19–23), he seems odd indeed. Is he a bit crazy, or do you see meaning in his ant speech?

3. What does Ríos mean when he writes that his abuelo "speaks through all the mouths in my house" (line 10)? Could this be a positive notion?

4. Ríos seems convinced that his grandfather's "fever is cooled now" (line 36). Should we take this literally?

5. Do you agree that Ríos wants to continue conversing with his dead abuelo? Why? Can we see this as a metaphor?

≣ MAKING COMPARISONS

1. Compare Ríos's attitude toward his grandfather with the attitudes shown in the poems by Giovanni, Hogan, and Soto.

2. Which of the grandparents featured in these poems would you like to meet? Why?

3. Do all the poems have a sense that grandparents possess some special experience or knowledge?

JUDITH ORTIZ COFER

Claims

Judith Ortiz Cofer (b. 1952) was born in Puerto Rico but spent most of her childhood traveling between Paterson, New Jersey, and Hormigueros, Puerto Rico. The constant shifting of languages and cultures influenced most of her early work, especially two volumes of poetry: Reaching for the Mainland *and* Terms of Survival, *both published in 1987. Her first novel,* The Line of the Sun *(1989), the first novel ever published by the University of Georgia Press, was widely praised and was nominated for the Pulitzer Prize. Her themes center on the pressures of migratory life and the cultural importance of male-female relationships.* Woman in Front of the Sun *was published in 2000. Her latest book is* A Love Story Beginning in Spanish *(2005). Cofer is a faculty member at the University of Georgia in Athens and is a Regents and Franklin Professor of English and Creative Writing.*

Last time I saw her, Grandmother
had grown seamed as a Bedouin tent.
She had claimed the right
to sleep alone, to own
her nights, to never bear   5
the weight of sex again nor to accept
its gift of comfort, for the luxury
of stretching her bones.
She'd carried eight children,
three had sunk in her belly, *naufragos*°   10
she called them, shipwrecked babies

10 *naufragos*: Victims of shipwrecks (Spanish).

drowned in her black waters.
Children are made in the night and
steal your days
for the rest of your life, amen. She said this   15
to each of her daughters in turn. Once she had made a pact
with man and nature and kept it. Now like the sea,
she is claiming back her territory.   [1987]

≡ THINKING ABOUT THE TEXT

1. To whom does the title refer?
2. What is the pact the grandmother made with "man and nature" (line 17)?
3. Comment on the simile "like the sea" Cofer uses in the last sentence. Has the reader been prepared for that comparison? Why, or why not?
4. What parts do duty and responsibility play in the grandmother's life? Does her quote (lines 13–15) suggest a negative view of children or sex?
5. Do you think the grandmother's response is typical or unusual?

≡ MAKING COMPARISONS

1. Is Cofer's attitude toward her grandmother more or less respectful than the other poets here?
2. Compare Cofer's grandmother with Soto's.
3. Which of the grandparents portrayed here might make the same decision about sex as Cofer's grandmother?

≡ WRITING ABOUT ISSUES

1. Pick one of the five preceding poems, and argue that it offers an appropriate view of grandparents.
2. Pick two of these poems, and argue that something of value is learned in each.
3. Which poem comes closest to your own experiences? Write a narrative that demonstrates this.
4. Do some research on over-sixty-five communities from a sociological point of view. Write a report about your findings. Include the impact of such places on the family and on the larger culture. Do you think they are a positive development or not?

■ Poetic Visions of Family: A Collection of Poems by Sharon Olds

SHARON OLDS, "I Go Back to May 1937"

SHARON OLDS, "My Son the Man"

SHARON OLDS, "First Thanksgiving"

SHARON OLDS, "Last Look"

Although Sharon Olds is one of contemporary poetry's leading voices, she claims she is not really a deep thinker, just a commentator on the events of ordinary life, from giving birth and nursing children to dealing with an alcoholic father and, as poet Alicia Ostriker puts it, "the erotics of family love and pain." Olds's first poem is a haunting and poignant fantasy, a kind of time travel wish to prevent her mother and father from inflicting pain on each other. In her poem about her son, she is stunned by the brevity of childhood, and her Houdini analogy is both clear and apt. The third poem, about her daughter's first Thanksgiving home from college, is both admiring of her daughter's maturity and bittersweet. The last and most recent poem, "Last Look," is from *Stag's Leap* (2012), which won the 2013 Pulitzer Prize for poetry. Olds says that once she wrote the title of this new collection she knew it would be about "the end of a long marriage—poems of divorce, loss, longing and healing." The critic Lisel Mueller notes that Olds's poems are "believable and touching. . . . [W]e hear a proud, urgent, human voice."

■ BEFORE YOU READ

If you were to write poems about your family, what topics would interest you? Would being honest be a problem for you? Would you want your family to read these poems?

SHARON OLDS

I Go Back to May 1937

Born in 1942 in San Francisco, Sharon Olds claims she was raised as a "hellfire Calvinist." She graduated from Stanford University and earned a Ph.D. in English from Columbia University. After receiving her doctorate, she vowed that she would become a poet who wrote in her own voice, no matter what. Her second volume, The Dead and the Living, won the 1983 Lamont Poetry Prize and the National Book Award. The Father (1992) is devoted entirely to her memories of her alcoholic father, who was abusive during her childhood but who expressed his love for her on his deathbed, and her struggle to reconcile with him. Her poems are often candid and explicit, prompting a range of critical estimations, from Michael Ondaatje's "pure fire

David Bartolomi

in the hands" to Helen Vendler's view that she is self-indulgent and sensationalist. Olds was the New York State poet laureate from 1998 to 2000. A recent collection of poems is One Sacred Thing *(2009). She teaches in the graduate creative writing program at New York University. "I Go Back to May 1937" was quoted in the popular 2007 film* Into the Wild.

I see them standing at the formal gates of their colleges,
I see my father strolling out
under the ochre sandstone arch, the
red tiles glinting like bent
plates of blood behind his head, I   5
see my mother with a few light books at her hip
standing at the pillar made of tiny bricks,
the wrought-iron gate still open behind her, its
sword-tips aglow in the May air,
they are about to graduate, they are about to get married,   10
they are kids, they are dumb, all they know is they are
innocent, they would never hurt anybody.
I want to go up to them and say Stop,
don't do it — she's the wrong woman,
he's the wrong man, you are going to do things   15
you cannot imagine you would ever do,

you are going to do bad things to children,
you are going to suffer in ways you have not heard of,
you are going to want to die. I want to go
up to them there in the late May sunlight and say it,   20
her hungry pretty face turning to me,
her pitiful beautiful untouched body,
his arrogant handsome face turning to me,
his pitiful beautiful untouched body,
but I don't do it. I want to live. I   25
take them up like the male and female
paper dolls and bang them together
at the hips, like chips of flint, as if to
strike sparks from them, I say
Do what you are going to do, and I will tell about it.   [1987] 30

☰ THINKING ABOUT THE TEXT

1. Although this is a fanciful poem involving time travel, it has a tone of grim resignation. What does Olds decide she is not able to do? What is she able to do?

2. Have you ever looked at a photograph of your parents when they were about to get married? What was your response? Does Olds's reaction seem odd?

3. Why do you think Olds uses the phrase "pitiful beautiful untouched body" (lines 22 and 24) for both parents? Does "pitiful" seem an unusual term? How about "dumb" (line 11)?

4. What do you think Olds means by referring to her father's face as "arrogant" (line 23) and her mother's as "hungry" (line 21)?

5. How might the last line be an indication of Olds's poetic mission?

SHARON OLDS
My Son the Man

"My Son the Man," which appeared in The Wellspring *(1996), reveals Sharon Olds's bittersweet feelings regarding her son's sudden maturity.*

Suddenly his shoulders get a lot wider,
the way Houdini would expand his body
while people were putting him in chains. It seems
no time since I would help him to put on his sleeper,
guide his calves into the gold interior,   5
zip him up and toss him up and
catch his weight. I cannot imagine him

no longer a child, and I know I must get ready,
get over my fear of men now my son
is going to be one. This was not   10
what I had in mind when he pressed up through me like a
sealed trunk through the ice of the Hudson,
snapped the padlock, unsnaked the chains,
and appeared in my arms. Now he looks at me
the way Houdini studied a box   15
to learn the way out, then smiled and let himself be manacled.   *[1995]*

≡ THINKING ABOUT THE TEXT

1. Explain how Olds uses the Houdini analogy to explain her feelings about her son.

2. Houdini, of course, was famous for amazing escapes. How does this idea figure in the poem?

3. Is Olds's "fear of men" (line 9) surprising? What other surprises appear in the poem?

4. What is Olds getting ready for?

5. Describe your reading of the last sentence.

≡ MAKING COMPARISONS

1. Compare Olds's use of metaphor and simile in these two poems.

2. Critics often comment on Olds's honesty. Do you think she is being honest in these two poems?

3. Compare the sentence "I cannot imagine him / no longer a child" (lines 7–8) with "they are kids, they are dumb, all they know is they are / in-nocent" (lines 11–12) in "I Go Back to May 1937."

SHARON OLDS
First Thanksgiving

In "First Thanksgiving," Sharon Olds uses her daughter's return home to ruminate on the joy of briefly containing something free and wild. This poem was published in Strike Sparks: Selected Poems, 1980–2002 *(2004).*

When she comes back, from college, I will see
the skin of her upper arms, cool,
matte, glossy. She will hug me, my old
soupy chest against her breasts,
I will smell her hair! She will sleep in this apartment,   5
her sleep like an untamed, good object,

like a soul in a body. She came into my life the
second great arrival, after him, fresh
from the other world — which lay, from within him,
within me. Those nights, I fed her to sleep,   10
week after week, the moon rising,
and setting, and waxing — whirling, over the months,
in a slow blur, around our planet.
Now she doesn't need love like that, she has
had it. She will walk in glowing, we will talk,   15
and then, when she's fast asleep, I'll exult
to have her in that room again,
behind that door! As a child, I caught
bees, by the wings, and held them, some seconds,
looked into their wild faces,   20
listened to them sing, then tossed them back
into the air — I remember the moment the
arc of my toss swerved, and they entered
the corrected curve of their departure.   *[1999]*

≡ THINKING ABOUT THE TEXT

1. Nostalgia plays an obvious part in this poem. What other emotions do you notice?

2. Poets often try to represent the complexity and the sometimes contradictory impulses of our feelings. How might that be true here?

3. Is Olds finally willing to come to peace with her daughter's departure?

4. Why does Olds use the phrase "behind that door" (line 18)?

5. Explain your understanding of the bee analogy in the last seven lines.

≡ MAKING COMPARISONS

1. Compare the effectiveness of the bee analogy in this poem with her use of Houdini in "My Son the Man."

2. What thematic similarities do you see in these two poems about her son and daughter?

3. Do you think this poem would have been different if she were talking about her son? Would the previous poem change if her daughter were the focus?

SHARON OLDS

Last Look

"Last Look," which first appeared in the American Poetry Review, *is, of course, about Sharon Olds's divorce, but it also makes a poignant connection to 9/11.*

In the last minutes of our marriage, I looked into
his eyes. All that day until then, I had been
comforting him, for the shock he was in
at his pain — the act of leaving me
took him back, to his own early   5
losses. But now it was time to go beyond
comfort, to part. And his eyes seemed to me,
still, like the first ocean, wherein
the blue-green algae came into their early
language, his sea-wide iris still   10
essential, for me, with the depths in which
our firstborn, and then our second, had turned,
on the sides of their tongues the taste buds for the moon-bland
nectar of our milk — *our* milk. In his gaze,
rooms of the dead; halls of loss; fog-   15
emerald; driven, dirty-rice snow:
he was in there somewhere, I looked for him,
and he gave me the gift, he let me in,
knowing he would never once, in this world or in
any other, have to do it again,   20
and I saw him, not as he really was, I was
still without the strength of anger, but I
saw him see me, even now
that dropping down into trust's affection
in his gaze, and I held it, some seconds, quiet,   25
and I said, Good-bye, and he said, Good-bye,
and I closed my eyes, and rose up out of the
passenger seat in a spiral like someone
coming up out of a car gone off a
bridge into deep water. And two and   30
three Septembers later, and even
the September after that, that September in New York,
I was glad I had looked at him. And when I
told a friend how glad I'd been,
she said, *Maybe it's like with the families*   35
of the dead, even the families of those
who died in the Towers — that need to see
the body, no longer inhabited

*by what made them the one we loved—somehow
it helps to say good-bye to the actual,*   40

and I saw again, how blessed my life has been,
first, to have been able to love,
then, to have the parting now behind me,
and not to have lost him when the kids were young,
and the kids now not at all to have lost him,   45
and not to have lost him when he loved me, and not to have
lost someone who could have loved me for life.   *[2012]*

≡ **THINKING ABOUT THE TEXT**

1. If you were to make a film of this poem, describe exactly what would be going on. What specific directions would you give to the actors?

2. Why does Olds use the phrase, "our milk" (line 14)?

3. What "gift" does she say her husband gave her (line 18)? What simile does she use for her final parting in the car? Why might this be an apt comparison?

4. What connection does Olds make between 9/11 and her parting from her husband? What is her friend's explanation?

5. This somber poem seems to end on a positive note. How is this the case? Which of the six reasons she gives seems to you the most important and why?

≡ **MAKING COMPARISONS**

1. Which of these four poems seems the most positive? The least? Why?

2. Compare the idea of departure in the last three poems.

3. Compare the effectiveness of the bee analogy ("First Thanksgiving") and the Houdini comparison ("My Son the Man") with the car image (lines 27-30) in "Last Look."

≡ **WRITING ABOUT ISSUES**

1. Write a personal essay involving your family that focuses on one of the emotions or insights that Olds describes in these four poems.

2. Write an essay that explores the idea that students and parents have different perceptions of their departure to and return from college.

3. Argue that Olds's insights into family life are either typical or unusual.

4. Argue that nonfiction writers, poets, and fiction writers have an artistic responsibility to describe specifically and honestly the joy and pain of family life.

≡ Gays and Lesbians in Families: Poems

ESSEX HEMPHILL, "Commitments"

AUDRE LORDE, "Who Said It Was Simple"

MINNIE BRUCE PRATT, "Two Small-Sized Girls"

RICHARD BLANCO, "Queer Theory: According to My Grandmother"

The late Essex Hemphill was gay, as is Richard Blanco; the late Audre Lorde was a lesbian, as is Minnie Bruce Pratt. All four writers in this cluster remind their audience that families may have gay or lesbian members, but the families depicted in most literature, films, television shows, and songs are heterosexual. Indeed, much of American society prefers this image. Throughout history, plenty of gays and lesbians have concealed their sexual identities from their families, fearing rejection. Families that do have gay or lesbian members may refuse to admit the fact, although most have grown more accepting of their loved ones' differences.

As increasing numbers of gays and lesbians "come out of the closet," many are also publicly claiming the term *family*. They seek acceptance by the families they were raised in and the right to form and raise families of their own. Some are working to get same-sex marriage legalized. In all these efforts, they have quite a few heterosexual allies, but they face heterosexual resistance too. In the 1990s, a lesbian mother, Sharon Bottoms, lost custody of her children for that reason. Also, gays and lesbians are far from winning a universal right to adopt. In 2004, Massachusetts became the first state to legalize same-sex marriage, but as arguments about it raged throughout the United States, the federal government sought to discourage it by passing the Defense of Marriage Act in 1996, and several states passed laws against it. Recently, however, the Supreme Court ruled that important parts of that law are unconstitutional. And as of the summer of 2014, more than half the states will soon permit same-sex marriages. Gays and lesbians still face difficulties with adoption and foster parenting, although there are indications that societal attitudes here are also changing, albeit slowly. Consider your own position on these matters as you read the following poems. Each refers to American society's widespread assumption that families are heterosexual; each also points out the suffering that can result from this belief.

≡ BEFORE YOU READ

What, at present, is your attitude toward gays and lesbians? Try to identify specific people, experiences, and institutions that have shaped your view. If it has changed over the years, explain how. Finally, describe an occasion that made you quite conscious of the attitude you now hold.

ESSEX HEMPHILL

Commitments

Before his untimely death from AIDS-related complications, Essex Hemphill (1957–1995) explored through prose, poetry, and film what it meant to live as a black gay man. The following poem comes from his 1992 book Ceremonies: Prose and Poetry. *His other books include a collection he edited,* Brother to Brother: New Writings by Black Gay Men *(1991). Hemphill also appeared in the documentaries* Looking for Langston *and* Tongues Untied.

I will always be there.
When the silence is exhumed.
When the photographs are examined
I will be pictured smiling
among siblings, parents,   5
nieces and nephews.

In the background of the photographs
the hazy smoke of barbecue,
a checkered red-and-white tablecloth
laden with blackened chicken,   10
glistening ribs, paper plates,
bottles of beer, and pop.

In the photos
the smallest children
are held by their parents.   15
My arms are empty, or around
the shoulders of unsuspecting aunts
expecting to throw rice at me someday.

Or picture tinsel, candles,
ornamented, imitation trees,   20
or another table, this one
set for Thanksgiving,
a turkey steaming the lens.

My arms are empty
in those photos, too,   25
so empty they would break

around a lover.
I am always there
for critical emergencies,
graduations,   30
the middle of the night.

I am the invisible son.
In the family photos
nothing appears out of character.
I smile as I serve my duty.

[1992]   35

≡ THINKING ABOUT THE TEXT

1. The speaker begins with the announcement "I will always be there," and yet later he says "I am the invisible son" (line 32). How can these two statements be reconciled? In the second line, he uses the word *exhumed*. Look up this word in a dictionary. What do you infer from the speaker's use of it?

2. Unlike the other stanzas, the second lacks verbs. Should Hemphill have included at least one verb there for the sake of consistency? Why, or why not? Is the scene described in the second stanza characteristic of your own family? Note similarities and differences.

3. What do you think the speaker means when he describes his arms in the photographs as "so empty they would break / around a lover" (lines 26–27)?

4. In line 34, the speaker refers to "character." How does he seem to define the term? He concludes the poem by noting, "I smile as I serve my duty." Should this line be taken as an indication of how he really feels about his family commitments? Why, or why not?

5. List some commitments that you think the speaker's family should be making toward him. What overall attitude of yours toward the family does your list suggest? What is your overall attitude toward the speaker?

AUDRE LORDE
Who Said It Was Simple

Audre Lorde (1934–1992), a prolific writer and speaker, was also active in the civil rights, women's, and gay and lesbian movements. She published several books of poetry, including Cables to Rage *(1970);* From a Land Where Other People Live *(1973), where the following poem appeared;* The New York Head Shop and Museum *(1974);* Coal *(1976);* The Black Unicorn *(1978); and* Our Dead behind Us *(1986). In addition, she wrote several works of nonfiction, including a memoir,* Zami: A New Spelling of My Name *(1982); a collection of essays and speeches,* Sister Outsider *(1984); and an account of her struggle with breast cancer,* The Cancer Journals *(1980). Her last book was* The Marvelous Arithmetic of Distance *(1993). Although Lorde was a lesbian, she had two children and described herself as "black, lesbian, mother, warrior, poet." Lorde was quite controversial, as she saw a clear link among sexism, racism, and homophobia. The key issue for her*

*was mainstream culture's intolerance of difference. This issue alienated her from
many white feminists who thought solidarity was crucial. Although Lorde certainly
believed in sisterhood, for her the metaphor of family had its limits, as the following
poem suggests.*

There are so many roots to the tree of anger
that sometimes the branches shatter
before they bear.

Sitting in Nedicks
the women rally before they march   5
discussing the problematic girls
they hire to make them free.
An almost white counterman passes
a waiting brother to serve them first
and the ladies neither notice nor reject   10
the slighter pleasures of their slavery.
But I who am bound by my mirror
as well as my bed
see causes in colour
as well as sex   15

and sit here wondering
which me will survive
all these liberations.   *[1973]*

≡ THINKING ABOUT THE TEXT

1. What is the thematic focus that Lorde announces with the tree metaphor of the first three lines?

2. What does the counterman do, and why does that annoy the speaker?

3. Why does Lorde use such a strong word as *slavery* (line 11) to describe
   the women at the counter who are served before the "brother"?

4. What does Lorde mean by being "bound by my mirror / as well as my
   bed" (lines 12–13)?

5. Do you see irony in Lorde's final stanza? Do you think Lorde is using
   "liberations" (line 18) sarcastically?

≡ MAKING COMPARISONS

1. Explain how both Lorde and Hemphill use the idea of invisibility.

2. Lorde mentions anger. Do you think Hemphill is angry, or do you sense
   other emotions?

3. Lorde was the mother of two children. Do you think that gave her a different perspective when protesting for gay rights?

MINNIE BRUCE PRATT
Two Small-Sized Girls

Minnie Bruce Pratt (b. 1946) has long been active in the women's movement. Her prose writings include Rebellion: Essays, 1980–1991 *(1991) and a 1995 volume of short pieces titled* S/HE. *As a poet, she has published* The Sound of One Fork *(1981);* Crime against Nature *(1990), which won the prestigious Lamont Prize of the American Academy of Poets; and* We Say We Love Each Other *(1992). Her latest books are* Walking Back Up Depot Street *(1999),* The Dirt She Ate *(2003), and* Inside the Money Machine *(2011). In divorce proceedings, Pratt lost custody of her two sons because she is a lesbian. Many of the poems in* Crime against Nature, *including the following, refer to this experience.*

1

Two small-sized girls, hunched in the corn crib,
skin prickly with heat and dust.   We rustle
in the corn husks and grab rough cobs gnawed
empty as bone.   We twist them with papery shreds.
Anyone passing would say we're making our dolls.   5

Almost sisters, like our mothers, we turn and shake
the shriveled beings.   We are not playing at babies.
We are doing, single-minded, what we've been watching
our grandmother do.   We are making someone.   We hunker
on splintered grey planks older than our mothers,   10
and ignore how the sun blazes across us, the straw husks,
the old door swung open for the new corn of the summer.

2

Here's the cherry spool bed from her old room,
the white bedspread crocheted by Grandma,
rough straw baskets hanging on the blank wall,   15
snapshots from her last trip home, ramshackle
houses eaten up by kudzu.   The same past
haunts us.   We have ended up in the same present

where I sit crosslegged with advice on how to keep
her children from being seized by their father   20
ten years after I lost my own.   The charge then:
crime against nature, going too far with women,
and not going back to men.   And hers?   Wanting
to have her small garden the way she wanted it,
and wanting to go her own way.   The memory: 25

   Her father's garden, immense rows of corn,
   cantaloupe and melon squiggling, us squatting,

late afternoon, cool in the four o'clocks;
waiting for them to open, making up stories,
anything might happen, waiting in the garden.   30

3

So much for the power of my ideas about oppression
and her disinterest in them.   In fact we've ended
in the same place.   Made wrong, knowing we've done
nothing wrong:
                    Like the afternoon we burned up   35
the backyard, wanting to see some fire.
The match's seed opened into straw, paper,
then bushes, like enormous red and orange
lantana flowers.   We chased the abrupt power
blooming around us down to charred straw,   40
and Grandma bathed us, scorched and ashy,
never saying a word.

                    Despite our raw hearts,
guilt from men who used our going to take our children,
we know we've done nothing wrong, to twist and search   45
for the kernels of fire deep in the body's shaken husk.   *[1990]*

≡ THINKING ABOUT THE TEXT

1. Do you think any behavior deserves to be called a "crime against nature" (line 22)? Explain your reasoning.

2. Ironically, one pattern in Pratt's poem is nature imagery. Do you consider some or all of this imagery to be symbolic, or do you accept the images simply as details of a physical scene? Refer to specific examples.

3. Compare the three sections of the poem. What are their common elements? How do they significantly differ from one another? Why does the speaker believe that she and her cousin have "ended / in the same place" (lines 32–33)?

4. How would you describe the two girls' relationship to their grandmother? Support your answer with specific details from the text.

5. Do you think this poem is an affirmation of family ties? A criticism of them? Both? Again, refer to specific details.

≡ MAKING COMPARISONS

1. Compare the tone of the three speakers in Hemphill's, Lorde's, and Pratt's poems.

2. Do you get the impression that all three speakers in this cluster are searching for Pratt's "kernels of fire deep in the body's shaken husk" (line 46)? Show how these words are or are not relevant in each case.

3. Do you sympathize with any of the three speakers more than the others? Why, or why not?

RICHARD BLANCO

Queer Theory: According to My Grandmother

Richard Blanco (b.1968) was born in Madrid and emigrated to Miami as an infant with his Cuban exiled family. He graduated from Florida International University with a B.S. in civil engineering and later received an M.F.A. in 1997. He was the fifth poet, first Latino, and first openly gay person to read at a presidential inauguration. At Barack Obama's second inauguration, Blanco read "One Today," a poem that affirms America's collective identity. He has taught at Georgetown and American Universities and continues to practice as a civil engineer in his home in Bethel, Maine. The following poem is taken from Looking for the Gulf Motel *(2012), published by the University of Pittsburgh Press. One critic notes that Blanco is "a virtuoso of art and craft who juggles the subjective and the objective beautifully."*

Never drink soda with a straw—
   milk shakes? Maybe.
Stop eyeing your mother's Avon catalog,
and the men's underwear in those Sears flyers.
   I've seen you . . .   5
Stay out of her Tupperware parties
and her perfume bottles—don't let her kiss you,
   she kisses you much too much.
Avoid hugging men, but if you must,
   pat them real hard   10
   on the back, even
   if it's your father.
Must you keep that cat? Don't pet him so much.
   Why don't you like dogs?
Never play house, even if you're the husband.   15
Quit hanging with that Henry kid, he's too pale,
   and I don't care what you call them
   those GI Joes of his
   are dolls.
Don't draw rainbows or flowers or sunsets.   20
   I've seen you . . .
Don't draw at all—no coloring books either.
Put away your crayons, your Play-Doh, your Legos.
   Where are your Hot Wheels,

your laser gun and handcuffs,   25
   the knives I gave you?
Never fly a kite or roller skate, but light
   all the firecrackers you want,
     kill all the lizards you can, cut up worms—
   feed them to that cat of yours.   30
Don't sit *Indian* style with your legs crossed—
   you're no Indian.
Stop click-clacking your sandals—
   you're no girl.
For God's sake, never pee sitting down.   35
   I've seen you . . .
Never take a bubble bath or wash your hair
with shampoo—shampoo is for women.
     So is conditioner.
     So is mousse.   40
     So is hand lotion.
Never file your nails or blow-dry your hair—
go to the barber shop with your grandfather—
   you're not *unisex*.
Stay out of the kitchen. Men don't cook—   45
they eat. Eat anything you want, except:
     deviled eggs
     Blow Pops
     croissants (Bagels? Maybe.)
     cucumber sandwiches   50
     petit fours
Don't watch *Bewitched* or *I Dream of Jeannie*.
Don't stare at *The Six-Million Dollar Man*.
   I've seen you . . .
Never dance alone in your room: 55
Donna Summer, Barry Manilow, the Captain
and Tennille, Bette Midler, and all musicals—
     forbidden.
Posters of kittens, *Star Wars*, or the Eiffel Tower—
     forbidden.   60
Those fancy books on architecture and art—
   I threw them in the trash.
You can't wear cologne or puka shells
and I better not catch you in clogs.
If I see you in a ponytail—I'll cut it off.   65
What? No, you can't pierce your ear,
     left or right side—
     I don't care—
you will not look like a goddamn queer,
   I've seen you . . .   70
even if you are one.   *[2012]*

≡ THINKING ABOUT THE TEXT

1. Blanco's grandmother has a fairly extensive forbidden list. Which ones surprised you, and why? Are some of these dated? Is the "gayness" of other items on the list unclear?

2. The grandmother seems to have fairly old-fashioned notions about what boys and girls should and should not do. How would you describe her version of male and female behavior?

3. How might the last three lines be seen as a compromise on the grandmother's part? Although egregious stereotyping is a serious topic, Blanco's poem is also meant to be humorous. Wherein does the humor lie? Is it effective?

4. The grandmother's assumption, not uncommon among some uneducated people, is that gay men like the same things that stereotypical girls do. How does this poem support that view? Where do you think such a misconception comes from? Does our culture encourage such views?

5. Perhaps Blanco is somewhat hyperbolic about his grandmother's forbidden list. Which items seem unlikely to have actually caught the grandmother's attention? Why might Blanco have included them?

≡ MAKING COMPARISONS

1. Compare the idea of "being oneself" in these four poems.

2. In her poem, Pratt uses the phrase "we know we've done nothing wrong." How would Essex Hemphill and Richard Blanco have responded to this idea?

3. What are the major ideas you see in these four poems?

≡ WRITING ABOUT ISSUES

1. Choose Hemphill's, Lorde's, or Pratt's poem, and write an essay arguing for or against a position held by someone in the poem. The person can be the speaker. Support your argument with specific details and examples.

2. Choose two of the poems in this cluster, and write an essay comparing how commitments figure in them. Be sure to cite specific words from each poem.

3. In the next week, observe and jot down things on your campus that you think might disturb a gay or lesbian student. (If you are a gay or lesbian student, you may have already thought about such matters.) Then write an essay addressing the issue of whether your campus is inviting to gay and lesbian students. In arguing for your position on this issue, refer to some of the observations you made. If you wish, refer as well to one or more of the poems in this cluster.

4. Increasingly, the United States is grappling with whether same-sex marriage should be legalized. Another debate is whether gays and lesbians should be allowed to become foster parents. Choose one of these issues, and read at least three articles about it. Then write an essay in which you not only put forth and support your own position on the issue but also state whether and how the articles affected your thinking. If you wish, you may refer as well to one or more of the poems in this cluster.

▤ Mothers and Daughters: Stories

TILLIE OLSEN, "I Stand Here Ironing"

AMY TAN, "Two Kinds"

ALICE WALKER, "Everyday Use"

We all know stories of parents who want to mold their children, stories of mothers and fathers who push their reluctant children to be fashion models or beauty queens or Little League stars. Some studies of adults playing musical instruments in orchestras say the biggest factor in their success was the commitment of their parents. But we also hear about tennis prodigies who burn out at sixteen because of parental pressure. Mothers and daughters have always struggled with each other over life goals and identity. How much guidance is enough? How much is too much? What is a reasonable balance between preparing a child for life's challenges and shaping a child to act out the mother's fantasy or her internal vision of what the good life is? And no matter where parents fall on this continuum, are there childhood events so powerful that we cannot get beyond them? The following three stories chart the difficulties mothers and daughters have with each other and with the social and cultural forces that influence our destiny.

▤ BEFORE YOU READ

Are your parents responsible for your successes? Your failures? Do you wish that your parents had pushed you to succeed more insistently? Are you annoyed that your parents set unreasonable standards for you?

TILLIE OLSEN
I Stand Here Ironing

Born in Omaha, Nebraska, to Russian immigrants of Jewish descent and socialist views, Tillie Olsen (1912–2007) was an activist in social and political causes all of her life, often choosing family, work, union, feminist, or other political causes over writing. Although her publishing record is short, its quality is greatly admired. In addition to critically respected short stories, Olsen wrote a novel, Yonnondio (1974), which paints a vivid picture of a coal-mining family during the Depression. Her essay collection, Silences (1978), stimulated debate about class and gender as factors in the creation of literature and led both directly and indirectly to the revived interest in works by women writers. The mother of four daughters, Olsen often wrote about generational relationships within families. "I Stand Here Ironing" is from her 1961 collection of stories, Tell Me a Riddle.

313

I stand here ironing, and what you asked me moves tormented back and forth with the iron.

"I wish you would manage the time to come in and talk with me about your daughter. I'm sure you can help me understand her. She's a youngster who needs help and whom I'm deeply interested in helping."

"Who needs help." . . . Even if I came, what good would it do? You think because I am her mother I have a key, or that in some way you could use me as a key? She has lived for nineteen years. There is all that life that has happened outside of me, beyond me.

And when is there time to remember, to sift, to weigh, to estimate, to total? I will start and there will be an interruption and I will have to gather it all together again. Or I will become engulfed with all I did or did not do, with what should have been and what cannot be helped.

She was a beautiful baby. The first and only one of our five that was beautiful at birth. You do not guess how new and uneasy her tenancy in her now-loveliness. You did not know her all those years she was thought homely, or see her poring over her baby pictures, making me tell her over and over how beautiful she had been — and would be, I would tell her — and was now, to the seeing eye. But the seeing eyes were few or nonexistent. Including mine. 5

I nursed her. They feel that's important nowadays. I nursed all the children, but with her, with all the fierce rigidity of first motherhood, I did like the books then said. Though her cries battered me to trembling and my breasts ached with swollenness, I waited till the clock decreed.

Why do I put that first? I do not even know if it matters, or if it explains anything.

She was a beautiful baby. She blew shining bubbles of sound. She loved motion, loved light, loved color and music and textures. She would lie on the floor in her blue overalls patting the surface so hard in ecstasy her hands and feet would blur. She was a miracle to me, but when she was eight months old I had to leave her daytimes with the woman downstairs to whom she was no miracle at all, for I worked or looked for work and for Emily's father, who "could no longer endure" (he wrote in his good-bye note) "sharing want with us."

I was nineteen. It was the pre-relief, pre-WPA world of the depression. I would start running as soon as I got off the streetcar, running up the stairs, the place smelling sour, and awake or asleep to startle awake, when she saw me she would break into a clogged weeping that could not be comforted, a weeping I can hear yet.

After a while I found a job hashing at night so I could be with her days, and it was better. But it came to where I had to bring her to his family and leave her. 10

It took a long time to raise the money for her fare back. Then she got chicken pox and I had to wait longer. When she finally came, I hardly knew her, walking quick and nervous like her father, looking like her father, thin, and dressed in a shoddy red that yellowed her skin and glared at the pockmarks. All the baby loveliness gone.

She was two. Old enough for nursery school they said, and I did not know then what I know now—the fatigue of the long day, and the lacerations of group life in the kinds of nurseries that are only parking places for children.

Except that it would have made no difference if I had known. It was the only place there was. It was the only way we could be together, the only way I could hold a job.

And even without knowing, I knew. I knew the teacher that was evil because all these years it has curdled into my memory, the little boy hunched in the corner, her rasp, "why aren't you outside, because Alvin hits you? that's no reason, go out, scaredy." I knew Emily hated it even if she did not clutch and implore "don't go Mommy" like the other children, mornings.

She always had a reason why we should stay home. Momma, you look   15
sick. Momma, I feel sick. Momma, the teachers aren't there today, they're sick. Momma, we can't go, there was a fire there last night. Momma, it's a holiday today, no school, they told me.

But never a direct protest, never rebellion. I think of our others in their three-, four-year-oldness—the explosions, the tempers, the denunciations, the demands—and I feel suddenly ill. I put the iron down. What in me demanded that goodness in her? And what was the cost, the cost to her of such goodness?

The old man living in the back once said in his gentle way: "You should smile at Emily more when you look at her." What *was* in my face when I looked at her? I loved her. There were all the acts of love.

It was only with the others I remembered what he said, and it was the face of joy, and not of care or tightness or worry I turned to them—too late for Emily. She does not smile easily, let alone almost always as her brothers and sisters do. Her face is closed and sombre, but when she wants, how fluid. You must have seen it in her pantomimes, you spoke of her rare gift for comedy on the stage that rouses laughter out of the audience so dear they applaud and applaud and do not want to let her go.

Where does it come from, that comedy? There was none of it in her when she came back to me that second time, after I had to send her away again. She had a new daddy now to learn to love, and I think perhaps it was a better time.

Except when we left her alone nights, telling ourselves she was old enough.   20

"Can't you go some other time, Mommy, like tomorrow?" she would ask. "Will it be just a little while you'll be gone? Do you promise?"

The time we came back, the front door open, the clock on the floor in the hall. She rigid awake. "It wasn't just a little while. I didn't cry. Three times I called you, just three times, and then I ran downstairs to open the door so you could come faster. The clock talked loud. I threw it away, it scared me what it talked."

She said the clock talked loud again that night I went to the hospital to have Susan. She was delirious with the fever that comes before red measles, but she was fully conscious all the week I was gone and the week after we were home when she could not come near the new baby or me.

She did not get well. She stayed skeleton thin, not wanting to eat, and night after night she had nightmares. She would call for me, and I would rouse from exhaustion to sleepily call back: "You're all right, darling, go to sleep, it's just a dream," and if she still called, in a sterner voice, "now go to sleep, Emily, there's nothing to hurt you." Twice, only twice, when I had to get up for Susan anyhow, I went in to sit with her.

Now when it is too late (as if she would let me hold her and comfort her like I do the others) I get up and go to her at once at her moan or restless stirring. "Are you awake, Emily? Can I get you something?" And the answer is always the same: "No, I'm all right, go back to sleep, Mother."   25

They persuaded me at the clinic to send her away to a convalescent home in the country where "she can have the kind of food and care you can't manage for her, and you'll be free to concentrate on the new baby." They still send children to that place. I see pictures on the society page of sleek young women planning affairs to raise money for it, or dancing at the affairs, or decorating Easter eggs or filling Christmas stockings for the children.

They never have a picture of the children so I do not know if the girls still wear those gigantic red bows and the ravaged looks on the every other Sunday when parents can come to visit "unless otherwise notified" — as we were notified the first six weeks.

Oh it is a handsome place, green lawns and tall trees and fluted flower beds. High up on the balconies of each cottage the children stand, the girls in their red bows and white dresses, the boys in white suits and giant red ties. The parents stand below shrieking up to be heard and the children shriek down to be heard, and between them the invisible wall "Not To Be Contaminated by Parental Germs or Physical Affection."

There was a tiny girl who always stood hand in hand with Emily. Her parents never came. One visit she was gone. "They moved her to Rose Cottage," Emily shouted in explanation. "They don't like you to love anybody here."

She wrote once a week, the labored writing of a seven-year-old. "I am fine.   30
How is the baby. If I write my leter nicly I will have a star. Love." There never was a star. We wrote every other day, letters she could never hold or keep but only hear read — once. "We simply do not have room for children to keep any personal possessions," they patiently explained when we pieced one Sunday's shrieking together to plead how much it would mean to Emily, who loved so to keep things, to be allowed to keep her letters and cards.

Each visit she looked frailer. "She isn't eating," they told us.

(They had runny eggs for breakfast or mush with lumps, Emily said later, I'd hold it in my mouth and not swallow. Nothing ever tasted good, just when they had chicken.)

It took us eight months to get her released home, and only the fact that she gained back so little of her seven lost pounds convinced the social worker.

I used to try to hold and love her after she came back, but her body would stay stiff, and after a while she'd push away. She ate little. Food sickened her, and I think much of life too. Oh she had physical lightness and brightness, twinkling by on skates, bouncing like a ball up and down up and down over the jump rope, skimming over the hill; but these were momentary.

She fretted about her appearance, thin and dark and foreign-looking at a   35 time when every little girl was supposed to look or thought she should look like a chubby blonde replica of Shirley Temple. The doorbell sometimes rang for her, but no one seemed to come and play in the house or to be a best friend. Maybe because we moved so much.

There was a boy she loved painfully through two school semesters. Months later she told me how she had taken pennies from my purse to buy him candy. "Licorice was his favorite and I brought him some every day, but he still liked Jennifer better'n me. Why, Mommy?" The kind of question for which there is no answer.

School was a worry for her. She was not glib or quick in a world where glibness and quickness were easily confused with ability to learn. To her overworked and exasperated teachers she was an overconscientious "slow learner" who kept trying to catch up and was absent entirely too often.

I let her be absent, though sometimes the illness was imaginary. How different from my now-strictness about attendance with the others. I wasn't working. We had a new baby. I was home anyhow. Sometimes, after Susan grew old enough, I would keep her home from school, too, to have them all together.

Mostly Emily had asthma, and her breathing, harsh and labored, would fill the house with a curiously tranquil sound. I would bring the two old dresser mirrors and her boxes of collections to her bed. She would select beads and single earrings, bottle tops and shells, dried flowers and pebbles, old postcards and scraps, all sorts of oddments; then she and Susan would play Kingdom, setting up landscapes and furniture, peopling them with action.

Those were the only times of peaceful companionship between her and   40
Susan. I have edged away from it, that poisonous feeling between them, that terrible balancing of hurts and needs I had to do between the two, and did so badly, those earlier years.

Oh there were conflicts between the others too, each one human, needing, demanding, hurting, taking — but only between Emily and Susan, no, Emily toward Susan that corroding resentment. It seems so obvious on the surface, yet it is not obvious; Susan, the second child, Susan, golden- and curly-haired and chubby, quick and articulate and assured, everything in appearance and manner Emily was not; Susan, not able to resist Emily's precious things, losing or sometimes clumsily breaking them; Susan telling jokes and riddles to company for applause while Emily sat silent (to say to me later: that was *my* riddle, Mother, I told it to Susan); Susan, who for all the five years' difference in age was just a year behind Emily in developing physically.

I am glad for that slow physical development that widened the difference between her and her contemporaries, though she suffered over it. She was too vulnerable for that terrible world of youthful competition, of preening and parading, of constant measuring of yourself against every other, of envy, "If I had that copper hair," "If I had that skin. . . ." She tormented herself enough about not looking like the others, there was enough of unsureness, the having to be conscious of words before you speak, the constant caring — what are they thinking of me? without having it all magnified by the merciless physical drives.

Ronnie is calling. He is wet and I change him. It is rare there is such a cry now. That time of motherhood is almost behind me when the ear is not one's own but must always be racked and listening for the child cry, the child call. We sit for a while and I hold him, looking out over the city spread in charcoal with its soft aisles of light. *"Shoogily,"* he breathes and curls closer. I carry him back to bed, asleep. *Shoogily.* A funny word, a family word, inherited from Emily, invented by her to say: *comfort.*

In this and other ways she leaves her seal, I say aloud. And startle at my saying it. What do I mean? What did I start to gather together, to try and make coherent? I was at the terrible, growing years. War years. I do not remember them well. I was working, there were four smaller ones now, there was not time for her. She had to help be a mother, and housekeeper, and shopper. She had to get her seal. Mornings of crisis and near hysteria trying to get lunches packed, hair combed, coats and shoes found, everyone to school or Child Care on time, the baby ready for transportation. And always the paper scribbled on by a smaller one, the book looked at by Susan then mislaid, the homework not done. Running out to that huge school where she was one, she was lost, she was a drop; suffering over the unpreparedness, stammering and unsure in her classes.

There was so little time left at night after the kids were bedded down. She   45
would struggle over books, always eating (it was in those years she developed her enormous appetite that is legendary in our family) and I would be ironing, or preparing food for the next day, or writing V-mail to Bill, or tending the baby. Sometimes, to make me laugh, or out of her despair, she would imitate happenings or types at school.

I think I said once: "Why don't you do something like this in the school amateur show?" One morning she phoned me at work, hardly understandable through the weeping: "Mother, I did it. I won, I won; they gave me first prize; they clapped and clapped and wouldn't let me go."

Now suddenly she was Somebody, and as imprisoned in her difference as she had been in anonymity.

She began to be asked to perform at other high schools, even in colleges, then at city and statewide affairs. The first one we went to, I only recognized her that first moment when thin, shy, she almost drowned herself into the curtains. Then: Was this Emily? The control, the command, the convulsing and deadly clowning, the spell, then the roaring, stamping audience, unwilling to let this rare and precious laughter out of their lives.

Afterwards: You ought to do something about her with a gift like that — but without money or knowing how, what does one do? We have left it all to her, and the gift has so often eddied inside, clogged and clotted, as been used and growing.

She is coming. She runs up the stairs two at a time with her light graceful   50
step, and I know she is happy tonight. Whatever it was that occasioned your call did not happen today.

"Aren't you ever going to finish the ironing, Mother? Whistler painted his mother in a rocker. I'd have to paint mine standing over an ironing board." This is one of her communicative nights and she tells me everything and nothing as she fixes herself a plate of food out of the icebox.

She is so lovely. Why did you want me to come in at all? Why were you concerned? She will find her way.

She starts up the stairs to bed. "Don't get me up with the rest in the morning." "But I thought you were having midterms." "Oh, those," she comes back in, kisses me, and says quite lightly, "in a couple of years when we'll all be atom-dead they won't matter a bit."

She has said it before. She *believes* it. But because I have been dredging the past, and all that compounds a human being is so heavy and meaningful in me, I cannot endure it tonight.

I will never total it all. I will never come in to say: She was a child seldom   55
smiled at. Her father left me before she was a year old. I had to work her first six years when there was work, or I sent her home and to his relatives. There were years she had care she hated. She was dark and thin and foreign-looking in a world where the prestige went to blondeness and curly hair and dimples, she was slow where glibness was prized. She was a child of anxious, not proud, love. We were poor and could not afford for her the soil of easy growth. I was a young mother, I was a distracted mother. There were other children pushing up, demanding. Her younger sister seemed all that she was not. There were years she did not want me to touch her. She kept too much in herself, her life was such she had to keep too much in herself. My wisdom came too late. She has much to her and probably little will come of it. She is a child of her age, of depression, of war, of fear.

Let her be. So all that is in her will not bloom — but in how many does it? There is still enough left to live by. Only help her to know — help make it so there is cause for her to know — that she is more than this dress on the ironing board, helpless before the iron.   *[1961]*

☰ THINKING ABOUT THE TEXT

1. Is Olsen's last paragraph optimistic or pessimistic about personal destiny? Is there some support in the story for both perspectives?

2. There is an old expression: "To know all is to forgive all." Does this statement apply to "I Stand Here Ironing"? Some critics want to privilege personal responsibility; others, social conditions. Do you blame Emily's mother? Or is she just a victim?

3. How might this story be different if told from Emily's perspective? From Susan's? From Emily's teacher's? What are the advantages and disadvantages of writing a story from one character's point of view?

4. How would you describe the voice or voices we hear in the story? What qualities, dimensions, or emotions can you infer? Does one dominate? Are you sympathetic to this voice? Is that what Olsen wanted?

5. Do you agree with the mother's decision not to visit the school for a conference? What are her reasons? Are they sound? What do you think the teacher wants to discuss? How involved in a child's life should a teacher be?

AMY TAN

Two Kinds

Born to Chinese immigrants in Oakland, California, Amy Tan (b. 1952) weaves intricate stories about generational and intercultural relationships among women in families, basing much of her writing on her own family history. She earned a double B.A., in English and linguistics, and an M.A. in linguistics at San Jose State University. Her novels dealing with mother-daughter relationships, The Joy Luck Club *(1989) and* The Kitchen God's Wife *(1991), have received awards and critical acclaim.* The Hundred Secret Senses *(1995) explores the relationship between sisters who grew up in different cultures. Her latest novel is* Valley of Amazement *(2013), and another book is a collection of nonfiction,* The Opposite of Fate *(2003). "Two Kinds" is excerpted from* The Joy Luck Club.

My mother believed you could be anything you wanted to be in America. You could open a restaurant. You could work for the government and get good retirement. You could buy a house with almost no money down. You could become rich. You could become instantly famous.

"Of course you can be prodigy, too," my mother told me when I was nine. "You can be best anything. What does Auntie Lindo know? Her daughter, she is only best tricky."

America was where all my mother's hopes lay. She had come here in 1949 after losing everything in China: her mother and father, her family home, her first husband, and two daughters, twin baby girls. But she never looked back with regret. There were so many ways for things to get better.

We didn't immediately pick the right kind of prodigy. At first my mother thought I could be a Chinese Shirley Temple. We'd watch Shirley's old movies on TV as though they were training films. My mother would poke my arm and say, "*Ni kan*" — You watch. And I would see Shirley tapping her feet, or singing a sailor song, or pursing her lips into a very round O while saying, "Oh my goodness."

"*Ni kan*," said my mother as Shirley's eyes flooded with tears. "You already know how. Don't need talent for crying!"   5

Soon after my mother got this idea about Shirley Temple, she took me to a beauty training school in the Mission district and put me in the hands of a student who could barely hold the scissors without shaking. Instead of getting big fat curls, I emerged with an uneven mass of crinkly black fuzz. My mother dragged me off to the bathroom and tried to wet down my hair.

"You look like Negro Chinese," she lamented, as if I had done this on purpose.

The instructor of the beauty training school had to lop off these soggy clumps to make my hair even again. "Peter Pan is very popular these days," the instructor assured my mother. I now had hair the length of a boy's, with straight-across bangs that hung at a slant two inches above my eyebrows. I liked the haircut and it made me actually look forward to my future fame.

In fact, in the beginning, I was just as excited as my mother, maybe even more so. I pictured this prodigy part of me as many different images, trying each one on for size. I was a dainty ballerina girl standing by the curtains, waiting to hear the right music that would send me floating on my tiptoes. I was like the Christ child lifted out of the straw manger, crying with holy indignity. I was Cinderella stepping from her pumpkin carriage with sparkly cartoon music filling the air.

In all of my imaginings, I was filled with a sense that I would soon become *perfect*. My mother and father would adore me. I would be beyond reproach. I would never feel the need to sulk for anything.

But sometimes the prodigy in me became impatient. "If you don't hurry up and get me out of here, I'm disappearing for good," it warned. "And then you'll always be nothing."

Every night after dinner, my mother and I would sit at the Formica kitchen table. She would present new tests, taking her examples from stories of amazing children she had read in *Ripley's Believe It or Not,* or *Good Housekeeping, Reader's Digest,* and a dozen other magazines she kept in a pile in our bathroom. My mother got these magazines from people whose houses she cleaned. And since she cleaned many houses each week, we had a great assortment. She would look through them all, searching for stories about remarkable children.

The first night she brought out a story about a three-year-old boy who knew the capitals of all the states and even most of the European countries. A teacher was quoted as saying the little boy could also pronounce the names of the foreign cities correctly.

"What's the capital of Finland?" my mother asked me, looking at the magazine story.

All I knew was the capital of California, because Sacramento was the name of the street we lived on in Chinatown. "Nairobi!" I guessed, saying the most foreign word I could think of. She checked to see if that was possibly one way to pronounce "Helsinki" before showing me the answer.

The tests got harder — multiplying numbers in my head, finding the queen of hearts in a deck of cards, trying to stand on my head without using my hands, predicting the daily temperatures in Los Angeles, New York, and London.

One night I had to look at a page from the Bible for three minutes and then report everything I could remember. "Now Jehoshaphat had riches and honor in abundance and . . . that's all I remember, Ma," I said.

And after seeing my mother's disappointed face once again, something inside of me began to die. I hated the tests, the raised hopes and failed expectations. Before going to bed that night, I looked in the mirror above the bathroom sink and when I saw only my face staring back — and that it would always be this ordinary face — I began to cry. Such a sad, ugly girl! I made high-pitched noises like a crazed animal, trying to scratch out the face in the mirror.

And then I saw what seemed to be the prodigy side of me — because I had never seen that face before. I looked at my reflection, blinking so I could see more clearly. The girl staring back at me was angry, powerful. This girl and I

were the same. I had new thoughts, willful thoughts, or rather thoughts filled
with lots of won'ts. I won't let her change me, I promised myself. I won't be
what I'm not.

So now on nights when my mother presented her tests, I performed list- 20
lessly, my head propped on one arm. I pretended to be bored. And I was. I got so
bored I started counting the bellows of the foghorns out on the bay while my
mother drilled me in other areas. The sound was comforting and reminded me
of the cow jumping over the moon. And the next day, I played a game with
myself, seeing if my mother would give up on me before eight bellows. After a
while I usually counted only one, maybe two bellows at most. At last she was
beginning to give up hope.

Two or three months had gone by without any mention of my being a prodigy
again. And then one day my mother was watching *The Ed Sullivan Show* on TV.
The TV was old and the sound kept shorting out. Every time my mother got
halfway up from the sofa to adjust the set, the sound would go back on and Ed
would be talking. As soon as she sat down, Ed would go silent again. She got up,
the TV broke into loud piano music. She sat down. Silence. Up and down, back
and forth, quiet and loud. It was like a stiff embraceless dance between her and
the TV set. Finally she stood by the set with her hand on the sound dial.

She seemed entranced by the music, a little frenzied piano piece with this
mesmerizing quality, sort of quick passages and then teasing lilting ones before
it returned to the quick playful parts.

"*Ni kan*," my mother said, calling me over with hurried hand gestures.
"Look here."

I could see why my mother was fascinated by the music. It was being
pounded out by a little Chinese girl, about nine years old, with a Peter Pan haircut. The girl had the sauciness of a Shirley Temple. She was proudly modest like
a proper Chinese child. And she also did this fancy sweep of a curtsy, so that the
fluffy skirt of her white dress cascaded slowly to the floor like the petals of a
large carnation.

In spite of these warning signs, I wasn't worried. Our family had no piano 25
and we couldn't afford to buy one, let alone reams of sheet music and piano
lessons. So I could be generous in my comments when my mother bad-mouthed
the little girl on TV.

"Play note right, but doesn't sound good! No singing sound," complained
my mother.

"What are you picking on her for?" I said carelessly. "She's pretty good.
Maybe she's not the best, but she's trying hard." I knew almost immediately I
would be sorry I said that.

"Just like you," she said. "Not the best. Because you not trying." She gave a
little huff as she let go of the sound dial and sat down on the sofa.

The little Chinese girl sat down also to play an encore of "Anitra's Dance"
by Grieg. I remember the song, because later on I had to learn how to play it.

Three days after watching *The Ed Sullivan Show*, my mother told me what my 30
schedule would be for piano lessons and piano practice. She had talked to Mr.

Chong, who lived on the first floor of our apartment building. Mr. Chong was a retired piano teacher and my mother had traded housecleaning services for weekly lessons and a piano for me to practice on every day, two hours a day, from four until six.

When my mother told me this, I felt as though I had been sent to hell. I whined and then kicked my foot a little when I couldn't stand it anymore.

"Why don't you like me the way I am? I'm *not* a genius! I can't play the piano. And even if I could, I wouldn't go on TV if you paid me a million dollars!" I cried.

My mother slapped me. "Who ask you be genius?" she shouted. "Only ask you be your best. For you sake. You think I want you be genius? Hnnh! What for! Who ask you!"

"So ungrateful," I heard her mutter in Chinese. "If she had as much talent as she has temper, she would be famous now."

Mr. Chong, whom I secretly nicknamed Old Chong, was very strange, always tapping his fingers to the silent music of an invisible orchestra. He looked ancient in my eyes. He had lost most of the hair on top of his head and he wore thick glasses and had eyes that always looked tired and sleepy. But he must have been younger than I thought, since he lived with his mother and was not yet married.

I met Old Lady Chong once and that was enough. She had this peculiar smell like a baby that had done something in its pants. And her fingers felt like a dead person's, like an old peach I once found in the back of the refrigerator; the skin just slid off the meat when I picked it up.

I soon found out why Old Chong had retired from teaching piano. He was deaf. "Like Beethoven!" he shouted to me. "We're both listening only in our head!" And he would start to conduct his frantic silent sonatas.

Our lessons went like this. He would open the book and point to different things, explaining their purpose: "Key! Treble! Bass! No sharps or flats! So this is C major! Listen now and play after me!"

And then he would play the C scale a few times, a simple chord, and then, as if inspired by an old, unreachable itch, he gradually added more notes and running trills and a pounding bass until the music was really something quite grand.

I would play after him, the simple scale, the simple chord, and then I just played some nonsense that sounded like a cat running up and down on top of garbage cans. Old Chong smiled and applauded and then said, "Very good! But now you must learn to keep time!"

So that's how I discovered that Old Chong's eyes were too slow to keep up with the wrong notes I was playing. He went through the motions in half-time. To help me keep rhythm, he stood behind me, pushing down on my right shoulder for every beat. He balanced pennies on top of my wrists so I would keep them still as I slowly played scales and arpeggios. He had me curve my hand around an apple and keep that shape when playing chords. He marched stiffly to show me how to make each finger dance up and down, staccato like an obedient little soldier.

He taught me all these things, and that was how I also learned I could be lazy and get away with mistakes, lots of mistakes. If I hit the wrong notes because I hadn't practiced enough, I never corrected myself. I just kept playing in rhythm. And Old Chong kept conducting his own private reverie.

So maybe I never really gave myself a fair chance. I did pick up the basics pretty quickly, and I might have become a good pianist at that young age. But I was so determined not to try, not to be anybody different that I learned to play only the most ear-splitting preludes, the most discordant hymns.

Over the next year, I practiced like this, dutifully in my own way. And then one day I heard my mother and her friend Lindo Jong both talking in a loud bragging tone of voice so others could hear. It was after church, and I was leaning against the brick wall wearing a dress with stiff white petticoats. Auntie Lindo's daughter, Waverly, who was about my age, was standing farther down the wall about five feet away. We had grown up together and shared all the closeness of two sisters squabbling over crayons and dolls. In other words, for the most part, we hated each other. I thought she was snotty. Waverly Jong had gained a certain amount of fame as "Chinatown's Littlest Chinese Chess Champion."

"She bring home too many trophy," lamented Auntie Lindo that Sunday.   45
"All day she play chess. All day I have no time do nothing but dust off her winnings." She threw a scolding look at Waverly, who pretended not to see her.

"You lucky you don't have this problem," said Auntie Lindo with a sigh to my mother.

And my mother squared her shoulders and bragged: "Our problem worser than yours. If we ask Jing-mei wash dish, she hear nothing but music. It's like you can't stop this natural talent."

And right then, I was determined to put a stop to her foolish pride.

A few weeks later, Old Chong and my mother conspired to have me play in a talent show which would be held in the church hall. By then, my parents had saved up enough to buy me a secondhand piano, a black Wurlitzer spinet with a scarred bench. It was the showpiece of our living room.

For the talent show, I was to play a piece called "Pleading Child" from   50
Schumann's *Scenes from Childhood*. It was a simple, moody piece that sounded more difficult than it was. I was supposed to memorize the whole thing, playing the repeat parts twice to make the piece sound longer. But I dawdled over it, playing a few bars and then cheating, looking up to see what notes followed. I never really listened to what I was playing. I daydreamed about being somewhere else, about being someone else.

The part I liked to practice best was the fancy curtsy: right foot out, touch the rose on the carpet with a pointed foot, sweep to the side, left leg bends, look up and smile.

My parents invited all the couples from the Joy Luck Club to witness my debut. Auntie Lindo and Uncle Tin were there. Waverly and her two older brothers had also come. The first two rows were filled with children both younger and older than I was. The littlest ones got to go first. They recited simple nursery rhymes, squawked out tunes on miniature violins, twirled Hula

Hoops, pranced in pink ballet tutus, and when they bowed or curtsied, the audience would sigh in unison, "Awww," and then clap enthusiastically.

When my turn came, I was very confident. I remember my childish excitement. It was as if I knew, without a doubt, that the prodigy side of me really did exist. I had no fear whatsoever, no nervousness. I remember thinking to myself, This is it! This is it! I looked out over the audience, at my mother's blank face, my father's yawn, Auntie Lindo's stiff-lipped smile, Waverly's sulky expression. I had on a white dress layered with sheets of lace, and a pink bow in my Peter Pan haircut. As I sat down I envisioned people jumping to their feet and Ed Sullivan rushing up to introduce me to everyone on TV.

And I started to play. It was so beautiful. I was so caught up in how lovely I looked that at first I didn't worry how I would sound. So it was a surprise to me when I hit the first wrong note and I realized something didn't sound quite right. And then I hit another and another followed that. A chill started at the top of my head and began to trickle down. Yet I couldn't stop playing, as though my hands were bewitched. I kept thinking my fingers would adjust themselves back, like a train switching to the right track. I played this strange jumble through two repeats, the sour notes staying with me all the way to the end.

When I stood up, I discovered my legs were shaking. Maybe I had just been   55 nervous and the audience, like Old Chong, had seen me go through the right motions and had not heard anything wrong at all. I swept my right foot out, went down on my knee, looked up and smiled. The room was quiet, except for Old Chong, who was beaming and shouting, "Bravo! Bravo! Well done!" But then I saw my mother's face, her stricken face. The audience clapped weakly, and as I walked back to my chair, with my whole face quivering as I tried not to cry, I heard a little boy whisper loudly to his mother, "That was awful," and the mother whispered back, "Well, she certainly tried."

And now I realized how many people were in the audience, the whole world it seemed. I was aware of eyes burning into my back. I felt the shame of my mother and father as they sat stiffly throughout the rest of the show.

We could have escaped during intermission. Pride and some strange sense of honor must have anchored my parents to their chairs. And so we watched it all: the eighteen-year-old boy with a fake mustache who did a magic show and juggled flaming hoops while riding a unicycle. The breasted girl with white makeup who sang from *Madama Butterfly* and got honorable mention. And the eleven-year-old boy who won first prize playing a tricky violin song that sounded like a busy bee.

After the show, the Hsus, the Jongs, and the St. Clairs from the Joy Luck Club came up to my mother and father.

"Lots of talented kids," Auntie Lindo said vaguely, smiling broadly.

"That was somethin' else," said my father, and I wondered if he was refer-   60 ring to me in a humorous way, or whether he even remembered what I had done.

Waverly looked at me and shrugged her shoulders. "You aren't a genius like me," she said matter-of-factly. And if I hadn't felt so bad, I would have pulled her braids and punched her stomach.

But my mother's expression was what devastated me: a quiet, blank look that said she had lost everything. I felt the same way, and it seemed as if everybody were now coming up, like gawkers at the scene of an accident, to see what parts were actually missing. When we got on the bus to go home, my father was humming the busy-bee tune and my mother was silent. I kept thinking she wanted to wait until we got home before shouting at me. But when my father unlocked the door to our apartment, my mother walked in and then went to the back, into the bedroom. No accusations. No blame. And in a way, I felt disappointed. I had been waiting for her to start shouting, so I could shout back and cry and blame her for all my misery.

I assumed my talent-show fiasco meant I never had to play the piano again. But two days later, after school, my mother came out of the kitchen and saw me watching TV.

"Four clock," she reminded me as if it were any other day. I was stunned, as though she were asking me to go through the talent-show torture again. I wedged myself more tightly in front of the TV.

"Turn off TV," she called from the kitchen five minutes later. 65

I didn't budge. And then I decided. I didn't have to do what my mother said anymore. I wasn't her slave. This wasn't China. I had listened to her before and look what happened. She was the stupid one.

She came out from the kitchen and stood in the arched entryway of the living room. "Four clock," she said once again, louder.

"I'm not going to play anymore," I said nonchalantly. "Why should I? I'm not a genius."

She walked over and stood in front of the TV. I saw her chest was heaving up and down in an angry way.

"No!" I said, and I now felt stronger, as if my true self had finally emerged. 70 So this was what had been inside me all along.

"No! I won't!" I screamed.

She yanked me by the arm, pulled me off the floor, snapped off the TV. She was frighteningly strong, half pulling, half carrying me toward the piano as I kicked the throw rugs under my feet. She lifted me up and onto the hard bench. I was sobbing by now, looking at her bitterly. Her chest was heaving even more and her mouth was open, smiling crazily as if she were pleased I was crying.

"You want me to be someone that I'm not!" I sobbed. "I'll never be the kind of daughter you want me to be!"

"Only two kinds of daughters," she shouted in Chinese. "Those who are obedient and those who follow their own mind! Only one kind of daughter can live in this house. Obedient daughter!"

"Then I wish I wasn't your daughter. I wish you weren't my mother," I 75 shouted. As I said these things I got scared. I felt like worms and toads and slimy things were crawling out of my chest, but it also felt good, as if this awful side of me had surfaced, at last.

"Too late change this," said my mother shrilly.

And I could sense her anger rising to its breaking point. I wanted to see it spill over. And that's when I remembered the babies she had lost in China, the ones we never talked about. "Then I wish I'd never been born!" I shouted. "I wish I were dead! Like them."

It was as if I had said the magic words, Alakazam! — and her face went blank, her mouth closed, her arms went slack, and she backed out of the room, stunned, as if she were blowing away like a small brown leaf, thin, brittle, lifeless.

It was not the only disappointment my mother felt in me. In the years that followed, I failed her so many times, each time asserting my own will, my right to fall short of expectations. I didn't get straight As. I didn't become class president. I didn't get into Stanford. I dropped out of college.

For unlike my mother, I did not believe I could be anything I wanted to be.   80
I could only be me.

And for all those years, we never talked about the disaster at the recital or my terrible accusations afterward at the piano bench. All that remained unchecked, like a betrayal that was now unspeakable. So I never found a way to ask her why she had hoped for something so large that failure was inevitable.

And even worse, I never asked her what frightened me the most: Why had she given up hope?

For after our struggle at the piano, she never mentioned my playing again. The lessons stopped, the lid to the piano was closed, shutting out the dust, my misery, and her dreams.

So she surprised me. A few years ago, she offered to give me the piano, for my thirtieth birthday. I had not played in all those years. I saw the offer as a sign of forgiveness, a tremendous burden removed.

"Are you sure?" I asked shyly. "I mean, won't you and Dad miss it?"   85

"No, this your piano," she said firmly. "Always your piano. You only one can play."

"Well, I probably can't play anymore," I said. "It's been years."

"You pick up fast," said my mother, as if she knew this was certain. "You have natural talent. You could been genius if you want to."

"No I couldn't."

"You just not trying," said my mother. And she was neither angry nor sad.   90
She said it as if to announce a fact that could never be disproved. "Take it," she said.

But I didn't at first. It was enough that she had offered it to me. And after that, every time I saw it in my parents' living room, standing in front of the bay windows, it made me feel proud, as if it were a shiny trophy I had won back.

Last week I sent a tuner over to my parents' apartment and had the piano reconditioned, for purely sentimental reasons. My mother had died a few months before and I had been getting things in order for my father, a little bit at a time.

I put the jewelry in special silk pouches. The sweaters she had knitted in yellow, pink, bright orange — all the colors I hated — I put those in moth-proof boxes. I found some old Chinese silk dresses, the kind with little slits up the sides. I rubbed the old silk against my skin, then wrapped them in tissue and decided to take them home with me.

After I had the piano tuned, I opened the lid and touched the keys. It sounded even richer than I remembered. Really, it was a very good piano. Inside the bench were the same exercise notes with handwritten scales, the same secondhand music books with their covers held together with yellow tape.

I opened up the Schumann book to the dark little piece I had played at the recital. It was on the left-hand side of the page, "Pleading Child." It looked more difficult than I remembered. I played a few bars, surprised at how easily the notes came back to me.

And for the first time, or so it seemed, I noticed the piece on the right-hand   95
side. It was called "Perfectly Contented." I tried to play this one as well. It had a lighter melody but the same flowing rhythm and turned out to be quite easy. "Pleading Child" was shorter but slower; "Perfectly Contented" was longer but faster. And after I played them both a few times, I realized they were two halves of the same song.   [1989]

≣ THINKING ABOUT THE TEXT

1. Most sons and daughters struggle to establish their own identities. Does this seem true in "Two Kinds"? Does the cultural difference between the immigrant mother and Americanized daughter intensify their struggle? Do you think you have different goals in life than your parents do?

2. Do you agree with the mother's belief that "you could be anything you wanted to be in America" (para. 1)? Does race matter? Gender? Ethnicity? Religion? Sexual orientation?

3. What do you believe each character learned from the argument at the piano bench the day after the recital?

4. How does Tan establish the differing personalities of her characters? Through details? Dialogue? Anecdotes? Do the main characters change significantly? Does she tell us or show us?

5. Do you sympathize with the mother or with the daughter? Should parents channel their children toward selected activities? Or should parents let their children choose their own paths? Can parents push their children too much? Why would they do this?

≣ MAKING COMPARISONS

1. Do you think Emily's mother in Olsen's story would want to be like the Chinese mother if given the opportunity? Which mother would you prefer to have? Why?

2. One mother seems to do too little, the other too much. Is this your reading of the two stories? Is the lesson of Olsen's and Tan's stories that
   mothers can't win no matter what they do? Or do you have a more optimistic interpretation?

3. Which daughter's life seems more difficult? How possible is it to say
   from the outside looking in?

ALICE WALKER
Everyday Use

A native of Eatonton, Georgia, Alice Walker (b. 1944) attended Spelman College and received her B.A. from Sarah Lawrence College in 1965. During the 1960s, she was active in the civil rights movement, an experience reflected in her 1976 novel Merid-ian *and in her autobiographical book,* The Way Forward Is with a Broken Heart *(2000). Walker is accomplished in many genres, and her essays, short stories, nov-els, and poems are widely read. She is perhaps best known for the novel* The Color Purple *(1976), which earned her both a Pulitzer Prize and an American Book Award and was made into a movie. Terming herself a "womanist" rather than a fem-inist in the essays of* In Search of Our Mothers' Gardens *(1983), Walker has confronted many issues concerning women, including abusive relationships, lesbian love, and the horrors of ritual genital mutilation in some African societies. Her daughter, Rebecca, has written her own memoir,* Black, White and Jewish, *dealing with her childhood and adolescence as the daughter of Alice Walker and activist law-yer Mel Leventhal, to whom Walker was married for nine years, after meeting him during voter registration drives in Mississippi in 1967. The short story "Everyday Use," from the collection* In Love and Trouble: Stories of Black Women *(1973), deals with definitions of history, heritage, and value in a changing world for African Americans in the mid-twentieth century. Her recent work includes a novel,* Now Is the Time to Open Your Heart *(2004);* We Are the Ones We've Been Waiting For *(2006), "a book of spiritual ruminations with a progressive political edge"; and* Hard Times Require Serious Dancing: New Poems *(2010). Her most recent col-lection is* The World Will Follow Joy: Turning Madness into Flowers *(2014).*

I will wait for her in the yard that Maggie and I made so clean and wavy yester-day afternoon. A yard like this is more comfortable than most people know. It is not just a yard. It is like an extended living room. When the hard clay is swept clean as a floor and the fine sand around the edges lined with tiny, irregular grooves anyone can come and sit and look up into the elm tree and wait for the breezes that never come inside the house.

Maggie will be nervous until after her sister goes: she will stand hopelessly in corners homely and ashamed of the burn scars down her arms and legs, eyeing her sister with a mixture of envy and awe. She thinks her sister has held life always in the palm of one hand, that "no" is a word the world never learned to say to her.

You've no doubt seen those TV shows where the child who has "made it" is confronted, as a surprise, by her own mother and father, tottering in weakly from backstage. (A pleasant surprise, of course: What would they do if parent and child came on the show only to curse out and insult each other?) On TV mother and child embrace and smile into each other's faces. Sometimes the mother and father weep, the child wraps them in her arms and leans across the table to tell how she would not have made it without their help. I have seen these programs.

Sometimes I dream a dream in which Dee and I are suddenly brought together on a TV program of this sort. Out of a dark and soft-seated limousine I am ushered into a bright room filled with many people. There I meet a smiling, gray, sporty man like Johnny Carson who shakes my hand and tells me what a fine girl I have. Then we are on the stage and Dee is embracing me with tears in her eyes. She pins on my dress a large orchid, even though she has told me once that she thinks orchids are tacky flowers.

In real life I am a large, big-boned woman with rough, man-working   5
hands. In the winter I wear flannel nightgowns to bed and overalls during the day. I can kill and clean a hog as mercilessly as a man. My fat keeps me hot in zero weather. I can work outside all day, breaking ice to get water for washing; I can eat pork liver cooked over the open fire minutes after it comes steaming from the hog. One winter I knocked a bull calf straight in the brain between the eyes with a sledge hammer and had the meat hung up to chill before nightfall. But of course all this does not show on television. I am the way my daughter would want me to be: a hundred pounds lighter, my skin like an uncooked barley pancake. My hair glistens in the hot bright lights. Johnny Carson has much to do to keep up with my quick and witty tongue.

But that is a mistake. I know even before I wake up. Who ever knew a Johnson with a quick tongue? Who can even imagine me looking a strange white man in the eye? It seems to me I have talked to them always with one foot raised in flight, with my head turned in whichever way is farthest from them. Dee, though. She would always look anyone in the eye. Hesitation was no part of her nature.

"How do I look, Mama?" Maggie says, showing just enough of her thin body enveloped in pink skirt and red blouse for me to know she's there, almost hidden by the door.

"Come out into the yard," I say.

Have you ever seen a lame animal, perhaps a dog run over by some careless person rich enough to own a car, sidle up to someone who is ignorant enough to be kind to him? That is the way my Maggie walks. She has been like this, chin on chest, eyes on ground, feet in shuffle, ever since the fire that burned the other house to the ground.

Dee is lighter than Maggie, with nicer hair and a fuller figure. She's a   10
woman now, though sometimes I forget. How long ago was it that the other house burned? Ten, twelve years? Sometimes I can still hear the flames and feel Maggie's arms sticking to me, her hair smoking and her dress falling off her in

little black papery flakes. Her eyes seemed stretched open, blazed open by the flames reflected in them. And Dee. I see her standing off under the sweet gum tree she used to dig gum out of; a look of concentration on her face as she watched the last dingy gray board of the house fall in toward the red-hot brick chimney. Why don't you do a dance around the ashes? I'd wanted to ask her. She had hated the house that much.

I used to think she hated Maggie, too. But that was before we raised the money, the church and me, to send her to Augusta to school. She used to read to us without pity; forcing words, lies, other folks' habits, whole lives upon us two, sitting trapped and ignorant underneath her voice. She washed us in a river of make-believe, burned us with a lot of knowledge we didn't necessarily need to know. Pressed us to her with the serious way she read, to shove us away at just the moment, like dimwits, we seemed about to understand.

Dee wanted nice things. A yellow organdy dress to wear to her graduation from high school; black pumps to match a green suit she'd made from an old suit somebody gave me. She was determined to stare down any disaster in her efforts. Her eyelids would not flicker for minutes at a time. Often I fought off the temptation to shake her. At sixteen she had a style of her own: and knew what style was.

I never had an education myself. After second grade the school was closed down. Don't ask me why: in 1927 colored asked fewer questions than they do now. Sometimes Maggie reads to me. She stumbles along good-naturedly but can't see well. She knows she is not bright. Like good looks and money, quickness passed her by. She will marry John Thomas (who has mossy teeth in an earnest face) and then I'll be free to sit here and I guess just sing church songs to myself. Although I never was a good singer. Never could carry a tune. I was always better at a man's job. I used to love to milk till I was hooked in the side in '49. Cows are soothing and slow and don't bother you, unless you try to milk them the wrong way.

I have deliberately turned my back on the house. It is three rooms, just like the one that burned, except the roof is tin; they don't make shingle roofs any more. There are no real windows, just some holes cut in the sides, like the portholes in a ship, but not round and not square, with rawhide holding the shutters up on the outside. This house is in a pasture, too, like the other one. No doubt when Dee sees it she will want to tear it down. She wrote me once that no matter where we "choose" to live, she will manage to come see us. But she will never bring her friends. Maggie and I thought about this and Maggie asked me, "Mama, when did Dee ever *have* any friends?"

She had a few. Furtive boys in pink shirts hanging about on washday after   15
school. Nervous girls who never laughed. Impressed with her they worshiped the well-turned phrase, the cute shape, the scalding humor that erupted like bubbles in lye. She read to them.

When she was courting Jimmy T she didn't have much time to pay to us, but turned all her faultfinding power on him. He *flew* to marry a cheap gal from a family of ignorant flashy people. She hardly had time to recompose herself.

*   *   *

When she comes I will meet — but there they are!

Maggie attempts to make a dash for the house, in her shuffling way, but I stay her with my hand. "Come back here," I say. And she stops and tries to dig a well in the sand with her toe.

It is hard to see them clearly through the strong sun. But even the first glimpse of leg out of the car tells me it is Dee. Her feet were always neat-looking, as if God himself had shaped them with a certain style. From the other side of the car comes a short, stocky man. Hair is all over his head a foot long and hanging from his chin like a kinky mule tail. I hear Maggie suck in her breath. "Uhnnnh," is what it sounds like. Like when you see the wriggling end of a snake just in front of your foot on the road. "Uhnnnh."

Dee next. A dress down to the ground, in this hot weather. A dress so loud   20
it hurts my eyes. There are yellows and oranges enough to throw back the light of the sun. I feel my whole face warming from the heat waves it throws out. Earrings gold, too, and hanging down to her shoulders. Bracelets dangling and making noises when she moves her arm up to shake the folds of the dress out of her armpits. The dress is loose and flows, and as she walks closer, I like it. I hear Maggie go "Uhnnnh" again. It is her sister's hair. It stands straight up like the wool on a sheep. It is black as night and around the edges are two long pig-tails that rope about like small lizards disappearing behind her ears.

"Wa-su-zo-Tean-o!" she says, coming on in that gliding way the dress makes her move. The short stocky fellow with the hair to his navel is all grin-ning and he follows up with "Asalamalakim, my mother and sister!" He moves to hug Maggie but she falls back, right up against the back of my chair. I feel her trembling there and when I look up I see the perspiration falling off her chin.

"Don't get up," says Dee. Since I am stout it takes something of a push. You can see me trying to move a second or two before I make it. She turns, showing white heels through her sandals, and goes back to the car. Out she peeks next with a Polaroid. She stoops down quickly and lines up picture after picture of me sitting there in front of the house with Maggie cowering behind me. She never takes a shot without making sure the house is included. When a cow comes nibbling around the edge of the yard she snaps it and me and Maggie *and* the house. Then she puts the Polaroid in the back seat of the car, and comes up and kisses me on the forehead.

Meanwhile Asalamalakim is going through the motions with Maggie's hand. Maggie's hand is as limp as a fish, and probably as cold, despite the sweat, and she keeps trying to pull it back. It looks like Asalamalakim wants to shake hands but wants to do it fancy. Or maybe he don't know how people shake hands. Anyhow, he soon gives up on Maggie.

"Well," I say. "Dee."

"No, Mama," she says. "Not 'Dee,' Wangero Leewanika Kemanjo!"   25

"What happened to 'Dee'?" I wanted to know.

"She's dead," Wangero said. "I couldn't bear it any longer being named after the people who oppress me."

"You know as well as me you was named after your aunt Dicie," I said. Dicie is my sister. She named Dee. We called her "Big Dee" after Dee was born.

"But who was *she* named after?" asked Wangero.

"I guess after Grandma Dee," I said.   30

"And who was she named after?" asked Wangero.

"Her mother," I said, and saw Wangero was getting tired. "That's about as far back as I can trace it," I said. Though, in fact, I probably could have carried it back beyond the Civil War through the branches.

"Well," said Asalamalakim, "there you are."

"Uhnnnh," I heard Maggie say.

"There I was not," I said, "before 'Dicie' cropped up in our family, so why   35
should I try to trace it that far back?"

He just stood there grinning, looking down on me like somebody inspecting a Model A car. Every once in a while he and Wangero sent eye signals over my head.

"How do you pronounce this name?" I asked.

"You don't have to call me by it if you don't want to," said Wangero.

"Why shouldn't I?" I asked. "If that's what you want us to call you, we'll call you."

"I know it might sound awkward at first," said Wangero.   40

"I'll get used to it," I said. "Ream it out again."

Well, soon we got the name out of the way. Asalamalakim had a name twice as long and three times as hard. After I tripped over it two or three times he told me to just call him Hakim-a-barber. I wanted to ask him was he a barber, but I didn't really think he was, so I didn't ask.

"You must belong to those beef-cattle peoples down the road," I said. They said "Asalamalakim" when they met you, too, but they didn't shake hands. Always too busy: feeding the cattle, fixing the fences, putting up salt-lick shelters, throwing down hay. When the white folks poisoned some of the herd the men stayed up all night with rifles in their hands. I walked a mile and a half just to see the sight.

Hakim-a-barber said, "I accept some of their doctrines, but farming and raising cattle is not my style." (They didn't tell me, and I didn't ask, whether Wangero [Dee] had really gone and married him.)

We sat down to eat and right away he said he didn't eat collards and pork   45
was unclean. Wangero, though, went on through the chitlins and corn bread, the greens and everything else. She talked a blue streak over the sweet potatoes. Everything delighted her. Even the fact that we still used the benches her daddy made for the table when we couldn't afford to buy chairs.

"Oh, Mama!" she cried. Then turned to Hakim-a-barber. "I never knew how lovely these benches are. You can feel the rump prints," she said, running her hands underneath her and along the bench. Then she gave a sigh and her hand closed over Grandma Dee's butter dish. "That's it!" she said. "I knew there was something I wanted to ask you if I could have." She jumped up from the table and went over in the corner where the churn stood, the milk in it clabber by now. She looked at the churn and looked at it.

"This churn top is what I need," she said. "Didn't Uncle Buddy whittle it out of a tree you all used to have?"

"Yes," I said.

"Uh huh," she said happily. "And I want the dasher, too."

"Uncle Buddy whittle that, too?" asked the barber.   50

Dee (Wangero) looked up at me.

"Aunt Dee's first husband whittled the dash," said Maggie so low you almost couldn't hear her. "His name was Henry, but they called him Stash."

"Maggie's brain is like an elephant's," Wangero said, laughing. "I can use the churn top as a centerpiece for the alcove table," she said, sliding a plate over the churn, "and I'll think of something artistic to do with the dasher."

When she finished wrapping the dasher the handle stuck out. I took it for a moment in my hands. You didn't even have to look close to see where hands pushing the dasher up and down to make butter had left a kind of sink in the wood. In fact, there were a lot of small sinks; you could see where thumbs and fingers had sunk into the wood. It was beautiful light yellow wood, from a tree that grew in the yard where Big Dee and Stash had lived.

After dinner Dee (Wangero) went to the trunk at the foot of my bed and   55
started rifling through it. Maggie hung back in the kitchen over the dishpan. Out came Wangero with two quilts. They had been pieced by Grandma Dee and then Big Dee and me had hung them on the quilt frames on the front porch and quilted them. One was in the Lone Star pattern. The other was Walk Around the Mountain. In both of them were scraps of dresses Grandma Dee had worn fifty and more years ago. Bits and pieces of Grandpa Jarrell's paisley shirts. And one teeny faded blue piece, about the size of a penny matchbox, that was from Great Grandpa Ezra's uniform that he wore in the Civil War.

"Mama," Wangero said sweet as a bird. "Can I have these old quilts?"

I heard something fall in the kitchen, and a minute later the kitchen door slammed.

"Why don't you take one or two of the others?" I asked. "These old things was just done by me and Big Dee from some tops your grandma pieced before she died."

"No," said Wangero. "I don't want those. They are stitched around the borders by machine."

"That'll make them last better," I said.   60

"That's not the point," said Wangero. "These are all pieces of dresses Grandma used to wear. She did all this stitching by hand. Imagine!" She held the quilts securely in her arms, stroking them.

"Some of the pieces, like those lavender ones, come from old clothes her mother handed down to her," I said, moving up to touch the quilts. Dee (Wangero) moved back just enough so that I couldn't reach the quilts. They already belonged to her.

"Imagine!" she breathed again, clutching them closely to her bosom.

"The truth is," I said, "I promised to give them quilts to Maggie, for when she marries John Thomas."

She gasped like a bee had stung her.   65

"Maggie can't appreciate these quilts!" she said. "She'd probably be backward enough to put them to everyday use."

"I reckon she would," I said. "God knows I been saving 'em for long enough with nobody using 'em. I hope she will!" I didn't want to bring up how I had offered Dee (Wangero) a quilt when she went away to college. Then she had told me they were old-fashioned, out of style.

"But they're *priceless*!" she was saying now, furiously; for she has a temper. "Maggie would put them on the bed and in five years they'd be in rags. Less than that!"

"She can always make some more," I said. "Maggie knows how to quilt."

Dee (Wangero) looked at me with hatred. "You just will not understand. 70
The point is these quilts, *these* quilts!"

"Well," I said, stumped. "What would *you* do with them?"

"Hang them," she said. As if that was the only thing you *could* do with quilts.

Maggie by now was standing in the door. I could almost hear the sound her feet made as they scraped over each other.

"She can have them, Mama," she said, like somebody used to never winning anything, or having anything reserved for her. "I can 'member Grandma Dee without the quilts."

I looked at her hard. She had filled her bottom lip with checkerberry snuff 75
and it gave her face a kind of dopey, hangdog look. It was Grandma Dee and Big Dee who taught her how to quilt herself. She stood there with her scarred hands hidden in the folds of her skirt. She looked at her sister with something like fear but she wasn't mad at her. This was Maggie's portion. This was the way she knew God to work.

When I looked at her like that something hit me in the top of my head and ran down to the soles of my feet. Just like when I'm in church and the spirit of God touches me and I get happy and shout. I did something I never had done before: hugged Maggie to me, then dragged her on into the room, snatched the quilts out of Miss Wangero's hands and dumped them into Maggie's lap. Maggie just sat there on my bed with her mouth open.

"Take one or two of the others," I said to Dee.

But she turned without a word and went out to Hakim-a-barber.

"You just don't understand," she said, as Maggie and I came out to the car.

"What don't I understand?" I wanted to know. 80

"Your heritage," she said. And then she turned to Maggie, kissed her, and said, "You ought to try to make something of yourself, too, Maggie. It's really a new day for us. But from the way you and Mama still live you'd never know it."

She put on some sunglasses that hid everything above the tip of her nose and her chin.

Maggie smiled; maybe at the sunglasses. But a real smile, not scared. After we watched the car dust settle I asked Maggie to bring me a dip of snuff. And then the two of us sat there just enjoying, until it was time to go in the house and go to bed. *[1973]*

≡ THINKING ABOUT THE TEXT

1. Be specific in arguing that Mama is more sympathetic to Maggie than to Dee. Is Mama hostile to Dee? What values are involved in the tension between Mama and Dee and Maggie?

2. Although many students seem to prefer Maggie to Dee, most would probably rather be Dee than Maggie. Is this true for you? Why?

3. Do you think Walker is against "getting back to one's roots"? Does she give a balanced characterization of Maggie? Of Dee? How might she portray Dee if she wanted to be more positive about her? Less positive?

4. Do you think it helps or hinders the social fabric to affirm ethnic differences? Do you think America is a melting pot? Is a quilt a better symbol to capture our diversity? Can you suggest another metaphor?

5. Do you think most mothers would side with daughters with whom they are more politically or culturally sympathetic? What might be the deciding factor? Are most mothers equally supportive of each of their children?

≡ MAKING COMPARISONS

1. How do you think Maggie would fare if she were the first child in "I Stand Here Ironing"? In "Two Kinds"?

2. Which relationship in the stories in this cluster is closest to your own? Explain.

3. Which one of the five daughters seems the kindest? The smartest? The most ambitious? The most troubled? The most likely to succeed? To find love? Do you think the mothers are responsible for how their daughters turn out?

≡ WRITING ABOUT ISSUES

1. After reading Olsen's story, as Emily's teacher, write a letter to Emily's mother persuading her that she should still come in for a conference. Acknowledge her excuses and her side of the issue, but offer objections.

2. Write a brief essay arguing that each of the mothers presented in Olsen's, Tan's, and Walker's stories is either a good or a bad model for parenting.

3. Write a personal-experience narrative about a time when your parents pushed you too hard or too little or wanted you to be someone you thought you were not. Conclude with your present view of the consequences of their action.

4. Ask six males and six females if they feel their parents tried to shape their personalities, behavior, choice of friends, and so forth. Were the parents' efforts successful? Do the sons and daughters resent it now? Conclude your brief report with some generalizations, including how relevant gender is.

■ Longing for a Father: Stories

JOHN CHEEVER, "REUNION"

DAGOBERTO GILB, "UNCLE ROCK"

Psychologically inclined critics seem to have no trouble unearthing subtle searches for father figures in literature and films of all sorts. They should have no problem finding that theme in the two stories printed here. Their interest, of course, is not idiosyncratic since the ideal father figure as a wise, strong, and caring protector is a staple of American cultural imagination. And while that might be the case for some, many fathers are decidedly less saintly. It's common for writers, perhaps drawing on their own experiences, to focus on the ways fictional fathers compare to the lofty, and perhaps unfair, iconic all-knowing, all-caring image. Growing-up narratives often deal with the tension between childhood expectations for the perfect father and the sometimes disappointing and painful reality. In these two stories, one boy is bitterly disappointed, while the other gradually comes to learn a lesson about the differences between his boyish views of masculinity and being a good partner and husband.

■ BEFORE YOU READ

What was your view of what made a good father when you were ten? How about at fifteen? What about now?

JOHN CHEEVER

Reunion

John Cheever (1912–1982), known as the "Chekhov of the suburbs," is widely regarded as one of the most significant short story writers of the twentieth century. Cheever left his private high school at age seventeen and wrote about it in a story called "Expelled" when he was eighteen. It was published in the New Republic. *After serving in the army, Cheever moved to New York City and published "The Enormous Radio," in* The New Yorker *in 1947, which was the beginning of a long and successful career. The Wapshot Chronicle was published in 1957 and Bullet Park in 1969. During this time, Cheever struggled for years with alcoholic depression. In March 1977, Cheever was featured on the cover of* Newsweek *as the author of* Falconer, *"a great American novel." Stories of John Cheever (1978) became one of the most successful story collections ever, winning numerous awards for its poised, elegant prose and insightful perspective on American life.*

The last time I saw my father was in Grand Central Station. I was going from my grandmother's in the Adirondacks to a cottage on the Cape that my mother had rented, and I wrote my father that I would be in New York between trains for an hour and a half, and asked if we could have lunch together. His secretary wrote to say that he would meet me at the information booth at noon, and at twelve o'clock sharp I saw him coming through the crowd. He was a stranger to me—my mother divorced him three years ago and I hadn't been with him since—but as soon as I saw him I felt that he was my father, my flesh and blood, my future and my doom. I knew that when I was grown I would be something like him; I would have to plan my campaigns within his limitations. He was a big, good-looking man, and I was terribly happy to see him again. He struck me on the back and shook my hand. "Hi Charlie," he said, "Hi, boy. I'd like to take you up to my club, but it's in the Sixties, and if you have to catch an early train I guess we'd better get something to eat around here." He put his arm around me, and I smelled my father the way my mother sniffs a rose. It was a rich compound of whiskey, after shave lotion, shoe polish, woolens, and the rankness of a mature male. I hoped that someone would see us together. I wished that we could be photographed. I wanted some record of our having been together.

We went out of the station and up a side street to a restaurant. It was still very early, and the place was empty. The bartender was quarreling with a delivery boy, and there was one very old waiter in a red coat down by the kitchen door. We sat down, and my father hailed the waiter in a loud voice. *"Kellner°!"* he shouted. *"Garçon°! Cameriere°! You!"* His boisterousness in the empty restaurant seemed out of place. "Could we have a little service here!" he shouted. "Chop-chop." Then he clapped his hands. This caught the waiter's attention, and he shuffled over to our table.

"Were you clapping your hands at me?" he asked.

"Calm down, calm down, *sommelier°*," my father said. "If it isn't too much to ask of you—if it wouldn't be too much above and beyond the call of duty, we would like a couple of Beefeater Gibsons°."

"I don't like to be clapped at," the waiter said.   5

"I should have brought my whistle," my father said. "I have a whistle that is audible only to the ears of old waiters. Now, take out your little pad and your little pencil and see if you can get this straight: two Beefeater Gibsons. Repeat after me: two Beefeater Gibsons."

"I think you'd better go somewhere else," the waiter said quietly.

"That," said my father, "is one of the most brilliant suggestions I have ever heard. Come on, Charlie, let's get the hell out of here."

I followed my father out of that restaurant and into another. He was not so boisterous this time. Our drinks came, and he cross-questioned me about the baseball season. He then struck the edge of his empty glass with his knife and began shouting again. *"Garçon! Kellner! Cameriere! You!* Could we trouble you to bring us two more of the same?"

"How old is the boy?" the waiter asked.   10

"That," my father said, "is none of your God-damned business."

Kellner: Barkeep; waiter (German).   ***Garçon:*** Waiter (French).   ***Cameriere:*** Waiter (Italian).   ***Sommelier:*** Wine steward.   ***Beefeater Gibson:*** A martini made with Beefeater gin.

"I'm sorry, sir," the waiter said, "but I won't serve the boy another drink."

"Well, I have some news for you," my father said. "I have some very interesting news for you. This doesn't happen to be the only restaurant in New York. They've opened another on the corner. C'mon, Charlie."

He paid the bill, and I followed him out of that restaurant into another. Here the waiters wore pink jackets like hunting coats, and there was a lot of horse tack on the walls. We sat down, and my father began to shout again.

"Master of the hounds! Tallyhoo and all that sort of thing. We'd like a little   15
something in the way of a stirrup cup. Namely, two Bibson Geefeaters."

"Two Bibson Geefeaters?" the waiter asked, smiling.

"You know damned well what I want," my father said angrily. "I want two Beefeater Gibsons, and make it snappy. Things have changed in jolly old England. So my friend the duke tells me. Let's see what England can produce in the way of a cocktail."

"This isn't England," the waiter said.

"Don't argue with me," my father said. "Just do as you're told."

"I just thought you might like to know where you are," the waiter said.   20

"If there is one thing I cannot tolerate," my father said, "it is an impudent domestic. C'mon, Charlie."

The fourth place we went to was Italian. "*Buon giorno*," my father said. "*Per favore, possiamo avere° due cocktail americani°, forti, forti. Molto gin, poco vermut.*"

"I don't understand Italian," the waiter said.

"Oh, come off it," my father said. "You understand Italian, and you know damned well you do. *Vogliamo due cocktail americani. Subito.*"

The waiter left us and spoke with the captain, who came over to our table   25
and said, "I'm sorry, sir, but this table is reserved."

"All right," my father said. "Get us another table."

"All the tables are reserved," the captain said.

"I get it," my father said. "You don't desire our patronage. Is that it? Well, the hell with you. *Vada all'inferno°*. Let's go, Charlie."

"I have to get my train," I said.

"I'm sorry, sonny," my father said. "I'm terribly sorry." He put his arm   30
around me and pressed me against him. "I'll walk you back to the station. If there had only been time to go up to my club."

"That's all right, Daddy," I said.

"I'll get you a paper," he said. "I'll get you a paper to read on the train."

Then he went up to a newsstand and said, "Kind sir, will you be good enough to favor me with one of your God-damned, no-good, ten-cent afternoon papers?" The clerk turned away from him and stared at a magazine cover. "Is it asking too much, kind sir," my father said, "is it asking too much for you to sell me one of your disgusting specimens of yellow journalism°?"

Per favore possiamo avere: Please can we have . . . (Italian). ***Due cocktail americani***: Two American cocktails (Italian). ***Vada all' inferno***: Go to hell (Italian). **Yellow journalism**: A style of newspaper reporting that emphasizes sensationalism over facts.

"I have to go, Daddy," I said. "It's late."

"Now, just wait a second, sonny," he said. "Just wait a second. I want to get   35
a rise out of this chap."

"Goodbye, Daddy," I said, and I went down the stairs and got my train, and
that was the last time I saw my father.   [1978]

≡ THINKING ABOUT THE TEXT

1. Filling in the gaps in this story, why do you think Charlie's mother divorced his father? Why hasn't Charlie seen his father in three years? Why hasn't he seen him since?

2. How would you characterize the father's behavior? Do you think his son's presence might have affected him?

3. How does the son's comment that he was "terribly happy to see him" (para. 2) and his calling his father "Daddy" (paras. 35–40) affect your attitude toward the father's behavior? Why does he hope that someone will "see us together" (para. 2)?

4. Explain what you think the son means when he says, "I would have to plan my campaigns within his limitations" (para. 2). Seen as an initiation story, what is it the boy learns from his reunion?

5. Why is the last thing his father says to him significant? The narrator, of course, is remembering an incident from his past. What do you think his attitude is toward this incident? What specific details suggest his attitude?

DAGOBERTO GILB
Uncle Rock

Dagoberto Gilb (b. 1950) was born in Los Angeles and raised by a single mother, a Mexican woman who came to the United States illegally. He graduated from the University of Santa Barbara, where he also received a master's degree in religious studies in 1976. His first full book of stories, The Magic of Blood, *was published in 1993 by the University of New Mexico Press. Recent books include a collection of stories,* Before the End, After the Beginning *(2011), and a novel,* The Flowers *(2008). He has won numerous awards, including a Guggenheim and the PEN/Hemingway and PEN/Faulkner Awards. The following story first appeared in* The New Yorker *and was selected for the PEN/O. Henry Prize Stories 2012. He lives in Austin, Texas.*

In the morning, at his favorite restaurant, Erick got to order his favorite American food, sausage and eggs and hash-brown *papitas°* fried crunchy on top. He'd

---

papitas: In Spanish, "little potato": probably French fries.

be sitting there, eating with his mother, not bothering anybody, and life was good, when a man started changing it all. Most of the time it was just a man staring too much—but then one would come over. Friendly, he'd put his thick hands on the table as if he were touching water, and squat low, so that he was at sitting level, as though he were being so polite, and he'd smile, with coffee-and-tobacco-stained teeth. He might wear a bolo tie and speak in a drawl. Or he might have a tan uniform on, a company logo on the back, an oval name patch on the front. Or he'd be in a nothing-special work shirt, white or striped, with a couple of pens clipped onto the left side pocket, tucked into a pair of jeans or chinos that were morning-clean still, with a pair of scuffed work boots that laced up higher than regular shoes. He'd say something about her earrings, or her bracelet, or her hair, or her eyes, and if she had on her white uniform how nice it looked on her. Or he'd come right out with it and tell her how pretty she was, how he couldn't keep himself from walking up, speaking to her directly, and could they talk again? Then he'd wink at Erick. Such a fine-looking boy! How old is he, eight or nine? Erick wasn't even small for an eleven-year-old. He tightened his jaw then, slanted his eyes up from his plate at his mom and not the man, definitely not this man he did not care for. Erick drove a fork into a goopy American egg yolk and bled it into his American potatoes. She wouldn't offer the man Erick's correct age, either, saying only that he was growing too fast.

She almost always gave the man her number if he was wearing a suit. Not a sports coat but a buttoned suit with a starched white shirt and a pinned tie meant something to her. Once in a while, Erick saw one of these men again at the front door of the apartment in Silverlake. The man winked at Erick as if they were buddies. Grabbed his shoulder or arm, squeezed the muscle against the bone. What did Erick want to be when he grew up? A cop, a jet-airplane mechanic, a travel agent, a court reporter? A dog groomer? Erick stood there, because his mom said that he shouldn't be impolite. His mom's date said he wanted to take Erick along with them sometime. The three of them. What kind of places did Erick think were fun? Erick said nothing. He never said anything when the men were around, and not because of his English, even if that was the excuse his mother gave for his silence. He didn't talk to any of the men and he didn't talk much to his mom, either. Finally they took off, and Erick's night was his alone. He raced to the grocery store and bought half a gallon of choco-late ice cream. When he got back, he turned on the TV, scooted up real close, as close as he could, and ate his dinner with a soup spoon. He was away from all the men. Even though a man had given the TV to them. He was a salesman in an appliance store who'd bragged that a rich customer had given it to him and so why shouldn't he give it to Erick's mom, who couldn't afford such a good TV otherwise?

When his mom was working as a restaurant hostess, and was going to marry the owner, Erick ate hot-fudge sundaes and drank chocolate shakes. When she worked at a trucking company, the owner of all the trucks told her he was getting a divorce. Erick climbed into the rigs, with their rooms full of dials and levers in the sky. Then she started working in an engineer's office. There was no food or fun there, but even he could see the money. He was not supposed to touch anything, but what was there to touch—the tubes full of paper? He and his mom were invited to the engineer's house, where he had two horses and a stable, a swimming pool, and two convertible sports cars. The engineer's family was there: his grown children, his gray-haired parents. They all sat down for dinner in a dining room that seemed bigger than Erick's apartment, with three candelabras on the table, and a tablecloth and cloth napkins. Erick's mom took him aside to tell him to be well mannered at the table and polite to everyone. Erick hadn't said anything. He never spoke anyway, so how could he have said anything wrong? She leaned into his ear and said that she wanted them to know that he spoke English. That whole dinner he was silent, chewing quietly, taking the smallest bites, because he didn't want them to think he liked their food.

When she got upset about days like that, she told Erick that she wished they could just go back home. She was tired of worrying. "Back," for Erick, meant mostly the stories he'd heard from her, which never sounded so good to him: She'd had to share a room with her brothers and sisters. They didn't have toilets. They didn't have electricity. Sometimes they didn't have enough food. He saw this Mexico as if it were the backdrop of a movie on afternoon TV, where children walked around barefoot in the dirt or on broken sidewalks and small men wore wide-brimmed straw hats and baggy white shirts and pants. The women went to church all the time and prayed to alcoved saints and, heads down, fearful, counted rosary beads. There were rocks everywhere, and scorpions and tarantulas and rattlesnakes, and vultures and no trees and not much water, and skinny dogs and donkeys, and ugly bad guys with guns and bullet vests who rode laughing into town to drink and shoot off their pistols and rifles, as if it were the Fourth of July, driving their horses all over town like dirt bikes on desert dunes. When they spoke English, they had stupid accents—his mom didn't have an accent like theirs. It didn't make sense to him that Mexico would only be like that, but what if it was close? He lived on paved, lighted city streets, and a bicycle ride away were the Asian drugstore and the Armenian grocery store and the corner where black Cubans drank coffee and talked Dodgers baseball.

When he was in bed, where he sometimes prayed, he thanked God for his   5
mom, who he loved, and he apologized to Him for not talking to her, or to anyone, really, except his friend Albert, and he apologized for her never going to church and for his never taking Holy Communion, as Albert did—though only to God would he admit that he wanted to because Albert did. He prayed for good to come, for his mom and for him, since God was like magic, and happiness might come the way of early morning, in the trees and bushes full of sparrows next to his open window, louder and louder when he listened hard, eyes closed.

The engineer wouldn't have mattered if Erick hadn't told Albert that he was his dad. Albert had just moved into the apartment next door and lived with both his mother and his father, and since Albert's mother already didn't like Erick's mom, Erick told him that his new dad was an engineer. Erick actually believed it, too, and thought that he might even get his own horse. When that didn't happen, and his mom was lying on her bed in the middle of the day, blowing her nose, because she didn't have the job anymore, that was when Roque came around again. Roque was nobody — or he was anybody. He wasn't special, he wasn't not. He tried to speak English to Erick, thinking that was the reason Erick didn't say anything when he was there. And Erick had to tell Albert that Roque was his uncle, because the engineer was supposed to be his new dad any minute. Uncle Rock, Erick said. His mom's brother, he told Albert. Roque worked at night and was around during the day, and one day he offered Erick and Albert a ride. When his mom got in the car, she scooted all the way over to Roque on the bench seat. Who was supposed to be her brother, Erick's Uncle Rock. Albert didn't say anything, but he saw what had happened, and that was it for Erick. Albert had parents, grandparents, and a brother and a sister, and he'd hang out only when one of his cousins wasn't coming by. Erick didn't need a friend like him.

What if she married Roque, his mom asked him one day soon afterward. She told Erick that they would move away from the apartment in Silverlake to a better neighborhood. He did want to move, but he wished that it weren't because of Uncle Rock. It wasn't just because Roque didn't have a swimming pool or horses or a big ranch house. There wasn't much to criticize except that he was always too willing and nice, too considerate, too generous. He wore nothing flashy or expensive, just ordinary clothes that were clean and ironed, and shoes he kept shined. He combed and parted his hair neatly. He didn't have a buzzcut like the men who didn't like kids. He moved slow, he talked slow, as quiet as night. He only ever said yes to Erick's mom. How could she not like him for that? He loved her so much — anybody could see his pride when he was with her. He signed checks and gave her cash. He knocked on their door carrying cans and fruit and meat. He was there when she asked, gone when she asked, back whenever, grateful. He took her out to restaurants on Sunset, to the movies in Hollywood, or on drives to the beach in rich Santa Monica.

Roque knew that Erick loved baseball. Did Roque like baseball? It was doubtful that he cared even a little bit — he didn't listen to games on the radio or TV, and he never looked at a newspaper. He loved boxing, though. He knew the names of all the Mexican fighters as if they lived here, as if they were Dodgers players, like Steve Sax or Steve Yeager, Dusty Baker, Kenny Landreaux or Mike Marshall, Pedro Guerrero. Roque did know about Fernando Valenzuela, as everyone did, even his mom, which is why she agreed to let Roque take them to a game. What Mexican didn't love Fernando? Dodger Stadium was close to their apartment. He'd been there once with Albert and his family — well, outside it, on a nearby hill, to see the fireworks for Fourth of July. His mom decided that all three of them would go on a Saturday afternoon, since Saturday night, Erick thought, she might want to go somewhere else, even with somebody else.

Roque, of course, didn't know who the Phillies were. He knew nothing about the strikeouts by Steve Carlton or the home runs by Mike Schmidt. He'd never heard of Pete Rose. It wasn't that Erick knew very much, either, but there was nothing that Roque could talk to him about, if they were to talk.

If Erick showed his excitement when they drove up to Dodger Stadium and   10
parked, his mom and Roque didn't really notice it. They sat in the bleachers,
and for him the green of the field was a magic light; the stadium decks surrounding them seemed as far away as Rome. His body was somewhere it had
never been before. The fifth inning? That's how late they were. Or were they
right on time, because they weren't even sure they were sitting in the right
seats yet when he heard the crack of the ball, saw the crowd around them rising as it came at them. Erick saw the ball. He had to stand and move and stretch
his arms and want that ball until it hit his bare hands and stayed there. Everybody saw him catch it with no bobble. He felt all the eyes and voices around him
as if they were every set of eyes and every voice in the stadium. His mom was
saying something, and Roque, too, and then, finally, it was just him and that
ball and his stinging hands. He wasn't even sure if it had been hit by Pete
Guerrero. He thought for sure it had been, but he didn't ask. He didn't watch
the game then—he couldn't. He didn't care who won. He stared at his official
National League ball, reimagining what had happened. He ate a hot dog and
drank a soda and he sucked the salted peanuts and the wooden spoon from his
chocolate-malt ice cream. He rubbed the bumpy seams of his home-run ball.

Game over, they were the last to leave. People were hanging around, not
going straight to their cars. Roque didn't want to leave. He didn't want to end it
so quickly, Erick thought, while he still had her with him. Then one of the Phillies came out of the stadium door and people swarmed—boys mostly, but also
men and some women and girls—and they got autographs before the player
climbed onto the team's bus. Joe Morgan, they said. Then Garry Maddox appeared. Erick clutched the ball but he didn't have a pen. He just watched, his
back to the gray bus the Phillies were getting into.

Then a window slid open. *Hey, big man,* a voice said. Erick really wasn't
sure. *Gimme the ball, la pelota,* the face in the bus said. *I'll have it signed, comprendes? Échalo°, just toss it to me.* Erick obeyed. He tossed it up to the hand that
was reaching out. The window closed. The ball was gone a while, so long that
his mom came up to him, worried that he'd lost it. The window slid open again
and the voice spoke to her. *We got the ball, Mom. It's not lost, just a few more.*
When the window opened once more, this time the ball was there. *Catch.* There
were all kinds of signatures on it, though none that he could really recognize
except for Joe Morgan and Pete Rose.

Then the voice offered more, and the hand threw something at him. *For
your mom, O.K.? Comprendes?* Erick stared at the asphalt lot where the object
lay, as if he'd never seen a folded-up piece of paper before. *Para tu mamá, bueno?°*
He picked it up, and he started to walk over to his mom and Roque, who were
so busy talking they hadn't noticed anything. Then he stopped. He opened the
note himself. No one had said he couldn't read it. It said, *I'd like to get to know
you. You are muy linda. Very beautiful and sexy. I don't speak Spanish very good, may
be you speak better English, pero No Importa. Would you come by tonite and let me
buy you a drink?* There was a phone number and a hotel-room number. A name,
too. A name that came at him the way that the home run had.

Comprendes Echalo?: Do you understand?   ***para tu mama, bueno?:*** For your Mom, OK?

Erick couldn't hear. He could see only his mom ahead of him. She was talking to Roque, Roque was talking to her. Roque was the proudest man, full of joy because he was with her. It wasn't his fault he wasn't an engineer. Now Erick could hear again. Like sparrows hunting seed, boys gathered round the bus, calling out, while the voice in the bus was yelling at him, *Hey, big guy! Give it to her!* Erick had the ball in one hand and the note in the other. By the time he reached his mom and Roque, the note was already somewhere on the asphalt parking lot. *Look*, he said in a full voice. *They all signed the ball.*   [2010]

≡ THINKING ABOUT THE TEXT

1. What are some reasons that Erick doesn't speak throughout the story? Why does he finally speak in the last line of the story?

2. This could be thought of as a coming-of-age narrative for Erick. What does he come to understand about adult life, especially men and women? How does his view of men change?

3. Why does Erick say he doesn't need a friend like Albert? What does Erick fear? What does he hope for?

4. What are Roque's strengths and weaknesses according to Erick? Does he change his mind about these? What is the significance of Uncle Rock becoming Roque?

5. Why does Erick throw the note from the ballplayer away? How can this be seen as a positive move for Erick?

≡ MAKING COMPARISONS

1. How are ideas about masculinity dealt with in these two stories?

2. What do both boys learn about men in these stories? Why, for example, are they disappointed in male behavior?

3. What might Erick think of Charlie's father? What might Charlie's father think of Roque?

≡ WRITING ABOUT ISSUES

1. Argue that Erick does or does not learn something important about adult relationships.

2. Argue that both stories are about a search for an appropriate father figure.

3. Argue that unpacking the titles of these two stories is a way to understand significant ideas about masculine role models.

4. Write an argument, based on your personal experience and on your familiarity with novels, films, and television shows, about appropriate role models for fatherhood provided by American culture.

≡ Siblings in Conflict: Stories

TOBIAS WOLFF, "The Rich Brother"

JAMES BALDWIN, "Sonny's Blues"

Although the expression "blood is thicker than water" suggests that brothers and sisters should support each other, the reality is often more complex. Children growing up together share intense emotional ties, but affection and loyalty sometimes conflict with hostility and jealousy. Children often feel they are competing for their parents' attention and love, a rivalry often played out over a lifetime and intensified as siblings choose different lifestyles. Well into adulthood, brothers and sisters often find their relationships with each other conflicted by unresolved issues of mutual responsibility and disparities in values as well as individual issues of financial success, self-esteem, and guilt. The siblings in the following two stories, separated by age and disparate occupations, engage in a psychologically complex dance that ebbs and flows over their lives. They struggle to understand each other and ultimately themselves, for, as with all of us, healthy relationships with siblings start with a healthy relationship with oneself.

≡ BEFORE YOU READ

How would you describe your relationship with your siblings? Did rivalry ever play a part? Does it now? Do you consider your siblings' futures as similar to yours? Is it important for brothers and sisters to look after each other? Or might that create more problems than it solves?

TOBIAS WOLFF

The Rich Brother

Tobias Wolff (b. 1945) is known chiefly for his short stories. The following piece comes from his second collection, Back in the World *(1985). He has produced two other volumes of stories,* In the Garden of the North American Martyrs *(1981) and* The Night in Question *(1996), and a short novel,* The Barracks Thief *(1984). His latest novel is* Old School *(2004). Wolff is also the author of two memoirs. In the first,* This Boy's Life *(1989), he recalls his parents' divorce and subsequent family dramas. These include wanderings with his mother through the West and Northwest; arguments with his abusive stepfather; occasional contact with his real father, who was a habitual liar later imprisoned for fraud; and years of separation from his brother, Geoffrey, who eventually became a writer himself. This Boy's Life won the Los Angeles Times Book Award for biography and later became a movie starring Robert De Niro as the stepfather and Leonardo DiCaprio as the young Toby. Wolff's second memoir,* In Pharaoh's Army: Memories of the Lost War *(1994), deals mostly with his military service in Vietnam. His most recent collection is* Our Story Begins: New and Selected Stories *(2008). Today, Wolff teaches creative writing at Stanford University.*

There were two brothers, Pete and Donald.

Pete, the older brother, was in real estate. He and his wife had a Century 21 franchise in Santa Cruz. Pete worked hard and made a lot of money, but not any more than he thought he deserved. He had two daughters, a sailboat, a house from which he could see a thin slice of the ocean, and friends doing well enough in their own lives not to wish bad luck on him. Donald, the younger brother, was still single. He lived alone, painted houses when he found the work, and got deeper in debt to Pete when he didn't.

No one would have taken them for brothers. Where Pete was stout and hearty and at home in the world, Donald was bony, grave, and obsessed with the fate of his soul. Over the years Donald had worn the images of two different Perfect Masters around his neck. Out of devotion to the second of these he entered an ashram in Berkeley, where he nearly died of undiagnosed hepatitis. By the time Pete finished paying the medical bills Donald had become a Christian. He drifted from church to church, then joined a pentecostal community that met somewhere in the Mission District to sing in tongues and swap prophecies.

Pete couldn't make sense of it. Their parents were both dead, but while they were alive neither of them had found it necessary to believe in anything. They managed to be decent people without making fools of themselves, and Pete had the same ambition. He thought that the whole thing was an excuse for Donald to take himself seriously.

The trouble was that Donald couldn't content himself with worrying about his own soul. He had to worry about everyone else's, and especially Pete's. He handed down his judgments in ways that he seemed to consider subtle: through significant silence, innuendo, looks of mild despair that said, *Brother, what have you come to?* What Pete had come to, as far as he could tell, was prosperity. That was the real issue between them. Pete prospered and Donald did not prosper. 5

At the age of forty Pete took up sky diving. He made his first jump with two friends who'd started only a few months earlier and were already doing stunts. He never would have used the word *mystical*, but that was how Pete felt about the experience. Later he made the mistake of trying to describe it to Donald, who kept asking how much it cost and then acted appalled when Pete told him.

"At least I'm trying something new," Pete said. "At least I'm breaking the pattern."

Not long after that conversation Donald also broke the pattern, by going to live on a farm outside Paso Robles. The farm was owned by several members of Donald's community, who had bought it and moved there with the idea of forming a family of faith. That was how Donald explained it in the first letter he sent. Every week Pete heard how happy Donald was, how "in the Lord." He told Pete that he was praying for him, he and the rest of Pete's brothers and sisters on the farm.

"I only have one brother," Pete wanted to answer, "and that's enough." But he kept this thought to himself.

In November the letters stopped. Pete didn't worry about this at first, but   10
when he called Donald at Thanksgiving Donald was grim. He tried to sound upbeat but he didn't try hard enough to make it convincing. "Now listen," Pete said, "you don't have to stay in that place if you don't want to."

"I'll be all right," Donald answered.

"That's not the point. Being all right is not the point. If you don't like what's going on up there, then get out."

"I'm all right," Donald said again, more firmly. "I'm doing fine."

But he called Pete a week later and said that he was quitting the farm. When Pete asked him where he intended to go, Donald admitted that he had no plan. His car had been repossessed just before he left the city, and he was flat broke.

"I guess you'll have to stay with us," Pete said.   15

Donald put up a show of resistance. Then he gave in. "Just until I get my feet on the ground," he said.

"Right," Pete said. "Check out your options." He told Donald he'd send him money for a bus ticket, but as they were about to hang up Pete changed his mind. He knew that Donald would try hitchhiking to save the fare. Pete didn't want him out on the road all alone where some head case would pick him up, where anything could happen to him.

"Better yet," he said, "I'll come and get you."

"You don't have to do that. I didn't expect you to do that," Donald said. He added, "It's a pretty long drive."

"Just tell me how to get there."   20

But Donald wouldn't give him directions. He said that the farm was too depressing, that Pete wouldn't like it. Instead, he insisted on meeting Pete at a service station called Jonathan's Mechanical Emporium.

"You must be kidding," Pete said.

"It's close to the highway," Donald said. "I didn't name it."

"That's one for the collection," Pete said.

The day before he left to bring Donald home, Pete received a letter from a man   25
who described himself as "head of household" at the farm where Donald had been living. From this letter Pete learned that Donald had not quit the farm, but had been asked to leave. The letter was written on the back of a mimeographed survey form asking people to record their response to a ceremony of some kind. The last question said:

What did you feel during the liturgy?
a) Being
b) Becoming
c) Being and Becoming

d) *None of the Above*
e) *All of the Above*

Pete tried to forget the letter. But of course he couldn't. Each time he thought of it he felt crowded and breathless, a feeling that came over him again when he drove into the service station and saw Donald sitting against a wall with his head on his knees. It was late afternoon. A paper cup tumbled slowly past Donald's feet, pushed by the damp wind.

Pete honked and Donald raised his head. He smiled at Pete, then stood and stretched. His arms were long and thin and white. He wore a red bandanna across his forehead, a T-shirt with a couple of words on the front. Pete couldn't read them because the letters were inverted.

"Grow up," Pete yelled. "Get a Mercedes."

Donald came up to the window. He bent down and said, "Thanks for coming. You must be totally whipped."

"I'll make it." Pete pointed at Donald's T-shirt. "What's that supposed to say?"   30

Donald looked down at his shirt front. "Try God. I guess I put it on backwards. Pete, could I borrow a couple of dollars? I owe these people for coffee and sandwiches."

Pete took five twenties from his wallet and held them out the window.

Donald stepped back as if horrified. "I don't need that much."

"I can't keep track of all these nickels and dimes," Pete said. "Just pay me back when your ship comes in." He waved the bills impatiently. "Go on — take it."

"Only for now." Donald took the money and went into the service station   35
office. He came out carrying two orange sodas, one of which he gave to Pete as he got into the car. "My treat," he said.

"No bags?"

"Wow, thanks for reminding me." Donald balanced his drink on the dashboard, but the slight rocking of the car as he got out tipped it onto the passenger's seat, where half its contents foamed over before Pete could snatch it up again. Donald looked on while Pete held the bottle out the window, soda running down his fingers.

"Wipe it up," Pete told him. "Quick!"

"With what?"

Pete stared at Donald. "That shirt. Use the shirt."   40

Donald pulled a long face but did as he was told, his pale skin puckering against the wind.

"Great, just great," Pete said. "We haven't even left the gas station yet."

Afterwards, on the highway, Donald said, "This is a new car, isn't it?"

"Yes. This is a new car."

"Is that why you're so upset about the seat?"   45

"Forget it, okay? Let's just forget about it."

"I said I was sorry."

Pete said, "I just wish you'd be more careful. These seats are made of leather. That stain won't come out, not to mention the smell. I don't see why I can't have leather seats that smell like leather instead of orange pop."

"What was wrong with the other car?"

Pete glanced over at Donald. Donald had raised the hood of the blue sweat-   50
shirt he'd put on. The peaked hood above his gaunt, watchful face gave him the look of an inquisitor.

"There wasn't anything wrong with it," Pete said. "I just happened to like this one better."

Donald nodded.

There was a long silence between them as Pete drove on and the day darkened toward evening. On either side of the road lay stubble-covered fields. A line of low hills ran along the horizon, topped here and there with trees black against the grey sky. In the approaching line of cars a driver turned on his headlights. Pete did the same.

"So what happened?" he asked. "Farm life not your bag?"

Donald took some time to answer, and at last he said, simply, "It was my   55
fault."

"What was your fault?"

"The whole thing. Don't play dumb, Pete. I know they wrote to you." Donald looked at Pete, then stared out the windshield again.

"I'm not playing dumb."

Donald shrugged.

"All I really know is they asked you to leave," Pete went on. "I don't know   60
any of the particulars."

"I blew it," Donald said. "Believe me, you don't want to hear the gory details."

"Sure I do," Pete said. He added, "Everybody likes the gory details."

"You mean everybody likes to hear how someone messed up."

"Right," Pete said. "That's the way it is here on Spaceship Earth."

Donald bent one knee onto the front seat and leaned against the door so   65
that he was facing Pete instead of the windshield. Pete was aware of Donald's scrutiny. He waited. Night was coming on in a rush now, filling the hollows of the land. Donald's long cheeks and deep-set eyes were dark with shadow. His brow was white. "Do you ever dream about me?" Donald asked.

"Do I ever dream about you? What kind of a question is that? Of course I don't dream about you," Pete said, untruthfully.

"What do you dream about?"

"Sex and money. Mostly money. A nightmare is when I dream I don't have any."

"You're just making that up," Donald said.

Pete smiled.   70

"Sometimes I wake up at night," Donald went on, "and I can tell you're dreaming about me."

"We were talking about the farm," Pete said. "Let's finish that conversation and then we can talk about our various out-of-body experiences and the interesting things we did during previous incarnations."

For a moment Donald looked like a grinning skull; then he turned serious again. "There's not much to tell," he said. "I just didn't do anything right."

"That's a little vague," Pete said.

"Well, like the groceries. Whenever it was my turn to get the groceries I'd   75
blow it somehow. I'd bring the groceries home and half of them would be missing, or I'd have all the wrong things, the wrong kind of flour or the wrong kind of chocolate or whatever. One time I gave them away. It's not funny, Pete."

Pete said, "Who did you give the groceries to?"

"Just some people I picked up on the way home. Some fieldworkers. They had about eight kids with them and they didn't even speak English — just nodded their heads. Still, I shouldn't have given away the groceries. Not all of them, anyway. I really learned my lesson about that. You have to be practical. You have to be fair to yourself." Donald leaned forward, and Pete could sense his excitement. "There's nothing actually wrong with being in business," he said. "As long as you're fair to other people you can still be fair to yourself. I'm thinking of going into business, Pete."

"We'll talk about it," Pete said. "So, that's the story? There isn't any more to it than that?"

"What did they tell you?" Donald asked.

"Nothing."   80

"They must have told you something."

Pete shook his head.

"They didn't tell you about the fire?" When Pete shook his head again Donald regarded him for a time, then folded his arms across his chest and slumped back into the corner. "Everybody had to take turns cooking dinner. I usually did tuna casserole or spaghetti with garlic bread. But this one night I thought I'd do something different, something really interesting." Donald looked sharply at Pete. "It's all a big laugh to you, isn't it?"

"I'm sorry," Pete said.

"You don't know when to quit. You just keep hitting away."   85

"Tell me about the fire, Donald."

Donald kept watching him. "You have this compulsion to make me look foolish."

"Come off it, Donald. Don't make a big thing out of this."

"I know why you do it. It's because you don't have any purpose in life. You're afraid to relate to people who do, so you make fun of them."

"Relate," Pete said.   90

"You're basically a very frightened individual," Donald said. "Very threatened. You've always been like that. Do you remember when you used to try to kill me?"

"I don't have any compulsion to make you look foolish, Donald — you do it yourself. You're doing it right now."

"You can't tell me you don't remember," Donald said. "It was after my operation. You remember that?"

"Sort of." Pete shrugged. "Not really."

"Oh yes," Donald said. "Do you want to see the scar?"   95

"I remember you had an operation. I don't remember the specifics, that's all. And I sure as hell don't remember trying to kill you."

"Oh yes," Donald repeated, maddeningly. "You bet your life you did. All the time. The thing was, I couldn't have anything happen to me where they sewed me up because then my intestines would come apart again and poison me. That was a big issue, Pete. Mom was always in a state about me climbing trees and so on. And you used to hit me there every chance you got."

"Mom was in a state every time you burped," Pete said. "I don't know. Maybe I bumped into you accidentally once or twice. I never did it deliberately."

"Every chance you got," Donald said. "Like when the folks went out at night and left you to baby-sit. I'd hear them say good night, and then I'd hear the car start up, and when they were gone I'd lie there and listen. After a while I would hear you coming down the hall, and I would close my eyes and pretend to be asleep. There were nights when you would stand outside the door, just stand there, and then go away again. But most nights you'd open the door and I would hear you in the room with me, breathing. You'd come over and sit next to me on the bed — you remember, Pete, you have to — you'd sit next to me on the bed and pull the sheets back. If I was on my stomach you'd roll me over. Then you would lift up my pajama shirt and start hitting me on my stitches. You'd hit me as hard as you could, over and over. I was afraid that you'd get mad if you knew I was awake. Is that strange or what? I was afraid that you'd get mad if you found out that I knew you were trying to kill me." Donald laughed. "Come on, you can't tell me you don't remember that."

"It might have happened once or twice. Kids do those things. I can't get all excited about something I maybe did twenty-five years ago."   100

"No maybe about it. You did it."

Pete said, "You're wearing me out with this stuff. We've got a long drive ahead of us and if you don't back off pretty soon we aren't going to make it. You aren't, anyway."

Donald turned away.

"I'm doing my best," Pete said. The self-pity in his own voice made the words sound like a lie. But they weren't a lie! He was doing his best.

The car topped a rise. In the distance Pete saw a cluster of lights that   105
blinked out when he started downhill. There was no moon. The sky was low and black.

"Come to think of it," Pete said, "I did have a dream about you the other night." Then he added, impatiently, as if Donald were badgering him, "A couple of other nights, too. I'm getting hungry," he said.

"The same dream?"

"Different dreams. I only remember one of them. There was something wrong with me, and you were helping out. Taking care of me. Just the two of us. I don't know where everyone else was supposed to be."

Pete left it at that. He didn't tell Donald that in this dream he was blind.

"I wonder if that was when I woke up," Donald said. He added, "I'm sorry   110
I got into that thing about my scar. I keep trying to forget it but I guess I never

will. Not really. It was pretty strange, having someone around all the time who wanted to get rid of me."

"Kid stuff," Pete said. "Ancient history."

They ate dinner at a Denny's on the other side of King City. As Pete was paying the check he heard a man behind him say, "Excuse me, but I wonder if I might ask which way you're going?" and Donald answer, "Santa Cruz."

"Perfect," the man said.

Pete could see him in the fish-eye mirror above the cash register: a red blazer with some kind of crest on the pocket, little black moustache, glossy black hair combed down on his forehead like a Roman emperor's. A rug, Pete thought. Definitely a rug.

Pete got his change and turned. "Why is that perfect?" he asked.   115

The man looked at Pete. He had a soft, ruddy face that was doing its best to express pleasant surprise, as if this new wrinkle were all he could have wished for, but the eyes behind the aviator glasses showed signs of regret. His lips were moist and shiny. "I take it you're together," he said.

"You got it," Pete told him.

"All the better, then," the man went on. "It so happens I'm going to Santa Cruz myself. Had a spot of car trouble down the road. The old Caddy let me down."

"What kind of trouble?" Pete asked.

"Engine trouble," the man said. "I'm afraid it's a bit urgent. My daughter is   120 sick. Urgently sick. I've got a telegram here." He patted the breast pocket of his blazer.

Before Pete could say anything Donald got into the act again. "No problem," Donald said. "We've got tons of room."

"Not that much room," Pete said.

Donald nodded. "I'll put my things in the trunk."

"The trunk's full," Pete told him.

"It so happens I'm traveling light," the man said. "This leg of the trip any-   125 way. In fact, I don't have any luggage at this particular time."

Pete said, "Left it in the old Caddy, did you?"

"Exactly," the man said.

"No problem," Donald repeated. He walked outside and the man went with him. Together they strolled across the parking lot, Pete following at a distance. When they reached Pete's car Donald raised his face to the sky, and the man did the same. They stood there looking up. "Dark night," Donald said.

"Stygian,°" the man said.

Pete still had it in his mind to brush him off, but he didn't do that. Instead   130 he unlocked the door for him. He wanted to see what would happen. It was an adventure, but not a dangerous adventure. The man might steal Pete's ashtrays but he wouldn't kill him. If Pete got killed on the road it would be by some spiritual person in a sweatsuit, someone with his eyes on the far horizon and a wet Try God T-shirt in his duffel bag.

Stygian: Unremittingly dark and frightening.

As soon as they left the parking lot the man lit a cigar. He blew a cloud of smoke over Pete's shoulder and sighed with pleasure. "Put it out," Pete told him.

"Of course," the man said. Pete looked in the rearview mirror and saw the man take another long puff before dropping the cigar out the window. "Forgive me," he said. "I should have asked. Name's Webster, by the way."

Donald turned and looked back at him. "First name or last?"

The man hesitated. "Last," he said finally.

"I know a Webster," Donald said. "Mick Webster."   135

"There are many of us," Webster said.

"Big fellow, wooden leg," Pete said.

Donald gave Pete a look.

Webster shook his head. "Doesn't ring a bell. Still, I wouldn't deny the connection. Might be one of the cousinry."

"What's your daughter got?" Pete asked.   140

"That isn't clear," Webster answered. "It appears to be a female complaint of some nature. Then again it may be tropical." He was quiet for a moment, and added: "If indeed it *is* tropical, I will have to assume some of the blame myself. It was my own vaulting ambition that first led us to the tropics and kept us in the tropics all those many years, exposed to every evil. Truly I have much to answer for. I left my wife there."

Donald said quietly, "You mean she died?"

"I buried her with these hands. The earth will be repaid, gold for gold."

"Which tropics?" Pete asked.

"The tropics of Peru."   145

"What part of Peru are they in?"

"The lowlands," Webster said.

"What's it like down there? In the lowlands."

"Another world," Webster said. His tone was sepulchral. "A world better imagined than described."

"Far out," Pete said.   150

The three men rode in silence for a time. A line of trucks went past in the other direction, trailers festooned with running lights, engines roaring.

"Yes," Webster said at last, "I have much to answer for."

Pete smiled at Donald, but Donald had turned in his seat again and was gazing at Webster. "I'm sorry about your wife," Donald said.

"What did she die of?" Pete asked.

"A wasting illness," Webster said. "The doctors have no name for it, but I   155
do." He leaned forward and said, fiercely, "*Greed*. My greed, not hers. She wanted no part of it."

Pete bit his lip. Webster was a find and Pete didn't want to scare him off by hooting at him. In a voice low and innocent of knowingness, he asked, "What took you there?"

"It's difficult for me to talk about."

"Try," Pete told him.

"A cigar would make it easier."

Donald turned to Pete and said, "It's okay with me."   160

"All right," Pete said. "Go ahead. Just keep the window rolled down."

"Much obliged." A match flared. There were eager sucking sounds.

"Let's hear it," Pete said.

"I am by training an engineer," Webster began. "My work has exposed me to all but one of the continents, to desert and alp and forest, to every terrain and season of the earth. Some years ago I was hired by the Peruvian government to search for tungsten in the tropics. My wife and daughter accompanied me. We were the only white people for a thousand miles in any direction, and we had no choice but to live as the Indians lived — to share their food and drink and even their culture."

Pete said, "You knew the lingo, did you?"   165

"We picked it up." The ember of the cigar bobbed up and down. "We were used to learning as necessity decreed. At any rate, it became evident after a couple of years that there was no tungsten to be found. My wife had fallen ill and was pleading to be taken home. But I was deaf to her pleas, because by then I was on the trail of another metal — a metal far more valuable than tungsten."

"Let me guess," Pete said. "Gold?"

Donald looked at Pete, then back at Webster.

"Gold," Webster said. "A vein of gold greater than the Mother Lode itself. After I found the first traces of it nothing could tear me away from my search — not the sickness of my wife or anything else. I was determined to uncover the vein, and so I did — but not before I laid my wife to rest. As I say, the earth will be repaid."

Webster was quiet. Then he said, "But life must go on. In the years since my   170 wife's death I have been making the arrangements necessary to open the mine. I could have done it immediately, of course, enriching myself beyond measure, but I knew what that would mean — the exploitation of our beloved Indians, the brutal destruction of their environment. I felt I had too much to atone for already." Webster paused, and when he spoke again his voice was dull and rushed, as if he had used up all the interest he had in his own words. "Instead I drew up a program for returning the bulk of the wealth to the Indians themselves. A kind of trust fund. The interest alone will allow them to secure their ancient lands and rights in perpetuity. At the same time, our investors will be rewarded a thousandfold. Two-thousandfold. Everyone will prosper together."

"That's great," said Donald. "That's the way it ought to be."

Pete said, "I'm willing to bet that you just happen to have a few shares left. Am I right?"

Webster made no reply.

"Well?" Pete knew that Webster was on to him now, but he didn't care. The story had bored him. He'd expected something different, something original, and Webster had let him down. He hadn't even tried. Pete felt sour and stale. His eyes burned from cigar smoke and the high beams of road-hogging truckers. "Douse the stogie," he said to Webster. "I told you to keep the window down."

"Got a little nippy back here."   175

Donald said, "Hey, Pete. Lighten up."

"Douse it!"

Webster sighed. He got rid of the cigar.

"I'm a wreck," Pete said to Donald. "You want to drive for a while?"

Donald nodded.   180

Pete pulled over and they changed places.

Webster kept his counsel in the back seat. Donald hummed while he drove, until Pete told him to stop. Then everything was quiet.

Donald was humming again when Pete woke up. Pete stared sullenly at the road, at the white lines sliding past the car. After a few moments of this he turned and said, "How long have I been out?"

Donald glanced at him. "Twenty, twenty-five minutes."

Pete looked behind him and saw that Webster was gone. "Where's our   185
friend?"

"You just missed him. He got out in Soledad. He told me to say thanks and good-bye."

"Soledad? What about his sick daughter? How did he explain her away?"

"He has a brother living there. He's going to borrow a car from him and drive the rest of the way in the morning."

"I'll bet his brother's living there," Pete said. "Doing fifty concurrent life sentences. His brother and his sister and his mom and his dad."

"I kind of liked him," Donald said.   190

"I'm sure you did," Pete said wearily.

"He was interesting. He's been places."

"His cigars had been places, I'll give you that."

"Come on, Pete."

"Come on yourself. What a phony."   195

"You don't know that."

"Sure I do."

"How? How do you know?"

Pete stretched. "Brother, there are some things you're just born knowing. What's the gas situation?"

"We're a little low."   200

"Then why didn't you get some more?"

"I wish you wouldn't snap at me like that," Donald said.

"Then why don't you use your head? What if we run out?"

"We'll make it," Donald said. "I'm pretty sure we've got enough to make it. You didn't have to be so rude to him," Donald added.

Pete took a deep breath. "I don't feel like running out of gas tonight, okay?"   205

Donald pulled in at the next station they came to and filled the tank while Pete went to the men's room. When Pete came back, Donald was sitting in the passenger's seat. The attendant came up to the driver's window as Pete got in behind the wheel. He bent down and said, "Twelve fifty-five."

"You heard the man," Pete said to Donald.

Donald looked straight ahead. He didn't move.

"Cough up," Pete said. "This trip's on you."

"I can't."   210

"Sure you can. Break out that wad."

Donald glanced up at the attendant, then at Pete. "Please," he said, "Pete, I don't have it anymore."

Pete took this in. He nodded, and paid the attendant.

Donald began to speak when they left the station but Pete cut him off. He said, "I don't want to hear from you right now. You just keep quiet or I swear to God I won't be responsible."

They left the fields and entered a tunnel of tall trees. The trees went on   215 and on. "Let me get this straight," Pete said at last. "You don't have the money I gave you."

"You treated him like a bug or something," Donald said.

"You don't have the money," Pete said again.

Donald shook his head.

"Since I bought dinner, and since we didn't stop anywhere in between, I assume you gave it to Webster. Is that right? Is that what you did with it?"

"Yes."   220

Pete looked at Donald. His face was dark under the hood but he still managed to convey a sense of remove, as if none of this had anything to do with him.

"Why?" Pete asked. "Why did you give it to him?" When Donald didn't answer, Pete said, "A hundred dollars. Gone. Just like that. I *worked* for that money, Donald."

"I know, I know," Donald said.

"You don't know! How could you? You get money by holding out your hand."

"I work too," Donald said.   225

"You work too. Don't kid yourself, brother."

Donald leaned toward Pete, about to say something, but Pete cut him off again.

"You're not the only one on the payroll, Donald. I don't think you understand that. I have a family."

"Pete, I'll pay you back."

"Like hell you will. A hundred dollars!" Pete hit the steering wheel with the   230 palm of his hand. "Just because you think I hurt some goofball's feelings. Jesus, Donald."

"That's not the reason," Donald said. "And I didn't just *give* him the money."

"What do you call it, then? What do you call what you did?"

"I *invested* it. I wanted a share, Pete." When Pete looked over at him Donald nodded and said again, "I wanted a share."

Pete said, "I take it you're referring to the gold mine in Peru."

"Yes," Donald said.   235

"You believe that such a gold mine exists?"

Donald looked at Pete, and Pete could see him just beginning to catch on. "You'll believe anything," Pete said. "Won't you? You really will believe anything at all."

"I'm sorry," Donald said, and turned away.

Pete drove on between the trees and considered the truth of what he had just said — that Donald would believe anything at all. And it came to him that it would be just like this unfair life for Donald to come out ahead in the end, by believing in some outrageous promise that would turn out to be true and that he, Pete, would reject out of hand because he was too wised up to listen to anybody's pitch anymore except for laughs. What a joke. What a joke if there really was a blessing to be had, and the blessing didn't come to the one who deserved it, the one who did all the work, but to the other.

And as if this had already happened Pete felt a shadow move upon him, darkening his thoughts. After a time he said, "I can see where all this is going, Donald."   240

"I'll pay you back," Donald said.

"No," Pete said. "You won't pay me back. You can't. You don't know how. All you've ever done is take. All your life."

Donald shook his head.

"I see exactly where this is going," Pete went on. "You can't work, you can't take care of yourself, you believe anything anyone tells you. I'm stuck with you, aren't I?" He looked over at Donald. "I've got you on my hands for good."

Donald pressed his fingers against the dashboard as if to brace himself. "I'll get out," he said.   245

Pete kept driving.

"Let me out," Donald said. "I mean it, Pete."

"Do you?"

Donald hesitated. "Yes," he said.

"Be sure," Pete told him. "This is it. This is for keeps."   250

"I mean it."

"All right. You made the choice." Pete braked the car sharply and swung it to the shoulder of the road. He turned off the engine and got out. Trees loomed on both sides, shutting out the sky. The air was cold and musty. Pete took Donald's duffel bag from the back seat and set it down behind the car. He stood there, facing Donald in the red glow of the taillights. "It's better this way," Pete said.

Donald just looked at him.

"Better for you," Pete said.

Donald hugged himself. He was shaking. "You don't have to say all that," he told Pete. "I don't blame you."   255

"Blame me? What the hell are you talking about? Blame me for what?"

"For anything," Donald said.

"I want to know what you mean by blame me."

"Nothing. Nothing, Pete. You'd better get going. God bless you."

"That's it," Pete said. He dropped to one knee, searching the packed dirt with his hands. He didn't know what he was looking for, his hands would know when they found it.   260

Donald touched Pete's shoulder. "You'd better go," he said.

Somewhere in the trees Pete heard a branch snap. He stood up. He looked at Donald, then went back to the car and drove away. He drove fast, hunched over the wheel, conscious of the way he was hunched and the shallowness of his breathing, refusing to look in the mirror above his head until there was nothing behind him but darkness.

Then he said, "A hundred dollars," as if there were someone to hear.

The trees gave way to fields. Metal fences ran beside the road, plastered with windblown scraps of paper. Tule fog hung above the ditches, spilling into the road, dimming the ghostly halogen lights that burned in the yards of the farms Pete passed. The fog left beads of water rolling up the windshield.

Pete rummaged among his cassettes. He found Pachelbel's Canon and   265
pushed it into the tape deck. When the violins began to play he leaned back and assumed an attentive expression as if he were really listening to them. He smiled to himself like a man at liberty to enjoy music, a man who has finished his work and settled his debts, done all things meet and due.

And in this way, smiling, nodding to the music, he went another mile or so and pretended that he was not already slowing down, that he was not going to turn back, that he would be able to drive on like this, alone, and have the right answer when his wife stood before him in the doorway of his home and asked, Where is he? Where is your brother?   *[1985]*

≡ THINKING ABOUT THE TEXT

1. Are you more sympathetic to Donald's side or to Pete's side in this story? Do you agree with the comment that "everybody likes to hear how someone messed up" (para. 63)? Does Donald get conned by Webster? Would you be angry with Donald for giving Webster your money? Does Pete want Donald to look foolish? Is Donald foolish?

2. How do you interpret Donald's story about Pete hitting his stitches? Was Pete trying to get rid of Donald? What could his reason have been?

3. Why doesn't Pete tell Donald he was blind in his dream? How do you interpret this dream? Is the heart of their dispute "prosperity," or is it something else?

4. In his recent book (*Our Story Begins: New and Selected Stories* [2008]), Wolff revises the end of this story. In paragraph 260, he deletes the last two sentences and adds instead, "and took a step toward Donald." Some readers were disappointed that he takes out what they see as an enigmatic action that adds mystery and complexity to the ending. Do you agree? Why do you think Wolff made this change?

5. Why would Pete turn around to get Donald? Why would he keep going? What would you do? Why?

JAMES BALDWIN
Sonny's Blues

James Baldwin (1924–1987) wanted to be a writer from the time he was a boy growing up in Harlem. He continued his writing through high school while also following in his foster father's footsteps by doing some preaching. On his own at age eighteen, Baldwin left Greenwich Village in 1948 and moved to Paris. He lived in France for eight years before returning to New York, where he wrote widely about the civil rights movement. Indeed, Baldwin's passionate and eloquent essays, like those in Notes of a Native Son *(1955) and* The Fire Next Time *(1963), exploring the place of African Americans in contemporary society are considered among the best nonfiction of his generation.*

Being an artist and an African American were lifelong central issues for Baldwin. His fiction confronts the psychological challenges that were inevitable for black writers searching for identity in America. Themes of responsibility, pain, identity, frustration, and bitterness are woven into his fiction along with understanding, equanimity, love, and tolerance. "Sonny's Blues," from Going to Meet the Man *(1965), is one of his strongest dramatizations of the struggles and achievements of black artists.*

I read about it in the paper, in the subway, on my way to work. I read it, and I couldn't believe it, and I read it again. Then perhaps I just stared at it, at the newsprint spelling out his name, spelling out the story. I stared at it in the swinging lights of the subway car, and in the faces and bodies of the people, and in my own face, trapped in the darkness which roared outside.

It was not to be believed and I kept telling myself that, as I walked from the subway station to the high school. And at the same time I couldn't doubt it. I was scared, scared for Sonny. He became real to me again. A great block of ice got settled in my belly and kept melting there slowly all day long, while I taught my classes algebra. It was a special kind of ice. It kept melting, sending trickles of ice water all up and down my veins, but it never got less. Sometimes it hardened and seemed to expand until I felt my guts were going to come spilling out or that I was going to choke or scream. This would always be at a moment when I was remembering some specific thing Sonny had once said or done.

When he was about as old as the boys in my classes his face had been bright and open, there was a lot of copper in it; and he'd had wonderfully direct brown eyes, and great gentleness and privacy. I wondered what he looked like now. He had been picked up, the evening before, in a raid on an apartment downtown, for peddling and using heroin.

I couldn't believe it: but what I mean by that is that I couldn't find any room for it anywhere inside me. I had kept it outside me for a long time. I hadn't wanted to know. I had had suspicions, but I didn't name them, I kept putting them away. I told myself that Sonny was wild, but he wasn't crazy. And he'd always been a good boy, he hadn't ever turned hard or evil or disrespectful, the way kids can, so quick, so quick, especially in Harlem. I didn't want to believe that I'd ever see my brother going down, coming to nothing, all that light in his face gone out, in the condition I'd already seen so many others. Yet it had happened and here I was, talking about algebra to a lot of boys who might, every one of them for all I knew, be popping off needles every time they went to the head°. Maybe it did more for them than algebra could.

I was sure that the first time Sonny had ever had horse,° he couldn't have   5
been much older than these boys were now. These boys, now, were living as we'd been living then, they were growing up with a rush and their heads bumped abruptly against the low ceiling of their actual possibilities. They were filled with rage. All they really knew were two darknesses, the darkness of their lives, which was now closing in on them, and the darkness of the movies, which had blinded them to that other darkness, and in which they now, vindictively, dreamed, at once more together than they were at any other time, and more alone.

When the last bell rang, the last class ended, I let out my breath. It seemed I'd been holding it for all that time. My clothes were wet — I may have looked as though I'd been sitting in a steam bath, all dressed up, all afternoon. I sat alone in the classroom a long time. I listened to the boys outside, downstairs, shouting and cursing and laughing. Their laughter struck me for perhaps the first time. It was not the joyous laughter which — God knows why — one associates with children. It was mocking and insular, its intent to denigrate. It was disenchanted, and in this, also, lay the authority of their curses. Perhaps I was listening to them because I was thinking about my brother and in them I heard my brother. And myself.

One boy was whistling a tune, at once very complicated and very simple, it seemed to be pouring out of him as though he were a bird, and it sounded very cool and moving through all that harsh, bright air, only just holding its own through all those other sounds.

I stood up and walked over to the window and looked down into the courtyard. It was the beginning of the spring and the sap was rising in the boys. A teacher passed through them every now and again, quickly, as though he or she couldn't wait to get out of that courtyard, to get those boys out of their sight and off their minds. I started collecting my stuff. I thought I'd better get home and talk to Isabel.

The courtyard was almost deserted by the time I got downstairs. I saw this boy standing in the shadow of a doorway, looking just like Sonny. I almost called his name. Then I saw that it wasn't Sonny, but somebody we used to know, a boy from around our block. He'd been Sonny's friend. He'd never been mine, having been too young for me, and, anyway, I'd never liked him. And now, even though he was a grown-up man, he still hung around that block, still spent hours on the street corners, was always high and raggy. I used to run into him from time to time and he'd often work around to asking me for a quarter or fifty cents. He always had some real good excuse, too, and I always gave it to him, I don't know why.

head: Slang for bathroom.   **horse:** Name for heroin in the 1950s.

But now, abruptly, I hated him. I couldn't stand the way he looked at me,   10
partly like a dog, partly like a cunning child. I wanted to ask him what the hell
he was doing in the school courtyard.

He sort of shuffled over to me, and he said, "I see you got the papers. So you
already know about it."

"You mean about Sonny? Yes, I already know about it. How come they
didn't get you?"

He grinned. It made him repulsive and it also brought to mind what he'd
looked like as a kid. "I wasn't there. I stay away from them people."

"Good for you." I offered him a cigarette and I watched him through the
smoke. "You come all the way down here just to tell me about Sonny?"

"That's right." He was sort of shaking his head and his eyes looked strange,   15
as though they were about to cross. The bright sun deadened his damp dark
brown skin and it made his eyes look yellow and showed up the dirt in his
kinked hair. He smelled funky. I moved a little away from him and I said, "Well,
thanks. But I already know about it and I got to get home."

"I'll walk you a little ways," he said. We started walking. There were a
couple of kids still loitering in the courtyard and one of them said goodnight to
me and looked strangely at the boy beside me.

"What're you going to do?" he asked me. "I mean, about Sonny?"

"Look. I haven't seen Sonny for over a year. I'm not sure I'm going to do
anything. Anyway, what the hell *can* I do?"

"That's right," he said quickly, "ain't nothing you can do. Can't much help
old Sonny no more, I guess."

It was what I was thinking and so it seemed to me he had no right to say it.   20

"I'm surprised at Sonny, though," he went on — he had a funny way of
talking, he looked straight ahead as though he were talking to himself — "I
thought Sonny was a smart boy, I thought he was too smart to get hung."

"I guess he thought so too," I said sharply, "and that's how he got hung.
And how about you? You're pretty goddamn smart, I bet."

Then he looked directly at me, just for a minute. "I ain't smart," he said. "If
I was smart, I'd have reached for a pistol a long time ago."

"Look. Don't tell *me* your sad story, if it was up to me, I'd give you one."
Then I felt guilty — guilty, probably, for never having supposed that the poor
bastard *had* a story of his own, much less a sad one, and I asked, quickly,
"What's going to happen to him now?"

He didn't answer this. He was off by himself some place. "Funny thing," he   25
said, and from his tone we might have been discussing the quickest way to get
to Brooklyn, "when I saw the papers this morning, the first thing I asked myself
was if I had anything to do with it. I felt sort of responsible."

I began to listen more carefully. The subway station was on the corner, just
before us, and I stopped. He stopped, too. We were in front of a bar and he
ducked slightly, peering in, but whoever he was looking for didn't seem to be
there. The juke box was blasting away with something black and bouncy and I
half watched the barmaid as she danced her way from the juke box to her place
behind the bar. And I watched her face as she laughingly responded to some-

thing someone said to her, still keeping time to the music. When she smiled one saw the little girl, one sensed the doomed, still-struggling woman beneath the battered face of the semi-whore.

"I never *give* Sonny nothing," the boy said finally, "but a long time ago I come to school high and Sonny asked me how it felt." He paused, I couldn't bear to watch him, I watched the barmaid, and I listened to the music which seemed to be causing the pavement to shake. "I told him it felt great." The music stopped, the barmaid paused and watched the juke box until the music began again. "It did."

All this was carrying me some place I didn't want to go. I certainly didn't want to know how it felt. It filled everything, the people, the houses, the music, the dark, quicksilver barmaid, with menace; and this menace was their reality.

"What's going to happen to him now?" I asked again.

"They'll send him away some place and they'll try to cure him." He shook   30
his head. "Maybe he'll even think he's kicked the habit. Then they'll let him loose" — he gestured, throwing his cigarette into the gutter. "That's all."

"What do you mean, that's *all?*"

But I knew what he meant.

"I *mean*, that's *all.*" He turned his head and looked at me, pulling down the corners of his mouth. "Don't you know what I mean?" he asked, softly.

"How the hell *would* I know what you mean?" I almost whispered it, I don't know why.

"That's right," he said to the air, "how would *he* know what I mean?" He   35
turned toward me again, patient and calm, and yet I somehow felt him shaking, shaking as though he were going to fall apart. I felt that ice in my guts again, the dread I'd felt all afternoon; and again I watched the barmaid, moving about the bar, washing glasses, and singing. "Listen. They'll let him out and then it'll just start all over again. That's what I mean."

"You mean — they'll let him out. And then he'll just start working his way back in again. You mean he'll never kick the habit. Is that what you mean?"

"That's right," he said, cheerfully. "*You* see what I mean."

"Tell me," I said at last, "why does he want to die? He must want to die, he's killing himself, why does he want to die?"

He looked at me in surprise. He licked his lips. "He don't want to die. He wants to live. Don't nobody want to die, ever."

Then I wanted to ask him — too many things. He could not have answered,   40
or if he had, I could not have borne the answers. I started walking. "Well, I guess it's none of my business."

"It's going to be rough on old Sonny," he said. We reached the subway station. "This is your station?" he asked. I nodded. I took one step down. "Damn!" he said, suddenly. I looked up at him. He grinned again. "Damn it if I didn't leave all my money home. You ain't got a dollar on you, have you? Just for a couple of days, is all."

All at once something inside gave and threatened to come pouring out of me. I didn't hate him any more. I felt that in another moment I'd start crying like a child.

"Sure," I said. "Don't sweat." I looked in my wallet and didn't have a dollar, I only had a five. "Here," I said. "That hold you?"

He didn't look at it — he didn't want to look at it. A terrible closed look came over his face, as though he were keeping the number on the bill a secret from him and me. "Thanks," he said, and now he was dying to see me go. "Don't worry about Sonny. Maybe I'll write him or something."

"Sure," I said. "You do that. So long."   45

"Be seeing you," he said. I went on down the steps.

And I didn't write Sonny or send him anything for a long time. When I finally did, it was just after my little girl died, he wrote me back a letter which made me feel like a bastard.

Here's what he said:

> Dear brother,
>
> You don't know how much I needed to hear from you. I wanted to write you many a time but I dug how much I must have hurt you and so I didn't write. But now I feel like a man who's been trying to climb up out of some deep, real deep and funky hole and just saw the sun up there, outside. I got to get outside.
>
> I can't tell you much about how I got here. I mean I don't know how to tell you. I guess I was afraid of something or I was trying to escape from something and you know I have never been very strong in the head (smile). I'm glad Mama and Daddy are dead and can't see what's happened to their son and I swear if I'd known what I was doing I would never have hurt you so, you and a lot of other fine people who were nice to me and who believed in me.
>
> I don't want you to think it had anything to do with me being a musician. It's more than that. Or maybe less than that. I can't get anything straight in my head down here and I try not to think about what's going to happen to me when I get outside again. Sometime I think I'm going to flip and never get outside and sometime I think I'll come straight back. I tell you one thing, though, I'd rather blow my brains out than go through this again. But that's what they all say, so they tell me. If I tell you when I'm coming to New York and if you could meet me, I sure would appreciate it. Give my love to Isabel and the kids and I was sure sorry to hear about little Gracie. I wish I could be like Mama and say the Lord's will be done, but I don't know it seems to me that trouble is the one thing that never does get stopped and I don't know what good it does to blame it on the Lord. But maybe it does some good if you believe it.
>
>   Your brother,
>   Sonny

Then I kept in constant touch with him and I sent him whatever I could and I went to meet him when he came back to New York. When I saw him many things I thought I had forgotten came flooding back to me. This was because I had begun, finally, to wonder about Sonny, about the life that Sonny lived inside. This life, whatever it was, had made him older and thinner and it had deepened the distant stillness in which he had always moved. He looked very unlike my baby brother. Yet, when he smiled, when we shook hands, the baby brother I'd never known looked out from the depths of his private life, like an animal waiting to be coaxed into the light.

"How you been keeping?" he asked me.

"All right. And you?"

"Just fine." He was smiling all over his face. "It's good to see you again."

"It's good to see you."

The seven years' difference in our ages lay between us like a chasm: I wondered if these years would ever operate between us as a bridge. I was remembering, and it made it hard to catch my breath, that I had been there when he was born; and I had heard the first words he had ever spoken. When he started to walk, he walked from our mother straight to me. I caught him just before he fell when he took the first steps he ever took in this world.

"How's Isabel?"

"Just fine. She's dying to see you."

"And the boys?"

"They're fine, too. They're anxious to see their uncle."

"Oh, come on. You know they don't remember me."

"Are you kidding? Of course they remember you."

He grinned again. We got into a taxi. We had a lot to say to each other, far too much to know how to begin.

As the taxi began to move, I asked, "You still want to go to India?"

He laughed. "You still remember that. Hell, no. This place is Indian enough for me."

"It used to belong to them," I said.

And he laughed again. "They damn sure knew what they were doing when they got rid of it."

Years ago, when he was around fourteen, he'd been all hipped on the idea of going to India. He read books about people sitting on rocks, naked, in all kinds of weather, but mostly bad, naturally, and walking barefoot through hot coals and arriving at wisdom. I used to say that it sounded to me as though they were getting away from wisdom as fast as they could. I think he sort of looked down on me for that.

"Do you mind," he asked, "if we have the driver drive alongside the park? On the west side — I haven't seen the city in so long."

"Of course not," I said. I was afraid that I might sound as though I were humoring him, but I hoped he wouldn't take it that way.

So we drove along, between the green of the park and the stony, lifeless elegance of hotels and apartment buildings, toward the vivid, killing streets of our childhood. These streets hadn't changed, though housing projects jutted up out of them now like rocks in the middle of a boiling sea. Most of the houses in which we had grown up had vanished, as had the stores from which we had stolen, the basements in which we had first tried sex, the rooftops from which we had hurled tin cans and bricks. But houses exactly like the houses of our past yet dominated the landscape, boys exactly like the boys we once had been found themselves smothering in these houses, came down into the streets for light and air and found themselves encircled by disaster. Some escaped the trap, most didn't. Those who got out always left something of themselves behind, as some animals amputate a leg and leave it in the trap. It might be said, perhaps, that I had escaped, after all, I was a school teacher; or that Sonny had, he hadn't lived in Harlem for years. Yet, as the cab moved uptown through streets which seemed, with a rush, to darken with dark people, and as I covertly studied Sonny's face, it came to me that what we both were seeking through our separate cab windows was that part of ourselves which had been left behind. It's always at the hour of trouble and confrontation that the missing member aches.

We hit 110th Street and started rolling up Lenox Avenue. And I'd known   70 this avenue all my life, but it seemed to me again, as it had seemed on the day I'd first heard about Sonny's trouble, filled with a hidden menace which was its very breath of life.

"We almost there," said Sonny.

"Almost." We were both too nervous to say anything more.

We live in a housing project. It hasn't been up long. A few days after it was up it seemed uninhabitably new, now, of course, it's already rundown. It looks like a parody of the good, clean, faceless life — God knows the people who live in it do their best to make it a parody. The beat-looking grass lying around isn't enough to make their lives green, the hedges will never hold out the streets, and they know it. The big windows fool no one, they aren't big enough to make space out of no space. They don't bother with the windows, they watch the TV screen instead. The playground is most popular with the children who don't play at jacks, or skip rope, or roller skate, or swing, and they can be found in it after dark. We moved in partly because it's not too far from where I teach, and partly for the kids; but it's really just like the houses in which Sonny and I grew up. The same things happen, they'll have the same things to remember. The moment Sonny and I started into the house I had the feeling that I was simply bringing him back into the danger he had almost died trying to escape.

Sonny has never been talkative. So I don't know why I was sure he'd be dying to talk to me when supper was over the first night. Everything went fine, the oldest boy remembered him, and the youngest boy liked him, and Sonny had remembered to bring something for each of them; and Isabel, who is really much nicer than I am, more open and giving, had gone to a lot of trouble about dinner and was genuinely glad to see him. And she's always been able to tease Sonny in a way that I haven't. It was nice to see her face so vivid again and to hear her laugh and watch her make Sonny laugh. She wasn't, or, anyway, she didn't seem to be, at all uneasy or embarrassed. She chatted as though there were no subject which had to be avoided and she got Sonny past his first, faint stiffness. And thank God she was there, for I was filled with that icy dread again. Everything I did seemed awkward to me, and everything I said sounded freighted with hidden meaning. I was trying to remember everything I'd heard about dope addiction and I couldn't help watching Sonny for signs. I wasn't doing it out of malice. I was trying to find out something about my brother. I was dying to hear him tell me he was safe.

"Safe!" my father grunted, whenever Mama suggested trying to move to a   75 neighborhood which might be safer for children. "Safe, hell! Ain't no place safe for kids, nor nobody."

He always went on like this, but he wasn't, ever, really as bad as he sounded, not even on weekends, when he got drunk. As a matter of fact, he was always on the lookout for "something a little better," but he died before he found it. He died suddenly, during a drunken weekend in the middle of the war, when Sonny was fifteen. He and Sonny hadn't ever got on too well. And this was partly because Sonny was the apple of his father's eye. It was because he loved Sonny so much and was frightened for him, that he was always fighting with him. It doesn't do any good to fight with Sonny. Sonny just moves back, inside himself, where he can't be reached. But the principal reason that they never hit it off is that they were so much alike. Daddy was big and rough and loud-talking, just the opposite of Sonny, but they both had — that same privacy.

Mama tried to tell me something about this, just after Daddy died. I was home on leave from the army.

This was the last time I ever saw my mother alive. Just the same, this picture gets all mixed up in my mind with pictures I had of her when she was younger. The way I always see her is the way she used to be on a Sunday afternoon, say, when the old folks were talking after the big Sunday dinner. I always see her wearing pale blue. She'd be sitting on the sofa. And my father would be sitting in the easy chair, not far from her. And the living room would be full of church folks and relatives. There they sit, in chairs all around the living room, and the night is creeping up outside, but nobody knows it yet. You can see the darkness growing against the windowpanes and you hear the street noises every now and again, or maybe the jangling beat of a tambourine from one of the churches close by, but it's real quiet in the room. For a moment nobody's talking, but every face looks darkening, like the sky outside. And my mother rocks a little from the waist, and my father's eyes are closed. Everyone is looking at something a child can't see. For a minute they've forgotten the children. Maybe a kid is lying on the rug, half asleep. Maybe somebody's got a kid in his lap and is absent-mindedly stroking the kid's head. Maybe there's a kid, quiet and big-eyed, curled up in a big chair in the corner. The silence, the darkness coming, and the darkness in the faces frightens the child obscurely. He hopes that the hand which strokes his forehead will never stop — will never die. He hopes that there will never come a time when the old folks won't be sitting around the living room, talking about where they've come from, and what they've seen, and what's happened to them and their kinfolk.

But something deep and watchful in the child knows that this is bound to end, is already ending. In a moment someone will get up and turn on the light. Then the old folks will remember the children and they won't talk any more that day. And when light fills the room, the child is filled with darkness. He knows that every time this happens he's moved just a little closer to that darkness outside. The darkness outside is what the old folks have been talking about. It's what they've come from. It's what they endure. The child knows that they won't talk any more because if he knows too much about what's happened to *them*, he'll know too much too soon, about what's going to happen to *him*.

The last time I talked to my mother, I remember I was restless. I wanted to get out and see Isabel. We weren't married then and we had a lot to straighten out between us.

80

There Mama sat, in black, by the window. She was humming an old church song, *Lord, you brought me from a long ways off.* Sonny was out somewhere. Mama kept watching the streets.

"I don't know," she said, "if I'll ever see you again, after you go off from here. But I hope you'll remember the things I tried to teach you."

"Don't talk like that," I said, and smiled. "You'll be here a long time yet."

She smiled, too, but she said nothing. She was quiet for a long time. And I said, "Mama, don't you worry about nothing. I'll be writing all the time, and you be getting the checks. . . ."

"I want to talk to you about your brother," she said, suddenly. "If anything   85
happens to me he ain't going to have nobody to look out for him."

"Mama," I said, "ain't nothing going to happen to you *or* Sonny. Sonny's all right. He's a good boy and he's got good sense."

"It ain't a question of his being a good boy," Mama said, "nor of his having good sense. It ain't only the bad ones, nor yet the dumb ones that gets sucked under." She stopped, looking at me. "Your Daddy once had a brother," she said, and she smiled in a way that made me feel she was in pain. "You didn't never know that, did you?"

"No," I said, "I never knew that," and I watched her face.

"Oh, yes," she said, "your Daddy had a brother." She looked out of the window again. "I know you never saw your Daddy cry. But *I* did — many a time, through all these years."

I asked her, "What happened to his brother? How come nobody's ever   90
talked about him?"

This was the first time I ever saw my mother look old.

"His brother got killed," she said, "when he was just a little younger than you are now. I knew him. He was a fine boy. He was maybe a little full of the devil, but he didn't mean nobody no harm."

Then she stopped and the room was silent, exactly as it had sometimes been on those Sunday afternoons. Mama kept looking out into the streets.

"He used to have a job in the mill," she said, "and, like all young folks, he just liked to perform on Saturday nights. Saturday nights, him and your father would drift around to different places, go to dances and things like that, or just sit around with people they knew, and your father's brother would sing, he had a fine voice, and play along with himself on his guitar. Well, this particular Saturday night, him and your father was coming home from some place, and they were both a little drunk and there was a moon that night, it was bright like day. Your father's brother was feeling kind of good, and he was whistling to himself, and he had his guitar slung over his shoulder. They was coming down a hill and beneath them was a road that turned off from the highway. Well, your father's brother, being always kind of frisky, decided to run down this hill, and he did, with that guitar banging and clanging behind him, and he ran across the road, and he was making water behind a tree. And your father was sort of amused at him and he was still coming down the hill, kind of slow. Then he heard a car motor and that same minute his brother stepped from behind the tree, into the road, in the moonlight. And he started to cross the road. And your father started to run down the hill, he says he don't know why. This car was full of white men. They was all drunk, and when they seen your father's brother they let out a great whoop and holler and they aimed the car straight at him. They was having fun, they just wanted to scare him, the way they do sometimes, you know. But they was drunk. And I guess the boy, being drunk, too, and scared, kind of lost his head. By the time he jumped it was too late. Your father says he heard his brother scream when the car rolled over him, and he heard the wood of that guitar when it give, and he heard them strings go flying, and he heard them white men shouting, and the car kept on a-going and it ain't stopped till this day. And, time your father got down the hill, his brother weren't nothing but blood and pulp."

Tears were gleaming on my mother's face. There wasn't anything I could say.   95

"He never mentioned it," she said, "because I never let him mention it before you children. Your Daddy was like a crazy man that night and for many a night thereafter. He says he never in his life seen anything as dark as that road after the lights of that car had gone away. Weren't nothing, weren't nobody on that road, just your Daddy and his brother and that busted guitar. Oh, yes. Your Daddy never did really get right again. Till the day he died he weren't sure but that every white man he saw was the man that killed his brother."

She stopped and took out her handkerchief and dried her eyes and looked at me.

"I ain't telling you all this," she said, "to make you scared or bitter or to make you hate nobody. I'm telling you this because you got a brother. And the world ain't changed."

I guess I didn't want to believe this. I guess she saw this in my face. She turned away from me, toward the window again, searching those streets.

"But I praise my Redeemer," she said at last, "that He called your Daddy   100 home before me. I ain't saying it to throw no flowers at myself, but, I declare, it keeps me from feeling too cast down to know I helped your father get safely through this world. Your father always acted like he was the roughest, strongest man on earth. And everybody took him to be like that. But if he hadn't had *me* there — to see his tears!"

She was crying again. Still, I couldn't move. I said, "Lord, Lord, Mama, I didn't know it was like that."

"Oh, honey," she said, "there's a lot that you don't know. But you are going to find it out." She stood up from the window and came over to me. "You got to hold on to your brother," she said, "and don't let him fall, no matter what it looks like is happening to him and no matter how evil you gets with him. You going to be evil with him many a time. But don't you forget what I told you, you hear?"

"I won't forget," I said. "Don't you worry, I won't forget. I won't let nothing happen to Sonny."

My mother smiled as though she were amused at something she saw in my face. Then, "You may not be able to stop nothing from happening. But you got to let him know you's *there*."

*   *   *

Two days later I was married, and then I was gone. And I had a lot of things on   105
my mind and I pretty well forgot my promise to Mama until I got shipped home
on a special furlough for her funeral.

And, after the funeral, with just Sonny and me alone in the empty kitchen,
I tried to find out something about him.

"What do you want to do?" I asked him.

"I'm going to be a musician," he said.

For he had graduated, in the time I had been away, from dancing to the
juke box to finding out who was playing what, and what they were doing with
it, and he had bought himself a set of drums.

"You mean, you want to be a drummer?" I somehow had the feeling that   110
being a drummer might be all right for other people but not for my brother
Sonny.

"I don't think," he said, looking at me very gravely, "that I'll ever be a good
drummer. But I think I can play a piano."

I frowned. I'd never played the role of the older brother quite so seriously
before, had scarcely ever, in fact, *asked* Sonny a damn thing. I sensed myself in
the presence of something I didn't really know how to handle, didn't understand. So I made my frown a little deeper as I asked: "What kind of musician do
you want to be?"

He grinned. "How many kinds do you think there are?"

"Be *serious*," I said.

He laughed, throwing his head back, and then looked at me. "I *am* serious."   115

"Well, then, for Christ's sake, stop kidding around and answer a serious
question. I mean, do you want to be a concert pianist, you want to play classical music and all that, or — or what?" Long before I finished he was laughing
again. "For Christ's *sake*, Sonny!"

He sobered, but with difficulty. "I'm sorry. But you sound so — *scared*!" and
he was off again.

"Well, you may think it's funny now, baby, but it's not going to be so funny
when you have to make your living at it, let me tell you *that*." I was furious because I knew he was laughing at me and I didn't know why.

"No," he said, very sober now, and afraid, perhaps, that he'd hurt me, "I
don't want to be a classical pianist. That isn't what interests me. I mean" — he
paused, looking hard at me, as though his eyes would help me to understand,
and then gestured helplessly, as though perhaps his hand would help — "I mean,
I'll have a lot of studying to do, and I'll have to study *everything*, but, I mean, I
want to play *with* — jazz musicians." He stopped. "I want to play jazz," he said.

Well, the word had never before sounded as heavy, as real, as it sounded   120
that afternoon in Sonny's mouth. I just looked at him and I was probably
frowning a real frown by this time. I simply couldn't see why on earth he'd
want to spend his time hanging around nightclubs, clowning around on band-
stands, while people pushed each other around a dance floor. It seemed —
beneath him, somehow. I had never thought about it before, had never been
forced to, but I suppose I had always put jazz musicians in a class with what
Daddy called "good-time people."

"Are you *serious?*"

"Hell, *yes,* I'm serious."

He looked more helpless than ever, and annoyed, and deeply hurt.

I suggested, helpfully: "You mean — like Louis Armstrong?"

His face closed as though I'd struck him. "No. I'm not talking about none   125
of that old-time, down home crap."

"Well, look, Sonny, I'm sorry, don't get mad. I just don't altogether get it,
that's all. Name somebody — you know, a jazz musician you admire."

"Bird."

"Who?"

"Bird! Charlie Parker! Don't they teach you nothing in the goddamn army?"

I lit a cigarette. I was surprised and then a little amused to discover that I   130
was trembling. "I've been out of touch," I said. "You'll have to be patient with
me. Now. Who's this Parker character?"

"He's just one of the greatest jazz musicians alive," said Sonny, sullenly, his
hands in his pockets, his back to me. "Maybe *the* greatest," he added, bitterly,
"that's probably why *you* never heard of him."

"All right," I said, "I'm ignorant. I'm sorry. I'll go out and buy all the cat's
records right away, all right?"

"It don't," said Sonny, with dignity, "make any difference to me. I don't
care what you listen to. Don't do me no favors."

I was beginning to realize that I'd never seen him so upset before. With
another part of my mind I was thinking that this would probably turn out to be
one of those things kids go through and that I shouldn't make it seem important by pushing it too hard. Still, I didn't think it would do any harm to ask:
"Doesn't all this take a lot of time? Can you make a living at it?"

He turned back to me and half leaned, half sat, on the kitchen table. "Ev-   135
erything takes time," he said, "and — well, yes, sure, I can make a living at it.
But what I don't seem to be able to make you understand is that it's the only
thing I want to do."

"Well, Sonny," I said, gently, "you know people can't always do exactly
what they *want* to do —"

"*No,* I don't know that," said Sonny, surprising me. "I think people *ought* to
do what they want to do, what else are they alive for?"

"You getting to be a big boy," I said desperately, "it's time you started thinking about your future."

"I'm thinking about my future," said Sonny, grimly. "I think about it all the
time."

I gave up. I decided, if he didn't change his mind, that we could always talk   140
about it later. "In the meantime," I said, "you got to finish school." We had already decided that he'd have to move in with Isabel and her folks. I knew this
wasn't the ideal arrangement because Isabel's folks are inclined to be dicty°
and they hadn't especially wanted Isabel to marry me. But I didn't know what
else to do. "And we have to get you fixed up at Isabel's."

dicty: Slang for snobbish.

There was a long silence. He moved from the kitchen table to the window. "That's a terrible idea. You know it yourself."

"Do you have a *better* idea?"

He just walked up and down the kitchen for a minute. He was as tall as I was. He had started to shave. I suddenly had the feeling that I didn't know him at all.

He stopped at the kitchen table and picked up my cigarettes. Looking at me with a kind of mocking, amused defiance, he put one between his lips. "You mind?"

"You smoking already?"   145

He lit the cigarette and nodded, watching me through the smoke. "I just wanted to see if I'd have the courage to smoke in front of you." He grinned and blew a great cloud of smoke to the ceiling. "It was easy." He looked at my face. "Come on, now. I bet you was smoking at my age, tell the truth."

I didn't say anything but the truth was on my face, and he laughed. But now there was something very strained in his laugh. "Sure. And I bet that ain't all you was doing."

He was frightening me a little. "Cut the crap," I said. "We already decided that you was going to go and live at Isabel's. Now what's got into you all of a sudden?"

"*You* decided it," he pointed out. "*I* didn't decide nothing." He stopped in front of me, leaning against the stove, arms loosely folded. "Look, brother. I don't want to stay in Harlem no more, I really don't." He was very earnest. He looked at me, then over toward the kitchen window. There was something in his eyes I'd never seen before, some thoughtfulness, some worry all his own. He rubbed the muscle of one arm. "It's time I was getting out of here."

"Where do you want to *go*, Sonny?"   150

"I want to join the army. Or the navy, I don't care. If I say I'm old enough, they'll believe me."

Then I got mad. It was because I was so scared. "You must be crazy. You goddamn fool, what the hell do you want to go and join the *army* for?"

"I just told you. To get out of Harlem."

"Sonny, you haven't even finished *school*. And if you really want to be a musician, how do you expect to study if you're in the *army*?"

He looked at me, trapped, and in anguish. "There's ways. I might be able to   155 work out some kind of deal. Anyway, I'll have the G.I. Bill when I come out."

"*If* you come out." We stared at each other. "Sonny, please. Be reasonable. I know the setup is far from perfect. But we got to do the best we can."

"I ain't learning nothing in school," he said. "Even when I go." He turned away from me and opened the window and threw his cigarette out into the narrow alley. I watched his back. "At least, I ain't learning nothing you'd want me to learn." He slammed the window so hard I thought the glass would fly out, and turned back to me. "And I'm sick of the stink of these garbage cans!"

"Sonny," I said, "I know how you feel. But if you don't finish school now, you're going to be sorry later that you didn't." I grabbed him by the shoulders. "And you only got another year. It ain't so bad. And I'll come back and I swear I'll help you do *whatever* you want to do. Just try to put up with it till I come back. Will you please do that? For me?"

He didn't answer and he wouldn't look at me.

"Sonny. You hear me?"   160

He pulled away. "I hear you. But you never hear anything *I* say."

I didn't know what to say to that. He looked out of the window and then back at me. "OK," he said, and sighed. "I'll try."

Then I said, trying to cheer him up a little, "They got a piano at Isabel's. You can practice on it."

And as a matter of fact, it did cheer him up for a minute. "That's right," he said to himself. "I forgot that." His face relaxed a little. But the worry, the thoughtfulness, played on it still, the way shadows play on a face which is staring into the fire.

But I thought I'd never hear the end of that piano. At first, Isabel would write   165
me, saying how nice it was that Sonny was so serious about his music and how, as soon as he came in from school, or wherever he had been when he was supposed to be at school, he went straight to that piano and stayed there until suppertime. And, after supper, he went back to that piano and stayed there until everybody went to bed. He was at the piano all day Saturday and all day Sunday. Then he bought a record player and started playing records. He'd play one record over and over again, all day long sometimes, and he'd improvise along with it on the piano. Or he'd play one section of the record, one chord, one change, one progression, then he'd do it on the piano. Then back to the record. Then back to the piano.

Well, I really don't know how they stood it. Isabel finally confessed that it wasn't like living with a person at all, it was like living with sound. And the sound didn't make any sense to her, didn't make any sense to any of them — naturally. They began, in a way, to be afflicted by this presence that was living in their home. It was as though Sonny were some sort of god, or monster. He moved in an atmosphere which wasn't like theirs at all. They fed him and he ate, he washed himself, he walked in and out of their door; he certainly wasn't nasty or unpleasant or rude, Sonny isn't any of those things; but it was as though he were all wrapped up in some cloud, some fire, some vision all his own; and there wasn't any way to reach him.

At the same time, he wasn't really a man yet, he was still a child, and they had to watch out for him in all kinds of ways. They certainly couldn't throw him out. Neither did they dare to make a great scene about that piano because even they dimly sensed, as I sensed, from so many thousands of miles away, that Sonny was at that piano playing for his life.

But he hadn't been going to school. One day a letter came from the school board and Isabel's mother got it — there had, apparently, been other letters but Sonny had torn them up. This day, when Sonny came in, Isabel's mother showed him the letter and asked where he'd been spending his time. And she finally got it out of him that he'd been down in Greenwich Village, with musicians and other characters, in a white girl's apartment. And this scared her and she started to scream at him and what came up, once she began — though she denies it to this day — was what sacrifices they were making to give Sonny a decent home and how little he appreciated it.

Sonny didn't play the piano that day. By evening, Isabel's mother had calmed down but then there was the old man to deal with, and Isabel herself. Isabel says she did her best to be calm but she broke down and started crying. She says she just watched Sonny's face. She could tell, by watching him, what was happening with him. And what was happening was that they penetrated his cloud, they had reached him. Even if their fingers had been a thousand times more gentle than human fingers ever are, he could hardly help feeling that they had stripped him naked and were spitting on that nakedness. For he also had to see that his presence, that music, which was life or death to him, had been torture for them and that they had endured it, not at all for his sake, but only for mine. And Sonny couldn't take that. He can take it a little better today than he could then but he's still not very good at it and, frankly, I don't know anybody who is.

The silence of the next few days must have been louder than the sound of   170 all the music ever played since time began. One morning, before she went to work, Isabel was in his room for something and she suddenly realized that all of his records were gone. And she knew for certain that he was gone. And he was. He went as far as the navy would carry him. He finally sent me a postcard from some place in Greece and that was the first I knew that Sonny was still alive. I didn't see him any more until we were both back in New York and the war had long been over.

He was a man by then, of course, but I wasn't willing to see it. He came by the house from time to time, but we fought almost every time we met. I didn't like the way he carried himself, loose and dreamlike all the time, and I didn't like his friends, and his music seemed to be merely an excuse for the life he led. It sounded just that weird and disordered.

Then we had a fight, a pretty awful fight, and I didn't see him for months. By and by I looked him up, where he was living, in a furnished room in the Village, and I tried to make it up. But there were lots of people in the room and Sonny just lay on his bed, and he wouldn't come downstairs with me, and he treated these other people as though they were his family and I weren't. So I got mad and then he got mad, and then I told him that he might just as well be dead as live the way he was living. Then he stood up and he told me not to worry about him any more in life, that he *was* dead as far as I was concerned. Then he pushed me to the door and the other people looked on as though nothing were happening, and he slammed the door behind me. I stood in the hallway, staring at the door. I heard somebody laugh in the room and then the tears came to my eyes. I started down the steps, whistling to keep from crying, I kept whistling to myself, *You going to need me, baby, one of these cold, rainy days.*

I read about Sonny's trouble in the spring. Little Grace died in the fall. She was a beautiful little girl. But she only lived a little over two years. She died of polio and she suffered. She had a slight fever for a couple of days, but it didn't seem like anything and we just kept her in bed. And we would certainly have called the doctor, but the fever dropped, she seemed to be all right. So we thought it had just been a cold. Then, one day, she was up, playing, Isabel was in the kitchen fixing lunch for the two boys when they'd come in from school, and she heard Grace fall down in the living room. When you have a lot of children you don't always start running when one of them falls, unless they start screaming or something. And, this time, Grace was quiet. Yet, Isabel says that when she heard that *thump* and then that silence, something happened in her to make her afraid. And she ran to the living room and there was little Grace on the floor, all twisted up, and the reason she hadn't screamed was that she couldn't get her breath. And when she did scream, it was the worst sound, Isabel says, that she'd ever heard in all her life, and she still hears it sometimes in her dreams. Isabel will sometimes wake me up with a low, moaning, strangled sound and I have to be quick to awaken her and hold her to me and where Isabel is weeping against me seems a mortal wound.

I think I may have written Sonny the very day that little Grace was buried. I was sitting in the living room in the dark, by myself, and I suddenly thought of Sonny. My trouble made his real.

One Saturday afternoon, when Sonny had been living with us, or, anyway, been in our house, for nearly two weeks, I found myself wandering aimlessly about the living room, drinking from a can of beer, and trying to work up the courage to search Sonny's room. He was out, he was usually out whenever I was home, and Isabel had taken the children to see their grandparents. Suddenly I was standing still in front of the living room window, watching Seventh Avenue. The idea of searching Sonny's room made me still. I scarcely dared to admit to myself what I'd be searching for. I didn't know what I'd do if I found it. Or if I didn't.

On the sidewalk across from me, near the entrance to a barbecue joint, some people were holding an old-fashioned revival meeting. The barbecue cook, wearing a dirty white apron, his conked hair° reddish and metallic in the pale sun, and a cigarette between his lips, stood in the doorway, watching them. Kids and older people paused in their errands and stood there, along with some older men and a couple of very tough-looking women who watched everything that happened on the avenue, as though they owned it, or were maybe owned by it. Well, they were watching this, too. The revival was being carried on by three sisters in black, and a brother. All they had were their voices and their Bibles and a tambourine. The brother was testifying and while he testified two of the sisters stood together, seeming to say, amen, and the third sister walked around with the tambourine outstretched and a couple of people dropped coins into it. Then the brother's testimony ended and the sister who had been taking up the collection dumped the coins into her palm and transferred them to the pocket of her long black robe. Then she raised both hands, striking the tambourine against the air, and then against one hand, and she started to sing. And the two other sisters and the brother joined in.

It was strange, suddenly, to watch, though I had been seeing these street meetings all my life. So, of course, had everybody else down there. Yet, they

conked hair: African-American straightened hair.

175

paused and watched and listened and I stood still at the window. "*Tis the old ship of Zion,*" they sang, and the sister with the tambourine kept a steady, jangling beat, "*it has rescued many a thousand!*" Not a soul under the sound of their voices was hearing this song for the first time, not one of them had been rescued. Nor had they seen much in the way of rescue work being done around them. Neither did they especially believe in the holiness of the three sisters and the brother, they knew too much about them, knew where they lived, and how. The woman with the tambourine, whose voice dominated the air, whose face was bright with joy, was divided by very little from the woman who stood watching her, a cigarette between her heavy, chapped lips, her hair a cuckoo's nest, her face scarred and swollen from many beatings, and her black eyes glittering like coal. Perhaps they both knew this, which was why, when, as rarely, they addressed each other, they addressed each other as Sister. As the singing filled the air the watching, listening faces underwent a change, the eyes focusing on something within; the music seemed to soothe a poison out of them; and time seemed, nearly, to fall away from the sullen, belligerent, battered faces, as though they were fleeing back to their first condition, while dreaming of their last. The barbecue cook half shook his head and smiled, and dropped his cigarette and disappeared into his joint. A man fumbled in his pockets for change and stood holding it in his hand impatiently, as though he had just remembered a pressing appointment further up the avenue. He looked furious. Then I saw Sonny, standing on the edge of the crowd. He was carrying a wide, flat notebook with a green cover, and it made him look, from where I was standing, almost like a schoolboy. The coppery sun brought out the copper in his skin, he was very faintly smiling, standing very still. Then the singing stopped, the tambourine turned into a collection plate again. The furious man dropped in his coins and vanished, so did a couple of the women, and Sonny dropped some change in the plate, looking directly at the woman with a little smile. He started across the avenue, toward the house. He has a slow, loping walk, something like the way Harlem hipsters walk, only he's imposed on this his own half-beat. I had never really noticed it before.

I stayed at the window, both relieved and apprehensive. As Sonny disappeared from my sight, they began singing again. And they were still singing when his key turned in the lock.

"Hey," he said.

"Hey, yourself. You want some beer?"   180

"No. Well, maybe." But he came up to the window and stood beside me, looking out. "What a warm voice," he said.

They were singing *If I could only hear my mother pray again!*

"Yes," I said, "and she can sure beat that tambourine."

"But what a terrible song," he said, and laughed. He dropped his notebook on the sofa and disappeared into the kitchen. "Where's Isabel and the kids?"

"I think they went to see their grandparents. You hungry?"   185

"No." He came back into the living room with his can of beer. "You want to come some place with me tonight?"

I sensed, I don't know how, that I couldn't possibly say no. "Sure. Where?"

He sat down on the sofa and picked up his notebook and started leafing through it. "I'm going to sit in with some fellows in a joint in the Village."

"You mean, you're going to play, tonight?"

"That's right." He took a swallow of his beer and moved back to the win- 190
dow. He gave me a sidelong look. "If you can stand it."

"I'll try," I said.

He smiled to himself and we both watched as the meeting across the way broke up. The three sisters and the brother, heads bowed, were singing *God be with you till we meet again.* The faces around them were very quiet. Then the song ended. The small crowd dispersed. We watched the three women and the lone man walk slowly up the avenue.

"When she was singing before," said Sonny, abruptly, "her voice reminded me for a minute of what heroin feels like sometimes — when it's in your veins. It makes you feel sort of warm and cool at the same time. And distant. And — and sure." He sipped his beer, very deliberately not looking at me. I watched his face. "It makes you feel — in control. Sometimes you've got to have that feeling."

"Do you?" I sat down slowly in the easy chair.

"Sometimes." He went to the sofa and picked up his notebook again. "Some 195
people do."

"In order," I asked, "to play?" And my voice was very ugly, full of contempt and anger.

"Well" — he looked at me with great, troubled eyes, as though, in fact, he hoped his eyes would tell me things he could never otherwise say — "they *think* so. And *if* they think so — !"

"And what do *you* think?" I asked.

He sat on the sofa and put his can of beer on the floor. "I don't know," he said, and I couldn't be sure if he were answering my question or pursuing his thoughts. His face didn't tell me. "It's not so much to *play.* It's to *stand* it, to be able to make it at all. On any level." He frowned and smiled: "In order to keep from shaking to pieces."

"But these friends of yours," I said, "they seem to shake themselves to 200
pieces pretty goddamn fast."

"Maybe." He played with the notebook. And something told me that I should curb my tongue, that Sonny was doing his best to talk, that I should listen. "But of course you only know the ones that've gone to pieces. Some don't — or at least they haven't *yet* and that's just about all *any* of us can say." He paused. "And then there are some who just live, really, in hell, and they know it and they see what's happening and they go right on. I don't know." He sighed, dropped the notebook, folded his arms. "Some guys, you can tell from the way they play, they on something *all* the time. And you can see that, well, it makes something real for them. But of course," he picked up his beer from the floor and sipped it and put the can down again, "they *want* to, too, you've got to see that. Even some of them that say they don't — *some,* not all."

"And what about you?" I asked — I couldn't help it. "What about you? Do *you* want to?"

He stood up and walked to the window and remained silent for a long time. Then he sighed. "Me," he said. Then: "While I was downstairs before, on my way here, listening to that woman sing, it struck me all of a sudden how much suffering she must have had to go through — to sing like that. It's *repulsive* to think you have to suffer that much."

I said: "But there's no way not to suffer — is there, Sonny?"

"I believe not," he said and smiled, "but that's never stopped anyone from   205
trying." He looked at me. "Has it?" I realized, with this mocking look, that there stood between us, forever, beyond the power of time or forgiveness, the fact that I had held silence — so long! — when he had needed human speech to help him. He turned back to the window. "No, there's no way not to suffer. But you try all kinds of ways to keep from drowning in it, to keep on top of it, and to make it seem — well, like *you*. Like you did something, all right, and now you're suffering for it. You know?" I said nothing. "Well you know," he said, impatiently, "why *do* people suffer? Maybe it's better to do something to give it a reason, *any* reason."

"But we just agreed," I said, "that there's no way not to suffer. Isn't it better, then, just to — take it?"

"But nobody just takes it," Sonny cried, "that's what I'm telling you! *Everybody* tries not to. You're just hung up on the *way* some people try — it's not *your* way!"

The hair on my face began to itch, my face felt wet. "That's not true," I said, "that's not true. I don't give a damn what other people do, I don't even care how they suffer." And he looked at me. "Please believe me," I said, "I don't want to see you — die — trying not to suffer."

"I won't," he said, flatly, "die trying not to suffer. At least, not any faster than anybody else."

"But there's no need," I said, trying to laugh, "is there? in killing yourself."   210

I wanted to say more, but I couldn't. I wanted to talk about will power and how life could be — well, beautiful. I wanted to say that it was all within; but was it? or, rather, wasn't that exactly the trouble? And I wanted to promise that I would never fail him again. But it would all have sounded — empty words and lies.

So I made the promise to myself and prayed that I would keep it.

"It's terrible sometimes, inside," he said, "that's what's the trouble. You walk these streets, black and funky and cold, and there's not really a living ass to talk to, and there's nothing shaking, and there's no way of getting it out — that storm inside. You can't talk it and you can't make love with it, and when you finally try to get with it and play it, you realize *nobody's* listening. So *you've* got to listen. You got to find a way to listen."

And then he walked away from the window and sat on the sofa again, as though all the wind had suddenly been knocked out of him. "Sometimes you'll do *anything* to play, even cut your mother's throat." He laughed and looked at me. "Or your brother's." Then he sobered. "Or your own." Then: "Don't worry. I'm all right now and I think I'll *be* all right. But I can't forget — where I've been. I don't mean just the physical place I've been, I mean where I've *been*. And *what* I've been."

"What have you been, Sonny?" I asked.   215

He smiled—but sat sideways on the sofa, his elbow resting on the back, his fingers playing with his mouth and chin, not looking at me. "I've been something I didn't recognize, didn't know I could be. Didn't know anybody could be." He stopped, looking inward, looking helplessly young, looking old. "I'm not talking about it now because I feel *guilty* or anything like that—maybe it would be better if I did, I don't know. Anyway, I can't really talk about it. Not to you, not to anybody," and now he turned and faced me. "Sometimes, you know, and it was actually when I was most *out* of the world, I felt that I was in it, that I was *with* it, really, and I could play or I didn't really have to *play*, it just came out of me, it was there. And I don't know how I played, thinking about it now, but I know I did awful things, those times, sometimes, to people. Or it wasn't that I *did* anything to them—it was that they weren't real." He picked up the beer can; it was empty; he rolled it between his palms: "And other times—well, I needed a fix, I needed to find a place to lean, I needed to clear a space to *listen*—and I couldn't find it, and I—went crazy, I did terrible things to *me*, I was terrible *for* me." He began pressing the beer can between his hands, I watched the metal begin to give. It glittered, as he played with it, like a knife, and I was afraid he would cut himself, but I said nothing. "Oh well. I can never tell you. I was all by myself at the bottom of something, stinking and sweating and crying and shaking, and I smelled it, you know? *my* stink, and I thought I'd die if I couldn't get away from it and yet, all the same, I knew that everything I was doing was just locking me in with it. And I didn't know," he paused, still flattening the beer can, "I didn't know, I still *don't* know, something kept telling me that maybe it was good to smell your own stink, but I didn't think that *that* was what I'd been trying to do—and—who can stand it?" and he abruptly dropped the ruined beer can, looking at me with a small, still smile, and then rose, walking to the window as though it were the lodestone rock. I watched his face, he watched the avenue. "I couldn't tell you when Mama died—but the reason I wanted to leave Harlem so bad was to get away from drugs. And then, when I ran away, that's what I was running from—really. When I came back, nothing had changed, I hadn't changed, I was just—older." And he stopped, drumming with his fingers on the windowpane. The sun had vanished, soon darkness would fall. I watched his face. "It can come again," he said, almost as though speaking to himself. Then he turned to me. "It can come again," he repeated. "I just want you to know that."

"All right," I said, at last. "So it can come again. All right."

He smiled, but the smile was sorrowful. "I had to try to tell you," he said.

"Yes," I said. "I understand that."

"You're my brother," he said, looking straight at me, and not smiling at all.   220

"Yes," I repeated, "yes. I understand that."

He turned back to the window, looking out. "All that hatred down there," he said, "all that hatred and misery and love. It's a wonder it doesn't blow the avenue apart."

We went to the only nightclub on a short, dark street, downtown. We squeezed through the narrow, chattering, jam-packed bar to the entrance of the big room, where the bandstand was. And we stood there for a moment, for the lights were very dim in this room and we couldn't see. Then, "Hello, boy," said a voice and an enormous black man, much older than Sonny or myself, erupted out of all that atmospheric lighting and put an arm around Sonny's shoulder. "I been sitting right here," he said, "waiting for you."

He had a big voice, too, and heads in the darkness turned toward us.

Sonny grinned and pulled a little away, and said, "Creole, this is my brother.   225
I told you about him."

Creole shook my hand. "I'm glad to meet you, son," he said, and it was clear that he was glad to meet me *there*, for Sonny's sake. And he smiled, "You got a real musician in *your* family," and he took his arm from Sonny's shoulder and slapped him, lightly, affectionately, with the back of his hand.

"Well. Now I've heard it all," said a voice behind us. This was another musician, and a friend of Sonny's, a coal-black, cheerful-looking man, built close to the ground. He immediately began confiding to me, at the top of his lungs, the most terrible things about Sonny, his teeth gleaming like a lighthouse and his laugh coming up out of him like the beginning of an earthquake. And it turned out that everyone at the bar knew Sonny, or almost everyone; some were musicians, working there, or nearby, or not working, some were simply hangers-on, and some were there to hear Sonny play. I was introduced to all of them and they were all very polite to me. Yet, it was clear that, for them, I was only Sonny's brother. Here, I was in Sonny's world. Or, rather: his kingdom. Here, it was not even a question that his veins bore royal blood.

They were going to play soon and Creole installed me, by myself, at a table in a dark corner. Then I watched them, Creole, and the little black man, and Sonny, and the others, while they horsed around, standing just below the bandstand. The light from the bandstand spilled just a little short of them and, watching them laughing and gesturing and moving about, I had the feeling that they, nevertheless, were being most careful not to step into that circle of light too suddenly: that if they moved into the light too suddenly, without thinking, they would perish in flame. Then, while I watched, one of them, the small, black man, moved into the light and crossed the bandstand and started fooling around with his drums. Then — being funny and being, also, extremely ceremonious — Creole took Sonny by the arm and led him to the piano. A woman's voice called Sonny's name and a few hands started clapping. And Sonny, also being funny and being ceremonious, and so touched, I think, that he could have cried, but neither hiding it nor showing it, riding it like a man, grinned, and put both hands to his heart and bowed from the waist.

Creole then went to the bass fiddle and a lean, very bright-skinned brown man jumped up on the bandstand and picked up his horn. So there they were, and the atmosphere on the bandstand and in the room began to change and tighten. Someone stepped up to the microphone and announced them. Then there were all kinds of murmurs. Some people at the bar shushed others. The waitress ran around, frantically getting in the last orders, guys and chicks got closer to each other, and the lights on the bandstand, on the quartet, turned to a kind of indigo. Then they all looked different there. Creole looked about him for the last time, as though he were making certain that all his chickens were in the coop, and then he — jumped and struck the fiddle. And there they were.

All I know about music is that not many people ever really hear it. And even then, on the rare occasions when something opens within, and the music enters, what we mainly hear, or hear corroborated, are personal, private, vanishing evocations. But the man who creates the music is hearing something else, is dealing with the roar rising from the void and imposing order on it as it hits the air. What is evoked in him, then, is of another order, more terrible because it has no words, and triumphant, too, for that same reason. And his triumph, when he triumphs, is ours. I just watched Sonny's face. His face was troubled, he was working hard, but he wasn't with it. And I had the feeling that, in a way, everyone on the bandstand was waiting for him, both waiting for him and pushing him along. But as I began to watch Creole, I realized that it was Creole who held them all back. He had them on a short rein. Up there, keeping the beat with his whole body, wailing on the fiddle, with his eyes half closed, he was listening to everything, but he was listening to Sonny. He was having a dialogue with Sonny. He wanted Sonny to leave the shoreline and strike out for the deep water. He was Sonny's witness that deep water and drowning were not the same thing — he had been there, and he knew. And he wanted Sonny to know. He was waiting for Sonny to do the things on the keys which would let Creole know that Sonny was in the water.

And, while Creole listened, Sonny moved, deep within, exactly like someone in torment. I had never before thought of how awful the relationship must be between the musician and his instrument. He has to fill it, this instrument, with the breath of life, his own. He has to make it do what he wants it to do. And a piano is just a piano. It's made out of so much wood and wires and little hammers and big ones, and ivory. While there's only so much you can do with it, the only way to find this out is to try; to try and make it do everything.

And Sonny hadn't been near a piano for over a year. And he wasn't on much better terms with his life, not the life that stretched before him now. He and the piano stammered, started one way, got scared, stopped; started another way, panicked, marked time, started again; then seemed to have found a direction, panicked again, got stuck. And the face I saw on Sonny I'd never seen before. Everything had been burned out of it, and, at the same time, things usually hidden were being burned in, by the fire and fury of the battle which was occurring in him up there.

Yet, watching Creole's face as they neared the end of the first set, I had the feeling that something had happened, something I hadn't heard. Then they finished, there was scattered applause, and then, without an instant's warning, Creole started into something else, it was almost sardonic, it was *Am I Blue*. And, as though he commanded, Sonny began to play. Something began to happen. And Creole let out the reins. The dry, low, black man said something awful on the drums, Creole answered, and the drums talked back. Then the horn insisted, sweet and high, slightly detached perhaps, and Creole listened, commenting now and then, dry, and driving, beautiful and calm and old. Then they all came together again, and Sonny was part of the family again. I could tell

230

this from his face. He seemed to have found, right there beneath his fingers, a damn brand-new piano. It seemed that he couldn't get over it. Then, for awhile, just being happy with Sonny, they seemed to be agreeing with him that brand-new pianos certainly were a gas.

Then Creole stepped forward to remind them that what they were playing was the blues. He hit something in all of them, he hit something in me, myself, and the music tightened and deepened, apprehension began to beat the air. Creole began to tell us what the blues were all about. They were not about anything very new. He and his boys up there were keeping it new, at the risk of ruin, destruction, madness, and death, in order to find new ways to make us listen. For, while the tale of how we suffer, and how we are delighted, and how we may triumph is never new, it always must be heard. There isn't any other tale to tell, it's the only light we've got in all this darkness.

And this tale, according to that face, that body, those strong hands on   235
those strings, has another aspect in every country, and a new depth in every generation. Listen, Creole seemed to be saying, listen. Now these are Sonny's blues. He made the little black man on the drums know it, and the bright, brown man on the horn. Creole wasn't trying any longer to get Sonny in the water. He was wishing him Godspeed. Then he stepped back, very slowly, filling the air with the immense suggestion that Sonny speak for himself.

Then they all gathered around Sonny and Sonny played. Every now and again one of them seemed to say, amen. Sonny's fingers filled the air with life, his life. But that life contained so many others. And Sonny went all the way back, he really began with the spare, flat statement of the opening phrase of the song. Then he began to make it his. It was very beautiful because it wasn't hurried and it was no longer a lament. I seemed to hear with what burning he had made it his, with what burning we had yet to make it ours, how we could cease lamenting. Freedom lurked around us and I understood, at last, that he could help us to be free if we would listen, that he would never be free until we did. Yet, there was no battle in his face now. I heard what he had gone through, and would continue to go through until he came to rest in earth. He had made it his: that long line, of which we knew only Mama and Daddy. And he was giving it back, as everything must be given back, so that, passing through death, it can live forever. I saw my mother's face again, and felt, for the first time, how the stones of the road she had walked on must have bruised her feet. I saw the moonlit road where my father's brother died. And it brought something else back to me, and carried me past it. I saw my little girl again and felt Isabel's tears again, and I felt my own tears begin to rise. And I was yet aware that this was only a moment, that the world waited outside, as hungry as a tiger, and that trouble stretched above us, longer than the sky.

Then it was over. Creole and Sonny let out their breath, both soaking wet, and grinning. There was a lot of applause and some of it was real. In the dark, the girl came by and I asked her to take drinks to the bandstand. There was a long pause, while they talked up there in the indigo light and after awhile I saw the girl put a Scotch and milk on top of the piano for Sonny. He didn't seem to notice it, but just before they started playing again, he sipped from it and looked toward me, and nodded. Then he put it back on top of the piano. For me, then, as they began to play again, it glowed and shook above my brother's head like the very cup of trembling.   *[1957]*

☰ THINKING ABOUT THE TEXT

1. Were you sympathetic to the older brother in the beginning of the story? Did this become more so or less so as the story progressed? Is Sonny a sympathetic character in the beginning? At the end?

2. In real life, what do you believe is the role of an older brother? Do you have a responsibility to the members of your family regardless of their behavior? Explain. What is Sonny's mother's view of this?

3. Baldwin refers to the "darkness outside" several times. What do you think this means for Sonny? For Sonny's mother and father? For the older brother?

4. Listening seems to play an important function for Sonny and his brother. Cite specific examples of how they do or do not listen to each other. What might be some definitions of "listening" in this context?

5. One might think that brothers would understand each other better than outsiders do. But is that the case here? In your experience? In other stories or movies? How might you account for this difficulty?

☰ MAKING COMPARISONS

1. The older brothers in "The Rich Brother" and "Sonny's Blues" struggle to understand their younger brothers. Which one seems more successful at understanding his younger brother? Why?

2. Both younger brothers in these two stories seem to march to different drummers. How would you describe their variations from the norm?

3. Some critics claim that these two stories are about responsibility; others claim they are about tolerance; still others see sibling rivalry, blind faith, or ego as the focus. What do you think, and why?

☰ WRITING ABOUT ISSUES

1. Baldwin shows us the letter Sonny writes to his older brother, but we do not see any of the older brother's letters to Sonny. Based on the older brother's insights about Sonny in the closing scene, write a letter to Sonny from the older brother's point of view, explaining the substance of his new understanding of Sonny's life and music.

2. Write an essay that compares the relationship between Pete and Donald to the one between Sonny and his brother. Be sure to comment on similarities and differences.

3. Write a personal essay based on a conflict you had with a sibling, explaining how the relationship evolved. Use at least two specific incidents, and describe how they fit into a larger pattern.

4. Do some library research on birth order as it affects sibling rivalry, especially between brothers. Write a report comparing your findings to the relationships depicted in these two stories.

TENNESSEE WILLIAMS, *The Glass Menagerie*

CHRISTOPHER DURANG, *For Whom the Southern Belle Tolls*

Tennessee Williams's play — performed in high schools, in colleges, and on professional stages for more than sixty years — is one of the most admired dramas in American literature. *The Glass Menagerie* is based on Williams's own life, especially the time he spent working at a shoe factory. Set in a dingy apartment in a poor section of St. Louis, Missouri, the story focuses on Tom and his relationships with his sister, Laura, who walks with a slight limp, and his mother, Amanda, whose illusions about her children are thwarted by their own desires and limitations.

Williams's own sister, Rose, suffered from a variety of mental disorders. His mother's decision to have doctors perform a lobotomy on her and his decision to leave home to pursue a career as a writer inspired the central conflict in his play and haunted Williams throughout his life.

When a play is as famous as *The Glass Menagerie*, it is often imitated and sometimes parodied. In *For Whom the Southern Belle Tolls*, Christopher Durang's humor is rarely subtle and often frivolous, even slapstick. Durang is clearly having fun with Williams's masterpiece when he makes Laura, one of the most fragile characters in American literature, into a self-absorbed, unimaginative male hypochondriac. If Williams's moving play touches on such serious ideas as familial responsibility, innocence, loss, and the inescapable sadness of life, Durang's parody often delights audiences with broad humor and stand-up comic routines. Durang's play is serious fun.

■ BEFORE YOU READ

Should your first loyalty be to yourself or to your family? What if you were expected to quit college and work in a factory to help support your mother and homebound sibling. Would you do it? Why?

TENNESSEE WILLIAMS
The Glass Menagerie

Thomas Lanier "Tennessee" Williams (1911–1983) wrote some of the most famous plays of the American stage, which took a frank look at adultery, mental illness, homosexuality, and incest. The Glass Menagerie *(1945),* A Streetcar Named Desire *(1948),* Cat on a Hot Tin Roof *(1955),* Suddenly Last Summer *(1958), and* The Night of the Iguana *(1961) were considered shocking when they were first staged but eventually were made into popular and acclaimed films. After a childhood that was "lonely and miserable" largely because of his domineering, alcoholic father*

© Bettmann/Corbis

and because of the taunts he endured for being small, sickly, and bookish, he gradu-
ated from the University of Iowa in 1939 and immediately began writing fiction and
drama. With The Glass Menagerie, *Williams won the first of his four New York*
Drama Critics' Circle Awards for the best play of the season. He received the first of
two Pulitzer Prizes in 1948 for A Streetcar Named Desire. *Williams struggled with*
depression most of his life. Addicted to prescription drugs and alcohol, he choked to
death on a bottle cap at his New York City apartment at the Hotel Elysee.

nobody, not even the rain, has such small hands
— e. e. cummings

LIST OF CHARACTERS

AMANDA WINGFIELD, *the mother. A little woman of great but confused vitality clinging*
frantically to another time and place. Her characterization must be carefully created,
not copied from type. She is not paranoiac, but her life is paranoia. There is much to
admire in Amanda, and as much to love and pity as there is to laugh at. Certainly she

has endurance and a kind of heroism, and though her foolishness makes her unwittingly cruel at times, there is tenderness in her slight person.

LAURA WINGFIELD, *her daughter. Amanda, having failed to establish contact with reality, continues to live vitally in her illusions, but Laura's situation is even graver. A childhood illness has left her crippled, one leg slightly shorter than the other, and held in a brace. This defect need not be more than suggested on the stage. Stemming from this, Laura's separation increases till she is like a piece of her own glass collection, too exquisitely fragile to move from the shelf.*

TOM WINGFIELD, *her son. And the narrator of the play. A poet with a job in a warehouse. His nature is not remorseless, but to escape from a trap he has to act without pity.*

JIM O'CONNOR, *the gentleman caller. A nice, ordinary, young man.*

SCENE: *An alley in St. Louis.*
PART I: *Preparation for a Gentleman Caller.*
PART II: *The Gentleman Calls.*
TIME: *Now and the Past.*

Scene 1

The Wingfield apartment is in the rear of the building, one of those vast hivelike conglomerations of cellular living-units that flower as warty growths in overcrowded urban centers of lower middle-class population and are symptomatic of the impulse of this largest and fundamentally enslaved section of American society to avoid fluidity and differentiation and to exist and function as one interfused mass of automatism.

The apartment faces an alley and is entered by a fire-escape, a structure whose name is a touch of accidental poetic truth, for all of these huge buildings are always burning with the slow and implacable fires of human desperation. The fire-escape is included in the set — that is, the landing of it and steps descending from it.

The scene is memory and is therefore nonrealistic. Memory takes a lot of poetic license. It omits some details; others are exaggerated, according to the emotional value of the articles it touches, for memory is seated predominantly in the heart. The interior is therefore rather dim and poetic.

At the rise of the curtain, the audience is faced with the dark, grim rear wall of the Wingfield tenement. This building, which runs parallel to the footlights, is flanked on both sides by dark, narrow alleys which run into murky canyons of tangled clotheslines, garbage cans, and the sinister latticework of neighboring fire-escapes. It is up and down these side alleys that exterior entrances and exits are made, during the play. At the end of Tom's opening commentary, the dark tenement wall slowly reveals (by means of a transparency) the interior of the ground floor Wingfield apartment.

Downstage is the living room, which also serves as a sleeping room for Laura, the sofa unfolding to make her bed. Upstage, center, and divided by a wide arch or second proscenium with transparent faded portieres (or second curtain), is the dining room. In an old-fashioned what-not in the living room are seen scores of transparent glass animals. A blown-up photograph of the father hangs on the wall of the living room, facing the audience, to the left of the archway. It is the face of a very handsome young man in a doughboy's First World War cap. He is gallantly smiling, ineluctably smiling, as if to say, "I will be smiling forever."

The audience hears and sees the opening scene in the dining room through both the transparent fourth wall of the building and the transparent gauze portieres of the dining-room arch. It is during this revealing scene that the fourth wall slowly ascends, out of sight. This transparent exterior wall is not brought down again until the very end of the play, during Tom's final speech.

The narrator is an undisguised convention of the play. He takes whatever license with dramatic convention as is convenient to his purposes.

Tom enters dressed as a merchant sailor from alley, stage left, and strolls across the front of the stage to the fire-escape. There he stops and lights a cigarette. He addresses the audience.

TOM: Yes, I have tricks in my pocket, I have things up my sleeve. But I am the opposite of a stage magician. He gives you illusion that has the appearance of truth. I give you truth in the pleasant disguise of illusion. To begin with, I turn back time. I reverse it to that quaint period, the thirties, when the huge middle class of America was matriculating in a school for the blind. Their eyes had failed them, or they had failed their eyes, and so they were having their fingers pressed forcibly down on the fiery Braille alphabet of a dissolving economy. In Spain there was revolution. Here there was only shouting and confusion. In Spain there was Guernica.° Here there were disturbances of labor, sometimes pretty violent, in otherwise peaceful cities such as Chicago, Cleveland, Saint Louis. . . . This is the social background of the play.

(Music.)

The play is memory. Being a memory play, it is dimly lighted, it is sentimental, it is not realistic. In memory everything seems to happen to music. That explains the fiddle in the wings. I am the narrator of the play, and also a character in it. The other characters are my mother, Amanda, my sister, Laura, and a gentleman caller who appears in the final scenes. He is the most realistic character in the play, being an emissary from a world of reality that we were somehow set apart from. But since I have a poet's weakness for symbols, I am using this character also as a symbol; he is the long delayed but always expected something that we live for. There is a fifth character in the play who doesn't appear except in this larger-than-life photograph over the mantel. This is our father who left us a long time ago. He was a telephone man who fell in love with long distances; he gave up his job with the telephone company and skipped the light fantastic out of town. . . . The last we heard of him was a picture post-card from Mazatlán, on the Pacific coast of Mexico, containing a message of two words — "Hello — Good-bye!" and no address. I think the rest of the play will explain itself. . . .

Guernica: A town in northern Spain destroyed by German bombers in 1937 during the Spanish civil war.

Amanda's voice becomes audible through the portieres.

(Legend on screen: "Où sont les neiges."°)

> *He divides the portieres and enters the upstage area.*
> *Amanda and Laura are seated at a drop-leaf table. Eating is indicated by gestures without food or utensils. Amanda faces the audience.*
> *Tom and Laura are seated in profile.*
> *The interior has lit up softly and through the scrim we see Amanda and Laura seated at the table in the upstage area.*

AMANDA *(calling)*: Tom?

TOM: Yes, Mother.

AMANDA: We can't say grace until you come to the table!

TOM: Coming, Mother. *(He bows slightly and withdraws, reappearing a few moments later in his place at the table.)*

AMANDA *(to her son)*: Honey, don't *push* with your *fingers*. If you have to push with something, the thing to push with is a crust of bread. And chew — chew! Animals have sections in their stomachs which enable them to digest food without mastication, but human beings are supposed to chew their food before they swallow it down. Eat food leisurely, son, and really enjoy it. A well-cooked meal has lots of delicate flavors that have to be held in the mouth for appreciation. So chew your food and give your salivary glands a chance to function!

Tom deliberately lays his imaginary fork down and pushes his chair back from the table.

TOM: I haven't enjoyed one bite of this dinner because of your constant directions on how to eat it. It's you that makes me rush through meals with your hawklike attention to every bite I take. Sickening — spoils my appetite — all this discussion of animals' secretion — salivary glands — mastication!

AMANDA *(lightly)*: Temperament like a Metropolitan star! *(He rises and crosses downstage.)* You're not excused from the table.

TOM: I am getting a cigarette.

AMANDA: You smoke too much.

Laura rises.

LAURA: I'll bring in the blanc mange.

He remains standing with his cigarette by the portieres during the following.

AMANDA *(rising)*: No, sister, no, sister — you be the lady this time and I'll be the darky.

LAURA: I'm already up.

AMANDA: Resume your seat, little sister — I want you to stay fresh and pretty — for gentlemen callers!

LAURA: I'm not expecting any gentlemen callers.

"Où sont les neiges": Part of a line from a poem by the French medieval writer François Villon (1431–c. 1463); the full line translates, "Where are the snows of yesteryear?"

AMANDA *(crossing out to kitchenette. Airily):*   Sometimes they come when they are least expected! Why, I remember one Sunday afternoon in Blue Mountain — *(Enters kitchenette.)*

TOM: I know what's coming!

LAURA: Yes. But let her tell it.

TOM: Again?

LAURA: She loves to tell it.

Amanda returns with bowl of dessert.

AMANDA: One Sunday afternoon in Blue Mountain — your mother received — seventeen! — gentlemen callers! Why, sometimes there weren't chairs enough to accommodate them all. We had to send the nigger over to bring in folding chairs from the parish house.

TOM *(remaining at portieres):*   How did you entertain those gentlemen callers?

AMANDA: I understood the art of conversation!

TOM: I bet you could talk.

AMANDA: Girls in those days knew how to talk, I can tell you.

TOM: Yes?

(Image: Amanda as a girl on a porch greeting callers.)

AMANDA: They knew how to entertain their gentlemen callers. It wasn't enough for a girl to be possessed of a pretty face and a graceful figure — although I wasn't slighted in either respect. She also needed to have a nimble wit and a tongue to meet all occasions.

TOM: What did you talk about?

AMANDA: Things of importance going on in the world! Never anything coarse or common or vulgar. *(She addresses Tom as though he were seated in the vacant chair at the table though he remains by portieres. He plays this scene as though he held the book.)* My callers were gentlemen — all! Among my callers were some of the most prominent young planters of the Mississippi Delta — planters and sons of planters!

Tom motions for music and a spot of light on Amanda.
Her eyes lift, her face glows, her voice becomes rich and elegiac.
(Screen legend: "Où sont les neiges.")

There was young Champ Laughlin who later became vice-president of the Delta Planters Bank. Hadley Stevenson who was drowned in Moon Lake and left his widow one hundred and fifty thousand in Government bonds. There were the Cutrere brothers, Wesley and Bates. Bates was one of my bright particular beaux! He got in a quarrel with that wild Wainright boy. They shot it out on the floor of Moon Lake Casino. Bates was shot through the stomach. Died in the ambulance on his way to Memphis. His widow was also well-provided for, came into eight or ten thousand acres, that's all. She married him on the rebound — never loved her — carried my picture on him the night he died! And there was that boy that every girl in the Delta had set her cap for! That beautiful, brilliant young Fitzhugh boy from Green County!

TOM: What did he leave his widow?

AMANDA: He never married! Gracious, you talk as though all of my old admirers had turned up their toes to the daisies!

TOM: Isn't this the first you mentioned that still survives?

AMANDA: That Fitzhugh boy went North and made a fortune — came to be known as the Wolf of Wall Street! He had the Midas touch, whatever he touched turned to gold! And I could have been Mrs. Duncan J. Fitzhugh, mind you! But — I picked your *father!*

LAURA *(rising)*: Mother, let me clear the table.

AMANDA: No dear, you go in front and study your typewriter chart. Or practice your shorthand a little. Stay fresh and pretty! — It's almost time for our gentlemen callers to start arriving. *(She flounces girlishly toward the kitchenette.)* How many do you suppose we're going to entertain this afternoon?

Tom throws down the paper and jumps up with a groan.

LAURA *(alone in the dining room)*: I don't believe we're going to receive any, Mother.

AMANDA *(reappearing, airily)*: What? No one — not one? You must be joking! *(Laura nervously echoes her laugh. She slips in a fugitive manner through the half-open portieres and draws them gently behind her. A shaft of very clear light is thrown on her face against the faded tapestry of the curtains.) (Music: "The Glass Menagerie" under faintly.) (Lightly.)* Not one gentleman caller? It can't be true! There must be a flood, there must have been a tornado!

LAURA: It isn't a flood, it's not a tornado, Mother. I'm just not popular like you were in Blue Mountain. . . . *(Tom utters another groan. Laura glances at him with a faint, apologetic smile. Her voice catching a little.)* Mother's afraid I'm going to be an old maid.

(The scene dims out with "Glass Menagerie" music.)

Scene 2

"Laura, Haven't You Ever Liked Some Boy?"

On the dark stage the screen is lighted with the image of blue roses.

Gradually Laura's figure becomes apparent and the screen goes out.

The music subsides.

Laura is seated in the delicate ivory chair at the small clawfoot table.

She wears a dress of soft violet material for a kimono — her hair tied back from her forehead with a ribbon.

She is washing and polishing her collection of glass.

Amanda appears on the fire-escape steps. At the sound of her ascent, Laura catches her breath, thrusts the bowl of ornaments away, and seats herself stiffly before the diagram of the typewriter keyboard as though it held her spellbound. Something has happened to Amanda. It is written in her face as she climbs to the landing: a look that is grim and hopeless and a little absurd.

She has on one of those cheap or imitation velvety-looking cloth coats with imitation fur collar. Her hat is five or six years old, one of those dreadful cloche hats that were worn in the late twenties, and she is clasping an enormous black patent-leather pocketbook with nickel clasp and initials. This is her full-dress outfit, the one she usually wears to the D.A.R.°

Before entering she looks through the door.

She purses her lips, opens her eyes wide, rolls them upward, and shakes her head.

Then she slowly lets herself in the door. Seeing her mother's expression Laura touches her lips with a nervous gesture.

LAURA: Hello, Mother, I was — *(She makes a nervous gesture toward the chart on the wall. Amanda leans against the shut door and stares at Laura with a martyred look.)*

AMANDA: Deception? Deception? *(She slowly removes her hat and gloves, continuing the swift suffering stare. She lets the hat and gloves fall on the floor — a bit of acting.)*

LAURA *(shakily)*: How was the D.A.R. meeting? *(Amanda slowly opens her purse and removes a dainty white handkerchief, which she shakes out delicately and delicately touches to her lips and nostrils.)* Didn't you go to the D.A.R. meeting, Mother?

AMANDA *(faintly, almost inaudibly)*: — No. — No. *(Then more forcibly.)* I did not have the strength — to go to the D.A.R. In fact, I did not have the courage! I wanted to find a hole in the ground and hide myself in it forever! *(She crosses slowly to the wall and removes the diagram of the typewriter keyboard. She holds it in front of her for a second, staring at it sweetly and sorrowfully — then bites her lips and tears it in two pieces.)*

LAURA *(faintly)*: Why did you do that, Mother? *(Amanda repeats the same procedure with the chart of the Gregg Alphabet.°)* Why are you —

AMANDA: Why? Why? How old are you, Laura?

LAURA: Mother, you know my age.

AMANDA: I thought that you were an adult; it seems that I was mistaken. *(She crosses slowly to the sofa and sinks down and stares at Laura.)*

LAURA: Please don't stare at me, Mother.

Amanda closes her eyes and lowers her head. Count ten.

AMANDA: What are we going to do, what is going to become of us, what is the future?

Count ten.

LAURA: Has something happened, Mother? *(Amanda draws a long breath and takes out the handkerchief again. Dabbing process.)* Mother, has — something happened?

AMANDA: I'll be all right in a minute. I'm just bewildered — *(count five)* — by life. . . .

D.A.R.: Daughters of the American Revolution; members must document that they have ancestors who served the patriots' cause in the Revolutionary War. **Gregg Alphabet:** System of shorthand symbols invented by John Robert Gregg.

LAURA: Mother, I wish that you would tell me what's happened.

AMANDA: As you know, I was supposed to be inducted into my office at the D.A.R. this afternoon. *(Image: A swarm of typewriters.)* But I stopped off at Rubicam's Business College to speak to your teachers about your having a cold and ask them what progress they thought you were making down there.

LAURA: Oh. . . .

AMANDA: I went to the typing instructor and introduced myself as your mother. She didn't know who you were. Wingfield, she said. We don't have any such student enrolled at the school! I assured her she did, that you had been going to classes since early in January. "I wonder," she said, "if you could be talking about that terribly shy little girl who dropped out of school after only a few days' attendance?" "No," I said, "Laura, my daughter, has been going to school every day for the past six weeks!" "Excuse me," she said. She took the attendance book out and there was your name, unmistakably printed, and all the dates you were absent until they decided that you had dropped out of school. I still said, "No, there must have been some mistake! There must have been some mix-up in the records!" And she said, "No — I remember her perfectly now. Her hand shook so that she couldn't hit the right keys! The first time we gave a speed-test, she broke down completely — was sick at the stomach and almost had to be carried into the wash-room! After that morning she never showed up any more. We phoned the house but never got any answer" — while I was working at Famous and Barr, I suppose, demonstrating those — Oh! I felt so weak I could barely keep on my feet. I had to sit down while they got me a glass of water! Fifty dollars' tuition, all of our plans — my hopes and ambitions for you — just gone up the spout, just gone up the spout like that. *(Laura draws a long breath and gets awkwardly to her feet. She crosses to the Victrola, and winds it up.)* What are you doing?

LAURA: Oh! *(She releases the handle and returns to her seat.)*

AMANDA: Laura, where have you been going when you've gone out pretending that you were going to business college?

LAURA: I've just been going out walking.

AMANDA: That's not true.

LAURA: It is. I just went walking.

AMANDA: Walking? Walking? In winter? Deliberately courting pneumonia in that light coat? Where did you walk to, Laura?

LAURA: It was the lesser of two evils, Mother. *(Image: Winter scene in park.)* I couldn't go back up. I — threw up — on the floor!

AMANDA: From half past seven till after five every day you mean to tell me you walked around in the park, because you wanted to make me think that you were still going to Rubicam's Business College?

LAURA: It wasn't as bad as it sounds. I went inside places to get warmed up.

AMANDA: Inside where?

LAURA: I went in the art museum and the bird-houses at the Zoo. I visited the penguins every day! Sometimes I did without lunch and went to the movies. Lately I've been spending most of my afternoons in the Jewel-box, that big glass house where they raise the tropical flowers.

AMANDA: You did all this to deceive me, just for the deception? *(Laura looks down.)* Why?

LAURA: Mother, when you're disappointed, you get that awful suffering look on your face, like the picture of Jesus' mother in the museum!

AMANDA: Hush!

LAURA: I couldn't face it.

Pause. A whisper of strings.
   (Legend: "The Crust of Humility.")

AMANDA *(hopelessly fingering the huge pocketbook)*:   So what are we going to do the rest of our lives? Stay home and watch the parades go by? Amuse ourselves with the glass menagerie, darling? Eternally play those worn-out phonograph records your father left as a painful reminder of him? We won't have a business career — we've given that up because it gave us nervous indigestion! *(Laughs wearily.)* What is there left but dependency all our lives? I know so well what becomes of unmarried women who aren't prepared to occupy a position. I've seen such pitiful cases in the South — barely tolerated spinsters living upon the grudging patronage of sister's husband or brother's wife! — stuck away in some little mousetrap of a room — encouraged by one in-law to visit another — little birdlike women without any nest — eating the crust of humility all their life! Is that the future that we've mapped out for ourselves? I swear it's the only alternative I can think of! It isn't a very pleasant alternative, is it? Of course — some girls *do marry. (Laura twists her hands nervously.)* Haven't you ever liked some boy?

LAURA: Yes. I liked one once. *(Rises.)* I came across his picture a while ago.

AMANDA *(with some interest)*:   He gave you his picture?

LAURA: No, it's in the year-book.

AMANDA *(disappointed)*:   Oh — a high-school boy.

(Screen image: Jim as a high-school hero bearing a silver cup.)

LAURA: Yes. His name was Jim. *(Laura lifts the heavy annual from the clawfoot table.)* Here he is in *The Pirates of Penzance.*

AMANDA *(absently)*:   The what?

LAURA: The operetta the senior class put on. He had a wonderful voice and we sat across the aisle from each other Mondays, Wednesdays, and Fridays in the Aud. Here he is with the silver cup for debating! See his grin?

AMANDA *(absently)*:   He must have had a jolly disposition.

LAURA: He used to call me — Blue Roses.

(Image: Blue roses.)

AMANDA: Why did he call you such a name as that?

LAURA: When I had that attack of pleurosis° — he asked me what was the matter when I came back. I said pleurosis — he thought that I said Blue

---

pleurosis: Also called pleurisy. A lung disease like pneumonia.

Roses! So that's what he always called me after that. Whenever he saw me, he'd holler, "Hello, Blue Roses!" I didn't care for the girl that he went out with. Emily Meisenbach. Emily was the best-dressed girl at Soldan. She never struck me, though, as being sincere. . . . It says in the Personal Section — they're engaged. That's — six years ago! They must be married by now.

AMANDA: Girls that aren't cut out for business careers usually wind up married to some nice man. *(Gets up with a spark of revival.)* Sister, that's what you'll do!

Laura utters a startled, doubtful laugh. She reaches quickly for a piece of glass.

LAURA: But, Mother —

AMANDA: Yes? *(Crossing to photograph.)*

LAURA *(in a tone of frightened apology)*:   I'm — crippled!

(Image: Screen.)

AMANDA: Nonsense! Laura, I've told you never, never to use that word. Why, you're not crippled, you just have a little defect — hardly noticeable, even! When people have some slight disadvantage like that, they cultivate other things to make up for it — develop charm — and vivacity — and — *charm*! That's all you have to do! *(She turns again to the photograph.)* One thing your father had *plenty of* — was *charm*!

Tom motions to the fiddle in the wings.
  (The scene fades out with music.)

Scene 3

(Legend on the screen: "After the Fiasco—")
  Tom speaks from the fire-escape landing.

TOM: After the fiasco at Rubicam's Business College, the idea of getting a gentleman caller for Laura began to play a more important part in Mother's calculations. It became an obsession. Like some archetype of the universal unconscious, the image of the gentleman caller haunted our small apartment. . . . *(Image: Young man at door with flowers.)* An evening at home rarely passed without some allusion to this image, this specter, this hope. . . . Even when he wasn't mentioned, his presence hung in Mother's preoccupied look and in my sister's frightened, apologetic manner — hung like a sentence passed upon the Wingfields! Mother was a woman of action as well as words. She began to take logical steps in the planned direction. Late that winter and in the early spring — realizing that extra money would be needed to properly feather the nest and plume the bird — she conducted a vigorous campaign on the telephone, roping in subscribers to one of those magazines for matrons called *The Home-maker's Companion*, the type of journal that features the serialized sublimations of ladies of letters who think in terms of delicate cuplike breasts, slim, tapering waists, rich, creamy thighs, eyes like wood-smoke in autumn, fingers that soothe and caress like strains of music, bodies as powerful as Etruscan sculpture.

(Screen image: Glamour *magazine cover.)*

Amanda enters with phone on long extension cord. She is spotted in the dim stage.

AMANDA: Ida Scott? This is Amanda Wingfield! We *missed* you at the D.A.R. last Monday! I said to myself: She's probably suffering with that sinus condition! How is that sinus condition? Horrors! Heaven have mercy! — You're a Christian martyr, yes, that's what you are, a Christian martyr! Well, I just now happened to notice that your subscription to the *Companion*'s about to expire! Yes, it expires with the next issue, honey! — just when that wonderful new serial by Bessie Mae Hopper is getting off to such an exciting start. Oh, honey, it's something that you can't miss! You remember how *Gone with the Wind* took everybody by storm? You simply couldn't go out if you hadn't read it. All everybody *talked* was Scarlett O'Hara. Well, this is a book that critics already compare to *Gone with the Wind.* It's the *Gone with the Wind* of the post–World War generation! — What? — Burning? — Oh, honey, don't let them burn, go take a look in the oven and I'll hold the wire! Heavens — I think she's hung up!

(Dim out.)

(Legend on screen: "You think I'm in love with Continental Shoemakers?")

Before the stage is lighted, the violent voices of Tom and Amanda are heard. They are quarreling behind the portieres. In front of them stands Laura with clenched hands and panicky expression.

A clear pool of light on her figure throughout this scene.

TOM: What in Christ's name am I —

AMANDA *(shrilly)*:   Don't you use that —

TOM: Supposed to do!

AMANDA: Expression! Not in my —

TOM: Ohhh!

AMANDA: Presence! Have you gone out of your senses?

TOM: I have, that's true, been *driven* out!

AMANDA: What is the matter with you, you — big — big — IDIOT!

TOM: Look — I've got *no thing,* no single thing —

AMANDA: Lower your voice!

TOM: In my life here that I can call my own! Everything is —

AMANDA: Stop that shouting!

TOM: Yesterday you confiscated my books! You had the nerve to —

AMANDA: I took that horrible novel back to the library — yes! That hideous book by that insane Mr. Lawrence.° *(Tom laughs wildly.)* I cannot control the output of diseased minds or people who cater to them — *(Tom laughs*

Mr. Lawrence: D. H. Lawrence (1885–1930), English poet and novelist who advocated sexual freedom.

still more wildly.) BUT I WON'T ALLOW SUCH FILTH BROUGHT INTO MY HOUSE! No, no, no, no, no!

TOM: House, house! Who pays rent on it, who makes a slave of himself to —

AMANDA *(fairly screeching)*:   Don't you DARE to —

TOM: No, no, *I* mustn't say things! *I've* got to just —

AMANDA: Let me tell you —

TOM: I don't want to hear any more! *(He tears the portieres open. The upstage area is lit with a turgid smoky red glow.)*

Amanda's hair is in metal curlers and she wears a very old bathrobe, much too large for her slight figure, a relic of the faithless Mr. Wingfield.

  An upright typewriter and a wild disarray of manuscripts are on the drop-leaf table. The quarrel was probably precipitated by Amanda's interruption of his creative labor. A chair lying overthrown on the floor.

  Their gesticulating shadows are cast on the ceiling by the fiery glow.

AMANDA: You *will* hear more, you —

TOM: No, I won't hear more, I'm going out!

AMANDA: You come right back in —

TOM: Out, out, out! Because I'm —

AMANDA: Come back here, Tom Wingfield! I'm not through talking to you!

TOM: Oh, go —

LAURA *(desperately)*:   Tom!

AMANDA: You're going to listen, and no more insolence from you! I'm at the end of my patience! *(He comes back toward her.)*

TOM: What do you think I'm at? Aren't I supposed to have any patience to reach the end of, Mother? I know, I know. It seems unimportant to you, what I'm *doing* — what I *want* to do — having a little *difference* between them! You don't think that —

AMANDA: I think you've been doing things that you're ashamed of. That's why you act like this. I don't believe that you go every night to the movies. Nobody goes to the movies night after night. Nobody in their right minds goes to the movies as often as you pretend to. People don't go to the movies at nearly midnight, and movies don't let out at two A.M. Come in stumbling. Muttering to yourself like a maniac! You get three hours' sleep and then go to work. Oh, I can picture the way you're doing down there. Moping, doping, because you're in no condition.

TOM *(wildly)*:   No, I'm in no condition!

AMANDA: What right have you got to jeopardize your job? Jeopardize the security of us all? How do you think we'd manage if you were —

TOM: Listen! You think I'm crazy *about* the *warehouse!* *(He bends fiercely toward her slight figure.)* You think I'm in love with the Continental Shoemakers? You think I want to spend fifty-five *years* down there in that — *celotex interior!* with — *fluorescent* — *tubes!* Look! I'd rather somebody picked up a crowbar and battered out my brains — than go back mornings! I go! Every time you come in yelling that God damn *"Rise and Shine!" "Rise and Shine!"* I say to myself "How *lucky dead* people are!" But I get up. I *go!* For sixty-five dollars a month I give up all that I dream of doing and being *ever*! And you say self — *self's* all I ever think of. Why, listen, if self is what I thought of, Mother, I'd be where he is — ! *(Pointing to father's picture.)* As far as the system of transportation reaches! *(He starts past her. She grabs his arm.)* Don't grab at me, Mother!

AMANDA: Where are you going?

TOM: I'm going to the *movies*!

AMANDA: I don't believe that lie!

TOM *(crouching toward her, overtowering her tiny figure. She backs away, gasping)*:   I'm going to opium dens! Yes, opium dens, dens of vice and criminals' hang-outs, Mother. I've joined the Hogan gang, I'm a hired assassin, I carry a tommy-gun in a violin case! I run a string of cat-houses in the Valley! They call me Killer, Killer Wingfield, I'm leading a double-life, a simple, honest warehouse worker by day, by night a dynamic *czar* of the *underworld, Mother.* I go to gambling casinos, I spin away fortunes on the roulette table! I wear a patch over one eye and a false mustache, sometimes I put on green whiskers. On those occasions they call me — *El Diablo!°* Oh, I could tell you things to make you sleepless! My enemies plan to dynamite this place. They're going to blow us all sky-high some night! I'll be glad, very happy, and so will you! You'll go up, up on a broomstick, over Blue Mountain with seventeen gentlemen callers! You ugly — babbling old — witch. . . . *(He goes through a series of violent, clumsy movements, seizing his overcoat, lunging to the door, pulling it fiercely open. The women watch him, aghast. His arm catches in the sleeve of the coat as he struggles to pull it on. For a moment he is pinioned by the bulky garment. With an outraged groan he tears the coat off again, splitting the shoulders of it, and hurls it across the room. It strikes against the shelf of Laura's glass collection, there is a tinkle of shattering glass. Laura cries out as if wounded.)*

(Music legend: "The Glass Menagerie.")

LAURA *(shrilly)*:   My glass! — menagerie. . . . *(She covers her face and turns away.)*

But Amanda is still stunned and stupefied by the "ugly witch" so that she barely notices this occurrence. Now she recovers her speech.

AMANDA *(in an awful voice)*:   I won't speak to you — until you apologize! *(She crosses through portieres and draws them together behind her. Tom is left with Laura. Laura clings weakly to the mantel with her face averted. Tom stares at her stupidly for a moment. Then he crosses to shelf. Drops awkwardly to his knees to collect the fallen glass, glancing at Laura as if he would speak but couldn't.)*

"The Glass Menagerie" steals in as
    (The scene dims out.)

El Diablo: The devil (Spanish).

Scene 4

The interior is dark. Faint light in the alley.

A deep-voiced bell in a church is tolling the hour of five as the scene commences.

Tom appears at the top of the alley. After each solemn boom of the bell in the tower, he shakes a little noise-maker or rattle as if to express the tiny spasm of man in contrast to the sustained power and dignity of the Almighty. This and the unsteadiness of his advance make it evident that he has been drinking.

As he climbs the few steps to the fire-escape landing light steals up inside. Laura appears in night-dress, observing Tom's empty bed in the front room.

Tom fishes in his pockets for the door-key, removing a motley assortment of articles in the search, including a perfect shower of movie-ticket stubs and an empty bottle. At last he finds the key, but just as he is about to insert it, it slips from his fingers. He strikes a match and crouches below the door.

TOM *(bitterly)*:   One crack — and it falls through!

Laura opens the door.

LAURA: Tom! Tom, what are you doing?

TOM: Looking for a door-key.

LAURA: Where have you been all this time?

TOM: I have been to the movies.

LAURA: All this time at the movies?

TOM: There was a very long program. There was a Garbo picture and a Mickey Mouse and a travelogue and a newsreel and a preview of coming attractions. And there was an organ solo and a collection for the milk-fund — simultaneously — which ended up in a terrible fight between a fat lady and an usher!

LAURA *(innocently)*:   Did you have to stay through everything?

TOM: Of course! And, oh, I forgot! There was a big stage show! The headliner on this stage show was Malvolio the Magician. He performed wonderful tricks, many of them, such as pouring water back and forth between pitchers. First it turned to wine and then it turned to beer and then it turned to whiskey. I know it was whiskey it finally turned into because he needed somebody to come up out of the audience to help him, and I came up — both shows! It was Kentucky Straight Bourbon. A very generous fellow, he gave souvenirs. *(He pulls from his back pocket a shimmering rainbow-colored scarf.)* He gave me this. This is his magic scarf. You can have it, Laura. You wave it over a canary cage and you get a bowl of gold-fish. You wave it over the gold-fish bowl and they fly away canaries. . . . But the wonderfullest trick of all was the coffin trick. We nailed him into a coffin and he got out of the coffin without removing one nail. *(He has come inside.)* There is a trick that would come in handy for me — get me out of this 2 by 4 situation! *(Flops onto bed and starts removing shoes.)*

LAURA: Tom — Shhh!

TOM: What you shushing me for?

LAURA: You'll wake up Mother.

TOM: Goody, goody! Pay 'er back for all those "Rise an' Shines." *(Lies down, groaning.)* You know it don't take much intelligence to get yourself into a nailed-up coffin, Laura. But who in hell ever got himself out of one without removing one nail?

As if in answer, the father's grinning photograph lights up.
    (Scene dims out.)
    Immediately following: The church bell is heard striking six. At the sixth stroke the alarm clock goes off in Amanda's room, and after a few moments we hear her calling: "Rise and Shine! Rise and Shine! Laura, go tell your brother to rise and shine!"

TOM *(sitting up slowly)*:   I'll rise — but I won't shine.

The light increases.

AMANDA: Laura, tell your brother his coffee is ready.

Laura slips into front room.

LAURA: Tom! it's nearly seven. Don't make Mother nervous. *(He stares at her stupidly. Beseechingly.)* Tom, speak to Mother this morning. Make up with her, apologize, speak to her!

TOM: She won't to me. It's her that started not speaking.

LAURA: If you just say you're sorry she'll start speaking.

TOM: Her not speaking — is that such a tragedy?

LAURA: Please — please!

AMANDA *(calling from kitchenette)*:   Laura, are you going to do what I asked you to do, or do I have to get dressed and go out myself?

LAURA: Going, going — soon as I get on my coat! *(She pulls on a shapeless felt hat with nervous, jerky movement, pleadingly glancing at Tom. Rushes awkwardly for coat. The coat is one of Amanda's, inaccurately made-over, the sleeves too short for Laura.)* Butter and what else?

AMANDA *(entering upstage)*:   Just butter. Tell them to charge it.

LAURA: Mother, they make such faces when I do that.

AMANDA: Sticks and stones may break my bones, but the expression on Mr. Garfinkel's face won't harm us! Tell your brother his coffee is getting cold.

LAURA *(at door)*:   Do what I asked you, will you, will you, Tom?

He looks sullenly away.

AMANDA: Laura, go now or just don't go at all!

LAURA *(rushing out)*:   Going — going! *(A second later she cries out. Tom springs up and crosses to the door. Amanda rushes anxiously in. Tom opens the door.)*

TOM: Laura?

LAURA: I'm all right. I slipped, but I'm all right.

AMANDA *(peering anxiously after her)*:   If anyone breaks a leg on those fire-escape steps, the landlord ought to be sued for every cent he possesses! *(She shuts door. Remembers she isn't speaking and returns to other room.)*

As Tom enters listlessly for his coffee, she turns her back to him and stands rigidly facing the window on the gloomy gray vault of the areaway. Its light on her face with its aged but childish features is cruelly sharp, satirical as a Daumier° print.

(Music under: "Ave Maria.")

Tom glances sheepishly but sullenly at her averted figure and slumps at the table. The coffee is scalding hot; he sips it and gasps and spits it back in the cup. At his gasp, Amanda catches her breath and half turns. Then catches herself and turns back to window.

Tom blows on his coffee, glancing sidewise at his mother. She clears her throat. Tom clears his. He starts to rise. Sinks back down again, scratches his head, clears his throat again. Amanda coughs. Tom raises his cup in both hands to blow on it, his eyes staring over the rim of it at his mother for several moments. Then he slowly sets the cup down and awkwardly and hesitantly rises from the chair.

TOM *(hoarsely)*: Mother. I — I apologize. Mother. *(Amanda draws a quick, shuddering breath. Her face works grotesquely. She breaks into childlike tears.)* I'm sorry for what I said, for everything that I said, I didn't mean it.

AMANDA *(sobbingly)*: My devotion has made me a witch and so I make myself hateful to my children!

TOM: No, you *don't.*

AMANDA: I worry so much, don't sleep, it makes me nervous!

TOM *(gently)*: I understand that.

AMANDA: I've had to put up a solitary battle all these years. But you're my right-hand bower! Don't fall down, don't fail!

TOM *(gently)*: I try, Mother.

AMANDA *(with great enthusiasm)*: Try and you will SUCCEED! *(The notion makes her breathless.)* Why, you — you're just full of natural endowments! Both of my children — they're *unusual* children! Don't you think I know it? I'm so — *proud*! Happy and — feel I've — so much to be thankful for but — Promise me one thing, son!

TOM: What, Mother?

AMANDA: Promise, son, you'll — never be a drunkard!

TOM *(turns to her grinning)*: I will never be a drunkard, Mother.

AMANDA: That's what frightened me so, that you'd be drinking! Eat a bowl of Purina!

TOM: Just coffee, Mother.

AMANDA: Shredded wheat biscuit?

TOM: No. No, Mother, just coffee.

AMANDA: You can't put in a day's work on an empty stomach. You've got ten minutes — don't gulp! Drinking too-hot liquids makes cancer of the stomach. . . . Put cream in.

TOM: No, thank you.

AMANDA: To cool it.

TOM: No! No, thank you, I want it black.

Daumier: Honoré Daumier (1808–1879), French caricaturist, lithographer, and painter who mercilessly satirized bourgeois society.

AMANDA: I know, but it's not good for you. We have to do all that we can to build ourselves up. In these trying times we live in, all that we have to cling to is — each other. . . . That's why it's so important to — Tom, I — I sent out your sister so I could discuss something with you. If you hadn't spoken I would have spoken to you. *(Sits down.)*

TOM *(gently)*:   What is it, Mother, that you want to discuss?

AMANDA: Laura!

Tom puts his cup down slowly.
    (Legend on screen: "Laura.")
    (Music: "The Glass Menagerie.")

TOM: — Oh. — Laura . . .

AMANDA *(touching his sleeve)*:   You know how Laura is. So quiet but — still water runs deep! She notices things and I think she — broods about them. *(Tom looks up.)* A few days ago I came in and she was crying.

TOM: What about?

AMANDA: You.

TOM: Me?

AMANDA: She has an idea that you're not happy here.

TOM: What gave her that idea?

AMANDA: What gives her any idea? However, you do act strangely. I — I'm not criticizing, understand *that*! I know your ambitions do not lie in the warehouse, that like everybody in the whole wide world — you've had to — make sacrifices, but — Tom — Tom — life's not easy, it calls for — Spartan endurance! There's so many things in my heart that I cannot describe to you! I've never told you but I — *loved* your father. . . .

TOM *(gently)*:   I know that, Mother.

AMANDA: And you — when I see you taking after his ways! Staying out late — and — well, you *had* been drinking the night you were in that — terrifying condition! Laura says that you hate the apartment and that you go out nights to get away from it! Is that true, Tom?

TOM: No. You say there's so much in your heart that you can't describe to me. That's true of me, too. There's so much in my heart that I can't describe to *you*! So let's respect each other's —

AMANDA: But, why — why, Tom — are you always so *restless*? Where do you go to, nights?

TOM: I — go to the movies.

AMANDA: Why do you go to the movies so much, Tom?

TOM: I go to the movies because — I like adventure. Adventure is something I don't have much of at work, so I go to the movies.

AMANDA: But, Tom, you go to the movies *entirely too much*!

TOM: I like a lot of adventure.

Amanda looks baffled, then hurt. As the familiar inquisition resumes he becomes hard and impatient again. Amanda slips back into her querulous attitude toward him.
    (Image on screen: Sailing vessel with Jolly Roger.)

AMANDA: Most young men find adventure in their careers.

TOM: Then most young men are not employed in a warehouse.

AMANDA: The world is full of young men employed in warehouses and offices and factories.

TOM: Do all of them find adventure in their careers?

AMANDA: They do or they do without it! Not everybody has a craze for adventure.

TOM: Man is by instinct a lover, a hunter, a fighter, and none of those instincts are given much play at the warehouse!

AMANDA: Man is by instinct! Don't quote instinct to me! Instinct is something that people have got away from! It belongs to animals! Christian adults don't want it!

TOM: What do Christian adults want, then, Mother?

AMANDA: Superior things! Things of the mind and the spirit! Only animals have to satisfy instincts! Surely your aims are somewhat higher than theirs! Than monkeys — pigs —

TOM: I reckon they're not.

AMANDA: You're joking. However, that isn't what I wanted to discuss.

TOM *(rising)*: I haven't much time.

AMANDA *(pushing his shoulders)*: Sit down.

TOM: You want me to punch in red° at the warehouse, Mother?

AMANDA: You have five minutes. I want to talk about Laura.

(Legend: "Plans and Provisions.")

TOM: All right! What about Laura?

AMANDA: We have to be making plans and provisions for her. She's older than you, two years, and nothing has happened. She just drifts along doing nothing. It frightens me terribly how she just drifts along.

TOM: I guess she's the type that people call home girls.

AMANDA: There's no such type, and if there is, it's a pity! That is unless the home is hers, with a husband!

TOM: What?

AMANDA: Oh, I can see the handwriting on the wall as plain as I see the nose in front of my face! It's terrifying! More and more you remind me of your father! He was out all hours without explanation — Then *left! Good-bye!* And me with the bag to hold. I saw that letter you got from the Merchant Marine. I know what you're dreaming of. I'm not standing here blindfolded. Very well, then. Then *do* it! But not till there's somebody to take your place.

TOM: What do you mean?

AMANDA: I mean that as soon as Laura has got somebody to take care of her, married, a home of her own, independent — why, then you'll be free to go wherever you please, on land, on sea, whichever way the wind blows! But until that time you've got to look out for your sister. I don't say me because

punch in red: Be late for work.

I'm old and don't matter! I say for your sister because she's young and dependent. I put her in business college — a dismal failure! Frightened her so it made her sick to her stomach. I took her over to the Young People's League at the church. Another fiasco. She spoke to nobody, nobody spoke to her. Now all she does is fool with those pieces of glass and play those worn-out records. What kind of a life is that for a girl to lead!

TOM: What can I do about it?

AMANDA: Overcome selfishness! Self, self, self is all that you ever think of! *(Tom springs up and crosses to get his coat. It is ugly and bulky. He pulls on a cap with earmuffs.)* Where is your muffler? Put your wool muffler on! *(He snatches it angrily from the closet and tosses it around his neck and pulls both ends tight.)* Tom! I haven't said what I had in mind to ask you.

TOM: I'm too late to —

AMANDA *(catching his arms — very importunately. Then shyly.)*:   Down at the warehouse, aren't there some — nice young men?

TOM: No!

AMANDA: There *must* be — *some.*

TOM: Mother —

Gesture.

AMANDA: Find out one that's clean-living — doesn't drink and — ask him out for sister!

TOM: What?

AMANDA: For *sister!* To *meet!* Get *acquainted!*

TOM *(stamping to door)*:   Oh, my *go-osh!*

AMANDA: Will you? *(He opens door. Imploringly.)* Will you? *(He starts down.)* Will you? *Will* you, dear?

TOM *(calling back)*:   YES!

Amanda closes the door hesitantly and with a troubled but faintly hopeful expression.
  (Screen image: Glamour magazine cover.)
  Spot Amanda at phone.

AMANDA: Ella Cartwright? This is Amanda Wingfield! How are you, honey? How is that kidney condition? *(Count five.)* Horrors! *(Count five.)* You're a Christian martyr, yes, honey, that's what you are, a Christian martyr! Well, I just happened to notice in my little red book that your subscription to the *Companion* has just run out! I knew that you wouldn't want to miss out on the wonderful serial starting in this new issue. It's by Bessie Mae Hopper, the first thing she's written since *Honeymoon for Three.* Wasn't that a strange and interesting story? Well, this one is even lovelier, I believe. It has a sophisticated society background. It's all about the horsey set on Long Island!

(Fade out.)

Scene 5

(Legend on screen: "Annunciation.") Fade with music.

   It is early dusk of a spring evening. Supper has just been finished in the Wingfield apartment. Amanda and Laura in light-colored dresses are removing dishes from the table, in the upstage area, which is shadowy, their movements formalized almost as a dance or ritual, their moving forms as pale and silent as moths.

   Tom, in white shirt and trousers, rises from the table and crosses toward the fire-escape.

AMANDA *(as he passes her):*   Son, will you do me a favor?

TOM: What?

AMANDA: Comb your hair! You look so pretty when your hair is combed! *(Tom slouches on sofa with evening paper. Enormous caption "Franco Triumphs."°)*

   There is only one respect in which I would like you to emulate your father.

TOM: What respect is that?

AMANDA: The care he always took of his appearance. He never allowed himself to look untidy. *(He throws down the paper and crosses to fire-escape.)* Where are you going?

TOM: I'm going out to smoke.

AMANDA: You smoke too much. A pack a day at fifteen cents a pack. How much would that amount to in a month? Thirty times fifteen is how much, Tom? Figure it out and you will be astounded at what you could save. Enough to give you a night-school course in accounting at Washington U! Just think what a wonderful thing that would be for you, son!

Tom is unmoved by the thought.

TOM: I'd rather smoke. *(He steps out on landing, letting the screen door slam.)*

AMANDA *(sharply):*   I know! That's the tragedy of it. . . . *(Alone, she turns to look at her husband's picture.)*

(Dance music: "All the World Is Waiting for the Sunrise!")

TOM *(to the audience):*   Across the alley from us was the Paradise Dance Hall. On evenings in spring the windows and doors were open and the music came outdoors. Sometimes the lights were turned out except for a large glass sphere that hung from the ceiling. It would turn slowly about and filter the dusk with delicate rainbow colors. Then the orchestra played a waltz or a tango, something that had a slow and sensuous rhythm. Couples would come outside, to the relative privacy of the alley. You could see them kissing behind ash-pits and telephone poles. This was the compensation for lives that passed like mine, without any change or adventure. Adventure and change were imminent in this year. They were waiting around the corner for all these kids. Suspended in the mist over the

---

"Franco Triumphs": In January 1939, the Republican forces of Francisco Franco (1892–1975) defeated the Loyalists, ending the Spanish civil war.

Berchtesgaden,° caught in the folds of Chamberlain's° umbrella — In Spain there was Guernica! But here there was only hot swing music and liquor, dance halls, bars, and movies, and sex that hung in the gloom like a chandelier and flooded the world with brief, deceptive rainbows. . . . All the world was waiting for bombardments!

Amanda turns from the picture and comes outside.

AMANDA (*sighing*):   A fire-escape landing's a poor excuse for a porch. (*She spreads a newspaper on a step and sits down, gracefully and demurely as if she were settling into a swing on a Mississippi veranda.*) What are you looking at?

TOM: The moon.

AMANDA: Is there a moon this evening?

TOM: It's rising over Garfinkel's Delicatessen.

AMANDA: So it is! A little silver slipper of a moon. Have you made a wish on it yet?

TOM: Um-hum.

AMANDA: What did you wish for?

TOM: That's a secret.

AMANDA: A secret, huh? Well, I won't tell mine either. I will be just as mysterious as you.

TOM: I bet I can guess what yours is.

AMANDA: Is my head so transparent?

TOM: You're not a sphinx.

AMANDA: No, I don't have secrets. I'll tell you what I wished for on the moon. Success and happiness for my precious children! I wish for that whenever there's a moon, and when there isn't a moon, I wish for it, too.

TOM: I thought perhaps you wished for a gentleman caller.

AMANDA: Why do you say that?

TOM: Don't you remember asking me to fetch one?

AMANDA: I remember suggesting that it would be nice for your sister if you brought home some nice young man from the warehouse. I think I've made that suggestion more than once.

TOM: Yes, you have made it repeatedly.

AMANDA: Well?

TOM: We are going to have one.

AMANDA: *What?*

TOM: A gentleman caller!

(*The Annunciation is celebrated with music.*)
    Amanda rises.
    (*Image on screen: Caller with bouquet.*)

AMANDA: You mean you have asked some nice young man to come over?

TOM: Yep. I've asked him to dinner.

Berchtesgaden: A resort in the German Alps where Adolf Hitler had a heavily protected villa.   **Chamberlain:** Neville Chamberlain (1869–1940), British prime minister who sought to avoid war with Hitler through a policy of appeasement.

AMANDA: You really did?

TOM: I did!

AMANDA: You did, and did he — *accept?*

TOM: He did!

AMANDA: Well, well — well, well! That's — lovely!

TOM: I thought that you would be pleased.

AMANDA: It's definite, then?

TOM: Very definite.

AMANDA: Soon?

TOM: Very soon.

AMANDA: For heaven's sake, stop putting on and tell me some things, will you?

TOM: What things do you want me to tell you?

AMANDA: Naturally I would like to know when he's *coming!*

TOM: He's coming tomorrow.

AMANDA: *Tomorrow?*

TOM: Yep. Tomorrow.

AMANDA: But, Tom!

TOM: Yes, Mother?

AMANDA: Tomorrow gives me no time!

TOM: Time for what?

AMANDA: Preparations! Why didn't you phone me at once, as soon as you asked him, the minute that he accepted? Then, don't you see, I could have been getting ready!

TOM: You don't have to make any fuss.

AMANDA: Oh, Tom, Tom, Tom, of course I have to make a fuss! I want things nice, not sloppy! Not thrown together. I'll certainly have to do some fast thinking, won't I?

TOM: I don't see why you have to think at all.

AMANDA: You just don't know. We can't have a gentleman caller in a pig-sty! All my wedding silver has to be polished, the monogrammed table linen ought to be laundered! The windows have to be washed and fresh curtains put up. And how about clothes? We have to *wear* something, don't we?

TOM: Mother, this boy is no one to make a fuss over!

AMANDA: Do you realize he's the first young man we've introduced to your sister? It's terrible, dreadful, disgraceful that poor little sister has never received a single gentleman caller! Tom, come inside! *(She opens the screen door.)*

TOM: What for?

AMANDA: I want to ask you some things.

TOM: If you're going to make such a fuss, I'll call it off, I'll tell him not to come.

AMANDA: You certainly won't do anything of the kind. Nothing offends people worse than broken engagements. It simply means I'll have to work like a Turk! We won't be brilliant, but we'll pass inspection. Come on inside. *(Tom follows, groaning.)* Sit down.

TOM: Any particular place you would like me to sit?

AMANDA: Thank heavens I've got that new sofa! I'm also making payments on a floor lamp I'll have sent out! And put the chintz covers on, they'll brighten things up! Of course I'd hoped to have these walls re-papered. . . . What is the young man's name?

TOM: His name is O'Connor.

AMANDA: That, of course, means fish — tomorrow is Friday! I'll have that salmon loaf — with Durkee's dressing! What does he do? He works at the warehouse?

TOM: Of course! How else would I —

AMANDA: Tom, he — doesn't drink?

TOM: Why do you ask me that?

AMANDA: Your father did!

TOM: Don't get started on that!

AMANDA: He does drink, then?

TOM: Not that I know of!

AMANDA: Make sure, be certain! The last thing I want for my daughter's a boy who drinks!

TOM: Aren't you being a little premature? Mr. O'Connor has not yet appeared on the scene!

AMANDA: But will tomorrow. To meet your sister, and what do I know about his character? Nothing! Old maids are better off than wives of drunkards!

TOM: Oh, my God!

AMANDA: Be still!

TOM *(leaning forward to whisper)*:   Lots of fellows meet girls whom they don't marry!

AMANDA: Oh, talk sensibly, Tom — and don't be sarcastic! *(She has gotten a hairbrush.)*

TOM: What are you doing?

AMANDA: I'm brushing that cow-lick down! What is this young man's position at the warehouse?

TOM *(submitting grimly to the brush and the interrogation)*:   This young man's position is that of a shipping clerk, Mother.

AMANDA: Sounds to me like a fairly responsible job, the sort of a job *you* would be in if you just had more *get-up*. What is his salary? Have you got any idea?

TOM: I would judge it to be approximately eighty-five dollars a month.

AMANDA: Well — not princely, but —

TOM: Twenty more than I make.

AMANDA: Yes, how well I know! But for a family man, eighty-five dollars a month is not much more than you can just get by on. . . .

TOM: Yes, but Mr. O'Connor is not a family man.

AMANDA: He might be, mightn't he? Some time in the future?

TOM: I see. Plans and provisions.

AMANDA: You are the only young man that I know of who ignores the fact that the future becomes the present, the present the past, and the past turns into everlasting regret if you don't plan for it!

TOM: I will think that over and see what I can make of it.

AMANDA: Don't be supercilious with your mother! Tell me some more about this — what do you call him?

TOM: James D. O'Connor. The D. is for Delaney.

AMANDA: Irish on *both* sides! *Gracious!* And doesn't drink?

TOM: Shall I call him up and ask him right this minute?

AMANDA: The only way to find out about those things is to make discreet inquiries at the proper moment. When I was a girl in Blue Mountain and it was suspected that a young man drank, the girl whose attentions he had been receiving, if any girl *was*, would sometimes speak to the minister of his church, or rather her father would if her father was living, and sort of feel him out on the young man's character. That is the way such things are discreetly handled to keep a young woman from making a tragic mistake!

TOM: Then how did you happen to make a tragic mistake?

AMANDA: That innocent look of your father's had everyone fooled! He *smiled* — the world was *enchanted*! No girl can do worse than put herself at the mercy of a handsome appearance! I hope that Mr. O'Connor is not too good-looking.

TOM: No, he's not too good-looking. He's covered with freckles and hasn't too much of a nose.

AMANDA: He's not right-down homely, though?

TOM: Not right-down homely. Just medium homely, I'd say.

AMANDA: Character's what to look for in a man.

TOM: That's what I've always said, Mother.

AMANDA: You've never said anything of the kind and I suspect you would never give it a thought.

TOM: Don't be suspicious of me.

AMANDA: At least I hope he's the type that's up and coming.

TOM: I think he really goes in for self-improvement.

AMANDA: What reason have you to think so?

TOM: He goes to night school.

AMANDA *(beaming)*:   Splendid! What does he do, I mean study?

TOM: Radio engineering and public speaking!

AMANDA: Then he has visions of being advanced in the world! Any young man who studies public speaking is aiming to have an executive job some day! And radio engineering? A thing for the future! Both of these facts are very illuminating. Those are the sort of things that a mother should know concerning any young man who comes to call on her daughter. Seriously or — not.

TOM: One little warning. He doesn't know about Laura. I didn't let on that we had dark ulterior motives. I just said, why don't you come have dinner with us? He said okay and that was the whole conversation.

AMANDA: I bet it was! You're eloquent as an oyster. However, he'll know about Laura when he gets here. When he sees how lovely and sweet and pretty she is, he'll thank his lucky stars he was asked to dinner.

TOM: Mother, you mustn't expect too much of Laura.

AMANDA: What do you mean?

TOM: Laura seems all those things to you and me because she's ours and we love her. We don't even notice she's crippled any more.

AMANDA: Don't say crippled! You know that I never allow that word to be used!

TOM: But face facts, Mother. She is and — that's not all —

AMANDA: What do you mean "not all"?

TOM: Laura is very different from other girls.

AMANDA: I think the difference is all to her advantage.

TOM: Not quite all — in the eyes of others — strangers — she's terribly shy and lives in a world of her own and those things make her seem a little peculiar to people outside the house.

AMANDA: Don't say peculiar.

TOM: Face the facts. She is.

(The dance-hall music changes to a tango that has a minor and somewhat ominous tone.)

AMANDA: In what way is she peculiar — may I ask?

TOM *(gently)*:   She lives in a world of her own — a world of — little glass ornaments, Mother. . . . *(Gets up. Amanda remains holding brush, looking at him, troubled.)* She plays old phonograph records and — that's about all — *(He glances at himself in the mirror and crosses to door.)*

AMANDA *(sharply)*:   Where are you going?

TOM: I'm going to the movies. *(Out screen door.)*

AMANDA: Not to the movies, every night to the movies! *(Follows quickly to screen door.)* I don't believe you always go to the movies! *(He is gone. Amanda looks worriedly after him for a moment. Then vitality and optimism return and she turns from the door. Crossing to portieres.)* Laura! Laura! *(Laura answers from kitchenette.)*

LAURA: Yes, Mother.

AMANDA: Let those dishes go and come in front! *(Laura appears with dish towel. Gaily.)* Laura, come here and make a wish on the moon!

LAURA *(entering)*:   Moon — moon?

AMANDA: A little silver slipper of a moon. Look over your left shoulder, Laura, and make a wish! *(Laura looks faintly puzzled as if called out of sleep. Amanda seizes her shoulders and turns her at angle by the door.)* Now! Now, darling, wish!

LAURA: What shall I wish for, Mother?

AMANDA *(her voice trembling and her eyes suddenly filling with tears)*:   Happiness! Good Fortune!

The violin rises and the stage dims out.

Scene 6

(Image: High-school hero.)

TOM: And so the following evening I brought Jim home to dinner. I had known Jim slightly in high school. In high school Jim was a hero. He had tremendous Irish good nature and vitality with the scrubbed and polished look of white chinaware. He seemed to move in a continual spotlight. He was a star in basketball, captain of the debating club, president of the senior class and the glee club and he sang the male lead in the annual light operas. He was always running or bounding, never just walking. He seemed always at the point of defeating the law of gravity. He was shooting with such velocity through his adolescence that you would logically expect him to arrive at nothing short of the White House by the time he was thirty. But Jim apparently ran into more interference after his graduation from Soldan. His speed had definitely slowed. Six years after he left high school he was holding a job that wasn't much better than mine.

(Image: Clerk.)

He was the only one at the warehouse with whom I was on friendly terms. I was valuable to him as someone who could remember his former glory, who had seen him win basketball games and the silver cup in debating. He knew of my secret practice of retiring to a cabinet of the washroom to work on poems when business was slack in the warehouse. He called me Shakespeare. And while the other boys in the warehouse regarded me with suspicious hostility, Jim took a humorous attitude toward me. Gradually his attitude affected the others, their hostility wore off, and they also began to smile at me as people smile at an oddly fashioned dog who trots across their paths at some distance.

I knew that Jim and Laura had known each other at Soldan, and I had heard Laura speak admiringly of his voice. I didn't know if Jim remembered her or not. In high school Laura had been as unobtrusive as Jim had been astonishing. If he did remember Laura, it was not as my sister, for when I asked him to dinner, he grinned and said, "You know, Shakespeare, I never thought of you as having folks!"

He was about to discover that I did. . . .

(Light upstage.)

(Legend on screen: "The Accent of a Coming Foot.")

Friday evening. It is about five o'clock of a late spring evening which comes "scattering poems in the sky."

A delicate lemony light is in the Wingfield apartment.

Amanda has worked like a Turk in preparation for the gentleman caller. The results are astonishing. The new floor lamp with its rose-silk shade is in place, a colored paper lantern conceals the broken light fixture in the ceiling, new billowing white curtains are at the windows, chintz covers are on chairs and sofa, a pair of new sofa pillows make their initial appearance.

Open boxes and tissue paper are scattered on the floor.

Laura stands in the middle with lifted arms while Amanda crouches before her, adjusting the hem of the new dress, devout and ritualistic. The dress is colored and designed by memory. The arrangement of Laura's hair is changed; it is softer and more becoming. A fragile, unearthly prettiness has come out in Laura: she is like a piece of translucent glass touched by light, given a momentary radiance, not actual, not lasting.

AMANDA *(impatiently)*: Why are you trembling?

LAURA: Mother, you've made me so nervous!

AMANDA: How have I made you nervous?

LAURA: By all this fuss! You make it seem so important!

AMANDA: I don't understand you, Laura. You couldn't be satisfied with just sitting home, and yet whenever I try to arrange something for you, you seem to resist it. *(She gets up.)* Now take a look at yourself. No, wait! Wait just a moment — I have an idea!

LAURA: What is it now?

Amanda produces two powder puffs which she wraps in handkerchiefs and stuffs in Laura's bosom.

LAURA: Mother, what are you doing?

AMANDA: They call them "Gay Deceivers"!

LAURA: I won't wear them!

AMANDA: You will!

LAURA: Why should I?

AMANDA: Because, to be painfully honest, your chest is flat.

LAURA: You make it seem like we were setting a trap.

AMANDA: All pretty girls are a trap, a pretty trap, and men expect them to be. *(Legend: "A Pretty Trap.")* Now look at yourself, young lady. This is the prettiest you will ever be! I've got to fix myself now! You're going to be surprised by your mother's appearance! *(She crosses through portieres, humming gaily.)*

Laura moves slowly to the long mirror and stares solemnly at herself.

A wind blows the white curtains inward in a slow, graceful motion and with a faint, sorrowful sighing.

AMANDA *(offstage):*   It isn't dark enough yet. *(She turns slowly before the mirror with a troubled look).*

(Legend on screen: "This Is My Sister: Celebrate Her with Strings!" Music.)

AMANDA *(laughing, off):* I'm going to show you something. I'm going to make a spectacular appearance!

LAURA: What is it, Mother?

AMANDA: Possess your soul in patience — you will see! Something I've resurrected from that old trunk! Styles haven't changed so terribly much after all. . . . *(She parts the portieres.)* Now just look at your mother! *(She wears a girlish frock of yellowed voile with a blue silk sash. She carries a bunch of jonquils — the legend of her youth is nearly revived. Feverishly.)* This is the dress in which I led the cotillion. Won the cakewalk twice at Sunset Hill, wore one spring to the Governor's ball in Jackson! See how I sashayed around the ballroom, Laura? *(She raises her skirt and does a mincing step around the room.)* I wore it on Sundays for my gentlemen callers! I had it on the day I met your father — I had malaria fever all that spring. The change of climate from East Tennessee to the Delta — weakened resistance — I had a little temperature all the time — not enough to be serious — just enough to make me restless and giddy! Invitations poured in — parties all over the Delta! — "Stay in bed," said Mother, "you have fever!" — but I just wouldn't. — I took quinine but kept on going, going! — Evenings, dances! — Afternoons, long, long rides! Picnics — lovely! — So lovely, that country in May. — All lacy with dogwood, literally flooded with jonquils! — That was the spring I had the craze for jonquils. Jonquils became an absolute obsession. Mother said, "Honey, there's no more room for jonquils." And still I kept bringing in more jonquils. Whenever, wherever I saw them, I'd say, "Stop! Stop! I see jonquils!" I made the young men help me gather the jonquils! It was a joke, Amanda and her jonquils! Finally there were no more vases to hold them, every available space was filled with jonquils. No vases to hold them? All right, I'll hold them myself! And then I — *(She stops in front of the picture.) (Music.)* met your father! Malaria fever and jonquils and then — this — boy.... *(She switches on the rose-colored lamp.)* I hope they get here before it starts to rain. *(She crosses upstage and places the jonquils in bowl on table.)* I gave your brother a little extra change so he and Mr. O'Connor could take the service car home.

LAURA *(with altered look)*:   What did you say his name was?

AMANDA: O'Connor.

LAURA: What is his first name?

AMANDA: I don't remember. Oh, yes, I do. It was — Jim!

Laura sways slightly and catches hold of a chair.

    (Legend on screen: "Not Jim!")

LAURA *(faintly)*:   Not — Jim!

AMANDA: Yes, that was it, it was Jim! I've never known a Jim that wasn't nice!

(Music: Ominous.)

LAURA: Are you sure his name is Jim O'Connor?

AMANDA: Yes. Why?

LAURA: Is he the one that Tom used to know in high school?

AMANDA: He didn't say so. I think he just got to know him at the warehouse.

LAURA: There was a Jim O'Connor we both knew in high school — *(Then, with effort.)* If that is the one that Tom is bringing to dinner — you'll have to excuse me, I won't come to the table.

AMANDA: What sort of nonsense is this?

LAURA: You asked me once if I'd ever liked a boy. Don't you remember I showed you this boy's picture?

AMANDA: You mean the boy you showed me in the year-book?

LAURA: Yes, that boy.

AMANDA: Laura, Laura, were you in love with that boy?

LAURA: I don't know, Mother. All I know is I couldn't sit at the table if it was him!

AMANDA: It won't be him! It isn't the least bit likely. But whether it is or not, you will come to the table. You will not be excused.

LAURA: I'll have to be, Mother.

AMANDA: I don't intend to humor your silliness, Laura. I've had too much from you and your brother, both! So just sit down and compose yourself till they come. Tom has forgotten his key so you'll have to let them in, when they arrive.

LAURA *(panicky)*:   Oh, Mother — *you* answer the door!

AMANDA *(lightly)*:   I'll be in the kitchen — busy!

LAURA: Oh, Mother, please answer the door, don't make me do it!

AMANDA *(crossing into kitchenette)*:   I've got to fix the dressing for the salmon. Fuss, fuss — silliness! — over a gentleman caller!

Door swings shut. Laura is left alone.

(Legend: "Terror!")

She utters a low moan and turns off the lamp — sits stiffly on the edge of the sofa, knotting her fingers together.

(Legend on screen: "The Opening of a Door!")

Tom and Jim appear on the fire-escape steps and climb to landing. Hearing their approach, Laura rises with a panicky gesture. She retreats to the portieres.

The doorbell. Laura catches her breath and touches her throat. Low drums.

AMANDA *(calling)*:   Laura, sweetheart! The door!

Laura stares at it without moving.

JIM: I think we just beat the rain.

TOM: Uh-huh. *(He rings again, nervously. Jim whistles and fishes for a cigarette.)*

AMANDA *(very, very gaily)*:   Laura, that is your brother and Mr. O'Connor! Will you let them in, darling?

Laura crosses toward kitchenette door.

LAURA *(breathlessly)*:   Mother — you go to the door!

Amanda steps out of kitchenette and stares furiously at Laura. She points imperiously at the door.

LAURA: Please, please!

AMANDA *(in a fierce whisper)*:   What is the matter with you, you silly thing?

LAURA *(desperately)*:   Please, you answer it, *please!*

AMANDA: I told you I wasn't going to humor you, Laura. Why have you chosen this moment to lose your mind?

LAURA: Please, please, please, you go!

AMANDA: You'll have to go to the door because I can't!

LAURA *(despairingly)*:   I can't either!

AMANDA: Why?

LAURA: I'm sick!

AMANDA: I'm sick, too — of your nonsense! Why can't you and your brother be normal people? Fantastic whims and behavior! *(Tom gives a long ring.)* Preposterous goings on! Can you give me one reason — *(Calls out lyrically.)* COMING! JUST ONE SECOND! — why should you be afraid to open a door? Now you answer it, Laura!

LAURA: Oh, oh, oh . . . *(She returns through the portieres. Darts to the Victrola and winds it frantically and turns it on.)*

AMANDA: Laura Wingfield, you march right to that door!

LAURA: Yes — yes, Mother!

A faraway, scratchy rendition of "Dardanella" softens the air and gives her strength to move through it. She slips to the door and draws it cautiously open.

Tom enters with the caller, Jim O'Connor.

TOM: Laura, this is Jim. Jim, this is my sister, Laura.

JIM *(stepping inside)*:   I didn't know that Shakespeare had a sister!

LAURA *(retreating stiff and trembling from the door)*:   How — how do you do?

JIM *(heartily extending his hand)*:   Okay!

Laura touches it hesitantly with hers.

JIM: Your hand's *cold*, Laura!

LAURA: Yes, well — I've been playing the Victrola . . .

JIM: Must have been playing classical music on it! You ought to play a little hot swing music to warm you up!

LAURA: Excuse me — I haven't finished playing the Victrola . . .

She turns awkwardly and hurries into the front room. She pauses a second by the Victrola. Then catches her breath and darts through the portieres like a frightened deer.

JIM *(grinning)*:   What was the matter?

TOM: Oh — with Laura? Laura is — terribly shy.

JIM: Shy, huh? It's unusual to meet a shy girl nowadays. I don't believe you ever mentioned you had a sister.

TOM: Well, now you know. I have one. Here is the *Post Dispatch.* You want a piece of it?

JIM: Uh-huh.

TOM: What piece? The comics?

JIM: Sports! *(Glances at it.)* Ole Dizzy Dean is on his bad behavior.

TOM *(disinterest)*:   Yeah? *(Lights cigarette and crosses back to fire-escape door.)*

JIM: Where are *you* going?

TOM: I'm going out on the terrace.

JIM *(goes after him)*:   You know, Shakespeare — I'm going to sell you a bill of goods!

TOM: What goods?

JIM: A course I'm taking.

TOM: Huh?

JIM: In public speaking! You and me, we're not the warehouse type.

TOM: Thanks — that's good news. But what has public speaking got to do with it?

JIM: It fits you for — executive positions!

TOM: Awww.

JIM: I tell you it's done a helluva lot for me.

(Image: Executive at desk.)

TOM: In what respect?

JIM: In every! Ask yourself what is the difference between you an' me and men in the office down front? Brains? — No! — Ability? — No! Then what? Just one little thing —

TOM: What is that one little thing?

JIM: Primarily it amounts to — social poise! Being able to square up to people and hold your own on any social level!

AMANDA (*offstage*):   Tom?

TOM: Yes, Mother?

AMANDA: Is that you and Mr. O'Connor?

TOM: Yes, Mother.

AMANDA: Well, you just make yourselves comfortable in there.

TOM: Yes, Mother.

AMANDA: Ask Mr. O'Connor if he would like to wash his hands.

JIM: Aw — no — no — thank you — I took care of that at the warehouse. Tom —

TOM: Yes?

JIM: Mr. Mendoza was speaking to me about you.

TOM: Favorably?

JIM: What do you think?

TOM: Well —

JIM: You're going to be out of a job if you don't wake up.

TOM: I am waking up —

JIM: You show no signs.

TOM: The signs are interior.

(Image on screen: The sailing vessel with Jolly Roger again.)

TOM: I'm planning to change. (*He leans over the rail speaking with quiet exhilaration. The incandescent marquees and signs of the first-run movie houses light his face from across the alley. He looks like a voyager.*) I'm right at the point of committing myself to a future that doesn't include the warehouse and Mr. Mendoza or even a night-school course in public speaking.

JIM: What are you gassing about?

TOM: I'm tired of the movies.

JIM: Movies!

TOM: Yes, movies! Look at them — (*A wave toward the marvels of Grand Avenue.*) All of those glamorous people — having adventures — hogging it all, gobbling the whole thing up! You know what happens? People go to the *movies* instead of *moving*! Hollywood characters are supposed to have all the adventures for everybody in America, while everybody in America sits in a dark room and watches them have them! Yes, until there's a war. That's when adventure becomes available to the masses! *Everyone's* dish, not only Gable's°! Then the people in the dark room come out of the dark room to have some adventures themselves — Goody, goody — It's our turn now, to go to the South Sea Island — to make a safari — to be exotic, far-

---

Gable: Clark Gable, a famous movie star of the 1940s and 1950s.

off — But I'm not patient. I don't want to wait till then. I'm tired of the movies and I am *about* to *move*!

JIM *(incredulously)*: Move?

TOM: Yes.

JIM: When?

TOM: Soon!

JIM: Where? Where?

(Theme three: Music seems to answer the question, while Tom thinks it over. He searches among his pockets.)

TOM: I'm starting to boil inside. I know I seem dreamy, but inside — well, I'm boiling! Whenever I pick up a shoe, I shudder a little thinking how short life is and what I am doing! — Whatever that means. I know it doesn't mean shoes — except as something to wear on a traveler's feet! *(Finds paper.)* Look —

JIM: What?

TOM: I'm a member.

JIM *(reading)*: The Union of Merchant Seamen.

TOM: I paid my dues this month, instead of the light bill.

JIM: You will regret it when they turn the lights off.

TOM: I won't be here.

JIM: How about your mother?

TOM: I'm like my father. The bastard son of a bastard! See how he grins? And he's been absent going on sixteen years!

JIM: You're just talking, you drip. How does your mother feel about it?

TOM: Shhh — Here comes Mother! Mother is not acquainted with my plans!

AMANDA *(enters portieres)*: Where are you all?

TOM: On the terrace, Mother.

They start inside. She advances to them. Tom is distinctly shocked at her appearance. Even Jim blinks a little. He is making his first contact with girlish Southern vivacity and in spite of the night-school course in public speaking is somewhat thrown off the beam by the unexpected outlay of social charm.

Certain responses are attempted by Jim but are swept aside by Amanda's gay laughter and chatter. Tom is embarrassed but after the first shock Jim reacts very warmly. Grins and chuckles, is altogether won over.

(Image: Amanda as a girl.)

AMANDA *(coyly smiling, shaking her girlish ringlets)*: Well, well, well, so this is Mr. O'Connor. Introductions entirely unnecessary. I've heard so much about you from my boy. I finally said to him, Tom — good gracious! — why don't you bring this paragon to supper? I'd like to meet this nice young man at the warehouse! — Instead of just hearing him sing your praises so much! I don't know why my son is so stand-offish — that's not Southern behavior! Let's sit down and — I think we could stand a little more air in here! Tom, leave the door open. I felt a nice fresh breeze a moment ago. Where has it gone? Mmm, so warm already! And not quite summer, even. We're going to burn up when summer really gets started. However, we're having — we're having a very light supper. I think light things are better fo' this time of year. The same as light clothes are. Light clothes an' light food are what warm weather calls fo'. You know our blood gets so thick during th' winter — it takes a while fo' us to *adjust* ou'selves! — when the season changes. . . . It's come so quick this year. I wasn't prepared. All of a sudden — heavens! Already summer! — I ran to the trunk an' pulled out this light dress — Terribly old! Historical almost! But feels so good — so good an' co-ol, y'know. . . .

TOM: Mother —

AMANDA: Yes, honey?

TOM: How about — supper?

AMANDA: Honey, you go ask Sister if supper is ready! You know that Sister is in full charge of supper! Tell her you hungry boys are waiting for it. *(To Jim.)* Have you met Laura?

JIM: She —

AMANDA: Let you in? Oh, good, you've met already! It's rare for a girl as sweet an' pretty as Laura to be domestic! But Laura is, thank heavens, not only pretty but also very domestic. I'm not at all. I never was a bit. I never could make a thing but angel-food cake. Well, in the South we had so many servants. Gone, gone, gone. All vestiges of gracious living! Gone completely! I wasn't prepared for what the future brought me. All of my gentlemen callers were sons of planters and so of course I assumed that I would be married to one and raise my family on a large piece of land with plenty of servants. But man proposes — and woman accepts the proposal! — To vary that old, old saying a little bit — I married no planter! I married a man who worked for the telephone company! — that gallantly smiling gentleman over there! *(Points to the picture.)* A telephone man who — fell in love with long distance! — Now he travels and I don't even know where! — But what am I going on for about my   tribulations! Tell me yours — I hope you don't have any! Tom?

TOM *(returning)*:   Yes, Mother?

AMANDA: Is supper nearly ready?

TOM: It looks to me like supper is on the table.

AMANDA: Let me look — *(She rises prettily and looks through portieres.)* Oh, lovely — But where is Sister?

TOM: Laura is not feeling well and she says that she thinks she'd better not come to the table.

AMANDA: What? — Nonsense! — Laura? Oh, Laura!

LAURA *(offstage, faintly)*:   Yes, Mother.

AMANDA: You really must come to the table. We won't be seated until you come to the table! Come in, Mr. O'Connor. You sit over there and I'll — Laura? Laura Wingfield! You're keeping us waiting, honey! We can't say grace until you come to the table!

The back door is pushed weakly open and Laura comes in. She is obviously quite faint, her lips trembling, her eyes wide and staring. She moves unsteadily toward the table.

(Legend: "Terror!")
   Outside a summer storm is coming abruptly. The white curtains billow inward at the windows and there is a sorrowful murmur and deep blue dusk.
   Laura suddenly stumbles — She catches at a chair with a faint moan.

TOM: Laura!

AMANDA: Laura! *(There is a clap of thunder.) (Legend: "Ah!") (Despairingly.)* Why, Laura, you *are* sick, darling! Tom, help your sister into the living room, dear! Sit in the living room, Laura — rest on the sofa. Well! *(To the gentleman caller.)* Standing over the hot stove made her ill! — I told her that it was just too warm this evening, but — *(Tom comes back in. Laura is on the sofa.)* Is Laura all right now?

TOM: Yes.

AMANDA: What *is* that? Rain? A nice cool rain has come up! *(She gives the gentleman caller a frightened look.)* I think we may — have grace — now . . . *(Tom looks at her stupidly.)* Tom, honey — you say grace!

TOM: Oh . . . "For these and all thy mercies — " *(They bow their heads, Amanda stealing a nervous glance at Jim. In the living room Laura, stretched on the sofa, clenches her hand to her lips, to hold back a shuddering sob.)* God's Holy Name be praised —

(The scene dims out.)

Scene 7

A Souvenir
   Half an hour later. Dinner is just being finished in the upstage area, which is concealed by the drawn portieres.
   As the curtain rises Laura is still huddled upon the sofa, her feet drawn under her, her head resting on a pale blue pillow, her eyes wide and mysteriously watchful. The new floor lamp with its shade of rose-colored silk gives a soft, becoming light to her face, bringing out the fragile, unearthly prettiness which usually escapes attention. There is a steady murmur of rain, but it is slackening and stops soon after the scene begins; the air outside becomes pale and luminous as the moon breaks out.
   A moment after the curtain rises, the lights in both rooms flicker and go out.

JIM: Hey, there, Mr. Light Bulb!

Amanda laughs nervously.
   (Legend: "Suspension of a Public Service.")

AMANDA: Where was Moses when the lights went out? Ha-ha. Do you know the answer to that one, Mr. O'Connor?

JIM: No, Ma'am, what's the answer?

AMANDA: In the dark! *(Jim laughs appreciatively.)* Everybody sit still. I'll light the candles. Isn't it lucky we have them on the table? Where's a match? Which of you gentlemen can provide a match?

JIM: Here.

AMANDA: Thank you, sir.

JIM: Not at all, Ma'am!

AMANDA: I guess the fuse has burnt out. Mr. O'Connor, can you tell a burnt-out fuse? I know I can't and Tom is a total loss when it comes to mechanics. *(Sound: Getting up: Voices recede a little to kitchenette.)* Oh, be careful you don't bump into something. We don't want our gentleman caller to break his neck. Now wouldn't that be a fine howdy-do?

JIM: Ha-ha! Where is the fuse-box?

AMANDA: Right here next to the stove. Can you see anything?

JIM: Just a minute.

AMANDA: Isn't electricity a mysterious thing? Wasn't it Benjamin Franklin who tied a key to a kite? We live in such a mysterious universe, don't we? Some people say that science clears up all the mysteries for us. In my opinion it only creates more! Have you found it yet?

JIM: No, Ma'am. All these fuses look okay to me.

AMANDA: Tom!

TOM: Yes, Mother?

AMANDA: That light bill I gave you several days ago. The one I told you we got the notices about?

TOM: Oh. — Yeah.

(Legend: "Ha!")

AMANDA: You didn't neglect to pay it by any chance?

TOM: Why, I —

AMANDA: Didn't! I might have known it!

JIM: Shakespeare probably wrote a poem on that light bill, Mrs. Wingfield.

AMANDA: I might have known better than to trust him with it! There's such a high price for negligence in this world!

JIM: Maybe the poem will win a ten-dollar prize.

AMANDA: We'll just have to spend the remainder of the evening in the nineteenth century, before Mr. Edison made the Mazda lamp!

JIM: Candlelight is my favorite kind of light.

AMANDA: That shows you're romantic! But that's no excuse for Tom. Well, we got through dinner. Very considerate of them to let us get through dinner before they plunged us into everlasting darkness, wasn't it, Mr. O'Connor?

JIM: Ha-ha!

AMANDA: Tom, as a penalty for your carelessness you can help me with the dishes.

JIM: Let me give you a hand.

AMANDA: Indeed you will not!

JIM: I ought to be good for something.

AMANDA: Good for something? *(Her tone is rhapsodic.)* You? Why, Mr. O'Connor, nobody, *nobody's* given me this much entertainment in years — as you have!

JIM: Aw, now, Mrs. Wingfield!

AMANDA: I'm not exaggerating, not one bit! But Sister is all by her lonesome. You go keep her company in the parlor! I'll give you this lovely old candelabrum that used to be on the altar at the church of the Heavenly Rest. It was melted a little out of shape when the church burnt down. Lightning struck it one spring. Gypsy Jones was holding a revival at the time and he intimated that the church was destroyed because the Episcopalians gave card parties.

JIM: Ha-ha.

AMANDA: And how about coaxing Sister to drink a little wine? I think it would be good for her! Can you carry both at once?

JIM: Sure. I'm Superman!

AMANDA: Now, Thomas, get into this apron!

The door of kitchenette swings closed on Amanda's gay laughter; the flickering light approaches the portieres.

Laura sits up nervously as he enters. Her speech at first is low and breathless from the almost intolerable strain of being alone with a stranger.

(Legend: "I Don't Suppose You Remember Me at All!")

In her first speeches in this scene, before Jim's warmth overcomes her paralyzing shyness, Laura's voice is thin and breathless as though she has run up a steep flight of stairs.

Jim's attitude is gently humorous. In playing this scene it should be stressed that while the incident is apparently unimportant, it is to Laura the climax of her secret life.

JIM: Hello, there, Laura.

LAURA *(faintly)*:   Hello. *(She clears her throat.)*

JIM: How are you feeling now? Better?

LAURA: Yes. Yes, thank you.

JIM: This is for you. A little dandelion wine. *(He extends it toward her with extravagant gallantry.)*

LAURA: Thank you.

JIM: Drink it — but don't get drunk! *(He laughs heartily. Laura takes the glass uncertainly; laughs shyly.)* Where shall I set the candles?

LAURA: Oh — oh, anywhere . . .

JIM: How about here on the floor? Any objections?

LAURA: No.

JIM: I'll spread a newspaper under to catch the drippings. I like to sit on the floor. Mind if I do?

LAURA: Oh, no.

JIM: Give me a pillow?

LAURA: What?

JIM: A pillow!

LAURA: Oh . . . *(Hands him one quickly.)*

JIM: How about you? Don't you like to sit on the floor?

LAURA: Oh — yes.

JIM: Why don't you, then?

LAURA: I — will.

JIM: Take a pillow! *(Laura does. Sits on the other side of the candelabrum. Jim crosses his legs and smiles engagingly at her.)* I can't hardly see you sitting way over there.

LAURA: I can — see you.

JIM: I know, but that's not fair, I'm in the limelight. *(Laura moves her pillow closer.)* Good! Now I can see you! Comfortable?

LAURA: Yes.

JIM: So am I. Comfortable as a cow. Will you have some gum?

LAURA: No, thank you.

JIM: I think that I will indulge, with your permission. *(Musingly unwraps it and holds it up.)* Think of the fortune made by the guy that invented the first piece of chewing gum. Amazing, huh? The Wrigley Building is one of the sights of Chicago. — I saw it summer before last when I went up to the Century of Progress. Did you take in the Century of Progress?

LAURA: No, I didn't.

JIM: Well, it was quite a wonderful exposition. What impressed me most was the Hall of Science. Gives you an idea of what the future will be in America, even more wonderful than the present time is! *(Pause. Smiling at her.)* Your brother tells me you're shy. Is that right, Laura?

LAURA: I — don't know.

JIM: I judge you to be an old-fashioned type of girl. Well, I think that's a pretty good type to be. Hope you don't think I'm being too personal — do you?

LAURA *(hastily, out of embarrassment)*:   I believe I *will* take a piece of gum, if you — don't mind. *(Clearing her throat.)* Mr. O'Connor, have you — kept up with your singing?

JIM: Singing? Me?

LAURA: Yes. I remember what a beautiful voice you had.

JIM: When did you hear me sing?

(Voice offstage in the pause.)

VOICE *(offstage)*:   O blow, ye winds, heigh-ho,
                         A-roving I will go!
                         I'm off to my love
                         With a boxing glove —
                         Ten thousand miles away!

JIM: You say you've heard me sing?

LAURA: Oh, yes! Yes, very often . . . I — don't suppose you remember me — at all?

JIM *(smiling doubtfully)*:   You know I have an idea I've seen you before. I had that idea soon as you opened the door. It seemed almost like I was about to remember your name. But the name that I started to call you — wasn't a name! And so I stopped myself before I said it.

LAURA: Wasn't it — Blue Roses?

JIM (*springs up, grinning*):   Blue Roses! My gosh, yes — Blue Roses! That's what I had on my tongue when you opened the door! Isn't it funny what tricks your memory plays? I didn't connect you with the high school somehow or other. But that's where it was; it was high school. I didn't even know you were Shakespeare's sister! Gosh, I'm sorry.

LAURA: I didn't expect you to. You — barely knew me!

JIM: But we did have a speaking acquaintance, huh?

LAURA: Yes, we — spoke to each other.

JIM: When did you recognize me?

LAURA: Oh, right away!

JIM: Soon as I came in the door?

LAURA: When I heard your name I thought it was probably you. I knew that Tom used to know you a little in high school. So when you came in the door — Well, then I was — sure.

JIM: Why didn't you *say* something, then?

LAURA (*breathlessly*):   I didn't know what to say, I was — too surprised!

JIM: For goodness' sakes! You know, this sure is funny!

LAURA: Yes! Yes, isn't it, though . . .

JIM: Didn't we have a class in something together?

LAURA: Yes, we did.

JIM: What class was that?

LAURA: It was — singing — Chorus!

JIM: Aw!

LAURA: I sat across the aisle from you in the Aud.

JIM: Aw.

LAURA: Mondays, Wednesdays, and Fridays.

JIM: Now I remember — you always came in late.

LAURA: Yes, it was so hard for me, getting upstairs. I had that brace on my leg — it clumped so loud!

JIM: I never heard any clumping.

LAURA (*wincing in the recollection*):   To me it sounded like — thunder!

JIM: Well, well, well. I never even noticed.

LAURA: And everybody was seated before I came in. I had to walk in front of all those people. My seat was in the back row. I had to go clumping all the way up the aisle with everyone watching!

JIM: You shouldn't have been self-conscious.

LAURA: I know, but I was. It was always such a relief when the singing started.

JIM: Aw, yes, I've placed you now! I used to call you Blue Roses. How was it that I got started calling you that?

LAURA: I was out of school a little while with pleurosis. When I came back you asked me what was the matter. I said I had pleurosis — you thought I said Blue Roses. That's what you always called me after that!

JIM: I hope you didn't mind.

LAURA: Oh, no — I liked it. You see, I wasn't acquainted with many — people....

JIM: As I remember you sort of stuck by yourself.

LAURA: I — I — never had much luck at — making friends.

JIM: I don't see why you wouldn't.

LAURA: Well, I — started out badly.

JIM: You mean being —

LAURA: Yes, it sort of — stood between me —

JIM: You shouldn't have let it!

LAURA: I know, but it did, and —

JIM: You were shy with people!

LAURA: I tried not to be but never could —

JIM: Overcome it?

LAURA: No, I — I never could!

JIM: I guess being shy is something you have to work out of kind of gradually.

LAURA *(sorrowfully)*:   Yes — I guess it —

JIM: Takes time!

LAURA: Yes —

JIM: People are not so dreadful when you know them. That's what you have to remember! And everybody has problems, not just you, but practically everybody has got some problems. You think of yourself as having the only problems, as being the only one who is disappointed. But just look around you and you will see lots of people as disappointed as you are. For instance, I hoped when I was going to high school that I would be further along at this time, six years later, than I am now — You remember that wonderful write-up I had in *The Torch*?

LAURA: Yes! *(She rises and crosses to table.)*

JIM: It said I was bound to succeed in anything I went into! *(Laura returns with the annual.)* Holy Jeez! The Torch! *(He accepts it reverently. They smile across it with mutual wonder. Laura crouches beside him and they begin to turn through it. Laura's shyness is dissolving in his warmth.)*

LAURA: Here you are in *Pirates of Penzance*!

JIM *(wistfully)*:   I sang the baritone lead in that operetta.

LAURA *(rapidly)*:   So — beautifully!

JIM *(protesting)*:   Aw —

LAURA: Yes, yes — beautifully — beautifully!

JIM: You heard me?

LAURA: All three times!

JIM: No!

LAURA: Yes!

JIM: All three performances?

LAURA *(looking down)*:   Yes.

JIM: Why?

LAURA: I — wanted to ask you to — autograph my program.

JIM: Why didn't you ask me to?

LAURA: You were always surrounded by your own friends so much that I never had a chance to.

JIM: You should have just —

LAURA: Well, I — thought you might think I was —

JIM: Thought I might think you was — what?

LAURA: Oh —

JIM *(with reflective relish):*   I was beleaguered by females in those days.

LAURA: You were terribly popular!

JIM: Yeah —

LAURA: You had such a — friendly way —

JIM: I was spoiled in high school.

LAURA: Everybody — liked you!

JIM: Including you?

LAURA: I — yes, I — I did, too — *(She gently closes the book in her lap.)*

JIM: Well, well, well! — Give me that program, Laura. *(She hands it to him. He signs it with a flourish.)* There you are — better late than never!

LAURA: Oh, I — what a — surprise!

JIM: My signature isn't worth very much right now. But someday — maybe — it will increase in value! Being disappointed is one thing and being discouraged is something else. I am disappointed but I'm not discouraged. I'm twenty-three years old. How old are you?

LAURA: I'll be twenty-four in June.

JIM: That's not old age.

LAURA: No, but —

JIM: You finished high school?

LAURA *(with difficulty):*   I didn't go back.

JIM: You mean you dropped out?

LAURA: I made bad grades in my final examinations. *(She rises and replaces the book and the program. Her voice strained.)* How is — Emily Meisenbach getting along?

JIM: Oh, that kraut-head!

LAURA: Why do you call her that?

JIM: That's what she was.

LAURA: You're not still — going with her?

JIM: I never see her.

LAURA: It said in the Personal Section that you were — engaged!

JIM: I know, but I wasn't impressed by that — propaganda!

LAURA: It wasn't — the truth?

JIM: Only in Emily's optimistic opinion!

LAURA: Oh —

(Legend: "What Have You Done Since High School?")

> *Jim lights a cigarette and leans indolently back on his elbows smiling at Laura with a warmth and charm which light her inwardly with altar candles. She remains by the table and turns in her hands a piece of glass to cover her tumult.*

JIM *(after several reflective puffs on a cigarette):*   What have you done since high school? *(She seems not to hear him.)* Huh? *(Laura looks up.)* I said what have you done since high school, Laura?

LAURA: Nothing much.

JIM: You must have been doing something these six long years.

LAURA: Yes.

JIM: Well, then, such as what?

LAURA: I took a business course at business college —

JIM: How did that work out?

LAURA: Well, not very — well — I had to drop out, it gave me — indigestion —

Jim laughs gently.

JIM: What are you doing now?

LAURA: I don't do anything — much. Oh, please don't think I sit around doing nothing! My glass collection takes up a good deal of my time. Glass is something you have to take good care of.

JIM: What did you say — about glass?

LAURA: Collection I said — I have one — *(She clears her throat and turns away again, acutely shy.)*

JIM *(abruptly)*:   You know what I judge to be the trouble with you? Inferiority complex! Know what that is? That's what they call it when someone low-rates himself! I understand it because I had it, too. Although my case was not so aggravated as yours seems to be. I had it until I took up public speaking, developed my voice, and learned that I had an aptitude for science. Before that time I never thought of myself as being outstanding in any way whatsoever! Now I've never made a regular study of it, but I have a friend who says I can analyze people better than doctors that make a profession of it. I don't claim that to be necessarily true, but I can sure guess a person's psychology, Laura! *(Takes out his gum.)* Excuse me, Laura. I always take it out when the flavor is gone. I'll use this scrap of paper to wrap it in. I know how it is to get it stuck on a shoe. Yep — that's what I judge to be your principal trouble. A lack of confidence in yourself as a person. You don't have the proper amount of faith in yourself. I'm basing that fact on a number of your remarks and also on certain observations I've made. For instance that clumping you thought was so awful in high school. You say that you even dreaded to walk into class. You see what you did? You dropped out of school, you gave up an education because of a clump, which as far as I know was practically nonexistent! A little physical defect is what you have. Hardly noticeable even! Magnified thousands of times by imagination! You know what my strong advice to you is? Think of yourself as *superior* in some way!

LAURA: In what way would I think?

JIM: Why, man alive, Laura! Just look about you a little. What do you see? A world full of common people! All of 'em born and all of 'em going to die! Which of them has one-tenth of your good points! Or mine! Or anyone else's, as far as that goes — Gosh! Everybody excels in some one thing. Some in many! *(Unconsciously glances at himself in the mirror.)* All you've got to do is discover in *what!* Take me, for instance. *(He adjusts his tie at the mirror.)* My interest happened to lie in electrodynamics. I'm taking a course in radio engineering at night school, Laura, on top of a fairly responsible job at the warehouse. I'm taking that course and studying public speaking.

LAURA: Ohhhh.

JIM: Because I believe in the future of television! *(Turning back to her.)* I wish to be ready to go up right along with it. Therefore I'm planning to get in on the ground floor. In fact, I've already made the right connections and all that remains is for the industry itself to get under way! Full steam — *(His eyes are starry.)* Knowledge — Zzzzzp! Money — Zzzzzzp! — Power! That's the cycle democracy is built on! *(His attitude is convincingly dynamic. Laura stares at him, even her shyness eclipsed in her absolute wonder. He suddenly grins.)* I guess you think I think a lot of myself!

LAURA: No — o-o-o, I —

JIM: Now how about you? Isn't there something you take more interest in than anything else?

LAURA: Well, I do — as I said — have my — glass collection —

A peal of girlish laughter from the kitchen.

JIM: I'm not right sure I know what you're talking about. What kind of glass is it?

LAURA: Little articles of it, they're ornaments mostly! Most of them are little animals made out of glass, the tiniest little animals in the world. Mother calls them a glass menagerie! Here's an example of one, if you'd like to see it! This one is one of the oldest. It's nearly thirteen. *(He stretches out his hand.)* *(Music: "The Glass Menagerie.")* Oh, be careful — if you breathe, it breaks!

JIM: I'd better not take it. I'm pretty clumsy with things.

LAURA: Go on, I trust you with him! *(Places it in his palm.)* There now — you're holding him gently! Hold him over the light, he loves the light! You see how the light shines through him?

JIM: It sure does shine!

LAURA: I shouldn't be partial, but he is my favorite one.

JIM: What kind of thing is this one supposed to be?

LAURA: Haven't you noticed the single horn on his forehead?

JIM: A unicorn, huh?

LAURA: Mmm-hmmm!

JIM: Unicorns, aren't they extinct in the modern world?

LAURA: I know!

JIM: Poor little fellow, he must feel sort of lonesome.

LAURA *(smiling)*: Well, if he does he doesn't complain about it. He stays on a shelf with some horses that don't have horns and all of them seem to get along nicely together.

JIM: How do you know?

LAURA *(lightly)*: I haven't heard any arguments among them!

JIM *(grinning)*: No arguments, huh? Well, that's a pretty good sign! Where shall I set him?

LAURA: Put him on the table. They all like a change of scenery once in a while!

JIM *(stretching)*: Well, well, well, well — Look how big my shadow is when I stretch!

LAURA: Oh, oh, yes — it stretches across the ceiling!

JIM *(crossing to door)*:   I think it's stopped raining. *(Opens fire-escape door.)* Where does the music come from?

LAURA: From the Paradise Dance Hall across the alley.

JIM: How about cutting the rug a little, Miss Wingfield?

LAURA: Oh, I —

JIM: Or is your program filled up? Let me have a look at it. *(Grasps imaginary card.)* Why, every dance is taken! I'll have to scratch some out. *(Waltz music: "La Golondrina.")* Ahhh, a waltz! *(He executes some sweeping turns by himself then holds his arms toward Laura.)*

LAURA *(breathlessly)*:   I — can't dance!

JIM: There you go, that inferiority stuff!

LAURA: I've never danced in my life!

JIM: Come on, try!

LAURA: Oh, but I'd step on you!

JIM: I'm not made out of glass.

LAURA: How — how — how do we start?

JIM: Just leave it to me. You hold your arms out a little.

LAURA: Like this?

JIM: A little bit higher. Right. Now don't tighten up, that's the main thing about it — relax.

LAURA *(laughing breathlessly)*:   It's hard not to.

JIM: Okay.

LAURA: I'm afraid you can't budge me.

JIM: What do you bet I can't? *(He swings her into motion.)*

LAURA: Goodness, yes, you can!

JIM: Let yourself go, now, Laura, just let yourself go.

LAURA: I'm —

JIM: Come on!

LAURA: Trying.

JIM: Not so stiff — Easy does it!

LAURA: I know but I'm —

JIM: Loosen th' backbone! There now, that's a lot better.

LAURA: Am I?

JIM: Lots, lots better! *(He moves her about the room in a clumsy waltz.)*

LAURA: Oh, my!

JIM: Ha-ha!

LAURA: Goodness, yes you can!

JIM: Ha-ha-ha! *(They suddenly bump into the table. Jim stops.)* What did we hit on?

LAURA: Table.

JIM: Did something fall off it? I think —

LAURA: Yes.

JIM: I hope it wasn't the little glass horse with the horn!

LAURA: Yes.

JIM: Aw, aw, aw. Is it broken?

LAURA: Now it is just like all the other horses.

JIM: It's lost its —

LAURA: Horn! It doesn't matter. Maybe it's a blessing in disguise.

JIM: You'll never forgive me. I bet that that was your favorite piece of glass.

LAURA: I don't have favorites much. It's no tragedy, Freckles. Glass breaks so easily. No matter how careful you are. The traffic jars the shelves and things fall off them.

JIM: Still I'm awfully sorry that I was the cause.

LAURA *(smiling)*:   I'll just imagine he had an operation. The horn was removed to make him feel less — freakish! *(They both laugh.)* Now he will feel more at home with the other horses, the ones that don't have horns . . .

JIM: Ha-ha, that's very funny! *(Suddenly serious.)* I'm glad to see that you have a sense of humor. You know — you're — well — very different! Surprisingly different from anyone else I know! *(His voice becomes soft and hesitant with a genuine feeling.)* Do you mind me telling you that? *(Laura is abashed beyond speech.)* You make me feel sort of — I don't know how to put it! I'm usually pretty good at expressing things, but — This is something that I don't know how to say! *(Laura touches her throat and clears it — turns the broken unicorn in her hands.)* *(Even softer.)* Has anyone ever told you that you were pretty?

Pause: Music.

(Laura looks up slowly, with wonder, and shakes her head.) Well, you are! In a very different way from anyone else. And all the nicer because of the difference, too. *(His voice becomes low and husky. Laura turns away, nearly faint with the novelty of her emotions.)* I wish that you were my sister. I'd teach you to have some confidence in yourself. The different people are not like other people, but being different is nothing to be ashamed of. Because other people are not such wonderful people. They're one hundred times one thousand. You're one times one! They walk all over the earth. You just stay here. They're common as — weeds, but — you — well, you're — Blue Roses!

(Image on screen: Blue Roses.)
   (Music changes.)

LAURA: But blue is wrong for — roses . . .

JIM: It's right for you — You're — pretty!

LAURA: In what respect am I pretty?

JIM: In all respects — believe me! Your eyes — your hair — are pretty! Your hands are pretty! *(He catches hold of her hand.)* You think I'm making this up because I'm invited to dinner and have to be nice. Oh, I could do that! I could put on an act for you, Laura, and say lots of things without being very sincere. But this time I am. I'm talking to you sincerely. I happened to notice you had this inferiority complex that keeps you from feeling comfortable with people. Somebody needs to build your confidence up and make you proud instead of shy and turning away and — blushing — Somebody ought to — ought to — *kiss* you, Laura! *(His hand slips slowly up her arm to her shoulder.) (Music swells tumultuously.) (He suddenly turns her about and kisses her on the lips. When he releases her Laura sinks on the sofa with a bright, dazed look. Jim backs away and fishes in his pocket for a cigarette.) (Legend on screen: "Souvenir.")* Stumble-john! *(He lights the cigarette, avoiding her look. There is a peal of girlish laughter from Amanda in the kitchen. Laura slowly raises and opens her hand. It still contains the little broken glass animal. She looks at it with a tender, bewildered expression.)* Stumble-john! I shouldn't have done that — That was way off the beam. You don't smoke, do you? *(She looks up, smiling, not hearing the question. He sits beside her a little gingerly. She looks at him speechlessly — waiting. He coughs decorously and moves a little farther aside as he considers the situation and senses her feelings, dimly, with perturbation. Gently.)* Would you — care for a — mint? *(She doesn't seem to hear him but her look grows brighter even.)* Peppermint — Life Saver? My pocket's a regular drug store — wherever I go . . . *(He pops a mint in his mouth. Then gulps and decides to make a clean breast of it. He speaks slowly and gingerly.)* Laura, you know, if I had a sister like you, I'd do the same thing as Tom. I'd bring out fellows — introduce her to them. The right type of boys of a type to — appreciate her. Only — well — he made a mistake about me. Maybe I've got no call to be saying this. That may not have been the idea in having me over. But what if it was? There's nothing wrong about that. The only trouble is that in my case — I'm not in a situation to — do the right thing. I can't take down your number and say I'll phone. I can't call up next week and — ask for a date. I thought I had better explain the situation in case you misunderstood it and — hurt your feelings. . . . *(Pause. Slowly, very slowly, Laura's look changes, her eyes returning slowly from his to the ornament in her palm.)*

Amanda utters another gay laugh in the kitchen.

LAURA *(faintly)*:   You — won't — call again?

JIM: No, Laura, I can't. *(He rises from the sofa.)* As I was just explaining, I've — got strings on me, Laura, I've — been going steady! I go out all the time with a girl named Betty. She's a home-girl like you, and Catholic, and Irish, and in a great many ways we — get along fine. I met her last summer on a moonlight boat trip up the river to Alton, on the *Majestic.* Well — right away from the start it was — love! *(Legend: Love!) (Laura sways slightly forward and grips the arm of the sofa. He fails to notice, now enrapt in his own comfortable being.)* Being in love has made a new man of me! *(Leaning stiffly forward, clutching the arm of the sofa, Laura struggles visibly with her storm. But Jim is oblivious, she is a long way off.)* The power of love is really pretty tremendous! Love is something that — changes the whole world, Laura! *(The storm abates a little and Laura leans back. He notices her again.)* It happened that Betty's aunt took sick, she got a wire and had to go to Centralia. So Tom — when he asked me to dinner — I naturally just accepted the invitation, not knowing that you — that he — that I — *(He stops awkwardly.)* Huh — I'm a stumble-john! *(He flops back on the sofa. The holy candles in the altar of Laura's face have been snuffed out! There is a look of almost infinite desolation. Jim glances at her uneasily.)* I wish that you would — say something. *(She bites her lip which was trembling and then bravely smiles. She opens her hand again on the broken glass ornament. Then she gently takes his hand and raises it level with her own. She carefully places the unicorn in the palm of his hand, then pushes his fingers closed upon it.)* What are you — doing that for? You want me to have him? — Laura? *(She nods.)* What for?

LAURA: A — souvenir . . .

She rises unsteadily and crouches beside the Victrola to wind it up.

   (Legend on screen: "Things Have a Way of Turning Out So Badly.")
   (Or image: "Gentleman caller waving good-bye! — Gaily.")

   At this moment Amanda rushes brightly back in the front room. She bears a pitcher of fruit punch in an old-fashioned cut-glass pitcher and a plate of macaroons. The plate has a gold border and poppies painted on it.

AMANDA: Well, well, well! Isn't the air delightful after the shower? I've made you children a little liquid refreshment. *(Turns gaily to the gentleman caller.)* Jim, do you know that song about lemonade?
"Lemonade, lemonade
Made in the shade and stirred with a spade —
Good enough for any old maid!"

JIM *(uneasily)*:   Ha-ha! No — I never heard it.

AMANDA: Why, Laura! You look so serious!

JIM: We were having a serious conversation.

AMANDA: Good! Now you're better acquainted!

JIM *(uncertainly)*:   Ha-ha! Yes.

AMANDA: You modern young people are much more serious-minded than my generation. I was so gay as a girl!

JIM: You haven't changed, Mrs. Wingfield.

AMANDA: Tonight I'm rejuvenated! The gaiety of the occasion, Mr. O'Connor! *(She tosses her head with a peal of laughter. Spills lemonade.)* Oooo! I'm baptizing myself!

JIM: Here — let me —

AMANDA *(setting the pitcher down)*:   There now. I discovered we had some maraschino cherries. I dumped them in, juice and all!

JIM: You shouldn't have gone to that trouble, Mrs. Wingfield.

AMANDA: Trouble, trouble? Why it was loads of fun! Didn't you hear me cutting up in the kitchen? I bet your ears were burning! I told Tom how outdone with him I was for keeping you to himself so long a time! He should have brought you over much, much sooner! Well, now that you've found your way, I want you to be a very frequent caller! Not just occasional but all the time. Oh, we're going to have a lot of gay times together! I see them coming! Mmm, just breathe that air! So fresh, and the moon's so pretty! I'll skip back out — I know where my place is when young folks are having a — serious conversation!

JIM: Oh, don't go out, Mrs. Wingfield. The fact of the matter is I've got to be going.

AMANDA: Going, now? You're joking! Why, it's only the shank of the evening, Mr. O'Connor!

JIM: Well, you know how it is.

AMANDA: You mean you're a young workingman and have to keep working-men's hours. We'll let you off early tonight. But only on the condition that next time you stay later. What's the best night for you? Isn't Saturday night the best night for you workingmen?

JIM: I have a couple of time-clocks to punch, Mrs. Wingfield. One at morning, another one at night!

AMANDA: My, but you *are* ambitious! You work at night, too?

JIM: No, Ma'am, not work but — Betty! *(He crosses deliberately to pick up his hat. The band at the Paradise Dance Hall goes into a tender waltz.)*

AMANDA: Betty? Betty? Who's — Betty! *(There is an ominous cracking sound in the sky.)*

JIM: Oh, just a girl. The girl I go steady with! *(He smiles charmingly. The sky falls.)*

(Legend: "The Sky Falls.")

AMANDA *(a long-drawn exhalation)*:   Ohhhh . . . Is it a serious romance, Mr. O'Connor?

JIM: We're going to be married the second Sunday in June.

AMANDA: Ohhhh — how nice! Tom didn't mention that you were engaged to be married.

JIM: The cat's not out of the bag at the warehouse yet. You know how they are. They call you Romeo and stuff like that. *(He stops at the oval mirror to put on his hat. He carefully shapes the brim and the crown to give a discreetly dashing effect.)* It's been a wonderful evening, Mrs. Wingfield. I guess this is what they mean by Southern hospitality.

AMANDA: It really wasn't anything at all.

JIM: I hope it don't seem like I'm rushing off. But I promised Betty I'd pick her up at the Wabash depot, an' by the time I get my jalopy down there her train'll be in. Some women are pretty upset if you keep 'em waiting.

AMANDA: Yes, I know — The tyranny of women! *(Extends her hand.)* Good-bye, Mr. O'Connor. I wish you luck — and happiness — and success! All three of them, and so does Laura — Don't you, Laura?

LAURA: Yes!

JIM *(taking her hand)*:   Good-bye, Laura. I'm certainly going to treasure that sou-venir. And don't you forget the good advice I gave you. *(Raises his voice to a cheery shout.)* So long, Shakespeare! Thanks again, ladies — Good night!

He grins and ducks jauntily out.

Still bravely grimacing, Amanda closes the door on the gentleman caller. Then she turns back to the room with a puzzled expression. She and Laura don't dare to face each other. Laura crouches beside the Victrola to wind it.

AMANDA *(faintly)*:   Things have a way of turning out so badly. I don't believe that I would play the Victrola. Well, well — well — Our gentleman caller was engaged to be married! Tom!

TOM *(from back)*:   Yes, Mother?

AMANDA: Come in here a minute. I want to tell you something awfully funny.

TOM *(enters with macaroon and a glass of the lemonade)*: Has the gentleman caller gotten away already?

AMANDA: The gentleman caller has made an early departure. What a wonderful joke you played on us!

TOM: How do you mean?

AMANDA: You didn't mention that he was engaged to be married.

TOM: Jim? Engaged?

AMANDA: That's what he just informed us.

TOM: I'll be jiggered! I didn't know about that.

AMANDA: That seems very peculiar.

TOM: What's peculiar about it?

AMANDA: Didn't you call him your best friend down at the warehouse?

TOM: He is, but how did I know?

AMANDA: It seems extremely peculiar that you wouldn't know your best friend was going to be married!

TOM: The warehouse is where I work, not where I know things about people!

AMANDA: You don't know things anywhere! You live in a dream; you manufacture illusions! *(He crosses to door.)* Where are you going?

TOM: I'm going to the movies.

AMANDA: That's right, now that you've had us make such fools of ourselves. The effort, the preparations, all the expense! The new floor lamp, the rug, the clothes for Laura! All for what? To entertain some other girl's fiancé! Go to the movies, go! Don't think about us, a mother deserted, an unmarried sister who's crippled and has no job! Don't let anything interfere with your selfish pleasure! Just go, go, go — to the movies!

TOM: All right, I will! The more you shout about my selfishness to me the quicker I'll go, and I won't go to the movies!

AMANDA: Go, then! Then go to the moon — you selfish dreamer!

Tom smashes his glass on the floor. He plunges out on the fire-escape, slamming the door. Laura screams — cut by door.

Dance-hall music up. Tom goes to the rail and grips it desperately, lifting his face in the chill white moonlight penetrating the narrow abyss of the alley.

(Legend on screen: "And So Good-Bye . . .")

Tom's closing speech is timed with the interior pantomime. The interior scene is played as though viewed through sound-proof glass. Amanda appears to be making a comforting speech to Laura who is huddled upon the sofa. Now that we cannot hear the mother's speech, her silliness is gone and she has dignity and tragic beauty. Laura's dark hair hides her face until at the end of the speech she lifts it to smile at her mother. Amanda's gestures are slow and graceful, almost dancelike, as she comforts the daughter. At the end of her speech she glances a moment at the father's picture — then withdraws through the portieres. At close of Tom's speech, Laura blows out the candles, ending the play.

TOM: I didn't go to the moon, I went much further — for time is the longest distance between two places — Not long after that I was fired for writing a poem on the lid of a shoe-box. I left Saint Louis. I descended the steps of this fire-escape for a last time and followed, from then on, in my father's footsteps, attempting to find in motion what was lost in space — I traveled around a great deal. The cities swept about me like dead leaves, leaves that were brightly colored but torn away from the branches. I would have stopped, but I was pursued by something. It always came upon me un-awares, taking me altogether by surprise. Perhaps it was a familiar bit of music. Perhaps it was only a piece of transparent glass — Perhaps I am walking along a street at night, in some strange city, before I have found companions. I pass the lighted window of a shop where perfume is sold. The window is filled with pieces of colored glass, tiny transparent bottles in delicate colors, like bits of a shattered rainbow. Then all at once my sister touches my shoulder. I turn around and look into her eyes. . . . Oh, Laura, Laura, I tried to leave you behind me, but I am more faithful than I intended to be! I reach for a cigarette, I cross the street, I run into the movies or a bar, I buy a drink, I speak to the nearest stranger — anything that can blow your candles out! *(Laura bends over the candles.)* — for nowa-days the world is lit by lightning! Blow out your candles, Laura — and so good-bye . . .

She blows the candles out.
(The Scene Dissolves.)   [1945]

≡ THINKING ABOUT THE TEXT

1. Is Amanda just overprotective, or does her devotion to Laura's eventual marriage suggest a more serious issue? If you were a close friend of Amanda, how would you advise her to behave toward Laura?

2. Why does Laura keep the glass menagerie? Why does she give Jim her broken unicorn? Is this a positive sign?

3. This is a play about love, guilt, pity, regret, cruelty, and self-loathing. Can you cite concrete examples of these emotions in this play? Did you notice any other emotions? Is this a realistic portrait of family life, or is it an exaggeration?

4. Critics are divided over Williams's motivation in this play. Is he trying to get rid of Laura's memory (based on his sister Rose, who went mad and whom he deserted), or is he replaying the traumatic leaving? Which makes the most sense to you? How do you read the last line, "Blow out your candles, Laura — and so good-bye . . ."?

5. Do you blame Tom for leaving? Does he abandon his responsibilities? What do you think of Tom's priorities? Does he have a duty to take the place of his absent father? What would have happened if Tom had stayed? What would you do?

CHRISTOPHER DURANG
For Whom the Southern Belle Tolls

Born in Montclair, New Jersey, in 1949, Christopher Durang graduated from Harvard University and the Yale School of Drama. He has won numerous awards, fellowships, and grants, including Obie awards for Sister Mary Ignatius Explains It All for You *(1980) and* The Marriage of Betty and Boo *(1985). The former, one of his most popular plays, focuses on a nun who is proud of the righteousness of her students. But this turns to dark comedy when her former charges appear and reveal that they despise her and her dogmatic ways. The play is insightful, violent, and hilarious. His latest work is* Vanya and Sonia and Masha and Spike *(2012). Durang has taught playwriting at Yale and is currently cochair of the playwriting program at the Juilliard School in New York City.*

CHARACTERS

AMANDA, *the mother*
LAWRENCE, *the son*
TOM, *the other son*
GINNY

Lights up on a fussy living room setting. Enter Amanda, the Southern belle mother.

AMANDA: Rise and shine! Rise and shine! *(Calls off.)* Lawrence, honey, come on out here and let me have a look at you!

Enter Lawrence, who limps across the room. He is very sensitive, and is wearing what are clearly his dress clothes. Amanda fiddles with his bow tie and stands back to admire him.

AMANDA: Lawrence, honey, you look lovely.

LAWRENCE: No, I don't mama. I have a pimple on the back of my neck.

AMANDA: Don't say the word "pimple," honey, it's common. Now your brother Tom is bringing home a girl from the warehouse for you to meet, and I want you to make a good impression, honey.

LAWRENCE: It upsets my stomach to meet people, mama.

AMANDA: Oh, Lawrence honey, you're so sensitive it makes me want to hit you.

LAWRENCE: I don't need to meet people, mama. I'm happy just by myself, playing with my collection of glass cocktail stirrers.

Lawrence limps over to a table on top of which sits a glass jar filled with glass swizzle sticks.

AMANDA: Lawrence, you are a caution. Only retarded people and alcoholics are interested in glass cocktail stirrers.

LAWRENCE *(picking up some of them)*: Each one of them has a special name, mama. This one is called Stringbean because it's long and thin; and this one is called Stringbean because it's long and thin; and this one is called Blue because it's blue.

© Chris Barth/Star
Ledger/Corbis

AMANDA: All my children have such imagination, why was I so blessed? Oh,
Lawrence, honey, how are you going to get on in the world if you just stay
home all day, year after year, playing with your collection of glass cocktail
stirrers?

LAWRENCE: I don't like the world, mama, I like it here in this room.

AMANDA: I know you do, Lawrence honey, that's part of your charm. Some
days. But, honey, what about making a living?

LAWRENCE: I can't work, mama. I'm crippled. *(He limps over to the couch and
sits.)*

AMANDA: There is nothing wrong with your leg, Lawrence honey, all the doctors have told you that. This limping thing is an affectation.

LAWRENCE: I only know how I feel, mama.

AMANDA: Oh, if only I had connections in the Mafia, I'd have someone come
and break both your legs.

LAWRENCE: Don't try to make me laugh, mama. You know I have asthma.

AMANDA: Your asthma, your leg, your eczema. You're just a mess, Lawrence.

LAWRENCE: I have scabs from the itching, mama.

AMANDA: That's lovely, Lawrence. You must tell us more over dinner.

LAWRENCE: Alright.

AMANDA: That was a joke, Lawrence.

LAWRENCE: Don't try to make me laugh, mama. My asthma.

AMANDA: Now, Lawrence, I don't want you talking about your ailments to the feminine caller your brother Tom is bringing home from the warehouse, honey. No nice-bred young lady likes to hear a young man discussing his eczema, Lawrence.

LAWRENCE: What else can I talk about, mama?

AMANDA: Talk about the weather. Or Red China.

LAWRENCE: Or my collection of glass cocktail stirrers?

AMANDA: I suppose so, honey, if the conversation comes to some godawful standstill. Otherwise, I'd shut up about it. Conversation is an art, Lawrence. Back at Blue Mountain, when I had seventeen gentlemen callers, I was able to converse with charm and vivacity for six hours without stop and never once mention eczema or bone cancer or vivisection. Try to emulate me, Lawrence, honey. Charm and vivacity. And charm. And vivacity. And charm.

LAWRENCE: Well, I'll try, but I doubt it.

AMANDA: Me too, honey. But we'll go through the motions anyway, won't we?

LAWRENCE: I don't know if I want to meet some girl who works in a warehouse, mama.

AMANDA: Your brother Tom says she's a lovely girl with a nice personality. And where else does he meet girls except the few who work at the warehouse? He only seems to meet men at the movies. Your brother goes to the movies entirely too much. I must speak to him about it.

LAWRENCE: It's unfeminine for a girl to work at a warehouse.

AMANDA: Lawrence, honey, if you can't go out the door without getting an upset stomach or an attack of vertigo, then we got to find some nice girl who's willing to support you. Otherwise, how am I ever going to get you out of this house and off my hands?

LAWRENCE: Why do you want to be rid of me, mama?

AMANDA: I suppose it's unmotherly of me, dear, but you really get on my nerves. Limping around the apartment, pretending to have asthma. If only some nice girl would marry you and I knew you were taken care of, then I'd feel free to start to live again. I'd join Parents Without Partners, I'd go to dinner dances, I'd have a life again. Rather than just watch you mope about this stupid apartment. I'm not bitter, dear, it's just that I hate my life.

LAWRENCE: I understand, mama.

AMANDA: Do you, dear? Oh, you're cute. Oh listen, I think I hear them.

TOM (*from offstage*): Mother, I forgot my key.

LAWRENCE: I'll be in the other room. (*Starts to limp away.*)

AMANDA: I want you to let them in, Lawrence.

LAWRENCE: Oh, I couldn't mama. She'd see I limp.

AMANDA: Then don't limp, damn it.

TOM (*from off*): Mother, are you there?

AMANDA: Just a minute, Tom, honey. Now, Lawrence, you march over to that door or I'm going to break all your swizzle sticks.

LAWRENCE: Mama, I can't.

AMANDA: Lawrence, you're a grown boy. Now you answer that door like any normal person.

LAWRENCE: I can't.

TOM: Mother, I'm going to break the door down in a minute.

AMANDA: Just be patient, Tom. Now you're causing a scene, Lawrence. I want you to answer that door.

LAWRENCE: My eczema itches.

AMANDA: I'll itch it for you in a second, Lawrence.

TOM: Alright, I'm breaking it down.

Sound of door breaking down. Enter Tom and Ginny Bennett, a vivacious girl dressed in factory clothes.

AMANDA: Oh, Tom, you got in.

TOM: Why must we go through this every night? You know the stupid fuck won't open the door, so why don't you let him alone about it? *(To Ginny.)* My kid brother has a thing about answering doors. He thinks people will notice his limp and his asthma and his eczema.

LAWRENCE: Excuse me. I think I hear someone calling me in the other room. *(Limps off, calls to imaginary person.)* Coming!

AMANDA: Now see what you've done. He's probably going to refuse to come to the table due to your insensitivity. Oh, was any woman as cursed as I? With one son who's too sensitive and another one who's this big ox. I'm sorry, how rude of me. I'm Amanda Wingvalley. You must be Virginia Bennett from the warehouse. Tom has spoken so much about you I feel you're almost one of the family, preferably a daughter-in-law. Welcome, Virginia.

GINNY *(speaking very loudly)*:   Call me Ginny or Gin. But just don't call me late for dinner! *(Roars with laughter.)*

AMANDA: Oh, how amusing. *(Whispers to Tom.)* Why is she shouting? Is she deaf?

GINNY: You're asking why I am speaking loudly. It's so that I can be heard! I am taking a course in public speaking, and so far we've covered organizing your thoughts and speaking good and loud so the people in the back of the room can hear you.

AMANDA: Public speaking. How impressive. You must be interested in improving yourself.

GINNY *(truly not having heard)*:   What?

AMANDA *(loudly)*:   YOU MUST BE INTERESTED IN IMPROVING YOURSELF.

GINNY *(loudly and happily)*:   YES I AM!

TOM: When's dinner? I want to get this over with fast if everyone's going to shout all evening.

GINNY: What?

AMANDA *(to Ginny)*:   Dinner is almost ready, Ginny.

GINNY: Who's Freddy?

AMANDA: Oh, Lord. No, dear. DINNER IS READY.

GINNY: Oh good. I'm as hungry as a bear! *(Growls enthusiastically.)*

AMANDA: You must be very popular at the warehouse, Ginny.

GINNY: No popsicle for me, ma'am, although I will take you up on some gin.

AMANDA *(confused)*:   What?

GINNY *(loudly)*:   I WOULD LIKE SOME GIN.

AMANDA: Well, fine. I think I'd like to get drunk too. Tom, why don't you go and make two Southern ladies some nice summer gin and tonics? And see if your sister would like a lemonade.

TOM: Sister?

AMANDA: I'm sorry, did I say sister? I meant brother.

TOM *(calling as he exits)*:   Hey, four eyes, you wanna lemonade?

AMANDA: Tom's so amusing. He calls Lawrence four eyes even though he doesn't wear glasses.

GINNY: And does Lawrence wear glasses?

AMANDA *(confused)*:   What?

GINNY: You said Tom called Lawrence four eyes even though he doesn't wear glasses, and I wondered if Lawrence wore glasses. Because that would, you see, explain it.

AMANDA *(looks at her with despair)*:   Ah. I don't know. I'll have to ask Lawrence someday. Speaking of Lawrence, let me go check on the supper and see if I can convince him to come out here and make conversation with you.

GINNY: No, thank you, ma'am, I'll just have the gin.

AMANDA: What?

GINNY: What?

AMANDA: Never mind. I'll be back. Or with luck I won't.

Amanda exits. Ginny looks around uncomfortably, and crosses to the table with the collection of glass cocktail stirrers.

GINNY: They must drink a lot here.

Enter Tom with a glass of gin for Ginny.

TOM: Here's some gin for Ginny.

GINNY: What?

TOM: Here's your poison.

GINNY: No, thanks, I'll just wait here.

TOM: Have you ever thought all that loud machinery at the warehouse may be affecting your hearing?

GINNY: Scenery? You mean, like trees? Yeah, I like trees.

TOM: I like trees, too.

AMANDA *(from offstage)*:   Now you get out of that bed this minute, Lawrence Wingvalley, or I'm going to give that overbearing girl your entire collection of glass gobbledygook — is that clear?

Amanda pushes in Lawrence, who is wearing a nightshirt.

AMANDA: I believe Lawrence would like to visit with you, Ginny.

GINNY *(shows her drink)*:   Tom brought me my drink already, thank you, Mrs. Wingvalley.

AMANDA: You know a hearing aid isn't really all that expensive, dear, you might look into that.

GINNY: No, if I have the gin, I don't really want any Gatorade. Never liked the stuff anyway. But you feel free.

AMANDA: Thank you, dear. I will. Come, Tom, come to the kitchen and help me prepare the dinner. And we'll let the two young people converse. Remember, Lawrence. Charm and vivacity.

TOM: I hope this dinner won't take long, mother. I don't want to get to the movies too late.

AMANDA: Oh shut up about the movies.

Amanda and Tom exit. Lawrence stands still, uncomfortable. Ginny looks at him pleasantly. Silence for a while.

GINNY: Hi.

LAWRENCE: Hi. *(Pause.)* I'd gone to bed.

GINNY: I never eat bread. It's too fattening. I have to watch my figure if I want to get ahead in the world. Why are you wearing that nightshirt?

LAWRENCE: I'd gone to bed. I wasn't feeling well. My leg hurts and I have a headache, and I have palpitations of the heart.

GINNY: I don't know. Hum a few bars, and I'll see.

LAWRENCE: We've met before, you know.

GINNY: I've never seen snow. Is it exciting?

LAWRENCE: We were in high school together. You were voted Girl Most Likely To Succeed. We sat next to one another in glee club.

GINNY: I'm sorry, I really can't hear you. You're talking too softly.

LAWRENCE *(louder)*:   You used to call me BLUE ROSES.

GINNY: Blue Roses? Oh yes, I remember, sort of. Why did I do that?

LAWRENCE: I had been absent from school for several months, and when I came back, you asked me where I'd been, and I said I'd been sick with viral pneumonia, but you thought I said "blue roses."

GINNY: I didn't get much of that, but I remember you now. You used to make a spectacle of yourself every day in glee class, clumping up the aisle with this great big noisy leg brace on your leg. God, you made a racket.

LAWRENCE: I was always so afraid people were looking at me, and pointing. But then eventually mama wouldn't let me wear the leg brace anymore. She gave it to the Salvation Army.

GINNY: I've never been in the army. How long were you in for?

LAWRENCE: I've never been in the army. I have asthma.

GINNY: You do? May I see it?

LAWRENCE *(confused)*:   See it?

GINNY: Well, sure, unless you don't want to.

LAWRENCE: Maybe you want to see my collection of glass cocktail stirrers. *(He limps to the table, and limps back to her, holding his collection.)*

LAWRENCE *(holds up a stick)*:   I call this one Stringbean, because it's long and thin.

GINNY: Thank you. *(Puts it in her glass and stirs it.)*

LAWRENCE *(fairly appalled)*:   They're not for use. *(Takes it back from her.)* They're a collection.

GINNY: Well, I guess I stirred it enough.

LAWRENCE: They're my favorite thing in the world. *(Holds up another one.)* I call this one Q-tip, because I realized it looks like a Q-tip, except it's made out of glass and doesn't have little cotton swabs at the end of it. *(She looks blank.)* Q-TIPS.

GINNY: Really? *(She takes it and puts it in her ear.)*

LAWRENCE: No! Don't put it in your ear. *(Takes it back.)* Now it's disgusting.

GINNY: Well, I didn't think it was a Q-tip, but that's what you said it was.

LAWRENCE: I call it that. I think I'm going to throw it out now. *(Holds up another one.)* I call this one Pinocchio because if you hold it perpendicular to your nose it makes your nose look long. *(He holds it to his nose.)*

GINNY: Uh huh.

LAWRENCE: And I call this one Henry Kissinger, because he wears glasses and it's made of glass.

GINNY: Uh huh. *(Takes it and stirs her drink.)*

LAWRENCE: No! They're just for looking, not for stirring. Mama, she's making a mess with my collection.

AMANDA *(from off)*:   Oh shut up about your collection, honey, you're probably driving the poor girl bananas.

GINNY: No bananas, thank you! My nutritionist says I should avoid potassium. You know what I take your trouble to be, Lawrence?

LAWRENCE: Mama says I'm retarded.

GINNY: I know you're tired, I figured that's why you put on the nightshirt, but this won't take long. I judge you to be lacking in self-confidence. Am I right?

LAWRENCE: Well, I am afraid of people and things, and I have a lot of ailments.

GINNY: But that makes you special, Lawrence.

LAWRENCE: What does?

GINNY: I don't know. Whatever you said. And that's why you should present yourself with more confidence. Throw back your shoulders, and say, "HI! HOW YA DOIN'?" Now you try it.

LAWRENCE *(unenthusiastically, softly)*:   Hello, How are you?

GINNY *(looking at watch, in response to his supposed question)*:   I don't know, it's about 8:30, but this won't take long and then you can go to bed. Alright, now try it. *(Booming.)* "HI! HOW YA DOIN'?"

LAWRENCE: Hi. How ya doin'?

GINNY: Now swagger a bit. *(Kinda butch.)* HI. HOW YA DOIN'?

LAWRENCE *(imitates her fairly successfully)*:   HI. HOW YA DOIN'?

GINNY: Good, Lawrence. That's much better, Again.

Amanda and Tom enter from behind them and watch this.

GINNY *(continued)*:   HI! HOW YA DOIN'?

LAWRENCE: HI! HOW YA DOIN'?

GINNY: THE BRAVES PLAYED A HELLUVA GAME, DON'TCHA THINK?

LAWRENCE: THE BRAVES PLAYED A HELLUVA GAME, DON'TCHA THINK?

AMANDA: Oh God I feel sorry for their children. Is this the only girl who works at the warehouse, Tom?

GINNY: HI, MRS. WINGVALLEY. YOUR SON LAWRENCE AND I ARE GETTING ON JUST FINE. AREN'T WE, LAWRENCE?

AMANDA: Please, no need to shout, I'm not deaf, even if you are.

GINNY: What?

AMANDA: I'm glad you like Lawrence.

GINNY: What?

AMANDA: I'M GLAD YOU LIKE LAWRENCE.

GINNY: What?

AMANDA: WHY DON'T YOU MARRY LAWRENCE?

GINNY *(looks shocked; has heard this)*:   Oh.

LAWRENCE: Oh, mama.

GINNY: Oh dear, I see. So that's why Shakespeare asked me here.

AMANDA *(to Tom)*:   Shakespeare?

TOM: The first day of work she asked my name, and I said Tom Wingvalley, and she thought I said Shakespeare.

GINNY: Oh dear, Mrs. Wingvalley, if I had a young brother as nice and as special as Lawrence, I'd invite girls from the warehouse home to meet him too.

AMANDA: I'm sure I don't know what you mean.

GINNY: And you're probably hoping I'll say that I'll call again.

AMANDA: Really, we haven't even had dinner yet. Tom, shouldn't you be checkin' on the roast pigs feet?

TOM: I guess so. If anything interesting happens, call me. *(Exits.)*

GINNY: But I'm afraid I won't be calling on Lawrence again.

LAWRENCE: This is so embarrassing. I told you I wanted to stay in my room.

AMANDA: Hush up, Lawrence.

GINNY: But, Lawrence, I don't want you to think that I won't be calling because I don't like you. I do like you.

LAWRENCE: You do?

GINNY: Sure. I like everybody. But I got two time clocks to punch, Mrs. Wingvalley. One at the warehouse, and one at night.

AMANDA: At night? You have a second job? That is ambitious.

GINNY: Not a second job, ma'am. Betty.

AMANDA: Pardon?

GINNY: Now who's deaf, eh what? Betty. I'm involved with a girl named Betty. We've been going together for about a year. We're saving money so that we can buy a farmhouse and a tractor together. So you *(to Lawrence)* can see why I can't visit your son, though I wish I could. No hard feelings, Lawrence. You're a good kid.

LAWRENCE *(offers her another swizzle stick)*:   I want you to keep this. It's my very favorite one. I call it Thermometer because it looks like a thermometer.

GINNY: You want me to have this?

LAWRENCE: Yes, as a souvenir.

GINNY *(offended)*:   Well, there's no need to call me a queer. Fuck you and your stupid swizzle sticks. *(Throws the offered gift upstage.)*

LAWRENCE *(very upset)*:   You've broken it!

GINNY: What?

LAWRENCE: You've broken it. YOU'VE BROKEN IT.

GINNY: So I've broken it. Big fuckin' deal. You have twenty more of them here.

AMANDA: Well, I'm so sorry you have to be going.

GINNY: What?

AMANDA: Hadn't you better be going?

GINNY: What?

AMANDA: Go away!

GINNY: Well I guess I can tell when I'm not wanted. I guess I'll go now.

AMANDA: You and Betty must come over some evening. Preferably when we're out.

GINNY: I wasn't shouting. *(Calls off.)* So long, Shakespeare. See you at the warehouse. *(To Lawrence.)* So long, Lawrence. I hope your rash gets better.

LAWRENCE *(saddened, holding the broken swizzle stick)*:   You broke Thermometer.

GINNY: What?

LAWRENCE: YOU BROKE THERMOMETER!

GINNY: Well, what was a thermometer doing in with the swizzle sticks anyway?

LAWRENCE: Its name was Thermometer, you nitwit!

AMANDA: Let it go, Lawrence. There'll be other swizzle sticks. Good-bye, Virginia.

GINNY: I sure am hungry. Any chance I might be able to take a sandwich with me?

AMANDA: Certainly you can shake hands with me, if that will make you happy.

GINNY: I said I'm hungry.

AMANDA: Really, dear? What part of Hungary are you from?

GINNY: Oh never mind. I guess I'll go.

AMANDA: That's right. You have two time clocks. It must be getting near to when you punch in Betty.

GINNY: Well, so long, everybody. I had a nice time. *(Exits.)*

AMANDA: Tom, come in here please. Lawrence, I don't believe I would play the victrola right now.

LAWRENCE: What victrola?

AMANDA: Any victrola.

Enter Tom.

TOM: Yes, mother? Where's Ginny?

AMANDA: The feminine caller made a hasty departure.

TOM: Old four eyes bored her to death, huh?

LAWRENCE: Oh, drop dead.

TOM: We should have you institutionalized.

AMANDA: That's the first helpful thing you've said all evening, but first things first. You played a little joke on us, Tom.

TOM: What are you talking about?

AMANDA: You didn't mention that your friend is already spoken for.

TOM: Really? I didn't even think she liked men.

AMANDA: Yes, well. It seems odd that you know so little about a person you see everyday at the warehouse.

TOM: The warehouse is where I work, not where I know things about people.

AMANDA: The disgrace. The expense of the pigs feet, a new tie for Lawrence. And you — bringing a lesbian into this house. We haven't had a lesbian in this house since your grandmother died, and now you have the audacity to bring in that . . . that . . .

LAWRENCE: Dyke.

AMANDA: Thank you, Lawrence. That overbearing, booming-voiced bull dyke. Into a Christian home.

TOM: Oh look, who cares? No one in their right mind would marry four eyes here.

AMANDA: You have no Christian charity, or filial devotion, or fraternal affection.

TOM: I don't want to listen to this. I'm going to the movies.

AMANDA: You go to the movies to excess, Tom. It isn't healthy.

LAWRENCE: While you're out, could you stop at the liquor store and get me some more cocktail stirrers? She broke Thermometer, and she put Q-tip in her ear.

AMANDA: Listen to your brother, Tom. He's pathetic. How are we going to support ourselves once you go? And I know you want to leave. I've seen the brochure for the merchant marines in your underwear drawer. And the application to the Air Force. And your letter of inquiry to the Ballet Trockadero. So I'm not unaware of what you're thinking. But don't leave us until you fulfill your duties here, Tom. Help brother find a wife, or a job, or a doctor. Or consider euthanasia. But don't leave me here all alone, saddled with him.

LAWRENCE: Mama, don't you like me?

AMANDA: Of course, dear. I'm just making jokes.

LAWRENCE: Be careful of my asthma.

AMANDA: I'll try, dear. Now why don't you hold your breath in case you get a case of terminal hiccups?

LAWRENCE: Alright. *(Holds his breath.)*

TOM: I'm leaving.

AMANDA: Where are you going?

TOM: I'm going to the movies.

AMANDA: I don't believe you go to the movies. What did you see last night?

TOM: Hyapatia Lee in "Beaver City."

AMANDA: And the night before that?

TOM: I don't remember. "Humpy Busboys" or something.

AMANDA: Humpy what?

TOM: Nothing. Leave me alone.

AMANDA: These are not mainstream movies, Tom. Why can't you see a normal movie like "The Philadelphia Story." Or "The Bitter Tea of General Yen"?

TOM: Those movies were made in the 1930s.

AMANDA: They're still good today.

TOM: I don't want to have this conversation. I'm going to the movies.

AMANDA: That's right, go to the movies! Don't think about us, a mother alone, an unmarried brother who thinks he's crippled, and has no job. Stop holding your breath, Lawrence, mama was kidding. *(Back to Tom.)* Don't let anything interfere with your selfish pleasure. Go see your pornographic trash that's worse than anything Mr. D. H. Lawrence ever envisioned. Just go, go, go — to the movies!

TOM: Alright, I will! And the more you shout about my selfishness and my taste in movies the quicker I'll go, and I won't just go to the movies!

AMANDA: Go then! Go to the moon — you selfish dreamer!

Tom exits.

AMANDA *(continued)*: Oh Lawrence, honey, what's to become of us?

LAWRENCE: Tom forgot his newspaper, mama.

AMANDA: He forgot a lot more than that, Lawrence honey. He forgot his mama and brother.

Amanda and Lawrence stay in place. Tom enters down right and stands apart from them in a spot. He speaks to the audience.

TOM: I didn't go to the moon, I went to the movies. In Amsterdam. A long, lonely trip working my way on a freighter. They had good movies in Amsterdam. They weren't in English, but I didn't really care. And as for my mother and brother — well, I was adopted anyway. So I didn't miss them.

Or at least so I thought. For something pursued me. It always came upon me unawares, it always caught me by surprise. Sometimes it would be a swizzle stick in someone's vodka glass, or sometimes it would just be a jar of pigs feet. But then all of a sudden my brother touches my shoulder, and my mother puts her hands around my neck, and everywhere I look I am reminded of them. And in all the bars I go to there are those damn swizzle sticks everywhere. I find myself thinking of my brother Lawrence. And of his collection of glass. And of my mother. I begin to think that their story would maybe make a good novel, or even a play. A mother's hopes, a brother's dreams. Pathos, humor, even tragedy. But then I lose interest, I really haven't the energy. So I'll leave them both, dimly lit, in my memory. For nowadays the world is lit by lightning, and when we get those colored lights going, it feels like I'm on LSD. Or some other drug. Or maybe it's the trick of memory, and the fact that life is very, very sad. Play with your cocktail stirrers, Lawrence. And so, good-bye.

AMANDA *(calling over in Tom's direction)*: Tom, I hear you out on the porch talking. Who are you talking to?

TOM: No one, mother. I'm just on my way to the movies.

AMANDA: Well, try not to be too late, you have to work early at the warehouse tomorrow. And please don't bring home any visitors from the movies, I'm not up to it after that awful girl. Besides, if some sailor misses his boat, that's no reason you have to put him up in your room. You're too big-hearted, son.

TOM: Yes, mother. See you later. *(Exits.)*

LAWRENCE: Look at the light through the glass, mama. *(Looks through a swizzle stick.)* Isn't it amazin'?

AMANDA: Yes, I guess it is, Lawrence. Oh, but both my children are weird. What have I done, O Lord, to deserve them?

LAWRENCE: Just lucky, mama.

AMANDA: Don't make jokes, Lawrence. Your asthma. Your eczema. My life.

LAWRENCE: Don't be sad, mama. We have each other for company and amusement.

AMANDA: That's right. It's always darkest before the dawn. Or right before a typhoon sweeps up and kills everybody.

LAWRENCE: Oh, poor mama, let me try to cheer you up with my collection. Is that a good idea?

AMANDA: It's just great, Lawrence. Thank you.

LAWRENCE: I call this one Daffodil, because its yellow, and daffodils are yellow.

AMANDA: Uh huh.

LAWRENCE (holds up another one):   And I call this one Curtain Rod because it reminds me of a curtain rod.

AMANDA: Uh huh.

LAWRENCE: And I call this one Ocean, because it's blue, and the ocean is . . .

AMANDA: I THOUGHT YOU CALLED THE BLUE ONE BLUE, YOU IDIOT CHILD! DO I HAVE TO LISTEN TO THIS PATHETIC PRATTLING THE REST OF MY LIFE??? CAN'T YOU AT LEAST BE CONSISTENT???

LAWRENCE (pause, hurt):   No, I guess I can't.

AMANDA: Well, try, can't you? (Silence.) I'm sorry, Lawrence. I'm a little short-tempered today.

LAWRENCE: That's alright.

Silence.

AMANDA (trying to make up):   Do you have any other swizzle sticks with names, Lawrence?

LAWRENCE: Yes, I do. (Holds one up.) I call this one "Mama." (He throws it over his shoulder onto the floor.)

AMANDA: Well, that's lovely, Lawrence, thank you.

LAWRENCE: I guess I can be a little short-tempered too.

AMANDA: Yes, well, whatever. I think we won't kill each other this evening, alright?

LAWRENCE: Alright.

AMANDA: I'll just distract myself from my rage and despair, and read about other people's rage and despair in the newspaper, shall I? (Picks up Tom's newspaper.) Your brother has the worst reading and viewing taste of any living creature. This is just a piece of filth. (Reads.) Man Has Sex With Chicken, Then Makes Casserole. (Closes the paper.) Disgusting. Oh, Lawrence honey, look — it's the Evening Star. (She holds the paper out in front of them.) Let's make a wish on it, honey, shall we?

LAWRENCE: Alright, mama.

Amanda holds up the newspaper, and she and Lawrence close their eyes and make a wish.

AMANDA: What did you wish for, darlin'?

LAWRENCE: More swizzle sticks.

AMANDA: You're so predictable, Lawrence. It's part of your charm, I guess.

LAWRENCE: What did you wish for, mama?

AMANDA: The same thing, honey. Maybe just a little happiness, too, but mostly just some more swizzle sticks.

Sad music. Amanda and Lawrence look up at the Evening Star. Fade to black.

[1994]

≣ THINKING ABOUT THE TEXT

1. It is difficult to laugh at Laura, but why is it easy to laugh at Lawrence? What did you find amusing about Lawrence? Are there still boundaries here? That is, what changes would you suggest that would make it inappropriate to make fun of Lawrence?

2. Much of Durang's humor would be lost on those who have not read the Williams play. List some aspects of this play that rely for their effect on the context of the original.

3. Here the central symbol of the glass animals has been transformed into cocktail stirrers. Comment on this change. Do both say something about their collectors?

4. Durang keeps the basic outline of the original plot mostly intact. What changes does he make in the narrative? How do they affect your response to the parody?

5. The ending monologue by Tom in *The Glass Menagerie* is one of the most famous speeches in American theater. What makes it so, and how does Durang play off its themes, words, and emotional impact? What do you think Durang's main purpose is in this parody?

≣ MAKING COMPARISONS

1. Compare Tom's character in both plays. What makes one sympathetic and the other less so?

2. Compare Laura with Lawrence and Jim with Ginny. What changes did Durang make, and why? Are they effective changes in terms of parody?

3. What changes in Amanda's personality does Durang make, and why? Is she now more or less sympathetic?

≣ WRITING ABOUT ISSUES

1. Which play is more effective in fulfilling its purpose? Be specific in terms of character, narrative, and thematic concerns.

2. Critics claim that the following thematic strands are present in *The Glass Menagerie* — tenderness, illusions, illness, fragility, transformation,

emotion, nostalgia, and being trapped. Which seems the most important to you? Write a brief essay that explores the play's various themes.

3. Humor is often intuitive and difficult to explain, and sometimes it defies analysis. Look back on the four or five things that you found amusing in *For Whom the Southern Belle Tolls*. Then try to explain — perhaps to someone from another culture — why these things are humorous.

4. Argue either that we have a responsibility to society to develop our own talents or that we have a duty to try to meet the financial and emotional needs of our birth family.

■ A Family's Dreams: Cultural Contexts for a Play

LORRAINE HANSBERRY, *A Raisin in the Sun*

CULTURAL CONTEXTS:

THE CRISIS, "The Hansberrys of Chicago: They Join Business Acumen with Social Vision"

LORRAINE HANSBERRY, *Letter to the* New York Times *Editor, dated April 23, 1964*

ALAN EHRENHALT, From *The Lost City: Discovering the Forgotten Virtues of Community in the Chicago of the 1950s*

SIDNEY POITIER, From *The Measure of a Man: A Spiritual Autobiography*

Hansberry's title comes from the African American poet Langston Hughes's 1951 poem "Harlem," which begins by asking *"What happens to a dream deferred? / Does it dry up / Like a raisin in the sun?"* Hughes had in mind white America's continued thwarting of his own race's hopes for freedom, equality, and prosperity. This is a situation painfully familiar to the Youngers, the African American family of Hansberry's play, who live in a poor black Chicago neighborhood in the 1950s. Like many of the texts in Part One, the play deals with the topic of work. Most of the Youngers have survived by laboring for white people, though they have been stuck in near poverty all the same. Now, a large inheritance promises to fulfill their dreams at last—but these dreams conflict. Lena wants to buy a house, but her son Walter Lee wants to invest in a liquor store to escape his degrading job as a chauffeur. Much of the play's drama occurs as these two characters clash. Following the play, we include four cultural texts to help you place the drama in a specific historical moment. We hope they will help illuminate the social condition Hansberry wrote in.

■ BEFORE YOU READ

Think of your own family or another you know well. For outsiders to get a sense of this family, what do they have to know about its social and historical background? Do you think the phrase *a dream deferred* applies to this family? Why, or why not?

LORRAINE HANSBERRY

A Raisin in the Sun

The life of Lorraine Hansberry (1930–1965) was brief. She died of cancer the day that her second play, The Sign in Sidney Brustein's Window *(1964), closed on Broadway. But by then she had been immensely productive as a writer and gained a considerable reputation for her work. In 1959, her first play,* A Raisin in the Sun, *was the first by an African American woman to be produced on Broadway. Later that*

AP/Wide World Photos.

year, it became the first play by an African American to win the New York Drama Critics Circle Award. In part, the play was based on an experience that Hansberry's own family endured while she was growing up in Chicago. Her father, Carl Hansberry, a prominent real estate agent and banker, made history in 1938 when he moved his family to an all-white section of Chicago's Hyde Park neighborhood. After encountering white resistance there, he fought a series of legal battles that went all the way to the U.S. Supreme Court. In 1940, the Court ruled in his favor, but its decision largely was not enforced; housing remained basically segregated in Chicago and in most of the country. Embittered, Carl Hansberry considered moving his family permanently to Mexico, but before he could, he died there of a cerebral hemorrhage in 1946.

After attending the University of Wisconsin, Lorraine Hansberry moved to New York City. Besides plays, she wrote essays and articles on a variety of subjects, including homophobia and racism. She also wrote the screenplay for the 1961 film version of A Raisin in the Sun, *which featured the original Broadway cast (including Sidney Poitier as Walter Lee Younger). In 1969, her widower, Robert Nemiroff, combined various writings of hers into a play called* To Be Young, Gifted, and Black. *In 1970, a book version of it was published, and that same year there was a Broadway production of Hansberry's final play,* Les Blancs.

Harlem (A Dream Deferred)

What happens to a dream deferred?

Does it dry up
Like a raisin in the sun?
Or fester like a sore —
And then run?
Does it stink like rotten meat?
Or crust and sugar over —
Like a syrupy sweet?

Maybe it just sags
Like a heavy load.

Or does it explode?
                    — Langston Hughes

CHARACTERS (in order of appearance)

RUTH YOUNGER

TRAVIS YOUNGER

WALTER LEE YOUNGER, BROTHER

BENEATHA YOUNGER

LENA YOUNGER, MAMA

JOSEPH ASAGAI

GEORGE MURCHISON

MRS. JOHNSON

KARL LINDNER

BOBO

MOVING MEN

The action of the play is set in Chicago's Southside, sometime between World War II and the present.

ACT 1, Scene 1

[Friday morning.]

   The Younger living room would be a comfortable and well-ordered room if it were not for a number of indestructible contradictions to this state of being. Its furnishings are typical and undistinguished and their primary feature now is that they have clearly had to accommodate the living of too many people for too many years — and they are tired. Still, we can see that at some time, a time probably no longer remembered by the family (except perhaps for Mama), the furnishings of this room were actually selected with care and love and even hope — and brought to this apartment and arranged with taste and pride.

   That was a long time ago. Now the once loved pattern of the couch upholstery has to fight to show itself from under acres of crocheted doilies and couch covers which have themselves finally come to be more important than the upholstery. And here a table or a chair has been moved to disguise the worn places in the carpet; but the carpet has fought back by showing its weariness, with depressing uniformity, elsewhere on its surface.

Weariness has, in fact, won in this room. Everything has been polished, washed, sat on, used, scrubbed too often. All pretenses but living itself have long since vanished from the very atmosphere of this room.

Moreover, a section of this room, for it is not really a room unto itself, though the landlord's lease would make it seem so, slopes backward to provide a small kitchen area, where the family prepares the meals that are eaten in the living room proper, which must also serve as dining room. The single window that has been provided for these "two" rooms is located in this kitchen area. The sole natural light the family may enjoy in the course of a day is only that which fights its way through this little window.

At left, a door leads to a bedroom which is shared by Mama and her daughter, Beneatha. At right, opposite, is a second room (which in the beginning of the life of this apartment was probably a breakfast room) which serves as a bedroom for Walter and his wife, Ruth.

Time: Sometime between World War II and the present.

Place: Chicago's Southside.

At rise: It is morning dark in the living room. Travis is asleep on the make-down bed at center. An alarm clock sounds from within the bedroom at right, and presently Ruth enters from that room and closes the door behind her. She crosses sleepily toward the window. As she passes her sleeping son she reaches down and shakes him a little. At the window she raises the shade and a dusky Southside morning light comes in feebly. She fills a pot with water and puts it on to boil. She calls to the boy, between yawns, in a slightly muffled voice.

Ruth is about thirty. We can see that she was a pretty girl, even exceptionally so, but now it is apparent that life has been little that she expected, and disappointment has already begun to hang in her face. In a few years, before thirty-five even, she will be known among her people as a "settled woman."

She crosses to her son and gives him a good, final, rousing shake.

RUTH: Come on now, boy, it's seven thirty! *(Her son sits up at last, in a stupor of sleepiness.)* I say hurry up, Travis! You ain't the only person in the world got to use a bathroom! *(The child, a sturdy, handsome little boy of ten or eleven, drags himself out of the bed and almost blindly takes his towels and "today's clothes" from drawers and a closet and goes out to the bathroom, which is in an outside hall and which is shared by another family or families on the same floor. Ruth crosses to the bedroom door at right and opens it and calls in to her husband.)* Walter Lee! . . . It's after seven thirty! Lemme see you do some waking up in there now! *(She waits.)* You better get up from there, man! It's after seven thirty I tell you. *(She waits again.)* All right, you just go ahead and lay there and next thing you know Travis be finished and Mr. Johnson'll be in there and you'll be fussing and cussing round here like a madman! And be late too! *(She waits, at the end of patience.)* Walter Lee — it's time for you to GET UP!

She waits another second and then starts to go into the bedroom, but is apparently satisfied that her husband has begun to get up. She stops, pulls the door to, and returns to the kitchen area. She wipes her face with a moist cloth and runs her fingers through her sleep-disheveled hair in a vain effort and ties an apron around her housecoat. The bedroom door at right opens and her husband stands in the doorway in his pajamas, which are rumpled and mismated. He is a lean, intense young man in his middle thirties, inclined to quick nervous movements and erratic speech habits — and always in his voice there is a quality of indictment.

WALTER: Is he out yet?

RUTH: What you mean *out?* He ain't hardly got in there good yet.

WALTER *(wandering in, still more oriented to sleep than to a new day)*:   Well, what was you doing all that yelling for if I can't even get in there yet? *(Stopping and thinking.)* Check coming today?

RUTH: They *said* Saturday and this is just Friday and I hopes to God you ain't going to get up here first thing this morning and start talking to me 'bout no money — 'cause I 'bout don'want to hear it.

WALTER: Something the matter with you this morning?

RUTH: No — I'm just sleepy as the devil. What kind of eggs you want?

WALTER: Not scrambled. *(Ruth starts to scramble eggs.)* Paper come? *(Ruth points impatiently to the rolled up Tribune on the table, and he gets it and spreads it out and vaguely reads the front page.)* Set off another bomb yesterday.

RUTH *(maximum indifference)*:   Did they?

WALTER *(looking up)*:   What's the matter with you?

RUTH: Ain't nothing the matter with me. And don't keep asking me that this morning.

WALTER: Ain't nobody bothering you. *(Reading the news of the day absently again.)* Say Colonel McCormick is sick.

RUTH *(affecting tea-party interest)*:   Is he now? Poor thing.

WALTER *(sighing and looking at his watch)*:   Oh, me. *(He waits.)* Now what is that boy doing in that bathroom all this time? He just going to have to start getting up earlier. I can't be being late to work on account of him fooling around in there.

RUTH *(turning on him)*:   Oh, no he ain't going to be getting up no earlier no such thing! It ain't his fault that he can't get to bed no earlier nights 'cause he got a bunch of crazy good-for-nothing clowns sitting up running their mouths in what is supposed to be his bedroom after ten o'clock at night . . .

WALTER: That's what you mad about, ain't it? The things I want to talk about with my friends just couldn't be important in your mind, could they?

He rises and finds a cigarette in her handbag on the table and crosses to the little window and looks out, smoking and deeply enjoying this first one.

RUTH *(almost matter of factly, a complaint too automatic to deserve emphasis)*:   Why you always got to smoke before you eat in the morning?

WALTER *(at the window)*:   Just look at 'em down there . . . Running and racing to work . . . *(He turns and faces his wife and watches her a moment at the stove, and then, suddenly.)* You look young this morning, baby.

RUTH (*indifferently*):   Yeah?

WALTER: Just for a second — stirring them eggs. Just for a second it was — you looked real young again. (*He reaches for her; she crosses away. Then, drily.*) It's gone now — you look like yourself again!

RUTH: Man, if you don't shut up and leave me alone.

WALTER (*looking out to the street again*):   First thing a man ought to learn in life is not to make love to no colored woman first thing in the morning. You all some eeeevil people at eight o'clock in the morning.

Travis appears in the hall doorway, almost fully dressed and quite wide awake now, his towels and pajamas across his shoulders. He opens the door and signals for his father to make the bathroom in a hurry.

TRAVIS (*watching the bathroom*):   Daddy, come on!

Walter gets his bathroom utensils and flies out to the bathroom.

RUTH: Sit down and have your breakfast, Travis.

TRAVIS: Mama, this is Friday. (*Gleefully.*) Check coming tomorrow, huh?

RUTH: You get your mind off money and eat your breakfast.

TRAVIS (*eating*):   This is the morning we supposed to bring the fifty cents to school.

RUTH: Well, I ain't got no fifty cents this morning.

TRAVIS: Teacher say we have to.

RUTH: I don't care what teacher say. I ain't got it. Eat your breakfast, Travis.

TRAVIS: I *am* eating.

RUTH: Hush up now and just eat!

The boy gives her an exasperated look for her lack of understanding, and eats grudgingly.

TRAVIS: You think Grandmama would have it?

RUTH: No! And I want you to stop asking your grandmother for money, you hear me?

TRAVIS (*outraged*):   Gaaaleee! I don't ask her, she just gimme it sometimes!

RUTH: Travis Willard Younger — I got too much on me this morning to be —

TRAVIS: Maybe Daddy —

RUTH: Travis!

The boy hushes abruptly. They are both quiet and tense for several seconds.

TRAVIS (*presently*):   Could I maybe go carry some groceries in front of the supermarket for a little while after school then?

RUTH: Just hush, I said. (*Travis jabs his spoon into his cereal bowl viciously, and rests his head in anger upon his fists.*) If you through eating, you can get over there and make up your bed.

The boy obeys stiffly and crosses the room, almost mechanically, to the bed and more or less folds the bedding into a heap, then angrily gets his books and cap.

TRAVIS (*sulking and standing apart from her unnaturally*):   I'm gone.

RUTH (*looking up from the stove to inspect him automatically*):   Come here. (*He crosses to her and she studies his head.*) If you don't take this comb and fix this here head, you better! (*Travis puts down his books with a great sigh of oppression, and crosses to the mirror. His mother mutters under her breath*

about his *"slubbornness."*) 'Bout to march out of here with that head looking just like chickens slept in it! I just don't know where you get your
slubborn° ways . . . And get your jacket, too. Looks chilly out this morning.

TRAVIS *(with conspicuously brushed hair and jacket):* I'm gone.

RUTH: Get carfare and milk money — *(Waving one finger.)* — and not a single
penny for no caps, you hear me?

TRAVIS *(with sullen politeness):* Yes'm.

*He turns in outrage to leave. His mother watches after him as in his frustration he
approaches the door almost comically. When she speaks to him, her voice has become
a very gentle tease.*

RUTH *(mocking; as she thinks he would say it):* Oh, Mama makes me so mad
sometimes, I don't know what to do! *(She waits and continues to his back as
he stands stock-still in front of the door.)* I wouldn't kiss that woman good-bye
for nothing in this world this morning! *(The boy finally turns around and
rolls his eyes at her, knowing the mood has changed and he is vindicated; he does
not, however, move toward her yet.)* Not for nothing in this world! *(She finally
laughs aloud at him and holds out her arms to him and we see that it is a way
between them, very old and practiced. He crosses to her and allows her to embrace him warmly but keeps his face fixed with masculine rigidity. She holds
him back from her presently and looks at him and runs her fingers over the features of his face. With utter gentleness —.)* Now — whose little old angry
man are you?

TRAVIS *(the masculinity and gruffness start to fade at last):* Aw gaalee — Mama . . .

RUTH *(mimicking):* Aw — gaaaaalleeeee, Mama! *(She pushes him, with rough
playfulness and finality, toward the door.)* Get on out of here or you going to
be late.

TRAVIS *(in the face of love, new aggressiveness):* Mama, could I *please* go carry
groceries?

RUTH: Honey, it's starting to get so cold evenings.

WALTER *(coming in from the bathroom and drawing a make-believe gun from a make-
believe holster and shooting at his son):* What is it he wants to do?

RUTH: Go carry groceries after school at the supermarket.

WALTER: Well, let him go . . .

TRAVIS *(quickly, to the ally):* I have to — she won't gimme the fifty cents . . .

WALTER *(to his wife only):* Why not?

RUTH *(simply, and with flavor):* 'Cause we don't have it.

WALTER *(to Ruth only):* What you tell the boy things like that for? *(Reaching
down into his pants with a rather important gesture.)* Here, son —

*He hands the boy the coin, but his eyes are directed to his wife's. Travis takes the
money happily.*

TRAVIS: Thanks, Daddy.

*He starts out. Ruth watches both of them with murder in her eyes. Walter stands and
stares back at her with defiance, and suddenly reaches into his pocket again on an afterthought.*

slubborn: A made-up combination of "slovenly" and "stubborn."

WALTER (*without even looking at his son, still staring hard at his wife*):   In fact, here's another fifty cents . . . Buy yourself some fruit today — or take a taxicab to school or something!

TRAVIS: Whoopee —

He leaps up and clasps his father around the middle with his legs, and they face each other in mutual appreciation; slowly Walter Lee peeks around the boy to catch the violent rays from his wife's eyes and draws his head back as if shot.

WALTER: You better get down now — and get to school, man.

TRAVIS (*at the door*):   O.K. Good-bye.

He exits.

WALTER (*after him, pointing with pride*):   That's *my* boy. (*She looks at him in disgust and turns back to her work.*) You know what I was thinking 'bout in the bathroom this morning?

RUTH: No.

WALTER: How come you always try to be so pleasant!

RUTH: What is there to be pleasant 'bout!

WALTER: You want to know what I was thinking bout in the bathroom or not!

RUTH: I know what you thinking 'bout.

WALTER (*ignoring her*):   'Bout what me and Willy Harris was talking about last night.

RUTH (*immediately — a refrain*):   Willy Harris is a good-for-nothing loudmouth.

WALTER: Anybody who talks to me has got to be a good-for-nothing loudmouth, ain't he? And what you know about who is just a good-for-nothing loudmouth? Charlie Atkins was just a "good-for-nothing loudmouth" too, wasn't he! When he wanted me to go in the dry-cleaning business with him. And now — he's grossing a hundred thousand a year. A hundred thousand dollars a year! You still call *him* a loudmouth!

RUTH (*bitterly*):   Oh, Walter Lee . . .

She folds her head on her arms over the table.

WALTER (*rising and coming to her and standing over her*):   You tired, ain't you? Tired of everything. Me, the boy, the way we live — this beat-up hole — everything. Ain't you? (*She doesn't look up, doesn't answer.*) So tired — moaning and groaning all the time, but you wouldn't do nothing to help, would you? You couldn't be on my side that long for nothing, could you?

RUTH: Walter, please leave me alone.

WALTER: A man needs for a woman to back him up . . .

RUTH: Walter —

WALTER: Mama would listen to you. You know she listen to you more than she do me and Bennie. She think more of you. All you have to do is just sit down with her when you drinking your coffee one morning and talking 'bout things like you do and — (*He sits down beside her and demonstrates graphically what he thinks her methods and tone should be.*) — you just sip your coffee, see, and say easy like that you been thinking 'bout that deal Walter Lee is so interested in, 'bout the store and all, and sip some more coffee, like what you saying ain't really that important to you — And the next thing you know, she be listening good and asking you questions and when I come home — I can tell her the details. This ain't no fly-by-night proposition, baby. I mean we figured it out, me and Willy and Bobo.

RUTH *(with a frown)*:   Bobo?

WALTER: Yeah. You see, this little liquor store we got in mind cost seventy-five thousand and we figured the initial investment on the place be 'bout thirty thousand, see. That be ten thousand each. Course, there's a couple of hundred you got to pay so's you don't spend your life just waiting for them clowns to let your license get approved —

RUTH: You mean graft?

WALTER *(frowning impatiently)*:   Don't call it that. See there, that just goes to show you what women understand about the world. Baby, don't *nothing* happen for you in the world 'less you pay *somebody* off!

RUTH: Walter, leave me alone! *(She raises her head and stares at him vigorously — then says, more quietly.)* Eat your eggs, they gonna be cold.

WALTER *(straightening up from her and looking off)*:   That's it. There you are. Man say to his woman: I got me a dream. His woman say: Eat your eggs. *(Sadly, but gaining in power.)* Man say: I got to take hold of this here world, baby! And a woman will say: Eat your eggs and go to work. *(Passionately now.)* Man say: I got to change my life, I'm choking to death, baby! And his woman say — *(In utter anguish as he brings his fists down on his thighs.)* — Your eggs is getting cold!

RUTH *(softly)*:   Walter, that ain't none of our money.

WALTER *(not listening at all or even looking at her)*:   This morning, I was lookin' in the mirror and thinking about it . . . I'm thirty-five years old; I been married eleven years and I got a boy who sleeps in the living room — *(Very, very quietly.)* — and all I got to give him is stories about how rich white people live . . .

RUTH: Eat your eggs, Walter.

WALTER *(slams the table and jumps up)*:   — DAMN MY EGGS — DAMN ALL THE EGGS THAT EVER WAS!

RUTH: Then go to work.

WALTER *(looking up at her)*:   See — I'm trying to talk to you 'bout myself — *(Shaking his head with the repetition.)* — and all you can say is eat them eggs and go to work.

RUTH *(wearily)*:   Honey, you never say nothing new. I listen to you every day, every night and every morning, and you never say nothing new. *(Shrugging.)* So you would rather *be* Mr. Arnold than be his chauffeur. So — I would *rather* be living in Buckingham Palace.

WALTER: That is just what is wrong with the colored woman in this world . . . Don't understand about building their men up and making 'em feel like they somebody. Like they can do something.

RUTH *(drily, but to hurt)*:   There *are* colored men who do things.

WALTER: No thanks to the colored woman.

RUTH: Well, being a colored woman, I guess I can't help myself none.

She rises and gets the ironing board and sets it up and attacks a huge pile of rough-dried clothes, sprinkling them in preparation for the ironing and then rolling them into tight fat balls.

WALTER *(mumbling)*:   We one group of men tied to a race of women with small minds!

His sister Beneatha enters. She is about twenty, as slim and intense as her brother. She is not as pretty as her sister-in-law, but her lean, almost intellectual face has a handsomeness of its own. She wears a bright-red flannel nightie, and her thick hair stands wildly about her head. Her speech is a mixture of many things; it is different from the rest of the family's insofar as education has permeated her sense of English — and perhaps the Midwest rather than the South has finally — at last — won out in her inflection; but not altogether, because over all of it is a soft slurring and transformed use of vowels which is the decided influence of the Southside. She passes through the room without looking at either Ruth or Walter and goes to the outside door and looks, a little blindly, out to the bathroom. She sees that it has been lost to the Johnsons. She closes the door with a sleepy vengeance and crosses to the table and sits down a little defeated.

BENEATHA: I am going to start timing those people.

WALTER: You should get up earlier.

BENEATHA *(her face in her hands. She is still fighting the urge to go back to bed)*:   Really — would you suggest dawn? Where's the paper?

WALTER *(pushing the paper across the table to her as he studies her almost clinically, as though he has never seen her before)*:   You a horrible-looking chick at this hour.

BENEATHA *(drily)*:   Good morning, everybody.

WALTER *(senselessly)*:   How is school coming?

BENEATHA *(in the same spirit)*:   Lovely. Lovely. And you know, biology is the greatest. *(Looking up at him.)* I dissected something that looked just like you yesterday.

WALTER: I just wondered if you've made up your mind and everything.

BENEATHA *(gaining in sharpness and impatience)*:   And what did I answer yesterday morning — and the day before that?

RUTH *(from the ironing board, like someone disinterested and old)*:   Don't be so nasty, Bennie.

BENEATHA *(still to her brother)*:   And the day before that and the day before that!

WALTER *(defensively)*:   I'm interested in you. Something wrong with that? Ain't many girls who decide —

WALTER AND BENEATHA *(in unison)*:   — "to be a doctor."

Silence.

WALTER: Have we figured out yet just exactly how much medical school is going to cost?

RUTH: Walter Lee, why don't you leave that girl alone and get out of here to work?

BENEATHA *(exits to the bathroom and bangs on the door)*:   Come on out of there, please!

She comes back into the room.

WALTER *(looking at his sister intently)*:   You know the check is coming tomorrow.

BENEATHA *(turning on him with a sharpness all her own)*:   That money belongs to Mama, Walter, and it's for her to decide how she wants to use it. I don't care if she wants to buy a house or a rocket ship or just nail it up somewhere and look at it. It's hers. Not ours — *hers.*

WALTER *(bitterly)*:   Now ain't that fine! You just got your mother's interest at heart, ain't you, girl? You such a nice girl — but if Mama got that money she can always take a few thousand and help you through school too — can't she?

BENEATHA: I have never asked anyone around here to do anything for me!

WALTER: No! And the line between asking and just accepting when the time comes is big and wide — ain't it!

BENEATHA *(with fury)*:   What do you want from me, Brother — that I quit school or just drop dead, which!

WALTER: I don't want nothing but for you to stop acting holy 'round here. Me and Ruth done made some sacrifices for you — why can't you do something for the family?

RUTH: Walter, don't be dragging me in it.

WALTER: You are in it — Don't you get up and go work in somebody's kitchen for the last three years to help put clothes on her back?

RUTH: Oh, Walter — that's not fair . . .

WALTER: It ain't that nobody expects you to get on your knees and say thank you, Brother; thank you, Ruth; thank you, Mama — and thank you, Travis, for wearing the same pair of shoes for two semesters —

BENEATHA *(dropping to her knees)*:   Well — I *do* — all right? — thank everybody! And forgive me for ever wanting to be anything at all! *(Pursuing him on her knees across the floor.)* FORGIVE ME, FORGIVE ME, FORGIVE ME!

RUTH: Please stop it! Your mama'll hear you.

WALTER: Who the hell told you you had to be a doctor? If you so crazy 'bout messing 'round with sick people — then go be a nurse like other women — or just get married and be quiet . . .

BENEATHA: Well — you finally got it said . . . It took you three years but you finally got it said. Walter, give up; leave me alone — it's Mama's money.

WALTER: *He was my father, too!*

BENEATHA: So what? He was mine, too — and Travis' grandfather — but the insurance money belongs to Mama. Picking on me is not going to make her give it to you to invest in any liquor stores — *(Under breath, dropping into a chair.)* — and I for one say, God bless Mama for that!

WALTER *(to Ruth)*:   See — did you hear? Did you hear!

RUTH: Honey, please go to work.

WALTER: Nobody in this house is ever going to understand me.

BENEATHA: Because you're a nut.

WALTER: Who's a nut?

BENEATHA: You — you are a nut. Thee is mad, boy.

WALTER *(looking at his wife and his sister from the door, very sadly)*:   The world's most backward race of people, and that's a fact.

BENEATHA *(turning slowly in her chair)*:   And then there are all those prophets who would lead us out of the wilderness — *(Walter slams out of the house.)* — into the swamps!

RUTH: Bennie, why you always gotta be pickin' on your brother? Can't you be a little sweeter sometimes? *(Door opens. Walter walks in. He fumbles with his cap, starts to speak, clears throat, looks everywhere but at Ruth. Finally:)*

WALTER *(to Ruth)*:   I need some money for carfare.

RUTH *(looks at him, then warms; teasing, but tenderly)*:   Fifty cents? *(She goes to her bag and gets money.)* Here — take a taxi!

Walter exits. Mama enters. She is a woman in her early sixties, full-bodied and strong. She is one of those women of a certain grace and beauty who wear it so unob-trusively that it takes a while to notice. Her dark-brown face is surrounded by the total whiteness of her hair, and, being a woman who has adjusted to many things in life and overcome many more, her face is full of strength. She has, we can see, wit and faith of a kind that keep her eyes lit and full of interest and expectancy. She is, in a word, a beautiful woman. Her bearing is perhaps most like the noble bearing of the women of the Hereros of Southwest Africa — rather as if she imagines that as she walks she still bears a basket or a vessel upon her head. Her speech, on the other hand, is as careless as her carriage is precise — she is inclined to slur everything — but her voice is perhaps not so much quiet as simply soft.

MAMA: Who that 'round here slamming doors at this hour?

She crosses through the room, goes to the window, opens it, and brings in a feeble little plant growing doggedly in a small pot on the window sill. She feels the dirt and puts it back out.

RUTH: That was Walter Lee. He and Bennie was at it again.

MAMA: My children and they tempers. Lord, if this little old plant don't get more sun than it's been getting it ain't never going to see spring again. *(She turns from the window.)* What's the matter with you this morning, Ruth? You looks right peaked. You aiming to iron all them things? Leave some for me. I'll get to 'em this afternoon. Bennie honey, it's too drafty for you to be sitting 'round half dressed. Where's your robe?

BENEATHA: In the cleaners.

MAMA: Well, go get mine and put it on.

BENEATHA: I'm not cold, Mama, honest.

MAMA: I know — but you so thin . . .

BENEATHA *(irritably)*:   Mama, I'm not cold.

MAMA *(seeing the make-down bed as Travis has left it)*:   Lord have mercy, look at that poor bed. Bless his heart — he tries, don't he?

She moves to the bed Travis has sloppily made up.

RUTH: No — he don't half try at all 'cause he knows you going to come along behind him and fix everything. That's just how come he don't know how to do nothing right now — you done spoiled that boy so.

MAMA *(folding bedding)*: Well — he's a little boy. Ain't supposed to know 'bout housekeeping. My baby, that's what he is. What you fix for his breakfast this morning?

RUTH *(angrily)*: I feed my son, Lena!

MAMA: I ain't meddling — *(Under breath; busy-bodyish.)* I just noticed all last week he had cold cereal, and when it starts getting this chilly in the fall a child ought to have some hot grits or something when he goes out in the cold —

RUTH *(furious)*: I gave him hot oats — is that all right!

MAMA: I ain't meddling. *(Pause.)* Put a lot of nice butter on it? *(Ruth shoots her an angry look and does not reply.)* He likes lots of butter.

RUTH *(exasperated)*: Lena —

MAMA *(to Beneatha. Mama is inclined to wander conversationally sometimes)*: What was you and your brother fussing 'bout this morning?

BENEATHA: It's not important, Mama.

She gets up and goes to look out at the bathroom, which is apparently free, and she picks up her towels and rushes out.

MAMA: What was they fighting about?

RUTH: Now you know as well as I do.

MAMA *(shaking her head)*: Brother still worrying hisself sick about that money?

RUTH: You know he is.

MAMA: You had breakfast?

RUTH: Some coffee.

MAMA: Girl, you better start eating and looking after yourself better. You almost thin as Travis.

RUTH: Lena —

MAMA: Un-hunh?

RUTH: What are you going to do with it?

MAMA: Now don't you start, child. It's too early in the morning to be talking about money. It ain't Christian.

RUTH: It's just that he got his heart set on that store —

MAMA: You mean that liquor store that Willy Harris want him to invest in?

RUTH: Yes —

MAMA: We ain't no business people, Ruth. We just plain working folks.

RUTH: Ain't nobody business people till they go into business. Walter Lee say colored people ain't never going to start getting ahead till they start gambling on some different kinds of things in the world — investments and things.

MAMA: What done got into you, girl? Walter Lee done finally sold you on investing.

RUTH: No. Mama, something is happening between Walter and me. I don't know what it is — but he needs something — something I can't give him any more. He needs this chance, Lena.

MAMA *(frowning deeply)*:   But liquor, honey —

RUTH: Well — like Walter say — I spec people going to always be drinking themselves some liquor.

MAMA: Well — whether they drinks it or not ain't none of my business. But whether I go into business selling it to 'em *is,* and I don't want that on my ledger this late in life. *(Stopping suddenly and studying her daughter-in-law.)* Ruth Younger, what's the matter with you today? You look like you could fall over right there.

RUTH: I'm tired.

MAMA: Then you better stay home from work today.

RUTH: I can't stay home. She'd be calling up the agency and screaming at them, "My girl didn't come in today — send me somebody! My girl didn't come in!" Oh, she just have a fit . . .

MAMA: Well, let her have it. I'll just call her up and say you got the flu —

RUTH *(laughing)*:   Why the flu?

MAMA: 'Cause it sounds respectable to 'em. Something white people get, too. They know 'bout the flu. Otherwise they think you been cut up or something when you tell 'em you sick.

RUTH: I got to go in. We need the money.

MAMA: Somebody would of thought my children done all but starved to death the way they talk about money here late. Child, we got a great big old check coming tomorrow.

RUTH *(sincerely, but also self-righteously)*:   Now that's your money. It ain't got nothing to do with me. We all feel like that — Walter and Bennie and me — even Travis.

MAMA *(thoughtfully, and suddenly very far away)*:   Ten thousand dollars —

RUTH: Sure is wonderful.

MAMA: Ten thousand dollars.

RUTH: You know what you should do, Miss Lena? You should take yourself a trip somewhere. To Europe or South America or someplace —

MAMA *(throwing up her hands at the thought)*:   Oh, child!

RUTH: I'm serious. Just pack up and leave! Go on away and enjoy yourself some. Forget about the family and have yourself a ball for once in your life —

MAMA *(drily)*:   You sound like I'm just about ready to die. Who'd go with me? What I look like wandering 'round Europe by myself?

RUTH: Shoot — these here rich white women do it all the time. They don't think nothing of packing up they suitcases and piling on one of them big steamships and — swoosh! — they gone, child.

MAMA: Something always told me I wasn't no rich white woman.

RUTH: Well — what are you going to do with it then?

MAMA: I ain't rightly decided. *(Thinking. She speaks now with emphasis.)* Some of it got to be put away for Beneatha and her schoolin' — and ain't nothing going to touch that part of it. Nothing. *(She waits several seconds, trying to make up her mind about something, and looks at Ruth a little tentatively before going on.)* Been thinking that we maybe could meet the notes on a little old two-story somewhere, with a yard where Travis could play in the summertime, if we use part of the insurance for a down payment and everybody kind of pitch in. I could maybe take on a little day work again, few days a week —

RUTH *(studying her mother-in-law furtively and concentrating on her ironing, anxious to encourage without seeming to)*:   Well, Lord knows, we've put enough rent into this here rat trap to pay for four houses by now . . .

MAMA *(looking up at the words "rat trap" and then looking around and leaning back and sighing — in a suddenly reflective mood—)*:   "Rat trap" — yes, that's all it is. *(Smiling.)* I remember just as well the day me and Big Walter moved in here. Hadn't been married but two weeks and wasn't planning on living here no more than a year. *(She shakes her head at the dissolved dream.)* We was going to set away, little by little, don't you know, and buy a little place out in Morgan Park. We had even picked out the house. *(Chuckling a little.)* Looks right dumpy today. But Lord, child, you should know all the dreams I had 'bout buying that house and fixing it up and making me a little garden in the back — *(She waits and stops smiling.)* And didn't none of it happen.

Dropping her hands in a futile gesture.

RUTH *(keeps her head down, ironing)*:   Yes, life can be a barrel of disappointments, sometimes.

MAMA: Honey, Big Walter would come in here some nights back then and slump down on that couch there and just look at the rug, and look at me and look at the rug and then back at me — and I'd know he was down then . . . really down. *(After a second very long and thoughtful pause; she is seeing back to times that only she can see.)* And then, Lord, when I lost that baby — little Claude — I almost thought I was going to lose Big Walter too. Oh, that man grieved hisself! He was one man to love his children.

RUTH: Ain't nothin' can tear at you like losin' your baby.

MAMA: I guess that's how come that man finally worked hisself to death like he done. Like he was fighting his own war with this here world that took his baby from him.

RUTH: He sure was a fine man, all right. I always liked Mr. Younger.

MAMA: Crazy 'bout his children! God knows there was plenty wrong with Walter Younger — hard-headed, mean, kind of wild with women — plenty wrong with him. But he sure loved his children. Always wanted them to have something — be something. That's where Brother gets all these notions, I reckon. Big Walter used to say, he'd get right wet in the eyes sometimes, lean his head back with the water standing in his eyes and say, "Seem like God didn't see fit to give the black man nothing but dreams — but He did give us children to make them dreams seem worthwhile." *(She smiles.)* He could talk like that, don't you know.

RUTH: Yes, he sure could. He was a good man, Mr. Younger.

MAMA: Yes, a fine man — just couldn't never catch up with his dreams, that's all.

Beneatha comes in, brushing her hair and looking up to the ceiling, where the sound of a vacuum cleaner has started up.

BENEATHA: What could be so dirty on that woman's rugs that she has to vacuum them every single day?

RUTH: I wish certain young women 'round here who I could name would take inspiration about certain rugs in a certain apartment I could also mention.

BENEATHA *(shrugging)*:   How much cleaning can a house need, for Christ's sakes.

MAMA *(not liking the Lord's name used thus)*:   Bennie!

RUTH: Just listen to her — just listen!

BENEATHA: Oh, God!

MAMA: If you use the Lord's name just one more time —

BENEATHA *(a bit of a whine)*:   Oh, Mama —

RUTH: Fresh — just fresh as salt, this girl!

BENEATHA *(drily)*:   Well — if the salt loses its savor —

MAMA: Now that will do. I just ain't going to have you 'round here reciting the scriptures in vain — you hear me?

BENEATHA: How did I manage to get on everybody's wrong side by just walking into a room?

RUTH: If you weren't so fresh —

BENEATHA: Ruth, I'm twenty years old.

MAMA: What time you be home from school today?

BENEATHA: Kind of late. *(With enthusiasm.)* Madeline is going to start my guitar lessons today.

Mama and Ruth look up with the same expression.

MAMA: Your *what* kind of lessons?

BENEATHA: Guitar.

RUTH: Oh, Father!

MAMA: How come you done taken it in your mind to learn to play the guitar?

BENEATHA: I just want to, that's all.

MAMA *(smiling)*:   Lord, child, don't you know what to do with yourself? How long it going to be before you get tired of this now — like you got tired of that little play-acting group you joined last year? *(Looking at Ruth.)* And what was it the year before that?

RUTH: The horseback-riding club for which she bought that fifty-five-dollar riding habit that's been hanging in the closet ever since!

MAMA *(to Beneatha)*:   Why you got to flit so from one thing to another, baby?

BENEATHA *(sharply)*:   I just want to learn to play the guitar. Is there anything wrong with that?

MAMA: Ain't nobody trying to stop you. I just wonders sometimes why you has to flit so from one thing to another all the time. You ain't never done nothing with all that camera equipment you brought home —

BENEATHA: I don't flit! I — I experiment with different forms of expression —

RUTH: Like riding a horse?

BENEATHA: — People have to express themselves one way or another.

MAMA: What is it you want to express?

BENEATHA *(angrily)*:   Me! *(Mama and Ruth look at each other and burst into raucous laughter.)* Don't worry — I don't expect you to understand.

MAMA *(to change the subject)*:   Who you going out with tomorrow night?

BENEATHA *(with displeasure)*:   George Murchison again.

MAMA *(pleased)*:   Oh — you getting a little sweet on him?

RUTH: You ask me, this child ain't sweet on nobody but herself — *(Under breath.)* Express herself!

They laugh.

BENEATHA: Oh — I like George all right, Mama. I mean I like him enough to go out with him and stuff, but —

RUTH *(for devilment)*:   What does *and stuff* mean?

BENEATHA: Mind your own business.

MAMA: Stop picking at her now, Ruth. *(She chuckles — then a suspicious sudden look at her daughter as she turns in her chair for emphasis.)* What DOES it mean?

BENEATHA *(wearily)*:   Oh, I just mean I couldn't ever really be serious about George. He's — he's so shallow.

RUTH: Shallow — what do you mean he's shallow? He's *rich!*

MAMA: Hush, Ruth.

BENEATHA: I know he's rich. He knows he's rich, too.

RUTH: Well — what other qualities a man got to have to satisfy you, little girl?

BENEATHA: You wouldn't even begin to understand. Anybody who married Walter could not possibly understand.

MAMA *(outraged)*:   What kind of way is that to talk about your brother?

BENEATHA: Brother is a flip — let's face it.

MAMA *(to Ruth, helplessly)*:   What's a flip?

RUTH *(glad to add kindling)*:   She's saying he's crazy.

BENEATHA: Not crazy. Brother isn't really crazy yet — he — he's an elaborate neurotic.

MAMA: Hush your mouth!

BENEATHA: As for George. Well. George looks good — he's got a beautiful car and he takes me to nice places and, as my sister-in-law says, he is probably the richest boy I will ever get to know and I even like him sometimes — but if the Youngers are sitting around waiting to see if their little Bennie is going to tie up the family with the Murchisons, they are wasting their time.

RUTH: You mean you wouldn't marry George Murchison if he asked you someday? That pretty, rich thing? Honey, I knew you was odd —

BENEATHA: No I would not marry him if all I felt for him was what I feel now. Besides, George's family wouldn't really like it.

MAMA: Why not?

BENEATHA: Oh, Mama — The Murchisons are honest-to-God-real-*live*-rich colored people, and the only people in the world who are more snobbish than rich white people are rich colored people. I thought everybody knew that. I've met Mrs. Murchison. She's a scene!

MAMA: You must not dislike people 'cause they well off, honey.

BENEATHA: Why not? It makes just as much sense as disliking people 'cause they are poor, and lots of people do that.

RUTH *(a wisdom-of-the-ages manner. To Mama)*:   Well, she'll get over some of this —

BENEATHA: Get over it? What are you talking about, Ruth? Listen, I'm going to be a doctor. I'm not worried about who I'm going to marry yet — if I ever get married.

MAMA AND RUTH: *If!*

MAMA: Now, Bennie —

BENEATHA: Oh, I probably will . . . but first I'm going to be a doctor, and George, for one, still thinks that's pretty funny. I couldn't be bothered with that. I am going to be a doctor and everybody around here better understand that!

MAMA *(kindly)*:   'Course you going to be a doctor, honey, God willing.

BENEATHA *(drily)*:   God hasn't got a thing to do with it.

MAMA: Beneatha — that just wasn't necessary.

BENEATHA: Well — neither is God. I get sick of hearing about God.

MAMA: Beneatha!

BENEATHA: I mean it! I'm just tired of hearing about God all the time. What has He got to do with anything? Does He pay tuition?

MAMA: You 'bout to get your fresh little jaw slapped!

RUTH: That's just what she needs, all right!

BENEATHA: Why? Why can't I say what I want to around here, like everybody else?

MAMA: It don't sound nice for a young girl to say things like that — you wasn't brought up that way. Me and your father went to trouble to get you and Brother to church every Sunday.

BENEATHA: Mama, you don't understand. It's all a matter of ideas, and God is just one idea I don't accept. It's not important. I am not going out and be immoral or commit crimes because I don't believe in God. I don't even think about it. It's just that I get tired of Him getting credit for all the things the human race achieves through its own stubborn effort. There simply is no blasted God — there is only man and it is *He* who makes miracles!

Mama absorbs this speech, studies her daughter, and rises slowly and crosses to Beneatha and slaps her powerfully across the face. After, there is only silence and the daughter drops her eyes from her mother's face, and Mama is very tall before her.

MAMA: Now — you say after me, in my mother's house there is still God. *(There is a long pause and Beneatha stares at the floor wordlessly. Mama repeats the phrase with precision and cool emotion.)* In my mother's house there is still God.

BENEATHA: In my mother's house there is still God.

A long pause.

MAMA *(walking away from Beneatha, too disturbed for triumphant posture. Stopping and turning back to her daughter):*   There are some ideas we ain't going to have in this house. Not long as I am at the head of this family.

BENEATHA: Yes, ma'am.

Mama walks out of the room.

RUTH *(almost gently, with profound understanding):*   You think you a woman, Bennie — but you still a little girl. What you did was childish — so you got treated like a child.

BENEATHA: I see. *(Quietly.)* I also see that everybody thinks it's all right for Mama to be a tyrant. But all the tyranny in the world will never put a God in the heavens!

She picks up her books and goes out. Pause.

RUTH *(goes to Mama's door):*   She said she was sorry.

MAMA *(coming out, going to her plant):*   They frightens me, Ruth. My children.

RUTH: You got good children, Lena. They just a little off sometimes — but they're good.

MAMA: No — there's something come down between me and them that don't let us understand each other and I don't know what it is. One done almost lost his mind thinking 'bout money all the time and the other done commence to talk about things I can't seem to understand in no form or fashion. What is it that's changing, Ruth.

RUTH *(soothingly, older than her years):*   Now . . . you taking it all too seriously. You just got strong-willed children and it takes a strong woman like you to keep 'em in hand.

MAMA *(looking at her plant and sprinkling a little water on it):*   They spirited all right, my children. Got to admit they got spirit — Bennie and Walter. Like this little old plant that ain't never had enough sunshine or nothing — and look at it . . .

She has her back to Ruth, who has had to stop ironing and lean against something and put the back of her hand to her forehead.

RUTH *(trying to keep Mama from noticing):*   You . . . sure . . . loves that little old thing, don't you? . . .

MAMA: Well, I always wanted me a garden like I used to see sometimes at the back of the houses down home. This plant is close as I ever got to having one. *(She looks out of the window as she replaces the plant.)* Lord, ain't nothing as dreary as the view from this window on a dreary day, is there? Why ain't you singing this morning, Ruth? Sing that "No Ways Tired." That song always lifts me up so — *(She turns at last to see that Ruth has slipped quietly to the floor, in a state of semiconsciousness.)* Ruth! Ruth honey — what's the matter with you . . . Ruth!

Curtain.

Scene 2

It is the following morning; a Saturday morning, and house cleaning is in progress at the Youngers'. Furniture has been shoved hither and yon and Mama is giving the kitchen-area walls a washing down. Beneatha, in dungarees, with a handkerchief tied around her face, is spraying insecticide into the cracks in the walls. As they work, the radio is on and a Southside disk-jockey program is inappropriately filling the house with a rather exotic saxophone blues. Travis, the sole idle one, is leaning on his arms, looking out of the window.

TRAVIS: Grandmama, that stuff Bennie is using smells awful. Can I go downstairs, please?

MAMA: Did you get all them chores done already? I ain't seen you doing much.

TRAVIS: Yes'm — finished early. Where did Mama go this morning?

MAMA *(looking at Beneatha)*:   She had to go on a little errand.

The phone rings. Beneatha runs to answer it and reaches it before Walter, who has entered from bedroom.

TRAVIS: Where?

MAMA: To tend to her business.

BENEATHA: Haylo . . . *(Disappointed.)* Yes, he is. *(She tosses the phone to Walter, who barely catches it.)* It's Willie Harris again.

WALTER *(as privately as possible under Mama's gaze)*:   Hello, Willie. Did you get the papers from the lawyer? . . . No, not yet. I told you the mailman doesn't get here till ten-thirty . . . No, I'll come there . . . Yeah! Right away. *(He hangs up and goes for his coat.)*

BENEATHA: Brother, where did Ruth go?

WALTER *(as he exits)*:   How should I know!

TRAVIS: Aw come on, Grandma. Can I go outside?

MAMA: Oh, I guess so. You stay right in front of the house, though, and keep a good lookout for the postman.

TRAVIS: Yes'm. *(He darts into bedroom for stickball and bat, reenters, and sees Beneatha on her knees spraying under sofa with behind upraised. He edges closer to the target, takes aim, and lets her have it. She screams.)* Leave them poor little cockroaches alone, they ain't bothering you none! *(He runs as she swings the spraygun at him viciously and playfully.)* Grandma! Grandma!

MAMA: Look out there, girl, before you be spilling some of that stuff on that child!

TRAVIS *(safely behind the bastion of Mama)*:   That's right — look out, now! *(He exits.)*

BENEATHA *(drily)*:   I can't imagine that it would hurt him — it has never hurt the roaches.

MAMA: Well, little boys' hides ain't as tough as Southside roaches. You better get over there behind the bureau. I seen one marching out of there like Napoleon yesterday.

BENEATHA: There's really only one way to get rid of them, Mama —

MAMA: How?

BENEATHA: Set fire to this building! Mama, where did Ruth go?

MAMA *(looking at her with meaning)*: To the doctor, I think.

BENEATHA: The doctor? What's the matter? *(They exchange glances.)* You don't think —

MAMA *(with her sense of drama)*: Now I ain't saying what I think. But I ain't never been wrong 'bout a woman neither.

The phone rings.

BENEATHA *(at the phone)*: Hay-lo . . . *(Pause, and a moment of recognition.)* Well — when did you get back! . . . And how was it? . . . Of course I've missed you — in my way . . . This morning? No . . . house cleaning and all that and Mama hates it if I let people come over when the house is like this . . . You *have?* Well, that's different . . . What is it — Oh, what the hell, come on over . . . Right, see you then. *Arrividerci.*

She hangs up.

MAMA *(who has listened vigorously, as is her habit)*: Who is that you inviting over here with this house looking like this? You ain't got the pride you was born with!

BENEATHA: Asagai doesn't care how houses look, Mama — he's an intellectual.

MAMA: *Who?*

BENEATHA: Asagai — Joseph Asagai. He's an African boy I met on campus. He's been studying in Canada all summer.

MAMA: What's his name?

BENEATHA: Asagai, Joseph. Ah-sah-guy . . . He's from Nigeria.

MAMA: Oh, that's the little country that was founded by slaves way back . . .

BENEATHA: No, Mama — that's Liberia.

MAMA: I don't think I never met no African before.

BENEATHA: Well, do me a favor and don't ask him a whole lot of ignorant questions about Africans. I mean, do they wear clothes and all that —

MAMA: Well, now, I guess if you think we so ignorant 'round here maybe you shouldn't bring your friends here —

BENEATHA: It's just that people ask such crazy things. All anyone seems to know about when it comes to Africa is Tarzan —

MAMA *(indignantly)*: Why should I know anything about Africa?

BENEATHA: Why do you give money at church for the missionary work?

MAMA: Well, that's to help save people.

BENEATHA: You mean save them from *heathenism* —

MAMA *(innocently)*: Yes.

BENEATHA: I'm afraid they need more salvation from the British and the French.

Ruth comes in forlornly and pulls off her coat with dejection. They both turn to look at her.

RUTH *(dispiritedly)*: Well, I guess from all the happy faces — everybody knows.

BENEATHA: You pregnant?

MAMA: Lord have mercy, I sure hope it's a little old girl. Travis ought to have a sister.

Beneatha and Ruth give her a hopeless look for this grandmotherly enthusiasm.

BENEATHA: How far along are you?

RUTH: Two months.

BENEATHA: Did you mean to? I mean did you plan it or was it an accident?

MAMA: What do you know about planning or not planning?

BENEATHA: Oh, Mama.

RUTH *(wearily)*:   She's twenty years old, Lena.

BENEATHA: Did you plan it, Ruth?

RUTH: Mind your own business.

BENEATHA: It is my business — where is he going to live, on the *roof*? *(There is silence following the remark as the three women react to the sense of it.)* Gee — I didn't mean that, Ruth, honest. Gee, I don't feel like that at all. I — I think it is wonderful.

RUTH *(dully)*:   Wonderful.

BENEATHA: Yes — really.

MAMA *(looking at Ruth, worried)*:   Doctor say everything going to be all right?

RUTH *(far away)*:   Yes — she says everything is going to be fine . . .

MAMA *(immediately suspicious)*:   "She" — What doctor you went to?

Ruth folds over, near hysteria.

MAMA *(worriedly hovering over Ruth)*:   Ruth honey — what's the matter with you — you sick?

Ruth has her fists clenched on her thighs and is fighting hard to suppress a scream that seems to be rising in her.

BENEATHA: What's the matter with her, Mama?

MAMA *(working her fingers in Ruth's shoulders to relax her)*:   She be all right. Women gets right depressed sometimes when they get her way. *(Speaking softly, expertly, rapidly.)* Now you just relax. That's right . . . just lean back, don't think 'bout nothing at all . . . nothing at all —

RUTH: I'm all right . . .

The glassy-eyed look melts and then she collapses into a fit of heavy sobbing. The bell rings.

BENEATHA: Oh, my God — that must be Asagai.

MAMA *(to Ruth)*:   Come on now, honey. You need to lie down and rest awhile . . . then have some nice hot food.

They exit, Ruth's weight on her mother-in-law. Beneatha, herself profoundly disturbed, opens the door to admit a rather dramatic-looking young man with a large package.

ASAGAI: Hello, Alaiyo —

BENEATHA *(holding the door open and regarding him with pleasure)*:   Hello . . . *(Long pause.)* Well — come in. And please excuse everything. My mother was very upset about my letting anyone come here with the place like this.

ASAGAI *(coming into the room)*: You look disturbed too . . . Is something wrong?

BENEATHA *(still at the door, absently)*: Yes . . . we've all got acute ghetto-itus. *(She smiles and comes toward him, finding a cigarette and sitting.)* So — sit down! No! Wait! *(She whips the spraygun off sofa where she had left it and puts the cushions back. At last perches on arm of sofa. He sits.)* So, how was Canada?

ASAGAI *(a sophisticate)*: Canadian.

BENEATHA *(looking at him)*: Asagai, I'm very glad you are back.

ASAGAI *(looking back at her in turn)*: Are you really?

BENEATHA: Yes — very.

ASAGAI: Why? — you were quite glad when I went away. What happened?

BENEATHA: You went away.

ASAGAI: Ahhhhhhhh.

BENEATHA: Before — you wanted to be so serious before there was time.

ASAGAI: How much time must there be before one knows what one feels?

BENEATHA *(stalling this particular conversation. Her hands pressed together, in a deliberately childish gesture)*: What did you bring me?

ASAGAI *(handing her the package)*: Open it and see.

BENEATHA *(eagerly opening the package and drawing out some records and the colorful robes of a Nigerian woman)*: Oh Asagai! . . . You got them for me! . . . How beautiful . . . and the records too! *(She lifts out the robes and runs to the mirror with them and holds the drapery up in front of herself.)*

ASAGAI *(coming to her at the mirror)*: I shall have to teach you how to drape it properly. *(He flings the material about her for the moment and stands back to look at her.)* Ah — Oh-pay-gay-day, oh-gbah-mu-shay. *(A Yoruba exclamation for admiration.)* You wear it well . . . very well . . . mutilated hair and all.

BENEATHA *(turning suddenly)*: My hair — what's wrong with my hair?

ASAGAI *(shrugging)*: Were you born with it like that?

BENEATHA *(reaching up to touch it)*: No . . . of course not.

She looks back to the mirror, disturbed.

ASAGAI *(smiling)*: How then?

BENEATHA: You know perfectly well how . . . as crinkly as yours . . . that's how.

ASAGAI: And it is ugly to you that way?

BENEATHA *(quickly)*: Oh, no — not ugly . . . *(More slowly, apologetically.)* But it's so hard to manage when it's, well — raw.

ASAGAI: And so to accommodate that — you mutilate it every week?

BENEATHA: It's not mutilation!

ASAGAI *(laughing aloud at her seriousness)*: Oh . . . please! I am only teasing you because you are so very serious about these things. *(He stands back from her and folds his arms across his chest as he watches her pulling at her hair and frowning in the mirror.)* Do you remember the first time you met me at school? . . . *(He laughs.)* You came up to me and you said — and I thought you were the most serious little thing I had ever seen — you said: *(He imitates her.)* "Mr. Asagai—I want very much to talk with you. About Africa. You see, Mr. Asagai, I am looking for my *identity*!"

He laughs.

BENEATHA *(turning to him, not laughing):* Yes—

Her face is quizzical, profoundly disturbed.

ASAGAI *(still teasing and reaching out and taking her face in his hands and turning her profile to him):* Well . . . it is true that this is not so much a profile of a Hollywood queen as perhaps a queen of the Nile—*(A mock dismissal of the importance of the question.)* But what does it matter? Assimilationism is so popular in your country.

BENEATHA *(wheeling, passionately, sharply):* I am not an assimilationist!

ASAGAI *(the protest hangs in the room for a moment and Asagai studies her, his laughter fading):* Such a serious one. *(There is a pause.)* So—you like the robes? You must take excellent care of them—they are from my sister's personal wardrobe.

BENEATHA *(with incredulity):* You—you sent all the way home—for me?

ASAGAI *(with charm):* For you—I would do much more . . . Well, that is what I came for. I must go.

BENEATHA: Will you call me Monday?

ASAGAI: Yes . . . We have a great deal to talk about. I mean about identity and time and all that.

BENEATHA: Time?

ASAGAI: Yes. About how much time one needs to know what one feels.

BENEATHA: You see! You never understood that there is more than one kind of feeling which can exist between a man and a woman—or, at least, there should be.

ASAGAI *(shaking his head negatively but gently):* No. Between a man and a woman there need be only one kind of feeling. I have that for you . . . Now even . . . right this moment . . .

BENEATHA: I know—and by itself—it won't do. I can find that anywhere.

ASAGAI: For a woman it should be enough.

BENEATHA: I know—because that's what it says in all the novels that men write. But it isn't. Go ahead and laugh—but I'm not interested in being someone's little episode in America or—*(With feminine vengeance.)*—one of them! *(Asagai has burst into laughter again.)* That's funny as hell, huh!

ASAGAI: It's just that every American girl I have known has said that to me. White—black—in this you are all the same. And the same speech, too!

BENEATHA *(angrily):* Yuk, yuk, yuk!

ASAGAI: It's how you can be sure that the world's most liberated women are not liberated at all. You all talk about it too much!

Mama enters and is immediately all social charm because of the presence of a guest.

BENEATHA: Oh—Mama—this is Mr. Asagai.

MAMA: How do you do?

ASAGAI *(total politeness to an elder)*:   How do you do, Mrs. Younger. Please forgive me for coming at such an outrageous hour on a Saturday.

MAMA: Well, you are quite welcome. I just hope you understand that our house don't always look like this. *(Chatterish.)* You must come again. I would love to hear all about — *(Not sure of the name.)* — your country. I think it's so sad the way our American Negroes don't know nothing about Africa 'cept Tarzan and all that. And all that money they pour into these churches when they ought to be helping you people over there drive out them French and Englishmen done taken away your land.

The mother flashes a slightly superior look at her daughter upon completion of the recitation.

ASAGAI *(taken aback by this sudden and acutely unrelated expression of sympathy)*:   Yes . . . yes . . .

MAMA *(smiling at him suddenly and relaxing and looking him over)*:   How many miles is it from here to where you come from?

ASAGAI: Many thousands.

MAMA *(looking at him as she would Walter)*:   I bet you don't half look after yourself, being away from your mama either. I spec you better come 'round here from time to time to get yourself some decent homecooked meals . . .

ASAGAI *(moved)*:   Thank you. Thank you very much. *(They are all quiet, then —)* Well . . . I must go. I will call you Monday, Alaiyo.

MAMA: What's that he call you?

ASAGAI: Oh — "Alaiyo." I hope you don't mind. It is what you would call a nickname, I think. It is a Yoruba word. I am a Yoruba.

MAMA *(looking at Beneatha)*:   I — I thought he was from — *(Uncertain.)*

ASAGAI *(understanding)*:   Nigeria is my country. Yoruba is my tribal origin —

BENEATHA: You didn't tell us what Alaiyo means . . . for all I know, you might be calling me Little Idiot or something . . .

ASAGAI: Well . . . let me see . . . I do not know how just to explain it . . . The sense of a thing can be so different when it changes languages.

BENEATHA: You're evading.

ASAGAI: No — really it is difficult . . . *(Thinking.)* It means . . . it means One for Whom Bread — Food — Is Not Enough. *(He looks at her.)* Is that all right?

BENEATHA *(understanding, softly)*:   Thank you.

MAMA *(looking from one to the other and not understanding any of it)*:   Well . . . that's nice . . . You must come see us again — Mr. —

ASAGAI: Ah-sah-guy . . .

MAMA: Yes . . . Do come again.

ASAGAI: Good-bye.

He exits.

MAMA *(after him)*:   Lord, that's a pretty thing just went out here! *(Insinuatingly, to her daughter.)* Yes, I guess I see why we done commence to get so interested in Africa 'round here. Missionaries my aunt Jenny!

She exits.

BENEATHA: Oh, Mama! . . .

She picks up the Nigerian dress and holds it up to her in front of the mirror again. She sets the headdress on haphazardly and then notices her hair again and clutches at it and then replaces the headdress and frowns at herself. Then she starts to wriggle in front of the mirror as she thinks a Nigerian woman might. Travis enters and stands regarding her.

TRAVIS: What's the matter, girl, you cracking up?

BENEATHA: Shut up.

She pulls the headdress off and looks at herself in the mirror and clutches at her hair again and squinches her eyes as if trying to imagine something. Then, suddenly, she gets her raincoat and kerchief and hurriedly prepares for going out.

MAMA *(coming back into the room):*   She's resting now. Travis, baby, run next door and ask Miss Johnson to please let me have a little kitchen cleanser. This here can is empty as Jacob's kettle.

TRAVIS: I just came in.

MAMA: Do as you told. *(He exits and she looks at her daughter.)* Where you going?

BENEATHA *(halting at the door):*   To become a queen of the Nile!

She exits in a breathless blaze of glory. Ruth appears in the bedroom doorway.

MAMA: Who told you to get up?

RUTH: Ain't nothing wrong with me to be lying in no bed for. Where did Bennie go?

MAMA *(drumming her fingers):*   Far as I could make out — to Egypt. *(Ruth just looks at her.)* What time is it getting to?

RUTH: Ten twenty. And the mailman going to ring that bell this morning just like he done every morning for the last umpteen years.

Travis comes in with the cleanser can.

TRAVIS: She say to tell you that she don't have much.

MAMA *(angrily):*   Lord, some people I could name sure is tight-fisted! *(Directing her grandson.)* Mark two cans of cleanser on the list there. If she that hard up for kitchen cleanser, I sure don't want to forget to get her none!

RUTH: Lena — maybe the woman is just short on cleanser —

MAMA *(not listening):*   —Much baking powder as she done borrowed from me all these years, she could of done gone into the baking business!

The bell sounds suddenly and sharply and all three are stunned — serious and silent — midspeech. In spite of all the other conversations and distractions of the morning, this is what they have been waiting for, even Travis, who looks helplessly from his mother to his grandmother. Ruth is the first to come to life again.

RUTH *(to Travis):*   Get down them steps, boy!

Travis snaps to life and flies out to get the mail.

MAMA *(her eyes wide, her hand to her breast):*   You mean it done really come?

RUTH *(excited):*   Oh, Miss Lena!

MAMA *(collecting herself)*:   Well . . . I don't know what we all so excited about 'round here for. We known it was coming for months.

RUTH: That's a whole lot different from having it come and being able to hold it in your hands . . . a piece of paper worth ten thousand dollars . . . *(Travis bursts back into the room. He holds the envelope high above his head, like a little dancer, his face is radiant and he is breathless. He moves to his grandmother with sudden slow ceremony and puts the envelope into her hands. She accepts it, and then merely holds it and looks at it.)* Come on! Open it . . . Lord have mercy, I wish Walter Lee was here!

TRAVIS: Open it, Grandmama!

MAMA *(staring at it)*:   Now you all be quiet. It's just a check.

RUTH: Open it . . .

MAMA *(still staring at it)*:   Now don't act silly . . . We ain't never been no people to act silly 'bout no money —

RUTH *(swiftly)*:   We ain't never had none before — OPEN IT!

Mama finally makes a good strong tear and pulls out the thin blue slice of paper and inspects it closely. The boy and his mother study it raptly over Mama's shoulders.

MAMA: Travis! *(She is counting off with doubt.)* Is that the right number of zeros?

TRAVIS: Yes'm . . . ten thousand dollars. Gaalee, grandmama, you rich.

MAMA *(She holds the check away from her, still looking at it. Slowly her face sobers into a mask of unhappiness)*:   Ten thousand dollars. *(She hands it to Ruth.)* Put it away somewhere, Ruth. *(She does not look at Ruth; her eyes seem to be seeing something somewhere very far off.)* Ten thousand dollars they give you. Ten thousand dollars.

TRAVIS *(to his mother, sincerely)*:   What's the matter with Grandmama — don't she want to be rich?

RUTH *(distractedly)*:   You go on out and play now, baby. *(Travis exits. Mama starts wiping dishes absently, humming intently to herself. Ruth turns to her, with kind exasperation.)* You've gone and got yourself upset.

MAMA *(not looking at her)*:   I spec if it wasn't for you all . . . I would just put that money away or give it to the church or something.

RUTH: Now what kind of talk is that. Mr. Younger would just be plain mad if he could hear you talking foolish like that.

MAMA *(stopping and staring off)*:   Yes . . . he sure would. *(Sighing.)* We got enough to do with that money, all right. *(She halts then, and turns and looks at her daughter-in-law hard; Ruth avoids her eyes and Mama wipes her hands with finality and starts to speak firmly to Ruth.)* Where did you go today, girl?

RUTH: To the doctor.

MAMA *(impatiently)*:   Now, Ruth . . . you know better than that. Old Doctor Jones is strange enough in his way but there ain't nothing 'bout him make somebody slip and call him "she" — like you done this morning.

RUTH: Well, that's what happened — my tongue slipped.

MAMA: You went to see that woman, didn't you?

RUTH *(defensively, giving herself away)*:   What woman you talking about?

MAMA *(angrily)*: That woman who —

Walter enters in great excitement.

WALTER: Did it come?

MAMA *(quietly)*: Can't you give people a Christian greeting before you start asking about money?

WALTER *(to Ruth)*: Did it come? *(Ruth unfolds the check and lays it quietly before him, watching him intently with thoughts of her own. Walter sits down and grasps it close and counts off the zeros.)* Ten thousand dollars — *(He turns suddenly, frantically to his mother and draws some papers out of his breast pocket.)* Mama — look. Old Willy Harris put everything on paper —

MAMA: Son — I think you ought to talk to your wife . . . I'll go on out and leave you alone if you want —

WALTER: I can talk to her later — Mama, look —

MAMA: Son —

WALTER: WILL SOMEBODY PLEASE LISTEN TO ME TODAY!

MAMA *(quietly)*: I don't 'low no yellin' in this house, Walter Lee, and you know it — *(Walter stares at them in frustration and starts to speak several times.)* And there ain't going to be no investing in no liquor stores.

WALTER: But, Mama, you ain't even looked at it.

MAMA: I don't aim to have to speak on that again.

A long pause.

WALTER: You ain't looked at it and you don't aim to have to speak on that again? You ain't even looked at it and *you* have decided — *(Crumpling his papers.)* Well, *you* tell that to my boy tonight when you put him to sleep on the living-room couch . . . . *(Turning to Mama and speaking directly to her.)* Yeah — and tell it to my wife, Mama, tomorrow when she has to go out of here to look after somebody else's kids. And tell it to *me*, Mama, every time we need a new pair of curtains and I have to watch *you* go out and work in somebody's kitchen. Yeah, you tell me then!

Walter starts out.

RUTH: Where you going?

WALTER: I'm going out!

RUTH: Where?

WALTER: Just out of this house somewhere —

RUTH *(getting her coat)*: I'll come too.

WALTER: I don't want you to come!

RUTH: I got something to talk to you about, Walter.

WALTER: That's too bad.

MAMA *(still quietly)*: Walter Lee — *(She waits and he finally turns and looks at her.)* Sit down.

WALTER: I'm a grown man, Mama.

MAMA: Ain't nobody said you wasn't grown. But you still in my house and my presence. And as long as you are — you'll talk to your wife civil. Now sit down.

RUTH *(suddenly):*   Oh, let him go on out and drink himself to death! He makes me sick to my stomach! *(She flings her coat against him and exits to bedroom.)*

WALTER *(violently flinging the coat after her):*   And you turn mine too, baby! *(The door slams behind her.)* That was my biggest mistake —

MAMA *(still quietly):*   Walter, what is the matter with you?

WALTER: Matter with me? Ain't nothing the matter with *me!*

MAMA: Yes there is. Something eating you up like a crazy man. Something more than me not giving you this money. The past few years I been watching it happen to you. You get all nervous acting and kind of wild in the eyes — *(Walter jumps up impatiently at her words.)* I said sit there now, I'm talking to you!

WALTER: Mama — I don't need no nagging at me today.

MAMA: Seem like you getting to a place where you always tied up in some kind of knot about something. But if anybody ask you 'bout it you just yell at 'em and bust out the house and go out and drink somewheres. Walter Lee, people can't live with that. Ruth's a good, patient girl in her way — but you getting to be too much. Boy, don't make the mistake of driving that girl away from you.

WALTER: Why — what she do for me?

MAMA: She loves you.

WALTER: Mama — I'm going out. I want to go off somewhere and be by myself for a while.

MAMA: I'm sorry 'bout your liquor store, son. It just wasn't the thing for us to do. That's what I want to tell you about —

WALTER: I got to go out, Mama —

He rises.

MAMA: It's dangerous, son.

WALTER: What's dangerous?

MAMA: When a man goes outside his home to look for peace.

WALTER *(beseechingly):*   Then why can't there never be no peace in this house then?

MAMA: You done found it in some other house?

WALTER: No — there ain't no woman! Why do women always think there's a woman somewhere when a man gets restless. *(Picks up the check.)* Do you know what this money means to me? Do you know what this money can do for us? *(Puts it back.)* Mama — Mama — I want so many things . . .

MAMA: Yes, son —

WALTER: I want so many things that they are driving me kind of crazy . . . Mama — look at me.

MAMA: I'm looking at you. You a good-looking boy. You got a job, a nice wife, a fine boy, and —

WALTER: A job. *(Looks at her.)* Mama, a job? I open and close car doors all day long. I drive a man around in his limousine and I say, "Yes, sir; no, sir; very good, sir; shall I take the Drive, sir?" Mama, that ain't no kind of job . . . that ain't nothing at all. *(Very quietly.)* Mama, I don't know if I can make you understand.

MAMA: Understand what, baby?

WALTER *(quietly)*:   Sometimes it's like I can see the future stretched out in front of me — just plain as day. The future, Mama. Hanging over there at the edge of my days. Just waiting for me — a big, looming blank space — full of *nothing.* Just waiting for *me.* But it don't have to be. *(Pause. Kneeling beside her chair.)* Mama — sometimes when I'm downtown and I pass them cool, quiet-looking restaurants where them white boys are sitting back and talking 'bout things . . . sitting there turning deals worth millions of dollars . . . sometimes I see guys don't look much older than me —

MAMA: Son — how come you talk so much 'bout money?

WALTER *(with immense passion)*:   Because it is life, Mama!

MAMA *(quietly)*:   Oh — *(Very quietly.)* So now it's life. Money is life. Once upon a time freedom used to be life — now it's money. I guess the world really do change . . .

WALTER: No — it was always money, Mama. We just didn't know about it.

MAMA: No . . . something has changed. *(She looks at him.)* You something new, boy. In my time we was worried about not being lynched and getting to the North if we could and how to stay alive and still have a pinch of dignity too . . . Now here come you and Beneatha — talking 'bout things we ain't never even thought about hardly, me and your daddy. You ain't satisfied or proud of nothing we done. I mean that you had a home; that we kept you out of trouble till you was grown; that you don't have to ride to work on the back of nobody's streetcar — You my children — but how different we done become.

WALTER *(a long beat. He pats her hand and gets up)*:   You just don't understand, Mama, you just don't understand.

MAMA: Son — do you know your wife is expecting another baby? *(Walter stands, stunned, and absorbs what his mother has said.)* That's what she wanted to talk to you about. *(Walter sinks down into a chair.)* This ain't for me to be telling — but you ought to know. *(She waits.)* I think Ruth is thinking 'bout getting rid of that child.

WALTER *(slowly understanding)*:   — No — no — Ruth wouldn't do that.

MAMA: When the world gets ugly enough — a woman will do anything for her family. *The part that's already living.*

WALTER: You don't know Ruth, Mama, if you think she would do that.

Ruth opens the bedroom door and stands there a little limp.

RUTH *(beaten)*:   Yes I would too, Walter. *(Pause.)* I gave her a five-dollar down payment.

There is total silence as the man stares at his wife and the mother stares at her son.

MAMA *(presently)*:   Well — *(Tightly.)* Well — son, I'm waiting to hear you say something . . . *(She waits.)* I'm waiting to hear how you be your father's son. Be the man he was . . . *(Pause. The silence shouts.)* Your wife say she going to destroy your child. And I'm waiting to hear you talk like him and say we a people who give children life, not who destroys them — *(She rises.)* I'm waiting to see you stand up and look like your daddy and say we done give up one baby to poverty and that we ain't going to give up nary another one . . . I'm waiting.

WALTER: Ruth — *(He can say nothing.)*

MAMA: If you a son of mine, tell her! *(Walter picks up his keys and his coat and walks out. She continues, bitterly.)* You . . . you are a disgrace to your father's memory. Somebody get me my hat!

Curtain.

ACT 2, Scene 1

Time: Later the same day.

At rise: Ruth is ironing again. She has the radio going. Presently Beneatha's bedroom door opens and Ruth's mouth falls and she puts down the iron in fascination.

RUTH: What have we got on tonight!

BENEATHA *(emerging grandly from the doorway so that we can see her thoroughly robed in the costume Asagai brought)*:   You are looking at what a well-dressed Nigerian woman wears — *(She parades for Ruth, her hair completely hidden by the headdress; she is coquettishly fanning herself with an ornate oriental fan, mistakenly more like Butterfly than any Nigerian that ever was.)* Isn't it beautiful? *(She promenades to the radio and, with an arrogant flourish, turns off the good loud blues that is playing.)* Enough of this assimilationist junk! *(Ruth follows her with her eyes as she goes to the phonograph and puts on a record and turns and waits ceremoniously for the music to come up. Then, with a shout —)* OCOMOGOSIAY!

Ruth jumps. The music comes up, a lovely Nigerian melody. Beneatha listens, enraptured, her eyes far way — "back to the past." She begins to dance. Ruth is dumfounded.

RUTH: What kind of dance is that?

BENEATHA: A folk dance.

RUTH *(Pearl Bailey)*:   What kind of folks do that, honey?

BENEATHA: It's from Nigeria. It's a dance of welcome.

RUTH: Who you welcoming?

BENEATHA: The men back to the village.

RUTH: Where they been?

BENEATHA: How should I know — out hunting or something. Anyway, they are coming back now . . .

RUTH: Well, that's good.

BENEATHA *(with the record)*:

Alundi, alundi
Alundi alunya
Jop pu a jeepua
Ang gu sooooooooooo
Ai yai yae . . .
Ayehaye —
alundi . . .

Walter comes in during this performance; he has obviously been drinking. He leans against the door heavily and watches his sister, at first with distaste. Then his eyes look off — "back to the past" — as he lifts both his fists to the roof, screaming.

WALTER: YEAH . . . AND ETHIOPIA STRETCH FORTH HER HANDS AGAIN! . . .

RUTH *(drily, looking at him)*:   Yes — and Africa sure is claiming her own tonight. *(She gives them both up and starts ironing again.)*

WALTER *(all in a drunken, dramatic shout)*:   Shut up! . . . I'm diggin them drums . . . them drums move me! . . . *(He makes his weaving way to his wife's face and leans in close to her.)* In my *heart of hearts* — *(He thumps his chest.)* — I am much warrior!

RUTH *(without even looking up)*:   In your heart of hearts you are much drunkard.

WALTER *(coming away from her and starting to wander around the room, shouting)*:   Me and Jomo . . . *(Intently, in his sister's face. She has stopped dancing to watch him in this unknown mood.)* That's my man, Kenyatta. *(Shouting and thumping his chest.)* FLAMING SPEAR! HOT DAMN! *(He is suddenly in possession of an imaginary spear and actively spearing enemies all over the room.)* OCOMOGOSIAY . . .

BENEATHA *(to encourage Walter, thoroughly caught up with this side of him)*:   OCOMOGOSIAY, FLAMING SPEAR!

WALTER: THE LION IS WAKING . . . OWIMOWEH!

He pulls his shirt open and leaps up on the table and gestures with his spear.

BENEATHA: OWIMOWEH!

WALTER *(on the table, very far gone, his eyes pure glass sheets. He sees what we cannot, that he is a leader of his people, a great chief, a descendant of Chaka, and that the hour to march has come)*:   Listen, my black brothers —

BENEATHA: OCOMOGOSIAY!

WALTER: — Do you hear the waters rushing against the shores of the coastlands —

BENEATHA: OCOMOGOSIAY!

WALTER: — Do you hear the screeching of the cocks in yonder hills beyond where the chiefs meet in council for the coming of the mighty war —

BENEATHA: OCOMOGOSIAY!

And now the lighting shifts subtly to suggest the world of Walter's imagination, and the mood shifts from pure comedy. It is the inner Walter speaking: the Southside chauffeur has assumed an unexpected majesty.

WALTER: — Do you hear the beating of the wings of the birds flying low over the mountains and the low places of our land —

BENEATHA: OCOMOGOSIAY!

WALTER: — Do you hear the singing of the women, singing the war songs of our fathers to the babies in the great houses? Singing the sweet war songs! *(The doorbell rings.)* OH, DO YOU HEAR, MY *BLACK* BROTHERS!

BENEATHA *(completely gone)*:   We hear you, Flaming Spear —

Ruth shuts off the phonograph and opens the door. George Murchison enters.

WALTER: Telling us to prepare for the GREATNESS OF THE TIME! *(Lights back to normal. He turns and sees George.)* Black Brother!

He extends his hand for the fraternal clasp.

GEORGE: Black Brother, hell!

RUTH *(having had enough, and embarrassed for the family)*: Beneatha, you got company — what's the matter with you? Walter Lee Younger, get down off that table and stop acting like a fool . . .

Walter comes down off the table suddenly and makes a quick exit to the bathroom.

RUTH: He's had a little to drink . . . I don't know what her excuse is.

GEORGE *(to Beneatha)*: Look honey, we're going to the theater — we're not going to be *in* it . . . so go change, huh?

Beneatha looks at him and slowly, ceremoniously, lifts her hands and pulls off the headdress. Her hair is close-cropped and unstraightened. George freezes mid-sentence and Ruth's eyes all but fall out of her head.

GEORGE: What in the name of —

RUTH *(touching Beneatha's hair)*: Girl, you done lost your natural mind? Look at your head!

GEORGE: What have you done to your head — I mean your hair!

BENEATHA: Nothing — except cut it off.

RUTH: Now that's the truth — it's what ain't been done to it! You expect this boy to go out with you with your head all nappy like that?

BENEATHA *(looking at George)*: That's up to George. If he's ashamed of his heritage —

GEORGE: Oh, don't be so proud of yourself, Bennie — just because you look eccentric.

BENEATHA: How can something that's natural be eccentric?

GEORGE: That's what being eccentric means — being natural. Get dressed.

BENEATHA: I don't like that, George.

RUTH: Why must you and your brother make an argument out of everything people say?

BENEATHA: Because I hate assimilationist Negroes!

RUTH: Will somebody please tell me what assimila-whoever means!

GEORGE: Oh, it's just a college girl's way of calling people Uncle Toms — but that isn't what it means at all.

RUTH: Well, what does it mean?

BENEATHA *(cutting George off and staring at him as she replies to Ruth)*: It means someone who is willing to give up his own culture and submerge himself completely in the dominant, and in this case *oppressive* culture!

GEORGE: Oh, dear, dear, dear! Here we go! A lecture on the African past! On our Great West African Heritage! In one second we will hear all about the great Ashanti empires; the great Songhay civilizations; and the great sculpture of Bénin — and then some poetry in the Bantu — and the whole monologue will end with the word *heritage*! *(Nastily.)* Let's face it, baby, your heritage is nothing but a bunch of raggedy-assed spirituals and some grass huts!

BENEATHA: GRASS HUTS! *(Ruth crosses to her and forcibly pushes her toward the bedroom.)* See there . . . you are standing there in your splendid ignorance talking about people who were the first to smelt iron on the face of the earth! *(Ruth is pushing her through the door.)* The Ashanti were performing surgical operations when the English — *(Ruth pulls the door to, with Beneatha on the other side, and smiles graciously at George. Beneatha opens the door and shouts the end of the sentence defiantly at George.)* — were still tatooing themselves with blue dragons! *(She goes back inside.)*

RUTH: Have a seat, George. *(They both sit. Ruth folds her hands rather primly on her lap, determined to demonstrate the civilization of the family.)* Warm, ain't it? I mean for September. *(Pause.)* Just like they always say about Chicago weather: if it's too hot or cold for you, just wait a minute and it'll change. *(She smiles happily at this cliché of clichés.)* Everybody say it's got to do with them bombs and things they keep setting off. *(Pause.)* Would you like a nice cold beer?

GEORGE: No, thank you. I don't care for beer. *(He looks at his watch.)* I hope she hurries up.

RUTH: What time is the show?

GEORGE: It's an eight-thirty curtain. That's just Chicago, though. In New York standard curtain time is eight forty.

He is rather proud of this knowledge.

RUTH *(properly appreciating it):*   You get to New York a lot?

GEORGE *(offhand):*   Few times a year.

RUTH: Oh — that's nice. I've never been to New York.

Walter enters. We feel he has relieved himself, but the edge of unreality is still with him.

WALTER: New York ain't got nothing Chicago ain't. Just a bunch of hustling people all squeezed up together — being "Eastern."

He turns his face into a screw of displeasure.

GEORGE: Oh — you've been?

WALTER: *Plenty* of times.

RUTH *(shocked at the lie):*   Walter Lee Younger!

WALTER *(staring her down):*   Plenty! *(Pause.)* What we got to drink in this house? Why don't you offer this man some refreshment. *(To George.)* They don't know how to entertain people in this house, man.

GEORGE: Thank you — I don't really care for anything.

WALTER *(feeling his head; sobriety coming):*   Where's Mama?

RUTH: She ain't come back yet.

WALTER *(looking Murchison over from head to toe, scrutinizing his carefully casual tweed sports jacket over cashmere V-neck sweater over soft eyelet shirt and tie, and soft slacks, finished off with white buckskin shoes):*   Why all you college boys wear them faggoty-looking white shoes?

RUTH: Walter Lee!

George Murchison ignores the remark.

WALTER *(to Ruth)*: Well, they look crazy as hell — white shoes, cold as it is.

RUTH *(crushed)*: You have to excuse him —

WALTER: No he don't! Excuse me for what? What you always excusing me for! I'll excuse myself when I needs to be excused! *(A pause.)* They look as funny as them black knee socks Beneatha wears out of here all the time.

RUTH: It's the college *style*, Walter.

WALTER: Style, hell. She looks like she got burnt legs or something!

RUTH: Oh, Walter —

WALTER *(an irritable mimic)*: Oh, Walter! Oh, Walter! *(To Murchison.)* How's your old man making out? I understand you all going to buy that big hotel on the Drive? *(He finds a beer in the refrigerator, wanders over to Murchison, sipping and wiping his lips with the back of his hand, and straddling a chair backwards to talk to the other man.)* Shrewd move. Your old man is all right, man. *(Tapping his head and half winking for emphasis.)* I mean he knows how to operate. I mean he thinks *big*, you know what I mean, I mean for a *home*, you know? But I think he's kind of running out of ideas now. I'd like to talk to him. Listen, man, I got some plans that could turn this city upside down. I mean think like he does. *Big*. Invest big, gamble big, hell, lose *big* if you have to, you know what I mean. It's hard to find a man on this whole Southside who understands my kind of thinking — you dig? *(He scrutinizes Murchison again, drinks his beer, squints his eyes, and leans in close, confidential, man to man.)* Me and you ought to sit down and talk sometimes, man. Man, I got me some ideas . . .

MURCHISON *(with boredom)*: Yeah — sometimes we'll have to do that, Walter.

WALTER *(understanding the indifference, and offended)*: Yeah — well, when you get the time, man. I know you a busy little boy.

RUTH: Walter, please —

WALTER *(bitterly, hurt)*: I know ain't nothing in this world as busy as you colored college boys with your fraternity pins and white shoes . . .

RUTH *(covering her face with humiliation)*: Oh, Walter Lee —

WALTER: I see you all all the time — with the books tucked under your arms — going to your *(British A — a mimic.)* "clahsses." And for what! What the hell you learning over there? Filling up your heads — *(Counting off on his fingers.)* — with the sociology and the psychology — but they teaching you how to be a man? How to take over and run the world? They teaching you how to run a rubber plantation or a steel mill? Naw — just to talk proper and read books and wear them faggoty-looking white shoes . . .

GEORGE *(looking at him with distaste, a little above it all)*: You're all wacked up with bitterness, man.

WALTER *(intently, almost quietly, between the teeth, glaring at the boy)*: And you — ain't you bitter, man? Ain't you just about had it yet? Don't you see no stars gleaming that you can't reach out and grab? You happy? — You contented son-of-a-bitch — you happy? You got it made? Bitter? Man, I'm a volcano. Bitter? Here I am a giant — surrounded by ants! Ants who can't even understand what it is the giant is talking about.

RUTH *(passionately and suddenly)*: Oh, Walter — ain't you with nobody!

WALTER *(violently)*:   No! 'Cause ain't nobody with me! Not even my own mother!

RUTH: Walter, that's a terrible thing to say!

Beneatha enters, dressed for the evening in a cocktail dress and earrings, hair natural.

GEORGE: Well — hey — *(Crosses to Beneatha; thoughtful, with emphasis, since this is a reversal.)* You look great!

WALTER *(seeing his sister's hair for the first time)*:   What's the matter with your head?

BENEATHA *(tired of the jokes now)*:   I cut it off, Brother.

WALTER *(coming close to inspect it and walking around her)*:   Well, I'll be damned. So that's what they mean by the African bush . . .

BENEATHA: Ha ha. Let's go, George.

GEORGE *(looking at her)*:   You know something? I like it. It's sharp. I mean it really is. *(Helps her into her wrap.)*

RUTH: Yes — I think so, too. *(She goes to the mirror and starts to clutch at her hair.)*

WALTER: Oh no! You leave yours alone, baby. You might turn out to have a pin-shaped head or something!

BENEATHA: See you all later.

RUTH: Have a nice time.

GEORGE: Thanks. Good night. *(Half out the door, he reopens it. To Walter.)* Good night, Prometheus!

Beneatha and George exit.

WALTER *(to Ruth)*:   Who is Prometheus?

RUTH: I don't know. Don't worry about it.

WALTER *(in fury, pointing after George)*:   See there — they get to a point where they can't insult you man to man — they got to go talk about something ain't nobody never heard of!

RUTH: How do you know it was an insult? *(To humor him.)* Maybe Prometheus is a nice fellow.

WALTER: Prometheus! I bet there ain't even no such thing! I bet that simple-minded clown —

RUTH: Walter —

She stops what she is doing and looks at him.

WALTER *(yelling)*:   Don't start!

RUTH: Start what?

WALTER: Your nagging! Where was I? Who was I with? How much money did I spend?

RUTH *(plaintively)*:   Walter Lee — why don't we just try to talk about it . . .

WALTER *(not listening)*:   I been out talking with people who understand me. People who care about the things I got on my mind.

RUTH *(wearily)*:   I guess that means people like Willy Harris.

WALTER: Yes, people like Willy Harris.

RUTH *(with a sudden flash of impatience)*:   Why don't you all just hurry up and go into the banking business and stop talking about it!

WALTER: Why? You want to know why? 'Cause we all tied up in a race of people that don't know how to do nothing but moan, pray, and have babies!

The line is too bitter even for him and he looks at her and sits down.

RUTH: Oh, Walter . . . *(Softly.)* Honey, why can't you stop fighting me?

WALTER *(without thinking)*:   Who's fighting you? Who even cares about you?

This line begins the retardation of his mood.

RUTH: Well — *(She waits a long time, and then with resignation starts to put away her things.)* I guess I might as well go on to bed . . . *(More or less to herself.)* I don't know where we lost it . . . but we have . . . *(Then, to him.)* I — I'm sorry about this new baby, Walter. I guess maybe I better go on and do what I started . . . I guess I just didn't realize how bad things was with us . . . I guess I just didn't really realize — *(She starts out to the bedroom and stops.)* You want some hot milk?

WALTER: Hot milk?

RUTH: Yes — hot milk.

WALTER: Why hot milk?

RUTH: 'Cause after all that liquor you come home with you ought to have something hot in your stomach.

WALTER: I don't want no milk.

RUTH: You want some coffee then?

WALTER: No, I don't want no coffee. I don't want nothing hot to drink. *(Almost plaintively.)* Why you always trying to give me something to eat?

RUTH *(standing and looking at him helplessly)*:   What *else* can I give you, Walter Lee Younger?

She stands and looks at him and presently turns to go out again. He lifts his head and watches her going away from him in a new mood which began to emerge when he asked her "Who cares about you?"

WALTER: It's been rough, ain't it, baby? *(She hears and stops but does not turn around and he continues to her back.)* I guess between two people there ain't never as much understood as folks generally thinks there is. I mean like between me and you — *(She turns to face him.)* How we gets to the place where we scared to talk softness to each other. *(He waits, thinking hard himself.)* Why you think it got to be like that? *(He is thoughtful, almost as a child would be.)* Ruth, what is it gets into people ought to be close?

RUTH: I don't know, honey. I think about it a lot.

WALTER: On account of you and me, you mean? The way things are with us. The way something done come down between us.

RUTH: There ain't so much between us, Walter . . . Not when you come to me and try to talk to me. Try to be with me . . . a little even.

WALTER *(total honesty)*:   Sometimes . . . sometimes . . . I don't even know how to try.

RUTH: Walter —

WALTER: Yes?

RUTH *(coming to him, gently and with misgiving, but coming to him)*:   Honey . . . life don't have to be like this. I mean sometimes people can do things so that things are better . . . You remember how we used to talk when Travis was born . . . about the way we were going to live . . . the kind of house . . . *(She is stroking his head.)* Well, it's all starting to slip away from us . . .

He turns her to him and they look at each other and kiss, tenderly and hungrily. The door opens and Mama enters — Walter breaks away and jumps up. A beat.

WALTER: Mama, where have you been?

MAMA: My — them steps is longer than they used to be. Whew! *(She sits down and ignores him.)* How you feeling this evening, Ruth?

Ruth shrugs, disturbed at having been interrupted and watching her husband knowingly.

WALTER: Mama, where have you been all day?

MAMA *(still ignoring him and leaning on the table and changing to more comfortable shoes)*:   Where's Travis?

RUTH: I let him go out earlier and he ain't come back yet. Boy, is he going to get it!

WALTER: Mama!

MAMA *(as if she has heard him for the first time)*:   Yes, son?

WALTER: Where did you go this afternoon?

MAMA: I went downtown to tend to some business that I had to tend to.

WALTER: What kind of business?

MAMA: You know better than to question me like a child, Brother.

WALTER *(rising and bending over the table)*:   Where were you, Mama? *(Bringing his fists down and shouting.)* Mama, you didn't go do something with that insurance money, something crazy?

The front door opens slowly, interrupting him, and Travis peeks his head in, less than hopefully.

TRAVIS *(to his mother)*:   Mama, I —

RUTH: "Mama I" nothing! You're going to get it, boy! Get on in that bedroom and get yourself ready!

TRAVIS: But I —

MAMA: Why don't you all never let the child explain hisself.

RUTH: Keep out of it now, Lena.

Mama clamps her lips together, and Ruth advances toward her son menacingly.

RUTH: A thousand times I have told you not to go off like that —

MAMA *(holding out her arms to her grandson)*:   Well — at least let me tell him something. I want him to be the first one to hear . . . Come here, Travis. *(The boy obeys, gladly.)* Travis — *(She takes him by the shoulder and looks into his face.)* — you know that money we got in the mail this morning?

TRAVIS: Yes'm —

MAMA: Well — what you think your grandmama gone and done with that money?

TRAVIS: I don't know, Grandmama.

MAMA *(putting her finger on his nose for emphasis)*: She went out and she bought you a house! *(The explosion comes from Walter at the end of the revelation and he jumps up and turns away from all of them in a fury. Mama continues, to Travis.)* You glad about the house? It's going to be yours when you get to be a man.

TRAVIS: Yeah — I always wanted to live in a house.

MAMA: All right, gimme some sugar then — *(Travis puts his arms around her neck as she watches her son over the boy's shoulder. Then, to Travis, after the embrace.)* Now when you say your prayers tonight, you thank God and your grandfather — 'cause it was him who give you the house — in his way.

RUTH *(taking the boy from Mama and pushing him toward the bedroom)*: Now you get out of here and get ready for your beating.

TRAVIS: Aw, Mama —

RUTH: Get on in there — *(Closing the door behind him and turning radiantly to her mother-in-law.)* So you went and did it!

MAMA *(quietly, looking at her son with pain)*: Yes, I did.

RUTH *(raising both arms classically)*: PRAISE GOD! *(Looks at Walter a moment, who says nothing. She crosses rapidly to her husband.)* Please, honey — let me be glad . . . you be glad too. *(She has laid her hands on his shoulders, but he shakes himself free of her roughly, without turning to face her.)* Oh, Walter . . . a home . . . a home. *(She comes back to Mama.)* Well — where is it? How big is it? How much it going to cost?

MAMA: Well —

RUTH: When we moving?

MAMA *(smiling at her)*: First of the month.

RUTH *(throwing back her head with jubilance)*: Praise God!

MAMA *(tentatively, still looking at her son's back turned against her and Ruth)*: It's — it's a nice house too . . . *(She cannot help speaking directly to him. An imploring quality in her voice, her manner, makes her almost like a girl now.)* Three bedrooms — nice big one for you and Ruth . . . Me and Beneatha still have to share our room, but Travis have one of his own — and *(With difficulty.)* I figure if the — new baby — is a boy, we could get one of them double-decker outfits . . . And there's a yard with a little patch of dirt where I could maybe get to grow me a few flowers . . . And a nice big basement . . .

RUTH: Walter honey, be glad —

MAMA *(still to his back, fingering things on the table)*: 'Course I don't want to make it sound fancier than it is . . . It's just a plain little old house — but it's made good and solid — and it will be *ours*. Walter Lee — it makes a difference in a man when he can walk on floors that belong to *him* . . .

RUTH: Where is it?

MAMA *(frightened at this telling)*: Well — well — it's out there in Clybourne Park —

Ruth's radiance fades abruptly, and Walter finally turns slowly to face his mother with incredulity and hostility.

RUTH: Where?

MAMA *(matter-of-factly)*:   Four o six Clybourne Street, Clybourne Park.

RUTH: Clybourne Park? Mama, there ain't no colored people living in Clybourne Park.

MAMA *(almost idiotically)*:   Well, I guess there's going to be some now.

WALTER *(bitterly)*:   So that's the peace and comfort you went out and bought for us today!

MAMA *(raising her eyes to meet his finally)*:   Son — I just tried to find the nicest place for the least amount of money for my family.

RUTH *(trying to recover from the shock)*:   Well — well — 'course I ain't one never been 'fraid of no crackers, mind you — but — well, wasn't there no other houses nowhere?

MAMA: Them houses they put up for colored in them areas way out all seem to cost twice as much as other houses. I did the best I could.

RUTH *(struck senseless with the news, in its various degrees of goodness and trouble, she sits a moment, her fists propping her chin in thought, and then she starts to rise, bringing her fists down with vigor, the radiance spreading from cheek to cheek again)*:   Well — well — All I can say is — if this is my time in life — MY TIME — to say good-bye — (And she builds with momentum as she starts to circle the room with an exuberant, almost tearfully happy release.) — to these Goddamned cracking walls! — (She pounds the walls.) — and these marching roaches! — (She wipes at an imaginary army of marching roaches.) — and this cramped little closet which ain't now or never was no kitchen! . . . then I say it loud and good, HALLELUJAH! AND GOOD-BYE MISERY . . . I DON'T NEVER WANT TO SEE YOUR UGLY FACE AGAIN! (She laughs joyously, having practically destroyed the apartment, and flings her arms up and lets them come down happily, slowly, reflectively, over her abdomen, aware for the first time perhaps that the life therein pulses with happiness and not despair.) Lena?*

MAMA *(moved, watching her happiness)*:   Yes, honey?

RUTH *(looking off)*:   Is there — is there a whole lot of sunlight?

MAMA *(understanding)*:   Yes, child, there's a whole lot of sunlight.

Long pause.

RUTH *(collecting herself and going to the door of the room Travis is in)*:   Well — I guess I better see 'bout Travis. *(To Mama.)* Lord, I sure don't feel like whipping nobody today!

She exits.

MAMA *(the mother and son are left alone now and the mother waits a long time, considering deeply, before she speaks)*:   Son — you — you understand what I done, don't you? *(Walter is silent and sullen.)* I — I just seen my family falling apart today . . . just falling to pieces in front of my eyes . . . We couldn't of gone on like we was today. We was going backwards 'stead of forwards — talking 'bout killing babies and wishing each other was dead . . . When it gets like that in life — you just got to do something different, push on out and do something bigger . . . *(She waits.)* I wish you say something, son . . . I wish you'd say how deep inside you you think I done the right thing —

WALTER *(crossing slowly to his bedroom door and finally turning there and speaking measuredly)*: What you need me to say you done right for? *You* the head of this family. You run our lives like you want to. It was your money and you did what you wanted with it. So what you need for me to say it was all right for? *(Bitterly, to hurt her as deeply as he knows is possible.)* So you butchered up a dream of mine — you — who always talking 'bout your children's dreams . . .

MAMA: Walter Lee —

He just closes the door behind him. Mama sits alone, thinking heavily.

Curtain.

Scene 2

Time: Friday night, a few weeks later.

At rise: Packing crates mark the intention of the family to move. Beneatha and George come in, presumably from an evening out again.

GEORGE: O.K. . . . O.K., whatever you say . . . *(They both sit on the couch. He tries to kiss her. She moves away.)* Look, we've had a nice evening; let's not spoil it, huh? . . .

He again turns her head and tries to nuzzle in and she turns away from him, not with distaste but with momentary lack of interest; in a mood to pursue what they were talking about.

BENEATHA: I'm *trying* to talk to you.

GEORGE: We always talk.

BENEATHA: Yes — and I love to talk.

GEORGE *(exasperated; rising)*: I know it and I don't mind it sometimes . . . I want you to cut it out, see — The moody stuff, I mean. I don't like it. You're a nice-looking girl . . . all over. That's all you need, honey, forget the atmosphere. Guys aren't going to go for the atmosphere — they're going to go for what they see. Be glad for that. Drop the Garbo routine. It doesn't go with you. As for myself, I want a nice — *(Groping.)* — simple *(Thoughtfully.)* — sophisticated girl . . . not a poet — O.K.?

He starts to kiss her, she rebuffs him again and he jumps up.

BENEATHA: Why are you angry, George?

GEORGE: Because this is stupid! I don't go out with you to discuss the nature of "quiet desperation" or to hear all about your thoughts — because the world will go on thinking what it thinks regardless —

BENEATHA: Then why read books? Why go to school?

GEORGE *(with artificial patience, counting on his fingers)*:   It's simple. You read books — to learn facts — to get grades — to pass the course — to get a degree. That's all — it has nothing to do with thoughts.

A long pause.

BENEATHA: I see. *(He starts to sit.)* Good night, George.

George looks at her a little oddly, and starts to exit. He meets Mama coming in.

GEORGE: Oh — hello, Mrs. Younger.

MAMA: Hello, George, how you feeling?

GEORGE: Fine — fine, how are you?

MAMA: Oh, a little tired. You know them steps can get you after a day's work. You all have a nice time tonight?

GEORGE: Yes — a fine time. A fine time.

MAMA: Well, good night.

GEORGE: Good night. *(He exits. Mama closes the door behind her.)* Hello, honey. What you sitting like that for?

BENEATHA: I'm just sitting.

MAMA: Didn't you have a nice time?

BENEATHA: No.

MAMA: No? What's the matter?

BENEATHA: Mama, George is a fool — honest. *(She rises.)*

MAMA *(hustling around unloading the packages she has entered with. She stops)*:   Is he, baby?

BENEATHA: Yes.

Beneatha makes up Travis's bed as she talks.

MAMA: You sure?

BENEATHA: Yes.

MAMA: Well — I guess you better not waste your time with no fools.

Beneatha looks up at her mother, watching her put groceries in the refrigerator. Finally she gathers up her things and starts into the bedroom. At the door she stops and looks back at her mother.

BENEATHA: Mama —

MAMA: Yes, baby —

BENEATHA: Thank you.

MAMA: For what?

BENEATHA: For understanding me this time.

She exits quickly and the mother stands, smiling a little, looking at the place where Beneatha just stood. Ruth enters.

RUTH: Now don't you fool with any of this stuff, Lena —

MAMA: Oh, I just thought I'd sort a few things out. Is Brother here?

RUTH: Yes.

MAMA *(with concern)*:   Is he —

RUTH *(reading her eyes)*:   Yes.

Mama is silent and someone knocks on the door. Mama and Ruth exchange weary and knowing glances and Ruth opens it to admit the neighbor, Mrs. Johnson,° who is a rather squeaky wide-eyed lady of no particular age, with a newspaper under her arm.

MAMA *(changing her expression to acute delight and a ringing cheerful greeting)*:   Oh — hello there, Johnson.

JOHNSON *(this is a woman who decided long ago to be enthusiastic about EVERYTHING in life and she is inclined to wave her wrist vigorously at the height of her exclamatory comments)*:   Hello there, yourself! H'you this evening, Ruth?

RUTH *(not much of a deceptive type)*:   Fine, Mis' Johnson, h'you?

JOHNSON: Fine. *(Reaching out quickly, playfully, and patting Ruth's stomach.)* Ain't you starting to poke out none yet! *(She mugs with delight at the over familiar remark and her eyes dart around looking at the crates and packing preparation; Mama's face is a cold sheet of endurance.)* Oh, ain't we getting ready round here, though! Yessir! Lookathere! I'm telling you the Youngers is really getting ready to "move on up a little higher!" — Bless God!

MAMA *(a little drily, doubting the total sincerity of the Blesser)*:   Bless God.

JOHNSON: He's good, ain't He?

MAMA: Oh yes, He's good.

JOHNSON: I mean sometimes He works in mysterious ways . . . but He works, don't He!

MAMA *(the same)*:   Yes, He does.

JOHNSON: I'm just soooooo happy for y'all. And this here child — *(About Ruth.)* looks like she could just pop open with happiness, don't she. Where's all the rest of the family?

MAMA: Bennie's gone to bed —

JOHNSON: Ain't no . . . *(The implication is pregnancy.)* sickness done hit you — I hope . . . ?

MAMA: No — she just tired. She was out this evening.

JOHNSON *(all is a coo, an emphatic coo)*:   Aw — ain't that lovely. She still going out with the little Murchison boy?

MAMA *(drily)*:   Ummmm huh.

JOHNSON: That's lovely. You sure got lovely children, Younger. Me and Isaiah talks all the time 'bout what fine children you was blessed with. We sure do.

MAMA: Ruth, give Mis' Johnson a piece of sweet potato pie and some milk.

JOHNSON: Oh honey, I can't stay hardly a minute — I just dropped in to see if there was anything I could do. *(Accepting the food easily.)* I guess y'all seen the news what's all over the colored paper this week . . .

MAMA: No — didn't get mine yet this week.

JOHNSON *(lifting her head and blinking with the spirit of catastrophe)*:   You mean you ain't read 'bout them colored people that was bombed out their place out there?

Mrs. Johnson: This character and the scene of her visit were cut from the original production and early editions of the play.

Ruth straightens with concern and takes the paper and reads it. Johnson notices her and feeds commentary.

JOHNSON: Ain't it something how bad these here white folks is getting here in Chicago! Lord, getting so you think you right down in Mississippi! *(With a tremendous and rather insincere sense of melodrama.)* 'Course I thinks it's wonderful how our folk keeps on pushing out. You hear some of these Negroes round here talking 'bout how they don't go where they ain't wanted and all that — but not me, honey! *(This is a lie.)* Wilhemenia Othella Johnson goes anywhere, any time she feels like it! *(With head movement for emphasis.)* Yes I do! Why if we left it up to these here crackers, the poor niggers wouldn't have nothing — *(She clasps her hand over her mouth.)* Oh, I always forgets you don't 'low that word in your house.

MAMA *(quietly, looking at her)*:   No — I don't 'low it.

JOHNSON *(vigorously again)*:   Me neither! I was just telling Isaiah yesterday when he come using it in front of me — I said, "Isaiah, it's just like Mis' Younger says all the time —"

MAMA: Don't you want some more pie?

JOHNSON: No — no thank you; this was lovely. I got to get on over home and have my midnight coffee. I hear some people say it don't let them sleep but I finds I can't close my eyes right lessen I done had that laaaast cup of coffee . . . *(She waits. A beat. Undaunted.)* My Goodnight coffee, I calls it!

MAMA *(with much eye-rolling and communication between herself and Ruth)*:   Ruth, why don't you give Mis' Johnson some coffee.

Ruth gives Mama an unpleasant look for her kindness.

JOHNSON *(accepting the coffee)*:   Where's Brother tonight?

MAMA: He's lying down.

JOHNSON: Mmmmmmm, he sure gets his beauty rest, don't he? Good-looking man. Sure is a good-looking man! *(Reaching out to pat Ruth's stomach again.)* I guess that's how come we keep on having babies around here. *(She winks at Mama.)* One thing 'bout Brother, he always know how to have a *good* time. And sooooo ambitious! I bet it was his idea y'all moving out to Clybourne Park. Lord — I bet this time next month y'all's names will have been in the papers plenty — *(Holding up her hands to mark off each word of the headline she can see in front of her.)* "NEGROES INVADE CLYBOURNE PARK — BOMBED!"

MAMA *(she and Ruth look at the woman in amazement)*:   We ain't exactly moving out there to get bombed.

JOHNSON: Oh honey — you know I'm praying to God every day that don't nothing like that happen! But you have to think of life like it is — and these here Chicago peckerwoods is some baaaad peckerwoods.

MAMA *(wearily)*:   We done thought about all that Mis' Johnson.

Beneatha comes out of the bedroom in her robe and passes through to the bathroom. Mrs. Johnson turns.

JOHNSON: Hello there, Bennie!

BENEATHA *(crisply)*:   Hello, Mrs. Johnson.

JOHNSON: How is school?

BENEATHA *(crisply)*:   Fine, thank you. *(She goes out.)*

JOHNSON *(insulted)*:   Getting so she don't have much to say to nobody.

MAMA: The child was on her way to the bathroom.

JOHNSON: I know — but sometimes she act like ain't got time to pass the time of day with nobody ain't been to college. Oh — I ain't criticizing her none. It's just — you know how some of our young people gets when they get a little education. *(Mama and Ruth say nothing, just look at her.)* Yes — well. Well, I guess I better get on home. *(Unmoving.)* 'Course I can understand how she must be proud and everything — being the only one in the family to make something of herself. I know just being a chauffeur ain't never satisfied Brother none. He shouldn't feel like that, though. Ain't nothing wrong with being a chauffeur.

MAMA: There's plenty wrong with it.

JOHNSON: What?

MAMA: Plenty. My husband always said being any kind of a servant wasn't a fit thing for a man to have to be. He always said a man's hands was made to make things, or to turn the earth with — not to drive nobody's car for 'em — or — *(She looks at her own hands.)* carry they slop jars. And my boy is just like him — he wasn't meant to wait on nobody.

JOHNSON *(rising, somewhat offended)*:   Mmmmmmmmm. The Youngers is too much for me! *(She looks around.)* You sure one proud-acting bunch of colored folks. Well — I always thinks like Booker T. Washington° said that time — "Education has spoiled many a good plow hand" —

MAMA: Is that what old Booker T. said?

JOHNSON: He sure did.

MAMA: Well, it sounds just like him. The fool.

JOHNSON *(indignantly)*:   Well — he was one of our great men.

MAMA: Who said so?

JOHNSON *(nonplussed)*:   You know, me and you ain't never agreed about some things, Lena Younger. I guess I better be going —

RUTH *(quickly)*:   Good night.

JOHNSON: Good night. Oh — *(Thrusting it at her.)* You can keep the paper! *(With a trill.)* 'Night.

MAMA: Good night, Mis' Johnson.

Mrs. Johnson exits.

RUTH: If ignorance was gold . . .

MAMA: Shush. Don't talk about folks behind their backs.

RUTH: You do.

MAMA: I'm old and corrupted. *(Beneatha enters.)* You was rude to Mis' Johnson, Beneatha, and I don't like it at all.

Booker T. Washington: Dominant leader in the African-American community (1890–1915). Emphasized self-help over agitation for civil rights in a segregated America.

BENEATHA *(at her door)*:   Mama, if there are two things we, as a people, have got to overcome, one is the Klu Klux Klan — and the other is Mrs. Johnson. *(She exits.)*

MAMA: Smart aleck.

The phone rings.

RUTH: I'll get it.

MAMA: Lord, ain't this a popular place tonight.

RUTH *(at the phone)*:   Hello — Just a minute. *(Goes to door.)* Walter, it's Mrs. Arnold. *(Waits. Goes back to the phone. Tense.)* Hello. Yes, this is his wife speaking . . . He's lying down now. Yes . . . well, he'll be in tomorrow. He's been very sick. Yes — I know we should have called, but we were so sure he'd be able to come in today. Yes — yes, I'm very sorry. Yes . . . Thank you very much. *(She hangs up. Walter is standing in the doorway of the bedroom behind her.)* That was Mrs. Arnold.

WALTER *(indifferently)*:   Was it?

RUTH: She said if you don't come in tomorrow that they are getting a new man . . .

WALTER: Ain't that sad — ain't that crying sad.

RUTH: She said Mr. Arnold has had to take a cab for three days . . . Walter, you ain't been to work for three days! *(This is a revelation to her.)* Where you been, Walter Lee Younger? *(Walter looks at her and starts to laugh.)* You're going to lose your job.

WALTER: That's right . . . *(He turns on the radio.)*

RUTH: Oh, Walter, and with your mother working like a dog every day —

A steamy, deep blues pours into the room.

WALTER: That's sad too — Everything is sad.

MAMA: What you been doing for these three days, son?

WALTER: Mama — you don't know all the things a man what got leisure can find to do in this city . . . What's this — Friday night? Well — Wednesday I borrowed Willy Harris's car and I went for a drive . . . just me and myself and I drove and drove . . . Way out . . . way past South Chicago, and I parked the car and I sat and looked at the steel mills all day long. I just sat in the car and looked at them big black chimneys for hours. Then I drove back and I went to the Green Hat. *(Pause.)* And Thursday — Thursday I borrowed the car again and I got in it and I pointed it the other way and I drove the other way — for hours — way, way up to Wisconsin, and I looked at the farms. I just drove and looked at the farms. Then I drove back and I went to the Green Hat. *(Pause.)* And today — today I didn't get the car. Today I just walked. All over the Southside. And I looked at the Negroes and they looked at me and finally I just sat down on the curb at Thirty-ninth and South Parkway and I just sat there and watched the Negroes go by. And then I went to the Green Hat. You all sad? You all depressed? And you know where I am going right now —

Ruth goes out quietly.

MAMA: Oh, Big Walter, is this the harvest of our days?

WALTER: You know what I like about the Green Hat? I like this little cat they got there who blows a sax . . . He blows. He talks to me. He ain't but 'bout five feet tall and he's got a conked head° and his eyes is always closed and he's all music —

MAMA *(rising and getting some papers out of her handbag)*: Walter —

WALTER: And there's this other guy who plays the piano . . . and they got a sound. I mean they can work on some music . . . They got the best little combo in the world in the Green Hat . . . You can just sit there and drink and listen to them three men play and you realize that don't nothing matter worth a damn, but just being there —

MAMA: I've helped do it to you, haven't I, son? Walter, I been wrong.

WALTER: Naw — you ain't never been wrong about nothing, Mama.

MAMA: Listen to me, now. I say I been wrong, son. That I been doing to you what the rest of the world been doing to you. *(She turns off the radio.)* Walter — *(She stops and he looks up slowly at her and she meets his eyes pleadingly.)* What you ain't never understood is that I ain't got nothing, don't own nothing, ain't never really wanted nothing that wasn't for you. There ain't nothing as precious to me . . . There ain't nothing worth holding on to, money, dreams, nothing else — if it means — if it means it's going to destroy my boy. *(She takes an envelope out of her handbag and puts it in front of him and he watches her without speaking or moving.)* I paid the man thirty-five hundred dollars down on the house. That leaves sixty-five hundred dollars. Monday morning I want you to take this money and take three thousand dollars and put it in a savings account for Beneatha's medical schooling. The rest you put in a checking account — with your name on it. And from now on any penny that come out of it or that go in it is for you to look after. For you to decide. *(She drops her hands a little helplessly.)* It ain't much, but it's all I got in the world and I'm putting it in your hands. I'm telling you to be the head of this family from now on like you supposed to be.

WALTER *(stares at the money)*: You trust me like that, Mama?

MAMA: I ain't never stop trusting you. Like I ain't never stop loving you.

She goes out, and Walter sits looking at the money on the table. Finally, in a decisive gesture, he gets up, and, in mingled joy and desperation, picks up the money. At the same moment, Travis enters for bed.

TRAVIS: What's the matter, Daddy? You drunk?

WALTER *(sweetly, more sweetly than we have ever known him)*: No, Daddy ain't drunk. Daddy ain't going to never be drunk again . . .

TRAVIS: Well, good night, Daddy.

The father has come from behind the couch and leans over, embracing his son.

WALTER: Son, I feel like talking to you tonight.

TRAVIS: About what?

WALTER: Oh, about a lot of things. About you and what kind of man you going to be when you grow up . . . Son — son, what do you want to be when you grow up?

conked head: A straightened hair style for men.

TRAVIS: A bus driver.

WALTER *(laughing a little)*:   A what? Man, that ain't nothing to want to be!

TRAVIS: Why not?

WALTER: 'Cause, man — it ain't big enough — you know what I mean.

TRAVIS: I don't know then. I can't make up my mind. Sometimes Mama asks me that too. And sometimes when I tell her I just want to be like you — she says she don't want me to be like that and sometimes she says she does. . . .

WALTER *(gathering him up in his arms)*:   You know what, Travis? In seven years you going to be seventeen years old. And things is going to be very different with us in seven years, Travis. . . . One day when you are seventeen I'll come home — home from my office downtown somewhere —

TRAVIS: You don't work in no office, Daddy.

WALTER: No — but after tonight. After what your daddy gonna do tonight, there's going to be offices — a whole lot of offices. . . .

TRAVIS: What you gonna do tonight, Daddy?

WALTER: You wouldn't understand yet, son, but your daddy's gonna make a transaction . . . a business transaction that's going to change our lives. . . . That's how come one day when you 'bout seventeen years old I'll come home and I'll be pretty tired, you know what I mean, after a day of conferences and secretaries getting things wrong the way they do . . . 'cause an executive's life is hell, man — *(The more he talks the farther away he gets.)* And I'll pull the car up on the driveway . . . just a plain black Chrysler, I think, with white walls — no — black tires. More elegant. Rich people don't have to be flashy . . . though I'll have to get something a little sportier for Ruth — maybe a Cadillac convertible to do her shopping in. . . . And I'll come up the steps to the house and the gardener will be clipping away at the hedges and he'll say, "Good evening, Mr. Younger." And I'll say, "Hello, Jefferson, how are you this evening?" And I'll go inside and Ruth will come downstairs and meet me at the door and we'll kiss each other and she'll take my arm and we'll go up to your room to see you sitting on the floor with the catalogues of all the great schools in America around you. . . . All the great schools in the world! And — and I'll say, all right son — it's your seventeenth birthday, what is it you've decided? . . . Just tell me where you want to go to school and you'll *go.* Just tell me, what it is you want to be — and you'll *be* it. . . . Whatever you want to be — Yessir! *(He holds his arms open for Travis.)* You just name it, son . . . *(Travis leaps into them.)* and I hand you the world!

Walter's voice has risen in pitch and hysterical promise and on the last line he lifts Travis high.

   Blackout.

Scene 3

Time: Saturday, moving day, one week later.

   Before the curtain rises, Ruth's voice, a strident, dramatic church alto, cuts through the silence.

It is, in the darkness, a triumphant surge, a penetrating statement of expectation: "Oh, Lord, I don't feel no ways tired! Children, oh, glory hallelujah!"

As the curtain rises we see that Ruth is alone in the living room, finishing up the family's packing. It is moving day. She is nailing crates and tying cartons. Beneatha enters, carrying a guitar case, and watches her exuberant sister-in-law.

RUTH: Hey!

BENEATHA *(putting away the case)*:   Hi.

RUTH *(pointing at a package)*:   Honey — look in that package there and see what I found on sale this morning at the South Center. *(Ruth gets up and moves to the package and draws out some curtains.)* Lookahere — hand-turned hems!

BENEATHA: How do you know the window size out there?

RUTH *(who hadn't thought of that)*:   Oh — Well, they bound to fit something in the whole house. Anyhow, they was too good a bargain to pass up. *(Ruth slaps her head, suddenly remembering something.)* Oh, Bennie — I meant to put a special note on that carton over there. That's your mama's good china and she wants 'em to be very careful with it.

BENEATHA: I'll do it.

Beneatha finds a piece of paper and starts to draw large letters on it.

RUTH: You know what I'm going to do soon as I get in that new house?

BENEATHA: What?

RUTH: Honey — I'm going to run me a tub of water up to here . . . *(With her fingers practically up to her nostrils.)* And I'm going to get in it — and I am going to sit . . . and sit . . . and sit in that hot water and the first person who knocks to tell *me* to hurry up and come out —

BENEATHA: Gets shot at sunrise.

RUTH *(laughing happily)*:   You said it, sister! *(Noticing how large Beneatha is absent-mindedly making the note)*:   Honey, they ain't going to read that from no airplane.

BENEATHA *(laughing herself)*:   I guess I always think things have more emphasis if they are big, somehow.

RUTH *(looking up at her and smiling)*:   You and your brother seem to have that as a philosophy of life. Lord, that man — done changed so 'round here. You know — you know what we did last night? Me and Walter Lee?

BENEATHA: What?

RUTH *(smiling to herself)*:   We went to the movies. *(Looking at Beneatha to see if she understands.)* We went to the movies. You know the last time me and Walter went to the movies together?

BENEATHA: No.

RUTH: Me neither. That's how long it been. *(Smiling again.)* But we went last night. The picture wasn't much good, but that didn't seem to matter. We went — and we held hands.

BENEATHA: Oh, Lord!

RUTH: We held hands — and you know what?

BENEATHA: What?

RUTH: When we come out of the show it was late and dark and all the stores and things was closed up . . . and it was kind of chilly and there wasn't

many people on the streets . . . and we was still holding hands, me and
Walter.

BENEATHA: You're killing me.

*Walter enters with a large package. His happiness is deep in him; he cannot keep still
with his newfound exuberance. He is singing and wiggling and snapping his fingers.
He puts his package in a corner and puts a phonograph record, which he has brought
in with him, on the record player. As the music, soulful and sensuous, comes up he
dances over to Ruth and tries to get her to dance with him. She gives in at last to his
raunchiness and in a fit of giggling allows herself to be drawn into his mood. They dip
and she melts into his arms in a classic, body-melting "slow drag."*

BENEATHA *(regarding them a long time as they dance, then drawing in her breath for a
deeply exaggerated comment which she does not particularly mean):*   Talk
about — olddddddddddd-fashioneddddddd — Negroes!

WALTER *(stopping momentarily)*:   What kind of Negroes?

*He says this in fun. He is not angry with her today, nor with anyone. He starts to
dance with his wife again.*

BENEATHA: Old-fashioned.

WALTER *(as he dances with Ruth)*:   You know, when these *New Negroes* have their
convention — *(Pointing at his sister.)* — that is going to be the chairman of
the Committee on Unending Agitation. *(He goes on dancing, then stops.)*
Race, race, race! . . . Girl, I do believe you are the first person in the history
of the entire human race to successfully brainwash yourself. *(Beneatha
breaks up and he goes on dancing. He stops again, enjoying his tease.)* Damn,
even the N double A C P takes a holiday sometimes! *(Beneatha and Ruth
laugh. He dances with Ruth some more and starts to laugh and stops and pantomimes someone over an operating table.)* I can just see that chick someday
looking down at some poor cat on an operating table and before she starts
to slice him, she says . . . *(Pulling his sleeves back maliciously.)* "By the way,
what are your views on civil rights down there? . . ."

He laughs at her again and starts to dance happily. The bell sounds.

BENEATHA: Sticks and stones may break my bones but . . . words will never
hurt me!

*Beneatha goes to the door and opens it as Walter and Ruth go on with the clowning.
Beneatha is somewhat surprised to see a quiet-looking middle-aged white man in a
business suit holding his hat and a briefcase in his hand and consulting a small piece
of paper.*

MAN: Uh — how do you do, miss. I am looking for a Mrs. — *(He looks at the slip
of paper.)* Mrs. Lena Younger? *(He stops short, struck dumb at the sight of the
oblivious Walter and Ruth.)*

BENEATHA *(smoothing her hair with slight embarrassment)*:   Oh — yes, that's my
mother. Excuse me. *(She closes the door and turns to quiet the other two.)*
Ruth! Brother! *(Enunciating precisely but soundlessly: "There's a white man at
the door!" They stop dancing, Ruth cuts off the phonograph, Beneatha opens the
door. The man casts a curious quick glance at all of them.)* Uh — come in please.

MAN *(coming in)*:   Thank you.

BENEATHA: My mother isn't here just now. Is it business?

MAN: Yes . . . well, of a sort.

WALTER *(freely, the Man of the House)*:   Have a seat. I'm Mrs. Younger's son. I look after most of her business matters.

Ruth and Beneatha exchange amused glances.

MAN *(regarding Walter, and sitting)*:   Well — My name is Karl Lindner . . .

WALTER *(stretching out his hand)*:   Walter Younger. This is my wife — *(Ruth nods politely.)* — and my sister.

LINDNER: How do you do.

WALTER *(amiably, as he sits himself easily on a chair, leaning forward on his knees with interest and looking expectantly into the newcomer's face)*:   What can we do for you, Mr. Lindner!

LINDNER *(some minor shuffling of the hat and briefcase on his knees)*:   Well — I am a representative of the Clybourne Park Improvement Association —

WALTER *(pointing)*:   Why don't you sit your things on the floor?

LINDNER: Oh — yes. Thank you. *(He slides the briefcase and hat under the chair.)* And as I was saying — I am from the Clybourne Park Improvement Association and we have had it brought to our attention at the last meeting that you people — or at least your mother — has bought a piece of residential property at — *(He digs for the slip of paper again.)* — four o six Clybourne Street . . .

WALTER: That's right. Care for something to drink? Ruth, get Mr. Lindner a beer.

LINDNER *(upset for some reason)*:   Oh — no, really. I mean thank you very much, but no thank you.

RUTH *(innocently)*:   Some coffee?

LINDNER: Thank you, nothing at all.

Beneatha is watching the man carefully.

LINDNER: Well, I don't know how much you folks know about our organization. *(He is a gentle man; thoughtful and somewhat labored in his manner.)* It is one of these community organizations set up to look after — oh, you know, things like block upkeep and special projects and we also have what we call our New Neighbors Orientation Committee . . .

BENEATHA *(drily)*:   Yes — and what do they do?

LINDNER *(turning a little to her and then returning the main force to Walter)*:   Well — it's what you might call a sort of welcoming committee, I guess. I mean they, we — I'm the chairman of the committee — go around and see the new people who move into the neighborhood and sort of give them the low-down on the way we do things out in Clybourne Park.

BENEATHA *(with appreciation of the two meanings, which escape Ruth and Walter)*:   Un-huh.

LINDNER: And we also have the category of what the association calls — *(He looks elsewhere.)* — uh — special community problems . . .

BENEATHA: Yes — and what are some of those?

WALTER: Girl, let the man talk.

LINDNER *(with understated relief)*:   Thank you. I would sort of like to explain this thing in my own way. I mean I want to explain to you in a certain way.

WALTER: Go ahead.

LINDNER: Yes. Well. I'm going to try to get right to the point. I'm sure we'll all appreciate that in the long run.

BENEATHA: Yes.

WALTER: Be still now!

LINDNER: Well —

RUTH *(still innocently)*:   Would you like another chair — you don't look comfortable.

LINDNER *(more frustrated than annoyed)*:   No, thank you very much. Please. Well — to get right to the point, I — *(A great breath, and he is off at last.)* I am sure you people must be aware of some of the incidents which have happened in various parts of the city when colored people have moved into certain areas — *(Beneatha exhales heavily and starts tossing a piece of fruit up and down in the air.)* Well — because we have what I think is going to be a unique type of organization in American community life — not only do we deplore that kind of thing — but we are trying to do something about it. *(Beneatha stops tossing and turns with a new and quizzical interest to the man.)* We feel — *(gaining confidence in his mission because of the interest in the faces of the people he is talking to.)* — we feel that most of the trouble in this world, when you come right down to it — *(He hits his knee for emphasis.)* — most of the trouble exists because people just don't sit down and talk to each other.

RUTH *(nodding as she might in church, pleased with the remark)*:   You can say that again, mister.

LINDNER *(more encouraged by such affirmation)*:   That we don't try hard enough in this world to understand the other fellow's problem. The other guy's point of view.

RUTH: Now that's right.

Beneatha and Walter merely watch and listen with genuine interest.

LINDNER: Yes — that's the way we feel out in Clybourne Park. And that's why I was elected to come here this afternoon and talk to you people. Friendly like, you know, the way people should talk to each other and see if we couldn't find some way to work this thing out. As I say, the whole business is a matter of *caring* about the other fellow. Anybody can see that you are a nice family of folks, hard working and honest I'm sure. *(Beneatha frowns slightly, quizzically, her head tilted regarding him.)* Today everybody knows what it means to be on the outside of *something.* And of course, there is always somebody who is out to take advantage of people who don't always understand.

WALTER: What do you mean?

LINDNER: Well — you see our community is made up of people who've worked hard as the dickens for years to build up that little community. They're not rich and fancy people; just hard-working, honest people who don't really have much but those little homes and a dream of the kind of community they want to raise their children in. Now, I don't say we are perfect and there is a lot wrong in some of the things they want. But you've got to admit that a man, right or wrong, has the right to want to have the neighborhood he lives in a certain kind of way. And at the moment the overwhelming majority of our people out there feel that people get along better, take more of a common interest in the life of the community, when they share a common background. I want you to believe me when I tell you that race prejudice simply doesn't enter into it. It is a matter of the people of Clybourne Park believing, rightly or wrongly, as I say, that for the happiness of all concerned that our Negro families are happier when they live in their *own* communities.

BENEATHA *(with a grand and bitter gesture)*: This, friends, is the Welcoming Committee!

WALTER *(dumfounded, looking at Lindner)*: Is this what you came marching all the way over here to tell us?

LINDNER: Well, now we've been having a fine conversation. I hope you'll hear me all the way through.

WALTER *(tightly)*: Go ahead, man.

LINDNER: You see — in the face of all the things I have said, we are prepared to make your family a very generous offer . . .

BENEATHA: Thirty pieces and not a coin less!

WALTER: Yeah?

LINDNER *(putting on his glasses drawing a form out of the briefcase)*: Our association is prepared, through the collective effort of our people, to buy the house from you at a financial gain to your family.

RUTH: Lord have mercy, ain't this the living gall!

WALTER: All right, you through?

LINDNER: Well, I want to give you the exact terms of the financial arrangement —

WALTER: We don't want to hear no exact terms of no arrangements. I want to know if you got any more to tell us 'bout getting together?

LINDNER *(taking off his glasses)*: Well — I don't suppose that you feel . . .

WALTER: Never mind how I feel — you got any more to say 'bout how people ought to sit down and talk to each other? . . . Get out of my house, man.

He turns his back and walks to the door.

LINDNER *(looking around at the hostile faces and reaching and assembling his hat and briefcase)*: Well — I don't understand why you people are reacting this way. What do you think you are going to gain by moving into a neighborhood where you just aren't wanted and where some elements — well — people can get awful worked up when they feel that their whole way of life and everything they've ever worked for is threatened.

WALTER: Get out.

LINDNER *(at the door, holding a small card)*: Well — I'm sorry it went like this.

WALTER: Get out.

LINDNER *(almost sadly regarding Walter)*:   You just can't force people to change their hearts, son.

He turns and puts his card on a table and exits. Walter pushes the door to with stinging hatred, and stands looking at it. Ruth just sits and Beneatha just stands. They say nothing. Mama and Travis enter.

MAMA: Well — this all the packing got done since I left out of here this morning. I testify before God that my children got all the energy of the *dead!* What time the moving men due?

BENEATHA: Four o'clock. You had a caller, Mama.

She is smiling, teasingly.

MAMA: Sure enough — who?

BENEATHA *(her arms folded saucily)*:   The Welcoming Committee.

Walter and Ruth giggle.

MAMA *(innocently)*:   Who?

BENEATHA: The Welcoming Committee. They said they're sure going to be glad to see you when you get there.

WALTER *(devilishly)*:   Yeah, they said they can't hardly wait to see your face.

Laughter.

MAMA *(sensing their facetiousness)*:   What's the matter with you all?

WALTER: Ain't nothing the matter with us. We just telling you 'bout the gentleman who came to see you this afternoon. From the Clybourne Park Improvement Association.

MAMA: What he want?

RUTH *(in the same mood as Beneatha and Walter)*:   To welcome you, honey.

WALTER: He said they can't hardly wait. He said the one thing they don't have, that they just *dying* to have out there is a fine family of fine colored people! *(To Ruth and Beneatha.)* Ain't that right!

RUTH *(mockingly)*:   Yeah! He left his card —

BENEATHA *(handing card to Mama)*:   In case.

Mama reads and throws it on the floor — understanding and looking off as she draws her chair up to the table on which she has put her plant and some sticks and some cord.

MAMA: Father, give us strength. *(Knowingly — and without fun.)* Did he threaten us?

BENEATHA: Oh — Mama — they don't do it like that any more. He talked Brotherhood. He said everybody ought to learn how to sit down and hate each other with good Christian fellowship.

She and Walter shake hands to ridicule the remark.

MAMA *(sadly)*:   Lord, protect us . . .

RUTH: You should hear the money those folks raised to buy the house from us. All we paid and then some.

BENEATHA: What they think we going to do — eat 'em?

RUTH: No, honey, marry 'em.

MAMA (*shaking her head*):   Lord, Lord, Lord . . .

RUTH: Well — that's the way the crackers crumble. (*A beat.*) Joke.

BENEATHA (*laughingly noticing what her mother is doing*):   Mama, what are you doing?

MAMA: Fixing my plant so it won't get hurt none on the way . . .

BENEATHA: Mama, you going to take *that* to the new house?

MAMA: Un-huh —

BENEATHA: That raggedy-looking old thing?

MAMA (*stopping and looking at her*):   It expresses ME!

RUTH (*with delight, to Beneatha*):   So there, Miss Thing!

Walter comes to Mama suddenly and bends down behind her and squeezes her in his arms with all his strength. She is overwhelmed by the suddenness of it and, though delighted, her manner is like that of Ruth and Travis.

MAMA: Look out now, boy! You make me mess up my thing here!

WALTER (*his face lit, he slips down on his knees beside her, his arms still about her*):   Mama . . . you know what it means to climb up in the chariot?

MAMA (*gruffly, very happy*):   Get on away from me now . . .

RUTH (*near the gift-wrapped package, trying to catch Walter's eye*):   Psst —

WALTER: What the old song say, Mama . . .

RUTH: Walter — Now?

She is pointing at the package.

WALTER (*speaking the lines, sweetly, playfully, in his mother's face*):

> I got wings . . . you got wings . . .
> All God's children got wings . . .

MAMA: Boy — get out of my face and do some work . . .

WALTER:

> When I get to heaven gonna put on my wings,
> Gonna fly all over God's heaven . . .

BENEATHA (*teasingly, from across the room*):   Everybody talking 'bout heaven ain't going there!

WALTER (*to Ruth, who is carrying the box across to them*):   I don't know, you think we ought to give her that . . . Seems to me she ain't been very appreciative around here.

MAMA (*eyeing the box, which is obviously a gift*):   What is that?

WALTER (*taking it from Ruth and putting it on the table in front of Mama*):   Well — what you all think? Should we give it to her?

RUTH: Oh — she was pretty good today.

MAMA: I'll good you —

She turns her eyes to the box again.

BENEATHA: Open it, Mama.

She stands up, looks at it, turns and looks at all of them, and then presses her hands together and does not open the package.

WALTER (*sweetly*):   Open it, Mama. It's for you. (*Mama looks in his eyes. It is the first present in her life without its being Christmas. Slowly she opens her package and lifts out, one by one, a brand-new sparkling set of gardening tools. Walter continues, prodding.)* Ruth made up the note — read it . . .

MAMA *(picking up the card and adjusting her glasses)*:   "To our own Mrs. Miniver° — Love from Brother, Ruth, and Beneatha." Ain't that lovely . . .

TRAVIS *(tugging at his father's sleeve)*:   Daddy, can I give her mine now?

WALTER: All right, son. *(Travis flies to get his gift.)*

MAMA: Now I don't have to use my knives and forks no more . . .

WALTER: Travis didn't want to go in with the rest of us, Mama. He got his own. *(Somewhat amused.)* We don't know what it is . . .

TRAVIS *(racing back in the room with a large hatbox and putting it in front of his grandmother)*:   Here!

MAMA: Lord have mercy, baby. You done gone and bought your grandmother a hat?

TRAVIS *(very proud)*:   Open it!

She does and lifts out an elaborate, but very elaborate, wide gardening hat, and all the adults break up at the sight of it.

RUTH: Travis, honey, what is that?

TRAVIS *(who thinks it is beautiful and appropriate)*:   It's a gardening hat! Like the ladies always have on in the magazines when they work in their gardens.

BENEATHA *(giggling fiercely)*:   Travis — we were trying to make Mama Mrs. Miniver — not Scarlett O'Hara!

MAMA *(indignantly)*:   What's the matter with you all! This here is a beautiful hat! *(Absurdly.)* I always wanted me one just like it!

She pops it on her head to prove it to her grandson, and the hat is ludicrous and considerably oversized.

RUTH: Hot dog! Go, Mama!

WALTER *(doubled over with laughter)*:   I'm sorry, Mama — but you look like you ready to go out and chop you some cotton sure enough!

They all laugh except Mama, out of deference to Travis's feelings.

MAMA *(gathering the boy up to her)*:   Bless your heart — this is the prettiest hat I ever owned — *(Walter, Ruth, and Beneatha chime in — noisily, festively, and insincerely congratulating Travis on his gift.)* What are we all standing around here for? We ain't finished packin' yet. Bennie, you ain't packed one book.

The bell rings.

BENEATHA: That couldn't be the movers . . . it's not hardly two good yet —

Beneatha goes into her room. Mama starts for door.

WALTER *(turning, stiffening)*:   Wait — wait — I'll get it.

He stands and looks at the door.

MAMA: You expecting company, son?

Mrs. Miniver: A much-admired fictional character who appeared in newspaper columns and then in a popular World War II movie (1942).

WALTER *(just looking at the door)*:   Yeah — yeah . . .

Mama looks at Ruth, and they exchange innocent and unfrightened glances.

MAMA *(not understanding)*:   Well, let them in, son.

BENEATHA *(from her room)*:   We need some more string.

MAMA: Travis — you run to the hardware and get me some string cord.

Mama goes out and Walter turns and looks at Ruth. Travis goes to a dish for money.

RUTH: Why don't you answer the door, man?

WALTER *(suddenly bounding across the floor to embrace her)*:   'Cause sometimes it hard to let the future begin! *(Stooping down in her face.)*

> I got wings! You got wings!
> All God's children got wings!

He crosses to the door and throws it open. Standing there is a very slight little man in a not-too-prosperous business suit and with haunted frightened eyes and a hat pulled down tightly, brim up, around his forehead. Travis passes between the men and exits. Walter leans deep in the man's face, still in his jubilance.

> When I get to heaven gonna put on my wings,
> Gonna fly all over God's heaven . . .

The little man just stares at him.

> Heaven —

Suddenly he stops and looks past the little man into the empty hallway.

Where's Willy, man?

BOBO: He ain't with me.

WALTER *(not disturbed)*:   Oh — come on in. You know my wife.

BOBO *(dumbly, taking off his hat)*:   Yes — h'you, Miss Ruth.

RUTH *(quietly, a mood apart from her husband already, seeing Bobo)*:   Hello, Bobo.

WALTER: You right on time today . . . Right on time. That's the way! *(He slaps Bobo on his back.)* Sit down . . . lemme hear.

Ruth stands stiffly and quietly in back of them, as though somehow she senses death, her eyes fixed on her husband.

BOBO *(his frightened eyes on the floor, his hat in his hands)*:   Could I please get a drink of water, before I tell you about it, Walter Lee?

Walter does not take his eyes off the man. Ruth goes blindly to the tap and gets a glass of water and brings it to Bobo.

WALTER: There ain't nothing wrong, is there?

BOBO: Lemme tell you —

WALTER: Man — didn't nothing go wrong?

BOBO: Lemme tell you — Walter Lee. *(Looking at Ruth and talking to her more than to Walter.)* You know how it was. I got to tell you how it was. I mean first I got to tell you how it was all the way . . . I mean about the money I put in, Walter Lee . . .

WALTER *(with taut agitation now)*:   What about the money you put in?

BOBO: Well — it wasn't much as we told you — me and Willy — *(He stops.)* I'm sorry, Walter. I got a bad feeling about it. I got a real bad feeling about it . . .

WALTER: Man, what you telling me about all this for? . . . Tell me what happened in Springfield . . .

BOBO: Springfield.

RUTH *(like a dead woman)*:   What was supposed to happen in Springfield?

BOBO *(to her)*:   This deal that me and Walter went into with Willy — Me and Willy was going to go down to Springfield and spread some money 'round so's we wouldn't have to wait so long for the liquor license . . . That's what we were going to do. Everybody said that was the way you had to do, you understand, Miss Ruth?

WALTER: Man — what happened down there?

BOBO *(a pitiful man, near tears)*:   I'm trying to tell you, Walter.

WALTER *(screaming at him suddenly)*:   THEN TELL ME, GODDAMMIT . . . WHAT'S THE MATTER WITH YOU?

BOBO: Man . . . I didn't go to no Springfield, yesterday.

WALTER *(halted, life hanging in the moment)*:   Why not?

BOBO *(the long way, the hard way to tell)*:   'Cause I didn't have no reasons to . . .

WALTER: Man, what are you talking about!

BOBO: I'm talking about the fact that when I got to the train station yesterday morning — eight o'clock like we planned . . . Man — *Willy didn't never show up.*

WALTER: Why . . . where was he . . . where is he?

BOBO: That's what I'm trying to tell you . . . I don't know . . . I waited six hours . . . I called his house . . . and I waited . . . six hours . . . I waited in that train station six hours . . . *(Breaking into tears.)* That was all the extra money I had in the world . . . *(Looking up at Walter with the tears running down his face.)* Man, *Willy is gone.*

WALTER: Gone, what you mean Willy is gone? Gone where? You mean he went by himself. You mean he went off to Springfield by himself — to take care of getting the license — *(Turns and looks anxiously at Ruth.)* You mean maybe he didn't want too many people in on the business down there? *(Looks to Ruth again, as before.)* You know Willy got his own ways. *(Looks back to Bobo.)* Maybe you was late yesterday and he just went on down there without you. Maybe — maybe — he's been callin' you at home tryin' to tell you what happened or something. Maybe — maybe — he just got sick. He's somewhere — he's got to be somewhere. We just got to find him — me and you got to find him. *(Grabs Bobo senselessly by the collar and starts to shake him.)* We got to!

BOBO *(in sudden angry, frightened agony)*:   What's the matter with you, Walter! *When a cat take off with your money he don't leave you no road maps!*

WALTER *(turning madly, as though he is looking for Willy in the very room)*:   Willy! . . . Willy . . . don't do it . . . Please don't do it . . . Man, not with that money . . . Man, please, not with that money . . . Oh, God . . . Don't let it be true . . . *(He is wandering around, crying out for Willy and looking for him or perhaps for help from God.)* Man . . . I trusted you . . . Man, I put my life in your hands . . . *(He starts to crumple down on the floor as Ruth just covers her face in horror. Mama opens the door and comes into the room, with Beneatha behind her.)* Man . . . *(He starts to pound the floor with his fists, sobbing wildly.)* THAT MONEY IS MADE OUT OF MY FATHER'S FLESH —

BOBO *(standing over him helplessly)*: I'm sorry, Walter . . . *(only Walter's sobs reply. Bobo puts on his hat.)* I had my life staked on this deal, too . . .

He exits.

MAMA *(to Walter)*: Son — *(She goes to him, bends down to him, talks to his bent head.)* Son . . . Is it gone? Son, I gave you sixty-five hundred dollars. Is it gone? All of it? Beneatha's money too?

WALTER *(lifting his head slowly)*: Mama . . . I never . . . went to the bank at all . . .

MAMA *(not wanting to believe him)*: You mean . . . your sister's school money . . . you used that too . . . Walter? . . .

WALTER: Yessss! All of it . . . It's all gone . . .

There is total silence. Ruth stands with her face covered with her hands; Beneatha leans forlornly against a wall, fingering a piece of red ribbon from the mother's gift. Mama stops and looks at her son without recognition and then, quite without thinking about it, starts to beat him senselessly in the face. Beneatha goes to them and stops it.

BENEATHA: Mama!

Mama stops and looks at both of her children and rises slowly and wanders vaguely, aimlessly away from them.

MAMA: I seen . . . him . . . night after night . . . come in . . . and look at that rug . . . and then look at me . . . the red showing in his eyes . . . the veins moving in his head . . . I seen him grow thin and old before he was forty . . . working and working and working like somebody's old horse . . . killing himself . . . and you — you give it all away in a day — *(She raises her arms to strike him again.)*

BENEATHA: Mama —

MAMA: Oh, God . . . *(She looks up to Him.)* Look down here — and show me the strength.

BENEATHA: Mama —

MAMA *(folding over)*: Strength . . .

BENEATHA *(plaintively)*: Mama . . .

MAMA: Strength!

Curtain.

Act 3

Time: An hour later.

    At curtain, there is a sullen light of gloom in the living room, gray light not unlike that which began the first scene of Act 1. At left we can see Walter within his room, alone with himself. He is stretched out on the bed, his shirt out and open, his arms under his head. He does not smoke, he does not cry out, he merely lies there, looking up at the ceiling, much as if he were alone in the world.

In the living room Beneatha sits at the table, still surrounded by the now almost ominous packing crates. She sits looking off. We feel that this is a mood struck perhaps an hour before, and it lingers now, full of the empty sound of profound disappointment. We see on a line from her brother's bedroom the sameness of their attitudes. Presently the bell rings and Beneatha rises without ambition or interest in answering. It is Asagai, smiling broadly, striding into the room with energy and happy expectation and conversation.

ASAGAI: I came over . . . I had some free time. I thought I might help with the packing. Ah, I like the look of packing crates! A household in preparation for a journey! It depresses some people . . . but for me . . . it is another feeling. Something full of the flow of life, do you understand? Movement, progress . . . It makes me think of Africa.

BENEATHA: Africa!

ASAGAI: What kind of a mood is this? Have I told you how deeply you move me?

BENEATHA: He gave away the money, Asagai . . .

ASAGAI: Who gave away what money?

BENEATHA: The insurance money. My brother gave it away.

ASAGAI: Gave it away?

BENEATHA: He made an investment! With a man even Travis wouldn't have trusted with his most worn-out marbles.

ASAGAI: And it's gone?

BENEATHA: Gone!

ASAGAI: I'm very sorry . . . And you, now?

BENEATHA: Me? . . . Me? . . . Me, I'm nothing . . . Me. When I was very small . . . we used to take our sleds out in the wintertime and the only hills we had were the ice-covered stone steps of some houses down the street. And we used to fill them in with snow and make them smooth and slide down them all day . . . and it was very dangerous, you know . . . far too steep . . . and sure enough one day a kid named Rufus came down too fast and hit the sidewalk and we saw his face just split open right there in front of us . . . And I remember standing there looking at his bloody open face thinking that was the end of Rufus. But the ambulance came and they took him to the hospital and they fixed the broken bones and they sewed it all up . . . and the next time I saw Rufus he just had a little line down the middle of his face . . . I never got over that . . .

ASAGAI: What?

BENEATHA: That that was what one person could do for another, fix him up — sew up the problem, make him all right again. That was the most marvelous thing in the world . . . I wanted to do that. I always thought it was the one concrete thing in the world that a human being could do. Fix up the sick, you know — and make them whole again. This was truly being God . . .

ASAGAI: You wanted to be God?

BENEATHA: No — I wanted to cure. It used to be so important to me. I wanted to cure. It used to matter. I used to care. I mean about people and how their bodies hurt . . .

ASAGAI: And you've stopped caring?

BENEATHA: Yes — I think so.

ASAGAI: Why?

BENEATHA *(bitterly)*:   Because it doesn't seem deep enough, close enough to what ails mankind! It was a child's way of seeing things — or an idealist's.

ASAGAI: Children see things very well sometimes — and idealists even better.

BENEATHA: I know that's what you think. Because you are still where I left off. You with all your talk and dreams about Africa! You still think you can patch up the world. Cure the Great Sore of Colonialism — *(Loftily, mocking it.)* with the Penicillin of Independence — !

ASAGAI: Yes!

BENEATHA: Independence *and then what?* What about all the crooks and thieves and just plain idiots who will come into power and steal and plunder the same as before — only now they will be black and do it in the name of the new Independence — WHAT ABOUT THEM?!

ASAGAI: That will be the problem for another time. First we must get there.

BENEATHA: And where does it end?

ASAGAI: End? Who even spoke of an end? To life? To living?

BENEATHA: An end to misery! To stupidity! Don't you see there isn't any real progress, Asagai, there is only one large circle that we march in, around and around, each of us with our own little picture in front of us — our own little mirage that we think is the future.

ASAGAI: That is the mistake.

BENEATHA: What?

ASAGAI: What you just said — about the circle. It isn't a circle — it is simply a long line — as in geometry, you know, one that reaches into infinity. And because we cannot see the end — we also cannot see how it changes. And it is very odd but those who see the changes — who dream, who will not give up — are called idealists . . . and those who see only the circle — we call *them* the "realists"!

BENEATHA: Asagai, while I was sleeping in that bed in there, people went out and took the future right out of my hands! And nobody asked me, nobody consulted me — they just went out and changed my life!

ASAGAI: Was it your money?

BENEATHA: What?

ASAGAI: Was it your money he gave away?

BENEATHA: It belonged to all of us.

ASAGAI: But did you earn it? Would you have had it at all if your father had not died?

BENEATHA: No.

ASAGAI: Then isn't there something wrong in a house — in a world — where all dreams, good or bad, must depend on the death of a man? I never thought to see *you* like this, Alaiyo. You! Your brother made a mistake and you are grateful to him so that now you can give up the ailing human race on account of it! You talk about what good is struggle, what good is anything! Where are we all going and why are we bothering!

BENEATHA: AND YOU CANNOT ANSWER IT!

ASAGAI *(shouting over her)*:   *I LIVE THE ANSWER! (Pause.)* In my village at home it is the exceptional man who can even read a newspaper . . . or who ever sees a book at all. I will go home and much of what I will have to say will seem strange to the people of my village. But I will teach and work and things will happen, slowly and swiftly. At times it will seem that nothing changes at all . . . and then again the sudden dramatic events which make history leap into the future. And then quiet again. Retrogression even. Guns, murder, revolution. And I even will have moments when I wonder if the quiet was not better than all that death and hatred. But I will look about my village at the illiteracy and disease and ignorance and I will not wonder long. And perhaps . . . perhaps I will be a great man . . . I mean perhaps I will hold on to the substance of truth and find my way always with the right course . . . and perhaps for it I will be butchered in my bed some night by the servants of empire . . .

BENEATHA: *The martyr!*

ASAGAI *(he smiles)*:   . . . or perhaps I shall live to be a very old man, respected and esteemed in my new nation . . . And perhaps I shall hold office and this is what I'm trying to tell you, Alaiyo: perhaps the things I believe now for my country will be wrong and outmoded, and I will not understand and do terrible things to have things my way or merely to keep my power. Don't you see that there will be young men and women — not British soldiers then, but my own black countrymen — to step out of the shadows some evening and slit my then useless throat? Don't you see they have always been there . . . that they always will be. And that such a thing as my own death will be an advance? They who might kill me even . . . actually replenish all that I was.

BENEATHA: Oh, Asagai, I know all that.

ASAGAI: Good! Then stop moaning and groaning and tell me what you plan to do.

BENEATHA: Do?

ASAGAI: I have a bit of a suggestion.

BENEATHA: What?

ASAGAI *(rather quietly for him)*:   That when it is all over — that you come home with me —

BENEATHA *(staring at him and crossing away with exasperation)*:   Oh — Asagai — at this moment you decide to be romantic!

ASAGAI *(quickly understanding the misunderstanding)*:   My dear, young creature of the New World — I do not mean across the city — I mean across the ocean: home — to Africa.

BENEATHA *(slowly understanding and turning to him with murmured amazement)*: To Africa?

ASAGAI: Yes! . . . *(smiling and lifting his arms playfully.)* Three hundred years later the African Prince rose up out of the seas and swept the maiden back across the middle passage over which her ancestors had come —

BENEATHA *(unable to play)*: To — to Nigeria?

ASAGAI: Nigeria. Home. *(Coming to her with genuine romantic flippancy.)* I will show you our mountains and our stars; and give you cool drinks from gourds and teach you the old songs and the ways of our people — and, in time, we will pretend that — *(Very softly.)* — you have only been away for a day. Say that you'll come — *(He swings her around and takes her full in his arms in a kiss which proceeds to passion.)*

BENEATHA *(pulling away suddenly)*: You're getting me all mixed up —

ASAGAI: Why?

BENEATHA: Too many things — too many things have happened today. I must sit down and think. I don't know what I feel about anything right this minute.

She promptly sits down and props her chin on her fist.

ASAGAI *(charmed)*: All right, I shall leave you. No — don't get up. *(Touching her, gently, sweetly.)* Just sit awhile and think . . . Never be afraid to sit awhile and think. *(He goes to door and looks at her.)* How often I have looked at you and said, "Ah — so this is what the New World hath finally wrought . . ."

He exits. Beneatha sits on alone. Presently Walter enters from his room and starts to rummage through things, feverishly looking for something. She looks up and turns in her seat.

BENEATHA *(hissingly)*: Yes — just look at what the New World hath wrought! . . . Just look! *(She gestures with bitter disgust.)* There he is! *Monsieur le petit bourgeois noir*° — himself! There he is — Symbol of a Rising Class! Entrepreneur! Titan of the system! *(Walter ignores her completely and continues frantically and destructively looking for something and hurling things to floor and tearing things out of their place in his search. Beneatha ignores the eccentricity of his actions and goes on with the monologue of insult.)* Did you dream of yachts on Lake Michigan, Brother? Did you see yourself on that Great Day sitting down at the Conference Table, surrounded by all the mighty bald-headed men in America? All halted, waiting, breathless, waiting for your pronouncements on industry? Waiting for you — Chairman of the Board! *(Walter finds what he is looking for — a small piece of white paper — and pushes it in his pocket and puts on his coat and rushes out without ever having looked at her. She shouts after him.)* I look at you and I see the final triumph of stupidity in the world!

The door slams and she returns to just sitting again. Ruth comes quickly out of Mama's room.

RUTH: Who was that?

BENEATHA: Your husband.

Monsieur le petit bourgeois noir: Mr. Black Bourgeoisie (French).

RUTH: Where did he go?

BENEATHA: Who knows — maybe he has an appointment at U.S. Steel.

RUTH *(anxiously, with frightened eyes)*:   You didn't say nothing bad to him, did you?

BENEATHA: Bad? Say anything bad to him? No — I told him he was a sweet boy and full of dreams and everything is strictly peachy keen, as the ofay° kids say!

Mama enters from her bedroom. She is lost, vague, trying to catch hold, to make some sense of her former command of the world, but it still eludes her. A sense of waste overwhelms her gait; a measure of apology rides on her shoulders. She goes to her plant, which has remained on the table, looks at it, picks it up and takes it to the window sill and sits it outside, and she stands and looks at it a long moment. Then she closes the window, straightens her body with effort and turns around to her children.

MAMA: Well — ain't it a mess in here, though? *(A false cheerfulness, a beginning of something.)* I guess we all better stop moping around and get some work done. All this unpacking and everything we got to do. *(Ruth raises her head slowly in response to the sense of the line; and Beneatha in similar manner turns very slowly to look at her mother.)* One of you all better call the moving people and tell 'em not to come.

RUTH: Tell 'em not to come?

MAMA: Of course, baby. Ain't no need in 'em coming all the way here and having to go back. They charges for that too. *(She sits down, fingers to her brow, thinking.)* Lord, ever since I was a little girl, I always remembers people saying, "Lena — Lena Eggleston, you aims too high all the time. You needs to slow down and see life a little more like it is. Just slow down some." That's what they always used to say down home — "Lord, that Lena Eggleston is a high-minded thing. She'll get her due one day!"

RUTH: No, Lena . . .

MAMA: Me and Big Walter just didn't never learn right.

RUTH: Lena, no! We gotta go. Bennie — tell her . . .

She rises and crosses to Beneatha with her arms outstretched. Beneatha doesn't respond.

Tell her we can still move . . . the notes ain't but a hundred and twenty-five a month. We got four grown people in this house — we can work . . .

MAMA *(to herself)*:   Just aimed too high all the time —

RUTH *(turning and going to Mama fast — the words pouring out with urgency and desperation)*:   Lena — I'll work . . . I'll work twenty hours a day in all the kitchens in Chicago . . . I'll strap my baby on my back if I have to and scrub all the floors in America and wash all the sheets in America if I have to — but we got to MOVE! We got to get OUT OF HERE!!

Mama reaches out absently and pats Ruth's hand.

ofay: Derogatory term for a white person.

MAMA: No — I sees things differently now. Been thinking 'bout some of the things we could do to fix this place up some. I seen a second-hand bureau over on Maxwell Street just the other day that could fit right there. *(She points to where the new furniture might go. Ruth wanders away from her.)* Would need some new handles on it and then a little varnish and it look like something brand-new. And — we can put up them new curtains in the kitchen . . . Why this place be looking fine. Cheer us all up so that we forget trouble ever come . . . *(To Ruth.)* And you could get some nice screens to put up in your room round the baby's bassinet . . . *(She looks at both of them pleadingly.)* Sometimes you just got to know when to give up some things . . . and hold on to what you got . . .

Walter enters from the outside, looking spent and leaning against the door, his coat hanging from him.

MAMA: Where you been, son?

WALTER *(breathing hard)*:   Made a call.

MAMA: To who, son?

WALTER: To The Man. *(He heads for his room.)*

MAMA: What man, baby?

WALTER *(stops in the door)*:   The Man, Mama. Don't you know who The Man is?

RUTH: Walter Lee?

WALTER: *The Man.* Like the guys in the streets say — The Man. Captain Boss — Mistuh Charley . . . Old Cap'n Please Mr. Bossman . . .

BENEATHA *(suddenly)*:   Lindner!

WALTER: That's right! That's good. I told him to come right over.

BENEATHA *(fiercely, understanding)*:   For what? What do you want to see him for!

WALTER *(looking at his sister)*:   We going to do business with him.

MAMA: What you talking 'bout, son?

WALTER: Talking 'bout life, Mama. You all always telling me to see life like it is. Well — I laid in there on my back today . . . and I figured it out. Life just like it is. Who gets and who don't get. *(He sits down with his coat on and laughs.)* Mama, you know it's all divided up. Life is. Sure enough. Between the takers and the "tooken." *(He laughs.)* I've figured it out finally. *(He looks around at them.)* Yeah. Some of us always getting "tooken." *(He laughs.)* People like Willy Harris, they don't never get "tooken." And you know why the rest of us do? 'Cause we all mixed up. Mixed up bad. We get to looking 'round for the right and the wrong; and we worry about it and cry about it and stay up nights trying to figure out 'bout the wrong and the right of things all the time . . . And all the time, man, them takers is out there operating, just taking and taking. Willy Harris? Shoot — Willy Harris don't even count. He don't even count in the big scheme of things. But I'll say one thing for old Willy Harris . . . he's taught me something. He's taught me to keep my eye on what counts in this world. Yeah — *(Shouting out a little.)* Thanks, Willy!

RUTH: What did you call that man for, Walter Lee?

WALTER: Called him to tell him to come on over to the show. Gonna put on a show for the man. Just what he wants to see. You see, Mama, the man came here today and he told us that them people out there where you want us to move — well they so upset they willing to pay us *not* to move! *(He laughs again.)* And — and oh, Mama — you would of been proud of the way me and Ruth and Bennie acted. We told him to get out . . . Lord have mercy! We told the man to get out! Oh, we was some proud folks this afternoon, yeah. *(He lights a cigarette.)* We were still full of that old-time stuff . . .

RUTH *(coming toward him slowly)*:   You talking 'bout taking them people's money to keep us from moving in that house?

WALTER: I ain't just talking 'bout it, baby — I'm telling you that's what's going to happen!

BENEATHA: Oh, God! Where is the bottom! Where is the real honest-to-God bottom so he can't go any farther!

WALTER: See — that's the old stuff. You and that boy that was here today. You all want everybody to carry a flag and a spear and sing some marching songs, huh? You wanna spend your life looking into things and trying to find the right and the wrong part, huh? Yeah. You know what's going to happen to that boy someday — he'll find himself sitting in a dungeon, locked in forever — and the takers will have the key! Forget it, baby! There ain't no causes — there ain't nothing but taking in this world, and he who takes most is smartest — and it don't make a damn bit of difference *how.*

MAMA: You making something inside me cry, son. Some awful pain inside me.

WALTER: Don't cry, Mama. Understand. That white man is going to walk in that door able to write checks for more money than we ever had. It's important to him and I'm going to help him . . . I'm going to put on the show, Mama.

MAMA: Son — I come from five generations of people who was slaves and sharecroppers — but ain't nobody in my family never let nobody pay 'em no money that was a way of telling us we wasn't fit to walk the earth. We ain't never been that poor. *(Raising her eyes and looking at him.)* We ain't never been that — dead inside.

BENEATHA: Well — we are dead now. All the talk about dreams and sunlight that goes on in this house. It's all dead now.

WALTER: What's the matter with you all! I didn't make this world! It was give to me this way! Hell, yes, I want me some yachts someday! Yes, I want to hang some real pearls 'round my wife's neck. Ain't she supposed to wear no pearls? Somebody tell me — tell me, who decides which women is suppose to wear pearls in this world. I tell you I am a *man* — and I think my wife should wear some pearls in this world!

This last line hangs a good while and Walter begins to move about the room. The word "Man" has penetrated his consciousness; he mumbles it to himself repeatedly between strange agitated pauses as he moves about.

MAMA: Baby, how you going to feel on the inside?

WALTER: Fine! . . . Going to feel fine . . . a man . . .

MAMA: You won't have nothing left then, Walter Lee.

WALTER *(coming to her)*:   I'm going to feel fine, Mama. I'm going to look that son-of-a-bitch in the eyes and say — *(He falters.)* — and say, "All right, Mr. Lindner — *(He falters even more.)* — that's *your* neighborhood out there! You got the right to keep it like you want! You got the right to have it like you want! Just write the check and — the house is yours." And — and I am going to say — *(His voice almost breaks.)* "And you — you people just put the money in my hand and you won't have to live next to this bunch of stinking niggers! . . ." *(He straightens up and moves away from his mother, walking around the room.)* And maybe — maybe I'll just get down on my black knees . . . *(He does so; Ruth and Bennie and Mama watch him in frozen horror.)* "Captain, Mistuh, Bossman — *(Groveling and grinning and wringing his hands in profoundly anguished imitation of the slow-witted movie stereotype.)* A-hee-hee-hee! Oh, yassuh boss! Yasssssuh! Great white — *(Voice breaking, he forces himself to go on.)* — Father, just gi' ussen de money, fo' God's sake, and we's — we's ain't gwine come out deh and dirty up yo' white folks neighborhood . . ." *(He breaks down completely.)* And I'll feel fine! Fine! FINE! *(He gets up and goes into the bedroom.)*

BENEATHA: That is not a man. That is nothing but a toothless rat.

MAMA: Yes — death done come in this here house. *(She is nodding, slowly, reflectively.)* Done come walking in my house on the lips of my children. You what supposed to be my beginning again. You — what supposed to be my harvest. *(To Beneatha.)* You — you mourning your brother?

BENEATHA: He's no brother of mine.

MAMA: What you say?

BENEATHA: I said that that individual in that room is no brother of mine.

MAMA: That's what I thought you said. You feeling like you better than he is today? *(Beneatha does not answer.)* Yes? What you tell him a minute ago? That he wasn't a man? Yes? You give him up for me? You done wrote his epitaph too — like the rest of the world? Well, who give you the privilege?

BENEATHA: Be on my side for once! You saw what he just did, Mama! You saw him — down on his knees. Wasn't it you who taught me to despise any man who would do that? Do what he's going to do?

MAMA: Yes — I taught you that. Me and your daddy. But I thought I taught you something else too . . . I thought I taught you to love him.

BENEATHA: Love him? There is nothing left to love.

MAMA: There is *always* something left to love. And if you ain't learned that, you ain't learned nothing. *(Looking at her.)* Have you cried for that boy today? I don't mean for yourself and for the family 'cause we lost the money. I mean for him: what he been through and what it done to him. Child, when do you think is the time to love somebody the most? When they done good and made things easy for everybody? Well then, you ain't through learning — because that ain't the time at all. It's when he's at his lowest and can't believe in hisself 'cause the world done whipped him so! When you starts measuring somebody, measure him right, child, measure him right. Make sure you done taken into account what hills and valleys he come through before he got to wherever he is.

Travis bursts into the room at the end of the speech, leaving the door open.

TRAVIS: Grandmama—the moving men are downstairs! The truck just pulled up.

MAMA *(turning and looking at him):*   Are they, baby? They downstairs?

She sighs and sits. Lindner appears in the doorway. He peers in and knocks lightly, to gain attention, and comes in. All turn to look at him.

LINDNER *(hat and briefcase in hand):*   Uh—hello . . .

Ruth crosses mechanically to the bedroom door and opens it and lets it swing open freely and slowly as the lights come up on Walter within, still in his coat, sitting at the far corner of the room. He looks up and out through the room to Lindner.

RUTH: He's here.

A long minute passes and Walter slowly gets up.

LINDNER *(coming to the table with efficiency, putting his briefcase on the table and starting to unfold papers and unscrew fountain pens):*   Well, I certainly was glad to hear from you people. *(Walter has begun the trek out of the room, slowly and awkwardly, rather like a small boy, passing the back of his sleeve across his mouth from time to time.)* Life can really be so much simpler than people let it be most of the time. Well—with whom do I negotiate? You, Mrs. Younger, or your son here? *(Mama sits with her hands folded on her lap and her eyes closed as Walter advances. Travis goes closer to Lindner and looks at the papers curiously.)* Just some official papers, sonny.

RUTH: Travis, you go downstairs—

MAMA *(opening her eyes and looking into Walter's):*   No. Travis, you stay right here. And you make him understand what you doing, Walter Lee. You teach him good. Like Willy Harris taught you. You show where our five generations done come to. *(Walter looks from her to the boy, who grins at him innocently.)* Go ahead, son— *(She folds her hands and closes her eyes.)* Go ahead.

WALTER *(at last crosses to Lindner, who is reviewing the contract):*   Well, Mr. Lindner. *(Beneatha turns away.)* We called you— *(There is a profound, simple groping quality in his speech.)* —because, well, me and my family *(He looks around and shifts from one foot to the other.)* Well—we are very plain people . . .

LINDNER: Yes—

WALTER: I mean—I have worked as a chauffeur most of my life—and my wife here, she does domestic work in people's kitchens. So does my mother. I mean—we are plain people . . .

LINDNER: Yes, Mr. Younger—

WALTER *(really like a small boy, looking down at his shoes and then up at the man):*   And—uh—well, my father, well, he was a laborer most of his life. . . .

LINDNER *(absolutely confused):*   Uh, yes—yes, I understand. *(He turns back to the contract.)*

WALTER *(a beat; staring at him):*   And my father— *(With sudden intensity.)* My father almost *beat a man to death* once because this man called him a bad name or something, you know what I mean?

LINDNER *(looking up, frozen)*:   No, no, I'm afraid I don't —

WALTER *(a beat. The tension hangs; then Walter steps back from it)*:   Yeah. Well — what I mean is that we come from people who had a lot of *pride*. I mean — we are very proud people. And that's my sister over there and she's going to be a doctor — and we are very proud —

LINDNER: Well — I am sure that is very nice, but —

WALTER: What I am telling you is that we called you over here to tell you that we are very proud and that this — *(Signaling to Travis.)* Travis, come here. *(Travis crosses and Walter draws him before him facing the man.)* This is my son, and he makes the sixth generation our family in this country. And we have all thought about your offer —

LINDNER: Well, good . . . good —

WALTER: And we have decided to move into our house because my father — my father — he earned it for us brick by brick. *(Mama has her eyes closed and is rocking back and forth as though she were in church, with her head nodding the Amen yes.)* We don't want to make no trouble for nobody or fight no causes, and we will try to be good neighbors. And that's *all* we got to say about that. *(He looks the man absolutely in the eyes.)* We don't want your money. *(He turns and walks away.)*

LINDNER *(looking around at all of them)*:   I take it then — that you have decided to occupy . . .

BENEATHA: That's what the man said.

LINDNER *(to Mama in her reverie)*:   Then I would like to appeal to you, Mrs. Younger. You are older and wiser and understand things better I am sure . . .

MAMA: I am afraid you don't understand. My son said we was going to move and there ain't nothing left for me to say. *(Briskly.)* You know how these young folks is nowadays, mister. Can't do a thing with 'em! *(As he opens his mouth, she rises.)* Good-bye.

LINDNER *(folding up his materials)*:   Well — if you are that final about it . . . there is nothing left for me to say. *(He finishes, almost ignored by the family, who are concentrating on Walter Lee. At the door Lindner halts and looks around.)* I sure hope you people know what you're getting into.

He shakes his head and exits.

RUTH *(looking around and coming to life)*:   Well, for God's sake — if the moving men are here — LET'S GET THE HELL OUT OF HERE!

MAMA *(into action)*:   Ain't it the truth! Look at all this here mess. Ruth, put Travis's good jacket on him . . . Walter Lee, fix your tie and tuck your shirt in, you look like somebody's hoodlum! Lord have mercy, where is my plant? *(She flies to get it amid the general bustling of the family, who are deliberately trying to ignore the nobility of the past moment.)* You all start on down . . . Travis child, don't go empty-handed . . . Ruth, where did I put that box with my skillets in it? I want to be in charge of it myself . . . I'm going to make us the biggest dinner we ever ate tonight . . . Beneatha, what's the matter with them stockings? Pull them things up, girl . . .

The family starts to file out as two moving men appear and begin to carry out the heavier pieces of furniture, bumping into the family as they move about.

BENEATHA: Mama, Asagai asked me to marry him today and go to Africa —

MAMA *(in the middle of her getting-ready activity)*:   He did? You ain't old enough to marry nobody — *(Seeing the moving men lifting one of her chairs precariously.)* Darling, that ain't no bale of cotton, please handle it so we can sit in it again! I had that chair twenty-five years . . .

The movers sigh with exasperation and go on with their work.

BENEATHA *(girlishly and unreasonably trying to pursue the conversation)*:   To go to Africa, Mama — be a doctor in Africa . . .

MAMA *(distracted)*:   Yes, baby —

WALTER: *Africa!* What he want you to go to Africa for?

BENEATHA: To practice there . . .

WALTER: Girl, if you don't get all them silly ideas out your head! You better marry yourself a man with some loot . . .

BENEATHA *(angrily, precisely as in the first scene of the play)*:   What have you got to do with who I marry!

WALTER: Plenty. Now I think George Murchison —

BENEATHA: *George Murchison!* I wouldn't marry him if he was Adam and I was Eve!

Walter and Beneatha go out yelling at each other vigorously and the anger is loud and real till their voices diminish. Ruth stands at the door and turns to Mama and smiles knowingly.

MAMA *(fixing her hat at last)*:   Yeah — they something all right, my children . . .

RUTH: Yeah — they're something. Let's go, Lena.

MAMA *(stalling, starting to look around at the house)*:   Yes — I'm coming. Ruth —

RUTH: Yes?

MAMA *(quietly, woman to woman)*:   He finally come into his manhood today, didn't he? Kind of like a rainbow after the rain . . .

RUTH *(biting her lip lest her own pride explode in front of Mama)*:   Yes, Lena.

Walter's voice calls for them raucously.

WALTER *(offstage)*:   Y'all come on! These people charges by the hour, you know!

MAMA *(waving Ruth out vaguely)*:   All right, honey — go on down. I be down directly.

Ruth hesitates, then exits. Mama stands, at last alone in the living room, her plant on the table before her as the lights start to come down. She looks around at all the walls and ceilings and suddenly, despite herself, while the children call below, a great heaving thing rises in her and she puts her fist to her mouth to stifle it, takes a final desperate look, pulls her coat about her, pats her hat, and goes out. The lights dim down. The door opens and she comes back in, grabs her plant, and goes out for the last time.

Curtain.   [1959]

☰ THINKING ABOUT THE TEXT

1. The play's main characters are Walter Lee, Mama, Ruth, and Beneatha. List three or more adjectives to describe each of these characters. What basic values does each character seem to express during the arguments that occur in their family? Do you sympathize with them equally? Why, or why not? What, evidently, was Walter Lee's father like?

2. At the end of the play, speaking to Ruth about Walter Lee, Mama says "He finally come into his manhood today, didn't he?" How does Mama appear to be defining *manhood*? What other possible definitions of *manhood* come up directly or indirectly in the play? Identify places where characteristics of *womanhood* are brought up. In general, would you say that gender is at least as important in this play as race is? Why, or why not?

3. Analyze Asagai's conversations with Beneatha and the rest of her family. What does Hansberry suggest about the relations of Africans and African Americans in the late 1950s?

4. Although there is a white character, he makes only two relatively brief appearances, and no other white characters are shown. Why do you suppose Hansberry keeps the presence of whites minimal?

5. Do you think this play is universal in its truths and concerns, or are you more inclined to see it as specifically about African Americans? Explain. In what ways is this 1959 play relevant to life in the United States today?

THE CRISIS

The Hansberrys of Chicago: They Join Business Acumen with Social Vision

The following article appeared in the April 1941 issue of The Crisis, *the journal of the National Association for the Advancement of Colored People (NAACP). The photographs to which the article refers are omitted. The NAACP was established in 1909 and* The Crisis *a year later, its founder and first editor being the noted African American intellectual W. E. B. Du Bois. This article pays tribute to Lorraine Hansberry's parents; it notes their successful real estate business, the foundation they established to get civil rights laws enforced, and their 1940 U.S. Supreme Court victory. The Court's decision was meant to erode at least some racial covenants, policies by which white neighborhoods kept out blacks. However, the decision was not enforced, and very little changed.*

Mr. and Mrs. Carl A. Hansberry of Chicago, Illinois, have the distinction not only of conducting one of the largest real estate enterprises in the country operated by Negroes but they are unique business people because they are spending much of their wealth to safeguard the civil rights of colored citizens in their city, state, and nation.

The properties shown on these pages are a part of the $250,000.00 worth of Chicago real estate from which The Hansberry Enterprises and The Hansberry Foundation receive a gross annual income of $100,000.00. The real estate firm makes available to Negroes with limited income apartments within their economic reach, while the profits from this enterprise are used to safeguard the Negro's civil rights and to make additional housing available to him. The Hansberrys played a very significant role in the recent Chicago restrictive covenant case before the United States Supreme Court whose decision opened blocks of houses and apartment buildings from which Negroes formerly had been excluded.

The Hansberry Enterprises

The Hansberry Enterprises is a real estate syndicate founded by Mr. Hansberry in 1929. From a very modest beginning, the business has grown to be one of the largest in the Mid-West. The property owned and controlled by the company is in excess of $250,000 in value and accommodates four hundred families. During the past ten years the payroll and commissions have aggregated more than $350,000.00.

The offices of the Hansberry Enterprises are located at 4247 Indiana Avenue, Chicago, Illinois.

The Hansberry Foundation

The Hansberry Foundation was established in 1936 by Mrs. N. Louise Hansberry, and her husband, Carl A. Hansberry, with substantial grants of the interest from the Hansberry Enterprises. Mr. Hansberry is the Director. The Foundation was set up as a Trust Fund and only the members of the immediate Hansberry family may contribute to this Fund. A provision of the Trust provides "That during the first ten (10) years only 60 percent of the income of the trust may be used, thereafter, both the income and the principal may be used, but at no time shall the principal be reduced to less than Ten Thousand ($10,000.00) dollars."

5

The purpose of the Foundation is to encourage and promote respect for all laws, and especially those laws as related to the Civil Rights of American citizens. The following paragraph taken from a letter to the Cook County Bar Association under date of April 27, 1937, gives a precise statement of the purpose and scope of the Hansberry Foundation:

> The Creators of the Hansberry Foundation believe that the Illinois Civil Rights Law represents the crystallized views of the best citizens of Illinois and were made in the best interest of the whole people of Illinois. They therefore believed, that the Civil Rights Code should be enforced; that the passiveness of any citizen should cease. Because of and in view of the foregoing premises, the Hansberry Foundation was created and now

therefore announces its desire to cooperate with sympathetic public officials, associations, or organizations, likewise interested in the active enforcement of the Civil Rights Laws of Illinois and throughout the Nation. The Foundation will assume (at its discretion) a part, or all of the costs of prosecuting violations of the law wherever, and/or whenever, the authorities willfully neglect or refuse to act; and where the victims are financially unable to protect themselves.

[1941]

☰ THINKING ABOUT THE TEXT

1. What do you sense is the main rhetorical purpose of *The Crisis* in publishing this article? Does anyone in *A Raisin in the Sun* share the values expressed by the article? To what extent do you aim to "join business acumen with social vision"?

2. Much of the article consists of quotations from legal documents associated with the Hansberry Foundation. What do you think of this rhetorical strategy?

3. The article makes clear that when Lorraine Hansberry's family sought to live in an all-white part of Chicago, they were wealthier than the Youngers. What would you say to someone who argued that it would have been more honest of Hansberry to focus her play on a family as well-off as hers?

LORRAINE HANSBERRY
Letter to the New York Times *Editor, dated April 23, 1964*

Here is part of a letter by Lorraine Hansberry written five years after A Raisin in the Sun. *Once again, she quotes the poem by Langston Hughes containing her play's title. Now, however, she is expressing approval of civil rights activists' aggressive tactics, including attempts by the Congress of Racial Equality (CORE) to block traffic. In her letter, Hansberry also recalls her family's fight against racial covenants and her father's subsequent death in Mexico. Although the* New York Times *never published Hansberry's letter, some of it was included by her husband, Robert Nemiroff, in his 1969 compilation of her writings,* To Be Young, Gifted, and Black.

April 23, 1964

To the Editor,
The New York Times:
    . . . My father was typical of a generation of Negroes who believed that the "American way" could successfully be made to work to democratize the United States. Thus, twenty-five years ago, he spent a small personal fortune, his considerable talents, and many years of his life fighting, in association with

NAACP attorneys, Chicago's "restrictive covenants" in one of this nation's ugliest ghettoes.

That fight also required that our family occupy the disputed property in a hellishly hostile "white neighborhood" in which, literally, howling mobs surrounded our house. One of their missiles almost took the life of the then eight-year-old signer of this letter. My memories of this "correct" way of fighting white supremacy in America include being spat at, cursed, and pummeled in the daily trek to and from school. And I also remember my desperate and courageous mother, patrolling our house all night with a loaded German luger, doggedly guarding her four children, while my father fought the respectable part of the battle in the Washington court.

The fact that my father and the NAACP "won" a Supreme Court decision, in a now famous case which bears his name in the lawbooks, is — ironically — the sort of "progress" our satisfied friends allude to when they presume to deride the more radical means of struggle. The cost, in emotional turmoil, time, and money, which led to my father's early death as a permanently embittered exile in a foreign country when he saw that after such sacrificial efforts the Negroes of Chicago were as ghetto-locked as ever, does not seem to figure in their calculations.

That is the reality that I am faced with when I now read that some Negroes my own age and younger say that we must now lie down in the streets, tie up traffic, do whatever we can — take to the hills with guns if necessary — and fight back. Fatuous people remark these days on our "bitterness." Why, of course we are bitter. The entire situation suggests that the nation be reminded of the too little noted final lines of Langston Hughes's mighty poem:

> *What happens to a dream deferred?*
>
> Does it dry up
> Like a raisin in the sun?
> Or fester like a sore —
> And then run?
> Does it stink like rotten meat?
> Or crust and sugar over —
> Like a syrupy sweet?
>
> Maybe it just sags
> Like a heavy load.
>
> *Or does it explode?*

Sincerely,
Lorraine Hansberry
[1964]

≡ **THINKING ABOUT THE TEXT**

1. Hansberry indicates that she is "bitter." Is *bitter* a word that you associate with the author of *A Raisin in the Sun?* Why, or why not? Do you get

the sense that the bitterness she refers to in her letter is justified? Why, or why not?

2. Does Hansberry's play give you the impression that the family in it will suffer the same kinds of things described in the second paragraph of Hansberry's letter? Support your answer with details from the play.

3. In the letter, Hansberry seems to condone acts of civil disobedience. In what kinds of cases, if any, do you think people are justified in breaking the law?

ALAN EHRENHALT

From *The Lost City: Discovering the Forgotten Virtues of Community in the Chicago of the 1950s*

Alan Ehrenhalt (b. 1947) is the executive editor of Governing *magazine and was formerly political editor of* Congressional Quarterly. *In much of his writing, he argues that Americans will achieve true democracy only if they regain the sense of community they once had. This is the basic claim of Ehrenhalt's first book,* The United States of Ambition: Politicians, Power, and the Pursuit of Office *(1991). In his second,* The Lost City: Discovering the Forgotten Virtues of Community in the Chicago of the 1950s *(1995), he extends his concern with community spirit by focusing on the role it played in Chicago during the 1950s. His latest book is* Governing *(2005). The following excerpts deal with Bronzeville, the South Side ghetto where Lorraine Hansberry grew up and where her 1959 play* A Raisin in the Sun *takes place.*

If St. Nick's parish° was a world of limited choices, a far more limited world existed five miles further east, where the bulk of Chicago's black community — hundreds of thousands of people — lived together in Bronzeville, a neighborhood they were all but prohibited from escaping.

Any discussion of the city we have lost during the past generation must eventually confront the issue of Bronzeville, and the question that may be most troublesome of all: Have we lost something important that existed even in the worst place that the Chicago of the 1950s had to offer?

Anybody who did not live in a black ghetto is bound to be leery of asking the question, with its implied assumption that segregation hid its good points. But the fact remains, long after Bronzeville's disappearance from the map, that a remarkable number of people who did live there find themselves asking it.

"Fifty-first and Dearborn was a bunch of shacks," Alice Blair wrote thirty years later, after she had become Chicago's deputy superintendent of education.

St. Nick's parish: St. Nicholas of Tolentine parish, a postimmigrant, working-class neighborhood of Chicago.

"We didn't have hot water — and the houses were torn down for slum clearance to build Robert Taylor Homes. But in those shacks, there was something different from what is there now."

What was it, exactly? Several things. "People took a great deal of pride in just being where they were," says John Stroger, the first black president of the Cook County Board of Commissioners. "It was economically poor, but spiritually and socially rich. People had hope that things would be better." Stroger echoes what Vernon Jarrett, the longtime Chicago newspaper columnist, said rather hauntingly a few years ago. "The ghetto used to have something going for it. It had a beat, it had a certain rhythm, and it was all hope. I don't care how rough things were."

Then there is the bluntness of Timuel Black, a lifelong civil rights activist, looking back at age seventy-five on the South Side as it used to be and as it has become: "I would say," he declares at the end of a long conversation, "at this point in my life and experience, that we made a mistake leaving the ghetto."

These fragments prove nothing. To many who read them, they will suggest merely that nostalgia is not only powerful but dangerous, that late in life it can generate a fondness for times and places that should be properly remembered with nothing more than relief that they are gone. And yet something valuable did die with Bronzeville, and we can learn something about community and authority, faith and hope, by tracing their presence even in what was, by common agreement, an unjust and constricted corner of the world.

What Bronzeville had, and so many of its graduates continue to mourn, was a sense of posterity — a feeling that, however difficult the present might be, the future was worth thinking about and planning for in some detail. Most of the inhabitants of Bronzeville were farsighted people, able to focus on events and ideas whose outlines were hazy and whose arrival might still be very far away. They were looking forward to a time in which it would be possible to break free of the constrictions and indignities of the moment.

Forty years later, in a time-shortened world hooked on fax machines, microwave popcorn, and MTV, the word *posterity* carries far less meaning than it once did. Its gradual disappearance is one of the genuine losses of modern life. To find the concept so vibrant and well entrenched in a place as deprived as Bronzeville in the 1950s seems to mock the freer but far less anchored world that most of us inhabit today.

The indignities of life for a black person on the South Side in the 1950s are unlikely to come as news to very many readers of any race, but some details are worth dredging up. They reveal the triumphs and comforts of Bronzeville society to have been that much more impressive.

It was, for example, uncommonly dangerous for a black Chicagoan to get sick. Of the seventy-seven hospitals in the metropolitan area, only six would accept black patients at all, and five of those had quotas, so that once a certain small number of beds were occupied by blacks, the next black patient would be turned away, no matter how ill he or she was. It was not unusual for blacks who could perfectly well afford private hospital care to be taken to Cook County Hospital, the spartan and overcrowded charity institution on the West Side.

Most of the time, though, even in an emergency, they would be rushed to Provident, the city's only "black" hospital, sometimes speeding past one white facility after another to get to the Provident emergency room. In 1956, Provident saw an emergency patient every nineteen minutes, five times the average for the city's other hospitals. And it was, of course, the only place where a black doctor could aspire to practice; the other hospitals did their hiring on a strict Jim Crow basis.

Getting stopped for a traffic ticket on the South Side was not the same experience for blacks that it was for whites. Until 1958, all traffic tickets in Chicago mentioned the race of the driver. The police maintained a special task force, known to just about everybody as the "flying squad," which was supposed to zero in on high-crime neighborhoods but in fact spent a good deal of its time harassing black citizens, middle-class as well as poor. It was standard practice for flying squad officers to stop black motorists for traffic violations, frisk them, and search their cars before writing the ticket, often abusing them verbally and physically in the process. The abuses nearly always took place when someone was driving alone, so there were rarely any witnesses.

The force that patrolled these neighborhoods was still mostly white, and the supervisors were essentially all white. There were 1,200 black police officers in Chicago in 1957, but only one black captain, and no lieutenants. In the Englewood district, where many of the new recruits were sent, black patrolmen were nearly always given the most tedious assignments: guard duty night after night, or a motorcycle beat in the depths of winter. The two-man teams were all segregated; blacks and whites were not allowed to work together.

Meanwhile, the public schools were not only segregated but demonstrably unequal. Most of the white elementary schools on the South Side were underused, while the black ones were jammed far beyond capacity. Some black schools in Bronzeville were handling more than 2,000 pupils a day on a double-shift basis, with one set of children in attendance from 8 A.M. to noon and another from noon to 4 P.M. At the same time, there were nearly 300 vacant classrooms elsewhere in the city and more than 1,000 classrooms being used for nonessential activities of one sort or another. But the school board did not want to adjust the district lines to permit black kids to take advantage of the space that existed beyond the racial borders.

The incidents of hospital bias, police harassment, and school inequity pointed up just how indifferent Jim Crow was to class distinctions in the 1950s: having money was simply no help in these situations. There was a fourth indignity that somehow makes this point even clearer, and it had to do with travel and vacations.

For $20 a year in 1957, a black family could join an organization called the Tourist Motor Club. What they received in return was a list of hotels and restaurants where blacks would be allowed inside the door, and a guarantee of $500 in bond money in case they found themselves being arrested for making the wrong choice. "Are you ready for any traveling emergency — even in a

15

hostile town?" the Tourist Motor Club asked in its ads, and not unreasonably. "What would you do if you were involved in a highway accident in a hostile town — far away from home. You could lose your life savings — you could be kept in jail without adequate reason. You could lose your entire vacation fighting unjust prejudice."

Vacations were for those who could afford them. The problem that united everyone in the black community — wealthy, working class, and poor — was housing. Unlike St. Nick's or any other white community in Chicago, the ghetto was almost impossible to move out of. The rules of segregation simply made it difficult for a black family to live anywhere else, whether it could afford to or not.

By 1957, that had begun to change. Chicago's South Side black population was expanding, block by block, into what had been white working-class territory on its southern and western borders, and a new, separate black enclave had emerged a few miles west of downtown. But as a practical matter, the number of decent housing opportunities opening up for blacks was far smaller than the number needed. Thus, most of the city's black community remained where it had been since the 1920s: in a narrow strip south of Twenty-third Street, roughly eight miles long and still no more than two or three miles wide.

This ghetto had been badly overcrowded by the time of World War II, and in the years since then it had grown more crowded still. The number of black people in Chicago had increased nearly 40 percent between 1950 and 1956, while the white population was declining. And the newcomers were simply stacking up on top of one another. The Kenwood-Oakland neighborhood, centered around Forty-seventh Street, had gone from 13,000 white residents to 80,000 blacks in a matter of a few years. "A new Negro reaches this sprawling city every fifteen minutes," the young black journalist Carl Rowan wrote in 1957, seeming a little overwhelmed himself. Parts of the South Side that had once been relatively spacious and comfortable now held more people than anyone had imagined possible.

The physical world that those migrants confronted was the world of the infamous "kitchenette" — a one-room flat with an icebox, a bed, and a hotplate, typically in an ancient building that once held a few spacious apartments but had been cut up into the tiniest possible pieces to bring the landlord more money. The bathroom and stove were shared with neighbors, a dozen or more people taking turns with the same meager facilities. . . .

In Bronzeville, hope and authority tended to come out of the same package. If the ultimate authority figures were wealthy white people somewhere far away, the most familiar and important ones were right there, inside the community. They were people who had maneuvered their way through the currents of segregated life, made careers and often fortunes for themselves, and remained in the neighborhood, hammering home the message that there were victories to strive for. They were employers and entrepreneurs of all sorts: businessmen,

20

politicians, and entertainers, gambling czars and preachers of the Gospel. They were people whose moral flaws and weaknesses were no secret to those around them, and those weaknesses were a frequent topic of discussion in the community. But they were leaders nevertheless. They led by command, sometimes rather crudely, and they also led by example.

It is easy to forget, forty years later, just how many successful black-owned businesses there were in Chicago. There were black entrepreneurs all up and down the commercial streets in the 1950s, able to stay afloat because they were guaranteed a clientele. They provided services that white businesses simply did not want to provide to blacks. They ran barber shops and beauty parlors, restaurants and taverns, photography studios and small hotels. Many of them were mom-and-pop operations but quite a few evolved into sizable corporations. "Business," as Dempsey Travis says, "was the pillar of optimism."

The nation's largest black-owned bank was at Forty-seventh Street and Cottage Grove Avenue. Parker House Sausage Company, at Forty-sixth and State, called itself the "Jackie Robinson of meat-packing." At Twenty-seventh and Wabash, S. B. Fuller operated a giant cosmetics business that touted three hundred different products, maintained thirty-one branches all over the country, and employed five thousand salesmen. "Anyone can succeed," Fuller used to say, "if he has the desire."

But the great symbols of the entrepreneurial spirit in Bronzeville were the funeral parlors and the insurance companies. In many cases they were related businesses, a legacy of the burial insurance associations that had existed among black sharecroppers in Mississippi and Arkansas early in the century. Undertakers were the largest single source of advertising in the *Defender*; they were also, like their white counterparts elsewhere in the city, mainstays of every community organization: lodges, churches, social clubs. 25

The opening of a new funeral parlor was a community event in itself. In the spring of 1957, the Jackson funeral home opened a state-of-the art facility on Cottage Grove Avenue, complete, with three large chapels, slumber rooms, a powder room, and a smoking lounge. On the first day, three thousand people came to see it. The Jackson family also owned Jackson Mutual, the fifth largest insurance company in Bronzeville, employing one hundred and twenty people and writing nearly $2 million worth of policies every year.

Insurance actually was a service that white corporations were willing to provide to black customers. Thousands of Bronzeville residents had policies with Metropolitan Life, paying a dollar or two every month to an agent who came by door-to-door to collect. But this was one case where black firms could compete fairly easily. Met Life charged black families more than it charged whites for the same policies, its agents didn't like to come at night when customers were home, and they often seemed to resent having to be there at all. There were billboards all over the neighborhood urging people to buy their insurance from a Negro company.

The result was that by the mid-1950s, the five largest black-owned insurance companies in Chicago had nearly $50 million in assets and more than two thousand employees among them. "Negro life insurance companies," said

Walter Lowe, one of the leading agents, "represent the core of Negro economic life. It is the axis upon which are revolved the basic financial activities of a world constricted by the overpowering forces of discrimination."

But it was more than that. It was the underwriter of the extended time horizons that made life in Bronzeville tolerable in the first place. It was the primary symbol of hope for people burdened with a difficult present but unwilling to abandon their focus on the future. In 1954, *Ebony* magazine, published in Chicago, took a survey of its black readership and found that 42 percent owned washing machines, 44 percent owned cars, and 60 percent owned television sets. But 86 percent said they carried life insurance.

The *Defender*'s tribute to the life insurance companies was reprinted every year to coincide with National Negro Insurance Week: "I am the destroyer of poverty and the enemy of crime," it said. "I bring sunshine and happiness wherever I am given half the welcome I deserve. I do not live for the day nor for the morrow but for the unfathomable future. I am your best friend — I am life insurance." ...

Overcoming evil was a job at which most of Bronzeville worked very hard every Sunday, in congregations that ranged in size from tiny to immense. There were five churches whose sanctuary had a seating capacity of two thousand or more, and at least two churches had more than ten thousand people on their membership rolls. But a majority of the churches in the community, even in the late 1950s, were basically storefront operations — often a couple of dozen worshipers or even fewer than that.

In the bigger churches, Sunday worship was an all-day affair: Sunday school at nine in the morning and the main service at eleven; an evening musicale later on, with the full choir and Gospel chorus; and then, for many of the faithful, a radio sermon from one of the big-name Bronzeville preachers before retiring for the night. Music was at the heart of the experience. Most churches had choirs that accompanied the pastor when he preached as a guest in another pulpit, which all of them did. Some choirs spent considerable time traveling outside the city.

Between Sundays, the odds were that a larger congregation would be busy with some social activity every single night. All these churches had a wide variety of auxiliary organizations — youth groups, missionary societies, sewing circles — and some had as many as two dozen different ones in existence at the same time. Of all the Bronzeville social institutions of the 1950s, the churches were the most uniformly successful and self-reliant. "In their own churches in their own denominational structures," the historian C. Eric Lincoln was to write in retrospect, "black Christians had become accustomed to a sense of dignity and self-fulfillment impossible even to contemplate in the white church in America. . . . To be able to say that 'I belong to Mount Nebo Baptist' or 'We go to Mason's Chapel Methodist' was the accepted way of establishing identity and status."

The storefront churches had to make do without the elaborate network of groups and social involvement. But the key distinction was not the size of the

30

facility; it was the style of worship and particularly the level of emotion. Many of the storefronts, perhaps most, were Holiness or Pentecostal churches — Holy Rollers, as the outside world had already come to know them. The service combined shouting, faith healing, and speaking in tongues; as much as three hours of singing, accompanied by guitar, drum, and tambourine; and vivid storytelling sermons about such things as the fiery furnace or the prodigal son. Some churches employed attendants in white uniforms to calm the shouting worshipers when they became too excited. In a liturgy that devoted a great deal of its time to discussing the nature and consequences of sin — and the specific sins of alcohol, tobacco, profanity, gambling, and adultery — there was intense joy as well. "I have known the sisters and the brothers to become so happy," one woman told Horace Cayton and St. Clair Drake in *Black Metropolis*, "that persons around them are in actual danger of getting knocked in the face."

The popularity of these storefronts was something of a problem for the   35
mainline Baptist and African Methodist Episcopal (AME) congregations that aimed for what they saw as a higher level of decorum and dignity. Some ministers used to upbraid their worshipers for becoming too emotional during the service. By the mid-1950s, however, the liturgical distinction between the storefronts and the mainline institutions was blurring. Dozens of preachers who had begun with nothing had built their churches into successful operations, all without departing significantly from the Holiness or Pentecostal script.

The mid-1950s were an exciting time for Bronzeville churches of all varieties. Congregations were growing, debts were being paid, and churches everywhere seemed to be moving into larger, more elaborate facilities: the shouters as well as the elite. . . .

Bronzeville no longer exists. That is not merely because no one would use such a name anymore, but because most of the buildings that comprised the neighborhood have long since been leveled. With the completion in 1962 of Robert Taylor Homes, the nation's largest public housing project and quite possibly its most squalid, the area once called Bronzeville ceased to run the gamut from worn-out but respectable apartment buildings to gruesome kitchenettes. It became a much more uniform high-rise slum, punctuated every half-mile or so by decrepit commercial strips, hosting intermittent taverns, barbecues, and convenience stores and suggesting only a remnant of the much more thriving business streets that once existed.

Bronzeville is long gone not only physically but socially; it passed out of existence as a community as soon as the middle class left, which was as soon as it was permitted to leave with the lifting of segregation. By 1960, the middle-class exodus had already begun, and by 1970, it was virtually complete. Thousands of families who had been the pillars of Bronzeville society returned at most once a week, for church on Sunday.

So much has been written about the impact of middle-class departure on the life of the ghetto that it seems unnecessary to belabor the point. Perhaps it is sufficient to say that Bronzeville was a community unique in America, that its uniqueness depended on the presence of people from all classes and with all sorts of values, living and struggling together, and that with the disappearance of that diversity, the community could not have continued to exist, even if there had been no physical changes at all.

In thinking about what has disappeared, however, there is no shortage of ironies to ponder. The policy racket is legal now, run neither by local black gamblers nor by the Mafia but by the state of Illinois, which calls it a lottery. The game that was once considered an emblem of sin by much of white Chicago is now depended upon as a contributor to the financing of public education. Policy is merely a business now, managed by a colorless bureaucracy far away — it is no longer a cult or a neighborhood institution. There is no demand for dream books anymore on the South Side, no circus-like drawings in crowded basements with a light over the entrance. People play the legal numbers game with a humorless compulsiveness that has little in common with the old-fashioned emotional experience.   40

Legal businesses have fared almost as badly as illegal ones. Notwithstanding Earl Dickerson's prediction that Supreme Liberty Life would thrive under integration to become a billion-dollar insurance business by the end of the century, the company was simply absorbed into United of America, becoming a piece of a gigantic white institution, and a rather small and inconspicuous piece at that. Not that there was anything racist about such a consolidation; plenty of smaller white-owned insurance companies suffered the same fate. But the cumulative effect on black economic life was powerful: the old life insurance companies were the one significant engine of capital in Chicago's black community, and by 1990, not a single firm was left.

The *Chicago Defender* remains in business at the same location it occupied in the 1950s, published by the same man, John Sengstacke. But it never really found a coherent role to play as a voice of its people in an integrated city. Once the white newspapers began printing news about blacks on the South Side, the paper lost its franchise as virtually the sole source of information within the community. It played a surprisingly passive role in the civil rights confrontations of the 1960s, serving neither as a conspicuous engine of militant activism nor as a persistent critic. By the 1970s, the *Defender* had essentially been superseded as a forum for political debate by the plethora of black radio stations that had sprung up on the South Side. The Bud Billiken parade is still held each summer in Washington Park, attracting a huge contingent of Chicago politicians, white as well as black, but it is no longer the signature event of a powerful black journalistic institution: it is a reminder of the influence that institution once had.

Of all the fixtures of Bronzeville life, the churches come the closest to having survived in recognizable form. Olivet Baptist stands as an impressive edifice at Thirty-first Street and King Drive, its front lawn dominated by a statue of the Reverend J. H. Jackson, pugnacious in stone as he was in life, along with quotations from some of his sermons and praise for him from around the world. Olivet, South Park Baptist, and some of the other Bronzeville churches still turn out crowds at services on Sunday morning, attracting families who return from the far South Side and the suburbs, senior citizens who have remained in the neighborhood, and a sprinkling of children and adults from the projects nearby.

Some of the churches still maintain choirs, Sunday schools, Bible study groups, and social outreach programs, struggling rather heroically against the social disorganization that is all around them. But they have ceased to be voices of clear authority. No preacher can deliver instruction and expect compliance in the way that J. H. Jackson could in his prime. And while sin remains a familiar topic in the South Side black churches on Sundays — a more important topic than at St. Nick's or Elmhurst Presbyterian — the subject no longer has the hold over its listeners that it had a generation ago.

Only in politics can one really argue that Bronzeville has gained more than   45
it has lost. William L. Dawson was a power broker and even a role model of sorts, but he was a leader whose rewards from the white machine were disappointingly meager, somehow not commensurate with the job he did in guaranteeing the election of Richard J. Daley and other white politicians. Dawson's machine yielded in the 1980s to something truly remarkable — a citywide coalition that made possible the election of Harold Washington as the city's first black mayor. Washington's victory in 1983, in a campaign with "Our Turn" as its most conspicuous slogan, was a psychological triumph far beyond anything the old Dawson organization could possibly accomplish, perhaps beyond anything blacks had experienced in any American city. And while the extent of Washington's tangible achievements in office can be debated, the fact that he died in 1987 with his heroic status in the black community intact, and his respect growing even among whites, represented a victory comparable in its way to the first one.

Black political power in Chicago, however, seemed to disappear almost as suddenly as it emerged. Ten years after Washington's first election, Chicago was again being governed by a white mayor, Richard M. Daley, son of the old boss, and by a majority coalition in which Hispanics, not blacks, were the significant minority partner. Meanwhile, the black community was deeply divided over whom to follow and how to proceed, seemingly years away from the level of influence it had had in city politics in the mid-1980s.

In the black community, unlike the white working-class neighborhoods or white suburbia, it may seem perverse — or at least misleading — to dwell on the losses of the past generation. At the individual level, there have been so many gains — in personal freedom, in job opportunities, in income. Today's black middle class is far larger in proportional terms than the one that existed in Bronzeville in the 1950s, much of it living comfortably in neighborhoods scattered all across the Chicago metropolitan area.

When it comes to community institutions, however, the losses are no less real for Chicago's blacks than for white ethnics or for the split-level suburbanites of the 1950s generation. If anything, they are more real. Nearly all of the things that gave texture and coherence to life in Bronzeville, demeaning as that life often was, are simply not reproducible in the freer, more individualistic, more bewildering world of the 1990s.   *[1995]*

≡ **THINKING ABOUT THE TEXT**

1. Does reading these passages from Ehrenhalt's book make you think differently about any of the events and characters in *A Raisin in the Sun?* Why, or why not?

2. To what extent does the neighborhood described by Ehrenhalt resemble where you grew up? Identify specific similarities and differences.

3. Note Ehrenhalt's last sentence. While he recognizes that Bronzeville was segregated, evidently he feels some regret over its passing, mourning in particular what he sees as the death of its community spirit. Does his attitude make sense to you? Explain your reasoning. What do you think he might say about the Younger family's decision to leave the neighborhood? How much does it matter to you that this historian of Bronzeville is white?

SIDNEY POITIER
From *The Measure of a Man: A Spiritual Autobiography*

Raised in the Bahamas, Sidney Poitier (b. 1927) became the leading African American film star of his generation. For his 1963 movie Lilies of the Field, *he won the Academy Award for best actor, the first African American to do so. He has also acted in such important films as* The Blackboard Jungle *(1955),* The Defiant Ones *(1958),* A Patch of Blue *(1965),* Guess Who's Coming to Dinner *(1967),* In the Heat of the Night *(1967),* To Sir, With Love *(1967), and* A Raisin in the Sun *(1961), where he again portrayed Walter Lee Younger, his role in the play's original production. In the following excerpt from his memoir,* The Measure of a Man: A Spiritual Autobiography *(2000; selected by Oprah's Book Club in 2007), Poitier recalls that first staging, especially his struggle in getting other members of the company to accept his view of the play.*

I finished a six-month run, but by the time I left the production the actress who played the mother wasn't speaking to me. She hated me. Need I tell you that this is a difficult position to find yourself in as the member of an ensemble of actors?

Claudia McNeil, a fine performer, was in complete dominance over most of the other members of the cast. Naturally enough, she perceived the play as being best when it unfolded from the mother's point of view. *I* perceived the play as being best when it unfolded from the son's point of view, however, and I argued that position. In fact, we argued constantly.

I prevailed, I guess because I was considered the principal player who was responsible for getting the piece mounted. I suppose there might have been some who didn't agree with me but simply acquiesced to my position. But I wasn't just throwing my weight around. I was not, and am not, in the habit of doing that. I genuinely felt that when tragedy fell on the family in *Raisin*, the most devastating effects were visited upon the son, because the mother was such a towering figure.

In my opinion, it was the son who carried the theatrical obligation as the force between the audience and the play. The eyes of those watching were on the son to see if the tragedy would destroy him, would blow him apart beyond recovery. And it was also my opinion that there was no such feeling between the audience and the mother. The audience witnessed the sadness that was visited on her. They saw that her family was in disarray, but they also saw her as a force beyond that kind of vulnerability. If they were to vote, they would say, "Oh, but she's going to be okay."

So where's the drama in the piece?   5

The drama asks an audience to *care*. This was my argument to the playwright and the director and the producer, all of whom were my friends. If you're going to ask that audience to care, you're going to have to take them to the place where the most damage is possible so they can feel that pain.

If you keep them focused on the mother, they're going to say, "Oh, that's too bad that happened — but listen, that family's going to be okay."

Well, I had learned in my experience as an actor and as a theater participant that wherever there's threatened destruction of a human being, that's where the focus is; and the only existence that was threatened in *Raisin* was the son's. There was simply no guarantee that he would survive. It was fifty-fifty that this boy couldn't do it, wouldn't be able to bounce back. It was highly probable that he wouldn't have the resilience, the guts, the stamina, or the determination. Or, looked at another way, it was possible that he wouldn't be able to experience the catharsis as fully as necessary for him to be reborn. That's what the audience had to see to be fully engaged: the rebirth of this person.

Now, there was no ego in that. I mean, I was a theater person. I had spent most of my early years in theater — not on Broadway necessarily, but I had done many, many off-Broadway shows. I'd seen dozens and dozens of plays, I'd *worked* in dozens of plays, so I felt comfortable in my sense of what drama is made of, both in theatrical terms and in life terms.

So that was my position, and I was fought tooth and nail on it by the direc-   10
tor and the writer and the producer. Ruby Dee and I saw more eye to eye than did either of us with the others, so it was my intent, and she concurred, that I would play the drama on opening night the way I believed it *should* be played. That didn't require changing the words, only making a fundamental change in the attitude of the individual.

Now, this gets to the very core of what acting is. How do you shift the emphasis of a play when, as is the case in *A Raisin in the Sun*, there are two characters who are very forceful and quite strong? Here's how: if you see the son's need as not just personal but a need on behalf of his family, then the emotional center shifts, and it becomes a different play.

The action of the play turns on the death of the father, and the fact that the mother receives ten thousand dollars in insurance money because her husband was killed in an accident on the job. The son wants to use the money in the most constructive way he can think of, which is to start a business, to move the family in some structural way up from where they are.

The mother, on the other hand, wants to use the money to buy a house. But the son says to her, in effect, "The money used to buy a house wouldn't affect the family circumstances in that I'd still chauffeur for somebody else, my wife still works as a maid, and you'd still work as a maid. There'd be no shifting of dynamics here. But there could be, with some sweat and tears, there could be some shifting of dynamics if that money were used as down payment for a business that we could all work at. Then in two years or five years, what we'd have done would be substantial enough for us to be thinking about getting a house and, hopefully, then the business would grow and we could have two such businesses or three such businesses in ten years by the time my son is ready for college."

That's his argument, and the mother's argument runs something like, "You want to spend that money to open a liquor store?" She insists, "My husband's memory is not going to be tied in with the selling of liquor. I'm going to use that money to buy a house, to put a roof over our heads."

He says to his mother, "Isn't it better that my father's death advances the   15
family? You have a daughter who's going off to college, hopefully, but where is the money coming from? I have a son who is going to be soon a young man. What are the lessons in this for him? I am a chauffeur. Where are we going to be down the line? Am I going to be a chauffeur at the age of sixty, and is my son going to take over chauffeuring?"

So that's the heart of it. Therefore, the playing of this man has to be such that the audience believes that his need for his family is absolutely elemental, and that this is the last chance, *his* last chance. If he fails now, he'll never be able to gather the steam, gather the courage and the determination to spend himself again in a losing effort. He just won't be able to.

It's this sense of possible destruction that prepares the audience for tragedy when the mother *does* give him the money, after he really fights and struggles for it, and the money is lost. All of it.

The audience is primed to see either total destruction of this man or his resurrection, you follow? But there's no resurrection for the mother, regardless. She gives the money to her son because she finally decides to let him have his shot at being a man, his own man — and then he fucks it up. Well, sad as it might be for her as a mother, there's no great tragedy in that for her as an individual. She loses ten grand that she didn't really have in the first place.

But this young man — he's destroyed. That's what the audience assumes. But in the third act he comes out of the ashes, and that's where the real drama is, because he looks at that boy of his, and he talks to him. In fact, he's talking to the audience *through* the boy; and when he speaks, the audience just goes nuts. I mean, it's so *dramatic*.

Well, that was my position — the position I acted from. The other position,   20
as I said, was held very strongly by the actress who played the mother, as well as by the producer, the director, and the playwright — my friends. When I left

the fold to go make movies and they had to replace me, the several men who, over time, took the part had to play it the other way, the mother's way, because the continued success of the play depended on having Claudia McNeil.

Well, the audiences didn't seem to mind one bit. The play continued to work well because it had garnered such recognition by then. And the guys who took over the part were all very fine actors, all extremely fine actors, one of whom was Ruby Dee's husband, Ossie Davis.

So what was the lesson in all this?

I would say that sometimes convictions firmly held can cost more than we're willing to pay. And irrevocable change occurs when we're not up to paying, and irrevocable change occurs when we *are* up to paying. Either way, we have to live with the consequences. If I'm up to paying the price in a certain situation, I walk away from the experience with some kind of self-respect because I took the heat. And if I go the other way, feeling that the cost is too high, then however bright the situation turns out, I feel that something is missing.

For an actor to go onstage every night with the sort of hostile undercurrent we experienced with *A Raisin in the Sun* — it can only be described as being like a bad marriage. I felt that Claudia McNeil wasn't giving me what I needed. She knew where my big moments were, and she knew when to hold back and take the air out — and I lived through that opposition for months.

It was very painful for me to know the effect our disagreement was having on my colleagues. If you're a producer, certainly you're irritated by dissension that threatens to interrupt the life of a hit play. Now, my friend Philip Rose, the producer, disagreed with me completely, and I believe that his disagreement was genuine, because I've known the man all these years, and today he's still one of my closest friends. But at the time, I was leaving his play. He had a play that would run, if he could hold it together and keep Claudia McNeil happy, for years and years. So he wasn't especially sympathetic to my concerns.

The playwright's sympathies were completely against me. She saw the play as weighted toward the mother; that's how she'd *written* it. She was a very intelligent young black woman, and she came from a family of achievers. Her whole family were achievers, especially the women, and she had a certain mindset about women and their potential, especially black women in America. So she wrote a play about a matriarch faced with this dilemma. But in that formulation the son is just a ne'er-do-well. He's a fuckup, not a tragic figure, not a man whose life is on the line. I simply couldn't do it that way, because in my mind the dramatic possibilities were so much greater the other way.

Then, of course, there was the director, Lloyd Richards. Again, a very close friend with whom I had very little quarrel on the question, because his first responsibility was to the work by the playwright. He had gone inside the play with her; she had taken him on an excursion into the inner selves of these characters. So he saw the play as she conceived it, and when he put it together, he put it together that way. He didn't have any conflict with it. But I did — because I had to face an audience, you know? — and I just couldn't face an audience playing it with less than the attitude I thought was necessary for this drama.

25

Out of town in New Haven I played it their way, but I was looking for answers. I wasn't altogether comfortable. We went on to Philadelphia. Same thing. The play was working fine, but there was something missing. It was working overall, but I wasn't really there. We went to Chicago. Same thing. So Ruby Dee and I started exploring, and in Chicago magic started to happen. Wham! And I started to play differently.

Then we went to New York, and on opening night the energy was at its apex. The director saw it, but he wouldn't characterize the added excitement he sensed as coming from the way I had played the role. The producer saw it too, but he said it was just a great night. The playwright was in the audience, and I went out and helped her up on the stage so that all the world could see this magnificent young woman, this gifted person. She assumed that the incredible night of theater we'd all just experienced was as she wrote it.

Well, I say it played well because there was something special in the conviction I held, and I carried it from Chicago to New York.   30

There's a special moment in the third act, just before the end. They had put a down payment on a house before they lost the money, but a man comes to tell them that they're not wanted in that neighborhood. My character, the son, has to stand up and talk to this man. He's talking to this man about his family. After a given point in the speech, he says, "This is my mother." Then he says, "This is my sister." And then he says. "This is my wife, — and she is" — pride, pain, and love overpower him and he's not able to get her name out. And by the time he turns to his son, his emotions are more than any words could express. The tears roll down his cheeks and he begins to cry. He gestures to the boy, but the words won't come out, and finally he forces out the words. He says, "This is my son," and the house goes nuts, you hear me?

I know from my own experience that when a guy is just afraid, and he wishes to succeed *because he's afraid of failure*, that's not much of a commitment. But there's another kind of drive to succeed. I think of my father, going from bar to bar selling his cigars, probing my arm because he's worried that I'm not getting enough to eat. Then sitting down to write a letter to his eldest son, telling him that he's no longer able to control and guide his youngest, that he needs help. You find a man like that, with a need to do something that's over and above his own ego-requirement — a need that's for his *family*, as he sees it — and you get every ounce of his energy. When a man says, "This is for my *child*," you get over and above that which he thinks he's capable of.

My father was with me every moment as I performed in *A Raisin in the Sun*. The themes, too, seemed like so many threads from my own life. The days in Nassau and Miami and New York when I seemed to be in such a downward spiral and there was no promise of resurrection. All the risks I took, all the brushes with destruction. I know how much it pained my family, but there was nothing they could do. It was this art form that saved me. Ultimately, by taking even greater risks — by going to New York and then by choosing a life in the theater — I came through. And it wasn't just for myself. It was for Reggie too.   *[2000]*

≡ THINKING ABOUT THE TEXT

1. Poitier's experience with the play was very much that of an actor involved in performing it. Does his account make you aware of anything that you did not realize when you simply *read* the play? If so, what?

2. Poitier reports that even the author, Lorraine Hansberry, disagreed with his view of the play. In such cases, do you think the performer should usually defer to the playwright? Why, or why not?

3. Does Poitier succeed in persuading you that his view of the play made more sense than its rival? Specify things that affect your response to his argument.

≡ WRITING ABOUT ISSUES

1. Choose a particular moment in *A Raisin in the Sun* when characters disagree. Then write an essay analyzing their disagreement. More specifically, identify the different positions they take, the warrants or assumptions that seem to underlie their positions, the outcome of their disagreement, your own evaluation of their views, and the relationship of this moment to the rest of the play. Be sure to quote from the text.

2. Imagine that Hansberry's play is being republished and that you are asked to edit it. Imagine further that the publisher asks you to introduce the play with one of the four background documents in this cluster. Write an essay stating which document you would choose and why.

3. Choose a family you know well, and write an essay comparing it with the Younger family. Above all, consider whether your chosen family, too, has conflicting dreams.

4. Spend time in the library examining newspapers and magazines from 1959, the year *A Raisin in the Sun* opened on Broadway. In particular, try to identify a variety of events and trends that might have affected an American family that year. Next, imagine a specific American family living in 1959. Finally, write an essay describing a play that might be written about your imagined family's reaction to a specific event or trend back then. Give details of the plot, the family's social background, and its members' personalities. If you wish, present some dialogue.

RUTH REICHL, "The Queen of Mold"

DAVID SEDARIS, "Tasteless"

CHANG RAE LEE, "Coming Home Again"

Food occupies a ubiquitous and central place in the customs and rituals of all cultures. If the pragmatic reasons are obvious, perhaps the innumerable variations in the types of food and the complex and often inscrutable manner of its consumption are not so clear. Professionally trained anthropologists believe you can tell a lot about a culture by studying its eating habits, but even casual observers know that what you eat and how you eat it are windows into personality. And we all have stories of how we first encounter food. Perhaps some of the earliest stories we can remember revolve around our behavior at the family dinner table. As a source of despair or pleasure, these memories form many of the narratives we tell about ourselves over a lifetime. It is no wonder then, that memoirists tell many stories about how food shaped their lives. In the three selections here, one is by a noted food critic, one by an acclaimed humorist, and the other by a well-received novelist. All three offer interesting and insightful accounts of how food influenced their lives.

■ BEFORE YOU READ

In one way or another, food is part of the stories all families tell. Recall stories you've heard someone in your family tell or perhaps ones you've told yourself. What do these stories say about your family or about your view of your family?

RUTH REICHL
The Queen of Mold

Ruth Reichl (b. 1948), one of America's most famous food writers, was born in Greenwich Village in New York City. She graduated from the University of Michigan in 1970 with an M.A. in art history. She and her husband moved to Berkeley, California, and took part in the culinary revolution happening there. She became the food and restaurant critic for the Los Angeles Times *and later the* New York Times. *She has won the James Beard Award (restaurant criticism's highest honor) four times. Her most recent paperback is* For you, Mom. Finally. *(2009). The following is taken from her successful first memoir,* Tender at the Bone: Growing Up at the Table *(1998).*

This is a true story.

Imagine a New York City apartment at six in the morning. It is a modest apartment in Greenwich Village. Coffee is bubbling in an electric percolator. On the table is a basket of rye bread, an entire coffee cake, a few cheeses, a platter of cold cuts. My mother has been making breakfast—a major meal in our house, one where we sit down to fresh orange juice every morning, clink our glasses as if they held wine, and toast each other with "Cheerio. Have a nice day."

Right now she is the only one awake, but she is getting impatient for the day to begin and she cranks WQXR up a little louder on the radio, hoping that the noise will rouse everyone else. But Dad and I are good sleepers, and when the sounds of martial music have no effect she barges into the bedroom and shakes my father awake.

"Darling," she says, "I need you. Get up and come into the kitchen."

My father, a sweet and accommodating person, shuffles sleepily down the   5
hall. He is wearing loose pajamas, and the strand of hair he combs over his bald spot stands straight up. He leans against the sink, holding on to it a little, and obediently opens his mouth when my mother says, "Try this."

Later, when he told the story, he attempted to convey the awfulness of what she had given him. The first time he said that it tasted like cat toes and rotted barley, but over the years the description got better. Two years later it had turned into pigs' snouts and mud and five years later he had refined the flavor into a mixture of antique anchovies and moldy chocolate.

Whatever it tasted like, he said it was the worst thing he had ever had in his mouth, so terrible that it was impossible to swallow, so terrible that he leaned over and spit it into the sink and then grabbed the coffeepot, put the spout into his mouth, and tried to eradicate the flavor.

My mother stood there watching all this. When my father finally put the coffeepot down she smiled and said, "Just as I thought. Spoiled!"

And then she threw the mess into the garbage can and sat down to drink her orange juice.

For the longest time I thought I had made this story up. But my brother insists   10
that my father told it often, and with a certain amount of pride. As far as I know, my mother was never embarrassed by the telling, never even knew that she should have been. It was just the way she was.

Which was taste-blind and unafraid of rot. "Oh, it's just a little mold," I can remember her saying on the many occasions she scraped the fuzzy blue stuff off some concoction before serving what was left for dinner. She had an iron stomach and was incapable of understanding that other people did not.

This taught me many things. The first was that food could be dangerous, especially to those who loved it. I took this very seriously. My parents entertained a great deal, and before I was ten I had appointed myself guardian of the guests. My mission was to keep Mom from killing anybody who came to dinner.

Her friends seemed surprisingly unaware that they took their lives in their hands each time they ate with us. They chalked their ailments up to the weather, the flu, or one of my mother's more unusual dishes. "No more sea urchins for me," I imagined Burt Langner saying to his wife, Ruth, after a dinner at our house, "they just don't agree with me." Little did he know that it was not the sea urchins that had made him ill, but that bargain beef my mother had found so irresistible.

"I can make a meal out of anything," Mom told her friends proudly. She liked to brag about "Everything Stew," a dish invented while she was concocting a casserole out of a two-week-old turkey carcass. (The very fact that my mother confessed to cooking with two-week-old turkey says a lot about her.) She put the turkey and a half can of mushroom soup into the pot. Then she began rummaging around in the refrigerator. She found some leftover broccoli and added that. A few carrots went in, and then a half carton of sour cream. In a hurry, as usual, she added green beans and cranberry sauce. And then, somehow, half an apple pie slipped into the dish. Mom looked momentarily horrified. Then she shrugged and said, "Who knows? Maybe it will be good." And she began throwing everything in the refrigerator in along with it—leftover pâté, some cheese ends, a few squishy tomatoes.

That night I set up camp in the dining room. I was particularly worried   15
about the big eaters, and I stared at my favorite people as they approached the buffet, willing them away from the casserole. I actually stood directly in front of Burt Langner so he couldn't reach the turkey disaster. I loved him, and I knew that he loved food.

Unknowingly I had started sorting people by their tastes. Like a hearing child born to deaf parents, I was shaped by my mother's handicap, discovering that food could be a way of making sense of the world.

At first I paid attention only to taste, storing away the knowledge that my father preferred salt to sugar and my mother had a sweet tooth. Later I also began to note how people ate, and where. My brother liked fancy food in fine surroundings, my father only cared about the company, and Mom would eat anything so long as the location was exotic. I was slowly discovering that if you watched people as they ate, you could find out who they were.

Then I began listening to the way people talked about food, looking for clues to their personalities. "What is she really saying?" I asked myself when Mom bragged about the invention of her famous corned beef ham.

"I was giving a party," she'd begin, "and as usual I left everything for the last minute." Here she'd look at her audience, laughing softly at herself. "I asked Ernst to do the shopping, but you know how absentminded he is! Instead of picking up a ham he brought me corned beef." She'd look pointedly at Dad, who would look properly sheepish.

"What could I do?" Mom asked. "I had people coming in a couple of hours.   20
I had no choice. I simply pretended it was a ham." With that Dad would look admiringly at my mother, pick up his carving knife, and start serving the masterpiece.   *[1998]*

MIRIAM REICHL'S CORNED BEEF HAM

4 pounds whole corned beef	¼ cup brown sugar
5 bay leaves	Whole cloves
1 onion, chopped	1 can (1 pound 15 ounces)
1 tablespoon prepared mustard	spiced peaches

Cover corned beef with water in a large pot. Add bay leaves and onion. Cook over medium heat about 3 hours, until meat is very tender.

While meat is cooking, mix mustard and brown sugar.

Preheat oven to 325°.

Take meat from water and remove all visible fat. Insert cloves into meat as if it were ham. Cover the meat with the mustard mixture and bake 1 hour, basting frequently with the peach syrup.

Surround meat with spiced peaches and serve.

Serves 6.

≡ THINKING ABOUT THE TEXT

1. What does Reichl's father's changing description tell you about the nature of many details in memoirs?

2. How would you unpack the comment Reichl makes about her mother: "It was just the way she was" (para. 10)?

3. Why is "The Queen of Mold" an appropriate title for this brief essay?

4. What do you think Reichl means when she says, "I was shaped by my mother's handicap, discovering that food could be a way of making sense of the world" (para. 16)? Give an example of this from your own experience.

5. What does the final anecdote say about Reichl's parents?

DAVID SEDARIS

Tasteless

David Sedaris (b. 1956) is one of America's most famous humorists. His books have sold seven million copies. Sedaris was born in Binghamton, New York, and grew up in Raleigh, North Carolina. He graduated from the School of the Art Institute of Chicago in 1987. While he was performing in a Chicago club, he was discovered by Ira Glass, current host of the National Public Radio program This American Life. *Sedaris's radio essays made him famous. His first book of stories and essays,* Barrel Fever, *was published in 1994. In 2001,* Time *magazine named him "Humorist of the Year."* Dress Your Family in Corduroy and Denim *rose to number one on the* New York Times *nonfiction best-seller list in June 2004. Sedaris's most recent book,* Let's Explore Diabetes with Owls, *was published in April 2013.*

One of the things they promise when you quit smoking is that food will regain its flavor. Taste buds paved beneath decades of tar will spring back to life, and an entire sense will be restored. I thought it would be like putting on a pair of glasses — something dramatic that makes you say, "Whoa!" — but it's been six months now, and I have yet to notice any significant change.

Part of the problem might be me. I've always been in touch with my stomach, but my mouth and I don't really speak. Oh, it chews all right. It helps me form words and holds stuff when my hands are full, but it doesn't do any of these things very well. It's third-rate at best—fifth if you take my teeth into consideration.

Even before I started smoking, I was not a remarkably attentive eater. "Great fried fish," I'd say to my mother, only to discover that I was eating a chicken breast or, just as likely, a veal cutlet. She might as well have done away with names and identified our meals by color: "Golden brown." "Red." "Beige with some pink in it."

I am a shoveller, a quantity man, and I like to keep going until I feel sick. It's how a prisoner might eat, one arm maneuvering the fork and the other encircling the plate like a fence: head lowered close to my food, eyes darting this way and that; even if I don't particularly like it, it's *mine*, God damn it.

Some of this has to do with coming from a large family. Always afraid that   5
I wouldn't get enough, I'd start worrying about more long before I finished what was in front of me. We'd be at the dinner table, and, convict-like, out of one side of my mouth, I'd whisper to my sister Amy.

"What'll you take for that chicken leg?"

"You mean my barbecued rib?"

"Call it what you like, just give me your asking price."

"Oh gosh," she'd say. "A quarter?"

"Twenty-five cents! What do you think this is—a restaurant?"   10

She'd raise the baton of meat to her face and examine it for flaws. "A dime."

"A nickel," I'd say, and before she could argue I'd have snatched it away.

I should have been enormous, the size of a panda, but I think that the fear of going without—the anxiety that this produced—acted like a kind of furnace, and burned off the calories before I could gain weight. Even after learning how to make my own meals, I remained, if not skinny, then at least average. My older sister Lisa and I were in elementary school when our mother bought us our first cookbook. The recipes were fairly simple—lots of Jell-O-based desserts and a wheel-shaped meat loaf cooked in an angel-food-cake pan. This last one was miraculous to me. "A meat loaf—with a hole in it!" I kept saying. I guess I thought that as it baked the cavity would fill itself with rubies or butterscotch pudding. How else to explain my disappointment the first dozen times I made it?

In high school, I started cooking pizzas—"from scratch," I liked to say, "the ol' fashioned way." On Saturday afternoons, I'd make my dough, place it in a cloth-covered bowl, and set it in the linen closet to rise. We'd have our dinner at seven or so, and four hours later, just as "Shock Theater," our local horror-movie program, came on, I'd put my pizzas in the oven. It might have been all right if this were just *part* of my evening, but it was everything: all I knew about being young had canned Parmesan cheese on it. While my classmates were taking acid and having sex in their cars, I was arranging sausage buttons and sliced peppers into smiley faces.

"The next one should look mad," my younger brother would say. And, as 15
proof of my versatility, I would create a frown.

To make it all that much sadder, things never got any better than this.
Never again would I take so many chances or feel such giddy confidence in my
abilities. This is not to say that I stopped cooking, just that I stopped trying.

Between the year that I left my parents' house and the year that I met
Hugh, I made myself dinner just about every night. I generally alternated between three or four simple meals, but if forced to name my signature dish I'd
probably have gone with my Chicken and Linguine with Grease on It. I don't
know that I ever had an actual recipe; rather, like my Steak and Linguine with
Blood on It, I just sort of played it by ear. The good thing about those meals was
that they had only two ingredients. Anything more than that and I'm like
Hugh's mother buying Christmas presents. "I look at the list, I go to the store,
and then I just freeze," she says.

I suggest that it's nothing to get worked up about, and see in her eyes the
look I give when someone says, "It's only a dinner party," or "Can we have
something *with* the Chicken and Linguine with Grease on It?"

I cook for myself when I'm alone; otherwise, Hugh takes care of it, and
happily, too. People tell me that he's a real chef, and something about the way
they say it, a tone of respect and envy, leads me to believe them. I know that the
dinners he prepares are correct. If something is supposed to be hot, it is. If it
looks rust-colored in pictures, it looks rust-colored on the plate. I'm always
happy to eat Hugh's cooking, but when it comes to truly tasting, to discerning
the subtleties I hear others talking about, it's as if my tongue were wearing a
mitten.

That's why fine restaurants are wasted on me. I suppose I can appreciate 20
the lighting, or the speed with which my water glass is refilled, but, as far as the
food is concerned, if I can't distinguish between a peach and an apricot I really
can't tell the difference between an excellent truffle and a mediocre one. Then,
too, the more you pay the less they generally give you to eat. French friends
visiting the United States are floored by the size of the portions. "Plates the size
of hubcaps!" they cry. "No wonder the Americans are so fat."

"I know," I say. "Isn't it awful?" Then I think of Claim Jumper, a California-
based chain that serves a massive hamburger called the Widow Maker. I ordered a side of creamed spinach there, and it came in what looked like a mixing
bowl. It was like being miniaturized, shrunk to the height of a leprechaun or a
doll and dropped in the dining room of regular-sized people. Even the salt and
pepper shakers seemed enormous. I ate at Claim Jumper only once, and it was
the first time in years that I didn't corral my plate. For starters, my arm wasn't
long enough, but even if it had been I wouldn't have felt the need. There was
plenty to go around, some of it brown, some of it green, and some a color I've
come to think of, almost dreamily, as enough. *[2013]*

≡ **THINKING ABOUT THE TEXT**

1. What does Sedaris claim is the result of growing up in a large family? Is this meant to be taken at face value or is he being hyperbolic for humorous effect?

2. What is the relationship between the opening two paragraphs and the closing sentence?

3. Sedaris is noted for his humor. Point out two or three places where you think he is deliberately funny. How does this increase or decrease the content of the text?

4. What is the effect of Sedaris's self-deprecating humor? Does it increase or decrease his narrative persona?

5. What is the point of his anecdote about his partner's mother? Is being a good cook a matter of attitude or personality? What answer does the story suggest?

≡ **MAKING COMPARISONS**

1. Compare the attitudes of both narrators toward cooking as a child.

2. How would Sedaris as a child have fared if he'd had Reichl's mother?

3. Compare the significance of the titles in each memoir.

CHANG RAE LEE
Coming Home Again

Chang Rae Lee (b.1965) was born in South Korea. He came to the United States shortly thereafter and was raised in Westchester County, a suburb outside New York City. He graduated from Yale University and has an M.F.A. in writing from the University of Oregon. His first novel, Native Speaker *(1995), won the prestigious PEN/Hemingway Award.* A Gesture Life *(1999) was also critically acclaimed. His novel* The Surrendered *(2010) was a finalist for the Pulitzer Prize for fiction. His latest novel is* On Such a Full Sea, *published in 2014.*

When my mother began using the electronic pump that fed her liquids and medication, we moved her to the family room. The bedroom she shared with my father was upstairs, and it was impossible to carry the machine up and down all day and night. The pump itself was attached to a metal stand on casters, and she pulled it along wherever she went. From anywhere in the house, you could hear the sound of the wheels clicking out a steady time over the grout lines of the slate-tiled foyer, her main thoroughfare to the bathroom and the kitchen. Sometimes you would hear her halt after only a few steps, to catch her breath or steady her balance, and whatever you were doing was instantly suspended by a pall of silence.

I was usually in the kitchen, preparing lunch or dinner, poised over the butcher block with her favorite chef's knife in my hand and her old yellow apron slung around my neck. I'd be breathless in the sudden quiet, and, having ceased my mincing and chopping, would stare blankly at the brushed sheen of the blade. Eventually, she would clear her throat or call out to say she was fine, then begin to move again, starting her rhythmic *ka-jug*; and only then could I go on with my cooking, the world of our house turning once more, wheeling through the black.

I wasn't cooking for my mother but for the rest of us. When she first moved downstairs she was still eating, though scantily, more just to taste what we were having than from any genuine desire for food. The point was simply to sit together at the kitchen table and array ourselves like a family again. My mother would gently set herself down in her customary chair near the stove. I sat across from her, my father and sister to my left and right, and crammed in the center was all the food I had made—a spicy codfish stew, say, or a casserole of gingery beef, dishes that in my youth she had prepared for us a hundred times.

It had been ten years since we'd all lived together in the house, which at fifteen I had left to attend boarding school in New Hampshire. My mother would sometimes point this out, by speaking of our present time as being "just like before Exeter," which surprised me, given how proud she always was that I was a graduate of the school.

My going to such a place was part of my mother's not so secret plan to change my character, which she worried was becoming too much like hers. I was clever and able enough, but without outside pressure I was readily given to sloth and vanity. The famous school—which none of us knew the first thing about—would prove my mettle. She was right, of course, and while I was there I would falter more than a few times, academically and otherwise. But I never thought that my leaving home then would ever be a problem for her, a private quarrel she would have even as her life waned.

Now her house was full again. My sister had just resigned from her job in New York City, and my father, who typically saw his psychiatric patients until eight or nine in the evening, was appearing in the driveway at four-thirty. I had been living at home for nearly a year and was in the final push of work on what would prove a dismal failure of a novel. When I wasn't struggling over my prose, I kept occupied with the things she usually did—the daily errands, the grocery shopping, the vacuuming and the cleaning, and, of course, all the cooking.

When I was six or seven years old, I used to watch my mother as she prepared our favorite meals. It was one of my daily pleasures. She shooed me away in the beginning, telling me that the kitchen wasn't my place, and adding, in her half-proud, half-deprecating way, that her kind of work would only serve to weaken me. "Go out and play with your friends," she'd snap in Korean, "or better yet, do your reading and homework." She knew that I had already done both, and that as the evening approached there was no place to go save her small and tidy kitchen, from which the clatter of her mixing bowls and pans would ring through the house.

I would enter the kitchen quietly and stand beside her, my chin lodging upon the point of her hip. Peering through the crook of her arm, I beheld the movements of her hands. For *kalbi*, she would take up a butchered short rib in her narrow hand, the flinty bone shaped like a section of an airplane wing and deeply embedded in gristle and flesh, and with the point of her knife cut so that the bone fell away, though not completely, leaving it connected to the meat by the barest opaque layer of tendon. Then she methodically butterflied the flesh, cutting and unfolding, repeating the action until the meat lay out on her board, glistening and ready for seasoning. She scored it diagonally, then sifted sugar into the crevices with her pinched fingers, gently rubbing in the crystals. The sugar would tenderize as well as sweeten the meat. She did this with each rib, and then set them all aside in a large shallow bowl. She minced a half-dozen cloves of garlic, a stub of gingerroot, sliced up a few scallions, and spread it all over the meat. She wiped her hands and took out a bottle of sesame oil, and, after pausing for a moment, streamed the dark oil in two swift circles around the bowl. After adding a few splashes of soy sauce, she thrust her hands in and kneaded the flesh, careful not to dislodge the bones. I asked her why it mattered that they remain connected. "The meat needs the bone nearby," she said, "to borrow its richness." She wiped her hands clean of the marinade, except for her little finger, which she would flick with her tongue from time to time, because she knew that the flavor of a good dish developed not at once but in stages.

Whenever I cook, I find myself working just as she would, readying the ingredients—a mash of garlic, a julienne of red peppers, fantails of shrimp—and pilling them in little mounds about the cutting surface. My mother never left me any recipes, but this is how I learned to make her food, each dish coming not from a list or a card but from the aromatic spread of a board.

I've always thought it was particularly cruel that the cancer was in her   10
stomach and that for a long time at the end she couldn't eat. The last meal I made for her was on New Year's Eve, 1990. My sister suggested that instead of a rib roast or a bird, or the usual overflow of Korean food, we make all sorts of finger dishes that our mother might fancy and pick at.

We set the meal out on the glass coffee table in the family room. I prepared a tray of smoked-salmon canapés, fried some Korean bean cakes, and made a few other dishes I thought she might enjoy. My sister supervised me, arranging the platters, and then with some pomp carried each dish in to our parents. Finally, I brought out a bottle of champagne in a bucket of ice. My mother had moved to the sofa and was sitting up, surveying the low table. "It looks pretty nice," she said. "I think I'm feeling hungry."

This made us all feel good, especially me, for I couldn't remember the last time she had felt any hunger or had eaten something I cooked. We began to eat. My mother picked up a piece of salmon toast and took a tiny corner in her mouth. She rolled it around for a moment and then pushed it out with the tip of her tongue, letting it fall back onto her plate. She swallowed hard, as if to quell a gag, then glanced up to see if we had noticed. Of course we all had. She attempted a bean cake, some cheese, and then a slice of fruit, but nothing was any use.

She nodded at me anyway, and said, "Oh, it's very good." But I was already feeling lost and I put down my plate abruptly, nearly shattering it on the thick glass. There was an ugly pause before my father asked me in a weary, gentle voice if anything was wrong, and I answered that it was nothing, it was the last night of a long year, and we were together, and I was simply relieved. At midnight, I poured out glasses of champagne, even one for my mother, who took a deep sip. Her manner grew playful and light, and I helped her shuffle to her mattress, and she lay down in the place where in a brief week she was dead.

My mother could whip up most anything, but during our first years of living in this country we ate only Korean foods. At my haranguelike behest, my mother set herself to learning how to cook exotic American dishes. Luckily, a kind neighbor, Mrs. Churchill, a tall, florid young woman with flaxen hair, taught my mother her most trusted recipes. Mrs. Churchill's two young sons, palish, weepy boys with identical crewcuts, always accompanied her, and though I liked them well enough, I would slip away from them after a few minutes, for I knew that the real action would be in the kitchen, where their mother was playing guide. Mrs. Churchill hailed from the state of Maine, where the finest Swedish meatballs and tuna casserole and angel-food cake in America are made. She readily demonstrated certain techniques—how to layer wet sheets of pasta for a lasagna or whisk up a simple roux, for example. She often brought gift shoeboxes containing curious ingredients like dried oregano, instant yeast, and cream-of-mushroom soup. The two women, though at ease and jolly with each other, had difficulty communicating, and this was made worse by the often confusing terminology of Western cuisine ("corned beef," "devilled eggs"). Although I was just learning the language myself, I'd gladly play the interlocutor, jumping back and forth between their places at the counter, dipping my fingers into whatever sauce lay about.

I was an insistent child, and, being my mother's firstborn, much too prized. My mother could say no to me, and did often enough, but anyone who knew us—particularly my father and sister—could tell how much the denying pained her. And if I was overconscious of her indulgence even then, and suffered the rushing pangs of guilt that she could inflict upon me with the slightest wounded turn of her lip, I was too happily obtuse and venal to let her cease. She reminded me daily that I was her sole son, her reason for living, and that if she were to lose me, in either body or spirit, she wished that God would mercifully smite her down like a weak branch. 15

In the traditional fashion, she was the house accountant, the maid, the launderer, the disciplinarian, the driver, the secretary, and of course, the cook. She was also my first basketball coach. In South Korea, where girls' high-school basketball is a popular spectator sport, she had been a star, the point guard for the national high-school team that once won the all-Asia championships. I learned this one Saturday during the summer, when I asked my father if he would go down to the school yard and shoot some baskets with me. I had just finished the fifth grade, and wanted desperately to make the middle-school team the coming fall. He called for my mother and sister to come along. When we arrived, my sister immediately ran off to the swings, and I recall being annoyed that my mother wasn't following her. I dribbled clumsily around the key, on the verge of losing control of the ball, and flung a flat shot that caromed wildly off the rim. The ball bounced to my father, who took a few not so graceful dribbles and made an easy layup. He dribbled out and then drove to the hoop for a layup on the other side. He rebounded his shot and passed the ball to my mother, who had been watching us from the foul line. She turned from the basket and began heading the other way.

"Um-mah," I cried at her, my exasperation already bubbling over, "the basket's over *here!*"

After a few steps she turned around, and from where the professional three-point line must be now, she effortlessly flipped the ball up in a two-handed set shot, its flight truer and higher than I'd witnessed from any boy or man. The ball arced cleanly into the hoop, stiffly popping the chain-link net. All afternoon, she rained in shot after shot, as my father and I scrambled after her.

When we got home from the playground, my mother showed me the photograph album of her team's championship run. For years, I kept it in my room, on the same shelf that housed the scrapbooks I made of basketball stars, with magazine clippings of slick players like Bubbles Hawkins and Pistol Pete and George (the Iceman) Gervin.

It puzzled me how much she considered her own history to be immaterial,   20 and if she never patently diminished herself, she was able to finesse a kind of self-removal by speaking of my father whenever she could. She zealously recounted his excellence as a student in medical school and reminded me, each night before I started my homework, of how hard he drove himself in his work to make a life for us. She said that because of his Asian face and imperfect English, he was "working two times the American doctors." I knew that she was building him up, buttressing him with both genuine admiration and her own brand of anxious braggadocio, and that her overarching concern was that I might fail to see him as she wished me to — in the most dawning light, his pose steadfast and solitary.

In the year before I left for Exeter, I became weary of her oft-repeated accounts of my father's success. I was a teen-ager, and so ever inclined to be dismissive and bitter toward anything that had to do with family and home. Often enough, my mother was the object of my derision. Suddenly, her life seemed so small to me. She was there and sometimes, I thought, *always* there, as if she were confined to the four walls of our house. I would even complain about her cooking. Mostly, though, I was getting more and more impatient with the difficulty she encountered in doing everyday things. I was afraid for her. One day, we got into a terrible argument when she asked me to call the bank, to question a discrepancy she had discovered in the monthly statement. I asked her why she couldn't call herself. I was stupid and brutal, and I knew exactly how to wound her.

"Whom do I talk to?" she said. She would mostly speak to me in Korean, and I would answer in English.

"The bank manager, who else?"

"What do I say?"

"Whatever you want to say."   25

"Don't speak to me like that!" she cried.

"It's just that you should be able to do it yourself," I said.

"You know how I feel about this!"

"Well, maybe then you should consider it *practice*," I answered lightly, using the Korean word to make sure she understood.

Her face blanched, and her neck suddenly became rigid, as if I were throt-   30
tling her. She nearly struck me right then, but instead she bit her lip and ran upstairs. I followed her, pleading for forgiveness at her door. But it was the one time in our life that I couldn't convince her, melt her resolve with the blandishments of a spoiled son.

When my mother was feeling strong enough, or was in particularly good spirits, she would roll her machine into the kitchen and sit at the table and watch me work. She wore pajamas day and night, mostly old pairs of mine.

She said, "I can't tell, what are you making?"

"*Mahn-doo* filling."

"You didn't salt the cabbage and squash."

"Was I supposed to?"   35

"Of course. Look, it's too wet. Now the skins will get soggy before you can fry them."

"What should I do?"

"It's too late. Maybe it'll be O.K. if you work quickly. Why didn't you ask me?"

"You were finally sleeping."

"You should have woken me."   40

"No way."

She sighed, as deeply as her weary lungs would allow.

"I don't know how you were going to make it without me."

"I don't know, either. I'll remember the salt next time."

"You better. And not too much."   45

We often talked like this, our tone decidedly matter-of-fact, chin up, just this side of being able to bear it. Once, while inspecting a potato-fritter batter I was making, she asked me if she had ever done anything that I wished she hadn't done. I thought for a moment, and told her no. In the next breath, she wondered aloud if it was right of her to have let me go to Exeter, to live away from the house while I was so young. She tested the batter's thickness with her finger and called for more flour. Then she asked if, given a choice, I would go to Exeter again.

I wasn't sure what she was getting at, and I told her that I couldn't be certain, but probably, yes, I would. She snorted at this and said it was my leaving home that had once so troubled our relationship. "Remember how I had so much difficulty talking to you? Remember?"

She believed back then that I had found her more and more ignorant each time I came home. She said she never blamed me, for this was the way she knew it would be with my wonderful new education. Nothing I could say seemed to quell the notion. But I knew that the problem wasn't simply the *education*; the first time I saw her again after starting school, barely six weeks later, when she and my father visited me on Parents Day, she had already grown nervous and distant. After the usual campus events, we had gone to the motel where they were staying in a nearby town and sat on the beds in our room. She seemed to sneak looks at me, as though I might discover a horrible new truth if our eyes should meet.

My own secret feeling was that I had missed my parents greatly, my mother especially, and much more than I had anticipated. I couldn't tell them that these first weeks were a mere blur to me, that I felt completely overwhelmed by all the studies and my much brighter friends and the thousand irritating details of living alone, and that I had really learned nothing, save perhaps how to put on a necktie while sprinting to class. I felt as if I had plunged too deep into the world, which, to my great horror, was much larger than I had ever imagined.

I welcomed the lull of the motel room. My father and I had nearly dozed off   50
when my mother jumped up excitedly, murmured how stupid she was, and hurried to the closet by the door. She pulled out our old metal cooler and dragged it between the beds. She lifted the top and began unpacking plastic containers, and I thought she would never stop. One after the other they came out, each with a dish that traveled well — a salted stewed meat, rolls of Korean-style sushi. I opened a container of radish kimchi and suddenly the room bloomed with its odor, and I reveled in the very peculiar sensation (which perhaps only true kimchi lovers know) of simultaneously drooling and gagging as I breathed it all in. For the next few minutes, they watched me eat. I'm not certain that I was even hungry. But after weeks of pork parmigiana and chicken patties and wax beans, I suddenly realized that I had lost all the savor in my life. And it seemed I couldn't get enough of it back. I ate and I ate, so much and so fast that I actually went to the bathroom and vomited. I came out dizzy and sated with the phantom warmth of my binge.

And beneath the face of her worry, I thought, my mother was smiling.

From that day, my mother prepared a certain meal to welcome me home. It was always the same. Even as I rode the school's shuttle bus from Exeter to Logan airport, I could already see the exact arrangement of my mother's table.

I knew that we would eat in the kitchen, the table brimming with plates. There was the *kalbi*, of course, broiled or grilled depending on the season. Leaf lettuce, to wrap the meat with. Bowls of garlicky clam broth with miso and tofu and fresh spinach. Shavings of cod dusted in flour and then dipped in egg wash and fried. Glass noodles with onions and shiitake. Scallion-and-hot-pepper pancakes. Chilled steamed shrimp. Seasoned salads of bean sprouts, spinach, and white radish. Crispy squares of seaweed. Steamed rice with barley and red beans. Homemade kimchi. It was all there — the old flavors I knew, the beautiful salt, the sweet, the excellent taste.

After the meal, my father and I talked about school, but of course I could never say enough for it to make any sense. My father would often recall his high-school principal, who had gone to England to study the methods and traditions of the public schools, and regaled students with stories of the great Eton man. My mother sat with us, paring fruit, not saying a word but taking everything in. When it was time to go to bed, my father said good night first. I usually watched television until the early morning. My mother would sit with me for an hour or two, perhaps until she was accustomed to me again, and only then would she kiss me and head upstairs to sleep.

During the following days, it was always the cooking that started our conversations. She'd hold an inquest over the cold leftovers we ate at lunch, discussing each dish in terms of its balance of flavors or what might have been prepared differently. But mostly I begged her to leave the dishes alone. I wish I had paid more attention. After her death, when my father and I were the only ones left in the house, drifting through the rooms like ghosts, I sometimes tried to make that meal for him. Though it was too much for two, I made each dish anyway, taking as much care as I could. But nothing turned out quite right — not the color, not the smell. At the table, neither of us said much of anything. And we had to eat the food for days.

I remember washing rice in the kitchen one day, and my mother's saying in English, from her usual seat, "I made a big mistake."

"About Exeter?"

"Yes, I made a big mistake. You should be with us for that time. I should never let you go there."

"So why did you?" I said.

"Because I didn't know I was going to die."

I let her words pass. For the first time in her life, she was letting herself speak her full mind, so what else could I do?

"But you know what?" she spoke up. "It was better for you. If you stayed home, you would not like me so much now."

I suggested that maybe I would like her even more.

She shook her head. "Impossible."

Sometimes I still think about what she said, about having made a mistake. I would have left home for college, that was never in doubt, but those years I was away at boarding school grew more precious to her as her illness progressed. After many months of exhaustion and pain and the haze of the drugs, I thought that her mind was beginning to fade, for more and more it seemed that she was seeing me again as her fifteen-year-old boy, the one she had dropped off in New Hampshire on a cloudy September afternoon.

I remember the first person I met, another student, named Zack, who walked to the welcome picnic with me. I had planned to eat with my parents — my mother had brought a coolerful of food even that first day — but I learned of the cookout and told her that I should probably go. I wanted to go, of course. I was excited, and no doubt fearful and nervous, and I must have thought I was only thinking ahead. She agreed wholeheartedly, saying I certainly should. I walked them to the car, and perhaps I hugged them, before saying goodbye. One day, after she died, my father told me what happened on the long drive home to Syracuse.

He was driving the car, looking straight ahead. Traffic was light on the Massachusetts Turnpike, and the sky was nearly dark. They had driven for more than two hours and had not yet spoken a word. He then heard a strange sound from her, a kind of muffled chewing noise, as if something inside her were grinding its way out.

"So, what's the matter?" he said, trying to keep an edge to his voice.

She looked at him with her ashen face and she burst into tears. He began to cry himself, and pulled the car over onto the narrow shoulder of the turnpike, where they stayed for the next half hour or so, the blank-faced cars droning by them in the cold, onrushing night.

Every once in a while, when I think of her, I'm driving alone somewhere on   70
the highway. In the twilight, I see their car off to the side, a blue Olds coupe with a landau top, and as I pass them by I look back in the mirror and I see them again, the two figures huddling together in the front seat. Are they sleeping? Or kissing? Are they all right?   [1995]

≡ **THINKING ABOUT THE TEXT**

1. Why does Lee's mother smile in the motel on Parents' Day?

2. Why do Lee's parents pull off the highway after they drop him off at Exeter? Why does he still imagine them "in the twilight . . . their car off to the side" (para. 70)?

3. What significance does the coming-home meal have for Lee?

4. What effect does Lee's going to the prestigious prep school have on his mother? On Lee? On the family? Why isn't Lee completely honest about his experience there?

5. Why is Lee so specific about his mother's preparation of the Korean dish *kalbi*? What are some specific things Lee admires about his mother?

≡ **MAKING COMPARISONS**

1. Compare the mothers' attitudes toward food in Reichl's and Lee's memoirs.

2. Compare Reichl's and Lee's attitudes toward their mothers.

3. Point out instances of honesty in the memoirs of these three narrators. What effect do they have on you?

≡ **WRITING ABOUT ISSUES**

1. Based on your own experience, agree or disagree with Reichl's observation that, "if you watched people as they ate, you could find out who they were" (para. 17).

2. Write an essay that researches the cultural significance of the "family meal" in at least two societies.

3. Read a chapter in Reichl's *Tender at the Bone* other than "The Queen of Mold" and discuss the significance of food in Reichl's early life.

4. Write a narrative that demonstrates the significance of food in your early life.

≡ Fateful Decisions about Parenthood: Across Genres

T. CORAGHESSAN BOYLE, "The Love of My Life" (story)

MAXINE HONG KINGSTON, "No Name Woman" (essay)

Ambitious politicians are not the only voices extolling the virtues of family life. Millennia of images and narratives have socialized us to accept the naturalness of motherhood and fatherhood and to see parenthood as a concept that is nearly beyond critique, beyond questioning. We look askance at those who fail in their roles as loving, supportive parents — and sometimes even at couples who decide that they do not want children or at least not as a result of a particular pregnancy. Even though the right to terminate a pregnancy is still an emotionally contested political and ethical issue, there is almost universal condemnation — in America, at least — for parents who harm infants. Our culture does not seem to forgive such behavior, often condemning it regardless of the circumstances. And in Kingston's harrowing tale, the circumstances are so oppressive that Kingston's aunt seems a set-upon victim without recourse. Her fateful decision is, of course, tragically haunting, but we also wonder how many choices she really has.

But serious writers are not in the habit of shying away from the dark corners of human experience, and we can profitably turn to writers like T. Coraghessan Boyle and Maxine Hong Kingston to shine the artist's light on disturbing stories of family life gone awry. In his notes on "The Love of My Life," Boyle writes that at its essence the world "remains a dark and mysterious place. I write fiction to address and measure my response to that darkness and mystery." With Boyle and Kingston, we can try to sort out the inevitably conflicting feelings we have about the actions of the characters in the following stories.

≡ BEFORE YOU READ

Respond to the following statement: "Neonaticide (the killing of an infant less than a day old) has been going on for centuries. Some societies have allowed the practice if done under extreme stress. Some modern philosophers also agree with this position."

T. CORAGHESSAN BOYLE
The Love of My Life

T. Coraghessan Boyle (b. 1948), who says that his middle name is pronounced with the stress on the second syllable and that his friends call him Tom, has written more than twenty books of fiction, including Drop City *(2003),* The Inner Circle *(2004),*

Ulf Andersen /Getty
Images

Tooth and Claw *(2005), and* Talk, Talk *(2006). His novel* The Women *(2009) focuses on the women in Frank Lloyd Wright's life.* Wild Child and Other Stories *was published in 2010 and* When the Killing's Done *was published in 2011. His latest book is* T.C. Boyle Stories II *(2013). After graduating from the State University of New York, Potsdam, with a B.A. in English and history, Boyle taught for several years at the high school that he had attended as a teenager, though he continued to follow his interests in creative writing. In the early 1970s, he attended the prestigious University of Iowa Writers' Workshop and went on to receive a Ph.D. in nineteenth-century British literature from the University of Iowa in 1977. His list of awards and publications is long, and he received the O. Henry Award in 2001 for the short story reprinted here. Boyle says that the story is based on a news event of a few years ago that "should break your heart. I know it broke mine."*

They wore each other like a pair of socks. He was at her house, she was at his. Everywhere they went — to the mall, to the game, to movies and shops and the classes that structured their days like a new kind of chronology — their fingers were entwined, their shoulders touching, their hips joined in the slow triumphant sashay of love. He drove her car, slept on the couch in the family room at her parents' house, played tennis and watched football with her father on the big, thirty-six-inch TV in the kitchen. She went shopping with his mother and hers, a triumvirate of tastes, and she would have played tennis with his father, if it came to it, but his father was dead. "I love you," he told her, because he did, because there was no feeling like this, no triumph, no high — it was like being immortal and unconquerable, like floating. And a hundred times a day she said it, too: "I love you. I love you."

They were together at his house one night when the rain froze on the streets and sheathed the trees in glass. It was her idea to take a walk and feel it in their hair and on the glistening shoulders of their parkas, an other-worldly drumming of pellets flung down out of the troposphere, alien and familiar at the same time, and they glided the length of the front walk and watched the way the power lines bellied and swayed. He built a fire when they got back, while she towelled her hair and made hot chocolate laced with Jack Daniel's. They'd rented a pair of slasher movies for the ritualized comfort of them — "Teens have sex," he said, "and then they pay for it in body parts" — and the maniac had just climbed out of the heating vent, with a meat hook dangling from the recesses of his empty sleeve, when the phone rang.

It was his mother, calling from the hotel room in Boston where she was curled up — shacked up? — for the weekend with the man she'd been dating. He tried to picture her, but he couldn't. He even closed his eyes a minute, to concentrate, but there was nothing there. Was everything all right? she wanted to know. With the storm and all? No, it hadn't hit Boston yet, but she saw on the Weather Channel that it was on its way. Two seconds after he hung up — before she could even hit the Start button on the VCR — the phone rang again, and this time it was her mother. Her mother had been drinking. She was calling from the restaurant, and China could hear a clamor of voices in the background. "Just stay put," her mother shouted into the phone. "The streets are like a skating rink. Don't you even think of getting in that car."

Well, she wasn't thinking of it. She was thinking of having Jeremy to herself, all night, in the big bed in his mother's room. They'd been having sex ever since they started going together at the end of their junior year, but it was always sex in the car or sex on a blanket or the lawn, hurried sex, nothing like she wanted it to be. She kept thinking of the way it was in the movies, where the stars ambushed each other on beds the size of small planets and then did it again and again until they lay nestled in a heap of pillows and blankets, her head on his chest, his arm flung over her shoulder, the music fading away to individual notes plucked softly on a guitar and everything in the frame glowing as if it had been sprayed with liquid gold. That was how it was supposed to be. That was how it was going to be. At least for tonight.

She'd been wandering around the kitchen as she talked, dancing with the phone in an idle slow saraband, watching the frost sketch a design on the window over the sink, no sound but the soft hiss of the ice pellets on the roof, and now she pulled open the freezer door and extracted a pint box of ice cream. She was in her socks, socks so thick they were like slippers, and a pair of black leggings under an oversize sweater. Beneath her feet, the polished floorboards were as slick as the sidewalk outside, and she liked the feel of that, skating indoors in her big socks. "Uh-huh," she said into the phone. "Uh-huh. Yeah,

5

we're watching a movie." She dug a finger into the ice cream and stuck it in her mouth.

"Come on," Jeremy called from the living room, where the maniac rippled menacingly over the Pause button. "You're going to miss the best part."

"O.K., Mom, O.K.," she said into the phone, parting words, and then she hung up. "You want ice cream?" she called, licking her finger.

Jeremy's voice came back at her, a voice in the middle range, with a con-genital scratch in it, the voice of a nice guy, a very nice guy who could be the star of a TV show about nice guys: "What kind?" He had a pair of shoulders and pumped-up biceps, too, a smile that jumped from his lips to his eyes, and close-cropped hair that stood up straight off the crown of his head. And he was always singing — she loved that — his voice so true he could do any song, and there was no lyric he didn't know, even on the oldies station. She scooped ice cream and saw him in a scene from last summer, one hand draped casually over the wheel of his car, the radio throbbing, his voice raised in perfect synch with Billy Corgan's, and the night standing still at the end of a long dark street overhung with maples.

"Chocolate. Swiss-chocolate almond."

"O.K.," he said, and then he was wondering if there was any whipped   10
cream, or maybe hot fudge — he was sure his mother had a jar stashed away somewhere, *Look behind the mayonnaise on the top row* — and when she turned around he was standing in the doorway.

She kissed him — they kissed whenever they met, no matter where or when, even if one of them had just stepped out of the room, because that was love, that was the way love was — and then they took two bowls of ice cream into the liv-ing room and, with a flick of the remote, set the maniac back in motion.

It was an early spring that year, the world gone green overnight, the thermom-eter twice hitting the low eighties in the first week of March. Teachers were holding sessions outside. The whole school, even the halls and the cafeteria, smelled of fresh-mowed grass and the unfolding blossoms of the fruit trees in the development across the street, and students — especially seniors — were cutting class to go out to the quarry or the reservoir or to just drive the back-streets with the sunroof and the windows open wide. But not China. She was hitting the books, studying late, putting everything in its place like pegs in a board, even love, even that. Jeremy didn't get it. "Look, you've already been ac-cepted at your first-choice school, you're going to wind up in the top ten G.P.A.-wise, and you've got four years of tests and term papers ahead of you, and grad school after that. You'll only be a high-school senior once in your life. Relax. Enjoy it. Or at least *experience* it."

He'd been accepted at Brown, his father's alma mater, and his own G.P.A. would put him in the top ten percent of their graduating class, and he was content with that, skating through his final semester, no math, no science, tak-ing art and music, the things he'd always wanted to take but never had time for — and Lit., of course, A.P. History, and Spanish 5. "*Tú eres el amor de mi vida,*" he would tell her when they met at her locker or at lunch or when he picked her up for a movie on Saturday nights.

"*Y tú también,*" she would say, "or is it '*yo también*'?" — French was her language. "But I keep telling you it really matters to me, because I know I'll never catch Margery Yu or Christian Davenport, I mean they're a lock for val and salut, but it'll kill me if people like Kerry Sharp or Jalapy Seegrand finish ahead of me — you should know that, you of all people —"

It amazed him that she actually brought her books along when they went   15
backpacking over spring break. They'd planned the trip all winter and through the long wind tunnel that was February, packing away freeze-dried entrées, PowerBars, Gore-Tex windbreakers, and matching sweatshirts, weighing each item on a handheld scale with a dangling hook at the bottom of it. They were going up into the Catskills, to a lake he'd found on a map, and they were going to be together, without interruption, without telephones, automobiles, parents, teachers, friends, relatives, and pets, for five full days. They were going to cook over an open fire, they were going to read to each other and burrow into the double sleeping bag with the connubial zipper up the seam he'd found in his mother's closet, a relic of her own time in the lap of nature. It smelled of her, of his mother, a vague scent of her perfume that had lingered there dormant all these years, and maybe there was the faintest whiff of his father, too, though his father had been gone so long he didn't even remember what he looked like, let alone what he might have smelled like. Five days. And it wasn't going to rain, not a drop. He didn't even bring his fishing rod, and that was love.

When the last bell rang down the curtain on Honors Math, Jeremy was waiting at the curb in his mother's Volvo station wagon, grinning up at China through the windshield while the rest of the school swept past with no thought for anything but release. There were shouts and curses, T-shirts in motion, slashing legs, horns bleating from the seniors' lot, the school buses lined up like armored vehicles awaiting the invasion — chaos, sweet chaos — and she stood there a moment to savor it. "Your mother's car?" she said, slipping in beside him and laying both arms over his shoulders to pull him to her for a kiss. He'd brought her jeans and hiking boots along, and she was going to change as they drove, no need to go home, no more circumvention and delay, a stop at McDonald's, maybe, or Burger King, and then it was the sun and the wind and the moon and the stars. Five days. Five whole days.

"Yeah," he said, in answer to her question, "my mother said she didn't want to have to worry about us breaking down in the middle of nowhere —"

"So she's got your car? She's going to sell real estate in your car?"

He just shrugged and smiled. "Free at last," he said, pitching his voice down low till it was exactly like Martin Luther King's. "Thank God Almighty, we are free at last."

It was dark by the time they got to the trailhead, and they wound up camp-   20
ing just off the road in a rocky tumble of brush, no place on earth less likely or less comfortable, but they were together, and they held each other through the damp whispering hours of the night and hardly slept at all. They made the lake

by noon the next day, the trees just coming into leaf, the air sweet with the smell of the sun in the pines. She insisted on setting up the tent, just in case — it could rain, you never knew — but all he wanted to do was stretch out on a gray neoprene pad and feel the sun on his face. Eventually, they both fell asleep in the sun, and when they woke they made love right there, beneath the trees, and with the wide blue expanse of the lake giving back the blue of the sky. For dinner, it was étouffée and rice, out of the foil pouch, washed down with hot chocolate and a few squirts of red wine from Jeremy's bota bag.

The next day, the whole day through, they didn't bother with clothes at all. They couldn't swim, of course — the lake was too cold for that — but they could bask and explore and feel the breeze out of the south on their bare legs and the places where no breeze had touched before. She would remember that always, the feel of that, the intensity of her motions, the simple unrefined pleasure of living in the moment. Wood smoke. Duelling flashlights in the night. The look on Jeremy's face when he presented her with the bag of finger-size crayfish he'd spent all morning collecting.

What else? The rain, of course. It came midway through the third day, clouds the color of iron filings, the lake hammered to iron, too, and the storm that crashed through the trees and beat at their tent with a thousand angry fists. They huddled in the sleeping bag, sharing the wine and a bag of trail mix, reading to each other from a book of Donne's love poems (she was writing a paper for Mrs. Masterson called "Ocular Imagery in the Poetry of John Donne") and the last third of a vampire novel that weighed eighteen-point-one ounces.

And the sex. They were careful, always careful — *I will never, never be like those breeders that bring their puffed-up squalling little red-faced babies to class*, she told him, and he agreed, got adamant about it, even, until it became a running theme in their relationship, the breeders overpopulating an overpopulated world and ruining their own lives in the process — but she had forgotten to pack her pills and he had only two condoms with him, and it wasn't as if there were a drugstore around the corner.

In the fall — or the end of August, actually — they packed their cars separately and left for college, he to Providence and she to Binghamton. They were separated by three hundred miles, but there was the telephone, there was e-mail, and for the first month or so there were Saturday nights in a motel in Danbury, but that was a haul, it really was, and they both agreed that they should focus on their course work and cut back to every second or maybe third week. On the day they'd left — and no, she didn't want her parents driving her up there, she was an adult and she could take care of herself — Jeremy followed her as far as the Bear Mountain Bridge and they pulled off the road and held each other till the sun fell down into the trees. She had a poem for him, a Donne poem, the saddest thing he'd ever heard. It was something about the moon. *More than moon*, that was it, lovers parting and their tears swelling like an ocean till the girl — the woman, the female — had more power to raise the tides than the moon itself, or some such. More than moon. That's what he called her after that, because she was white and round and getting rounder, and it was no joke, and it was no term of endearment.

She was pregnant. Pregnant, they figured, since the camping trip, and it was their secret, a new constant in their lives, a fact, an inescapable fact that never varied no matter how many home-pregnancy kits they went through. Baggy clothes, that was the key, all in black, cargo pants, flowing dresses, a jacket even in summer. They went to a store in the city where nobody knew them and she got a girdle, and then she went away to school in Binghamton and he went to Providence. "You've got to get rid of it," he told her in the motel room that had become a prison. "Go to a clinic," he told her for the hundredth time, and outside it was raining — or, no, it was clear and cold that night, a foretaste of winter. "I'll find the money — you know I will."

She wouldn't respond. Wouldn't even look at him. One of the *Star Wars* movies was on TV, great flat thundering planes of metal roaring across the screen, and she was just sitting there on the edge of the bed, her shoulders hunched and hair hanging limp. Someone slammed a car door — two doors in rapid succession — and a child's voice shouted, "Me! Me first!"

"China," he said. "Are you listening to me?"

"I can't," she murmured, and she was talking to her lap, to the bed, to the floor. "I'm scared. I'm so scared." There were footsteps in the room next door, ponderous and heavy, then the quick tattoo of the child's feet and a sudden thump against the wall. "I don't want anyone to know," she said.

He could have held her, could have squeezed in beside her and wrapped her in his arms, but something flared in him. He couldn't understand it. He just couldn't. "What are you thinking? Nobody'll know. He's a doctor, for Christ's sake, sworn to secrecy, the doctor-patient compact and all that. What are you going to do, keep it? Huh? Just show up for English 101 with a baby on your lap and say, 'Hi, I'm the Virgin Mary'?"

She was crying. He could see it in the way her shoulders suddenly crumpled and now he could hear it, too, a soft nasal complaint that went right through him. She lifted her face to him and held out her arms and he was there beside her, rocking her back and forth in his arms. He could feel the heat of her face against the hard fibre of his chest, a wetness there, fluids, her fluids. "I don't want a doctor," she said.

And that colored everything, that simple negative: life in the dorms, roommates, bars, bullshit sessions, the smell of burning leaves and the way the light fell across campus in great wide smoking bands just before dinner, the unofficial skateboard club, films, lectures, pep rallies, football — none of it mattered. He couldn't have a life. Couldn't be a freshman. Couldn't wake up in the morning and tumble into the slow steady current of the world. All he could think of was her. Or not simply her — her and him, and what had come between them. Because they argued now, they wrangled and fought and debated, and it was no pleasure to see her in that motel room with the queen-size bed and the big color TV and the soaps and shampoos they made off with as if they were treasure. She was pig-headed, stubborn, irrational. She was spoiled, he could see

25

30

that now, spoiled by her parents and their standard of living and the socio-economic expectations of her class—of his class—and the promise of life as you like it, an unscrolling vista of pleasure and acquisition. He loved her. He didn't want to turn his back on her. He would be there for her no matter what, but why did she have to be so *stupid?*

Big sweats, huge sweats, sweats that drowned and engulfed her, that was her campus life, sweats and the dining hall. Her dorm mates didn't know her, and so what if she was putting on weight? Everybody did. How could you shovel down all those carbohydrates, all that sugar and grease and the puddings and nachos and all the rest, without putting on ten or fifteen pounds the first semester alone? Half the girls in the dorm were waddling around like the Dough-boy, their faces bloated and blotched with acne, with crusting pimples and whiteheads fed on fat. So she was putting on weight. Big deal. "There's more of me to love," she told her roommate, "and Jeremy likes it that way. And, really, he's the only one that matters." She was careful to shower alone, in the early morning, long before the light had begun to bump up against the windows.

On the night her water broke—it was mid-December, almost nine months, as best as she could figure—it was raining. Raining hard. All week she'd been having tense rasping sotto-voce debates with Jeremy on the phone—arguments, fights—and she told him that she would die, creep out into the woods like some animal and bleed to death, before she'd go to a hospital. "And what am I supposed to do?" he demanded in a high childish whine, as if he were the one who'd been knocked up, and she didn't want to hear it, she didn't.

"Do you love me?" she whispered. There was a long hesitation, a pause you could have poured all the affirmation of the world into.

"Yes," he said finally, his voice so soft and reluctant it was like the last gasp   35
of a dying old man.

"Then you're going to have to rent the motel."

"And then what?"

"Then—I don't know." The door was open, her roommate framed there in the hall, a burst of rock and roll coming at her like an assault. "I guess you'll have to get a book or something."

By eight, the rain had turned to ice and every branch of every tree was coated with it, the highway littered with glistening black sticks, no moon, no stars, the tires sliding out from under her, and she felt heavy, big as a sumo wrestler, heavy and loose at the same time. She'd taken a towel from the dorm and put it under her, on the seat, but it was a mess, everything was a mess. She was cramping. Fidgeting with her hair. She tried the radio, but it was no help, nothing but songs she hated, singers that were worse. Twenty-two miles to Danbury and the first of the contractions came like a seizure, like a knife blade thrust into her spine. Her world narrowed to what the headlights would show her.

Jeremy was waiting for her at the door to the room, the light behind him a   40
pale rinse of nothing, no smile on his face, no human expression at all. They didn't kiss—they didn't even touch—and then she was on the bed, on her back, her face clenched like a fist. She heard the rattle of the sleet at the win-

dow, the murmur of TV: *I can't let you go like this,* a man protested, and she could picture him, angular and tall, a man in a hat and overcoat in a black-and-white world that might have been another planet, *I just can't.* "Are you —?" Jeremy's voice drifted into the mix, and then stalled. "Are you ready? I mean, is it time? Is it coming now?"

She said one thing then, one thing only, her voice as pinched and hollow as the sound of the wind in the gutters: "Get it out of me."

It took a moment, and then she could feel his hands fumbling with her sweats.

Later, hours later, when nothing had happened but pain, a parade of pain with drum majors and brass bands and penitents crawling on their hands and knees till the streets were stained with their blood, she cried out and cried out again. "It's like *Alien,*" she gasped, "like that thing in *Alien* when it, it —"

"It's O.K.," he kept telling her, "it's O.K.," but his face betrayed him. He looked scared, looked as if he'd been drained of blood in some evil experiment in yet another movie, and a part of her wanted to be sorry for him, but another part, the part that was so commanding and fierce it overrode everything else, couldn't begin to be.

He was useless, and he knew it. He'd never been so purely sick at heart and terrified in all his life, but he tried to be there for her, tried to do his best, and when the baby came out, the baby girl all slick with blood and mucus and the lumped white stuff that was like something spilled at the bottom of a garbage can, he was thinking of the ninth grade and how close he'd come to fainting while the teacher went around the room to prick their fingers one by one so they each could smear a drop of blood across a slide. He didn't faint now. But he was close to it, so close he could feel the room dodging away under his feet. And then her voice, the first intelligible thing she'd said in an hour: "Get rid of it. Just get rid of it."

45

Of the drive back to Binghamton he remembered nothing. Or practically nothing. They took towels from the motel and spread them across the seat of her car, he could remember that much . . . and the blood, how could he forget the blood? It soaked through her sweats and the towels and even the thick cotton bathmat and into the worn fabric of the seat itself. And it all came from inside her, all of it, tissue and mucus and the shining bright fluid, no end to it, as if she'd been turned inside out. He wanted to ask her about that, if that was normal, but she was asleep the minute she slid out from under his arm and dropped into the seat. If he focused, if he really concentrated, he could remember the way her head lolled against the doorframe while the engine whined and the car rocked and the slush threw a dark blanket over the windshield every time a truck shot past in the opposite direction. That and the exhaustion. He'd never been so tired, his head on a string, shoulders slumped, his arms like two pillars of concrete. And what if he'd nodded off? What if he'd gone into a skid and hurtled over an embankment into the filthy gray accumulation of the worst day of his life? What then?

She made it into the dorm under her own power, nobody even looked at her, and, no, she didn't need his help. "Call me," she whispered, and they kissed, her lips so cold it was like kissing a steak through the plastic wrap, and then he parked her car in the student lot and walked to the bus station. He made Danbury late that night, caught a ride out to the motel, and walked right through the "Do Not Disturb" sign on the door. Fifteen minutes. That was all it took. He bundled up everything, every trace, left the key in the box at the desk, and stood scraping the ice off the windshield of his car while the night opened up above him to a black glitter of sky. He never gave a thought to what lay discarded in the Dumpster out back, itself wrapped in plastic, so much meat, so much cold meat.

He was at the very pinnacle of his dream, the river dressed in its currents, the deep hole under the cutbank, and the fish like silver bullets swarming to his bait, when they woke him — when Rob woke him, Rob Greiner, his roommate, Rob with a face of crumbling stone and two policemen there at the door behind him and the roar of the dorm falling away to a whisper. And that was strange, policemen, a real anomaly in that setting, and at first — for the first thirty seconds, at least — he had no idea what they were doing there. Parking tickets? Could that be it? But then they asked him his name, just to confirm it, joined his hands together behind his back, and fitted two loops of naked metal over his wrists, and he began to understand. He saw McCaffrey and Tuttle from across the hall staring at him as if he were Jeffrey Dahmer or something, and the rest of them, all the rest, every head poking out of every door up and down the corridor, as the police led him away.

"What's all this about?" he kept saying, the cruiser nosing through the dark streets to the station house, the man at the wheel and the man beside him as incapable of speech as the seats or the wire mesh or the gleaming black dashboard that dragged them forward into the night. And then it was up the steps and into an explosion of light, more men in uniform, stand here, give me your hand, now the other one, and then the cage and the questions. Only then did he think of that thing in the garbage sack and the sound it had made — its body had made — when he flung it into the Dumpster like a sack of flour and the lid slammed down on it. He stared at the walls, and this was a movie, too. He'd never been in trouble before, never been inside a police station, but he knew his role well enough, because he'd seen it played out a thousand times on the tube: deny everything. Even as the two detectives settled in across from him at the bare wooden table in the little box of the overlit room he was telling himself just that: *Deny it, deny it all.*

The first detective leaned forward and set his hands on the table as if he'd come for a manicure. He was in his thirties, or maybe his forties, a tired-looking man with the scars of the turmoil he'd witnessed gouged into the flesh under his eyes. He didn't offer a cigarette ("I don't smoke," Jeremy was prepared to say, giving them that much at least), and he didn't smile or soften his eyes. And when he spoke his voice carried no freight at all, not outrage or threat or cajolery — it was just a voice, flat and tired. "Do you know a China Berkowitz?" he said.

And she. She was in the community hospital, where the ambulance had deposited her after her roommate had called 911 in a voice that was like a bone

50

stuck in the back of her throat, and it was raining again. Her parents were there, her mother red-eyed and sniffling, her father looking like an actor who has forgotten his lines, and there was another woman there, too, a police-woman. The policewoman sat in an orange plastic chair in the corner, dipping her head to the knitting in her lap. At first, China's mother had tried to be pleas-ant to the woman, but pleasant wasn't what the circumstances called for, and now she ignored her, because the very unpleasant fact was that China was be-ing taken into custody as soon as she was released from the hospital.

For a long while no one said anything — everything had already been said, over and over, one long flood of hurt and recrimination — and the antiseptic silence of the hospital held them in its grip while the rain beat at the windows and the machines at the foot of the bed counted off numbers. From down the hall came a snatch of TV dialogue, and for a minute China opened her eyes and thought she was back in the dorm. "Honey," her mother said, raising a purga-torial face to her, "are you all right? Can I get you anything?"

"I need to — I think I need to pee."

"Why?" her father demanded, and it was the perfect non sequitur. He was up out of the chair, standing over her, his eyes liked cracked porcelain. "Why didn't you tell us, or at least tell your mother — or Dr. Fredman? Dr. Fredman, at least. He's been — he's like a family member, you know that, and he could have, or he would have . . . What were you *thinking*, for Christ's sake?"

Thinking? She wasn't thinking anything, not then and not now. All she   55
wanted — and she didn't care what they did to her, beat her, torture her, drag her weeping through the streets in a dirty white dress with "Baby Killer" stitched over her breast in scarlet letters — was to see Jeremy. Just that. Because what really mattered was what he was thinking.

The food at the Sarah Barnes Cooper Women's Correctional Institute was ex-actly what they served at the dining hall in college, heavy on the sugars, starches, and bad cholesterol, and that would have struck her as ironic if she'd been there under other circumstances — doing community outreach, say, or researching a paper for sociology class. But given the fact that she'd been locked up for more than a month now, the object of the other girls' threats, scorn, and just plain *nastiness*, given the fact that her life was ruined beyond any hope of redemption, and every newspaper in the country had her shrunken white face plastered across its front page under a headline that screamed "MOTEL MOM," she didn't have much use for irony. She was scared twenty-four hours a day. Scared of the present, scared of the future, scared of the reporters waiting for the judge to set bail so that they could swarm all over her the minute she stepped out the door. She couldn't concentrate on the books and magazines her mother brought her, or even on the TV in the rec room. She sat in her room — it was a room, just like a dorm room, except that they locked you in at night — and stared at the walls, eating peanuts, M&M's, sunflower seeds by the handful, chewing for the pure animal gratification of it. She was putting on more weight, and what did it matter?

Jeremy was different. He'd lost everything — his walk, his smile, the muscles of his upper arms and shoulders. Even his hair lay flat now, as if he couldn't bother with a tube of gel and a comb. When she saw him at the arraignment, saw him for the first time since she'd climbed out of the car and limped into the dorm with the blood wet on her legs, he looked like a refugee, like a ghost. The room they were in — the courtroom — seemed to have grown up around them, walls, windows, benches, lights, and radiators already in place, along with the judge, the American flag, and the ready-made spectators. It was hot. People coughed into their fists and shuffled their feet, every sound magnified. The judge presided, his arms like bones twirled in a bag, his eyes searching and opaque as he peered over the top of his reading glasses.

China's lawyer didn't like Jeremy's lawyer, that much was evident, and the state prosecutor didn't like anybody. She watched him — Jeremy, only him — as the reporters held their collective breath and the judge read off the charges and her mother bowed her head and sobbed into the bucket of her hands. And Jeremy was watching her, too, his eyes locked on hers as if he defied them all, as if nothing mattered in the world but her, and when the judge said *First-degree murder* and *Murder by abuse or neglect* he never flinched.

She sent him a note that day — "I love you, will always love you no matter what, More than Moon" — and in the hallway, afterward, while their lawyers fended off the reporters and the bailiffs tugged impatiently at them, they had a minute, just a minute, to themselves. "What did you tell them?" he whispered. His voice was a rasp, almost a growl; she looked at him, inches away, and hardly recognized him.

"I told them it was dead."   60

"My lawyer — Mrs. Teagues? — she says they're saying it was alive when we, when we put it in the bag." His face was composed, but his eyes were darting like insects trapped inside his head.

"It was dead."

"It looked dead," he said, and already he was pulling away from her and some callous shit with a camera kept annihilating them with flash after flash of light, "and we certainly didn't — I mean, we didn't slap it or anything to get it breathing. . . ."

And then the last thing he said to her, just as they were pulled apart, and it was nothing she wanted to hear, nothing that had any love in it, or even the hint of love: "You told me to get rid of it."

There was no elaborate name for the place where they were keeping him. It was   65
known as Drum Hill Prison, period. No reform-minded notions here, no verbal gestures toward rehabilitation or behavior modification, no benefactors, may-ors, or role models to lend the place their family names, but then who in his right mind would want a prison named after him anyway? At least they kept him separated from the other prisoners, the gangbangers and dope dealers and sexual predators and the like. He was no longer a freshman at Brown, not offi-cially, but he had his books and his course notes and he tried to keep up as best he could. Still, when the screams echoed through the cell block at night and the walls dripped with the accumulated breath of eight and a half thousand

terminally angry sociopaths, he had to admit it wasn't the sort of college experience he'd bargained for.

And what had he done to deserve it? He still couldn't understand. That thing in the Dumpster — and he refused to call it human, let alone a baby — was nobody's business but his and China's. That's what he'd told his attorney, Mrs. Teagues, and his mother and her boyfriend, Howard, and he'd told them over and over again: *I didn't do anything wrong.* Even if it was alive, and it was, he knew in his heart that it was, even before the state prosecutor presented evidence of blunt-force trauma and death by asphyxiation and exposure, it didn't matter, or shouldn't have mattered. There was no baby. There was nothing but a mistake, a mistake clothed in blood and mucus. When he really thought about it, thought it through on its merits and dissected all his mother's pathetic arguments about where he'd be today if she'd felt as he did when she was pregnant herself, he hardened like a rock, like sand turning to stone under all the pressure the planet can bring to bear. Another unwanted child in an overpopulated world? They should have given him a medal.

It was the end of January before bail was set — three hundred and fifty thousand dollars his mother didn't have — and he was released to house arrest. He wore a plastic anklet that set off an alarm if he went out the door, and so did she, so did China, imprisoned like some fairy-tale princess at her parents' house. At first, she called him every day, but mostly what she did was cry — "I want to see it," she sobbed. "I want to see our daughter's *grave*." That froze him inside. He tried to picture her — her now, China, the love of his life — and he couldn't. What did she look like? What was her face like, her nose, her hair, her eyes and breasts and the slit between her legs? He drew a blank. There was no way to summon her the way she used to be or even the way she was in court, because all he could remember was the thing that had come out of her, four limbs and the equipment of a female, shoulders rigid and eyes shut tight, as if she were a mummy in a tomb . . . and the breath, the shuddering long gasping rattle of a breath he could feel ringing inside her even as the black plastic bag closed over her face and the lid of the Dumpster opened like a mouth.

He was in the den, watching basketball, a drink in his hand (7UP mixed with Jack Daniel's in a ceramic mug, so no one would know he was getting shit-faced at two o'clock on a Sunday afternoon), when the phone rang. It was Sarah Teagues. "Listen, Jeremy," she said in her crisp, equitable tones, "I thought you ought to know — the Berkowitzes are filing a motion to have the case against China dropped."

His mother's voice on the portable, too loud, a blast of amplified breath and static: "On what grounds?"

"She never saw the baby, that's what they're saying. She thought she had a miscarriage."

"Yeah, right," his mother said.

Sarah Teagues was right there, her voice as clear and present as his mother's. "Jeremy's the one that threw it in the Dumpster, and they're saying he acted alone. She took a polygraph test day before yesterday."

70

He could feel his heart pounding like it used to when he plodded up that last agonizing ridge behind the school with the cross-country team, his legs sapped, no more breath left in his body. He didn't say a word. Didn't even breathe.

"She's going to testify against him."

Outside was the world, puddles of ice clinging to the lawn under a weak after-   75
noon sun, all the trees stripped bare, the grass dead, the azalea under the window reduced to an armload of dead brown twigs. She wouldn't have wanted to go out today anyway. This was the time of year she hated most, the long interval between the holidays and spring break, when nothing grew and nothing changed — it didn't even seem to snow much anymore. What was out there for her anyway? They wouldn't let her see Jeremy, wouldn't even let her talk to him on the phone or write him anymore, and she wouldn't be able to show her face at the mall or even the movie theater without somebody shouting out her name as if she were a freak, as if she were another Monica Lewinsky or Heidi Fleiss. She wasn't China Berkowitz, honor student, not anymore — she was the punch line to a joke, a footnote to history.

She wouldn't mind going for a drive, though — that was something she missed, just following the curves out to the reservoir to watch the way the ice cupped the shore, or up to the turnout on Route 9 to look out over the river where it oozed through the mountains in a shimmering coil of light. Or to take a walk in the woods, just that. She was in her room, on her bed, posters of bands she'd outgrown staring down from the walls, her high-school books on two shelves in the corner, the closet door flung open on all the clothes she'd once wanted so desperately she could have died for each individual pair of boots or the cashmere sweaters that felt so good against her skin. At the bottom of her left leg, down there at the foot of the bed, was the anklet she wore now, the plastic anklet with the transmitter inside, no different, she supposed, than the collars they put on wolves to track them across all those miles of barren tundra or the bears sleeping in their dens. Except that hers had an alarm on it.

For a long while she just lay there gazing out the window, watching the rinsed-out sun slip down into the sky that had no more color in it than a TV tuned to an unsubscribed channel, and then she found herself picturing things the way they were an eon ago, when everything was green. She saw the azalea bush in bloom, the leaves knifing out of the trees, butterflies — or were they cabbage moths? — hovering over the flowers. Deep green. That was the color of the world. And she was remembering a night, summer before last, just after she and Jeremy started going together, the crickets thrumming, the air thick with humidity, and him singing along with the car radio, his voice so sweet and pure it was as if he'd written the song himself, just for her. And when they got to where they were going, at the end of that dark lane overhung with trees, to a place where it was private and hushed and the night fell in on itself as if it couldn't support the weight of the stars, he was as nervous as she was. She moved into his arms and they kissed, his lips groping for hers in the dark, his fingers trembling over the thin yielding silk of her blouse. He was Jeremy. He was the love of her life. And she closed her eyes and clung to him as if that were all that mattered.

[2000]

≡ THINKING ABOUT THE TEXT

1. Both China and Jeremy are condemned by their peers in this story (as they were in real life). Is that your response, too? How does Boyle persuade you to see how such an event is possible? What is the most reasonable way to understand how such an event is possible? What is the least plausible explanation for such behavior?

2. After reading the first few pages of the exposition, what do you think Boyle's purpose is in this opening scene? Is the sentence "Teens have sex . . . and then they pay for it in body parts" (para. 2) clever or perhaps even cruel?

3. Look again at the fourth paragraph. What does it tell you about China's frame of mind? Her sense of reality?

4. How might Boyle be trying to make an argument about the power of the media? The obliviousness of teens? The power of first love?

5. How might China's and Jeremy's lives have been irreparably ruined? Boyle ends the story with China remembering a summer night shortly after she started dating Jeremy. How might this memory save the relationship, or is it proof of her blindness?

MAXINE HONG KINGSTON
No Name Woman

Born in Stockton, California, to Chinese immigrants, Maxine Hong Kingston's (b. 1940) first language was Say Yup, a dialect of Cantonese. As a member of a close-knit community, many of whose members came from the same village in China, she was immersed in the storytelling tradition of her particular Chinese culture and soon became a gifted writer in her second language, English. Winning eleven scholarships, Kingston began her education at the University of California at Berkeley as an engineering major but soon moved into English literature, receiving her B.A. in 1962 and her teaching certificate in 1965. After teaching in Hawaii for ten years, Kingston published her first book, The Woman Warrior: Memoirs of a Girlhood among Ghosts *(1976), from which the following selection comes. This volume won the National Book Critics Circle Award for nonfiction. Kingston's reinterpretation of oral traditions is continued in her later works, including* Tripmaster Monkey: His Fake Book *(1989),* Hawai'i One Summer *(1998),* To Be a Poet *(2003),* The Fifth Book of Peace *(2003), an edited volume of contemporary soldiers' memoirs entitled* Veterans of War, Veterans of Peace *(2006), and* I Love a Broad Margin to My Life *(2011), a book of poems.*

Jack Sotomayor / Getty Images

"You must not tell anyone," my mother said, "what I am about to tell you. In China your father had a sister who killed herself. She jumped into the family well. We say that your father has all brothers because it is as if she had never been born.

"In 1924 just a few days after our village celebrated seventeen hurry-up weddings—to make sure that every young man who went 'out on the road' would responsibly come home—your father and his brothers and your grandfather and his brothers and your aunt's new husband sailed for America, the Gold Mountain. It was your grandfather's last trip. Those lucky enough to get contracts waved good-bye from the decks. They fed and guarded the stowaways and helped them off in Cuba, New York, Bali, Hawaii. 'We'll meet in California next year,' they said. All of them sent money home.

"I remember looking at your aunt one day when she and I were dressing; I had not noticed before that she had such a protruding melon of a stomach. But I did not think, 'She's pregnant,' until she began to look like other pregnant women, her shirt pulling and the white tops of her black pants showing. She could not have been pregnant, you see, because her husband had been gone for years. No one said anything. We did not discuss it. In early summer she was ready to have the child, long after the time when it could have been possible."

"The village had also been counting. On the night the baby was to be born the villagers raided our house. Some were crying. Like a great saw, teeth strung with lights, files of people walked zigzag across our land, tearing the rice. Their lanterns doubled in the disturbed black water, which drained away through the broken bunds. As the villagers closed in, we could see that some of them, probably men and women we knew well, wore white masks. The people with long hair hung it over their faces. Women with short hair made it stand up on end. Some had tied white bands around their foreheads, arms, and legs.

"At first they threw mud and rocks at the house. Then they threw eggs and began slaughtering our stock. We could hear the animals scream their deaths—the roosters, the pigs, a last great roar from the ox. Familiar wild heads flared in our night windows; the villagers encircled us. Some of the faces stopped to peer at us, their eyes rushing like searchlights. The hands flattened against the panes, framed heads, and left red prints.

"The villagers broke in the front and the back doors at the same time, even though we had not locked the doors against them. Their knives dripped with the blood of our animals. They smeared blood on the doors and walls. One woman swung a chicken, whose throat she had slit, splattering blood in red arcs about her. We stood together in the middle of our house, in the family hall with the pictures and tables of the ancestors around us, and looked straight ahead.

"At that time the house had only two wings. When the men came back, we would build two more to enclose our courtyard and a third one to begin a second courtyard. The villagers pushed through both wings, even your grandparents' rooms, to find your aunt's, which was also mine until the men returned. From this room a new wing for one of the younger families would grow. They ripped up her clothes and shoes and broke her combs, grinding them underfoot. They tore her work from the loom. They scattered the cooking fire and rolled the new weaving in it. We could hear them in the kitchen breaking our bowls and banging the pots. They overturned the great waist-high earthenware jugs; duck eggs, pickled fruits, vegetables burst out and mixed in acrid torrents. The old woman from the next field swept a broom through the air and loosed the spirits-of-the-broom over our heads. 'Pig.' 'Ghost.' 'Pig,' they sobbed and scolded while they ruined our house.

"When they left, they took sugar and oranges to bless themselves. They cut pieces from the dead animals. Some of them took bowls that were not broken and clothes that were not torn. Afterward we swept up the rice and sewed it back up into sacks. But the smells from the spilled preserves lasted. Your aunt gave birth in the pigsty that night. The next morning when I went for the water, I found her and the baby plugging up the family well.

"Don't let your father know that I told you. He denies her. Now that you have started to menstruate, what happened to her could happen to you. Don't humiliate us. You wouldn't like to be forgotten as if you had never been born. The villagers are watchful."

Whenever she had to warn us about life, my mother told stories that ran like this one, a story to grow up on. She tested our strength to establish realities. Those in the emigrant generations who could not reassert brute survival

died young and far from home. Those of us in the first American generations
have had to figure out how the invisible world the emigrants built around our
childhoods fits in solid America.

The emigrants confused the gods by diverting their curses, misleading
them with crooked streets and false names. They must try to confuse their offspring as well, who, I suppose, threaten them in similar ways—always trying
to get things straight, always trying to name the unspeakable. The Chinese I
know hide their names; sojourners take new names when their lives change
and guard their real names with silence.

Chinese-Americans, when you try to understand what things in you are
Chinese, how do you separate what is peculiar to childhood, to poverty, insani-
ties, one family, your mother who marked your growing with stories, from
what is Chinese? What is Chinese tradition and what is the movies?

If I want to learn what clothes my aunt wore, whether flashy or ordinary,
I would have to begin, "Remember Father's drowned-in-the-well sister?" I cannot ask that. My mother has told me once and for all the useful parts. She
will add nothing unless powered by Necessity, a riverbank that guides her life.
She plants vegetable gardens rather than lawns; she carries the odd-shaped
tomatoes home from the fields and eats food left for the gods.

Whenever we did frivolous things, we used up energy; we flew high kites.
We children came up off the ground over the melting cones our parents
brought home from work and the American movie on New Year's Day—*Oh,
You Beautiful Doll* with Betty Grable one year, and *She Wore a Yellow Ribbon* with
John Wayne another year. After the one carnival ride each, we paid in guilt;
our tired father counted his change on the dark walk home.

Adultery is extravagance. Could people who hatch their own chicks and   15
eat the embryos and the heads for delicacies and boil the feet in vinegar for
party food, leaving only the gravel, eating even the gizzard lining—could such
people engender a prodigal aunt? To be a woman, to have a daughter in starva-
tion time was a waste enough. My aunt could not have been the lone romantic
who gave up everything for sex. Women in the old China did not choose. Some
man had commanded her to lie with him and be his secret evil. I wonder
whether he masked himself when he joined the raid on her family.

Perhaps she had encountered him in the fields or on the mountain where
the daughters-in-law collected fuel. Or perhaps he first noticed her in the marketplace. He was not a stranger because the village housed no strangers. She
had to have dealings with him other than sex. Perhaps he worked an adjoining
field, or he sold her the cloth for the dress she sewed and wore. His demand
must have surprised, then terrified her. She obeyed him; she always did as she
was told.

When the family found a young man in the next village to be her husband,
she had stood tractably beside the best rooster, his proxy, and promised before
they met that she would be his forever. She was lucky that he was her age and
she would be the first wife, an advantage secure now. The night she first saw
him, he had sex with her. Then he left for America. She had almost forgotten

what he looked like. When she tried to envision him, she only saw the black and white face in the group photograph the men had had taken before leaving.

The other man was not, after all, much different from her husband. They both gave orders: she followed. "If you tell your family, I'll beat you. I'll kill you. Be here again next week." No one talked sex, ever. And she might have separated the rapes from the rest of living if only she did not have to buy her oil from him or gather wood in the same forest. I want her fear to have lasted just as long as rape lasted so that the fear could have been contained. No drawn-out fear. But women at sex hazarded birth and hence lifetimes. The fear did not stop but permeated everywhere. She told the man, "I think I'm pregnant." He organized the raid against her.

On nights when my mother and father talked about their life back home, sometimes they mentioned an "outcast table" whose business they still seemed to be settling, their voices tight. In a commensal tradition, where food is precious, the powerful older people made wrongdoers eat alone. Instead of letting them start separate new lives like the Japanese, who could become samurais and geishas, the Chinese family, faces averted but eyes glowering sideways, hung on to the offenders and fed them leftovers. My aunt must have lived in the same house as my parents and eaten at an outcast table. My mother spoke about the raid as if she had seen it, when she and my aunt, a daughter-in-law to a different household, should not have been living together at all. Daughters-in-law lived with their husbands' parents, not their own; a synonym for marriage in Chinese is "taking a daughter-in-law." Her husband's parents could have sold her, mortgaged her, stoned her. But they had sent her back to her own mother and father, a mysterious act hinting at disgraces not told me. Perhaps they had thrown her out to deflect the avengers.

She was the only daughter; her four brothers went with her father, husband, and uncles "out on the road" and for some years became Western men. When the goods were divided among the family, three of the brothers took land, and the youngest, my father, chose an education. After my grandparents gave their daughter away to her husband's family, they had dispensed all the adventure and all the property. They expected her alone to keep the traditional ways, which her brothers, now among the barbarians, could fumble without detection. The heavy, deep-rooted women were to maintain the past against the flood, safe for returning. But the rare urge west had fixed upon our family, and so my aunt crossed boundaries not delineated in space. 20

The work of preservation demands that the feelings playing about in one's guts not be turned into action. Just watch their passing like cherry blossoms. But perhaps my aunt, my forerunner, caught in a slow life, let dreams grow and fade and after some months or years went toward what persisted. Fear at the enormities of the forbidden kept her desires delicate, wire and bone. She looked at a man because she liked the way the hair was tucked behind his ears, or she liked the question-mark line of a long torso curving at the shoulder and straight at the hip. For warm eyes or a soft voice or a slow walk—that's all—a few hairs, a line, a brightness, a sound, a pace, she gave up family. She offered us up for a charm that vanished with tiredness, a pigtail that didn't toss when the wind died. Why, the wrong lighting could erase the dearest thing about him.

It could very well have been, however, that my aunt did not take subtle enjoyment of her friend, but, a wild woman, kept rollicking company. Imagining her free with sex doesn't fit, though. I don't know any women like that, or men either. Unless I see her life branching into mine, she gives me no ancestral help.

To sustain her being in love, she often worked at herself in the mirror, guessing at the colors and shapes that would interest him, changing them frequently in order to hit on the right combination. She wanted him to look back.

On a farm near the sea, a woman who tended her appearance reaped a reputation for eccentricity. All the married women blunt-cut their hair in flaps about their ears or pulled it back in tight buns. No nonsense. Neither style blew easily into heart-catching tangles. And at their weddings they displayed themselves in their long hair for the last time. "It brushed the backs of my knees," my mother tells me. "It was braided, and even so, it brushed the backs of my knees."

At the mirror my aunt combined individuality into her bob. A bun could   25
have been contrived to escape into black streamers blowing in the wind or in quiet wisps about her face, but only the older women in our picture album wear buns. She brushed her hair back from her forehead, tucking the flaps behind her ears. She looped a piece of thread, knotted into a circle between her index fingers and thumbs, and ran the double strand across her forehead. When she closed her fingers as if she were making a pair of shadow geese bite, the string twisted together catching the little hairs. Then she pulled the thread away from her skin, ripping the hairs out neatly, her eyes watering from the needles of pain. Opening her fingers, she cleaned the thread, then rolled it along her hairline and the tops of her eyebrows. My mother did the same to me and my sisters and herself. I used to believe that the expression "caught by the short hairs" meant a captive held with a depilatory string. It especially hurt at the temples, but my mother said we were lucky we didn't have to have our feet bound when we were seven. Sisters used to sit on their beds and cry together, she said, as their mothers or their slave removed the bandages for a few minutes each night and let the blood gush back into their veins. I hope that the man my aunt loved appreciated a smooth brow, that he wasn't just a tits-and-ass man.

Once my aunt found a freckle on her chin, at a spot that the almanac said predestined her for unhappiness. She dug it out with a hot needle and washed the wound with peroxide.

More attention to her looks than these pullings of hairs and pickings at spots would have caused gossip among the villagers. They owned work clothes and good clothes, and they wore good clothes for feasting the new seasons. But since a woman combing her hair hexes beginnings, my aunt rarely found an occasion to look her best. Women looked like great sea snails—the corded wood, babies, and laundry they carried were the whorls on their backs. The Chinese did not admire a bent back; goddesses and warriors stood straight. Still there must have been a marvelous freeing of beauty when a worker laid down her burden and stretched and arched.

Such commonplace loveliness, however, was not enough for my aunt. She dreamed of a lover for the fifteen days of New Year's, the time for families to exchange visits, money, and food. She plied her secret comb. And sure enough she cursed the year, the family, the village, and herself.

Even as her hair lured her imminent lover, many other men looked at her. Uncles, cousins, nephews, brothers would have looked, too, had they been home between journeys. Perhaps they had already been restraining their curiosity, and they left, fearful that their glances, like a field of nesting birds, might be startled and caught. Poverty hurt, and that was their first reason for leaving. But another, final reason for leaving the crowded house was the never-said.

She may have been unusually beloved, the precious only daughter, spoiled and mirror gazing because of the affection the family lavished on her. When her husband left, they welcomed the chance to take her back from the in-laws; she could live like the little daughter for just a while longer. There are stories that my grandfather was different from other people, "crazy ever since the little Jap bayoneted him in the head." He used to put his naked penis on the dinner table, laughing. And one day he brought home a baby girl, wrapped up inside his brown Western-style greatcoat. He had traded one of his sons, probably my father, the youngest, for her. My grandmother made him trade back. When he finally got a daughter of his own, he doted on her. They must have all loved her, except perhaps my father, the only brother who never went back to China, having once been traded for a girl.

Brothers and sisters, newly men and women, had to efface their sexual color and present plain miens. Disturbing hair and eyes, a smile like no other, threatened the ideal of five generations living under one roof. To focus blurs, people shouted face to face and yelled from room to room. The immigrants I know have loud voices, unmodulated to American tones even after years away from the village where they called their friendships out across the fields. I have not been able to stop my mother's screams in public libraries or over telephones. Walking erect (knees straight, toes pointed forward, not pigeon-toed, which is Chinese-feminine) and speaking in an inaudible voice, I have tried to turn myself American-feminine. Chinese communication was loud, public. Only sick people had to whisper. But at the dinner table, where the family members came nearest one another, no one could talk, not the outcasts nor any eaters. Every word that falls from the mouth is a coin lost. Silently they gave and accepted food with both hands. A preoccupied child who took his bowl with one hand got a sideways glare. A complete moment of total attention is due everyone alike. Children and lovers have no singularity here, but my aunt used a secret voice, a separate attentiveness.

She kept the man's name to herself throughout her labor and dying; she did not accuse him that he be punished with her. To save her inseminator's name she gave silent birth.

He may have been somebody in her own household, but intercourse with a man outside the family would have been no less abhorrent. All the village

30

were kinsmen, and the titles shouted in loud country voices never let kinship be forgotten. Any man within visiting distance would have been neutralized as a lover—"brother," "younger brother," "older brother"—one hundred and fifteen relationship titles. Parents researched birth charts probably not so much to assure good fortune as to circumvent incest in a population that has but one hundred surnames. Everybody has eight million relatives. How useless then sexual mannerisms, how dangerous.

As if it came from an atavism deeper than fear, I used to add "brother" silently to boys' names. It hexed the boys, who would or would not ask me to dance, and made them less scary and as familiar and deserving of benevolence as girls.

But, of course, I hexed myself also—no dates. I should have stood up, both arms waving, and shouted out across libraries, "Hey, you! Love me back." I had no idea, though, how to make attraction selective, how to control its direction and magnitude. If I made myself American-pretty so that the five or six Chinese boys in the class fell in love with me, everyone else—the Caucasian, Negro, and Japanese boys—would too. Sisterliness, dignified and honorable, made much more sense.

Attraction eludes control so stubbornly that whole societies designed to organize relationships among people cannot keep order, not even when they bind people to one another from childhood and raise them together. Among the very poor and the wealthy, brothers married their adopted sisters, like doves. Our family allowed some romance, paying adult brides' prices and providing dowries so that their sons and daughters could marry strangers. Marriage promises to turn strangers into friendly relatives—a nation of siblings.

In the village structure, spirits shimmered among the live creatures, balanced and held in equilibrium by time and land. But one human being flaring up into violence could open up a black hole, a maelstrom that pulled in the sky. The frightened villagers, who depended on one another to maintain the real, went to my aunt to show her a personal, physical representation of the break she had made in the "roundness." Misallying couples snapped off the future, which was to be embodied in true offspring. The villagers punished her for acting as if she could have a private life, secret and apart from them.

If my aunt had betrayed the family at a time of large grain yields and peace, when many boys were born, and wings were being built on many houses, perhaps, she might have escaped such severe punishment. But the men—hungry, greedy, tired of planting in dry soil—had been forced to leave the village in order to send food-money home. There were ghost plagues, bandit plagues, wars with the Japanese, floods. My Chinese brother and sister had died of an unknown sickness. Adultery, perhaps only a mistake during good times, became a crime when the village needed food.

The round moon cakes and round doorways, the round tables of graduated size that fit one roundness inside another, round windows and rice bowls—these talismans had lost their power to warn this family of the law: a family must be whole, faithfully keeping the descent line by having sons to feed

35

the old and the dead, who in turn look after the family. The villagers came to show my aunt and her lover-in-hiding a broken house. The villagers were speeding up the circling of events because she was too shortsighted to see that her infidelity had already harmed the village, that waves of consequences would return unpredictably, sometimes in disguise, as now, to hurt her. This roundness had to be made coin-sized so that she would see its circumference: punish her at the birth of her baby. Awaken her to the inexorable. People who refused fatalism because they could invent small resources insisted on culpability. Deny accidents and wrest fault from the stars.

After the villagers left, their lanterns now scattering in various directions toward home, the family broke their silence and cursed her. "Aiaa, we're going to die. Death is coming. Death is coming. Look what you've done. You've killed us. Ghost! Dead ghost! Ghost! You've never been born." She ran out into the fields, far enough from the house so that she could no longer hear their voices, and pressed herself against the earth, her own land no more. When she felt the birth coming, she thought that she had been hurt. Her body seized together. "They've hurt me too much," she thought. "This is gall, and it will kill me." With forehead and knees against the earth, her body convulsed and then relaxed. She turned on her back, lay on the ground. The black well of sky and stars went out and out and out forever; her body and her complexity seemed to disappear. She was one of the stars, a bright dot in blackness, without home, without a companion, in eternal cold and silence. An agoraphobia rose in her, speeding higher and higher, bigger and bigger; she would not be able to contain it; there would be no end to fear.

Flayed, unprotected against space, she felt pain return, focusing her body. This pain chilled her — a cold, steady kind of surface pain. Inside, spasmodically, the other pain, the pain of the child, heated her. For hours she lay on the ground, alternately body and space. Sometimes a vision of normal comfort obliterated reality: she saw the family in the evening gambling at the dinner table, the young people massaging their elders' backs. She saw them congratulating one another, high joy on the mornings the rice shoots came up. When these pictures burst, the stars drew yet further apart. Black space opened.

She got to her feet to fight better and remembered that old-fashioned women gave birth in their pigsties to fool the jealous, pain-dealing gods, who do not snatch piglets. Before the next spasms could stop her, she ran to the pigsty, each step a rushing out into emptiness. She climbed over the fence and knelt in the dirt. It was good to have a fence enclosing her, a tribal person alone.

Laboring, this woman who had carried her child as a foreign growth that sickened her every day, expelled it at last. She reached down to touch the hot, wet, moving mass, surely smaller than anything human, and could feel that it was human after all — fingers, toes, nails, nose. She pulled it up on to her belly, and it lay curled there, butt in the air, feet precisely tucked one under the other. She opened her loose shirt and buttoned the child inside. After resting, it squirmed and thrashed and she pushed it up to her breast. It turned its head this way and that until it found her nipple. There, it made little snuffling

40

noises. She clenched her teeth at its preciousness, lovely as a young calf, a pig-let, a little dog.

She may have gone to the pigsty as a last act of responsibility: she would protect this child as she had protected its father. It would look after her soul, leaving supplies on her grave. But how would this tiny child without family find her grave when there would be no marker for her anywhere, neither in the earth nor the family hall? No one would give her a family hall name. She had taken the child with her into the wastes. At its birth the two of them had felt the same raw pain of separation, a wound that only the family pressing tight could close. A child with no descent line would not soften her life but only trail after her, ghostlike, begging her to give it purpose. At dawn the villagers on their way to the fields would stand around the fence and look.

Full of milk, the little ghost slept. When it awoke, she hardened her breasts against the milk that crying loosens. Toward morning she picked up the baby and walked to the well.   45

Carrying the baby to the well shows loving. Otherwise abandon it. Turn its face into the mud. Mothers who love their children take them along. It was probably a girl; there is some hope of forgiveness for boys.

"Don't tell anyone you had an aunt. Your father does not want to hear her name. She has never been born." I have believed that sex was unspeakable and words so strong and fathers so frail that "aunt" would do my father myste-rious harm. I have thought that my family, having settled among immigrants who had also been their neighbors in the ancestral land, needed to clean their name, and a wrong word would incite the kinspeople even here. But there is more to this silence: they want me to participate in her punishment. And I have.

In the twenty years since I heard this story I have not asked for details nor said my aunt's name; I do not know it. People who can comfort the dead can also chase after them to hurt them further — a reverse ancestor worship. The real punishment was not the raid swiftly inflicted by the villagers, but the fam-ily's deliberately forgetting her. Her betrayal so maddened them, they saw to it that she would suffer forever, even after death. Always hungry, always need-ing, she would have to beg food from other ghosts, snatch and steal it from those whose living descendants give them gifts. She would have to fight the ghosts massed at crossroads for the buns a few thoughtful citizens leave to de-coy her away from village and home so that the ancestral spirits could feast unharassed. At peace, they could act like gods, not ghosts, their descent lines providing them with paper suits and dresses, spirit money, paper houses, paper automobiles, chicken, meat, and rice into eternity — essences delivered up in smoke and flames, steam and incense rising from each rice bowl. In an attempt to make the Chinese care for people outside the family, Chairman Mao encour-ages us now to give our paper replicas to the spirits of outstanding soldiers and workers, no matter whose ancestors they may be. My aunt remains forever hungry. Goods are not distributed evenly among the dead.

My aunt haunts me — her ghost drawn to me because now, after fifty years of neglect, I alone devote pages of paper to her, though not origamied into houses and clothes. I do not think she always means me well. I am telling on her, and she was a spite suicide, drowning herself in the drinking water. The Chinese are always very frightened of the drowned one, whose weeping ghost, wet hair hanging and skin bloated, waits silently by the water to pull down a substitute.   [1976]

≡ THINKING ABOUT THE TEXT

1. This cautionary tale is meant to persuade Kingston to conform to her parents' values. What is the argument behind the narrative the mother tells? Does it make sense to you? What might be a contemporary argument in a middle-class American family?

2. Were you ever put at an "outcast table" (para. 19) or anything comparable in your house or school? Have you ever heard of such a ritual? What did happen when you were punished? What kinds of things were you punished for? Why do you think these specific things were chosen?

3. Is this also a tale about gender inequality? How does Kingston suggest this? How are relations between men and women portrayed here?

4. How do ghosts and spirits function in this essay? Which parts of this piece seem true to you, and which seem fictional? Why do you suppose Kingston blends these elements?

5. Sexual mores change over time and from country to country. What specifically about the aunt's context made her transgression so severe? How would her "crime" be viewed in contemporary America? Why? What do you think an ideal response would be?

≡ MAKING COMPARISONS

1. Discuss the reasons China Berkowitz and Kingston's aunt keep their pregnancies secret.

2. What explanations are there for the difference in China and Jeremy's fateful decision and Kingston's aunt's decision?

3. Discuss the idea of community in both narratives.

≡ WRITING ABOUT ISSUES

1. Some philosophers argue that neonaticide should not be a criminal offense. Write an argument essay that agrees or disagrees.

2. Write an essay that compares the notion of choice in both these narratives.

3. In the conclusion of Boyle's story, Jeremy thinks: "And what had he done to deserve it? He still couldn't understand" (para. 66). Write a brief comparison of this position with that of Kingston's aunt.

4. In *Intimate Reading*, her study of the memoir, Janet Ellerby claims that reading memoirs of women who keep secrets "will help those people who rush to damn unfortunate adolescent girls to understand why these desperate girls hide their pregnancies from their families . . . and themselves . . . and help others understand how a panicked and forsaken girl in unimaginable pain might hysterically abandon the newborn she has steadfastly denied, whether she gives birth in a delivery room or a high school bathroom . . . [and] will help our culture understand that we have not yet solved the physical and psychological obstacles that adolescent girls must brave when faced with unwanted pregnancies." Write an essay that agrees or disagrees with this position.

CHAPTER 8

Love

Our culture makes many claims about love: stories of the rejected lover who dies of a broken heart abound. Modern kings give up the throne, ancient cities go to war—all for love. Love is thought to be such a powerful emotion that its loss may even make one want to die or to kill. (In some countries, finding one's wife or husband in bed with a lover is a legal excuse for murder.) Men and women seem willing to radically change their lives to be near their beloved. These are a few examples of love's powerful influence on our behavior and our understanding of who we are.

Yet a serious discussion about the nature of love is often frustratingly difficult. We can all make a list of things we love: a cold beer in summer, a great science-fiction film, a new car, a quiet dinner with a good friend, a walk in fresh snow, a football game when our favorite team comes from behind for a dramatic victory. We love our parents, our siblings, our best friends. How can one word cover such diversity?

When we try to generalize about love, we find ourselves relying on specific incidents because giving examples is easier than giving definitions. If clarifying the essence of love seems difficult, perhaps it is because our stories, myths, and songs are filled with contradictions. Love conquers all, we say, but doesn't love fade? We profess our undying love, but divorce statistics soar. Love is complex and frustrating to pin down. Our culture even identifies different types of love: true love, platonic love, maternal love, erotic love. Yet opinions about love are strong; we all have evidence for what it is and isn't that we find persuasive.

But the evidence we find so convincing is influenced by cultural assumptions, probably more than we know. It would be naive to claim otherwise when we are bombarded with so many movies, songs, and stories about love. Indeed, some critics argue that romantic love is only a socially constructed illusion, merely an elaborate rationalization for physical desire. Once the carnal attraction fades, we get restless. At least, this is one argument, and probably not a popular one among college students in search of love. Because we know what we feel about those we love, we often grow impatient with other people's perspectives. We are likely to ignore friends who say, "He wouldn't treat you like that if he really loved you." Perhaps nothing arouses our interest more than a discussion of our hopes and dreams about love.

Our engagement with stories and poems about love is equally complex and ambivalent. Although the stories in this chapter often illuminate the sometimes dark passageways we take in our romantic journeys, there is no consensus about the final destination. Arguing about love stories engages us as much as it may also baffle us. As you read, rely on your own experience, ethical positions, and literary judgment in determining whether specific characters are indeed in love, whether they should continue their relationship, whether they need more commitment or less. The wise and the foolish seem equally perplexed in matters of the heart.

The first five clusters comprise poems about love. Four expressions of true love, two passionate love poems, three poems about melancholy love, and three poems about seductions lead up to Matthew Arnold's haunting "Dover Beach" and three cultural contexts for thinking about the poem. Three stories of romantic illusions are next, followed by a collection of stories by Kate Chopin and then two modern stories, in which a canonical tale by Raymond Carver is paired with Nathan Englander's homage. One of the world's great plays about jealousy, *Othello*, is next along with interesting critical commentary. Two essays about places of the heart follow. The penultimate cluster presents two essays that make an argument about marriage. The last cluster presents a poem and a story about arranged marriages that happened a hundred years ago that still elicit our compassion.

≡ True Love: Poems

WILLIAM SHAKESPEARE, "Let me not to the marriage of true minds"

JOHN KEATS, "Bright Star"

ELIZABETH BARRETT BROWNING, "How Do I Love Thee?"

E. E. CUMMINGS, "somewhere i have never travelled"

Think about the term *true love*. Why *true*? Does *love* need this modification? Isn't love supposed to be true? Is there a *false* love? Or is something else implied that *love* doesn't convey by itself? Might it be something like *the one-and-only*? Some writers seem committed to the idea that true love lasts forever, for better or worse, regardless of circumstances. Is this just a fantasy, something we hope will be true? Or is it a reality, delivered to those who are lucky or who work hard to make it true? See if you agree with the four poets in this cluster, some of whom are direct and clear about the possibilities of true love, while others take a more indirect, even playful tone.

≡ BEFORE YOU READ

Do you believe in true love? How would you describe it? How has the idea been portrayed in books and films you are familiar with?

WILLIAM SHAKESPEARE

Let me not to the marriage of true minds

William Shakespeare (1564–1616) is best known to modern readers as a dramatist; however, there is evidence that both he and his contemporaries valued his poetry above the plays. In 1598, for example, a writer praised Shakespeare's "sugared sonnets among his private friends." As with other aspects of his life and work, questions about how much autobiographical significance to attach to Shakespeare's subject matter continue to arise. Regardless of the discussion, there can be no doubt that the sonnets attributed to Shakespeare, at times directed to a man and at others directed to a woman, address the subject of love. Sonnet 116, which was written in 1609 and proposes a "marriage of true minds," is no exception.

Let me not to the marriage of true minds,
Admit impediments. Love is not love
Which alters when it alteration finds,
Or bends with the remover to remove:
Oh, no! it is an ever-fixèd mark,   5
That looks on tempests and is never shaken;
It is the star to every wandering bark,°   *small ship*

Whose worth's unknown, although his height be taken.
Love's not Time's fool, though rosy lips and cheeks
Within his bending sickle's compass come;   10
Love alters not with his brief hours and weeks,
But bears it out even to the edge of doom.
If this be error and upon me proved,
I never writ, nor no man ever loved.   *[1609]*

≡ THINKING ABOUT THE TEXT

1. Why would you be pleased if your beloved wrote you this sonnet? Is he professing his love or giving a definition of true love as unchanging?

2. What if love didn't last "even to the edge of doom" (line 12)? Why might it then be ordinary?

3. Shakespeare uses images to describe true love. Which one strikes you as apt? Can you suggest an image of your own?

4. The concluding couplet seems to be saying something like "I'm absolutely right." Do you think Shakespeare is? Can you think of a situation in which love should bend or alter?

5. The world seems to demonstrate that true love seldom lasts forever. Why then do writers of all kinds profess the opposite? If you really believe that true love does not exist, would you still marry? If your beloved asked you if your love would last forever, would you truthfully answer, "Only time will tell"?

JOHN KEATS
Bright Star

John Keats (1795–1821) was born into a working-class family. He hoped to be a physician but decided that poetry was his calling. His narrative poem Endymion *(1818) received poor reviews, but he was totally committed to his work. He was stricken with tuberculosis shortly after the poem's publication and went to Italy to recover. He died in Rome at age twenty-five.*

In 2009, Jane Campion directed Bright Star, *a film based on the last three years of Keats's life. The film focuses on his intense relationship with Fanny Brawne. Lines from many of his most famous poems are recited, including "La Belle Dame Sans Merci" and "Ode on Melancholy," as well as lines from his poetic letters to Fanny. On his tombstone is his own inscription: "Here lies one whose name was writ in water." Today Keats is considered one of literature's greatest poets.*

Bright star, would I were stedfast as thou art—
Not in lone splendour hung aloft the night

And watching, with eternal lids apart,
Like nature's patient, sleepless Eremite,°   *A Christian hermit*
The moving waters at their priestlike task   5
Of pure ablution round earth's human shores,
Or gazing on the new soft-fallen mask
Of snow upon the mountains and the moors —
No — yet still stedfast, still unchangeable,
Pillow'd upon my fair love's ripening breast,   10
To feel for ever its soft fall and swell,
Awake for ever in a sweet unrest,
Still, still to hear her tender-taken breath,
And so live ever — or else swoon to death.   *[1819]*

☰ THINKING ABOUT THE TEXT

1. Discuss how the speaker wants to be like the bright star in some ways, but not in others.

2. Is the speaker trying to stop time (as the pop star Jim Croce sang, "If I could save time in a bottle"), or is he hoping that his love will never change?

3. "Sweet unrest" (line 12) seems to be a contradiction. Is it? What is Keats trying to get at?

4. Is it psychologically healthy to want to have an unchanging love for someone forever? Is it realistic? Is it simply a kind of ritual to say such things?

5. Keats was quite sickly at the end of his short life. Do you think awareness of his serious illness influenced the theme of his poem?

☰ MAKING COMPARISONS

1. Compare the images of change that both Shakespeare and Keats use.

2. Compare Shakespeare's and Keats's use of the star metaphor.

3. Do both poets have similar notions of true love?

ELIZABETH BARRETT BROWNING
How Do I Love Thee?

Elizabeth Barrett Browning (1806–1861) was a prominent Victorian poet whose work was well received in England and the United States. She was raised in a wealthy family and was a studious, precocious child who read widely in classic and contemporary literature. Her first collection of poems, An Essay on Mind, with Other Poems, *was published in 1826. Elizabeth battled illness her whole life and often depended on opium and morphine. She married the poet Robert Browning in 1846, and they moved to Italy for her health. They had a son nicknamed Pen, Two verse novels,* Aurora Leigh *(1856) and* Sonnets from the Portuguese *(1850), which are both still highly regarded works, made her famous. "How Do I Love Thee?" is the popular title of the forty-third of her* Sonnets from the Portuguese.

How do I love thee? Let me count the ways.
I love thee to the depth and breath and height
My soul can reach, when feeling out of sight
For the ends of being and ideal grace.
I love thee to the level of every day's   5
Most quiet need, by sun and candle-light.
I love thee freely, as men strive for right.
I love thee purely, as they turn from praise.
I love thee with the passion put to use
In my old griefs, and with my childhood's faith.   10
I love thee with a love I seemed to lose
With my lost saints. I love thee with the breath,
Smiles, tears, of all my life; and, if God choose,
I shall but love thee better after death.   *[1845]*

≡ **THINKING ABOUT THE TEXT**

1. Explain the lines, ". . . when feeling out of sight / For the ends of being and ideal grace" (lines 3–4).

2. How would you translate ". . . to the level of every day's / Most quiet need, by sun and candle-light" (lines 5–6) into everyday prose?

3. How would you define these terms that Browning uses: "freely" (line 7), "purely" (line 8), and "childhood's faith" (line 10)?

4. How do you interpret Browning's idea that she loves with a love "I seemed to lose / With my lost saints" (lines 11–12)?

5. What other topics besides love are considered in Browning's sonnet?

≡ **MAKING COMPARISONS**

1. How would you describe the kind of love Browning writes about? Spiritual, physical, erotic, platonic, sentimental? Compare this love to that in Shakespeare and Keats.

2. Compare the theme of Browning's poem with Keats's and Shakespeare's themes.

3. How is death dealt with in these poems?

E. E. CUMMINGS
somewhere i have never travelled

E. E. Cummings is the pen name of Edward Estlin Cummings (1894–1962), and though he experimented with language on every level, he did not legally change his name to lowercase and preferred the usual uppercase. Born in Cambridge, Massachusetts, and educated at Harvard, he tried his hand at essays, plays, and other types of prose; in fact, it was a novel based on a World War I concentration camp experience in France, The Enormous Room *(1922), that first brought Cummings attention. It is his poetry, however, that most readers immediately recognize for its eccentric use of typography and punctuation, its wordplay and slang usage, its jazz rhythms, and its childlike foregrounding of the concrete above the abstract. Cummings hated pretension and would only agree to deliver the prestigious Eliot lectures at Harvard in 1953 if they were called* nonlectures. *His two large volumes of* The Complete Poems, 1913–1962, *published in 1972, include humor, understated satire, and celebrations of love and sex.*

somewhere i have never travelled, gladly beyond
any experience, your eyes have their silence:
in your most frail gesture are things which enclose me,
or which i cannot touch because they are too near

your slightest look easily will unclose me   5
though i have closed myself as fingers,
you open always petal by petal myself as Spring opens
(touching skilfully, mysteriously) her first rose
or if your wish be to close me, i and
my life will shut very beautifully, suddenly,   10

as when the heart of this flower imagines
the snow carefully everywhere descending;

nothing which we are to perceive in this world equals
the power of your intense fragility: whose texture
compels me with the colour of its countries,   15
rendering death and forever with each breathing

(i do not know what it is about you that closes
and opens; only something in me understands
the voice of your eyes is deeper than all roses)
nobody, not even the rain, has such small hands   *[1931]*   20

≡ THINKING ABOUT THE TEXT

1. In your own words, what is Cummings saying about the effect love has on him? Is this hyperbolic? Why?

2. Does love open us up? In what ways? Can you give a personal example of what a strong feeling did to you?

3. Is this a poem about love or obsession or romantic infatuation? What is the difference?

4. What do you think "the power of your intense fragility" (line 14) might mean? Is this a contradiction?

5. When Cummings says "something in me understands" (line 18), what might he mean? Is love located inside us somewhere? In our hearts? Our brains?

≡ MAKING COMPARISONS

1. Is Cummings's flower imagery more effective than the images that Shakespeare and Keats use?

2. Is this poem closer in theme to Keats's poem or to Browning's?

3. What do you imagine Shakespeare and Keats would think about Cummings's sentence structure? His images?

≡ WRITING ABOUT ISSUES

1. Translate the Cummings poem into concrete prose. Try not to use images; just explain the individual lines as simply as you can.

2. Write a comparison of the effects these four poems had on you.

3. Write a position paper arguing for or against the reality of true love. Make reference to two of the poems given here.

4. Find three more love poems by William Shakespeare or John Keats and write a report about the issues of love that this poet raises.

≡ Passionate Love: Poems

MICHAEL S. HARPER, "Discovery"

SUSAN MINOT, "My Husband's Back"

A brief online search will turn up scores of sites about love in all its variety and complexity. There are three types or five types or seven types, depending on the site. The Greeks started this confusing classification with eros, or unconditional love, and storge, or affectionate love. The list goes on: mania, infatuation, puppy love, and so forth. Although we have used the term passionate love for these two poems, think about how you would label the deep feelings in Harper's and Minot's poems.

≡ BEFORE YOU READ

Describe recent examples of passionate love you have read about or seen on television or in films.

MICHAEL S. HARPER
Discovery

Born in Brooklyn, New York, in 1951 to working-class parents, Michael S. Harper and his family soon moved to a predominantly white Los Angeles neighborhood. While attending college in Los Angeles, he worked as a postal worker, where he met educated black men like his father who came of age before the civil rights movement and had not been able to advance economically. Harper received an M.F.A. from the University of Iowa's creative writing program. His first book of poems, Dear John, Dear Coltrane *(1970), from which this selection is taken, was nominated for the National Book Award. He has received many writing awards, including a Guggenheim. Among his ten books of poetry are the recent* Songlines in Michaeltree: New and Collected Poems *(2000) and* Use Trouble *(2009). He is a professor of English at Brown University.*

We lay together, darkness all around,
I listen to her constant breath,
and when I thought she slept,
I too fell asleep.
But something stirred me, why I . . .   5
she was staring at me with her eyes,
her breasts still sturdy,
her thigh warming mine.
And I, a little shaken as she stroked
my skin and kissed my brow,   10

reached for the light turned on,
feeling for the heat which would
reveal how long she had looked
and cared.
The bulb was hot. It burned my hand.   *[1970]*   15

≡ THINKING ABOUT THE TEXT

1. The last sentence seems literal. But how might you read it metaphorically?

2. Why do you think Harper used the ellipsis in line 5? Is this an effective
   device, or should he have tried to say what the "something" was?

3. Why was the speaker "a little shaken" (line 9)? Would you feel that way
   in a similar situation, or would your response be something else? Surprise? Satisfaction?

4. Why did he want to know "how long she had looked / and cared" (lines
   13–14)? Why might it matter to him? Would it to you?

5. Would you interpret the staring as evidence of passionate love? Would
   you interpret the speaker's behavior as true love or something else?

SUSAN MINOT

My Husband's Back

Susan Minot (b. 1956) was born in Boston and grew up in Manchester-by-the-Sea,
Massachusetts. She studied writing and painting at Brown University and received an
M.F.A. from Columbia University. Minot was an editor of the literary journal Grant
Street. *Her first book,* Monkeys *(1986), is a collection of nine stories about a large*
New England family. Minot's female protagonists are searching for love, usually un-
successfully. Her best-selling collection Lust and Other Stories *(1989) focuses on*
romantic love, although one critic cautions readers not to "look for a happy, mutual,
heterosexual relationship in Minot. You will not find it." Her novel Evening *(1998)*
was made into a popular film in 2007 starring Vanessa Redgrave, Meryl Streep, and
Claire Danes. Her novel about war-torn Africa, Thirty Girls, *was published in 2014.*
A volume of her verse, Poems 4am, *was published in 2002. The women in these*
poems seem more optimistic about love than do those in her fiction.

Sunday evening.
Breakdown hour. Weeping into
a pot of burnt rice. Sun dimmed
like a light bulb gone out
behind a gray lawn of snow.   5
The baby flushed with the flu
asleep on a pillow.

The fire won't catch.
The wet wood's caked
with ice. Sitting   10
on the couch my spine
collides with all its bones
and I watch my husband
peer past the glass grate
and blow.   15
His back in a snug plaid shirt
gray and white
leaning into the woodstove
is firm and compact
like a young man's back.   20

And the giant world which swirls
in my head
stopping most thought
suddenly ceases
to spin. It sits   25
right there, the back I love,
animal and gamine,° leaning
on one arm.
I could crawl on it forever
the one point in the world   30
turns out
I have traveled everywhere
to get to.   *[2005]*

gamine: Untamed and mischievous.

≡ **THINKING ABOUT THE TEXT**

1. Why is the speaker "Weeping" (line 2)? Is she unhappy? Frustrated? Overwhelmed?

2. Why does "the giant world" (line 21) cease to spin?

3. What do you think the speaker means in the last two lines when she says she has "traveled everywhere / to get to" (lines 32–33)?

4. Do you think being in love can help a person deal with global tragedies? Domestic frustration? Cosmic gloom?

5. Do you think Minot's feelings of love are momentary, caused by the "Breakdown hour" (line 2)?

≡ **MAKING COMPARISONS**

1. Which of the two characters in "Discovery" might Minot's narrator be? Why?

2. Compare the use of light bulbs in these two poems.

3. How would you describe the two women's attitudes toward love?

≡ WRITING ABOUT ISSUES

1. Write an essay that discusses the complexity of passionate love in these two poems.

2. Write an essay that discusses Minot's narrator's idea that love can be an antidote to life's difficulties.

3. Argue that the passion exhibited by Harper's partner and Minot's narrator is good or bad for a relationship.

4. Research the different kinds of love, including romantic, sentimental, erotic, platonic, spiritual, and so forth. Write an essay that discusses some of these, giving examples from your reading and film watching.

EDNA ST. VINCENT MILLAY, "What Lips My Lips Have Kissed, and Where, and Why"

PABLO NERUDA, "The Song of Despair"

ROBIN BECKER, "Morning Poem"

It is not uncommon, of course, for a romantic relationship to evolve from intense physical attraction or erotic love in the beginning to sadness or melancholy at the end. Naturally, poets have written about all stages of love in all their complexity, from joy and wonder to resignation and despair. Few of us would prefer to suffer than to exult in love, but perhaps Tennyson's lines " 'Tis better to have loved and lost than never to have loved at all" captures the pragmatic attitude that understands that love is a risk worth taking. Although at different times in history melancholy was embraced as an appropriate attitude toward the vagaries of love, most of us probably hope to recover, not wallow in the sorrow of a failed romance. In our selections, Edna St. Vincent Millay and Pablo Neruda offer us memorable variations on love lost, whereas Robin Becker's narrator tries to deal with the implications of "while nothing lasts" even in the midst of a passionate affair.

EDNA ST. VINCENT MILLAY
What Lips My Lips Have Kissed, and Where, and Why

Edna St. Vincent Millay (1892–1950) was born in Rockland, Maine. Her mother encouraged her to be ambitious and self-sufficient and taught her about literature at an early age. On the strength of her early poems, Millay won a scholarship to Vassar, where she became a romantic legend for breaking the "hearts of half the undergraduate class." She also soon became wildly famous for her love poetry, giving readings in large auditoriums across the country, much like a contemporary rock star. She was openly bisexual, and her fame, talent, beauty, and bohemian aura was said to have driven her many admirers to distraction. A biography by Nancy Milford, Savage Beauty *(2001), quotes from dozens of letters to Millay, whining, pleading, and groveling for her favors. Milford writes that "she gave the Jazz Age its lyric voice." In fact, we still use a phrase that Salon.com says Millay "invented to describe a life of impudent abandon":*

> *My candle burns at both ends;*
> *It will not last the night;*
> *But oh, my foes, and oh, my friends —*
> *It gives a lovely light!*

Once called "the greatest female poet since Sappho," Millay's reputation in academic circles has fallen off somewhat. Perhaps her work seems a bit obvious compared to the cerebral and allusive free verse of poets like T. S. Eliot. But some critics still think of her as America's "most illustrious love poet." The title poem of Renascence and Other Poems (1917) *ranks as a landmark of modern literature, and the collection itself is ranked fifth on the New York Public Library's Books of the Century. The following poem is from* Collected Poems (1956).

What lips my lips have kissed, and where, and why,
I have forgotten, and what arms have lain
Under my head till morning; but the rain
Is full of ghosts tonight, that tap and sigh
Upon the glass and listen for reply,   5
And in my heart there stirs a quiet pain
For unremembered lads that not again
Will turn to me at midnight with a cry.
Thus in winter stands the lonely tree,
Nor knows what birds have vanished one by one,   10
Yet knows its boughs more silent than before:
I cannot say what loves have come and gone,
I only know that summer sang in me
A little while, that in me sings no more.   *[1923]*

≡ THINKING ABOUT THE TEXT

1. What is it the speaker misses if she can't remember who her lovers were?

2. What does Millay mean by "a quiet pain" (line 6)?

3. Is Millay the "lonely tree" in winter (line 9)? Does it surprise you that she was only thirty-one when she wrote this poem?

4. Do you read the last two lines as saying that the speaker is no longer in love?

5. How would you describe the tone of this poem? Is it wistful or nostalgic? Appropriate? Regretful or sentimental? Bittersweet or simply sad?

PABLO NERUDA
The Song of Despair

Pablo Neruda (1904–1973), a Nobel Prize–winning poet, was born in Chile and began writing at a young age. He was publishing essays at thirteen, and his most famous collection, from which our poem is selected, Twenty Love Poems and a Song of Despair, *gave him an international reputation at twenty. Neruda was intensely political during most of his adult life, supporting leftist causes. As a result, he spent years in exile from Chile because of his Communist sympathies. He did, however, also spend many years in the diplomatic service, which is a traditional way in Latin America of honoring leading poets. He was widely known as the "people's poet." Gabriel García Márquez, a renowned Colombian novelist, called Neruda "the greatest poet of the twentieth century in any language."*

Translated by W. S. Merwin

The memory of you emerges from the night around me.
The river mingles its stubborn lament with the sea.

Deserted like the wharves at dawn.
It is the hour of departure, oh deserted one!

Cold flower heads are raining over my heart.   5
Oh pit of debris, fierce cave of the shipwrecked.

In you the wars and the flights accumulated.
From you the wings of the song birds rose.

You swallowed everything, like distance.
Like the sea, like time. In you everything sank!   10

It was the happy hour of assault and the kiss.
The hour of the spell that blazed like a lighthouse.

Pilot's dread, fury of a blind diver,
turbulent drunkenness of love, in you everything sank!

In the childhood of mist my soul, winged and wounded.   15
Lost discoverer, in you everything sank!

You girdled sorrow, you clung to desire,
sadness stunned you, in you everything sank!

I made the wall of shadow draw back,
beyond desire and act, I walked on.   20

Oh flesh, my own flesh, woman whom I loved and lost,
I summon you in the moist hour, I raise my song to you.

Like a jar you housed the infinite tenderness,
and the infinite oblivion shattered you like a jar.

There was the black solitude of the islands,   25
and there, woman of love, your arms took me in.

There were thirst and hunger, and you were the fruit.
There were grief and the ruins, and you were the miracle.

Ah woman, I do not know how you could contain me
in the earth of your soul, in the cross of your arms!   30

How terrible and brief was my desire of you!
How difficult and drunken, how tensed and avid.

Cemetery of kisses, there is still fire in your tombs,
still the fruited boughs burn, pecked at by birds.

Oh the bitten mouth, oh the kissed limbs,   35
oh the hungering teeth, oh the entwined bodies.

Oh the mad coupling of hope and force
in which we merged and despaired.

And the tenderness, light as water and as flour.
And the word scarcely begun on the lips.   40

This was my destiny and in it was the voyage of my longing,
and in it my longing fell, in you everything sank!

Oh pit of debris, everything fell into you,
what sorrow did you not express, in what sorrow are you not drowned!

From billow to billow you still called and sang.   45
Standing like a sailor in the prow of a vessel.

You still flowered in songs, you still broke in currents.
Oh pit of debris, open and bitter well.

Pale blind diver, luckless slinger,
lost discoverer, in you everything sank!   50

It is the hour of departure, the hard cold hour
which the night fastens to all the timetables.

The rustling belt of the sea girdles the shore.
Cold stars heave up, black birds migrate.

Deserted like the wharves at dawn.   55
Only the tremulous shadow twists in my hands.

Oh farther than everything. Oh farther than everything.
It is the hour of departure. Oh abandoned one.   *[1969]*

≣ **THINKING ABOUT THE TEXT**

1. The narrator clearly misses someone who was once his beloved. What
   images suggest this? What lines most clearly suggest his feelings?

2. How do you read Neruda's repeated phrase "in you everything sank"?

3. What does Neruda seem to be doing "in the moist hour" (line 22)? How
   do you read the lines "How terrible and brief was my desire of you! /
   How difficult and drunken, how tensed and avid" (lines 31–32)?

4. Explain what is meant by the couplet: "Cemetery of kisses, there is still
   fire in your tombs / still the fruited boughs burn, pecked at by birds"
   (lines 33–34). Translate these lines into simple prose.

5. Give several examples and explain Neruda's reasons for using contradictory images and feelings in the poem.

≡ MAKING COMPARISONS

1. Compare the use of nature imagery to suggest mood in Millay's and Neruda's poems.
2. Compare the use of birds in both poems.
3. Compare the use of memory in both poems.

ROBIN BECKER
Morning Poem

Robin Becker (b. 1951) was born in Philadelphia, Pennsylvania, and received her B.A. (1973) and M.A. (1976) from Boston University. She taught for many years at the Massachusetts Institute of Technology. She has been teaching at Penn State since 1994. She has published seven books of poetry, including Domain of Perfect Affection *(2006), a collection informed by feminist and lesbian sympathies. She was appointed Penn State Laureate in 2010. The noted poet Maxine Kumin says Becker's poetry has a "controlled ironic intelligence."*

Listen. It's morning. Soon I'll see your hand reach
for my watch, the water will agitate in the kettle,
but listen. Traffic. I want your dreams first. And
to slide my leg beneath yours before the day opens.
Wait. We slept late. You'll be moody, the phone   5
will ring, someone wanting something. Let me put
my hands in your hair. Who I was last night I would
be again. This is how the future holds me, how depression
wakes with us; my body shelters it. Let me
put my head on your breast. I know nothing lasts.   10
I would try to hold you back, not out of meanness
but fear. Oh my practical, my worldly-wise. You
know how the body falters, falls in on itself. Tell me
that we will never want from each other what we
cannot have. Lie. It's morning.   *[2008]*   15

≡ THINKING ABOUT THE TEXT

1. Why does the speaker say that "depression wakes with us" (lines 8–9)?
2. What does the narrator mean by "I would try to hold you back" (line 11)?

3. How do the following words or phrases suggest the narrator's mood: "watch," "agitate," "Traffic," "slept late," "moody," "the phone will ring" (lines 2–6)?

4. How might "lie" in the last line be ambiguous? How is the meaning of the phrase "It's morning" in the last line different from the opening line?

5. What do you think the narrator means when she says "who I was last night I would / be again" (lines 7–8)?

≡ MAKING COMPARISONS

1. Compare the use of night in these poems.

2. Compare the line "I know nothing lasts" (line 10) in "Morning Poem" with the last two lines of Millay's poem.

3. Compare the attitudes of the three narrators toward loss.

≡ WRITING ABOUT ISSUES

1. Write a narrative that translates Neruda's poem into prose and that tells the story of the love affair from beginning to end, from "your arms took me in" (line 26) to "the hour of departure" (line 51). Include the various moods the speaker moves through.

2. Write a brief essay that argues that Millay has or does not have a healthier attitude toward love affairs than either Becker or Neruda.

3. Argue that the attitude of one of these poets toward love affairs is closer to that of today's college students than the others. Refer to specific lines or ideas in all three poems.

4. Read John Keats's classic poem "Ode on Melancholy," and write an essay that compares Keats's views on melancholic love with Neruda's.

JOHN DONNE, "The Flea"

ANDREW MARVELL, "To His Coy Mistress"

T. S. ELIOT, "The Love Song of J. Alfred Prufrock"

Surely the idea of men trying to convince women to sleep with them is neither new nor surprising. As the line from the Talking Heads has it, "Same as it ever was." Naturally such impulses have found their way into literature, from the Greeks to the present. It was the Roman poet Horace, after all, who made famous the term *carpe diem*, or "seize the day," an attitude that became quite popular among poets in the seventeenth century. Their rhetorical strategy was simple: sleep with me before time runs out. If the logic is somewhat dubious, their poetic sophistication and inventiveness perhaps make up for the flawed logic. And, of course, women at the time were expected to be virgins until marriage, and their marriage prospects and options in general were seriously diminished if they were not. Perhaps the most famous of these poems is Andrew Marvell's "To His Coy Mistress." And while not technically a carpe diem poem, John Donne's obvious seductive intentions have made "The Flea" famous for its wildly imaginative attempts to bring logic to his physical urges.

We also include here one of the most famous poems of the twentieth century, "The Love Song of J. Alfred Prufrock," because Prufrock's journey is often viewed as an attempt to either propose marriage or engage in a seduction. But Prufrock vacillates so much and is so uncertain about love and seems so fearful and so anxious that we wonder if he is up to the task. Prufrock is often seen as a modern antihero who reflects our own doubts and lack of self-esteem about love. Prufrock seems alienated in a meaningless world and as such is surely an ironic modern counterpoint to the confident and heedless narrator of Marvell's poem.

≡ BEFORE YOU READ

Are seduction poems (or songs or letters) effective? Is such an offer more effectively made in person? What would the difference be? Could you say some things in a letter, say, that you couldn't (or wouldn't) say in person?

JOHN DONNE

The Flea

Long regarded as a major English writer, John Donne (1572–1631) was also trained as a lawyer and clergyman. Around 1594, he converted from Catholicism to Anglicanism; in 1615, he was ordained; and in 1621, he was appointed to the prestigious position of dean of St. Paul's Cathedral in London. Today, his sermons continue to be studied as literature, yet he is more known for his poetry. When he was a young man, he often wrote about love, but later he focused on religious themes. In the following classic poem—a complex combination of poetic sophistication and persuasive rhetoric (if somewhat ridiculous logic)—the narrator tries to convince a lady to sleep with him. His clever and seemingly serious argument hinges on a flea having bitten both the speaker and his mistress, and thus their blood is joined. Actually, at the time, it was believed that blood was exchanged during intercourse. The speaker's insistence is both amusing and shocking.

Mark but this flea, and mark in this,
How little that which thou deniest me is;
It sucked me first, and now sucks thee,
And in this flea our two bloods mingled be;
Thou know'st that this cannot be said   5
A sin, nor shame, nor loss of maidenhead,
    Yet this enjoys before it woo,
    And pampered swells with one blood made of two,
    And this, alas, is more than we would do.

Oh stay, three lives in one flea spare,   10
Where we almost, nay more than married are.
This flea is you and I, and this
Our mariage bed, and marriage temple is;
Though parents grudge, and you, w'are met,
And cloistered in these living walls of jet.   15
    Though use make you apt to kill me,
    Let not to that, self-murder added be,
    And sacrilege, three sins in killing three.

Cruel and sudden, hast thou since
Purpled thy nail, in blood of innocence?   20
Wherein could this flea guilty be,
Except in that drop which it sucked from thee?
Yet thou triumph'st, and say'st that thou
Find'st not thy self, nor me the weaker now;
    'Tis true; then learn how false, fears be: 25
    Just so much honor, when thou yield'st to me,
    Will waste, as this flea's death took life from thee.   *[1633]*

☰ THINKING ABOUT THE TEXT

1. Using straightforward prose, explain why the narrator thinks his mistress should have sex with him.

2. Besides "kill" and "death," words often used in Donne's time for sexual intercourse, what other terms in the poem have a sexual connotation or double meaning?

3. Choose several metaphors in the poem and explain their significance.

4. How does the narrator turn the argument against his beloved in the conclusion?

5. Probably not many women either then or now would be persuaded by this argument. The narrator seems so clever and sophisticated that he must know that. Do you agree? Are his motives as simple as they seem? What might his thinking be? Since it appears that his love might have killed the flea ("Purpled thy nail, in blood of innocence" [line 20]), what do you imagine her response to him is?

ANDREW MARVELL

To His Coy Mistress

Andrew Marvell (1621–1678) was famous in his own time as an adroit politician and a writer of satire, but modern readers admire him for the style and content of his lyric, metaphysical poetry. Born into a Protestant family, Marvell was tolerant of Catholicism from a young age, and his willingness to somehow circumvent the religious prejudices of seventeenth-century England allowed his continued success. He traveled to Holland, France, Italy, and Spain — possibly to avoid the English civil war as a young man and undoubtedly to spy for England in later years. He tutored Cromwell's ward and later served on his Council of State but was influential enough during the Restoration to get his fellow poet and mentor, John Milton, released from prison. Although admired by the Romantic poets of the early nineteenth century, Marvell's poetry (much of it published after his death) was revived in the twentieth century by T. S. Eliot and has been widely read for its ironic approach to the conventions of love.

Had we but world enough, and time,
This coyness, lady, were no crime.
We would sit down, and think which way
To walk, and pass our long love's day.
Thou by the Indian Ganges'° side   5
Shouldst rubies find; I by the tide
Of Humber° would complain.° I would
Love you ten years before the Flood,
And you should, if you please, refuse
Till the conversion of the Jews.   10
My vegetable love should grow°
Vaster than empires, and more slow;
An hundred years should go to praise

---

5 Ganges: A river in India sacred to the Hindus.   **7 Humber:** An estuary that flows through Marvell's native town, Hull.   **complain:** Sing love songs.   **11 My vegetable love . . . grow:** A slow, insensible growth, like that of a vegetable.

Thine eyes and on thy forehead gaze,
Two hundred to adore each breast,   15
But thirty thousand to the rest:
An age at least to every part,
And the last age should show your heart.
For, lady, you deserve this state,
Nor would I love at lower rate.   20
     But at my back I always hear
Time's wingèd chariot hurrying near;
And yonder all before us lie
Deserts of vast eternity.
Thy beauty shall no more be found,   25
Nor in thy marble vault shall sound
My echoing song; then worms shall try
That long preserved virginity,
And your quaint honor turn to dust,
And into ashes all my lust.   30
The grave's a fine and private place,
But none, I think, do there embrace.
     Now, therefore, while the youthful hue
Sits on thy skin like morning dew,
And while thy willing soul transpires°   35
At every pore with instant fires,
Now let us sport us while we may,
And now, like amorous birds of prey,
Rather at once our time devour
Than languish in his slow-chapped° power.   40
Let us roll all our strength and all
Our sweetness up into one ball,
And tear our pleasures with rough strife
Thorough° the iron gates of life.
Thus, though we cannot make our sun   45
Stand still, yet we will make him run.   *[1681]*

35 transpires: Breathes forth.   **40 slow-chapped:** Slow-jawed.   **44 Thorough:** Through.

≣ THINKING ABOUT THE TEXT

1. Considered as both an intellectual and an emotional argument, what is the narrator's goal, and what specific claims does he make? Are they convincing? Do you think they were in 1681? Do you think women three hundred years ago worried about virginity? Why?

2. What does this poem say about the needs of Marvell's audience? What assumptions about women does the poem make?

3. How many sections does this poem have? What is the purpose of each?

How is the concluding couplet in each related to that section? Is the rhyme scheme related to the meaning of these couplets?

4. Is the speaker passionate? Sincere? How do you make such a decision? Do you look at his language or at his message?

5. Some feminist readers see in the last ten lines a kind of indirect threat, a suggestion of force through the use of violent images. Is this a plausible reading? If this is the case, what do you now think of the narrator's pleading?

≡ MAKING COMPARISONS

1. Compare the logic of seduction in Donne's and Marvell's poems.

2. Compare the use of a woman's honor in both poems.

3. Compare the tone of both poems. Is one more likely to achieve its goal than the other?

T. S. ELIOT

The Love Song of J. Alfred Prufrock

One of the most respected intellectuals of his time, Thomas Stearns Eliot (1888–1965) was a poet, playwright (Murder in the Cathedral), and critic (The Sacred Wood). His poem "The Waste Land" (1922), considered a modernist masterpiece, is perhaps the last century's most influential poem. The long-running Broadway musical Cats is based on some of Eliot's lighter poems. Born in America and educated at Harvard, Eliot lived his mature life in England. He was awarded the Nobel Prize for literature in 1948.

> *S'io credesse che mia risposta fosse*
> *A persona che mai tornasse al mondo,*
> *Questa fiamma staria senza più scosse.*
> *Ma perciocchè giammai di questo fondo*
> *Non tornò vivo alcun, s'i'odo il vero,*
> *Senza tema d'infamia ti rispondo.*°

Let us go then, you and I,
When the evening is spread out against the sky
Like a patient etherized upon a table;
Let us go, through certain half-deserted streets,
The muttering retreats   5
Of restless nights in one-night cheap hotels

EPIGRAPH: **S'io . . . rispondo:** In Dante's *Inferno,* a sufferer in hell says, "If I thought I was talking to someone who might return to earth, this flame would cease; but if what I have heard is true, no one does return; therefore, I can speak to you without fear of infamy."

And sawdust restaurants with oyster-shells:
Streets that follow like a tedious argument
Of insidious intent

To lead you to an overwhelming question . . .   10
Oh, do not ask, "What is it?"
Let us go and make our visit.

In the room the women come and go
Talking of Michelangelo.

    The yellow fog that rubs its back upon the window panes,   15
The yellow smoke that rubs its muzzle on the window panes
Licked its tongue into the corners of the evening,
Lingered upon the pools that stand in drains,
Let fall upon its back the soot that falls from chimneys,
Slipped by the terrace, made a sudden leap,   20
And seeing that it was a soft October night,
Curled once about the house, and fell asleep.

    And indeed there will be time°
For the yellow smoke that slides along the street,
Rubbing its back upon the window panes;   25
There will be time, there will be time
To prepare a face to meet the faces that you meet;
There will be time to murder and create,
And time for all the works and days° of hands
That lift and drop a question on your plate: 30
Time for you and time for me,
And time yet for a hundred indecisions,
And for a hundred visions and revisions,
Before the taking of a toast and tea.
In the room the women come and go   35
Talking of Michelangelo.
    And indeed there will be time
To wonder, "Do I dare?" and, "Do I dare?" —
Time to turn back and descend the stair,
With a bald spot in the middle of my hair —   40
(They will say: "How his hair is growing thin!")
My morning coat, my collar mounting firmly to the chin,
My necktie rich and modest, but asserted by a simple pin —
(They will say: "But how his arms and legs are thin!")
Do I dare   45
Disturb the universe?

---

23 there will be time: An allusion to Ecclesiastes 3:1–8: "To everything there is a season, and a time to every purpose under heaven." **29 works and days:** Hesiod's eighth-century B.C.E. poem gave practical advice.

In a minute there is time
For decisions and revisions which a minute will reverse.

    For I have known them all already, known them all:
Have known the evenings, mornings, afternoons,   50
I have measured out my life with coffee spoons;
I know the voices dying with a dying fall
Beneath the music from a farther room.
      So how should I presume?

    And I have known the eyes already, known them all —   55
The eyes that fix you in a formulated phrase,
And when I am formulated, sprawling on a pin,
When I am pinned and wriggling on the wall,
Then how should I begin
To spit out all the butt-ends of my days and ways?   60
      And how should I presume?

    And I have known the arms already, known them all —
Arms that are braceleted and white and bare
(But in the lamplight, downed with light brown hair!)
      Is it perfume from a dress   65
      That makes me so digress?
Arms that lie along a table, or wrap about a shawl.
      And should I then presume?
      And how should I begin?

    Shall I say, I have gone at dusk through narrow streets,   70
And watched the smoke that rises from the pipes
Of lonely men in shirtsleeves, leaning out of windows? . . .
I should have been a pair of ragged claws
Scuttling across the floors of silent seas.

    And the afternoon, the evening, sleeps so peacefully!   75
Smoothed by long fingers,
Asleep . . . tired . . . or it malingers,
Stretched on the floor, here beside you and me.
Should I, after tea and cakes and ices,
Have the strength to force the moment to its crisis?   80
But though I have wept and fasted, wept and prayed,
Though I have seen my head (grown slightly bald) brought in upon a
      platter,°
I am no prophet — and here's no great matter;
I have seen the moment of my greatness flicker,
And I have seen the eternal Footman hold my coat, and snicker,   85
      And in short, I was afraid.

82 head . . . platter: Like John the Baptist (Matt. 14:1–12).

And would it have been worth it, after all,
After the cups, the marmalade, the tea,
Among the porcelain, among some talk of you and me,
Would it have been worth while   90
To have bitten off the matter with a smile,
To have squeezed the universe into a ball°
To roll it toward some overwhelming question,
To say: "I am Lazarus,° come from the dead,
Come back to tell you all, I shall tell you all" —   95
If one, settling a pillow by her head,
    Should say: "That is not what I meant at all;
    That is not it, at all."

And would it have been worth it, after all,
Would it have been worth while,   100
After the sunsets and the dooryards and the sprinkled streets,
After the novels, after the teacups, after the skirts that trail along the
    floor —
And this, and so much more? —
It is impossible to say just what I mean!
But as if a magic lantern° threw the nerves in patterns on a screen: 105
Would it have been worth while
If one, settling a pillow or throwing off a shawl,
And turning toward the window, should say:
    "That is not it at all,
    That is not what I meant, at all."   110

No! I am not Prince Hamlet, nor was meant to be;
Am an attendant lord,° one that will do
To swell a progress,° start a scene or two
Advise the prince: withal, an easy tool,
Deferential, glad to be of use,   115
Politic, cautious, and meticulous;
Full of high sentence, but a bit obtuse;
At times, indeed, almost ridiculous —
Almost, at times, the Fool.
I grow old . . . I grow old . . .   120
I shall wear the bottoms of my trowsers rolled.

    Shall I part my hair behind?° Do I dare to eat a peach°?
I shall wear white flannel trowsers, and walk upon the beach.
I have heard the mermaids singing, each to each.

---

92 squeezed . . . ball: See lines 41–42 of Marvell's "To His Coy Mistress" (p. 599).   **94 "I
am Lazarus":** Raised from the dead by Jesus.   **105 magic lantern:** Precursor of the slide
projector.   **112 attendant lord:** Like Polonius in Shakespeare's *Hamlet*.   **113 progress:** State procession.   **121–122 trowsers rolled . . . part my hair behind:** The latest
fashion. **eat a peach:** Considered a risky fruit.

I do not think that they will sing to me.   125

I have seen them riding seaward on the waves,
Combing the white hair of the waves blown back
When the wind blows the water white and black.

We have lingered in the chambers of the sea
By seagirls wreathed with seaweed red and brown,   130
Till human voices wake us, and we drown.   *[1917]*

≣ THINKING ABOUT THE TEXT

1. Do you think Prufrock is on a journey to propose marriage, to have a sexual rendezvous, or to do something else?

2. Is Prufrock enchanted with women (lines 62–67) or wary of them (lines 55–61)? What other lines might help to answer this question?

3. How do you interpret the questions "Do I dare" (lines 38, 45), "So how should I presume?" (line 54), and "And how should I begin?" (line 69)?

4. How old do you think Prufrock is? Can you cite some evidence in the text? How might his age (young man? middle-aged man?) be a factor in the purpose for his journey toward marriage, casual sex, or something else?

5. Why do you think Prufrock ends his poem with fantasies about mermaids? Do you read this as an admission of failure?

≣ MAKING COMPARISONS

1. Compare the narrators in these three poems.

2. Compare the use of time in Marvell's and Eliot's poems.

3. What do you suspect Donne and Marvell would have thought of Prufrock's "Do I dare"?

≣ WRITING ABOUT ISSUES

1. Argue that Prufrock does or does not represent contemporary concerns about romantic relationships.

2. Write a letter to Donne or Marvell explaining why contemporary readers of his poem might find his proposal objectionable.

3. Write a letter to Prufrock explaining why you think his attitude toward love is either accurate or ill-founded.

4. Argue that contemporary social networks like Facebook and Twitter make verbal seduction easier or more difficult.

☰ Love as a Haven: Cultural Contexts for a Poem

MATTHEW ARNOLD, "Dover Beach"

CULTURAL CONTEXTS:

CHARLES DICKENS, From *Hard Times*

FRIEDRICH ENGELS, From *The Condition of the Working Class in England*

JAMES ELI ADAMS, "Narrating Nature: Darwin"

Considered one of the greatest poems of the Victorian period, Matthew Arnold's "Dover Beach" expresses the spiritual malaise troubling many educated people in the middle of the nineteenth century. Although England was becoming the most powerful country in the world, there were serious social problems left unattended as it focused on its empire. And Matthew Arnold was keenly aware of them. He was educated to be an educational reformer, to promote a rich intellectual and ethical spirit in English society. Moral and social issues were crucial for him, and he championed the study of the best that was said and thought. But there was such a class division in England that only a small fraction of the population was able to reap the rewards Arnold thought a humanistic education could deliver. Such injustice troubled him.

Industrialization brought power and wealth to some and great poverty to many others. It is difficult to educate children when they are starving and cold. Prostitution was also a huge social problem, compounded by disease and poverty. Child labor was also widespread, and hundreds of thousands of nine- and ten-year-olds were working sixty hours a week under gruesomely unsafe and brutal conditions. To add to Arnold's ethical discomfort, scientific advances in geology and biology seemed to many to be in direct contradiction to the natural history found in the first book of the Bible, Genesis. Scientific evidence was demonstrating that the earth was millions of years old, not six thousand. Although his ideas had been well-known in scientific circles for a while, Charles Darwin's *On the Origin of the Species* (1859) dealt a body blow to traditional religious ideas of creation with the theory that all life had evolved over millions of years through a process that put an emphasis on chance and randomness over a clear divine plan. If the Bible was so wrong about these facts, perhaps the whole basis of Christianity should be called into question. Such thoughts produced a crisis of faith for many thinkers like Arnold.

"Dover Beach" reflects a sense of spiritual ambiguity and abandonment as Arnold contemplates the "turbid ebb and flow / Of human misery." Although a progressive who supported objective scientific investigation and discovery, Arnold was disturbed by the reality that we might be on our own in the universe. He hears the "melancholy, long, withdrawing roar" of traditional faith and looks to love for solace in a world that is not as simple and comforting as it once seemed. And so, like so many before and after him, he hopes that love, or maybe simply loyalty, can be an antidote to his discontented soul. Although many critics see the other person in the room with Arnold as the reader, feminists object that the person never speaks, just listens. Such a patriarchal view, that women should comfort men in their world-weariness was quite common in Victorian England but is problematic in today's world where men and women must confront the disturbing issues of the day equally.

We have included three cultural contexts for Arnold's poem that address some of the issues troubling Arnold and his contemporaries—one by the novelist Charles Dickens who, like Arnold, opposed the kind of utilitarian education portrayed in the opening chapters of *Hard Times*. Friedrich Engels gives us an eyewitness account of the kind of poverty that Arnold would have seen everywhere. And, finally, a brief selection from *A History of Victorian Literature* comments on the impact of evolution.

≡ BEFORE YOU READ

How does our culture promote the idea that love is an antidote to a depressing world? What social, political, or scientific issue would you say affects your generation the most?

MATTHEW ARNOLD

Dover Beach

Victorian poet Matthew Arnold (1822–1889) was the eldest son of Thomas Arnold, an influential clergyman and historian and headmaster of Rugby, one of England's most prestigious college preparatory schools. He grew up in an educational milieu in which religious, political, and social issues were discussed in depth. He went on to Oxford, where he eventually achieved success despite his irreverence and eccentricity. In 1851, he became an inspector of schools and served in this capacity for thirty-five years. He drew on his experiences with people of diverse social classes to become a keen critic of British education and culture, and he expressed his views of society in critical essays on literary, social, and religious issues as well as in poems. "Dover Beach" may have been written during the months just before or just after Arnold's marriage and honeymoon, which included a ferry ride from Dover, England, to Calais, France.

The sea is calm tonight.
The tide is full, the moon lies fair
Upon the straits; — on the French coast the light
Gleams and is gone; the cliffs of England stand,
Glimmering and vast, out in the tranquil bay.   5
Come to the window, sweet is the night-air!
Only, from the long line of spray
Where the sea meets the moon-blanched land,
Listen! you hear the grating roar
Of pebbles which the waves draw back, and fling,   10

Getty Images

At their return, up the high strand,
Begin, and cease, and then again begin,
With tremulous cadence slow, and bring
The eternal note of sadness in.

Sophocles long ago   15
Heard it on the Aegean, and it brought
Into his mind the turbid ebb and flow
Of human misery;° we
Find also in the sound a thought,
Hearing it by this distant northern sea.   20

The Sea of Faith
Was once, too, at the full, and round earth's shore
Lay like the folds of a bright girdle furled.
But now I only hear
Its melancholy, long, withdrawing roar,   25
Retreating, to the breath

Of the night-wind, down the vast edges drear
And naked shingles° of the world.

Ah, love, let us be true
To one another! for the world, which seems   30
To lie before us like a land of dreams,
So various, so beautiful, so new,
Hath really neither joy, nor love, nor light,
Nor certitude, nor peace, nor help for pain;
And we are here as on a darkling plain   35
Swept with confused alarms of struggle and flight,
Where ignorant armies clash by night.   *[1867]*

15–18 Sophocles . . . misery: In *Antigone*, Sophocles compares the disasters that beset the house of Oedipus to a mounting tide.   **28 shingles:** Pebble beach.

≣ THINKING ABOUT THE TEXT

1. In trying to re-create this scene — say, for a movie script — what would you have the lovers look like? Where would the couple be positioned? If you were the director, how would you explain the scene to the actors — that is, what is the speaker saying? Put another way, what argument is being made?

2. Arnold uses the sea as a metaphor. What do you think it represents? What other metaphors and similes are used? Are they effective in making his point?

3. What specifically triggers Arnold's despondency? What was comforting about the "Sea of Faith"? What do you think Arnold meant by the sentence beginning with "But now I only hear . . ." (line 24)?

4. In the film *The Anniversary Party*, Kevin Kline's character reads the last stanza of this poem to a couple celebrating their sixth wedding anniversary. Some critics saw it as an ironic joke, others as a parody of a "sweet" love poem. What is it about the poem that seems to make it inappropriate for such an occasion? Would you send it to your beloved? Why, or why not?

5. What specific reasons does the speaker give for the lovers to be true to each other, beginning with "for the world" (line 30)? Is this an attitude you share? Do you know others who agree? Is this an extreme position? What would the opposite view be? Is this extreme, as well? How does this poem express a contemporary feeling? If you were Arnold's editor, what changes would you suggest to reflect contemporary ideas about relationships between lovers?

CHARLES DICKENS
From *Hard Times*

Charles Dickens (1812–1870), one of the most famous, prolific, and respected nov-
elists in English literature, was born into a family of modest means and had to begin
work at twelve years old, an event that would have a profound effect on his thinking
and writing. The appalling conditions he experienced find their way into his great
novels, including Oliver Twist, David Copperfield, *and* Great Expectations. *Most*
of his novels were commercially successful as serializations in monthly magazines,
which was a common means of publishing at the time. At the height of his fame,
Dickens travelled widely, giving readings in Europe and America. He read voraciously
and was intensely interested in the political and social issues of the day. The excerpt
here, the first two chapters of Hard Times *(1859), is a parody-like critique of Jer-*
emy Bentham's utilitarianism, which promoted the idea of the greatest happiness for
the greatest number. Like Matthew Arnold, Dickens opposed an education of bare
facts, a dehumanized education that did little else but prepare children for the further
dehumanization of the factory. On his tomb in Poet's Corner in Westminster Abbey
is inscribed the following: "He was a sympathiser to the poor, the sick, and the op-
pressed; and by his death, one of England's greatest writers is lost to the world."

"Now, what I want is, Facts. Teach these boys and girls nothing but Facts. Facts
alone are wanted in life. Plant nothing else, and root out everything else. You can
only form the minds of reasoning animals upon Facts: nothing else will ever be
of any service to them. This is the principle on which I bring up my own children,
and this is the principle on which I bring up these children. Stick to Facts, sir!"

The scene was a plain, bare, monotonous vault of a school-room, and the
speaker's square forefinger emphasized his observations by underscoring every
sentence with a line on the schoolmaster's sleeve. The emphasis was helped by
the speaker's square wall of a forehead, which had his eyebrows for its base,
while his eyes found commodious cellarage in two dark caves, overshadowed
by the wall. The emphasis was helped by the speaker's mouth, which was wide,
thin, and hard set. The emphasis was helped by the speaker's voice, which was
inflexible, dry, and dictatorial. The emphasis was helped by the speaker's hair,
which bristled on the skirts of his bald head, a plantation of firs to keep the
wind from its shining surface, all covered with knobs, like the crust of a plum
pie, as if the head had scarcely warehouse-room for the hard facts stored inside.
The speaker's obstinate carriage, square coat, square legs, square shoulders, —
nay, his very neckcloth, trained to take him by the throat with an unaccom-
modating grasp, like a stubborn fact, as it was, — all helped the emphasis.

"In this life, we want nothing but Facts, sir; nothing but Facts!"

The speaker, and the schoolmaster, and the third grown person present, all
backed a little, and swept with their eyes the inclined plane of little vessels then
and there arranged in order, ready to have imperial gallons of facts poured into
them until they were full to the brim. [. . .]

*   *   *

Thomas Gradgrind, sir. A man of realities. A man of facts and calculations. A   5
man who proceeds upon the principle that two and two are four, and nothing
over, and who is not to be talked into allowing for anything over. Thomas
Gradgrind, sir—peremptorily Thomas—Thomas Gradgrind. With a rule and
a pair of scales, and the multiplication table always in his pocket, sir, ready
to weigh and measure any parcel of human nature, and tell you exactly what
it comes to. It is a mere question of figures, a case of simple arithmetic. You
might hope to get some other nonsensical belief into the head of George
Gradgrind, or Augustus Gradgrind, or John Gradgrind, or Joseph Gradgrind
(all supposititious, non-existent persons), but into the head of Thomas
Gradgrind—no, sir!

In such terms Mr. Gradgrind always mentally introduced himself, whether
to his private circle of acquaintance, or to the public in general. In such terms,
no doubt, substituting the words "boys and girls," for "sir," Thomas Gradgrind
now presented Thomas Gradgrind to the little pitchers before him, who were to
be filled so full of facts.

Indeed, as he eagerly sparkled at them from the cellarage before mentioned, he seemed a kind of cannon loaded to the muzzle with facts, and prepared to blow them clean out of the regions of childhood at one discharge. He
seemed a galvanizing apparatus, too, charged with a grim mechanical substitute for the tender young imaginations that were to be stormed away.

"Girl number twenty," said Mr. Gradgrind, squarely pointing with his
square forefinger, "I don't know that girl. Who is that girl?"

"Sissy Jupe, sir," explained number twenty, blushing, standing up, and
curtseying.

"Sissy is not a name," said Mr. Gradgrind. "Don't call yourself Sissy. Call   10
yourself Cecilia."

"It's father as calls me Sissy, sir," returned the young girl in a trembling
voice, and with another curtsey.

"Then he has no business to do it," said Mr. Gradgrind. "Tell him he
mustn't. Cecilia Jupe. Let me see. What is your father?"

"He belongs to the horse-riding, if you please, sir."

Mr. Gradgrind frowned, and waved off the objectionable calling with his
hand.

"We don't want to know anything about that, here. You mustn't tell us   15
about that, here. Your father breaks horses, don't he?"

"If you please, sir, when they can get any to break, they do break horses in
the ring, sir."

"You mustn't tell us about the ring, here. Very well, then. Describe your
father as a horsebreaker. He doctors sick horses, I dare say?"

"Oh yes, sir."

"Very well, then. He is a veterinary surgeon, a farrier, and horsebreaker.
Give me your definition of a horse."

(Sissy Jupe thrown into the greatest alarm by this demand.)   20

"Girl number twenty unable to define a horse!" said Mr. Gradgrind, for the
general behoof of all the little pitchers. "Girl number twenty possessed of no

facts, in reference to one of the commonest of animals! Some boy's definition of a horse. Bitzer, yours."

The square finger, moving here and there, lighted suddenly on Bitzer, perhaps because he chanced to sit in the same ray of sunlight which, darting in at one of the bare windows of the intensely white-washed room, irradiated Sissy. For, the boys and girls sat on the face of the inclined plane in two compact bodies, divided up the centre by a narrow interval; and Sissy, being at the corner of a row on the sunny side, came in for the beginning of a sunbeam, of which Bitzer, being at the corner of a row on the other side, a few rows in advance, caught the end. But, whereas the girl was so dark-eyed and dark-haired, that she seemed to receive a deeper and more lustrous colour from the sun, when it shone upon her, the boy was so light-eyed and light-haired that the self-same rays appeared to draw out of him what little colour he ever possessed. His cold eyes would hardly have been eyes, but for the short ends of lashes which, by bringing them into immediate contrast with something paler than themselves, expressed their form. His short-cropped hair might have been a mere continuation of the sandy freckles on his forehead and face. His skin was so unwholesomely deficient in the natural tinge, that he looked as though, if he were cut, he would bleed white.

"Bitzer," said Thomas Gradgrind. "Your definition of a horse."

"Quadruped. Graminivorous. Forty teeth, namely twenty-four grinders, four eye-teeth, and twelve incisive. Sheds coat in the spring; in marshy countries, sheds hoofs, too. Hoofs hard, but requiring to be shod with iron. Age known by marks in mouth." Thus (and much more) Bitzer.

"Now girl number twenty," said Mr. Gradgrind. "You know what a horse is."   25

She curtseyed again, and would have blushed deeper, if she could have blushed deeper than she had blushed all this time. Bitzer, after rapidly blinking at Thomas Gradgrind with both eyes at once, and so catching the light upon his quivering ends of lashes that they looked like the antennæ of busy insects, put his knuckles to his freckled forehead, and sat down again.

The third gentleman now stepped forth. A mighty man at cutting and drying, he was; a government officer; in his way (and in most other people's too), a professed pugilist; always in training, always with a system to force down the general throat like a bolus, always to be heard of at the bar of his little Public-office, ready to fight all England. To continue in fistic phraseology, he had a genius for coming up to the scratch, wherever and whatever it was, and proving himself an ugly customer. He would go in and damage any subject whatever with his right, follow up with his left, stop, exchange, counter, bore his opponent (he always fought All England) to the ropes, and fall upon him neatly. He was certain to knock the wind out of common sense, and render that unlucky adversary deaf to the call of time. And he had it in charge from high authority to bring about the great public-office Millennium, when Commissioners should reign upon earth.

"Very well," said this gentleman, briskly smiling, and folding his arms. "That's a horse. Now, let me ask you girls and boys, Would you paper a room with representations of horses?"

After a pause, one half of the children cried in chorus, "Yes, sir!" Upon which the other half, seeing in the gentleman's face that Yes was wrong, cried out in chorus, "No, sir" — as the custom is, in these examinations.

"Of course, No. Why wouldn't you?" 30

A pause. One corpulent slow boy, with a wheezy manner of breathing, ventured the answer, Because he wouldn't paper a room at all, but would paint it.

"You *must* paper it," said the gentleman, rather warmly.

"You must paper it," said Thomas Gradgrind, "whether you like it or not. Don't tell us you wouldn't paper it. What do you mean, boy?"

"I'll explain to you, then," said the gentleman, after another and a dismal pause, "why you wouldn't paper a room with representations of horses. Do you ever see horses walking up and down the sides of rooms in reality — in fact? Do you?"

"Yes, sir!" from one half. "No, sir!" from the other. 35

"Of course no," said the gentleman, with an indignant look at the wrong half. "Why, then, you are not to see anywhere, what you don't see in fact; you are not to have anywhere, what you don't have in fact. What is called Taste, is only another name for Fact." Thomas Gradgrind nodded his approbation.

"This is a new principle, a discovery, a great discovery," said the gentleman. "Now, I'll try you again. Suppose you were going to carpet a room. Would you use a carpet having a representation of flowers upon it?"

There being a general conviction by this time that "No, sir!" was always the right answer to this gentleman, the chorus of No was very strong. Only a few feeble stragglers said Yes: among them Sissy Jupe.

"Girl number twenty," said the gentleman, smiling in the calm strength of knowledge.

Sissy blushed, and stood up. 40

"So you would carpet your room — or your husband's room, if you were a grown woman, and had a husband — with representations of flowers, would you?" said the gentleman. "Why would you?"

"If you please, sir, I am very fond of flowers," returned the girl.

"And is that why you would put tables and chairs upon them, and have people walking over them with heavy boots?"

"It wouldn't hurt them, sir. They wouldn't crush and wither, if you please, sir. They would be the pictures of what was very pretty and pleasant, and I would fancy —"

"Ay, ay, ay! But you mustn't fancy," cried the gentleman, quite elated by 45 coming so happily to his point. "That's it! You are never to fancy."

"You are not, Cecilia Jupe," Thomas Gradgrind solemnly repeated, "to do anything of that kind."

"Fact, fact, fact!" said the gentleman. And "Fact, fact, fact!" repeated Thomas Gradgrind.

"You are to be in all things regulated and governed," said the gentleman, "by fact. We hope to have, before long, a board of fact, composed of commissioners of fact, who will force the people to be a people of fact, and of nothing but fact. You must discard the word Fancy altogether. You have nothing to do with it. You are not to have, in any object of use or ornament, what would be a contradiction in fact. You don't walk upon flowers in fact; you cannot be allowed to walk upon flowers in carpets. You don't find that foreign birds and butterflies come and perch upon your crockery; you cannot be permitted to paint foreign birds and butterflies upon your crockery. You never meet with quadrupeds going up and down walls; you must not have quadrupeds represented upon walls. You must use," said the gentleman, "for all these purposes, combinations and modifications (in primary colours) of mathematical figures which are susceptible of proof and demonstration. This is the new discovery. This is fact. This is taste."

The girl curtseyed, and sat down. She was very young, and she looked as if she were frightened by the matter-of-fact prospect the world afforded.

"Now, if Mr. M'Choakumchild," said the gentleman, "will proceed to give   50
his first lesson here, Mr. Gradgrind, I shall be happy, at your request, to observe his mode of procedure."

Mr. Gradgrind was much obliged. "Mr. M'Choakumchild, we only wait for you."

So, Mr. M'Choakumchild began in his best manner. He and some one hundred and forty other schoolmasters, had been lately turned at the same time, in the same factory, on the same principles, like so many pianoforte legs. He had been put through an immense variety of paces, and had answered volumes of head-breaking questions. Orthography, etymology, syntax, and prosody, biography, astronomy, geography, and general cosmography, the sciences of compound proportion, algebra, land-surveying and levelling, vocal music, and drawing from models, were all at the ends of his ten chilled fingers. He had worked his stony way into Her Majesty's most Honourable Privy Council's Schedule B, and had taken the bloom off the higher branches of mathematics and physical science, French, German, Latin, and Greek. He knew all about all the Water Sheds of all the world (whatever they are), and all the histories of all the peoples, and all the names of all the rivers and mountains, and all the productions, manners, and customs of all the countries, and all their boundaries and bearings on the two and thirty points of the compass. Ah, rather overdone, M'Choakumchild. If he had only learnt a little less, how infinitely better he might have taught much more!   *[1859]*

≡ THINKING ABOUT THE TEXT

1. What is ironic about Sissy not being able to define a horse to Gradgrind's satisfaction? Why is Bitzer's definition more appealing to Gradgrind?

2. What do you think Dickens means by "Ah . . . M'Choakumchild. If he had only learnt a little less, how infinitely better he might have taught much more!" (para. 52)?

3. What is your reading of the last question in the selection? How does Dickens make it fairly obvious that he means us to laugh (wince?) at the two educators?

FRIEDRICH ENGELS
From *The Condition of the Working Class in England*

Friedrich Engels (1820–1995) was born in Germany to wealthy parents who expected him to have a career in business. But early on, Engels had a strong interest in revolutionary politics. When he was twenty-two, his father sent him to Manchester, England, to learn the textile business. Instead, he met a young radical, Mary Burns, who gave him a tour of the horrors of environmental destruction, child labor, and numbing poverty in the slums of Manchester. His observations became the influential text from which our selection is taken. Engels went on to collaborate with Karl Marx on The German Ideology *(1846; published 1932) and* The Communist Manifesto *(1848) and to help him write* Das Kapital *(1867). Engels is considered one of the great social scientists and political theorists of the nineteenth century.*

I may mention just here that the mills almost all adjoin the rivers or the different canals that ramify throughout the city, before I proceed at once to describe the labouring quarters. First of all, there is the old town of Manchester, which lies between the northern boundary of the commercial district and the Irk. Here the streets, even the better ones, are narrow and winding, as Todd Street, Long Mill-gate, Withy Grove, and Shude Hill, the houses dirty, old, and tumbledown, and the construction of the side streets utterly horrible. Going from the Old Church to Long Millgate, the stroller has at once a row of old-fashioned houses at the right, of which not one has kept its original level; these are remnants of the old pre-manufacturing Manchester, whose former inhabitants have removed with their descendants into better-built districts, and have left the houses, which were not good enough for them, to a population strongly mixed with Irish blood. Here one is in an almost undisguised working-men's quarter, for even the shops and beer-houses hardly take the trouble to exhibit a trifling degree of cleanliness. But all this is nothing in comparison with the courts and lanes which lie behind, to which access can be gained only through covered passages, in which no two human beings can pass at the same time. Of the irregular cramming together of dwellings in ways which defy all rational plan, of the tangle in which they are crowded literally one upon the other, it is impossible to convey an idea. And it is not the buildings surviving from the old times of Manchester which are to blame for this; the confusion has only recently reached its height when every scrap of space left by the old way of building has been filled up and patched over until not a foot of land is left to be further occupied.

The south bank of the Irk is here very steep and between fifteen and thirty feet high. On this declivitous hillside there are planted three rows of houses, of which the lowest rise directly out of the river, while the front walls of the highest stand on the crest of the hill in Long Millgate. Among them are mills on the river, in short, the method of construction is as crowded and disorderly here as in the lower part of Long Millgate. Right and left a multitude of covered passages lead from the main street into numerous courts, and he who turns in thither gets into a filth and disgusting grime, the equal of which is not to be found—especially in the courts which lead down to the Irk, and which contain unqualifiedly the most horrible dwellings which I have yet beheld. In one of these courts there stands directly at the entrance, at the end of the covered passage, a privy without a door, so dirty that the inhabitants can pass into and out of the court only by passing through foul pools of stagnant urine and excrement. This is the first court on the Irk above Ducie Bridge—in case any one should care to look into it. Below it on the river there are several tanneries which fill the whole neighbourhood with the stench of animal putrefaction. Below Ducie Bridge the only entrance to most of the houses is by means of narrow, dirty stairs and over heaps of refuse and filth. The first court below Ducie Bridge, known as Allen's Court, was in such a state at the time of the cholera that the sanitary police ordered it evacuated, swept, and disinfected with chloride of lime. Dr. Kay gives a terrible description of the state of this court at that time. Since then, it seems to have been partially torn away and rebuilt; at least looking down from Ducie Bridge, the passer-by sees several ruined walls and heaps of débris with some newer houses. The view from this bridge, mercifully concealed from mortals of small stature by a parapet as high as a man, is characteristic for the whole district. At the bottom flows, or rather stagnates, the Irk, a narrow, coal-black, foul-smelling stream, full of débris and refuse, which it deposits on the shallower right bank. In dry weather, a long string of the most disgusting, blackish-green, slime pools are left standing on this bank, from the depths of which bubbles of miasmatic gas constantly arise and give forth a stench unendurable even on the bridge forty or fifty feet above the surface of the stream. But besides this, the stream itself is checked every few paces by high weirs, behind which slime and refuse accumulate and rot in thick masses. Above the bridge are tanneries, bonemills, and gasworks, from which all drains and refuse find their way into the Irk, which receives further the contents of all the neighbouring sewers and privies. It may be easily imagined, therefore, what sort of residue the stream deposits. Below the bridge you look upon the piles of débris, the refuse, filth, and offal from the courts on the steep left bank; here each house is packed close behind its neighbour and a piece of each is visible, all black, smoky, crumbling, ancient, with broken panes and window frames. The background is furnished by old barrack-like factory buildings. On the lower right bank stands a long row of houses and mills; the second house being a ruin without a roof, piled with débris; the third stands so low that the lowest floor is uninhabitable, and therefore without windows or doors. Here the background embraces the pauper burial-ground, the station of the Liverpool and Leeds railway, and, in the rear of this, the Workhouse, the "Poor-Law Bastille" of Manchester, which, like a citadel, looks threateningly down from behind its high walls and parapets on the hilltop, upon the working-people's quarter below.

Above Ducie Bridge, the left bank grows more flat and the right bank steeper, but the condition of the dwellings on both banks grows worse rather than better. He who turns to the left here from the main street, Long Millgate, is lost; he wanders from one court to another, turns countless corners, passes nothing but narrow, filthy nooks and alleys, until after a few minutes he has lost all clue, and knows not whither to turn. Everywhere half or wholly ruined buildings, some of them actually uninhabited, which means a great deal here; rarely a wooden or stone floor to be seen in the houses, almost uniformly broken, ill-fitting windows and doors, and a state of filth! Everywhere heaps of débris, refuse, and offal; standing pools for gutters, and a stench which alone would make it impossible for a human being in any degree civilised to live in such a district. The newly-built extension of the Leeds railway, which crosses the Irk here, has swept away some of these courts and lanes, laying others completely open to view. Immediately under the railway bridge there stands a court, the filth and horrors of which surpass all the others by far, just because it was hitherto so shut off, so secluded that the way to it could not be found without a good deal of trouble. I should never have discovered it myself, without the breaks made by the railway, though I thought I knew this whole region thoroughly. Passing along a rough bank, among stakes and washing-lines, one penetrates into this chaos of small one-storied, one-roomed huts, in most of which there is no artificial floor; kitchen, living and sleeping-room all in one. In such a hole, scarcely five feet long by six broad, I found two beds — and such bedsteads and beds! — which, with a staircase and chimney-place, exactly filled the room. In several others I found absolutely nothing, while the door stood open, and the inhabitants leaned against it. Everywhere before the doors refuse and offal; that any sort of pavement lay underneath could not be seen but only felt, here and there, with the feet. This whole collection of cattle-sheds for human beings was surrounded on two sides by houses and a factory, and on the third by the river, and besides the narrow stair up the bank, a narrow doorway alone led out into another almost equally ill-built, ill-kept labyrinth of dwellings.

Enough! The whole side of the Irk is built in this way, a planless, knotted chaos of houses, more or less on the verge of uninhabitableness, whose unclean interiors fully correspond with their filthy external surroundings. And how could the people be clean with no proper opportunity for satisfying the most natural and ordinary wants? Privies are so rare here that they are either filled up every day, or are too remote for most of the inhabitants to use. How can people wash when they have only the dirty Irk water at hand, while pumps and water pipes can be found in decent parts of the city alone? In truth, it cannot be charged to the account of these helots of modern society if their dwellings are not more cleanly than the pig-sties which are here and there to be seen among them. The landlords are not ashamed to let dwellings like the six or seven cellars on the quay directly below Scotland Bridge, the floors of which stand at least two feet below the low-water level of the Irk that flows not six feet away from them; or like the upper floor of the corner-house on the opposite shore directly above the bridge, where the ground floor, utterly uninhabitable, stands deprived of all fittings for doors and windows, a case by no means rare in this region, when this open ground floor is used as a privy by the whole neighbourhood for want of other facilities!   *[1844]*

≡ THINKING ABOUT THE TEXT

1. What specific details of Engels's description of the slums would have upset Matthew Arnold?

2. What indication of the class conflicts, which Engels would highlight in later books, is most present here?

3. Where is Engels's rage at these deplorable conditions most clear?

JAMES ELI ADAMS
Narrating Nature: Darwin

James Eli Adams (b. 1956) is a professor of English at Columbia University. He received degrees from the Massachusetts Institute of Technology and Oxford University and his Ph.D. from Cornell University in 1987. He writes on a range of issues in Victorian studies. He is the general editor of the Encyclopedia of the Victorian Era, *among many other books and articles. The following excerpt is from* A History of Victorian Literature *(2009), named by* Choice *as an Outstanding Academic Book.*

Even as Mill was inveighing against intellectual cowardice and the decline of individual genius, a country squire was putting the final touches on arguably the most daring and unsettling book of the century. Charles Darwin's *On the Origin of Species By Means of Natural Selection, or Preservation of Favoured Races in the Struggle for Life* (1859) has had an impact so far-ranging and many-faceted that it confounds brief summary. Darwin's theory did not constitute a radical break with prevailing science; evolution had been "in the air" for decades, so much so that Tennyson's In Memoriam (much influenced by Chamber's Vestiges of Creation) seemed to be arguing with Darwin a decade before the Origin appeared. Indeed, Darwin was spurred to write up his long-pondered theory (the main ideas were in place as early as 1839) only after a fellow naturalist, A. R. Wallace, presented a paper anticipating some of its central claims. Darwin's theory also was far from the first to undermine the idea of divine creation most influentially set forth in Genesis. The geologist Charles Lyell, on whom Darwin drew heavily, during the 1830s had argued that natural forces acted uniformly over time, constantly reshaping the face of the planet, and left an ongoing history of its power in "the evidence of the rocks"!—a record which included those fossils of extinct species that so haunted Tennyson. As John Tyndall in his 1874 Belfast address would put it, "the strength of the doctrine of Evolution consists, not in an experimental demonstration . . . but in its general harmony with scientific thought" (Tyndall 1905: ii.206). Indeed, Darwin lacked any concept of genetics, and thus any plausible account of why variations occurred (as distinct from how they might establish new species). Thus at the heart of this theory, as critics pointed out, there was something of a black box. But Darwin nonetheless provided the most intricate, persuasive, and lucid account to date not only of extinction but also of the emergence of new species over time. The Newtonian world did not change; Darwinian nature was inherently, emphatically historical.

Darwin, then, tells a compelling story, a narrative at once expansive and intricately detailed, which reached all of educated Britain, and was appropriated to many, often conflicting ends. The idea of "struggle" between different species and their environment seemed to some commentators readily transferable to the analysis of society. This was a superficially plausible gesture (and one encouraged by Darwin's own subtitle). Darwin's theory resembles an extension to the animal and vegetable world of laissez-faire economics, or the intellectual marketplace of Millian liberalism. Thus Herbert Spencer, most influentially, coined the phrase "survival of the fittest" in order to describe social competition—with the clear implication that class hierarchies were underwritten by nature itself. In *The Principles of Sociology* (1876), Spencer (1820–1903) argued that societies are themselves organisms that evolve from "primitive" to more complex forms. This view would have an enormous impact in emergent sciences of anthropology and sociology, which typically formulated schemes of racial and cultural development grounded on a similar logic. But Spencer, like many commentators since, smuggled into his evolutionary scheme a sense of direction that Darwinian evolution does not provide. Spencer's "social Darwinism" (which persists in some forms of "evolutionary psychology") is closer to earlier Lamarckian schemes, whereby (for example) giraffes develop long necks in order to reach more food. This suggestion that evolutionary changes arise to meet a pre-existent need obscures one of the most disconcerting aspects of Darwin's theory: evolution offers no overarching direction, no governing telos. The present moment is not the culmination of the past, but one moment in an endless process of change. An animal happened to appear with a longer neck than its fellows, which in a particular milieu made it better adapted to survival; the same variation in another environment might prove fatal. The new species is "better" only in a strenuously relativist sense: the word that Darwin uses is not "progress" but "adaptation." As T. H. Huxley would insist in a famous 1893 essay, evolution provides no ethics.

Clearly this randomness was as much a blow to traditional faith as was the more obvious conflict with biblical schemes of creation. Yet Darwin's theory also provided a narrative model, as recent commentators have pointed out, that had much in common with those engaging a more familiar storyteller, the novelist. Not only does Darwinian theory incorporate history, it takes up familiar mythic themes of transformation and metamorphosis; it foregrounds the idea of kinship; it puts great stress (unlike, say, classical mechanics) on the particularity of the world, its sheer abundance and variety, as well as its subtle gradations and modulations (Beer 2000). Perhaps most suggestively, Darwinism discovers unifying structure without teleology. Victorian novelists likewise began with the assumption that the world they described was intelligible and coherent. But the efforts to embody that coherence in novelistic form—most obviously through coincidence and other residues of the so-called "providential plot"—were increasingly liable to seem either unrealistic, too obvious a simplification of the flux of experience, or to seem a deadening abridgement of human agency, in which the power of choice was thoroughly circumscribed by external forces. Thus Darwin leads back to another version of Mill's worry, which is also Estella's: we are not free, you and I. It would be some while before this impact was fully grasped by poets and novelists, but in the latter decades of the century, the impact would be immense.   *[2009]*

≡ THINKING ABOUT THE TEXT

1. What are some ways in which Darwin's famous text was interpreted then and now? How do you think Matthew Arnold read Darwin?

2. How do you think religious Victorians responded to what Adams calls "one of the most disconcerting aspects of Darwin's theory: evolution offers no overarching direction, no governing telos" (para. 2)?

3. How might Adams's notion of Darwinian randomness have influenced "Dover Beach"? How might the idea he mentions in the penultimate sentence, "we are not free, you and I" have affected Arnold's outlook?

≡ WRITING ABOUT ISSUES

1. Write an argument based on Thomas H. Huxley's famous observation in an 1893 essay: "Evolution provides no ethics."

2. Write an analysis of "Dover Beach" that traces the narrator's thinking through the different sections of the poem. Be explicit about his concerns and his possible remedy.

3. Argue that love should or should not be used as a haven against the world. Refer to "Dover Beach" and other texts or films to support your claims.

■ Romantic Dreams: Stories

JAMES JOYCE, "Araby"

JOHN UPDIKE, "A & P"

LESLIE MARMON SILKO, "Yellow Woman"

Although centuries old, the cliché that the human heart is a mystery still seems valid. We still wonder if falling in love is natural: Is love our inborn impulse to seek romance, or is it simply a physical attraction spurred on by our evolutionary need to procreate? Perhaps Western culture has socialized us to believe in the power of romantic love and the often irrational behavior that follows. Might it serve some deep psychological need to find a substitute for a beloved parent? Is it a giving emotion? A selfish one? Is it a psychological malady or the one thing worth giving up everything for? Do we need to believe in it whether or not it exists? Since we are often driven to irrational behavior, delusions, and heartbreak, might we be better off without romantic love? Or might life without it be intolerably flat?

In the following cluster, three fiction writers explore the ways romantic love can sometimes cloud judgment, encouraging us to act against our best interests.

Joyce shows us a boy in the throes of romantic idealism; Updike gives us a memorable picture of how an indifferent world responds to romantic gestures; and Silko shows us a woman torn between myth and reality.

■ BEFORE YOU READ

Can people be truly happy without being in love? Is there one person in the world who is your true love? Or are there only certain types of people you could love? If your love didn't make you "float on a cloud," would you be disappointed? Is true love unconditional? Have you ever been fooled by romantic dreams?

JAMES JOYCE
Araby

James Joyce (1882–1941) is regarded as one of the most innovative and influential writers of the modernist movement of the early twentieth century. His use of interior monologue, wordplay, complex allusions, and other techniques variously delighted, offended, or puzzled readers. Joyce's work demanded attention and was often subject to censorship during his lifetime. A Portrait of the Artist as a Young Man *(1916), set in Joyce's native Dublin, is largely autobiographical. Like his hero at the end of the novel, Joyce left Ireland at the age of twenty to spend the remainder of his life in Paris and other European cities. His long, complex novel* Ulysses *(1922), also set in Dublin, takes the reader through one day in the life of its protagonist and his city. In "Araby," published in* Dubliners *(1914), as in other stories in the collection, Joyce pictures the limited life of his character and leads him toward a sudden insight, or epiphany.*

North Richmond Street, being blind, was a quiet street except at the hour when the Christian Brothers' School set the boys free. An uninhabited house of two storeys stood at the blind end, detached from its neighbors in a square ground. The other houses of the street, conscious of decent lives within them, gazed at one another with brown imperturbable faces.

The former tenant of our house, a priest, had died in the back drawing-room. Air, musty from having been long enclosed, hung in all the rooms, and the waste room behind the kitchen was littered with old useless papers. Among these I found a few paper-covered books, the pages of which were curled and damp: *The Abbot,* by Walter Scott, *The Devout Communicant,* and *The Memoirs of Vidocq.* I liked the last best because its leaves were yellow. The wild garden behind the house contained a central apple-tree and a few straggling bushes under one of which I found the late tenant's rusty bicycle-pump. He had been a very charitable priest; in his will he had left all his money to institutions and the furniture of his house to his sister.

When the short days of winter came dusk fell before we had well eaten our dinners. When we met in the street the houses had grown sombre. The space of sky above us was the color of ever-changing violet and towards it the lamps of the street lifted their feeble lanterns. The cold air stung us and we played till our bodies glowed. Our shouts echoed in the silent street. The career of our play brought us through the dark muddy lanes behind the houses where we ran the gauntlet of the rough tribes from the cottages, to the back doors of the dark dripping gardens where odors arose from the ashpits, to the dark odorous stables where a coachman smoothed and combed the horse or shook music from the buckled harness. When we returned to the street light from the kitchen windows had filled the areas. If my uncle was seen turning the corner we hid in the shadow until we had seen him safely housed. Or if Mangan's sister came out on the doorstep to call her brother in to his tea we watched her from our shadow peer up and down the street. We waited to see whether she would remain or go in and, if she remained, we left our shadow and walked up to Mangan's steps resignedly. She was waiting for us, her figure defined by the light from the half-opened door. Her brother always teased her before he obeyed and I stood by the railings looking at her. Her dress swung as she moved her body and the soft rope of her hair tossed from side to side.

Every morning I lay on the floor in the front parlor watching her door. The blind was pulled down to within an inch of the sash so that I could not be seen. When she came out on the doorstep my heart leaped. I ran to the hall, seized my books, and followed her. I kept her brown figure always in my eye and, when we came near the point at which our ways diverged, I quickened my pace and passed her. This happened morning after morning. I had never spoken to her, except for a few casual words, and yet her name was like a summons to all my foolish blood.

Her image accompanied me even in places the most hostile to romance. On Saturday evenings when my aunt went marketing I had to go to carry some of the parcels. We walked through the flaring streets, jostled by drunken men and bargaining women, amid the curses of laborers, the shrill litanies of shop-boys who stood on guard by the barrel of pigs' cheeks, the nasal chanting of street-singers, who sang a *come-all-you* about O'Donovan Rossa,° or a ballad about the troubles in our native land. These noises converged in a single sensation of life for me: I imagined that I bore my chalice safely through a throng of foes. Her name sprang to my lips at moments in strange prayers and praises which I myself did not understand. My eyes were often full of tears (I could not tell why) and at times a flood from my heart seemed to pour itself out into my bosom. I thought little of the future. I did not know whether I would ever speak to her or not or, if I spoke to her, how I could tell her of my confused adoration. But my body was like a harp and her words and gestures were like fingers running upon the wires.

One evening I went into the back drawing-room in which the priest had died. It was a dark rainy evening and there was no sound in the house. Through one of the broken panes I heard the rain impinge upon the earth, the fine incessant needles of water playing in the sodden beds. Some distant lamp or lighted window gleamed below me. I was thankful that I could see so little. All my senses seemed to desire to veil themselves and, feeling that I was about to slip from them, I pressed the palms of my hands together until they trembled, murmuring: "*O love! O love!*" many times.

At last she spoke to me. When she addressed the first words to me I was so confused that I did not know what to answer. She asked me was I going to *Araby.* I forgot whether I answered yes or no. It would be a splendid bazaar, she said she would love to go.

"And why can't you?" I asked.

While she spoke she turned a silver bracelet round and round her wrist. She could not go, she said, because there would be a retreat that week in her convent. Her brother and two other boys were fighting for their caps and I was alone at the railings. She held one of the spikes, bowing her head towards me. The light from the lamp opposite our door caught the white curve of her neck, lit up her hair that rested there and, falling, lit up the hand upon the railing. It fell over one side of her dress and caught the white border of a petticoat, just visible as she stood at ease.

"It's well for you," she said.

"If I go," I said, "I will bring you something."

What innumerable follies laid waste my waking and sleeping thoughts after that evening! I wished to annihilate the tedious intervening days. I chafed against the work of school. At night in my bedroom and by day in the

---

O'Donovan Rossa: Jeremiah O'Donovan (1831–1915) was nicknamed "Dynamite Rossa" for advocating violent means to achieve Irish independence.

classroom her image came between me and the page I strove to read. The syllables of the word *Araby* were called to me through the silence in which my soul luxuriated and cast an Eastern enchantment over me. I asked for leave to go to the bazaar on Saturday night. My aunt was surprised and hoped it was not some Freemason° affair. I answered few questions in class. I watched my master's face pass from amiability to sternness; he hoped I was not beginning to idle. I could not call my wandering thoughts together. I had hardly any patience with the serious work of life which, now that it stood between me and my desire, seemed to me child's play, ugly monotonous child's play.

On Saturday morning I reminded my uncle that I wished to go to the bazaar in the evening. He was fussing at the hallstand, looking for the hat-brush, and answered me curtly:

"Yes, boy, I know."

As he was in the hall I could not go into the front parlor and lie at the window. I left the house in bad humor and walked slowly towards the school. The air was pitilessly raw and already my heart misgave me.   15

When I came home to dinner my uncle had not yet been home. Still it was early. I sat staring at the clock for some time and, when its ticking began to irritate me, I left the room. I mounted the staircase and gained the upper part of the house. The high cold empty gloomy rooms liberated me and I went from room to room singing. From the front window I saw my companions playing below in the street. Their cries reached me weakened and indistinct and, leaning my forehead against the cool glass, I looked over at the dark house where she lived. I may have stood there for an hour, seeing nothing but the brown-clad figure cast by my imagination, touched discreetly by the lamplight at the curved neck, at the hand upon the railings, and at the border below the dress.

When I came downstairs again I found Mrs. Mercer sitting at the fire. She was an old garrulous woman, a pawnbroker's widow, who collected used stamps for some pious purpose. I had to endure the gossip of the tea-table. The meal was prolonged beyond an hour and still my uncle did not come. Mrs. Mercer stood up to go: she was sorry she couldn't wait any longer, but it was after eight o'clock and she did not like to be out late, as the night air was bad for her. When she had gone I began to walk up and down the room, clenching my fists. My aunt said:

"I'm afraid you may put off your bazaar for this night of Our Lord."

At nine o'clock I heard my uncle's latchkey in the halldoor. I heard him talking to himself and heard the hallstand rocking when it had received the weight of his overcoat. I could interpret these signs. When he was midway through his dinner I asked him to give me the money to go to the bazaar. He had forgotten.

"The people are in bed and after their first sleep now," he said.   20

I did not smile. My aunt said to him energetically:

Freemason: A Protestant fraternal society that was in the past viewed by Catholics as hostile.

"Can't you give him the money and let him go? You've kept him late enough as it is."

My uncle said he was very sorry he had forgotten. He said he believed in the old saying: "All work and no play makes Jack a dull boy." He asked me where I was going and, when I had told him a second time he asked me did I know *The Arab's Farewell to His Steed.* When I left the kitchen he was about to recite the opening lines of the piece to my aunt.

I held a florin° tightly in my hand as I strode down Buckingham Street towards the station. The sight of the streets thronged with buyers and glaring with gas recalled to me the purpose of my journey. I took my seat in a third-class carriage of a deserted train. After an intolerable delay the train moved out of the station slowly. It crept onward among ruinous houses and over the twinkling river. At Westland Row Station a crowd of people pressed to the carriage doors; but the porters moved them back, saying that it was a special train for the bazaar. I remained alone in the bare carriage. In a few minutes the train drew up beside an improvised wooden platform. I passed out on to the road and saw by the lighted dial of a clock that it was ten minutes to ten. In front of me was a large building which displayed the magical name.

I could not find any sixpenny entrance and, fearing that the bazaar would   25
be closed, I passed in quickly through a turnstile, handing a shilling to a weary-looking man. I found myself in a big hall girdled at half its height by a gallery. Nearly all the stalls were closed and the greater part of the hall was in darkness. I recognized a silence like that which pervades a church after a service. I walked into the center of the bazaar timidly. A few people were gathered about the stalls which were still open. Before a curtain, over which the words *Café Chantant* were written in colored lamps, two men were counting money on a salver. I listened to the fall of the coins.

Remembering with difficulty why I had come I went over to one of the stalls and examined porcelain vases and flowered tea-sets. At the door of the stall a young lady was talking and laughing with two young gentlemen. I remarked their English accents and listened vaguely to their conversation.

"O, I never said such a thing!"

"O, but you did!"

"O, but I didn't!"

"Didn't she say that?"   30

"Yes. I heard her."

"O, there's a . . . fib!"

Observing me the young lady came over and asked me did I wish to buy anything. The tone of her voice was not encouraging; she seemed to have spoken to me out of a sense of duty. I looked humbly at the great jars that stood like eastern guards at either side of the dark entrance to the stall and murmured:

"No, thank you."

---

florin: A silver coin worth two shillings.

The young lady changed the position of one of the vases and went back to   35
the two young men. They began to talk of the same subject. Once or twice the
young lady glanced at me over her shoulder.

I lingered before her stall, though I knew my stay was useless, to make my
interest in her wares seem the more real. Then I turned away slowly and walked
down the middle of the bazaar. I allowed the two pennies to fall against the
sixpence in my pocket. I heard a voice call from one end of the gallery that the
light was out. The upper part of the hall was now completely dark.

Gazing up into the darkness I saw myself as a creature driven and derided
by vanity; and my eyes burned with anguish and anger.   [1914]

≡ THINKING ABOUT THE TEXT

1. Why do the boy's eyes burn with anguish and anger? Has he learned
   something about romantic love? Was he in love with Mangan's sister?
   Give evidence.

2. If this story is partly autobiographical, what is Joyce's attitude toward
   his younger self? Are you sympathetic or critical of your own initiations
   into the complexities of relationships?

3. Reread the first and last paragraphs. In what ways might they be
   connected?

4. Find examples of religious imagery. What do you think is its purpose?

5. Do you think the boy's quest has symbolic meaning? Do you think cultures can also search for something?

JOHN UPDIKE
A & P

*John Updike (1932–2009) was born in Shillington, Pennsylvania, an only child of
a father who taught high-school algebra and a mother who wrote short stories and
novels. After graduating from Harvard, Updike studied art in England and later joined
the staff of* The New Yorker. *In 1959, he published his first novel,* The Poorhouse
Fair, *and moved to Massachusetts. His many novels are notable for their lyrical and
accurate depiction of the details and concerns of modern America.* Rabbit Run
(1960) and the sequels Rabbit Redux *(1971),* Rabbit Is Rich *(1981), and* Rabbit
at Rest *(1990) are considered important and insightful records of American life. His
other works include the novels* Villages *(2004) and* Terrorist *(2006);* Due Considerations: Essays and Criticism *(2007);* The Maples Stories *(2009); and* Hub
Fans Bid Kid Adieu: John Updike on Ted Williams *(2010). "A & P" comes from*
Pigeon Feathers and Other Stories *(1962).*

In walks these three girls in nothing but bathing suits. I'm in the third check-
out slot, with my back to the door, so I don't see them until they're over by the

bread. The one that caught my eye first was the one in the plaid green two-piece. She was a chunky kid, with a good tan and a sweet broad soft-looking can with those two crescents of white just under it, where the sun never seems to hit, at the top of the backs of her legs. I stood there with my hand on a box of HiHo crackers trying to remember if I rang it up or not. I ring it up again and the customer starts giving me hell. She's one of these cash-register-watchers, a witch about fifty with rouge on her cheekbones and no eyebrows, and I know it made her day to trip me up. She'd been watching cash registers for fifty years and probably never seen a mistake before.

By the time I got her feathers smoothed and her goodies into a bag — she gives me a little snort in passing, if she'd been born at the right time they would have burned her over in Salem — by the time I get her on her way the girls had circled around the bread and were coming back, without a pushcart, back my way along the counters, in the aisle between the checkouts and the Special bins. They didn't even have shoes on. There was this chunky one, with the two-piece — it was bright green and the seams on the bra were still sharp and her belly was still pretty pale so I guessed she just got it (the suit) — there was this one, with one of those chubby berry-faces, the lips all bunched together under her nose, this one, and a tall one, with black hair that hadn't quite frizzed right, and one of these sunburns right across under the eyes, and a chin that was too long — you know, the kind of girl other girls think is very "striking" and "attractive" but never quite makes it, as they very well know, which is why they like her so much — and then the third one, that wasn't quite so tall. She was the queen. She kind of led them, the other two peeking around and making their shoulders round. She didn't look around, not this queen, she just walked straight on slowly, on these long white prima-donna legs. She came down a little hard on her heels, as if she didn't walk in her bare feet that much, putting down her heels and then letting the weight move along to her toes as if she was testing the floor with every step, putting a little deliberate extra action into it. You never know for sure how girls' minds work (do you really think it's a mind in there or just a little buzz like a bee in a glass jar?) but you got the idea she had talked the other two into coming in here with her, and now she was showing them how to do it, walk slow and hold yourself straight.

She had on a kind of dirty-pink — beige maybe, I don't know — bathing suit with a little nubble all over it, and what got me, the straps were down. They were off her shoulders looped loose around the cool tops of her arms, and I guess as a result the suit had slipped a little on her, so all around the top of the cloth there was this shining rim. If it hadn't been there you wouldn't have known there could have been anything whiter than those shoulders. With the straps pushed off, there was nothing between the top of the suit and the top of her head except just *her*, this clean bare plane of the top of her chest down from the shoulder bones like a dented sheet of metal tilted in the light. I mean, it was more than pretty.

She had sort of oaky hair that the sun and salt had bleached, done up in a bun that was unravelling, and a kind of prim face. Walking into the A & P with your straps down, I suppose it's the only kind of face you *can* have. She held her head so high her neck, coming up out of those white shoulders, looked kind of stretched, but I didn't mind. The longer her neck was, the more of her there was.

She must have felt in the corner of her eye me and over my shoulder   5
Stokesie in the second slot watching, but she didn't tip. Not this queen. She kept her eyes moving across the racks, and stopped, and turned so slow it made my stomach rub the inside of my apron, and buzzed to the other two, who kind of huddled against her for relief, and then they all three of them went up the cat-and-dog-food-breakfast-cereal-macaroni-rice-raisins-seasonings-spreads-spaghetti-soft-drinks-crackers-and-cookies aisle. From the third slot I look straight up this aisle to the meat counter, and I watched them all the way. The fat one with the tan sort of fumbled with the cookies, but on second thought she put the package back. The sheep pushing their carts down the aisle — the girls were walking against the usual traffic (not that we have one-way signs or anything) — were pretty hilarious. You could see them, when Queenie's white shoulders dawned on them, kind of jerk, or hop, or hiccup, but their eyes snapped back to their own baskets and on they pushed. I bet you could set off dynamite in an A & P and the people would by and large keep reaching and checking oatmeal off their lists and muttering "Let me see, there was a third thing, began with A, asparagus, no, ah, yes, applesauce!" or whatever it is they do mutter. But there was no doubt, this jiggled them. A few houseslaves in pin curlers even looked around after pushing their carts past to make sure what they had seen was correct.

You know, it's one thing to have a girl in a bathing suit down on the beach, where what with the glare nobody can look at each other much anyway, and another thing in the cool of the A & P, under the fluorescent lights, against all those stacked packages, with her feet paddling along naked over our check-board green-and-cream rubber-tile floor.

"Oh Daddy," Stokesie said beside me. "I feel so faint."

"Darling," I said. "Hold me tight." Stokesie's married, with two babies chalked up on his fuselage already, but as far as I can tell that's the only difference. He's twenty-two, and I was nineteen this April.

"Is it done?" he asks, the responsible married man finding his voice. I forgot to say he thinks he's going to be manager some sunny day, maybe in 1990 when it's called the Great Alexandrov and Petrooshki Tea Company or something.

What he meant was, our town is five miles from a beach, with a big sum-   10
mer colony out on the Point, but we're right in the middle of town, and the women generally put on a shirt or shorts or something before they get out of the car into the street. And anyway these are usually women with six children and varicose veins mapping their legs and nobody, including them, could care less. As I say, we're right in the middle of town, and if you stand at our front doors you can see two banks and the Congregational church and the newspaper store and three real-estate offices and about twenty-seven old freeloaders tearing up Central Street because the sewer broke again. It's not as if we're on the Cape; we're north of Boston and there's people in this town haven't seen the ocean for twenty years.

The girls had reached the meat counter and were asking McMahon something. He pointed, they pointed, and they shuffled out of sight behind a pyramid of Diet Delight peaches. All that was left for us to see was old McMahon patting his mouth and looking after them sizing up their joints. Poor kids, I began to feel sorry for them, they couldn't help it.

Now here comes the sad part of the story, at least my family says it's sad, but I don't think it's so sad myself. The store's pretty empty, it being Thursday afternoon, so there was nothing much to do except lean on the register and wait for the girls to show up again. The whole store was like a pinball machine and I didn't know which tunnel they'd come out of. After a while they come around out of the far aisle, around the light bulbs, records at discount of the Caribbean Six or Tony Martin Sings or some such gunk you wonder they waste the wax on, sixpacks of candy bars, and plastic toys done up in cellophane that fall apart when a kid looks at them anyway. Around they come, Queenie still leading the way, and holding a little gray jar in her hand. Slots Three through Seven are unmanned and I could see her wondering between Stokes and me, but Stokesie with his usual luck draws an old party in baggy gray pants who stumbles up with four giant cans of pineapple juice (what do these bums *do* with all that pineapple juice? I've often asked myself) so the girls come to me. Queenie puts down the jar and I take it into my fingers icy cold. Kingfish Fancy Herring Snacks in Pure Sour Cream: 49¢. Now her hands are empty, not a ring or a bracelet, bare as God made them, and I wonder where the money's coming from. Still with that prim look she lifts a folded dollar bill out of the hollow at the center of her nubbled pink top. The jar went heavy in my hand. Really, I thought that was so cute.

Then everybody's luck begins to run out. Lengel comes in from haggling with a truck full of cabbages on the lot and is about to scuttle into that door marked manager behind which he hides all day when the girls touch his eye. Lengel's pretty dreary, teaches Sunday school and the rest, but he doesn't miss that much. He comes over and says, "Girls, this isn't the beach."

Queenie blushes, though maybe it's just a brush of sunburn I was noticing for the first time, now that she was so close. "My mother asked me to pick up a jar of herring snacks." Her voice kind of startled me, the way voices do when you see the people first, coming out so flat and dumb yet kind of tony, too, the way it ticked over "pick up" and "snacks." All of a sudden I slid right down her voice into her living room. Her father and the other men were standing around in ice-cream coats and bow ties and the women were in sandals picking up herring snacks on toothpicks off a big glass plate and they were all holding drinks the color of water with olives and sprigs of mint in them. When my parents have somebody over they get lemonade and if it's a real racy affair Schlitz in tall glasses with "They'll Do It Every Time" cartoons stencilled on.

"That's all right," Lengel said. "But this isn't the beach." His repeating this struck me as funny, as if it had just occurred to him, and he had been thinking all these years the A & P was a great big sand dune and he was the head lifeguard. He didn't like my smiling — as I say he doesn't miss much — but he concentrates on giving the girls that sad Sunday-school-superintendent stare.

15

Queenie's blush is no sunburn now, and the plump one in plaid, that I liked better from the back — a really sweet can — pipes up, "We weren't doing any shopping. We just came in for the one thing."

"That makes no difference," Lengel tells her, and I could see from the way his eyes went that he hadn't noticed she was wearing a two-piece before. "We want you decently dressed when you come in here."

"We *are* decent," Queenie says suddenly, her lower lip pushing, getting sore now that she remembers her place, a place from which the crowd that runs the A & P must look pretty crummy. Fancy Herring Snacks flashed in her very blue eyes.

"Girls, I don't want to argue with you. After this come in here with your shoulders covered. It's our policy." He turns his back. That's policy for you. Policy is what the kingpins want. What the others want is juvenile delinquency.

All this while, the customers had been showing up with their carts but, you know, sheep, seeing a scene, they had all bunched up on Stokesie, who shook open a paper bag as gently as peeling a peach, not wanting to miss a word. I could feel in the silence everybody getting nervous, most of all Lengel, who asks me, "Sammy, have you rung up their purchase?"   20

I thought and said "No" but it wasn't about that I was thinking. I go through the punches, 4, 9, groc, tot — it's more complicated than you think, and after you do it often enough, it begins to make a little song, that you hear words to, in my case "Hello (*bing*) there, you (*gung*) hap-py *pee*-pul (*splat*)!" — the *splat* being the drawer flying out. I uncrease the bill, tenderly as you may imagine, it just having come from between the two smoothest scoops of vanilla I had ever known were there, and pass a half and a penny into her narrow pink palm, and nestle the herrings in a bag and twist its neck and hand it over, all the time thinking.

The girls, and who'd blame them, are in a hurry to get out, so I say "I quit" to Lengel enough for them to hear, hoping they'll stop and watch me, their unsuspected hero. They keep right on going, into the electric eye; the door flies open and they flicker across the lot to their car, Queenie and Plaid and Big Tall Goony-Goony (not that as raw material she was so bad), leaving me with Lengel and a kink in his eyebrow.

"Did you say something, Sammy?"

"I said I quit."

"I thought you did."   25

"You didn't have to embarrass them."

"It was they who were embarrassing us."

I started to say something that came out "Fiddle-de-doo." It's a saying of my grandmother's, and I know she would have been pleased.

"I don't think you know what you're saying," Lengel said.

"I know you don't," I said. "But I do." I pull the bow at the back of my apron and start shrugging it off my shoulders. A couple customers that had been heading for my slot begin to knock against each other, like scared pigs in a chute.   30

Lengel sighs and begins to look very patient and old and gray. He's been a friend of my parents for years. "Sammy, you don't want to do this to your Mom and Dad," he tells me. It's true, I don't. But it seems to me that once you begin a gesture it's fatal not to go through with it. I fold the apron, "Sammy" stitched in red on the pocket, and put it on the counter, and drop the bow tie on top of it. The bow tie is theirs, if you've ever wondered. "You'll feel this for the rest of your life," Lengel says, and I know that's true, too, but remembering how he made that pretty girl blush makes me so scrunchy inside I punch the No Sale tab and the machine whirs "pee-pul" and the drawer splats out. One advantage to this scene taking place in summer, I can follow this up with a clean exit, there's no fumbling around getting your coat and galoshes, I just saunter into the electric eye in my white shirt that my mother ironed the night before, and the door heaves itself open, and outside the sunshine is skating around on the asphalt.

I look around for my girls, but they're gone, of course. There wasn't anybody but some young married screaming with her children about some candy they didn't get by the door of a powder-blue Falcon station wagon. Looking back in the big windows, over the bags of peat moss and aluminum lawn furniture stacked on the pavement, I could see Lengel in my place in the slot, checking the sheep through. His face was dark gray and his back stiff, as if he'd just had an injection of iron, and my stomach kind of fell as I felt how hard the world was going to be to me hereafter.   [1961]

≡ THINKING ABOUT THE TEXT

1. Why do you think Sammy quits? Make a list of several plausible answers.

2. What would you do if you were in Sammy's position? What would your priorities be in this situation?

3. When Sammy hears Queenie's voice, he imagines an elegant cocktail party that he contrasts to his parents' "real racy affair" (para. 14) with lemonade and beer. What does this scene say about Sammy's attitude toward the girls? Toward his own social status?

4. Some critics have objected to Sammy's comment in the last sentence of paragraph 2 about "girls' minds." Is this a sexist observation? Does the time frame of the story figure in your opinion? Should it?

5. Comment on the last paragraph. What is the significance of the young married woman? Why does Sammy mention "sheep"? Why does Sammy think the world will be hard on him? Do you agree? What does "hard" mean?

≡ MAKING COMPARISONS

1. Which character's views about romance are most compatible with yours when you were, say, thirteen? With yours presently?

2. Compare the last paragraphs of "Araby" and "A & P." What attitudes do they express?

3. Make a case for one narrator being wiser or happier than the other by the end of the stories.

LESLIE MARMON SILKO

Yellow Woman

Leslie Marmon Silko (b. 1948) is a major figure in the American Indian Renaissance. Raised in "Old Laguna" on the Pueblo Reservation near Albuquerque, New Mexico, Silko weaves the mythology of her matrilineal society into stories that move freely through what she calls an "ocean of time." The Yellow Woman character appears frequently in Silko's writing, both as a traditional figure, closely connected with nature and heterosexuality, and as a female character awakening to her cultural and sexual identity. Silko writes both poetry and fiction, often synthesizing the two genres into a single text. Her novels include Storyteller *(1981), in which "Yellow Woman" appears;* Ceremony *(1977); and* Almanac of the Dead *(1991). Her latest book is* The Turquoise Ledge *(2010). She formerly taught at the University of Arizona at Tucson.*

1

My thigh clung to his with dampness, and I watched the sun rising up through the tamaracks and willows. The small brown water birds came to the river and hopped across the mud, leaving brown scratches in the alkali-white crust. They bathed in the river silently. I could hear the water, almost at our feet where the narrow fast channel bubbled and washed green ragged moss and fern leaves. I looked at him beside me, rolled in the red blanket on the white river sand. I cleaned the sand out of the cracks between my toes, squinting because the sun was above the willow trees. I looked at him for the last time, sleeping on the white river sand.

I felt hungry and followed the river south the way we had come the afternoon before, following our footprints that were already blurred by the lizard tracks and bug trails. The horses were still lying down, and the black one whinnied when he saw me but he did not get up — maybe it was because the corral was made out of thick cedar branches and the horses had not yet felt the sun like I had. I tried to look beyond the pale red mesas to the pueblo. I knew it was there, even if I could not see it, on the sand rock hill above the river, the same river that moved past me now and had reflected the moon last night.

The horse felt warm underneath me. He shook his head and pawed the sand. The bay whinnied and leaned against the gate trying to follow, and I remembered him asleep in the red blanket beside the river. I slid off the horse and tied him close to the other horse. I walked north with the river again, and the white sand broke loose in footprints over footprints.

"Wake up."

He moved in the blanket and turned his face to me with his eyes still closed.   5
I knelt down to touch him.

"I'm leaving."

He smiled now, eyes still closed. "You are coming with me, remember?" He sat up now with his bare dark chest and belly in the sun.

"Where?"

"To my place."

"And will I come back?"   10

He pulled his pants on. I walked away from him, feeling him behind me and smelling the willows.

"Yellow Woman," he said.

I turned to face him. "Who are you?" I asked.

He laughed and knelt on the low, sandy bank, washing his face in the river. "Last night you guessed my name, and you knew why I had come."

I stared past him at the shallow moving water and tried to remember the   15
night, but I could only see the moon in the water and remember his warmth around me.

"But I only said that you were him and that I was Yellow Woman — I'm not really her — I have my own name and I come from the pueblo on the other side of the mesa. Your name is Silva and you are a stranger I met by the river yesterday afternoon."

He laughed softly. "What happened yesterday has nothing to do with what you will do today, Yellow Woman."

"I know — that's what I'm saying — the old stories about the ka'tsina spirit° and Yellow Woman can't mean us."

My old grandpa liked to tell those stories best. There is one about Badger and Coyote who went hunting and were gone all day, and when the sun was going down they found a house. There was a girl living there alone, and she had light hair and eyes and she told them that they could sleep with her. Coyote wanted to be with her all night so he sent Badger into a prairie-dog hole, telling him he thought he saw something in it. As soon as Badger crawled in, Coyote blocked up the entrance with rocks and hurried back to Yellow Woman.

"Come here," he said gently.   20

He touched my neck and I moved close to him to feel his breathing and to hear his heart. I was wondering if Yellow Woman had known who she was — if she knew that she would become part of the stories. Maybe she'd had another name that her husband and relatives called her so that only the ka'tsina from the north and the storytellers would know her as Yellow Woman. But I didn't go on; I felt him all around me, pushing me down into the white river sand.

Yellow Woman went away with the spirit from the north and lived with him and his relatives. She was gone for a long time, but then one day she came back and she brought twin boys.

"Do you know the story?"

ka'tsina spirit: A mountain spirit of the Laguna Pueblo Indians.

"What story?" He smiled and pulled me close to him as he said this. I was afraid lying there on the red blanket. All I could know was the way he felt, warm, damp, his body beside me. This is the way it happens in the stories, I was thinking, with no thought beyond the moment she meets the ka'tsina spirit and they go.

"I don't have to go. What they tell in stories was real only then, back in   25 time immemorial, like they say."

He stood up and pointed at my clothes tangled in the blanket. "Let's go," he said.

I walked beside him, breathing hard because he walked fast, his hand around my wrist. I had stopped trying to pull away from him, because his hand felt cool and the sun was high, drying the river bed into alkali. I will see someone, eventually I will see someone, and then I will be certain that he is only a man — some man from nearby — and I will be sure that I am not Yellow Woman. Because she is from out of time past and I live now and I've been to school and there are highways and pickup trucks that Yellow Woman never saw.

It was an easy ride north on horseback. I watched the change from the cottonwood trees along the river to the junipers that brushed past us in the foothills, and finally there were only piñons, and when I looked up at the rim of the mountain plateau I could see pine trees growing on the edge. Once I stopped to look down, but the pale sandstone had disappeared and the river was gone and the dark lava hills were all around. He touched my hand, not speaking, but always singing softly a mountain song and looking into my eyes.

I felt hungry and wondered what they were doing at home now — my mother, my grandmother, my husband, and the baby. Cooking breakfast, saying, "Where did she go? — maybe kidnapped," and Al going to the tribal police with the details: "She went walking along the river."

The house was made with black lava rock and red mud. It was high above   30 the spreading miles of arroyos and long mesas. I smelled a mountain smell of pitch and buck brush. I stood there beside the black horse, looking down on the small, dim country we had passed, and I shivered.

"Yellow Woman, come inside where it's warm."

2

He lit a fire in the stove. It was an old stove with a round belly and an enamel coffeepot on top. There was only the stove, some faded Navajo blankets, and a bedroll and cardboard box. The floor was made of smooth adobe plaster, and there was one small window facing east. He pointed at the box.

"There's some potatoes and the frying pan." He sat on the floor with his arms around his knees pulling them close to his chest and he watched me fry the potatoes. I didn't mind him watching me because he was always watching me — he had been watching me since I came upon him sitting on the river bank trimming leaves from a willow twig with his knife. We ate from the pan and he wiped the grease from his fingers on his Levis.

"Have you brought women here before?" He smiled and kept chewing, so I said, "Do you always use the same tricks?"

"What tricks?" He looked at me like he didn't understand.   35

"The story about being a ka'tsina from the mountains. The story about Yellow Woman."

Silva was silent; his face was calm.

"I don't believe it. Those stories couldn't happen now," I said.

He shook his head and said softly, "But someday they will talk about us, and they will say, 'Those two lived long ago when things like that happened.'"

He stood up and went out. I ate the rest of the potatoes and thought about   40
things — about the noise the stove was making and the sound of the mountain wind outside. I remembered yesterday and the day before, and then I went outside.

I walked past the corral to the edge where the narrow trail cut through the black rim rock. I was standing in the sky with nothing around me but the wind that came down from the blue mountain peak behind me. I could see faint mountain images in the distance miles across the vast spread of mesas and valleys and plains. I wondered who was over there to feel the mountain wind on those sheer blue edges — who walks on the pine needles in those blue mountains.

"Can you see the pueblo?" Silva was standing behind me.

I shook my head. "We're too far away."

"From here I can see the world." He stepped out on the edge. "The Navajo reservation begins over there." He pointed to the east. "The Pueblo boundaries are over here." He looked below us to the south, where the narrow trail seemed to come from. "The Texans have their ranches over there, starting with that valley, the Concho Valley. The Mexicans run some cattle over there too."

"Do you ever work for them?"   45

"I steal from them," Silva answered. The sun was dropping behind us and shadows were filling the land below. I turned away from the edge that dropped forever into the valleys below.

"I'm cold," I said; "I'm going inside." I started wondering about this man who could speak the Pueblo language so well but who lived on a mountain and rustled cattle. I decided that this man Silva must be Navajo, because Pueblo men didn't do things like that.

"You must be a Navajo."

Silva shook his head gently. "Little Yellow Woman," he said, "you never give up, do you? I have told you who I am. The Navajo people know me, too." He knelt down and unrolled the bedroll and spread the extra blankets out on a piece of canvas. The sun was down, and the only light in the house came from outside — the dim orange light from sundown.

I stood there and waited for him to crawl under the blankets.   50

"What are you waiting for?" he said, and I lay down beside him. He undressed me slowly like the night before beside the river — kissing my face gently and running his hands up and down my belly and legs. He took off my pants and then he laughed.

"Why are you laughing?"

"You are breathing so hard."

I pulled away from him and turned my back to him.

He pulled me around and pinned me down with his arms and chest. "You   55
don't understand, do you, little Yellow Woman? You will do what I want."

And again he was all around me with his skin slippery against mine, and I
was afraid because I understood that his strength could hurt me. I lay underneath him and I knew that he could destroy me. But later, while he slept beside
me, I touched his face and I had a feeling — the kind of feeling for him that
overcame me that morning along the river. I kissed him on the forehead and he
reached out for me.

When I woke up in the morning he was gone. It gave me a strange feeling
because for a long time I sat there on the blankets and looked around the little
house for some object of his — some proof that he had been there or maybe
that he was coming back. Only the blankets and the cardboard box remained.
The .30–30° that had been leaning in the corner was gone, and so was the
knife I had used the night before. He was gone, and I had my chance to go now.
But first I had to eat, because I knew it would be a long walk home.

I found some dried apricots in the cardboard box, and I sat down on a rock
at the edge of the plateau rim. There was no wind and the sun warmed me. I
was surrounded by silence. I drowsed with apricots in my mouth, and I didn't
believe that there were highways or railroads or cattle to steal.

When I woke up, I stared down at my feet in the black mountain dirt. Little
black ants were swarming over the pine needles around my foot. They must
have smelled the apricots. I thought about my family far below me. They would
be wondering about me, because this had never happened to me before. The
tribal police would file a report. But if old Grandpa weren't dead he would tell
them what happened — he would laugh and say, "Stolen by a ka'tsina, a mountain spirit. She'll come home — they usually do." There are enough of them to
handle things. My mother and grandmother will raise the baby like they raised
me. Al will find someone else, and they will go on like before, except that there
will be a story about the day I disappeared while I was walking along the river.
Silva had come for me; he said he had. I did not decide to go. I just went. Moon-
flowers blossom in the sand hills before dawn, just as I followed him. That's
what I was thinking as I wandered along the trail through the pine trees.

It was noon when I got back. When I saw the stone house I remembered   60
that I had meant to go home. But that didn't seem important any more, maybe
because there were little blue flowers growing in the meadow behind the stone
house and the gray squirrels were playing in the pines next to the house. The
horses were standing in the corral, and there was a beef carcass hanging on
the shady side of a big pine in front of the house. Flies buzzed around the clotted blood that hung from the carcass. Silva was washing his hands in a bucket
full of water. He must have heard me coming because he spoke to me without
turning to face me.

.30–30: A rifle.

"I've been waiting for you."

"I went walking in the big pine trees."

I looked into the bucket full of bloody water with brown-and-white animal hairs floating in it. Silva stood there letting his hand drip, examining me intently.

"Are you coming with me?"

"Where?" I asked him.

"To sell the meat in Marquez."

"If you're sure it's O.K."

"I wouldn't ask you if it wasn't," he answered.

He sloshed the water around in the bucket before he dumped it out and set the bucket upside down near the door. I followed him to the corral and watched him saddle the horses. Even beside the horses he looked tall, and I asked him again if he wasn't Navajo. He didn't say anything; he just shook his head and kept cinching up the saddle.

"But Navajos are tall."

"Get on the horse," he said, "and let's go."

The last thing he did before we started down the steep trail was to grab the .30–30 from the corner. He slid the rifle into the scabbard that hung from his saddle.

"Do they ever try to catch you?" I asked.

"They don't know who I am."

"Then why did you bring the rifle?"

"Because we are going to Marquez where the Mexicans live."

3

The trail leveled out on a narrow ridge that was steep on both sides like an animal spine. On one side I could see where the trail went around the rocky gray hills and disappeared into the southeast where the pale sandrock mesas stood in the distance near my home. On the other side was a trail that went west, and as I looked far into the distance I thought I saw the little town. But Silva said no, that I was looking in the wrong place, that I just thought I saw houses. After that I quit looking off into the distance; it was hot and the wildflowers were closing up their deep-yellow petals. Only the waxy cactus flowers bloomed in the bright sun, and I saw every color that a cactus blossom can be; the white ones and the red ones were still buds, but the purple and the yellow were blossoms, open full and the most beautiful of all.

Silva saw him before I did. The white man was riding a big gray horse, coming up the trail toward us. He was traveling fast and the gray horse's feet sent rocks rolling off the trail into the dry tumbleweeds. Silva motioned for me to stop and we watched the white man. He didn't see us right away, but finally his horse whinnied at our horses and he stopped. He looked at us briefly before he loped the gray horse across the three hundred yards that separated us. He stopped his horse in front of Silva, and his young fat face was shadowed by the brim of his hat. He didn't look mad, but his small, pale eyes moved from the blood-soaked gunny sacks hanging from my saddle to Silva's face and then back to my face.

"Where did you get the fresh meat?" the white man asked.

"I've been hunting," Silva said, and when he shifted his weight in the saddle the leather creaked.   80

"The hell you have, Indian. You've been rustling cattle. We've been looking for the thief for a long time."

The rancher was fat, and sweat began to soak through his white cowboy shirt and the wet cloth stuck to the thick rolls of belly fat. He almost seemed to be panting from the exertion of talking, and he smelled rancid, maybe because Silva scared him.

Silva turned to me and smiled. "Go back up the mountain, Yellow Woman."

The white man got angry when he heard Silva speak in a language he couldn't understand. "Don't try anything, Indian. Just keep riding to Marquez. We'll call the state police from there."

The rancher must have been unarmed because he was very frightened and   85
if he had a gun he would have pulled it out then. I turned my horse around and the rancher yelled, "Stop!" I looked at Silva for an instant and there was something ancient and dark — something I could feel in my stomach — in his eyes, and when I glanced at his hand I saw his finger on the trigger of the .30–30 that was still in the saddle scabbard. I slapped my horse across the flank and the sacks of raw meat swung against my knees as the horse leaped up the trail. It was hard to keep my balance, and once I thought I felt the saddle slipping backward; it was because of this that I could not look back.

I didn't stop until I reached the ridge where the trail forked. The horse was breathing deep gasps and there was a dark film of sweat on its neck. I looked down in the direction I had come from, but I couldn't see the place. I waited. The wind came up and pushed warm air past me. I looked up at the sky, pale blue and full of thin clouds and fading vapor trails left by jets.

I think four shots were fired — I remember hearing four hollow explosions that reminded me of deer hunting. There could have been more shots after that, but I couldn't have heard them because my horse was running again and the loose rocks were making too much noise as they scattered around his feet.

Horses have a hard time running downhill, but I went that way instead of uphill to the mountain because I thought it was safer. I felt better with the horse running southeast past the round gray hills that were covered with cedar trees and black lava rock. When I got to the plain in the distance I could see the dark green patches of tamaracks that grew along the river; and beyond the river I could see the beginning of the pale sandrock mesas. I stopped the horse and looked back to see if anyone was coming; then I got off the horse and turned the horse around, wondering if it would go back to its corral under the pines on the mountain. It looked back at me for a moment and then plucked a mouthful of green tumbleweeds before it trotted back up the trail with its ears pointed forward, carrying its head daintily to one side to avoid stepping on the dragging reins. When the horse disappeared over the last hill, the gunny sacks full of meat were still swinging and bouncing.

4

I walked toward the river on a wood-hauler's road that I knew would eventually lead to the paved road. I was thinking about waiting beside the road for someone to drive by, but by the time I got to the pavement I had decided it wasn't very far to walk if I followed the river back the way Silva and I had come.

The river water tasted good, and I sat in the shade under a cluster of silvery willows. I thought about Silva, and I felt sad at leaving him; still, there was something strange about him, and I tried to figure it out all the way back home. 90

I came back to the place on the river bank where he had been sitting the first time I saw him. The green willow leaves that he had trimmed from the branch were still lying there, wilted in the sand. I saw the leaves and I wanted to go back to him — to kiss him and to touch him — but the mountains were too far away now. And I told myself, because I believe it, he will come back sometime and be waiting again by the river.

I followed the path up from the river into the village. The sun was getting low, and I could smell supper cooking when I got to the screen door of my house. I could hear their voices inside — my mother was telling my grandmother how to fix the Jell-O and my husband, Al, was playing with the baby. I decided to tell them that some Navajo had kidnapped me, but I was sorry that old Grandpa wasn't alive to hear my story because it was the Yellow Woman stories he liked to tell best.   *[1974]*

≡ **THINKING ABOUT THE TEXT**

1. Why does Yellow Woman run away with Silva? Does it have something to do with the coyote stories? What stories in your own culture have persuaded you to trust in romantic love?

2. How do myths and stories differ? Are they based on reality or on fantasy? What are the social or cultural purposes of stories about love?

3. Do you trust the narrator's judgment? Sincerity? On what textual evidence are you basing this evaluation? What bearing does her cultural heritage have on your analysis of her?

4. What specific details of Silko's story do you remember? Is the narrator a careful observer? Explain. What effect does the narrator's "noticing little things" have on you as a reader?

5. Has Yellow Woman learned her lesson? Do societies change their views of romantic love? How?

≡ **MAKING COMPARISONS**

1. Compare the growth of the boy in "Araby" or Sammy in "A & P" with that of the wife in "Yellow Woman."

2. Make explicit the insight or epiphany the boy or Sammy comes to at the end. What would be a comparable epiphany for the wife in "Yellow Woman"?

3. Is one ending more realistic than the others? Explain.

≡ WRITING ABOUT ISSUES

1. Choose either the boy in "Araby," Sammy, or Yellow Woman and argue that this character was or was not really in love. Support your argument with references to the text and your own cultural experience.

2. Write an essay that defends or denies the idea that romantic love is irrational. Use two of the stories from this cluster.

3. Would any of the characters in this cluster have been comfortable in the cultural context you were raised in? (Consider movies, books, TV, family narratives, and so forth in analyzing your culture.) Write a brief analysis of how well one or more of these characters would "fit in."

4. Look up information about Native American culture and the coyote stories referred to in "Yellow Woman." Do they help to explain her attitudes? Do the same for the culture of Joyce's Ireland, especially religion and romance. How about America in the middle of the twentieth century? In a brief essay, argue that each story is understood more fully when the cultural context is provided.

▤ The Appearance of Love: A Collection of Stories by Kate Chopin

KATE CHOPIN, "The Storm"

KATE CHOPIN, "The Story of an Hour"

KATE CHOPIN, "Désirée's Baby"

People at weddings often remark how happy and in love the bridal couple looks. But people can *appear* to be in love. Indeed, psychologists tell us that someone can play a loving role for years, at times actually believing the part he or she is playing. To a limited extent, this is true for all of us. We learn what it means to be in love from watching movies, reading books, and absorbing other clues from our culture. A man proposing marriage on one knee is just one cultural notion of how we should act when we are in love.

Suppose a woman acts lovingly toward her husband and then has a passionate sexual encounter with an old boyfriend. Which is her true self? Which is the appearance and which the reality? Sometimes a society's conventions about marriage are so strong that men and women have little choice but to conform. If we were to judge the behavior of a woman toward her husband a hundred years ago, we might not get an accurate reading of how much she loved him. Likewise, people can believe their lives to be quite harmonious until they find out that one of them has a surprising past. William Shakespeare wrote of love that would not change when difficulties arose, but such is not always the case. Does that mean that one's love is not deep enough? Or when a loved one does not live up to expectations, is it natural to readjust one's heart?

The following three stories take on controversial topics. Kate Chopin was not a conformist thinker, and her stories are filled with views of desire, love, and relationships meant to provoke her late-nineteenth-century readers. Indeed, they continue to provoke audiences today.

▤ BEFORE YOU READ

Would you change your mind about loving someone if you found out he or she was having an affair? If that person lied about his or her religion or race? Is it possible to love someone and at the same time want to be free?

KATE CHOPIN

The Storm

Kate Chopin (1851–1904) is known for her evocations of the unique, multiethnic Creole and Cajun societies of late-nineteenth-century Louisiana; however, her characters transcend the limitation of regional genre writing, striking a particularly resonant note among feminist readers. Born Katherine O'Flaherty in St. Louis, Missouri,

Missouri History
Museum, St. Louis

she married Oscar Chopin in 1870 and went to live with him in New Orleans and on his plantation along the Mississippi River. Her short stories were collected in Bayou Folk *(1894) and* A Night in Acadie *(1897). Chopin's last novel,* The Awakening, *scandalized readers at the time of its publication in 1899 because of its frank portrayal of female sexuality in the context of an extramarital affair. Long ignored by readers and critics, her work was revived in the 1960s and continues to provoke heated discussion of her female characters: are they women who seek freedom in the only ways available to them, or are they willing participants in their own victimhood?*

"The Storm" was written about 1898, but because of its provocative content, Chopin probably did not even try to find a magazine that would risk the publicity.

1

The leaves were so still that even Bibi thought it was going to rain. Bobinôt, who was accustomed to converse on terms of perfect equality with his little son, called the child's attention to certain sombre clouds that were rolling with sinister intention from the west, accompanied by a sullen, threatening roar. They were at Friedheimer's store and decided to remain there till the storm had passed. They sat within the door on two empty kegs. Bibi was four years old and looked very wise.

"Mama'll be 'fraid, yes," he suggested with blinking eyes.

"She'll shut the house. Maybe she got Sylvie helpin' her this evenin'," Bobinôt responded reassuringly.

"No; she ent got Sylvie. Sylvie was helpin' her yistiday," piped Bibi.

Bobinôt arose and going across to the counter purchased a can of shrimps, 5 of which Calixta was very fond. Then he returned to his perch on the keg and sat stolidly holding the can of shrimps while the storm burst. It shook the wooden store and seemed to be ripping great furrows in the distant field. Bibi laid his little hand on his father's knee and was not afraid.

2

Calixta, at home, felt no uneasiness for their safety. She sat at a side window sewing furiously on a sewing machine. She was greatly occupied and did not notice the approaching storm. But she felt very warm and often stopped to mop her face on which the perspiration gathered in beads. She unfastened her white sacque at the throat. It began to grow dark, and suddenly realizing the situation she got up hurriedly and went about closing windows and doors.

Out on the small front gallery she had hung Bobinôt's Sunday clothes to air and she hastened out to gather them before the rain fell. As she stepped outside, Alcée Laballière rode in at the gate. She had not seen him very often since her marriage, and never alone. She stood there with Bobinôt's coat in her hands, and the big rain drops began to fall. Alcée rode his horse under the shelter of a side projection where the chickens had huddled and there were plows and a harrow piled up in the corner.

"May I come and wait on your gallery till the storm is over, Calixta?" he asked.

"Come 'long in, M'sieur Alcée."

His voice and her own startled her as if from a trance, and she seized 10 Bobinôt's vest. Alcée, mounting to the porch, grabbed the trousers and snatched Bibi's braided jacket that was about to be carried away by a sudden gust of wind. He expressed an intention to remain outside, but it was soon apparent that he might as well have been out in the open: the water beat in upon the boards in driving sheets, and he went inside, closing the door after him. It was even necessary to put something beneath the door to keep the water out.

"My! what a rain! It's good two years sence it rain' like that," exclaimed Calixta as she rolled up a piece of bagging and Alcée helped her to thrust it beneath the crack.

She was a little fuller of figure than five years before when she married; but she had lost nothing of her vivacity. Her blue eyes still retained their melting quality; and her yellow hair, dishevelled by the wind and rain, kinked more stubbornly than ever about her ears and temples.

The rain beat upon the low, shingled roof with a force and clatter that threatened to break an entrance and deluge them there. They were in the dining room — the sitting room — the general utility room. Adjoining was her bed room, with Bibi's couch along side her own. The door stood open, and the room with its white, monumental bed, its closed shutters, looked dim and mysterious.

Alcée flung himself into a rocker and Calixta nervously began to gather up from the floor the lengths of a cotton sheet which she had been sewing.

"If this keeps up, *Dieu sait*° if the levees goin' to stan' it!" she exclaimed.   15

"What have you got to do with the levees?"

"I got enough to do! An' there's Bobinôt with Bibi out in that storm — if he only didn' left Friedheimer's!"

"Let us hope, Calixta, that Bobinôt's got sense enough to come in out of a cyclone."

She went and stood at the window with a greatly disturbed look on her face. She wiped the frame that was clouded with moisture. It was stiflingly hot. Alcée got up and joined her at the window, looking over her shoulder. The rain was coming down in sheets obscuring the view of far-off cabins and enveloping the distant wood in a gray mist. The playing of the lightning was incessant. A bolt struck a tall chinaberry tree at the edge of the field. It filled all visible space with a blinding glare and the crash seemed to invade the very boards they stood upon.

Calixta put her hands to her eyes, and with a cry, staggered backward.   20
Alcée's arm encircled her, and for an instant he drew her close and spasmodically to him.

"*Bonté!*"° she cried, releasing herself from his encircling arm and retreating from the window, "the house'll go next! If I only knew w'ere Bibi was!" She would not compose herself; she would not be seated. Alcée clasped her shoulders and looked into her face. The contact of her warm, palpitating body when he had unthinkingly drawn her into his arm, had aroused all the old-time infatuation and desire for her flesh.

"Calixta," he said, "don't be frightened. Nothing can happen. The house is too low to be struck, with so many tall trees standing about. There! aren't you going to be quiet? say, aren't you?" He pushed her hair back from her face that was warm and steaming. Her lips were as red and moist as pomegranate seed. Her white neck and a glimpse of her full, firm bosom disturbed him powerfully. As she glanced up at him the fear in her liquid blue eyes had given place to a drowsy gleam that unconsciously betrayed a sensuous desire. He looked down into her eyes and there was nothing for him to do but to gather her lips in a kiss. It reminded him of Assumption.

"Do you remember — in Assumption, Calixta?" he asked in a low voice broken by passion. Oh! she remembered; for in Assumption he had kissed her and kissed and kissed her; until his senses would well nigh fail, and to save her he would resort to a desperate flight. If she was not an immaculate dove in those days, she was still inviolate; a passionate creature whose very defenselessness had made her defense, against which his honor forbade him to prevail.

Dieu sait: God knows.   *Bonté*: Goodness.

Now — well, now — her lips seemed in a manner free to be tasted, as well as her round, white throat and her whiter breasts.

They did not heed the crashing torrents, and the roar of the elements made her laugh as she lay in his arms. She was a revelation in that dim, mysterious chamber; as white as the couch she lay upon. Her firm, elastic flesh that was knowing for the first time its birthright, was like a creamy lily that the sun invites to contribute its breath and perfume to the undying life of the world.

The generous abundance of her passion, without guile or trickery, was like   25 a white flame which penetrated and found response in depths of his own sensuous nature that had never yet been reached.

When he touched her breasts they gave themselves up in quivering ecstasy, inviting his lips. Her mouth was a fountain of delight. And when he possessed her, they seemed to swoon together at the very borderland of life's mystery.

He stayed cushioned upon her, breathless, dazed, enervated, with his heart beating like a hammer upon her. With one hand she clasped his head, her lips lightly touching his forehead. The other hand stroked with a soothing rhythm his muscular shoulders.

The growl of the thunder was distant and passing away. The rain beat softly upon the shingles, inviting them to drowsiness and sleep. But they dared not yield.

The rain was over; and the sun was turning the glistening green world into a palace of gems. Calixta, on the gallery, watched Alcée ride away. He turned and smiled at her with a beaming face; and she lifted her pretty chin in the air and laughed aloud.

3

Bobinôt and Bibi, trudging home, stopped without at the cistern to make them-   30 selves presentable.

"My! Bibi, w'at will yo' mama say! You ought to be ashame'. You oughtn' put on those good pants. Look at 'em! An' that mud on yo' collar! How you got that mud on yo' collar, Bibi? I never saw such a boy!" Bibi was the picture of pathetic resignation. Bobinôt was the embodiment of serious solicitude as he strove to remove from his own person and his son's the signs of their tramp over heavy roads and through wet fields. He scraped the mud off Bibi's bare legs and feet with a stick and carefully removed all traces from his heavy brogans. Then, prepared for the worst — the meeting with an over-scrupulous housewife, they entered cautiously at the back door.

Calixta was preparing supper. She had set the table and was dripping coffee at the hearth. She sprang up as they came in.

"Oh, Bobinôt! You back! My! but I was uneasy. W'ere you been during the rain? An' Bibi? he ain't wet? he ain't hurt?" She had clasped Bibi and was kissing him effusively. Bobinôt's explanations and apologies which he had been composing all along the way, died on his lips as Calixta felt him to see if he were dry, and seemed to express nothing but satisfaction at their safe return.

"I brought you some shrimps, Calixta," offered Bobinôt, hauling the can from his ample side pocket and laying it on the table.

"Shrimps! Oh, Bobinôt! you too good fo' anything!" and she gave him a   35
smacking kiss on the cheek that resounded. *"J'vous réponds,*° we'll have a feas' to-night! umph-umph!"

Bobinôt and Bibi began to relax and enjoy themselves, and when the three seated themselves at table they laughed much and so loud that anyone might have heard them as far away as Laballière's.

4

Alcée Laballière wrote to his wife, Clarisse, that night. It was a loving letter, full of tender solicitude. He told her not to hurry back, but if she and the babies liked it at Biloxi, to stay a month longer. He was getting on nicely; and though he missed them, he was willing to bear the separation a while longer — realizing that their health and pleasure were the first things to be considered.

5

As for Clarisse, she was charmed upon receiving her husband's letter. She and the babies were doing well. The society was agreeable; many of her old friends and acquaintances were at the bay. And the first free breath since her marriage seemed to restore the pleasant liberty of her maiden days. Devoted as she was to her husband, their intimate conjugal life was something which she was more than willing to forego for a while.

So the storm passed and every one was happy.   [1898]

J'vous réponds: I'm telling you.

≡ THINKING ABOUT THE TEXT

1. Does Calixta truly love Bobinôt? What explains the sudden passion of Calixta and Alcée? Are they in love?

2. Are you bothered by the happy ending? Are stories supposed to reinforce the dominant values of a society? What do you think would (or should) have happened in real life?

3. Can you recall other stories, novels, films, or television programs in which someone who is sexually transgressive is not punished?

4. Are the injured parties in this story really injured; that is, if they never find out, will they still suffer somehow?

5. Should extramarital affairs be illegal? Is Chopin suggesting that they are not so terrible, or is she simply saying something about passion?

KATE CHOPIN
The Story of an Hour

"The Story of an Hour" was first published in Bayou Folk (1894). It is typical of Chopin's controversial works and caused a sensation among the reading public.

Knowing that Mrs. Mallard was afflicted with a heart trouble, great care was taken to break to her as gently as possible the news of her husband's death.

It was her sister Josephine who told her, in broken sentences; veiled hints that revealed in half concealing. Her husband's friend Richards was there, too, near her. It was he who had been in the newspaper office when intelligence of the railroad disaster was received, with Brently Mallard's name leading the list of "killed." He had only taken the time to assure himself of its truth by a second telegram, and had hastened to forestall any less careful, less tender friend in bearing the sad message.

She did not hear the story as many women have heard the same, with a paralyzed inability to accept its significance. She wept at once, with sudden, wild abandonment, in her sister's arms. When the storm of grief had spent itself she went away to her room alone. She would have no one follow her.

There stood, facing the open window, a comfortable, roomy armchair. Into this she sank, pressed down by a physical exhaustion that haunted her body and seemed to reach into her soul.

She could see in the open square before her house the tops of trees that   5 were all aquiver with the new spring life. The delicious breath of rain was in the air. In the street below a peddler was crying his wares. The notes of a distant song which some one was singing reached her faintly, and countless sparrows were twittering in the eaves.

There were patches of blue sky showing here and there through the clouds that had met and piled one above the other in the west facing her window.

She sat with her head thrown back upon the cushion of the chair, quite motionless, except when a sob came up into her throat and shook her, as a child who had cried itself to sleep continues to sob in its dreams.

She was young, with a fair, calm face, whose lines bespoke repression and even a certain strength. But now there was a dull stare in her eyes, whose gaze was fixed away off yonder on one of those patches of blue sky. It was not a glance of reflection, but rather indicated a suspension of intelligent thought.

There was something coming to her and she was waiting for it, fearfully. What was it? She did not know; it was too subtle and elusive to name. But she felt it, creeping out of the sky, reaching toward her through the sounds, the scents, the color that filled the air.

Now her bosom rose and fell tumultuously. She was beginning to recog-   10 nize this thing that was approaching to possess her, and she was striving to beat it back with her will — as powerless as her two white slender hands would have been.

When she abandoned herself a little whispered word escaped her slightly parted lips. She said it over and over under her breath: "free, free, free!" The vacant stare and the look of terror that had followed it went from her eyes. They stayed keen and bright. Her pulses beat fast, and the coursing blood warmed and relaxed every inch of her body.

She did not stop to ask if it were or were not a monstrous joy that held her. A clear and exalted perception enabled her to dismiss the suggestion as trivial.

She knew that she would weep again when she saw the kind, tender hands folded in death; the face that had never looked save with love upon her, fixed and gray and dead. But she saw beyond that bitter moment a long procession of years to come that would belong to her absolutely. And she opened and spread her arms out to them in welcome.

There would be no one to live for her during those coming years: she would live for herself. There would be no powerful will bending hers in that blind persistence with which men and women believe they have a right to impose a private will upon a fellow-creature. A kind intention or a cruel intention made the act seem no less a crime as she looked upon it in that brief moment of illumination.

And yet she had loved him — sometimes. Often she had not. What did it   15
matter! What could love, the unsolved mystery, count for in face of this possession of self-assertion which she suddenly recognized as the strongest impulse of her being!

"Free! Body and soul free!" she kept whispering.

Josephine was kneeling before the closed door with her lips to the keyhole, imploring for admission. "Louise, open the door! I beg; open the door — you will make yourself ill. What are you doing, Louise? For heaven's sake open the door."

"Go away. I am not making myself ill." No; she was drinking in a very elixir of life through that open window.

Her fancy was running riot along those days ahead of her. Spring days, and summer days, and all sorts of days that would be her own. She breathed a quick prayer that life might be long. It was only yesterday she had thought with a shudder that life might be long.

She arose at length and opened the door to her sister's importunities. There   20
was a feverish triumph in her eyes, and she carried herself unwittingly like a goddess of Victory. She clasped her sister's waist, and together they descended the stairs. Richards stood waiting for them at the bottom.

Some one was opening the front door with a latchkey. It was Brently Mallard who entered, a little travel-stained, composedly carrying his gripsack and umbrella. He had been far from the scene of accident, and did not even know there had been one. He stood amazed at Josephine's piercing cry; at Richards's quick motion to screen him from the view of his wife.

But Richards was too late.

When the doctors came they said she had died of heart disease — of joy that kills.   *[1894]*

≡ THINKING ABOUT THE TEXT

1. Is Louise Mallard really in love with her husband? Regardless of your answer, would she ever leave him? Is it possible to confuse love with duty?
2. Is it possible to assign blame for this tragedy? To Mr. Mallard? Mrs. Mallard? The culture?
3. Why did Chopin keep the story so brief? What would you like to know more about?
4. What specifically do you think Mrs. Mallard was thinking about in the room?
5. Do you think this situation was common during Chopin's time? Is it today?

≡ MAKING COMPARISONS

1. Compare Mrs. Mallard and Calixta. Do you think Mrs. Mallard would have an extramarital affair?
2. Is Chopin sympathetic to Mrs. Mallard and Calixta? Is she judgmental?
3. Calixta and Bobinôt seem to be on more equal terms than Mr. and Mrs. Mallard. Do you think this is the case? Explain why this might be so.

KATE CHOPIN
Désirée's Baby

"Désirée's Baby" was written in 1892 and published in Bayou Folk *(1894). The story reflects Chopin's experience among the French Creoles in Louisiana.*

As the day was pleasant, Madame Valmondé drove over to L'Abri to see Désirée and the baby.

It made her laugh to think of Désirée with a baby. Why, it seemed but yesterday that Désirée was little more than a baby herself; when Monsieur in riding through the gateway of Valmondé had found her lying asleep in the shadow of the big stone pillar.

The little one awoke in his arms and began to cry for "Dada." That was as much as she could do or say. Some people thought she might have strayed there of her own accord, for she was of the toddling age. The prevailing belief was that she had been purposely left by a party of Texans, whose canvas-covered wagon, late in the day, had crossed the ferry that Coton Maïs kept, just below the plantation. In time Madame Valmondé abandoned every speculation but the one that Désirée had been sent to her by a beneficent Providence to be the child of her affection, seeing that she was without child of the flesh. For the girl grew to be beautiful and gentle, affectionate and sincere, — the idol of Valmondé.

It was no wonder, when she stood one day against the stone pillar in whose shadow she had lain asleep, eighteen years before, that Armand Aubigny riding by and seeing her there, had fallen in love with her. That was the way all the Aubignys fell in love, as if struck by a pistol shot. The wonder was that he had not loved her before; for he had known her since his father brought him home from Paris, a boy of eight, after his mother died there. The passion that awoke in him that day, when he saw her at the gate, swept along like an avalanche, or like a prairie fire, or like anything that drives headlong over all obstacles.

Monsieur Valmondé grew practical and wanted things well considered: 5
that is, the girl's obscure origin. Armand looked into her eyes and did not care. He was reminded that she was nameless. What did it matter about a name when he could give her one of the oldest and proudest in Louisiana? He ordered the *corbeille*° from Paris, and contained himself with what patience he could until it arrived; then they were married.

Madame Valmondé had not seen Désirée and the baby for four weeks. When she reached L'Abri she shuddered at the first sight of it, as she always did. It was a sad looking place, which for many years had not known the gentle presence of a mistress, old Monsieur Aubigny having married and buried his wife in France, and she having loved her own land too well ever to leave it. The roof came down steep and black like a cowl, reaching out beyond the wide galleries that encircled the yellow stuccoed house. Big, solemn oaks grew close to it, and their thick-leaved, far-reaching branches shadowed it like a pall. Young Aubigny's rule was a strict one, too, and under it his negroes had forgotten how to be gay, as they had been during the old master's easy-going and indulgent lifetime.

The young mother was recovering slowly, and lay full length, in her soft white muslins and laces, upon a couch. The baby was beside her, upon her arm, where he had fallen sleep, at her breast. The yellow nurse woman sat beside a window fanning herself.

Madame Valmondé bent her portly figure over Désirée and kissed her, holding her an instant tenderly in her arms. Then she turned to the child.

"This is not the baby!" she exclaimed, in startled tones. French was the language spoken at Valmondé in those days.

"I knew you would be astonished," laughed Désirée, "at the way he has   10
grown. The little *cochon de lait!*° Look at his legs, mamma, and his hands and fingernails, — real fingernails. Zandrine had to cut them this morning. Isn't it true, Zandrine?"

The woman bowed her turbaned head majestically, "Mais si, Madame."

"And the way he cries," went on Désirée, "is deafening. Armand heard him the other day as far away as La Blanche's cabin."

Madame Valmondé had never removed her eyes from the child. She lifted it and walked with it over to the window that was lightest. She scanned the baby

---

***corbeille*:** Double bed.   ***cochon de lait*:** French for "suckling pig"; an endearment.

narrowly, then looked as searchingly at Zandrine, whose face was turned to gaze across the fields.

"Yes, the child has grown, has changed," said Madame Valmondé, slowly, as she replaced it beside its mother. "What does Armand say?"

Désirée's face became suffused with a glow that was happiness itself.   15

"Oh, Armand is the proudest father in the parish, I believe, chiefly because it is a boy, to bear his name; though he says not, — that he would have loved a girl as well. But I know it isn't true. I know he says that to please me. And mamma," she added, drawing Madame Valmondé's head down to her and speaking in a whisper, "he hasn't punished one of them — not one of them — since baby is born. Even Négrillon, who pretended to have burnt his leg that he might rest from work — he only laughed, and said Négrillon was a great scamp. Oh, mamma, I'm so happy; it frightens me."

What Désirée said was true. Marriage, and later the birth of his son had softened Armand Aubigny's imperious and exacting nature greatly. This was what made the gentle Désirée so happy, for she loved him desperately. When he frowned she trembled, but loved him. When he smiled, she asked no greater blessing of God. But Armand's dark, handsome face had not often been disfigured by frowns since the day he fell in love with her.

When the baby was about three months old, Désirée awoke one day to the conviction that there was something in the air menacing her peace. It was at first too subtle to grasp. It had only been a disquieting suggestion; an air of mystery among the blacks; unexpected visits from far-off neighbors who could hardly account for their coming. Then a strange, an awful change in her husband's manner, which she dared not ask him to explain. When he spoke to her, it was with averted eyes, from which the old love-light seemed to have gone out. He absented himself from home; and when there, avoided her presence and that of her child, without excuse. And the very spirit of Satan seemed suddenly to take hold of him in his dealings with the slaves. Désirée was miserable enough to die.

She sat in her room, one hot afternoon, in her *peignoir*, listlessly drawing through her fingers the strands of her long, silky brown hair that hung about her shoulders. The baby, half naked, lay asleep upon her own great mahogany bed, that was like a sumptuous throne, with its satin-lined half-canopy. One of La Blanche's little quadroon boys — half naked too — stood fanning the child slowly with a fan of peacock feathers. Désirée's eyes had been fixed absently and sadly upon the baby, while she was striving to penetrate the threatening mist that she felt closing about her. She looked from her child to the boy who stood beside him, and back again; over and over. "Ah!" It was a cry that she could not help; which she was not conscious of having uttered. The blood turned like ice in her veins, and a clammy moisture gathered upon her face.

She tried to speak to the little quadroon boy; but no sound would come, at   20
first. When he heard his name uttered, he looked up, and his mistress was pointing to the door. He laid aside the great, soft fan, and obediently stole away, over the polished floor, on his bare tiptoes.

She stayed motionless, with gaze riveted upon her child, and her face the picture of fright.

Presently her husband entered the room, and without noticing her, went to a table and began to search among some papers which covered it.

"Armand," she called to him, in a voice which must have stabbed him, if he was human. But he did not notice. "Armand," she said again. Then she rose and tottered towards him. "Armand," she panted once more, clutching his arm, "look at our child. What does it mean? tell me."

He coldly but gently loosened her fingers from about his arm and thrust the hand away from him. "Tell me what it means!" she cried despairingly.

"It means," he answered lightly, "that the child is not white; it means that   25
you are not white."

A quick conception of all that this accusation meant for her nerved her with unwonted courage to deny it. "It is a lie; it is not true, I am white! Look at my hair, it is brown; and my eyes are gray, Armand, you know they are gray. And my skin is fair," seizing his wrist. "Look at my hand; whiter than yours, Armand," she laughed hysterically.

"As white as La Blanche's," he returned cruelly; and went away leaving her alone with their child.

When she could hold a pen in her hand, she sent a despairing letter to Madame Valmondé.

"My mother, they tell me I am not white. Armand has told me I am not white. For God's sake tell them it is not true. You must know it is not true. I shall die. I must die. I cannot be so unhappy, and live."

The answer that came was as brief: 30

"My own Désirée: Come home to Valmondé; back to your mother who loves you. Come with your child."

When the letter reached Désirée she went with it to her husband's study, and laid it open upon the desk before which he sat. She was like a stone image: silent, white, motionless after she placed it there.

In silence he ran his cold eyes over the written words. He said nothing. "Shall I go, Armand?" she asked in tones sharp with agonized suspense.

"Yes, go."

"Do you want me to go?"   35

"Yes, I want you to go."

He thought Almighty God had dealt cruelly and unjustly with him; and felt, somehow, that he was paying Him back in kind when he stabbed thus into his wife's soul. Moreover he no longer loved her, because of the unconscious injury she had brought upon his home and his name.

She turned away like one stunned by a blow, and walked slowly towards the door, hoping he would call her back.

"Good-by, Armand," she moaned.

He did not answer her. That was his last blow at fate.   40

Désirée went in search of her child. Zandrine was pacing the sombre gallery with it. She took the little one from the nurse's arms with no word of explanation, and descending the steps, walked away, under the live-oak branches.

It was an October afternoon; the sun was just sinking. Out in the still fields the negroes were picking cotton.

Désirée had not changed the thin white garment nor the slippers which she wore. Her hair was uncovered and the sun's rays brought a golden gleam from its brown meshes. She did not take the broad, beaten road which led to the far-off plantation of Valmondé. She walked across a deserted field, where the stubble bruised her tender feet, so delicately shod, and tore her thin gown to shreds.

She disappeared among the reeds and willows that grew thick along the banks of the deep, sluggish bayou; and she did not come back again.

Some weeks later there was a curious scene enacted at L'Abri. In the center of the smoothly swept back yard was a great bonfire. Armand Aubigny sat in the wide hallway that commanded a view of the spectacle; and it was he who dealt out to a half dozen negroes the material which kept this fire ablaze. 45

A graceful cradle of willow, with all its dainty furbishings, was laid upon the pyre, which had already been fed with the richness of a priceless *layette.* Then there were silk gowns, and velvet and satin ones added to these; laces, too, and embroideries; bonnets and gloves; for the *corbeille* had been of rare quality.

The last thing to go was a tiny bundle of letters; innocent little scribblings that Désirée had sent to him during the days of their espousal. There was the remnant of one back in the drawer from which he took them. But it was not Désirée's; it was part of an old letter from his mother to his father. He read it. She was thanking God for the blessing of her husband's love: —

"But, above all," she wrote, "night and day, I thank the good God for having so arranged our lives that our dear Armand will never know that his mother, who adores him, belongs to the race that is cursed with the brand of slavery."

[1892]

≣ THINKING ABOUT THE TEXT

1. Does Armand really love Désirée? Explain.

2. Armand seems to have fallen in love "at first sight." Is this possible? Can love conquer all, even racial bias? Is Chopin skeptical?

3. What would you have done if you were Désirée? What will Armand do now that he knows his own racial background?

4. Are we able to break free of our cultural heritage? What are the ways society tries to keep us in line? How do some people break free? Is there a danger in disregarding societal norms? Are there benefits?

5. Could this story happen this way today?

≡ **MAKING COMPARISONS**

1. Which female character — Calixta, Louise, or Désirée — possesses true love for her husband? Do the husbands love their wives more? In different ways?

2. Which one of these marriages seems the strongest? Why?

3. Compare Chopin's attitude toward marriage in these three stories. Does she support all aspects of marriage? Since she wrote over a century ago, would she be pleased with the present state of marriage (including divorce)?

≡ **WRITING ABOUT ISSUES**

1. Which ending seems more ethically questionable? Write a brief position paper suggesting that one of Chopin's endings should be changed (or remain the same) for moral reasons before junior high students read it.

2. Compare Alcée and Armand. Write a brief justification for or refutation of the behavior of one of them.

3. Argue that complete honesty is or is not the best policy in a relationship. Use the stories here or other stories, novels, and films that you know.

4. Chopin's works shocked American audiences. Research the ways sex, love, and relationships were dealt with in the 1890s in America. Write a brief explanation of why Chopin was ahead of her time.

RAYMOND CARVER, "What We Talk About When We Talk About Love"

NATHAN ENGLANDER, "What We Talk About When We Talk About
Anne Frank"

Unless you're a philosopher, most conversations about love quickly turn from abstract definitions to concrete examples, from generalizations to specifics, from what love might be or should be to the actual behavior of our friends or ourselves. Being concrete seems our most comfortable way to talk about such a baffling, complex, and compelling topic as love. And this is just what happens in Carver's "What We Talk About When We Talk About Love." The four characters rely mostly on personal experience to get a foothold on the slippery slopes of love's reality. There is some agreement but lots of "That's not love; it's something else." Of course the difficulties are compounded when we add such qualifiers or intensifiers as "true" or "real" or "everlasting." Carver's couples, after a night of drinking and talking, seem stupefied. Nathan Englander, who admires Carver's story, writes what is sometimes called an homage, changing the title to substitute "Anne Frank" for "Love." One critic called his story a "cordial, stoned salute to Raymond Carver." There are obvious similarities, but Englander has a host of ideas on his mind, from squabbles over secular and religious Jews, to the impact of the Holocaust on contemporary life, to upsetting stereotypes. But finally he seems to home in on questions of trust in relationships and, like Carver, on how difficult or impossible it is to know what is locked away in another's heart. Both stories force us to consider how little we know about such mysteries as love and trust.

RAYMOND CARVER
What We Talk About
When We Talk About Love

Raymond Carver (1938–1988) re-creates in what has been called a "stripped-down and muscular prose style" the minutiae of everyday life in mid-twentieth-century America. Brought up in the Pacific Northwest in a working-class family, Carver began writing in high school and married early. While both he and his young wife worked at low-paying jobs, Carver took college courses and struggled to find time to write. In 1958, he studied fiction writing with John Gardner and graduated in 1963 from what is now the California State University at Humboldt. He received national recognition in 1967 when a story was included in the Best American Short Stories annual anthology. Although Carver was a National Endowment for the Arts fellow in poetry in 1971, fiction remained his primary genre, earning him numerous awards and fellowships, including O. Henry awards in 1974, 1975, and 1980.

Marion Ettlinger

Despite his success as a writer, alcoholism plagued Carver for most of his life until with the help of Alcoholics Anonymous he stopped drinking in 1982, soon after his divorce. "What We Talk About When We Talk About Love" was the title story in his 1981 collection.

My friend Mel McGinnis was talking. Mel McGinnis is a cardiologist, and sometimes that gives him the right.

The four of us were sitting around his kitchen table drinking gin. Sunlight filled the kitchen from the big window behind the sink. There were Mel and me and his second wife, Teresa — Terri, we called her — and my wife, Laura. We lived in Albuquerque then. But we were all from somewhere else.

There was an ice bucket on the table. The gin and the tonic water kept going around, and we somehow got on the subject of love. Mel thought real love was nothing less than spiritual love. He said he'd spent five years in a seminary before quitting to go to medical school. He said he still looked back on those years in the seminary as the most important years in his life.

Terri said the man she lived with before she lived with Mel loved her so much he tried to kill her. Then Terri said, "He beat me up one night. He dragged me around the living room by my ankles. He kept saying, 'I love you, I love you,

you bitch.' He went on dragging me around the living room. My head kept knocking on things." Terri looked around the table. "What do you do with love like that?"

She was a bone-thin woman with a pretty face, dark eyes, and brown hair   5
that hung down her back. She liked necklaces made of turquoise, and long pendant earrings.

"My God, don't be silly. That's not love, and you know it," Mel said. "I don't know what you'd call it, but I sure know you wouldn't call it love."

"Say what you want to, but I know it was," Terri said. "It may sound crazy to you, but it's true just the same. People are different, Mel. Sure, sometimes he may have acted crazy. Okay. But he loved me. In his own way maybe, but he loved me. There was love there, Mel. Don't say there wasn't."

Mel let out his breath. He held his glass and turned to Laura and me. "The man threatened to kill me," Mel said. He finished his drink and reached for the gin bottle. "Terri's a romantic. Terri's of the kick-me-so-I'll-know-you-love-me school. Terri, hon, don't look that way." Mel reached across the table and touched Terri's cheek with his fingers. He grinned at her.

"Now he wants to make up," Terri said.

"Make up what?" Mel said. "What is there to make up? I know what I know.   10
That's all."

"How'd we get started on this subject, anyway?" Terri said. She raised her glass and drank from it. "Mel always has love on his mind," she said. "Don't you, honey?" She smiled, and I thought that was the last of it.

"I just wouldn't call Ed's behavior love. That's all I'm saying, honey," Mel said. "What about you guys?" Mel said to Laura and me. "Does that sound like love to you?"

"I'm the wrong person to ask," I said. "I didn't even know the man. I've only heard his name mentioned in passing. I wouldn't know. You'd have to know the particulars. But I think what you're saying is that love is an absolute."

Mel said, "The kind of love I'm talking about is. The kind of love I'm talking about, you don't try to kill people."

Laura said, "I don't know anything about Ed, or anything about the situa-   15
tion. But who can judge anyone else's situation?"

I touched the back of Laura's hand. She gave me a quick smile. I picked up Laura's hand. It was warm, the nails polished, perfectly manicured. I encircled the broad wrist with my fingers, and I held her.

"When I left, he drank rat poison," Terri said. She clasped her arms with her hands. "They took him to the hospital in Santa Fe. That's where we lived then, about ten miles out. They saved his life. But his gums went crazy from it. I mean they pulled away from his teeth. After that, his teeth stood out like fangs. My God," Terri said. She waited a minute, then let go of her arms and picked up her glass.

"What people won't do!" Laura said.

"He's out of the action now," Mel said. "He's dead."

Mel handed me the saucer of limes. I took a section, squeezed it over my   20
drink, and stirred the ice cubes with my finger.

"It gets worse," Terri said. "He shot himself in the mouth. But he bungled that too. Poor Ed," she said. Terri shook her head.

"Poor Ed nothing," Mel said. "He was dangerous."

Mel was forty-five years old. He was tall and rangy with curly soft hair. His face and arms were brown from the tennis he played. When he was sober, his gestures, all his movements, were precise, very careful.

"He did love me though, Mel. Grant me that," Terri said. "That's all I'm asking. He didn't love me the way you love me. I'm not saying that. But he loved me. You can grant me that, can't you?"

"What do you mean, he bungled it?" I said.   25

Laura leaned forward with her glass. She put her elbows on the table and held her glass in both hands. She glanced from Mel to Terri and waited with a look of bewilderment on her open face, as if amazed that such things happened to people you were friendly with.

"How'd he bungle it when he killed himself?" I said.

"I'll tell you what happened," Mel said. "He took this twenty-two pistol he'd bought to threaten Terri and me with. Oh, I'm serious, the man was always threatening. You should have seen the way we lived in those days. Like fugitives. I even bought a gun myself. Can you believe it? A guy like me? But I did. I bought one for self-defense and carried it in the glove compartment. Sometimes I'd have to leave the apartment in the middle of the night. To go to the hospital, you know? Terri and I weren't married then, and my first wife had the house and kids, the dog, everything, and Terri and I were living in this apartment here. Sometimes, as I say, I'd get a call in the middle of the night and have to go in to the hospital at two or three in the morning. It'd be dark out there in the parking lot, and I'd break into a sweat before I could even get to my car. I never knew if he was going to come up out of the shrubbery or from behind a car and start shooting. I mean, the man was crazy. He was capable of wiring a bomb, anything. He used to call my service at all hours and say he needed to talk to the doctor, and when I'd return the call, he'd say, 'Son of a bitch, your days are numbered.' Little things like that. It was scary, I'm telling you."

"I still feel sorry for him," Terri said.

"It sounds like a nightmare," Laura said. "But what exactly happened after   30
he shot himself?"

Laura is a legal secretary. We'd met in a professional capacity. Before we knew it, it was a courtship. She's thirty-five, three years younger than I am. In addition to being in love, we like each other and enjoy one another's company. She's easy to be with.

"What happened?" Laura said.

Mel said, "He shot himself in the mouth in his room. Someone heard the shot and told the manager. They came in with a passkey, saw what had happened, and called an ambulance. I happened to be there when they brought him in, alive but past recall. The man lived for three days. His head swelled up to twice the size of a normal head. I'd never seen anything like it, and I hope I never do again. Terri wanted to go in and sit with him when she found out about it. We had a fight over it. I didn't think she should see him like that. I didn't think she should see him, and I still don't."

"Who won the fight?" Laura said.

"I was in the room with him when he died," Terri said. "He never came up   35
out of it. But I sat with him. He didn't have anyone else."

"He was dangerous," Mel said. "If you call that love, you can have it."

"It was love," Terri said. "Sure, it's abnormal in most people's eyes. But he was willing to die for it. He did die for it."

"I sure as hell wouldn't call it love," Mel said. "I mean, no one knows what he did it for. I've seen a lot of suicides, and I couldn't say anyone ever knew what they did it for."

Mel put his hands behind his neck and tilted his chair back. "I'm not interested in that kind of love," he said. "If that's love, you can have it."

Terri said, "We were afraid. Mel even made a will out and wrote to his   40
brother in California who used to be a Green Beret. Mel told him who to look for if something happened to him."

Terri drank from her glass. She said, "But Mel's right — we lived like fugitives. We were afraid. Mel was, weren't you, honey? I even called the police at one point, but they were no help. They said they couldn't do anything until Ed actually did something. Isn't that a laugh?" Terri said.

She poured the last of the gin into her glass and waggled the bottle. Mel got up from the table and went to the cupboard. He took down another bottle.

"Well, Nick and I know what love is," Laura said. "For us, I mean," Laura said. She bumped my knee with her knee. "You're supposed to say something now," Laura said, and turned her smile on me.

For an answer, I took Laura's hand and raised it to my lips. I made a big production out of kissing her hand. Everyone was amused.

"We're lucky," I said.   45

"You guys," Terri said. "Stop that now. You're making me sick. You're still on the honeymoon, for God's sake. You're still gaga, for crying out loud. Just wait. How long have you been together now? How long has it been? A year? Longer than a year?"

"Going on a year and a half," Laura said, flushed and smiling.

"Oh, now," Terri said. "Wait awhile."

She held her drink and gazed at Laura.

"I'm only kidding," Terri said.   50

Mel opened the gin and went around the table with the bottle.

"Here, you guys," he said. "Let's have a toast. I want to propose a toast. A toast to love. To true love," Mel said.

We touched glasses.

"To love," we said.

Outside in the backyard, one of the dogs began to bark. The leaves of the aspen   55
that leaned past the window ticked against the glass. The afternoon sun was like a presence in this room, the spacious light of ease and generosity. We

could have been anywhere, somewhere enchanted. We raised our glasses again and grinned at each other like children who had agreed on something forbidden.

"I'll tell you what real love is," Mel said. "I mean, I'll give you a good example. And then you can draw your own conclusions." He poured more gin into his glass. He added an ice cube and a sliver of lime. We waited and sipped our drinks. Laura and I touched knees again. I put a hand on her warm thigh and left it there.

"What do any of us really know about love?" Mel said. "It seems to me we're just beginners at love. We say we love each other and we do, I don't doubt it. I love Terri and Terri loves me, and you guys love each other too. You know the kind of love I'm talking about now. Physical love, that impulse that drives you to someone special, as well as love of the other person's being, his or her essence, as it were. Carnal love and, well, call it sentimental love, the day-to-day caring about the other person. But sometimes I have a hard time accounting for the fact that I must have loved my first wife too. But I did, I know I did. So I suppose I am like Terri in that regard. Terri and Ed." He thought about it and then he went on. "There was a time when I thought I loved my first wife more than life itself. But now I hate her guts. I do. How do you explain that? What happened to that love? What happened to it, is what I'd like to know. I wish someone could tell me. Then there's Ed. Okay, we're back to Ed. He loves Terri so much he tries to kill her and he winds up killing himself." Mel stopped talking and swallowed from his glass. "You guys have been together eighteen months and you love each other. It shows all over you. You glow with it. But you both loved other people before you met each other. You've both been married before, just like us. And you probably loved other people before that too, even. Terri and I have been together five years, been married for four. And the terrible thing, the terrible thing is, but the good thing too, the saving grace, you might say, is that if something happened to one of us—excuse me for saying this—but if something happened to one of us tomorrow I think the other one, the other person, would grieve for a while, you know, but then the surviving party would go out and love again, have someone else soon enough. All this, all of this love we're talking about, it would just be a memory. Maybe not even a memory. Am I wrong? Am I way off base? Because I want you to set me straight if you think I'm wrong. I want to know. I mean, I don't know anything, and I'm the first one to admit it."

"Mel, for God's sake," Terri said. She reached out and took hold of his wrist. "Are you getting drunk? Honey? Are you drunk?"

"Honey, I'm just talking," Mel said. "All right? I don't have to be drunk to say what I think. I mean, we're all just talking, right?" Mel said. He fixed his eyes on her.

"Sweetie, I'm not criticizing," Terri said.

She picked up her glass.

"I'm not on call today," Mel said. "Let me remind you of that. I am not on call," he said.

"Mel, we love you," Laura said.

60

Mel looked at Laura. He looked at her as if he could not place her, as if she was not the woman she was.

"Love you too, Laura," Mel said. "And you, Nick, love you too. You know   65
something?" Mel said. "You guys are our pals," Mel said.

He picked up his glass.

Mel said, "I was going to tell you about something. I mean, I was going to prove a point. You see, this happened a few months ago, but it's still going on right now, and it ought to make us feel ashamed when we talk like we know what we're talking about when we talk about love."

"Come on now," Terri said. "Don't talk like you're drunk if you're not drunk."

"Just shut up for once in your life," Mel said very quietly. "Will you do me a favor and do that for a minute? So as I was saying, there's this old couple who had this car wreck out on the interstate. A kid hit them and they were all torn to shit and nobody was giving them much chance to pull through."

Terri looked at us and then back at Mel. She seemed anxious, or maybe   70
that's too strong a word.

Mel was handing the bottle around the table.

"I was on call that night," Mel said. "It was May or maybe it was June. Terri and I had just sat down to dinner when the hospital called. There'd been this thing out on the interstate. Drunk kid, teenager, plowed his dad's pickup into this camper with this old couple in it. They were up in their midseventies, that couple. The kid — eighteen, nineteen, something — he was DOA. Taken the steering wheel through his sternum. The old couple, they were alive, you understand. I mean, just barely. But they had everything. Multiple fractures, internal injuries, hemorrhaging, contusions, lacerations, the works, and they each of them had themselves concussions. They were in a bad way, believe me. And, of course, their age was two strikes against them. I'd say she was worse off than he was. Ruptured spleen along with everything else. Both kneecaps broken. But they'd been wearing their seatbelts and, God knows, that's what saved them for the time being."

"Folks, this is an advertisement for the National Safety Council," Terri said. "This is your spokesman, Dr. Melvin R. McGinnis, talking." Terri laughed. "Mel," she said, "sometimes you're just too much. But I love you, hon," she said.

"Honey, I love you," Mel said.

He leaned across the table. Terri met him halfway. They kissed.   75

"Terri's right," Mel said as he settled himself again. "Get those seatbelts on. But seriously, they were in some shape, those oldsters. By the time I got down there, the kid was dead, as I said. He was off in a corner, laid out on a gurney. I took one look at the old couple and told the ER nurse to get me a neurologist and an orthopedic man and a couple of surgeons down there right away."

He drank from his glass. "I'll try to keep this short," he said. "So we took the two of them up to the OR and worked like fuck on them most of the night. They had these incredible reserves, those two. You see that once in a while. So we did everything that could be done, and toward morning we're giving them a fifty-fifty chance, maybe less than that for her. So here they are, still alive the next morning. So, okay, we move them into the ICU, which is where they both kept plugging away at it for two weeks, hitting it better and better on all the scopes. So we transfer them out to their own room."

Mel stopped talking. "Here," he said, "let's drink this cheapo gin the hell up. Then we're going to dinner, right? Terri and I know a new place. That's where we'll go, to this new place we know about. But we're not going until we finish up this cut-rate, lousy gin."

Terri said, "We haven't actually eaten there yet. But it looks good. From the outside, you know."

"I like food," Mel said. "If I had it to do all over again, I'd be a chef, you   80
know? Right, Terri?" Mel said.

He laughed. He fingered the ice in his glass.

"Terri knows," he said. "Terri can tell you. But let me say this. If I could come back again in a different life, a different time and all, you know what? I'd like to come back as a knight. You were pretty safe wearing all that armor. It was all right being a knight until gunpowder and muskets and pistols came along."

"Mel would like to ride a horse and carry a lance," Terri said.

"Carry a woman's scarf with you everywhere," Laura said.

"Or just a woman," Mel said.   85

"Shame on you," Laura said.

Terri said, "Suppose you came back as a serf. The serfs didn't have it so good in those days," Terri said.

"The serfs never had it good," Mel said. "But I guess even the knights were vessels to someone. Isn't that the way it worked? But then everyone is always a vessel to someone. Isn't that right? Terri? But what I liked about knights, besides their ladies, was that they had that suit of armor, you know, and they couldn't get hurt very easy. No cars in those days, you know? No drunk teenagers to tear into your ass."

"Vassals," Terri said.

"What?" Mel said.   90

"Vassals," Terri said. "They were called vassals, not vessels."

"Vassals, vessels," Mel said, "what the fuck's the difference? You knew what I meant anyway. All right," Mel said. "So I'm not educated. I learned my stuff. I'm a heart surgeon, sure, but I'm just a mechanic. I go in and I fuck around and I fix things. Shit," Mel said.

"Modesty doesn't become you," Terri said.

"He's just a humble sawbones," I said. "But sometimes they suffocated in all that armor, Mel. They'd even have heart attacks if it got too hot and they were too tired and worn out. I read somewhere that they'd fall off their horses and not be able to get up because they were too tired to stand with all that armor on them. They got trampled by their own horses sometimes."

"That's terrible," Mel said. "That's a terrible thing, Nicky. I guess they'd   95
just lay there and wait until somebody came along and made a shish kebab out of them."

"Some other vessel," Terri said.

"That's right," Mel said. "Some vassal would come along and spear the bastard in the name of love. Or whatever the fuck it was they fought over in those days."

"Same things we fight over these days," Terri said.

Laura said, "Nothing's changed."

The color was still high in Laura's cheeks. Her eyes were bright. She brought her glass to her lips.   100

Mel poured himself another drink. He looked at the label closely as if studying a long row of numbers. Then he slowly put the bottle down on the table and slowly reached for the tonic water.

"What about the old couple?" Laura said. "You didn't finish that story you started."

Laura was having a hard time lighting her cigarette. Her matches kept going out.

The sunshine inside the room was different now, changing, getting thinner. But the leaves outside the window were still shimmering, and I stared at the pattern they made on the panes and on the Formica counter. They weren't the same patterns, of course.

"What about the old couple?" I said.   105

"Older but wiser," Terri said.

Mel stared at her.

Terri said, "Go on with your story, hon. I was only kidding. Then what happened?"

"Terri, sometimes," Mel said.

"Please, Mel," Terri said. "Don't always be so serious, sweetie. Can't you   110
take a joke?"

"Where's the joke?" Mel said.

He held his glass and gazed steadily at his wife.

"What happened?" Laura said.

Mel fastened his eyes on Laura. He said, "Laura, if I didn't have Terri and if I didn't love her so much, and if Nick wasn't my best friend, I'd fall in love with you, I'd carry you off, honey," he said.

"Tell your story," Terri said. "Then we'll go to that new place, okay?"   115

"Okay," Mel said. "Where was I?" he said. He stared at the table and then he began again.

"I dropped in to see each of them every day, sometimes twice a day if I was up doing other calls anyway. Casts and bandages, head to foot, the both of them. You know, you've seen it in the movies. That's just the way they looked, just like in the movies. Little eye-holes and nose-holes and mouth-holes. And she had to have her legs slung up on top of it. Well, the husband was very depressed for the longest while. Even after he found out that his wife was going to pull through, he was still very depressed. Not about the accident, though. I mean, the accident was one thing, but it wasn't everything. I'd get up to his mouth-hole, you know, and he'd say no, it wasn't the accident exactly but it was because he couldn't see her through his eye-holes. He said that was what was making him feel so bad. Can you imagine? I'm telling you, the man's heart was breaking because he couldn't turn his goddamn head and *see* his goddamn wife."

Mel looked around the table and shook his head at what he was going to say.

"I mean, it was killing the old fart just because he couldn't *look* at the fucking woman."

We all looked at Mel.   120

"Do you see what I'm saying?" he said.

Maybe we were a little drunk by then. I know it was hard keeping things in focus. The light was draining out of the room, going back through the window where it had come from. Yet nobody made a move to get up from the table to turn on the overhead light.

"Listen," Mel said. "Let's finish this fucking gin. There's about enough left here for one shooter all around. Then let's go eat. Let's go to the new place."

"He's depressed," Terri said. "Mel, why don't you take a pill?"

Mel shook his head. "I've taken everything there is."   125

"We all need a pill now and then," I said.

"Some people are born needing them," Terri said.

She was using her finger to rub at something on the table. Then she stopped rubbing.

"I think I want to call my kids," Mel said. "Is that all right with everybody? I'll call my kids," he said.

Terri said, "What if Marjorie answers the phone? You guys, you've heard   130
us on the subject of Marjorie? Honey, you know you don't want to talk to Marjorie. It'll make you feel even worse."

"I don't want to talk to Marjorie," Mel said. "But I want to talk to my kids."

"There isn't a day goes by that Mel doesn't say he wishes she'd get married again. Or else die," Terri said. "For one thing," Terri said, "she's bankrupting us. Mel says it's just to spite him that she won't get married again. She has a boyfriend who lives with her and the kids, so Mel is supporting the boyfriend too."

"She's allergic to bees," Mel said. "If I'm not praying she'll get married again, I'm praying she'll get herself stung to death by a swarm of fucking bees."

"Shame on you," Laura said.

"Bzzzzzzz," Mel said, turning his fingers into bees and buzzing them at   135
Terri's throat. Then he let his hands drop all the way to his sides.

"She's vicious," Mel said. "Sometimes I think I'll go up there dressed like a beekeeper. You know, that hat that's like a helmet with the plate that comes down over your face, the big gloves, and the padded coat? I'll knock on the door and let loose a hive of bees in the house. But first I'd make sure the kids were out, of course."

He crossed one leg over the other. It seemed to take him a lot of time to do it. Then he put both feet on the floor and leaned forward, elbows on the table, his chin cupped in his hands.

"Maybe I won't call the kids, after all. Maybe it isn't such a hot idea. Maybe we'll just go eat. How does that sound?"

"Sounds fine to me," I said. "Eat or not eat. Or keep drinking. I could head right on out into the sunset."

"What does that mean, honey?" Laura said.   140

"It just means what I said," I said. "It means I could just keep going. That's all it means."

"I could eat something myself," Laura said. "I don't think I've ever been so hungry in my life. Is there something to nibble on?"

"I'll put out some cheese and crackers," Terri said.

But Terri just sat there. She did not get up to get anything.

Mel turned his glass over. He spilled it out on the table.   145

"Gin's gone," Mel said.

Terri said, "Now what?"

I could hear my heart beating. I could hear everyone's heart. I could hear the human noise we sat there making, not one of us moving, not even when the room went dark.   *[1981]*

≡ THINKING ABOUT THE TEXT

1. The argument between the couples seems to be about the nature of love. Which character's ideas make the most sense to you? What kinds of love are discussed? Are these demonstrated in the story? Do you think true love is an illusion?

2. Do you see similarities between Mel and Ed? Do any of the characters seem aware of any similarities? Is Mel a perceptive person? What are his problems? Is he in love with Terri? How do you interpret his fantasy with the bees and Marjorie?

3. Why does Mel seem so interested in knights? Is this symbolic? Are there other symbols here (light? dark? cardiologist?)? What do you make of the last paragraph? Why does it end with beating hearts and silence?

4. Is this story optimistic or pessimistic about true love? Is the old couple a positive or a negative example of true love? What about Nick and Laura? What about Ed? Could you argue that he was in love?

5. What does the title mean? Be specific, especially about the first word. Do you tell stories about love? Have you heard some recently? What lessons or information do they give about love?

NATHAN ENGLANDER

What We Talk About
When We Talk About Anne Frank

Nathan Englander (b. 1970) was born and grew up on Long Island outside New York City. He graduated from SUNY Binghamton and the Writer's Workshop at the University of Iowa. His successful short story collection For the Relief of Unbearable Urges *was published in 1999. His second collection,* What We Talk About When We Talk About Anne Frank *(2012), won the Frank O'Connor International Short Story Award and was a finalist for the Pulitzer Prize in fiction. He has won other prestigious prizes, and his work has appeared a number of times in the O. Henry Prize Stories and the Best American Short Stories collections. He has also written a novel and a play. Of his recent collection, the celebrated novelist Michael Chabon said it contains "certifiable masterpieces of contemporary short story art." He is currently the Distinguished Writer-in-Residence at New York University and lives in Brooklyn, New York, and Madison, Wisconsin.*

They're in our house maybe ten minutes and already Mark's lecturing us on the Israeli occupation. Mark and Lauren live in Jerusalem, and people from there think it gives them the right.

Mark is looking all stoic and nodding his head. "If we had what you have down here in South Florida," he says, and trails off. "Yup," he says, and he's nodding again. "We'd have no troubles at all."

"You do have what we have," I tell him. "All of it. Sun and palm trees. Old Jews and oranges and the worst drivers around. At this point, we've probably got more Israelis than you." Debbie, my wife, puts a hand on my arm — her signal that I'm either taking a tone, interrupting someone's story, sharing something private, or making an inappropriate joke. That's my cue, and I'm surprised, considering how often I get it, that she ever lets go of my arm.

"Yes, you've got everything now," Mark says. "Even terrorists."

I look at Lauren. She's the one my wife has the relationship with — the one who should take charge. But Lauren isn't going to give her husband any signal. She and Mark ran off to Israel twenty years ago and turned Hasidic, and neither of them will put a hand on the other in public. Not for this. Not to put out a fire.   5

"Wasn't Mohamed Atta living right here before 9/11?" Mark says, and now he pantomimes pointing out houses. "Goldberg, Goldberg, Goldberg — Atta. How'd you miss him in this place?"

"Other side of town," I say.

"That's what I'm talking about. That's what you have that we don't. Other sides of town. Wrong sides of the tracks. Space upon space." And now he's fingering the granite countertop in our kitchen, looking out into the living room and the dining room, staring through the kitchen windows at the pool. "All this house," he says, "and one son? Can you imagine?"

Barbara Zanon /Getty Images

"No," Lauren says. And then she turns to us, backing him up. "You should see how we live with ten."

"Ten kids," I say. "We could get you a reality show with that here in the States. Help you get a bigger place."

The hand is back pulling at my sleeve. "Pictures," Debbie says. "I want to see the girls." We all follow Lauren into the den for her purse.

"Do you believe it?" Mark says. "Ten girls!" And the way it comes out of his mouth, it's the first time I like the guy. The first time I think about giving him a chance.

Facebook and Skype brought Deb and Lauren back together. They were glued at the hip growing up. Went all the way through school together. Yeshiva school. All girls. Out in Queens till high school and then riding the subway together to one called Central in Manhattan. They stayed best friends until I married Deb and turned her secular, and soon after that Lauren met Mark and they went off to the Holy Land and shifted from Orthodox to *ultra-*Orthodox, which to me sounds like a repackaged detergent — ORTHODOX ULTRA®, now with more deep-healing power. Because of that, we're supposed to call them Shoshana and Yerucham now. Deb's been doing it. I'm just not saying their names.

"You want some water?" I offer. "Coke in the can?"

" 'You'—which of us?" Mark says.   15

"You both," I say. "Or I've got whiskey. Whiskey's kosher too, right?"

"If it's not, I'll kosher it up real fast," he says, pretending to be easygoing. And right then he takes off that big black hat and plops down on the couch in the den.

Lauren's holding the verticals aside and looking out at the yard. "Two girls from Forest Hills," she says. "Who ever thought we'd be the mothers of grownups?"

"Trevor's sixteen," Deb says. "You may think he's a grownup, and he may think he's grownup—but we are not convinced."

Right then is when Trev comes padding into the den, all six feet of him,   20
plaid pajama bottoms dragging on the floor and T-shirt full of holes. He's just woken up, and you can tell he's not sure if he's still dreaming. We told him we had guests. But there's Trev, staring at this man in the black suit, a beard resting on his belly. And Lauren, I met her once before, right when Deb and I got married, but ten girls and a thousand Shabbos dinners later—well, she's a big woman, in a bad dress and a giant blond Marilyn Monroe wig.° Seeing them at the door, I can't say I wasn't shocked myself.

"Hey," he says.

And then Deb's on him, preening and fixing his hair and hugging him. "Trevy, this is my best friend from childhood," she says. "This is Shoshana, and this is—"

"Mark," I say.

"Yerucham," Mark says, and sticks out a hand. Trev shakes it. Then Trev sticks out his hand, polite, to Lauren. She looks at it, just hanging there in the air.

"I don't shake," she says. "But I'm so happy to see you. Like meeting my   25
own son. I mean it." And here she starts to cry, and then she and Deb are hugging. And the boys, we just stand there until Mark looks at his watch and gets himself a good manly grip on Trev's shoulder.

"Sleeping until three on a Sunday? Man, those were the days," Mark says. "A regular little Rumpleforeskin." Trev looks at me, and I want to shrug, but Mark's also looking, so I don't move. Trev just gives us both his best teenage glare and edges out of the room. As he does, he says, "Baseball practice," and takes my car keys off the hook by the door to the garage.

"There's gas," I say.

"They let them drive here at sixteen?" Mark says. "Insane."

"So what brings you here after all these years?" I say.

"My mother," Mark says. "She's failing, and my father's getting old—and   30
they come to us for Sukkot° every year. You know?"

---

wig: Some Orthodox women wear wigs after they are married as a religious practice.
Sukkot: The Jewish harvest holiday.

"I know the holidays."

"They used to fly out to us. For Sukkot and Pesach°, both. But they can't fly now, and I just wanted to get over while things are still good. We haven't been in America—"

"Oh, gosh," Lauren says. "I'm afraid to think how long it's been. More than ten years. Twelve," she says. "With the kids, it's just impossible until enough of them are big."

"How do you do it?" Deb says. "Ten kids? I really do want to hear."

That's when I remember. "I forgot your drink," I say to Mark.   35

"Yes, his drink. That's how," Lauren says. "That's how we cope."

And that's how the four of us end up back at the kitchen table with a bottle of vodka between us. I'm not one to get drunk on a Sunday afternoon, but, I tell you, when the plan is to spend the day with Mark I jump at the chance. Deb's drinking too, but not for the same reason. I think she and Lauren are reliving a little bit of the wild times. The very small window when they were together, barely grown up, two young women living in New York on the edge of two worlds.

Deb says, "This is really racy for us. I mean, *really* racy. We try not to drink much at all these days. We think it sets a bad example for Trevor. It's not good to drink in front of them right at this age when they're all transgressive. He's suddenly so interested in that kind of thing."

"I'm just happy when he's interested in something," I say.

Deb slaps at the air. "I just don't think it's good to make drinking look like   40
it's fun with a teenager around."

Lauren smiles and straightens her wig. "Does anything we do look fun to our kids?"

I laugh at that. Honestly, I'm liking her more and more.

"It's the age limit that does it," Mark says. "It's the whole American puritanical thing, the twenty-one-year-old drinking age and all that. We don't make a big deal about it in Israel, and so the kids, they don't even notice alcohol. Except for the foreign workers on Fridays, you hardly see anyone drunk at all."

"The workers and the Russians," Lauren says.

"The Russian immigrants," he says, "that's a whole separate matter. Most   45
of them, you know, not even Jews."

"What does that mean?" I say.

"It means matrilineal descent, is what it means," Mark says. "With the Ethiopians there were conversions."

But Deb wants to keep us away from politics, and the way we're arranged, me in between them and Deb opposite (it's a round table, our kitchen table), she practically has to throw herself across to grab hold of my arm. "Fix me another," she says.

And here she switches the subject to Mark's parents. "How's the visit been going?" she says, her face all somber. "How are your folks holding up?"

Pesach: The Jewish holiday of Passover.

Deb is very interested in Mark's parents. They're Holocaust survivors. And   50
Deb has what can only be called an unhealthy obsession with the idea of that
generation being gone. Don't get me wrong. It's important to me too. All I'm
saying is there's healthy and unhealthy, and my wife, she gives the subject a *lot*
of time.

"What can I say?" Mark says. "My mother's a very sick woman. And my
father, he tries to keep his spirits up. He's tough guy."

"I'm sure," I say. Then I look down at my drink, all serious, and give a shake
of my head. "They really are amazing."

"Who?" Mark says. "Fathers?"

I look back up and they're all staring at me. "Survivors," I say, realizing I
jumped the gun.

"There's good and bad," Mark says. "Like anyone else."   55

Lauren says, "The whole of Carmel Lake Village, it's like a D.P. camp with
a billiards room."

"One tells the other, and they follow," Mark says. "From Europe to New
York, and now, for the end of their lives, again the same place."

"Tell them that crazy story, Yuri," Lauren says.

"Tell us," Deb says.

"So you can picture my father," Mark says. "In the old country, he went to   60
heder°, had the *peyes*° and all that. But in America a classic *galusmonger*°. He
looks more like you than me. It's not from him that I get this," he says, pointing
at his beard. "Shoshana and I—"

"We know," I say.

"So my father. They've got a nice nine-hole course, a driving range, some
greens for the practice putting. And my dad's at the clubhouse. I go with him.
He wants to work out in the gym, he says. Tells me I should come. Get some
exercise. And he tells me"—and here Mark points at his feet, sliding a leg out
from under the table so we can see his big black clodhoppers—"'You can't
wear those Shabbos shoes on the treadmill. You need the sneakers. You know,
sports shoes?' And I tell him, 'I know what sneakers are. I didn't forget my
English any more than your Yiddish is gone.' So he says, '*Ah shaynem dank dir in
pupik*°.' Just to show me who's who."

"Tell them the point," Lauren says.

"He's sitting in the locker room, trying to pull a sock on, which is, at that age,
basically the whole workout in itself. It's no quick business. And I see, while I'm
waiting, and I can't believe it—I nearly pass out. The guy next to him, the number on his arm, it's three before my father's number. You know, in sequence."

"What do you mean?" Deb says.   65

"I mean the number tattooed. It's the same as my father's camp number,
digit for digit, but my father's ends in an eight. And this guy's, it ends in a five.
That's the only difference. I mean, they're separated by two people. So I say,

Heder: Jewish elementary school.   **Peyes:** Sidecurls.   **Galusmonger:** Probably a negative term for someone excessively focused on the Jewish diaspora and fear of persecution.
Ah shaynem dank dir in pupik: Thanks for nothing (Yiddish).

'Excuse me, sir.' And the guy just says, 'You with the Chabad? I don't want anything but to be left alone. I already got candles at home.' I tell him, 'No. I'm not. I'm here visiting my father.' And to my father I say, 'Do you know this gentleman? Have you two met? I'd really like to introduce you, if you haven't.' And they look each other over for what, I promise you, is minutes. Actual minutes. It is—with *kavod* I say this, with respect for my father—but it is like watching a pair of big beige manatees sitting on a bench, each with one sock on. They're just looking each other up and down, everything slow. And then my father says, 'I seen him. Seen him around.' The other guy, he says, 'Yes, I've seen.' 'You're both survivors,' I tell them. 'Look. The numbers.' And they look. 'They're the same,' I say. And they both hold out their arms to look at the little ashen tattoos. To my father I say, 'Do you get it? The same, except his—it's right ahead of yours. Look! Compare.' So they look. They compare." Mark's eyes are popping out of his head. "Think about it," he says. "Around the world, surviving the unsurvivable, these two old guys end up with enough money to retire to Carmel Lake and play golf every day. So I say to my dad, 'He's right ahead of you. Look, a five,' I say. 'And yours is an eight.' And my father says, 'All that means is he cut ahead of me in line. There same as here. This guy's a cutter. I just didn't want to say.' 'Blow it out your ear,' the other guy says. And that's it. Then they get back to putting on socks."

Deb looks crestfallen. She was expecting something empowering. Some story with which to educate Trevor, to reaffirm her belief in the humanity that, from inhumanity, forms.

But me, I love that kind of story. I'm starting to take a real shine to these two, and not just because I'm suddenly feeling sloshed.

"Good story, Yuri," I say, copying his wife. "Yerucham, that one's got zing."

Yerucham hoists himself up from the table, looking proud. He checks the   70
label of our white bread on the counter, making sure it's kosher. He takes a slice, pulls off the crust, and rolls the white part against the countertop with the palm of his hand, making a little ball. He comes over and pours himself a shot and throws it back. Then he eats that crazy dough ball. Just tosses it in his mouth, as if it's the bottom of his own personal punctuation mark—you know, to underline his story.

"Is that good?" I say.

"Try it," he says. He goes to the counter and pitches me a slice of white bread, and says, "But first pour yourself a shot."

I reach for the bottle and find that Deb's got her hands around it, and her head's bowed down, like the bottle is anchoring her, keeping her from tipping back.

"Are you okay, Deb?" Lauren says.

"It's because it was funny," I say.   75

"Honey!" Deb says.

"She won't tell you, but she's a little obsessed with the Holocaust. That story—no offense, Mark—it's not what she had in mind."

I should leave it be, I know. But it's not like someone from Deb's high school is around every day offering insights.

672   CHAPTER 8   Love

672   CHAPTER 8   Love

"It's like she's a survivor's kid, my wife. It's crazy, that education they give them. Her grandparents were all born in the Bronx, and here we are twenty minutes from downtown Miami but it's like it's 1937 and we live on the edge of Berlin."

"That's not it!" Deb says, openly defensive, her voice super high up in the register. "I'm not upset about that. It's the alcohol. All this alcohol. It's that and seeing Lauren. Seeing Shoshana, after all this time."

"Oh, she was always like this in high school," Shoshana says. "Sneak one drink, and she started to cry. You want to know what used to get her going, what would make her truly happy?" Shoshana says. "It was getting high. That's what always did it. Smoking up. It would make her laugh for hours and hours."

And, I tell you, I didn't see it coming. I'm as blindsided as Deb was by that numbers story.

"Oh, my God," Deb says, and she's pointing at me. "Look at my big bad secular husband. He really can't handle it. He can't handle his wife's having any history of naughtiness at all — Mr. Liberal Open-Minded." To me she says, "How much more chaste a wife can you dream of than a modern-day yeshiva girl who stayed a virgin until twenty-one? Honestly. What did you think Shoshana was going to say was so much fun?"

"Honestly-honestly?" I say. "I don't want to. It's embarrassing."

"Say it!" Deb says, positively glowing.

"Honestly, I thought you were going to say it was something like competing in the Passover Nut Roll, or making sponge cake. Something like that." I hang my head. And Shoshana and Deb are laughing so hard they can't breathe. They're grabbing at each other so that I can't tell if they're holding each other up or pulling each other down.

"I can't believe you told him about the nut roll," Shoshana says.

"And I can't believe," Deb says, "you just told my husband of twenty-two years how much we used to get high. I haven't touched a joint since before we were married," she says. "Have we, honey? Have we smoked since we got married?"

"No," I say. "It's been a very long time."

"So come on, Shosh. When was it? When was the last time you smoked?"

Now, I know I mentioned the beard on Mark. But I don't know if I mentioned how hairy a guy he is. That thing grows right up to his eyeballs. Like having eyebrows on top and bottom both. So when Deb asks the question, the two of them, Shosh and Yuri, are basically giggling like children, and I can tell, in the little part that shows, in the bit of skin I can see, that Mark's eyelids and earlobes are in full blush.

"When Shoshana said we drink to get through the days," Mark says, "she was kidding about the drinking."

"We don't drink much," Shoshana says.

"It's smoking that she means," he says.

"We still get high," Shoshana says. "I mean, all the time."

"Hasidim!" Deb screams. "You're not allowed!"

"Everyone does in Israel. It's like the sixties there," Mark says. "It's the highest country in the world. Worse than Holland and India and Thailand put together. Worse than anywhere, even Argentina—though they may have us tied."

"Well, maybe that's why the kids aren't interested in alcohol," I say.

"Do you want to get high now?" Deb says. And we all three look at her. Me, with surprise. And those two with straight longing.

"We didn't bring," Shoshana says. "Though it's pretty rare anyone at customs peeks under the wig."   100

"Maybe you guys can find your way into the glaucoma underground over at Carmel Lake," I say. "I'm sure that place is rife with it."

"That's funny," Mark says.

"I'm funny," I say, now that we're all getting on.

"We've got pot," Deb says.

"We do?" I say. "I don't think we do."   105

Deb looks at me and bites at the cuticle on her pinkie.

"You're not secretly getting high all these years?" I say. I really don't feel well at all.

"Our son," Deb says. "He has pot."

"Our son?"   110

"Trevor," she says.

"Yes," I say. "I know which one."

It's a lot for one day, that kind of news. And it feels to me a lot like betrayal. Like my wife's old secret and my son's new secret are bound up together, and I've somehow been wronged. Also, I'm not one to recover quickly from any kind of slight from Deb—not when there are people around. I really need to talk stuff out. Some time alone, even five minutes, would fix it. But it's super apparent that Deb doesn't need any time alone with me. She doesn't seem troubled at all. What she seems is focused. She's busy at the counter, using a paper tampon wrapper to roll a joint.

"It's an emergency-preparedness method we came up with in high school," Shoshana says. "The things teenage girls will do when they're desperate."

"Do you remember that nice boy that we used to smoke in front of?" Deb   115 says. "He'd just watch us. There'd be six or seven of us in a circle, girls and boys not touching—we were so religious. Isn't that crazy?" Deb is talking to me, as Shoshana and Mark don't think it's crazy at all. "The only place we touched was passing the joint, at the thumbs. And this boy, we had a nickname for him."

"Passover!" Shoshana yells.

"Yes," Deb says, "that's it. All we ever called him was Passover. Because every time the joint got to him he'd just pass it over to the next one of us. Passover Rand."

Shoshana takes the joint and lights it with a match, sucking deep. "It's a miracle when I remember anything these days," she says. "After my first was born, I forgot half of everything I knew. And then half again with each one after. Just last night, I woke up in a panic. I couldn't remember if there were fifty-two cards in a deck or fifty-two weeks in a year. The recall errors—I'm up all night worrying over them, just waiting for the Alzheimer's to kick in."

"It's not that bad," Mark tells her. "It's only everyone on one side of your family that has it."

"That's true," she says, passing her husband the joint. "The other side is   120 blessed only with dementia. Anyway, which is it? Weeks or cards?"

"Same, same," Mark says, taking a hit.

When it's Deb's turn, she holds the joint and looks at me, like I'm supposed to nod or give her permission in some husbandly anxiety-absolving way. But instead of saying, "Go ahead," I pretty much bark at Deb. "When were you going to tell me about our son?"

At that, Deb takes a long hit, holding it deep, like an old pro.

"Really, Deb. How could you not tell me you knew?"

Deb walks over and hands me the joint. She blows the smoke in my face,   125 not aggressive, just blowing.

"I've only known five days," she says. "I was going to tell you. I just wasn't sure how, or if I should talk to Trevy first, maybe give him a chance," she says.

"A chance to what?" I ask.

"To let him keep it as a secret between us. To let him know he could have my trust if he promised to stop."

"But he's the son," I say. "I'm the father. Even if it's a secret with him, it should be a double secret between me and you. I should always get to know— even if I pretend not to know—any secret with him."

"Do that double part again," Mark says. But I ignore him.   130

"That's how it's always been," I say to Deb. And, because I'm desperate and unsure, I follow it up with "Hasn't it?"

I mean, we really trust each other, Deb and I. And I can't remember feeling like so much has hung on one question in a long time. I'm trying to read her face, and something complex is going on, some formulation. And then she sits right there on the floor, at my feet.

"Oh, my God," she says. "I'm so fucking high. Like instantly. Like, like," and then she starts laughing. "Like, Mike," she says. "Like, kike," she says, turning completely serious. "Oh, my God, I'm really messed up."

"We should have warned you," Shoshana says.

As she says this, I'm holding my first hit in, and already trying to fight off   135 the paranoia that comes rushing behind that statement.

"Warned us what?" I say, my voice high, and the smoke still sweet in my nose.

"This isn't your father's marijuana," Mark says. "The THC levels. One hit of this new hydroponic stuff, it's like if maybe you smoked a pound of the stuff we had when we were kids."

"I feel it," I say. And I do. I sit down with Deb on the floor and take her hands. I feel nice. Though I'm not sure if I thought that or said it, so I try it again, making sure it's out loud. "I feel nice," I say.

"I found the pot in the laundry hamper," Deb says. "Leave it to a teenage boy to think that's the best place to hide something. His clean clothes show up folded in his room, and it never occurs to him that someone empties that hamper. To him, it's the loneliest, most forgotten space in the world. Point is I found an Altoids tin at the bottom, stuffed full." Deb gives my hands a squeeze. "Are we good now?"

"We're good," I say. And it feels like we're a team again, like it's us against   140
them. Because Deb says, "Are you sure you guys are allowed to smoke pot that comes out of a tin that held non-kosher candy? I really don't know if that's okay." And it's just exactly the kind of thing I'm thinking.

"First of all, we're not eating it. We're smoking it," Shoshana says. "And even so, it's cold contact, so it's probably all right either way."

" 'Cold contact'?" I say.

"It's a thing," Shoshana says. "Just forget about it and get up off the floor. Chop-chop." And they each offer us a hand and get us standing. "Come, sit back at the table," Shoshana says.

"I'll tell you," Mark says. "That's got to be the number-one most annoying thing about being Hasidic in the outside world. Worse than the rude stuff that gets said is the constant policing by civilians. Everywhere we go, people are checking on us. Ready to make some sort of liturgical citizen's arrest."

"Strangers!" Shoshana says. "Just the other day, on the way in from the   145
airport. Yuri pulled into a McDonald's to pee, and some guy in a trucker hat came up to him as he went in and said, 'You allowed to go in there, brother?' Just like that."

"Not true!" Deb says.

"It's not that I don't see the fun in that," Mark says. "The allure. You know, we've got Mormons in Jerusalem. They've got a base there. A seminary. The rule is—the deal with the government—they can have their place, but they can't do outreach. No proselytizing. Anyway, I do some business with one of their guys."

"From Utah?" Deb says.

"From Idaho. His name is Jebediah, for real—do you believe it?"

"No, Yerucham and Shoshana," I say. "Jebediah is a very strange name."   150
Mark rolls his eyes at that, handing me what's left of the joint. Without even asking, he gets up and gets the tin and reaches into his wife's purse for another tampon. And I'm a little less comfortable with this than with the white bread, with a guest coming into the house and smoking up all our son's pot. Deb must be thinking something similar, as she says, "After this story, I'm going to text Trev and make sure he's not coming back anytime soon."

"So when Jeb's at our house," Mark says, "when he comes by to eat and pours himself a Coke, I do that same religious-police thing. I can't resist. I say, 'Hey, Jeb, you allowed to have that?' People don't mind breaking their own rules, but they're real strict about someone else's."

"So are they allowed to have Coke?" Deb says.

"I don't know," Mark says. "All Jeb ever says back is 'You're thinking of coffee, and mind your own business, either way.' "

And then my Deb. She just can't help herself. "You heard about the scandal? The Mormons going through the Holocaust list."

"Like in *Dead Souls*," I say, explaining. "Like in the Gogol book, but real."   155
"Do you think we read that?" Mark says. "As Hasidim, or before?"
"They took the records of the dead," Deb says, "and they started running through them. They took these people who died as Jews and started converting them into Mormons. Converting the six million against their will."
"And this is what keeps an American Jew up at night?" Mark says.
"What does that mean?" Deb says.
"It means — " Mark says.   160
But Shoshana interrupts him. "Don't tell them what it means, Yuri. Just leave it unmeant."
"We can handle it," I say. "We are interested, even, in handling it."
"Your son, he seems like a nice boy."
"Do not talk about their son," Shoshana says.
"Do not talk about our son," Deb says. This time I reach across and lay a   165
hand on her elbow.
"Talk," I say.
"He does not," Mark says, "seem Jewish to me."
"How can you say that?" Deb says. "What is wrong with you?" But Deb's upset draws less attention than my response. I'm laughing so hard that everyone turns toward me.
"What?" Mark says.
"Jewish to you?" I say. "The hat, the beard, the blocky shoes. A lot of pres-   170
sure, I'd venture, to look Jewish to you. Like, say, maybe Ozzy Osbourne, or the guys from Kiss, like them telling Paul Simon, 'You do not look like a musician to me.' "
"It is not about the outfit," Mark says. "It's about building life in a vacuum. Do you know what I saw on the drive over here? Supermarket, supermarket, adult bookstore, supermarket, supermarket, firing range."
"Floridians do like their guns and porn," I say. "And their supermarkets."
"What I'm trying to say, whether you want to take it seriously or not, is that you can't build Judaism only on the foundation of one terrible crime," Mark says. "It's about this obsession with the Holocaust as a necessary sign of identity. As your only educational tool. Because for the children there is no connection otherwise. Nothing Jewish that binds."
"Wow, that's offensive," Deb says. "And closed-minded. There is such a thing as Jewish culture. One can live a culturally rich life."
"Not if it's supposed to be a Jewish life. Judaism is a religion. And with reli-   175
gion comes ritual. Culture is nothing. Culture is some construction of the modern world. It is not fixed; it is ever changing, and a weak way to bind generations. It's like taking two pieces of metal, and instead of making a nice weld you hold them together with glue."
"What does that even mean?" Deb says. "Practically."
Mark raises a finger to make his point, to educate. "In Jerusalem we don't need to busy ourselves with symbolic efforts to keep our memories in place. Because we live exactly as our parents lived before the war. And

this serves us in all things, in our relationships too, in our marriages and parenting."

"Are you saying your marriage is better than ours?" Deb says. "Really? Just because of the rules you live by?"

"I'm saying your husband would not have the long face, worried his wife is keeping secrets. And your son, he would not get into the business of smoking without first coming to you. Because the relationships, they are defined. They are clear."

"Because they are welded together," I say, "and not glued."   180

"Yes," he says. "And I bet Shoshana agrees." But Shoshana is distracted. She is working carefully with an apple and a knife. She is making a little apple pipe, all the tampons gone.

"Did your daughters?" Deb says. "If they tell you everything, did they come to you first, before they smoked?"

"Our daughters do not have the taint of the world we grew up in. They have no interest in such things."

"So you think," I say.

"So I know," he says. "Our concerns are different, our worries."   185

"Let's hear 'em," Deb says.

"Let's not," Shoshana says. "Honestly, we're drunk, we're high, we are having a lovely reunion."

"Every time you tell him not to talk," I say, "it makes me want to hear what he's got to say even more."

"Our concern," Mark says, "is not the past Holocaust. It is the current one. The one that takes more than fifty percent of the Jews of this generation. Our concern is intermarriage. It's the Holocaust that's happening now. You don't need to be worrying about some Mormons doing hocus-pocus on the murdered six million. You need to worry that your son marries a Jew."

"Oh, my God," Deb says. "Are you calling intermarriage a Holocaust?"   190

"You ask my feeling, that's my feeling. But this, no, it does not exactly apply to you, except in the example you set for the boy. Because you're Jewish, your son, he is as Jewish as me. No more, no less."

"I went to yeshiva too, Born-Again Harry! You don't need to explain the rules to me."

"Did you just call me 'Born-Again Harry'?" Mark asks.

"I did," Deb says. And she and he, they start to laugh at that. They think "Born-Again Harry" is the funniest thing they've heard in a while. And Shoshana laughs, and then I laugh, because laughter is infectious — and it is doubly so when you're high.

"You don't really think our family, my lovely, beautiful son, is headed for a   195
Holocaust, do you?" Deb says. "Because that would really cast a pall on this beautiful day."

"No, I don't," Mark says. "It's a lovely house and a lovely family, a beautiful home that you've made for that strapping young man. You're a real *balabusta*," Mark says.

"That makes me happy," Deb says. And she tilts her head nearly ninety degrees to show her happy, sweet smile. "Can I hug you? I'd really like to give you a hug."

"No," Mark says, though he says it really politely. "But you can hug my wife. How about that?"

"That's a great idea," Deb says. Shoshana gets up and hands the loaded apple to me, and I smoke from the apple as the two women hug a tight, deep, dancing-back-and-forth hug, tilting this way and that, so, once again, I'm afraid they might fall.

"It is a beautiful day," I say.   200

"It is," Mark says. And both of us look out the window, and both of us watch the perfect clouds in a perfect sky, so that we're both starting out as the sky suddenly darkens. It is a change so abrupt that the ladies undo their hug to watch.

"It's like that here," Deb says. And the clouds open up and torrential tropical rain drops straight down, battering. It is loud against the roof, and loud against the windows, and the fronds of the palm trees bend, and the floaties in the pool jump as the water boils.

Shoshana goes to the window. And Mark passes Deb the apple and goes to the window. "Really, it's always like this here?" Shoshana says.

"Sure," I say. "Every day. Stops as quick as it starts."

And both of them have their hands pressed up against the window. And   205
they stay like that for some time, and when Mark turns around, harsh guy, tough guy, we see that he is weeping.

"You do not know," he says. "I forget what it's like to live in a place rich with water. This is a blessing above all others."

"If you had what we had," I say.

"Yes," he says, wiping his eyes.

"Can we go out?" Shoshana says. "In the rain?"

"Of course," Deb says. Then Shoshana tells me to close my eyes. Only me.   210
And I swear I think she's going to be stark naked when she calls, "Open up."

She's taken off her wig is all, and she's wearing one of Trev's baseball caps in its place.

"I've only got the one wig this trip," she says. "If Trev won't mind."

"He won't mind," Deb says. And this is how the four of us find ourselves in the back yard, on a searingly hot day, getting pounded by all this cool, cool rain. It's just about the best feeling in the world. And, I have to say, Shoshana looks twenty years younger in that hat.

We do not talk in the rain. We are too busy frolicking and laughing and jumping around. And that's how it happens that I'm holding Mark's hand and sort of dancing, and Deb is holding Shoshana's hand, and they're doing their own kind of jig. And when I take Deb's hand, though neither Mark nor Shoshana is touching the other, somehow we've formed a broken circle. We've started dancing our own kind of hora in the rain.

It is the silliest and freest and most glorious I can remember feeling in   215
years. Who would think that's what I'd be saying with these strict, suffocat-

ingly austere people visiting our house? And then my Deb, my love, once again she is thinking what I'm thinking, and she says, face up into the rain, all of us spinning, "Are you sure this is okay, Shoshana? That it's not mixed dancing? I don't want anyone feeling bad after."

"We'll be just fine," Shoshana says. "We will live with the consequences." The question slows us, and stops us, though no one has yet let go.

"It's like the old joke," I say. Without waiting for anyone to ask which one, I say, "Why don't Hasidim have sex standing up?"

"Why?" Shoshana says.

"Because it might lead to mixed dancing."

Deb and Shoshana pretend to be horrified as we let go of hands, as we   220
recognize that the moment is over, the rain disappearing as quickly as it came.
Mark stands there staring into the sky, lips pressed tight. "That joke is very, very old," he says. "And mixed dancing makes me think of mixed nuts, and mixed grill, and *insalata mista*.° The sound of 'mixed dancing' has made me wildly hungry. And I'm going to panic if the only kosher thing in the house is that loaf of bleached American bread."

"You have the munchies," I say.

"Diagnosis correct," he says.

Deb starts clapping at that, tiny claps, her hands held to her chest in prayer. She says to him, absolutely beaming, "You will not even believe what riches await."

The four of us stand in the pantry, soaking wet, hunting through the shelves and dripping on the floor. "Have you ever seen such a pantry?" Shoshana says, reaching her arms out. "It's gigantic." It is indeed large, and it is indeed stocked, an enormous amount of food, and an enormous selection of sweets, befitting a home that is often host to a swarm of teenage boys.

"Are you expecting a nuclear winter?" Shoshana says.   225

"I'll tell you what she's expecting," I say. "You want to know how Holocaust-obsessed she really is? I mean, to what degree?"

"To no degree," Deb says. "We are done with the Holocaust."

"Tell us," Shoshana says.

"She's always plotting our secret hiding place," I say.

"No kidding," Shoshana says.   230

"Like, look at this. At the pantry, with a bathroom next to it, and the door to the garage. If you sealed it all up—like put drywall at the entrance to the den—you'd never suspect. If you covered that door inside the garage up good with, I don't know—if you hung your tools in front of it and hid hinges behind, maybe leaned the bikes and the mower against it, you'd have this closed area, with running water and a toilet and all this food. I mean, if someone sneaked into the garage to replenish things, you could rent out the house. Put in another family without their having any idea."

Insalata mista: Mixed salad.

"Oh, my God," Shoshana says. "My short-term memory may be gone from having all those children—"

"And from the smoking," I say.

"And from that too. But I remember from when we were kids," Shoshana says, turning to Deb. "You were always getting me to play games like that. To pick out spaces. And even worse, even darker—"

"Don't," Deb says.   235

"I know what you're going to say," I tell her, and I'm honestly excited. "The game, yes? She played that crazy game with you?"

"No," Deb says. "Enough. Let it go."

And Mark—who is utterly absorbed in studying kosher certifications, who is tearing through hundred-calorie snack packs and eating handfuls of roasted peanuts, and who has said nothing since we entered the pantry except "What's a Fig Newman?"—he stops and says, "I want to play this game."

"It's not a game," Deb says.

And I'm happy to hear her say that, as it's just what I've been trying to get   240
her to admit for years. That it's not a game. That it's dead serious, and a kind of preparation, and an active pathology that I prefer not to indulge.

"It's the Anne Frank game," Shoshana says. "Right?"

Seeing how upset my wife is, I do my best to defend her. I say, "No, it's not a game. It's just what we talk about when we talk about Anne Frank."

"How do we play this non-game?" Mark says. "What do we do?"

"It's the Righteous Gentile game," Shoshana says.

"It's Who Will Hide Me?" I say.   245

"In the event of a second Holocaust," Deb says, giving in. "It's a serious exploration, a thought experiment that we engage in."

"That you play," Shoshana says.

"That, in the event of an American Holocaust, we sometimes talk about which of our Christian friends would hide us."

"I don't get it," Mark says.

"Of course you do," Shoshana says. "It's like this. If there was a Shoah, if   250
it happened again—say we were in Jerusalem, and it's 1941 and the Grand Mufti got his way, what would Jebediah do?"

"What could he do?" Mark says.

"He could hide us. He could risk his life and his family's and everyone's around him. That's what the game is: would he—for real—would he do that for you?"

"He'd be good for that, a Mormon," Mark says. "Forget this pantry. They have to keep a year of food stored in case of the Rapture, or something like that. Water too. A year of supplies. Or maybe it's that they have sex through a sheet. No, wait. I think that's supposed to be us."

"All right," Deb says. "Let's not play. Really, let's go back to the kitchen. I can order in from the glatt kosher place. We can eat outside, have a real dinner and not just junk."

"No, no," Mark says. "I'll play. I'll take it seriously."   255

"So would the guy hide you?" I say.

"The kids too?" Mark says. "I'm supposed to pretend that in Jerusalem he's got a hidden motel or something where he can put the twelve of us?"

"Yes," Shoshana says. "In their seminary or something. Sure."

Mark thinks about this for a long, long time. He eats Fig Newmans and considers, and you can tell that he's taking it seriously—serious to the extreme.

"Yes," Mark says, looking choked up. "Jeb would do that for us. He would   260
risk it all."

Shoshana nods. "Now you go," she says to us. "You take a turn."

"But we don't know any of the same people anymore," Deb says. "We usually just talk about the neighbors."

"Our across-the-street neighbors," I tell them. "They're the perfect example. Because the husband, Mitch, he would hide us. I know it. He'd lay down his life for what's right. But that wife of his."

"Yes," Deb says. "Mitch would hide us, but Gloria, she'd buckle. When he was at work one day, she'd turn us in."

"You could play against yourselves," Shoshana says. "What if one of you   265
wasn't Jewish? Would you hide the other?"

"I'll do it," I say. "I'll be the Gentile, because I could pass best. A grown woman with an ankle-length denim skirt in her closet—they'd catch you in a flash."

"Fine," Deb says. And I stand up straight, put my shoulders back, like maybe I'm in a lineup. I stand there with my chin raised so my wife can study me. So she can decide if her husband really has what it takes. Would I have the strength, would I care enough—and it is not a light question, not a throwaway question—to risk my life to save her and our son?

Deb stares, and Deb smiles, and gives me a little push to my chest. "Of course he would," Deb says. She takes the half stride that's between us and gives me a tight hug that she doesn't release. "Now you," Deb says. "You and Yuri go."

"How does that even make sense?" Mark says. "Even for imagining."

"Sh-h-h," Shoshana says. "Just stand over there and be a good Gentile   270
while I look."

"But if I weren't Jewish I wouldn't be me."

"That's for sure," I say.

"He agrees," Mark says. "We wouldn't even be married. We wouldn't have kids."

"Of course you can imagine it," Shoshana says. "Look," she says, and goes over and closes the pantry door. "Here we are, caught in South Florida for the second Holocaust. You're not Jewish, and you've got the three of us hiding in your pantry."

"But look at me!" he says.   275

"I've got a fix," I say. "You're a background singer for ZZ Top. You know that band?"

Deb lets go of me so she can give my arm a slap.

"Really," Shoshana says. "Look at the three of us like it's your house and we're your charges, locked up in this room."

"And what're you going to do while I do that?" Mark says.

"I'm going to look at you looking at us. I'm going to imagine."   280

"Okay," he says. "*Nu*, get to it. I will stand, you imagine."

And that's what we do, the four of us. We stand there playing our roles, and we really get into it. I can see Deb seeing him, and him seeing us, and Shoshana just staring at her husband.

We stand there so long I can't tell how much time has passed, though the light changes ever so slightly—the sun outside again dimming—in the crack under the pantry door.

"So would I hide you?" he says. And for the first time that day he reaches out, as my Deb would, and puts his hand to his wife's hand. "Would I, Shoshi?"

And you can tell that Shoshana is thinking of her kids, though that's not   285
part of the scenario. You can tell that she's changed part of the imagining. And she says, after a pause, yes, but she's not laughing. She says yes, but to him it sounds as it does to us, so that he is now asking and asking. But wouldn't I? Wouldn't I hide you? Even if it was life and death—if it would spare you, and they'd kill me alone for doing it? Wouldn't I?

Shoshana pulls back her hand.

She does not say it. And he does not say it. And of the four of us no one will say what cannot be said—that this wife believes her husband would not hide her. What to do? What will come of it? And so we stand like that, the four of us trapped in that pantry. Afraid to open the door and let out what we've locked inside.   *[2012]*

≡ THINKING ABOUT THE TEXT

1. Besides the dramatic concluding conversation, what other topics do the characters engage in? How do these discussions differentiate the narrator and Debbie from Yuri (Mark) and Shoshana (Lauren)?

2. What is your interpretation of Yuri's story of the two Holocaust survivors meeting in the locker room? Why is Debbie disappointed? Why isn't our narrator?

3. The difference between the couples seems obvious in the beginning, but there are surprises. What are they, and what significance do they have for understanding secular and religious Jews? What stereotypes are being called into question?

4. When playing the "Anne Frank game," Shoshana at first halfheartedly agrees that her husband, Yuri, would hide her. But something in her voice makes the others dubious. Describe what you think will happen when the four of them finally speak. Has Yuri discovered something im-

portant about their relationship? Will they all pass it off as a game? Will they simply never speak of it again?

5. Of course the characters never do explicitly talk about Anne Frank. What is it, then, that they do talk about? Is Anne Frank a metaphor? Locate foreshadowings of this ending.

≡ MAKING COMPARISONS

1. Compare the first and last paragraphs in both stories. What specific connections are there? Do they serve the same function in both stories?

2. Compare the narrators in both stories. Do they have similar attitudes? Compare Laura and Debbie. How would you describe their relationships to their husbands?

3. Compare the use of alcohol in both stories. Would both stories be different without alcohol?

≡ WRITING ABOUT ISSUES

1. Write an essay that asserts that the ending of Carver's story is either optimistic or pessimistic.

2. Research various types of love (e.g., unconditional, erotic, infatuation, affectionate, sentimental, passionate), and write an essay that uses these ideas to discuss the kinds of love found in Carver's story.

3. Write an essay that compares and contrasts the characters and themes of Carver's and Englander's stories. Be sure to include the endings of both.

4. Write an analysis of Englander's story, focusing on the title, the religious conflicts, the significance of the Holocaust, and the implications of Shoshana's belief that her "husband would not hide her" (para. 286).

▤ Jealous Love: Critical Commentaries on a Play

WILLIAM SHAKESPEARE, *Othello*

CRITICAL COMMENTARIES:

A. C. BRADLEY, "The Noble Othello"

MILLICENT BELL, "Othello's Jealousy"

JEFFRIE G. MURPHY, "Jealousy, Shame, and the Rival"

Of all the great tragedies of Shakespeare, *Othello* seems the closest to our own lives. Hamlet is a prince, and Lear and Macbeth are kings with the fate of their nations tied to their destiny. It is sometimes hard for contemporary readers to relate to their struggles or to regicide. But *Othello* is more domesticated, more about a relationship we can understand; few of us would claim that we have never been jealous. We know that relationships thrive on trust and openness, but even if we trust our partner, jealousy can find its way into our consciousness and might especially do so if we are prompted to doubt by a close friend.

Psychologists suggest that insecure people are prone to jealousy, perhaps because their low esteem suggests to them that they are not worthy of love. Is this the case with Othello? Although at first he seems filled with confidence and authority, he is considered a Moorish outsider in Venetian society and as such might be tempted to think that his wife, Desdemona, might find Cassio, one of her "own kind," attractive and desirable. The innocent and devoted Desdemona does not, but the seeds of distrust that are planted early on by Brabantio ("She deceived her father, and may thee") are diabolically nurtured by Iago, "an inhuman dog." The speed with which a great love is destroyed leaves the reader stunned by the potential darkness within us all.

The three essays that follow the play focus on jealousy, but they have different ideas about where that emotion comes from and how it alters our view of Othello's character and the play. A. C. Bradley develops the idea that Othello remains a noble soul and so we admire him to the end. This admiration increases our pity and the force of catharsis, which leaves us "for the moment free from pain, and exulting in the power of 'love and man's unconquerable mind.'" Millicent Bell sees jealousy as connected to philosophical ideas about truth and seeming and connects the play to ideas about skepticism in Elizabethan England and contemporary America. Jeffrie G. Murphy takes a more psychological view of jealousy as personal disintegration strongly linked to shame.

▤ BEFORE YOU READ

Do you think jealousy is a natural emotion? If you loved someone deeply, would you trust him or her? Are only insecure people jealous? Are there any positive elements to jealousy?

Barbara Zanon/Getty
Images

WILLIAM SHAKESPEARE
Othello

William Shakespeare's reputation as the greatest dramatist in the English language is built on his five major tragedies: Romeo and Juliet *(1594),* Hamlet *(1600),* Othello *(1604),* Macbeth *(1605), and* King Lear *(1605). But he was also a master in other genres, including comedies (*As You Like It *in 1599), histories (*Henry IV *in 1597), and romances (*The Tempest *in 1611). And his collection of sonnets is considered art of the highest order.*

Very little is known about Shakespeare's personal life. He attended the grammar school at Stratford-upon-Avon, where he was born in 1564. He married Anne Hathaway in 1582 and had three children. Around 1590 he moved to London, where he became an actor and began writing plays. He was an astute businessperson, becoming a shareholder in London's famous Globe Theatre. After writing thirty-seven plays, he retired to Stratford in 1611. When he died in 1616, he left behind the most respected body of work in literature. Shakespeare's ability to use artistic language to convey a wide range of humor and emotion is perhaps unsurpassed.

THE NAMES OF THE ACTORS

OTHELLO, *the Moor*
BRABANTIO, *father to Desdemona*
CASSIO, *an honorable lieutenant [to Othello]*
IAGO *[Othello's ancient,] a villain*
RODERIGO, *a gulled gentleman*
DUKE OF VENICE
SENATORS OF VENICE
MONTANO, *governor of Cyprus*
LODOVICO AND GRATIANO, *[kinsmen to Brabantio,] two noble Venetians*
SAILORS
CLOWNS
DESDEMONA, *wife to Othello*
EMILIA, *wife to Iago*
BIANCA, *a courtesan*
[Messenger, Herald, Officers, Venetian Gentlemen, Musicians, Attendants
scene: Venice and Cyprus]

[ACT I, Scene I: A street in Venice.]

Enter Roderigo and Iago.

RODERIGO: Tush, never tell me! I take it much unkindly
    That thou, Iago, who hast had my purse
    As if the strings were thine, shouldst know of this.°
IAGO: 'Sblood,° but you'll not hear me!
    If ever I did dream of such a matter,   5
    Abhor me.
RODERIGO: Thou told'st me thou didst hold him in thy hate.
IAGO: Despise me if I do not. Three great ones of the city,
    In personal suit to make me his lieutenant,
    Off-capped to him;° and, by the faith of man,   10
    I know my price; I am worth no worse a place.
    But he, as loving his own pride and purposes,
    Evades them with a bombast circumstance.°
    Horribly stuffed with epithets of war;
    [And, in conclusion,]   15
    Nonsuits° my mediators; for, "Certes," says he,
    "I have already chose my officer."
    And what was he?
    Forsooth, a great arithmetician,°

ACT I, SCENE I.   **3 this:** I.e., Desdemona's elopement.   **4 'Sblood:** By God's blood.   **10**
him: I.e., Othello.   **13 a bombast circumstance:** Pompous circumlocutions.   **16**
Nonsuits: Rejects.   **19 arithmetician:** Theoretician.

One Michael Cassio, a Florentine   20
(A fellow almost damned in a fair wife°)
That never set a squadron in the field,
Nor the division of a battle knows
More than a spinster; unless the bookish theoric,
Wherein the togèd consuls can propose   25
As masterly as he. Mere prattle without practice
Is all his soldiership. But he, sir, had th' election;
And I (of whom his eyes had seen the proof
At Rhodes, at Cyprus, and on other grounds
Christian and heathen) must be belee'd and calmed°   30
By debitor and creditor; this counter-caster,°
He, in good time, must his lieutenant be,
And I — God bless the mark! — his Moorship's ancient.°
RODERIGO: By heaven, I rather would have been his hangman.
IAGO: Why, there's no remedy; 'tis the curse of service.   35
Preferment goes by letter and affection,°
And not by old gradation, where each second
Stood heir to th' first. Now, sir, be judge yourself,
Whether I in any just term am affined°
To love the Moor.
RODERIGO: I would not follow him then.   40
IAGO: O, sir, content you;
I follow him to serve my turn upon him.
We cannot all be masters, nor all masters
Cannot be truly followed. You shall mark
Many a duteous and knee-crooking knave   45
That, doting on his own obsequious bondage,
Wears out his time, much like his master's ass,
For naught but provender; and when he's old, cashiered.°
Whip me such honest knaves! Others there are
Who, trimmed° in forms and visages of duty,   50
Keep yet their hearts attending on themselves;
And, throwing but shows of service on their lords,
Do well thrive by them, and when they have lined their coats,
Do themselves homage. These fellows have some soul;
And such a one do I profess myself. For, sir,   55
It is as sure as you are Roderigo,
Were I the Moor, I would not be Iago.
In following him, I follow but myself;
Heaven is my judge, not I for love and duty,

---

21 almost . . . wife: (An obscure allusion; Cassio is unmarried, but see IV.i.12).   **30 belee'd and calmed:** Left in the lurch.   **31 counter-caster:** Bookkeeper.   **33 ancient:**
Ensign.   **36 affection:** Favoritism.   **39 affined:** Obliged.   **48 cashiered:** Turned off.
50 trimmed: Dressed up.

But seeming so, for my peculiar end;   60
For when my outward action doth demonstrate
The native act and figure of my heart°
In compliment extern,° 'tis not long after
But I will wear my heart upon my sleeve
For daws to peck at; I am not what I am.   65

RODERIGO: What a full fortune does the thick-lips° owe°
If he can carry't thus!

IAGO: Call up her father,
Rouse him. Make after him, poison his delight,
Proclaim him in the streets. Incense her kinsmen,
And though he in a fertile climate dwell,   70
Plague him with flies; though that his joy be joy,
Yet throw such changes of vexation on't
As it may lose some color.

RODERIGO: Here is her father's house. I'll call aloud.

IAGO: Do, with like timorous° accent and dire yell   75
As when, by night and negligence, the fire
Is spied in populous cities.

RODERIGO: What, ho, Brabantio! Signior Brabantio, ho!

IAGO: Awake! What, ho, Brabantio! Thieves! thieves! thieves!
Look to your house, your daughter, and your bags!   80
Thieves! thieves!

Brabantio at a window.°

BRABANTIO *(above)*:   What is the reason of this terrible summons?
What is the matter there?

RODERIGO: Signior, is all your family within?

IAGO: Are your doors locked?

BRABANTIO: Why, wherefore ask you this?   85

IAGO: Zounds, sir, y' are robbed! For shame, put on your gown!
Your heart is burst; you have lost half your soul.
Even now, now, very now, an old black ram
Is tupping your white ewe. Arise, arise!
Awake the snorting° citizens with the bell.   90
Or else the devil will make a grandsire of you.
Arise, I say!

BRABANTIO: What, have you lost your wits?

RODERIGO: Most reverend signior, do you know my voice?

BRABANTIO: Not I. What are you?   95

RODERIGO: My name is Roderigo.

BRABANTIO: The worser welcome!

---

62 The . . . heart: What I really believe and intend.   **63 compliment extern:** Outward appearance.   **66 thick-lips:** An Elizabethan epithet for blacks, including Moors; **owe:** Own.   **75 timorous:** Terrifying.   ***Brabantio at a window:*** (added from quarto).
90 snorting: Snoring.

I have charged thee not to haunt about my doors.
In honest plainness thou hast heard me say
My daughter is not for thee; and now, in madness,
Being full of supper and distemp'ring draughts,   100
Upon malicious knavery dost thou come
To start my quiet.

RODERIGO: Sir, sir, sir —

BRABANTIO: But thou must needs be sure
My spirit and my place have in them power   105
To make this bitter to thee.

RODERIGO: Patience, good sir.

BRABANTIO: What tell'st thou me of robbing? This is Venice;
My house is not a grange.°

RODERIGO: Most grave Brabantio,
In simple and pure soul I come to you.

IAGO: Zounds, sir, you are one of those that will not serve God if the devil bid   110
you. Because we come to do you service, and you think we are ruffians,
you'll have your daughter covered with a Barbary horse; you'll have your
nephews° neigh to you; you'll have coursers for cousins, and gennets for
germans.°

BRABANTIO: What profane wretch art thou?   115

IAGO: I am one, sir, that comes to tell you your daughter and the Moor are now
making the beast with two backs.

BRABANTIO: Thou are a villain.

IAGO: You are — a senator.

BRABANTIO: This thou shalt answer. I know thee, Roderigo.

RODERIGO: Sir, I will answer anything. But I beseech you,   120
If 't be your pleasure and most wise consent,
As partly I find it is, that your fair daughter,
At this odd-even° and dull watch o' th' night,
Transported, with no worse nor better guard
But with a knave of common hire, a gondolier,   125
To the gross clasps of a lascivious Moor —
If this be known to you, and your allowance,°
We then have done you bold and saucy wrongs;
But if you know not this, my manners tell me
We have your wrong rebuke. Do not believe   130
That, from the sense° of all civility,
I thus would play and trifle with your reverence.
Your daughter, if you have not given her leave,
I say again, hath made a gross revolt,
Tying her duty, beauty, wit, and fortunes   135

---

108 grange: Isolated farmhouse.   **113 nephews:** I.e., grandsons.   **113–14 gennets
for germans:** Spanish horses for near kinsmen.   **123 odd-even:** Between night and
morning.   **127 allowance:** Approval.   **131 from the sense:** In violation.

In an extravagant and wheeling° stranger
Of here and everywhere. Straight satisfy yourself.
If she be in her chamber, or your house,
Let loose on me the justice of the state
For thus deluding you.

BRABANTIO: Strike on the tinder, ho!   140
Give me a taper! Call up all my people!
This accident° is not unlike my dream.
Belief of it oppresses me already.

Light, I say! light!   *Exit [above].*

IAGO: Farewell, for I must leave you.
It seems not meet, nor wholesome to my place,   145
To be produced — as, if I stay, I shall —
Against the Moor. For I do know the state,
However this may gall him with some check,°
Cannot with safety cast° him; for he's embarked
With such loud reason to the Cyprus wars,   150
Which even now stand in act,° that for their souls
Another of his fathom° they have none
To lead their business; in which regard,
Though I do hate him as I do hell-pains,
Yet, for necessity of present life,   155
I must show out a flag and sign of love,
Which is indeed but sign. That you shall surely find him,
Lead to the Sagittary° the raisèd search;
And there will I be with him. So farewell.   *Exit.*

Enter [below] Brabantio in his nightgown,° and Servants with torches.

BRABANTIO: It is too true an evil. Gone she is;   160
And what's to come of my despisèd time
Is naught but bitterness. Now, Roderigo,
Where didst thou see her? — O unhappy girl! —
With the Moor, say'st thou? — Who would be a father? —
How didst thou know 'twas she! — O, she deceives me   165
Past thought! — What said she to you? — Get moe° tapers!
Raise all my kindred! — Are they married, think you?

RODERIGO: Truly I think they are.

BRABANTIO: O heaven! How got she out? O treason of the blood!
Fathers, from hence trust not your daughters' minds   170
By what you see them act. Is there not charms
By which the property° of youth and maidhood

---

136 extravagant and wheeling: Expatriate and roving.   **142 accident:** Occurrence.
148 check: Reprimand.   **149 cast:** Discharge.   **151 stand in act:** Are going on.
152 fathom: Capacity.   **158 Sagittary:** An inn.   **nightgown:** Dressing gown.   **166
moe:** More.   **172 property:** Nature.

May be abused? Have you not read, Roderigo,
Of some such thing?
RODERIGO: Yes, sir, I have indeed.
BRABANTIO: Call up my brother. — O, would you had had her! —   175
Some one way, some another. — Do you know
Where we may apprehend her and the Moor?
RODERIGO: I think I can discover him, if you please
To get good guard and go along with me.
BRABANTIO: I pray you lead on. At every house I'll call;   180
I may command at most. — Get weapons, ho!
And raise some special officers of night. —
On, good Roderigo; I'll deserve° your pains.   *Exeunt.*

[Scene II: Before the lodgings of Othello.]

Enter Othello, Iago, and Attendants with torches.

IAGO: Though in the trade of war I have slain men,
Yet do I hold it very stuff o' th' conscience
To do no contrived murther. I lack iniquity
Sometimes to do me service. Nine or ten times
I had thought t' have yerked° him here under the ribs.   5
OTHELLO: 'Tis better as it is.
IAGO: Nay, but he prated,
And spoke such scurvy and provoking terms
Against your honor
That with the little godliness I have
I did full hard forbear him. But I pray you, sir,   10
Are you fast° married? Be assured of this,
That the magnifico° is much beloved,
And hath in his effect a voice potential°
As double° as the Duke's. He will divorce you,
Or put upon you what restraint and grievance   15
The law, with all his might to enforce it on,
Will give him cable.
OTHELLO: Let him do his spite.
My services which I have done the signiory°
Shall out-tongue his complaints. 'Tis yet to know° —
Which, when I know that boasting is an honor,   20
I shall promulgate — I fetch my life and being
From men of royal siege;° and my demerits°

183 deserve: Show gratitude for. **SCENE II. 5 yerked:** Stabbed. **11 fast:** Securely.
12 magnifico: Grandee (Brabantio). **13 potential:** Powerful. **14 double:** Doubly influential. **18 signiory:** Venetian government. **19 yet to know:** Still not generally
known. **22 siege:** Rank. **demerits:** Deserts.

May speak unbonneted to as proud a fortune
As this that I have reached.° For know, Iago,
But that I love the gentle Desdemona,   25
I would not my unhousèd° free condition
Put into circumscription and confine
For the sea's worth. But look what lights come yond?

IAGO: Those are the raisèd father and his friends.
You were best go in.

OTHELLO: Not I; I must be found.   30
My parts, my title, and my perfect soul°
Shall manifest me rightly. Is it they?

IAGO: By Janus, I think no.

Enter Cassio, with torches, Officers.

OTHELLO: The servants of the Duke, and my lieutenant.
The goodness of the night upon you, friends!   35
What is the news?

CASSIO: The Duke does greet you, general;
And he requires your haste-post-haste appearance
Even on the instant.

OTHELLO: What's the matter, think you?

CASSIO: Something from Cyprus, as I may divine.
It is a business of some heat. The galleys   40
Have sent a dozen sequent° messengers
This very night at one another's heels,
And many of the consuls, raised and met,
Are at the Duke's already. You have been hotly called for;
When, being not at your lodging to be found,   45
The Senate hath sent about three several quests
To search you out.

OTHELLO: 'Tis well I am found by you.
I will but spend a word here in the house,
And go with you.   *[Exit.]*

CASSIO: Ancient, what makes he here?

IAGO: Faith, he to-night hath boarded a land carack.°   50
If it prove lawful prize, he's made for ever.

CASSIO: I do not understand.

IAGO: He's married.

CASSIO: To who?

[Enter Othello.]

IAGO: Marry, to — Come, captain, will you go?

OTHELLO: Have with you.

23–24 May speak . . . reached: Are equal, I modestly assert, to those of Desdemona's family. **26 unhousèd:** Unrestrained. **31 perfect soul:** Stainless conscience. **41 sequent:** Consecutive. **50 carack:** Treasure ship.

CASSIO: Here comes another troop to seek for you.

Enter Brabantio, Roderigo, and others with lights and weapons.

IAGO: It is Brabantio. General, be advised.   55
    He comes to bad intent.

OTHELLO: Holla! stand there!

RODERIGO: Signior, it is the Moor.

BRABANTIO: Down with him, thief!

[They draw on both sides.]

IAGO: You, Roderigo! Come, sir, I am for you.

OTHELLO: Keep up° your bright swords, for the dew will rust them.
    Good signior, you shall more command with years   60
    Than with your weapons.

BRABANTIO: O thou foul thief, where hast thou stowed my daughter?
    Damned as thou art, thou hast enchanted her!
    For I'll refer me to all things of sense,
    If she in chains of magic were not bound,   65
    Whether a maid so tender, fair, and happy,
    So opposite to marriage that she shunned
    The wealthy curlèd darlings of our nation,
    Would ever have, t' incur a general mock,
    Run from her guardage to the sooty bosom   70
    Of such a thing as thou — to fear, not to delight.
    Judge me the world if 'tis not gross in sense°
    That thou hast practiced on her with foul charms,
    Abused her delicate youth with drugs or minerals
    That weaken motion.° I'll have't disputed on;   75
    'Tis probable, and palpable to thinking.
    I therefore apprehend and do attach° thee
    For an abuser of the world, a practicer
    Of arts inhibited and out of warrant.
    Lay hold upon him. If he do resist,   80
    Subdue him at his peril.

OTHELLO: Hold your hands,
    Both you of my inclining and the rest.
    Were it my cue to fight, I should have known it
    Without a prompter. Where will you that I go
    To answer this your charge?

BRABANTIO: To prison, till fit time   85
    Of law and course of direct session°
    Call thee to answer.

OTHELLO: What if I do obey?
    How may the Duke be therewith satisfied,

59 Keep up: I.e., sheath.   **72 gross in sense:** Obvious.   **75 motion:** Perception.
77 attach: Arrest.   **86 direct session:** Regular trial.

Whose messengers are here about my side
Upon some present business of the state   90
To bring me to him?
OFFICER: 'Tis true, most worthy signior.
The Duke's in council, and your noble self
I am sure is sent for.
BRABANTIO: How? The Duke in council?
In this time of the night? Bring him away.
Mine's not an idle° cause. The Duke himself,   95
Or any of my brothers of the state,
Cannot but feel this wrong as 'twere their own;
For if such actions may have passage free,
Bondslaves and pagans shall our statesmen be.   *Exeunt.*

[Scene III: The Venetian Senate Chamber.]

Enter Duke and Senators, set at a table, with lights and Attendants.

DUKE: There is no composition° in these news
That gives them credit.
1. SENATOR: Indeed they are disproportioned.
My letters say a hundred and seven galleys.
DUKE: And mine a hundred forty.
2. SENATOR: And mine two hundred.
But though they jump° not on a just account —   5
As in these cases where the aim° reports
'Tis oft with difference — yet do they all confirm
A Turkish fleet, and bearing up to Cyprus.
DUKE: Nay, it is possible enough to judgment.
I do not so secure me° in the error   10
But the main article° I do approve°
In fearful sense.
SAILOR *(within):*   What, ho! what, ho! what, ho!
OFFICER: A messenger from the galleys.

Enter Sailor.

DUKE: Now, what's the business?
SAILOR: The Turkish preparation makes for Rhodes.
So was I bid report here to the state   15
By Signior Angelo.
DUKE: How say you by this change?
1. SENATOR: This cannot be
By no assay° of reason. 'Tis a pageant
To keep us in false gaze.° When we consider

95 idle: Trifling.   **SCENE III.   1 composition:** Consistency.   **5 jump:** Agree.
6 aim: Conjecture.   **10 so secure me:** Take such comfort.   **11 article:** Substance;
approve: Accept.   **18 assay:** Test.   **19 in false gaze:** Looking the wrong way.

Th' importancy of Cyprus to the Turk,   20
And let ourselves again but understand
That, as it more concerns the Turk than Rhodes,
So may he with more facile question bear° it,
For that it stands not in such warlike brace,°
But altogether lacks th' abilities   25
That Rhodes is dressed in — if we make thought of this,
We must not think the Turk is so unskillful
To leave that latest which concerns him first,
Neglecting an attempt of ease and gain
To wake and wage° a danger profitless.   30
DUKE: Nay, in all confidence, he's not for Rhodes.
OFFICER: Here is more news.

Enter a Messenger.

MESSENGER: The Ottomites, reverend and gracious,
Steering with due course toward the isle of Rhodes,
Have there injointed them with an after fleet.   35
1. SENATOR: Ay, so I thought. How many, as you guess?
MESSENGER: Of thirty sail; and now they do restem°
Their backward course, bearing with frank appearance
Their purposes toward Cyprus, Signior Montano,
Your trusty and most valiant servitor,   40
With his free duty recommends you thus,
And prays you to believe him.
DUKE: 'Tis certain then for Cyprus.
Marcus Luccicos,° is not he in town?
1. SENATOR: He's now in Florence.   45
DUKE: Write from us to him; post, post-haste dispatch.
1. SENATOR: Here comes Brabantio and the valiant Moor.

Enter Brabantio, Othello, Cassio, Iago, Roderigo, and Officers.

DUKE: Valiant Othello, we must straight employ you
Against the general enemy Ottoman.   *[To Brabantio.]*
I did not see you. Welcome, gentle signior.   50
We lacked your counsel and your help to-night.
BRABANTIO: So did I yours. Good your grace, pardon me.
Neither my place, nor aught I heard of business,
Hath raised me from my bed; nor doth the general care
Take hold on me; for my particular grief   55
Is of so floodgate° and o'erbearing nature
That it engluts° and swallows other sorrows,
And it is still itself.

---

23 with . . . bear: More easily capture.   **24 brace:** Posture of defense.   **30 wake and wage:** Rouse and risk.   **37 restem:** Steer again.   **44 Marcus Luccicos:** (Presumably a Venetian envoy).   **56 floodgate:** Torrential.   **57 engluts:** Devours.

DUKE: Why, what's the matter?
BRABANTIO: My daughter! O, my daughter!
ALL: Dead?
BRABANTIO: Ay, to me.
　　She is abused, stol'n from me, and corrupted   60
　　By spells and medicines bought of mountebanks;
　　For nature so prepost'rously to err,
　　Being not deficient,° blind, or lame of sense,
　　Sans witchcraft could not.
DUKE: Whoe'er he be that in this foul proceeding   65
　　Hath thus beguiled your daughter of herself,
　　And you of her, the bloody book of law
　　You shall yourself read in the bitter letter
　　After your own sense; yea, though our proper° son
　　Stood in your action.°
BRABANTIO: Humbly I thank your grace.   70
　　Here is the man — this Moor, whom now, it seems,
　　Your special mandate for the state affairs
　　Hath hither brought.
ALL: We are very sorry for't.
DUKE [to Othello]:   What, in your own part, can you say to this?
BRABANTIO: Nothing, but this is so.   75
OTHELLO: Most potent, grave, and reverend signiors,
　　My very noble, and approved° good masters,
　　That I have ta'en away this old man's daughter,
　　It is most true; true I have married her.
　　The very head and front of my offending   80
　　Hath this extent, no more. Rude° am I in my speech,
　　And little blessed with the soft phrase of peace;
　　For since these arms of mine had seven years' pith°
　　Till now some nine moons wasted, they have used
　　Their dearest action in the tented field;   85
　　And little of this great world can I speak
　　More than pertains to feats of broil and battle;
　　And therefore little shall I grace my cause
　　In speaking for myself. Yet, by your gracious patience,
　　I will a round° unvarnished tale deliver   90
　　Of my whole course of love — what drugs, what charms,
　　What conjuration, and what mighty magic
　　(For such proceeding am I charged withal)
　　I won his daughter.

---

63 deficient: Feeble-minded.   **69 our proper:** My own.   **70 Stood in your action:**
Were accused by you.   **77 approved:** Tested by experience.   **81 Rude:** Unpolished.
83 pith: Strength.   **90 round:** Plain.

BRABANTIO: A maiden never bold;
    Of spirit so still and quiet that her motion   95
    Blushed° at herself; and she — in spite of nature,
    Of years, of country, credit, everything —
    To fall in love with what she feared to look on!
    It is a judgment maimed and most imperfect
    That will confess perfection so could err   100
    Against all rules of nature, and must be driven
    To find out practices° of cunning hell
    Why this should be. I therefore vouch° again
    That with some mixtures pow'rful o'er the blood,°
    Or with some dram, conjured to this effect,   105
    He wrought upon her.
DUKE: To vouch this is no proof,
    Without more certain and more overt test
    Than these thin habits° and poor likelihoods
    Of modern seeming° do prefer against him.
1. SENATOR: But, Othello, speak.   110
    Did you by indirect and forcèd° courses
    Subdue and poison this young maid's affections?
    Or came it by request, and such fair question°
    As soul to soul affordeth?
OTHELLO: I do beseech you,
    Send for the lady to the Sagittary   115
    And let her speak of me before her father.
    If you do find me foul in her report,
    The trust, the office, I do hold of you
    Not only take away, but let your sentence
    Even fall upon my life.
DUKE: Fetch Desdemona hither.   120
OTHELLO: Ancient, conduct them; you best know the place.

                                 Exit [Iago, with] two or three [Attendants].

    And till she come, as truly as to heaven
    I do confess the vices of my blood,
    So justly to your grave ears I'll present
    How I did thrive in this fair lady's love,   125
    And she in mine.
DUKE: Say it, Othello.
OTHELLO: Her father loved me, oft invited me;
    Still° questioned me the story of my life
    From year to year — the battles, sieges, fortunes   130

95–96 her motion Blushed: Her own emotions caused her to blush.   **102 practices:**
Plots.   **103 vouch:** Assert.   **104 blood:** Passions.   **108 thin habits:** Slight appearances.   **109 modern seeming:** Everyday supposition.   **111 forcèd:** Violent.   **113 question:** Conversation.   **129 Still:** Continually.

That I have passed.
I ran it through, even from my boyish days
To th' very moment that he bade me tell it.
Wherein I spoke of most disastrous chances,
Of moving accidents by flood and field;   135
Of hairbreadth scapes i' th' imminent deadly breach;
Of being taken by the insolent foe
And sold to slavery; of my redemption thence
And portance° in my travels' history;
Wherein of anters° vast and deserts idle,   140
Rough quarries, rocks, and hills whose heads touch heaven,
It was my hint° to speak — such was the process;
And of the Cannibals that each other eat,
The Anthropophagi,° and men whose heads
Do grow beneath their shoulders. This to hear   145
Would Desdemona seriously incline;
But still the house affairs would draw her thence;
Which ever as she could with haste dispatch,
She'ld come again, and with a greedy ear
Devour up my discourse. Which I observing,   150
Took once a pliant° hour, and found good means
To draw from her a prayer of earnest heart
That I would all my pilgrimage dilate,°
Whereof by parcels° she had something heard,
But not intentively.° I did consent,   155
And often did beguile her of her tears
When I did speak of some distressful stroke
That my youth suffered. My story being done,
She gave me for my pains a world of sighs.
She swore, i' faith, 'twas strange, 'twas passing strange;   160
'Twas pitiful, 'twas wondrous pitiful.
She wished she had not heard it; yet she wished
That heaven had made her such a man. She thanked me;
And bade me, if I had a friend that loved her,
I should but teach him how to tell my story,   165
And that would woo her. Upon this hint° I spake.
She loved me for the dangers I had passed,
And I loved her that she did pity them.
This only is the witchcraft I have used.
Here comes the lady. Let her witness it.   170

Enter Desdemona, Iago, Attendants.

139 portance: Behavior.   **140 anters:** Caves.   **142 hint:** Occasion.   **144 Anthropophagi:** Man-eaters.   **151 pliant:** Propitious.   **153 dilate:** Recount in full. **154 parcels:** Portions.   **155 intentively:** With full attention.   **166 hint:** Opportunity.

DUKE: I think this tale would win my daughter too.
　　　　Good Brabantio,
　　　　Take up this mangled matter at the best.
　　　　Men do their broken weapons rather use
　　　　Than their bare hands.
BRABANTIO: I pray you hear her speak.   175
　　　　If she confess that she was half the wooer,
　　　　Destruction on my head if my bad blame
　　　　Light on the man! Come hither, gentle mistress.
　　　　Do you perceive in all this noble company
　　　　Where most you owe obedience?
DESDEMONA: My noble father,   180
　　　　I do perceive here a divided duty.
　　　　To you I am bound for life and education;°
　　　　My life and education both do learn me
　　　　How to respect you: you are the lord of duty;
　　　　I am hitherto your daughter. But here's my husband;   185
　　　　And so much duty as my mother showed
　　　　To you, preferring you before her father,
　　　　So much I challenge° that I may profess
　　　　Due to the Moor my lord.
BRABANTIO: God be with you! I have done.
　　　　Please it your grace, on to the state affairs.   190
　　　　I had rather to adopt a child than get° it.
　　　　Come hither, Moor.
　　　　I here do give thee that with all my heart
　　　　Which, but thou hast already, with all my heart
　　　　I would keep from thee. For your sake,° jewel,   195
　　　　I am glad at soul I have no other child;
　　　　For thy escape° would teach me tyranny,
　　　　To hang clogs on them. I have done, my lord.
DUKE: Let me speak like yourself° and lay a sentence°
　　　　Which, as a grise° or step, may help these lovers   200
　　　　[Into your favor.]
　　　　When remedies are past, the griefs are ended
　　　　By seeing the worst, which late on hopes depended.
　　　　To mourn a mischief that is past and gone
　　　　Is the next way to draw new mischief on.   205
　　　　What cannot be preserved when fortune takes,
　　　　Patience her injury a mock'ry makes.
　　　　The robbed that smiles steals something from the thief;
　　　　He robs himself that spends a bootless grief.

---

182 education: Upbringing. **188 challenge:** Claim the right. **191 get:** Beget. **195 For your sake:** Because of you. **197 escape:** Escapade. **199 like yourself:** As you should; **sentence:** Maxim. **200 grise:** Step.

BRABANTIO: So let the Turk of Cyprus us beguile: 210
 We lose it not so long as we can smile.
 He bears the sentence well that nothing bears
 But the free comfort which from thence he hears;
 But he bears both the sentence and the sorrow
 That to pay grief must of poor patience borrow.   215
 These sentences, to sugar, or to gall,
 Being strong on both sides, are equivocal.
 But words are words. I never yet did hear
 That the bruisèd heart was piercèd through the ear.
 Beseech you, now to the affairs of state.   220

DUKE: The Turk with a most mighty preparation makes for Cyprus. Othello, the fortitude° of the place is best known to you; and though we have there a substitute of most allowed° sufficiency, yet opinion,° a more sovereign mistress of effects, throws a more safer voice on you. You must therefore be content to slubber° the gloss of your new fortunes with this more stubborn   225 and boist'rous expedition.

OTHELLO: The tyrant custom, most grave senators,
 Hath made the flinty and steel couch of war
 My thrice-driven bed of down. I do agnize
 A natural and prompt alacrity   230
 I find in hardness;° and do undertake
 These present wars against the Ottomites.
 Most humbly, therefore, bending to your state,
 I crave fit disposition for my wife,
 Due reference of place, and exhibition,°   235
 With such accommodation and besort°
 As levels° with her breeding.

DUKE: If you please,
 Be't at her father's.

BRABANTIO: I will not have it so.

OTHELLO: Nor I.

DESDEMONA: Nor I. I would not there reside,   240
 To put my father in impatient thoughts
 By being in his eye. Most gracious Duke,
 To my unfolding lend your prosperous° ear,
 And let me find a charter in your voice,
 T' assist my simpleness.°   245

DUKE: What would you, Desdemona?

DESDEMONA: That I did love the Moor to live with him,

---

222 fortitude: Fortification.   **223 allowed:** Acknowledged;   **opinion:** Public opinion.   **225 slubber:** Sully.   **229–31 agnize . . . hardness:** Recognize in myself a natural and easy response to hardship.   **235 exhibition:** Allowance of money.   **236 besort:** Suitable company.   **237 levels:** Corresponds.   **243 prosperous:** Favorable.   **245 simpleness:** Lack of skill.

My downright violence, and storm of fortunes,
May trumpet to the world. My heart's subdued
Even to the very quality of my lord.   250
I saw Othello's visage in his mind,
And to his honors and his valiant parts
Did I my soul and fortunes consecrate.
So that, dear lords, if I be left behind,
A moth of peace, and he go to the war,   255
The rites for which I love him are bereft me,
And I a heavy interim shall support
By his dear absence. Let me go with him.

OTHELLO: Let her have your voice.
Vouch with me, heaven, I therefore beg it not   260
To please the palate of my appetite,
Not to comply with heat° — the young affects°
In me defunct — and proper satisfaction;
But to be free and bounteous to her mind;
And heaven defend your good souls that you think   265
I will your serious and great business scant
When she is with me. No, when light-winged toys
Of feathered Cupid seel° with wanton dullness
My speculative and officed instruments,°
That° my disports corrupt and taint my business,   270
Let housewives make a skillet of my helm,
And all indign° and base adversities
Make head against my estimation!°

DUKE: Be it as you shall privately determine,
Either for her stay or going. Th' affair cries haste,   275
And speed must answer it.

1. SENATOR: You must away to-night.

OTHELLO: With all my heart.

DUKE: At nine i' th' morning here we'll meet again.
Othello, leave some officer behind,
And he shall our commission bring to you,   280
With such things else of quality and respect
As doth import° you.

OTHELLO: So please your grace, my ancient;
A man he is of honesty and trust
To his conveyance I assign my wife,
With what else needful your good grace shall think   285
To be sent after me.

DUKE: Let it be so.

---

262 heat: Passions; **young affects:** Tendencies of youth. **268 seel:** Blind. **269 My . . . instruments:** My perceptive and responsible faculties. **270 That:** So that. **272 indign:** Unworthy. **273 estimation:** Reputation. **282 import:** Concern.

Good night to every one.
[To Brabantio.]   And, noble signior,
If virtue no delighted° beauty lack,
Your son-in-law is far more fair than black.

1. SENATOR: Adieu, brave Moor. Use Desdemona well.   290

BRABANTIO: Look to her, Moor, if thou hast eyes to see:
She has deceived her father, and may thee.

Exeunt [Duke, Senators, Officers, &c.].

OTHELLO: My life upon her faith! — Honest Iago,
My Desdemona must I leave to thee.
I prithee let thy wife attend on her,   295
And bring them after in the best advantage.°
Come, Desdemona. I have but an hour
Of love, of worldly matters and direction,
To spend with thee. We must obey the time.

Exit Moor and Desdemona.

RODERIGO: Iago, —   300

IAGO: What say'st thou, noble heart?

RODERIGO: What will I do, think'st thou?

IAGO: Why, go to bed and sleep.

RODERIGO: I will incontinently° drown myself.

IAGO: If thou dost, I shall never love thee after. Why, thou silly gentleman!   305

RODERIGO: It is silliness to live when to live is torment; and then have we a prescription to die when death is our physician.

IAGO: O villainous! I have looked upon the world for four times seven years;
and since I could distinguish betwixt a benefit and an injury, I never found
man that knew how to love himself. Ere I would say I would drown myself   310
for the love of a guinea hen, I would change my humanity with a baboon.

RODERIGO: What should I do? I confess it is my shame to be so fond, but it is not
in my virtue to amend it.

IAGO: Virtue? a fig! 'Tis in ourselves that we are thus or thus. Our bodies are
our gardens, to which our wills are gardeners; so that if we will plant   315
nettles or sow lettuce, set hyssop and weed up thyme, supply it with one
gender° of herbs or distract it with many — either to have it sterile with
idleness or manured with industry — why, the power and corrigible
authority° of this lies in our wills. If the balance of our lives had not one
scale of reason to poise° another of sensuality, the blood and baseness° of   320
our natures would conduct us to most preposterous conclusions. But we
have reason to cool our raging motions,° our carnal strings, our unbitted°
lusts; whereof I take this that you call love to be a sect or scion.°

288 delighted: Delightful.   **296 in the best advantage:** At the best opportunity.
304 incontinently: Forthwith.   **317 gender:** Species.   **318–19 corrigible
authority:** Corrective power.   **320 poise:** Counterbalance;   **blood and baseness:**
Animal instincts.   **322 motions:** Appetites;   **unbitted:** Uncontrolled.   **323 sect or
scion:** Offshoot, cutting.

RODERIGO: It cannot be.

IAGO: It is merely a lust of the blood and a permission of the will. Come, be a   325
man! Drown thyself? Drown cats and blind puppies! I have professed me
thy friend, and I confess me knit to thy deserving with cables of perdurable
toughness. I could never better stead thee than now. Put money in thy
purse. Follow thou the wars; defeat thy favor° with an usurped beard. I say,
put money in thy purse. It cannot be that Desdemona should long con-   330
tinue her love to the Moor — put money in thy purse — nor he his to her.
It was a violent commencement in her, and thou shalt see an answerable
sequestration° — put but money in thy purse. These Moors are changeable in their wills — fill thy purse with money. The food that to him now is
as luscious as locusts shall be to him shortly as bitter as coloquintida.° She   335
must change for youth: when she is sated with his body, she will find the
error of her choice. [She must have change, she must.] Therefore put
money in thy purse. If thou wilt needs damn thyself, do it a more delicate
way than drowning. Make° all the money thou canst. If sanctimony and a
frail vow betwixt an erring° barbarian and a supersubtle Venetian be not   340
too hard for my wits and all the tribe of hell, thou shalt enjoy her. Therefore make money. A pox of drowning thyself! 'Tis clean out of the way.
Seek thou rather to be hanged in compassing thy joy than to be drowned
and go without her.

RODERIGO: Wilt thou be fast to my hopes, if I depend on the issue?   345

IAGO: Thou art sure of me. Go, make money. I have told thee often, and I retell
thee again and again, I hate the Moor. My cause is hearted;° thine hath no
less reason. Let us be conjunctive in our revenge against him. If thou canst
cuckold him, thou dost thyself a pleasure, me a sport. There are many
events in the womb of time, which will be delivered. Traverse,° go, provide   350
thy money! We will have more of this to-morrow. Adieu.

RODERIGO: Where shall we meet i' th' morning?

IAGO: At my lodging.

RODERIGO: I'll be with thee betimes.

IAGO: Go to, farewell — Do you hear, Roderigo?   355

RODERIGO: What say you?

IAGO: No more of drowning, do you hear?

RODERIGO: I am changed.

IAGO: Go to, farewell. Put money enough in your purse.

RODERIGO: I'll sell all my land.   *Exit.*   360

IAGO: Thus do I ever make my fool my purse;
For I mine own gained knowledge should profane
If I would time expend with such a snipe°
But for my sport and profit. I hate the Moor;

---

329 defeat thy favor: Spoil thy appearance.   **333 sequestration:** Estrangement.
335 coloquintida: A medicine.   **339 Make:** Raise.   **340 erring:** Wandering.
347 My cause is hearted: My heart is in it.   **350 Traverse:** Forward march.   **363
snipe:** Fool.

And it is thought abroad that 'twixt my sheets   365
H'as done my office. I know not if 't be true;
But I, for mere suspicion in that kind,
Will do as if for surety. He holds me well;°
The better shall my purpose work on him.
Cassio's a proper man. Let me see now: 370
To get his place, and to plume up° my will
In double knavery — How, how? — Let's see: —
After some time, to abuse Othello's ears
That he is too familiar with his wife.
He hath a person and a smooth dispose°   375
To be suspected — framed to make women false.
The Moor is of a free° and open nature
That thinks men honest that but seem to be so;
And will as tenderly be led by th' nose
As asses are.   380
I have't! It is engend'red! Hell and night
Must bring this monstrous birth to the world's light.   *Exit.*

[ACT II, Scene I: An open place in Cyprus, near the harbor.]

Enter Montano and two Gentlemen.

MONTANO: What from the cape can you discern at sea?
1. GENTLEMAN: Nothing at all: it is a high-wrought flood.
    I cannot 'twixt the heaven and the main
    Descry a sail.
MONTANO: Methinks the wind hath spoke aloud at land;   5
    A fuller blast ne'er shook our battlements.
    If it hath ruffianed so upon the sea,
    What ribs of oak, when mountains melt on them,
    Can hold the mortise?° What shall we hear of this?
2. GENTLEMAN: A segregation° of the Turkish fleet.   10
    For do but stand upon the foaming shore,
    The chidden billow seems to pelt the clouds;
    The wind-shaked surge, with high and monstrous mane,
    Seems to cast water on the burning Bear
    And quench the Guards° of th' ever-fixèd pole.°   15
    I never did like molestation° view
    On the enchafèd flood.
MONTANO: If that the Turkish fleet

---

368 well: In high regard.   **371 plume up:** Gratify.   **375 dispose:** Manner.   **377 free:** Frank.   **ACT II, SCENE I. 9 hold the mortise:** Hold their joints together.   **10 segregation:** Scattering.   **15 Guards:** Stars near the North Star; **pole:** Polestar.   **16 molestation:** Tumult.

Be not ensheltered and embayed, they are drowned;
It is impossible to bear it out.

Enter a third Gentleman.

3. GENTLEMAN: News, lads! Our wars are done.   20
    The desperate tempest hath so banged the Turks
    That their designment halts.° A noble ship of Venice
    Hath seen a grievous wrack and sufferance°
    On most part of their fleet.
MONTANO: How? Is this true?
3. GENTLEMAN: The ship is here put in,   25
    A Veronesa;° Michael Cassio,
    Lieutenant to the warlike Moor Othello,
    Is come on shore; the Moor himself at sea,
    And is in full commission here for Cyprus.
MONTANO: I am glad on't. 'Tis a worthy governor.   30
3. GENTLEMAN: But his same Cassio, though he speak of comfort
    Touching the Turkish loss, yet he looks sadly
    And prays the Moor be safe, for they were parted
    With foul and violent tempest.
MONTANO: Pray heaven he be;
    For I have served him, and the man commands   35
    Like a full soldier. Let's to the seaside, ho!
    As well to see the vessel that's come in
    As to throw out our eyes for brave Othello,
    Even till we make the main and th' aerial blue
    An indistinct regard.°   40
3. GENTLEMAN: Come, let's do so;
    For every minute is expectancy
    Of more arrivance.

Enter Cassio.

CASSIO: Thanks, you the valiant of this warlike isle,
    That so approve the Moor! O, let the heavens
    Give him defense against the elements,   45
    For I have lost him on a dangerous sea!
MONTANO: Is he well shipped?
CASSIO: His bark is stoutly timbered, and his pilot
    Of very expert and approved allowance;
    Therefore my hopes, not surfeited to death,°   50
    Stand in bold cure.°
    (Within.)   A sail, a sail, a sail!   *Enter a messenger.*
CASSIO: What noise?

---

22 designment halts: Plan is crippled.   **23 sufferance:** Disaster.   **26 Veronesa:** Ship furnished by Verona.   **40 An indistinct regard:** Indistinguishable.   **50 surfeited to death:** Overindulged.   **51 in bold cure:** A good chance of fulfillment.

MESSENGER: The town is empty; on the brow o' th' sea
 Stand ranks of people, and they cry "A sail!"

CASSIO: My hopes do shape him for the governor.   55

A shot.

2. GENTLEMAN: They do discharge their shot of courtesy:
 Our friends at least.

CASSIO: I pray you, sir, go forth
 And give us truth who 'tis that is arrived.

2. GENTLEMAN: I shall.   *Exit.*

MONTANO: But, good lieutenant, is your general wived? 60

CASSIO: Most fortunately. He hath achieved a maid
 That paragons° description and wild fame;
 One that excels the quirks° of blazoning° pens,
 And in th' essential vesture of creation
 Does tire the ingener.°

Enter Second Gentleman.

       How now? Who has put in? 65

2. GENTLEMAN: 'Tis one Iago, ancient to the general.

CASSIO: H'as had most favorable and happy speed:
 Tempests themselves, high seas, and howling winds,
 The guttered° rocks and congregated sands,
 Traitors ensteeped° to clog the guiltless keel, 70
 As having sense of beauty, do omit
 Their mortal° natures, letting go safely by
 The divine Desdemona.

MONTANO: What is she?

CASSIO: She that I spake of, our great captain's captain,
 Left in the conduct of the bold Iago, 75
 Whose footing° here anticipates our thoughts
 A se'nnight's° speed. Great Jove, Othello guard,
 And swell his sail with thine own pow'rful breath,
 That he may bless this bay with his tall ship,
 Make love's quick pants in Desdemona's arms, 80
 Give renewed fire to our extincted spirits,
 [And bring all Cyprus comfort!]

Enter Desdemona, Iago, Roderigo, and Emilia [with Attendants].

       O, behold!
 The riches of the ship is come on shore!
 You men of Cyprus, let her have your knees.°

---

62 paragons: Surpasses. **63 quirks:** Ingenuities; **blazoning:** Describing.
64–65 And . . . ingener: Merely to describe her as God made her exhaust her praiser.
69 guttered: Jagged. **70 ensteeped:** Submerged. **72 mortal:** Deadly. **76
footing:** Landing. **77 se'nnight's:** Week's. **84 knees:** I.e., kneeling.

Hail to thee, lady! and the grace of heaven,   85
Before, behind thee, and on every hand,
Enwheel thee round!
DESDEMONA: I thank you, valiant Cassio.
What tidings can you tell me of my lord?
CASSIO: He is not yet arrived; nor know I aught
But that he's well and will be shortly here.   90
DESDEMONA: O but I fear! How lost you company?
CASSIO: The great contention of the sea and skies
Parted our fellowship.
(Within.)   A sail, a sail! [A shot.]
                              But hark. A sail!
2. GENTLEMAN: They give their greeting to the citadel;
This likewise is a friend.
CASSIO: See for the news.   95

                                              [Exit Gentleman.]

Good ancient, you are welcome.
[To Emilia.]   Welcome, mistress. —
Let it not gall your patience, good Iago,
That I extend my manners. 'Tis my breeding
That gives me this bold show of courtesy.

[Kisses Emilia.°]

IAGO: Sir, would she give you so much of her lips   100
As of her tongue she oft bestows on me,
You would have enough.
DESDEMONA: Alas, she has no speech!
IAGO: In faith, too much.
I find it still when I have list to sleep.
Marry, before your ladyship, I grant,   105
She puts her tongue a little in her heart
And chides with thinking.
EMILIA: You have little cause to say so.
IAGO: Come on, come on! You are pictures out of doors,
Bells in your parlors, wildcats in your kitchens,   110
Saints in your injuries, devils being offended,
Players in your housewifery,° and housewives° in your beds.
DESDEMONA: O, fie upon thee, slanderer!
IAGO: Nay, it is true, or else I am a Turk:
You rise to play, and go to bed to work.   115
EMILIA: You shall not write my praise.
IAGO: No, let me not.

Kisses Emilia: (Kissing was a common Elizabethan form of social courtesy).   **112 housewifery:** Housekeeping;   **housewives:** Hussies.

DESDEMONA: What wouldst thou write of me, if thou shouldst praise me?

IAGO: O gentle lady, do not put me to't,
For I am nothing if not critical.

DESDEMONA: Come on, assay.° — There's one gone to the harbor?   120

IAGO: Ay, madam.

DESDEMONA: I am not merry; but I do beguile
The thing I am by seeming otherwise. —
Come, how wouldst thou praise me?

IAGO: I am about it; but indeed my invention   125
Comes from my pate as birdlime° does from frieze° —
It plucks out brains and all. But my Muse labors,
And thus she is delivered:
If she be fair and wise, fairness and wit —
The one's for use, the other useth it.   130

DESDEMONA: Well praised! How if she be black° and witty?

IAGO: If she be black, and thereto have a wit,
She'll find a white that shall her blackness fit.

DESDEMONA: Worse and worse!

EMILIA: How if fair and foolish?   135

IAGO: She never yet was foolish that was fair,
For even her folly° helped her to an heir.

DESDEMONA: These are old fond° paradoxes to make fools laugh i' th' alehouse.
What miserable praise hast thou for her that's foul° and foolish?

IAGO: There's none so foul, and foolish thereunto,   140
But does foul pranks which fair and wise ones do.

DESDEMONA: O heavy ignorance! Thou praisest the worst best. But what praise
couldst thou bestow on a deserving woman indeed — one that in the
authority of her merit did justly put on the vouch° of very malice itself?

IAGO: She that was ever fair, and never proud;   145
Had tongue at will, and yet was never loud;
Never lacked gold, and yet went never gay;
Fled from her wish, and yet said "Now I may";
She that, being ang'red, her revenge being nigh,
Bade her wrong stay, and her displeasure fly;   150
She that in wisdom never was so frail
To change the cod's head for the salmon's tail;°
She that could think, and ne'er disclose her mind;
See suitors following, and not look behind:
She was a wight (if ever such wight were) —   155

DESDEMONA: To do what?

IAGO: To suckle fools and chronicle small beer.°

---

120 assay: Try.   **126 birdlime:** A sticky paste; **frieze:** Rough cloth.   **131 black:**
Brunette.   **137 folly:** Wantonness.   **138 fond:** Foolish.   **139 foul:** Ugly.   **144 put
on the vouch:** Compel the approval.   **152 To . . . tail:** I.e., to exchange the good for
the poor but expensive.   **157 chronicle small beer:** Keep petty household accounts.

DESDEMONA: O most lame and impotent conclusion! Do not learn of him, Emilia, though he be thy husband. How say you, Cassio? Is he not a most profane and liberal° counsellor? 160

CASSIO: He speaks home,° madam. You may relish him more in the soldier than in the scholar.

IAGO *[aside]*: He takes her by the palm. Ay, well said, whisper! With as little a web as this will I ensnare as great a fly as Cassio. Ay, smile upon her, do! I will gyve thee in thine own courtship.° — You say true; 'tis so, indeed! — If 165 such tricks as these strip you out of your lieutenantry, it had been better you had not kissed your three fingers so oft — which now again you are most apt to play the sir° in. Very good! well kissed! an excellent courtesy! 'Tis so, indeed. Yet again your fingers to your lips? Would they were clyster pipes° for your sake! (Trumpet within.) 170
The Moor! I know his trumpet.

CASSIO: 'Tis truly so.

DESDEMONA: Let's meet him and receive him.

CASSIO: Lo, where he comes.

Enter Othello and Attendants.

OTHELLO: O my fair warrior!

DESDEMONA: My dear Othello! 175

OTHELLO: It gives me wonder great as my content
    To see you here before me. O my soul's joy!
    If after every tempest come such calms,
    May the winds blow till they have wakened death!
    And let the laboring bark climb hills of seas 180
    Olympus-high, and duck again as low
    As hell's from heaven! If it were now to die,
    'Twere now to be most happy;° for I fear
    My soul hath her content so absolute
    That not another comfort like to this 185
    Succeeds in unknown fate.

DESDEMONA: The heavens forbid
    But that our loves and comforts should increase
    Even as our days do grow.

OTHELLO: Amen to that, sweet powers!
    I cannot speak enough of this content;
    It stops me here; it is too much of joy. 190
    And this, and this, the greatest discords be

They kiss.

That e'er our hearts shall make!

IAGO *[aside]*:   O, you are well tuned now!

---

160 profane and liberal: Worldly and licentious. **161 home:** Bluntly. **165 gyve . . . courtship:** Manacle you by means of your courtly manners. **168 sir:** Courtly gentleman. **169–70 clyster pipes:** Syringes. **183 happy:** Fortunate.

But I'll set down° the pegs that make this music,
As honest as I am.
OTHELLO: Come, let us to the castle.
News, friends! Our wars are done; the Turks are drowned.   195
How does my old acquaintance of this isle? —
Honey, you shall be well desired° in Cyprus;
I have found great love amongst them. O my sweet,
I prattle out of fashion, and I dote
In mine own comforts. I prithee, good Iago,   200
Go to the bay and disembark my coffers.
Bring thou the master° to the citadel;
He is a good one, and his worthiness
Does challenge° much respect. — Come, Desdemona,
Once more well met at Cyprus.   205

> *Exit Othello [with all but Iago and Roderigo].*

IAGO [*to an Attendant, who goes out*]:   Do thou meet me presently at the harbor.
[*To Roderigo.*] Come hither. If thou be'st valiant (as they say base men
being in love have then a nobility in their natures more than is native to
them), list me. The lieutenant to-night watches on the court of guard.°
First, I must tell thee this: Desdemona is directly in love with him.   210
RODERIGO: With him? Why, 'tis not possible.
IAGO: Lay thy finger thus,° and let thy soul be instructed. Mark me with
what violence she first loved the Moor, but for bragging and telling her
fantastical lies; and will she love him still for prating? Let not thy discreet
heart think it. Her eye must be fed; and what delight shall she have to look   215
on the devil? When the blood is made dull with the act of sport, there
should be, again to inflame it and to give satiety a fresh appetite, loveliness
in favor, sympathy in years, manners, and beauties; all which the Moor is
defective in. Now for want of these required conveniences,° her delicate
tenderness will find itself abused, begin to heave the gorge,° disrelish and   220
abhor the Moor. Very nature will instruct her in it and compel her to some
second choice. Now, sir, this granted — as it is a most pregnant° and
unforced position — who stands so eminent in the degree of this fortune as
Cassio does? A knave very voluble; no further conscionable° than in
putting on the mere form of civil and humane° seeming for the better   225
compassing of his salt° and most hidden loose affection? Why, none! why,
none! A slipper° and subtle knave; a finder-out of occasions; that has an
eye can stamp and counterfeit advantages, though true advantage never
present itself; a devilish knave! Besides, the knave is handsome, young, and

---

193 set down: Loosen.   **197 well desired:** Warmly welcomed.   **202 master:** Ship
captain.   **204 challenge:** Deserve.   **209 court of guard:** Headquarters.   **212 thus:** I.e.,
on your lips.   **219 conveniences:** Compatibilities.   **220 heave the gorge:** Be nauseated.
222 pregnant: Evident.   **224 conscionable:** Conscientious.   **225 humane:** Polite.
226 salt: Lecherous.   **227 slipper:** Slippery.

hath all those requisites in him that folly and green minds look after. A   230
pestilent complete knave! and the woman hath found him already.

RODERIGO: I cannot believe that in her; she's full of most blessed condition.°

IAGO: Blessed fig's-end! The wine she drinks is made of grapes. If she had been
blessed, she would never have loved the Moor. Blessed pudding! Didst thou
not see her paddle with the palm of his hand? Didst not mark that?   235

RODERIGO: Yes, that I did; but that was but courtesy.

IAGO: Lechery, by this hand! an index and obscure prologue to the history of
lust and foul thoughts. They met so near with their lips that their breaths
embraced together. Villainous thoughts, Roderigo! When these mutuali-
ties° so marshal the way, hard at hand comes the master and main exer-   240
cise, th' incorporate° conclusion. Pish! But, sir, be you ruled by me: I have
brought you from Venice. Watch you to-night; for the command, I'll lay't
upon you. Cassio knows you not. I'll not be far from you: do you find some
occasion to anger Cassio, either by speaking too loud, or tainting° his discipline, or from what other course you please which the time shall more fa-   245
vorably minister.

RODERIGO: Well.

IAGO: Sir, he's rash and very sudden in choler,° and haply with his truncheon
may strike at you. Provoke him that he may; for even out of that will I
cause these of Cyprus to mutiny; whose qualification° shall come into no   250
true taste° again but by the displanting of Cassio. So shall you have a
shorter journey to your desires by the means I shall then have to prefer°
them; and the impediment most profitably removed with-out the which
there were no expectation of our prosperity.

RODERIGO: I will do this if you can bring it to any opportunity.   255

IAGO: I warrant thee. Meet me by and by at the citadel; I must fetch his necessaries ashore. Farewell.

RODERIGO: Adieu.   ·*Exit.*

IAGO: That Cassio loves her, I do well believe't;
That she loves him, 'tis apt° and of great credit.   260
The Moor, howbeit that I endure him not,
Is of a constant, loving, noble nature,
And I dare think he'll prove to Desdemona
A most dear husband. Now I do love her too;
Not out of absolute lust, though peradventure   265
I stand accountant° for as great a sin,
But partly led to diet° my revenge,
For that I do suspect the lusty Moor
Hath leaped into my seat; the thought whereof
Doth, like a poisonous mineral, gnaw my inwards;   270

---

232 condition: Character.   **239–240 mutualities:** Exchanges.   **241 incorporate:** Carnal.   **244 tainting:** Discrediting.   **248 sudden in choler:** Violent in anger.
250 qualification: Appeasement.   **251 true taste:** Satisfactory state.   **252 prefer:**
Advance.   **260 apt:** Probable.   **266 accountant:** Accountable.   **267 diet:** Feed.

And nothing can or shall content my soul
Till I am evened with him, wife for wife;
Or failing so, yet that I put the Moor
At least into a jealousy so strong
That judgment cannot cure. Which thing to do,   275
If this poor trash of Venice, whom I trash°
For° his quick hunting, stand the putting on,°
I'll have our Michael Cassio on the hip,°
Abuse him to the Moor in the rank garb°
(For I fear Cassio with my nightcap too),   280
Make the Moor thank me, love me, and reward me
For making him egregiously an ass
And practicing upon° his peace and quiet
Even to madness. 'Tis here, but yet confused:
Knavery's plain face is never seen till used.   *Exit.*   285

[Scene II: A street in Cyprus.]

Enter Othello's Herald, with a proclamation.

HERALD: It is Othello's pleasure, our noble and valiant general, that, upon certain tidings now arrived, importing the mere perdition° of the Turkish fleet,
every man put himself into triumph; some to dance, some to make bonfires,
each man to what sport and revels his addiction leads him. For, besides
these beneficial news, it is the celebration of his nuptial. So much was his   5
pleasure should be proclaimed. All offices° are open, and there is full liberty
of feasting from the present hour of five till the bell have told eleven. Heaven
bless the isle of Cyprus and our noble general Othello!   *Exit.*

[Scene III: The Cyprian Castle.]

Enter Othello, Desdemona, Cassio, and Attendants.

OTHELLO: Good Michael, look you to the guard to-night.
Let's teach ourselves that honorable stop,
Not to outsport discretion.
CASSIO: Iago hath direction what to do;
But not withstanding, with my personal eye   5
Will I look to't.
OTHELLO: Iago is most honest.
Michael, good night. To-morrow with your earliest
Let me have speech with you.

276 **I trash:** I weight down (in order to keep under control).   277 **For:** In order to
develop;   **stand the putting on:** Responds to my inciting.   278 **on the hip:** At my
mercy.   279 **rank garb:** Gross manner.   283 **practicing upon:** Plotting against.
SCENE II. 2 **mere perdition:** Complete destruction.   6 **offices:** Kitchens and storerooms.

[*To Desdemona.*]   Come, my dear love.
The purchase made, the fruits are to ensue;
That profit's yet to come 'tween me and you. —   10
Good night.

                    Exit [Othello with Desdemona and Attendants].

Enter Iago.

CASSIO: Welcome, Iago. We must to the watch.

IAGO: Not this hour, lieutenant; 'tis not yet ten o' th' clock. Our general cast°
us thus early for the love of his Desdemona; who let us not therefore
blame. He hath not yet made wanton the night with her, and she is sport   15
for Jove.

CASSIO: She's a most exquisite lady.

IAGO: And, I'll warrant her, full of game.

CASSIO: Indeed, she's a most fresh and delicate creature.

IAGO: What an eye she has! Methinks it sounds a parley to provocation.   20

CASSIO: An inviting eye; and yet methinks right modest.

IAGO: And when she speaks, is it not an alarum to love?

CASSIO: She is indeed perfection.

IAGO: Well, happiness to their sheets! Come, lieutenant, I have a stoup° of
wine, and here without are a brace of Cyprus gallants that would fain have   25
a measure to the health of black Othello.

CASSIO: Not to-night, good Iago. I have very poor and unhappy brains for
drinking; I could well wish courtesy would invent some other custom of
entertainment.

IAGO: O, they are our friends. But one cup! I'll drink for you.   30

CASSIO: I have drunk but one cup to-night, and that was craftily qualified° too;
and behold what innovation° it makes here. I am unfortunate in the infirmity and dare not task my weakness with any more.

IAGO: What, man! 'Tis a night of revels: the gallants desire it.

CASSIO: Where are they?   35

IAGO: Here at the door; I pray you call them in.

CASSIO: I'll do't, but it dislikes me.   *Exit.*

IAGO: If I can fasten but one cup upon him
With that which he hath drunk to-night already,
He'll be as full of quarrel and offense   40
As my young mistress' dog. Now my sick fool Roderigo,
Whom love hath turned almost the wrong side out,
To Desdemona hath to-night caroused
Potations pottle-deep;° and he's to watch.
Three lads of Cyprus — noble swelling spirits,   45
That hold their honors in a wary distance,°
The very elements° of this warlike isle —

SCENE III. **14 cast:** Dismissed.   **24 stoup:** Two-quart tankard.   **31 qualified:** Diluted.
32 innovation: Disturbance.   **44 pottle-deep:** Bottoms up.   **46 That . . . distance:**
Very sensitive about their honor.   **47 very elements:** True representatives.

Have I to-night flustered with flowing cups,
And they watch too. Now, 'mongst this flock of drunkards
Am I to put our Cassio in some action   50
That may offend the isle.

Enter Cassio, Montano, and Gentlemen [; Servants following with wine].

But here they come.
If consequence do but approve my dream,
My boat sails freely, both with wind and stream.
CASSIO: 'Fore God, they have given me a rouse° already.
MONTANO: Good faith, a little one; not past a pint, as I am a soldier.   55
IAGO: Some wine, ho!

   [Sings.]   And let me the canakin clink, clink;
               And let me the canakin clink
                  A soldier's a man;
                  A life's but a span,   60
               Why then, let a soldier drink.

Some wine, boys!
CASSIO: 'Fore God, an excellent song!
IAGO: I learned it in England, where indeed they are most potent in potting.
Your Dane, your German, and your swag-bellied Hollander — Drink,   65
ho! — are nothing to your English.
CASSIO: Is your Englishman so expert in his drinking?
IAGO: Why, he drinks you with facility your Dane dead drunk; he sweats not
to overthrow your Almain; he gives your Hollander a vomit ere the next
pottle can be filled.   70
CASSIO: To the health of our general!
MONTANO: I am for it, lieutenant, and I'll do you justice.
IAGO: O sweet England!

   [Sings.]   King Stephen was a worthy peer;
               His breeches cost him but a crown;   75
              He held 'em sixpence all too dear,
               With that he called the tailor lown.°
              He was a wight of high renown,
               And thou art but of low degree.
              'Tis pride that pulls the country down;   80
               Then take thine auld cloak about thee.

Some wine, ho!
CASSIO: 'Fore God, this is a more exquisite song than the other.
IAGO: Will you hear't again?
CASSIO: No, for I hold him to be unworthy of his place that does those things.°   85
Well, God's above all; and there be souls must be saved, and there be souls
must not be saved.
IAGO: It's true, good lieutenant.

54 rouse: Bumper.   **77 lown:** Rascal.   **85 does...things:** I.e., behaves in this fashion.

CASSIO: For mine own part — no offense to the general, nor any man of quality — I hope to be saved.   90
IAGO: And so do I too, lieutenant.
CASSIO: Ay, but, by your leave, not before me. The lieutenant is to be saved
before the ancient. Let's have no more of this; let's to our affairs. — God forgive us our sins! — Gentlemen, let's look to our business. Do not think, gentlemen, I am drunk. This is my ancient; this is my right hand, and this is my
left. I am not drunk now. I can stand well enough, and I speak well enough.
ALL: Excellent well!
CASSIO: Why, very well then. You must not think then that I am drunk.

                                                                                    Exit.

MONTANO: To th' platform, masters. Come, let's set the watch.
IAGO: You see this fellow that is gone before.   100
      He's a soldier fit to stand by Caesar
      And give direction; and do but see his vice.
      'Tis to his virtue a just equinox,°
      The one as long as th' other. 'Tis pity of him.
      I fear the trust Othello puts him in,   105
      On some odd time of his infirmity,
      Will shake this island.
MONTANO: But is he often thus?
IAGO: 'Tis evermore his prologue to his sleep:
      He'll watch the horologe a double set°
      If drink rock not his cradle.
MONTANO: It were well   110
      The general were put in mind of it.
      Perhaps he sees it not, or his good nature
      Prizes the virtue that appears in Cassio
      And looks not on his evils. Is not this true?

Enter Roderigo.

IAGO [*aside to him*]:   How now, Roderigo?   115
      I pray you after the lieutenant, go!   *Exit Roderigo.*
MONTANO: And 'tis great pity that the noble Moor
      Should hazard such a place as his own second
      With one of an ingraft° infirmity.
      It were an honest action to say   120
      So to the Moor.
IAGO: Not I, for this fair island!
      I do love Cassio well and would do much
      To cure him of this evil.
            (*Within.*) Help! help!
                        But hark! What noise?

103 **just equinox:** Exact equivalent.   **109 watch . . . set:** Stay awake twice around
the clock.   **119 ingraft:** I.e., ingrained.

Enter Cassio, driving in Roderigo.

CASSIO: Zounds, you rogue! you rascal!   125
MONTANO: What's the matter, lieutenant?
CASSIO: A knave to teach me my duty?
    I'll beat the knave into a twiggen° bottle.
RODERIGO: Beat me?
CASSIO: Dost thou prate, rogue? *[Strikes him.]*
MONTANO: Nay, good lieutenant!

                                        [Stays him.]

    I pray you, sir, hold your hand.
CASSIO: Let me go, sir,
    Or I'll knock you o'er the mazzard.°
MONTANO: Come, come, you're drunk!   130
CASSIO: Drunk?

They fight.

IAGO *[aside to Roderigo]:*   Away, I say! Go out and cry a mutiny!

                                    Exit Roderigo.

    Nay, good lieutenant. God's will, gentlemen!
    Help, ho! — lieutenant — sir — Montano — sir —
    Help, masters! — Here's a goodly watch indeed!   135

A bell rung.

    Who's that which rings the bell? Diablo, ho!
    The town will rise.° God's will, lieutenant, hold!
    You'll be shamed for ever.

Enter Othello and Gentlemen with weapons.

OTHELLO: What is the matter here?
MONTANO: Zounds, I bleed still. I am hurt to th' death.
    He dies!   140
OTHELLO: Hold for your lives!
IAGO: Hold, hold! Lieutenant — sir — Montano — gentlemen!
    Have you forgot all sense of place and duty?
    Hold! The general speaks to you. Hold, for shame!
OTHELLO: Why, how now ho? From whence ariseth this?   145
    Are we turned Turks, and to ourselves do that
    Which heaven hath forbid the Ottomites?
    For Christian shame put by this barbarous brawl!
    He that stirs next to carve for° his own rage.
    Holds his soul light; he dies upon his motion.   150
    Silence that dreadful bell! It frights the isle
    From her propriety.° What is the matter, masters?
    Honest Iago, that looks dead with grieving,

127 twiggen: Wicker-covered.   **130 mazzard:** Head.   **137 rise:** Grow riotous.
149 carve for: Indulge.   **152 propriety:** Proper self.

Speak. Who began this? On thy love, I charge thee.

IAGO: I do not know. Friends all, but now, even now,   155
In quarter,° and in terms like bride and groom
Devesting them for bed; and then, but now —
As if some planet had unwitted men —
Swords out, and tilting one at other's breast
In opposition bloody. I cannot speak   160
Any beginning to this peevish odds,°
And would in action glorious I had lost
Those legs that brought me to a part of it!

OTHELLO: How comes it, Michael, you are thus forgot?

CASSIO: I pray you pardon me; I cannot speak.   165

OTHELLO: Worthy Montano, you were wont to be civil;
The gravity and stillness of your youth
The world hath noted, and your name is great
In months of wisest censure.° What's the matter
That you unlace° your reputation thus   170
And spend your rich opinion° for the name
Of a night-brawler? Give me answer to it.

MONTANO: Worthy Othello, I am hurt to danger.
Your officer, Iago, can inform you,
While I spare speech, which something now offends° me,   175
Of all that I do know; nor know I aught
By me that's said or done amiss this night,
Unless self-charity be sometimes a vice,
And to defend ourselves it be a sin
When violence assails us.

OTHELLO: Now, by heaven,   180
My blood° begins my safer guides to rule,
And passion, having my best judgment collied,°
Assays° to lead the way. If I once stir
Or do but lift this arm, the best of you
Shall sink in my rebuke. Give me to know   185
How this foul rout began, who set it on;
And he that is approved in° this offense,
Though he had twinned with me, both at a birth,
Shall lose me. What! in a town of war,
Yet wild, the people's hearts brimful of fear,   190
To manage° private and domestic quarrel?
In night, and on the court and guard of safety?
'Tis monstrous. Iago, who began't?

---

156 quarter: Friendliness.   **161 peevish odds:** Childish quarrel.   **169 censure:**
Judgment.   **170 unlace:** Undo.   **171 rich   opinion:** High   reputation.   **175 offends:** Pains.   **181 blood:** Passion.   **182 collied:** Darkened.   **183 Assays:** Tries.
187 approved in: Proved guilty of.   **191 manage:** Carry on.

MONTANO: If partially affined, or leagued in office,°
    Thou dost deliver more or less than truth,   195
    Thou art no soldier.
IAGO: Touch me not so near.
    I had rather have this tongue cut from my mouth
    Than it should do offense to Michael Cassio;
    Yet I persuade myself, to speak the truth
    Shall nothing wrong him. This it is, general.   200
    Montano and myself being in speech,
    There comes a fellow crying out for help,
    And Cassio following him with determined sword
    To execute° upon him. Sir, this gentleman
    Steps in to Cassio and entreats his pause.   205
    Myself the crying fellow did pursue,
    Lest by his clamor — as it so fell out —
    The town might fall in fright. He, swift of foot,
    Outran my purpose; and I returned then rather
    For that I heard the clink and fall of swords,   210
    And Cassio high in oath;° which till to-night
    I ne'er might say before. When I came back —
    For this was brief — I found them close together
    At blow and thrust, even as again they were
    When you yourself did part them.   215
    More of this matter cannot I report;
    But men are men; the best sometimes forget.
    Though Cassio did some little wrong to him,
    As men in rage strike those that wish them best,
    Yet surely Cassio I believe received   220
    From him that fled some strange indignity,
    Which patience could not pass.°
OTHELLO: I know, Iago,
    Thy honesty and love doth mince this matter,
    Making it light to Cassio. Cassio, I love thee;
    But never more be officer of mine.   225

Enter Desdemona, attended.

    Look if my gentle love be not raised up!
    I'll make thee an example.
DESDEMONA: What's the matter?
OTHELLO: All's well now, sweeting; come away to bed.
    [To Montano.]
    Sir, for your hurts, myself will be your surgeon.
    Lead him off.   230

---

194 partially . . . office: Prejudiced by comradeship or official relations.   **204 execute:** Work his will.   **211 high in oath:** Cursing.   **222 pass:** Pass over, ignore.

[Montano is led off.]

> Iago, look with care about the town
> And silence those whom this vile brawl distracted.°
> Come, Desdemona; 'tis the soldiers' life
> To have their balmy slumbers waked with strife.

Exit [with all but Iago and Cassio].

IAGO: What, are you hurt, lieutenant?   235

CASSIO: Ay, past all surgery.

IAGO: Marry, God forbid!

CASSIO: Reputation, reputation, reputation! O, I have lost my reputation! I have lost the immortal part of myself, and what remains is bestial. My reputation, Iago, my reputation!   240

IAGO: As I am an honest man, I thought you had received some bodily wound. There is more sense in that than in reputation. Reputation is an idle and most false imposition; oft got without merit and lost without deserving. You have lost no reputation at all unless you repute yourself such a loser. What, man! there are ways to recover° the general again. You are but now   245 cast in his mood° — a punishment more in policy than in malice, even so as one would beat his offenseless dog to affright an imperious lion. Sue to him again, and he's yours.

CASSIO: I will rather sue to be despised than to deceive so good a commander with so slight, so drunken, and so indiscreet an officer. Drunk! and speak   250 parrot!° and squabble! swagger! swear! and discourse fustian° with one's own shadow! O thou invisible spirit of wine, if thou hast no name to be known by, let us call thee devil!

IAGO: What was he that you followed with your sword? What had he done to you?   255

CASSIO: I know not.

IAGO: Is't possible?

CASSIO: I remember a mass of things, but nothing distinctly; a quarrel, but nothing wherefore. O God, that men should put an enemy in their mouths to steal away their brains! that we should with joy, pleasance, revel, and   260 applause° transform ourselves into beasts!

IAGO: Why, but you are now well enough. How came you thus recovered?

CASSIO: It hath pleased the devil drunkenness to give place to the devil wrath. One unperfectness shows me another, to make me frankly despise myself.

IAGO: Come, you are too severe a moraler. As the time, the place, and the con-   265 dition of this country stands, I could heartily wish this had not so befall'n; but since it is as it is, mend it for your own good.

CASSIO: I will ask him for my place again: he shall tell me I am a drunkard! Had I as many mouths as Hydra,° such an answer would stop them all. To

---

232 distracted: Excited.   **245 recover:** Regain favor with.   **246 in his mood:** Dismissed because of his anger.   **251 parrot:** Meaningless phrases.   **fustian:** Bombastic nonsense.   **261 applause:** Desire to please.   **269 Hydra:** Monster with many heads.

be now a sensible man, by and by a fool, and presently a beast! O strange!   270
Every inordinate cup is unblest, and the ingredient° is a devil.

IAGO: Come, come, good wine is a good familiar creature if it be well used.
Exclaim no more against it. And, good lieutenant, I think you think I
love you.

CASSIO: I have well approved° it, sir. I drunk!   275

IAGO: You or any man living may be drunk at some time, man. I'll tell you
what you shall do. Our general's wife is now the general. I may say so in
this respect, for that he hath devoted and given up himself to the contemplation, mark, and denotement of her parts and graces. Confess yourself
freely to her; importune her help to put you in your place again. She is of so   280
free,° so kind, so apt, so blessed a disposition she holds it a vice in her goodness not to do more than she is requested. This broken joint between you
and her husband entreat her to splinter;° and my fortunes against any lay°
worth naming, this crack of your love shall grow stronger than it was
before.   285

CASSIO: You advise me well.

IAGO: I protest, in the sincerity of love and honest kindness.

CASSIO: I think it freely; and betimes in the morning will I beseech the virtuous Desdemona to undertake for me. I am desperate of my fortunes if they
check me here.   290

IAGO: You are in the right. Good night, lieutenant; I must to the watch.

CASSIO: Good night, honest Iago.   *Exit Cassio.*

IAGO: And what's he then that says I play the villain,
When this advice is free I give and honest,
Probal° to thinking, and indeed the course   295
To win the Moor again? For 'tis most easy
Th' inclining Desdemona to subdue°
In an honest suit; she's framed as fruitful
As the free elements. And then for her
To win the Moor — were't to renounce his baptism,   300
All seals and symbols of redeemèd sin —
His soul is so enfettered to her love
That she may make, unmake, do what she list,
Even as her appetite shall play the god
With his weak function. How am I then a villain   305
To counsel Cassio to this parallel° course,
Directly to his good? Divinity° of hell!
When devils will the blackest sins put on,°
They do suggest at first with heavenly shows,
As I do now. For whiles this honest fool   310
Plies Desdemona to repair his fortunes,

271 ingredient: Contents.   **275 approved:** Proved.   **281 free:** Bounteous.
283 splinter: Bind up with splints;   **lay:** Wager.   **295 Probal:** Probable.   **297 subdue:** Persuade.   **306 parallel:** Corresponding.   **307 Divinity:** Theology.   **308
put on:** Incite.

And she for him pleads strongly to the Moor,
I'll pour this pestilence into his ear,
That she repeals him° for her body's lust;
And by how much she strives to do him good,   315
She shall undo her credit with the Moor.
So will I turn her virtue into pitch,
And out of her own goodness make the net
That shall enmesh them all.

Enter Roderigo.

                        How, now, Roderigo?

RODERIGO: I do follow here in the chase, not like a hound that hunts, but one   320
that fills up the cry.° My money is almost spent; I have been to-night
exceedingly well cudgelled; and I think the issue will be — I shall have so
much experience for my pains; and so, with no money at all, and a little
more wit, return again to Venice.

IAGO: How poor are they that have not patience!   325
What wound did ever heal but by degrees?
Thou know'st we work by wit, and not by witchcraft;
And wit depends on dilatory time.
Does't not go well? Cassio hath beaten thee,
And thou by that small hurt hast cashiered Cassio.°   330
Though other things grow fair against the sun,
Yet fruits that blossom first will first be ripe.
Content thyself awhile. By the mass, 'tis morning!
Pleasure and action make the hours seem short.
Retire thee; go where thou art billeted.   335
Away, I say! Thou shalt know more hereafter.
Nay, get thee gone!   *Exit Roderigo.*
                    Two things are to be done:
My wife must move for Cassio to her mistress;
I'll set her on;
Myself the while to draw the Moor apart   340
And bring him jump° when he may Cassio find
Soliciting his wife. Ay, that's the way!
Dull no device by coldness and delay.   *Exit.*

[ACT III, Scene I: Before the chamber of Othello and Desdemona.]

Enter Cassio, with Musicians and the Clown.

CASSIO: Masters, play here, I will content° your pains:
Something that's brief; and bid "Good morrow, general."

314 repeals him: Seeks his recall. **321 cry:** Pack. **330 cashiered Cassio:**
Maneuvered Cassio's discharge. **341 jump:** At the exact moment. **ACT III, SCENE I. 1
content:** Reward.

[They play.]

CLOWN: Why, masters, ha' your instruments been in Naples,° that they speak
    i' th' nose thus?

MUSICIAN: How, sir, how?   5

CLOWN: Are these, I pray you, called wind instruments?

MUSICIAN: Ay, marry, are they, sir.

CLOWN: O, thereby hangs a tail.

MUSICIAN: Whereby hangs a tail, sir?

CLOWN: Marry, sir, by many a wind instrument that I know. But, masters,   10
    here's money for you; and the general so likes your music that he desires
    you, for love's sake, to make no more noise with it.

MUSICIAN: Well, sir, we will not.

CLOWN: If you have any music that may not be heard, to't again: but, as they
    say, to hear music the general does not greatly care.   15

MUSICIAN: We have none such, sir.

CLOWN: Then put up your pipes in your bag, for I'll away. Go, vanish into air,
    away!   *Exit Musician [with his fellows].*

CASSIO: Dost thou hear, my honest friend?

CLOWN: No, I hear not your honest friend. I hear you.   20

CASSIO: Prithee keep up thy quillets.° There's a poor piece of gold for thee. If
    the gentlewoman that attends the general's wife be stirring, tell her there's
    one Cassio entreats her a little favor of speech. Wilt thou do this?

CLOWN: She is stirring sir. If she will stir hither, I shall seem to notify unto her.

CASSIO: [Do, good my friend.]   *Exit Clown.*

Enter Iago.

                              In happy time,° Iago.   25

IAGO: You have not been abed then?

CASSIO: Why, no; the day had broke
    Before we parted. I have made bold, Iago,
    To send in to your wife: my suit to her
    Is that she will to virtuous Desdemona   30
    Procure me some access.

IAGO: I'll send her to you presently;
    And I'll devise a mean to draw the Moor
    Out of the way, that your converse and business
    May be more free.

CASSIO: I humbly thank you for't.   *Exit [Iago].*

                              I never knew   35
    A Florentine° more kind and honest.

Enter Emilia.

EMILIA: Good morrow, good lieutenant. I am sorry

---

3 Naples: (Notorious for its association with venereal disease).   **21 quillets:** Quips.
25 In happy time: Well met.   **36 Florentine:** I.e., even a Florentine (like Cassio; Iago
was a Venetian).

For your displeasure: but all will sure be well.
The general and his wife are talking of it,
And she speaks for you stoutly. The Moor replied   40
That he you hurt is of great fame in Cyprus
And great affinity,° and that in wholesome wisdom
He might not but refuse you; but he protests he loves you,
And needs no other suitor but his likings
[To take the safest occasion° by the front°]   45
To bring you in again.

CASSIO: Yet I beseech you,
If you think fit, or that it may be done,
Give me advantage of some brief discourse
With Desdemona alone.

EMILIA: Pray you come in.
I will bestow you where you shall have time   50
To speak your bosom° freely.

CASSIO: I am much bound to you.   *Exeunt.*

[Scene II: The castle.]

Enter Othello, Iago, and Gentlemen.

OTHELLO: These letters give, Iago, to the pilot
And by him do my duties to the Senate.
That done, I will be walking on the works;°
Repair there to me.

IAGO: Well, my good lord, I'll do't.

OTHELLO: This fortification, gentlemen, shall we see't?   5

GENTLEMEN: We'll wait upon your lordship.   *Exeunt.*

[Scene III: The castle grounds.]

Enter Desdemona, Cassio, and Emilia.

DESDEMONA: Be thou assured, good Cassio, I will do
All my abilities in thy behalf.

EMILIA: Good madam, do. I warrant it grieves my husband
As if the cause were his.

DESDEMONA: O, that's an honest fellow. Do not doubt, Cassio,   5
But I will have my lord and you again
As friendly as you were.

CASSIO: Bounteous madam,
Whatever shall become of Michael Cassio,
He's never anything but your true servant.

DESDEMONA: I know't; I thank you. You do love my lord;   10

---

42 affinity: Family connections.   **45 occasion:** Opportunity;   **front:** Forelock.   **51 your bosom:** Your inmost thoughts.   **SCENE II. 3 works:** Fortifications.

You have known him long; and be you well assured
He shall in strangeness° stand no farther off
Than in a politic distance.°

CASSIO: Ay, but, lady,
That policy may either last so long,
Or feed upon such nice and waterish diet,°   15
Or breed itself so out of circumstance,
That, I being absent, and my place supplied,
My general will forget my love and service.

DESDEMONA: Do not doubt° that; before Emilia here
I give thee warrant of thy place. Assure thee,   20
If I do vow a friendship, I'll perform it
To the last article. My lord shall never rest;
I'll watch him tame° and talk him out of patience;
His bed shall seem a school, his board a shrift;°
I'll intermingle everything he does   25
With Cassio's suit. Therefore be merry, Cassio,
For thy solicitor shall rather die
Than give thy cause away.

Enter Othello and Iago [at a distance].

EMILIA: Madam, here comes my lord.
CASSIO: Madam, I'll take my leave.   30
DESDEMONA: Why, stay, and hear me speak.
CASSIO: Madam, not now: I am very ill at ease,
    Unfit for mine own purposes.
DESDEMONA: Well, do your discretion.   *Exit Cassio.*
IAGO: Ha! I like not that.
OTHELLO: What dost thou say?   35
IAGO: Nothing, my lord; or if — I know not what.
OTHELLO: Was not that Cassio parted from my wife?
IAGO: Cassio, my lord? No, sure, I cannot think it,
    That he would steal away so guilty-like,
    Seeing your coming.
OTHELLO: I do believe 'twas he.   40
DESDEMONA: How now, my lord?
    I have been talking with a suitor here,
    A man that languishes in your displeasure.
OTHELLO: What is't you mean?
DESDEMONA: Why, your lieutenant, Cassio. Good my lord,   45
    If I have any grace or power to move you,
    His present° reconciliation take;
    For if he be not one that truly loves you,

SCENE III.   **12 strangeness:** Aloofness.   **13 Than . . . distance:** Than wise policy
requires.   **15 Or . . . diet:** Or be continued for such slight reasons.   **19 doubt:** Fear.
23 watch him tame: Keep him awake until he gives in.   **24 shrift:** Confessional.   **47
present:** Immediate.

That errs in ignorance, and not in cunning,
I have no judgment in an honest face,   50
I prithee call him back.
OTHELLO: Went he hence now?
DESDEMONA: Yes, faith; so humbled
That he hath left part of his grief with me
To suffer with him. Good love, call him back.
OTHELLO: Not now, sweet Desdemon; some other time.   55
DESDEMONA: But shall't be shortly?
OTHELLO: The sooner, sweet, for you.
DESDEMONA: Shall't be to-night at supper?
OTHELLO: No, not to-night.
DESDEMONA: To-morrow dinner then?
OTHELLO: I shall not dine at home;
I meet the captains at the citadel.
DESDEMONA: Why then, to-morrow night, or Tuesday morn,   60
On Tuesday noon or night, or Wednesday morn.
I prithee name the time, but let it not
Exceed three days. I' faith, he's penitent;
And yet his trespass, in our common reason
(Save that, they say, the wars must make examples   65
Out of their best), is not almost° a fault
T' incur a private check.° When shall he come?
Tell me, Othello. I wonder in my soul
What you could ask me that I should deny
Or stand so mamm'ring on.° What? Michael Cassio,   70
That came a-wooing with you, and so many a time,
When I have spoke of you dispraisingly,
Hath ta'en your part — to have so much to do
To bring him in? By'r Lady, I could do much —
OTHELLO: Prithee no more. Let him come when he will!   75
I will deny thee nothing.
DESDEMONA: Why, this is not a boon;
'Tis as I should entreat you wear your gloves,
Or feed on nourishing dishes, or keep you warm,
Or sue to you to do a peculiar profit
To your own person. Nay, when I have a suit   80
Wherein I mean to touch your love indeed,
It shall be full of poise and difficult weight,
And fearful° to be granted.
OTHELLO: I will deny thee nothing!
Whereon I do beseech thee grant me this,
To leave me but a little to myself.   85

---

66 not almost: Hardly.   **67 a private check:** Even a private reprimand.   **70 mamm'ring on:** Hesitating about.   **83 fearful:** Dangerous.

DESDEMONA: Shall I deny you? No. Farewell, my lord.

OTHELLO: Farewell, my Desdemon: I'll come to thee straight.

DESDEMONA: Emilia, come. — Be as your fancies teach you;
    Whate'er you be, I am obedient.   *Exit [with Emilia].*

OTHELLO: Excellent wretch!° Perdition catch my soul   90
    But I do love thee! and when I love thee not,
    Chaos is come again.

IAGO: My noble lord —

OTHELLO: What dost thou say, Iago?

IAGO: Did Michael Cassio, when you wooed my lady,
    Know of your love?   95

OTHELLO: He did, from first to last. Why dost thou ask?

IAGO: But for a satisfaction of my thought;
    No further harm.

OTHELLO: Why of thy thought, Iago?

IAGO: I did not think he had been acquainted with her.

OTHELLO: O, yes, and went between us° very oft.   100

IAGO: Indeed?

OTHELLO: Indeed? Ay, indeed! Discern'st thou aught in that?
    Is he not honest?

IAGO: Honest, my lord?

OTHELLO: Honest. Ay, honest.

IAGO: My lord, for aught I know.

OTHELLO: What dost thou think?

IAGO: Think, my lord?

OTHELLO: Think, my lord?   105
    By heaven, he echoes me,
    As if there were some monster in his thought
    Too hideous to be shown. Thou dost mean something:
    I heard thee say even now, thou lik'st not that,
    When Cassio left my wife. What didst not like?   110
    And when I told thee he was of my counsel
    In my whole course of wooing, thou cried'st "Indeed?"
    And didst contract and purse thy brow together,
    As if thou then hadst shut up in thy brain
    Some horrible conceit.° If thou dost love me,   115
    Show me thy thought

IAGO: My lord, you know I love you.

OTHELLO: I think thou dost;
    And, for I know thou'rt full of love and honesty
    And weigh'st thy words before thou giv'st them breath,
    Therefore these stops of thine fright me the more;   120
    For such things in a false disloyal knave

---

90 wretch: (A term of endearment).   **100 went . . . us:** (I.e., as messenger).   **115
conceit:** Fancy.

Are tricks of custom; but in a man that's just
They are close dilations, working from the heart
That passion cannot rule.°
IAGO: For Michael Cassio,
   I dare be sworn I think that he is honest.   125
OTHELLO: I think so too.
IAGO: Men should be what they seem;
   Or those that be not, would they might seem none!°
OTHELLO: Certain, men should be what they seem.
IAGO: Why then, I think Cassio's an honest man.
OTHELLO: Nay, yet there's more in this.   130
   I prithee speak to me as to thy thinkings,
   As thou dost ruminate, and give thy worst of thoughts
   The worst of words.
IAGO: Good my lord, pardon me:
   Though I am bound to every act of duty,
   I am not bound to that all slaves are free to.°   135
   Utter my thoughts? Why, say they are vile and false,
   As where's that palace whereinto foul things
   Sometimes intrude not? Who has a breast so pure
   But some uncleanly apprehensions
   Keep leets and law days,° and in Sessions sit   140
   With meditations lawful?
OTHELLO: Thou dost conspire against thy friend, Iago,
   If thou but think'st him wronged, and mak'st his ear
   A stranger to thy thoughts.
IAGO: I do beseech you —
   Though I perchance am vicious in my guess   145
   (As I confess it is my nature's plague
   To spy into abuses, and oft my jealousy°
   Shapes faults that are not), that your wisdom yet
   From one that so imperfectly conjects°
   Would take no notice, nor build yourself a trouble   150
   Out of his scattering and unsure observance.
   It were not for your quiet nor your good,
   Nor for my manhood, honesty, and wisdom,
   To let you know my thoughts.
OTHELLO: What dost thou mean?
IAGO: Good name in man and woman, dear my lord,   155
   Is the immediate° jewel of their souls.

123–24 close dilations . . . rule: Secret emotions that well up in spite of restraint.
127 seem none: I.e., not pretend to be men when they are really monsters.   **135
bound . . . free to:** Bound to tell that which even slaves are allowed to keep to themselves.
140 leets and law days: Sittings of the courts.   **147 jealousy:** Suspicion.   **149
conjects:** Conjectures.   **156 immediate:** Nearest the heart.

Who steals my purse steals trash; 'tis something, nothing;
'Twas mine, 'tis his, and has been slave to thousands;
But he that filches from me my good name
Robs me of that which not enriches him   160
And makes me poor indeed.
OTHELLO: By heaven, I'll know thy thoughts!
IAGO: You cannot, if my heart were in your hand;
Nor shall not whilst 'tis in my custody.
OTHELLO: Ha!
IAGO: O, beware, my lord, of jealousy!   165
It is the green-eyed monster, which doth mock°
The meat it feeds on. That cuckold lives in bliss
Who, certain of his fate, loves not his wronger;
But O, what damnèd minutes tells he o'er
Who dotes, yet doubts — suspects, yet strongly loves!   170
OTHELLO: O misery!
IAGO: Poor and content is rich, and rich enough;
But riches fineless° is as poor as winter
To him that ever fears he shall be poor.
Good God, the souls of all my tribe defend
From jealousy!   175
OTHELLO: Why, why is this?
Think'st thou I'ld make a life of jealousy,
To follow still the changes of the moon
With fresh suspicions? No! To be once in doubt
Is once to be resolved. Exchange me for a goat   180
When I shall turn the business of my soul
To such exsufflicate and blown° surmises,
Matching this inference. 'Tis not to make me jealous
To say my wife is fair, feeds well, loves company,
Is free of speech, sings, plays, and dances;   185
Where virtue is, these are more virtuous.
Nor from mine own weak merits will I draw
The smallest fear or doubt of her revolt,°
For she had eyes, and chose me. No, Iago;
I'll see before I doubt; when I doubt, prove;   190
And on the proof there is no more but this —
Away at once with love or jealousy!
IAGO: I am glad of this; for now I shall have reason
To show the love and duty that I bear you
With franker spirit. Therefore, as I am bound,   195
Receive it from me. I speak not yet of proof.
Look at your wife; observe her well with Cassio;

---

166 mock: Play with, like a cat with a mouse. **173 fineless:** Unlimited. **182 exsufflicate and blown:** Spat out and flyblown. **188 revolt:** Unfaithfulness.

Wear your eyes thus, not jealous nor secure:°
I would not have your free and noble nature,
Out of self-bounty,° be abused. Look to't.   200
I know our country disposition well:
In Venice they do let God see the pranks
They dare not show their husbands; their best conscience
Is not to leave't undone, but keep't unknown.
OTHELLO: Dost thou say so?   205
IAGO: She did deceive her father, marrying you;
And when she seemed to shake and fear your looks,
She loved them most.
OTHELLO: And so she did.
IAGO: Why, go to then!
She that, so young, could give out such a seeming
To seel° her father's eyes up close as oak° —   210
He thought 'twas witchcraft — but I am much to blame.
I humbly do beseech you of your pardon
For too much loving you.
OTHELLO: I am bound to thee for ever.
IAGO: I see this hath a little dashed your spirits.
OTHELLO: Not a jot, not a jot.   215
IAGO: I' faith, I fear it has.
I hope you will consider what is spoke
Comes from my love. But I do see y' are moved.
I am to pray you not to strain my speech
To grosser issues° nor to larger reach
Than to suspicion.   220
OTHELLO: I will not.
IAGO: Should you do so, my lord,
My speech should fall into such vile success°
As my thoughts aim not at. Cassio's my worthy friend —
My lord, I see y' are moved.
OTHELLO: No, not much moved:
I do not think but Desdemona's honest.°   225
IAGO: Long live she so! and long live you to think so!
OTHELLO: And yet, how nature erring from itself —
IAGO: Ay, there's the point! as (to be bold with you)
Not to affect many proposèd matches
Of her own clime, complexion, and degree,   230
Whereto we see in all things nature tends —
Foh! one may smell in such a will most rank,
Foul disproportions, thought unnatural —

---

198 secure: Overconfident.   **200 self-bounty:** Natural goodness.   **210 seel:** Close;
oak: Oak grain.   **219 To grosser issues:** To mean something more monstrous.   **222
vile success:** Evil outcome.   **225 honest:** Chaste.

But pardon me — I do not in position°
Distinctly speak of her; though I may fear   235
Her will, recoiling° to her better judgment,
May fall to match° you with her country forms,
And happily° repent.
OTHELLO: Farewell, farewell!
If more thou dost perceive, let me know more.
Set on thy wife to observe. Leave me, Iago.   240
IAGO: My lord, I take my leave.   *[Going.]*
OTHELLO: Why did I marry? This honest creature doubtless
Sees and knows more, much more, than he unfolds.
IAGO *[returns]*:   My lord, I would I might entreat your honor
To scan this thing no further: leave it to time.   245
Although 'tis fit that Cassio have his place,
For sure he fills it up with great ability,
Yet, if you please to hold off a while,
You shall by that perceive him and his means.
Note if your lady strain his entertainment°   250
With any strong or vehement importunity;
Much will be seen in that. In the mean time
Let me be thought too busy° in my fears
(As worthy cause I have to fear I am)
And hold her free,° I do beseech your honor.   255
OTHELLO: Fear not my government.°
IAGO: I once more take my leave.   *Exit.*
OTHELLO: This fellow's of exceeding honesty,
And knows all qualities,° with a learned spirit
Of° human dealings. If I do prove her haggard,°   260
Though that her jesses° were my dear heartstrings,
I'd whistle her off and let her down the wind
To prey at fortune.° Haply, for I am black
And have not those soft parts of conversation°
That chamberers° have, or for I am declined   265
Into the vale of years — yet that's not much —
She's gone. I am abused, and my relief
Must be to loathe her. O curse of marriage,
That we can call these delicate creatures ours,
And not their appetites! I had rather be a toad   270

---

234 position: Definite assertion.   **236 recoiling:** Reverting.   **237 fall to match:** Happen to compare.   **238 happily:** Haply, perhaps.   **250 strain his entertainment:** Urge his recall.   **253 busy:** Meddlesome.   **255 hold her free:** Consider her guiltless.   **256 government:** Self-control.   **259 qualities:** Natures.   **259–60 learned spirit Of:** Mind informed about.   **260 haggard:** A wild hawk.   **261 jesses:** Thongs for controlling a hawk.   **262–63 whistle . . . fortune:** Turn her out and let her take care of herself.   **264 soft . . . conversation:** Ingratiating manners.   **265 chamberers:** Courtiers.

And live upon the vapor of a dungeon
Than keep a corner in the thing I love
For others' uses. Yet 'tis the plague of great ones;°
Prerogatived° are they less than the base.
'Tis destiny unshunnable, like death.   275
Even then this forkèd plague° is fated to us
When we do quicken.° Look where she comes.

Enter Desdemona and Emilia.

If she be false, O, then heaven mocks itself!
I'll not believe't.
DESDEMONA: How now, my dear Othello?
Your dinner, and the generous° islanders   280
By you invited, do attend your presence.
OTHELLO: I am to blame.
DESDEMONA: Why do you speak so faintly?
Are you not well?
OTHELLO: I have a pain upon my forehead, here.
DESDEMONA: Faith, that's with watching;° 'twill away again.   285
Let me but bind it hard, within this hour
It will be well.
OTHELLO: Your napkin° is too little;

[He pushes the handkerchief from him, and it falls unnoticed.]

Let it° alone. Come, I'll go in with you.
DESDEMONA: I am very sorry that you are not well.   *Exit [with Othello].*
EMILIA: I am glad I have found this napkin;   290
This was her first remembrance from the Moor,
My wayward husband hath a hundred times
Wooed me to steal it; but she so loves the token
(For he conjured her she should ever keep it)
That she reserves it evermore about her   295
To kiss and talk to. I'll have the work ta'en out°
And give't Iago.
What he will do with it heaven knows, not I;
I nothing but to please his fantasy.°

Enter Iago.

IAGO: How now? What do you here alone?   300
EMILIA: Do not you chide; I have a thing for you.
IAGO: A thing for me? It is a common thing —
EMILIA: Ha?
IAGO: To have a foolish wife.

---

273 great   ones: Prominent   men.   **274 Prerogatived:** Privileged.   **276 forkèd
plague:** I.e., horns of a cuckold.   **277 do quicken:** Are born.   **280 generous:**
Noble.   **285 watching:** Working late.   **287 napkin:** Handkerchief.   **288 it:** I.e., his
forehead.   **296 work ta'en out:** Pattern copied.   **299 fantasy:** Whim.

EMILIA: O, is that all? What will you give me now   305
    For that same handkerchief?
IAGO: What handkerchief?
EMILIA: What handkerchief!
    Why, that the Moor first gave to Desdemona;
    That which so often you did bid me steal.
IAGO: Hast stol'n it from her?   210
EMILIA: No, faith; she let it drop by negligence,
    And to th' advantage,° I, being here, took't up.
    Look, here it is.
IAGO: A good wench! Give it me.
EMILIA: What will you do with't, that you have been so earnest
    To have me filch it?
IAGO: Why, what is that to you?   315

[Snatches it.]

EMILIA: If it be not for some purpose of import,°
    Give't me again. Poor lady, she'll run mad
    When she shall lack it.
IAGO: Be not acknown on't;° I have use for it.
    Go, leave me.   *Exit Emilia.*   320
    I will in Cassio's lodgings lose this napkin
    And let him find it. Trifles light as air
    Are to the jealous confirmations strong
    As proofs of holy writ. This may do something.
    The Moor already changes with my poison: 325
    Dangerous conceits° are in their nature poisons,
    Which at the first are scarce found to distaste,
    But with a little act upon the blood
    Burn like the mines of sulphur.

Enter Othello.

                         I did say so.
    Look where he comes! Not poppy nor mandragora,°   330
    Nor all the drowsy syrups of the world,
    Shall ever med'cine thee to that sweet sleep
    Which thou owedst yesterday.
OTHELLO: Ha! ha! false to me?
IAGO: Why, how now, general? No more of that!
OTHELLO: Avaunt! be gone! Thou hast set me on the rack.   335
    I swear 'tis better to be much abused
    Than but to know't a little.
IAGO: How now, my lord?
OTHELLO: What sense had I of her stol'n hours of lust?

312 to th' advantage: Opportunely.   **316 import:** Importance.   **319 Be . . . on't:**
Do not acknowledge it.   **326 conceits:** Ideas.   **330 mandragora:** A narcotic.

I saw't not, thought it not, it harmed not me;
I slept the next night well, fed well, was free° and merry;   340
I found not Cassio's kisses on her lips
He that is robbed, not wanting° what is stol'n,
Let him not know't, and he's not robbed at all.
IAGO: I am sorry to hear this.
OTHELLO: I had been happy if the general camp,   345
Pioneers° and all, had tasted her sweet body,
So I had nothing known. O, now for ever
Farewell the tranquil mind! farewell content!
Farewell the plumèd troop, and the big° wars
That make ambition virtue! O, farewell!   350
Farewell the neighing steed and the shrill trump,
The spirit-stirring drum, th' ear-piercing fife,
The royal banner, and all quality,
Pride, pomp, and circumstance° of glorious war!
And O you mortal engines° whose rude throats   355
Th' immortal Jove's dread clamors counterfeit,°
Farewell! Othello's occupation's gone!
IAGO: Is't possible, my lord?
OTHELLO: Villain, be sure thou prove my love a whore!
Be sure of it; give me the ocular proof;   360
Or, by the worth of mine eternal soul,
Thou hadst been better have been born a dog
Than answer my waked wrath!
IAGO: Is't come to this?
OTHELLO: Make me to see't; or at the least so prove it
That the probation° bear no hinge nor loop   365
To hang a doubt on — or woe upon thy life!
IAGO: My noble lord —
OTHELLO: If thou dost slander her and torture me,
Never pray more; abandon all remorse;
On horror's head horrors accumulate;   370
Do deeds to make heaven weep, all earth amazed;
For nothing canst thou to damnation add
Greater than that.
IAGO: O grace! O heaven forgive me!
Are you a man? Have you a soul or sense? —
God b' wi' you! take mine office. O wretched fool,   375
That liv'st to make thine honesty a vice!
O monstrous world! Take note, take note, O world,
To be direct and honest is not safe.

---

340 free: Carefree.   **342 wanting:** Missing.   **346 Pioneers:** Sappers, laborers.
349 big: Stately.   **354 circumstance:** Pageantry.   **355 mortal engines:** Deadly artillery.   **356 counterfeit:** Imitate.   **365 probation:** Proof.

I thank you for this profit;° and from hence
I'll love no friend, sith love breeds such offense.   380
OTHELLO: Nay, stay. Thou shouldst be honest.
IAGO: I should be wise; for honesty's a fool
     And loses that it works for.
OTHELLO: By the world,
     I think my wife be honest, and think she is not;
     I think that thou art just, and think thou art not.   385
     I'll have some proof. Her name, that was as fresh
     As Dian's visage, is now begrimed and black
     As mine own face. If there be cords, or knives,
     Poison, or fire, or suffocating streams,
     I'll not endure it. Would I were satisfied!°   390
IAGO: I see, sir, you are eaten up with passion:
     I do repent me that I put it to you.
     You would be satisfied?
OTHELLO: Would? Nay, I will.
IAGO: And may; but how? how satisfied, my lord?
     Would you, the supervisor,° grossly gape on?   395
     Behold her topped?
OTHELLO: Death and damnation! O!
IAGO: It were a tedious difficulty, I think,
     To bring them to that prospect. Damn them then,
     If ever mortal eyes do see them bolster°
     More than their own! What then? How then?   400
     What shall I say? Where's satisfaction?
     It is impossible you should see this,
     Were they as prime° as goats, as hot as monkeys,
     As salt° as wolves in pride,° and fools as gross
     As ignorance made drunk. But yet, I say,   405
     If imputation and strong circumstances
     Which lead directly to the door of truth
     Will give you satisfaction, you may have't.
OTHELLO: Give me a living reason she's disloyal.
IAGO: I do not like the office.   410
     But sith I am ent'red in this cause so far,
     Pricked to't by foolish honesty and love,
     I will go on. I lay with Cassio lately,
     And being troubled with a raging tooth,
     I could not sleep.   415
     There are a kind of men so loose of soul
     That in their sleeps will mutter their affairs.

---

379 profit: Profitable lesson.   **390 satisfied:** Completely informed.   **395 supervisor:**
Spectator.   **399 bolster:** Lie together.   **403 prime:** Lustful.   **404 salt:** Lecherous; **pride:**
Heat.

One of this kind is Cassio.
In sleep I heard him say, "Sweet Desdemona,
Let us be wary, let us hide our loves!"   420
And then, sir, would he gripe and wring my hand,
Cry "O sweet creature!" and then kiss me hard,
As if he plucked up kisses by the roots
That grew upon my lips; then laid his leg
Over my thigh, and sighed, and kissed, and then   425
Cried "Cursèd fate that gave thee to the Moor!"

OTHELLO: O monstrous! monstrous!

IAGO: Nay, this was but his dream.

OTHELLO: But this denoted a foregone conclusion;°
'Tis a shrewd doubt,° though it be but a dream.

IAGO: And this may help to thicken other proofs   430
That do demonstrate thinly.

OTHELLO: I'll tear her all to pieces!

IAGO: Nay, but be wise. Yet we see nothing done;
She may be honest yet. Tell me but this —
Have you not sometimes seen a handkerchief
Spotted with strawberries in your wife's hand?   435

OTHELLO: I gave her such a one; 'twas my first gift.

IAGO: I know not that; but such a handkerchief —
I am sure it was your wife's — did I to-day
See Cassio wipe his beard with.

OTHELLO: If it be that —

IAGO: If it be that, or any that was hers,   440
It speaks against her with the other proofs.

OTHELLO: O, that the slave had forty thousand lives!
One is too poor, too weak for my revenge.
Now do I see 'tis true. Look here, Iago:
All my fond love thus do I blow to heaven.   445
'Tis gone.
Arise, black vengeance, from the hollow hell!
Yield up, O love, thy crown and hearted throne
To tyrannous hate! Swell, bosom, with thy fraught,°
For 'tis of aspics'° tongues!

IAGO: Yet be content.   450

OTHELLO: O, blood, blood, blood!

IAGO: Patience, I say. Your mind perhaps may change.

OTHELLO: Never, Iago. Like to the Pontic sea,°
Whose icy current and compulsive course
Ne'er feels retiring ebb, but keeps due on   455

---

428 foregone conclusion: Previous experience. **429 a shrewd doubt:** Cursedly
suspicious. **449 fraught:** Burden. **450 aspics:** Deadly poisonous snakes. **453 Pontic sea:** Black Sea.

To the Propontic and the Hellespont,
Even so my bloody thoughts, with violent pace,
Shall ne'er look back, ne'er ebb to humble love,
Till that a capable° and wide revenge
Swallow them up.
    (He kneels.)   Now, by yond marble heaven,   460
In the due reverence of a sacred vow
I here engage my words.

IAGO: Do not rise yet.

(Iago kneels.)

Witness, you ever-burning lights above,
You elements that clip° us round about,
Witness that here Iago doth give up   465
The execution° of his wit,° hands, heart
To wronged Othello's service! Let him command,
And to obey shall be in me remorse,°
What bloody business ever.

[They rise.]

OTHELLO: I greet thy love,
Not with vain thanks but with acceptance bounteous,   470
And will upon the instant put thee to't.
Within these three days let me hear thee say
That Cassio's not alive.

IAGO: My friend is dead; 'tis done at your request.
But let her live.   475

OTHELLO: Damn her, lewd minx! O, damn her! damn her!
Come, go with me apart. I will withdraw
To furnish me with some swift means of death
For the fair devil. Now art thou my lieutenant.

IAGO: I am your own forever.   *Exeunt.*   480

[Scene IV: The environs of the castle.]

Enter Desdemona, Emilia, and Clown.

DESDEMONA: Do you know, sirrah, where Lieutenant Cassio lies?°
CLOWN: I dare not say he lies anywhere.
DESDEMONA: Why, man?
CLOWN: He's a soldier, and for me to say a soldier lies is stabbing.
DESDEMONA: Go to. Where lodges he?   5
CLOWN: To tell you where he lodges is to tell you where I lie.
DESDEMONA: Can anything be made of this?

459 capable: All-embracing.   **464 clip:** Encompass.   **466 execution:** Activities;
wit: Mind.   **468 remorse:** Pity.   SCENE IV. **1 lies:** Lives, lodges.

CLOWN: I know not where he lodges; and for me to devise a lodging, and say he
    lies here or he lies there, were to lie in mine own throat.

DESDEMONA: Can you enquire him out, and be edified by report?   10

CLOWN: I will catechize the world for him; that is, make questions, and by
    them answer.

DESDEMONA: Seek him, bid him come hither. Tell him I have moved° my lord on
    his behalf and hope all will be well.

CLOWN: To do this is within the compass of man's wit, and therefore I'll   15
    attempt the doing of it.   *Exit.*

DESDEMONA: Where should I lose that handkerchief, Emilia?

EMILIA: I know not, madam.

DESDEMONA: Believe me, I had rather have lost my purse
    Full of crusadoes;° and but my noble Moor
    Is true of mind, and made of no such baseness   20
    As jealous creatures are, it were enough
    To put him to ill thinking.

EMILIA: Is he not jealous?

DESDEMONA: Who? he? I think the sun where he was born
    Drew all such humors° from him.

Enter Othello.

EMILIA: Look where he comes.   25

DESDEMONA: I will not leave him now till Cassio
    Be called to him — How is't with you, my lord?

OTHELLO: Well, my good lady. [*Aside.*] O, hardness to dissemble! —
    How do you, Desdemona?

DESDEMONA: Well, my good lord.

OTHELLO: Give me your hand. This hand is moist, my lady.   30

DESDEMONA: It yet hath felt no age nor known no sorrow.

OTHELLO: This argues fruitfulness and liberal heart.
    Hot, hot, and moist. This hand of yours requires
    A sequester° from liberty, fasting and prayer,
    Much castigation, exercise devout;   35
    For here's a young and sweating devil here
    That commonly rebels. 'Tis a good hand,
    A frank one.

DESDEMONA: You may, indeed, say so;
    For 'twas that hand that gave away my heart.   40

OTHELLO: A liberal hand! The hearts of old gave hands;
    But our new heraldry° is hands, not hearts.

DESDEMONA: I cannot speak of this. Come now, your promise!

OTHELLO: What promise, chuck?

DESDEMONA: I have sent to bid Cassio come speak with you.   45

---

13 moved: Made proposals to.   **20 crusadoes:** Portuguese gold coins.   **25 humors:**
Inclinations.   **34 sequester:** Removal.   **42 heraldry:** Heraldic symbolism.

OTHELLO: I have a salt and sorry rheum° offends me.
   Lend me thy handkerchief.
DESDEMONA: Here, my lord.
OTHELLO: That which I gave you.
DESDEMONA: I have it not about me.
OTHELLO: Not?
DESDEMONA: No, faith, my lord.
OTHELLO: That's a fault.
   That handkerchief   50
   Did an Egyptian° to my mother give.
   She was a charmer,° and could almost read
   The thoughts of people. She told her, while she kept it,
   'Twould make her amiable° and subdue my father
   Entirely to her love; but if she lost it   55
   Or made a gift of it, my father's eye
   Should hold her loathèd, and his spirits should hunt
   After new fancies. She, dying, gave it me,
   And bid me, when my fate would have me wive;
   To give it her. I did so; and take heed on't;   60
   Make it a darling like your precious eye.
   To lose't or give't away were such perdition°
   As nothing else could match.
DESDEMONA: Is't possible?
OTHELLO: 'Tis true. There's magic in the web of it.
   A sibyl that had numb'red in the world   65
   The sun to course two hundred compasses,°
   In her prophetic fury sewed the work;
   The worms were hallowed that did breed the silk;
   And it was dyed in mummy° which the skillful
   Conserved of maidens' hearts.
DESDEMONA: I' faith? Is't true?   70
OTHELLO: Most veritable. Therefore look to't well.
DESDEMONA: Then would to God that I had never seen't!
OTHELLO: Ha! Wherefore?
DESDEMONA: Why do you speak so startingly and rash?
OTHELLO: Is't lost? Is't gone? Speak, is it out o' th' way?   75
DESDEMONA: Heaven bless us!
OTHELLO: Say you?
DESDEMONA: It is not lost. But what an if it were?
OTHELLO: How?
DESDEMONA: I say it is not lost.
OTHELLO: Fetch't, let me see't!   80

---

46 salt . . . rheum: Distressing head cold.   **51 Egyptian:** Gypsy.   **52 charmer:**
Sorceress.   **54 amiable:** Lovable.   **62 perdition:** Disaster.   **66 compasses:**
Annual rounds.   **69 mummy:** A drug made from mummies.

DESDEMONA: Why, so I can, sir; but I will not now.
   This is a trick to put° me from my suit:
   Pray you let Cassio be received again.
OTHELLO: Fetch me the handkerchief! My mind misgives.
DESDEMONA: Come, come!   85
   You'll never meet a more sufficient man.
OTHELLO: The handkerchief!
DESDEMONA: I pray talk me of Cassio.
OTHELLO: The handkerchief!
DESDEMONA: A man that all his time°
   Hath founded his good fortunes on your love,
   Shared dangers with you —   90
OTHELLO: The handkerchief!
DESDEMONA: I' faith, you are to blame.
OTHELLO: Zounds!   *Exit Othello.*
EMILIA: Is not this man jealous?
DESDEMONA: I ne'er saw this before.   95
   Sure there's some wonder in this handkerchief;
   I am most unhappy in the loss of it.
EMILIA: 'Tis not a year or two shows us a man.
   They are all but stomachs, and we all but food;
   They eat us hungerly, and when they are full,   100
   They belch us.

Enter Iago and Cassio.

          Look you — Cassio and my husband!
IAGO: There is no other way; 'tis she must do't.
   And lo the happiness!° Go and importune her.
DESDEMONA: How now, good Cassio? What's the news with you?
CASSIO: Madam, my former suit. I do beseech you   105
   That by your virtuous means I may again
   Exist, and be a member of his love
   Whom I with all the office of my heart
   Entirely honor. I would not be delayed.
   If my offense be of such mortal kind   110
   That neither service past, nor present sorrows,
   Nor purposed merit in futurity,
   Can ransom me into his love again,
   But to know so must be my benefit.
   So shall I clothe me in a forced content,   115
   And shut myself up in° some other course,
   To fortune's alms.
DESDEMONA: Alas, thrice-gentle Cassio!

---

82 put: Divert.   **88 all . . . time:** During his whole career.   **103 happiness:** Good
luck.   **116 shut myself up in:** Confine myself to.

My advocation° is not now in tune.
My lord is not my lord; nor should I know him,
Were he in favor° as in humor altered.   120
So help me every spirit sanctified
As I have spoken for you all my best
And stood within the blank° of his displeasure
For my free speech! You must a while be patient.
What I can do I will; and more I will   125
Than for myself I dare. Let that suffice you.

IAGO: Is my lord angry?

EMILIA: He went hence but now,
And certainly in strange unquietness.

IAGO: Can he be angry? I have seen the cannon
When it hath blown his ranks into the air   130
And, like the devil, from his very arm
Puffed his own brother — and is he angry?
Something of moment then. I will go meet him.
There's matter in't indeed if he be angry.

DESDEMONA: I prithee do so.   *Exit [Iago].*
                         Something sure of state,°   135
Either from Venice or some unhatched practice°
Made demonstrable here in Cyprus to him,
Hath puddled° his clear spirit; and in such cases
Men's natures wrangle with inferior things,
Though great ones are their object. 'Tis even so;   140
For let our finger ache, and it endues°
Our other, healthful members even to a sense
Of pain. Nay, we must think men are not gods,
Nor of them look for such observancy
As fits the bridal. Beshrew me much, Emilia,   145
I was, unhandsome warrior° as I am,
Arraigning his unkindness with my soul;°
But now I find I had suborned the witness,
And he's indicted falsely.

EMILIA: Pray heaven it be state matters, as you think,   150
And no conception nor no jealous toy°
Concerning you.

DESDEMONA: Alas the day! I never gave him cause.

EMILIA: But jealous souls will not be answered so;
They are not ever jealous for the cause,   155

---

118 advocation: Advocacy.   **120 favor:** Appearance.   **123 blank:** Bull's-eye of the
target.   **135 state:** Public affairs.   **136 unhatched practice:** Budding plot.   **138
puddled:** Muddied.   **141 endues:** Brings.   **146 unhandsome warrior:** Inadequate
soldier.   **147 Arraigning . . . soul:** Indicting his unkindness before the bar of my soul.
151 toy: Fancy.

But jealous for they're jealous. 'Tis a monster
Begot upon itself,° born on itself.
DESDEMONA: Heaven keep that monster from Othello's mind!
EMILIA: Lady, amen.
DESDEMONA: I will go seek him. Cassio, walk here about: 160
If I do find him fit, I'll move your suit
And seek to effect it to my uttermost.
CASSIO: I humbly thank your ladyship.

Exeunt Desdemona and Emilia.

Enter Bianca.

BIANCA: Save you, friend Cassio!
CASSIO: What make you from home?
How is't with you, my most fair Bianca?   165
I' faith, sweet love, I was coming to your house.
BIANCA: And I was going to your lodging, Cassio.
What, keep a week away? seven days and nights?
Eightscore eight hours? and lovers' absent hours,
More tedious than the dial° eightscore times?   170
O weary reck'ning!
CASSIO: Pardon me, Bianca:
I have this while with leaden thoughts been pressed;
But I shall in a more continuate° time
Strike off this score of absence. Sweet Bianca,

[Gives her Desdemona's handkerchief.]

Take me this work out.°
BIANCA: O Cassio, whence came this?   175
This is some token from a newer friend.
To the felt absence now I feel a cause.
Is't come to this? Well, well.
CASSIO: Go to, woman!
Throw your vile guesses in the devil's teeth,
From whence you have them. You are jealous now   180
That this is from some mistress, some remembrance.
No, by my faith, Bianca.
BIANCA: Why, whose is it?
CASSIO: I know not, sweet; I found it in my chamber.
I like the work° well; ere it be demanded,
As like enough it will, I'd have it copied.   185
Take it and do't, and leave me for this time.
BIANCA: Leave you? Wherefore?
CASSIO: I do attend here on the general

---

157 Begot ... itself: Self-engendered.   **170 dial:** Clock.   **173 continuate:** Uninter-
rupted.   **175 Take ... out:** Copy this embroidery for me.   **184 work:** Needlework.

And think it no addition, nor my wish,
To have him see me womaned.
BIANCA: Why, I pray you?   190
CASSIO: Not that I love you not.
BIANCA: But that you do not love me!
I pray you bring me on the way a little,
And say if I shall see you soon at night.
CASSIO: 'Tis but a little way that I can bring you,
For I attend here; but I'll see you soon.   195
BIANCA: 'Tis very good. I must be circumstanced.°   *Exeunt.*

[ACT IV, Scene I: The environs of the castle.]

Enter Othello and Iago.

IAGO: Will you think so?
OTHELLO: Think so, Iago?
IAGO: What,
      To kiss in private?
OTHELLO: An unauthorized kiss.
IAGO: Or to be naked with her friend in bed
      An hour or more, not meaning any harm?
OTHELLO: Naked in bed, Iago, and not mean harm?   5
      It is hypocrisy against the devil.°
      They that mean virtuously, and yet do so,
      The devil their virtue tempts, and they tempt heaven.
IAGO: So they do nothing, 'tis a venial slip.
      But if I give my wife a handkerchief —   10
OTHELLO: What then?
IAGO: Why, then 'tis hers, my lord; and being hers,
      She may, I think, bestow't on any man.
OTHELLO: She is protectress of her honor too;
      May she give that?   15
IAGO: Her honor is an essence that's not seen;
      They have it very oft that have it not.
      But for the handkerchief —
OTHELLO: By heaven, I would most gladly have forgot it!
      Thou said'st — O, it comes o'er my memory   20
      As doth the raven o'er the infected° house,
      Boding to all! — he had my handkerchief.
IAGO: Ay, what of that?
OTHELLO: That's not so good now.
IAGO: What

196 circumstanced: Governed by circumstances.   **Act IV, Scene I. 6 hypocrisy . . .
devil:** I.e., feigned sin instead of feigned virtue.   **21 infected:** Plague-stricken.

If I had said I had seen him do you wrong?
Or heard him say — as knaves be such abroad   25
Who having, by their own importunate suit,
Or voluntary dotage of some mistress,
Convincèd or supplied° them, cannot choose
But they must blab —
OTHELLO: Hath he said anything?
IAGO: He hath, my lord; but be you well assured,   30
No more than he'll unswear.
OTHELLO: What hath he said?
IAGO: Faith, that he did — I know not what he did.
OTHELLO: What? what?
IAGO: Lie —
OTHELLO: With her?
IAGO: With her, on her; what you will.   35
OTHELLO: Lie with her? lie on her? — We say lie on her when they belie her. —
Lie with her! Zounds, that's fulsome. — Handkerchief — confessions —
handkerchief! — To confess, and be hanged for his labor — first to be
hanged, and then to confess! I tremble at it. Nature would not invest herself
in such shadowing passion without some instruction.° It is not words that   40
shakes me thus. — Pish! Noses, ears, and lips? Is't possible? — Confess? —
Handkerchief? — O devil!

(Falls in a trance.)

IAGO: Work on,
My med'cine, work! Thus credulous fools are caught,
And many worthy and chaste dames even thus,   45
All guiltless, meet reproach. — What, ho! my lord!
My lord, I say! Othello!
Enter Cassio.   How now, Cassio?
CASSIO: What's the matter?
IAGO: My lord is fall'n into an epilepsy.
This is his second fit; he had one yesterday.   50
CASSIO: Rub him about the temples.
IAGO: No, forbear.
The lethargy° must have his quiet course.
If not, he foams at mouth, and by and by
Breaks out to savage madness. Look, he stirs.
Do you withdraw yourself a little while.   55
He will recover straight. When he is gone,
I would on great occasion speak with you.   *[Exit Cassio.]*
How is it, general? Have you not hurt your head?
OTHELLO: Dost thou mock me?

---

28 Convincèd or supplied: Overcome or gratified.   **39–40 Nature . . . instruction:**
My natural faculties would not be so overcome by passion without reason.   **52 lethargy:**
Coma.

IAGO: I mock you? No, by heaven.
    Would you would bear your fortune like a man!   60
OTHELLO: A hornèd man's° a monster and a beast.
IAGO: There's many a beast then in a populous city,
    And many a civil monster.
OTHELLO: Did he confess it?
IAGO: Good sir, be a man.
    Think every bearded fellow that's but yoked   65
    May draw with you. There's millions now alive
    That nightly lie in those unproper° beds
    Which they dare swear peculiar:° your case is better.
    O, 'tis the spite of hell, the fiend's arch-mock,
    To lip a wanton in a secure° couch,   70
    And to suppose her chaste! No, let me know;
    And knowing what I am, I know what she shall be.
OTHELLO: O, thou art wise! 'Tis certain.
IAGO: Stand you awhile apart;
    Confine yourself but in a patient list.°
    Whilst you were here, o'erwhelmèd with your grief —   75
    A passion most unsuiting such a man —
    Cassio came hither. I shifted him away
    And laid good 'scuse upon your ecstasy;°
    Bade him anon return, and here speak with me;
    The which he promised. Do but encave° yourself   80
    And mark the fleers, the gibes, and notable scorns
    That dwell in every region of his face;
    For I will make him tell the tale anew —
    Where, how, how oft, how long ago, and when
    He hath, and is again to cope° your wife.   85
    I say, but mark his gesture. Marry, patience!
    Or I shall say y'are all in all in spleen,°
    And nothing of a man.
OTHELLO: Dost thou hear, Iago?
    I will be found most cunning in my patience;
    But — dost thou hear? — most bloody.
IAGO: That's not amiss: 90
    But yet keep time in all. Will you withdraw?

                                [Othello retires.]

    Now will I question Cassio of Bianca,
    A huswife° that by selling her desires
    Buys herself bread and clothes. It is a creature

---

61 hornèd man: Cuckold.   **67 unproper:** Not exclusively their own.   **68 peculiar:**
Exclusively their own.   **70 secure:** Free from fear of rivalry.   **74 in a patient list:** With-
in the limits of self-control.   **78 ecstasy:** Trance.   **80 encave:** Conceal.   **85 cope:**
Meet.   **87 all in all in spleen:** Wholly overcome by your passion.   **93 huswife:** Hussy.

That dotes on Cassio, as 'tis the strumpet's plague   95
To beguile many and be beguiled by one.
He, when he hears of her, cannot refrain
From the excess of laughter. Here he comes.

Enter Cassio.

As he shall smile, Othello shall go mad;
And his unbookish° jealousy must conster°   100
Poor Cassio's smiles, gestures, and light behavior
Quite in the wrong. How do you now, lieutenant?
CASSIO: The worser that you give me the addition°
Whose want even kills me.
IAGO: Ply Desdemona well, and you are sure on't.   105
Now, if this suit lay in Bianca's power,
How quickly should you speed!
CASSIO: Alas, poor caitiff!°
OTHELLO: Look how he laughs already!
IAGO: I never knew a woman love man so.
CASSIO: Alas, poor rogue! I think, i' faith, she loves me.   110
OTHELLO: Now he denies it faintly, and laughs it out.
IAGO: Do you hear, Cassio?
OTHELLO: Now he importunes him
To tell it o'er. Go to! Well said, well said!
IAGO: She gives out that you shall marry her.
Do you intend it?   115
CASSIO: Ha, ha, ha!
OTHELLO: Do you triumph, Roman? Do you triumph?
CASSIO: I marry her? What, a customer?° Prithee bear some charity to my wit;
do not think it so unwholesome. Ha, ha, ha!
OTHELLO: So, so, so, so! They laugh that win!   120
IAGO: Faith, the cry goes that you shall marry her.
CASSIO: Prithee say true.
IAGO: I am a very villain else.
OTHELLO: Have you scored me?° Well.
CASSIO: This is the monkey's own giving out. She is persuaded I will marry   125
her out of her own love and flattery, not out of my promise.
OTHELLO: Iago beckons° me; now he begins the story.
CASSIO: She was here even now; she haunts me in every place. I was t' other
day talking on the sea bank with certain Venetians, and thither comes the
bauble,° and, by this hand, she falls me thus about my neck —   130
OTHELLO: Crying "O dear Cassio!" as it were. His gesture imports it.
CASSIO: So hangs, and lolls, and weeps upon me; so shakes and pulls me! Ha,
ha, ha!

---

100 unbookish: Uninstructed;   **conster:** Construe, interpret.   **103 addition:** Title.
107 caitiff: Wretch.   **118 customer:** Prostitute.   **124 scored me:** Settled my account (?).   **127 beckons:** Signals.   **130 bauble:** Plaything.

OTHELLO: Now he tells how she plucked him to my chamber. O, I see that nose
of yours, but not that dog I shall throw it to.   135

CASSIO: Well, I must leave her company.

Enter Bianca.

IAGO: Before me! Look where she comes.

CASSIO: 'Tis such another fitchew!° marry, a perfumed one. What do you
mean by this haunting of me?

BIANCA: Let the devil and his dam haunt you! What did you mean by that   140
same handkerchief you gave me even now? I was a fine fool to take it. I
must take out the whole work? A likely piece of work that you should find it
in your chamber and know not who left it there! This is some minx's token,
and I must take out the work? There! Give it your hobby-horse.° Whereso-
ever you had it, I'll take out no work on't.   145

CASSIO: How now, my sweet Bianca? How now? how now?

OTHELLO: By heaven, that should be my handkerchief!

BIANCA: An you'll come to supper to-night, you may; an you will not, come
when you are next prepared for.   *Exit.*

IAGO: After her, after her!   150

CASSIO: Faith, I must; she'll rail in the street else.

IAGO: Will you sup there?

CASSIO: Yes, I intend so.

IAGO: Well, I may chance to see you; for I would very fain speak with you.

CASSIO: Prithee come. Will you?   155

IAGO: Go to! say no more.   *Exit Cassio.*

OTHELLO *[comes forward]*:   How shall I murder him, Iago?

IAGO: Did you perceive how he laughed at his vice?°

OTHELLO: O Iago!

IAGO: And did you see the handkerchief?   160

OTHELLO: Was that mine?

IAGO: Your, by this hand! And to see how he prizes° the foolish woman your
wife! She gave it him, and he hath giv'n it his whore.

OTHELLO: I would have him nine years a-killing — A fine woman! a fair
woman! a sweet woman!   165

IAGO: Nay, you must forget that.

OTHELLO: Ay, let her rot, and perish, and be damned to-night; for she shall not
live. No, my heart is turned to stone; I strike it, and it hurts my hand. O, the
world hath not a sweeter creature! She might lie by an emperor's side and
command him tasks.   170

IAGO: Nay, that's not your way.

OTHELLO: Hang her! I do but say what she is. So delicate with her needle! an
admirable musician! O, she will sing the savageness out of a bear! Of so
high and plenteous wit and invention° —

---

138 fitchew: Polecat (slang for whore).   **144 hobby-horse:** Harlot.   **158 vice:** I.e., vicious conduct.   **162 prizes:** Values.   **174 invention:** Imagination.

IAGO: She's the worse for all this.   175

OTHELLO: O, a thousand thousand times! And then, of so gentle a condition!°

IAGO: Ay, too gentle.

OTHELLO: Nay, that's certain. But yet the pity of it, Iago! O Iago, the pity of it, Iago!

IAGO: If you are so fond over her iniquity, give her patent° to offend; for if it   180
touch not you, it comes near nobody.

OTHELLO: I will chop her into messes! Cuckold me!

IAGO: O, 'tis foul in her.

OTHELLO: With mine officer!

IAGO: That's fouler.   185

OTHELLO: Get me some poison, Iago, this night. I'll not expostulate with her,
lest her body and beauty unprovide° my mind again. This night, Iago!

IAGO: Do it not with poison. Strangle her in her bed, even the bed she hath
contaminated.

OTHELLO: Good, good! The justice of it pleases. Very good!   190

IAGO: And for Cassio, let me be his undertaker;° you shall hear more by
midnight.

OTHELLO: Excellent good!

A trumpet.

What trumpet is that same?

IAGO: I warrant something from Venice.

Enter Lodovico, Desdemona, and Attendants.

'Tis Lodovico.   195
This comes from the Duke; and see, your wife is with him.

LODOVICO: God save you, worthy general!

OTHELLO: With all my heart, sir.

LODOVICO: The Duke and senators of Venice greet you.

[Gives him a letter.]

OTHELLO: I kiss the instrument of their pleasures.

[Opens the letter and reads.]

DESDEMONA: And what's the news, good cousin Lodovico?   200

IAGO: I am very glad to see you, signior.
Welcome to Cyprus.

LODOVICO: I thank you. How does Lieutenant Cassio?

IAGO: Lives, sir.

DESDEMONA: Cousin, there's fall'n between him and my lord
An unkind breach; but you shall make all well.   205

OTHELLO: Are you sure of that?

DESDEMONA: My lord?

OTHELLO [*reads*]:   "This fail you not to do, as you will —"

---

176 condition: Disposition.   **180 patent:** License.   **187 unprovide:** Disarm.
191 be his undertaker: Undertake to deal with him.

LODOVICO: He did not call; he's busy in the paper.
    Is there division 'twixt thy lord and Cassio?   210
DESDEMONA: A most unhappy one. I would do much
    T' atone° them, for the love I bear to Cassio.
OTHELLO: Fire and brimstone!
DESDEMONA: My lord?
OTHELLO: Are you wise?
DESDEMONA: What, is he angry?
LODOVICO: May be the letter moved him;
    For, as I think, they do command him home,   215
    Deputing Cassio in his government.
DESDEMONA: By my troth, I am glad on't.
OTHELLO: Indeed?
DESDEMONA: My lord?
OTHELLO: I am glad to see you mad.°
DESDEMONA: Why, sweet Othello —
OTHELLO: Devil!

[Strikes her.]

DESDEMONA: I have not deserved this.   220
LODOVICO: My lord, this would not be believed in Venice,
    Though I should swear I saw't. 'Tis very much.
    Make her amends; she weeps.
OTHELLO: O devil, devil!
    If that the earth could teem° with woman's tears,
    Each drop she falls would prove a crocodile.°   225
    Out of my sight!
DESDEMONA: I will not stay to offend you.   *[Going.]*
LODOVICO: Truly, an obedient lady.
    I do beseech your lordship call her back.
OTHELLO: Mistress!
DESDEMONA: My lord?
OTHELLO: What would you with her, sir?   230
LODOVICO: Who? I, my lord?
OTHELLO: Ay! You did wish that I would make her turn.
    Sir, she can turn, and turn, and yet go on
    And turn again; and she can weep, sir, weep;
    And she's obedient; as you say, obedient,   235
    Very obedient. — Proceed you in your tears. —
    Concerning this, sir — O well-painted passion!° —
    I am commanded home. — Get you away;
    I'll send for you anon. — Sir, I obey the mandate
    And will return to Venice. — Hence, avaunt!   240

---

212 atone: Reconcile.   **218 mad:** I.e., waggish.   **224 teem:** Breed.   **225 crocodile:** Crocodiles were supposed to shed hypocritical tears to lure men to destruction.   **237 passion:** Grief.

[Exit Desdemona.]

Cassio shall have my place. And, sir, to-night
I do entreat that we may sup together.
You are welcome, sir, to Cyprus — Goats and monkeys!

Exit.

LODOVICO: Is this the noble Moor whom our full Senate
    Call all in all sufficient? Is this the nature   245
    Whom passion could not shake? whose solid virtue
    The shot of accident nor dart of chance
    Could neither graze nor pierce?
IAGO: He is much changed.
LODOVICO: Are his wits safe? Is he not light of brain?
IAGO: He's that he is; I may not breathe my censure.   250
    What he might be — if what he might he is not —
    I would to heaven he were!
LODOVICO: What, strike his wife?
IAGO: Faith, that was not so well; yet would I knew
    That stroke would prove the worst!
LODOVICO: Is it his use?°
    Or did the letters work upon his blood   255
    And new-create this fault?
IAGO: Alas, alas!
    It is not honesty in me to speak
    What I have seen and known. You shall observe him,
    And his own courses will denote him so
    That I may save my speech. Do but go after   260
    And mark how he continues.
LODOVICO: I am sorry that I am deceived in him.   *Exeunt.*

[Scene II: Within the castle.]

Enter Othello and Emilia.

OTHELLO: You have seen nothing then?
EMILIA: Nor ever heard, nor ever did suspect.
OTHELLO: Yes, you have seen Cassio and she together.
EMILIA: But then I saw no harm, and then I heard
    Each syllable that breath made up between them.   5
OTHELLO: What, did they never whisper?
EMILIA: Never, my lord.
OTHELLO: Nor send you out o' th' way?
EMILIA: Never.
OTHELLO: To fetch her fan, her gloves, her mask, nor nothing?

254 use: Custom.

EMILIA: Never, my lord.   10
OTHELLO: That's strange.
EMILIA: I durst, my lord, to wager she is honest,
    Lay down my soul at stake. If you think other,
    Remove your thought; it doth abuse your bosom.°
    If any wretch have put this in your head,   15
    Let heaven requite it with the serpent's curse!°
    For if she be not honest, chaste, and true,
    There's no man happy; the purest of their wives
    Is foul as slander.
OTHELLO: Bid her come hither. Go.   *Exit Emilia.*
    She says enough; yet she's a simple bawd   20
    That cannot say as much. This is a subtle whore,
    A closet lock and key of villainous secrets;
    And yet she'll kneel and pray; I have seen her do't.

Enter Desdemona and Emilia.

DESDEMONA: My lord, what is your will?
OTHELLO: Pray, chuck, come hither.
DESDEMONA: What is your pleasure?
OTHELLO: Let me see your eyes.   25
    Look in my face.
DESDEMONA: What horrible fancy's this?
OTHELLO *[to Emilia]*:   Some of your function, mistress.
    Leave procreants° alone and shut the door;
    Cough or cry hem if anybody come.
    Your mystery, your mystery!° Nay, dispatch!   30
                                     Exit Emilia.

DESDEMONA: Upon my knees, what doth your speech import?
    I understand a fury in your words,
    [But not the words.]
OTHELLO: Why, what art thou?
DESDEMONA: Your wife, my lord; your true
    And loyal wife.
OTHELLO: Come, swear it, damn thyself;   35
    Lest, being like one of heaven,° the devils themselves
    Should fear to seize thee. Therefore be double-damned —
    Swear thou art honest.°
DESDEMONA: Heaven doth truly know it.
OTHELLO: Heaven truly knows that thou art false as hell.
DESDEMONA: To whom, my lord? With whom? How am I false?   40
OTHELLO: Ah, Desdemona! away! away! away!

SCENE II. **14 abuse . . . bosom:** Deceive your heart. **16 serpent's curse:** (cf. Genesis 3:14). **28 procreants:** Mating couples. **30 mystery:** Trade, occupation. **36 being . . . heaven:** Looking like an angel. **38 honest:** Chaste.

DESDEMONA: Alas the heavy day! Why do you weep?
    Am I the motive of these tears, my lord?
    If haply you my father do suspect
    An instrument° of this your calling back,   45
    Lay not your blame on me. If you have lost him,
    Why, I have lost him too.
OTHELLO: Had it pleased heaven
    To try me with affliction, had they rained
    All kinds of sores and shames on my bare head,
    Steeped me in poverty to the very lips,   50
    Given to captivity me and my utmost hopes,
    I should have found in some place of my soul
    A drop of patience. But, alas, to make me
    A fixèd figure for the time of scorn°
    To point his slow unmoving finger at!   55
    Yet could I bear that too; well, very well.
    But there where I have garnered up my heart,
    Where either I must live or bear no life,
    The fountain from the which my current runs
    Or else dries up — to be discarded thence,   60
    Or keep it as a cistern for foul toads
    To knot and gender in — turn thy complexion there,°
    Patience, thou young and rose-lipped cherubin!
    Ay, there look grim as hell!
DESDEMONA: I hope my noble lord esteems me honest.   65
OTHELLO: O, ay; as summer flies are in the shambles,°
    That quicken° even with blowing. O thou weed,
    Who art so lovely fair, and smell'st so sweet,
    That the sense aches at thee, would thou hadst ne'er been born!
DESDEMONA: Alas, what ignorant sin have I committed?   70
OTHELLO: Was this fair paper, this most goodly book,
    Made to write "whore" upon? What committed?
    Committed? O thou public commoner!°
    I should make very forges of my cheeks
    That would to cinders burn up modesty,   75
    Did I but speak thy deeds. What committed?
    Heaven stops the nose at it, and the moon winks;°
    The bawdy wind, that kisses all it meets,
    Is hushed within the hollow mine of earth
    And will not hear it. What committed?   80
    Impudent strumpet!
DESDEMONA: By heaven, you do me wrong!

---

45 An instrument: To be the cause.   **54 time of scorn:** Scornful world.   **62 turn thy complexion there:** Change your color at that point.   **66 shambles:** Slaughterhouse. **67 quicken:** Come to life.   **73 commoner:** Harlot.   **77 winks:** Closes her eyes.

OTHELLO: Are not you a strumpet?

DESDEMONA: No, as I am a Christian!
    If to preserve this vessel for my lord
    From any other foul unlawful touch
    Be not to be a strumpet, I am none.   85

OTHELLO: What, not a whore?

DESDEMONA: No, as I shall be saved!

OTHELLO: Is't possible?

DESDEMONA: O, heaven forgive us!

OTHELLO: I cry you mercy° then.
    I took you for that cunning whore of Venice
    That married with Othello. — *[Calling.]* You, mistress,   90
    That have the office opposite to Saint Peter
    And keep the gate of hell!

Enter Emilia.

                    You, you, ay, you!
    We have done our course; there's money for your pains:
    I pray you turn the key, and keep our counsel.   *Exit.*

EMILIA: Alas, what does this gentleman conceive?   95
    How do you, madam? How do you, my good lady?

DESDEMONA: Faith, half asleep.°

EMILIA: Good madam, what's the matter with my lord?

DESDEMONA: With who?

EMILIA: Why, with my lord, madam.   100

DESDEMONA: Who is thy lord?

EMILIA: He that is yours, sweet lady.

DESDEMONA: I have none. Do not talk to me, Emilia.
    I cannot weep; nor answer have I none
    But what should go by water. Prithee to-night
    Lay on my bed my wedding sheets, remember;   105
    And call thy husband hither.

EMILIA: Here's a change indeed!   *Exit.*

DESDEMONA: 'Tis meet I should be used so, very meet.
    How have I been behaved, that he might stick
    The small'st opinion° on my least misuse?°

Enter Iago and Emilia.

IAGO: What is your pleasure, madam? How is't with you?   110

DESDEMONA: I cannot tell. Those that do teach young babes
    Do it with gentle means and easy tasks:
    He might have chid me so; for, in good faith,
    I am a child to chiding.

IAGO: What is the matter, lady?

---

88 cry you mercy: Beg your pardon.   **97 half asleep:** I.e., stunned.   **109 small'st opinion:** Least suspicion;   **least misuse:** Slightest misconduct.

EMILIA: Alas, Iago, my lord hath so bewhored her,   115
　　　Thrown such despite and heavy terms upon her
　　　As true hearts cannot bear.
DESDEMONA: Am I that name, Iago?
IAGO: What name, fair lady?
DESDEMONA: Such as she said my lord did say I was.
EMILIA: He called her whore. A beggar in his drink   120
　　　Could not have laid such terms upon his callet.°
IAGO: Why did he so?
DESDEMONA: I do not know; I am sure I am none such.
IAGO: Do not weep, do not weep. Alas the day!
EMILIA: Hath she forsook so many noble matches,   125
　　　Her father and her country, and her friends,
　　　To be called whore? Would it not make one weep?
DESDEMONA: It is my wretched fortune.
IAGO: Beshrew him for't!
　　　How comes this trick° upon him?
DESDEMONA: Nay, heaven doth know.
EMILIA: I will be hanged if some eternal villain,   130
　　　Some busy and insinuating rogue,
　　　Some cogging, cozening° slave, to get some office,
　　　Have not devised this slander. I'll be hanged else.
IAGO: Fie, there is no such man! It is impossible.
DESDEMONA: If any such there be, heaven pardon him!   135
EMILIA: A halter pardon him! and hell gnaw his bones!
　　　Why should he call her whore? Who keeps her company?
　　　What place? what time? what form? what likelihood?
　　　The Moor 's abused by some most villainous knave,
　　　Some base notorious knave, some scurvy fellow.   140
　　　O heaven, that such companions° thou 'dst unfold,°
　　　And put in every honest hand a whip
　　　To lash the rascals naked through the world
　　　Even from the east to th' west!
IAGO: Speak within door.°
EMILIA: O, fie upon them! Some such squire he was   145
　　　That turned your wit the seamy side without
　　　And made you to suspect me with the Moor.
IAGO: You are a fool. Go to.
DESDEMONA: Alas, Iago,
　　　What shall I do to win my lord again?
　　　Good friend, go to him; for, by this light of heaven,   150
　　　I know not how I lost him. Here I kneel:

---

121 callet: Whore.   **129 trick:** Freakish behavior.   **132 cogging, cozening:** Cheating, defrauding.   **141 companions:** Rogues;   **unfold:** Expose.   **144 within door:** With restraint.

If e'er my will did trespass 'gainst his love
Either in discourse° of thought or actual deed,
Or that mine eyes, mine ears, or any sense
Delighted them in any other form,   155
Or that I do not yet, and ever did,
And ever will (though he do shake me off
To beggarly divorcement) love him dearly,
Comfort forswear° me! Unkindness may do much;
And his unkindness may defeat° my life,   160
But never taint my love. I cannot say "whore."
It does abhor me now I speak the word;
To do the act that might the addition earn
Not the world's mass of vanity could make me.
IAGO: I pray you be content. 'Tis but his humor.   165
  The business of the state does him offense,
  [And he does chide with you.]
DESDEMONA: If 'twere no other —
IAGO: 'Tis but so, I warrant.

[Trumpets within.]

  Hark how these instruments summon you to supper.
  The messengers of Venice stay the meat: 170
  Go in, and weep not. All things shall be well.
                              Exeunt Desdemona and Emilia.

Enter Roderigo.

  How now, Roderigo?
RODERIGO: I do not find that thou deal'st justly with me.
IAGO: What in the contrary?
RODERIGO: Every day thou daff'st me with some device,° Iago, and rather, as it   175
  seems to me now, keep'st from me all conveniency° than suppliest me with
  the least advantage of hope. I will indeed no longer endure it; nor am I yet
  persuaded to put up in peace what already I have foolishly suffered.
IAGO: Will you hear me, Roderigo?
RODERIGO: Faith, I have heard too much; for your words and performances are   180
  no kin together.
IAGO: You charge me most unjustly.
RODERIGO: With naught but truth. I have wasted myself out of my means. The
  jewels you have had from me to deliver to Desdemona would half have
  corrupted a votarist.° You have told me she hath received them, and   185
  returned me expectations and comforts of sudden respect° and acquaintance; but I find none.

---

153 discourse: Course.   **159 Comfort forswear:** Happiness forsake.   **160 defeat:** Destroy.   **175 thou . . . device:** You put me off with some trick.   **176 conveniency:** Favorable opportunities.   **185 votarist:** Nun.   **186 sudden respect:** Immediate notice.

IAGO: Well, go to; very well.

RODERIGO: Very well! go to! I cannot go to, man; nor 'tis not very well. By this
 hand, I say 'tis very scurvy, and begin to find myself fopped° in it.   190

IAGO: Very well.

RODERIGO: I tell you 'tis not very well. I will make myself known to Desdemona.
 If she will return me my jewels, I will give over my suit and repent my unlawful solicitation; if not, assure yourself I will seek satisfaction of you.

IAGO: You have said now.   195

RODERIGO: Ay, and said nothing but what I protest intendment of doing.

IAGO: Why, now I see there's mettle in thee; and even from this instant do
 build on thee a better opinion than ever before. Give me thy hand,
 Roderigo. Thou has taken against me a most just exception; but yet I
 protest I have dealt most directly° in thy affair.   200

RODERIGO: It hath not appeared.

IAGO: I grant indeed it hath not appeared, and your suspicion is not without
 wit and judgment. But, Roderigo, if thou hast that in thee indeed which I
 have greater reason to believe now than ever, I mean purpose, courage,
 and valor, this night show it. If thou the next night following enjoy not   205
 Desdemona, take me from this world with treachery and devise engines
 for° my life.

RODERIGO: Well, what is it? Is it within reason and compass?

IAGO: Sir, there is especial commission come from Venice to depute Cassio in
 Othello's place.   210

RODERIGO: Is that true? Why, then Othello and Desdemona return again to
 Venice.

IAGO: O, no; he goes into Mauritania and takes away with him the fair Desdemona, unless his abode be lingered here° by some accident; wherein none
 can be so determinate° as the removing of Cassio.   215

RODERIGO: How do you mean removing of him?

IAGO: Why, by making him uncapable of Othello's place — knocking out his
 brains.

RODERIGO: And that you would have me to do?

IAGO: Ay, if you dare do yourself a profit and a right. He sups to-night with a 220
 harlotry, and thither will I go to him. He knows not yet of his honorable
 fortune. If you will watch his going thence, which I will fashion to fall out
 between twelve and one, you may take him at your pleasure. I will be near
 to second your attempt, and he shall fall between us. Come, stand not
 amazed at it, but go along with me. I will show you such a necessity in his   225
 death that you shall think yourself bound to put it on him. It is now high
 supper time, and the night grows to waste. About it!

RODERIGO: I will hear further reason for this.

IAGO: And you shall be satisfied.   *Exeunt.*

---

190 fopped: Duped.   **200 directly:** Straightforwardly.   **207 engines for:** Plots against.
214 abode . . . here: Stay here be extended.   **215 determinate:** Effective.

[Scene III: Within the castle.]

Enter Othello, Lodovico, Desdemona, Emilia, and Attendants.

LODOVICO: I do beseech you, sir, trouble yourself no further.

OTHELLO: O, pardon me; 'twill do me good to walk.

LODOVICO: Madam, good night. I humbly thank your ladyship.

DESDEMONA: Your honor is most welcome.

OTHELLO: Will you walk, sir?

O, Desdemona —   5

DESDEMONA: My lord?

OTHELLO: Get you to bed on th' instant; I will be returned forthwith. Dismiss
your attendant there. Look't be done.

DESDEMONA: I will, my lord.

Exit [Othello, with Lodovico and Attendants].

EMILIA: How goes it now? He looks gentler than he did.   10

DESDEMONA: He says he will return incontinent.°

He hath commanded me to go to bed,

And bade me to dismiss you.

EMILIA: Dismiss me?

DESDEMONA: It was his bidding; therefore, good Emilia,

Give me my nightly wearing, and adieu.   15

We must not now displease him.

EMILIA: I would you had never seen him!

DESDEMONA: So would not I. My love doth so approve him

That even his stubbornness,° his checks,° his frowns —

Prithee unpin me — have grace and favor in them.   20

EMILIA: I have laid those sheets you bade me on the bed.

DESDEMONA: All's one. Good faith, how foolish are our minds!

If I do die before thee, prithee shroud me

In one of those same sheets.

EMILIA: Come, come! You talk.

DESDEMONA: My mother had a maid called Barbary.   25

She was in love; and he she loved proved mad°

And did forsake her. She had a song of "Willow";

An old thing 'twas; but it expressed her fortune,

And she died singing it. That song to-night

Will not go from my mind; I have much to do   30

But to go hang my head all at one side

And sing it like poor Barbary. Prithee dispatch.

EMILIA: Shall I go fetch your nightgown?°

DESDEMONA: No, unpin me here.

This Lodovico is a proper man.

SCENE III.   **11 incontinent:** At once.   **19 stubbornness:** Roughness;   **checks:** Rebukes.   **26 mad:** Wild, faithless.   **33 nightgown:** Dressing gown.

EMILIA: A very handsome man.   35
DESDEMONA: He speaks well.
EMILIA: I know a lady in Venice would have walked barefoot to Palestine for a
    touch of his nether lip.
DESDEMONA *(sings)*:   "The poor soul sat sighing by a sycamore tree
          Sing all a green willow;   40
      Her hand on her bosom, her head on her knee,
          Sing willow, willow, willow.
      The fresh streams ran by her and murmured her moans;
          Sing willow, willow, willow;
      Her salt tears fell from her, and soft'ned the stones" —   45
  Lay by these.

      "Sing willow, willow, willow" —
  Prithee hie thee;° he'll come anon.
      "Sing all a green willow must be my garland.
      Let nobody blame him; his scorn I approve" —   50
  Nay, that's not next. Hark! who is't that knocks?
EMILIA: It's the wind.
DESDEMONA *(sings)*:   "I call my love false love; but what said he then?
      "Sing willow, willow, willow" —
      If I court moe women, you'll couch with moe men."   55
  So get thee gone; good night. Mine eyes do itch.
  Doth that bode weeping?
EMILIA: 'Tis neither here nor there.
DESDEMONA: I have heard it said so. O, these men, these men!
  Dost thou in conscience think — tell me, Emilia —
  That there be women do abuse their husbands   60
  In such gross kind?
EMILIA: There be some such, no question.
DESDEMONA: Wouldst thou do such a deed for all the world?
EMILIA: Why, would not you?
DESDEMONA: No, by this heavenly light!
EMILIA: Nor I neither by this heavenly light.
  I might do't as well i' th' dark.   65
DESDEMONA: Wouldst thou do such a deed for all the world?
EMILIA: The world's a huge thing; it is a great price for a small vice.
DESDEMONA: In troth, I think thou wouldst not.
EMILIA: In troth, I think I should; and undo't when I had done it. Marry, I
    would not do such a thing for a joint-ring,° nor for measures of lawn, nor   70
    for gowns, petticoats, nor caps, nor any petty exhibition;° but, for all the
    whole world — 'Ud's pity! who would not make her husband a cuckold to
    make him a monarch? I should venture purgatory for't.
DESDEMONA: Beshrew me if I would do such a wrong

48 hie thee: Hurry.   **70 joint-ring:** Ring made in separable halves.   **71 exhibition:**
Gift.

For the whole world.   75

EMILIA: Why, the wrong is but a wrong i' th' world; and having the world
for your labor, 'tis a wrong in your own world, and you might quickly make
it right.

DESDEMONA: I do not think there is any such woman.

EMILIA: Yes, a dozen; and as many to th' vantage° as   80
would store° the world they played for.
But I do think it is their husbands' faults
If wives do fall. Say that they slack their duties
And pour our treasures into foreign laps;
Or else break out in peevish° jealousies,   85
Throwing restraint upon us; or say they strike us,
Or scant our former having° in despite —
Why, we have galls;° and though we have some grace,
Yet have we some revenge. Let husbands know
Their wives have sense like them. They see, and smell,   90
And have their palates both for sweet and sour,
As husbands have. What is it that they do
When they change us for others? Is it sport?
I think it is. And doth affection breed it?
I think it doth. Is't frailty that thus errs?   95
It is so too. And have not we affections,
Desires for sport, and frailty, as men have?
Then let them use us well; else let them know,
The ills we do, their ills instruct us so.

DESDEMONA: Good night, good night. God me such usage° send,   100
Not to pick bad from bad, but by bad mend!   *Exeunt.*

[ACT V, Scene I: A street in Cyprus]

Enter Iago and Roderigo.

IAGO: Here, stand behind this bulk;° straight will he come.
Wear thy good rapier bare, and put it home.
Quick, quick! Fear nothing; I'll be at thy elbow.
It makes us, or it mars us — think on that,
And fix most firm thy resolution.   5

RODERIGO: Be near at hand; I may miscarry in't.

IAGO: Here, at thy hand. Be bold, and take thy stand.

[Stands aside.]

RODERIGO: I have no great devotion to the deed,
And yet he hath given me satisfying reasons.

80 to th' vantage: Besides. **81 store:** Populate. **85 peevish:** Senseless. **87 having:**
Allowance. **88 galls:** Spirits to resent. **100 usage:** Habits. ACT V, SCENE I. **1 bulk:**
Projecting shop-front.

'Tis but a man gone. Forth my sword! He dies!   10

IAGO: I have rubbed this young quat° almost to the sense,°
    And he grows angry. Now whether he kill Cassio,
    Or Cassio him, or each do kill the other,
    Every way makes my gain. Live Roderigo,
    He calls me to a restitution large   15
    Of gold and jewels that I bobbed° from him
    As gifts to Desdemona.
    It must not be. If Cassio do remain,
    He hath a daily beauty in his life
    That makes me ugly; and besides, the Moor   20
    May unfold me to him; there stand I in much peril.
    No, he must die. Be't so! I hear him coming.

Enter Cassio.

RODERIGO: I know his gait. 'Tis he. Villain, thou diest!

[Makes a pass at Cassio.]

CASSIO: That thrust had been mine enemy indeed
    But that my coat° is better than thou know'st.   25
    I will make proof of thine.

[Draws, and wounds Roderigo.]

RODERIGO: O, I am slain!

[Iago darts from concealment behind Cassio, wounds him in the leg, and exit.]

CASSIO: I am maimed for ever. Help, ho! Murder! murder!

[Falls.]

Enter Othello.

OTHELLO: The voice of Cassio. Iago keeps his word.
RODERIGO: O, villain that I am!
OTHELLO: It is even so.
CASSIO: O, help, ho! light! a surgeon!   30
OTHELLO: 'Tis he. O brave Iago, honest and just,
    That hast such noble sense of thy friend's wrong!
    Thou teachest me. Minion,° your dear lies dead,
    And your unblest fate hies.° Strumpet, I come.
    Forth of my heart those charms, thine eyes, are blotted.   35
    Thy bed, lust-stained, shall with lust's blood be spotted.

                                              Exit Othello.

Enter Lodovico and Gratiano.

CASSIO: What, ho? No watch? No passage?° Murder! murder!
GRATIANO: 'Tis some mischance. The cry is very direful.

11 quat: Pimple; **sense:** Quick.   **16 bobbed:** Swindled.   **25 coat:** Undershirt of
mail.   **33 Minion:** Mistress.   **34 hies:** Hurries on.   **37 passage:** Passersby.

CASSIO: O, help!

LODOVICO: Hark!   40

RODERIGO: O wretched villain!

LODOVICO: Two or three groan. It is a heavy° night.

    These may be counterfeits. Let's think't unsafe

    To come in to the cry without more help.

RODERIGO: Nobody come? Then shall I bleed to death.   45

LODOVICO: Hark!

Enter Iago, with a light.

GRATIANO: Here's one comes in his shirt, with light and weapons.

IAGO: Who's there? Whose noise is this that cries on° murder?

LODOVICO: We do not know.

IAGO: Did not you hear a cry?

CASSIO: Here, here! For heaven's sake, help me!

IAGO: What's the matter?   50

GRATIANO: This is Othello's ancient, as I take it.

LODOVICO: The same indeed, a very valiant fellow.

IAGO: What are you here that cry so grievously?

CASSIO: Iago? O, I am spoiled, undone by villains!

    Give me some help.   55

IAGO: O me, lieutenant! What villains have done this?

CASSIO: I think that one of them is hereabout

    And cannot make° away.

IAGO: O treacherous villains!

[To Lodovico and Gratiano.]

    What are you there? Come in, and give some help.

RODERIGO: O, help me here!   60

CASSIO: That's one of them.

IAGO: O murd'rous slave! O villain!

[Stabs Roderigo.]

RODERIGO: O damned Iago! O inhuman dog!

IAGO: Kill men i' th' dark? — Where be these bloody thieves? —

    How silent is this town! — Ho! murder! murder! —

    What may you be? Are you of good or evil?   65

LODOVICO: As you shall prove us, praise us.

IAGO: Signior Lodovico?

LODOVICO: He, sir.

IAGO: I cry you mercy. Here's Cassio hurt by villains.

GRATIANO: Cassio?   70

IAGO: How is't, brother?

CASSIO: My leg is cut in two.

IAGO: Marry,° heaven forbid!

    Light, gentlemen. I'll bind it with my shirt.

---

42 heavy: Cloudy, dark.   **48 cries on:** Raises the cry of.   **58 make:** Get.   **72 Marry:**
(From "By Mary").

Enter Bianca.

BIANCA: What is the matter, ho? Who is't that cried?
IAGO: Who is't that cried?   75
BIANCA: O my dear Cassio! my sweet Cassio!
　　　O Cassio, Cassio, Cassio!
IAGO: O notable strumpet! — Cassio, may you suspect
　　　Who they should be that have thus mangled you?
CASSIO: No.   80
GRATIANO: I am sorry to find you thus. I have been to seek you.
IAGO: Lend me a garter. So. O for a chair°
　　　To bear him easily hence!
BIANCA: Alas, he faints! O Cassio, Cassio, Cassio!
IAGO: Gentlemen all, I do suspect this trash   85
　　　To be a party in this injury. —
　　　Patience a while, good Cassio. — Come, come!
　　　Lend me a light. Know we this face or no?
　　　Alas, my friend and my dear countryman
　　　Roderigo? No — Yes, sure. — O heaven, Roderigo!   90
GRATIANO: What, of Venice?
IAGO: Even he, sir. Did you know him?
GRATIANO: Know him? Ay.
IAGO: Signior Gratiano? I cry your gentle pardon.
　　　These bloody accidents must excuse my manners
　　　That so neglected you.
GRATIANO: I am glad to see you.   95
IAGO: How do you, Cassio? — O, a chair, a chair!
GRATIANO: Roderigo?
IAGO: He, he, 'tis he!

[A chair brought in.]

　　　O, that's well said;° the chair.
　　　Some good man bear him carefully from hence.   100
　　　I'll fetch the general's surgeon. *[To Bianca.]* For you, mistress,
　　　Save you your labor. — He that lies slain here, Cassio,
　　　Was my dear friend. What malice was between you?
CASSIO: None in the world; nor do I know the man.
IAGO *[to Bianca]*:   What, look you pale? — O, bear him out o' th' air.   105

　　　　　　　　　　　　　　　　　　[Cassio and Roderigo are borne off.]

　　　Stay you, good gentlemen. — Look you pale, mistress? —
　　　Do you perceive the gastness° of her eye? —
　　　Nay, if you stare, we shall hear more anon.
　　　Behold her well; I pray you look upon her.
　　　Do you see, gentlemen? Nay, guiltiness will speak.   110
　　　Though tongues were out of use.

---

82 chair: Litter.   **99 well said:** Well done.   **107 gastness:** Terror.

Enter Emilia.

EMILIA: 'Las, what's the matter? What's the matter, husband?
IAGO: Cassio hath here been set on in the dark
    By Roderigo, and fellows that are scaped.
    He's almost slain, and Roderigo dead.   115
EMILIA: Alas, good gentlemen! alas, good Cassio!
IAGO: This is the fruits of whoring. Prithee, Emilia,
    Go know of Cassio where he supped to-night.

[To Bianca.]

    What, do you shake at that?
BIANCA: He supped at my house; but I therefore shake not.   120
IAGO: O, did he so? I charge you go with me.
EMILIA: Fie, fie upon thee, strumpet!
BIANCA: I am no strumpet, but of life as honest°
    As you that thus abuse me.
EMILIA: As I? Foh! fie upon thee!
IAGO: Kind gentlemen, let's go see poor Cassio dressed.   125

[To Bianca.]

    Come, mistress, you must tell's another tale.
    Emilia, run you to the citadel
    And tell my lord and lady what hath happed.

[Exit Emilia.]

    Will you go on afore?   *Exeunt [all but Iago].*
    This is the night
    That either makes me or fordoes° me quite.   *[Exit.]*   130

[Scene II: A bedchamber in the castle.]

Desdemona [asleep] in her bed. Enter Othello with a light.

OTHELLO: It is the cause, it is the cause,° my soul.
    Let me not name it to you, you chaste stars!
    It is the cause. Yet I'll not shed her blood,
    Nor scar that whiter skin of hers than snow,
    And smooth as monumental alabaster.   5
    Yet she must die, else she'll betray more men.
    Put out the light, and then put out the light.
    If I quench thee, thou flaming minister,°
    I can again thy former light restore,
    Should I repent me; but once put out thy light,   10
    Thou cunning'st pattern of excelling nature,
    I know not where is that Promethean heat°

---

123 honest: Chaste.   **130 fordoes:** Destroys.   **SCENE II. 1 cause:** Cause of justice.
8 minister: Servant.   **12 Promethean heat:** Divine fire.

That can thy light relume.° When I have plucked the rose,
I cannot give it vital growth again;
It needs must wither. I'll smell thee on the tree.   15

(He kisses her.)

O balmy breath, that dost almost persuade
Justice to break her sword! One more, one more!
Be thus when thou art dead, and I will kill thee,
And love thee after. One more, and that's the last!
So sweet was ne'er so fatal. I must weep,   20
But they are cruel tears. This sorrow's heavenly;
It strikes where it doth love. She wakes.

DESDEMONA: Who's there? Othello?

OTHELLO: Ay, Desdemona.

DESDEMONA: Will you come to bed, my lord?

OTHELLO: Have you prayed to-night, Desdemona?

DESDEMONA: Ay, my lord.   25

OTHELLO: If you bethink yourself of any crime°
Unreconciled as yet to heaven and grace,
Solicit for it straight.

DESDEMONA: Alack, my lord, what may you mean by that?

OTHELLO: Well, do it, and be brief; I will walk by.   30
I would not kill thy unpreparèd spirit.
No, heaven forfend!° I would not kill thy soul.

DESDEMONA: Talk you of killing?

OTHELLO: Ay, I do.

DESDEMONA: Then heaven
Have mercy on me!

OTHELLO: Amen, with all my heart!

DESDEMONA: If you say so, I hope you will not kill me.   35

OTHELLO: Hum!

DESDEMONA: And yet I fear you; for you're fatal then
When your eyes roll so. Why I should fear I know not,
Since guiltiness I know not; but yet I feel I fear.

OTHELLO: Think on thy sins.

DESDEMONA: They are loves I bear to you.   40

OTHELLO: Ay, and for that thou diest.

DESDEMONA: That death's unnatural that kills for loving.
Alas, why gnaw you so your nether lip?
Some bloody passion shakes your very frame.
These are portents,° but yet I hope, I hope,   45
They do not point on me.

OTHELLO: Peace and be still!

DESDEMONA: I will so. What's the matter?

---

13 relume: Relight.   **26 crime:** Sin.   **32 forfend:** Forbid.   **45 portents:** Signs of
impending violence.

OTHELLO: That handkerchief which I so loved and gave thee
    Thou gav'st to Cassio.
DESDEMONA: No, by my life and soul!
    Send for the man and ask him.
OTHELLO: Sweet soul, take heed,   50
    Take heed of perjury; thou art on thy deathbed.
DESDEMONA: Ay, but not yet to die.
OTHELLO: Yes, presently.°
    Therefore confess thee freely of thy sin;
    For to deny each article with oath
    Cannot remove nor choke the strong conception°   55
    That I do groan withal. Thou art to die.
DESDEMONA: Then Lord have mercy on me!
OTHELLO: I say amen.
DESDEMONA: And have you mercy too! I never did
    Offend° you in my life; never loved Cassio
    But with such general warranty of heaven   60
    As I might love. I never gave him token.
OTHELLO: By heaven, I saw my handkerchief in's hand!
    O perjured woman! thou dost stone my heart,°
    And mak'st me call what I intend to do
    A murder, which I thought a sacrifice.   65
    I saw the handkerchief.
DESDEMONA: He found it then.
    I never gave it him. Send for him hither.
    Let him confess a truth.
OTHELLO: He hath confessed.
DESDEMONA: What, my lord?
OTHELLO: That he hath used thee.
DESDEMONA: How? Unlawfully?
OTHELLO: Ay.   70
DESDEMONA: He will not say so.
OTHELLO: No, his mouth is stopped.
    Honest Iago hath ta'en order° for't.
DESDEMONA: O, my fear interprets. What, is he dead?
OTHELLO: Had all his hairs been lives, my great revenge
    Had stomach for them all.   75
DESDEMONA: Alas, he is betrayed, and I undone!
OTHELLO: Out, strumpet! Weep'st thou for him to my face?
DESDEMONA: O, banish me, my lord, but kill me not!
OTHELLO: Down, strumpet!
DESDEMONA: Kill me to-morrow; let me live to-night!   80
OTHELLO: Nay, if you strive —

52 presently: At once.   **55 conception:** Belief.   **59 Offend:** Wrong.   **63 stone my
heart:** Turn my heart to stone.   **72 ta'en order:** Taken measures.

DESDEMONA: But half an hour!

OTHELLO: Being done, there is no pause.

DESDEMONA: But while I say one prayer!

OTHELLO: It is too late.

                                        (Smothers her.)

DESDEMONA: [O Lord, Lord, Lord!]

Emilia at the door.

EMILIA *(calls within):*   My lord, my lord! What, ho! my lord, my lord!   85

OTHELLO: What noise is this? Not dead? not yet quite dead?

    I that am cruel am yet merciful;

    I would not have thee linger in thy pain.

    So, so.

EMILIA *(within):*   What, ho! my lord, my lord!

OTHELLO: Who's there?   90

EMILIA *(within):*   O, good my lord, I would speak a word with you!

OTHELLO: Yes, 'tis Emilia. — By and by.° — She's dead. —

    'Tis like she comes to speak of Cassio's death.

    The noise was here. Ha! no more moving?

    Still as the grave. — Shall she come in? Were't good! —   95

    I think she stirs again. No. — What's best to do?

    If she come in, she'll sure speak to my wife.

    My wife! my wife! what wife? I have no wife.

    O, insupportable! O heavy hour!

    Methinks it should be now a huge eclipse   100

    Of sun and moon, and that th' affrighted globe

    Should yawn° at alteration.

EMILIA *(within):*   I do beseech you

    That I may speak with you, O good my lord!

OTHELLO: I had forgot thee. O, come in, Emilia.

    Soft, by and by. — Let me the curtains draw. —   105

[Closes the bed-curtains.]

    Where art thou?

[Opens the door.]

Enter Emilia.

               What's the matter with thee now?

EMILIA: O my good lord, yonder's foul murder done!

OTHELLO: What? Now?

EMILIA: But now, my lord.

OTHELLO: It is the very error° of the moon.   110

    She comes more nearer earth than she was wont

    And makes men mad.

92 By and by: Just a moment (addressed to Emilia).   **102 yawn:** Open, as in an earthquake.   **110 error:** Straying off course.

EMILIA: Cassio, my lord, hath killed a young Venetian
    Called Roderigo.
OTHELLO: Roderigo killed?
    And Cassio killed?
EMILIA: No, Cassio is not killed.   115
OTHELLO: Not Cassio killed? Then murder's out of tune,
    And sweet revenge grows harsh.
DESDEMONA: O, falsely, falsely murdered?
EMILIA: O, Lord! what cry is that?
OTHELLO: That? What?
EMILIA: Out and alas! that was my lady's voice.   120
    Help! help, ho! help! O lady, speak again!
    Sweet Desdemona! O sweet mistress, speak!
DESDEMONA: A guiltless death I die.
EMILIA: O, who hath done this deed?
DESDEMONA: Nobody — I myself. Farewell.   125
    Commend° me to my kind lord. O, farewell!

(She dies.)

OTHELLO: Why, how should she be murd'red?
EMILIA: Alas, who knows?
OTHELLO: You heard her say herself, it was not I.
EMILIA: She said so. I must needs report the truth.
OTHELLO: She's like a liar gone to burning hell!   130
    'Twas I that killed her.
EMILIA: O, the more angel she,
    And you the blacker devil!
OTHELLO: She turned to folly, and she was a whore.
EMILIA: Thou dost belie her, and thou art a devil.
OTHELLO: She was false as water.°
EMILIA: Thou art rash as fire to say   135
    That she was false. O, she was heavenly true!
OTHELLO: Cassio did top her. Ask thy husband else.
    O, I were damned beneath all depth in hell
    But that I did proceed upon just grounds
    To this extremity. Thy husband knew it all.   140
EMILIA: My husband?
OTHELLO: Thy husband.
EMILIA: That she was false to wedlock?
OTHELLO: Ay, with Cassio. Nay, had she been true,
    If heaven would make me such another world   145
    Of one entire and perfect chrysolite,°
    I'ld not have sold her for it.

---

126 Commend: Remember.   **135 water:** (Which is yielding).   **146 chrysolite:** (Precious topaz).

EMILIA: My husband?
OTHELLO: Ay 'twas he that told me first.
An honest man he is, and hates the slime
That sticks on filthy deeds.
EMILIA: My husband?   150
OTHELLO: What needs this iterance,° woman? I say thy husband.
EMILIA: O mistress, villainy hath made mocks with love!
My husband say that she was false?
OTHELLO: He, woman.
I say, thy husband. Dost understand the word?
My friend, thy husband; honest, honest Iago.   155
EMILIA: If he say so, may his pernicious soul
Rot half a grain a day! he lies to th' heart.
She was too fond of her most filthy bargain.
OTHELLO: Ha!
EMILIA: Do thy worst.   160
This deed of thine is no more worthy heaven
Than thou wast worthy her.
OTHELLO: Peace, you were best.
EMILIA: Thou hast not half the power to do me harm
As I have to be hurt.° O gull! O dolt!
As ignorant as dirt! thou hast done a deed —   165
I care not for thy sword; I'll make thee known,
Though I lost twenty lives. Help! help! Ho! help!
The Moor hath killed my mistress! Murder! murder!

Enter Montano, Gratiano, Iago, and others.

MONTANO: What is the matter? How now, general?
EMILIA: O, are you come, Iago? You have done well,   170
That men must lay their murders on your neck.
GRATIANO: What is the matter?
EMILIA: Disprove this villain, if thou be'st a man.
He says thou told'st him that his wife was false.
I know thou didst not; thou'rt not such a villain.   175
Speak, for my heart is full.
IAGO: I told him what I thought, and told no more
Than what he found himself was apt and true.
EMILIA: But did you ever tell him she was false?
IAGO: I did.   180
EMILIA: You told a lie, an odious damnèd lie!
Upon my soul, a lie! a wicked lie!
She false with Cassio? Did you say with Cassio?
IAGO: With Cassio, mistress. Go to, charm° your tongue.

---

151 iterance: Repetition.   **164 to be hurt:** To endure hurt.   **184 charm:** Cast a spell on.

EMILIA: I will not charm my tongue; I am bound to speak: 185
    My mistress here lies murdered in her bed —
ALL: O heavens forfend!
EMILIA: And your reports have set the murder on.
OTHELLO: Nay, stare not, masters. It is true indeed.
GRATIANO: 'Tis a strange truth.   190
MONTANO: O monstrous act!
EMILIA: Villainy, villainy, villainy!
    I think upon't — I think I smell't! — O villainy!
    I thought so then. — I'll kill myself for grief. —
    O villainy, villainy!
IAGO: What, are you mad? I charge you get you home.   195
EMILIA: Good gentlemen, let me have leave to speak.
    'Tis proper I obey him, but not now.
    Perchance, Iago, I will ne'er go home.
OTHELLO: O! O! O!   *(Falls on the bed.)*
EMILIA: Nay, lay thee down and roar!
    For thou hast killed the sweetest innocent   200
    That e'er did lift up eye.
OTHELLO: O, she was foul!
[Rises.]

    I scarce did know you, uncle. There lies your niece,
    Whose breath, indeed, these hands have newly stopped.
    I know this act shows° horrible and grim.
GRATIANO: Poor Desdemon! I am glad thy father's dead.   205
    Thy match was mortal to him, and pure grief
    Shore his old thread in twain. Did he live now,
    This sight would make him do a desperate turn;°
    Yea, curse his better angel from his side,
    And fall to reprobation.°   210
OTHELLO: 'Tis pitiful; but yet Iago knows
    That she with Cassio hath the act of shame
    A thousand times committed. Cassio confessed it;
    And she did gratify° his amorous works
    With that recognizance° and pledge of love   215
    Which I first gave her. I saw it in his hand.
    It was a handkerchief, an antique token
    My father gave my mother.
EMILIA: O God! O heavenly God!
IAGO: Zounds, hold your peace!
EMILIA: 'Twill out, 'twill out! I peace?   220

---

204 shows: Appears. **208 turn:** Act. **210 reprobation:** Rejection by God, damnation. **214 gratify:** Reward. **215 recognizance:** Token.

No, I will speak as liberal as the north,°
Let heaven and men and devils, let them all,
All, all, cry shame against me, yet I'll speak.
IAGO: Be wise, and get you home.
EMILIA: I will not.

[Iago draws and threatens Emilia.]

GRATIANO: Fie!
Your sword upon a woman?   225
EMILIA: O thou dull Moor, that handkerchief thou speak'st of
I found by fortune, and did give my husband;
For often with a solemn earnestness —
More than indeed belonged to such a trifle —
He begged of me to steal't.
IAGO: Villainous whore!   230
EMILIA: She give it Cassio? No, alas, I found it,
And I did give't my husband.
IAGO: Filth, thou liest!
EMILIA: By heaven, I do not, I do not, gentlemen.
O murd'rous coxcomb! what should such a fool
Do with so good a wife?
OTHELLO: Are there no stones° in heaven   235
But what serves for the thunder? Precious villain!

The Moor runs at Iago [but is disarmed by Montano].

Iago kills his wife.

GRATIANO: The woman falls. Sure he hath killed his wife.
EMILIA: Ay, ay. O, lay me by my mistress' side.   *Exit Iago.*
GRATIANO: He's gone, but his wife's killed.
MONTANO: 'Tis a notorious° villain. Take you this weapon,   240
Which I have here recovered from the Moor.
Come, guard the door without. Let him not pass,
But kill him rather. I'll after that same villain,
For 'tis a damnèd slave.

                    Exit [Montano, with all but Othello and Emilia].

OTHELLO: I am not valiant neither;
But every puny whipster° gets my sword.   245
But why should honor outlive honesty?
Let it go all.
EMILIA: What did thy song bode, lady?
Hark, canst thou hear me? I will play the swan,
And die in music. *[Sings.]* "Willow, willow, willow."

---

221 liberal as the north: Unchecked as the north wind blows.   **235 stones:** Bolts like those used for thunderbolts.   **240 notorious:** Notable.   **245 puny whipster:** Whippersnapper.

Moor, she was chaste. She loved thee, cruel Moor: 250
So come my soul to bliss as I speak true.
So speaking as I think, alas, I die.

(She dies.)

OTHELLO: I have another weapon in this chamber;
It is a sword of Spain, the ice brook's° temper.
O, here it is. — Uncle, I must come forth.   255
GRATIANO *(within)*:   If thou attempt it, it will cost thee dear.
Thou hast no weapon, and perforce must suffer.
OTHELLO: Look in upon me then and speak with me,
Or, naked° as I am, I will assault thee.

[Enter Gratiano.]

GRATIANO: What is the matter?
OTHELLO: Behold, I have a weapon;   260
A better never did itself sustain
Upon a soldier's thigh. I have seen the day
That with this little arm and this good sword
I have made my way through more impediments
Than twenty times your stop.° But O vain boast!   265
Who can control his fate? 'Tis not so now.
Be not afraid, though you do see me weaponed.
Here is my journey's end, here is my butt,°
And very seamark° of my utmost sail:
Do you go back dismayed? 'Tis a lost° fear.   270
Man but a rush° against Othello's breast,
And he retires. Where should Othello go?
Now, how dost thou look now? O ill-starred wench!
Pale as thy smock! When we shall meet at compt,°
This look of thine will hurl my soul from heaven,   275
And fiends will snatch at it. Cold, cold, my girl?
Even like thy chastity.
O cursèd, cursèd slave! Whip me, ye devils,
From the possession of this heavenly sight!
Blow me about in winds! roast me in sulphur!   280
Wash me in steep-down gulfs of liquid fire!
Oh Desdemon! dead Desdemon! dead! Oh! Oh!

Enter Lodovico, Montano, Iago [as prisoner], and Officers; Cassio in a chair.

LODOVICO: Where is this rash and most unfortunate man?
OTHELLO: That's he that was Othello. Here I am.

---

254 ice brook: I.e., a Spanish blade, tempered in cold running water. **259 naked:**
Disarmed. **265 stop:** Power to stop. **268 butt:** Limit. **269 seamark:** Beacon, des-
tination. **270 lost:** Wasted. **271 Man but a rush:** Wield only a reed. **274 compt:**
Final accounting, Last Judgment.

LODOVICO: Where is that viper? Bring the villain forth.   285
OTHELLO: I look down towards his feet° — but that's a fable.
    If that thou be'st a devil, I cannot kill thee.

[Wounds Iago.]

LODOVICO: Wrench his sword from him.

[Othello is disarmed.]

IAGO: I bleed, sir, but not killed.
OTHELLO: I am not sorry neither. I'ld have thee live;
    For in my sense, 'tis happiness to die.   290
LODOVICO: O thou Othello that wert once so good,
    Fall'n in the practice° of a damnèd slave,
    What shall be said to thee?
OTHELLO: Why, anything;
    An honorable murderer, if you will;
    For naught did I in hate, but all in honor.   295
LODOVICO: This wretch hath part confessed his villainy.
    Did you and he consent in° Cassio's death?
OTHELLO: Ay.
CASSIO: Dear general, I never gave you cause.
OTHELLO: I do believe it, and I ask your pardon.   300
    Will you, I pray, demand that demi-devil
    Why he hath thus ensnared my soul and body?
IAGO: Demand me nothing. What you know, you know.
    From this time forth I never will speak word.
LODOVICO: What, not to pray?
GRATIANO: Torments will ope your lips.   305
OTHELLO: Well, thou dost best.
LODOVICO: Sir, you shall understand what hath befall'n,
    Which, as I think, you know not. Here is a letter
    Found in the pocket of the slain Roderigo;
    And here another. The one of them imports   310
    The death of Cassio to be undertook
    By Roderigo.
OTHELLO: O villain!
CASSIO: Most heathenish and most gross!
LODOVICO: Now here's another discontented paper
    Found in the pocket too; and this, it seems,   315
    Roderigo meant t' have sent this damnèd villain;
    But that, belike, Iago in the nick°
    Came in and satisfied him.
OTHELLO: O thou pernicious caitiff! —

---

286 I . . . feet: I.e., to see if they are cloven, like the Devil's. **292 practice:** Plot.
297 consent in: Agree upon.   **317 nick:** Nick of time.

How came you, Cassio, by that handkerchief
That was my wife's?

CASSIO: I found it in my chamber;   320
And he himself confessed but even now
That there he dropped it for a special purpose
Which wrought to his desire.

OTHELLO: O fool! fool! fool!

CASSIO: There is besides in Roderigo's letter,
How he upbraids Iago that he made him   325
Brave me upon the watch; whereon it came
That I was cast;° and even but now he spake,
After long seeming dead — Iago hurt him,
Iago set him on.

LODOVICO: You must forsake this room and go with us.   330
Your power and your command is taken off,
And Cassio rules in Cyprus. For this slave,
If there be any cunning cruelty
That can torment him much and hold him long,
It shall be his. You shall close prisoner rest   335
Till that the nature of your fault be known
To the Venetian state. Come, bring away.

OTHELLO: Soft you! a word or two before you go.
I have done the state some service, and they know't.
No more of that. I pray you, in your letters,   340
When you shall these unlucky° deeds relate,
Speak of me as I am. Nothing extenuate,
Nor set down aught in malice. Then must you speak
Of one that loved not wisely, but too well;
Of one not easily jealous, but, being wrought,   345
Perplexed° in the extreme; of one whose hand,
Like the base Judean,° threw a pearl away
Richer than all his tribe; of one whose subdued° eyes,
Albeit unusèd to the melting mood,
Drop tears as fast as the Arabian trees   350
Their med'cinable gum. Set you down this.
And say besides that in Aleppo once,
Where a malignant and a turbaned Turk
Beat a Venetian and traduced the state,
I took by th' throat the circumcisèd dog   355
And smote him — thus.

(He stabs himself.)

---

327 cast: Dismissed. **341 unlucky:** Fatal. **346 Perplexed:** Distracted. **347 Judean:** Judas Iscariot (?) (quarto reads "Indian"). **348 subdued:** I.e., conquered by grief.

LODOVICO: O bloody period!°
GRATIANO: All that's spoke is marred.
OTHELLO: I kissed thee ere I killed thee. No way but this,
    Killing myself, to die upon a kiss.

(He [falls upon the bed and] dies.)

CASSIO: This did I fear, but thought he had no weapon;   360
    For he was great of heart.
LODOVICO *[to Iago]*:   O Spartan dog,
    More fell° than anguish, hunger, or the sea!
    Look on the tragic loading of this bed.
    This is thy work. The object poisons sight;
    Let it be hid.° Gratiano, keep the house,   365
    And seize upon° the fortunes of the Moor,
    For they succeed on you. To you, lord governor,
    Remains the censure° of this hellish villain,
    The time, the place, the torture. O, enforce it!
    Myself will straight aboard, and to the state   370
    This heavy act with heavy heart relate.

Exeunt.

357 period: Ending.   **362 fell:** Cruel.   **365 Let it be hid:** I.e., draw the bed curtains.   **366 seize upon:** Take legal possession of.   **368 censure:** Judicial sentence.

≡ THINKING ABOUT THE TEXT

1. Jealousy is one of the central motifs in this play. What characters are jealous and for what reasons?

2. Is Iago diabolically devious and clever, or is Othello especially gullible? How would you respond if a trusted friend made similar accusations against someone whom you cared for deeply?

3. Is Othello's tragic flaw — the quality that leads to his downfall — jealousy or something else, perhaps credulity?

4. Is it possible for Othello's love to turn so quickly into hate?

5. How might the end of the play and the final resolution of the characters' fates be seen as Shakespeare's commentary on jealousy?

A. C. BRADLEY
The Noble Othello

A. C. Bradley (1851–1935), a British literary critic and highly influential Shakespearean scholar, was the youngest boy among twenty-one children. His father was a well-regarded preacher. Bradley attended Balliol College at Oxford University and later was a professor at the University of Liverpool and at Oxford. His books include Oxford Lectures on Poetry *(1909) and* Shakespearean Tragedy *(1904), where "The Noble Othello" appeared. The essays published in both books were originally lectures delivered by Bradley. Upon his death, Bradley's will established a fellowship for English literary scholars. Here, Bradley refutes the common notion that Othello was unjustifiably and easily jealous by considering how Othello's character diminishes only in light of the evidence Iago provides regarding Desdemona's supposed affair.*

This character is so noble, Othello's feelings and actions follow so inevitably from it and from the forces brought to bear on it, and his sufferings are so heart-rending, that he stirs, I believe, in most readers a passion of mingled love and pity which they feel for no other hero in Shakespeare, and to which not even Mr. Swinburne can do more than justice. Yet there are some critics and not a few readers who cherish a grudge against him. They do not merely think that in the later stages of his temptation he showed a certain obtuseness, and that, to speak pedantically, he acted with unjustifiable precipitance and violence; no one, I suppose, denies that. But, even when they admit that he was not of a jealous temper, they consider that he *was* "easily jealous"; they seem to think that it was inexcusable in him to feel any suspicion of his wife at all; and they blame him for never suspecting Iago or asking him for evidence. I refer to this attitude of mind chiefly in order to draw attention to certain points in the story. It comes partly from mere inattention (for Othello did suspect Iago and did ask him for evidence); partly from a misconstruction of the text which makes Othello appear jealous long before he really is so; and partly from failure to realise certain essential facts. I will begin with these.

(1) Othello, we have seen, was trustful, and thorough in his trust. He put entire confidence in the honesty of Iago, who had not only been his companion in arms, but, as he believed, had just proved his faithfulness in the matter of the marriage. This confidence was misplaced, and we happen to know it; but it was no sign of stupidity in Othello. For his opinion of Iago was the opinion of practically everyone who knew him: and that opinion was that Iago was before all things "honest," his very faults being those of excess in honesty. This being so, even if Othello had not been trustful and simple, it would have been quite unnatural in him to be unmoved by the warnings of so honest a friend, warnings offered with extreme reluctance and manifestly from a sense of a friend's duty. *Any* husband would have been troubled by them.

(2) Iago does not bring these warnings to a husband who had lived with a wife for months and years and knew her like his sister or his bosom-friend. Nor is there any ground in Othello's character for supposing that, if he had been such a man, he would have felt and acted as he does in the play. But he was newly married; in the circumstances he cannot have known much of Desdemona before his marriage; and further he was conscious of being under the spell of a feeling which can give glory to the truth but can also give it to a dream.

(3) This consciousness in any imaginative man is enough, in such circumstances, to destroy his confidence in his powers of perception. In Othello's case,

after a long and most artful preparation, there now comes, to reinforce its effect, the suggestions that he is not an Italian, nor even a European; that he is totally ignorant of the thoughts and the customary morality of Venetian women; that he had himself seen in Desdemona's deception of her father how perfect an actress she could be. As he listens in horror, for a moment at least the past is revealed to him in a new and dreadful light, and the ground seems to sink under his feet. These suggestions are followed by a tentative but hideous and humiliating insinuation of what his honest and much-experienced friend fears may be the true explanation of Desdemona's rejection of acceptable suitors, and of her strange, and naturally temporary, preference for a black man. Here Iago goes too far. He sees something in Othello's face that frightens him, and he breaks off. Nor does this idea take any hold of Othello's mind. But it is not surprising that his utter powerlessness to repel it on the ground of knowledge of his wife, or even of that instinctive interpretation of character which is possible between persons of the same race, should complete his misery, so that he feels he can bear no more, and abruptly dismisses his friend (III. iii. 238).

Now I repeat that *any* man situated as Othello was would have been disturbed by Iago's communications, and I add that many men would have been made wildly jealous. But up to this point, where Iago is dismissed, Othello, I must maintain, does not show jealousy. His confidence is shaken, he is confused and deeply troubled, he feels even horror; but he is not yet jealous in the proper sense of that word. In his soliloquy (III. iii. 258ff.) the beginning of this passion may be traced; but it is only after an interval of solitude, when he has had time to dwell on the idea presented to him, and especially after statements of fact, not mere general grounds of suspicion, are offered, that the passion lays hold of him. Even then, however, and indeed to the very end, he is quite unlike the essentially jealous man, quite unlike Leontes. No doubt the thought of another man's possessing the woman he loves is intolerable to him; no doubt the sense of insult and the impulse of revenge are at times most violent; and these are the feelings of jealousy proper. But these are not the chief or the deepest source of Othello's suffering. It is the wreck of his faith and his love. It is the feeling,

> If she be false, oh then Heaven mocks itself;

the feeling,

> O Iago, the pity of it, Iago!

the feeling,

> But there where I have garner'd up my heart,
> Where either I must live, or bear no life;
> The fountain from the which my current runs,
> Or else dries up — to be discarded thence. . . .

You will find nothing like this in Leontes.

Up to this point, it appears to me, there is not a syllable to be said against Othello. But the play is a tragedy, and from this point we may abandon the ungrateful and undramatic task of awarding praise and blame. When Othello, after a brief interval, re-enters (III. iii. 329), we see at once that the poison has been at work, and "burns like the mines of sulphur."

> Look where he comes! Not poppy, nor mandragora,
> Nor all the drowsy syrups of the world,
> Shall ever medicine thee to that sweet sleep
> Which thou owedst yesterday.

He is "on the rack," in an agony so unbearable that he cannot endure the sight of Iago. Anticipating the probability that Iago has spared him the whole truth, he feels that in that case his life is over and his "occupation gone" with all its glories. But he has not abandoned hope. The bare possibility that his friend is deliberately deceiving him — though such a deception would be a thing so monstrously wicked that he can hardly conceive it credible — is a kind of hope. He furiously demands proof, ocular proof. And when he is compelled to see that he is demanding an impossibility he still demands evidence. He forces it from the unwilling witness, and hears the maddening tale of Cassio's dream. It is enough. And if it were not enough, has he not sometimes seen a handkerchief spotted with strawberries in his wife's hand? Yes, it was his first gift to her.

> I know not that; but such a handkerchief —
> I am sure it was your wife's — did I to-day
> See Cassio wipe his beard with.

"If it be that," he answers — but what need to test the fact? The "madness of revenge" is in his blood, and hesitation is a thing he never knew. He passes judgment, and controls himself only to make his sentence a solemn vow.

The Othello of the Fourth Act is Othello in his fall. His fall is never complete, but he is much changed. Towards the close of the Temptation-scene he becomes at times most terrible, but his grandeur remains almost undiminished. Even in the following scene (III. iv.), where he goes to test Desdemona in the matter of the handkerchief, and receives a fatal confirmation of her guilt, our sympathy with him is hardly touched by any feeling of humiliation. But in the Fourth Act "Chaos has come." A slight interval of time may be admitted here. It is but slight; for it was necessary for Iago to hurry on, and terribly dangerous to leave a chance for a meeting of Cassio with Othello; and his insight into Othello's nature taught him that his plan was to deliver blow on blow, and never to allow his victim to recover from the confusion of the first shock. Still there is a slight interval; and when Othello reappears we see at a glance that he is a changed man. He is physically exhausted, and his mind is dazed. He sees everything blurred through a mist of blood and tears. He has actually forgotten the incident of the handkerchief, and has to be reminded of it. When Iago, perceiving that he can now risk almost any lie, tells him that Cassio has confessed his guilt, Othello, the hero who has seemed to us only second to Coriolanus in physical power, trembles all over; he mutters disjointed words; a blackness suddenly intervenes between his eyes and the world; he takes it for the shuddering testimony of nature to the horror he has just heard, and he falls senseless to the ground. When he recovers it is to watch Cassio, as he imagines, laughing over his shame. It is an imposition so gross, and should have been one so perilous, that Iago would never have ventured it before. But he is safe now. The sight only adds to the confusion of intellect the madness of rage; and a ravenous thirst for revenge, contending with motions of infinite longing and regret, conquers them. The delay till night-fall is torture to him. His self-control has wholly deserted him, and he strikes his wife in the presence of the Venetian envoy. He is so lost to all sense of reality that he never asks himself what will follow the deaths of Cassio and his wife. An ineradicable instinct of justice, rather than any last quiver of hope, leads him to question Emilia; but nothing could convince him now, and there follows the dreadful scene of accusation; and then, to allow us the relief of burning hatred and burning tears, the interview of Desdemona with Iago, and that last talk of hers with Emilia, and her last song.

But before the end there is again a change. The supposed death of Cassio (V. i.) satiates the thirst for vengeance. The Othello who enters the bed-chamber with the words,

> It is the cause, it is the cause, my soul,

is not the man of the Fourth Act. The deed he is bound to do is no murder, but a sacrifice. He is to save Desdemona from herself, not in hate but in honour; in honour, and also in love. His anger has passed; a boundless sorrow has taken its place; and

> this sorrow's heavenly:
> It strikes where it doth love.

Even when, at the sight of her apparent obduracy, and at the hearing of words which by a crowning fatality can only reconvince him of her guilt, these feelings give way to others, it is to righteous indignation they give way, not to rage; and, terribly painful as this scene is, there is almost nothing here to diminish the admiration and love which heighten pity. And pity itself vanishes, and love and admiration alone remain, in the majestic dignity and sovereign ascendancy of the close. Chaos has come and gone; and the Othello of the Council-chamber and the quay of Cyprus has returned, or a greater and nobler Othello still. As he speaks those final words in which all the glory and agony of his life — long ago in India and Arabia and Aleppo, and afterwards in Venice, and now in Cyprus — seem to pass before us, like the pictures that flash before the eyes of a drowning man, a triumphant scorn for the fetters of the flesh and the littleness of all the lives that must survive him sweeps our grief away, and when he dies upon a kiss the most painful of all tragedies leaves us for the moment free from pain, and exulting in the power of "love and man's unconquerable mind."   *[1904]*

MILLICENT BELL
Othello's Jealousy

Millicent Bell is a professor emerita in the English department at Boston University and a frequent contributor to The New York Review of Books. *She is the author of the books* Marquand: An American Life *(1979),* Meaning in Henry James *(1993), and* Shakespeare's Tragic Skepticism *(2002), where this essay appeared after first publication in the* Yale Review *(1997). In "Othello's Jealousy," Bell delves into how the notion of "seeing is believing" drives Othello to madness as what he sees in life and what he sees in his imagination are used by Iago to disturb his trust in Desdemona.*

Oh, yes, the chief subject of *Othello* is sexual jealousy. Most dramatic represen-tations seize upon and emphasize the way this condition, like a fatal disease, grows on the hero and destroys him until the recovery of sanity and dignity arrives at the tragic end. The more directly we see and hear him the more we almost share the madness that mounts in his mind until it reaches a point in which he appears to hallucinate, seeing what is not there, writhing before the inner vision of his wife's betrayal. In the recent Kenneth Branagh film this in-ner vision reaches the screen and the viewer is briefly unable to distinguish between what is and what is imagined as he or she sees — for a terrifying mo-ment, like a clip from a porn film — Cassio's lips meeting Desdemona's, their naked bodies twining together. Film's hallucinatory power, its ability to make virtual what words have only suggested, its ability to make us voyeurs who desire to witness the last detail of a scene, particularly an erotic scene, adds something that goes beyond stage presentation. The movie's powerful lan-guage of the visible provides — delusively even to us, though we know Othello is deluded — that ultimate visibility which goes beyond the evidence Iago has manipulated to "prove" Othello's love a whore.

But the greater reserve of the play as we read it, and even the reserve of stage presentation, which works such tricks awkwardly if at all, reminds us that jealousy feeds, precisely, upon what is *not* witnessed but only imagined. Othello, desperately swinging between belief in his wife's innocence and con-viction of her guilt, pleads for visible proof: "I'll see before I doubt," he cries. He thinks he can trust Desdemona, "for she had eyes and chose me," he tells Iago, who responds, "Look to your wife. Observe her well with Cassio; wear your eyes thus: not jealous, nor secure.... Look to't.... In Venice they do let God see the pranks / They dare not show their husbands." "Make me to see't," Othello pleads.

He groans, "Would I were satisfied!" but his tormentor observes — in an age before hidden video cameras and paparazzi — "but how? How satisfied, my Lord? / Would you the supervisor, grossly gape on? / Behold her topped?" and summons into inner view the dreadful vision, after all. But Iago says, at the same time,

It is impossible you should see this,
Were they as prime as goats, as hot as monkeys,
As salt as wolves in pride, and fools as gross
As Ignorance made drunk.

Iago will continue throughout the travail of Othello's jealousy to induce such hallucinations, to make Othello's own imagination set them forth on his inner stage. By the time we have reached the opening of the fourth act, the process is complete, and inner and outer vision are indistinguishable.

IAGO: Will you think so?
OTHELLO: Think so, Iago!
IAGO: What!
    To kiss in private?
OTHELLO: An unauthorized kiss!
IAGO: Or to be naked with her friend in bed
    An hour or more, not meaning any harm?
OTHELLO: Naked in bed, Iago, and not mean harm?

Othello is driven mad by what, by the force of suggestion, he *inwardly* sees, and yet he craves a certainty that can be satisfied only by outward sight — the sense that most convincingly assures us that we know what is before us. The central utterance in the play is, surely, Othello's anguished "Give me the ocular proof." But he craves confirmation of suspicion to end the agony aroused by what he cannot really see. For, as Iago says, "Her honor is an essence that's not seen." If he could witness the pair in bed together it might still not be enough. He is plagued by the realization that truth cannot be directly known; what we perceive is only *seeming.* "Seeing" and "seeming" are significantly repeated words that underline this problem thoughout the play.

    Othello, I want to argue against many of the play's critics, is the *most* intel-   5
lectual of all Shakespeare's tragedies, including *Hamlet*, despite its concern with elementary personal emotion. In a genuine sense, the play is a "domestic tragedy," as it is frequently termed. But this is not at all to say that it simply shows the evolution of wife-murder, a version of the O. J. Simpson case. Harley Granville-Barker said it was "a tragedy without meaning," and A. C. Bradley thought it inferior to Shakespeare's other tragedies for lacking "the power of dilating the imagination by vague suggestions of huge universal powers working in the world of individual fate and passion." The editor of the New Cambridge Shakespeare edition, Norman Sanders, calls it "the most private of the great tragedies," though he insists that "to complain of its lack of supernatural reference or its limited metaphysical range is to miss the point." "The object poisons sight; / Let it be hid," says Lodovico when Othello and Desdemona lie dead together on their bed. Sanders says this "is the only possible end, because the arena for the struggle the protagonists have lived through is best symbolized by the curtained bed." But I shall insist that the play is not the less philosophical for that. "Sight" is indeed "poisoned" — yet not merely because of the

spectacle of a love that has made such horror, but because this ending has shown the inadequacy of human vision.

Shakespeare, as is his habit, is always telling us a number of things at once. The power of the theme of sexual jealousy obscures other subjects in the play. Race and the divisive role of prejudice seem much more central than used to be conceded by critics who could not imagine how the Elizabethan world provided Shakespeare with so strong a sense of the most acute social problem of modern societies — expressed by the symbolic fantasy of miscegenation, the monstrous union of the socially separated. Shakespeare's treatment of marital violence also contains much that we respond to with recognition, seeing this problem rooted, then as now, in false notions of the differentiations of gender. Jealousy is also rooted in the unnaturalness of *any* love inordinate in its expectations, because each of us is just one and no more, and the single "beast with two backs" — that frightening visibility with which Iago arouses the rage of Brabantio — is a monster created only in an instant of sensual joy. Jealousy is evidence of the doubt that lies at the bottom of love's desire for knowledge of another, the doubt beneath love's refusal to accept the difference between one's perception and another's reality. The torment of Othello is epistemological, a condition of doubt of which sexual jealousy is only a specific illustration or consequence.

That Othello is so vulnerable to suggestion, passing so readily from hypothesis to certainty, has bothered those who have complained that he does not connect, as a character, with what happens; his noble strength, the slowness to anger that rules his early responses to Brabantio and to the drunken scuffle that awakens him from his wedded bliss in Cyprus, the majesty of his language — none of this prepares us for the speed with which he casts reason and refinement aside and becomes brutal and coarse. But it is precisely because jealousy cannot be satisfied by any degree of proof that it is a representation of the effect of skepticism, the specter that haunted the Renaissance imagination.

At the end of the sixteenth century, natural science was becoming more empirical. The view the educated person took of human history and of an individual life was apt to distinguish more consciously between certainty and probability, to discriminate among different kinds of evidence, whereas what "truth" was had become problematic. Though the truth of received religion was still a matter of faith, only a few kinds of certainty — like the certainty of mathematical proofs — were practically attainable. Shakespeare's great contemporary, Sir Francis Bacon, aspired with his grand inductive program to the ultimate restitution of "moral certainty," a concept borrowed from theology by which one might be sure about most things after observing and evaluating the facts. Bacon's effort was directed against the devastating view expressed by Montaigne that nothing could be known. A response to the problem of Montaigne's radical disbelief has been noted in Shakespeare's best writing — the sonnets and the great tragedies. Florio's translation into English of Montaigne's *Essais* was published in 1603, the year before *Othello* appeared on the stage. Perhaps, even, as Stanley Cavell argues, Shakespeare intuitively anticipated the terrifying culmination of Renaissance skepticism in René Descartes, who would make the issue "no longer, or not alone, as with earlier skepticism, how to conduct oneself in an uncertain world; the issue suggested is how to live at all in a groundless world."

In *Othello*, Iago is the source of skepticism; his nihilism links him in Shakespeare's works with Thersites and Edmund. But Othello's mind is the theater in which faith in the unseen and unseeable contends with the doubt that demands physical seeing and yet is never convinced it sees enough. Because Othello becomes the victim of his desire to know by seeing, his almost unbelievable collapse, his too-swift descent from composure and confidence to panic and disbelief, can be understood. But we are not meant to view him altogether in terms of realistic psychology — though nothing seems more real than his actual feelings when they overtake him.

If we do try to explain his fall realistically, we find ourselves in the crossfire   10
of critical tradition. F. R. Leavis was able to make a devastating case against Bradley's view that Othello's perfect nature — noble, strong-minded, self-disciplined — is destroyed by Iago's inhuman malice and intellect. Leavis discovered grounds for seeing Othello as a man infatuated with his own ideal view of himself, and *self*-destroyed. More recent psychological views suggest that Othello's great love, expressed in majestic, romantic hyperbole, may be the bluster of the untried bridegroom whose fear of inadequacy already rouses him from his nuptial bed along with the shouts of Iago and Roderigo in the opening scene. But neither a completely heroic nor a fatuous or secretly vulnerable Othello accounts adequately for the way this hero affects us. Perhaps Othello's improbable gullibility and precipitate fall depends, then, as E. E. Stoll claimed, on the literary convention of the "calumniator believed." We need to remember how commonplace and even farcical are some of the delusionary tricks that destroy Othello's faith in Desdemona; in Shakespeare's own *Much Ado About Nothing*, another ex-soldier, Claudio, is tricked by similar means into believing in the wantonness of his innocent betrothed. But Othello, unlike the lightweight Claudio, is really undone by an idea, though he is hardly philosopher enough himself to formulate it. Shakespeare makes us experience — through Othello's trauma — the absolute difference between a trust in appearances and the loss of that trust. . . .

Throughout *Othello*, Shakespeare's strong interest in the law is also evident in language full of legal terms drawn from the procedures of court trials that those who have hoped to detect more about his life from such elusive traces can suppose that he had had some training in the law. But English court trials were open to the public, forms of entertainment like the theater, and the audience for both was likely to contain persons who were amateur experts, like recent viewers of televised trials. Iago complains that Othello turned a deaf ear to those who urged his advancement; he "non-suites my Mediators," he says — that is, he rules their case out of court. When he refuses to tell Othello his private thoughts, he asks if anyone has "a breast so pure, / But some un-cleanly apprehensions / Keep leets and law-days, and in sessions sit / With meditations lawful," "leets and law-days" being court sessions to certify the good behavior of a community. Pleading Cassio's case with Othello, Desdemona insists that the handkerchief business is but "a trick to put me from my suit." She chides herself for "Arraigning his unkindness with my soul; / But now I find I had suborned the witness / And he's indicted falsely," a reference to the crime of subornation of perjury. What is important to note, among these ob-scurities, is the way words that have a common usage as well as a specific legal sense seem to reverberate with a courtroom meaning — as when Othello's handkerchief, the central symbolic object that is the mark of the troth between him and Desdemona, is called "the recognizance and pledge of love," where "recognizance" is the *legal* word for a binding bond.

It is appropriate to the preoccupation of the play with a general epistemo-logical crisis that the issue of proof is expressed as a legal question. The general evolution of thought in the sixteenth and seventeenth centuries is connected with the fact that English common law established in this period a foundation of rules of evidence that persists to this day. Brabantio's charges and Othello's refutation reflect current controversy over trials for witchcraft. In 1597, James I of England[1] had felt called upon to attempt in his *Demonologie* to refute Reginald Scott's attack (*Discoverie of Witchcraft*, 1584) on the procedures for trying those accused of witchcraft. Yet James I soon developed doubts and cen-sured judges who rushed to judgment without adequate proof. A general move-ment had begun in the courts to develop proper modes of establishing this crime. Along with that skeptical doubt that caused some, like Montaigne, to doubt the existence of witchcraft altogether, the trial of witches was changing from the search for a hidden character — established only by confession, for-merly extracted by torture, if necessary — to a weighing of visible effects, testi-fied to by witnesses. The shift is epistemological.

The courtroom, like the stage, was for the Elizabethans a place where the dynamics of changing concepts of the self were being enacted, being tried. How might one argue from crime to criminal — or reverse the process? By what evidence might the play connect plot and character? In the courtroom it was not enough to argue from "reputation" in deciding probable guilt — as it is not enough for Iago to convict Desdemona by referring to her "Venetian" char-acter — but the prosecution might add plausibility to its case by presenting, as Iago does, a narrative of events leading to her crime, by "imputation." Beyond this, how might guilt be proven? Circumstantial evidence in criminal cases was becoming the most usual basis of conviction. Iago protests that he cannot en-able Othello to see his wife in her lover's arms, but adds,

> If imputation and strong circumstances,
> Which lead directly to the door of truth,
> Will give you satisfaction, you might have't.

---

[1] Before becoming James I of England in 1603, he was James VI of Scotland from 1567–1603. [Eds.]

The paradigm of a trial of law, invoked at the start by an actual trial, is replicated in the structure of the play, a trial of Desdemona that ends in her execution. In a terrible parody of judicial sentence, in the second scene of the last act, Othello enters with a speech of deliberate dignity:

> It is the cause, it is the cause, my soul:
> Let me not name it to you, you chaste stars.
> It is the cause. Yet I'll not shed her blood,
> Nor scar that whiter skin of hers than snow,
> And smooth as monumental alabaster —
> Yet she must die, else she'll betray more men.

"Cause" is a legal term in addition to meaning simply a reason for an oc- 15
currence. To seek a cause is to seek a motive to increase the probability of guilt, while the accused may claim for his deed that he had *just* cause. Iago has begun by telling Roderigo, "I hate the Moor. My cause is hearted; thine hath no less reason." He has begun the motive-hunting that Coleridge deemed motiveless; his search for his own motive is a legal procedure to reinforce belief. A cause may be a general purpose, even a high principle to which one is attached; the cause of a heavenly ideal of chastity for which, Othello declares, Desdemona must die. But a cause is also, simply, a suit, as Desdemona called her effort to win pardon for Cassio, acting as his "solicitor." And Othello's charge against Desdemona is a suit in which he becomes prosecutor, judge, and, finally, executioner under a rule of human law aimed not only at punishment but to protect society from further crimes by the criminal ("else she'll betray more men").

Proof as in a law court is what Othello so mistakenly has asked Iago to produce. When Othello says, "I'll see before I doubt; when I doubt prove," Iago says, "I speak not yet of proof," but urges him to watch Desdemona for some self-betrayal and sets forth, meanwhile, her record as a practiced deceiver who has known how to make seeing her directly impossible: "She that so young could give out such a seeming / To seal her father's eyes up close as oak." Perhaps this would not be enough — though Othello is already frantic — but prompt to his purpose, Desdemona reappears to drop the handkerchief that Iago will seize and enter into evidence. "Trifles light as air / Are to the jealous confirmations strong / As proofs of holy writ" — though a just judge and dispassionate jury might not take them so. The handkerchief, for Othello, is the exhibit brought into the courtroom, a piece of the accused's clothing found at the scene of the crime, "ocular proof" — not of the unseeable act but circumstantial evidence, so that "the probation [or determining test] bear no hinge nor loop to hang a doubt on."

Feebly, Othello clings to his faith that Desdemona is honest and asks for presumptive motive: "Give me a living reason she's disloyal," but Iago ignores this. He testifies that he has observed Cassio relive in sleep his secret moments with Desdemona. And when Othello protests that this was but a dream, Iago says, "this may help to thicken other proofs / That do demonstrate thinly." And what are these? Iago saw Cassio wipe his beard with the handkerchief. "It speaks against her with the other proofs."

So, as the fourth act opens, Iago provokingly drives the question of proof to its most paradoxical extreme — with the assurance that, although absolute knowledge is impossible, circumstances will convict. There is no direct witness to adultery between Cassio and Desdemona — but after all, how could there be? What if you found them naked and kissing in bed together for an hour or more? Would it *prove* they were "meaning any harm? . . . if they do nothing, 'tis a venial slip." As though the case would be similar, Iago asks if giving a hand-kerchief away need convict a woman of much — knowing that Othello will conclude that it is as circumstantially damning as a sight of the lovers fla-grantly embracing. But the time has come for Iago to offer the confirming proof of confession, though, of course, it is confession reported at second hand — Cassio has supposedly confessed to *him*. It is not quite enough, and Iago will repair the defect in his case, or appear to; Othello will think he witnesses Cassio boasting how "he hath and is again to cope" Desdemona when Cassio really is talking about his mistress, who appears on cue, handkerchief in hand.

It is no use for Desdemona to defend herself. Or for Emilia to protest in a logical way, "Who keeps her company? What place, what time, what form, what likelihood?" But Emilia as defense witness arrives too late, discovering her husband's perfidy only after the death of her mistress. Before Othello executes his sentence, he asks Desdemona if she has repented of crime, as condemned criminals generally were asked, for the rescue of her soul and also to confirm the sentence by the strongest of proofs: "Take heed of perjury: thou art on thy death bed."

She maintains her innocence, having nothing to confess. Iago, who has everything to tell, withholds *his* confession, but Emilia will dispose of the false evidence of the handkerchief by revealing that she stole it for him, and docu-mentary proof, letters from Iago found on Roderigo, close the case — unneces-sarily for the audience but in keeping with the judicial process that governs the play.   20

But if the legal conceptualization of *Othello* relates it to the whole issue of the nature of truth, it is really an ironic parody of real legal inquiry. The search for evidentiary proof is, in fact, constantly mocked despite all the talk of proofs and making the wronged husband "see." Iago's pseudo-legal demonstration of Cassio's and Desdemona's guilt is conducted in the Cyprus world ruled by "seeming" — a world that makes such deceptions possible by demonic magic. Emilia's "what place, what time, what form, what likelihood" reminds us of the sleights that the playwright has himself exercised, not the least by that famous deception of "double time" that allows no time or opportunity — though we fail to notice it — for an affair between Cassio and Desdemona. Iago has merely to repeat Brabantio's charges that there was something "unnatural" in Desdemona's love to get Othello's assent to an idea he had serenely rejected in the Venetian court. He says Cassio's declarations, in sleep, of his love for Desdemona, reported by Iago, "denoted a foregone conclusion," and it is enough for him to have heard that Cassio has the handkerchief to be convinced that she would betray him sexually, accepting the false analogy: may she not just as freely give away her invisible honor? Othello does not have to hear Cassio's actual conversation with Iago about Bianca to assume that his wife is the subject.

There is a subtle slippage that merges supposition with ascertained fact. When Iago says, "What if I had said I had seen him do you wrong?" or heard Cassio "blab" of his conquest, the "what if" glides by as though never uttered. Othello reaches vainly for his sanity: "Hath he said anything?" *Then,* Iago slips in the knife — "He hath my lord" — only to assure Othello that Cassio would deny it. When Othello asks, "What hath he said?" he receives the riddling answer "what he did — I know not what he did," and to Othello's "with her?" the reply is a verbal quibble that throws his victim into his swoon, "With her, on her, what you will."

As we attend this collapse of logic, the difference between the world of illusion and the real world in which fact and appearance are distinguishable dissolves, for we are ourselves swept along by the play's hypnotic persuasion to jealousy, which banishes such distinctions. When Desdemona wonders at the "cause" for Othello's rage, Emilia rightly says,

> . . . jealous souls will not be answered so.
> They are not ever jealous for the cause,
> But jealous for they're jealous. 'Tis a monster
> Begot upon itself, born on itself.

But as I have been suggesting, jealousy becomes, in this extraordinary play, just a way of exhibiting a change of mind that equalizes the effect of all impressions. Othello may well say that contentedness in deception is best; it annihilates the reality that gives pain: "He that is robbed, not wanting what is stolen, / Let him not know't and he's not robbed at all."

It is often pointed out that the play exhibits contrasted viewpoints in the language of Othello and Iago — there is the poetic "Othello music," as L. C. Knights called it, sounded in words that seem to arise from a sense of the ordered cosmos and the hero's place in it. And there is the language of Iago, prosaically intelligent without any element of the ideal. Only Leavis and a few others have felt that Iago had some right to complain of Othello as "loving his own pride and purposes" and apt to employ "bombast circumstance" and "stuff'd" epithets. But it must be said that Othello's is the half of language most vulnerable to skepticism. Iago's version of Othello's tragedy is not the one most readers and viewers of the play embrace — he sees it as comedy, the leveling of preposterous presumption. His view goes down in defeat, we assume, as we listen to Othello's last grand speech as he prepares to kill himself — even though one suspects that T. S. Eliot was right in pointing out that the "honorable murderer" whom Emilia has called a "gull" and a "dolt" is simply trying to cheer himself up. Where Shakespeare stood is, as usual, not evident.

But if we see Othello's fall as a telescoped representation of the mind overtaken by its own epistemological distrust of appearances — and the paradoxical trust *only* in appearances — we can see that what overcomes Othello, or rather what is represented *through* Othello's mad jealousy, is a trembling of the

25

universal spheres, a perturbation from which recovery comes only at the cost of deadly anguish. It is not mere hyperbole that causes him to tell Desdemona, out of her hearing, "When I love thee not, / Chaos is come again," to exclaim, "If she be false, O then heaven mocks itself," or to say, in later confirmation of this prediction,

> O heavy hour!
> Methinks it should be now a huge eclipse
> Of sun and moon, and that th'affrighted globe
> Should yawn at alteration.   *[1997]*

JEFFRIE G. MURPHY
Jealousy, Shame, and the Rival

Jeffrie G. Murphy (b. 1941) is a distinguished legal and moral philosopher. He has published a number of books, including Getting Even: Forgiveness and Mercy *(2004) and most recently* Retribution Reconsidered: More Essays in the Philosophy of Law *(2010). His essay, "Jealousy, Shame, and the Rival," which appeared in the journal* Philosophical Studies, *is essentially a critique of Jerome Neu's work on jealousy in* A Tear Is an Intellectual Thing *(2000). Murphy maintains that Othello's acts of jealousy stem not from a fear of loss of love (as Neu's definition of jealousy requires) but from a fear of the shame brought on by that loss.*

When Jerome Neu's essay "Jealous Thoughts" was published in 1980, jealousy was widely regarded — at least in leftist intellectual and cultural circles — as an irrational and even evil "bourgeois" passion — one tied to a capitalistic market conception of human relations. The jealous person — according to this view — regards the loved person as a kind of object — as owned property over which the lover has rights. Jealousy is thus a kind of property fear — analogous to the fear of theft. The fear intrinsically involves the belief that one risks losing a possessed loved object to whose love one has a right.

Neu — rightly in my judgment — rejects this account of jealousy as psychologically shallow. He argues — in "Jealous Thoughts" and in the later "Jealous Afterthoughts" — that psychoanalytic theory teaches us that love gets its initial life and draws its basic character from the Oedipal situation. The child so needs and depends upon the mother that loss of the mother's love would appear both as biological and psychological annihilation — psychological because the very self of the child is identified with that of the mother. Any perceived rival for the mother's affections (initially the father) is seen as a threat to security and thus provokes in the child a fear of loss of love. It is here that love and jealousy begin, develop through what Winnicott calls "transitional objects," and assume forms that will persist in adult life. To love is, at least in part, to be so identified with another person that the loss of that person's love will be perceived as loss or annihilation of one's very self or personality. Jealousy, then, is simply the fear that one will lose the love of a person with whom one is psychologically identified — an instance of the fear of annihilation. "If others do not love us," Neu writes, "we will disintegrate."

This fear is not, according to Neu, grounded in a bourgeois or possessive model of human relations, for one can fear the loss of love without believing that one owns the loved person or that one has a right to that person's love. All that is required is that one has the love. Love, then, in part involves self identi- fication — when we lose it we lose ourselves, having our vulnerabilities open and unsupported. All human beings, regardless of social setting — bourgeois or communitarian — fear the exposure of vulnerabilities and the resulting loss of self. According to Neu, this fear is jealousy. Thus jealousy and love are neces- sarily connected — we cannot get rid of the former without losing the latter.

There are some questions that I immediately want to raise about this anal- ysis. First, what about unrequited love? There are surely intense cases of jeal- ousy where the jealous person knows full well that the love he feels is not returned. Not having it, he cannot fear its loss. Thus it cannot be literally true to say, as Neu does in the first essay, that "to be jealous over someone, you must believe that they love you or have loved you."

Unrequited love thus presents a problem for Neu's original analysis, but I   5
think that the problem can be rather easily fixed. One might draw on some of the instructive things that Neu has to say in the later essay about the role of illusion and projection in erotic love, or one might suggest (think of the John Hinckley/Jodie Foster case) that what the jealous unrequited lover fears is not the loss of love (which he clearly does not have) but the loss of the *possibility* of love (which he may still hope for).

There is also, of course, the problem of jealousy over love that one believes is already hopelessly lost. Othello — often presented (as he is by Neu) as a para- digm of a jealous person — is frequently thought to be most jealous *after* he believes that he has lost Desdemona's love to Cassio. But surely this cannot be understood simply as the fear of loss of love, for how can one fear to lose what one has already lost?

In keeping with the spirit — if not the exact letter — of Neu's analysis, one might try to deal with the Othello case in this way: The fear that constitutes Othello's jealousy should not be seen as the fear of the loss of love (it is simply too late for *that* fear) but rather as the fear of the personal disintegration that may result from that loss.

Perhaps killing or other acts of revenge against the lost lover are strategies to defend against this possible consequence. Perhaps they are preventive strate- gies that seek the prevention, not of the loss of love, but rather of the dire con- sequences that — according to Neu — may flow from that loss. Or perhaps they are *retributive* strategies — seeking to inflict punishment on the person who has caused such personal disruption and pain at the core of one's very self. Thus it is possible that the jealous person who inflicts pain over love lost is somewhat like the lover of a murder victim who believes (sometimes rightly, sometimes wrongly) that a kind of closure will result from the execution of the killer.

We are all, alas, familiar with newspaper reports that read "He killed her in a jealous rage." Such a phrase might well describe Othello, but I am not sure. He was surely jealous when he suspected Desdemona of infidelity, but was he jealous at the time he murdered her? Perhaps he was simply vindictive. However, if such murderous rage is properly to be identified as "jealous," it surely cannot be motivated by the fear of losing love since the surest way permanently to lose love is to kill the lover. Dead people cannot love. So what goes on in these cases is either not jealousy at all but rather something else — vengeance perhaps — or it is jealousy motivated by something other than the fear of losing love. Perhaps it is motivated by a deep aversion to certain *consequences* of losing love. Neu would stress the consequence of annihilation or disintegration — since that is so integral to his analysis of love — but I shall later argue that one of these consequences may be *shame.* . . .

It is a perhaps sad but surely true claim that, to a substantial degree, people   10 derive their sense of self worth from the judgments of others. If we love a person, we tend to take that person's judgments in these matters quite seriously — i.e., we take them in some sense to be accurate judges of our own worth. (The mentally healthy among us — if there are any — would not follow Groucho Marx in contemptuously refusing to join any club that would have us for members; nor would we deeply mistrust the judgment of any person who could love us.) If we add to this the fact that non-moral judgments of worth are generally comparative, then the fact that a judge whom we trust prefers someone over us may make us doubt our own worth or value. So jealousy may stand as testimony, not merely to our need for love and attention, but also to our need for validation by another. We are thus shamed by rejection.

It is, of course, not merely the judgment of the loved person who matters. The judgment of a wider circle of people matters as well, for even the strongest of us needs validation from some relevant reference group. Consider Achilles. His rage over the loss of Briseis to Agamemnon is to a substantial degree based on his loss of honor — face and standing — in the eyes of his fellow warriors. He has been shamed by having the girl taken from him.

I think that similar shame may be found in many contemporary cases of jealousy and loss. The jilted lover is often ashamed to report this to others — thinking that it casts some bad reflection on his or her worth or standing. (Sometimes — for similar reasons I suspect — people are reluctant even to admit that they are divorced.) Being a victim of infidelity is, among other unpleasant things, shameful and embarrassing. Perhaps this in part explains the rage that is often found in those who have been jilted — a rage that may provoke expensive and vicious lawsuits, small or even major acts of retribution, and sometimes even murder. Why do people do these things? These acts will not get the love back, but they may go a long way — at least in the eyes of the perpetrator — toward saving face, restoring lost status and honor, and thus overcoming the shame of it all. If one believes that he has been brought down by another, he may find it therapeutic — or think he will find it therapeutic — to bring that person down as well. I am not, of course, saying that such a response is justified, only that it is — unfortunately — not unusual (particularly among men). As Norman Mailer (who ought to know) has asked: "Isn't human nature depressing?"

To summarize and conclude: I think that Neu has provided us with many profound insights on jealousy and its relation to love. Indeed, if I were asked to recommend just one philosophical essay on jealousy, it would be Neu's. It is, I think, the best place to start — for its insights, the framework it provides, and the provocative questions it forces us to raise.

In raising these questions, however, I have come to think that Neu's account of jealousy needs to be supplemented in certain ways. In particular, I have suggested that *shame* needs to be stressed in order fully to account for the role of the rival in jealousy.   *[2002]*

≡ MAKING COMPARISONS

1. Murphy focuses on jealousy as having a psychological basis, arguing that jealousy is "the fear that one will lose the love of a person with whom one is psychologically identified" (para. 2) and later adds shame into the mix of jealousy. Bell, however, seems to think jealousy has more to do with philosophy, with appearances and reality, with the distinction "between seeming and true seeing" — indeed, with the very nature of truth itself. Explain why one of these interpretations helps you understand *Othello* better.

2. Bradley claims that the true source of Othello's suffering is "the wreck of his faith and love" (para. 5). Do you think Bell and Murphy agree?

3. From each essay, choose a sentence or two that impresses you as offering an interesting insight into the play. How did each one deepen your understanding of *Othello*?

≡ WRITING ABOUT ISSUES

1. Write an argument that Bradley's last paragraph captures your feelings as you read the last scene.

2. In a brief essay, agree or disagree with Bell's comment that "the power of the theme of sexual jealousy obscures other subjects in the play" (para. 6).

3. Most critics think of Othello as noble in thought and action, and he is often seen as authoritative, disciplined, human, and eloquent. But if we heard the outline of this play on today's news — "General kills wife suspected of adultery, then kills self" — we might not think highly of him. Write an essay that explores this disparity. You might want to take into consideration the nature and purpose of tragedy.

4. Write an essay about your response to *Othello* that focuses on the familiar idea "There, but for the grace of God, go I." That is, is the tragedy of the Moor and "the green-eyed monster" one we could all succumb to?

N. SCOTT MOMADAY, "The Way to Rainy Mountain"

BARRY LOPEZ, "Emancipation"

The meaning of the environment has been a lively topic for discussion in intellectual circles for decades. As the natural world becomes domesticated at an
alarming rate every year, philosophers worry that we will lose a crucial connection to our own identity, to our place in history, and an understanding of
our planet. Some people want the land to provide, as Barry Lopez suggests,
"something marketable." If it doesn't provide for us, then what good is it? But
there is a backlash to this extremely utilitarian view that the land must serve us
or else. Lopez claims that environmentalism has emerged "as a movement for
the emancipation of land." Out of their love for wild lands, the two writers
presented here understand the importance of these natural places. In an interview, the environmentalist Terry Tempest Williams echoes the thinking of our
writers when she says: "Our national parks are not only our best idea, but our
highest ideal of what it means to live with an enduring grace that will survive
us. . . . We remember the sacredness of life. We remember that this is the open
space of democracy. And it is, as John Muir has reminded us, the beginning of
creation. This is what we loved, and now they are in your hands. We entrust
these sacred lands to you."

■ BEFORE YOU READ

Do you have a special wild place that stays in your memory? What is it
about that place that makes it memorable? Is there a place in your region
you would like to see made into a national park? Why?

N. SCOTT MOMADAY
The Way to Rainy Mountain

*Born in 1934 into a Native American family living next to Rainy Mountain in
Oklahoma, N. Scott Momaday grew up on a family farm and later on several reserva-
tions. Momaday graduated from the University of New Mexico and earned his Ph.D.
at Stanford University. He has taught writing at the University of California at
Berkeley and at Stanford and currently teaches at the University of Arizona. Momaday
is a poet and novelist as well as an accomplished essayist and painter. He won the
Pulitzer Prize in 1969 for* House Made of Dawn. *Momaday's work celebrates his
Native American heritage, about which he writes with reverence and artistic subtlety.
His most recent book is* Again the Far Morning: New and Selected Poems *(2011).
The following essay appeared as the introduction to* The Way to Rainy Mountain
(1969), a collection of Kiowa legends.

A single knoll rises out of the plain in Oklahoma, north and west of the Wichita range. For my people, the Kiowas, it is an old landmark, and they gave it the name Rainy Mountain. The hardest weather in the world is there. Winter brings blizzards, hot tornadic winds arise in the spring, and in summer the prairie is an anvil's edge. The grass turns brittle and brown, and it cracks beneath your feet. There are green belts along the rivers and creeks, linear groves of hickory and pecan, willow and witch hazel. At a distance in July or August the steaming foliage seems almost to writhe in fire. Great green and yellow grasshoppers are everywhere in the tall grass, popping up like corn to sting the flesh, and tortoises crawl about on the red earth, going nowhere in the plenty of time. Loneliness is an aspect of the land. All things in the plain are isolate; there is no confusion of objects in the eye, but *one* hill or *one* tree or *one* man. To look upon that landscape in the early morning, with the sun at your back, is to lose the sense of proportion. Your imagination comes to life, and this, you think, is where Creation was begun.

I returned to Rainy Mountain in July. My grandmother had died in the spring, and I wanted to be at her grave. She had lived to be very old and at last infirm. Her only living daughter was with her when she died, and I was told that in death her face was that of a child.

I like to think of her as a child. When she was born, the Kiowas were living the last great moment of their history. For more than a hundred years they had controlled the open range from the Smoky Hill River to the Red, from the headwaters of the Canadian to the fork of the Arkansas and Cimarron. In alliance with the Comanches, they had ruled the whole of the Southern Plains. War was their sacred business, and they were the finest horsemen the world has ever known. But warfare for the Kiowas was pre-eminently a matter of disposition rather than of survival, and they never understood the grim, unrelenting advance of the U.S. Cavalry. When at last, divided and ill provisioned, they were driven onto the Staked Plains in the cold of autumn, they fell into panic. In Palo Duro Canyon they abandoned their crucial stores to pillage and had nothing then but their lives. In order to save themselves, they surrendered to the soldiers at Fort Sill and were imprisoned in the old stone corral that now stands as a military museum. My grandmother was spared the humiliation of those high gray walls by eight or ten years, but she must have known from birth the affliction of defeat, the dark brooding of old warriors.

Her name was Aho, and she belonged to the last culture to evolve in North America. Her forebears came down from the high country in western Montana nearly three centuries ago. They were a mountain people, a mysterious tribe of hunters whose language has never been classified in any major group. In the late seventeenth century they began a long migration to the south and east. It was a journey toward the dawn, and it led to a golden age. Along the way the Kiowas were befriended by the Crows, who gave them the culture and religion of the Plains. They acquired horses, and their ancient nomadic spirit was suddenly free of the ground. They acquired Tai-me, the sacred sun-dance doll, from that moment the object and symbol of their worship, and so shared in the divinity of the sun. Not least, they acquired the sense of destiny, therefore courage and pride. When they entered upon the Southern Plains they had been transformed. No longer were they slaves to the simple necessity of survival; they were a lordly and dangerous society of fighters and thieves, hunters and priests of the sun. According to their origin myth, they entered the world through a hollow log. From one point of view, their migration was the fruit of an old prophecy, for indeed they emerged from a sunless world.

Though my grandmother lived out her long life in the shadow of Rainy Mountain, the immense landscape of the continental interior lay like memory in her blood. She could tell of the Crows, whom she had never seen, and of the Black Hills, where she had never been. I wanted to see in reality what she had seen more perfectly in the mind's eye, and drove fifteen hundred miles to begin my pilgrimage.   5

A dark mist lay over the Black Hills, and the land was like iron. At the top of a ridge I caught sight of Devil's Tower upthrust against the gray sky as if in the birth of time the core of the earth had broken through its crust and the motion of the world was begun. There are things in nature that engender an awful quiet in the heart of man; Devil's Tower is one of them. Two centuries ago, because of their need to explain it, the Kiowas made a legend at the base of the rock. My grandmother said:

"Eight children were there at play, seven sisters and their brother. Suddenly the boy was struck dumb; he trembled and began to run upon his hands and feet. His fingers became claws, and his body was covered with fur. There was a bear where the boy had been. The sisters were terrified; they ran, and the bear after them. They came to the stump of a great tree, and the tree spoke to them. It bade them climb upon it, and as they did so, it began to rise into the air. The bear came to kill them, but they were just beyond its reach. It reared against the tree and scored the bark all around with its claws. The seven sisters were borne into the sky, and they became the stars of the Big Dipper." From that moment, and so long as the legend lives, the Kiowas have kinsmen in the night sky. Whatever they were in the mountains, they could be no more. However tenuous their well-being, however much they had suffered and would suffer again, they had found a way out of the wilderness.

My grandmother had a reverence for the sun, a holy regard that now is all but gone out of mankind. There was a wariness in her, and an ancient awe. She was a Christian in her later years, but she had come a long way about, and she never forgot her birthright. As a child she had been to the sun dances; she had taken part in that annual rite, and by it she had learned the restoration of her people in the presence of Tai-me. She was about seven when the last Kiowa sun dance was held in 1887 on the Washita River above Rainy Mountain Creek. The buffalo were gone. In order to consummate the ancient sacrifice — to impale the head of a buffalo bull upon the Tai-me tree — a delegation of old men journeyed into Texas, there to beg and barter for an animal from the Goodnight herd. She was ten when the Kiowas came together for the last time as a living sun-dance culture. They could find no buffalo; they had to hang an old hide from the sacred tree. Before the dance could begin, a company of soldiers rode out from Fort Sill under orders to disperse the tribe. Forbidden without cause the essential act of their faith, having seen the wild herds slaughtered and left to rot upon the ground, the Kiowas backed away forever from the tree. That was July 20, 1890, at the great bend of the Washita. My grandmother was there. Without bitterness, and for as long as she lived, she bore a vision of deicide.

Now that I can have her only in memory, I see my grandmother in the several postures that were peculiar to her: standing at the wood stove on a winter morning and turning meat in a great iron skillet; sitting at the south window, bent above her beadwork, and afterwards, when her vision failed, looking down for a long time into the fold of her hands; going out upon a cane, very slowly as she did when the weight of age came upon her; praying. I remember her most often at prayer. She made long, rambling prayers out of suffering and hope, having seen many things. I was never sure that I had the right to hear, so exclusive were they of all mere custom and company. The last time I saw her she prayed standing by the side of the bed at night, naked to the waist, the light of a kerosene lamp moving upon her dark skin. Her long black hair, always drawn and braided in the day, lay upon her shoulders and against her breasts like a shawl. I do not speak Kiowa, and I never understood her prayers, but there was something inherently sad in the sound, some merest hesitation upon the syllables of sorrow. She began in a high and descending pitch, exhausting her breath to silence; then again and again — and always the same intensity of effort, of something that is, and is not, like urgency in the human voice. Transported so in the dancing light among the shadows of her room, she seemed beyond the reach of time. But that was illusion; I think I knew then that I should not see her again.

Houses are like sentinels in the plain, old keepers of the weather watch.   10
There, in a very little while, wood takes on the appearance of great age. All colors wear soon away in the wind and rain, and then the wood is burned gray and the grain appears and the nails turn red with rust. The window panes are black and opaque; you imagine there is nothing within, and indeed there are many ghosts, bones given up to the land. They stand here and there against the sky, and you approach them for a longer time than you expect. They belong in the distance; it is their domain.

Once there was a lot of sound in my grandmother's house, a lot of coming and going, feasting and talk. The summers there were full of excitement and reunion. The Kiowas are a summer people; they abide the cold and keep to themselves, but when the season turns and the land becomes warm and vital they cannot hold still; an old love of going returns upon them. The aged visitors who came to my grandmother's house when I was a child were made of lean and leather, and they bore themselves upright. They wore great black hats and bright ample shirts that shook in the wind. They rubbed fat upon their hair and wound their braids with strips of colored cloth. Some of them painted their faces and carried the scars of old and cherished enmities. They were an old council of warlords, come to remind and be reminded of who they were. Their wives and daughters served them well. The women might indulge themselves; gossip was at once the mark and compensation of their servitude. They made loud and elaborate talk among themselves, full of jest and gesture, fright and false alarm. They went abroad in fringed and flowered shawls, bright beadwork and German silver. They were at home in the kitchen, and they prepared meals that were banquets.

There were frequent prayer meetings, and nocturnal feasts. When I was a child I played with my cousins outside, where the lamplight fell upon the ground and the singing of the old people rose up around us and carried away into the darkness. There were a lot of good things to eat, a lot of laughter and surprise. And afterwards, when the quiet returned, I lay down with my grandmother and could hear the frogs away by the river and feel the motion of the air.

Now there is a funereal silence in the rooms, the endless wake of some final word. The walls have closed in upon my grandmother's house. When I returned to it in mourning, I saw for the first time in my life how small it was. It was late at night, and there was a white moon, nearly full. I sat for a long time on the stone steps by the kitchen door. From there I could see out across the land; I could see the long row of trees by the creek, the low light upon the rolling plains, and the stars of the Big Dipper. Once I looked at the moon and caught sight of a strange thing. A cricket had perched upon the handrail, only a few inches away. My line of vision was such that the creature filled the moon like a fossil. It had gone there, I thought to live and die, for there, of all places, was its small definition made whole and eternal. A warm wind rose up and purled like the longing within me.

The next morning, I awoke at dawn and went out on the dirt road to Rainy Mountain. It was already hot and the grasshoppers began to fill the air. Still, it was early in the morning, and birds sang out of the shadows. The long yellow grass on the mountain shone in the bright light, and a scissortail hied above the land. There, where it ought to be, at the end of a long and legendary way, was my grandmother's grave. She had at last succeeded to that holy ground. Here and there on the dark stones were ancestral names. Looking back once, I saw the mountain and came away.   [1969]

≡ THINKING ABOUT THE TEXT

1. Momaday wants to "see in reality" the things his grandmother described, so he travels "fifteen hundred miles to begin [his] pilgrimage" (para. 5). Is he successful in this quest? What does it mean to see as someone else has seen? How would you know if you had succeeded?

2. Momaday mixes memoir, folklore, myth, history, and personal reflections in this essay. Does he successfully blend these genres? What is Momaday's aim in each? How does he achieve coherence?

3. Critics claim that Momaday treats his grandmother's memory with tenderness and reverence. Can you cite specific examples of this attitude?

4. Reread the opening as well as the last two paragraphs. Why might Momaday and his ancestors think of Rainy Mountain as a holy place?

5. Can you think of a comparable place in your own family's history or in your personal experience? What makes it special to you?

BARRY LOPEZ

Emancipation

Barry Lopez (b. 1945) grew up in California and New York City. He received a B.A. (1966) and an M.A. (1968) from the University of Notre Dame. Widely regarded as one of the most important writers on the environment, Lopez won the National Book Award for Arctic Dreams *in 1986. His focus is often on the relationship between human culture and physical landscape. He has also written fiction, including the award-winning* Resistance *(2004). His highly respected essays are published in the collections* Crossing Open Ground *(1988) and* About This Life *(1998). His most recent book is* Home Ground: Language for an American Landscape *(2006), a dictionary of regional landscape terms, which he edited with Debra Gwartney. "Landscapes of the Shamans" appeared in* Orion *in July 2013. He has won many awards and fellowships and taught at Notre Dame and Texas Tech. He lives in western Oregon.*

Who can say how the break between nature and cultural man came about? Or when. Historians of the West might trace it back to the rise of agriculture among early Sumerians, 7,000 years ago in the Tigris-Euphrates valley. Anthropologists tell us, though, the breach is no neat rift, that it has no single cause; central to the separation, though, wherever and whenever it occurs, is a shift in humanity's attitude toward its place. When one's home landscape — its animals, waters, plants, and earths — comes to be regarded as a servant, a producer of wealth and surfeit, the divide has opened. When the man who once plucked a few wild berries while traveling across a landscape he belonged to, a specific place which occupied the heart of his daily prayer, evolves into a strategist for profit, the split has occurred.

In essence, one's home land, once included like a member of a family in the reciprocities of life, has become a thing, an object no longer part of the owner's moral universe. Once a part of the face of God, it is now chattel.

These breaks, of course, occurred long ago in the West. In corners of Australia and Brazil, however, in Greenland, Mongolia, and other *aboriginum refugia*, we believe the mutual obligations and courtesies that historically obtained in the human relationship with place have not been completely abrogated. We imagine we can still inquire hopefully here about our prospects.

Time is short, though. If there is wisdom to serve the billions of us in Sydney, Buenos Aires, Mumbai, and Los Angeles, if the outline of a different moral practice is to be had by listening to Navajo, Pitjantjatjara, Hadza, or Inuit tradition keepers, we need to be at it quickly.

In the meantime, we find ourselves in the Visa, CNN, AK-47 present, slightly alarmed by the weather, wondering how to ensure that the last few buttons of undisturbed land remain free of their putative new owners' social and economic scheming. We must somehow counter the entrenched philosophy of the contemporary investor — corporate, individual, or governmental: the belief that every parcel of land must pay its way. If it cannot provide something marketable, they say, what's to be gained by keeping it inviolate? If it can't serve, why care for it?

Land as serf. In nineteenth-century New World terms, the land as Negro.

In the long line of emancipations that have unfolded in the West since the Enlightenment — the abolition of slavery; one man/one woman, one vote; independence thrown up in the face of colonialism — environmentalism has emerged as a movement for the emancipation of land. Wild land — "nature without an audience," as the writer Jay Griffiths calls it — is without equal as a symbol of unhindered life. Those who seek its manumission are the same women and men who once drafted the most eloquent of arguments against slavery, colonial subjugation, and corporate exploitation and thievery.

Global climate change is the great leveler in the environmental debate. Leaving our own fate out of it for the moment, it is now instructive to wonder how wild land will respond. Beautifully, one has to think. Adaptation is its history, its legacy. No matter the stress — bolide impact, monocultured forests, rerouted rivers — adaptation is its eternal answer. Wild land exists without regret, has no plan for improvement, no goal outside its own integrity. It is attractive to us partly because it has no defense against the laceration of road building, the penetration of mines, the scarifying of machinery. It is also attractive to us, strangely, because we intuit wild land is apt to meet global climate change with more equanimity than our labyrinthine cities, our drought-stricken fields.

Wild lands, of course, can give some empire builders pause. If he or she sees fresh land as more than a warehouse of goods or a mean wall between himself and other riches, the pause will do us all good. Wilderness is a warning to those who dream of controlling nature: short-term triumphs — bumper crops, fire suppression, brimming reservoirs — are no more than that. Good in the short term only. Further, untrampled land, its innate worth defended by conservationists, offers yet another sort of warning to the would-be plunderer: when strongly tempted by the promise of profit, some people will still choose to hold such ground for the next generation.

If the question remains, Why preserve these areas?, the answer can't any longer be for tourism or the promise of new medicines, or for the sake of scientific discoveries, or even to preserve minerals or timber for future use. Not if we have in mind the sense of integrity we claim the work of conservation implies. It has to be for emancipation. It has to be because every pleader for preservation knows somewhere deep in his or her psyche that the effort to protect un-disturbed lands is an effort to break the stranglehold industrial man has put on the Earth. It is an effort to reduce the reach of corporate muscle, an effort to staunch the bleeding of the brutalized oceans and their continents. It's a plea to reconcile. It's a call for principles that take us beyond the adolescent urge to plunder, to overpower, to win. In defending wild lands, we reclaim our dignity.

The real work of preservation, then, is our own salvation. It is not to save nature. Nature will save itself, no matter what climatic or nuclear hell we plunge ourselves into.

One spring I took the Indian Pacific from Sydney to Perth. Most of the way I was able to ride in the locomotive's cab with the engineers, and so take in the full sweep of the countryside. Crossing the Nullarbor Plain one morning we ran into a violent storm, sheets of rain so dense there was no view forward through the windscreen and but pale views to either side. I reveled in the fury and insouciance of the storm. And then it was gone. Ahead and to the south the span of a double rainbow materialized in the mist, an entity the breadth of Perth itself. The ionized air tore through open windows on either side of us. Neither the engineers nor I spoke a word. We nodded confidently to one an-other. Yes, we were in it now, an apparition of the wild that lay outside any human control or language. To the north, kangaroos bounded as if in fright or glee, radiating across the Nullarbor in streaks, and the three of us in the cab knew we could sail on like this for days, with no thought of sleep or nourish-ment. We were feeding on the food of our ancestors, those who had not aban-doned nature in order to discover man but who had gone deep into nature to discover the Eden of which man is a part.

We felt emancipated.   *[2009]*

≡ THINKING ABOUT THE TEXT

1. What shift in our attitude toward place concerns Lopez?

2. What does Lopez think we can learn from the tradition keepers of, for example, the Navajo and Inuit?

3. What would you say is the attitude toward place in your neighborhood at home? At school? In your city?

4. What is Lopez's sense of environmentalism? What is yours?

5. How effective is Lopez's closing anecdote in advancing his argument? Do you find his claim persuasive?

≡ MAKING COMPARISONS

1. Why might Rainy Mountain make Lopez feel emancipated?

2. How do think Momaday would respond to Lopez's claim that "in de-fending wild lands, we reclaim our dignity" (para. 10)?

3. How would Momaday respond to the next-to-last sentence of this essay, especially the idea of ancestors?

≡ WRITING ABOUT ISSUES

1. Argue that our culture does or does not appreciate the value of wild places.

2. Write a personal narrative in which you describe an early outing in nature and what you thought then and what you think now about that experience.

3. Write an essay that answers Lopez's question, "Why preserve these [wild] areas?" (para. 10).

4. Research the ideas of the early environmentalist John Muir, and then write a report on your findings.

≡ Arguments about Love: Essays

LAURA KIPNIS, "Against Love"

MEGHAN O'ROURKE, "The Marriage Trap"

Ever since Shakespeare's comedies, marriage has been one of the most popular endings for plays, novels, and films. And it is assumed by almost everybody, including both heterosexual and same-sex partners, that the happy couple, having found true love at last, will be lovers and friends for a lifetime. But according to some skeptics, the facts should make us believe otherwise. After all, the divorce rate has almost doubled since the 1960s, and considerably less than half of married couples say they are happy in their marriages. Some critics blame our inflated expectations about love's durability. Others see a kind of conspiracy to keep marriages together for economic reasons. And there are those who think we should give up the ghost and look for other less permanent arrangements. Laura Kipnis and Meghan O'Rourke develop witty, provocative, and often conflicting arguments about love and marriage.

≡ BEFORE YOU READ

Why do you think true love should last forever? Why do you think love fades? Why do you think so many couples feel trapped in their marriages? Why do so many marriages end in divorce? Why do married people have affairs? Why might monogamy be unnatural?

LAURA KIPNIS

Against Love

Laura Kipnis (b. 1956) is a professor at Northwestern University outside of Chicago, where she teaches courses on gender, popular culture, and sexual politics. She has an M.F.A. from Nova Scotia College of Art and Design. The following essay appeared in the New York Times Magazine *in October 2001 as a prelude to her book* Against Love: A Polemic *(2003). Her latest book is* How to Become a Scandal: Adventures in Bad Behavior *(2010). She has been praised for her "sharp analysis" and "blistering wit" in challenging contemporary notions of love and sex.*

Love is, as we know, a mysterious and controlling force. It has vast power over our thoughts and life decisions. It demands our loyalty, and we, in turn, freely comply. Saying no to love isn't simply heresy; it is tragedy—the failure to achieve what is most essentially human. So deeply internalized is our obedience to this most capricious despot that artists create passionate odes to its cruelty, and audiences seem never to tire of the most deeply unoriginal mass spectacles devoted to rehearsing the litany of its torments, fixating their very beings on the narrowest glimmer of its fleeting satisfactions.

Yet despite near total compliance, a buzz of social nervousness attends the subject. If a society's lexicon of romantic pathologies reveals its particular anxieties, high on our own list would be diagnoses like "inability to settle down" or "immaturity," leveled at those who stray from the norms of domestic coupledom either by refusing entry in the first place or, once installed, pursuing various escape routes: excess independence, ambivalence, "straying," divorce. For the modern lover, "maturity" isn't a depressing signal of impending decrepitude but a sterling achievement, the sine qua non of a lover's qualifications to love and be loved.

This injunction to achieve maturity—synonymous in contemporary usage with 30-year mortgages, spreading waistlines, and monogamy—obviously finds its raison d'être in modern love's central anxiety, that structuring social contradiction the size of the San Andreas Fault: namely, the expectation that romance and sexual attraction can last a lifetime of coupled togetherness despite much hard evidence to the contrary.

Ever optimistic, heady with love's utopianism, most of us eventually pledge ourselves to unions that will, if successful, far outlast the desire that impelled them into being. The prevailing cultural wisdom is that even if sexual desire tends to be a short-lived phenomenon, "mature love" will kick in to save the day when desire flags. The issue that remains unaddressed is whether cutting off other possibilities of romance and sexual attraction for the more muted pleasures of mature love isn't similar to voluntarily amputating a healthy limb: a lot of anesthesia is required and the phantom pain never entirely abates. But if it behooves a society to convince its citizenry that wanting change means personal failure or wanting to start over is shameful or simply wanting more satisfaction than what you have is an illicit thing, clearly grisly acts of self-mutilation will be required.

There hasn't always been quite such optimism about love's longevity. For   5
the Greeks, inventors of democracy and a people not amenable to being pushed around by despots, love was a disordering and thus preferably brief experience. During the reign of courtly love, love was illicit and usually fatal. Passion meant suffering: the happy ending didn't yet exist in the cultural imagination. As far as togetherness as an eternal ideal, the twelfth-century advice manual *De Amore et Amor is Remedio* (*On Love and the Remedies of Love*) warned that too many opportunities to see or chat with the beloved would certainly decrease love.

The innovation of happy love didn't even enter the vocabulary of romance until the seventeenth century. Before the eighteenth century—when the family was primarily an economic unit of production rather than a hothouse of Oedipal tensions—marriages were business arrangements between families; participants had little to say on the matter. Some historians consider romantic love a learned behavior that really only took off in the late eighteenth century along with the new fashion for reading novels, though even then affection between a husband and wife was considered to be in questionable taste.

Historians disagree, of course. Some tell the story of love as an eternal and unchanging essence; others, as a progress narrative over stifling social conventions. (Sometimes both stories are told at once; consistency isn't required.) But has modern love really set us free? Fond as we are of projecting our own emotional quandaries back through history, construing vivid costume dramas featuring medieval peasants or biblical courtesans sharing their feelings with the post-Freudian savvy of lifelong analysands, our amatory predecessors clearly didn't share all our particular aspirations about their romantic lives.

We, by contrast, feel like failures when love dies. We believe it could be otherwise. Since the cultural expectation is that a state of coupled permanence is achievable, uncoupling is experienced as crisis and inadequacy — even though such failures are more the norm than the exception.

As love has increasingly become the center of all emotional expression in the popular imagination, anxiety about obtaining it in sufficient quantities — and for sufficient duration — suffuses the population. Everyone knows that as the demands and expectations on couples escalated, so did divorce rates. And given the current divorce statistics (roughly 50 percent of all marriages end in divorce), all indications are that whomever you love today — your beacon of hope, the center of all your optimism — has a good chance of becoming your worst nightmare tomorrow. (Of course, that 50 percent are those who actually leave their unhappy marriages and not a particularly good indication of the happiness level or nightmare potential of those who remain.) Lawrence Stone, a historian of marriage, suggests — rather jocularly, you can't help thinking — that today's rising divorce rates are just a modern technique for achieving what was once taken care of far more efficiently by early mortality.

Love may or may not be a universal emotion, but clearly the social forms it   10
takes are infinitely malleable. It is our culture alone that has dedicated itself to allying the turbulence of romance and the rationality of the long-term couple, convinced that both love and sex are obtainable from one person over the course of decades, that desire will manage to sustain itself for 30 or 40 or 50 years, and that the supposed fate of social stability is tied to sustaining a fleeting experience beyond its given life span.

Of course, the parties involved must "work" at keeping passion alive (and we all know how much fun that is), the presumption being that even after living in close proximity to someone for a historically unprecedented length of time, you will still muster the requisite desire to achieve sexual congress on a regular basis. (Should passion fizzle out, just give up sex. Lack of desire for a mate is never an adequate rationale for "looking elsewhere.") And it is true, many couples do manage to perform enough psychic retooling to reshape the anarchy of desire to the confines of the marriage bed, plugging away at the task year after year (once a week, same time, same position) like diligent assembly-line workers, aided by the occasional fantasy or two to help get the old motor to turn over, or keep running, or complete the trip. And so we have the erotic life of a nation of workaholics: if sex seems like work, clearly you're not working hard enough at it.

But passion must not be allowed to die! The fear — or knowledge — that it does shapes us into particularly conflicted psychological beings, perpetually in search of prescriptions and professional interventions, regardless of cost or consequence. Which does have its economic upside, at least. Whole new sectors of the economy have been spawned, with massive social investment in new technologies from Viagra to couples' porn: capitalism's Lourdes for dying marriages.

There are assorted low-tech solutions to desire's dilemmas too. Take advice. In fact, take more and more advice. Between print, airwaves, and the therapy industry, if there were any way to quantify the G.N.P. in romantic counsel, it would be a staggering number. Desperate to be cured of love's temporality, a love-struck populace has molded itself into an advanced race of advice receptacles, like some new form of miracle sponge that can instantly absorb many times its own body weight in wetness.

Inexplicably, however, a rebellious breakaway faction keeps trying to leap over the wall and emancipate themselves, not from love itself — unthinkable! — but from love's domestic confinements. The escape routes are well trodden — love affairs, midlife crises — though strewn with the left-behind luggage of those who encountered unforeseen obstacles along the way (panic, guilt, self-engineered exposures) and beat self-abashed retreats to their domestic gulags, even after pledging body and soul to newfound loves in the balmy utopias of nondomesticated romances. Will all the adulterers in the audience please stand up? You know who you are. Don't be embarrassed! Adulterers aren't just "playing around." These are our home-grown closet social theorists, because adultery is not just a referendum on the sustainability of monogamy; it is a veiled philosophical discussion about the social contract itself. The question on the table is this: "How much renunciation of desire does society demand of us, versus the degree of gratification it provides?" Clearly, the adulterer's answer, following a long line of venerable social critics, would be, "Too much."

But what exactly is it about the actual lived experience of modern domestic   15
love that would make flight such a compelling option for so many? Let us briefly examine those material daily life conditions.

Fundamentally, to achieve love and qualify for entry into that realm of salvation and transcendence known as the couple (the secular equivalent of entering a state of divine grace), you must be a lovable person. And what precisely does being lovable entail? According to the tenets of modern love, it requires an advanced working knowledge of the intricacies of mutuality.

Mutuality means recognizing that your partner has needs and being prepared to meet them. This presumes, of course, that the majority of those needs can and should be met by one person. (Question this, and you question the very foundations of the institution. So don't.) These needs of ours run deep, a tangled underground morass of ancient, gnarled roots, looking to ensnarl any hapless soul who might accidentally trod upon their outer radices.

Still, meeting those needs is the most effective way to become the object of another's desire, thus attaining intimacy, which is required to achieve the state known as psychological maturity. (Despite how closely it reproduces the affective conditions of our childhoods, since trading compliance for love is the earliest social lesson learned; we learn it in our cribs.)

You, in return, will have your own needs met by your partner in matters large and small. In practice, many of these matters turn out to be quite small. Frequently, it is the tensions and disagreements over the minutiae of daily living that stand between couples and their requisite intimacy. Taking out the garbage, tone of voice, a forgotten errand—these are the rocky shoals upon which intimacy so often founders.

Mutuality requires communication, since in order to be met, these needs   20
must be expressed. (No one's a mind reader, which is not to say that many of us don't expect this quality in a mate. Who wants to keep having to tell someone what you need?) What you need is for your mate to understand you—your desires, your contradictions, your unique sensitivities, what irks you. (In practice, that means what about your mate irks you.) You, in turn, must learn to understand the mate's needs. This means being willing to hear what about yourself irks your mate. Hearing is not a simple physiological act performed with the ears, as you will learn. You may think you know how to hear, but that doesn't mean that you know how to listen.

With two individuals required to coexist in enclosed spaces for extended periods of time, domesticity requires substantial quantities of compromise and adaptation simply to avoid mayhem. Yet with the post-Romantic ideal of unconstrained individuality informing our most fundamental ideas of the self, this can prove a perilous process. Both parties must be willing to jettison whatever aspects of individuality might prove irritating while being simultaneously allowed to retain enough individuality to feel their autonomy is not being sacrificed, even as it is being surgically excised.

Having mastered mutuality, you may now proceed to advanced intimacy. Advanced intimacy involves inviting your partner "in" to your most interior self. Whatever and wherever our "inside" is, the widespread—if somewhat metaphysical—belief in its existence (and the related belief that whatever is in there is dying to get out) has assumed a quasi-medical status. Leeches once served a similar purpose. Now we "express our feelings" in lieu of our fluids because everyone knows that those who don't are far more prone to cancer, ulcers, or various dire ailments.

With love as our culture's patent medicine, prescribed for every ill (now even touted as a necessary precondition for that other great American obsession, longevity), we willingly subject ourselves to any number of arcane procedures in its quest. "Opening up" is required for relationship health, so lovers fashion themselves after doctors wielding long probes to penetrate the tender regions. Try to think of yourself as one big orifice: now stop clenching and relax. If the procedure proves uncomfortable, it just shows you're not open enough. Psychotherapy may be required before sufficient dilation can be achieved: the world's most expensive lubricant.

Needless to say, this opening-up can leave you feeling quite vulnerable, lying there psychically spread-eagled and shivering on the examining table of your relationship. (A favored suspicion is that your partner, knowing exactly where your vulnerabilities are, deliberately kicks you there—one reason this opening-up business may not always feel as pleasant as advertised.) And as anyone who has spent much time in—or just in earshot of—a typical couple knows, the "expression of needs" is often the Trojan horse of intimate warfare, since expressing needs means, by definition, that one's partner has thus far failed to meet them.

In any long-term couple, this lexicon of needs becomes codified over time   25
into a highly evolved private language with its own rules. Let's call this couple grammar. Close observation reveals this as a language composed of one recurring unit of speech: the interdiction—highly nuanced, mutually imposed commands and strictures extending into the most minute areas of household affairs, social life, finances, speech, hygiene, allowable idiosyncrasies, and so on. From bathroom to bedroom, car to kitchen, no aspect of coupled life is not subject to scrutiny, negotiation, and codes of conduct.

A sample from an inexhaustible list, culled from interviews with numerous members of couples of various ages, races, and sexual orientations:

You can't leave the house without saying where you're going. You can't not say what time you'll return. You can't go out when the other person feels like staying at home. You can't be a slob. You can't do less than 50 percent of the work around the house, even if the other person wants to do 100 percent more cleaning than you find necessary or even reasonable. You can't leave the dishes for later, load them the way that seems best to you, drink straight from the carton, or make crumbs. You can't leave the bathroom door open—it's offensive. You can't leave the bathroom door closed—your partner needs to get in. You can't not shave your underarms or legs. You can't gain weight. You can't watch soap operas. You can't watch infomercials or the pregame show or Martha Stewart. You can't eat what you want—goodbye Marshmallow Fluff; hello tofu meatballs. You can't spend too much time on the computer. And stay out of those chat rooms. You can't take risks, unless they are agreed-upon risks, which somewhat limits the concept of "risk." You can't make major purchases alone, or spend money on things the other person considers excesses. You can't blow money just because you're in a bad mood, and you can't be in a bad mood without being required to explain it. You can't begin a sentence with "You always. . . ." You can't begin a sentence with "I never. . . ." You can't be simplistic, even when things are simple. You can't say what you really think of that outfit or color combination or cowboy hat. You can't be cynical about things the other person is sincere about. You can't drink without the other person counting your drinks. You can't have the wrong laugh. You can't bum cigarettes when you're out because it embarrasses your mate, even though you've explained the unspoken fraternity between smokers. You can't tailgate, honk, or listen to talk radio in the car. And so on. The specifics don't matter. What matters is that the operative word is "can't."

Thus is love obtained.

Certainly, domesticity offers innumerable rewards: companionship, child-rearing convenience, reassuring predictability, and many other benefits too varied to list. But if love has power over us, domesticity is its enforcement wing:

the iron dust mop in the velvet glove. The historian Michel Foucault has argued that modern power made its mark on the world by inventing new types of enclosures and institutions, places like factories, schools, barracks, prisons, and asylums, where individuals could be located, supervised, processed, and subjected to inspection, order, and the clock. What current social institution is more enclosed than modern intimacy? What offers greater regulation of movement and time, or more precise surveillance of body and thought, to a greater number of individuals?

Of course, it is your choice—as if any of us could really choose not to desire love or not to feel like hopeless losers should we fail at it. We moderns are beings yearning to be filled, yearning to be overtaken by love's mysterious power. We prostrate ourselves at love's portals, like social strivers waiting at the rope line outside some exclusive club hoping to gain admission and thereby confirm our essential worth. A life without love lacks an organizing narrative. A life without love seems so barren, and it might almost make you consider how empty the rest of the world is, as if love were vital plasma and everything else just tap water.

Exchanging obedience for love comes naturally—after all, we all were once children whose survival depended on the caprices of love. And there you have the template for future intimacies. If you love me, you'll do what I want—or need, or demand—and I'll love you in return. We all become household dictators, petty tyrants of the private sphere, who are, in our turn, dictated to.

And why has modern love developed in such a way as to maximize submission and minimize freedom, with so little argument about it? No doubt a citizenry schooled in renouncing desire instead of imagining there could be something more would be, in many respects, advantageous. After all, wanting more is the basis for utopian thinking, a path toward dangerous social demands, even toward imagining the possibilities for altogether different social arrangements. But if the most elegant forms of social control are those that came packaged in the guise of individual needs and satisfactions, so wedded to the individual psyche that any opposing impulse registers as the anxiety of unlovability, who needs a soldier on every corner? We are more than happy to police ourselves and those we love and call it living happily ever after. Perhaps a secular society needed another metaphysical entity to subjugate itself to after the death of God, and love was available for the job. But isn't it a little depressing to think we are somehow incapable of inventing forms of emotional life based on anything other than subjugation?

Steve (top): "When we got together, we immediately merged our finances. Chuck owned a lovely home in Sausalito, and to my total astonishment, he made me joint tenant with him. We have always maintained one checking account, and all of our investments and everything are in both our names. That is about as formal as a gay couple can get. And I think, like a lot of couples, it has helped us get through rough spots in life. When your lives are totally intertwined, it makes more sense to resolve issues than to start cutting things apart most of the time.

"At this point, after thirty years, Chuck and I have very few rules in our relationship. We don't have a rule, for instance, that you can never go out on

the other one. We realized from time to time the opportunity would present itself, and we also realized that if we turned down every opportunity that presented itself to us, eventually we might begin to resent each other. So we said,
O.K., you can go ahead and do it, but never make a date that leaves me sitting
at home while you are out with someone else. And we have never done that.
From time to time we have had affairs with other people, or moments of sexual
release, but they were recreational."

Chuck: "Jealousy probably breaks up more gay people than anything in   35
the world. I guess that goes for all couples. And jealousy is caused by a lack of
trust. The one who lacks trust the most and is accusing the other of cheating,
he's usually the one who is cheating. Jealousy is based on guilt, an awful lot.
But if you are absolutely convinced that the person you are with is totally open
to you, that nothing is hidden, there won't be problems, ever. I know that Brad
Pitt could not walk in this house and take Steve away from me. I am absolutely
convinced of that.

I have total confidence in that. In my case, it is Michael York, but I go way
back. And when you know that, sex is really an unimportant aspect, in terms
of the deep emotions of your relationship. There is a movie called *Relax . . . It's
Just Sex*—I love that title. It is only sex; it has no deep-seated meaning. It may
seem to be a part of romance—certainly it jump-starts it—but as the years go
by, it becomes more of a bonus to the relationship. There are no earthquakes
that can happen as a result of sex."   *[2001]*

≡ THINKING ABOUT THE TEXT

1. Clearly Kipnis believes love doesn't last. In what ways does your personal experience and your cultural experience (reading novels, watching
   television and films) confirm, deny, or make problematic this belief?

2. In what specific ways does Kipnis answer her own question: "But has
   modern love really set us free" (para. 7)? Describe how one can answer
   this question positively.

3. Kipnis uses a number of clever and provocative metaphors to bring
   home her point about love's temporality, including the claim that Viagra
   and pornography are "capitalism's Lourdes for dying marriages" (para.
   12). What does she mean here? Explain her use of other metaphors,
   such as "like diligent assembly-line workers" (para. 11); "some new form
   of miracle sponge" (para. 13); "rocky shoals upon which intimacy so often
   founders" (para. 19); "leeches once served a similar purpose" (para. 22).

4. Kipnis claims "hard evidence to the contrary" (para. 3) that romance
   and sexual attraction can last a lifetime. What "evidence" does she cite?
   What does she mean by "hard"? Why might some of this "evidence" be
   considered interpretation or subjective?

5. Explain Kipnis's counterintuitive claim that adulterers are "our home-
   grown closet social theorists" (para. 14). How does this fit into her argument? Kipnis claims in several places that we learn about love in

childhood. What specifically do we learn, and how does this play into her argument?

MEGHAN O'ROURKE
The Marriage Trap

Meghan O'Rourke (b. 1976) is a poet and critic who has been widely published, winning numerous prizes and fellowships. She was a fiction editor at The New Yorker, *served as poetry editor at the* Paris Review, *and is a contributor to the* New York Times. *Her first book of poems,* Halflife *(2007), was published by W. W. Norton, and her memoir about the death of her mother,* The Long Goodbye *(2011), was critically acclaimed. She graduated from Yale University, has taught at New York University and Princeton University, and currently lives in Brooklyn, New York. O'Rourke posted her essay on* Slate *in September 2003 as a review of and response to Kipnis's* Against Love: A Polemic.

The classic 1960s feminist critique of marriage was that it suffocated women by tying them to the home and stifling their identity. The hope was that in a non-sexist society marriage could be a harmonious, genuine connection of minds. But forty years after Betty Friedan, Laura Kipnis has arrived with a new jeremiad, *Against Love: A Polemic*, to tell us that this hope was forlorn: Marriage, she suggests, belongs on the junk heap of human folly. It is an equal-opportunity oppressor, trapping men and women in a life of drudgery, emotional anesthesia, and a tug-of-war struggle to balance vastly different needs.

The numbers seem to back up her thesis: Modern marriage doesn't work for the majority of people. The rate of divorce has roughly doubled since the 1960s. Half of all marriages end in divorce. And as sketchy as poll data can be, a recent Rutgers University poll found that only 38 percent of married couples describe themselves as happy.

What's curious, though, is that even though marriage doesn't seem to make Americans very happy, they keep getting married (and remarried). Kipnis's essential question is: Why? Why, in what seems like an age of great social freedom, would anyone willingly consent to a life of constricting monogamy? Why has marriage (which she defines broadly as any long-term monogamous relationship) remained a polestar even as ingrained ideas about race, gender, and sexuality have been overturned?

Kipnis's answer is that marriage is an insidious social construct, harnessed by capitalism to get us to have kids and work harder to support them. Her quasi-Marxist argument sees desire as inevitably subordinated to economics. And the price of this subordination is immense: Domestic cohabitation is a "gulag"; marriage is the rough equivalent of a credit card with 0 percent APR that, upon first misstep, zooms to a punishing 30 percent and compounds daily. You feel you owe something, or you're afraid of being alone, and so you "work" at your relationship, like a prisoner in Siberia ice-picking away at the erotic permafrost.

Kipnis's ideological tack might easily have been as heavy as Frederick Engels's in *The Origins of the Family, Private Property, and the State*, but she possesses the gleeful, viperish wit of a Dorothy Parker and the energetic charisma of a cheerleader. She is dead-on about the everyday exhaustion a relationship can produce. And she's diagnosed something interesting about the public discourse of marriage. People are more than happy to talk about how unhappy their individual marriages are, but public discussion assumes that in each case there is something wrong with *the* marriage—not marriage itself.

Take the way infidelity became a prime-time political issue in the '90s: Even as we wondered whether a politician who was not faithful to his or her spouse could be "faithful" to the country, no one was interested in asking whether marital fidelity was realistic or desirable.

Kipnis's answer to that question is a resounding no. The connection between sex and love, she argues, doesn't last as long as the need for each. And we probably shouldn't invest so much of *our own* happiness in the idea that someone else can help us sustain it—or spend so much time trying to make unhappy relationships "work." We should just look out for ourselves, perhaps mutually—more like two people gazing in the same general direction than two people expecting they want to look in each other's eyes for the rest of their (now much longer) lives. For this model to work, she argues, our social decisions need to start reflecting the reality of declining marriage rates—not the fairy-tale "happily ever after all" version.

Kipnis's vision of a good relationship may sound pretty vague. In fact, she doesn't really offer an alternative so much as diagnose the problems, hammering us into submission: Do we need a new way of thinking about love and domesticity? Marriage could be a form of renewable contract, as she idly wonders (and as Goethe proposed almost 200 years ago in *Elective Affinities*, his biting portrait of a marriage blighted by monogamy). Might it be possible to envision committed nonmonogamous heterosexual relationships?

Kipnis's book derives its *frisson* from the fact that she's asking questions no one seems that interested in entertaining. As she notes, even in a post-feminist age of loose social mores we are still encouraged, from the time we are children, to think of marriage as the proper goal of a well-lived life. I was first taught to play at the marriage fantasy in a Manhattan commune that had been formed explicitly to reject traditional notions of marriage; faced with a gaggle of eight-year-old girls, one of the women gave us a white wedding gown and invited us to imagine the heartthrob whom we wanted to devote ourselves to. Even radicals have a hard time banishing the dream of an enduring true love.

Let's accept that the resolute public emphasis on fixing ourselves, not marriage, can seem grim, and even sentimentally blinkered in its emphasis on ending divorce. Yet Kipnis's framing of the problem is grim, too. While she usefully challenges our assumptions about commitment, it's not evident that we'd be better off in the lust-happy world she envisions, or that men and women really want the exact same sexual freedoms. In its ideal form, marriage seems to reify all that's best about human exchange. Most people don't want to be alone at home with a cat, and everyone but Kipnis worries about the effects of divorce on children. "Work," in her lexicon, is always the drudgery of self-denial, not the challenge of extending yourself beyond what you knew you could do. But we usually mean two things when we say "work": The slog we endure purely to put food on the table, and the kind we do because we like it — are drawn to it, even.

While it's certainly true that people stay in an unhappy relationship longer than they should, it's not yet clear that monogamy is more "unnatural" than sleeping around but finding that the hum of your refrigerator is your most constant companion. And Kipnis spends scant time thinking about the fact that marriage is a hardy social institution several thousand years old, spanning many cultures — which calls into question, to say the least, whether its presence in our lives today has mostly to do with the insidious chokehold capitalism has on us.

While Kipnis's exaggerated polemic romp is wittily invigorating, it may not actually be as radical as it promises to be: These days, even sitcoms reflect her way of thinking. There's an old episode of *Seinfeld* in which Jerry and Kramer anticipate most of Kipnis's critique of domesticity; Kramer asks Jerry if he and his girlfriend are thinking about marriage and family, and then cuts him off: "They're prisons! Man-made prisons! You're doin' time! You get up in the morning — she's there. You go to sleep at night — she's there. It's like you gotta ask permission to, to use the bathroom: *Is it all right if I use the bathroom now?*" Still, love might indeed get a better name if we were as attentive to the intellectual dishonesties of the public debate over its failings as we are to the emotional dishonesties of adulterers.   *[2003]*

≡ **THINKING ABOUT THE TEXT**

1. O'Rourke claims that as a culture we are happy to talk about unhappy individual marriages but not about marriage itself. In what ways do your personal experience and your cultural experience (reading novels, watching films and television) support or contradict this observation?

2. O'Rourke seems to agree with Kipnis that we are socialized to think of marriage as "the proper goal of a well-lived life" (para. 9). In what specific ways is this true from your personal and cultural experience?

3. In what ways does O'Rourke support marriage? What objections does she have to Kipnis's idea of working at a relationship? O'Rourke praises Kipnis for her "gleeful, viperish wit" (para. 5). Point out examples of where the same could be said of O'Rourke.

4. What is O'Rourke's position on the connection between sex and love?

5. Paraphrase O'Rourke's position on marriage.

≡ MAKING COMPARISONS

1. How does O'Rourke summarize the key elements of Kipnis's argument? What features of the argument does she seem most impressed with?

2. What are some objections O'Rourke has to Kipnis's essay? O'Rourke seems to save her main critique of Kipnis until the last paragraph. What is it? What is the rhetorical effect of "still" in the last sentence?

3. Kipnis's tone is often biting and ironic. How would you describe O'Rourke's tone? What are the advantages and disadvantages of using various tones, such as ironic, sarcastic, sincere, witty, clever, and confident?

≡ WRITING ABOUT ISSUES

1. Write an argument that agrees or disagrees with the idea that "marriage . . . belongs on the junk heap of human folly." Be sure to cite specific support and make reference to both Kipnis and O'Rourke.

2. Write an analysis of Kipnis's argument, focusing on the clarity of the claim, the adequacy of her supporting evidence, her attention to the opposition, and the idea of fairness.

3. Write an argument that focuses on the idea that our culture should be more honest about the failings of love. Give concrete suggestions about how this might happen and what the consequences might be.

4. In August 1989, the *New Republic* published Andrew Sullivan's "Here Comes the Groom," an influential essay that made (as the subtitle said) "a conservative case for gay marriage" that seemed radical to most readers. Now, decades later, a growing number of states have legalized same-sex marriage. And more and more Americans support such legislation. Read Sullivan's essay and write an analysis of his argument. Be sure to include contemporary voices both pro and con.

CHITRA BANERJEE DIVAKARUNI, "The Brides Come to Yuba City" (poem)

JULIE OTSUKA, "Come Japanese!" (story)

Sometimes called "picture brides" or, later, mail-order brides, thousands of young women in the early decades of the twentieth century left their homes in Asia to marry men they knew only through letters and photographs. Often desperately poor or unable to find suitable husbands, these women, sometimes young teenagers, endured cramped and squalid conditions on ships taking them to America. Many came from Japan and India, hoping for a fresh start in the land of opportunity. But most knew very little either about the realities of American culture or who their husbands-to-be actually were. And their previous socialization had prepared them for a culture completely at odds with the California of a hundred years ago to which they were headed. To make matters worse, there was little reality to the letters and pictures most men seeking brides sent. Expecting the fulfillment of their fantasies, the "picture brides" immediately encountered the grim realization that their futures would be arduous and hardly romantic. Chitra Banerjee Divakaruni in a poem and Julie Otsuka in a story present us with a detailed and harrowing glimpse of youthful and innocent women waking from hopeful dreams to a life none of them were prepared for.

■ BEFORE YOU READ

Imagine you're a woman who was to be sent halfway around the world to Japan or India to marry someone based on a picture and a letter. Or imagine you're a man who will marry a woman from Japan or India you have never met until the day she arrives in America. Imagine you have no choice. What would you be thinking? What would you do?

CHITRA BANERJEE DIVAKARUNI
The Brides Come to Yuba City

Chitra Banerjee Divakaruni (b. 1956) was born in Calcutta, India, and graduated from the University of Calcutta with a B.A. in 1976. Shortly thereafter, she moved to the United States, receiving an M.A. from Wright State University and a Ph.D. from the University of California, Berkeley in 1985. Her short fiction has been widely published, and her novels, including The Mistress of Spices *(1997) and* Queen of Dreams *(2004), have received high praise. Her novel* The Palace of Illusions *(2008) is a retelling of a famous Indian epic,* The Mahabharata. *She has also won awards for her poetry. "The Brides Come to Yuba City" is from* Black Candle *(2000) and focuses on the lives of South Asian women. Her latest book is a novel,* Oleander Girl *(2013). She teaches at the University of Houston.*

GREGORY URQUIAGA
KRT/Newscom

The sky is hot and yellow, filled
with blue screaming birds. The train
heaved us from its belly
and vanished in shrill smoke.
Now only the tracks   5
gleam dull in the heavy air,
a ladder to eternity, each receding rung
cleaved from our husbands' ribs.
Mica°-flecked, the platform
dazzles, burns up through thin   10
chappal° soles, lurches
like the ship's dark hold,
blurred month of nights, smell of vomit,
a porthole like the bleached iris
of a giant unseeing eye.   15

Red-veiled, we lean into each other,
press damp palms, try
broken smiles. The man

___

mica: Aluminum silicate, characteristically shiny and found in igneous and metamorphic rocks.   **chappal:** Leather sandals.

who met us at the ship whistles
a restless *Angrezi°* tune   20
and scans the fields. Behind us,
the black wedding trunks, sharp-edged,
shiny, stenciled with strange men-names
our bodies do not fit into:
Mrs. Baldev Johl, Mrs. Kanwal Bains.   25
Inside, folded like wings,
bright *salwar kameezes°* scented
with sandalwood. For the men,
kurtas° and thin white gauze
to wrap their uncut hair.   30
Laddus° from Jullundhar, sugar-crusted,
six kinds of lentils, a small bag
of *bajra°* flour. Labeled in our mothers'
hesitant hands, pickled mango and lime,
packets of seeds—*methi°*, *karela°*, *saag°*—   35
to burst from this new soil
like green stars.

He gives a shout, waves
at the men, their slow
uneven approach. We crease our eyes   40
through the veils' red film,
cannot breathe. Thirty years
since we saw them. Or never,
like Harvinder, married last year
at Hoshiarpur to her husband's photo,   45
which she clutches tight to her
to stop the shaking. He is fifty-two,
she sixteen. Tonight—like us all—
she will open her legs to him.

The platform is endless-wide.   50
The men walk and walk
without advancing. Their lined,
wavering mouths, their
eyes like drowning lights.
We cannot recognize a single face.   *[1991]*   55

Note: Yuba City in northern California was settled largely by Indian railroad workers around the 1900s. Due to immigration restrictions, many of them were unable to bring their families over—or, in the case of single men, go back to get married—until the 1940s.

Angrezi: An Indian slang word for "English."   ***salwar kameezes:*** Traditional dress of South and Central Asia.   ***kurtas:*** Upper garment.   ***Laddus:*** A ball-shaped sweet.   ***bajra:*** Pearl millet.   ***methi:*** Fenugreek. A culinary spice.   ***karela:*** Bitter melon.   ***saag:*** Spinach.

≡ THINKING ABOUT THE TEXT

1. How do the detailed descriptions in the first stanza prepare us for the narrator's attitudes toward the marriages?

2. What is meant by the line, "each receding rung / cleaved from our husbands' ribs" (lines 7–8)? (See the note following the poem.)

3. What cultural information about the women and men can be gleaned from the poem?

4. What feeling does the poet hope to convey with the lines, "The men walk and walk / without advancing" (lines 51–52)?

5. Describe the point of view of the poem. Why do you think Divakaruni chose this unusual perspective? What does she hope to convey here? How might the wedding be described?

JULIE OTSUKA
Come, Japanese!

Julie Otsuka (b. 1962) was born in Palo Alto, California, to parents of Japanese descent. Otsuka graduated from Yale University and later received an M.F.A. from Columbia University. She has won numerous awards for her fiction, including the PEN/ Faulkner Award and a Guggenheim Fellowship. She was also a finalist for the National Book Award. Her first novel, When the Emperor Was Divine *(2002), tells the story of a Japanese American family sent to an internment camp during World War II. The following story is from* The Buddha in the Attic *(2011) about Japanese "picture brides" who, a hundred years ago, sailed to America to marry men they had never seen. The* New York Times *called Otsuka's novel "a resonant and beautifully nuanced achievement."*

On the boat we were mostly virgins. We had long black hair and flat wide feet and we were not very tall. Some of us had eaten nothing but rice gruel as young girls and had slightly bowed legs, and some of us were only fourteen years old and were still young girls ourselves. Some of us came from the city, and wore stylish city clothes, but many more of us came from the country and on the boat we wore the same old kimonos we'd been wearing for years—faded hand-me-downs from our sisters that had been patched and re-dyed many times. Some of us came from the mountains and had never before seen the sea, except for in pictures, and some of us were the daughters of fishermen who had been around the sea all our lives. Perhaps we had lost a brother or father to the sea, or a fiancé, or perhaps someone we loved had jumped into the water one unhappy morning and simply swam away, and now it was time for us, too, to move on.

On the boat the first thing we did—before deciding who we liked and didn't like, before telling each other which one of the islands we were from, and

Ulf Andersen/Getty
Images

why we were leaving, before even bothering to learn each other's names — was to compare photographs of our husbands. They were handsome young men with dark eyes and full heads of hair and skin that was smooth and unblemished. Their chins were strong. Their posture, good. Their noses were straight and high. They looked like our brothers and fathers back home, only better dressed, in grey frock coats and fine Western three-piece suits. Some of them were standing on sidewalks in front of wooden A-frame houses with white picket fences and neatly mowed lawns, and some were leaning in driveways against Model T Fords. Some were sitting in studios on stiff high-backed chairs with their hands neatly folded and staring straight into the camera, as though they were ready to take on the world. All of them had promised to be there, waiting for us, in San Francisco, when we sailed into port.

On the boat we often wondered: Would we like them? Would we love them? Would we recognize them from their pictures when we first saw them on the dock?

On the boat we slept down below, in steerage, where it was filthy and dim. Our beds were narrow metal racks stacked one on top of the other and our mattresses were hard and thin and darkened with the stains of other journeys, other lives. Our pillows were stuffed with dried wheat hulls. Scraps of food littered the passageways between berths and the floors were wet and slick. There was one porthole and in the evening, after the hatch was closed, the darkness filled with whispers. *Will it hurt?* Bodies tossed and turned beneath the blankets. The sea rose and fell. The damp air stifled. At night we dreamed of our husbands. We dreamed of new wooden sandals and endless bolts of indigo silk and of living, one day, in a house with a chimney. We dreamed we were lovely and tall. We dreamed we were back in the rice paddies, which we had so desperately wanted to escape. The rice paddy dreams were always nightmares. We dreamed of our older and prettier sisters, who had been sold to the geisha houses by our fathers so that the rest of us might eat, and when we woke we were gasping for air. *For a second I thought I was her.*

Our first few days on the boat we were seasick and could not keep down our food, and had to make repeated trips to the railing. Some of us were so dizzy we could not even walk and lay in our berths in a dull stupor, unable to remember our own names, not to mention those of our new husbands. *Remind me one more time, I'm Mrs Who?* Some of us clutched our stomachs and prayed out loud to Kannon, the goddess of mercy—*Where are you?*—while others of us preferred to turn silently green. And often, in the middle of the night, we were jolted awake by a violent swell and for a brief moment we had no idea where we were, or why our beds would not stop moving, or why our hearts were pounding with such dread. *Earthquake*, was the first thought that usually came to our minds. We reached out for our mothers then, in whose arms we had slept until the day we'd left home. Were they sleeping now? Were they dreaming? Were they thinking of us all the time? Were they still walking three steps behind our fathers on the streets with their arms full of packages while our fathers carried nothing at all? Were they secretly envious of us for sailing away? *Didn't I give you everything?* Had they remembered to air out our old kimonos? Had they remembered to feed the cats? Had they made sure to tell us everything we needed to know? *Hold your teacup with both hands, stay out of the sun, never say more than you have to.*

Most of us on the boat were accomplished, and were sure we would make good wives. We knew how to cook and sew. We knew how to serve tea and arrange flowers and sit quietly on our flat wide feet for hours, saying absolutely nothing of substance at all. *A girl must blend into a room: she must be present without appearing to exist.* We knew how to behave at funerals, and how to write short, melancholy poems about the passing of autumn that were exactly seventeen syllables long. We knew how to pull weeds and chop kindling and haul water and one of us—the rice miller's daughter—knew how to walk two miles into town with an eighty-pound sack of rice on her back without once breaking into a sweat. *It's all in the way you breathe.* Most of us had good manners and were extremely polite, except for when we got mad and cursed like sailors. Most of us spoke like ladies most of the time, with our voices pitched high, and pretended to know much less than we did, and whenever we walked past the deckhands we made sure to take small, mincing steps with our toes turned properly in. Because how many times had our mothers told us: *Walk like the city, not like the farm!*

5

On the boat we crowded into each other's bunks every night and stayed up for hours discussing the unknown continent ahead of us. The people there were said to eat nothing but meat, and their bodies were covered with hair (we were mostly Buddhist, and did not eat meat, and only had hair in the appropriate places). The trees were enormous. The plains were vast. The women were loud and tall—a full head taller, we had heard, than the tallest of our men. The language was ten times as difficult as our own and the customs were unfathomably strange. Books were read from back to front and soap was used in the bath. Noses were blown on dirty cloths that were stuffed back into pockets only to be taken out later and used again and again. The opposite of white was not red, but black. What would become of us, we wondered, in such an alien land? We imagined ourselves—an unusually small people armed only with our guidebooks—entering a country of giants. Would we be laughed at? Spat on? Or, worse yet, would we not be taken seriously at all? But even the most reluctant of us had to admit that it was better to marry a stranger in America than grow old with a farmer from the village. Because in America the women did not have to work in the fields and there was plenty of rice and firewood for all. And wherever you went the men held open the doors and tipped their hats and called out, "Ladies first," and "After you."

Some of us on the boat were from Kyoto, and were delicate and fair, and had lived our entire lives in darkened rooms at the back of the house. Some of us were from Nara, and we prayed to our ancestors three times a day, and swore we could still hear the temple bells ringing. Some of us were farmers' daughters from Yamaguchi with thick wrists and broad shoulders who had never gone to bed after nine. Some of us were from a small mountain hamlet in Yamanashi and had only recently seen our first train. Some of us were from Tokyo and had seen everything, and spoke beautiful Japanese, and did not mix much with any of the others. Many more of us were from Kagoshima and spoke in a thick southern dialect that those of us from Tokyo pretended we could not understand. Some of us were from Hokkaido, where it was snowy and cold, and would dream of that white landscape for years. Some of us were from Hiroshima, which would later explode, and were lucky to be on the boat at all though of course we did not then know it. The youngest of us was twelve, and from the eastern shore of Lake Biwa, and had not yet begun to bleed. *My parents married me off for the betrothal money.* The oldest of us was thirty-seven, and from Niigata, and had spent her entire life taking care of her invalid father, whose recent death made her both happy and sad. *I knew I could only marry if he died.* One of us was from Kumamoto, where there were no more eligible men—they had all left the year before to find work in Manchuria—and felt fortunate to have found any kind of husband at all. *I took one look at his photograph and told the matchmaker, "He'll do."* One of us was from a silk-weaving village in Fukushima, and had lost her first husband to the flu, and her second to a younger and prettier woman who lived on the other side of the hill, and now she was sailing to America to marry her third. *He's healthy, he doesn't drink, he doesn't gamble, that's all I needed to know.* One of us was a former dancing girl from Nagoya who dressed beautifully, and had translucent white skin, and knew everything there was to know about men, and it was to her we turned every night with our questions. How long will it last? With the lamp lit or in the dark? Legs up or down? Eyes open or closed? What if I can't breathe? What if I get thirsty? What if he is too heavy? What if he is too big? What if he does not want me at all? 'Men are really quite simple,' she told us. And then she began to explain.

On the boat we sometimes lay awake for hours in the swaying damp darkness of the hold, filled with longing and dread, and wondered how we would last another three weeks.

On the boat we carried with us in our trunks all the things we would need 10 for our new lives: white silk kimonos for our wedding night, colourful cotton kimonos for everyday wear, plain cotton kimonos for when we grew old, calligraphy brushes, thick black sticks of ink, thin sheets of rice paper on which to write long letters home, tiny brass Buddhas, ivory statues of the fox god, dolls we had slept with since we were five, bags of brown sugar with which to buy favours, bright cloth quilts, paper fans, English phrase books, flowered silk sashes, smooth black stones from the river that ran behind our house, a lock of hair from a boy we had once touched, and loved, and promised to write, even though we knew we never would, silver mirrors given to us by our mothers, whose last words still rang in our ears. *You will see: women are weak, but mothers are strong.*

On the boat we complained about everything. Bedbugs. Lice. Insomnia. The constant dull throb of the engine, which worked its way even into our dreams. We complained about the stench from the latrines—huge, gaping holes that opened out onto the sea—and our own slowly ripening odour, which seemed to grow more pungent by the day. We complained about Kazuko's aloofness, Chiyo's throat-clearing, Fusayo's incessant humming of the "Teapicker's Song", which was slowly driving us all crazy. We complained about our disappearing hairpins—who among us was the thief?—and how the girls from first class had never once said hello from beneath their violet silk parasols in all the times they had walked past us up above on the deck. Just who do they think they are? We complained about the heat. The cold. The scratchy wool blankets. We complained about our own complaining. Deep down, though, most of us were really very happy, for soon we would be in America with our new husbands, who had written to us many times over the months. *I have bought a beautiful house. You can plant tulips in the garden. Daffodils. Whatever you like. I own a farm. I operate a hotel. I am the president of a large bank. I left Japan several years ago to start my own business and can provide for you well. I am 179 centimetres tall and do not suffer from leprosy or lung disease and there is no history of madness in my family. I am a native of Okayama. Of Hyogo. Of Miyagi. Of Shizuoka. I grew up in the village next to yours and saw you once years ago at a fair. I will send you the money for your passage as soon as I can.*

On the boat we carried our husbands' pictures in tiny oval lockets that hung on long chains around our necks. We carried them in silk purses and old tea tins and red lacquer boxes and in the thick brown envelopes from America in which they had originally been sent. We carried them in the sleeves of our kimonos, which we touched often, just to make sure they were still there. We carried them pressed flat between the pages of *Come, Japanese!* and *Guidance for Going to America* and *Ten Ways to Please a Man* and old, well-worn volumes of the Buddhist sutras, and one of us, who was Christian, and ate meat, and prayed to a different and longer-haired god, carried hers between the pages of a King James Bible. And when we asked her which man she liked better — the man in the photograph or the Lord Jesus Himself — she smiled mysteriously and replied, "Him, of course."

Several of us on the boat had secrets, which we swore we would keep from our husbands for the rest of our lives. Perhaps the real reason we were sailing to America was to track down a long-lost father who had left the family years before. *He went to Wyoming to work in the coal mines and we never heard from him again.* Or perhaps we were left behind a young daughter who had been born to a man whose face we could now barely recall — a travelling storyteller who had spent a week in the village, or a wandering Buddhist priest who had stopped by the house late one night on his way to Mount Fuji. And even though we knew our parents would care for her well — *If you stay here in the village,* they had warned us, *you will never marry at all* — we still felt guilty for having chosen our own life over hers, and on the boat we wept for her every night for many nights in a row and then one morning we woke up and dried our eyes and said, "That's enough," and began to think of other things. Which kimono to wear when we landed. How to fix our hair. What to say when we first saw him. Because we were on the boat now, the past was behind us, and there was no going back.

On the boat we had no idea we would dream of our daughter every night until the day that we died, and that in our dreams she would always be three and as she was when we last saw her: a tiny figure in a dark red kimono squatting at the edge of a puddle, utterly entranced by the sight of a dead floating bee.

On the boat we ate the same food every day and every day we breathed the same stale air. We sang the same songs and laughed at the same jokes and in the morning, when the weather was mild, we climbed up out of the cramped quarters of the hold and strolled the deck in our wooden sandals and light summer kimonos, stopping, every now and then, to gaze out at the same endless blue sea. Sometimes a flying fish would land at our feet, flopping and out of breath, and one of us — usually it was one of the fishermen's daughters — would pick it up and toss it back into the water. Or a school of dolphins would appear out of nowhere and leap alongside the boat for hours. One calm, windless morning when the sea was flat as glass and the sky a brilliant shade of blue, the smooth black flank of a whale suddenly rose up out of the water and then disappeared and for a moment we forgot to breathe. *It was like looking into the eye of the Buddha.*

On the boat we often stood on the deck for hours with the wind in our hair, watching the other passengers go by. We saw turbaned Sikhs from the Punjab who were fleeing to Panama from their native land. We saw wealthy White Russians who were fleeing from the revolution. We saw Chinese labourers from Hong Kong who were going to work in the cotton fields of Peru. We saw King

15

Lee Uwanowich and his famous band of gypsies, who owned a large cattle ranch in Mexico and were rumoured to be the richest band of gypsies in the world. We saw a trio of sunburned German tourists and a handsome Spanish priest and a tall, ruddy Englishman named Charles, who appeared at the railing every afternoon at quarter past three and walked several brisk lengths of the deck. Charles was travelling in first class, and had dark green eyes and a sharp, pointy nose, and spoke perfect Japanese, and was the first white person many of us had ever seen. He was a professor of foreign languages at the university in Osaka, and had a Japanese wife, and a child, and had been to America many times, and was endlessly patient with our questions. Was it true that Americans had a strong animal odour? (Charles laughed and said, "Well, do I?" and let us lean in close for a sniff.) And just how hairy *were* they? ("About as hairy as I am," Charles replied, and then he rolled up his sleeve to show us his arms, which were covered with dark brown hairs that made us shiver.) And did they really grow hair on their chests? (Charles blushed, and said he could not show us his chest, and we blushed and explained that we had not asked him to.) And were there still savage tribes of Red Indians wandering all over the prairies? (Charles told us that all the Red Indians had been taken away, and we breathed a sigh of relief.) And was it true that the women in America did not have to kneel down before their husbands or cover their mouths when they laughed? (Charles stared at a passing ship on the horizon and then sighed and said, "Sadly, yes.") And did the men and women there really dance cheek to cheek all night long? (Only on Saturdays, Charles explained.) And were the dance steps very difficult? (Charles said they were easy, and gave us a moonlit lesson in the foxtrot the following evening on the deck. *Slow, slow, quick, quick.*) And was downtown San Francisco truly bigger than the Ginza? (Why, of course.) And were the houses in America really three times the size of our own? (Indeed they were.) And did each house have a piano in the front parlour? (Charles said it was more like every other house.) And did he think we would be happy there? (Charles took off his glasses and looked down at us with his lovely green eyes and said, "Oh, yes, very.")

Some of us on the boat could not resist becoming friendly with the deckhands, who came from the same villages as we did, and knew all the words to our songs, and were constantly asking us to marry them. We already *are* married, we would explain, but a few of us fell in love with them anyway. And when they asked if they could see us alone—that very same evening, say, on the 'tween deck, at quarter past ten—we stared down at our feet for a moment and then took a deep breath and said, "Yes," and this was another thing we would never tell our husbands. *It was the way he looked at me*, we would think to ourselves later. Or, *He had a nice smile.*

One of us on the boat became pregnant but did not know it and when the baby was born nine months later the first thing she would notice was how much it resembled her new husband. *He's got your eyes.* One of us jumped overboard after spending the night with a sailor and leaving behind a short note on her pillow: "*After him, there can be no other.*" Another of us fell in love with a returning Methodist missionary she had met on the deck and even though he begged her to leave her husband for him when they got to America she told him that she could not. "I must remain true to my fate," she said to him. But for the rest of her life she would wonder about the life that could have been.

Some of us on the boat were brooders by nature, and preferred to stay to ourselves, and spent most of the voyage lying face down in our berths, thinking of all the men we had left behind. The fruit seller's son, who always pretended not to notice us, but gave us an extra tangerine whenever his mother was not minding the store. Or the married man for whom we had once waited, on a bridge, in the rain, late at night, for two hours. And for what? A kiss and a promise. "I'll come again tomorrow," he had said. And even though we never saw him again we knew we would do it all over in an instant, because being with him was like being alive for the very first time, only better. And often, as we were falling asleep, we found ourselves thinking of the peasant boy we had talked to every afternoon on our way home from school—the beautiful young boy in the next village whose hands could coax up even the most stubborn of seedlings from the soil—and how our mother, who knew everything, and could often read our mind, had looked at us as though we were crazy. *Do you want to spend the rest of your life crouched over a field?* (We had hesitated and almost said yes, for hadn't we always dreamed of becoming our mother? Wasn't that all we had ever once wanted to be?)

On the boat we each had to make choices. Where to sleep and who to trust   20 and who to befriend and how to befriend her. Whether or not to say something to the neighbour who snored, or talked in her sleep, or to the neighbour whose feet smelled even worse than our own, and whose dirty clothes were strewn all over the floor. And if somebody asked us if she looked good when she wore her hair in a certain way—in the "eaves" style, say, which seemed to be taking the boat by storm—and she did not, it made her head look too big, did we tell her the truth, or did we tell her she had never looked better? And was it all right to complain about the cook, who came from China, and only knew how to make one dish—rice curry—which he served to us day after day? But if we said something and he was sent back to China, where on many days you might not get any kind of rice at all, would it then be our fault? And was anybody listening to us anyway? Did anybody care?

Somewhere on the boat there was a captain, from whose cabin a beautiful young girl was said to emerge every morning at dawn. And of course we were all dying to know: was she one of us, or one of the girls from first class?

On the boat we sometimes crept into each other's berths late at night and lay quietly side by side, talking about all the things we remembered from home: the smell of roasted sweet potatoes in early autumn, picnics in the bamboo grove, playing shadows and demons in the crumbling temple courtyard, the day our father went out to fetch a bucket of water from the well and did not return, and how our mother never mentioned him even once after that. *It was as though he never even existed. I stared down into that well for years.* We discussed favourite face creams, the benefits of leaden powder, the first time we saw our husband's photograph. *He looked like an earnest person, so I figured he was good enough for me.* Sometimes we found ourselves saying things we had never said to anyone, and once we got started it was impossible to stop, and sometimes we grew suddenly silent and lay tangled in each other's arms until dawn, when one of us would pull away from the other and ask, "But will it last?" And that was another choice we had to make. If we said yes, it would last, and went back to her—if not that night, then the next, or the night after that—then we told ourselves that whatever we did would be forgotten the minute we got off the boat. And it was all good practice for our husbands anyway.

A few of us on the boat never did get used to being with a man, and if there had been a way of going to America without marrying one, we would have figured it out.

On the boat we could not have known that when we first saw our husbands we would have no idea who they were. That the crowd of men in knit caps and shabby black coats waiting for us down below on the dock would bear no resemblance to the handsome young men in the photographs. That the photographs we had been sent were twenty years old. That the letters we had been written had been written to us by people other than our husbands, professional people with beautiful handwriting whose job it was to tell lies and win hearts. That when we first heard our names being called out across the water one of us would cover her eyes and turn away—*I want to go home*—but the rest of us would lift our heads and smooth down the skirts of our kimonos and walk down the gangplank and step out into the still warm day. *This is America,* we would say to ourselves, *there is no need to worry.* And we would be wrong.

[2011]

≡ THINKING ABOUT THE TEXT

1. Given the details the narrator reveals, what seems to be the difference between Japanese and American culture around 1920? What are the specific "abilities" these young women possess?

2. What are the specific expectations of the "picture brides"? How well do they match the expectations of their husbands? Why do you assume men would arrange marriages with Japanese women they had never seen?

3. What is the significance of the encounter with the Englishman Charles? Is he honest in his replies? Why does he answer "Sadly, yes" (para. 16)? Why does Charles say they will be happy? How does this jibe with the last two sentences of the story?

4. In what way could the boat journey be seen as a foreshadowing of the brides' new life in America?

5. What references are there to love in the story? What do they tell you about the mindset of these young women? What references, direct and indirect, are there to sex? What do they tell you about the experiences or cultural attitudes of these women?

≡ MAKING COMPARISONS

1. Compare the point of view in the story and poem. What are the advantages of such a choice? What might the limitations be?

2. How is the thinking of the women on the boat and those on the train similar?

3. How would you summarize these two authors' attitudes toward pre-arranged marriage?

≡ WRITING ABOUT ISSUES

1. Although Divakaruni and Otsuka are from different countries, as are the young women they write about, there are surprising similarities. Write an essay that compares these two texts, pointing out the brides' socialization, their expectations, and other similarities in outlook.

2. Write an essay that analyzes the story and the poem, focusing on the specific descriptions and foreshadowing devices that suggest what the future holds for these women.

3. Write two letters from one of the men waiting for his bride in "Come, Japanese!" One, addressed to his potential bride, tells her what she wants to hear, what will rhetorically convince her to come. The second, which he would never send, tells her the absolute truth about his agenda and the conditions of himself and his home she will find upon her arrival.

4. Research Japanese "picture brides" as well as Otsuka's *Buddha in the Attic* and write a report about who the brides were, who their husbands were, and the problems they actually faced in America. When did the practice decline? Is there something comparable today?

CHAPTER 9

Freedom and Confinement

Like most abstract and frequently used terms, *freedom* means many things to many people. In countries in the West, freedom is usually associated with political and religious choice, with the ability to dissent publicly from government policy, and even with an ability to dye our hair orange and paint our lips black. Indeed, freedom involves the right not to conform to conventional ideas about who we are and how we should behave as well as the right not to be stereotyped by a culture's demeaning, limiting, and distorted images and assumptions.

Readers of nineteenth-century fiction by women are familiar with the rigid cultural expectations that constricted the lives of most women. Excluded from public life and confined almost exclusively to domestic spaces, many women felt trapped in helping roles constructed for them by men. The consequences for the mental and physical health of thousands of would-be writers, artists, scientists, and intellectuals were often severe. Today many minorities in America also feel limited by the confining legacies of both racial and gender stereotypes. Children, who are especially vulnerable to the negative images that adults from the dominant culture have of them, have few defenses against internalizing damaging stereotypes that can adversely affect them well into adulthood. And when an entire culture constructs invidious stereotypes, as German Nazis did about European Jews, the consequences can be deadly.

The chapter opens with six poems that explore the painful consequences of stereotyping, followed by five poets who remember the horrors of the Holocaust. A selection of poems by one of the giants in American literature, Emily Dickinson, is next, followed by three translations of a famous poem by Rainer Maria Rilke. Three stories about the darker side of tradition comprise the fifth cluster. The difficulties of returning home after war are the focus of the next cluster. Willa Cather's classic story "Paul's Case" and a cluster of critical commentaries responding to that text are followed by Henrik Ibsen's play *A Doll's House* and contextual documents that illuminate its controversial appeal. Three essays that deal with surveillance are next, and then the chapter concludes with a story, a poem, and an excerpt from a speech that try to come to grips with the historical troubles in Ireland.

≡ Struggling against Stereotypes: Poems

CHRYSTOS, "Today Was a Bad Day like TB"

DWIGHT OKITA, "In Response to Executive Order 9066"

DAVID HERNANDEZ, "Pigeons"

PAT MORA, "Legal Alien"

TOI DERRICOTTE, "Black Boys Play the Classics"

NAOMI SHIHAB NYE, "Blood"

When pressed, thoughtful people would agree that each of us has an individual personality and attributes that make us different from others. No one is an exact duplicate: even identical twins have both subtle and significant differences. Even so, cultures tend to lump together whole groups under dubious but convenient generalizations: used car dealers are dishonest, surfers are laidback slackers, and computer geniuses are geeks. Usually based on limited, anecdotal, and often highly contextual historical and cultural evidence, these generalizations have a way of taking hold in a society long after the original context has disappeared (if there ever was one). Does anyone really think that dumb-blond jokes had any original validity? Is considering each person on his or her own merits too complicated?

When ethnic groups are stereotyped, their members may suffer consequences that are significantly more severe than those endured by, say, absent-minded professors. Some stereotypes are benign: as children growing up in New York, we routinely heard about industrious Chinese or hardworking Germans. But we also heard many negative generalizations that went hand in hand with racial discrimination and psychological damage. Members of the dominant groups in America are often oblivious to the ways that members of minority groups internalize destructive and distorted images of themselves, often seeing themselves as inferior to the dominant group and irredeemably other. They become trapped in images rampant in the culture and struggle daily to overcome the limited reality these stereotypes portray. The following seven poems represent aspects of this struggle in various ways — some with anger, resentment, and despair, others with thoughtful reflection, but all with an awareness of the pain that thoughtless stereotypes have on millions of Americans.

≡ BEFORE YOU READ

Do you think of yourself as an ethnic American? Have you ever seen the term *English American* or *Dutch American*? What's the difference between those terms and *African American* or *Irish American*? Do you think ethnic traditions should be preserved, or should they be replaced with American traditions? Can these traditions coexist?

CHRYSTOS
Today Was a Bad Day like TB

Born in San Francisco of a Lithuanian/Alsace-Lorraine mother and a Native American father of the Menominee tribe, Chrystos (b. 1946) writes in the outsider traditions of her ancestry, her lesbian perspective, and her geographical position on Bainbridge Island off the coast of the Pacific Northwest. She is a women's and native rights advocate, a working artist, and a poet. Her poetry collections include Not Vanishing *(1988),* Dream On *(1991),* In Her I Am *(1993),* Fire Power *(1995), and the 1994 winner of the Audre Lorde International Poetry Competition,* Fugitive Colors. *In 2007, she published* Some Poems by People I Like. *She is a Lannan Foundation fellow and the 1995 recipient of the Sappho Award of Distinction. The poem reprinted here is from* Not Vanishing.

    For Amanda White
Saw whites clap during a sacred dance
Saw young blond hippie boy with a red stone pipe°
    My eyes burned him up
He smiled   *This is a Sioux pipe* he said from his sportscar
    Yes   I hiss   *I'm wondering how you got it*   5
    & the name is Lakota not Sioux
I'll tell you he said all friendly & liberal as only
    those with no pain can be
    I turned away   Can't charm me   can't bear to know
thinking of the medicine bundle I saw opened up in a glass case   10
    with a small white card beside it
    naming the rich whites who say they
    "own" it
Maybe they have an old Indian grandma back in time
    to excuse themselves   15
Today was a day I wanted to beat up the smirking man wearing
    a pack with a Haida design from Moe's bookstore
Listen Moe's   How many Indians do you have working there?
How much money are you sending the Haida people
to use their sacred Raven design?   20
    You probably have an Indian grandma too
    whose name you don't know
    Today was a day like TB
    you cough & cough trying to get it out
        all that comes   25
            is blood & spit   *[1988]*

2 red stone pipe: Traditionally, sacred peace pipes were made of red catlinite, a fine-grained stone.

☰ THINKING ABOUT THE TEXT

1. What argument about the ways whites relate to Native Americans is Chrystos making? What assumptions about whites does Chrystos seem to have? What stereotypes does she seem to harbor?

2. Might you have clapped during a Lakota dance? During a Catholic Mass? What is the "it" in line 24 that the poet is trying to get out? Do you think she is angry with her readers?

3. Is the ending too stark or perhaps too crude? Might the language have been more indirect and subtle, or is it appropriate to the theme?

4. Americans who are part of the "mainstream" — that is, white, male, middle class, or heterosexual — sometimes get annoyed when those who are not complain about bias, probably because the offense was inadvertent. (Think of Atlanta Braves fans doing "the tomahawk chop.") The young man in this poem, for example, seems quite oblivious of giving offense. Who determines who is right in these situations?

5. What other stereotypes can you think of that mainstream America harbors?

DWIGHT OKITA

In Response to Executive Order 9066

A third-generation Japanese American, poet and playwright Dwight Okita (b. 1958) won an Illinois Art Council Fellowship for poetry in 1988. Although Crossing with the Light *(1992), from which this poem is taken, is his first book of poetry, Okita has been more active in promoting the performance of poetry than the printing of it, and he is well known as a "slam" poet at open-mike readings in Chicago. A member of the large Japanese American community that developed in Chicago as a result of the migration from the West after the bitter experience of the internment camps during World War II, Okita expresses his family history in his poetry and plays. His dramas include* The Rainy Season *(1992) and* The Salad Bowl Dance *(1993). His book* The Prospect of My Arrival *(2008) was nominated for the Amazon Breakthrough Novel Award.*

> All Americans of Japanese Descent
> Must Report to Relocation Centers

Dear Sirs:
Of course I'll come. I've packed my galoshes
and three packets of tomato seeds. Denise calls them
love apples. My father says where we're going
they won't grow.   5

I am a fourteen-year-old girl with bad spelling
and a messy room. If it helps any, I will tell you

I have always felt funny using chopsticks
and my favorite food is hot dogs.
My best friend is a white girl named Denise —   10
we look at boys together. She sat in front of me
all through grade school because of our names:
O'Connor, Ozawa. I know the back of Denise's head very well.

I tell her she's going bald. She tells me I copy on tests.
We're best friends.   15

I saw Denise today in Geography class.
She was sitting on the other side of the room.
"You're trying to start a war," she said, "giving secrets
away to the Enemy. Why can't you keep your big
mouth shut?"   20

I didn't know what to say.
I gave her a packet of tomato seeds
and asked her to plant them for me, told her
when the first tomato ripened
she'd miss me.   *[1992]*   25

≡ THINKING ABOUT THE TEXT

1. What claim is Okita making in the last stanza? On what assumption about friendship is it based?

2. During the U.S. government's internment of Japanese American citizens, thousands were told to leave their homes to live in relocation centers for the duration of the war. To represent this complex historical event, why do you think it is effective to have a young girl writing a letter about being shunned by her best friend?

3. Explain Okita's use of the tomato seeds throughout the poem (lines 3, 22). What about other concrete words: *galoshes* (line 2), *chopsticks* (line 8), *hot dogs* (line 9)?

4. Since there was no evidence that Japanese American citizens ever gave any "secrets / away to the Enemy" (lines 18–19) during World War II, why do you think Denise and millions of other Americans made that assumption?

5. What current situations seem comparable to the theme of this poem?

≡ MAKING COMPARISONS

1. Compare the tones of Okita's and Chrystos's poems. What emotions do you see in each?

2. Okita creates a young female narrator to speak for him. Does this make his poem less direct than Chrystos's?

3. Is the alienation described by Okita more or less painful than that described by Chrystos?

DAVID HERNANDEZ

Pigeons

An active member of Chicago's arts community, David Hernandez (1946–2013) published several books of poetry, including Despertando / Waking Up *(1991),* Satin City Lullaby *(1986), and* Rooftop Piper *(1991), from which this poem is taken. He wrote, recited, and taught poetry for more than thirty years and was commissioned to write a poem for Chicago's 150th anniversary in 1987.*

Pigeons are the spiks of Birdland.
   They are survivors of blood, fire and stone.
      They can't afford to fly south
         or a Florida winter home.

Most everybody passing up a pigeon pack   5
tries to break it up because they move funny
and seem to be dancing like young street thugs
with an 18-foot, 10-speaker Sanyo book box radio
on a 2-foot red shoulder strap.
              Pigeons have feathers of a different color.   10
              They are too bright to be dull
              and too dull to be bright
              so they are not accepted anywhere.
     Nobody wants to give pigeons a job.
     Parakeets, canaries and parrots   15
     have the market sewn up as far as that goes.
     They live in fancy cages, get 3 meals a day
     for a song and dance routine.
     When was the last time you saw a pigeon
     in someone's home?   20
     Unless they bleach their feathers white
     and try to pass off as doves,
     you will never see pet pigeons.
     Besides, their accents give them away
     when they start cooing.   25

Once in a while, some creature will treat them decent.
   They are known as pigeon ladies, renegades,
      or bleeding-heart Liberals.
              What they do is build these wooden cages
                on rooftops that look like huge   30
            pigeon housing projects
         where they freeze during the winters
        and get their little claws stuck in tar
      on hot summer days

No wonder they are pigeon-toed.   35
I tell you,
            Pigeons are the spiks of Birdland.   *[1991]*

≡ **THINKING ABOUT THE TEXT**

1. Hernandez uses the pigeon simile to comment on the place of Latinos in Birdland/America. What specific comparisons does he make? What is his larger argument?

2. Is this poem a complaint or an accusation of Birdland/America? Do you see some validity in what Hernandez says?

3. Does he press the bird comparison too far? Not far enough? What about attempts to eradicate pigeons or their reputation as disease carriers? How far should a poet carry such similes or metaphors? How far should the reader?

4. Is *spiks* an appropriate word to use in a poem? What if a white person (a dove?) used the term? What does Hernandez mean by "pigeon-toed" (line 35)?

5. Is the poet being ironic about those who try to treat the pigeons decently? What would he have preferred?

≡ **MAKING COMPARISONS**

1. How would you compare Hernandez's complaint against the liberals with Chrystos's against the hippie?

2. Hernandez's poem seems more ambitious than the other poems. Do you think he is trying to paint a fuller picture of discrimination?

3. Which of the poetic devices in these first three poems strikes you as the most effective? The least? Why?

PAT MORA

Legal Alien

Pat Mora (b. 1942) was born in El Paso, Texas. She earned a B.A. from Texas Western College in 1963 and an M.A. from the University of Texas, El Paso, in 1967. She is a versatile writer of many children's books, essays, and poems. Her poems are, according to the New York Times, *"proudly bilingual." Her sixth collection,* Adobe Odes *(2006), was praised for turning its back on hopelessness, "finding a way to delight in the sensual world as well as its people," and a "must-have for libraries serving Latino communities." Her latest collection is* Dizzy in Your Eyes *(2010). Mora lives in Santa Fe, New Mexico. "Legal Alien" is from* Chants *(1984) and focuses on a common Chicana theme: the difficulties of living in two cultures simultaneously.*

Bi-lingual, Bi-cultural,
able to slip from "How's life?"
to *"Me'stan volviendo loca,"*°
able to sit in a paneled office
drafting memos in smooth English,   5
able to order in fluent Spanish
at a Mexican restaurant,
American but hyphenated,
viewed by Anglos as perhaps exotic,
perhaps inferior, definitely different,   10
viewed by Mexicans as alien,
(their eyes say, "You may speak
Spanish but you're not like me")
an American to Mexicans
a Mexican to Americans   15
a handy token
sliding back and forth
between the fringes of both worlds
by smiling
by masking the discomfort   20
of being pre-judged
Bi-laterally.   *[1984]*

3 *"Me'stan volviendo loca"*: They're driving me crazy (Spanish).

≡ THINKING ABOUT THE TEXT

1. Was your first response to the opening line to think that such a situation is an advantage? Is that Mora's intent?

2. What advantages does being bicultural have? What disadvantages?

3. What other Americans are referred to as "hyphenated"? Do you think the same pluses and minuses apply?

4. Is the title appropriate? Explain.

5. Explain the significance of the "token" metaphor in line 16.

≡ MAKING COMPARISONS

1. Mora sees some advantage to being bicultural. Do any of the other poets?

2. Compare Mora's tone with Chrystos's.

3. Which of the stereotypes in these poems seems the most psychologically damaging? Why?

TOI DERRICOTTE

Black Boys Play the Classics

Toi Derricotte (b. 1941) was born in Louisiana and was influenced as a child by her Creole and Catholic background. She graduated from Wayne State University in 1965. The first of her six books, The Empress of the Death House, *was published in 1978. Her latest collection of poems and stories,* The Undertaker's Daughter, *was published in 2011. Often compared to Sylvia Plath and Anne Sexton, Derricotte writes poems that, according to the poet and critic Marilyn Hacker, are "honest, fine-boned, deceptively simple . . . and deadly accurate." She is currently a professor of English at the University of Pittsburgh. The following poem is from* Tender *(1997).*

The most popular "act" in
Penn Station
is the three black kids in ratty
sneakers & T-shirts playing
two violins and a cello — Brahms.   5
White men in business suits
have already dug into their pockets
as they pass and they toss in
a dollar or two without stopping.
Brown men in work-soiled khakis   10
stand with their mouths open,
arms crossed on their bellies
as if they themselves have always
wanted to attempt those bars.
One white boy, three, sits   15
cross-legged in front of his
idols — in ecstasy —
their slick, dark faces,
their thin, wiry arms,
who must begin to look   20
like angels!
Why does this trembling
pull us?
A: *Beneath the surface we are one.*
B: *Amazing! I did not think that they could speak this tongue.*   [1997]   25

≡ THINKING ABOUT THE TEXT

1. Why do the "brown men" (line 10) respond as they do? Why do the "white men" (line 6)?

2. Why does the poet offer a description of the boys' clothes? Does it have to do with our stereotyped expectations?

3. What are some possible meanings for "pull us" (line 23)?

4. Explain what you think Derricotte means by the last line.

5. How would you state the theme of this poem? Do you agree with it? Who is the "we" in the next-to-last line?

≡ MAKING COMPARISONS

1. How does Derricotte's tone differ from Chrystos's tone? From Hernandez's?

2. How does the end of this poem differ from the ends of the other poems in this cluster? Is it more effective or less effective?

3. If you were to rewrite "Black Boys Play the Classics" as a first-person poem (as Okita's poem demonstrates), which character from this poem would you choose, and why? How would a different point of view change the poem?

NAOMI SHIHAB NYE
Blood

Naomi Shihab Nye (b. 1952) was born to a Lutheran German American mother and a Muslim Palestinian American father in St. Louis. Her parents moved to the Middle East near Jerusalem, where her father edited the Jerusalem Times, *for which Nye, at fourteen, wrote a weekly column. Eventually turmoil forced their return to America. They settled in Texas, and Nye graduated from Trinity University in San Antonio in 1974. She has published books for children and adolescents with subject matter she hopes will dispel stereotypes and foster an understanding of "difference." Her poetic focus is often on the Palestinian Diaspora and on themes of our common humanity. Her books include* 19 Varieties of Gazelle *(2002) and* You and Yours: Poems *(2005). "Blood" is from* Yellow Glove *(1986).*

"A true Arab knows how to catch a fly in his hands,"
my father would say. And he'd prove it,
cupping the buzzer instantly
while the host with the swatter stared.

In the spring our palms peeled like snakes.   5
True Arabs believed watermelon could heal fifty ways.
I changed these to fit the occasion.

Years before, a girl knocked,
wanted to see the Arab.
I said we didn't have one.   10
After that, my father told me who he was,

"Shihab" — "shooting star" —
a good name, borrowed from the sky.
Once I said, "When we die, we give it back?"
He said that's what a true Arab would say.　　　　　　　　　15

Today the headlines clot in my blood.
A little Palestinian dangles a truck on the front page.
Homeless fig, this tragedy with a terrible root
is too big for us. What flag can we wave?
I wave the flag of stone and seed,　　　　　　　　　20
table mat stitched in blue.

I call my father, we talk around the news.
It is too much for him,
neither of his two languages can reach it.
I drive into the country to find sheep, cows,　　　　　　　　　25
to plead with the air:
Who calls anyone *civilized*?
Where can the crying heart graze?
What does a true Arab do now?　　　　　　　　　*[1986]*

≡ THINKING ABOUT THE TEXT

1. What is your response to the girl who comes looking "to see the Arab" (line 9)? What is the speaker's response?

2. What do you think the father means by "a true Arab"? Is there a true American? A true man? Woman? Texan?

3. What is the father's response to the news about the Middle East? What is the speaker's? What is yours?

4. What is the purpose of the speaker's drive into the country?

5. How would you answer the questions the speaker asks in the last stanza?

≡ MAKING COMPARISONS

1. Compare Nye's bicultural perspective to Mora's. Is Nye's status more precarious than Mora's in contemporary America?

2. Which of the speakers in all these poems seems angriest? Saddest? The most understanding?

3. What seems to be the most common theme among the poems?

≡ WRITING ABOUT ISSUES

1. Write a journal entry from either Chrystos's or Okita's perspective that comments on the writing of the poem, what you (as the author) were

trying to do, how you feel about stereotyping, and what response you are hoping for from readers.

2. Write an essay that compares the stereotyping that occurs in "Pigeons" and "Legal Alien." Comment on its origins, consequences, and possible solutions.

3. Write an essay that explores the kind of stereotyping you were exposed to as a child and as an adolescent in your family, in your peer group, or in the larger culture.

4. After doing research on an ethnic group not represented here, locate a poet from that group and write a brief report on his or her work.

≡ Remembering the Death Camps: Poems

MARTIN NIEMÖLLER, "First They Came for the Jews"

NELLY SACHS, "Chorus of the Rescued"

MARIANNE COHN, "I Shall Betray Tomorrow"

KAREN GERSHON, "Race"

ANNE SEXTON, "After Auschwitz"

Being shunned by neighbors because of religion, race, gender, or ethnicity creates painful psychological alienation for victims of such treatment. But what if your religion, cultural heritage, or sexual orientation were deemed dangerous to the well-being of your country? What if the powerful so dehumanized you that you were thought of as vermin to be disposed of? This would be more than alienation; this would be putting respect for human life beyond normal moral restraints. As in war, the different ones become the enemy who is less than human and who can be destroyed with impunity.

Of course, this describes exactly what happened during the Holocaust when the Nazis murdered millions of Jews. Thousands of eyewitness accounts have been written about this tragedy, but writers who were not there feel equally compelled to write about the events of the Holocaust. It is impossible to adequately represent such horrors: some writers are furious; others are disciplined and controlled. It is one of a writer's challenges to try to express in words what is truly beyond description.

≡ BEFORE YOU READ

Have you seen photographs of Holocaust survivors? Have you seen films, read books, or heard stories about these events? What are your feelings? Can you explain how systematic genocide is possible? Do such things still happen in the world?

MARTIN NIEMÖLLER
First They Came for the Jews

A German Protestant theologian and pastor, Martin Niemöller (1892–1984), who won the Iron Cross as a submarine commander in World War I, is best known as an outspoken critic of Adolf Hitler and Nazism preceding and during World War II. As the pastor of the Berlin congregation of the Evangelical Church from 1931, Niemöller led a group of clergy working to counter Nazism and earned Hitler's hatred. From 1937 to 1945, he was interned at the Dachau and Sachsenhausen concentration camps. After the war, he focused his efforts on international disarmament and the recovery of the German church. He served as president of the World Council of Churches from 1961 to 1968.

> First they came for the Jews
> and I did not speak out
> because I was not a Jew.
> Then they came for the Communists
> and I did not speak out   5
> because I was not a Communist.
> Then they came for the trade unionists
> and I did not speak out
> because I was not a trade unionist.
> Then they came for me   10
> and there was no one left
> to speak out for me.   *[1945]*

≡ THINKING ABOUT THE TEXT

1. The poem seems to merely narrate a sequence of events, but is there an implicit argument here? Should the writer have been more explicit?

2. As you read this poem, do you think, "He's talking to me"? Do you think that might be Niemöller's intention?

3. Many poems are lyrical, filled with beautiful images and imaginative phrases. Would this poem be improved by moving in this direction?

4. Often in poetry, people and situations can be taken both literally and as symbols for something else. Do you think that is the case here with the Jews and Communists?

5. Most societies, even democracies, have insiders and outsiders, those with power and privilege and those with no influence. In your experience, does literature relate the feelings and experiences of both equally? Should this anthology balance the poems in this cluster with the experience of insiders?

NELLY SACHS
Chorus of the Rescued

Translated by Ruth and Matthew Mead

A poet and playwright born in Berlin of Jewish parents, Nelly Sachs (1891–1970) escaped from Nazi Germany in 1940 to Stockholm, where she became a Swedish citizen and eventually won the Nobel Prize for literature in 1966. First published as a poet in Germany in 1921, she later used biblical forms and motifs and empathized with the millions who suffered in the Holocaust. Her best-known play, Eli: A Mystery Play of the Sufferings of Israel, *epitomizes this style, as does the following poem, which uses pathos to evoke sympathy.*

We, the rescued,
From whose hollow bones death had begun to whittle his flutes,
And on whose sinews he had already stroked his bow —
Our bodies continue to lament
With their mutilated music.   5
We, the rescued,
The nooses would for our necks still dangle
Before us in the blue air —
Hourglasses still fill with our dripping blood.
We, the rescued,   10
The worms of fear still feed on us.
Our constellation is buried in dust.
We, the rescued,
Beg you:
Show us your sun, but gradually.   15
Lead us from star to star, step by step.
Be gentle when you teach us to live again.
Lest the song of a bird,
Or a pail being filled at the well,
Let our badly sealed pain burst forth again   20
And carry us away —
We beg you:
Do not show us an angry dog, not yet —
It could be, it could be
That we will dissolve into dust —   25
Dissolve into dust before your eyes.
For what binds our fabric together?
We whose breath vacated us,
Whose soul fled to Him out of that midnight?
Long before our bodies were rescued   30
Into the arc of the moment.
We, the rescued,
We press your hand
We look into your eye —
But all that binds us together now is leave-taking.   35
The leave-taking in the dust
Binds us together with you.   *[1967]*

≡ THINKING ABOUT THE TEXT

1. What is your reading of "Show us your sun" (line 15)?
2. What is meant by "Do not show us an angry dog, not yet" (line 23)?

3. How would you describe the emotional state of the narrator?

4. The poet uses metaphors throughout the poem, but particularly in the first twelve lines. How would you paraphrase the poet's descriptions?

5. According to the last three lines, what finally binds the poet to the reader?

≡ **MAKING COMPARISONS**

1. Even though both Niemöller's and Sachs's poems are about the Holocaust, are you able to relate to them from your own experiences?

2. With its metaphors, Sachs's poem seems more typically poetic. Would Niemöller's poem have been improved with more poetic devices? Might Sachs's poem have been improved with fewer?

3. One might argue that these two poems are causally connected. Explain.

MARIANNE COHN

I Shall Betray Tomorrow

Marianne Cohn (1922–1944) was born in Mannheim, Germany. Her family went into exile in Spain in 1934. Marianne joined the Resistance in France, taking Jewish children to territories outside Nazi control. In 1943, she was imprisoned for three months in Nice, where she wrote this poem. She was arrested again in 1944 with a group of twenty-eight children and tortured. Then, in July, she was murdered by the Gestapo. The children were eventually saved.

I shall betray tomorrow, not today.
Today, pull out my fingernails,
I shall not betray.
You do not know the limits of my courage,
I, I do.   5
You are five hands, harsh and full of rings,
Wearing hob-nailed boots.
I shall betray tomorrow, not today.
I need the night to make up my mind.
I need at least one night,   10
To disown, to abjure, to betray.
To disown my friends,
To abjure bread and wine,
To betray life,
To die.   15
I shall betray tomorrow, not today.
The file is under the window-pane.
The file is not [meant] for the window-bars,

The file is not [meant] for the executioner,
The file is for my own wrists.   20
Today, I have nothing to say,
I shall betray tomorrow.   *[1943]*

≡ THINKING ABOUT THE TEXT

1. Is the title meant ironically? How do you know?
2. What seems to be the most pronounced attitude of the narrator?
3. Does anything suggest that she is contemplating suicide?
4. The narrator seems quite confident about her ability to resist torture. Do you think she really is? Would you be able to resist torture?
5. Do you think other prisoners would be inspired or dispirited by this poem?

≡ MAKING COMPARISONS

1. Compare your response to the attitude of the speakers in Sachs's and Cohn's poems.
2. What do you think is the purpose of each of the three poems?
3. Do you think Cohn might have written a poem like "Chorus of the Rescued" had she survived?

KAREN GERSHON
Race

Later known by her married name, Karen Tripp, Gershon (1923–1993) escaped from Nazi Germany in 1939 as a teenager. Sent to England without her family, she wrote in her poetry of this experience and the loss of her parents, who died in the Holocaust. Gershon published eight books, contributed to numerous periodicals, and won much recognition, including the British Arts Council Award in 1967. Her poetry was widely read in the 1960s and later, perhaps influencing contemporaries Anne Sexton and Sylvia Plath, who borrowed the imagery of Holocaust survivors to describe family conflict and inner turmoil. "Race" is from Selected Poems *(1966).*

When I returned to my home town
believing that no one would care
who I was and what I thought
it was as if the people caught
an echo of me everywhere   5
they knew my story by my face
and I who am always alone
became a symbol of my race

Like every living Jew I have
in imagination seen   10
the gas-chamber the mass-grave
the unknown body which was mine
and found in every German face
behind the mask the mark of Cain
I will not make their thoughts my own   15
by hating people for their race.   *[1966]*

≡ THINKING ABOUT THE TEXT

1. Is Gershon imagining or actually describing her reception? How can you
   tell?

2. Do you mind the poet speaking for "every living Jew" (line 9)? Do you
   think this is accurate? Can someone be a symbol of their race?

3. Does the title refer to Jews or to Germans? Why is neither group mentioned in the title?

4. Gershon writes fairly straightforward poetry, letting her content speak
   for itself. What specific poetic devices does she employ? Should she use
   more?

5. Do you find the last four lines ambiguous? Does she see Germans as
   murderers, or does she reject such invidious generalizations? Should
   Germans be held accountable for the Holocaust? Should Americans be
   held accountable for slavery? Are only the people who specifically par-
   take in evil deeds responsible, or is the whole culture that "allowed" it
   guilty as well?

≡ MAKING COMPARISONS

1. Compare Gershon's attitude in the last two lines of her poem with
   Sachs's attitude in the last three lines of her poem.

2. Had Cohn lived, might she have written "Chorus of the Rescued" or
   "Race"?

3. Describe the emotions you find in all four poems.

ANNE SEXTON
After Auschwitz

*Growing up in New England and attending elite boarding and finishing schools during
the years of World War II, Anne Sexton (1928–1974) had an emotional connection
with the Holocaust rather than a firsthand one: her obsession with images of death
and degradation and her "confessional" poetic stance blend seamlessly with such a
theme. "After Auschwitz" is from* The Awful Rowing toward God *(1977).*

Anger,
as black as a hook,
overtakes me.
Each day,
each Nazi   5
took, at 8.00 a.m., a baby
and sautéed him for breakfast
in his frying pan.

And death looks on with a casual eye
and picks at the dirt under his fingernail.   10

Man is evil,
I say aloud.
Man is a flower
that should be burnt,
I say aloud.   15
Man
is a bird full of mud,
I say aloud.

And death looks on with a casual eye
and scratches his anus.   20

Man with his small pink toes,
with his miraculous fingers
is not a temple
but an outhouse,
I say aloud.   25
Let man never again raise his teacup.
Let man never again write a book.
Let man never again put on his shoe.
Let man never again raise his eyes,
on a soft July night.   30
Never. Never. Never. Never. Never.
I say these things aloud.

I beg the Lord not to hear.   [1977]

≡ THINKING ABOUT THE TEXT

1. What is Sexton's purpose here if she really does not want God to listen?

2. What is your response to the image of Nazi cannibalism in lines 4–8? What about her inclusive accusation that "Man is evil" (line 11)?

3. As Sexton's editor, would you suggest that she change any specific words or phrases? Should she control the generally angry tone?

4. Sexton personifies death. Why? Why do you think she refers to man's "pink toes" and "miraculous fingers" in lines 21 and 22?

5. Sexton sees the Holocaust as an indictment of everyone. Do you agree with her?

≡ MAKING COMPARISONS

1. Compare the ambivalence at the end of Sexton's poem with the last sentence in Sachs's poem.
2. Do you think Gershon's poem would be improved by Sexton's explicit anger?
3. Which of these five poets comes closest to expressing your feelings about the Holocaust?

≡ WRITING ABOUT ISSUES

1. Argue that Sexton's indictment of humankind is either hyperbolic or accurate.
2. Make a case in a brief essay that "First They Came for the Jews" leads to "I Shall Betray Tomorrow."
3. Write a brief personal response explaining your feelings about the Holocaust or suggesting what such an event tells us about human nature, if anything.
4. Rent a film about the Holocaust such as Steven Spielberg's *Schindler's List* or Roman Polanski's *The Pianist*. Write a review expressing your feelings and thoughts about its contents and its representation of the Holocaust. Include a comparison to the poems you read.

▤ A Creative Confinement: A Collection of Poems by Emily Dickinson

Although Emily Dickinson was considered an eccentric recluse by many of her provincial neighbors, history has interpreted her life in various ways, changing with the thinking of the times. Once considered isolated, she is now seen by many critics as vitally connected to the issues and literature of her age. Feminist and queer studies scholars now see the once-shy figure as an active champion who defied gender stereotypes. Although she has often been described as nunlike and passive, critics today see her as a nonconformist, mistrustful of power and dogma, and as someone who questioned any kind of received opinion, even popular views on religion and the afterlife. And although it may seem paradoxical to many, the artistic freedom necessary for a focused creative life is often achieved by isolation, by physically removing oneself from the temptation and distractions of social life. If ever there was an example of confinement nurturing the creative impulse, it is the life and poems of Emily Dickinson.

EMILY DICKINSON
Wild Nights — Wild Nights!

Emily Dickinson (1830–1886) spent most of her life in her father's house in Amherst, Massachusetts. Except for a year of college and several brief excursions to Philadelphia and Washington, D.C., Dickinson lived a quiet, reclusive life in a house she described as "pretty much all sobriety." Although a few poems were published during her lifetime, Dickinson wrote almost two thousand poems on love, death, immortality, and nature that are universally judged to be some of the most original, lyrical, and artistic works in American literature. Although the specific person to whom Dickinson wrote her love poems is unclear, many critics today believe her interests were both lesbian and heterosexual. As the four poems below suggest, Dickinson, although outwardly retiring and isolated, lived a lively, rich, and passionate life in her poetry.

> Wild Nights — Wild Nights!
> Were I with thee
> Wild Nights should be
> Our luxury!

Boston Globe via Getty Images

Futile — the Winds —   5
To a Heart in port —
Done with the Compass —
Done with the Chart!

Rowing in Eden —
Ah, the Sea!   10
Might I but moor — Tonight —
In Thee   *[c. 1861]*

≣ THINKING ABOUT THE TEXT

1. Many critics see this poem as an erotic fantasy, perhaps a surprising subject for a reclusive spinster. Are there indications that this is not a poem about a real sexual encounter?

2. Comment on the imagery of the ocean and port. Could the port be Dickinson's isolation? The ocean, the actual consummation?

3. How do you read the speaker's claim that she is done with the compass and chart? Is she rejecting convention?

4. What are some ways to interpret "Eden" in line 9?

5. What does the image of "moor[ing] . . . In Thee" (lines 11–12) suggest about her erotic desire?

EMILY DICKINSON

Tell all the truth but tell it slant—

Tell all the truth but tell it slant—
Success in Circuit lies
Too bright for our infirm Delight
The Truth's superb surprise

As Lightning to the Children eased   5
With explanation kind
The Truth must dazzle gradually
Or every man be blind—   *[1868]*

≡ THINKING ABOUT THE TEXT

1. What is the primary dictionary definition of "slant"? What does Dickinson mean by slant?
2. Why does Dickinson say we shouldn't be direct in telling the truth?
3. What similarity between the truth and lightning does Dickinson want us to make?
4. What is it about poetry that makes indirection a better path to truth?
5. How does this poem embody Dickinson's advice?

≡ MAKING COMPARISONS

1. How might both poems be about freedom and confinement?
2. Compare the images in both poems. Are they apt?
3. To whom is each poem addressed?

EMILY DICKINSON

Much Madness is divinest Sense—

Much Madness is divinest Sense—
To a discerning Eye—
Much Sense—the starkest Madness—
'Tis the Majority
In this, as all, prevail—   5
Assent—and you are sane—
Demur—you're straightway dangerous—
And handled with a Chain—   *[1871]*

≡ THINKING ABOUT THE TEXT

1. What does Dickinson suggest is one way to lose your freedom?

2. How might this poem be an example of Dickinson's own biography? (See also the introduction on p. 844.)

3. Why does Dickinson use "Demur" (line 7)? What synonyms might she have used?

4. Why does she use "divinest sense" (line 1)? Why does she say the majority is usually wrong? Why does she use the dramatic image of a chain? Is this an indication of her mood?

5. In your experience, how is Dickinson's idea that the majority is intolerant of dissent true?

≡ MAKING COMPARISONS

1. How might Dickinson be telling the truth in "Much Madness is divinest Sense" at a slant?

2. Why might Dickinson's "tell it slant" be necessary given the last two lines of "Much Madness is divinest Sense"?

3. Compare the idea that there is freedom in confinement with the themes of these poems.

EMILY DICKINSON
I'm Nobody! Who are you?

I'm Nobody! Who are you?
Are you — Nobody — too?
Then there's a pair of us!
Don't tell! they'd advertise — you know!

How dreary — to be — Somebody!   5
How public — like a Frog —
To tell one's name — the livelong June —
To an admiring Bog! —   *[1891]*

≡ THINKING ABOUT THE TEXT

1. How might this poem be about Dickinson's own life?

2. Why does Dickinson use "Bog" (line 8)? In what way is this an appropriate image for her theme? Why does she pick a frog and not something else — say, a robin or a horse?

3. Is this poem meant to be comical or satirical? Why does she invite the reader to identify with her?

4. How would you describe what the poet means by "Nobody" (line 1) and "Somebody" (line 5)?

5. How might this poem be applicable to fame in today's culture?

≡ MAKING COMPARISONS

1. How might the theme of "Much Madness is divinest Sense" be a reason for Dickinson's declaration, "I'm Nobody"?

2. Compare the intended audience for all four poems.

3. Compare the implications of "an admiring Bog" in "I'm Nobody! Who are you" with "Majority" in "Much Madness is divinest Sense."

≡ WRITING ABOUT ISSUES

1. Write an analysis of these four poems as examples of the ideas mentioned in the introduction to this chapter (p. 824) and in the biographical note about Dickinson (p. 844).

2. Write an analysis of these four poems, focusing on the imagery Dickinson uses to support her themes.

3. Research Dickinson's poetry and choose two other poems that develop similar themes to those given here. Write an essay that demonstrates how freedom is developed in these two poems.

4. Argue that Dickinson's ideas about nonconformity and fame are relevant in today's culture.

RAINER MARIA RILKE, "Der Panther"

ROBERT BLY, "The Panther"

J. B. LEISHMAN, "The Panther"

STEPHEN MITCHELL, "The Panther"

Translating simple, objective prose from one language to another is more difficult than it seems, but it pales in comparison to, say, translating German poetry into English. By its very nature, poetry with its figurative language is indirect and suggestive, its themes dependent on subtle shades of meaning, on subjective connotations. It is difficult enough translating a lyrical poem into prose, and a daunting task, indeed, translating the complex, abstract, and nuanced poetry of someone like Rainer Maria Rilke. And there will always be differences of opinion about the intent of the writer, as well as the problem of determining the comparable meaning of the poet's words and images in the translator's culture.

It is for these reasons that there are scores of translations of Ranier Maria Rilke's "Der Panther." So much depends on the linguistic and poetic skill of the translators and on their interpretation of the poem itself. Some will want to stick as closely as possible to the denotation of the words, others will want to give free rein to their creative imaginations with the connotations of words. Being true to the spirit of the poem will to some be more "accurate" than a faithful word-by-word rendering. Perhaps all translation decisions will depend on the mood the translator thinks the poet wants to evoke.

Rilke's friend, the great sculptor August Rodin, urged him to go to the Jardin des Plantes in Paris and intensely study one of the animals in the zoo there so that he could know it deeply, in all its movements and moods. The resulting poem is considered one of Rilke's greatest achievements.

■ BEFORE YOU READ

Have you ever felt sorry for an animal in a zoo? What changes in its life would you make? Is it possible to have a "humane" zoo?

RAINER MARIA RILKE

Der Panther

Rainer Maria Rilke (1875–1926) is considered one of the greatest modern German poets. Rilke, who was born in Prague (now in the Czech Republic), is known for his lyrical and mystical writings about the difficulties of existence. His poems are still widely read, especially by those who appreciate Khalil Gibran and the Sufi poet Rumi. In Paris, Rilke was involved with the leading artists of the day, including August

Getty Images

Rodin and Paul Cézanne. He also lived in Switzerland and Italy, where his two most famous works, Duino Elegies *(1922) and* Sonnets to Orpheus *(1922) were written. His elegies are religious and mystical, with many symbolic references to angels and salvation. The sonnets are highly metaphorical and mythical. He is often cited as having been influential in the poetic outlooks of W. H. Auden, Robert Bly, Galway Kinnell, and many others. Rilke wrote his own epitaph: "Rose, oh pure contradiction, delight / of being no one's sleep under so / many lids."*

Sein Blick ist vomVorübergehn der Stäbe
so müd geworden, daß er nichts mehr hält.
Ihm ist, als ob es tausend Stäbe gäbe
und hinter tausend Stäben keine Welt.

Der weiche Gang geschmeidig starker Schritte,   5
der sich im allerkleinsten Kreise dreht,
ist wie ein Tanz von Kraft um eine Mitte,
in der betäubt ein großer Wille steht.

Nur manchmal schiebt der Vorhang der Pupille
sich lautlos auf — dann geht ein Bild hinein,   10
geht durch der Glieder angespannte Stille —
und hört im Herzen auf zu sein.   *[1902]*

ROBERT BLY
The Panther

Robert Bly (b. 1926) grew up in western Minnesota and graduated from Harvard in 1950. He travelled to Norway on a Fulbright grant, where he developed an interest in translation. He won the National Book Award for The Light Around the Body *in 1967. Perhaps his most famous text is* Iron John: A Book About Men *(1990), an international bestseller that used traditional mythology to restore the idea of healthy masculinity, which, in his view, had been damaged by contemporary culture. His latest book of poems is* Talking into the Ear of a Donkey *(2011).*

From seeing the bars, his seeing is so exhausted
that it no longer holds anything anymore.
To him the world is bars, a hundred thousand
bars, and behind the bars, nothing.

The lithe swinging of that rhythmical easy stride   5
which circles down to the tiniest hub
is like a dance of energy around a point
in which a great will stands stunned and numb.

Getty Images

Only at times the curtains of the pupil rise
without a sound—then a shape enters,   10
slips through the tightened silence of the shoulders,
reaches the heart, and dies.   *[1981]*

≡ THINKING ABOUT THE TEXT

1. What is the main mood of the poem? What feelings are evoked by "stunned and numb" (line 8); "reaches the heart, and dies" (line 12)?
2. Why does Bly imply that the panther doesn't want to see any further than the bars?
3. What idea is Bly trying to suggest about the panther's movements?
4. What happens in the last stanza?
5. What metaphorical idea about humans is suggested by the panther's plight?

J. B. LEISHMAN
The Panther

J. B. Leishman (1902–1963) taught for many years at Oxford University, where he was a Lecturer in English Literature. He published widely on John Donne, Shakespeare, and Andrew Marvell. His was the most popular translation of Rilke for decades. His translation of Possibility of Being: A Selection of Poems *by Rainer Maria Rilke was published in 1977.*

His gaze those bars keep passing is so misted
with tiredness, it can take in nothing more.
He feels as though a thousand bars existed,
and no more world beyond them before.

Those supply-powerful paddings, turning there   5
in the tiniest of circles, well might be
the dance of forces round a center where
some mighty will stands paralyticly.

Just now and then the pupil's noiseless shutter
is lifted—then an image will indart,   10
down through the limbs' intensive stillness flutter,
and end its being in the heart.   *[1964]*

≡ THINKING ABOUT THE TEXT

1. What is gained and lost by Leishman's rhyme scheme?

2. What do you assume happened in the panther's cage or outside of it for the poet to write "the pupil's noiseless shutter / is lifted . . ." (lines 9–10)?

3. What happens to the "image" mentioned in line 10?

4. What is meant by lines 7 and 8? What might the "center" be? What do you assume "paralyticly" means?

5. What do you think Leishman thinks of the panther's situation? Where is that the clearest?

☰ MAKING COMPARISONS

1. What seems to be the most significant difference between the two translations? Which do you prefer, and why?

2. What is the difference between Bly's lines 8, "in which a great will stands stunned and numb" and Leishman's, "some mighty will stands paralyticly"?

3. Why do you prefer either "exhausted" (Bly, line 1) or "tiredness" (Leishman, line 2) in referring to the panther? How about Bly's "dies" versus Leishman's "end its being" (line 12)?

STEPHEN MITCHELL

The Panther

Stephen Mitchell (b. 1943) was born in Brooklyn, New York, and studied at Amherst, Colby, University of Paris, and Yale. He is a poet and scholar and fluent in many languages, having translated The Iliad *and* The Odyssey, *as well as* The Selected Poetry of Rainer Maria Rilke.

His vision, from the constantly passing bars,
has grown so weary that it cannot hold
anything else. It seems to him there are
a thousand bars, and behind the bars, no world.

As he paces in cramped circles, over and over,   5
the movement of his powerful soft strides
is like a ritual dance around a center
in which a mighty will stands paralyzed.

Only at times, the curtain of the pupils
lifts, quietly — an image enters in,   10
rushes down through the tensed, arrested muscles,
plunges into the heart and is gone.   *[1980]*

Scott London

≡ THINKING ABOUT THE TEXT

1. What is most disturbing to the panther?

2. Would you choose the phrase "ritual dance" or "dance of forces" (Leishman) or "dance of energy" (Bly) in line 7? Which best conveys your feeling about the panther?

3. Are there moments of hope in the life of this panther?

4. What is the word you would use to convey the panther's own sense of his situation? What about your feeling after finishing the poem?

5. Is there a suggestion that the panther is like a man in prison? Or a person metaphorically trapped? Explain.

≡ MAKING COMPARISONS

1. Give specific reasons why you prefer one translation over the other two.

2. What are the most poetic images in the three versions?

3. Why do you prefer one of these three: *exhausted, tiredness, weary* (line 1, 2)? How about *seeing, gaze,* and *vision* (line 1); or *dies, ends its being,* or *gone* (line 12)?

≡ WRITING ABOUT ISSUES

1. Locate one of Rilke's sonnets and write an analysis of its themes.

2. Research the history of zoos. How have they changed since Rilke's time? Are there different philosophies about what a zoo should be? Write an essay that focuses on the problem Rilke writes about and some possible solutions.

3. Write an analysis of the poem, focusing on the description, mood, and movement of the panther and the possible analogy to confinement in human society.

4. Research online translations of Rilke's "Der Panther." Choose two additional versions, and in an essay, compare them to the three selections.

■ Where Tradition Is a Trap: Stories

SHIRLEY JACKSON, "The Lottery"

URSULA K. LE GUIN, "The Ones Who Walk Away from Omelas"

CAITLIN HORROCKS, "The Sleep"

Often our fondest memories of childhood involve family and community traditions, from public events like Thanksgiving, Halloween, and Fourth of July celebrations, to religious holidays like Christmas and Hanukkah, to private celebrations like birthdays and anniversaries. These rituals give our lives structure and create a sense of belonging. They give us psychological comfort and security and a ready-made identity of belonging with like-minded people who share our values. We acquire a sense of our adult roles, our goals, our understanding of the meaning of life, birth, death, love, and hate. Traditions and their accompanying rituals offer guidance as we address the complex question of how to "be" in the world.

Once a tradition starts, however, it may be difficult to change. Perhaps that is not so significant when we are thinking of birthday and graduation ceremonies, but it is life altering when traditions govern whom we may marry, what roles we can play in society, how we understand justice and freedom, and when our lives begin and end.

In some societies, traditions have been in place for thousands of years. They are difficult to change since they are woven into individuals' sense of self. People often feel that their own traditions are normal, even though anthropologists claim that few traditions are universal among cultures.

How does one change a time-honored tradition? What if the reason for the tradition has been lost to history? What if some members of the community feel their own values and morality are offended by the tradition? Can we look to the law for change? Or to community pressure? Maybe we just endure the ritual. Or maybe the sense of outrage is so great that we must leave the community. Then what? The three authors in this cluster confront these and other dilemmas when honored traditions are questioned. Sixty-five years after its publication, Shirley Jackson's "The Lottery" is still one of the most controversial stories ever printed in *The New Yorker*. When the story was banned in South Africa, Jackson said, "Well, at least they understood it." Ursula K. Le Guin's tale of a utopia with a terrible secret is an excellent example of the insidious snares of tradition. In both stories, the origins of the rituals are lost in deep history, but interestingly, Caitlin Horrocks's tale lets us in on its inauguration. First, one small-town family decides to sleep the winter away. But after a while, others are drawn to its benefits. Using a bit of magical realism, Horrocks's story begins to seem plausible. Its matter-of-fact style will remind you of "The Lottery" without the horrific ritualistic ending. But the allegorical implications are just as rich.

≣ **BEFORE YOU READ**

Recall incidents from the past when you felt uncomfortable being involved in a tradition or ritual. How did you respond? What specific traditions in our culture could easily be eliminated? Are there harmful traditions in our culture that should be changed? Explain.

SHIRLEY JACKSON

The Lottery

Shirley Jackson (1919–1965) was born in San Francisco and grew up in the affluent suburb of Burlingame. Her family moved to Rochester, New York, in 1939, and she graduated from Syracuse University in 1940. Jackson wrote of her life: "I was married in 1940 to Stanley Edgar Hyman, critic and numismatist, and we live in Vermont, in a quiet rural community with fine scenery and comfortably away from city life. Our major export are books and children, both of which we produce in abundance." She received a National Book Award nomination for The Haunting of Hill House *(1959), which was adapted for film twice (1963 and 1999); this popular book is often cited as one of the best horror novels of the twentieth century and as an influence on contemporary masters of that genre such as Stephen King.*

The morning of June 27th was clear and sunny, with the fresh warmth of a full-summer day; the flowers were blossoming profusely and the grass was richly green. The people of the village began to gather in the square, between the post office and the bank, around ten o'clock; in some towns there were so many people that the lottery took two days and had to be started on June 26th, but in this village, where there were only about three hundred people, the whole lottery took less than two hours, so it could begin at ten o'clock in the morning and still be through in time to allow the villagers to get home for noon dinner.

The children assembled first, of course. School was recently over for the summer, and the feeling of liberty sat uneasily on most of them; they tended to gather together quietly for a while before they broke into boisterous play, and their talk was still of the classroom and teacher, of books and reprimands. Bobby Martin had already stuffed his pockets full of stones, and the other boys soon followed his example, selecting the smoothest and roundest stones; Bobby and Harry Jones and Dickie Delacroix—the villagers pronounced this name "Dellacroy"—eventually made a great pile of stones in one corner of the square and guarded it against the raids of the other boys. The girls stood aside, talking among themselves, looking over their shoulders at the boys, and the very small children rolled in the dust or clung to the hands of their older brothers or sisters.

Soon the men began to gather, surveying their own children, speaking of planting and rain, tractors and taxes. They stood together, away from the pile of stones in the corner, and their jokes were quiet and they smiled rather than laughed. The women, wearing faded house dresses and sweaters, came shortly after their menfolk. They greeted one another and exchanged bits of gossip as they went to join their husbands. Soon the women, standing by their husbands, began to call to their children, and the children came reluctantly, having to be called four or five times. Bobby Martin ducked under his mother's grasping hand and ran, laughing, back to the pile of stones. His father spoke up sharply, and Bobby came quickly and took his place between his father and his oldest brother.

The lottery was conducted—as were the square dances, the teenage club, the Halloween program—by Mr. Summers, who had time and energy to devote to civic activities. He was a round-faced, jovial man and he ran the coal business, and people were sorry for him, because he had no children and his wife was a scold. When he arrived in the square, carrying the black wooden box, there was a murmur of conversation among the villagers, and he waved and called, "Little late today, folks." The postmaster, Mr. Graves, followed him, carrying a three-legged stool, and the stool was put in the center of the square and Mr. Summers set the black box down on it. The villagers kept their distance, leaving a space between themselves and the stool, and when Mr. Summers said, "Some of you fellows want to give me a hand?" there was a hesitation before two men, Mr. Martin and his oldest son, Baxter, came forward to hold the box steady on the stool while Mr. Summers stirred up the papers inside it.

The original paraphernalia for the lottery had been lost long ago, and the black box now resting on the stool had been put into use even before Old Man Warner, the oldest man in town, was born. Mr. Summers spoke frequently to the villagers about making a new box, but no one liked to upset even as much tradition as was represented by the black box. There was a story that the present box had been made with some pieces of the box that had preceded it, the one that had been constructed when the first people settled down to make a village here. Every year, after the lottery, Mr. Summers began talking again about a new box, but every year the subject was allowed to fade off without anything's being done. The black box grew shabbier each year; by now it was no longer completely black but splintered badly along one side to show the original wood color, and in some places faded or stained.

Mr. Martin and his oldest son, Baxter, held the black box securely on the stool until Mr. Summers had stirred the papers thoroughly with his hand. Because so much of the ritual had been forgotten or discarded, Mr. Summers had been successful in having slips of paper substituted for the chips of wood that had been used for generations. Chips of wood, Mr. Summers had argued, had been all very well when the village was tiny, but now that the population was more than three hundred and likely to keep on growing, it was necessary to use something that would fit more easily into the black box. The night before the lottery, Mr. Summers and Mr. Graves made up the slips of paper and put them in the box, and it was then taken to the safe of Mr. Summers's coal company and locked up until Mr. Summers was ready to take it to the square next morning. The rest of the year, the box was put away, sometimes one place, sometimes

5

another; it had spent one year in Mr. Graves's barn and another year underfoot in the post office, and sometimes it was set on a shelf in the Martin grocery and left there.

There was a great deal of fussing to be done before Mr. Summers declared the lottery open. There were the lists to make up—of heads of families, heads of households in each family, members of each household in each family. There was the proper swearing-in of Mr. Summers by the postmaster, as the official of the lottery; at one time, some people remembered, there had been a recital of some sort, performed by the official of the lottery, a perfunctory, tuneless chant that had been rattled off duly each year; some people believed that the official of the lottery used to stand just so when he said or sang it, others believed that he was supposed to walk among the people, but years and years ago this part of the ritual had been allowed to lapse. There had been, also, a ritual salute, which the official of the lottery had had to use in addressing each person who came up to draw from the box, but this also had changed with time, until now it was felt necessary only for the official to speak to each person approaching. Mr. Summers was very good at all this; in his clean white shirt and blue jeans, with one hand resting carelessly on the black box, he seemed very proper and important as he talked interminably to Mr. Graves and the Martins.

Just as Mr. Summers finally left off talking and turned to the assembled villagers, Mrs. Hutchinson came hurriedly along the path to the square, her sweater thrown over her shoulders, and slid into place in the back of the crowd. "Clean forgot what day it was," she said to Mrs. Delacroix, who stood next to her, and they both laughed softly. "Thought my old man was out back stacking wood," Mrs. Hutchinson went on, "and then I looked out the window and the kids was gone, and then I remembered it was the twenty-seventh and came a-running." She dried her hands on her apron, and Mrs. Delacroix said, "You're in time, though. They're still talking away up there."

Mrs. Hutchinson craned her neck to see through the crowd and found her husband and children standing near the front. She tapped Mrs. Delacroix on the arm as a farewell and began to make her way through the crowd. The people separated good-humoredly to let her through; two or three people said, in voices just loud enough to be heard across the crowd, "Here comes your Missus, Hutchinson," and "Bill, she made it after all." Mrs. Hutchinson reached her husband, and Mr. Summers, who had been waiting, said cheerfully, "Thought we were going to have to get on without you, Tessie." Mrs. Hutchinson said, grinning, "Wouldn't have me leave m'dishes in the sink, now, would you, Joe?" and soft laughter ran through the crowd as the people stirred back into position after Mrs. Hutchinson's arrival.

"Well, now," Mr. Summers said soberly, "guess we better get started, get this over with, so's we can go back to work. Anybody ain't here?"   10

"Dunbar," several people said. "Dunbar; Dunbar."

Mr. Summers consulted his list. "Clyde Dunbar," he said. "That's right. He's broke his leg, hasn't he? Who's drawing for him?"

"Me, I guess," a woman said, and Mr. Summers turned to look at her. "Wife draws for her husband," Mr. Summers said. "Don't you have a grown boy to do it for you, Janey?" Although Mr. Summers and everyone else in the village knew the answer perfectly well, it was the business of the official of the lottery to ask such questions formally. Mr. Summers waited with an expression of polite interest while Mrs. Dunbar answered.

"Horace's not but sixteen yet," Mrs. Dunbar said regretfully. "Guess I gotta fill in for the old man this year."

"Right," Mr. Summers said. He made a note on the list he was holding. 15
Then he asked, "Watson boy drawing this year?"

A tall boy in the crowd raised his hand. "Here," he said. "I'm drawing for m'mother and me." He blinked his eyes nervously and ducked his head as several voices in the crowd said things like "Good fellow, Jack," and "Glad to see your mother's got a man to do it."

"Well," Mr. Summers said, "guess that's everyone. Old Man Warner make it?"

"Here," a voice said, and Mr. Summers nodded.

A sudden hush fell on the crowd as Mr. Summers cleared his throat and looked at the list. "All ready?" he called. "Now, I'll read the names—heads of families first—and the men come up and take a paper out of the box. Keep the paper folded in your hand without looking at it until everyone has had a turn. Everything clear?"

The people had done it so many times that they only half listened to the 20
directions; most of them were quiet, wetting their lips, not looking around. Then Mr. Summers raised one hand high and said, "Adams." A man disengaged himself from the crowd and came forward. "Hi, Steve," Mr. Summers said, and Mr. Adams said, "Hi, Joe." They grinned at one another humorlessly and nervously. Then Mr. Adams reached into the black box and took out a folded paper. He held it firmly by one corner as he turned and went hastily back to his place in the crowd, where he stood a little apart from his family, not looking down at his hand.

"Allen," Mr. Summers said, "Anderson. . . . Bentham."

"Seems like there's no time at all between lotteries any more," Mrs. Delacroix said to Mrs. Graves in the back row. "Seems like we got through with the last one only last week."

"Time sure goes fast," Mrs. Graves said.

"Clark. . . . Delacroix."

"There goes my old man," Mrs. Delacroix said. She held her breath while 25
her husband went forward.

"Dunbar," Mr. Summers said, and Mrs. Dunbar went steadily to the box while one of the women said, "Go on, Janey," and another said, "There she goes."

"We're next," Mrs. Graves said. She watched while Mr. Graves came around from the side of the box, greeted Mr. Summers gravely, and selected a slip of paper from the box. By now, all through the crowd there were men holding the small folded papers in their large hands, turning them over and over nervously. Mrs. Dunbar and her two sons stood together, Mrs. Dunbar holding the slip of paper.

"Harburt. . . . Hutchinson."

"Get up there, Bill," Mrs. Hutchinson said, and the people near her laughed.
"Jones."   30

"They do say," Mr. Adams said to Old Man Warner, who stood next to him,
"that over in the north village they're talking of giving up the lottery."

Old Man Warner snorted. "Pack of crazy fools," he said. "Listening to the
young folks, nothing's good enough for *them*. Next thing you know, they'll be
wanting to go back to living in caves, nobody work any more, live *that* way for
a while. Used to be a saying about 'Lottery in June, corn be heavy soon.' First
thing you know, we'd all be eating stewed chickweed and acorns. There's
always been a lottery," he added petulantly. "Bad enough to see young Joe
Summers up there joking with everybody."

"Some places have already quit lotteries," Mrs. Adams said.

"Nothing but trouble in *that*," Old Man Warner said stoutly. "Pack of
young fools."

"Martin." And Bobby Martin watched his father go forward. "Overdyke. . . .   35
Percy."

"I wish they'd hurry," Mrs. Dunbar said to her older son. "I wish they'd
hurry."

"They're almost through," her son said.

"You get ready to run tell Dad," Mrs. Dunbar said.

Mr. Summers called his own name and then stepped forward precisely and
selected a slip from the box. Then he called, "Warner."

"Seventy-seventh year I been in the lottery," Old Man Warner said as he   40
went through the crowd. "Seventy-seventh time."

"Watson." The tall boy came awkwardly through the crowd. Someone
said, "Don't be nervous, Jack," and Mr. Summers said, "Take your time, son."

"Zanini."

After that, there was a long pause, a breathless pause, until Mr. Summers,
holding his slip of paper in the air, said, "All right, fellows." For a minute, no
one moved, and then all the slips of paper were opened. Suddenly, all the
women began to speak at once, saying, "Who is it?" "Who's got it?" "Is it the
Dunbars?" "Is it the Watsons?" Then the voices began to say, "It's Hutchinson.
It's Bill," "Bill Hutchinson's got it."

"Go tell your father," Mrs. Dunbar said to her older son.

People began to look around to see the Hutchinsons. Bill Hutchinson   45
was standing quiet, staring down at the paper in his hand. Suddenly, Tessie
Hutchinson shouted to Mr. Summers, "You didn't give him time enough to take
any paper he wanted. I saw you. It wasn't fair!"

"Be a good sport, Tessie," Mrs. Delacroix called, and Mrs. Graves said, "All
of us took the same chance."

"Shut up, Tessie," Bill Hutchinson said.

"Well, everyone," Mr. Summers said, "that was done pretty fast, and now
we've got to be hurrying a little more to get done in time." He consulted his next
list. "Bill," he said, "you draw for the Hutchinson family. You got any other
households in the Hutchinsons?"

"There's Don and Eva," Mrs. Hutchinson yelled. "Make *them* take their chance!"

"Daughters drew with their husbands' families, Tessie," Mr. Summers said   50
gently. "You know that as well as anyone else."

"It wasn't *fair,*" Tessie said.

"I guess not, Joe," Bill Hutchinson said regretfully. "My daughter draws with her husband's family, that's only fair. And I've got no other family except the kids."

"Then, as far as drawing for families is concerned, it's you," Mr. Summers said in explanation, "and as far as drawing for households is concerned, that's you, too. Right?"

"Right," Bill Hutchinson said.

"How many kids, Bill?" Mr. Summers asked formally.   55

"Three," Bill Hutchinson said. "There's Bill Jr., and Nancy, and little Dave. And Tessie and me."

"All right, then," Mr. Summers said. "Harry, you got their tickets back?"

Mr. Graves nodded and held up the slips of paper. "Put them in the box, then," Mr. Summers directed. "Take Bill's and put it in."

"I think we ought to start over," Mrs. Hutchinson said, as quietly as she could. "I tell you it wasn't *fair.* You didn't give him time enough to choose. *Every*body saw that."

Mr. Graves had selected the five slips and put them in the box, and he   60
dropped all the papers but those onto the ground, where the breeze caught them and lifted them off.

"Listen, everybody," Mrs. Hutchinson was saying to the people around her.

"Ready, Bill?" Mr. Summers asked, and Bill Hutchinson, with one quick glance around at his wife and children, nodded.

"Remember," Mr. Summers said, "take the slips and keep them folded until each person has taken one. Harry, you help little Dave." Mr. Graves took the hand of the little boy, who came willingly with him up to the box. "Take a paper out of the box, Davy," Mr. Summers said. Davy put his hand into the box and laughed. "Take just *one* paper," Mr. Summers said. "Harry, you hold it for him." Mr. Graves took the child's hand and removed the folded paper from the tight fist and held it while little Dave stood next to him and looked up at him wonderingly.

"Nancy next," Mr. Summers said. Nancy was twelve, and her school friends breathed heavily as she went forward, switching her skirt, and took a slip daintily from the box. "Bill Jr.," Mr. Summers said, and Billy, his face red and his feet overlarge, nearly knocked the box over as he got a paper out. "Tessie," Mr. Summers said. She hesitated for a minute, looking around defiantly, and then set her lips and went up to the box. She snatched a paper out and held it behind her.

"Bill," Mr. Summers said, and Bill Hutchinson reached into the box and felt   65
around, bringing his hand out at last with the slip of paper in it.

The crowd was quiet. A girl whispered, "I hope it's not Nancy," and the sound of the whisper reached the edges of the crowd.

"It's not the way it used to be," Old Man Warner said clearly. "People ain't the way they used to be."

"All right," Mr. Summers said. "Open the papers. Harry, you open little Dave's."

Mr. Graves opened the slip of paper and there was a general sigh through the crowd as he held it up and everyone could see that it was blank. Nancy and Bill Jr. opened theirs at the same time, and both beamed and laughed, turning around to the crowd and holding their slips of paper above their heads.

"Tessie," Mr. Summers said. There was a pause, and then Mr. Summers   70
looked at Bill Hutchinson, and Bill unfolded his paper and showed it. It was blank.

"It's Tessie," Mr. Summers said, and his voice was hushed. "Show us her paper, Bill."

Bill Hutchinson went over to his wife and forced the slip of paper out of her hand. It had a black spot on it, the black spot Mr. Summers had made the night before with the heavy pencil in the coal-company office. Bill Hutchinson held it up and there was a stir in the crowd.

"All right, folks," Mr. Summers said. "Let's finish quickly."

Although the villagers had forgotten the ritual and lost the original black box, they still remembered to use stones. The pile of stones the boys had made earlier was ready; there were stones on the ground with the blowing scraps of paper that had come out of the box. Mrs. Delacroix selected a stone so large she had to pick it up with both hands and turned to Mrs. Dunbar. "Come on," she said. "Hurry up."

Mrs. Dunbar had small stones in both hands, and she said, gasping for   75
breath, "I can't run at all. You'll have to go ahead and I'll catch up with you."

The children had stones already, and someone gave little Davy Hutchinson a few pebbles.

Tessie Hutchinson was in the center of a cleared space by now, and she held her hands out desperately as the villagers moved in on her. "It isn't fair," she said. A stone hit her on the side of the head.

Old Man Warner was saying, "Come on, come on, everyone." Steve Adams was in the front of the crowd of villagers, with Mrs. Graves beside him.

"It isn't fair, it isn't right," Mrs. Hutchinson screamed and then they were upon her.   [1948]

≡ THINKING ABOUT THE TEXT

1. At what point in the story did you suspect that something was amiss in this bucolic village? How does Jackson both prepare you for and surprise you with her ending?

2. Make a list of the characters' names in the story. What symbolic significance might they have?

3. What do the phrase "Lottery in June, corn be heavy soon" and the pile of stones suggest about the origins of the lottery?

4. Critics often mention scapegoating, man's inherent evil, and the destructive consequence of hanging on to ancient and outdated rituals as the principal themes of this story. Do you agree? What are some other themes suggested by the story?

5. What contemporary issues does "The Lottery" bring to mind?

URSULA K. LE GUIN

The Ones Who Walk Away from Omelas

Ursula K. Le Guin (b. 1929) was born and raised in Berkeley, California, where she began writing at eleven, unsuccessfully submitting a story to Astounding Science Fiction. *She graduated from Radcliffe College (Phi Beta Kappa) in 1951 and received her M.A. from Columbia University a year later. She became famous with the publication of* The Left Hand of Darkness *(1969), an exploration of a hermaphroditic race that most critics see as a comment on contemporary gender politics. The novel won science fiction's highest awards: the Hugo and the Nebula.* The Farthest Shore *(1972) won the National Book Award, and* Tehanu: The Last Book of Earthsea *(1990) won the prestigious Nebula Award. More recently,* Powers *won the Nebula Award for 2008, and* Lavinia *won the 2009 Locus Award for Best Fantasy Novel. Besides her twenty novels, Le Guin has also published scores of short stories, books for children, nonfiction, and six volumes of poems. In 2000, Le Guin received the Library of Congress Living Legends award for her "significant contribution to America's heritage."*

With a clamor of bells that set the swallows soaring, the Festival of Summer came to the city Omelas, bright-towered by the sea. The rigging of the boats in harbor sparkled with flags. In the streets between houses with red roofs and painted walls, between old moss-grown gardens and under avenues of trees, past great parks and public buildings, processions moved. Some were decorous: old people in long stiff robes of mauve and gray, grave master workmen, quiet, merry women carrying their babies and chatting as they walked. In other streets the music beat faster, a shimmering of gong and tambourine, and the people went dancing, the procession was a dance. Children dodged in and out, their high calls rising like the swallows' crossing flights over the music and the singing. All the processions wound towards the north side of the city, where on the great water-meadow called the Green Fields boys and girls, naked in the bright air, with mudstained feet and ankles and long, lithe arms, exercised their restive horses before the race. The horses wore no gear at all but a halter without bit. Their manes were braided with streamers of silver, gold, and green. They flared their nostrils and pranced and boasted to one another; they were vastly excited, the horse being the only animal who has adopted our ceremonies as his own. Far off to the north and west the mountains stood up half encircling Omelas on her bay. The air of morning was so clear that the snow still crowning the Eighteen Peaks burned with white-gold fire across the miles of sunlit air, under the dark blue of the sky. There was just enough wind to make the banners that marked the racecourse snap and flutter now and then. In the silence of the broad green meadows one could hear the music winding through the city streets, farther and nearer and ever approaching, a cheerful faint sweetness of the air that from time to time trembled and gathered together and broke out into the great joyous clanging of the bells.

Joyous! How is one to tell about joy? How describe the citizens of Omelas?

They were not simple folk, you see, though they were happy. But we do not say the words of cheer much any more. All smiles have become archaic. Given a description such as this one tends to make certain assumptions. Given a description such as this one tends to look next for the King, mounted on a splendid stallion and surrounded by his noble knights, or perhaps in a golden litter borne by great-muscled slaves. But there was no king. They did not use swords, or keep slaves. They were not barbarians. I do not know the rules and laws of their society, but I suspect that they were singularly few. As they did without monarchy and slavery, so they also got on without the stock exchange, the advertisement, the secret police, and the bomb. Yet I repeat that these were not simple folk, not dulcet shepherds, noble savages, bland utopians. They were not less complex than us. The trouble is that we have a bad habit, encouraged by pedants and sophisticates, of considering happiness as something rather stupid. Only pain is intellectual, only evil interesting. This is the treason of the artist: a refusal to admit the banality of evil and the terrible boredom of pain. If you can't lick 'em, join 'em. If it hurts, repeat it. But to praise despair is to condemn delight, to embrace violence is to lose hold of everything else. We have almost lost hold, we can no longer describe a happy man, nor make any celebration of joy. How can I tell you about the people of Omelas? They were not naive and happy children — though their children were, in fact, happy. They were mature, intelligent, passionate adults whose lives were not wretched. O miracle! But I wish I could describe it better. I wish I could convince you. Omelas sounds in my words like a city in a fairy tale, long ago and far away, once upon a time. Perhaps it would be best if you imagined it as your own fancy bids, assuming it will rise to the occasion, for certainly I cannot suit you all. For instance, how about technology? I think that there would be no cars or helicopters in and above the streets; this follows from the fact that the people of Omelas are happy people. Happiness is based on a just discrimination of what is necessary, what is neither necessary nor destructive, and what is destructive. In the middle category, however — that of the unnecessary but undestructive, that of comfort, luxury, exuberance, etc. — they could perfectly well have central heating, subway trains, washing machines, and all kinds of marvelous devices not yet invented here, floating light-sources, fuelless power, a cure for the common cold. Or they could have none of that: it doesn't matter. As you like it. I incline to think that people from towns up and down the coast have been coming in to Omelas during the last days before the Festival on very fast little trains and double-decked trams, and that the train station of Omelas is actually the handsomest building in town, though plainer than the magnificent Farmers'

Market. But even granted trains, I fear that Omelas so far strikes some of you as goody-goody. Smiles, bells, parades, horses, bleh. If so, please add an orgy. If an orgy would help, don't hesitate. Let us not, however, have temples from which issue beautiful nude priests and priestesses already half in ecstasy and ready to copulate with any man or woman, lover or stranger, who desires union with the deep godhead of the blood, although that was my first idea. But really it would be better not to have any temples in Omelas — at least, not manned temples. Religion yes, clergy no. Surely the beautiful nudes can just wander about, offering themselves like divine soufflés to the hunger of the needy and the rapture of the flesh. Let them join the processions. Let tambourines be struck above the copulations, and the glory of desire be proclaimed upon the gongs, and (a not unimportant point) let the offspring of these delightful rituals be beloved and looked after by all. One thing I know there is none of in Omelas is guilt. But what else should there be? I thought that first there were no drugs, but that is puritanical. For those who like it, the faint insistent sweetness of *drooz* may perfume the ways of the city, *drooz* which first brings a great lightness and brilliance to the mind and limbs, and then after some hours a dreamy languor, and wonderful visions at last of the very arcana and inmost secrets of the Universe, as well as exciting the pleasure of sex beyond all belief; and it is not habit-forming. For more modest tastes I think there ought to be beer. What else, what else belongs in the joyous city? The sense of victory, surely, the celebration of courage. But as we did without clergy, let us do without soldiers. The joy built upon successful slaughter is not the right kind of joy; it will not do; it is fearful and it is trivial. A boundless and generous contentment, a magnanimous triumph felt not against some outer enemy but in communion with the finest and fairest in the souls of all men everywhere and the splendor of the world's summer: this is what swells the hearts of the people of Omelas, and the victory they celebrate is that of life. I really don't think many of them need to take *drooz*.

Most of the processions have reached the Green Fields by now. A marvelous smell of cooking goes forth from the red and blue tents of the provisioners. The faces of small children are amiably sticky; in the benign grey beard of a man a couple of crumbs of rich pastry are entangled. The youths and girls have mounted their horses and are beginning to group around the starting line of the course. An old woman, small, fat, and laughing, is passing out flowers from a basket, and tall young men wear her flowers in their shining hair. A child of nine or ten sits at the edge of the crowd, alone, playing on a wooden flute. People pause to listen, and they smile, but they do not speak to him, for he never ceases playing and never sees them, his dark eyes wholly rapt in the sweet, thin magic of the tune.

He finishes, and slowly lowers his hands holding the wooden flute.   5

As if that little private silence were the signal, all at once a trumpet sounds from the pavilion near the starting line: imperious, melancholy, piercing. The horses rear on their slender legs, and some of them neigh in answer. Soberfaced, the young riders stroke the horses' necks and soothe them, whispering, "Quiet, quiet, there my beauty, my hope. . . ." They begin to form in rank along the starting line. The crowds along the racecourse are like a field of grass and flowers in the wind. The Festival of Summer has begun.

Do you believe? Do you accept the festival, the city, the joy? No? Then let me describe one more thing.

In a basement under one of the beautiful public buildings of Omelas, or perhaps in the cellar of one of its spacious private homes, there is a room. It has one locked door, and no window. A little light seeps in dustily between cracks in the boards, secondhand from a cobwebbed window somewhere across the cellar. In one corner of the little room a couple of mops, with stiff, clotted, foul-smelling heads, stand near a rusty bucket. The floor is dirt, a little damp to the touch, as cellar dirt usually is. The room is about three paces long and two wide: a mere broom closet or disused tool room. In the room a child is sitting. It could be a boy or a girl. It looks about six, but actually is nearly ten. It is feeble-minded. Perhaps it was born defective, or perhaps it has become imbecile through fear, malnutrition, and neglect. It picks its nose and occasionally fumbles vaguely with its toes or genitals, as it sits hunched in the corner far-thest from the bucket and the two mops. It is afraid of the mops. It finds them horrible. It shuts its eyes, but it knows the mops are still standing there; and the door is locked; and nobody will come. The door is always locked; and nobody ever comes, except that sometimes — the child has no understanding of time or interval — sometimes the door rattles terribly and opens, and a person, or several people, are there. One of them may come in and kick the child to make it stand up. The others never come close, but peer in at it with frightened, dis-gusted eyes. The food bowl and the water jug are hastily filled, the door is locked, the eyes disappear. The people at the door never say anything, but the child, who has not always lived in the tool room, and can remember sunlight and its mother's voice, sometimes speaks. "I will be good," it says. "Please let me out. I will be good!" They never answer. The child used to scream for help at night, and cry a good deal, but now it only makes a kind of whining, "eh-haa, eh-haa," and it speaks less and less often. It is so thin there are no calves to its legs; its belly protrudes; it lives on a half-bowl of corn meal and grease a day. It is naked. Its buttocks and thighs are a mass of festered sores, as it sits in its own excrement continually.

They all know it is there, all the people of Omelas. Some of them have come to see it, others are content merely to know it is there. They all know that it has to be there. Some of them understand why, and some do not, but they all un-derstand that their happiness, the beauty of their city, the tenderness of their friendships, the health of their children, the wisdom of their scholars, the skill of their makers, even the abundance of their harvest and the kindly weathers of their skies, depend wholly on this child's abominable misery.

This is usually explained to children when they are between eight and twelve, whenever they seem capable of understanding; and most of those who come to see the child are young people, though often enough an adult comes, or comes back, to see the child. No matter how well the matter has been ex-plained to them, these young spectators are always shocked and sickened at the sight. They feel disgust, which they had thought themselves superior to. They

10

feel anger, outrage, impotence, despite all the explanations. They would like to do something for the child. But there is nothing they can do. If the child were brought up into the sunlight out of that vile place, if it were cleaned and fed and comforted, that would be a good thing, indeed; but if it were done, in that day and hour all the prosperity and beauty and delight of Omelas would wither and be destroyed. Those are the terms. To exchange all the goodness and grace of every life in Omelas for that single, small improvement: to throw away the happiness of thousands for the chance of the happiness of one: that would be to let guilt within the walls indeed.

The terms are strict and absolute; there may not even be a kind word spoken to the child.

Often the young people go home in tears, or in a tearless rage, when they have seen the child and faced this terrible paradox. They may brood over it for weeks or years. But as time goes on they begin to realize that even if the child could be released, it would not get much good of its freedom: a little vague pleasure of warmth and food, no doubt, but little more. It is too degraded and imbecile to know any real joy. It has been afraid too long ever to be free of fear. Its habits are too uncouth for it to respond to humane treatment. Indeed, after so long it would probably be wretched without walls about it to protect it, and darkness for its eyes, and its own excrement to sit in. Their tears at the bitter injustice dry when they begin to perceive the terrible justice of reality, and to accept it. Yet it is their tears and anger, the trying of their generosity and the acceptance of their helplessness, which are perhaps the true source of the splendor of their lives. Theirs is no vapid, irresponsible happiness. They know that they, like the child, are not free. They know compassion. It is the existence of the child, and their knowledge of its existence, that makes possible the nobility of their architecture, the poignancy of their music, the profundity of their science. It is because of the child that they are so gentle with children. They know that if the wretched one were not there snivelling in the dark, the other one, the flute-player, could make no joyful music as the young riders line up in their beauty for the race in the sunlight of the first morning of summer.

Now do you believe in them? Are they not more credible? But there is one more thing to tell, and this is quite incredible.

At times one of the adolescent girls or boys who go to see the child does not go home to weep or rage, does not, in fact, go home at all. Sometimes also a man or woman much older falls silent for a day or two, and then leaves home. These people go out into the street, and walk down the street alone. They keep walking, and walk straight out of the city of Omelas, through the beautiful gates. They keep walking across the farmlands of Omelas. Each one goes alone, youth or girl, man or woman. Night falls; the traveler must pass down village streets, between the houses with yellow-lit windows, and on out into the darkness of the fields. Each alone, they go west or north, towards the mountains. They go on. They leave Omelas, they walk ahead into the darkness, and they do not come back. The place they go towards is a place even less imaginable to most of us than the city of happiness. I cannot describe it at all. It is possible that it does not exist. But they seem to know where they are going, the ones who walk away from Omelas.   [1973]

≡ THINKING ABOUT THE TEXT

1. The opening three paragraphs make Omelas sound idyllic. Would some-place like this be your idea of utopia? What would you add? Subtract? Is such a world possible?

2. Is life inherently unfair? Are some destined to prosper and be happy and others destined for a life of toil and hardship? Does this tale touch on this idea?

3. How is Le Guin trying, in this dark fairy tale/allegory, to say something about our own culture? How is our happiness and comfort based on the pain or inconvenience of others?

4. What would your response be to the suffering outcast? Would you be outraged? Would you, like most of those in Omelas, come to accept the necessity of the solution?

5. Speculate on the reasons why some walk away from Omelas. Where are they going? How come they seem so resolute?

≡ MAKING COMPARISONS

1. In what ways are the worlds of Omelas and "The Lottery" similar and different?

2. Compare those who reject the central ritual in both stories.

3. How does the concept of scapegoating apply to both stories?

CAITLIN HORROCKS
The Sleep

Caitlin Horrocks (b. 1980) is a professor of writing at Grand Valley State University and lives in Grand Rapids, Michigan. She graduated from Kenyon College and received an M.F.A. from Arizona State University. She is the fiction editor of the Kenyon Review. Her fiction has been published in such prestigious journals as the Paris Review and Tin House, as well as the Atlantic, The New Yorker, and the PEN/O. Henry Prize Stories. Her latest book is the collection This Is Not Your City (2011). The following story appears in The Best American Short Stories 2011.

The snow came early that first year, and so heavy that when Albert Rasmussen invited the whole town over, we had to park around the corner from his unplowed street. We staggered through the drifts, across the lawns, down the neat sidewalks where a few of Al's neighbors owned snowblowers. Mr. Kajaamaki and the Lutven boys were still out huffing and puffing with shovels. We waved as we passed, and they nodded.

Al stood that November in his family room, arms outstretched, knee-deep in a nest of mattresses and bedding: flannels and florals mixed with Bobby Rasmussen's NASCAR pillowcases, Dee's Disney-princess comforter. The sideboard had a hot plate and an electric kettle plugged into a power strip. Al opened drawers filled with crackers, tinned soup, bags of pink-frosted animal cookies, vitamin C pills and canned juice to prevent scurvy. "Hibernation" he announced. "Human hibernation."

This was before the cameras, before the sleep, before the outsiders, and the plan sounded as strange to us then as it would to anybody. Our town had always wintered the way towns do: gas bills and window plastic, blankets and boots. We bought cream for our cracked skin and socks for our numb feet. We knew how we felt when our extremities faded temporarily away, and we knew how much we hurt when they prickled back to life.

Al showed off a heater he'd built that ran on used grease, and the filter that sieved out the hash browns and hamburger. Al had always been handy. He'd been the smartest kid in school, back when Bounty still had its own high school. He was the senior everyone called "college material" until he decided to stay, and then we called him "ours." Our Albert, Albert and his girl Jeannie, who were confident that everything they could want in the world was right here in Bounty. We went to their wedding, the Saturday after graduation, and then stood by, helpless, when Albert's parents lost the farm three years later. Maybe the family should have gotten out then, moved away and never looked back. Al might have found a job that paid better than fence repair, and Jeannie might not have been killed by Reggie Lapham, seventeen years old and driving drunk on Highway 51 eight months before Al's November invitation. Al might never have struck on hibernation, and we might all have gone along the way we'd been going, for better or worse.

But they had stayed, and Jeannie had died, and Reggie had been sent to a   5
juvenile detention facility downstate. The accident happened in early spring, when patches of snow were still dissolving on the roads, and what no one would say within Al's earshot was that the weather had killed her as much as Reggie had. Al needed something small enough to blame, and Reggie, skinny as a weed and driving his father's truck, served as well as anything could. Al had always seemed older than he was, had transitioned easily from high school basketball star to assistant coach. Now, in his thirties, he looked twenty years older, bent and exhausted. We wondered if the weight on his shoulders was truly Jeannie, or if he'd been carrying, for more years than we'd realized, some piece of Bounty, and he'd invited us over to make sure we understood that he was putting it down.

We'd all stayed in Bounty the way Al had stayed, had carried it as best we could. When our high school shut down, we sent our children to the next town over, then to the county consolidated when that one closed too. They came home with their textbooks about westward expansion, about the gold rush, the tin rush, the copper rush, the wheat farms, the corn farms, the feedlots. About land that gave until it couldn't give, and the chumps who kept trying to live on it. Our children came home and told us that we were the suckers of the last century.

"But what if you love it here?" we asked them. "What if you don't want to leave?"

"What's to love?" our children asked, in surly disbelief: What kind of mo-
rons hustle for jobs that don't even pay for cable television? What kind of
people spend twenty years buying beer at the Hop-In and drinking in the quarry,
the next thirty drinking at the Pointes, the last sodden ten at the Elks Lodge?

Our kind of people, we thought.

"Sleep," Al said, there in his living room, and explained how in the old days 10
in Russia people sacked out around a stove when the snows came, waking to
munch a piece of rye bread, feed the fire, slump back into sleep. Only so much
food could be laid in, and the thinking went that unless a man could come up
with something to do in the cold and the dark that justified the calories he'd
expend doing it, he was better off doing nothing. The Russians would wake up
skinny and hungry, but they'd wake up alive.

We worried that maybe the Rasmussens were harder up than we had
thought. Times were tough for everybody, but others weren't shutting down
their houses and lives and planning to warm their kids with burger grease.
"What do we do all winter?" Al asked, the kind of question we knew he considered rhetorical. "Why work like dogs all summer to keep the television on, the
furnace cranked, noodles on the stove? Why scrape off the car to burn fuel to
go to the store to buy more noodles? That's pointless."

Mrs. Pekola, of Pekola Downtown Antiques, opened her mouth for a moment, as if she were going to point out that that routine wasn't much different
from plenty of people's autumns and springs and maybe summers, in which
case Al was saying that we might as well all blow our brains out and have done
with it. But she stayed silent, probably because she thought of many things we
didn't need to hear.

"What about Christmas?" Mrs. Drausmann, the librarian, offered.

"We're staying awake for it. Just doing a two-month trial run this year,
January and February," Al explained.

"School," Bill and Valeer Simmons said. "Your kids." 15

Al shrugged. Both his kids were bright and ahead of their classes. At seven,
Dee read at a sixth-grade level. Bobby was nine and the best speller at Bounty
Elementary. Al had picked up copies of the upcoming curriculum: long divi-
sion, suffixes, photosynthesis, cursive.

"We're having a sleepover instead," Dee said.

"You know what Mrs. Fiske has planned for February? Fractions!" Bobby
yelled, and the kids bopped around the room until Al chased them upstairs.

"They'll get caught up in spring," Al said. "I don't think they'll have
difficulty."

He looked around at us, his old compatriots, the parents of the handful of 20
children still enrolled at the school, and apologized. "I didn't mean anything by
that," he said. "I don't think they're special. But they probably won't miss
much."

We nodded. Being the children of a dying town had taught us that none of
us was special. Whatever our various talents, we'd all ended up here, in the
Rasmussens' family room.

"Don't try to convince me anything worthwhile happens in this town during January and February. I've lived here as long as you have," Al said. We could tell he meant to joke, but nobody laughed. "I'm not crazy. NASA studies this stuff. They're planning for astronauts to hibernate through long voyages. So they don't go stircrazy and kill each other, bust out the shuttle walls." Al's fingers twitched a bit, and we looked at his walls: scuffed beige paint, three china plates with pictures of Holsteins, a family portrait taken at the JCPenney in Bullhorn when Jeannie was still alive, and a single round hole at the height of a man's fist, sloppily covered with paint and plaster. His walls looked a lot like our walls, and all of a sudden we were tempted to jam our fists in and pull them down.

"You think we're like that?" Nils Andersen asked from the back of the crowd, all the way in the front foyer, and people parted to let him come closer. He'd been a point guard to Al's shooting guard on the old high school basketball team. The two still sometimes took practice shots into the hoop on Al's garage.

"Like what?"

"Russians and astronauts. You think we've got two options, asleep or dead?"   25

Al started to shake his head, because we're not a town that likes to offend. Then he paused, ran his big hands through his hair, and let them drop to his sides. Fair and broad and tall, like his parents and grandparents and Norwegian great-grandparents, like a lot of the rest of us, he looked suddenly large and unwieldy. As if he could only ever fit in this little room curled up asleep, and we'd all been crazy to hope otherwise. He hunched his shoulders and looked down at the floor. "Maybe," he said. "This is about my family. I never meant any of you had to be involved. But maybe."

We'd thought our town's silence had been stoic; we glimpsed now how much we simply hadn't wanted to say. We rustled in the blankets but kept our mouths shut, put on our shoes, and drifted out into the snow. Some of us drove straight home. Others took longer routes down Main Street, past First Lutheran, the Pointes, the Elks Lodge, Mrs. Pekola's antiques store, the single-screen movie theater with the marquee still announcing CLOSED, as if the closing were news. The public library was housed in the old pharmacy; we checked out our books at the prescriptions counter and bought our prescriptions thirty miles down the road. We looked at all the shuttered stores and tried to remember what each one had sold.

We cruised back and forth like bored teenagers on Saturday nights, watching the road run quickly from empty storefronts to clapboard frame houses and tiny brick ranches. We turned around at the Hop-In at the west end of town, near the park with its silent gray bandstand. We drove east until we passed the elementary school and empty high school, then turned into the parking lot of the old farm supply store, the beams of its collapsed roof poking skyward and its windows like eyes. Bounty had never been a pretty town, but we'd tried to be proud of it. Now we examined it carefully, looking for new reasons to stay awake. One by one we gave up, peeled off, and drove home. We turned into our shoveled driveways in the tiny grid of residential streets, or took spokes of blacktop and gravel out to scattered farmhouses in little islands of yard, their old acreage spreading behind them like a taunt. Bounty was an assertion, an act of faith. It looked best left unexamined.

A few of us met back at the Pointes that night for beer and darts. The hours went by, but no one said a thing about Al Rasmussen, and we were all waiting for it. "Fucking *grease*," Nils finally said. "Like fucking *Russians*." We were able to laugh then and walk out to the parking lot, slapping each other's backs and leaving trails of footprints in the snow. We felt better about ourselves, sitting side by side in our idling cars, waiting for the engines to warm.

On New Year's Day, the Rasmussens made neighborhood rounds, dropping   30
off house keys and perishables: a gallon of milk and some apples for the Lutven boys, carrots for Valeer Simmons, a bag of shredded cheese and half a loaf of bread for Mr. Kajaamaki. We wished them luck and hung the keys on pegs.

We could have robbed them blind while they slept, but we knew they didn't have anything worth taking. We tiptoed in ones and twos to watch the family sleep, to see how this hibernation thing was working out. The kids looked peaceful. The food disappeared in barely perceptible increments. The room was stuffy by late February, smelling of night sweat and canned soup, but the Rasmussens didn't seem to mind. Mrs. Pekola lit a lavender-scented candle on the sideboard and found it blown out the next day. All in all, they looked cozy.

In March the children woke first, bounding out the front door in their pajamas. Spring hadn't really started yet; dirty snow was still melting into mud. But the fiercest part of winter was over. Al looked rested for the first time since Jeannie's death, the terrible tension gone from his shoulders. His body looked more like that of the man most of us had known for years, but his eyes looked like a stranger's. No one could place the expression, except those of us whose children or grandchildren had left Bounty, gone off for college or work. When the children came back, we said, their eyes looked like that, like departure. *Imagine*, we thought: *Albert had found that look in his sleep.*

He asked for all the updates. A blizzard in early February had blown the roof off the old hardware store. Mr. Fiske had had a heart attack one morning in the barn with his livestock. One of the grain elevator operators had died of cirrhosis, and half the town had applied for his job. The youngest Suarez boy had tried to hitch home from work at the rendering plant in Piric one evening, but nobody stopped. He decided to walk and disappeared into the snow. We drove poles down, walking across the fields in formation, bracing ourselves to strike flesh. We never found him; now that spring had come, we probably would.

"Anything good?" Al asked.

We struggled. We hadn't thought about how dark the winter had been   35
when we were in its midst. "One of the Thao girls had a baby," we said.

Al smiled, although half of the town thought the Thaos belonged to us, and half wanted nothing to do with them. "That's something."

"What did *you* do?" we asked, and before he could say "I slept," we specified: "What was it like? How did it feel?"

"I had these long dreams," he said. "Unfolding over days. I dreamed I was in Eden, but it was mine. My farm. I picked pineapples every day."

Al Rasmussen had wintered in Eden, we thought. We started to feel a little like suckers.

Bobby and Dee had boundless energy, and spent a lot of it recounting   40
dreams to their schoolmates. Soon many of the children were planning for their own long sleep, and the ones who weren't were calculating how scary empty classrooms might get, how the forest of raised hands would thin and they'd get called on over and over, expected to know the right answers. They pictured how lonely the playground would be, all lopsided seesaws and un-pushed swings, and soon all the children of Bounty were begging to spend the next winter asleep.

Quite a few of them got their way. The Lutven boys were happy not to catch the bus in the dark, standing around in 20 below. The pudgy Sanderson girl, all bushy hair and braces, woke up with her teeth straighter and her belly flat. She showed off her new smile for Lucy Simmons, and Lucy confessed that her pe-riod had started sometime in early February. How easily, they thought, so much of the hard work of growing up had happened while they were asleep, while no one could make fun of them for it.

Mrs. Sanderson fit into clothes she hadn't worn since high school. The styles had changed, but she paraded around in her high-waisted, acid-washed jeans just so we could admire what sleep had done for her. Mr. Sanderson had started off awake, reporting to the John Deere dealership north of town at nine every morning, the way he'd done for years. But suddenly he saw the unfair-ness, his creaking out of bed while his wife rolled over with a slack, content smile. "Our food costs were way down," he said at the Pointes one night the next spring. "The heat bills. Gas. For once my daughter wasn't pestering for a new pair of jeans. I asked for a temporary leave. They said sales were down so far I'd be doing them a favor."

A lot of us lived in houses our parents or grandparents had owned; mort-gages weren't usually our problem. Just the daily costs of living, and the closer those got to zero, the less we needed to work. John Deere lost three more before the winter was over. Other folks didn't have any employers to apologize to. The families that still kept animals thought we were all a bunch of pansies, at least according to Nils, but then we imagined him slogging to the barn every morn-ing at five for the feeding and the milking, his fingers stiff and snot frozen in his mustache, and we mostly just felt smart.

Mrs. Drausmann, the town librarian, hated the sleep even more than Nils. She cornered Bobby and Dee after story time, near the shelves that once held skin creams and now held paperbacks, and threatened: "This will be like Nar-nia under the White Witch. Always winter and never Christmas."

"After Christmas," Dee asked her, "what's there to like? What do *you* do?"   45

"I keep the library open," she said. "So everyone has books. They come and use the computers and get their music and their movies."

"If you're dreaming, you have your own movies," Dee said gravely, and Mrs. Drausmann sighed. We tried to make it up to her, registered for her sum-mer reading program and attended fall story time. But Dee was right. Sleeping folk needed almost nothing—a little food, a little water, air, and warmth. They definitely didn't need DVDs.

That second winter, the road crews noticed less traffic, and some of the plow drivers' hours were cut. Several decided to screw it and just sleep, and by the time the county and the drivers were done sniping at each other, the budget for next year's salting and plowing was half what it had been. The harder leaving your driveway was, the easier the choice to stay home.

The third year, a family died of carbon monoxide poisoning from an unventilated gas heater. An electric space heater started a fire at the Simmonses'. They got out, but the house was a loss. Al staggered into the snow bleary-eyed, called his neighbors dumbasses, and then invited them to pile on into his family room. When he woke up for real in March, he announced that if we were all going to do this thing, we should do it right. He didn't have enough old grease for everyone, so he charged hourly for consultations about different compact heating systems, then for assembly and installation, and soon he was doing well enough to quit fence repair.

We were glad Al had the new business, because that October, Reggie 50 Lapham came home. He'd been seventeen when he hit Jeannie three and a half years earlier, and as young as that was, as much as we remembered the ice on the road and the evenings we'd gotten behind the wheel when we shouldn't have, we weren't sure how to forgive him. Our hearts went out to Reggie and then to Jeannie and then to Al and Bobby and Dee and then back to Reggie, until we couldn't keep our hearts straight and peaceful in our own chests. They were all ours, and we were too much like all of them. We needed men like Al to lead us, and we needed young people like Reggie to stay. We looked to Al for permission to take Reggie back.

But Reggie seemed to know Al wasn't going to give it, at least not that autumn, because he walked from his parents' van into his house and wouldn't come out again. We spoke to Mrs. Lapham at the Hop-In. "He's looking forward to the sleep," she said. "That's really all he wants to do. I don't think he would have come back if he had to—"

She broke off, and we wondered, *Had to what? Leave the house? Talk to people? Get a job?* The family went to bed a few days after Thanksgiving. Mrs. Lapham said that seemed like the easiest way to get through what had to be gotten through. Then we heard that Al had put his kids to bed early too, without Christmas, and then some of us started calculating the money we could save not buying presents. Those of us without small children, or without extended families, had to admit that the holidays were a downer as often as not. We knew that the Laphams and Rasmussens weren't sleeping for the healthiest of reasons, but we understood the urge.

Mrs. Drausmann called in to a radio psychologist when everyone woke up the next spring, about whether sleeping through four months of strife was sanity or just denial. She talked her way past the producers, but Dr. Joe wouldn't believe her. "Sure, excessive sleeping is a sign of depression," he said. "But no one hibernates." Then he hung up.

Several of us heard the call, and it prompted some soul-searching, both about why so many of us were listening to *The Dr. Joe Show* and about what our town might look like to outsiders. We started to wonder if Reggie Lapham should maybe be talking to somebody. If Al and Reggie needed help, we weren't giving it to them, because sleeping was easier for us too.

A woman from the *Piric Gazette* heard *The Dr. Joe Show* that night and came   55 to ask Mrs. Drausmann some questions. We braced ourselves for the story, but the reporter apparently couldn't figure out whom to believe or what the heck was going on, and before she hit on the answer, the Gannett Company shut down the paper. We saw Nils Andersen and Al having a beer together at the Pointes a few weeks later, the first time they'd been social together in years. "She came to interview me," Nils said. "I told her the hibernation business was bullshit."

"I know you think the sleeping's bullshit," Al said. "You don't need to tell me."

"I told her Drausmann was bullshit. I told her nothing was going on in this town that was any of Dr. Joe's business or the *Piric Gazette*'s. I told her to leave you alone." Nils shook his head and clinked the neck of his bottle against Al's. "I figured you've always known what you needed. Crazy fucker."

A few weeks later, we watched the grease heater leave the Rasmussen house in parts, the foam-taped exhaust pipe, the burger filter. The mattresses came out, Bobby's and Dee's sheets, graduated now from NASCAR and Disney to plain solids, navy and lavender. We worried Al was abandoning the cause, until we found out he'd reassembled it all at the Andersen farm. With more people to share shifts taking care of the animals, Al explained, everyone could get some sleep.

More people economized like this, throwing in their lots with friends, neighbors. The Simmonses rebuilt their burned house with a single large room on the ground floor, an energy-efficient heat stove in the center, with nonflammable tile around the base. They went to ask Al's permission and then invited the Laphams to spend the next winter. They knew what a chill felt like, they said, as well as to be given shelter when nothing but cold was around you.

Mrs. Drausmann stayed awake. She had her books; she had her own kind   60 of dreaming. She and Mrs. Pekola would walk up and down the streets, Mrs. Drausmann's snow boots and Mrs. Pekola's orthopedics the only prints for miles. Mrs. Pekola's faith wouldn't let her sleep. She walked to the Lutheran church every December 24 to light the Christ candle. "I'm sorry," she whispered to God. "They don't mean anything by it. They don't mean to disrespect you." She tried to tell us in spring how lonely our church looked, a single candle alight in the empty sanctuary.

In the first years, the reverend turned the electricity back on whenever the temperature hit 45, but then someone hit on the idea of Easter. We flipped the switch on the day that Christ rose. "Alleluia, alleluia," we sang, uttering the word we had denied ourselves for Lent, one of the first words to pass our lips since waking. The Rasmussens and the Laphams stood in their old pews, just across the aisle from each other. They didn't embrace at the greeting-neighbors part of the service, didn't say "Peace be with you" or "And also with you," but they didn't flee. Al stood between his children, with an arm draped over each of them, and we realized with surprise that Bobby was fourteen now and nearly as tall as his father. He would have been good at basketball too, if he'd been awake for the season. Dee's pale hair had darkened to a dirty blond, and her face was spotted with acne. The kids leaned into their father, facing forward, until Dee looked to her right and nodded at Mrs. Lapham. Just then, Reggie turned his head to peer anxiously over his mother, and we saw Dee freeze and then slowly nod at him too. We all nodded our pale faces at each other, and that seemed like enough.

In the end, the Hop-In is what brought the outsiders. Corporate couldn't understand why winter-quarter sales were down 95 percent from five years earlier. A regional manager came out, and then his supervisors, and finally news crews from Fargo. The satellite vans were hard to miss, and we stayed up that night for the eleven o'clock news. We hadn't expected the story they chose to tell: it wasn't a human-interest piece about ingenuity or survival. Our hibernation practice was horrible, the anchors announced, from up and down the state, then across the country. Horrifying. Another product of the recession. A new economic indicator: in addition to tumbling home prices and soaring unemployment, a town was going to sleep. A blond reporter asked the Sandersons if they were making a statement.

"We get tired," they said. "Is that a statement?"

We were annoyed at how they filmed the shabbiest parts of our town, until we flipped through the newscasts and realized that together they'd filmed nearly all of our town and that it all looked equally shabby. We were used to our potholes and tumbledown barns, and now alongside those were cracked sidewalks and collapsing houses. The gray bandstand in the park leaned heavily to one side; the flat roof of the old high school had caved in under last year's snow. Raccoons and groundhogs hibernated in some of the downtown buildings and chased each other up and down Main Street in their spring excitement. A few had gotten into Mrs. Pekola's antiques store, either for burrow bedding or just to be troublesome, and we were plagued by a video clip of skinny raccoons bursting out the store's front door, trailing gnawed-up christening dresses and crib quilts. A badger birthed a spring litter in the church basement on a pile of old Sunday school workbooks. We told ourselves that none of this mattered. We weren't using the buildings anyway: the barns, the high school, most of downtown. We reminded ourselves that Bounty had never been a pretty place. It was built for function, not ornament, and as long as it functioned the way we wanted, we shouldn't be ashamed. We had never had any great architecture in Bounty, and the certainty that we never would didn't seem a sacrifice.

We might have become a tourist attraction, except that getting to us when we were sleeping was so hard. The snow accumulated in giant drifts. We put a big stick out by the WELCOME TO BOUNTY sign and let it measure how deeply we were buried. People could come in on the highway, as far as the county plowed it, and then see a wall of snow taller than their car greeting them at the entrance.

65

That was the establishing shot, a tiny car next to a wall of snow, when the documentary was released. On the tenth anniversary of the sleep, the state public television channel contacted us and said they planned to take a more balanced approach than the news crews. We liked that they promised to hold the premiere in Bounty, projected after dark onto the wall of the farm supply store, since the old movie theater had been condemned.

They interviewed Bobby in his dorm room in the last weeks of the fall semester. The state university had offered him a small baseball scholarship. He was a one-sport kid. "I'm not sure where I'll go for Christmas break," he said. "I haven't had Christmas in years. My dad and my sister won't even be awake." He was broad like his father, a young man there in his cramped college room, and we wondered if Jeannie would even have recognized him.

The Lutven boys had already finished college, worked for a year in St. Paul, and then come home. They liked the pace of life here, they said. They liked the way winter gave you a chance to catch your breath. One of them married the Sanderson girl, who'd taken over the antiques store and chased the raccoons out. Even after two Lutven babies, ten-pound Scandinavian boys, she fit into the shop's old clothes, the slim, fitted dresses. She liked the quiet way her boys were growing up, she said, polite and calm and curled for five months like warm puppies at her side.

Mrs. Pekola had passed away, which we knew, but we hadn't known her family blamed us. Her eldest daughter was living in Florida, and the filmmakers had gone down to interview her about how her mother had died alone in a church pew, frozen to death in a wool coat and orthopedic shoes. "No one found her till spring," the woman said, her anger fresh and righteous.

Mrs. Fiske had taught all the Pekola girls over the years. "Fractions," she   70
whispered in the audience. "That girl just hated fractions."

Dee had never left Bounty, never expressed any interest in going anywhere else. She was "ours," like her father before her, despite her faraway look most days, her eyes the color of the ice that froze over the flooded quarry. Her dirty-blond hair had darkened to brown, and her teenage acne had faded into a nearly translucent paleness. She volunteered at the library with Mrs. Drausmann and took over story time. The film showed her sitting in a rocking chair with books far too advanced for the children gathered cross-legged around her. "He heard the snow falling faintly through the universe and faintly falling, like the descent of their last end, upon all the living and the dead," she read, as the children squirmed. She wasn't very good at story time, but Mrs. Drausmann had grown hoarse and weary over the years.

One by one we tried to explain for the cameras. Why stay? What is Bounty worth? Three months? Four? Half your life spent asleep? Our people had moved to Bounty because the land was there and it was empty, and now all we had was the emptiness and each other. We had a wide sky and tall grass and a sun that felt good when you'd waited for it half the year. We had our children, the ones we'd feared for, feared their boredom and their recklessness and their hunger for somewhere else. We'd feared becoming Jeannie Rasmussen, and we'd feared becoming Reggie Lapham. We'd feared wanting too much and ending up with less than what we already had. Now Al and Nils dreamed of the sound of a basketball bouncing off the warped, snow-soaked floor of the high school gymnasium. Al dreamed of nights asleep in Jeannie's arms. Reggie Lapham probably dreamed his life differently too, but he seemed content with what he had: he was interviewed with his son on his lap, a boy who had never made a snowman, never opened a Christmas present. He spoke about that first year back, about how the sleep had saved him, and when his voice foundered, his wife, Nkauj Thao-Lapham, reached over to squeeze his hand.

Dr. Joe, interviewed, said that the sleep was profoundly unhealthy, that legislation should be passed before the custom could spread. The documentary included interviews with American history professors at the state university, experts on westward expansion, on what had happened to our county over the past two centuries. Someone in a bow tie said he was dismayed by what had happened to our immigrant spirit, to our desire to press on and out to something better. Our congressman pointed out that the immigrant spirit might have pushed us all the way on out of the state, further west or back east. Instead, we'd found a way to stay, and the census didn't ask if you were awake or asleep. It just asked where you lived, and now, more than ever, we were proud to say we lived in Bounty.

"*Sisu*," old Mr. Kajaamaki grunted for the camera, with his hand held in front of his mouth; his teeth had fallen out, but he'd never bothered with dentures, and we felt a bit guilty that no one had insisted on driving him to Piric to get some fitted. Our people were shabby, like our houses, our streets, our ancient coats and boots. But our ancestors had come, and they had stopped, and we persisted. Persistence, Mr. Kajaamaki's old-world word for it. The endurance of a people who had once starved and eaten bark and come across an ocean to a flat sea of snow, to make new ways of life when the old ones seemed insufficient.

"But do you regret their decision? Your father's?" the interviewer, off-camera, 75 prodded. The film cut back to Dee and Al standing together. They were outside, walking down the shuttered main street of our town, the sky blue and endlessly wide. Dee squinted in the light, and Al squinted at his daughter. He'd been quiet in front of the cameras, tentative to the point of taciturn, and as we watched the movie from lawn chairs in the farm supply store parking lot, we could see him fidgeting, turning his head to check the expression on his children's faces, turning around in his seat to look at the people he'd led into sleep.

"I barely remember what our life was like before. I remember being cold."

"And now?"

Dee looked baffled, not able to find words sufficient to explain half her life, the happier, more perfect half. The camera turned to Al, but his face was unreadable. "Now?" Dee said. "Now I guess we're not."

Now we are the people of Bounty, the farmers of dust and cold, the harvesters of dreams. After the lumber, after the mines, after the railroad, after the interstate, after the crops, after the cows, after the jobs. We're better neighbors in warm beds than we ever were awake. The suckers of the last century, but not of this one.

[2011]

☰ THINKING ABOUT THE TEXT

1. Explain why the sleep is a good or a bad thing, or perhaps both. What seems to be the narrator's opinion?

2. What triggers Al's initial decision? Why do others join the sleep?

3. What seem to be the positive aspects of living in a small town? Why do people stay? How could you demonstrate that the narrator is proud of Bounty?

4. How might the sleep be an escape from pain? How does it help some?

5. Why does the narrator say, "We're better neighbors in warm beds than we ever were awake" (para. 79)? Do you agree with the last sentence? Why or why not?

☰ MAKING COMPARISONS

1. Besides taking place in a small town, what other similarities are there between Horrocks's story and "The Lottery"?

2. In Jackson's and Le Guin's stories, the custom is long-standing. Why do you think the sleep will or will not endure?

3. Explain why one of these customs seems the most dangerous to the community.

☰ WRITING ABOUT ISSUES

1. Argue that one of these stories is still, or even more, relevant to contemporary concerns.

2. Write an essay that argues that certain accepted traditions/rituals/customs should be abandoned.

3. Argue that these three stories are allegories.

4. Read Shirley Jackson's essay "Biography of a Story" from her book *Come Along with Me* and write a report highlighting what you feel are her most interesting ideas. Take a position on whether the story's reception would be similar or different if it were written today.

ERNEST HEMINGWAY, "Soldier's Home"

LOUISE ERDRICH, "The Red Convertible"

Among the earliest narratives in literature are those that chart the perilous journey of the soldier from home to battle and then home again. Although most of us probably assume that the physical dangers of war are the most harrowing, it is sometimes the case that, for returning warriors, the transition to a previous life can be even more gruesomely traumatic. The anticipated freedom from war is often a bitter disappointment as the inevitable psychological scars of war do not heal fast enough, if at all. Soldiers, having experienced the horrors of war, return significantly changed. They are often so afflicted by trauma that their families are bewildered and powerless to help. Writers since Homer have given us vivid stories of the troubled freedom damaged soldiers and their anxious families endure when the transition from war to home goes badly.

Ernest Hemingway's classic tale highlights the difficulties an alienated soldier has reconnecting with his family after World War I. Louise Erdrich's haunting story reminds us of the emotional toll the Vietnam War soldiers had to pay as they struggled, many in vain, to find some small measure of peace and stability at home.

▤ BEFORE YOU READ

What stories have you heard about soldiers returning home from Vietnam or Iraq or Afghanistan? Why do you suppose that veterans have such an abnormally high rate of suicide and homelessness?

ERNEST HEMINGWAY
Soldier's Home

One of the most influential writers of the first half of the twentieth century, Ernest Hemingway (1898–1961) was born in a suburb of Chicago but felt most alive at his parents' summer home in the woods of Michigan, where he could indulge his enthusiastic love of hunting, fishing, and camping. After high school, where he was an active and excellent student, Hemingway decided to become a journalist instead of going to college and worked successfully for the Kansas City Star. *He signed up as an ambulance driver for the Red Cross during World War I and was seriously wounded in Italy. After moving to Paris after the war, he wrote his first important book,* In Our Time *(1925). It was well received, and the next year* The Sun Also Rises, *about the "lost generation," made him a celebrity. He published several popular novels, including* For Whom the Bell Tolls *(1949) and* The Old Man and the Sea *(1952). He received the Nobel Prize for literature in 1954 and committed suicide after difficult mental and physical problems. Always full of contradictions, Hemingway was at once an inveterate sportsman and an omnivorous reader; he loved life while also being obsessed with death, especially his father's suicide. Most people think of him as a famous and intensely masculine writer of adventure tales of big game hunting, fishing, and war. While this is true, he was also a dedicated and intricate stylist of great delicacy and power. The following story is a good example of Hemingway's technique. He was a believer in compression, using an analogy to an iceberg to explain his narrative method: "There is seven-eighths of it under water for every part that shows." His laconic style continues to influence today's writers.*

Krebs went to the war from a Methodist college in Kansas. There is a picture which shows him among his fraternity brothers, all of them wearing exactly the same height and style collar. He enlisted in the Marines in 1917 and did not return to the United States until the second division returned from the Rhine in the summer of 1919.

There is a picture which shows him on the Rhine with two German girls and another corporal. Krebs and the corporal look too big for their uniforms. The German girls are not beautiful. The Rhine does not show in the picture.

By the time Krebs returned to his home town in Oklahoma the greeting of heroes was over. He came back much too late. The men from the town who had been drafted had all been welcomed elaborately on their return. There had been a great deal of hysteria. Now the reaction had set in. People seemed to think it was rather ridiculous for Krebs to be getting back so late, years after the war was over.

At first Krebs, who had been at Belleau Wood, Soissons, the Champagne, St. Mihiel, and in the Argonne° did not want to talk about the war at all. Later he felt the need to talk but no one wanted to hear about it. His town had heard too many atrocity stories to be thrilled by actualities. Krebs found that to be listened to at all he had to lie, and after he had done this twice he, too, had a reaction against the war and against talking about it. A distaste for everything that had happened to him in the war set in because of the lies he had told. All of the times that had been able to make him feel cool and clear inside himself when he thought of them; the times so long back when he had done the one thing, the only thing for a man to do, easily and naturally, when he might have done something else, now lost their cool, valuable quality and then were lost themselves.

His lies were quite unimportant lies and consisted in attributing to himself   5
things other men had seen, done, or heard of, and stating as facts certain apocryphal incidents familiar to all soldiers. Even his lies were not sensational at the pool room. His acquaintances, who had heard detailed accounts of German women found chained to machine guns in the Argonne forest and who could not comprehend, or were barred by their patriotism from interest in, any German machine gunners who were not chained, were not thrilled by his stories.

Krebs acquired the nausea in regard to experience that is the result of untruth or exaggeration, and when he occasionally met another man who had

Belleau Wood ... Argonne: Battle sites in World War I.

really been a soldier and they talked a few minutes in the dressing room at a dance he fell into the easy pose of the old soldier among other soldiers: that he had been badly, sickeningly frightened all the time. In this way he lost everything.

During this time, it was late summer, he was sleeping late in bed, getting up to walk down town to the library to get a book, eating lunch at home, reading on the front porch until he became bored, and then walking down through the town to spend the hottest hours of the day in the cool dark of the pool room. He loved to play pool.

In the evening he practiced on his clarinet, strolled down town, read, and went to bed. He was still a hero to his two young sisters. His mother would have given him breakfast in bed if he had wanted it. She often came in when he was in bed and asked him to tell her about the war, but her attention always wandered. His father was noncommittal.

Before Krebs went away to the war he had never been allowed to drive the family motor car. His father was in the real estate business and always wanted the car to be at his command when he required it to take clients out into the country to show them a piece of farm property. The car always stood outside the First National Bank building where his father had an office on the second floor. Now, after the war, it was still the same car.

Nothing was changed in the town except that the young girls had grown up. But they lived in such a complicated world of already defined alliances and shifting feuds that Krebs did not feel the energy or the courage to break into it. He liked to look at them, though. There were so many good-looking young girls. Most of them had their hair cut short. When he went away only little girls wore their hair like that or girls that were fast. They all wore sweaters and shirt waists with round Dutch collars. It was a pattern. He liked to look at them from the front porch as they walked on the other side of the street. He liked to watch them walking under the shade of the trees. He liked the round Dutch collars above their sweaters. He liked their silk stockings and flat shoes. He liked their bobbed hair and the way they walked.

When he was in town their appeal to him was not very strong. He did not like them when he saw them in the Greek's ice cream parlor. He did not want them themselves really. They were too complicated. There was something else. Vaguely he wanted a girl but he did not want to have to work to get her. He would have liked to have a girl but he did not want to have to spend a long time getting her. He did not want to get into the intrigue and the politics. He did not want to have to do any courting. He did not want to tell any more lies. It wasn't worth it.

He did not want any consequences. He did not want any consequences ever again. He wanted to live alone without consequences. Besides he did not really need a girl. The army had taught him that. It was all right to pose as though you had to have a girl. Nearly everybody did that. But it wasn't true. You did not need a girl. That was the funny thing. First a fellow boasted how girls mean nothing to him, that he never thought of them, that they could not touch him. Then a fellow boasted that he could not get along without girls, that he had to have them all the time, that he could not go to sleep without them.

That was all a lie. It was all a lie both ways. You did not need a girl unless you thought about them. He learned that in the army. Then sooner or later you always got one. When you were really ripe for a girl you always got one. You did not have to think about it. Sooner or later it would come. He had learned that in the army.

Now he would have liked a girl if she had come to him and not wanted to talk. But here at home it was all too complicated. He knew he could never get through it all again. It was not worth the trouble. That was the thing about French girls and German girls. There was not all this talking. You couldn't talk much and you did not need to talk. It was simple and you were friends. He thought about France and then he began to think about Germany. On the whole he had liked Germany better. He did not want to leave Germany. He did not want to come home. Still, he had come home. He sat on the front porch.

He liked the girls that were walking along the other side of the street. He   15
liked the look of them much better than the French girls or the German girls. But the world they were in was not the world he was in. He would like to have one of them. But it was not worth it. They were such a nice pattern. He liked the pattern. It was exciting. But he would not go through all the talking. He did not want one badly enough. He liked to look at them all, though. It was not worth it. Not now when things were getting good again.

He sat there on the porch reading a book on the war. It was a history and he was reading about all the engagements he had been in. It was the most interesting reading he had ever done. He wished there were more maps. He looked forward with a good feeling to reading all the really good histories when they would come out with good detail maps. Now he was really learning about the war. He had been a good soldier. That made a difference.

One morning after he had been home about a month his mother came into his bedroom and sat on the bed. She smoothed her apron.

"I had a talk with your father last night, Harold," she said. "and he is willing for you to take the car out in the evenings."

"Yeah?" said Krebs, who was not fully awake. "Take the car out? Yeah?"

"Yes. Your father has felt for some time that you should be able to take the   20
car out in the evenings whenever you wished but we only talked it over last night."

"I'll bet you made him," Krebs said.

"No. It was your father's suggestion that we talk the matter over."

"Yeah. I'll bet you made him," Krebs sat up in bed.

"Will you come down to breakfast, Harold?" his mother said.

"As soon as I get my clothes on," Krebs said.   25

His mother went out of the room and he could hear her frying something downstairs while he washed, shaved, and dressed to go down into the dining-room for breakfast. While he was eating breakfast his sister brought in the mail.

"Well, Hare," she said. "You old sleepyhead. What do you ever get up for?"

Krebs looked at her. He liked her. She was his best sister.

"Have you got the paper?" he asked.

She handed him the Kansas City *Star* and he shucked off its brown wrap- 30
per and opened it to the sporting page. He folded the *Star* open and propped it
against the water pitcher with his cereal dish to steady it, so he could read while
he ate.

"Harold," his mother stood in the kitchen doorway, "Harold, please don't
muss up the paper. Your father can't read his Star if it's been mussed."

"I won't muss it," Krebs said.

His sister sat down at the table and watched him while he read.

"We're playing indoor over at school this afternoon," she said. "I'm going
to pitch."

"Good," said Krebs. "How's the old wing?" 35

"I can pitch better than lots of the boys. I tell them all you taught me. The
other girls aren't much good."

"Yeah?" said Krebs.

"I tell them all you're my beau. Aren't you my beau, Hare?"

"You bet."

"Couldn't your brother really be your beau just because he's your brother?" 40

"I don't know."

"Sure you know. Couldn't you be my beau, Hare, if I was old enough and if
you wanted to?"

"Sure. You're my girl now."

"Am I really your girl?"

"Sure." 45

"Do you love me?"

"Uh, huh."

"Will you love me always?"

"Sure."

"Will you come over and watch me play indoor?" 50

"Maybe."

"Aw, Hare, you don't love me. If you loved me, you'd want to come over and
watch me play indoor."

Krebs's mother came into the dining-room from the kitchen. She carried a
plate with two fried eggs and some crisp bacon on it and a plate of buckwheat
cakes.

"You run along, Helen," she said. "I want to talk to Harold."

She put the eggs and bacon down in front of him and brought in a jug of 55
maple syrup for the buckwheat cakes. Then she sat down across the table from
Krebs.

"I wish you'd put down the paper a minute, Harold," she said.

Krebs took down the paper and folded it.

"Have you decided what you are going to do yet, Harold?" his mother said,
taking off her glasses.

"No," said Krebs.

"Don't you think it's about time?" His mother did not say this in a mean 60
way. She seemed worried.

"I hadn't thought about it," Krebs said.

"God has some work for everyone to do," his mother said. "There can be no idle hands in His Kingdom."

"I'm not in His Kingdom," Krebs said.

"We are all of us in His Kingdom."

Krebs felt embarrassed and resentful as always.   65

"I've worried about you so much, Harold," his mother went on. "I know the temptations you must have been exposed to. I know how weak men are. I know what your own dear grandfather, my own father, told us about the Civil War and I have prayed for you. I pray for you all day long, Harold."

Krebs looked at the bacon fat hardening on his plate.

"Your father is worried, too," his mother went on. "He thinks you have lost your ambition, that you haven't got a definite aim in life. Charley Simmons, who is just your age, has a good job and is going to be married. The boys are all settling down; they're all determined to get somewhere; you can see that boys like Charley Simmons are on their way to being really a credit to the community."

Krebs said nothing.

"Don't look that way, Harold," his mother said. "You know we love you   70 and I want to tell you for your own good how matters stand. Your father does not want to hamper your freedom. He thinks you should be allowed to drive the car. If you want to take some of the nice girls out riding with you, we are only too pleased. We want you to enjoy yourself. But you are going to have to settle down to work, Harold. Your father doesn't care what you start in at. All work is honorable as he says. But you've got to make a start at something. He asked me to speak to you this morning and then you can stop in and see him at his office."

"Is that all?" Krebs said.

"Yes. Don't you love your mother, dear boy?"

"No," Krebs said.

His mother looked at him across the table. Her eyes were shiny. She started crying.

"I don't love anybody," Krebs said.   75

It wasn't any good. He couldn't tell her, he couldn't make her see it. It was silly to have said it. He had only hurt her. He went over and took hold of her arm. She was crying with her head in her hands.

"I didn't mean it," he said. "I was just angry at something. I didn't mean I didn't love you."

His mother went on crying. Krebs put his arm on her shoulder.

"Can't you believe me, mother?"

His mother shook her head.   80

"Please, please, mother. Please believe me."

"All right," his mother said chokily. She looked up at him. "I believe you, Harold."

Krebs kissed her hair. She put her face up to him.

"I'm your mother," she said. "I held you next to my heart when you were a tiny baby."

Krebs felt sick and vaguely nauseated.   85
"I know, Mummy," he said. "I'll try and be a good boy for you."
"Would you kneel and pray with me, Harold?" his mother asked.
They knelt down beside the dining-room table and Krebs's mother prayed.
"Now, you pray, Harold," she said.
"I can't," Krebs said.   90
"Try, Harold."
"I can't."
"Do you want me to pray for you?"
"Yes."

So his mother prayed for him and then they stood up and Krebs kissed his   95
mother and went out of the house. He had tried so to keep his life from being
complicated. Still, none of it had touched him. He had felt sorry for his mother
and she had made him lie. He would go to Kansas City and get a job and she
would feel all right about it. There would be one more scene maybe before he
got away. He would not go down to his father's office. He would miss that one.
He wanted his life to go smoothly. It had just gotten going that way. Well, that
was all over now, anyway. He would go over to the schoolyard and watch Helen
play indoor baseball.   *[1925]*

≡ THINKING ABOUT THE TEXT

1. Why does Krebs stay in Europe so long? Why is Krebs upset with himself? What specific behaviors does he regret?

2. Why doesn't Krebs want a close relationship with the girls he watches?
   In what way might this be quite understandable?

3. What does Krebs mean by his frequent use of "complicated"?

4. What seems to be Krebs's plan for the future? Why does he feel he must
   leave home? How might he be successful?

5. What specific details could you use to argue that Hemingway means
   Krebs to be or not to be a sympathetic figure?

LOUISE ERDRICH
The Red Convertible

*Born in Little Falls, Minnesota, Louise Erdrich (b. 1954) is a member of the Turtle
Mountain Band of the Chippewa tribe. Her parents taught at the Bureau of Indian
Affairs Boarding School in North Dakota, where Erdrich worked as a beet weeder,
waitress, and teacher. She earned a B.A. from Dartmouth College in 1976 and an
M.A. from the writing program at Johns Hopkins University in 1979 and has won
many awards and fellowships for her writing, including the National Book Critics
Circle Award in 1984 for her first novel,* Love Medicine. *Although she writes both
poetry and nonfiction, she has received the most acclaim for her novels, which include*

The Beet Queen *(1986),* Tracks *(1988),* The Bingo Palace *(1994), and* Tales of Burning Love *(1996). Some recent novels are* The Master Butchers Singing Club *(2003),* Four Souls *(2004),* Shadow Tag *(2010), and* The Round House *(2012).* The Game of Silence, *a children's book, was published in 2005. The following story is a chapter from* Love Medicine *(1984; revised 1993; revised 2009), a novel about Native American families on a reservation in North Dakota between 1934 and 1984.*

Lyman Lamartine

I was the first one to drive a convertible on my reservation. And of course it was red, a red Olds. I owned that car along with my brother Henry Junior. We owned it together until his boots filled with water on a windy night and he bought out my share. Now Henry owns the whole car, and his younger brother Lyman (that's myself), Lyman walks everywhere he goes.

How did I earn enough money to buy my share in the first place? My own talent was I could always make money. I had a touch for it, unusual in a Chippewa. From the first I was different that way, and everyone recognized it. I was the only kid they let in the American Legion Hall to shine shoes, for example, and one Christmas I sold spiritual bouquets for the mission door to door. The nuns let me keep a percentage. Once I started, it seemed the more money I made the easier the money came. Everyone encouraged it. When I was fifteen I got a job washing dishes at the Joliet Café, and that was where my first big break happened.

It wasn't long before I was promoted to busing tables, and then the short-order cook quit and I was hired to take her place. No sooner than you know it I was managing the Joliet. The rest is history. I went on managing. I soon became part owner, and of course there was no stopping me then. It wasn't long before the whole thing was mine.

After I'd owned the Joliet for one year, it blew over in the worst tornado ever seen around here. The whole operation was smashed to bits. A total loss. The fryalator was up in a tree, the grill torn in half like it was paper. I was only sixteen. I had it all in my mother's name, and I lost it quick, but before I lost it I had every one of my relatives, and their relatives, to dinner, and I also bought that red Olds I mentioned, along with Henry.

The first time we saw it! I'll tell you when we first saw it. We had gotten a ride up to Winnipeg, and both of us had money. Don't ask me why, because we never mentioned a car or anything, we just had all our money. Mine was cash, a big bankroll from the Joliet's insurance. Henry had two checks—a week's extra pay for being laid off, and his regular check from the Jewel Bearing Plant.

We were walking down Portage anyway, seeing the sights, when we saw it. There it was, parked, large as life. Really as if it was alive. I thought of the word *repose,* because the car wasn't simply stopped, parked, or whatever. That car reposed, calm and gleaming, a for sale sign in its left front window. Then, before

5

we had thought it over at all, the car belonged to us and our pockets were empty. We had just enough money for gas back home.

We went places in that car, me and Henry. We took off driving all one whole summer. We started off toward the Little Knife River and Mandaree in Fort Berthold and then we found ourselves down in Wakpala somehow, and then suddenly we were over in Montana on the Rocky Boy, and yet the summer was not even half over. Some people hang on to details when they travel, but we didn't let them bother us and just lived our everyday lives here to there.

I do remember this one place with willows. I remember I laid under those trees and it was comfortable. So comfortable. The branches bent down all around me like a tent or a stable. And quiet, it was quiet, even though there was a powwow close enough so I could see it going on. The air was not too still, not too windy either. When the dust rises up and hangs in the air around the dancers like that, I feel good. Henry was asleep with his arms thrown wide. Later on, he woke up and we started driving again. We were somewhere in Montana, or maybe on the Blood Reserve — it could have been anywhere. Anyway it was where we met the girl.

All her hair was in buns around her ears, that's the first thing I noticed about her. She was posed alongside the road with her arm out, so we stopped. That girl was short, so short her lumber shirt looked comical on her, like a nightgown. She had jeans on and fancy moccasins and she carried a little suitcase.

"Hop on in," says Henry. So she climbs in between us.   10

"We'll take you home," I says. "Where do you live?"

"Chicken," she says.

"Where the hell's that?" I ask her.

"Alaska."

"Okay," says Henry, and we drive.   15

We got up there and never wanted to leave. The sun doesn't truly set there in summer, and the night is more a soft dusk. You might doze off, sometimes, but before you know it you're up again, like an animal in nature. You never feel like you have to sleep hard or put away the world. And things would grow up there. One day just dirt or moss, the next day flowers and long grass. The girl's name was Susy. Her family really took to us. They fed us and put us up. We had our own tent to live in by their house, and the kids would be in and out of there all day and night. They couldn't get over me and Henry being brothers, we looked so different. We told them we knew we had the same mother, anyway.

One night Susy came in to visit us. We sat around in the tent talking of this and that. The season was changing. It was getting darker by that time, and the cold was even getting just a little mean. I told her it was time for us to go. She stood up on a chair.

"You never seen my hair," Susy said.

That was true. She was standing on a chair, but still, when she unclipped her buns the hair reached all the way to the ground. Our eyes opened. You couldn't tell how much hair she had when it was rolled up so neatly. Then my brother Henry did something funny. He went up to the chair and said, "Jump on my shoulders." So she did that, and her hair reached down past his waist, and he started twirling, this way and that, so her hair was flung out from side to side.

"I always wondered what it was like to have long pretty hair," Henry says.   20
Well we laughed. It was a funny sight, the way he did it. The next morning we got up and took leave of those people.

On to greener pastures, as they say. It was down through Spokane and across Idaho then Montana and very soon we were racing the weather right along under the Canadian border through Columbus, Des Lacs, and then we were in Bottineau County and soon home. We'd made most of the trip, that summer, without putting up the car hood at all. We got home just in time, it turned out, for the army to remember Henry had signed up to join it.

I don't wonder that the army was so glad to get my brother that they turned him into a Marine. He was built like a brick outhouse anyway. We liked to tease him that they really wanted him for his Indian nose. He had a nose big and sharp as a hatchet, like the nose on Red Tomahawk, the Indian who killed Sitting Bull, whose profile is on signs all along the North Dakota highways. Henry went off to training camp, came home once during Christmas, then the next thing you know we got an overseas letter from him. It was 1970, and he said he was stationed up in the northern hill country. Whereabouts I did not know. He wasn't such a hot letter writer, and only got off two before the enemy caught him. I could never keep it straight, which direction those good Vietnam soldiers were from.

I wrote him back several times, even though I didn't know if those letters would get through. I kept him informed all about the car. Most of the time I had it up on blocks in the yard or half taken apart, because that long trip did a hard job on it under the hood.

I always had good luck with numbers, and never worried about the draft myself. I never even had to think about what my number was. But Henry was never lucky in the same way as me. It was at least three years before Henry came home. By then I guess the whole war was solved in the government's mind, but for him it would keep on going. In those years I'd put his car into almost perfect shape. I always thought of it as his car while he was gone, even though when he left he said, "Now it's yours," and threw me his key.

"Thanks for the extra key," I'd said. "I'll put it up in your drawer just in case   25
I need it." He laughed.

When he came home, though, Henry was very different, and I'll say this: the change was no good. You could hardly expect him to change for the better, I know. But he was quiet, so quiet, and never comfortable sitting still anywhere but always up and moving around. I thought back to times we'd sat still for whole afternoons, never moving a muscle, just shifting our weight along the ground, talking to whoever sat with us, watching things. He'd always had a joke, then, too, and now you couldn't get him to laugh, or when he did it was more the sound of a man choking, a sound that stopped up the throats of other people around him. They got to leaving him alone most of the time, and I didn't blame them. It was a fact: Henry was jumpy and mean.

I'd bought a color TV set for my mom and the rest of us while Henry was away. Money still came very easy. I was sorry I'd ever bought it though, because of Henry. I was also sorry I'd bought color, because with black-and-white the pictures seem older and farther away. But what are you going to do? He sat in front of it, watching it, and that was the only time he was completely still. But it was the kind of stillness that you see in a rabbit when it freezes and before it will bolt. He was not easy. He sat in his chair gripping the armrests with all his might, as if the chair itself was moving at a high speed and if he let go at all he would rocket forward and maybe crash right through the set.

Once I was in the room watching TV with Henry and I heard his teeth click at something. I looked over, and he'd bitten through his lip. Blood was going down his chin. I tell you right then I wanted to smash that tube to pieces. I went over to it but Henry must have known what I was up to. He rushed from his chair and shoved me out of the way, against the wall. I told myself he didn't know what he was doing.

My mom came in, turned the set off real quiet, and told us she had made something for supper. So we went and sat down. There was still blood going down Henry's chin, but he didn't notice it and no one said anything, even though every time he took a bite of his bread his blood fell onto it until he was eating his own blood mixed in with the food.

While Henry was not around we talked about what was going to happen   30
to him. There were no Indian doctors on the reservation, and my mom was afraid of trusting the old man, Moses Pillager, because he courted her long ago and was jealous of her husbands. He might take revenge through her son. We were afraid that if we brought Henry to a regular hospital they would keep him.

"They don't fix them in those places," Mom said; "they just give them drugs."

"We wouldn't get him there in the first place," I agreed, "so let's just forget about it."

Then I thought about the car.

Henry had not even looked at the car since he'd gotten home, though like I said, it was in tip-top condition and ready to drive. I thought the car might bring the old Henry back somehow. So I bided my time and waited for my chance to interest him in the vehicle.

One night Henry was off somewhere. I took myself a hammer. I went out   35
to that car and I did a number on its underside. Whacked it up. Bent the tail pipe double. Ripped the muffler loose. By the time I was done with the car it looked worse than any typical Indian car that has been driven all its life on reservation roads, which they always say are like government promises—full of holes. It just about hurt me, I'll tell you that! I threw dirt in the carburetor and I ripped all the electric tape off the seats. I made it look just as beat up as I could. Then I sat back and waited for Henry to find it.

Still, it took him over a month. That was all right, because it was just getting warm enough, not melting, but warm enough to work outside.

"Lyman," he says, walking in one day, "that red car looks like shit."

"Well it's old," I says. "You got to expect that."

"No way!" says Henry. "That car's a classic! But you went and ran the piss right out of it, Lyman, and you know it don't deserve that. I kept that car in A-one shape. You don't remember. You're too young. But when I left, that car was running like a watch. Now I don't even know if I can get it to start again, let alone get it anywhere near its old condition."

"Well you try," I said, like I was getting mad, "but I say it's a piece of junk."   40

Then I walked out before he could realize I knew he'd strung together more than six words at once.

After that I thought he'd freeze himself to death working on that car. He was out there all day, and at night he rigged up a little lamp, ran a cord out the window, and had himself some light to see by while he worked. He was better than he had been before, but that's still not saying much. It was easier for him to do the things the rest of us did. He ate more slowly and didn't jump up and down during the meal to get this or that or look out the window. I put my hand in the back of the TV set, I admit, and fiddled around with it good, so that it was almost impossible now to get a clear picture. He didn't look at it very often anyway. He was always out with that car or going off to get parts for it. By the time it was really melting outside, he had it fixed.

I had been feeling down in the dumps about Henry around this time. We had always been together before. Henry and Lyman. But he was such a loner now that I didn't know how to take it. So I jumped at the chance one day when Henry seemed friendly. It's not that he smiled or anything. He just said, "Let's take that old shitbox for a spin." Just the way he said it made me think he could be coming around.

We went out to the car. It was spring. The sun was shining very bright. My only sister, Bonita, who was just eleven years old, came out and made us stand together for a picture. Henry leaned his elbow on the red car's windshield, and he took his other arm and put it over my shoulder, very carefully, as though it was heavy for him to lift and he didn't want to bring the weight down all at once.

"Smile," Bonita said, and he did.   45

That picture, I never look at it anymore. A few months ago, I don't know why, I got his picture out and tacked it on the wall. I felt good about Henry at the time, close to him. I felt good having his picture on the wall, until one night when I was looking at television. I was a little drunk and stoned. I looked up at the wall and Henry was staring at me. I don't know what it was, but his smile had changed, or maybe it was gone. All I know is I couldn't stay in the same room with that picture. I was shaking. I got up, closed the door, and went into the kitchen. A little later my friend Ray came over and we both went back into that room. We put the picture in a brown bag, folded the bag over and over tightly, then put it way back in a closet.

I still see that picture now, as if it tugs at me, whenever I pass that closet door. The picture is very clear in my mind. It was so sunny that day Henry had to squint against the glare. Or maybe the camera Bonita held flashed like a mirror, blinding him, before she snapped the picture. My face is right out in the sun, big and round. But he might have drawn back, because the shadows on his face are deep as holes. There are two shadows curved like little hooks around the ends of his smile, as if to frame it and try to keep it there—that one, first smile that looked like it might have hurt his face. He has his field jacket on and the worn-in clothes he'd come back in and kept wearing ever since. After Bonita took the picture, she went into the house and we got into the car. There was a full cooler in the trunk. We started off, east, toward Pembina and the Red River because Henry said he wanted to see the high water.

The trip over there was beautiful. When everything starts changing, drying up, clearing off, you feel like your whole life is starting. Henry felt it, too. The top was down and the car hummed like a top. He'd really put it back in shape, even the tape on the seats was very carefully put down and glued back in layers. It's not that he smiled again or even joked, but his face looked to me as if it was clear, more peaceful. It looked as though he wasn't thinking of anything in particular except the bare fields and windbreaks and houses we were passing.

The river was high and full of winter trash when we got there. The sun was still out, but it was colder by the river. There were still little clumps of dirty snow here and there on the banks. The water hadn't gone over the banks yet, but it would, you could tell. It was just at its limit, hard swollen glossy like an old gray scar. We made ourselves a fire, and we sat down and watched the current go. As I watched it I felt something squeezing inside me and tightening and trying to let go all at the same time. I knew I was not just feeling it myself; I knew I was feeling what Henry was going through at that moment. Except that I couldn't stand it, the closing and opening. I jumped to my feet. I took Henry by the shoulders and I started shaking him. "Wake up," I says, "wake up, wake up, wake up!" I didn't know what had come over me. I sat down beside him again.

His face was totally white and hard. Then it broke, like stones break all of a 50 sudden when water boils up inside them.

"I know it," he says. "I know it. I can't help it. It's no use."

We start talking. He said he knew what I'd done with the car. It was obvious it had been whacked out of shape and not just neglected. He said he wanted to give the car to me for good now, it was no use. He said he'd fixed it just to give it back and I should take it.

"No way," I says, "I don't want it."

"That's okay," he says, "you take it."

"I don't want it, though," I says back to him, and then to emphasize, just 55 to emphasize, you understand, I touch his shoulder. He slaps my hand off.

"Take that car," he says.

"No," I say. "Make me," I say, and then he grabs my jacket and rips the arm loose. That jacket is a class act, suede with tags and zippers. I push Henry backwards, off the log. He jumps up and bowls me over. We go down in a clinch and come up swinging hard, for all we're worth, with our fists. He socks my jaw so hard I feel like it swings loose. Then I'm at his rib cage and land a good one under his chin so his head snaps back. He's dazzled. He looks at me and I look at him and then his eyes are full of tears and blood and at first I think he's crying. But no, he's laughing. "Ha! Ha!" he says. "Ha! Ha! Take good care of it."

"Okay," I says, "okay, no problem. Ha! Ha!"

I can't help it, and I start laughing, too. My face feels fat and strange, and after a while I get a beer from the cooler in the trunk, and when I hand it to Henry he takes his shirt and wipes my germs off. "Hoof-and-mouth disease," he says. For some reason this cracks me up, and so we're really laughing for a while, and then we drink all the rest of the beers one by one and throw them in the river and see how far, how fast, the current takes them before they fill up and sink.

"You want to go on back?" I ask after a while. "Maybe we could snag a   60
couple nice Kashpaw girls."

He says nothing. But I can tell his mood is turning again.

"They're all crazy, the girls up here, every damn one of them."

"You're crazy too," I say, to jolly him up. "Crazy Lamartine boys!"

He looks as though he will take this wrong at first. His face twists, then clears, and he jumps up on his feet. "That's right!" he says. "Crazier 'n hell. Crazy Indians!"

I think it's the old Henry again. He throws off his jacket and starts swing-   65
ing his legs out from the knees like a fancy dancer. He's down doing something between a grass dance and a bunny hop, no kind of dance I ever saw before, but neither has anyone else on all this green growing earth. He's wild. He wants to pitch whoopee! He's up and at me and all over. All this time I'm laughing so hard, so hard my belly is getting tied up in a knot.

"Got to cool me off!" he shouts all of a sudden. Then he runs over to the river and jumps in.

There's boards and other things in the current. It's so high. No sound comes from the river after the splash he makes, so I run right over. I look around. It's getting dark. I see he's halfway across the water already, and I know he didn't swim there but the current took him. It's far. I hear his voice, though, very clearly across it.

"My boots are filling," he says.

He says this in a normal voice, like he just noticed and he doesn't know what to think of it. Then he's gone. A branch comes by. Another branch. And I go in.

By the time I get out of the river, off the snag I pulled myself onto, the sun is   70
down. I walk back to the car, turn on the high beams, and drive it up the bank. I put it in first gear and then I take my foot off the clutch. I get out, close the door, and watch it plow softly into the water. The headlights reach in as they go down, searching, still lighted even after the water swirls over the back end. I wait. The wires short out. It is all finally dark. And then there is only the water, the sound of it going and running and going and running and running.   *[1984]*

≣ **THINKING ABOUT THE TEXT**

1. In what way is the red convertible symbolic? Why is it red? Why does Lyman damage it?

2. Assuming that Henry was traumatized in the Vietnam War, what specific symptoms does he exhibit?

3. Why do you think Erdrich decides to tell this story mostly from Lyman's point of view? What would be the benefits and drawbacks of telling it from Henry's perspective?

4. What is the significance of the scene when Henry and Lyman are watching TV and then go in to supper (paras. 28–29)?

5. How do you interpret the last paragraph; specifically, why does Lyman drive the car into the river?

≣ **MAKING COMPARISONS**

1. Compare the responses of Henry and Krebs in readjusting to civilian life.

2. How would you compare the self-awareness of Henry and Krebs?

3. Compare the roles of Helen and Lyman in the stories.

≣ **WRITING ABOUT ISSUES**

1. After doing research online, write an essay that describes the difficulties faced by soldiers returning home from the Civil War, World War I, World War II, the Vietnam War, Iraq, and Afghanistan. How were these difficulties similar? How were they different?

2. Write an essay that focuses on the families of the returning soldiers. What do the stories suggest are the problems? How well do all three families deal with them? Do the stories seem sympathetic or critical of the families' responses?

3. Research the symptoms of Post Traumatic Stress Disorder, its causes, and suggested therapy. Write an essay that uses this information to discuss the behavior of Krebs and Henry.

4. Read another story about a returning veteran—for example, Hamlin Garland's "The Return of a Private" or Tim O'Brien's "Speaking of Courage"—and compare the ideas and themes raised there to the stories in this cluster.

▤ Unendurable Confinement: Critical Commentaries on a Story

WILLA CATHER, "Paul's Case"

CRITICAL COMMENTARIES:

SARAH KANE, "Narcissistic Personality Disorder in Willa Cather's 'Paul's Case'"

LORETTA WASSERMAN, From *Willa Cather: A Study of the Short Fiction*

JOHN P. ANDERS, From *Willa Cather's Sexual Aesthetics and the Male Homosexual Literary Tradition*

SHARON O'BRIEN, From *Willa Cather: The Emerging Voice*

Since we are such social beings, most of us would probably find the confinement of prison an emotional catastrophe. Indeed, being physically isolated and shunned by society is considered such a serious punishment that it is reserved only for criminals. But there are other kinds of isolation and confinement, some of which have nothing to do with physical walls. At times all of us can feel out of step with our culture, with its values, its traditions and politics, its ways of defining success or failure. But to most of us these might be minor annoyances, simply part of making our peace with an imperfect society. But for some, these inevitable conflicts between society and the individual are life-altering struggles. Whether from ideological principles, or sexual orientation, or religious conviction, or gender identification, or perhaps from temperament, they cannot conform. They have, as Paul does in the following story, a "shudder of loathing" for ordinary life. They find school repulsive, their daily tasks dreary, their surroundings ugly, and their peers dull and monotonous. They feel trapped, confined, and hopelessly alienated from mainstream life. And like Paul, they may long for a world of beauty and mystery, a fantasy world never to be found. And tragically for Paul, when he realizes that his revolt against the world is a "losing game," life becomes unendurable.

▤ BEFORE YOU READ

Did you ever feel frustrated by your life as a teenager? Why? What did you do about it? Do you still feel the same? Do you know anyone who took dramatic steps to escape? What did they do, and how did you respond?

WILLA CATHER
Paul's Case

Willa Cather (1873–1947) was born in Virginia, but her family moved to Red Cloud, a small town on the Nebraska frontier, when she was nine. After she graduated from the University of Nebraska, she moved to Pittsburgh and, while teaching En-

Getty Images

glish and Latin in various high schools, she also wrote for women's magazines and published some of her most famous stories, "Paul's Case," and "A Wagner Matinee." She then moved to New York City and spent most of her life there, publishing her most critically acclaimed novels about the harsh pioneer life on the prairie, O Pioneers! (1913) and My Ántonia (1918). During her life, Cather's primary emotional attachments were to women. Although she herself did not label herself as a lesbian, most (but not all) contemporary critics see her this way. Cather's novels were quite popular in her day, appealing to both readers and critics with her clear literary style and her sensitive and sympathetic narratives of thwarted quests, spiritual despair, and the resilience of the artistic imagination, all themes present in "Paul's Case."

We have included four different critical commentaries on Cather's story. The first offers a detailed psychological, even clinical, assessment of Paul's character. The next excerpt from Loretta Wasserman confronts the tension in the story between nature and nurture, freedom and determinism. The next essay sees the story as Cather's representative gay text, while the brief excerpt from Sharon O'Brien's critical biography combines several approaches that demonstrate the complexity of Cather's beautiful and tragic tale.

It was Paul's afternoon to appear before the faculty of the Pittsburgh High School to account for his various misdemeanors. He had been suspended a week ago, and his father had called at the Principal's office and confessed his perplexity about his son. Paul entered the faculty room suave and smiling. His clothes were a trifle outgrown and the tan velvet on the collar of his open overcoat was frayed and worn; but for all that there was something of the dandy about him, and he wore an opal pin in his neatly knotted black four-in-hand°, and a red carnation in his buttonhole. This latter adornment the faculty somehow felt was not properly significant of the contrite spirit befitting a boy under the ban of suspension.

Paul was tall for his age and very thin, with high, cramped shoulders and a narrow chest. His eyes were remarkable for a certain hysterical brilliancy and he continually used them in a conscious, theatrical sort of way, peculiarly offensive in a boy. The pupils were abnormally large, as though he were addicted to belladonna, but there was a glassy glitter about them which that drug does not produce.

When questioned by the Principal as to why he was there, Paul stated, politely enough, that he wanted to come back to school. This was a lie, but Paul was quite accustomed to lying; found it, indeed, indispensable for overcoming friction. His teachers were asked to state their respective charges against him, which they did with such a rancor and aggrievedness as evinced that this was not a usual case. Disorder and impertinence were among the offenses named, yet each of his instructors felt that it was scarcely possible to put into words the real cause of the trouble, which lay in a sort of hysterically defiant manner of the boy's; in the contempt which they all knew he felt for them, and which he seemingly made not the least effort to conceal. Once, when he had been making a synopsis of a paragraph at the blackboard, his English teacher had stepped to his side and attempted to guide his hand. Paul had started back with a shudder and thrust his hands violently behind him. The astonished woman could scarcely have been more hurt and embarrassed had he struck at her. The insult was so involuntary and definitely personal as to be unforgettable. In one way and another, he had made all his teachers, men and women alike, conscious of the same feeling of physical aversion. In one class he habitually sat with his hand shading his eyes; in another he always looked out of the window during the recitation; in another he made a running commentary on the lecture, with humorous intention.

His teachers felt this afternoon that his whole attitude was symbolized by his shrug and his flippantly red carnation flower, and they fell upon him without mercy, his English teacher leading the pack. He stood through it smiling, his pale lips parted over his white teeth. (His lips were continually twitching, and he had a habit of raising his eyebrows that was contemptuous and irritating to the last degree.) Older boys than Paul had broken down and shed tears under that baptism of fire, but his set smile did not once desert him, and his only sign of discomfort was the nervous trembling of the fingers that toyed with the buttons of his overcoat, and an occasional jerking of the other hand that held his hat. Paul was always smiling, always glancing about him, seeming to feel that people might be watching him and trying to detect something. This conscious expression, since it was as far as possible from boyish mirthfulness, was usually attributed to insolence or "smartness."

---

four-in-hand: a necktie tied in a loose knot with two hanging ends, popular in the late nineteenth and early twentieth centuries.

As the inquisition proceeded, one of his instructors repeated an imperti-   5
nent remark of the boy's, and the Principal asked him whether he thought that
a courteous speech to make to a woman. Paul shrugged his shoulders slightly
and his eyebrows twitched.

"I don't know," he replied. "I didn't mean to be polite or impolite, either. I
guess it's a sort of way I have of saying things regardless."

The Principal, who was a sympathetic man, asked him whether he didn't
think that a way it would be well to get rid of. Paul grinned and said he guessed
so. When he was told that he could go, he bowed gracefully and went out. His
bow was but a repetition of the scandalous red carnation.

His teachers were in despair, and his drawing master voiced the feeling of
them all when he declared there was something about the boy which none of
them understood. He added: "I don't really believe that smile of his comes altogether from insolence; there's something sort of haunted about it. The boy is
not strong, for one thing. I happen to know that he was born in Colorado, only
a few months before his mother died out there of a long illness. There is something wrong about the fellow."

The drawing master had come to realize that, in looking at Paul, one saw
only his white teeth and the forced animation of his eyes. One warm afternoon
the boy had gone to sleep at his drawing-board, and his master had noted with
amazement what a white, blue-veined face it was; drawn and wrinkled like an
old man's about the eyes, the lips twitching even in his sleep, and stiff with a
nervous tension that drew them back from his teeth.

His teachers left the building dissatisfied and unhappy; humiliated to have   10
felt so vindictive toward a mere boy, to have uttered this feeling in cutting
terms, and to have set each other on, as it were, in the gruesome game of intemperate reproach. Some of them remembered having seen a miserable street
cat set at bay by a ring of tormentors.

As for Paul, he ran down the hill whistling the Soldiers' Chorus from *Faust*,
looking wildly behind him now and then to see whether some of his teachers
were not there to writhe under this light-heartedness. As it was now late in the
afternoon and Paul was on duty that evening as usher at Carnegie Hall, he
decided that he would not go home to supper. When he reached the concert
hall the doors were not yet open and, as it was chilly outside, he decided to go
up into the picture gallery—always deserted at this hour—where there were
some of Raffelli's gay studies of Paris streets and an airy blue Venetian scene or
two that always exhilarated him. He was delighted to find no one in the gallery
but the old guard, who sat in one corner, a newspaper on his knee, a black
patch over one eye and the other closed. Paul possessed himself of the place
and walked confidently up and down, whistling under his breath. After a while
he sat down before a blue Rico and lost himself. When he bethought him to
look at his watch, it was after seven o'clock, and he rose with a start and ran
downstairs, making a face at Augustus, peering out from the cast-room, and
an evil gesture at the Venus of Milo as he passed her on the stairway.

When Paul reached the ushers' dressing-room half-a-dozen boys were
there already, and he began excitedly to tumble into his uniform. It was one of
the few that at all approached fitting, and Paul thought it very becoming—

though he knew that the tight, straight coat accentuated his narrow chest, about which he was exceedingly sensitive. He was always considerably excited while he dressed, twanging all over to the tuning of the strings and the preliminary flourishes of the horns in the music-room; but tonight he seemed quite beside himself, and he teased and plagued the boys until, telling him that he was crazy, they put him down on the floor and sat on him.

Somewhat calmed by his suppression, Paul dashed out to the front of the house to seat the early comers. He was a model usher; gracious and smiling he ran up and down the aisles; nothing was too much trouble for him; he carried messages and brought programmes as though it were his greatest pleasure in life, and all the people in his section thought him a charming boy, feeling that he remembered and admired them. As the house filled, he grew more and more vivacious and animated, and the color came to his cheeks and lips. It was very much as though this were a great reception and Paul were the host. Just as the musicians came out to take their places, his English teacher arrived with checks for the seats which a prominent manufacturer had taken for the season. She betrayed some embarrassment when she handed Paul the tickets, and a *hauteur* which subsequently made her feel very foolish. Paul was startled for a moment, and had the feeling of wanting to put her out; what business had she here among all these fine people and gay colors? He looked her over and decided that she was not appropriately dressed and must be a fool to sit downstairs in such togs. The tickets had probably been sent her out of kindness, he reflected as he put down a seat for her, and she had about as much right to sit there as he had.

When the symphony began Paul sank into one of the rear seats with a long sigh of relief, and lost himself as he had done before the Rico. It was not that symphonies, as such, meant anything in particular to Paul, but the first sigh of the instruments seemed to free some hilarious and potent spirit within him; something that struggled there like the Genius in the bottle found by the Arab fisherman. He felt a sudden zest of life; the lights danced before his eyes and the concert hall blazed into unimaginable splendor. When the soprano soloist came on, Paul forgot even the nastiness of his teacher's being there and gave himself up to the peculiar stimulus such personages always had for him. The soloist chanced to be a German woman, by no means in her first youth, and the mother of many children; but she wore an elaborate gown and a tiara, and above all she had that indefinable air of achievement, that world-shine upon her, which, in Paul's eyes, made her a veritable queen of Romance.

After a concert was over Paul was always irritable and wretched until he   15
got to sleep, and tonight he was even more than usually restless. He had the feeling of not being able to let down, of its being impossible to give up this delicious excitement which was the only thing that could be called living at all. During the last number he withdrew and, after hastily changing his clothes in the dressing-room, slipped out to the side door where the soprano's carriage stood. Here he began pacing rapidly up and down the walk, waiting to see her come out.

Over yonder the Schenley, in its vacant stretch, loomed big and square through the fine rain, the windows of its twelve stories glowing like those of a lighted cardboard house under a Christmas tree. All the actors and singers of the better class stayed there when they were in the city, and a number of the big manufacturers of the place lived there in the winter. Paul had often hung about the hotel, watching the people go in and out, longing to enter and leave school-masters and dull care behind him forever.

At last the singer came out, accompanied by the conductor, who helped her into her carriage and closed the door with a cordial *auf wiedersehen* which set Paul to wondering whether she were not an old sweetheart of his. Paul followed the carriage over to the hotel, walking so rapidly as not to be far from the en-trance when the singer alighted and disappeared behind the swinging glass doors that were opened by a negro in a tall hat and a long coat. In the moment that the door was ajar it seemed to Paul that he, too, entered. He seemed to feel himself go after her up the steps, into the warm, lighted building, into an exotic, a tropical world of shiny, glistening surfaces and basking ease. He reflected upon the mysterious dishes that were brought into the dining-room, the green bottles in buckets of ice, as he had seen them in the supper party pictures of the *Sunday World* supplement. A quick gust of wind brought the rain down with sudden ve-hemence, and Paul was startled to find that he was still outside in the slush of the gravel driveway; that his boots were letting in the water and his scanty overcoat was clinging wet about him; that the lights in front of the concert hall were out, and that the rain was driving in sheets between him and the orange glow of the windows above him. There it was, what he wanted—tangibly before him, like the fairy world of a Christmas pantomime, but mocking spirits stood guard at the doors, and, as the rain beat in his face, Paul wondered whether he were destined always to shiver in the black night outside, looking up at it.

He turned and walked reluctantly toward the car tracks. The end had to come sometime; his father in his night-clothes at the top of the stairs, explana-tions that did not explain, hastily improvised fictions that were forever tripping him up, his upstairs room and its horrible yellow wall-paper, the creaking bu-reau with the greasy plush collar-box, and over his painted wooden bed the pictures of George Washington and John Calvin, and the framed motto, "Feed my Lambs," which had been worked in red worsted by his mother.

Half an hour later, Paul alighted from his car and went slowly down one of the side streets off the main thoroughfare. It was a highly respectable street, where all the houses were exactly alike, and where businessmen of moderate means begot and reared large families of children, all of whom went to Sabbath-school and learned the shorter catechism, and were interested in arithmetic; all of whom were as exactly alike as their homes, and of a piece of the monot-ony in which they lived. Paul never went up Cordelia Street without a shudder of loathing. His home was next to the house of the Cumberland minister. He approached it tonight with the nerveless sense of defeat, the hopeless feeling of sinking back forever into ugliness and commonness that he had always had when he came home. The moment he turned into Cordelia Street he felt the waters close above his head. After each of these orgies of living, he experienced all the physical depression which follows a debauch; the loathing of respect-able beds, of common food, of a house penetrated by kitchen odors; a shudder-ing repulsion for the flavorless, colorless mass of every-day existence; a morbid desire for cool things and soft lights and fresh flowers.

The nearer he approached the house, the more absolutely unequal Paul   20
felt to the sight of it all; his ugly sleeping chamber; the cold bathroom with the
grimy zinc tub, the cracked mirror, the dripping spiggots; his father, at the top
of the stairs, his hairy legs sticking out from his night-shirt, his feet thrust into
carpet slippers. He was so much later than usual that there would certainly be
inquiries and reproaches. Paul stopped short before the door. He felt that he
could not be accosted by his father tonight; that he could not toss again on that
miserable bed. He would not go in. He would tell his father that he had no car
fare, and it was raining so hard he had gone home with one of the boys and
stayed all night.

Meanwhile, he was wet and cold. He went around to the back of the house
and tried one of the basement windows, found it open, raised it cautiously, and
scrambled down the cellar wall to the floor. There he stood, holding his breath,
terrified by the noise he had made, but the floor above him was silent, and there
was no creak on the stairs. He found a soap-box, and carried it over to the soft
ring of light that streamed from the furnace door, and sat down. He was horribly afraid of rats, so he did not try to sleep, but sat looking distrustfully at the
dark, still terrified lest he might have awakened his father. In such reactions,
after one of the experiences which made days and nights out of the dreary
blanks of the calendar, when his senses were deadened, Paul's head was always
singularly clear. Suppose his father had heard him getting in at the window
and had come down and shot him for a burglar? Then, again, suppose his father had come down, pistol in hand, and he had cried out in time to save himself, and his father had been horrified to think how nearly he had killed him?
Then, again, suppose a day should come when his father would remember that
night, and wish there had been no warning cry to stay his hand? With this last
supposition Paul entertained himself until daybreak.

The following Sunday was fine; the sodden November chill was broken by
the last flash of autumnal summer. In the morning Paul had to go to church
and Sabbath-school, as always. On seasonable Sunday afternoons the bur-
ghers of Cordelia Street always sat out on their front "stoops," and talked to
their neighbors on the next stoop, or called to those across the street in neigh-
borly fashion. The men usually sat on gay cushions placed upon the steps that
led down to the sidewalk, while the women, in their Sunday "waists," sat in
rockers on the cramped porches, pretending to be greatly at their ease. The
children played in the streets; there were so many of them that the place resembled the recreation grounds of a kindergarten. The men on the steps—all
in their shirt sleeves, their vests unbuttoned—sat with their legs well apart,
their stomachs comfortably protruding, and talked of the prices of things, or
told anecdotes of the sagacity of their various chiefs and overlords. They occasionally looked over the multitude of squabbling children, listened affectionately to their high-pitched, nasal voices, smiling to see their own proclivities
reproduced in their offspring, and interspersed their legends of the iron kings
with remarks about their sons' progress at school, their grades in arithmetic,
and the amounts they had saved in their toy banks.

On this last Sunday of November, Paul sat all the afternoon on the lowest step of his "stoop," staring into the street, while his sisters, in their rockers, were talking to the minister's daughters next door about how many shirt-waists they had made in the last week, and how many waffles some one had eaten at the last church supper. When the weather was warm, and his father was in a particularly jovial frame of mind, the girls made lemonade, which was always brought out in a red-glass pitcher, ornamented with forget-me-nots in blue enamel. This the girls thought very fine, and the neighbors always joked about the suspicious color of the pitcher.

Today Paul's father sat on the top step, talking to a young man who shifted a restless baby from knee to knee. He happened to be the young man who was daily held up to Paul as a model, and after whom it was his father's dearest hope that he would pattern. This young man was of a ruddy complexion, with a compressed, red mouth, and faded, near-sighted eyes, over which he wore thick spectacles, with gold bows that curved about his ears. He was clerk to one of the magnates of a great steel corporation, and was looked upon in Cordelia Street as a young man with a future. There was a story that, some five years ago—he was now barely twenty-six—he had been a trifle dissipated but in order to curb his appetites and save the loss of time and strength that a sowing of wild oats might have entailed, he had taken his chief's advice, oft reiterated to his employees, and at twenty-one had married the first woman whom he could persuade to share his fortunes. She happened to be an angular school-mistress, much older than he, who also wore thick glasses, and who had now borne him four children, all near-sighted, like herself.

The young man was relating how his chief, now cruising in the Mediter- 25 ranean, kept in touch with all the details of the business, arranging his office hours on his yacht just as though he were at home, and "knocking off work enough to keep two stenographers busy." His father told, in turn, the plan his corporation was considering, of putting in an electric railway plant at Cairo. Paul snapped his teeth; he had an awful apprehension that they might spoil it all before he got there. Yet he rather liked to hear these legends of the iron kings, that were told and retold on Sundays and holidays; these stories of pal-aces in Venice, yachts on the Mediterranean, and high play at Monte Carlo appealed to his fancy, and he was interested in the triumphs of these cash boys who had become famous, though he had no mind for the cash-boy stage.

After supper was over, and he had helped to dry the dishes, Paul nervously asked his father whether he could go to George's to get some help in his geom-etry, and still more nervously asked for car fare. This latter request he had to repeat, as his father, on principle, did not like to hear requests for money, whether much or little. He asked Paul whether he could not go to some boy who lived nearer, and told him that he ought not to leave his school work until Sunday; but he gave him the dime. He was not a poor man, but he had a worthy ambition to come up in the world. His only reason for allowing Paul to usher was, that he thought a boy ought to be earning a little.

Paul bounded upstairs, scrubbed the greasy odor of the dish-water from his hands with the ill-smelling soap he hated, and then shook over his fingers a few drops of violet water from the bottle he kept hidden in his drawer. He left the house with his geometry conspicuously under his arm, and the moment he got out of Cordelia Street and boarded a downtown car, he shook off the lethargy of two deadening days, and began to live again.

The leading juvenile of the permanent stock company which played at one of the downtown theatres was an acquaintance of Paul's, and the boy had been invited to drop in at the Sunday-night rehearsals whenever he could. For more than a year Paul had spent every available moment loitering about Charley Edwards's dressing-room. He had won a place among Edwards's following not only because the young actor, who could not afford to employ a dresser, often found him useful, but because he recognized in Paul something akin to what churchmen term "vocation."

It was at the theatre and at Carnegie Hall that Paul really lived; the rest was but a sleep and a forgetting. This was Paul's fairy tale, and it had for him all the allurement of a secret love. The moment he inhaled the gassy, painty, dusty odor behind the scenes, he breathed like a prisoner set free, and felt within him the possibility of doing or saying splendid, brilliant, poetic things. The moment the cracked orchestra beat out the overture from *Martha*, or jerked at the serenade from *Rigoletto*, all stupid and ugly things slid from him, and his senses were deliciously, yet delicately fired.

Perhaps it was because, in Paul's world, the natural nearly always wore   30
the guise of ugliness, that a certain element of artificiality seemed to him necessary in beauty. Perhaps it was because his experience of life elsewhere was so full of Sabbath-school picnics, petty economies, wholesome advice as to how to succeed in life, and the unescapable odors of cooking, that he found this existence so alluring, these smartly-clad men and women so attractive, that he was so moved by these starry apple orchards that bloomed perennially under the lime-light.

It would be difficult to put it strongly enough how convincingly the stage entrance of that theatre was for Paul the actual portal of Romance. Certainly none of the company ever suspected it, least of all Charley Edwards. It was very like the old stories that used to float about London of fabulously rich Jews, who had subterranean halls there, with palms, and fountains, and soft lamps and richly apparelled women who never saw the disenchanting light of London day. So, in the midst of that smoke-palled city, enamored of figures and grimy toil, Paul had his secret temple, his wishing carpet, his bit of blue-and-white Mediterranean shore bathed in perpetual sunshine.

Several of Paul's teachers had a theory that his imagination had been perverted by garish fiction, but the truth was that he scarcely ever read at all. The books at home were not such as would either tempt or corrupt a youthful mind, and as for reading the novels that some of his friends urged upon him—well, he got what he wanted much more quickly from music; any sort of music, from an orchestra to a barrel organ. He needed only the spark, the indescribable thrill that made his imagination master of his senses, and he could make plots and pictures enough of his own. It was equally true that he was not stage struck—not, at any rate, in the usual acceptation of that expression. He had no desire to become an actor, any more than he had to become a musician. He felt no necessity to do any of these things; what he wanted was to see, to be in the atmosphere, float on the wave of it, to be carried out, blue league after blue league, away from everything.

After a night behind the scenes, Paul found the school-room more than ever repulsive; the bare floors and asked naked walls; the prosy men who never wore frock coats, or violets in their buttonholes; the women with their dull gowns, shrill voices, and pitiful seriousness about prepositions that govern the dative. He could not bear to have the other pupils think, for a moment, that he took these people seriously; he must convey to them that he considered it all trivial, and was there only by way of a jest, anyway. He had autographed pictures of all the members of the stock company which he showed his classmates, telling them the most incredible stories of his familiarity with these people, of his acquaintance with the soloists who came to Carnegie Hall, his suppers with them and the flowers he sent them. When these stories lost their effect, and his audience grew listless, he became desperate and would bid all the boys good-bye, announcing that he was going to travel for a while; going to Naples, to Venice, to Egypt. Then, next Monday, he would slip back, conscious and nervously smiling; his sister was ill, and he should have to defer his voyage until spring.

Matters went steadily worse with Paul at school. In the itch to let his instructors know how heartily he despised them and their homilies, and how thoroughly he was appreciated elsewhere, he mentioned once or twice that he had no time to fool with theorems; adding—with a twitch of the eyebrows and a touch of that nervous bravado which so perplexed them—that he was helping the people down at the stock company; they were old friends of his.

The upshot of the matter was that the Principal went to Paul's father, and   35
Paul was taken out of school and put to work. The manager at Carnegie Hall was told to get another usher in his stead; the door-keeper at the theatre was warned not to admit him to the house; and Charley Edwards remorsefully promised the boy's father not to see him again.

The members of the stock company were vastly amused when some of Paul's stories reached them—especially the women. They were hard-working women, most of them supporting indigent husbands or brothers, and they laughed rather bitterly at having stirred the boy to such fervid and florid inventions. They agreed with the faculty and with his father that Paul's was a bad case.

The east-bound train was ploughing through a January snow-storm; the dull dawn was beginning to show grey when the engine whistled a mile out of Newark. Paul started up from the seat where he had lain curled in uneasy slumber, rubbed the breath-misted window glass with his hand, and peered out. The snow was whirling in curling eddies above the white bottom lands, and the drifts lay already deep in the fields and along the fences, while here and there the long dead grass and dried weed stalks protruded black above it. Lights shone from the scattered houses, and a gang of laborers who stood beside the track waved their lanterns.

Paul had slept very little, and he felt grimy and uncomfortable. He had made the all-night journey in a day coach, partly because he was ashamed, dressed as he was, to go into a Pullman, and partly because he was afraid of being seen there by some Pittsburgh businessman, who might have noticed him in Denny & Carson's office. When the whistle awoke him, he clutched quickly at his breast pocket, glancing about him with an uncertain smile. But the little, clay-bespattered Italians were still sleeping, the slatternly women across the aisle were in open-mouthed oblivion, and even the crumby, crying babies were for the nonce stilled. Paul settled back to struggle with his impatience as best he could.

When he arrived at the Jersey City station, he hurried through his breakfast, manifestly ill at ease and keeping a sharp eye about him. After he reached the Twenty-third Street station, he consulted a cabman, and had himself driven to a men's furnishing establishment that was just opening for the day. He spent upward of two hours there, buying with endless reconsidering and great care. His new street suit he put on in the fitting-room; the frock coat and dress clothes he had bundled into the cab with his linen. Then he drove to a hatter's and a shoe house. His next errand was at Tiffany's, where he selected his silver and a new scarf-pin. He would not wait to have his silver marked, he said. Lastly, he stopped at a trunk shop on Broadway, and had his purchases packed into various travelling bags.

It was a little after one o'clock when he drove up to the Waldorf, and after   40
settling with the cabman, went into the office. He registered from Washington; said his mother and father had been abroad, and that he had come down to await the arrival of their steamer. He told his story plausibly and had no trouble, since he volunteered to pay for them in advance, in engaging his rooms; a sleeping-room, sitting-room, and bath.

Not once, but a hundred times Paul had planned this entry into New York. He had gone over every detail of it with Charley Edwards, and in his scrap book at home there were pages of description about New York hotels, cut from the Sunday papers. When he was shown to his sitting-room on the eight floor, he saw at a glance that everything was as it should be; there was but one detail in his mental picture that the place did not realize, so he rang for the bell boy and sent him down for flowers. He moved about nervously until the boy returned, putting away his new linen and fingering it delightedly as he did so. When the flowers came, he put them hastily into water, and then tumbled into a hot bath. Presently he came out of his white bath-room, resplendent in his new silk underwear, and playing with the tassels of his red robe. The snow was whirling so fiercely outside his windows that he could scarcely see across the street, but within the air was deliciously soft and fragrant. He put the violets and jonquils on the taboret° beside the couch, and threw himself down, with a long sigh, covering himself with a Roman blanket. He was throughly tired; he had been in such haste, he had stood up to such a strain, covered so much ground in the last twenty-four hours, that he wanted to think how it had all come about. Lulled by the sound of the wind, the warm air, and the cool fragrance of the flowers, he sank into deep, drowsy retrospection.

taboret: A low stool or small table.

It had been wonderfully simple; when they had shut him out of the theatre and concert hall, when they had taken away his bone, the whole thing was virtually determined. The rest was a mere matter of opportunity. The only thing that at all surprised him was his own courage—for he realized well enough that he had always been tormented by fear, a sort of apprehensive dread that, of late years, as the meshes of the lies he had told closed about him, had been pulling the muscles of his body tighter and tighter. Until now, he could not remember the time when he had not been dreading something. Even when he was a little boy, it was always there—behind him, or before, or on either side. There had always been the shadowed corner, the dark place into which he dared not look, but from which something seemed always to be watching him—and Paul had done things that were not pretty to watch, he knew.

But now he had a curious sense of relief, as though he had at last thrown down the gauntlet to the thing in the corner.

Yet it was but a day since he had been sulking in the traces; but yesterday afternoon that he had been sent to the bank with Denny & Carson's deposit, as usual—but this time he was instructed to leave the book to be balanced. There was above two thousand dollars in checks, and nearly a thousand in the bank notes which he had taken from the book and quietly transferred to his pocket. At the bank he had made out a new deposit slip. His nerves had been steady enough to permit of his returning to the office, where he had finished his work and asked for a full day's holiday tomorrow, Saturday, giving a perfectly reasonable pretext. The bank book, he knew, would not be returned before Monday or Tuesday, and his father would be out of town for the next week. From the time he slipped the bank notes into his pocket until he boarded the night train for New York, he had not known a moment's hesitation. It was not the first time Paul had steered through treacherous waters.

How astonishingly easy it had all been; here he was, the thing done; and this time there would be no awakening, no figure at the top of the stairs. He watched the snow flakes whirling by his window until he fell asleep.

When he awoke, it was three o'clock in the afternoon. He bounded up with a start; half of one of his precious days gone already! He spent more than an hour in dressing, watching every stage of his toilet carefully in the mirror. Everything was quite perfect; he was exactly the kind of boy he had always wanted to be.

When he went downstairs, Paul took a carriage and drove up Fifth Avenue toward the Park. The snow had somewhat abated; carriages and tradesmen's wagons were hurrying soundlessly to and fro in the winter twilight; boys in woollen mufflers were shovelling off the doorsteps; the avenue stages made fine spots of color against the white street. Here and there on the corners were stands, with whole flower gardens blooming under glass cases, against the sides of which the snow flakes stuck and melted; violets, roses, carnations, lilies of the valley—somewhat vastly more lovely and alluring that they blossomed thus unnaturally in the snow. The Park itself was a wonderful stage winterpiece.

When he returned, the pause of the twilight had ceased, and the tune of the streets had changed. The snow was falling faster, lights streamed from the hotels that reared their dozen stories fearlessly up into the storm, defying the

45

raging Atlantic winds. A long, black stream of carriages poured down the avenue, intersected here and there by other streams; tending horizontally. There were a score of cabs about the entrance of his hotel, and his driver had to wait. Boys in livery were running in and out of the awning stretched across the sidewalk, up and down the red velvet carpet laid from the door to the street. Above, about, within it all was the rumble and roar, the hurry and toss of thousands of human beings as hot for pleasure as himself, and on every side of him towered the glaring affirmation of the omnipotence of wealth.

The boy set his teeth and drew his shoulders together in a spasm of realization: the plot of all dramas, the text of all romances, the nerve-stuff of all sensations was whirling about him like the snow flakes. He burnt like a faggot in a tempest.

When Paul went down to dinner, the music of the orchestra came floating   50
up the elevator shaft to greet him. His head whirled as he stepped into the thronged corridor, and he sank back into one of the chairs against the wall to get his breath. The lights, the chatter, the perfumes, the bewildering medley of color—he had, for a moment, the feeling of not being able to stand it. But only for a moment; these were his own people, he told himself. He went slowly about the corridors, through the writing-rooms, smoking-rooms, reception-rooms, as though he were exploring the chambers of an enchanted palace, built and peopled for him alone.

When he reached the dining-room he sat down at a table near a window. The flowers, the white linen, the many-colored wine glasses, the gay toilettes of the women, the low popping of corks, the undulating repetitions of the *Blue Danube* from the orchestra, all flooded Paul's dream with bewildering radiance. When the roseate tinge of his champagne was added—that cold, precious, bubbling stuff that creamed and foamed in his glass—Paul wondered that there were honest men in the world at all. This was what all the world was fighting for, he reflected; this was what all the struggle was about. He doubted the reality of his past. Had he ever known a place called Cordelia Street, a place where fagged-looking businessmen got on the early car; mere rivets in a machine they seemed to Paul—sickening men, with combings of children's hair always hanging to their coats, and the smell of cooking in their clothes. Cordelia Street—Ah! that belonged to another time and country; had he not always been thus, had he not sat here night after night, from as far back as he could remember, looking pensively over just such shimmering textures, and slowly twirling the stem of a glass like this one between his thumb and middle finger? He rather thought he had.

He was not in the least abashed or lonely. He had no especial desire to meet or to know any of these people; all he demanded was the right to look on and conjecture, to watch the pageant. The mere stage properties were all he contended for. Nor was he lonely later in the evening, in his loge at the Metropolitan. He was now entirely rid of his nervous misgivings, of his forced aggressiveness, of the imperative desire to show himself different from his surroundings. He felt now that his surroundings explained him. Nobody questioned the purple; he had only to wear it passively. He had only to glance down at his attire to reassure himself that here it would be impossible for anyone to humiliate him.

He found it hard to leave his beautiful sitting-room to go to bed that night, and sat long watching the raging storm from his turret window. When he went to sleep it was with the lights turned on in his bedroom; partly because of his old timidity, and partly so that, if he should wake in the night, there would be no wretched moment of doubt, no horrible suspicion of yellow wall-paper, or of Washington or Calvin above his bed.

Sunday morning the city was practically snow-bound. Paul breakfasted late, and in the afternoon he fell in with a wild San Francisco boy, a freshman at Yale, who said he had run down for a "little flyer" over Sunday. The young man offered to show Paul the night side of the town, and the two boys went out together after dinner, not returning to the hotel until seven o'clock the next morning. They had started out in the confiding warmth of a champagne friendship, but their parting in the elevator was singularly cool. The freshman pulled himself together to make his train, and Paul went to bed. He awoke at two o'clock in the afternoon, very thirsty and dizzy, and rang for ice-water, coffee, and the Pittsburgh papers.

On the part of the hotel management, Paul excited no suspicion. There was this to be said for him, that he wore his spoils with dignity and in no way made himself conspicuous. Even under the glow of his wine he was never boisterous, though he found the stuff like a magician's wand for wonder-building. His chief greediness lay in his ears and eyes, and his excesses were not offensive ones. His dearest pleasures were the grey winter twilights in his sitting-room; his quiet enjoyment of his flowers, his clothes, his wide divan, his cigarette, and his sense of power. He could not remember a time when he had felt so at peace with himself. The mere release from the necessity of petty lying, lying every day and every day, restored his self-respect. He had never lied for pleasure, even at school; but to be noticed and admired, to assert his difference from other Cordelia Street boys; and he felt a good deal more manly, more honest, even, now that he had no need for boastful pretensions, now that he could, as his actor friends used to say, "dress the part." It was characteristic that remorse did not occur to him. His golden days went by without a shadow, and he made each as perfect as he could.

On the eighth day after his arrival in New York, he found the whole affair exploited in the Pittsburgh papers, exploited with a wealth of detail which indicated that local news of a sensational nature was at a low ebb. The firm of Denny & Carson announced that the boy's father had refunded the full amount of the theft, and that they had no intention of prosecuting. The Cumberland minister had been interviewed, and expressed his hope of yet reclaiming the motherless lad, and his Sabbath-school teacher declared that she would spare no effort to that end. The rumor had reached Pittsburgh that the boy had been seen in a New York hotel, and his father had gone East to find him and bring him home.

Paul had just come in to dress for dinner; he sank into a chair, weak to the knees, and clasped his head in his hands. It was to be worse than jail, even; the tepid waters of Cordelia Street were to close over him finally and forever. The grey monotony stretched before him in hopeless, unrelieved years; Sabbath-school, Young People's Meeting, the yellow-papered room, the damp dish-towels; it all rushed back upon him with a sickening vividness. He had the old feeling that the orchestra had suddenly stopped, the sinking sensation that the play was over. The sweat broke out on his face, and he sprang to his feet, looked about him with his white, conscious smile, and winked at himself in the mirror. With something of the old childish belief in miracles with which he had so often gone to class, all his lessons unlearned, Paul dressed and dashed whistling down the corridor to the elevator.

He had no sooner entered the dining-room and caught the measure of the music than his remembrance was lightened by his old elastic power of claiming the moment, mounting with it, and finding it all sufficient. The glare and glitter about him, the mere scenic accessories had again, and for the last time, their old potency. He would show himself that he was game, he would finish the thing splendidly. He doubted, more than ever, the existence of Cordelia Street, and for the first time he drank his wine recklessly. Was he not, after all, one of those fortunate beings born to the purple, was he not still himself and in his own place? He drummed a nervous accompaniment to the Pagliacci music and looked about him, telling himself over and over that it had paid.

He reflected drowsily, to the swell of the music and the chill sweetness of his wine, that he might have done it more wisely. He might have caught an outboard steamer and been well out of their clutches before now. But the other side of the world had seemed too far away and too uncertain then; he could not have waited for it; his need had been too sharp. If he had to choose over again, he would do the same thing tomorrow. He looked affectionately about the dining-room, now gilded with a soft mist. Ah, it had paid indeed!

Paul was awakened next morning by a painful throbbing in his head and feet. He had thrown himself across the bed without undressing, and had slept with his shoes on. His limbs and hands were lead heavy, and his tongue and throat were parched and burnt. There came upon him one of those fateful attacks of clear-headedness that never occurred except when he was physically exhausted and his nerves hung loose. He lay still and closed his eyes and let the tide of things wash over him.   60

His father was in New York; "stopping at some joint or other," he told himself. The memory of successive summers on the front stoop fell upon him like a weight of black water. He had not a hundred dollars left; and he knew now, more than ever, that money was everything, the wall that stood between all he loathed and all he wanted. The thing was winding itself up; he had thought of that on his first glorious day in New York, and had even provided a way to snap the thread. It lay on his dressing-table now; he had got it out last night when he came blindly up from dinner, but the shiny metal hurt his eyes, and he disliked the looks of it.

He rose and moved about with a painful effort, succumbing now and again to attacks of nausea. It was the old depression exaggerated; all the world had become Cordelia Street. Yet somehow he was not afraid of anything, was absolutely calm; perhaps because he had looked into the dark corner at last and knew. It was bad enough, what he saw there, but somehow not so bad as his long fear of it had been. He saw everything clearly now. He had a feeling that he had made the best of it, that he had lived the sort of life he was meant to live, and for half an hour he sat staring at the revolver. But he told himself that was not the way, so he went downstairs and took a cab to the ferry.

When Paul arrived at Newark, he got off the train and took another cab, directing the driver to follow the Pennsylvania tracks out of the town. The snow lay heavy on the roadways and had drifted deep in the open fields. Only here and there the dead grass or dried weed stalks projected, singularly black, above it. Once well into the country, Paul dismissed the carriage and walked, floundering along the tracks, his mind a medley of irrelevant things. He seemed to hold in his brain an actual picture of everything he had seen that morning. He remembered every feature of both his drivers, of the toothless old woman from whom he had bought the red flowers in his coat, the agent from whom he had got his ticket, and all of his fellow-passengers on the ferry. His mind, unable to cope with vital matters near at hand, worked feverishly and deftly at sorting and grouping these images. They made for him a part of the ugliness of the world, of the ache in his head, and the bitter burning on his tongue. He stopped and put a handful of snow into his mouth as he walked, but that, too, seemed hot. When he reached a little hillside, where the tracks ran through a cut some twenty feet below him, he stopped and sat down.

The carnations in his coat were drooping with the cold, he noticed; their red glory all over. It occurred to him that all the flowers he had seen in the glass cases that first night must have gone the same way, long before this. It was only one splendid breath they had, in spite of their brave mockery at the winter outside the glass; and it was a losing game in the end, it seemed, this revolt against the homilies by which the world is run. Paul took one of the blossoms carefully from his coat and scooped a little hole in the snow, where he covered it up. Then he dozed a while, from his weak condition, seemingly insensible to the cold.

The sound of an approaching train awoke him, and he started to his feet, 65 remembering only his resolution, and afraid lest he should be too late. He stood watching the approaching locomotive, his teeth chattering, his lips drawn away from them in a frightened smile; once or twice he glanced nervously sidewise, as though he were being watched. When the right moment came, he jumped. As he fell, the folly of his haste occurred to him with merciless clearness, the vastness of what he had left undone. There flashed through his brain, clearer than ever before, the blue of Adriatic water, the yellow of Algerian sands.

He felt something strike his chest, and that his body was being thrown swiftly through the air, on and on, immeasurably far and fast, while his limbs were gently relaxed. Then, because the picture making mechanism was crushed, the disturbing visions flashed into black, and Paul dropped back into the immense design of things. *[1905]*

≡ THINKING ABOUT THE TEXT

1. How does the description of Paul in the exposition, that is, in the first three or four paragraphs, prepare us for his later behavior? Is his suicide anywhere prepared for? His stealing?

2. What are Paul's major objections to his life? Which of these seem typical for an adolescent, and which seem unconventional?

3. What pleases Paul the most about his hotel adventure? Which of these seem normal to you, and which do not? What does his behavior here tell you about his personality?

4. What would make a difference in Paul's happiness? If Paul had survived, what do you think he would have done, that is, has he learned something about himself that might have made a difference?

5. Paul thinks at the end, "Money was everything, the wall that stood between all he loathed and all he wanted" (para. 61). Is this really true for Paul? Explain. Do you think many people feel the same way? Explain.

WILLA CATHER

Narcissistic Personality Disorder in Willa Cather's "Paul's Case"

Sarah Kane (b. 1988) was a senior English major at SUNY Cortland in 2010 when her essay on "Paul's Case" won a college-wide writing contest.

Willa Cather's "Paul's Case: A Study in Temperament" (1905) invites the reader to wonder, "What really is Paul's case?" Cather provides us with ample clues and descriptions of Paul's temperament with remarkable detail and insight into the human psyche considering that she had no formal background in psychology and that she was writing when Sigmund Freud was just beginning to publish his theories and was therefore writing by intuitive observation rather than by using a scientific approach. Because "Paul's Case" is written much like a descriptive analysis or case study in a patient's temperament, the reader is left with several details about Paul that are mysterious and psychiatrically and medically unexplained. The lack of a diagnosis for Paul has led many critics to develop their own diagnosis — some say Paul is a stereotypical homosexual, has Asperger's Syndrome or Autism, or that he has a combination of depression and anxiety. In my opinion, however, the most likely diagnosis for Paul is that he suffers from Narcissistic Personality Disorder.

According to the DSM-IV, people with Narcissistic Personality Disorder are "preoccupied with fantasies of unlimited success, power, brilliance, beauty, or ideal love" (Criterion 2) and believe that they are " 'special' and unique and can only be understood by, or should be associated with, other special or high-status people" (Criterion 3). Paul's clothing gives us our first clue to his narcissistic attitudes about himself; in Cather's description of Paul's dress, it is apparent that Paul is attempting to rise above his lower-class status by mimicking the upper class' appearance. The collar of Paul's overcoat is velvet, and "there was something of the dandy about him, and he wore an opal pin in his neatly knotted four-in-hand, and a red carnation in his buttonhole" (685). According to the DSM-IV, narcissistic people typically "ruminate about 'long overdue' admiration and privilege and compare themselves favorably with famous or privileged people" (714). They also have a strong sense of entitlement, and "begrudge others of their success or possessions, feeling that they better deserve those achievements, admirations, or privileges" (715). Paul evidently has the desire to be a part of the privileged upper class, or at least play the role, perhaps because it makes him feel more comfortable to be luxurious, or perhaps because he enjoys being "special, or unique" (714) in comparison to those around him.

Also related is Criterion 1, which states that people with Narcissistic Personality Disorder have "a grandiose sense of self-importance (e.g., exaggerates achievements and talents, expects to be recognized as superior without commensurate achievements)" (717). Paul certainly feels superior to his living situation with his father on Cordelia Street. Paul never goes home "without a shudder of loathing," because he had an overwhelming sensation, every time he approached the street, of "sinking back forever into ugliness and commonness" (688). He preferred a neighboring street that was respectable, and filled with businessmen and large families with children who went to Sabbath school and were interested in arithmetic (688).

Paul's inner conflict as a person suffering from Narcissistic Personality Disorder is his intense dissatisfaction with his common lifestyle and a strong desire for and a sense of entitlement to a more lavish one. This dilemma fits perfectly with Criterion 5, which states that people with Narcissistic Personality Disorder have "a sense of entitlement, i.e., unreasonable expectations of especially favorable treatment or automatic compliance with his or her expectations" (717).

Because life does not meet Paul's lavish expectations, he seeks them himself. He escapes his "flavorless, colorless mass of everyday existence" (688) on Cordelia Street and takes a train to New York City, a symbol of ultimate glamour and sophistication, and a place of acceptance of the unorthodox and fantastical. He takes refuge from a snowstorm inside a grand hotel where the environment is as luxurious and as aesthetically pleasing as he had always wanted his life to be. Having plenty of money that he stole from his father's account, Paul chooses the most high-end hotel in the city: the Waldorf. There, he is surrounded by the sights, sounds, and smells that only the privileged are able to experience. Paul reminds himself that the people in the Waldorf are "his own people" (693). And as he explores the inside of the Waldorf, it is as if "he were exploring the chambers of an enchanted palace, built and peopled for him alone" (693). Paul is definitely experiencing some delusions of grandeur here, as he thinks that he is inherently superior to the rest of the population and belongs in the upper crust, and the fact that he thinks all the pleasures surrounding him are meant especially for him is a sure sign of narcissism.

Criterion 4 states that a person with Narcissistic Personality Disorder "requires excessive admiration" (717), which explains why Paul takes so much delight in his job as an usher at his local theater; "He was a model usher; gracious and smiling he ran up and down the aisles; nothing was too much trouble for him; he carried messages and brought programmes as though it were his greatest pleasure in life; and all the people in his section thought him a charming boy. . . . It was very much as though this were a great reception and Paul were the host" (686–687). Though Paul does not wish to become an actor, he performs his duties so thoroughly and theatrically that it is clear that Paul loves to be the center of attention and in social situations in which he receives a lot of praise for performance.

Criterion 9 of the DSM-IV's description of Narcissistic Personality Disorder cites that people with this disorder are arrogant and show "haughty behaviors or attitudes" (717). The faculty who are present at Paul's hearing for his misdemeanors find the carnation in his buttonhole to be "not properly significant of the contrite spirit befitting a boy under the ban of suspension" (685). In other words, the faculty takes the carnation as a sign of Paul's arrogance and his contempt for them and the entire situation, and they are offended that Paul is not more regretful of his ill behavior. In addition to arrogance and haughtiness, people with Narcissistic Personality Disorder "often display snobbish, disdainful, or patronizing attitudes" (715). All of these Criterion 9 characteristics are evident in Paul's classroom behavior: "In one class he habitually sat with his hand shielding his eyes . . . in another, he made a running commentary on the lecture, with humorous intention" (685). Paul's shielding of the eyes clearly indicates that he is arrogant enough to blatantly ignore his teacher. This behavior also symbolizes Paul's attempt to dissociate himself from the average people where he lives that he devaluates. And turning his teacher's lecture into a comical mockery is a definite example of his patronizing attitude and behavior.

In a sense, this arrogance and patronization can be directly related to the lack of empathy among narcissistic people. Criterion 7 cites that people with Narcissistic Personality Disorder "have difficulty recognizing the desires, subjective experiences, and feelings of others . . . and are often contemptuous and impatient of others who talk about their own problems and concerns" (715). Paul is certainly impatient and contemptuous during the hearing, most likely because he is emotionally unable to understand why his teachers are upset with him or the seriousness of the situation in the first place. In his mind, there is a great divide between his concerns and the concerns of others, so Paul disregards the concerns of others and maintains his haughty attitude throughout the hearing by smiling and toying with the buttons of his coat (685).

Because of his lack of empathy for others, Paul is able to take advantage of people because he is only interested in his self-gain. Criterion 6 states that a person with Narcissistic Personality Disorder is "interpersonally exploitive, i.e., takes advantage of others to achieve his or her own ends" (717). During Paul's hearing, he tells the faculty members a lie when he states that he wants to come back to school. Apparently, "Paul was quite accustomed to lying; found it, indeed, indispensable for overcoming friction" (685). Later, Paul abuses his privilege of helping his father handle his bank deposits, and steals the money from his father's account. Paul uses the money for his extravagant trip to New York City.

There are some critics, like Larry Rubin, who argue that Cather's short   10
story contains a strong homosexual motif throughout. This is undoubtedly a
valid hypothesis if we look at Paul's especially flamboyant behavior and appearance (the red carnation, his love of theater and the arts, his fascination
with the female soprano who we may interpret to be not a love interest but an
example of feminine beauty that Paul aspires to, and his relationships with
other boys). However, homosexuality is not the only "diagnosis" for all of Paul's
behaviors, and it does not sufficiently account for any of Paul's attitudes or
behaviors that have already been discussed in this paper. During his stay in the
city, Paul spends some time with "a wild San Francisco boy" who has come to
the city for "a little flyer." The way that Cather describes this boy sounds as if he
is gay and is looking for a partner for the weekend. The boy offers to "show Paul
the night side of the town" (694), and the two stay out until 7 o'clock in the
morning. However, when they leave each other that morning, their parting is
"singularly cool" (694). Critic Larry Rubin asserts that his encounter with the
San Francisco boy is undoubtedly a homosexual one. In my reading, however,
there is clear evidence of the San Francisco boy's homosexuality, but no evidence that Paul was attracted to this wild boy for sexual reasons. Rubin hy-
pothesizes that "Paul wanted something [sexual] from his companion that the
latter was unprepared to give" (130), but this interpretation is reversed. Rubin
previously admits that Cather's description of the San Francisco boy indicates
his homosexuality and his intent to have sexual relations with a partner that
weekend, so there is no reason that the boy would be unprepared to have sex
with Paul. It seems more likely that Paul mistook the wild boy for a potentially
exciting and cultured tour guide of the big city, and when the wild boy attempts
something more intimate with Paul, the relationship between the two goes
sour, as is evident in the elevator when they leave each other.

Cather's writing about Paul is remarkable because of its intuitive insight
into human behavior, especially considering that Cather was writing about a
social disorder that had not yet been identified or studied. Despite the lack of
knowledge about Narcissistic Personality Disorder when Cather wrote this
short story, she provides readers with plenty of details to diagnose the boy
themselves. Narcissism is the only diagnosis that can explain all of Paul's attitudes and behaviors, and that is why it is the disorder that he must be suffering
from.   [2010]

Works Cited

Diagnostic and Statistical Manual of Mental Disorders DSM-IV. Arlington, VA.:
American Psychiatric Association, 2007. Print.

Larry Rubin. "The Homosexual Motif in Willa Cather's 'Paul's Case'" *Studies in
Short Fiction* (1975): 127–31. Print.

Perkins, Barbara, Robyn Warhol-Down, and George B. Perkins. "Paul's Case: A
Study in Temperament." *Women's Work: An Anthology of American Literature* New York: McGrawHill, 1994. Print.

LORETTA WASSERMAN

From *Willa Cather: A Study of the Short Fiction*

Loretta Wasserman (1924–2011) was a professor of English at Grand Valley State University, where she published widely on Willa Cather's life and work.

The story falls into two parts. In the first Paul is facing expulsion from high school for what seem minor kinds of insubordination and disrespect, the underlying cause being his exasperating contempt (as the teachers see it) toward the whole educational enterprise. In the opening scene he is called before a disciplinary committee to explain himself. The teachers are not unkind, but Paul's insouciant air (he enters "suave and smiling" with a red carnation in his buttonhole) both baffles and angers them. At the end of the hearing, they leave feeling "dissatisfied and unhappy; humiliated to have felt so vindictive toward a mere boy."[29] Paul rushes off to his ushering job at Carnegie Hall, first going up to the picture gallery in the Hall, where "he sat down before a blue Rico and lost himself" (*TG*, 104). Later, after helping patrons to their seats, he falls into a similar dreamy state as the symphony begins ("he lost himself as he had before the Rico" [105]).

The concert over, Paul delays long enough to follow the singer's carriage and watch her enter her hotel: "he seemed to feel himself go after her up the steps, into the warm, lighted building, into an exotic, a tropical world of shiny, glistening surfaces and basking ease" (107). A gust of cold wind and rain in his face rouses him, and he takes the cars to Cordelia Street, "where all the houses were exactly alike" (107). He pictures to himself his upstairs room, with its "horrible yellow wallpaper, . . . and over his painted wooden bed the pictures of George Washington and John Calvin, and the framed motto 'Feed My Lambs,' which had been worked in red worsted by his mother" (107). His father, with his endless questions and complaints, will be standing at the top of the stairs. (Paul's mother died when he was a baby, and Paul lives with his father and sisters, shadowy girls who barely appear in the story.)

When the school principal reports that Paul has not improved following the faculty hearing, Paul's father takes him out of school and finds a place for him as a cash boy with Denny & Carson—the first step, as Cordelia Street sees it, to a solid future. Further, Paul is required to quit ushering, and the doorkeeper is to see that he does not enter the theater.

The second half of the story begins with Paul on a train to New York. On arrival he takes a cab to an expensive men's furnishing establishment, where he outfits himself with street and dress clothes, then to Tiffany's for a scarfpin and silver articles, and last to a trunk shop where his purchases are put in traveling bags. He registers at the Waldorf for a sleeping room, sitting room, and bath. In a brief flashback we learn that Paul has quietly stolen almost a thousand dollars in cash from Denny & Carson. It had been "astonishingly easy," and now Paul looks ahead with relief to a few "precious days" of case: "This time there would be no awakening, no figure at the top of the stairs" (115). He luxuriates in his surroundings—the lavishly furnished hotel, hothouse flowers, the music in the dining room, and the city itself, including a night out with a freshman from Yale and an evening in a loge at the Metropolitan: "Everything was quite perfect; he was exactly the kind of boy he had always wanted to be" (115). On the eighth day he learns from the Pittsburgh papers that his theft has been discovered, and that his father is in New York looking for him: "It was to be worse than jail, even; the tepid waters of Cordelia Street were to close over him finally and forever. The grey monotony stretched before him in hopeless, unrelieved years; Sabbath-school, Young People's Meeting, the yellow-papered room, the damp dish-towels" (118). He enjoys one last evening in the hotel dining room, drinking more wine than usual, drumming nervously to the *Pagliacci* music in the background—a sound track signaling the inevitable tragedy and also the sad clownishness of the deluded boy in his masquerade. (Revising the story, Cather cut the reference to *Pagliacci*, possibly to remove the suggestion that Paul's true self was hidden, rather than revealed, by his new clothes.)[30] The next day Paul takes the ferry to New Jersey, then hires a horse cab to drive him into the countryside by the railroad track, where he dismisses the cab, walks to a high bank, and launches himself before an oncoming train. Before he jumps he takes one of the red flowers he has been wearing in his coat and buries it in the snow.

Critics generally follow the lead of Cather's title, which seems to hint that this is a "case study," a sociological or clinical examination of a completed, enclosed incident or pathological state. The most frequent reading sees a sensitive, artistically inclined youth crushed by a withering environment, the dreary rigidities of Pittsburgh Presbyterianism and the physical ugliness of Paul's home ("the cold bathroom with the grimy zinc tub, the cracked mirror, the dripping spiggots" [107]). Adherents to this view in its most extreme form hold that in this story "environment is consistently portrayed as the inexhaustible determiner of human lives."[31] The two faces over his bed, Washington and Calvin, represent the failures of state (high school) and church.

Countering interpretations point out that Paul gives no evidence of suppressed talent or even fine-grained love of art; in fact, he appears to use art only as a vehicle for escapist dreams. Paul himself is the "case," and the story poses a psychological question: what is the etiology of such maladjustment? Early deprivation, the loss of his mother, is one explanation ("he could not remember the time when he had not been dreading something. Even when he was a little boy, it was always there—behind him or before, or on either side" [114]). The motto embroidered by his mother, "Feed My Lambs," symbolizes his poignant longing for love, a need not met by his father, a figure of judgment and punishment. In accord with this view of Paul as emotionally infantile, Cordelia Street is interpreted as an ordinary working-class community, full of children and plans for the future, its dreariness and ugliness a reflection of Paul's distorting vision. Possibly an older psychology, one less attuned to the importance of early childhood experiences, is behind Cather's portrait. Reading William James, Cather would have come across his discussion of types of "diseased will," including cases marked by an inability to plan or act. She would have been particularly sensitive to his speculation that too much theatergoing, or too much music listening, has a debilitating effect on forming constructive life habits (James, especially chapters 1, "Habit," and 17, "Will").

That "Paul's Case" responds to such contrasting readings is sufficient evidence that Cather succeeded in balancing the competing claims of the old arguments between nature and nurture, heredity and environment, freedom and determinism, and that the beauty of the story inheres in just this tension. Reflecting on the story, readers must reluctantly side with Paul's teachers (voices for the best understanding his culture could provide), admitting, as each does, "that it was scarcely possible to put into words the real cause of the trouble" (102).

More remains to be said. Accomplished as the whole story is, its real glory lies in the second half —the realization of the dream. Here is the source of the fascination the story continues to exert on the young and the not-so-young: to win without desert or guilt, to be queen-for-a-day, to be the lost heir. Against all odds, this wish is indeed fulfilled in the story, however temporarily. All the little failures that could have spoiled Paul's week are avoided. He *does* know that he wants, and he enjoys fully the feel of his clothes, the white linen, the flowers blooming under glass, the red velvet carpets, the sound of popping corks. He is not embarrassed or gauche, as an uneducated, callow boy might be in such surroundings ("he wore his spoils with dignity and in no way made himself conspicuous. . . . His chief greediness lay in his ears and eyes, and his excesses were not offensive ones" [117]). The experienced clerks at the Waldorf take him at his own estimation; apparently he could spend an evening with a college boy without betraying his ignorance. Most intriguing of all is his mental poise ("He was not the least abashed or lonely. . . . He could not remember a time when he had felt so at peace with himself" [117]). No qualms about his crime disturb him; apparently the long lessons of Sabbath School gained no niche in his consciousness—in fact, he feels virtuous ("The mere release from the necessity of petty lying, lying every day and every day, restored his self-respect. . . . He felt a good deal more manly, more honest, even" [117]). Later, facing death, he still "had a feeling that he had made the best of it" (119). What he believes now with even greater certainty is "that money was everything" (119).

In giving Paul this irreverent final thought, Cather is doubtless playing with discreet irony against the sentimental moralists of her day, who would have anticipated a wave of guilt and remorse (in this regard, at least, she is like her admired Mark Twain). That this is her intent is underscored when Paul, falling before the train, sees "the folly of his haste . . . with merciless clarity"; but the "folly" is not his crime, not his suicide, not his false moral sense; rather, it is his failure to escape further, to more distant lands, to "the blue of Adriatic water, the yellow of Algerian sands" (121).

Modern psychologists say that we excuse, even find amusing, the extreme narcissists, who can take and enjoy without conscience (comic figures like Falstaff; great criminals), because deep down we understand these longings embedded in us from early infancy. Cather evokes these long-suppressed desires, and we accept as humanly right the forgiveness implicit in the delicate compassion of the lines ending Paul's story (not really a "case" at all): "Then, because the picture making mechanism was crushed, the disturbing visions flashed into black, and Paul dropped back into the immense design of things" (121).

Among the many delicate touches in the narration of Paul's story are a few

10

hints that his apparent self-destructiveness is rather his fidelity to some dimly felt ultimacy, the "immense design of things." When Paul is forced to give up the theater, Charley Edwards, the stock company juvenile, feels sorry because "he recognized in Paul something akin to what churchmen term 'vocation'" (110). An odd term, *vocation*, for the boy's obsession. The suggestion of a religious votive appears also as the narrator describes the childish dream of escape to another world that Paul builds to comfort himself through school and work. "So, in the midst of that smoke-palled city, enamoured of figures and grimy toil, Paul had his secret temple, his wishing carpet, his bit of blue-and-white Mediterranean shore bathed in perpetual sunshine" (111). The vision of sand and blue water that blesses Paul's final hour is the "secret temple" that has sustained him, and to which, in his fashion, he has been faithful.   [1992]

JOHN P. ANDERS

From *Willa Cather's Sexual Aesthetics and the Male Homosexual Literary Tradition*

John P. Anders (b. 1948) received his Ph.D. in English from the University of Nebraska in 1993.

Since its publication "Paul's Case" has become Cather's most recognizable short fiction; likewise, it has gradually emerged as her representative gay text. In fact, it has become something of a critical commonplace to read homosexuality in the story, and in doing so, critics have discovered the indirect manner in which Cather treats the subject as well as the contributions it makes to her art. Larry Rubin first identified a homosexual motif in "Paul's Case" in 1975, paying close attention to the manner in which it moves the story away from the clinical aura of a case study toward subtle, psychological portraiture. Rubin collects what he considers to be clues to Paul's sexual nature, such as his physical appearance, social relationships, personal habits, and inner feelings, all of which, he stresses, indirectly hint at "Paul's deviation from what the culture of [Cather's] day . . . would consider the sexual norm" (129). Specific examples in the story include Paul's theatrically expressive eyes, "remarkable for a certain hysterical brilliancy . . . peculiarly offensive in a boy" (TTG 102), his use of violet water, friendships with boys his own age or slightly older, and an "apprehensive dread" of "the thing in the corner" (114). Particularly interesting among these suggestive details is Paul's encounter with the "wild" (117) freshman from Yale. As they embark upon a night on the town together, their relationship is cordial; their parting in the morning, however, is "singularly cool" (117)—an event that leaves the reader, as Rubin suggests, "with an unshakable sense of innuendo" (130).

    Such details build a convincing argument for Paul's unstated sexuality. But homosexuality does more in "Paul's Case" than describe its protagonist's nature, and it is here that readers begin to feel the effects of Cather's sexual aesthetics. Rubin explains:

> The importance of all this for a balanced critical evaluation of the story lies not so much in the fact that Paul is very probably homosexual by nature and temperament, but that Cather is trying to show us the tragic consequences of the conflict between a sensitive and hence alienated temperament, on the one hand, and a narrowly "moral," bourgeois environment, on the other. It is one of her more familiar themes, and has been widely dealt with by critics; but here it would seem important to be aware of the homosexuality of the sensitive protagonist in order to comprehend the full depth of his alienation from the "normal" American society in which he feels trapped and hence the full pathos of his situation. (131)

Cather's subtle treatment of homosexuality in this early story intensifies her skill at narrative indirection and positions "Paul's Case" more securely with her mature work than with her apprentice fiction.

Building upon Rubin's observations, Claude J. Summers sees homosexuality in "Paul's Case" as more than simply a metaphor for alienation. He places the story in the forefront of modern gay fiction and argues that its homosexual aspects enable Cather to make a powerful social commentary. As Rubin distances "Paul's Case" from the clinical and criminal implications of its title, Summers begins his argument by emphasizing the sexual connotations of its subtitle, "A Study in Temperament."[2] Extending Rubin's list of sexual clues, Summers stresses the subliminal impact of Cather's language:

> Throughout the story, Cather repeatedly uses diction suggestive of homosexuality. Although in almost every instance the words are used with no specific allusion to homosexuality, the startling number and pervasiveness of such terms as *gay* (used four times), *fairy, faggot, fagged, queen, loitering, tormented, unnatural, haunted, different, perverted, secret love,* and so forth create a verbal ambiance that subtly but persistently calls attention to the issue. However innocently used, these words and phrases appear too often to be merely coincidental. They function to help establish the overtone by which the ear divines homosexuality in the text. (*Gay Fictions* 67)

Summers goes beyond the surface details of the story to reveal its symbolic importance that for him lies in Cather's response to Oscar Wilde — his life, his trial, and his posthumous *De Profundis*. For Summers, "The reaction of the teachers to Paul parallels Cather's own excessive reaction to Wilde's mocking manner in the 1890's, and may reflect the author's mature reconsideration of her own earlier lack of imagination in not dealing charitably with Wilde in his disgrace" (69). Consequently, "Paul's Case" becomes both an indictment of Wildean aestheticism and an alternative to its limitations.

Paul is Cather's Wildean aesthete. His dandified appearance, his "scandalous red carnation" (TTG 103), and his loathing of the commonplace associate him with what Cather perceived to be the negative attributes of aestheticism. Most damning, however, Paul lacks sympathy for others. In criticizing Paul's deficiency, Cather strongly indicts the aesthetic movement for its lack of imagination, but rather than the position Wilde offers in *De Profundis*, which calls for the homosexual to reject society, Cather advocates human sympathy. Summers finds this implicit in the optimistic motto "Feed my Lambs" (TTG 107), which "haunts the story as an unnamed presence that promises the possibility of integrating outcasts like Paul—and like Wilde and other homosexuals—into the community, and doing so without violating their individuality" (*Gay Fictions* 74). Although O'Brien sees Cather still subordinating herself to the male tradition in "Paul's Case," part of the story's maturity is its questioning of masculine ideals, and important in this social critique is Oscar Wilde's role in helping Cather convey the need for diversity and acceptance. "As a gay fiction," Summers writes, " 'Paul's Case' is complex and resonant. . . . subtly implying alternatives to alienation and suicide and envisioning possibilities implicit in those homilies by which the world is run" (76).

By envisioning alternatives, Cather's story breaks with the obligatory treatment of homosexuality, which prescribes death or prolonged despair. Homosexuality in "Paul's Case" is not the reason for Paul's tragedy, and his suicide is not the stereotypical tragic ending for gay characters. Rather, as Summers explains, the cause of Paul's unhappiness and suicide is "his inability to integrate his homosexuality into real life" (*Gay Fictions* 68). The subject of homosexuality thus allows Cather poignantly to dramatize her appeal for human sympathy, which is necessary in life and in art.   *[1999]*

SHARON O'BRIEN
From *Willa Cather: The Emerging Voice*

Sharon O'Brien (b. 1946) received her B.A. from Radcliffe College in 1967 and her Ph.D. from Harvard in 1975. She is a noted biographer of Willa Cather and frequently publishes critical essays in scholarly journals on Cather's work. She is currently the John Hope Caldwell Professor of American Cultures at Dickinson College.

In "Paul's Case," however, Cather found a momentary and happy resolution to the tension between disclosure and concealment, life and art. Placed last (and seventh) in *The Troll Garden*, the story eludes categorization. Although set in the East, it does not romanticize Eastern culture and denigrate Western; a psychological study of a romantic temperament—a subject dear to Henry James—it is not Jamesian. In this beautifully crafted story, the high-water mark of her early fiction, Cather draws upon her observations of Presbyteria and Bohemia, her memories of a gifted and unhappy student in her Latin class, and her own adolescent rebellion. The result is neither unmediated self-disclosure not protective imitation, but a controlled work of art that does seem, as she said of Sarah Orne Jewett's Maine stories, to resemble "life itself" (*CPF*, p. 6). Long the favorite of critics, this was Cather's first choice as well, and in later years the only short story she allowed to be anthologized. [. . .]

Cather looks back at an earlier self in "Paul's Case"—William Cather, Jr.—as she portrays another imaginative, sensitive youth at odds with a repressive society. Paul's enemy is the emotionally and aesthetically bankrupt middle-class world devoted to the gods of money and respectability. Cordelia Street, his dreary home where the ugliness of petty-bourgeois life is symbolized by the "horrible yellow wallpaper," the bathroom's grimy zinc tub and dripping spiggots, and his father's hairy legs and carpet slippers, is Cather's Presbyteria. Paul's alternative world of fairy-tale allure—his troll garden—is the concert hall and theater where he feasts on delicious sensations, a version of Cather's Bohemia. Repulsed by the sordid vulgarity he sees around him, Paul plays the dandy's role to signify his citizenship in Bohemia, sporting an opal pin in his frayed coat and wearing a red carnation as his badge of defiance and kinship with the fin-de-siècle aesthetes and decadents.

In many ways Paul is a male version of Willa Cather. In addition to the adolescent rebellion, she grants him her love for music and theater; her distaste for the mundane and the conventional; and her repudiation of the expected gender role, expressed in the story by Paul's distaste for the Horatio Alger values. Another resemblance may be Paul's probable homosexuality, hinted by his similarity to Oscar Wilde and later by his ambiguous night on the town with a "wild" freshman from Yale.[13] And yet Paul is a separate fictional creation whom Cather regards critically as well as sympathetically, as when she suggests that there is something unhealthy in his nature. His eyes have a "hysterical brilliancy," the pupils "abnormally large, as though he were addicted to belladonna." Paul is addicted, we discover, although not to belladonna. He is wedded to the artificial world of the theater and concert hall where he indulges in "orgies of living" and "debauches" of sensation.

Paul has to be a glutton in Bohemia because he is famished for spiritual, aesthetic, and emotional food in Presbyteria. The portraits of John Calvin and George Washington over his bed embody the grim, repressive patriarchal values of the national religion of financial success, the Protestant ethic allied with a patriotic capitalism. These beliefs—Paul's paternal inheritance—offer him no sustenance, while the one legacy from his dead mother (the framed motto "Feed my Lambs" embroidered in red worsted) offers him only the inadequate nurturance of a feminized Christianity. The nourishment he absorbs during his other life as usher at Carnegie Hall and hanger-on at the local repertory company is evident in the transformation he undergoes in these magical realms; he becomes more "vivacious and animated," and the "colour came to his cheeks and lips." Like Katherine Gaylord, however, Paul is the parasite-vampire greedily drawing life from an external source, and his physical appearance reveals that such food is not wholesome. Like the "thirsty, cankered, goblin-ridden" Laura in Rossetti's poem or the dying Katherine, Paul is emaciated, with "high, cramped shoulders and a narrow chest," and despite his youth his "white blue-veined face" is "drawn and wrinkled like an old man's."

The story is subtitled "A Study in Temperament," and as Cather progressively makes clear, Paul's is not the artistic temperament. Delicately and consistently, she separates her point of view from his. She demonstrates the distorting power of Paul's excitable, greedy imagination, as when she shows us the dis-

5

crepancy between his vision of an opera singer as a "veritable queen of Romance" and the mundane reality: the singer is a tired woman well past her first youth, and singing is just another job for her. In addition, Paul is no connoisseur of music; he can derive the escape he desires from anything from an "orchestra to a barrel organ." Symphonies and operas mean nothing to him as art forms. What he wants is to "lose himself." to "float on the wave of [music], to be carried out, blue league after blue league, away from everything."

Although Carter associated such loss of self with the creative process, Paul's self-dissolution is not the artist's desire to create, but the child's regressive yearning to regain the preoedipal union with the mother. He uses music to enter a solipsistic realm where he passively absorbs the sensations he craves. Cather creates parallels to the regressive William of "The Burglar's Christmas," who also sought the infant's gratifications, when she has Paul follow the opera singer to her hotel. As he shivers outside in the cold (as did William in "The Burglar's Christmas"), the singer enters the elegant, welcoming building. Paul accompanies her in his imagination:

> He seemed to feel himself go after her up the steps, into the warm, lighted building, into an exotic, a tropical world of shiny glistening surfaces and basking ease. He reflected upon the mysterious dishes that were brought into the dining room. the green bottles in buckets of ice. as he had seen them in the supper party pictures of the *Sunday World* supplement.

Like William, Paul gains this idyllic space when he becomes a thief: he steals money from his employers to finance his trip to New York, desperate to enter the world of "basking ease" into which the opera singer has vanished. His week-long orgy of gratification further demonstrates Cather's intention to portray his temperament as regressive rather than artistic. Entering his own expensive hotel. Paul gains the house of his dreams, a protected, expensive world where the air is "deliciously soft and fragrant," magically safe from the winter storm outside. Commenting on the artificiality and precariousness of Paul's hothouse world through her use of space and metaphor, Cather connects his womblike hotel room—seemingly a refuge from the howling January blizzard—with a flower stand where "flower gardens [were] blooming under glass cases, against the sides of which the snow flakes stuck and melted; violets, roses, carnations, lilies of the valley—somehow vastly more lovely and alluring that they blossomed thus unnaturally in the snow."

The pleasures Paul seeks during his brief stay in the luxurious hotel also reveal the regressiveness of his journey. Despite his love for music he attends the opera only once, since he can attain his real goal—passive gratification—without music's aid. He spends most of his time sleeping, eating, and drinking. His most enjoyable waking moments are those passed in the sitting room, where he drowsily contemplates his delicate flowers, elegant new clothes, and gracious surroundings, or in the hotel dining room where he tastes unfamiliar delicacies and savors champagne.

When the theft is discovered and his money runs out, Paul envisions returning to Pittsburgh—its Sabbath schools, yellowing wallpaper, and cooking smells—in images of drowning, as he senses the "tepid waters of Cordelia

Street" about to "close over him finally and forever." He finds this loss of self as terrifying as his floating "blue league after blue league" on the billows of gratification had been delectable. So he chooses to lose himself in death, a decision Cather links metaphorically and psychologically with all the forms of self-dissolution he has pursued. After the artificial garden disappears. Paul's quest for annihilation leads him to a snow-covered wasteland beside the train tracks. He throws himself in front of the train — as had Anna Karenina, whose romanticism Cather also criticized — and "dropped back into the immense design of things" (CSF, pp. 243–61).

Although "Paul's Case" does not comment directly on the woman artist's   10
plight, as do several of the other stories, it does show Cather's condemnation of conventional gender arrangements. Paul's alienation is connected with the polarized sex roles that Willa Cather had also confronted in adolescence; he is William Cather, Jr.'s opposite and double, as much in conflict with the male role as she had been with the female. Cather's sympathetic portrayal of this "girl-boy" who resembles Ethelbert Nevin reveals how far she was moving from male identification. Even though Cather was still subordinating herself to the male literary tradition, she had rejected the cult of virility once exemplified by Kipling and football. Androgynous or feminine men could be oppressive to women. And yet Cather's ability to create Paul, who is destroyed by the male world she had once wanted to enter, shows her awareness that men as well as women could be victims of masculine — and heterosexual — roles and values.   [1986]

≡ MAKING COMPARISONS

1. What similarities and differences in viewpoint about narcissism do you see in Kane's and Wasserman's essays?

2. How do O'Brien and Anders deal with the episode of the wild freshman from Yale?

3. How do you think Anders would respond to the last sentence in O'Brien's essay? How do their discussions of Paul as a gay character differ?

≡ WRITING ABOUT ISSUES

1. Write an essay that analyzes Paul's behavior. Use at least one of the critics given here and one other.

2. Locate Larry Rubin's essay on Paul's homosexuality. Write an argument that agrees or disagrees with his conclusions.

3. Read Cather's brief story "A Wagner Matinee," and write an essay comparing this story to "Paul's Case."

4. In Sharon O'Brien's biography, read her discussion about Cather calling herself "William" in high school. Find another biography of Cather and write a brief essay comparing the two biographies' discussions of this episode. Which one makes the most sense to you? Why?

≡ A Door to Freedom: Cultural Contexts for a Play

HENRIK IBSEN, *A Doll's House*

CULTURAL CONTEXTS:
HENRIK IBSEN, Memorandum

AUGUST STRINDBERG, "Woman in a Doll's House"

EMMA GOLDMAN, Review of *A Doll's House*

JOAN TEMPLETON, From *"The* Doll House *Backlash: Criticism, Feminism, and Ibsen"*

SUSANNA RUSTIN, "Why *A Doll's House* by Henrik Ibsen Is More Relevant Than Ever"

The writer and scientist Loren Eiseley notes that "to grow is a gain, an enlargement of life. . . . Yet it is also a departure." Eiseley's seems a more sophisticated idea than one portraying personal and social progress as only positive. Life is more complicated than that. Most of us eagerly anticipate becoming adults and embracing adult responsibilities and privileges. But our literature is filled with nostalgia for the innocence and wonder of childhood. We have a sense that we have lost something as our culture, technology, and lifestyles have advanced. There is no going back, but to some the old ways sometimes seem simpler. Our grandparents longed to leave the limitations of small-town life, but fifty years later their urban grandchildren idealize small communities. Women agonized over the legal and personal restrictions of Victorian marriages, but contemporary women understand that divorce is often painful and difficult. No reasonable thinker would want women to return to the childlike position that wives were expected to inhabit a hundred years ago, but that does not mean we cannot acknowledge that divorce often comes with a steep emotional and practical price.

It appears that Henrik Ibsen understood this when he wrote *A Doll's House* in 1879. It was an era of great political and social change, and Ibsen believed that writers could be instrumental in affecting the way people thought about the great issues of the day. His realistic problem plays confronted topical and controversial issues. Among the most debated was the status of women in society, especially their legal and emotional subjugation within marriage. To a contemporary audience, Nora, the main character of *A Doll's House*, is treated like a child. Although that disturbs most women today, Ibsen's female audience tended not to sympathize with Nora. The play's unsettling conclusion outraged most men. Changes in accepted thinking are always contested. But although most critics today see Ibsen as a social visionary who championed equality in marriage, he was not naive enough to think that great sacrifice and pain would not also accompany freedom and equality. The solution of one problem often creates new problems. When Nora begins to question the old ways, her future starts to grow uncertain. Knowing what she knows, can she really remain in a marriage that seems to her a cruel and unjust trap?

We have included several works that provide context for the play, but we have selected ones that focus especially on Nora. Over the past hundred years or so, Nora has been seen as either a villain or a hero, depending on the cultural context. If you support feminist ideals, you will probably see Nora in a positive light and support her dramatic departure as necessary and liberating. If you are not particularly sympathetic to feminist principles, you will most likely see Nora negatively and condemn her as vain, cruel, and self-centered. It would be unusual for a present-day critic not to empathize with Nora's plight, but that was clearly not always the case. Many critics early in the century and into the fifties and sixties were not at all sympathetic. Some were even hostile. Nora's situation may seem clearly unjust to a progressive twenty-first-century consciousness, but that was certainly not obvious to those in the past who saw her marriage as perfectly acceptable, normal, and desirable and her behavior as deceitful, abnormal, and neurotic. In many ways, we are all children of our time, subject to the prevailing thinking about relationships, marriage, gender equality, parental responsibility, and so on. Audiences in Ibsen's day were upset by *A Doll's House*. And if there is currently a consensus about the necessity of Nora's actions, that shift in perspective happened exceedingly slowly and incrementally.

≡ BEFORE YOU READ

When do you think a woman can be justified in leaving her children? Why do you think equality is or is not necessary for love to exist in a marriage?

HENRIK IBSEN

A Doll's House

Translated by B. Farquharson Sharp

Henrik Ibsen (1828–1906) was born into a family with money in a small town in Norway, but his father soon went bankrupt. Ibsen later remembered this genteel poverty by writing about issues of social injustice that he experienced firsthand. At fifteen Ibsen was apprenticed to a pharmacist, a profession he had no interest in. He soon was drawn to the theater, working to establish a Norwegian national theater. But this led to frustration, and Ibsen spent almost thirty years in a self-imposed exile in Italy and Germany, where he wrote some of his most famous plays. Ibsen's plays are often performed today and still provoke controversy. They include Ghosts *(1881),* An Enemy of the People *(1882),* Hedda Gabler *(1890), and* When We Dead Awaken *(1899).*

DRAMATIS PERSONAE

TORVALD HELMER
NORA, *his wife*

Mondadori via Getty Images

DOCTOR RANK
MRS. LINDE
NILS KROGSTAD
Helmer's three young children
ANNE, *their nurse*
A Housemaid
A Porter

SCENE: *The action takes place in Helmer's house.*

ACT I

SCENE: *A room furnished comfortably and tastefully, but not extravagantly. At the back, a door to the right leads to the entrance-hall, another to the left leads to Helmer's study. Between the doors stands a piano. In the middle of the left-hand wall is a door, and beyond it a window. Near the window are a round table, arm-chairs, and a small sofa. In the right-hand wall, at the farther end, another door; and on the same side, nearer the footlights, a stove, two easy chairs, and a rocking-chair; between the stove and the door, a small table. Engravings on the walls; a cabinet with china and other small objects; a small book-case with well-bound books. The floors are carpeted, and a fire burns in the stove. It is winter.*

A bell rings in the hall; shortly afterwards the door is heard to open. Enter Nora, humming a tune and in high spirits. She is in outdoor dress and carries a number of parcels; these she lays on the table to the right. She leaves the outer door open after her, and through it is seen a Porter who is carrying a Christmas Tree and a basket, which he gives to the Maid who has opened the door.

NORA: Hide the Christmas Tree carefully, Helen. Be sure the children do not see it until this evening, when it is dressed. (*To the Porter, taking out her purse.*) How much?

PORTER: Sixpence.

NORA: There is a shilling. No, keep the change. (*The Porter thanks her, and goes out. Nora shuts the door. She is laughing to herself, as she takes off her hat and coat. She takes a packet of macaroons from her pocket and eats one or two; then goes cautiously to her husband's door and listens.*) Yes, he is in. (*Still humming, she goes to the table on the right.*)

HELMER (*calls out from his room*):   Is that my little lark twittering out there?

NORA (*busy opening some of the parcels*):   Yes, it is!

HELMER: Is it my little squirrel bustling about?

NORA: Yes!

HELMER: When did my squirrel come home?

NORA: Just now. (*Puts the bag of macaroons into her pocket and wipes her mouth.*) Come in here, Torvald, and see what I have bought.

HELMER: Don't disturb me. (*A little later, he opens the door and looks into the room, pen in hand.*) Bought, did you say? All these things? Has my little spendthrift been wasting money again?

NORA: Yes but, Torvald, this year we really can let ourselves go a little. This is the first Christmas that we have not needed to economise.

HELMER: Still, you know, we can't spend money recklessly.

NORA: Yes, Torvald, we may be a wee bit more reckless now, mayn't we? Just a tiny wee bit! You are going to have a big salary and earn lots and lots of money.

HELMER: Yes, after the New Year; but then it will be a whole quarter before the salary is due.

NORA: Pooh! we can borrow until then.

HELMER: Nora! (*Goes up to her and takes her playfully by the ear.*) The same little featherhead! Suppose, now, that I borrowed fifty pounds to-day, and you spent it all in the Christmas week, and then on New Year's Eve a slate fell on my head and killed me, and—

NORA (*putting her hands over his mouth*):   Oh! don't say such horrid things.

HELMER: Still, suppose that happened,—what then?

NORA: If that were to happen, I don't suppose I should care whether I owed money or not.

HELMER: Yes, but what about the people who had lent it?

NORA: They? Who would bother about them? I should not know who they were.

HELMER: That is like a woman! But seriously, Nora, you know what I think about that. No debt, no borrowing. There can be no freedom or beauty about a home life that depends on borrowing and debt. We two have kept bravely on the straight road so far, and we will go on the same way for the short time longer that there need be any struggle.

NORA (*moving towards the stove*):   As you please, Torvald.

HELMER (*following her*):   Come, come, my little skylark must not droop her wings. What is this! Is my little squirrel out of temper? (*Taking out his purse.*) Nora, what do you think I have got here?

NORA (*turning round quickly*):   Money!

HELMER: There you are. (*Gives her some money.*) Do you think I don't know what a lot is wanted for housekeeping at Christmas-time?

NORA (*counting*):   Ten shillings—a pound—two pounds! Thank you, thank you, Torvald; that will keep me going for a long time.

HELMER: Indeed it must.

NORA: Yes, yes, it will. But come here and let me show you what I have bought. And all so cheap! Look, here is a new suit for Ivar, and a sword; and a horse and a trumpet for Bob; and a doll and dolly's bedstead for Emmy,—they are very plain, but anyway she will soon break them in pieces. And here are dress-lengths and handkerchiefs for the maids; old Anne ought really to have something better.

HELMER: And what is in this parcel?

NORA (*crying out*):   No, no! you mustn't see that until this evening.

HELMER: Very well. But now tell me, you extravagant little person, what would you like for yourself ?

NORA: For myself ? Oh, I am sure I don't want anything.

HELMER: Yes, but you must. Tell me something reasonable that you would particularly like to have.

NORA: No, I really can't think of anything—unless, Torvald—

HELMER: Well?

NORA (*playing with his coat buttons, and without raising her eyes to his*):   If you really want to give me something, you might—you might—

HELMER: Well, out with it!

NORA (*speaking quickly*):   You might give me money, Torvald. Only just as much as you can afford; and then one of these days I will buy something with it.

HELMER: But, Nora—

NORA: Oh, do! dear Torvald; please, please do! Then I will wrap it up in beautiful gilt paper and hang it on the Christmas Tree. Wouldn't that be fun?

HELMER: What are little people called that are always wasting money?

NORA: Spendthrifts—I know. Let us do as you suggest, Torvald, and then I shall have time to think what I am most in want of. That is a very sensible plan, isn't it?

HELMER (*smiling*):   Indeed it is—that is to say, if you were really to save out of the money I give you, and then really buy something for yourself. But if you spend it all on the housekeeping and any number of unnecessary things, then I merely have to pay up again.

NORA: Oh but, Torvald—

HELMER: You can't deny it, my dear little Nora. (*Puts his arm round her waist.*)

It's a sweet little spendthrift, but she uses up a deal of money. One would hardly believe how expensive such little persons are!

NORA: It's a shame to say that. I do really save all I can.

HELMER (*laughing*):   That's very true,—all you can. But you can't save anything!

NORA (*smiling quietly and happily*):   You haven't any idea how many expenses we skylarks and squirrels have, Torvald.

HELMER: You are an odd little soul. Very like your father. You always find some new way of wheedling money out of me, and, as soon as you have got it, it seems to melt in your hands. You never know where it has gone. Still, one must take you as you are. It is in the blood; for indeed it is true that you can inherit these things, Nora.

NORA: Ah, I wish I had inherited many of papa's qualities.

HELMER: And I would not wish you to be anything but just what you are, my sweet little skylark. But, do you know, it strikes me that you are looking rather—what shall I say—rather uneasy today?

NORA: Do I?

HELMER: You do, really. Look straight at me.

NORA (*looks at him*):   Well?

HELMER (*wagging his finger at her*):   Hasn't Miss Sweet Tooth been breaking rules in town today?

NORA: No; what makes you think that?

HELMER: Hasn't she paid a visit to the confectioner's?

NORA: No, I assure you, Torvald—

HELMER: Not been nibbling sweets?

NORA: No, certainly not.

HELMER: Not even taken a bite at a macaroon or two?

NORA: No, Torvald, I assure you really—

HELMER: There, there, of course I was only joking.

NORA (*going to the table on the right*):   I should not think of going against your wishes.

HELMER: No, I am sure of that; besides, you gave me your word—(*Going up to her.*) Keep your little Christmas secrets to yourself, my darling. They will all be revealed to-night when the Christmas Tree is lit, no doubt.

NORA: Did you remember to invite Doctor Rank?

HELMER: No. But there is no need; as a matter of course he will come to dinner with us. However, I will ask him when he comes in this morning. I have ordered some good wine. Nora, you can't think how I am looking forward to this evening.

NORA: So am I! And how the children will enjoy themselves, Torvald!

HELMER: It is splendid to feel that one has a perfectly safe appointment, and a big enough income. It's delightful to think of, isn't it?

NORA: It's wonderful!

HELMER: Do you remember last Christmas? For a full three weeks beforehand you shut yourself up every evening until long after midnight, making ornaments for the Christmas Tree, and all the other fine things that were to be a surprise to us. It was the dullest three weeks I ever spent!

NORA: I didn't find it dull.

HELMER (*smiling*):   But there was precious little result, Nora.

NORA: Oh, you shouldn't tease me about that again. How could I help the cat's going in and tearing everything to pieces?

HELMER: Of course you couldn't, poor little girl. You had the best of intentions to please us all, and that's the main thing. But it is a good thing that our hard times are over.

NORA: Yes, it is really wonderful.

HELMER: This time I needn't sit here and be dull all alone, and you needn't ruin your dear eyes and your pretty little hands—

NORA (*clapping her hands*):   No, Torvald, I needn't any longer, need I! It's wonderfully lovely to hear you say so! (*Taking his arm.*) Now I will tell you how I have been thinking we ought to arrange things, Torvald. As soon as Christmas is over—(*A bell rings in the hall.*) There's the bell. (*She tidies the room a little.*) There's some one at the door. What a nuisance!

HELMER: If it is a caller, remember I am not at home.

MAID (*in the doorway*):   A lady to see you, ma'am,—a stranger.

NORA: Ask her to come in.

MAID (*to Helmer*):   The doctor came at the same time, sir.

HELMER: Did he go straight into my room?

MAID: Yes, sir.

Helmer goes into his room. The Maid ushers in Mrs. Linde, who is in travelling dress, and shuts the door.

MRS. LINDE (*in a dejected and timid voice*):   How do you do, Nora?

NORA (*doubtfully*):   How do you do—

MRS. LINDE: You don't recognise me, I suppose.

NORA: No, I don't know—yes, to be sure, I seem to—(*Suddenly.*) Yes! Christine! Is it really you?

MRS. LINDE: Yes, it is I.

NORA: Christine! To think of my not recognising you! And yet how could I—(*In a gentle voice.*) How you have altered, Christine!

MRS. LINDE: Yes, I have indeed. In nine, ten long years—

NORA: Is it so long since we met? I suppose it is. The last eight years have been a happy time for me, I can tell you. And so now you have come into the town, and have taken this long journey in winter—that was plucky of you.

MRS. LINDE: I arrived by steamer this morning.

NORA: To have some fun at Christmas-time, of course. How delightful! We will have such fun together! But take off your things. You are not cold, I hope. (*Helps her.*) Now we will sit down by the stove, and be cosy. No, take this armchair; I will sit here in the rocking-chair. (*Takes her hands.*) Now you look like your old self again; it was only the first moment—You are a little paler, Christine, and perhaps a little thinner.

MRS. LINDE: And much, much older, Nora.

NORA: Perhaps a little older; very, very little; certainly not much. (*Stops *suddenly and speaks seriously.*) What a thoughtless creature I am, chattering away like this. My poor, dear Christine, do forgive me.

MRS. LINDE: What do you mean, Nora?

NORA (*gently*):   Poor Christine, you are a widow.

MRS. LINDE: Yes; it is three years ago now.

NORA: Yes, I knew; I saw it in the papers. I assure you, Christine, I meant ever so often to write to you at the time, but I always put it off and something always prevented me.

MRS. LINDE: I quite understand, dear.

NORA: It was very bad of me, Christine. Poor thing, how you must have suffered. And he left you nothing?

MRS. LINDE: No.

NORA: And no children?

MRS. LINDE: No.

NORA: Nothing at all, then.

MRS. LINDE: Not even any sorrow or grief to live upon.

NORA (*looking incredulously at her*):   But, Christine, is that possible?

MRS. LINDE (*smiles sadly and strokes her hair*):   It sometimes happens, Nora.

NORA: So you are quite alone. How dreadfully sad that must be. I have three lovely children. You can't see them just now, for they are out with their nurse. But now you must tell me all about it.

MRS. LINDE: No, no; I want to hear about you.

NORA: No, you must begin. I mustn't be selfish today; today I must only think of your affairs. But there is one thing I must tell you. Do you know we have just had a great piece of good luck?

MRS. LINDE: No, what is it?

NORA: Just fancy, my husband has been made manager of the Bank!

MRS. LINDE: Your husband? What good luck!

NORA: Yes, tremendous! A barrister's profession is such an uncertain thing, especially if he won't undertake unsavoury cases; and naturally Torvald has never been willing to do that, and I quite agree with him. You may imagine how pleased we are! He is to take up his work in the Bank at the New Year, and then he will have a big salary and lots of commissions. For the future we can live quite differently — we can do just as we like. I feel so relieved and so happy, Christine! It will be splendid to have heaps of money and not need to have any anxiety, won't it?

MRS. LINDE: Yes, anyhow I think it would be delightful to have what one needs.

NORA: No, not only what one needs, but heaps and heaps of money.

MRS. LINDE (*smiling*):   Nora, Nora, haven't you learned sense yet? In our school-days you were a great spendthrift.

NORA (*laughing*):   Yes, that is what Torvald says now. (*Wags her finger at her.*) But "Nora, Nora" is not so silly as you think. We have not been in a position for me to waste money. We have both had to work.

MRS. LINDE: You too?

NORA: Yes; odds and ends, needlework, crotchet-work, embroidery, and that kind of thing. (*Dropping her voice.*) And other things as well. You know

Torvald left his office when we were married? There was no prospect of promotion there, and he had to try and earn more than before. But during the first year he over-worked himself dreadfully. You see, he had to make money every way he could, and he worked early and late; but he couldn't stand it, and fell dreadfully ill, and the doctors said it was necessary for him to go south.

MRS. LINDE: You spent a whole year in Italy, didn't you?

NORA: Yes. It was no easy matter to get away, I can tell you. It was just after Ivar was born; but naturally we had to go. It was a wonderfully beautiful journey, and it saved Torvald's life. But it cost a tremendous lot of money, Christine.

MRS. LINDE: So I should think.

NORA: It cost about two hundred and fifty pounds. That's a lot, isn't it?

MRS. LINDE: Yes, and in emergencies like that it is lucky to have the money.

NORA: I ought to tell you that we had it from papa.

MRS. LINDE: Oh, I see. It was just about that time that he died, wasn't it?

NORA: Yes; and, just think of it, I couldn't go and nurse him. I was expecting little Ivar's birth every day and I had my poor sick Torvald to look after. My dear, kind father—I never saw him again, Christine. That was the saddest time I have known since our marriage.

MRS. LINDE: I know how fond you were of him. And then you went off to Italy?

NORA: Yes; you see we had money then, and the doctors insisted on our going, so we started a month later.

MRS. LINDE: And your husband came back quite well?

NORA: As sound as a bell!

MRS. LINDE: But—the doctor?

NORA: What doctor?

MRS. LINDE: I thought your maid said the gentleman who arrived here just as I did, was the doctor?

NORA: Yes, that was Doctor Rank, but he doesn't come here professionally. He is our greatest friend, and comes in at least once everyday. No, Torvald has not had an hour's illness since then, and our children are strong and healthy and so am I. (*Jumps up and claps her hands.*) Christine! Christine! it's good to be alive and happy!—But how horrid of me; I am talking of nothing but my own affairs. (*Sits on a stool near her, and rests her arms on her knees.*) You mustn't be angry with me. Tell me, is it really true that you did not love your husband? Why did you marry him?

MRS. LINDE: My mother was alive then, and was bedridden and helpless, and I had to provide for my two younger brothers; so I did not think I was justified in refusing his offer.

NORA: No, perhaps you were quite right. He was rich at that time, then?

MRS. LINDE: I believe he was quite well off. But his business was a precarious one; and, when he died, it all went to pieces and there was nothing left.

NORA: And then?—

MRS. LINDE: Well, I had to turn my hand to anything I could find—first a small shop, then a small school, and so on. The last three years have seemed like one long working-day, with no rest. Now it is at an end, Nora. My poor mother needs me no more, for she is gone; and the boys do not need me either; they have got situations and can shift for themselves.

NORA: What a relief you must feel it—

MRS. LINDE: No, indeed; I only feel my life unspeakably empty. No one to live for anymore. (*Gets up restlessly.*) That was why I could not stand the life in my little backwater any longer. I hope it may be easier here to find something which will busy me and occupy my thoughts. If only I could have the good luck to get some regular work—office work of some kind—

NORA: But, Christine, that is so frightfully tiring, and you look tired out now. You had far better go away to some watering-place.

MRS. LINDE (*walking to the window*):   I have no father to give me money for a journey, Nora.

NORA (*rising*):   Oh, don't be angry with me!

MRS. LINDE (*going up to her*):   It is you that must not be angry with me, dear. The worst of a position like mine is that it makes one so bitter. No one to work for, and yet obliged to be always on the lookout for chances. One must live, and so one becomes selfish. When you told me of the happy turn your fortunes have taken—you will hardly believe it—I was delighted not so much on your account as on my own.

NORA: How do you mean?—Oh, I understand. You mean that perhaps Torvald could get you something to do.

MRS. LINDE: Yes, that was what I was thinking of.

NORA: He must, Christine. Just leave it to me; I will broach the subject very cleverly—I will think of something that will please him very much. It will make me so happy to be of some use to you.

MRS. LINDE: How kind you are, Nora, to be so anxious to help me! It is doubly kind in you, for you know so little of the burdens and troubles of life.

NORA: I—? I know so little of them?

MRS. LINDE (*smiling*):   My dear! Small household cares and that sort of thing!—You are a child, Nora.

NORA (*tosses her head and crosses the stage*):   You ought not to be so superior.

MRS. LINDE: No?

NORA: You are just like the others. They all think that I am incapable of anything really serious—

MRS. LINDE: Come, come—

NORA: —that I have gone through nothing in this world of cares.

MRS. LINDE: But, my dear Nora, you have just told me all your troubles.

NORA: Pooh!—those were trifles. (*Lowering her voice.*) I have not told you the important thing.

MRS. LINDE: The important thing? What do you mean?

NORA: You look down upon me altogether, Christine—but you ought not to. You are proud, aren't you, of having worked so hard and so long for your mother?

MRS. LINDE: Indeed, I don't look down on anyone. But it is true that I am both proud and glad to think that I was privileged to make the end of my mother's life almost free from care.

NORA: And you are proud to think of what you have done for your brothers?

MRS. LINDE: I think I have the right to be.

NORA: I think so, too. But now, listen to this; I too have something to be proud and glad of.

MRS. LINDE: I have no doubt you have. But what do you refer to?

NORA: Speak low. Suppose Torvald were to hear! He mustn't on any account—no one in the world must know, Christine, except you.

MRS. LINDE: But what is it?

NORA: Come here. (*Pulls her down on the sofa beside her.*) Now I will show you that I too have something to be proud and glad of. It was I who saved Torvald's life.

MRS. LINDE: "Saved"? How?

NORA: I told you about our trip to Italy. Torvald would never have recovered if he had not gone there—

MRS. LINDE: Yes, but your father gave you the necessary funds.

NORA (*smiling*):   Yes, that is what Torvald and all the others think, but—

MRS. LINDE: But—

NORA: Papa didn't give us a shilling. It was I who procured the money.

MRS. LINDE: You? All that large sum?

NORA: Two hundred and fifty pounds. What do you think of that?

MRS. LINDE: But, Nora, how could you possibly do it? Did you win a prize in the Lottery?

NORA (*contemptuously*):   In the Lottery? There would have been no credit in that.

MRS. LINDE: But where did you get it from, then?

NORA (*humming and smiling with an air of mystery*):   Hm, hm! Aha!

MRS. LINDE: Because you couldn't have borrowed it.

NORA: Couldn't I? Why not?

MRS. LINDE: No, a wife cannot borrow without her husband's consent.

NORA (*tossing her head*):   Oh, if it is a wife who has any head for business—a wife who has the wit to be a little bit clever—

MRS. LINDE: I don't understand it at all, Nora.

NORA: There is no need you should. I never said I had borrowed the money. I may have got it some other way. (*Lies back on the sofa.*) Perhaps I got it from some other admirer. When anyone is as attractive as I am—

MRS. LINDE: You are a mad creature.

NORA: Now, you know you're full of curiosity, Christine.

MRS. LINDE: Listen to me, Nora dear. Haven't you been a little bit imprudent?

NORA (*sits up straight*):   Is it imprudent to save your husband's life?

MRS. LINDE: It seems to me imprudent, without his knowledge, to—

NORA: But it was absolutely necessary that he should not know! My goodness, can't you understand that? It was necessary he should have no idea what a dangerous condition he was in. It was to me that the doctors came and said that his life was in danger, and that the only thing to save him was to live in the south. Do you suppose I didn't try, first of all, to get what I wanted as if it were for myself? I told him how much I should love to travel abroad like other young wives; I tried tears and entreaties with him; I told him that he ought to remember the condition I was in, and that he ought to be kind and indulgent to me; I even hinted that he might raise a loan. That nearly made him angry, Christine. He said I was thoughtless, and that it was his duty as my husband not to indulge me in my whims and caprices—as I believe he called them. Very well, I thought, you must be saved—and that was how I came to devise a way out of the difficulty—

MRS. LINDE: And did your husband never get to know from your father that the money had not come from him?

NORA: No, never. Papa died just at that time. I had meant to let him into the secret and beg him never to reveal it. But he was so ill then—alas, there never was any need to tell him.

MRS. LINDE: And since then have you never told your secret to your husband?

NORA: Good Heavens, no! How could you think so? A man who has such strong opinions about these things! And besides, how painful and humiliating it would be for Torvald, with his manly independence, to know that he owed me anything! It would upset our mutual relations altogether; our beautiful happy home would no longer be what it is now.

MRS. LINDE: Do you mean never to tell him about it?

NORA (*meditatively, and with a half smile*):   Yes—someday, perhaps, after many years, when I am no longer as nice-looking as I am now. Don't laugh at me! I mean, of course, when Torvald is no longer as devoted to me as he is now; when my dancing and dressing-up and reciting have palled on him; then it may be a good thing to have something in reserve—(*Breaking off.*) What nonsense! That time will never come. Now, what do you think of my great secret, Christine? Do you still think I am of no use? I can tell you, too, that this affair has caused me a lot of worry. It has been by no means easy for me to meet my engagements punctually. I may tell you that there is something that is called, in business, quarterly interest, and another thing called payment in installments, and it is always so dreadfully difficult to manage them. I have had to save a little here and there, where I could, you understand. I have not been able to put aside much from my housekeeping money, for Torvald must have a good table. I couldn't let my children be shabbily dressed; I have felt obliged to use up all he gave me for them, the sweet little darlings!

MRS. LINDE: So it has all had to come out of your own necessaries of life, poor Nora?

NORA: Of course. Besides, I was the one responsible for it. Whenever Torvald has given me money for new dresses and such things, I have never spent more than half of it; I have always bought the simplest and cheapest things. Thank Heaven, any clothes look well on me, and so Torvald has never noticed it. But it was often very hard on me, Christine—because it is delightful to be really well dressed, isn't it?

MRS. LINDE: Quite so.

NORA: Well, then I have found other ways of earning money. Last winter I was lucky enough to get a lot of copying to do; so I locked myself up and sat writing every evening until quite late at night. Many a time I was desperately tired; but all the same it was a tremendous pleasure to sit there working and earning money. It was like being a man.

MRS. LINDE: How much have you been able to pay off in that way?

NORA: I can't tell you exactly. You see, it is very difficult to keep an account of a business matter of that kind. I only know that I have paid every penny that I could scrape together. Many a time I was at my wits' end. (*Smiles.*) Then I used to sit here and imagine that a rich old gentleman had fallen in love with me—

MRS. LINDE: What! Who was it?

NORA: Be quiet!—that he had died; and that when his will was opened it contained, written in big letters, the instruction: "The lovely Mrs. Nora Helmer is to have all I possess paid over to her at once in cash."

MRS. LINDE: But, my dear Nora—who could the man be?

NORA: Good gracious, can't you understand? There was no old gentleman at all; it was only something that I used to sit here and imagine, when I couldn't think of any way of procuring money. But it's all the same now; the tiresome old person can stay where he is, as far as I am concerned; I don't care about him or his will either, for I am free from care now. (*Jumps up.*) My goodness, it's delightful to think of, Christine! Free from care! To be able to be free from care, quite free from care; to be able to play and romp with the children; to be able to keep the house beautifully and have every-thing just as Torvald likes it! And, think of it, soon the spring will come and the big blue sky! Perhaps we shall be able to take a little trip—perhaps I shall see the sea again! Oh, it's a wonderful thing to be alive and be happy. (*A bell is heard in the hall.*)

MRS. LINDE (*rising*):   There is the bell; perhaps I had better go.

NORA: No, don't go; no one will come in here; it is sure to be for Torvald.

SERVANT (*at the hall door*):   Excuse me, ma'am—there is a gentleman to see the master, and as the doctor is with him—

NORA: Who is it?

KROGSTAD (*at the door*):   It is I, Mrs. Helmer (*Mrs. Linde starts, trembles, and turns to the window.*)

NORA (*takes a step towards him, and speaks in a strained, low voice*):   You? What is it? What do you want to see my husband about?

KROGSTAD: Bank business—in a way. I have a small post in the Bank, and I hear your husband is to be our chief now—

NORA: Then it is—

KROGSTAD: Nothing but dry business matters, Mrs. Helmer; absolutely noth-ing else.

NORA: Be so good as to go into the study, then. (*She bows indifferently to him and shuts the door into the hall; then comes back and makes up the fire in the stove.*)

MRS. LINDE: Nora—who was that man?

NORA: A lawyer, of the name of Krogstad.

MRS. LINDE: Then it really was he.

NORA: Do you know the man?

MRS. LINDE: I used to—many years ago. At one time he was a solicitor's clerk in our town.

NORA: Yes, he was.

MRS. LINDE: He is greatly altered.

NORA: He made a very unhappy marriage.

MRS. LINDE: He is a widower now, isn't he?

NORA: With several children. There now, it is burning up. (*Shuts the door of the stove and moves the rocking-chair aside.*)

MRS. LINDE: They say he carries on various kinds of business.

NORA: Really! Perhaps he does; I don't know anything about it. But don't let us think of business; it is so tiresome.

DOCTOR RANK (*comes out of Helmer's study. Before he shuts the door he calls to him*):   No, my dear fellow, I won't disturb you; I would rather go in to your wife for a little while. (*Shuts the door and sees Mrs. Linde.*) I beg your pardon; I am afraid I am disturbing you too.

NORA: No, not at all. (*Introducing him.*) Doctor Rank, Mrs. Linde.

RANK: I have often heard Mrs. Linde's name mentioned here. I think I passed you on the stairs when I arrived, Mrs. Linde?

MRS. LINDE: Yes, I go up very slowly; I can't manage stairs well.

RANK: Ah! some slight internal weakness?

MRS. LINDE: No, the fact is I have been overworking myself.

RANK: Nothing more than that? Then I suppose you have come to town to amuse yourself with our entertainments?

MRS. LINDE: I have come to look for work.

RANK: Is that a good cure for overwork?

MRS. LINDE: One must live, Doctor Rank.

RANK: Yes, the general opinion seems to be that it is necessary.

NORA: Look here, Doctor Rank—you know you want to live.

RANK: Certainly. However wretched I may feel, I want to prolong the agony as long as possible. All my patients are like that. And so are those who are morally diseased; one of them, and a bad case too, is at this very moment with Helmer—

MRS. LINDE (*sadly*):   Ah!

NORA: Whom do you mean?

RANK: A lawyer of the name of Krogstad, a fellow you don't know at all. He suffers from a diseased moral character, Mrs. Helmer; but even he began talking of its being highly important that he should live.

NORA: Did he? What did he want to speak to Torvald about?

RANK: I have no idea; I only heard that it was something about the Bank.

NORA: I didn't know this—what's his name—Krogstad had anything to do with the Bank.

RANK: Yes, he has some sort of appointment there. (*To Mrs. Linde.*) I don't know whether you find also in your part of the world that there are certain people who go zealously snuffing about to smell out moral corruption, and, as soon as they have found some, put the person concerned into some lucrative position where they can keep their eye on him. Healthy natures are left out in the cold.

MRS. LINDE: Still I think the sick are those who most need taking care of.

RANK (*shrugging his shoulders*):   Yes, there you are. That is the sentiment that is turning Society into a sick-house.

Nora, who has been absorbed in her thoughts, breaks out into smothered laughter and claps her hands.

RANK: Why do you laugh at that? Have you any notion what Society really is?

NORA: What do I care about tiresome Society? I am laughing at something quite different, something extremely amusing. Tell me, Doctor Rank, are all the people who are employed in the Bank dependent on Torvald now?

RANK: Is that what you find so extremely amusing?

NORA (*smiling and humming*):   That's my affair! (*Walking about the room.*) It's perfectly glorious to think that we have—that Torvald has so much power over so many people. (*Takes the packet from her pocket.*) Doctor Rank, what do you say to a macaroon?

RANK: What, macaroons? I thought they were forbidden here.

NORA: Yes, but these are some Christine gave me.

MRS. LINDE: What! I?—

NORA: Oh, well, don't be alarmed! You couldn't know that Torvald had forbidden them. I must tell you that he is afraid they will spoil my teeth. But, bah!—once in a way—That's so, isn't it, Doctor Rank? By your leave! (*Puts a macaroon into his mouth.*) You must have one too, Christine. And I shall have one, just a little one—or at most two. (*Walking about.*) I am tremendously happy. There is just one thing in the world now that I should dearly love to do.

RANK: Well, what is that?

NORA: It's something I should dearly love to say, if Torvald could hear me.

RANK: Well, why can't you say it?

NORA: No, I daren't; it's so shocking.

MRS. LINDE: Shocking?

RANK: Well, I should not advise you to say it. Still, with us you might. What is it you would so much like to say if Torvald could hear you?

NORA: I should just love to say—Well, I'm damned!

RANK: Are you mad?

MRS. LINDE: Nora, dear—!

RANK: Say it, here he is!

NORA (*hiding the packet*):   Hush! Hush! Hush! (*Helmer comes out of his room, with his coat over his arm and his hat in his hand.*)

NORA: Well, Torvald dear, have you got rid of him?

HELMER: Yes, he has just gone.

NORA: Let me introduce you—this is Christine, who has come to town.

HELMER: Christine—? Excuse me, but I don't know—

NORA: Mrs. Linde, dear; Christine Linde.

HELMER: Of course. A school friend of my wife's, I presume?

MRS. LINDE: Yes, we have known each other since then.

NORA: And just think, she has taken a long journey in order to see you.

HELMER: What do you mean?

MRS. LINDE: No, really, I—

NORA: Christine is tremendously clever at book-keeping, and she is frightfully anxious to work under some clever man, so as to perfect herself —

HELMER: Very sensible, Mrs. Linde.

NORA: And when she heard you had been appointed manager of the Bank — the news was telegraphed, you know — she travelled here as quick as she could. Torvald, I am sure you will be able to do something for Christine, for my sake, won't you?

HELMER: Well, it is not altogether impossible. I presume you are a widow, Mrs. Linde?

MRS. LINDE: Yes.

HELMER: And have had some experience of book-keeping?

MRS. LINDE: Yes, a fair amount.

HELMER: Ah! well, it's very likely I may be able to find something for you —

NORA (*clapping her hands*):   What did I tell you? What did I tell you?

HELMER: You have just come at a fortunate moment, Mrs. Linde.

MRS. LINDE: How am I to thank you?

HELMER: There is no need. (*Puts on his coat.*) But to-day you must excuse me —

RANK: Wait a minute; I will come with you. (*Brings his fur coat from the hall and warms it at the fire.*)

NORA: Don't be long away, Torvald dear.

HELMER: About an hour, not more.

NORA: Are you going too, Christine?

MRS. LINDE (*putting on her cloak*):   Yes, I must go and look for a room.

HELMER: Oh, well then, we can walk down the street together.

NORA (*helping her*):   What a pity it is we are so short of space here; I am afraid it is impossible for us —

MRS. LINDE: Please don't think of it! Good-bye, Nora dear, and many thanks.

NORA: Good-bye for the present. Of course you will come back this evening. And you too, Dr. Rank. What do you say? If you are well enough? Oh, you must be! Wrap yourself up well. (*They go to the door all talking together. Children's voices are heard on the staircase.*)

NORA: There they are! There they are! (*She runs to open the door. The Nurse comes in with the children.*) Come in! Come in! (*Stoops and kisses them.*) Oh, you sweet blessings! Look at them, Christine! Aren't they darlings?

RANK: Don't let us stand here in the draught.

HELMER: Come along, Mrs. Linde; the place will only be bearable for a mother now!

Rank, Helmer, and Mrs. Linde go downstairs. The Nurse comes forward with the children; Nora shuts the hall door.

NORA: How fresh and well you look! Such red cheeks like apples and roses. (*The children all talk at once while she speaks to them.*) Have you had great fun? That's splendid! What, you pulled both Emmy and Bob along on the sledge? — both at once? — that was good. You are a clever boy, Ivar. Let me take her for a little, Anne. My sweet little baby doll! (*Takes the baby from the Maid and dances it up and down.*) Yes, yes, mother will dance with

Bob too. What! Have you been snowballing? I wish I had been there too!
No, no, I will take their things off, Anne; please let me do it, it is such fun.
Go in now, you look half frozen. There is some hot coffee for you on the
stove.

*The Nurse goes into the room on the left. Nora takes off the children's things and
throws them about, while they all talk to her at once.*

NORA: Really! Did a big dog run after you? But it didn't bite you? No, dogs don't
bite nice little dolly children. You mustn't look at the parcels, Ivar. What
are they? Ah, I daresay you would like to know. No, no—it's something
nasty! Come, let us have a game! What shall we play at? Hide and Seek?
Yes, we'll play Hide and Seek. Bob shall hide first. Must I hide? Very well, I'll
hide first. (*She and the children laugh and shout, and romp in and out of the
room; at last Nora hides under the table, the children rush in and out for her, but
do not see her; they hear her smothered laughter, run to the table, lift up the cloth
and find her. Shouts of laughter. She crawls forward and pretends to frighten
them. Fresh laughter. Meanwhile there has been a knock at the hall door, but
none of them has noticed it. The door is half opened, and Krogstad appears. He
waits a little; the game goes on.*)

KROGSTAD: Excuse me, Mrs. Helmer.

NORA (*with a stifled cry, turns round and gets up on to her knees*):   Ah! what do
you want?

KROGSTAD: Excuse me, the outer door was ajar; I suppose someone forgot to
shut it.

NORA (*rising*):   My husband is out, Mr. Krogstad.

KROGSTAD: I know that.

NORA: What do you want here, then?

KROGSTAD: A word with you.

NORA: With me?—(*To the children, gently.*) Go in to nurse. What? No, the
strange man won't do mother any harm. When he has gone we will have
another game. (*She takes the children into the room on the left, and shuts the
door after them.*) You want to speak to me?

KROGSTAD: Yes, I do.

NORA: To-day? It is not the first of the month yet.

KROGSTAD: No, it is Christmas Eve, and it will depend on yourself what sort of
a Christmas you will spend.

NORA: What do you mean? To-day it is absolutely impossible for me—

KROGSTAD: We won't talk about that until later on. This is something different.
I presume you can give me a moment?

NORA: Yes—yes, I can—although—

KROGSTAD: Good. I was in Olsen's Restaurant and saw your husband going
down the street—

NORA: Yes?

KROGSTAD: With a lady.

NORA: What then?

KROGSTAD: May I make so bold as to ask if it was a Mrs. Linde?

NORA: It was.

KROGSTAD: Just arrived in town?

NORA: Yes, to-day.

KROGSTAD: She is a great friend of yours, isn't she?

NORA: She is. But I don't see—

KROGSTAD: I knew her too, once upon a time.

NORA: I am aware of that.

KROGSTAD: Are you? So you know all about it; I thought as much. Then I can ask you, without beating about the bush—is Mrs. Linde to have an appointment in the Bank?

NORA: What right have you to question me, Mr. Krogstad?—You, one of my husband's subordinates! But since you ask, you shall know. Yes, Mrs. Linde *is* to have an appointment. And it was I who pleaded her cause, Mr. Krogstad, let me tell you that.

KROGSTAD: I was right in what I thought, then.

NORA (*walking up and down the stage*):   Sometimes one has a tiny little bit of influence, I should hope. Because one is a woman, it does not necessarily follow that—. When anyone is in a subordinate position, Mr. Krogstad, they should really be careful to avoid offending anyone who—who—

KROGSTAD: Who has influence?

NORA: Exactly.

KROGSTAD (*changing his tone*):   Mrs. Helmer, you will be so good as to use your influence on my behalf.

NORA: What? What do you mean?

KROGSTAD: You will be so kind as to see that I am allowed to keep my subordinate position in the Bank.

NORA: What do you mean by that? Who proposes to take your post away from you?

KROGSTAD: Oh, there is no necessity to keep up the pretence of ignorance. I can quite understand that your friend is not very anxious to expose herself to the chance of rubbing shoulders with me; and I quite understand, too, whom I have to thank for being turned off.

NORA: But I assure you—

KROGSTAD: Very likely; but, to come to the point, the time has come when I should advise you to use your influence to prevent that.

NORA: But, Mr. Krogstad, I *have* no influence.

KROGSTAD: Haven't you? I thought you said yourself just now—

NORA: Naturally I did not mean you to put that construction on it. What should make you think I have any influence of that kind with my husband?

KROGSTAD: Oh, I have known your husband from our student days. I don't suppose he is any more unassailable than other husbands.

NORA: If you speak slightingly of my husband, I shall turn you out of the house.

KROGSTAD: You are bold, Mrs. Helmer.

NORA: I am not afraid of you any longer. As soon as the New Year comes, I shall in a very short time be free of the whole thing.

KROGSTAD (*controlling himself*):   Listen to me, Mrs. Helmer. If necessary, I am prepared to fight for my small post in the Bank as if I were fighting for my life.

NORA: So it seems.

KROGSTAD: It is not only for the sake of the money; indeed, that weighs least with me in the matter. There is another reason — well, I may as well tell you. My position is this. I daresay you know, like everybody else, that once, many years ago, I was guilty of an indiscretion.

NORA: I think I have heard something of the kind.

KROGSTAD: The matter never came into court; but every way seemed to be closed to me after that. So I took to the business that you know of. I had to do something; and, honestly, I don't think I've been one of the worst. But now I must cut myself free from all that. My sons are growing up; for their sake I must try and win back as much respect as I can in the town. This post in the Bank was like the first step up for me — and now your husband is going to kick me downstairs again into the mud.

NORA: But you must believe me, Mr. Krogstad; it is not in my power to help you at all.

KROGSTAD: Then it is because you haven't the will; but I have means to compel you.

NORA: You don't mean that you will tell my husband that I owe you money?

KROGSTAD: Hm! — suppose I were to tell him?

NORA: It would be perfectly infamous of you. (*Sobbing.*) To think of his learning my secret, which has been my joy and pride, in such an ugly, clumsy way — that he should learn it from you! And it would put me in a horribly disagreeable position —

KROGSTAD: Only disagreeable?

NORA (*impetuously*):   Well, do it, then! — and it will be the worse for you. My husband will see for himself what a blackguard you are, and you certainly won't keep your post then.

KROGSTAD: I asked you if it was only a disagreeable scene at home that you were afraid of?

NORA: If my husband does get to know of it, of course he will at once pay you what is still owing, and we shall have nothing more to do with you.

KROGSTAD (*coming a step nearer*):   Listen to me, Mrs. Helmer. Either you have a very bad memory or you know very little of business. I shall be obliged to remind you of a few details.

NORA: What do you mean?

KROGSTAD: When your husband was ill, you came to me to borrow two hundred and fifty pounds.

NORA: I didn't know anyone else to go to.

KROGSTAD: I promised to get you that amount —

NORA: Yes, and you did so.

KROGSTAD: I promised to get you that amount, on certain conditions. Your mind was so taken up with your husband's illness, and you were so anxious to get the money for your journey, that you seem to have paid no attention to the conditions of our bargain. Therefore it will not be amiss if I remind you of them. Now, I promised to get the money on the security of a bond which I drew up.

NORA: Yes, and which I signed.

KROGSTAD: Good. But below your signature there were a few lines constituting your father a surety for the money; those lines your father should have signed.

NORA: Should? He did sign them.

KROGSTAD: I had left the date blank; that is to say, your father should himself have inserted the date on which he signed the paper. Do you remember that?

NORA: Yes, I think I remember —

KROGSTAD: Then I gave you the bond to send by post to your father. Is that not so?

NORA: Yes.

KROGSTAD: And you naturally did so at once, because five or six days afterwards you brought me the bond with your father's signature. And then I gave you the money.

NORA: Well, haven't I been paying it off regularly?

KROGSTAD: Fairly so, yes. But — to come back to the matter in hand — that must have been a very trying time for you, Mrs. Helmer.

NORA: It was, indeed.

KROGSTAD: Your father was very ill, wasn't he?

NORA: He was very near his end.

KROGSTAD: And he died soon afterwards?

NORA: Yes.

KROGSTAD: Tell me, Mrs. Helmer, can you by any chance remember what day your father died? — on what day of the month, I mean.

NORA: Papa died on the 29th of September.

KROGSTAD: That is correct; I have ascertained it for myself. And, as that is so, there is a discrepancy (*taking a paper from his pocket*) which I cannot account for.

NORA: What discrepancy? I don't know —

KROGSTAD: The discrepancy consists, Mrs. Helmer, in the fact that your father signed this bond three days after his death.

NORA: What do you mean? I don't understand —

KROGSTAD: Your father died on the 29th of September. But, look here; your father has dated his signature the 2nd of October. It is a discrepancy, isn't it? (*Nora is silent.*) Can you explain it to me? (*Nora is still silent.*) It is a remarkable thing, too, that the words "2nd of October," as well as the year, are not written in your father's handwriting but in one that I think I know. Well, of course it can be explained; your father may have forgotten to date his signature, and someone else may have dated it haphazard before they knew of his death. There is no harm in that. It all depends on the signature of the name; and *that* is genuine, I suppose, Mrs. Helmer? It was your father himself who signed his name here?

NORA (*after a short pause, throws her head up and looks defiantly at him*):   No, it was not. It was I that wrote papa's name.

KROGSTAD: Are you aware that is a dangerous confession?

NORA: In what way? You shall have your money soon.

KROGSTAD: Let me ask you a question; why did you not send the paper to your father?

NORA: It was impossible; papa was so ill. If I had asked him for his signature, I should have had to tell him what the money was to be used for; and when he was so ill himself I couldn't tell him that my husband's life was in danger—it was impossible.

KROGSTAD: It would have been better for you if you had given up your trip abroad.

NORA: No, that was impossible. That trip was to save my husband's life; I couldn't give that up.

KROGSTAD: But did it never occur to you that you were committing a fraud on me?

NORA: I couldn't take that into account; I didn't trouble myself about you at all. I couldn't bear you, because you put so many heartless difficulties in my way, although you knew what a dangerous condition my husband was in.

KROGSTAD: Mrs. Helmer, you evidently do not realise clearly what it is that you have been guilty of. But I can assure you that my one false step, which lost me all my reputation, was nothing more or nothing worse than what you have done.

NORA: You? Do you ask me to believe that you were brave enough to run a risk to save your wife's life?

KROGSTAD: The law cares nothing about motives.

NORA: Then it must be a very foolish law.

KROGSTAD: Foolish or not, it is the law by which you will be judged, if I produce this paper in court.

NORA: I don't believe it. Is a daughter not to be allowed to spare her dying father anxiety and care? Is a wife not to be allowed to save her husband's life? I don't know much about law; but I am certain that there must be laws permitting such things as that. Have you no knowledge of such laws— you who are a lawyer? You must be a very poor lawyer, Mr. Krogstad.

KROGSTAD: Maybe. But matters of business—such business as you and I have had together—do you think I don't understand that? Very well. Do as you please. But let me tell you this—if I lose my position a second time, you shall lose yours with me. (*He bows, and goes out through the hall.*)

NORA (*appears buried in thought for a short time, then tosses her head*):   Nonsense! Trying to frighten me like that!—I am not so silly as he thinks. (*Begins to busy herself putting the children's things in order.*) And yet—? No, it's impossible! I did it for love's sake.

CHILDREN (*in the doorway on the left*):   Mother, the stranger man has gone out through the gate.

NORA: Yes, dears, I know. But, don't tell anyone about the stranger man. Do you hear? Not even papa.

CHILDREN: No, mother; but will you come and play again?

NORA: No, no,—not now.

CHILDREN: But, mother, you promised us.

NORA: Yes, but I can't now. Run away in; I have such a lot to do. Run away in, my sweet little darlings. (*She gets them into the room by degrees and shuts the door on them; then sits down on the sofa, takes up a piece of needlework and sews a few stitches, but soon stops.*) No! (*Throws down the work, gets up, goes to the hall door and calls out.*) Helen! bring the Tree in. (*Goes to the table on the left, opens a drawer, and stops again.*) No, no! it is quite impossible!

MAID (*coming in with the Tree*):   Where shall I put it, ma'am?

NORA: Here, in the middle of the floor.

MAID: Shall I get you anything else?

NORA: No, thank you. I have all I want.   (*Exit Maid.*)

NORA (*begins dressing the tree*):   A candle here—and flowers here—. The horrible man! It's all nonsense—there's nothing wrong. The Tree shall be splendid! I will do everything I can think of to please you, Torvald!—I will sing for you, dance for you—(*Helmer comes in with some papers under his arm.*) Oh! are you back already?

HELMER: Yes. Has anyone been here?

NORA: Here? No.

HELMER: That is strange. I saw Krogstad going out of the gate.

NORA: Did you? Oh yes, I forgot, Krogstad was here for a moment.

HELMER: Nora, I can see from your manner that he has been here begging you to say a good word for him.

NORA: Yes.

HELMER: And you were to appear to do it of your own accord; you were to conceal from me the fact of his having been here; didn't he beg that of you too?

NORA: Yes, Torvald, but—

HELMER: Nora, Nora, and you would be a party to that sort of thing? To have any talk with a man like that, and give him any sort of promise? And to tell me a lie into the bargain?

NORA: A lie—?

HELMER: Didn't you tell me no one had been here? (*Shakes his finger at her.*) My little song-bird must never do that again. A song-bird must have a clean beak to chirp with—no false notes! (*Puts his arm around her waist.*) That is so, isn't it? Yes, I am sure it is. (*Lets her go.*) We will say no more about it. (*Sits down by the stove.*) How warm and snug it is here! (*Turns over his papers.*)

NORA (*after a short pause, during which she busies herself with the Christmas Tree*):   Torvald!

HELMER: Yes.

NORA: I am looking forward tremendously to the fancy-dress ball at the Stenborgs' the day after to-morrow.

HELMER: And I am tremendously curious to see what you are going to surprise me with.

NORA: It was very silly of me to want to do that.

HELMER: What do you mean?

NORA: I can't hit upon anything that will do; everything I think of seems so silly and insignificant.

HELMER: Does my little Nora acknowledge that at last?

NORA (*standing behind his chair with her arms on the back of it*):   Are you very busy, Torvald?

HELMER: Well—

NORA: What are all those papers?

HELMER: Bank business.

NORA: Already?

HELMER: I have got authority from the retiring manager to undertake the necessary changes in the staff and in the rearrangement of the work; and I
must make use of the Christmas week for that, so as to have everything in
order for the new year.

NORA: Then that was why this poor Krogstad—

HELMER: Hm!

NORA (*leans against the back of his chair and strokes his hair*):   If you hadn't been
so busy I should have asked you a tremendously big favour, Torvald.

HELMER: What is that? Tell me.

NORA: There is no one has such good taste as you. And I do so want to look
nice at the fancy-dress ball. Torvald, couldn't you take me in hand and
decide what I shall go as, and what sort of a dress I shall wear?

HELMER: Aha! so my obstinate little woman is obliged to get someone to come
to her rescue?

NORA: Yes, Torvald, I can't get along a bit without your help.

HELMER: Very well, I will think it over, we shall manage to hit upon something.

NORA: That is nice of you. (*Goes to the Christmas Tree. A short pause.*) How pretty
the red flowers look—. But, tell me, was it really something very bad that
this Krogstad was guilty of ?

HELMER: He forged someone's name. Have you any idea what that means?

NORA: Isn't it possible that he was driven to do it by necessity?

HELMER: Yes; or, as in so many cases, by imprudence. I am not so heartless as
to condemn a man altogether because of a single false step of that kind.

NORA: No, you wouldn't, would you, Torvald?

HELMER: Many a man has been able to retrieve his character, if he has openly
confessed his fault and taken his punishment.

NORA: Punishment—?

HELMER: But Krogstad did nothing of that sort; he got himself out of it by a
cunning trick, and that is why he has gone under altogether.

NORA: But do you think it would—?

HELMER: Just think how a guilty man like that has to lie and play the hypocrite
with every one, how he has to wear a mask in the presence of those near
and dear to him, even before his own wife and children. And about the
children—that is the most terrible part of it all, Nora.

NORA: How?

HELMER: Because such an atmosphere of lies infects and poisons the whole life
of a home. Each breath the children take in such a house is full of the
germs of evil.

NORA (*coming nearer him*):   Are you sure of that?

HELMER: My dear, I have often seen it in the course of my life as a lawyer. Almost
everyone who has gone to the bad early in life has had a deceitful mother.

NORA: Why do you only say—mother?

HELMER: It seems most commonly to be the mother's influence, though

naturally a bad father's would have the same result. Every lawyer is familiar with the fact. This Krogstad, now, has been persistently poisoning his
own children with lies and dissimulation; that is why I say he has lost all
moral character. (*Holds out his hands to her.*) That is why my sweet little
Nora must promise me not to plead his cause. Give me your hand on it.
Come, come, what is this? Give me your hand. There now, that's settled. I
assure you it would be quite impossible for me to work with him; I literally
feel physically ill when I am in the company of such people.

NORA (*takes her hand out of his and goes to the opposite side of the Christmas
Tree*):   How hot it is in here; and I have such a lot to do.

HELMER (*getting up and putting his papers in order*):   Yes, and I must try and
read through some of these before dinner; and I must think about your
costume, too. And it is just possible I may have something ready in gold
paper to hang up on the Tree. (*Puts his hand on her head.*) My precious little
singing-bird! (*He goes into his room and shuts the door after him.*)

NORA (*after a pause, whispers*):   No, no—it isn't true. It's impossible; it must be
impossible.

The Nurse opens the door on the left.

NURSE: The little ones are begging so hard to be allowed to come in to mamma.

NORA: No, no, no! Don't let them come in to me! You stay with them, Anne.

NURSE: Very well, ma'am. (*Shuts the door.*)

NORA (*pale with terror*):   Deprave my little children? Poison my home? (*A short
pause. Then she tosses her head.*) It's not true. It can't possibly be true.

ACT II

THE SAME SCENE: *The Christmas Tree is in the corner by the piano, stripped of its ornaments and with burnt-down candle-ends on its dishevelled branches. Nora's cloak
and hat are lying on the sofa. She is alone in the room, walking about uneasily. She
stops by the sofa and takes up her cloak.*

NORA (*drops her cloak*):   Someone is coming now! (*Goes to the door and listens.*)
No—it is no one. Of course, no one will come to-day, Christmas Day—nor
to-morrow either. But, perhaps—(*opens the door and looks out*). No, nothing in the letter-box; it is quite empty. (*Comes forward.*) What rubbish! of
course he can't be in earnest about it. Such a thing couldn't happen; it is
impossible—I have three little children.

Enter the Nurse from the room on the left, carrying a big cardboard box.

NURSE: At last I have found the box with the fancy dress.

NORA: Thanks; put it on the table.

NURSE (*doing so*):   But it is very much in want of mending.

NORA: I should like to tear it into a hundred thousand pieces.

NURSE: What an idea! It can easily be put in order—just a little patience.

NORA: Yes, I will go and get Mrs. Linde to come and help me with it.

NURSE: What, out again? In this horrible weather? You will catch cold, ma'am, and make yourself ill.

NORA: Well, worse than that might happen. How are the children?

NURSE: The poor little souls are playing with their Christmas presents, but—

NORA: Do they ask much for me?

NURSE: You see, they are so accustomed to have their mamma with them.

NORA: Yes, but, nurse, I shall not be able to be so much with them now as I was before.

NURSE: Oh well, young children easily get accustomed to anything.

NORA: Do you think so? Do you think they would forget their mother if she went away altogether?

NURSE: Good heavens!—went away altogether?

NORA: Nurse, I want you to tell me something I have often wondered about— how could you have the heart to put your own child out among strangers?

NURSE: I was obliged to, if I wanted to be little Nora's nurse.

NORA: Yes, but how could you be willing to do it?

NURSE: What, when I was going to get such a good place by it? A poor girl who has got into trouble should be glad to. Besides, that wicked man didn't do a single thing for me.

NORA: But I suppose your daughter has quite forgotten you.

NURSE: No, indeed she hasn't. She wrote to me when she was confirmed, and when she was married.

NORA (*putting her arms round her neck*):   Dear old Anne, you were a good mother to me when I was little.

NURSE: Little Nora, poor dear, had no other mother but me.

NORA: And if my little ones had no other mother, I am sure you would—What nonsense I am talking! (*Opens the box.*) Go in to them. Now I must—. You will see to-morrow how charming I shall look.

NURSE: I am sure there will be no one at the ball so charming as you, ma'am. (*Goes into the room on the left.*)

NORA (*begins to unpack the box, but soon pushes it away from her*):   If only I dared go out. If only no one would come. If only I could be sure nothing would happen here in the meantime. Stuff and nonsense! No one will come. Only I mustn't think about it. I will brush my muff. What lovely, lovely gloves! Out of my thoughts, out of my thoughts! One, two, three, four, five, six— (*Screams.*) Ah! there is someone coming—. (*Makes a movement towards the door, but stands irresolute.*)

Enter Mrs. Linde from the hall, where she has taken off her cloak and hat.

NORA: Oh, it's you, Christine. There is no one else out there, is there? How good of you to come!

MRS. LINDE: I heard you were up asking for me.

NORA: Yes, I was passing by. As a matter of fact, it is something you could help me with. Let us sit down here on the sofa. Look here. To-morrow evening there is to be a fancy-dress ball at the Stenborgs', who live above us;

and Torvald wants me to go as a Neapolitan fisher-girl, and dance the Tarantella that I learned at Capri.

MRS. LINDE: I see; you are going to keep up the character.

NORA: Yes, Torvald wants me to. Look, here is the dress; Torvald had it made for me there, but now it is all so torn, and I haven't any idea—

MRS. LINDE: We will easily put that right. It is only some of the trimming come unsewn here and there. Needle and thread? Now then, that's all we want.

NORA: It *is* nice of you.

MRS. LINDE (*sewing*):   So you are going to be dressed up to-morrow, Nora. I will tell you what—I shall come in for a moment and see you in your fine feathers. But I have completely forgotten to thank you for a delightful evening yesterday.

NORA (*gets up, and crosses the stage*):   Well, I don't think yesterday was as pleasant as usual. You ought to have come to town a little earlier, Christine. Certainly Torvald does understand how to make a house dainty and attractive.

MRS. LINDE: And so do you, it seems to me; you are not your father's daughter for nothing. But tell me, is Doctor Rank always as depressed as he was yesterday?

NORA: No; yesterday it was very noticeable. I must tell you that he suffers from a very dangerous disease. He has consumption of the spine, poor creature. His father was a horrible man who committed all sorts of excesses; and that is why his son was sickly from childhood, do you understand?

MRS. LINDE (*dropping her sewing*):   But, my dearest Nora, how do you know anything about such things?

NORA (*walking about*):   Pooh! When you have three children, you get visits now and then from—from married women, who know something of medical matters, and they talk about one thing and another.

MRS. LINDE: (*goes on sewing. A short silence*) Does Doctor Rank come here everyday?

NORA: Everyday regularly. He is Torvald's most intimate friend, and a great friend of mine too. He is just like one of the family.

MRS. LINDE: But tell me this—is he perfectly sincere? I mean, isn't he the kind of man that is very anxious to make himself agreeable?

NORA: Not in the least. What makes you think that?

MRS. LINDE: When you introduced him to me yesterday, he declared he had often heard my name mentioned in this house; but afterwards I noticed that your husband hadn't the slightest idea who I was. So how could Doctor Rank—?

NORA: That is quite right, Christine. Torvald is so absurdly fond of me that he wants me absolutely to himself, as he says. At first he used to seem almost jealous if I mentioned any of the dear folk at home, so naturally I gave up doing so. But I often talk about such things with Doctor Rank, because he likes hearing about them.

MRS. LINDE: Listen to me, Nora. You are still very like a child in many things, and I am older than you in many ways and have a little more experience. Let me tell you this—you ought to make an end of it with Doctor Rank.

NORA: What ought I to make an end of?

MRS. LINDE: Of two things, I think. Yesterday you talked some nonsense about a rich admirer who was to leave you money—

NORA: An admirer who doesn't exist, unfortunately! But what then?

MRS. LINDE: Is Doctor Rank a man of means?

NORA: Yes, he is.

MRS. LINDE: And has no one to provide for?

NORA: No, no one; but—

MRS. LINDE: And comes here everyday?

NORA: Yes, I told you so.

MRS. LINDE: But how can this well-bred man be so tactless?

NORA: I don't understand you at all.

MRS. LINDE: Don't prevaricate, Nora. Do you suppose I don't guess who lent you the two hundred and fifty pounds?

NORA: Are you out of your senses? How can you think of such a thing! A friend of ours, who comes here everyday! Do you realise what a horribly painful position that would be?

MRS. LINDE: Then it really isn't he?

NORA: No, certainly not. It would never have entered into my head for a moment. Besides, he had no money to lend then; he came into his money afterwards.

MRS. LINDE: Well, I think that was lucky for you, my dear Nora.

NORA: No, it would never have come into my head to ask Doctor Rank. Although I am quite sure that if I had asked him—

MRS. LINDE: But of course you won't.

NORA: Of course not. I have no reason to think it could possibly be necessary. But I am quite sure that if I told Doctor Rank—

MRS. LINDE: Behind your husband's back?

NORA: I must make an end of it with the other one, and that will be behind his back too. I *must* make an end of it with him.

MRS. LINDE: Yes, that is what I told you yesterday, but—

NORA (*walking up and down*): A man can put a thing like that straight much easier than a woman—

MRS. LINDE: One's husband, yes.

NORA: Nonsense! (*Standing still.*) When you pay off a debt you get your bond back, don't you?

MRS. LINDE: Yes, as a matter of course.

NORA: And can tear it into a hundred thousand pieces, and burn it up—the nasty dirty paper!

MRS. LINDE (*looks hard at her, lays down her sewing and gets up slowly*): Nora, you are concealing something from me.

NORA: Do I look as if I were?

MRS. LINDE: Something has happened to you since yesterday morning. Nora, what is it?

NORA (*going nearer to her*): Christine! (*Listens.*) Hush! there's Torvald come home. Do you mind going in to the children for the present? Torvald can't bear to see dressmaking going on. Let Anne help you.

MRS. LINDE (*gathering some of the things together*): Certainly—but I am not going away from here until we have had it out with one another. (*She goes into the room on the left, as Helmer comes in from the hall.*)

NORA (*going up to Helmer*):   I have wanted you so much, Torvald dear.

HELMER: Was that the dressmaker?

NORA: No, it was Christine; she is helping me to put my dress in order. You will see I shall look quite smart.

HELMER: Wasn't that a happy thought of mine, now?

NORA: Splendid! But don't you think it is nice of me, too, to do as you wish?

HELMER: Nice?—because you do as your husband wishes? Well, well, you little rogue, I am sure you did not mean it in that way. But I am not going to disturb you; you will want to be trying on your dress, I expect.

NORA: I suppose you are going to work.

HELMER: Yes. (*Shows her a bundle of papers.*) Look at that. I have just been into the bank. (*Turns to go into his room.*)

NORA: Torvald.

HELMER: Yes.

NORA: If your little squirrel were to ask you for something very, very prettily—?

HELMER: What then?

NORA: Would you do it?

HELMER: I should like to hear what it is, first.

NORA: Your squirrel would run about and do all her tricks if you would be nice, and do what she wants.

HELMER: Speak plainly.

NORA: Your skylark would chirp about in every room, with her song rising and falling—

HELMER: Well, my skylark does that anyhow.

NORA: I would play the fairy and dance for you in the moonlight, Torvald.

HELMER: Nora—you surely don't mean that request you made to me this morning?

NORA (*going near him*):   Yes, Torvald, I beg you so earnestly—

HELMER: Have you really the courage to open up that question again?

NORA: Yes, dear, you *must* do as I ask; you *must* let Krogstad keep his post in the bank.

HELMER: My dear Nora, it is his post that I have arranged Mrs. Linde shall have.

NORA: Yes, you have been awfully kind about that; but you could just as well dismiss some other clerk instead of Krogstad.

HELMER: This is simply incredible obstinacy! Because you chose to give him a thoughtless promise that you would speak for him, I am expected to—

NORA: That isn't the reason, Torvald. It is for your own sake. This fellow writes in the most scurrilous newspapers; you have told me so yourself. He can do you an unspeakable amount of harm. I am frightened to death of him—

HELMER: Ah, I understand; it is recollections of the past that scare you.

NORA: What do you mean?

HELMER: Naturally you are thinking of your father.

NORA: Yes—yes, of course. Just recall to your mind what these malicious creatures wrote in the papers about papa, and how horribly they slandered him. I believe they would have procured his dismissal if the Department had not sent you over to inquire into it, and if you had not been so kindly disposed and helpful to him.

HELMER: My little Nora, there is an important difference between your father and me. Your father's reputation as a public official was not above suspicion. Mine is, and I hope it will continue to be so, as long as I hold my office.

NORA: You never can tell what mischief these men may contrive. We ought to be so well off, so snug and happy here in our peaceful home, and have no cares—you and I and the children, Torvald! That is why I beg you so earnestly—

HELMER: And it is just by interceding for him that you make it impossible for me to keep him. It is already known at the Bank that I mean to dismiss Krogstad. Is it to get about now that the new manager has changed his mind at his wife's bidding—

NORA: And what if it did?

HELMER: Of course!—if only this obstinate little person can get her way! Do you suppose I am going to make myself ridiculous before my whole staff, to let people think that I am a man to be swayed by all sorts of outside influence? I should very soon feel the consequences of it, I can tell you! And besides, there is one thing that makes it quite impossible for me to have Krogstad in the Bank as long as I am manager.

NORA: Whatever is that?

HELMER: His moral failings I might perhaps have overlooked, if necessary—

NORA: Yes, you could—couldn't you?

HELMER: And I hear he is a good worker, too. But I knew him when we were boys. It was one of those rash friendships that so often prove an incubus in afterlife. I may as well tell you plainly, we were once on very intimate terms with one another. But this tactless fellow lays no restraint on himself when other people are present. On the contrary, he thinks it gives him the right to adopt a familiar tone with me, and every minute it is "I say, Helmer, old fellow!" and that sort of thing. I assure you it is extremely painful for me. He would make my position in the Bank intolerable.

NORA: Torvald, I don't believe you mean that.

HELMER: Don't you? Why not?

NORA: Because it is such a narrow-minded way of looking at things.

HELMER: What are you saying? Narrow-minded? Do you think I am narrow-minded?

NORA: No, just the opposite, dear—and it is exactly for that reason.

HELMER: It's the same thing. You say my point of view is narrow-minded, so I must be so too. Narrow-minded! Very well—I must put an end to this. (*Goes to the hall door and calls.*) Helen!

NORA: What are you going to do?

HELMER (*looking among his papers*):   Settle it. (*Enter Maid.*) Look here; take this letter and go downstairs with it at once. Find a messenger and tell him to deliver it, and be quick. The address is on it, and here is the money.

MAID: Very well, sir. (*Exit with the letter.*)

HELMER (*putting his papers together*):   Now then, little Miss Obstinate.

NORA (*breathlessly*):   Torvald — what was that letter?

HELMER: Krogstad's dismissal.

NORA: Call her back, Torvald! There is still time. Oh Torvald, call her back! Do it for my sake — for your own sake — for the children's sake! Do you hear me, Torvald? Call her back! You don't know what that letter can bring upon us.

HELMER: It's too late.

NORA: Yes, it's too late.

HELMER: My dear Nora, I can forgive the anxiety you are in, although really it is an insult to me. It is, indeed. Isn't it an insult to think that I should be afraid of a starving quill-driver's vengeance? But I forgive you nevertheless, because it is such eloquent witness to your great love for me. (*Takes her in his arms.*) And that is as it should be, my own darling Nora. Come what will, you may be sure I shall have both courage and strength if they be needed. You will see I am man enough to take everything upon myself.

NORA (*in a horror-stricken voice*):   What do you mean by that?

HELMER: Everything, I say —

NORA (*recovering herself*):   You will never have to do that.

HELMER: That's right. Well, we will share it, Nora, as man and wife should. That is how it shall be. (*Caressing her.*) Are you content now? There! there! — not these frightened dove's eyes! The whole thing is only the wildest fancy! — Now, you must go and play through the Tarantella and practise with your tambourine. I shall go into the inner office and shut the door, and I shall hear nothing; you can make as much noise as you please. (*Turns back at the door.*) And when Rank comes, tell him where he will find me. (*Nods to her, takes his papers and goes into his room, and shuts the door after him.*)

NORA (*bewildered with anxiety, stands as if rooted to the spot, and whispers*):   He was capable of doing it. He will do it. He will do it in spite of everything. — No, not that! Never, never! Anything rather than that! Oh, for some help, some way out of it! (*The door-bell rings.*) Doctor Rank! Anything rather than that — anything, whatever it is! (*She puts her hands over her face, pulls herself together, goes to the door and opens it. Rank is standing without, hanging up his coat. During the following dialogue it begins to grow dark.*)

NORA: Good-day, Doctor Rank. I knew your ring. But you mustn't go in to Torvald now; I think he is busy with something.

RANK: And you?

NORA (*brings him in and shuts the door after him*):   Oh, you know very well I always have time for you.

RANK: Thank you. I shall make use of as much of it as I can.

NORA: What do you mean by that? As much of it as you can?

RANK: Well, does that alarm you?

NORA: It was such a strange way of putting it. Is anything likely to happen?

RANK: Nothing but what I have long been prepared for. But I certainly didn't expect it to happen so soon.

NORA (*gripping him by the arm*):   What have you found out? Doctor Rank, you must tell me.

RANK (*sitting down by the stove*):   It is all up with me. And it can't be helped.

NORA (*with a sigh of relief*):   Is it about yourself?

RANK: Who else? It is no use lying to one's self. I am the most wretched of all my patients, Mrs. Helmer. Lately I have been taking stock of my internal economy. Bankrupt! Probably within a month I shall lie rotting in the churchyard.

NORA: What an ugly thing to say!

RANK: The thing itself is cursedly ugly, and the worst of it is that I shall have to face so much more that is ugly before that. I shall only make one more examination of myself; when I have done that, I shall know pretty certainly when it will be that the horrors of dissolution will begin. There is something I want to tell you. Helmer's refined nature gives him an unconquerable disgust at everything that is ugly; I won't have him in my sick-room.

NORA: Oh, but, Doctor Rank—

RANK: I won't have him there. Not on any account. I bar my door to him. As soon as I am quite certain that the worst has come, I shall send you my card with a black cross on it, and then you will know that the loathsome end has begun.

NORA: You are quite absurd to-day. And I wanted you so much to be in a really good humour.

RANK: With death stalking beside me?—To have to pay this penalty for another man's sin? Is there any justice in that? And in every single family, in one way or another, some such inexorable retribution is being exacted—

NORA (*putting her hands over her ears*):   Rubbish! Do talk of something cheerful.

RANK: Oh, it's a mere laughing matter, the whole thing. My poor innocent spine has to suffer for my father's youthful amusements.

NORA (*sitting at the table on the left*):   I suppose you mean that he was too partial to asparagus and pâté de foie gras, don't you?

RANK: Yes, and to truffles.

NORA: Truffles, yes. And oysters too, I suppose?

RANK: Oysters, of course, that goes without saying.

NORA: And heaps of port and champagne. It is sad that all these nice things should take their revenge on our bones.

RANK: Especially that they should revenge themselves on the unlucky bones of those who have not had the satisfaction of enjoying them.

NORA: Yes, that's the saddest part of it all.

RANK (*with a searching look at her*):   Hm!—

NORA (*after a short pause*):   Why did you smile?

RANK: No, it was you that laughed.

NORA: No, it was you that smiled, Doctor Rank!

RANK (*rising*):   You are a greater rascal than I thought.

NORA: I am in a silly mood to-day.

RANK: So it seems.

NORA (*putting her hands on his shoulders*):   Dear, dear Doctor Rank, death mustn't take you away from Torvald and me.

RANK: It is a loss you would easily recover from. Those who are gone are soon forgotten.

NORA (*looking at him anxiously*):   Do you believe that?

RANK: People form new ties, and then—

NORA: Who will form new ties?

RANK: Both you and Helmer, when I am gone. You yourself are already on the high road to it, I think. What did that Mrs. Linde want here last night?

NORA: Oho!—you don't mean to say you are jealous of poor Christine?

RANK: Yes, I am. She will be my successor in this house. When I am done for, this woman will—

NORA: Hush! don't speak so loud. She is in that room.

RANK: To-day again. There, you see.

NORA: She has only come to sew my dress for me. Bless my soul, how unreasonable you are! (*Sits down on the sofa.*) Be nice now, Doctor Rank, and to-morrow you will see how beautifully I shall dance, and you can imagine I am doing it all for you—and for Torvald too, of course. (*Takes various things out of the box.*) Doctor Rank, come and sit down here, and I will show you something.

RANK (*sitting down*):   What is it?

NORA: Just look at those!

RANK: Silk stockings.

NORA: Flesh-coloured. Aren't they lovely? It is so dark here now, but to-morrow—. No, no, no! you must only look at the feet. Oh well, you may have leave to look at the legs too.

RANK: Hm!—

NORA: Why are you looking so critical? Don't you think they will fit me?

RANK: I have no means of forming an opinion about that.

NORA (*looks at him for a moment*):   For shame! (*Hits him lightly on the ear with the stockings.*) That's to punish you. (*Folds them up again.*)

RANK: And what other nice things am I to be allowed to see?

NORA: Not a single thing more, for being so naughty. (*She looks among the things, humming to herself.*)

RANK (*after a short silence*):   When I am sitting here, talking to you as intimately as this, I cannot imagine for a moment what would have become of me if I had never come into this house.

NORA (*smiling*):   I believe you do feel thoroughly at home with us.

RANK (*in a lower voice, looking straight in front of him*):   And to be obliged to leave it all—

NORA: Nonsense, you are not going to leave it.

RANK (*as before*):   And not be able to leave behind one the slightest token of one's gratitude, scarcely even a fleeting regret—nothing but an empty place which the first comer can fill as well as any other.

NORA: And if I asked you now for a—? No!

RANK: For what?

NORA: For a big proof of your friendship—

RANK: Yes, yes!

NORA: I mean a tremendously big favour.

RANK: Would you really make me so happy for once?

NORA: Ah, but you don't know what it is yet.

RANK: No—but tell me.

NORA: I really can't, Doctor Rank. It is something out of all reason; it means
advice, and help, and a favour—

RANK: The bigger a thing it is the better. I can't conceive what it is you mean.
Do tell me. Haven't I your confidence?

NORA: More than anyone else. I know you are my truest and best friend, and so
I will tell you what it is. Well, Doctor Rank, it is something you must help me
to prevent. You know how devotedly, how inexpressibly deeply Torvald loves
me; he would never for a moment hesitate to give his life for me.

RANK (*leaning towards her*):   Nora—do you think he is the only one—?

NORA (*with a slight start*):   The only one—?

RANK: The only one who would gladly give his life for your sake.

NORA (*sadly*):   Is that it?

RANK: I was determined you should know it before I went away, and there will
never be a better opportunity than this. Now you know it, Nora. And now
you know, too, that you can trust me as you would trust no one else.

NORA (*rises, deliberately and quietly*):   Let me pass.

RANK (*makes room for her to pass him, but sits still*):   Nora!

NORA (*at the hall door*):   Helen, bring in the lamp. (*Goes over to the stove.*) Dear
Doctor Rank, that was really horrid of you.

RANK: To have loved you as much as anyone else does? Was that horrid?

NORA: No, but to go and tell me so. There was really no need—

RANK: What do you mean? Did you know—? (*Maid enters with lamp, puts it
down on the table, and goes out.*) Nora—Mrs. Helmer—tell me, had you any
idea of this?

NORA: Oh, how do I know whether I had or whether I hadn't? I really can't tell
you—To think you could be so clumsy, Doctor Rank! We were getting on
so nicely.

RANK: Well, at all events you know now that you can command me, body and
soul. So won't you speak out?

NORA (*looking at him*):   After what happened?

RANK: I beg you to let me know what it is.

NORA: I can't tell you anything now.

RANK: Yes, yes. You mustn't punish me in that way. Let me have permission to
do for you whatever a man may do.

NORA: You can do nothing for me now. Besides, I really don't need any help at
all. You will find that the whole thing is merely fancy on my part. It really
is so—of course it is! (*Sits down in the rocking-chair, and looks at him with a
smile.*) You are a nice sort of man, Doctor Rank!—don't you feel ashamed
of yourself, now the lamp has come?

RANK: Not a bit. But perhaps I had better go—for ever?

NORA: No, indeed, you shall not. Of course you must come here just as before. You know very well Torvald can't do without you.

RANK: Yes, but you?

NORA: Oh, I am always tremendously pleased when you come.

RANK: It is just that, that put me on the wrong track. You are a riddle to me. I have often thought that you would almost as soon be in my company as in Helmer's.

NORA: Yes—you see there are some people one loves best, and others whom one would almost always rather have as companions.

RANK: Yes, there is something in that.

NORA: When I was at home, of course I loved papa best. But I always thought it tremendous fun if I could steal down into the maids' room, because they never moralised at all, and talked to each other about such entertaining things.

RANK: I see—it is *their* place I have taken.

NORA (*jumping up and going to him*):   Oh, dear, nice Doctor Rank, I never meant that at all. But surely you can understand that being with Torvald is a little like being with papa—

Enter Maid from the hall.

MAID: If you please, ma'am. (*Whispers and hands her a card.*)

NORA (*glancing at the card*):   Oh! (*Puts it in her pocket.*)

RANK: Is there anything wrong?

NORA: No, no, not in the least. It is only something—it is my new dress—

RANK: What? Your dress is lying there.

NORA: Oh, yes, that one; but this is another. I ordered it. Torvald mustn't know about it—

RANK: Oho! Then that was the great secret.

NORA: Of course. Just go in to him; he is sitting in the inner room. Keep him as long as—

RANK: Make your mind easy; I won't let him escape. (*Goes into Helmer's room.*)

NORA (*to the Maid*):   And he is standing waiting in the kitchen?

MAID: Yes; he came up the back stairs.

NORA: But didn't you tell him no one was in?

MAID: Yes, but it was no good.

NORA: He won't go away?

MAID: No; he says he won't until he has seen you, ma'am.

NORA: Well, let him come in—but quietly. Helen, you mustn't say anything about it to anyone. It is a surprise for my husband.

MAID: Yes, ma'am, I quite understand. (*Exit.*)

NORA: This dreadful thing is going to happen! It will happen in spite of me! No, no, no, it can't happen—it shan't happen! (*She bolts the door of Helmer's room. The Maid opens the hall door for Krogstad and shuts it after him. He is wearing a fur coat, high boots and a fur cap.*)

NORA (*advancing towards him*):   Speak low—my husband is at home.

KROGSTAD: No matter about that.

NORA: What do you want of me?

KROGSTAD: An explanation of something.

NORA: Make haste then. What is it?

KROGSTAD: You know, I suppose, that I have got my dismissal.

NORA: I couldn't prevent it, Mr. Krogstad. I fought as hard as I could on your side, but it was no good.

KROGSTAD: Does your husband love you so little, then? He knows what I can expose you to, and yet he ventures—

NORA: How can you suppose that he has any knowledge of the sort?

KROGSTAD: I didn't suppose so at all. It would not be the least like our dear Torvald Helmer to show so much courage—

NORA: Mr. Krogstad, a little respect for my husband, please.

KROGSTAD: Certainly—all the respect he deserves. But since you have kept the matter so carefully to yourself, I make bold to suppose that you have a little clearer idea, than you had yesterday, of what it actually is that you have done?

NORA: More than you could ever teach me.

KROGSTAD: Yes, such a bad lawyer as I am.

NORA: What is it you want of me?

KROGSTAD: Only to see how you were, Mrs. Helmer. I have been thinking about you all day long. A mere cashier, a quill-driver, a—well, a man like me— even he has a little of what is called feeling, you know.

NORA: Show it, then; think of my little children.

KROGSTAD: Have you and your husband thought of mine? But never mind about that. I only wanted to tell you that you need not take this matter too seriously. In the first place there will be no accusation made on my part.

NORA: No, of course not; I was sure of that.

KROGSTAD: The whole thing can be arranged amicably; there is no reason why anyone should know anything about it. It will remain a secret between us three.

NORA: My husband must never get to know anything about it.

KROGSTAD: How will you be able to prevent it? Am I to understand that you can pay the balance that is owing?

NORA: No, not just at present.

KROGSTAD: Or perhaps that you have some expedient for raising the money soon?

NORA: No expedient that I mean to make use of.

KROGSTAD: Well, in any case, it would have been of no use to you now. If you stood there with ever so much money in your hand, I would never part with your bond.

NORA: Tell me what purpose you mean to put it to.

KROGSTAD: I shall only preserve it—keep it in my possession. No one who is not concerned in the matter shall have the slightest hint of it. So that if the thought of it has driven you to any desperate resolution—

NORA: It has.

KROGSTAD: If you had it in your mind to run away from your home—

NORA: I had.

KROGSTAD: Or even something worse—

NORA: How could you know that?

KROGSTAD: Give up the idea.

NORA: How did you know I had thought of *that?*

KROGSTAD: Most of us think of that at first. I did, too—but I hadn't the courage.

NORA (*faintly*):   No more had I.

KROGSTAD (*in a tone of relief*):   No, that's it, isn't it—you hadn't the courage either?

NORA: No, I haven't—I haven't.

KROGSTAD: Besides, it would have been a great piece of folly. Once the first storm at home is over—. I have a letter for your husband in my pocket.

NORA: Telling him everything?

KROGSTAD: In as lenient a manner as I possibly could.

NORA (*quickly*):   He mustn't get the letter. Tear it up. I will find some means of getting money.

KROGSTAD: Excuse me, Mrs. Helmer, but I think I told you just now—

NORA: I am not speaking of what I owe you. Tell me what sum you are asking my husband for, and I will get the money.

KROGSTAD: I am not asking your husband for a penny.

NORA: What do you want, then?

KROGSTAD: I will tell you. I want to rehabilitate myself, Mrs. Helmer; I want to get on; and in that your husband must help me. For the last year and a half I have not had a hand in anything dishonourable, and all that time I have been struggling in most restricted circumstances. I was content to work my way up step by step. Now I am turned out, and I am not going to be satisfied with merely being taken into favour again. I want to get on, I tell you. I want to get into the Bank again, in a higher position. Your husband must make a place for me—

NORA: That he will never do!

KROGSTAD: He will; I know him; he dare not protest. And as soon as I am in there again with him, then you will see! Within a year I shall be the manager's right hand. It will be Nils Krogstad and not Torvald Helmer who manages the Bank.

NORA: That's a thing you will never see!

KROGSTAD: Do you mean that you will—?

NORA: I have courage enough for it now.

KROGSTAD: Oh, you can't frighten me. A fine, spoilt lady like you—

NORA: You will see, you will see.

KROGSTAD: Under the ice, perhaps? Down into the cold, coal-black water? And then, in the spring, to float up to the surface, all horrible and unrecognisable, with your hair fallen out—

NORA: You can't frighten me.

KROGSTAD: Nor you me. People don't do such things, Mrs. Helmer. Besides, what use would it be? I should have him completely in my power all the same.

NORA: Afterwards? When I am no longer—

KROGSTAD: Have you forgotten that it is I who have the keeping of your reputation? (*Nora stands speechlessly looking at him.*) Well, now, I have warned you. Do not do anything foolish. When Helmer has had my letter, I shall expect a message from him. And be sure you remember that it is your husband himself who has forced me into such ways as this again. I will never forgive him for that. Good-bye, Mrs. Helmer. (*Exit through the hall.*)

NORA (*goes to the hall door, opens it slightly and listens*):   He is going. He is not putting the letter in the box. Oh no, no! that's impossible! (*Opens the door by degrees.*) What is that? He is standing outside. He is not going downstairs. Is he hesitating? Can he—? (*A letter drops into the box; then Krogstad's footsteps are heard, till they die away as he goes downstairs. Nora utters a stifled cry, and runs across the room to the table by the sofa. A short pause.*)

NORA: In the letter-box. (*Steals across to the hall door.*) There it lies—Torvald, Torvald, there is no hope for us now!

Mrs. Linde comes in from the room on the left, carrying the dress.

MRS. LINDE: There, I can't see anything more to mend now. Would you like to try it on—?

NORA (*in a hoarse whisper*):   Christine, come here.

MRS. LINDE (*throwing the dress down on the sofa*):   What is the matter with you? You look so agitated!

NORA: Come here. Do you see that letter? There, look—you can see it through the glass in the letter-box.

MRS. LINDE: Yes, I see it.

NORA: That letter is from Krogstad.

MRS. LINDE: Nora—it was Krogstad who lent you the money!

NORA: Yes, and now Torvald will know all about it.

MRS. LINDE: Believe me, Nora, that's the best thing for both of you.

NORA: You don't know all. I forged a name.

MRS. LINDE: Good heavens—!

NORA: I only want to say this to you, Christine—you must be my witness.

MRS. LINDE: Your witness? What do you mean? What am I to—?

NORA: If I should go out of my mind—and it might easily happen—

MRS. LINDE: Nora!

NORA: Or if anything else should happen to me—anything, for instance, that might prevent my being here—

MRS. LINDE: Nora! Nora! you are quite out of your mind.

NORA: And if it should happen that there were some one who wanted to take all the responsibility, all the blame, you understand—

MRS. LINDE: Yes, yes—but how can you suppose—?

NORA: Then you must be my witness, that it is not true, Christine. I am not out of my mind at all! I am in my right senses now, and I tell you no one else has known anything about it; I, and I alone, did the whole thing. Remember that.

MRS. LINDE: I will, indeed. But I don't understand all this.

NORA: How should you understand it? A wonderful thing is going to happen!

MRS. LINDE: A wonderful thing?

NORA: Yes, a wonderful thing!—But it is so terrible, Christine; it *mustn't* happen, not for all the world.

MRS. LINDE: I will go at once and see Krogstad.

NORA: Don't go to him; he will do you some harm.

MRS. LINDE: There was a time when he would gladly do anything for my sake.

NORA: He?

MRS. LINDE: Where does he live?

NORA: How should I know—? Yes (*feeling in her pocket*), here is his card. But the letter, the letter—!

HELMER (*calls from his room, knocking at the door*):   Nora!

NORA (*cries out anxiously*):   Oh, what's that? What do you want?

HELMER: Don't be so frightened. We are not coming in; you have locked the door. Are you trying on your dress?

NORA: Yes, that's it. I look so nice, Torvald.

MRS. LINDE (*who has read the card*):   I see he lives at the corner here.

NORA: Yes, but it's no use. It is hopeless. The letter is lying there in the box.

MRS. LINDE: And your husband keeps the key?

NORA: Yes, always.

MRS. LINDE: Krogstad must ask for his letter back unread, he must find some pretence—

NORA: But it is just at this time that Torvald generally—

MRS. LINDE: You must delay him. Go in to him in the meantime. I will come back as soon as I can. (*She goes out hurriedly through the hall door.*)

NORA (*goes to Helmer's door, opens it and peeps in*):   Torvald!

HELMER (*from the inner room*):   Well? May I venture at last to come into my own room again? Come along, Rank, now you will see—(*Halting in the doorway.*) But what is this?

NORA: What is what, dear?

HELMER: Rank led me to expect a splendid transformation.

RANK (*in the doorway*):   I understood so, but evidently I was mistaken.

NORA: Yes, nobody is to have the chance of admiring me in my dress until tomorrow.

HELMER: But, my dear Nora, you look so worn out. Have you been practising too much?

NORA: No, I have not practised at all.

HELMER: But you will need to—

NORA: Yes, indeed I shall, Torvald. But I can't get on a bit without you to help me; I have absolutely forgotten the whole thing.

HELMER: Oh, we will soon work it up again.

NORA: Yes, help me, Torvald. Promise that you will! I am so nervous about it—all the people—. You must give yourself up to me entirely this evening. Not the tiniest bit of business—you mustn't even take a pen in your hand. Will you promise, Torvald dear?

HELMER: I promise. This evening I will be wholly and absolutely at your service, you helpless little mortal. Ah, by the way, first of all I will just—(*Goes towards the hall door.*)

NORA: What are you going to do there?

HELMER: Only see if any letters have come.

NORA: No, no! don't do that, Torvald!

HELMER: Why not?

NORA: Torvald, please don't. There is nothing there.

HELMER: Well, let me look. (*Turns to go to the letter-box. Nora, at the piano, plays the first bars of the Tarantella. Helmer stops in the doorway.*) Aha!

NORA: I can't dance tomorrow if I don't practise with you.

HELMER (*going up to her*):   Are you really so afraid of it, dear?

NORA: Yes, so dreadfully afraid of it. Let me practise at once; there is time now, before we go to dinner. Sit down and play for me, Torvald dear; criticise me, and correct me as you play.

HELMER: With great pleasure, if you wish me to. (*Sits down at the piano.*)

NORA (*takes out of the box a tambourine and a long variegated shawl. She hastily drapes the shawl round her. Then she springs to the front of the stage and calls out*):   Now play for me! I am going to dance!

Helmer plays and Nora dances. Rank stands by the piano behind Helmer, and looks on.

HELMER (*as he plays*):   Slower, slower!

NORA: I can't do it any other way.

HELMER: Not so violently, Nora!

NORA: This is the way.

HELMER (*stops playing*):   No, no—that is not a bit right.

NORA (*laughing and swinging the tambourine*):   Didn't I tell you so?

RANK: Let me play for her.

HELMER (*getting up*):   Yes, do. I can correct her better then.

Rank sits down at the piano and plays. Nora dances more and more wildly. Helmer has taken up a position beside the stove, and during her dance gives her frequent instructions. She does not seem to hear him; her hair comes down and falls over her shoulders; she pays no attention to it, but goes on dancing. Enter Mrs. Linde.

MRS. LINDE (*standing as if spell-bound in the doorway*):   Oh!—

NORA (*as she dances*):   Such fun, Christine!

HELMER: My dear darling Nora, you are dancing as if your life depended on it.

NORA: So it does.

HELMER: Stop, Rank; this is sheer madness. Stop, I tell you! (*Rank stops playing, and Nora suddenly stands still. Helmer goes up to her.*) I could never have believed it. You have forgotten everything I taught you.

NORA (*throwing away the tambourine*):   There, you see.

HELMER: You will want a lot of coaching.

NORA: Yes, you see how much I need it. You must coach me up to the last minute. Promise me that, Torvald!

HELMER: You can depend on me.

NORA: You must not think of anything but me, either to-day or to-morrow; you mustn't open a single letter—not even open the letter-box—

HELMER: Ah, you are still afraid of that fellow —

NORA: Yes, indeed I am.

HELMER: Nora, I can tell from your looks that there is a letter from him lying there.

NORA: I don't know; I think there is; but you must not read anything of that kind now. Nothing horrid must come between us until this is all over.

RANK (*whispers to Helmer*):   You mustn't contradict her.

HELMER (*taking her in his arms*):   The child shall have her way. But to-morrow night, after you have danced —

NORA: Then you will be free. (*The Maid appears in the doorway to the right.*)

MAID: Dinner is served, ma'am.

NORA: We will have champagne, Helen.

MAID: Very good, ma'am.   [*Exit.*]

HELMER: Hullo! — are we going to have a banquet?

NORA: Yes, a champagne banquet until the small hours. (*Calls out.*) And a few macaroons, Helen — lots, just for once!

HELMER: Come, come, don't be so wild and nervous. Be my own little skylark, as you used.

NORA: Yes, dear, I will. But go in now and you too, Doctor Rank. Christine, you must help me to do up my hair.

RANK (*whispers to Helmer as they go out*):   I suppose there is nothing — she is not expecting anything?

HELMER: Far from it, my dear fellow; it is simply nothing more than this child-ish nervousness I was telling you of. (*They go into the right-hand room.*)

NORA: Well!

MRS. LINDE: Gone out of town.

NORA: I could tell from your face.

MRS. LINDE: He is coming home to-morrow evening. I wrote a note for him.

NORA: You should have let it alone; you must prevent nothing. After all, it is splendid to be waiting for a wonderful thing to happen.

MRS. LINDE: What is it that you are waiting for?

NORA: Oh, you wouldn't understand. Go in to them, I will come in a moment. (*Mrs. Linde goes into the dining-room. Nora stands still for a little while, as if to compose herself. Then she looks at her watch.*) Five o'clock. Seven hours until midnight; and then four-and-twenty hours until the next midnight. Then the Tarantella will be over. Twenty-four and seven? Thirty-one hours to live.

HELMER (*from the doorway on the right*):   Where's my little skylark?

NORA (*going to him with her arms outstretched*):   Here she is!

ACT III

THE SAME SCENE: *The table has been placed in the middle of the stage, with chairs round it. A lamp is burning on the table. The door into the hall stands open. Dance music is heard in the room above. Mrs. Linde is sitting at the table idly turning over the leaves of a book; she tries to read, but does not seem able to collect her thoughts. Every now and then she listens intently for a sound at the outer door.*

MRS. LINDE (*looking at her watch*):   Not yet—and the time is nearly up. If only he does not—. (*Listens again.*) Ah, there he is. (*Goes into the hall and opens the outer door carefully. Light footsteps are heard on the stairs. She whispers.*) Come in. There is no one here.

KROGSTAD (*in the doorway*):   I found a note from you at home. What does this mean?

MRS. LINDE: It is absolutely necessary that I should have a talk with you.

KROGSTAD: Really? And is it absolutely necessary that it should be here?

MRS. LINDE: It is impossible where I live; there is no private entrance to my rooms. Come in; we are quite alone. The maid is asleep, and the Helmers are at the dance upstairs.

KROGSTAD (*coming into the room*):   Are the Helmers really at a dance to-night?

MRS. LINDE: Yes, why not?

KROGSTAD: Certainly—why not?

MRS. LINDE: Now, Nils, let us have a talk.

KROGSTAD: Can we two have anything to talk about?

MRS. LINDE: We have a great deal to talk about.

KROGSTAD: I shouldn't have thought so.

MRS. LINDE: No, you have never properly understood me.

KROGSTAD: Was there anything else to understand except what was obvious to all the world—a heartless woman jilts a man when a more lucrative chance turns up?

MRS. LINDE: Do you believe I am as absolutely heartless as all that? And do you believe that I did it with a light heart?

KROGSTAD: Didn't you?

MRS. LINDE: Nils, did you really think that?

KROGSTAD: If it were as you say, why did you write to me as you did at the time?

MRS. LINDE: I could do nothing else. As I had to break with you, it was my duty also to put an end to all that you felt for me.

KROGSTAD (*wringing his hands*):   So that was it. And all this—only for the sake of money!

MRS. LINDE: You must not forget that I had a helpless mother and two little brothers. We couldn't wait for you, Nils; your prospects seemed hopeless then.

KROGSTAD: That may be so, but you had no right to throw me over for anyone else's sake.

MRS. LINDE: Indeed I don't know. Many a time did I ask myself if I had the right to do it.

KROGSTAD (*more gently*):   When I lost you, it was as if all the solid ground went from under my feet. Look at me now—I am a shipwrecked man clinging to a bit of wreckage.

MRS. LINDE: But help may be near.

KROGSTAD: It *was* near; but then you came and stood in my way.

MRS. LINDE: Unintentionally, Nils. It was only to-day that I learned it was your place I was going to take in the Bank.

KROGSTAD: I believe you, if you say so. But now that you know it, are you not going to give it up to me?

MRS. LINDE: No, because that would not benefit you in the least.

KROGSTAD: Oh, benefit, benefit — I would have done it whether or no.

MRS. LINDE: I have learned to act prudently. Life, and hard, bitter necessity have taught me that.

KROGSTAD: And life has taught me not to believe in fine speeches.

MRS. LINDE: Then life has taught you something very reasonable. But deeds you must believe in?

KROGSTAD: What do you mean by that?

MRS. LINDE: You said you were like a shipwrecked man clinging to some wreckage.

KROGSTAD: I had good reason to say so.

MRS. LINDE: Well, I am like a shipwrecked woman clinging to some wreckage — no one to mourn for, no one to care for.

KROGSTAD: It was your own choice.

MRS. LINDE: There was no other choice — then.

KROGSTAD: Well, what now?

MRS. LINDE: Nils, how would it be if we two shipwrecked people could join forces?

KROGSTAD: What are you saying?

MRS. LINDE: Two on the same piece of wreckage would stand a better chance than each on their own.

KROGSTAD: Christine!

MRS. LINDE: What do you suppose brought me to town?

KROGSTAD: Do you mean that you gave me a thought?

MRS. LINDE: I could not endure life without work. All my life, as long as I can remember, I have worked, and it has been my greatest and only pleasure. But now I am quite alone in the world — my life is so dreadfully empty and I feel so forsaken. There is not the least pleasure in working for one's self. Nils, give me someone and something to work for.

KROGSTAD: I don't trust that. It is nothing but a woman's overstrained sense of generosity that prompts you to make such an offer of yourself.

MRS. LINDE: Have you ever noticed anything of the sort in me?

KROGSTAD: Could you really do it? Tell me — do you know all about my past life?

MRS. LINDE: Yes.

KROGSTAD: And do you know what they think of me here?

MRS. LINDE: You seemed to me to imply that with me you might have been quite another man.

KROGSTAD: I am certain of it.

MRS. LINDE: Is it too late now?

KROGSTAD: Christine, are you saying this deliberately? Yes, I am sure you are. I see it in your face. Have you really the courage, then — ?

MRS. LINDE: I want to be a mother to someone, and your children need a mother. We two need each other. Nils, I have faith in your real character — I can dare anything together with you.

KROGSTAD (*grasps her hands*):   Thanks, thanks, Christine! Now I shall find a way to clear myself in the eyes of the world. Ah, but I forgot —

MRS. LINDE (*listening*):   Hush! The Tarantella! Go, go!

KROGSTAD: Why? What is it?

MRS. LINDE: Do you hear them up there? When that is over, we may expect them back.

KROGSTAD: Yes, yes—I will go. But it is all no use. Of course you are not aware what steps I have taken in the matter of the Helmers.

MRS. LINDE: Yes, I know all about that.

KROGSTAD: And in spite of that have you the courage to—?

MRS. LINDE: I understand very well to what lengths a man like you might be driven by despair.

KROGSTAD: If I could only undo what I have done!

MRS. LINDE: You cannot. Your letter is lying in the letter-box now.

KROGSTAD: Are you sure of that?

MRS. LINDE: Quite sure, but—

KROGSTAD (*with a searching look at her*):   Is that what it all means?—that you want to save your friend at any cost? Tell me frankly. Is that it?

MRS. LINDE: Nils, a woman who has once sold herself for another's sake, doesn't do it a second time.

KROGSTAD: I will ask for my letter back.

MRS. LINDE: No, no.

KROGSTAD: Yes, of course I will. I will wait here until Helmer comes; I will tell him he must give me my letter back—that it only concerns my dismissal— that he is not to read it—

MRS. LINDE: No, Nils, you must not recall your letter.

KROGSTAD: But, tell me, wasn't it for that very purpose that you asked me to meet you here?

MRS. LINDE: In my first moment of fright, it was. But twenty-four hours have elapsed since then, and in that time I have witnessed incredible things in this house. Helmer must know all about it. This unhappy secret must be disclosed; they must have a complete understanding between them, which is impossible with all this concealment and falsehood going on.

KROGSTAD: Very well, if you will take the responsibility. But there is one thing I can do in any case, and I shall do it at once.

MRS. LINDE (*listening*):   You must be quick and go! The dance is over; we are not safe a moment longer.

KROGSTAD: I will wait for you below.

MRS. LINDE: Yes, do. You must see me back to my door.

KROGSTAD: I have never had such an amazing piece of good fortune in my life! (*Goes out through the outer door. The door between the room and the hall remains open.*)

MRS. LINDE (*tidying up the room and laying her hat and cloak ready*):   What a difference! what a difference! Some-one to work for and live for—a home to bring comfort into. That I will do, indeed. I wish they would be quick and come—(*Listens.*) Ah, there they are now. I must put on my things. (*Takes up her hat and cloak. Helmer's and Nora's voices are heard outside; a key is turned, and Helmer brings Nora almost by force into the hall. She is in an Italian costume with a large black shawl around her; he is in evening dress, and a black domino° which is flying open.*)

NORA (*hanging back in the doorway, and struggling with him*):   No, no, no!— don't take me in. I want to go upstairs again; I don't want to leave so early.

HELMER: But, my dearest Nora—

NORA: Please, Torvald dear—please, *please*—only an hour more.

HELMER: Not a single minute, my sweet Nora. You know that was our agreement. Come along into the room; you are catching cold standing there. (*He brings her gently into the room, in spite of her resistance.*)

MRS. LINDE: Good-evening.

NORA: Christine!

HELMER: You here, so late, Mrs. Linde?

MRS. LINDE: Yes, you must excuse me; I was so anxious to see Nora in her dress.

NORA: Have you been sitting here waiting for me?

MRS. LINDE: Yes, unfortunately I came too late, you had already gone upstairs; and I thought I couldn't go away again without having seen you.

HELMER (*taking off Nora's shawl*):   Yes, take a good look at her. I think she is worth looking at. Isn't she charming, Mrs. Linde?

MRS. LINDE: Yes, indeed she is.

HELMER: Doesn't she look remarkably pretty? Everyone thought so at the dance. But she is terribly self-willed, this sweet little person. What are we to do with her? You will hardly believe that I had almost to bring her away by force.

NORA: Torvald, you will repent not having let me stay, even if it were only for half an hour.

HELMER: Listen to her, Mrs. Linde! She had danced her Tarantella, and it had been a tremendous success, as it deserved—although possibly the performance was a trifle too realistic—a little more so, I mean, than was strictly compatible with the limitations of art. But never mind about that! The chief thing is, she had made a success—she had made a tremendous success. Do you think I was going to let her remain there after that, and spoil the effect? No, indeed! I took my charming little Capri maiden—my capricious little Capri maiden, I should say—on my arm; took one quick turn round the room; a curtsey on either side, and, as they say in novels, the beautiful apparition disappeared. An exit ought always to be effective, Mrs. Linde; but that is what I cannot make Nora understand. Pooh! this room is hot. (*Throws his domino on a chair, and opens the door of his room.*) Hullo! it's all dark in here. Oh, of course—excuse me—. (*He goes in, and lights some candles.*)

NORA (*in a hurried and breathless whisper*):   Well?

MRS. LINDE (*in a low voice*):   I have had a talk with him.

NORA: Yes, and—

MRS. LINDE: Nora, you must tell your husband all about it.

NORA (*in an expressionless voice*):   I knew it.

---

domino: A loose cloak, worn with a mask for the upper part of the face at masquerades.

MRS. LINDE: You have nothing to be afraid of as far as Krogstad is concerned; but you must tell him.

NORA: I won't tell him.

MRS. LINDE: Then the letter will.

NORA: Thank you, Christine. Now I know what I must do. Hush—!

HELMER (*coming in again*):   Well, Mrs. Linde, have you admired her?

MRS. LINDE: Yes, and now I will say good-night.

HELMER: What, already? Is this yours, this knitting?

MRS. LINDE (*taking it*):   Yes, thank you, I had very nearly forgotten it.

HELMER: So you knit?

MRS. LINDE: Of course.

HELMER: Do you know, you ought to embroider.

MRS. LINDE: Really? Why?

HELMER: Yes, it's far more becoming. Let me show you. You hold the embroidery thus in your left hand, and use the needle with the right—like this—with a long, easy sweep. Do you see?

MRS. LINDE: Yes, perhaps—

HELMER: But in the case of knitting—that can never be anything but ungraceful; look here—the arms close together, the knitting-needles going up and down—it has a sort of Chinese effect—. That was really excellent champagne they gave us.

MRS. LINDE: Well,—good-night, Nora, and don't be self-willed any more.

HELMER: That's right, Mrs. Linde.

MRS. LINDE: Good-night, Mr. Helmer.

HELMER (*accompanying her to the door*):   Good-night, good-night. I hope you will get home all right. I should be very happy to—but you haven't any great distance to go. Good-night, good-night. (*She goes out; he shuts the door after her, and comes in again.*) Ah!—at last we have got rid of her. She is a frightful bore, that woman.

NORA: Aren't you very tired, Torvald?

HELMER: No, not in the least.

NORA: Nor sleepy?

HELMER: Not a bit. On the contrary, I feel extraordinarily lively. And you?—you really look both tired and sleepy.

NORA: Yes, I am very tired. I want to go to sleep at once.

HELMER: There, you see it was quite right of me not to let you stay there any longer.

NORA: Everything you do is quite right, Torvald.

HELMER (*kissing her on the forehead*):   Now my little skylark is speaking reasonably. Did you notice what good spirits Rank was in this evening?

NORA: Really? Was he? I didn't speak to him at all.

HELMER: And I very little, but I have not for a long time seen him in such good form. (*Looks for a while at her and then goes nearer to her.*) It is delightful to be at home by ourselves again, to be all alone with you—you fascinating, charming little darling!

NORA: Don't look at me like that, Torvald.

HELMER: Why shouldn't I look at my dearest treasure?—at all the beauty that is mine, all my very own?

NORA (*going to the other side of the table*):   You mustn't say things like that to me to-night.

HELMER (*following her*):   You have still got the Tarantella in your blood, I see. And it makes you more captivating than ever. Listen—the guests are beginning to go now. (*In a lower voice.*) Nora—soon the whole house will be quiet.

NORA: Yes, I hope so.

HELMER: Yes, my own darling Nora. Do you know, when I am out at a party with you like this, why I speak so little to you, keep away from you, and only send a stolen glance in your direction now and then?—do you know why I do that? It is because I make believe to myself that we are secretly in love, and you are my secretly promised bride, and that no one suspects there is anything between us.

NORA: Yes, yes—I know very well your thoughts are with me all the time.

HELMER: And when we are leaving, and I am putting the shawl over your beautiful young shoulders—on your lovely neck—then I imagine that you are my young bride and that we have just come from the wedding, and I am bringing you for the first time into our home—to be alone with you for the first time—quite alone with my shy little darling! All this evening I have longed for nothing but you. When I watched the seductive figures of the Tarantella, my blood was on fire; I could endure it no longer, and that was why I brought you down so early—

NORA: Go away, Torvald! You must let me go. I won't—

HELMER: What's that? You're joking, my little Nora! You won't—you won't? Am I not your husband—? (*A knock is heard at the outer door.*)

NORA (*starting*):   Did you hear—?

HELMER (*going into the hall*):   Who is it?

RANK (*outside*):   It is I. May I come in for a moment?

HELMER (*in a fretful whisper*):   Oh, what does he want now? (*Aloud.*) Wait a minute! (*Unlocks the door.*) Come, that's kind of you not to pass by our door.

RANK: I thought I heard your voice, and felt as if I should like to look in. (*With a swift glance round.*) Ah, yes!—these dear familiar rooms. You are very happy and cosy in here, you two.

HELMER: It seems to me that you looked after yourself pretty well upstairs too.

RANK: Excellently. Why shouldn't I? Why shouldn't one enjoy everything in this world?—at any rate as much as one can, and as long as one can. The wine was capital—

HELMER: Especially the champagne.

RANK: So you noticed that too? It is almost incredible how much I managed to put away!

NORA: Torvald drank a great deal of champagne to-night too.

RANK: Did he?

NORA: Yes, and he is always in such good spirits afterwards.

RANK: Well, why should one not enjoy a merry evening after a well-spent day?

HELMER: Well spent? I am afraid I can't take credit for that.

RANK (*clapping him on the back*): But I can, you know!

NORA: Doctor Rank, you must have been occupied with some scientific investigation to-day.

RANK: Exactly.

HELMER: Just listen!—little Nora talking about scientific investigations!

NORA: And may I congratulate you on the result?

RANK: Indeed you may.

NORA: Was it favourable, then?

RANK: The best possible, for both doctor and patient—certainty.

NORA (*quickly and searchingly*): Certainty?

RANK: Absolute certainty. So wasn't I entitled to make a merry evening of it after that?

NORA: Yes, you certainly were, Doctor Rank.

HELMER: I think so too, so long as you don't have to pay for it in the morning.

RANK: Oh well, one can't have anything in this life without paying for it.

NORA: Doctor Rank—are you fond of fancy-dress balls?

RANK: Yes, if there is a fine lot of pretty costumes.

NORA: Tell me—what shall we two wear at the next?

HELMER: Little featherbrain!—are you thinking of the next already?

RANK: We two? Yes, I can tell you. You shall go as a good fairy—

HELMER: Yes, but what do you suggest as an appropriate costume for that?

RANK: Let your wife go dressed just as she is in everyday life.

HELMER: That was really very prettily turned. But can't you tell us what you will be?

RANK: Yes, my dear friend, I have quite made up my mind about that.

HELMER: Well?

RANK: At the next fancy-dress ball I shall be invisible.

HELMER: That's a good joke!

RANK: There is a big black hat—have you never heard of hats that make you invisible? If you put one on, no one can see you.

HELMER (*suppressing a smile*): Yes, you are quite right.

RANK: But I am clean forgetting what I came for. Helmer, give me a cigar—one of the dark Havanas.

HELMER: With the greatest pleasure. (*Offers him his case.*)

RANK (*takes a cigar and cuts off the end*): Thanks.

NORA (*striking a match*): Let me give you a light.

RANK: Thank you. (*She holds the match for him to light his cigar.*) And now good-bye!

HELMER: Good-bye, good-bye, dear old man!

NORA: Sleep well, Doctor Rank.

RANK: Thank you for that wish.

NORA: Wish me the same.

RANK: You? Well, if you want me to sleep well! And thanks for the light. (*He nods to them both and goes out.*)

HELMER (*in a subdued voice*): He has drunk more than he ought.

NORA (*absently*):   Maybe. (*Helmer takes a bunch of keys out of his pocket and goes into the hall.*) Torvald! what are you going to do there?

HELMER: Empty the letter-box; it is quite full; there will be no room to put the newspaper in to-morrow morning.

NORA: Are you going to work to-night?

HELMER: You know quite well I'm not. What is this? Someone has been at the lock.

NORA: At the lock—?

HELMER: Yes, someone has. What can it mean? I should never have thought the maid—. Here is a broken hairpin. Nora, it is one of yours.

NORA (*quickly*):   Then it must have been the children—

HELMER: Then you must get them out of those ways. There, at last I have got it open. (*Takes out the contents of the letter-box, and calls to the kitchen.*) Helen!—Helen, put out the light over the front door. (*Goes back into the room and shuts the door into the hall. He holds out his hand full of letters.*) Look at that—look what a heap of them there are. (*Turning them over.*) What on earth is that?

NORA (*at the window*):   The letter—No! Torvald, no!

HELMER: Two cards—of Rank's.

NORA: Of Doctor Rank's?

HELMER (*looking at them*):   Doctor Rank. They were on the top. He must have put them in when he went out.

NORA: Is there anything written on them?

HELMER: There is a black cross over the name. Look there—what an uncomfortable idea! It looks as if he were announcing his own death.

NORA: It is just what he is doing.

HELMER: What? Do you know anything about it? Has he said anything to you?

NORA: Yes. He told me that when the cards came it would be his leave-taking from us. He means to shut himself up and die.

HELMER: My poor old friend! Certainly I knew we should not have him very long with us. But so soon! And so he hides himself away like a wounded animal.

NORA: If it has to happen, it is best it should be without a word—don't you think so, Torvald?

HELMER (*walking up and down*):   He had so grown into our lives. I can't think of him as having gone out of them. He, with his sufferings and his loneliness, was like a cloudy background to our sunlit happiness. Well, perhaps it is best so. For him, anyway. (*Standing still.*) And perhaps for us too, Nora. We two are thrown quite upon each other now. (*Puts his arms round her.*) My darling wife, I don't feel as if I could hold you tight enough. Do you know, Nora, I have often wished that you might be threatened by some great danger, so that I might risk my life's blood, and everything, for your sake.

NORA (*disengages herself, and says firmly and decidedly*):   Now you must read your letters, Torvald.

HELMER: No, no; not to-night. I want to be with you, my darling wife.

NORA: With the thought of your friend's death—

HELMER: You are right, it has affected us both. Something ugly has come between us—the thought of the horrors of death. We must try and rid our
minds of that. Until then—we will each go to our own room.

NORA (*hanging on his neck*):   Good-night, Torvald—Good-night!

HELMER (*kissing her on the forehead*):   Good-night, my little singing-bird. Sleep
sound, Nora. Now I will read my letters through. (*He takes his letters and
goes into his room, shutting the door after him.*)

NORA (*gropes distractedly about, seizes Helmer's domino, throws it round her, while
she says in quick, hoarse, spasmodic whispers*):   Never to see him again.
Never! Never! (*Puts her shawl over her head.*) Never to see my children again
either—never again. Never! Never!—Ah! the icy, black water—the unfathomable depths—If only it were over! He has got it now—now he is
reading it. Good-bye, Torvald and my children! (*She is about to rush out
through the hall, when Helmer opens his door hurriedly and stands with an open
letter in his hand.*)

HELMER: Nora!

NORA: Ah!—

HELMER: What is this? Do you know what is in this letter?

NORA: Yes, I know. Let me go! Let me get out!

HELMER (*holding her back*):   Where are you going?

NORA (*trying to get free*):   You shan't save me, Torvald!

HELMER (*reeling*):   True? Is this true, that I read here? Horrible! No, no—it is
impossible that it can be true.

NORA: It is true. I have loved you above everything else in the world.

HELMER: Oh, don't let us have any silly excuses.

NORA (*taking a step towards him*):   Torvald—!

HELMER: Miserable creature—what have you done?

NORA: Let me go. You shall not suffer for my sake. You shall not take it upon
yourself.

HELMER: No tragedy airs, please. (*Locks the hall door.*) Here you shall stay and
give me an explanation. Do you understand what you have done? Answer
me! Do you understand what you have done?

NORA (*looks steadily at him and says with a growing look of coldness in her
face*):   Yes, now I am beginning to understand thoroughly.

HELMER (*walking about the room*):   What a horrible awakening! All these eight
years—she who was my joy and pride—a hypocrite, a liar—worse,
worse—a criminal! The unutterable ugliness of it all!—For shame! For
shame! (*Nora is silent and looks steadily at him. He stops in front of her.*) I
ought to have suspected that something of the sort would happen. I ought
to have foreseen it. All your father's want of principle—be silent!—all
your father's want of principle has come out in you. No religion, no morality, no sense of duty—. How I am punished for having winked at what he
did! I did it for your sake, and this is how you repay me.

NORA: Yes, that's just it.

HELMER: Now you have destroyed all my happiness. You have ruined all my
future. It is horrible to think of! I am in the power of an unscrupulous

man; he can do what he likes with me, ask anything he likes of me, give me any orders he pleases—I dare not refuse. And I must sink to such miserable depths because of a thoughtless woman!

NORA: When I am out of the way, you will be free.

HELMER: No fine speeches, please. Your father had always plenty of those ready, too. What good would it be to me if you were out of the way, as you say? Not the slightest. He can make the affair known everywhere; and if he does, I may be falsely suspected of having been a party to your criminal action. Very likely people will think I was behind it all—that it was I who prompted you! And I have to thank you for all this—you whom I have cherished during the whole of our married life. Do you understand now what it is you have done for me?

NORA (*coldly and quietly*):   Yes.

HELMER: It is so incredible that I can't take it in. But we must come to some understanding. Take off that shawl. Take it off, I tell you. I must try and appease him some way or another. The matter must be hushed up at any cost. And as for you and me, it must appear as if everything between us were just as before—but naturally only in the eyes of the world. You will still remain in my house, that is a matter of course. But I shall not allow you to bring up the children; I dare not trust them to you. To think that I should be obliged to say so to one whom I have loved so dearly, and whom I still—. No, that is all over. From this moment happiness is not the question; all that concerns us is to save the remains, the fragments, the appearance—

A ring is heard at the front-door bell.

HELMER (*with a start*):   What is that? So late! Can the worst—? Can he—? Hide yourself, Nora. Say you are ill.

Nora stands motionless. Helmer goes and unlocks the hall door.

MAID (*half-dressed, comes to the door*):   A letter for the mistress.

HELMER: Give it to me. (*Takes the letter, and shuts the door.*) Yes, it is from him. You shall not have it; I will read it myself.

NORA: Yes, read it.

HELMER (*standing by the lamp*):   I scarcely have the courage to do it. It may mean ruin for both of us. No, I must know. (*Tears open the letter, runs his eye over a few lines, looks at a paper enclosed, and gives a shout of joy.*) Nora! (*She looks at him questioningly.*) Nora!—No, I must read it once again—. Yes, it is true! I am saved! Nora, I am saved!

NORA: And I?

HELMER: You too, of course; we are both saved, both you and I. Look, he sends you your bond back. He says he regrets and repents—that a happy change in his life—never mind what he says! We are saved, Nora! No one can do anything to you. Oh, Nora, Nora!—no, first I must destroy these hateful things. Let me see—. (*Takes a look at the bond.*) No, no, I won't look at it. The whole thing shall be nothing but a bad dream to me. (*Tears up the bond*

and both letters, throws them all into the stove, and watches them burn.)
There—now it doesn't exist any longer. He says that since Christmas Eve
you—. These must have been three dreadful days for you, Nora.

NORA: I have fought a hard fight these three days.

HELMER: And suffered agonies, and seen no way out but—. No, we won't call
any of the horrors to mind. We will only shout with joy, and keep saying,
"It's all over! It's all over!" Listen to me, Nora. You don't seem to realise that
it is all over. What is this?—such a cold, set face! My poor little Nora, I
quite understand; you don't feel as if you could believe that I have forgiven
you. But it is true, Nora, I swear it; I have forgiven you everything. I know
that what you did, you did out of love for me.

NORA: That is true.

HELMER: You have loved me as a wife ought to love her husband. Only you
had not sufficient knowledge to judge of the means you used. But do
you suppose you are any the less dear to me, because you don't understand
how to act on your own responsibility? No, no; only lean on me; I will advise you and direct you. I should not be a man if this womanly helplessness
did not just give you a double attractiveness in my eyes. You must not think
anymore about the hard things I said in my first moment of consternation,
when I thought everything was going to overwhelm me. I have forgiven
you, Nora; I swear to you I have forgiven you.

NORA: Thank you for your forgiveness. (*She goes out through the door to the
right.*)

HELMER: No, don't go—. (*Looks in.*) What are you doing in there?

NORA (*from within*): Taking off my fancy dress.

HELMER (*standing at the open door*): Yes, do. Try and calm yourself, and make
your mind easy again, my frightened little singing-bird. Be at rest, and feel
secure; I have broad wings to shelter you under. (*Walks up and down by the
door.*) How warm and cosy our home is, Nora. Here is shelter for you; here
I will protect you like a hunted dove that I have saved from a hawk's claws;
I will bring peace to your poor beating heart. It will come, little by little,
Nora, believe me. To-morrow morning you will look upon it all quite differently; soon everything will be just as it was before. Very soon you won't
need me to assure you that I have forgiven you; you will yourself feel the
certainty that I have done so. Can you suppose I should ever think of such
a thing as repudiating you, or even reproaching you? You have no idea
what a true man's heart is like, Nora. There is something so indescribably
sweet and satisfying, to a man, in the knowledge that he has forgiven his
wife—forgiven her freely, and with all his heart. It seems as if that had
made her, as it were, doubly his own; he has given her a new life, so to
speak; and she has in a way become both wife and child to him. So you
shall be for me after this, my little scared, helpless darling. Have no anxiety
about anything, Nora; only be frank and open with me, and I will serve as
will and conscience both to you—. What is this? Not gone to bed? Have
you changed your things?

NORA (*in everyday dress*): Yes, Torvald, I have changed my things now.

HELMER:　But what for?—so late as this.

NORA:　I shall not sleep to-night.

HELMER:　But, my dear Nora—

NORA (*looking at her watch*):　It is not so very late. Sit down here, Torvald. You and I have much to say to one another. (*She sits down at one side of the table.*)

HELMER:　Nora—what is this?—this cold, set face?

NORA:　Sit down. It will take some time; I have a lot to talk over with you.

HELMER (*sits down at the opposite side of the table*):　You alarm me, Nora!—and I don't understand you.

NORA:　No, that is just it. You don't understand me, and I have never understood you either—before to-night. No, you mustn't interrupt me. You must simply listen to what I say. Torvald, this is a settling of accounts.

HELMER:　What do you mean by that?

NORA (*after a short silence*):　Isn't there one thing that strikes you as strange in our sitting here like this?

HELMER:　What is that?

NORA:　We have been married now eight years. Does it not occur to you that this is the first time we two, you and I, husband and wife, have had a serious conversation?

HELMER:　What do you mean by serious?

NORA:　In all these eight years—longer than that—from the very beginning of our acquaintance, we have never exchanged a word on any serious subject.

HELMER:　Was it likely that I would be continually and forever telling you about worries that you could not help me to bear?

NORA:　I am not speaking about business matters. I say that we have never sat down in earnest together to try and get at the bottom of anything.

HELMER:　But, dearest Nora, would it have been any good to you?

NORA:　That is just it; you have never understood me. I have been greatly wronged, Torvald—first by papa and then by you.

HELMER:　What! By us two—by us two, who have loved you better than anyone else in the world?

NORA (*shaking her head*):　You have never loved me. You have only thought it pleasant to be in love with me.

HELMER:　Nora, what do I hear you saying?

NORA:　It is perfectly true, Torvald. When I was at home with papa, he told me his opinion about everything, and so I had the same opinions; and if I differed from him I concealed the fact, because he would not have liked it. He called me his doll-child, and he played with me just as I used to play with my dolls. And when I came to live with you—

HELMER:　What sort of an expression is that to use about our marriage?

NORA (*undisturbed*):　I mean that I was simply transferred from papa's hands into yours. You arranged everything according to your own taste, and so I got the same tastes as you—or else I pretended to, I am really not quite sure which—I think sometimes the one and sometimes the other. When I look back on it, it seems to me as if I had been living here like a poor woman—just from hand to mouth. I have existed merely to perform tricks for you, Torvald. But you would have it so. You and papa have committed a great sin against me. It is your fault that I have made nothing of my life.

HELMER: How unreasonable and how ungrateful you are, Nora! Have you not been happy here?

NORA: No, I have never been happy. I thought I was, but it has never really been so.

HELMER: Not—not happy!

NORA: No, only merry. And you have always been so kind to me. But our home has been nothing but a playroom. I have been your doll-wife, just as at home I was papa's doll-child; and here the children have been my dolls. I thought it great fun when you played with me, just as they thought it great fun when I played with them. That is what our marriage has been, Torvald.

HELMER: There is some truth in what you say—exaggerated and strained as your view of it is. But for the future it shall be different. Playtime shall be over, and lesson-time shall begin.

NORA: Whose lessons? Mine, or the children's?

HELMER: Both yours and the children's, my darling Nora.

NORA: Alas, Torvald, you are not the man to educate me into being a proper wife for you.

HELMER: And you can say that!

NORA: And I—how am I fitted to bring up the children?

HELMER: Nora!

NORA: Didn't you say so yourself a little while ago—that you dare not trust me to bring them up?

HELMER: In a moment of anger! Why do you pay any heed to that?

NORA: Indeed, you were perfectly right. I am not fit for the task. There is another task I must undertake first. I must try and educate myself—you are not the man to help me in that. I must do that for myself. And that is why I am going to leave you now.

HELMER (*springing up*):   What do you say?

NORA: I must stand quite alone, if I am to understand myself and everything about me. It is for that reason that I cannot remain with you any longer.

HELMER: Nora, Nora!

NORA: I am going away from here now, at once. I am sure Christine will take me in for the night—

HELMER: You are out of your mind! I won't allow it! I forbid you!

NORA: It is no use forbidding me anything any longer. I will take with me what belongs to myself. I will take nothing from you, either now or later.

HELMER: What sort of madness is this!

NORA: To-morrow I shall go home—I mean, to my old home. It will be easiest for me to find something to do there.

HELMER: You blind, foolish woman!

NORA: I must try and get some sense, Torvald.

HELMER: To desert your home, your husband and your children! And you don't consider what people will say!

NORA: I cannot consider that at all. I only know that it is necessary for me.

HELMER: It's shocking. This is how you would neglect your most sacred duties.

NORA: What do you consider my most sacred duties?

HELMER: Do I need to tell you that? Are they not your duties to your husband and your children?

NORA: I have other duties just as sacred.

HELMER: That you have not. What duties could those be?

NORA: Duties to myself.

HELMER: Before all else, you are a wife and a mother.

NORA: I don't believe that any longer. I believe that before all else I am a reasonable human being, just as you are—or, at all events, that I must try and become one. I know quite well, Torvald, that most people would think you right, and that views of that kind are to be found in books; but I can no longer content myself with what most people say, or with what is found in books. I must think over things for myself and get to understand them.

HELMER: Can you not understand your place in your own home? Have you not a reliable guide in such matters as that?—have you no religion?

NORA: I am afraid, Torvald, I do not exactly know what religion is.

HELMER: What are you saying?

NORA: I know nothing but what the clergyman said, when I went to be confirmed. He told us that religion was this, and that, and the other. When I am away from all this, and am alone, I will look into that matter too. I will see if what the clergyman said is true, or at all events if it is true for me.

HELMER: This is unheard of in a girl of your age! But if religion cannot lead you aright, let me try and awaken your conscience. I suppose you have some moral sense? Or—answer me—am I to think you have none?

NORA: I assure you, Torvald, that is not an easy question to answer. I really don't know. The thing perplexes me altogether. I only know that you and I look at it in quite a different light. I am learning, too, that the law is quite another thing from what I supposed; but I find it impossible to convince myself that the law is right. According to it a woman has no right to spare her old dying father, or to save her husband's life. I can't believe that.

HELMER: You talk like a child. You don't understand the conditions of the world in which you live.

NORA: No, I don't. But now I am going to try. I am going to see if I can make out who is right, the world or I.

HELMER: You are ill, Nora; you are delirious; I almost think you are out of your mind.

NORA: I have never felt my mind so clear and certain as to-night.

HELMER: And is it with a clear and certain mind that you forsake your husband and your children?

NORA: Yes, it is.

HELMER: Then there is only one possible explanation.

NORA: What is that?

HELMER: You do not love me anymore.

NORA: No, that is just it.

HELMER: Nora!—and you can say that?

NORA: It gives me great pain, Torvald, for you have always been so kind to me, but I cannot help it. I do not love you any more.

HELMER (*regaining his composure*):   Is that a clear and certain conviction too?

NORA: Yes, absolutely clear and certain. That is the reason why I will not stay here any longer.

HELMER: And can you tell me what I have done to forfeit your love?

NORA: Yes, indeed I can. It was to-night, when the wonderful thing did not happen; then I saw you were not the man I had thought you.

HELMER: Explain yourself better. I don't understand you.

NORA: I have waited so patiently for eight years; for, goodness knows, I knew very well that wonderful things don't happen every day. Then this horrible misfortune came upon me; and then I felt quite certain that the wonderful thing was going to happen at last. When Krogstad's letter was lying out there, never for a moment did I imagine that you would consent to accept this man's conditions. I was so absolutely certain that you would say to him: Publish the thing to the whole world. And when that was done—

HELMER: Yes, what then?—when I had exposed my wife to shame and disgrace?

NORA: When that was done, I was so absolutely certain, you would come forward and take everything upon yourself, and say: I am the guilty one.

HELMER: Nora—!

NORA: You mean that I would never have accepted such a sacrifice on your part? No, of course not. But what would my assurances have been worth against yours? That was the wonderful thing which I hoped for and feared; and it was to prevent that, that I wanted to kill myself.

HELMER: I would gladly work night and day for you, Nora—bear sorrow and want for your sake. But no man would sacrifice his honour for the one he loves.

NORA: It is a thing hundreds of thousands of women have done.

HELMER: Oh, you think and talk like a heedless child.

NORA: Maybe. But you neither think nor talk like the man I could bind myself to. As soon as your fear was over—and it was not fear for what threatened me, but for what might happen to you—when the whole thing was past, as far as you were concerned it was exactly as if nothing at all had happened. Exactly as before, I was your little skylark, your doll, which you would in future treat with doubly gentle care, because it was so brittle and fragile. (*Getting up.*) Torvald—it was then it dawned upon me that for eight years I had been living here with a strange man, and had borne him three children—. Oh, I can't bear to think of it! I could tear myself into little bits!

HELMER (*sadly*):   I see, I see. An abyss has opened between us—there is no denying it. But, Nora, would it not be possible to fill it up?

NORA: As I am now, I am no wife for you.

HELMER: I have it in me to become a different man.

NORA: Perhaps—if your doll is taken away from you.

HELMER: But to part!—to part from you! No, no, Nora, I can't understand that idea.

NORA (*going out to the right*):   That makes it all the more certain that it must be done. (*She comes back with her cloak and hat and a small bag which she puts on a chair by the table.*)

HELMER: Nora, Nora, not now! Wait until to-morrow.

NORA (*putting on her cloak*):   I cannot spend the night in a strange man's room.

HELMER: But can't we live here like brother and sister—?

NORA (*putting on her hat*):   You know very well that would not last long. (*Puts the shawl round her.*) Good-bye, Torvald. I won't see the little ones. I know they are in better hands than mine. As I am now, I can be of no use to them.

HELMER: But some day, Nora—some day?

NORA: How can I tell? I have no idea what is going to become of me.

HELMER: But you are my wife, whatever becomes of you.

NORA: Listen, Torvald. I have heard that when a wife deserts her husband's house, as I am doing now, he is legally freed from all obligations towards her. In any case, I set you free from all your obligations. You are not to feel yourself bound in the slightest way, any more than I shall. There must be perfect freedom on both sides. See, here is your ring back. Give me mine.

HELMER: That too?

NORA: That too.

HELMER: Here it is.

NORA: That's right. Now it is all over. I have put the keys here. The maids know all about everything in the house—better than I do. To-morrow, after I have left her, Christine will come here and pack up my own things that I brought with me from home. I will have them sent after me.

HELMER: All over! All over!—Nora, shall you never think of me again?

NORA: I know I shall often think of you, the children, and this house.

HELMER: May I write to you, Nora?

NORA: No—never. You must not do that.

HELMER: But at least let me send you—

NORA: Nothing—nothing—

HELMER: Let me help you if you are in want.

NORA: No. I can receive nothing from a stranger.

HELMER: Nora—can I never be anything more than a stranger to you?

NORA (*taking her bag*):   Ah, Torvald, the most wonderful thing of all would have to happen.

HELMER: Tell me what that would be!

NORA: Both you and I would have to be so changed that—. Oh, Torvald, I don't believe any longer in wonderful things happening.

HELMER: But I will believe in it. Tell me! So changed that—?

NORA: That our life together would be a real wedlock. Good-bye. (*She goes out through the hall.*)

HELMER (*sinks down on a chair at the door and buries his face in his hands*):   Nora! Nora! (*Looks round, and rises.*) Empty. She is gone. (*A hope flashes across his mind.*) The most wonderful thing of all—?

The sound of a door shutting is heard from below.   [1879]

≣ THINKING ABOUT THE TEXT

1. Critics disagree about the necessity for Nora's leaving. What would your advice to her be? One critic thinks she has to leave because Torvald is impossible. What do you think?

2. Do you find credible the change in Nora's character from the first scene to the last? Do you know people who have transformed themselves?

3. Is Torvald in love with Nora in the first act? Explain. Is Nora in love with him in the first act? What is your idea of love in a marriage?

4. An early critic of the play claims that it is a comedy. Is this possible? How would you characterize it? Is it an optimistic or a pessimistic play? Is it tragic?

5. A few critics think Nora will return. Do you think this is possible? Under what conditions would you counsel her to do so? Do you think the "door heard 'round the world" had a positive or a negative effect on marriage?

HENRIK IBSEN
Memorandum

Ibsen's intentions in writing A Doll's House *have been widely debated from the opening of the play in 1879. In a speech given to the Norwegian Association for Women's Rights twenty years later, Ibsen claimed he was not specifically working for women's rights, but rather trying to give a "description of humanity." Nevertheless, the following, written before the production, clearly seems to contradict that.*

Here is the first memorandum:

NOTES FOR THE TRAGEDY OF TO-DAY

ROME, 19/10/78.

There are two kinds of spiritual laws, two kinds of conscience, one in men and a quite different one in women. They do not understand each other; but the woman is judged in practical life according to the man's law, as if she were not a woman but a man.

The wife in the play finds herself at last entirely at sea as to what is right and what wrong; natural feeling on the one side, and belief in authority on the other, leave her in utter bewilderment.

A woman cannot be herself in the society of to-day, which is exclusively a masculine society, with laws written by men, and with accusers and judges who judge feminine conduct from the masculine standpoint.   *[1878]*

≡ **THINKING ABOUT THE TEXT**

1. How can Torvald be a good example of Ibsen's point in the last paragraph?

2. Give a specific example from the play that illustrates Ibsen's point about Nora in the second paragraph.

3. How might Ibsen's point still be applicable today?

AUGUST STRINDBERG
Woman in a Doll's House

August Strindberg (1849–1912), one of the most celebrated writers in Swedish literature, was born in Stockholm and described his childhood as subject to "emotional insecurity, poverty, religious fanaticism and neglect." Strindberg is known primarily as a naturalist playwright. Miss Julie *(1888) and* The Stronger *(1889) are his most famous dramas. Eugene O'Neill, in his Nobel Prize acceptance speech said Strindberg was "that greatest genius of all modern dramatists." Strindberg had a troubled relationship with women, and some critics see him as misogynistic. The following essay was written as a preface to* Getting Married *(1884), a collection of stories. Some critics believe Strindberg was furious with Ibsen for encouraging "the new woman of the nineteenth century to focus on the injustices of marriage in a male-dominant society."*

Let us now take a look at how, for some unknown and incomprehensible reason, Ibsen has caricatured the cultured man and woman in his play *A Doll's House*, which has become the gospel of all the zealots for the Woman Question.

A Doll's House is a play. Perhaps it was written for a great actress whose performance of a sphinx-like part could be guaranteed to be a success. The author has done the husband a great injustice. He has done nothing to help him by making excuses for him on the grounds of inherited characteristics, as he has for his wife, and the excuses he makes for her he presses home over and over again when he talks about her father. But let us carefully examine this Nora, whom all our depraved cultured women have adopted as their ideal.

In the first act she lies to her husband. She conceals her forgery, she smuggles away some cakes, she behaves shiftily over all kinds of simple matters, apparently because she has a taste for lying. Her husband, on the other hand, openly confides everything to her, even the affairs of his Bank, which shows that he treats her as his true wife. She, not he, is the one who never tells anything. It is consequently a lie to say that he treats her like a doll, but true to say that she treats him like one. Surely no one believes that Nora did not know what she was doing when she committed forgery? Perhaps when they sit in the stalls and see an appealing actress in the footlights. I do not believe myself that she committed forgery *exclu-*

sively for her husband's sake, for she tells us herself how tremendously she enjoyed their journey to Italy. No law, and no lawyer would accept that as an excuse. Thus we see that Nora is no saint; at best she is an accomplice who has also enjoyed the fruits of the theft. She incriminates herself. The author unintentionally gives her husband a further opportunity of showing how much he trusts and respects his wife when he lets him discuss with Nora the question of filling a vacancy at the Bank. But what a tyrant he is when he refuses to engage a forger as Head Clerk! What would Nora have said if Mr. Helmer had wanted to dismiss a maid? That would have been a very different story.

Then comes the scene in which she wants to borrow money from the syphilitic Dr. Rank. Nora really is sweet in this scene. As a prelude to her negotiations about the money she shows him her flesh-colored stockings.

> *Nora:* "Aren't they pretty? Of course it's dark in here now, but tomorrow.—No no, no, you're only allowed to see the feet. Oh well, I'll let you see the upper part too!"
>
> *Rank:* "Hm!"
>
> *Nora:* "Why are you looking so disapproving? Don't you think they'll suit me?"
>
> *Rank:* "I'm not qualified to express an opinion on that subject."
>
> *Nora:* (looks at him for a moment) "Shame on you!" (strikes him lightly on the ear with the stockings). "Take this then!" (Packs up the stockings.)
>
> *Rank:* "What are the other delights I'm to be allowed to see?"
>
> *Nora:* "You're so naughty I shan't let you see another thing." (She hums a little and looks for something in the box.)

As far as I can see Nora is offering herself—in return for hard cash. That   5
is idealistic and charming, of course. All done out of love for her husband. To save him! But go to her husband and confess her dilemma, oh no, that would be too much for her pride! In Nora's language: she was not yet quite certain that he would respond by showing her the miracle of miracles.

Then comes the tarantella scene, which is introduced in order to throw a distorting light upon Helmer. The audience forgets that Nora is a hussy whom Helmer treats as a sensible woman, and is only allowed to see Helmer treating her *merely* as a doll. This is a dishonest scene, but it is very effective. In a word: it is good *theatre*.

That Helmer woos his wife that night simply shows that he is young, and that she is young. But the author makes it show that Helmer—who has not the least suspicion of the dirty game that Nora is playing—is nothing more than a sensual creature, sensual through and through, who has no appreciation whatever of his excellent wife's spiritual qualities, which she has not deigned to reveal, and this gives Nora a false halo of martyrdom. This is the most dishonest scene that Ibsen has ever written. After it comes the dénouement, which is a fine muddle, with a great deal of misrepresentation and many lies. Mr. Helmer wakes up, and finds that the wife to whom he is bound is a liar and a hypocrite. But the audience has been so impregnated with compassion for Nora that it thinks Helmer is wrong. If Helmer had witnessed the scene with the stockings he would not have begged Nora to stay, but of course he had not. Helmer learns that he, his wife, and his children have escaped social death and ruin. This makes him happy. Put your hand on your heart, you father of a family, and ask yourself if you would not be happy if you heard that your beloved wife, the mother of your children, was not going to be put into prison after all. But these feelings are too mundane. You must reach higher. Right up to the idealist's heaven of lies. Helmer must be chastised. He is the criminal. Yet all the same he speaks kindly to his deceitful wife. — "Oh," he says, "these must have been three dreadful days for you, Nora." But then the author regrets having been fair to the poor fellow, and puts some untrue words into his mouth. Of course it is clumsy of Helmer to tell Nora that he forgives her. And for her to accept forgiveness from one who has always trusted her, while she has lied to him would be far too simple-minded. No, Nora has grander ideas. She is so magnanimous about forgetting the past that she forgets everything that happened in the first act. This is what she now says, and the stalls have forgotten the first act too, for their handkerchiefs are out.

> *Nora:* "Doesn't it occur to you that this is the first time that we two, husband and wife, have talked seriously to one another?"

Helmer is so taken aback by this mendacious question that he (or the author!) answers: "Seriously — what do you mean by seriously?" — The author has achieved his object, Helmer has been made to look a fool. He should have answered: "No, my little pet, it doesn't occur to me at all. We talked very seriously together when our children were born, for we talked about their future. We talked very seriously when you wanted to install the forger, Krogstad, as head clerk in the Bank. We talked very seriously when my life was in danger, and about giving Mrs. Linde a job, and about running the house, and about your dead father, and our syphilitic friend Dr. Rank. We have talked seriously for eight long years, but we have joked too, and we were right to do so, for life isn't only a serious business. We could indeed have had more serious talk if you'd been kind enough to tell me of your worries, but you were too proud, for you preferred to be my doll rather than my friend." But Mr. Ibsen does not allow Helmer to say these sensible things, for he must be shown to be a fool, and Nora must be allowed her most brilliant answer, which will be quoted for twenty-five years. This is her reply:

> *Nora:* "For eight (8!) long years — why longer — from the very first time we met, we have never exchanged a serious word on a serious matter."

—But now, true to his unfortunate role of fool, Mr. Helmer answers: "Would you have liked me to be forever telling you of problems that you wouldn't have been able to help me with?" It is kind of Helmer to say this, but it is not honest, for he should have turned on her for not confiding in him. This scene is absurdly false. After it Nora has some very fine (French) replies, which consist of such hollow wisdom that they vanish when you blow at them.

> *Nora:* "You have never loved me. You have only thought it amusing to be in love with me!"

What is the difference? She also says: "You have never understood me!" 10
Not an easy thing for Helmer to do as she has always deceived him. Then poor
Helmer is made to say some very stupid things, like: "I'm going to educate you."
That is surely the last thing a man should say to a woman. But Mr. Helmer
must be stupid, for the end is drawing near, and Nora is going to "turn the
screw." At that Helmer weakens. He begs for forgiveness; forgiveness because
she has committed forgery, because she has lied, for all her faults.

Then Nora says a few sensible things. She wants to give up her marriage in
order to find herself. The question is whether she could not do that just as well
in the same house as her children, in contact with the realities of life, and while
struggling with her love for Helmer, for her love will not die instantaneously
any more than any other love. But this is a question of taste. When she says
that she is unfit to bring up her children she is lying, for not long before she had
put herself on a pretty high pedestal when castigating the innocent Helmer. To
be logical she ought to have stayed with her children if she really thought her
husband was such a dolt that he would not be able to grasp the "miracle." For
how could she leave the education of her children to such a poor specimen? All
her babbling about the "miracle" that would have happened if Helmer had
taken the blame for her crime upon himself is such romantic nonsense that it
does not deserve discussion. That "hundreds of thousands of women" have
sacrificed themselves for their husbands is a compliment to the ladies that
Ibsen should be too old to pay. Nora rambles on pell-mell: she has loved him, he
has loved her, and yet she can say that for eight years she has been a stranger
to him, and borne three children to a man who has been a stranger to her.
Helmer agrees that he has not been perfect, and promises to reform. This is
handsome of him and there seems to be every guarantee that things will be
better in the future than they have been in the past. But of course this will not
do in a play. The curtain must come down on a Bang. So Nora proves (?) that
she has been a doll. Had it not been Helmer who decided where the furniture
should stand? Maybe. But if only the mistress of the house had deigned to make
her wishes known there would have been no doubt about who was the master.

Why did she not do so? Probably because she thought it did not matter, and
she may have been right. If Nora was a doll, then upon my word it was not
Helmer's fault, for he had always shown that he trusted her as a man should
trust his wife. But this was not what Ibsen wanted to prove, he wanted to prove
the opposite, but he was not strong enough to do so, for he did not believe in his
task, and his sense of justice broke through from time to time.

What its author himself really meant by *A Doll's House* we shall never know.
The fact that it gave the impression of being, and was generally accepted as a
manifesto for the oppressed woman, immediately raised a storm in which the
steadiest people lost their heads. For the play proves the direct opposite of what it
is intended to prove. Or is it that the whole play is a proof of the danger of writing
plays on serious subjects? Or, to take another point of view altogether: is it in fact
not a defense of the oppressed woman, but simply an illustration of the effect of
heredity upon character? If this is the case then the author should have been
honorable enough to give Helmer's heredity as an excuse for his behavior. Or is it

Nora's bad upbringing? She herself places a lot of the blame on this. Why then cannot Helmer blame his bad upbringing? Or is it nothing more than a play, pure and simple, an example of our modern courtship of the ladies? If so it should be put among the plays classed as "Public Entertainments," and not be regarded as a matter for serious discussion, still less have the honor of setting the two halves of humanity against each other.   [1884]

≡ THINKING ABOUT THE TEXT

1. What specific evidence is there that Strindberg might be misogynistic?
2. Point out instances of Strindberg's sarcasm and irony.
3. What are some specific complaints Strindberg has against Nora? What do you think of their validity?

EMMA GOLDMAN
Review of *A Doll's House*

Emma Goldman (1869–1940), a leading radical activist, thinker, and writer in the first half of the twentieth century, was born in Russia and immigrated to the United States in 1885. She agitated passionately for women's and worker's rights. She was deported to Russia in 1919 for being an anarchist but left, eventually becoming a British citizen. She began the radical journal Mother Earth *and wrote influential books such as* Anarchism and Other Essays *(1910) and* The Social Significance of the Modern Drama *(1914), from which the following selection is taken.*

In *A Doll's House* Ibsen returns to the subject so vital to him — the Social Lie and Duty — this time as manifesting themselves in the sacred institution of the home and in the position of woman in her gilded cage.

   Nora is the beloved, adored wife of *Torvald Helmer*. He is an admirable man, rigidly honest, of high moral ideals, and passionately devoted to his wife and children. In short, a good man and an enviable husband. Almost every mother would be proud of such a match for her daughter, and the latter would consider herself fortunate to become the wife of such a man.

   Nora, too, considers herself fortunate. Indeed, she worships her husband, believes in him implicitly, and is sure that if ever her safety should be menaced, *Torvald*, her idol, her god, would perform the miracle.

   When a woman loves as *Nora* does, nothing else matters; least of all, social, legal, or moral considerations. Therefore, when her husband's life is threatened, it is no effort, it is joy for *Nora* to forge her father's name to a note and borrow 800 cronen on it, in order to take her sick husband to Italy.

   In her eagerness to serve her husband, and in perfect innocence of the legal aspect of her act, she does not give the matter much thought, except for her   5 anxiety to shield him from any emergency that may call upon him to perform the miracle in her behalf. She works hard, and saves every penny of her pin-money to pay back the amount she borrowed on the forged check.

Nora is light-hearted and gay, apparently without depth. Who, indeed, would expect depth of a doll, a "squirrel," a song-bird? Her purpose in life is to be happy for her husband's sake, for the sake of the children; to sing, dance, and play with them. Besides, is she not shielded, protected, and cared for? Who, then, would suspect *Nora* of depth? But already in the opening scene, when *Torvald* inquires what his precious "squirrel" wants for a Christmas present, *Nora* quickly asks him for money. Is it to buy macaroons or finery? In her talk with *Mrs. Linde*, *Nora* reveals her inner self, and forecasts the inevitable debacle of her doll's house.

After telling her friend how she had saved her husband, Nora says: "When Torvald gave me money for clothes and so on, I never used more than half of it; I always bought the simplest things. . . . Torvald never noticed anything. But it was often very hard, Christina dear. For it's nice to be beautifully dressed. Now, isn't it? . . . Well, and besides that, I made money in other ways. Last winter I was so lucky—I got a heap of copying to do. I shut myself up every evening and wrote far into the night. Oh, sometimes I was so tired, so tired. And yet it was splendid to work in that way and earn money. I almost felt as if I was a man."

Down deep in the consciousness of *Nora* there evidently slumbers person-ality and character, which could come into full bloom only through a great miracle—not the kind *Nora* hopes for, but a miracle just the same.

Nora had borrowed the money from *Nils Krogstad*, a man with a shady past in the eyes of the community and of the righteous moralist, *Torvald Helmer*. So long as *Krogstad* is allowed the little breathing space a Christian people grants to him who has once broken its laws, he is reasonably human. He does not molest *Nora*. But when *Helmer* becomes director of the bank in which *Krogstad* is employed, and threatens the man with dismissal, *Krogstad* naturally fights back. For as he says to *Nora*: "If need be, I shall fight as though for my life to keep my little place in the bank. . . . It's not only for the money: that matters least to me. It's something else. Well, I'd better make a clean breast of it. Of course you know, like every one else, that some years ago I—got into trou-ble. . . . The matter never came into court; but from that moment all paths were barred to me. Then I took up the business you know about. I was obliged to grasp at something; and I don't think I've been one of the worst. But now I must clear out of it all. My sons are growing up; for their sake I must try to win back as much respectability as I can. This place in the bank was the first step, and now your husband wants to kick me off the ladder, back into the mire. Mrs. Helmer, you evidently have no idea what you have really done. But I can assure you that it was nothing more and nothing worse that made me an outcast from society. . . . But this I may tell you, that if I'm flung into the gutter a second time, you shall keep me company."

Even when *Nora* is confronted with this awful threat, she does not fear for herself, only for *Torvald*—so good, so true, who has such an aversion to debts, but who loves her so devotedly that for her sake he would take the blame upon

10

himself. But this must never be. *Nora*, too, begins a fight for life, for her husband's life and that of her children. Did not *Helmer* tell her that the very presence of a criminal like *Krogstad* poisons the children? And is she not a criminal?

Torvald Helmer assures her, in his male conceit, that "early corruption generally comes from the mother's side, but of course the father's influence may act in the same way. And this Krogstad has been poisoning his own children for years past by a life of lies and hypocrisy — that's why I call him morally ruined."

Poor *Nora*, who cannot understand why a daughter has no right to spare her dying father anxiety, or why a wife has no right to save her husband's life, is surely not aware of the true character of her idol. But gradually the veil is lifted. At first, when in reply to her desperate pleading for *Krogstad*, her husband discloses the true reason for wanting to get rid of him: "The fact is, he was a college chum of mine — there was one of those rash friendships between us that one so often repents later. I don't mind confessing it — he calls me by my Christian name; and he insists on doing it even when others are present. He delights in putting on airs of familiarity — Torvald here, Torvald there! I assure you it's most painful to me. He would make my position at the bank perfectly unendurable."

And then again when the final blow comes. For forty-eight hours *Nora* battles for her ideal, never doubting *Torvald* for a moment. Indeed, so absolutely sure is she of her strong oak, her lord, her god, that she would rather kill herself than have him take the blame for her act. The end comes, and with it the doll's house tumbles down, and *Nora* discards her doll's dress — she sheds her skin, as it were. *Torvald Helmer* proves himself a petty Philistine, a bully and a coward, as so many good husbands when they throw off their respectable cloak.

Helmer's rage over *Nora's* crime subsides the moment the danger of publicity is averted — proving that *Helmer*, like many a moralist, is not so much incensed at *Nora's* offense as by the fear of being found out. Not so *Nora*. Finding out is her salvation. It is then that she realizes how much she has been wronged, that she is only a plaything, a doll to *Helmer*. In her disillusionment she says, "You have never loved me. You only thought it amusing to be in love with me. [. . .] I think that before all else I am a human being, just as much as you are — or, at least, I will try to become one. I know that most people agree with you, Torvald, and that they say so in books. But henceforth I can't be satisfied with what most people say, and what is in books. I must think things out for myself and try to get clear about them. . . . I had been living here these eight years with a strange man, and had borne him three children — Oh! I can't bear to think of it — I could tear myself to pieces!. . . . I can't spend the night in a strange man's house.

Is there anything more degrading to woman than to live with a stranger,   15
and bear him children? Yet, the lie of the marriage institution decrees that she shall continue to do so, and the social conception of duty insists that for the sake of that lie she need be nothing else than a plaything, a doll, a nonentity.

When *Nora* closes behind her the door of her doll's house, she opens wide the gate of life for woman, and proclaims the revolutionary message that only perfect freedom and communion make a true bond between man and woman, meeting in the open, without lies, without shame, free from the bondage of duty.   *[1914]*

☰ THINKING ABOUT THE TEXT

1. What idea of Nora's does Goldman seem most impressed by?
2. What is Goldman's view of moralists? What does Nora mean by "a strange man"?
3. What specifically do you think Goldman meant in 1914 when referring to "the bondage of duty" (para. 16)?

JOAN TEMPLETON
From *The* Doll House *Backlash: Criticism, Feminism, and Ibsen*

Joan Templeton (b. 1942) received her undergraduate degree at Centenary College and her Ph.D. from the University of Oregon. She is a noted Ibsen scholar who has published widely on the dramatist and others. Her books include Ibsen's Women *(1997) and* Munch's Ibsen *(2008). She taught for many years at Long Island University where she was professor of English and comparative literature. The following selection is from "The* Doll House *Backlash: Criticism, Feminism, and Ibsen," published in PMLA in 1989. Interestingly, most of the critics she cites as attacking Nora are men who wrote in an era when feminist thinking was largely disparaged.*

For over a hundred years, Nora has been under direct siege as exhibiting the most perfidious characteristics of her sex; the original outcry of the 1880s is swollen now to a mighty chorus of blame. She is denounced as an irrational and frivolous narcissist; an "abnormal" woman, a "hysteric"; a vain, unloving egoist who abandons her family in a paroxysm of selfishness. The proponents of the last view would seem to think Ibsen had in mind a housewife Medea, whose cruelty to husband and children he tailored down to fit the framed, domestic world of realist drama.

The first attacks were launched against Nora on moral grounds and against Ibsen, ostensibly, on "literary" ones. The outraged reviewers of the premiere claimed that *A Doll House* did not have to be taken as a serious statement about women's rights because the heroine of act 3 is an incomprehensible transformation of the heroine of acts 1 and 2. This reasoning provided an ideal way to dismiss Nora altogether; nothing she said needed to be taken seriously, and her door slamming could be written off as silly theatrics (Marker and Marker 85–87).

The argument for the two Noras, which still remains popular,[1] has had its most determined defender in the Norwegian scholar Else Høst, who argues that Ibsen's carefree, charming "lark" could never have become the "newly fledged feminist." In any case it is the "childish, expectant, ecstatic, broken-hearted Nora" who makes A Doll House immortal (28; my trans.); the other one, the unfeeling woman of act 3 who coldly analyzes the flaws in her marriage, is psychologically unconvincing and wholly unsympathetic.

The most unrelenting attempt on record to trivialize Ibsen's protagonist, and a favorite source for Nora's later detractors, is Hermann Weigand's.[2] In a classic 1925 study, Weigand labors through forty-nine pages to demonstrate that Ibsen conceived of Nora as a silly, lovable female. At the beginning, Weigand confesses, he was, like all men, momentarily shaken by the play: "Having had the misfortune to be born of the male sex, we slink away in shame, vowing to mend our ways." The chastened critic's remorse is short-lived, however, as a "clear male voice, irreverently breaking the silence," stuns with its critical acumen: " 'The meaning of the final scene,' the voice says, 'is epitomized by Nora's remark: "Yes, Torvald. Now I have changed my dress." ' " With this epiphany as guide, Weigand spends the night poring over the "little volume." Dawn arrives, bringing with it the return of "masculine self-respect" (26–27). For there is only one explanation for the revolt of "this winsome little woman" (52) and her childish door slamming: Ibsen meant A Doll House as comedy. Nora's erratic behavior at the curtain's fall leaves us laughing heartily, for there is no doubt that she will return home to "revert, imperceptibly, to her role of song-bird and charmer" (68). After all, since Nora is

> an irresistibly bewitching piece of femininity, an extravagant poet and romancer, utterly lacking in sense of fact, and endowed with a natural gift for play-acting which makes her instinctively dramatize her experiences: how can the settlement fail of a fundamentally comic appeal?   (64)

The most popular way to render Nora inconsequential has been to attack   5
her morality; whatever the vocabulary used, the arguments have remained much the same for over a century. Oswald Crawford, writing in the *Fortnightly Review* in 1891, scolded that while Nora may be "charming as doll-women may be charming," she is "unprincipled" (732). A half century later, after Freudianism had produced a widely accepted "clinical" language of disapproval, Nora could be called "abnormal." Mary McCarthy lists Nora as one of the "neurotic" women whom Ibsen, she curiously claims, was the first playwright to put on stage (80). For Maurice Valency, Nora is a case study of female hysteria, a willful, unwomanly woman: "Nora is a carefully studied example of what we have come to know as the hysterical personality—bright, unstable, impulsive, romantic, quite immune from feelings of guilt, and, at bottom, not especially feminine" (151–52).

---

[1]See, for example, Robert Brustein (49) and Marvin Rosenberg, whose article is a rehash of Høst's points, although Rosenberg seems unacquainted with her well-known essay.
[2]For a thoroughgoing defense of Weigand by a much later critic who understands that "A Doll House is not a feminist play," see R. F. Dietrich.

More recent assaults on Nora have argued that her forgery to obtain the money to save her husband's life proves her irresponsibility and egotism. Brian Johnston condemns Nora's love as "unintelligent" and her crime as "a trivial act which nevertheless turns to evil because it refused to take the universal ethical realm into consideration at all" (97); Ibsen uses Torvald's famous pet names for Nora—lark, squirrel—to give her a "strong 'animal' identity" and to underscore her inability to understand the ethical issues faced by human beings (97). Evert Sprinchorn argues that Nora had only to ask her husband's kindly friends (entirely missing from the play) for the necessary money: ". . . any other woman would have done so. But Nora knew that if she turned to one of Torvald's friends for help, she would have had to share her role of savior with someone else" (124).

Even Nora's sweet tooth is evidence of her unworthiness, as we see her "surreptitiously devouring the forbidden [by her husband] macaroons," even "brazenly offer[ing] macaroons to Doctor Rank, and finally lying in her denial that the macaroons are hers"; eating macaroons in secret suggests that "Nora is deceitful and manipulative from the start" and that her exit thus "reflects only a petulant woman's irresponsibility" (Schlueter 64–65). As she eats the cookies, Nora adds insult to injury by declaring her hidden wish to say "death and damnation" in front of her husband, thus revealing, according to Brian Downs, of Christ's College, Cambridge, "something a trifle febrile and morbid" in her nature (Downs 130).

Much has been made of Nora's relationship with Doctor Rank, the surest proof, it is argued, of her dishonesty. Nora is revealed as *la belle dame sans merci* when she "suggestively queries Rank whether a pair of silk stockings will fit her" (Schlueter 65); she "flirts cruelly with [him] and toys with his affection for her, drawing him on to find out how strong her hold over him actually is" (Sprinchorn 124).

Nora's detractors have often been, from the first, her husband's defenders. In an argument that claims to rescue Nora and Torvald from "the campaign for the liberation of women" so that they "become vivid and disturbingly real," Evert Sprinchorn pleads that Torvald "has given Nora all the material things and all the sexual attention that any young wife could reasonably desire. He loves beautiful things, and not least his pretty wife" (121). Nora is incapable of appreciating her husband because she "is not a normal woman. She is compulsive, highly imaginative, and very much inclined to go to extremes." Since it is she who has acquired the money to save his life, Torvald, and not Nora, is really the "wife in the family," although he "has regarded himself as the breadwinner . . . the main support of his wife and children, as any decent husband would like to regard himself" (122). In another defense, John Chamberlain argues that Torvald deserves our sympathy because he is no "mere common or garden chauvinist." If Nora were less the actress Weigand has proved her to be, "the woman in her might observe what the embarrassingly naive feminist overlooks or ignores, namely, the indications that Torvald, for all his faults, is taking her at least as seriously as he can—and perhaps even as seriously as she deserves" (85).

All female, or no woman at all, Nora loses either way. Frivolous, deceitful, or unwomanly, she qualifies neither as a heroine nor as a spokeswoman for feminism. Her famous exit embodies only "the latest and shallowest notion of emancipated womanhood, abandoning her family to go out into the world in search of 'her true identity' " (Freedman 4). And in any case, it is only naive Nora who believes she might make a life for herself; "the audience," argues an essayist in *College English*, "can see most clearly how Nora is exchanging a practical doll's role for an impractical one" (Pearce 343). We are back to the high condescension of the Victorians and Edward Dowden:

> Inquires should be set on foot to ascertain whether a manuscript may not lurk in some house in Christiania [Oslo] entitled *Nora Helmer's Reflections in Solitude*; it would be a document of singular interest, and probably would conclude with the words, "Tomorrow I return to Torvald; have been exactly one week away; shall insist on a free woman's right to unlimited macaroons as test of his reform."   (248)

In the first heady days of *A Doll House* Nora was rendered powerless by   10
substituted denouements and sequels that sent her home to her husband. Now Nora's critics take the high-handed position that all the fuss was unnecessary, since Nora is not a feminist heroine. And yet in the twentieth-century case against her, whether Nora is judged childish, "neurotic," or unprincipled and whether her accuser's tone is one of witty derision, clinical sobriety, or moral earnestness, the purpose behind the verdict remains that of Nora's frightened contemporaries: to destroy her credibility and power as a representative of women. The demon in the house, the modern "half-woman," as Strindberg called her in the preface to *Miss Julie*, who, "now that she has been discovered has begun to make a noise" (65), must be silenced, her heretical forces destroyed, so that *A Doll House* can emerge a safe classic, rescued from feminism, and Ibsen can assume his place in the pantheon of true artists, unsullied by the "woman question" and the topical taint of history.   *[1989]*

Works Cited

Brustein, Robert. *The Theatre of Revolt*. New York: Little, 1962.

Chamberlain, John. *Ibsen: The Open Vision*. London: Athlone, 1982.

Crawford, Oswald. "The Ibsen Question." *Fortnightly Review* 55 (1891): 727–40.

Dietrich, R. F. "Nora's Change of Dress: Weigand Revisited." *Theatre Annual* 36 (1981): 20–40.

Dowden, Edward. "Henrik Ibsen." Ibsen, *Works* 3: 219–58.

Downs, Brian. *A Study of Six Plays by Ibsen*. 1959. New York: Octagon, 1978.

Freedman, Morris. *The Moral Impulse: Modern Drama from Ibsen to the Present*. Carbondale: Southern Illinois UP, 1967.

Høst, Else. "Nora." *Edda* 46 (1946): 13–48.

Ibsen, Henrik. *Ibsens Samlede Verker*. Vol. 3. Oslo: Gyldendal, 1978. 3 vols.

———. *The Works of Henrik Ibsen.* Ed. and trans. William Archer. 13 vols. New York: Scribner's, 1917.

Johnston, Brian. *The Ibsen Cycle.* Boston: Hall, 1975.

Marker, Frederick, and Lisa-Lone Marker. "The First Nora: Notes on the World Premiere of *A Doll's House.*" *Ibsenårboken* 11 (1970–71): 84–100.

McCarthy, Mary. "The Will and Testament of Ibsen." *Partisan Review* 23 (1956): 74–80.

Pearce, Richard. "The Limits of Realism." *College English* 31 (1970): 335–43.

Rosenberg, Marvin. "Ibsen versus Ibsen: Or, Two Versions of *A Doll House.*" *Modern Drama* 12 (1969): 187–96.

Schlueter, June. "How to Get into *A Doll House*: Ibsen's Play as an Introduction to Drama." *Shafer* 63–68.

Sprinchorn, Evert. "Ibsen and the Actors." *Ibsen and the Theatre.* Ed. Errol Durbach. New York: New York UP, 1980. 118–30.

Strindberg, August. Author's Foreword. *Miss Julie. Six Plays of Strindberg.* Trans. Elizabeth Sprigge. Garden City: Doubleday, 1955. 61–73.

Valency, Maurice. *The Flower and the Castle: An Introduction to Modern Drama.* 1963. New York: Schocken, 1982.

Weigand, Hermann. *The Modern Ibsen: A Reconsideration.* New York: Holt, 1925.

≡ THINKING ABOUT THE TEXT

1. What is your response to the Weigand block quote (para. 4)?

2. Templeton argues that critics, mostly men, wanted to make the play "a safe classic" (para. 10). How might our selection support the claim?

3. Explain why one of these critics seems to you to be misguided.

SUSANNA RUSTIN

Why *A Doll's House* by Henrik Ibsen Is More Relevant Than Ever

Susanna Rustin (b. 1971) is a features writer and editor for the Guardian. She grew up in London and studied at York University. She is active in local politics, having run for the Green Party ticket.

When, next Wednesday evening, Hattie Morahan picks up an armful of Christmas shopping and steps on stage to open a run of Ibsen's *A Doll's House*, it will be for the third time in just over a year. Morahan first starred as Nora, the 1870s Norwegian wife and mother who realises her life is a sham, at the Young Vic last July, but such is the production's popularity that this is its second revival. Moreover, two other, brand new productions have been seen in recent months: in May an adaptation by Bryony Lavery received rave reviews at the

Royal Exchange in Manchester, and in April Zinnie Harris's version, set in Edwardian London and first seen at the Donmar Warehouse in London with Gillian Anderson in the lead role, was staged by the National Theatre of Scotland in Edinburgh.

Three such high-profile productions in the space of a few months is unusual. Morahan has already won the Evening Standard and Critics' Circle awards for her performance and was unlucky to miss out to Helen Mirren at the Oliviers. But the combination of the play's brisk and thriller-like plotting, and the sense shared by everyone involved that the play still speaks to audiences in ways that feel fresh and interesting, means there is no fear of overkill.

In fact, Morahan, speaking to me just before Thursday's dress rehearsal, says she feels "liberated" to be occupying the role again, while director Carrie Cracknell says that even the last few days of rehearsals have thrown up new insights into Ibsen's endlessly complex characters. "There is something timeless about it," Morahan says, "which is what's so shocking. You try to keep it in its box of 19th-century Scandinavia, but the things Ibsen writes mean it ceases to be about a particular milieu and becomes about marriage (or partnership) and money. These are universal anxieties, and it seems from talking to people that it resonates in the most visceral way, especially if they are or have been in a difficult relationship. Someone said to me the other night, 'That's the play that broke my parents' marriage up.' It shines a very harsh light on the messy heart of relationships, and how difficult it can be to be honest with another human being even if you love them."

The play, hugely controversial when first published and performed in Copenhagen in 1879, is about the unravelling of a family. Nora and Torvald Helmer believe they are happily married and on the brink of a blissful new phase of life: Torvald has been promoted to bank manager and their money worries are over. But Nora has a secret debt, incurred with good intentions and a forged signature, and with her husband's new power comes the threat of blackmail.

Over three acts the illusion of bourgeois contentment unravels, and the play culminates in a spectacular scene between the couple as Nora's lie is exposed and Torvald first blames, then forgives her — and is finally abandoned as Nora recognises the truth of her situation. She accuses her husband, and her father before him, of having used her as a doll, and declares herself unfit to be a wife or mother until she has learned to be herself. Ibsen's final stage direction, of the door closing behind her, is one of the most famous ever written.

Unsurprisingly, feminist contemporaries of Ibsen welcomed the play, although, as theatre critic Caroline McGinn points out, when he was invited to speak at a women's congress, he told them he wasn't a feminist himself. The first German production notoriously altered the ending so that Nora did not leave home, when leading woman Hedwig Niemann-Raabe refused to act the part as written, an amendment Ibsen later described as "a barbaric outrage." In the century and more since, the play and the role of Nora have taken on iconic status; Unesco's Memory of the World register calls Nora "a symbol throughout the world, for women fighting for liberation and equality."

She is also a symbol for female actors, both of what is possible and of how much they still have to fight for, when most plays and films still feature more male than female characters and work famously dries up for older women unless they are among a lucky handful of national treasures. Cush Jumbo, star of the Royal Exchange's production, says "it's a role a lot of actresses have on their list—if they have a wish list—because it's a very challenging part. It's Ibsen's Rosalind [the heroine of Shakespeare's *As You Like It*], I suppose. You never leave the stage and the journey she goes on is epic."

"I would compare it to Hamlet," says Morahan, whose interpretation has been described as a career-changing breakthrough. Janet McTeer experienced a similar effect two decades ago when her tempestuous, 6ft Nora, deeply in love with her husband and completely broken by his betrayal, won plaudits in London and then on Broadway, where the *New York Times* theatre critic Ben Brantley called McTeer's "the single most compelling performance I have ever seen."

McTeer's take on the play was to sweep away some of the feminist baggage it carried—it doesn't work for Torvald's "sweet little skylark" to suddenly turn into Emily Pankhurst,° she decided—and to treat it as the story not of a woman, but of a marriage. Anthony Page, who directed, says "she was very unexpected casting, being tall and strong-looking, but it heightened the idiocy of the false identity she was living under. She had a wonderful way of playing it very naturalistically, and she and Owen Teale [as Torvald] were playing off each other. Sometimes it got a bit out of hand. They were throwing chairs at each other, which had to be stopped, but they were remarkable."

But it is hard to ignore the play's strong feminist resonances in a culture   10
where it is blindingly obvious that any woman who puts herself in the public eye will become a target for abuse. Some complain that social media have given misogynists—such as those who have been in the news this week after threatening the MP Stella Creasy, or sending death threats to female journalists—a platform they don't deserve. Others argue they have simply revealed a woman-hating streak that has always been with us. Either way, it seems difficult to deny that virulent prejudice against women and the pressure on them to behave in certain ways still exist. Ibsen himself wrote in a note on his work-in-progress that women can't be themselves in an "exclusively male society, with laws made by men and with prosecutors and judges who assess feminine conduct from a masculine standpoint"—which felt startlingly pertinent when I read it shortly after learning of the male prosecutor and judge who this week labelled a 13-year-old child a sexual predator and suspended the prison sentence of the 41-year-old man convicted of abusing her.

Which is why some of the current generation of women acting, directing, and adapting *A Doll's House* have sought to reassert its feminist credentials. Director Carrie Cracknell made a short film that imagined Nora as an overstretched modern mother, her life a nightmare of spilled porridge, missed appointments, and hurriedly applied makeup. She says working on the play made her acutely aware of the ideas about gender that shaped her parenting of her

Emily Pankhurst: Militant Victorian activist.

two young children. "We live in a culture in which the way we represent women is becoming narrower. I think we have a generation of women growing up who understand that power is linked to how we look."

But all those I spoke to agree that the central dilemma the play presents, of how to be yourself and true to yourself, while being married and being a parent, is not exclusive to women. "In a sense," says Caroline McGinn, "Nora's famous dramatic exit [leaving home and children to work and pursue self-fulfilment] is something many parents do five days a week."

And perhaps this is the play's most radical aspect: that it presents a woman's dilemma as a human dilemma, relevant to both sexes, when so often women's stories are treated as a special subject of concern only to women (evidence of which can be seen everywhere in culture, from the small number of men who read books by and about women to the girl-heavy audience for the RSC's smash-hit musical *Matilda*, when there is no equivalent gender bias at *Charlie and the Chocolate Factory* down the road).

"I feel really strongly that we still obsess around male protagonists," Cracknell says. "There's a thousands-of-years-long legacy of storytelling in which men have been the protagonists—we go back to telling their stories over and over." McGinn says *A Doll's House* remains thrilling as a critic because "you go to new plays all the time where the ratio of men to women is 80/20."

Jumbo, who is currently starring in her own play about the singer Josephine   15
Baker at the Bush Theatre in London, also acted in Phyllida Lloyd's all-female production of Julius Caesar earlier this year and found "it opened people's minds to the idea that it's not that there aren't any roles for us, it's that plays aren't produced in that way. Quite a lot of the time you are the minority sex in a cast, because most stories that are told are male-driven. So it's a case of telling more women-driven stories, or being open to casting things in different ways."

Or, as Zinnie Harris puts it: "Nora's departure started a journey, and it's incumbent on us to keep going."   [2013]

≡ THINKING ABOUT THE TEXT

1. What does Rustin think the most radical aspect of the play is? What do you think of her evidence? Can you give other examples?

2. In your experience, is the Cracknell quote (para. 14) right about the ratio of men to women being 80/20 in films and TV shows?

3. What is your answer the question of why this play is so enduringly popular?

≡ WRITING ABOUT ISSUES

1. The feminist thinker and activist Gloria Steinem writes about the "big click," a kind of epiphany, a moment when a woman realizes her true position in a patriarchal society. Write an essay that uses Steinem's idea to argue that Nora's transformation in act 3 is realistic or not.

2. In her review, Rustin claims that the most radical aspect of the play is that a woman's dilemma is treated as a human dilemma rather than as an exclusively women's concern. She claims that this is not usually the case. Write an essay that agrees or disagrees with this position, offering support from popular culture, including films and TV shows.

3. Argue that Nora will or will not return.

4. Write an essay that argues that *A Doll's House* is or is not still relevant today.

Confining Surveillance: Essays

MICHEL FOUCAULT, "Panopticon"

JEFFREY TOOBIN, "Edward Snowden's Real Impact"

PETER LUDLOW, "The Banality of Systemic Evil"

A recent survey of PEN, an organization of American writers, found that a "majority of its members are deeply concerned about . . . government surveillance of email and phone records." Seventy-three percent said they were "never as worried about privacy rights and freedom of the press as they are today." Some said they now avoid writing or speaking on certain controversial topics. Some critics interpret this trepidation as a result of Edward Snowden's disclosures of widespread surveillance by the National Security Agency (NSA). If so, this situation reinforces an idea developed by the French philosopher Michel Foucault about the nature and scope of power. In modern democracies, he claims, it is no longer necessary to exert coercive force to compel conformity to approved values. Through socialization at home, in schools, in the community, and in the culture at large, we readily adopt ideas about right and wrong, about what acceptable behavior is, about the consequences of deviance. Why do those writers feel wary? Certainly not because they were threatened directly in any way. Because the leaked information by Snowden seemed to suggest that the NSA was spying on practically everybody, the writers felt they could easily be monitored. And it is just this possibility that keeps us in line. Foucault called it the *panopticon*, and it will be the focus of the first selection. Next is Jeffrey Toobin's negative take on Snowden's disclosures, which is then followed by Peter Ludlow's warning about the chilling effect surveillance has on our freedom.

☰ BEFORE YOU READ

What limitations would you place on the government's surveillance abilities? Do you know people who spy on/monitor others? What is your position on Edward Snowden's disclosures? On WikiLeaks?

MICHEL FOUCAULT

Panopticon, from *Discipline and Punish*

Michel Foucault (1926–1984) was a French philosopher and social theorist and one of the most important intellectuals of the second half of the twentieth century. He received his doctorate in 1959 and subsequently taught at the most prestigious universities in France. His influential books include The History of Sexuality *(1984) and* Archaeology of Knowledge *(1969). In* Discipline and Punish: The Birth of the

Prison, *he claims that all institutions discipline the body to be docile through surveil-lance, both real and imagined, which leads to the psychological control of individuals.*

The following excerpt is from Discipline and Punish *(1975), where Foucault has been discussing "the constant division between the normal and the abnormal." Although he is specifically discussing prisons, he means for the reader to make con-nections to society at large.*

Bentham's Panopticon is the architectural figure of this composition. We know the principle on which it was based: at the periphery, an annular building; at the centre, a tower; this tower is pierced with wide windows that open onto the inner side of the ring; the peripheric building is divided into cells, each of which extends the whole width of the building; they have two windows, one on the inside, corresponding to the windows of the tower; the other, on the outside, allows the light to cross the cell from one end to the other. All that is needed, then, is to place a supervisor in a central tower and to shut up in each cell a madman, a patient, a condemned man, a worker, or a schoolboy. By the effect of backlighting, one can observe from the tower, standing out precisely against the light, the small captive shadows in the cells of the periphery. They are like so many cages, so many small theatres, in which each actor is alone, perfectly individualized and constantly visible. The panoptic mechanism arranges spa-tial unities that make it possible to see constantly and to recognize immediately. In short, it reverses the principle of the dungeon; or rather of its three func-tions—to enclose, to deprive of light, and to hide—it preserves only the first and eliminates the other two. Full lighting and the eye of a supervisor capture better than darkness, which ultimately protected. Visibility is a trap.

To begin with, this made it possible—as a negative effect—to avoid those compact, swarming, howling masses that were to be found in places of con-finement, those painted by Goya or described by Howard. Each individual, in his place, is securely confined to a cell from which he is seen from the front by the supervisor; but the side walls prevent him from coming into contact with his companions. He is seen, but he does not see; he is the object of information, never a subject in communication. The arrangement of his room, opposite the central tower, imposes on him an axial visibility; but the divisions of the ring, those separated cells, imply a lateral invisibility. And this invisibility is a guar-antee of order. If the inmates are convicts, there is no danger of a plot, an at-tempt at collective escape, the planning of new crimes for the future, bad reciprocal influences; if they are patients, there is no danger of contagion; if they are madmen there is no risk of their committing violence upon one an-other; if they are schoolchildren, there is no copying, no noise, no chatter, no waste of time; if they are workers, there are no disorders, no theft, no coali-tions, none of those distractions that slow down the rate of work, make it less perfect or cause accidents. The crowd, a compact mass, a locus of multiple ex-changes, individualities merging together, a collective effect, is abolished and replaced by a collection of separated individualities. From the point of view of the guardian, it is replaced by a multiplicity that can be numbered and supervised; from the point of view of the inmates, by a sequestered and observed solitude (Bentham, 60–64).

Hence the major effect of the Panopticon: to induce in the inmate a state of conscious and permanent visibility that assures the automatic functioning of power. So to arrange things that the surveillance is permanent in its effects, even if it is discontinuous in its action; that the perfection of power should tend to render its actual exercise unnecessary; that this architectural apparatus should be a machine for creating and sustaining a power relation independent of the person who exercises it; in short, that the inmates should be caught up in a power situation of which they are themselves the bearers. To achieve this, it is at once too much and too little that the prisoner should be constantly observed by an inspector: too little, for what matters is that he knows himself to be observed; too much, because he has no need in fact of being so. In view of this, Bentham laid down the principle that power should be visible and unverifiable. Visible: the inmate will constantly have before his eyes the tall outline of the central tower from which he is spied upon. Unverifiable: the inmate must never know whether he is being looked at any one moment; but he must be sure that he may always be so. In order to make the presence or absence of the inspector unverifiable, so that the prisoners, in their cells, cannot even see a shadow, Bentham envisaged not only venetian blinds on the windows of the central observation hall, but, on the inside, partitions that intersected the hall at right angles and, in order to pass from one quarter to the other, not doors but zig-zag openings; for the slightest noise, a gleam of light, a brightness in a half-opened door would betray the presence of the guardian. The Panopticon is a machine for dissociating the see/being seen dyad: in the peripheric ring, one is totally seen, without ever seeing; in the central tower, one sees everything without ever being seen.

It is an important mechanism, for it automatizes and disindividualizes power. Power has its principle not so much in a person as in a certain concerted distribution of bodies, surfaces, lights, gazes; in an arrangement whose internal mechanisms produce the relation in which individuals are caught up. The ceremonies, the rituals, the marks by which the sovereign's surplus power was manifested are useless. There is a machinery that assures dissymmetry, disequilibrium, difference. Consequently, it does not matter who exercises power. Any individual, taken almost at random, can operate the machine: in the absence of the director, his family, his friends, his visitors, even his servants (Bentham, 45). Similarly, it does not matter what motive animates him: the curiosity of the indiscreet, the malice of a child, the thirst for knowledge of a philosopher who wishes to visit this museum of human nature, or the perversity of those who take pleasure in spying and punishing. The more numerous those anonymous and temporary observers are, the greater the risk for the inmate of being surprised and the greater his anxious awareness of being observed. The Panopticon is a marvellous machine which, whatever use one may wish to put it to, produces homogeneous effects of power.   *[1975]*

≡ THINKING ABOUT THE TEXT

1. What exactly is the purpose of the architecture, especially the tower that Foucault describes?

2. How is the surveillance "permanent in its effects" (para. 3)? How are the prisoners themselves the bearers of power?

3. Why is it important that the prisoners never know whether someone is looking at them at any given moment? What specific relevance does the idea of panopticon have to modern surveillance, say, by the NSA?

JEFFREY TOOBIN
Edward Snowden's Real Impact

Jeffrey Toobin (b. 1960) was born in New York City and attended Harvard College. He received a degree from Harvard Law School in 1986. He gave up the law after a controversial case in which he was accused of taking classified documents to write a book about the Iran–Contra Affair. He spent six years as a television legal analyst for ABC News and received a 2000 Emmy Award for his reporting. He is currently a staff writer for The New Yorker *and a senior analyst for CNN. His book,* The Nine: Inside the Secret World of the Supreme Court *(2007) has won numerous awards. His latest book is* The Oath: The Obama White House and The Supreme Court *(2012). The following article appeared in* The New Yorker *in August 2013.*

The assassinations of Martin Luther King, Jr., and Robert F. Kennedy led directly to the passage of a historic law, the Gun Control Act of 1968. Does that change your view of the assassinations? Should we be grateful for the deaths of these two men?

Of course not. That's lunatic logic. But the same reasoning is now being applied to the actions of Edward Snowden. Yes, the thinking goes, Snowden may have violated the law, but the outcome has been so worthwhile. According to Glenn Greenwald, the journalist who was one of the primary vehicles for Snowden's disclosures, Snowden "is very pleased with the debate that is arising in many countries around the world on Internet privacy and U.S. spying. It is exactly the debate he wanted to inform."

In this debate, Snowden himself says, those who followed the law were nothing better than Nazis: "I believe in the principle declared at Nuremberg, in 1945: 'Individuals have international duties which transcend the national obligations of obedience. Therefore individual citizens have the duty to violate domestic laws to prevent crimes against peace and humanity from occurring.'"

To be sure, Snowden has prompted an international discussion about surveillance, but it's worthwhile to note that this debate is no academic exercise. It has real costs. Consider just a few.

What if Snowden's wrong? What if there is no pervasive illegality in the Na-   5
tional Security Agency's surveillance programs?

Indeed, for all the excitement generated by Snowden's disclosures, there is
no proof of any systemic, deliberate violations of law. Based on the ruling in a
1979 Supreme Court case, Smith v. Maryland, it is well established that individuals do not have an expectation of privacy in the phone numbers they call.
This is not entirely surprising; we all know that we're already sharing that information with the phone company. In the same way, it's long established that
the government has great latitude in intercepting communications between
the United States and other countries. It's true, too, that while the Foreign Intelligence Surveillance Act court is largely toothless, it has, on occasion, rejected some N.S.A. procedures, and the agency has made adjustments in
response. That is not the act of an entirely lawless agency.

It is true that, as the Washington Post's Barton Gellman recently reported,
the N.S.A. sometimes went beyond its authority. According to Gellman, the
agency privately admits to two thousand seven hundred and seventy-six incidents of unauthorized collection of data within a twelve-month period. This is
bad — but it's not clear how bad. If it's that many incidents out of a total of, say,
three thousand initiatives, then it's very bad. But if — as is far more likely — it's
two thousand seven hundred and seventy-six incidents out of many millions,
then the errors are less serious. There should be no mistakes, of course. But
government surveillance, like any human activity, is going to have errors, and
it's far from clear, at this point, that the N.S.A. 's errors amounted to a major
violation of law or an invasion of privacy.

What are the actual dollar costs of Snowden's disclosures?

The United States, like any great power, is always going to have an intelligence operation, and some electronic surveillance is obligatory in the modern
world. But, because of Snowden's disclosures, the government will almost certainly have to spend billions of dollars, and thousands of people will have to
spend thousands of hours, reworking our procedures. This is all because a
thirty-year-old self-appointed arbiter of propriety decided to break the law and
disclose what he had sworn to protect. That judgment — in my view — was not
Snowden's to make. And it is simply grotesque that Snowden compares these
thousands of government workers — all doing their jobs to protect the United
States — to the Nazi war criminals at Nuremberg.

What did China and Russia learn about American surveillance operations from   10
Snowden — and what will they do with this information?

As part of Snowden's flight from American justice, he went to two of the
most repressive and technologically sophisticated countries on earth. (Hong
Kong is, of course, part of China.) In an interview with Greenwald, Snowden
said that the authorities in those countries behaved like perfect gentlemen.

"I never gave any information to either government, and they never took
anything from my laptops," Snowden said.

Oh, really? Is he serious? Should anyone believe a word of this? China and
Russia spend billions of dollars conducting counterintelligence against the
United States. An American citizen walks into their countries bearing the keys

to our most secret programs, and both — both! — China and Russia decline to take even a peek. That is a preposterous proposition. Even assuming that Snowden believes he had control of his computers 24/7 (he never slept?), there is simply no way that China and Russia would pass up that kind of bounty.

There is obviously some legitimate debate to be had about the extent and the legality of American surveillance operations. But there is no doubt about the nature of China and Russia. Snowden's pious invocation of the Nuremberg trials will probably be small comfort to the dissidents and the political prisoners whose cell doors may be locked a little tighter today because of what these authoritarian governments may have learned from his hard drive.   [2013]

≡ THINKING ABOUT THE TEXT

1. Do you think Snowden is right that the Nuremburg analogy is valid, that is, that we have a higher duty than "national obligations of obedience" (para. 3)?

2. Which of the "costs" Toobin cites makes the most sense to you? Why?

3. What exactly is Toobin's objection to Snowden's actions? Is the surveillance debate just about legality? What might be some larger issues?

PETER LUDLOW
The Banality of Systemic Evil

Peter Ludlow (b. 1957) is a professor of philosophy at Northwestern University. He received a Ph.D. in philosophy from Columbia University. His academic interests are in linguistics and philosophy and theories of meanings in linguistic semantics. His nonacademic interests focus on the hacktivist culture and WikiLeaks. He has also written widely on issues regarding cyberspace. This article appeared in the New York Times *in September 2013.*

In recent months there has been a visible struggle in the media to come to grips with the leaking, whistle-blowing, and hacktivism that has vexed the United States military and the private and government intelligence communities. This response has run the gamut. It has involved attempts to condemn, support, demonize, psychoanalyze, and in some cases canonize figures like Aaron Swartz, Jeremy Hammond, Chelsea Manning, and Edward Snowden.

In broad terms, commentators in the mainstream and corporate media have tended to assume that all of these actors needed to be brought to justice, while independent players on the Internet and elsewhere have been much more supportive. Tellingly, a recent *Time* magazine cover story has pointed out a marked generational difference in how people view these matters: 70 percent of those age 18 to 34 sampled in a poll said they believed that Snowden "did a good thing" in leaking the news of the National Security Agency's surveillance program.

So has the younger generation lost its moral compass?

No. In my view, just the opposite.

Clearly, there is a moral principle at work in the actions of the leakers,   5
whistle-blowers, and hacktivists and those who support them. I would also argue that that moral principle has been clearly articulated, and it may just save
us from a dystopian future.

In "Eichmann in Jerusalem," one of the most poignant and important
works of 20th-century philosophy, Hannah Arendt made an observation
about what she called "the banality of evil." One interpretation of this holds
that it was not an observation about what a regular guy Adolf Eichmann
seemed to be, but rather a statement about what happens when people play
their "proper" roles within a system, following prescribed conduct with respect
to that system, while remaining blind to the moral consequences of what the
system was doing—or at least compartmentalizing and ignoring those consequences.

A good illustration of this phenomenon appears in "Moral Mazes," a book
by the sociologist Robert Jackall that explored the ethics of decision making
within several corporate bureaucracies. In it, Jackall made several observations that dovetailed with those of Arendt. The mid-level managers that he
spoke with were not "evil" people in their everyday lives, but in the context of
their jobs, they had a separate moral code altogether, what Jackall calls the
"fundamental rules of corporate life":

> (1) You never go around your boss. (2) You tell your boss what he wants to
> hear, even when your boss claims that he wants dissenting views. (3) If
> your boss wants something dropped, you drop it. (4) You are sensitive to
> your boss's wishes so that you anticipate what he wants; you don't force
> him, in other words, to act as a boss. (5) Your job is not to report some-
> thing that your boss does not want reported, but rather to cover it up. You
> do your job and you keep your mouth shut.

Jackall went through case after case in which managers violated this code
and were drummed out of a business (for example, for reporting wrongdoing
in the cleanup at the Three Mile Island nuclear power plant).

Aaron Swartz counted "Moral Mazes" among his "very favorite books."
Swartz was the Internet wunderkind who was hounded by a government prosecution threatening him with 35 years in jail for illicitly downloading academic journals that were behind a pay wall. Swartz, who committed suicide in
January at age 26 (many believe because of his prosecution), said that "Moral
Mazes" did an excellent job of "explaining how so many well-intentioned
people can end up committing so much evil."

Swartz argued that it was sometimes necessary to break the rules that required obedience to the system in order to avoid systemic evil. In Swartz's case
the system was not a corporation but a system for the dissemination of bottled
up knowledge that should have been available to all. Swartz engaged in an act
of civil disobedience to liberate that knowledge, arguing that "there is no jus-

tice in following unjust laws. It's time to come into the light and, in the grand tradition of civil disobedience, declare our opposition to this private theft of public culture."

Chelsea Manning, the United States Army private incarcerated for leaking   10
classified documents from the Departments of Defense and State, felt a similar pull to resist the internal rules of the bureaucracy. In a statement at her trial she described a case where she felt this was necessary. In February 2010, she received a report of an event in which the Iraqi Federal Police had detained 15 people for printing "anti-Iraqi" literature. Upon investigating the matter, Manning discovered that none of the 15 had previous ties to anti-Iraqi actions or suspected terrorist organizations. Manning had the allegedly anti-Iraqi literature translated and found that, contrary to what the federal police had said, the published literature in question "detailed corruption within the cabinet of Prime Minister Nuri Kamal al-Maliki's government and the financial impact of his corruption on the Iraqi people."

When Manning reported this discrepancy to the officer in charge (OIC), she was told to "drop it," she recounted.

Manning could not play along. As she put it, she knew if she "continued to assist the Baghdad Federal Police in identifying the political opponents of Prime Minister al-Maliki, those people would be arrested and in the custody of the Special Unit of the Baghdad Federal Police and very likely tortured and not seen again for a very long time—if ever." When her superiors would not address the problem, she was compelled to pass this information on to WikiLeaks.

Snowden too felt that, confronting what was clearly wrong, he could not play his proper role within the bureaucracy of the intelligence community. As he put it,

> [W]hen you talk to people about [abuses] in a place like this where this is the normal state of business people tend not to take them very seriously and move on from them. But over time that awareness of wrongdoing sort of builds up and you feel compelled to talk about [them]. And the more you talk about [them] the more you're ignored. The more you're told it's not a problem until eventually you realize that these things need to be determined by the public and not by somebody who was simply hired by the government.

The bureaucracy was telling him to shut up and move on (in accord with the five rules in "Moral Mazes"), but Snowden felt that doing so was morally wrong.

In a June Op-Ed in The Times, David Brooks made a case for why he thought Snowden was wrong to leak information about the Prism surveillance program. His reasoning cleanly framed the alternative to the moral code endorsed by Swartz, Manning, and Snowden. "For society to function well," he wrote, "there have to be basic levels of trust and cooperation, a respect for institutions and deference to common procedures. By deciding to unilaterally leak secret N.S.A. documents, Snowden has betrayed all of these things."

The complaint is eerily parallel to one from a case discussed in "Moral   15
Mazes," where an accountant was dismissed because he insisted on reporting
"irregular payments, doctored invoices, and shuffling numbers." The complaint against the accountant by the other managers of his company was that
"by insisting on his own moral purity . . . he eroded the fundamental trust and
understanding that makes cooperative managerial work possible."

But wasn't there arrogance or hubris in Snowden's and Manning's decisions to leak the documents? After all, weren't there established procedures
determining what was right further up the organizational chart? Weren't these
ethical decisions better left to someone with a higher pay grade? The former
United States ambassador to the United Nations, John Bolton, argued that
Snowden "thinks he's smarter and has a higher morality than the rest of
us . . . that he can see clearer than other 299, 999, 999 of us, and therefore he
can do what he wants. I say that is the worst form of treason."

For the leaker and whistleblower the answer to Bolton is that there can be
no expectation that the system will act morally of its own accord. Systems are
optimized for their own survival and preventing the system from doing evil
may well require breaking with organizational niceties, protocols, or laws. It
requires stepping outside of one's assigned organizational role. The chief executive is not in a better position to recognize systemic evil than is a middle
level manager or, for that matter, an IT contractor. Recognizing systemic evil
does not require rank or intelligence, just honesty of vision.

Persons of conscience who step outside their assigned organizational roles
are not new. There are many famous earlier examples, including Daniel Ellsberg
(the Pentagon Papers), John Kiriakou (of the Central Intelligence Agency), and
several former N.S.A. employees, who blew the whistle on what they saw as an
unconstitutional and immoral surveillance program (William Binney, Russ
Tice, and Thomas Drake, for example). But it seems that we are witnessing a
new generation of whistleblowers and leakers, which we might call generation
W (for the generation that came of age in the era of WikiLeaks, and now the
war on whistleblowing).

The media's desire to psychoanalyze members of generation W is natural
enough. They want to know why these people are acting in a way that they,
members of the corporate media, would not. But sauce for the goose is sauce
for the gander; if there are psychological motivations for whistleblowing, leaking, and hacktivism, there are likewise psychological motivations for closing
ranks with the power structure within a system—in this case a system in
which corporate media plays an important role. Similarly it is possible that the
system itself is sick, even though the actors within the organization are behaving in accord with organizational etiquette and respecting the internal bonds
of trust.

Just as Hannah Arendt saw that the combined action of loyal managers   20
can give rise to unspeakable systemic evil, so too generation W has seen that
complicity within the surveillance state can gives rise to evil as well—not the
horrific evil that Eichmann's bureaucratic efficiency brought us, but still an
Orwellian future that must be avoided at all costs.   *[2013]*

≡ THINKING ABOUT THE TEXT

1. What does Arendt's phrase "the banality of evil" mean (para. 6)? Give examples from your experience or from history.

2. What is the connection between the panopticon and the five rules of corporate life (para. 7)?

3. How does Ludlow suggest that we can avoid an Orwellian future?

≡ WRITING ABOUT ISSUES

1. Write an argument that agrees or disagrees with the statement that Snowden "did a good thing" (para. 2) in leaking information about the NSA's surveillance program.

2. Research Hannah Arendt's "banality of evil" or the Nuremburg Trials of 1945, and write an essay that explains the moral issues involved and whether you agree or disagree with the principles at stake.

3. Write a personal narrative about a time when you or someone you know stepped outside of an assigned role because of an ethical or moral issue.

4. Research one of the people mentioned (Daniel Ellsberg, John Kiriakou, Chelsea Manning, William Benney, Russ Tice) who defied the "surveillance state," and write a report about what they did, the principles involved, and the outcome.

≡ A Deadly Quest for Freedom: Across Genres

FRANK O'CONNOR, "Guests of the Nation" (story)

SEAMUS HEANEY, "Casualty" (poem)

SEAMUS HEANEY, From "Crediting Poetry" (speech)

It is a painful paradox that often those who fight for freedom have their own freedom confined by the bitter realities of their struggle. Freedom fighters often deny freedom to those they oppose; soldiers for a just cause often commit atrocities, finding they have little choice in their decisions about who lives and who dies. Such contradictions are nowhere clearer than in the Irish struggle for independence over the past several centuries. The Irish people have longed for freedom from British rule since the seventeenth century. That freedom started to become real in the early part of the twentieth century with the Easter Rising of 1916 and a resulting insurgency that gave the Catholic southern part of Ireland partial and, later, full independence. But Northern Ireland, which was mostly Protestant, remained a part of the British Empire. There were deep religious and nationalist differences among the Catholics and Protestants in the North, with the Catholics protesting blatant civil rights violations. The struggle intensified in the late sixties and lasted until the Good Friday Agreement of 1988, which, except for sporadic violence, has held until the present. A catalyst for what are known as "the Troubles" was the killing of thirteen unarmed Catholic protestors on Bloody Sunday in 1972 by British paratroopers. The decades-long unrest that ensued cost over 3,600 lives and injured thousands more in a population of less than two million.

Frank O'Connor's story takes place during the Irish Republican Army's (IRA) struggle with the British in the War of Independence in the early 1920s. The IRA fighters were seen as terrorists by England, and as freedom fighters by most Catholics. Seamus Heaney's poem and the excerpt from his Nobel speech refer to the intense violence of the 1970s and 1980s. Although both authors were Catholics sympathetic to the IRA in its anticolonial struggle, both see the horrific cost in human life and humanistic values, especially as the innocent are devastated by the inevitable cycle of violence and revenge followed by more violence and more revenge.

FRANK O'CONNOR

Guests of the Nation

During the 1920s, Ireland was torn by various levels of armed conflict. The main opponents were England, who had been ruling the country, and Irish militants seeking to free it. Early in the decade, the southern part of Ireland did become semi-independent. Yet in many ways it remained under England's control and Northern Ireland gained no freedom at all. Therefore, the Irish Republican Army and other groups initially

CBS via Getty Images

fought against the new state as well as against the English government. One of the rebels was a clerk from Cork named Michael Donovan (1903–1955), who was eventually captured and sentenced to prison. After his release, he launched what became a long and distinguished career as a fiction writer, taking the pen name Frank O'Connor. Today, he is chiefly known for his short stories. The following one appeared in his first published collection, also entitled Guests of the Nation *(1931).*

1

At dusk the big Englishman, Belcher, would shift his long legs out of the ashes and say "Well. chums, what about it?" and Noble or me would say "All right, chum" (for we had picked up some of their curious expressions), and the little Englishman, Hawkins, would light the lamp and bring out the cards. Sometimes Jeremiah Donovan would come up and supervise the game and get excited over Hawkins's cards, which he always played badly, and shout at him as if he was one of our own "Ah, you divil, you, why didn't you play the tray?"

But ordinarily Jeremiah was a sober and contented poor devil like the big Englishman, Belcher, and was looked up to only because he was a fair hand at documents, though he was slow enough even with them. He wore a small cloth hat and big gaiters over his long pants, and you seldom saw him with his hands out of his pockets. He reddened when you talked to him, tilting from toe to heel and back, and looking down all the time at his big farmer's feet. Noble and me used to make fun of his broad accent, because we were from the town.

I couldn't at the time see the point of me and Noble guarding Belcher and Hawkins at all, for it was my belief that you could have planted that pair down anywhere from this to Claregalway and they'd have taken root there like a native weed. I never in my short experience seen two men to take to the country as they did.

They were handed on to us by the Second Battalion when the search for them became too hot, and Noble and myself, being young, took over with a natural feeling of responsibility, but Hawkins made us look like fools when he showed that he knew the country better than we did.

"You're the bloke they calls Bonaparte," he says to me. "Mary Brigid O'Connell told me to ask you what you done with the pair of her brother's socks you borrowed."   5

For it seemed, as they explained it, that the Second used to have little evenings, and some of the girls of the neighborhood turned in, and, seeing they were such decent chaps, our fellows couldn't leave the two Englishmen out of them. Hawkins learned to dance "The Walls of Limerick," "The Siege of Ennis," and "The Waves of Tory" as well as any of them, though, naturally, he couldn't return the compliment, because our lads at that time did not dance foreign dances on principle.

So whatever privileges Belcher and Hawkins had with the Second they just naturally took with us, and after the first day or two we gave up all pretense of keeping a close eye on them. Not that they could have got far, for they had accents you could cut with a knife and wore khaki tunics and overcoats with civilian pants and boots. But it's my belief that they never had any idea of escaping and were quite content to be where they were.

It was a treat to see how Belcher got off with the old woman of the house where we were staying. She was a great warrant to scold, and cranky even with us, but before ever she had a chance of giving our guests, as I may call them, a lick of her tongue, Belcher had made her his friend for life. She was breaking sticks, and Belcher, who hadn't been more than ten minutes in the house, jumped up from his seat and went over to her.

"Allow me, madam," he says, smiling his queer little smile, "please allow me"; and he takes the bloody hatchet. She was struck too paralytic to speak, and after that, Belcher would be at her heels, carrying a bucket, a basket, or a load of turf, as the case might be. As Noble said, he got into looking before she leapt, and hot water, or any little thing she wanted, Belcher would have it ready for her. For such a huge man (and though I am five foot ten myself I had to look up at him) he had an uncommon shortness or should I say lack? of speech. It took us some time to get used to him, walking in and out, like a ghost, without a word. Especially because Hawkins talked enough for a platoon, it was strange to hear big Belcher with his toes in the ashes come out with a solitary "Excuse me, chum" or "That's right, chum." His one and only passion was cards, and I will say for him that he was a good card-player. He could have fleeced myself and Noble, but whatever we lost to him Hawkins lost to us, and Hawkins played with the money Belcher gave him.

Hawkins lost to us because he had too much old gab, and we probably lost to Belcher for the same reason. Hawkins and Noble would spit at one another about religion into the early hours of the morning, and Hawkins worried the soul out of Noble, whose brother was a priest, with a string of questions that would puzzle a cardinal. To make it worse even in treating of holy subjects, Hawkins had a deplorable tongue. I never in all my career met a man who could mix such a variety of cursing and bad language into an argument. He was a terrible man, and a fright to argue. He never did a stroke of work, and when he had no one else to talk to, he got stuck in the old woman.

He met his match in her, for one day when he tried to get her to complain profanely of the drought, she gave him a great come-down by blaming it entirely on Jupiter Pluvius (a deity neither Hawkins nor I have ever heard of, though Noble said that among the pagans it was believed that he had something to do with the rain). Another day he was swearing at the capitalists for starting the German war when the old lady laid down her iron, puckered up her little crab's mouth, and said: "Mr. Hawkins, you can say what you like about the war, and think you'll deceive me because I'm only a simple poor countrywoman, but I know what started the war. It was the Italian Count that stole the heathen divinity out of the temple in Japan. Believe me, Mr. Hawkins, nothing but sorrow and want can follow the people that disturb the hidden powers."

A queer old girl, all right.

2

We had our tea one evening, and Hawkins lit the lamp and we all sat into cards. Jeremiah Donovan came in too, and sat down and watched us for a while, and it suddenly struck me that he had no great love for the two Englishmen. It came as a great surprise to me, because I hadn't noticed anything about him before.

Late in the evening a really terrible argument blew up between Hawkins and Noble, about capitalists and priests and love of your country.

"The capitalists," says Hawkins with an angry gulp, "pays the priests to tell you about the next world so as you won't notice what the bastards are up to in this."

"Nonsense, man!" says Noble, losing his temper. "Before ever a capitalist was thought of, people believed in the next world."

Hawkins stood up as though he was preaching a sermon.

"Oh, they did, did they?" he says with a sneer. "They believed all the things you believe, isn't that what you mean? And you believe that God created Adam, and Adam created Shem, and Shem created Jehoshophat. You believe all that silly old fairytale about Eve and Eden and the apple. Well, listen to me, chum. If you're entitled to hold a silly belief — like that, I'm entitled to hold my silly belief which is that the first thing your God created was a bleeding capitalist, with morality and Rolls-Royce complete. Am I right, chum?" he says to Belcher.

"You're right, chum," says Belcher with his amused smile, and got up from the table to stretch his long legs into the fire and stroke his moustache. So, seeing that Jeremiah Donovan was going, and that there was no knowing when the argument about religion would be over, I went out with him. We strolled down to the village together, and then he stopped and started blushing and mumbling and saying I ought to be behind, keeping guard on the prisoners. I didn't like the tone he took with me, and anyway I was bored with life in the cottage, so I replied by asking him what the hell we wanted guarding them at all for. I told him I'd talked it over with Noble, and that we'd both rather be out with a fighting column.

"What use are those fellows to us?" says I.   20

He looked at me in surprise and said: "I thought you knew we were keeping them as hostages."

"Hostages?" I said.

"The enemy have prisoners belonging to us," he says, "and now they're talking of shooting them. If they shoot our prisoners, we'll shoot theirs."

"Shoot them?" I said.

"What else did you think we were keeping them for?" he says.   25

"Wasn't it very unforeseen of you not to warn Noble and myself of that in the beginning?" I said.

"How was it?" says he. "You might have known it."

"We couldn't know it, Jeremiah Donovan," says I. "How could we when they were on our hands so long?"

"The enemy have our prisoners as long and longer." says he.

"That's not the same thing at all," says I.   30

"What difference is there?" says he.

I couldn't tell him, because I knew he wouldn't understand. If it was only an old dog that was going to the vet's, you'd try and not get too fond of him, but Jeremiah Donovan wasn't a man that would ever be in danger of that.

"And when is this thing going to be decided?" says I.

"We might hear tonight," he says. "Or tomorrow or the next day at latest. So if it's only hanging round here that's a trouble to you, you'll be free soon enough."

It wasn't the hanging round that was a trouble to me at all by this time. I   35
had worse things to worry about. When I got back to the cottage the argument was still on. Hawkins was holding forth in his best style, maintaining that there was no next world, and Noble was maintaining that there was; but I could see that Hawkins had had the best of it.

"Do you know what, chum?" he was saying with a saucy smile. "I think you're just as big a bleeding unbeliever as I am. You say you believe in the next world, and you know just as much about the next world as I do, which is sweet damn-all. What's heaven? You don't know. Where's heaven? You don't know. You know sweet damn-all! I ask you again, do they wear wings?"

"Very well, then," says Noble, "they do. Is that enough for you? They do wear wings."

"Where do they get them, then? Who makes them? Have they a factory for wings? Have they a sort of store where you hands in your chit and takes your bleeding wings?"

"You're an impossible man to argue with," says Noble. "Now, listen to me—" And they were off again.

It was long after midnight when we locked up and went to bed. As I blew out the candle I told Noble what Jeremiah Donovan was after telling me. Noble took it very quietly. When we'd been in bed about an hour he asked me did I think we ought to tell the Englishmen. I didn't think we should, because it was more than likely that the English wouldn't shoot our men, and even if they did, the brigade officers, who were always up and down with the Second Battalion and knew the Englishmen well, wouldn't be likely to want them plugged. "I think so too," says Noble. "It would be great cruelty to put the wind up them now."

"It was very unforeseen of Jeremiah Donovan anyhow," says I.

It was next morning that we found it so hard to face Belcher and Hawkins. We went about the house all day scarcely saying a word. Belcher didn't seem to notice; he was stretched into the ashes as usual, with his usual look of waiting in quietness for something unforeseen to happen, but Hawkins noticed and put it down to Noble's being beaten in the argument of the night before.

"Why can't you take a discussion in the proper spirit?" he says severely. "You and your Adam and Eve! I'm a Communist, that's what I am. Communist or anarchist, it all comes to much the same thing." And for hours he went round the house, muttering when the fit took him. "Adam and Eve! Adam and Eve! Nothing better to do with their time than picking bleeding apples!"

3

I don't know how we got through that day, but I was very glad when it was over, the tea things were cleared away, and Belcher said in his peaceable way: "Well, chums, what about it?" We sat round the table and Hawkins took out the cards, and just then I heard Jeremiah Donovan's footstep on the path and a dark presentiment crossed my mind. I rose from the table and caught him before he reached the door.

"What do you want?" I asked.

"I want those two soldier friends of yours," he says, getting red.

"Is that the way, Jeremiah Donovan?" I asked.

"That's the way. There were four of our lads shot this morning, one of them a boy of sixteen."

"That's bad," I said.

At that moment Noble followed me out, and the three of us walked down the path together, talking in whispers. Feeney, the local intelligence officer, was standing by the gate.

"What are you going to do about it?" I asked Jeremiah Donovan.

"I want you and Noble to get them out; tell them they're being shifted again; that'll be the quietest way."

"Leave me out of that," says Noble under his breath.

40

45

50

Jeremiah Donovan looks at him hard.

"All right," he says. "You and Feeney get a few tools from the shed and dig   55
a hole by the far end of the bog. Bonaparte and myself will be after you. Don't
let anyone see you with the tools. I wouldn't like it to go beyond ourselves."

We saw Feeney and Noble go round to the shed and went in ourselves. I left
Jeremiah Donovan to do the explanations. He told them that he had orders to
send them back to the Second Battalion. Hawkins let out a mouthful of curses,
and you could see that though Belcher didn't say anything, he was a bit upset
too. The old woman was for having them stay in spite of us, and she didn't stop
advising them until Jeremiah Donovan lost his temper and turned on her. He
had a nasty temper. I noticed. It was pitch-dark in the cottage by this time, but
no one thought of lighting the lamp, and in the darkness the two Englishmen
fetched their topcoats and said good-bye to the old woman.

"Just as a man makes a home of a bleeding place, some bastard at headquarters thinks you're too cushy and shunts you off," says Hawkins, shaking
her hand.

"A thousand thanks, madam, " says Belcher. "A thousand thanks for everything" — as though he'd made it up.

We went round to the back of the house and down towards the bog. It was
only then that Jeremiah Donovan told them. He was shaking with excitement.

"There were four of our fellows shot in Cork this morning and now you're   60
to be shot as a reprisal."

"What are you talking about?" snaps Hawkins. "It's bad enough being
mucked about as we are without having to put up with your funny jokes."

"It isn't a joke," says Donovan. "I'm sorry, Hawkins, but it's true," and begins on the usual rigmarole about duty and how unpleasant it is.

I never noticed that people who talk a lot about duty find it much of a
trouble to them.

"Oh, cut it out!" says Hawkins.

"Ask Bonaparte," says Donovan, seeing that Hawkins isn't taking him seri-   65
ously. "Isn't it true, Bonaparte?"

"It is," I say, and Hawkins stops.

"Ah, for Christ's sake, chum!"

"I mean it, chum," I say.

"You don't sound as if you mean it."

"If he doesn't mean it, I do," says Donovan, working himself up.   70

"What have you against me, Jeremiah Donovan?"

"I never said I had anything against you. But why did your people take out
four of our prisoners and shoot them in cold blood?"

He took Hawkins by the arm and dragged him on, but it was impossible to
make him understand that we were in earnest. I had the Smith and Wesson in
my pocket and I kept fingering it and wondering what I'd do if they put up a
fight for it or ran, and wishing to God they'd do one or the other. I knew if they
did run for it, that I'd never fire on them. Hawkins wanted to know was Noble
in it, and when we said yes, he asked us why Noble wanted to plug him. Why

did any of us want to plug him? What had he done to us? Weren't we all chums? Didn't we understand him and didn't he understand us? Did we imagine for an instant that he'd shoot us for all the so-and-so officers in the so-and-so British Army?

By this time we'd reached the bog, and I was so sick I couldn't even answer him. We walked along the edge of it in the darkness, and every now and then Hawkins would call a halt and begin all over again, as if he was wound up, about our being chums, and I knew that nothing but the sight of the grave would convince him that we had to do it. And all the time I was hoping that something would happen; that they'd run for it or that Noble would take over the responsibility from me. I had the feeling that it was worse on Noble than on me.

4

At last we saw the lantern in the distance and made towards it. Noble was carrying it, and Feeney was standing somewhere in the darkness behind him, and the picture of them so still and silent in the bogland brought it home to me that we were in earnest, and banished the last bit of hope I had.

Belcher, on recognizing Noble, said: "Hallo, chum," in his quiet way, but Hawkins flew at him at once, and the argument began all over again, only this time Noble had nothing to say for himself and stood with his head down, holding the lantern between his legs.

It was Jeremiah Donovan who did the answering. For the twentieth time, as though it was haunting his mind, Hawkins asked if anybody thought he'd shoot Noble.

"Yes, you would," says Jeremiah Donovan.

"No, I wouldn't, damn you!"

"You would, because you'd know you'd be shot for not doing it."

"I wouldn't, not if I was to be shot twenty times over. I wouldn't shoot a pal. And Belcher wouldn't—isn't that right, Belcher?"

"That's right, chum," Belcher said, but more by way of answering the question than of joining in the argument. Belcher sounded as though whatever unforeseen thing he'd always been waiting for had come at last.

"Anyway, who says Noble would be shot if I wasn't? What do you think I'd do if I was in his place, out in the middle of a blasted bog?"

"What would you do?" asks Donovan.

"I'd go with him wherever he was going, of course. Share my last bob with him and stick by him through thick and thin. No one can ever say of me that I let down a pal."

"We had enough of this," says Jeremiah Donovan, cocking his revolver. "Is there any message you want to send?"

"No, there isn't."

"Do you want to say your prayers?"

Hawkins came out with a cold-blooded remark that even shocked me and turned on Noble again.

75

80

85

"Listen to me, Noble," he says. "You and me are chums. You can't come   90
over to my side, so I'll come over to your side. That show you I mean what I say?
Give me a rifle and I'll go along with you and the other lads."

Nobody answered him. We knew that was no way out.

"Hear what I'm saying?" he says. "I'm through with it. I'm a deserter or
anything else you like. I don't believe in your stuff, but it's no worse than mine.
That satisfy you?"

Noble raised his head, but Donovan began to speak and he lowered it again
without replying.

"For the last time, have you any messages to send?" says Donovan in a
cool, excited sort of voice.

"Shut up, Donovan! You don't understand me, but these lads do. They're   95
not the sort to make a pal and kill a pal. They're not the tools of any capitalist."

I alone of the crowd saw Donovan raise his Webley to the back of Hawkins's
neck, and as he did so I shut my eyes and tried to pray. Hawkins had begun to
say something else when Donovan fired, and as I opened my eyes at the bang. I
saw Hawkins stagger at the knees and lie out flat at Noble's feet, slowly and as
quiet as a kid falling asleep, with the lantern-light on his lean legs and bright
farmer's boots. We all stood very still, watching him settle out in the last agony.

Then Belcher took out a handkerchief and began to tie it about his own
eyes (in our excitement we'd forgotten to do the same for Hawkins), and, seeing
it wasn't big enough, turned and asked for the loan of mine. I gave it to him and
he knotted the two together and pointed with his foot at Hawkins.

"He's not quite dead," he says. "Better give him another."

Sure enough. Hawkins's left knee is beginning to rise. I bend down and put
my gun to his head; then, recollecting myself. I get up again. Belcher understands what's in my mind.

"Give him his first," he says. "I don't mind. Poor bastard, we don't know   100
what's happening to him now."

I knelt and fired. By this time I didn't seem to know what I was doing.
Belcher, who was fumbling a bit awkwardly with the handkerchiefs, came out
with a laugh as he heard the shot. It was the first time I heard him laugh and it
sent a shudder down my back; it sounded so unnatural.

"Poor bugger!" he said quietly. "And last night he was so curious about it
all. It's very queer, chums, I always think. Now he knows as much about it as
they'll ever let him know, and last night he was all in the dark."

Donovan helped him to tie the handkerchiefs about his eyes. "Thanks,
chum," he said. Donovan asked if there were any messages he wanted sent.

"No, chum," he says, "not for me. If any of you would like to write to
Hawkins's mother, you'll find a letter from her in his pocket. He and his mother
were great chums. But my missus left me eight years ago. Went away with another fellow and took the kid with her. I like the feeling of a home, as you may
have noticed, but I couldn't start again after that."

It was an extraordinary thing, but in those few minutes Belcher said more   105
than in all the weeks before. It was just as if the sound of the shot had started a
flood of talk in him and he could go on the whole night like that, quite happily,

talking about himself. We stood round like fools now that he couldn't see us any longer. Donovan looked at Noble, and Noble shook his head. Then Donovan raised his Webley, and at that moment Belcher gives his queer laugh again. He may have thought we were talking about him, or perhaps he noticed the same thing I'd noticed and couldn't understand it.

"Excuse me, chums," he says. "I feel I'm talking the hell of a lot, and so silly, about my being so handy about a house and things like that. But this thing came on me suddenly. You'll forgive me, I'm sure."

"You don't want to say a prayer?" asks Donovan.

"No, chum," he says. "I don't think it would help. I'm ready, and you boys want to get it over."

"You understand that we're only doing our duty?" says Donovan.

Belcher's head was raised like a blind man's, so that you could only see his   110
chin and the tip of his nose in the lantern-light.

"I never could make out what duty was myself," he said. "I think you're all good lads, if that's what you mean. I'm not complaining."

Noble, just as if he couldn't bear any more of it, raised his fist at Donovan, and in a flash Donovan raised his gun and fired. The big man went over like a sack of meal, and this time there was no need of a second shot.

I don't remember much about the burying, but that it was worse than all the rest because we had to carry them to the grave. It was all mad lonely with nothing but a patch of lantern-light between ourselves and the dark, and birds hooting and screeching all round, disturbed by the guns. Noble went through Hawkins's belongings to find the letter from his mother, and then joined his hands together. He did the same with Belcher. Then, when we'd filled the grave, we separated from Jeremiah Donovan and Feeney and took our tools back to the shed. All the way we didn't speak a word. The kitchen was dark and cold as we'd left it, and the old woman was sitting over the hearth, saying her beads. We walked past her into the room, and Noble struck a match to light the lamp. She rose quietly and came to the doorway with all her cantankerousness gone.

"What did ye do with them?" she asked in a whisper, and Noble started so that the match went out in his hand.

"What's that?" he asked without turning around.   115

"I heard ye." she said.

"What did you hear?" asked Noble.

"I heard ye. Do ye think I didn't hear ye, putting the spade back in the houseen?"

Noble struck another match and this time the lamp lit for him.

"Was that what ye did to them?" she asked.   120

Then, by God, in the very doorway, she fell on her knees and began praying, and after looking at her for a minute or two Noble did the same by the fireplace. I pushed my way out past her and left them at it. I stood at the door, watching the stars and listening to the shrieking of the birds dying out over the bags. It is so strange what you feel at times like that that you can't describe it. Noble says he saw everything ten times the size, as though there were nothing in the whole world but that little patch of bog with the two Englishmen stiffening into it, but with me it was as if the patch of bog where the Englishmen were was a million miles away, and even Noble and the old woman, mumbling behind me, and the birds and the bloody stars were all far away, and I was somehow very small and very lost and lonely like a child astray in the snow. And anything that happened to me afterwards, I never felt the same about again.   *[1931, 1954]*

≡ THINKING ABOUT THE TEXT

1. What thoughts are expressed about duty in this story? What do these thoughts indicate to you about the characters who express them? Does the story lead you to conclude that any duty is worthwhile? If so, what specific duty or duties do you see it as endorsing?

2. Do you think there is anything Bonaparte can and should have done that he didn't do? Explain. How does his response to the executions differ from Noble's and the woman's? State the difference in your own words.

3. Identify references to the "unforeseen." Which characters were surprised by the execution order? Which, if any, foresaw it? Did the ending surprise you? Why, or why not?

4. Through much of the story, Hawkins argues against religion and capitalism. What do you think of his arguments? Near the end, he argues against his own execution. Should readers agree with the case he makes? Why, or why not? Compare Hawkins and Belcher. Which ultimately strikes you more, their similarities or their differences?

5. Before you read the story, what did you know about conflicts between the English and the Irish? Does O'Connor provide enough historical background for you? If not, what additional sorts of details should he have incorporated into his story? Where in the world are there conflicts today that could produce situations like the one O'Connor depicts?

SEAMUS HEANEY
Casualty

For his distinguished career as a poet, Seamus Heaney (1939–2013) won the Nobel Prize for literature in 1995. He was raised as a Catholic in Northern Ireland, where Protestants remained in the majority and frequently conflicted with Catholics. Until the Peace Accord of 1997, the region was controlled by the British government, whereas now it is ruled by a mixed body representing both religions. Several of Heaney's poems deal with Catholic resistance to the longtime British domination of his native land. Heaney moved to Dublin, in the Republic of Ireland, in the early 1970s, but he often visited the United States, even holding an appointment as Boylston Professor of Rhetoric at Harvard University. The following poem appears in Opened Ground: Selected Poems 1966–1996 *(1998). It is set in Northern*

Boston Globe via Getty Images

Ireland in 1972 after Bloody Sunday, where thirteen civil rights protesters from the Catholic Bogside neighborhood were killed by British troops. The poem is a kind of elegy for an innocent friend of Heaney who was accidentally killed in the terrible aftermath of that massacre, probably by the IRA, seeking revenge. The Irish writer Colm Tóibín wrote, "In a time of burnings and bombings Heaney used poetry to offer an alternative world."

I

He would drink by himself
And raise a weathered thumb
Towards the high shelf,
Calling another rum
And blackcurrant, without   5
Having to raise his voice,
Or order a quick stout
By a lifting of the eyes
And a discreet dumb-show
Of pulling off the top;   10
At closing time would go
In waders and peaked cap

Into the showery dark,
A dole-kept breadwinner
But a natural for work.   15
I loved his whole manner,
Sure-footed but too sly,
His deadpan sidling tact,
His fisherman's quick eye
And turned observant back.   20

Incomprehensible
To him, my other life.
Sometimes, on the high stool,
Too busy with his knife
At a tobacco plug   25
And not meeting my eye,
In the pause after a slug
He mentioned poetry.
We would be on our own
And, always politic   30
And shy of condescension,
I would manage by some trick
To switch the talk to eels
Or lore of the horse and cart
Or the Provisionals.   35

But my tentative art
His turned back watches too:
He was blown to bits
Out drinking in a curfew
Others obeyed, three nights   40
After they shot dead
The thirteen men in Derry.
PARAS THIRTEEN, the walls said,
BOGSIDE NIL. That Wednesday
Everyone held   45
His breath and trembled.

II

It was a day of cold
Raw silence, wind-blown
surplice and soutane:
Rained-on, flower-laden   50
Coffin after coffin
Seemed to float from the door
Of the packed cathedral
Like blossoms on slow water.

The common funeral   55
Unrolled its swaddling band,
Lapping, tightening
Till we were braced and bound
Like brothers in a ring.

But he would not be held   60
At home by his own crowd
Whatever threats were phoned,
Whatever black flags waved.
I see him as he turned
In that bombed offending place,   65
Remorse fused with terror
In his still knowable face,
His cornered outfaced stare
Blinding in the flash.

He had gone miles away   70
For he drank like a fish
Nightly, naturally
Swimming towards the lure
Of warm lit-up places,
The blurred mesh and murmur   75
Drifting among glasses
In the gregarious smoke.
How culpable was he
That last night when he broke
Our tribe's complicity?   80
'Now, you're supposed to be
An educated man,'
I hear him say. 'Puzzle me
The right answer to that one.'

III

I missed his funeral,   85
Those quiet walkers
And sideways talkers
Shoaling out of his lane
To the respectable
Purring of the hearse . . .   90
They move in equal pace
With the habitual
Slow consolation
Of a dawdling engine,
The line lifted, hand   95
Over fist, cold sunshine

On the water, the land
Banked under fog: that morning
I was taken in his boat,
The Screw purling, turning   100
Indolent fathoms white,
I tasted freedom with him.
To get out early, haul
Steadily off the bottom,
Dispraise the catch, and smile   105
As you find a rhythm
Working you, slow mile by mile,
Into your proper haunt
Somewhere, well out, beyond . . .

Dawn-sniffing revenant,   110
Plodder through midnight rain,
Question me again.   *[1998]*

≡ THINKING ABOUT THE TEXT

1. How specifically is Heaney's friend (Louis O'Neill) described in the first stanza? Translate the description after "whole manner" (line 16) into simple prose.

2. What do the friends talk about? What does the speaker do when the fisherman mentions poetry (line 28)?

3. In what specific ways are the lines in stanza seven that begin, "To get out early . . ." (line 103) a possible comparison between fishing and writing poetry? Why is this an apt connection?

4. Part II begins with the funeral of those killed on Bloody Sunday, which the speaker refers to in the closing lines of stanza three. How is the funeral described? What poetic devices are used?

5. Apparently the IRA gave warnings that Louis did not heed. Are any reasons given? Heaney imagines Louis asking him a question (stanza 6, lines 81–84). What is it, and what might an answer be? How does this relate to the poem's last three lines?

SEAMUS HEANEY
From *Crediting Poetry*

Awarded the prestigious Nobel Prize for literature in 1995 for his "works of lyrical beauty and ethical depth," Heaney spoke mostly about his poetic life but also focused on the Troubles and the ubiquitous violence that was "productive of nothing but retaliatory violence." He does not diminish the brutality of the IRA bombings, but he also reminds us of the grave injustices suffered by the Catholic minority in Northern Ireland. The following excerpt from his Nobel acceptance speech makes clear his heartbreaking frustration at the callousness of his homeland's sectarian violence.

One of the most harrowing moments in the whole history of the harrowing of the heart in Northern Ireland came when a minibus full of workers being driven home one January evening in 1976 was held up by armed and masked men and the occupants of the van ordered at gunpoint to line up at the side of the road. Then one of the masked executioners said to them, "Any Catholics among you, step out here." As it happened, this particular group, with one exception, were all Protestants, so the presumption must have been that the masked men were Protestant paramilitaries about to carry out a tit-for-tat sectarian killing of the Catholic as the odd man out, the one who would have been presumed to be in sympathy with the IRA and all its actions. It was a terrible moment for him, caught between dread and witness, but he did make a motion to step forward. Then, the story goes, in that split second of decision, and in the relative cover of the winter evening darkness, he felt the hand of the Protestant worker next to him take his hand and squeeze it in a signal that said no, don't move, we'll not betray you, nobody need know what faith or party you belong to. All in vain, however, for the man stepped out of the line; but instead of finding a gun at his temple, he was thrown backward and away as the gunmen opened fire on those remaining in the line, for these were not Protestant terrorists, but members, presumably, of the Provisional IRA.

It is difficult at times to repress the thought the history is about as instructive as an abattoir; that Tacitus was right and that peace is merely the desolation left behind after the decisive operations of merciless power. I remember, for example, shocking myself with a thought I had about that friend who was imprisoned in the seventies upon suspicion of having been involved with a political murder: I shocked myself by thinking that even if he were guilty, he might still perhaps be helping the future to be born, breaking the repressive forms and liberating new potential in the only way that worked, that is to say the violent way — which therefore became, by extension, the right way. It was like a moment of exposure to interstellar cold, a reminder of the scary element, both inner and outer, in which human beings must envisage and conduct their lives. But it was only a moment. The birth of the future we desire is surely in the contraction which that terrified Catholic felt on the roadside when another hand gripped his hand, not in the gunfire that followed, so absolute and so desolate, if also so much a part of the music of what happens.   *[1995]*

≡ THINKING ABOUT THE TEXT

1. Why does Heaney claim that "history is as instructive as an abattoir" (slaughterhouse) (para. 2)?

2. Why does Heaney say he shocked himself?

3. Describe what Heaney means by the idea that the future he desires is in "the contraction which that terrified Catholic felt . . ." (para. 2).

4. How would you describe Heaney's position on revolutionary violence?

5. What is the "scary element" Heaney mentions (para. 2)? Is this something all of us are capable of, depending on the context? Explain.

≡ WRITING ABOUT ISSUES

1. Argue that the members of the IRA in "Guests of the Nation" were terrorists or freedom fighters or perhaps something else. Take into consideration Heaney's poem and speech.

2. Write a review of one of the following films: *Bloody Sunday* (2002) about the massacre mentioned in "Casualty"; *The Wind That Shakes the Barley* (2006) about the closing days of the War of Independence focused on in "Guests of the Nation"; Neil Jordan's *The Crying Game* (1992), a film that imagines a continuation of O'Connor's story in surprising and controversial ways.

3. Change "Casualty" to a narrative that tells the story of Louis O'Neill in prose, using either a first person or omniscient point of view.

4. Read William Butler Yeats's poem, "Easter, 1916," and write an essay that compares its themes, topics, characters, metaphors, and tone to "Casualty" and the Nobel lecture.

CHAPTER 10

Crime and Justice

Thinking about literature involves making judgments about other people's views. Throughout your course, you have been making judgments as you interpret and evaluate written works, including the texts in this book and those produced by the class. You have been deciding also how you feel about positions expressed by your teacher and classmates. In all these acts of judgment, you have considered where you stand on general issues of aesthetics, ethics, politics, religion, and law.

Outside school, you judge things all the time, though you may not always be aware that you are doing so. You may be more conscious of your judgments when other people disagree with you, when you face multiple options, when you are trying to understand something complex, when your decisions will have significant consequences, or when you must review an act you have already committed. Some people are quite conscious that they make judgments because they have the political, professional, or institutional authority to enforce their will. Of course, these people may wind up being judged by whomever they dominate, and they may even face active revolt.

A term closely related to *judgment* is *justice*, which many people associate with judgments that are wise, fair, and sensitive to the parties involved. In this sense, justice is an ideal, which may not always be achieved in real life. Indeed, though communities hope their police departments and courts will act soundly, sometimes representatives of our legal institutions are accused of violating justice instead of upholding it. Much, of course, depends on how *justice* is defined in any particular case, and equally crucial is who defines it. The same is true of the word *crime*. Many works of literature have challenged laws of the society in which they were written, while others have at least questioned or complicated the notions of justice prevailing in their culture. Often, literature has probed the complexities of situations that in real life are resolved as clear victories for one particular party. In this respect, literature draws attention to issues that we may normally oversimplify or overlook.

Through poems by D. H. Lawrence, Elizabeth Bishop, and William Stafford, the opening cluster in this chapter treats the issue of how human beings should apply the concept of justice to animals. How to define *justice*—especially with respect to conditions for workers—is a dominant question in the cluster that follows: a set of poems by Philip Levine, Marge Piercy, Jimmy Santiago Baca, and Philip Schultz. In the subsequent section, poems by Countee Cullen and

Natasha Trethewey—both entitled "Incident"—present speakers confronted by racial injustice. Then come three poems that examine the responsibilities of people who inflict, witness, or learn about punishments. The ensuing cluster uses poems by William Blake, Mark Jarman, and Maurice Manning to imagine what a world of ideal justice would be like. These works are followed by a pair of poems whose speakers assert their own sense of justice by taking revenge against their spouses. In Robert Browning's classic "My Last Duchess," the speaker is a vengeful man, while Gabriel Spera's contemporary poem "My Ex-Husband" offers the reverse perspective.

The single-author cluster in this chapter focuses on writings by Langston Hughes, who repeatedly called for his society to treat African Americans more justly. After our Hughes collection come stories by Jessamyn West and Toni Cade Bambara that probe the psychological changes that youths may experience when they sense great injustice for the first time. Stories by William Faulkner and Edward J. Delaney, however, remind their readers that crimes can be committed in secret, the perpetrators unexposed. The same point is subsequently reinforced by Edgar Allan Poe's and Andre Dubus's stories about revenge. The next two clusters also focus on criminal activities that seem to go unpunished. The first features Joyce Carol Oates's well-known story "Where Are You Going, Where Have You Been?" along with texts that help situate the work in cultural contexts; the second highlights Flannery O'Connor's story "A Good Man is Hard to Find" along with commentaries on it. Then we juxtapose two plays written almost a hundred years apart, Susan Glaspell's *Trifles* and Lynn Nottage's *POOF!*, to focus on crimes that can occur within marriage or a similar relationship. The consequences of a real-life crime are examined in the cluster that follows, where we present essays by Bruce Shapiro and Emily Bernard that recall a stabbing attack each writer suffered. The chapter concludes by drawing on works widely separated in history—Sophocles' play *Antigone* and Martin Luther King Jr.'s "Letter from Birmingham Jail"—to get you thinking about when, if ever, people are justified in committing civil disobedience.

D. H. LAWRENCE, "Snake"

ELIZABETH BISHOP, "The Fish"

WILLIAM STAFFORD, "Traveling Through the Dark"

The last few decades have given rise to numerous organizations and social movements that fight for animal rights. But for centuries, literature has raised the issue of how best to treat animals. The following poems center in turn on human behavior toward a snake, a fish, and a deer. They encourage you to wonder what it means to give these specific creatures justice. At the same time, the poems' ethical implications extend beyond these species. In general, should the term *justice* apply to animals the same ways it applies to humans? Do animals indeed have "rights"? What is "fair" and "decent" conduct toward them? What sorts of acts would be "crimes" against them?

≡ BEFORE YOU READ

Describe at least one encounter you have had with wildlife, noting how you behaved at the time and what influenced your conduct. What is your attitude toward people who like to hunt or fish? What forms of wildlife, if any, do you think people are justified in fearing or despising? Do you think the notion of animal rights has merit? Identify particular values that your answers reflect.

D. H. LAWRENCE
Snake

David Herbert Lawrence (1885–1930) was a leading novelist and short-story writer in the first half of the twentieth century. The son of a coal miner and a former schoolteacher, he describes his English working-class upbringing in his autobiographical novel Sons and Lovers *(1913). Probably he remains best known for his 1928 novel* Lady Chatterley's Lover. *For many years, it was banned in England and the United States because it explicitly described the sexual relationship between an aristocratic woman and her husband's gamekeeper. In most of his work, Lawrence endorses human passion, although he argued that people needed to exist in harmony with nature as well as with one another. Besides writing fiction, he painted and wrote poetry. "Snake," published in 1913, is based on Lawrence's stay in Sicily, one of the many places he went as he searched for a land friendly to his ideals.*

A snake came to my water-trough
On a hot, hot day, and I in pyjamas for the heat,
To drink there.

In the deep, strange-scented shade of the great dark carob-tree
I came down the steps with my pitcher   5
And must wait, must stand and wait, for there he was at the trough
    before me.

He reached down from a fissure in the earth-wall in the gloom
And trailed his yellow-brown slackness soft-bellied down, over the edge
    of the stone trough
And rested his throat upon the stone bottom,
And where the water had dripped from the tap, in a small clearness,   10
He sipped with his straight mouth,
Softly drank through his straight gums, into his slack long body,
Silently.

Someone was before me at my water-trough,
And I, like a second comer, waiting.   15

He lifted his head from his drinking, as cattle do,
And looked at me vaguely, as drinking cattle do,
And flickered his two-forked tongue from his lips, and mused a moment,
And stooped and drank a little more,
Being earth-brown, earth-golden from the burning bowels of the earth   20
On the day of Sicilian July, with Etna smoking.

The voice of my education said to me
He must be killed,
For in Sicily the black, black snakes are innocent, the gold are
    venomous.

And voices in me said, If you were a man   25
You would take a stick and break him now, and finish him off.

But must I confess how I liked him,
How glad I was he had come like a guest in quiet, to drink at my
    water-trough
And depart peaceful, pacified, and thankless,
Into the burning bowels of this earth?   30

Was it cowardice, that I dared not kill him?
Was it perversity, that I longed to talk to him?
Was it humility, to feel so honoured?
I felt so honoured.

And yet those voices: 35
If you were not afraid, you would kill him!

And truly I was afraid, I was most afraid,
But even so, honoured still more
That he should seek my hospitality
From out the dark door of the secret earth.   40

He drank enough
And lifted his head, dreamily, as one who has drunken,
And flickered his tongue like a forked night on the air, so black;
Seeming to lick his lips,
And looked around like a god, unseeing, into the air,   45
And slowly turned his head,
And slowly, very slowly, as if thrice adream,
Proceeded to draw his slow length curving round
And climb again the broken bank of my wall-face.

And as he put his head into that dreadful hole,   50
And as he slowly drew up, snake-easing his shoulders, and entered
        farther,
A sort of horror, a sort of protest against his withdrawing into that
        horrid black hole,
Deliberately going into the blackness, and slowly drawing himself after,
Overcame me now his back was turned.

I looked round, I put down my pitcher,   55
I picked up a clumsy log
And threw it at the water-trough with a clatter.

I think it did not hit him,
But suddenly that part of him that was left behind convulsed in
        undignified haste,
Writhed like lightning, and was gone   60
Into the black hole, the earth-lipped fissure in the wall-front,
At which, in the intense still noon, I stared with fascination.

And immediately I regretted it.
I thought how paltry, how vulgar, what a mean act!
I despised myself and the voices of my accursed human education.   65

And I thought of the albatross,°
And I wished he would come back, my snake.

For he seemed to me again like a king,
Like a king in exile, uncrowned in the underworld,
Now due to be crowned again.   70

And so, I missed my chance with one of the lords
Of life.
And I have something to expiate;
A pettiness.   *[1913]*

---

66 albatross: In Samuel Taylor Coleridge's "Rime of the Ancient Mariner," a seaman
brings misfortune to the crew of his ship by killing an albatross, an ocean bird.

≣ THINKING ABOUT THE TEXT

1. What did you associate with snakes before reading this poem? Does Lawrence push you to look at snakes differently, or does his poem endorse the view you already had? Develop your answer by referring to specific lines.

2. Discuss the poem as an argument involving various "voices." How do you think you would have reacted to the snake if you had been the speaker? What "voices" might you have heard inside your own mind? What people or institutions would these "voices" have come from?

3. Why does the speaker throw the log just as the snake is leaving? Note the explanation the speaker gives as well as the judgment he then makes about his act. Do both make sense to you? Why, or why not?

4. Lawrence begins many lines with the word *and*. What is the effect of his doing so?

5. In "Snake," Lawrence writes positively about an animal that is often feared. Think of a similar poem that you might write. What often-feared animal would you choose? What positive qualities would you point out or suggest in describing this animal? If you wish, try actually writing such a poem.

ELIZABETH BISHOP

The Fish

Although she also wrote short stories, Elizabeth Bishop (1911–1979) is primarily known for her poetry, winning both the Pulitzer Prize and the National Book Award for it. Born in Worcester, Massachusetts, she spent much of her youth in Nova Scotia. As an adult, she lived in various places, including New York City, Florida, Mexico, and Brazil. Much of her poetry observes and reflects on a particular object or figure. Such is the case with "The Fish," which Bishop wrote in 1940 and then included in her 1946 book North and South.

I caught a tremendous fish
and held him beside the boat
half out of water, with my hook
fast in a corner of his mouth.
He didn't fight.   5
He hadn't fought at all.
He hung a grunting weight,
battered and venerable
and homely. Here and there
his brown skin hung in strips   10
like ancient wall-paper,

and its pattern of darker brown
was like wall-paper:
shapes like full-blown roses
stained and lost through age.   15
He was speckled with barnacles,
fine rosettes of lime,
and infested
with tiny white sea-lice,
and underneath two or three   20
rags of green weed hung down.
While his gills were breathing in
the terrible oxygen
—the frightening gills,
fresh and crisp with blood,   25
that can cut so badly—
I thought of the coarse white flesh
packed in like feathers,
the big bones and the little bones,
the dramatic reds and blacks   30
of his shiny entrails,
and the pink swim-bladder
like a big peony.
I looked into his eyes
which were far larger than mine   35
but shallower, and yellowed,
the irises backed and packed
with tarnished tinfoil
seen through the lenses
of old scratched isinglass.°   40
They shifted a little, but not
to return my stare.
—It was more like the tipping
of an object toward the light.
I admired his sullen face,   45
the mechanism of his jaw,
and then I saw
that from his lower lip
—if you could call it a lip—
grim, wet, and weapon-like,   50
hung five old pieces of fish-line,
or four and a wire leader
with the swivel still attached,
with all their five big hooks
grown firmly in his mouth.   55

---

40 isinglass: A substitute for glass made from mica.

A green line, frayed at the end
where he broke it, two heavier lines,
and a fine black thread
still crimped from the strain and snap
when it broke and he got away.   60
Like medals with their ribbons
frayed and wavering,
a five-haired beard of wisdom
trailing from his aching jaw.
I stared and stared   65
and victory filled up
the little rented boat,
from the pool of bilge
where oil had spread a rainbow
around the rusted engine   70
to the bailer rusted orange,
the sun-cracked thwarts,
the oarlocks on their strings,
the gunnels—until everything
was rainbow, rainbow, rainbow!   75
And I let the fish go.   *[1946]*

≡ THINKING ABOUT THE TEXT

1. Does the speaker change her attitude toward the fish, or does it stay pretty much the same? Support your reasoning by referring to specific lines. Are you surprised that the speaker lets the fish go? Why, or why not? How effective a conclusion is her release of the fish?

2. To what extent is the speaker describing the fish objectively? In what ways, if any, does her description of him seem to reflect her own particular values? Refer to specific lines.

3. The speaker reports that "victory filled up / the little rented boat" (lines 66–67). Whose victory might she have in mind? Why might she use this word? Often, a victory for one is a defeat for another. Is that the case here?

4. Where does the poem refer to acts and instruments of seeing? What conclusions might be drawn from these references?

5. How significant is it that the fish is male?

≡ MAKING COMPARISONS

1. What would you say to someone who argues that Bishop's speaker is more admirable than Lawrence's speaker because she lets the animal go free?

2. With both Lawrence's and Bishop's poems, consider what you learn about the speaker's own state of mind. Does one poem tell you more than the other about its speaker's thoughts? Support your answer by referring to specific lines.

3. Bishop's poem is one long, continuous stanza, whereas Lawrence divides his into several stanzas. Does this difference in strategy lead to a significant difference in effect? Do you consider one of these strategies better than the other? Explain your reasoning.

WILLIAM STAFFORD
Traveling through the Dark

Besides being a poet himself, William Stafford (1914–1995) was a mentor to many others. During World War II, he was a conscientious objector. Later, he wrote and taught poetry at a variety of places in the United States, eventually settling in Oregon. The following poem was written in 1960 and subsequently appeared in a 1962 collection of Stafford's poems, also entitled Traveling through the Dark, *which won the National Book Award in 1963. He went on to publish over fifty more volumes of poetry and prose. He taught at Lewis and Clark College until his retirement in 1980. Like those of Robert Frost, to whom Stafford is often compared, his poems are deceptively simple. On closer examination, however, they reveal themselves to be complex and highly suggestive of deeper concerns.*

Traveling through the dark I found a deer
dead on the edge of the Wilson River road.
It is usually best to roll them into the canyon:
that road is narrow; to swerve might make more dead.

By glow of the tail-light I stumbled back of the car   5
and stood by the heap, a doe, a recent killing;
she had stiffened already, almost cold.
I dragged her off; she was large in the belly.

My fingers touching her side brought me the reason —
her side was warm; her fawn lay there waiting,   10
alive, still, never to be born.
Beside that mountain road I hesitated.

The car aimed ahead its lowered parking lights;
under the hood purred the steady engine.
I stood in the glare of the warm exhaust turning red;   15
around our group I could hear the wilderness listen.

I thought hard for us all — my only swerving —
then pushed her over the edge into the river.   *[1962]*

≡ THINKING ABOUT THE TEXT

1. What would you say to someone who argues that the situation in this poem is too unusual to be relevant for most readers?

2. What does the speaker conceivably mean in saying "I could hear the wilderness listen" (line 16)? What do you infer from his use of the word "purred" in line 14?

3. What are possible interpretations of the title — in particular, of the word "dark"?

4. Why do you think the narrator "hesitated" (line 12)? How would you define "swerve" as used in line 4? How about as it is used in the penultimate line?

5. How sensible do you find the choice that the speaker makes at the end? Explain your reasoning.

≡ MAKING COMPARISONS

1. Bishop's and Stafford's speakers make decisions. Does Lawrence's speaker make one, too? Explain what you mean by *decision*.

2. Stafford's speaker reports that "I thought hard for us all" (line 17). Can this statement apply to Lawrence's and Bishop's speakers as well? Why, or why not?

3. Does time of day matter equally in all three poems? Refer to their specific circumstances.

≡ WRITING ABOUT ISSUES

1. What does it mean to treat an animal with justice? Choose Lawrence's, Bishop's, or Stafford's poem, and write an essay that interprets it as an answer to this question. Make clear in your analysis how you yourself define *justice*.

2. How important is setting in each of these poems? Choose two of them, and write an essay in which you consider whether their particular locations are equally important.

3. Write an essay recalling an occasion when you found it hard to decide what's involved in treating an animal with justice. What definition of *justice* did you end up with? If you wish, refer to one or more of the poems in this cluster.

4. Find a case in the news that centers on the issue of how best to treat animals, and then write an essay that develops your own position on the case by referring to at least one of the poems in this cluster.

PHILIP LEVINE, "What Work Is"

MARGE PIERCY, "The Secretary Chant"

JIMMY SANTIAGO BACA, "So Mexicans Are Taking Jobs from Americans"

PHILIP SHULTZ, "Greed"

During the 1930s, the world suffered a great economic depression. Millions who wanted employment couldn't find it. Today, things are significantly better. Many hold stable, well-paying, and fulfilling positions. Still, not everyone thrives. To compete in the new global economy, corporations cut budgets, relocate plants, outsource services, and automate facilities. As a result, large numbers of people have lost their jobs, others work for low wages, and even college graduates worry about their prospects for careers. Though defenses of capitalism continue to be voiced, protests against it like Occupy Wall Street burst forth. Whatever their political stance, social activists and average citizens ponder how to define *justice* for workers and what policies would promote it. In effect, the following poems also raise these issues, by depicting conditions of work at various times in modern American history.

■ BEFORE YOU READ

What are the characteristics of your ideal job? In what ways, if any, have your real jobs fallen short?

PHILIP LEVINE
What Work Is

In his long career as a poet, Philip Levine (b. 1928) has often written about working-class culture in Detroit, Michigan, his native city. At an early age and then at later times in his life, he himself worked in car manufacturing there. For thirty years, however, he taught at California State University in Fresno, and he has been a visiting professor at several other schools. Levine was appointed to serve as U.S. poet laureate in 2011–2012 and received the Pulitzer Prize in poetry for his book The Simple Truth *(1994). The following selection is the title poem from his book* What Work Is *(1991). His many other volumes of poetry include* News of the World *(2009),* Stranger to Nothing: Selected Poems *(2006),* Breath *(2004),* The Mercy *(1999),* The Names of the Lost *(1976),* They Feed They Lion *(1972),* and On the Edge *(1963).*

> We stand in the rain in a long line
> waiting at Ford Highland Park. For work.

You know what work is — if you're
old enough to read this you know what
work is, although you may not do it.   5
Forget you. This is about waiting,
shifting from one foot to another.
Feeling the light rain falling like mist
into your hair, blurring your vision
until you think you see your own brother   10
ahead of you, maybe ten places.
You rub your glasses with your fingers,
and of course it's someone else's brother,
narrower across the shoulders than
yours but with the same sad slouch, the grin   15
that does not hide the stubbornness,
the sad refusal to give in to
rain, to the hours wasted waiting,
to the knowledge that somewhere ahead
a man is waiting who will say, "No,   20
we're not hiring today," for any
reason he wants. You love your brother,
now suddenly you can hardly stand
the love flooding you for your brother,
who's not beside you or behind or   25
ahead because he's home trying to
sleep off a miserable night shift
at Cadillac so he can get up
before noon to study his German.
Works eight hours a night so he can sing   30
Wagner, the opera you hate most,
the worst music ever invented.
How long has it been since you told him
you loved him, held his wide shoulders,
opened your eyes wide and said those words,   35
and maybe kissed his cheek? You've never
done something so simple, so obvious,
not because you're too young or too dumb,
not because you're jealous or even mean
or incapable of crying in   40
the presence of another man, no,
just because you don't know what work is.   *[1991]*

≡ **THINKING ABOUT THE TEXT**

1. In the third line, the speaker declares, "You know what work is," but at
   the very end he declares, "you don't know what work is" (line 42). How

do you explain this shift? What definition of *work*, if any, does the poem leave you with?

2. In line 6, the speaker claims that "this is about waiting." Identify the multiple places where the word *waiting* appears in the poem. In what sense(s) can a poem about work be about waiting, too?

3. How is this poem also about the ability to see?

4. What is the significance of the poem's beginning "We"? Who is the "you" that the speaker proceeds to address?

5. What image of his brother does the speaker create? How would you describe the relationship between these brothers?

MARGE PIERCY
The Secretary Chant

Like Philip Levine, Marge Piercy (b. 1936) is originally from the working-class community of Detroit, Michigan, though she now lives in Wellfleet, Massachusetts. In addition to being a well-known author, she has played major roles in political movements, including feminism, environmentalism, and antiwar protests. She is prolific not only as a poet, but also as a novelist. Her novels include the widely read Woman on the Edge of Time *(1976) as well as* The Longings of Women *(1994),* Gone to Soldiers *(1987),* Fly Away Home *(1984),* Braided Lives *(1982),* Vida *(1980),* The High Cost of Living *(1978), and* Small Changes *(1973). The following poem is included in the 1982 collection* Circles on the Water: Selected Poems of Marge Piercy. *Among her many other volumes of poetry are* The Crooked Inheritance *(2006),* Available Light *(1988),* The Moon is Always Female *(1980),* The Twelve-Spoked Wheel Flashing *(1978),* To Be of Use *(1973),* Hard Loving *(1969), and* Breaking Camp *(1968). In recent years, Piercy has focused especially on Jewish history, theology, and culture, in part through her service as poetry editor of the magazine* Tikkun *and through her book* The Art of Blessing the Day: Poems with a Jewish Theme *(1999).*

My hips are a desk.
From my ears hang
chains of paper clips.
Rubber bands form my hair.

My breasts are wells of mimeograph ink.   5
My feet bear casters.
Buzz. Click.
My head is a badly organized file.
My head is a switchboard

where crossed lines crackle.   10
Press my fingers

and in my eyes appear
credit and debit.
Zing. Tinkle.

My navel is a reject button.   15
From my mouth issue canceled reams.
Swollen, heavy, rectangular
I am about to be delivered
of a baby

Xerox machine.   20
File me under W
because I wonce
was
a woman.   *[1973]*

≡ THINKING ABOUT THE TEXT

1. Note the poem's title. What do you associate with chanting? What features of Piercy's text strike you as chant-like?

2. Note where Piercy uses *enjambment*—places, that is, where a sentence spills over from one line to the next. What is the technique's effect at these moments?

3. In the last stanza, Piercy spells the word *once* as "wonce" (line 22). Why, do you think? The very last word of the poem is *woman*. But how gender-specific is this text? How much would you have to alter it, and in what ways, if you wanted to make it clearly about a male worker?

4. What indications, if any, are there that Piercy wrote this poem in the 1970s? What elements of the poem, if any, fit today's world?

5. What would you say to someone who argues that the speaker simply suffers from a poor self-perception and has the power within herself to change it?

≡ MAKING COMPARISONS

1. Is Levine's poem as gender-specific as Piercy's is? Explain your reasoning.

2. How can Piercy's poem be seen as responding to the issue of definition raised by Levine's title, "What Work Is"?

3. In what way might *waiting*, a key word in Levine's poem, be applied to Piercy's?

JIMMY SANTIAGO BACA

So Mexicans Are Taking Jobs from Americans

Originally from Santa Fe, New Mexico, Jimmy Santiago Baca (b. 1952) is a poet, autobiographer, and social activist whose writing often reflects his Chicano and Apache heritage. He candidly acknowledges his experience in prison, where he spent five years after being convicted of drug charges in 1973. After teaching himself literacy there, he eventually earned a B.A. in English at the University of New Mexico. The following poem appears in the 1991 edition of his collection Immigrants in Our Own Land *(first published in 1979). Other books of his include* Spring Poems Along the Rio Grande *(2007),* Winter Poems Along the Rio Grande *(2004),* C-Train & 13 Mexicans *(2002),* Healing Earthquakes *(2001), and* A Place to Stand *(2001), a memoir that won the International Prize. Baca is the founder of Cedar Tree, which runs educational programs for various groups—including people who have served time in prison and those who are still incarcerated.*

O Yes? do they come on horses
with rifles, and say,
    Ese, gringo, gimmee your job?
And do you, gringo, take off your ring,
drop your wallet into a blanket   5
spread over the ground, and walk away?

I hear Mexicans are taking your jobs away.
Do they sneak into town at night,
and as you're walking home with a whore,
do they mug you, a knife at your throat,   10
saying, I want your job?

Even on TV, an asthmatic leader
crawls turtle heavy, leaning on an assistant,
and from a nest of wrinkles on his face,
a tongue paddles through flashing waves   15
of lightbulbs, of cameramen, rasping,
"They're taking our jobs away."

Well, I've gone about trying to find them,
asking just where the hell are these fighters.

The rifles I hear sound in the night   20
are white farmers shooting blacks and browns
whose ribs I see jutting out
and starving children,
I see the poor marching for a little work,
I see small white farmers selling out   25
to clean-suited farmers living in New York,
who've never been on a farm,

don't know the look of a hoof or the smell
of a woman's body bending all day long in fields.

I see this, and I hear only a few people   30
got all the money in this world, the rest
count their pennies to buy bread and butter.

Below that cool green sea of money,
millions and millions of people fight to live,
search for pearls in the darkest depths   35
of their dreams, hold their breath for years
trying to cross poverty to just having something.

The children are dead already. We are killing them,
that is what America should be saying;
on TV, in the streets, in offices, should be saying,   40
"We aren't giving the children a chance to live."

    Mexicans are taking our jobs, they say instead.
    What they really say is, let them die,
    and the children too.   [1982]

≣ THINKING ABOUT THE TEXT

1. How would you describe the audience that the poem's speaker is addressing? Refer to specific lines.

2. What argument does the speaker make as a response to the claim in the poem's title? How does the speaker support his own argument through pathos, the rhetorical strategy that uses emotional appeals to persuade an audience? Again, refer to specific lines.

3. Where does the poem bring up class (social divisions based on wealth), not just nationality?

4. Note places where the speaker reports what "I see" and "I hear." How accurate do you consider his testimony? Do you "see" and "hear" the same things he does?

5. Where does the speaker use metaphor? Do you find the technique effective in this poem? Why, or why not?

≣ MAKING COMPARISONS

1. What would you say to someone who argues that Levine's, Piercy's, and Baca's poems are all full of despair? Do any of these poems express at least *some* optimism or propose at least *some* constructive action?

2. Baca's speaker challenges a claim made in the poem's title. What claims might Levine's and Piercy's speakers be challenging?

3. In Baca's poem, a significant shift—a turning point—comes with the fourth stanza. From then on, the speaker presents what he considers a reality that challenges the poem's title claim. Are there turning points in Levine's and Piercy's poems, too? If so, where?

PHILIP SCHULTZ

Greed

A native of Rochester, New York, Philip Schultz (b. 1945) has produced numerous volumes of poetry. They include The Wherewithal *(2014),* The God of Loneliness: Selected and New Poems *(2010),* Living in the Past *(2004),* The Holy Worm of Praise *(2002),* Deep Within the Ravine *(1984),* Like Wings *(1978), and* Failure *(2007), which won the Pulitzer Prize. He has also written a memoir,* My Dyslexia *(2011). Schultz founded and continues to direct The Writers Studio, which offers programs in the writing of both poetry and fiction. The following poem was published in the July/August 2013 issue of* Poetry *magazine.*

My ocean town struggles
to pick up leaves,
offer summer school,
and keep our library open.
Every day now   5
more men stand
at the railroad station,
waiting to be chosen for work.
Because it's thought
the Hispanics will work for less   10
they get picked first,
while the whites and blacks
avoid the terror
in one another's eyes.
Our handyman, Santos,   15
who expects only
what his hands earn,
is proud of his half acre in Guatemala,
where he plans to retire.
His desire to proceed with dignity   20
is admirable, but he knows
that now no one retires,
everyone works harder.
My father imagined a life
more satisfying than the one   25
he managed to lead.

He didn't see himself as uneducated,
thwarted, or bitter,
but soon-to-be rich.
Being rich was his right, he believed.   30
Happiness, I used to think,
was a necessary illusion.
Now I think it's just
precious moments of relief,
like dreams of Guatemala.   35
Sometimes, at night,
in winter, surrounded by
the significant silence
of empty mansions,
which once were cottages,   40
where people lived their lives,
and now are owned by banks
and the absent rich,
I like to stand at my window,
looking for a tv's futile flickering,   45
always surprised to see
instead
the quaint, porous face
of my reflection,
immersed   50
in its one abundance.   *[2013]*

≡ THINKING ABOUT THE TEXT

1. Despite being the title, the word *greed* never appears in the poem. What lines, if any, do you think it applies to? Why might Schultz have chosen to omit it from his actual text?

2. Although the poem is a single stanza, it makes a number of shifts as it proceeds. What are these? Given that it can be divided into stages, why do you suppose Schultz decided not to break the poem into multiple stanzas?

3. The speaker reports that he has changed his definition of happiness. State this change in your own words. Does it make sense to you? Why, or why not?

4. Where does the speaker call our attention to things *not* present? Refer to specific lines.

5. The poem begins by referring to the speaker's community, but it ends with him looking at his own reflection. Is it fair to say, then, that the speaker becomes increasingly self-absorbed? Explain your reasoning.

≡ MAKING COMPARISONS

1. As a single stanza, Schultz's poem resembles Levine's. In what other ways are these two poems similar? What would you say to someone who argues that Schultz is *too* influenced by Levine?

2. To what extent are Levine's, Piercy's, and Baca's poems also about greed?

3. Of the four poems in this cluster, Schultz's is by far the newest, published in 2013. If you didn't know these poems' publication dates, would you be able to tell that Schultz's is the most recent? Why, or why not?

≡ WRITING ABOUT ISSUES

1. Choose one of the poems in this cluster, and write an essay explaining how it seems to define *justice* for workers. Make clear your own understanding of this concept.

2. Choose two of the poems, and write an essay comparing the attention they give to the speaker's self. To what extent do these poems' speakers look beyond themselves to offer insights into the larger world?

3. Recall an occasion when you or someone you know suffered unjust working conditions and yet failed to challenge them right away. Then, write an essay in which you analyze the sufferer's state of mind — the thoughts and feelings that this person had at the time, including any psychological changes that he or she went through. If you wish, refer to one or more poems in this cluster.

4. Write an essay in which you apply the title of one of this cluster's poems to a recent news report. What major aspects of the report does the poem's title fit? What major aspects, if any, does the title not cover?

▬ Racial Injustice: Poems

COUNTEE CULLEN, "Incident"

NATASHA TRETHEWEY, "Incident"

Throughout literary history, writers have called attention to the injustices of racial oppression. The following pair of poems, both entitled "Incident," remind us that racial prejudice could be blatant and vicious both early in the twentieth century and toward its end. Indeed, the subject is not likely to die out even now, when laws blatantly permitting slavery or segregation have ceased to exist. Racism continues in various forms, though perhaps subtler ones. As you read these poems, consider what recent "incidents" might be topics of similar texts.

▬ BEFORE YOU READ

How do you define *racism*? What, for you, are possible signs of it?

COUNTEE CULLEN
Incident

Countee Cullen (1903–1946) was one of the leading writers of the Harlem Renaissance, a New York-based movement of African American authors, artists, and intellectuals that flourished from World War I to the Great Depression. Cullen's place of birth may have been Baltimore, Louisville, or New York, but by 1918 he was living in New York as the adopted son of a Methodist minister. Cullen wrote poetry and received prizes for it even as he attended New York University. In 1925, while pursuing a master's degree from Harvard, he published his first book of poems, Color, which contained "Incident." His later books include Copper Sun (1927), The Black Christ and Other Poems (1929), a translation of Euripides' play Medea (1935), and a children's book, The Lost Zoo (1940). Cullen gained much attention when, in 1928, he wed the daughter of famed African American writer and scholar W. E. B. DuBois, but their marriage ended just two years later. During the 1930s, Cullen's writing did not earn him enough to live on, so he taught English and French at Frederick Douglass High School. At the time of his death in 1946, he was collaborating on the Broadway musical St. Louis Woman. In part because he died relatively young, Cullen's reputation faded. Langston Hughes became much better known as a Harlem Renaissance figure. "Incident," however, has been consistently anthologized, and today Cullen is being rediscovered along with other contributors to African American literature.

Once riding in old Baltimore
    Heart-filled, head-filled with glee,
I saw a Baltimorean
    Keep looking straight at me.

Now I was eight and very small,   5
    And he was no whit bigger,
And so I smiled, but he poked out
    His tongue and called me, "Nigger."

I saw the whole of Baltimore
    From May until December: 10
Of all the things that happened there
    That's all that I remember.   *[1925]*

≡ THINKING ABOUT THE TEXT

1. Why do you think the speaker calls attention to his heart *and* his head in the second line? Might referring to just one of these things have been enough?

2. "Baltimorean" (line 3) seems a rather unusual and abstract term for the boy that the speaker encountered. How do you explain its presence in the poem? How important is it that the speaker name the city where the incident occurred?

3. Although the incident that the speaker recalls must have been painful for him, why do you think he does not state his feelings about it more explicitly? What is the effect of his relative reticence about it?

4. The rhythm of this poem is rather singsongy. Why do you think Cullen made it so?

5. The speaker states that he was eight at the time of the incident. How old might he be now? How important is his age?

NATASHA TRETHEWEY

Incident

The child of an interracial marriage, Natasha Trethewey (b. 1966) graduated from the University of Georgia and earned a master's degree at Hollins College in Virginia. Now she teaches creative writing at Emory University in Atlanta, Georgia. She is the author of several volumes of poetry, such as Domestic Work *(2000),* Bellocq's Ophelia *(2002), and* Native Guard *(2006), which won the Pulitzer Prize and includes the following poem. Her latest books are another poetry collection,* Thrall *(2102), and* Beyond Katrina: A Meditation on the Mississippi Gulf Coast *(2010), a combination of memoir and reportage that also mixes prose with verse. Trethewey was appointed to serve as U.S. poet laureate for 2012–2014.*

We tell the story every year—
how we peered from the windows, shades drawn—
though nothing really happened,
the charred grass now green again.

We peered from the windows, shades drawn,   5
at the cross trussed like a Christmas tree,
the charred grass still green. Then
we darkened our rooms, lit the hurricane lamps.

At the cross trussed like a Christmas tree,
a few men gathered, white as angels in their gowns.   10
We darkened our rooms and lit hurricane lamps,
the wicks trembling in their fonts of oil.

It seemed the angels had gathered, white men in their gowns.
When they were done, they left quietly. No one came.
The wicks trembled all night in their fonts of oil;   15
by morning the flames had all dimmed.

When they were done, the men left quietly. No one came.
Nothing really happened.
By morning all the flames had dimmed.
We tell the story every year.   [2006]   20

≣ THINKING ABOUT THE TEXT

1. Trethewey has acknowledged that this poem is a *pantoum*. This form of verse consists of *quatrains* (stanzas of four lines each); also, the second and fourth lines of a quatrain are repeated as the first and third lines of the following quatrain, with the final line of the entire poem repeating its very first line. It's a difficult type of poem to write. Why do you think Trethewey attempted it here?

2. How does the poem use religious imagery?

3. What information does the poet leave out? Why do you think she omits it?

4. Why do you think the "we" of the poem "tell[s] the story every year"? Why tell the story at all? Why not tell it more often?

5. Twice, the speaker claims that "nothing really happened." Do you agree with her? Why, or why not?

≣ MAKING COMPARISONS

1. In giving her poem the title "Incident," Trethewey is surely aware of Cullen's poem. What other connections between these two texts do you feel encouraged by her to make?

2. Which of the two poems, Cullen's or Trethewey's, strikes you as more abstract? Does this difference lead to a difference in effect? Why, or why not?

3. Do the speakers in these two poems strike you as using pretty much the same tone? Refer to specific lines in each work.

≡ WRITING ABOUT ISSUES

1. Choose either Cullen's poem or Trethewey's, and write an essay in which you examine what the poem suggests about the act of *remembering* an incident of race-related injustice.

2. Cullen's poem is famous; does Trethewey's deserve to be equally well known? Write an essay addressing this question for your audience, making clear your criteria for artistic success.

3. Take a line from either Cullen's poem or Trethewey's, and write an essay showing how the line is applicable to an "incident" that you recently witnessed or saw being reported in the media.

4. Find and read at least three articles on racial discrimination in early twentieth-century Baltimore or on American laws against interracial marriage. Then write an essay explaining how these articles illuminate the "incident" described in Cullen's or Trethewey's poem.

SEAMUS HEANEY, "Punishment"

CAROLYN FORCHÉ, "The Colonel"

SHERMAN ALEXIE, "Capital Punishment"

Acts of punishment may be just or unjust: in any case, a punishment reflects the decisions and values of the person ordering it and the ethics of the person willing to carry it out. Even people who merely learn about a punishment wind up judging it. Consciously or unconsciously, they choose to praise it, criticize it, or passively tolerate it. Each of these three poems deals with judgments made by punishers and by those who are, in some sense, their audience. Think about the actions you are taking and the principles you are expressing as you judge the people you encounter here.

■ BEFORE YOU READ

Recall a particular punishment that you considered unjust. What were the circumstances? What experiences, values, and reasoning led you to disapprove of the punishment? Could you have done anything to prevent it or to see that similarly unfair punishments did not recur? If so, what?

SEAMUS HEANEY
Punishment

For his distinguished career as a poet, Seamus Heaney (1939–2013) won the Nobel Prize for literature in 1995. He was raised as a Catholic in Northern Ireland, where Protestants remained in the majority and frequently conflicted with Catholics. Until the Peace Accord of 1997, the region was controlled by the British government, whereas now it is ruled by a mixed body representing both religions. Several of Heaney's poems deal with Catholic resistance to the longtime British domination of his native land. Heaney moved to Dublin, in the Republic of Ireland, in the early 1970s, but he often visited the United States, even holding an appointment as Boylston Professor of Rhetoric at Harvard University. The following poem appears in Heaney's 1975 book North. *It is part of a whole sequence of poems based on P. V. Glob's 1969 book* The Bog People. *Heaney was drawn to Glob's photographs of Iron Age people whose preserved bodies were discovered in bogs of Denmark and other European countries.*

> I can feel the tug
> of the halter at the nape

of her neck, the wind
on her naked front.

It blows her nipples   5
to amber beads,
it shakes the frail rigging
of her ribs.

I can see her drowned
body in the bog,   10
the weighing stone,
the floating rods and boughs.

Under which at first
she was a barked sapling
that is dug up   15
oak-bone, brain-firkin°:

her shaved head
like a stubble of black corn,
her blindfold a soiled bandage,
her noose a ring   20

to store
the memories of love.
Little adulteress,
before they punished you

you were flaxen-haired,   25
undernourished, and your
tar-black face was beautiful.
My poor scapegoat,

I almost love you
but would have cast, I know, 30
the stones of silence.°
I am the artful voyeur

of your brain's exposed
and darkened combs,
your muscles' webbing   35
and all your numbered bones:

I who have stood dumb
when your betraying sisters,

16 firkin: A small cask.   **30–31 would have cast . . . of silence:** In John 8:7–9, Jesus confronts a mob about to stone an adulterous woman and makes the famous statement "He that is without sin among you, let him first cast a stone at her." The crowd retreats, "being convicted by their own conscience."

cauled in tar,
wept by the railings,°   40

who would connive
in civilized outrage
yet understand the exact
and tribal, intimate revenge.   *[1975]*

37–40 I who . . . by the railings: In 1969, the British army became highly visible occupiers of Northern Ireland. In Heaney's native city of Belfast, the Irish Republican Army
retaliated against Irish Catholic women who dated British soldiers. Punishments included
shaving the women's heads, stripping and tarring them, and handcuffing them to the city's
railings.

☰ THINKING ABOUT THE TEXT

1. Summarize your impression of the bog woman. Where does the speaker
   begin addressing her directly? Why do you suppose Heaney has him refrain from addressing her right away?

2. Who is the main subject of this poem? The bog woman? The "betraying
   sisters" (line 38)? The speaker? Some combination of these people?

3. The speaker refers to himself as a "voyeur" (line 32). Consult a dictionary definition of this word. How might it apply to the speaker? Do you
   think it is ultimately the best label for him? Explain. Do you feel like a
   voyeur reading this poem? Why, or why not?

4. What are the speaker's thoughts in the last stanza? What connotation
   do you attach to the word *connive*? (You might want to consult a dictionary definition of it.) What is the speaker's attitude toward "the exact /
   and tribal, intimate revenge"? Do you see him as tolerating violence?

5. What words in this poem, if any, are unfamiliar to you? What is their
   effect on you? Each stanza has four lines. Does this pattern create a
   steady rhythm or one more fragmented than harmonious? Try reading it
   aloud.

CAROLYN FORCHÉ
The Colonel

*In her poetry, Carolyn Forché (b. 1950) often addresses contemporary abuses of
power. Her first book of poems,* Gathering the Tribes *(1976), won the Yale Series
of Younger Poets competition. The following poem is from her second,* The Country
between Us *(1981), which won the Lamont Award from the Academy of American
Poets. Much of this book is based on Forché's experiences during her stay in
El Salvador, which at the time was beset by civil war. She has edited two anthologies,*
Poetry of Witness: The Tradition in English, 1500–2001 *(2014) and* Against
Forgetting: Twentieth-Century Poetry of Witness *(1993). Her own latest book*

of poetry is The Blue Hour *(2003). She is currently a professor of English at Georgetown University in Washington, D.C.*

What you have heard is true. I was in his house. His wife carried a tray of coffee and sugar. His daughter filed her nails, his son went out for the night. There were daily papers, pet dogs, a pistol on the cushion beside him. The moon swung bare on its black cord over the house. On the television was a cop show. It was in English. Broken bottles were embedded in the walls around the house   5
to scoop the kneecaps from a man's legs or cut his hands to lace. On the windows there were gratings like those in liquor stores. We had dinner, rack of lamb, good wine, a gold bell was on the table for calling the maid. The maid brought green mangoes, salt, a type of bread. I was asked how I enjoyed the country. There was a brief commercial in Spanish. His wife took everything   10
away. There was some talk then of how difficult it had become to govern. The parrot said hello on the terrace. The colonel told it to shut up, and pushed himself from the table. My friend said to me with his eyes: say nothing. The colonel returned with a sack used to bring groceries home. He spilled many human ears on the table. They were like dried peach halves. There is no other way to   15
say this. He took one of them in his hands, shook it in our faces, dropped it into a water glass. It came alive there. I am tired of fooling around he said. As for the rights of anyone, tell your people they can go fuck themselves. He swept the ears to the floor with his arm and held the last of his wine in the air. Something for your poetry, no? he said. Some of the ears on the floor caught this scrap of   20
his voice. Some of the ears on the floor were pressed to the ground.   *[1978]*

≡ THINKING ABOUT THE TEXT

1. How do you characterize the colonel? List a number of specific adjectives and supporting details. Does your impression of him change as you read, or does it stay pretty much the same? Explain.

2. Forché calls this text a poem, and yet it seems to consist of one long prose paragraph. Here is an issue of genre: Is it *really* a poem? Support your answer by identifying what you think are characteristics of poetry. What is the effect of Forché's presenting the text as a poem? Note what the colonel says about poetry. How might this text be considered a response to him?

3. Forché uses many short sentences here. What is the effect of this strategy? Even though she quotes the colonel, she does not use quotation marks. What is the effect of this choice?

4. The poem begins, "What you have heard is true." Do you think the situation it describes really occurred? Identify some assumptions that influence your answer. Where else does the poem refer to hearing? How might it be seen as being about audiences and their responses?

5. Forché wrote "The Colonel" after a stay in El Salvador, and so it is reasonable for her audience to conclude that the poem is set in that country. Yet she does not actually specify the setting. Should she have done so? Why, or why not?

≡ MAKING COMPARISONS

1. Do you find the punishments alluded to in Heaney's and Forché's poems equally disturbing? Note specific details that influence your impressions.

2. To what extent does each of these two poems seem an effort to imagine the mind of someone who inflicts punishment?

3. Which, if any, of the situations referred to in these two poems could happen in the contemporary United States?

SHERMAN ALEXIE
Capital Punishment

Born in Spokane, Washington, Sherman Alexie (b. 1966) is a member of the Spokane/ Coeur d'Alene tribe. His fiction includes the novels Reservation Blues *(1996),* Indian Killer *(1997),* Flight *(2007), and* The Absolutely True Diary of a Part-Time Indian *(2007). He has produced five collections of short stories:* Blasphemy: New and Selected Stories *(2013),* War Dances *(2010),* The Toughest Indian in the World *(2001),* Ten Little Indians *(2003), and* The Lone Ranger and Tonto Fistfight in Heaven *(1994), which he adapted for the acclaimed 1998 film* Smoke Signals. *Alexie is a poet, too, with his collections of verse including* The Business of Fancy Dancing *(1992),* Old Shirts & New Skins *(1993),* First Indian on the Moon *(1993), and* One Stick Song *(2000). "Capital Punishment" appeared in a 1995 issue of* Indiana Review *and, that same year, in Alexie's collection* The Summer of Black Widows. *It was also selected for the 1996 edition of* The Best American Poetry. *Alexie wrote the poem after reading media coverage of an actual execution in the state of Washington.*

I prepare the last meal
for the Indian man to be executed

but this killer doesn't want much:
baked potato, salad, tall glass of ice water.

(I am not a witness)   5

It's mostly the dark ones
who are forced to sit in the chair

especially when white people die.
It's true, you can look it up

and this Indian killer pushed   10
his fists all the way down

a white man's throat, just to win a bet
about the size of his heart.

Those Indians are always gambling.
Still, I season this last meal   15

with all I have. I don't have much
but I send it down the line

with the handsome guard
who has fallen in love

with the Indian killer.   20
I don't care who loves whom.

(I am not a witness)

I don't care if I add too much
salt or pepper to the warden's stew.

He can eat what I put in front of him.   25
I just cook for the boss

but I cook just right
for the Indian man to be executed.

The temperature is the thing.
I once heard a story   30

about a black man who was electrocuted
in that chair and lived to tell about it

before the court decided to sit him back down
an hour later and kill him all over again.

I have an extra sandwich hidden away   35
in the back of the refrigerator

in case this Indian killer survives
that first slow flip of the switch

and gets hungry while he waits
for the engineers to debate the flaws.   40

(I am not a witness)

I prepare the last meal for free
just like I signed up for the last war.

I learned how to cook
by lasting longer than any of the others.   45

Tonight, I'm just the last one left
after the handsome guard takes the meal away.

I turn off the kitchen lights
and sit alone in the dark

because the whole damn prison dims   50
when the chair is switched on.

You can watch a light bulb flicker
on a night like this

and remember it too clearly
like it was your first kiss   55

or the first hard kick to your groin.
It's all the same

when I am huddled down here
trying not to look at the clock

look at the clock, no, don't   60
look at the clock, when all of it stops

making sense: a salad, a potato
a drink of water all taste like heat.

(I am not a witness)

I want you to know I tasted a little   65
of that last meal before I sent it away.

It's the cook's job, to make sure
and I was sure I ate from the same plate

and ate with the same fork and spoon
that the Indian killer used later   70

in his cell. Maybe a little bit of me
lodged in his stomach, wedged between

his front teeth, his incisors, his molars
when he chewed down on the bit

and his body arced like modern art   75
curving organically, smoke rising

from his joints, wispy flames decorating
the crown of his head, the balls of his feet.

(I am not a witness)

I sit here in the dark kitchen   80
when they do it, meaning

when they kill him, kill
and add another definition of the word

to the dictionary. America fills
its dictionary. We write down *kill* and everybody   85

in the audience shouts out exactly how
they spell it, what it means to them

and all of the answers are taken down
by the pollsters and secretaries

who take care of the small details: 90
time of death, pulse rate, press release.

I heard a story once about some reporters
at a hanging who wanted the hood removed

from the condemned's head, so they could look
into his eyes and tell their readers   95

what they saw there. What did they expect?
All of the stories should be simple.

1 death + 1 death = 2 deaths.
But we throw the killers in one grave

and victims in another. We form sides   100
and have two separate feasts.

(I am a witness)

I prepared the last meal
for the Indian man who was executed

and have learned this: If any of us   105
stood for days on top of a barren hill

during an electrical storm
then lightning would eventually strike us

and we'd have no idea for which of our sins
we were reduced to headlines and ash.   *[1996]* 110

≣ THINKING ABOUT THE TEXT

1. Alexie reports that in writing this poem, he aimed "to call for the abolition of the death penalty." In reading the poem, do you sense that this
   is his aim? Why, or why not? In what respects might the poem be seen
   as arguing against the death penalty? State how you viewed capital punishment before and after you read it. Did Alexie affect your attitude? If
   so, how?

2. Why do you think Alexie cast the speaker as the condemned man's cook? How do you explain the speaker's shift from denying that he is a witness to acknowledging that he is one? Identify how he seems to define the term *witness*. What would you say to someone who argues that the speaker is unreasonably stretching the meaning of this word because apparently he didn't directly observe the execution?

3. How does race figure in this poem? Should people consider race when discussing capital punishment? If so, what about race should they especially ponder? In examining Alexie's poem, should readers bear in mind that the author is Native American? Why, or why not?

4. The film *Dead Man Walking* (1995), which deals with arguments about capital punishment, shows in chilling detail an execution by injection. Yet at the moment the condemned man dies, the film also shows the faces of his two victims. By contrast, Alexie doesn't refer to the victim of the executed man after line 12. Should he have mentioned this victim again? Identify some of the values reflected in your answer.

5. Summarize and evaluate the lesson delivered by the speaker at the end of the poem. What do you think headlines might say about you if you were killed in the manner he describes?

≡ MAKING COMPARISONS

1. Forché's first sentence is "What you have heard is true." After noting that "It's mostly the dark ones / who are forced to sit in the chair / especially when white people die" (lines 6–8), Alexie's speaker declares, "It's true, you can look it up" (line 9). What do these lines imply about each poem's readers?

2. In his last three lines, Alexie's speaker refers to "us," a pronoun that apparently refers to society in general. Do Forché's and Heaney's also seem to have this "us" in mind? If so, do all three speakers seem to be making the same point about this "us"? Support your answers with details from the poems.

3. Of all the punishments mentioned in these three poems, only the one discussed in Alexie's—capital punishment—is currently authorized by law in the United States. Should this fact make his poem the most relevant to American readers? Why, or why not?

≡ WRITING ABOUT ISSUES

1. Choose one of the poems in this cluster. Then write an essay explaining how it can be seen as a poem about witnessing *or* about how people may be somehow involved with events that they haven't directly observed. If your essay refers to witnessing, make clear your definition of the term.

2. Even when people are not literally guilty of a crime or an atrocity, they may still *feel* guilty in a psychological sense. Choose two of the poems in this cluster, and write an essay arguing that one poem's main speaker evidently feels more guilt than the other poem's main speaker does. Refer to specific lines in both texts.

3. Write an essay in which you discuss whether the phrase "cruel and unusual punishment" applies to the event described in this paragraph from the March 26, 1997, issue of the *Washington Post*:

   > Moments after convicted killer Pedro Medina was strapped into Florida's electric chair and 2,000 volts of electricity surged into his body this morning, flames leapt from the inmate's head, filling the death chamber with smoke and horrifying two dozen witnesses.

   Does Medina's execution amount to "cruel and unusual punishment"? If you need additional information before firmly deciding, what do you need to know?

4. Today, Amnesty International and PEN International, a writers' organization, regularly bring to the American public's attention cases of what they deem unjust punishment. In fact, Amnesty International has criticized all instances of capital punishment in the United States. Research one of the cases reported by these organizations. Then write an article for your school newspaper in which you (a) present the basic facts of the case, (b) identify values and principles you think your audience should apply to it, and (c) point out anything you believe can and should be done about it. If you wish, refer to any of the poems in this cluster.

WILLIAM BLAKE, "The Chimney Sweeper"

MARK JARMAN, "If I Were Paul"

MAURICE MANNING, "The Hill People"

The next three poems invite readers to imagine what a more just world than the current one would be like. Such a vision involves defining what *justice* means in the first place. It also involves identifying what the leading examples of present injustice are. Directly or indirectly, each poem in this cluster points to moral blights that its speaker hopes to cure. Whether or not utopia can ever be achieved, these literary works encourage their audiences to identify and challenge existing social ills.

■ BEFORE YOU READ

When you think about major types of injustice today, what specifically comes to your mind?

WILLIAM BLAKE
The Chimney Sweeper

His contemporaries largely dismissed him as eccentric, even mad, but William Blake (1757–1827) is now regarded as a major figure in British Romanticism. In part, Blake was a printer and an engraver, lavishly illustrating his own editions of his poems. Through both his visual and his verbal art, Blake promoted his own self-devised religion, which incorporated stories and characters from the Bible. The following poem appears in his 1789 collection Songs of Innocence. *In 1794, he produced a counterpart volume,* Songs of Experience.

When my mother died I was very young,
And my father sold me while yet my tongue
Could scarcely cry "'weep! 'weep! 'weep! 'weep!"
So your chimneys I sweep & in soot I sleep.

There's little Tom Dacre, who cried when his head   5
That curled like a lamb's back, was shaved, so I said,
"Hush, Tom! never mind it, for when your head's bare,
You know that the soot cannot spoil your white hair."

And so he was quiet, & that very night,
As Tom was a-sleeping he had such a sight!   10

That thousands of sweepers, Dick, Joe, Ned, & Jack,
Were all of them locked up in coffins of black;

And by came an Angel who had a bright key,
And he opened the coffins & set them all free;
Then down a green plain, leaping, laughing they run,   15
And wash in a river and shine in the Sun.

Then naked & white, all their bags left behind,
They rise upon clouds, and sport in the wind.
And the Angel told Tom, if he'd be a good boy,
He'd have God for his father & never want joy.   20

And so Tom awoke; and we rose in the dark
And got with our bags & our brushes to work.
Though the morning was cold, Tom was happy & warm;
So if all do their duty, they need not fear harm.   *[1789]*

≡ THINKING ABOUT THE TEXT

1. How do colors matter in this poem?

2. What is the effect of the poem's obvious rhyming?

3. Why do you think that Blake made the dream Tom's rather than the speaker's?

4. As an imaginative vision of a better world, how unusual does Tom's dream strike you?

5. Do you assume that the author himself agrees with the last line? Why, or why not? In general, how much of what the speaker says do you think Blake wants his readers to accept? Explain.

MARK JARMAN
If I Were Paul

Mark Jarman (b. 1952) is Centennial Professor of English at Vanderbilt University in Nashville, Tennessee. The author of two essay collections, The Secret of Poetry *(2001) and* Body and Soul *(2002), he has also produced several books of verse, including* Questions for Ecclesiastes *(1998),* Unholy Sonnets *(2000),* To the Green Man *(2004),* Bone Fires: New and Selected Poems *(2011), and* Epistles *(2007), which begins with the following poem. In the Bible, the genre of the epistle is associated with Paul of Tarsus. It is a type of letter that he supposedly wrote to first-century churches in various cities, addressing issues they faced. Martin Luther King Jr.'s "Letter from Birmingham Jail" (see this chapter's "Civil Disobedience" cluster) has been viewed as a modern-day Pauline epistle.*

Consider how you were made.

Consider the loving geometry that sketched your bones, the passionate symmetry that sewed flesh to your skeleton, and the cloudy zenith whence your soul descended in shimmering rivulets across pure granite to pour as a single braided stream into the skull's cup.

Consider the first time you conceived of justice, engendered mercy, brought parity into being, coaxed liberty like a marten from its den to uncoil its limber spine in a sunny clearing, how you understood the inheritance of first principles, the legacy of noble thought, and built a city like a forest in the forest, and erected temples like thunderheads.

Consider, as if it were penicillin or the speed of light, the discovery of another's hands, his oval field of vision, her muscular back and hips, his nerve-jarred neck and shoulders, her bleeding gums and dry elbows and knees, his baldness and cauterized skin cancers, her lucid and forgiving gaze, his healing touch, her mind like a prairie. Consider the first knowledge of otherness. How it felt.

Consider what you were meant to be in the egg, in your parents' arms,   5
under a sky full of stars.

Now imagine what I have to say when I learn of your enterprising viciousness, the discipline with which one of you turns another into a robot or a parasite or a maniac or a body strapped to a chair. Imagine what I have to say.

Do the impossible. Restore life to those you have killed, wholeness to those you have maimed, goodness to what you have poisoned, trust to those you have betrayed.

Bless each other with the heart and soul, the hand and eye, the head and foot, the lips, tongue, and teeth, the inner ear and the outer ear, the flesh and spirit, the brain and bowels, the blood and lymph, the heel and toe, the muscle and bone, the waist and hips, the chest and shoulders, the whole body, clothed and naked, young and old, aging and growing up.

I sent you this not knowing if you will receive it, or if having received it, you will read it, or if having read it, you will know that it contains my blessing.   [2008]

≡ THINKING ABOUT THE TEXT

1. Paul was an early Christian. Do you see Jarman's poem as addressed primarily to people of this faith? Why, or why not?

2. Note the first line. Why, in order to correct injustice, might it be important to "Consider how you were made"?

3. The next three stanzas are pretty dense in their language. Try to express in your own words the main ideas they convey. Should Jarman have used much simpler wording than he does? Why, or why not?

4. In the sixth stanza, the speaker accuses his audience of "enterprising viciousness." In the next stanza, he says that they have "killed," "maimed," "poisoned," and "betrayed" people. What would you say to someone who argues that language like this would merely offend readers rather than persuade them to share the speaker's ideals?

5. What, in general, does the speaker emphasize in his next-to-last stanza when he calls for things to be blessed?

≡ MAKING COMPARISONS

1. Does the last line of Blake's poem ("So if all do their duty, they need not fear harm") have any relevance to Jarman's poem? If so, in what respect?

2. Does Blake's chimney sweeper seem capable of expressing any of the anger that Jarman's speaker does? Explain your reasoning.

3. Do you think that Blake's chimney sweeper would be shocked by much of what Jarman's speaker says? Why, or why not?

MAURICE MANNING
The Hill People

Maurice Manning (b. 1966) teaches at Transylvania University in Lexington, Kentucky, his native state. His first volume of poetry, Lawrence Booth's Book of Visions *(2001), won the Yale Series of Younger Poets Competition. His subsequent collections include* A Companion for Owls *(2004),* Bucolics *(2007),* The Gone and The Going Away *(2013), and* The Common Man *(2010), which was a finalist for the Pulitzer Prize. In addition to writing, Manning has been active in campaigns against environmentally destructive practices of coal mining in Appalachia. "The Hill People" was published in the Winter 2013 issue of the journal* Appalachian Heritage.

And then the hill people came down
riding mules flanked by dogs
some feist some liver-spotted hounds
and they were ghosts the men and women
and their ash-faced children their mules   5
and dogs were ghosts come down from the place
where they had lived in scant array
like lint in the pockets of their dark land

and the men were gaunt and the women were thin
and the children had hayseed flung   10
in their hair and the dogs tracked back and forth
and they came to the town which wasn't a town
but a circle of nothing surrounding nowhere
no river no trees no shadows no time
for darkness no slow crawl   15
toward love or death or after death
the nowhere town was fast and the people
who lived there only wanted more
whatever it was and the next thing
after that they had appetite   20
but not desire and they didn't come
from anywhere and didn't know
they lived in a place that wasn't a place
and the hill people with their haunted faces
said to the people of the town   25
you have taken everything there is
and heaped it into a god a god
who gives you nothing not even
a tree no shade behind the tree
no wind to carry the birdsong   30
no branch to quiver with the bird
no doubt no hope no lie no mirth
no tenderness no shame no knowing
hill or horizon or the hand
behind it or why no silence nothing   35
no end this was the vision I had.   [2013]

≡ THINKING ABOUT THE TEXT

1. Manning has written thirty-six lines without a clear, punctuated sentence break until the very end. Why do you think he employs this strategy? What is its effect?

2. Note the poem's last words. Why do you think Manning delays letting us know that what we are reading is someone's personal "vision"?

3. Trace the poem's repetitions of the word *no*. What is the effect of these? In what sense can a town be "a circle of nothing" (line 13) if there are people living there?

4. What do you suppose turned the hill people into "ghosts" (line 4)? Do you take Manning to be implying that their way of life was ideal? Why, or why not?

5. Beginning with line 26, the hill people make an accusation against the community they have come to. Put this accusation in your own words. What might be the community's response?

≣ **MAKING COMPARISONS**

1. How might Blake's chimney sweeper interpret the "vision" had by Manning's speaker?

2. What specific lines in Jarman's poem, if any, express sentiments that resemble those of Manning's hill people?

3. Can all three poems in this cluster be considered epistles? Why, or why not?

≣ **WRITING ABOUT ISSUES**

1. Choose one of the poems in this cluster, and write an essay in which you identify what are, in general, the injustice(s) that the poem considers. Refer to specific lines.

2. The three poems in this cluster differ markedly in the number and kinds of stanzas they use. Choose two of the poems, and write an essay in which you explain how the different ways they use stanzas produce major differences in effect.

3. Write your own epistle, in prose or verse, to a specific group of people who in your view have committed a particular injustice. In your letter, do not simply accuse your readers of a moral failing and demand that they correct it; explain *why* you are disturbed by something they have done, as well as *how* it amounts to an injustice in your definition of the term. If you wish, refer to any of the poems in this cluster.

4. Choose a recent speech, editorial, or blog entry that you see as identifying an injustice and as imagining a world in which it no longer exists. Write an essay analyzing the strategies of persuasion the speaker or writer uses. If you wish, refer to any of the poems in this cluster.

ROBERT BROWNING, "My Last Duchess"

GABRIEL SPERA, "My Ex-Husband"

Although the terms *justice* and *injustice* are most often applied to developments that affect entire groups, these words can also prove relevant to personal relationships. In particular, two people may quit being a couple because at least one of them feels that the other has done an injustice to him or her. Of course, the two parties may define *justice* differently, and they may disagree as well about which of them is in the wrong. Together, the following poems illustrate such a conflict of views. Indeed, they present a he said/she said scenario. In the first poem, Robert Browning's famous "My Last Duchess," the speaker explains how his wife's allegedly unjust behavior forced him to get rid of her. In the second poem, Gabriel Spera's more recent "My Ex-Husband," the speaker recalls how her former spouse's injustices drove her to divorce him. Notice the specific ways that Spera's re-vision of Browning's poem forces us to consider differences in perspective.

≡ BEFORE YOU READ

Think of two people you know who have broken off a relationship they had with each other. To what extent do these people see the breakup the same way? How, if at all, do their views of it differ?

ROBERT BROWNING
My Last Duchess

*Today, Robert Browning (1812–1889) is regarded as one of the greatest poets of nineteenth-century England, but in his own time he was not nearly as celebrated as his wife, the poet Elizabeth Barrett Browning. He is chiefly known for his achievements with the **dramatic monologue**, a genre of poetry that emphasizes the speaker's own distinct personality. Often Browning's speakers are his imaginative re-creations of people who once existed in real life. He was especially interested in religious, political, and artistic figures from the Renaissance. The following poem, perhaps Browning's most famous, was written in 1842, and its speaker, the Duke of Ferrara, was an actual man.*

© Bettmann/Corbis

Ferrara°

That's my last Duchess painted on the wall,
Looking as if she were alive. I call
That piece a wonder, now: Frà Pandolf's° hands
Worked busily a day, and there she stands.
Will't please you sit and look at her? I said   5
"Frà Pandolf" by design, for never read
Strangers like you that pictured countenance,
The depth and passion of its earnest glance,
But to myself they turned (since none puts by
The curtain I have drawn for you, but I)   10
And seemed as they would ask me, if they durst,
How such a glance came there; so, not the first
Are you to turn and ask thus. Sir, 'twas not
Her husband's presence only, called that spot
Of joy into the Duchess' cheek: perhaps   15

EPIGRAPH Ferrara: In the sixteenth century, the duke of this Italian city arranged to marry a second time after the mysterious death of his very young first wife.   **3 Frà Pandolf:** A fictitious artist.

Frà Pandolf chanced to say "Her mantle laps
Over my lady's wrist too much," or "Paint
Must never hope to reproduce the faint
Half-flush that dies along her throat": such stuff
Was courtesy, she thought, and cause enough   20
For calling up that spot of joy. She had
A heart—how shall I say?—too soon made glad,
Too easily impressed; she liked whate'er
She looked on, and her looks went everywhere.
Sir, 'twas all one! My favor at her breast,   25
The dropping of the daylight in the West,
The bough of cherries some officious fool
Broke in the orchard for her, the white mule
She rode with round the terrace—all and each
Would draw from her alike the approving speech,   30
Or blush, at least. She thanked men,—good! but thanked
Somehow—I know not how—as if she ranked
My gift of a nine-hundred-years-old name
With anybody's gift. Who'd stoop to blame
This sort of trifling? Even had you skill   35
In speech—which I have not—to make your will
Quite clear to such an one, and say, "Just this
Or that in you disgusts me; here you miss,
Or there exceed the mark"—and if she let
Herself be lessoned so, nor plainly set   40
Her wits to yours, forsooth, and made excuse,
—E'en then would be some stooping; and I choose
Never to stoop. Oh sir, she smiled, no doubt,
Whene'er I passed her; but who passed without
Much the same smile? This grew; I gave commands;   45
Then all smiles stopped together. There she stands
As if alive. Will't please you rise? We'll meet
The company below, then. I repeat,
The Count your master's known munificence
Is ample warrant that no just pretense   50
Of mine for dowry will be disallowed;
Though his fair daughter's self, as I avowed
At starting, is my object. Nay, we'll go
Together down, sir. Notice Neptune, though,
Taming a sea-horse, thought a rarity,   55
Which Claus of Innsbruck° cast in bronze for me!   *[1842]*

56 Claus of Innsbruck: A fictitious artist.

≡ THINKING ABOUT THE TEXT

1. The duke offers a history of his first marriage. Summarize his story in your own words, including the reasons he gives for his behavior. How would you describe him? Do you admire anything about him? If so, what?

2. Try to reconstruct the rhetorical situation in which the duke is making his remarks. Who might be his audience? What might be his goals? What strategies is he using to accomplish them? Cite details that support your conjectures.

3. When you read the poem aloud, how conscious are you of its rhymes? What is its rhyme scheme? What is the effect of Browning's using just one stanza rather than breaking the poem into several?

4. Going by this example of the genre, what are the advantages of writing a poem as a dramatic monologue? What are the disadvantages?

5. Browning suggests that the setting of this poem is Renaissance Italy. What relevance might his poem have had for readers in mid-nineteenth-century England? What relevance might it have for audiences in the United States today?

GABRIEL SPERA
My Ex-Husband

Raised in New Jersey, Gabriel Spera (b. 1966) graduated from Cornell University and earned an M.F.A. from the University of North Carolina at Greensboro. He has worked as a technical writer for several years, most recently for a California aerospace firm. At the same time, he has published many poems, including the following one, which first appeared in the journal Poetry *in 1992. It also appears in his book* The Standing Wave *(2003), which was chosen for the National Poetry Series and also won the PEN-USA West Literary Book Award for Poetry. More recently, Spera has published another volume of poetry,* The Rigid Body *(2012).*

> That's my ex-husband pictured on the shelf,
> Smiling as if in love. I took it myself
> With his Leica, and stuck it in that frame
> We got for our wedding. Kind of a shame
> To waste it on him, but what could I do?   5
> (Since I haven't got a photograph of you.)
> I know what's on your mind — you want to know
> Whatever could have made me let him go —
> He seems like any woman's perfect catch,
> What with his ruddy cheeks, the thin mustache,   10
> Those close-set, baggy eyes, that tilted grin.

Photo by Rachel Lee

But snapshots don't show what's beneath the skin!
He had a certain charm, charisma, style,
That passionate, earnest glance he struck, meanwhile
Whispering the sweetest things, like "Your lips   15
Are like plump rubies, eyes like diamond chips,"
Could flush the throat of any woman, not
Just mine. He blew the most romantic spots
In town, where waiters, who all knew his face,
Reserved an intimately dim-lit place   20
Half-hidden in a corner nook. Such stuff
Was all too well rehearsed, I soon enough
Found out. He had an attitude—how should
I put it—smooth, self-satisfied, too good
For the rest of the world, too easily   25
Impressed with his officious self. And he
flirted—fine! but flirted somehow a bit
Too ardently, too blatantly, as if,

If someone ever noticed, no one cared
How slobbishly he carried on affairs.   30
Who'd lower herself to put up with shit
Like that? Even if you'd the patience—which
I have not—to go and see some counsellor
And say, "My life's a living hell," or
"Everything he does disgusts, the lout!"—   35
And even if you'd somehow worked things out,
Took a long trip together, made amends,
Let things get back to normal, even then
You'd still be on the short end of the stick;
And I choose never ever to get stuck.   40
Oh, no doubt, it always made my limbs go
Woozy when he kissed me, but what bimbo
In the steno pool went without the same
Such kisses? So, I made some calls, filed some claims,
All kisses stopped together. There he grins,   45
Almost lovable. Shall we go? I'm in
The mood for Chez Pierre's, perhaps, tonight,
Though anything you'd like would be all right
As well, of course, though I'd prefer not to go
To any place with checkered tables. No,   50
We'll take my car. By the way, have I shown
You yet these lovely champagne flutes, hand blown,
Imported from Murano, Italy,
Which Claus got in the settlement for me!   *[1992]*

≣ THINKING ABOUT THE TEXT

1. Why, evidently, did the speaker get divorced? What would you say to
   someone who argues that because she still thinks about her former husband, keeps his photograph on the shelf, and clearly has not forgiven
   him, she remains "stuck" (line 40) in that relationship?

2. How reliable do you think the speaker's account of her former husband is?

3. Where does the speaker shift the kind of language she's been using? Do
   you think her feelings are consistent despite this shifting? Explain.

4. Who do you think the "you" (line 6) in this poem is? In what ways, if
   any, does the presence of this "you" seem to influence what the speaker
   says and how she says it?

5. Although the speaker is a woman, poet Gabriel Spera is a man. Does
   this poem lead you to believe that a man can, in fact, write from a woman's point of view? Why, or why not?

≡ MAKING COMPARISONS

1. Where in his poem does Spera closely echo Browning's poem? Refer to specific lines in both texts. What is the effect of the changes in wording that Spera makes?

2. Do you sympathize more with Spera's speaker than with Browning's? Why, or why not? Explain.

3. Do the listeners in these two poems both seem passive? Refer to specific details of both texts.

≡ WRITING ABOUT ISSUES

1. Choose either of the poems in this cluster, and write an essay analyzing what you consider to be its most significant line. Be sure to explain why you find your chosen line important.

2. To what extent and in what ways does Spera's poem seem more "modern" than Browning's? Write an essay in which you answer this question. Refer to specific details from both poems, and define clearly what you mean by *modern*.

3. Write an essay analyzing a relationship that you broke off because you thought the other person had acted unjustly. To what extent do you still brood about this relationship? How much have you forgiven the other person? What meaning of the term *justice* seems applicable here?

4. Write a dialogue between the speakers of these two poems, or write a dialogue between the listeners in them. Shape the dialogue so that it emphasizes ideas and principles that the two people have in common. Then write a brief essay in which you analyze the conversation you have constructed. What do you want your readers to conclude from it?

≡ Dreams of Justice: A Collection of Works by Langston Hughes

Inspired by two of the great poetic voices of American life, Walt Whitman and Carl Sandburg, Langston Hughes is often thought of as the African American poet laureate, a writer who is able to sing eloquently about the reality and idealism of democracy in America. He was committed to telling the truth about the lives of black people. The introduction to *The Collected Poems of Langston Hughes* notes that Hughes wrote of "the joys and sorrows, the trials and triumphs, of ordinary black folk, in the language of their typical speech and composed out of a genuine love of these people."

In response to the Depression of the 1930s, Hughes became radicalized by the poverty and injustice he saw everywhere in black America. His poems from this period are radical indeed. "Let America Be America Again" poignantly laments the wide gulf that often existed between the idealistic rhetoric of democracy and the appalling social reality of segregation. Although he later became less radical in his poetry, "Theme for English B" and "Harlem" still reflect his belief that poetry is a form of social action. At the heart of all Hughes's poetry was the deferred dream of African Americans to achieve the freedom and equality promised to all in America. Not restricting himself to verse, he pursued this concern through drama and fiction as well, as you will see in his mid-1930s short story "On the Road."

≡ BEFORE YOU READ

Can you imagine what would have happened to your personality if a dream of yours (perhaps going to college, playing a sport, or marrying someone you loved deeply) were denied? What would you do if America was not living up to its stated ideals or if those ideals were suddenly altered significantly? Would you express your disappointment publicly or only privately?

LANGSTON HUGHES

Let America Be America Again

Langston Hughes (1902–1967) has long been regarded as a major African American writer and is increasingly seen as an important contributor to American literature in general. Like Countee Cullen, Hughes was actively involved in the 1920s

© Corbis

movement called the Harlem Renaissance. Then and later, he worked in various genres, including fiction, drama, and autobiography. Nevertheless, he is primarily known for his poems. The version of "Let America Be America Again" we present here was first published in Esquire *magazine in 1936. A longer version then appeared in a 1938 pamphlet by Hughes entitled* A New Song, *which was published by a socialist organization named the International Workers Order. Hughes was critical of capitalism and sympathetic toward Communism, as were many other writers during the Great Depression. During the late 1930s, Communism in the United States entered a phase called the Popular Front, which linked Marxist principles to traditional American ideas and values. The title of Hughes's poem reflects this attempt at connection. Note, too, that within the poem Hughes sees African Americans as part of a larger population suffering from poverty and powerlessness. Indeed, the Depression led many writers to connect racism with other kinds of oppression, especially inequalities of class.*

Let America be America again.
Let it be the dream it used to be.

Let it be the pioneer on the plain
Seeking a home where he himself is free.

(America never was America to me.)   5

Let America be the dream the dreamers dreamed—
Let it be that great strong land of love
Where never kings connive nor tyrants scheme
That any man be crushed by one above.

(It never was America to me.)   10

O, let my land be a land where Liberty
Is crowned with no false patriotic wreath,
But opportunity is real, and life is free,
Equality is in the air we breathe.

(There's never been equality for me,   15
Nor freedom in this "homeland of the free.")

Say who are you that mumbles in the dark?
And who are you that draws your veil across the stars?

I am the poor white, fooled and pushed apart,
I am the red man driven from the land.
I am the refugee clutching the hope I seek—   20
But finding only the same old stupid plan
Of dog eat dog, of mighty crush the weak.
I am the Negro, "problem" to you all.
I am the people, humble, hungry, mean—   25
Hungry yet today despite the dream.
Beaten yet today—O, Pioneers!
I am the man who never got ahead,
The poorest worker bartered through the years.
Yet I'm the one who dreamt our basic dream   30
In that Old World while still a serf of kings,
Who dreamt a dream so strong, so brave, so true,
That even yet its mighty daring sings
In every brick and stone, in every furrow turned
That's made America the land it has become.   35
O, I'm the man who sailed those early seas
In search of what I meant to be my home—
For I'm the one who left dark Ireland's shore,
And Poland's plain, and England's grassy lea,
And torn from Black Africa's strand I came   40
To build a "homeland of the free."

The free?
Who said the free? Not me?

Surely not me? The millions on relief today?
The millions who have nothing for our pay   45
For all the dreams we've dreamed
And all the songs we've sung
And all the hopes we've held
And all the flags we've hung,
The millions who have nothing for our pay—   50
Except the dream we keep alive today.

O, let America be America again—
The land that never has been yet—
And yet must be—the land where *every* man is free.
The land that's mine—the poor man's, Indian's, Negro's, ME—   55

Who made America,
Whose sweat and blood, whose faith and pain,
Whose hand at the foundry, whose plow in the rain,
Must bring back our mighty dream again.

    O, yes,   60
    I say it plain,
    America never was America to me,
    And yet I swear this oath—
    America will be!   *[1938]*

≡ THINKING ABOUT THE TEXT

1. In the title and in the first line comes the plea "Let America be America again." At several points in the poem, however, the speaker indicates that America has never lived up to its ideals, especially about freedom and equality. Identify these points. How can we reconcile them with the opening plea?

2. When this poem was written in 1938, what do you think the response to the poem would have been among poor blacks? Poor whites? Members of Congress? Intellectuals? Religious groups in the South? The North? How would you answer this question in today's America?

3. What other oppressed peoples does the speaker refer to besides African Americans? Does he succeed in convincing you that all these groups belong together in the poem? What significant differences among them, if any, do you think he overlooks?

4. Although the speaker uses "I" a lot, sometimes he refers to "we." What is the effect of this shift? Should he have used one of these pronouns more than he does? Explain.

5. What lines of this poem seem to reflect the specific period of the Depression? What lines, if any, strike you as still relevant today?

LANGSTON HUGHES
Theme for English B

Langston Hughes wrote "Theme for English B" in 1949, when he was twenty-five years older than the poem's speaker. As a young man, he had attended a "college on the hill above Harlem": Columbia University.

The instructor said,

> *Go home and write*
> *a page tonight.*
> *And let that page come out of you—*
> *Then, it will be true.*   5

I wonder if it's that simple?
I am twenty-two, colored, born in Winston-Salem.
I went to school there, then Durham, then here
to this college on the hill above Harlem.
I am the only colored student in my class.   10
The steps from the hill lead down into Harlem,
through a park, then I cross St. Nicholas,
Eighth Avenue, Seventh, and I come to the Y,
the Harlem Branch Y, where I take the elevator
up to my room, sit down, and write this page: 15

It's not easy to know what is true for you or me
at twenty-two, my age. But I guess I'm what
I feel and see and hear, Harlem, I hear you:
hear you, hear me—we two—you, me, talk on this page.
(I hear New York, too.) Me—who?   20
Well, I like to eat, sleep, drink, and be in love.
I like to work, read, learn, and understand life.
I like a pipe for a Christmas present,
or records—Bessie,° bop, or Bach.
I guess being colored doesn't make me *not* like   25
the same things other folks like who are other races.
So will my page be colored that I write?
Being me, it will not be white.
But it will be
a part of you, instructor.   30
You are white—
yet a part of me, as I am part of you.
That's American.
Sometimes perhaps you don't want to be a part of me.
Nor do I often want to be a part of you.   35

---

24 Bessie: Bessie Smith (1894–1937), the famous American blues singer.

But we are, that's true!
As I learn from you,
I guess you learn from me—
although you're older—and white—
and somewhat more free.   40
This is my page for English B.   *[1949]*

≡ THINKING ABOUT THE TEXT

1. What do you think the instructor's response to "my page" (line 41) would be? What would yours be?

2. What do you think the instructor was hoping for? On what basis does the narrator seem to critique the assignment?

3. What do you think the narrator means by "American" in line 33? After more than sixty years, does it mean something different?

4. What do you think he means by the line "It's not easy to know what is true for you or me / at twenty-two" (lines 16–17)? Do you agree?

5. The emphasis on freedom here seems more indirect than in the previous poem. What do you think Hughes means by "free" in the next-to-last line? Would you agree with him then (1949)? Now?

≡ MAKING COMPARISONS

1. Compare the tone of this poem with the tone of "Let America Be America Again." Which is more aggressive? Refer to specific lines of both texts.

2. While the "I" of "Let America Be America Again" identifies himself as various people, the "I" of "Theme for English B" seems to be one particular individual. Does the poem seem less wide in its relevance as a result? Why, or why not?

3. The speaker in "Theme for English B" addresses a particular person—the white teacher. Does the speaker in "Let America Be America Again" seem to have a specific audience in mind, or do the two poems differ in this respect?

LANGSTON HUGHES

Harlem

Sometimes called "A Dream Deferred," "Harlem" is Hughes's most anthologized poem and has become synonymous with African Americans' long struggle for freedom and equality. Lorraine Hansberry drew upon the third line for the title of her play A Raisin in the Sun *(see Chapter 7).*

What happens to a dream deferred?

> Does it dry up
> like a raisin in the sun?
> Or fester like a sore —
> And then run?   5
> Does it stink like rotten meat?
> Or crust and sugar over —
> like a syrupy sweet?

> Maybe it just sags
> like a heavy load.   10

Or does it explode?   [1951]

≣ **THINKING ABOUT THE TEXT**

1. The inspiration for Lorraine Hansberry's famous play, *A Raisin in the Sun* (p. 449), Hughes's brief poem asks a question and then answers it with more questions. Is this technique effective? Should he have made his own thinking plainer?

2. What is the "dream deferred" (line 1)?

3. The alternatives given are specific and concrete metaphors, presumably embodied in people. What kind of person would be "like a raisin in the sun" (line 3)?

4. How do you explain the presence of the word "sweet" (line 8) amidst others that seem for the most part negative?

5. What would you say to someone who argues that no poem should end by threatening violence?

≣ **MAKING COMPARISONS**

1. Why do you think "Harlem" is the most popular of the three poems presented here?

2. Are there hints in the previous two poems of the ideas developed in "Harlem"?

3. Which poem would you recommend to someone from another country who is trying to understand our racial history? Why?

LANGSTON HUGHES

On the Road

Although chiefly known for his poetry, Langston Hughes also wrote plays and short stories. The following story was published in the January 1935 issue of Esquire *magazine, at the height of the Great Depression. Evidently Hughes based the story on experiences he himself had gone through in Reno, Nevada, the year before.*

He was not interested in snow. When he got off the freight, one early evening during the depression, Sargeant never even noticed the snow. But he must have felt it seeping down his neck, cold, wet, sopping in his shoes. But if you had asked him, he wouldn't have known it was snowing. Sargeant didn't see the snow, not even under the bright lights of the main street, falling white and flaky against the night. He was too hungry, too sleepy, too tired.

The Reverend Mr. Dorset, however, saw the snow when he switched on his porch light, opened the front door of his parsonage, and found standing there-before him a big black man with snow on his face, a human piece of night with snow on his face — obviously unemployed.

Said the Reverend Mr. Dorset before Sargeant even realized he'd opened his mouth: "I'm sorry. No! Go right on down this street four blocks and turn to your left, walk up seven and you'll see the Relief Shelter. I'm sorry. No!" He shut the door.

Sargeant wanted to tell the holy man that he had already been to the Relief Shelter, been to hundreds of relief shelters during the depression years, the beds were always gone and supper was over, the place was full, and they drew the color line anyhow. But the minister said, "No," and shut the door. Evidently he didn't want to hear about it. And he *had* a door to shut.

The big black man turned away. And even yet he didn't see the snow, walk-   5
ing right into it. Maybe he sensed it, cold, wet, sticking to his jaws, wet on his black hands, sopping in his shoes. He stopped and stood on the sidewalk hunched over — hungry, sleepy, cold — looking up and down. Then he looked right where he was — in front of a church! Of course! A church! Sure, right next to a parsonage, certainly a church.

It had *two* doors.

Broad white steps in the night all snowy white. Two high arched doors with slender stone pillars on either side. And way up, a round lacy window with a stone crucifix in the middle and Christ on the crucifix in stone. All this was pale in the street lights, solid and stony pale in the snow.

Sargeant blinked. When he looked up, the snow fell into his eyes. For the first time that night he saw the snow. He shook his head. He shook the snow from his coat sleeves, felt hungry, felt lost, felt not lost, felt cold. He walked up the steps of the church. He knocked at the door. No answer. He tried the handle. Locked. He put his shoulder against the door and his long black body slanted like a ramrod. He pushed. With loud rhythmic grunts, like the grunts in a chaingang song, he pushed against the door.

"I'm tired . . . Huh! . . . Hongry . . . Uh! . . . I'm sleepy . . . Huh! I'm cold . . . I got to sleep somewheres," Sargeant said. "This here is a church, ain't it? Well, uh!"

He pushed against the door.   10

Suddenly, with an undue cracking and screaking, the door began to give way to the tall black Negro who pushed ferociously against it.

By now two or three white people had stopped in the street, and Sargeant was vaguely aware of some of them yelling at him concerning the door. Three or four more came running, yelling at him.

"Hey!" they said. "Hey!"

"Uh-huh," answered the big tall Negro, "I know it's a white folks' church, but I got to sleep somewhere." He gave another lunge at the door. "Huh!" And the door broke open.

But just when the door gave way, two white cops arrived in a car, ran up   15
the steps with their clubs, and grabbed Sargeant. But Sargeant for once had no intention of being pulled or pushed away from the door.

Sargeant grabbed, but not for anything so weak as a broken door. He grabbed for one of the tall stone pillars beside the door, grabbed at it and caught it. And held it. The cops pulled Sargeant pulled. Most of the people in the street got behind the cops and helped them pull.

"A big black unemployed Negro holding onto our church!" thought the people. "The idea!"

The cops began to beat Sargeant over the head, and nobody protested. But he held on.

And then the church fell down.

Gradually, the big stone front of the church fell down, the walls and the   20
rafters, the crucifix and the Christ. Then the whole thing fell down, covering the cops and the people with bricks and stones and debris. The whole church fell down in the snow.

Sargeant got out from under the church and went walking on up the street with the stone pillar on his shoulder. He was under the impression that he had buried the parsonage and the Reverend Mr. Dorset who said, "No!" So he laughed, and threw the pillar six blocks up the street and went on.

Sargeant thought he was alone, but listening to the crunch, crunch, crunch on the snow of his own footsteps, he heard other footsteps, too, doubling his own. He looked around, and there was Christ walking along beside him, the same Christ that had been on the cross on the church—still stone with a rough stone surface, walking along beside him just like he was broken off the cross when the church fell down.

"Well, I'll be dogged," said Sargeant. "This here's the first time I ever seed you off the cross."

"Yes," said Christ, crunching his feet in the snow. "You had to pull the church down to get me off the cross."

"You glad?" said Sargeant.   25

"I sure am," said Christ.

They both laughed.

"I'm a hell of a fellow, ain't I?" said Sargeant. "Done pulled the church down!"

"You did a good job," said Christ. "They have kept me nailed on a cross for nearly two thousand years."

"Whee-ee-e!" said Sargeant. "I know you are glad to get off."   30

"I sure am," said Christ.

They walked on in the snow. Sargeant looked at the man of stone.

"And you have been up there two thousand years?"

"I sure have," Christ said.

"Well, if I had a little cash," said Sargeant, "I'd show you around a bit."   35

"I been around," said Christ.

"Yeah, but that was a long time ago."

"All the same," said Christ, "I've been around."

They walked on in the snow until they came to the railroad yards. Sargeant was tired, sweating and tired.

"Where you goin'?" Sargeant said, stopping by the tracks. He looked at   40
Christ. Sargeant said, "I'm just a bum on the road. How about you? Where you goin'?"

"God knows" Christ said, "but I'm leavin' here."

They saw the red and green lights of the railroad yard half veiled by the snow that fell out of the night. Away down the track they saw a fire in a hobo jungle.

"I can go there and sleep," Sargeant said.

"You can?"

"Sure," said Sargeant. "That place ain't got no doors."   45

Outside the town, along the tracks, there were barren trees and bushes below the embankment, snow-gray in the dark. And down among the trees and bushes there were makeshift houses made out of boxes and tin and old pieces of wood and canvas. You couldn't see them in the dark, but you knew they were there if you'd ever been on the road, if you had ever lived with the homeless and hungry in a depression.

"I'm side-tracking," Sargeant said. "I'm tired."

"I'm gonna make it on to Kansas City," said Christ.

"O.K.," Sargeant said. "So long!"

He went down into the hobo jungle and found himself a place to sleep.   50
He never did see Christ no more. About six a.m. a freight came by. Sargeant scrambled out of the jungle with a dozen or so more hobos and ran along the track, grabbing at the freight. It was dawn, early dawn, cold and gray.

"Wonder where Christ is by now?" Sargeant thought. "He musta gone on way on down the road. He didn't sleep in this jungle."

Sargeant grabbed the train and started to pull himself up into a moving coal car, over the edge of a wheeling coal car. But strangely enough, the car was full of cops. The nearest cop rapped Sargeant soundly across the knuckles with his night stick. Wham! Rapped his big black hands for clinging to the top of the car. Wham! But Sargeant did not turn loose. He clung on and tried to pull himself into the car. He hollered at the top of his voice, "Damn it, lemme in this car!"

"Shut up," barked the cop. "You crazy coon!" He rapped Sargeant across the knuckles and punched him in the stomach. "You ain't out in no jungle now. This ain't no train. You in jail."

Wham! across his bare black fingers clinging to the bars of his cell. Wham! between the steel bars low down against his shins.

Suddenly Sargeant realized that he really was in jail. He wasn't on no   55
train. The blood of the night before had dried on his face, his head hurt terribly,

and a cop outside in the corridor was hitting him across the knuckles for holding onto the door, yelling and shaking the cell door.

"They musta took me to jail for breaking down the door last night," Sargeant thought, "that church door."

Sargeant went over and sat on a wooden bench against the cold stone wall. He was emptier than ever. His clothes were wet, clammy cold wet, and shoes sloppy with snow water. It was just about dawn. There he was, locked up behind a cell door, nursing his bruised fingers.

The bruised fingers were his, but not the *door*.

Not the *club*, but the fingers.

"You wait," mumbled Sargeant, black against the jail wall. "I'm gonna break down this door, too." 60

"Shut up—or I'll paste you one," said the cop.

"I'm gonna break down this door," yelled Sargeant as he stood up in his cell.

Then he must have been talking to himself because he said, "I wonder where Christ's gone? I wonder if he's gone to Kansas City?" *[1935]*

≡ THINKING ABOUT THE TEXT

1. What would you say is the genre of this story?

2. What do you think the story implies about Christianity?

3. Is social class as important in the story as race is? Explain your reasoning.

4. How much do you sympathize with Sargeant?

5. What would you say to someone who argues that even though this story was written in the mid-1930s, it is relevant to the situation of homeless people today?

≡ MAKING COMPARISONS

1. What lines in "Let America Be America Again" strike you as applying to someone like Sargeant?

2. In what respect might this story concern, as "Harlem" does, "a dream deferred"?

3. What would you say to someone who argues that even though Sargeant and the speaker in "Theme for English B" are both African American, they otherwise have very little in common? Explain your reasoning.

≡ WRITING ABOUT ISSUES

1. Choose one of the texts in this cluster, and write an essay that explains how it brings a perspective to American racism that not every African American writer might employ.

2. Write an essay explaining how "On the Road" develops an idea present in one of the poems in this cluster.

3. Write an essay in which you apply Hughes's term "a dream deferred" to someone you know. Focus in particular on the extent to which, and the ways in which, unjust social circumstances thwarted this person's ambition.

4. Identify a current American social problem, and then write an essay in which you argue that properly addressing it requires America to "be America again." Be sure to specify the ideals and practices you think are needed to deal with the problem adequately. If you wish, refer to one or more texts in this cluster.

≣ Lessons in Injustice: Stories

JESSAMYN WEST, "The Lesson"

TONI CADE BAMBARA, "The Lesson"

Much fiction depicts characters encountering injustice they have not been aware of or have tried to ignore. Many of these characters are youths who find, often reluctantly, that the world is not as humane or reasonable as they have wished it to be. In Jessamyn West's 1951 short story "The Lesson," a farm boy must confront a terrible fact about his community: it will auction off his beloved steer to butchers, who will turn his pet into meat. Meanwhile, the boy's older sister must cope with other things that seem cruelly unfair: her mother's death and her father's frozen grief. In Toni Cade Bambara's story of the same title from 1972, the narrator is an African American girl who must decide what to think when a woman of her race tries to teach her that whites monopolize society's wealth. Both stories prod their readers to consider what lessons young people should learn about the world's imperfections. How should children define *injustice*? Which forms of it should they come to accept, and which should they resist?

≣ BEFORE YOU READ

In his memoir *Fatheralong* (1994), John Edgar Wideman notes that his father's attitude toward society differs from that of his late mother. "The first rule of my father's world," Wideman writes, "is that you stand alone. Alone, alone, alone. . . . Accept the bottom line, icy clarity, of the one thing you can rely on: nothing" (50). On the other hand, "My mother's first rule was love. She refused to believe she was alone. *Be not dismayed, what e'er betides / God will take care of you*" (51). What were you taught about society as you were growing up? What specific messages were you given about it by your parents or the people who raised you? How did they convey these messages to you?

JESSAMYN WEST

The Lesson

Though she was born in Indiana and set much of her fiction there, Jessamyn West (1902–1984) grew up in California. A major turning point in her life occurred while she was in graduate school: she was stricken with tuberculosis, from which she nearly died. Upon recovering, she launched what turned out to be a long writing career. West is best known for her 1945 novel The Friendly Persuasion, *which became a celebrated movie in 1956. Reflecting West's own religious upbringing, the book focuses on a nineteenth-century family of Quakers. West did not limit herself to a single genre; she also wrote poetry, memoirs, and short stories. The following story first appeared in the August 11, 1951, issue of* The New Yorker. *It gained new attention in 2012, when writer Sherman Alexie read and discussed it during one of the magazine's podcasts. West retitled the story "Learn to Say Good-bye" when she included it in* Collected Stories of Jessamyn West *(1986).*

John Thomas had awakened thinking of Curly — or, rather, when he woke up, he did not stop thinking of Curly, for all night he had been with the young steer, encouraging him, patting him on his curling forelock, leading him before the admiring judges. The boy was wide awake now, yet Curly's image was still as strongly with him as in the dream — the heavy shoulders, the great barrel, the short legs, the red coat shining with health and with the many brushings John Thomas had given it. And Curly's face! The boy's own face crinkled happily as he thought of it, and then turned scornful as he thought of the people who said one baby beef was just like another. Curly looked at you with intelligence. His eyes weren't just hairless spots on his head, like the eyes of most baby beeves. They showed that Curly knew when eating time had come and that he understood the difference between being told he was a lazy old cuss and a prize-winning baby beef. You had only to say to him, "You poor old steer," and he put his head down and looked at you as much as to say he knew it was true and not to kid him about it. John Thomas remembered a hundred humors and shrewdnesses of Curly's, and lay in bed smiling about them — the way he had of getting the last bite of mash out of his feed pail, and his cleverness in evading the vet, and how he would lunge at Wolf when the collie barked at him.

"This is the day!" John Thomas said aloud. "This is the day!"

Across the hall came a girl's sleepy voice. "Johnny, you promised to be quiet."

John Thomas didn't answer. No use arguing with Jo when she was sleepy. He sat up and slipped his arms into the sleeves of his bathrobe, and then stepped onto the floor boards, which were so much cooler than the air, and walked slowly, because he wanted so much to walk fast, to the window.

There Curly was, standing with his nose over the corral fence looking up   5
toward John Thomas's window. Curly acts as if he knows, the boy thought. I bet he does know.

"Hey, Curly!" he called softly. "How you feel this morning? Feel like a prize baby beef? Feel like the best steer in California? First prize for Curly?" Curly swished his tail. "Don't you worry, Curly. You *are* the best."

John Thomas knew he was going to have to go in and talk to Jo, even though she'd be mad at being waked so early. If he stood another minute looking at Curly — so beautiful in his clean corral, with the long blue early-morning shadows of the eucalyptus falling across it — and listening to the meadow larks off in the alfalfa and remembering that this was the day, he'd give a whoop, and that would make both Jo and Pop mad. He tiptoed across the hall, opened his sister's door, and looked at her room with distaste. Grown-up girls like Jo, almost twenty, ought to be neater. All girls ought to be neater. The clothes Jo had taken off before she went to sleep made a path from her door to her bed, starting with her shoes and hat and ending with her underwear. Curly's corral's neater, he thought, and said, "It's time to get up, Jo!"

Jo rolled over on her face and groaned. John Thomas stepped over Jo's clothes and sat down on the edge of the bed.

Jo groaned again. "*Please* don't wake me up yet, Johnny," she said.

"You're already awake. You're talking."   10

"I'm talking in my sleep."

"I don't care if you don't wake up, if you'll talk. I've seen Curly already. He looks pretty good. He looks like he knows it's the day."

"He's dead wrong, then. It's still the night."

John Thomas laughed. If he got Jo to arguing, she'd wake up. "It's six o'clock," he said.

Jo, still face down, raised herself on one elbow and looked at her wrist-   15
watch. Then she whirled onto her back, stuck one leg out from under the sheet, and gave her brother a kick that set him down on the floor with a thud. "Why, John Thomas Hobhouse!" she said indignantly. "It's only five-fifteen and Nicky didn't get me home until two. You're so kind to that damned old steer of yours, but you don't care whether your own sister gets any sleep or not."

John Thomas bounced back onto the bed. Jo looked at him sharply and he knew what was to come.

"What have you got on under that bathrobe, John Thomas Hobhouse?" she demanded. "Did you sleep in your underwear last night?"

"I slept in my shorts."

"That's a filthy thing to do."

"You say it's filthy if I don't wear them in the daytime and filthy if I do wear   20
them at night. What's daylight or dark got to do with it? Now, if I—"

"Look, Johnny, let's not get started on that. There are some things you're going to have to do that aren't reasonable. Once school starts, you'll be spend-ing some nights with the other boys, and their mothers will be saying I don't look after you, and let you sleep in your underwear."

"I don't do it away from home, Jo, but it was so hot last night. You tell Mrs. Henny to do my ducks up special for today? Boy, wait till you see me and Curly go by the grandstand! Wait till you see us in the ring when Curly wins!"

"When Curly wins! Maybe he won't win, Johnny."

"Maybe the judges *won't* see he's best—but they will if they're any good."

John Thomas lay on his stomach, hanging his head over the edge of the   25
bed until his long pompadour spread out on the floor like a dust mop and his face was out of Jo's sight. "I prayed about today," he said.

"Did you, Johnny?"

"Yep, but I didn't think it was fair to pray for Curly to win." He heaved him-self up and down, so that his hair flicked back and forth across the floor. "A lot of kids probably did pray they'd win, though."

Jo regarded him with tenderness and amazement. "I never would have thought most of the kids who go to the fair had ever heard of praying," she said.

"Oh, sure, they all heard of it," Johnny said. "And when it comes to something important like this, they all think you ought to try everything. But I didn't ask for Curly to win. I just prayed the judges would be good and know their stuff. If they do, Curly will get the blue ribbon, all right. With everyone else asking to win, I thought maybe that would kind of make an impression on God."

It made an impression on Jo. Lord, she thought, I'm a heathen. "What do you care whether or not Curly wins, if you know he's best?" she asked.   30

John Thomas heaved his head and shoulders up onto the bed and lay on his stomach with his face near Jo's. "How can you wear those tin things in your hair?" he asked. Then he answered her question. "I know for sure Curly's best, but *he* don't. He knows he's good, but he don't know he's that good. I want him to win so he can have the blue ribbon on his halter and walk up in front of the people while all the other baby beeves watch him."

"You going to walk with him, kid?" Jo asked.

"Yep, I got to."

"Kinda nice to have the other kids watch, too?"

This slyness tickled John Thomas and he laughed. No use trying to fool Jo   35
about anything. "Anyway, it's mostly Curly," he said.

Jo started taking the curlers out of her hair. She tucked them, one by one, into Johnny's bush of hair as she took them out. "Remember when Curly got bloated?" she asked. "You weren't much help then. You cried and didn't want the vet to stick him."

"Yeah, but, Jo, it looked so awful. To take a knife and stick it inside him. And Curly was so darned scared." He spoke dreamily, with the satisfaction and relief of dangers past. "He looked like he was going to have a calf, didn't he? And I guess it hurt more."

"Yep, Johnny. A cow's made to have a calf, but a steer isn't made to have gas. Hand me my comb. Top left-hand drawer."

John Thomas got up and stood looking at himself in the mirror. His hair was thick enough to keep the curlers from dropping out.

"You look like an African Bushman," Jo said. "Come on, get that comb."   40

When John Thomas handed it to her, she began loosening her sausagelike curls. He watched her turn the fat little sausages into big frankfurters.

"Time to get dressed, kid," she said. "Jump into your ducks. They're all done up fresh and hanging in your closet."

"Do you think I've been giving him too much mash, Jo?" Johnny asked. "Does he look kind of soft to you? Too fat?"

"He looks just right to me. But it's all over now. No use worrying any more. This time tomorrow, he'll be someone else's problem."

John Thomas sat down on the window sill and looked out at the tank   45
house. The sunlight lay on it in a slab as heavy and yellow as a bar of naphtha soap. There was already a dance of heat out across the alfalfa fields. White clouds were boiling up from behind purple Tahquitz. The morning-glories were beginning to shut themselves against the sun. This was the day all right, but he could not think ahead until tomorrow, when Curly would have been sold.

The boy made the width of the room in three jack-rabbit hops, and banged the door behind him.

Jo swung herself out of her bed and her nightgown in a single looping movement and stood before her mirror. I guess it's hell to be thirteen and not have a mother, and to love a steer that's going to be beefsteak in forty-eight hours, she thought sombrely. I ought to take better care of Johnny, and Dad ought to wake up from remembering Mother. He's been that way ever since she died.

But the air flowed like liquid silk about her naked body, and she lifted her arms and tautened her body, thinking no longer of John Thomas but of Nicky. She regarded her image with affection and pride. I don't know where I would change it, she thought. The sound of Johnny's leaps down the stairs—four house-shuddering thuds—and his cracked voice calling out to Mrs. Henny made her look at her watch. Almost six. Jo grabbed fresh underwear from the drawer and ran for the bathroom.

When Jo came downstairs, ten minutes later, all dressed except for putting on the scarf and belt that were hanging over her shoulders, she saw her father, seated at the table on the screened porch where they ate breakfast in summer and reading the morning paper. She was fond of her father, but in one respect he was unsatisfactory: She didn't like his appearance. He didn't look fatherly to her. There wasn't any gray in his black hair or any stoop to his shoulders, and her girl friends exasperated her by saying, "I could go for your old man."

He called to her now, "Tell Mrs. Henny we're ready to eat."   50

Jo went through the porch door into the sunny kitchen, where Mrs. Henny was slicing peaches for breakfast. She was already dressed for the fair, in a lavender dotted swiss with a lavender ribbon through her bobbed gray hair. "Hello, Mrs. Henny," Jo said. "Dad says let's eat. Gee, you look swell!"

"I thought I'd better wear something light," Mrs. Henny said. "It's going to be hot as a little red wagon today. Take these peaches out with you. Time you've finished them, everything else will be ready."

Jo stopped to buckle on her belt and tie her scarf. Then she took the peaches out to the porch. Her father put the Los Angeles *Times* under his chair and took his dish of peaches out of her hand. "Well, Josephine," he said, "considering you only had three hours' sleep last night, you don't look so bad."

"You hear me come in?"

"Nope, but I heard that fellow drive away. He ran into everything loose and   55
bangable on the place. What's wrong with him?"

"Blind with love, I guess," Jo said lightly.

Her father held his third spoonful of sugar poised over his peaches. "I take it that you have no impairment in your eyesight," he said.

"Things look a little rosy, but the outline's still plain, I think."

Mrs. Henny came in with the eggs and bacon and muffins. "I don't want to hurry you," she said, pausing, on her way out, at the kitchen door, "but it's not getting any earlier."

"Where did Johnny go?" Jo asked. "He ought to be eating. He'll be sick this   60 afternoon if he doesn't eat." She took two muffins, buttered them, and put them on Johnny's plate.

"He's out talking to Curly. You'd better call him."

"Dad, what's Johnny going to do about not having Curly any more after today?" Jo asked. "You know he acts as if Curly were a dog—or a brother."

"Oh, Johnny's all right. He knows what the score is," her father said, with his mouth full of muffin and scrambled eggs. "But call him, call him. We've less than an hour to eat and load the steer. I ought to have taken him down last night, but John Thomas was afraid Curly would look peaked today if he spent a night away from home."

"Remember John Thomas's kitten?"

"Kitten?" said her father grumpily. "He's had a dozen."   65

"This was the one he had when he broke his leg. Don't you remember? He said, 'Let's never let her see herself in a mirror, and then she'll think she's just like us, only smaller.' He's that way about Curly now, you know. He never lets Curly know there's any other difference than size between them."

"Doesn't he know where Curly'll be tomorrow?"

"He *must* know it, but he hasn't felt it yet."

"Well, call him, call him," her father said. He got up from the table and stood with his back to her. "Her can't learn to say goodbye any earlier."

He's thinking of Mama, Jo thought, and walked slowly out through the   70
screen door and down the steps into the sunshine, eating a muffin-and-bacon sandwich as she went. She stopped at the foot of the steps to pick up the cat, and balanced him, heavy and purring, on her shoulder, and let him lick the last of the muffin crumbs from her fingers. "Oh, Nicky, Nicky," she murmured, pressing her face close against the cat's soft, furry side. Then she saw Johnny, sitting hunched up on the top rail of the corral, looking at Curly. "Well, bud," she called out, "he looks like silk!"

"He's kind of rough on the left flank," Johnny said as she came and stood beside him. "Been rubbing against something. Can you notice it? I been working on it."

"Can't see a thing," Jo said. "Now, look here, John Thomas, you're going to make him nervous, sitting there staring at him—give him the jitters before he ever gets to the fair. You'll spoil his morale. Dad let you keep him here till this morning when he didn't want to, so don't you gum things up now."

John Thomas slid to the ground. "So long, Curly," he said. "I got to eat now." And he ran for the house.

A little before eight, they all drove in to Verdant, the county seat—Mr. Hobhouse and Mrs. Henny and Jo and Johnny in the car, and Curly in the trailer behind them. "Awnings up early this morning," said Mr. Hobhouse as they moved slowly forward in the already long line of cars. "Going to be a scorcher, I guess. Flags look dead when there isn't any wind, don't they?"

Jo, who was riding beside her father in the front seat, nodded, but noth-   75
ing looked dead to her. She loved the beginning-again look of a town in the morning—the sidewalks sluiced down, the vegetables fresh and shining, the storekeepers in clean shirts, the feeling that nothing that had been spilled or

broken or hurt or wronged the day before need be carried over into the new day. The heat made her sleepy, and because she wouldn't be seeing Nicky until evening, the day seemed dreamlike, unimportant. She would move through it, be kind to Johnny, and wait for evening and Nicky again. Her father swerved sharply to avoid hitting a car that had swung, without signalling, out of the line of cars heading for the fair.

"Hey, Pop, take it easy!" John Thomas yelled anxiously from the back seat, where he sat with Mrs. Henny. "You almost busted Curly's ribs then."

"John Thomas ought to be riding back there with that steer," declared Mrs. Henny. "Or else I wish I could have rid in the trailer and the steer could have set here with John Thomas. The boy hasn't done a thing since we started but put his feet in my lunch basket and squirm, till I've got a rash watching him."

"Hold out five minutes longer, both of you, and we'll be there," Mr. Hobhouse said.

Jo roused herself, lifted her eyelids, which seemed weighed down with the heat, and turned around. "Hi ya, Johnny," she murmured.

As soon as they were well inside the fairgrounds, her father maneuvered   80
out of the line of cars and stopped. "Jo, you and Mrs. Henny had better get out here," he said. "It'll take me and Johnny some time to get Curly unloaded."

As Jo climbed out, John Thomas touched her arm. "You'll sure be there, won't you, Sis?" he asked.

"Where?"

"In the grandstand for the parade at ten-thirty. All the baby beeves."

"Johnny, where'd you think I'd be then? Looking at the pickle exhibit, maybe? Of course I'll be there. Just you and Curly listen when you go by the stand. You'll hear me roar."

"Hurry up, you two," said her father. "It's getting late."   85

"When's the judging, Johnny?" Jo asked.

"Two-thirty. Front of the Agriculture Pavilion," he replied.

"I'll see you then. Don't worry. I think the judges are going to know their business." She poked a finger through the trailer's bars and touched Curly. "So long, Curly. You do your stuff!"

Her father edged the car and trailer back into the line of traffic. Mrs. Henny lumbered off, with a campstool on one arm and the lunch basket on the other, and Jo was left alone. The day was already blistering and she was glad. She took no pleasure in a moderately warm day, but a record breaker, one that challenged her ability to survive, elated her. She went into one of the exhibition buildings and walked through acres of handiwork, wondering if she would ever find life so empty that she would need to fill it with the making of such ugly and useless articles. Children whimpered as mothers jerked them doggedly through the heat. Oh, Nicky, I promise you never to be like them, Jo thought.

She was in the grandstand at ten-thirty when a voice from the loudspeaker   90
announced, "Ladies and gentlemen! The Future Farmers of Riverbank County and their baby beeves will now pass in front of the grandstand for your inspection. At two-thirty, the final judging will take place in front of the Agriculture Pavilion, and after that the steers will be auctioned to the highest bidders. I'm proud to announce that there isn't a first-rate hotel in Los Angeles that hasn't

a representative here to bid in one or more of these famous Riverbank beeves. There they come now, ladies and gentlemen, through the west gate. Let's give them a big hand—the Future Farmers of Riverbank County!"

Jo craned forward to watch the long line of steers and boys move proudly in review before the grandstand. The steers were mostly Herefords, shining like bright-russet leather in the blazing sun. Jo had not realized how thoroughly John Thomas had convinced her of Curly's superiority. She looked down the long line, expecting Curly, by some virtue of size or spirit, to be distinct from all the others.

A woman leaned heavily against her to nudge a friend in the row below them. "There they are!" she said excitedly.

Jo followed their glances before it occurred to her that they were not talking about John Thomas and Curly. Finally, she saw them, well along toward the end of the line, the steer like the other red steers, the boy like the other white-clothed boys. But unlike, too, for surely no other boy walked with the sensitive, loving pride of her brother. Then she saw that Johnny was the only boy who did not lead his animal by a halter or a rope. He walked beside Curly, with only a hand on his neck. Idiot, thought Jo, he's put something over on somebody; he ought not to be doing that.

She stood up and, to fulfill her promise, shouted, over and over, "Hi, Johnny! Hi, Curly!," until a man behind her jerked her skirt and said, "Sit down, Sis, you're not made of cellophane."

After the boys and the steers had circled the grandstand and passed   95
through the west gate again and out of sight, Jo closed her eyes and half slept, hearing as in a dream the announcement of the next event. She fully awakened, though, when someone wedged himself into the narrow space that separated her from the stair railing on her right.

"Dad! Where did you come from?" she exclaimed.

"I was up above you," her father said. "Well, the boy's having his day. You're half asleep, Jo."

"More than half. Where's the car? I think I'll go and sleep in it until the judging. I've seen all the Yo-yo pillows and canned apricots I can take in one day."

"I don't know whether you can find the car or not," her father said. "It's over in the first nine or ten rows of cars back of the dining tents. Here's the key, and don't forget to lock it when you leave."

Jo slept for a long time, doubled up on the back seat of the car, and then awak-   100
ened with a sudden sick start. She seemed to be drowning in heat, and the velours of the seat she was sleeping on was a quicksand that held her down. She looked at her watch and saw with consternation that it was after four o'clock.

She had a long way to go to reach the Agriculture Pavilion, and because she was so angry with herself and still so sleepy, she ran clumsily, bumping into people. I'm so full of fair promises, she accused herself bitterly, and now I've let poor Johnny down. She wanted to hurt herself running—punish herself— and she finally reached the Pavilion with a sick, cutting pain in her side and a taste of sulphur in her throat. A deep circle of onlookers stood around the judging ring, laughing and talking quietly. At last, she saw Johnny and her father in the front line of the circle, a little to her left. Paying no heed to the sour looks she got, she pushed her way to them. John Thomas saw what she had done and frowned. "You oughtn't to do that, Jo," he said. "People'll think we can get away with anything just because we own the winner."

"Has Curly won already?" Jo asked.

"No, not yet," Johnny said. "Couldn't you see the judging from where you were?"

"Not very well," Jo said. "No, I couldn't see a thing."

She looked now at the animals that were still in the ring, and saw that   105
Curly was there with three other Herefords and an enormous black Ayrshire.
He was wearing a halter now, and one of the judge's assistants was leading
him. Unless one of the five steers had a cast in his eye or a tick in his ear, Jo did
not see how any man living could say that one was an iota better than another.
She knew the points in judging as well as Johnny himself; she had stood by the
corral many half hours after breakfast while Johnny recounted them for her,
but while she knew them well, her eye could not limn them out in the living
beasts.

"Why're you so sure Curly will win?" she asked Johnny.

"Higgins said he would."

"Who's Higgins?"

Johnny shook his head, too absorbed to answer her question. The judge,
an old, bowlegged fellow in a pale-blue sweater, had stopped examining the
animals and was reading over some notes he had taken on the back of a dirty
envelope. He walked over for another look at the Ayrshire. Seemingly satisfied
by what he saw, he took off his gray felt hat and, with the back of his hand,
wiped away the sweat that had accumulated under the sweatband. He set his
hat on the back of his head, stuffed his envelope in a hip pocket, stepped to the
edge of the ring, and began to speak.

"Ladies and gentlemen, it gives me great pleasure to be able to announce   110
to you the winner of the Eighteenth Annual Riverbank Baby Beef Contest."

There was a hush as the spectators stopped talking, and Jo tried to find in
her father's face some hint of what he thought the decision would be. She saw
nothing there but concern. Johnny, though, had a broad and assured smile. His
eyes were sparkling; the hour of Curly's recognition had come.

"And I may say," continued the judge, enjoying the suspense he was creating, "that in a lifetime of cattle judging I have never seen an animal that compares with today's winner."

The fool, thought Jo, the damn fool orator! What's got into him? They
never do this. Why can't he speak out?

But Johnny looked as if he enjoyed it, as if he knew whose name would be
announced when people's ears had become so strained to hear it that it would
seem to be articulated not by another's lips but by their own heartbeats.

"The winner, ladies and gentlemen, is that very fine animal, John Thomas   115
Hobhouse's Hereford, Curly!" said the judge.

There was a lot of good-natured hand clapping. A few boys yelled "Nerts!,"
but the choice was popular with the crowd, most of whom knew and liked the

Hobhouses. The judge went on to name the second- and third-prize winners and the honorable mentions. Then he called out, "I would like to present to you Curly's owner, John Thomas Hobhouse himself. Come take a bow, Johnny!"

Jo was proud of the easy, happy way Johnny ran over to his side. The judge put out a hand intended for the boy's shoulder, but before it could settle there, Johnny was pressing his cheek against Curly's big, flat jowl. The steer seemed actually to lower his head for the caress and to move his cheek against Johnny's in loving recognition. This delighted the spectators, who laughed and cheered again.

"Now, ladies and gentlemen, the show's almost over," said the judge. "Only one thing left—the auctioning of these animals—and, believe you me, the enjoyment you've had here is nothing to the enjoyment you're going to have when you bite into one of these big, juicy baby-beef steaks. Now if you'll all just clear the ring. Ladies and gentlemen, may I present that silver-tongued Irish auctioneer, Terence O'Flynn. Terence, the show is all yours."

The non-prize-winners were disposed of first and in short order. They fetched fancy prices, but nothing like what would be paid for the prize-winners. The big Los Angeles hotels and the Riverbank Inn liked to be able to advertise "Steaks from Riverbank's Prize Baby Beeves." Jo felt sick at her stomach during the auction. This talk of club steaks and top sirloins seemed indecent to her, in front of animals of whom these cuts were still integral parts. But Johnny seemed unaffected by the auction. "Bet you Curly will get more than that," he said whenever a high price was bid.

"He'll fetch top price," his father answered him shortly. "You'll have a big   120
check tonight, besides your blue ribbon, Johnny." The prize-winners were auctioned last. All of them except Curly went to Los Angeles hotels, but the Riverbank Inn, determined not to let outside counties get all the prize-winners, bid Curly in for itself.

"I'm not a Riverbank citizen," boomed O'Flynn, "but I don't mind admitting, folks, that I'm going to come back the day my good friend Chef Rossi of the Riverbank Inn serves steak from Curly. I know that baby beef is going to yield juices that haven't been equalled since Abel broiled the first steak. If *I* was young Hobhouse, I'd never sell that animal. I'd barbecue it and pick its bones myself."

Most of the animals had already been led into slaughterhouse vans and trucks, and the rest were being quickly loaded. A van belonging to Mack's Market, the Riverbank Inn's butchers, backed up to the ring, which now held only Curly and the Ayrshire. As O'Flynn finished speaking, two young fellows in jumpers marked "Mack's" leaped out and came over to give Curly a congratulatory pat before sending him up the runway.

"Well, kid," one said pleasantly to John Thomas, "you got a fine animal here."

Johnny didn't hear him. He was looking at O'Flynn, hearing those last words of his.

Now it's come, thought Jo. Now he's really taken in what he's been prepar-   125
ing Curly for. Now he knows for the first time. Don't look that way, Johnny, she

pleaded silently. Oh, Johnny, you *must* know you can't keep Curly—you can't keep a fat pet steer.

But Johnny didn't smile. He walked over and stood with one arm about Curly's neck, staring incredulously at O'Flynn. "Nobody's going to pick Curly's bones," he said to the auctioneer. Then he turned to the steer. "Don't you worry, Curly. That guy hasn't got anything to do with you."

There was a sympathetic murmur among the bystanders. "The poor kid's made a pet of him," one man said. "Too bad. Well, he can't learn any earlier."

The men from Mack's Market tried to take the matter lightly. "Look here, bud," said one of them. "Get yourself a canary. This steer don't want to be nobody's pet. He wants to be beefsteaks." And he put a hand on Curly's halter.

Johnny struck it down. "Don't touch Curly!" he shouted. "He's going home, where he belongs! He's won the prize! That's all he came here to do!"

The circle of onlookers came closer, augmented by passersby whose ears   130
had caught in Johnny's voice the sound of passion and hurt. The buzzards, Jo thought. She saw Johnny press himself still more closely against Curly, keeping his eyes all the time on O'Flynn. She gripped her father's arm. "Dad, do something!" she cried. "Let Johnny take Curly home. There's plenty of food and room. Johnny wouldn't feel this way about him except for you and me. It's our fault!" She was half crying.

"Yes, this nonsense can't go on," her father agreed, and went quickly over to Johnny.

Jo couldn't hear what he said or see his face, for he stood with his back to her, but she could see Johnny's face, and its anguish and disbelief. At last, the boy turned and threw both arms around Curly's neck and buried his face against the steer's heavy muscles. Jo saw his thin shoulder blades shaking.

When her father turned and came toward her, eyes to the ground, she found she could not say to him any of the bitter things that had been on her tongue's tip.

"Dad," she said, and put her hand out to him.

"There's no use, Jo."   135

"But he loves Curly so."

"Oh, love!" her father said, and then added more quietly, "It's better to learn to say goodbye early than late, Jo."

"I'm going to the car," Jo said, and she turned and ran blindly through the crowd. Because Dad's had to learn, why must Johnny, she thought bitterly.

She got into the front seat and leaned across the wheel, without any attempt to stop crying. Then, as the sobs let up, she pounded the wheel. "No, sir!" she said aloud. "I *won't* learn! I refuse to learn! I'll be an exception!"   *[1951]*

☰ THINKING ABOUT THE TEXT

1. Although the story begins by focusing on John Thomas and, at the climax, dramatizes his torment, much of the text is from Jo's point of view. What would you say to someone who argues that Jo is therefore the story's main character?

2. Although the children's mother has recently died, West tells us virtually nothing about her life or about the circumstances of her death. Why do you think West withholds this information?

3. West eventually retitled this story "Learn to Say Good-bye." Where do these words appear within the text? What "good-byes" do the characters have to make?

4. Do you think the father is cruel when he forces John Thomas to give up Curly? Why, or why not?

5. At the end of the story, Jo declares, "I'll be an exception!" In what sense does she mean this? How realistic is her assertion?

TONI CADE BAMBARA
The Lesson

Toni Cade Bambara (1939–1995) taught at various colleges and worked as a community activist. She edited The Black Woman *(1970), a collection of essays that became a landmark of contemporary black feminism. Bambara wrote two novels:* The Salt Eaters *(1980), which won the American Book Award, and* Those Bones Are Not My Child *(2000), a posthumously published work about the murders of several African American children in late 1970s Atlanta. She also produced several collections of short stories. "The Lesson" comes from her first,* Gorilla, My Love *(1972).*

Back in the days when everyone was old and stupid or young and foolish and me and Sugar were the only ones just right, this lady moved on our block with nappy hair and proper speech and no makeup. And quite naturally we laughed at her, laughed the way we did at the junk man who went about his business like he was some big-time president and his sorry-ass horse his secretary. And we kinda hated her too, hated the way we did the winos who cluttered up our parks and pissed on our handball walls and stank up our hallways and stairs so you couldn't halfway play hide-and-seek without a goddamn gas mask. Miss Moore was her name. The only woman on the block with no first name. And she was black as hell, cept for her feet, which were fish-white and spooky. And she was always planning these boring-ass things for us to do, us being my cousin, mostly, who lived on the block cause we all moved North the same time and to the same apartment then spread out gradual to breathe. And our parents would yank our heads into some kinda shape and crisp up our clothes so we'd be presentable for travel with Miss Moore, who always looked like she was going to church, though she never did. Which is just one of the things the grownups talked about when they talked behind her back like a dog. But when she came calling with some sachet she'd sewed up or some gingerbread she'd made or some book, why then they'd all be too embarrassed to turn her down and we'd get handed over all spruced up. She'd been to college and said it was only right that she should take responsibility for the young ones' education, and she not even related by marriage or blood. So they'd go for it. Specially Aunt Gretchen. She was the main gofer in the family. You got some ole dumb shit foolishness you want somebody to go for, you send for Aunt Gretchen. She been screwed into the go-along for so long, it's a blood-deep natural thing with her. Which is how she got saddled with me and Sugar and Junior in the first place while our mothers were in a la-de-da apartment up the block having a good ole time.

So this one day, Miss Moore rounds us all up at the mailbox and it's puredee hot and she's knockin herself out about arithmetic. And school suppose to let up in summer I heard, but she don't never let up. And the starch in my pinafore scratching the shit outta me and I'm really hating this nappy-head bitch and her goddamn college degree. I'd much rather go to the pool or to the show where it's cool. So me and Sugar leaning on the mailbox being surly, which is a Miss Moore word. And Flyboy checking out what everybody brought for lunch. And Fat Butt already wasting his peanut-butter-and-jelly sandwich like the pig he is. And Junebug punchin on Q.T.'s arm for potato chips. And Rosie Giraffe shifting from one hip to the other waiting for somebody to step on her foot or ask her if she from Georgia so she can kick ass, preferably Mercedes's. And Miss Moore asking us do we know what money is, like we a bunch of retards. I mean real money, she say, like it's only poker chips or monopoly papers we lay on the grocer. So right away I'm tired of this and say so. And would much rather snatch Sugar and go to the Sunset and terrorize the West Indian kids and take their hair ribbons and their money too. And Miss Moore files that remark away for next week's lesson on brotherhood, I can tell. And finally I say we oughta get to the subway cause it's cooler and besides we might meet some cute boys. Sugar done swiped her mama's lipstick, so we ready.

So we heading down the street and she's boring us silly about what things cost and what our parents make and how much goes for rent and how money ain't divided up right in this country. And then she gets to the part about we all poor and live in the slums, which I don't feature. And I'm ready to speak on that, but she steps out in the street and hails two cabs just like that. Then she hustles half the crew in with her and hands me a five-dollar bill and tells me to calculate 10 percent tip for the driver. And we're off. Me and Sugar and Junebug and Flyboy hangin out the window and hollering to everybody, putting lipstick on each other cause Flyboy a faggot anyway, and making farts with our sweaty armpits. But I'm mostly trying to figure how to spend this money. But they all fascinated with the meter ticking and Junebug starts laying bets as to how much it'll read when Flyboy can't hold his breath no more. Then Sugar lays bets as to how much it'll be when we get there. So I'm stuck. Don't nobody want to go for my plan, which is to jump out at the next light and run off to the first bar-b-que we can find. Then the driver tells us to get the hell out cause we there already. And the meter reads eighty-five cents. And I'm stalling to figure out the tip and Sugar say give him a dime. And I decide he don't need it bad as I do, so later for him. But then he tries to take off with Junebug foot still in the door so we talk about his mama something ferocious. Then we check out that we on Fifth Avenue and everybody dressed up in stockings. One lady in a fur coat, hot as it is. White folks crazy.

"This is the place," Miss Moore say, presenting it to us in the voice she uses at the museum. "Let's look in the windows before we go in."

"Can we steal?" Sugar asks very serious like she's getting the ground rules 5 squared away before she plays. "I beg your pardon," say Miss Moore, and we fall out. So she leads us around the windows of the toy store and me and Sugar screamin, "This is mine, that's mine, I gotta have that, that was made for me, I was born for that," till Big Butt drowns us out.

"Hey, I'm goin to buy that there."

"That there? You don't even know what it is, stupid."

"I do so," he say punchin on Rosie Giraffe. "It's a microscope."

"Whatcha gonna do with a microscope, fool?"

"Look at things." 10

"Like what, Ronald?" ask Miss Moore. And Big Butt ain't got the first notion. So here go Miss Moore gabbing about the thousands of bacteria in a drop of water and the somethinorother in a speck of blood and the million and one living things in the air around us is invisible to the naked eye. And what she say that for? Junebug go to town on that "naked" and we rolling. Then Miss Moore ask what it cost. So we all jam into the window smudgin it up and the price tag say $300. So then she ask how long'd take for Big Butt and Junebug to save up their allowances. "Too long," I say. "Yeh," adds Sugar, "outgrown it by that time." And Miss Moore say no, you never outgrow learning instruments. "Why, even medical students and interns and," blah, blah, blah. And we ready to choke Big Butt for bringing it up in the first damn place.

"This here costs four hundred eighty dollars," says Rosie Giraffe. So we pile up all over her to see what she pointin out. My eyes tell me it's a chunk of glass cracked with something heavy, and different-color inks dripped into the splits, then the whole thing put into a oven or something. But for $480 it don't make sense.

"That's a paperweight made of semi-precious stones fused together under tremendous pressure," she explains slowly, with her hands doing the mining and all the factory work.

"So what's a paperweight?" asks Rosie Giraffe.

"To weigh paper with, dumbbell," say Flyboy, the wise man from the East. 15

"Not exactly," say Miss Moore, which is what she say when you warm or way off too. "It's to weigh paper down so it won't scatter and make your desk untidy." So right away me and Sugar curtsy to each other and then to Mercedes who is more the tidy type.

"We don't keep paper on top of the desk in my class," say Junebug, figuring Miss Moore crazy or lyin one.

"At home, then," she say. "Don't you have a calendar and pencil case and a blotter and a letter-opener on your desk at home where you do your homework?" And she know damn well what our homes look like cause she nosys around in them every chance she gets.

"I don't even have a desk," say Junebug. "Do we?"

"No. And I don't get no homework neither," says Big Butt.   20

"And I don't even have a home," say Flyboy like he do at school to keep the white folks off his back and sorry for him. Send this poor kid to camp posters, is his specialty.

"I do," says Mercedes. "I have a box of stationery on my desk and a picture of my cat. My godmother bought the stationery and the desk. There's a big rose on each sheet and the envelopes smell like roses."

"Who wants to know about your smelly-ass stationery," say Rosie Giraffe fore I can get my two cents in.

"It's important to have a work area all your own so that . . ."

"Will you look at this sailboat, please," say Flyboy, cuttin her off and   25 pointin to the thing like it was his. So once again we tumble all over each other to gaze at this magnificent thing in the toy store which is just big enough to maybe sail two kittens across the pond if you strap them to the posts tight. We all start reciting the price tag like we in assembly. "Handcrafted sailboat of fiberglass at one thousand one hundred ninety-five dollars."

"Unbelievable," I hear myself say and am really stunned. I read it again for myself just in case the group recitation put me in a trance. Same thing. For some reason this pisses me off. We look at Miss Moore and she lookin at us, waiting for I dunno what.

"Who'd pay all that when you can buy a sailboat set for a quarter at Pop's, a tube of glue for a dime, and a ball of string for eight cents? It must have a motor and a whole lot else besides," I say. "My sailboat cost me about fifty cents."

"But will it take water?" say Mercedes with her smart ass.

"Took mine to Alley Pond Park once," say Flyboy. "String broke. Lost it. Pity."

"Sailed mine in Central Park and it keeled over and sank. Had to ask my   30 father for another dollar."

"And you got the strap," laugh Big Butt. "The jerk didn't even have a string on it. My old man wailed on his behind."

Little Q.T. was staring hard at the sailboat and you could see he wanted it bad. But he too little and somebody'd just take it from him. So what the hell. "This boat for kids, Miss Moore?"

"Parents silly to buy something like that just to get all broke up," say Rosie Giraffe.

"That much money it should last forever," I figure.

"My father'd buy it for me if I wanted it."   35

"Your father, my ass," say Rosie Giraffe getting a chance to finally push Mercedes.

"Must be rich people shop here," say Q.T.

"You are a very bright boy," say Flyboy. "What was your first clue?" And he rap him on the head with the back of his knuckles, since Q.T. the only one he could get away with. Though Q.T. liable to come up behind you years later and get his licks in when you half expect it.

"What I want to know is," I says to Miss Moore though I never talk to her, I wouldn't give the bitch that satisfaction, "is how much a real boat costs? I figure a thousand'd get you a yacht any day."

"Why don't you check that out," she says, "and report back to the group?"   40 Which really pains my ass. If you gonna mess up a perfectly good swim day least you could do is have some answers. "Let's go in," she say like she got something up her sleeve. Only she don't lead the way. So me and Sugar turn the corner to where the entrance is, but when we get there I kinda hang back. Not that I'm scared, what's there to be afraid of, just a toy store. But I feel funny, shame. But what I got to be shamed about? Got as much right to go in as anybody. But somehow I can't seem to get hold of the door, so I step away from Sugar to lead. But she hangs back too. And I look at her and she looks at me and this is ridiculous. I mean, damn, I have never ever been shy about doing nothing or going nowhere. But then Mercedes steps up and then Rosie Giraffe and Big Butt crowd in behind and shove, and next thing we all stuffed into the doorway with only Mercedes squeezing past us, smoothing out her jumper and walking right down the aisle. Then the rest of us tumble in like a glued-together jigsaw done all wrong. And people lookin at us. And it's like the time me and Sugar crashed into the Catholic church on a dare. But once we got in there and everything so hushed and holy and the candles and the bowin and the handkerchiefs on all the drooping heads, I just couldn't go through with the plan. Which was for me to run up to the altar and do a tap dance while Sugar played the nose flute and messed around in the holy water. And Sugar kept givin me the elbow. Then later teased me so bad I tied her up in the shower and turned it on and locked her in. And she'd be there till this day if Aunt Gretchen hadn't finally figured I was lying about the boarder takin a shower.

Same thing in the store. We all walkin on tiptoe and hardly touchin the games and puzzles and things. And I watched Miss Moore who is steady watchin us like she waitin for a sign. Like Mama Drewery watches the sky and sniffs the air and takes note of just how much slant is in the bird formation. Then me and Sugar bump smack into each other, so busy gazing at the toys, 'specially the sailboat. But we don't laugh and go into our fat-lady bump-stomach routine. We just stare at that price tag. Then Sugar run a finger over the whole boat. And I'm jealous and want to hit her. Maybe not her, but I sure want to punch somebody in the mouth.

"Watcha bring us here for, Miss Moore?"

"You sound angry, Sylvia. Are you mad about something?" Givin me one of them grins like she tellin a grown-up joke that never turns out to be funny. And she's lookin very closely at me like maybe she plannin to do my portrait from memory. I'm mad, but I won't give her that satisfaction. So I slouch around the store bein very bored and say, "Let's go."

Me and Sugar at the back of the train watchin the tracks whizzin by large then small then getting gobbled up in the dark. I'm thinkin about this tricky toy I saw in the store. A clown that somersaults on a bar then does chin-ups just cause you yank lightly at his leg. Cost $35. I could see me askin my mother for a $35 birthday clown. "You wanna who that costs what?" she'd say, cocking her head to the side to get a better view of the hole in my head. Thirty-five dollars could buy new bunk beds for Junior and Gretchen's boy. Thirty-five dollars and the whole household could go visit Grand-daddy Nelson in the country. Thirty-five dollars would pay for the rent and the piano bill too. Who are these people that spend that much for performing clowns and $1000 for toy sailboats? What kinda work they do and how they live and how come we ain't in on it? Where we are is who we are, Miss Moore always pointin out. But it don't necessarily have to be that way, she always adds then waits for somebody to say that poor people have to wake up and demand their share of the pie and don't none of us know what kind of pie she talking about in the first damn place. But she ain't so smart cause I still got her four dollars from the taxi and she sure ain't gettin it. Messin up my day with this shit. Sugar nudges me in my pocket and winks.

Miss Moore lines us up in front of the mailbox where we started from, seem   45
like years ago, and I got a headache for thinkin so hard. And we lean all over each other so we can hold up under the draggy-ass lecture she always finishes us off with at the end before we thank her for borin us to tears. But she just looks at us like she readin tea leaves. Finally she say, "Well, what did you think of F. A. O. Schwarz?"

Rosie Giraffe mumbles, "White folks crazy."

"I'd like to go there again when I get my birthday money," says Mercedes, and we shove her out the pack so she has to lean on the mailbox by herself.

"I'd like a shower. Tiring day," say Flyboy.

Then Sugar surprises me by sayin, "You know, Miss Moore, I don't think all of us here put together eat in a year what that sailboat costs." And Miss Moore lights up like somebody goosed her. "And?" she say, urging Sugar on. Only I'm standin on her foot so she don't continue.

"Imagine for a minute what kind of society it is in which some people   50
can spend on a toy what it would cost to feed a family of six or seven. What do you think?"

"I think," say Sugar pushing me off her feet like she never done before, cause I whip her ass in a minute, "that this is not much of a democracy if you ask me. Equal chance to pursue happiness means an equal crack at the dough, don't it?" Miss Moore is beside herself and I am disgusted with Sugar's treachery. So I stand on her foot one more time to see if she'll shove me. She shuts up, and Miss Moore looks at me, sorrowfully I'm thinkin. And somethin weird is goin on, I can feel it in my chest.

"Anybody else learn anything today?" lookin dead at me. I walk away and Sugar has to run to catch up and don't even seem to notice when I shrug her arm off my shoulder.

"Well, we got four dollars anyway," she says.

"Uh hunh."

"We could go to Hascombs and get half a chocolate layer and then go to   55
the Sunset and still have plenty money for potato chips and ice cream sodas."

"Un hunh."

"Race you to Hascombs," she say.

We start down the block and she gets ahead which is O.K. by me cause I'm going to the West End and then over to the Drive to think this day through. She can run if she want to and even run faster. But ain't nobody gonna beat me at nuthin. *[1972]*

≡ THINKING ABOUT THE TEXT

1. Bambara's story begins with "Back in the days," which suggests that Sylvia is significantly older now than she was then. How much time do you think has passed since the events she recalls? Does it matter to you how old she is now? Why, or why not?

2. Miss Moore is not officially a teacher. Nor is she a relative of the children she instructs. Is it right, then, for her to "take responsibility for the young ones' education" (para. 1)? Make arguments for and against her doing so.

3. Consider Miss Moore herself as making an argument. What are her claims? Which of her strategies, if any, seem effective in persuading her audience? Which, if any, seem ineffective?

4. What statements by the children articulate the lesson that Miss Moore teaches? Are all these statements saying pretty much the same thing? At the end of the story, is Sylvia ready to agree with all of them? Explain.

5. Do class and race seem equally important in this story, or does one seem more important than the other? Elaborate your reasoning.

≡ MAKING COMPARISONS

1. Bambara's "The Lesson" is more humorous than West's story. Do you therefore take it less seriously? Why, or why not?

2. A key concept in West's story, and its eventual title, is "learn to say good-bye." How relevant are these words to Bambara's story? Is there any sense in which Sylvia must "learn to say good-bye"?

3. Is Sylvia the "exception" that Jo intends to be? Why, or why not?

≡ WRITING ABOUT ISSUES

1. Choose West's story or Bambara's and write an essay in which you argue a claim about its setting (in the first case, a farm community; in the second case, New York City). How important is the story's location? Might the story have taken place just as easily somewhere else? Why, or why not?

2. Do West's character Jo and Bambara's character Sylvia both change over the course of the stories they are in? Write an essay in which you address this question. What signs of change, if any, does each character show? In what ways might each remain the same?

3. Write an essay recalling an occasion when someone you knew or read about was intent on resisting a lesson. Moreover, let this occasion be one that left you with mixed feelings. Then write an essay that identifies the issues you thought were at stake and also expresses and supports your view of the outcome. If you wish, refer to one or both of the stories in this cluster.

4. Imagine that you are giving a brief speech about West's "The Lesson" at a conference of animal-rights activists or a brief speech about Bambara's "The Lesson" at a workshop for elementary-school teachers. Write this speech, making clear the main point that you are using the story to illustrate.

WILLIAM FAULKNER, "A Rose for Emily"

EDWARD J. DELANEY, "Clean"

We like to think that everyone who commits a crime is caught, convicted, sentenced, and suitably punished. But of course things don't always turn out this way. Many a crime goes unsolved or isn't discovered in the first place. Many a criminal goes unidentified or manages to flee. In such cases, the perpetrators are left with their own thoughts, which may be tranquil, remorseful, or a blend of satisfaction and guilt. The two stories in this cluster suggest that someone who gets away with a crime may be a cauldron of feelings. Their minds may be hard for others to grasp—and perhaps a chaos to themselves as well. In William Faulkner's classic "A Rose for Emily," the title character is a frustrating mystery for the people of her town, who realize the brutality she is capable of only after her death. In Edward J. Delaney's more recent story "Clean," the narrator pulls off a murder when he is young but then struggles with his conscience in the years that follow.

■ BEFORE YOU READ

Do you think it is possible for someone to commit murder and not feel guilty at all? Identify specific cases that come to mind when you consider this question.

WILLIAM FAULKNER

A Rose for Emily

William Faulkner (1897–1962) is recognized as a great American novelist and storyteller and a major figure of world literature, having won the Nobel Prize in 1949. This acclaim failed to impress the people of his hometown, however, where his genteel poverty and peculiar ways earned him the title "Count No Count." Born in New Albany, Mississippi, and raised in Oxford, the home of the University of Mississippi, Faulkner briefly attended college there after World War I but was reduced to working odd jobs while continuing his writing. His fiction is most often set in Yoknapatawpha County, a created world whose history, geography, and complex genealogies parallel those of the American South. His many novels and stories blend the grotesquely comic with the appallingly tragic. The Sound and the Fury (1929) is often considered his finest work. In later years, Faulkner's "odd jobs" included scriptwriting for Hollywood movies, speaking at universities, and writing magazine articles. "A Rose for Emily," first published in Forum, presents a story of secret crime as told by citizens of Yoknapatawpha County.

1

When Miss Emily Grierson died, our whole town went to her funeral: the men through a sort of respectful affection for a fallen monument, the women mostly out of curiosity to see the inside of her house, which no one save an old man-servant — a combined gardener and cook — had seen in at least ten years.

It was a big, squarish frame house that had once been white, decorated with cupolas and spires and scrolled balconies in the heavily lightsome style of the seventies, set on what had once been our most select street. But garages and cotton gins had encroached and obliterated even the august names of that neighborhood; only Miss Emily's house was left, lifting its stubborn and co-quettish decay above the cotton wagons and the gasoline pumps — an eyesore among eyesores. And now Miss Emily had gone to join the representatives of those august names where they lay in the cedar-bemused cemetery among the ranked and anonymous graves of Union and Confederate soldiers who fell at the battle of Jefferson.

Alive, Miss Emily had been a tradition, a duty, and a care; a sort of heredi-tary obligation upon the town, dating from that day in 1894 when Colonel Sartoris, the mayor — he who fathered the edict that no Negro woman should appear on the streets without an apron — remitted her taxes, the dispensation dating from the death of her father on into perpetuity. Not that Miss Emily would have accepted charity. Colonel Sartoris invented an involved tale to the effect that Miss Emily's father had loaned money to the town, which the town, as a matter of business, preferred this way of repaying. Only a man of Colonel Sartoris's generation and thought could have invented it, and only a woman could have believed it.

When the next generation, with its more modern ideas, became mayors and aldermen, this arrangement created some little dissatisfaction. On the first of the year they mailed her a tax notice. February came, and there was no re-ply. They wrote her a formal letter, asking her to call at the sheriff's office at her convenience. A week later the mayor wrote her himself, offering to call or to send his car for her, and received in reply a note on paper of an archaic shape, in a thin, flowing calligraphy in faded ink, to the effect that she no longer went out at all. The tax notice was also enclosed, without comment.

They called a special meeting of the Board of Aldermen. A deputation waited upon her, knocked at the door through which no visitor had passed since she ceased giving china-painting lessons eight or ten years earlier. They were admitted by the old Negro into a dim hall from which a stairway mounted into still more shadow. It smelled of dust and disuse — a close, dank smell. The Negro led them into the parlor. It was furnished in heavy, leather-covered fur-niture. When the Negro opened the blinds of one window, they could see that the leather was cracked; and when they sat down, a faint dust rose sluggishly about their thighs, spinning with slow motes in the single sun-ray. On a tar-nished gilt easel before the fireplace stood a crayon portrait of Miss Emily's father.

They rose when she entered — a small, fat woman in black, with a thin

5

gold chain descending to her waist and vanishing into her belt, leaning on an ebony cane with a tarnished gold head. Her skeleton was small and spare; perhaps that was why what would have been merely plumpness in another was obesity in her. She looked bloated, like a body long submerged in motionless water, and of that pallid hue. Her eyes, lost in the fatty ridges of her face, looked like two small pieces of coal pressed into a lump of dough as they moved from one face to another while the visitors stated their errand.

She did not ask them to sit. She just stood in the door and listened quietly until the spokesman came to a stumbling halt. Then they could hear the invisible watch ticking at the end of the gold chain.

Her voice was dry and cold. "I have no taxes in Jefferson. Colonel Sartoris explained it to me. Perhaps one of you can gain access to the city records and satisfy yourselves."

"But we have. We are the city authorities, Miss Emily. Didn't you get a notice from the sheriff, signed by him?"

"I received a paper, yes," Miss Emily said. "Perhaps he considers himself   10
the sheriff. . . . I have no taxes in Jefferson."

"But there is nothing on the books to show that, you see. We must go by the—"

"See Colonel Sartoris. I have no taxes in Jefferson."

"But, Miss Emily—"

"See Colonel Sartoris." (Colonel Sartoris had been dead almost ten years.) "I have no taxes in Jefferson. Tobe!" The Negro appeared. "Show these gentlemen out."

2

So she vanquished them, horse and foot, just as she had vanquished their fa-   15
thers thirty years before about the smell. That was two years after her father's death and a short time after her sweetheart—the one we believed would marry her—had deserted her. After her father's death she went out very little; after her sweetheart went away, people hardly saw her at all. A few of the ladies had the temerity to call, but were not received, and the only sign of life about the place was the Negro man—a young man then—going in and out with a market basket.

"Just as if a man—any man—could keep a kitchen properly," the ladies said; so they were not surprised when the smell developed. It was another link between the gross, teeming world and the high and mighty Griersons.

A neighbor, a woman, complained to the mayor, Judge Stevens, eighty years old.

"But what will you have me do about it, madam?" he said.

"Why, send her word to stop it," the woman said. "Isn't there a law?"

"I'm sure that won't be necessary," Judge Stevens said. "It's probably just a   20
snake or a rat that nigger of hers killed in the yard. I'll speak to him about it."

The next day he received two more complaints, one from a man who came in diffident deprecation. "We really must do something about it, Judge. I'd be the last one in the world to bother Miss Emily, but we've got to do something."

That night the Board of Aldermen met—three graybeards and one younger man, a member of the rising generation.

"It's simple enough," he said. "Send her word to have her place cleaned up. Give her a certain time to do it in, and if she don't. . . ."

"Dammit, sir," Judge Stevens said, "will you accuse a lady to her face of smelling bad?"

So the next night, after midnight, four men crossed Miss Emily's lawn and slunk about the house like burglars, sniffing along the base of the brickwork and at the cellar openings while one of them performed a regular sowing motion with his hand out of a sack slung from his shoulder. They broke open the cellar door and sprinkled lime there, and in all the outbuildings. As they recrossed the lawn, a window that had been dark was lighted and Miss Emily sat in it, the light behind her, and her upright torso motionless as that of an idol. They crept quietly across the lawn and into the shadow of the locusts that lined the street. After a week or two the smell went away.

That was when people had begun to feel really sorry for her. People in our town, remembering how old lady Wyatt, her great-aunt, had gone completely crazy at last, believed that the Griersons held themselves a little too high for what they really were. None of the young men were quite good enough for Miss Emily and such. We had long thought of them as a tableau, Miss Emily a slender figure in white in the background, her father a spraddled silhouette in the foreground, his back to her and clutching a horsewhip, the two of them framed by the backflung front door. So when she got to be thirty and was still single, we were not pleased exactly, but vindicated; even with insanity in the family she wouldn't have turned down all of her chances if they had really materialized.

When her father died, it got about that the house was all that was left to her; and in a way, people were glad. At last they could pity Miss Emily. Being left alone, and a pauper, she had become humanized. Now she too would know the old thrill and the old despair of a penny more or less.

The day after his death all the ladies prepared to call at the house and offer condolence and aid, as is our custom. Miss Emily met them at the door, dressed as usual and with no trace of grief on her face. She told them that her father was not dead. She did that for three days, with the ministers calling on her, and the doctors, trying to persuade her to let them dispose of the body. Just as they were about to resort to law and force, she broke down, and they buried her father quickly.

We did not say she was crazy then. We believed she had to do that. We remembered all the young men her father had driven away, and we knew that with nothing left, she would have to cling to that which had robbed her, as people will.

3

She was sick for a long time. When we saw her again, her hair was cut short, making her look like a girl, with a vague resemblance to those angels in colored church windows—sort of tragic and serene.

The town had just let the contracts for paving the sidewalks, and in the   30
summer after her father's death they began the work. The construction company came with niggers and mules and machinery, and a foreman named
Homer Barron, a Yankee—a big, dark, ready man, with a big voice and eyes
lighter than his face. The little boys would follow in groups to hear him cuss the
niggers, and the niggers singing in time to the rise and fall of picks. Pretty soon
he knew everybody in town. Whenever you heard a lot of laughing anywhere
about the square, Homer Barron would be in the center of the group. Presently,
we began to see him and Miss Emily on Sunday afternoons driving in the
yellow-wheeled buggy and the matched team of bays from the livery stable.

At first we were glad that Miss Emily would have an interest, because the
ladies all said, "Of course a Grierson would not think seriously of a Northerner,
a day laborer." But there were still others, older people, who said that even grief
could not cause a real lady to forget *noblesse oblige*—without calling it *noblesse
oblige.* They just said, "Poor Emily. Her kinsfolk should come to her." She had
some kin in Alabama; but years ago her father had fallen out with them over
the estate of old lady Wyatt, the crazy woman, and there was no communication between the two families. They had not even been represented at the
funeral.

And as soon as the old people said, "Poor Emily," the whispering began.
"Do you suppose it's really so?" they said to one another. "Of course it is. What
else could. . . ." This behind their hands; rustling of craned silk and satin behind jalousies closed upon the sun of Sunday afternoon as the thin, swift clop-
clop-clop of the matched team passed: "Poor Emily."

She carried her head high enough—even when we believed that she was
fallen. It was as if she demanded more than ever the recognition of her dignity
as the last Grierson; as if it had wanted that touch of earthiness to reaffirm her
imperviousness. Like when she bought the rat poison, the arsenic. That was
over a year after they had begun to say "Poor Emily," and while the two female
cousins were visiting her.

"I want some poison," she said to the druggist. She was over thirty then,
still a slight woman, though thinner than usual, with cold, haughty black eyes
in a face the flesh of which was strained across the temples and about the eye-
sockets as you imagine a lighthouse-keeper's face ought to look. "I want some
poison," she said.

"Yes, Miss Emily. What kind? For rats and such? I'd recom——"   35

"I want the best you have. I don't care what kind."

The druggist named several. "They'll kill anything up to an elephant. But
what you want is——"

"Arsenic," Miss Emily said. "Is that a good one?"

"Is . . . arsenic? Yes, ma'am. But what you want——"

"I want arsenic."   40

The druggist looked down at her. She looked back at him, erect, her face
like a strained flag. "Why, of course," the druggist said. "If that's what you
want. But the law requires you to tell what you are going to use it for."

Miss Emily just stared at him, her head tilted back in order to look him eye for eye, until he looked away and went and got the arsenic and wrapped it up. The Negro delivery boy brought her the package; the druggist didn't come back. When she opened the package at home there was written on the box, under the skull and bones: "For rats."

4

So the next day we all said, "She will kill herself"; and we said it would be the best thing. When she had first begun to be seen with Homer Barron, we had said, "She will marry him." Then we said, "She will persuade him yet," because Homer himself had remarked—he liked men, and it was known that he drank with the younger men in the Elks' Club—that he was not a marrying man. Later we said, "Poor Emily" behind the jalousies as they passed on Sunday afternoon in the glittering buggy, Miss Emily with her head high and Homer Barron with his hat cocked and a cigar in his teeth, reins and whip in a yellow glove.

Then some of the ladies began to say that it was a disgrace to the town and a bad example to the young people. The men did not want to interfere, but at last the ladies forced the Baptist minister—Miss Emily's people were Episcopal—to call upon her. He would never divulge what happened during that interview, but he refused to go back again. The next Sunday they again drove about the streets, and the following day the minister's wife wrote to Miss Emily's relations in Alabama.

So she had blood-kin under her roof again and we sat back to watch developments. At first nothing happened. Then we were sure that they were to be married. We learned that Miss Emily had been to the jeweler's and ordered a man's toilet set in silver, with the letters H.B. on each piece. Two days later we learned that she had bought a complete outfit of men's clothing, including a nightshirt, and we said, "They are married." We were really glad. We were glad because the two female cousins were even more Grierson than Miss Emily had ever been.

So we were not surprised when Homer Barron—the streets had been finished some time since—was gone. We were a little disappointed that there was not a public blowing-off, but we believed that he had gone on to prepare for Miss Emily's coming, or to give her a chance to get rid of the cousins. (By that time it was a cabal, and we were all Miss Emily's allies to help circumvent the cousins.) Sure enough, after another week they departed. And, as we had expected all along, within three days Homer Barron was back in town. A neighbor saw the Negro man admit him at the kitchen door at dusk one evening.

And that was the last we saw of Homer Barron. And of Miss Emily for some time. The Negro man went in and out with the market basket, but the front door remained closed. Now and then we would see her at the window for a moment, as the men did that night when they sprinkled the lime, but for almost six months she did not appear on the streets. Then we knew that this was to be expected too; as if that quality of her father which had

45

thwarted her woman's life so many times had been too virulent and too furious to die.

When we next saw Miss Emily, she had grown fat and her hair was turning gray. During the next few years it grew grayer and grayer until it attained an even pepper-and-salt iron-gray, when it ceased turning. Up to the day of her death at seventy-four it was still that vigorous iron-gray, like the hair of an active man.

From that time on her front door remained closed, save during a period of six or seven years, when she was about forty, during which she gave lessons in china-painting. She fitted up a studio in one of the downstairs rooms, where the daughters and granddaughters of Colonel Sartoris's contemporaries were sent to her with the same regularity and in the same spirit that they were sent to church on Sundays with a twenty-five-cent piece for the collection plate. Meanwhile her taxes had been remitted.

Then the newer generation became the backbone and the spirit of the   50
town, and the painting pupils grew up and fell away and did not send their children to her with boxes of color and tedious brushes and pictures cut from the ladies' magazines. The front door closed upon the last one and remained closed for good. When the town got free postal delivery, Miss Emily alone refused to let them fasten the metal numbers above her door and attach a mailbox to it. She would not listen to them.

Daily, monthly, yearly we watched the Negro grow grayer and more stooped, going in and out with the market basket. Each December we sent her a tax notice, which would be returned by the post office a week later, unclaimed. Now and then we would see her in one of the downstairs windows — she had evidently shut up the top floor of the house — like the carven torso of an idol in a niche, looking or not looking at us, we could never tell which. Thus she passed from generation to generation — dear, inescapable, impervious, tranquil, and perverse.

And so she died. Fell ill in the house filled with dust and shadows, with only a doddering Negro man to wait on her. We did not even know she was sick; we had long since given up trying to get any information from the Negro. He talked to no one, probably not even to her, for his voice had grown harsh and rusty, as if from disuse.

She died in one of the downstairs rooms, in a heavy walnut bed with a curtain, her gray head propped on a pillow yellow and moldy with age and lack of sunlight.

5

The Negro met the first of the ladies at the front door and let them in, with their hushed, sibilant voices and their quick, curious glances, and then he disappeared. He walked right through the house and out the back and was not seen again.

The two female cousins came at once. They held the funeral on the second   55
day, with the town coming to look at Miss Emily beneath a mass of bought flow-

ers, with the crayon face of her father musing profoundly above the bier and the ladies sibilant and macabre; and the very old men — some in their brushed Confederate uniforms — on the porch and the lawn, talking of Miss Emily as if she had been a contemporary of theirs, believing that they had danced with her and courted her perhaps, confusing time with its mathematical progression, as the old do, to whom all the past is not a diminishing road but, instead, a huge meadow which no winter ever quite touches, divided from them now by the narrow bottleneck of the most recent decade of years.

Already we knew that there was one room in that region above stairs which no one had seen in forty years, and which would have to be forced. They waited until Miss Emily was decently in the ground before they opened it.

The violence of breaking down the door seemed to fill this room with pervading dust. A thin, acrid pall as of the tomb seemed to lie everywhere upon this room decked and furnished as for a bridal: upon the valance curtains of faded rose color, upon the rose-shaded lights, upon the dressing table, upon the delicate array of crystal and the man's toilet things backed with tarnished silver, silver so tarnished that the monogram was obscured. Among them lay a collar and tie, as if they had just been removed, which, lifted, left upon the surface a pale crescent in the dust. Upon a chair hung the suit, carefully folded; beneath it the two mute shoes and the discarded socks.

The man himself lay in the bed.

For a long while we just stood there, looking down at the profound and fleshless grin. The body had apparently once lain in the attitude of an embrace, but now the long sleep that outlasts love, that conquers even the grimace of love, had cuckolded him. What was left of him, rotted beneath what was left of the nightshirt, had become inextricable from the bed in which he lay; and upon him and upon the pillow beside him lay that even coating of the patient and biding dust.

Then we noticed that in the second pillow was the indentation of a head. 60 One of us lifted something from it, and leaning forward, that faint and invisible dust dry and acrid in the nostrils, we saw a long strand of iron-gray hair.

[1931]

≡ **THINKING ABOUT THE TEXT**

1. Who seems to be the "we" that narrates this story? Why would Faulkner tell the story from this perspective? Why not from Emily's?

2. List the events of the story in chronological order. Why do you think Faulkner doesn't follow this order in telling the story?

3. Look at the last sentence of paragraph 51. How does each of the five adjectives there conceivably apply to Emily? What additional adjectives would you apply to her? Do you feel any sympathy for her? Why, or why not? Would you say that she loved Homer? Define what you mean by "love."

4. What does Faulkner imply about the culture of the South in Emily's era?

5. Reread the story. How does your knowledge of the ending affect your second reading? What details of the narrative stand out for you this second time around?

EDWARD J. DELANEY
Clean

Edward J. Delaney (b. 1957) is a journalist and a producer of documentaries as well as a writer of fiction. Newspapers he has worked for include the Denver Post *and the* Chicago Tribune. *With Dustin Pedroia of the Boston Red Sox, he wrote the nonfiction book* Born to Play *(2009). One of his films,* The Times Were Never So Bad *(2007), is about Andre Dubus, author of the short story "Killings" that appears elsewhere in this chapter. Delaney's works of fiction include the novels* Broken Irish *(2011) and* Warp & Weft *(2004) along with a short story collection,* The Drowning: And Other Stories *(1999). He teaches creative writing at Roger Williams University in Providence, Rhode Island. The following story appeared in the November 2012 issue of* The Atlantic *magazine.*

You think of that night endlessly from your imprisonment, the decisions made, the chain of mistakes. It had begun with your two buddies, a fifth of cheap vodka, and half a gallon of orange juice; one of these friends had suggested the confrontation. He said this kid, Barry, was cutting in on your girl—well, she wasn't even really your girl yet, the flirtation was just in its formative moments—something that you, at sixteen, had no intention of allowing.

He'd been walking home, at night. He worked at a burger place in town and, even drunk, you'd known a spot to intercept him. Again, at the suggestion of your friends. There he was, his backpack slung over his shoulder, looking at you as if not even sure who you were. You'd decided you would rough him up, and he'd decided to fight back, and you'd picked up a rock, and you'd swung it at his head. A minute later he was on the ground, dead.

You think of how, as drunk as you had been, you instantly sobered. The discussion was quick, and its determinations would last a lifetime. You waited for him to somehow come to; soon enough he was irredeemably cold. But you three had decided by then. No one would tell. No one would try to explain that the moment was one of passion and mistakes. In your long memory, telling wasn't even part of that shaky conversation, your voices all gone weepy and scared.

You took the rock, with its rime of blood, and threw it in a pond. You filled Barry's backpack with other rocks and into the pond that went, too. You were driving your old Pontiac, and the first odd decision was to drive home, go in your bedroom, and strip the top sheet off your bed, to bring it back to the scene as your buddies waited, hidden in the nearby woods with Barry, the body dragged in by the feet. You got your mother's gardening trowel from the nail in the garage. Then her garden claw.

By the time you drove up, watching for headlights, you had calmed a bit. 5 You were thinking now, your head clicking with logic and forethought that were a revelation in themselves. Your buddies had kicked the blood under dirt, and you wondered as you came back if they had been talking of turning you in. Apparently they had not.

You wrapped the body in the sheet and drove to a place you thought would work. Again, the choices made: A place close to your house, less than half a mile. But a place far enough away from other houses, and with somewhat yielding ground. The three of you, all high-school athletes, did not tire that night, rotating through the clawing and digging, going deeper, no sloppy shallow grave here. When his sheet-wrapped body went into the groundwater that had gathered at the bottom, you felt for that glorious instant as if the problem was now solved. You all filled the hole with dirt and stomped it down, then drove to the ocean at dawn and walked into the surf, fully clothed, emerging salty and bloodless.

This was '72. You think of forty years gone past, and the girl. For days after, you did the calculus, of risk and probability. You realized in that panicky first day that his wallet had gone into the ground with him; everything had not been fully considered. You and the other two never spoke of it directly again, and you weighed the human factors you could not control. You sensed, by the light of day, some shrill and growing prospect of being caught. Then you got lucky. Barry, the aspiring hippie, had been trying to get her to take off with him, hitchhiking with backpacks, cross-country. He did not get along with his parents; he craved adventure and escape. She told the police she guessed he must have gone, then she keened at her presumed abandonment. You heard about that at school and felt a surge of both relief and fury, that Barry had made the plan and that she had apparently considered it. You hated her for choosing him.

The conclusion was simple. Barry was deemed just another wandering soul, a longhair, a dreamer. He'd return in due time. The only thing was that your mother could not stop going on about the missing bedsheet. Where did it go? How do you lose a bedsheet? "Now you've broken up the set," she said. You heard her telling the neighbor about her son's mysteriously losing a sheet, and you wanted to make her stop.

The girl: Barry gone, you dated her for a few months, but found you had nothing to talk about. She turned out, in fact, to be mildly irritating, and that was that.

Senior year: Thinking back over the decades, you are appalled to consider 10 how little you worried about what had happened. In fact, you barely thought about it at all. In your mind, It (you could not bring yourself to use the more specific word) wasn't even your fault. You'd been egged on, drunk, by the other two. You met other girls, and you played your games, and you avoided the vicinity of the grave. You were an adolescent; you did not dwell on things that might ruin your fun.

Your buddies: you realized that they would not talk, even when drunk. Besides, the three of you were no longer that friendly. Typical teenagers, you all had found other interests, other friends.

College: those were the years when you needed to tell yourself what you were, and what you were not. So: You were a good person. You were not violent. Indeed, in those years you became milder and milder, almost as if shedding the ill-thought fashions of your youth like a bad sweater. Changing times. You held that memory in your stomach, but you functioned, actually, *well*. It had been three years then, and no one was going to find out. Then you went home for Thanksgiving and you saw bulldozers edged up toward that place. A new housing tract. You spent the weekend sleepless, telling yourself that even when the body emerged, the police would have no suspects, no motive. But the soft ground in which your secret lay was wetland. New environmental laws had been passed, and the housing tract stopped fewer than a hundred yards from where the body lay buried. The next spring, you told your parents you were going to stay on at your distant school, do summer classes, accelerate, and when you were done with that, you stayed on as a grad student. When those unbidden memories occurred, those predawn panics, you pushed deeper into your studies, forcing the ghosts away. You graduated with your parents and sisters smiling at your side for the picture, and then you moved farther west still.

In love, you married. Some nights you felt so intimate with her that you wanted to tell her, felt you had to. Felt she would hold your secret and love you still. But then one odd night, an awkward dinner, and you weren't so sure you two were always in tune. The marriage evened into something mellow and a bit more distant, and the impulse passed. When you had children, you tried to be good. The business flourished, and the money came in without much struggle.

Why, in your thirties, did you begin to obsess about the hidden crime? When you read the articles about DNA, and how it could tell of a long-past crime, did you begin to see a story that hadn't been completely written? You became an insomniac. You played that one minute of your life in an endless loop on the pale wall of your skull. The phone suddenly felt as if it would go off. You would see a police car thousands of miles from your hometown and feel on edge. You worried in those years that your unmasking was imminent, but then nothing happened. During the holidays, you had your parents out for a visit to a warmer climate. Sometimes, your mother would start in about the missing sheet. You'd all laugh in reminiscence.

Your father died, and you flew back to take care of things. You went through his desk, sorting out his papers, tending to your mother. At the bottom of a drawer was a yellowed bit of newspaper, clipped down to a tiny headline and one-paragraph item. *Local boy reported missing.* Strangely, the photo in the paper, though blurred, didn't match the memory in your head, of that face on the side of the road, turning to meet the judgment of your headlights.

Why had your father kept this? What did he guess? Did you make noise that night as you came and went? At the funeral, a Navy ensign played taps, and your mother got the triangled flag. Your father went into that neat, nearly

15

surgically cut hole with his own secrets. You burned the newspaper in his kettle grill on the back deck, igniting some charcoal and then making a steak.

That evening, you left your mother's house near dark and went walking in those woods. Twenty years had passed, more. You'd built a life now. In this cold ground was what would always threaten to change it. You had an exact memory of the spot he was buried, but that memory failed you, too. You could find no place that was at all like the place you remembered.

Flying home, you realized someone had to have been following all this. Were the police so sure of the hitchhiking story, even in 1972? Could they not have tried to look into it? Who was assigned to the case, and could he have known of you? But you saw no signs of any investigation. Maybe when Barry eventually did not return home, too much time had passed. Maybe they just didn't care that much. But you knew a file must have been kept at the police station, and your desire to open that file and see what was written became instantly unbearable. You were 35,000 feet in the air, over the arrayed pivot-circles of Kansas, heading toward the sun. By the time you landed, you felt the anxiety was finally over. In long-term parking, you slipped into the leather seat of your German car as if it were a glove that fit you perfectly.

In your forties, you thought of the boy less, but when the memory came to you, it gave you an unremitting ache. You could barely remember who you were then, what urges drove you, or what aspirations you'd had. The indisputable irony was that the aftermath of it all had given you focus, and direction. Who would you have become instead, if It had not happened? You also felt a welling anger at Barry himself. If he was going to leave, why didn't he just leave? Was this talk of hitchhiking just something to woo his wanted girl, or was he really going to do it? You thought about how, if he'd decamped a day sooner, or if you three had not drunk that plastic jug of orange juice and that bottle of vodka, that night would just be something forgotten, rather than a specific date on the calendar you suffered through each year, and from which you could count, to the very minute, your growing remove. The colors faded like a washed-out Kodachrome.

In the eleventh year of your marriage, you found out your wife had been 20 having an affair. She confessed; you were shocked. Boredom, she told you tearfully. Someone else had offered escape, she said.

"I love you," she said, "but you're a dull, passionless person. You have no fire."

She was right, but now wrong. You knew who the man was. For the first time in thirty years, the familiar urge came back to you, for the same reasons. The careful decades of telling yourself you were different now crumbled, in an instant. You could have done it again, right then, had you decided to. But you did not.

Instead you got up from the couch and went out on your deck with a drink (good wine, never the hard stuff) and looked at the sky and thought about the careful, boring man you had sculpted yourself into. No passion at all. Later, your tearstained wife came out and sat with you in the wind of sunset and said she wanted to try to work things out, for your daughters. Her love of your daughters made her want to stay with you and find the middle ground. You wanted badly to offer your forgiveness, as you badly wanted forgiveness for yourself.

Yes, you'd had chances for affairs, but you always held back. Your reason wasn't strict morality, more the fear of the weight of yet another secret. The thought of that was just too heavy. You accepted life as it was, and you walked in the evening, to get air.

One night, a few years later, the phone rang and your wife held it in front of you, saying "It's Dennis." Dennis who? You heard the voice and you were back to that night. Dennis, your long-ago buddy, was not well. Lymphoma. Three or four months. He had the urge to tell, to unburden. He had thought about that night every day of his life, he said into the phone. He'd spoken of it many times over the years, he said, in the darkness of the confessional. Father Shea had told him his soul was now clean, even as it felt not.

"Dennis, I can't tell you what to do," you said to him. "We're all different people now. Do what you feel you must. I would understand."

"Thank you for that," he said. "I guess telling would be easy for me now. I'll be dead before I have to face the consequences. But I think we all should have." You had the phone to your ear, listening to him. He was a stranger. As Barry had been. Someone about whom you knew nothing.

Dennis asked about your family then, and you told him. He said he had not heard from Jeff in years, no idea where he'd gone. When you hung up, you were giddy that the secret might come out. You were surprised, and gratified, at the relief you felt. For weeks you sat at your desk and prepared things, just in case. You slept straight through each night. You got on the computer and read about juvenile law. You were all sixteen when It happened. Had the three of you gone to the police that night, explained you'd been in a fight that went out of control, you probably would have been out by the age of eighteen. Now you quietly imagined the neat rectangle of a cell, with a thin mattress. The thought didn't seem as foreboding as it had when you were young and felt the possibilities of life. This future now seemed orderly, calm. You had forgiven your wife, and you imagined and craved her own understanding. You had never given her the opportunity, never shared the secret. You concluded that this was why, in your entire life, you'd never felt true intimacy.

That night, you Googled Barry's name, and found nothing. So many years had passed; who'd remember? Where would Barry's name have been preserved? He seemed to have never existed. You remembered back in '75, when word had quietly come that his parents had moved away, some new job, or escape from worries. But now, so long after, people would remember him. You lay down in bed against your sleeping wife and felt the powerful promise of the simplicity, and the real facts of your life.

But your conversation had apparently given Dennis the peace not to speak, or perhaps he had simply died before he had a chance. No one told you anything. After a long stretch of months in which a tap did not come on your door, you went to the online obituaries and saw that he was gone. You checked on Father Shea, and he too had passed, years before. Your younger daughter walked in the room, said you looked weird, and walked out. By dinner, you were who you were again.

Later that year, your mother succumbed, the story of the missing bedsheet forever silenced. Back in town to close the house, you now did not venture into the dark woods. You and your sisters sorted things out and renewed bonds. You promised to stay in touch, knowing you probably would not.

That evening, at a hotel by the airport, you watched local TV. To your shock, you saw a vaguely familiar face. A woman, real estate. She was the girl, from all those years before. You'd nearly forgotten her name. She was, like you, an aging person. Now she sold high-end real estate, and seemed to have had some ineffectual cosmetic surgery. She had a horsey, drawn face, and wore a giant rock on her left ring finger. Did she ever think of Barry? He'd only been a boy who made her promises then went off hitchhiking, leaving her out of his adventure. You wondered about it as you tried to sleep.

You flew home and idly considered the third of you, Jeff, somewhere out there with the other half of your secret. You sat on your deck and drank some wine and watched the sun set over the Pacific. Another day had elapsed between you and that night. You had come to this place, imprisoned by what you were, what you had done, never able fully to be inside the life you made. You imagined how you would feel to just live.

The irony of getting away with something was that you were your own keeper. You were the executioner: in a pang of remorse, you could just open your mouth and change your life. You felt almost as if you would. But, greedy, you always wanted to savor one more day, even as that day turned leaden with a memory that no longer went away. It could not be put aside as it was your senior year of high school, when something that had happened the year before may as well have never happened at all. Who were you? How did you find the way to make it just not be? Now, an older man, you decided that if the time came to tell, you would edit Dennis and Jeff from the story, a small act of charity.

The vast ocean shimmered below you, endless expanses in which things could be effortlessly hidden, even as what you looked at was only a knife's edge along greater stretches past the distant horizon. Even as the silver surface only whispered of the dark depths, the things you could not see. This was your life now, orderly, calm. This was how things were now. Clean. You knew you would sleep as well as one might be expected to, all of us with our own given histories.   *[2012]*

35

≡ THINKING ABOUT THE TEXT

1. It is fairly unusual for a story to be narrated in the second person ("you"). Why do you think Delaney uses this technique?

2. The story is entitled "Clean," and that word appears in the final paragraph. But how helpful is it as a guide to the story? Other than the ending, what specific passages does it connect to?

3. What, specifically, are the effects on the protagonist of his murder and of his failure to confess? How guilty does he seem to feel about the murder he has committed? Use specific passages to support your answer. How well does he seem to understand himself?

4. With the last words of the story—"all of us with our own given histories"—the protagonist seems to imply that many people go through comparable experiences. How typical a person does he strike you as being? Is he unusually bad? To what extent can you sympathize with him?

5. Did you think that after the phone conversation with Dennis the protagonist's secret would go public and his guilt would be revealed? Why, or why not?

≣ MAKING COMPARISONS

1. Do you think that after murdering Homer, Faulkner's Emily would have at least some of the same troubled thoughts as Delaney's protagonist has? Why, or why not? What would you say to someone who argues that these characters become equally detached from the world? Cite specific passages from both stories in responding to this claim.

2. Does the killing done by Delaney's protagonist seem more excusable than the murder that Emily commits? Explain your reasoning.

3. How different would "A Rose for Emily" be if it were narrated by a "you," the point of view that Delaney employs? Try rewriting some of Faulkner's passages to test this idea.

≣ WRITING ABOUT ISSUES

1. Is Emily or the protagonist of Delaney's story the type of person who would *ever* confess? Choose one of the two characters, and write an essay that answers this question. Refer to specific passages in the story you discuss.

2. In the first sentence of Delaney's story, the protagonist refers to his "imprisonment." Does the word apply just as much to Emily as it does to him? Write an essay addressing this question, referring to specific passages in both stories.

3. Recall an occasion when you agreed to keep a secret, though you felt guilty about doing so. (Choose a secret that you are willing to reveal now.) Then, write an essay in which you identify the issues that arose for you at the time. If you wish, refer to one or both of the stories in this cluster.

4. Research a real-life criminal case that is as yet unsolved—perhaps one in your local community. Then, write an essay in which you speculate about how the perpetrator(s) of this crime thinks. If you wish, refer to one or both of the stories in this cluster.

EDGAR ALLAN POE, "The Cask of Amontillado"

ANDRE DUBUS, "Killings"

Many people automatically consider revenge abhorrent. They hold that wrong-doers should be forgiven, left to the judgment of God ("Vengeance is mine, saith the Lord"), or dealt with through the supposedly fair and rational processes of the judicial system. Yet others believe that in some circumstances, getting even may be legitimate. They may tolerate or encourage certain acts of revenge or retaliate themselves against perceived offenders, in effect following the ancient principle of "an eye for an eye, a tooth for a tooth." Several works of literature focus on avengers who seem not simply villainous but rather complex. Whether or not the reader comes to sympathize with these characters, their approach to issues of crime and justice demands analysis. They resist being easily labeled or condemned. The protagonists of the following two stories — a classic tale and a more recent piece — are cases in point.

■ BEFORE YOU READ

Do you believe it is ever justifiable for someone to avenge a crime or wrong-doing by going outside the law? What specific cases do you think about as you address this issue?

EDGAR ALLAN POE

The Cask of Amontillado

The life of Edgar Allan Poe (1809–1849) was relatively brief, its end tragically has-tened by his alcohol and drug abuse, but his contributions to literature were unique. As a book reviewer, he produced pieces of literary criticism and theory that are still widely respected. As a poet, he wrote such classics as "The Raven" (1845), "The Bells" (1849), and "Annabel Lee" (1849). Moreover, his short fiction was ground-breaking and continues to be popular, a source for many films and television shows. With works such as "The Murders in the Rue Morgue" (1841), "The Gold Bug" (1843), and "The Purloined Letter" (1844), he pioneered the modern detective story. Some of Poe's other tales are masterpieces of horror, including "The Fall of the House of Usher" (1842), "The Pit and the Pendulum" (1842), and the following story, one of Poe's most famous. It was first published in an 1846 issue of Godey's Lady's Book *and was then included in a posthumous 1850 collection of Poe's writings.*

The thousand injuries of Fortunato I had borne as I best could; but when he ventured upon insult, I vowed revenge. You, who so well know the nature of my soul, will not suppose, however, that I gave utterance to a threat. *At length* I would be avenged; this was a point definitely settled—but the very definitiveness with which it was resolved precluded the idea of risk. I must not only punish, but punish with impunity. A wrong is unredressed when retribution overtakes its redresser. It is equally unredressed when the avenger fails to make himself felt as such to him who has done the wrong.

It must be understood, that neither by word nor deed had I given Fortunato cause to doubt my good-will. I continued, as was my wont, to smile in his face, and he did not perceive that my smile *now* was at the thought of his immolation.

He had a weak point—this Fortunato—although in other regards he was a man to be respected and even feared. He prided himself on his connoisseurship in wine. Few Italians have the true virtuoso spirit. For the most part their enthusiasm is adopted to suit the time and opportunity—to practice imposture upon the British and Austrian *millionnaires.* In painting and gemmary Fortunato, like his countrymen, was a quack—but in the matter of old wines he was sincere. In this respect I did not differ from him materially: I was skillful in the Italian vintages myself, and bought largely whenever I could.

It was about dusk, one evening during the supreme madness of the carnival season, that I encountered my friend. He accosted me with excessive warmth, for he had been drinking much. The man wore motley. He had on a tight-fitting parti-striped dress, and his head was surmounted by the conical cap and bells. I was so pleased to see him, that I thought I should never have done wringing his hand.

I said to him: "My dear Fortunato, you are luckily met. How remarkably   5
well you are looking to-day! But I have received a pipe° of what passes for Amontillado, and I have my doubts."

"How?" said he. "Amontillado? A pipe? Impossible! And in the middle of the carnival!"

"I have my doubts," I replied; "and I was silly enough to pay the full Amontillado price without consulting you in the matter. You were not to be found, and I was fearful of losing a bargain."

"Amontillado!"

"I have my doubts."

"Amontillado!"   10

"And I must satisfy them."

"Amontillado!"

"As you are engaged, I am on my way to Luchesi. If any one has a critical turn, it is he. He will tell me——"

"Luchesi cannot tell Amontillado from Sherry."

"And yet some fools will have it that his taste is a match for your own."   15

"Come, let us go."

"Whither?"

---

pipe: A large cask.

"To your vaults."

"My friend, no; I will not impose upon your good nature. I perceive you have an engagement. Luchesi——"

"I have no engagement;—come."   20

"My friend, no. It is not the engagement, but the severe cold with which I perceive you are afflicted. The vaults are insufferably damp. They are encrusted with niter°."

"Let us go, nevertheless. The cold is merely nothing. Amontillado! You have been imposed upon. And as for Luchesi, he cannot distinguish Sherry from Amontillado."

Thus speaking, Fortunato possessed himself of my arm. Putting on a mask of black silk, and drawing a *roquelaire*° closely about my person, I suffered him to hurry me to my palazzo.

There were no attendants at home; they had absconded to make merry in honor of the time. I had told them that I should not return until the morning, and had given them explicit orders not to stir from the house. These orders were sufficient, I well knew, to insure their immediate disappearance, one and all, as soon as my back was turned.

I took from their sconces two flambeaux, and giving one to Fortunato,   25
bowed him through several suites of rooms to the archway that led into the vaults. I passed down a long and winding staircase, requesting him to be cautious as he followed. We came at length to the foot of the descent, and stood together on the damp ground of the catacombs of the Montresors.

The gait of my friend was unsteady, and the bells upon his cap jingled as he strode.

"The pipe?" said he.

"It is farther on," said I; "but observe the white web-work which gleams from these cavern walls."

He turned toward me, and looked into my eyes with two filmy orbs that distilled the rheum of intoxication.

"Nitre?" he asked, at length.   30

"Nitre," I replied. "How long have you had that cough?"

"Ugh! ugh! ugh!—ugh! ugh! ugh!—ugh! ugh! ugh!—ugh! ugh! ugh!— ugh! ugh! ugh!"

My poor friend found it impossible to reply for many minutes.

"It is nothing," he said, at last.

"Come," I said, with decision, "we will go back; your health is precious.   35
You are rich, respected, admired, beloved; you are happy, as once I was. You are a man to be missed. For me it is no matter. We will go back; you will be ill, and I cannot be responsible. Besides, there is Luchesi——"

"Enough," he said; "the cough is a mere nothing; it will not kill me. I shall not die of a cough."

"True—true," I replied; "and, indeed, I had no intention of alarming you

niter: Potassium nitrate.   ***roqueclaire*:** A short cloak.

unnecessarily; but you should use all proper caution. A draught of this Medoc will defend us from the damps."

Here I knocked off the neck of a bottle which I drew from a long row of its fellows that lay upon the mold.

"Drink," I said, presenting him the wine.

He raised it to his lips with a leer. He paused and nodded to me familiarly, while his bells jingled.   40

"I drink," he said, "to the buried that repose around us."

"And I to your long life."

He again took my arm, and we proceeded.

"These vaults," he said, "are extensive."

"The Montresors," I replied, "were a great and numerous family."   45

"I forget your arms."

"A huge human foot d'or,° in a field azure; the foot crushes a serpent rampant whose fangs are imbedded in the heel."

"And the motto?"

"*Nemo me impune lacessit.*"°

"Good!" he said.   50

The wine sparkled in his eyes and the bells jingled. My own fancy grew warm with the Medoc. We had passed through walls of piled bones, with casks and puncheons intermingling into the inmost recesses of the catacombs. I paused again, and this time I made bold to seize Fortunato by an arm above the elbow.

"The nitre!" I said; "see, it increases. It hangs like moss upon the vaults. We are below the river's bed. The drops of moisture trickle among the bones. Come, we will go back ere it is too late. Your cough——"

"It is nothing," he said; "let us go on. But first, another draught of the Medoc."

I broke and reached him a flagon of De Grâve. He emptied it at a breath. His eyes flashed with a fierce light. He laughed and threw the bottle upward with a gesticulation I did not understand.

I looked at him in surprise. He repeated the movement—a grotesque one.   55

"You do not comprehend?" he said.

"Not I," I replied.

"Then you are not of the brotherhood."

"How?"

"You are not of the masons."   60

"Yes, yes," I said; "yes, yes."

"You? Impossible! A mason?"

"A mason," I replied.

"A sign," he said.

"It is this," I answered, producing a trowel from beneath the folds of my   65
roquelaire.

---

d'or: Of gold. **Nemo me impune lacessit:** "No one wounds me with impunity" is the motto on the royal arms of Scotland (Latin).

"You jest," he exclaimed, recoiling a few paces. "But let us proceed to the Amontillado."

"Be it so," I said, replacing the tool beneath the cloak, and again offering him my arm. He leaned upon it heavily. We continued our route in search of the Amontillado. We passed through a range of low arches, descended, passed on, and descending again, arrived at a deep crypt, in which the foulness of the air caused our flambeaux rather to glow than flame.

At the most remote end of the crypt there appeared another less spacious. Its walls had been lined with human remains, piled to the vault overhead, in the fashion of the great catacombs of Paris. Three sides of this interior crypt were still ornamented in this manner. From the fourth the bones had been thrown down, and lay promiscuously upon the earth, forming at one point a mound of some size. Within the wall thus exposed by the displacing of the bones, we perceived a still interior recess, in depth about four feet, in width three, in height six or seven. It seemed to have been constructed for no especial use within itself, but formed merely the interval between two of the colossal supports of the roof of the catacombs, and was backed by one of their circumscribing walls of solid granite.

It was in vain that Fortunato, uplifting his dull torch, endeavored to pry into the depth of the recess. Its termination the feeble light did not enable us to see.

"Proceed," I said; "herein is the Amontillado. As for Luchesi——"   70

"He is an ignoramus," interrupted my friend, as he stepped unsteadily forward, while I followed immediately at his heels. In an instant he had reached the extremity of the niche, and finding his progress arrested by the rock, stood stupidly bewildered. A moment more and I had fettered him to the granite. In its surface were two iron staples, distant from each other about two feet, horizontally. From one of these depended a short chain, from the other a padlock. Throwing the links about his waist, it was but the work of a few seconds to secure it. He was too much astounded to resist. Withdrawing the key I stepped back from the recess.

"Pass your hand," I said, "over the wall; you cannot help feeling the nitre. Indeed it is *very* damp. Once more let me *implore* you to return. No? Then I must positively leave you. But I must first render you all the little attentions in my power."

"The Amontillado!" ejaculated my friend, not yet recovered from his astonishment.

"True," I replied; "the Amontillado."

As I said these words I busied myself among the pile of bones of which   75
I have before spoken. Throwing them aside, I soon uncovered a quantity of building stone and mortar. With these materials and with the aid of my trowel, I began vigorously to wall up the entrance of the niche.

I had scarcely laid the first tier of the masonry when I discovered that the intoxication of Fortunato had in a great measure worn off. The earliest indication I had of this was a low moaning cry from the depth of the recess. It was *not* the cry of a drunken man. There was then a long and obstinate silence. I laid the second tier, and the third, and the fourth; and then I heard the furious vibrations of the chain. The noise lasted for several minutes, during which, that I might hearken to it with the more satisfaction, I ceased my labors and sat down upon the bones. When at last the clanking subsided, I resumed the trowel, and finished without interruption the fifth, the sixth, and the seventh tier. The wall was now nearly upon a level with my breast. I again paused, and holding the flambeaux over the masonwork, threw a few feeble rays upon the figure within.

A succession of loud and shrill screams, bursting suddenly from the throat of the chained form, seemed to thrust me violently back. For a brief moment I hesitated—I trembled. Unsheathing my rapier, I began to grope with it about the recess; but the thought of an instant reassured me. I placed my hand upon the solid fabric of the catacombs, and felt satisfied. I reapproached the wall. I replied to the yells of him who clamored. I reechoed—I aided—I surpassed them in volume and in strength. I did this, and the clamorer grew still.

It was now midnight, and my task was drawing to a close. I had completed the eighth, the ninth, and the tenth tier. I had finished a portion of the last and the eleventh; there remained but a single stone to be fitted and plastered in. I struggled with its weight; I placed it partially in its destined position. But now there came from out the niche a low laugh that erected the hairs upon my head. It was succeeded by a sad voice, which I had difficulty in recognizing as that of the noble Fortunato. The voice said—

"Ha! ha! ha!—he! he!—a very good joke indeed—an excellent jest. We will have many a rich laugh about it at the palazzo—he! he! he!—over our wine—he! he! he!"

"The Amontillado!" I said.   80

"He! he! he!—he! he! he!—yes, the Amontillado. But is it not getting late? Will not they be awaiting us at the palazzo, the Lady Fortunato and the rest? Let us be gone."

"Yes," I said, "let us be gone."

"*For the love of God, Montresor!*"

"Yes," I said, "for the love of God!"

But to these words I hearkened in vain for a reply. I grew impatient. I called   85
aloud:

"Fortunato!"

No answer. I called again:

"Fortunato!"

No answer still, I thrust a torch through the remaining aperture and let it fall within. There came forth in return only a jingling of the bells. My heart grew sick—on account of the dampness of the catacombs. I hastened to make an end of my labor. I forced the last stone into its position; I plastered it up. Against the new masonry I re-erected the old rampart of bones. For the half of a century no mortal has disturbed them. *In pace requiescat!*°   [1846]

In pace requiescat: In peace may he rest (Latin).

≣ THINKING ABOUT THE TEXT

1. Evidently Montresor is recounting the story of his revenge fifty years after it took place. To whom might he be speaking? With what purposes?

2. Montresor does not describe in detail any of the offenses that Fortunato has supposedly committed against him. In considering how to judge Montresor, do you need such information? Why, or why not? State in your own words the principles of revenge he lays out in the first paragraph.

3. What, if anything, does Poe achieve by having this story take place during a carnival? By repeating the word *amontillado* so much?

4. What does Montresor mean when he echoes Fortunato's words "for the love of God" (para. 84)? What might Fortunato be attempting to communicate with his final "jingling of the bells" (para. 89)?

5. Do you sympathize with Montresor? With Fortunato? Explain. What emotion did you mainly feel as you read the story? Identify specific features of it that led to this emotion.

ANDRE DUBUS
Killings

Andre Dubus (1936–1999) served five years in the Marine Corps, attaining the rank of captain before becoming a full-time writer of short stories. Dubus lived in Haverhill, Massachusetts, and much of his fiction is set in the Merrimack Valley north of Boston. This is true of the following story, which appeared in his collection Finding a Girl in America *(1980) and was reprinted in his* Selected Stories *(1988). In 1991, Dubus also published a collection of essays,* Broken Vessels. *In part, the book deals with a 1986 accident that changed his life. Getting out of his car to aid stranded motorists, he was struck by another car; he eventually lost most of one leg and power over the other. Though confined to a wheelchair, Dubus continued to work actively. In 1996, he published his last collection of stories,* Dancing After Hours, *and in 1998, another volume of essays entitled* Meditations from a Moveable Chair. *Two years after he died came a much-acclaimed film adaptation of "Killings," entitled* In the Bedroom *(2001).*

On the August morning when Matt Fowler buried his youngest son, Frank, who had lived for twenty-one years, eight months, and four days, Matt's older son, Steve, turned to him as the family left the grave and walked between their friends, and said: "I should kill him." He was twenty-eight, his brown hair starting to thin in front where he used to have a cowlick. He bit his lower lip, wiped his eyes, then said it again. Ruth's arm, linked with Matt's, tightened; he looked at her. Beneath her eyes there was swelling from the three days she had suffered. At the limousine Matt stopped and looked back at the grave, the casket, and the Congregationalist minister who he thought had probably had a difficult job with the eulogy though he hadn't seemed to, and the old funeral director who was saying something to the six young pallbearers. The grave was on a hill and overlooked the Merrimack, which he could not see from where he stood; he looked at the opposite bank, at the apple orchard with its symmetrically planted trees going up a hill.

Next day Steve drove with his wife back to Baltimore where he managed the branch office of a bank, and Cathleen, the middle child, drove with her husband back to Syracuse. They had left the grandchildren with friends. A month after the funeral Matt played poker at Willis Trottier's because Ruth, who knew this was the second time he had been invited, told him to go, he couldn't sit home with her for the rest of her life, she was all right. After the game Willis went outside to tell everyone good night and, when the others had driven away, he walked with Matt to his car. Willis was a short, silver-haired man who had opened a diner after World War II, his trade then mostly very early breakfast, which he cooked, and then lunch for the men who worked at the leather and shoe factories. He now owned a large restaurant.

"He walks the Goddamn streets," Matt said.

"I know. He was in my place last night, at the bar. With a girl."

"I don't see him. I'm in the store all the time. Ruth sees him. She sees him too much. She was at Sunnyhurst today getting cigarettes and aspirin, and there he was. She can't even go out for cigarettes and aspirin. It's killing her."   5

"Come back in for a drink."

Matt looked at his watch. Ruth would be asleep. He walked with Willis back into the house, pausing at the steps to look at the starlit sky. It was a cool summer night; he thought vaguely of the Red Sox, did not even know if they were at home tonight; since it happened he had not been able to think about any of the small pleasures he believed he had earned, as he had earned also what was shattered now forever: the quietly harried and quietly pleasurable days of fatherhood. They went inside. Willis's wife, Martha, had gone to bed hours ago, in the rear of the large house which was rigged with burglar and fire alarms. They went downstairs to the game room: the television set suspended from the ceiling, the pool table, the poker table with beer cans, cards, chips, filled ashtrays, and the six chairs where Matt and his friends had sat, the friends picking up the old banter as though he had only been away on vacation; but he could see the affection and courtesy in their eyes. Willis went behind the bar and mixed them each a Scotch and soda; he stayed behind the bar and looked at Matt sitting on the stool.

"How often have you thought about it?" Willis said.

"Every day since he got out. I didn't think about bail. I thought I wouldn't have to worry about him for years. She sees him all the time. It makes her cry."

"He was in my place a long time last night. He'll be back."   10

"Maybe he won't."

"The band. He likes the band."

"What's he doing now?"

"He's tending bar up to Hampton Beach. For a friend. Ever notice even the

worst bastard always has friends? He couldn't get work in town. It's just tourists and kids up to Hampton. Nobody knows him. If they do, they don't care.
They drink what he mixes."

"Nobody tells me about him."   15

"I hate him, Matt. My boys went to school with him. He was the same then.
Know what he'll do? Five at the most. Remember that woman about seven
years ago? Shot her husband and dropped him off the bridge in the Merrimack
with a hundred-pound sack of cement and said all the way through it that
nobody helped her. Know where she is now? She's in Lawrence now, a secretary. And whoever helped her, where the hell is he?"

"I've got a .38 I've had for years, I take it to the store now. I tell Ruth it's for
the night deposits. I tell her things have changed: we got junkies here now too.
Lots of people without jobs. She knows though."

"What does she know?"

"She knows I started carrying it after the first time she saw him in town.
She knows it's in case I see him, and there's some kind of a situation —"

He stopped, looked at Willis, and finished his drink. Willis mixed him   20
another.

"What kind of situation?"

"Where he did something to me. Where I could get away with it."

"How does Ruth feel about that?"

"She doesn't know."

"You said she does, she's got it figured out."   25

He thought of her that afternoon: when she went into Sunnyhurst, Strout
was waiting at the counter while the clerk bagged the things he had bought;
she turned down an aisle and looked at soup cans until he left.

"Ruth would shoot him herself, if she thought she could hit him."

"You got a permit?"

"No."

"I do. You could get a year for that."   30

"Maybe I'll get one. Or maybe I won't. Maybe I'll just stop bringing it to the
store."

Richard Strout was twenty-six years old, a high school athlete, football scholarship to the University of Massachusetts where he lasted for almost two semesters before quitting in advance of the final grades that would have forced
him not to return. People then said: Dickie can do the work; he just doesn't
want to. He came home and did construction work for his father but refused his
father's offer to learn the business; his two older brothers had learned it, so that
Strout and Sons trucks going about town, and signs on construction sites, now
slashed wounds into Matt Fowler's life. Then Richard married a young girl and
became a bartender, his salary and tips augmented and perhaps sometimes
matched by his father, who also posted his bond. So his friends, his enemies (he
had those: fist fights or, more often, boys and then young men who had not
fought him when they thought they should have), and those who simply knew
him by face and name, had a series of images of him which they recalled when

they heard of the killing: the high school running back, the young drunk in bars, the oblivious hard-hatted young man eating lunch at a counter, the bartender who could perhaps be called courteous but not more than that: as he tended bar, his dark eyes and dark, wide-jawed face appeared less sullen, near blank.

One night he beat Frank. Frank was living at home and waiting for September, for graduate school in economics, and working as a lifeguard at Salisbury Beach, where he met Mary Ann Strout, in her first month of separation. She spent most days at the beach with her two sons. Before ten o'clock one night Frank came home; he had driven to the hospital first, and he walked into the living room with stitches over his right eye and both lips bright and swollen.

"I'm all right," he said, when Matt and Ruth stood up, and Matt turned off the television, letting Ruth get to him first: the tall, muscled but slender suntanned boy. Frank tried to smile at them but couldn't because of his lips.

"It was her husband, wasn't it?" Ruth said.   35

"Ex," Frank said. "He dropped in."

Matt gently held Frank's jaw and turned his face to the light, looked at the stitches, the blood under the white of the eye, the bruised flesh.

"Press charges," Matt said.

"No."

"What's to stop him from doing it again? Did you hit him at all? Enough so   40
he won't want to next time?"

"I don't think I touched him."

"So what are you going to do?"

"Take karate," Frank said, and tried again to smile.

"That's not the problem," Ruth said.

"You know you like her," Frank said.   45

"I like a lot of people. What about the boys? Did they see it?"

"They were asleep."

"Did you leave her alone with him?"

"He left first. She was yelling at him. I believe she had a skillet in her hand."

"Oh for God's sake," Ruth said.   50

Matt had been dealing with that too: at the dinner table on evenings when Frank wasn't home, was eating with Mary Ann; or, on the other nights — and Frank was with her every night — he talked with Ruth while they watched television, or lay in bed with the windows open and he smelled the night air and imagined, with both pride and muted sorrow, Frank in Mary Ann's arms. Ruth didn't like it because Mary Ann was in the process of divorce, because she had two children, because she was four years older than Frank, and finally — she told this in bed, where she had during all of their marriage told him of her deepest feelings: of love, of passion, of fears about one of the children, of pain Matt had caused her or she had caused him — she was against it because of what she had heard: that the marriage had gone bad early, and for most of it Richard and Mary Ann had both played around.

"That can't be true," Matt said. "Strout wouldn't have stood for it."

"Maybe he loves her."

"He's too hot-tempered. He couldn't have taken that."

But Matt knew Strout had taken it, for he had heard the stories too. He   55
wondered who had told them to Ruth; and he felt vaguely annoyed and isolated:
living with her for thirty-one years and still not knowing what she talked about
with her friends. On these summer nights he did not so much argue with her as
try to comfort her, but finally there was no difference between the two: she had
concrete objections, which he tried to overcome. And in his attempt to do this,
he neglected his own objections, which were the same as hers, so that as he
spoke to her he felt as disembodied as he sometimes did in the store when he
helped a man choose a blouse or dress or piece of costume jewelry for his wife.

"The divorce doesn't mean anything," he said. "She was young and maybe
she liked his looks and then after a while she realized she was living with a
bastard. I see it as a positive thing."

"She's not divorced yet."

"It's the same thing. Massachusetts has crazy laws, that's all. Her age is no
problem. What's it matter when she was born? And that other business: even if
it's true, which it probably isn't, it's got nothing to do with Frank, and it's in the
past. And the kids are no problem. She's been married six years; she ought to
have kids. Frank likes them. He plays with them. And he's not going to marry
her anyway, so it's not a problem of money."

"Then what's he doing with her?"

"She probably loves him, Ruth. Girls always have. Why can't we just leave   60
it at that?"

"He got home at six o'clock Tuesday morning."

"I didn't know you knew. I've already talked to him about it."

Which he had: since he believed almost nothing he told Ruth, he went to
Frank with what he believed. The night before, he had followed Frank to the car
after dinner.

"You wouldn't make much of a burglar," he said.

"How's that?"   65

Matt was looking up at him; Frank was six feet tall, an inch and a half
taller than Matt, who had been proud when Frank at seventeen outgrew him;
he had only felt uncomfortable when he had to reprimand or caution him. He
touched Frank's bicep, thought of the young taut passionate body, believed he
could sense the desire, and again he felt the pride and sorrow and envy too, not
knowing whether he was envious of Frank or Mary Ann.

"When you came in yesterday morning, I woke up. One of these mornings
your mother will. And I'm the one who'll have to talk to her. She won't interfere with you. Okay? I know it means—" But he stopped, thinking: I know it
means getting up and leaving that suntanned girl and going sleepy to the car,
I know—

"Okay," Frank said, and touched Matt's shoulder and got into the car.

There had been other talks, but the only long one was their first one: a
night driving to Fenway Park, Matt having ordered the tickets so they could
talk, and knowing when Frank said yes, he would go, that he knew the talk was
coming too. It took them forty minutes to get to Boston, and they talked about

Mary Ann until they joined the city traffic along the Charles River, blue in the late sun. Frank told him all the things that Matt would later pretend to believe when he told them to Ruth.

"It seems like a lot for a young guy to take on," Matt finally said.   70

"Sometimes it is. But she's worth it."

"Are you thinking about getting married?"

"We haven't talked about it. She can't for over a year. I've got school."

"I *do* like her," Matt said.

He did. Some evenings, when the long summer sun was still low in the sky,   75
Frank brought her home; they came into the house smelling of suntan lotion and the sea, and Matt gave them gin and tonics and started the charcoal in the backyard, and looked at Mary Ann in the lawn chair: long and very light brown hair (Matt thinking that twenty years ago she would have dyed it blonde), and the long brown legs he loved to look at; her face was pretty; she had probably never in her adult life gone unnoticed into a public place. It was in her wide brown eyes that she looked older than Frank; after a few drinks Matt thought what he saw in her eyes was something erotic, testament to the rumors about her; but he knew it wasn't that, or all that: she had, very young, been through a sort of pain that his children, and he and Ruth, had been spared. In the moments of his recognizing that pain, he wanted to tenderly touch her hair, wanted with some gesture to give her solace and hope. And he would glance at Frank, and hope they would love each other, hope Frank would soothe that pain in her heart, take it from her eyes; and her divorce, her age, and her children did not matter at all. On the first two evenings she did not bring her boys, and then Ruth asked her to bring them the next time. In bed that night Ruth said, "She hasn't brought them because she's embarrassed. She shouldn't feel embarrassed."

Richard Strout shot Frank in front of the boys. They were sitting on the living room floor watching television, Frank sitting on the couch, and Mary Ann just returning from the kitchen with a tray of sandwiches. Strout came in the front door and shot Frank twice in the chest and once in the face with a 9 mm automatic. Then he looked at the boys and Mary Ann, and went home to wait for the police.

It seemed to Matt that from the time Mary Ann called weeping to tell him until now, a Saturday night in September, sitting in the car with Willis, parked beside Strout's car, waiting for the bar to close, that he had not so much moved through his life as wandered through it, his spirits like a dazed body bumping into furniture and corners. He had always been a fearful father: when his children were young, at the start of each summer he thought of them drowning in a pond or the sea, and he was relieved when he came home in the evenings and they were there; usually that relief was his only acknowledgment of his fear, which he never spoke of, and which he controlled within his heart. As he had when they were very young and all of them in turn, Cathleen too, were drawn to the high oak in the backyard, and had to climb it. Smiling, he watched them, imagining the fall: and he was poised to catch the small body before it hit the earth. Or his legs were poised; his hands were in his pockets or his arms were folded and, for the child looking down, he appeared relaxed and confident while his heart beat with the two words he wanted to call out but did not: *Don't fall.* In winter he was less afraid: he made sure the ice would hold him before they skated, and he brought or sent them to places where they could sled without ending in the street. So he and his children had survived their childhood, and he only worried about them when he knew they were driving a long distance, and then he lost Frank in a way no father expected to lose his son, and he felt that all the fears he had borne while they were growing up, and all the grief he had been afraid of, had backed up like a huge wave and struck him on the beach and swept him out to sea. Each day he felt the same and when he was able to forget how he felt, when he was able to force himself not to feel that way, the eyes of his clerks and customers defeated him. He wished those eyes were oblivious, even cold; he felt he was withering in their tenderness. And beneath his listless wandering, every day in his soul he shot Richard Strout in the face; while Ruth, going about town on errands, kept seeing him. And at night in bed she would hold Matt and cry, or sometimes she was silent and Matt would touch her tightening arm, her clenched fist.

As his own right fist was now, squeezing the butt of the revolver, the last of the drinkers having left the bar, talking to each other, going to their separate cars which were in the lot in front of the bar, out of Matt's vision. He heard their voices, their cars, and then the ocean again, across the street. The tide was in and sometimes it smacked the sea wall. Through the windshield he looked at the dark red side wall of the bar, and then to his left, past Willis, at Strout's car, and through its windows he could see the now-emptied parking lot, the road, the sea wall. He could smell the sea.

The front door of the bar opened and closed again and Willis looked at Matt then at the corner of the building; when Strout came around it alone Matt got out of the car, giving up the hope he had kept all night (and for the past week) that Strout would come out with friends, and Willis would simply drive away; thinking: *All right then. All right*; and he went around the front of Willis's car, and at Strout's he stopped and aimed over the hood at Strout's blue shirt ten feet away. Willis was aiming too, crouched on Matt's left, his elbow resting on the hood.

"Mr. Fowler," Strout said. He looked at each of them, and at the guns. "Mr. Trottier."   80

Then Matt, watching the parking lot and the road, walked quickly between the car and the building and stood behind Strout. He took one leather glove from his pocket and put it on his left hand.

"Don't talk. Unlock the front and back and get in."

Strout unlocked the front door, reached in and unlocked the back, then got in, and Matt slid into the back seat, closed the door with his gloved hand, and touched Strout's head once with the muzzle.

"It's cocked. Drive to your house."

When Strout looked over his shoulder to back the car, Matt aimed at his   85
temple and did not look at his eyes.

"Drive slowly," he said. "Don't try to get stopped."

They drove across the empty front lot and onto the road, Willis's headlights shining into the car; then back through town, the sea wall on the left hiding the beach, though far out Matt could see the ocean; he uncocked the revolver; on the right were the places, most with their neon signs off, that did so much business in summer: the lounges and cafés and pizza houses, the street itself empty of traffic, the way he and Willis had known it would be when they decided to take Strout at the bar rather than knock on his door at two o'clock one morning and risk that one insomniac neighbor. Matt had not told Willis he was afraid he could not be alone with Strout for very long, smell his smells, feel the presence of his flesh, hear his voice, and then shoot him. They left the beach town and then were on the high bridge over the channel: to the left the smacking curling white at the breakwater and beyond that the dark sea and the full moon, and down to his right the small fishing boats bobbing at anchor in the cove. When they left the bridge, the sea was blocked by abandoned beach cottages, and Matt's left hand was sweating in the glove. Out here in the dark in the car he believed Ruth knew. Willis had come to his house at eleven and asked if he wanted a nightcap; Matt went to the bedroom for his wallet, put the gloves in one trouser pocket and the .38 in the other and went back to the living room, his hand in his pocket covering the bulge of the cool cylinder pressed against his fingers, the butt against his palm. When Ruth said good night she looked at his face, and he felt she could see in his eyes the gun, and the night he was going to. But he knew he couldn't trust what he saw. Willis's wife had taken her sleeping pill, which gave her eight hours—the reason, Willis had told Matt, he had the alarms installed, for nights when he was late at the restaurant—and when it was all done and Willis got home he would leave ice and a trace of Scotch and soda in two glasses in the game room and tell Martha in the morning that he had left the restaurant early and brought Matt home for a drink.

"He was making it with my wife." Strout's voice was careful, not pleading.

Matt pressed the muzzle against Strout's head, pressed it harder than he wanted to, feeling through the gun Strout's head flinching and moving forward; then he lowered the gun to his lap.

"Don't talk," he said.   90

Strout did not speak again. They turned west, drove past the Dairy Queen closed until spring, and the two lobster restaurants that faced each other and were crowded all summer and were now also closed, onto the short bridge crossing the tidal stream, and over the engine Matt could hear through his open window the water rushing inland under the bridge; looking to his left he saw its swift moonlit current going back into the marsh which, leaving the bridge, they entered: the salt marsh stretching out on both sides, the grass tall in patches but mostly low and leaning earthward as though windblown, a large dark rock sitting as though it rested on nothing but itself, and shallow pools reflecting the bright moon.

Beyond the marsh they drove through woods, Matt thinking now of the hole he and Willis had dug last Sunday afternoon after telling their wives they were going to Fenway Park. They listened to the game on a transistor radio, but heard none of it as they dug into the soft earth on the knoll they had chosen because elms and maples sheltered it. Already some leaves had fallen. When the hole was deep enough they covered it and the piled earth with dead branches, then cleaned their shoes and pants and went to a restaurant farther up in New Hampshire where they ate sandwiches and drank beer and watched the rest of the game on television. Looking at the back of Strout's head he thought of Frank's grave; he had not been back to it; but he would go before winter, and its second burial of snow.

He thought of Frank sitting on the couch and perhaps talking to the children as they watched television, imagined him feeling young and strong, still warmed from the sun at the beach, and feeling loved, hearing Mary Ann moving about in the kitchen, hearing her walking into the living room; maybe he looked up at her and maybe she said something, looking at him over the tray of sandwiches, smiling at him, saying something the way women do when they offer food as a gift, then the front door opening and this son of a bitch coming in and Frank seeing that he meant the gun in his hand, this son of a bitch and his gun the last person and thing Frank saw on earth.

When they drove into town the streets were nearly empty: a few slow cars, a policeman walking his beat past the darkened fronts of stores. Strout and Matt both glanced at him as they drove by. They were on the main street, and all the stoplights were blinking yellow. Willis and Matt had talked about that too: the lights changed at midnight, so there would be no place Strout had to stop and where he might try to run. Strout turned down the block where he lived and Willis's headlights were no longer with Matt in the back seat. They had planned that too, had decided it was best for just the one car to go to the house, and again Matt had said nothing about his fear of being alone with Strout, especially in his house: a duplex, dark as all the houses on the street were, the street itself lit at the corner of each block. As Strout turned into the driveway Matt thought of the one insomniac neighbor, thought of some man or woman sitting alone in the dark living room, watching the all-night channel from Boston. When Strout stopped the car near the front of the house, Matt said: "Drive it to the back."

He touched Strout's head with the muzzle.   95

"You wouldn't have it cocked, would you? For when I put on the brakes."

Matt cocked it, and said: "It is now."

Strout waited a moment; then he eased the car forward, the engine doing little more than idling, and as they approached the garage he gently braked. Matt opened the door, then took off the glove and put it in his pocket. He stepped out and shut the door with his hip and said: "All right."

Strout looked at the gun, then got out, and Matt followed him across the grass, and as Strout unlocked the door Matt looked quickly at the row of small backyards on either side, and scattered tall trees, some evergreens, others not, and he thought of the red and yellow leaves on the trees over the hole, saw them falling soon, probably in two weeks, dropping slowly, covering. Strout stepped into the kitchen.

"Turn on the light."   100

Strout reached to the wall switch, and in the light Matt looked at his wide back, the dark blue shirt, the white belt, the red plaid pants.

"Where's your suitcase?"

"My suitcase?"

"Where is it?"

"In the bedroom closet."   105

"That's where we're going then. When we get to a door you stop and turn on the light."

They crossed the kitchen, Matt glancing at the sink and stove and refrigerator: no dishes in the sink or even the dish rack beside it, no grease splashings on the stove, the refrigerator door clean and white. He did not want to look at any more but he looked quickly at all he could see: in the living room magazines and newspapers in a wicker basket, clean ashtrays, a record player, the records shelved next to it, then down the hall where, near the bedroom door, hung a color photograph of Mary Ann and the two boys sitting on a lawn—there was no house in the picture—Mary Ann smiling at the camera or Strout or whoever held the camera, smiling as she had on Matt's lawn this summer while he waited for the charcoal and they all talked and he looked at her brown legs and at Frank touching her arm, her shoulder, her hair; he moved down the hall with her smile in his mind, wondering: was that when they were both playing around and she was smiling like that at him and they were happy, even sometimes, making it worth it? He recalled her eyes, the pain in them, and he was conscious of the circles of love he was touching with the hand that held the revolver so tightly now as Strout stopped at the door at the end of the hall.

"There's no wall switch."

"Where's the light?"

"By the bed."   110

"Let's go."

Matt stayed a pace behind, then Strout leaned over and the room was lighted: the bed, a double one, was neatly made; the ashtray on the bedside table clean, the bureau top dustless, and no photographs; probably so the girl—who *was* she?—would not have to see Mary Ann in the bedroom she believed was theirs. But because Matt was a father and a husband, though never an ex-husband, he knew (and did not want to know) that this bedroom had never been theirs alone. Strout turned around; Matt looked at his lips, his wide jaw, and thought of Frank's doomed and fearful eyes looking up from the couch.

"Where's Mr. Trottier?"

"He's waiting. Pack clothes for warm weather."

"What's going on?"   115

"You're jumping bail."

"Mr. Fowler—"

He pointed the cocked revolver at Strout's face. The barrel trembled but not much, not as much as he had expected. Strout went to the closet and got the suitcase from the floor and opened it on the bed. As he went to the bureau, he said: "He was making it with my wife. I'd go pick up my kids and he'd be there. Sometimes he spent the night. My boys told me."

He did not look at Matt as he spoke. He opened the top drawer and Matt stepped closer so he could see Strout's hands: underwear and socks, the socks rolled, the underwear folded and stacked. He took them back to the bed, arranged them neatly in the suitcase, then from the closet he was taking shirts and trousers and a jacket; he laid them on the bed and Matt followed him to the bathroom and watched from the door while he packed those things a person accumulated and that became part of him so that at times in the store Matt felt he was selling more than clothes.

"I wanted to try to get together with her again." He was bent over the suitcase. "I couldn't even talk to her. He was always with her. I'm going to jail for it; if I ever get out I'll be an old man. Isn't that enough?" 120

"You're not going to jail."

Strout closed the suitcase and faced Matt, looking at the gun. Matt went to his rear, so Strout was between him and the lighted hall; then using his handkerchief he turned off the lamp and said: "Let's go."

They went down the hall, Matt looking again at the photograph, and through the living room and kitchen, Matt turning off the lights and talking, frightened that he was talking, that he was telling this lie he had not planned: "It's the trial. We can't go through that, my wife and me. So you're leaving. We've got you a ticket, and a job. A friend of Mr. Trottier's. Out west. My wife keeps seeing you. We can't have that anymore."

Matt turned out the kitchen light and put the handkerchief in his pocket, and they went down the two brick steps and across the lawn. Strout put the suitcase on the floor of the back seat, then got into the front seat and Matt got in the back and put on his glove and shut the door.

"They'll catch me. They'll check passenger lists." 125

"We didn't use your name."

"They'll figure that out too. You think I wouldn't have done it myself if it was that easy?"

He backed into the street, Matt looking down the gun barrel but not at the profiled face beyond it.

"You were alone," Matt said. "We've got it worked out."

"There's no planes this time of night, Mr. Fowler." 130

"Go back through town. Then north on 125."

They came to the corner and turned, and now Willis's headlights were in the car with Matt.

"Why north, Mr. Fowler?"

"Somebody's going to keep you for a while. They'll take you to the airport." He uncocked the hammer and lowered the revolver to his lap and said wearily: "No more talking."

As they drove back through town, Matt's body sagged, going limp with his 135 spirit and its new and false bond with Strout, the hope his lie had given Strout. He had grown up in this town whose streets had become places of apprehension and pain for Ruth as she drove and walked, doing what she had to do; and for him too, if only in his mind as he worked and chatted six days a week in his store; he wondered now if his lie would have worked, if sending Strout away would have been enough; but then he knew that just thinking of Strout in Montana or whatever place lay at the end of the lie he had told, thinking of him walking the streets there, loving a girl there (who *was* she?) would be enough to slowly rot the rest of his days. And Ruth's. Again he was certain that she knew, that she was waiting for him.

They were in New Hampshire now, on the narrow highway, passing the shopping center at the state line, and then houses and small stores and sandwich shops. There were few cars on the road. After ten minutes he raised his trembling hand, touched Strout's neck with the gun, and said: "Turn in up here. At the dirt road."

Strout flicked on the indicator and slowed.

"Mr. Fowler?"

"They're waiting here."

Strout turned very slowly, easing his neck away from the gun. In the   140
moonlight the road was light brown, lighter and yellowed where the headlights shone; weeds and a few trees grew on either side of it, and ahead of them were the woods.

"There's nothing back here, Mr. Fowler."

"It's for your car. You don't think we'd leave it at the airport, do you?"

He watched Strout's large, big-knuckled hands tighten on the wheel, saw Frank's face that night: not the stitches and bruised eye and swollen lips, but his own hand gently touching Frank's jaw, turning his wounds to the light. They rounded a bend in the road and were out of sight of the highway: tall trees all around them now, hiding the moon. When they reached the abandoned gravel pit on the left, the bare flat earth and steep pale embankment behind it, and the black crowns of trees at its top, Matt said: "Stop here."

Strout stopped but did not turn off the engine. Matt pressed the gun hard against his neck, and he straightened in the seat and looked in the rearview mirror, Matt's eyes meeting his in the glass for an instant before looking at the hair at the end of the gun barrel.

"Turn it off."   145

Strout did, then held the wheel with two hands, and looked in the mirror.

"I'll do twenty years, Mr. Fowler; at least. I'll be forty-six years old."

"That's nine years younger than I am," Matt said, and got out and took off the glove and kicked the door shut. He aimed at Strout's ear and pulled back the hammer. Willis's headlights were off and Matt heard him walking on the soft thin layer of dust, the hard earth beneath it. Strout opened the door, sat for a moment in the interior light, then stepped out onto the road. Now his face was pleading. Matt did not look at his eyes, but he could see it in the lips.

"Just get the suitcase. They're right up the road."

Willis was beside him now, to his left. Strout looked at both guns. Then he   150
opened the back door, leaned in, and with a jerk brought the suitcase out. He was turning to face them when Matt said: "Just walk up the road. Just ahead."

Strout turned to walk, the suitcase in his right hand, and Matt and Willis followed; as Strout cleared the front of his car he dropped the suitcase and, ducking, took one step that was the beginning of a sprint to his right. The gun kicked in Matt's hand, and the explosion of the shot surrounded him, isolated him in a nimbus of sound that cut him off from all his time, all his history, isolated him standing absolutely still on the dirt road with the gun in his hand, looking down at Richard Strout squirming on his belly, kicking one leg behind him, pushing himself forward, toward the woods. Then Matt went to him and shot him once in the back of the head.

Driving south to Boston, wearing both gloves now, staying in the middle lane and looking often in the rearview mirror at Willis's headlights, he relived the suitcase dropping, the quick dip and turn of Strout's back, and the kick of the gun, the sound of the shot. When he walked to Strout, he still existed within the first shot, still trembled and breathed with it. The second shot and the burial seemed to be happening to someone else, someone he was watching. He and Willis each held an arm and pulled Strout face-down off the road and into the woods, his bouncing sliding belt white under the trees where it was so dark that when they stopped at the top of the knoll, panting and sweating, Matt could not see where Strout's blue shirt ended and the earth began. They pulled off the branches then dragged Strout to the edge of the hole and went behind him and lifted his legs and pushed him in. They stood still for a moment. The woods were quiet save for their breathing, and Matt remembered hearing the movements of birds and small animals after the first shot. Or maybe he had not heard them. Willis went down to the road. Matt could see him clearly out on the tan dirt, could see the glint of Strout's car and, beyond the road, the gravel pit. Willis came back up the knoll with the suitcase. He dropped it in the hole and took off his gloves and they went down to his car for the spades. They worked quietly. Sometimes they paused to listen to the woods. When they were finished Willis turned on his flashlight and they covered the earth with leaves and branches and then went down to the spot in front of the car, and while Matt held the light Willis crouched and sprinkled dust on the blood, backing up till he reached the grass and leaves, then he used leaves until they had worked up to the grave again. They did not stop. They walked around the grave and through the woods, using the light on the ground, looking up through the trees to where they ended at the lake. Neither of them spoke above the sounds of their heavy and clumsy strides through low brush and over fallen branches. Then they reached it: wide and dark, lapping softly at the bank, pine needles smooth under Matt's feet, moonlight on the lake, a small island near its middle, with black, tall evergreens. He took out the gun and threw for the island: taking two steps back on the pine needles, striding with the throw and going to one knee as he followed through, looking up to see the dark shapeless object arcing downward, splashing.

They left Strout's car in Boston, in front of an apartment building on Commonwealth Avenue. When they got back to town Willis drove slowly over the bridge and Matt threw the keys into the Merrimack. The sky was turning light. Willis let him out a block from his house, and walking home he listened for sounds from the houses he passed. They were quiet. A light was on in his living room.

He turned it off and undressed in there, and went softly toward the bedroom; in the hall he smelled the smoke, and he stood in the bedroom doorway and looked at the orange of her cigarette in the dark. The curtains were closed. He went to the closet and put his shoes on the floor and felt for a hanger.

"Did you do it?" she said.

He went down the hall to the bathroom and in the dark he washed his 155 hands and face. Then he went to her, lay on his back, and pulled the sheet up to his throat.

"Are you all right?" she said.

"I think so."

Now she touched him, lying on her side, her hand on his belly, his thigh.

"Tell me," she said.

He started from the beginning, in the parking lot at the bar; but soon with 160 his eyes closed and Ruth petting him, he spoke of Strout's house: the order, the woman presence, the picture on the wall.

"The way she was smiling," he said.

"What about it?"

"I don't know. Did you ever see Strout's girl? When you saw him in town?"

"No."

"I wonder who she was." 165

Then he thought: *not was: is. Sleeping now she is his girl.* He opened his eyes, then closed them again. There was more light beyond the curtains. With Ruth now he left Strout's house and told again his lie to Strout, gave him again that hope that Strout must have for a while believed, else he would have to believe only the gun pointed at him for the last two hours of his life. And with Ruth he saw again the dropping suitcase, the darting move to the right: and he told of the first shot, feeling her hand on him but his heart isolated still, beating on the road still in that explosion like thunder. He told her the rest, but the words had no images for him, he did not see himself doing what the words said he had done; he only saw himself on that road.

"We can't tell the other kids," she said. "It'll hurt them, thinking he got away. But we mustn't."

"No."

She was holding him, wanting him, and he wished he could make love with her but he could not. He saw Frank and Mary Ann making love in her bed, their eyes closed, their bodies brown and smelling of the sea; the other girl was faceless, bodiless, but he felt her sleeping now; and he saw Frank and Strout, their faces alive; he saw red and yellow leaves falling on the earth, then snow: falling and freezing and falling; and holding Ruth, his cheek touching her breast, he shuddered with a sob that he kept silent in his heart.   *[1979]*

≡ THINKING ABOUT THE TEXT

1. Here is an issue of cause and effect: Why, evidently, does Matt kill Richard Strout? Consider the possibility that he has more than one reason. Here is an issue of evaluation: To what extent should the reader

sympathize with Matt? Identify some things that readers should especially consider in addressing this question.

2. Identify the argument that Richard Strout makes as he tries to keep Matt
   from killing him. What assumptions does Strout use? How common is
   his way of thinking?

3. Why does Willis help Matt take revenge? To what extent does Ruth's
   thinking resemble her husband's?

4. What is Matt's view of Mary Ann, his late son's girlfriend?

5. After beginning with Frank's funeral, the story features several flashbacks. Only gradually does Dubus provide certain seemingly important
   facts, such as exactly how Matt's son died. ("Richard Strout shot Frank
   in front of the boys" [para. 76].) What do you think might have been
   Dubus's purpose(s) in refusing to be more straightforward? In the last
   several pages, the story *is* pretty straightforward, moving step-by-step
   through the night of Matt's revenge. Why do you suppose Dubus
   changed his method of storytelling?

≣ MAKING COMPARISONS

1. Does the way that Fortunato dies seem more horrible to you than the
   way that Richard Srout dies? Why, or why not? Do you feel more sympathetic toward one of these characters than the other? Why, or why not?

2. Do you think that, after committing revenge, Matt Fowler has more of a
   guilty conscience than Montresor does? Why, or why not?

3. Montresor narrates "The Cask of Amontillado." Could the story have
   had the same effect if it had an omniscient narrator? How significantly
   would "Killings" be changed if Matt Fowler narrated it?

≣ WRITING ABOUT ISSUES

1. Choose one of the two stories in this cluster, and write an essay explaining how its author encourages readers to take a complex view of the
   story's protagonist. Cite specific details of the text.

2. In her book *Bird by Bird: Some Instructions on Writing and Life*, Anne Lamott
   advises would-be fiction writers that a story must culminate in "a killing
   or a healing or a domination." She goes on to explain:

   It can be a real killing, a murder, or it can be a killing of the spirit, or
   of something terrible inside one's soul, or it can be a killing of a deadness within, after which the person becomes alive again. The healing
   may be about union, reclamation, the rescue of a fragile prize. But
   whatever happens, we need to feel that it was inevitable, that even
   though we may be amazed, it feels absolutely right, that of course
   things would come to this, of course they would shake down in
   this way.

Write an essay discussing the extent to which Poe and Dubus obey this advice. Refer to specific words in the passage from Lamott, as well as to specific details of the stories. If you wish, feel free to evaluate Lamott's advice. Do you think fiction writers ought to follow it?

3. Gerald Murphy, a famous socialite of the 1920s, once said that "living well is the best revenge." Murphy did not identify whom it was revenge against. Still, his statement is thought provoking in its suggestion that revenge is not always recognizable as such. "Living well" may be revenge in disguise. Write an essay showing how a specific action you are familiar with can be seen as an act of revenge, even though many people wouldn't realize this. In your essay, also evaluate the action. Do you approve of this act of revenge? Why, or why not?

4. Write an essay examining how at least three movie critics have responded to a particular film about revenge, such as *In the Bedroom* (the movie adaptation of "Killings"), *Kill Bill I* or *II*, *Django Unchained*, *The Dark Knight*, *The Godfather*, or *V for Vendetta*. To learn critics' responses, you will have to do research. A good Web site to consult is the Internet Movie Database at imdb.com. In your essay, point out a key issue that your chosen critics have raised, identify their positions on this issue, and develop a case for your own position.

▪ A Menacing Stalker: Cultural Contexts for a Story

JOYCE CAROL OATES, "Where Are You Going, Where Have You Been?"

CULTURAL CONTEXTS:

DON MOSER, "The Pied Piper of Tucson: He Cruised in a Golden Car, Looking for the Action"

JOYCE CAROL OATES, "*Smooth Talk*: Short Story into Film"

MARGARET TALBOT, From *"Gone Girl: The Extraordinary Resilience of Elizabeth Smart"*

The harrowing ending of Joyce Carol Oates's much-anthologized initiation tale of innocence versus evil may shock you. The fifteen-year-old Connie, focused on boys and pop music, seems defenseless against her menacing stalker. This 1966 story uses the prospect of violent crime to remind readers, in its own chilling way, that adolescence may be fraught with anxieties, challenges, and risks. Often, however, a literary text reflects and responds to specific cultural contexts. Such is the case with this one. Therefore, we include with Oates's story three other texts: the *Life* magazine article that evidently led Oates to conceive her work of fiction; a *New York Times* article she wrote when her story became the movie *Smooth Talk*; and an excerpt from Margaret Talbot's 2013 *New Yorker* magazine article on Elizabeth Smart, a real-life woman who drew much national interest when she was abducted from her home as a teenager and ultimately gained freedom from her kidnappers.

▪ BEFORE YOU READ

Many historians of literature and culture have pointed out that as far back as colonial times, Americans have been fascinated with narratives of female captivity. Why do you think this kind of story has engaged them?

JOYCE CAROL OATES

Where Are You Going, Where Have You Been?

Joyce Carol Oates (b. 1938) is perhaps the most prolific of major American writers, publishing about two books a year for more than forty years. Oates has won numerous awards, including a National Book Award for fiction (1970).

Oates grew up in the countryside of upstate New York. She started writing early and won a scholarship to Syracuse University, where she was valedictorian in 1960. She received her M.A. from the University of Wisconsin a year later. She taught at the University of Detroit and the University of Windsor before joining the faculty at Princeton, where she has taught since 1978. Like Flannery O'Connor's and William

Marion Ettlinger

Faulkner's work, Oates's is usually referred to as gothic, probably because of her vio- lent characters, many of whom are filled with enigmatic malice and tormented emo- tions. Working in the realistic tradition, the "Dark Lady of American Literature" writes compelling narratives about seemingly ordinary people who beneath the surface live in a nightmare world of unconscious forces and sometimes sensational events.

Oates claims the story printed here was written after listening to Bob Dylan's "It's All Over Now, Baby Blue." The story was inspired by the serial killer Charles Schmid, also known as "The Pied Piper of Tucson." Her recent books include the nov- els The Accursed *(2013),* Daddy Love *(2013), and* Mudwoman *(2012); a mem- oir,* A Widow's Story *(2011); and the short story collection* Give Me Your Heart: Tales of Mystery and Suspense *(2011).*

For Bob Dylan

Her name was Connie. She was fifteen and she had a quick nervous giggling habit of craning her neck to glance into mirrors, or checking other people's faces to make sure her own was all right. Her mother, who noticed everything and knew everything and who hadn't much reason any longer to look at her own face, always scolded Connie about it. "Stop gawking at yourself, who are you? You think you're so pretty?" she would say. Connie would raise her eyebrows at these familiar complaints and look right through her mother, into a shadowy vision of herself as she was right at that moment: she knew she was pretty and that was everything. Her mother had been pretty once too, if you could believe those old snapshots in the album, but now her looks were gone and that was why she was always after Connie.

"Why don't you keep your room clean like your sister? How've you got your hair fixed—what the hell stinks? Hair spray? You don't see your sister using that junk."

Her sister June was twenty-four and still lived at home. She was a secretary in the high school Connie attended, and if that wasn't bad enough—with her in the same building—she was so plain and chunky and steady that Connie had to hear her praised all the time by her mother and her mother's sisters. June did this, June did that, she saved money and helped clean the house and cooked and Connie couldn't do a thing, her mind was all filled with trashy daydreams. Their father was away at work most of the time and when he came home he wanted supper and he read the newspaper at supper and after supper he went to bed. He didn't bother talking much to them, but around his bent head Connie's mother kept picking at her until Connie wished her mother was dead and she herself was dead and it was all over. "She makes me want to throw up sometimes," she complained to her friends. She had a high, breathless, amused voice which made everything she said a little forced, whether it was sincere or not.

There was one good thing: June went places with girl friends of hers, girls who were just as plain and steady as she, and so when Connie wanted to do that her mother had no objections. The father of Connie's best girl friend drove the girls the three miles to town and left them off at a shopping plaza, so that they could walk through the stores or go to a movie, and when he came to pick them up again at eleven he never bothered to ask what they had done.

They must have been familiar sights, walking around that shopping plaza in their shorts and flat ballerina slippers that always scuffed the sidewalk, with charm bracelets jingling on their thin wrists; they would lean together to whisper and laugh secretly if someone passed by who amused or interested them. Connie had long dark blond hair that drew anyone's eye to it, and she wore part of it pulled up on her head and puffed out and the rest of it she let fall down her back. She wore a pullover jersey blouse that looked one way when she was at home and another way when she was away from home. Everything about her had two sides to it, one for home and one for anywhere that was not home: her walk that could be childlike and bobbing, or languid enough to make anyone think she was hearing music in her head, her mouth which was pale and smirking most of the time, but bright and pink on these evenings out, her laugh which was cynical and drawling at home—"Ha, ha, very funny"—but high-pitched and nervous anywhere else, like the jingling of the charms on her bracelet.

Sometimes they did go shopping or to a movie, but sometimes they went across the highway, ducking fast across the busy road, to a drive-in restaurant where older kids hung out. The restaurant was shaped like a big bottle, though squatter than a real bottle, and on its cap was a revolving figure of a grinning boy who held a hamburger aloft. One night in midsummer they ran across, breathless with daring, and right away someone leaned out a car window and invited them over, but it was just a boy from high school they didn't like. It made them feel good to be able to ignore him. They went up through the maze of parked and cruising cars to the bright-lit, fly-infested restaurant, their faces pleased and expectant as if they were entering a sacred building that loomed out of the night to give them what haven and what blessing they yearned for. They sat at the counter and crossed their legs at the ankles, their thin shoulders rigid with excitement and listened to the music that made everything so good: the music was always in the background like music at a church service, it was something to depend upon.

A boy named Eddie came in to talk with them. He sat backwards on his stool, turning himself jerkily around in semi-circles and then stopping and turning again, and after a while he asked Connie if she would like something to eat. She said she did and so she tapped her friend's arm on her way out—her friend pulled her face up into a brave droll look—and Connie said she would meet her at eleven, across the way. "I just hate to leave her like that," Connie said earnestly, but the boy said that she wouldn't be alone for long. So they went out to his car and on the way Connie couldn't help but let her eyes wander over the windshields and faces all around her, her face gleaming with the joy that had nothing to do with Eddie or even this place; it might have been the music. She drew her shoulders up and sucked in her breath with the pure pleasure of being alive, and just at that moment she happened to glance at a face just a few feet from hers. It was a boy with shaggy black hair, in a convertible jalopy painted gold. He stared at her and then his lips widened into a grin. Connie slit her eyes at him and turned away, but she couldn't help glancing back and there he was still watching her. He wagged a finger and laughed and said, "Gonna get you, baby," and Connie turned away again without Eddie noticing anything.

She spent three hours with him, at the restaurant where they ate hamburgers and drank Cokes in wax cups that were always sweating, and then down an alley a mile or so away, and when he left her off at five to eleven only the movie house was still open at the plaza. Her girl friend was there, talking with a boy. When Connie came up the two girls smiled at each other and Connie said, "How was the movie?" and the girl said, "*You* should know." They rode off with the girl's father, sleepy and pleased, and Connie couldn't help but look at the darkened shopping plaza with its big empty parking lot and its signs that were faded and ghostly now, and over at the drive-in restaurant where cars were still circling tirelessly. She couldn't hear the music at this distance.

Next morning June asked her how the movie was and Connie said, "So-so."

She and that girl and occasionally another girl went out several times a week that way, and the rest of the time Connie spent around the house—it was

10

summer vacation—getting in her mother's way and thinking, dreaming, about the boys she met. But all the boys fell back and dissolved into a single face that was not even a face, but an idea, a feeling, mixed up with the urgent insistent pounding of the music and the humid night air of July. Connie's mother kept dragging her back to the daylight by finding things for her to do or saying suddenly, "What's this about the Pettinger girl?"

And Connie would say nervously, "Oh, her. That dope." She always drew thick clear lines between herself and such girls, and her mother was simple and kindly enough to believe her. Her mother was so simple, Connie thought, that it was maybe cruel to fool her so much. Her mother went scuffling around the house in old bedroom slippers and complained over the telephone to one sister about the other, then the other called up and the two of them complained about the third one. If June's name was mentioned her mother's tone was approving, and if Connie's name was mentioned it was disapproving. This did not really mean she disliked Connie and actually Connie thought that her mother preferred her to June because she was prettier, but the two of them kept up a pretense of exasperation, a sense that they were tugging and struggling over something of little value to either of them. Sometimes, over coffee, they were almost friends, but something would come up—some vexation that was like a fly buzzing suddenly around their heads—and their faces went hard with contempt.

One Sunday Connie got up at eleven—none of them bothered with church—and washed her hair so that it could dry all day long, in the sun. Her parents and sister were going to a barbecue at an aunt's house and Connie said no, she wasn't interested, rolling her eyes, to let mother know just what she thought of it. "Stay home alone then," her mother said sharply. Connie sat out back in a lawn chair and watched them drive away, her father quiet and bald, hunched around so that he could back the car out, her mother with a look that was still angry and not at all softened through the windshield, and in the back seat poor old June all dressed up as if she didn't know what a barbecue was, with all the running yelling kids and the flies. Connie sat with her eyes closed in the sun, dreaming and dazed with the warmth about her as if this were a kind of love, the caresses of love, and her mind slipped over onto thoughts of the boy she had been with the night before and how nice he had been, how sweet it always was, not the way someone like June would suppose but sweet, gentle, the way it was in movies and promised in songs; and when she opened her eyes she hardly knew where she was, the back yard ran off into weeds and a fenceline of trees and behind it the sky was perfectly blue and still. The asbestos "ranch house" that was now three years old startled her—it looked small. She shook her head as if to get awake.

It was too hot. She went inside the house and turned on the radio to drown out the quiet. She sat on the edge of her bed, barefoot, and listened for an hour and a half to a program called XYZ Sunday Jamboree, record after record of hard, fast, shrieking songs she sang along with, interspersed by exclamations from "Bobby King": "An' look here you girls at Napoleon's—Son and Charley want you to pay real close attention to this song coming up!"

And Connie paid close attention herself, bathed in a glow of slow-pulsed joy that seemed to rise mysteriously out of the music itself and lay languidly about the airless little room, breathed in and breathed out with each gentle rise and fall of her chest.

After a while she heard a car coming up the drive. She sat up at once, startled, because it couldn't be her father so soon. The gravel kept crunching all the way in from the road—the driveway was long—and Connie ran to the window. It was a car she didn't know. It was an open jalopy, painted a bright gold that caught the sun opaquely. Her heart began to pound and her fingers snatched at her hair, checking it, and she whispered "Christ. Christ," wondering how bad she looked. The car came to a stop at the side door and the horn sounded four short taps as if this were a signal Connie knew.

She went into the kitchen and approached the door slowly, then hung out the screen door, her bare toes curling down off the step. There were two boys in the car and now she recognized the driver: he had shaggy, shabby black hair that looked crazy as a wig and he was grinning at her.

"I ain't late, am I?" he said.

"Who the hell do you think you are?" Connie said.

"Toldja I'd be out, didn't I?"

"I don't even know who you are."

She spoke sullenly, careful to show no interest or pleasure, and he spoke in a fast bright monotone. Connie looked past him to the other boy, taking her time. He had fair brown hair, with a lock that fell onto his forehead. His sideburns gave him a fierce, embarrassed look, but so far he hadn't even bothered to glance at her. Both boys wore sunglasses. The driver's glasses were metallic and mirrored everything in miniature.

"You wanta come for a ride?" he said.

Connie smirked and let her hair fall loose over one shoulder.

"Don'tcha like my car? New paint job," he said. "Hey."

"What?"

"You're cute."

She pretended to fidget, chasing flies away from the door.

"Don'tcha believe me, or what?" he said.

"Look, I don't even know who you are," Connie said in disgust.

"Hey, Ellie's got a radio, see. Mine's broke down." He lifted his friend's arm and showed her the little transistor the boy was holding, and now Connie began to hear the music. It was the same program that was playing inside the house.

"Bobby King?" she said.

"I listen to him all the time. I think he's great."

"He's kind of great," Connie said reluctantly.

"Listen, that guy's *great*. He knows where the action is."

Connie blushed a little, because the glasses made it impossible for her to see just what this boy was looking at. She couldn't decide if she liked him or if he was just a jerk, and so she dawdled in the doorway and wouldn't come down or go back inside. She said, "What's all that stuff painted on your car?"

15

20

25

30

35

"Can'tcha read it?" He opened the door very carefully, as if he was afraid it might fall off. He slid out just as carefully, planting his feet firmly on the ground, the tiny metallic world in his glasses slowing down like gelatine hardening and in the midst of it Connie's bright green blouse. "This here is my name, to begin with," he said. ARNOLD FRIEND was written in tar-like black letters on the side, with a drawing of a round grinning face that reminded Connie of a pumpkin, except it wore sunglasses. "I wanta introduce myself, I'm Arnold Friend and that's my real name and I'm gonna be your friend, honey, and inside the car's Ellie Oscar, he's kinda shy." Ellie brought his transistor up to his shoulder and balanced it there. "Now these numbers are a secret code, honey," Arnold Friend explained. He read off the numbers 33, 19, 17 and raised his eyebrows at her to see what she thought of that, but she didn't think much of it. The left rear fender had been smashed and around it was written, on the gleaming gold background: DONE BY CRAZY WOMAN DRIVER. Connie had to laugh at that. Arnold Friend was pleased at her laughter and looked up at her. "Around the other side's a lot more—you wanta come and see them?"

"No."

"Why not?"

"Why should I?"

"Don'tcha wanta see what's on the car? Don'tcha wanta go for a ride?" 40

"I don't know."

"Why not?"

"I got things to do."

"Like what?"

"Things." 45

He laughed as if she had said something funny. He slapped his thighs. He was standing in a strange way, leaning back against the car as if he were balancing himself. He wasn't tall, only an inch or so taller than she would be if she came down to him. Connie liked the way he was dressed, which was the way all of them dressed: tight faded jeans stuffed into black, scuffed boots, a belt that pulled his waist in and showed how lean he was, and a white pullover shirt that was a little soiled and showed the hard small muscles of his arms and shoulders. He looked as if he probably did hard work, lifting and carrying things. Even his neck looked muscular. And his face was a familiar face, somehow: the jaw and chin and cheeks slightly darkened, because he hadn't shaved for a day or two, and the nose long and hawk-like, sniffing as if she were a treat he was going to gobble up and it was all a joke.

"Connie, you ain't telling the truth. This is your day set aside for a ride with me and you know it," he said, still laughing. The way he straightened and recovered from his fit of laughing showed that it had been all fake.

"How do you know what my name is?" she said suspiciously.

"It's Connie."

"Maybe and maybe not." 50

"I know my Connie," he said, wagging his finger. Now she remembered him even better, back at the restaurant, and her cheeks warmed at the thought of how she sucked in her breath just at the moment she passed him — how she must have looked to him. And he had remembered her. "Ellie and I come out here especially for you," he said. "Ellie can sit in back. How about it?"

"Where?"

"Where what?"

"Where're we going?"

He looked at her. He took off the sunglasses and she saw how pale the skin   55
around his eyes was, like holes that were not in shadow but instead in light. His eyes were like chips of broken glass that catch the light in an amiable way. He smiled. It was as if the idea of going for a ride somewhere, to some place, was a new idea to him.

"Just for a ride, Connie sweetheart."

"I never said my name was Connie," she said.

"But I know what it is. I know your name and all about you, lots of things," Arnold Friend said. He had not moved yet but stood still leaning back against the side of his jalopy. "I took a special interest in you, such a pretty girl, and found out all about you like I know your parents and sister are gone somewheres and I know where and how long they're going to be gone, and I know who you were with last night, and your best friend's name is Betty. Right?"

He spoke in a simple lilting voice, exactly as if he were reciting the words to a song. His smile assured her that everything was fine. In the car Ellie turned up the volume on his radio and did not bother to look around at them.

"Ellie can sit in the back seat," Arnold Friend said. He indicated his friend   60
with a casual jerk of his chin, as if Ellie did not count and she could not bother with him.

"How'd you find out all that stuff?" Connie said.

"Listen: Betty Schultz and Tony Fitch and Jimmy Pettinger and Nancy Pettinger," he said, in a chant. "Raymond Stanley and Bob Hutter —"

"Do you know all those kids?"

"I know everybody."

"Look, you're kidding. You're not from around here."   65

"Sure."

"But — how come we never saw you before?"

"Sure you saw me before," he said. He looked down at his boots, as if he were a little offended. "You just don't remember."

"I guess I'd remember you," Connie said.

"Yeah?" He looked up at this, beaming. He was pleased. He began to mark   70
time with the music from Ellie's radio, tapping his fists lightly together. Connie looked away from his smile to the car, which was painted so bright it almost hurt her eyes to look at it. She looked at that name, ARNOLD FRIEND. And up at the front fender was an expression that was familiar — MAN THE FLYING SAUCERS. It was an expression kids had used the year before, but didn't use this year. She looked at it for a while as if the words meant something to her that she did not yet know.

"What're you thinking about? Huh?" Arnold Friend demanded. "Not worried about your hair blowing around in the car, are you?"

"No."

"Think I maybe can't drive good?"

"How do I know?"

"You're a hard girl to handle. How come?" he said. "Don't you know I'm   75
your friend? Didn't you see me put my sign in the air when you walked by?"

"What sign?"

"My sign." And he drew an X in the air, leaning out toward her. They were maybe ten feet apart. After his hand fell back to his side the X was still in the air, almost visible. Connie let the screen door close and stood perfectly still inside it, listening to the music from her radio and the boy's blend together. She stared at Arnold Friend. He stood there so stiffly relaxed, pretending to be relaxed, with one hand idly on the door handle as if he were keeping himself up that way and had no intention of ever moving again. She recognized most things about him, the tight jeans that showed his thighs and buttocks and the greasy leather boots and the tight shirt, and even that slippery friendly smile of his, that sleepy dreamy smile that all the boys used to get across ideas they didn't want to put into words. She recognized all this and also the singsong way he talked, slightly mocking, kidding, but serious and a little melancholy, and she recognized the way he tapped one fist against the other in homage to the perpetual music behind him. But all these things did not come together.

She said suddenly, "Hey, how old are you?"

His smile faded. She could see then that he wasn't a kid, he was much older—thirty, maybe more. At this knowledge her heart began to pound faster.

"That's a crazy thing to ask. Can'tcha see I'm your own age?"   80

"Like hell you are."

"Or maybe a coupla years older, I'm eighteen."

"Eighteen?" she said doubtfully.

He grinned to reassure her and lines appeared at the corners of his mouth. His teeth were big and white. He grinned so broadly his eyes became slits and she saw how thick the lashes were, thick and black as if painted with a black tar-like material. Then he seemed to become embarrassed, abruptly, and looked over his shoulder at Ellie. "*Him,* he's crazy," he said. "Ain't he a riot, he's a nut, a real character." Ellie was still listening to the music. His sunglasses told nothing about what he was thinking. He wore a bright orange shirt unbuttoned halfway to show his chest, which was a pale, bluish chest and not muscular like Arnold Friend's. His shirt collar was turned up all around and the very tips of the collar pointed out past his chin as if they were protecting him. He was pressing the transistor radio up against his ear and sat there in a kind of daze, right in the sun.

"He's kinda strange," Connie said.   85

"Hey, she says you're kinda strange! Kinda strange!" Arnold Friend cried. He pounded on the car to get Ellie's attention. Ellie turned for the first time and Connie saw with shock that he wasn't a kid either—he had a fair, hairless face, cheeks reddened slightly as if the veins grew too close to the surface of his skin, the face of a forty-year-old baby. Connie felt a wave of dizziness rise in her at this sight and she stared at him as if waiting for something to change the shock of the moment, make it all right again. Ellie's lips kept shaping words, mumbling along with the words blasting his ear.

"Maybe you two better go away," Connie said faintly.

"What? How come?" Arnold Friend cried. "We come out here to take you for a ride. It's Sunday." He had the voice of the man on the radio now. It was the same voice, Connie thought. "Don'tcha know it's Sunday all day and honey, no matter who you were with last night today you're with Arnold Friend and don't you forget it! — Maybe you better step out here," he said, and this last was in a different voice. It was a little flatter, as if the heat was finally getting to him.

"No. I got things to do."

"Hey." 90

"You two better leave."

"We ain't leaving until you come with us."

"Like hell I am—"

"Connie, don't fool around with me. I mean — I mean, don't fool *around*," he said, shaking his head. He laughed incredulously. He placed his sunglasses on top of his head, carefully, as if he were indeed wearing a wig, and brought the stems down behind his ears. Connie stared at him, another wave of dizziness and fear rising in her so that for a moment he wasn't even in focus but was just a blur; standing there against his gold car, and she had the idea that he had driven up the driveway all right but had come from nowhere before that and belonged nowhere and that everything about him and even the music that was so familiar to her was only half real.

"If my father comes and sees you—" 95

"He ain't coming. He's at a barbecue."

"How do you know that?"

"Aunt Tillie's. Right now they're — uh — they're drinking. Sitting around," he said vaguely, squinting as if he were staring all the way to town and over to Aunt Tillie's back yard. Then the vision seemed to clear and he nodded energetically. "Yeah. Sitting around. There's your sister in a blue dress, huh? And high heels, the poor sad bitch — nothing like you, sweetheart! And your mother's helping some fat woman with the corn, they're cleaning the corn — husking the corn—"

"What fat woman?" Connie cried.

"How do I know what fat woman. I don't know every goddamn fat woman in the world!" Arnold Friend laughed. 100

"Oh, that's Mrs. Hornby. . . . Who invited her?" Connie said. She felt a little light-headed. Her breath was coming quickly.

"She's too fat. I don't like them fat. I like them the way you are, honey," he said, smiling sleepily at her. They stared at each other for a while, through the screen door. He said softly, "Now what you're going to do is this: you're going to come out that door. You're going to sit up front with me and Ellie's going to sit in the back, the hell with Ellie, right? This isn't Ellie's date. You're my date. I'm your lover, honey."

"What? You're crazy—"

"Yes, I'm your lover. You don't know what that is but you will," he said. "I know that too. I know all about you. But look: it's real nice and you couldn't ask for nobody better than me, or more polite. I always keep my word. I'll tell you how it is, I'm always nice at first, the first time. I'll hold you so tight you won't think you have to try to get away or pretend anything because you'll know you can't. And I'll come inside you where it's all secret and you'll give in to me and you'll love me—"

"Shut up! You're crazy!" Connie said. She backed away from the door. She   105
put her hands against her ears as if she'd heard something terrible, something not meant for her. "People don't talk like that, you're crazy," she muttered. Her heart was almost too big now for her chest and its pumping made sweat break out all over her. She looked out to see Arnold Friend pause and then take a step toward the porch lurching. He almost fell. But, like a clever drunken man, he managed to catch his balance. He wobbled in his high boots and grabbed hold of one of the porch posts.

"Honey?" he said. "You still listening?"

"Get the hell out of here!"

"Be nice, honey. Listen."

"I'm going to call the police—"

He wobbled again and out of the side of his mouth came a fast spat curse,   110
an aside not meant for her to hear. But even this "Christ!" sounded forced. Then he began to smile again. She watched this smile come, awkward as if he were smiling from inside a mask. His whole face was a mask, she thought wildly, tanned down onto his throat but then running out as if he had plastered make-up on his face but had forgotten about his throat.

"Honey—? Listen, here's how it is. I always tell the truth and I promise you this: I ain't coming in that house after you."

"You better not! I'm going to call the police if you—if you don't—"

"Honey," he said, talking right through her voice, "honey, I'm not coming in there but you are coming out here. You know why?"

She was panting. The kitchen looked like a place she had never seen before, some room she had run inside but which wasn't good enough, wasn't going to help her. The kitchen window had never had a curtain, after three years, and there were dishes in the sink for her to do—probably—and if you ran your hand across the table you'd probably feel something sticky there.

"You listening, honey? Hey?"   115

"—going to call the police—"

"Soon as you touch the phone I don't need to keep my promise and can come inside. You won't want that."

She rushed forward and tried to lock the door. Her fingers were shaking. "But why lock it," Arnold Friend said gently, talking right into her face. "It's just a screen door. It's just nothing." One of his boots was at a strange angle, as if his foot wasn't in it. It pointed out to the left, bent at the ankle. "I mean, any-body can break through a screen door and glass and wood and iron or any-thing else if he needs to, anybody at all and specially Arnold Friend. If the place got lit up with a fire, honey, you'd come runnin' out into my arms, right into my arms an' safe at home—like you knew I was your lover and'd stopped fooling around, I don't mind a nice shy girl but I don't like no fooling around." Part of those words were spoken with a slight rhythmic lilt, and Connie somehow recognized them—the echo of a song from last year, about a girl rushing into her boy friend's arms and coming home again—

Connie stood barefoot on the linoleum floor, staring at him. "What do you want?" she whispered.

"I want you," he said.   120

"What?"

"Seen you that night and thought, that's the one, yes sir. I never needed to look any more."

"But my father's coming back. He's coming to get me. I had to wash my hair first—" She spoke in a dry, rapid voice, hardly raising it for him to hear.

"No, your daddy is not coming and yes, you had to wash your hair and you washed it for me. It's nice and shining and all for me. I thank you, sweetheart," he said, with a mock bow, but again he almost lost his balance. He had to bend and adjust his boots. Evidently his feet did not go all the way down; the boots must have been stuffed with something so that he would seem taller. Connie stared out at him and behind him at Ellie in the car, who seemed to be looking off toward Connie's right, into nothing. Then Ellie said, pulling the words out of the air one after another as if he were just discovering them, "You want me to pull out the phone?"

"Shut your mouth and keep it shut," Arnold Friend said, his face red from   125
bending over or maybe from embarrassment because Connie had seen his boots. "This ain't none of your business."

"What—what are you doing? What do you want?" Connie said. "If I call the police they'll get you, they'll arrest you—"

"Promise was not to come in unless you touch that phone, and I'll keep that promise," he said. He resumed his erect position and tried to force his shoulders back. He sounded like a hero in a movie, declaring something important. He spoke too loudly and it was as if he were speaking to someone behind Connie. "I ain't made plans for coming in that house where I don't belong but just for you to come out to me, the way you should. Don't you know who I am?"

"You're crazy," she whispered. She backed away from the door but did not want to go into another part of the house, as if this would give him permission to come through the door. "What do you . . . You're crazy, you. . . ."

"Huh? What're you saying, honey?"

Her eyes darted everywhere in the kitchen. She could not remember what   130
it was, this room.

"This is how it is, honey: you come out and we'll drive away, have a nice ride. But if you don't come out we're gonna wait till your people come home and then they're all going to get it."

"You want that telephone pulled out?" Ellie said. He held the radio away from his ear and grimaced, as if without the radio the air was too much for him.

"I toldja shut up, Ellie," Arnold Friend said, "you're deaf, get a hearing aid, right? Fix yourself up. This little girl's no trouble and's gonna be nice to me, so

Ellie keep to yourself, this ain't your date—right? Don't hem in on me, don't hog, don't crush, don't bird dog, don't trail me," he said in a rapid, meaningless voice, as if he were running through all the expressions he'd learned but was no longer sure which one of them was in style, then rushing on to new ones, making them up with his eyes closed. "Don't crawl under my fence, don't squeeze in my chipmunk hole, don't sniff my glue, suck my popsicle, keep your own greasy fingers on yourself!" He shaded his eyes and peered in at Connie, who was backed against the kitchen table. "Don't mind him, honey, he's just a creep. He's a dope. Right? I'm the boy for you and like I said, you come out here nice like a lady and give me your hand, and nobody else gets hurt, I mean, your nice old bald-headed daddy and your mummy and your sister in her high heels. Because listen: why bring them in this?"

"Leave me alone," Connie whispered.

"Hey, you know that old woman down the road, the one with the chickens   135
and stuff—you know her?"

"She's dead!"

"Dead? What? You know her?" Arnold Friend said.

"She's dead—"

"Don't you like her?"

"She's dead—she's—she isn't here any more—"   140

"But don't you like her, I mean, you got something against her? Some grudge or something?" Then his voice dipped as if he were conscious of rudeness. He touched the sunglasses on top of his head as if to make sure they were still there. "Now you be a good girl."

"What are you going to do?"

"Just two things, or maybe three," Arnold Friend said. "But I promise it won't last long and you'll like me that way you get to like people you're close to. You will. It's all over for you here, so come on out. You don't want your people in any trouble, do you?"

She turned and bumped against a chair or something, hurting her leg, but she ran into the back room and picked up the telephone. Something roared in her ear, a tiny roaring, and she was so sick with fear that she could do nothing but listen to it—the telephone was clammy and very heavy and her fingers groped down to the dial but were too weak to touch it. She began to scream into the phone, into the roaring. She cried out, she cried for her mother, she felt her breath start jerking back and forth in her lungs as if it were something Arnold Friend was stabbing her with again and again with no tenderness. A noisy sorrowful wailing rose all about her and she was locked inside it the way she was locked inside this house.

After a while she could hear again. She was sitting on the floor, with her   145
wet back against the wall.

Arnold Friend was saying from the door, "That's a good girl. Put the phone back."

She kicked the phone away from her.

"No, honey. Pick it up. Put it back right."

She picked it up and put it back. The dial tone stopped.

"That's a good girl. Now you come outside."   150

She was hollow with what had been fear but what was now just an emptiness. All that screaming had blasted it out of her. She sat, one leg cramped under her, and deep inside her brain was something like a pinpoint of light that kept going and would not let her relax. She thought, I'm not going to see my mother again. She thought, I'm not going to sleep in my bed again. Her bright green blouse was all wet.

Arnold Friend said, in a gentle-loud voice that was like a stage voice, "The place where you came from ain't there any more, and where you had in mind to go is cancelled out. This place you are now — inside your daddy's house — is nothing but a cardboard box I can knock down any time. You know that and always did know it. You hear me?"

She thought, I have got to think. I have got to know what to do.

"We'll go out to a nice field, out in the country here where it smells so nice and it's sunny," Arnold Friend said. "I'll have my arms tight around you so you won't need to try to get away and I'll show you what love is like, what it does. The hell with this house! It looks solid all right," he said. He ran a fingernail down the screen and the noise did not make Connie shiver, as it would have the day before. "Now put your hand on your heart, honey. Feel that? That feels solid too but we know better. Be nice to me, be sweet like you can because what else is there for a girl like you but to be sweet and pretty and give in? — and get away before her people get back?"

She felt her pounding heart. Her hand seemed to enclose it. She thought for   155
the first time in her life that it was nothing that was hers, that belonged to her, but just a pounding, living thing inside this body that wasn't really hers either.

"You don't want them to get hurt," Arnold Friend went on. "Now get up, honey. Get up all by yourself."

She stood.

"Now turn this way. That's right. Come over to me — Ellie, put that away, didn't I tell you? You dope. You miserable creepy dope," Arnold Friend said. His words were not angry but only part of an incantation. The incantation was kindly. "Now come out through the kitchen to me honey and let's see a smile, try it, you're a brave sweet little girl and now they're eating corn and hotdogs cooked to bursting over an outdoor fire, and they don't know one thing about you and never did and honey you're better than them because not a one of them would have done this for you."

Connie felt the linoleum under her feet; it was cool. She brushed her hair back out of her eyes. Arnold Friend let go of the post tentatively and opened his arms for her, his elbows pointing in toward each other and his wrists limp, to show that this was an embarrassed embrace and a little mocking, he didn't want to make her self-conscious.

She put out her hand against the screen. She watched herself push the   160
door slowly open as if she were back safe somewhere in the other doorway, watching this body and this head of long hair moving out into the sunlight where Arnold Friend waited.

"My sweet little blue-eyed girl," he said in a half-sung sigh that had nothing to do with her brown eyes but was taken up just the same by the vast sunlit reaches of the land behind him and on all sides of him—so much land that Connie had never seen before and did not recognize except to know that she was going to it.   *[1966]*

≡ THINKING ABOUT THE TEXT

1. This story was first published in 1966. What still seems typical of fifteen-year-old Connie's behavior? What seems dated about her?

2. Is Oates making a comment about the effect music has on Connie? Should popular music be accountable for the behavior of its listeners? Can popular culture make us oblivious to the real dangers of the world? Can it make us suspicious and cynical?

3. The suggestions about what will happen to Connie when she leaves the protection of her home are not so subtle. What is your view of her future? What does Connie mean when she says, "'People don't talk like that, you're crazy'" (para. 105)? What is your reading of her response? Is Arnold Friend crazy?

4. A common response to this story is frustration with Connie's hesitation and her inability to take appropriate action in the face of serious danger. Was this your response? Why isn't she more assertive?

5. Could Connie have been better prepared for this encounter with evil? What evidence does the author give to show how prepared she is or isn't? What is her relationship with her parents? Is her social awareness primarily her parents' responsibility? If not, whose is it?

DON MOSER

The Pied Piper of Tucson: He Cruised in a Golden Car, Looking for the Action

Published in the March 4, 1966, issue of Life *magazine, this article by Don Moser (b. 1932) focuses on a real-life murderer who in major ways resembled Joyce Carol Oates's character Arnold Friend. Indeed, in the essay by Oates that follows, she indicates some familiarity with Moser's piece, although she claims that she didn't read it fully. However much his article inspired Oates to write her story, he illuminates American youth culture of the mid-1960s—including the role that deadly crime could play in it.*

> *Hey, c 'mon babe, follow me,*
> *I'm the Pied Piper, follow me,*
> *I'm the Pied Piper,*
> *And I'll show you where it's at.*
> —Popular song
> Tucson, winter 1965

At dusk in Tucson, as the stark, yellow-flared mountains begin to blur against the sky, the golden car slowly cruises Speedway. Smoothly it rolls down the long divided avenue, past the supermarkets, the gas stations, and the motels; past the twist joints, the sprawling drive-in restaurants. The car slows for an intersection, stops, then pulls away again. The exhaust mutters against the pavement as the young man driving takes the machine swiftly, expertly through the gears. A car pulls even with him; the teen-age girls in the front seat laugh, wave, and call his name. The young man glances toward the rearview mirror, turned always so he can look at his own reflection, and he appraises himself.

The face is his own creation; the hair dyed raven black, the skin darkened to a deep tan with pancake make-up, the lips whitened, the whole effect heightened by a mole he has painted on one cheek. But the deep-set blue eyes are all his own. Beautiful eyes, the girls say.

Approaching the Hi-Ho, the teen-agers' nightclub, he backs off on the accelerator, then slowly cruises on past Johnie's Drive-in. The cars are beginning to orbit and accumulate in the parking lot—near sharp cars with deep-throated mufflers and Maltese-cross decals on the windows. But it's early yet. Not much going on. The driver shifts up again through the gears, and the golden car slides away along the glitter and gimcrack of Speedway. Smitty keeps looking for the action.

Whether the juries in the two trials decide that Charles Howard Schmid Jr. did or did not brutally murder Alleen Rowe, Gretchen Fritz, and Wendy Fritz has from the beginning seemed of almost secondary importance to the people of Tucson. They are not indifferent. But what disturbs them far beyond the question of Smitty's guilt or innocence are the revelations about Tucson itself that have followed on the disclosure of the crimes. Starting from the bizarre circumstances of the killings and on through the ugly fragments of the plot—which in turn hint at other murders as yet undiscovered, at teen-age sex, blackmail, even connections with the Cosa Nostra—they have had to view their city in a new and unpleasant light. The fact is that Charles Schmid—who cannot be dismissed as a freak, an aberrant of no consequence—had for years functioned successfully as a member, even a leader, of the yeastiest stratum of Tucson's teen-age society.

As a high school student Smitty had been, as classmates remember, an outsider—but not that far outside. He was small but he was a fine athlete, and in his last year—1960—he was a state gymnastics champion. His grades were poor, but he was in no trouble to speak of until his senior year, when he was suspended for stealing tools from a welding class.

But Smitty never really left the school. After his suspension he hung around waiting to pick up kids in a succession of sharp cars which he drove fast and well. He haunted all the teen-age hangouts along Speedway, including the bowling alleys and the public swimming pool—and he put on spectacular driving exhibitions for girls far younger than he.

At the time of his arrest last November, Charles Schmid was 23 years old. He wore face make-up and dyed his hair. He habitually stuffed three or four inches of old rags and tin cans into the bottoms of his high-topped boots to make himself taller than his five-foot-three and stumbled about so awkwardly while walking that some people thought he had wooden feet. He pursed his lips and let his eyelids droop in order to emulate his idol, Elvis Presley. He bragged to girls that he knew 100 ways to make love, and that he ran dope, that he was a Hell's Angel. He talked about being a rough customer in a fight (he was, though he was rarely in one), and he always carried in his pocket tiny bottles of salt and pepper, which he said he used to blind his opponents. He liked to use high-falutin language and had a favorite saying, "I can manifest my neurotical emotions, emancipate an epicureal instinct, and elaborate on my heterosexual tendencies."

He occasionally shocked even those who thought they knew him well. A friend says that he once saw Smitty tie a string to the tail of his pet cat, swing it around his head and beat it bloody against a wall. Then he turned calmly and asked, "You feel compassion—why?"

Yet even while Smitty tried to create an exalted, heroic image of himself, he had worked on a pitiable one. "He thrived on feeling sorry for himself," recalls a friend, "and making others feel sorry for him." At various times Smitty told inmates that he had leukemia and didn't have long to live. He claimed that he was adopted, that his real name was Angel Rodriguez, that his father was a "bean" (local slang for Mexican, an inferior race in Smitty's view), and that his mother was a famous lawyer who would have nothing to do with him.

What made Smitty a hero to Tucson's youth?   10

Isn't Tucson—out there in the Golden West, in the grand setting where the skies are not cloudy all day—supposed to be a flowering of the American Dream? One envisions teen-agers who drink milk, wear crewcuts, go to bed at half past 9, say "Sir" and "Ma'am," and like to go fishing with Dad. Part of Tucson is like this—but the city is not yet Utopia. It is glass and chrome and well-weathered stucco; it is also gimcrack, ersatz, and urban sprawl at its worst. Its suburbs stretch for mile after mile—a level sea of bungalows, broken only by mammoth shopping centers, that ultimately peters out among the cholla and saguaro. The city has grown from 85,000 to 300,000 since World War II. Few who live there were born there, and a lot are just passing through. Its superb climate attracts the old and the infirm, many of whom, as one citizen put it, "have come here to retire from their responsibilities to life." Jobs are hard to find and there is little industry to stabilize employment. ("What do people do in Tucson?" the visitor asks. Answer: "They do each other's laundry.")

As for the youngsters, they must compete with the army of semi-retired who are willing to take on part-time work for the minimum wage. Schools are beautiful but overcrowded; and at those with split sessions, the kids are on the loose from noon on, or from 6 p.m. till noon the next day. When they get into trouble, Tucson teenagers are capable of getting into trouble in style: a couple of years ago they shocked the city fathers by throwing a series of beer-drinking parties in the desert, attended by scores of kids. The fests were called "boon-dockers" and if they were no more sinful than any other kid's drinking parties, they were at least on a magnificent scale. One statistic seems relevant: 50 runaways are reported to the Tucson police department each month.

Of an evening kids with nothing to do wind up on Speedway, looking for action. There is the teen-age nightclub ("Pickup Palace," the kids call it). There are the rock'n'roll beer joints (the owners check ages meticulously, but young girls can enter if they don't drink; besides, anyone can buy a phony I.D. card for $2.50 around the high schools) where they can Jerk, Swim, and Frug away the evening to the room-shaking electronic blare of *Hang on Sloopy*, *The Pied Piper*, and a number called *The Bo Diddley Rock*. At the drive-in hamburger and pizza stands their cars circle endlessly, mufflers rumbling, as they check each other over.

Here on Speedway you find Ritchie and Ronny, out of work and bored and with nothing to do. Here you find Debby and Jabron, from the wrong side of the tracks, aimlessly cruising in their battered old car looking for something — anything — to relieve the tedium of their lives, looking for somebody neat. ("Well if the boys look bitchin' you pull up next to them in your car and you roll down the window and say 'Hey, how about a dollar for gas?' and if they give you the dollar then maybe you let them take you to Johnie's for a coke.") Here you find Gretchen, pretty and rich and with problems, bad problems. Of a Saturday night, all of them cruising the long, bright street that seems endlessly in motion with the young. Smitty's people.

He had a nice car. He had plenty of money from his parents, who ran a nursing home, and he was always glad to spend it on anyone who'd listen to him. He had a pad of his own where he threw parties and he had impeccable manners. He was always willing to help a friend and he would send flowers to girls who were ill. He was older and more mature than most of his friends. He knew where the action was, and if he wore make-up — well, at least he was *different*. 15

Some of the older kids — those who worked, who had something else to do — thought Smitty was a creep. But to the youngsters — to the bored and the lonely, to the dropout and the delinquent, to the young girls with beehive hairdos and tight pants they didn't quite fill out, and to the boys with acne and no jobs — to these people, Smitty was a kind of folk hero. Nutty maybe, but at least more dramatic, more theatrical, more *interesting* than anyone else in their lives: a semi-ludicrous, sexy-eyed pied piper who, stumbling along in his rag-stuffed boots, led them up and down Speedway.

On the evening of May 31, 1964, Alleen Rowe prepared to go to bed early. She had to be in class by 6 a.m., and she had an examination the next day. Alleen was a pretty girl of 15, a better-than-average student who talked about going to college and becoming an oceanographer. She was also a sensitive child — given to reading romantic novels and taking long walks in the desert at night. Recently she had been going through a period of adolescent melancholia, often talking with her mother, a nurse, about death. She would, she hoped, be some day reincarnated as a cat.

On this evening, dressed in a black bathing suit and thongs, her usual costume around the house, she had watched the Beatles on TV and had tried to
teach her mother to dance the Frug. Then she took her bath, washed her hair,
and came out to kiss her mother good night. Norma Rowe, an attractive, womanly divorcee, was somehow moved by the girl's clean fragrance and said, "You
smell so good—are you wearing perfume?"

"No, Mom," the girl answered, laughing, "it's just me."

A little later Mrs. Rowe looked in on her daughter, found her apparently   20
sleeping peacefully, and then left for her job as a night nurse in a Tucson hospital. She had no premonition of danger, but she had lately been concerned
about Alleen's friendship with a neighbor girl named Mary French.

Mary and Alleen had been spending a good deal of time together, smoking
and giggling and talking girl talk in the Rowe backyard. Norma Rowe did not
approve. She particularly did not approve of Mary French's friends, a tall, gan-
gling boy of 19 named John Saunders and another named Charles Schmid.
She had seen Smitty racing up and down the street in his car and once, when
he came to call on Alleen and found her not at home, he had looked at Norma
so menacingly with his "pinpoint eyes" that she had been frightened.

Her daughter, on the other hand, seemed to have mixed feelings about
Smitty. "He's creepy," she once told her mother, "he just makes me crawl. But
he can be nice when he wants to."

At any rate, later that night—according to Mary French's sworn testi-
mony—three friends arrived at Alleen Rowe's house: Smitty, Mary French and
Saunders. Smitty had frequently talked with Mary French about killing the
Rowe girl by hitting her over the head with a rock. Mary French tapped on
Alleen's window and asked her to come out and drink beer with them. Wearing
a shift over her bathing suit, she came willingly enough.

Schmid's accomplices were strange and pitiable creatures. Each of them
was afraid of Smitty, yet each was drawn to him. As a baby, John Saunders had
been so afflicted with allergies that scabs encrusted his entire body. To keep him
from scratching himself his parents had tied his hands and feet to the crib each
night, and when eventually he was cured he was so conditioned that he could
not go to sleep without being bound hand and foot.

Later, a scrawny boy with poor eyesight ("Just a skinny little body with a   25
big head on it"), he was taunted and bullied by larger children; in turn he bullied those who were smaller. He also suffered badly from asthma and he had few
friends. In high school he was a poor student and constantly in minor trouble.

Mary French, 19, was—to put it straight—a frump. Her face, which
might have been pretty, seemed somehow lumpy, her body shapeless. She was
not dull but she was always a poor student, and she finally had simply stopped
going to high school. She was, a friend remembers, "fantastically in love with
Smitty. She just sat home and waited while he went out with other girls."

Now, with Smitty at the wheel, the four teen-agers headed for the desert,
which begins out Golf Links Road. It is spooky country, dry and empty, the yellow sand clotted with cholla and mesquite and stunted, strangely green palo
verde trees, and the great humanoid saguaro that hulk against the sky. Out

there at night you can hear the yip and ki-yi of coyotes, the piercing screams of wild creatures—cats, perhaps.

According to Mary French, they got out of the car and walked down into a wash, where they sat on the sand and talked for a while, the four of them. Schmid and Mary then started back to the car. Before they got there, they heard a cry and Schmid turned back toward the wash. Mary went on to the car and sat in it alone. After 45 minutes, Saunders appeared and said Smitty wanted her to come back down. She refused, and Saunders went away. Five or 10 minutes later, Smitty showed up. "He got into the car," says Mary, "and he said 'We killed her. I love you very much.' He kissed me. He was breathing real hard and seemed excited." Then Schmid got a shovel from the trunk of the car and they returned to the wash. "She was lying on her back and there was blood on her face and head," Mary French testified. Then the three of them dug a shallow grave and put the body in it and covered it up. Afterwards, they wiped Schmid's car clean of Alleen's fingerprints.

More than a year passed. Norma Rowe had reported her daughter missing and the police searched for her—after a fashion. At Mrs. Rowe's insistence they picked up Schmid, but they had no reason to hold him. The police, in fact, assumed that Alleen was just one more of Tucson's runaways.

Norma Rowe, however, had become convinced that Alleen had been killed 30 by Schmid, although she left her kitchen light on every night just in case Alleen did come home. She badgered the police and she badgered the sheriff until the authorities began to dismiss her as a crank. She began to imagine a high-level conspiracy against her. She wrote the state attorney general, the FBI, the U.S. Department of Health, Education and Welfare. She even contacted a New Jersey mystic, who said she could see Alleen's body out in the desert under a big tree.

Ultimately Norma Rowe started her own investigation, questioning Alleen's friends, poking around, dictating her findings to a tape recorder; she even tailed Smitty at night, following him in her car, scared stiff that he might spot her.

Schmid, during this time, acquired a little house of his own. There he held frequent parties, where people sat around amid his stacks of *Playboy* magazines, playing Elvis Presley records and drinking beer.

He read Jules Feiffer's novel, *Harry, the Rat with Women*, and said that his ambition was to be like Harry and have a girl commit suicide over him. Once, according to a friend, he went to see a minister, who gave him a Bible and told him to read the first three chapters of John. Instead Schmid tore the pages out and burned them in the street. "Religion is a farce," he announced. He started an upholstery business with some friends, called himself "founder and president," but then failed to put up the money he'd promised and the venture was short-lived.

He decided he liked blondes best, and took to dyeing the hair of various teen-age girls he went around with. He went out and bought two imitation diamond rings for about $13 apiece and then engaged himself, on the same day, both to Mary French and to a 15-year-old girl named Kathy Morath. His plan, he confided to a friend, was to put each of the girls to work and have them deposit their salaries in a bank account held jointly with him. Mary French did indeed go to work in the convalescent home Smitty's parents operated. When their bank account was fat enough, Smitty withdrew the money and bought a tape recorder.

By this time Smitty also had a girl from a higher social stratum than he usually was involved with. She was Gretchen Fritz, daughter of a prominent Tucson heart surgeon. Gretchen was a pretty, thin, nervous girl of 17 with a knack for trouble. A teacher described her as "erratic, subversive, a psychopathic liar." 35

At the horsy private school she attended for a time she was a misfit. She not only didn't care about horses, but she shocked her classmates by telling them they were foolish for going out with boys without getting paid for it. Once she even committed the unpardonable social sin of turning up at a formal dance accompanied by boys wearing what was described as beatnik dress. She cut classes, she was suspected of stealing and when, in the summer before her senior year, she got into trouble with juvenile authorities for her role in an attempted theft at a liquor store, the headmaster suggested she not return and then recommended she get psychiatric treatment.

Charles Schmid saw Gretchen for the first time at a public swimming pool in the summer of 1964. He met her by the simple expedient of following her home, knocking on the door and, when she answered, saying, "Don't I know you?" They talked for an hour. Thus began a fierce and stormy relationship. A good deal of what authorities know of the development of this relationship comes from the statements of a spindly scarecrow of a young man who wears pipestem trousers and Beatle boots: Richard Bruns. At the time Smitty was becoming involved with Gretchen, Bruns was 18 years old. He had served two terms in the reformatory at Fort Grant. He had been in and out of trouble his whole life, had never fit in anywhere. Yet, although he never went beyond the tenth grade in school and his credibility on many counts is suspect, he is clearly intelligent and even sensitive. He was, for a time, Smitty's closest friend and confidant, and he is today one of the mainstays of the state's case against Smitty. His story:

"He and Gretchen were always fighting," says Bruns. "She didn't want him to drink or go out with the guys or go out with other girls. She wanted him to stay home, call her on the phone, be punctual. First she would get suspicious of him, then he'd get suspicious of her. They were made for each other."

Their mutual jealousy led to sharp and continual arguments. Once she infuriated him by throwing a bottle of shoe polish on his car. Another time she was driving past Smitty's house and saw him there with some other girls. She jumped out of her car and began screaming. Smitty took off into the house, out the back, and climbed a tree in his backyard.

His feelings for her were an odd mixture of hate and adoration. He said he was madly in love with her, but he called her a whore. She would let Smitty in her bedroom window at night. Yet he wrote an anonymous letter to the Tucson Health Department accusing her of having venereal disease and spreading it 40 about town. But Smitty also went to enormous lengths to impress Gretchen, once shooting holes through the windows of his car and telling her that thugs, from whom he was protecting her, had fired at him. So Bruns described the relationship.

On the evening of Aug. 16, 1965, Gretchen Fritz left the house with her little sister Wendy, a friendly, lively 13-year-old, to go to a drive-in movie. Neither girl ever came home again. Gretchen's father, like Alleen Rowe's mother, felt sure that Charles Schmid had something to do with his daughters' disappearance, and eventually he hired Bill Heilig, a private detective, to handle the case. One of Heilig's men soon found Gretchen's red compact car parked behind a motel, but the police continued to assume that the girls had joined the ranks of Tucson's runaways.

About a week after Gretchen disappeared, Bruns was at Smitty's house. "We were sitting in the living room," Bruns recalls. "He was sitting on the sofa and I was in the chair by the window and we got on the subject of Gretchen. He said, 'You know I killed her?' I said I didn't, and he said 'You know where?' I said no. He said, 'I did it here in the living room. First I killed Gretchen, then Wendy was still going "*huh, huh, huh*," so I . . . [Here Bruns showed how Smitty made a garroting gesture.] Then I took the bodies and I put them in the trunk of the car. I put the bodies in the most obvious place I could think of because I just didn't care anymore. Then I ditched the car and wiped it clean.'"

Bruns was not particularly upset by Smitty's story. Months before, Smitty had told him of the murder of Alleen Rowe, and nothing had come of that. So he was not certain Smitty was telling the truth about the Fritz girls. Besides, Bruns detested Gretchen himself. But what happened next, still according to Bruns's story, did shake him up.

One night not long after, a couple of tough-looking characters, wearing sharp suits and smoking cigars, came by with Smitty and picked up Bruns. Smitty said they were Mafia, and that someone had hired them to look for Gretchen. Smitty and Bruns were taken to an apartment where several men were present whom Smitty later claimed to have recognized as local Cosa Nostra figures.

They wanted to know what had happened to the girls. They made no   45
threats, but the message, Bruns remembers, came across loud and clear. These were no street-corner punks: these were the real boys. In spite of the intimidating company, Schmid lost none of his insouciance. He said he didn't know where Gretchen was, but if she turned up hurt he wanted these men to help him get whoever was responsible. He added that she might have gone to California.

By the time Smitty and Bruns got back to Smitty's house, they were both a little shaky. Later that night, says Bruns, Smitty did the most unlikely thing imaginable: he called the FBI. First he tried the Tucson office and couldn't raise anyone. Then he called Phoenix and couldn't get an agent there either. Finally he put in a person-to-person call to J. Edgar Hoover in Washington. He didn't get Hoover, of course, but he got someone and told him that the Mafia was harassing him over the disappearance of a girl. The FBI promised to have someone in touch with him soon.

Bruns was scared and said so. It occurred to him now that if Smitty really had killed the Fritz girls and left their bodies in an obvious place, they were in very bad trouble indeed—with the Mafia on one hand and the FBI on the other. "Let's go bury them," Bruns said.

"Smitty stole the keys to his old man's station wagon," says Bruns, "and then we got a flat shovel—the only one we could find. We went to Johnie's and got a hamburger, and then we drove out to the old drinking spot [in the desert]—that's what Smitty meant when he said the most obvious place. It's where we used to drink beer and make out with girls.

"So we parked the car and got the shovel and walked down there, and we couldn't find anything. Then Smitty said, 'Wait, I smell something.' We went in opposite directions looking, and then I heard Smitty say, 'Come here.' I found him kneeling over Gretchen. There was a white rag tied around her legs. Her blouse was pulled up and she was wearing a white bra and Capris.

"Then he said, 'Wendy's up this way.' I sat there for a minute. Then I followed Smitty to where Wendy was. He'd had the decency to cover her—except for one leg, which was sticking up out of the ground.   50

"We tried to dig with the flat shovel. We each took turns. He'd dig for a while and then I'd dig for a while, but the ground was hard and we couldn't get anywhere with that flat shovel. We dug for twenty minutes and finally Smitty said we'd better do something because it's going to get light. So he grabbed the rag that was around Gretchen's legs and dragged her down in the wash. It made a noise like dragging a hollow shell. It stunk like hell. Then Smitty said wipe off her shoes, there might be fingerprints, so I wiped them off with my handkerchief and threw it away.

"We went back to Wendy. Her leg was sticking up with a shoe on it. He said take off her tennis shoe and throw it over there. I did, I threw it. Then he said, 'Now you're in this as deep as I am.'" By then, the sisters had been missing for about two weeks.

Early next morning Smitty did see the FBI. Nevertheless—here Bruns's story grows even wilder—that same day Smitty left for California, accompanied by a couple of Mafia types, to look for Gretchen Fritz. While there, he was picked up by the San Diego police on a complaint the he was impersonating an FBI officer. He was detained briefly, released and returned to Tucson.

But now, it seemed to Richard Bruns, Smitty began acting very strangely. He startled Bruns by saying, "I've killed—not three times, but four. Now it's your turn, Ritchie." He went berserk in his little house, smashing his fist through a wall, slamming doors, then rushing out into the backyard in nothing but his undershorts, where he ran through the night screaming, "God is going to punish me!" He also decided, suddenly, to get married—to a 15-year-old girl who was a stranger to most of his friends.

If Smitty seemed to Bruns to be losing his grip, Ritchie Bruns himself was not   55
in much better shape. His particular quirk revolved around Kathy Morath, the thin, pretty, 16-year-old daughter of a Tucson postman. Kathy had once been attracted to Smitty. He had given her one of his two cut-glass engagement rings. But Smitty never really took her seriously, and one day, in a fit of pique

and jealousy, she threw the ring back in his face. Ritchie Bruns comforted her and then started dating her himself. He was soon utterly and irrevocably smitten with goofy adoration.

Kathy accepted Bruns as a suitor, but halfheartedly. She thought him weird (oddly enough, she did not think Smitty in the least weird) and their romance was short-lived. After she broke up with him last July, Bruns went into a blue funk, a nosedive into romantic melancholy, and then, like some love-swacked Elizabethan poet, he started pouring out his heart to her on paper. He sent her poems, short stories, letters 24 pages long. ("My God, you should have read the stuff," says her perplexed father. "His letters were so romantic it was like 'Next week, East Lynne.'") Bruns even began writing a novel dedicated to "My Darling Kathy."

If Bruns had confined himself to literary catharsis, the murders of the Rowe and Fritz girls might never have been disclosed. But Ritchie went a little bit around the bend. He became obsessed with the notion that Kathy Morath was the next victim on Smitty's list. Someone had cut the Moraths' screen door, there had been a prowler around her house, and Bruns was sure that it was Smitty. (Kathy and her father, meantime, were sure it was Bruns.)

"I started having this dream," Bruns says. "It was the same dream every night. Smitty would have Kathy out in the desert and he'd be doing all those things to her, and strangling her, and I'd be running across the desert with a gun in my hand, but I could never get there."

If Bruns couldn't save Kathy in his dreams, he could, he figured, stop a walking, breathing Smitty. His scheme for doing so was so wild and so simple that it put the whole Morath family into a state of panic and very nearly landed Bruns in jail.

Bruns undertook to stand guard over Kathy Morath. He kept watch in front of her house, in the alley, and in the street. He patrolled the sidewalk from early in the morning till late at night, seven days a week. If Kathy was home he would be there. If she went out, he would follow her. Kathy's father called the police, and when they told Bruns he couldn't loiter around like that, Bruns fetched his dog and walked the animal up and down the block, hour after hour.   60

Bruns by now was wallowing in feelings of sacrifice and nobility—all of it unappreciated by Kathy Morath and her parents. At the end of October, he was finally arrested for harassing the Morath family. The judge, facing the obviously woebegone and smitten young man, told Bruns that he wouldn't be jailed if he'd agree to get out of town until he got over his infatuation.

Bruns agreed and a few days later went to Ohio to stay with his grandmother and try to get a job. It was hopeless. He couldn't sleep at night, and if he did doze off he had his old nightmare again.

One night he blurted out the whole story to his grandmother in their kitchen. She thought he had had too many beers and didn't believe him. "I hear beer does strange things to a person," she said comfortingly. At her words Bruns exploded, knocked over a chair and shouted, "The one time in my life when I need advice and what do I get?" A few minutes later he was on the phone to the Tucson police.

Things happened swiftly. At Bruns's frantic insistence, the police picked up Kathy Morath and put her in protective custody. They went into the desert and discovered—precisely as Bruns had described them—the grisly, skeletal remains of Gretchen and Wendy Fritz. They started the machinery that resulted in the arrest a week later of John Saunders and Mary French. They found Charles Schmid working in the yard of his little house, his face layered with make-up, his nose covered by a patch of adhesive plaster which he had worn for five months, boasting that his nose was broken in a fight, and his boots packed full of old rags and tin cans. He put up no resistance.

John Saunders and Mary French confessed immediately to their roles in the slaying of Alleen Rowe and were quickly sentenced, Mary French to four to five years, Saunders to life. When Smitty goes on trial for this crime, on March 15, they will be principal witnesses against him.   65

Meanwhile Ritchie Bruns, the perpetual misfit, waits apprehensively for the end of the Fritz trial, desperately afraid that Schmid will go free. "If he does," Bruns says glumly, "I'll be the first one he'll kill."

As for Charles Schmid, he has adjusted well to his period of waiting. He is polite and agreeable with all, though at the preliminary hearings he glared menacingly at Ritchie Bruns. Dressed tastefully, tie neatly knotted, hair carefully combed, his face scrubbed clean of make-up, he is a short, compact, darkly handsome young man with a wide, engaging smile and those deepset eyes.

The people of Tucson wait uneasily for what fresh scandal the two trials may develop. Civic leaders publicly cry that a slur has been cast on their community by an isolated crime. High school students have held rallies and written vehement editorials in the school papers, protesting that they all are being judged by the actions of a few oddballs and misfits. But the city reverberates with stories of organized teen-age crime and vice, in which Smitty is cast in the role of a minor-league underworld boss. None of these later stories has been substantiated.

One disclosure, however, has most disturbing implications: Smitty's boasts may have been heard not just by Bruns and his other intimates, but by other teen-agers as well. How many—and precisely how much they knew—it remains impossible to say. One authoritative source, however, having listened to the admissions of six high school students, says they unquestionably knew enough so that they should have gone to the police—but were either afraid to talk, or didn't want to rock the boat.

As for Smitty's friends, the thought of telling the police never entered their minds.   70

"I didn't know he killed her," said one, "and even if I had, I wouldn't have said anything. I wouldn't want to be a fink."

Out in the respectable Tucson suburbs parents have started to crack down on the youngsters and have declared Speedway hangouts off limits. "I thought my folks were bad before," laments one grounded 16-year-old, "but now they're just impossible."

As for the others—Smitty's people—most don't care very much. Things are duller without Smitty around, but things have always been dull.

"There's nothing to do in this town," says one of his girls, shaking her dyed blond hair. "The only other town I know is Las Vegas and there's nothing to do there either." For her, and for her friends, there's nothing to do in any town.

They are down on Speedway again tonight, cruising, orbiting the drive- 75
ins, stopping by the joints, where the words of *The Bo Diddley Rock* cut through the smoke and the electronic dissonance like some macabre reminder of their fallen hero:

> All you women stand in line,
> And I'll love you all in an hour's time. . . .
> I got a cobra snake for a necktie,
> I got a brand-new house on the roadside
> Covered with rattlesnake hide,
> I got a brand-new chimney made on top,
> Made out of human skulls.
> Come on baby, take a walk with me,
> And tell me, who do you love?
> Who do you love?
> Who do you love?
> Who do you love?   *[1966]*

≡ THINKING ABOUT THE TEXT

1. As his title implies, Moser analyzes Tucson at least as much as he analyzes Charles Schmid. What main points does he make about the city, especially about its youth? To what extent is setting similarly important in Oates's story?

2. Moser himself gave the name "the pied piper" to Charles Schmid. Why does Moser call Schmid this? How helpful is it to think of Arnold Friend as a "pied piper," too? (You may wish to look up details of the classic tale "The Pied Piper of Hamelin.")

3. After Moser's article was published, Charles Schmid pled guilty to second-degree murder of Alleen Rowe. For murdering the Fritz sisters, he received the death penalty, but he was spared execution when the state of Arizona abandoned capital punishment in 1971. Schmid remained in prison, where in 1975 he was stabbed to death by two other inmates. Does Oates's story leave you with the impression that Arnold Friend will meet a similar fate? Why, or why not?

JOYCE CAROL OATES
Smooth Talk: Short Story into Film

Joyce Carol Oates published the following article in the March 23, 1986, issue of the New York Times. She wrote it upon the release of Smooth Talk, *a film adaptation of "Where Are You Going, Where Have You Been?"*

Some years ago in the American Southwest there surfaced a tabloid psychopath known as "The Pied Piper of Tucson." I have forgotten his name, but his specialty was the seduction and occasional murder of teen-aged girls. He may or may not have had actual accomplices, but his bizarre activities were known among a circle of teenagers in the Tucson area; for some reason they kept his secret, deliberately did not inform parents or police. It was this fact, not the fact of the mass murderer himself, that struck me at the time. And this was a pre-Manson time, early or mid-1960s.

The Pied Piper mimicked teenagers in talk, dress, and behavior, but he was not a teenager—he was a man in his early thirties. Rather short, he stuffed rags in his leather boots to give himself height. (And sometimes walked unsteadily as a consequence: did none among his admiring constituency notice?) He charmed his victims as charismatic psychopaths have always charmed their victims, to the bewilderment of others who fancy themselves free of all lunatic attractions. The Pied Piper of Tucson: a trashy dream, a tabloid archetype, sheer artifice, comedy, cartoon—surrounded, however improbably, and finally tragically, by real people. You think that, if you look twice, he won't be there. But there he is.

I don't remember any longer where I first read about this Pied Piper—very likely in *Life* Magazine. I do recall deliberately not reading the full article because I didn't want to be distracted by too much detail. It was not after all the mass murderer himself who intrigued me, but the disturbing fact that a number of teenagers—from "good" families—aided and abetted his crimes. This is the sort of thing authorities and responsible citizens invariably call "inexplicable" because they can't find explanations for it. They would not have fallen under this maniac's spell, after all.

An early draft of my short story "Where Are You Going, Where Have You Been?"—from which the film *Smooth Talk* was adapted by Joyce Chopra and Tom Cole—had the rather too explicit title "Death and the Maiden." It was cast in a mode of fiction to which I am still partial—indeed, every third or fourth story of mine is probably in this mode—"realistic allegory," it might be called. It is Hawthornean, romantic, shading into parable. Like the medieval German engraving from which my title was taken, the story was minutely detailed yet clearly an allegory of the fatal attractions of death (or the devil). An innocent young girl is seduced by way of her own vanity; she mistakes death for erotic romance of a particularly American/trashy sort.

In subsequent drafts the story changed its tone, its focus, its language, its   5
title. It became "Where Are You Going, Where Have You Been?" Written at a time when the author was intrigued by the music of Bob Dylan, particularly the hauntingly elegiac song "It's All Over Now, Baby Blue," it was dedicated to Bob Dylan. The charismatic mass murderer drops into the background and his innocent victim, a fifteen-year-old, moves into the foreground. She becomes the true protagonist of the tale, courting and being courted by her fate, a self-styled 1950s pop figure, alternately absurd and winning. There is no suggestion in the published story that "Arnold Friend" has seduced and murdered other young girls, or even that he necessarily intends to murder Connie. Is his inter-

est "merely" sexual? (Nor is there anything about the complicity of other teen-agers. I saved that yet more provocative note for a current story, "Testimony.") Connie is shallow, vain, silly, hopeful, doomed—but capable nonetheless of an unexpected gesture of heroism at the story's end. Her smooth-talking seducer, who cannot lie, promises her that her family will be unharmed if she gives her-self to him; and so she does. The story ends abruptly at the point of her "cross-ing over." We don't know the nature of her sacrifice, only that she is generous enough to make it.

In adapting a narrative so spare and thematically foreshortened as "Where Are You Going, Where Have You Been?" film director Joyce Chopra and screen-writer Tom Cole were required to do a good deal of filling in, expanding, invent-ing. Connie's story becomes lavishly, and lovingly, textured; she is not an allegorical figure so much as a "typical" teenaged girl (if Laura Dern, spectacu-larly good-looking, can be so defined). Joyce Chopra, who has done documen-tary films on contemporary teenage culture and, yet more authoritatively, has an adolescent daughter of her own, creates in *Smooth Talk* a vivid and abso-lutely believable world for Connie to inhabit. Or worlds: as in the original story there is Connie-at-home, and there is Connie-with-her-friends. Two fifteen-year-old girls, two finely honed styles, two voices, sometimes but not often over-lapping. It is one of the marvelous visual features of the film that we *see* Connie and her friends transform themselves, once they are safely free of parental ob-servation. The girls claim their true identities in the neighborhood shopping mall. What freedom, what joy!

Smooth Talk is, in a way, as much Connie's mother's story as it is Connie's; its center of gravity, its emotional nexus, is frequently with the mother—warmly and convincingly played by Mary Kay Place. (Though the mother's sexual jealousy of her daughter is slighted in the film.) Connie's ambiguous relationship with her affable, somewhat mysterious father (well played by Levon Helm) is an excellent touch: I had thought, subsequent to the story's publication, that I should have built up the father, suggesting, as subtly as I could, an attraction there paralleling the attraction Connie feels for her se-ducer, Arnold Friend. And Arnold Friend himself — "A. Friend" as he says—is played with appropriately overdone sexual swagger by Treat Williams, who is perfect for the part; and just the right age. We see that Arnold Friend isn't a teenager even as Connie, mesmerized by his presumed charm, does not seem to see him at all. What is so difficult to accomplish in prose—nudging the reader to look over the protagonist's shoulder, so to speak—is accomplished with en-viable ease in film.

Treat Williams as Arnold Friend is supreme in his very awfulness, as, surely, the original Pied Piper of Tucson must have been. (Though no one in-volved in the film knew about the original source.) Mr. Williams flawlessly im-personates Arnold Friend as Arnold Friend impersonates—is it James Dean? James Dean regarding himself in mirrors, doing James Dean impersonations? That Connie's fate is so trashy is in fact her fate.

What is outstanding in Joyce Chopra's *Smooth Talk* is its visual freshness, its sense of motion and life; the attentive intelligence the director has brought to the semi-secret world of the American adolescent—shopping mall flirtations, drive-in restaurant romances, highway hitchhiking, the fascination of rock music played very, very loud. (James Taylor's music for the film is wonderfully appropriate. We hear it as Connie hears it; it is the music of her spiritual being.) Also outstanding, as I have indicated, and numerous critics have noted, are the acting performances. Laura Dern is so dazzlingly right as "my" Connie that I may come to think I modeled the fictitious girl on her, in the way that writers frequently delude themselves about notions of causality.

My difficulties with *Smooth Talk* have primarily to do with my chronic hes-   10
itation—about seeing/hearing work of mine abstracted from its contexture of language. All writers know that Language is their subject; quirky word choices, patterns of rhythm, enigmatic pauses, punctuation marks. Where the quick scanner sees "quick" writing, the writer conceals nine tenths of the iceberg. Of course we all have "real" subjects, and we will fight to the death to defend those subjects, but beneath the tale-telling it is the tale-telling that grips us so very fiercely. The writer works in a single dimension, the director works in three. I assume they are professionals to their fingertips; authorities in their medium as I am an authority (if I am) in mine. I would fiercely defend the placement of a semicolon in one of my novels but I would probably have deferred in the end to Joyce Chopra's decision to reverse the story's conclusion, turn it upside down, in a sense, so that the film ends not with death, not with a sleepwalker's crossing over to her fate, but upon a scene of reconciliation, rejuvenation.

A girl's loss of virginity, bittersweet but not necessarily tragic. Not today. A girl's coming-of-age that involves her succumbing to, but then rejecting, the "trashy dreams" of her pop teenage culture. "Where Are You Going, Where Have You Been?" defines itself as allegorical in its conclusion: Death and Death's chariot (a funky souped-up convertible) have come for the Maiden. Awakening is, in the story's final lines, moving out into the sunlight where Arnold Friend waits:

> "My sweet little blue-eyed girl," he said in a half-sung sigh that had nothing to do with [Connie's] brown eyes but was taken up just the same by the vast sunlit reaches of the land behind him and on all sides of him—so much land that Connie had never seen before and did not recognize except to know that she was going to it.

—a conclusion impossible to transfigure into film.   *[1986]*

≡ **THINKING ABOUT THE TEXT**

1. In discussing Moser's article and Joyce Chopra's film, Oates specifies various elements that she put into "Where Are You Going, Where Have You Been?" How accurate do you find her description of her story? What aspects of her text, if any, do you think she distorts or ignores?

2. At the end of the film *Smooth Talk*, Connie is alive. She returns home from her outing with Arnold Friend, and she dances with her sister to James Taylor's song "Handy Man." What does Oates seem to think of this ending? Do you object to it? Why, or why not?

3. To what extent should readers of a short story be guided by the author's explanation of it? Explain your reasoning, and refer to Oates's story as well as her article about it.

MARGARET TALBOT

From *Gone Girl: The Extraordinary Resilience of Elizabeth Smart*

Elizabeth Smart was fourteen years old when she was abducted from her Salt Lake City home on June 4, 2002. The kidnappers were a pair of religious cultists, Brian David Mitchell and his wife, Wanda Barzee. Smart remained their captive for almost a year, when she was finally rescued by police. In 2013, she published a book about her experience, My Story. *In her memoir, Smart discusses her enduring Mormon faith. She also responds to people who wonder why she didn't flee or reveal her identity when she went out with Mitchell and Barzee in public. The same topics come up in Margaret Talbot's October 21, 2013,* New Yorker *magazine article about Smart, based partly on an interview with her. As you read the following text, excerpted from Talbot's piece, think about the extent to which Smart differs from and resembles Oates's character Connie.*

One day at the downtown library, Mitchell, Barzee, and Smart were sitting at an out-of-the-way table on the second floor when a man came over and introduced himself as a homicide detective. Smart was "dizzy with hope and anticipation and gut-wrenching fear." Under the table, Barzee's hand clamped down on her leg. The fear won out. The detective asked them to remove Smart's veil, noting that the police had received phone calls from people who were concerned that she might be a kidnapping victim. Mitchell calmly insisted that Smart was his daughter, and that his religion forbade him to reveal her face to a strange man. Smart couldn't bring herself to speak. "Officer," Mitchell said, "if she were the person you were looking for, why would she just sit there?" The detective left.

Mitchell gloated as they left the library. Smart writes, "It was maybe the lowest I had ever felt." It's clear from Smart's memoir, and from those of other former captives, that incidents like this—in which an outsider asks questions but accepts dubious answers—are resoundingly significant. They confirm the captor's sense of invincibility and the captive's sense of invisibility.

In her book, Smart distinguishes such moments of terrified passivity from Stockholm syndrome—the idea that hostages sometimes become emotionally attached to their abductors. The term was coined, in 1973, by a Swedish criminologist who was trying to explain the behavior of four bank employees taken hostage in a robbery. During their six days in the bank, they had talked with the robbers, who had not harmed them. One hostage reported being more afraid of what police officers might do when they broke in. Since then, Stockholm syndrome has entered the parlance of pop psychology. No doubt, many hostages coöperate with their captors, or attempt to see their humanity. Some captives must sometimes feel a confusing rush of gratitude when they expect to be killed but aren't, or yearn, in the midst of unimaginable isolation, to talk to somebody—even their kidnappers. (Jaycee Dugard, in her memoir, acknowledges sometimes needing the companionship of the man who imprisoned her—especially before she had her daughters.) There is very little published academic research on Stockholm syndrome, and it has never been included in the *DSM*.

Smart argues that you don't need to have affection for a captor in order to be compliant—fear is enough. Throughout her captivity, she was afraid for her life and for her family; Mitchell frequently threatened to kill her, or them, if she screamed or ran away. As Smart knew, Mitchell didn't make idle threats: he told her that he once threw his own mother down a flight of stairs, prompting her to file a restraining order; while he was holding Smart captive, he tried, unsuccessfully, to kidnap a young cousin of hers. "My Story" goes a long way toward explaining how Mitchell's intimidation left Smart feeling hollowed out and paralyzed. "I am the living dead," she writes. "I am nothing but a shell."

David Finkelhor, a sociologist who directs the Crimes Against Children Research Center, at the University of New Hampshire, told me that he found Smart's critique of Stockholm syndrome persuasive: "She's right—fear and intimidation explain a lot more." Natascha Kampusch, in "3,096 Days in Captivity," writes that the Stockholm-syndrome diagnosis "turns victims into victims a second time, by taking from them the power to interpret their own story—and by turning the most significant experiences from their story into the product of a syndrome. The term places the very behavior that contributes significantly to the victim's survival that much closer to being objectionable. Getting closer to the kidnapper is not an illness. Creating a cocoon of normality within the framework of a crime is not a syndrome."

. . . On the cover of her memoir, Smart, in a peach-colored sweater, is bathed in a gauzy light, her hair shining, and in person she didn't look much different. In Park City and on the other occasions that we met, she wore crisp business-casual clothes that had girlish splashes of color or pattern. It was as though she had resolved never to look grubby again. Indeed, part of what audiences seemed to like about her was that she never did. It wasn't quite fair, but Smart's Breck-girl beauty had been part of what fascinated people about her kidnapping, and now that beauty seemed to confirm her triumph as a survivor.

We talked about the radKIDS self-defense classes, which are open to children in preschool through sixth grade. Smart cited a study, conducted by the National Center for Missing and Exploited Children, that looked at seven thousand failed abductions of children—mostly girls between the ages of ten and fourteen. Eighty-one percent of the time, the attempt was foiled by kids running away, yelling, or kicking. David Finkelhor, the sociologist, emphasized that some incidents that are classified as attempted abduction do not involve force. Still, he said, "Most people in the field would agree that, when kids say no and resist, it's usually successful."

Smart told me that she wishes that she'd been trained to put up a fuss if someone tried to make her do something against her will. When I asked her if she thought that would have made a difference the night that Mitchell broke into her house, she said, "Yes, but I'll never know. Because I never had that training." She went through the radKIDS program herself shortly after returning home, and said that she felt safer, and more powerful, as a result. She had a story that was "maybe a little silly," but made her point. As a college freshman, she'd been walking around the B.Y.U. campus with a guy she was dating, and a friend warned her that somebody in a scary clown mask was menacing other students. "So this kid with the mask did come up to us, and he got closer and closer to me," she said. "The guy I was with wasn't doing anything. And, well, I just don't take risks anymore. So I said, 'If you come one step closer, I'm going to kick you right where it counts.' And he took one step closer. And, because of my training, I felt empowered to kick him. He left me alone after that."

In her speeches, Smart reminds audiences of the need to watch out for one another and to report abuse when we suspect it, often observing that she was saved by whoever called the police in that suburb of Salt Lake City. After a talk, several people usually come up to her to say that they, too, were abused when they were young. Often, they tell her that she's the first person they've confided in. Smart responds that she's honored by their trust, but they must tell the authorities, too, because the person who hurt them is probably hurting someone else.

Smart always tells audiences about the "best advice" she has ever received.   10
When she came home, her mother said to her, "Elizabeth, what this man has done is terrible. There aren't any words that are strong enough to describe how wicked and evil he is! He has taken nine months of your life that you will never get back again. But the best punishment you could ever give him is to be happy. To move forward with your life. To do exactly what you want."

This counsel might seem overly optimistic, even unrealistic. Smart had an unusually supportive family that did not come apart under the stress of her abduction — even after they became criminal suspects for a time, as family members often do in such cases. Someone in Salt Lake City who knows the Smarts told me, "They are a prominent Mormon family, and a very tight one. Her family and her community folded her right back in." Smart remains close to all her relatives, and on the legislative issues she has lobbied for — like the national registry for sex offenders — she often works with her father, a former real-estate agent who now owns a furniture store.

Smart's return to emotional health may also be tied to the fact that Mitchell was, basically, a stranger. Most victims of sexual crimes are harmed by family members and acquaintances, and this violation of trust can be permanently debilitating. In "My Story," Smart writes about how lucky she is that her abusers are forever out of her life: "I don't have to go home every night and see them, or see pictures of them hanging on the wall, or know that, even though my family is so upset with what they might have done to me, there is still a piece of their hearts that cares and loves the abusers because they are their children, or parents, or brothers and sisters."

In our conversations, Smart emphasized that there is no right way to recover after a trauma like hers. She did not seek therapy, finding solace instead in playing the harp and in riding horses with her grandfather, an oncologist who died in 2006. She started high school the fall after she returned home, and graduated on schedule. "My parents were really good at resuming a normal routine, not singling me out, saying, 'Oh, Elizabeth can't do this or that anymore.'" Her parents also made it clear that if she wanted any kind of counselling or medication she would get it. Smart thinks that therapy is a good option for many people, and she has offered counsel to other victims—"some high profile, some nobody's ever heard of." But she would "never presume, never go out and push myself forward, because privacy and finding your own way are so precious."

Smart's greatest appeal as a public figure is her evident desire not to judge other women. Kristine Haglund, the editor of a journal about Mormonism, told me, "The interesting thing is that she is almost universally admired. Which is a tough thing for a Mormon woman to pull off. She had this terrible experience, and one that had weird and creepy Mormon overtones. Yet she still believes. She's entirely faithful. And while she's not part of the feminist ferment in Mormonism, and I doubt she'd call herself a feminist, she is strong in a way that feminists can admire. She emerged strong and whole, a modern woman able to address questions of sexuality directly and confidently."   *[2013]*

≣ THINKING ABOUT THE TEXT

1. What would you say to someone who argues that Connie suffers from "Stockholm syndrome"?

2. To what extent does Connie seem to have the personal resources that Elizabeth Smart had at the time of her kidnapping and has subsequently developed? Refer to specific passages in Oates's story and Talbot's article.

3. If Connie escaped from Arnold Friend or survived her encounter with him, what do you think she might say in a book entitled, like Elizabeth Smart's, *My Story*? Would her self-description be quite different from or similar to Smart's? Explain your reasoning.

≣ WRITING ABOUT ISSUES

1. Write an essay in which you explain how the title of Oates's story applies to it. Consider how Connie *thinks*, not just what she does. Where, psychologically, is Connie going? Where, psychologically, has she been?

2. To what extent does present-day American culture prepare its young women for the dangers of the world? Write an essay that addresses this question by referring to Oates's story and another text in this cluster.

3. Write an essay in which you imagine what Elizabeth Smart would say about Connie. Refer to both Oates's story and Talbot's article. If you wish, write your essay as if it is Elizabeth Smart speaking at a conference of young women.

4. Research another real-life case of female captivity: for example, the kidnapping of Patty Hearst, Jaycee Dugard, or the group of women who escaped from their abductor's Cleveland house in 2013. Then, write an essay in which you develop and support a claim about the media's coverage of your chosen case. If you wish, refer to any of the texts in this cluster.

≣ Misfit Justice: Critical Commentaries on a Story

FLANNERY O'CONNOR, "A Good Man Is Hard to Find"

CRITICAL COMMENTARIES:
FLANNERY O'CONNOR, From *Mystery and Manners*

MARTHA STEPHENS, From *The Question of Flannery O'Connor*

STEPHEN BANDY, From "'One of My Babies': The Misfit
and the Grandmother"

JOHN DESMOND, From *"Flannery O'Connor's Misfit and
the Mystery of Evil"*

Most of us are social beings; we long to fit in. The communities we form sustain us, giving us our moral compasses and our psychological bearings. But sometimes people voluntarily remove themselves from all traditional communities. Indeed, literature is filled with misfits. Their decisions may intrigue us but also perplex and trouble us, perhaps because they represent antisocial impulses in all of us. Especially interesting are those literary misfits who demand that their own sense of justice be satisfied. Probably the most notable example in post-World War II American fiction is a character in Flannery O'Connor's 1953 short story "A Good Man Is Hard to Find." This man actually calls himself The Misfit, and he turns violent as he challenges Christianity's belief in Jesus' ability to raise the dead. O'Connor's story has been widely read, in part because it is subject to various interpretations. Here, in addition to the story and O'Connor's own remarks about it, we present three critical commentaries that respond to her analysis.

≣ BEFORE YOU READ

What do you think you might find in a story by a practicing Roman Catholic author? What topics, themes, characters, and events might she write about?

FLANNERY O'CONNOR
A Good Man Is Hard to Find

Flannery O'Connor (1925–1964) spent most of her life in Millidgeville, Georgia, where she raised peacocks on a farm with her mother. She died of lupus at the age of thirty-nine, when she was at the peak of her creative powers. All of her fiction reflects her Roman Catholic faith and Southern heritage, as do her nonfiction writings, which were collected after her death in Mystery and Manners *(1969). Critics have often seen in her work Christian parables of grace and redemption in the face of random violence. Like other Southern writers such as William Faulkner and Carson McCullers, she uses grotesque characters to suggest our own morally flawed humanity. O'Connor's*

AP Photo

early stories won her a scholarship to the University of Iowa, where she received an M.F.A. She went on to produce two novels, Wise Blood *(1952) and* The Violent Bear It Away *(1960), but she is known and admired mostly for her short fiction. The following story was first published in the volume* Modern Writing 1 *in 1953. O'Connor then included it in her 1955 collection entitled* A Good Man Is Hard to Find and Other Stories. *The book won her national acclaim, as did a later collection, the posthumously published* Everything That Rises Must Converge *(1965). These two volumes were combined in 1979 as* The Complete Stories of Flannery O'Connor, *which won the National Book Award for fiction.*

> The dragon is by the side of the road, watching those who pass. Beware lest he devour you. We go to the Father of Souls, but it is necessary to pass by the dragon.
>
> —St. Cyril of Jerusalem

The grandmother didn't want to go to Florida. She wanted to visit some of her connections in east Tennessee and she was seizing at every chance to change Bailey's mind. Bailey was the son she lived with, her only boy. He was sitting on the edge of his chair at the table, bent over the orange sports section of the

Journal. "Now look here, Bailey," she said, "see here, read this," and she stood with one hand on her thin hip and the other rattling the newspaper at his bald head. "Here this fellow that calls himself The Misfit is aloose from the Federal Pen and headed toward Florida and you read here what it says he did to these people. Just you read it. I wouldn't take my children in any direction with a criminal like that aloose in it. I couldn't answer to my conscience if I did."

Bailey didn't look up from his reading so she wheeled around then and faced the children's mother, a young woman in slacks, whose face was as broad and innocent as a cabbage and was tied around with a green head-kerchief that had two points on the top like rabbit's ears. She was sitting on the sofa, feeding the baby his apricots out of a jar. "The children have been to Florida before," the old lady said. "You all ought to take them somewhere else for a change so they would see different parts of the world and be broad. They never have been to east Tennessee."

The children's mother didn't seem to hear her but the eight-year-old boy, John Wesley, a stocky child with glasses, said, "If you don't want to go to Florida, why dontcha stay at home?" He and the little girl, June Star, were reading the funny papers on the floor.

"She wouldn't stay at home to be queen for a day," June Star said without raising her yellow head.

"Yes and what would you do if this fellow, The Misfit, caught you?" the   5
grandmother asked.

"I'd smack his face," John Wesley said.

"She wouldn't stay at home for a million bucks," June Star said. "Afraid she'd miss something. She has to go everywhere we go."

"All right, Miss," the grandmother said. "Just remember that the next time you want me to curl your hair."

June Star said her hair was naturally curly.

The next morning the grandmother was the first one in the car, ready to   10
go. She had her big black valise that looked like the head of a hippopotamus in one corner, and underneath it she was hiding a basket with Pitty Sing, the cat, in it. She didn't intend for the cat to be left alone in the house for three days because he would miss her too much and she was afraid he might brush against one of the gas burners and accidentally asphyxiate himself. Her son, Bailey, didn't like to arrive at a motel with a cat.

She sat in the middle of the back seat with John Wesley and June Star on either side of her. Bailey and the children's mother and the baby sat in front and they left Atlanta at eight forty-five with the mileage on the car at 55890. The grandmother wrote this down because she thought it would be interesting to say how many miles they had been when they got back. It took them twenty minutes to reach the outskirts of the city.

The old lady settled herself comfortably, removing her white cotton gloves and putting them up with her purse on the shelf in front of the back window. The children's mother still had on slacks and still had her head tied up in a green kerchief, but the grandmother had on a navy blue straw sailor hat with a bunch of white violets on the brim and a navy blue dress with a small white dot in the print. Her collars and cuffs were white organdy trimmed with lace and at her neckline she had pinned a purple spray of cloth violets containing a sachet. In case of an accident, anyone seeing her dead on the highway would know at once that she was a lady.

She said she thought it was going to be a good day for driving, neither too hot nor too cold, and she cautioned Bailey that the speed limit was fifty-five miles an hour and that the patrolmen hid themselves behind billboards and small clumps of trees and sped out after you before you had a chance to slow down. She pointed out interesting details of the scenery: Stone Mountain; the blue granite that in some places came up to both sides of the highway; the brilliant red clay banks slightly streaked with purple; and the various crops that made rows of green lace-work on the ground. The trees were full of silver-white sunlight and the meanest of them sparkled. The children were reading comic magazines and their mother had gone back to sleep.

"Let's go through Georgia fast so we won't have to look at it much," John Wesley said.

"If I were a little boy," said the grandmother, "I wouldn't talk about my   15
native state that way. Tennessee has the mountains and Georgia has the hills."

"Tennessee is just a hillbilly dumping ground," John Wesley said, "and Georgia is a lousy state too."

"You said it," June Star said.

"In my time," said the grandmother, folding her thin veined fingers, "children were more respectful of their native states and their parents and everything else. People did right then. Oh look at the cute little pickaninny!" she said and pointed to a Negro child standing in the door of a shack. "Wouldn't that make a picture, now?" she asked and they all turned and looked at the little Negro out of the back window. He waved.

"He didn't have any britches on," June Star said.

"He probably didn't have any," the grandmother explained. "Little niggers   20
in the country don't have things like we do. If I could paint, I'd paint that picture," she said.

The children exchanged comic books.

The grandmother offered to hold the baby and the children's mother passed him over the front seat to her. She set him on her knee and bounced him and told him about the things they were passing. She rolled her eyes and screwed up her mouth and stuck her leathery thin face into his smooth bland one. Occasionally he gave her a faraway smile. They passed a large cotton field with five or six graves fenced in the middle of it, like a small island. "Look at the graveyard!" the grandmother said, pointing it out. "That was the old family burying ground. That belonged to the plantation."

"Where's the plantation?" John Wesley asked.

"Gone with the Wind," said the grandmother. "Ha. Ha."

When the children finished all the comic books they had brought, they   25
opened the lunch and ate it. The grandmother ate a peanut butter sandwich and an olive and would not let the children throw the box and the paper napkins out the window. When there was nothing else to do they played a game by

choosing a cloud and making the other two guess what shape it suggested. John Wesley took one the shape of a cow and June Star guessed a cow and John Wesley said, no, an automobile, and June Star said he didn't play fair, and they began to slap each other over the grandmother.

The grandmother said she would tell them a story if they would keep quiet. When she told a story, she rolled her eyes and waved her head and was very dramatic. She said once when she was a maiden lady she had been courted by a Mr. Edgar Atkins Teagarden from Jasper, Georgia. She said he was a very good-looking man and a gentleman and that he brought her a watermelon every Saturday afternoon with his initials cut in it, E. A. T. Well, one Saturday, she said, Mr. Teagarden brought the watermelon and there was nobody at home and he left it on the front porch and returned in his buggy to Jasper, but she never got the watermelon, she said, because a nigger boy ate it when he saw the initials, E. A. T.! This story tickled John Wesley's funny bone and he giggled and giggled but June Star didn't think it was any good. She said she wouldn't marry a man that just brought her a watermelon on Saturday. The grandmother said she would have done well to marry Mr. Teagarden because he was a gentleman and had bought Coca-Cola stock when it first came out and that he had died only a few years ago, a very wealthy man.

They stopped at The Tower for barbecued sandwiches. The Tower was a part stucco and part wood filling station and dance hall set in a clearing outside of Timothy. A fat man named Red Sammy Butts ran it and there were signs stuck here and there on the building and for miles up and down the highway saying, TRY RED SAMMY'S FAMOUS BARBECUE. NONE LIKE FAMOUS RED SAMMY'S! RED SAM! THE FAT BOY WITH THE HAPPY LAUGH. A VETERAN! RED SAMMY'S YOUR MAN!

Red Sammy was lying on the bare ground outside The Tower with his head under a truck while a gray monkey about a foot high, chained to a small chinaberry tree, chattered nearby. The monkey sprang back into the tree and got on the highest limb as soon as he saw the children jump out of the car and run toward him.

Inside, The Tower was a long dark room with a counter at one end and tables at the other and dancing space in the middle. They all sat down at a board table next to the nickelodeon and Red Sam's wife, a tall burnt-brown woman with hair and eyes lighter than her skin, came and took their order. The children's mother put a dime in the machine and played "The Tennessee Waltz," and the grandmother said that tune always made her want to dance. She asked Bailey if he would like to dance but he only glared at her. He didn't have a naturally sunny disposition like she did and trips made him nervous. The grandmother's brown eyes were very bright. She swayed her head from side to side and pretended she was dancing in her chair. June Star said play something she could tap to so the children's mother put in another dime and played a fast number and June Star stepped out onto the dance floor and did her tap routine.

"Ain't she cute?" Red Sam's wife said, leaning over the counter. "Would you like to come be my little girl?"   30

"No I certainly wouldn't," June Star said. "I wouldn't live in a broken-down place like this for a million bucks!" and she ran back to the table.

"Ain't she cute?" the woman repeated, stretching her mouth politely.

"Aren't you ashamed?" hissed the grandmother.

Red Sam came in and told his wife to quit lounging on the counter and hurry up with these people's order. His khaki trousers reached just to his hip bones and his stomach hung over them like a sack of meal swaying under his shirt. He came over and sat down at a table nearby and let out a combination sigh and yodel. "You can't win," he said. "You can't win," and he wiped his sweating red face off with a gray handkerchief. "These days you don't know who to trust," he said. "Ain't that the truth?"

"People are certainly not nice like they used to be," said the grandmother.   35

"Two fellers come in here last week," Red Sammy said, "driving a Chrysler. It was a old beat-up car but it was a good one and these boys looked all right to me. Said they worked at the mill and you know I let them fellers charge the gas they bought? Now why did I do that?"

"Because you're a good man!" the grandmother said at once.

"Yes'm, I suppose so," Red Sam said as if he were struck with this answer.

His wife brought the orders, carrying the five plates all at once without a tray, two in each hand and one balanced on her arm. "It isn't a soul in this green world of God's that you can trust," she said. "And I don't count nobody out of that, not nobody," she repeated, looking at Red Sammy.

"Did you read about that criminal, The Misfit, that's escaped?" asked the   40
grandmother.

"I wouldn't be a bit surprised if he didn't attack this place right here," said the woman. "If he hears about it being here, I wouldn't be none surprised to see him. If he hears it's two cent in the cash register, I wouldn't be a tall surprised if he . . ."

"That'll do," Red Sam said. "Go bring these people their Co'-Colas," and the woman went off to get the rest of the order.

"A good man is hard to find," Red Sammy said. "Everything is getting terrible. I remember the day you could go off and leave your screen door unlatched. Not no more."

He and the grandmother discussed better times. The old lady said that in her opinion Europe was entirely to blame for the way things were now. She said the way Europe acted you would think we were made of money and Red Sam said it was no use talking about it, she was exactly right. The children ran outside into the white sunlight and looked at the monkey in the lacy chinaberry tree. He was busy catching fleas on himself and biting each one carefully between his teeth as if it were a delicacy.

They drove off again into the hot afternoon. The grandmother took cat   45
naps and woke up every few minutes with her own snoring. Outside of Toombs-boro she woke up and recalled an old plantation that she had visited in this neighborhood once when she was a young lady. She said the house had six white columns across the front and that there was an avenue of oaks leading up to it and two little wooden trellis arbors on either side in front where you sat

down with your suitor after a stroll in the garden. She recalled exactly which road to turn off to get to it. She knew that Bailey would not be willing to lose any time looking at an old house, but the more she talked about it, the more she wanted to see it once again and find out if the little twin arbors were still standing. "There was a secret panel in this house," she said craftily, not telling the truth but wishing that she were, "and the story went that all the family silver was hidden in it when Sherman came through but it was never found . . ."

"Hey!" John Wesley said. "Let's go see it! We'll find it! We'll poke all the woodwork and find it! Who lives there? Where do you turn off at? Hey Pop, can't we turn off there?"

"We never have seen a house with a secret panel!" June Star shrieked. "Let's go to the house with the secret panel! Hey Pop, can't we go see the house with the secret panel!"

"It's not far from here, I know," the grandmother said. "It wouldn't take over twenty minutes."

Bailey was looking straight ahead. His jaw was as rigid as a horseshoe. "No," he said.

The children began to yell and scream that they wanted to see the house with the secret panel. John Wesley kicked the back of the front seat and June Star hung over her mother's shoulder and whined desperately into her ear that they never had any fun even on their vacation, that they could never do what THEY wanted to do. The baby began to scream and John Wesley kicked the back of the seat so hard that his father could feel the blows in his kidney.

"All right!" he shouted and drew the car to a stop at the side of the road. "Will you all shut up? Will you all just shut up for one second? If you don't shut up, we won't go anywhere."

"It would be very educational for them," the grandmother murmured.

"All right," Bailey said, "but get this: this is the only time we're going to stop for anything like this. This is the one and only time."

"The dirt road that you have to turn down is about a mile back," the grandmother directed. "I marked it when we passed."

"A dirt road," Bailey groaned.

After they had turned around and were headed toward the dirt road, the grandmother recalled other points about the house, the beautiful glass over the front doorway and the candle-lamp in the hall. John Wesley said that the secret panel was probably in the fireplace.

"You can't go inside this house," Bailey said. "You don't know who lives there."

"While you all talk to the people in front, I'll run around behind and get in a window," John Wesley suggested.

"We'll all stay in the car," his mother said.

They turned onto the dirt road and the car raced roughly along in a swirl of pink dust. The grandmother recalled the times when there were no paved roads and thirty miles was a day's journey. The dirt road was hilly and there were sudden washes in it and sharp curves on dangerous embankments. All at once they would be on a hill, looking down over the blue tops of trees for miles around, then the next minute, they would be in a red depression with the dust-coated trees looking down on them.

"This place had better turn up in a minute," Bailey said, "or I'm going to turn around."

The road looked as if no one had traveled on it in months.

"It's not much farther," the grandmother said and just as she said it, a horrible thought came to her. The thought was so embarrassing that she turned red in the face and her eyes dilated and her feet jumped up, upsetting her valise in the corner. The instant the valise moved, the newspaper top she had over the basket under it rose with a snarl and Pitty Sing, the cat, sprang onto Bailey's shoulder.

The children were thrown to the floor and their mother, clutching the baby, was thrown out the door onto the ground; the old lady was thrown into the front seat. The car turned over once and landed right-side-up in a gulch off the side of the road. Bailey remained in the driver's seat with the cat— gray-striped with a broad white face and an orange nose—clinging to his neck like a caterpillar.

As soon as the children saw they could move their arms and legs, they   65
scrambled out of the car, shouting, "We've had an ACCIDENT!" The grandmother was curled up under the dashboard, hoping she was injured so that Bailey's wrath would not come down on her all at once. The horrible thought she had had before the accident was that the house she had remembered so vividly was not in Georgia but in Tennessee.

Bailey removed the cat from his neck with both hands and flung it out the window against the side of a pine tree. Then he got out of the car and started looking for the children's mother. She was sitting against the side of the red gutted ditch, holding the screaming baby, but she only had a cut down her face and a broken shoulder. "We've had an ACCIDENT!" the children screamed in a frenzy of delight.

"But nobody's killed," June Star said with disappointment as the grandmother limped out of the car, her hat still pinned to her head but the broken front brim standing up at a jaunty angle and the violet spray hanging off the side. They all sat down in the ditch, except the children, to recover from the shock. They were all shaking.

"Maybe a car will come along," said the children's mother hoarsely.

"I believe I have injured an organ," said the grandmother, pressing her side, but no one answered her. Bailey's teeth were clattering. He had on a yellow sport shirt with bright blue parrots designed in it and his face was as yellow as the shirt. The grandmother decided that she would not mention that the house was in Tennessee.

The road was about ten feet above and they could only see the tops of the   70
trees on the other side of it. Behind the ditch they were sitting in there were more woods, tall and dark and deep. In a few minutes they saw a car some distance away on top of a hill, coming slowly as if the occupants were watching them. The grandmother stood up and waved both arms dramatically to attract their attention. The car continued to come on slowly, disappeared around

a bend and appeared again, moving even slower, on top of the hill they had gone over. It was a big black battered hearse-like automobile. There were three men in it.

It came to a stop just over them and for some minutes, the driver looked down with a steady expressionless gaze to where they were sitting, and didn't speak. Then he turned his head and muttered something to the other two and they got out. One was a fat boy in black trousers and a red sweat shirt with a silver stallion embossed on the front of it. He moved around on the right side of them and stood staring, his mouth partly open in a kind of loose grin. The other had on khaki pants and a blue striped coat and a gray hat pulled very low, hiding most of his face. He came around slowly on the left side. Neither spoke.

The driver got out of the car and stood by the side of it, looking down at them. He was an older man than the other two. His hair was just beginning to gray and he wore silver-rimmed spectacles that gave him a scholarly look. He had a long creased face and didn't have on any shirt or undershirt. He had on blue jeans that were too tight for him and was holding a black hat and a gun. The two boys also had guns.

"We've had an ACCIDENT!" the children screamed.

The grandmother had the peculiar feeling that the bespectacled man was someone she knew. His face was as familiar to her as if she had known him all her life but she could not recall who he was. He moved away from the car and began to come down the embankment, placing his feet carefully so that he wouldn't slip. He had on tan and white shoes and no socks, and his ankles were red and thin. "Good afternoon," he said. "I see you all had you a little spill."

"We turned over twice!" said the grandmother.   75

"Oncet," he corrected. "We seen it happen. Try their car and see will it run, Hiram," he said quietly to the boy with the gray hat.

"What you got that gun for?" John Wesley asked. "Whatcha gonna do with that gun?"

"Lady," the man said to the children's mother, "would you mind calling them children to sit down by you? Children make me nervous. I want all you all to sit down right together there where you're at."

"What are you telling US what to do for?" June Star asked.

Behind them the line of woods gaped like a dark open mouth. "Come here,"   80
said the mother.

"Look here now," Bailey began suddenly, "we're in a predicament! We're in . . ."

The grandmother shrieked. She scrambled to her feet and stood staring. "You're The Misfit!" she said. "I recognized you at once!"

"Yes'm," the man said, smiling slightly as if he were pleased in spite of himself to be known, "but it would have been better for all of you, lady, if you hadn't of reckernized me."

Bailey turned his head sharply and said something to his mother that shocked even the children. The old lady began to cry and The Misfit reddened.

"Lady," he said, "don't you get upset. Sometimes a man says things he   85
don't mean. I don't reckon he meant to talk to you thataway."

"You wouldn't shoot a lady, would you?" the grandmother said and removed a clean handkerchief from her cuff and began to slap at her eyes with it.

The Misfit pointed the toe of his shoe into the ground and made a little hole and then covered it up again. "I would hate to have to," he said.

"Listen," the grandmother almost screamed, "I know you're a good man. You don't look a bit like you have common blood. I know you must come from nice people!"

"Yes mam," he said, "finest people in the world." When he smiled he showed a row of strong white teeth. "God never made a finer woman than my mother and my daddy's heart was pure gold," he said. The boy with the red sweat shirt had come around behind them and was standing with his gun at his hip. The Misfit squatted down on the ground. "Watch them children, Bobby Lee," he said. "You know they make me nervous." He looked at the six of them huddled together in front of him and he seemed to be embarrassed as if he couldn't think of anything to say. "Ain't a cloud in the sky," he remarked, looking up at it. "Don't see no sun but don't see no cloud neither."

"Yes, it's a beautiful day," said the grandmother. "Listen," she said, "you shouldn't call yourself The Misfit because I know you're a good man at heart. I can just look at you and tell." 90

"Hush!" Bailey yelled. "Hush! Everybody shut up and let me handle this!" He was squatting in the position of a runner about to sprint forward but he didn't move.

"I pre-chate that, lady," The Misfit said and drew a little circle in the ground with the butt of his gun.

"It'll take a half a hour to fix this here car," Hiram called, looking over the raised hood of it.

"Well, first you and Bobby Lee get him and that little boy to step over yonder with you," The Misfit said, pointing to Bailey and John Wesley. "The boys want to ast you something," he said to Bailey. "Would you mind stepping back in them woods there with them?"

"Listen," Bailey began, "we're in a terrible predicament! Nobody realizes 95 what this is," and his voice cracked. His eyes were as blue and intense as the parrots in his shirt and he remained perfectly still.

The grandmother reached up to adjust her hat brim as if she were going to the woods with him but it came off in her hand. She stood staring at it and after a second she let it fall on the ground. Hiram pulled Bailey up by the arm as if he were assisting an old man. John Wesley caught hold of his father's hand and Bobby Lee followed. They went off toward the woods and just as they reached the dark edge, Bailey turned and supporting himself against a gray naked pine trunk, he shouted, "I'll be back in a minute, Mamma, wait on me!"

"Come back this instant!" his mother shrilled but they all disappeared into the woods.

"Bailey Boy!" the grandmother called in a tragic voice but she found she was looking at The Misfit squatting on the ground in front of her. "I just know you're a good man," she said desperately. "You're not a bit common!"

"Nome, I ain't a good man," The Misfit said after a second as if he had considered her statement carefully, "but I ain't the worst in the world neither. My daddy said I was a different breed of dog from my brothers and sisters. 'You know,' Daddy said, 'it's some that can live their whole life out without asking about it and it's others has to know why it is, and this boy is one of the latters. He's going to be into everything!'" He put on his black hat and looked up suddenly and then away deep into the woods as if he were embarrassed again. "I'm sorry I don't have on a shirt before you ladies," he said, hunching his shoulders slightly. "We buried our clothes that we had on when we escaped and we're just making do until we can get better. We borrowed these from some folks we met," he explained.

"That's perfectly all right," the grandmother said. "Maybe Bailey has an   100
extra shirt in his suitcase."

"I'll look and see terrectly," The Misfit said.

"Where are they taking him?" the children's mother screamed.

"Daddy was a card himself," The Misfit said. "You couldn't put anything over on him. He never got in trouble with the Authorities though. Just had the knack of handling them."

"You could be honest too if you'd only try," said the grandmother. "Think how wonderful it would be to settle down and live a comfortable life and not have to think about somebody chasing you all the time."

The Misfit kept scratching in the ground with the butt of his gun as if he   105
were thinking about it. "Yes'm, somebody is always after you," he murmured.

The grandmother noticed how thin his shoulder blades were just behind his hat because she was standing up looking down at him. "Do you ever pray?" she asked.

He shook his head. All she saw was the black hat wiggle between his shoulder blades. "Nome," he said.

There was a pistol shot from the woods, followed closely by another. Then silence. The old lady's head jerked around. She could hear the wind move through the tree tops like a long satisfied insuck of breath. "Bailey Boy!" she called.

"I was a gospel singer for a while," The Misfit said. "I been most everything. Been in the arm service, both land and sea, at home and abroad, been twict married, been an undertaker, been with the railroads, plowed Mother Earth, been in a tornado, seen a man burnt alive oncet," and he looked up at the children's mother and the little girl who were sitting close together, their faces white and their eyes glassy; "I even seen a woman flogged," he said.

"Pray, pray," the grandmother began, "pray, pray . . ."   110

"I never was a bad boy that I remember of," The Misfit said in an almost dreamy voice, "but somewheres along the line I done something wrong and got sent to the penitentiary. I was buried alive," and he looked up and held her attention to him by a steady stare.

"That's when you should have started to pray," she said. "What did you do to get sent to the penitentiary, that first time?"

"Turn to the right, it was a wall," The Misfit said, looking up again at the cloudless sky. "Turn to the left, it was a wall. Look up it was a ceiling, look down it was a floor. I forgot what I done, lady. I set there and set there, trying to remember what it was I done and I ain't recalled it to this day. Oncet in a while, I would think it was coming to me, but it never come."

"Maybe they put you in by mistake," the old lady said vaguely.

"Nome," he said. "It wasn't no mistake. They had the papers on me."   115

"You must have stolen something," she said.

The Misfit sneered slightly. "Nobody had nothing I wanted," he said. "It was a head-doctor at the penitentiary said what I had done was kill my daddy but I known that for a lie. My daddy died in nineteen ought nineteen of the epidemic flu and I never had a thing to do with it. He was buried in the Mount Hopewell Baptist churchyard and you can go there and see for yourself."

"If you would pray," the old lady said, "Jesus would help you."

"That's right," The Misfit said.

"Well then, why don't you pray?" she asked trembling with delight   120 suddenly.

"I don't want no hep," he said. "I'm doing all right by myself."

Bobby Lee and Hiram came ambling back from the woods. Bobby Lee was dragging a yellow shirt with bright blue parrots in it.

"Thow me that shirt, Bobby Lee," The Misfit said. The shirt came flying at him and landed on his shoulder and he put it on. The grandmother couldn't name what the shirt reminded her of. "No, lady," The Misfit said while he was buttoning it up, "I found out the crime don't matter. You can do one thing or you can do another, kill a man or take a tire off his car, because sooner or later you're going to forget what it was you done and just be punished for it."

The children's mother had begun to make heaving noises as if she couldn't get her breath. "Lady," he asked, "would you and that little girl like to step off yonder with Bobby Lee and Hiram and join your husband?"

"Yes, thank you," the mother said faintly. Her left arm dangled helplessly   125 and she was holding the baby, who had gone to sleep, in the other. "Hep that lady up, Hiram," The Misfit said as she struggled to climb out of the ditch, "and Bobby Lee, you hold onto that little girl's hand."

"I don't want to hold hands with him," June Star said. "He reminds me of a pig."

The fat boy blushed and laughed and caught her by the arm and pulled her off into the woods after Hiram and her mother.

Alone with The Misfit, the grandmother found that she had lost her voice. There was not a cloud in the sky nor any sun. There was nothing around her but woods. She wanted to tell him that he must pray. She opened and closed her mouth several times before anything came out. Finally she found herself saying, "Jesus. Jesus," meaning, Jesus will help you, but the way she was saying it, it sounded as if she might be cursing.

"Yes'm," The Misfit said as if he agreed. "Jesus thown everything off balance. It was the same case with Him as with me except He hadn't committed any crime and they could prove I had committed one because they had the papers on me. Of course," he said, "they never shown me my papers. That's why I sign myself now. I said long ago, you get you a signature and sign everything you do and keep a copy of it. Then you'll know what you done and you can hold up the crime to the punishment and see do they match and in the end you'll have something to prove you ain't been treated right. I call myself The Misfit," he said, "because I can't make what all I done wrong fit what all I gone through in punishment."

There was a piercing scream from the woods, followed closely by a pistol   130 report. "Does it seem right to you, lady, that one is punished a heap and another ain't punished at all?"

"Jesus!" the old lady cried. "You've got good blood! I know you wouldn't shoot a lady! I know you come from nice people! Pray! Jesus, you ought not to shoot a lady. I'll give you all the money I've got!"

"Lady," The Misfit said, looking beyond her far into the woods, "there never was a body that give the undertaker a tip."

There were two more pistol reports and the grandmother raised her head like a parched old turkey hen crying for water and called, "Bailey Boy, Bailey Boy!" as if her heart would break.

"Jesus was the only One that ever raised the dead," The Misfit continued, "and He shouldn't have done it. He thown everything off balance. If He did what He said, then it's nothing for you to do but thow away everything and follow Him, and if He didn't, then it's nothing for you to do but enjoy the few minutes you got left the best you can—by killing somebody or burning down his house or doing some other meanness to him. No pleasure but meanness," he said and his voice had become almost a snarl.

"Maybe He didn't raise the dead," the old lady mumbled, not knowing   135 what she was saying and feeling so dizzy that she sank down in the ditch with her legs twisted under her.

"I wasn't there so I can't say He didn't," The Misfit said. "I wisht I had of been there," he said, hitting the ground with his fist. "It ain't right I wasn't there because if I had of been there I would of known. Listen lady," he said in a high voice, "if I had of been there I would of known and I wouldn't be like I am now." His voice seemed about to crack and the grandmother's head cleared for an instant. She saw the man's face twisted close to her own as if he were going to cry and she murmured, "Why you're one of my babies. You're one of my own children!" She reached out and touched him on the shoulder. The Misfit sprang back as if a snake had bitten him and shot her three times through the chest. Then he put his gun down on the ground and took off his glasses and began to clean them.

Hiram and Bobby Lee returned from the woods and stood over the ditch, looking down at the grandmother who half sat and half lay in a puddle of blood with her legs crossed under her like a child's and her face smiling up at the cloudless sky.

Without his glasses, The Misfit's eyes were red-rimmed and pale and defenseless-looking. "Take her off and thow her where you thown the others," he said, picking up the cat that was rubbing itself against his leg.

"She was a talker, wasn't she?" Bobby Lee said, sliding down the ditch with a yodel.

"She would of been a good woman," The Misfit said, "if it had been some-   140
body there to shoot her every minute of her life."

"Some fun!" Bobby Lee said.

"Shut up, Bobby Lee," The Misfit said. "It's no real pleasure in life."

[1955]

≡ THINKING ABOUT THE TEXT

1. Although this story begins with comedy, ultimately it shocks many read-ers. Did it shock you? Why, or why not? What would you say to some-one who argues that the shift in tone is a flaw in the story?

2. Note places where the word *good* comes up in this story. How is it de-fined? Do the definitions change? Do you think the author has in mind a definition that does not occur to the characters? If so, what might that definition be?

3. What in his life history is The Misfit unsure about? Why do you think he is hazy about these matters? Should O'Connor have resolved for us all the issues of fact that bother him? Why, or why not?

4. Does The Misfit have any redeeming qualities? Does the grandmother? Explain. What do you think the grandmother means when she murmurs, "Why you're one of my babies. You're one of my own children!" (para. 136)? Why do you think The Misfit responds as he does?

5. There is much talk about Jesus and Christianity in this story. Should O'Connor have done more to help non-Christian readers see the story as relevant to them? Explain your reasoning.

FLANNERY O'CONNOR
From *Mystery and Manners*

For public presentations at colleges and other places, Flannery O'Connor often chose to read and comment on "A Good Man Is Hard to Find." The following remarks come from her introduction to the story when she read it at Hollins College in Virginia in 1963. After her death, the introduction was published as "On Her Own Work" in Mystery and Manners, *a 1969 collection of O'Connor's nonfiction pieces. Her comments on "A Good Man Is Hard to Find" encourage a religious analysis of it. How helpful, though, is her own interpretation? Many critics who have subsequently writ-ten about the story have raised and addressed this issue.*

It is true that the old lady is a hypocritical old soul; her wits are no match for the Misfit's, nor is her capacity for grace equal to his; yet I think the unprejudiced reader will feel that the Grandmother has a special kind of triumph in this story which instinctively we do not allow to someone altogether bad.

I often ask myself what makes a story work and what makes it hold up as a story, and I have decided that it is probably some action, some gesture of a character that is unlike any other in the story, one which indicates where the real heart of the story lies. This would have to be an action or a gesture which was both totally right and totally unexpected; it would have to be one that was both in character and beyond character; it would have to suggest both the world and eternity. The action or gesture I'm talking about would have to be on the anagogical level, that is, the level which has to do with the Divine life and our participation in it. It would be a gesture that transcended any neat allegory that might have been intended or any pat moral categories a reader could make. It would be a gesture which somehow made contact with mystery.

There is a point in this story where such a gesture occurs. The Grandmother is at last alone, facing the Misfit. Her head clears for an instant and she realizes, even in her limited way, that she is responsible for the man before her and joined to him by ties of kinship which have their roots deep in the mystery she has been merely prattling about so far. And at this point, she does the right thing, she makes the right gesture.

I find that students are often puzzled by what she says and does here, but I think myself that if I took out this gesture and what she says with it, I would have no story. What was left would not be worth your attention. Our age not only does not have a very sharp eye for the almost imperceptible intrusions of grace, it no longer has much feeling for the nature of the violences which precede and follow them. The devil's greatest wile, Baudelaire has said, is to convince us that he does not exist.

I suppose the reasons for the use of so much violence in modern fiction will differ with each writer who uses it, but in my own stories I have found that violence is strangely capable of returning my characters to reality and preparing them to accept their moment of grace. Their heads are so hard that almost nothing else will do the work. This idea, that reality is something to which we must be returned at considerable cost, is one which is seldom understood by the casual reader, but it is one which is implicit in the Christian view of the world.   5

I don't want to equate the Misfit with the devil. I prefer to think that, however unlikely this may seem, the old lady's gesture, like the mustard-seed, will grow to be a great crow-filled tree in the Misfit's heart and will be enough of a pain to him there to turn him into the prophet he was meant to become. But that's another story.

This story has been called grotesque, but I prefer to call it literal. A good story is literal in the same sense that a child's drawing is literal. When a child draws, he doesn't intend to distort but to set down exactly what he sees, and as his gaze is direct, he sees the lines that create motion. Now the lines of motion that interest the writer are usually invisible. They are lines of spiritual motion. And in this story you should be on the lookout for such things as the action of grace in the Grandmother's soul, and not for the dead bodies.   *[1963]*

MARTHA STEPHENS

From *The Question of Flannery O'Connor*

Martha Stephens is professor emeritus of English and comparative literature at the University of Cincinnati. After Flannery O'Connor's religious explanation of "A Good Man Is Hard to Find" was published in the 1969 volume Mystery and Manners, *other readers of the story began responding to her comments. Stephens's 1973 book* The Question of Flannery O'Connor *includes one of the earliest attempts to gauge the helpfulness of O'Connor's analysis. Stephens is disturbed by the story's apparent shift of tone as it moves from farce to violent tragedy. O'Connor's remarks clarify this shift, Stephens thinks, but the religious doctrine reflected in them is severe.*

An ordinary and undistinguished family, a family even comical in its dullness, ill-naturedness, and triviality, sets out on a trip to Florida and on an ordinary summer day meets with a terrible fate. In what would the interest of such a story normally lie? Perhaps, one might think, in something that is revealed about the family in the way it meets its death, in some ironical or interesting truth about the nature of those people or those relationships—something we had been prepared unbeknownst to see, at the end plainly dramatized by their final common travail and death. But obviously, as regards the family as a whole, no such thing happens. The family is shown to be in death just as ordinary and ridiculous as before. With the possible exception of the grandmother, we know them no better; nothing about them of particular significance is brought forth.

The grandmother, being as we have seen the last to die, suffers the deaths of all her family while carrying on the intermittent conversation with the Misfit, and any reader will have some dim sense that it is through this encounter that the story is trying to transform and justify itself. One senses that this conversation—even though our attention is in reality fastened upon the horrible acts that are taking place in the background (and apparently against the thrust of the story)—is meant to be the real center of the story and the part in which the "point," as it were, of the whole tale lies.

But what is the burden of that queer conversation between the Misfit and the grandmother; what power does it have, even when we retrospectively sift and weigh it line by line, to transform our attitude towards the seemingly gratuitous—in terms of the art of the tale—horror of the massacre? The uninitiated reader will not, most likely, be able to unravel the strange complaint of the killer without some difficulty, but when we see the convict's peculiar dilemma in the context of O'Connor's whole work and what is known of her religious thought, it is not difficult to explain.

The Misfit's most intriguing statement—the line that seemingly the reader must ponder, set as it is as the final pronouncement on the grandmother after her death—is from the final passage . . . . : "She would of been a good woman if it had been somebody there to shoot her every minute of her life." Certainly we know from the first half of the story that the grandmother has seen herself as a good woman—and a good woman in a day when good men and women are hard to find, when people are disrespectful and dishonest, when they are not nice like they used to be. The grandmother is not common but a lady; and at the end of the story we know that she will be found dead just as we know she wanted to be—in the costume of a lady. She was not common, and the Misfit, with his "scholarly spectacles," his courtly apology for not wearing a shirt, his yes ma'ams and no ma'ams, was not common either—she had believed, wanted to believe, or pretended to believe. "Why I can see you come from good people," she said, "not common at all." Yet the Misfit says of her that she *would* have been a good woman if somebody had been there to shoot her all her life. And if we take the Misfit's statement as the right one about the grandmother, how was she a good woman in her death?

A good woman, perhaps we are given to believe, is one who understands   5
the worthlessness and emptiness of being or not being a "lady," of having or not having Coca-Cola stock, of "being broad" and seeing the world, of good manners and genteel attire. "Woe to them," said Isaiah, "that are wise in their own eyes, and prudent in their own sight." The futility of all the grandmother's values, the story strives to encapsulate in this image of her disarray after the car has overturned and she has recognized the Misfit: "The grandmother reached up to adjust her hat brim as if she were going to the woods with him but it came off in her hand. She stood staring at it and after a second she let it fall on the ground."

The Misfit is a figure that seems, one must say to the story's credit, to have fascinated more readers than any other single O'Connor character, and it is by contrast with the tormented spiritual state of this seeming monster that the nature of the grandmother's futile values becomes evident. We learn that the center of the Misfit's thought has always been Jesus Christ, and what becomes clear as we study over the final scene is that the Misfit has, in the eyes of the author, the enormous distinction of having at least faced up to the problem of Christian belief. And everything he has done—everything he so monstrously does here—proceeds from his inability to accept Christ, to truly believe. This is the speech which opens the narrow and emotionally difficult route into the meaning of the story:

> "Jesus was the only One that ever raised the dead," The Misfit continued, "and He shouldn't have done it. He thown everything off balance. If He did what He said, then it's nothing for you to do but thow away everything and follow Him, and if He didn't, then it's nothing for you to do but enjoy the few minutes you got left the best way you can—by killing somebody or burning down his house or doing some other meanness to him. No pleasure but meanness," he said and his voice had become almost a snarl.

The Misfit has chosen, at least, whom he would serve—has followed the injunction of the prophet in I Kings 18:21: "And Elijah came unto all the people, and said, How long halt ye between two opinions? if the Lord be God, follow him: but if Baal, then follow him." The crucial modern text for the authorial view here, which belongs to a tradition in religio-literary thought sometimes referred to as the sanctification of the sinner, is T. S. Eliot's essay on Baudelaire, in which he states: "So far as we are human, what we do must be either evil or good; so far as we do evil or good, we are human; and it is better, in a paradoxical way, to do evil than to do nothing; at least, we exist. It is true that the glory of man is his capacity for salvation; it is also true to say that his glory is his capacity for damnation."

Thus observe how, in the context of these statements, "A Good Man Is Hard to Find" begins to yield its meaning. What O'Connor has done is to take, in effect, Eliot's maxim—"It is better, in a paradoxical way, to do evil than to do nothing"—and to stretch our tolerance of this idea to its limits. The conclusion that one cannot avoid is that the story depends, for its final effect, on our being able to appreciate—even to be startled by, to be pleasurably struck with—the notion of the essential moral superiority of the Misfit over his victims, who have lived without choice or commitment of any kind, who have in effect not "lived" at all.

But again, in what sense is the grandmother a "good woman" in her death, as the Misfit claims? Here even exegesis falters. Because in her terror she calls on the name of Jesus, because she exhorts the Misfit to pray? Is she "good" because as the old lady sinks fainting into the ditch, after the Misfit's Jesus speech recorded above, she mumbles, "Maybe he didn't raise the dead"? Are we to see her as at last beginning to face the central question of human existence: did God send his son to save the world? Perhaps there is a clue in the dead grandmother's final image: she is said to half lie and half sit "in a puddle of blood with her legs crossed under her like a child's and her face smiling up at the cloudless sky." For Christ said, after all, that "whosoever shall not receive the kingdom of God as a little child shall in no wise enter herein."

To see that the Misfit is really the one courageous and admirable figure in the story; that the grandmother was perhaps—even as he said—a better woman in her death than she had ever been; to see that the pain of the other members of the family, that any godless pain or pleasure that human beings may experience is, beside the one great question of existence, *unimportant*—to see all these things is to enter fully into the experience of the story. Not to see them is to find oneself pitted not only against the forces that torture and destroy the wretched subjects of the story, but against the story itself and its attitude of indifference to and contempt for human pain.

Now as it happens, "A Good Man Is Hard to Find" was a favorite story of O'Connor's. It was the story she chose to read whenever she was asked to read from her work, and clearly it held a meaning for her that was particularly important. Whenever she read the story, she closed by reading a statement giving her own explanation of it. (One version of that statement can now be read in the collection of O'Connor's incidental prose edited by Robert and Sally Fitzgerald titled *Mystery and Manners*.) She had come to realize that it was a story that readers found difficult, and she said in her statement that she felt that the reason the story was misunderstood was that the present age "not only does not have a very sharp eye for the almost imperceptible intrusions of grace, it no longer has much feeling for the nature of the violences which precede and follow them." The intrusion of grace in "A Good Man Is Hard to Find" comes, Miss O'Connor said, in that much-discussed passage in which the grandmother, her head suddenly clearing for a moment, murmurs to the Misfit, "Why, you're one of my babies. You're one of my own children!" and is shot just as she reaches out to touch him. The grandmother's gesture here is what, according to O'Connor, makes the story work; it shows that the grandmother realizes that "she is responsible for the man before her and joined to him by ties of kinship which have their roots deep in the mystery she has been merely prattling about so far," and it affords the grandmother "a special kind of triumph . . . which we instinctively do not allow to someone altogether bad."

This explanation does solve, in a sense, one of the riddles of this odd story—although, of course, one must say that while it is interesting to know the intent of the author, speaking outside the story and after the fact, such knowledge does not change the fact that the intent of the narrator manifested strictly within the story is damagingly unclear on this important point. And what is even more important here is that O'Connor's statement about the story, taken as a whole, only further confirms the fact that the only problem in this tale is really a function of our difficulty with O'Connor's formidable doctrine. About the Misfit, O'Connor says that while he is not to be seen as the hero of the story, yet his capacity for grace is far greater than the grandmother's and that the author herself prefers to think "that the old lady's gesture, like the mustard-seed, will grow to be a great crow-filled tree in the Misfit's heart, and will be enough of a pain to him there to turn him into the prophet he was meant to become." The capacity for grace of the other members of the family is apparently zero, and hence—Christian grace in O'Connor, one cannot help noting, is rather an expensive process—it is proper that their deaths should have no spiritual context whatever.   [1973]

STEPHEN BANDY

From *"One of My Babies"*:
The Misfit and the Grandmother

In an article published in a 1996 issue of Studies in Short Fiction, *Stephen Bandy strongly disagrees with O'Connor's interpretation of "A Good Man Is Hard to Find." In particular, he thinks that the grandmother is sentimental and vindictive, whereas O'Connor is sympathetic to the character and believes that she manifests grace. Following are excerpts from Bandy's analysis.*

Grasping at any appeal, and hardly aware of what she is saying, the Grandmother declares to the Misfit: " 'Why you're one of my babies. You're one of my own children!' " As she utters these shocking words, "She reached out and touched him on the shoulder. The Misfit sprang back as if a snake had bitten him and shot her three times through the chest."

Noting that some squeamish readers had found this ending too strong, O'Connor defended the scene in this way: "If I took out this gesture and what she says with it, I would have no story. What was left would not be worth your attention" (*Mystery and Manners* 112).[1] Certainly the scene is crucial to the story, and most readers, I think, grant its dramatic "rightness" as a conclusion. What is arguable is the meaning to the Grandmother's final words to the Misfit, as well as her "gesture," which seemed equally important to O'Connor. One's interpretation depends on one's opinion of the Grandmother.

What *are* we to think of this woman? At the story's beginning, she seems a harmless busybody, utterly self-absorbed but also amusing, in her way. And, in her way, she provides a sort of human Rorschach test of her readers. We readily forgive her so much, including her mindless racism — she points at the "cute little pickaninny" by the roadside, and entertains her grandchildren with a story in which a watermelon is devoured by "a nigger boy." She is filled with the prejudices of her class and her time. And so, some readers conclude, she is in spite of it all a "good" person. Somewhat more ominously, the Misfit — after he has fired three bullets into her chest — pronounces that she might have been "'a good woman . . . if it had been somebody there to shoot her every minute of her life'." We surmise that in the universe of this story, the quality of what is "good" (which is after all the key word of the story's title) depends greatly on who is using the term. I do not think the Misfit is capable of irony — he truly means what he says about her, even though he finds it necessary to kill her. Indeed, the opposing categories of "good" and "evil" are very much in the air throughout this story. But like most supposed opposites, they have an alarming tendency to merge. It is probably worth noting that the second line of the once-popular song that gave O'Connor her title is "You always get the other kind."

Much criticism of the story appears to take a sentimental view of the Grandmother largely because she *is* a grandmother. Flannery O'Connor herself, as we shall see shortly, found little to blame in this woman, choosing to wrap her in the comfortable mantle of elderly Southern womanhood. O'Connor applies this generalization so uncritically that we half suspect she is pulling our leg. In any case, we can be sure that such sentimentality (in the mind of either the writer or her character) is fatal to clear thinking. If the Grandmother is old (although she does not seem to be *that* old), grey-haired, and "respectable," it follows that she must be weak, gentle, and benevolent — precisely the Grandmother's opinion of herself, and she is not shy of letting others know it. Intentionally or not, O'Connor has etched the Grandmother's character with wicked irony, which makes it all the more surprising to read the author's response to a frustrated teacher whose (Southern) students persisted in favoring the Grandmother, despite his strenuous efforts to point out her flaws. O'Connor said,

> I had to tell him that they resisted . . . because they all had grandmothers
> or great-aunts just like her at home, and they knew, from personal experi-

[1] Flannery O'Connor, *Mystery and Manners: Occasional Prose*. Selected and Edited by Sally and Robert Fitzgerald (New York: Farrar, Straus, and Giroux, 1969).

ence, that the old lady lacked comprehension, but that she had a good heart.

O'Connor continued,

> The Southerner is usually tolerant of those weaknesses that proceed from innocence, and he knows that a taste for self-preservation can be readily combined with the missionary spirit. (*Mystery and Manners* 110)

What is most disappointing in this moral summary of the Grandmother, and her ilk, is its disservice to the spiky, vindictive woman of the story. There may be a purpose to O'Connor's betrayal of her own character: her phrase "missionary spirit" gives the game away. O'Connor is determined that the Grandmother shall be the Misfit's savior, even though she may not seem so in the story.

The Grandmother's role as grace-bringer is by now a received idea, largely because the author said it is so. But one must question the propriety of such tinkering with the character, after the fact. It reduces the fire-breathing woman who animates this story to nothing much more than a cranky maiden aunt. On the contrary, the Grandmother is a fierce fighter, never more so than in her final moments, nose-to-nose with the Misfit.

Granted, the Grandmother is not a homicidal monster like the Misfit, and she certainly does not deserve to die for her minor sins. And yet, does she quite earn absolution from any moral weakness beyond that of "a hypocritical old soul" (111)? For every reader who sees the image of his or her own grandmother printed on this character's cold face, as O'Connor suggested we might do, there are surely many others who can only be appalled by a calculating opportunist who is capable of embracing her family's murderer, to save her own skin. Where indeed is the "good heart" which unites this unprincipled woman with all those "grandmothers or great-aunts just like her at home"? The answer to that question can only be an affirmation of the "banality of evil," to use Hannah Arendt's well-known phrase. . . .

What does in fact happen in this part of the story is quite straightforward: the Grandmother, having exhausted all other appeals to the Misfit, resorts to her only remaining (though certainly imperfect) weapon: motherhood. Declaring to the Misfit that he is one of her babies, she sets out to conquer him. Perhaps she hopes that this ultimate flattery will melt his heart, and he will collapse in her comforting motherly embrace. Such are the stratagems of sentimentality. The moral shoddiness of her action is almost beyond description. If we had not already guessed the depths to which the Grandmother might sink, now we know. It is not easy to say who is the more evil, the Misfit or the Grandmother, and indeed that is the point. Her behavior is the manifest of her character.

It has been said that no action is without its redeeming aspect. Could this unspeakable act of selfishness carry within it the seeds of grace, acting, as it were, above the Grandmother? So Flannery O'Connor believed. But what is the precise movement of grace in this scene? It is surely straining the text to propose that the Grandmother has in this moment "seen the light." Are we to regard her as the unwitting agent of divine grace whose selfish intentions are somehow transfigured into a blessing? Such seems to have been O'Connor's opinion:

> ... however unlikely this may seem, the old lady's gesture, like the mustard-seed, will grow to be a great crow-filled tree in the Misfit's heart, and will be enough of a pain to him there to turn him into the prophet he was meant to become. (*Mystery and Manners* 113)

We are almost persuaded to forget that none of this happens in the story itself. If this can be so, then we can just as easily attribute any interpretation we like to the scene. But in fact he is in no way changed. There is no "later on" in fiction. We do not, and will not, see "created grace" in the spirit of the Misfit.

But more important, this is not the way grace works. As we read in the *New*   10 *Catholic Encyclopedia:*

> ... the spiritual creature must respond to this divine self-donation freely. Hence, the doctrine of grace supposes a creature already constituted in its own being in such wise that it has the possibility of entering into a free and personal relationship with the Divine Persons or of rejecting that relationship. (6:661)

If grace was extended to the Misfit, he refused it and that is the end. There can be no crow-filled tree, nor can there be the "lines of spiritual motion" leading to that tree, however attractive the image may be. Prudently, O'Connor added, "But that's another story" (*Mystery and Manners* 113)   [1996]

JOHN DESMOND
From *Flannery O'Connor's Misfit and the Mystery of Evil*

In an article published in a 2004 issue of Renascence, *a journal that examines religious issues in literature, John Desmond tends to support O'Connor's interpretation of "A Good Man Is Hard to Find." For help in understanding the climactic scene between The Misfit and the grandmother, he turns to the late French Catholic philosopher Simone Weil. The following is an excerpt from his analysis.*

This climactic scene, full of ambiguity, has occasioned a wealth of critical comment. O'Connor herself argued that the grandmother's final words and actions represent the mysterious action of grace (5). Some readers have viewed it more skeptically, even arguing that the grandmother's gesture may be a final desperate attempt to save her own life. Other critics have argued a middle ground, granting O'Connor's right to her theological view, while judging the scene as satisfactory or not on the basis of strictly literary criteria. My focus here is on what this climactic scene suggests about the mysterious interpenetration of good and evil.

What initially strikes the reader about the scene is the enormous gap or lacuna between the grandmother's statement of doubt—"Maybe He didn't raise the dead . . ."—and her reaching out fatally to touch the Misfit and embrace him as "one of my babies . . . ," one of "my own children." O'Connor explains nothing of what happens in the grandmother's mind and heart to bring her to this touch of kinship with the criminal, except to say that "her head cleared for an instant." The gap is mysterious, perhaps supernatural, yet also exactly right in the human sense. Such acts of metanoia,° while inexplicable, are totally within the range of human behavior. What is significant about her calling him "one of my babies . . . ," one of "my own children," and "touching him" is that her actions threaten to undermine his self-designation of himself as the Misfit, the name he chose to signify his difference from ordinary humanity. The Misfit rejects the communal world, just as his sense of "justice" is individualistic rather than communal. Significantly, he remarked earlier in that story that "children make me nervous." The grandmother's claim of kinship rejects his solitary identity, and instead places him within the community as a child of man, like any other. So also, her touching him threatens his proud, isolated self-created role as the Misfit, a threat he cannot tolerate. After all, if he is not the Misfit, what is he? An ordinary, frail, suffering creature. So what we view from the grandmother's perspective as a good act—her recognition of her own bond with an evil man, her complicity, yet also her compassion for his suffering—is viewed by the Misfit as evil: he springs back from her touch "as if a snake had bitten him. . . ."

Why does the Misfit regard the touch as evil, and then answer it with evil? We recall Simone Weil's maxim: "Evil is to love, what mystery is to the intelligence." The grandmother's touch brings the Misfit into direct contact with the good of charity. The touch of charity measures the gap between him and the good. He cannot abide such threatening contact because it would mean opening himself to an admission of failure, and more importantly, to the possibility of good within the human community. Instead, he chooses the "hell" of isolation and despair. The truth of compassion, and being named a child of the human community, is for the Misfit an "evil" he must escape. Once again, Weil's comments are insightful:

> The sin against the Spirit consists of knowing a thing to be good, and hating it because it is good. We experience the equivalent of it in the form of resistance every time we set our faces in the direction of good. For every contact with good leads to a knowledge of the distance between good and evil and the commencement of a painful effort of assimilation. It is something which hurts and we are afraid. This fear is perhaps the sign of the reality of the contact. The corresponding sin cannot come about unless a lack of hope makes the consciousness of the distance intolerable and changes the pain into hatred. (*Gravity and Grace* 67)

---

metanoia: A Greek term meaning repentance or spiritual conversion.

The Misfit's pain at the grandmother's touch is instantly transformed into a hatred of the gratuitous act of charity, which he then answers with a brutal execution. What the Misfit fears is the mystery of love, the demands of love which the grandmother mysteriously responded to when faced with the criminal's suffering, and her own impending death. In her case, evil issued finally in good, or as Weil expressed it, evil exposed the good. But if the encounter with evil exposed the good in the grandmother, the final predicament of the Misfit is more complicated, more mysterious.

As I noted earlier, the Misfit acts under the delusion that his actions are somehow good, i.e., good for him. Since he cannot make sense of his spiritual condition, he now tries to reduce ethical mystery to a perverse pleasure-pain principle. Initially he told the grandmother: "No pleasure but meanness." Yet his encounter with her touch has exposed his need, his human vulnerability. In his crucial final remark, he shifts from the earlier "No pleasure but meanness" to "It's no real pleasure in life." He has again failed to liberate himself from his predicament through violence, failed to "balance out" his deeds and find the meaning of his life. He himself is his own deepest mystery, a profoundly human condition which he can neither fathom nor abide. His last statement, that there is no "real pleasure" in life, shows that what he thought might bring pleasure, i.e., acts of meanness, has also proven to be bankrupt, a hollow illusion. 5

In the end, the Misfit's spiritual and mental suffering continues and intensifies, for with the failure of his code, his awareness of the gap between good and evil has widened. His violence is projected back onto himself as self-hatred. Perhaps at some future time his knowledge of this interior chasm will bring about the collapse of his self-begotten identity as a "Misfit," and an acceptance of his broken humanity. O'Connor suggested the possibility that he might ultimately be brought to such a conversion. She called the Misfit a "prophet gone wrong," and referred to the grandmother's touching him as "like the mustard-seed," which "will grow to be a great crow-filled tree in the Misfit's heart, and will be enough of a pain to him there to turn him into the prophet he was meant to become" (*Mystery and Manners* 110, 112–13). The grandmother's touch may bring him to the point where the mystery of good and evil is finally subsumed in the mystery of love. For the Misfit, evil may, in the end, through the grace of charity, bring about his ultimate good.

≡ MAKING COMPARISONS

1. Stephens believes that her interpretation of "A Good Man Is Hard to Find" is compatible with O'Connor's. Do you accept both? Why, or why not?

2. In what ways, if any, does Desmond's use of Simone Weil go beyond O'Connor's view of her story or complicate it? Do the other two critics, Stephens and Bandy, make you hesitate to accept O'Connor's account? In general, do you think readers should accept an author's interpretation of his or her work? Explain your reasoning.

3. All of these commentaries on the story focus on religious aspects of it, though not all of them agree on how much of a role, and what kind of a role, religion plays in it. Are you similarly inclined to put the story in a religious framework? Why, or why not?

≡ WRITING ABOUT ISSUES

1. The Misfit says that the grandmother " 'would of been a good woman . . . if it had been somebody there to shoot her every minute of her life' " (para. 140). Write an essay in which you argue for your own understanding of this claim. Is The Misfit right or just cruel? How should we define *good* in this context?

2. Choose one of the critics' interpretations featured in this cluster, and write an essay in which you imagine how O'Connor would respond to its points. Feel free to express and support your own views, too.

3. The man in O'Connor's story calls himself The Misfit " 'because I can't make what all I done wrong fit what all I gone through in punishment' " (para. 129). But plainly he is also a misfit in the sense that he has become alienated from society. Write an essay recalling someone you knew who seemed to be a misfit in this sense. More specifically, speculate on and try to describe this person's own perspective — what the person believed, how the person viewed the world, why he or she acted in certain ways. If you wish, your essay can be in the form of a letter to this person.

4. O'Connor promoted her version of Christianity in "A Good Man Is Hard to Find" and in her commentary on the story. On the basis of both texts, list various principles and concepts that she associates with her religion. Then do research on another religion, perhaps by reading two or three articles on it. Write an essay in which you compare O'Connor's theology with the religion you have researched. If you wish, you can focus your comparison by imagining what adherents to the other religion would say about "A Good Man Is Hard to Find."

SUSAN GLASPELL, *Trifles*

LYNN NOTTAGE, *POOF!*

When does brutality in a marriage, or in a similar relationship, deserve to be called criminal abuse? How might justice be served in this situation? What kinds of solidarity might women form with one another when their husbands or other partners abuse them? Almost a hundred years apart, Susan Glaspell and Lynn Nottage vividly brought up these issues in plays merely one act long. Although these plays employ different styles—Glaspell's is realistic, Nottage's fanciful—they are interestingly similar in focusing on a pair of women who must ponder together how crime and justice figure in *un*holy wedlock.

☰ BEFORE YOU READ

In what circumstances, if any, do you think an abused wife who takes criminal revenge on her husband deserves little or no punishment from the legal system?

SUSAN GLASPELL
Trifles

Susan Glaspell (1876–1948) is best known for the frequently anthologized play Trifles *and its short-story version, "A Jury of Her Peers." Surprisingly modern, Glaspell's work is in harmony with contemporary feminist concerns of identity, the difficulty of female expression in a patriarchal culture, the disillusion of marriage for gifted women, and the necessity for female support and understanding.*

Glaspell graduated from Drake University in 1899 and first worked as a journalist in Des Moines, Iowa. She soon began to publish short stories in prestigious magazines like Harper's *and* The American. *After she married novelist and playwright George Cram Cook, they moved to Greenwich Village, where they felt more comfortable with its freethinking attitudes. Glaspell continued to publish both stories and novels. She also began writing plays, and in 1916 she and her husband founded the Provincetown Players, an important source for innovative American drama. During the 1920s and 1930s, Glaspell published a number of best-selling novels, including* Brook Evans *(1928), which was turned into a successful movie. Her play* Alison's House *won the Pulitzer Prize in 1931, and her novel* The Morning Is Near *(1939) sold more than one hundred thousand copies. Today her significant successes in two genres, drama and fiction, are considered remarkable.*

CHARACTERS

GEORGE HENDERSON, *county attorney*
HENRY PETERS, *sheriff*

LEWIS HALE, *a neighboring farmer*
MRS. PETERS
MRS. HALE

SCENE: *The kitchen in the now-abandoned farmhouse of John Wright, a gloomy kitchen, and left without having been put in order—the walls covered with a faded wallpaper. Down right is a door leading to the parlor. On the right wall above this door is a built-in kitchen cupboard with shelves in the upper portion and drawers below. In the rear wall at right, up two steps is a door opening onto stairs leading to the second floor. In the rear wall at left is a door to the shed and from there to the outside. Between these two doors is an old-fashioned black iron stove. Running along the left wall from the shed door is an old iron sink and sink shelf, in which is set a hand pump. Downstage of the sink is an uncurtained window. Near the window is an old wooden rocker. Center stage is an unpainted wooden kitchen table with straight chairs on either side. There is a small chair down right. Unwashed pans under the sink, a loaf of bread outside the breadbox, a dish towel on the table—other signs of incompleted work. At the rear the shed door opens and the Sheriff comes in followed by the County Attorney and Hale. The Sheriff and Hale are men in middle life, the County Attorney is a young man; all are much bundled up and go at once to the stove. They are followed by the two women—the Sheriff's wife, Mrs. Peters, first; she is a slight wiry woman, a thin nervous face. Mrs. Hale is larger and would ordinarily be called more comfortable looking, but she is disturbed now and looks fearfully about as she enters. The women have come in slowly, and stand close together near the door.*

COUNTY ATTORNEY *(at stove rubbing his hands):* This feels good. Come up to the fire, ladies.
MRS. PETERS *(after taking a step forward):* I'm not—cold.
SHERIFF *(unbuttoning his overcoat and stepping away from the stove to right of table as if to mark the beginning of official business):* Now, Mr. Hale, before we move things about, you explain to Mr. Henderson just what you saw when you came here yesterday morning.
COUNTY ATTORNEY *(crossing down to left of the table):* By the way, has anything been moved? Are things just as you left them yesterday?
SHERIFF *(looking about):* It's just about the same. When it dropped below zero last night I thought I'd better send Frank out this morning to make a fire for us—*(sits right of center table)* no use getting pneumonia with a big case on, but I told him not to touch anything except the stove—and you know Frank.
COUNTY ATTORNEY: Somebody should have been left here yesterday.
SHERIFF: Oh—yesterday. When I had to send Frank to Morris Center for that man who went crazy—I want you to know I had my hands full yesterday. I knew you could get back from Omaha by today and as long as I went over everything here myself ——
COUNTY ATTORNEY: Well, Mr. Hale, tell just what happened when you came here yesterday morning.
HALE *(crossing down to above table):* Harry and I had started to town with a load of potatoes. We came along the road from my place and as I got here I

said, "I'm going to see if I can't get John Wright to go in with me on a party telephone." I spoke to Wright about it once before and he put me off, saying folks talked too much anyway, and all he asked was peace and quiet—I guess you know about how much he talked himself; but I thought maybe if I went to the house and talked about it before his wife, though I said to Harry that I didn't know as what his wife wanted made much difference to John——

COUNTY ATTORNEY: Let's talk about that later, Mr. Hale. I do want to talk about that, but tell now just what happened when you got to the house.

HALE: I didn't hear or see anything; I knocked at the door, and still it was all quiet inside. I knew they must be up, it was past eight o'clock. So I knocked again, and I thought I heard somebody say, "Come in." I wasn't sure, I'm not sure yet, but I opened the door—this door *(indicating the door by which the two women are still standing)* and there in that rocker— *(pointing to it)* sat Mrs. Wright. *(They all look at the rocker down left.)*

COUNTY ATTORNEY: What—was she doing?

HALE: She was rockin' back and forth. She had her apron in her hand and was kind of —pleating it.

COUNTY ATTORNEY: And how did she —look?

HALE: Well, she looked queer.

COUNTY ATTORNEY: How do you mean —queer?

HALE: Well, as if she didn't know what she was going to do next. And kind of done up.

COUNTY ATTORNEY *(takes out notebook and pencil and sits left of center table)*:   How did she seem to feel about your coming?

HALE: Why, I don't think she minded—one way or other. She didn't pay much attention. I said, "How do, Mrs. Wright, it's cold, ain't it?" And she said, "Is it?"—and went on kind of pleating at her apron. Well, I was surprised; she didn't ask me to come up to the stove, or to set down, but just sat there, not even looking at me, so I said, "I want to see John." And then she —laughed. I guess you would call it a laugh. I thought of Harry and the team outside, so I said a little sharp: "Can't I see John?" "No," she says, kind o' dull like. "Ain't he home?" says I. "Yes," says she, "he's home." "Then why can't I see him?" I asked her, out of patience. "'Cause he's dead," says she. "*Dead?*" says I. She just nodded her head, not getting a bit excited, but rockin' back and forth. "Why—where is he?" says I, not knowing what to say. She just pointed upstairs—like that. *(Himself pointing to the room above.)* I started for the stairs, with the idea of going up there. I walked from there to here—then I says, "Why, what did he die of?" "He died of a rope round his neck," says she, and just went on pleatin' at her apron. Well, I went out and called Harry. I thought I might—need help. We went upstairs and there he was lyin'——

COUNTY ATTORNEY: I think I'd rather have you go into that upstairs, where you can point it all out. Just go on now with the rest of the story.

HALE: Well, my first thought was to get that rope off. It looked . . . *(stops; his face twitches)* . . . but Harry, he went up to him, and he said, "No, he's dead all right, and we'd better not touch anything." So we went back down-stairs. She was still sitting that same way. "Has anybody been notified?" I asked. "No," says she, unconcerned. "Who did this, Mrs. Wright?" said Harry. He said it businesslike—and she stopped pleatin' of her apron. "I don't know," she says. "You don't *know*?" says Harry. "No," says she. "Weren't you sleepin' in the bed with him?" says Harry. "Yes," says she, "but I was on the inside." "Somebody slipped a rope round his neck and strangled him and you didn't wake up?" says Harry. "I didn't wake up," she said after him. We must 'a' looked as if we didn't see how that could be, for after a minute she said, "I sleep sound." Harry was going to ask her more questions but I said maybe we ought to let her tell her story first to the coroner, or the sheriff, so Harry went fast as he could to Rivers's place, where there's a telephone.

COUNTY ATTORNEY: And what did Mrs. Wright do when she knew that you had gone for the coroner?

HALE: She moved from the rocker to that chair over there *(pointing to a small chair in the down right corner)* and just sat there with her hands held to-gether and looking down. I got a feeling that I ought to make some conver-sation, so I said I had come in to see if John wanted to put in a telephone, and at that she started to laugh, and then she stopped and looked at me—scared. *(The County Attorney, who has had his notebook out, makes a note.)* I dunno, maybe it wasn't scared. I wouldn't like to say it was. Soon Harry got back, and then Dr. Lloyd came and you, Mr. Peters, and so I guess that's all I know that you don't.

COUNTY ATTORNEY *(rising and looking around)*: I guess we'll go upstairs first—and then out to the barn and around there. *(To the Sheriff.)* You're con-vinced that there was nothing important here—nothing that would point to any motive?

SHERIFF: Nothing here but kitchen things. *(The County Attorney, after again looking around the kitchen, opens the door of a cupboard closet in right wall. He brings a small chair from right—gets on it and looks on a shelf. Pulls his hand away, sticky.)*

COUNTY ATTORNEY: Here's a nice mess. *(The women draw nearer up center.)*

MRS. PETERS *(to the other woman)*: Oh, her fruit; it did freeze. *(To the Lawyer.)* She worried about that when it turned so cold. She said the fire'd go out and her jars would break.

SHERIFF *(rises)*: Well, can you beat the woman! Held for murder and worryin' about her preserves.

COUNTY ATTORNEY *(getting down from chair)*: I guess before we're through she may have something more serious than preserves to worry about. *(Crosses down right center.)*

HALE: —Well, women are used to worrying over trifles. *(The two women move a little closer together.)*

COUNTY ATTORNEY *(with the gallantry of a young politician)*: And yet, for all their worries, what would we do without the ladies? *(The women do not unbend. He goes below the center table to the sink, takes a dipperful of water from the pail, and pouring it into a basin, washes his hands. While he is doing this the Sheriff and Hale cross to cupboard, which they inspect. The County Attorney starts to wipe his hands on the roller towel, turns it for a cleaner place.)* Dirty towels! *(Kicks his foot against the pans under the sink.)* Not much of a housekeeper, would you say, ladies?

MRS. HALE *(stiffly)*:   There's a great deal of work to be done on a farm.

COUNTY ATTORNEY: To be sure. And yet *(with a little bow to her)* I know there are some Dickson County farmhouses which do not have such roller towels. *(He gives it a pull to expose its full-length again.)*

MRS. HALE: Those towels get dirty awful quick. Men's hands aren't always as clean as they might be.

COUNTY ATTORNEY: Ah, loyal to your sex, I see. But you and Mrs. Wright were neighbors. I suppose you were friends, too.

MRS. HALE *(shaking her head)*:   I've not seen much of her of late years. I've not been in this house — it's more than a year.

COUNTY ATTORNEY *(crossing to women up center)*:   And why was that? You didn't like her?

MRS. HALE: I liked her all well enough. Farmers' wives have their hands full, Mr. Henderson. And then——

COUNTY ATTORNEY: Yes——?

MRS. HALE *(looking about)*:   It never seemed a very cheerful place.

COUNTY ATTORNEY: No — it's not cheerful. I shouldn't say she had the homemaking instinct.

MRS. HALE: Well, I don't know as Wright had, either.

COUNTY ATTORNEY: You mean that they didn't get on very well?

MRS. HALE: No, I don't mean anything. But I don't think a place'd be any cheerfuller for John Wright's being in it.

COUNTY ATTORNEY: I'd like to talk more of that a little later. I want to get the lay of things upstairs now. *(He goes past the women to up right where steps lead to a stair door.)*

SHERIFF: I suppose anything Mrs. Peters does'll be all right. She was to take in some clothes for her, you know, and a few little things. We left in such a hurry yesterday.

COUNTY ATTORNEY: Yes, but I would like to see what you take, Mrs. Peters, and keep an eye out for anything that might be of use to us.

MRS. PETERS: Yes, Mr. Henderson. *(The men leave by up right door to stairs. The women listen to the men's steps on the stairs, then look about the kitchen.)*

MRS. HALE *(crossing left to sink)*:   I'd hate to have men coming into my kitchen, snooping around and criticizing. *(She arranges the pans under sink which the lawyer had shoved out of place.)*

MRS. PETERS: Of course it's no more than their duty. *(Crosses to cupboard up right.)*

MRS. HALE: Duty's all right, but I guess that deputy sheriff that came out to make the fire might have got a little of this on. *(Gives the roller towel a pull.)* Wish I'd thought of that sooner. Seems mean to talk about her for not having things slicked up when she had to come away in such a hurry. (*Crosses right to Mrs. Peters at cupboard.*)

MRS. PETERS (*who has been looking through cupboard, lifts one end of towel that covers a pan*):   She had bread set. (*Stands still.*)

MRS. HALE (*eyes fixed on a loaf of bread beside the breadbox, which is on a low shelf of the cupboard*):   She was going to put this in there. (*Picks up loaf, abruptly drops it. In a manner of returning to familiar things.*) It's a shame about her fruit. I wonder if it's all gone. (*Gets up on the chair and looks.*) I think there's some here that's all right, Mrs. Peters. Yes—here; (*holding it toward the window*) this is cherries, too. (*Looking again.*) I declare I believe that's the only one. (*Gets down, jar in her hand. Goes to the sink and wipes it off on the outside.*) She'll feel awful bad after all her hard work in the hot weather. I remember the afternoon I put up my cherries last summer. (*She puts the jar on the big kitchen table, center of the room. With a sigh, is about to sit down in the rocking chair. Before she is seated realizes what chair it is; with a slow look at it, steps back. The chair which she has touched rocks back and forth. Mrs. Peters moves to center table and they both watch the chair rock for a moment or two.*)

MRS. PETERS (*shaking off the mood which the empty rocking chair has evoked. Now in a businesslike manner she speaks*):   Well I must get those things from the front room closet. (*She goes to the door at the right but, after looking into the other room, steps back.*) You coming with me, Mrs. Hale? You could help me carry them. (*They go in the other room; reappear, Mrs. Peters carrying a dress, petticoat, and skirt, Mrs. Hale following with a pair of shoes.*) My, it's cold in there. (*She puts the clothes on the big table and hurries to the stove.*)

MRS. HALE (*right of center table examining the skirt*):   Wright was close. I think maybe that's why she kept so much to herself. She didn't even belong to the Ladies' Aid. I suppose she felt she couldn't do her part, and then you don't enjoy things when you feel shabby. I heard she used to wear pretty clothes and be lively, when she was Minnie Foster, one of the town girls singing in the choir. But that—oh, that was thirty years ago. This all you want to take in?

MRS. PETERS: She said she wanted an apron. Funny thing to want, for there isn't much to get you dirty in jail, goodness knows. But I suppose just to make her feel more natural. (*Crosses to cupboard.*) She said they was in the top drawer in this cupboard. Yes, here. And then her little shawl that always hung behind the door. (*Opens stair door and looks.*) Yes, here it is. (*Quickly shuts door leading upstairs.*)

MRS. HALE (*abruptly moving toward her*):   Mrs. Peters?

MRS. PETERS: Yes, Mrs. Hale? (*At up right door.*)

MRS. HALE: Do you think she did it?

MRS. PETERS (*in a frightened voice*):   Oh, I don't know.

MRS. HALE: Well, I don't think she did. Asking for an apron and her little shawl. Worrying about her fruit.

MRS. PETERS (*starts to speak, glances up, where footsteps are heard in the room above. In a low voice*):   Mr. Peters says it looks bad for her. Mr. Henderson is awful sarcastic in a speech and he'll make fun of her sayin' she didn't wake up.

MRS. HALE: Well, I guess John Wright didn't wake when they was slipping that rope under his neck.

MRS. PETERS *(crossing slowly to table and placing shawl and apron on table with other clothing)*:   No, it's strange. It must have been done awful crafty and still. They say it was such a—funny way to kill a man, rigging it all up like that.

MRS. HALE *(crossing to left of Mrs. Peters at table)*:   That's just what Mr. Hale said. There was a gun in the house. He says that's what he can't understand.

MRS. PETERS: Mr. Henderson said coming out that what was needed for the case was a motive; something to show anger, or—sudden feeling.

MRS. HALE *(who is standing by the table)*:   Well, I don't see any signs of anger around here. *(She puts her hand on the dish towel, which lies on the table, stands looking down at table, one-half of which is clean, the other half messy.)* It's wiped to here. *(Makes a move as if to finish work, then turns and looks at loaf of bread outside the breadbox. Drops towel. In that voice of coming back to familiar things.)* Wonder how they are finding things upstairs. *(Crossing below table to down right.)* I hope she had it a little more red-up° up there. You know, it seems kind of *sneaking.* Locking her up in town and then coming out here and trying to get her own house to turn against her!

MRS. PETERS: But, Mrs. Hale, the law is the law.

MRS. HALE: I s'pose 'tis. *(Unbuttoning her coat.)* Better loosen up your things, Mrs. Peters. You won't feel them when you go out. *(Mrs. Peters takes off her fur tippet, goes to hang it on chair back left of table, stands looking at the work basket on floor near down left window.)*

MRS. PETERS: She was piecing a quilt. *(She brings the large sewing basket to the center table and they look at the bright pieces, Mrs. Hale above the table and Mrs. Peters left of it.)*

MRS. HALE: It's a log cabin pattern. Pretty, isn't it? I wonder if she was goin' to quilt it or just knot it? *(Footsteps have been heard coming down the stairs. The Sheriff enters followed by Hale and the County Attorney.)*

SHERIFF: They wonder if she was going to quilt it or just knot it! *(The men laugh, the women look abashed.)*

COUNTY ATTORNEY *(rubbing his hands over the stove)*:   Frank's fire didn't do much up there, did it? Well, let's go out to the barn and get that cleared up. *(The men go outside by up left door.)*

MRS. HALE *(resentfully)*:   I don't know as there's anything so strange, our takin' up our time with little things while we're waiting for them to get the evidence. *(She sits in chair right of table smoothing out a block with decision.)* I don't see as it's anything to laugh about.

MRS. PETERS *(apologetically)*:   Of course they've got awful important things on their minds. *(Pulls up a chair and joins Mrs. Hale at the left of the table.)*

MRS. HALE *(examining another block)*:   Mrs. Peters, look at this one. Here, this is the one she was working on, and look at the sewing! All the rest of it has

---

red-up: To get ready or clean up.

been so nice and even. And look at this! It's all over the place! Why, it looks as if she didn't know what she was about! *(After she has said this they look at each other, then start to glance back at the door. After an instant Mrs. Hale has pulled at a knot and ripped the sewing.)*

MRS. PETERS: Oh, what are you doing, Mrs. Hale?

MRS. HALE *(mildly)*:   Just pulling out a stitch or two that's not sewed very good. *(Threading a needle.)* Bad sewing always made me fidgety.

MRS. PETERS *(with a glance at door, nervously)*:   I don't think we ought to touch things.

MRS. HALE: I'll just finish up this end. *(Suddenly stopping and leaning forward.)* Mrs. Peters?

MRS. PETERS: Yes, Mrs. Hale?

MRS. HALE: What do you suppose she was so nervous about?

MRS. PETERS: Oh — I don't know. I don't know as she was nervous. I sometimes sew awful queer when I'm just tired. *(Mrs. Hale starts to say something, looks at Mrs. Peters, then goes on sewing.)* Well, I must get these things wrapped up. They may be through sooner than we think. *(Putting apron and other things together.)* I wonder where I can find a piece of paper, and string. *(Rises.)*

MRS. HALE: In that cupboard, maybe.

MRS. PETERS *(crosses right looking in cupboard)*:   Why, here's a bird-cage. *(Holds it up.)* Did she have a bird, Mrs. Hale?

MRS. HALE: Why, I don't know whether she did or not — I've not been here for so long. There was a man around last year selling canaries cheap, but I don't know as she took one; maybe she did. She used to sing real pretty herself.

MRS. PETERS *(glancing around)*:   Seems funny to think of a bird here. But she must have had one, or why would she have a cage? I wonder what happened to it?

MRS. HALE: I s'pose maybe the cat got it.

MRS. PETERS: No, she didn't have a cat. She's got that feeling some people have about cats — being afraid of them. My cat got in her room and she was real upset and asked me to take it out.

MRS. HALE: My sister Bessie was like that. Queer, ain't it?

MRS. PETERS *(examining the cage)*:   Why, look at this door. It's broke. One hinge is pulled apart. *(Takes a step down to Mrs. Hale's right.)*

MRS. HALE *(looking too)*:   Looks as if someone must have been rough with it.

MRS. PETERS: Why, yes. *(She brings the cage forward and puts it on the table.)*

MRS. HALE *(glancing toward up left door)*:   I wish if they're going to find any evidence they'd be about it. I don't like this place.

MRS. PETERS: But I'm awful glad you came with me, Mrs. Hale. It would be lonesome for me sitting here alone.

MRS. HALE: It would, wouldn't it? *(Dropping her sewing.)* But I tell you what I do wish, Mrs. Peters. I wish I had come over sometimes when *she* was here. I — *(looking around the room)* — wish I had.

MRS. PETERS: But of course you were awful busy, Mrs. Hale — your house and your children.

MRS. HALE (*rises and crosses left*):   I could've come. I stayed away because it weren't cheerful—and that's why I ought to have come. I—(*looking out left window*)—I've never liked this place. Maybe because it's down in a hollow and you don't see the road. I dunno what it is, but it's a lonesome place and always was. I wish I had come over to see Minnie Foster sometimes. I can see now—(*Shakes her head.*)

MRS. PETERS (*left of table and above it*):   Well, you mustn't reproach yourself, Mrs. Hale. Somehow we just don't see how it is with other folks until—something turns up.

MRS. HALE: Not having children makes less work—but it makes a quiet house, and Wright out to work all day, and no company when he did come in. (*Turning from window.*) Did you know John Wright, Mrs. Peters?

MRS. PETERS: Not to know him; I've seen him in town. They say he was a good man.

MRS. HALE: Yes—good; he didn't drink, and kept his word as well as most, I guess, and paid his debts. But he was a hard man, Mrs. Peters. Just to pass the time of day with him—(*Shivers.*) Like a raw wind that gets to the bone. (*Pauses, her eye falling on the cage.*) I should think she would 'a' wanted a bird. But what do you suppose went with it?

MRS. PETERS: I don't know, unless it got sick and died. (*She reaches over and swings the broken door, swings it again, both women watch it.*)

MRS. HALE: You weren't raised round here, were you? (*Mrs. Peters shakes her head.*) You didn't know—her?

MRS. PETERS: Not till they brought her yesterday.

MRS. HALE: She—come to think of it, she was kind of like a bird herself—real sweet and pretty, but kind of timid and—fluttery. How—she—did—change. (*Silence: then as if struck by a happy thought and relieved to get back to everyday things. Crosses right above Mrs. Peters to cupboard, replaces small chair used to stand on to its original place down right.*) Tell you what, Mrs. Peters, why don't you take the quilt in with you? It might take up her mind.

MRS. PETERS: Why, I think that's a real nice idea, Mrs. Hale. There couldn't possibly be any objection to it could there? Now, just what would I take? I wonder if her patches are in here—and her things. (*They look in the sewing basket.*)

MRS. HALE (*crosses to right of table*):   Here's some red. I expect this has got sewing things in it. (*Brings out a fancy box.*) What a pretty box. Looks like something somebody would give you. Maybe her scissors are in here. (*Opens box. Suddenly puts her hand to her nose.*) Why——(*Mrs. Peters bends nearer, then turns her face away.*) There's something wrapped up in this piece of silk.

MRS. PETERS: Why, this isn't her scissors.

MRS. HALE (*lifting the silk*):   Oh, Mrs. Peters—it's——(*Mrs. Peters bends closer.*)

MRS. PETERS: It's the bird.

MRS. HALE: But, Mrs. Peters—look at it! Its neck! Look at its neck! It's all—other side *to.*

MRS. PETERS: Somebody—wrung—its—neck. (*Their eyes meet. A look of growing comprehension, of horror. Steps are heard outside. Mrs. Hale slips box under quilt pieces, and sinks into her chair. Enter Sheriff and County Attorney. Mrs. Peters steps down left and stands looking out of window.)*

COUNTY ATTORNEY *(as one turning from serious things to little pleasantries)*:   Well, ladies, have you decided whether she was going to quilt it or knot it? *(Crosses to center above table.)*

MRS. PETERS: We think she was going to—knot it. *(Sheriff crosses to right of stove, lifts stove lid, and glances at fire, then stands warming hands at stove.)*

COUNTY ATTORNEY: Well, that's interesting, I'm sure. *(Seeing the bird-cage.)* Has the bird flown?

MRS. HALE *(putting more quilt pieces over the box)*:   We think the—cat got it.

COUNTY ATTORNEY *(preoccupied)*:   Is there a cat? *(Mrs. Hale glances in a quick covert way at Mrs. Peters.)*

MRS. PETERS *(turning from window takes a step in)*:   Well, not now. They're superstitious, you know. They leave.

COUNTY ATTORNEY *(to Sheriff Peters, continuing an interrupted conversation)*:   No sign at all of anyone having come from the outside. Their own rope. Now let's go up again and go over it piece by piece. *(They start upstairs.)* It would have to have been someone who knew just the—— *(Mrs. Peters sits down left of table. The two women sit there not looking at one another, but as if peering into something and at the same time holding back. When they talk now it is in the manner of feeling their way over strange ground, as if afraid of what they are saying, but as if they cannot help saying it.)*

MRS. HALE *(hesitatively and in hushed voice)*:   She liked the bird. She was going to bury it in that pretty box.

MRS. PETERS *(in a whisper)*:   When I was a girl—my kitten—there was a boy took a hatchet, and before my eyes—and before I could get there—— *(Covers her face an instant.)* If they hadn't held me back I would have— *(catches herself, looks upstairs where steps are heard, falters weakly)*—hurt him.

MRS. HALE *(with a slow look around her)*:   I wonder how it would seem never to have had any children around. *(Pause.)* No, Wright wouldn't like the bird—a thing that sang. She used to sing. He killed that, too.

MRS. PETERS *(moving uneasily)*:   We don't know who killed the bird.

MRS. HALE: I knew John Wright.

MRS. PETERS: It was an awful thing was done in this house that night, Mrs. Hale. Killing a man while he slept, slipping a rope around his neck that choked the life out of him.

MRS. HALE: His neck. Choked the life out of him. *(Her hand goes out and rests on the bird-cage.)*

MRS. PETERS *(with rising voice)*:   We don't know who killed him. We don't know.

MRS. HALE *(her own feeling not interrupted)*:   If there'd been years and years of nothing, then a bird to sing to you, it would be awful—still, after the bird was still.

MRS. PETERS *(something within her speaking)*:   I know what stillness is. When we homesteaded in Dakota, and my first baby died—after he was two years old, and me with no other then——

MRS. HALE *(moving)*:　How soon do you suppose they'll be through looking for the evidence?

MRS. PETERS:　I know what stillness is. *(Pulling herself back.)* The law has got to punish crime, Mrs. Hale.

MRS. HALE *(not as if answering that)*:　I wish you'd seen Minnie Foster when she wore a white dress with blue ribbons and stood up there in the choir and sang. *(A look around the room.)* Oh, I *wish* I'd come over here once in a while! That was a crime! That was a crime! Who's going to punish that?

MRS. PETERS *(looking upstairs)*:　We mustn't—take on.

MRS. HALE:　I might have known she needed help! I know how things can be—for women. I tell you, it's queer, Mrs. Peters. We live close together and we live far apart. We all go through the same things—it's all just a different kind of the same thing. *(Brushes her eyes, noticing the jar of fruit, reaches out for it.)* If I was you I wouldn't tell her her fruit was gone. Tell her it *ain't.* Tell her it's all right. Take this in to prove it to her. She—she may never know whether it was broke or not.

MRS. PETERS *(takes the jar, looks about for something to wrap it in; takes petticoat from the clothes brought from the other room, very nervously begins winding this around the jar. In a false voice)*:　My, it's a good thing the men couldn't hear us. Wouldn't they just laugh! Getting all stirred up over a little thing like a—dead canary. As if that could have anything to do with—with— wouldn't they *laugh!* *(The men are heard coming downstairs.)*

MRS. HALE *(under her breath)*:　Maybe they would—maybe they wouldn't.

COUNTY ATTORNEY:　No, Peters, it's all perfectly clear except a reason for doing it. But you know juries when it comes to women. If there was some definite thing. *(Crosses slowly to above table. Sheriff crosses down right. Mrs. Hale and Mrs. Peters remain seated at either side of table.)* Something to show— something to make a story about—a thing that would connect up with this strange way of doing it—— *(The women's eyes meet for an instant. Enter Hale from outer door.)*

HALE *(remaining by door)*:　Well, I've got the team around. Pretty cold out there.

COUNTY ATTORNEY:　I'm going to stay awhile by myself. *(To the Sheriff.)* You can send Frank out for me, can't you? I want to go over everything. I'm not satisfied that we can't do better.

SHERIFF:　Do you want to see what Mrs. Peters is going to take in? *(The Lawyer picks up the apron, laughs.)*

COUNTY ATTORNEY:　Oh, I guess they're not very dangerous things the ladies have picked out. *(Moves a few things about, disturbing the quilt pieces which cover the box. Steps back.)* No, Mrs. Peters doesn't need supervising. For that matter a sheriff's wife is married to the law. Ever think of it that way, Mrs. Peters?

MRS. PETERS:　Not—just that way.

SHERIFF *(chuckling)*:　Married to the law. *(Moves to down right door to the other room.)* I just want you to come in here a minute, George. We ought to take a look at these windows.

COUNTY ATTORNEY *(scoffingly)*:　Oh, windows!

SHERIFF: We'll be right out, Mr. Hale. (*Hale goes outside. The Sheriff follows the County Attorney into the room. Then Mrs. Hale rises, hands tight together, looking intensely at Mrs. Peters, whose eyes make a slow turn, finally meeting Mrs. Hale's. A moment Mrs. Hale holds her, then her own eyes point the way to where the box is concealed. Suddenly Mrs. Peters throws back quilt pieces and tries to put the box in the bag she is carrying. It is too big. She opens box, starts to take bird out, cannot touch it, goes to pieces, stands there helpless. Sound of a knob turning in the other room. Mrs. Hale snatches the box and puts it in the pocket of her big coat. Enter County Attorney and Sheriff, who remains down right.*)

COUNTY ATTORNEY (*crosses to up left door facetiously*): Well, Henry, at least we found out that she was not going to quilt it. She was going to — what is it you call it, ladies?

MRS. HALE (*standing center below table facing front, her hand against her pocket*): We call it — knot it, Mr. Henderson.

Curtain.   *[1916]*

☰ THINKING ABOUT THE TEXT

1. Although much of this play is about Minnie Wright, Glaspell keeps her offstage. Why, do you think?

2. What does Glaspell imply about differences between men and women? Support your inference with details from the text.

3. What do Mrs. Hale and Mrs. Peters realize about themselves during the course of the play? To what extent should they feel guilty about their own past behavior?

4. Ultimately, Mrs. Hale and Mrs. Peters cover up evidence to protect Minnie Wright. They seem to act out of loyalty to their sex. How sympathetic are you to their stand? Do you feel there are times when you should be someone's ally because that person is of the same gender as you?

5. Is this play about freedom and confinement? About the injustice of male domination? About the bonds that hold women together? Or something else? Explain your answer.

LYNN NOTTAGE
POOF!

Lynn Nottage (b. 1964) is an American playwright and an activist focused on preventing violence against women. She grew up in New York City and attended Brown University and the Yale School of drama. She then worked for four years at Amnesty International. Ruined, *a play about Congolese women during civil war, was awarded the Pulitzer Prize for drama in 2009. Her plays have been performed in dozens of theaters. She has received a Guggenheim Fellowship and a MacArthur Grant. Her latest play is* By the Way, Meet Vera Stark *(2011).*

CHARACTERS

SAMUEL, *Loureen's husband*
LOUREEN, *a demure housewife, early thirties*
FLORENCE, *Loureen's best friend, early thirties*

TIME: *The present*
PLACE: *Kitchen*

A NOTE: *Nearly half the women on death row in the United States were convicted of killing abusive husbands. Spontaneous combustion is not recognized as a capital crime.*

Darkness.

SAMUEL (*In the darkness*):   WHEN I COUNT TO TEN I DON' WANT TO SEE YA! I DON' WANT TO HEAR YA! ONE, TWO, THREE, FOUR—
LOUREEN (*In the darkness*):   DAMN YOU TO HELL, SAMUEL!

A bright flash.
     Lights rise. A huge pile of smoking ashes rests in the middle of the kitchen. Loureen, a demure housewife in her early thirties, stares down at the ashes incredulously. She bends and lifts a pair of spectacles from the remains. She ever so slowly backs away.

> Samuel? Uh! (*Places the spectacles on the kitchen table*) Uh! . . . Samuel? (*Looks around*) Don't fool with me now. I'm not in the mood. (*Whispers*) Samuel? I didn't mean it really. I'll be good if you come back . . . Come on now, dinner's waiting. (*Chuckles, then stops abruptly*) Now stop your foolishness . . . And let's sit down. (*Examines the spectacles*) Uh! (*Softly*) Don't be cross with me. Sure I forgot to pick up your shirt for tomorrow. I can wash another, I'll do it right now. Right now! Sam? . . . (*Cautiously*) You hear me! (*Awaits a response*) Maybe I didn't ever intend to wash your shirt. (*Pulls back as though about to receive a blow; a moment*) Uh! (*Sits down and dials the telephone*) Florence, honey, could you come on down for a moment. There's been a . . . little . . . accident . . . Quickly please. Uh!

Loureen hangs up the phone. She gets a broom and a dust pan. She hesitantly approaches the pile of ashes. She gets down on her hands and knees and takes a closer look. A fatuous grin spreads across her face. She is startled by a sudden knock on the door. She slowly walks across the room like a possessed child. Loureen lets in Florence, her best friend and upstairs neighbor. Florence, also a housewife in her early thirties, wears a floral housecoat and a pair of oversized slippers. Without acknowledgment Loureen proceeds to saunter back across the room.

FLORENCE: HEY!
LOUREEN (*Pointing at the ashes*):   Uh! . . . (*She struggles to formulate words, which press at the inside of her mouth, not quite realized*) Uh! . . .

FLORENCE: You all right? What happened? (*Sniffs the air*) Smells like you burned something? (*Stares at the huge pile of ashes*) What the devil is that?

LOUREEN (*Hushed*):   Samuel . . . It's Samuel, I think.

FLORENCE: What's he done now?

LOUREEN: It's him. It's him. (*Nods her head repeatedly*)

FLORENCE: Chile, what's wrong with you? Did he finally drive you out your mind? I knew something was going to happen sooner or later.

LOUREEN: Dial 911, Florence!

FLORENCE: Why? You're scaring me!

LOUREEN: Dial 911!

Florence picks up the telephone and quickly dials.

I think I killed him.

Florence hangs up the telephone.

FLORENCE: What?

LOUREEN (*Whimpers*):   I killed him! I killed Samuel!

FLORENCE: Come again? . . . He's dead dead?

Loureen wrings her hands and nods her head twice, mouthing "dead dead." Florence backs away.

No, stop it, I don't have time for this. I'm going back upstairs. You know how Samuel hates to find me here when he gets home. You're not going to get me this time. (*Louder*) Y'all can have your little joke, I'm not part of it! (*A moment. She takes a hard look into Loureen's eyes; she squints*) Did you really do it this time?

LOUREEN (*Hushed*):   I don't know how or why it happened, it just did.

FLORENCE: Why are you whispering?

LOUREEN: I don't want to talk too loud—something else is liable to disappear.

FLORENCE: Where's his body?

LOUREEN (*Points to the pile of ashes*):   There! . . .

FLORENCE: You burned him?

LOUREEN: I DON'T KNOW! (*Covers her mouth as if to muffle her words; hushed*) I think so.

FLORENCE: Either you did or you didn't, what you mean you don't know? We're talking murder, Loureen, not oven settings.

LOUREEN: You think I'm playing?

FLORENCE: How many times have I heard you talk about being rid of him. How many times have we sat at this very table and laughed about the many ways we could do it and how many times have you done it? None.

LOUREEN (*Lifting the spectacles*):   A pair of cheap spectacles, that's all that's left. And you know how much I hate these. You ever seen him without them, no! . . . He counted to four and disappeared. I swear to God!

FLORENCE: Don't bring the Lord into this just yet! Sit down now . . . What you got to sip on?

LOUREEN: I don't know whether to have a stiff shot of scotch or a glass of champagne.

Florence takes a bottle of sherry out of the cupboard and pours them each a glass. Loureen downs hers, then holds out her glass for more.

He was . . .

FLORENCE: Take your time.

LOUREEN: Standing there.

FLORENCE: And?

LOUREEN: He exploded.

FLORENCE: Did that muthafucka hit you again?

LOUREEN: No . . . he exploded. Boom! Right in front of me. He was shouting like he does, being all colored, then he raised up that big crusty hand to hit me, and poof, he was gone . . . I barely got words out and I'm looking down at a pile of ash.

Florence belts back her sherry. She wipes her forehead and pours them both another.

FLORENCE: Chile, I'll give you this, in terms of color you've matched my husband Edgar, the story king. He came in at six Sunday morning, talking about he'd hit someone with his car, and had spent all night trying to outrun the police. I felt sorry for him. It turns out he was playing poker with his paycheck no less. You don't want to know how I found out . . . But I did.

LOUREEN: You think I'm lying?

FLORENCE: I certainly hope so, Loureen. For your sake and my heart's.

LOUREEN: Samuel always said if I raised my voice something horrible would happen. And it did. I'm a witch . . . the devil spawn!

FLORENCE: You've been watching too much television.

LOUREEN: Never seen anything like this on television. Wish I had, then I'd know what to do . . . There's no question, I'm a witch. (*Looks at her hands with disgust*)

FLORENCE: Chile, don't tell me you've been messing with them mojo women again? What did I tell ya.

Loureen, agitated, stands and sits back down.

LOUREEN: He's not coming back. Oh no, how could he? It would be a miracle! Two in one day . . . I could be canonized. Worse yet, he could be . . . All that needs to happen now is for my palms to bleed and I'll be eternally remembered as Saint Loureen, the patron of battered wives. Women from across the country will make pilgrimages to me, laying pies and pot roast at my feet and asking the good saint to make their husbands turn to dust. How often does a man like Samuel get damned to hell, and go?

She breaks down. Florence moves to console her friend, then realizes that Loureen is actually laughing hysterically.

FLORENCE: You smoking crack?

LOUREEN: Do I look like I am?

FLORENCE: Hell, I've seen old biddies creeping out of crack houses, talking about they were doing church work.

LOUREEN: Florence, please be helpful, I'm very close to the edge! . . . I don't know what to do next! Do I sweep him up? Do I call the police? Do I . . .

The phone rings.

Oh God.

FLORENCE: You gonna let it ring?

Loureen reaches for the telephone slowly.

LOUREEN: NO! (*Holds the receiver without picking it up, paralyzed*) What if it's his mother? . . . She knows!

The phone continues to ring. They sit until it stops. They both breathe a sigh of relief.

I should be mourning, I should be praying, I should be thinking of the burial, but all that keeps popping into my mind is what will I wear on television when I share my horrible and wonderful story with a studio audience . . . (*Whimpers*) He's made me a killer, Florence, and you remember what a gentle child I was. (*Whispers*) I'm a killer, I'm a killer, I'm a killer.

FLORENCE: I wouldn't throw that word about too lightly even in jest. Talk like that gets around.

LOUREEN: You think they'll lock me up? A few misplaced words and I'll probably get the death penalty, isn't that what they do with women like me, murderesses?

FLORENCE: Folks have done time for less.

LOUREEN: Thank you, just what I needed to hear!

FLORENCE: What did you expect, that I was going to throw up my arms and congratulate you? Why'd you have to go and lose your mind at this time of day, while I got a pot of rice on the stove and Edgar's about to walk in the door and wonder where his goddamn food is. (*Losing her cool*) And he's going to start in on me about all the nothing I've been doing during the day and why I can't work and then he'll mention how clean you keep your home. And I don't know how I'm going to look him in the eye without . . .

LOUREEN: I'm sorry, Florence. Really. It's out of my hands now.

She takes Florence's hand and squeezes it.

FLORENCE (*Regaining her composure*):   You swear on your right tit?

LOUREEN (*Clutching both breasts*):   I swear on both of them!

FLORENCE: Both your breasts, Loureen! You know what will happen if you're lying. (*Loureen nods; hushed*) Both your breasts Loureen?

LOUREEN: Yeah!

FLORENCE (*Examines the pile of ashes, then shakes her head*):   Oh sweet, sweet Jesus. He must have done something truly terrible.

LOUREEN: No more than usual. I just couldn't take being hit one more time.

FLORENCE: You've taken a thousand blows from that man, couldn't you've turned the cheek and waited? I'd have helped you pack. Like we talked about.

A moment.

LOUREEN: Uh! . . . I could blow on him and he'd disappear across the linoleum. (*Snaps her fingers*) Just like that. Should I be feeling remorse or regret or some other "R" word? I'm strangely jubilant, like on prom night when Samuel and I first made love. That's the feeling! (*The women lock eyes*) Uh!

FLORENCE: Is it . . .

LOUREEN: Like a ton of bricks been lifted from my shoulders, yeah.

FLORENCE: Really?

LOUREEN: Yeah!

Florence walks to the other side of the room.

FLORENCE: You bitch!

LOUREEN: What?

FLORENCE: We made a pact.

LOUREEN: I know.

FLORENCE: You've broken it . . . We agreed that when things got real bad for both of us we'd . . . you know . . . together . . . Do I have to go back upstairs to that? . . . What next?

LOUREEN: I thought you'd tell me! . . . I don't know!

FLORENCE: I don't know!

LOUREEN: I don't know!

Florence begins to walk around the room, nervously touching objects. Loureen sits, wringing her hands and mumbling softly to herself.

FLORENCE: Now you got me, Loureen, I'm truly at a loss for words.

LOUREEN: Everybody always told me, "Keep your place, Loureen." My place, the silent spot on the couch with a wine cooler in my hand and a pleasant smile that warmed the heart. All this time I didn't know why he was so afraid for me to say anything, to speak up. Poof! . . . I've never been by myself, except for them two weeks when he won the office pool and went to Reno with his cousin Mitchell. He wouldn't tell me where he was going until I got that postcard with the cowboy smoking a hundred cigarettes . . . Didn't Sonny Larkin look good last week at Caroline's? He looked good, didn't he . . .

Florence nods. She nervously picks up Samuel's jacket, which is hanging on the back of the chair. She clutches it unconsciously.

NO! No! Don't wrinkle that, that's his favorite jacket. He'll kill me. Put it back!

Florence returns the jacket to its perch. Loureen begins to quiver.

I'm sorry. (*She grabs the jacket and wrinkles it up*) There! (*She then digs into the coat pockets and pulls out his wallet and a movie stub*) Look at that, he said he didn't go to the movies last night. Working late. (*Frantically thumbs through his wallet*) Picture of his motorcycle, Social Security card, driver's license, and look at that from our wedding. (*Smiling*) I looked good, didn't I? (*She puts the pictures back in the wallet and holds the jacket up to her face*) There were some good things. (*She then sweeps her hand over the jacket to remove the wrinkles, and folds it ever so carefully, and finally throws it in the garbage*) And out of my mouth those words made him disappear. All these years and just words, Florence. That's all they were.

FLORENCE: I'm afraid I won't ever get those words out. I'll start resenting you, honey. I'm afraid won't anything change for me.

LOUREEN: I been to that place.

FLORENCE: Yeah? But now I wish I could relax these old lines (*Touches her fore-head*) for a minute maybe. Edgar has never done me the way Samuel did you, but he sure did take the better part of my life.

LOUREEN: Not yet, Florence.

FLORENCE (*Nods*):   I have the children to think of . . . right?

LOUREEN: You can think up a hundred things before . . .

FLORENCE: Then come upstairs with me . . . we'll wait together for Edgar and then you can spit out your words and . . .

LOUREEN: I can't do that.

FLORENCE: Yes you can. Come on now.

Loureen shakes her head no.

Well, I guess my mornings are not going to be any different.

LOUREEN: If you can say for certain, then I guess they won't be. I couldn't say that.

FLORENCE: But you got a broom and a dust pan, you don't need anything more than that . . . He was a bastard and nobody will care that he's gone.

LOUREEN: Phone's gonna start ringing soon, people are gonna start asking soon, and they'll care.

FLORENCE: What's your crime? Speaking your mind?

LOUREEN: Maybe I should mail him to his mother. I owe her that. I feel bad for her, she didn't understand how it was. I can't just throw him away and pretend like it didn't happen. Can I?

FLORENCE: I didn't see anything but a pile of ash. As far as I know you got a little careless and burned a chicken.

LOUREEN: He was always threatening not to come back.

FLORENCE: I heard him.

LOUREEN: It would've been me eventually.

FLORENCE: Yes.

LOUREEN: I should call the police, or someone.

FLORENCE: Why? What are you gonna tell them? About all those times they refused to help, about all those nights you slept in my bed 'cause you were afraid to stay down here? About the time he nearly took out your eye 'cause you flipped the television channel?

LOUREEN: No.

FLORENCE: You've got it, girl!

LOUREEN: Good-bye to the fatty meats and the salty food. Good-bye to the bour-bon and the bologna sandwiches. Good-bye to the smell of his feet, his breath and his bowel movements . . . (*A moment. She closes her eyes and, reliving a horrible memory, she shudders*) Good-bye. (*Walks over to the pile of ashes*) Samuel? . . . Just checking.

FLORENCE: Good-bye Samuel.

They both smile.

LOUREEN: I'll let the police know that he's missing tomorrow . . .

FLORENCE: Why not the next day?

LOUREEN: Chicken's warming in the oven, you're welcome to stay.

FLORENCE: Chile, I got a pot of rice on the stove, kids are probably acting out . . . and Edgar, well . . . Listen, I'll stop in tomorrow.

LOUREEN: For dinner?

FLORENCE: Edgar wouldn't stand for that. Cards maybe.

LOUREEN: Cards.

The women hug for a long moment. Florence exits. Loureen stands over the ashes for a few moments contemplating what to do. She finally decides to sweep them under the carpet, and then proceeds to set the table and sit down to eat her dinner.

END OF PLAY   [1993]

≡ THINKING ABOUT THE TEXT

1. How would you describe Loureen's relationship to her husband Samuel? What reason can you suggest for Loureen staying in that relationship?

2. What specific offenses does Samuel commit? Which would be violations of wedding vows? Which would be legal issues?

3. Describe the progression of Loureen's response to Samuel's death.

4. What evidence might there be that Loureen could become a model for battered women? What do you think about Edgar's future?

5. Even though Samuel dies, the play doesn't seem tragic. Point out the comic elements. How does Nottage get away with using humor in a play where someone loses his life?

≡ MAKING COMPARISONS

1. Do the comic elements of *POOF!* lead you to take Nottage's play less seriously than you do Glaspell's? Why, or why not?

2. Do Glaspell and Nottage show similar reasoning in keeping certain characters offstage, unseen? Explain.

3. To what extent, if any, does Nottage's play seem more racially specific than Glaspell's?

≡ WRITING ABOUT ISSUES

1. Choose either Glaspell's or Nottage's play. Then, write an essay in which you develop and support a claim about whether justice is served in the play you have selected. Make clear how you are defining *justice*.

2. On the basis of Glaspell's and Nottage's plays, would you say that marital problems have basically remained the same over the last hundred years, or do you think that they have significantly changed? Write an essay that answers this question by referring to specific passages in both texts.

3. Write an essay in which you explain how a mystical intervention (like the spontaneous combustion in *POOF!*) could occur in *Trifles*, or how the thorough realism of *Trifles* could be transferred to *POOF!* If you wish, substitute for this essay a script that you compose.

4. How can one tell that partners in a marriage, or in a similar relationship, have equal status? Write an essay specifying the features you have in mind. If you wish, refer to one or both of the plays in this cluster.

≡ Recalling a Violent Crime: Essays

BRUCE SHAPIRO, "One Violent Crime"

EMILY BERNARD, "Scar Tissue"

A crime, especially when violent, may leave its surviving victims suffering for years. Physically, they may be marked forever. Psychologically, they may sustain long-lasting trauma, haunted by memories of the event. In part, their mental pain may be caused by people other than the original perpetrator. These may include reporters and politicians who exploit criminal cases to promote their personal views. Several victims of violent crimes have tried to regain power over their lives by writing about what happened. They thereby make sure that *their* sense of what occurred becomes public record. Of course, even victims of the same crime will differ in their perspectives on it — not only at the moment, but also later on.

These effects are evident in the following two essays. Their authors were both victims of a stabbing attack in New Haven, Connecticut, on August 7, 1994. Bruce Shapiro wrote about his experience soon afterward. He was stirred to do so by government policies that he saw as misguided in their approach to crime and other social problems. Emily Bernard wrote about the attack, however, almost two decades later. Her essay acknowledges Shapiro's but mostly contemplates how this horrific incident scarred her own body and mind.

≡ BEFORE YOU READ

Have you or someone you know been the victim of a crime? If so, what were the psychological effects of it?

BRUCE SHAPIRO

One Violent Crime

Bruce Shapiro (b. 1959) is currently associated with two universities. At Yale, he teaches investigative journalism; at Columbia, he is executive director of the Dart Center for Journalism & Trauma. He has edited Shaking the Foundations: 200 Years of Investigative Journalism in America *(2003) and coauthored (with Jesse Jackson and Jesse Jackson Jr.)* Legal Lynching: The Death Penalty and America's Future *(2003). Shapiro is also a veteran reporter, having written for such publications as the* New York Times, *the* Los Angeles Times, *the* Guardian, Salon.com, *and* The Nation *magazine, whose April 3, 1995, issue is where "One Violent Crime" first appeared. Subsequently it was chosen for the volume* The Best American Essays 1996.

Alone in my home I am staring at the television screen and shouting. On the evening local news I have unexpectedly encountered video footage, several months old, of myself writhing on an ambulance gurney, bright green shirt open and drenched with blood, skin pale, knee raised, trying desperately and with utter futility to find relief from pain.

On the evening of August 7, 1994, I was among seven people stabbed and seriously wounded in a coffee bar a few blocks from my house. Any televised recollection of this incident would be upsetting. But the anger that has me shouting tonight is quite specific, and political, in origin: My picture is being shown on the news to illustrate why Connecticut's legislature plans to lock up more criminals for a longer time. A picture of my body, contorted and bleeding, has become a propaganda image in the crime war.

I had not planned to write about this assault. But for months now the politics of the nation have in large part been the politics of crime, from last year's federal crime bill through the fall elections through the Contract With America proposals currently awaiting action by the Senate. Among a welter of reactions to the attack, one feeling is clear: I am unwilling to be a silent poster child in this debate.

The physical and political truth about violence and crime lie in their specificity, so here is what happened: I had gone out for after-dinner coffee that evening with two friends and New Haven neighbors, Martin and Anna Broell Bresnick. At 9:45 we arrived at a recently opened coffeehouse on Audubon Street, a block occupied by an arts high school where Anna teaches, other community arts institutions, a few pleasant shops, and upscale condos. Entering, we said hello to another friend, a former student of Anna's named Cristina Koning, who the day before had started working behind the counter. We sat at a small table near the front of the cafe; about fifteen people were scattered around the room. Just before 10, the owner announced closing time. Martin stood up and walked a few yards to the counter for a final refill.

Suddenly there was chaos—as if a mortar shell had landed. I looked up,   5
heard Martin call Anna's name, saw his arm raised and a flash of metal and people leaping away from a thin bearded man with a ponytail. Tables and chairs toppled. Without thinking I shouted to Anna, "Get down!" and pulled her to the floor, between our table and the cafe's outer wall. She clung to my shirt. I to her shoulders, and, crouching, we pulled each other toward the door.

What actually happened I was only able to tentatively reconstruct many weeks later. Apparently, as Martin headed toward the counter the thin bearded man, whose name we later learned was Daniel Silva, asked the time from a young man named Richard Colberg, who answered and turned to leave.

Without any warning, Silva pulled out a hunting knife with a six-inch blade and stabbed in the lower back a woman leaving with Colberg, a medical technician named Kerstin Braig. Then he stabbed Colberg, severing an artery in his thigh. Silva was a slight man but he moved with demonic speed and force around the cafe's counter. He struck Martin in the thigh and in the arm he raised to protect his face. Our friend Cris Koning had in a moment's time pushed out the screen in a window and helped the wounded Kerstin Braig through it to safety. Cris was talking on the phone with the police when Silva lunged over the counter and stabbed her in the chest and abdomen. He stabbed Anna in the side as she and I pulled each other along the wall. He stabbed Emily Bernard, a graduate student who had been sitting quietly reading a book, in the abdomen as she tried to flee through the cafe's back door. All of this happened in about the time it has taken you to read this paragraph.

Meanwhile, I had made it out the cafe's front door onto the brick sidewalk with Anna, neither of us realizing yet that she was wounded. Seeing Martin through the window, I returned inside and we came out together. Somehow we separated, fleeing opposite ways down the street. I had gone no more than a few steps when I felt a hard punch in my back followed instantly by the unforgettable sensation of skin and muscle tissue parting. Silva had stabbed me about six inches above my waist, just beneath my rib cage. (That single deep stroke cut my diaphragm and sliced my spleen in half.) Without thinking, I clapped my left hand over the wound even before the knife was out and its blade caught my hand, leaving a slice across my palm and two fingers.

"Why are you doing this?" I cried out to Silva in the moment after feeling his knife punch in and yank out. As I fell to the street he leaned over my face; I vividly remember the knife's immense and glittering blade. He directed the point through my shirt into the flesh of my chest, beneath my left shoulder. I remember his brown beard, his clear blue-gray eyes looking directly into mine, the round globe of a street lamp like a halo above his head. Although I was just a few feet from a cafe full of people and although Martin and Anna were only yards away, the street, the city, the world felt utterly empty except for me and this thin bearded stranger with clear eyes and a bowie knife. The space around us — well-lit, familiar Audubon Street, where for six years I had taken a child to music lessons — seemed literally to have expanded into a vast and dark canyon.

"You killed my mother," he answered. My own desperate response: "Please   10
don't." Silva pulled the knifepoint out of my chest and disappeared. A moment later I saw him flying down the street on a battered, ungainly bicycle, back straight, vest flapping and ponytail flying.

After my assailant had gone I lay on the sidewalk, hand still over the wound on my back, screaming. Pain ran over me like an express train; it felt as though every muscle in my back was locked and contorted; breathing was excruciating. A security guard appeared across the street from me; I called out to him but he stood there frozen, or so it seemed. (A few minutes later, he would help police chase Silva down.) I shouted to Anna, who was hiding behind a car down the street. Still in shock and unaware of her own injury, she ran for help, eventually collapsing on the stairs of a nearby brownstone where a prayer group that was meeting upstairs answered her desperate ringing of the doorbell. From where I was lying, I saw a second-floor light in the condo complex across the way. A woman's head appeared in the window. "Please help me," I implored. "He's gone. Please help me." She shouted back that she had called the police, but she did not come to the street. I was suddenly aware of a blond woman—Kerstin Braig, though I did not know her name then—in a white-and-gray plaid dress, sitting on the curb. I asked her for help. "I'm sorry, I've done all I can," she muttered. She raised her hand, like a medieval icon; it was covered with blood. So was her dress. She sank into a kind of stupor. Up the street I saw a police car's flashing blue lights, then another's, then I saw an officer with a concerned face and a cracking radio crouched beside me. I stayed conscious as the medics arrived and I was loaded into an ambulance—being filmed for television, as it turns out, though I have no memory of the crew's presence.

Being a victim is a hard idea to accept, even while lying in a hospital bed with tubes in veins, chest, penis, and abdomen. The spirit rebels against the idea of oneself as fundamentally powerless. So I didn't think much for the first few days about the meaning of being a victim; I saw no political dimension to my experience.

As I learned in more detail what had happened I thought, in my jumbled-up, anesthetized state, about my injured friends—although everyone survived, their wounds ranged from quite serious to critical—and about my wounds and surgery. I also thought about my assailant. A few facts about him are worth repeating. Until August 7 Daniel Silva was a self-employed junk dealer and a homeowner. He was white. He lived with his mother and several dogs. He had no arrest record. A New Haven police detective who was hospitalized across the hall from me recalled Silva as a socially marginal neighborhood character. He was not, apparently, a drug user. He had told neighbors about much violence in his family—indeed not long before August 7 he showed one neighbor a scar on his thigh he said was from a stab wound.

A week earlier, Silva's 79-year-old mother had been hospitalized for diabetes. After a few days the hospital moved her to a new room; when Silva saw his mother's empty bed he panicked, but nurses swiftly took him to her new location. Still, something seemed to have snapped. Earlier on the day of the stabbings, police say, Silva released his beloved dogs, set fire to his house, and rode away on his bicycle as it burned. He arrived on Audubon Street with a single dog on a leash, evidently convinced his mother was dead. (She actually did die a few weeks after Silva was jailed.)

While I lay in the hospital, the big story on CNN was the federal crime bill then being debated in Congress. Even fogged by morphine I was aware of the irony. I was flat on my back, the result of a particularly violent assault, while Congress eventually passed the anti-crime package I had editorialized against in *The Nation* just a few weeks earlier. Night after night hospital, unable to sleep, I watched the crime bill debate replayed and heard Republicans and Democrats (who had sponsored the bill in the first place) fall over each other to prove who could be the toughest on crime.   15

The bill passed on August 21, a few days after I returned home. In early autumn I actually read the entire text of the crime bill—all 412 pages. What I found was perhaps obvious, yet under the circumstances compelling: Not a single one of those 412 pages would have protected me or Anna or Martin or any of the others from our assailant. Not the enhanced prison terms, not the forty-four new death penalty offenses, not the three-strikes-you're-out requirements, not the summary deportations of criminal aliens. And the new tougher-than-tough anti-crime provisions of the Contract With America, like the proposed abolition of the Fourth Amendment's search and seizure protections, offer no more practical protection.

On the other hand, the mental-health and social-welfare safety net shredded by Reaganomics and conservatives of both parties might have made a difference in the life of someone like my assailant—and thus in the life of someone like me. My assailant's growing distress in the days before August 7 was obvious to his neighbors. He had muttered darkly about relatives planning to burn down his house. A better-funded, more comprehensive safety net might just have saved me and six others from untold pain and trouble.

From my perspective—the perspective of a crime victim—the Contract With America and its conservative Democratic analogs are really blueprints for making the streets even less safe. Want to take away that socialistic income subsidy called welfare? Fine. Connecticut Governor John Rowland proposes cutting off all benefits after eighteen months. So more people in New Haven and other cities will turn to the violence-breeding economy of crack, or emotionally implode from sheer desperation. Cut funding for those soft-headed social workers? Fine; let more children be beaten without the prospect of outside intervention, more Daniel Silvas carrying their own traumatic scars into violent adulthood. Get rid of the few amenities prisoners enjoy, like sports equipment, musical instruments, and the right to get college degrees, as proposed by the Congressional right? Fine; we'll make sure that those inmates are released to their own neighborhoods tormented with unchanneled rage.

One thing I could not properly appreciate in the hospital was how deeply many friends, neighbors, and acquaintances were shaken by the coffeehouse stabbings, let alone strangers who took the time to write. The reaction of most was a combination of decent horrified empathy and a clear sense that their own presumption of safety was undermined.

But some people who didn't bother to aquaint themselves with the facts   20
used the stabbings as a sort of Rorschach test on which they projected their own preconceptions about crime, violence, and New Haven. Some present and former Yale students, for instance, were desperate to see in my stabbing evidence of the great dangers of New Haven's inner city. One student newspaper wrote about "New Haven's image as a dangerous town fraught with violence." A student reporter from another Yale paper asked if I didn't think the attack proved New Haven needs better police protection. Given the random nature of this assault—it could as easily have happened in wealthy, suburban Greenwich, where a friend of mine was held up at an ATM at the point of an assault rifle—it's tempting to dismiss such sentiments as typical products of an insular urban campus. But city-hating is central to today's political culture. Newt Gingrich excoriates cities as hopelessly pestilential, crime-ridden, and corrupt.

Fear of urban crime and of the dark-skinned people who live in cities is the right's basic text, and defunding cities a central agenda item for the new Congressional majority.

Yet in no small measure it was the institutions of an urban community that saved my life last August 7. That concerned police officer who found me and Kerstin Braig on the street was joined in a moment by enough emergency workers to handle the carnage in and around the coffeehouse, and his backups arrived quickly enough to chase down my assailant three blocks away. In minutes I was taken to Yale–New Haven hospital less than a mile away—built in part with the kind of public funding so hated by the right. As I was wheeled into the E.R., several dozen doctors and nurses descended to handle all the wounded.

By then my abdomen had swelled from internal bleeding. Dr. Gerard Burns, a trauma surgeon, told me a few weeks later that I arrived on his operating table white as a ghost; my prospects, he said, would have been poor had I not been delivered so quickly, and to an E.R. with the kind of trauma team available only at a large metropolitan hospital. In other words, if my stabbing had taken place in the suburbs I would have bled to death.

"Why didn't anyone try to stop him?" That question was even more common than the reflexive city-bashing. I can't even begin to guess the number of times I had to answer it. Each time, I repeated that Silva moved too fast, that it was simply too confusing. And each time, I found the question not just foolish but offensive.

"Why didn't anyone stop him?" To understand that question is to understand, in some measure, why crime is such a potent political issue. To begin with, the question carries not empathy but an implicit burden of blame; it really asks "Why didn't *you* stop him?" It is asked because no one likes to imagine oneself a victim. It's far easier to graft onto oneself the aggressive power of the attacker, to embrace the delusion of oneself as Arnold Schwarzenegger defeating a multitude single-handedly. *If I am tough enough and strong enough I can take out the bad guys.*

The country is at present suffering from a huge version of this same delusion. This myth is buried deep in the political culture, nurtured in the historical tales of frontier violence and vigilantism and by the action-hero fantasies of film and television. Now, bolstered by the social Darwinists of the right, who see society as an unfettered marketplace in which the strongest individuals flourish, this delusion frames the crime debate.

I also felt that the question "Why didn't anybody stop him?" implied only two choices: Rambo-like heroism or abject victimhood. To put it another way, it suggests that the only possible responses to danger are the individual biological imperatives of fight or flight. And people don't want to think of themselves as on the side of flight. This is a notion whose political moment has arrived. In last year's debate over the crime bill, conservatives successfully portrayed themselves as those who would stand and fight; liberals were portrayed as ineffectual cowards.

25

"Why didn't anyone stop him?" That question and its underlying implications see both heroes and victims as lone individuals. But on the receiving end of a violent attack, the fight-or-flight dichotomy didn't apply. Nor did that radically individualized notion of survival. At the coffeehouse that night, at the moments of greatest threat, there were no Schwarzeneggers, no stand-alone heroes. (In fact I doubt anyone could have "taken out" Silva; as with most crimes, his attack came too suddenly.) But neither were there abject victims. Instead, in the confusion and panic of life-threatening attack, *people reached out to one another.* This sounds simple; yet it suggests there is an instinct for mutual aid that poses a profound challenge to the atomized individualism of the right. Cristina Koning helped the wounded Kerstin Braig to escape, and Kerstin in turn tried to bring Cristina along. Anna and I, and then Martin and I, clung to each other, pulling one another toward the door. And just as Kerstin found me on the sidewalk rather than wait for help alone, so Richard and Emily, who had never met before, together sought a hiding place around the corner. Three of us even spoke with Silva either the moment before or the instant after being stabbed. My plea to Silva may or may not have been what kept him from pushing his knife all the way through my chest and into my heart; it's impossible to know what was going through his mind. But this impulse to communicate, to establish human contact across a gulf of terror and insanity, is deeper and more subtle than the simple formulation of fight or flight, courage or cowardice, would allow.

I have never been in a war, but I now think I understand a little the intense bond among war veterans who have survived awful carnage. It is not simply the common fact of survival but the way in which the presence of these others seemed to make survival itself possible. There's evidence, too, that those who try to go it alone suffer more. In her insightful study *Trauma and Recovery,* Judith Herman, a psychiatrist, writes about rape victims, Vietnam War veterans, political prisoners, and other survivors of extreme violence. "The capacity to preserve social connection . . . ," she concludes, "even in the face of extremity, seems to protect people to some degree against the later development of post-traumatic syndromes. For example, among survivors of a disaster at sea, the men who had managed to escape by cooperating with other showed relatively little evidence of post-traumatic stress afterward." On the other hand, she reports that the "highly symptomatic" ones among those survivors were " 'Rambos,' men who had plunged into impulsive, isolated action and not affiliated with others."

The political point here is that the Rambo justice system proposed by the right is rooted in that dangerous myth of the individual fighting against a hostile world. Recently that myth got another boost from several Republican-controlled state legislatures, which have made it much easier to carry concealed handguns. But the myth has nothing to do with the reality of violent crime, the ways to prevent it, or the needs of survivors. Had Silva been carrying a handgun instead of a knife on August 7, there would have been a massacre.

I do understand the rage and frustration behind the crime-victim movement, and I can see how the right has harnessed it. For weeks I thought obsessively and an-   30 grily of those minutes on Audubon Street, when first the nameless woman in the window and then the security guard refused to approach me—as if I, wounded and helpless, were the dangerous one. There was also a subtle shift in my consciousness a few days after the stabbing. Up until that point, the legal process and press attention seemed clearly centered on my injuries and experience, and those of my fellow victims. But once Silva was arraigned and the formal process of prosecution began, it became *his* case, not mine. I experienced an overnight sense of marginalization, a feeling of helplessness bordering on irrelevance.

Sometimes that got channeled into outrage, fear and panic. After arraignment, Silva's bail was set at $700,000. That sounds high, but just 10 percent of that amount in cash, perhaps obtained through some relative with home equity, would have bought his pretrial release. I was frantic at even this remote prospect of Silva walking the streets. So were the six other victims and our families. We called the prosecutor virtually hourly to request higher bail. It was eventually raised to $800,000, partly because of our complaints and partly because an arson charge was added. Silva remains in the Hartford Community Correctional Center awaiting trial.

Near the six-month anniversary of the stabbings I called the prosecutor and learned that in December Silva's lawyer filed papers indicating he intends to claim a "mental disease or defect" defense. If successful it would send him to a maximum-security hospital for the criminally insane for the equivalent of the maximum criminal penalty. In February the court was still awaiting a report from Silva's psychiatrist. Then the prosecution will have him examined by its own psychiatrist. "There's a backlog," I was told; the case is not likely to come to trial until the end of 1995 at the earliest. Intellectually, I understand that Silva is securely behind bars, that the court system is overburdened, that the delay makes no difference in the long-term outcome. But emotionally, viscerally, the delay is devastating.

Another of my bursts of victim-consciousness involved the press. Objectively, I know that many people who took the trouble to express their sympathy to me found out only through news stories. And sensitive reporting can for the crime victim be a kind of ratification of the seriousness of an assault, a reflection of the community's concern. One reporter for the daily *New Haven Register*, Josh Kovner, did produce level-headed and insightful stories about the Audubon Street attack. But most other reporting was exploitative, intrusive, and inaccurate. I was only a few hours out of surgery, barely able to speak, when the calls from television stations and papers started coming to my hospital room. Anna and Martin, sent home to recover, were ambushed by a Hartford TV crew as they emerged from their physician's office, and later rousted from their beds by reporters from another TV station ringing their doorbell. The *Register*'s editors enraged all seven victims by printing our home addresses (a company policy, for some reason) and running spectacularly distressing full-color photos of the crime scene complete with the coffee bar's bloody windowsill.

Such press coverage inspired in all of us a rage it is impossible to convey. In a study commissioned by the British Broadcasting Standards Council, survivors of violent crimes and disasters "told story after story of the hurt they suffered through the timing of media attention, intrusion into their privacy and harassment, through inaccuracy, distortion and distasteful detail in what was reported." This suffering is not superficial. To the victim of violent crime the press may reinforce the perception that the world is an uncomprehending and dangerous place.

The very same flawed judgments about "news value" contribute significantly to a public conception of crime that is as completely divorced from the facts as a Schwarzenegger movie. One study a few years ago found that reports on crime and justice constitute 22-28 percent of newspaper stories, "nearly three times as much attention as the presidency or the Congress or the state of the economy." And the most spectacular crimes — the stabbing of seven people in an upscale New Haven coffee bar, for instance — are likely to be the most "newsworthy" even though they are statistically the least likely. "The image of crime presented in the media is thus a reverse image of reality," writes sociologist Mark Warr in a study commissioned by the National Academy of Sciences.

Media coverage also brings us to another crucial political moral: The "seriousness" of crime is a matter of race and real estate. This has been pointed out before, but it can't be said too often. Seven people stabbed in a relatively affluent, mostly white neighborhood near Yale University — this was big news on a slow news night. It went national over the A.P. wires and international over CNN's *Headline News*. It was covered by *The New York Times*, and words of sympathy came to New Haven from as far as Prague and Santiago. Because a graduate student and a professor were among those wounded, the university sent representatives to the emergency room. The morning after, New Haven Mayor John DeStefano walked the neighborhood to reassure merchants and office workers. For more than a month the regional press covered every new turn in the case.

Horrendous as it was, though, no one was killed. Four weeks later, a 15-year-old girl named Rashawnda Crenshaw was driving with two friends about a mile from Audubon Street. As the car in which she was a passenger turned a corner she was shot through the window and killed. Apparently her assailants mistook her for someone else. Rashawnda Crenshaw was black and her shooting took place in the Hill, the New Haven neighborhood with the highest poverty rate. No Yale officials showed up at the hospital to comfort Crenshaw's mother or cut through red tape. *The New York Times* did not come calling; there were certainly no bulletins flashed around the world on CNN. The local news coverage lasted just long enough for Rashawnda Crenshaw to be buried.

Anyone trying to deal with the reality of crime, as opposed to the fantasies peddled to win elections, needs to understand the complex suffering of those who are survivors of traumatic crimes, and the suffering and turmoil of their families. I have impressive physical scars: There is a broad purple line from my breastbone to the top of my pubic bone, an X-shaped cut into my side where the chest tube entered, a thick pink mark on my chest where the point of Silva's

35

knife rested on a rib. Then on my back is the unevenly curving horizontal scar where Silva thrust the knife in and yanked it out, leaving what looks like a crooked smile. But the disruption of my psyche is, day in and day out, more noticeable. For weeks after leaving the hospital I awoke nightly agitated, drenched with perspiration. For two months I was unable to write; my brain simply refused to concentrate. Into any moment of mental repose would rush images from the night of August 7; or alternatively, my mind would simply not tune in at all. My reactions are still out of balance and disproportionate. I shut a door on my finger, not too hard, and my body is suddenly flooded with adrenaline and I nearly faint. Walking on the arm of my partner, Margaret, one evening I abruptly shove her to the side of the road; I have seen a tall, lean shadow on the block where we are headed and am alarmed out of all proportion. I get into an argument and find myself quaking with rage for an hour afterward, completely unable to restore calm. Though to all appearances normal, I feel at a long arm's remove from all the familiar sources of pleasure, comfort and anger that shaped my daily life before August 7.

What psychologists call post-traumatic stress disorder is, among other things, a profoundly political state in which the world has gone wrong, in which you feel isolated from the broader community by the inarticulable extremity of experience. I have spent a lot of time in the past few months thinking about what the world must look like to those who have survived repeated violent attacks, whether children battered in their homes or prisoners beaten or tortured behind bars; as well as those, like rape victims, whose assaults are rarely granted public ratification.

The right owes much of its success to the anger of crime victims and the argument that government should do more for us. This appeal is epitomized by the rise of restitution laws—statutes requiring offenders to compensate their targets. On February 7 the House of Representatives passed, by a vote of 431 to 0, the Victim Restitution Act, a plank of the Contract With America that would supposedly send back to jail offenders who don't make good on their debts to their victims. In my own state, Governor Rowland recently proposed a restitution amendment to the state Constitution. 40

On the surface it is hard to argue with the principle of reasonable restitution—particularly since it implies community recognition of the victim's suffering. But I wonder if these laws really will end up benefiting someone like me—or if they are just empty, vote-getting devices that exploit victims and could actually hurt our chances of getting speedy, substantive justice. H. Scott Wallace, former counsel to the Senate Judiciary Subcommittee on Juvenile Justice, writes in *Legal Times* that the much-touted Victim Restitution Act is "unlikely to put a single dollar into crime victims' pockets, would tie up the federal courts with waves of new damages actions, and would promote unconstitutional debtors' prisons."

I also worry that the rhetoric of restitution confuses—as does so much of the imprisonment-and-execution mania dominating the political landscape—the goals of justice and revenge. Revenge, after all, is just another version of the individualized, take-out-the-bad-guys myth. Judith Herman believes indulging fantasies of revenge actually worsens the psychic suffering of trauma survivors: "The desire for revenge . . . arises out of the victim's experience of complete helplessness," and forever ties the victim's fate to the perpetrator's. Real recovery from the cataclysmic isolation of trauma comes only when "the survivor comes to understand the issues of principle that transcend her personal grievance against the perpetrator . . . [a] principle of social justice that connects the fate of others to her own." The survivors and victims' families of the Long Island Rail Road massacre have banded together not to urge that Colin Ferguson be executed but to work for gun control.

What it all comes down to is this: What do survivors of violent crime really need? What does it mean to create a safe society? Do we need courts so overburdened by nonviolent drug offenders that Daniel Silvas go untried for eighteen months, delays that leave victims and suspects alike in limbo? Do we need to throw nonviolent drug offenders into mandatory-sentence proximity with violent sociopaths and career criminals? Do we need the illusory bravado of a Schwarzenegger film—or the real political courage of those L.I.R.R. survivors?

If the use of my picture on television unexpectedly brought me face to face with the memory of August 7, some part of the attack is relived for me daily as I watch the gruesome, voyeuristically reported details of the stabbing deaths of two people in California, Nicole Brown Simpson and Ronald Goldman. It was relived even more vividly by the televised trial of Colin Ferguson. (One night recently after watching Ferguson on the evening news I dreamed that I was on the witness stand and Silva, like Ferguson, was representing himself and questioning me.) Throughout the trial, as Ferguson spoke of falling asleep and having someone else fire his gun, I heard neither cowardly denial nor what his first lawyer called "black rage"; I heard Daniel Silva's calm, secure voice telling me I killed his mother. And when I hear testimony by the survivors of that massacre—on a train as comfortable and familiar to them as my neighborhood coffee bar—I feel a great and incommunicable fellowship.

But the public obsession with these trials, I am convinced, has no more to do with the real experience of crime victims than does the anti-crime posturing of politicians. I do not know what made my assailant act as he did. Nor do I think crime and violence can be reduced to simple political categories. I do know that the answers will not be found in social Darwinism and atomized individualism, in racism, in dismantling cities and increasing the destitution of the poor. To the contrary: Every fragment of my experience suggests that the best protections from crime and the best aid to victims are the very social institutions most derided by the right. As crime victim and citizen what I want is the reality of a safe community—not a politician's fantasyland of restitution and revenge. That is my testimony.   *[1995]*

45

≡ THINKING ABOUT THE TEXT

1. Shapiro concludes by announcing that he has written a "testimony." What do you think are typical features of this genre? In what ways, spe-

cifically, does Shapiro's essay belong to it? Do you think that "testi-mony" is indeed the best genre label for his text? Why, or why not?

2. Where are you especially conscious that Shapiro is relying on ethos — that is, using his personal experience of crime to present himself as an authority on issues of social policy? Refer to specific passages. Do you think it is fair for him to claim authority in this way? Explain your rea-soning.

3. Where are you especially conscious that Shapiro is relying on pathos — that is, emphasizing his own emotions to get his readers feeling as he does? Again, refer to specific passages, and discuss whether you find his strategy persuasive.

4. What, specifically, are Shapiro's main criticisms of how government and the press treat crime? Evaluate at least two of these criticisms, providing support for your attitude toward them.

5. Shapiro seems especially critical of political conservatives, and the *Nation* (where his essay first appeared) is known for being a left-wing magazine. Could someone who is conservative nevertheless agree with at least some of his ideas? If so, which?

EMILY BERNARD

Scar Tissue

Born in Nashville, Tennessee, in 1967, Emily Bernard teaches English and U.S. Ethnic Studies at the University of Vermont. A scholar of the modern cultural move-ment known as the Harlem Renaissance, she has published a book on its most famous photographer, Carl Van Vechten and the Harlem Renaissance: A Portrait in Black and White *(2012). She has also edited* Remember Me to Harlem: The Letters of Langston Hughes and Carl Van Vechten *(2001) and* Some of My Best Friends: Writers on Interracial Friendship *(2004). With Deborah Willis, she co-authored the 2009 volume* Michelle Obama: The First Lady in Photographs. *Bernard has distinguished herself as an essayist, too, with repeated inclusion in* The Best American Essays *series. She was a graduate student when Daniel Silva stabbed her, Bruce Shapiro, and others. Unlike Shapiro, she waited many years before writing about the attack. "Scar Tissue" first appeared in the summer 2012 issue of* The American Scholar *magazine.*

I have been telling this story for years, but telling is a different animal from writing. In the telling and retelling, I have shaped a version of it, one that fits neatly in my hand, something to pull out of my pocket at will, to display, and to tuck away when I'm ready, like a shell or a stone or a molded piece of clay. The story that I have honed over the years is as neat as my scar; it is smooth, and tender, and conceals more than it reveals.

Here is how the newspaper tells the story:

Stabbing spree sends 7 to hospitals

Seven people were wounded, two with life-threatening injuries, when a man pulled a knife at an Audubon Street coffeehouse late Sunday and began stabbing people.

The attack, occurring about 10 p.m., caused pandemonium and a virtual blood bath at Koffee? at 104 Audubon St. . . .

There was no apparent provocation, police said.

The two victims most seriously hurt were covered with blood, and it was difficult to tell how many times they were stabbed, police said.

"There was a lot of blood," said Detective Sgt. Robert Lawlor. "There were some very serious injuries." . . .

Bloody handprints were visible on a window, where one of the victims apparently climbed out. Numerous trails of blood led from the coffeehouse, which is in the city's arts district, near the Creative Arts Workshop and Neighborhood Music School.

"We have no idea what provoked him," Lawlor said. There were about 10 people in the coffeehouse at the time, he said.

—New Haven Register, Monday, August 8, 1994

The first time I read this article I laughed when I got to "blood bath." Blood bath? It sounded like a trailer for a slasher movie. But it wasn't a movie, and there *was* a lot of blood, evidently, although I don't remember that part. I remember it differently.

On the night of August 7, 1994, I walked into a coffee shop called Koffee? on Audubon Street in New Haven, Connecticut. I was a graduate student in the American Studies Program at Yale University, and I was there to work. I had James Weldon Johnson with me, specifically his 1912 novel, *The Autobiography of an Ex-Colored Man*, about which I was writing a paper. I was having a hard time concentrating that night so I went out to the shop, which was not far from where I lived, and was one of the many places in New Haven where students went to read and write and talk. It was a typical coffee shop in a typical college town.

I was frustrated with my work, so frustrated with my inability to concentrate that I was giving the evening only one last chance. It was late, nearly nine o'clock. Maybe too late, maybe just call it a night. I debated with myself, walking slowly the three yards from my car to the door of the shop. I was probably talking to myself, as I do all the time, muttering about everything I had to do. A man on a bicycle arrived at the door at the same time I did. Beside him stood an average-size, average-looking brown dog on a leash. The man was listing on the bike, rocking back and forth, as if he himself had not made the commitment to go inside (*maybe, maybe not*). Our eyes met. He looked like Gallagher, the 1970s comedian—the same long hair and bald pate, the same thick mustache. Or at least that's what I remember. To this day, when I think of Daniel Silva, I think of Gallagher, whom I rarely—if ever—thought about before that night.

5

I don't remember who went in first, but I remember making the decision not to let the oddness of this stranger bother me. Because he was odd. It was the way he was listing on his bicycle; it was the strange way he looked at me. His look was familiar, or too aware — not the passing glance of a stranger. Even now, I have a hard time describing it. He was odd; it was instinct. I *knew* something was wrong with him. Or maybe this is just the cliché of hindsight speaking. After all, we're talking about a university town, and a coffee shop full of nerds off in their own odd little worlds, people who routinely talk to themselves out loud, as I had been doing.

Here I have lingered longer than I lingered in the moment, which passed as quickly as the proverbial blink of an eye. I looked at the man, made the unconscious association with the comic, went in to get my coffee, and planted myself at a table. I put my keys on the table. I pulled out my book and notepad. I took off my glasses and my watch. No distractions, just me and the page, as naked as I allow myself to get in public.

At some point, I looked up and noticed that the strange man had settled into a chair not far from me. I was aware of him as he watched a table full of young girls next to me, presumably undergraduates. They were talking about sex, a sexual encounter one of them had had recently. The girls were loud, sexy, and full of swagger. I had been feeling annoyed by them and their devil-may-care bluster, but now I looked up and saw that the man was staring at them, obviously and (I assumed) salaciously. I felt intimidated by his frank stare, but the girls didn't seem to care, which made me proud of them, and emboldened for myself. Go ahead, talk about sex, I thought. Don't let this freak scare you. Eventually the girls left.

When they did, the man seemed to turn his attention to a young woman I assumed to be medical student or a law student, judging by the size of her very official-looking textbooks. She tried to engage him in conversation, said something like, Hi. I didn't hear his response, but I do know that not long after this exchange, the woman gathered up her books and left.

What happened next? Here's what I told Detective C. Willougby at 1:30 a.m. on August 8, 1994 (for whatever reason, Detective Willougby recorded this in all-caps): 10

> THIS DETECTIVE THEN SPOKE WITH _____ WHO STATED THAT SHE WAS SITTING INSIDE THE RESTAURANT WHEN A WHITE MALE CAME IN WHO HAD A DOG. SHE THEN STATED THAT HE WALKED THE DOG OUTSIDE AND HE THEN RETURNED, HE THEN PULLED OUT A KNIFE AND STARTED STABBING PEOPLE IN THE RESTAURANT. SHE STATED THAT HE STAB HER ONCE IN THE STOMACH AND SHE THEN FLED THE RESTAURANT. SHE THEN STATED THAT SHE HAD NEVER SEEN THE WHITE MALE SUBJECT BEFORE AND SHE DOES NOT KNOW HIM.

What I remember about the moments before it happened is stillness, the hum of low voices and the lights, bright yet soothing, like the talk surrounding me. People talking and laughing quietly. Students, professors, writers; I was the only black person present at that time, but these were people just like me, people who looked like me. So many moments like these over the years in coffee shops in so many cities; all forgettable, ordinary, uneventful. But these particular moments on this particular evening stay with me more palpably than any other moments from that long night. The stillness, the quiet, the hum of low pleasant talk. The sensation of being inside those moments—it is the only *real* memory I retain from that night. Yet, just beyond the border of that quiet, pleasant memory, I can still hear the rhythmic, continuous sound of a dog barking outside, like a warning.

Suddenly, chaos. Pandemonium. Bedlam. Topsy-turvy. Madhouse. A holy mess. All hell broke loose. The room turned upside down, on its back, inside out, went crazy, flipped out. Other words, other clichés. Fear erupted like a seismic shift in the earth's surface, and then charged and pierced and saturated the room like smoke. Fear—a good friend to me that night—chased me toward the back door. But even in the midst of this utter confusion, I paused and listened for gunshots—this was America, after all. I paused not only to listen for the gunshots but to brace myself—literally to tense my shoulders and grit my teeth, searching inside somewhere for the pain, for the tearing impact of a bullet. When I completed that brief inventory, and discovered no bullet, I was overcome with a feeling of relief. Hope, luck. A chance. And a door right behind me—and I *ran*.

And then I was outside in back of the coffeehouse. There were no lights; it was as dark as the bottom of a pocket. Others rushed by me—I don't remember if they were speaking, shouting, screaming, or crying. What I remember was silence, which seemed inexplicable to me even then. I would find out later that what felt like silence was the adrenaline pounding in my ears and deafening me.

I don't know how long I watched the others rush past me before I walked back toward the coffee shop. I don't remember how long I stood there, trying to understand, before everything in me *rejected* what I saw and I charged back into the shop, to retrieve my watch, my keys and glasses, so that I could drive home. Why would I have done this? Nothing about it makes any sense. But however I try to explain it to myself—my stubborn West Indian heritage, a Freudian state of denial—the same thing happened next.

I found myself face to face with the odd man, and he had a knife in his hand. At this point the knife would have had a substantial amount of blood on it. I don't remember the blood. I do remember asking him not to kill me. I meant it, of course, but it also just seemed like the thing to say. I felt that I was playing a role; I felt that the die was cast. I had turned and met my fate. But I was watching as much as I was experiencing. My witnessing was involuntary. In *The Autobiography of an Ex-Colored Man*, the narrator recalls being "fixed to the spot" when he watches a white mob lynch a black man. Like that narrator, I was fixed to the spot.

Why? I did not move because I did not want to excite this man. I did not move because I had to see what was going to happen next. I did not move because I was afraid. I did not move because I was free from fear, as many report feeling in the moments before death. I did not move because I knew that he would hurt me if I did. I did not move because I knew he would not kill me. I did not move because I didn't believe he had the knife I saw in front of me. I did not move because I did not know what to do.

I saw the knife before it entered me. But I have no specific memory of it, the instrument that has determined much of the course of the past 17 years of my life. It went in and out swiftly. What was the sensation upon impact? I don't remember. But I do remember that when he pulled it out of my gut, I fell to the ground. What did it feel like? Strange. Weird. Unusual. Lying on the ground, I beseeched God for help. When I neither felt nor heard a thundering reply, I started to laugh. I knew that I needed a hospital, not God. But I call this my "God moment" anyway, because when I laughed, my wound gaped open, and I looked down and saw and then felt the thick, warm blood rush over my fingers. It is time to get to a hospital, God was saying. I got up, and ran again.

I was more afraid of being in the dark without my glasses than I was of running into the man with the knife a second time. I had never been out on a city street alone without my glasses. I have been wearing eyeglasses since I was eight years old. The last time I had gone without glasses in public, I was not allowed to walk down a street without holding on to the hand of an adult. I was on the eve of my 27th birthday when I was stabbed. The last time I had been out in public without my glasses, I was not permitted to be awake at just before 10:24, which is the time it has become at this point in the story.

A figure ran toward me, a man; I was afraid. I stopped, and he must have seen my fear, this man, because he waved his hands in the air and shouted, "I'm a good Samaritan! A good Samaritan!" I trusted his words, his biblical reference. I let him lead me to some steps across the street.

From Officer Pitoniak's Incident Report, 10:44, on August 7, 1994:   20

> This investigating officer did find one white male subject and one Black
> female subject on the stairs of a apartment complex located across the
> street from 24 Whitney Avenue. Both subjects had stab wounds to the
> stomach areas and Bleeding Profusely. Due to extent of injuries and call-
> ing for medical assistance this officer was not able to obtain any identifica-
> tion of victims.

What's your name? What's your social security number? I fired these questions at the white male subject shortly before Officer Pitoniak arrived. The young white man, whom I had never seen before, was sitting on the steps a few feet away from me. He was going into shock, and I was trying to keep him from doing so. I kept up my round of questioning, and he mumbled some answers. "I'm going out, I'm going out," he said, and fainted. It was only then that I really looked at him. He's white as a sheet, I thought. Literally, *white as a sheet.* This is what it looks like, I thought. He had pale skin, light blond hair, and wore a white oxford shirt. The contrast between the blood and his skin, hair, and shirt must have been dramatic, but I don't remember the blood. I watched him. The more he faded away, the less I was able to ignore what was happening just under my hand. An EMT came close to me and asked about the young man, and I answered him. I talked and talked, told my story, posed as a witness, even as I was seeing sparks and hearing static and the man's badge started to blur. The EMT, trained to recognize the signs of shock, cradled my head and took my hand away from my side. His gloved hand, like my bare hand, became wet with my blood. He said something to his partner — who was tending to the white male subject — and suddenly there was a commotion around me. He laid me down carefully on the steps. He held my bloody hand as his team moved me onto the gurney. At some point, we met eyes and we laughed. The more I laughed, the more I came to. The more I laughed, the more my wound gaped open, which made us laugh even harder. It was all so *absurd*.

> Emily Bernard, 26, is listed in serious condition at Yale-New Haven Hospital. Her birthday is Thursday. — from "The Victims," *New Haven Register*, Tuesday, August 9, 1994

On my birthday, a middle-aged white couple brought chocolates to my hospital room. "It just seemed so sad that you had to spend your birthday in the hospital," said the woman, while her husband looked on sympathetically. I began to cry, not only because of the purity of their kindness, but also because of the morphine. The morphine was there to shield me from the pain, a consequence of healing, my body reassembling itself. A word about the pain: it didn't hurt, the knife. That and the surprising fact that no one died are the two things I always make sure to say in my version of the story.

I did experience terrible pain on the night of August 7. The person responsible for it was the surgeon on call that night. I lay on a gurney, feeling helpless and afraid. A surgeon walked over and without saying a word to me, or even looking in my direction, plunged his fingers into my gaping wound. I gasped and instinctively grabbed his hand. It was only then that the man looked at me, and said icily, "Don't. Touch. My. Hand." His eyes were Aryan blue and as cold as his voice. I asked questions about what was happening, and he refused to respond. Only the attending nurses treated me with any kindness or respect. Whenever I tell the story of the night I got stabbed, I always say that the person who did the most injury to me, who left the deepest wounds, was not Daniel Silva, but the surgeon.

If my story is about pain, it's also about rage. Rage is a physical condition, I've learned from this experience. I feel it now, when I recount the story of the surgeon and recall his face, his voice, his hands.

It also happens unconsciously when I am out in the world. A few months ago, I was walking in downtown New Haven when a young man — presumably a Yale student — suddenly broke into a run. This happens all the time. People run because they're in a hurry to get somewhere; they run to cross the street before the light changes; they run to greet someone they are happy to see. Which was the case on this day.   25

This happens every day. But every time it happens to me, alarms go off, blood rushes to my ears. Adrenaline spills through my bloodstream like lighter fluid. My heart pounds, my pulse races, my temple throbs. Fight or flight — I'm ready to *fight*; the machine inside switches into gear. It doesn't make any sense: I'm watching a young brown-skinned man in an argyle sweater and clunky glasses hug a young white woman in a flouncy white skirt. Such a sight would normally fill me with happiness, but my body is bursting with rage. He hugs her tightly and lifts her off the ground. She wiggles her feet, and they laugh. I smile and come down.

But it takes a while for the machine to grind down and my body to feel normal again. This reaction always throws me. More than my scar, it reminds me of how much of this story I carry inside me.

"You never get angry about it," a therapist once said to me during a conversation about the stabbing. "In all these years, you've never expressed any anger over it." I explained to her, as I have explained to many people over the years, that I did not look into the eyes of someone who was really there, that — and I know this sounds odd — it wasn't *personal*.

John, my husband, knew the story of the stabbing before he knew me, having read an essay about the incident by Bruce Shapiro, who was also stabbed that night. "One Violent Crime" was first published in *The Nation* and then reprinted in *Best American Essays*. I don't know when this came up in the course of our dating, but I remember feeling both a little weirded-out and also reassured: weirded-out because it always feels strange to have people know something intimate about you before they know you, reassured because it's one less thing about yourself, about your past, that you will have to explain.

Even though John was already acquainted with this chapter of my history   30
by the time we met, he has had to sit through numerous renditions of it over the years. Once, not long after we got engaged, we were in New York. I had just given a talk to promote my first book, and after the talk, we met up with a couple of people from my publishing house in the bar of the hotel where we were staying. I had recently begged out of another event because of abdominal pain due to adhesions. Twice before, in the years since the stabbing, adhesions had sent me back to the hospital. Each time this happens, simply, my intestines get locked in a complex dance with my scar tissue. Most likely, the dance gains in intensity for years without my knowing it. Then the dancing stops but the dancers are still intertwined. I can no longer process food. I find myself vomiting, stream upon stream of thick yellow bile. And the pain — it is like being ripped in two, tissue by tissue; I *am* being ripped in two, no similes necessary. Then, as mysteriously as these episodes begin, they simply end.

That night at the bar, Brian, my editor's assistant, asked me how I was feeling. I explained to Susan, the publicist who was there with him, that I suspected the pains had something to do with the stabbing, although no doctor had yet confirmed that. Susan said she didn't know I'd been stabbed, and Brian said I'd never told the whole story. So off I went.

Having had a couple of cocktails, I had become tone deaf. So I told the story in all its glory, lingering on the gruesome details. At some point, John got up abruptly and walked away from the table. Brian looked concerned, but I was sure that my fiancé was only going to the bathroom. I turned back to the table, and to my story, but Brian kept his eye on John, who suddenly fell backward on the floor of the bar, flat as a domino.

It was remarkable. John, my John — so solid, strong and steady — falling backward like a tree having met an ax. His head went *thunk* as it hit the marble floor. The lights in the bar came up so swiftly that it was as if God himself had flipped the switch. Brian was suddenly at his side, cradling his head, pelting questions like "What's your name? What's your social security number? Who's the president?" Brian and I must have watched the same TV shows. John lay on his back on the floor in his suit jacket. His eyes were dazed, straining to register Brian's face, the words coming out of his mouth. It was all that talk of blood, he would tell me later, the blood that I don't remember, the blood that was, according to police reports, all over the walls. Brian said it was the most romantic thing he'd ever witnessed, but I think the fainting had to do with being a man — women, after all, become well acquainted with blood over the course of our lives. At any rate, the story of my stabbing belongs to John, too.

This story also belongs to my twin daughters, Giulia and Isabella, now five and full actors in the world, careful observers of and frequent travelers across the terrain of their mother's body. They have questions. Their questions about the scar, lead, inevitably, to a knife. What happened, Mommy? A man hurt me, he was sick. Why, Mommy? He was really sick. Like he had a stomachache, Mommy? Yes, a really bad stomachache, but it was in his mind, and he didn't have any medicine. The girls fall silent, worry tightening their foreheads. It will never happen to you, I say, and it will never happen to me again.

Being a parent brings up the question of what to call this story. Over the years: The incident. The accident. The stabbing. *My* stabbing. What do my daughters call it? *Your face, Mommy. Your face.*   35

The girls were two and a half years old when I was taken to Yale-New Haven in the fall of 2008 with one of my bouts with adhesions. It was late at night when John and I finally realized that I would have to go to the hospital. We had to ask a friend to come over and stay with the girls while John took me to the emergency room. I can't know what it was like for my daughters to wake up in the morning and find me gone. Gone I remained for seven full days. What sense could this make to a two-year-old? Once I was stable, John brought them to see me in the hospital. What did I look like? Hair wild; eyes glassy from morphine; an IV in my arm; an NG tube in my nose. The nasogastric tube goes through the nose, down the throat, and into the stomach. It is as unpleasant as it sounds, and it has saved my life three times now. It was there to decompress my bowel, which was in distress, and it was held in place by several rudimentary pieces of masking tape. It hurt, and it looked terrible.

I could tell how bad it looked from the expression on Isabella's face. True to form, Giulia, who never takes anything very seriously, who has a "well, that's life" way of approaching the world, hopped right up on my hospital bed and began fooling around with the call button. Isabella, however, clung to her father, her impossibly big brown eyes even impossibly bigger. She said nothing and stared at the wild-haired creature, and shook her head when I held my arms out. She was "fixed to the spot." Even now, when she remembers the hospital, remembers what it was like for her to see me there, what her five-year-old mind seizes upon, what she may continue to seize upon for the rest of her life, regardless of her own wishes or mine, what she remembers is captured in a single phrase she repeats over and over again, which she first uttered as she sat in her car seat a couple of weeks after I was home, back from gone, taking her home from school. She repeated it recently when studying my scar and asking me to explain the *how* of it once again: "Your face, Mommy. Your face."

Seventeen years ago, I was stabbed in the gut by a stranger in a coffee shop. I have proof: a scar (puffy and wormlike, over the points of entry and exit); another scar, similar in texture but much longer, that covers the work of two surgeons (so far); it covers the points of entry and exit of their knives. A midline incision, it's called, and it begins just under my breastbone and ends at my pubic bone, stem to stern, fore to aft. Reminders. Every morning and every night. Evidence. I have police and hospital records, newspaper articles, and Bruce's prize-winning essay, my memories and the memories of others close to me. This happened to me.

I've been telling this story since the night of August 7, 1994. That night, I told the story to doctors, nurses, police officers, family, and friends. Since then, I have told it to gynecologists, a dermatologist, dentists, ophthalmologists, general practitioners, even a podiatrist, and of course, emergency room physicians — all of these men and women in white coats, and their assistants, too. "Have you ever been hospitalized?" reads every single form in every single doctor's waiting room. It's either "yes" or "no." There's no box for "I'd rather not get into it today, thank you very much." So, I tell what happened: in 1994, I was stabbed in the gut by a stranger in a coffee shop. I raise my shirt and reveal my wound. I reassure my listener: it didn't hurt; no one died.

It's the same story, and it isn't true. In the story I tell, there is little blood;   40
the police reports say otherwise. In the story I tell, I wasn't badly hurt; newspaper accounts and hospital records have me in serious condition. In the story I tell, there is no anger; my body begs to differ. Memory lies. To this day, when I speak of the knife, my mind conjures up a butter knife, a small thin blade, flat and tidy. It is a quick, involuntary association, like Daniel Silva and the '70s comic. By chance, several years ago, I saw a hunting knife in a glass cabinet. I got close to the six-inch blade, and shook my head. No, that has nothing to do with me.

But surely the knife, as well as this story, has everything to do with Daniel Silva, to whom this story also belongs.

Not long ago, I received an email that included a link to an article from Renee, a friend in New Haven. "Is this you, Emily?" read the subject field. I opened the link:

> Daniel Silva, who burned down his house, then stabbed seven people with a knife at a New Haven coffee shop, pleaded guilty to second-degree arson Tuesday and received a suspended 10-year sentence that will allow him to eventually be placed in a halfway house.
>
> During a hearing at Superior Court in Waterbury, Silva, now 53, apologized to the stabbing victims and said he was not in a rational "state of mind" on that day in August 1994. Senior Assistant State's Attorney

Gary Nicholson told Judge Richard Damiani that the state recommended
the plea arrangement, which includes five years of probation and a list of
conditions, because Silva has been confined at Connecticut Valley Hospital since the assaults and arson.

Nicholson noted Silva had been repeatedly ruled incompetent to
stand trial for the assaults. Those first-degree assault charges were dismissed in 2000 because, under state law, a defendant facing such charges
must be restored to competency within five years. No such limitation applies to first-degree arson. Last month, Silva was ruled competent to stand
trial on the arson charges, based on testimony from an assistant clinical
professor at Yale School of Medicine who interviewed him. . . .

Silva, dressed in a coat and tie, is bearded and balding. He rose and
told Damiani, "I apologize to the court and to the people that were hurt. I
never meant to do what I did. If I hadn't been in that state of mind, it
never would have occurred."

—*New Haven Register*, September 9, 2009

Yes, Renee. It's me.   *[2012]*

☰ THINKING ABOUT THE TEXT

1. Note places in her essay where Bernard quotes other "texts" about her
   stabbing, including excerpts from official reports. Why, evidently, does
   she incorporate these records?

2. Looking back, what does Bernard think about how she and others acted
   that night, both during and immediately after Silva's stabbing spree?

3. In what ways, specifically, did being stabbed leave Bernard with *psychological* scars?

4. At the start of her essay, Bernard acknowledges that "I have been telling
   this story for years" (para. 1). How does she now view her willingness to
   talk about her stabbing repeatedly? To what extent does she regret having conversed about it so much? Refer to specific passages. What do
   you think she hopes to accomplish by now *writing* about the experience?

5. Where does Bernard use **anaphora**—the technique of beginning several
   consecutive sentences with the same words? Why do you think she
   resorts to this rhetorical strategy at such times? How effective do you
   find it?

☰ MAKING COMPARISONS

1. Bernard wrote about the stabbing attack many years after Shapiro
   wrote about it. How do their essays differ as a result?

2. Does Bernard seem to find any political implications in her experience,
   or is she completely different from Shapiro in this respect? Refer to specific passages in both texts.

3. Shapiro reports feeling anger. Does Bernard ever seem as angry in her essay, or does she appear less driven by emotion than Shapiro is?

≡ WRITING ABOUT ISSUES

1. Write an essay identifying ways in which either Shapiro or Bernard resists being seen *solely* as a victim. Be sure to make clear how you are defining the term *victim*.

2. In recalling details of the attack for their readers, do Shapiro and Bernard similarly emphasize the night's chaos and confusion? Answer this question by writing an essay that refers to specific passages in both texts.

3. On November 8, 2012, Shapiro and Bernard publically discussed their stabbing experience, at a forum sponsored by the Dart Center (where Shapiro is executive director). Watch this discussion online by going to the center's Web site. Then, imagine that you were asked to be a guest respondent at this event. Write a ten-minute speech you would give — the comment you would make on the two writers' conversation. Refer at least briefly to their essays.

4. Write an essay explaining how Shapiro's and Bernard's essays influence your view of a recent violent crime committed by someone who seemed to have mental problems. Possible cases include the 2007 massacre at Virginia Tech; the 2012 shootings at an Aurora, Colorado movie theater; the 2012 killings in Newtown, Massachusetts; and the 2014 killings near the campus of the University of California at Santa Barbara.

The Possible Virtue of Disobeying the Law: Across Genres

SOPHOCLES, *Antigone* (play)

MARTIN LUTHER KING JR., "Letter from Birmingham Jail" (letter)

Many people assume that the legal systems they live under are fair and moral. At various times and places, however, individuals and social movements have objected to certain laws, declaring them unethical and perhaps even condemning the entire government behind them. History has seen numerous occasions when such criticism has turned violent, even becoming outright revolt. At other moments, though, the protest has taken the form of civil disobedience. This is usually defined as the use of relatively *nonviolent* means to defy a law, on behalf of what the protestors claim is a higher principle. Contemporary examples in the United States have included mass demonstrations by foes of capitalism at economic summits, as well as the blocking of abortion clinics by right-to-life groups. Of course, civil disobedience has also occurred in other countries. Mahatma Gandhi famously practiced it in working for the independence of India. More recently, rallies have defied oppressive regimes in the Mideast, while smaller circles of dissidents continue to challenge the leaders of Communist China.

Paired in this cluster are two of the most well-known texts that examine the possible virtue of disobeying the law. In Sophocles' ancient Greek tragedy *Antigone*, the title character buries her dead brother even when forbidden to by the head of state. The play's audience must consider whether family obligations can indeed outweigh government decrees. Martin Luther King Jr.'s 1963 "Letter from Birmingham Jail" is perhaps the most famous modern argument for nonviolent resistance to laws that maintain racial inequality. Both of these works leave you, their current reader, having to decide how you would identify and deal with the differences between "just" and "unjust" legal systems.

≣ BEFORE YOU READ

Civil disobedience is usually defined as a form of protest: specifically, the use of nonviolent means to defy a law on behalf of a supposedly higher moral principle. Under what circumstances, if any, do you think civil disobedience is justified? What particular historical and contemporary events come to mind as you think about this issue?

SOPHOCLES

Antigone

Translated by Robert Fagles

Along with Aeschylus and Euripides, Sophocles (496? B.C.E.–406? B.C.E.) is considered one of the greatest writers of tragedy in ancient Athens. During his lifetime, he

© Bettmann/Corbis

was much respected in the city, often winning its dramatic competitions. Evidently he wrote over a hundred plays, but only seven survive complete. As a practitioner of tragedy, Sophocles was innovative. Among other things, he increased the number of actors on stage from two to three, while reducing the chorus from fifty to fifteen. Productions of his plays did remain traditional in that the performers wore masks and were exclusively male. Oedipus the King *and* Antigone *continue to be much performed today; moreover, through the centuries there have been numerous adaptations of them, such as Jean Anouilh's 1944 version of* Antigone, *a challenge to the Nazi occupiers of Paris.*

Antigone *was produced in 441* B.C.E., *the first of three interrelated plays now known as the Oedipus cycle.* Oedipus the King *was produced between 430 and 427* B.C.E., *and* Oedipus at Colonus *was posthumously produced in 401* B.C.E. *Scholars know that the plots of both these plays were familiar to Sophocles' audience. Less clear is whether that audience was familiar with the story of* Antigone, *which comes last in terms of plot chronology. The title character of* Oedipus the King *is Antigone's father, the ruler of Thebes. In the play, Oedipus blinds himself and leaves Thebes when he discovers that he has unknowingly fulfilled a terrible prophecy—that he would kill his own father and marry his mother.* Oedipus at Colonus *focuses on his death.*

CHARACTERS

ANTIGONE, *daughter of Oedipus and Jocasta*
ISMENE, *sister of Antigone*

A CHORUS *of old Theban citizens and their* LEADER
CREON, *king of Thebes, uncle of Antigone and Ismene*
A SENTRY
HAEMON, *son of Creon and Eurydice*
TIRESIAS, *a blind prophet*
A MESSENGER
EURYDICE, *wife of Creon*
GUARDS, ATTENDANTS, AND A BOY

TIME AND SCENE: *The royal house of Thebes. It is still night, and the invading armies of Argos have just been driven from the city. Fighting on opposite sides, the sons of Oedipus, Eteocles and Polynices, have killed each other in combat. Their uncle, Creon, is now king of Thebes.*

    Enter Antigone, slipping through the central doors of the palace. She motions to her sister, Ismene, who follows her cautiously toward an altar at the center of the stage.

ANTIGONE: My own flesh and blood—dear sister, dear Ismene,
    how many griefs our father Oedipus handed down!
    Do you know one, I ask you, one grief
    that Zeus° will not perfect for the two of us
    while we still live and breathe? There's nothing,   5
    no pain—our lives are pain—no private shame,
    no public disgrace, nothing I haven't seen
    in your griefs and mine. And now this:
    an emergency decree, they say, the Commander
    has just declared for all of Thebes.   10
    What, haven't you heard? Don't you see?
    The doom reserved for enemies
    marches on the ones we love the most.
ISMENE: Not I, I haven't heard a word, Antigone.
    Nothing of loved ones,   15
    no joy or pain has come my way, not since
    the two of us were robbed of our two brothers,
    both gone in a day, a double blow—
    not since the armies of Argos vanished,
    just this very night. I know nothing more,   20
    whether our luck's improved or ruin's still to come.
ANTIGONE: I thought so. That's why I brought you out here,
    past the gates, so you could hear in private.
ISMENE: What's the matter? Trouble, clearly . . .
    you sound so dark, so grim.   25
ANTIGONE: Why not? Our own brothers' burial!

---

4 Zeus: The highest Olympian deity.

Hasn't Creon graced one with all the rites,
disgraced the other? Eteocles, they say,
has been given full military honors,
rightly so — Creon's laid him in the earth   30
and he goes with glory down among the dead.
But the body of Polynices, who died miserably —
why, a city-wide proclamation, rumor has it,
forbids anyone to bury him, even mourn him.
He's to be left unwept, unburied, a lovely treasure   35
for birds that scan the field and feast to their heart's content.

Such, I hear, is the martial law our good Creon
lays down for you and me — yes, me, I tell you —
and he's coming here to alert the uninformed
in no uncertain terms,   40
and he won't treat the matter lightly. Whoever
disobeys in the least will die, his doom is sealed:
stoning to death inside the city walls!

There you have it. You'll soon show what you are,
worth your breeding, Ismene, or a coward —   45
for all your royal blood.
ISMENE: My poor sister, if things have come to this,
who am I to make or mend them, tell me,
what good am I to you?
ANTIGONE: Decide.
Will you share the labor, share the work?   50
ISMENE: What work, what's the risk? What do you mean?
ANTIGONE:

Raising her hands.

Will you lift up his body with these bare hands
and lower it with me?
ISMENE: What? You'd bury him —
when a law forbids the city?
ANTIGONE: Yes!
He is my brother and — deny it as you will —   55
your brother too.
No one will ever convict me for a traitor.
ISMENE: So desperate, and Creon has expressly —
ANTIGONE: No,
he has no right to keep me from my own.
ISMENE: Oh my sister, think —   60
think how our own father died, hated,
his reputation in ruins, driven on
by the crimes he brought to light himself
to gouge out his eyes with his own hands —

then mother . . . his mother and wife, both in one,   65
mutilating her life in the twisted noose—
and last, our two brothers dead in a single day,
both shedding their own blood, poor suffering boys,
battling out their common destiny hand-to-hand.
Now look at the two of us, left so alone . . .   70
think what a death we'll die, the worst of all
if we violate the laws and override
the fixed decree of the throne, its power—
we must be sensible. Remember we are women,
we're not born to contend with men. Then too,   75
we're underlings, ruled by much stronger hands,
so we must submit in this, and things still worse.

I, for one, I'll beg the dead to forgive me—
I'm forced, I have no choice—I must obey
the ones who stand in power. Why rush to extremes?   80
It's madness, madness.
ANTIGONE: I won't insist,
no, even if you should have a change of heart,
I'd never welcome you in the labor, not with me.
So, do as you like, whatever suits you best—
I'll bury him myself.   85
And even if I die in the act, that death will be a glory.
I'll lie with the one I love and loved by him—
an outrage sacred to the gods! I have longer
to please the dead than please the living here:
in the kingdom down below I'll lie forever.   90
Do as you like, dishonor the laws
the gods hold in honor.
ISMENE: I'd do them no dishonor . . .
but defy the city? I have no strength for that.
ANTIGONE: You have your excuses. I am on my way,
I'll raise a mound for him, for my dear brother.   95
ISMENE: Oh Antigone, you're so rash—I'm so afraid for you!
ANTIGONE: Don't fear for me. Set your own life in order.
ISMENE: Then don't, at least, blurt this out to anyone.
Keep it a secret. I'll join you in that, I promise.
ANTIGONE: Dear god, shout it from the rooftops. I'll hate you   100
all the more for silence—tell the world!
ISMENE: So fiery—and it ought to chill your heart.
ANTIGONE: I know I please where I must please the most.
ISMENE: Yes, if you can, but you're in love with impossibility.
ANTIGONE: Very well then, once my strength gives out   105
I will be done at last.
ISMENE: You're wrong from the start,

you're off on a hopeless quest.

ANTIGONE: If you say so, you will make me hate you,
and the hatred of the dead, by all rights,
will haunt you night and day.   110
But leave me to my own absurdity, leave me
to suffer this—dreadful thing. I'll suffer
nothing as great as death without glory.

Exit to the side.

ISMENE: Then go if you must, but rest assured,
wild, irrational as you are, my sister,   115
you are truly dear to the ones who love you.

*Withdrawing to the palace. Enter a Chorus, the old citizens of Thebes, chanting as
the sun begins to rise.*

CHORUS: Glory!—great beam of sun, brightest of all
that ever rose on the seven gates of Thebes,
you burn through night at last!
Great eye of the golden day,   120
mounting the Dirce's° banks you throw him back—
the enemy out of Argos, the white shield, the man of bronze—
he's flying headlong now
the bridle of fate stampeding him with pain!

And he had driven against our borders,   125
launched by the warring claims of Polynices—
like an eagle screaming, winging havoc
over the land, wings of armor
shielded white as snow,
a huge army massing,   130
crested helmets bristling for assault.

He hovered above our roofs, his vast maw gaping
closing down around our seven gates,
his spears thirsting for the kill
but now he's gone, look,   135
before he could glut his jaws with Theban blood
or the god of fire put our crown of towers to the torch.

He grappled the Dragon none can master—Thebes—
the clang of our arms like thunder at his back!

Zeus hates with a vengeance all bravado,   140
the mighty boasts of men. He watched them
coming on in a rising flood, the pride
of their golden armor ringing shrill—

121 the Dirce: A river near Thebes.

and brandishing his lightning
blasted the fighter just at the goal,   145
rushing to shout his triumph from our walls.

Down from the heights he crashed, pounding down on the earth!
And a moment ago, blazing torch in hand—
          mad for attack, ecstatic
he breathed his rage, the storm   150
    of his fury hurling at our heads!
But now his high hopes have laid him low
and down the enemy ranks the iron god of war
          deals his rewards, his stunning blows—Ares°
          rapture of battle, our right arm in the crisis.   155

          Seven captains marshaled at seven gates
          seven against their equals, gave
          their brazen trophies up to Zeus,
          god of the breaking rout of battle,
          all but two: those blood brothers,   160
          one father, one mother—matched in rage,
          spears matched for the twin conquest—
          clashed and won the common prize of death.

But now for Victory! Glorious in the morning,
joy in her eyes to meet our joy   165
          she is winging down to Thebes,
our fleets of chariots wheeling in her wake—
          Now let us win oblivion from the wars,
thronging the temples of the gods
in singing, dancing choirs through the night!   170
          Lord Dionysus,° god of the dance
          that shakes the land of Thebes, now lead the way!

Enter Creon from the palace, attended by his guard.

          But look, the king of the realm is coming,
          Creon, the new man for the new day,
          whatever the gods are sending now . . .   175
          what new plan will he launch?
          Why this, this special session?
          Why this sudden call to the old men
          summoned at one command?
CREON: My countrymen,
          the ship of state is safe. The gods who rocked her,   180
after a long, merciless pounding in the storm,
have righted her once more.

154 Ares: God of war.   **171 Dionysus:** God of fertility and wine.

Out of the whole city
I have called you here alone. Well I know,
first, your undeviating respect
for the throne and royal power of King Laius.   185
Next, while Oedipus steered the land of Thebes,
and even after he died, your loyalty was unshakable,
you still stood by their children. Now then,
since the two sons are dead — two blows of fate
in the same day, cut down by each other's hands,   190
both killers, both brothers stained with blood —
as I am next in kin to the dead,
I now possess the throne and all its powers.

Of course you cannot know a man completely,
his character, his principles, sense of judgment,   195
not till he's shown his colors, ruling the people,
making laws. Experience, there's the test.
As I see it, whoever assumes the task,
the awesome task of setting the city's course,
and refuses to adopt the soundest policies   200
but fearing someone, keeps his lips locked tight,
he's utterly worthless. So I rate him now,
I always have. And whoever places a friend
above the good of his own country, he is nothing:
I have no use for him. Zeus my witness,   205
Zeus who sees all things, always —
I could never stand by silent, watching destruction
march against our city, putting safety to rout,
nor could I ever make that man a friend of mine
who menaces our country. Remember this: 210
our country *is* our safety.
Only while she voyages true on course
can we establish friendships, truer than blood itself.
Such are my standards. They make our city great.

Closely akin to them I have proclaimed,   215
just now, the following decree to our people
concerning the two sons of Oedipus.
Eteocles, who died fighting for Thebes,
excelling all in arms: he shall be buried,
crowned with a hero's honors, the cups we pour   220
to soak the earth and reach the famous dead.

But as for his blood brother, Polynices,
who returned from exile, home to his father-city
and the gods of his race, consumed with one desire —

to burn them roof to roots—who thirsted to drink   225
his kinsmen's blood and sell the rest to slavery:
that man—a proclamation has forbidden the city
to dignify him with burial, mourn him at all.
No, he must be left unburied, his corpse
carrion for the birds and dogs to tear,   230
an obscenity for the citizens to behold!
These are my principles. Never at my hands
will the traitor be honored above the patriot.
But whoever proves his loyalty to the state:
I'll prize that man in death as well as life.   235

LEADER: If this is your pleasure, Creon, treating
our city's enemy and our friend this way . . .
The power is yours, I suppose, to enforce it
with the laws, both for the dead and all of us,
the living.

CREON: Follow my orders closely then,   240
be on your guard.

LEADER: We're too old.
Lay that burden on younger shoulders.

CREON: No, no,
I don't mean the body—I've posted guards already.

LEADER: What commands for us then? What other service?

CREON: See that you never side with those who break my orders. 245

LEADER: Never. Only a fool could be in love with death.

CREON: Death is the price—you're right. But all too often
the mere hope of money has ruined many men.

A Sentry enters from the side.

SENTRY: My lord,
I can't say I'm winded from running, or set out
with any spring in my legs either—no sir,   250
I was lost in thought, and it made me stop, often,
dead in my tracks, wheeling, turning back,
and all the time a voice inside me muttering,
"Idiot, why? You're going straight to your death."
Then muttering, "Stopped again, poor fool?   255
If somebody gets the news to Creon first,
what's to save your neck?"
                          And so,
mulling it over, on I trudged, dragging my feet,
you can make a short road take forever . . .
but at last, look, common sense won out,   260
I'm here, and I'm all yours,
and even though I come empty-handed
I'll tell my story just the same, because

I've come with a good grip on one hope,
what will come will come, whatever fate—   265
CREON: Come to the point!
What's wrong—why so afraid?
SENTRY: First, myself, I've got to tell you,
I didn't do it, didn't see who did—
Be fair, don't take it out on me.   270
CREON: You're playing it safe, soldier,
barricading yourself from any trouble.
It's obvious, you've something strange to tell.
SENTRY: Dangerous too, and danger makes you delay
for all you're worth.   275
CREON: Out with it—then dismiss!
SENTRY: All right, here it comes. The body—
someone's just buried it, then run off . . .
sprinkled some dry dust on the flesh,
given it proper rites.
CREON: What?   280
What man alive would dare—
SENTRY: I've no idea, I swear it.
There was no mark of a spade, no pickaxe there,
no earth turned up, the ground packed hard and dry,
unbroken, no tracks, no wheelruts, nothing,
the workman left no trace. Just at sunup   285
the first watch of the day points it out—
it was a wonder! We were stunned . . .
a terrific burden too, for all of us, listen:
you can't see the corpse, not that it's buried,
really, just a light cover of road-dust on it,   290
as if someone meant to lay the dead to rest
and keep from getting cursed.
Not a sign in sight that dogs or wild beasts
had worried the body, even torn the skin.

But what came next! Rough talk flew thick and fast,   295
guard grilling guard—we'd have come to blows
at last, nothing to stop it; each man for himself
and each the culprit, no one caught red-handed,
all of us pleading ignorance, dodging the charges,
ready to take up red-hot iron in our fists,   300
go through fire, swear oaths to the gods—
"I didn't do it, I had no hand in it either,
not in the plotting, not in the work itself!"

Finally, after all this wrangling came to nothing,
one man spoke out and made us stare at the ground,   305

hanging our heads in fear. No way to counter him,
no way to take his advice and come through
safe and sound. Here's what he said:
"Look, we've got to report the facts to Creon,
we can't keep this hidden." Well, that won out,   310
and the lot fell on me, condemned me,
unlucky as ever, I got the prize. So here I am,
against my will and yours too, well I know—
no one wants the man who brings bad news.

LEADER: My king,
ever since he began I've been debating in my mind,   315
could this possibly be the work of the gods?

CREON: Stop—
before you make me choke with anger—the gods!
You, you're senile, must you be insane?
You say—why it's intolerable—say the gods
could have the slightest concern for that corpse?   320
Tell me, was it for meritorious service
they proceeded to bury him, prized him so? The hero
who came to burn their temples ringed with pillars,
their golden treasures—scorch their hallowed earth
and fling their laws to the winds.   325
Exactly when did you last see the gods
celebrating traitors? Inconceivable!

No, from the first there were certain citizens
who could hardly stand the spirit of my regime,
grumbling against me in the dark, heads together,   330
tossing wildly, never keeping their necks beneath
the yoke, loyally submitting to their king.
These are the instigators, I'm convinced—
they've perverted my own guard, bribed them
to do their work.

                          Money! Nothing worse   335
in our lives, so current, rampant, so corrupting.
Money—you demolish cities, root men from their homes,
you train and twist good minds and set them on
to the most atrocious schemes. No limit,
you make them adept at every kind of outrage,   340
every godless crime—money!
                              Everyone—
the whole crew bribed to commit this crime,
they've made one thing sure at least:
sooner or later they will pay the price.

Wheeling on the Sentry.

You— 345
I swear to Zeus as I still believe in Zeus,
if you don't find the man who buried that corpse,
the very man, and produce him before my eyes,
simple death won't be enough for you,
not till we string you up alive 350
and wring the immorality out of you.
Then you can steal the rest of your days,
better informed about where to make a killing.
You'll have learned, at last, it doesn't pay
to itch for rewards from every hand that beckons. 355
Filthy profits wreck most men, you'll see—
they'll never save your life.

SENTRY: Please,
    may I say a word or two, or just turn and go?

CREON: Can't you tell? Everything you say offends me.

SENTRY: Where does it hurt you, in the ears or in the heart? 360

CREON: And who are you to pinpoint my displeasure?

SENTRY: The culprit grates on your feelings,
    I just annoy your ears.

CREON: Still talking?
    You talk too much! A born nuisance—

SENTRY: Maybe so,
    but I never did this thing, so help me!

CREON: Yes you did— 365
    what's more, you squandered your life for silver!

SENTRY: Oh it's terrible when the one who does the judging
    judges things all wrong.

CREON: Well now,
    you just be clever about your judgments—
    if you fail to produce the criminals for me, 370
    you'll swear your dirty money brought you pain.

Turning sharply, reentering the palace.

SENTRY: I hope he's found. Best thing by far.
    But caught or not, that's in the lap of fortune;
    I'll never come back, you've seen the last of me.
    I'm saved, even now, and I never thought, 375
    I never hoped—
    dear gods, I owe you all my thanks!

Rushing out.

CHORUS: Numberless wonders
    terrible wonders walk the world but none the match for man—
    that great wonder crossing the heaving gray sea,
            driven on by the blasts of winter 380

on through breakers crashing left and right,
    holds his steady course
and the oldest of the gods he wears away—
the Earth, the immortal, the inexhaustible—
as his plows go back and forth, year in, year out   385
    with the breed of stallions turning up the furrows.
And the blithe, lightheaded race of birds he snares,
the tribes of savage beasts, the life that swarms the depths—
       with one fling of his nets
woven and coiled tight, he takes them all,   390
    man the skilled, the brilliant!
He conquers all, taming with his techniques
the prey that roams the cliffs and wild lairs,
training the stallion, clamping the yoke across
    his shaggy neck, and the tireless mountain bull.   395
And speech and thought, quick as the wind
and the mood and mind for law that rules the city—
    all these he has taught himself
and shelter from the arrows of the frost
when there's rough lodging under the cold clear sky   400
and the shafts of lashing rain—
       ready, resourceful man!
         Never without resources
never an impasse as he marches on the future—
only Death, from Death alone he will find no rescue   405
but from desperate plagues he has plotted his escapes.

Man the master, ingenious past all measure
past all dreams, the skills within his grasp—
    he forges on, now to destruction
now again to greatness. When he weaves in   410
the laws of the land, and the justice of the gods
that binds his oaths together
       he and his city rise high—
        but the city casts out
that man who weds himself to inhumanity   415
thanks to reckless daring. Never share my hearth
never think my thoughts, whoever does such things.

Enter Antigone from the side, accompanied by the Sentry.

    Here is a dark sign from the gods—
    what to make of this? I know her,
    how can I deny it? That young girl's Antigone!   420
    Wretched, child of a wretched father,
    Oedipus. Look, is it possible?
    They bring you in like a prisoner—

why? did you break the king's laws?
Did they take you in some act of mad defiance?   425
SENTRY: She's the one, she did it single-handed—
we caught her burying the body. Where's Creon?

Enter Creon from the palace.

LEADER: Back again, just in time when you need him.
CREON: In time for what? What is it?
SENTRY: My king,
there's nothing you can swear you'll never do—   430
second thoughts make liars of us all.
I could have sworn I wouldn't hurry back
(what with your threats, the buffeting I just took),
but a stroke of luck beyond our wildest hopes,
what a joy, there's nothing like it. So,   435
back I've come, breaking my oath, who cares?
I'm bringing in our prisoner—this young girl—
we took her giving the dead the last rites.
But no casting lots this time; this is *my* luck,
my prize, no one else's.
                                      Now, my lord,   440
here she is. Take her, question her,
cross-examine her to your heart's content.
But set me free, it's only right—
I'm rid of this dreadful business once for all.
CREON: Prisoner! Her? You took her—where, doing what?   445
SENTRY: Burying the man. That's the whole story.
CREON: What?
You mean what you say, you're telling me the truth?
SENTRY: She's the one. With my own eyes I saw her
bury the body, just what you've forbidden.
There. Is that plain and clear?   450
CREON: What did you see? Did you catch her in the act?
SENTRY: Here's what happened. We went back to our post,
those threats of yours breathing down our necks—
we brushed the corpse clean of the dust that covered it,
stripped it bare . . . it was slimy, going soft,   455
and we took to high ground, backs to the wind
so the stink of him couldn't hit us;
jostling, baiting each other to keep awake,
shouting back and forth—no napping on the job,
not this time. And so the hours dragged by   460
until the sun stood dead above our heads,
a huge white ball in the noon sky, beating,
blazing down, and then it happened—
suddenly, a whirlwind!

Twisting a great dust-storm up from the earth,   465
a black plague of the heavens, filling the plain,
ripping the leaves off every tree in sight,
choking the air and sky. We squinted hard
and took our whipping from the gods.

And after the storm passed—it seemed endless—   470
there, we saw the girl!
And she cried out a sharp, piercing cry,
like a bird come back to an empty nest,
peering into its bed, and all the babies gone . . .
Just so, when she sees the corpse bare   475
she bursts into a long, shattering wail
and calls down withering curses on the heads
of all who did the work. And she scoops up dry dust,
handfuls, quickly, and lifting a fine bronze urn,
lifting it high and pouring, she crowns the dead   480
with three full libations.
                             Soon as we saw
we rushed her, closed on the kill like hunters,
and she, she didn't flinch. We interrogated her,
charging her with offenses past and present—
she stood up to it all, denied nothing. I tell you,   485
it made me ache and laugh in the same breath.
It's pure joy to escape the worst yourself,
it hurts a man to bring down his friends.
But all that, I'm afraid, means less to me
than my own skin. That's the way I'm made.

CREON:

Wheeling on Antigone.

                                                    You,   490
with your eyes fixed on the ground—speak up.
Do you deny you did this, yes or no?
ANTIGONE: I did it. I don't deny a thing.
CREON:

To the Sentry.

You, get out, wherever you please—
you're clear of a very heavy charge.   495

He leaves; Creon turns back to Antigone.

You, tell me briefly, no long speeches—
were you aware a decree had forbidden this?
ANTIGONE: Well aware. How could I avoid it? It was public.
CREON: And still you had the gall to break this law?

ANTIGONE: Of course I did. It wasn't Zeus, not in the least,   500
  who made this proclamation—not to me.
  Nor did that Justice, dwelling with the gods
  beneath the earth, ordain such laws for men.
  Nor did I think your edict had such force
  that you, a mere mortal, could override the gods,   505
  the great unwritten, unshakable traditions.
  They are alive, not just today or yesterday:
  they live forever, from the first of time,
  and no one knows when they first saw the light.

  These laws—I was not about to break them,   510
  not out of fear of some man's wounded pride,
  and face the retribution of the gods.
  Die I must, I've known it all my life—
  how could I keep from knowing?—even without
  your death-sentence ringing in my ears.   515
  And if I am to die before my time
  I consider that a gain. Who on earth,
  alive in the midst of so much grief as I,
  could fail to find his death a rich reward?
  So for me, at least, to meet this doom of yours   520
  is precious little pain. But if I had allowed
  my own mother's son to rot, an unburied corpse—
  that would have been an agony! This is nothing.
  And if my present actions strike you as foolish,
  let's just say I've been accused of folly   525
  by a fool.
LEADER: Like father like daughter,
  passionate, wild . . .
  she hasn't learned to bend before adversity.
CREON: No? Believe me, the stiffest stubborn wills
  fall the hardest; the toughest iron,   530
  tempered strong in the white-hot fire,
  you'll see it crack and shatter first of all.
  And I've known spirited horses you can break
  with a light bit—proud, rebellious horses.
  There's no room for pride, not in a slave,   535
  not with the lord and master standing by.

  This girl was an old hand at insolence
  when she overrode the edicts we made public.
  But once she'd done it—the insolence,
  twice over—to glory in it, laughing,   540
  mocking us to our face with what she'd done.

I'm not the man, not now: she is the man
if this victory goes to her and she goes free.

Never! Sister's child or closer in blood
than all my family clustered at my altar   545
worshiping Guardian Zeus—she'll never escape,
she and her blood sister, the most barbaric death.
Yes, I accuse her sister of an equal part
in scheming this, this burial.

To his attendants.

                       Bring her here!
I just saw her inside, hysterical, gone to pieces.   550
It never fails: the mind convicts itself
in advance, when scoundrels are up to no good,
plotting in the dark. Oh but I hate it more
when a traitor, caught red-handed,
tries to glorify his crimes.   555
ANTIGONE: Creon, what more do you want
   than my arrest and execution?
CREON: Nothing. Then I have it all.
ANTIGONE: Then why delay? Your moralizing repels me,
   every word you say—pray god it always will.   560
   So naturally all I say repels you too.
                           Enough.
Give me glory! What greater glory could I win
than to give my own brother decent burial?
These citizens here would all agree,

To the Chorus.

   they'd praise me too   565
   if their lips weren't locked in fear.

Pointing to Creon.

   Lucky tyrants—the perquisites of power!
   Ruthless power to do and say whatever pleases *them.*
CREON: You alone, of all the people in Thebes,
   see things that way.
ANTIGONE: They see it just that way   570
   but defer to you and keep their tongues in leash.
CREON: And you, aren't you ashamed to differ so from them?
   So disloyal!
ANTIGONE: Not ashamed for a moment,
   not to honor my brother, my own flesh and blood.
CREON: Wasn't Eteocles a brother too—cut down, facing him?   575
ANTIGONE: Brother, yes, by the same mother, the same father.
CREON: Then how can you render his enemy such honors,

such impieties in his eyes?
ANTIGONE: He'll never testify to that,
    Eteocles dead and buried.
CREON: He will—   580
    if you honor the traitor just as much as him.
ANTIGONE: But it was his brother, not some slave that died—
CREON: Ravaging our country!—
    but Eteocles died fighting in our behalf.
ANTIGONE: No matter—Death longs for the same rites for all.   585
CREON: Never the same for the patriot and the traitor.
ANTIGONE: Who, Creon, who on earth can say the ones below
    don't find this pure and uncorrupt?
CREON: Never. Once an enemy, never a friend,
    not even after death.   590
ANTIGONE: I was born to join in love, not hate—
    that is my nature.
CREON: Go down below and love,
    if love you must—love the dead! While I'm alive,
    no woman is going to lord it over me.

Enter Ismene from the palace, under guard.

CHORUS: Look,
    Ismene's coming, weeping a sister's tears,   595
    loving sister, under a cloud . . .
    her face is flushed, her cheeks streaming.
    Sorrow puts her lovely radiance in the dark.
CREON: You—
    in my house, you viper, slinking undetected,
    sucking my life-blood! I never knew   600
    I was breeding twin disasters, the two of you
    rising up against my throne. Come, tell me,
    will you confess your part in the crime or not?
    Answer me. Swear to me.
ISMENE: I did it, yes—
    if only she consents—I share the guilt,   605
    the consequences too.
ANTIGONE: No,
    Justice will never suffer that—not you,
    you were unwilling. I never brought you in.
ISMENE: But now you face such dangers . . . I'm not ashamed
    to sail through trouble with you,   610
    make your troubles mine.
ANTIGONE: Who did the work?
    Let the dead and the god of death bear witness!
    I've no love for a friend who loves in words alone.
ISMENE: Oh no, my sister, don't reject me, please,

	let me die beside you, consecrating	615
	the dead together.	
ANTIGONE:	Never share my dying,	
	don't lay claim to what you never touched.	
	My death will be enough.	
ISMENE:	What do I care for life, cut off from you?	
ANTIGONE:	Ask Creon. Your concern is all for him.	620
ISMENE:	Why abuse me so? It doesn't help you now.	
ANTIGONE:	You're right—	
	if I mock you, I get no pleasure from it,	
	only pain.	
ISMENE:	Tell me, dear one,	
	what can I do to help you, even now?	
ANTIGONE:	Save yourself. I don't grudge you your survival.	625
ISMENE:	Oh no, no, denied my portion in your death?	
ANTIGONE:	You chose to live, I chose to die.	
ISMENE:	Not, at least,	
	without every kind of caution I could voice.	
ANTIGONE:	Your wisdom appealed to one world—mine, another.	
ISMENE:	But look, we're both guilty, both condemned to death.	630
ANTIGONE:	Courage! Live your life. I gave myself to death,	
	long ago, so I might serve the dead.	
CREON:	They're both mad, I tell you, the two of them.	
	One's just shown it, the other's been that way	
	since she was born.	
ISMENE:	True, my king,	635
	the sense we were born with cannot last forever . . .	
	commit cruelty on a person long enough	
	and the mind begins to go.	
CREON:	Yours did,	
	when you chose to commit your crimes with her.	
ISMENE:	How can I live alone, without her?	
CREON:	Her?	640
	Don't even mention her—she no longer exists.	
ISMENE:	What? You'd kill your own son's bride?	
CREON:	Absolutely:	
	there are other fields for him to plow.	
ISMENE:	Perhaps,	
	but never as true, as close a bond as theirs.	
CREON:	A worthless woman for my son? It repels me.	645
ISMENE:	Dearest Haemon, your father wrongs you so!	
CREON:	Enough, enough—you and your talk of marriage!	
ISMENE:	Creon—you're really going to rob your son of Antigone?	
CREON:	Death will do it for me—break their marriage off.	
LEADER:	So, it's settled then? Antigone must die?	650
CREON:	Settled, yes—we both know that.	

To the guards.

> Stop wasting time. Take them in.
> From now on they'll act like women.
> Tie them up, no more running loose;
> even the bravest will cut and run,   655
> once they see Death coming for their lives.

The guards escort Antigone and Ismene into the palace. Creon remains while the old citizens form their chorus.

CHORUS: Blest, they are the truly blest who all their lives
> have never tasted devastation. For others, once
> the gods have rocked a house to its foundations
>   the ruin will never cease, cresting on and on   660
> from one generation on throughout the race—
> like a great mounting tide
> driven on by savage northern gales,
>   surging over the dead black depths
> roiling up from the bottom dark heaves of sand   665
> and the headlands, taking the storm's onslaught full-force,
> roar, and the low moaning
>   echoes on and on
>   and now
> as in ancient times I see the sorrows of the house,
> the living heirs of the old ancestral kings,
> piling on the sorrows of the dead   670
>   and one generation cannot free the next—
> some god will bring them crashing down,
> the race finds no release.
> And now the light, the hope
>   springing up from the late last root   675
> in the house of Oedipus, that hope's cut down in turn
> by the long, bloody knife swung by the gods of death
> by a senseless word
>   by fury at the heart.
>   Zeus,
> yours is the power, Zeus, what man on earth
> can override it, who can hold it back?   680
> Power that neither Sleep, the all-ensnaring
>   no, nor the tireless months of heaven
> can ever overmaster—young through all time,
> mighty lord of power, you hold fast
>   the dazzling crystal mansions of Olympus.   685
> And throughout the future, late and soon
> as through the past, your law prevails:
> no towering form of greatness
>   enters into the lives of mortals

free and clear of ruin.

                                                    True,   690
our dreams, our high hopes voyaging far and wide
bring sheer delight to many, to many others
        delusion, blithe, mindless lusts
and the fraud steals on one slowly . . . unaware
till he trips and puts his foot into the fire.   695
        He was a wise old man who coined
the famous saying: "Sooner or later
foul is fair, fair is foul
to the man the gods will ruin" —
        He goes his way for a moment only   700
                        free of blinding ruin.

Enter Haemon from the palace.

        Here's Haemon now, the last of all your sons.
        Does he come in tears for his bride,
        his doomed bride, Antigone —
        bitter at being cheated of their marriage?   705
CREON: We'll soon know, better than seers could tell us.

Turning to Haemon.

        Son, you've heard the final verdict on your bride?
        Are you coming now, raving against your father?
        Or do you love me, no matter what I do?
HAEMON: Father, I'm your *son* . . . you in your wisdom   710
        set my bearings for me — I obey you.
        No marriage could ever mean more to me than you,
        whatever good direction you may offer.
CREON: Fine, Haemon.
        That's how you ought to feel within your heart,
        subordinate to your father's will in every way.   715
        That's what a man prays for: to produce good sons —
        households full of them, dutiful and attentive,
        so they can pay his enemy back with interest
        and match the respect their father shows his friend.
        But the man who rears a brood of useless children,   720
        what has he brought into the world, I ask you?
        Nothing but trouble for himself, and mockery
        from his enemies laughing in his face.
                                Oh Haemon,
        never lose your sense of judgment over a woman.
        The warmth, the rush of pleasure, it all goes cold   725
        in your arms, I warn you . . . a worthless woman
        in your house, a misery in your bed.
        What wound cuts deeper than a loved one

turned against you? Spit her out,
like a mortal enemy—let the girl go. 730
Let her find a husband down among the dead.

Imagine it: I caught her in naked rebellion,
the traitor, the only one in the whole city.
I'm not about to prove myself a liar,
not to my people, no, I'm going to kill her! 735
That's right—so let her cry for mercy, sing her hymns
to Zeus who defends all bonds of kindred blood.
Why, if I bring up my own kin to be rebels,
think what I'd suffer from the world at large.
Show me the man who rules his household well: 740
I'll show you someone fit to rule the state.
That good man, my son,
I have every confidence he and he alone
can give commands and take them too. Staunch
in the storm of spears he'll stand his ground, 745
a loyal, unflinching comrade at your side.

But whoever steps out of line, violates the laws
or presumes to hand out orders to his superiors,
he'll win no praise from me. But that man
the city places in authority, his orders 750
must be obeyed, large and small,
right and wrong.
           Anarchy—
show me a greater crime in all the earth!
She, she destroys cities, rips up houses,
breaks the ranks of spearmen into headlong rout. 755
But the ones who last it out, the great mass of them
owe their lives to discipline. Therefore
we must defend the men who live by law,
never let some woman triumph over us.
Better to fall from power, if fall we must, 760
at the hands of a man—never be rated
inferior to a woman, never.

LEADER: To us,
unless old age has robbed us of our wits,
you seem to say what you have to say with sense.

HAEMON: Father, only the gods endow a man with reason, 765
the finest of all their gifts, a treasure.
Far be it from me—I haven't the skill,
and certainly no desire, to tell you when,
if ever, you make a slip in speech . . . though
someone else might have a good suggestion. 770

Of course it's not for you,
in the normal run of things, to watch
whatever men say or do, or find to criticize.
The man in the street, you know, dreads your glance,
he'd never say anything displeasing to your face.   775
But it's for me to catch the murmurs in the dark,
the way the city mourns for this young girl.
"No woman," they say, "ever deserved death less,
and such a brutal death for such a glorious action.
She, with her own dear brother lying in his blood—   780
she couldn't bear to leave him dead, unburied,
food for the wild dogs or wheeling vultures.
Death? She deserves a glowing crown of gold!"
So they say, and the rumor spreads in secret,
darkly . . .
        I rejoice in your success, father—   785
nothing more precious to me in the world.
What medal of honor brighter to his children
than a father's growing glory? Or a child's
to his proud father? Now don't, please,
be quite so single-minded, self-involved,   790
or assume the world is wrong and you are right.
Whoever thinks that he alone possesses intelligence,
the gift of eloquence, he and no one else,
and character too . . . such men, I tell you,
spread them open—you will find them empty.
                  No,   795
it's no disgrace for a man, even a wise man,
to learn many things and not to be too rigid.
You've seen trees by a raging winter torrent,
how many sway with the flood and salvage every twig,
but not the stubborn—they're ripped out, roots and all.   800
Bend or break. The same when a man is sailing:
haul your sheets too taut, never give an inch,
you'll capsize, go the rest of the voyage
keel up and the rowing-benches under.

Oh give way. Relax your anger—change!   805
I'm young, I know, but let me offer this:
it would be best by far, I admit,
if a man were born infallible, right by nature.
If not—and things don't often go that way,
it's best to learn from those with good advice.   810
LEADER: You'd do well, my lord, if he's speaking to the point,
    to learn from him,

Turning to Haemon.

and you, my boy, from him.
You both are talking sense.

CREON: So,
men our age, we're to be lectured, are we? —
schooled by a boy his age?   815

HAEMON: Only in what is right. But if I seem young,
look less to my years and more to what I do.

CREON: Do? Is admiring rebels an achievement?

HAEMON: I'd never suggest that you admire treason.

CREON: Oh? —
isn't that just the sickness that's attacked her?   820

HAEMON: The whole city of Thebes denies it, to a man.

CREON: And is Thebes about to tell me how to rule?

HAEMON: Now, you see? Who's talking like a child?

CREON: Am I to rule this land for others — or myself?

HAEMON: It's no city at all, owned by one man alone.   825

CREON: What? The city *is* the king's — that's the law!

HAEMON: What a splendid king you'd make of a desert island —
you and you alone.

CREON:

To the Chorus.

                                        This boy, I do believe,
is fighting on her side, the woman's side.

HAEMON: If you are a woman, yes;   830
my concern is all for you.

CREON: Why, you degenerate — bandying accusations,
threatening me with justice, your own father!

HAEMON: I see my father offending justice — wrong.

CREON: Wrong?
To protect my royal rights?

HAEMON: Protect your rights?   835
When you trample down the honors of the gods?

CREON: You, you soul of corruption, rotten through —
woman's accomplice!

HAEMON: That may be,
but you'll never find me accomplice to a criminal.

CREON: That's what *she* is,   840
and every word you say is a blatant appeal for her —

HAEMON: And you, and me, and the gods beneath the earth.

CREON: You'll never marry her, not while she's alive.

HAEMON: Then she'll die . . . but her death will kill another.

CREON: What, brazen threats? You go too far!

HAEMON: What threat?   845
Combating your empty, mindless judgments with a word?

CREON: You'll suffer for your sermons, you and your empty wisdom!

HAEMON: If you weren't my father, I'd say you were insane.

CREON: Don't flatter me with Father—you woman's slave!

HAEMON: You really expect to fling abuse at me   850
　　　and not receive the same?

CREON: Is that so!
　　　Now, by heaven, I promise you, you'll pay—
　　　taunting, insulting me! Bring her out,
　　　that hateful—she'll die now, here,
　　　in front of his eyes, beside her groom!   855

HAEMON: No, no, she will never die beside me—
　　　don't delude yourself. And you will never
　　　see me, never set eyes on my face again.
　　　Rage your heart out, rage with friends
　　　who can stand the sight of you.   860

Rushing out.

LEADER: Gone, my king, in a burst of anger.
　　　A temper young as his . . . hurt him once,
　　　he may do something violent.

CREON: Let him do—
　　　dream up something desperate, past all human limit!
　　　Good riddance. Rest assured,   865
　　　he'll never save those two young girls from death.

LEADER: Both of them, you really intend to kill them both?

CREON: No, not her, the one whose hands are clean;
　　　you're quite right.

LEADER: But Antigone—
　　　what sort of death do you have in mind for her?   870

CREON: I'll take her down some wild, desolate path
　　　never trod by men, and wall her up alive
　　　in a rocky vault, and set out short rations,
　　　just a gesture of piety
　　　to keep the entire city free of defilement.   875
　　　There let her pray to the one god she worships:
　　　Death—who knows?—may just reprieve her from death.
　　　Or she may learn at last, better late than never,
　　　what a waste of breath it is to worship Death.

Exit to the palace.

CHORUS: Love, never conquered in battle   880
　　　Love the plunderer laying waste the rich!
　　　Love standing the night-watch
　　　　　　　　guarding a girl's soft cheek,
　　　you range the seas, the shepherds' steadings off in the wilds—
　　　not even the deathless gods can flee your onset,   885
　　　nothing human born for a day—

whoever feels your grip is driven mad.
Love
you wrench the minds of the righteous into outrage,
swerve them to their ruin — you have ignited this,
this kindred strife, father and son at war   890
and Love alone the victor —
warm glance of the bride triumphant, burning with desire!
Throned in power, side-by-side with the mighty laws!
Irresistible Aphrodite,° never conquered —
Love, you mock us for your sport.   895

Antigone is brought from the palace under guard.

> But now, even I'd rebel against the king,
> I'd break all bounds when I see this —
> I fill with tears, can't hold them back,
> not any more . . . I see Antigone make her way
> to the bridal vault where all are laid to rest.   900

ANTIGONE: Look at me, men of my fatherland,
> setting out on the last road
looking into the last light of day
the last I'll ever see . . .
the god of death who puts us all to bed   905
takes me down to the banks of Acheron° alive —
> denied my part in the wedding-songs,
no wedding-song in the dusk has crowned my marriage —
I go to wed the lord of the dark waters.

CHORUS: Not crowned with glory, crowned with a dirge,   910
> you leave for the deep pit of the dead.
> No withering illness laid you low,
> no strokes of the sword — a law to yourself,
> alone, no mortal like you, ever, you go down
> to the halls of Death alive and breathing.   915

ANTIGONE: But think of Niobe° — well I know her story —
> think what a living death she died,
Tantalus's daughter, stranger queen from the east:
there on the mountain heights, growing stone
binding as ivy, slowly walled her round   920
and the rains will never cease, the legends say
the snows will never leave her . . .
> wasting away, under her brows the tears
showering down her breasting ridge and slopes —
a rocky death like hers puts me to sleep.   925

---

894 Aphrodite: Goddess of love. **906 Acheron:** A river in the underworld, to which the dead go. **916 Niobe:** A queen of Thebes who was punished by the gods for her pride and was turned into stone.

CHORUS: But she was a god, born of gods,
    and we are only mortals born to die.
    And yet, of course, it's a great thing
    for a dying girl to hear, just hear
    she shares a destiny equal to the gods,   930
    during life and later, once she's dead.

ANTIGONE: O you mock me!
  Why, in the name of all my fathers' gods
  why can't you wait till I am gone—
    must you abuse me to my face?
  O my city, all your fine rich sons!   935
  And you, you springs of the Dirce,
  holy grove of Thebes where the chariots gather,
    you at least, you'll bear me witness, look,
  unmourned by friends and forced by such crude laws
  I go to my rockbound prison, strange new tomb—   940
    always a stranger, O dear god,
    I have no home on earth and none below,
      not with the living, not with the breathless dead.

CHORUS: You went too far, the last limits of daring—
    smashing against the high throne of Justice!   945
      Your life's in ruins, child—I wonder . . .
    do you pay for your father's terrible ordeal?

ANTIGONE: There—at last you've touched it, the worst pain
  the worst anguish! Raking up the grief for father
    three times over, for all the doom   950
  that's struck us down, the brilliant house of Laius.
  O mother, your marriage-bed
  the coiling horrors, the coupling there—
    you with your own son, my father—doomstruck mother!
  Such, such were my parents, and I their wretched child.   955
  I go to them now, cursed, unwed, to share their home—
    I am a stranger! O dear brother, doomed
    in your marriage—your marriage murders mine,
    your dying drags me down to death alive!

Enter Creon.

CHORUS: Reverence asks some reverence in return—   960
    but attacks on power never go unchecked,
      not by the man who holds the reins of power.
    Your own blind will, your passion has destroyed you.

ANTIGONE: No one to weep for me, my friends,
    no wedding-song—they take me away   965
    in all my pain . . . the road lies open, waiting.
    Never again, the law forbids me to see
    the sacred eye of day. I am agony!

No tears for the destiny that's mine,
no loved one mourns my death.

CREON: Can't you see?   970
   If a man could wail his own dirge *before* he dies,
   he'd never finish.

To the guards.

                     Take her away, quickly!
   Wall her up in the tomb, you have your orders.
   Abandon her there, alone, and let her choose—
   death or a buried life with a good roof for shelter.   975
   As for myself, my hands are clean. This young girl—
   dead or alive, she will be stripped of her rights,
   her stranger's rights, here in the world above.

ANTIGONE: O tomb, my bridal-bed—my house, my prison
   cut in the hollow rock, my everlasting watch!   980
   I'll soon be there, soon embrace my own,
   the great growing family of our dead
   Persephone° has received among her ghosts.

                                                I,
   the last of them all, the most reviled by far,
   go down before my destined time's run out.   985
   But still I go, cherishing one good hope:
   my arrival may be dear to father,
   dear to you, my mother,
   dear to you, my loving brother, Eteocles—
   When you died I washed you with my hands,   990
   I dressed you all, I poured the cups
   across your tombs. But now, Polynices,
   because I laid your body out as well,
   this, this is my reward. Nevertheless
   I honored you—the decent will admit it—   995
   well and wisely too.

                     Never, I tell you,
   if I had been the mother of children
   or if my husband died, exposed and rotting—
   I'd never have taken this ordeal upon myself,
   never defied our people's will. What law,   1000
   you ask, do I satisfy with what I say?
   A husband dead, there might have been another.
   A child by another too, if I had lost the first.
   But mother and father both lost in the halls of Death,
   no brother could ever spring to light again.   1005
   For this law alone I held you first in honor.
   For this, Creon, the king, judges me a criminal

983 Persephone: Queen of the underworld.

guilty of dreadful outrage, my dear brother!
And now he leads me off, a captive in his hands,
with no part in the bridal-song, the bridal-bed,   1010
denied all joy of marriage, raising children —
deserted so by loved ones, struck by fate,
I descend alive to the caverns of the dead.
What law of the mighty gods have I transgressed?
Why look to the heavens any more, tormented as I am?   1015
Whom to call, what comrades now? Just think,
my reverence only brands me for irreverence!
Very well: if this is the pleasure of the gods,
once I suffer I will know that I was wrong.
But if these men are wrong, let them suffer   1020
nothing worse than they mete out to me —
these masters of injustice!

LEADER: Still the same rough winds, the wild passion
raging through the girl.

CREON:

To the guards.

                Take her away.
You're wasting time — you'll pay for it too.   1025

ANTIGONE: Oh god, the voice of death. It's come, it's here.

CREON: True. Not a word of hope — your doom is sealed.

ANTIGONE: Land of Thebes, city of all my fathers —
O you gods, the first gods of the race!
They drag me away, now, no more delay.   1030
Look on me, you noble sons of Thebes —
the last of a great line of kings,
I alone, see what I suffer now
at the hands of what breed of men —
all for reverence, my reverence for the gods!   1035

She leaves under guard; the Chorus gathers.

CHORUS: Danaë, Danaë° —
even she endured a fate like yours,
    in all her lovely strength she traded
the light of day for the bolted brazen vault —
buried within her tomb, her bridal-chamber,   1040
wed to the yoke and broken.
    But she was of glorious birth
              my child, my child
and treasured the seed of Zeus within her womb,
the cloudburst streaming gold!   1045

1036 Danaë: Locked in a cell by her father because it was prophesied that her son would kill him, but visited by Zeus in the form of a shower of gold. Their son was Perseus.

The power of fate is a wonder,
dark, terrible wonder—
neither wealth nor armies
towered walls nor ships
black hulls lashed by the salt   1050
can save us from that force.
The yoke tamed him too
    young Lycurgus° flaming in anger
king of Edonia, all for his mad taunts
Dionysus clamped him down, encased   1055
in the chain-mail of rock
    and there his rage
                    his terrible flowering rage burst—
sobbing, dying away . . . at last that madman
came to know his god—   1060
    the power he mocked, the power
    he taunted in all his frenzy
    trying to stamp out
    the women strong with the god—
    the torch, the raving sacred cries—   1065
    enraging the Muses° who adore the flute.

And far north where the Black Rocks
    cut the sea in half
and murderous straits
split the coast of Thrace   1070
    a forbidding city stands
where once, hard by the walls
the savage Ares thrilled to watch
a king's new queen, a Fury rearing in rage
    against his two royal sons—   1075
        her bloody hands, her dagger-shuttle
stabbing out their eyes—cursed, blinding wounds—
their eyes blind sockets screaming for revenge!

They wailed in agony, cries echoing cries
        the princes doomed at birth . . .   1080
and their mother doomed to chains,
walled off in a tomb of stone—
    but she traced her own birth back
to a proud Athenian line and the high gods
and off in caverns half the world away,   1085
born of the wild North Wind
    she sprang on her father's gales,

1053 Lycurgus: Punished by Dionysus because he would not worship him.   **1066 Muses:** Goddesses of the arts.

        racing stallions up the leaping cliffs —
  child of the heavens. But even on her the Fates
  the gray everlasting Fates rode hard   1090
  my child, my child.

Enter Tiresias, the blind prophet, led by a boy.

TIRESIAS: Lords of Thebes,
  I and the boy have come together,
  hand in hand. Two see with the eyes of one . . .
  so the blind must go, with a guide to lead the way.
CREON: What is it, old Tiresias? What news now?   1095
TIRESIAS: I will teach you. And you obey the seer.
CREON: I will,
  I've never wavered from your advice before.
TIRESIAS: And so you kept the city straight on course.
CREON: I owe you a great deal, I swear to that.
TIRESIAS: Then reflect, my son: you are poised,   1100
  once more, on the razor-edge of fate.
CREON: What is it? I shudder to hear you.
TIRESIAS: You will learn
  when you listen to the warnings of my craft.
  As I sat on the ancient seat of augury,°
  in the sanctuary where every bird I know   1105
  will hover at my hands — suddenly I heard it,
  a strange voice in the wingbeats, unintelligible,
  barbaric, a mad scream! Talons flashing, ripping,
  they were killing each other — that much I knew —
  the murderous fury whirring in those wings   1110
  made that much clear!
                 I was afraid,
  I turned quickly, tested the burnt-sacrifice,
  ignited the altar at all points — but no fire,
  the god in the fire never blazed.
  Not from those offerings . . . over the embers   1115
  slid a heavy ooze from the long thighbones,
  smoking, sputtering out, and the bladder
  puffed and burst — spraying gall into the air —
  and the fat wrapping the bones slithered off
  and left them glistening white. No fire!   1120
  The rites failed that might have blazed the future
  with a sign. So I learned from the boy here;
  he is my guide, as I am guide to others.
              And it's you —
  your high resolve that sets this plague on Thebes.
  The public altars and sacred hearths are fouled,   1125

1104 seat of augury: Where Tiresias looked for omens among birds.

one and all, by the birds and dogs with carrion
torn from the corpse, the doomstruck son of Oedipus!
And so the gods are deaf to our prayers, they spurn
the offerings in our hands, the flame of holy flesh.
No birds cry out an omen clear and true—   1130
they're gorged with the murdered victim's blood and fat.
Take these things to heart, my son, I warn you.
All men make mistakes, it is only human.
But once the wrong is done, a man
can turn his back on folly, misfortune too,   1135
if he tries to make amends, however low he's fallen,
and stops his bullnecked ways. Stubbornness
brands you for stupidity—pride is a crime.
No, yield to the dead!
Never stab the fighter when he's down.   1140
Where's the glory, killing the dead twice over?

I mean you well. I give you sound advice.
It's best to learn from a good adviser
when he speaks for your own good:
it's pure gain.
CREON: Old man—all of you! So,   1145
you shoot your arrows at my head like archers at the target—
I even have *him* loosed on me, this fortune-teller.
Oh his ilk has tried to sell me short
and ship me off for years. Well,
drive your bargains, traffic—much as you like—   1150
in the gold of India, silver-gold of Sardis.
You'll never bury that body in the grave,
not even if Zeus's eagles rip the corpse
and wing their rotten pickings off to the throne of god!
Never, not even in fear of such defilement   1155
will I tolerate his burial, that traitor.
Well I know, we can't defile the gods—
no mortal has the power.
                    No,
reverend old Tiresias, all men fall,
it's only human, but the wisest fall obscenely   1160
when they glorify obscene advice with rhetoric—
all for their own gain.
TIRESIAS: Oh god, is there a man alive
who knows, who actually believes . . .
CREON: What now?
What earth-shattering truth are you about to utter?   1165
TIRESIAS: . . . just how much a sense of judgment, wisdom
is the greatest gift we have?

CREON: Just as much, I'd say,
    as a twisted mind is the worst affliction going.
TIRESIAS: You are the one who's sick, Creon, sick to death.
CREON: I am in no mood to trade insults with a seer.   1170
TIRESIAS: You have already, calling my prophecies a lie.
CREON: Why not?
    You and the whole breed of seers are mad for money!
TIRESIAS: And the whole race of tyrants lusts to rake it in.
CREON: This slander of yours—
    are you aware you're speaking to the king?   1175
TIRESIAS: Well aware. Who helped you save the city?
CREON: You—
    you have your skills, old seer, but you lust for injustice!
TIRESIAS: You will drive me to utter the dreadful secret in my heart.
CREON: Spit it out! Just don't speak it out for profit.
TIRESIAS: Profit? No, not a bit of profit, not for you.   1180
CREON: Know full well, you'll never buy off my resolve.
TIRESIAS: Then know this too, learn this by heart!
    The chariot of the sun will not race through
    so many circuits more, before you have surrendered
    one born of your own loins, your own flesh and blood,   1185
    a corpse for corpses given in return, since you have thrust
    to the world below a child sprung for the world above,
    ruthlessly lodged a living soul within the grave—
    then you've robbed the gods below the earth,
    keeping a dead body here in the bright air,   1190
    unburied, unsung, unhallowed by the rites.

    You, you have no business with the dead,
    nor do the gods above—this is violence
    you have forced upon the heavens.
    And so the avengers, the dark destroyers late   1195
    but true to the mark, now lie in wait for you,
    the Furies sent by the gods and the god of death
    to strike you down with the pains that you perfected!

    There. Reflect on that, tell me I've been bribed.
    The day comes soon, no long test of time, not now,   1200
    that wakes the wails for men and women in your halls.
    Great hatred rises against you—
    cities in tumult, all whose mutilated sons
    the dogs have graced with burial, or the wild beasts,
    some wheeling crow that wings the ungodly stench of carrion   1205
    back to each city, each warrior's hearth and home.

    These arrows for your heart! Since you've raked me
    I loose them like an archer in my anger,

arrows deadly true. You'll never escape
their burning, searing force.   1210

Motioning to his escort.

Come, boy, take me home.
So he can vent his rage on younger men,
and learn to keep a gentler tongue in his head
and better sense than what he carries now.

Exit to the side.

LEADER: The old man's gone, my king—   1215
terrible prophecies. Well I know,
since the hair on this old head went gray,
he's never lied to Thebes.
CREON: I know it myself—I'm shaken, torn.
It's a dreadful thing to yield . . . but resist now?   1220
Lay my pride bare to the blows of ruin?
That's dreadful too.
LEADER: But good advice,
Creon, take it now, you must.
CREON: What should I do? Tell me . . . I'll obey.
LEADER: Go! Free the girl from the rocky vault   1225
and raise a mound for the body you exposed.
CREON: That's your advice? You think I should give in?
LEADER: Yes, my king, quickly. Disasters sent by the gods
cut short our follies in a flash.
CREON: Oh it's hard.
giving up the heart's desire . . . but I will do it—   1230
no more fighting a losing battle with necessity.
LEADER: Do it now, go, don't leave it to others.
CREON: Now—I'm on my way! Come, each of you,
take up axes, make for the high ground,
over there, quickly! I and my better judgment   1235
have come round to this—I shackled her,
I'll set her free myself. I am afraid . . .
it's best to keep the established laws
to the very day we die.

Rushing out, followed by his entourage. The Chorus clusters around the altar.

CHORUS: God of a hundred names!
                              Great Dionysus—   1240
              Son and glory of Semele! Pride of Thebes—
Child of Zeus whose thunder rocks the clouds—
Lord of the famous lands of evening—
King of the Mysteries!
                    King of Eleusis, Demeter's plain°

1244 Demeter's plain: The goddess of grain was worshipped at Eleusis, near Athens.

her breasting hills that welcome in the world—   1245
Great Dionysus!
    Bacchus,° living in Thebes
the mother-city of all your frenzied women—
        Bacchus
   living along the Ismenus's° rippling waters
standing over the field sown with the Dragon's teeth!

You—we have seen you through the flaring smoky fires,   1250
  your torches blazing over the twin peaks
where nymphs of the hallowed cave climb onward
     fired with you, your sacred rage—
we have seen you at Castalia's running spring°
and down from the heights of Nysa° crowned with ivy   1255
the greening shore rioting vines and grapes
   down you come in your storm of wild women
    ecstatic, mystic cries—
      Dionysus—
down to watch and ward the roads of Thebes!

First of all cities, Thebes you honor first   1260
you and your mother, bride of the lightning—
come, Dionysus! now your people lie
in the iron grip of plague,
come in your racing, healing stride
    down Parnassus's° slopes   1265
or across the moaning straits.
      Lord of the dancing—
dance, dance the constellations breathing fire!
Great master of the voices of the night!
Child of Zeus, God's offspring, come, come forth!
Lord, king, dance with your nymphs, swirling, raving   1270
arm-in-arm in frenzy through the night
   they dance you, Iacchus°—
      Dance, Dionysus
 giver of all good things!

Enter a Messenger from the side.

MESSENGER: Neighbors,
 friends of the house of Cadmus° and the kings,
 there's not a thing in this life of ours   1275

1246 Bacchus: Another name for Dionysus. **1248 Ismenus:** A river near Thebes where the founders of the city were said to have sprung from a dragon's teeth. **1254 Castalia's running spring:** The sacred spring of Apollo's oracle at Delphi. **1255 Nysa:** A mountain where Dionysus was worshipped. **1265 Parnassus:** A mountain in Greece that was sacred to Dionysus as well as other gods and goddesses. **1272 Iacchus:** Dionysus. **1274 Cadmus:** The legendary founder of Thebes.

I'd praise or blame as settled once for all.
Fortune lifts and Fortune fells the lucky
and unlucky every day. No prophet on earth
can tell a man his fate. Take Creon:
there was a man to rouse your envy once,   1280
as I see it. He saved the realm from enemies;
taking power, he alone, the lord of the fatherland,
he set us true on course—flourished like a tree
with the noble line of sons he bred and reared . . .
and now it's lost, all gone.

                            Believe me,   1285
when a man has squandered his true joys,
he's good as dead, I tell you, a living corpse.
Pile up riches in your house, as much as you like—
live like a king with a huge show of pomp,
but if real delight is missing from the lot,   1290
I wouldn't give you a wisp of smoke for it,
not compared with joy.
LEADER: What now?
What new grief do you bring the house of kings?
MESSENGER: Dead, dead—and the living are guilty of their death!
LEADER: Who's the murderer? Who is dead? Tell us.   1295
MESSENGER: Haemon's gone, his blood spilled by the very hand—
LEADER: His father's or his own?
MESSENGER: His own . . .
raging mad with his father for the death—
LEADER: Oh great seer,
you saw it all, you brought your word to birth!
MESSENGER: Those are the facts. Deal with them as you will.   1300

As he turns to go, Eurydice enters from the palace.

LEADER: Look, Eurydice. Poor woman, Creon's wife,
so close at hand. By chance perhaps,
unless she's heard the news about her son.
EURYDICE: My countrymen,
all of you—I caught the sound of your words
as I was leaving to do my part,   1305
to appeal to queen Athena° with my prayers.
I was just loosing the bolts, opening the doors,
when a voice filled with sorrow, family sorrow,
struck my ears, and I fell back, terrified,
into the women's arms—everything went black.   1310
Tell me the news, again, whatever it is . . .
sorrow and I are hardly strangers;
I can bear the worst.

1306 Athena: Goddess of wisdom and protector of Greek cities.

MESSENGER: I—dear lady,
  I'll speak as an eye-witness. I was there.
  And I won't pass over one word of the truth.   1315
  Why should I try to soothe you with a story,
  only to prove a liar in a moment?
  Truth is always best.
               So,
  I escorted your lord, I guided him
  to the edge of the plain where the body lay,   1320
  Polynices, torn by the dogs and still unmourned.
  And saying a prayer to Hecate of the Crossroads,
  Pluto° too, to hold their anger and be kind,
  we washed the dead in a bath of holy water
  and plucking some fresh branches, gathering . . .   1325
  what was left of him, we burned them all together
  and raised a high mound of native earth, and then
  we turned and made for that rocky vault of hers,
  the hollow, empty bed of the bride of Death.
  And far off, one of us heard a voice,   1330
  a long wail rising, echoing
  out of that unhallowed wedding-chamber;
  he ran to alert the master and Creon pressed on,
  closer—the strange, inscrutable cry came sharper,
  throbbing around him now, and he let loose   1335
  a cry of his own, enough to wrench the heart,
  "Oh god, am I the prophet now? going down
  the darkest road I've ever gone? My son—
  it's *his* dear voice, he greets me! Go, men,
  closer, quickly! Go through the gap,   1340
  the rocks are dragged back—
  right to the tomb's very mouth—and look,
  see if it's Haemon's voice I think I hear,
  or the gods have robbed me of my senses."

  The king was shattered. We took his orders,   1345
  went and searched, and there in the deepest,
  dark recesses of the tomb we found her . . .
  hanged by the neck in a fine linen noose,
  strangled in her veils—and the boy,
  his arms flung around her waist,   1350
  clinging to her, wailing for his bride,
  dead and down below, for his father's crimes
  and the bed of his marriage blighted by misfortune.
  When Creon saw him, he gave a deep sob,

1322–23 Hecate, Pluto: Gods of the underworld.

he ran in, shouting, crying out to him,   1355
"Oh my child—what have you done? what seized you,
what insanity? what disaster drove you mad?
Come out, my son! I beg you on my knees!"
But the boy gave him a wild burning glance,
spat in his face, not a word in reply,   1360
he drew his sword—his father rushed out,
running as Haemon lunged and missed!—
and then, doomed, desperate with himself,
suddenly leaning his full weight on the blade,
he buried it in his body, halfway to the hilt.   1365
And still in his senses, pouring his arms around her,
he embraced the girl and breathing hard,
released a quick rush of blood,
bright red on her cheek glistening white.
And there he lies, body enfolding body . . .   1370
he has won his bride at last, poor boy,
not here but in the houses of the dead.

Creon shows the world that of all the ills
afflicting men the worst is lack of judgment.

Eurydice turns and reenters the palace.

LEADER: What do you make of that? The lady's gone,   1375
  without a word, good or bad.
MESSENGER: I'm alarmed too
  but here's my hope—faced with her son's death,
  she finds it unbecoming to mourn in public.
  Inside, under her roof, she'll set her women
  to the task and wail the sorrow of the house.   1380
  She's too discreet. She won't do something rash.
LEADER: I'm not so sure. To me, at least,
  a long heavy silence promises danger,
  just as much as a lot of empty outcries.
MESSENGER: We'll see if she's holding something back,   1385
  hiding some passion in her heart.
  I'm going in. You may be right—who knows?
  Even too much silence has its dangers.

*Exit to the palace. Enter Creon from the side, escorted by attendants carrying
Haemon's body on a bier.*

LEADER: The king himself! Coming toward us,
   look, holding the boy's head in his hands.   1390
   Clear, damning proof, if it's right to say so—
   proof of his own madness, no one else's,
    no, his own blind wrongs.
CREON: Ohhh,

so senseless, so insane . . . my crimes,
my stubborn, deadly—   1395
Look at us, the killer, the killed,
father and son, the same blood—the misery!
My plans, my mad fanatic heart,
my son, cut off so young!
Ai, dead, lost to the world,   1400
not through your stupidity, no, my own.

LEADER: Too late,
    too late, you see what justice means.

CREON: Oh I've learned
    through blood and tears! Then, it was then,
    when the god came down and struck me—a great weight
    shattering, driving me down that wild savage path,   1405
    ruining, trampling down my joy. Oh the agony,
        the heartbreaking agonies of our lives.

Enter the Messenger from the palace.

MESSENGER: Master,
    what a hoard of grief you have, and you'll have more.
    The grief that lies to hand you've brought yourself—

Pointing to Haemon's body.

    the rest, in the house, you'll see it all too soon.   1410

CREON: What now? What's worse than this?

MESSENGER: The queen is dead.
    The mother of this dead boy . . . mother to the end—
    poor thing, her wounds are fresh.

CREON: No, no,
    harbor of Death, so choked, so hard to cleanse!—
    why me? why are you killing me?   1415
    Herald of pain, more words, more grief?
    I died once, you kill me again and again!
    What's the report, boy . . . some news for me?
    My wife dead? O dear god!
    Slaughter heaped on slaughter?

The doors open; the body of Eurydice is brought out on her bier.

MESSENGER: See for yourself: 1420
    now they bring her body from the palace.

CREON: Oh no,
    another, a second loss to break the heart.
    What next, what fate still waits for me?
    I just held my son in my arms and now,
    look, a new corpse rising before my eyes—   1425
        wretched, helpless mother—O my son!

MESSENGER: She stabbed herself at the altar,
       then her eyes went dark, after she'd raised
       a cry for the noble fate of Megareus,° the hero
       killed in the first assault, then for Haemon,   1430
       then with her dying breath she called down
       torments on your head — you killed her sons.
CREON: Oh the dread,
              I shudder with dread! Why not kill me too? —
              run me through with a good sharp sword?
              Oh god, the misery, anguish —   1435
              I, I'm churning with it, going under.
MESSENGER: Yes, and the dead, the woman lying there,
       piles the guilt of all their deaths on you.
CREON: How did she end her life, what bloody stroke?
MESSENGER: She drove home to the heart with her own hand,   1440
       once she learned her son was dead . . . that agony.
CREON: And the guilt is all mine —
              can never be fixed on another man,
              no escape for me. I killed you,
              I, god help me, I admit it all!   1445

To his attendants.

              Take me away, quickly, out of sight.
              I don't even exist — I'm no one. Nothing.
LEADER: Good advice, if there's any good in suffering.
       Quickest is best when troubles block the way.
CREON:

Kneeling in prayer.

              Come, let it come! — that best of fates for me   1450
              that brings the final day, best fate of all.
              Oh quickly, now —
              so I never have to see another sunrise.
LEADER: That will come when it comes;
       we must deal with all that lies before us.
       The future rests with the ones who tend the future.   1455
CREON: That prayer — I poured my heart into that prayer!
LEADER: No more prayers now. For mortal men
       there is no escape from the doom we must endure.
CREON: Take me away, I beg you, out of sight.   1460
              A rash, indiscriminate fool!
              I murdered you, my son, against my will —
              you too, my wife . . .

1429 Megareus: A son of Creon and Eurydice; he died when Thebes was attacked.

                     Wailing wreck of a man,
       whom to look to? where to lean for support?

Desperately turning from Haemon to Eurydice on their biers.

          Whatever I touch goes wrong—once more   1465
          a crushing fate's come down upon my head.

The Messenger and attendants lead Creon into the palace.

CHORUS: Wisdom is by far the greatest part of joy,
          and reverence toward the gods must be safeguarded.
          The mighty words of the proud are paid in full
          with mighty blows of fate, and at long last   1470
          those blows will teach us wisdom.

The old citizens exit to the side.   *[c. 441 B.C.E.]*

≡ THINKING ABOUT THE TEXT

1. Describe Antigone with at least three adjectives of your own. How much do you sympathize with her? Do you consider her morally superior to Creon? Identify specific things that influence your view of her. Do your feelings about her shift during the course of the play? If so, when and how?

2. Do you feel any sympathy for Creon? For Ismene? Explain your reasoning. What values seem to be in conflict as Antigone argues with each?

3. Where, if anywhere, do you see the chorus as expressing wisdom? Where, if anywhere, do the members of the chorus strike you as imperfect people?

4. Here is an issue of genre: ever since the ancient Greek philosopher Aristotle analyzed tragedy in his *Poetics*, a common definition of this kind of play is that its central character has a fatal flaw. How well does this definition fit *Antigone*? Must it be altered to accommodate Sophocles' play? Explain. Here is another issue of genre: in the *Poetics*, Aristotle also argued that a tragedy ends in catharsis. After arousing pity and fear in the audience, a tragedy relieves the audience of these feelings. How well does Aristotle's observation apply in the case of *Antigone*?

5. As was customary in Greek tragedy, the violent events in this play occur offstage and are merely reported. Had they occurred onstage, how might the audience's reaction have been different? Today, many films and television shows directly confront their audience with violence. Do you prefer this directness to Greek tragedy's way of dealing with violence? Support your answer by comparing some contemporary presentations of violence with *Antigone*'s.

MARTIN LUTHER KING JR.

Letter from Birmingham Jail°

A native of Atlanta, Martin Luther King Jr. (1929–1968) was the son of a Baptist minister and a schoolteacher. After graduating from Morehouse College in Atlanta, he studied at several universities before receiving a Ph.D. in theology from Boston University. He married Coretta Scott in 1955 and had four children. In 1959, he resigned his position as pastor of a church in Alabama to move back to Atlanta to direct the activities of the Southern Christian Leadership Conference. From 1960 until his death, he was copastor with his father at Ebenezer Baptist Church in Atlanta.

Dr. King was a central figure in the civil rights movement. Pivotal in the successful Montgomery bus boycott in 1956, he was arrested more than thirty times for his participation in nonviolent demonstrations. His charismatic leadership and eloquent speeches stirred and inspired the conscience of a generation. Dr. King's idea of "somebodiness" gave black and poor people a new sense of worth and dignity, and his philosophy of nonviolent direct action helped change the nation's attitudes and priorities. His famous "I have a dream" speech at the Lincoln Memorial in 1963 and the classic "Letter" printed here (composed the same year) are among the most important documents in American history. At thirty-five, he was the youngest person to win the Nobel Prize for peace. His assassination in 1968 set off riots in more than a hundred cities. Today the nation honors his birthday as a holiday.

My Dear Fellow Clergymen:

While confined here in the Birmingham city jail, I came across your recent statement calling my present activities "unwise and untimely." Seldom do I pause to answer criticism of my work and ideas. If I sought to answer all the criticisms that cross my desk, my secretaries would have little time for anything other than such correspondence in the course of the day, and I would have no time for constructive work. But since I feel that you are men of genuine good will and that your criticisms are sincerely set forth, I want to try to answer your statement in what I hope will be patient and reasonable terms.

I think I should indicate why I am here in Birmingham, since you have been influenced by the view which argues against "outsiders coming in." I have the honor of serving as president of the Southern Christian Leadership Conference, an organization operating in every southern state, with headquarters in Atlanta, Georgia. We have some eighty-five affiliated organizations across the

---

Letter from Birmingham Jail: This response to a published statement by eight fellow clergymen from Alabama (Bishop C. C. J. Carpenter, Bishop Joseph A. Durick, Rabbi Hilton L. Grafman, Bishop Paul Hardin, Bishop Holan B. Harmon, the Reverend George M. Murray, the Reverend Edward V. Ramage, and the Reverend Earl Stallings) was composed under somewhat constricting circumstances. Begun on the margins of the newspaper in which the statement appeared while I was in jail, the letter was continued on scraps of writing paper supplied by a friendly Negro trusty, and concluded on a pad my attorneys were eventually permitted to leave me. Although the text remains in substance unaltered, I have indulged in the author's prerogative of polishing it for publication. [King's note.]

Time & Life Pictures/
Getty Images

South, and one of them is the Alabama Christian Movement for Human Rights. Frequently we share staff, educational, and financial resources with our affiliates. Several months ago the affiliate here in Birmingham asked us to be on call to engage in a nonviolent direct-action program if such were deemed necessary. We readily consented, and when the hour came we lived up to our promise. So I, along with several members of my staff, am here because I was invited here. I am here because I have organizational ties here.

But more basically, I am in Birmingham because injustice is here. Just as the prophets of the eighth century B.C. left their villages and carried their "thus saith the Lord" far beyond the boundaries of their home towns, and just as the Apostle Paul left his village of Tarsus° and carried the gospel of Jesus Christ to the far corners of the Greco-Roman world, so am I compelled to carry the gospel of freedom beyond my own home town. Like Paul, I must constantly respond to the Macedonian call for aid.°

Moreover, I am cognizant of the interrelatedness of all communities and states. I cannot sit idly by in Atlanta and not be concerned about what happens in Birmingham. Injustice anywhere is a threat to justice everywhere. We are caught in an inescapable network of mutuality, tied in a single garment of des-

Tarsus: Present-day Turkey, birthplace of St. Paul.   **Macedonian . . . aid:** The Christian community in Macedonia often called on Paul for aid.

tiny. Whatever affects one directly, affects all indirectly. Never again can we afford to live with the narrow, provincial "outside agitator" idea. Anyone who lives inside the United States can never be considered an outsider anywhere within its bounds.

You deplore the demonstrations taking place in Birmingham. But your statement, I am sorry to say, fails to express a similar concern for the conditions that brought about the demonstrations. I am sure that none of you would want to rest content with the superficial kind of social analysis that deals merely with effects and does not grapple with the underlying causes. It is unfortunate that demonstrations are taking place in Birmingham, but it is even more unfortunate that the city's white power structure left the Negro community with no alternative.

In any nonviolent campaign there are four basic steps: collection of the facts to determine whether injustices exist; negotiation; self-purification; and direct action. We have gone through all these steps in Birmingham. There can be no gainsaying the fact that racial injustice engulfs this community. Birmingham is probably the most thoroughly segregated city in the United States. Its ugly record of brutality is widely known. Negroes have experienced grossly unjust treatment in the courts. There have been more unsolved bombings of Negro homes and churches in Birmingham than in any other city in the nation. These are the hard, brutal facts of the case. On the basis of these conditions, Negro leaders sought to negotiate with the city fathers. But the latter consistently refused to engage in good-faith negotiation.

Then, last September, came the opportunity to talk with leaders of Birmingham's economic community. In the course of the negotiations, certain promises were made by the merchants—for example, to remove the stores' humiliating racial signs. On the basis of these promises, the Reverend Fred Shuttlesworth and the leaders of the Alabama Christian Movement for Human Rights agreed to a moratorium on all demonstrations. As the weeks and months went by, we realized that we were the victims of a broken promise. A few signs, briefly removed, returned; the others remained.

As in so many past experiences, our hopes had been blasted, and the shadow of deep disappointment settled upon us. We had no alternative except to prepare for direct action, whereby we would present our very bodies as a means of laying our case before the conscience of the local and the national community. Mindful of the difficulties involved, we decided to undertake a process of self-purification. We began a series of workshops on nonviolence, and we repeatedly asked ourselves: "Are you able to accept blows without retaliating?" "Are you able to endure the ordeal of jail?" We decided to schedule our direct-action program for the Easter season, realizing that except for Christmas, this is the main shopping period of the year. Knowing that a strong economic-withdrawal program would be the by-product of direct action, we felt that this would be the best time to bring pressure to bear on the merchants for the needed change.

Then it occurred to us that Birmingham's mayoral election was coming up in March, and we speedily decided to postpone action until after election-day.

When we discovered that the Commissioner of Public Safety, Eugene "Bull" Connor, had piled up enough votes to be in the run-off, we decided again to postpone action until the day after the run-off so that the demonstrations could not be used to cloud the issues. Like many others, we waited to see Mr. Connor defeated, and to this end we endured postponement after postponement. Having aided in this community need, we felt that our direct-action program could be delayed no longer.

You may well ask, "Why direct action? Why sit-ins, marches, and so forth? Isn't negotiation a better path?" You are quite right in calling for negotiation. Indeed, this is the very purpose of direct action. Nonviolent direct action seeks to create such a crisis and foster such a tension that a community which has constantly refused to negotiate is forced to confront the issue. It seeks so to dramatize the issue that it can no longer be ignored. My citing the creation of tension as part of the work of the nonviolent-resister may sound rather shocking. But I must confess that I am not afraid of the word "tension." I have earnestly opposed violent tension, but there is a type of constructive, nonviolent tension which is necessary for growth. Just as Socrates° felt that it was necessary to create a tension in the mind so that individuals could rise from the bondage of myths and half-truths to the unfettered realm of creative analysis and objective appraisal, so must we see the need for nonviolent gadflies to create the kind of tension in society that will help men rise from the dark depths of prejudice and racism to the majestic heights of understanding and brotherhood.

The purpose of our direct-action program is to create a situation so crisis-packed that it will inevitably open the door to negotiation. I therefore concur with you in your call for negotiation. Too long has our beloved Southland been bogged down in a tragic effort to live in monologue rather than dialogue.

One of the basic points in your statement is that the action that I and my associates have taken in Birmingham is untimely. Some have asked: "Why didn't you give the new city administration time to act?" The only answer that I can give to this query is that the new Birmingham administration must be prodded about as much as the outgoing one, before it will act. We are sadly mistaken if we feel that the election of Albert Boutwell as mayor will bring the millennium to Birmingham. While Mr. Boutwell is a much more gentle person than Mr. Connor, they are both segregationists, dedicated to maintenance of the status quo. I have hoped that Mr. Boutwell will be reasonable enough to see the futility of massive resistance to desegregation. But he will not see this without pressure from devotees of civil rights. My friends, I must say to you that we have not made a single gain in civil rights without determined legal and nonviolent pressure. Lamentably, it is an historical fact that privileged groups seldom give up their privileges voluntarily. Individuals may see the moral light and voluntarily give up their unjust posture; but, as Reinhold Niebuhr° has reminded us, groups tend to be more immoral than individuals.

Socrates (469–399 B.C.E.): The Greek philosopher would feign ignorance to expose the errors in his opponent's arguments.   **Reinhold Niebuhr (1892–1971):** American theologian.

We know through painful experience that freedom is never voluntarily given by the oppressor; it must be demanded by the oppressed. Frankly, I have yet to engage in a direct-action campaign that was "well timed" in the view of those who have not suffered unduly from the disease of segregation. For years now I have heard the word "Wait!" It rings in the ear of every Negro with piercing familiarity. This "Wait" has almost always meant "Never." We must come to see, with one of our distinguished jurists, that "justice too long delayed is justice denied."

We have waited for more than 340 years for our constitutional and God-given rights. The nations of Asia and Africa are moving with jetlike speed toward gaining political independence, but we still creep at horse-and-buggy pace toward gaining a cup of coffee at a lunch counter. Perhaps it is easy for those who have never felt the stinging darts of segregation to say, "Wait." But when you have seen vicious mobs lynch your mothers and fathers at will and drown your sisters and brothers at whim; when you have seen hate-filled policemen curse, kick, and even kill your black brothers and sisters; when you see the vast majority of your twenty million Negro brothers smothering in an airtight cage of poverty in the midst of an affluent society; when you suddenly find your tongue twisted and your speech stammering as you seek to explain to your six-year-old daughter why she can't go to the public amusement park that has just been advertised on television, and see tears welling up in her eyes when she is told that Funtown is closed to colored children, and see ominous clouds of inferiority beginning to form in her little mental sky, and see her beginning to distort her personality by developing an unconscious bitterness toward white people; when you have to concoct an answer for a five-year-old son who is asking, "Daddy, why do white people treat colored people so mean?"; when you take a cross-country drive and find it necessary to sleep night after night in the uncomfortable corners of your automobile because no motel will accept you; when you are humiliated day in and day out by nagging signs reading "white" and "colored"; when your first name becomes "nigger," your middle name becomes "boy" (however old you are), and your last name becomes "John," and your wife and mother are never given the respected title "Mrs."; when you are harried by day and haunted by night by the fact that you are a Negro, living constantly at tiptoe stance, never quite knowing what to expect next, and are plagued with inner fears and outer resentments; when you are forever fighting a degenerating sense of "nobodiness"—then you will understand why we find it difficult to wait. There comes a time when the cup of endurance runs over, and men are no longer willing to be plunged into the abyss of despair. I hope, sirs, you can understand our legitimate and unavoidable impatience.

You express a great deal of anxiety over our willingness to break laws. This   15
is certainly a legitimate concern. Since we so diligently urge people to obey the Supreme Court's decision of 1954 outlawing segregation in the public schools, at first glance it may seem rather paradoxical for us consciously to break laws. One may well ask: "How can you advocate breaking some laws and obeying others?" The answer lies in the fact that there are two types of laws: just and

unjust. I would be the first to advocate obeying just laws. One has not only a legal but a moral responsibility to obey just laws. Conversely, one has a moral responsibility to disobey unjust laws. I would agree with St. Augustine that "an unjust law is no law at all."

Now, what is the difference between the two? How does one determine whether a law is just or unjust? A just law is a man-made code that squares with the moral law or the law of God. An unjust law is a code that is out of harmony with the moral law. To put it in the terms of St. Thomas Aquinas: An unjust law is a human law that is not rooted in eternal law and natural law. Any law that uplifts human personality is just. Any law that degrades human personality is unjust. All segregation statutes are unjust because segregation distorts the soul and damages the personality. It gives the segregator a false sense of superiority and the segregated a false sense of inferiority. Segregation, to use the terminology of the Jewish philosopher Martin Buber, substitutes an "I-it" relationship for an "I-thou" relationship and ends up relegating persons to the status of things. Hence segregation is not only politically, economically, and sociologically unsound, it is morally wrong and sinful. Paul Tillich has said that sin is separation. Is not segregation an existential expression of man's tragic separation, his awful estrangement, his terrible sinfulness? Thus it is that I can urge men to obey the 1954 decision of the Supreme Court, for it is morally right; and I can urge them to disobey segregation ordinances, for they are morally wrong.

Let us consider a more concrete example of just and unjust laws. An unjust law is a code that a numerical or power majority group compels a minority group to obey but does not make binding on itself. This is *difference* made legal. By the same token, a just law is a code that a majority compels a minority to follow and that it is willing to follow itself. This is *sameness* made legal.

Let me give another explanation. A law is unjust if it is inflicted on a minority that, as a result of being denied the right to vote, had no part in enacting or devising the law. Who can say that the legislature of Alabama which set up that state's segregation laws was democratically elected? Throughout Alabama all sorts of devious methods are used to prevent Negroes from becoming registered voters, and there are some counties in which, even though Negroes constitute a majority of the population, not a single Negro is registered. Can any law enacted under such circumstances be considered democratically structured?

Sometimes a law is just on its face and unjust in its application. For instance, I have been arrested on a charge of parading without a permit. Now, there is nothing wrong in having an ordinance which requires a permit for a parade. But such an ordinance becomes unjust when it is used to maintain segregation and to deny citizens the First-Amendment privilege of peaceful assembly and protest.

I hope you are able to see the distinction I am trying to point out. In no sense   20
do I advocate evading or defying the law, as would the rabid segregationist. That would lead to anarchy. One who breaks an unjust law must do so openly, lovingly, and with a willingness to accept the penalty. I submit that an individual who breaks a law that conscience tells him is unjust, and who willingly accepts

the penalty of imprisonment in order to arouse the conscience of the community over its injustice, is in reality expressing the highest respect for law.

Of course, there is nothing new about this kind of civil disobedience. It was evidenced sublimely in the refusal of Shadrach, Meshach, and Abednego to obey the laws of Nebuchadnezzar, on the ground that a higher moral law was at stake.° It was practiced superbly by the early Christians, who were willing to face hungry lions and the excruciating pain of chopping blocks rather than submit to certain unjust laws of the Roman Empire. To a degree, academic freedom is a reality today because Socrates practiced civil disobedience. In our own nation, the Boston Tea Party represented a massive act of civil disobedience.

We should never forget that everything Adolf Hitler did in Germany was "legal" and everything the Hungarian freedom fighters did in Hungary was "illegal." It was "illegal" to aid and comfort a Jew in Hitler's Germany. Even so, I am sure that, had I lived in Germany at the time, I would have aided and comforted my Jewish brothers. If today I lived in a Communist country where certain principles dear to the Christian faith are suppressed, I would openly advocate disobeying that country's anti-religious laws.

I must make two honest confessions to you, my Christian and Jewish brothers. First, I must confess that over the past few years I have been gravely disappointed with the white moderate. I have almost reached the regrettable conclusion that the Negro's great stumbling block in his stride toward freedom is not the white Citizen's Counciler° or the Ku Klux Klanner, but the white moderate, who is more devoted to "order" than to justice; who prefers a negative peace which is the absence of tension to a positive peace which is the presence of justice; who constantly says, "I agree with you in the goal you seek, but I cannot agree with your methods of direct action"; who paternalistically believes he can set the timetable for another man's freedom; who lives by a mythical concept of time and who constantly advises the Negro to wait for a "more convenient season." Shallow understanding from people of good will is more frustrating than absolute misunderstanding from people of ill will. Lukewarm acceptance is much more bewildering than outright rejection.

I had hoped that the white moderate would understand that law and order exist for the purpose of establishing justice and that when they fail in this purpose they become the dangerously structured dams that block the flow of social progress. I had hoped that the white moderate would understand that the present tension in the South is a necessary phase of the transition from an obnoxious negative peace, in which the Negro passively accepted his unjust plight, to a substantive and positive peace, in which all men will respect the dignity and worth of human personality. Actually, we who engage in nonviolent direct action are not the creators of tension. We merely bring to the surface the hidden tension that is already alive. We bring it out in the open, where it can be seen and dealt with. Like a boil that can never be cured so long as it is

Shadrach . . . : See the book of Daniel in the Hebrew Scriptures (1:7–3:30).   **White Citizen's Councils:** Resisted desegregation after the U.S. Supreme Court declared segregated education unconstitutional in 1954.

covered up but must be opened with all its ugliness to the natural medicines of air and light, injustice must be exposed, with all the tension its exposure creates, to the light of human conscience and the air of national opinion, before it can be cured.

In your statement you assert that our actions, even though peaceful, must 25 be condemned because they precipitate violence. But is this a logical assertion? Isn't this like condemning a robbed man because his possession of money precipitated the evil act of robbery? Isn't this like condemning Socrates because his unswerving commitment to truth and his philosophical inquiries precipitated the act by the misguided populace in which they made him drink hemlock? Isn't this like condemning Jesus because his unique God-consciousness and never-ceasing devotion to God's will precipitated the evil act of crucifixion? We must come to see that, as the federal courts have consistently affirmed, it is wrong to urge an individual to cease his efforts to gain his basic constitutional rights because the quest may precipitate violence. Society must protect the robbed and punish the robber.

I had also hoped that the white moderate would reject the myth concerning time in relation to the struggle for freedom. I have just received a letter from a white brother in Texas. He writes: "All Christians know that the colored people will receive greater equal rights eventually, but it is possible that you are in too great a religious hurry. It has taken Christianity almost two thousand years to accomplish what it has. The teachings of Christ take time to come to earth." Such an attitude stems from a tragic misconception of time, from the strangely irrational notion that there is something in the very flow of time that will inevitably cure all ills. Actually, time itself is neutral; it can be used either destructively or constructively. More and more I feel that the people of ill will have used time much more effectively than have the people of good will. We will have to repent in this generation not merely for the hateful words and actions of the bad people, but for the appalling silence of the good people. Human progress never rolls in on wheels of inevitability; it comes through the tireless efforts of men willing to be co-workers with God, and without this hard work, time itself becomes an ally of the forces of social stagnation. We must use time creatively, in the knowledge that the time is always ripe to do right. Now is the time to make real the promise of democracy and transform our pending national elegy into a creative psalm of brotherhood. Now is the time to lift our national policy from the quicksand of racial injustice to the solid rock of human dignity.

You speak of our activity in Birmingham as extreme. At first I was rather disappointed that fellow clergymen would see my nonviolent efforts as those of an extremist. I began thinking about the fact that I stand in the middle of two opposing forces in the Negro community. One is a force of complacency, made up in part of Negroes, who, as a result of long years of oppression, are so drained of self-respect and a sense of "somebodiness" that they have adjusted to segregation; and in part of a few middle-class Negroes who, because of a degree of academic and economic security and because in some ways they profit by segregation, have become insensitive to the problems of the masses.

The other force is one of bitterness and hatred, and it comes perilously close to advocating violence. It is expressed in the various black nationalist groups that are springing up across the nation, the largest and best-known being Elijah Muhammad's Muslim movement.° Nourished by the Negro's frustration over the continued existence of racial discrimination, this movement is made up of people who have lost faith in America, who have absolutely repudiated Christianity, and who have concluded that the white man is an incorrigible "devil."

I have tried to stand between these two forces, saying that we need emulate neither the "do-nothingism" of the complacent nor the hatred and despair of the black nationalist. For there is the more excellent way of love and nonviolent protest. I am grateful to God that, through the influence of the Negro church, the way of nonviolence became an integral part of our struggle.

If this philosophy had not emerged, by now many streets of the South would, I am convinced, be flowing with blood. And I am further convinced that if our white brothers dismiss as "rabble-rousers" and "outside agitators" those of us who employ nonviolent direct action, and if they refuse to support our nonviolent efforts, millions of Negroes will, out of frustration and despair, seek solace and security in black-nationalist ideologies — a development that would inevitably lead to a frightening racial nightmare.

Oppressed people cannot remain oppressed forever. The yearning for free-   30
dom eventually manifests itself, and that is what has happened to the American Negro. Something within has reminded him of his birthright of freedom, and something without has reminded him that it can be gained. Consciously or unconsciously, he has been caught up by the *Zeitgeist*,° and with his black brothers of Africa and his brown and yellow brothers of Asia, South America, and the Caribbean, the United States Negro is moving with a sense of great urgency toward the promised land of racial justice. If one recognizes this vital urge that has engulfed the Negro community, one should readily understand why public demonstrations are taking place. The Negro has many pent-up resentments and latent frustrations, and he must release them. So let him march; let him make prayer pilgrimages to the city hall; let him go on freedom rides° — and try to understand why he must do so. If his repressed emotions are not released in nonviolent ways, they will seek expression through violence; this is not a threat but a fact of history. So I have not said to my people, "Get rid of your discontent." Rather, I have tried to say that this normal and healthy discontent can be channeled into the creative outlet of nonviolent direct action. And now this approach is being termed extremist.

But though I was initially disappointed at being categorized as an extremist, as I continued to think about the matter I gradually gained a measure of satisfaction from the label. Was not Jesus an extremist for love: "Love your enemies, bless them that curse you, do good to them that hate you, and pray for

Elijah Muhammad (1897–1975): Leader of the Nation of Islam, a Muslim religious group that called on African Americans to reject integration and establish their own nation. **Zeitgeist:** The spirit of the age (German).   **freedom rides:** In 1961, the Congress of Racial Equality (CORE) directed activists to flout race laws in the South that mandated segregation in buses and bus terminals.

them that despitefully use you, and persecute you." Was not Amos an extremist for justice: "Let justice roll down like waters and righteousness like an everflowing stream." Was not Paul an extremist for the Christian gospel: "I bear in my body the marks of the Lord Jesus." Was not Martin Luther an extremist: "Here I stand; I cannot do otherwise, so help me God." And John Bunyan: "I will stay in jail to the end of my days before I make a butchery of my conscience." And Abraham Lincoln: "This nation cannot survive half slave and half free." And Thomas Jefferson: "We hold these truths to be self-evident, that all men are created equal. . . ." So the question is not whether we will be extremists, but what kind of extremists we will be. Will we be extremists for the preservation of injustice or for the extension of justice? In that dramatic scene on Calvary's hill three men were crucified. We must never forget that all three were crucified for the same crime—the crime of extremism. Two were extremists for immorality, and thus fell below their environment. The other, Jesus Christ, was an extremist for love, truth, and goodness, and thereby rose above his environment. Perhaps the South, the nation, and the world are in dire need of creative extremists.

I had hoped that the white moderate would see this need. Perhaps I was too optimistic; perhaps I expected too much. I suppose I should have realized that few members of the oppressor race can understand the deep groans and passionate yearnings of the oppressed race, and still fewer have the vision to see that injustice must be rooted out by strong, persistent, and determined action. I am thankful, however, that some of our white brothers in the South have grasped the meaning of this social revolution and committed themselves to it. They are still all too few in quantity, but they are big in quality. Some—such as Ralph McGill, Lillian Smith, Harry Golden, James McBride Dabbs, Ann Braden, and Sarah Patton Boyle—have written about our struggle in eloquent and prophetic terms. Others have marched with us down nameless streets of the South. They have languished in filthy, roach-infested jails, suffering the abuse and brutality of policemen who view them as "dirty nigger-lovers." Unlike so many of their moderate brothers and sisters, they have recognized the urgency of the moment and sensed the need for powerful "action" antidotes to combat the disease of segregation.

Let me take note of my other major disappointment. I have been so greatly disappointed with the white church and its leadership. Of course, there are some notable exceptions. I am not unmindful of the fact that each of you has taken some significant stands on this issue. I commend you, Reverend Stallings, for your Christian stand on this past Sunday, in welcoming Negroes to your worship service on a nonsegregated basis. I commend the Catholic leaders of this state for integrating Spring Hill College several years ago.

But despite these notable exceptions, I must honestly reiterate that I have been disappointed with the church. I do not say this as one of those negative critics who can always find something wrong with the church. I say this as a minister of the gospel, who loves the church; who was nurtured in its bosom; who has been sustained by its spiritual blessings and who will remain true to it as long as the cord of life shall lengthen.

When I was suddenly catapulted into the leadership of the bus protest in   35
Montgomery, Alabama, a few years ago, I felt we would be supported by the
white church. I felt that the white ministers, priests, and rabbis of the South
would be among our strongest allies. Instead, some have been outright opponents,
refusing to understand the freedom movement and misrepresenting its leaders;
all too many others have been more cautious than courageous and have remained silent behind the anesthetizing security of stained-glass windows.

In spite of my shattered dreams, I came to Birmingham with the hope that
the white religious leadership of this community would see the justice of our
cause and, with deep moral concern, would serve as the channel through
which our just grievances could reach the power structure. I had hoped that
each of you would understand. But again I have been disappointed.

I have heard numerous southern religious leaders admonish their worshipers to comply with a desegregation decision because it is the law, but I have
longed to hear white ministers declare: "Follow this decree because integration is morally right and because the Negro is your brother." In the midst of
blatant injustices inflicted upon the Negro, I have watched white churchmen
stand on the sideline and mouth pious irrelevancies and sanctimonious trivi-
alities. In the midst of a mighty struggle to rid our nation of racial and economic injustice, I have heard many ministers say: "Those are social issues,
with which the gospel has no real concern." And I have watched many
churches commit themselves to a completely otherworldly religion which
makes a strange, unbiblical distinction between body and soul, between the
sacred and the secular.

I have traveled the length and breadth of Alabama, Mississippi, and all the
other southern states. On sweltering summer days and crisp autumn mornings
I have looked at the South's beautiful churches with their lofty spires pointing
heavenward. I have beheld the impressive outlines of her massive religious-
education buildings. Over and over I have found myself asking: "What kind of
people worship here? Who is their God? Where were their voices when the lips
of Governor Barnett dripped with words of interposition and nullification?
Where were they when Governor Wallace gave a clarion call for defiance and
hatred? Where were their voices of support when bruised and weary Negro
men and women decided to rise from the dark dungeons of complacency to the
bright hills of creative protest?"

Yes, these questions are still in mind. In deep disappointment I have wept
over the laxity of the church. But be assured that my tears have been tears of
love. There can be no deep disappointment where there is not deep love. Yes, I
love the church. How could I do otherwise? I am in the rather unique position
of being the son, the grandson, and the great-grandson of preachers. Yes, I see
the church as the body of Christ. But, oh! How we have blemished and scarred
the body through social neglect and through fear of being nonconformists.

There was a time when the church was very powerful—in the time when   40
the early Christians rejoiced at being deemed worthy to suffer for what they
believed. In those days the church was not merely a thermometer that transformed the mores of society. Whenever the early Christians entered a town,

the people in power became disturbed and immediately sought to convict the Christians for being "disturbers of the peace" and "outside agitators." But the Christians pressed on, in the conviction that they were "a colony of heaven," called to obey God rather than man. Small in number, they were big in commitment. They were too God-intoxicated to be "astronomically intimidated." By their effort and example they brought an end to such ancient evils as infanticide and gladiatorial contests.

Things are different now. So often the contemporary church is a weak, ineffectual voice with an uncertain sound. So often it is an archdefender of the status quo. Far from being disturbed by the presence of the church, the power structure of the average community is consoled by the church's silent—and often even vocal—sanction of things as they are.

But the judgment of God is upon the church as never before. If today's church does not recapture the sacrificial spirit of the early church, it will lose its authenticity, forfeit the loyalty of millions, and be dismissed as an irrelevant social club with no meaning for the twentieth century. Every day I meet young people whose disappointment with the church has turned into outright disgust.

Perhaps I have once again been too optimistic. Is organized religion too inextricably bound to the status quo to save our nation and the world? Perhaps I must turn my faith to the inner spiritual church, the church within the church, as the true *ekklesia°* and the hope of the world. But again I am thankful to God that some noble souls from the ranks of organized religion have broken loose from the paralyzing chains of conformity and joined us as active partners in the struggle for freedom. They have left their secure congregations and walked the streets of Albany, Georgia, with us. They have gone down the highways of the South on tortuous rides for freedom. Yes, they have gone to jail with us. Some have been dismissed from their churches, have lost the support of their bishops and fellow ministers. But they have acted in the faith that right defeated is stronger than evil triumphant. Their witness has been the spiritual salt that has preserved the true meaning of the gospel in these troubled times. They have carved a tunnel of hope through the dark mountain of disappointment.

I hope that the church as a whole will meet the challenge of this decisive hour. But even if the church does not come to the aid of justice, I have no despair about the future. I have no fear about the outcome of our struggle in Birmingham, even if our motives are at present misunderstood. We will reach the goal of freedom in Birmingham and all over the nation, because the goal of America is freedom. Abused and scorned though we may be, our destiny is tied up with America's destiny. Before the pilgrims landed at Plymouth, we were here. Before the pen of Jefferson etched the majestic words of the Declaration of Independence across the pages of history, we were here. For more than two centuries our forebears labored in this country without wages; they made cotton king; they built the homes of their masters while suffering gross injustice and shameful humiliation—and yet out of a bottomless vitality they contin-

---

ekklesia: The ancient Greek term for "people's assembly." It was chosen by early Christians to describe their gatherings or church.

ued to thrive and develop. If the inexpressible cruelties of slavery could not stop us, the opposition we now face will surely fail. We will win our freedom because the sacred heritage of our nation and the eternal will of God are embodied in our echoing demands.

Before closing I feel impelled to mention one other point in your statement that has troubled me profoundly. You warmly commended the Birmingham police force for keeping "order" and "preventing violence." I doubt that you would have so warmly commended the police force if you had seen its dogs sinking their teeth into unarmed, nonviolent Negroes. I doubt that you would so quickly commend the policemen if you were to observe their ugly and inhumane treatment of Negroes here in the city jail; if you were to watch them push and curse old Negro women and young Negro girls; if you were to see them slap and kick old Negro men and young boys; if you were to observe them, as they did on two occasions, refuse to give us food because we wanted to sing our grace together. I cannot join you in your praise of the Birmingham police department.   45

It is true that the police have exercised a degree of discipline in handling the demonstrators. In this sense they have conducted themselves rather "non-violently" in public. But for what purpose? To preserve the evil system of segregation. Over the past few years I have consistently preached that nonviolence demands that the means we use must be as pure as the ends we seek. I have tried to make clear that it is wrong to use immoral means to attain moral ends. But now I must affirm that it is just as wrong, or perhaps even more so, to use moral means to preserve immoral ends. Perhaps Mr. Connor and his policemen have been rather nonviolent in public, as was Chief Pritchett in Albany, Georgia, but they have used the moral means of nonviolence to maintain the immoral end of racial injustice. As T. S. Eliot° has said, "The last temptation is the greatest treason: to do the right deed for the wrong reason."

I wish you had commended the Negro sit-inners and demonstrators of Birmingham for their sublime courage, their willingness to suffer, and their amazing discipline in the midst of great provocation. One day the South will recognize its real heroes. They will be the James Merediths,° with the noble sense of purpose that enables them to face jeering and hostile mobs, and with the agonizing loneliness that characterizes the life of the pioneer. They will be old, oppressed, battered Negro women, symbolized in a seventy-two-year-old woman in Montgomery, Alabama, who rose up with a sense of dignity and with her people decided not to ride segregated buses, and who responded with ungrammatical profundity to one who inquired about her weariness: "My feets is tired, but my soul is at rest." They will be the young high school and college students, the young ministers of the gospel and a host of their elders, courageously and nonviolently sitting in at lunch counters and willingly going to jail for conscience' sake. One day the South will know that when these disinherited

---

Thomas Stearns Eliot (1888–1965): American-born poet and literary critic.   **James Meredith (b. 1933):** The first African American student to be admitted to the University of Mississippi.

children of God sat down at lunch counters, they were in reality standing up for what is best in the American dream and for the most sacred values in our Judaeo-Christian heritage, thereby bringing our nation back to those great wells of democracy which were dug deep by the founding fathers in their formulation of the Constitution and the Declaration of Independence.

Never before have I written so long a letter. I'm afraid it is much too long to take your precious time. I can assure you that it would have been much shorter if I had been writing from a comfortable desk, but what else can one do when he is alone in a narrow jail cell, other than write long letters, think long thoughts, and pray long prayers?

If I have said anything in this letter that overstates the truth and indicates an unreasonable impatience, I beg you to forgive me. If I have said anything that understates the truth and indicates my having a patience that allows me to settle for anything less than brotherhood, I beg God to forgive me.

I hope this letter finds you strong in the faith. I hope that circumstances   50
will soon make it possible for me to meet each of you, not as an integrationist or a civil-rights leader but as a fellow clergyman and a Christian brother. Let us all hope that the dark clouds of a racial prejudice will soon pass away and the deep fog of misunderstanding will be lifted from our fear-drenched communities, and in some not too distant tomorrow the radiant stars of love and brotherhood will shine over our great nation with all their scintillating beauty.

Yours for the cause of Peace and Brotherhood,
Martin Luther King Jr.   *[1963]*

≡ THINKING ABOUT THE TEXT

1. King wrote his letter in response to a published statement by eight clergymen from Alabama, who — as he points out in his first sentence — felt that his actions in Birmingham were "unwise and untimely." In what passages does he seem to be addressing this particular audience of religious leaders, referring to their specific accusation as well as to other ideas and texts that they would be especially familiar with? What are some passages where he seems to be addressing a larger audience, perhaps American society as a whole?

2. In one of the letter's most famous sections, King distinguishes between just and unjust laws (paras. 16–22). How does he define each of these two categories? To what extent do you find helpful the differences he draws between them?

3. In the middle of his letter (beginning in para. 23), King criticizes at length "the white moderate." What are his main observations about this kind of person? Why, apparently, does he devote his central section to *this* figure rather than to the extreme segregationist, who many people would think is his biggest enemy?

4. How would you describe King's tone? What impression of himself does he evidently seek to convey with it? Identify specific passages where you

are especially conscious of his tone, perhaps because you are aware that another writer in his situation might have used a different one.

5. Among the rhetorical devices that King employs is anaphora, a pattern of repetition in which consecutive sentences all start with the same word or words. For example, in paragraph 25, King begins three sentences in a row with the words "Isn't this." Where else in his letter does he use the technique? How effective do you find it?

≡ MAKING COMPARISONS

1. Do you think King would recognize Antigone as a kindred spirit? Why, or why not?

2. King argues that in the situation he writes about, resisting the law is virtuous. Does Sophocles make clear that Antigone's disobedience of the law is also virtuous, or is he more ambiguous than that? Explain.

3. How do religious references function in both Sophocles' play and King's "Letter"? Refer to specific passages in the two texts.

≡ WRITING ABOUT ISSUES

1. Choose *Antigone* or King's "Letter" and write an essay explaining how it treats prison or physical confinement as a *psychological* condition, too.

2. Is civil disobedience for King a more carefully reasoned decision than it is for Antigone? Write an essay that develops and supports your response to this question.

3. Write an essay in which you recall and analyze an occasion when you were inclined to disobey a law, rule, or regulation that you thought was unjust. Perhaps you did engage in disobedience; then again, perhaps you ultimately decided not to. Besides giving details of the incident, explain what criteria you used in determining the "right" thing to do. If you wish, refer to one or both of the texts in this cluster. Especially helpful may be the distinctions they draw between "just" and "unjust" government policies.

4. Choose a recent case of civil disobedience that the media has reported on, and read some opinion columns that have been published about it. Then, write an essay in which you analyze and evaluate at least two of these arguments. If you wish, refer to one or both of the texts in this cluster. Again, you may want to consider the distinctions they draw between "just" and "unjust" government policies.

CHAPTER 11

Journeys

Perhaps no impulse is as ancient and as natural as the desire to leave one's home, to journey out of the village to unknown lands. Ancient epics like the *Iliad* and the *Odyssey* and more modern tales like Mark Twain's *Adventures of Huckleberry Finn* and Jack Kerouac's *On the Road* are narratives of wandering, encountering the strange and the wondrous. Sometimes the journey has a specific goal, a quest for riches, for fame, or for adventure. Sometimes the journey is simply for escape, for curiosity's sake, for an understanding of the wider world. Of course the idea of the journey easily lends itself to both the literal and the metaphorical, to quests external and internal. We all take journeys of self-discovery from childhood to adolescence to adulthood and eventually to death. Life as a journey is a notion deeply woven into our cultural understanding from Greek mythology, epics, novels, religious beliefs, and popular culture.

It is no surprise then that writers for thousands of years have written about their perilous journeys to dangerous places, their contemplative journeys to self-reflection and wisdom, as well as their imaginative treks to dystopic futures. Our selections in this chapter work with an expansive idea of the journey, featuring work from Eudora Welty's classic short story "A Worn Path" to Kurt Vonnegut's journey to a harrowing future. For some the journey is quite literal; for others the path is decidedly metaphorical. Like the dancers in the Eagles' song "Hotel California," some writers journey to remember, others to forget. Whether the journey is the writer's own or a fictional one a character takes, the creative leap is always thoughtful, illuminating, and moving.

The chapter opens with a series of poetry clusters focused on journeys real and imagined. Four iconic poems of journeys taken and not by Robert Frost initiate our selections, followed by classic poems by Samuel Taylor Coleridge, Percy Bysshe Shelley, and William Butler Yeats. Then Alfred Lord Tennyson and Adrienne Rich take us on mythic journeys. Five poems about our final journey comprise the next cluster, followed by three poems involving interesting and poignant ferry rides. Phoenix Jackson's arduous journey in Eudora Welty's "A Worn Path" is paired with a doctor's surprising journey to a personal crisis. The seventh cluster pairs Nathaniel Hawthorne's harrowing depiction of Young Goodman Brown's disturbing journey with Sherman Alexie's narrative of two Native Americans' redemptive journey to bury a dead father. Next we present three science fiction masters: Ray Bradbury, Arthur C. Clarke, and Kurt Vonnegut, whose tales are always strange and provocative. Three variations on the classic fairy tale "Little Red Riding Hood" follow. And then we present the first chapter of Ralph Ellison's *Invisible Man*, a terrifying tale of a young man's brutal initiation into an unjust society. This story is illuminated by three pieces that provide cultural context about racial issues. In the eleventh cluster, Oscar Wilde's often-produced *The Importance of Being Ernest* is followed by critical commentaries on his comic masterpiece. Two essays by Hispanic Americans discussing their difficulties in crossing boundaries form the penultimate cluster. And lastly, a poem by the great poet of WWI, Wilfred Owen, a story by Tim O'Brien, and an essay by Michael Herr explore the horrific experience of battle. These thirteen clusters offer literary texts that are illuminating, inspiring, and sometimes unsettling, but we hope the journey will be worthwhile.

▪ Roads Taken: A Collection of Poems by Robert Frost

ROBERT FROST, "Stopping by Woods on a Snowy Evening"

ROBERT FROST, "The Road Not Taken"

ROBERT FROST, "Acquainted with the Night"

ROBERT FROST, "The Gift Outright"

Critic Randall Jarrell saw Robert Frost as "the subtlest and saddest of poets." Although many readers thought of this esteemed, pastoral poet as the optimistic voice of the common man, his lyrical vision is actually quite tragic, a quality President Kennedy thought helped strengthen his own presidential character. Alert readers should be careful about equating Frost's simple language and rural settings with lack of depth. The four poems assembled here (and "Mending Wall," p. 71) use the common motif of an external journey to comment on the internal burdens of adult responsibility, the anxiety inherent in making choices, and the loneliness of the human heart. The language of these journeys is beautifully crafted and evocative, able to be read profitably by both schoolchildren and sophisticated critics.

≡ BEFORE YOU READ

Do you remember reading a Frost poem in high school? What is your memory of that reading and discussion in class?

ROBERT FROST

Stopping by Woods on a Snowy Evening

Robert Frost (1874–1963) was perhaps the best-known American poet of the twentieth century: winning four Pulitzer Prizes, garnering more than forty honorary degrees, and being widely anthologized throughout the world. His popular image, perhaps forever fixed by his reading at John Kennedy's inauguration, is of a white-haired New Englander fond of simple, homey descriptions of nature. Actually, Frost was born in San Francisco, and most critics think his poetry is anything but simple.

Frost spent his childhood in California and later moved with his mother to eastern Massachusetts, where he grew up in the small city of Lawrence. He briefly attended Dartmouth College and married in 1895. Frost and his wife taught school together, but they soon moved to a farm in New Hampshire, where he worked and wrote poetry. In 1912, he moved to a town outside London and soon published his first book of poetry, A Boy's Will, in 1913. The book was well received, and a few years later Frost moved to Franconia, New Hampshire, and began a lifelong career of

© Bettmann/Corbis

writing and teaching. For more than twenty years, he was a professor at Amherst College and for decades taught summers at the Bread Loaf School in Vermont.

Frost's most popular poems, including those printed here, deal with complex social issues in a seemingly natural manner. But even a casual search of essays interpreting "Mending Wall," for example, demonstrates that critics see in Frost's poems a sophisticated, searching, and often dark commentary on the human condition.

"The Gift Outright" was published in 1941, but became famous when Frost read it at President Kennedy's inauguration in 1961. Frost had planned to read a poem written specifically for the event, but he had difficulty seeing in the bright winter glare, so he recited this poem, which he knew well. It tells of the American journey from colonial days to the westward expansion. Some see it as a celebration of Manifest Destiny, while others point to the statement in parentheses as suggesting something darker.

Whose woods these are I think I know.
His house is in the village, though;
He will not see me stopping here
To watch his woods fill up with snow.

My little horse must think it queer
To stop without a farmhouse near   5
Between the woods and frozen lake
The darkest evening of the year.

He gives his harness bells a shake
To ask if there is some mistake   10
The only other sound's the sweep
Of easy wind and downy flake.

The woods are lovely, dark and deep,
But I have promises to keep,
And miles to go before I sleep,   15
And miles to go before I sleep.   *[1923]*

≣ THINKING ABOUT THE TEXT

1. Why does the narrator seem so concerned that someone will notice him watching "woods fill up with snow" (line 4)?

2. Is the "darkest evening" (line 8) meant literally or metaphorically or both?

3. Notice the alliteration in lines 11–12. What effect is Frost trying to achieve with this poetic device?

4. Some critics see the narrator's pause and the lure of woods that "are lovely, dark and deep" (line 13) as something like a death wish. Do you agree?

5. How do you interpret the last lines? Are they a literal or a figurative statement? Why the repetition?

ROBERT FROST

The Road Not Taken

Two roads diverged in a yellow wood,
And sorry I could not travel both
And be one traveler, long I stood
And looked down one as far as I could
To where it bent in the undergrowth;   5

Then took the other, as just as fair,
And having perhaps the better claim,
Because it was grassy and wanted wear;
Though as for that the passing there
Had worn them really about the same,   10

And both that morning equally lay
In leaves no step had trodden black.

Oh, I kept the first for another day!
Yet knowing how way leads on to way,
I doubted if I should ever come back.   15

I shall be telling this with a sigh
Somewhere ages and ages hence:
Two roads diverged in a wood, and I —
I took the one less traveled by,
And that has made all the difference.   *[1916]*   20

≣ THINKING ABOUT THE TEXT

1. Is it odd that the title would refer to a road *not* taken?
2. This is clearly a poem about a journey. Did you ever think of your life as a journey on a particular path? How far can you see your future on this path?
3. Critics have noticed that although the narrator says he has taken the path less traveled, he also says the paths were worn about the same. How might you account for this?
4. The conventional interpretation of this poem is that it is about nonconformity. Does this make sense? Why? Given the issue in the previous question, might there be other interpretations?
5. Why does the narrator "sigh" in the last stanza? Is it due to boredom? Regret? Resignation? Nostalgia?

≣ MAKING COMPARISONS

1. Compare the moods of the speakers in both poems.
2. Both poems touch on the future. In what ways?
3. Is the tone of "Stopping by Woods on a Snowy Evening" more pessimistic than that of "The Road Not Taken"?

ROBERT FROST

Acquainted with the Night

I have been one acquainted with the night.
I have walked out in rain — and back in rain.
I have outwalked the furthest city light.

I have looked down the saddest city lane.
I have passed by the watchman on his beat   5
And dropped my eyes, unwilling to explain.

I have stood still and stopped the sound of feet
When far away an interrupted cry
Came over houses from another street,

But not to call me back or say good-by;   10
And further still at an unearthly height
One luminary clock against the sky

Proclaimed the time was neither wrong nor right.
I have been one acquainted with the night.   *[1928]*

≡ THINKING ABOUT THE TEXT

1. When the narrator passes the watchman, he drops his eyes (lines 5–6). Why?

2. It seems that the cry (line 8) has nothing to do with the narrator. Is this detail a key to his psychological and emotional state?

3. The narrator says the "time was neither wrong nor right" (line 13). What is he trying to suggest? What might the "time was right" suggest?

4. Why does the narrator choose the night for his walks? Why not walk during the day?

5. Although the first and last lines are identical, do you sense a difference in meaning?

≡ MAKING COMPARISONS

1. Which of these three journeys in Frost's poems seems the most hopeful?

2. Is the speaker in "Acquainted with the Night" more honest than the other speakers? Why?

3. Which line in the three poems seems the most enigmatic? Why?

ROBERT FROST

The Gift Outright

The land was ours before we were the land's.
She was our land more than a hundred years
Before we were her people. She was ours
In Massachusetts, in Virginia,
But we were England's, still colonials,   5
Possessing what we still were unpossessed by,
Possessed by what we now no more possessed.
Something we were withholding made us weak
Until we found out that it was ourselves
We were withholding from our land of living,   10
And forthwith found salvation in surrender.
Such as we were we gave ourselves outright
(The deed of gift was many deeds of war)

To the land vaguely realizing westward,
But still unstoried, artless, unenhanced,   15
Such as she was, such as she would become.   *[1923]*

≣ THINKING ABOUT THE TEXT

1. What does the first sentence mean? How might America's early history figure into Frost's observation?

2. Some critics see a connection between our possession of the land and lovers possessing one another. How could this interpretation be plausible?

3. Frost uses "our" a number of times. Some critics see this as aggressive possession of a land that was, after all, inhabited by hundreds of thousands of Native Americans. How might this be a plausible reading?

4. How can this poem be seen as narrating a journey? Does Frost suggest the journey is over or not?

5. How do you read line 13? What, for example, are the many deeds of war he references? How might this change the tone of the poem? Do you, for example, think he is celebrating these wars, making excuses for them, or bemoaning them? Explain.

≣ MAKING COMPARISONS

1. How is this journey different from the other three?

2. Compare the idea of the future in the last line with the last lines in "Stopping by Woods on a Snowy Evening" and "The Road Not Taken."

3. Compare the idea of the land in all four poems.

≣ WRITING ABOUT ISSUES

1. Write an essay about a decision you made that you assumed would make a difference in your life.

2. All four poems involve journeys. Write an essay that compares the four journeys in terms of purpose, mood, and meaning.

3. Write an essay about a significant and recent journey that you have taken. Did you learn something about yourself? Did you change?

4. Another Frost poem, "Mending Wall," appears in the first part of this book (p. 71). Write an essay that compares the attitude of that speaker with the four speakers in this cluster. Which one is he the closest to? The most distant from?

SAMUEL TAYLOR COLERIDGE, "Kubla Khan"

PERCY BYSSHE SHELLEY, "Ozymandias"

WILLIAM BUTLER YEATS, "Sailing to Byzantium"

Perhaps the idea of a visionary poet conjures up in your mind one who can see the future, or one who can imagine a better future with a more humane and just society, or perhaps one who has a vision of fantasy worlds like those ancient and exotic lands visited by Marco Polo, with Mongol emperors and his entourage in vast and elaborate palaces and gardens. If so, then Samuel Taylor Coleridge's "Kubla Khan" and William Butler Yeats's "Sailing to Byzantium" fit the bill. Coleridge's poem is one of the strangest and most well-known poems in English. Mysterious and haunting, the visionary Xanadu was conjured in an opium dream. No less compelling is Yeats's wish to sail to Byzantium, where he hopes to leave his natural body and become a work of art that could sing forever, much like the poet in "Kubla Khan" who would amaze us all with songs fueled by "the milk of Paradise." And in Shelley's poem "Ozymandias," the poet paints a vision of a statue in the desert decaying after thousands of years, a vision that reminds us of mortality, even for the most powerful rulers of empires.

SAMUEL TAYLOR COLERIDGE
Kubla Khan

Samuel Taylor Coleridge (1772–1834) was one of the romantic movement's most influential poets and thinkers. In "The Rime of the Ancient Mariner," and "Kubla Khan," he sought to make the strange, the mystical, and the supernatural seem real. He was born in a remote section of England. He excelled at academics and was an outstanding student at Cambridge University. He became friends with the poet William Wordsworth, and their poetic collaboration inspired both to produce some of their best work, including their masterpiece, Lyrical Ballads *(1798). He believed that culture, and particularly literature, could be a positive unifying force in the life of a country, combating the materialistic and fragmented society he saw all around him.*

Coleridge claimed that his famous poem "Kubla Khan" was written after he woke from a dream influenced by opium, a drug commonly prescribed at the time for various ailments. But his furiously written remembrance was interrupted by a man visiting on business. When the visitor left, Coleridge could not recapture the dream-poem, and so it was left as a fragment. This mysterious and enigmatic tale focuses on a Mongol emperor, Kubla Khan, and the palace he built, surrounded by strange, perhaps demonic forces. In his vision, Coleridge sees a woman playing an instrument which inspires him in interesting ways. He recalls past visions and sees Kubla Khan, a figure with flashing eyes. The meaning of the poem has been debated ever since it appeared, but perhaps the most common is that it is about the creative process and the power of the unconscious to produce art. As you read the poem, you can make your own judgments.

Or, a vision in a dream. A Fragment.

In Xanadu did Kubla Khan
A stately pleasure-dome decree:
Where Alph, the sacred river, ran
Through caverns measureless to man
    Down to a sunless sea.   5
So twice five miles of fertile ground
With walls and towers were girdled round;
And there were gardens bright with sinuous rills,
Where blossomed many an incense-bearing tree;
And here were forests ancient as the hills,   10
Enfolding sunny spots of greenery.

But oh! that deep romantic chasm which slanted
Down the green hill athwart a cedarn cover!
A savage place! as holy and enchanted
As e'er beneath a waning moon was haunted   15
By woman wailing for her demon-lover!
And from this chasm, with ceaseless turmoil seething,
As if this earth in fast thick pants were breathing,
A mighty fountain momently was forced:
Amid whose swift half-intermitted burst   20
Huge fragments vaulted like rebounding hail,
Or chaffy grain beneath the thresher's flail:
And mid these dancing rocks at once and ever
It flung up momently the sacred river.
Five miles meandering with a mazy motion   25
Through wood and dale the sacred river ran,
Then reached the caverns measureless to man,
And sank in tumult to a lifeless ocean;
And 'mid this tumult Kubla heard from far
Ancestral voices prophesying war!   30
    The shadow of the dome of pleasure
    Floated midway on the waves;
    Where was heard the mingled measure
    From the fountain and the caves.
It was a miracle of rare device,   35
A sunny pleasure-dome with caves of ice!

    A damsel with a dulcimer
    In a vision once I saw:

It was an Abyssinian maid
   And on her dulcimer she played,   40
   Singing of Mount Abora.
   Could I revive within me
     Her symphony and song,
      To such a deep delight 'twould win me,
That with music loud and long,   45
I would build that dome in air,
That sunny dome! those caves of ice!
And all who heard should see them there,
And all should cry, Beware! Beware!
His flashing eyes, his floating hair!   50
Weave a circle round him thrice,
And close your eyes with holy dread
For he on honey-dew hath fed,
And drunk the milk of Paradise.   *[1797]*

☰ THINKING ABOUT THE TEXT

1. Describe what Coleridge calls "A savage place" (line 14). Why does he use that term?

2. What does Coleridge say is the result of hearing the Abyssinian maid (line 39)? What might that have to do with poetry?

3. How can critics claim that the poem draws a contrast between the man-made and the natural world?

4. Why would people cry, "Beware! Beware!" (line 49)? Some critics think Coleridge is speaking of himself in the last lines. What might he be saying?

5. What lines seem the most enigmatic to you? What might some possible interpretations be? What is the most interesting line or phrase? Why? What is the most memorable line? Why?

PERCY BYSSHE SHELLEY
Ozymandias

Before his untimely death by drowning, Percy Bysshe Shelley (1792–1822) composed many poems that are now regarded as masterpieces of British romanticism such as "Ode to the West Wind" and "To a Skylark." Shelley published the following poem in 1818 after a visit to the British Museum. On exhibit there were artifacts from the tomb of the ancient Egyptian pharaoh Rameses II, called Ozymandias by many of Shelley's contemporaries. These objects included a broken statue of the pharaoh.

I met a traveler from an antique land
Who said: Two vast and trunkless legs of stone
Stand in the desert. . . . Near them, on the sand,
Half sunk, a shattered visage lies, whose frown,
And wrinkled lip, and sneer of cold command,   5
Tell that its sculptor well those passions read
Which yet survive, stamped on these lifeless things,
The hand that mocked them, and the heart that fed:
And on the pedestal these words appear:
"My name is Ozymandias, King of Kings: 10
Look on my works, ye Mighty, and despair!"
Nothing beside remains. Round the decay
Of that colossal wreck, boundless and bare
The lone and level sands stretch far away.   *[1818]*

≡ THINKING ABOUT THE TEXT

1. "Ozymandias" is a sonnet, a poem consisting of fourteen lines. Often there is a significant division in content between a sonnet's first eight lines and its last six. Is there such a division in Shelley's poem? Explain.

2. How is the poem a comment on the epitaph it quotes from the statue's pedestal? Describe Ozymandias by listing at least three adjectives for him, and identify the specific lines that make you think of them.

3. Although the poem begins by referring to "I," this is not the main speaker of the poem; soon we are presented with the report of the "traveler." Shelley could have had the traveler narrate the whole poem. Why might he have begun with the "I"?

4. Both Shelley and the sculptor are artists. To what extent do they resemble each other? Note that the poem describes the sculptor as someone who "well those passions read" (line 6). Why does Shelley associate him with the act of reading?

5. According to this poem, what survives? What does not?

≡ MAKING COMPARISONS

1. Compare the attitudes of the poets toward Ozymandias and Kubla Khan.

2. What might you infer about their personalities from the building projects of Ozymandias and Kubla Khan?

3. Compare the last two lines of "Ozymandias" with the last two lines of the first stanza in "Kubla Khan."

WILLIAM BUTLER YEATS

Sailing to Byzantium

William Butler Yeats (1865–1939) was one of the most revered and influential modern poets, winning the Nobel Prize for literature in 1923. He was born in Dublin, Ireland, and although he spent part of his childhood in London, he is closely associated with his native country. Besides writing poetry, he cofounded Dublin's Abbey Theatre and wrote books of literary criticism along with treatises on mystical philosophy. Yeats was also strongly involved in Irish politics. Both in his literary works and in his civic life, he was dedicated to resurrecting Irish folklore traditions and overthrowing British rule. In 1922, he was even elected as a senator for the newly established Irish Free Republic.

In comments about the following poem, Yeats said he was "trying to write about the state of my soul. . . . When Irishmen were illuminating the Book of Kells, and making the jeweled croziers in the National Museum, Byzantium [Istanbul] was the centre of European civilization and the source of its spiritual philosophy, so I symbolize the search for the spiritual life by a journey to that city."

That is no country for old men. The young
In one another's arms, birds in the trees
—Those dying generations—at their song,
The salmon-falls, the mackerel-crowded seas,
Fish, flesh, or fowl, commend all summer long   5
Whatever is begotten, born, and dies.
Caught in that sensual music all neglect
Monuments of unageing intellect.

An aged man is but a paltry thing,
A tattered coat upon a stick, unless   10
Soul clap its hands and sing, and louder sing
For every tatter in its mortal dress,
Nor is there singing school but studying
Monuments of its own magnificence;
And therefore I have sailed the seas and come   15
To the holy city of Byzantium.

O sages standing in God's holy fire
As in the gold mosaic of a wall,
Come from the holy fire, perne in a gyre,
And be the singing-masters of my soul.   20
Consume my heart away; sick with desire
And fastened to a dying animal
It knows not what it is; and gather me
Into the artifice of eternity.

Once out of nature I shall never take   25
My bodily form from any natural thing,

But such a form as Grecian goldsmiths make
Of hammered gold and gold enamelling
To keep a drowsy Emperor awake;
Or set upon a golden bough to sing   30
To lords and ladies of Byzantium
Of what is past, or passing, or to come.   *[1928]*

☰ THINKING ABOUT THE TEXT

1. Why does the poet say this "is no country for old men" (line 1)? What are the neglected monuments of "unageing intellect" (line 8)? Who is caught in "that sensual music" (line 7)?

2. Why does he want to go to Byzantium and not someplace else?

3. What is the "dying animal" (line 22)? What does the poet hope will happen to it?

4. What is the meaning of "perne" and "gyre" (line 19)? Who does the poet want to be the "singing-masters" of his soul (line 20)? What does this mean?

5. What will the speaker never reclaim? What does the poet hope to spend his days doing?

☰ MAKING COMPARISONS

1. Compare the singing mentioned at the end of Yeats's poem with Coleridge's lines 45ff., especially, "I would build that dome in air . . ." (line 46).

2. Compare Byzantium and Xanadu.

3. Compare ideas of time in "Sailing to Byzantium" and "Ozymandias."

☰ WRITING ABOUT ISSUES

1. Write a comparison of "Kubla Khan" and "Sailing to Byzantium," noting thematic, metaphorical, and descriptive similarities and differences.

2. Read either Coleridge's "The Rime of the Ancient Mariner" or Yeats's "The Second Coming," and write an analysis of its themes. Make reference to the poet's other poem presented here.

3. Research information on such poets as William Blake, Arthur Rimbaud, Charles Baudelaire, and Pablo Neruda. Write a report on at least two of these, comparing them to the three poets presented here. The focus of your essay could be: what constitutes a visionary poet?

4. Do research on recent criticism of "Kubla Khan" (a good place to start is the extensive Wikipedia Web site), and write a review of what contemporary critics are saying about the poem. Include your own evaluation of these ideas.

≡ Mythic Journeys: Poems

ALFRED LORD TENNYSON, "Ulysses"

ADRIENNE RICH, "Diving into the Wreck"

In Joseph Campbell's influential book *The Hero with a Thousand Faces*, he finds that the idea of a hero who sacrifices for the good of others is present in almost all cultures. In Western culture, of course, the heroes of Greek mythology loom large, influencing writers from Homer to Dante to Tennyson and Adrienne Rich. The hero often goes on a journey, seeking wealth, power, adventure, or even self-knowledge, wisdom, and redemption. In Homer's The *Iliad* and *The Odyssey*, Ulysses helps the Greeks succeed in the Trojan War and returns to rule in Ithaca. Writers ever since have used this myth for their own purposes. Dante has Ulysses dying because he wandered too far. In Victorian England, Alfred Lord Tennyson, suffering from the death of a close friend, has Ulysses longing in his old age for an escape on the open seas. His poem about the Greek hero became a kind of rallying cry among Victorians eager for adventure, conquest, and glory. Nearly a century later, the feminist thinker and lesbian activist, Adrienne Rich uses the idea of a journey as a metaphor to explore her own journey to understand the place of women in human history. Before she descends into the sea of history, she reads "the book of myths," which readers have often interpreted as the false history of women as written by men. This is the wreck, and she wants to cut away at this distorted account so she can write the truth. Both poems describe literal journeys but both suggest more philosophical and psychological journeys into self-knowledge and self-discovery.

ALFRED, LORD TENNYSON

Ulysses

Alfred, Lord Tennyson (1809–1892), one of the great poets of the nineteenth century, served as poet laureate of England longer than any other poet before or since. He was born into a wealthy family and early on demonstrated a gift for verse. He was quite popular with all classes in Victorian England and is one of the most quoted poets in English. Many schoolchildren were and still are asked to memorize "The Charge of the Light Brigade" with its famous "Theirs not reason why, / Theirs but to do and die." But perhaps his most well-known quote is "'Tis better to have loved and lost / Than never to have loved at all." Another is the last line of the following poem, which became a motto for confident Victorians: "To strive, to seek, to find, and not to yield." Tennyson often wrote about classical mythological figures, such as Ulysses (Odysseus). In his poem, he combines stories about the famous Greek hero from both Homer and Dante. In his version, Ulysses is a rebel bored with conformity and, even in his old age, seeking adventures in a mythological dimension "beyond the sunset."

It little profits that an idle king,
By this still hearth, among these barren crags,
Match'd with an aged wife, I mete and dole
Unequal laws unto a savage race,
That hoard, and sleep, and feed, and know not me.   5
I cannot rest from travel: I will drink
Life to the lees: All times I have enjoy'd
Greatly, have suffer'd greatly, both with those
That loved me, and alone, on shore, and when
Thro' scudding drifts the rainy Hyades   10
Vext the dim sea: I am become a name;
For always roaming with a hungry heart
Much have I seen and known; cities of men
And manners, climates, councils, governments,
Myself not least, but honour'd of them all;   15
And drunk delight of battle with my peers,
Far on the ringing plains of windy Troy.
I am a part of all that I have met;
Yet all experience is an arch wherethro'
Gleams that untravell'd world whose margin fades   20
For ever and forever when I move.
How dull it is to pause, to make an end,
To rust unburnish'd, not to shine in use!
As tho' to breathe were life! Life piled on life
Were all too little, and of one to me   25
Little remains: but every hour is saved
From that eternal silence, something more,
A bringer of new things; and vile it were
For some three suns to store and hoard myself,
And this gray spirit yearning in desire   30
To follow knowledge like a sinking star,
Beyond the utmost bound of human thought.

     This is my son, mine own Telemachus,
To whom I leave the sceptre and the isle, —
Well-loved of me, discerning to fulfil   35
This labour, by slow prudence to make mild
A rugged people, and thro' soft degrees
Subdue them to the useful and the good.
Most blameless is he, centred in the sphere
Of common duties, decent not to fail   40
In offices of tenderness, and pay
Meet adoration to my household gods,
When I am gone. He works his work, I mine.

     There lies the port; the vessel puffs her sail:
There gloom the dark, broad seas. My mariners,   45

Souls that have toil'd, and wrought, and thought with me—
That ever with a frolic welcome took
The thunder and the sunshine, and opposed
Free hearts, free foreheads—you and I are old;
Old age hath yet his honour and his toil;   50
Death closes all: but something ere the end,
Some work of noble note, may yet be done,
Not unbecoming men that strove with Gods.
The lights begin to twinkle from the rocks:
The long day wanes: the slow moon climbs: the deep   55
Moans round with many voices. Come, my friends,
'T is not too late to seek a newer world.
Push off, and sitting well in order smite
The sounding furrows; for my purpose holds
To sail beyond the sunset, and the baths   60
Of all the western stars, until I die.
It may be that the gulfs will wash us down:
It may be we shall touch the Happy Isles,
And see the great Achilles, whom we knew.
Tho' much is taken, much abides; and tho'   65
We are not now that strength which in old days
Moved earth and heaven, that which we are, we are;
One equal temper of heroic hearts,
Made weak by time and fate, but strong in will
To strive, to seek, to find, and not to yield.   *[1854]*   70

≡ THINKING ABOUT THE TEXT

1. In this dramatic monologue, spoken by Ulysses, what comments about himself and his plans tell us something about his character?

2. What has Ulysses done that he is proud of? What do you think the phrase "a hungry heart" (line 12) means?

3. What specific lines suggest his boredom and disdain for conformity? What lines suggest a rebellious spirit?

4. What is Ulysses' attitude toward his son, Telemachus? What does he ask of him? What is your judgment about Ulysses' plans for his city, his family, and his companions?

5. The last stanza is addressed to Ulysses' fellow mariners. What is he asking of them? What are his reasons for his request? How would you evaluate this last stanza as an act of persuasion?

ADRIENNE RICH

Diving into the Wreck

Adrienne Rich (1929–2012) is one of the most celebrated poets of the past fifty years. She was also a renowned public intellectual whose books on feminism, politics, sexual identity, and literature were learned, controversial, and influential. Rich was born in Baltimore and educated at home and in private schools. She graduated from Radcliffe University and soon married an economics professor from Harvard. They had three children. She published her first poetry collection, A Change of the World *in 1951, her last year of college. She moved to New York City in the mid-1960s and became active in the civil rights, anti-war, and feminist movements. Ten years later, she separated from her husband and started a lifelong relationship with the poet Michelle Cliff. During this tumultuous period, Rich produced some of her most famous work. Her reputation as a first-class thinker was assured with her essay collections,* On Lies, Secrets, and Silence: Selected Prose, 1966–1978 *(1979) and* Of Woman Born: Motherhood as Experience and Institution *(1976), both of which were called "erudite, lucid, and poetic." Rich pursued a humane, progressive agenda for equality for women and lesbians and passionately insisted on human dignity and social justice for all. The following title poem from her most famous collection,* Diving into the Wreck *(1973), which won the National Book Award, uses the extended metaphor referred to in the title to comment on Rich's symbolic poetic journey of self-discovery. Among her numerous awards and honors is the McArthur ("Genius") Fellowship, The National Medal of Arts (refused), a Guggenheim Fellowship, and the Griffin Poetry Prize. Her last book is* Later Poems Selected and New: 1971–2012 *(2012).*

First having read the book of myths,
and loaded the camera,
and checked the edge of the knife-blade,
I put on
the body-armor of black rubber   5
the absurd flippers
the grave and awkward mask.
I am having to do this
not like Cousteau with his
assiduous team   10
aboard the sun-flooded schooner
but here alone.

There is a ladder.
The ladder is always there
hanging innocently   15
close to the side of the schooner.
We know what it is for,
we who have used it.

Otherwise
it is a piece of maritime floss
some sundry equipment.   20

I go down.
Rung after rung and still
the oxygen immerses me
the blue light   25
the clear atoms
of our human air.
I go down.
My flippers cripple me,
I crawl like an insect down the ladder   30
and there is no one
to tell me when the ocean
will begin.

First the air is blue and then
it is bluer and then green and then   35
black I am blacking out and yet
my mask is powerful
it pumps my blood with power
the sea is another story
the sea is not a question of power   40
I have to learn alone
to turn my body without force
in the deep element.

And now: it is easy to forget
what I came for   45
among so many who have always
lived here
swaying their crenellated fans
between the reefs
and besides   50
you breathe differently down here.

I came to explore the wreck.
The words are purposes.
The words are maps.
I came to see the damage that was done   55
and the treasures that prevail.
I stroke the beam of my lamp
slowly along the flank
of something more permanent
than fish or weed   60

the thing I came for:
the wreck and not the story of the wreck

the thing itself and not the myth
the drowned face always staring
toward the sun   65
the evidence of damage
worn by salt and sway into this threadbare beauty
the ribs of the disaster
curving their assertion
among the tentative haunters.   70

This is the place.
And I am here, the mermaid whose dark hair
streams black, the merman in his armored body.
We circle silently
about the wreck   75
we dive into the hold.
I am she: I am he

whose drowned face sleeps with open eyes
whose breasts still bear the stress
whose silver, copper, vermeil cargo lies   80
obscurely inside barrels
half-wedged and left to rot
we are the half-destroyed instruments
that once held to a course
the water-eaten log   85
the fouled compass

We are, I am, you are
by cowardice or courage
the one who find our way
back to this scene   90
carrying a knife, a camera
a book of myths
in which
our names do not appear.   *[1973]*

≡ **THINKING ABOUT THE TEXT**

1. What specific things does Rich do before setting off? What symbolic
   significance do you think they have? Why, for example, does she check
   "the edge of the knife-blade" (line 3)?

2. What are some possible meanings for the wreck as metaphor? Could it
   be, for example, history written by men? Or obsolete myths about
   women, or lesbians, or Jews? (Rich's father was Jewish, although she
   was raised as a Christian.) Or perhaps something else?

3. Critics have noted the seemingly genderless (androgynous) being in
   stanza eight. What is your reading of this stanza?

4. How would you describe the purpose of the poet's journey? What might Rich mean when she says "our names do not appear" (line 94) in the "book of myths" (line 92)?

5. Translate the central idea of these ten stanzas into prose, recounting the steps, equipment, and activity in Rich's journey.

≡ MAKING COMPARISONS

1. Compare the purpose of each journey.

2. Compare the attitudes and characters of each poem's narrator.

3. Discuss the place of myth in each poem.

≡ WRITING ABOUT ISSUES

1. Write an analysis of "Diving into the Wreck," paying particular attention to the specific details of the speaker's journey. Consult two outside sources, and integrate them into your essay.

2. Write a comparison between Tennyson's and Rich's mythic journeys. Be sure to note the purpose of each, the speakers' attitudes toward the society they live in, and the metaphors used.

3. In the *Oxford Dictionary of Quotations*, locate five quotations from Tennyson and write an analysis of their relevance (or not) for today's world.

4. Read Rich's essay, "Compulsory Heterosexuality and Lesbian Existence" and write an analysis of its main ideas, noting comparisons to "Diving into the Wreck."

MARY OLIVER, "When Death Comes"

JOHN DONNE, "Death Be Not Proud"

DYLAN THOMAS, "Do Not Go Gentle into That Good Night"

WISŁAWA SYMBORSKA, "On Death, without Exaggeration"

EMILY DICKINSON, "Because I could not stop for Death"

For many cultures, death seems more than a metaphorical journey. This is especially true of the Greeks, in whose mythology Charon, the ferryman of the underworld, is literally charged with taking the dead across the river Styx, where they will continue their trek for better or worse. Contemporary poets tend to see death's journey differently than the ancients did, but their appreciation of the mysteries and power of death is enduring. And poets reflect on death's presence in our lives in lyrical and illuminating ways.

Mary Oliver uses a series of interesting similes both to describe death's arrival ("like the hungry bear") and to prepare herself for its inevitability. John Donne sneers at death, perhaps to demonstrate its power, and Dylan Thomas wants to resist that power. Reducing the significance of death was probably on Emily Dickinson's mind when she described Death as a civil carriage driver who kindly stops for her on the way to eternity. Death has intrigued and puzzled poets for centuries, perhaps because, as Shakespeare reminds us, it is a country from which no traveler returns.

■ BEFORE YOU READ

Does our society have a particular attitude toward death? Can you point to films that might reveal such a cultural inclination? Does your religion have a specific take on death? What is your general attitude toward death, and where does it come from?

MARY OLIVER
When Death Comes

Mary Oliver (b. 1935) was born in Maple Heights, Ohio, and briefly attended Ohio State University. She was strongly influenced by the poet Edna St. Vincent Millay. Her collection No Voyage and Other Poems *(1963) was the first of numerous volumes, including* New and Selected Poems *(1992), which won the National Book Award, and* American Primitive *(1984), which won the Pulitzer Prize for poetry. She has taught at Bucknell University and Sweet Briar College. Her most recent poetry collections are* Dog Songs *(2013) and* A Thousand Mornings *(2012). The poet Maxine Kumin calls Oliver "an undefatigable guide to the natural world."*

When death comes
like the hungry bear in autumn;
when death comes and takes all the bright coins from his purse

to buy me, and snaps the purse shut;
when death comes   5
like the measles-pox;

when death comes
like an iceberg between the shoulder blades,

I want to step through the door full of curiosity, wondering:
what is it going to be like, that cottage of darkness?   10

And therefore I look upon everything
as a brotherhood and a sisterhood,
and I look upon time as no more than an idea,
and I consider eternity as another possibility,

and I think of each life as a flower, as common   15
as a field daisy, and as singular,
and each name a comfortable music in the mouth
tending as all music does, toward silence,

and each body a lion of courage, and something
precious to the earth.   20

When it's over, I want to say: all my life
I was a bride married to amazement.
I was the bridegroom, taking the world into my arms.

When it is over, I don't want to wonder
if I have made of my life something particular, and real.   25
I don't want to find myself sighing and frightened,
or full of argument.

I don't want to end up simply having visited this world.   *[1992]*

≡ THINKING ABOUT THE TEXT

1. How would you describe what the narrator wants to avoid when death comes?

2. The poet uses a number of similes to describe death's coming. Explain why any one of these seems particularly apt.

3. How does Oliver's view of death influence the way she lives her life?

4. Unpack "visited" in the last line.

5. Does our culture have a particular view of death? What might that be? Does your religion have an attitude toward death that may have influenced you? Is there evidence for a cultural view of death in movies? In popular songs? On TV shows?

JOHN DONNE
Death Be Not Proud

Long regarded as a major English writer, John Donne (1572–1631) was also trained as a lawyer and clergyman. Around 1594, he converted from Catholicism to Anglicanism; in 1615, he was ordained; and in 1621, he was appointed to the prestigious position of dean of St. Paul's Cathedral in London. Today, his sermons continue to be studied as literature, yet he is more known for his poetry. When he was a young man, he often wrote about love, but later he focused on religious themes. The following poem, one of Donne's "holy sonnets," is from 1611.

Death be not proud, though some have callèd thee	
Mighty and dreadful, for thou art not so;	
For those whom thou think'st thou dost overthrow	
Die not, poor Death, nor yet canst thou kill me.	
From rest and sleep, which but thy pictures° be,	*images* 5
Much pleasure; then from thee much more must flow,	
And soonest our best men with thee do go,	
Rest of their bones, and soul's delivery.°	*deliverance*
Thou art slave to Fate, Chance, kings, and desperate men,	
And dost with Poison, War, and Sickness dwell;	10
And poppy or charms can make us sleep as well,	
And better than thy stroke; why swell'st° thou then?	*swell with pride*
One short sleep past, we wake eternally	
And death shall be no more; Death, thou shalt die.	*[1611]*

☰ THINKING ABOUT THE TEXT

1. In a sense, Death is the speaker's audience. But presumably Donne expected the living to read his poem. What reaction might he have wanted from this audience?

2. Is the speaker proud? Define what you mean by the term.

3. Evidently the speaker believes in an afterlife. What would you say to people who consider the speaker naive and the poem irrelevant because they don't believe that "we wake eternally" (line 13)? How significant is this warrant or assumption? Do you share it?

4. What are the arguments the narrator uses to diminish Death?

5. Imagine Death writing a sonnet in response to the speaker. Perhaps it would be entitled "Life Be Not Proud." What might Death say in it?

☰ MAKING COMPARISONS

1. Is death more or less fearsome in Donne's poem than in Oliver's?

2. Do both speakers refuse to be afraid of death?

3. What optimistic stance do both speakers take?

DYLAN THOMAS
Do Not Go Gentle into That Good Night

Dylan Thomas (1914–1953) was a Welsh poet, short-story writer, and playwright. Among his most enduring works are his radio dramas Under Milk Wood *(1954) and* A Child's Christmas in Wales *(1955). A frequent visitor to the United States, Thomas built a devoted audience in this country through his electrifying public readings. Unfortunately, he was also well known for his alcoholism, which killed him at a relatively young age. He wrote the following poem in 1952, not long before his own death. It takes the form of a* villanelle, *which consists of nineteen lines: five tercets (three-line stanzas) followed by a quatrain (four-line stanza). The first and third lines of the opening tercet are used alternately to conclude each succeeding tercet, and they are joined to form a rhyme at the poem's end.*

Do not go gentle into that good night,
Old age should burn and rave at close of day;
Rage, rage against the dying of the light.

Though wise men at their end know dark is right,
Because their words had forked no lightning they   5
Do not go gentle into that good night.

Good men, the last wave by, crying how bright
Their frail deeds might have danced in a green bay,
Rage, rage against the dying of the light.

Wild men who caught and sang the sun in flight,   10
And learn, too late, they grieved it on its way,
Do not go gentle into that good night.

Grave men, near death, who see with blinding sight
Blind eyes could blaze like meteors and be gay,
Rage, rage against the dying of the light.   15

And you, my father, there on the sad height,
Curse, bless, me now with your fierce tears, I pray.
Do not go gentle into that good night.
Rage, rage against the dying of the light.   *[1952]*

≡ THINKING ABOUT THE TEXT

1. In what sense could the night possibly be "good," given that people are supposed to "rage" at it?

2. Why do you think Thomas has his speaker refer to "the dying of the light" instead of simply to "dying"? What other parts of the poem relate to the word *light*?

3. The speaker refers to four kinds of "men." Restate in your own words the description given of each. Should Thomas's language about them have been less abstract? Why, or why not?

4. What is the effect of climaxing the poem with a reference to "you, my father" (line 16)? If the father had been introduced in the first or second stanzas, would the effect have been quite different? If so, how?

5. What is the effect of the villanelle form? Judging by Thomas's poem, do you think it is worthwhile for a poet to write in this way, despite the technical challenges of the form? Should teachers of poetry writing push their students to write a villanelle? Explain your reasoning.

≡ MAKING COMPARISONS

1. Is this poem an affirmation of life? Could Oliver's or Donne's poem be considered as such?

2. Compare the speaker's attitude in this poem to that in Oliver's.

3. Which poet seems most at peace with death?

WISŁAWA SZYMBORSKA
On Death, without Exaggeration

Translated by Stanislaw Baranczak and Clare Cavanagh

Although she had written several volumes of poetry, Wisława Szymborska (1923–2012) was little known outside of her native Poland until she won the Nobel Prize for literature in 1996. Since then, readers in various countries have come to admire the blend of simplicity, wit, and wisdom in her writing. The Polish version of the following poem appeared in Szymborska's 1986 book The People on the Bridge. *Subsequently, Stanislaw Baranczak and Clare Cavanagh included it in their 1995 English collection of Szymborska's poems,* View with a Grain of Sand. *We present their translation of the text. Her last two books are* Enough *(2012) and* The Glimmer of a Revolver *(2013).*

It can't take a joke,
find a star, make a bridge.
It knows nothing about weaving, mining, farming,
building ships, or baking cakes.

In our planning for tomorrow,   5
it has the final word,
which is always beside the point.

It can't even get the things done
that are part of its trade:

dig a grave,   10
make a coffin,
clean up after itself.

Preoccupied with killing,
it does the job awkwardly,
without system or skill.   15
As though each of us were its first kill.

Oh, it has its triumphs,
but look at its countless defeats,
missed blows,
and repeat attempts!   20

Sometimes it isn't strong enough
to swat a fly from the air.
Many are the caterpillars
that have outcrawled it.

All those bulbs, pods,   25
tentacles, fins, tracheae,
nuptial plumage, and winter fur
show that it has fallen behind
with its halfhearted work.

Ill will won't help   30
and even our lending a hand with wars and coups d'état
is so far not enough.

Hearts beat inside eggs.
Babies' skeletons grow.
Seeds, hard at work, sprout their first tiny pair of leaves   35
and sometimes even tall trees fall away.

Whoever claims that it's omnipotent
is himself living proof
that it's not.

There's no life   40
that couldn't be immortal
if only for a moment.

Death
always arrives by that very moment too late.

In vain it tugs at the knob   45
of the invisible door.
As far as you've come
can't be undone.   *[1986]*

≡ THINKING ABOUT THE TEXT

1. Although the word *death* appears in the title, it doesn't appear in the text of the poem until the next-to-last stanza. Up to that point, death is repeatedly referred to as "it." What is the effect of this pronoun? What might be the effect had Szymborska referred to death more explicitly throughout the text?

2. Evidently the speaker is trying not to exaggerate death. What sorts of remarks about death might the speaker see as an exaggeration of it? Define what you mean by *exaggeration*.

3. What images of death does the speaker create? Refer to specific lines.

4. In the eighth stanza, the speaker mentions that human beings are "lending a hand" to death. Do you take the speaker to be criticizing humanity at this point? Why, or why not?

5. Does the order of the stanzas matter? Could the speaker's observations about death appear in any order and have the same effect? Explain your reasoning.

≡ MAKING COMPARISONS

1. Do all four poems speak of death "without exaggeration"? Define what you mean by the phrase.

2. Does Szymborska's poem strike you as lighter, less serious than Donne's and Thomas's? Refer to specific lines in each text.

3. If you didn't know the authors of the four poems, could you guess which two were written by women? What evidence supports your position?

EMILY DICKINSON
Because I could not stop for Death

Although Emily Dickinson (1830–1886) was considered an eccentric recluse by many of her provincial neighbors, history has interpreted Emily Dickinson's life in various ways, according to the thinking of the times. Once considered isolated, she is now seen by many critics as connected to the issues and literature of her age. And feminist and queer studies scholars now see the once-shy figure as an active champion who defied gender stereotypes. Although she has often been described as nunlike and passive, critics today see her as a nonconformist, mistrustful of power and dogma, and as someone who questioned any kind of received opinion, even popular views on religion and the afterlife.

The following much-discussed poem has intrigued and puzzled critics for generations. Its elusive meaning and its combination of Christian promises and Gothic imagery has allowed critics to see the poem as everything from an acceptance of New

England Protestant dogma to a rejection of religion in favor of the immortality of art.
The poem was originally published in 1890 as "The Chariot."

Because I could not stop for Death—
He kindly stopped for me—
The Carriage held but just Ourselves—
And Immortality.

We slowly drove—He knew no haste   5
And I had put away
My labor and my leisure too,
For His Civility—

We passed the School, where Children strove
At Recess—in the Ring—   10
We passed the Fields of Gazing Grain—
We passed the Setting Sun—

Or rather—He passed us—
The Dews drew quivering and Chill—
For only Gossamer, my Gown—   15
My Tippet—only Tulle—

We paused before a House that seemed
A Swelling of the Ground—
The Roof was scarcely visible—
The Cornice—in the Ground—   20

Since then—'tis Centuries—and yet
Feels shorter than the Day
I first surmised the Horses' Heads
Were toward Eternity—   [1890]

≡ THINKING ABOUT THE TEXT

1. Who are the passengers in the carriage? What is the effect of "kindly" in line 2? How might we imagine Immortality? Fear of death was a common theme in nineteenth-century sermons. How might this poem be a rejection of that fear?

2. How might the second stanza be an acceptance of death? Why does Death drive slowly?

3. What might the three images in the third stanza stand for?

4. Critics have debated the reference for "He" in stanza 4. What do you think she means? What do "gossamer," "tippet," and "tulle" mean?

5. What suggests that the narrator might already be dead? What might "House" in the fifth stanza refer to?

☰ MAKING COMPARISONS

1. Using just a phrase or a word, how would you characterize the attitude of these five poems toward death?

2. What do you assume Donne's response to Dickinson's poem would be? How about Oliver's response?

3. Explain which of the five poems seem the most religious and which seem the most secular.

☰ WRITING ABOUT ISSUES

1. Choose one of the five poems about death, and write an essay analyzing it as an argument for a certain position on death. Specify the main claim and the evidence given in support of it. Feel free to evaluate the argument you discuss, although keep in mind that the artistic success of the poem may or may not depend on whether its argument is fully developed.

2. Write an essay comparing two of the poems in this cluster, focusing on the issue of whether they are basically similar or significantly different in the ideas and feelings they express. Refer to specific lines from each text.

3. Write an essay recalling a specific occasion when you had difficulty deciding whether to accept something as inevitable. In your essay, give details of the occasion, the difficulty, and your ultimate conclusion. Indicate as well what your final decision revealed about you. Perhaps you will want to distinguish between the self you were then and the self you are now. If you wish, refer to any of the poems in this cluster.

4. Imagine that you are on the staff of a nursing home. At a staff meeting, the chief administrator asks you and your colleagues to consider framing and hanging one of these five poems in the recreation room. Write a letter to the administrator in which you favor one of these poems or reject them all as inappropriate. Be sure to give reasons for your view.

≡ Crossing the Waters: Poems

KATIA KAPOVICH, "The Ferry"

LINDA PASTAN, "Leaving the Island"

MARK DOTY, "Night Ferry"

For some reason, journeys on ferries seem to put us in a wistful, meditative frame of mind. Especially for a writer, this trip seems more symbolic than those in cars or on planes. It often brings to mind previous outings, perhaps from childhood, or sometimes it might remind us that "all life," as Arthur Miller wrote, is a "leave taking." And, of course, there is the larger metaphor that our life is a kind of ferry ride between the shores of life and death. The three poets included here take advantage of these notions, adding their own lyrical perspectives. Katia Kapovich, for example, muses on time passing, Linda Pastan on rituals repeated, and Mark Doty on mysteries as deep as the seas. As Pastan writes, "The ferry is no simple pleasure boat."

≡ BEFORE YOU READ

Why do you think ferries evoke meditative responses that planes or cars usually do not elicit? Have you ever taken a ferry ride? What was your response?

KATIA KAPOVICH

The Ferry

Katia Kapovich (b. 1960) was born in Moldova in the former Soviet Union, where as a young intellectual artist she was under considerable pressure to conform. As a member of an underground literary dissident movement, she was in constant conflict with an oppressive government. During a demonstration for intellectual freedom at a university in Leningrad, she was arrested after clashing with police. She was briefly confined and later immigrated to America. For the past nearly twenty years, she has lived in Boston, where she teaches Russian literature and writes in both Russian and English. Her poems have been described as exquisitely crafted and quite complex. She and her husband edit the journal Fulcrum. *Her latest book of poems is* Cossacks and Bandits *(2008). The following poem is from* The Best American Poetry 2006.

> I'm jotting down these lines,
> having borrowed a pen from a waitress
> in this roadside restaurant. Three rusty pines

prod up the sky in the windows.
My soup gets cold, which implies   5

I'll eat it cold. Soon I too
will leave a tip on the table, merge
into the beehive of travelers
and board one of the ferries,
where there's always a line to the loo   10
and no one knows where the captain is.

Slightly seasick, I keep on writing
of the wind rose and lobster traps,
seagulls, if any — and there always are.
Check the air and you'll see them   15
above straw hats and caps.
The sun at noon glides like a monstrous star-

fish through clouds. Others drink iced tea,
training binoculars on a tugboat.
When I finish this letter, I'll take a gulp   20
from the flask you gave me for the road
in days when I was too young to care about
those on the pier who waved goodbye.

I miss them now: cousins in linen dresses,
my mother, you, boys in light summer shirts.   25
Life is too long. The compass needle dances.
Everything passes by. The ferry passes
by ragged yellow shores.
                                                      [2006]

≡ THINKING ABOUT THE TEXT

1. Who might the "you" referred to in lines 21 and 25 be? Is there a difference between missing one's mother and missing "cousins in linen
   dresses" (line 24) and "boys in light summer shirts" (line 25)?

2. How do the details in the first three stanzas (rusty pines, cold soup, long
   lines, seasickness) suggest the narrator's mood?

3. The poem shifts from the present to the past in stanza 4. What thought
   comes first to the narrator's mind? How old do you think the narrator is?

4. Is the claim that "[l]ife is too long" (line 26) surprising? Are the following two sentences (lines 26–27) evidence of this?

5. Do ferry rides (as opposed to bridge crossings or tunnel passages) seem
   to make you reflective or nostalgic? Why?

LINDA PASTAN
Leaving the Island

Linda Pastan (b. 1932) was born in the Bronx and graduated from Radcliffe Col-
lege; she later received her M.A. from Brandeis University. The recipient of numer-
ous prestigious awards and nominations for the National Book Award, Pastan has
published several volumes of poetry, including Carnival Evening: New and Selected
Poems 1968–1998 *(1998),* Queen of a Rainy Country *(2006), and* Traveling
Light *(2011). The poet May Sarton has praised Pastan for her integrity, noting her*
"unsentimental acceptance of hard work." Pastan was poet laureate of Maryland
(1991–1995) and for twenty years taught at the noted Bread Loaf Writers Confer-
ence sponsored by Middlebury College in Vermont.

We roll up rugs and strip the beds by rote,
summer expires as it has done before.
The ferry is no simple pleasure boat

nor are we simply cargo, though we'll float
alongside heavy trucks — their stink and roar.   5
We roll up rugs and strip the beds by rote.

This bit of land whose lines the glaciers wrote
becomes the muse of memory once more;
the ferry is no simple pleasure boat.

I'll trade my swimsuit for a woolen coat;   10
the torch of autumn has but small allure.

We roll up rugs and strip the beds by rote.

The absences these empty shells denote
suggest the losses winter has in store.
The ferry is no simple pleasure boat.   15

The songs of summer dwindle to one note:
the fog horn's blast (which drowns this closing door).
We rolled up rugs and stripped the beds by rote.
The ferry is no simple pleasure boat.   *[2004]*

≡ **THINKING ABOUT THE TEXT**

1. How would you describe the narrator's mood? Is it temporary?
   What effects does the repetition of "We roll up rugs and strip the
   beds by rote" and "The ferry is no simple pleasure boat" have on the
   reader?

2. Is this a poem about summer's passing or about something more
   general — say, time passing or aging?

3. Why does summer seem the best of times for the narrator? Is it for you? Do losses happen mostly in the winter?

4. Do you remember a childhood vacation? Is your memory positive? Were you sad when it ended?

5. How would you expand on the refrain "The ferry is no simple pleasure boat"? Is "simple" the key idea?

☰ MAKING COMPARISONS

1. Compare the mood or the tone of the speakers in these two poems.

2. Is nostalgia part of the poems? How does a poet avoid being too sentimental about the past? Do these poets succeed in that regard?

3. Note the rhyme scheme in both poems. Does the pattern work better in Pastan's poem than in Kapovich's? Why, or why not?

MARK DOTY
Night Ferry

Mark Doty (b. 1953) was born in Tennessee, but his father, who was a builder working for the Army Corps of Engineers, was a man who could not get along with supervisors and often moved the family. In the autobiographical Firebird *(1999), Doty describes growing up as "a sissy" in a Southern Gothic family. He attended high school in Tucson, Arizona, where he first developed an interest in writing. Then he briefly attended the University of Tucson, but dropped out and married when he was eighteen. In the 1970s, he attended Drake University in Iowa, where he and his wife published chapbooks of poetry together. In 1981, he dissolved his marriage when he acknowledged his homosexuality. He received his M.F.A. at Goddard College in Vermont and taught there, eventually moving with his partner to Provincetown, Massachusetts. After his partner died from complications of AIDS in 1984, Doty's poetry took on a new intensity and significance. Doty has taught at several universities and now teaches at Rutgers University. He has published five poetry collections and two memoirs. His awards and fellowships include the National Book Critics Award and the T. S. Eliot Prize in 1993 for* My Alexandria. *His recent books include* School of the Arts: Poems *(2005),* Dog Years: A Memoir *(2007),* Theories and Apparitions *(2008), and* Paragon Park *(2012).*

We're launched into the darkness,
half a load of late passengers
   gliding onto the indefinite
      black surface, a few lights vague

  and shimmering on the island shore.   5
Behind us, between the landing's twin flanks

(wooden pylons strapped with old tires),
　　　the docklights shatter in our twin,

folding wakes, their colors
on the roughened surface combed   10
　　　like the patterns of Italian bookpaper,
　　　　　lustrous and promising. The narrative

of the ferry begins and ends brilliantly,
and its text is this moving out
　　　into what is soon before us   15
　　　　　and behind: the night going forward,

sentence by sentence, as if on faith,
into whatever takes place.
　　　It's strange how we say things *take place,*
　　　　　as if occurrence were a location —   20

the dark between two shores,
for instance, where for a little while
　　　we're on no solid ground. Twelve minutes,
　　　　　precisely, the night ferry hurries

across the lake. And what happens   25
is always the body of water,
　　　its skin like the wrong side of satin.
　　　　　I love to stand like this,

where the prow pushes blunt into the future,
knowing, more than seeing, how   30
　　　the surface rushes and doesn't even break
　　　　　but simply slides under us.

Lake melds into shoreline,
one continuous black moiré;°
　　　the boatmen follow the one course they know   35
　　　　　toward a dock nearly the mirror

of the first, mercury lamps vaporing
over the few late birds
　　　attending the pier. Even the bored men
　　　　　at the landing, who wave   40

their flashlights for the last travelers,
steering us toward the road, will seem
　　　the engineers of our welcome,
　　　　　their red-sheathed lights marking

the completion of our, or anyone's, crossing.   45
Twelve dark minutes. Love,

34 *moiré*: Wavy pattern.

we are between worlds, between
     unfathomed water and I don't know how much

light-flecked black sky, the fogged circles
of island lamps. I am almost not afraid   50
     on this good boat, breathing its good smell
          of grease and kerosene,

warm wind rising up the stairwell
from the engine's serious study.
     There's no beautiful binding   55
          for this story, only the temporary,

liquid endpapers of the hurried water,
shot with random color. But in the gliding forward's
     a scent so quick and startling
          it might as well be blowing   60

off the stars. Now, just before we arrive,
the wind carries a signal and a comfort,
     lovely, though not really meant for us:
          woodsmoke risen from the chilly shore.   *[1993]*

▤ THINKING ABOUT THE TEXT

1. The poem seems to be a sustained metaphor for life's journey. In
   what ways does this comparison make sense? What other significant
   metaphor is developed?

2. As symbols, what do the following images suggest — "a few lights vague
   / and shimmering" (lines 4–5), "like the patterns of Italian bookpaper, /
   lustrous and promising" (lines 11–12), "no beautiful binding / for this
   story, only the temporary, / liquid endpapers of the hurried water, / shot
   with random color" (lines 55–58)?

3. How did you evaluate the speaker's attitude when he says, "I am almost not afraid / on this good boat, breathing its good smell" (lines
   50–51)?

4. Does the image of "a scent . . . / . . . blowing / off the stars" (lines 59–
   61) seem more mysterious than Doty's other images? What idea might
   the poet be after with such imagery?

5. Can we sustain the journey-of-life metaphor into the last stanza? Where
   might the passengers be arriving? What is the signal "not really meant
   for us" (line 63)? Why woodsmoke? Why "the chilly shore" (line 64)?

▤ MAKING COMPARISONS

1. Is Doty's poem more melancholy than the other poems? Why, or why not?

2. Is Doty's poem more metaphorical than the others? Why, or why not?

3. Which line or lines in these three poems do you find the most lyrical? The most mysterious? The most suggestive?

≡ WRITING ABOUT ISSUES

1. Which of these three poems most closely reflects your own sense of what life's journey is like? Write an essay in which you make the case for your poem in comparison with one or both of the other poems.

2. Write a brief essay defending the idea that ferry rides in literature often have symbolic value. Use the poems here as evidence.

3. Write a brief personal essay about a ferry trip you took, noting your thoughts about it.

4. Read Walt Whitman's famous poem "Crossing Brooklyn Ferry," and write a brief analysis of Whitman's response to his ride.

■ Errands of Mercy: Stories

WILLIAM CARLOS WILLIAMS, "The Use of Force"

EUDORA WELTY, "A Worn Path"

Although both of the well-known stories in this cluster start out as errands of mercy, they have quite different endings. Doctors are almost always portrayed in a favorable light in popular culture. And because they are sometimes the difference between life and death, they enjoy an elevated status in the culture. We think highly of them and expect them, perhaps unfairly, to be both paragons of compassion and professionally dispassionate. William Carlos Williams's story, however, reminds us that doctors are also human and can act in unprofessional ways, even with the best of intentions. "The Use of Force" is a disturbing tale that typically elicits a wide range of responses from readers. Perhaps Eudora Welty's tale of mercy, "A Worn Path," is not as unsettling as Williams's story, but it is as open to widely different interpretation. Phoenix Jackson, one of literature's most memorable characters, endures her difficult trek at Christmastime to buy medicine for her grandson, who may or may not be alive. Seen as everything from religious pilgrimage to civil rights allegory, Phoenix is a symbol for many things to many readers.

■ BEFORE YOU READ

In what ways does our popular culture portray doctors? What specific guidance were you given as a child in regard to mercy or compassion or self-sacrifice? How does our culture reward mercy and compassion? Recount an incident where you were forced to do something "for your own good." What was your response?

WILLIAM CARLOS WILLIAMS
The Use of Force

William Carlos Williams (1883–1963) was an American poet and fiction writer usually thought of as a modernist closely associated with the imagists. His brief poem, "The Red Wheelbarrow," is one of the most famous in literature. Williams was born in New Jersey and received his medical degree from the University of Pennsylvania in 1906. His first book, Poems, was published in 1909. Williams's main occupation was as a family doctor, but he had a successful literary career and was well known and respected among the leading writers of the day. He championed poetry as "equipment for living" and felt his own career was overshadowed by the highly intellectual and allusive style of T. S. Eliot, especially the highly influential "The Waste Land." Williams also wrote a number of novels and short story and essay collections. The following popular story was published on the eve of World War II and explores themes of responsibility, restraint, domination, submission, and the consequences of violence.

They were new patients to me, all I had was the name, Olson. Please come down as soon as you can, my daughter is very sick. When I arrived I was met by the mother, a big startled looking woman, very clean and apologetic who merely said, Is this the doctor? and let me in. In the back, she added. You must excuse us, doctor, we have her in the kitchen where it is warm. It is very damp here sometimes.

The child was fully dressed and sitting on her father's lap near the kitchen table. He tried to get up, but I motioned for him not to bother, took off my overcoat and started to look things over. I could see that they were all very nervous, eyeing me up and down distrustfully. As often, in such cases, they weren't telling me more than they had to, it was up to me to tell them; that's why they were spending three dollars on me.

The child was fairly eating me up with her cold, steady eyes, and no expression to her face whatever. She did not move and seemed, inwardly, quiet; an unusually attractive little thing, and as strong as a heifer in appearance. But her face was flushed, she was breathing rapidly, and I realized that she had a high fever. She had magnificent blond hair, in profusion. One of those picture children often reproduced in advertising leaflets and the photogravure sections of the Sunday papers.

She's had a fever for three days, began the father and we don't know what it comes from. My wife has given her things, you know, like people do, but it don't do no good. And there's been a lot of sickness around. So we tho't you'd better look her over and tell us what is the matter.

As doctors often do I took a trial shot at it as a point of departure. Has she   5
had a sore throat?

Both parents answered me together, No . . . No, she says her throat don't hurt her.

Does your throat hurt you? added the mother to the child. But the little girl's expression didn't change nor did she move her eyes from my face.

Have you looked?

I tried to, said the mother, but I couldn't see.

As it happens we had been having a number of cases of diphtheria in the   10
school to which the child went during that month and we were all, quite apparently, thinking of that, though no one had as yet spoken of the thing.

Well, I said, suppose we take a look at the throat first. I smiled in my best professional manner and asking for the child's first name I said, come on, Mathilda, open your mouth and let's take a look at your throat.

Nothing doing.

Aw, come on, I coaxed, just open your mouth wide and let me take a look. Look, I said opening both hands wide, I haven't anything in my hands. Just open up and let me see.

Such a nice man, put in the mother. Look how kind he is to you. Come on, do what he tells you to, he won't hurt you.

At that I ground my teeth in disgust. If only they wouldn't use the word   15
"hurt" I might be able to get somewhere. But I did not allow myself to be hurried or disturbed but speaking quietly and slowly I approached the child again.

As I moved my chair a little nearer suddenly with one catlike movement both her hands clawed instinctively for my eyes and she almost reached them too. In fact she knocked my glasses flying and they fell, though unbroken, several feet away from me on the kitchen floor.

Both the mother and father almost turned themselves inside out in embarrassment and apology. You bad girl, said the mother, taking her and shaking her by one arm. Look what you've done. The nice man . . .

For heaven's sake, I broke in. Don't call me a nice man to her. I'm here to look at her throat on the chance that she might have diphtheria and possibly die of it. But that's nothing to her. Look here, I said to the child, we're going to look at your throat. You're old enough to understand what I'm saying. Will you open it now by yourself or shall we have to open it for you?

Not a move. Even her expression hadn't changed. Her breaths however were coming faster and faster. Then the battle began. I had to do it. I had to have a throat culture for her own protection. But first I told the parents that it was entirely up to them. I explained the danger but said that I would not insist on a throat examination so long as they would take the responsibility.

If you don't do what the doctor says you'll have to go to the hospital, the   20
mother admonished her severely.

Oh yeah? I had to smile to myself. After all, I had already fallen in love with the savage brat, the parents were contemptible to me. In the ensuing struggle they grew more and more abject, crushed, exhausted while she surely rose to magnificent heights of insane fury of effort bred of her terror of me.

The father tried his best, and he was a big man but the fact that she was his daughter, his shame at her behavior and his dread of hurting her made him release her just at the critical times when I had almost achieved success, till I wanted to kill him. But his dread also that she might have diphtheria made him tell me to go on, go on though he himself was almost fainting, while the mother moved back and forth behind us raising and lowering her hands in an agony of apprehension.

Put her in front of you on your lap, I ordered, and hold both her wrists.

But as soon as he did the child let out a scream. Don't, you're hurting me. Let go of my hands. Let them go I tell you. Then she shrieked terrifyingly, hysterically. Stop it! Stop it! You're killing me!

Do you think she can stand it, doctor! said the mother.   25

You get out, said the husband to his wife. Do you want her to die of diphtheria?

Come on now, hold her, I said.

Then I grasped the child's head with my left hand and tried to get the wooden tongue depressor between her teeth. She fought, with clenched teeth, desperately! But now I also had grown furious—at a child. I tried to hold myself down but I couldn't. I know how to expose a throat for inspection. And I did my best. When finally I got the wooden spatula behind the last teeth and just the point of it into the mouth cavity, she opened up for an instant but before I could see anything she came down again and gripped the wooden blade between her molars. She reduced it to splinters before I could get it out again.

Aren't you ashamed, the mother yelled at her. Aren't you ashamed to act like that in front of the doctor?

Get me a smooth-handled spoon of some sort, I told the mother. We're go-   30
ing through with this. The child's mouth was already bleeding. Her tongue was cut and she was screaming in wild hysterical shrieks. Perhaps I should have desisted and come back in an hour or more. No doubt it would have been better. But I have seen at least two children lying dead in bed of neglect in such cases, and feeling that I must get a diagnosis now or never I went at it again. But the worst of it was that I too had got beyond reason. I could have torn the child apart in my own fury and enjoyed it. It was a pleasure to attack her. My face was burning with it.

The damned little brat must be protected against her own idiocy, one says to one's self at such times. Others must be protected against her. It is a social necessity. And all these things are true. But a blind fury, a feeling of adult shame, bred of a longing for muscular release are the operatives. One goes on to the end.

In the final unreasoning assault I overpowered the child's neck and jaws. I forced the heavy silver spoon back of her teeth and down her throat till she gagged. And there it was—both tonsils covered with membrane. She had fought valiantly to keep me from knowing her secret. She had been hiding that sore throat for three days at least and lying to her parents in order to escape just such an outcome as this.

Now truly she was furious. She had been on the defensive before but now she attacked. Tried to get off her father's lap and fly at me while tears of defeat blinded her eyes.   *[1938]*

≡ THINKING ABOUT THE TEXT

1. Describe the conflicting emotions of the doctor and the little girl.

2. What can be said to justify the doctor's actions? What can be said to criticize the doctor's actions? What can be said to justify the girl's actions? What can be said to criticize the girl's actions?

3. Why would some critics think the idea of being blind in all its literal and metaphorical meanings is a key idea in this story?

4. Explain the doctor's relationship to the child's parents. Why at one point does the doctor say about the father, "I wanted to kill him" (para. 22)?

5. What possible comment on human nature does the story make? What might the story be saying about the consequence of violence?

EUDORA WELTY

A Worn Path

Eudora Welty (1909–2001)—who was born, raised, and died in Jackson, Missis-
sippi—is considered one of the twentieth century's most gifted short-story writ-
ers. She studied at the University of Wisconsin and Columbia University and worked
for the New York Times Book Review *during World War II. During this time, she*
began writing stories for the Southern Review. *Soon after one of her stories ap-*
peared in the Atlantic Monthly, *she published her first collection in 1941,* A Curtain of Green, *which was followed by* The Wide Net and Other Stories *(1943).*
Her first novel was Delta Wedding *(1946). Another novel,* The Optimist's Daughter *(1972), won the Pulitzer Prize. Although Welty herself admitted that she led a*
sheltered life, her critics have always been impressed by her lyrical portrayal of the
complexities of the heart's emotional truths. "A Worn Path" received an O. Henry
Award in 1941.

It was December—a bright frozen day in the early morning. Far out in the country there was an old Negro woman with her head tied in a red rag, coming along a path through the pinewoods. Her name was Phoenix Jackson. She was very old and small and she walked slowly in the dark pine shadows, moving a little from side to side in her steps, with the balanced heaviness and lightness of a pendulum in a grandfather clock. She carried a thin, small cane made from an umbrella, and with this she kept tapping the frozen earth in front of her. This made a grave and persistent noise in the still air, that seemed meditative like the chirping of a solitary little bird.

She wore a dark striped dress reaching down to her shoe tops, and an equally long apron of bleached sugar sacks, with a full pocket: all neat and tidy, but every time she took a step she might have fallen over her shoelaces, which dragged from her unlaced shoes. She looked straight ahead. Her eyes were blue with age. Her skin had a pattern all its own of numberless branching wrinkles and as though a whole little tree stood in the middle of her forehead, but a golden color ran underneath, and the two knobs of her cheeks were illumined by a yellow burning under the dark. Under the red rag her hair came down on her neck in the frailest of ringlets, still black, and with an odor like copper.

Now and then there was a quivering in the thicket. Old Phoenix said, "Out of my way, all you foxes, owls, beetles, jack rabbits, coons, and wild animals! . . . Keep out from under these feet, little bobwhites. . . . Keep the big wild hogs out of my path. Don't let none of those come running my direction. I got a long way." Under her small black-freckled hand her cane, limber as a buggy whip, would switch at the brush as if to rouse up any hiding things.

On she went. The woods were deep and still. The sun made the pine needles almost too bright to look at, up where the wind rocked. The cones dropped as light as feathers. Down in the hollow was the mourning dove—it was not too late for him.

The path ran up a hill. "Seem like there is chains about my feet, time I   5
get this far," she said, in the voice of argument old people keep to use with
themselves. "Something always take a hold of me on this hill—pleads I
should stay."

After she got to the top she turned and gave a full, severe look behind her
where she had come. "Up through pines," she said at length. "Now down
through oaks."

Her eyes opened their widest, and she started down gently. But before she
got to the bottom of the hill a bush caught her dress.

Her fingers were busy and intent, but her skirts were full and long, so that
before she could pull them free in one place they were caught in another. It was
not possible to allow the dress to tear. "I in the thorny bush," she said. "Thorns,
you doing your appointed work. Never want to let folks pass, no sir. Old eyes
thought you was a pretty little *green* bush."

Finally, trembling all over, she stood free, and after a moment dared to
stoop for her cane.

"Sun so high!" she cried, leaning back and looking, while the thick tears   10
went over her eyes. "The time getting all gone here."

At the foot of this hill was a place where a log was laid across the creek.

"Now comes the trial," said Phoenix.

Putting her right foot out, she mounted the log and shut her eyes. Lifting
her skirt, leveling her cane fiercely before her, like a festival figure in some parade, she began to march across. Then she opened her eyes and she was safe on
the other side.

"I wasn't as old as I thought," she said.

But she sat down to rest. She spread her skirts on the bank around her and   15
folded her hands over her knees. Up above her was a tree in a pearly cloud of
mistletoe. She did not dare to close her eyes, and when a little boy brought her
a plate with a slice of marble-cake on it she spoke to him. "That would be acceptable," she said. But when she went to take it there was just her own hand
in the air.

So she left that tree, and had to go through a barbed-wire fence. There she
had to creep and crawl, spreading her knees and stretching her fingers like a
baby trying to climb the steps. But she talked loudly to herself: she could not let
her dress be torn now, so late in the day, and she could not pay for having her
arm or her leg sawed off if she got caught fast where she was.

At last she was safe through the fence and risen up out in the clearing. Big
dead trees, like black men with one arm, were standing in the purple stalks of
the withered cotton field. There sat a buzzard.

"Who you watching?"

In the furrow she made her way along.

"Glad this not the season for bulls," she said, looking sideways, "and the   20
good Lord made his snakes to curl up and sleep in the winter. A pleasure I don't
see no two-headed snake coming around that tree, where it come once. It took
a while to get by him, back in the summer."

She passed through the old cotton and went into a field of dead corn. It whispered and shook and was taller than her head. "Through the maze now," she said, for there was no path.

Then there was something tall, black, and skinny there, moving before her.

At first she took it for a man. It could have been a man dancing in the field. But she stood still and listened, and it did not make a sound. It was as silent as a ghost.

"Ghost," she said sharply, "who be you the ghost of? For I have heard of nary death close by."

But there was no answer—only the ragged dancing in the wind.   25

She shut her eyes, reached out her hand, and touched a sleeve. She found a coat and inside that an emptiness, cold as ice.

"You scarecrow," she said. Her face lighted. "I ought to be shut up for good," she said with laughter. "My senses is gone. I too old. I the oldest people I ever know. Dance, old scarecrow," she said, "while I dancing with you."

She kicked her foot over the furrow, and with mouth drawn down, shook her head once or twice in a little strutting way. Some husks blew down and whirled in streamers about her skirts.

Then she went on, parting her way from side to side with the cane, through the whispering field. At last she came to the end, to a wagon track where the silver grass blew between the red ruts. The quail were walking around like pullets, seeming all dainty and unseen.

"Walk pretty," she said. "This the easy place. This the easy going."   30

She followed the track, swaying through the quiet bare fields, through the little strings of trees silver in their dead leaves, past cabins silver from weather, with the doors and windows boarded shut, all like old women under a spell sitting there. "I walking in their sleep," she said, nodding her head vigorously.

In a ravine she went where a spring was silently flowing through a hollow log. Old Phoenix bent and drank. "Sweet-gum makes the water sweet," she said, and drank more. "Nobody know who made this well, for it was here when I was born."

The track crossed a swampy part where the moss hung as white as lace from every limb. "Sleep on, alligators, and blow your bubbles." Then the track went into the road.

Deep, deep the road went down between the high green-colored banks. Overhead the live-oaks met, and it was as dark as a cave.

A black dog with a lolling tongue came up out of the weeds by the ditch.   35
She was meditating, and not ready, and when he came at her she only hit him a little with her cane. Over she went in the ditch, like a little puff of milkweed.

Down there, her senses drifted away. A dream visited her, and she reached her hand up, but nothing reached down and gave her a pull. So she lay there and presently went to talking. "Old woman," she said to herself, "that black dog come up out of the weeds to stall you off, and now there he sitting on his fine tail, smiling at you."

A white man finally came along and found her—a hunter, a young man, with his dog on a chain.

"Well, Granny!" he laughed. "What are you doing there?"

"Lying on my back like a June-bug waiting to be turned over, mister," she said, reaching up her hand.

He lifted her up, gave her a swing in the air, and set her down. "Anything 40 broken, Granny?"

"No sir, them old dead weeds is springy enough," said Phoenix, when she had got her breath. "I thank you for your trouble."

"Where do you live, Granny?" he asked, while the two dogs were growling at each other.

"Away back yonder, sir, behind the ridge. You can't even see it from here."

"On your way home?"

"No sir, I going to town." 45

"Why, that's too far! That's as far as I walk when I come out myself, and I get something for my trouble." He patted the stuffed bag he carried, and there hung down a little closed claw. It was one of the bobwhites, with its beak hooked bitterly to show it was dead. "Now you go on home, Granny!"

"I bound to go to town, mister," said Phoenix. "The time come around."

He gave another laugh, filling the whole landscape. "I know you old colored people! Wouldn't miss going to town to see Santa Claus!"

But something held old Phoenix very still. The deep lines in her face went into a fierce and different radiation. Without warning, she had seen with her own eyes a flashing nickel fall out of the man's pocket onto the ground.

"How old are you, Granny?" he was saying. 50

"There is no telling, mister," she said, "no telling."

Then she gave a little cry and clapped her hands and said, "Git on away from here, dog! Look! Look at that dog!" She laughed as if in admiration. "He ain't scared of nobody. He a big black dog." She whispered, "Sic him!"

"Watch me get rid of that cur," said the man. "Sic him, Pete! Sic him!"

Phoenix heard the dogs fighting, and heard the man running and throwing sticks. She even heard a gunshot. But she was slowly bending forward by that time, further and further forward, the lid stretched down over her eyes, as if she were doing this in her sleep. Her chin was lowered almost to her knees. The yellow palm of her hand came out from the fold of her apron. Her fingers slid down and along the ground under the piece of money with the grace and care they would have in lifting an egg from under a setting hen. Then she slowly straightened up, she stood erect, and the nickel was in her apron pocket. A bird flew by. Her lips moved. "God watching me the whole time. I come to stealing."

The man came back, and his own dog panted about them. "Well, I scared 55 him off that time," he said, and then he laughed and lifted his gun and pointed it at Phoenix.

She stood straight and faced him.

"Doesn't the gun scare you?" he said, still pointing it.

"No, sir, I seen plenty go off closer by, in my day, and for less than what I done," she said, holding utterly still.

He smiled, and shouldered the gun. "Well, Granny," he said, "you must be a hundred years old, and scared of nothing. I'd give you a dime if I had any money with me. But you take my advice and stay home, and nothing will happen to you."

"I bound to go on my way, mister," said Phoenix. She inclined her head in   60
the red rag. Then they went in different directions, but she could hear the gun shooting again and again over the hill.

She walked on. The shadows hung from the oak trees to the road like curtains. Then she smelled wood-smoke, and smelled the river, and she saw a steeple and the cabins on their steep steps. Dozens of little black children whirled around her. There ahead was Natchez shining. Bells were ringing. She walked on.

In the paved city it was Christmas time. There were red and green electric lights strung and crisscrossed everywhere, and all turned on in the daytime. Old Phoenix would have been lost if she had not distrusted her eyesight and depended on her feet to know where to take her.

She paused quietly on the sidewalk where people were passing by. A lady came along in the crowd, carrying an armful of red-, green-, and silver-wrapped presents; she gave off perfume like the red roses in hot summer, and Phoenix stopped her.

"Please, missy, will you lace up my shoe?" She held up her foot.

"What do you want, Grandma?"   65

"See my shoe," said Phoenix. "Do all right for out in the country, but wouldn't look right to go in a big building."

"Stand still then, Grandma," said the lady. She put her packages down on the sidewalk beside her and laced and tied both shoes tightly.

"Can't lace 'em with a cane," said Phoenix. "Thank you, missy. I doesn't mind asking a nice lady to tie up my shoe, when I gets out on the street."

Moving slowly and from side to side, she went into the big building, and into a tower of steps, where she walked up and around and around until her feet knew to stop.

She entered a door, and there she saw nailed up on the wall the document   70
that had been stamped with the gold seal and framed in the gold frame, which matched the dream that was hung up in her head.

"Here I be," she said. There was a fixed and ceremonial stiffness over her body.

"A charity case, I suppose," said an attendant who sat at the desk before her.

But Phoenix only looked above her head. There was sweat on her face, the wrinkles in her skin shone like a bright net.

"Speak up, Grandma," the woman said. "What's your name? We must have your history, you know. Have you been here before? What seems to be the trouble with you?"

Old Phoenix only gave a twitch to her face as if a fly were bothering her.   75

"Are you deaf?" cried the attendant.

But then the nurse came in.

"Oh, that's just old Aunt Phoenix," she said. "She doesn't come for herself — she has a little grandson. She makes these trips just as regular as clockwork. She lives away back off the Old Natchez Trace." She bent down. "Well, Aunt Phoenix, why don't you just take a seat? We won't keep you standing after your long trip." She pointed.

The old woman sat down, bolt upright in the chair.

"Now, how is the boy?" asked the nurse.   80

Old Phoenix did not speak.

"I said, how is the boy?"

But Phoenix only waited and stared straight ahead, her face very solemn and withdrawn into rigidity.

"Is his throat any better?" asked the nurse. "Aunt Phoenix, don't you hear me? Is your grandson's throat any better since the last time you came for the medicine?"

With her hands on her knees, the old woman waited, silent, erect, and motionless, just as if she were in armor.   85

"You mustn't take up our time this way, Aunt Phoenix," the nurse said. "Tell us quickly about your grandson, and get it over. He isn't dead, is he?"

At last there came a flicker and then a flame of comprehension across her face, and she spoke.

"My grandson. It was my memory had left me. There I sat and forgot why I made my long trip."

"Forgot?" The nurse frowned. "After you came so far?"

Then Phoenix was like an old woman begging a dignified forgiveness for   90
waking up frightened in the night. "I never did go to school, I was too old at the Surrender,"° she said in a soft voice. "I'm an old woman without an education. It was my memory fail me. My little grandson, he is just the same, and I forgot it in the coming."

"Throat never heals, does it?" said the nurse, speaking in a loud, sure voice to old Phoenix. By now she had a card with something written on it, a little list. "Yes. Swallowed lye. When was it? — January — two, three years ago —"

Phoenix spoke unasked now. "No, missy, he not dead, he just the same. Every little while his throat began to close up again, and he not able to swallow. He not get his breath. He not able to help himself. So the time come around, and I go on another trip for the soothing medicine."

"All right. The doctor said as long as you came to get it, you could have it," said the nurse. "But it's an obstinate case."

"My little grandson, he sit up there in the house all wrapped up, waiting by himself," Phoenix went on. "We is the only two left in the world. He suffer and it don't seem to put him back at all. He got a sweet look. He going to last. He wear a little patch quilt and peep out holding his mouth open like a little bird. I remembers so plain now. I not going to forget him again, no, the whole enduring time. I could tell him from all the others in creation."

"All right." The nurse was trying to hush her now. She brought her a bottle 95
of medicine. "Charity," she said, making a check mark in a book.

---

the Surrender: On April 9, 1865, General Robert E. Lee surrendered to General Ulysses S. Grant, at Appomattox, Virginia, ending the Civil War.

Old Phoenix held the bottle close to her eyes, and then carefully put it into her pocket.

"I thank you," she said.

"It's Christmas time, Grandma," said the attendant. "Could I give you a few pennies out of my purse?"

"Five pennies is a nickel," said Phoenix stiffly.

"Here's a nickel," said the attendant.   100

Phoenix rose carefully and held out her hand. She received the nickel and then fished the other nickel out of her pocket and laid it beside the new one. She stared at her palm closely, with her head on one side.

Then she gave a tap with her cane on the floor.

"This is what come to me to do," she said. "I going to the store and buy my child a little windmill they sells, made out of paper. He going to find it hard to believe there such a thing in the world. I'll march myself back where he waiting, holding it straight up in this hand."

She lifted her free hand, gave a little nod, turned around, and walked out of the doctor's office. Then her slow step began on the stairs, going down.

                                                                    [1941]

≡ THINKING ABOUT THE TEXT

1. Comment on the old woman's name; in a tale about a journey, it seems to have allegorical significance.

2. Phoenix meets a hunter on her trek. Comment on the significant details of their encounter.

3. Phoenix speaks directly to a number of things. What are they, and what allegorical significance might they have?

4. Welty has claimed that the most frequent question she was asked about this story was whether Phoenix's grandson is really dead. Her answer is that, either way, the meaning of this story would not be affected. What do you think she means?

5. Google "A Worn Path" and look at the scores of images associated with the story. Describe three of them, and explain why they are apt.

≡ MAKING COMPARISONS

1. Compare the errands of mercy of Phoenix and the doctor.

2. In "The Use of Force" the doctor says, "One goes on to the end" (para. 31). Compare the significance of this idea in both stories.

3. Both Phoenix and the doctor start their journey with the best of intentions. It may be that Phoenix's specific mission is in vain. It may also be that the doctor's mission has mixed results. Explain these ideas.

≣ WRITING ABOUT ISSUES

1. Argue that the doctor is or is not at fault in "The Use of Force."

2. Write an essay that sees symbolic significance in the journey of Phoenix Jackson. Be sure to use specific incidents from the story to support your position.

3. Write an essay that compares the errands of mercy of Phoenix and the doctor. Make a judgment about their goals, their ethics, their missions, their characters, and anything else that seems relevant.

4. Locate and read Eudora Welty's essay, "Is Phoenix Jackson's Grandson Really Dead?" and write an argumentative essay that either agrees or disagrees with her conclusion. (The essay originally appeared in the September 1974 issue of *Critical Inquiry*.)

NATHANIEL HAWTHORNE, "Young Goodman Brown"

SHERMAN ALEXIE, "This Is What It Means to Say Phoenix, Arizona"

The quest motif is universal in almost all cultures, from ancient epics to contemporary novels and films, from *The Iliad* and *The Odyssey* to *Huckleberry Finn*, *On the Road*, and *Star Wars*. Some quests are motivated by clear and obvious goals, for wealth, power, adventure, and glory. Others are not so clear. Hawthorne's protagonist, Young Goodman Brown, leaves his wife, Faith, and begins an uncertain journey into an allegorical forest of witches, devils, and the unknown. For him the consequences are disastrous. The protagonists in Sherman Alexie's tale also begin an uncertain journey to retrieve a dead father, but along the way they grow in understanding and compassion. They both enter an uncertain future but are perhaps more self-aware.

NATHANIEL HAWTHORNE

Young Goodman Brown

Nathaniel Hawthorne (1804–1864) was born in Salem, Massachusetts, into a family that was descended from New England's Puritan colonists. This lineage troubled Hawthorne, especially because his ancestor John Hathorne was involved as a judge in the Salem witch trials. After graduating from Maine's Bowdoin College in 1825, Hawthorne returned to Salem and began his career as a writer. In 1832, he self-published his first novel, Fanshawe, *but considered it an artistic as well as a commercial failure and tried to destroy all unsold copies of it. He was more successful with his 1832 short-story collection* Twice-Told Tales *(reprinted and enlarged in 1842). In the early 1840s, Hawthorne worked as a surveyor in the Boston Custom House, briefly joined the Utopian community of Brook Farm, and then moved to Concord. There he published several children's books and lived with his wife, Sophia, in writer Ralph Waldo Emerson's former home, the Old Manse. In 1846, he produced a second collection of short stories,* Mosses from an Old Manse. *For the next three years, Hawthorne worked in a custom house in his hometown of Salem before publishing his most famous analysis of Puritan culture,* The Scarlet Letter *(1850). Later novels included* The House of the Seven Gables *(1851),* The Blithedale Romance *(an 1852 satire on Brook Farm), and* The Marble Faun *(1860). When his friend Franklin Pierce became president of the United States, Hawthorne served as American consul in Liverpool, England, for four years and then traveled in Italy for two more. At his death in 1864, he was already highly respected as a writer. Much of his fiction deals with conflicted characters whose hearts and souls are torn by sin, guilt, pride, and isolation. Indeed, his good friend Herman Melville, author of* Moby-Dick, *praised "the power of blackness" he found in Hawthorne's works. The allegorical story "Young Goodman Brown" is an especially memorable example of this power. Hawthorne wrote the tale in 1835 and later included it in* Mosses from an Old Manse.

Young Goodman Brown came forth at sunset into the street at Salem village; but put his head back, after crossing the threshold, to exchange a parting kiss with his young wife. And Faith, as the wife was aptly named, thrust her own pretty head into the street, letting the wind play with the pink ribbons of her cap while she called to Goodman Brown.

"Dearest heart," whispered she, softly and rather sadly, when her lips were close to his ear, "prithee put off your journey until sunrise and sleep in your own bed to-night. A lone woman is troubled with such dreams and such thoughts that she's afeared of herself sometimes. Pray tarry with me this night, dear husband, of all nights in the year."

"My love and my Faith," replied young Goodman Brown, "of all nights in the year, this one night must I tarry away from thee. My journey, as thou callest it, forth and back again, must needs be done 'twixt now and sunrise. What, my sweet, pretty wife, dost thou doubt me already, and we but three months married?"

"Then God bless you!" said Faith, with the pink ribbons; "and may you find all well when you come back."

"Amen!" cried Goodman Brown. "Say thy prayers, dear Faith, and go to bed at dusk, and no harm will come to thee." 5

So they parted; and the young man pursued his way until, being about to turn the corner by the meeting-house, he looked back and saw the head of Faith still peeping after him with a melancholy air, in spite of her pink ribbons.

"Poor little Faith!" thought he, for his heart smote him. "What a wretch am I to leave her on such an errand! She talks of dreams, too. Methought as she spoke there was trouble in her face, as if a dream had warned her what work is to be done to-night. But no, no; 't would kill her to think it. Well, she's a blessed angel on earth, and after this one night I'll cling to her skirts and follow her to heaven."

With this excellent resolve for the future, Goodman Brown felt himself justified in making more haste on his present evil purpose. He had taken a dreary road, darkened by all the gloomiest trees of the forest, which barely stood aside to let the narrow path creep through, and closed immediately behind. It was all as lonely as could be; and there is this peculiarity in such a solitude, that the traveller knows not who may be concealed by the innumerable trunks and the thick boughs overhead; so that with lonely footsteps he may yet be passing through an unseen multitude.

"There may be a devilish Indian behind every tree," said Goodman Brown to himself; and he glanced fearfully behind him as he added, "What if the devil himself should be at my very elbow!"

His head being turned back, he passed a crook of the road, and, looking forward again, beheld the figure of a man, in grave and decent attire, seated at the foot of an old tree. He arose at Goodman Brown's approach and walked onward side by side with him. 10

"You are late, Goodman Brown," said he. "The clock of the Old South was striking as I came through Boston, and that is full fifteen minutes agone."

"Faith kept me back a while," replied the young man, with a tremor in his voice, caused by the sudden appearance of his companion, though not wholly unexpected.

It was now deep dusk in the forest, and deepest in that part of it where these two were journeying. As nearly as could be discerned, the second traveller was about fifty years old, apparently in the same rank of life as Goodman Brown, and bearing a considerable resemblance to him, though perhaps more in expression than features. Still they might have been taken for father and son. And yet, though the elder person was as simply clad as the younger, and as simple in manner too, he had an indescribable air of one who knew the world, and who would not have felt abashed at the governor's dinner table or in King William's court, were it possible that his affairs should call him thither. But the only thing about him that could be fixed upon as remarkable was his staff, which bore the likeness of a great black snake, so curiously wrought that it might almost be seen to twist and wriggle itself like a living serpent. This, of course, must have been an ocular deception, assisted by the uncertain light.

"Come, Goodman Brown," cried his fellow-traveller, "this is a dull pace for the beginning of a journey. Take my staff, if you are so soon weary."

"Friend," said the other, exchanging his slow pace for a full stop, "having   15
kept covenant by meeting thee here, it is my purpose now to return whence I came. I have scruples touching the matter thou wot'st of."

"Sayest thou so?" replied he of the serpent, smiling apart. "Let us walk on, nevertheless, reasoning as we go; and if I convince thee not thou shalt turn back. We are but a little way in the forest yet."

"Too far! too far!" exclaimed the goodman, unconsciously resuming his walk. "My father never went into the woods on such an errand, nor his father before him. We have been a race of honest men and good Christians since the days of the martyrs; and shall I be the first of the name of Brown that ever took this path and kept" —

"Such company, thou wouldst say," observed the elder person, interpreting his pause. "Well said, Goodman Brown! I have been as well acquainted with your family as with ever a one among the Puritans; and that's no trifle to say. I helped your grandfather, the constable, when he lashed the Quaker woman so smartly through the streets of Salem; and it was I that brought your father a pitch-pine knot, kindled at my own hearth, to set fire to an Indian village, in King Philip's war.° They were my good friends, both; and many a pleasant walk have we had along this path, and returned merrily after midnight. I would fain be friends with you for their sake."

"If it be as thou sayest," replied Goodman Brown, "I marvel they never spoke of these matters; or, verily, I marvel not, seeing that the least rumor of the sort would have driven them from New England. We are a people of prayer, and good works to boot, and abide no such wickedness."

"Wickedness or not," said the traveller with the twisted staff, "I have a very   20
general acquaintance here in New England. The deacons of many a church

King Philip's war: King Philip, a Wampanoag chief, waged a bloody war against the New England colonists from 1675 to 1676.

have drunk the communion wine with me; the selectmen of divers towns make me their chairman; and a majority of the Great and General Court are firm supporters of my interest. The governor and I, too — But these are state secrets."

"Can this be so?" cried Goodman Brown, with a stare of amazement at his undisturbed companion. "Howbeit, I have nothing to do with the governor and council; they have their own ways, and are no rule for a simple husbandman like me. But, were I to go on with thee, how should I meet the eye of that good old man, our minister, at Salem village? Oh, his voice would make me tremble both Sabbath day and lecture day."

Thus far the elder traveller had listened with due gravity; but now burst into a fit of irrepressible mirth, shaking himself so violently that his snake-like staff actually seemed to wriggle in sympathy.

"Ha! ha! ha!" shouted he again and again; then composing himself, "Well, go on, Goodman Brown, go on; but, prithee, don't kill me with laughing."

"Well, then, to end the matter at once," said Goodman Brown, considerably nettled, "there is my wife, Faith. It would break her dear little heart; and I'd rather break my own."

"Nay, if that be the case," answered the other, "e'en go thy ways, Goodman   25
Brown. I would not for twenty old women like the one hobbling before us that
Faith should come to any harm."

As he spoke he pointed his staff at a female figure on the path, in whom Goodman Brown recognized a very pious and exemplary dame, who had taught him his catechism in youth, and was still his moral and spiritual adviser, jointly with the minister and Deacon Gookin.

"A marvel, truly that Goody Cloyse should be so far in the wilderness at nightfall," said he. "But with your leave, friend, I shall take a cut through the woods until we have left this Christian woman behind. Being a stranger to you, she might ask whom I was consorting with and whither I was going."

"Be it so," said his fellow-traveller. "Betake you to the woods, and let me keep the path."

Accordingly the young man turned aside, but took care to watch his companion, who advanced softly along the road until he had come within a staff's length of the old dame. She, meanwhile, was making the best of her way, with singular speed for so aged a woman, and mumbling some indistinct words — a prayer, doubtless — as she went. The traveller put forth his staff and touched her withered neck with what seemed the serpent's tail.

"The devil!" screamed the pious old lady.   30

"Then Goody Cloyse knows her old friend?" observed the traveller, confronting her and leaning on his writhing stick.

"Ah, forsooth, and is it your worship indeed?" cried the good dame. "Yea, truly is it, and in the very image of my old gossip, Goodman Brown, the grandfather of the silly fellow that now is. But — would your worship believe it? — my broomstick hath strangely disappeared, stolen, as I suspect, by that unhanged witch, Goody Cory, and that, too, when I was all anointed with the juice of smallage, and cinquefoil, and wolf's bane" —

"Mingled with fine wheat and the fat of a new-born babe," said the shape of old Goodman Brown.

"Ah, your worship knows the recipe," cried the old lady, cackling aloud.
"So, as I was saying, being all ready for the meeting, and no horse to ride on,
I made up my mind to foot it; for they tell me there is a nice young man to be
taken into communion to-night. But now your good worship will lend me your
arm, and we shall be there in a twinkling."

"That can hardly be," answered her friend. "I may not spare you my arm,   35
Goody Cloyse; but here is my staff, if you will."

So saying, he threw it down at her feet, where, perhaps, it assumed life, being one of the rods which its owner had formerly lent to the Egyptian magi. Of
this fact, however, Goodman Brown could not take cognizance. He had cast up
his eyes in astonishment, and, looking down again, beheld neither Goody
Cloyse nor the serpentine staff, but his fellow-traveller alone, who waited for
him as calmly as if nothing had happened.

"That old woman taught me my catechism," said the young man; and
there was a world of meaning in this simple comment.

They continued to walk onward, while the elder traveller exhorted his
companion to make good speed and persevere in the path, discoursing so aptly
that his arguments seemed rather to spring up in the bosom of his auditor than
to be suggested by himself. As they went, he plucked a branch of maple to serve
for a walking stick, and began to strip it of the twigs and little boughs, which
were wet with evening dew. The moment his fingers touched them they became strangely withered and dried up as with a week's sunshine. Thus the pair
proceeded, at a good free pace, until suddenly, in a gloomy hollow of the road,
Goodman Brown sat himself down on the stump of a tree and refused to go any
farther.

"Friend," he said, stubbornly, "my mind is made up. Not another step will I
budge on this errand. What if a wretched old woman do choose to go to the
devil when I thought she was going to heaven: is that any reason why I should
quit my dear Faith and go after her?"

"You will think better of this by and by," said his acquaintance, compos-   40
edly. "Sit here and rest yourself a while; and when you feel like moving again,
there is my staff to help you along."

Without more words, he threw his companion the maple stick, and was as
speedily out of sight as if he had vanished into the deepening gloom. The young
man sat a few moments by the roadside, applauding himself greatly, and thinking with how clear a conscience he should meet the minister in his morning
walk, nor shrink from the eye of good old Deacon Gookin. And what calm sleep
would be his that very night, which was to have been spent so wickedly, but so
purely and sweetly now, in the arms of Faith! Amidst these pleasant and praise-
worthy meditations, Goodman Brown heard the tramp of horses along the
road, and deemed it advisable to conceal himself within the verge of the forest,
conscious of the guilty purpose that had brought him thither, though now so
happily turned from it.

On came the hoof tramps and the voices of the riders, two grave old voices,
conversing soberly as they drew near. These mingled sounds appeared to pass
along the road, within a few yards of the young man's hiding-place; but, owing
doubtless to the depth of the gloom at that particular spot, neither the travellers

nor their steeds were visible. Though their figures brushed the small boughs by the wayside, it could not be seen that they intercepted, even for a moment, the faint gleam from the strip of bright sky athwart which they must have passed. Goodman Brown alternately crouched and stood on tiptoe, pulling aside the branches and thrusting forth his head as far as he durst without discerning so much as a shadow. It vexed him the more, because he could have sworn, were such a thing possible, that he recognized the voices of the minister and Deacon Gookin, jogging along quietly, as they were wont to do, when bound to some ordination or ecclesiastical council. While yet within hearing, one of the riders stopped to pluck a switch.

"Of the two, reverend sir," said the voice like the deacon's, "I had rather miss an ordination dinner than to-night's meeting. They tell me that some of our community are to be here from Falmouth and beyond, and others from Connecticut and Rhode Island, besides several of the Indian powwows, who, after their fashion, know almost as much deviltry as the best of us. Moreover, there is a goodly young woman to be taken into communion."

"Mighty well, Deacon Gookin!" replied the solemn old tones of the minister. "Spur up, or we shall be late. Nothing can be done, you know, until I get on the ground."

The hoofs clattered again; and the voices, talking so strangely in the empty air, passed on through the forest, where no church had ever been gathered or solitary Christian prayed. Whither, then, could these holy men be journeying so deep into the heathen wilderness? Young Goodman Brown caught hold of a tree for support, being ready to sink down on the ground, faint and overburdened with the heavy sickness of his heart. He looked up to the sky, doubting whether there really was a heaven above him. Yet there was the blue arch, and the stars brightening in it.

"With heaven above and Faith below, I will yet stand firm against the devil!" cried Goodman Brown.

While he still gazed upward into the deep arch of the firmament and had lifted his hands to pray, a cloud, though no wind was stirring, hurried across the zenith and hid the brightening stars. The blue sky was still visible, except directly overhead, where this black mass of cloud was sweeping swiftly northward. Aloft in the air, as if from the depths of the cloud, came a confused and doubtful sound of voices. Once the listener fancied that he could distinguish the accents of towns-people of his own, men and women, both pious and ungodly, many of whom he had met at the communion table, and had seen others rioting at the tavern. The next moment, so indistinct were the sounds, he doubted whether he had heard aught but the murmur of the old forest, whispering without a wind. Then came a stronger swell of those familiar tones, heard daily in the sunshine at Salem village, but never until now from a cloud of night. There was one voice, of a young woman, uttering lamentations, yet with an uncertain sorrow, and entreating for some favor, which, perhaps, it would grieve her to obtain; and all the unseen multitude, both saints and sinners, seemed to encourage her onward.

"Faith!" shouted Goodman Brown, in a voice of agony and desperation;

45

and the echoes of the forest mocked him, crying, "Faith! Faith!" as if bewildered wretches were seeking her all through the wilderness.

The cry of grief, rage, and terror was yet piercing the night, when the unhappy husband held his breath for a response. There was a scream, drowned immediately in a louder murmur of voices, fading into far-off laughter, as the dark cloud swept away, leaving the clear and silent sky above Goodman Brown. But something fluttered lightly down through the air and caught on the branch of a tree. The young man seized it, and beheld a pink ribbon.

"My Faith is gone!" cried he after one stupefied moment. "There is no good on earth; and sin is but a name. Come, devil; for to thee is this world given." 50

And, maddened with despair, so that he laughed loud and long, did Goodman Brown grasp his staff and set forth again, at such a rate that he seemed to fly along the forest path rather than to walk or run. The road grew wilder and drearier and more faintly traced, and vanished at length, leaving him in the heart of the dark wilderness, still rushing onward with the instinct that guides mortal man to evil. The whole forest was peopled with frightful sounds — the creaking of the trees, the howling of wild beasts, and the yell of Indians; while sometimes the wind tolled like a distant church bell, and sometimes gave a broad roar around the traveller, as if all Nature were laughing him to scorn. But he was himself the chief horror of the scene, and shrank not from its other horrors.

"Ha! ha! ha!" roared Goodman Brown when the wind laughed at him. "Let us hear which will laugh loudest. Think not to frighten me with your deviltry. Come witch, come wizard, come Indian powwow, come devil himself, and here comes Goodman Brown. You may as well fear him as he fear you."

In truth, all through the haunted forest there could be nothing more frightful than the figure of Goodman Brown. On he flew among the black pines, brandishing his staff with frenzied gestures, now giving vent to an inspiration of horrid blasphemy, and now shouting forth such laughter as set all the echoes of the forest laughing like demons around him. The fiend in his own shape is less hideous than when he rages in the breast of man. Thus sped the demoniac on his course, until, quivering among the trees, he saw a red light before him, as when the felled trunks and branches of a clearing have been set on fire, and throw up their lurid blaze against the sky, at the hour of midnight. He paused, in a lull of the tempest that had driven him onward, and heard the swell of what seemed a hymn, rolling solemnly from a distance with the weight of many voices. He knew the tune; it was a familiar one in the choir of the village meeting-house. The verse died heavily away, and was lengthened by a chorus, not of human voices, but of all the sounds of the benighted wilderness pealing in awful harmony together. Goodman Brown cried out, and his cry was lost to his own ear by its unison with the cry of the desert.

In the interval of silence he stole forward until the light glared full upon his eyes. At one extremity of an open space, hemmed in by the dark wall of the forest, arose a rock, bearing some rude, natural resemblance either to an altar or a pulpit, and surrounded by four blazing pines, their tops aflame, their stems untouched, like candles at an evening meeting. The mass of foliage that had overgrown the summit of the rock was all on fire, blazing high into the night and fitfully illuminating the whole field. Each pendent twig and leafy festoon was in a blaze. As the red light arose and fell, a numerous congregation alternately shone forth, then disappeared in shadow, and again grew, as it were, out of the darkness, peopling the heart of the solitary woods at once.

"A grave and dark-clad company," quoth Goodman Brown.   55

In truth they were such. Among them, quivering to and fro between gloom and splendor, appeared faces that would be seen next day at the council board of the province, and others which, Sabbath after Sabbath, looked devoutly heavenward, and benignantly over the crowded pews, from the holiest pulpits in the land. Some affirm that the lady of the governor was there. At least there were high dames well known to her, and wives of honored husbands, and widows, a great multitude, and ancient maidens, all of excellent repute, and fair young girls, who trembled lest their mothers should espy them. Either the sudden gleams of light flashing over the obscure field bedazzled Goodman Brown, or he recognized a score of the church members of Salem village famous for their especial sanctity. Good old Deacon Gookin had arrived, and waited at the skirts of that venerable saint, his revered pastor. But, irreverently consorting with these grave, reputable, and pious people, these elders of the church, these chaste dames and dewy virgins, there were men of dissolute lives and women of spotted fame, wretches given over to all mean and filthy vice, and suspected even of horrid crimes. It was strange to see that the good shrank not from the wicked, nor were the sinners abashed by the saints. Scattered also among their pale-faced enemies were the Indian priests, or powwows, who had often scared their native forest with more hideous incantations than any known to English witchcraft.

"But where is Faith?" thought Goodman Brown; and, as hope came into his heart, he trembled.

Another verse of the hymn arose, a slow and mournful strain, such as the pious love, but joined to words which expressed all that our nature can conceive of sin, and darkly hinted at far more. Unfathomable to mere mortals is the lore of fiends. Verse after verse was sung; and still the chorus of the desert swelled between like the deepest tone of a mighty organ; and with the final peal of that dreadful anthem there came a sound, as if the roaring wind, the rushing streams, the howling beasts, and every other voice of the unconcerted wilderness were mingling and according with the voice of guilty man in homage to the prince of all. The four blazing pines threw up a loftier flame, and obscurely discovered shapes and visages of horror on the smoke wreaths above the impious assembly. At the same moment the fire on the rock shot redly forth and formed a flowing arch above its base, where now appeared a figure. With reverence be it spoken, the figure bore no slight similitude, both in garb and manner, to some grave divine of the New England churches.

"Bring forth the converts!" cried a voice that echoed through the field and rolled into the forest.

At the word, Goodman Brown stepped forth from the shadow of the trees   60
and approached the congregation, with whom he felt a loathful brotherhood by the sympathy of all that was wicked in his heart. He could have well-nigh

sworn that the shape of his own dead father beckoned him to advance, looking downward from a smoke wreath, while a woman, with dim features of despair, threw out her hand to warn him back. Was it his mother? But he had no power to retreat one step, nor to resist, even in thought, when the minister and good old Deacon Gookin seized his arms and led him to the blazing rock. Thither came also the slender form of a veiled female, led between Goody Cloyse, that pious teacher of the catechism, and Martha Carrier, who had received the devil's promise to be queen of hell. A rampant hag was she. And there stood the proselytes beneath the canopy of fire.

"Welcome, my children," said the dark figure, "to the communion of your race. Ye have found thus young your nature and your destiny. My children, look behind you!"

They turned; and flashing forth, as it were, in a sheet of flame, the fiend worshippers were seen; the smile of welcome gleamed darkly on every visage.

"There," resumed the sable form, "are all whom ye have reverenced from youth. Ye deemed them holier than yourselves and shrank from your own sin, contrasting it with their lives of righteousness and prayerful aspirations heavenward. Yet here are they all in my worshipping assembly. This night it shall be granted you to know their secret deeds: how hoary-bearded elders of the church have whispered wanton words to the young maids of their households; how many a woman, eager for widows' weeds, has given her husband a drink at bedtime and let him sleep his last sleep in her bosom; how beardless youths have made haste to inherit their fathers' wealth; and how fair damsels — blush not, sweet ones — have dug little graves in the garden, and bidden me, the sole guest, to an infant's funeral. By the sympathy of your human hearts for sin ye shall scent out all the places — whether in church, bedchamber, street, field, or forest — where crime has been committed, and shall exult to behold the whole earth one stain of guilt, one mighty blood spot. Far more than this. It shall be yours to penetrate, in every bosom, the deep mystery of sin, the fountain of all wicked arts, and which inexhaustibly supplies more evil impulses than human power — than my power at its utmost — can make manifest in deeds. And now, my children, look upon each other."

They did so; and, by the blaze of the hell-kindled torches, the wretched man beheld his Faith, and the wife her husband, trembling before that unhallowed altar.

"Lo, there ye stand, my children," said the figure, in a deep and solemn tone, almost sad with its despairing awfulness, as if his once angelic nature could yet mourn for our miserable race. "Depending upon one another's hearts, ye had still hoped that virtue were not all a dream. Now are ye undeceived. Evil is the nature of mankind. Evil must be your only happiness. Welcome again, my children, to the communion of your race."

"Welcome," repeated the fiend worshippers, in one cry of despair and triumph.

And there they stood, the only pair, as it seemed, who were yet hesitating on the verge of wickedness in this dark world. A basin was hallowed, naturally, in the rock. Did it contain water, reddened by the lurid light? or was it blood? or,

65

perchance, a liquid flame? Herein did the shape of evil dip his hand and prepare to lay the mark of baptism upon their foreheads, that they might be partakers of the mystery of sin, more conscious of the secret guilt of others, both in deed and thought, than they could now be of their own. The husband cast one look at his pale wife, and Faith at him. What polluted wretches would the next glance show them to each other, shuddering alike at what they disclosed and what they saw!

"Faith! Faith!" cried the husband, "look up to heaven, and resist the wicked one."

Whether Faith obeyed he knew not. Hardly had he spoken when he found himself amid calm night and solitude, listening to a roar of the wind which died heavily away through the forest. He staggered against the rock, and felt it chill and damp; while a hanging twig, that had been all on fire, besprinkled his cheek with the coldest dew.

The next morning young Goodman Brown came slowly into the street   70 of Salem village, staring around him like a bewildered man. The good old minister was taking a walk along the graveyard to get an appetite for breakfast and meditate his sermon, and bestowed a blessing, as he passed, on Goodman Brown. He shrank from the venerable saint as if to avoid an anathema. Old Deacon Gookin was at domestic worship, and the holy words of his prayer were heard through the open window. "What God doth the wizard pray to?" quoth Goodman Brown. Goody Cloyse, that excellent old Christian, stood in the early sunshine at her own lattice, catechizing a little girl who had brought her a pint of morning's milk. Goodman Brown snatched away the child as from the grasp of the fiend himself. Turning the corner by the meeting-house, he spied the head of Faith, with the pink ribbons, gazing anxiously forth, and bursting into such joy at sight of him that she skipped along the street and almost kissed her husband before the whole village. But Goodman Brown looked sternly and sadly into her face, and passed on without a greeting.

Had Goodman Brown fallen asleep in the forest and only dreamed a wild dream of a witch-meeting?

Be it so if you will; but, alas! it was a dream of evil omen for young Goodman Brown. A stern, a sad, a darkly meditative, a distrustful, if not a desperate man did he become from the night of that fearful dream. On the Sabbath day, when the congregation were singing a holy psalm, he could not listen because an anthem of sin rushed loudly upon his ear and drowned all the blessed strain. When the minister spoke from the pulpit with power and fervid eloquence, and, with his hand on the open Bible, of the sacred truths of our religion, and of saint-like lives and triumphant deaths, and of future bliss or misery unutterable, then did Goodman Brown turn pale, dreading lest the roof should thunder down upon the gray blasphemer and his hearers. Often, awaking suddenly at midnight, he shrank from the bosom of Faith; and at morning or eventide, when the family knelt down at prayer, he scowled and muttered to himself, and gazed sternly at his wife, and turned away. And when he had lived long, and was borne to his grave a hoary corpse, followed by Faith, an aged woman, and children and grandchildren, a goodly procession, besides neighbors not a few, they carved no hopeful verse upon his tombstone, for his dying hour was gloom. *[1835]*

≡ THINKING ABOUT THE TEXT

1. "Young Goodman Brown" seems quite allegorical, with journeys in the night woods and statements like "My Faith is gone!" (para. 50). How would you explain this allegorical story? What is Brown looking for? What does he find out? How does he deal with his discoveries?

2. If you were a good friend of Brown's, what might you tell him to try to save him from a life of gloom?

3. The devil suggests that there is more evil in the human heart "than my power at its utmost" (para. 63). Do you agree? If so, is this a message to despair about?

4. The devil says he is well acquainted with Brown's family. What has his family done? Is Brown innocent and naive, or perhaps stubborn and arrogant, in his refusal to admit that evil exists all around us?

5. Do you suspect that Brown merely dreamed or imagined his experience in the woods? Or do you think it really took place? Refer to specific details of the text.

SHERMAN ALEXIE

This Is What It Means to Say Phoenix, Arizona

Born in Spokane, Washington, Sherman Alexie (b. 1966) is a member of the Spokane/ Coeur d'Alene tribe. His fiction includes the novels Reservation Blues *(1996),* Indian Killer *(1997),* Flight *(2007), and* The Absolutely True Diary of a Part-Time Indian *(2007). He has also produced three collections of short stories:* The Toughest Indian in the World *(2001),* Ten Little Indians *(2003), and* The Lone Ranger and Tonto Fistfight in Heaven *(1994), which he adapted for the acclaimed 1998 film* Smoke Signals. *Alexie is a poet, too, with his collections of verse including* The Business of Fancy Dancing *(1992),* Old Shirts & New Skins *(1993),* First Indian on the Moon *(1993), and* One Stick Song *(2000). His latest book is* Blasphemy: New and Selected Stories *(2013).*

Just after Victor lost his job at the BIA,° he also found out that his father had died of a heart attack in Phoenix, Arizona. Victor hadn't seen his father in a few years, only talked to him on the telephone once or twice, but there still was

The Bureau of Indian Affairs: A division of the U.S. Department of the Interior that oversees the administration of federal programs for American Indians, Indian tribes, and Alaskan natives.

a genetic pain, which was soon to be pain as real and immediate as a broken bone.

Victor didn't have any money. Who does have money on a reservation, except the cigarette and fireworks salespeople? His father had a savings account waiting to be claimed, but Victor needed to find a way to get to Phoenix. Victor's mother was just as poor as he was, and the rest of his family didn't have any use at all for him. So Victor called the Tribal Council.

"Listen," Victor said. "My father just died. I need some money to get to Phoenix to make arrangements."

"Now, Victor," the council said. "You know we're having a difficult time financially."

"But I thought the council had special funds set aside for stuff like this."   5

"Now, Victor, we do have some money available for the proper return of tribal members' bodies. But I don't think we have enough to bring your father all the way back from Phoenix."

"Well," Victor said. "It ain't going to cost all that much. He had to be cremated. Things were kind of ugly. He died of a heart attack in his trailer and nobody found him for a week. It was really hot, too. You get the picture."

"Now, Victor, we're sorry for your loss and the circumstances. But we can really only afford to give you one hundred dollars."

"That's not even enough for a plane ticket."

"Well, you might consider driving down to Phoenix."   10

"I don't have a car. Besides, I was going to drive my father's pickup back up here."

"Now, Victor," the council said. "We're sure there is somebody who could drive you to Phoenix. Or is there somebody who could lend you the rest of the money?"

"You know there ain't nobody around with that kind of money."

"Well, we're sorry, Victor, but that's the best we can do."

Victor accepted the Tribal Council's offer. What else could he do? So he   15
signed the proper papers, picked up his check, and walked over to the Trading Post to cash it.

While Victor stood in line, he watched Thomas Builds-the-Fire standing near the magazine rack, talking to himself. Like he always did. Thomas was a storyteller that nobody wanted to listen to. That's like being a dentist in a town where everybody has false teeth.

Victor and Thomas Builds-the-Fire were the same age, had grown up and played in the dirt together. Ever since Victor could remember, it was Thomas who always had something to say.

Once, when they were seven years old, when Victor's father still lived with the family, Thomas closed his eyes and told Victor this story: "Your father's heart is weak. He is afraid of his own family. He is afraid of you. Late at night he sits in the dark. Watches the television until there's nothing but that white noise. Sometimes he feels like he wants to buy a motorcycle and ride away. He wants to run and hide. He doesn't want to be found."

Thomas Builds-the-Fire had known that Victor's father was going to leave, knew it before anyone. Now Victor stood in the Trading Post with a one-hundred-dollar check in his hand, wondering if Thomas knew that Victor's father was dead, if he knew what was going to happen next.

Just then Thomas looked at Victor, smiled, and walked over to him.   20

"Victor, I'm sorry about your father," Thomas said.

"How did you know about it?" Victor asked.

"I heard it on the wind. I heard it from the birds. I felt it in the sunlight. Also, your mother was just in here crying."

"Oh," Victor said and looked around the Trading Post. All the other Indians stared, surprised that Victor was even talking to Thomas. Nobody talked to Thomas anymore because he told the same damn stories over and over again. Victor was embarrassed, but he thought that Thomas might be able to help him. Victor felt a sudden need for tradition.

"I can lend you the money you need," Thomas said suddenly. "But you   25
have to take me with you."

"I can't take your money," Victor said. "I mean, I haven't hardly talked to you in years. We're not really friends anymore."

"I didn't say we were friends. I said you had to take me with you."

"Let me think about it."

Victor went home with his one hundred dollars and sat at the kitchen table. He held his head in his hands and thought about Thomas Builds-the-Fire, remembered little details, tears and scars, the bicycle they shared for a summer, so many stories.

Thomas Builds-the-Fire sat on the bicycle, waited in Victor's yard. He was ten   30
years old and skinny. His hair was dirty because it was the Fourth of July.

"Victor," Thomas yelled. "Hurry up. We're going to miss the fireworks."

After a few minutes, Victor ran out of his house, jumped the porch railing, and landed gracefully on the sidewalk.

"And the judges award him a 9.95, the highest score of the summer," Thomas said, clapped, laughed.

"That was perfect, cousin," Victor said. "And it's my turn to ride the bike."

Thomas gave up the bike and they headed for the fairgrounds. It was nearly   35
dark and the fireworks were about to start.

"You know," Thomas said. "It's strange how us Indians celebrate the Fourth of July. It ain't like it was *our* independence everybody was fighting for."

"You think about things too much," Victor said. "It's just supposed to be fun. Maybe Junior will be there."

"Which Junior? Everybody on this reservation is named Junior."

And they both laughed.

The fireworks were small, hardly more than a few bottle rockets and a   40
fountain. But it was enough for two Indian boys. Years later, they would need much more.

Afterwards, sitting in the dark, fighting off mosquitoes, Victor turned to Thomas Builds-the-Fire.

"Hey," Victor said. "Tell me a story."

Thomas closed his eyes and told this story: "There were these two Indian boys who wanted to be warriors. But it was too late to be warriors in the old way. All the horses were gone. So the two Indian boys stole a car and drove to the city. They parked the stolen car in front of the police station and then hitch-hiked back home to the reservation. When they got back, all their friends cheered and their parents' eyes shone with pride. *You were very brave*, every-body said to the two Indian boys. *Very brave*."

"Ya-hey," Victor said. "That's a good one. I wish I could be a warrior."

"Me, too," Thomas said.   45

They went home together in the dark, Thomas on the bike now, Victor on foot. They walked through shadows and light from streetlamps.

"We've come a long ways," Thomas said. "We have outdoor lighting."

"All I need is the stars," Victor said. "And besides, you still think about things too much."

They separated then, each headed for home, both laughing all the way.

Victor sat at his kitchen table. He counted his one hundred dollars again and   50
again. He knew he needed more to make it to Phoenix and back. He knew he needed Thomas Builds-the-Fire. So he put his money in his wallet and opened the front door to find Thomas on the porch.

"Ya-hey, Victor," Thomas said. "I knew you'd call me."

Thomas walked into the living room and sat down on Victor's favorite chair.

"I've got some money saved up," Thomas said. "It's enough to get us down there, but you have to get us back."

"I've got this hundred dollars," Victor said. "And my dad had a savings ac-count I'm going to claim."

"How much in your dad's account?"   55

"Enough. A few hundred."

"Sounds good. When we leaving?"

When they were fifteen and had long since stopped being friends, Victor and Thomas got into a fistfight. That is, Victor was really drunk and beat Thomas up for no reason at all. All the other Indian boys stood around and watched it happen. Junior was there and so were Lester, Seymour, and a lot of others. The beating might have gone on until Thomas was dead if Norma Many Horses hadn't come along and stopped it.

"Hey, you boys," Norma yelled and jumped out of her car. "Leave him alone."

If it had been someone else, even another man, the Indian boys would've   60
just ignored the warnings. But Norma was a warrior. She was powerful. She could have picked up any two of the boys and smashed their skulls together. But worse than that, she would have dragged them all over to some tipi and made them listen to some elder tell a dusty old story.

The Indian boys scattered, and Norma walked over to Thomas and picked him up.

"Hey, little man, are you okay?" she asked.

Thomas gave her a thumbs up.

"Why they always picking on you?"

Thomas shook his head, closed his eyes, but no stories came to him, no   65
words or music. He just wanted to go home, to lie in his bed and let his dreams
tell his stories for him.

Thomas Builds-the-Fire and Victor sat next to each other in the airplane, coach
section. A tiny white woman had the window seat. She was busy twisting her
body into pretzels. She was flexible.

"I have to ask," Thomas said, and Victor closed his eyes in embarrassment.

"Don't" Victor said.

"Excuse me, miss," Thomas asked. "Are you a gymnast or something?"

"There's no something about it," she said. "I was first alternate on the   70
1980 Olympic team."

"Really?" Thomas asked.

"Really."

"I mean, you used to be a world-class athlete?" Thomas asked.

"My husband still thinks I am."

Thomas Builds-the-Fire smiled. She was a mental gymnast, too. She pulled   75
her leg straight up against her body so that she could've kissed her kneecap.

"I wish I could do that," Thomas said.

Victor was ready to jump out of the plane. Thomas, that crazy Indian
storyteller with ratty old braids and broken teeth, was flirting with a beautiful Olympic gymnast. Nobody back home on the reservation would ever believe it.

"Well," the gymnast said. "It's easy. Try it."

Thomas grabbed at his leg and tried to pull it up into the same position as
the gymnast. He couldn't even come close, which made Victor and the gymnast laugh.

"Hey," she asked. "You two are Indian, right?"   80

"Full-blood," Victor said.

"Not me," Thomas said. "I'm half magician on my mother's side and half
clown on my father's."

They all laughed.

"What are your names?" she asked.

"Victor and Thomas."   85

"Mine is Cathy. Pleased to meet you all."

The three of them talked for the duration of the flight. Cathy the gymnast
complained about the government, how they screwed the 1980 Olympic team
by boycotting.°

"Sounds like you all got a lot in common with Indians." Thomas said.

Nobody laughed.

boycotting: The United States withdrew from the 1980 Olympics in Moscow to protest the
Soviet Union's invasion of Afghanistan in 1979.

After the plane landed in Phoenix and they had all found their way to the   90
terminal, Cathy the gymnast smiled and waved good-bye.

"She was really nice," Thomas said.

"Yeah, but everybody talks to everybody on airplanes," Victor said. "It's
too bad we can't always be that way."

"You always used to tell me I think too much." Thomas said. "Now it
sounds like you do."

"Maybe I caught it from you."

"Yeah."   95

Thomas and Victor rode in a taxi to the trailer where Victor's father died.

"Listen," Victor said as they stopped in front of the trailer. "I never told you
I was sorry for beating you up that time."

"Oh, it was nothing. We were just kids and you were drunk."

"Yeah, but I'm still sorry."

"That's all right."   100

Victor paid for the taxi and the two of them stood in the hot Phoenix summer. They could smell the trailer.

"This ain't going to be nice," Victor said. "You don't have to go in."

"You're going to need help."

Victor walked to the front door and opened it. The stink rolled out and
made them both gag. Victor's father had lain in that trailer for a week in hun-
dred-degree temperatures before anyone found him. And the only reason anyone found him was because of the smell. They needed dental records to identify
him. That's exactly what the coroner said. They needed dental records.

"Oh, man," Victor said. "I don't know if I can do this."   105

"Well, then don't."

"But there might be something valuable in there."

"I thought his money was in the bank."

"It is. I was talking about pictures and letters and stuff like that."

"Oh," Thomas said as he held his breath and followed Victor into the trailer.   110

When Victor was twelve, he stepped into an underground wasp nest. His foot
was caught in the hole, and no matter how hard he struggled, Victor couldn't
pull free. He might have died there, stung a thousand times, if Thomas Builds-
the-Fire had not come by.

"Run," Thomas yelled and pulled Victor's foot from the hole. They ran
then, hard as they ever had, faster than Billy Mills, faster than Jim Thorpe,
faster than the wasps could fly.

Victor and Thomas ran until they couldn't breathe, ran until it was cold
and dark outside, ran until they were lost and it took hours to find their way
home. All the way back, Victor counted his stings.

"Seven," Victor said. "My lucky number."

Victor didn't find much to keep in the trailer. Only a photo album and a stereo.   115
Everything else had that smell stuck in it or was useless anyway.

"I guess this is all," Victor said. "It ain't much."

"Better than nothing," Thomas said.

"Yeah, and I do have the pickup."

"Yeah," Thomas said. "It's in good shape."

"Dad was good about that stuff."   120

"Yeah, I remember your dad."

"Really?" Victor asked. "What do you remember?"

Thomas Builds-the-Fire closed his eyes and told this story: "I remember when I had this dream that told me to go to Spokane, to stand by the Falls in the middle of the city and wait for a sign. I knew I had to go there but I didn't have a car. Didn't have a license. I was only thirteen. So I walked all the way, took me all day, and I finally made it to the Falls. I stood there for an hour waiting. Then your dad came walking up. *What the hell are you doing here?* he asked me. I said, *Waiting for a vision.* Then your father said, *All you're going to get here is mugged.* So he drove me over to Denny's bought me dinner, and then drove me home to the reservation. For a long time I was mad because I thought my dreams had lied to me. But they didn't. Your dad was my vision. *Take care of each other* is what my dreams were saying. Take care of each other."

Victor was quiet for a long time. He searched his mind for memories of his father, found the good ones, found a few bad ones, added it all up, and smiled.

"My father never told me about finding you in Spokane," Victor said.   125

"He said he wouldn't tell anybody. Didn't want me to get in trouble. But he said I had to watch out for you as part of the deal."

"Really?"

"Really. Your father said you would need the help. He was right."

"That's why you came down here with me, isn't it?" Victor asked.

"I came because of your father."   130

Victor and Thomas climbed into the pickup, drove over to the bank, and claimed the three hundred dollars in the savings account.

Thomas Builds-the-Fire could fly.

Once, he jumped off the roof of the tribal school and flapped his arms like a crazy eagle. And he flew. For a second, he hovered, suspended above all the other Indian boys who were too smart or too scared to jump.

"He's flying," Junior yelled, and Seymour was busy looking for the trick wires or mirrors. But it was real. As real as the dirt when Thomas lost altitude and crashed to the ground.

He broke his arm in two places.   135

"He broke his wing," Victor chanted, and the other Indian boys joined in, made it a tribal song.

"He broke his wing, he broke his wing, he broke his wing," all the Indian boys chanted as they ran off, flapping their wings, wishing they could fly, too. They hated Thomas for his courage, his brief moment as a bird. Everybody has dreams about flying. Thomas flew.

One of his dreams came true for just a second, just enough to make it real.

Victor's father, his ashes, fit in one wooden box with enough left over to fill a cardboard box.

"He always was a big man," Thomas said.   140

Victor carried part of his father and Thomas carried the rest out to the
pickup. They set him down carefully behind the seats, put a cowboy hat on the
wooden box and a Dodgers cap on the cardboard box. That's the way it was
supposed to be.

"Ready to head back home?" Victor asked.

"It's going to be a long drive."

"Yeah, take a couple days, maybe."

"We can take turns," Thomas said.   145

"Okay," Victor said, but they didn't take turns. Victor drove for sixteen
hours straight north, made it halfway up Nevada toward home before he finally pulled over.

"Hey, Thomas," Victor said. "You got to drive for a while."

"Okay."

Thomas Builds-the-Fire slid behind the wheel and started off down the
road. All through Nevada, Thomas and Victor had been amazed at the lack of
animal life, at the absence of water, of movement.

"Where is everything?" Victor had asked more than once.   150

Now when Thomas was finally driving they saw the first animal, maybe
the only animal in Nevada. It was a long-eared jackrabbit.

"Look," Victor yelled. "It's alive."

Thomas and Victor were busy congratulating themselves on their discovery when the jackrabbit darted out into the road and under the wheels of the
pickup.

"Stop the goddamn car," Victor yelled, and Thomas did stop, backed the
pickup to the dead jackrabbit.

"Oh, man, he's dead," Victor said as he looked at the squashed animal.   155

"Really dead."

"The only thing alive in this whole state and we just killed it."

"I don't know," Thomas said. "I think it was suicide."

Victor looked around the desert, sniffed the air, felt the emptiness and loneliness, and nodded his head.

"Yeah," Victor said. "It had to be suicide."   160

"I can't believe this," Thomas said. "You drive for a thousand miles and
there ain't even any bugs smashed on the windshield. I drive for ten seconds
and kill the only living thing in Nevada."

"Yeah," Victor said. "Maybe I should drive."

"Maybe you should."

Thomas Builds-the-Fire walked through the corridors of the tribal school by
himself. Nobody wanted to be anywhere near him because of all those stories.
Story after story.

Thomas closed his eyes and this story came to him: "We are all given one   165
thing by which our lives are measured, one determination. Mine are the stories
which can change or not change the world. It doesn't matter which as long as
I continue to tell the stories. My father, he died on Okinawa in World War II,
died fighting for this country, which had tried to kill him for years. My mother,

she died giving birth to me, died while I was still inside her. She pushed me out into the world with her last breath. I have no brothers or sisters. I have only my stories which came to me before I even had the words to speak. I learned a thousand stories before I took my first thousand steps. They are all I have. It's all I can do."

Thomas Builds-the-Fire told his stories to all those who would stop and listen. He kept telling them long after people had stopped listening.

Victor and Thomas made it back to the reservation just as the sun was rising. It was the beginning of a new day on earth, but the same old shit on the reservation.

"Good morning," Thomas said.

"Good morning."

The tribe was waking up, ready for work, eating breakfast, reading the   170
newspaper, just like everybody else does. Willene LeBret was out in her garden wearing a bathrobe. She waved when Thomas and Victor drove by.

"Crazy Indians made it," she said to herself and went back to her roses.

Victor stopped the pickup in front of Thomas Builds-the-Fire's HUD house.° They both yawned, stretched a little, shook dust from their bodies.

"I'm tired," Victor said.

"Of everything," Thomas added.

They both searched for words to end the journey. Victor needed to thank   175
Thomas for his help, for the money, and make the promise to pay it all back.

"Don't worry about the money," Thomas said. "It don't make any difference anyhow."

"Probably not, enit?"

"Nope."

Victor knew that Thomas would remain the crazy storyteller who talked to dogs and cars, who listened to the wind and pine trees. Victor knew that he couldn't really be friends with Thomas, even after all that had happened. It was cruel but it was real. As real as the ashes, as Victor's father, sitting behind the seats.

"I know how it is," Thomas said. "I know you ain't going to treat me any   180
better than you did before. I know your friends would give you too much shit about it."

Victor was ashamed of himself. Whatever happened to the tribal ties, the sense of community? The only real thing he shared with anybody was a bottle and broken dreams. He owed Thomas something, anything.

"Listen," Victor said and handed Thomas the cardboard box which contained half of his father. "I want you to have this."

Thomas took the ashes and smiled, closed his eyes, and told this story: "I'm going to travel to Spokane Falls one last time and toss these ashes into the water. And your father will rise like a salmon, leap over the bridge, over me, and

---

HUD house: The Department of Housing and Urban Development, an agency of the U.S. government, provides subsidized housing for low-income persons.

find his way home. It will be beautiful. His teeth will shine like silver, like a rainbow. He will rise. Victor, he will rise."

Victor smiled.

"I was planning on doing the same thing with my half," Victor said. "But I   185 didn't imagine my father looking anything like a salmon. I thought it'd be like cleaning the attic or something. Like letting things go after they've stopped having any use."

"Nothing stops, cousin," Thomas said. "Nothing stops."

Thomas Builds-the-Fire got out of the pickup and walked up his driveway. Victor started the pickup and began the drive home.

"Wait," Thomas yelled suddenly from his porch. "I just got to ask one favor."

Victor stopped the pickup, leaned out the window, and shouted back. "What do you want?"

"Just one time when I'm telling a story somewhere, why don't you stop and   190 listen?" Thomas asked.

"Just once?"

"Just once."

Victor waved his arms to let Thomas know that the deal was good. It was a fair trade, and that was all Victor had ever wanted from his whole life. So Victor drove his father's pickup toward home while Thomas went into his house, closed the door behind him, and heard a new story come to him in the silence afterwards.   [1994]

≡ THINKING ABOUT THE TEXT

1. Why does Victor feel "a sudden need for tradition" (para. 24)? What is significant about the "cowboy hat" and the "Dodgers cap" that Victor and Thomas put behind their car seat (para. 141)?

2. What is the significance of Thomas's story about the "two Indian boys who wanted to be warriors" (para. 43)?

3. Point out and explain instances of irony, sarcasm, and intentional humor in the story. What is Alexie's purpose in using these devices?

4. What relationship does Thomas have with Victor's father? What purpose does Thomas's story about Victor's father serve for himself? For his community? For Victor?

5. Explain the tension between the past and the present, between traditional Indian culture and modern American culture in the story.

≡ MAKING COMPARISONS

1. Compare the place of dreams or visions in both stories.

2. Compare Young Goodman Brown's and Thomas Builds-the-Fire's relationships to their communities.

3. Compare the stories as allegories.

≡ WRITING ABOUT ISSUES

1. Write an analysis of Hawthorne's story, taking into account Brown's journey, his interpretation of what happened, his changes, and what ideas about morality and community concerned Hawthorne.

2. Argue that the Alexie story is about a society's need for narratives.

3. Read Hawthorne's "The Minister's Black Veil" or Alexie's "What You Pawn I Will Redeem," and write an essay that compares the story you choose with the author's other story printed here.

4. Argue that both stories are quest allegories.

▤ Journeys to a Dark Place: Stories

RAY BRADBURY, "Mars Is Heaven!"

ARTHUR C. CLARKE, "The Nine Billion Names of God"

KURT VONNEGUT, "Harrison Bergeron"

Ever since H. G. Wells and through the golden age of Ray Bradbury, Isaac Asimov, Robert Heinlein, and Kurt Vonnegut to recent masters like William Gibson and Philip K. Dick, literary science fiction has been used to make serious and critical observations about society. Aldous Huxley in his famous *Brave New World* (1932), for example, was fearful of government's power to control all aspects of our lives, even determining at birth who would collect garbage and who would be future bureaucrats. Indeed, the depiction of Big Brother in George Orwell's *1984* (1948) is still a chilling image of governing authority taken to the extreme.

Much of science fiction uses satire's technique of exaggerating a contemporary concern and transporting it to the future. Because of this, most science fiction is seen as a warning. If this trend continues, it cautions, this is where we might end up. And here science fiction joins with another popular genre — the utopian vision. A utopia is an ideal society, a kind of earthly paradise. Famous examples are Plato's *Republic* and the book that coined the term, Thomas More's *Utopia*. Often initiated by idealism, historical attempts to create perfect societies, such as the French and Russian revolutions, have turned repressive and authoritarian. Perhaps this is why science fiction, like the three stories here, more often than not depict the flip side of utopia — a fictional dystopian world. Ray Bradbury's story creates a seemingly idealized vision of childhood memories, but the illusion has serious consequences. Arthur C. Clarke takes us to a remote corner of the world to a kind of utopian monastery where Western science and Eastern spirituality converge. And Vonnegut's dystopic society is clearly about our own society's inclinations to move toward a dark place.

▤ BEFORE YOU READ

What would be some features of your perfect utopian world? What are some aspects of our present culture that could develop into a future dystopian society? Is there a skepticism in our culture of Eastern religions?

RAY BRADBURY

Mars Is Heaven!

Ray Bradbury (1920–2012), perhaps the most well-known American science fiction writer, was born in Waukegan, Illinois, a beloved town often represented in his fiction as a comforting metaphor for safety, especially in his dangerous fictional dystopias. Although he did not go to college, Bradbury was well read. His professional career began in 1941 with the publication of "Pendulum" in Super Science Stories. *In 1947, his first collection of stories,* Dark Carnival, *appeared. His reputation as a literary science fiction writer was assured in 1950 with the publication of* The Martian Chronicles. *This masterpiece uses a fictional attempt to colonize Mars to comment on American society and its racial, political, and psychological struggles in the 1950s.* Fahrenheit 451 *(1953), another widely praised novel, is set in a dystopic future where books are burned by a totalitarian regime. His best work is characterized by a vivid imagination and the psychological complexity and depth of his characters. He has won numerous awards, including the Nebula Grand Master Award in 1989. The haunting story printed here, from* The Martian Chronicles, *builds its suspense from a masterful blend of hope and suspicion. We want the nostalgic and sentimental vision of the astronauts to be true, but we wisely fear the worst.*

The ship came down from space. It came from the stars and the black velocities, and the shining movements, and the silent gulfs of space. It was a new ship; it had fire in its body and men in its metal cells, and it moved with a clean silence, fiery and warm. In it were seventeen men, including a captain. The crowd at the Ohio field had shouted and waved their hands up into the sunlight, and the rocket had bloomed out great flowers of heat and color and run away into space on the *third* voyage to Mars!

Now it was decelerating with metal efficiency in the upper Martian atmospheres. It was still a thing of beauty and strength. It had moved in the midnight waters of space like a pale sea leviathan; it had passed the ancient moon and thrown itself onward into one nothingness following another. The men within it had been battered, thrown about, sickened, made well again, each in his turn. One man had died, but now the remaining sixteen, with their eyes clear in their heads and their faces pressed to the thick glass ports, watched Mars swing up under them.

"Mars! Mars! Good old Mars, here we are!" cried Navigator Lustig.

"Good old Mars!" said Samuel Hinkston, archaeologist.

"Well," said Captain John Black.   5

The ship landed softly on a lawn of green grass. Outside, upon the lawn, stood an iron deer. Further up the lawn, a tall brown Victorian house sat in the quiet sunlight, all covered with scrolls and rococo, its windows made of blue and pink and yellow and green colored glass. Upon the porch were hairy geraniums and an old swing which was hooked into the porch ceiling and which now swung back and forth, back and forth, in a little breeze. At the top of the house was a cupola with diamond, leaded-glass windows, and a dunce-cap roof! Through the front window you could see an ancient piano with yellow keys and a piece of music titled *Beautiful Ohio* sitting on the music rest.

Around the rocket in four directions spread the little town, green and motionless in the Martian spring. There were white houses and red brick ones, and tall elm trees blowing in the wind, and tall maples and horse chestnuts. And church steeples with golden bells silent in them.

The men in the rocket looked out and saw this. Then they looked at one another and then they looked out again. They held on to each other's elbows, suddenly unable to breathe, it seemed. Their faces grew pale and they blinked constantly, running from glass port to glass port of the ship.

"I'll be damned," whispered Lustig, rubbing his face with his numb fingers, his eyes wet. "I'll be damned, damned, damned."

"It can't be, it just can't be," said Samuel Hinkston.   10

"Lord," said Captain John Black.

There was a call from the chemist. "Sir, the atmosphere is fine for breathing, sir."

Black turned slowly. "Are you sure?"

"No doubt of it, sir."

"Then we'll go out," said Lustig.   15

"Lord, yes," said Samuel Hinkston.

"Hold on," said Captain John Black. "Just a moment. Nobody gave any orders."

"But, sir—"

"Sir, nothing. How do we know what this is?"

"We know what it is, sir," said the chemist. "It's a small town with good air   20
in it, sir."

"And it's a small town the like of Earth towns," said Samuel Hinkston, the archaeologist. "Incredible. It can't be, but it is."

Captain John Black looked at him, idly. "Do you think that the civilizations of two planets can progress at the same rate and evolve in the same way, Hinkston?"

"I wouldn't have thought so, sir."

Captain Black stood by the port. "Look out there. The geraniums. A specialized plant. That specific variety has only been known on Earth for fifty years. Think of the thousands of years of time it takes to evolve plants. Then tell me if it is logical that the Martians should have: one, leaded glass windows; two, cupolas; three, porch swings; four, an instrument that looks like a piano and probably is a piano; and, five, if you look closely, if a Martian composer would have published a piece of music titled, strangely enough, *Beautiful Ohio*. All of which means that we have an Ohio River here on Mars!"

"It is quite strange, sir."   25

"Strange, hell, it's absolutely impossible, and I suspect the whole bloody shooting setup. Something's wrong here, and I'm not leaving the ship until I know what it is."

"Oh, sir," said Lustig.

"Darn it," said Samuel Hinkston. "Sir, I want to investigate this at first hand. It may be that there are similar patterns of thought, movement, civilization on *every* planet in our system. We may be on the threshold of the great psychological and metaphysical discovery in our time, sir, don't you think?"

"I'm willing to wait a moment," said Captain John Black.

"It may be, sir, that we are looking upon a phenomenon that, for the first time, would absolutely prove the existence of a God, sir."   30

"There are many people who are of good faith without such proof, Mr. Hinkston."

"I'm one myself, sir. But certainly a thing like this, out there," said Hinkston, "could not occur without divine intervention, sir. It fills me with such terror and elation I don't know whether to laugh or cry, sir."

"Do neither, then, until we know what we're up against."

"Up against, sir?" inquired Lustig. "I see that we're up against nothing. It's a good quiet, green town, much like the one I was born in, and I like the looks of it."

"When were you born, Lustig?"   35

"In 1910, sir."

"That makes you fifty years old, now, doesn't it?"

"This being 1960, yes, sir."

"And you, Hinkston?"

"1920, sir. In Illinois. And this looks swell to me, sir."   40

"This couldn't be Heaven," said the captain, ironically. "Though, I must admit, it looks peaceful and cool, and pretty much like Green Bluff, where I was born, in 1915." He looked at the chemist. "The air's all right, is it?"

"Yes, sir."

"Well, then, tell you what we'll do. Lustig, you and Hinkston and I will fetch ourselves out to look this town over. The other 14 men will stay aboard ship. If anything untoward happens, lift the ship and get the hell out, do you hear what I say, Craner?"

"Yes, sir. The hell out we'll go, sir. Leaving *you?*"

"A loss of three men's better than a whole ship. If something bad happens   45 get back to Earth and warn the next Rocket, that's Lingle's Rocket, I think, which will be completed and ready to take off some time around next Christmas, what he has to meet up with. If there's something hostile about Mars we certainly want the next expedition to be well armed."

"So are we, sir. We've got a regular arsenal with us."

"Tell the men to stand by the guns, then, as Lustig and Hinkston and I go out."

"Right, sir."

"Come along, Lustig, Hinkston."

The three men walked together, down through the levels of the ship.   50

It was a beautiful spring day. A robin sat on a blossoming apple tree and sang continuously. Showers of petal snow sifted down when the wind touched the apple tree, and the blossom smell drifted upon the air. Somewhere in the town, somebody was playing the piano and the music came and went, came and went, softly, drowsily. The song was *Beautiful Dreamer.* Somewhere else, a phonograph, scratchy and faded, was hissing out a record of *Roamin' in the Gloamin'*, sung by Harry Lauder.

The three men stood outside the ship. The port closed behind them. At every window, a face pressed, looking out. The large metal guns pointed this way and that, ready.

Now the phonograph record being played was:

> "Oh give me a June night
> The moonlight and you — "

Lustig began to tremble. Samuel Hinkston did likewise.

Hinkston's voice was so feeble and uneven that the captain had to ask him   55
to repeat what he had said. "I said, sir, that I think I have solved this, all of this, sir!"

"And what is the solution, Hinkston?"

The soft wind blew. The sky was serene and quiet and somewhere a stream of water ran through the cool caverns and tree-shadings of a ravine. Somewhere a horse and wagon trotted and rolled by, bumping.

"Sir, it must be, it has to be, this is the *only* solution! Rocket travel began to Mars in the years before the first World War, sir!"

The captain stared at his archaeologist. "No!"

"But, yes, sir! You must admit, look at all of this! How else to explain it, the   60
houses, the lawns, the iron deer, the flowers, the pianos, the music!"

"Hinkston, Hinkston, oh," and the captain put his hand to his face, shaking his head, his hand shaking now, his lips blue.

"Sir, listen to me." Hinkston took his elbow persuasively and looked up into the captain's face, pleading. "Say that there were some people in the year 1905, perhaps, who hated wars and wanted to get away from Earth and they got together, some scientists, in secret, and built a rocket and came out here to Mars."

"No, no, Hinkston."

"Why not? The world was a different place in 1905, they could have kept it a secret much more easily."

"But the work, Hinkston, the work of building a complex thing like a   65
rocket, oh, no, no." The captain looked at his shoes, looked at his hands, looked at the houses, and then at Hinkston.

"And they came up here, and naturally the houses they built were similar to Earth houses because they brought the cultural architecture with them, and here it is!"

"And they've lived here all these years?" said the captain.

"In peace and quiet, sir, yes. Maybe they made a few trips, to bring enough people here for one small town, and then stopped, for fear of being discovered. That's why the town seems so old-fashioned. I don't see a thing, myself, that is older than the year 1927, do you?"

"No frankly, I don't, Hinkston."

"These are *our* people, sir. This is an American city; it's definitely not   70
European!"

"That — that's right, too, Hinkston."

"Or maybe, just maybe, sir, rocket travel is older than we think. Perhaps it
started in some part of the world hundreds of years ago, was discovered and
kept secret by a small number of men, and they came to Mars, with only occasional visits to Earth over the centuries."

"You make it sound almost reasonable."

"It is, sir. It has to be. We have the proof here before us, all we have to do
now, is find some people and verify it!"

"You're right there, of course. We can't just stand here and talk. Did you   75
bring your gun?"

"Yes, but we won't need it."

"We'll see about it. Come along, we'll ring that doorbell and see if anyone
is home."

Their boots were deadened of all sound in the thick green grass. It smelled
from a fresh mowing. In spite of himself, Captain John Black felt a great peace
come over him. It had been thirty years since he had been in a small town, and
the buzzing of spring bees on the air lulled and quieted him, and the fresh look
of things was a balm to the soul.

Hollow echoes sounded from under the boards as they walked across the porch
and stood before the screen door. Inside, they could see a bead curtain hung
across the hall entry, and a crystal chandelier and a Maxfield Parrish painting
framed on one wall over a comfortable Morris Chair. The house smelled old,
and of the attic, and infinitely comfortable. You could hear the tinkle of ice rattling in a lemonade pitcher. In a distant kitchen, because of the heat of the day,
someone was preparing a soft, lemon drink.

Captain John Black rang the bell.   80

Footsteps, dainty and thin, came along the hall and a kind faced lady of
some forty years, dressed in the sort of dress you might expect in the year 1909,
peered out at them.

"Can I help you?" she asked.

"Beg your pardon," said Captain Black, uncertainly. "But we're looking for,
that is, could you help us, I mean." He stopped. She looked out at him with dark
wondering eyes.

"If you're selling something," she said, "I'm much too busy and I haven't
time." She turned to go.

"No, *wait*," he cried, bewilderedly. "What town is this?"   85

She looked him up and down as if he were crazy. "What do you mean, what
town is it? How could you be in a town and not know what town it was?"

The captain looked as if he wanted to go sit under a shady apple tree. "I beg
your pardon," he said. "But we're strangers here. We're from Earth, and we
want to know how this town got here and you got here."

"Are you census takers?" she asked.

"No," he said.

"What do you want then?" she demanded.   90

"Well," said the captain.

"Well?" she asked.

"How long has this town been here?" he wondered.

"It was built in 1868," she snapped at them. "Is this a game?"

"No, not a game," cried the captain. "Oh, God," he said. "Look here. We're   95
from Earth!"

"From *where*?" she said.

"From Earth!" he said.

"Where's that?" she said.

"From Earth," he cried.

"Out of the ground, do you mean?"   100

"No, from the planet Earth!" he almost shouted. "Here," he insisted, "come
out on the porch and I'll show you."

"No," she said. "I won't come out there, you are all evidently quite mad
from the sun."

Lustig and Hinkston stood behind the captain. Hinkston now spoke up.
"Mrs.," he said. "We came in a flying ship across space, among the stars. We
came from the third planet from the sun, Earth, to this planet, which is Mars.
Now do you understand, Mrs.?"

"Mad from the sun," she said, taking hold of the door. "Go away now, before I call my husband who's upstairs taking a nap, and he'll beat you all with
his fists."

"But — " said Hinkston. "This is Mars, is it not?"   105

"This," explained the woman, as if she were addressing a child, "is Green
Lake, Wisconsin, on the continent of America, surrounded by the Pacific and
Atlantic Oceans, on a place called the world, or sometimes, the Earth. Go away
now. Good-bye!"

She slammed the door.

The three men stood before the door with their hands up in the air toward
it, as if pleading with her to open it once more.

They looked at one another.

"Let's knock the door down," said Lustig.   110

"We can't," sighed the captain.

"Why not?"

"She didn't do anything bad, did she? We're the strangers here. This is private property. Good God, Hinkston!" He went and sat down on the porchstep.

"What, sir?"

"Did it ever strike you, that maybe we got ourselves, somehow, some way,   115
fouled up. And, by accident, came back and landed on Earth!"

"Oh, sir, oh, sir, oh oh, sir." And Hinkston sat down numbly and thought
about it.

Lustig stood up in the sunlight. "How could we have done that?"

"I don't know, just let me think."

Hinkston said, "But we checked every mile of the way, and we saw Mars and our chronometers said so many miles gone, and we went past the moon and out into space and here we are, on Mars. I'm sure we're on Mars, sir."

Lustig said, "But, suppose, just suppose that, by accident, in space, in time, or something, we landed on a planet in space, in another time. Suppose this is Earth, thirty or fifty years ago? Maybe we got lost in the dimensions, do you think?"

"Oh, go away, Lustig."

"Are the men in the ship keeping an eye on us, Hinkston?"

"At their guns, sir."

Lustig went to the door, rang the bell. When the door opened again, he asked, "What year is this?"

"1926, of course!" cried the woman, furiously, and slammed the door again.

"Did you hear that?" Lustig ran back to them, wildly. "She said 1926! We *have* gone back in time! This *is* Earth!"

Lustig sat down and the three men let the wonder and terror of the thought afflict them. Their hands stirred fitfully on their knees. The wind blew, nodding the locks of hair on their heads.

The captain stood up, brushing off his pants. "I never thought it would be like this. It scares the hell out of me. How can a thing like this happen?"

"Will anybody in the whole town believe us?" wondered Hinkston. "Are we playing around with something dangerous? Time, I mean. Shouldn't we just take off and go home?"

"No. We'll try another house."

They walked three houses down to a little white cottage under an oak tree. "I like to be as logical as I can get," said the captain. He nodded at the town. "How does this sound to you, Hinkston? Suppose, as you said originally, that rocket travel occurred years ago. And when the Earth people had lived here a number of years they began to get homesick for Earth. First a mild neurosis about it, then a full fledged psychosis. Then, threatened insanity. What would you do, as a psychiatrist, if faced with such a problem?"

Hinkston thought. "Well, I think I'd re-arrange the civilization on Mars so it resembled Earth more and more each day. If there was any way of reproducing every plant, every road and every lake, and even an ocean, I would do so. Then I would, by some vast crowd hypnosis, theoretically anyway, convince everyone in a town this size that this really *was* Earth, not Mars at all."

"Good enough, Hinkston. I think we're on the right track now. That woman in that house back there, just *thinks* she's living on Earth. It protects her sanity. She and all the others in this town are the patients of the greatest experiment in migration and hypnosis you will ever lay your eyes on in your life."

"That's it, sir!" cried Lustig.

"Well," the captain sighed. "Now we're getting somewhere. I feel better. It all sounds a bit more logical now. This talk about time and going back and forth and traveling in time turns my stomach upside down. But, *this* way—" He actually smiled for the first time in a month. "Well. It looks as if we'll be fairly welcome here."

"Or, will we, sir?" said Lustig. "After all, like the Pilgrims, these people came here to escape Earth. Maybe they won't be too happy to see us, sir. Maybe they'll try to drive us out or kill us?"

"We have superior weapons if that should happen. Anyway, all we can do is try. This next house now. Up we go."

But they had hardly crossed the lawn when Lustig stopped and looked off across the town, down the quiet, dreaming afternoon street. "Sir," he said.

"What is it, Lustig?" asked the captain.

"Oh, sir, sir, what I see, what I do see now before me, oh, oh — " said Lustig, and he began to cry. His fingers came up, twisting and trembling, and his face was all wonder and joy and incredulity. He sounded as if any moment he might go quite insane with happiness. He looked down the street and he began to run, stumbling, awkwardly, falling, picking himself up, and running on. "Oh, God, God, thank you, God! Thank you!" 140

"Don't let him get away!" The captain broke into a run.

Now Lustig was running at full speed, shouting. He turned into a yard half way down the little shady side street and leaped up upon the porch of a large green house with an iron rooster on the roof.

He was beating upon the door, shouting and hollering and crying when Hinkston and the captain ran up and stood in the yard.

The door opened. Lustig yanked the screen wide and in a high wail of discovery and happiness, cried out, "Grandma! Grandpa!"

Two old people stood in the doorway, their faces lighting up. 145

"Albert!" Their voices piped and they rushed out to embrace and pat him on the back and move around him. "Albert, oh, Albert, it's been so many years! How you've grown, boy, how big you are, boy, oh, Albert boy, how are you!"

"Grandma, Grandpa!" sobbed Albert Lustig. "Good to see you! You look fine, fine! Oh, fine!" He held them, turned them, kissed them, hugged them, cried on them, held them out again, blinked at the little old people. The sun was in the sky, the wind blew, the grass was green, the screen door stood open.

"Come in, lad, come in, there's lemonade for you, fresh, lots of it!"

"Grandma, Grandpa, good to see you! I've got friends down here! Here!" Lustig turned and waved wildly at the captain and Hinkston, who, all during the adventure on the porch, had stood in the shade of a tree, holding onto each other. "Captain, captain, come up, come up, I want you to meet my grandfolks!"

"Howdy," said the folks. "Any friend of Albert's is ours, too! Don't stand there with your mouths open! Come on!" 150

In the living room of the old house it was cool and a grandfather clock ticked high and long and bronzed in one corner. There were soft pillows on large couches and walls filled with books and a rug cut in a thick rose pattern and antimacassars pinned to furniture, and lemonade in the hand, sweating, and cool on the thirsty tongue.

"Here's to our health." Grandma tipped her glass to her porcelain teeth.

"How long have you *been* here, Grandma?" said Lustig.

"A good many years," she said, tartly. "Ever since we died."

"Ever since you what?" asked Captain John Black, putting his drink down.   155

"Oh, yes," Lustig looked at his captain. "They've been dead thirty years."

"And you *sit* there, calmly!" cried the captain.

"Tush," said the old woman, and winked glitteringly at John Black. "Who are we to question what happens? Here we are. What's life, anyways? Who does what for why and where? All we know is here we are, alive again, and no questions asked. A second chance." She toddled over and held out her thin wrist to Captain John Black. "Feel." He felt. "Solid, ain't I?" she asked. He nodded. "You hear my voice don't you?" she inquired. Yes, he did. "Well, then," she said in triumph, "why go around questioning?"

"Well," said the captain, "it's simply that we never thought we'd find a thing like this on Mars."

"And now you've found it. I dare say there's lots on every planet that'll   160 show you God's infinite ways."

"Is this Heaven?" asked Hinkston.

"Nonsense, no. It's a world and we get a second chance. Nobody told us why. But then nobody told us why we were on Earth, either. That *other* Earth, I mean. The one you came from. How do we know there wasn't *another* before *that* one?"

"A good question," said the captain.

The captain stood up and slapped his hand on his leg in an off-hand fashion. "We've got to be going. It's been nice. Thank you for the drinks."

He stopped. He turned and looked toward the door, startled.   165

Far away, in the sunlight, there was a sound of voices, a crowd, a shouting and a great hello.

"What's that?" asked Hinkston.

"We'll soon find out!" And Captain John Black was out the front door abruptly, jolting across the green lawn and into the street of the Martian town.

He stood looking at the ship. The ports were open and his crew were streaming out, waving their hands. A crowd of people had gathered and in and through and among these people the members of the crew were running, talking, laughing, shaking hands. People did little dances. People swarmed. The rocket lay empty and abandoned.

A brass band exploded in the sunlight, flinging off a gay tune from up-   170 raised tubas and trumpets. There was a bang of drums and a shrill of fifes. Little girls with golden hair jumped up and down. Little boys shouted, "Hooray!" And fat men passed around ten-cent cigars. The mayor of the town made a speech. Then, each member of the crew with a mother on one arm, a father or sister on the other, was spirited off down the street, into little cottages or big mansions and doors slammed shut.

The wind rose in the clear spring sky and all was silent. The brass band had banged off around a corner leaving the rocket to shine and dazzle alone in the sunlight.

"Abandoned!" cried the captain. "Abandoned the ship, they did! I'll have their skins, by God! They had orders!"

"Sir," said Lustig. "Don't be too hard on them. Those were all old relatives and friends."

"That's no excuse!"

"Think how they felt, captain, seeing familiar faces outside the ship!"   175

"I would have obeyed orders! I would have — " The captain's mouth remained open.

Striding along the sidewalk under the Martian sun, tall, smiling, eyes blue, face tan, came a young man of some twenty-six years.

"John!" the man cried, and broke into a run.

"What?" said Captain John Black. He swayed.

"John, you old beggar, you!"   180

The man ran up and gripped his hand and slapped him on the back.

"It's you," said John Black.

"Of course, who'd you *think* it was!"

"Edward!" The captain appealed now to Lustig and Hinkston, holding the stranger's hand. "This is my brother Edward. Ed, meet my men, Lustig, Hinkston! My brother!"

They tugged at each other's hands and arms and then finally embraced.   185
"Ed!" "John, you old bum, you!" "You're looking fine, Ed, but, Ed, what is this? You haven't changed over the years. You died, I remember, when you were twenty-six, and I was nineteen, oh God, so many years ago, and here you are, and, Lord, what goes on, what goes on?"

Edward Black gave him a brotherly knock on the chin. "Mom's waiting," he said.

"Mom?"

"And Dad, too."

"And Dad?" The captain almost fell to earth as if hit upon the chest with a mighty weapon. He walked stiffly and awkwardly, out of coordination. He stuttered and whispered and talked only one or two words at a time. "Mom alive? Dad? Where?"

"At the old house on Oak Knoll Avenue."   190

"The old house." The captain stared in delighted amazement. "Did you *hear* that, Lustig, Hinkston?"

"I know it's hard for you to believe."

"But alive. Real."

"Don't I *feel* real?" The strong aim, the firm grip, the white smile. The light, curling hair.

Hinkston was gone. He had seen his own house down the street and was   195
running for it. Lustig was grinning. "Now you understand, sir, what happened to everybody on the ship. They couldn't help themselves."

"Yes. Yes," said the captain, eyes shut. "Yes." He put out his hand. "When I open my eyes, you'll be gone." He opened his eyes. "You're still here. God, Edward, you look fine!"

"Come along, lunch is waiting for you. I told Mom."

Lustig said, "Sir, I'll be with my grandfolks if you want me."

"What? Oh, fine, Lustig. Later, then."

Edward grabbed his arm and marched him. "You need support." 200

"I do. My knees, all funny. My stomach, loose. God."

"There's the house. Remember it?"

"Remember it? Hell! I can beat you to the front porch!"

They ran. The wind roared over Captain John Black's ears. The earth roared under his feet. He saw the golden figure of Edward Black pull ahead of him in the amazing dream of reality. He saw the house rush forward, the door open, the screen swing back. "Beat you!" cried Edward, bounding up the steps. "I'm an old man," panted the captain, "and you're still young. But, then, you *always* beat me, I remember!"

In the doorway, Mom, pink and plump and bright. And behind her, pepper 205 grey, Dad, with his pipe in his hand.

"Mom, Dad!"

He ran up the steps like a child, to meet them.

It was a fine long afternoon. They finished lunch and they sat in the living room and he told them all about his rocket and his being captain and they nodded and smiled upon him and Mother was just the same, and Dad bit the end off a cigar and lighted it in his old fashion. Mom brought in some iced tea in the middle of the afternoon. Then, there was a big turkey dinner at night and time flowing on. When the drumsticks were sucked clean and lay brittle upon the plates, the captain leaned back in his chair and exhaled his deep contentment. Dad poured him a small glass of dry sherry. It was seven-thirty in the evening. Night was in all the trees and coloring the sky, and the lamps were halos of dim light in the gentle house. From all the other houses down the streets came sounds of music, pianos playing, laughter.

Mom put a record on the victrola and she and Captain John Black had a dance. She was wearing the same perfume he remembered from the summer when she and Dad had been killed in the train accident. She was very real in his arms as they danced lightly to the music.

"I'll wake in the morning," said the captain. "And I'll be in my rocket in 210 space, and all this will be gone."

"No, no, don't think that," she cried, softly, pleadingly. "We're here. Don't question. God is good to us. Let's be happy."

The record ended with a circular hissing.

"You're tired, son," said Dad. He waved his pipe. "You and Ed go on upstairs. Your old bedroom is waiting for you."

"The old one?"

"The brass bed and all," laughed Edward. 215

"But I should report my men in."

"Why?" Mother was logical.

"Why? Well, I don't know. No reason, I guess. No, none at all. What's the difference?" He shook his head. "I'm not being very logical these days."

"Good night, son." She kissed his cheek.

"'Night, Mom."   220

"Sleep tight, son." Dad shook his hand.

"Same to you, Pop."

"It's good to have you home."

"It's good to *be* home."

He left the land of cigar smoke and perfume and books and gentle light   225
and ascended the stairs, talking, talking with Edward. Edward pushed a door
open and there was the yellow brass bed and the old semaphore banners from
college days and a very musty raccoon coat which he petted with strange,
muted affection. "It's too much," he said faintly. "Like being in a thunder
shower without an umbrella. I'm soaked to the skin with emotion. I'm numb.
I'm tired."

"A night's sleep between cool clean sheets for you, my bucko." Edward
slapped wide the snowy linens and flounced the pillows. Then he put up a window and let the night blooming jasmine float in. There was moonlight and the
sound of distant dancing and whispering.

"So this is Mars," said the captain undressing.

"So this is Mars," Edward undressed in idle, leisurely moves, drawing his
shirt off over his head, revealing golden shoulders and the good muscular neck.

The lights were out, they were into bed, side by side, as in the days, how
many decades ago? The captain lolled and was nourished by the night wind
pushing the lace curtains out upon the dark room air. Among the trees, upon
a lawn, someone had cranked up a portable phonograph and now it was playing softly. "I'll be loving you, always, with a love that's true, always."

The thought of Anna came to his mind. "Is Anna here?"   230

His brother, lying straight out in the moonlight from the window, waited
and then said, "Yes. She's out of town. But she'll be here in the morning."

The captain shut his eyes. "I want to see Anna very much."

The room was square and quiet except for their breathing. "Good
night, Ed."

A pause. "Good night, John."

He lay peacefully, letting his thoughts float. For the first time the stress of   235
the day was moved aside, all of the excitement was calmed. He could think
logically now. It had all been emotion. The bands playing, the sight of familiar
faces, the sick pounding of your heart. But — now . . .

How? He thought. How was all this made? And why? For what purpose?
Out of the goodness of some kind God? Was God, then, really that fine and
thoughtful of his children? How and why and what for?

He thought of the various theories advanced in the first heat of the afternoon by Hinkston and Lustig. He let all kinds of new theories drop in lazy
pebbles down through his mind, as through a dark water, now, turning, throwing out dull flashes of white light. Mars. Earth. Mom. Dad. Edward. Mars.
Martians.

Who had lived here a thousand years ago on Mars? Martians? Or had this
always been like this? Martians. He repeated the word quietly, inwardly.

He laughed out loud, almost. He had the most ridiculous theory, all of a sudden. It gave him a kind of chilled feeling. It was really nothing to think of, of course. Highly improbable. Silly. Forget it. Ridiculous.

But, he thought, just suppose. Just *suppose* now, that there were Martians living   240 on Mars and they saw our ship coming and saw us inside our ship and hated us. Suppose, now, just for the hell of it, that they wanted to destroy us, as invaders, as unwanted ones, and they wanted to do it in a very clever way, so that we would be taken off guard. Well, what would the best weapon be that a Martian could use against Earth-men with atom weapons?

The answer was interesting. Telepathy, hypnosis, memory, and imagination.

Suppose all these houses weren't real at all, this bed not real, but only figments of my own imagination, given substance by telepathy and hypnosis by the Martians.

Suppose these houses are really some other shape, a Martian shape, but, by playing on my desires and wants, these Martians have made this seem like my old home town, my old house, to lull me out of my suspicions? What better way to fool a man, by his own emotions.

And suppose those two people in the next room, asleep, are not my mother and father at all. But two Martians, incredibly brilliant, with the ability to keep me under this dreaming hypnosis all of the time?

And that brass band, today? What a clever plan it would be. First, fool   245 Lustig, then fool Hinkston, then gather a crowd around the rocket ship and wave. And all the men in the ship, seeing mothers, aunts, uncles, sweethearts dead ten, twenty years ago, naturally, disregarding orders, would rush out and abandon the ship. What more natural? What more unsuspecting? What more simple? A man doesn't ask too many questions when his mother is suddenly brought back to life; he's much too happy. And the brass band played and everybody was taken off to private homes. And here we all are, tonight, in various houses, in various beds, with no weapons to protect us, and the rocket lies in the moonlight, empty. And wouldn't it be horrible and terrifying to discover that all of this was part of some great clever plan by the Martians to divide and conquer us, and kill us. Some time during the night, perhaps, my brother on this bed, will change form, melt, shift, and become a one-eyed, green and yellow-toothed Martian. It would be very simple for him just to turn over in bed and put a knife into my heart. And in all those other houses down the street a dozen other brothers or fathers suddenly melting away and taking out knives and doing things to the unsuspecting, sleeping men of Earth.

His hands were shaking under the covers. His body was cold. Suddenly it was not a theory. Suddenly he was very afraid. He lifted himself in bed and listened. The night was very quiet. The music had stopped. The wind had died. His brother (?) lay sleeping beside him.

Very carefully he lifted the sheets, rolled them back. He slipped from bed and was walking softly across the room when his brother's voice said, "Where are you going?"

"What?"

His brother's voice was quite cold. "I said, where do you think you're going?"

"For a drink of water."   250

"But you're not thirsty."

"Yes, yes, I am."

"No, you're not."

Captain John Black broke and ran across the room. He screamed. He screamed twice.

He never reached the door.   255

In the morning, the brass band played a mournful dirge. From every house in the street came little solemn processions bearing long boxes and along the sun-filled street, weeping and changing, came the grandmas and grandfathers and mothers and sisters and brothers, walking to the churchyard, where there were open holes dug freshly and new tombstones installed. Seventeen holes in all, and seventeen tombstones. Three of the tombstones said, CAPTAIN JOHN BLACK, ALBERT LUSTIG, and SAMUEL HINKSTON.

The mayor made a little sad speech, his face sometimes looking like the mayor, sometimes looking like something else.

Mother and Father Black were there, with Brother Edward, and they cried, their faces melting now from a familiar face into something else.

Grandpa and Grandma Lustig were there, weeping, their faces also shifting like wax, shivering as a thing does in waves of heat on a summer day.

The coffins were lowered. Somebody murmured about "the unexpected   260
and sudden deaths of seventeen fine men during the night—"

Earth was shoveled in on the coffin tops.

After the funeral the brass band slammed and banged back into town and the crowd stood around and waved and shouted as the rocket was torn to pieces and strewn about and blown up.   [1948]

≡ THINKING ABOUT THE TEXT

1. What was your first response to the Victorian town? The captain says that "it's absolutely impossible" (para. 26). Did you think he is right?

2. What was your response to the attempted explanations for the town's appearance? Isn't seeing believing? Did you think that perhaps time travel is involved?

3. Comment on the thematic significance of the line "the buzzing of spring bees on the air lulled and quieted him, and the fresh look of things was a balm to the soul" (para. 78).

4. After Captain Black recovers from being "soaked to the skin with emotion" (para. 225), he begins thinking logically. At this point, as you sense the ending is near, what logical explanation did you suspect was coming—something about illusion, or perhaps delusion? What is ironic about the astronauts' coming armed with atomic weapons?

5. Readers are often puzzled by the ending. Indeed, it is strange that the Martians would hold a human funeral. After all, if the men are dead, why continue the charade? Why do you think they perform the ritual?

ARTHUR C. CLARKE
The Nine Billion Names of God

Arthur C. Clarke (1917–2008) is one of the giants of twentieth-century science fiction. His novels, including Childhood's End *(1953) and* Rendezvous with Rama *(1972), have been translated into dozens of languages. Clarke's family could not afford to send him to university, so instead he worked and served as a radar specialist during World War II, all the while pursuing his scientific interests and writing. In 1946, his story "Rescue Party" became his first published fiction piece. He eventually graduated from King's College with honors in physics and mathematics in 1948. He is widely credited with predicting satellite communication twenty years before it became a reality. In 1968, Clarke and Stanley Kubrick shared an Oscar nomination for the screenplay of* 2001: A Space Odyssey. *He has won science fiction's highest awards, The Hugo and The Nebula, several times. As in the following story, spirituality and religion were frequent themes in his work. Although he considered himself an atheist, he wrote "Any path to knowledge is a path to God—or Reality, whichever word one prefers to use."*

"This is a slightly unusual request," said Dr. Wagner, with what he hoped was commendable restraint. "As far as I know, it's the first time anyone's been asked to supply a Tibetan monastery with an Automatic Sequence Computer. I don't wish to be inquisitive, but I should hardly have thought that your—ah—establishment had much use for such a machine. Could you explain just what you intend to do with it?"

"Gladly," replied the lama, readjusting his silk robes and carefully putting away the slide rule he had been using for currency conversions. "Your Mark V Computer can carry out any routine mathematical operation involving up to ten digits. However, for our work we are interested in *letters*, not numbers. As we wish you to modify the output circuits, the machine will be printing words, not columns of figures."

"I don't quite understand. . . ."

"This is a project on which we have been working for the last three centuries—since the lamasery was founded, in fact. It is somewhat alien to your way of thought, so I hope you will listen with an open mind while I explain it."

"Naturally."

"It is really quite simple. We have been compiling a list which shall contain all the possible names of God."

"I beg your pardon?"

"We have reason to believe," continued the lama imperturbably, "that all

5

such names can be written with not more than nine letters in an alphabet we have devised."

"And you have been doing this for three centuries?"

"Yes: we expected it would take us about fifteen thousand years to com-   10
plete the task."

"Oh," Dr. Wagner looked a little dazed. "Now I see why you wanted to hire one of our machines. But exactly what is the *purpose* of this project?"

The lama hesitated for a fraction of a second, and Wagner wondered if he had offended him. If so, there was no trace of annoyance in the reply.

"Call it ritual, if you like, but it's a fundamental part of our belief. All the many names of the Supreme Being — God, Jehovah, Allah, and so on — they are only man-made labels. There is a philosophical problem of some difficulty here, which I do not propose to discuss, but somewhere among all the possible combinations of letters that can occur are what one may call the real names of God. By systematic permutation of letters, we have been trying to list them all."

"I see. You've been starting at AAAAAAA . . . and working up to ZZZZZZZZ. . . ."

"Exactly — though we use a special alphabet of our own. Modifying the   15
electromatic typewriters to deal with this is, of course, trivial. A rather more interesting problem is that of devising suitable circuits to eliminate ridiculous combinations. For example, no letter must occur more than three times in succession."

"Three? Surely you mean two."

"Three is correct: I am afraid it would take too long to explain why, even if you understood our language."

"I'm sure it would," said Wagner hastily. "Go on."

"Luckily, it will be a simple matter to adapt your Automatic Sequence Computer for this work, since once it has been programed properly it will permute each letter in turn and print the result. What would have taken us fifteen thousand years it will be able to do in a hundred days."

Dr. Wagner was scarcely conscious of the faint sounds from the Manhat-   20
tan streets far below. He was in a different world, a world of natural, not man-made, mountains. High up in their remote aeries these monks had been patiently at work, generation after generation, compiling their lists of meaningless words. Was there any limit to the follies of mankind? Still, he must give no hint of his inner thoughts. The customer was always right. . . .

"There's no doubt," replied the doctor, "that we can modify the Mark V to print lists of this nature. I'm much more worried about the problem of installation and maintenance. Getting out to Tibet, in these days, is not going to be easy."

"We can arrange that. The components are small enough to travel by air — that is one reason why we chose your machine. If you can get them to India, we will provide transport from there."

"And you want to hire two of our engineers?"

"Yes, for the three months that the project should occupy."

"I've no doubt that Personnel can manage that." Dr. Wagner scribbled a   25
note on his desk pad. "There are just two other points—"

Before he could finish the sentence the lama had produced a small slip of paper.

"This is my certified credit balance at the Asiatic Bank."

"Thank you. It appears to be—ah—adequate. The second matter is so trivial that I hesitate to mention it—but it's surprising how often the obvious gets overlooked. What source of electrical energy have you?"

"A diesel generator providing fifty kilowatts at a hundred and ten volts. It was installed about five years ago and is quite reliable. It's made life at the lamasery much more comfortable, but of course it was really installed to provide power for the motors driving the prayer wheels."

"Of course," echoed Dr. Wagner. "I should have thought of that."   30

The view from the parapet was vertiginous, but in time one gets used to anything. After three months, George Hanley was not impressed by the two-thousand-foot swoop into the abyss or the remote checkerboard of fields in the valley below. He was leaning against the wind-smoothed stones and staring morosely at the distant mountains whose names he had never bothered to discover.

This, thought George, was the craziest thing that had ever happened to him. "Project Shangri-La," some wit back at the labs had christened it. For weeks now the Mark V had been churning out acres of sheets covered with gibberish. Patiently, inexorably, the computer had been rearranging letters in all their possible combinations, exhausting each class before going on to the next. As the sheets had emerged from the electromatic typewriters, the monks had carefully cut them up and pasted them into enormous books. In another week, heaven be praised, they would have finished. Just what obscure calculations had convinced the monks that they needn't bother to go on to words of ten, twenty, or a hundred letters. George didn't know. One of his recurring nightmares was that there would be some change of plan, and that the high lama (whom they'd naturally called Sam Jaffe, though he didn't look a bit like him) would suddenly announce that the project would be extended to approximately A.D. 2060. They were quite capable of it.

George heard the heavy wooden door slam in the wind as Chuck came out onto the parapet beside him. As usual, Chuck was smoking one of the cigars that made him so popular with the monks—who, it seemed, were quite willing to embrace all the minor and most of the major pleasures of life. That was one thing in their favor: they might be crazy, but they weren't bluenoses. Those frequent trips they took down to the village, for instance . . .

"Listen, George," said Chuck urgently. "I've learned something that means trouble."

"What's wrong? Isn't the machine behaving?" That was the worst contin-   35
gency George could imagine. It might delay his return, and nothing could be more horrible. The way he felt now, even the sight of a TV commercial would seem like manna from heaven. At least it would be some link with home.

"No—it's nothing like that." Chuck settled himself on the parapet, which was unusual because normally he was scared of the drop. "I've just found what all this is about."

"What d'ya mean? I thought we knew."

"Sure—we know what the monks are trying to do. But we didn't know why. It's the craziest thing—"

"Tell me something new," growled George.

"—but old Sam's just come clean with me. You know the way he drops in   40
every afternoon to watch the sheets roll out. Well, this time he seemed rather excited, or at least as near as he'll ever get to it. When I told him that we were on the last cycle he asked me, in that cute English accent of his, if I'd ever wondered what they were trying to do. I said, 'Sure'—and he told me."

"Go on: I'll buy it."

"Well, they believe that when they have listed all His names—and they reckon that there are about nine billion of them—God's purpose will be achieved. The human race will have finished what it was created to do, and there won't be any point in carrying on. Indeed, the very idea is something like blasphemy."

"Then what do they expect us to do? Commit suicide?"

"There's no need for that. When the list's completed, God steps in and simply winds things up . . . bingo!"

"Oh, I get it. When we finish our job, it will be the end of the world." Chuck   45
gave a nervous little laugh.

"That's just what I said to Sam. And do you know what happened? He looked at me in a very queer way, like I'd been stupid in class, and said, 'It's nothing as trivial as *that*.'"

George thought this over for a moment.

"That's what I call taking the Wide View," he said presently. "But what d'you suppose we should do about it? I don't see that it makes the slightest difference to us. After all, we already knew that they were crazy."

"Yes—but don't you see what may happen? When the list's complete and the Last Trump doesn't blow—or whatever it is they expect—we may get the blame. It's our machine they've been using. I don't like the situation one little bit."

"I see," said George slowly. "You've got a point there. But this sort of thing's   50
happened before, you know. When I was a kid down in Louisiana we had a crackpot preacher who once said the world was going to end next Sunday. Hundreds of people believed him—even sold their homes. Yet when nothing happened, they didn't turn nasty, as you'd expect. They just decided that he'd made a mistake in his calculations and went right on believing. I guess some of them still do."

"Well, this isn't Louisiana, in case you hadn't noticed. There are just two of us and hundreds of these monks. I like them, and I'll be sorry for old Sam when his lifework backfires on him. But all the same, I wish I was somewhere else."

"I've been wishing that for weeks. But there's nothing we can do until the contract's finished and the transport arrives to fly us out."

"Of course," said Chuck thoughtfully, "we could always try a bit of sabotage."

"Like hell we could! That would make things worse."

"Not the way I meant. Look at it like this. The machine will finish its run   55
four days from now, on the present twenty-hours-a-day basis. The transport calls in a week. O.K.—then all we need to do is to find something that needs replacing during one of the overhaul periods—something that will hold up the works for a couple of days. We'll fix it of course, but not too quickly. If we time matters properly, we can be down at the airfield when the last name pops out of the register. They won't be able to catch us then."

"I don't like it," said George. "It will be the first time I ever walked out on a job. Besides, it would make them suspicious. No, I'll sit tight and take what comes."

"I *still* don't like it," he said, seven days later, as the tough little mountain ponies carried them down the winding road. "And don't you think I'm running away because I'm afraid. I'm just sorry for those poor old guys up there, and I don't want to be around when they find what suckers they've been. Wonder how Sam will take it?"

"It's funny," replied Chuck, "but when I said good-by I got the idea he knew we were walking out on him—and that he didn't care because he knew the machine was running smoothly and that the job would soon be finished. After that—well, of course, for him there just isn't any After That. . . ."

George turned in his saddle and stared back up the mountain road. This was the last place from which one could get a clear view of the lamasery. The squat, angular buildings were silhouetted against the afterglow of the sunset: here and there, lights gleamed like portholes in the side of an ocean liner. Electric lights, of course, sharing the same circuit as the Mark V. How much longer would they share it? wondered George. Would the monks smash up the computer in their rage and disappointment? Or would they just sit down quietly and begin their calculations all over again?

He knew exactly what was happening up on the mountain at this very mo-   60
ment. The high lama and his assistants would be sitting in their silk robes, inspecting the sheets as the junior monks carried them away from the typewriters and pasted them into the great volumes. No one would be saying anything. The only sound would be the incessant patter, the never-ending rainstorm of the keys hitting the paper, for the Mark V itself was utterly silent as it flashed through its thousands of calculations a second. Three months of this, thought George, was enough to start anyone climbing up the wall.

"There she is!" called Chuck, pointing down into the valley. "Ain't she beautiful!"

She certainly was, thought George. The battered old DC3 lay at the end of the runway like a tiny silver cross. In two hours she would be bearing them away to freedom and sanity. It was a thought worth savoring like a fine liqueur. George let it roll round his mind as the pony trudged patiently down the slope.

The swift night of the high Himalayas was now almost upon them. Fortunately, the road was very good, as roads went in that region, and they were both carrying torches. There was not the slightest danger, only a certain discomfort from the bitter cold. The sky overhead was perfectly clear, and ablaze with the familiar, friendly stars. At least there would be no risk, thought George, of the pilot being unable to take off because of weather conditions. That had been his only remaining worry.

He began to sing, but gave it up after a while. This vast arena of mountains, gleaming like whitely hooded ghosts on every side, did not encourage such ebullience. Presently George glanced at his watch.

"Should be there in an hour," he called back over his shoulder to Chuck.   65
Then he added, in an afterthought: "Wonder if the computer's finished its run. It was due about now."

Chuck didn't reply, so George swung round in his saddle. He could just see Chuck's face, a white oval turned toward the sky.

"Look," whispered Chuck, and George lifted his eyes to heaven. (There is always a last time for everything.)

Overhead, without any fuss, the stars were going out.   [1953]

≡ THINKING ABOUT THE TEXT

1. What are Dr. Wagner's attitudes toward the monks? Did you share his viewpoint?

2. Where in the story can you find indications that stereotypes about the monks are suspect?

3. Why did "some wit" label the request as "Project Shangri-La" (para. 32)? Who is Sam Jaffe (para. 32)?

4. Point out various examples of sarcasm and irony on Chuck's and George's part. Why does Clarke have them make such comments?

5. What was your first response to the last sentence? This is obviously a story with a surprise or twist ending. What do you think Clarke wants you to think about the ending? How might this story be more about us than the monks?

≡ MAKING COMPARISONS

1. Compare the endings of the two stories. Were you prepared for them? In what way?

2. How is arrogance a factor in the stories?

3. How would you describe Captain Black and Chuck and George? Are they heroes? Villains? Naive? Prideful? Something else?

KURT VONNEGUT

Harrison Bergeron

Kurt Vonnegut (1922–2007), one of the best-known science fiction writers in America, was widely popular in the 1960s and 1970s, mostly for his darkly ironic, antiwar novel Slaughterhouse-Five *(1969), a tale based on Vonnegut's own experiences as a prisoner of war in Dresden. Vonnegut survived the massive Allied firebombing that killed more than 130,000 people, mostly civilians. The mental anguish he suffered there haunted him for years. His novel of these events became a best-seller, and Vonnegut became a hero of the anti–Vietnam War movement.*

    Vonnegut was born in Indianapolis and attended Cornell University before entering World War II. His other works include the novel The Breakfast of Champions *(1973) and his short-story collection* Welcome to the Monkey House *(1968), which solidified his iconic status in America's counterculture as a comic genius with an urgent moral vision. In his last book,* A Man without a Country *(2005), he focuses his bitter satire on the Bush administration, the Iraq War, and conformist Americans. The novel was a best-seller.*

The year was 2081, and everybody was finally equal. They weren't only equal before God and the law. They were equal every which way. Nobody was smarter than anybody else. Nobody was better looking than anybody else. Nobody was stronger or quicker than anybody else. All this equality was due to the 211th, 212th, and 213th Amendments to the Constitution, and to the unceasing vigilance of agents of the United States Handicapper General.

Some things about living still weren't quite right, though. April, for instance, still drove people crazy by not being springtime. And it was in that clammy month that the H-G men took George and Hazel Bergeron's fourteen-year-old son, Harrison, away.

It was tragic, all right, but George and Hazel couldn't think about it very hard. Hazel had a perfectly average intelligence, which meant she couldn't think about anything except in short bursts. And George, while his intelligence was way above normal, had a little mental handicap radio in his ear. He was required by law to wear it at all times. It was tuned to a government transmitter. Every twenty seconds or so, the transmitter would send out some sharp noise to keep people like George from taking unfair advantage of their brains.

George and Hazel were watching television. There were tears on Hazel's cheeks, but she'd forgotten for the moment what they were about.

On the television screen were ballerinas. 5

A buzzer sounded in George's head. His thoughts fled in panic, like bandits from a burglar alarm.

"That was a real pretty dance, that dance they just did," said Hazel.

"Huh?" said George.

"That dance—it was nice," said Hazel.

"Yup," said George. He tried to think a little about the ballerinas. They 10 weren't really very good—no better than anybody else would have been, anyway. They were burdened with sash-weights and bags of birdshot, and their faces were masked, so that no one, seeing a free and graceful gesture or a pretty face, would feel like something the cat dragged in. George was toying with the vague notion that maybe dancers shouldn't be handicapped. But he didn't get very far with it before another noise in his ear radio scattered his thoughts.

George winced. So did two out of the eight ballerinas.

Hazel saw him wince. Having no mental handicap herself, she had to ask George what the latest sound had been.

"Sounded like somebody hitting a milk bottle with a ball peen hammer," said George.

"I'd think it would be real interesting, hearing all the different sounds," said Hazel, a little envious. "All the things they think up."

"Um," said George.   15

"Only, if I was Handicapper General, you know what I would do?" said Hazel. Hazel, as a matter of fact, bore a strong resemblance to the Handicapper General, a woman named Diana Moon Glampers. "If I was Diana Moon Glampers," said Hazel, "I'd have chimes on Sunday—just chimes. Kind of in honor of religion."

"I could think, if it was just chimes," said George.

"Well—maybe make 'em real loud," said Hazel. "I think I'd make a good Handicapper General."

"Good as anybody else," said George.

"Who knows better'n I do what normal is?" said Hazel.   20

"Right," said George. He began to think glimmeringly about his abnormal son who was now in jail, about Harrison, but a twenty-one-gun salute in his head stopped that.

"Boy!" said Hazel, "that was a doozy, wasn't it?"

It was such a doozy that George was white and trembling, and tears stood on the rims of his red eyes. Two of the eight ballerinas had collapsed to the studio floor, were holding their temples.

"All of a sudden you look so tired," said Hazel. "Why don't you stretch out on the sofa, so's you can rest your handicap bag on the pillows, honeybunch." She was referring to the forty-seven pounds of birdshot in a canvas bag, which was padlocked around George's neck. "Go on and rest the bag for a little while," she said. "I don't care if you're not equal to me for a while."

George weighed the bag with his hands. "I don't mind it," he said. "I don't   25
notice it any more. It's just a part of me."

"You been so tired lately—kind of wore out," said Hazel. "If there was just some way we could make a little hole in the bottom of the bag, and just take out a few of them lead balls. Just a few."

"Two years in prison and two thousand dollars fine for every ball I took out," said George. "I don't call that a bargain."

"If you could just take a few out when you came home from work," said Hazel. "I mean—you don't compete with anybody around here. You just set around."

"If I tried to get away with it," said George, "then other people'd get away with it — and pretty soon we'd be right back to the dark ages again, with everybody competing against everybody else. You wouldn't like that, would you?"

"I'd hate it," said Hazel.

"There you are," said George. "The minute people start cheating on laws, what do you think happens to society?"

If Hazel hadn't been able to come up with an answer to this question, George couldn't have supplied one. A siren was going off in his head.

"Reckon it'd fall all apart," said Hazel.

"What would?" said George blankly.

"Society," said Hazel uncertainly. "Wasn't that what you just said?"

"Who knows?" said George.

The television program was suddenly interrupted for a news bulletin. It wasn't clear at first as to what the bulletin was about, since the announcer, like all announcers, had a serious speech impediment. For about half a minute, and in a state of high excitement, the announcer tried to say, "Ladies and gentlemen —"

He finally gave up, handed the bulletin to a ballerina to read.

"That's all right —" Hazel said of the announcer, "he tried. That's the big thing. He tried to do the best he could with what God gave him. He should get a nice raise for trying so hard."

"Ladies and gentlemen —" said the ballerina, reading the bulletin. She must have been extraordinarily beautiful, because the mask she wore was hideous. And it was easy to see that she was the strongest and most graceful of all the dancers, for her handicap bags were as big as those worn by two-hundred-pound men.

And she had to apologize at once for her voice, which was a very unfair voice for a woman to use. Her voice was a warm, luminous, timeless melody. "Excuse me —" she said, and she began again, making her voice absolutely uncompetitive.

"Harrison Bergeron, age fourteen," she said in a grackle squawk, "has just escaped from jail, where he was held on suspicion of plotting to overthrow the government. He is a genius and an athlete, is under-handicapped, and should be regarded as extremely dangerous."

A police photograph of Harrison Bergeron was flashed on the screen — upside down, then sideways, upside down again, then right side up. The picture showed the full length of Harrison against a background calibrated in feet and inches. He was exactly seven feet tall.

The rest of Harrison's appearance was Halloween and hardware. Nobody had ever borne heavier handicaps. He had outgrown hindrances faster than the H-G men could think them up. Instead of a little ear radio for a mental handicap, he wore a tremendous pair of earphones, and spectacles with thick wavy lenses. The spectacles were intended to make him not only half blind, but to give him whanging headaches besides.

Scrap metal was hung all over him. Ordinarily, there was a certain symmetry, a military neatness to the handicaps issued to strong people, but

Harrison looked like a walking junkyard. In the race of life, Harrison carried three hundred pounds.

And to offset his good looks, the H-G men required that he wear at all times a red rubber ball for a nose, keep his eyebrows shaved off, and cover his even white teeth with black caps at snaggle-tooth random.

"If you see this boy," said the ballerina, "do not—I repeat, do not—try to reason with him."

There was the shriek of a door being torn from its hinges.

Screams and barking cries of consternation came from the television set. The photograph of Harrison Bergeron on the screen jumped again and again, as though dancing to the tune of an earthquake.

George Bergeron correctly identified the earthquake, and well he might   50
have—for many was the time his own home had danced to the same crashing tune. "My God—" said George, "that must be Harrison!"

The realization was blasted from his mind instantly by the sound of an automobile collision in his head.

When George could open his eyes again, the photograph of Harrison was gone. A living, breathing Harrison filled the screen.

Clanking, clownish, and huge, Harrison stood in the center of the studio. The knob of the uprooted studio door was still in his hand. Ballerinas, technicians, musicians, and announcers cowered on their knees before him, expecting to die.

"I am the Emperor!" cried Harrison. "Do you hear? I am the Emperor! Everybody must do what I say at once!" He stamped his foot and the studio shook.

"Even as I stand here—" he bellowed, "crippled, hobbled, sickened—I am   55
a greater ruler than any man who ever lived! Now watch me become what I *can* become!"

Harrison tore the straps of his handicap harness like wet tissue paper, tore straps guaranteed to support five thousand pounds.

Harrison's scrap-iron handicaps crashed to the floor.

Harrison thrust his thumbs under the bar of the padlock that secured his head harness. The bar snapped like celery. Harrison smashed his headphones and spectacles against the wall.

He flung away his rubber-ball nose, revealed a man that would have awed Thor, the god of thunder.

"I shall now select my Empress!" he said, looking down on the cowering   60
people. "Let the first woman who dares rise to her feet claim her mate and her throne!"

A moment passed, and then a ballerina arose, swaying like a willow.

Harrison plucked the mental handicap from her ear, snapped off her physical handicaps with marvellous delicacy. Last of all, he removed her mask.

She was blindingly beautiful.

"Now—" said Harrison, taking her hand, "shall we show the people the meaning of the word dance? Music!" he commanded.

The musicians scrambled back into their chairs, and Harrison stripped   65
them of their handicaps, too. "Play your best," he told them, "and I'll make you barons and dukes and earls."

The music began. It was normal at first — cheap, silly, false. But Harrison snatched two musicians from their chairs, waved them like batons as he sang the music as he wanted it played. He slammed them back into their chairs.

The music began again and was much improved.

Harrison and his Empress merely listened to the music for a while — listened gravely, as though synchronizing their heartbeats with it.

They shifted their weights to their toes.

Harrison placed his big hands on the girl's tiny waist, letting her sense the weightlessness that would soon be hers. 70

And then, in an explosion of joy and grace, into the air they sprang!

Not only were the laws of the land abandoned, but the law of gravity and the laws of motion as well.

They reeled, whirled, swiveled, flounced, capered, gamboled, and spun.

They leaped like deer on the moon.

The studio ceiling was thirty feet high, but each leap brought the dancers nearer to it. 75

It became their obvious intention to kiss the ceiling.

They kissed it.

And then, neutralizing gravity with love and pure will, they remained suspended in air inches below the ceiling, and they kissed each other for a long, long time.

It was then that Diana Moon Glampers, the Handicapper General, came into the studio with a double-barreled ten-gauge shotgun. She fired twice, and the Emperor and the Empress were dead before they hit the floor.

Diana Moon Glampers loaded the gun again. She aimed it at the musicians and told them they had ten seconds to get their handicaps back on. 80

It was then that the Bergerons' television tube burned out.

Hazel turned to comment about the blackout to George. But George had gone out into the kitchen for a can of beer.

George came back in with the beer, paused while a handicap signal shook him up. And then he sat down again. "You been crying?" he said to Hazel.

"Yup," she said.

"What about?" he said.

"I forget," she said. "Something real sad on television." 85

"What was it?" he said.

"It's all kind of mixed up in my mind," said Hazel.

"Forget sad things," said George.

"I always do," said Hazel. 90

"That's my girl," said George. He winced. There was the sound of a riveting gun in his head.

"Gee — I could tell that one was a doozy," said Hazel.

"You can say that again," said George.

"Gee —" said Hazel, "I could tell that one was a doozy." *[1961]*

≡ THINKING ABOUT THE TEXT

1. The famous nineteenth-century French historian Alexis de Tocqueville was impressed by American democracy but worried about its tendency to gravitate toward centrism, especially in small towns. Is this story a satire or a parody of that pressure to conform?

2. Does our culture have difficulty with difference, with those, say, with a very low or a very high IQ or with rebels, saints, and eccentrics? Give examples to support your answer.

3. If you read just the first sentence, would you assume that this is a story about a utopia? Since it is not, what is being satirized? Affirmative action? Authoritarian governments? Fear of difference?

4. What does "all men are created equal" mean? Do you think the meaning of this statement has changed over time?

5. What impulse does Harrison demonstrate when he rebels? Why does Glampers kill him?

≡ MAKING COMPARISONS

1. How is Harrison more or less of a hero than Captain Black?

2. Compare the reasons for death at the end of all three stories.

3. How could any of the victims in these stories have avoided their fates?

≡ WRITING ABOUT ISSUES

1. Write a comparison between "Mars is Heaven!" and "The Nine Billion Names of God," focusing on the thinking of the space explorers and the scientists in the stories.

2. Write an essay that explores the interplay of science and religion in both Bradbury's and Clarke's stories.

3. Write an essay that argues that "Harrison Bergeron" is perhaps an attack on conservative or liberal ideas — that is, that the story satirizes the quest for equality, or that it is actually about the danger of the authoritarian mind, or that perhaps Vonnegut had something else on his mind.

4. Read Harlan Ellison's dystopic story "'Repent, Harlequin!' Said the Ticktockman," and write a comparison to "Harrison Bergeron," focusing on the idea of the rebel in society.

≡ Fairy Tale Journeys: Re-Visions of a Story

CHARLES PERRAULT, "Little Red Riding Hood"

JACOB AND WILHELM GRIMM, "Little Red Cap"

ANGELA CARTER, "The Company of Wolves"

The story of Little Red Riding Hood is still told to children throughout the world. Her adventure in facing mortal danger is part of their education. What, though, do they learn from this narrative? Scholars have suggested various interpretations, many of which hold that the tale helps its young readers face their own childhood fears. Among the best-known and most provocative interpreters of the story is the psychoanalyst Bruno Bettelheim, who sees it as a symbolic treatment of a girl's effort to understand her sexual development. In this view, the story teaches girls to work through adolescent anxieties. But whatever decoding the tale receives, two aspects of it remain important. First, it depicts a child's journey from innocence to experience, however these terms are defined. Little Red Riding Hood learns something from her encounters with the murderous wolf, and she does so largely on her own. Several versions of her story exist. Because this tale of a perilous journey is so popular and has circulated in various forms, we invite you to compare three versions of it: Charles Perrault's from the seventeenth century, the Brothers Grimm's from the nineteenth century, and Angela Carter's modern variation. Note that the Grimms' tale does not stray too far from Perrault's, at least not in representing Little Red Riding Hood as an innocent in need of male protection. Under the influence of contemporary feminism, however, Carter feels no need to conform to the fairy-tale tradition. As a result, Little Red Riding Hood is freed not only from genre conventions but also from a centuries-old stereotype about passive females.

≡ BEFORE YOU READ

Write down what you remember about the story of Little Red Riding Hood, and then compare your version with those of your classmates. What elements of the story do your class's various renditions have in common? What differences, if any, emerge? Why do you think the story has been so popular?

CHARLES PERRAULT
Little Red Riding Hood

Along with the Brothers Grimm, Charles Perrault (1628–1703) was the most influential teller of the fairy tales many of us learned as children. Born in Paris to a fairly wealthy family, Perrault was trained as a lawyer. For his literary and

© Bettmann/Corbis

© Bettmann/Corbis   © Sophie Bassouls/Sygma/Corbis

philosophical achievements, however, Perrault was elected to the prestigious Acadé-
mie Française in 1671. During his lifetime, he and others were involved in a major
cultural dispute over the relative merits of ancient authors and modern ones, with
Perrault favoring the more up-to-date group. Later generations remember him best,
though, for his 1697 book Stories or Tales from Times Past, with Morals: Tales of
Mother Goose. *This collection included "Le Petit Chaperon Rouge," which English-*
speaking readers have come to know as "Little Red Riding Hood." This story did not
completely originate with Perrault; probably he had heard folktales containing some
of its narrative elements. Nevertheless, his version became popular on publication
and has remained so ever since.

Once upon a time there lived in a certain village a little country girl, the petti-
est creature who was ever seen. Her mother was excessively fond of her, and
her grandmother doted on her still more. This good woman had a little red riding hood made for her. It suited the girl so extremely well that everybody called
her Little Red Riding Hood.

One day her mother, having made some cakes, said to her, "Go, my dear, and see how your grandmother is doing, for I hear she has been very ill. Take her a cake, and this little pot of butter."

Little Red Riding Hood set out immediately to go to her grandmother, who lived in another village.

As she was going through the wood, she met with a wolf, who had a very great mind to eat her up, but he dared not, because of some woodcutters working nearby in the forest. He asked her where she was going. The poor child, who did not know that it was dangerous to stay and talk to a wolf, said to him, "I am going to see my grandmother and carry her a cake and a little pot of butter from my mother."

"Does she live far off?" said the wolf.   5

"Oh I say," answered Little Red Riding Hood. "It is beyond that mill you see there, at the first house in the village."

"Well," said the wolf, "and I'll go and see her too. I'll go this way and go you that, and we shall see who will be there first."

The wolf ran as fast as he could, taking the shortest path, and the little girl took a roundabout way, entertaining herself by gathering nuts, running after butterflies, and gathering bouquets of little flowers. It was not long before the wolf arrived at the old woman's house. He knocked at the door: tap, tap.

"Who's there?"

"Your grandchild, Little Red Riding Hood," replied the wolf, counterfeiting   10
her voice, "who has brought you a cake and a little pot of butter sent you by Mother."

The good grandmother, who was in bed because she was somewhat ill, cried out, "Pull the bobbin, and the latch will go up."

The wolf pulled the bobbin, and the door opened, and then he immediately fell upon the good woman and ate her up in a moment, for it had been more than three days since he had eaten. He then shut the door and got into the grandmother's bed, expecting Little Red Riding Hood, who came some time afterwards and knocked at the door: tap, tap.

"Who's there?"

Little Red Riding Hood, hearing the big voice of the wolf, was at first afraid but, believing her grandmother had a cold and was hoarse, answered, "It is your grandchild Little Red Riding Hood, who has brought you a cake and a little pot of butter Mother sends you."

The wolf cried out to her, softening his voice as much as he could, "Pull the   15
bobbin, and the latch will go up."

Little Red Riding Hood pulled the bobbin, and the door opened.

The wolf, seeing her come in, said to her, hiding himself under the bedclothes, "Put the cake and the little pot of butter upon the stool, and come get into bed with me."

Little Red Riding Hood took off her clothes and got into bed. She was greatly amazed to see how her grandmother looked in her nightclothes and said to her, "Grandmother, what big arms you have!"

"All the better to hug you with, my dear."

"Grandmother, what big legs you have!"   20
"All the better to run with, my child."
"Grandmother, what big ears you have!"
"All the better to hear with, my child."
"Grandmother, what big eyes you have!"
"All the better to see with, my child."   25
"Grandmother, what big teeth you have got!"
"All the better to eat you up with."
And saying these words, this wicked wolf fell upon Little Red Riding Hood,
and ate her all up.

Moral: Children, especially attractive, well-bred young ladies, should never talk
to strangers, for if they should do so, they may well provide dinner for a wolf. I
say "wolf," but there are various kinds of wolves. There are also those who
are charming, quiet, polite, unassuming, complacent, and sweet, who pursue
young women at home and in the streets. And unfortunately, it is these gentle
wolves who are the most dangerous ones of all.   *[1697]*

≡ THINKING ABOUT THE TEXT

1. To what extent does it matter to the story that Little Red Riding Hood is
   pretty? Would your reaction be the same if you learned she was homely
   or if you did not know how she looked? Explain.

2. The two main female characters are Little Red Riding Hood and her
   grandmother. Although the girl's mother appears briefly at the start,
   she then disappears from the narrative. What purposes are served by
   Perrault's leaving her out?

3. How would you describe Little Red Riding Hood as Perrault depicts her?
   Refer to specific details of the text.

4. In this version, Little Red Riding Hood dies. Would you draw different
   ideas from the text if she had lived? If so, what?

5. Does Perrault's moral seem well connected to the preceding story? Why,
   or why not? What metaphoric wolves might this moral apply to?

JACOB AND WILHELM GRIMM
Little Red Cap

*Jacob Grimm (1785–1863) and Wilhelm Grimm (1786–1859) were born in
Hanau, Germany, and studied law at Marburg University. They served as linguistics
professors at Göttingen University and made major contributions to the historical
study of language. The Grimms began to collect folktales from various oral European
traditions for their friends but later published their efforts for both children and
adults. Their methods became a model for the scientific collection of folktales and folk*

songs. Today they are known best for their volume Children's and Household Tales, *which was first published in 1812 and went through six more editions, the last in 1857. Their book included their version of the Little Red Riding Hood story, although their title for it was (in English translation) "Little Red Cap."*

Once upon a time there was a sweet little girl. Everyone who saw her liked her, but most of all her grandmother, who did not know what to give the child next. Once she gave her a little cap made of red velvet. Because it suited her so well, and she wanted to wear it all the time, she came to be known as Little Red Cap.

One day her mother said to her, "Come Little Red Cap. Here is a piece of cake and a bottle of wine. Take them to your grandmother. She is sick and weak, and they will do her well. Mind your manners, and give her my greetings. Behave yourself on the way, and do not leave the path, or you might fall down and break the glass, and then there will be nothing for your grandmother. And when you enter her parlor, don't forget to say 'Good morning,' and don't peer into all the corners first."

"I'll do everything just right," said Little Red Cap, shaking her mother's hand.

The grandmother lived out in the woods, a half hour from the village. When Little Red Cap entered the woods, a wolf came up to her. She did not know what a wicked animal he was and was not afraid of him.

"Good day to you, Little Red Cap." 5

"Thank you, wolf."

"Where are you going so early, Little Red Cap?"

"To Grandmother's."

"And what are you carrying under your apron?"

"Grandmother is sick and weak, and I am taking her some cake and wine. 10 We baked yesterday, and they should be good for her and give her strength."

"Little Red Cap, just where does your grandmother live?"

"Her house is a good quarter hour from here in the woods, under the three large oak trees. There's a hedge of hazel bushes there. You must know the place," said Little Red Cap.

The wolf thought to himself, "Now that sweet young thing is a tasty bite for me. She will taste even better than the old woman. You must be sly, and you can catch them both."

He walked along a little while with Little Red Cap. Then he said, "Little Red Cap, just look at the beautiful flowers that are all around us. Why don't you go and take a look? And I don't believe you can hear how beautifully the birds are singing. You are walking along as though you were on your way to school. It is very beautiful in the woods."

Little Red Cap opened her eyes, and when she saw the sunbeams dancing 15 to and fro through the trees and how the ground was covered with beautiful flowers, she thought, "If I take a fresh bouquet to Grandmother, she will be very pleased. Anyway, it is still early, and I'll be home on time." And she ran off the path into the woods looking for flowers. Each time she picked one, she thought that she could see an even more beautiful one a little way off, and she ran after it, going farther and farther into the woods. But the wolf ran straight to the grandmother's house and knocked on the door.

"Who's there?"

"Little Red Cap. I'm bringing you some cake and wine. Open the door."

"Just press the latch," called out the grandmother. "I'm too weak to get up."

The wolf pressed the latch, and the door opened. He stepped inside, went straight to the grandmother's bed, and ate her up. Then he put on her clothes, put her cap on his head, got into her bed, and pulled the curtains shut.

Little Red Cap had run after the flowers. After she had gathered so many   20
that she could not carry any more, she remembered her grandmother and then continued on her way to her house. She found, to her surprise, that the door was open. She walked into the parlor, and everything looked so strange that she thought, "Oh, my God, why am I so afraid? I usually like it at Grandmother's."

She called out, "Good morning!" but received no answer.

Then she went to the bed and pulled back the curtains. Grandmother was lying there with her cap pulled down over her face and looking very strange.

"Oh, Grandmother, what big ears you have!"

"All the better to hear you with."

"Oh, Grandmother, what big eyes you have!"   25

"All the better to see you with."

"Oh, Grandmother, what big hands you have!"

"All the better to grab you with!"

"Oh, Grandmother, what a horribly big mouth you have!"

"All the better to eat you with!"   30

The wolf had scarcely finished speaking when he jumped from the bed with a single leap and ate up poor Little Red Cap. As soon as the wolf had satisfied his desires, he climbed back into bed, fell asleep, and began to snore very loudly.

A huntsman was just passing by. He thought, "The old woman is snoring so loudly. You had better see if something is wrong with her."

He stepped into the parlor, and when he approached the bed, he saw the wolf lying there. "So here I find you, you old sinner," he said. "I have been hunting for you a long time."

He was about to aim his rifle when it occurred to him that the wolf might have eaten the grandmother and that she still might be rescued. So instead of shooting, he took a pair of scissors and began to cut open the wolf's belly. After a few cuts he saw the red cap shining through, and after a few more cuts the girl jumped out, crying, "Oh, I was so frightened! It was so dark inside the wolf's body!"

And then the grandmother came out as well, alive but hardly able to   35
breathe. Then Little Red Cap fetched some large stones. She filled the wolf's body with them, and when he woke up and tried to run away, the stones were so heavy that he immediately fell down dead.

The three of them were happy. The huntsman skinned the wolf and went home with the pelt. The grandmother ate the cake and drank the wine that

Little Red Cap had brought. And Little Red Cap thought, "As long as I live, I will never leave the path and run off into the woods by myself if Mother tells me not to."

They also tell how Little Red Cap was taking some baked things to her grandmother another time, when another wolf spoke to her and wanted her to leave the path. But Little Red Cap took care and went straight to Grandmother's. She told her that she had seen the wolf and that he had wished her a good day but had stared at her in a wicked manner. "If we hadn't been on a public road, he would have eaten me up," she said.

"Come," said the grandmother. "Let's lock the door, so he can't get in."

Soon afterward the wolf knocked on the door and called out, "Open up, Grandmother. It's Little Red Cap, and I'm bringing you some baked things."

They remained silent and did not open the door. Gray-Head crept around   40
the house several times and finally jumped onto the roof. He wanted to wait until Little Red Cap went home that evening and then follow her and eat her up in the darkness. But the grandmother saw what he was up to. There was a large stone trough in front of the house.

"Fetch a bucket, Little Red Cap," she said to the child. "Yesterday I cooked some sausage. Carry the water that I boiled them with to the trough." Little Red Cap carried water until the large, large trough was clear full. The smell of sausage arose into the wolf's nose. He sniffed and looked down, stretching his neck so long that he could no longer hold himself, and he began to slide. He slid off the roof, fell into the trough, and drowned. And Little Red Cap returned home happily, and no one harmed her.   *[1857]*

≡ THINKING ABOUT THE TEXT

1. Why do you think that, at the beginning of the tale, the Grimms emphasize how sweet and likable Little Red Cap is?

2. To what extent do you blame Little Red Cap for being distracted by the beauty of nature? Explain your reasoning.

3. The Grimms have Little Red Cap and her grandmother rescued by a hunter. Do you agree or disagree that the Grimm's story implies that women always need help from a man?

4. The wolf dies because Little Red Cap has filled his body with stones. Why do you think the Grimms did not have the huntsman simply shoot the wolf after freeing Little Red Cap and her grandmother?

5. Why do you think the Grimms added the second story? What is its effect?

≡ MAKING COMPARISONS

1. Does Little Red Riding Hood seem basically the same in both Perrault's version and the Grimms' version? Refer to specific details from both texts.

2. In Perrault's tale, the wolf persuades Little Red Riding Hood to take off her clothes and get into bed with him. In the Grimms' account, the wolf jumps up from the bed and eats her. How significant is this difference between the two versions?

3. In Perrault's version, Little Red Riding Hood and her grandmother die. In the Grimms' tale, on the other hand, they are rescued. Do you therefore see these two versions as putting forth different views of life? Explain.

ANGELA CARTER
The Company of Wolves

A native of Sussex, England, Angela Carter (1940–1991) worked in various genres, writing novels, short stories, screenplays, essays, and newspaper articles. Her fiction is most known for imaginatively refashioning classic tales of fantasy, including supernatural and gothic thrillers as well as fairy tales. Often, Carter rewrote these narratives from a distinctly female point of view, challenging what she saw as their patriarchal values and using them to explore the psychology of both genders. "The Company of Wolves," her version of the Little Red Riding Hood tale, was first published in the journal Bananas *in 1977. It then appeared in Carter's short-story volume* The Bloody Chamber *(1979) and was reprinted in* Burning Your Boats *(1995), a posthumous collection of all her stories. This tale also served as the basis for a 1984 film of the same title, which Carter wrote with director Neil Jordan.*

One beast and only one howls in the woods by night.

The wolf is carnivore incarnate, and he's as cunning as he is ferocious; once he's had a taste of flesh then nothing else will do.

At night, the eyes of wolves shine like candle flames, yellowish, reddish, but that is because the pupils of their eyes fatten on darkness and catch the light from your lantern to flash it back to you — red for danger; if a wolf's eyes reflect only moonlight, then they gleam a cold and unnatural green, a mineral, a piercing color. If the benighted traveler spies those luminous, terrible sequins stitched suddenly on the black thickets, then he knows he must run, if fear has not struck him stock-still.

But those eyes are all you will be able to glimpse of the forest assassins as they cluster invisibly round your smell of meat as you go through the wood unwisely late. They will be like shadows, they will be like wraiths, gray members of a congregation of nightmare; hark! his long, wavering howl . . . an aria of fear made audible.

The wolfsong is the sound of the rending you will suffer, in itself a murdering.   5

It is winter and cold weather. In this region of mountain and forest, there is now nothing for the wolves to eat. Goats and sheep are locked up in the byre,° the deer departed for the remaining pasturage on the southern slopes — wolves grow lean and famished. There is so little flesh on them that you could count the starveling ribs through their pelts, if they gave you time before they pounced. Those slavering jaws; the lolling tongue; the rime of saliva on the grizzled chops — of all the teeming perils of the night and the forest, ghosts, hobgoblins, ogres that grill babies upon gridirons, witches that fatten their captives in cages for cannibal tables, the wolf is worst for he cannot listen to reason.

You are always in danger in the forest, where no people are. Step between the portals of the great pines where the shaggy branches tangle about you, trapping the unwary traveler in nets as if the vegetation itself were in a plot with the wolves who live there, as though the wicked trees go fishing on behalf of their friends — step between the gateposts of the forest with the greatest trepidation and infinite precautions, for if you stray from the path for one instant, the wolves will eat you. They are gray as famine, they are as unkind as plague.

The grave-eyed children of the sparse villages always carry knives with them when they go out to tend the little flocks of goats that provide the homesteads with acrid milk and rank, maggoty cheeses. Their knives are half as big as they are, the blades are sharpened daily.

But the wolves have ways of arriving at your own hearthside. We try and try but sometimes we cannot keep them out. There is no winter's night the cottager does not fear to see a lean, gray, famished snout questing under the door, and there was a woman once bitten in her own kitchen as she was straining the macaroni.

Fear and flee the wolf; for, worst of all, the wolf may be more than he   10
seems.

There was a hunter once, near here, that trapped a wolf in a pit. This wolf had massacred the sheep and goats; eaten up a mad old man who used to live by himself in a hut halfway up the mountain and sing to Jesus all day; pounced on a girl looking after the sheep, but she made such a commotion that men came with rifles and scared him away and tried to track him into the forest but he was cunning and easily gave them the slip. So this hunter dug a pit and put a duck in it, for bait, all alive-oh; and he covered the pit with straw smeared with wolf dung. Quack, quack! went the duck and a wolf came slinking out of the forest, a big one, a heavy one, he weighed as much as a grown man, and the straw gave way beneath him — into the pit he tumbled. The hunter jumped down after him, slit his throat, cut off all his paws for a trophy.

And then no wolf at all lay in front of the hunter but the bloody trunk of a man, headless, footless, dying, dead.

A witch from up the valley once turned an entire wedding party into wolves because the groom had settled on another girl. She used to order them to visit her, at night, from spite, and they would sit and howl around her cottage for her, serenading her with their misery.

byre: Barn or shed.

Not so very long ago, a young woman in our village married a man who vanished clean away on her wedding night. The bed was made with new sheets and the bride lay down in it; the groom said, he was going out to relieve himself, insisted on it, for the sake of decency, and she drew the coverlet up to her chin and she lay there. And she waited and she waited and then she waited again — surely he's been gone a long time? Until she jumps up in bed and shrieks to hear a howling, coming on the wind from the forest.

That long-drawn, wavering howl has, for all its fearful resonance, some   15
inherent sadness in it, as if the beasts would love to be less beastly if only they knew how and never cease to mourn their own condition. There is a vast melancholy in the canticles° of the wolves, melancholy infinite as the forest, endless as these long nights of winter and yet that ghastly sadness, that mourning for their own, irremediable appetites, can never move the heart for not one phrase in it hints at the possibility of redemption; grace could not come to the wolf from its own despair, only through some external mediator, so that, sometimes, the beast will look as if he half welcomes the knife that dispatches him.

The young woman's brothers searched the outhouses and the haystacks but never found any remains, so the sensible girl dried her eyes and found herself another husband not too shy to piss into a pot who spent the nights indoors. She gave him a pair of bonny babies and all went right as a trivet until, one freezing night, the night of the solstice, the hinge of the year when things do not fit together as well as they should, the longest night, her first good man came home again.

A great thump on the door announced him as she was stirring the soup for the father of her children, and she knew him the moment she lifted the latch to him although it was years since she'd worn black for him and now he was in rags and his hair hung down his back and never saw a comb, alive with lice.

"Here I am again, missus," he said. "Get me my bowl of cabbage and be quick about it."

Then her second husband came in with wood for the fire and when the first one saw she'd slept with another man and, worse, clapped his red eyes on her little children who'd crept into the kitchen to see what all the din was about, he shouted: "I wish I were a wolf again, to teach this whore a lesson!" So a wolf he instantly became and tore off the eldest boy's left foot before he was chopped up with the hatchet they used for chopping logs. But when the wolf lay bleeding and gasping its last, the pelt peeled off again and he was just as he had been, years ago, when he ran away from his marriage bed, so that she wept and her second husband beat her.

They say there's an ointment the Devil gives you that turns you into a wolf the   20
minute you rub it on. Or that he was born feet first and had a wolf for his father and his torso is a man's but his legs and genitals are a wolf's. And he has a wolf's heart.

canticles: Songs or chants.

Seven years is a werewolf's natural span but if you burn his human clothing you condemn him to wolfishness for the rest of his life, so old wives hereabouts think it some protection to throw a hat or an apron at the werewolf, as if clothes made the man. Yet by the eyes, those phosphorescent eyes, you know him in all his shapes; the eyes alone unchanged by metamorphosis.

Before he can become a wolf, the lycanthrope° strips stark naked. If you spy a naked man among the pines, you must run as if the Devil were after you.

It is midwinter and the robin, the friend of man, sits on the handle of the gardener's spade and sings. It is the worst time in all the year for wolves, but this strong-minded child insists she will go off through the wood. She is quite sure the wild beasts cannot harm her although, well-warned, she lays a carving knife in the basket her mother has packed with cheeses. There is a bottle of harsh liquor distilled from brambles; a batch of flat oatcakes baked on the hearthstone; a pot or two of jam. The flaxen-haired girl will take these delicious gifts to a reclusive grandmother so old the burden of her years is crushing her to death. Granny lives two hours' trudge through the winter woods; the child wraps herself up in her thick shawl, draws it over her head. She steps into her stout wooden shoes; she is dressed and ready and it is Christmas Eve. The malign door of the solstice still swings upon its hinges, but she has been too much loved ever to feel scared.

Children do not stay young for long in this savage country. There are no toys for them to play with, so they work hard and grow wise, but this one, so pretty and the youngest of her family, a little late-comer, had been indulged by her mother and the grandmother who'd knitted her the red shawl that, today, has the ominous if brilliant look of blood on snow. Her breasts have just begun to swell; her hair is like lint, so fair it hardly makes a shadow on her pale forehead; her cheeks are an emblematic scarlet and white and she has just started her woman's bleeding, the clock inside her that will strike, henceforward, once a month.

She stands and moves within the invisible pentacle° of her own virginity. 25
She is an unbroken egg; she is a sealed vessel; she has inside her a magic space the entrance to which is shut tight with a plug of membrane; she is a closed system; she does not know how to shiver. She has her knife and she is afraid of nothing.

Her father might forbid her, if he were home, but he is away in the forest, gathering wood, and her mother cannot deny her.

The forest closed upon her like a pair of jaws.

There is always something to look at in the forest, even in the middle of winter — the huddled mounds of birds, succumbed to the lethargy of the season, heaped on the creaking boughs and too forlorn to sing; the bright frills of the winter fungi on the blotched trunks of the trees; the cuneiform° slots of rabbits and deer, the herringbone tracks of the birds, a hare as lean as a rasher of bacon streaking across the path where the thin sunlight dapples the russet brakes of last year's bracken.

---

lycanthrope: Werewolf.   **pentacle:** Five-pointed star; also called a pentagram.   **cuneiform:** Wedge-shaped.

When she heard the freezing howl of a distant wolf, her practiced hand sprang to the handle of her knife, but she saw no sign of a wolf at all, nor of a naked man, neither, but then she heard a clattering among the brushwood and there sprang on to the path a fully clothed one, a very handsome young one, in the green coat and wide-awake hat of a hunter, laden with carcasses of game birds. She had her hand on her knife at the first rustle of twigs, but he laughed with a flash of white teeth when he saw her and made her a comic yet flattering little bow; she'd never seen such a fine fellow before, not among the rustic clowns of her native village. So on they went together, through the thickening light of the afternoon.

Soon they were laughing and joking like old friends. When he offered to   30
carry her basket, she gave it to him although her knife was in it because he told her his rifle would protect them. As the day darkened, it began to snow again; she felt the first flakes settle on her eyelashes, but now there was only half a mile to go and there would be a fire, and hot tea, and a welcome, a warm one, surely, for the dashing huntsman as well as for herself.

This young man had a remarkable object in his pocket. It was a compass. She looked at the little round glass face in the palm of his hand and watched the wavering needle with a vague wonder. He assured her this compass had taken him safely through the wood on his hunting trip because the needle always told him with perfect accuracy where the north was. She did not believe it; she knew she should never leave the path on the way through the wood or else she would be lost instantly. He laughed at her again; gleaming trails of spittle clung to his teeth. He said, if he plunged off the path into the forest that surrounded them, he could guarantee to arrive at her grandmother's house a good quarter of an hour before she did, plotting his way through the undergrowth with his compass, while she trudged the long way, along the winding path.

I don't believe you. Besides, aren't you afraid of the wolves?

He only tapped the gleaming butt of his rifle and grinned.

Is it a bet? he asked her. Shall we make a game of it? What will you give me if I get to your grandmother's house before you?

What would you like? she asked disingenuously.   35

A kiss.

Commonplaces of a rustic seduction; she lowered her eyes and blushed.

He went through the undergrowth and took her basket with him but she forgot to be afraid of the beasts, although now the moon was rising, for she wanted to dawdle on her way to make sure the handsome gentleman would win his wager.

Grandmother's house stood by itself a little way out of the village. The freshly falling snow blew in eddies about the kitchen garden, and the young man stepped delicately up the snowy path to the door as if he were reluctant to get his feet wet, swinging his bundle of game and the girl's basket and humming a little tune to himself.

There is a faint trace of blood on his chin; he has been snacking on his catch.   40

He rapped upon the panels with his knuckles.

Aged and frail, granny is three-quarters succumbed to the mortality the ache in her bones promises her and almost ready to give in entirely. A boy came out from the village to build up her hearth for the night an hour ago and the kitchen crackles with busy firelight. She has her Bible for company, she is a pious old woman. She is propped up on several pillows in the bed set into the wall peasant-fashion, wrapped up in the patchwork quilt she made before she was married, more years ago than she cares to remember. Two china spaniels with liver-colored blotches on their coats and black noses sit on either side of the fireplace. There is a bright rug of woven rags on the pantiles. The grandfather clock ticks away her eroding time.

We keep the wolves outside by living well.

He rapped upon the panels with his hairy knuckles.

It is your granddaughter, he mimicked in a high soprano.   45

Lift up the latch and walk in, my darling.

You can tell them by their eyes, eyes of a beast of prey, nocturnal, devastating eyes as red as a wound; you can hurl your Bible at him and your apron after, granny, you thought that was a sure prophylactic against these infernal vermin . . . now call on Christ and his mother and all the angels in heaven to protect you but it won't do you any good.

His feral muzzle is sharp as a knife; he drops his golden burden of gnawed pheasant on the table and puts down your dear girl's basket, too. Oh, my God, what have you done with her?

Off with his disguise, that coat of forest-colored cloth, the hat with the feather tucked into the ribbon; his matted hair streams down his white shirt and she can see the lice moving in it. The sticks in the hearth shift and hiss; night and the forest has come into the kitchen with darkness tangled in its hair.

He strips off his shirt. His skin is the color and texture of vellum. A crisp   50
stripe of hair runs down his belly, his nipples are ripe and dark as poison fruit, but he's so thin you could count the ribs under his skin if only he gave you the time. He strips off his trousers and she can see how hairy his legs are. His genitals, huge. Ah! huge.

The last thing the old lady saw in all this world was a young man, eyes like cinders, naked as a stone, approaching her bed.

The wolf is carnivore incarnate.

When he had finished with her, he licked his chops and quickly dressed himself again, until he was just as he had been when he came through her door. He burned the inedible hair in the fireplace and wrapped the bones up in a napkin that he hid away under the bed in the wooden chest in which he found a clean pair of sheets. These he carefully put on the bed instead of the tell-tale stained ones he stowed away in the laundry basket. He plumped up the pillows and shook out the patchwork quilt, he picked up the Bible from the floor, closed it and laid it on the table. All was as it had been before except that grandmother was gone. The sticks twitched in the grate, the clock ticked and the young man sat patiently, deceitfully beside the bed in granny's nightcap.

Rat-a-tap-tap.

Who's there, he quavers in granny's antique falsetto.   55

Only your granddaughter.

So she came in, bringing with her a flurry of snow that melted in tears on the tiles, and perhaps she was a little disappointed to see only her grandmother sitting beside the fire. But then he flung off the blanket and sprang to the door, pressing his back against it so that she could not get out again.

The girl looked round the room and saw there was not even the indentation of a head on the smooth cheek of the pillow and how, for the first time she'd seen it so, the Bible lay closed on the table. The tick of the clock cracked like a whip. She wanted her knife from her basket, but she did not dare reach for it because his eyes were fixed upon her — huge eyes that now seemed to shine with a unique, interior light, eyes the size of saucers, saucers full of Greek fire, diabolic phosphorescence.

What big eyes you have.

All the better to see you with.   60

No trace at all of the old woman except for a tuft of white hair that had caught in the bark of an unburned log. When the girl saw that, she knew she was in danger of death.

Where is my grandmother?

There's nobody here but we two, my darling.

Now a great howling rose up all around them, near, very near, as close as the kitchen garden, the howling of a multitude of wolves; she knew the worst wolves are hairy on the inside and she shivered, in spite of the scarlet shawl she pulled more closely round herself as if it could protect her although it was as red as the blood she must spill.

Who has come to sing us carols, she said.   65

Those are the voices of my brothers, darling; I love the company of wolves. Look out of the window and you'll see them.

Snow half-caked the lattice and she opened it to look into the garden. It was a white night of moon and snow; the blizzard whirled round the gaunt, grey beasts who squatted on their haunches among the rows of winter cabbage, pointing their sharp snouts to the moon and howling as if their hearts would break. Ten wolves; twenty wolves — so many wolves she could not count them, howling in concert as if demented or deranged. Their eyes reflected the light from the kitchen and shone like a hundred candles.

It is very cold, poor things, she said; no wonder they howl so.

She closed the window on the wolves' threnody° and took off her scarlet shawl, the color of poppies, the color of sacrifices, the color of her menses, and, since her fear did her no good, she ceased to be afraid.

What shall I do with my shawl?   70

Throw it on the fire, dear one. You won't need it again.

She bundled up her shawl and threw it on the blaze, which instantly consumed it. Then she drew her blouse over her head; her small breasts gleamed as if the snow had invaded the room.

What shall I do with my blouse?

threnody: Lament or dirge.

Into the fire with it, too, my pet.

The thin muslin went flaring up the chimney like a magic bird and now   75
off came her skirt, her woolen stockings, her shoes, and on to the fire they went,
too, and were gone for good. The firelight shone through the edges of her skin;
now she was clothed only in her untouched integument° of flesh. This dazzling,
naked she combed out her hair with her fingers; her hair looked white as the snow
outside. Then went directly to the man with red eyes in whose unkempt mane the
lice moved; she stood up on tiptoe and unbuttoned the collar of his shirt.

What big arms you have.

All the better to hug you with.

Every wolf in the world now howled a prothalamion° outside the window
as she freely gave the kiss she owed him.

What big teeth you have!

She saw how his jaw began to slaver and the room was full of the clamor of   80
the forest's Liebestod° but the wise child never flinched, even when he answered:

All the better to eat you with.

The girl burst out laughing; she knew she was nobody's meat. She laughed
at him full in the face, she ripped off his shirt for him and flung it into the fire,
in the fiery wake of her own discarded clothing. The flames danced like dead
souls on Walpurgisnacht,° and the old bones under the bed set up a terrible
clattering, but she did not pay them any heed.

Carnivore incarnate, only immaculate flesh appeases him.

She will lay his fearful head on her lap and she will pick out the lice from
his pelt and perhaps she will put the lice into her mouth and eat them, as he
will bid her, as she would do in a savage marriage ceremony.

The blizzard will die down.   85

The blizzard died down, leaving the mountains as randomly covered with
snow as if a blind woman had thrown a sheet over them, the upper branches of
the forest pines limed, creaking, swollen with the fall.

Snowlight, moonlight, a confusion of paw-prints.

All silent, all still.

Midnight; and the clock strikes. It is Christmas Day, the werewolves' birthday, the door of the solstice stands wide open; let them all sink through.

See! sweet and sound she sleeps in granny's bed, between the paws of the   90
tender wolf.   [1977]

integument: Outer covering, such as animal skin or seed coat.   **prothalamion:** Wed-
ding song.   **Liebestod:** Final aria in Richard Wagner's opera *Tristan und Isolde*, in which
Isolde sings over Tristan's dead body and ultimately dies herself.   **Walpurgisnacht:** May
Day eve, the medieval witches' sabbath.

≡ THINKING ABOUT THE TEXT

1. The story begins with a section about wolves before it gets to the Little
   Red Riding Hood narrative. What image of wolves does this prologue
   convey? What in particular seems the purpose of the extended anecdote
   about the wife with two husbands?

2. Point out various places where Carter diverges from the conventions of the fairy tale.

3. Do you find it surprising that the girl does not get to her grandmother's house first? Do you suspect that the girl is not so innocent?

4. Obviously this is not a story for children. What traditional ideas about females and sexuality is Carter revising?

5. What do you conclude about the girl from her behavior at the end of the story? To what extent is "savage marriage ceremony" (para. 84) indeed an apt term for what occurs?

≡ MAKING COMPARISONS

1. To what extent is Carter's image of wolves different from Perrault's and the Grimms'? Refer to details from all three texts.

2. Several critics have described Carter's versions of fairy tales as feminist. To what extent can this term be applied to Perrault's and the Grimms' narratives as well as to hers? Define what you mean by *feminist*.

3. Would you say Carter's writing style is more realistic than that of Perrault and the Grimms? Or is the term *realism* completely irrelevant in the case of fairy tales? Explain.

≡ WRITING ABOUT ISSUES

1. Choose one of these versions of the Little Red Riding Hood story, and write an essay in which you elaborate a moral that modern *adults* might learn from it. Or write an essay in which you explain what an adolescent might learn from Carter's version.

2. Does Carter's version radically depart from Perrault's and the Grimms', or does it basically resemble them? Write an essay that addresses this question by focusing on Carter's story and one of the other two.

3. Write an essay explaining what you think you learned from a fairy tale or other fictional story that you heard as a child. If you want to contrast your thinking about the story now with your thinking about it then, do so. Feel free to compare the story you focus on with any of the versions of Little Red Riding Hood in this cluster.

4. Write your own version of the story of Little Red Riding Hood, and on a separate piece of paper write the moral you think should be drawn from your text. Then give your version to a classmate, and see if he or she can guess your moral.

■ Keep This Boy Running: Cultural Contexts for a Story

RALPH ELLISON, "Battle Royal"

CULTURAL CONTEXTS:

BOOKER T. WASHINGTON, "Atlanta Exposition Address (The Atlanta Compromise)"

W. E. B. DU BOIS, "Of Mr. Booker T. Washington"

GUNNAR MYRDAL, "Social Equality"

More than forty years after the civil rights movement of the 1960s, our national awareness of how brutal discrimination was against African Americans is diminished. Although educational and economic equality has not been completely attained, progress has been made, especially in eliminating official policies and gestures of bias. Before World War II, however, overt discrimination was common, especially in the small towns of the segregated South and the rural Midwest. African Americans were rarely allowed to hold anything other than menial jobs in small towns, and most middle-class whites knew African Americans only as maids, gardeners, and servants. African Americans were completely outside the established power structure and rarely able to complain about or obtain justice for their many grievances. Public protest was out of the question. Many African Americans even avoided private protest against their outsider status because they feared that it would worsen their situation. Among African American intellectuals and ordinary citizens, debates raged about which strategy to pursue: cooperate with the white establishment, hoping to modify hostility, or agitate for change. Generations of blacks followed the first course until the 1960s, when the nonviolent sit-ins of the civil rights movement ushered in the public protests that ended state-sanctioned segregation. Ralph Ellison's story takes place in the era of segregation and graphically portrays how marginalized African Americans were and how difficult they found it to decide on an effective strategy for progress. At the story's end, the main character, like Ellison himself, begins a lifelong journey from racism toward social justice.

≡ BEFORE YOU READ

Have you ever been in a situation in which you felt discriminated against because of your race, religion, gender, sexual orientation, or age? Did you ever see someone else suffer discrimination? Did you feel powerless? What was your strategy for dealing with this feeling?

National Archives

RALPH ELLISON
Battle Royal

Born in Oklahoma to an activist mother and an intellectual father, Ralph Ellison (1914–1994) was well grounded in literary and social matters by the time he entered Tuskegee Institute to study music in 1933. Finding the conservatism and accommodationism of Tuskegee limiting, Ellison read modernist poets like T. S. Eliot and in 1936 moved to New York, where he met writers Langston Hughes and Richard Wright. Inspired by Wright and by the works of Conrad, Dostoyevsky, and other writers of fiction, Ellison began drafting his novel Invisible Man *(1952) while he was serving in the merchant marine during World War II. Published as a short story in 1947, "Battle Royal" became the first chapter of this National Book Award–winning novel.*

It goes a long way back, some twenty years. All my life I had been looking for something, and everywhere I turned someone tried to tell me what it was. I accepted their answers too, though they were often in contradiction and even self-contradictory. I was naive. I was looking for myself and asking everyone except myself questions which I, and only I, could answer. It took me a long time and much painful boomeranging of my expectations to achieve a realization everyone else appears to have been born with: that I am nobody but myself. But first I had to discover that I am an invisible man!

And yet I am no freak of nature, not of history. I was in the cards, other things having been equal (or unequal) eighty-five years ago. I am not ashamed of my grandparents for having been slaves. I am only ashamed of myself for having at one time been ashamed. About eighty-five years ago they were told that they were free, united with others of our country in everything pertaining to the common good, and, in everything social, separate like the fingers of the hand. And they believed it. They exulted in it. They stayed in their place, worked hard, and brought up my father to do the same. But my grandfather is the one. He was an odd old guy, my grandfather, and I am told I take after him. It was he who caused the trouble. On his deathbed he called my father to him and said, "Son, after I'm gone I want you to keep up the good fight. I never told you, but our life is a war and I have been a traitor all my born days, a spy in the enemy's country ever since I give up my gun back in the Reconstruction. Live with your head in the lion's mouth. I want you to overcome 'em with yeses, undermine 'em with grins, agree 'em to death and destruction, let 'em swoller you till they vomit or bust wide open." They thought the old man had gone out of his mind. He had been the meekest of men. The younger children were rushed from the room, the shades drawn and the flame of the lamp turned so low that it sputtered on the wick like the old man's breathing. "Learn it to the younguns," he whispered fiercely; then he died.

But my folks were more alarmed over his last words than over his dying. It was as though he had not died at all, his words caused so much anxiety. I was warned emphatically to forget what he had said and, indeed, this is the first time it has been mentioned outside the family circle. It had a tremendous effect upon me, however. I could never be sure of what he meant. Grandfather had been a quiet old man who never made any trouble, yet on his deathbed he had called himself a traitor and a spy, and he had spoken of his meekness as a dangerous activity. It became a constant puzzle which lay unanswered in the back of my mind. And whenever things went well for me I remembered my grandfather and felt guilty and uncomfortable. It was as though I was carrying out his advice in spite of myself. And to make it worse, everyone loved me for it. I was praised by the most lily-white men of the town. I was considered an example of desirable conduct — just as my grandfather had been. And what puzzled me was that the old man had defined it as *treachery*. When I was praised for my conduct I felt a guilt that in some way I was doing something that was really against the wishes of the white folks, that if they had understood they would have desired me to act just the opposite, that I should have been sulky and mean, and that that really would have been what they wanted, even though they were fooled and thought they wanted me to act as I did. It made me afraid that some day they would look upon me as a traitor and I would be lost. Still I was more afraid to act any other way because they didn't like that at all. The old man's words were like a curse. On my graduation day I delivered an oration in which I showed that humility was the secret, indeed, the very essence of progress.

(Not that I believed this — how could I, remembering my grandfather? — I only believed that it worked.) It was a great success. Everyone praised me and I was invited to give the speech at a gathering of the town's leading white citizens. It was a triumph for our whole community.

It was in the main ballroom of the leading hotel. When I got there I discovered that it was on the occasion of a smoker, and I was told that since I was to be there anyway I might as well take part in the battle royal to be fought by some of my schoolmates as part of the entertainment. The battle royal came first.

All of the town's big shots were there in their tuxedoes, wolfing down the buffet foods, drinking beer and whiskey, and smoking black cigars. It was a large room with a high ceiling. Chairs were arranged in neat rows around three sides of a portable boxing ring. The fourth side was clear, revealing a gleaming space of polished floor. I had some misgivings over the battle royal, by the way. Not from a distaste for fighting, but because I didn't care too much for the other fellows who were to take part. They were tough guys who seemed to have no grandfather's curse worrying their minds. No one could mistake their toughness. And besides, I suspected that fighting a battle royal might detract from the dignity of my speech. In those pre-invisible days I visualized myself as a potential Booker T. Washington. But the other fellows didn't care too much for me either, and there were nine of them. I felt superior to them in my way, and I didn't like the manner in which we were all crowded together into the servants' elevator. Nor did they like my being there. In fact, as the warmly lighted floors flashed past the elevator we had words over the fact that I, by taking part in the fight, had knocked one of their friends out of a night's work.

We were led out of the elevator through a rococo hall into an anteroom and told to get into our fighting togs. Each of us was issued a pair of boxing gloves and ushered out into the big mirrored hall, which we entered looking cautiously about us and whispering, lest we might accidentally be heard above the noise of the room. It was foggy with cigar smoke. And already the whiskey was taking effect. I was shocked to see some of the most important men of the town quite tipsy. They were all there — bankers, lawyers, judges, doctors, fire chiefs, teachers, merchants. Even one of the more fashionable pastors. Something we could not see was going on up front. A clarinet was vibrating sensuously and the men were standing up and moving eagerly forward. We were a small tight group, clustered together, our bare upper bodies touching and shining with anticipatory sweat; while up front the big shots were becoming increasingly excited over something we still could not see. Suddenly I heard the school superintendent, who had told me to come, yell, "Bring up the shines, gentlemen! Bring up the little shines!"

We were rushed up to the front of the ballroom, where it smelled even more strongly of tobacco and whiskey. Then we were pushed into place. I almost wet my pants. A sea of faces, some hostile, some amused, ringed around us, and in the center, facing us, stood a magnificent blonde — stark naked. There was dead silence. I felt a blast of cold air chill me. I tried to back away, but they were behind me and around me. Some of the boys stood with lowered heads, trembling. I felt a wave of irrational guilt and fear. My teeth chattered,

5

my skin turned to goose flesh, my knees knocked. Yet I was strongly attracted and looked in spite of myself. Had the price of looking been blindness, I would have looked. The hair was yellow like that of a circus kewpie doll, the face heavily powdered and rouged, as though to form an abstract mask, the eyes hollow and smeared a cool blue, the color of a baboon's butt. I felt a desire to spit upon her as my eyes brushed slowly over her body. Her breasts were firm and round as the domes of East Indian temples, and I stood so close as to see the fine skin texture and beads of pearly perspiration glistening like dew around the pink and erected buds of her nipples. I wanted at one and the same time to run from the room, to sink through the floor, or go to her and cover her from my eyes and the eyes of the others with my body; to feel the soft thighs, to caress her and destroy her, to love her and murder her, to hide from her, and yet to stroke where below the small American flag tattooed upon her belly her thighs formed a capital V. I had a notion that of all in the room she saw only me with her impersonal eyes.

And then she began to dance, a slow sensuous movement; the smoke of a hundred cigars clinging to her like the thinnest of veils. She seemed like a fair bird-girl girdled in veils calling to me from the angry surface of some gray and threatening sea. I was transported. Then I became aware of the clarinet playing and the big shots yelling at us. Some threatened us if we looked and others if we did not. On my right I saw one boy faint. And now a man grabbed a silver pitcher from a table and stepped close as he dashed ice water upon him and stood him up and forced two of us to support him as his head hung and moans issued from his thick bluish lips. Another boy began to plead to go home. He was the largest of the group, wearing dark red fighting trunks much too small to conceal the erection which projected from him as though in answer to the insinuating low-registered moaning of the clarinet. He tried to hide himself with his boxing gloves.

And all the while the blonde continued dancing, smiling faintly at the big shots who watched her with fascination, and faintly smiling at our fear. I noticed a certain merchant who followed her hungrily, his lips loose and drooling. He was a large man who wore diamond studs in a shirtfront which swelled with the ample paunch underneath, and each time the blonde swayed her undulating hips he ran his hand through the thin hair of his bald head and, with his arms upheld, his posture clumsy like that of an intoxicated panda, wound his belly in a slow and obscene grind. This creature was completely hypnotized. The music had quickened. As the dancer flung herself about with a detached expression on her face, the men began reaching out to touch her. I could see their beefy fingers sink into the soft flesh. Some of the others tried to stop them as she began to move around the floor in graceful circles, as they gave chase, slipping and sliding over the polished floor. It was mad. Chairs went crashing, drinks were spilt, as they ran laughing and howling after her. They caught her just as she reached a door, raised her from the floor, and tossed her as college boys are tossed at a hazing, and above her red, fixed-smiling lips I saw the terror and disgust in her eyes, almost like my own terror and that which I saw in some of the other boys. As I watched, they tossed her twice and her soft breasts seemed to flatten against the air and her legs flung wildly as she spun. Some of the more sober ones helped her to escape. And I started off the floor, heading for the anteroom with the rest of the boys.

Some were still crying in hysteria. But as we tried to leave we were stopped   10 and ordered to get into the ring. There was nothing to do but what we were told. All ten of us climbed under the ropes and allowed ourselves to be blindfolded with broad bands of white cloth. One of the men seemed to feel a bit sympathetic and tried to cheer us up as we stood with our backs against the ropes. Some of us tried to grin. "See that boy over there?" one of the men said. "I want you to run across at the bell and give it to him right in the belly. If you don't get him, I'm going to get you. I don't like his looks." Each of us was told the same. The blindfolds were put on. Yet even then I had been going over my speech. In my mind each word was as bright as flame. I felt the cloth pressed into place, and frowned so that it would be loosened when I relaxed.

But now I felt a sudden fit of blind terror. I was unused to darkness. It was as though I had suddenly found myself in a dark room filled with poisonous cotton-mouths. I could hear the bleary voices yelling insistently for the battle royal to begin.

"Get going in there!"

"Let me at that big nigger!"

I strained to pick up the school superintendent's voice, as though to squeeze some security out of that slightly more familiar sound.

"Let me at those black sonsabitches!" someone yelled.   15

"No, Jackson, no!" another voice yelled. "Here, somebody, help me hold Jack."

"I want to get at that ginger-colored nigger. Tear him limb from limb," the first voice yelled.

I stood against the ropes trembling. For in those days I was what they called ginger-colored, and he sounded as though he might crunch me between his teeth like a crisp ginger cookie.

Quite a struggle was going on. Chairs were being kicked about and I could hear voices grunting as with a terrific effort. I wanted to see, to see more desperately than ever before. But the blindfold was tight as a thick skin-puckering scab and when I raised my gloved hands to push the layers of white aside a voice yelled, "Oh, no you don't, black bastard! Leave that alone!"

"Ring the bell before Jackson kills him a coon!" someone boomed in the   20 sudden silence. And I heard the bell clang and the sound of the feet scuffling forward.

A glove smacked against my head. I pivoted, striking out stiffly as someone went past, and felt the jar ripple along the length of my arm to my shoulder. Then it seemed as though all nine of the boys had turned upon me at once. Blows pounded me from all sides while I struck out as best I could. So many blows landed upon me that I wondered if I were not the only blindfolded fighter in the ring, or if the man called Jackson hadn't succeeded in getting me after all.

Blindfolded, I could no longer control my motions. I had no dignity. I stumbled about like a baby or a drunken man. The smoke had become thicker and with each new blow it seemed to sear and further restrict my lungs. My saliva became like hot bitter glue. A glove connected with my head, filling my mouth with warm blood. It was everywhere. I could not tell if the moisture I felt upon my body was sweat or blood. A blow landed hard against the nape of my neck. I felt myself going over, my head hitting the floor. Streaks of blue light filled the black world behind the blindfold. I lay prone, pretending that I was knocked out, but felt myself seized by hands and yanked to my feet. "Get going, black boy! Mix it up!" My arms were like lead, my head smarting from blows. I managed to feel my way to the ropes and held on, trying to catch my breath. A glove landed in my mid-section and I went over again, feeling as though the smoke had become a knife jabbed into my guts. Pushed this way and that by the legs milling around me, I finally pulled erect and discovered that I could see the black, sweat-washed forms weaving in the smoky-blue atmosphere like drunken dancers weaving to the rapid drumlike thuds of blows.

Everyone fought hysterically. It was complete anarchy. Everybody fought everybody else. No group fought together for long. Two, three, four, fought one, then turned to fight each other, were themselves attacked. Blows landed below the belt and in the kidney, with the gloves open as well as closed, and with my eye partly opened now there was not so much terror. I moved carefully, avoiding blows, although not too many to attract attention, fighting from group to group. The boys groped about like blind, cautious crabs crouching to protect their mid-sections, their heads pulled in short against their shoulders, their arms stretched nervously before them, with their fists testing the smoke-filled air like the knobbed feelers of hypersensitive snails. In one corner I glimpsed a boy violently punching the air and heard him scream in pain as he smashed his hand against a ring post. For a second I saw him bent over holding his hand, then going down as a blow caught his unprotected head. I played one group against the other, slipping in and throwing a punch then stepping out of range while pushing the others into the melee to take the blows blindly aimed at me. The smoke was agonizing and there were no rounds, no bells at three minute intervals to relieve our exhaustion. The room spun round me, a swirl of lights, smoke, sweating bodies surrounded by tense white faces. I bled from both nose and mouth, the blood spattering upon my chest.

The men kept yelling, "Slug him, black boy! Knock his guts out!"

"Uppercut him! Kill him! Kill that big boy!"   25

Taking a fake fall, I saw a boy going down heavily beside me as though we were felled by a single blow, saw a sneaker-clad foot shoot into his groin as the two who had knocked him down stumbled upon him. I rolled out of range, feeling a twinge of nausea.

The harder we fought the more threatening the men became. And yet, I had begun to worry about my speech again. How would it go? Would they recognize my ability? What would they give me?

I was fighting automatically when suddenly I noticed that one after another of the boys was leaving the ring. I was surprised, filled with panic, as though I had been left alone with an unknown danger. Then I understood. The boys had arranged it among themselves. It was the custom for the two men left in the ring to slug it out for the winner's prize. I discovered this too late. When the bell sounded two men in tuxedoes leaped into the ring and removed the blindfold. I found myself facing Tatlock, the biggest of the gang. I felt sick at my stomach. Hardly had the bell stopped ringing in my ears than it clanged again and I saw him moving swiftly toward me. Thinking of nothing else to do I hit him smash on the nose. He kept coming, bringing the rank sharp violence of stale sweat. His face was a black blank of a face, only his eyes alive — with hate of me and aglow with a feverish terror from what had happened to us all. I became anxious. I wanted to deliver my speech and he came at me as though he meant to beat it out of me. I smashed him again and again, taking his blows as they came. Then on a sudden impulse I struck him lightly and as we clinched, I whispered, "Fake like I knocked you out, you can have the prize."

"I'll break your behind," he whispered hoarsely.

"For *them?*"   30

"For *me*, sonofabitch!"

They were yelling for us to break it up and Tatlock spun me half around with a blow, and as a joggled camera sweeps in a reeling scene, I saw the howling red faces crouching tense beneath the cloud of blue-gray smoke. For a moment the world wavered, unraveled, flowed, then my head cleared and Tatlock bounced before me. That fluttering shadow before my eyes was his jabbing left hand. Then falling forward, my head against his damp shoulder, I whispered,

"I'll make it five dollars more."

"Go to hell!"

But his muscles relaxed a trifle beneath my pressure and I breathed, "Seven?"   35

"Give it to your ma," he said, ripping me beneath the heart.

And while I still held him I butted him and moved away. I felt myself bombarded with punches. I fought back with hopeless desperation. I wanted to deliver my speech more than anything else in the world, because I felt that only these men could judge truly my ability, and now this stupid clown was ruining my chances. I began fighting carefully now, moving in to punch him and out again with my greater speed. A lucky blow to his chin and I had him going too — until I heard a loud voice yell, "I got my money on the big boy."

Hearing this, I almost dropped my guard. I was confused: Should I try to win against the voice out there? Would not this go against my speech, and was not this a moment for humility, for nonresistance? A blow to my head as I danced about sent my right eye popping like a jack-in-the-box and settled my dilemma. The room went red as I fell. It was a dream fall, my body languid and fastidious as to where to land, until the floor became impatient and smashed up to meet me. A moment later I came to. An hypnotic voice said FIVE, emphatically. And I lay there, hazily watching a dark red spot of my own blood shaping itself into a butterfly, glistening and soaking into the soiled gray world of the canvas.

When the voice drawled TEN I was lifted up and dragged to a chair. I sat dazed. My eye pained and swelled with each throb of my pounding heart and I wondered if now I would be allowed to speak, I was wringing wet, my mouth still bleeding. We were grouped along the wall now. The other boys ignored me as they congratulated Tatlock and speculated as to how much they would be paid. One boy whimpered over his smashed hand. Looking up front, I saw attendants in white jackets rolling the portable ring away and placing a small square rug in the vacant space surrounded by chairs. Perhaps, I thought, I will stand on the rug to deliver my speech.

Then the M.C. called to us, "Come on up here boys and get your money." 40
We ran forward to where the men laughed and talked in their chairs, waiting. Everyone seemed friendly now.

"There it is on the rug," the man said. I saw the rug covered with coins of all dimensions and a few crumpled bills. But what excited me, scattered here and there, were the gold pieces.

"Boys, it's all yours," the man said. "You get all you grab."

"That's right, Sambo," a blond man said, winking at me confidentially.

I trembled with excitement, forgetting my pain. I would get the gold and the bills, I thought. I would use both hands. I would throw my body against the boys nearest me to block them from the gold.

"Get down around the rug now," the man commanded, "and don't anyone 45
touch it until I give the signal."

"This ought to be good," I heard.

As told, we got around the square rug on our knees. Slowly the man raised his freckled hand as we followed it upward with our eyes.

I heard, "These niggers look like they're about to pray!"

Then, "Ready," the man said. "Go!"

I lunged for a yellow coin lying on the blue design of the carpet, touching 50
it and sending a surprised shriek to join those rising around me. I tried frantically to remove my hand but could not let go. A hot, violent force tore through my body, shaking me like a wet rat. The rug was electrified. The hair bristled up on my head as I shook myself free. My muscles jumped, my nerves jangled, writhed. But I saw that this was not stopping the other boys. Laughing in fear and embarrassment, some were holding back and scooping up the coins knocked off by the painful contortions of the others. The men roared above us as we struggled.

"Pick it up, goddamnit, pick it up!" someone called like a bass-voiced parrot. "Go on, get it!"

I crawled rapidly around the floor, picking up the coins, trying to avoid the coppers and to get greenbacks and the gold. Ignoring the shock by laughing, as I brushed the coins off quickly, I discovered that I could contain the electricity — a contradiction, but it works. Then the men began to push us onto the rug. Laughing embarrassedly, we struggled out of their hands and kept after the coins. We were all wet and slippery and hard to hold. Suddenly I saw a boy lifted into the air, glistening with sweat like a circus seal, and dropped, his wet back landing flush upon the charged rug, heard him yell and saw him literally dance upon his back, his elbows beating a frenzied tattoo upon the floor, his muscles twitching like the flesh of a horse stung by many flies. When he finally rolled off, his face was gray and no one stopped him when he ran from the floor amid booming laughter.

"Get the money," the M.C. called. "That's good hard American cash!"

And we snatched and grabbed, snatched and grabbed. I was careful not to come too close to the rug now, and when I felt the hot whiskey breath descend upon me like a cloud of foul air I reached out and grabbed the leg of a chair. It was occupied and I held on desperately.

"Leggo, nigger! Leggo!"   55

The huge face wavered down to mine as he tried to push me free. But my body was slippery and he was too drunk. It was Mr. Colcord, who owned a chain of movie houses and "entertainment palaces." Each time he grabbed me I slipped out of his hands. It became a real struggle. I feared the rug more than I did the drunk, so I held on, surprising myself for a moment by trying to topple *him* upon the rug. It was such an enormous idea that I found myself actually carrying it out. I tried not to be obvious, yet when I grabbed his leg, trying to tumble him out of the chair, he raised up roaring with laughter, and, looking at me with soberness dead in the eye, kicked me viciously in the chest. The chair leg flew out of my hand and I felt myself going and rolled. It was as though I had rolled through a bed of hot coals. It seemed a whole century would pass before I would roll free, a century in which I was seared through the deepest levels of my body to the fearful breath within me and the breath seared and heated to the point of explosion. It'll all be over in a flash, I thought as I rolled clear. It'll all be over in a flash.

But not yet, the men on the other side were waiting, red faces swollen as though from apoplexy as they bent forward in their chairs. Seeing their fingers coming toward me I rolled away as a fumbled football rolls off the receiver's fingertips, back into the coals. That time I luckily sent the rug sliding out of place and heard the coins ringing against the floor and the boys scuffling to pick them up and the M.C. calling, "All right, boys, that's all. Go get dressed and get your money."

I was limp as a dish rag. My back felt as though it had been beaten with wires.

When we had dressed the M.C. came in and gave us each five dollars, except Tatlock, who got ten for being last in the ring. Then he told us to leave. I was not to get a chance to deliver my speech, I thought. I was going out into the dim alley in despair when I was stopped and told to go back. I returned to the ballroom, where the men were pushing back their chairs and gathering in groups to talk.

The M.C. knocked on a table for quiet. "Gentlemen," he said, "we almost   60
forgot an important part of the program. A most serious part, gentlemen. This boy was brought here to deliver a speech which he made at his graduation yesterday . . ."

"Bravo!"

"I'm told that he is the smartest boy we've got out there in Greenwood. I'm told that he knows more big words than a pocket-sized dictionary."

Much applause and laughter.

"So now, gentlemen, I want you to give him your attention."

There was still laughter as I faced them, my mouth dry, my eye throbbing.   65
I began slowly, but evidently my throat was tense, because they began shouting, "Louder! Louder!"

"We of the younger generation extol the wisdom of that great leader and
educator," I shouted, "who first spoke these flaming words of wisdom: 'A ship
lost at sea for many days suddenly sighted a friendly vessel. From the mast of
the unfortunate vessel was seen a signal: "Water, water; we die of thirst!" The
answer from the friendly vessel came back: "Cast down your bucket where you
are." The captain of the distressed vessel, at last heeding the injunction, cast
down his bucket, and it came up full of fresh sparkling water from the mouth
of the Amazon River.' And like him I say, and in his words, 'To those of my race
who depend upon bettering their condition in a foreign land, or who underestimate the importance of cultivating friendly relations with the Southern white
man, who is his next-door neighbor, I would say: "Cast down your bucket
where you are" — cast it down in making friends in every manly way of the
people of all races by whom we are surrounded . . .' "

I spoke automatically and with such fervor that I did not realize that the
men were still talking and laughing until my dry mouth, filling up with blood
from the cut, almost strangled me. I coughed, wanting to stop and go to one of
the tall brass, sand-filled spittoons to relieve myself, but a few of the men, especially the superintendent, were listening and I was afraid. So I gulped it down,
blood, saliva, and all, and continued. (What powers of endurance I had during
those days! What enthusiasm! What a belief in the rightness of things!) I spoke
even louder in spite of the pain. But still they talked and still they laughed, as
though deaf with cotton in dirty ears. So I spoke with greater emotional emphasis. I closed my ears and swallowed blood until I was nauseated. The speech
seemed a hundred times as long as before, but I could not leave out a single
word. All had to be said, each memorized nuance considered, rendered. Nor
was that all. Whenever I uttered a word of three or more syllables a group of
voices would yell for me to repeat it. I used the phrase "social responsibility"
and they yelled:

"What's that word you say, boy?"

"Social responsibility," I said.

"What?"   70

"Social . . ."

"Louder."

". . . responsibility."

"More!"

"Respon —"   75

"Repeat!"

"— sibility."

The room filled with the uproar of laughter until, no doubt, distracted by
having to gulp down my blood, I made a mistake and yelled a phrase I had often
seen denounced in newspaper editorials, heard debated in private.

"Social . . ."

"What?" they yelled.   80

". . . equality —"

The laughter hung smokelike in the sudden stillness. I opened my eyes, puzzled. Sounds of displeasure filled the room. The M.C. rushed forward. They shouted hostile phrases at me. But I did not understand.

A small dry mustached man in the front row blared out, "Say that slowly, son!"

"What, sir?"

"What you just said!"   85

"Social responsibility, sir," I said.

"You weren't being smart, were you, boy?" he said, not unkindly.

"No, sir!"

"You sure that about 'equality' was a mistake?"

"Oh, yes, sir," I said. "I was swallowing blood."   90

"Well, you had better speak more slowly so we can understand. We mean to do right by you, but you've got to know your place at all times. All right, now, go on with your speech."

I was afraid. I wanted to leave but I wanted also to speak and I was afraid they'd snatch me down.

"Thank you, sir," I said, beginning where I had left off, and having them ignore me as before.

Yet when I finished there was a thunderous applause. I was surprised to see the superintendent come forth with a package wrapped in white tissue paper, and, gesturing for quiet, address the men.

"Gentlemen, you see that I did not overpraise this boy. He makes a good   95
speech and some day he'll lead his people in the proper paths. And I don't have to tell you that that is important in these days and times. This is a good, smart boy, and so to encourage him in the right direction, in the name of the Board of Education I wish to present him a prize in the form of this . . ."

He paused, removing the tissue paper and revealing a gleaming calfskin brief case.

". . . in the form of this first-class article from Shad Whitmore's shop."

"Boy," he said, addressing me, "take this prize and keep it well. Consider it a badge of office. Prize it. Keep developing as you are and some day it will be filled with important papers that will help shape the destiny of your people."

I was so moved that I could hardly express my thanks. A rope of bloody saliva forming a shape like an undiscovered continent drooled upon the leather and I wiped it quickly away. I felt an importance that I had never dreamed.

"Open it and see what's inside," I was told.   100

My fingers a-tremble, I complied, smelling the fresh leather and finding an official-looking document inside. It was a scholarship to the state college for Negroes. My eyes filled with tears and I ran awkwardly off the floor.

I was overjoyed; I did not even mind when I discovered that the gold pieces I had scrambled for were brass pocket tokens advertising a certain make of automobile.

When I reached home everyone was excited. Next day the neighbors came to congratulate me. I even felt safe from grandfather, whose deathbed curse usually spoiled my triumphs. I stood beneath his photograph with my brief case in hand and smiled triumphantly into his stolid black peasant's face. It was a face that fascinated me. The eyes seemed to follow everywhere I went.

That night I dreamed I was at a circus with him and that he refused to laugh at the clowns no matter what they did. Then later he told me to open my brief case and read what was inside and I did, finding an official envelope stamped with the state seal; and inside the envelope I found another and another, endlessly, and I thought I would fall of weariness. "Them's years," he said. "Now open that one." And I did and in it I found an engraved document containing a short message in letters of gold. "Read it," my grandfather said. "Out loud!"

"To Whom It May Concern," I intoned. "Keep This Nigger-Boy Running." 105
I awoke with the old man's laughter ringing in my ears.

(It was a dream I was to remember and dream again for many years after. But at that time I had no insight into its meaning. First I had to attend college.)   *[1947]*

≡ THINKING ABOUT THE TEXT

1. Some critics have seen the events at the smoker as symbolic or perhaps as an allegory of the plight of African Americans in the segregated South. Pick at least two specific events from the story. How are they meant to explain certain aspects of the African American experience before the civil rights movement of the 1960s?

2. Some readers are surprised by the bizarre and cruel behavior of the town's leaders. Are you? How do you explain what goes on there?

3. How do you interpret the narrator's dream (paras. 104–06)? Why would his grandfather be laughing?

4. Reread paragraphs 1 through 3. How is this opening section connected to the story? To the last paragraph? What might Ellison's narrator mean when he says in paragraph 1 that he is "an invisible man"?

5. The grandfather's deathbed advice in paragraph 2 causes quite a stir. In your own words, what is his advice? Why are his relatives surprised? What might be some alternatives for dealing with oppression? Which "solution" sounds like the one you would have promoted for our society during Ellison's boyhood?

BOOKER T. WASHINGTON

Atlanta Exposition Address (The Atlanta Compromise)

Recognized in his time as the major spokesman for his race, Booker T. Washington (1856–1915) is often seen today as an accommodationist whose insistence on grad-ual progress and vocational rather than intellectual education played into the hands of the white power structure, delaying racial equality. He founded and served as pres-ident of Tuskegee Institute, wrote twelve books (including the autobiographical Up from Slavery *in 1901), controlled much of the Negro press, and spoke in cities throughout the nation. His speech at the Atlanta Cotton States and International Exposition in 1895, in which he praised the South, condoned segregation and the glory of "common labor" for his race, and called for harmony and cooperation be-tween the races, is often called "The Atlanta Compromise."*

One-third of the population of the South is of the Negro race. No enterprise seek-ing the material, civil, or moral welfare of this section can disregard this element of our population and reach the highest success. I but convey to you, Mr. Presi-dent and Directors, the sentiment of the masses of my race when I say that in no way have the value and manhood of the American Negro been more fittingly and generously recognized than by the managers of this magnificent Exposition at every stage of its progress. It is a recognition that will do more to cement the friendship of the two races than any occurrence since the dawn of our freedom.

Not only this, but the opportunity here afforded will awaken among us a new era of industrial progress. Ignorant and inexperienced, it is not strange that in the first years of our new life we began at the top instead of at the bot-tom; that a seat in Congress or the state legislature was more sought than real estate or industrial skill; that the political convention or stump speaking had more attractions than starting a dairy farm or truck garden.

A ship lost at sea for many days suddenly sighted a friendly vessel. From the mast of the unfortunate vessel was seen a signal, "Water, water; we die of thirst!" The answer from the friendly vessel at once came back, "Cast down your bucket where you are." A second time the signal, "Water, water, send us water!" ran up from the distressed vessel, and was answered, "Cast down your bucket where you are." And a third and fourth signal for water was answered, "Cast down your bucket where you are." The captain of the distressed vessel, at last heeding the injunction, cast down his bucket, and it came up full of fresh, sparkling water from the mouth of the Amazon River. To those of my race who depend on bettering their condition in a foreign land or who underestimate the importance of cultivating friendly relations with the Southern white man, who is their next-door neighbor, I would say: "Cast down your bucket where you are" — cast it down in making friends in every manly way of the people of all races by whom we are surrounded.

Cast it down in agriculture, mechanics, in commerce, in domestic service, and in the professions. And in this connection it is well to bear in mind that whatever other sins the South may be called to bear, when it comes to business, pure and simple, it is in the South that the Negro is given a man's chance in the commercial world, and in nothing is this Exposition more eloquent than in emphasizing this chance. Our greatest danger is that in the great leap from slavery to freedom we may overlook the fact that the masses of us are to live by the productions of our hands, and fail to keep in mind that we shall prosper in proportion as we learn to dignify and glorify common labor and put brains and skill into the common occupations of life; shall prosper in proportion as we learn to draw the line between the superficial and the substantial, the ornamental gewgaws of life and the useful. No race can prosper till it learns that there is as much dignity in tilling a field as in writing a poem. It is at the bottom of life we must begin, and not at the top. Nor should we permit our grievances to overshadow our opportunities.

To those of the white race who look to the incoming of those of foreign birth and strange tongue and habits for the prosperity of the South, were I permitted I would repeat what I say to my own race, "Cast down your bucket where you are." Cast it down among the eight millions of Negroes whose habits you know, whose fidelity and love you have tested in days when to have proved treacherous meant the ruin of your firesides. Cast down your bucket among these people who have, without strikes and labor wars, tilled your fields, cleared your forests, builded your railroads and cities, and brought forth treasures from the bowels of the earth, and helped make possible this magnificent representation of the progress of the South. Casting down your bucket among my people, helping and encouraging them as you are doing on these grounds, and to education of head, hand, and heart, you will find that they will buy your surplus land, make blossom the waste places in your fields, and run your factories. While doing this, you can be sure in the future, as in the past, that you and your families will be surrounded by the most patient, faithful, law-abiding, and unresentful people that the world has seen. As we have proved our loyalty to you in the past, in nursing your children, watching by the sick-bed of your mothers and fathers, and often following them with tear-dimmed eyes to their graves, so in the future, in our humble way, we shall stand by you with a devotion that no foreigner can approach, ready to lay down our lives, if need be, in defense of yours, interlacing our industrial, commercial, civil, and religious life with yours in a way that shall make the interests of both races one. In all things that are purely social we can be as separate as the fingers, yet one as the hand in all things essential to mutual progress.

There is no defense or security for any of us except in the highest intelligence and development of all. If anywhere there are efforts tending to curtail the fullest growth of the Negro, let these efforts be turned into stimulating, encouraging, and making him the most useful and intelligent citizen. Effort or means so invested will pay a thousand per cent interest. These efforts will be twice blessed — "blessing him that gives and him that takes."

There is no escape through law of man or God from the inevitable: —

> The laws of changeless justice bind
> Oppressor with oppressed;

5

> And close as sin and suffering joined
> We march to fate abreast.

Nearly sixteen millions of hands will aid you in pulling the load upward, or they will pull against you the load downward. We shall constitute one-third and more of the ignorance and crime of the South, or one-third its intelligence and progress; we shall contribute one-third to the business and industrial prosperity of the South, or we shall prove a veritable body of death, stagnating, depressing, retarding every effort to advance the body politic.

Gentlemen of the Exposition, as we present to you our humble effort at an exhibition of our progress, you must not expect overmuch. Starting thirty years ago with ownership here and there in a few quilts and pumpkins and chickens (gathered from miscellaneous sources), remember the path that has led from these to the inventions and production of agricultural implements, buggies, steam-engines, newspapers, books, statuary, carving, paintings, the management of drug-stores and banks, has not been trodden without contact with thorns and thistles. While we take pride in what we exhibit as a result of our independent efforts, we do not for a moment forget that our part in this exhibition would fall far short of your expectations but for the constant help that has come to our educational life, not only from the Southern states, but especially from Northern philanthropists who have made their gifts a constant stream of blessing and encouragement.

The wisest among my race understand that the agitation of questions of social equality is the extremest folly, and that progress in the enjoyment of all the privileges that will come to us must be the result of severe and constant struggle rather than of artificial forcing. No race that has anything to contribute to the markets of the world is long in any degree ostracized. It is important and right that all privileges of the law be ours, but it is vastly more important that we be prepared for the exercises of these privileges. The opportunity to earn a dollar in a factory just now is worth infinitely more than the opportunity to spend a dollar in an opera-house.

In conclusion, may I repeat that nothing in thirty years has given us more hope and encouragement, and drawn us so near to you of the white race, as this opportunity offered by the Exposition; and here bending, as it were, over the altar that represents the results of the struggles of your race and mine, both starting practically empty-handed three decades ago, I pledge that in your effort to work out the great and intricate problem which God has laid at the doors of the South, you shall have at all times the patient, sympathetic help of my race; only let this be constantly in mind, that, while from representations in these buildings of the product of field, of forest, of mine, of factory, letters, and art, much good will come, yet far above and beyond material benefits will be that higher good, that, let us pray God, will come, in a blotting out of sectional differences and racial animosities and suspicions, in a determination to administer absolute justice, in a willing obedience among all classes to the mandates of law. This, this, coupled with our material prosperity, will bring into our beloved South a new heaven and a new earth.   *[1895]*

≣ THINKING ABOUT THE TEXT

1. Cite two passages from Washington's speech that would probably have had an impact on the African American characters in "Battle Royal."

2. Do you think Washington is right in saying, "No race can prosper till it learns that there is as much dignity in tilling a field as in writing a poem" (para. 4)?

3. Are you surprised that Washington pledges "the patient, sympathetic help of my race" as those whites in power "work out the great and intricate problem which God has laid at the doors of the South" (para. 11)? What might contemporary black leaders think of this attitude?

W. E. B. DU BOIS

Of Mr. Booker T. Washington

W. E. B. Du Bois (1868–1963) was a driving force in the movement for equality for people of color in America and throughout the world well into his nineties. He was born in Massachusetts soon after the Civil War, and his death in Africa coincided with the March on Washington in 1963. Du Bois was educated at Fisk, Berlin, and Harvard universities, receiving a Ph.D. from Harvard in 1895 for his dissertation on the history of the slave trade. He is best known for his work with the National Association for the Advancement of Colored People (NAACP), serving as editor of The Crisis *from 1910 to 1932. As a scholar, writer, and intellectual, Du Bois openly opposed policies such as those supported by Booker T. Washington that kept social, political, and educational opportunities from most African Americans.* The Souls of Black Folk *(1903), from which our reading is taken, is perhaps the most influential of his many writings.*

Easily the most striking thing in the history of the American Negro since 1876 is the ascendancy of Mr. Booker T. Washington. It began at the time when war memories and ideals were rapidly passing; a day of astonishing commercial development was dawning; a sense of doubt and hesitation overtook the freedmen's sons, — then it was that his leading began. Mr. Washington came, with a simple definite programme, at the psychological moment when the nation was a little ashamed of having bestowed so much sentiment on Negroes, and was concentrating its energies on Dollars. His programme of industrial education, conciliation of the South, and submission and silence as to civil and political rights, was not wholly original; the Free Negroes from 1830 up to wartime had striven to build industrial schools, and the American Missionary Association had from the first taught various trades; and Price° and others had sought a way of honorable alliance with the best of the Southerners. But

Price: Joseph C. Price (1854–1893), founder of Zion Wesley College and Livingstone College, was a prominent African American educator and championed liberal-arts education.

Mr. Washington first indissolubly linked these things; he put enthusiasm, unlimited energy, and perfect faith into this programme, and changed it from a by-path into a veritable Way of Life. And the tale of the methods by which he did this is a fascinating study of human life.

It startled the nation to hear a Negro advocating such a programme after many decades of bitter complaint; it startled and won the applause of the South, it interested and won the admiration of the North; and after a confused murmur of protest, it silenced if it did not convert the Negroes themselves.

To gain the sympathy and cooperation of the various elements comprising the white South was Mr. Washington's first task; and this, at the time Tuskegee was founded, seemed, for a black man, well-nigh impossible. And yet ten years later it was done in the word spoken at Atlanta: "In all things purely social we can be as separate as the five fingers, and yet one as the hand in all things essential to mutual progress." This "Atlanta Compromise" is by all odds the most notable thing in Mr. Washington's career. The South interpreted it in different ways: the radicals received it as a complete surrender of the demand for civil and political equality; the conservatives, as a generously conceived working basis for mutual understanding. So both approved it, and today its author is certainly the most distinguished Southerner since Jefferson Davis, and the one with the largest personal following. . . .

Mr. Washington represents in Negro thought the old attitude of adjustment and submission; but adjustment at such a peculiar time as to make his programme unique. This is an age of unusual economic development, and Mr. Washington's programme naturally takes an economic cast, becoming a gospel of Work and Money to such an extent as apparently almost completely to over-shadow the higher aims of life. Moreover, this is an age when the more advanced races are coming in closer contact with the less developed races, and the race-feeling is therefore intensified; and Mr. Washington's programme practically accepts the alleged inferiority of the Negro races. Again, in our own land, the reaction from the sentiment of war time has given impetus to race-prejudice against Negroes, and Mr. Washington withdraws many of the high demands of Negroes as men and American citizens. In other periods of intensified prejudice all the Negro's tendency to self-assertion has been called forth; at this period a policy of submission is advocated. In the history of nearly all other races and people the doctrine preached at such crises has been that manly self-respect is worth more than lands and houses, and that a people who voluntarily surrender such respect, or cease striving for it, are not worth civilizing.

In answer to this, it has been claimed that the Negro can survive only   5
through submission. Mr. Washington distinctly asks that black people give up, at least for the present, three things —

First, political power,

Second, insistence on civil rights,

Third, higher education of Negro youth, —

and concentrate all their energies on industrial education, the accumulation of wealth, and the conciliation of the South. This policy has been courageously and insistently advocated for over fifteen years, and has been triumphant for perhaps ten years. As a result of this tender of the palm-branch, what has been the return? In these years there have occurred:

1. The disfranchisement of the Negro.
2. The legal creation of a distinct status of civil inferiority for the Negro.
3. The steady withdrawal of aid from institutions for the higher training of the Negro.

These movements are not, to be sure, direct results of Mr. Washington's teachings; but his propaganda has, without a shadow of doubt, helped their speedier accomplishment. The question then comes: Is it possible, and probable, that nine millions of men can make effective progress in economic lines if they are deprived of political rights, made a servile caste, and allowed only the most meager chance for developing their exceptional men? If history and reason give any distinct answer to these questions, it is an emphatic *No*. . . .

In failing thus to state plainly and unequivocally the legitimate demands of their people, even at the cost of opposing an honored leader the thinking classes of American Negroes would shirk a heavy responsibility, — a responsibility to themselves, a responsibility to struggling masses, a responsibility to the darker races of men whose future depends so largely on this American experiment, but especially a responsibility to this nation, — this common Fatherland. It is wrong to encourage a man or a people in evil-doing; it is wrong to aid and abet a national crime simply because it is unpopular not to do so. The growing spirit of kindliness and reconciliation between the North and South after the frightful differences of a generation ago ought to be a source of deep congratulation to all, and especially to those whose mistreatment caused the war; but if that reconciliation is to be marked by the industrial slavery and civic death of those same black men, with permanent legislation into a position of inferiority, then those black men, if they are really men, are called upon by every consideration of patriotism and loyalty to oppose such a course by all civilized methods, even though such opposition involves disagreement with Mr. Booker T. Washington. We have no right to sit silently by while the inevitable seeds are sown for a harvest of disaster to our children, black and white.

First, it is the duty of black men to judge the South discriminatingly. The present generation of Southerners are not responsible for the past, and they should not be blindly hated or blamed for it. Furthermore, to no class is the indiscriminate endorsement of the recent course of the South toward Negroes more nauseating than to the best thought of the South. The South is not "solid"; it is a land in the ferment of social change, wherein forces of all kinds are fighting for supremacy; and to praise the ill the South is today perpetrating is just as wrong as to condemn the good. Discriminating and broad-minded criticism is what the South needs, — needs it for the sake of her own white sons and daughters, and for the insurance of robust, healthy mental and moral development.

Today even the attitude of the Southern whites toward the blacks is not, as so many assume, in all cases the same; the ignorant Southerner hates the

Negro, the workingmen fear his competition, the money-makers wish to use him as a laborer, some of the educated see a menace in his upward development, while others, — usually the sons of the masters — wish to help him to rise. National opinion has enabled this last class to maintain the Negro common schools, and to protect the Negro partially in property, life, and limb. Through the pressure of the money-makers, the Negro is in danger of being reduced to semi-slavery, especially in the country districts; the workingmen, and those of the educated who fear the Negro, have united to disfranchise him, and some have urged his deportation; while the passions of the ignorant are easily aroused to lynch and abuse any black man. To praise this intricate whirl of thought and prejudice is nonsense, to inveigh indiscriminately against "the South" is unjust; but to use the same breath in praising Governor Aycock, exposing Senator Morgan, arguing with Mr. Thomas Nelson Page, and denouncing Senator Ben Tillman, is not only sane, but the imperative duty of thinking black men.

It would be unjust to Mr. Washington not to acknowledge that in several   10
instances he has opposed movements in the South which were unjust to the Negro; he sent memorials to the Louisiana and Alabama constitutional conventions, he has spoken against lynching, and in other ways has openly or silently set his influence against sinister schemes and unfortunate happenings. Notwithstanding this, it is equally true to assert that on the whole the distinct impression left by Mr. Washington's propaganda is, first, that the South is justified in its present attitude toward the Negro because of the Negro's degradation; secondly, that the prime cause of the Negro's failure to rise more quickly is his wrong education in the past; and, thirdly, that his future rise depends primarily on his own efforts. Each of these propositions is a dangerous half-truth. The supplementary truths must never be lost sight of: first, slavery and race-prejudice are potent if not sufficient causes of the Negro's position; second, industrial and common-school training were necessarily slow in planting because they had to await the black teachers trained by higher institutions, — it being extremely doubtful if any essentially different development was possible, and certainly a Tuskegee was unthinkable before 1880; and, third, while it is a great truth to say that the Negro must strive and strive mightily to help himself, it is equally true that unless his striving be not simply seconded, but rather aroused and encouraged, by the initiative of the richer and wiser environing group, he cannot hope for great success.

In his failure to realize and impress this last point, Mr. Washington is especially to be criticized. His doctrine has tended to make the whites, North and South, shift the burden of the Negro problem to the Negro's shoulders and stand aside as critical and rather pessimistic spectators; when in fact the burden belongs to the nation, and the hands of none of us are clean if we bend not our energies to righting these great wrongs.

The South ought to be led, by candid and honest criticism, to assert her better self and do her full duty to the race she has cruelly wronged and is still wronging. The North — her copartner in guilt — cannot salve her conscience by plastering it with gold. We cannot settle this problem by diplomacy and suaveness, by "policy" alone. If worse come to worst, can the moral fiber of this country survive the slow throttling and murder of nine millions of men?

The black men of America have a duty to perform, a duty stern and delicate, — a forward movement to oppose a part of the work of their greatest leader. So far as Mr. Washington preaches Thrift, Patience, and Industrial Training for the masses, we must hold up his hands and strive with him, rejoicing in his honors and glorying in the strength of this Joshua called of God and of man to lead the headless host. But so far as Mr. Washington apologizes for injustice, North or South, does not rightly value the privilege and duty of voting, belittles the emasculating effects of caste distinctions, and opposes the higher training and ambition of our brighter minds, — so far as he, the South, or the Nation, does this, — we must unceasingly and firmly oppose them. By every civilized and peaceful method we must strive for the rights which the world accords to men, clinging unwaveringly to those great words which the sons of the Fathers would fain forget: "We hold these truths to be self-evident: that all men are created equal; that they are endowed by their Creator with certain unalienable rights; that among these are life, liberty, and the pursuit of happiness."   *[1903]*

≡ **THINKING ABOUT THE TEXT**

1. Du Bois is clearly upset with Washington. What is his main objection to the Atlanta Compromise? Do you agree with him?

2. Is the narrator of "Battle Royal" still under Washington's influence, or has the thinking of Du Bois made some inroads?

3. What might the grandfather in "Battle Royal" think of Du Bois's last paragraph?

GUNNAR MYRDAL
Social Equality

A Swedish economist who with his wife, Alva Myrdal (winner of the 1982 Nobel Peace Prize), established a model social-welfare system for Sweden in the 1930s, Gunnar Myrdal (1898–1987) was asked by the Carnegie Foundation in 1938 to study racism in the United States. "Social Equality" is an excerpt from the book that elaborated on the results of his study, An American Dilemma: The Negro Problem and Modern Democracy *(1944). In* Cultural Contexts for Ralph Ellison's "Invisible Man," *historian Eric Sundquist points out that for the white men in "Battle Royal," the term* social equality *would have included sexual relations and marriage between black men and white women, which was then an important cultural taboo.*

In his first encounter with the American Negro problem, perhaps nothing perplexes the outside observer more than the popular term and the popular theory of "no social equality." He will be made to feel from the start that it has concrete implications and a central importance for the Negro problem in America. But, nevertheless, the term is kept vague and elusive, and the theory loose and ambiguous. One moment it will be stretched to cover and justify every form of social segregation and discrimination, and, in addition, all the inequalities in justice, politics, and breadwinning. The next moment it will be narrowed to express only the denial of close personal intimacies and intermarriage. The very lack of precision allows the notion of "no social equality" to rationalize the rather illogical and wavering system of color caste in America.

The kernel of the popular theory of "no social equality" will, when pursued, be presented as a firm determination on the part of the whites to block amalgamation and preserve "the purity of the white race." The white man identifies himself with "the white race" and feels that he has a stake in resisting the dissipation of its racial identity. Important in this identification is the notion of "the absolute and unchangeable superiority of the white race." From this racial dogma will often be drawn the *direct* inference that the white man shall dominate in all spheres. But when the logic of this inference is inquired about, the inference will be made *indirect* and will be made to lead over to the danger of amalgamation, or, as it is popularly expressed, "intermarriage."

It is further found that the ban on intermarriage is focused on white women. For them it covers both formal marriage and illicit intercourse. In regard to white men it is taken more or less for granted that they would not stoop to marry Negro women, and that illicit intercourse does not fall under the same intense taboo. Their offspring, under the popular doctrine that maternity is more certain than paternity, become Negroes anyway, and the white race easily avoids pollution with Negro blood. To prevent "intermarriage" in this specific sense of sex relations between white women and Negro men, it is not enough to apply legal and social sanctions against it — so the popular theory runs. In using the danger of intermarriage as a defense for the whole caste system, it is assumed both that Negro men have a strong desire for "intermarriage," and that white women would be open to proposals from Negro men, *if* they are not guarded from even meeting them on an equal plane. The latter assumption, of course, is never openly expressed, but is logically implicit in the popular theory. The conclusion follows that the whole system of segregation and discrimination is justified. Every single measure is defended as necessary to block "social equality" which in its turn is held necessary to prevent "intermarriage."

The basic role of the fear of amalgamation in white attitudes to the race problem is indicated by the popular magical concept of "blood." Educated white Southerners, who know everything about modern genetic and biological research, confess readily that they actually feel an irrational or "instinctive" repugnance in thinking of "intermarriage." These measures of segregation and discrimination are often of the type found in the true taboos, and in the notion "not to be touched" of primitive religion. The specific taboos are characterized, further, by a different degree of excitement which attends their violation and a different degree of punishment to the violator: the closer the act to sexual association, the more furious is the public reaction. Sexual association itself is punished by death and is accompanied by tremendous public excitement; the other social relations meet decreasing degrees of public fury. Sex becomes in this popular theory the principle around which the whole structure of segregation of the Negroes — down to disfranchisement and denial of equal opportunities on the labor market — is organized. The reasoning is this: "For, say what we will, may not all the equalities be ultimately based on potential social equality, and that in turn on intermarriage? Here we reach the real *crux* of the question." In cruder language, but with the same logic, the Southern man on the street responds to any plea for social equality: "Would you like to have your daughter marry a Negro?"

This theory of color caste centering around the aversion to amalgamation determines, as we have just observed, the white man's rather definite rank order of the various measures of segregation and discrimination against Negroes. The relative significance attached to each of those measures is dependent upon their degree of expediency or necessity — in the view of white people — as means of upholding the ban on "intermarriage." In this rank order, (1) the ban on intermarriage and other sex relations involving white women and colored men takes precedence before everything else. It is the end for which the other restrictions are arranged as means. Thereafter follow: (2) all sorts of taboos and etiquettes in personal contacts; (3) segregation in schools and churches; (4) segregation in hotels, restaurants, and theaters, and other public places where people meet socially; (5) segregation in public conveyances; (6) discrimination in public services; and, finally, inequality in (7) politics, (8) justice, and (9) breadwinning and relief.

The degree of liberalism on racial matters in the white South can be designated mainly by the point on this rank order where a man stops because he believes further segregation and discrimination are not necessary to prevent "intermarriage." We have seen that white liberals in the South of the present day, as a matter of principle, rather unanimously stand up against inequality in breadwinning, relief, justice, and politics. These fields of discrimination form the chief battleground and considerable changes in them are, as we have seen, on the way. When we ascend to the higher ranks which concern social relations in the narrow sense, we find the Southern liberals less prepared to split off from the majority opinion of the region. Hardly anybody in the South is prepared to go the whole way and argue that even the ban on intermarriage should be lifted. Practically all agree, not only upon the high desirability of preventing "intermarriage," but also that a certain amount of separation between the two groups is expedient and necessary to prevent it. Even the one who has his philosophical doubts on the point must, if he is reasonable, abstain from ever voicing them. The social pressure is so strong that it would be foolish not to conform. Conformity is a political necessity for having any hope of influence; it is, in addition, a personal necessity for not meeting social ostracism. . . .

The fixation on the purity of white womanhood, and also part of the intensity of emotion surrounding the whole sphere of segregation and discrimination, are to be understood as the backwashes of the sore conscience on the part of white men for their own or their compeers' relations with, or desires for, Negro women. These psychological effects are greatly magnified because of the puritan *milieu* of America and especially of the South. The upper class men in a less puritanical people could probably have indulged in sex relations with, and sexual day-dreams of, lower caste women in a more matter-of-course way and without generating so much pathos about white womanhood. The Negro people have to carry the burden not only of the white men's sins but also of their virtues. The virtues of the honest, democratic, puritan white Americans in the South are great, and the burden upon the Negroes becomes ponderous.

Our practical conclusion is that it would have cleansing effects on race relations in America, and particularly in the South, to have an open and sober discussion in rational terms of this ever present popular theory of "intermarriage" and "social equality," giving matters their factual ground, true proportions and logical relations. Because it is, to a great extent, an opportunistic rationalization, and because it refers directly and indirectly to the most touchy spots in American life and American morals, tremendous inhibitions have been built up against a detached and critical discussion of this theory. But such inhibitions are gradually overcome when, in the course of secularized education, people become rational about their life problems. It must never be forgotten that in our increasingly intellectualized civilization even the plain citizen feels an urge for truth and objectivity, and that this rationalistic urge is increasingly competing with the opportunistic demands for rationalization and escape.

There are reasons to believe that a slow but steady cleansing of the American mind is proceeding as the cultural level is raised. The basic racial inferiority doctrine is being undermined by research and education. For a white man to have illicit relations with Negro women is increasingly meeting disapproval. Negroes themselves are more and more frowning upon such relations. This all must tend to dampen the emotional fires around "social equality." Sex and race fears are, however, even today the main defense for segregation and, in fact, for the whole caste order. The question shot at the interviewer touching any point of this order is still: "Would you like to have your daughter (sister) marry a Negro?"   [1944]

≣ THINKING ABOUT THE TEXT

1. Look back at the smoker section in "Battle Royal," especially when the narrator during his speech says "social equality" instead of "social responsibility." Why do you think there was a "sudden stillness" in the room (paras. 81–82)?

2. Based on his ideas about white sexual fears, how might Myrdal read the part of the smoker dealing with the naked dancer?

3. Myrdal writes that "conformity is a political necessity for having any hope of influence; it is, in addition, a personal necessity for not meeting social ostracism" (para. 6). Does this insight help your understanding of the world of the smoker?

≡ WRITING ABOUT ISSUES

1. Argue that the episode at the smoker is or is not evidence that the grandfather's advice in "Battle Royal" to " 'overcome 'em with yeses, undermine 'em with grins, agree 'em to death and destruction' " (para. 2) will not work.

2. Analyze the arguments of Washington and Du Bois in terms of the claims they both make, the assumptions they base their claims on, the evidence they use as support for their assumptions, and the effectiveness of their claims with the intended audience. Which writer do you find more persuasive?

3. Write a personal narrative detailing an experience either when you were the victim of bias because of your race, sex, age, religion, ethnicity, sexual preference, or any other personal dynamic or when you were part of a group that held biased views. Be specific about what happened, how you felt then, how you feel now, and what you learned from the experience.

≡ From City to Country: Critical Commentaries on a Play

OSCAR WILDE, *The Importance of Being Earnest*

CRITICAL COMMENTARIES:

SOS ELTIS, From *Revising Wilde: Society and Subversion in the Plays of Oscar Wilde*

TIRTHANKAR BOSE, From "Oscar Wilde's Game of Being Earnest"

PATRICIA FLANAGAN BEHRENDT, From *Oscar Wilde: Eros and Aesthetics*

CHARLES ISHERWOOD, "A Stylish Monster Conquers at a Glance"

Many literary plots have centered on trips from city to country or vice versa. In traveling from one of these places to the other, characters often go through experiences that force them to reexamine their identities, relationships, assumptions, and goals. What they find in their new setting needn't be traumatic, of course; they may even fall in love. In the modern theater, one of the most celebrated and discussed plays about a journey from city to country is Oscar Wilde's 1895 comedy *The Importance of Being Earnest*. Acclaimed when it opened, it is still much performed today, with audience after audience relishing its wit. Meanwhile, more than ever, scholars of literature speculate about what Wilde hoped to convey through his script. They suspect that by subtitling the play "A Trivial Comedy for Serious People," he was signaling that major social criticisms lurked beneath its humorous surface. In part, these analysts of *Earnest* are influenced by their knowledge of what happened to Wilde soon after its premiere. Under England's repressive legal system of the time, he was criminally convicted for the homosexual affairs he had been conducting in secret. But to what extent, and in what ways, *is* the play autobiographical? The question lacks a clear answer; the result is continued debate. Here we encourage *you* to enter the conversation. We do so by presenting multiple lenses on Wilde's text: excerpts by three critics who have analyzed *Earnest*, along with a review of a 2011 Broadway production of it.

≡ BEFORE YOU READ

In the United States or in another nation you know well, do you think urban communities and rural communities still differ significantly, or do you sense that they have grown pretty much alike? Identify specific features of these communities that come to your mind as you consider this question.

Heritage Images/Getty Images

OSCAR WILDE
The Importance of Being Earnest

A Trivial Comedy for Serious People

Oscar Wilde (1854–1900) was born in Dublin, Ireland, but graduated from Oxford University in England and then moved to London, where he became one of the most acclaimed playwrights of his day. He was also well known in the United States, especially during a lecture tour he made there in 1882. Wilde wrote in other literary genres besides drama: verse, such as his 1881 book Poems; *fiction, most notably his novel* The Picture of Dorian Gray *(1891); and essays, such as "The Soul of Man under Socialism" and "The Decay of Lying" (both 1891). But his theatrical comedies are what chiefly comprise his literary legacy today. They include* Lady Windermere's Fan *(1892),* A Woman of No Importance *(1893), and* An Ideal Husband *(1895).* The Importance of Being Earnest, *his last and most performed play, debuted in 1895. Despite its immediate success, however, Wilde plunged into serious trouble with the law that same year. Although married, he had been conducting an affair with Lord Alfred Douglas, in an era when homosexuality was officially a crime. When accused of this by Douglas's father, the Marquis of Queensberry, Wilde sued him for libel, but lost the case when the facts of his private life emerged. Wilde was then convicted of "gross indecency" and subsequently served two years in prison. During his confinement, he wrote an anguished autobiographical letter to Douglas, eventually published as "De Profundis." When Wilde was released in 1897, he was still notorious and also broke. He died three years later in Paris, after writing a poem about his prison ordeal entitled "The Ballad of Reading Gaol" (1898).*

THE PERSONS OF THE PLAY

JOHN WORTHING, J.P., *of the Manor House, Woolton, Hertfordshire*
ALGERNON MONCRIEFF, *his friend*
REV. CANON CHASUBLE, *D.D., rector of Woolton*
MERRIMAN, *butler to Mr. Worthing*
LANE, *Mr. Moncrieff's manservant*
LADY BRACKNELL
HON. GWENDOLEN FAIRFAX, *her daughter*
CECILY CARDEW, *John Worthing's ward*
MISS PRISM, *her governess*

THE SCENES OF THE PLAY

ACT I: *Algernon Moncrieff's Flat in Half Moon Street, W.*
ACT II: *The Garden at the Manor House, Woolton*
ACT III: *Morning Room at the Manor House, Woolton*

ACT I

(Scene: Morning room in Algernon's flat in Half Moon Street. The room is luxuriously and artistically furnished. The sound of a piano is heard in the adjoining room. Lane is arranging afternoon tea on the table, and after the music has ceased, Algernon enters.)

ALGERNON: Did you hear what I was playing, Lane?
LANE: I didn't think it polite to listen, sir.
ALGERNON: I'm sorry for that, for your sake. I don't play accurately — anyone can play accurately — but I play with wonderful expression. As far as the piano is concerned, sentiment is my forte. I keep science for Life.
LANE: Yes, sir.
ALGERNON: And, speaking of the science of Life, have you got the cucumber sandwiches cut for Lady Bracknell?
LANE: Yes, sir.   *(Hands them on a salver°.)*
ALGERNON *(inspects them, takes two, and sits down on the sofa)*:   Oh! — by the way, Lane, I see from your book that on Thursday night, when Lord Shoreham

---

salver: A flat tray, often made of silver.

and Mr. Worthing were dining with me, eight bottles of champagne are entered as having been consumed.

LANE: Yes, sir; eight bottles and a pint.

ALGERNON: Why is it that at a bachelor's establishment the servants invariably drink the champagne? I ask merely for information.

LANE: I attribute it to the superior quality of the wine, sir. I have often observed that in married households the champagne is rarely of a first-rate brand.

ALGERNON: Good heavens! Is marriage so demoralizing as that?

LANE: I believe it *is* a very pleasant state, sir. I have had very little experience of it myself up to the present. I have only been married once. That was in consequence of a misunderstanding between myself and a young person.

ALGERNON (*languidly*):   I don't know that I am much interested in your family life, Lane.

LANE: No, sir; it is not a very interesting subject. I never think of it myself.

ALGERNON: Very natural, I am sure. That will do, Lane, thank you.

LANE: Thank you, sir.   (*Lane goes out.*)

ALGERNON: Lane's views on marriage seem somewhat lax. Really, if the lower orders don't set us a good example, what on earth is the use of them? They seem, as a class, to have absolutely no sense of moral responsibility.

(*Enter Lane.*)

LANE: Mr. Ernest Worthing.

(*Enter Jack. Lane goes out.*)

ALGERNON: How are you, my dear Ernest? What brings you up to town?

JACK: Oh, pleasure, pleasure! What else should bring one anywhere? Eating as usual, I see, Algy!

ALGERNON (*Stiffly*):   I believe it is customary in good society to take some slight refreshment at five o'clock. Where have you been since last Thursday?

JACK (*sitting down on the sofa*):   In the country.

ALGERNON: What on earth do you do there?

JACK (*pulling off his gloves*):   When one is in town one amuses oneself. When one is in the country one amuses other people. It is excessively boring.

ALGERNON: And who are the people you amuse?

JACK (*airily*):   Oh, neighbors, neighbors.

ALGERNON: Got nice neighbors in your part of Shropshire?

JACK: Perfectly horrid! Never speak to one of them.

ALGERNON: How immensely you must amuse them! (*Goes over and takes sandwich.*) By the way, Shropshire is your country, is it not?

JACK: Eh? Shropshire? Yes, of course. Hallo! Why all these cups? Why cucumber sandwiches? Why such reckless extravagance in one so young? Who is coming to tea?

ALGERNON: Oh! merely Aunt Augusta and Gwendolen.

JACK: How perfectly delightful!

ALGERNON: Yes, that is all very well; but I am afraid Aunt Augusta won't quite approve of your being here.

JACK: May I ask why?

ALGERNON: My dear fellow, the way you flirt with Gwendolen is perfectly disgraceful. It is almost as bad as the way Gwendolen flirts with you.

JACK: I am in love with Gwendolen. I have come up to town expressly to propose to her.

ALGERNON: I thought you had come up for pleasure?—I call that business.

JACK: How utterly unromantic you are!

ALGERNON: I really don't see anything romantic in proposing. It is very romantic to be in love. But there is nothing romantic about a definite proposal.
Why, one may be accepted. One usually is, I believe. Then the excitement is
all over. The very essence of romance is uncertainty. If ever I get married,
I'll certainly try to forget the fact.

JACK: I have no doubt about that, dear Algy. The Divorce Court was specially
invented for people whose memories are so curiously constituted.

ALGERNON: Oh! there is no use speculating on that subject. Divorces are made
in heaven—(*Jack puts out his hand to take a sandwich. Algernon at once inter-
feres.*) Please don't touch the cucumber sandwiches. They are ordered specially for Aunt Augusta. (*Takes one and eats it.*)

JACK: Well, you have been eating them all the time.

ALGERNON: That is quite a different matter. She is my aunt. (*Takes plate from
below.*) Have some bread and butter. The bread and butter is for Gwendolen. Gwendolen is devoted to bread and butter.

JACK (*advancing to table and helping himself*):   And very good bread and butter it
is too.

ALGERNON: Well, my dear fellow, you need not eat as if you were going to eat it
all. You behave as if you were married to her already. You are not married
to her already, and I don't think you ever will be.

JACK: Why on earth do you say that?

ALGERNON: Well, in the first place, girls never marry the men they flirt with.
Girls don't think it right.

JACK: Oh, that is nonsense!

ALGERNON: It isn't. It is a great truth. It accounts for the extraordinary number of bachelors that one sees all over the place. In the second place, I don't
give my consent.

JACK: Your consent!

ALGERNON: My dear fellow, Gwendolen is my first cousin. And before I allow
you to marry her, you will have to clear up the whole question of Cecily.

(*Rings bell.*)

JACK: Cecily! What on earth do you mean? What do you mean, Algy, by Cecily? I don't know anyone of the name of Cecily.

(*Enter Lane.*)

ALGERNON: Bring me that cigarette case Mr. Worthing left in the smoking
room the last time he dined here.

LANE: Yes, sir. (*Lane goes out.*)

JACK: Do you mean to say you have had my cigarette case all this time? I wish to goodness you had let me know. I have been writing frantic letters to Scotland Yard about it. I was very nearly offering a large reward.

ALGERNON: Well, I wish you would offer one. I happen to be more than usually hard up.

JACK: There is no good offering a large reward now that the thing is found.

(Enter Lane with the cigarette case on a salver. Algernon takes it at once. Lane goes out.)

ALGERNON: I think that is rather mean of you, Ernest, I must say. (*Opens case and examines it.*) However, it makes no matter, for, now that I look at the inscription inside, I find that the thing isn't yours after all.

JACK: Of course it's mine. (*Moving to him.*) You have seen me with it a hundred times, and you have no right whatsoever to read what is written inside. It is a very ungentlemanly thing to read a private cigarette case.

ALGERNON: Oh! it is absurd to have a hard-and-fast rule about what one should read and what one shouldn't. More than half of modern culture depends on what one shouldn't read.

JACK: I am quite aware of the fact, and I don't propose to discuss modern culture. It isn't the sort of thing one should talk of in private. I simply want my cigarette case back.

ALGERNON: Yes; but this isn't your cigarette case. This cigarette case is a present from someone of the name of Cecily, and you said you didn't know anyone of that name.

JACK: Well, if you want to know, Cecily happens to be my aunt.

ALGERNON: Your aunt!

JACK: Yes. Charming old lady she is, too. Lives at Tunbridge Wells. Just give it back to me, Algy.

ALGERNON (*retreating to back of sofa*):   But why does she call herself little Cecily if she is your aunt and lives at Tunbridge Wells? (*Reading.*) "From little Cecily with her fondest love."

JACK (*moving to sofa and kneeling upon it*):   My dear fellow, what on earth is there in that? Some aunts are tall, some aunts are not tall. That is a matter that surely an aunt may be allowed to decide for herself. You seem to think that every aunt should be exactly like your aunt! That is absurd! For heaven's sake give me back my cigarette case.

(Follows Algernon round the room.)

ALGERNON: Yes. But why does your aunt call you her uncle? "From little Cecily, with her fondest love to her dear Uncle Jack." There is no objection, I admit, to an aunt being a small aunt, but why an aunt, no matter what her size may be, should call her own nephew her uncle, I can't quite make out. Besides, your name isn't Jack at all; it is Ernest.

JACK: It isn't Ernest; it's Jack.

ALGERNON: You have always told me it was Ernest. I have introduced you to everyone as Ernest. You answer to the name of Ernest. You look as if your name was Ernest. You are the most earnest looking person I ever saw in my life. It is perfectly absurd your saying that your name isn't Ernest. It's on your cards. Here is one of them (*taking it from case*) "Mr. Ernest Worthing, B.4, The Albany." I'll keep this as a proof that your name is Ernest if ever you attempt to deny it to me, or to Gwendolen, or to anyone else.

(Puts the card in his pocket.)

JACK: Well, my name is Ernest in town and Jack in the country, and the cigarette case was given to me in the country.

ALGERNON: Yes, but that does not account for the fact that your small Aunt Cecily, who lives at Tunbridge Wells, calls you her dear uncle. Come, old boy, you had much better have the thing out at once.

JACK: My dear Algy, you talk exactly as if you were a dentist. It is very vulgar to talk like a dentist when one isn't a dentist. It produces a false impression.

ALGERNON: Well, that is exactly what dentists always do. Now, go on! Tell me the whole thing. I may mention that I have always suspected you of being a confirmed and secret Bunburyist; and I am quite sure of it now.

JACK: Bunburyist? What on earth do you mean by a Bunburyist?

ALGERNON: I'll reveal to you the meaning of that incomparable expression as soon as you are kind enough to inform me why you are Ernest in town and Jack in the country.

JACK: Well, produce my cigarette case first.

ALGERNON: Here it is. (*Hands cigarette case.*) Now produce your explanation, and pray make it improbable.

(Sits on sofa.)

JACK: My dear fellow, there is nothing improbable about my explanation at all. In fact it's perfectly ordinary. Old Mr. Thomas Cardew, who adopted me when I was a little boy, made me in his will guardian to his granddaughter, Miss Cecily Cardew. Cecily, who addresses me as her uncle from motives of respect that you could not possibly appreciate, lives at my place in the country under the charge of her admirable governess, Miss Prism.

ALGERNON: Where is that place in the country, by the way?

JACK: That is nothing to you, dear boy. You are not going to be invited—I may tell you candidly that the place is not in Shropshire.

ALGERNON: I suspected that, my dear fellow! I have Bunburyed all over Shropshire on two separate occasions. Now, go on. Why are you Ernest in town and Jack in the country?

JACK: My dear Algy, I don't know whether you will be able to understand my real motives. You are hardly serious enough. When one is placed in the position of guardian, one has to adopt a very high moral tone on all subjects. It's one's duty to do so. And as a high moral tone can hardly be said to conduce very much to either one's health or one's happiness, in order to get up to town I have always pretended to have a younger brother of the name of Ernest, who lives in the Albany, and gets into the most dreadful scrapes. That, my dear Algy, is the whole truth pure and simple.

ALGERNON: The truth is rarely pure and never simple. Modern life would be very tedious if it were either and modern literature a complete impossibility!

JACK: That wouldn't be at all a bad thing.

ALGERNON: Literary criticism is not your forte, my dear fellow. Don't try it. You should leave that to people who haven't been at a university. They do it so well in the daily papers. What you really are is a Bunburyist. I was quite right in saying you were a Bunburyist. You are one of the most advanced Bunburyists I know.

JACK: What on earth do you mean?

ALGERNON: You have invented a very useful younger brother called Ernest, in order that you may be able to come up to town as often as you like. I have invented an invaluable permanent invalid called Bunbury, in order that I may be able to go down into the country whenever I choose. Bunbury is perfectly invaluable. If it wasn't for Bunbury's extraordinary bad health, for instance, I wouldn't be able to dine with you at Willis's tonight, for I have been really engaged to Aunt Augusta for more than a week.

JACK: I haven't asked you to dine with me anywhere tonight.

ALGERNON: I know. You are absurdly careless about sending out invitations. It is very foolish of you. Nothing annoys people so much as not receiving invitations.

JACK: You had much better dine with your Aunt Augusta.

ALGERNON: I haven't the smallest intention of doing anything of the kind. To begin with, I dined there on Monday, and once a week is quite enough to dine with one's own relations. In the second place, whenever I do dine there I am always treated as a member of the family, and sent down with° either no woman at all, or two. In the third place, I know perfectly well whom she will place me next to, tonight. She will place me next Mary Farquhar, who always flirts with her own husband across the dinner table. That is not very pleasant. Indeed, it is not even decent—and that sort of thing is enormously on the increase. The amount of women in London who flirt with their own husbands is perfectly scandalous. It looks so bad. It is simply washing one's clean linen in public. Besides, now that I know you to be a confirmed Bunburyist I naturally want to talk to you about Bunburying. I want to tell you the rules.

JACK: I'm not a Bunburyist at all. If Gwendolen accepts me, I am going to kill my brother, indeed I think I'll kill him in any case. Cecily is a little too much interested in him. It is rather a bore. So I am going to get rid of Ernest. And I strongly advise you to do the same with Mr.—with your invalid friend who has the absurd name.

ALGERNON: Nothing will induce me to part with Bunbury, and if you ever get married, which seems to me extremely problematic, you will be very glad to know Bunbury. A man who marries without knowing Bunbury has a very tedious time of it.

JACK: That is nonsense. If I marry a charming girl like Gwendolen, and she is the only girl I ever saw in my life that I would marry, I certainly won't want to know Bunbury.

---

sent down with: Assigned a woman to escort into the dining room for dinner.

ALGERNON: Then your wife will. You don't seem to realize, that in married life three is company and two is none.

JACK (*sententiously*):   That, my dear young friend, is the theory that the corrupt French drama has been propounding for the last fifty years.

ALGERNON: Yes; and that the happy English home has proved in half the time.

JACK: For heaven's sake, don't try to be cynical. It's perfectly easy to be cynical.

ALGERNON: My dear fellow, it isn't easy to be anything nowadays. There's such a lot of beastly competition about. (*The sound of an electric bell is heard.*) Ah! that must be Aunt Augusta. Only relatives, or creditors, ever ring in that Wagnerian° manner. Now, if I get her out of the way for ten minutes, so that you can have an opportunity for proposing to Gwendolen, may I dine with you tonight at Willis's?

JACK: I suppose so, if you want to.

ALGERNON: Yes, but you must be serious about it. I hate people who are not serious about meals. It is so shallow of them.

(*Enter Lane.*)

LANE: Lady Bracknell and Miss Fairfax.

(*Algernon goes forward to meet them. Enter Lady Bracknell and Gwendolen.*)

LADY BRACKNELL: Good afternoon, dear Algernon, I hope you are behaving very well.

ALGERNON: I'm feeling very well, Aunt Augusta.

LADY BRACKNELL: That's not quite the same thing. In fact the two things rarely go together.

(*Sees Jack and bows to him with icy coldness.*)

ALGERNON (*to Gwendolen*):   Dear me, you are smart!

GWENDOLEN: I am always smart! Aren't I, Mr. Worthing?

JACK: You're quite perfect, Miss Fairfax.

GWENDOLEN: Oh! I hope I am not that. It would leave no room for developments, and I intend to develop in many directions.

(*Gwendolen and Jack sit down together in the corner.*)

LADY BRACKNELL: I'm sorry if we are a little late Algernon, but I was obliged to call on dear Lady Harbury. I hadn't been there since her poor husband's death. I never saw a woman so altered; she looks quite twenty years younger. And now I'll have a cup of tea, and one of those nice cucumber sandwiches you promised me.

ALGERNON: Certainly, Aunt Augusta.

(*Goes over to tea table.*)

LADY BRACKNELL: Won't you come and sit here, Gwendolen?

GWENDOLEN: Thanks, Mama, I'm quite comfortable where I am.

ALGERNON (*picking up empty plate in horror*):   Good heavens! Lane! Why are there no cucumber sandwiches? I ordered them specially.

Wagnerian: Referring to the operas of Richard Wagner (1813–1883), whose music was popularly thought to be loud.

LANE (*gravely*):   There were no cucumbers in the market this morning, sir. I went down twice.

ALGERNON: No cucumbers?

LANE: No, sir. Not even for ready money.

ALGERNON: That will do, Lane, thank you.

LANE: Thank you, sir.   (*Goes out.*)

ALGERNON: I am greatly distressed, Aunt Augusta, about there being no cucumbers, not even for ready money.

LADY BRACKNELL: It really makes no matter, Algernon. I had some crumpets with Lady Harbury, who seems to me to be living entirely for pleasure now.

ALGERNON: I hear her hair has turned quite gold from grief.

LADY BRACKNELL: It certainly has changed its color. From what cause I, of course, cannot say. (*Algernon crosses and hands tea.*) Thank you. I've quite a treat for you tonight, Algernon. I am going to send you down with Mary Farquhar. She is such a nice woman, and so attentive to her husband. It's delightful to watch them.

ALGERNON: I am afraid, Aunt Augusta, I shall have to give up the pleasure of dining with you tonight after all.

LADY BRACKNELL (*frowning*):   I hope not, Algernon. It would put my table completely out. Your uncle would have to dine upstairs. Fortunately he is accustomed to that.

ALGERNON: It is a great bore, and, I need hardly say, a terrible disappointment to me, but the fact is I have just had a telegram to say that my poor friend Bunbury is very ill again. (*Exchanges glances with Jack.*) They seem to think I should be with him.

LADY BRACKNELL: It is very strange. This Mr. Bunbury seems to suffer from curiously bad health.

ALGERNON: Yes; poor Bunbury is a dreadful invalid.

LADY BRACKNELL: Well, I must say, Algernon, that I think it is high time that Mr. Bunbury made up his mind whether he was going to live or to die. This shilly-shallying with the question is absurd. Nor do I in any way approve of the modern sympathy with invalids. I consider it morbid. Illness of any kind is hardly a thing to be encouraged in others. Health is the primary duty of life. I am always telling that to your poor uncle, but he never seems to take much notice — as far as any improvement in his ailments goes. I should be much obliged if you would ask Mr. Bunbury, from me, to be kind enough not to have a relapse on Saturday, for I rely on you to arrange my music for me. It is my last reception, and one wants something that will encourage conversation, particularly at the end of the season when everyone has practically said whatever they had to say, which, in most cases, was probably not much.

ALGERNON: I'll speak to Bunbury, Aunt Augusta, if he is still conscious, and I think I can promise you he'll be all right by Saturday. Of course the music is a great difficulty. You see, if one plays good music, people don't listen, and if one plays bad music people don't talk. But I'll run over the program I've drawn out, if you will kindly come into the next room for a moment.

LADY BRACKNELL: Thank you, Algernon. It is very thoughtful of you. (*Rising, and following Algernon.*) I'm sure the program will be delightful, after a few expurgations. French songs I cannot possibly allow. People always seem to think that they are improper, and either look shocked, which is vulgar, or laugh, which is worse. But German sounds a thoroughly respectable language, and indeed, I believe is so. Gwendolen, you will accompany me.

GWENDOLEN: Certainly, Mama.

(Lady Bracknell and Algernon go into the music room. Gwendolen remains behind.)

JACK: Charming day it has been, Miss Fairfax.

GWENDOLEN: Pray don't talk to me about the weather Mr. Worthing. Whenever people talk to me about the weather, I always feel quite certain that they mean something else. And that makes me so nervous.

JACK: I do mean something else.

GWENDOLEN: I thought so. In fact, I am never wrong.

JACK: And I would like to be allowed to take advantage of Lady Bracknell's temporary absence—

GWENDOLEN: I would certainly advise you to do so. Mama has a way of coming back suddenly into a room that I have often had to speak to her about.

JACK (*nervously*):   Miss Fairfax, ever since I met you I have admired you more than any girl—I have ever met since—I met you.

GWENDOLEN: Yes, I am quite aware of the fact. And I often wish that in public, at any rate, you had been more demonstrative. For me you have always had an irresistible fascination. Even before I met you I was far from indifferent to you. (*Jack looks at her in amazement.*) We live, as I hope you know Mr. Worthing, in an age of ideals. The fact is constantly mentioned in the more expensive monthly magazines, and has reached the provincial pulpits I am told; and my ideal has always been to love someone of the name of Ernest. There is something in that name that inspires absolute confidence. The moment Algernon first mentioned to me that he had a friend called Ernest, I knew I was destined to love you.

JACK: You really love me, Gwendolen?

GWENDOLEN: Passionately!

JACK: Darling! You don't know how happy you've made me.

GWENDOLEN: My own Ernest!

JACK: But you don't mean to say that you couldn't love me if my name wasn't Ernest?

GWENDOLEN: But your name is Ernest.

JACK: Yes, I know it is. But supposing it was something else? Do you mean to say you couldn't love me then?

GWENDOLEN (*glibly*):   Ah! that is clearly a metaphysical speculation, and like most metaphysical speculations has very little reference at all to the actual facts of real life, as we know them.

JACK: Personally, darling, to speak quite candidly, I don't much care about the name of Ernest—I don't think the name suits me at all.

GWENDOLEN: It suits you perfectly. It is a divine name. It has a music of its own. It produces vibrations.

JACK: Well, really, Gwendolen, I must say that I think there are lots of other much nicer names. I think Jack, for instance, a charming name.

GWENDOLEN: Jack?—No, there is very little music in the name Jack, if any at all, indeed. It does not thrill. It produces absolutely no vibrations—I have known several Jacks, and they all, without exception, were more than usually plain. Besides, Jack is a notorious domesticity for John! And I pity any woman who is married to a man called John. She would probably never be allowed to know the entrancing pleasure of a single moment's solitude. The only really safe name is Ernest.

JACK: Gwendolen, I must get christened at once—I mean we must get married at once. There is no time to be lost.

GWENDOLEN: Married, Mr. Worthing?

JACK (*astounded*):   Well—surely. You know that I love you, and you led me to believe, Miss Fairfax, that you were not absolutely indifferent to me.

GWENDOLEN: I adore you. But you haven't proposed to me yet. Nothing has been said at all about marriage. The subject has not even been touched on.

JACK: Well—may I propose to you now?

GWENDOLEN: I think it would be an admirable opportunity. And to spare you any possible disappointment, Mr. Worthing, I think it only fair to tell you quite frankly beforehand that I am fully determined to accept you.

JACK: Gwendolen!

GWENDOLEN: Yes, Mr. Worthing, what have you got to say to me?

JACK: You know what I have got to say to you.

GWENDOLEN: Yes, but you don't say it.

JACK: Gwendolen, will you marry me?

(Goes on his knees.)

GWENDOLEN: Of course I will, darling. How long you have been about it! I am afraid you have had very little experience in how to propose.

JACK: My own one, I have never loved anyone in the world but you.

GWENDOLEN: Yes, but men often propose for practice. I know my brother Gerald does. All my girlfriends tell me so. What wonderfully blue eyes you have, Ernest! They are quite, quite blue. I hope you will always look at me just like that, especially when there are other people present.

(Enter Lady Bracknell.)

LADY BRACKNELL: Mr. Worthing! Rise, sir, from this semirecumbent posture. It is most indecorous.

GWENDOLEN: Mama! (*He tries to rise; she restrains him.*) I must beg you to retire. This is no place for you. Besides, Mr. Worthing has not quite finished yet.

LADY BRACKNELL: Finished what, may I ask?

GWENDOLEN: I am engaged to Mr. Worthing, Mama.

(They rise together.)

LADY BRACKNELL: Pardon me, you are not engaged to anyone. When you do become engaged to someone, I, or your father, should his health permit him, will inform you of the fact. An engagement should come on a young girl as a surprise, pleasant or unpleasant, as the case may be. It is hardly a matter that she could be allowed to arrange for herself — And now I have a few questions to put to you, Mr. Worthing. While I am making these inquiries, you, Gwendolen, will wait for me below in the carriage.

GWENDOLEN (*reproachfully*):   Mama!

LADY BRACKNELL: In the carriage, Gwendolen! (*Gwendolen goes to the door. She and Jack blow kisses to each other behind Lady Bracknell's back. Lady Bracknell looks vaguely about as if she could not understand what the noise was. Finally turns round.*) Gwendolen, the carriage!

GWENDOLEN: Yes, Mama.

(*Goes out, looking back at Jack.*)

LADY BRACKNELL (*sitting down*):   You can take a seat, Mr. Worthing.

(*Looks in her pocket for notebook and pencil.*)

JACK: Thank you, Lady Bracknell, I prefer standing.

LADY BRACKNELL (*pencil and notebook in hand*):   I feel bound to tell you that you are not down on my list of eligible young men, although I have the same list as the dear Duchess of Bolton has. We work together, in fact. However, I am quite ready to enter your name, should your answers be what a really affectionate mother requires. Do you smoke?

JACK: Well, yes, I must admit I smoke.

LADY BRACKNELL: I am glad to hear it. A man should always have an occupation of some kind. There are far too many idle men in London as it is. How old are you?

JACK: Twenty-nine.

LADY BRACKNELL: A very good age to be married at. I have always been of opinion that a man who desires to get married should know either everything or nothing. Which do you know?

JACK (*after some hesitation*):   I know nothing, Lady Bracknell.

LADY BRACKNELL: I am pleased to hear it. I do not approve of anything that tampers with natural ignorance. Ignorance is like a delicate exotic fruit; touch it and the bloom is gone. The whole theory of modern education is radically unsound. Fortunately in England, at any rate, education produces no effect whatsoever. If it did, it would prove a serious danger to the upper classes, and probably lead to acts of violence in Grosvenor Square. What is your income?

JACK: Between seven and eight thousand a year.

LADY BRACKNELL (*makes a note in her book*):   In land, or in investments?

JACK: In investments, chiefly.

LADY BRACKNELL: That is satisfactory. What between the duties expected of one during one's lifetime, and the duties exacted from one after one's death, land has ceased to be either a profit or a pleasure. It gives one position, and prevents one from keeping it up. That's all that can be said about land.

JACK: I have a country house with some land, of course, attached to it, about fifteen hundred acres, I believe; but I don't depend on that for my real income. In fact, as far as I can make out, the poachers are the only people who make anything out of it.

LADY BRACKNELL: A country house! How many bedrooms? Well, that point can be cleared up afterwards. You have a town house, I hope? A girl with a simple, unspoiled nature, like Gwendolen, could hardly be expected to reside in the country.

JACK: Well, I own a house in Belgrave Square, but it is let by the year to Lady Bloxham. Of course, I can get it back whenever I like, at six months' notice.

LADY BRACKNELL: Lady Bloxham? I don't know her.

JACK: Oh, she goes about very little. She is a lady considerably advanced in years.

LADY BRACKNELL: Ah, nowadays that is no guarantee of respectability of character. What number in Belgrave Square?

JACK: 149.

LADY BRACKNELL (*shaking her head*):   The unfashionable side. I thought there was something. However, that could easily be altered.

JACK: Do you mean the fashion, or the side?

LADY BRACKNELL (*sternly*):   Both, if necessary, I presume. What are your politics?

JACK: Well, I am afraid I really have none. I am a Liberal Unionist.

LADY BRACKNELL: Oh, they count as Tories. They dine with us. Or come in the evening, at any rate. Now to minor matters. Are your parents living?

JACK: I have lost both my parents.

LADY BRACKNELL: Both? To lose one parent may be regarded as a misfortune — to lose *both* seems like carelessness. Who was your father? He was evidently a man of some wealth. Was he born in what the Radical papers call the purple of commerce, or did he rise from the ranks of the aristocracy?

JACK: I am afraid I really don't know. The fact is, Lady Bracknell, I said I had lost my parents. It would be nearer the truth to say that my parents seem to have lost me — I don't actually know who I am by birth. I was — well, I was found.

LADY BRACKNELL: Found!

JACK: The late Mr. Thomas Cardew, an old gentleman of a very charitable and kindly disposition, found me, and gave me the name of Worthing, because he happened to have a first-class ticket for Worthing in his pocket at the time. Worthing is a place in Sussex. It is a seaside resort.

LADY BRACKNELL: Where did the charitable gentleman who had a first-class ticket for this seaside resort find you?

JACK (*gravely*):   In a handbag.

LADY BRACKNELL: A handbag?

JACK (*very seriously*):   Yes, Lady Bracknell. I was in a handbag — a somewhat large, black leather handbag, with handles to it — an ordinary handbag in fact.

LADY BRACKNELL: In what locality did this Mr. James, or Thomas, Cardew come across this ordinary handbag?

JACK: In the cloakroom at Victoria Station. It was given to him in mistake for his own.

LADY BRACKNELL: The cloakroom at Victoria Station?

JACK: Yes. The Brighton line.

LADY BRACKNELL: The line is immaterial. Mr. Worthing, I confess I feel somewhat bewildered by what you have just told me. To be born, or at any rate bred, in a handbag, whether it had handles or not, seems to me to display a contempt for the ordinary decencies of family life that reminds one of the worst excesses of the French Revolution. And I presume you know what that unfortunate movement led to? As for the particular locality in which the handbag was found, a cloakroom at a railway station might serve to conceal a social indiscretion—has probably, indeed, been used for that purpose before now—but it could hardly be regarded as an assured basis for a recognized position in good society.

JACK: May I ask you then what you would advise me to do? I need hardly say I would do anything in the world to ensure Gwendolen's happiness.

LADY BRACKNELL: I would strongly advise you, Mr. Worthing, to try and acquire some relations as soon as possible, and to make a definite effort to produce at any rate one parent of either sex, before the season is quite over.

JACK: Well, I don't see how I could possibly manage to do that. I can produce the handbag at any moment. It is in my dressing room at home. I really think that should satisfy you, Lady Bracknell.

LADY BRACKNELL: Me, sir! What has it to do with me? You can hardly imagine that I and Lord Bracknell would dream of allowing our only daughter—a girl brought up with the utmost care—to marry into a cloakroom, and form an alliance with a parcel? Good morning, Mr. Worthing!

(Lady Bracknell sweeps out in majestic indignation.)

JACK: Good morning! (*Algernon, from the other room, strikes up the Wedding March. Jack looks perfectly furious, and goes to the door.*) For goodness' sake don't play that ghastly tune, Algy! How idiotic you are!

(The music stops, and Algernon enters cheerily.)

ALGERNON: Didn't it go off all right, old boy? You don't mean to say Gwendolen refused you? I know it is a way she has. She is always refusing people. I think it is most ill-natured of her.

JACK: Oh, Gwendolen is as right as a trivet. As far as she is concerned, we are engaged. Her mother is perfectly unbearable. Never met such a Gorgon°— I don't really know what a Gorgon is like, but I am quite sure that Lady Bracknell is one. In any case, she is a monster, without being a myth, which is rather unfair. I beg your pardon, Algy, I suppose I shouldn't talk about your own aunt in that way before you.

ALGERNON: My dear boy, I love hearing my relations abused. It is the only thing that makes me put up with them at all. Relations are simply a tedious pack

---

Gorgon: In Greek myth, one of three very ugly sisters who had, among other characteristics, serpents for hair.

of people, who haven't got the remotest knowledge of how to live, nor the smallest instinct about when to die.

JACK: Oh, that is nonsense!

ALGERNON: It isn't!

JACK: Well, I won't argue about the matter. You always want to argue about things.

ALGERNON: That is exactly what things were originally made for.

JACK: Upon my word, if I thought that, I'd shoot myself — (*A pause.*) You don't think there is any chance of Gwendolen becoming like her mother in about a hundred and fifty years, do you Algy?

ALGERNON: All women become like their mothers. That is their tragedy. No man does. That's his.

JACK: Is that clever?

ALGERNON: It is perfectly phrased! and quite as true as any observation in civilized life should be.

JACK: I am sick to death of cleverness. Everybody is clever nowadays. You can't go anywhere without meeting clever people. The thing has become an absolute public nuisance. I wish to goodness we had a few fools left.

ALGERNON: We have.

JACK: I should extremely like to meet them. What do they talk about?

ALGERNON: The fools? Oh! about the clever people, of course.

JACK: What fools!

ALGERNON: By the way, did you tell Gwendolen the truth about your being Ernest in town, and Jack in the country?

JACK (*in a very patronizing manner*):   My dear fellow, the truth isn't quite the sort of thing one tells to a nice sweet refined girl. What extraordinary ideas you have about the way to behave to a woman!

ALGERNON: The only way to behave to a woman is to make love to her if she is pretty, and to someone else if she is plain.

JACK: Oh, that is nonsense.

ALGERNON: What about your brother? What about the profligate Ernest?

JACK: Oh, before the end of the week I shall have got rid of him. I'll say he died in Paris of apoplexy. Lots of people die of apoplexy, quite suddenly, don't they?

ALGERNON: Yes, but it's hereditary, my dear fellow. It's a sort of thing that runs in families. You had much better say a severe chill.

JACK: You are sure a severe chill isn't hereditary, or anything of that kind?

ALGERNON: Of course it isn't!

JACK: Very well, then. My poor brother Ernest is carried off suddenly in Paris, by a severe chill. That gets rid of him.

ALGERNON: But I thought you said that — Miss Cardew was a little too much interested in your poor brother Ernest? Won't she feel his loss a good deal?

JACK: Oh, that is all right. Cecily is not a silly romantic girl, I am glad to say. She has got a capital appetite, goes on long walks, and pays no attention at all to her lessons.

ALGERNON: I would rather like to see Cecily.

JACK: I will take very good care you never do. She is excessively pretty, and she
is only just eighteen.

ALGERNON: Have you told Gwendolen yet that you have an excessively pretty
ward who is only just eighteen?

JACK: Oh! one doesn't blurt these things out to people. Cecily and Gwendolen are
perfectly certain to be extremely great friends. I'll bet you anything you like
that half an hour after they have met, they will be calling each other sister.

ALGERNON: Women only do that when they have called each other a lot of
other things first. Now, my dear boy, if we want to get a good table at Willis's, we really must go and dress. Do you know it is nearly seven?

JACK (*irritably*):   Oh! it always is nearly seven.

ALGERNON: Well, I'm hungry.

JACK: I never knew you when you weren't—

ALGERNON: What shall we do after dinner? Go to a theater?

JACK: Oh, no! I loathe listening.

ALGERNON: Well, let us go to the Club?

JACK: Oh, no! I hate talking.

ALGERNON: Well, we might trot round to the Empire° at ten?

JACK: Oh, no! I can't bear looking at things. It is so silly.

ALGERNON: Well, what shall we do?

JACK: Nothing!

ALGERNON: It is awfully hard work doing nothing. However, I don't mind hard
work where there is no definite object of any kind.

(Enter Lane.)

LANE: Miss Fairfax.

(Enter Gwendolen. Lane goes out.)

ALGERNON: Gwendolen, upon my word!

GWENDOLEN: Algy, kindly turn your back. I have something very particular to
say to Mr. Worthing.

ALGERNON: Really, Gwendolen, I don't think I can allow this at all.

GWENDOLEN: Algy, you always adopt a strictly immoral attitude towards life.
You are not quite old enough to do that.

(Algernon retires to the fireplace.)

JACK: My own darling!

GWENDOLEN: Ernest, we may never be married. From the expression on Mama's face I fear we never shall. Few parents nowadays pay any regard to
what their children say to them. The old-fashioned respect for the young is
fast dying out. Whatever influence I ever had over Mama, I lost at the age
of three. But although she may prevent us from becoming man and wife,
and I may marry someone else, and marry often, nothing that she can possibly do can alter my eternal devotion to you.

JACK: Dear Gwendolen!

GWENDOLEN: The story of your romantic origin, as related to me by Mama,

Empire: Empire Theatre, a London music hall that was also a rendezvous for prostitutes.

with unpleasing comments, has naturally stirred the deeper fibers of my nature. Your Christian name has an irresistible fascination. The simplicity of your character makes you exquisitely incomprehensible to me. Your town address at the Albany I have. What is your address in the country?

JACK: The Manor House, Woolton, Hertfordshire.

(Algernon, who has been carefully listening, smiles to himself, and writes the address on his shirt cuff. Then picks up the Railway Guide.)

GWENDOLEN: There is a good postal service, I suppose? It may be necessary to do something desperate. That of course will require serious consideration. I will communicate with you daily.

JACK: My own one!

GWENDOLEN: How long do you remain in town?

JACK: Till Monday.

GWENDOLEN: Good! Algy, you may turn round now.

ALGERNON: Thanks, I've turned round already.

GWENDOLEN: You may also ring the bell.

JACK: You will let me see you to your carriage, my own darling?

GWENDOLEN: Certainly.

JACK *(to Lane, who now enters)*:   I will see Miss Fairfax out.

LANE: Yes, sir.   *(Jack and Gwendolen go off.)*

(Lane presents several letters on a salver to Algernon. It is to be surmised that they are bills, as Algernon, after looking at the envelopes, tears them up.)

ALGERNON: A glass of sherry, Lane.

LANE: Yes, sir.

ALGERNON: Tomorrow, Lane, I'm going Bunburying.

LANE: Yes, sir.

ALGERNON: I shall probably not be back till Monday. You can put up my dress clothes, my smoking jacket, and all the Bunbury suits — ,

LANE: Yes, sir.   *(Handing sherry.)*

ALGERNON: I hope tomorrow will be a fine day, Lane.

LANE: It never is, sir.

ALGERNON: Lane, you're a perfect pessimist.

LANE: I do my best to give satisfaction, sir.

(Enter Jack. Lane goes off.)

JACK: There's a sensible, intellectual girl! the only girl I ever cared for in my life. *(Algernon is laughing immoderately.)* What on earth are you so amused at?

ALGERNON: Oh, I'm a little anxious about poor Bunbury, that is all.

JACK: If you don't take care, your friend Bunbury will get you into a serious scrape some day.

ALGERNON: I love scrapes. They are the only things that are never serious.

JACK: Oh, that's nonsense, Algy. You never talk anything but nonsense.

ALGERNON: Nobody ever does.

(Jack looks indignantly at him, and leaves the room. Algernon lights a cigarette, reads his shirt cuff, and smiles.)

ACT II

(Scene: Garden at the Manor House. A flight of gray stone steps leads up to the house. The garden, an old-fashioned one, full of roses. Time of year, July. Basket chairs, and a table covered with books, are set under a large yew tree. Miss Prism discovered seated at the table. Cecily is at the back watering flowers.)

MISS PRISM *(calling)*:   Cecily, Cecily! Surely such a utilitarian occupation as the watering of flowers is rather Moulton's duty than yours? Especially at a moment when intellectual pleasures await you. Your German grammar is on the table. Pray open it at page fifteen. We will repeat yesterday's lesson.

CECILY *(coming over very slowly)*:   But I don't like German. It isn't at all a becoming language. I know perfectly well that I look quite plain after my German lesson.

MISS PRISM: Child, you know how anxious your guardian is that you should improve yourself in every way. He laid particular stress on your German, as he was leaving for town yesterday. Indeed, he always lays stress on your German when he is leaving for town.

CECILY: Dear Uncle Jack is so very serious! Sometimes he is so serious that I think he cannot be quite well.

MISS PRISM *(drawing herself up)*:   Your guardian enjoys the best of health, and his gravity of demeanor is especially to be commended in one so comparatively young as he is. I know no one who has a higher sense of duty and responsibility.

CECILY: I suppose that is why he often looks a little bored when we three are together.

MISS PRISM: Cecily! I am surprised at you. Mr. Worthing has many troubles in his life. Idle merriment and triviality would be out of place in his conversation. You must remember his constant anxiety about that unfortunate young man his brother.

CECILY: I wish Uncle Jack would allow that unfortunate young man, his brother, to come down here sometimes. We might have a good influence over him, Miss Prism. I am sure you certainly would. You know German, and geology, and things of that kind influence a man very much.

(Cecily begins to write in her diary.)

MISS PRISM *(shaking her head)*:   I do not think that even I could produce any effect on a character that according to his own brother's admission is irretrievably weak and vacillating. Indeed I am not sure that I would desire to reclaim him. I am not in favor of this modern mania for turning bad people into good people at a moment's notice. As a man sows so let him reap. You must put away your diary, Cecily. I really don't see why you should keep a diary at all.

CECILY: I keep a diary in order to enter the wonderful secrets of my life. If I didn't write them down I should probably forget all about them.

MISS PRISM: Memory, my dear Cecily, is the diary that we all carry about with us.

CECILY: Yes, but it usually chronicles the things that have never happened, and couldn't possibly have happened. I believe that Memory is responsible for nearly all the three-volume novels that Mudie° sends us.

MISS PRISM: Do not speak slightingly of the three-volume novel, Cecily. I wrote one myself in earlier days.

CECILY: Did you really, Miss Prism? How wonderfully clever you are! I hope it did not end happily? I don't like novels that end happily. They depress me so much.

MISS PRISM: The good ended happily, and the bad unhappily. That is what Fiction means.

CECILY: I suppose so. But it seems very unfair. And was your novel ever published?

MISS PRISM: Alas! no. The manuscript unfortunately was abandoned. I use the word in the sense of lost or mislaid. To your work, child, these speculations are profitless.

CECILY (smiling):   But I see dear Dr. Chasuble coming up through the garden.

MISS PRISM (rising and advancing):   Dr. Chasuble! This is indeed a pleasure.

(Enter Canon Chasuble.)

CHASUBLE: And how are we this morning? Miss Prism, you are, I trust, well?

CECILY: Miss Prism has just been complaining of a slight headache. I think it would do her so much good to have a short stroll with you in the park, Dr. Chasuble.

MISS PRISM: Cecily, I have not mentioned anything about a headache.

CECILY: No, dear Miss Prism, I know that, but I felt instinctively that you had a headache. Indeed I was thinking about that, and not about my German lesson, when the Rector came in.

CHASUBLE: I hope, Cecily, you are not inattentive.

CECILY: Oh, I am afraid I am.

CHASUBLE: That is strange. Were I fortunate enough to be Miss Prism's pupil, I would hang upon her lips. (Miss Prism glares.) I spoke metaphorically.— My metaphor was drawn from bees. Ahem! Mr. Worthing, I suppose, has not returned from town yet?

MISS PRISM: We do not expect him till Monday afternoon.

CHASUBLE: Ah yes, he usually likes to spend his Sunday in London. He is not one of those whose sole aim is enjoyment, as, by all accounts, that unfortunate young man his brother seems to be. But I must not disturb Egeria° and her pupil any longer.

MISS PRISM: Egeria? My name is Laetitia, Doctor.

CHASUBLE (bowing):   A classical allusion merely, drawn from the Pagan authors. I shall see you both no doubt at Evensong?

MISS PRISM: I think, dear Doctor, I will have a stroll with you. I find I have a headache after all, and a walk might do it good.

CHASUBLE: With pleasure, Miss Prism, with pleasure. We might go as far as the schools and back.

Mudie: A well-known lending library of the time, established by Charles Edward Mudie.
Egeria: Roman goddess of water.

MISS PRISM: That would be delightful. Cecily, you will read your Political Economy in my absence. The chapter on the Fall of the Rupee° you may omit. It is somewhat too sensational. Even these metallic problems have their melodramatic side.

(Goes down the garden with Dr. Chasuble.)

CECILY (*picks up books and throws them back on table*):   Horrid Political Economy! Horrid Geography! Horrid, horrid German!

(Enter Merriman with a card on a salver.)

MERRIMAN: Mr. Ernest Worthing has just driven over from the station. He has brought his luggage with him.

CECILY (*takes the card and reads it*):   "Mr. Ernest Worthing, B.4, The Albany, W." Uncle Jack's brother! Did you tell him Mr. Worthing was in town?

MERRIMAN: Yes, Miss. He seemed very much disappointed. I mentioned that you and Miss Prism were in the garden. He said he was anxious to speak to you privately for a moment.

CECILY: Ask Mr. Ernest Worthing to come here. I suppose you had better talk to the housekeeper about a room for him.

MERRIMAN: Yes, Miss. (*Merriman goes off.*)

CECILY: I have never met any really wicked person before. I feel rather frightened. I am so afraid he will look just like everyone else.

(Enter Algernon, very gay and debonair.)

He does!

ALGERNON (*raising his hat*):   You are my little cousin Cecily, I'm sure.

CECILY: You are under some strange mistake. I am not little. In fact, I believe I am more than usually tall for my age. (*Algernon is rather taken aback.*) But I am your cousin Cecily. You, I see from your card, are Uncle Jack's brother, my cousin Ernest, my wicked cousin Ernest.

ALGERNON: Oh! I am not really wicked at all, Cousin Cecily. You mustn't think that I am wicked.

CECILY: If you are not, then you have certainly been deceiving us all in a very inexcusable manner. I hope you have not been leading a double life, pretending to be wicked and being really good all the time. That would be hypocrisy.

ALGERNON (*looks at her in amazement*):   Oh! Of course I have been rather reckless.

CECILY: I am glad to hear it.

ALGERNON: In fact, now you mention the subject, I have been very bad in my own small way.

CECILY: I don't think you should be so proud of that, though I am sure it must have been very pleasant.

ALGERNON: It is much pleasanter being here with you.

CECILY: I can't understand how you are here at all. Uncle Jack won't be back till Monday afternoon.

Fall of the Rupee: Reference to the Indian rupee, whose steady deflation between 1873 and 1893 caused the Indian government finally to close the mints.

ALGERNON: That is a great disappointment. I am obliged to go up by the first train on Monday morning. I have a business appointment that I am anxious— to miss.

CECILY: Couldn't you miss it anywhere but in London?

ALGERNON: No: the appointment is in London.

CECILY: Well, I know, of course, how important it is not to keep a business engagement, if one wants to retain any sense of the beauty of life, but still I think you had better wait till Uncle Jack arrives. I know he wants to speak to you about your emigrating.

ALGERNON: About my what?

CECILY: Your emigrating. He has gone up to buy your outfit.

ALGERNON: I certainly wouldn't let Jack buy my outfit. He has no taste in neckties at all.

CECILY: I don't think you will require neckties. Uncle Jack is sending you to Australia.

ALGERNON: Australia! I'd sooner die.

CECILY: Well, he said at dinner on Wednesday night, that you would have to choose between this world, the next world, and Australia.

ALGERNON: Oh, well! The accounts I have received of Australia and the next world are not particularly encouraging. This world is good enough for me, Cousin Cecily.

CECILY: Yes, but are you good enough for it?

ALGERNON: I'm afraid I'm not that. That is why I want you to reform me. You might make that your mission, if you don't mind, Cousin Cecily.

CECILY: I'm afraid I've no time, this afternoon.

ALGERNON: Well, would you mind my reforming myself this afternoon?

CECILY: It is rather quixotic° of you. But I think you should try.

ALGERNON: I will. I feel better already.

CECILY: You are looking a little worse.

ALGERNON: That is because I am hungry.

CECILY: How thoughtless of me. I should have remembered that when one is going to lead an entirely new life, one requires regular and wholesome meals. Won't you come in?

ALGERNON: Thank you. Might I have a buttonhole° first? I never have any appetite unless I have a buttonhole first.

CECILY: A Maréchal Niel?°

ALGERNON: No, I'd sooner have a pink rose.

CECILY: Why?   (Cuts a flower.)

ALGERNON: Because you are like a pink rose, Cousin Cecily.

CECILY: I don't think it can be right for you to talk to me like that. Miss Prism never says such things to me.

ALGERNON: Then Miss Prism is a shortsighted old lady. (Cecily puts the rose in his buttonhole.) You are the prettiest girl I ever saw.

---

quixotic: Foolishly impractical, from the idealistic hero of Cervantes' Don Quixote.   **buttonhole:** Boutonniere.   **Maréchal Niel:** A yellow rose.

CECILY: Miss Prism says that all good looks are a snare.

ALGERNON: They are a snare that every sensible man would like to be caught in.

CECILY: Oh! I don't think I would care to catch a sensible man. I shouldn't know what to talk to him about.

> *(They pass into the house. Miss Prism and Dr. Chasuble return.)*

MISS PRISM: You are too much alone, dear Dr. Chasuble. You should get married. A misanthrope I can understand—a womanthrope, never!

CHASUBLE (*with a scholar's shudder*):   Believe me, I do not deserve so neologistic a phrase. The precept as well as the practice of the Primitive Church was distinctly against matrimony.

MISS PRISM (*sententiously*):   That is obviously the reason why the Primitive Church has not lasted up to the present day. And you do not seem to realize, dear Doctor, that by persistently remaining single, a man converts himself into a permanent public temptation. Men should be more careful; this very celibacy leads weaker vessels astray.

CHASUBLE: But is a man not equally attractive when married?

MISS PRISM: No married man is ever attractive except to his wife.

CHASUBLE: And often, I've been told, not even to her.

MISS PRISM: That depends on the intellectual sympathies of the woman. Maturity can always be depended on. Ripeness can be trusted. Young women are green. (*Dr. Chasuble starts.*) I spoke horticulturally. My metaphor was drawn from fruits. But where is Cecily?

CHASUBLE: Perhaps she followed us to the schools.

(Enter Jack slowly from the back of the garden. He is dressed in the deepest mourning, with crepe hatband and black gloves.)

MISS PRISM: Mr. Worthing!

CHASUBLE: Mr. Worthing?

MISS PRISM: This is indeed a surprise. We did not look for you till Monday afternoon.

JACK (*shakes Miss Prism's hand in a tragic manner*):   I have returned sooner than I expected. Dr. Chasuble, I hope you are well?

CHASUBLE: Dear Mr. Worthing, I trust this garb of woe does not betoken some terrible calamity?

JACK: My brother.

MISS PRISM: More shameful debts and extravagance?

CHASUBLE: Still leading his life of pleasure?

JACK (*shaking his head*):   Dead!

CHASUBLE: Your brother Ernest dead?

JACK: Quite dead.

MISS PRISM: What a lesson for him! I trust he will profit by it.

CHASUBLE: Mr. Worthing, I offer you my sincere condolence. You have at least the consolation of knowing that you were always the most generous and forgiving of brothers.

JACK: Poor Ernest! He had many faults, but it is a sad, sad blow.

CHASUBLE: Very sad indeed. Were you with him at the end?

JACK: No. He died abroad, in Paris, in fact. I had a telegram last night from the manager of the Grand Hotel.

CHASUBLE: Was the cause of death mentioned?

JACK: A severe chill, it seems.

MISS PRISM: As a man sows, so shall he reap.

CHASUBLE (*raising his hand*):   Charity, dear Miss Prism, charity! None of us are perfect. I myself am peculiarly susceptible to drafts. Will the interment take place here?

JACK: No. He seemed to have expressed a desire to be buried in Paris.

CHASUBLE: In Paris! (*Shakes his head.*) I fear that hardly points to any very serious state of mind at the last. You would no doubt wish me to make some slight allusion to this tragic domestic affliction next Sunday. (*Jack presses his hand convulsively.*) My sermon on the meaning of the manna in the wilderness can be adapted to almost any occasion, joyful, or, as in the present case, distressing. (*All sigh.*) I have preached it at harvest celebrations, christenings, confirmations, on days of humiliation and festal days. The last time I delivered it was in the Cathedral, as a charity sermon on behalf of the Society for the Prevention of Discontent among the Upper Orders. The Bishop, who was present, was much struck by some of the analogies I drew.

JACK: Ah! that reminds me, you mentioned christenings I think, Dr. Chasuble? I suppose you know how to christen all right? (*Dr. Chasuble looks astounded.*) I mean, of course, you are continually christening, aren't you?

MISS PRISM: It is, I regret to say, one of the Rector's most constant duties in this parish. I have often spoken to the poorer classes on the subject. But they don't seem to know what thrift is.

CHASUBLE: But is there any particular infant in whom you are interested, Mr. Worthing? Your brother was, I believe, unmarried, was he not?

JACK: Oh yes.

MISS PRISM (*bitterly*):   People who live entirely for pleasure usually are.

JACK: But it is not for any child, dear Doctor. I am very fond of children. No! the fact is, I would like to be christened myself, this afternoon, if you have nothing better to do.

CHASUBLE: But surely, Mr. Worthing, you have been christened already?

JACK: I don't remember anything about it.

CHASUBLE: But have you any grave doubts on the subject?

JACK: I certainly intend to have. Of course I don't know if the thing would bother you in any way, or if you think I am a little too old now.

CHASUBLE: Not at all. The sprinkling, and, indeed, the immersion of adults is a perfectly canonical practice.

JACK: Immersion!

CHASUBLE: You need have no apprehensions. Sprinkling is all that is necessary, or indeed I think advisable. Our weather is so changeable. At what hour would you wish the ceremony performed?

JACK: Oh, I might trot round about five if that would suit you.

CHASUBLE: Perfectly, perfectly! In fact I have two similar ceremonies to perform at that time. A case of twins that occurred recently in one of the outlying cottages on your own estate. Poor Jenkins the carter, a most hardworking man.

JACK: Oh! I don't see much fun in being christened along with other babies. It would be childish. Would half-past five do?

CHASUBLE: Admirably! Admirably! (*Takes out watch.*) And now, dear Mr. Worthing, I will not intrude any longer into a house of sorrow. I would merely beg you not to be too much bowed down by grief. What seem to us bitter trials are often blessings in disguise.

MISS PRISM: This seems to me a blessing of an extremely obvious kind.

(*Enter Cecily from the house.*)

CECILY: Uncle Jack! Oh, I am pleased to see you back. But what horrid clothes you have got on! Do go and change them.

MISS PRISM: Cecily!

CHASUBLE: My child! my child!

(*Cecily goes towards Jack; he kisses her brow in a melancholy manner.*)

CECILY: What is the matter, Uncle Jack? Do look happy! You look as if you had toothache, and I have got such a surprise for you. Who do you think is in the dining room? Your brother!

JACK: Who?

CECILY: Your brother Ernest. He arrived about half an hour ago.

JACK: What nonsense! I haven't got a brother.

CECILY: Oh, don't say that. However badly he may have behaved to you in the past he is still your brother. You couldn't be so heartless as to disown him. I'll tell him to come out. And you will shake hands with him, won't you, Uncle Jack?

(*Runs back into the house.*)

CHASUBLE: These are very joyful tidings.

MISS PRISM: After we had all been resigned to his loss, his sudden return seems to me peculiarly distressing.

JACK: My brother is in the dining room? I don't know what it all means. I think it is perfectly absurd.

(*Enter Algernon and Cecily hand in hand. They come slowly up to Jack.*)

JACK: Good heavens!   (*Motions Algernon away.*)

ALGERNON: Brother John, I have come down from town to tell you that I am very sorry for all the trouble I have given you, and that I intend to lead a better life in the future.

(*Jack glares at him and does not take his hand.*)

CECILY: Uncle Jack, you are not going to refuse your own brother's hand?

JACK: Nothing will induce me to take his hand. I think his coming down here disgraceful. He knows perfectly well why.

CECILY: Uncle Jack, do be nice. There is some good in everyone. Ernest has just been telling me about his poor invalid friend Mr. Bunbury whom he goes to visit so often. And surely there must be much good in one who is kind to an invalid, and leaves the pleasures of London to sit by a bed of pain.

JACK: Oh! he has been talking about Bunbury has he?

CECILY: Yes, he has told me all about poor Mr. Bunbury, and his terrible state of health.

JACK: Bunbury! Well, I won't have him talk to you about Bunbury or about anything else. It is enough to drive one perfectly frantic.

ALGERNON: Of course I admit that the faults were all on my side. But I must say that I think that Brother John's coldness to me is peculiarly painful. I expected a more enthusiastic welcome, especially considering it is the first time I have come here.

CECILY: Uncle Jack, if you don't shake hands with Ernest I will never forgive you.

JACK: Never forgive me?

CECILY: Never, never, never!

JACK: Well, this is the last time I shall ever do it.

(Shakes hands with Algernon and glares.)

CHASUBLE: It's pleasant, is it not, to see so perfect a reconciliation? I think we might leave the two brothers together.

MISS PRISM: Cecily, you will come with us.

CECILY: Certainly, Miss Prism. My little task of reconciliation is over.

CHASUBLE: You have done a beautiful action today, dear child.

MISS PRISM: We must not be premature in our judgments.

CECILY: I feel very happy.   *(They all go off.)*

JACK: You young scoundrel, Algy, you must get out of this place as soon as possible. I don't allow any Bunburying here.

(Enter Merriman.)

MERRIMAN: I have put Mr. Ernest's things in the room next to yours, sir. I suppose that is all right?

JACK: What?

MERRIMAN: Mr. Ernest's luggage, sir. I have unpacked it and put it in the room next to your own.

JACK: His luggage?

MERRIMAN: Yes, sir. Three portmanteaus, a dressing case, two hatboxes, and a large luncheon basket.

ALGERNON: I am afraid I can't stay more than a week this time.

JACK: Merriman, order the dog cart at once. Mr. Ernest has been suddenly called back to town.

MERRIMAN: Yes, sir.   *(Goes back into the house.)*

ALGERNON: What a fearful liar you are, Jack. I have not been called back to town at all.

JACK: Yes, you have.

ALGERNON: I haven't heard anyone call me.

JACK: Your duty as a gentleman calls you back.

ALGERNON: My duty as a gentleman has never interfered with my pleasures in the smallest degree.

JACK: I can quite understand that.

ALGERNON: Well, Cecily is a darling.

JACK: You are not to talk of Miss Cardew like that. I don't like it.

ALGERNON: Well, I don't like your clothes. You look perfectly ridiculous in them. Why on earth don't you go up and change? It is perfectly childish to be in deep mourning for a man who is actually staying for a whole week in your house as a guest. I call it grotesque.

JACK: You are certainly not staying with me for a whole week as a guest or anything else. You have got to leave — by the four-five train.

ALGERNON: I certainly won't leave you so long as you are in mourning. It would be most unfriendly. If I were in mourning you would stay with me, I suppose. I should think it very unkind if you didn't.

JACK: Well, will you go if I change my clothes?

ALGERNON: Yes, if you are not too long. I never saw anybody take so long to dress, and with such little result.

JACK: Well, at any rate, that is better than being always overdressed as you are.

ALGERNON: If I am occasionally a little overdressed, I make up for it by being always immensely overeducated.

JACK: Your vanity is ridiculous, your conduct an outrage, and your presence in my garden utterly absurd. However, you have got to catch the four-five, and I hope you will have a pleasant journey back to town. This Bunburying, as you call it, has not been a great success for you.

(Goes into the house.)

ALGERNON: I think it has been a great success. I'm in love with Cecily, and that is everything.

(Enter Cecily at the back of the garden. She picks up the can and begins to water the flowers.)

But I must see her before I go, and make arrangements for another Bunbury. Ah, there she is.

CECILY: Oh, I merely came back to water the roses. I thought you were with Uncle Jack.

ALGERNON: He's gone to order the dog cart for me.

CECILY: Oh, is he going to take you for a nice drive?

ALGERNON: He's going to send me away.

CECILY: Then have we got to part?

ALGERNON: I am afraid so. It's a very painful parting.

CECILY: It is always painful to part from people whom one has known for a very brief space of time. The absence of old friends one can endure with equanimity. But even a momentary separation from anyone to whom one has just been introduced is almost unbearable.

ALGERNON: Thank you.

(Enter Merriman.)

MERRIMAN: The dog cart is at the door, sir.

(Algernon looks appealingly at Cecily.)

CECILY: It can wait, Merriman — for — five minutes.

MERRIMAN: Yes, miss.   *(Exit Merriman.)*

ALGERNON: I hope, Cecily, I shall not offend you if I state quite frankly and openly that you seem to me to be in every way the visible personification of absolute perfection.

CECILY: I think your frankness does you great credit, Ernest. If you will allow me I will copy your remarks into my diary.

(Goes over to table and begins writing in diary.)

ALGERNON: Do you really keep a diary? I'd give anything to look at it. May I?

CECILY: Oh no. *(Puts her hand over it.)* You see, it is simply a very young girl's record of her own thoughts and impressions, and consequently meant for publication. When it appears in volume form I hope you will order a copy. But pray, Ernest, don't stop. I delight in taking down from dictation. I have reached "absolute perfection." You can go on. I am quite ready for more.

ALGERNON *(somewhat taken aback)*:   Ahem! Ahem!

CECILY: Oh, don't cough, Ernest. When one is dictating one should speak fluently and not cough. Besides, I don't know how to spell a cough.

(Writes as Algernon speaks.)

ALGERNON *(speaking very rapidly)*:   Cecily, ever since I first looked upon your wonderful and incomparable beauty, I have dared to love you wildly, passionately, devotedly, hopelessly.

CECILY: I don't think that you should tell me that you love me wildly, passionately, devotedly, hopelessly. Hopelessly doesn't seem to make much sense, does it?

ALGERNON: Cecily!

(Enter Merriman.)

MERRIMAN: The dog cart is waiting, sir.

ALGERNON: Tell it to come round next week, at the same hour.

MERRIMAN *(looks at Cecily, who makes no sign)*:   Yes, sir.

(Merriman retires.)

CECILY: Uncle Jack would be very much annoyed if he knew you were staying on till next week, at the same hour.

ALGERNON: Oh, I don't care about Jack. I don't care for anybody in the whole world but you. I love you, Cecily. You will marry me, won't you?

CECILY: You silly boy! Of course. Why, we have been engaged for the last three months.

ALGERNON: For the last three months?

CECILY: Yes, it will be exactly three months on Thursday.

ALGERNON: But how did we become engaged?

CECILY: Well, ever since dear Uncle Jack first confessed to us that he had a younger brother who was very wicked and bad, you of course have formed the chief topic of conversation between myself and Miss Prism. And of course a man who is much talked about is always very attractive. One feels there must be something in him after all. I daresay it was foolish of me, but I fell in love with you, Ernest.

ALGERNON: Darling! And when was the engagement actually settled?

CECILY: On the 14th of February last. Worn out by your entire ignorance of my existence, I determined to end the matter one way or the other, and after a long struggle with myself I accepted you under this dear old tree here. The next day I bought this little ring in your name, and this is the little bangle with the true lovers' knot I promised you always to wear.

ALGERNON: Did I give you this? It's very pretty, isn't it?

CECILY: Yes, you've wonderfully good taste, Ernest. It's the excuse I've always given for your leading such a bad life. And this is the box in which I keep all your dear letters.

(Kneels at table, opens box, and produces letters tied up with blue ribbon.)

ALGERNON: My letters! But my own sweet Cecily, I have never written you any letters.

CECILY: You need hardly remind me of that, Ernest. I remember only too well that I was forced to write your letters for you. I wrote always three times a week, and sometimes oftener.

ALGERNON: Oh, do let me read them, Cecily!

CECILY: Oh, I couldn't possibly. They would make you far too conceited. (*Replaces box.*) The three you wrote me after I had broken off the engagement are so beautiful, and so badly spelled, that even now I can hardly read them without crying a little.

ALGERNON: But was our engagement ever broken off?

CECILY: Of course it was. On the 22nd of last March. You can see the entry if you like. (*Shows diary.*) "Today I broke off my engagement with Ernest. I feel it is better to do so. The weather still continues charming."

ALGERNON: But why on earth did you break it off? What had I done? I had done nothing at all. Cecily, I am very much hurt indeed to hear you broke it off. Particularly when the weather was so charming.

CECILY: It would hardly have been a really serious engagement if it hadn't been broken off at least once. But I forgave you before the week was out.

ALGERNON (*crossing to her, and kneeling*):   What a perfect angel you are, Cecily.

CECILY: You dear romantic boy. (*He kisses her; she puts her fingers through his hair.*) I hope your hair curls naturally, does it?

ALGERNON: Yes, darling, with a little help from others.

CECILY: I am so glad.

ALGERNON: You'll never break off our engagement again, Cecily?

CECILY: I don't think I could break it off now that I have actually met you. Besides, of course, there is the question of your name.

ALGERNON (*nervously*):   Yes, of course.

CECILY: You must not laugh at me, darling, but it had always been a girlish dream of mine to love someone whose name was Ernest. (*Algernon rises, Cecily also.*) There is something in that name that seems to inspire absolute confidence. I pity any poor married woman whose husband is not called Ernest.

ALGERNON: But, my dear child, do you mean to say you could not love me if I had some other name?

CECILY: But what name?

ALGERNON: Oh, any name you like—Algernon—for instance—

CECILY: But I don't like the name of Algernon.

ALGERNON: Well, my own dear, sweet, loving little darling, I really can't see why you should object to the name of Algernon. It is not at all a bad name. In fact, it is rather an aristocratic name. Half of the chaps who get into the Bankruptcy Court are called Algernon. But seriously, Cecily—(*moving to her*)—if my name was Algy, couldn't you love me?

CECILY (*rising*):   I might respect you, Ernest, I might admire your character, but I fear that I should not be able to give you my undivided attention.

ALGERNON: Ahem! Cecily! (*Picking up hat.*) Your Rector here is, I suppose, thoroughly experienced in the practice of all the rites and ceremonials of the Church?

CECILY: Oh yes. Dr. Chasuble is a most learned man. He has never written a single book, so you can imagine how much he knows.

ALGERNON: I must see him at once on a most important christening—I mean on most important business.

CECILY: Oh!

ALGERNON: I shan't be away more than half an hour.

CECILY: Considering that we have been engaged since February the 14th, and that I only met you today for the first time, I think it is rather hard that you should leave me for so long a period as half an hour. Couldn't you make it twenty minutes?

ALGERNON: I'll be back in no time.

(*Kisses her and rushes down the garden.*)

CECILY: What an impetuous boy he is! I like his hair so much. I must enter his proposal in my diary.

(*Enter Merriman.*)

MERRIMAN: A Miss Fairfax has just called to see Mr. Worthing. On very important business Miss Fairfax states.

CECILY: Isn't Mr. Worthing in his library?

MERRIMAN: Mr. Worthing went over in the direction of the Rectory some time ago.

CECILY: Pray ask the lady to come out here; Mr. Worthing is sure to be back soon. And you can bring tea.

MERRIMAN: Yes, miss.   (*Goes out.*)

CECILY: Miss Fairfax! I suppose one of the many good elderly women who are associated with Uncle Jack in some of his philanthropic work in London. I don't quite like women who are interested in philanthropic work. I think it is so forward of them.

(*Enter Merriman.*)

MERRIMAN: Miss Fairfax.

(*Enter Gwendolen. Exit Merriman.*)

CECILY (*advancing to meet her*):   Pray let me introduce myself to you. My name is Cecily Cardew.

GWENDOLEN: Cecily Cardew? (*Moving to her and shaking hands.*) What a very sweet name! Something tells me that we are going to be great friends. I like you already more than I can say. My first impressions of people are never wrong.

CECILY: How nice of you to like me so much after we have known each other such a comparatively short time. Pray sit down.

GWENDOLEN (*still standing up*):   I may call you Cecily, may I not?

CECILY: With pleasure!

GWENDOLEN: And you will always call me Gwendolen, won't you?

CECILY: If you wish.

GWENDOLEN: Then that is all quite settled, is it not?

CECILY: I hope so.

(A pause. They both sit down together.)

GWENDOLEN: Perhaps this might be a favorable opportunity for my mentioning who I am. My father is Lord Bracknell. You have never heard of Papa, I suppose?

CECILY: I don't think so.

GWENDOLEN: Outside the family circle, Papa, I am glad to say, is entirely unknown. I think that is quite as it should be. The home seems to me to be the proper sphere for the man. And certainly once a man begins to neglect his domestic duties he becomes painfully effeminate, does he not? And I don't like that. It makes men so very attractive. Cecily, Mama, whose views on education are remarkably strict, has brought me up to be extremely short-sighted; it is part of her system, so do you mind my looking at you through my glasses?

CECILY: Oh! not at all, Gwendolen. I am very fond of being looked at.

GWENDOLEN (*after examining Cecily carefully through a lorgnette*):   You are here on a short visit I suppose?

CECILY: Oh no! I live here.

GWENDOLEN (*severely*):   Really? Your mother, no doubt, or some female relative of advanced years, resides here also?

CECILY: Oh no! I have no mother, nor, in fact, any relations.

GWENDOLEN: Indeed?

CECILY: My dear guardian, with the assistance of Miss Prism, has the arduous task of looking after me.

GWENDOLEN: Your guardian?

CECILY: Yes, I am Mr. Worthing's ward.

GWENDOLEN: Oh! It is strange he never mentioned to me that he had a ward. How secretive of him! He grows more interesting hourly. I am not sure, however, that the news inspires me with feelings of unmixed delight. (*Rising and going to her.*) I am very fond of you, Cecily; I have liked you ever since I met you! But I am bound to state that now that I know that you are Mr. Worthing's ward, I cannot help expressing a wish you were—well just a little older than you seem to be—and not quite so very alluring in appearance. In fact, if I may speak candidly—

CECILY: Pray do! I think that whenever one has anything unpleasant to say, one should always be quite candid.

GWENDOLEN: Well, to speak with perfect candor, Cecily, I wish that you were fully forty-two, and more than usually plain for your age. Ernest has a strong upright nature. He is the very soul of truth and honor. Disloyalty would be as impossible to him as deception. But even men of the noblest possible moral character are extremely susceptible to the influence of the physical charms of others. Modern, no less than Ancient History, supplies us with many most painful examples of what I refer to. If it were not so, indeed, History would be quite unreadable.

CECILY: I beg your pardon, Gwendolen, did you say Ernest?

GWENDOLEN: Yes.

CECILY: Oh, but it is not Mr. Ernest Worthing who is my guardian. It is his brother — his elder brother.

GWENDOLEN (*sitting down again*):   Ernest never mentioned to me that he had a brother.

CECILY: I am sorry to say they have not been on good terms for a long time.

GWENDOLEN: Ah! that accounts for it. And now that I think of it I have never heard any man mention his brother. The subject seems distasteful to most men. Cecily, you have lifted a load from my mind. I was growing almost anxious. It would have been terrible if any cloud had come across a friendship like ours, would it not? Of course you are quite, quite sure that it is not Mr. Ernest Worthing who is your guardian?

CECILY: Quite sure. (*A pause.*) In fact, I am going to be his.

GWENDOLEN (*inquiringly*):   I beg your pardon?

CECILY (*rather shy and confidingly*):   Dearest Gwendolen, there is no reason why I should make a secret of it to you. Our little county newspaper is sure to chronicle the fact next week. Mr. Ernest Worthing and I are engaged to be married.

GWENDOLEN (*quite politely, rising*):   My darling Cecily, I think there must be some slight error. Mr. Ernest Worthing is engaged to me. The announcement will appear in the *Morning Post* on Saturday at the latest.

CECILY (*very politely, rising*):   I am afraid you must be under some misconception. Ernest proposed to me exactly ten minutes ago.   (*Shows diary.*)

GWENDOLEN (*examines diary through her lorgnette carefully*):   It is certainly very curious, for he asked me to be his wife yesterday afternoon at 5:30. If you would care to verify the incident, pray do so. (*Produces diary of her own.*) I never travel without my diary. One should always have something sensational to read in the train. I am so sorry, dear Cecily, if it is any disappointment to you, but I am afraid *I* have the prior claim.

CECILY: It would distress me more than I can tell you, dear Gwendolen, if it caused you any mental or physical anguish, but I feel bound to point out that since Ernest proposed to you he clearly has changed his mind.

GWENDOLEN (*meditatively*):   If the poor fellow has been entrapped into any foolish promise I shall consider it my duty to rescue him at once, and with a firm hand.

CECILY (*thoughtfully and sadly*):   Whatever unfortunate entanglement my dear boy may have got into, I will never reproach him with it after we are married.

GWENDOLEN: Do you allude to me, Miss Cardew, as an entanglement? You are presumptuous. On an occasion of this kind it becomes more than a moral duty to speak one's mind. It becomes a pleasure.

CECILY: Do you suggest, Miss Fairfax, that I entrapped Ernest into an engagement? How dare you? This is no time for wearing the shallow mask of manners. When I see a spade I call it a spade.

GWENDOLEN (*satirically*):   I am glad to say that I have never seen a spade. It is obvious that our social spheres have been widely different.

(*Enter Merriman, followed by the Footman. He carries a salver, tablecloth, and plate stand. Cecily is about to retort. The presence of the servants exercises a restraining influence, under which both girls chafe.*)

MERRIMAN: Shall I lay tea here as usual, miss?

CECILY (*sternly, in a calm voice*):   Yes, as usual.

(*Merriman begins to clear table and lay cloth. A long pause. Cecily and Gwendolen glare at each other.*)

GWENDOLEN: Are there many interesting walks in the vicinity, Miss Cardew?

CECILY: Oh! Yes! a great many. From the top of one of the hills quite close one can see five counties.

GWENDOLEN: Five counties! I don't think I should like that. I hate crowds.

CECILY (*sweetly*):   I suppose that is why you live in town?

(*Gwendolen bites her lip, and beats her foot nervously with her parasol.*)

GWENDOLEN (*looking round*):   Quite a well-kept garden this is, Miss Cardew.

CECILY: So glad you like it, Miss Fairfax.

GWENDOLEN: I had no idea there were any flowers in the country.

CECILY: Oh, flowers are as common here, Miss Fairfax, as people are in London.

GWENDOLEN: Personally I cannot understand how anybody manages to exist in the country, if anybody who is anybody does. The country always bores me to death.

CECILY: Ah! This is what the newspapers call agricultural depression, is it not? I believe the aristocracy are suffering very much from it just at present. It is almost an epidemic amongst them, I have been told. May I offer you some tea, Miss Fairfax?

GWENDOLEN (*with elaborate politeness*):   Thank you. (*Aside.*) Detestable girl! But I require tea!

CECILY (*sweetly*):   Sugar?

GWENDOLEN (*superciliously*):   No, thank you. Sugar is not fashionable anymore.

(*Cecily looks angrily at her, takes up the tongs, and puts four lumps of sugar into the cup.*)

CECILY (*severely*):   Cake or bread and butter?

GWENDOLEN (*in a bored manner*):   Bread and butter, please. Cake is rarely seen at the best houses nowadays.

CECILY (*cuts a very large slice of cake, and puts it on the tray*):   Hand that to Miss Fairfax.

(*Merriman does so, and goes out with Footman. Gwendolen drinks the tea and makes a grimace. Puts down cup at once, reaches out her hand to the bread and butter, looks at it, and finds it is cake. Rises in indignation.*)

GWENDOLEN: You have filled my tea with lumps of sugar, and though I asked most distinctly for bread and butter, you have given me cake. I am known for the gentleness of my disposition, and the extraordinary sweetness of my nature, but I warn you, Miss Cardew, you may go too far.

CECILY (*rising*):   To save my poor, innocent, trusting boy from the machinations of any other girl there are no lengths to which I would not go.

GWENDOLEN: From the moment I saw you I distrusted you. I felt that you were false and deceitful. I am never deceived in such matters. My first impressions of people are invariably right.

CECILY: It seems to me, Miss Fairfax, that I am trespassing on your valuable time. No doubt you have many other calls of a similar character to make in the neighborhood.

(*Enter Jack.*)

GWENDOLEN (*catching sight of him*):   Ernest! My own Ernest!

JACK: Gwendolen! Darling!   (*Offers to kiss her.*)

GWENDOLEN (*drawing back*):   A moment! May I ask if you are engaged to be married to this young lady? (*Points to Cecily.*)

JACK (*laughing*):   To dear little Cecily! Of course not! What could have put such an idea into your pretty little head?

GWENDOLEN: Thank you. You may!

(*Offers her cheek.*)

CECILY (*very sweetly*):   I knew there must be some misunderstanding, Miss Fairfax. The gentleman whose arm is at present round your waist is my dear guardian, Mr. John Worthing.

GWENDOLEN: I beg your pardon?

CECILY: This is Uncle Jack.

GWENDOLEN (*receding*):   Jack! Oh!

(*Enter Algernon.*)

CECILY: Here is Ernest.

ALGERNON (*goes straight over to Cecily without noticing anyone else*):   My own love!

(*Offers to kiss her.*)

CECILY (*drawing back*):   A moment, Ernest! May I ask you — are you engaged to be married to this young lady?

ALGERNON (*looking round*):   To what young lady? Good heavens! Gwendolen!

CECILY: Yes! to good heavens, Gwendolen, I mean to Gwendolen.

ALGERNON (*laughing*):   Of course not! What could have put such an idea into your pretty little head?

CECILY: Thank you. (*Presenting her cheek to be kissed.*) You may.

(*Algernon kisses her.*)

GWENDOLEN: I felt there was some slight error, Miss Cardew. The gentleman who is now embracing you is my cousin, Mr. Algernon Moncrieff.

CECILY (*breaking away from Algernon*):   Algernon Moncrieff! Oh!

(*The two girls move towards each other and put their arms round each other's waists as if for protection.*)

CECILY: Are you called Algernon?

ALGERNON: I cannot deny it.

CECILY: Oh!

GWENDOLEN: Is your name really John?

JACK (*standing rather proudly*):   I could deny it if I liked. I could deny anything if I liked. But my name certainly is John. It has been John for years.

CECILY (*to Gwendolen*):   A gross deception has been practiced on both of us.

GWENDOLEN: My poor wounded Cecily!

CECILY: My sweet wronged Gwendolen!

GWENDOLEN (*slowly and seriously*):   You will call me sister, will you not?

(*They embrace. Jack and Algernon groan and walk up and down.*)

CECILY (*rather brightly*):   There is just one question I would like to be allowed to ask my guardian.

GWENDOLEN: An admirable idea! Mr. Worthing, there is just one question I would like to be permitted to put to you. Where is your brother Ernest? We are both engaged to be married to your brother Ernest, so it is a matter of some importance to us to know where your brother Ernest is at present.

JACK (*slowly and hesitatingly*):   Gwendolen—Cecily—it is very painful for me to be forced to speak the truth. It is the first time in my life that I have ever been reduced to such a painful position, and I am really quite inexperienced in doing anything of the kind. However I will tell you quite frankly that I have no brother Ernest. I have no brother at all. I never had a brother in my life, and I certainly have not the smallest intention of ever having one in the future.

CECILY (*surprised*):   No brother at all?

JACK (*cheerily*):   None!

GWENDOLEN (*severely*):   Had you never a brother of any kind?

JACK (*pleasantly*):   Never. Not even of any kind.

GWENDOLEN: I am afraid it is quite clear, Cecily, that neither of us is engaged to be married to anyone.

CECILY: It is not a very pleasant position for a young girl suddenly to find herself in. Is it?

GWENDOLEN: Let us go into the house. They will hardly venture to come after us there.

CECILY: No, men are so cowardly, aren't they?

(*They retire into the house with scornful looks.*)

JACK: This ghastly state of things is what you call Bunburying, I suppose?

ALGERNON: Yes, and a perfectly wonderful Bunbury it is. The most wonderful Bunbury I have ever had in my life.

JACK: Well, you've no right whatsoever to Bunbury here.

ALGERNON: That is absurd. One has a right to Bunbury anywhere one chooses. Every serious Bunburyist knows that.

JACK: Serious Bunburyist! Good heavens!

ALGERNON: Well, one must be serious about something, if one wants to have any amusement in life. I happen to be serious about Bunburying. What on earth you are serious about I haven't got the remotest idea. About everything, I should fancy. You have such an absolutely trivial nature.

JACK: Well, the only small satisfaction I have in the whole of this wretched business is that your friend Bunbury is quite exploded. You won't be able to run down to the country quite so often as you used to do, dear Algy. And a very good thing too.

ALGERNON: Your brother is a little off color, isn't he, dear Jack? You won't be able to disappear to London quite so frequently as your wicked custom was. And not a bad thing either.

JACK: As for your conduct towards Miss Cardew, I must say that your taking in a sweet, simple, innocent girl like that is quite inexcusable. To say nothing of the fact that she is my ward.

ALGERNON: I can see no possible defense at all for your deceiving a brilliant, clever, thoroughly experienced young lady like Miss Fairfax. To say nothing of the fact that she is my cousin.

JACK: I wanted to be engaged to Gwendolen, that is all. I love her.

ALGERNON: Well, I simply wanted to be engaged to Cecily. I adore her.

JACK: There is certainly no chance of your marrying Miss Cardew.

ALGERNON: I don't think there is much likelihood, Jack, of you and Miss Fairfax being united.

JACK: Well, that is no business of yours.

ALGERNON: If it was my business, I wouldn't talk about it. (*Begins to eat muffins.*) It is very vulgar to talk about one's business. Only people like stockbrokers do that, and then merely at dinner parties.

JACK: How you can sit there, calmly eating muffins when we are in this horrible trouble. I can't make out. You seem to me to be perfectly heartless.

ALGERNON: Well, I can't eat muffins in an agitated manner. The butter would probably get on my cuffs. One should always eat muffins quite calmly. It is the only way to eat them.

JACK: I say it's perfectly heartless your eating muffins at all, under the circumstances.

ALGERNON: When I am in trouble, eating is the only thing that consoles me. Indeed, when I am in really great trouble, as anyone who knows me intimately will tell you, I refuse everything except food and drink. At the present moment I am eating muffins because I am unhappy. Besides, I am particularly fond of muffins.

(Rising.)

JACK (*rising*):   Well, that is no reason why you should eat them all in that greedy way.

(Takes muffins from Algernon.)

ALGERNON *(offering tea cake)*:   I wish you would have tea cake instead. I don't like tea cake.

JACK: Good heavens! I suppose a man may eat his own muffins in his own garden.

ALGERNON: But you have just said it was perfectly heartless to eat muffins.

JACK: I said it was perfectly heartless of you, under the circumstances. That is a very different thing.

ALGERNON: That may be, but the muffins are the same.

(He seizes the muffin dish from Jack.)

JACK: Algy, I wish to goodness you would go.

ALGERNON: You can't possibly ask me to go without having some dinner. It's absurd. I never go without my dinner. No one ever does, except vegetarians and people like that. Besides I have just made arrangements, with Dr. Chasuble to be christened at a quarter to six under the name of Ernest.

JACK: My dear fellow, the sooner you give up that nonsense the better. I made arrangements this morning with Dr. Chasuble to be christened myself at 5:30, and I naturally will take the name of Ernest. Gwendolen would wish it. We can't both be christened Ernest. It's absurd. Besides, I have a perfect right to be christened if I like. There is no evidence at all that I ever have been christened by anybody. I should think it extremely probable I never was, and so does Dr. Chasuble. It is entirely different in your case. You have been christened already.

ALGERNON: Yes, but I have not been christened for years.

JACK: Yes, but you have been christened. That is the important thing.

ALGERNON: Quite so. So I know my constitution can stand it. If you are not quite sure about your ever having been christened, I must say I think it rather dangerous your venturing on it now. It might make you very unwell. You can hardly have forgotten that someone very closely connected with you was very nearly carried off this week in Paris by a severe chill.

JACK: Yes, but you said yourself that a severe chill was not hereditary.

ALGERNON: It usen't to be, I know — but I daresay it is now. Science is always making wonderful improvements in things.

JACK *(picking up the muffin dish)*:   Oh, that is nonsense; you are always talking nonsense.

ALGERNON: Jack, you are at the muffins again! I wish you wouldn't. There are only two left. *(Takes them.)* I told you I was particularly fond of muffins.

JACK: But I hate tea cake.

ALGERNON: Why on earth then do you allow tea cake to be served up for your guests? What ideas you have of hospitality!

JACK: Algernon! I have already told you to go. I don't want you here. Why don't you go!

ALGERNON: I haven't quite finished my tea yet! and there is still one muffin left.

(Jack groans, and sinks into a chair. Algernon still continues eating.)

ACT III

(Scene: Morning room at the Manor House. Gwendolen and Cecily are at the window, looking out into the garden.)

GWENDOLEN: The fact that they did not follow us at once into the house, as anyone else would have done, seems to me to show that they have some sense of shame left.

CECILY: They have been eating muffins. That looks like repentance.

GWENDOLEN (*after a pause*):   They don't seem to notice us at all. Couldn't you cough?

CECILY: But I haven't got a cough.

GWENDOLEN: They're looking at us. What effrontery!

CECILY: They're approaching. That's very forward of them.

GWENDOLEN: Let us preserve a dignified silence.

CECILY: Certainly. It's the only thing to do now.

(Enter Jack followed by Algernon. They whistle some dreadful popular air from a British opera.)

GWENDOLEN: This dignified silence seems to produce an unpleasant effect.

CECILY: A most distasteful one.

GWENDOLEN: But we will not be the first to speak.

CECILY: Certainly not.

GWENDOLEN: Mr. Worthing, I have something very particular to ask you. Much depends on your reply.

CECILY: Gwendolen, your common sense is invaluable. Mr. Moncrieff, kindly answer me the following question. Why did you pretend to be my guardian's brother?

ALGERNON: In order that I might have an opportunity of meeting you.

CECILY (*to Gwendolen*):   That certainly seems a satisfactory explanation, does it not?

GWENDOLEN: Yes, dear, if you can believe him.

CECILY: I don't. But that does not affect the wonderful beauty of his answer.

GWENDOLEN: True. In matters of grave importance, style, not sincerity is the vital thing. Mr. Worthing, what explanation can you offer to me for pretending to have a brother? Was it in order that you might have an opportunity of coming up to town to see me as often as possible?

JACK: Can you doubt it, Miss Fairfax?

GWENDOLEN: I have the gravest doubts upon the subject. But I intend to crush them. This is not the moment for German skepticism. (*Moving to Cecily.*) Their explanations appear to be quite satisfactory, especially Mr. Worthing's. That seems to me to have the stamp of truth upon it.

CECILY: I am more than content with what Mr. Moncrieff said. His voice alone inspires one with absolute credulity.

GWENDOLEN: Then you think we should forgive them?

CECILY: Yes. I mean no.

GWENDOLEN: True! I had forgotten. There are principles at stake that one cannot surrender. Which of us should tell them? The task is not a pleasant one.

CECILY: Could we not both speak at the same time?

GWENDOLEN: An excellent idea! I nearly always speak at the same time as other people. Will you take the time from me?

CECILY: Certainly.

(Gwendolen beats time with uplifted finger.)

GWENDOLEN AND CECILY (*speaking together*):   Your Christian names are still an insuperable barrier. That is all!

JACK AND ALGERNON (*speaking together*):   Our Christian names! Is that all? But we are going to be christened this afternoon.

GWENDOLEN (*to Jack*):   For my sake you are prepared to do this terrible thing?

JACK: I am!

CECILY (*to Algernon*):   To please me you are ready to face this fearful ordeal?

ALGERNON: I am!

GWENDOLEN: How absurd to talk of the equality of the sexes! Where questions of self-sacrifice are concerned, men are infinitely beyond us.

JACK: We are! (*Clasps hands with Algernon.*)

CECILY: They have moments of physical courage of which we women know absolutely nothing.

GWENDOLEN (*to Jack*):   Darling!

ALGERNON (*to Cecily*):   Darling!

(They fall into each other's arms.)

(Enter Merriman. When he enters he coughs loudly, seeing the situation.)

MERRIMAN: Ahem! Ahem! Lady Bracknell!

JACK: Good heavens!

(Enter Lady Bracknell. The couples separate, in alarm. Exit Merriman.)

LADY BRACKNELL: Gwendolen! What does this mean?

GWENDOLEN: Merely that I am engaged to be married to Mr. Worthing, Mama.

LADY BRACKNELL: Come here. Sit down. Sit down immediately. Hesitation of any kind is a sign of mental decay in the young, of physical weakness in the old. (*Turns to Jack.*) Apprised, sir, of my daughter's sudden flight by her trusty maid, whose confidence I purchased by means of a small coin, I followed her at once by a luggage train. Her unhappy father is, I am glad to say, under the impression that she is attending a more than usually lengthy lecture by the University Extension Scheme on the influence of a permanent income on thought. I do not propose to undeceive him. Indeed I have never undeceived him on any question. I would consider it wrong. But of course, you will clearly understand that all communication between yourself and my daughter must cease immediately from this moment. On this point, as indeed on all points, I am firm.

JACK: I am engaged to be married to Gwendolen, Lady Bracknell!

LADY BRACKNELL: You are nothing of the kind, sir. And now, as regards Algernon! — Algernon!

ALGERNON: Yes, Aunt Augusta.

LADY BRACKNELL: May I ask if it is in this house that your invalid friend Mr. Bunbury resides?

ALGERNON (*stammering*):   Oh! No! Bunbury doesn't live here. Bunbury is somewhere else at present. In fact, Bunbury is dead.

LADY BRACKNELL: Dead! When did Mr. Bunbury die? His death must have been extremely sudden.

ALGERNON (*airily*):   Oh! I killed Bunbury this afternoon. I mean poor Bunbury died this afternoon.

LADY BRACKNELL: What did he die of?

ALGERNON: Bunbury? Oh, he was quite exploded.

LADY BRACKNELL: Exploded! Was he the victim of a revolutionary outrage? I was not aware that Mr. Bunbury was interested in social legislation. If so, he is well punished for his morbidity.

ALGERNON: My dear Aunt Augusta, I mean he was found out! The doctors found out that Bunbury could not live, that is what I mean—so Bunbury died.

LADY BRACKNELL: He seems to have had great confidence in the opinion of his physicians. I am glad, however, that he made up his mind at the last to some definite course of action, and acted under proper medical advice. And now that we have finally got rid of this Mr. Bunbury, may I ask, Mr. Worthing, who is that young person whose hand my nephew Algernon is now holding in what seems to me a peculiarly unnecessary manner?

JACK: That lady is Miss Cecily Cardew, my ward.

(Lady Bracknell bows coldly to Cecily.)

ALGERNON: I am engaged to be married to Cecily, Aunt Augusta.

LADY BRACKNELL: I beg your pardon?

CECILY: Mr. Moncrieff and I are engaged to be married, Lady Bracknell.

LADY BRACKNELL (*with a shiver, crossing to the sofa and sitting down*):   I do not know whether there is anything peculiarly exciting in the air of this particular part of Hertfordshire, but the number of engagements that go on seems to me considerably above the proper average that statistics have laid down for our guidance. I think some preliminary inquiry on my part would not be out of place. Mr. Worthing, is Miss Cardew at all connected with any of the larger railway stations in London? I merely desire information. Until yesterday I had no idea that there were any families or persons whose origin was a Terminus.

(Jack looks perfectly furious, but restrains himself.)

JACK (*in a clear, cold voice*):   Miss Cardew is the granddaughter of the late Mr. Thomas Cardew of 149, Belgrave Square, S. W.; Gervase Park, Dorking, Surrey; and the Sporran, Fifeshire, N.B.

LADY BRACKNELL: That sounds not unsatisfactory. Three addresses always inspire confidence, even in tradesmen. But what proof have I of their authenticity?

JACK: I have carefully preserved the Court Guides of the period. They are open to your inspection, Lady Bracknell.

LADY BRACKNELL (*grimly*):   I have known strange errors in that publication.

JACK: Miss Cardew's family solicitors are Messrs. Markby, Markby, and Markby.

LADY BRACKNELL: Markby, Markby, and Markby? A firm of the very highest position in their profession. Indeed I am told that one of the Mr. Markbys is occasionally to be seen at dinner parties. So far I am satisfied.

JACK (*very irritably*):   How extremely kind of you, Lady Bracknell! I have also in my possession, you will be pleased to hear, certificates of Miss Cardew's birth, baptism, whooping cough, registration, vaccination, confirmation, and the measles; both the German and the English variety.

LADY BRACKNELL: Ah! A life crowded with incident I see; though perhaps somewhat too exciting for a young girl. I am not myself in favor of premature experiences. (*Rises, looks at her watch.*) Gwendolen! the time approaches for our departure. We have not a moment to lose. As a matter of form, Mr. Worthing, I had better ask you if Miss Cardew has any little fortune?

JACK: Oh! about a hundred and thirty thousand pounds in the Funds. That is all. Good-bye, Lady Bracknell. So pleased to have seen you.

LADY BRACKNELL (*sitting down again*):   A moment, Mr. Worthing. A hundred and thirty thousand pounds! And in the Funds! Miss Cardew seems to me a most attractive young lady, now that I look at her. Few girls of the present day have any really solid qualities, any of the qualities that last, and improve with time. We live, I regret to say, in an age of surfaces. (*To Cecily.*) Come over here, dear. (*Cecily goes across.*) Pretty child! your dress is sadly simple, and your hair seems almost as Nature might have left it. But we can soon alter all that. A thoroughly experienced French maid produces a really marvelous result in a very brief space of time: I remember recommending one to young Lady Lancing, and after three months her own husband did not know her.

JACK (*aside*):   And after six months nobody knew her.

LADY BRACKNELL (*glares at Jack for a few moments. Then bends, with a practiced smile, to Cecily*):   Kindly turn round, sweet child. (*Cecily turns completely round.*) No, the side view is what I want. (*Cecily presents her profile.*) Yes, quite as I expected. There are distinct social possibilities in your profile. The two weak points in our age are its want of principle and its want of profile. The chin a little higher, dear. Style largely depends on the way the chin is worn. They are worn very high, just at present. Algernon!

ALGERNON: Yes, Aunt Augusta!

LADY BRACKNELL: There are distinct social possibilities in Miss Cardew's profile.

ALGERNON: Cecily is the sweetest, dearest, prettiest girl in the whole world. And I don't care twopence about social possibilities.

LADY BRACKNELL: Never speak disrespectfully of Society, Algernon. Only people who can't get into it do that. (*To Cecily.*) Dear child, of course you know that Algernon has nothing but his debts to depend upon. But I do not approve of mercenary marriages. When I married Lord Bracknell I had no fortune of any kind. But I never dreamed for a moment of allowing that to stand in my way. Well, I suppose I must give my consent.

ALGERNON: Thank you, Aunt Augusta.

LADY BRACKNELL: Cecily, you may kiss me!

CECILY (*kisses her*):   Thank you, Lady Bracknell.

LADY BRACKNELL: You may also address me as Aunt Augusta for the future.

CECILY: Thank you, Aunt Augusta.

LADY BRACKNELL: The marriage, I think, had better take place quite soon.

ALGERNON: Thank you, Aunt Augusta.

CECILY: Thank you, Aunt Augusta.

LADY BRACKNELL: To speak frankly, I am not in favor of long engagements. They give people the opportunity of finding out each other's character before marriage, which I think is never advisable.

JACK: I beg your pardon for interrupting you, Lady Bracknell, but this engagement is quite out of the question. I am Miss Cardew's guardian, and she cannot marry without my consent until she comes of age. That consent I absolutely decline to give.

LADY BRACKNELL: Upon what grounds may I ask? Algernon is an extremely, I may almost say an ostentatiously, eligible young man. He has nothing, but he looks everything. What more can one desire?

JACK: It pains me very much to have to speak frankly to you, Lady Bracknell, about your nephew, but the fact is that I do not approve at all of his moral character. I suspect him of being untruthful.

(Algernon and Cecily look at him in indignant amazement.)

LADY BRACKNELL: Untruthful! My nephew Algernon? Impossible! He is an Oxonian.°

JACK: I fear there can be no possible doubt about the matter. This afternoon, during my temporary absence in London on an important question of romance, he obtained admission to my house by means of the false pretense of being my brother. Under an assumed name he drank, I've just been informed by my butler, an entire pint bottle of my Perrier-Jouêt, Brut, '89; a wine I was specially reserving for myself. Continuing his disgraceful deception, he succeeded in the course of the afternoon in alienating the affections of my only ward. He subsequently stayed to tea, and devoured every single muffin. And what makes his conduct all the more heartless is, that he was perfectly well aware from the first that I have no brother, that I never had a brother, and that I don't intend to have a brother, not even of any kind. I distinctly told him so myself yesterday afternoon.

LADY BRACKNELL: Ahem! Mr. Worthing, after careful consideration I have decided entirely to overlook my nephew's conduct to you.

JACK: That is very generous of you, Lady Bracknell. My own decision, however, is unalterable. I decline to give my consent.

LADY BRACKNELL (*to Cecily*):   Come here, sweet child. (*Cecily goes over.*) How old are you, dear?

CECILY: Well, I am really only eighteen, but I always admit to twenty when I go to evening parties.

Oxonian: Educated at Oxford University.

LADY BRACKNELL: You are perfectly right in making some slight alteration. Indeed, no woman should ever be quite accurate about her age. It looks so calculating — (*In a meditative manner.*) Eighteen but admitting to twenty at evening parties. Well, it will not be very long before you are of age and free from the restraints of tutelage. So I don't think your guardian's consent is, after all, a matter of any importance.

JACK: Pray excuse me, Lady Bracknell, for interrupting you again, but it is only fair to tell you that according to the terms of her grandfather's will Miss Cardew does not come legally of age till she is thirty-five.

LADY BRACKNELL: That does not seem to me to be a grave objection. Thirty-five is a very attractive age. London society is full of women of the very highest birth who have, of their own free choice, remained thirty-five for years. Lady Dumbleton is an instance in point. To my own knowledge she has been thirty-five ever since she arrived at the age of forty, which was many years ago now. I see no reason why our dear Cecily should not be even still more attractive at the age you mention than she is at present. There will be a large accumulation of property.

CECILY: Algy, could you wait for me till I was thirty-five?

ALGERNON: Of course I could, Cecily. You know I could.

CECILY: Yes, I felt it instinctively, but I couldn't wait all that time. I hate waiting even five minutes for anybody. It always makes me rather cross. I am not punctual myself, I know, but I do like punctuality in others, and waiting, even to be married, is quite out of the question.

ALGERNON: Then what is to be done, Cecily?

CECILY: I don't know, Mr. Moncrieff.

LADY BRACKNELL: My dear Mr. Worthing, as Miss Cardew states positively that she cannot wait till she is thirty-five — a remark which I am bound to say seems to me to show a somewhat impatient nature — I would beg of you to reconsider your decision.

JACK: But my dear Lady Bracknell, the matter is entirely in your own hands. The moment you consent to my marriage with Gwendolen, I will most gladly allow your nephew to form an alliance with my ward.

LADY BRACKNELL (*rising and drawing herself up*):   You must be quite aware that what you propose is out of the question.

JACK: Then a passionate celibacy is all that any of us can look forward to.

LADY BRACKNELL: That is not the destiny I propose for Gwendolen. Algernon, of course, can choose for himself. (*Pulls out her watch.*) Come, dear; (*Gwendolen rises*) we have already missed five, if not six, trains. To miss any more might expose us to comment on the platform.

(*Enter Dr. Chasuble.*)

CHASUBLE: Everything is quite ready for the christenings.

LADY BRACKNELL: The christenings, sir! Is not that somewhat premature?

CHASUBLE (*looking rather puzzled, and pointing to Jack and Algernon*):   Both these gentlemen have expressed a desire for immediate baptism.

LADY BRACKNELL: At their age? The idea is grotesque and irreligious! Algernon,

I forbid you to be baptized. I will not hear of such excesses. Lord Bracknell would be highly displeased if he learned that that was the way in which you wasted your time and money.

CHASUBLE: Am I to understand then that there are to be no christenings at all this afternoon?

JACK: I don't think that, as things are now, it would be of much practical value to either of us, Dr. Chasuble.

CHASUBLE: I am grieved to hear such sentiments from you, Mr. Worthing. They savor of the heretical views of the Anabaptists,° views that I have completely refuted in four of my unpublished sermons. However, as your present mood seems to be one peculiarly secular, I will return to the church at once. Indeed, I have just been informed by the pew opener that for the last hour and a half Miss Prism has been waiting for me in the vestry.

LADY BRACKNELL (*starting*):   Miss Prism! Did I hear you mention a Miss Prism?

CHASUBLE: Yes, Lady Bracknell. I am on my way to join her.

LADY BRACKNELL: Pray allow me to detain you for a moment. This matter may prove to be one of vital importance to Lord Bracknell and myself. Is this Miss Prism a female of repellent aspect, remotely connected with education?

CHASUBLE (*somewhat indignantly*):   She is the most cultivated of ladies, and the very picture of respectability.

LADY BRACKNELL: It is obviously the same person. May I ask what position she holds in your household?

CHASUBLE (*severely*):   I am a celibate, madam.

JACK (*interposing*):   Miss Prism, Lady Bracknell, has been for the last three years Miss Cardew's esteemed governess and valued companion.

LADY BRACKNELL: In spite of what I hear of her, I must see her at once. Let her be sent for.

CHASUBLE (*looking off*):   She approaches; she is nigh.

(Enter Miss Prism hurriedly.)

MISS PRISM: I was told you expected me in the vestry, dear Canon. I have been waiting for you there for an hour and three-quarters.

(Catches sight of Lady Bracknell who has fixed her with a stony glare. Miss Prism grows pale and quails. She looks anxiously round as if desirous to escape.)

LADY BRACKNELL (*in a severe, judicial voice*):   Prism! (*Miss Prism bows her head in shame.*) Come here, Prism! (*Miss Prism approaches in a humble manner.*) Prism! Where is that baby? (*General consternation. The Canon starts back in horror. Algernon and Jack pretend to be anxious to shield Cecily and Gwendolen from hearing the details of a terrible public scandal.*) Twenty-eight years ago, Prism, you left Lord Bracknell's house, Number 104, Upper Grosvenor Street, in charge of a perambulator that contained a baby, of the male sex. You never returned. A few weeks later, through the elaborate investigations of

---

Anabaptists: A religious sect founded in the sixteenth century and advocating adult baptism and church membership for adults only.

the Metropolitan police, the perambulator was discovered at midnight, standing by itself in a remote corner of Bayswater. It contained the manuscript of a three-volume novel of more than usually revolting sentimentality. (*Miss Prism starts in involuntary indignation.*) But the baby was not there! (*Everyone looks at Miss Prism.*) Prism! Where is that baby?

(A pause.)

MISS PRISM: Lady Bracknell, I admit with shame that I do not know. I only wish I did. The plain facts of the case are these. On the morning of the day you mention, a day that is forever branded on my memory, I prepared as usual to take the baby out in its perambulator. I had also with me a somewhat old, but capacious handbag in which I had intended to place the manuscript of a work of fiction that I had written during my few unoccupied hours. In a moment of mental abstraction, for which I never can forgive myself, I deposited the manuscript in the bassinette, and placed the baby in the handbag.

JACK (*who has been listening attentively*):   But where did you deposit the handbag?

MISS PRISM: Do not ask me, Mr. Worthing.

JACK: Miss Prism, this is a matter of no small importance to me. I insist on knowing where you deposited the handbag that contained that infant.

MISS PRISM: I left it in the cloakroom of one of the larger railway stations in London.

JACK: What railway station?

MISS PRISM (*quite crushed*):   Victoria. The Brighton line.

(Sinks into a chair.)

JACK: I must retire to my room for a moment. Gwendolen, wait here for me.

GWENDOLEN: If you are not too long, I will wait here for you all my life.

(Exit Jack in great excitement.)

CHASUBLE: What do you think this means, Lady Bracknell?

LADY BRACKNELL: I dare not even suspect, Dr. Chasuble. I need hardly tell you that in families of high position strange coincidences are not supposed to occur. They are hardly considered the thing.

(*Noises heard overhead as if someone was throwing trunks about. Everyone looks up.*)

CECILY: Uncle Jack seems strangely agitated.

CHASUBLE: Your guardian has a very emotional nature.

LADY BRACKNELL: This noise is extremely unpleasant. It sounds as if he was having an argument. I dislike arguments of any kind. They are always vulgar, and often convincing.

CHASUBLE (*looking up*):   It has stopped now.

(The noise is redoubled.)

LADY BRACKNELL: I wish he would arrive at some conclusion.

GWENDOLEN: This suspense is terrible. I hope it will last.

(*Enter Jack with a handbag of black leather in his hand.*)

JACK (*rushing over to Miss Prism*):   Is this the handbag, Miss Prism? Examine it carefully before you speak. The happiness of more than one life depends on your answer.

MISS PRISM (*calmly*): It seems to be mine. Yes, here is the injury it received through the upsetting of a Gower Street omnibus in younger and happier days. Here is the stain on the lining caused by the explosion of a temperance beverage, an incident that occurred at Leamington. And here, on the lock, are my initials. I had forgotten that in an extravagant mood I had had them placed there. The bag is undoubtedly mine. I am delighted to have it so unexpectedly restored to me. It has been a great inconvenience being without it all these years.

JACK (*in a pathetic voice*): Miss Prism, more is restored to you than this handbag. I was the baby you placed in it.

MISS PRISM (*amazed*): You?

JACK (*embracing her*): Yes—mother!

MISS PRISM (*recoiling in indignant astonishment*): Mr. Worthing! I am unmarried!

JACK: Unmarried! I do not deny that is a serious blow. But after all, who has the right to cast a stone against one who has suffered? Cannot repentance wipe out an act of folly? Why should there be one law for men, and another for women? Mother, I forgive you. (*Tries to embrace her again.*)

MISS PRISM (*still more indignant*): Mr. Worthing, there is some error. (*Pointing to Lady Bracknell.*) There is the lady who can tell you who you really are.

JACK (*after a pause*): Lady Bracknell, I hate to seem inquisitive, but would you kindly inform me who I am?

LADY BRACKNELL: I am afraid that the news I have to give you will not altogether please you. You are the son of my poor sister, Mrs. Moncrieff, and consequently Algernon's elder brother.

JACK: Algy's elder brother! Then I have a brother after all. I knew I had a brother! I always said I had a brother! Cecily,—how could you have ever doubted that I had a brother. (*Seizes hold of Algernon.*) Dr. Chasuble, my unfortunate brother. Miss Prism, my unfortunate brother. Gwendolen, my unfortunate brother. Algy, you young scoundrel, you will have to treat me with more respect in the future. You have never behaved to me like a brother in all your life.

ALGERNON: Well, not till today, old boy, I admit. I did my best, however, though I was out of practice.

(*Shakes hands.*)

GWENDOLEN (*to Jack*): My own! But what own are you? What is your Christian name, now that you have become someone else?

JACK: Good heavens!—I had quite forgotten that point. Your decision on the subject of my name is irrevocable, I suppose?

GWENDOLEN: I never change, except in my affections.

CECILY: What a noble nature you have, Gwendolen!

JACK: Then the question had better be cleared up at once. Aunt Augusta, a moment. At the time when Miss Prism left me in the handbag, had I been christened already?

LADY BRACKNELL: Every luxury that money could buy, including christening, had been lavished upon you by your fond and doting parents.

JACK: Then I was christened! That is settled. Now, what name was I given? Let me know the worst.

LADY BRACKNELL: Being the eldest son you were naturally christened after your father.

JACK (*irritably*):   Yes, but what was my father's Christian name?

LADY BRACKNELL (*meditatively*):   I cannot at the present moment recall what the General's Christian name was. But I have no doubt he had one. He was eccentric, I admit. But only in later years. And that was the result of the Indian climate, and marriage, and indigestion, and other things of that kind.

JACK: Algy! Can't you recollect what our father's Christian name was?

ALGERNON: My dear boy, we were never even on speaking terms. He died before I was a year old.

JACK: His name would appear in the Army Lists of the period, I suppose, Aunt Augusta?

LADY BRACKNELL: The General was essentially a man of peace, except in his domestic life. But I have no doubt his name would appear in any military directory.

JACK: The Army Lists of the last forty years are here. These delightful records should have been my constant study. (*Rushes to bookcase and tears the books out.*) M. Generals — Mallam, Maxbohm, Magley, what ghastly names they have — Markby, Migsby, Mobbs, Moncrieff! Lieutenant 1840, Captain, Lieutenant-Colonel, Colonel, General 1869, Christian names, Ernest John. (*Puts book very quietly down and speaks quite calmly.*) I always told you, Gwendolen, my name was Ernest, didn't I? Well, it is Ernest after all. I mean it naturally is Ernest.

LADY BRACKNELL: Yes, I remember now that the General was called Ernest. I knew I had some particular reason for disliking the name.

GWENDOLEN: Ernest! My own Ernest! I felt from the first that you could have no other name!

JACK: Gwendolen, it is a terrible thing for a man to find out suddenly that all his life he has been speaking nothing but the truth. Can you forgive me?

GWENDOLEN: I can. For I feel that you are sure to change.

JACK: My own one!

CHASUBLE (*to Miss Prism*):   Laetitia! (*Embraces her.*)

MISS PRISM (*enthusiastically*):   Frederick! At last!

ALGERNON: Cecily! (*Embraces her.*) At last!

JACK: Gwendolen! (*Embraces her.*) At last!

LADY BRACKNELL: My nephew, you seem to be displaying signs of triviality.

JACK: On the contrary, Aunt Augusta, I've now realized for the first time in my life the vital Importance of Being Earnest.   [1895]

≡ THINKING ABOUT THE TEXT

1. Are city and country significantly different "worlds" in this play, or do they seem basically the same? Refer to specific elements of both settings.

2. To a great extent, the play's humor results from the characters saying things that challenge conventional wisdom. What are some examples? Another comic element is the speed with which characters make major decisions. What are some of these moments?

3. In what ways other than biological are Jack and Algernon "brothers"? Gwendolen and Cecily "sisters"?

4. In what respects, if any, does this play seem "modern" to you? Define what you mean by the term. In what respects, if any, do you think it relies on age-old theatrical conventions?

5. If you were staging or filming this play, whom would you cast in its major roles? Why?

SOS ELTIS

From *Revising Wilde: Society and Subversion in the Plays of Oscar Wilde*

Sos Eltis is a Tutorial Fellow in English at Oxford University's Brasenose College. She has written numerous academic articles as well as Acts of Desire: Women and Sex on Stage, 1800–1930 *(2013). The excerpt below comes from her 1996 book about Oscar Wilde's plays. She emphasizes how* The Importance of Being Earnest *affirms the spirit of anarchy.*

The Importance of Being Earnest was to all appearances a conventional nineteenth-century farce. As with Wilde's previous plays, most of the basic ingredients of the plot were familiar from innumerable other farces: misplaced parents, forbidden engagements, false identities, overbearing mothers, and the copious consumption of food were all clichés of the comic stage. Yet Wilde used his material to highly unconventional ends, for the world of *Earnest* is an anarchic one.

All farce contains an element of anarchy. Pinero's° farces are a perfect example of controlled comic chaos, where a figure of authority—schoolmistress, magistrate, or dean—disrupts the proper order by pursuing improper pastimes—singing comic operas, drinking after hours, or betting on horses. The disruption spreads as respectable persons are forced to lie, steal, and assume false identities to cover up their indiscretions. Yet, ultimately, law, order, and the *status quo* are re-established. The disorder is short-lived and the only aftereffects are that the errant figures of authority have been led to a more sympathetic understanding of human error. The spirit of anarchy is constantly opposed by the ruling spirit of civilized society, and civilized society eventually

Pinero: Sir Arthur Wing Pinero (1855–1934), English actor, stage director, and dramatist whose comedies include *The Schoolmistress* (1886), *The Magistrate* (1885), and *Dandy Dick* (1887).

achieves an impressive victory. In Wilde's farce, however, there is no division between chaos and order, fact and fiction. It is not a civilized society temporarily disrupted, but a perfect anarchic state in which the characters live, luxuriating in its benevolent lack of rules, morals, and principles. . . .

. . . *The Importance of Being Earnest* is remarkable less for any specific satire within it than for the fact that the play itself is the perfect realization of all Wilde's anarchist ideals; it is the society of "The Soul of Man under Socialism" made real°. In his political essay Wilde condemns all authority as degrading; in *Earnest* he reduces all authority to an absurdity. It is a utopia where all attempts to assert authority are doomed to failure. Its characters are free to realize themselves perfectly, for there are no harsh laws to intervene. It is an idyll of wish-fulfilment, where Cecily has only to dream she is engaged to Ernest for it to come true. Jack declares he is called Ernest and, sure enough, he is. Algy pretends to be Jack's younger brother, and by the end of the afternoon, this fantasy too has materialized. Nothing stands in the way of their self-creation, for reality itself is infinitely adaptable. So, when Lady Bracknell pronounces that Jack lives on the unfashionable side of Belgrave Square, the solution is simple:

> LADY BRACKNELL. I thought there was something. However, that could easily be altered.
>
> JACK. Do you mean the fashion, or the side?
>
> LADY BRACKNELL. Both, if necessary, I presume.

In this magical world, the perfect state of anarchy is realized, for the individual may pursue "The Soul of Man," his own desires without obstructing those of his neighbor. Wilde declared: "Selfishness is not living as one wishes to live, it is asking others to live as one wishes to live. And unselfishness is letting other people's lives alone, not interfering with them." So Gwendolen, Jack, Algy, and Cecily forge ahead, oblivious to anyone else's desires, and yet, in spite of Jack's determination to forbid Cecily's marriage unless he be allowed to marry Gwendolen, each achieves his or her goal without interfering with the others. Even Lady Bracknell, the one character who seeks to impose her own standards on everyone else, is transformed from a gorgon into the play's fairy godmother: contrary to her intentions, she finds herself playing the *dea ex machina* and granting the other characters' wishes.

This anarchic freedom, in which the characters are at liberty to create themselves, once again separates *Earnest* from other, more conventional, farces. The double lives led by Algernon, Jack, Cecily (through her diary), and even Miss Prism (via her abandoned three-volume novel) are another means by which they liberate themselves from the formal strictures of society. Characters have assumed false identities in almost every farce ever written. In Brandon Thomas's extremely popular *Charley's Aunt* (1892), for example, the unfortu-

---

The Soul of Man: Wilde expounded a social anarchist philosophy in his 1891 essay "The Soul of Man under Socialism."

nate Lord Fancourt Babberley is forced by friends to assume the guise of Charley's aunt from Brazil, in order to provide a chaperon for their female guests. The young students spend the next three acts desperately trying to sustain the pretense in the face of innumerable complications. In the last act Fancourt Babberley is released from the constrictions of his disguise and returned to his true identity. No such unmasking ends *The Importance of Being Earnest*; Cecily, Algy, and Jack become their own fantastic doubles, permanently granted the freedom which their fictions allowed them. Wilde, whose own sexuality was outlawed by the rigid and inhuman legislation of Victorian society, had created a fantasy world in which such laws had no power and double lives like his own no longer had to be kept secret.   *[1996]*

TIRTHANKAR BOSE
From *"Oscar Wilde's Game of Being Earnest"*

Tirthankar Bose taught English at Simon Fraser University in Canada. The following excerpt comes from his article on The Importance of Being Earnest *that appeared in the Spring 1978 issue of the journal* Modern Drama. *As the article's title suggests, Bose sees the play's characters as playing games with one another.*

What we observe is a reversion to an ancient archetype of mating behaviour. A common custom of tribal societies is that a suitor must prove his love, and more important, his manhood, by performing some extraordinary feat or by presenting some precious gift. This custom is precisely the demand that the girls make upon the men. This sense, implicit at first, becomes explicit and unambiguous at the end, when the girls term the men's decision to be rechristened "this terrible thing" and "this fearful ordeal," and reward them for their "self-sacrifice" and "physical courage" (Act III). The utterly nonsensical nature of the issue is of course the basis of laughter, and it can be sustained only within a very special framework of character conception, a framework made up of centuries-old male notions of female willfulness. What gives satiric edge to the laughter is the ambivalence of that framework in conforming both to the nineteenth-century mores and to the behavioral archetypes of the species.

As a theatrical image, the ritual of courtship is singularly effective. The men approach the girls and are rejected. Then, through a sequence of question and response, they are accepted, only to be rejected again through a second sequence of question and response; they are then given a task of symbolic value, and on its performance (actually on the mere promise of performance, as in codified rituals) they are finally accepted. All verbal exchanges, gestures, and movements of which the ritual is composed require total stylization through exact matching and counterpoise. Each group uses the same language, goes through the same motions, and strikes the same attitudes. As examples of counterpoising, we may cite several pieces of the stage action. While Gwendolen and Cecily embrace and stand still and silent, Jack and Algy "*groan and walk up and down*" (stage direction, Act II). To Gwendolen's "severe" question, "Had you never a brother of any kind?" Jack returns the cheery answer, "Never" (*Ibid.*). When Cecily and Gwendolen "*preserve a dignified silence*," Jack and Algernon "*whistle some dreadful popular air from a British opera*" (stage direction, Act III). The whole sequence comes to an operatic finale as the girls, "*speaking together*," say — while Gwendolen "*beats time with uplifted finger*" — "Your Christian names are still an insuperable barrier! That is all!" The men reply, "*speaking together*," "Our Christian names! Is that all?" And soon thereafter they "*fall into each other's arms*" (Act III).

Structurally, then, the play may be seen as a societal model simulating a courtship ritual which identifies the sexual drive of man as the controlling force in social relationships. Such an understanding could conceivably enrich a production of the play by replacing the evanescent world of the comedy of manners with the more durable framework of anthropological archetypes. But conspicuous as the ritual format is, it is possible to perceive the superimposition on it of yet another kind of archetypal design, that of a game of combat. *Earnest* begins, like most plays, with situations involving conflicts of interest; but it reveals its game characteristics in the layout of the situations. The design is made up of matched elements, the strategy of matching not confined to a specific sequence of action but determining to an ever-increasing degree the unfolding of the entire action. It is thus the real principle of structure. Conflicts arise between Jack and Algernon, and between Jack and Lady Bracknell. These situations are matched against each other. Jack obstructs Algernon while Lady Bracknell obstructs Jack. The object of the game is constant: to capture a closely guarded woman. The strategies are the same: the attacker pretends to be someone else; the defender refuses to move out of his square. This growing similarity between the two lines of play naturally brings them together and leads them to a joint climax in the second and the third acts when, after a mêlée, viable partnerships are formed. This part of the game makes deliberate use of a courtship format, for that is what the actual life situation requires. The game situation is: pursuit, capture, surrender, confrontation, reversed surrender, coalition. The men pursue and seize the women who, after a momentary surrender, confront the men with the discovery of their vulnerability, that is, their pretended identity. The men surrender to the women's demands by consenting to be re-christened, and partnerships are formed. Now we enter the second phase of the game in which the initial situation matches that of the first act: Lady Bracknell obstructs Jack and Jack obstructs Algernon. At the same time, Lady Bracknell is a supplicant before Jack just as he is before her. Both as opponents and supplicants, Jack and Lady Bracknell are evenly matched, and under these conditions the game has to end in a draw. Miss Prism, a new player, now enters the game and alters its balance by strengthening Jack, whereupon he demolishes all opposition, the conflict relating to him ends, and the new circumstances in turn terminate Algernon's problem.   *[1978]*

PATRICIA FLANAGAN BEHRENDT

From *Oscar Wilde: Eros and Aesthetics*

Before retiring, Patricia Flanagan Behrendt taught theater arts at the University of Nebraska in Lincoln. She has also served as editor of the journal American Theatre. *In this except from her 1991 book on Oscar Wilde, she joins several other Wilde scholars in hypothesizing that* The Importance of Being Earnest *touches on issues related to homosexuality.*

While *The Importance of Being Earnest* perpetuates the dandy's vision of the ridiculousness of relations between men and women as it had been put forth in the earlier plays, it simultaneously reveals a matrix of allusions to the complex problems of homosexual identity. The title, which is traditionally interpreted as a pun on the importance of being Ernest as well as earnest, embodies a pun of a far more significant nature. Karl Heinrich Ulrichs (1825–95), a German sexologist who studied the phenomenon of homosexuality, applied the term *Urning* to males with homosexual tendencies, a condition which he felt reflected a female spirit in a male body. Proof that Wilde was familiar with one English equivalent of Urning — Uranian — is his use of the term in a letter to Robert Ross (*Letters*, 705). More important, however, considering Wilde's expertise in French and his familiarity with things French, is the fact that, while the English equivalent of *Urning* is Uranian, the French equivalent is *Uraniste* — a term whose pronunciation clearly suggests the name Ernest. The fact that Wilde was probably familiar with the French term suggests that the title of his play may not only propose the importance of being Ernest or earnest but may also propose the importance of being *Uraniste* as well — a sentiment which refers to the intellectually superior role that Wilde had assigned to his dandies throughout his work, to the private delight of the coterie of the green carnation°.

The play's concerns with complex problems of identity, suggested by the title, are encoded within further references to homosexuality. For example . . . Algernon's conversation with the butler, Lane, in the opening moments of the play is significant in relation to his own piano playing. Algernon asks Lane if he has heard what he was playing. Lane replies, "I didn't think it polite to listen, sir." For the Victorian audience, Lane's is the seemingly guarded response of the domestic servant expressing his detached view of the household activities. However, the fact that the term "musical" was an 1890s code word for homosexuality illuminates quite another aspect of the scene. When Lane announces that he did not think it polite to acknowledge Algernon's musicianship, he represents through encoded verbal allusion Victorian society's refusal to acknowledge behaviors which it knows exist and which affront its moral codes and

---

coterie of the green carnation: Followers of Wilde wore this flower, which they dyed green.

assumptions, even when that society and its attitudes are challenged directly, as Algernon challenges Lane. In order to maintain his detached role as one who supposedly does not observe beyond his station, Lane is forced into the hypocritical and absurd position of denying his own senses. In his witty exchange with Lane, Algernon affirms the power of dandy language to manipulate characters into revealing the inherent absurdity of their poses by saying (or doing) things which they know contradict a reality which they otherwise acknowledge.

For the Victorian audience in general, the subsequent events of the play ostensibly concern merely the humorous frustrations of two couples on the complicated route to marriage. However, while appearing to poke fun at courtship, Wilde's play depicts the destructive effects of Jack's pursuit of marriage on his initially stable sense of personal identity. The conversation between Jack and Algernon in the opening scene reveals that Jack has been maintaining a complicated existence, successfully balancing two identities. In the country he is the country gentleman, Jack Worthing, who is responsible enough to have been made guardian to his own benefactor's granddaughter. In the city, however, where he casts off responsibility in favor of the pursuit of pleasure, he calls himself Ernest Worthing. Jack's situation is under control until he announces to Algernon that he has come to town to propose to Algernon's cousin Gwendolyn. Algernon suggests that proposals of marriage constitute business rather than pleasure, a conclusion which recalls Wilde's earlier associations of marriage with ulterior motives and secret pursuits. After discovering Jack's intentions, Algernon who has known Jack only as Ernest reveals that he has found a cigarette case left behind by Jack (Ernest) during an earlier visit and inscribed "To Uncle Jack from his ward Cecily (sic)." From this development, Algernon learns not only of Jack's double identity — as Ernest in town and Jack in the country — but also of the fact that Jack pretends that Ernest is a profligate younger brother who lives "in the Albany and gets into the most dreadful scrapes." At this point Algernon upsets Jack's satisfaction with his compartmentalized existence by accusing him of being a Bunburyist. The term, he says, comes from the name of his own imaginary invalid friend whom he "visits" when he wants to get out of other obligations. Algernon refers to himself as one who has "Bunburyed all over Shropshire." The phrase blatantly calls forth the image of a promiscuous sodomite and foreshadows the epithet "somdomite" [sic] applied to Wilde by Lord Alfred Douglas's father, the Marquis of Queensberry, only weeks after the play opened.

Infuriated by Algernon's suggestion that he is a hypocrite, Jack concludes that, if Gwendolyn accepts him, he will kill off Ernest. Algernon questions the wisdom of eliminating Ernest and adds his own doubts about Jack's identity as a married man. He says, ". . . if you ever get married, which seems to me extremely problematic, you will be very glad to know Bunbury. A man who marries without knowing Bunbury has a very tedious time of it." The subtext of these otherwise humorous lines concerns the fact that from the moment Jack announces his intention to marry Gwendolyn, his identity becomes the subject of greater and greater confusion. Having revealed his double identity as his imaginary younger brother which Algernon recognizes as his alter ego, Jack is forced into the position of defending his identity and his sense of himself against the accusation that he is a Bunburyist. The important aspect of his ardent self-defense is that Algernon's initial recognition that Jack is a Bunburyist — because he has a second identity as "Ernest" designed to mask certain activities — will prove to be true at the end of the play when Jack discovers that his name really is Ernest. In other words, within the context of the play, once Jack announces his pursuit of marriage, his understanding of his own identity undergoes a process of deconstruction until he realizes that he is exactly the person whom he most denied being in the opening scene. This reinforces our understanding of Algernon's intellectual superiority, since what he has pre-dicted is proved in fact to be true.

The second assault upon Jack's identity occurs when he proposes to 5 Gwendolyn in the next scene. She announces that her "ideal has always been to love someone of the name of Ernest." To his horror, Jack discovers that she will love only someone who bears the name of the very identity that he was going to "kill off" if she agreed to marry him. Given the homosexual connota-tion of musicality, an ironic note is added when she says that Ernest "is a divine name. It has a music of its own." To further undermine Jack's sense of himself, she repudiates his suggestion that Jack or John might be acceptable. She adds, "I pity any woman who is married to a man called John. She would probably never be allowed to know the entrancing pleasure of a single moment's solitude. The only really safe name is Ernest." In these complicated lines, Gwendolyn is already intimating, prior to marriage, that she anticipates the need for solitude and that she would prefer a certain level of uninterest in a husband. Moments ear-lier she had told Jack that she would prefer that he be more demonstrative to-ward her in public, implying that the public manifestations of their engagement are more important than their relationship in private. One begins to suspect that, when Gwendolyn speaks of "the only really safe" husband, she is refer-ring to one who will affect a high level of uninterest in her behind closed doors while putting up a facade of attentiveness in public.

Since it is the sexual aspect of marriage that is conducted in private, and since Gwendolyn seems to prefer an uninterested husband in private, we can assume that she is implying that she would prefer a husband with only limited interest in the sexual sphere of marriage. Since Wilde has already given the name Ernest overtones of homosexuality by having Gwendolyn observe that it has "music of its own," we might wonder if Wilde is not implying that Gwendolyn's own subconscious idea of "the ideal husband" is one who wears the attentive mask of the devoted husband in public but has no intention of making sexual demands in private. In such a situation, which would have ap-peared ideal to Wilde himself, both parties are free to pursue their own inter-ests, protected from public scrutiny by the conventional facade of marriage.

The idea that Gwendolyn is attracted specifically to men of questionable sexual preferences is substantiated in the second act, when she suggests that "once a man begins to neglect his domestic duties he becomes painfully effemi-nate, does he not? And I don't like that." Since "effeminate" is also a code word for homosexuality in the period, Gwendolyn would appear to be signalling her antipathy toward the type until she adds the seemingly paradoxical statement that being painfully effeminate "makes men so very attractive." The attraction that the effeminate man would hold for Gwendolyn would be his lack of sexual interest in her. Once again Wilde introduces the theme of the dandy who is both attractive to women and yet sexually uninterested in them as a woman's own vision of "the ideal husband." While Jack's discovery at the end of the play that he is actually Ernest makes him an ideal husband for Gwendolyn according to Lady Bracknell's standards, it is Jack's discovery of his identity as Ernest "the Bunburyist" that makes him an ideal husband by Wilde's standards.

The first two scenes of the play reveal Jack's deteriorating sense of identity in the wake of his announcement of his intention to marry Gwendolyn. While Algernon accuses Jack of not being who he pretends to be, Gwendolyn believes Jack to be the very person that he is not. What he has denied himself to Algernon to be—that he is Ernest and therefore a Bunburyist—he must become in order to please Gwendolyn. Under the cover of humor, Wilde once again reveals that marriage results in compromising one's identity. Most important, it is the dandy, Algernon, who, like Cecil Graham in conversation with Lord Darlington°, aggressively challenges the wisdom of Jack's pursuit of a woman by predicting that it will be "extremely problematic." The dandy's insight is correct, as usual.

After his interview with Algernon and Gwendolyn, Jack is confronted by Lady Bracknell, Algernon's aunt and soon to be revealed as Jack's aunt as well. She demands that Jack find some respectable relations if he intends to be considered a serious suitor for Gwendolyn. Lady Bracknell is the voice of authority whom everyone must please. Her description of her own marriage reveals that she dominates her husband to the point of making him eat upstairs when his presence will create an uneven table at dinner. When Wilde has Jack ask Algernon if Gwendolyn will become like her mother in a hundred years, he foreshadows Jack's grim destiny, for which Bunburying is the only recourse according to Algernon. After all, Gwendolyn has already revealed her ability to dominate Jack by making it impossible for him even to expose the simple fact that his name is not Ernest.

The fact that Lady Bracknell has usurped the traditionally masculine role   10 of dominating the household and of granting permission for Gwendolyn to marry accounts for the tendency to cast a man in her role, thereby revealing the hypocrisy of marriage in which the woman has absorbed the role of the male. Additional humor is added to the blurring of Lady Bracknell's gender by her designation as the "aunt." The word "aunt" or "auntie" was typical 1890s slang for a homosexual among homosexuals.

In terms of the structure of the play, Algernon's condemning remarks in the first scene about the unattractiveness of marriage pass at first as witty cynicism but are proved to be absolutely true to the reality of the play. The play is

Cecil Graham; Lord Darlington: Characters in the Oscar Wilde play *Lady Windermer's Fan.*

designed to reveal the truth, of Algernon's warning to Jack in the opening scene that a second identity — which makes Jack a Bunburyist — is essential to marital happiness. Jack discovers as the play progresses that in order to achieve the happiness of being accepted by Gwendolyn he must become Ernest, his Bunbury alter ego. The complication reveals that the dandy knows the other characters better than they know themselves.

In the tradition of Wilde's plays, the comedy ends in the country setting with Jack and Algernon engaged to marry Gwendolyn and Cecily respectively. Echoing the relationship between Lord Goring and Lord Chiltern in *An Ideal Husband*, Algernon's possessive interests in Jack's affairs have led him to the country to meet Jack's ward, to whom he becomes engaged. The country setting is significant in that it is always associated in Wilde's works with impulsive actions. Just as Lord Goring's marriage to Mabel ensures his access to Chiltern, Algernon's engagement to Jack's ward ensures Algernon's access to Jack. Wilde cements their ties when Jack's discovery that his name is Ernest results also in the discovery that he is Algernon's older brother. Part of the vanity of Algernon's intense interest in Jack, therefore, stems from the fact that he clearly sees himself reflected in Jack, like Narcissus° yearning for his own image in the pool. His attention to Jack is a typical measure of dandy self-centeredness. However, since Algernon has already indicated that he will never give up Bun-burying and since Jack has discovered that he *is* a Bunburyist, we see that the two are one of a kind and have merely capitulated to the compromises required for marriage. Their future is filled with the promise of hypocrisy heaped upon hypocrisy behind the mask of domestic tranquility. As in each of the plays, the role of the dandy is to expose the chilling — if not morbid — nature of heterosexual relations while revealing genuine good will, affection, human bonding, fun, and intellectual exchange which are played out between men.   [1991]

Narcissus: A famous youth in Greek mythology who fell in love with his own reflection when he looked in a pool.

CHARLES ISHERWOOD
A Stylish Monster Conquers at a Glance

Charles Isherwood is a theater critic for the New York Times, *where the following review appeared on January 13, 2011. Isherwood evaluates a Broadway production of* The Importance of Being Earnest *that he saw earlier at Canada's Stratford Shakespeare Festival. On the whole, he praises this staging — in particular, its director and star, Brian Bedford. Much to Isherwood's delight, Bedford has cast himself as Lady Bracknell. He isn't the only man to have played this female character on stage — others include Geoffrey Rush — and as Isherwood suggests, a cross-gendered performance like this can bring out dimensions of Wilde's play that more conventional renditions might not.*

Sara Krulwich/The New York Times/Redux

Within seconds of sweeping onstage, and with a wordless gesture as funny as it is subtle, the great actor Brian Bedford proves beyond question that gender is of no importance whatsoever in portraying the imposing Lady Bracknell in Oscar Wilde's greatest comedy, *The Importance of Being Earnest*.

Mr. Bedford's Lady Bracknell enters the drawing room of her nephew Algernon Moncrieff (Santino Fontana) as she would enter any room, with the authority of one who believes firmly in her right to be welcomed anywhere, preferably with tea and cucumber sandwiches. Advancing to greet Algernon, she registers the presence of his friend Jack Worthing (David Furr).

She pauses in dismay, and the grim aspect becomes a little grimmer. The icy blue eyes sweep and pierce, and then the lids slowly descend in a gesture as expressive of disgust as it is possible to imagine. Clearly Lady Bracknell would be most gratified—possibly not surprised, either—if she opened her eyes to discover that Mr. Worthing had had the good breeding to obey her unspoken command and disappear.

This magnificent gorgon, "a monster, without being a myth," as the horrified Jack describes her at one point, has perhaps never been more imperious, more indomitable—or more delectably entertaining—than in Mr. Bedford's brilliant portrayal, the highlight of this effervescent revival of Wilde's 1895 comedy of manners.

Originating at the Stratford Shakespeare Festival in Ontario, Canada, where I saw it about a year and a half ago, the production, which opened on Thursday night at the American Airlines Theater, courtesy of the Roundabout

5

Theater Company, is also directed by Mr. Bedford, with the same crystalline sharpness he brings to his turn in the play's most celebrated role.

It is not necessarily rare for actors—male actors, that is—to take on the role of Wilde's arch parody of a paragon of high Victorian propriety. I've seen two other productions with men in the part, including an all-male version at the Abbey Theater in Dublin. But Mr. Bedford is truly playing the role, not working a gimmick.

A classical actor particularly celebrated for his performances of Shakespeare and Molière, he is a versatile, conscientious stylist who has no interest in winning laughs by winking references to the gender switch. Mr. Bedford is aware that when portrayed with the seriousness of purpose that she deserves—or should I say demands?—Lady Bracknell is more than capable of keeping an audience breathless with laughter, thank you very much.

Beneath hats that vaguely suggest menacing birds ready to peck, Mr. Bedford's expressive face manages to twist itself into any number of memorable grimaces. Causes of distress are myriad, as Lady Bracknell contemplates the peculiar provenance of Mr. Worthing, the handbag-bred fellow who has the temerity to propose marriage to her daughter, Gwendolen Fairfax (Sara Topham), and the sudden infatuation of Algernon for Jack's young ward, Cecily Cardew (Charlotte Parry).

Mr. Bedford's stiff posture and serene bustling suggest a woman bearing her rectitude like a suit of armor and her trials with the surety of the righteous. But it is in the expert handling of Wilde's filigreed language that his portrayal most enchants. Here is a rare stage performance in which, truly, every word is made to count. Mr. Bedford earns hearty laughter when he has just one or two at his disposal—"Found?" or "A handbag?"—and when he is spinning out one of Lady Bracknell's priceless upside-down aphorisms, like her immortal observation that "to lose one parent, Mr. Worthing, may be regarded as a misfortune; to lose both looks like carelessness." . . .

. . . *The Importance of Being Earnest* is the rare work of art that achieves   10
perfection on its own terms. When viewed through the illuminating frame of a fine performance it dazzles both with its light touch and with its sturdy construction, like a cathedral made of spun sugar.

Mr. Bedford's production is not entirely effortless—Wilde's rococo style can be daunting even to experienced classicists—but it is more buoyant and consistently funny than any I've seen. And as Lady Bracknell, Mr. Bedford presides at the cathedral's altar with supreme skill and stylishness—and a hint of substance too. It's one of the great performances of the season; to miss it would most definitely look like carelessness.   *[2011]*

≡ **MAKING COMPARISONS**

1. While reading the play, did you look at it as Eltis, Bose, and Behrendt do? Why, or why not? Do you find one of these interpretations more illuminating than the others? Explain.

2. Are the lenses that Eltis, Bose, and Behrendt use compatible with one another? Is it possible for a reader of the play to agree with all three of these critics? Why, or why not?

3. If Eltis, Bose, and Behrendt had been familiar with Brian Bedford's performance as Lady Bracknell, how might it figure in their interpretations of the play? How does Isherwood's review affect *your* understanding of the play?

☰ WRITING ABOUT ISSUES

1. Choose a bit of dialogue—perhaps one line, perhaps a few—that for you conveys much of what is important about the journey from city to country in *The Importance of Being Earnest*. Then, write an essay explaining why the dialogue you have selected is significant.

2. How useful is knowledge of Wilde's life for an understanding of *The Importance of Being Earnest*? Write an essay that answers this question by referring to Behrendt and at least one other critic.

3. Suppose that you are the casting director of a new production of *The Importance of Being Earnest*. What would you say to someone who argues that casting a star as Lady Bracknell—whether the star is a man or a woman—risks making that character seem more important than she actually is? Write an essay that states and supports your response. If you wish, refer to Isherwood's review and any of the excerpts in this cluster.

4. Choose a specific film—perhaps a romantic comedy—that seems less original to you than it did before you read *The Importance of Being Earnest*. How does your new knowledge of Wilde's play make the movie seem less fresh? Answer in an essay.

RICHARD RODRIGUEZ, "Aria"

JOSE ANTONIO VARGAS, "My Life as an Undocumented Immigrant"

Although both Richard Rodriguez and Jose Antonio Vargas grew up in immigrant families around San Francisco, their responses to the cultural and language boundaries each had to negotiate were quite different. Rodriguez agonized over his childhood fluency in English. He felt Spanish was the comforting and solidifying language of family life. As he learned the public language of the majority, he felt his family life changed. In a way, his growing proficiency in English and gradual socialization into American culture distanced him from the family life he so loved as a child. His progress was also a loss. Despite this sense of loss, Rodriguez opposes bilingual education and affirmative action and favors immersing students in English. As a result of this controversial position against students using their native languages in school, he was widely criticized as a traitor to Mexican Americans. Caught between two cultures, not belonging completely in either, Rodriguez claims he is "a comic victim of two cultures."

Jose Vargas also has a foothold in both cultures, but he seems not to have suffered the emotional family turmoil that Rodriguez recounts. Vargas has assimilated into American culture with eloquence and excellence. His problem is a technical one. As he explains, "I am an American. I just don't have the right papers." Vargas's essay tells of his attempts to cross the boundary from immigrant to American citizen without official approval. That he is so successful is in itself an example of the American Dream.

■ BEFORE YOU READ

Recall incidents from your past when you felt you had to cross or negotiate various boundaries. How did you feel? Recall stories or films about people crossing boundaries, whether geographical, linguistic, class, religious, or other. How did you respond?

RICHARD RODRIGUEZ
Aria

A native of San Francisco, California, Richard Rodriguez (b. 1944) is the son of Mexican immigrants. Until he entered school at the age of six, he spoke primarily Spanish. His 1982 memoir, Hunger of Memory, *describes how English-language instruction distanced him from his parents' native culture. Rodriguez went on to attend Stanford University and the University of California at Berkeley, where he earned a doctorate in English Renaissance literature. He is also the author of* Days of Obligation: An Argument with My Mexican Father *(1992) and* Brown: The

Last Discovery of America *(2002). His essay "The God of the Desert" was published in* The Best American Essays 2009. *Currently Rodriguez is a contributing editor for* Harper's *magazine and a commentator on public television's* NewsHour.

1

I remember to start with that day in Sacramento — a California now nearly thirty years past — when I first entered a classroom, able to understand some fifty stray English words.

The third of four children, I had been preceded to a neighborhood Roman Catholic school by an older brother and sister. But neither of them had revealed very much about their classroom experiences. Each afternoon they returned, as they left in the morning, always together, speaking in Spanish as they climbed the five steps of the porch. And their mysterious books, wrapped in shopping-bag paper, remained on the table next to the door, closed firmly behind them.

An accident of geography sent me to a school where all my classmates were white, many the children of doctors and lawyers and business executives. All my classmates certainly must have been uneasy on that first day of school — as most children are uneasy — to find themselves apart from their families in the first institution of their lives. But I was astonished.

The nun said, in a friendly but oddly impersonal voice, "Boys and girls, this is Richard Rodriguez." (I heard her sound out: *Rich-heard Road-ree-guess.*) It was the first time I had heard anyone name me in English. "Richard," the nun repeated more slowly, writing my name down in her black leather book. Quickly I turned to see my mother's face dissolve in a watery blur behind the pebbled glass door.

Many years later there is something called bilingual education — a scheme proposed in the late 1960s by Hispanic-American social activists, later endorsed by a congressional vote. It is a program that seeks to permit non-English-speaking children, many from lower-class homes, to use their family language as the language of school. (Such is the goal its supporters announce.) I hear them and am forced to say no: it is not possible for a child — any child — ever to use his family's language in school. Not to understand this is to misunderstand the public uses of schooling and to trivialize the nature of intimate life — a family's "language."   5

Memory teaches me what I know of these matters; the boy reminds the adult. I was a bilingual child, a certain kind — socially disadvantaged — the son of working-class parents, both Mexican immigrants.

In the early years of my boyhood, my parents coped very well in America. My father had steady work. My mother managed at home. They were nobody's victims. Optimism and ambition led them to a house (our home) many blocks from the Mexican south side of town. We lived among *gringos* and only a block from the biggest, whitest houses. It never occurred to my parents that they couldn't live wherever they chose. Nor was the Sacramento of the fifties bent on teaching them a contrary lesson. My mother and father were more annoyed than intimidated by those two or three neighbors who tried initially to make us unwelcome. ("Keep your brats away from my sidewalk!") But despite all they achieved, perhaps because they had so much to achieve, any deep feeling of ease, the confidence of "belonging" in public was withheld from them both. They regarded the people at work, the faces in crowds, as very distant from us. They were the others, *los gringos*. That term was interchangeable in their speech with another, even more telling, *los americanos*.

I grew up in a house where the only regular guests were my relations. For one day, enormous families of relatives would visit and there would be so many people that the noise and the bodies would spill out to the backyard and front porch. Then, for weeks, no one came by. (It was usually a salesman who rang the doorbell.) Our house stood apart. A gaudy yellow in a row of white bungalows. We were the people with the noisy dog. The people who raised pigeons and chickens. We were the foreigners on the block. A few neighbors smiled and waved. We waved back. But no one in the family knew the names of the old couple who lived next door; until I was seven years old, I did not know the names of the kids who lived across the street.

In public, my father and mother spoke a hesitant, accented, not always grammatical English. And they would have to strain — their bodies tense — to catch the sense of what was rapidly said by *los gringos*. At home they spoke Spanish. The language of their Mexican past sounded in counterpoint to the English of public society. The words would come quickly, with ease. Conveyed through those sounds was the pleasing, soothing, consoling reminder of being at home.

During those years when I was first conscious of hearing, my mother and   10
father addressed me only in Spanish; in Spanish I learned to reply. By contrast, English (*inglés*), rarely heard in the house, was the language I came to associate with *gringos*. I learned my first words of English overhearing my parents speak to strangers. At five years of age, I knew just enough English for my mother to trust me on errands to stores one block away. No more.

I was a listening child, careful to hear the very different sounds of Spanish and English. Wide-eyed with hearing, I'd listen to sounds more than words. First, there were English (*gringo*) sounds. So many words were still unknown that when the butcher or the lady at the drugstore said something to me, exotic polysyllabic sounds would bloom in the midst of their sentences. Often, the speech of people in public seemed to me very loud, booming with confidence. The man behind the counter would literally ask, "What can I do for you?" But by being so firm and so clear, the sound of his voice said that he was a *gringo*; he belonged in public society.

I would also hear then the high nasal notes of middle-class American speech. The air stirred with sound. Sometimes, even now, when I have been traveling abroad for several weeks, I will hear what I heard as a boy. In hotel lobbies or airports, in Turkey or Brazil, some Americans will pass, and suddenly I will hear it again — the high sound of American voices. For a few seconds I will hear it with pleasure, for it is now the sound of *my* society — a reminder of home. But inevitably — already on the flight headed for home — the sound fades with repetition. I will be unable to hear it anymore.

When I was a boy, things were different. The accent of *los gringos* was never pleasing nor was it hard to hear. Crowds at Safeway or at bus stops would be noisy with sound. And I would be forced to edge away from the chirping chatter above me.

I was unable to hear my own sounds, but I knew very well that I spoke English poorly. My words could not stretch far enough to form complete thoughts. And the words I did speak I didn't know well enough to make into distinct sounds. (Listeners would usually lower their heads, better to hear what I was trying to say.) But it was one thing for *me* to speak English with difficulty. It was more troubling for me to hear my parents speak in public: their high-whining vowels and guttural consonants; their sentences that got stuck with "eh" and "ah" sounds; the confused syntax; the hesitant rhythm of sounds so different from the way *gringos* spoke. I'd notice, moreover, that my parents' voices were softer than those of *gringos* we'd meet.

I am tempted now to say that none of this mattered. In adulthood I am embarrassed by childhood fears. And in a way, it didn't matter very much that my parents could not speak English with ease. Their linguistic difficulties had no serious consequences. My mother and father made themselves understood at the county hospital clinic and at government offices. And yet, in another way, it mattered very much — it was unsettling to hear my parents struggle with English. Hearing them, I'd grow nervous, my clutching trust in their protection and power weakened.   15

There were many times like the night at a brightly lit gasoline station (a blaring white memory) when I stood uneasily, hearing my father. He was talking to a teenaged attendant. I do not recall what they were saying, but I cannot forget the sounds my father made as he spoke. At one point his words slid together to form one word — sounds as confused as the threads of blue and green oil in the puddle next to my shoes. His voice rushed through what he had left to say. And, toward the end, reached falsetto notes, appealing to his listener's understanding. I looked away to the lights of passing automobiles. I tried not to hear anymore. But I heard only too well the calm, easy tones in the attendant's reply. Shortly afterward, walking toward home with my father, I shivered when he put his hand on my shoulder. The very first chance that I got, I evaded his grasp and ran on ahead into the dark, skipping with feigned boyish exuberance.

But then there was Spanish. *Español*: my family's language. *Español*: the language that seemed to me a private language. I'd hear strangers on the radio and in the Mexican Catholic church across town speaking in Spanish, but I couldn't really believe that Spanish was a public language, like English. Spanish speakers, rather, seemed related to me, for I sensed that we shared — through our language — the experience of feeling apart from *los gringos*. It was thus a ghetto Spanish that I heard and I spoke. Like those whose lives are bound by a barrio, I was reminded by Spanish of my separateness from *los otros, los gringos* in power. But more intensely than for most barrio children — because I did not live in a barrio — Spanish seemed to me the language of home. (Most days it was only at home that I'd hear it.) It became the language of joyful return.

A family member would say something to me and I would feel myself specially recognized. My parents would say something to me and I would feel embraced by the sounds of their words. Those sounds said: *I am speaking with ease in Spanish. I am addressing you in words I never use with* los gringos. *I recognize you as someone special, close, like no one outside. You belong with us. In the family.*

(*Ricardo.*)

At the age of five, six, well past the time when most other children no   20
longer easily notice the difference between sounds uttered at home and words spoken in public, I had a different experience. I lived in a world magically compounded of sounds. I remained a child longer than most; I lingered too long, poised at the edge of language — often frightened by the sounds of *los gringos*, delighted by the sounds of Spanish at home. I shared with my family a language that was startlingly different from that used in the great city around us.

For me there were none of the gradations between public and private society so normal to a maturing child. Outside the house was public society; inside the house was private. Just opening or closing the screen door behind me was an important experience. I'd rarely leave home all alone or without reluctance. Walking down the sidewalk, under the canopy of tall trees, I'd warily notice the — suddenly — silent neighborhood kids who stood warily watching me. Nervously, I'd arrive at the grocery store to hear there the sounds of the *gringo* — foreign to me — reminding me that in this world so big, I was a foreigner. But then I'd return. Walking back toward our house, climbing the steps from the sidewalk, when the front door was open in summer, I'd hear voices beyond the screen door talking in Spanish. For a second or two, I'd stay, linger there, listening. Smiling, I'd hear my mother call out, saying in Spanish (words): "Is that you, Richard?" All the while her sounds would assure me: *You are home now; come closer; inside. With us.*

"*Sí,*" I'd reply.

Once more inside the house I would resume (assume) my place in the family. The sounds would dim, grow harder to hear. Once more at home, I would grow less aware of that fact. It required, however, no more than the blurt of the doorbell to alert me to listen to sounds all over again. The house would turn instantly still while my mother went to the door. I'd hear her hard English sounds. I'd wait to hear her voice return to soft-sounding Spanish, which assured me, as surely as did the clicking tongue of the lock on the door, that the stranger was gone.

Plainly, it is not healthy to hear such sounds so often. It is not healthy to distinguish public words from private sounds so easily. I remained cloistered by sounds, timid and shy in public, too dependent on voices at home. And yet it needs to be emphasized: I was an extremely happy child at home. I remember many nights when my father would come back from work, and I'd hear him call out to my mother in Spanish, sounding relieved. In Spanish, he'd sound light and free notes he never could manage in English. Some nights I'd jump up just at hearing his voice. With *mis hermanos* I would come running into the room where he was with my mother. Our laughing (so deep was the pleasure!) became screaming. Like others who know the pain of public alienation, we transformed the knowledge of our public separateness and made it consoling—the reminder of intimacy. Excited, we joined our voices in a celebration of sounds. *We are speaking now the way we never speak out in public. We are alone—together,* voices sounded, surrounded to tell me. Some nights, no one seemed willing to loosen the hold sounds had on us. At dinner, we invented new words. (Ours sounded Spanish, but made sense only to us.) We pieced together new words by taking, say, an English verb and giving it Spanish endings. My mother's instructions at bedtime would be lacquered with mock-urgent tones. Or a word like *sí* would become, in several notes, able to convey added measures of feeling. Tongues explored the edges of words, especially the fat vowels. And we happily sounded that military drum roll, the twirling roar of the Spanish *r.* Family language: my family's sounds. The voices of my parents and sisters and brother. Their voices insisting: *You belong here. We are family members. Related. Special to one another. Listen!* Voices singing and sighing, rising, straining, then surging, teeming with pleasure that burst syllables into fragments of laughter. At times it seemed there was steady quiet only when, from another room, the rustling whispers of my parents faded and I moved closer to sleep.

2

Supporters of bilingual education today imply that students like me miss a great   25
deal by not being taught in their family's language. What they seem not to recognize is that, as a socially disadvantaged child, I considered Spanish to be a private language. What I needed to learn in school was that I had the right— and the obligation—to speak the public language of *los gringos.* The odd truth is that my first-grade classmates could have become bilingual, in the conventional sense of that word, more easily than I. Had they been taught (as upper-middle-class children are often taught early) a second language like Spanish or French, they could have regarded it simply as that: another public language. In my case such bilingualism could not have been so quickly achieved. What I did not believe was that I could speak a single public language.

Without question, it would have pleased me to hear my teachers address me in Spanish when I entered the classroom. I would have felt much less afraid. I would have trusted them and responded with ease. But I would have delayed— for how long postponed?—having to learn the language of public society. I would have evaded—and for how long could I have afforded to delay?— learning the great lesson of school, that I had a public identity.

Fortunately, my teachers were unsentimental about their responsibility. What they understood was that I needed to speak a public language. So their voices would search me out, asking me questions. Each time I'd hear them, I'd look up in surprise to see a nun's face frowning at me. I'd mumble, not really meaning to answer. The nun would persist, "Richard, stand up. Don't look at the floor. Speak up. Speak to the entire class, not just to me!" But I couldn't believe that the English language was mine to use. (In part, I did not want to believe it.) I continued to mumble. I resisted the teacher's demands. (Did I somehow suspect that once I learned public language my pleasing family life would be changed?) Silent, waiting for the bell to sound, I remained dazed, diffident, afraid.

Because I wrongly imagined that English was intrinsically a public language and Spanish an intrinsically private one, I easily noted the difference between classroom language and the language of home. At school, words were directed to a general audience of listeners. ("Boys and girls.") Words were meaningfully ordered. And the point was not self-expression alone but to make oneself understood by many others. The teacher quizzed: "Boys and girls, why do we use that word in this sentence? Could we think of a better word to use there? Would the sentence change its meaning if the words were differently arranged? And wasn't there a better way of saying much the same thing?" (I couldn't say. I wouldn't try to say.)

Three months. Five. Half a year passed. Unsmiling, ever watchful, my teachers noted my silence. They began to connect my behavior with the difficult progress my older sister and brother were making. Until one Saturday morning three nuns arrived at the house to talk to our parents. Stiffly, they sat on the blue living room sofa. From the doorway of another room, spying the visitors, I noted the incongruity — the clash of two worlds, the faces and voices of school intruding upon the familiar setting of home. I overheard one voice gently wondering, "Do your children speak only Spanish at home, Mrs. Rodriguez?" While another voice added, "That Richard especially seems so timid and shy."

That Rich-heard!   30

With great tact the visitors continued, "Is it possible for you and your husband to encourage your children to practice their English when they are home?" Of course, my parents complied. What would they not do for their children's well-being? And how could they have questioned the Church's authority which those women represented? In an instant, they agreed to give up the language (the sounds) that had revealed and accentuated our family's closeness. The moment after the visitors left, the change was observed. "*Ahora*, speak to us *en inglés*," my father and mother united to tell us.

At first, it seemed a kind of game. After dinner each night, the family gathered to practice "our" English. (It was still then *inglés*, a language foreign to us, so we felt drawn as strangers to it.) Laughing, we would try to define words we could not pronounce. We played with strange English sounds, often overanglicizing our pronunciations. And we filled the smiling gaps of our sentences with familiar Spanish sounds. But that was cheating, somebody shouted. Everyone laughed. In school, meanwhile, like my brother and sister, I was required to attend a daily tutoring session. I needed a full year of special attention. I also needed my teachers to keep my attention from straying in class by calling out, *Rich-heard* — their English voices slowly prying loose my ties to my other name, its three notes, *Ri-car-do*. Most of all I needed to hear my mother and father speak to me in a moment of seriousness in broken — suddenly heartbreaking — English. The scene was inevitable: one Saturday morning I entered the kitchen where my parents were talking in Spanish. I did not realize that they were talking in Spanish however until, at the moment they saw me, I heard their voices change to speak English. Those *gringo* sounds they uttered startled me. Pushed me away. In that moment of trivial misunderstanding and profound insight, I felt my throat twisted by unsounded grief. I turned quickly and left the room. But I had no place to escape to with Spanish. (The spell was broken.) My brother and sisters were speaking English in another part of the house.

Again and again in the days following, increasingly angry, I was obliged to hear my mother and father: "Speak to us *en inglés.*" (*Speak.*) Only then did I determine to learn classroom English. Weeks after, it happened: one day in school I raised my hand to volunteer an answer. I spoke out in a loud voice. And I did not think it remarkable when the entire class understood. That day, I moved very far from the disadvantaged child I had been only days earlier. The belief, the calming assurance that I belonged in public, had at last taken hold.

Shortly after, I stopped hearing the high and loud sounds of *los gringos.* A more and more confident speaker of English, I didn't trouble to listen to *how* strangers sounded, speaking to me. And there simply were too many English-speaking people in my day for me to hear American accents anymore. Conversations quickened. Listening to persons who sounded eccentrically pitched voices, I usually noted their sounds for an initial few seconds before I concentrated on *what* they were saying. Conversations became content-full. Transparent. Hearing someone's *tone* of voice—angry or questioning or sarcastic or happy or sad—I didn't distinguish it from the words it expressed. Sound and word were thus tightly wedded. At the end of a day, I was often bemused, always relieved, to realize how "silent," though crowded with words, my day in public had been. (This public silence measured and quickened the change in my life.)

At last, seven years old, I came to believe what had been technically true since my birth: I was an American citizen.   35

But the special feeling of closeness at home was diminished by then. Gone was the desperate, urgent, intense feeling of being at home; rare was the experience of feeling myself individualized by family intimates. We remained a loving family, but one greatly changed. No longer so close; no longer bound tight by the pleasing and troubling knowledge of our public separateness. Neither my older brother nor sister rushed home after school anymore. Nor did I. When I arrived home there would often be neighborhood kids in the house. Or the house would be empty of sounds.

Following the dramatic Americanization of their children, even my parents grew more publicly confident. Especially my mother. She learned the names of all the people on our block. And she decided we needed to have a telephone installed in the house. My father continued to use the word *gringo.* But it was no longer charged with the old bitterness or distrust. (Stripped of any emotional content, the word simply became a name for those Americans not of Hispanic descent.) Hearing him, sometimes, I wasn't sure if he was pronouncing the Spanish word *gringo* or saying gringo in English.

Matching the silence I started hearing in public was a new quiet at home. The family's quiet was partly due to the fact that, as we children learned more and more English, we shared fewer and fewer words with our parents. Sentences needed to be spoken slowly when a child addressed his mother or father. (Often the parent wouldn't understand.) The child would need to repeat himself. (Still the parent misunderstood.) The young voice, frustrated, would end up saying, "Never mind" — the subject was closed. Dinners would be noisy with the clinking of knives and forks against dishes. My mother would smile softly between her remarks; my father at the other end of the table would chew and chew at his food, while he stared over the heads of his children.

My *mother*! My *father*! After English became my primary language, I no longer knew what words to use in addressing my parents. The old Spanish words (those tender accents of sound) I had used earlier — *mamá* and *papá* — I couldn't use anymore. They would have been too painful reminders of how much had changed in my life. On the other hand, the words I heard neighborhood kids call *their* parents seemed equally unsatisfactory. *Mother* and *Father*; *Ma, Papa, Pa, Dad, Pop* (how I hated the all-American sound of that last word especially) — all these terms I felt were unsuitable, not really terms of address for *my* parents. As a result, I never used them at home. Whenever I'd speak to my parents, I would try to get their attention with eye contact alone. In public conversations, I'd refer to "my parents" or "my mother and father."

My mother and father, for their part, responded differently, as their children spoke to them less. She grew restless, seemed troubled and anxious at the scarcity of words exchanged in the house. It was she who would question me about my day when I came home from school. She smiled at small talk. She pried at the edges of my sentences to get me to say something more. (What?) She'd join conversations she overheard, but her intrusions often stopped her children's talking. By contrast, my father seemed reconciled to the new quiet. Though his English improved somewhat, he retired into silence. At dinner he spoke very little. One night his children and even his wife helplessly giggled at his garbled English pronunciation of the Catholic Grace before Meals. Thereafter he made his wife recite the prayer at the start of each meal, even on formal occasions, when there were guests in the house. Hers became the public voice of the family. On official business, it was she, not my father, one would usually hear on the phone or in stores, talking to strangers. His children grew so accustomed to his silence that, years later, they would speak routinely of his shyness. (My mother would often try to explain: both his parents died when he was eight. He was raised by an uncle who treated him like little more than a menial servant. He was never encouraged to speak. He grew up alone. A man of few words.) But my father was not shy, I realized, when I'd watch him speaking Spanish with relatives. Using Spanish, he was quickly effusive. Especially when talking with other men, his voice would spark, flicker, flare alive with sounds. In Spanish, he expressed ideas and feelings he rarely revealed in English. With firm Spanish sounds, he conveyed confidence and authority English would never allow him.

The silence at home, however, was finally more than a literal silence. Fewer words passed between parent and child, but more profound was the silence that resulted from my inattention to sounds. At about the time I no longer

40

bothered to listen with care to the sounds of English in public, I grew careless about listening to the sounds family members made when they spoke. Most of the time I heard someone speaking at home and didn't distinguish his sounds from the words people uttered in public. I didn't even pay much attention to my parents' accented and ungrammatical speech. At least not at home. Only when I was with them in public would I grow alert to their accents. Though, even then, their sounds caused me less and less concern. For I was increasingly confident of my own public identity.

I would have been happier about my public success had I not sometimes recalled what it had been like earlier, when my family had conveyed its intimacy through a set of conveniently private sounds. Sometimes in public, hearing a stranger, I'd hark back to my past. A Mexican farmworker approached me downtown to ask directions to somewhere. "¿Hijito . . . ?" he said. And his voice summoned deep longing. Another time, standing beside my mother in the visiting room of a Carmelite convent, before the dense screen which rendered the nuns shadowy figures, I heard several Spanish-speaking nuns — their busy, singsong overlapping voices — assure us that yes, yes, we were remembered, all our family was remembered in their prayers. (Their voices echoed faraway family sounds.) Another day, a dark-faced old woman — her hand light on my shoulder — steadied herself against me as she boarded a bus. She murmured something I couldn't quite comprehend. Her Spanish voice came near, like the face of a never-before-seen relative in the instant before I was kissed. Her voice, like so many of the Spanish voices I'd hear in public, recalled the golden age of my youth. Hearing Spanish then, I continued to be a careful, if sad, listener to sounds. Hearing a Spanish-speaking family walking behind me, I turned to look. I smiled for an instant, before my glance found the Hispanic-looking faces of strangers in the crowd going by.

Today I hear bilingual educators say that children lose a degree of "individuality" by becoming assimilated into public society. (Bilingual schooling was popularized in the seventies, that decade when middle-class ethnics began to resist the process of assimilation — the American melting pot.) But the bilingualists simplistically scorn the value and necessity of assimilation. They do not seem to realize that there are *two* ways a person is individualized. So they do not realize that while one suffers a diminished sense of *private* individuality by becoming assimilated into public society, such assimilation makes possible the achievement of *public* individuality.

The bilingualists insist that a student should be reminded of his difference from others in mass society, his heritage. But they equate mere separateness with individuality. The fact is that only in private — with intimates — is separateness from the crowd a prerequisite for individuality. (An intimate draws me apart, tells me that I am unique, unlike all others.) In public, by contrast, full individuality is achieved, paradoxically, by those who are able to consider themselves members of the crowd. Thus it happened for me: only when I was able to think of myself as an American, no longer an alien in *gringo* society, could I seek the rights and opportunities necessary for full public individuality.

The social and political advantages I enjoy as a man result from the day that I came to believe that my name, indeed, is *Rich-heard Road-ree-guess.* It is true that my public society today is often impersonal. (My public society is usually mass society.) Yet despite the anonymity of the crowd and despite the fact that the individuality I achieve in public is often tenuous — because it depends on my being one in a crowd — I celebrate the day I acquired my new name. Those middle-class ethnics who scorn assimilation seem to me filled with decadent self-pity, obsessed by the burden of public life. Dangerously, they romanticize public separateness and they trivialize the dilemma of the socially disadvantaged.

My awkward childhood does not prove the necessity of bilingual education. My story discloses instead an essential myth of childhood — inevitable pain. If I rehearse here the changes in my private life after my Americanization, it is finally to emphasize the public gain. The loss implies the gain: the house I returned to each afternoon was quiet. Intimate sounds no longer rushed to the door to greet me. There were other noises inside. The telephone rang. Neighborhood kids ran past the door of the bedroom where I was reading my schoolbooks — covered with shopping-bag paper. Once I learned public language, it would never again be easy for me to hear intimate family voices. More and more of my day was spent hearing words. But that may only be a way of saying that the day I raised my hand in class and spoke loudly to an entire roomful of faces, my childhood started to end.   *[1982]*

45

≡ THINKING ABOUT THE TEXT

1. What distinctions does Rodriguez make between the "private" and "public" worlds of his childhood? Ultimately, he brings up the possibility of "*public* individuality" (para. 43). What does he mean by this? Does this concept make sense to you?

2. What, according to Rodriguez, were the changes he experienced? With what tone does he recall these changes? Consider in particular the way he describes his changing relationship to his parents.

3. Do you agree with Rodriguez that the changes he went through were necessary? To what extent is your answer influenced by your own social position?

4. Rodriguez declares, "Those middle-class ethnics who scorn assimilation seem to me filled with decadent self-pity, obsessed by the burden of public life. Dangerously, they romanticize public separateness and they trivialize the dilemma of the socially disadvantaged" (para. 44). Evaluate this claim. Would you say that you are a "middle-class ethnic"? Why, or why not?

5. Rodriguez suggests that a student must speak up in class to succeed in school. Do you agree? Rodriguez indicates that matters of language play a crucial role in a child's education. Have you found this true? Be specific.

JOSE ANTONIO VARGAS
My Life as an Undocumented Immigrant

Jose Antonio Vargas (b. 1981) is a journalist, filmmaker, and immigrant activist. He was born in the Philippines and at the age of twelve was sent to the U.S. to live with his grandparents, but without official authorization. He became interested in journalism in high school and became a copy boy with the San Francisco Chronicle. *After graduating from San Francisco State University, he began writing at the* Washington Post. *Vargas was part of a team working on the story of the Virginia Tech shootings that earned him a Pulitzer Prize. In 2009 he joined the staff of the* Huffington Post. *The following essay was published in the* New York Times Sunday Magazine *and won the June 2011 Sidney Award as an "outstanding piece of socially conscious journalism." He continues to be an activist for immigrant issues.*

One August morning nearly two decades ago, my mother woke me and put me in a cab. She handed me a jacket. "*Baka malamig doon*" were among the few words she said. ("It might be cold there.") When I arrived at the Philippines' Ninoy Aquino International Airport with her, my aunt, and a family friend, I was introduced to a man I'd never seen. They told me he was my uncle. He held my hand as I boarded an airplane for the first time. It was 1993, and I was twelve.

My mother wanted to give me a better life, so she sent me thousands of miles away to live with her parents in America—my grandfather (*Lolo* in Tagalog) and grandmother (*Lola*). After I arrived in Mountain View, California, in the San Francisco Bay Area, I entered sixth grade and quickly grew to love my new home, family, and culture. I discovered a passion for language, though it was hard to learn the difference between formal English and American slang. One of my early memories is of a freckled kid in middle school asking me, "What's up?" I replied, "The sky," and he and a couple of other kids laughed. I won the eighth-grade spelling bee by memorizing words I couldn't properly pronounce. (The winning word was "indefatigable.")

One day when I was sixteen, I rode my bike to the nearby D.M.V. office to get my driver's permit. Some of my friends already had their licenses, so I figured it was time. But when I handed the clerk my green card as proof of U.S. residency, she flipped it around, examining it. "This is fake," she whispered. "Don't come back here again."

Confused and scared, I pedaled home and confronted Lolo. I remember him sitting in the garage, cutting coupons. I dropped my bike and ran over to him, showing him the green card. "*Peke ba ito?*" I asked in Tagalog. ("Is this fake?") My grandparents were naturalized American citizens—he worked as a security guard, she as a food server—and they had begun supporting my mother and me financially when I was three, after my father's wandering eye and inability to properly provide for us led to my parents' separation. Lolo was a proud man, and I saw the shame on his face as he told me he purchased the card, along with other fake documents, for me. "Don't show it to other people," he warned.

I decided then that I could never give anyone reason to doubt I was an   5
American. I convinced myself that if I worked enough, if I achieved enough, I would be rewarded with citizenship. I felt I could earn it.

I've tried. Over the past fourteen years, I've graduated from high school and college and built a career as a journalist, interviewing some of the most famous people in the country. On the surface, I've created a good life. I've lived the American dream.

But I am still an undocumented immigrant. And that means living a different kind of reality. It means going about my day in fear of being found out. It means rarely trusting people, even those closest to me, with who I really am. It means keeping my family photos in a shoebox rather than displaying them on shelves in my home, so friends don't ask about them. It means reluctantly, even painfully, doing things I know are wrong and unlawful. And it has meant relying on a sort of twenty-first-century underground railroad of supporters, people who took an interest in my future and took risks for me.

Last year I read about four students who walked from Miami to Washington to lobby for the Dream Act, a nearly decade-old immigration bill that would provide a path to legal permanent residency for young people who have been educated in this country. At the risk of deportation — the Obama administration has deported almost 800,000 people in the last two years — they are speaking out. Their courage has inspired me.

There are believed to be 11 million undocumented immigrants in the United States. We're not always who you think we are. Some pick your strawberries or care for your children. Some are in high school or college. And some, it turns out, write news articles you might read. I grew up here. This is my home. Yet even though I think of myself as an American and consider America my country, my country doesn't think of me as one of its own.

My first challenge was the language. Though I learned English in the Philip-   10
pines, I wanted to lose my accent. During high school, I spent hours at a time watching television (especially *Frasier*, *Home Improvement*, and reruns of *The Golden Girls*) and movies (from *Goodfellas* to *Anne of Green Gables*), pausing the VHS to try to copy how various characters enunciated their words. At the local library, I read magazines, books, and newspapers — anything to learn how to write better. Kathy Dewar, my high-school English teacher, introduced me to journalism. From the moment I wrote my first article for the student paper, I convinced myself that having my name in print — writing in English, interviewing Americans — validated my presence here.

The debates over "illegal aliens" intensified my anxieties. In 1994, only a year after my flight from the Philippines, Governor Pete Wilson was re-elected in part because of his support for Proposition 187, which prohibited undocumented immigrants from attending public school and accessing other services. (A federal court later found the law unconstitutional.) After my encounter at the D.M.V.

in 1997, I grew more aware of anti-immigrant sentiments and stereotypes: *they don't want to assimilate, they are a drain on society.* They're not talking about me, I would tell myself. I have something to contribute.

To do that, I had to work—and for that, I needed a Social Security number. Fortunately, my grandfather had already managed to get one for me. Lolo had always taken care of everyone in the family. He and my grandmother emigrated legally in 1984 from Zambales, a province in the Philippines of rice fields and bamboo houses, following Lolo's sister, who married a Filipino American serving in the American military. She petitioned for her brother and his wife to join her. When they got here, Lolo petitioned for his two children—my mother and her younger brother—to follow them. But instead of mentioning that my mother was a married woman, he listed her as single. Legal residents can't petition for their married children. Besides, Lolo didn't care for my father. He didn't want him coming here too.

But soon Lolo grew nervous that the immigration authorities reviewing the petition would discover my mother was married, thus derailing not only her chances of coming here but those of my uncle as well. So he withdrew her petition. After my uncle came to America legally in 1991, Lolo tried to get my mother here through a tourist visa, but she wasn't able to obtain one. That's when she decided to send me. My mother told me later that she figured she would follow me soon. She never did.

The "uncle" who brought me here turned out to be a coyote°, not a relative, my grandfather later explained. Lolo scraped together enough money—I eventually learned it was $4,500, a huge sum for him—to pay him to smuggle me here under a fake name and fake passport. (I never saw the passport again after the flight and have always assumed that the coyote kept it.) After I arrived in America, Lolo obtained a new fake Filipino passport, in my real name this time, adorned with a fake student visa, in addition to the fraudulent green card.

Using the fake passport, we went to the local Social Security Administration office and applied for a Social Security number and card. It was, I remember, a quick visit. When the card came in the mail, it had my full, real name, but it also clearly stated: "Valid for work only with I.N.S. authorization."   15

When I began looking for work, a short time after the D.M.V. incident, my grandfather and I took the Social Security card to Kinko's, where he covered the "I.N.S. authorization" text with a sliver of white tape. We then made photocopies of the card. At a glance, at least, the copies would look like copies of a regular, unrestricted Social Security card.

Lolo always imagined I would work the kind of low-paying jobs that undocumented people often take. (Once I married an American, he said, I would get my real papers, and everything would be fine.) But even menial jobs require documents, so he and I hoped the doctored card would work for now. The more documents I had, he said, the better.

While in high school, I worked part time at Subway, then at the front desk

coyote: A person who smuggles undocumented aliens across the border into the United States, usually for a fee.

of the local Y.M.C.A., then at a tennis club, until I landed an unpaid internship at the *Mountain View Voice*, my hometown newspaper. First I brought coffee and helped around the office; eventually I began covering city-hall meetings and other assignments for pay.

For more than a decade of getting part-time and full-time jobs, employers have rarely asked to check my original Social Security card. When they did, I showed the photocopied version, which they accepted. Over time, I also began checking the citizenship box on my federal I-9 employment eligibility forms. (Claiming full citizenship was actually easier than declaring permanent resident "green card" status, which would have required me to provide an alien registration number.)

This deceit never got easier. The more I did it, the more I felt like an impostor, the more guilt I carried — and the more I worried that I would get caught. But I kept doing it. I needed to live and survive on my own, and I decided this was the way.   20

Mountain View High School became my second home. I was elected to represent my school at school-board meetings, which gave me the chance to meet and befriend Rich Fischer, the superintendent for our school district. I joined the speech and debate team, acted in school plays, and eventually became co-editor of the *Oracle*, the student newspaper. That drew the attention of my principal, Pat Hyland. "You're at school just as much as I am," she told me. Pat and Rich would soon become mentors, and over time, almost surrogate parents for me.

After a choir rehearsal during my junior year, Jill Denny, the choir director, told me she was considering a Japan trip for our singing group. I told her I couldn't afford it, but she said we'd figure out a way. I hesitated, and then decided to tell her the truth. "It's not really the money," I remember saying. "I don't have the right passport." When she assured me we'd get the proper documents, I finally told her. "I can't get the right passport," I said. "I'm not supposed to be here."

She understood. So the choir toured Hawaii instead, with me in tow. (Mrs. Denny and I spoke a couple of months ago, and she told me she hadn't wanted to leave any student behind.)

Later that school year, my history class watched a documentary on Harvey Milk, the openly gay San Francisco city official who was assassinated. This was 1999, just six months after Matthew Shepard's body was found tied to a fence in Wyoming. During the discussion, I raised my hand and said something like: "I'm sorry Harvey Milk got killed for being gay. . . . I've been meaning to say this. . . . I'm gay."

I hadn't planned on coming out that morning, though I had known that I   25
was gay for several years. With that announcement, I became the only openly gay student at school, and it caused turmoil with my grandparents. Lolo kicked me out of the house for a few weeks. Though we eventually reconciled, I had disappointed him on two fronts. First, as a Catholic, he considered homosexuality a sin and was embarrassed about having "*ang apo na bakla*" ("a grandson who is gay"). Even worse, I was making matters more difficult for myself, he said. I needed to marry an American woman in order to gain a green card.

Tough as it was, coming out about being gay seemed less daunting than coming out about my legal status. I kept my other secret mostly hidden.

While my classmates awaited their college acceptance letters, I hoped to get a full-time job at the *Mountain View Voice* after graduation. It's not that I didn't want to go to college, but I couldn't apply for state and federal financial aid. Without that, my family couldn't afford to send me.

But when I finally told Pat and Rich about my immigration "problem" — as we called it from then on — they helped me look for a solution. At first, they even wondered if one of them could adopt me and fix the situation that way, but a lawyer Rich consulted told him it wouldn't change my legal status because I was too old. Eventually they connected me to a new scholarship fund for high-potential students who were usually the first in their families to attend college. Most important, the fund was not concerned with immigration status. I was among the first recipients, with the scholarship covering tuition, lodging, books, and other expenses for my studies at San Francisco State University.

As a college freshman, I found a job working part time at the *San Francisco Chronicle*, where I sorted mail and wrote some freelance articles. My ambition was to get a reporting job, so I embarked on a series of internships. First I landed at the *Philadelphia Daily News*, in the summer of 2001, where I covered a drive-by shooting and the wedding of the 76ers star Allen Iverson. Using those articles, I applied to the *Seattle Times* and got an internship for the following summer.

But then my lack of proper documents became a problem again. The   30
Times's recruiter, Pat Foote, asked all incoming interns to bring certain paper-work on their first day: a birth certificate, or a passport, or a driver's license plus an original Social Security card. I panicked, thinking my documents wouldn't pass muster. So before starting the job, I called Pat and told her about my legal status. After consulting with management, she called me back with the answer I feared: I couldn't do the internship.

This was devastating. What good was college if I couldn't then pursue the career I wanted? I decided then that if I was to succeed in a profession that is all about truth-telling, I couldn't tell the truth about myself.

After this episode, Jim Strand, the venture capitalist who sponsored my scholarship, offered to pay for an immigration lawyer. Rich and I went to meet her in San Francisco's financial district.

I was hopeful. This was in early 2002, shortly after Senators Orrin Hatch, the Utah Republican, and Dick Durbin, the Illinois Democrat, introduced the Dream Act — Development, Relief, and Education for Alien Minors. It seemed like the legislative version of what I'd told myself: If I work hard and contribute, things will work out.

But the meeting left me crushed. My only solution, the lawyer said, was to go back to the Philippines and accept a ten-year ban before I could apply to return legally.

If Rich was discouraged, he hid it well. "Put this problem on a shelf," he   35
told me. "Compartmentalize it. Keep going."

And I did. For the summer of 2003, I applied for internships across the country. Several newspapers, including the *Wall Street Journal*, the *Boston Globe*, and the *Chicago Tribune*, expressed interest. But when the *Washington Post* offered me a spot, I knew where I would go. And this time, I had no intention of acknowledging my "problem."

The *Post* internship posed a tricky obstacle: It required a driver's license. (After my close call at the California D.M.V., I'd never gotten one.) So I spent an afternoon at the Mountain View Public Library, studying various states' requirements. Oregon was among the most welcoming — and it was just a few hours' drive north.

Again, my support network came through. A friend's father lived in Portland, and he allowed me to use his address as proof of residency. Pat, Rich, and Rich's longtime assistant, Mary Moore, sent letters to me at that address. Rich taught me how to do three-point turns in a parking lot, and a friend accompanied me to Portland.

The license meant everything to me — it would let me drive, fly, and work. But my grandparents worried about the Portland trip and the Washington internship. While Lola offered daily prayers so that I would not get caught, Lolo told me that I was dreaming too big, risking too much.

I was determined to pursue my ambitions. I was twenty-two, I told them,   40 responsible for my own actions. But this was different from Lolo's driving a confused teenager to Kinko's. I knew what I was doing now, and I knew it wasn't right. But what was I supposed to do?

I was paying state and federal taxes, but I was using an invalid Social Security card and writing false information on my employment forms. But that seemed better than depending on my grandparents or on Pat, Rich, and Jim — or returning to a country I barely remembered. I convinced myself all would be O.K. if I lived up to the qualities of a "citizen": hard work, self-reliance, love of my country.

At the D.M.V. in Portland, I arrived with my photocopied Social Security card, my college I.D., a pay stub from the *San Francisco Chronicle*, and my proof of state residence — the letters to the Portland address that my support network had sent. It worked. My license, issued in 2003, was set to expire eight years later, on my thirtieth birthday, on February 3, 2011. I had eight years to succeed professionally, and to hope that some sort of immigration reform would pass in the meantime and allow me to stay.

It seemed like all the time in the world.

My summer in Washington was exhilarating. I was intimidated to be in a major newsroom but was assigned a mentor — Peter Perl, a veteran magazine writer — to help me navigate it. A few weeks into the internship, he printed out one of my articles, about a guy who recovered a long-lost wallet, circled the first two paragraphs, and left it on my desk. "Great eye for details — awesome!" he wrote. Though I didn't know it then, Peter would become one more member of my network.

At the end of the summer, I returned to the *San Francisco Chronicle*. My   45 plan was to finish school — I was now a senior — while I worked for the *Chronicle* as a reporter for the city desk. But when the *Post* beckoned again, offering me a full-time, two-year paid internship that I could start when I graduated in June 2004, it was too tempting to pass up. I moved back to Washington.

About four months into my job as a reporter for the *Post*, I began feeling increasingly paranoid, as if I had "illegal immigrant" tattooed on my forehead—and in Washington, of all places, where the debates over immigration seemed never-ending. I was so eager to prove myself that I feared I was annoying some colleagues and editors—and worried that any one of these professional journalists could discover my secret. The anxiety was nearly paralyzing. I decided I had to tell one of the higher-ups about my situation. I turned to Peter.

By this time, Peter, who still works at the *Post*, had become part of management as the paper's director of newsroom training and professional development. One afternoon in late October, we walked a couple of blocks to Lafayette Square, across from the White House. Over some twenty minutes, sitting on a bench, I told him everything: the Social Security card, the driver's license, Pat and Rich, my family.

Peter was shocked. "I understand you 100 times better now," he said. He told me that I had done the right thing by telling him, and that it was now our shared problem. He said he didn't want to do anything about it just yet. I had just been hired, he said, and I needed to prove myself. "When you've done enough," he said, "we'll tell Don and Len together." (Don Graham is the chairman of the Washington Post Company; Leonard Downie Jr. was then the paper's executive editor.) A month later, I spent my first Thanksgiving in Washington with Peter and his family.

In the five years that followed, I did my best to "do enough." I was promoted to staff writer, reported on video-game culture, wrote a series on Washington's H.I.V./AIDS epidemic, and covered the role of technology and social media in the 2008 presidential race. I visited the White House, where I interviewed senior aides and covered a state dinner—and gave the Secret Service the Social Security number I obtained with false documents.

I did my best to steer clear of reporting on immigration policy but couldn't   50
always avoid it. On two occasions, I wrote about Hillary Clinton's position on driver's licenses for undocumented immigrants. I also wrote an article about Senator Mel Martinez of Florida, then the chairman of the Republican National Committee, who was defending his party's stance toward Latinos after only one Republican presidential candidate—John McCain, the coauthor of a failed immigration bill—agreed to participate in a debate sponsored by Univision, the Spanish-language network.

It was an odd sort of dance: I was trying to stand out in a highly competitive newsroom, yet I was terrified that if I stood out too much, I'd invite unwanted scrutiny. I tried to compartmentalize my fears, distract myself by reporting on the lives of other people, but there was no escaping the central conflict in my life. Maintaining a deception for so long distorts your sense of self. You start wondering who you've become, and why.

In April 2008, I was part of a *Post* team that won a Pulitzer Prize for the paper's coverage of the Virginia Tech shootings a year earlier. Lolo died a year earlier, so it was Lola who called me the day of the announcement. The first thing she said was, *"Anong mangyayari kung malaman ng mga tao?"*

What will happen if people find out?

I couldn't say anything. After we got off the phone, I rushed to the bathroom on the fourth floor of the newsroom, sat down on the toilet, and cried.

In the summer of 2009, without ever having had that follow-up talk with top *Post* management, I left the paper and moved to New York to join the *Huffington Post*. I met Arianna Huffington at a Washington Press Club Foundation dinner I was covering for the *Post* two years earlier, and she later recruited me to join her news site. I wanted to learn more about Web publishing, and I thought the new job would provide a useful education.

Still, I was apprehensive about the move: many companies were already using E-Verify, a program set up by the Department of Homeland Security that checks if prospective employees are eligible to work, and I didn't know if my new employer was among them. But I'd been able to get jobs in other newsrooms, I figured, so I filled out the paperwork as usual and succeeded in landing on the payroll.

While I worked at the *Huffington Post*, other opportunities emerged. My H.I.V./AIDS series became a documentary film called "The Other City," which opened at the Tribeca Film Festival last year and was broadcast on Showtime. I began writing for magazines and landed a dream assignment: profiling Facebook's Mark Zuckerberg for *The New Yorker*.

The more I achieved, the more scared and depressed I became. I was proud of my work, but there was always a cloud hanging over it, over me. My old eight-year deadline—the expiration of my Oregon driver's license—was approaching.

After slightly less than a year, I decided to leave the *Huffington Post*. In part, this was because I wanted to promote the documentary and write a book about online culture—or so I told my friends. But the real reason was, after so many years of trying to be a part of the system, of focusing all my energy on my professional life, I learned that no amount of professional success would solve my problem or ease the sense of loss and displacement I felt. I lied to a friend about why I couldn't take a weekend trip to Mexico. Another time I concocted an excuse for why I couldn't go on an all-expenses-paid trip to Switzerland. I have been unwilling, for years, to be in a long-term relationship because I never wanted anyone to get too close and ask too many questions. All the while, Lola's question was stuck in my head: What will happen if people find out?

Early this year, just two weeks before my thirtieth birthday, I won a small reprieve: I obtained a driver's license in the state of Washington. The license is valid until 2016. This offered me five more years of acceptable identification—but also five more years of fear, of lying to people I respect and institutions that trusted me, of running away from who I am.

I'm done running. I'm exhausted. I don't want that life anymore.

So I've decided to come forward, own up to what I've done, and tell my story to the best of my recollection. I've reached out to former bosses and em-

55

60

ployers and apologized for misleading them—a mix of humiliation and liberation coming with each disclosure. All the people mentioned in this article gave
me permission to use their names. I've also talked to family and friends about
my situation and am working with legal counsel to review my options. I don't
know what the consequences will be of telling my story.

I do know that I am grateful to my grandparents, my Lolo and Lola, for giving me the chance for a better life. I'm also grateful to my other family—the
support network I found here in America—for encouraging me to pursue my
dreams.

It's been almost eighteen years since I've seen my mother. Early on, I was
mad at her for putting me in this position, and then mad at myself for being
angry and ungrateful. By the time I got to college, we rarely spoke by phone. It
became too painful; after a while it was easier to just send money to help support her and my two half-siblings. My sister, almost two years old when I left, is
almost twenty now. I've never met my fourteen-year-old brother. I would love
to see them.

Not long ago, I called my mother. I wanted to fill the gaps in my memory   65
about that August morning so many years ago. We had never discussed it. Part
of me wanted to shove the memory aside, but to write this article and face the
facts of my life, I needed more details. Did I cry? Did she? Did we kiss goodbye?

My mother told me I was excited about meeting a stewardess, about getting on a plane. She also reminded me of the one piece of advice she gave me
for blending in: If anyone asked why I was coming to America, I should say I
was going to Disneyland.   [2011]

≡ WRITING ABOUT THE TEXT

1. Who is the audience for this essay? What response do you think Vargas
   wants? What likely response will he get? What is your response to this
   confession?

2. Why does Vargas mention the incident where he asserts that he is gay?
   Do you think this will make him more or less sympathetic?

3. Comment on the tension between Vargas telling the truth and fulfilling
   his dream. Mention at least three specific examples and say why you
   think he made the right or wrong choice.

4. If this essay were to be considered an attempt at persuasion, point out
   two or three incidents and say why you think they are persuasive.

5. Why do you think Vargas opens and closes with accounts of his mother?
   What significance do you think should be attributed to Vargas's mention of Disneyland in the last sentence?

≡ MAKING COMPARISONS

1. Compare Rodriguez's and Vargas's childhood views of English.

2. Rodriguez has generally been criticized by the immigrant activists while Vargas has been praised. Point to attitudes in these two essays that might account for such a difference.

3. What lessons have Rodriguez's and Vargas's childhoods taught them?

≡ WRITING ABOUT ISSUES

1. Argue that either Rodriguez or Vargas has more successfully crossed the boundary between immigrant and mainstream culture.

2. Write an essay that argues that Vargas should or should not be allowed to become an American citizen.

3. There is a complex and emotional debate in Congress over illegal immigrants. What seem to you to be the most cogent arguments on both sides? Explain why.

4. Locate Vargas's cover story for *Time* (June 15, 2012) on undocumented immigrants and argue that he does or does not offer a compelling solution.

WILFRED OWEN, "Dulce et Decorum Est" (poem)

TIM O'BRIEN, "The Things They Carried" (story)

MICHAEL HERR, "Scream a Lot" (essay)

Contrary to the evidence from those who have actually fought in war, there is a tendency in our popular culture to glorify and mythologize the courage of those who died. While it is natural for patriotic feelings to support soldiers, it is a distortion to ignore the brutality and the horrors of battle. Somehow we forget history and the lessons of countless writers who have detailed the grim realities of pain, suffering, and death. One of the most gruesome aspects of World War I was trench warfare, and perhaps no one depicts its graphic terrors better than Wilfred Owen, who was tragically shot in the head one week before the end of the war. Tim O'Brien and Michael Herr continue Owens's work with "tough, profane, relentless, and elegant" narratives of what William Burroughs called the "bare bones of fear, war, and death."

WILFRED OWEN
Dulce et Decorum Est

English poet and soldier Wilfred Owen (1893–1918) is regarded as the best war poet of the First World War, known for his frank and disturbingly realistic depictions of the horrors of trench and gas warfare. He attended what is now the University of Reading for a while and taught at the Berlitz School of Languages in Bordeaux. He enlisted in the war in 1915 and was commissioned as a second lieutenant. He was wounded and suffered "shell shock." He was sent home but returned to the front and was killed one week before the Armistice. He is often linked with his mentor and fellow poet Siegfried Sassoon, who inspired Owen's gritty realism and his focus on showing the "the pity of war."

Bent double, like old beggars under sacks,
Knock-kneed, coughing like hags, we cursed through sludge,
Till on the haunting flares we turned our backs
And towards our distant rest began to trudge.
Men marched asleep. Many had lost their boots   5
But limped on, blood-shod. All went lame; all blind;
Drunk with fatigue; deaf even to the hoots
Of disappointed shells that dropped behind.

GAS! Gas! Quick, boys! — An ecstasy of fumbling,
Fitting the clumsy helmets just in time;   10
But someone still was yelling out and stumbling
And floundering like a man in fire or lime. —

Getty Images

Dim, through the misty panes and thick green light
As under a green sea, I saw him drowning.

In all my dreams, before my helpless sight,   15
He plunges at me, guttering, choking, drowning.

If in some smothering dreams you too could pace
Behind the wagon that we flung him in,
And watch the white eyes writhing in his face,
His hanging face, like a devil's sick of sin;   20
If you could hear, at every jolt, the blood
Come gargling from the froth-corrupted lungs,
Obscene as cancer, bitter as the cud
Of vile, incurable sores on innocent tongues, —
My friend, you would not tell with such high zest   25
To children ardent for some desperate glory,
The old Lie: Dulce et decorum est
Pro patria mori.   *[1920]*

≡ THINKING ABOUT THE TEXT

1. What does the Latin quote that ends the poem mean? Why do you think
   Owen chose Latin?

2. Which images seem particularly gruesome to you? What do you think
   Owen's purpose is in being so graphic?

3. Most poets don't directly address the reader. Owen does, making a request, hoping the reader will do something. What is it? Do you agree with him? In what ways is this poem an act of persuasion? Is it effective?

4. What statement about war do you think Owen would agree with?

5. In the opening lines of the last stanza, Owen seems to be saying that if you experienced war, it would change your mind. Do you think there are other ways to convince people of war's horrors?

TIM O'BRIEN
The Things They Carried

A native of Minnesota, Tim O'Brien (b. 1946) was drafted after he graduated from Macalester College. Subsequently, he served in the Vietnam War, during which he received a Purple Heart. In one way or another, practically all of his fiction deals with the war, although he has been repeatedly ambiguous about how and when his work incorporates his own Vietnam experiences. O'Brien's novels include If I Die in a Combat Zone *(1973),* Going After Cacciato *(which won the National Book Award in 1979),* In the Lake of the Woods *(a 1994 book that touches on the massacre at My Lai),* Tomcat in Love *(1998), and* July, July *(2002). Originally published in* Esquire *magazine, the following story was reprinted in* The Best American Short Stories 1987. *It then appeared along with related stories by O'Brien in a 1990 book also entitled* The Things They Carried.

First Lieutenant Jimmy Cross carried letters from a girl named Martha, a junior at Mount Sebastian College in New Jersey. They were not love letters, but Lieutenant Cross was hoping, so he kept them folded in plastic at the bottom of his rucksack. In the late afternoon, after a day's march, he would dig his foxhole, wash his hands under a canteen, unwrap the letters, hold them with the tips of his fingers, and spend the last hour of light pretending. He would imagine romantic camping trips into the White Mountains in New Hampshire. He would sometimes taste the envelope flaps, knowing her tongue had been there. More than anything, he wanted Martha to love him as he loved her, but the letters were mostly chatty, elusive on the matter of love. She was a virgin, he was almost sure. She was an English major at Mount Sebastian, and she wrote beautifully about her professors and roommates and midterm exams, about her respect for Chaucer and her great affection for Virginia Woolf. She often quoted lines of poetry; she never mentioned the war, except to say, Jimmy, take care of yourself. The letters weighed ten ounces. They were signed "Love, Martha," but Lieutenant Cross understood that "Love" was only a way of signing and did not mean what he sometimes pretended it meant. At dusk, he would carefully return the letters to his rucksack. Slowly, a bit distracted, he would get up and

Photo by Bill Giduz

move among his men, checking the perimeter, then at full dark he would return to his hole and watch the night and wonder if Martha was a virgin.

The things they carried were largely determined by necessity. Among the necessities or near necessities were P-38 can openers, pocket knives, heat tabs, wrist watches, dog tags, mosquito repellant, chewing gum, candy, cigarettes, salt tablets, packets of Kool-Aid, lighters, matches, sewing kits, Military Payment Certificates, C rations, and two or three canteens of water. Together, these items weighed between fifteen and twenty pounds, depending upon a man's habits or rate of metabolism. Henry Dobbins, who was a big man, carried extra rations; he was especially fond of canned peaches in heavy syrup over pound cake. Dave Jensen, who practiced field hygiene, carried a toothbrush, dental floss, and several hotel-size bars of soap he'd stolen on R&R in Sydney, Australia. Ted Lavender, who was scared, carried tranquilizers until he was shot in the head outside the village of Than Khe in mid-April. By necessity and because it was SOP,° they all carried steel helmets that weighed five pounds including the liner and camouflage cover. They carried the standard fatigue jackets and trousers. Very few carried underwear. On their feet they carried jungle boots — 2.1 pounds — and Dave Jensen carried three pairs of socks and a can of Dr. Scholl's foot powder as a precaution against trench foot. Until he was shot, Ted Lavender carried six or seven ounces of premium dope, which for him was a necessity.

SOP: Standard operating procedure.

Mitchell Sanders, the RTO,° carried condoms. Norman Bowker carried a diary. Rat Kiley carried comic books. Kiowa, a devout Baptist, carried an illustrated New Testament that had been presented to him by his father, who taught Sunday school in Oklahoma City, Oklahoma. As a hedge against bad times, however, Kiowa also carried his grandmother's distrust of the white man, his grandfather's old hunting hatchet. Necessity dictated. Because the land was mined and booby-trapped, it was SOP for each man to carry a steel-centered, nylon-covered flak jacket, which weighed 6.7 pounds, but which on hot days seemed much heavier. Because you could die so quickly, each man carried at least one large compress bandage, usually in the helmet band for easy access. Because the nights were cold, and because the monsoons were wet, each carried a green plastic poncho that could be used as a raincoat or ground sheet or makeshift tent. With its quilted liner, the poncho weighed almost two pounds, but it was worth every ounce. In April, for instance, when Ted Lavender was shot, they used his poncho to wrap him up, then to carry him across the paddy, then to lift him into the chopper that took him away.

They were called legs or grunts.

To carry something was to "hump" it, as when Lieutenant Jimmy Cross humped his love for Martha up the hills and through the swamps. In its intransitive form, "to hump" meant "to walk," or "to march," but it implied burdens far beyond the intransitive.

Almost everyone humped photographs. In his wallet, Lieutenant Cross   5
carried two photographs of Martha. The first was a Kodachrome snapshot signed "Love," though he knew better. She stood against a brick wall. Her eyes were gray and neutral, her lips slightly open as she stared straight-on at the camera. At night, sometimes, Lieutenant Cross wondered who had taken the picture, because he knew she had boyfriends, because he loved her so much, and because he could see the shadow of the picture taker spreading out against the brick wall. The second photograph had been clipped from the 1968 Mount Sebastian yearbook. It was an action shot — women's volleyball — and Martha was bent horizontal to the floor, reaching, the palms of her hands in sharp focus, the tongue taut, the expression frank and competitive. There was no visible sweat. She wore white gym shorts. Her legs, he thought, were almost certainly the legs of a virgin, dry and without hair, the left knee cocked and carrying her entire weight, which was just over one hundred pounds. Lieutenant Cross remembered touching that left knee. A dark theater, he remembered, and the movie was *Bonnie and Clyde*, and Martha wore a tweed skirt, and during the final scene, when he touched her knee, she turned and looked at him in a sad, sober way that made him pull his hand back, but he would always remember the feel of the tweed skirt and the knee beneath it and the sound of the gunfire that killed Bonnie and Clyde, how embarrassing it was, how slow and oppressive. He remembered kissing her good night at the dorm door. Right then, he thought, he should've done something brave. He should've carried her

---

RTO: Radiotelephone operator.

up the stairs to her room and tied her to the bed and touched that left knee all night long. He should've risked it. Whenever he looked at the photographs, he thought of new things he should've done.

What they carried was partly a function of rank, partly of field specialty.

As a first lieutenant and platoon leader, Jimmy Cross carried a compass, maps, code books, binoculars, and a .45-caliber pistol that weighed 2.9 pounds fully loaded. He carried a strobe light and the responsibility for the lives of his men.

As an RTO, Mitchell Sanders carried the PRC-25 radio, a killer, twenty-six pounds with its battery.

As a medic, Rat Kiley carried a canvas satchel filled with morphine and plasma and malaria tablets and surgical tape and comic books and all the things a medic must carry, including M&M's for especially bad wounds, for a total weight of nearly twenty pounds.

As a big man, therefore a machine gunner, Henry Dobbins carried the M-60, which weighed twenty-three pounds unloaded, but which was almost always loaded. In addition, Dobbins carried between ten and fifteen pounds of ammunition draped in belts across his chest and shoulders.

As PFCs or Spec 4s, most of them were common grunts and carried the standard M-16 gas-operated assault rifle. The weapon weighed 7.5 pounds unloaded, 8.2 pounds with its full twenty-round magazine. Depending on numerous factors, such as topography and psychology, the riflemen carried anywhere from twelve to twenty magazines, usually in cloth bandoliers, adding on another 8.4 pounds at minimum, fourteen pounds at maximum. When it was available, they also carried M-16 maintenance gear — rods and steel brushes and swabs and tubes of LSA oil — all of which weighed about a pound. Among the grunts, some carried the M-79 grenade launcher, 5.9 pounds unloaded, a reasonably light weapon except for the ammunition, which was heavy. A single round weighed ten ounces. The typical load was twenty-five rounds. But Ted Lavender, who was scared, carried thirty-four rounds when he was shot and killed outside Than Khe, and he went down under an exceptional burden, more than twenty pounds of ammunition, plus the flak jacket and helmet and rations and water and toilet paper and tranquilizers and all the rest, plus the unweighed fear. He was dead weight. There was no twitching or flopping. Kiowa, who saw it happen, said it was like watching a rock fall, or a big sandbag or something — just boom, then down — not like the movies where the dead guy rolls around and does fancy spins and goes ass over teakettle — not like that, Kiowa said, the poor bastard just flat-fuck fell. Boom. Down. Nothing else. It was a bright morning in mid-April, Lieutenant Cross felt the pain. He blamed himself. They stripped off Lavender's canteens and ammo, all the heavy things, and Rat Kiley said the obvious, the guy's dead, and Mitchell Sanders used his radio to report one U.S. KIA° and to request a chopper. Then they wrapped Lavender in his poncho. They carried him out to a dry paddy, established security,

10

KIA: Killed in action.

and sat smoking the dead man's dope until the chopper came. Lieutenant Cross kept to himself. He pictured Martha's smooth young face, thinking he loved her more than anything, more than his men, and now Ted Lavender was dead because he loved her so much and could not stop thinking about her. When the dust-off arrived, they carried Lavender aboard. Afterward they burned Than Khe. They marched until dusk, then dug their holes, and that night Kiowa kept explaining how you had to be there, how fast it was, how the poor guy just dropped like so much concrete. Boom-down, he said. Like cement.

In addition to the three standard weapons — the M-60, M-16, and M-79 — they carried whatever presented itself, or whatever seemed appropriate as a means of killing or staying alive. They carried catch-as-catch-can. At various times, in various situations, they carried M-14s and CAR-15s and Swedish Ks and grease guns and captured AK-47s and Chi-Coms and RPGs and Simonov carbines and black-market Uzis and .38-caliber Smith & Wesson handguns and 66 mm LAWs and shotguns and silencers and blackjacks and bayonets and C-4 plastic explosives. Lee Strunk carried a slingshot; a weapon of last resort, he called it. Mitchell Sanders carried brass knuckles. Kiowa carried his grandfather's feathered hatchet. Every third or fourth man carried a Claymore antipersonnel mine — 3.5 pounds with its firing device. They all carried fragmentation grenades — fourteen ounces each. They all carried at least one M-18 colored smoke grenade — twenty-four ounces. Some carried CS or tear-gas grenades. Some carried white-phosphorus grenades. They carried all they could bear, and then some, including a silent awe for the terrible power of the things they carried.

In the first week of April, before Lavender died, Lieutenant Jimmy Cross received a good-luck charm from Martha. It was a simple pebble, an ounce at most. Smooth to the touch, it was a milky-white color with flecks of orange and violet, oval-shaped, like a miniature egg. In the accompanying letter, Martha wrote that she had found the pebble on the Jersey shoreline, precisely where the land touched water at high tide, where things came together but also separated. It was this separate-but-together quality, she wrote, that had inspired her to pick up the pebble and to carry it in her breast pocket for several days, where it seemed weightless, and then to send it through the mail, by air, as a token of her truest feelings for him. Lieutenant Cross found this romantic. But he wondered what her truest feelings were, exactly, and what she meant by separate-but-together. He wondered how the tides and waves had come into play on that afternoon along the Jersey shoreline when Martha saw the pebble and bent down to rescue it from geology. He imagined bare feet. Martha was a poet, with the poet's sensibilities, and her feet would be brown and bare, the toenails unpainted, the eyes chilly and somber like the ocean in March, and though it was painful, he wondered who had been with her that afternoon. He imagined a pair of shadows moving along the strip of sand where things came together but also separated. It was phantom jealousy, he knew, but he couldn't help himself. He loved her so much. On the march, through the hot days of early April, he carried the pebble in his mouth, turning it with his tongue, tasting sea salts and moisture. His mind wandered. He had difficulty keeping his attention on the war. On occasion he would yell at his men to spread out the column, to keep their eyes open, but then he would slip away into daydreams, just pretending, walking barefoot along the Jersey shore, with Martha, carrying nothing. He would feel himself rising. Sun and waves and gentle winds, all love and lightness.

What they carried varied by mission.

When a mission took them to the mountains, they carried mosquito netting, machetes, canvas tarps, and extra bug juice.   15

If a mission seemed especially hazardous, or if it involved a place they knew to be bad, they carried everything they could. In certain heavily mined AOs,° where the land was dense with Toe Poppers and Bouncing Betties, they took turns humping a twenty-eight-pound mine detector. With its headphones and big sensing plate, the equipment was a stress on the lower back and shoulders, awkward to handle, often useless because of the shrapnel in the earth, but they carried it anyway, partly for safety, partly for the illusion of safety.

On ambush, or other night missions, they carried peculiar little odds and ends. Kiowa always took along his New Testament and a pair of moccasins for silence. Dave Jensen carried night-sight vitamins high in carotin. Lee Strunk carried his slingshot; ammo, he claimed, would never be a problem. Rat Kiley carried brandy and M&M's. Until he was shot, Ted Lavender carried the starlight scope, which weighed 6.3 pounds with its aluminum carrying case. Henry Dobbins carried his girlfriend's pantyhose wrapped around his neck as a comforter. They all carried ghosts. When dark came, they would move out single file across the meadows and paddies to their ambush coordinates, where they would quietly set up the Claymores and lie down and spend the night waiting.

Other missions were more complicated and required special equipment. In mid-April, it was their mission to search out and destroy the elaborate tunnel complexes in the Than Khe area south of Chu Lai. To blow the tunnels, they carried one-pound blocks of pentrite high explosives, four blocks to a man, sixty-eight pounds in all. They carried wiring, detonators, and battery-powered clackers. Dave Jensen carried earplugs. Most often, before blowing the tunnels, they were ordered by higher command to search them, which was considered bad news, but by and large they just shrugged and carried out orders. Because he was a big man, Henry Dobbins was excused from tunnel duty. The others would draw numbers. Before Lavender died there were seventeen men in the platoon, and whoever drew the number seventeen would strip off his gear and crawl in head first with a flashlight and Lieutenant Cross's .45-caliber pistol. The rest of them would fan out as security. They would sit down or kneel, not facing the hole, listening to the ground beneath them, imagining cobwebs and ghosts, whatever was down there — the tunnel walls squeezing in — how the flashlight seemed impossibly heavy in the hand and how it was tunnel vision in the very strictest sense, compression in all ways, even time, and how you had to

AOs: Areas of operations.

wiggle in — ass and elbows — a swallowed-up feeling — and how you found yourself worrying about odd things — will your flashlight go dead? Do rats carry rabies? If you screamed, how far would the sound carry? Would your buddies hear it? Would they have the courage to drag you out? In some respects, though not many, the waiting was worse than the tunnel itself. Imagination was a killer.

On April 16, when Lee Strunk drew the number seventeen, he laughed and muttered something and went down quickly. The morning was hot and very still. Not good, Kiowa said. He looked at the tunnel opening, then out across a dry paddy toward the village of Than Khe. Nothing moved. No clouds or birds or people. As they waited, the men smoked and drank Kool-Aid, not talking much, feeling sympathy for Lee Strunk but also feeling the luck of the draw. You win some, you lose some, said Mitchell Sanders, and sometimes you settle for a rain check. It was a tired line and no one laughed.

Henry Dobbins ate a tropical chocolate bar. Ted Lavender popped a tran-   20
quilizer and went off to pee.

After five minutes, Lieutenant Jimmy Cross moved to the tunnel, leaned down, and examined the darkness. Trouble, he thought — a cave-in maybe. And then suddenly, without willing it, he was thinking about Martha. The stresses and fractures, the quick collapse, the two of them buried alive under all that weight. Dense, crushing love. Kneeling, watching the hole, he tried to concentrate on Lee Strunk and the war, all the dangers, but his love was too much for him, he felt paralyzed, he wanted to sleep inside her lungs and breathe her blood and be smothered. He wanted her to be a virgin and not a virgin, all at once. He wanted to know her. Intimate secrets: Why poetry? Why so sad? Why the grayness in her eyes? Why so alone? Not lonely, just alone — riding her bike across campus or sitting off by herself in the cafeteria. Even dancing, she danced alone — and it was the aloneness that filled him with love. He remembered telling her that one evening. How she nodded and looked away. And how, later, when he kissed her, she received the kiss without returning it, her eyes wide open, not afraid, not a virgin's eyes, just flat and uninvolved.

Lieutenant Cross gazed at the tunnel. But he was not there. He was buried with Martha under the white sand at the Jersey shore. They were pressed together, and the pebble in his mouth was her tongue. He was smiling. Vaguely, he was aware of how quiet the day was, the sullen paddies, yet he could not bring himself to worry about matters of security. He was beyond that. He was just a kid at war, in love. He was twenty-two years old. He couldn't help it.

A few moments later Lee Strunk crawled out of the tunnel. He came up grinning, filthy but alive. Lieutenant Cross nodded and closed his eyes while the others clapped Strunk on the back and made jokes about rising from the dead.

Worms, Rat Kiley said. Right out of the grave. Fuckin' zombie.

The men laughed. They all felt great relief.   25

Spook City, said Mitchell Sanders.

Lee Strunk made a funny ghost sound, a kind of moaning, yet very happy, and right then, when Strunk made that high happy moaning sound, when he went *Ahhooooo*, right then Ted Lavender was shot in the head on his way back from peeing. He lay with his mouth open. The teeth were broken. There was a swollen black bruise under his left eye. The cheekbone was gone. Oh shit, Rat Kiley said, the guy's dead. The guy's dead, he kept saying, which seemed profound — the guy's dead. I mean really.

The things they carried were determined to some extent by superstition. Lieutenant Cross carried his good-luck pebble. Dave Jensen carried a rabbit's foot. Norman Bowker, otherwise a very gentle person, carried a thumb that had been presented to him as a gift by Mitchell Sanders. The thumb was dark brown, rubbery to the touch, and weighed four ounces at most. It had been cut from a VC corpse, a boy of fifteen or sixteen. They'd found him at the bottom of an irrigation ditch, badly burned, flies in his mouth and eyes. The boy wore black shorts and sandals. At the time of his death he had been carrying a pouch of rice, a rifle, and three magazines of ammunition.

You want my opinion, Mitchell Sanders said, there's a definite moral here.

He put his hand on the dead boy's wrist. He was quiet for a time, as if counting a pulse, then he patted the stomach, almost affectionately, and used Kiowa's hunting hatchet to remove the thumb.   30

Henry Dobbins asked what the moral was.

Moral?

You know. *Moral.*

Sanders wrapped the thumb in toilet paper and handed it across to Norman Bowker. There was no blood. Smiling, he kicked the boy's head, watched the flies scatter, and said, It's like with that old TV show — Paladin. Have gun, will travel.

Henry Dobbins thought about it.   35

Yeah, well, he finally said. I don't see no moral.

There it *is*, man.

Fuck off.

They carried USO stationery and pencils and pens. They carried Sterno, safety pins, trip flares, signal flares, spools of wire, razor blades, chewing tobacco, liberated joss sticks and statuettes of the smiling Buddha, candles, grease pencils, *The Stars and Stripes*, fingernail clippers, Psy Ops° leaflets, bush hats, bolos, and much more. Twice a week, when the resupply choppers came in, they carried hot chow in green Mermite cans and large canvas bags filled with iced beer and soda pop. They carried plastic water containers, each with a two-gallon capacity. Mitchell Sanders carried a set of starched tiger fatigues for special occasions. Henry Dobbins carried Black Flag insecticide. Dave Jensen carried empty sandbags that could be filled at night for added protection. Lee Strunk carried tanning lotion. Some things they carried in common. Taking turns, they carried the big PRC-77 scrambler radio, which weighed thirty pounds with its battery. They shared the weight of memory. They took up what others could no longer bear. Often, they carried each other, the wounded or weak.

Psy Ops: Psychological operations.

They carried infections. They carried chess sets, basketballs, Vietnamese-English dictionaries, insignia of rank, Bronze Stars and Purple Hearts, plastic cards imprinted with the Code of Conduct. They carried diseases, among them malaria and dysentery. They carried lice and ringworm and leeches and paddy algae and various rots and molds. They carried the land itself — Vietnam, the place, the soil — a powdery orange-red dust that covered their boots and fatigues and faces. They carried the sky. The whole atmosphere, they carried it, the humidity, the monsoons, the stink of fungus and decay, all of it, they carried gravity. They moved like mules. By daylight they took sniper fire, at night they were mortared, but it was not battle, it was just the endless march, village to village, without purpose, nothing won or lost. They marched for the sake of the march. They plodded along slowly, dumbly, leaning forward against the heat, unthinking, all blood and bone, simple grunts, soldiering with their legs, toiling up the hills and down into the paddies and across the rivers and up again and down, just humping, one step and then the next and then another, but no volition, no will, because it was automatic, it was anatomy, and the war was entirely a matter of posture and carriage, the hump was everything, a kind of inertia, a kind of emptiness, a dullness of desire and intellect and conscience and hope and human sensibility. Their principles were in their feet. Their calculations were biological. They had no sense of strategy or mission. They searched the villages without knowing what to look for, not caring, kicking over jars of rice, frisking children and old men, blowing tunnels, sometimes setting fires and sometimes not, then forming up and moving on to the next village, then other villages, where it would always be the same. They carried their own lives. The pressures were enormous. In the heat of early afternoon, they would remove their helmets and flak jackets, walking bare, which was dangerous but which helped ease the strain. They would often discard things along the route of march. Purely for comfort, they would throw away rations, blow their Claymores and grenades, no matter, because by nightfall the resupply choppers would arrive with more of the same, then a day or two later still more, fresh watermelons and crates of ammunition and sunglasses and woolen sweaters — the resources were stunning — sparklers for the Fourth of July, colored eggs for Easter. It was the great American war chest — the fruits of science, the smokestacks, the canneries, the arsenals at Hartford, the Minnesota forests, the machine shops, the vast fields of corn and wheat — they carried like freight trains, they carried it on their backs and shoulders — and for all the ambiguities of Vietnam, all the mysteries and unknowns, there was at least the single abiding certainty that they would never be at a loss for things to carry.

After the chopper took Lavender away, Lieutenant Jimmy Cross led his men 40
into the village of Than Khe. They burned everything. They shot chickens and dogs, they trashed the village well, they called in artillery and watched the wreckage, then they marched for several hours through the hot afternoon, and then at dusk, while Kiowa explained how Lavender died, Lieutenant Cross found himself trembling.

He tried not to cry. With his entrenching tool, which weighed five pounds, he began digging a hole in the earth.

He felt shame. He hated himself. He had loved Martha more than his men, and as a consequence Lavender was now dead, and this was something he would have to carry like a stone in his stomach for the rest of the war.

All he could do was dig. He used his entrenching tool like an ax, slashing, feeling both love and hate, and then later, when it was full dark, he sat at the bottom of his foxhole and wept. It went on for a long while. In part, he was grieving for Ted Lavender, but mostly it was for Martha, and for himself, because she belonged to another world, which was not quite real, and because she was a junior at Mount Sebastian College in New Jersey, a poet and a virgin and uninvolved, and because he realized she did not love him and never would.

Like cement, Kiowa whispered in the dark. I swear to God — boom, down. Not a word.

I've heard this, said Norman Bowker.   45

A pisser, you know? Still zipping himself up. Zapped while zipping.

All right, fine. That's enough.

Yeah, but you had to see it, the guy just —

I *heard*, man. Cement. So why not shut the fuck *up*?

Kiowa shook his head sadly and glanced over at the hole where Lieutenant   50
Jimmy Cross sat watching the night. The air was thick and wet. A warm, dense fog had settled over the paddies and there was the stillness that precedes rain.

After a time Kiowa sighed.

One thing for sure, he said. The Lieutenant's in some deep hurt. I mean that crying jag — the way he was carrying on — it wasn't fake or anything, it was real heavy-duty hurt. The man cares.

Sure, Norman Bowker said.

Say what you want, the man does care.

We all got problems.   55

Not Lavender.

No, I guess not, Bowker said. Do me a favor, though.

Shut up?

That's a smart Indian. Shut up.

Shrugging, Kiowa pulled off his boots. He wanted to say more, just to   60
lighten up his sleep, but instead he opened his New Testament and arranged it beneath his head as a pillow. The fog made things seem hollow and unattached. He tried not to think about Ted Lavender, but then he was thinking how fast it was, no drama, down and dead, and how it was hard to feel anything except surprise. It seemed un-Christian. He wished he could find some great sadness, or even anger, but the emotion wasn't there and he couldn't make it happen. Mostly he felt pleased to be alive. He liked the smell of the New Testament under his cheek, the leather and ink and paper and glue, whatever the chemicals were. He liked hearing the sounds of night. Even his fatigue, it felt fine, the stiff muscles and the prickly awareness of his own body, a floating feeling. He enjoyed not being dead. Lying there, Kiowa admired Lieutenant Jimmy Cross's capacity for grief. He wanted to share the man's pain, he wanted to care as Jimmy Cross cared. And yet when he closed his eyes, all he could think was Boom-down, and all he could feel was the pleasure of having his boots off and

the fog curling in around him and the damp soil and the Bible smells and the plush comfort of night.

After a moment Norman Bowker sat up in the dark.

What the hell, he said. You want to talk, *talk*. Tell it to me.

Forget it.

No, man, go on. One thing I hate, it's a silent Indian.

For the most part they carried themselves with poise, a kind of dignity. Now 65 and then, however, there were times of panic, when they squealed or wanted to squeal but couldn't, when they twitched and made moaning sounds and covered their heads and said Dear Jesus and flopped around on the earth and fired their weapons blindly and cringed and sobbed and begged for the noise to stop and went wild and made stupid promises to themselves and to God and to their mothers and fathers, hoping not to die. In different ways, it happened to all of them. Afterward, when the firing ended, they would blink and peek up. They would touch their bodies, feeling shame, then quickly hiding it. They would force themselves to stand. As if in slow motion, frame by frame, the world would take on the old logic — absolute silence, then the wind, then sunlight, then voices. It was the burden of being alive. Awkwardly, the men would reassemble themselves, first in private, then in groups, becoming soldiers again. They would repair the leaks in their eyes. They would check for casualties, call in dust-offs, light cigarettes, try to smile, clear their throats and spit and begin cleaning their weapons. After a time someone would shake his head and say, No lie, I almost shit my pants, and someone else would laugh, which meant it was bad, yes, but the guy had obviously not shit his pants, it wasn't that bad, and in any case nobody would ever do such a thing and then go ahead and talk about it. They would squint into the dense, oppressive sunlight. For a few moments, perhaps, they would fall silent, lighting a joint and tracking its passage from man to man, inhaling, holding in the humiliation. Scary stuff, one of them might say. But then someone else would grin or flick his eyebrows and say, Roger-dodger, almost cut me a new asshole, *almost*.

There were numerous such poses. Some carried themselves with a sort of wistful resignation, others with pride or stiff soldierly discipline or good humor or macho zeal. They were afraid of dying but they were even more afraid to show it.

They found jokes to tell.

They used a hard vocabulary to contain the terrible softness. *Greased*, they'd say. *Offed, lit up, zapped while zipping*. It wasn't cruelty, just stage presence. They were actors and the war came at them in 3-D. When someone died, it wasn't quite dying, because in a curious way it seemed scripted, and because they had their lines mostly memorized, irony mixed with tragedy, and because they called it by other names, as if to encyst and destroy the reality of death itself. They kicked corpses. They cut off thumbs. They talked grunt lingo. They told stories about Ted Lavender's supply of tranquilizers, how the poor guy didn't feel a thing, how incredibly tranquil he was.

There's a moral here, said Mitchell Sanders.

They were waiting for Lavender's chopper, smoking the dead man's dope.   70

The moral's pretty obvious, Sanders said, and winked. Stay away from drugs. No joke, they'll ruin your day every time.

Cute, said Henry Dobbins.

Mind-blower, get it? Talk about wiggy — nothing left, just blood and brains.

They made themselves laugh.

There it is, they'd say, over and over, as if the repetition itself were an act of   75 poise, a balance between crazy and almost crazy, knowing without going. There it is, which meant be cool, let it ride, because oh yeah, man, you can't change what can't be changed, there it is, there it absolutely and positively and fucking well *is*.

They were tough.

They carried all the emotional baggage of men who might die. Grief, terror, love, longing — these were intangibles, but the intangibles had their own mass and specific gravity, they had tangible weight. They carried shameful memories. They carried the common secret of cowardice barely restrained, the instinct to run or freeze or hide, and in many respects this was the heaviest burden of all, for it could never be put down, it required perfect balance and perfect posture. They carried their reputations. They carried the soldier's greatest fear, which was the fear of blushing. Men killed, and died, because they were embarrassed not to. It was what had brought them to the war in the first place, nothing positive, no dreams of glory or honor, just to avoid the blush of dishonor. They died so as not to die of embarrassment. They crawled into tunnels and walked point and advanced under fire. Each morning, despite the unknowns, they made their legs move. They endured. They kept humping. They did not submit to the obvious alternative, which was simply to close the eyes and fall. So easy, really. Go limp and tumble to the ground and let the muscles unwind and not speak and not budge until your buddies picked you up and lifted you into the chopper that would roar and dip its nose and carry you off to the world. A mere matter of falling, yet no one ever fell. It was not courage, exactly; the object was not valor. Rather, they were too frightened to be cowards.

By and large they carried these things inside, maintaining the masks of composure. They sneered at sick call. They spoke bitterly about guys who had found release by shooting off their own toes or fingers. Pussies, they'd say. Candyasses. It was fierce, mocking talk, with only a trace of envy or awe, but even so, the image played itself out behind their eyes.

They imagined the muzzle against flesh. They imagined the quick, sweet pain, then the evacuation to Japan, then a hospital with warm beds and cute geisha nurses.

They dreamed of freedom birds.   80

At night, on guard, staring into the dark, they were carried away by jumbo jets. They felt the rush of takeoff. *Gone!* they yelled. And then velocity, wings and engines, a smiling stewardess — but it was more than a plane, it was a real bird, a big sleek silver bird with feathers and talons and high screeching. They were flying. The weights fell off, there was nothing to bear. They laughed and held on tight, feeling the cold slap of wind and altitude, soaring, thinking *It's over, I'm gone!* — they were naked, they were light and free — it was all lightness, bright and fast and buoyant, light as light, a helium buzz in the brain, a giddy bubbling in the lungs as they were taken up over the clouds and the war, beyond duty, beyond gravity and mortification and global entanglements — *Sin loi!*° they yelled, *I'm sorry, motherfuckers, but I'm out of it. I'm goofed, I'm on a space cruise, I'm gone!* — and it was a restful, disencumbered sensation, just riding the light waves, sailing that big silver freedom bird over the mountains and oceans, over America, over the farms and great sleeping cities and cemeteries and highways and the golden arches of McDonald's. It was flight, a kind of fleeing, a kind of falling, falling higher and higher, spinning off the edge of the earth and beyond the sun and through the vast, silent vacuum where there were no burdens and where everything weighed exactly nothing. *Gone!* they screamed, *I'm sorry but I'm gone!* And so at night, not quite dreaming, they gave themselves over to lightness, they were carried, they were purely borne.

On the morning after Ted Lavender died, First Lieutenant Jimmy Cross crouched at the bottom of his foxhole and burned Martha's letters. Then he burned the two photographs. There was a steady rain falling, which made it difficult, but he used heat tabs and Sterno to build a small fire, screening it with his body, holding the photographs over the tight blue flame with the tips of his fingers.

He realized it was only a gesture. Stupid, he thought. Sentimental, too, but mostly just stupid.

Lavender was dead. You couldn't burn the blame.

Besides, the letters were in his head. And even now, without photographs,   85
Lieutenant Cross could see Martha playing volleyball in her white gym shorts and yellow T-shirt. He could see her moving in the rain.

When the fire died out, Lieutenant Cross pulled his poncho over his shoulders and ate breakfast from a can.

There was no great mystery, he decided.

In those burned letters Martha had never mentioned the war, except to say, Jimmy, take care of yourself. She wasn't involved. She signed the letters "Love," but it wasn't love, and all the fine lines and technicalities did not matter.

The morning came up wet and blurry. Everything seemed part of everything else, the fog and Martha and the deepening rain.

It was a war, after all.   90

Half smiling, Lieutenant Jimmy Cross took out his maps. He shook his head hard, as if to clear it, then bent forward and began planning the day's march. In ten minutes, or maybe twenty, he would rouse the men and they would pack up and head west, where the maps showed the country to be green and inviting. They would do what they had always done. The rain might add some weight, but otherwise it would be one more day layered upon all the other days.

He was realistic about it. There was that new hardness in his stomach.

Sin loi!: "Sorry about that."

No more fantasies, he told himself.

Henceforth, when he thought about Martha, it would be only to think that she belonged elsewhere. He would shut down the daydreams. This was not Mount Sebastian, it was another world, where there were no pretty poems or midterm exams, a place where men died because of carelessness and gross stupidity. Kiowa was right. Boom-down, and you were dead, never partly dead.

Briefly, in the rain, Lieutenant Cross saw Martha's gray eyes gazing back at him.   95

He understood.

It was very sad, he thought. The things men carried inside. The things men did or felt they had to do.

He almost nodded at her, but didn't.

Instead he went back to his maps. He was now determined to perform his duties firmly and without negligence. It wouldn't help Lavender, he knew that, but from this point on he would comport himself as a soldier. He would dispose of his good-luck pebble. Swallow it, maybe, or use Lee Strunk's slingshot, or just drop it along the trail. On the march he would impose strict field discipline. He would be careful to send out flank security, to prevent straggling or bunching up, to keep his troops moving at the proper pace and at the proper interval. He would insist on clean weapons. He would confiscate the remainder of Lavender's dope. Later in the day, perhaps, he would call the men together and speak to them plainly. He would accept the blame for what had happened to Ted Lavender. He would be a man about it. He would look them in the eyes, keeping his chin level, and he would issue the new SOPs in a calm, impersonal tone of voice, an officer's voice, leaving no room for argument or discussion. Commencing immediately, he'd tell them, they would no longer abandon equipment along the route of march. They would police up their acts. They would get their shit together, and keep it together, and maintain it neatly and in good working order.

He would not tolerate laxity. He would show strength, distancing himself.   100

Among the men there would be grumbling, of course, and maybe worse, because their days would seem longer and their loads heavier, but Lieutenant Cross reminded himself that his obligation was not to be loved but to lead. He would dispense with love; it was not now a factor. And if anyone quarreled or complained, he would simply tighten his lips and arrange his shoulders in the correct command posture. He might give a curt little nod. Or he might not. He might just shrug and say Carry on, then they would saddle up and form into a column and move out toward the villages of Than Khe.   *[1986]*

≡ THINKING ABOUT THE TEXT

1. What specific psychological and emotional "things" do the soldiers carry into battle? Did any of these surprise you? Explain.

2. In three or four sentences, how would you describe the experience of war, using this story as a basis?

3. What are some significant differences, if any, among the soldiers under Jimmy Cross's command?

4. What is your attitude toward Jimmy Cross's apparent obsession with Martha?

5. Jimmy Cross seems to feel guilty about Ted Lavender's death. To what extent does his feeling seem rational? *Should* he feel guilty, in your view? Why, or why not? In the final two paragraphs, he makes a number of resolutions. Which, if any, do you think that he is capable of keeping?

≡ MAKING COMPARISONS

1. Critics see "Dulce et Decorum Est" as clearly an antiwar poem. How might such a judgment be more complicated with O'Brien's story?

2. Compare the descriptions of the man who was gassed in "Dulce et Decorum Est" with Ted Lavender's death in "The Things They Carried."

3. What do you think O'Brien would say the men in the first two stanzas of Owen's poem were carrying?

MICHAEL HERR
Scream a Lot

Michael Herr (b. 1940) was a correspondent during the Vietnam War for Esquire *magazine.* Dispatches, *a memoir of that experience, won high praise from critics and readers. John le Carré, the spy novelist, said it was "the best book I have ever read on men and war in our time." The following is an excerpt from that memoir. Herr also worked on the films* Full Metal Jacket *with Stanley Kubrick and* Apocalypse Now *with Francis Ford Coppola. His other books are* Walter Winchell: A Novel *(1990) and* Kubrick *(2000).*

You could make all the ritual moves, carry your lucky piece, wear your magic jungle hat, kiss your thumb knuckle smooth as stones under running water, the Inscrutable Immutable was still out there, and you kept on or not at its pitiless discretion. All you could say that wasn't fundamentally lame was something like, "He who bites it this day is safe from the next," and that was exactly what nobody wanted to hear.

After enough time passed and memory receded and settled, the name itself became a prayer, coded like all prayer to go past the extremes of petition and gratitude: Vietnam Vietnam Vietnam, say again, until the word lost all its old loads of pain, pleasure, horror, guilt, nostalgia. Then and there, everyone was just trying to get through it, existential crunch, no atheists in foxholes like you wouldn't believe. Even bitter refracted faith was better than none at all, like the black Marine I'd heard about during heavy shelling at Con Thien who said, "Don't worry, baby, God'll think of something."

Dudley Reed/
Getty Images

Flip religion, it was so far out, you couldn't blame anybody for believing anything. Guys dressed up in Batman fetishes, I saw a whole squad like that, it gave them a kind of dumb esprit. Guys stuck the ace of spades in their helmet bands, they picked relics off of an enemy they'd killed, a little transfer of power; they carried around five-pound Bibles from home, crosses, St. Christophers, mezuzahs, locks of hair, girlfriends' underwear, snaps of their families, their wives, their dogs, their cows, their cars, pictures of John Kennedy, Lyndon Johnson, Martin Luther King, Huey Newton, the Pope, Che Guevara, the Beatles, Jimi Hendrix, wiggier than cargo cultists. One man was carrying an oatmeal cookie through his tour, wrapped up in foil and plastic and three pair of socks. He took a lot of shit about it ("When you go to sleep we're gonna eat your . . . cookie"), but his wife had baked it and mailed it to him, he wasn't kidding.

On operations you'd see men clustering around the charmed grunt that many outfits created who would take himself and whoever stayed close enough through a field of safety, at least until he rotated home or got blown away, and then the outfit would hand the charm to someone else. If a bullet creased your head or you'd stepped on a dud mine or a grenade rolled between your feet and just lay there, you were magic enough. If you had any kind of extra-sense capacity, if you could smell VC° or their danger the way hunting guides smelled

---

VC: Military jargon for Viet Cong, or Vietnamese Communists.

the coming weather, if you had special night vision, or great ears, you were magic too; anything bad that happened to you could leave the men in your outfit pretty depressed. I met a man in the Cav . . . one afternoon, sound asleep in a huge tent with thirty cots inside, all empty but his, when some mortar rounds came in, tore the tent down to canvas slaw and put frags through every single cot but his, he was still high out of his mind from it, speedy, sure and lucky. The Soldier's Prayer came in two versions: Standard, printed on a plastic-coated card by the Defense Department, and Standard Revised, impossible to convey because it got translated outside of language, into chaos—screams, begging, promises, threats, sobs, repetitions of holy names until their throats were cracked and dry, until some men had bitten through their collar points and rifle straps and even their dog-tag chains.

Varieties of religious experience, good news and bad news; a lot of men found their compassion in the war, some found it and couldn't live with it, war-washed shutdown of feeling, . . . People retreated into positions of hard irony, cynicism, despair, some saw the action and declared for it, only heavy killing could make them feel so alive. And some just went insane, followed the black-light arrow around the bend and took possession of the madness that had been waiting there in trust for them for eighteen or twenty-five or fifty years. Every time there was combat you had a license to go maniac, everyone snapped over the line at least once there and nobody noticed, they hardly noticed if you forgot to snap back again.

One afternoon at Khe Sanh a Marine opened the door of a latrine and was killed by a grenade that had been rigged on the door. The Command tried to blame it on a North Vietnamese infiltrator, but the grunts knew what had happened: "Like a gook is really gonna tunnel all the way in here to booby-trap a shithouse, right? Some guy just flipped out is all." And it became another one of those stories that moved across the DMZ°, making people laugh and shake their heads and look knowingly at each other, but shocking no one. They'd talk about physical wounds in one way and psychic wounds in another, each man in a squad would tell you how crazy everyone else in the squad was, everyone knew grunts who'd gone crazy in the middle of a firefight, gone crazy on patrol, gone crazy back at camp, gone crazy on R&R, gone crazy during their first month home. Going crazy was built into the tour, the best you could hope for was that it didn't happen around you, the kind of crazy that made men empty clips into strangers or fix grenades on latrine doors. That was *really* crazy; anything less was almost standard, as standard as the vague prolonged stares and involuntary smiles, common as ponchos or 16's or any other piece of war issue. If you wanted someone to know you'd gone insane you really had to sound off like you had a pair, "Scream a lot, and all the time."   *[1977]*

DMZ: Military jargon for demilitarized zone.

≡ **THINKING ABOUT THE TEXT**

1. What do you think Herr means by the "Inscrutable Immutable" (para. 1)?

2. Explain the significance of Herr's statement, "You couldn't blame any-body for believing anything" (para. 3).

3. Explain what you think is the significance of some of the concrete things the soldiers carried. Do you or anyone you know carry comparable things? Why?

4. Which specific passages are the most convincing about the horrors of war? Explain.

5. What is Herr's point of view in this selection, that is, is he journalistically neutral, sympathetic, critical? Explain.

☰ MAKING COMPARISONS

1. Compare the things the soldiers carried in O'Brien's and Herr's texts.

2. What passage in Herr is closest in spirit to Owen's poem? Explain.

3. Which of the three selections would you give to someone whom you didn't want to join the army? Explain.

☰ WRITING ABOUT ISSUES

1. Write an essay that focuses on Jimmy Cross and his growth in "The Things They Carried."

2. In an essay, compare all three texts, noting the similarities and differ-ences in their treatment of heroism and fear.

3. Read O'Brien's story "How to Tell a True War Story," and in an essay, apply the ideas in that story to "The Things They Carried."

4. Read Owen's "Anthem for a Doomed Youth" and Sassoon's "After-math" and compare these war poems to "Dulce et Decorum Est."

Critical Approaches to Literature

Exploring the topics of literary criticism can help readers understand the various ways literature can matter. One popular way to investigate critical approaches to literature is to group critics into schools. Critics who are concerned primarily with equality for women, for example, are often classified as feminist critics, and those concerned with the responses of readers are classified as reader-response critics. Likewise, critics who focus on the unconscious are said to belong to the psychoanalytic school, and those who analyze class conflicts belong to the Marxist school.

Classifying critics in this way is probably more convenient than precise. Few critics like to be pigeonholed or thought predictable, and many professional readers tend to be eclectic — that is, they use ideas from various schools to help them illuminate the text. Nevertheless, knowing something about contemporary schools of criticism can make you a more informed reader and help literature matter to you even more.

There is a commonsense belief that words mean just what they say — that to understand a certain passage in a text a reader simply needs to know what the words mean. But meaning is rarely straightforward. Scholars have been arguing over the meaning of passages in the Bible, in the Constitution, and in Shakespeare's plays for centuries without reaching agreement. Pinning down the exact meaning of words like *sin, justice,* and *love* is almost impossible, but even more daunting is the unacknowledged theory of reading that each person brings to any text, including literature. Some people who read the Bible or the Constitution, for example, believe in the literal meaning of the words, and some think the real meaning lies in the original intention of the writer, while others believe that the only meaning we can be sure of is our own perspective. For these latter readers, there is no objective meaning, and no absolutely true meaning is possible.

Indeed, a good deal of what a text means depends on the perspective that readers bring with them. Passages can be read effectively from numerous points of view. A generation ago most English professors taught their students to pay attention to the internal aspects of a poem and not to the poem's larger social and political contexts. So oppositions, irony, paradox, and coherence — not gender equality or social justice — were topics of discussion. Proponents of this approach were said to belong to the New Critical school. In the last twenty-five years or so, however, professors have put much more emphasis on the external aspects of interpretation, stressing social, political, cultural, sexual, and gender-based perspectives. Each one of these perspectives can give us a valuable window on a text, helping us see the rich possibilities of literature. Even though each approach can provide insights into a text, it can also be blind to other textual elements. When we read in too focused a way, we can sometimes miss the opportunity to see what others see.

In this appendix, however, we want to present our interpretation in a clear, logical, and reflective manner as we take a position and try to persuade others of its reasonableness. Since there are many possible lenses to see a text through, you can be sure your classmates will see things differently. Part of the excitement and challenge of making arguments that matter is your ability to analyze and clarify your ideas, gather and organize your evidence, and present your claim in carefully revised and edited prose.

Contemporary Schools of Criticism

The following nine approaches are just a few of the many different literary schools or perspectives a reader can use in engaging a text. Think of them as intellectual tools or informed lenses that you can employ to enhance your interpretation of a particular literary text:

- New Criticism
- Feminist criticism
- Psychoanalytic criticism
- Marxist criticism
- Deconstruction
- Reader-response criticism
- Postcolonial criticism
- New Historicism
- Queer theory

NEW CRITICISM

New Criticism was developed about seventy years ago as a way to focus on "the text itself." Although it is no longer as popular as it once was, some of its principles are still widely accepted, especially the use of specific examples from the text as evidence for a particular interpretation. Sometimes called *close reading*, this approach does not see either the writer's intention or the reader's personal response as relevant. It is also uninterested in the text's social context, the spirit of the age, or its relevance to issues of gender, social justice, or oppression. These critics are interested, for example, in a poem's internal structure, images, symbols, metaphors, point of view, plot, and characterizations. Emphasis is placed on literary language—on the ways connotation, ambiguity, irony, and paradox all reinforce the meaning. In fact, *how* a poem means is inseparable from *what* it means. The primary method for judging the worth of a piece of literature is its organic unity or the complex way all the elements of a text contribute to the poem's meaning.

Critics often argue that their interpretations are the most consistent with textual evidence. A popular approach is to note the oppositions in the text and to focus on tensions, ironies, and paradoxes. Typically a paradox early in the text is shown at the end not to be that contradictory after all. The critic then argues that all the elements of the text can be seen as contributing to this resolution.

FEMINIST CRITICISM

Feminist criticism developed during the 1970s as an outgrowth of a resurgent women's movement. The goals of the feminist critic and the feminist political activist are similar—to contest the patriarchal point of view as the standard for all moral, aesthetic, political, and intellectual judgments and to assert that gender roles are primarily learned, not universal. They hope to uncover and challenge essentialist attitudes that hold it is normal for women to be kept in domestic, secondary, and subservient roles, and they affirm the value of a woman's experiences and perspectives in understanding the world. Recently both female and male critics have become interested in gender studies, a branch of theory concerned with the ways cultural practices socialize us to act in certain ways because of our gender. Focused primarily on issues of identity, gender criticism looks at the ways characters in literary texts are represented, or how they are constructed in a particular culture as feminine or masculine. Like the broader area of feminism, many gender specialists hope that studying the arbitrary ways we are expected to dress, walk, talk, and behave can help us widen the conventional notions of gender.

PSYCHOANALYTIC CRITICISM

Psychoanalytic criticism began with Sigmund Freud's theories of the unconscious, especially the numerous repressed wounds, fears, unresolved conflicts, and guilty desires from childhood that can significantly affect behavior and mental health in our adult lives. Freud developed the tripart division of the mind into the ego (the conscious self), the superego (the site of what our culture has taught us about good and bad), and the id (the primitive unconscious and source of our sexual drive). Psychoanalytic critics often see literature as a kind of dream, filled with symbolic elements that often mask their real meaning. Freud also theorized that young males were threatened by their fathers in the competition for the affection of their mothers. Critics are alert to the complex ways this Oedipal drama unfolds in literature.

MARXIST CRITICISM

Marxist criticism is based on the political and economic theories of Karl Marx. Marxists think that a society is propelled by its economy, which is manipulated by a class system. Most people, especially blue-collar workers (the proletariat), do not understand the complex ways their lives are subject to economic forces beyond their control. This false consciousness about history and material well-being prevents workers from seeing that their values have been socially constructed to keep them in their place. What most interests contemporary Marxists is the way ideology shapes our consciousness. And since literature both represents and projects ideology, Marxist critics see it as a way to unmask our limited view of society's structures.

DECONSTRUCTION

Deconstruction is really more a philosophical movement than a school of literary criticism, but many of its techniques have been used by Marxist and feminist literary critics to uncover important concepts they believe are hidden in texts. Made famous by the French philosopher Jacques Derrida, deconstruction's main tenet is that Western thought has divided the world into binary opposites. To gain a semblance of control over the complexity of human experience, we have constructed a worldview in which good is clearly at one end of a continuum and bad at the other. Additional examples of binary opposites include masculine and feminine, freedom and slavery, objective and subjective, mind and body, and presence and absence. According to Derrida, however, this arbitrary and illusory construct simply reflects the specific ideology of one culture. Far from being opposed to each other, masculinity and femininity, for example, are intimately interconnected, and traces of the feminine are to be found within the masculine. The concepts need each other for meaning to occur, an idea referred to as *différance.* Derrida also notes that language, far from being a neutral medium of communication, is infused with our biases, assumptions, and values—which leads some of us to refer to sexually active women as "sluts" and to sexually active men as "studs." One term ("sluts") is marginalized, and the other ("studs") is privileged because our culture grants men more power than women in shaping the language that benefits them.

Thus, language filters, distorts, and alters our perception of the world. For deconstructors or deconstructive critics, language is not stable or reliable, and when closely scrutinized, it becomes slippery and ambiguous, constantly overflowing with implications, associations, and contradictions. For Derrida, this endless freeplay of meaning suggests that language is always changing, always in flux—especially so when we understand that words can be viewed from almost endless points of view or contexts. That is why deconstructionists claim that texts (or individuals or systems of thought) have no fixed definition, no center, no absolute meaning. And so one way to deconstruct or lay bare the arbitrary construction of a text is to show that the oppositions in the text are not really absolutely opposed, that outsiders can be seen to be insiders, and that words that seem to mean one thing can mean many things.

READER-RESPONSE CRITICISM

Reader-response criticism is often misunderstood to be simply giving one's opinion about a text: "I liked it," "I hate happy endings," "I think the characters were unrealistic." But reader-response criticism is actually more interested in why readers have certain responses. The central assumption is that texts do not come alive and do not mean anything until active readers engage them with specific assumptions about what reading is. New Critics think a reader's response is irrelevant because a text's meaning is timeless. But response critics, including feminists and Marxists, maintain that what a text means cannot be separated from the reading process used by readers as they draw on personal and literary experiences to make meaning. In other words, the text is not an object but an event that occurs in readers over time.

Response criticism includes critics who think that the reader's contribution to the making of meaning is quite small as well as critics who think that readers play a primary role in the process. Louise Rosenblatt is a moderate response critic since she thinks the contributions are about equal. Her transactive theory claims that the text guides our response, like a printed musical score that we adjust as we move through the text. She allows for a range of acceptable meanings as long as she can find reasonable textual support in the writing.

Response critics like Stanley Fish downplay individual responses, focusing instead on how communities influence our responses to texts. We probably all belong to a number of these interpretive communities (such as churches, universities, neighborhoods, political parties, and social class) and have internalized their interpretive strategies, their discourse, or their way of reading texts of all kinds. Fish's point is that we all come to texts already predisposed to read them in a certain way: we do not interpret stories, but we create them by using the reading tools and cultural assumptions we bring with us. Our reading then reveals what is in us more than what is in the text. We find what we expect to see.

POSTCOLONIAL CRITICISM

Postcolonial criticism, like feminist criticism, has developed because of the dramatic shrinking of the world and the increasing multicultural cast of our own country. It is mainly interested in the ways nineteenth-century European political domination affects the lives of people living in former colonies, especially the way the dominant culture becomes the norm and those without power are portrayed as inferior. Postcolonial critics often look for stereotypes in texts as well as in characters whose self-image has been damaged by being forced to see themselves as Other, as less than. As oppressed people try to negotiate life in both the dominant and the oppressed cultures, they can develop a double consciousness that leads to feelings of alienation and deep conflicts.

Literary critics often argue that being caught between the demands of two cultures — one dominant and privileged, the other marginalized and scorned — causes a character to be "unhomed," a psychological refugee who is uncomfortable everywhere.

NEW HISTORICISM

New Historicism was developed because critics were dissatisfied with the old historicism, a long-standing traditional approach that viewed history simply as a background for understanding the literary text. History was thought to be an accurate record of what happened because the professional historian used objective and proven methods. But most literary critics no longer hold to this view of history. Instead, history is now thought to be just one perspective among many possibilities, inevitably subjective and biased. Influenced by the theorist Michel Foucault, history is seen as one of many discourses that can shed light on the past. But the dominant view is that all of us, including historians, writers, and critics, live in a particular culture and cannot escape its influences. And since these social, cultural, literary, economic, and political influences are all interrelated, all texts can tell us something important. Stories, histories, diaries, laws, speeches, newspapers, and magazines are all relevant. Culture permeates all texts, influencing everyone to see society's view of reality, of what's right and wrong and which values, assumptions, and truths are acceptable. Critics and historians try to interpret a vast web of interconnected discourses and forces in order to understand an era. Naturally, since many of these forces are competing for power, critics are always looking for power struggles among discourses. Think of the present struggle over the amount of influence religion should have in politics or who has the right to marry. Literature is one of the texts in a culture that shapes our views and which critics investigate to unearth these competing ideas.

QUEER THEORY

Influenced by the social, cultural, and academic advances of feminist theory in the 1980s, gay and lesbian critics in the 1990s began to join the critical conversation taking place in universities. Besides uncovering the possible homosexuality or bisexuality of canonical authors (such as Christopher Marlowe, Willa Cather, Emily Dickinson, and Henry James), these critics sought to reveal and discredit long-held stereotypes of gay and lesbian fictional characters. By challenging the homophobic prejudice they found in literature and society, lesbian and gay critics hoped to raise awareness of the complex ways society privileges heterosexual behavior and marginalizes any deviation from its norms. Adrienne Rich, an influential lesbian theorist, popularized the term "compulsive heterosexuality" to suggest the subtle and explicit ways the dominant straight culture unthinkingly socializes us to see heterosexuality as a given, the taken-for-granted default sexual identity for all. As a result, same-sex relationships suffer the disempowering injustices allotted to those judged abnormal. Therefore another concern of gay and lesbian critics has been to suggest that sexual identity is not a stable or an absolute given. Again, Adrienne Rich is helpful with her idea of a "lesbian continuum" where sexual identity is not absolute but is best seen as contextual and fluid, ranging from young girls holding hands (homosocial), to same-sex flirting and kissing (homoerotic), to genital sex (homosexual).

The idea of sexual identity as fluid and contingent can be seen as a bridge to Queer Theory, an umbrella term that became popular in the 1990s in the Lesbian-Gay-Bisexual-Transgender-Questioning-Intersex-Asexual (LGBTQIA) community. Although queer had been a term of homophobic abuse, it was rehabilitated to refer to whatever is at odds with the norm, the accepted, and the dominant. Practitioners of queer theory want to challenge the many institutions in which heteronormativity is so deeply embedded. Like deconstructionists, queer theorists do not believe in stable identities; consequently, they always debunk and question conventional gender identity and roles. Performance is more important than what you are; action counts, not biology.

Working with the Critical Approaches

Keep these brief descriptions of the critical approaches in mind as you read the following story by James Joyce, one of the most important writers of the twentieth century. Joyce (1882–1941) was born in Ireland, although he spent most of his life in self-imposed exile on the European continent. "Counterparts" is from *Dubliners* (1914), a collection of stories set in the Irish city of his childhood years. (For more on James Joyce, see his story "Araby," on p. 621.)

JAMES JOYCE

Counterparts

The bell rang furiously and, when Miss Parker went to the tube, a furious voice called out in a piercing North of Ireland accent:

—Send Farrington here!

Miss Parker returned to her machine, saying to a man who was writing at a desk:

—Mr Alleyne wants you upstairs.

The man muttered *Blast him!* under his breath and pushed back his chair   5
to stand up. When he stood up he was tall and of great bulk. He had a hanging face, dark wine-coloured, with fair eyebrows and moustache: his eyes bulged forward slightly and the whites of them were dirty. He lifted up the counter and, passing by the clients, went out of the office with a heavy step.

He went heavily upstairs until he came to the second landing, where a door bore a brass plate with the inscription *Mr Alleyne.* Here he halted, puffing with labor and vexation, and knocked. The shrill voice cried:

—Come in!

The man entered Mr Alleyne's room. Simultaneously Mr Alleyne, a little man wearing gold-rimmed glasses on a cleanshaven face, shot his head up over a pile of documents. The head itself was so pink and hairless that it seemed like a large egg reposing on the papers. Mr Alleyne did not lose a moment:

—Farrington? What is the meaning of this? Why have I always to complain of you? May I ask you why you haven't made a copy of that contract between Bodley and Kirwan? I told you it must be ready by four o'clock.

—But Mr Shelley said, sir—   10

—*Mr Shelley said, sir. . . .* Kindly attend to what I say and not to what *Mr Shelley says, sir.* You have always some excuse or another for shirking work.

Let me tell you that if the contract is not copied before this evening I'll lay the matter before Mr Crosbie. . . . Do you hear me now?

—Yes, sir.

—Do you hear me now? . . . Ay and another little matter! I might as well be talking to the wall as talking to you. Understand once for all that you get a half an hour for your lunch and not an hour and a half. How many courses do you want, I'd like to know. . . . Do you mind me, now?

—Yes, sir.

Mr Alleyne bent his head again upon his pile of papers. The man stared   15
fixedly at the polished skull which directed the affairs of Crosbie & Alleyne, gauging its fragility. A spasm of rage gripped his throat for a few moments and then passed, leaving after it a sharp sensation of thirst. The man recognized the sensation and felt that he must have a good night's drinking. The middle of the month was passed and, if he could get the copy done in time, Mr Alleyne might give him an order on the cashier. He stood still, gazing fixedly at the head upon the pile of papers. Suddenly Mr Alleyne began to upset all the papers, searching for something. Then, as if he had been unaware of the man's presence till that moment, he shot up his head again, saying:

—Eh? Are you going to stand there all day? Upon my word, Farrington, you take things easy!

—I was waiting to see . . .

—Very good, you needn't wait to see. Go downstairs and do your work.

The man walked heavily towards the door and, as he went out of the room, he heard Mr Alleyne cry after him that if the contract was not copied by evening Mr Crosbie would hear of the matter.

He returned to his desk in the lower office and counted the sheets which   20
remained to be copied. He took up his pen and dipped it in the ink but he continued to stare stupidly at the last words he had written: *In no case shall the said Bernard Bodley be.* . . . The evening was falling and in a few minutes they would be lighting the gas: then he could write. He felt that he must slake the thirst in his throat. He stood up from his desk and, lifting the counter as before, passed out of the office. As he was passing out the chief clerk looked at him inquiringly.

—It's all right, Mr Shelley, said the man, pointing with his finger to indicate the objective of his journey.

The chief clerk glanced at the hat-rack but, seeing the row complete, offered no remark. As soon as he was on the landing the man pulled a shepherd's plaid cap out of his pocket, put it on his head and ran quickly down the rickety stairs. From the street door he walked on furtively on the inner side of the path towards the corner and all at once dived into a doorway. He was now safe in the dark snug of O'Neill's shop, and, filling up the little window that looked into the bar with his inflamed face, the color of dark wine or dark meat, he called out:

—Here, Pat, give us a g.p., like a good fellow.

The curate brought him a glass of plain porter. The man drank it at a gulp and asked for a caraway seed. He put his penny on the counter and, leaving the curate to grope for it in the gloom, retreated out of the snug as furtively as he had entered it.

Darkness, accompanied by a thick fog, was gaining upon the dusk of   25
February and the lamps in Eustace Street had been lit. The man went up by the
houses until he reached the door of the office, wondering whether he could
finish his copy in time. On the stairs a moist pungent odor of perfumes saluted
his nose: evidently Miss Delacour had come while he was out in O'Neill's. He
crammed his cap back again into his pocket and re-entered the office assuming
an air of absent-mindedness.

—Mr Alleyne has been calling for you, said the chief clerk severely. Where
were you?

The man glanced at the two clients who were standing at the counter as if
to intimate that their presence prevented him from answering. As the clients
were both male the chief clerk allowed himself a laugh.

—I know that game, he said. Five times in one day is a little bit. . . . Well,
you better look sharp and get a copy of our correspondence in the Delacour
case for Mr Alleyne.

This address in the presence of the public, his run upstairs, and the porter
he had gulped down so hastily confused the man and, as he sat down at his
desk to get what was required, he realized how hopeless was the task of finishing his copy of the contract before half past five. The dark damp night was
coming and he longed to spend it in the bars, drinking with his friends amid the
glare of gas and the clatter of glasses. He got out the Delacour correspondence
and passed out of the office. He hoped Mr Alleyne would not discover that the
last two letters were missing.

The moist pungent perfume lay all the way up to Mr Alleyne's room. Miss   30
Delacour was a middle-aged woman of Jewish appearance. Mr Alleyne was
said to be sweet on her or on her money. She came to the office often and stayed
a long time when she came. She was sitting beside his desk now in an aroma
of perfumes, smoothing the handle of her umbrella, and nodding the great
black feather in her hat. Mr Alleyne had swivelled his chair round to face her
and thrown his right foot jauntily upon his left knee. The man put the correspondence on the desk and bowed respectfully but neither Mr Alleyne nor
Miss Delacour took any notice of his bow. Mr Alleyne tapped a finger on the
correspondence and then flicked it towards him as if to say: *That's all right: you
can go.*

The man returned to the lower office and sat down again at his desk. He
stared intently at the incomplete phrase: *In no case shall the said Bernard Bodley
be . . .* and thought how strange it was that the last three words began with the
same letter. The chief clerk began to hurry Miss Parker, saying she would never
have the letters typed in time for post. The man listened to the clicking of the
machine for a few minutes and then set to work to finish his copy. But his head
was not clear and his mind wandered away to the glare and rattle of the public-
house. It was a night for hot punches. He struggled on with his copy, but when
the clock struck five he had still fourteen pages to write. Blast it! He couldn't
finish it in time. He longed to execrate aloud, to bring his fist down on something violently. He was so enraged that he wrote *Bernard Bernard* instead of
Bernard Bodley and had to begin again on a clean sheet.

He felt strong enough to clear out the whole office singlehanded. His body ached to do something, to rush out and revel in violence. All the indignities of his life enraged him. . . . Could he ask the cashier privately for an advance? No, the cashier was no good, no damn good: he wouldn't give an advance. . . . He knew where he would meet the boys: Leonard and O'Halloran and Nosey Flynn. The barometer of his emotional nature was set for a spell of riot.

His imagination had so abstracted him that his name was called twice before he answered. Mr Alleyne and Miss Delacour were standing outside the counter and all the clerks had turned round in anticipation of something. The man got up from his desk. Mr Alleyne began a tirade of abuse, saying that two letters were missing. The man answered that he knew nothing about them, that he had made a faithful copy. The tirade continued: it was so bitter and violent that the man could hardly restrain his fist from descending upon the head of the manikin before him.

—I know nothing about any other two letters, he said stupidly.

—You—know—nothing. Of course you know nothing, said Mr Alleyne.   35
Tell me, he added, glancing first for approval to the lady beside him, do you take me for a fool? Do you think me an utter fool?

The man glanced from the lady's face to the little egg-shaped head and back again; and, almost before he was aware of it, his tongue had found a felicitous moment:

—I don't think, sir, he said, that that's a fair question to put to me.

There was a pause in the very breathing of the clerks. Everyone was astounded (the author of the witticism no less than his neighbors) and Miss Delacour, who was a stout amiable person, began to smile broadly. Mr Alleyne flushed to the hue of a wild rose and his mouth twitched with a dwarf's passion. He shook his fist in the man's face till it seemed to vibrate like the knob of some electric machine:

—You impertinent ruffian! You impertinent ruffian! I'll make short work of you! Wait till you see! You'll apologize to me for your impertinence or you'll quit the office instanter! You'll quit this, I'm telling you, or you'll apologize to me!

He stood in a doorway opposite the office watching to see if the cashier would   40
come out alone. All the clerks passed out and finally the cashier came out with the chief clerk. It was no use trying to say a word to him when he was with the chief clerk. The man felt that his position was bad enough. He had been obliged to offer an abject apology to Mr Alleyne for his impertinence but he knew what a hornet's nest the office would be for him. He could remember the way in which Mr Alleyne had hounded little Peake out of the office in order to make room for his own nephew. He felt savage and thirsty and revengeful, annoyed with himself and with everyone else. Mr Alleyne would never give him an hour's rest; his life would be a hell to him. He had made a proper fool of himself this time. Could he not keep his tongue in his cheek? But they had never pulled together from the first, he and Mr Alleyne, ever since the day Mr Alleyne had overheard him mimicking his North of Ireland accent to amuse Higgins and

Miss Parker: that had been the beginning of it. He might have tried Higgins for the money, but sure Higgins never had anything for himself. A man with two establishments to keep up, of course he couldn't. . . .

He felt his great body again aching for the comfort of the public-house. The fog had begun to chill him and he wondered could he touch Pat in O'Neill's. He could not touch him for more than a bob—and a bob was no use. Yet he must get money somewhere or other: he had spent his last penny for the g.p. and soon it would be too late for getting money anywhere. Suddenly, as he was fingering his watch-chain, he thought of Terry Kelly's pawn-office in Fleet Street. That was the dart! Why didn't he think of it sooner?

He went through the narrow alley of Temple Bar quickly, muttering to himself that they could all go to hell because he was going to have a good night of it. The clerk in Terry Kelly's said *A crown!* but the consignor held out for six shillings; and in the end the six shillings was allowed him literally. He came out of the pawn-office joyfully, making a little cylinder of the coins between his thumb and fingers. In Westmoreland Street the footpaths were crowded with young men and women returning from business and ragged urchins ran here and there yelling out the names of the evening editions. The man passed through the crowd, looking on the spectacle generally with proud satisfaction and staring masterfully at the office-girls. His head was full of the noises of tram-gongs and swishing trolleys and his nose already sniffed the curling fumes of punch. As he walked on he preconsidered the terms in which he would narrate the incident to the boys:

—So, I just looked at him—coolly, you know, and looked at her. Then I looked back at him again—taking my time, you know. *I don't think that that's a fair question to put to me,* says I.

Nosey Flynn was sitting up in his usual corner of Davy Byrne's and, when he heard the story, he stood Farrington a half-one, saying it was as smart a thing as ever he heard. Farrington stood a drink in his turn. After a while O'Halloran and Paddy Leonard came in and the story was repeated to them. O'Halloran stood tailors of malt, hot, all round and told the story of the retort he had made to the chief clerk when he was in Callan's of Fownes's Street; but, as the retort was after the manner of the liberal shepherds in the eclogues, he had to admit that it was not so clever as Farrington's retort. At this Farrington told the boys to polish off that and have another.

Just as they were naming their poisons who should come in but Higgins!   45 Of course he had to join in with the others. The men asked him to give his version of it, and he did so with great vivacity for the sight of five small hot whiskies was very exhilarating. Everyone roared laughing when he showed the way in which Mr Alleyne shook his fist in Farrington's face. Then he imitated Farrington, saying, *And here was my nabs, as cool as you please,* while Farrington looked at the company out of his heavy dirty eyes, smiling and at times drawing forth stray drops of liquor from his moustache with the aid of his lower lip.

When that round was over there was a pause. O'Halloran had money but neither of the other two seemed to have any; so the whole party left the shop somewhat regretfully. At the corner of Duke Street Higgins and Nosey Flynn bevelled off to the left while the other three turned back towards the city. Rain was drizzling down on the cold streets and, when they reached the Ballast Office, Farrington suggested the Scotch House. The bar was full of men and loud with the noise of tongues and glasses. The three men pushed past the whining match-sellers at the door and formed a little party at the corner of the counter. They began to exchange stories. Leonard introduced them to a young fellow named Weathers who was performing at the Tivoli as an acrobat and knockabout *artiste*. Farrington stood a drink all round. Weathers said he would take a small Irish and Apollinaris. Farrington, who had definite notions of what was what, asked the boys would they have an Apollinaris too; but the boys told Tim to make theirs hot. The talk became theatrical. O'Halloran stood a round and then Farrington stood another round, Weathers protesting that the hospitality was too Irish. He promised to get them in behind the scenes and introduce them to some nice girls. O'Halloran said that he and Leonard would go but that Farrington wouldn't go because he was a married man; and Farrington's heavy dirty eyes leered at the company in token that he understood he was being chaffed. Weathers made them all have just one little tincture at his expense and promised to meet them later on at Mulligan's in Poolbeg Street.

When the Scotch House closed they went round to Mulligan's. They went into the parlor at the back and O'Halloran ordered small hot specials all round. They were all beginning to feel mellow. Farrington was just standing another round when Weathers came back. Much to Farrington's relief he drank a glass of bitter this time. Funds were running low but they had enough to keep them going. Presently two young women with big hats and a young man in a check suit came in and sat at a table close by. Weathers saluted them and told the company that they were out of the Tivoli. Farrington's eyes wandered at every moment in the direction of one of the young women. There was something striking in her appearance. An immense scarf of peacock-blue muslin was wound round her hat and knotted in a great bow under her chin; and she wore bright yellow gloves, reaching to the elbow. Farrington gazed admiringly at the plump arm which she moved very often and with much grace; and when, after a little time, she answered his gaze he admired still more her large dark brown eyes. The oblique staring expression in them fascinated him. She glanced at him once or twice and, when the party was leaving the room, she brushed against his chair and said *O, pardon!* in a London accent. He watched her leave the room in the hope that she would look back at him, but he was disappointed. He cursed his want of money and cursed all the rounds he had stood, particularly all the whiskies and Apollinaris which he had stood to Weathers. If there was one thing that he hated it was a sponge. He was so angry that he lost count of the conversation of his friends.

When Paddy Leonard called him he found that they were talking about feats of strength. Weathers was showing his biceps muscle to the company and boasting so much that the other two had called on Farrington to uphold the national honor. Farrington pulled up his sleeve accordingly and showed his biceps muscle to the company. The two arms were examined and compared and finally it was agreed to have a trial of strength. The table was cleared and the two men rested their elbows on it, clasping hands. When Paddy Leonard said *Go!* each was to try to bring down the other's hand on to the table. Farrington looked very serious and determined.

The trial began. After about thirty seconds Weathers brought his opponent's hand slowly down on to the table. Farrington's dark wine-coloured face flushed darker still with anger and humiliation at having been defeated by such a stripling.

—You're not to put the weight of your body behind it. Play fair, he said.   50

—Who's not playing fair? said the other.

—Come on again. The two best out of three.

The trial began again. The veins stood out on Farrington's forehead, and the pallor of Weathers' complexion changed to peony. Their hands and arms trembled under the stress. After a long struggle Weathers again brought his opponent's hand slowly on to the table. There was a murmur of applause from the spectators. The curate, who was standing beside the table, nodded his red head towards the victor and said with loutish familiarity:

—Ah! that's the knack!

—What the hell do you know about it? said Farrington fiercely, turning on   55
the man. What do you put in your gab for?

—Sh, sh! said O'Halloran, observing the violent expression of Farrington's face. Pony up, boys. We'll have just one little smahan more and then we'll be off.

A very sullen-faced man stood at the corner of O'Connell Bridge waiting for the little Sandymount tram to take him home. He was full of smouldering anger and revengefulness. He felt humiliated and discontented; he did not even feel drunk; and he had only twopence in his pocket. He cursed everything. He had done for himself in the office, pawned his watch, spent all his money; and he had not even got drunk. He began to feel thirsty again and he longed to be back again in the hot reeking public-house. He had lost his reputation as a strong man, having been defeated twice by a mere boy. His heart swelled with fury and, when he thought of the woman in the big hat who had brushed against him and said *Pardon!* his fury nearly choked him.

His tram let him down at Shelbourne Road and he steered his great body along in the shadow of the wall of the barracks. He loathed returning to his home. When he went in by the side-door he found the kitchen empty and the kitchen fire nearly out. He bawled upstairs:

—Ada! Ada!

His wife was a little sharp-faced woman who bullied her husband when he   60
was sober and was bullied by him when he was drunk. They had five children. A little boy came running down the stairs.

—Who is that? said the man, peering through the darkness.

—Me, pa.

—Who are you? Charlie?

—No, pa. Tom.

—Where's your mother?   65

—She's out at the chapel.

—That's right. . . . Did she think of leaving any dinner for me?

—Yes, pa. I—

—Light the lamp. What do you mean by having the place in darkness? Are the other children in bed?

The man sat down heavily on one of the chairs while the little boy lit the lamp. He began to mimic his son's flat accent, saying half to himself: *At the chapel. At the chapel, if you please!* When the lamp was lit he banged his fist on the table and shouted:

—What's for my dinner?

—I'm going . . . to cook it, pa, said the little boy.

The man jumped up furiously and pointed to the fire.

—On that fire! You let the fire out! By God, I'll teach you to do that again!

He took a step to the door and seized the walking-stick which was standing behind it.

—I'll teach you to let the fire out! he said, rolling up his sleeve in order to give his arm free play.

The little boy cried *O, pa!* and ran whimpering round the table, but the man followed him and caught him by the coat. The little boy looked about him wildly but, seeing no way of escape fell upon his knees.

—Now, you'll let the fire out the next time! said the man, striking at him viciously with the stick. Take that, you little whelp!

The boy uttered a squeal of pain as the stick cut his thigh. He clasped his hands together in the air and his voice shook with fright.

—O, pa! he cried. Don't beat me, pa! And I'll . . . I'll say a *Hail Mary* for you. . . . I'll say a *Hail Mary* for you, pa, if you don't beat me. . . . I'll say a *Hail Mary*. . . .   *[1914]*

A thorough critical analysis of "Counterparts" using any one of these approaches would take dozens of pages. The following are brief suggestions for how such a reading might proceed.

NEW CRITICISM

A New Critic might want to demonstrate the multiple ways the title holds the narrative together, giving it unity and coherence—for example, Farrington and his son Tom are counterparts since Tom is the victim of his father's bullying just as Farrington is bullied by Mr. Alleyne at work. You can also probably spot other counterparts: Farrington and his wife, for example, trade off bullying each other, and their means of escaping from the drudgery of their lives, the bar and the church, are also parallel. And naturally when Weathers, the acrobat, defeats the much larger Farrington in arm wrestling, we are reminded of the verbal beating Farrington must endure from his equally diminutive boss, Mr. Alleyne. New Critics are fond of finding the ways all the elements of a text reinforce one another.

A New Critic might argue that these counterparts or oppositions introduce tensions into the story from the first few lines when the "bell rang furiously" for Farrington to report to Mr. Alleyne for a dressing-down. The irony is that Farrington is big and Alleyne is small, that Farrington is powerful and Alleyne is fragile as an egg. But it is Mr. Alleyne who breaks Farrington; it is Farrington who is weak. Throughout the story, tensions, oppositions, and ironies continue, for example, when Farrington is defeated by the smaller Weathers. In the last scene, the tension is finally resolved when the larger Farrington beats his small son, making him a counterpart to both Alleyne and Weathers in oppressing the weak. The final evidence that Farrington is ethically powerless is cruelly obvious as the son promises to pray for his abusing father.

FEMINIST CRITICISM

Feminist critics and their first cousins, gender critics, would naturally be struck by the violent masculinity of Farrington, his fantasies of riot and abuse, his savage feelings of revenge, and his "smouldering anger" (para. 57). Farrington is depicted not only as crude and brutish but also as a kind of perverse stereotype of male vanity, self-centeredness, and irresponsibility. His obsession with obtaining money for drinking completely disregards his role as the provider for a large family, and, of course, the beatings of his son are a cruel parody of his role as paternal protector. And if he had not wasted his money on drink, Farrington would also be a womanizer ("Farrington's eyes wandered at every moment in the direction of one of the young women," para. 47). Gender critics would be interested in the social and cultural mechanisms that could construct such primitive masculinity.

A reasonable argument might focus on the representation of women in the story. Miss Parker, Miss Delacour, Farrington's wife, and the performer Farrington sees in the bar are marginal characters. One student made the following claim: "The women in Farrington's world, and Irish society in general, have no agency: they are prevented from taking an active part in determining their lives and futures." Another student argued differently, saying, "While women in general are oppressed by the raw and brutal masculinity represented by Farrington, the women in this story do hold a degree of power over men." Based on their own analysis and interpretations, these students demonstrated that there was reasonable textual evidence to support their claims.

PSYCHOANALYTIC CRITICISM

A psychoanalytic critic would first notice the extreme pattern of behavior Farrington exhibits, as he repeatedly withdraws from his adult work responsibilities and as he fantasizes about being physically violent against his supervisors. Critics would argue that such behavior is typical of Farrington's repressed wounds and his unresolved conflicts with his own father. Farrington seems to be playing out painful childhood experiences. Given the violent displacement (taking it out on someone else) visited on Tom, we can imagine that Farrington is beating not only his boss, Mr. Alleyne, but also perhaps his own abusive father. The fantasies at work in Farrington also suggest the psychological defense of projection, since Farrington is blaming his problems on Mr. Alleyne and his job. Although his tasks do seem to be tedious, they certainly cannot account for his "spasm of rage" (para. 15) or his desire "to clear out the whole office single-handed" (para. 32). When Farrington feels "humiliated and discontented" (para. 57), it is only in part because of his immediate context. It is the return of the repressed that plagues Farrington, a resurfacing of a buried pain. These ideas should also be tied to Farrington's death wish, especially his stunningly self-destructive behavior at work. Freudian critics would also argue that these specific actions are related to other core issues that would include intense loss of self-esteem, fear of intimacy, and betrayal.

MARXIST CRITICISM

A Marxist critic would be interested in focusing on the specific historical moment of "Counterparts" and not on Farrington's individual psyche, which can only distract us from the real force that affects human experience—the economic system in which Farrington is trapped. Economic power—not the Oedipal drama or gender—is the crucial human motivator. Farrington's material circumstances and not timeless values are the key to understanding his behavior. The real battle lines are drawn between Crosbie and Alleyne (the "haves") and Farrington (a "have-not")—that is, between the bourgeoisie and the proletariat, between those who control economic resources and those who perform the labor that fills the coffers of the rich. In a Marxist analysis, critics would argue that Farrington is a victim of class warfare. His desperation, his humiliation, his rage, his cruel violence are all traceable to classism—an ideology that determines people's worth according to their economic class. Although Farrington does appear shiftless and irresponsible, it is not because of his class; it is because of the meaninglessness of his work and the demeaning hierarchy that keeps him at the bottom. In his alienation, he reverts to a primitive physical masculinity, a false consciousness that only further diminishes his sense of his worth.

Marxists are often interested in what lies beneath the text in its political unconscious. To get at the unconscious, Marxists, like psychoanalytic critics, look for symptoms on the surface that suggest problems beneath. Typically, such symptomatic readings reveal class conflicts that authors are sometimes unaware of themselves. Marxist critics might debate whether Joyce himself understood that the root cause of Farrington's aberrant behavior was economic and not psychological. This makes sense since for Marxists both reader and writer are under the sway of the same ideological system that they see as natural.

One student made the following claim: "Farrington's role as proletarian results in his feelings of inferiority, resentment over lack of entitlement, and an expectation of disappointment." This same student, like many Marxist critics who see the function of literature through a pragmatic lens, concluded her essay with an appeal toward change, arguing that "The remedy does not lie in changing Farrington's consciousness, but rather in changing the economic and political discourse of power that has constituted him."

DECONSTRUCTION

One of many possible deconstructions of "Counterparts" would involve focusing on a troubling or puzzling point called an *aporia*. Some deconstructive critics have looked at the incomplete phrase that Farrington copies, *"In no case shall the said Bernard Bodley be . . ."* as an aporia, an ambiguous and not completely understandable textual puzzle but one that might be a way into the story's meaning. The oppositions that are being deconstructed or laid bare here are *presence* and *absence, word* and *reality.* Working off the implications of the title "Counterparts," Bernard Bodley can be seen as a double or counterpart for Farrington, a character like Bodley whose existence is in doubt. Although Farrington's size suggests that he is very much physically present, his behavior might suggest otherwise. He spends his time copying other people's words and has a compelling need to repeat the narrative of his encounter with Mr. Alleyne, as if he must demonstrate his own existence through repetition. He does not have a viable inner life, an authentic identity. Farrington's essence is not present but absent. His identity is insubstantial. He tries to fill the emptiness at the center of his being with camaraderie and potency, but his efforts produce the opposite — escape, loneliness, and weakness. In other words, the said Farrington does not really exist and cannot be. In this way, we can deconstruct "Counterparts" as a story in which presence is absence, strength is weakness, Farrington's actions lead only to paralysis and repetition, and Farrington's frustration with his impotence makes his oppressors more powerful.

One student working with similar interpretations of "Counterparts" noted other oppositions, especially between male and female, escape and confinement. She argued that Farrington spends most of his time trying to avoid being thought of as stereotypically feminine. However, the more exaggerated his masculine aggression, drinking, violence, and irresponsibility become, the weaker, the more stereotypically feminine he becomes. Similarly, the more Farrington tries to escape, the more ensnared he is. In this way, the student argued, our conventional understandings of these opposing terms are deconstructed, so that we are no longer confident about the meaning of escape, masculinity, or strength.

READER-RESPONSE CRITICISM

Willa Ervinman, a student, was asked to respond to the story by using Stanley Fish's ideas and noting the conflicts between the interpretive or discourse communities Willa belonged to and those depicted in the story. The following are excerpts from her response journal:

> I was upset by Farrington's lack of responsibility at work. He is completely unreliable and demonstrates very little self-esteem. He must know that the people he works with consider him a slacker and a fake. I was raised in a middle-class home where both my parents worked hard in a bank from 9 to 5. Just the idea that they would sneak out of work to drink in dark bars is absurd. My belief in the

discourse of middle-class responsibility or perhaps the Protestant work ethic makes it almost impossible for me to see Farrington with sympathy even though I can see that his work is probably completely mechanical and unfulfilling. . . .

Farrington's domestic violence against his son is such a violation of the discourse of domesticity that it is hard to understand any other response. Someone in my response group thought that Farrington was a victim of his working-class discourse of masculinity. I can see how he was humiliated by the smaller men, Mr. Alleyne and Weathers, but beating his innocent son as a kind of revenge cannot be forgiven. My grandmother tells me that it was common for children to be physically punished in her day, but in the interpretive community I was raised in, there is no excuse for domestic violence. It is more than a character flaw; it is criminal behavior, and I judge Farrington to be a social menace, beyond compassion.

Willa went on to argue that Farrington's violent behavior is inexcusable, interpreting our current understandings of domestic violence and responsible masculinity as evidence. She blended this personal view with textual support. Her warrant for her claim was that historical circumstances and norms should not be used to excuse reprehensible behavior.

POSTCOLONIAL CRITICISM

"Counterparts" was written in the early twentieth century at a time when the Ireland Joyce writes about was still a colony of the British Empire. Farrington is, then, a colonial subject and subject to political domination. At the story's opening, Farrington, a Catholic from the south of Ireland, is summoned by a "furious voice" from Northern Ireland, a stronghold of British sympathy and Protestant domination. The tension is announced early because it is crucial to Farrington's behavior and his internalized and colonized mindset. Many colonials have a negative self-image because they are alienated from their own indigenous culture. Indeed, Farrington seems completely ill suited to the office copying task he is relegated to. He seems more suited to some physical endeavor, but given the difficult economics of Dublin, he probably has few career options.

Farrington is the Other in the discourse of colonialism, and he is made to seem inferior at every turn, from the verbal lashing of Mr. Alleyne to the physical defeat by Weathers, who is probably British. Symbolically, Farrington tries to resist his subjugation by the British establishment but fails. He is what postcolonial theorists refer to as *unhomed* or *displaced*. He is uncomfortable at work, in the bars where he seeks solace, and finally in his ultimate refuge, a place unprepared even to feed him. Indeed, in an act likely to perpetuate abuse upon future generations, Farrington turns on his own family, becoming, through his enraged attack on his child Tom, a metaphor for the conflicted, tormented, and defeated Ireland. When a colonial is not "at home" even in his own home, he is truly in psychological agony and exile. Joyce represents the trauma of British domination through one subject's self-destructive and self-hating journey, a journey made even more cruelly ironic by Farrington's attack—in a mimicry of British aggression and injustice—on his own sub- jected son.

NEW HISTORICISM

A critic influenced by Foucault and New Historicism might argue that Farrington is a victim of an inflexible discourse of masculinity, that he has been socialized by working-class norms of how a man should behave to such an extent that he cannot change. Growing up in a working-class culture, Farrington would have received high marks among his peers for his size and strength, just as Mr. Alleyne would be diminished in status for his. And in another context, say, on a construction site, Farrington's sense of masculinity might be a plus. But in an office, his aggressive masculinity is a liability. In all cultures, people are subject to multiple discourses that pull them one way then another. Farrington's sarcasm, his drinking, his longing for camaraderie, and his resort- ing to violence to solve problems are the results of being too enmeshed in a discourse of masculinity from working-class Dublin and not enough in the middle-class business assumptions about discipline, responsibility, and concen- tration. Farrington is defeated at work, in the pubs, and at home because he is unable to move from one discourse to another. He is stuck in a subject position that only reinforces his powerlessness. His self-esteem is so damaged by the end of the story that he even violates his own code of masculinity by beating a de- fenseless child.

QUEER THEORY

Because queer theorists are as concerned with gender identities as they are with sexuality, they would be interested in the asymmetrical power relation- ship between Farrington's "great bulk" (para. 5) and Mr. Allyne's "little man" with a "pink and hairless head" (para. 8) Farrington is surely performing as a queer character when he betrays his traditional masculine role by being thor- oughly emasculated at work; he is incompetent at simple tasks, and his status in the hierarchy is diminishing. And the reader knows that Farrington's occu- pation as a copier will soon be obsolete, replaced by legions of female typists. He is a queer figure in a queer job. However, his sexuality is less of an issue than the idea that heterosexuality as a pervasive and rigid institution causes Farrington intense humiliation and anguish as he fails at every traditional (al- beit arbitrary) masculine standard.

Farrington seeks solace and escape from his newfound queerness in the male homosocial pubs of Dublin. Here he does seem to perform masterfully with the retelling of his witty put-down of his boss. But the reader is well aware that Farrington has queered the real narrative of his confrontation with Mr. Allyne. In actuality, he was forced to apologize abjectly for his remarks and will pay dearly for not knowing his place. It is also here in his beloved pub space that he receives the greatest blow to what remains of his masculinity. He is humiliated in a contest of strength by an "artiste," "a mere boy" (para. 56).

When as an alienated outcast he returns home in rage and anger, and "viciously" (para. 78) beats his own son in a traditionally female space, the kitchen, his impotence is complete. In a good example of fluid gender roles, his wife, Ada, "who bullied [Farrington] when he was sober and was bullied by him when he was drunk" (para. 60) temporarily abandons her traditional role of caring for him. Their relationship is indeed queer. Farrington's performative queerness is never clearer than in his final violent undoing of the conventional role of the protective father, making a mockery of masculine decency, compassion, and fairness.

Alert to the inconsistencies, contradictions, and ambiguities of conventional gender behaviors, protocols, and values, queer theorists offer provocative and enriching readings that remind readers how easy it is to oversimplify the bewildering complexities of being men and women.

Sample Student Essay

The following essay was written by a first-year student using a postcolonial perspective.

Molly Frye
Prof. Christine Hardee
English 102
10 May - - - -

A Refugee at Home

It is difficult to argue that Farrington, the main character in James Joyce's "Counterparts," should be seen in a sympathetic light. After all, he seems an extreme stereotype of an aggressive, irresponsible drinker. Although his character traits certainly do not conform to our modern standards of mature masculinity, I want to argue that although we do not want to condone Farrington's brutal behavior, we can find it understandable. As an Irish subject in the British Empire, Farrington is more sinned against than sinner, more victim than victimizer. Farrington is not simply an obnoxious male since his actions can be understood as stemming from his colonial consciousness in struggling vainly against his powerlessness. His frustrations are especially clear in the three spaces Farrington inhabits: his office, the bars, and his home.

After setting up a context, states her claim supported by three examples.

Farrington's first appearance is telling. Because of his poor job performance, his boss demands to see him: "Send Farrington here!" Farrington, who most often is referred to as "the man," mutters his first words, "Blast him!" This typical antagonistic relationship in a colonial context foreshadows the rest of the story. Farrington is the working-class subject caught in a menial and unsatisfying job he can never complete under a boss who has social and cultural power. This counterpart relationship is similar to the positions of Ireland and England where the colony is disparaged and oppressed by the empire. In his office run by Protestants loyal to the British, Farrington is ironically "tall and of great bulk," while his boss, Mr. Alleyne, is "a little man" whose head, "pink and hairless," resembles a "large egg." Farrington's only asset, his size and strength, is irrelevant because he is so economically and socially weak. This disparity only increases Farrington's frustration and precipitates fantasies of violence against his oppressor. When Mr. Alleyne rebukes him, "Do you mind me now," Farrington is sent into a "spasm of rage." He cannot, of course, act on his aggressive urges, so he represses these feelings by rationalizing that he must have a "good night's drinking." Thus begins a pattern of self-destructive behavior that only increases Farrington's marginal position in society.

First concrete example of Farrington as frustrated colonial subject.

Transition to explanation of Farrington's failures at work.

Farrington is so uncomfortable at work, a postcolonial condition known as being unhomed, that he cannot concentrate on anything but drinking. He seems quite unsuited for the tedious task of copying legal documents, staring "stupidly at the last words he has written," knowing he will never finish his task, never advance, never get anywhere. Farrington is paralyzed by his alienation. He feels his only recourse is sneaking out to drink, which only exacerbates his poverty and powerlessness. When he attempts to cover up his inability to concentrate and finish copying letters for Mr. Alleyne, he is caught and confronted. Instead of acknowledging his underling position, he attempts a witticism which, of course, backfires. Even though he is forced to apologize, his job now seems in jeopardy. Mr. Alleyne humiliates him by calling him an "impertinent ruffian," a status that seems to him the most he can hope for. As a colonial subject, Farrington is plagued by a double consciousness. He longs for the masculine status his physical strength should give him in his working-class culture, but he must suffer indignities at the hands of Mr. Alleyne because of his inability to perform a simple task a competent child could do. Farrington should probably be working in construction as a laborer, not an office worker where discipline, patience, and mental concentration are necessary.

Uses postcolonial ideas to explain Farrington's behavior.

When Farrington finally leaves work, he expects to find some solace in the Dublin pubs. He has hocked his watch for

Transition to second example of Farrington as colonized.

drinking money, a clear indication of how desperate he is to escape the confines of regimented office work. The camaraderie of Paddy Leonard and Nosey Flynn is temporary, and Farrington is not at home in these public spaces either. He runs out of money he would have spent drinking and womanizing, and he is finally humiliated by another small British man. Called on to "uphold the national honor," Farrington's loss in an arm-wrestling contest with Weathers leaves him "full of smouldering anger and revengefulness. He is humiliated and discontented . . . His heart swelled with fury. . . ." His longing for escape from the confinement and disappointment of work has taken a disastrous turn. Farrington's already damaged self-esteem is degraded, and his repressed anger at his oppressor is near the breaking point. Perhaps his self-destructive behavior can be redirected at his home, his last possibility for comfort and acceptance.

Transition to last example.

For the unhomed colonized, however, this is not to be. Farrington enters the kitchen to find it symbolically empty, "the fire nearly out." His wife is at chapel, his five children in bed, and his dinner is cold. His agonies continue. Having internalized the humiliations suffered at work and in the pubs, Farrington has no resources left. And so in a bitter irony, he beats his son for not attending to the fire, "striking at him viciously with a stick. 'Take that, you little whelp!'" Farrington the oppressed becomes Farrington the oppressor. His role as provider and protector is cruelly turned upside-down. Farrington compensates for his defeats at the hands of Mr. Alleyne and Weathers by beating his son, and in doing so, mimics the cycle of oppression prevalent in countries dominated by the empire. Farrington is not only a cog in the bureaucratic wheel at work; he is also a pathetic, but understandable cog crushed by the wheel of power even in his own home.

Uses all three examples in concluding.

≡ FOR THINKING AND WRITING

1. Using a feminist critique of Joyce, one student claimed that "Joyce's text indulges dominance over submission." Do you think there is textual evidence to support this assertion?

2. How might various critics (postcolonial, feminist, Marxist, psychoanalytical) interpret these lines from "Counterparts":

   ■ "The man passed through the crowd, looking on the spectacle generally with proud satisfaction and staring masterfully at the office-girls" (para. 42).

- "His heart swelled with fury and, when he thought of the woman in the big hat who had brushed against him and said *Pardon!* his fury nearly choked him" (para. 57).
- "What's for my dinner?" (para. 71).

3. Influenced by New Critical ideas, one student wrote, "'Counterparts' is filled with parallel scenes and emotions that reflect one another." What textual evidence would help support this notion?

4. Engaging in a Marxist critique, one student wrote, "His unfair work conditions so distract him that he does not even know the names of his children." What is the warrant behind such an assertion? What work conditions might the student think "fair"?

5. Using a New Historicist approach, what might you learn about this story from doing research on the elementary-school curriculum in Dublin, the pay scale in a law office, the legal rights of women, the laws on domestic violence, the unemployment rate? What other practices and texts do you think would illuminate the story?

≡ A WRITING EXERCISE

Now you try. After reading the following story, construct an argument influenced by one or more of the following critical approaches: postcolonial, Marxist, reader-response, or feminist.

JAMES JOYCE
Eveline

Like "Counterparts," "Eveline" is from Dubliners *(1914). For more on James Joyce, see his story "Araby" on page 621.*

She sat at the window watching the evening invade the avenue. Her head was leaned against the window curtains and in her nostrils was the odor of dusty cretonne. She was tired.

Few people passed. The man out of the last house passed on his way home; she heard his footsteps clacking along the concrete pavement and afterwards crunching on the cinder path before the new red houses. One time there used to be a field there in which they used to play every evening with other people's children. Then a man from Belfast bought the field and built houses in it — not like their little brown houses but bright brick houses with shining roofs. The children of the avenue used to play together in that field — the Devines, the Waters, the Dunns, little Keogh the cripple, she and her brothers and sisters. Ernest, however, never played: he was too grown up. Her father used often to hunt them in out of the field with his blackthorn stick; but usually little Keogh used to keep *nix* and call out when he saw her father coming. Still they seemed to have been rather happy then. Her father was not so bad then; and besides, her mother was alive. That was a long time ago; she and her brothers and sisters were all grown up; her mother was dead. Tizzie Dunn was dead, too, and the Waters had gone back to England. Everything changes. Now she was going to go away like the others, to leave her home.

Home! She looked round the room, reviewing all its familiar objects which she had dusted once a week for so many years, wondering where on earth all the dust came from. Perhaps she would never see again those familiar objects from which she had never dreamed of being divided. And yet during all those years she had never found out the name of the priest whose yellowing photograph hung on the wall above the broken harmonium beside the colored print of the promises made to Blessed Margaret Mary Alacoque. He had been a school friend of her father. Whenever he showed the photograph to a visitor her father used to pass it with a casual word:

— He is in Melbourne now.

She had consented to go away, to leave her home. Was that wise? She tried to weigh each side of the question. In her home anyway she had shelter and food; she had those whom she had known all her life about her. Of course she had to work hard both in the house and at business. What would they say of her in the Stores when they found out that she had run away with a fellow? Say she was a fool, perhaps; and her place would be filled up by advertisement. Miss Gavan would be glad. She had always had an edge on her, especially whenever there were people listening.   5

— Miss Hill, don't you see these ladies are waiting?

— Look lively, Miss Hill, please.

She would not cry many tears at leaving the Stores.

But in her new home, in a distant unknown country, it would not be like that. Then she would be married — she, Eveline. People would treat her with respect then. She would not be treated as her mother had been. Even now, though she was over nineteen, she sometimes felt herself in danger of her father's violence. She knew it was that that had given her the palpitations. When they were growing up he had never gone for her, like he used to go for Harry and Ernest, because she was a girl; but latterly he had begun to threaten her and say what he would do to her only for her dead mother's sake. And now she had nobody to protect her. Ernest was dead and Harry, who was in the church decorating business, was nearly always down somewhere in the country. Besides, the invariable squabble for money on Saturday nights had begun to weary her unspeakably. She always gave her entire wages — seven shillings — and Harry always sent up what he could but the trouble was to get any money from her father. He said she used to squander the money, that she had no head, that he wasn't going to give her his hard-earned money to throw about the streets, and much more, for he was usually fairly bad of a Saturday night. In the end he would give her the money and ask her had she any intention of buying Sunday's dinner. Then she had to rush out as quickly as she could and do her marketing, holding her black leather purse tightly in her hand as she elbowed her way through the crowds and returning home late under her load of provisions. She had hard work to keep the house together and to see that the two young children who had been left to her charge went to school regularly and got their meals regularly. It was hard work—a hard life—but now that she was about to leave it she did not find it a wholly undesirable life.

She was about to explore another life with Frank. Frank was very kind, manly, open-hearted. She was to go away with him by the night-boat to be his wife and to live with him in Buenos Aires where he had a home waiting for her. How well she remembered the first time she had seen him; he was lodging in a house on the main road where she used to visit. It seemed a few weeks ago. He was standing at the gate, his peaked cap pushed back on his head and his hair tumbled forward over a face of bronze. Then they had come to know each other. He used to meet her outside the Stores every evening and see her home. He took her to see *The Bohemian Girl* and she felt elated as she sat in an unaccustomed part of the theater with him. He was awfully fond of music and sang a little. People knew that they were courting and, when he sang about the lass that loves a sailor, she always felt pleasantly confused. He used to call her Poppens out of fun. First of all it had been an excitement for her to have a fellow and then she had begun to like him. He had tales of distant countries. He had started as a deck boy at a pound a month on a ship of the Allan Line going out to Canada. He told her the names of the ships he had been on and the names of the different services. He had sailed through the Straits of Magellan and he told her stories of the terrible Patagonians. He had fallen on his feet in Buenos Aires, he said, and had come over to the old country just for a holiday. Of course, her father had found out the affair and had forbidden her to have anything to say to him.

—I know these sailor chaps, he said.

One day he had quarreled with Frank and after that she had to meet her lover secretly.

The evening deepened in the avenue. The white of two letters in her lap grew indistinct. One was to Harry; the other was to her father. Ernest had been her favorite but she liked Harry too. Her father was becoming old lately, she noticed; he would miss her. Sometimes he could be very nice. Not long before, when she had been laid up for a day, he had read her out a ghost story and made toast for her at the fire. Another day, when their mother was alive, they had all gone for a picnic to the Hill of Howth. She remembered her father putting on her mother's bonnet to make the children laugh.

Her time was running out but she continued to sit by the window, leaning her head against the window curtain, inhaling the odor of dusty cretonne. Down far in the avenue she could hear a street organ playing. She knew the air. Strange that it should come that very night to remind her of the promise to her mother, her promise to keep the home together as long as she could. She remembered the last night of her mother's illness; she was again in the close dark room at the other side of the hall and outside she heard a melancholy air of Italy. The organ-player had been ordered to go away and given sixpence. She remembered her father strutting back into the sickroom saying:

10

—Damned Italians! coming over here!   15

As she mused the pitiful vision of her mother's life laid its spell on the very quick of her being — that life of commonplace sacrifices closing in final craziness. She trembled as she heard again her mother's voice saying constantly with foolish insistence:

—Derevaun Seraun! Derevaun Seraun!°

She stood up in a sudden impulse of terror. Escape! She must escape! Frank would save her. He would give her life, perhaps love, too. But she wanted to live. Why should she be unhappy? She had a right to happiness. Frank would take her in his arms, fold her in his arms. He would save her.

She stood among the swaying crowd in the station at the North Wall. He held her hand and she knew that he was speaking to her, saying something about the passage over and over again. The station was full of soldiers with brown baggages. Through the wide doors of the sheds she caught a glimpse of the black mass of the boat, lying in beside the quay wall, with illumined portholes. She answered nothing. She felt her cheek pale and cold and, out of a maze of distress, she prayed to God to direct her, to show her what was her duty. The boat blew a long mournful whistle into the mist. If she went, tomorrow she would be on the sea with Frank, steaming toward Buenos Aires. Their passage had been booked. Could she still draw back after all he had done for her? Her distress awoke a nausea in her body and she kept moving her lips in silent fervent prayer.

A bell clanged upon her heart. She felt him seize her hand: 20
—Come!

All the seas of the world tumbled about her heart. He was drawing her into them: he would drown her. She gripped with both hands at the iron railing.
—Come!

No! No! No! It was impossible. Her hands clutched the iron in frenzy. Amid the seas she sent a cry of anguish!

—Eveline! Evvy!   25

He rushed beyond the barrier and called to her to follow. He was shouted at to go on but he still called to her. She set her white face to him, passive, like a helpless animal. Her eyes gave him no sign of love or farewell or recognition.

[1914]

≣ FOR THINKING AND WRITING

1. There is a French expression that says to understand all is to forgive all. Given the ending of "Eveline," argue for or against this idea.

2. Compare "Counterparts" and "Eveline" (see "Strategies for Writing a Comparative Paper," p. 105), arguing that Joyce has or has not prepared us for the endings.

Derevaun Seraun!: Gaelic for "The end of pleasure is pain."

Acknowledgments *(continued from page iv)*

James Eli Adams. "Narrating Nature: Darwin" from *A History of Victorian Literature* by James Eli Adams. Copyright © 2012 by James Eli Adams. Reprinted by permission of the author.

Sherman Alexie. "Capital Punishment" from *The Summer of Black Widows* by Sherman Alexie. Copyright © 1996 by Sherman Alexie. Reprinted with the permission of Hanging Loose Press.

Sherman Alexie. "This Is What It Means to Say Phoenix, Arizona" from *The Lone Ranger and Tonto Fistfight in Heaven* by Sherman Alexie. Copyright © 1993, 2005 by Sherman Alexie. Used by permission of Grove/Atlantic, Inc. Any third party use of this material, outside of this publication, is prohibited.

John P. Anders. Excerpt reprinted from *Willa Cather's Sexual Aesthetics and the Male Homosexual Literary Tradition* by John P. Anders by permission of the University of Nebraska Press. Copyright © 1999 by the University of Nebraska Press.

W. H. Auden. "Musée des Beaux Arts" from *W. H. Auden: Collected Poems* by W. H. Auden. Copyright © 1940 and renewed 1968 by W. H. Auden. Used by permission of Random House, an imprint and division of Random House LLC. All rights reserved. Any third party use of this material, outside of this publication, is prohibited. Interested parties must apply directly to Random House LLC for permission.

Steven Gould Axelrod. Excerpt from *Sylvia Plath: The Wound and the Cure of Words*, pp. 1–8. Copyright © 1990 by The Johns Hopkins University Press. Reprinted with permission of The Johns Hopkins University Press.

Jimmy Santiago Baca. "So Mexicans Are Taking Jobs from Americans" from *Immigrants in Our Own Land*. Copyright © 1979 by Jimmy Santiago Baca. Reprinted by permission of New Directions Publishing Corp.

James Baldwin. "Sonny's Blues" was originally published in *Partisan Review*. Collected in *Going to Meet the Man*, published by Vintage Books. Copyright © 1957 by James Baldwin. Copyright renewed. Used by arrangement with the James Baldwin Estate.

Toni Cade Bambara. "The Lesson" from *Gorilla, My Love* by Toni Cade Bambara. Copyright © 1972 by Toni Cade Bambara. Used by permission of Random House, an imprint and division of Random House LLC. All rights reserved. Any third party use of this material, outside of this publication, is prohibited. Interested parties must apply directly to Random House LLC for permission.

Stephen C. Bandy. Excerpt from " 'One of My Babies': The Misfit and the Grandmother." Originally published in *Studies in Short Fiction* 33.1 (Winter 1996). Copyright © 1996 by Stephen Bandy. Reprinted with permission.

Robin Becker. "Morning Poem" from *Backtalk*. Copyright © 1982 by Robin Becker. Reprinted with the permission of The Permissions Company, Inc., on behalf of Alice James Books, www.alicejamesbooks.org.

Patricia Flanagan Behrendt. Excerpt from *Oscar Wilde: Eros and Aesthetics* by Patricia Flanagan Behrendt, published 1991 Palgrave Macmillan. Copyright © 1991 by Patricia Flanagan Behrendt. Reproduced with permission of Palgrave Macmillan.

Millicent Bell. "Othello's Jealousy" from the *Yale Review* 85.2 (April 1997). Copyright © 1997 by Yale University. Reprinted with permission of Blackwell Publishing Ltd.

Emily Bernard. "Scar Tissue," *American Scholar* 80.4 (Autumn 2011). Copyright © 2011 by Emily Bernard. Reprinted by permission of the author.

Elizabeth Bishop. "The Fish" from *The Complete Poems, 1927–1979* by Elizabeth Bishop. Copyright © 1979, 1983 by Alice Helen Methfessel. Reprinted by permission of Farrar, Straus and Giroux, LLC.

Richard Blanco. "Queer Theory: According to My Grandmother" from *Looking for the Gulf Motel* by Richard Blanco. Copyright © 2012 by Richard Blanco. Reprinted by permission of the University of Pittsburgh Press.

Robert Bly. "The Panther" from *Selected Poems of Rainer Maria Rilke,* translated by Robert Bly (New York: HarperCollins, 1981). Copyright © 1981 by Robert Bly. Reprinted by permission of the author.

Tirthankar Bose. Excerpt from "Oscar Wilde's Game of Being Earnest," *Modern Drama* 21.1 (Spring 1978): 81–86. Copyright © 1978 by Tirthankar Bose. Reprinted by permission of the author.

T. Coraghessan Boyle. "The Love of My Life" from *After the Plague* by T. Coraghessan Boyle. Copyright © 2001 by T. Coraghessan Boyle. Used by permission of Penguin, a division of Penguin Group (USA) LLC.

Ray Bradbury. "Mars Is Heaven!" from *Planet Stories,* June 1, 1948. Copyright © 1948 by Love Romances, Inc., renewed 1975 by Ray Bradbury. Reprinted by permission of Don Congdon Associates, Inc.

Mary Lynn Broe. Excerpt from "A Performing Self: 'the theatrical / comeback in broad day' " in *Protean Poetic: The Poetry of Sylvia Plath.* Copyright © 1980 by the Curators of the University of Missouri. Reprinted by permission of the author.

Lynda K. Bundtzen. From *Plath's Incarnations: Woman and the Creative Process* by Lynda K. Bundtzen, published by the University of Michigan Press in 1989. Reprinted by permission of the University of Michigan Press.

Angela Carter. "The Company of Wolves" from *The Bloody Chamber* by Angela Carter. Copyright © 1979 by Angela Carter. Reproduced by the permission of the Estate of Angela Carter c/o Rogers, Coleridge & White Ltd., 20 Powis Mews, London W11 1JN.

Raymond Carver. "What We Talk About When We Talk About Love" from *What We Talk About When We Talk About Love* by Raymond Carver. Copyright © 1974, 1976, 1978, 1980, 1981 by Raymond Carver. Used by permission of Alfred A. Knopf, an imprint of the Knopf Doubleday Publishing Group, a division of Random House LLC. All rights reserved. Any third party use of this material, outside of this publication, is prohibited. Interested parties must apply directly to Random House LLC for permission.

Victoria Chang. "Edward Hopper's *Conference at Night*" from *The Boss* by Victoria Chang (McSweeney's Poetry Series, August 2013). First appeared in the *Missouri Review,* December 13, 2011.

John Cheever. "Reunion" from *The Stories of John Cheever* by John Cheever. Copyright © 1978 by John Cheever. Used by permission of Alfred A. Knopf, an imprint of the Knopf Doubleday Publishing Group, a division of Random House LLC. All rights reserved. Any third party use of this material, outside of this publication, is prohibited. Interested parties must apply directly to Random House LLC for permission.

Kate Chopin. "The Storm" from *The Complete Works of Kate Chopin.* Published by Louisiana State University Press in 1969. Reprinted by permission of Louisiana State University Press.

Chrystos. "Today Was a Bad Day like TB." Copyright © 1993. Used by permission of the author.

Arthur C. Clarke. "The Nine Billion Names of God" from *The Nine Billion Names of God* by Arthur C. Clarke (Harcourt, 1967). Copyright © 1953 by Arthur C. Clarke. Reprinted by permission of the author's estate and the author's agents, Scovil Galen Ghosh Literary Agency, Inc.

Lucille Clifton. "forgiving my father" from *The Collected Poems of Lucille Clifton, 1965–2010,* published by BOA Editions (2012). First appeared in *two-headed woman,* published by University of Massachusetts Press. Copyright © 1980 by Lucille Clifton. Reprinted by permission of Curtis Brown, Ltd.

Judith Ortiz Cofer. "Claims" from *Reaching for the Mainland & Selected New Poems* by Judith Ortiz Cofer. Copyright © 1987. Reprinted by permission of Bilingual Press/Editorial Bilingüe, Arizona State University, Tempe, AZ.

The Crisis. "The Hansberrys of Chicago: They Join Business Acumen with Social Vision" from *The Crisis,* April 1941. The author wishes to thank the Crisis Publishing Co., Inc., the publisher of the magazine of the National Association for the Advancement of Colored People, for the use of this material.

Shirley Jackson. "The Lottery" from *The Lottery* by Shirley Jackson. Copyright © 1948, 1949 by Shirley Jackson. Copyright renewed 1976, 1977 by Laurence Hyman, Barry Hyman, Mrs. Sarah Webster, and Mrs. Joanne Schnurer. Reprinted by permission of Farrar, Straus & Giroux, LLC.

Mark Jarman. "If I Were Paul" from *Epistles*. Copyright © 2008 by Mark Jarman. Reprinted with the permission of The Permissions Company, Inc., on behalf of Sarabande Books, www.sarabandebooks.org.

June Jordan. "Many Rivers to Cross" from *On Call: Political Essays* by June Jordan (Boston: South End Press, 1985). Copyright © 2014 by the June Jordan Literary Estate Trust. Reprinted by permission. www.junejordan.com

Sarah Kane. "Narcissistic Personality Disorder in Willa Cather's 'Paul's Case.'" Copyright © 2010 by Sarah Kane. Reprinted by permission of the author.

Katia Kapovich. "The Ferry." Published in *The Harvard Review: Best Poetry 2006*, pp. 63–64. Reprinted by permission of the author.

Tim Kendall. Excerpt from "The Theatrical Comeback: Repetition and Performance in *Ariel*" from *Sylvia Plath: A Critical Study* by Tim Kendall. Copyright © 2001 by Tim Kendall. Reprinted by permission of Faber and Faber Inc., an affiliate of Farrar, Straus & Giroux, LLC, and Faber and Faber Ltd.

X. J. Kennedy. "Death of a Window Washer" from *In a Prominent Bar in Secaucus: New and Selected Poems, 1955–2007*. Copyright © 2007 by X. J. Kennedy. Reprinted with permission of The Johns Hopkins University Press.

Jamaica Kincaid. "Girl" from *At the Bottom of the River* by Jamaica Kincaid. Copyright © 1983 by Jamaica Kincaid. Reprinted by permission of Farrar, Straus & Giroux, LLC.

Martin Luther King Jr. "Letter from Birmingham Jail." Copyright © 1963 Dr. Martin Luther King Jr., copyright © renewed 1991 by Coretta Scott King. Reprinted by arrangement with The Heirs to the Estate of Martin Luther King Jr., c/o Writers House as agent for the proprietor, New York, NY.

Maxine Hong Kingston. "No Name Woman" from *The Woman Warrior: Memoir of a Girlhood among Ghosts* by Maxine Hong Kingston. Copyright © 1975, 1976 by Maxine Hong Kingston. Used by permission of Alfred A. Knopf, an imprint of the Knopf Doubleday Publishing Group, a division of Random House LLC. All rights reserved. Any third party use of this material, outside of this publication, is prohibited. Interested parties must apply directly to Random House LLC for permission.

Laura Kipnis. "Love in the 21st Century—Against Love," *New York Times*, October 14, 2001. Copyright © 2001 The New York Times Company. All rights reserved. Used by permission and protected by the Copyright Laws of the United States. The printing, copying, redistribution, or retransmission of this Content without express written permission is prohibited.

Yusef Komunyakaa. "Blackberries" from *Pleasure Dome: New and Collected Poems*. Copyright © 2001 by Yusef Komunyakaa. Reprinted with the permission of Wesleyan University Press, www.wesleyan.edu/wespress.

Maxine Kumin. "Woodchucks" from *Selected Poems 1960–1990* by Maxine Kumin. Copyright © 1972, 1997 by Maxine Kumin. Used by permission of W. W. Norton & Company, Inc.

Chang-Rae Lee. "Coming Home Again." Copyright © 1995 by Chang Rae Lee. Originally published in the *New Yorker*, October 16, 1995. Used by permission. All rights reserved.

Li-Young Lee. "My Father, in Heaven, Is Reading Out Loud" from *The City in Which I Love You*. Copyright © 1990 by Li-Young Lee. Reprinted with the permission of The Permissions Company, Inc., on behalf of BOA Editions, Ltd., www.boaeditions.org.

Ursula K. Le Guin. "The Ones Who Walk Away from Omelas" from *The Wind's Twelve Quarters*, published by HarperCollins in 1975. First appeared in *New Dimensions* 3. Copyright © 1973 by Ursula K. Le Guin. Reprinted by permission of Curtis Brown, Ltd.

Sharon Olds. "My Son the Man" from *Wellspring: Poems* by Sharon Olds. Copyright © 1996 by Sharon Olds. Used by permission of Alfred A. Knopf, an imprint of the Knopf Doubleday Publishing Group, a division of Random House LLC. All rights reserved. Any third party use of this material, outside of this publication, is prohibited. Interested parties must apply directly to Random House LLC for permission.

Mary Oliver. "Singapore" from *House of Light* by Mary Oliver. Published by Beacon Press, Boston. Copyright © 1990 by Mary Oliver. Reprinted by permission of the Charlotte Sheedy Literary Agency, Inc.

Mary Oliver. "When Death Comes" from *New and Selected Poems, Volume One* by Mary Oliver. Published by Beacon Press, Boston. Copyright © 1992 by Mary Oliver. Reprinted by permission of the Charlotte Sheedy Literary Agency, Inc.

Tillie Olsen. "I Stand Here Ironing" from *Tell Me a Riddle, Requa I, and Other Works* by Tillie Olsen. Copyright © 1961 by Tillie Olsen. Reprinted by permission of the University of Nebraska Press.

Meghan O'Rourke. "The Marriage Trap," *Slate*, September 3, 2003, http://www.slate.com/articles/arts/books/2003/09/the_marriage_trap.single.html. Copyright © 2003 The Slate Group. All rights reserved. Used by permission and protected by the copyright laws of the United States. The printing, copying, redistribution, or retransmission of the material without express written permission is prohibited.

Daniel Orozco. "Orientation" from *Orientation and Other Stories* by Daniel Orozco. Copyright © 2011 by Daniel Orozco. Reprinted by permission of Faber and Faber Inc., an affiliate of Farrar, Straus & Giroux, LLC.

Julie Otsuka. "Come, Japanese!" from *The Buddha in the Attic* by Julie Otsuka. Copyright © 2011 by Julie Otsuka, Inc. Used by permission of Alfred A. Knopf, an imprint of the Knopf Doubleday Publishing Group, a division of Random House LLC. All rights reserved. Any third party use of this material, outside of this publication, is prohibited. Interested parties must apply directly to Random House LLC for permission.

Linda Pastan. "Ethics" from *Waiting for My Life* by Linda Pastan. Copyright © 1981 by Linda Pastan. Used by permission of W. W. Norton & Company, Inc.

Linda Pastan. "Leaving the Island" from *Queen of a Rainy Country* by Linda Pastan. Copyright © 2004 by Linda Pastan. Used by permission of W. W. Norton & Company, Inc.

Don Paterson. "Two Trees" from *Rain* by Don Paterson. Copyright © 2009 by Don Paterson. Reprinted by permission of Farrar, Straus & Giroux, LLC, and by the permission of the author c/o Rogers, Coleridge & White Ltd., 20 Powis Mews, London W11 1JN.

Rolando Perez. "Office at Night" from *The Lining of Our Souls: Excursions into Selected Paintings of Edward Hopper* by Rolando Perez. Cool Grove Press. Copyright © 2002. Reprinted by permission of Cool Grove Publishing.

Marge Piercy. "The Secretary Chant" from *Circles on the Water* by Marge Piercy. Copyright © 1982 by Middlemarsh, Inc. Used by permission of Alfred A. Knopf, an imprint of the Knopf Doubleday Publishing Group, a division of Random House LLC. All rights reserved. Any third party use of this material, outside of this publication, is prohibited. Interested parties must apply directly to Random House LLC for permission.

Sylvia Plath. All lines from "Daddy" from *Ariel* by Sylvia Plath. Copyright © 1963 by Ted Hughes. Also from *Collected Poems* by Sylvia Plath. Reprinted by permission of HarperCollins Publishers and Faber and Faber Ltd.

Sidney Poitier. Pages 150–58, entire, from *The Measure of a Man: A Spiritual Autobiography* by Sidney Poitier. Copyright © 2000 by Sidney Poitier. Reprinted by permission of HarperCollins Publishers.

Minnie Bruce Pratt. "Two Small-Sized Girls" from *Crime Against Nature* by Minnie Bruce Pratt. Copyright © 1992. Reprinted by permission of the author.

Ruth Reichl. "The Queen of Mold" and "Miriam Reichl's Corned Beef Ham recipe," from *Tender at*

Index of Authors, Titles, First Lines, and Key Terms

Key terms page numbers are in bold.